AREA OF COVERAGE

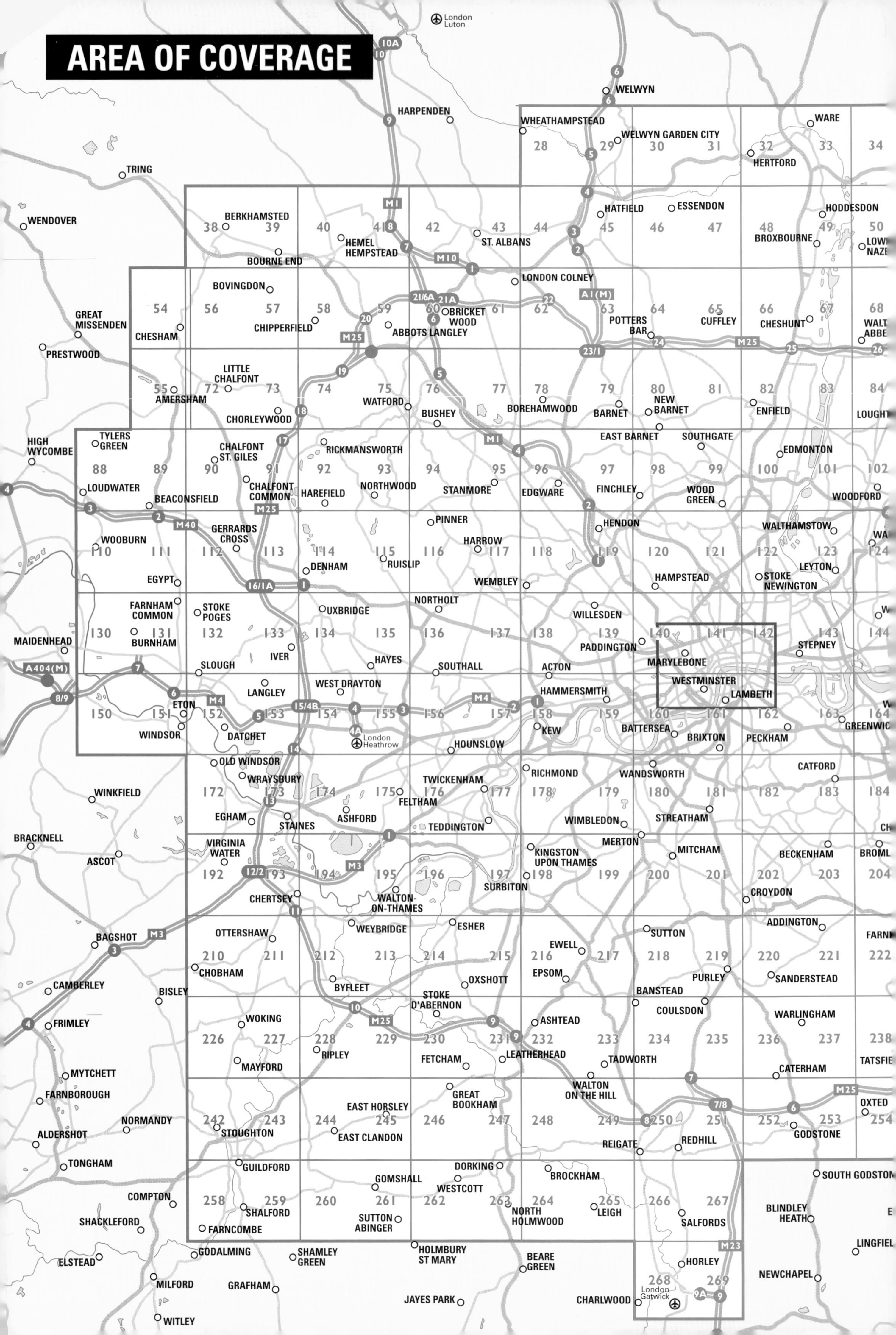

London Luton

10A
10

WELWYN
6
6
WHEATHAMPSTEAD
HARPENDEN
9
28   29   WELWYN GARDEN CITY   WARE
5   30   31   32   33   34
HERTFORD
HODDESDON
BERKHAMSTED   4   HATFIELD   ESSENDON
38   39   40   41   42   43   44   3   45   46   47   48   49   50
M1   8   2   BROXBOURNE   LOW NAZE
BOURNE END   7   ST. ALBANS
HEMEL HEMPSTEAD
M10   1
BOVINGDON   LONDON COLNEY
54   56   57   58   59   60   61   62   63   64   65   66   67   68
GREAT MISSENDEN   21/6A   21A   A1(M)   CUFFLEY   CHESHUNT   WALT ABBE
CHESHAM   CHIPPERFIELD   20   BRICKET WOOD   POTTERS BAR   24   M25   25   26
6   ABBOTS LANGLEY   23/1
PRESTWOOD   M25   19
LITTLE CHALFONT
55   72   73   74   75   76   77   78   79   80   81   82   83   84
AMERSHAM   18   WATFORD   5   BOREHAMWOOD   BARNET   NEW BARNET   ENFIELD   LOUGHT
CHORLEYWOOD   BUSHEY   M1
HIGH WYCOMBE   TYLERS GREEN   17   RICKMANSWORTH   4   EAST BARNET   SOUTHGATE   EDMONTON
88   89   90   91   92   93   94   95   96   97   98   99   100   101   102
CHALFONT ST. GILES   NORTHWOOD   STANMORE   EDGWARE   FINCHLEY   WOOD GREEN   WOODFORD
LOUDWATER   CHALFONT COMMON   HAREFIELD   2   WALTHAMSTOW
BEACONSFIELD   M25   PINNER   HENDON   WA
4   3   2   GERRARDS CROSS   HAMPSTEAD   LEYTON
WOOBURN   110   111   112   113   114   115   116   117   118   119   120   121   122   123   124
M40   DENHAM   RUISLIP   HARROW   i   STOKE NEWINGTON
EGYPT   16/1A   1   WEMBLEY   HAMPSTEAD
FARNHAM COMMON   NORTHOLT   WILLESDEN
130   131   132   133   134   135   136   137   138   139   140   141   142   143   144
MAIDENHEAD   STOKE POGES   UXBRIDGE   PADDINGTON   STEPNEY   W
A404(M)   BURNHAM   IVER   HAYES   SOUTHALL   ACTON   MARYLEBONE
150   151   152   153   154   155   156   157   158   159   160   161   162   163   164
7   SLOUGH   WEST DRAYTON   WESTMINSTER   LAMBETH   GREENWICH
8/9   6   ETON   LANGLEY   M4   HAMMERSMITH
M4   15/4B   4   3   2   1   KEW   BATTERSEA   BRIXTON   PECKHAM
WINDSOR   DATCHET   5   53   4A   London Heathrow   HOUNSLOW   BATTERSEA
14   OLD WINDSOR
WRAYSBURY   RICHMOND   WANDSWORTH   CATFORD
WINKFIELD   172   173   174   175   176   177   178   179   180   181   182   183   184
13   TWICKENHAM   FELTHAM   WIMBLEDON   STREATHAM
EGHAM   ASHFORD   TEDDINGTON
STAINES   1   MERTON   MITCHAM   BECKENHAM   BROML
VIRGINIA WATER   KINGSTON UPON THAMES
BRACKNELL   192   193   194   195   196   197   198   199   200   201   202   203   204
ASCOT   12/2   M3   SURBITON   CROYDON
CHERTSEY   WALTON-ON-THAMES   SUTTON   ADDINGTON   FARN
BAGSHOT   11   WEYBRIDGE   ESHER
M3   OTTERSHAW   EWELL   218   219   220   221   222
3   210   211   212   213   214   215   216   217   PURLEY   SANDERSTEAD
CHOBHAM   BYFLEET   OXSHOTT   EPSOM   BANSTEAD
CAMBERLEY   BISLEY   COULSDON   WARLINGHAM
4   FRIMLEY   10   STOKE D'ABERNON   9   ASHTEAD   226 227 228 229 230 231 232 233 234 235 236 237 238
WOKING   M25   9   LEATHERHEAD   TADWORTH   CATERHAM   TATSFIE
MYTCHETT   RIPLEY   FETCHAM   7
FARNBOROUGH   MAYFORD   WALTON ON THE HILL   7/8   M25   OXTED
NORMANDY   EAST HORSLEY   GREAT BOOKHAM   242 243 244 245 246 247 248 249 250 251 252 253 254
ALDERSHOT   STOUGHTON   EAST CLANDON   8   6   GODSTONE
TONGHAM   GUILDFORD   REIGATE   REDHILL
COMPTON   GOMSHALL   DORKING   BROCKHAM   SOUTH GODSTON
SHACKLEFORD   258 259 260 261 262 263 264 265 266 267   BLINDLEY HEATH
SHALFORD   WESTCOTT   NORTH HOLMWOOD   LEIGH   SALFORDS   LINGFIEL
FARNCOMBE   SUTTON ABINGER
ELSTEAD   GODALMING   SHAMLEY GREEN   HOLMBURY ST MARY   BEARE GREEN   M23
MILFORD   GRAFHAM   JAYES PARK   268   269   HORLEY   NEWCHAPEL
WITLEY   London Gatwick   9A   9   CHARLWOOD

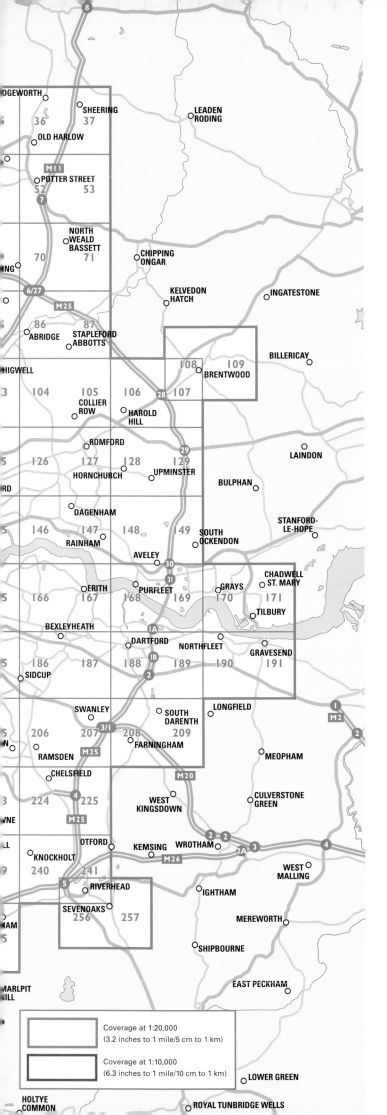

Published by Collins
An imprint of HarperCollins*Publishers*
77-85 Fulham Palace Road
Hammersmith
London W6 8JB

The HarperCollins website address is: www.**fire**and**water**.com
Copyright © HarperCollins*Publishers* Ltd 2002
First published by Geographia Ltd 1977
Mapping © Bartholomew Ltd 15th edition 2002

Collins® is a registered trademark of
HarperCollins*Publishers* Limited

Collins
An imprint of HarperCollins*Publishers*

Mapping generated from Bartholomew digital databases
Bartholomew website: www.bartholomewmaps.com

London Underground Map by permission of Transport
Trading Limited Registered User No. 02/3682

Printed in Italy

ISBN 0 00 713345 6 (paperback) Imp 001 OM11107 NDC
ISBN 0 00 713346 4 (hardback)   Imp 001 OM11108 NDC

The maps in this product are also available for purchase in
digital format, from Bartholomew Data Sales

e-mail: bartholomew@harpercollins.co.uk
Tel: +44 (0) 1242 258154
Fax: +44 (0) 1242 222725

e-mail: roadcheck@harpercollins.co.uk

Queries concerning this product to be addressd to:
    The Publisher,
    HarperCollins*Cartographic,*
    4, Manchester Park,
    Tewkesbury Road,
    Cheltenham,
    GL51 9EJ

LONDON WEB-SITES

TRAVEL

Transport for London
www.londontransport.co.uk

Car parks
www.ncp.co.uk

Traffic reports
www.rac.co.uk

Railways
www.railtrack.co.uk

London Underground
www.thetube.com

WEATHER

Weather forecasts
www.bbc.co.uk/weather
weather.yahoo.com

LONDON GUIDES

www.citiesforfree.com
www.uktravel.com/index.asp
www.timeout.com
www.netlondon.com
www.londonnet.co.uk
www.officiallondontheatre.co.uk
www.free-guide-london.com
www.londonpass.com

Official London Tourist Board site
www.londontown.com

London pubs
www.fancyapint.com

Club guide
www.clubinlondon.co.uk

LONDON TOURS

Sightseeing London's attractions via an open top bus
www.theoriginaltour.com
www.marksman.co.uk

Walks
www.talkingtour.co.uk/ripper.htm
www.zigzagtours.com
www.walks.com

Private guided tours
www.cruising-america.com/londontours

Virtual tours
www.vrlondon.com/vr/london

River trips
www.citycruises.com

PLACES OF INTEREST

Madam Tussaud's
www.madame-tussauds.co.uk

London Eye
www.londoneye.com

London Zoo
www.londonzoo.co.uk

The Tower of London
www.tower-of-london.com

Westminster Abbey
www.westminster-abbey.org

St Paul's Cathedral
www.stpauls.london.anglican.org

Royal Botanic Gardens, Kew
www.rbgkew.org.uk

The London Dungeon
www.london-dungeon.com

MUSEUMS

British Museum
www.british-museum.ac.uk

Natural History Museum
www.nhm.ac.uk

Museum of London
www.museumoflondon.org.uk

Science Museum
www.sciencemuseum.org.uk

Victoria and Albert Museum
www.vam.ac.uk

ART GALLERIES

Guildhall Art Gallery
www.guildhall-art-gallery.org.uk

National Gallery
www.nationalgallery.org.uk

Tate Britain/Modern
www.tate.org.uk

National Portrait Gallery
www.npg.org.uk/live/index.asp

ROYAL LONDON

Royal London
www.royal.gov.uk

Official web-site for visitors to the
Queen's Official Residencies
www.royalresidences.com

Official site of the Historic Royal Residencies
www.hrp.org.uk

MARKETS

Markets
www.camdenlock.net/markets
www.lfm.org.uk
www.uxbridge-craft-market.co.uk
www.demon.co.uk/hotel-uk/markets.html

HOTEL BOOKING AGENTS

Booking Bed and Breakfasts in London and UK
www.beduk.co.uk

Budget London accommodation
www.londonhomestay.co.uk/budget.htm

Web-Hotels.com provides you with a comprehensive
'no fee' one-stop London travel site
www.web-hotels.com/WebHotels

Book London hotels on-line
www.hotelbreaks.com/london.htm

Reservation facility for central London offering
discounted rates for over 100 venues
www.hotel-assist.com/london&hotels.html

The hotel register
www.hotelregister.co.uk/londonhotels.asp

YHA London accommodation
www.yha.org.uk

HEALTH

Health
www.medinet.co.uk
www.surflondon.co.uk/emergencies/hospitals

LONDON RADIO STATIONS

BBC London Live 94.9 FM
www.bbc.co.uk/london

Capital FM 95.8 FM
www.capitalfm.com

News Direct 97.3 FM
www.newsdirect.co.uk

Kiss 100.0 FM
www.kiss100.com

LBC 1152MW
www.lbc.co.uk

Christian radio. Religious worship 1305FM
www.premier.org.uk

Capital Gold (London) 1548 MW
www.capitalgold.com

LONDON COUNCILS

Barking & Dagenham
www.barking-dagenham.gov.uk

Barnet
www.barnet.gov.uk

Bexley
www.bexley.gov.uk

Brent
www.brent.gov.uk

Bromley
www.bromley.gov.uk

Camden
www.camden.gov.uk

Corporation of London
www.cityoflondon.gov.uk

Croydon
www.croydon.gov.uk

Ealing
www.ealing.gov.uk

Enfield
www.enfield.gov.uk

Greenwich
www.greenwich.gov.uk

Hackney
www.hackney.gov.uk

Hammersmith and Fulham
www.lbhf.gov.uk

Haringey
www.haringey.gov.uk

Harrow
www.harrow.gov.uk

Havering
www.havering.gov.uk

Hillingdon
www.hillingdon.gov.uk

Hounslow
www.hounslow.gov.uk

Islington
www.islington.gov.uk

Kensington and Chelsea
www.rbkc.gov.uk

Kingston
www.kingston.gov.uk

Lambeth
www.lambeth.gov.uk

Lewisham
www.lewisham.gov.uk

Merton
www.merton.gov.uk

Newham
www.newham.gov.uk

Redbridge
www.redbridge.gov.uk

Richmond upon Thames
www.richmond.gov.uk

Southwark
www.southwark.gov.uk

Sutton
www.sutton.gov.uk

Tower Hamlets
www.towerhamlets.gov.uk

Waltham Forest
www.lbwf.gov.uk

Wandsworth
www.wandsworth.gov.uk

Westminster
www.westminster.gov.uk

Greater London Authority
www.london.gov.uk

GREATER LONDON STREET ATLAS

CONTENTS

M25 LONDON ORBITAL MOTORWAY

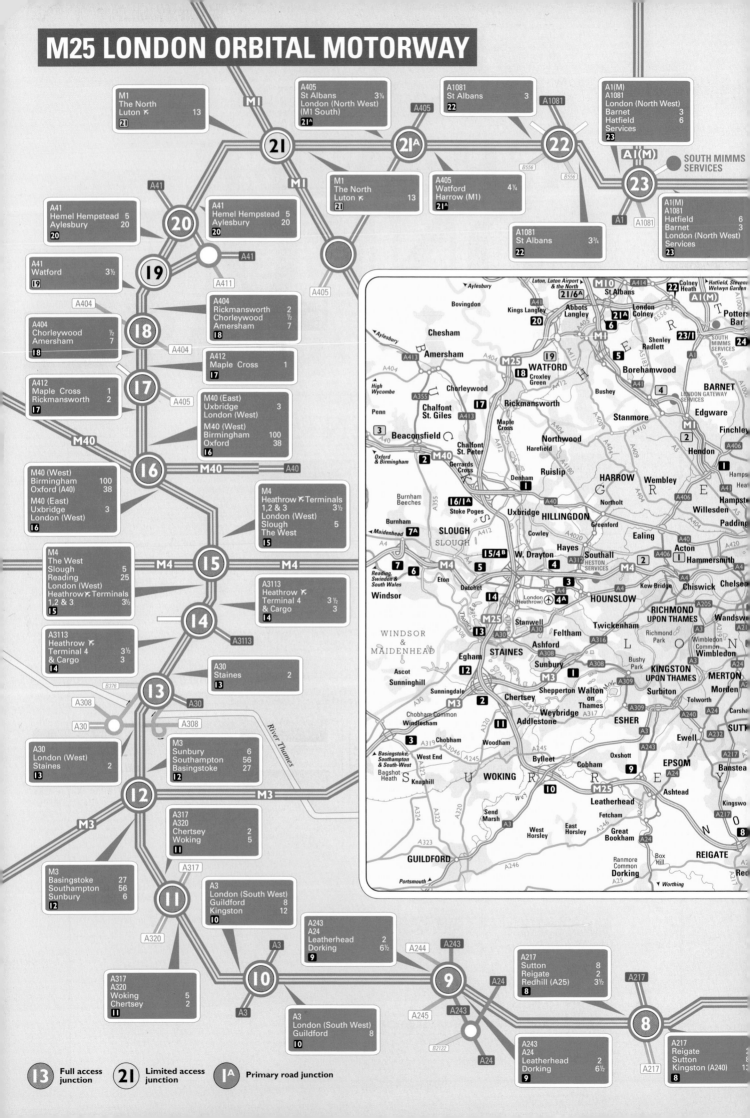

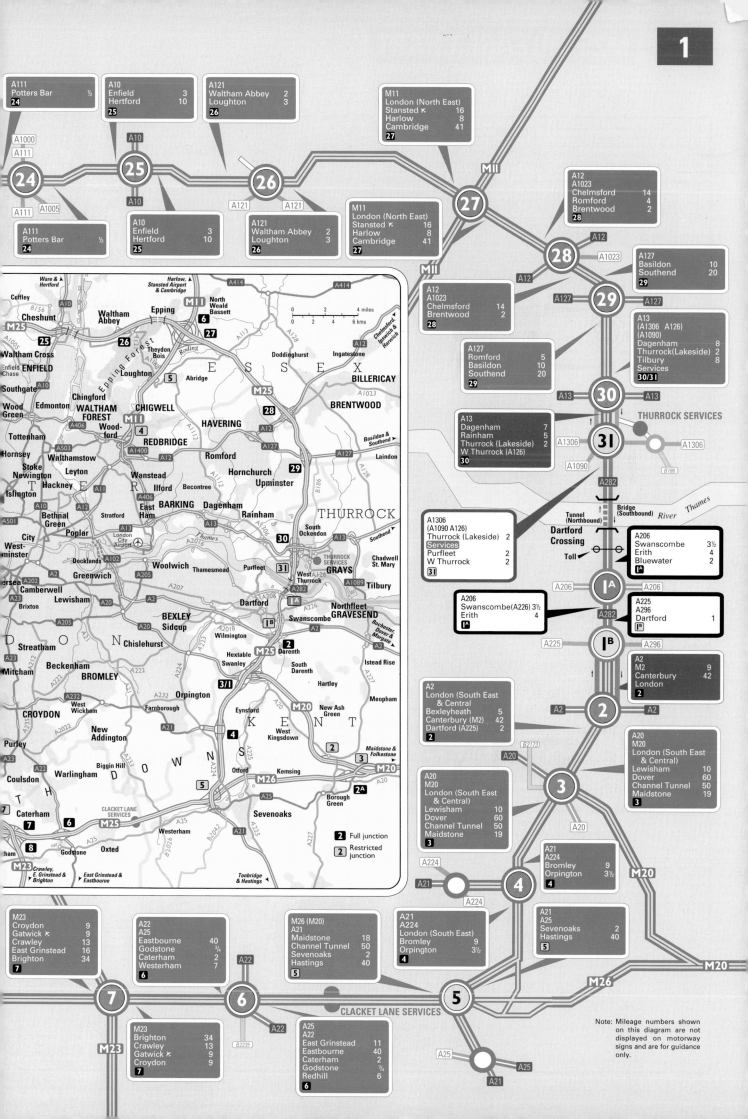

M25 MILEAGE CHART

JUNCTION OF EXIT (columns) × **JUNCTION OF ENTRY** (rows)

#	Junction	1	2	3	4	5	6	7	8	9	10	11	12	13	14	15	16	17	18	19	20	21	22	23	24	25	26	27	28	29	30	31
1	DARTFORD		1	4	8	12	22	25	28	35	41	46	48	51	53	55	59	53	52	51	48	45	40	37	34	28	25	21	13	10	5	4
2	A2	1		3	7	11	21	24	27	34	40	45	47	50	52	54	58	54	53	52	49	46	41	38	35	29	26	22	14	11	6	5
3	M20	4	3		4	8	18	21	24	31	37	42	44	47	49	51	55	57	56	55	52	49	44	41	38	32	29	25	17	14	9	8
4	A21	8	7	4		4	14	17	20	27	33	38	40	43	45	47	51	57	58	59	56	53	48	45	42	36	33	29	21	18	13	12
5	M26	12	11	8	4		10	13	16	23	29	34	36	39	41	43	47	53	54	55	58	57	52	49	46	40	37	33	25	22	17	16
6	A22	22	21	18	14	10		3	6	13	19	24	26	29	31	33	37	43	44	45	48	51	56	59	56	50	47	43	35	32	27	26
7	M23	25	24	21	17	13	3		3	10	16	21	23	26	28	30	34	40	41	42	45	48	53	56	59	53	50	46	38	35	30	29
8	REIGATE	28	27	24	20	16	6	3		7	13	18	20	23	25	27	31	37	38	39	42	45	50	53	56	56	53	49	41	38	33	32
9	LEATHERHEAD	35	34	31	27	23	13	10	7		6	11	13	16	18	20	24	30	31	32	35	38	43	46	49	55	58	56	48	45	40	39
10	A3	41	40	37	33	29	19	16	13	6		5	7	10	12	14	18	24	25	26	29	32	37	40	43	49	52	56	54	51	46	45
11	CHERTSEY	46	45	42	38	34	24	21	18	11	5		2	5	7	9	13	19	20	21	24	27	32	35	38	44	47	51	59	56	51	50
12	M3	48	47	44	40	36	26	23	20	13	7	2		3	5	7	11	17	18	19	22	25	30	33	36	42	45	49	57	58	53	52
13	A30	51	50	47	43	39	29	26	23	16	10	5	3		2	4	8	14	15	16	19	22	27	30	33	39	42	46	54	57	56	55
14	HEATHROW 4	53	52	49	45	41	31	28	25	18	12	7	5	2		2	6	12	13	14	17	20	25	28	31	37	40	44	52	55	58	57
15	M4, HEATHROW 1-3	55	54	51	47	43	33	30	27	20	14	9	7	4	2		4	10	11	12	15	18	23	26	29	35	38	42	50	53	58	59
16	M40	59	58	55	51	47	37	34	31	24	18	13	11	8	6	4		6	7	8	11	14	19	22	25	31	34	38	46	49	54	55
17	RICKMANSWORTH	53	54	57	57	53	43	40	37	30	24	19	17	14	12	10	6		1	2	5	8	13	16	19	25	28	32	40	43	48	49
18	A404	52	53	56	58	54	44	41	38	31	25	20	18	15	13	11	7	1		1	4	7	12	15	18	24	27	31	39	42	47	48
19	WATFORD	51	52	55	59	55	45	42	39	32	26	21	19	16	14	12	8	2	1		3	6	11	14	17	23	26	30	38	41	46	47
20	A41	48	49	52	56	58	48	45	42	35	29	24	22	19	17	15	11	5	4	3		3	8	11	14	20	23	27	35	38	43	44
21	M1	45	46	49	53	57	51	48	45	38	32	27	25	22	20	18	14	8	7	6	3		5	8	11	17	20	24	32	35	40	41
22	ST. ALBANS	40	41	44	48	52	56	53	50	43	37	32	30	27	25	23	19	13	12	11	8	5		3	6	12	15	19	27	30	35	36
23	A1 (M)	37	38	41	45	49	59	56	53	46	40	35	33	30	28	26	22	16	15	14	11	8	3		3	9	12	16	24	27	32	33
24	A111	34	35	38	42	46	56	59	56	49	43	38	36	33	31	29	25	19	18	17	14	11	6	3		6	9	13	21	24	29	30
25	A10	28	29	32	36	40	50	53	56	55	49	44	42	39	37	35	31	25	24	23	20	17	12	9	6		3	7	15	18	23	24
26	EPPING	25	26	29	33	37	47	50	53	58	52	47	45	42	40	38	34	28	27	26	23	20	15	12	9	3		4	12	15	20	21
27	M11	21	22	25	29	33	43	46	49	56	56	51	49	46	44	42	38	32	31	30	27	24	19	16	13	7	4		8	11	16	17
28	A12	13	14	17	21	25	35	38	41	48	54	59	57	54	52	50	46	40	39	38	35	32	27	24	21	15	12	8		3	8	9
29	A127	10	11	14	18	22	32	35	38	45	51	56	58	57	55	53	49	43	42	41	38	35	30	27	24	18	15	11	3		5	6
30	A13	5	6	9	13	17	27	30	33	40	46	51	53	56	58	58	54	48	47	46	43	40	35	32	29	23	20	16	8	5		1
31	A13	4	5	8	12	16	26	29	32	39	45	50	52	55	57	59	55	49	48	47	44	41	36	33	30	24	21	17	9	6	1	

Mileage Clockwise

Mileage AntiClockwise

Note: This chart shows the shortest distance between junctions. The colours indicate distance clockwise or anticlockwise and grey boxes indicate where access is not possible. The total distance around the M25 is approximately 117 miles.

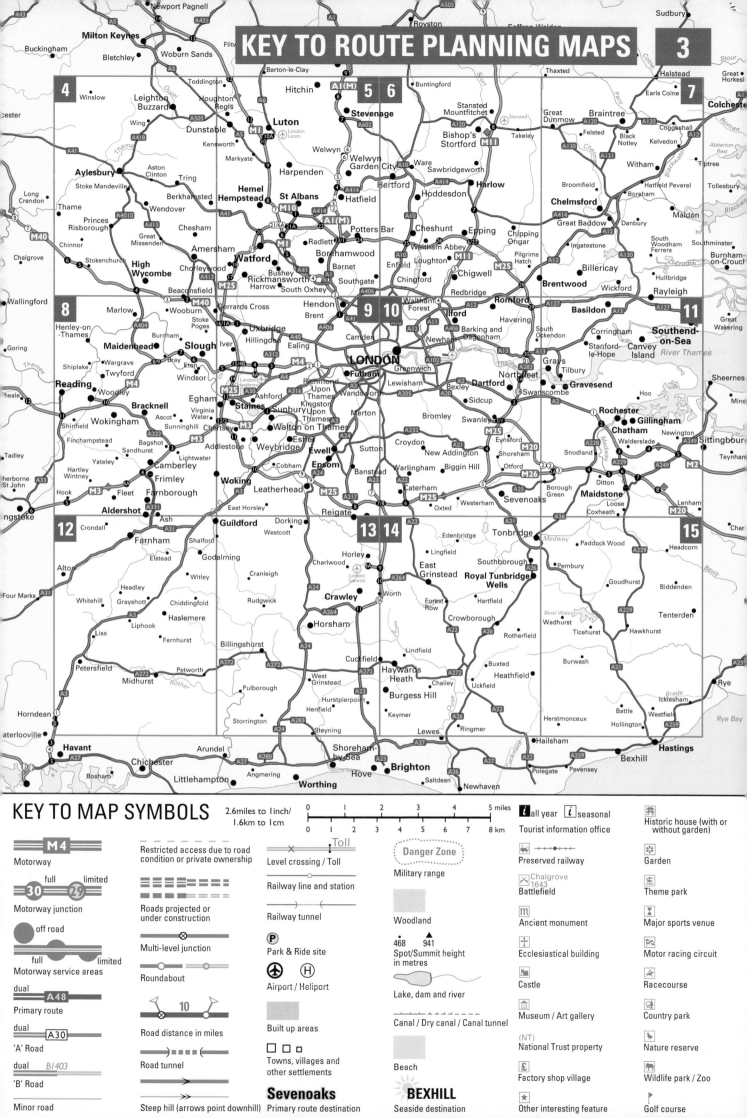

KEY TO ROUTE PLANNING MAPS

3

4 **5** **6** **7**

8 **9** **10** **11**

12 **13** **14** **15**

KEY TO MAP SYMBOLS

2.6 miles to 1 inch/
1.6km to 1cm

0 1 2 3 4 5 miles
0 1 2 3 4 5 6 7 8 km

M4
Motorway

30 **29**
full   limited
Motorway junction

off road
full   limited
Motorway service areas

dual **A48**
Primary route

dual **A30**
'A' Road

dual *B1403*
'B' Road

Minor road

Restricted access due to road
condition or private ownership

Roads projected or
under construction

Multi-level junction

Roundabout

10
Road distance in miles

Road tunnel

Steep hill (arrows point downhill)

Level crossing / Toll

Railway line and station

Railway tunnel

P Park & Ride site

Airport / Heliport

Built up areas

□ ▢ ▫
Towns, villages and
other settlements

Sevenoaks
Primary route destination

Danger Zone
Military range

Woodland

468   ▲ 941
Spot/Summit height
in metres

Lake, dam and river

Canal / Dry canal / Canal tunnel

Beach

BEXHILL
Seaside destination

i all year   *i* seasonal
Tourist information office

Preserved railway

Chalgrove 1643
Battlefield

Ancient monument

Ecclesiastical building

Castle

Museum / Art gallery

(NT)
National Trust property

Factory shop village

Other interesting feature

Historic house (with or
without garden)

Garden

Theme park

Major sports venue

Motor racing circuit

Racecourse

Country park

Nature reserve

Wildlife park / Zoo

Golf course

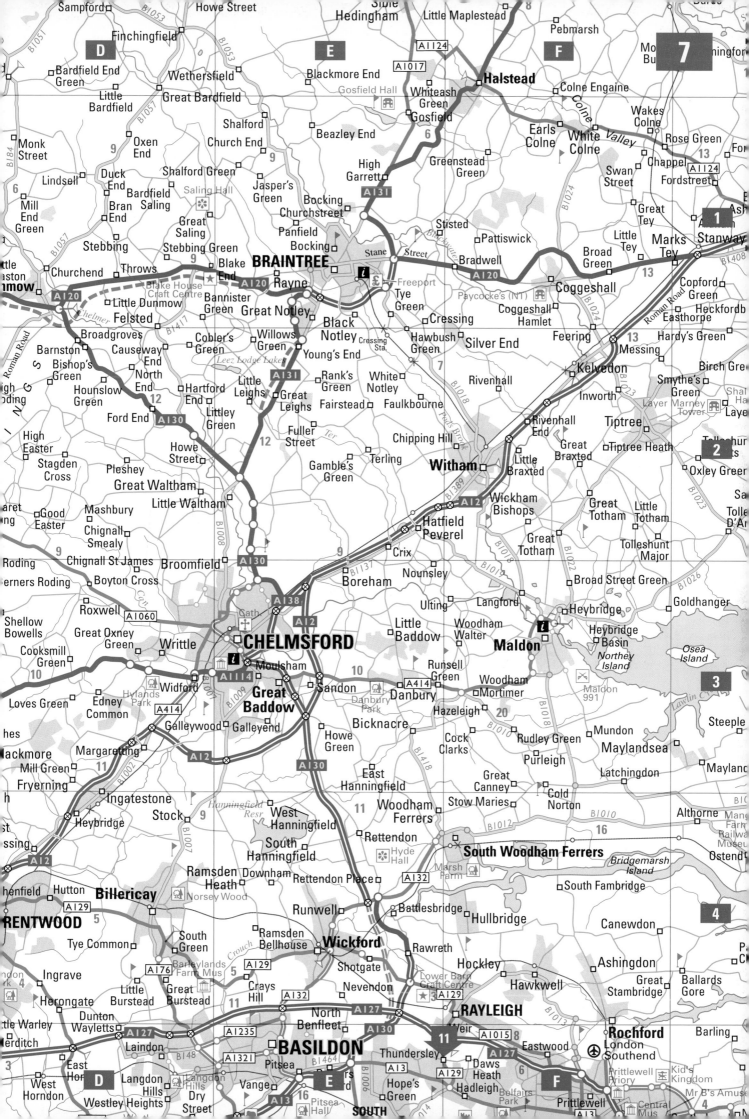

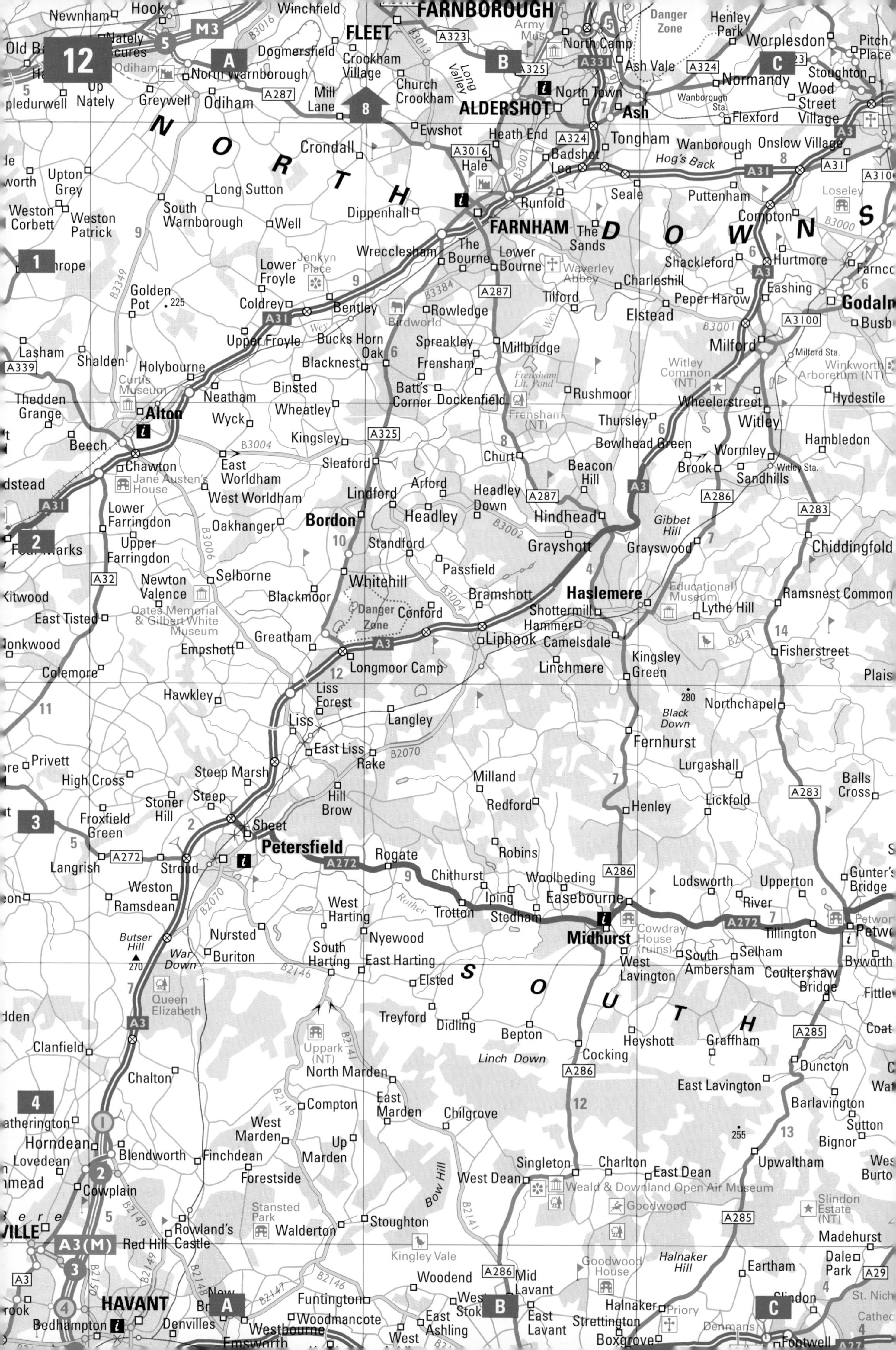

FARNBOROUGH

FLEET

Newnham Hook Winchfield

Danger Zone

Henley Park

Pitch Place

Worplesdon

M3 5 A Dogmersfield A323 Army Mus North Camp 5 C 23

Old Ba Nately Odiham North Warnborough Crookham Village B A325 A331 Ash Vale A324 Normandy Stoughton

Up Nately Greywell Odiham Mill Lane Church Crookham ALDERSHOT North Town Ash A31 Flexford Wood Street Village

pledurwell A287 8 Ewshot Heath End A324 Tongham Wanborough Onslow Village A3

Weston Corbett Crondall A3016 Badshot Lea Hog's Back A31 8 A31 A310

Weston Patrick 9 South Warnborough Well Dippenhall Hale Runfold Seale Puttenham Compton Loseley Farnco

1 hrope Long Sutton Wrecclesham The Bourne Lower Bourne Waverley Abbey Charleshill Shackleford Hurtmore Eashing 6

Lasham Lower Froyle Jenkyn Place FARNHAM The Sands Tilford Peper Harow Elstead A3 Godalm

Shalden Coldrey Bentley Rowledge Millbridge Frensham Lit. Pond Witley Common Milford Milford Sta. Busb

Thedden Grange A31 Upper Froyle Bucks Horn Oak Spreakley Frensham Rushmoor A3100 Winkworth Arboretum

Beech Holybourne Neatham Blacknest Batt's Corner Dockenfield Frensham Wheelerstreet Witley Hydestile

Chawton Wyck Wheatley East Worldham Kingsley A325 Churt Thursley Bowlhead Green Wormley Hambledon

Jane Austen's House West Worldham Sleaford Lindford Arford Headley Down Beacon Hill Hindhead Brook Witley Sta. Sandhills

Lower Farringdon Oakhanger Bordon Headley Grayshott Gibbet Hill Grayswood Chiddingfold

2 Fear Marks Upper Farringdon Selborne Standford Passfield Haslemere Ramsnest Common

Kitwood Newton Valence Blackmoor Whitehill Conford Bramshott Shottermill Educational Museum Lythe Hill 14

East Tisted Oates Memorial & Gilbert White Museum Greatham Danger Zone Liphook Hammer Fisherstreet

onkwood Empshott A3 Longmoor Camp Camelsdale Kingsley Green Plais

Colemore Hawkley Liss Forest Langley Linchmere Northchapel

11 Liss East Liss Rake B2070 Black Down Fernhurst Lurgashall Balls Cross

Privett High Cross Steep Marsh Milland Redford Henley Lickfold A283

Froxfield Green Stoner Hill Steep Hill Brow Woolbeding Lodsworth Upperton Gunter's Bridge

Sheet Rogate Robins Easebourne River Petwor

3 Langrish A272 Stroud PETERSFIELD Chithurst Iping A272 Tillington

Weston Ramsdean West Harting Trotton Stedham MIDHURST Cowdray House (ruins) Selham Byworth

Butser Hill Nursted South Harting Nyewood East Harting West Lavington South Ambersham Coultershaw Bridge Fittle

War Down Buriton B2146 Elsted SOUTH Coat

Queen Elizabeth Treyford Didling Bepton Heyshott Graffham A285

Clanfield Uppark (NT) North Marden Linch Down Cocking A286 East Lavington Duncton

Chalton Compton East Marden Chilgrove Barlavington Sutton

4 atherington West Marden Singleton Charlton East Dean Upwaltham Bignor

Horndean Blendworth Finchdean Up Marden West Dean Weald & Downland Open Air Museum East Lavington

Lovedean Forestside Goodwood A285 Slindon Estate (NT) Madehurst

mead Cowplain Stansted Park Dale Park A29

A3(M) Red Hill Castle Kingley Vale Woodend A286 Mid Lavant Goodwood House Halnaker Hill Eartham Slindon

HAVANT A Funtington Woodmancote West Stok B East Lavant Halnaker Priory Strettington Denmans C

Bedhampton Denvilles Westbourne West East Ashling Boxgrove Footwell St. Nich

Emsworth

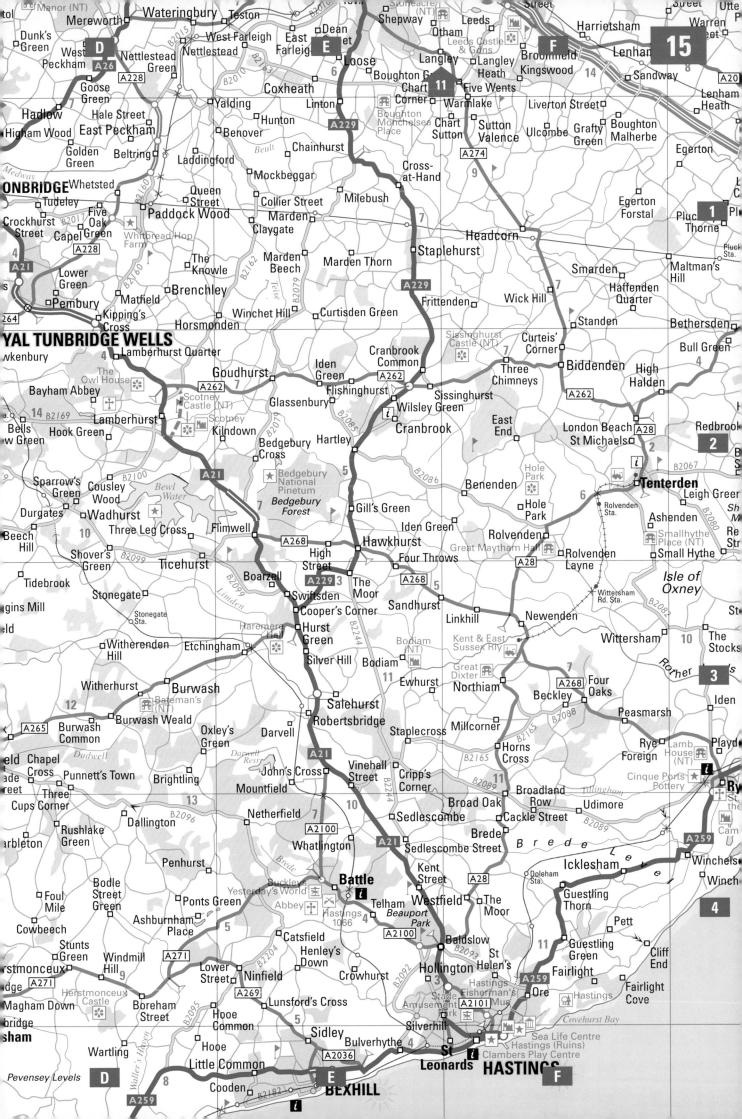

KEY TO MAP SYMBOLS

- [i] Tourist information centre
- [P] Short stay car park
- [P] Long stay car park
- ⊕ Railway station
- ⊖ London underground station
- 🚌 Bus station

LUTON

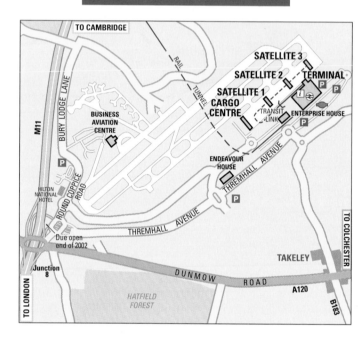

Tel. 01582 405100

STANSTED

Tel. 0870 000 0303

HEATHROW

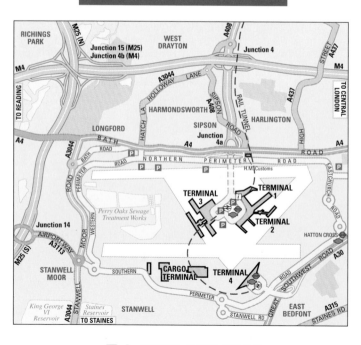

Tel. 0870 000 0123

GATWICK

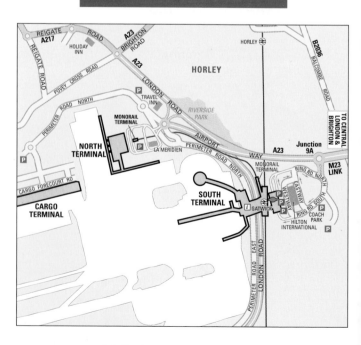

Tel. 0870 000 2468

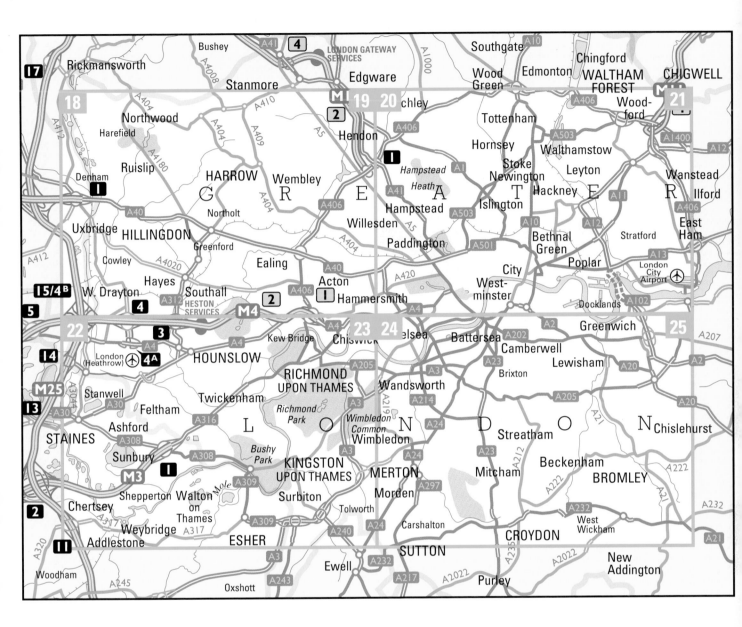

KEY TO MAP SYMBOLS

M25 tunnel	Motorway
4 restricted access **2**	Junction numbers
dual **A5** projected/under constr.	Primary route
dual **A4251** projected/under constr.	'A' road
dual **B652** projected/under constr.	'B' road
——————	Other road
▪▪▪▪▪▪▪▪▪	Restricted access
─○──○─	Roundabouts
▪ ▪ ▪ ─ ─	Tunnelled roads
Toll ─┼──→	Toll / One way street
▬▬▬ ▬ ▬	County / Borough boundary
– – – – – – –	Car ferry
┴┴┴┴┴┴┴	Canal
─── ─ ─ tunnel	Railway
⇌	Railway station
⊖	London Regional Transport station
•	Light railway/Tramway station
Ⓗ	Heliport
◭ 25	Page continuation number
▨	Open space / Park / Sports ground
▨	Woods
⚑	Golf course
✿	Garden
🏛	Historic house
🏛	Museum
🐘	Wildlife park or zoo
▦	Theme park
ⓘ	Information centre
🏃	Racecourse
★	Other interesting feature
★	Landmark public house

Scale 1: 50,000
1 inch to 0.8 miles / 2 cm to 1 km

0   1   2 miles
0   1   2   3 km

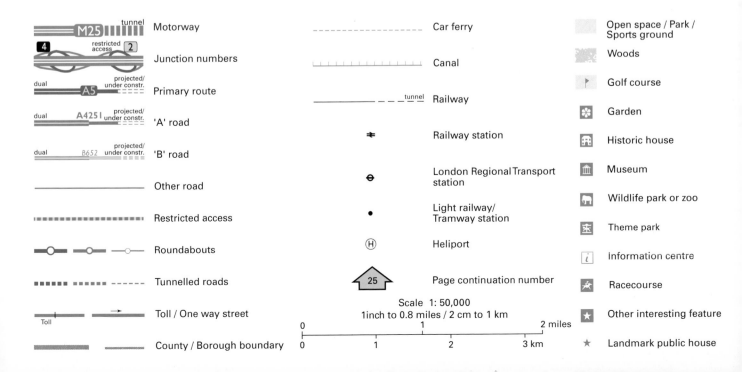

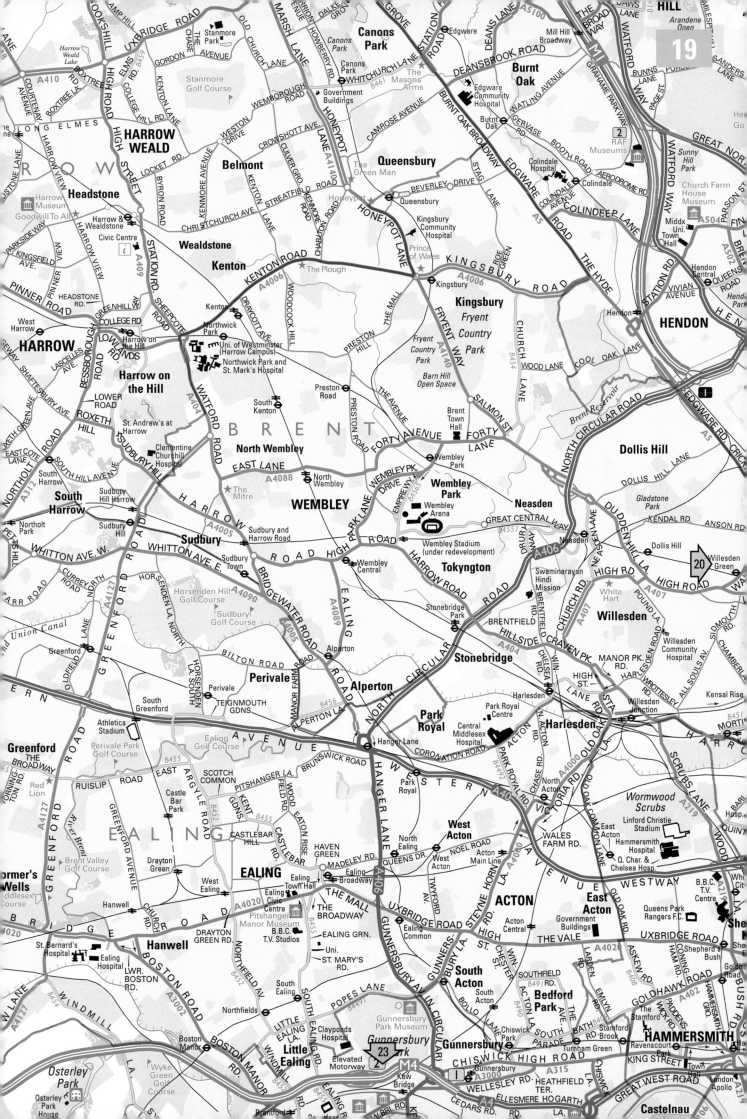

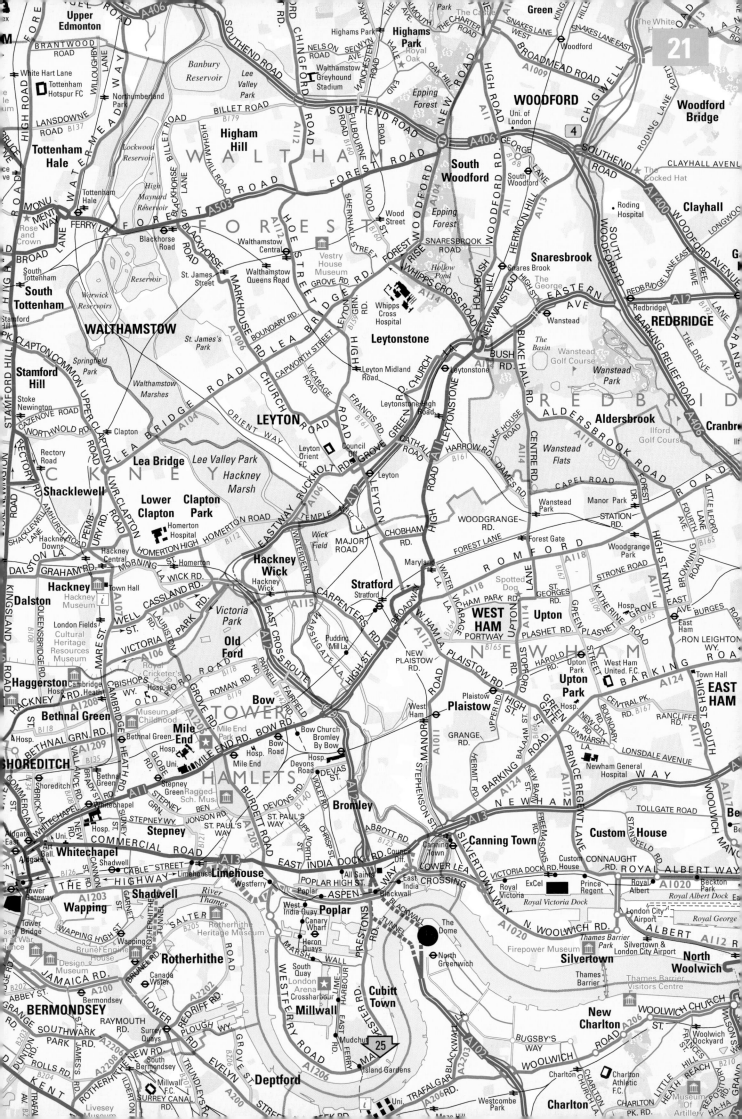

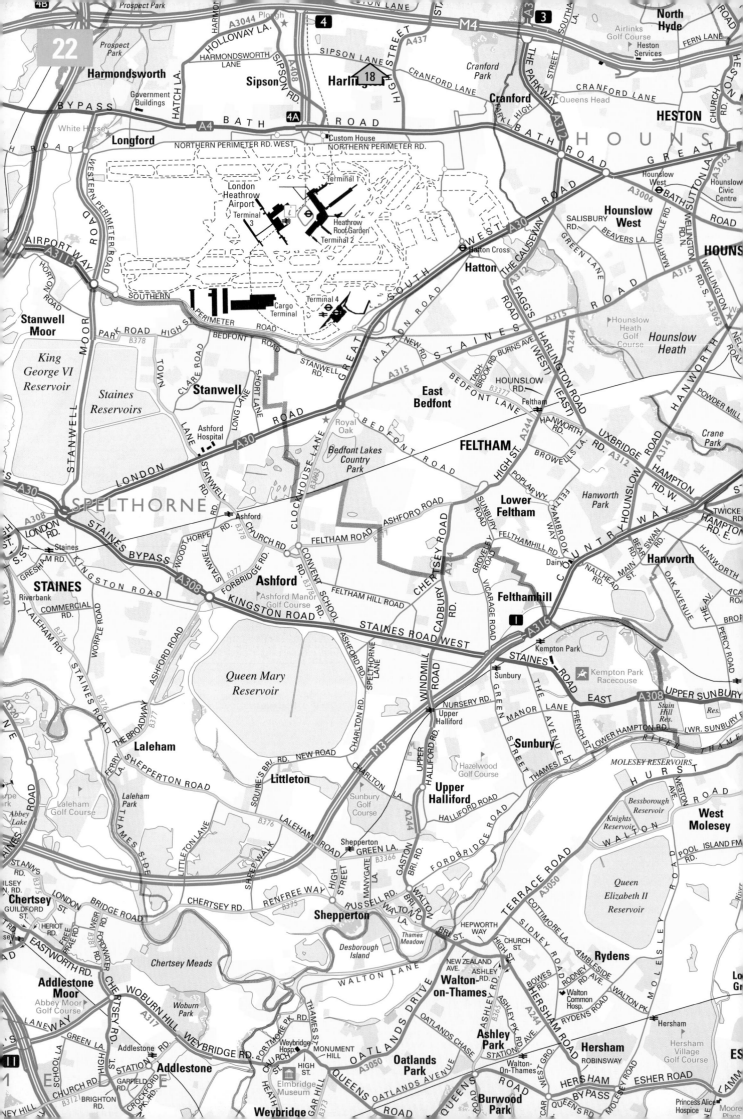

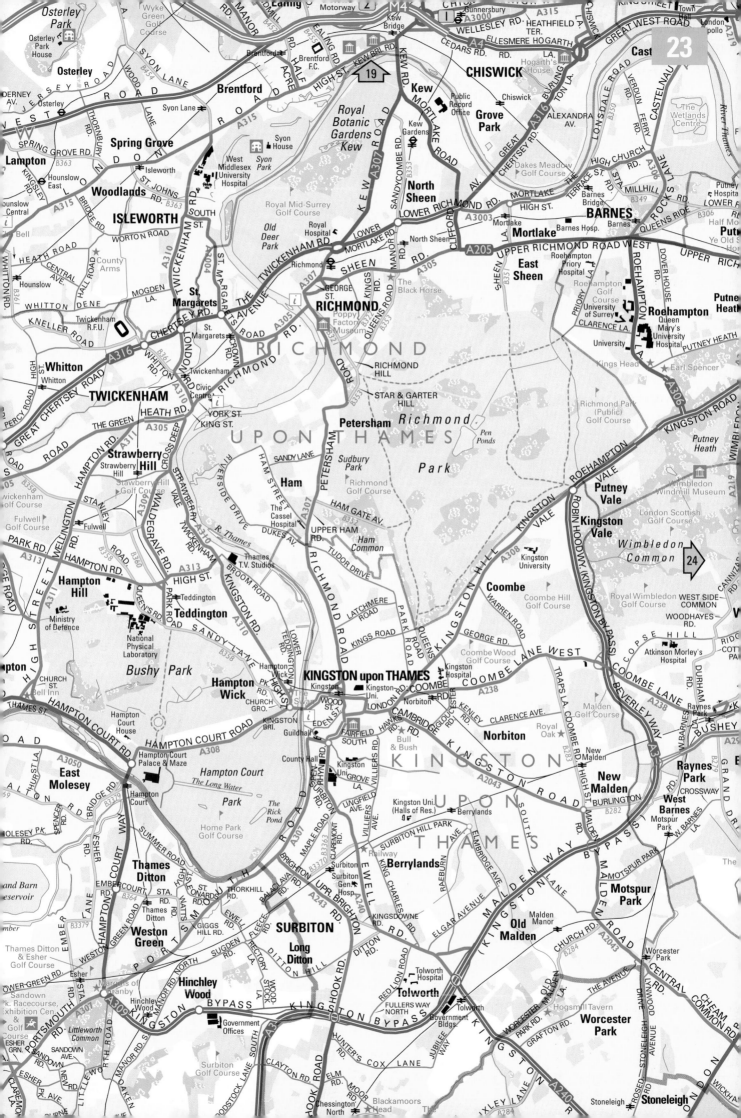

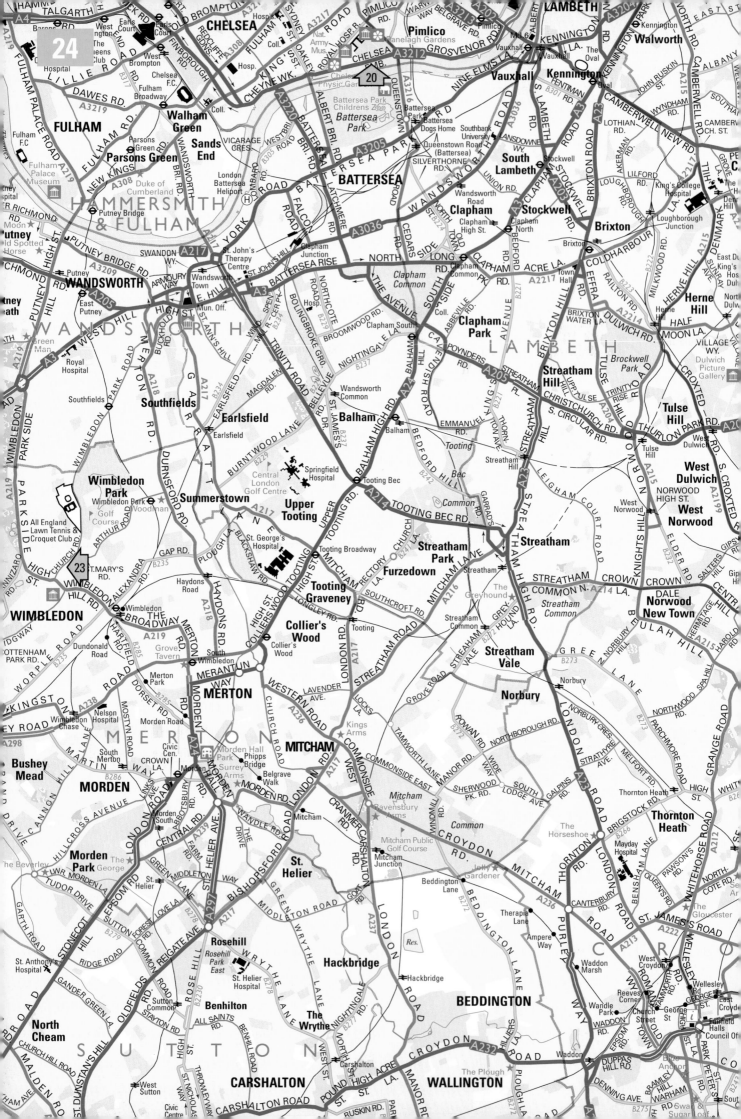

London Luton

WELWYN

HARPENDEN

WHEATHAMPSTEAD
WELWYN GARDEN CITY
WARE
28 29 30 31 32 33 34
HERTFORD

BERKHAMSTED
HATFIELD ESSENDON
HODDESDON
38 39 40 41 42 43 44 45 46 47 48 49 50
HEMEL HEMPSTEAD ST. ALBANS BROXBOURNE LOW NAZ

BOURNE END

BOVINGDON
LONDON COLNEY
54 56 57 58 59 60 61 62 63 64 65 66 67 68
CHESHAM CHIPPERFIELD BRICKET WOOD POTTERS BAR CUFFLEY CHESHUNT WALT ABBE
ABBOTS LANGLEY

PRESTWOOD

GREAT MISSENDEN

LITTLE CHALFONT
55 72 73 74 75 76 77 78 79 80 81 82 83 84
AMERSHAM WATFORD BOREHAMWOOD BARNET NEW BARNET ENFIELD LOUGH
CHORLEYWOOD BUSHEY

TYLERS GREEN
CHALFONT ST. GILES
RICKMANSWORTH
EAST BARNET SOUTHGATE
EDMONTON
88 89 90 91 92 93 94 95 96 97 98 99 100 101 102
LOUDWATER CHALFONT COMMON HAREFIELD NORTHWOOD STANMORE EDGWARE FINCHLEY WOOD GREEN WOODFORD
BEACONSFIELD

HIGH WYCOMBE

WOOBURN
PINNER
HENDON
WALTHAMSTOW
110 111 112 113 114 115 116 117 118 119 120 121 122 123 124
GERRARDS CROSS HARROW HAMPSTEAD STOKE NEWINGTON LEYTON WA
EGYPT DENHAM RUISLIP WEMBLEY

FARNHAM COMMON
STOKE POGES
UXBRIDGE
NORTHOLT
WILLESDEN
130 131 132 133 134 135 136 137 138 139 140 141 142 143 144
MAIDENHEAD BURNHAM HAYES SOUTHALL ACTON PADDINGTON MARYLEBONE STEPNEY W
SLOUGH IVER

WEST DRAYTON
WESTMINSTER LAMBETH
150 151 152 153 154 155 156 157 158 159 160 161 162 163 164
ETON LANGLEY HAMMERSMITH GREENWIC
WINDSOR DATCHET London Heathrow HOUNSLOW KEW BATTERSEA BRIXTON PECKHAM

OLD WINDSOR
WRAYSBURY
TWICKENHAM
RICHMOND
CATFORD
WANDSWORTH
172 173 174 175 176 177 178 179 180 181 182 183 184
WINKFIELD EGHAM FELTHAM
STAINES ASHFORD TEDDINGTON WIMBLEDON STREATHAM

BRACKNELL

VIRGINIA WATER
MERTON MITCHAM BECKENHAM BROML
ASCOT KINGSTON UPON THAMES
192 193 194 195 196 197 198 199 200 201 202 203 204
CHERTSEY WALTON-ON-THAMES SURBITON CROYDON
ADDINGTON
OTTERSHAW WEYBRIDGE ESHER SUTTON FARN
BAGSHOT
210 211 212 213 214 215 216 217 218 219 220 221 222
CHOBHAM EWELL PURLEY SANDERSTEAD
BISLEY BYFLEET OXSHOTT EPSOM
CAMBERLEY BANSTEAD

STOKE D'ABERNON
COULSDON
WOKING WARLINGHAM
FRIMLEY ASHTEAD
226 227 228 229 230 231 232 233 234 235 236 237 238
RIPLEY LEATHERHEAD TADWORTH CATERHAM TATSFIE
MAYFORD FETCHAM

MYTCHETT
FARNBOROUGH
GREAT BOOKHAM
WALTON ON THE HILL
NORMANDY EAST HORSLEY
242 243 244 245 246 247 248 249 250 251 252 253 254
ALDERSHOT STOUGHTON EAST CLANDON REIGATE REDHILL GODSTONE OXTED
TONGHAM

GUILDFORD
DORKING
BROCKHAM
SOUTH GODSTON
COMPTON GOMSHALL WESTCOTT LEIGH SALFORDS
258 259 260 261 262 263 264 265 266 267 BLINDLEY HEATH E
SHACKLEFORD SHALFORD NORTH HOLMWOOD
FARNCOMBE SUTTON ABINGER
ELSTEAD LINGFIEL

GODALMING SHAMLEY GREEN HOLMBURY ST MARY BEARE GREEN CHARLWOOD HORLEY NEWCHAPEL
MILFORD GRAFHAM 268 269
WITLEY JAYES PARK London Gatwick

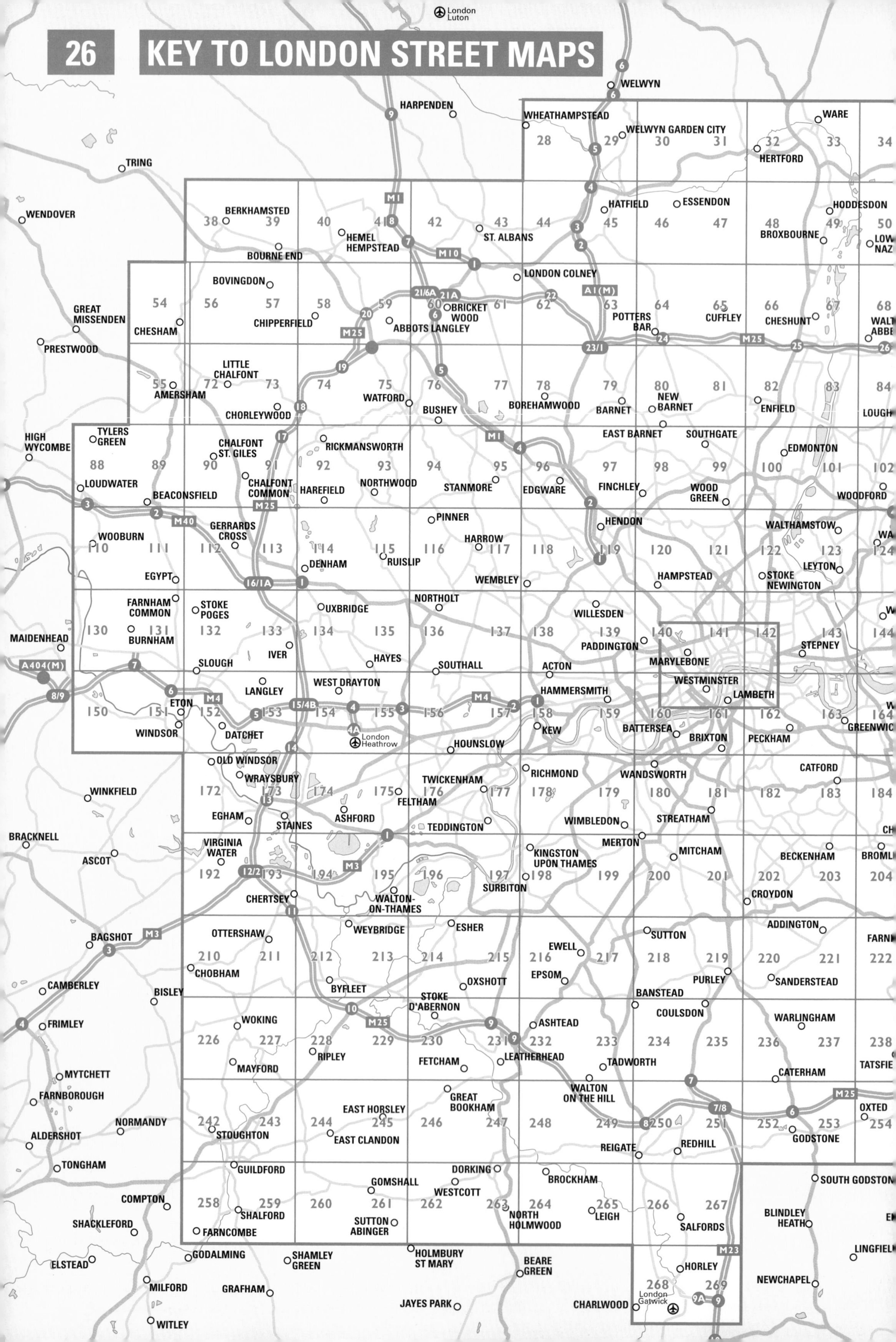

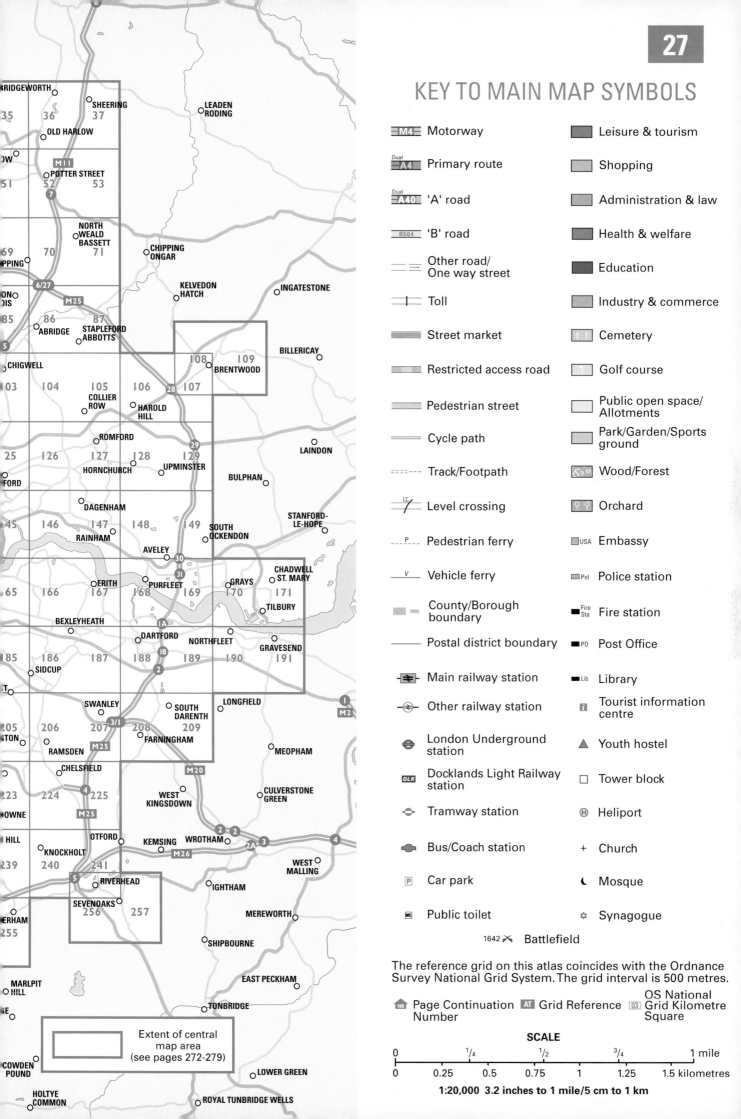

KEY TO MAIN MAP SYMBOLS

M4 Motorway

A4 Primary route

A40 'A' road

B504 'B' road

Other road/One way street

Toll

Street market

Restricted access road

Pedestrian street

Cycle path

Track/Footpath

Level crossing

Pedestrian ferry

Vehicle ferry

County/Borough boundary

Postal district boundary

Main railway station

Other railway station

London Underground station

Docklands Light Railway station

Tramway station

Bus/Coach station

Car park

Public toilet

Leisure & tourism

Shopping

Administration & law

Health & welfare

Education

Industry & commerce

Cemetery

Golf course

Public open space/Allotments

Park/Garden/Sports ground

Wood/Forest

Orchard

Embassy

Police station

Fire station

Post Office

Library

Tourist information centre

Youth hostel

Tower block

Heliport

Church

Mosque

Synagogue

1642 Battlefield

The reference grid on this atlas coincides with the Ordnance Survey National Grid System. The grid interval is 500 metres.

Page Continuation Number | Grid Reference | OS National Grid Kilometre Square

SCALE

0 — 1/4 — 1/2 — 3/4 — 1 mile

0 — 0.25 — 0.5 — 0.75 — 1 — 1.25 — 1.5 kilometres

1:20,000 3.2 inches to 1 mile/5 cm to 1 km

Extent of central map area (see pages 272-279)

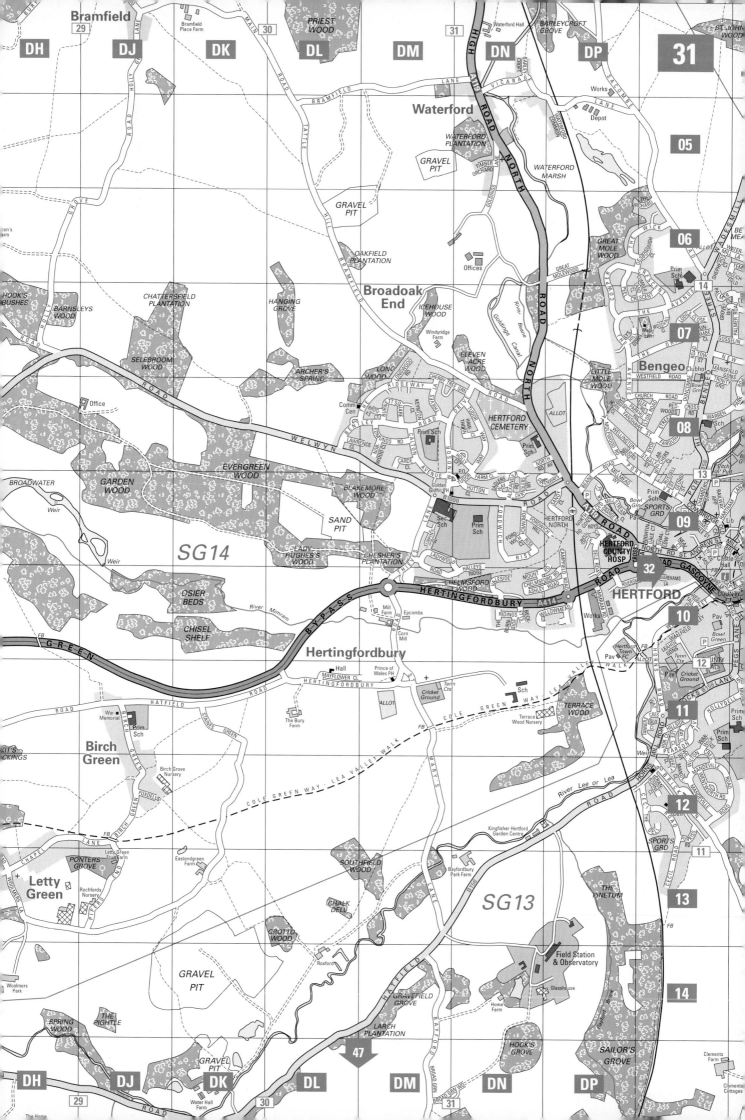

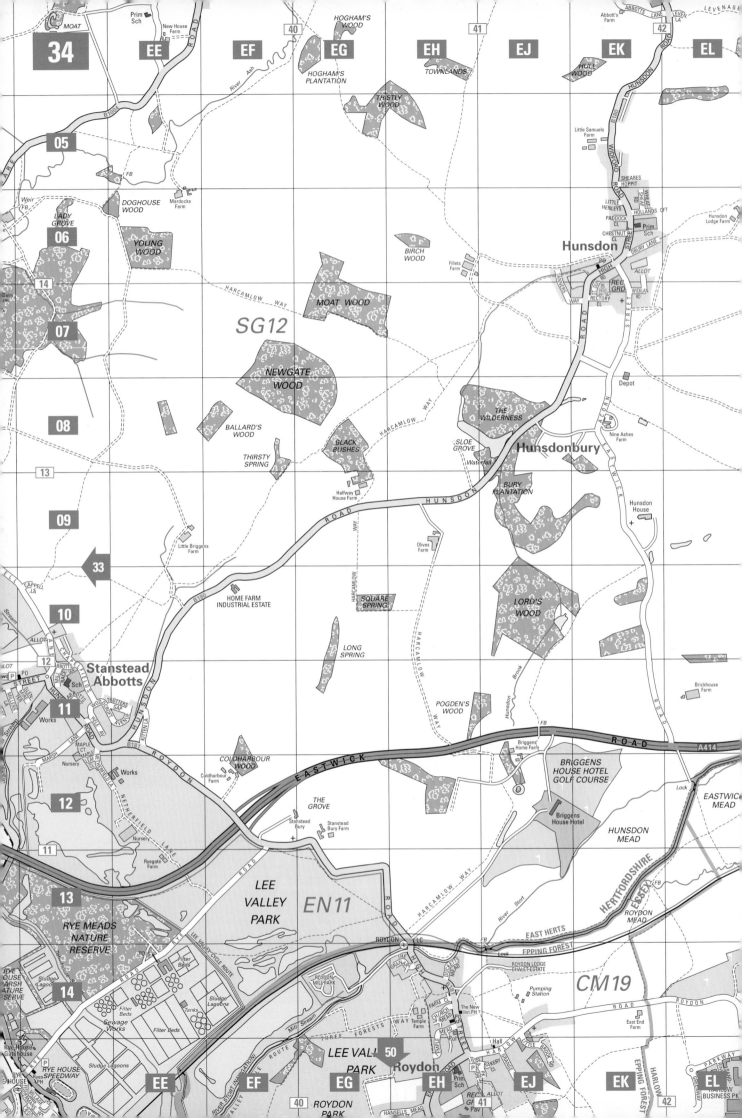

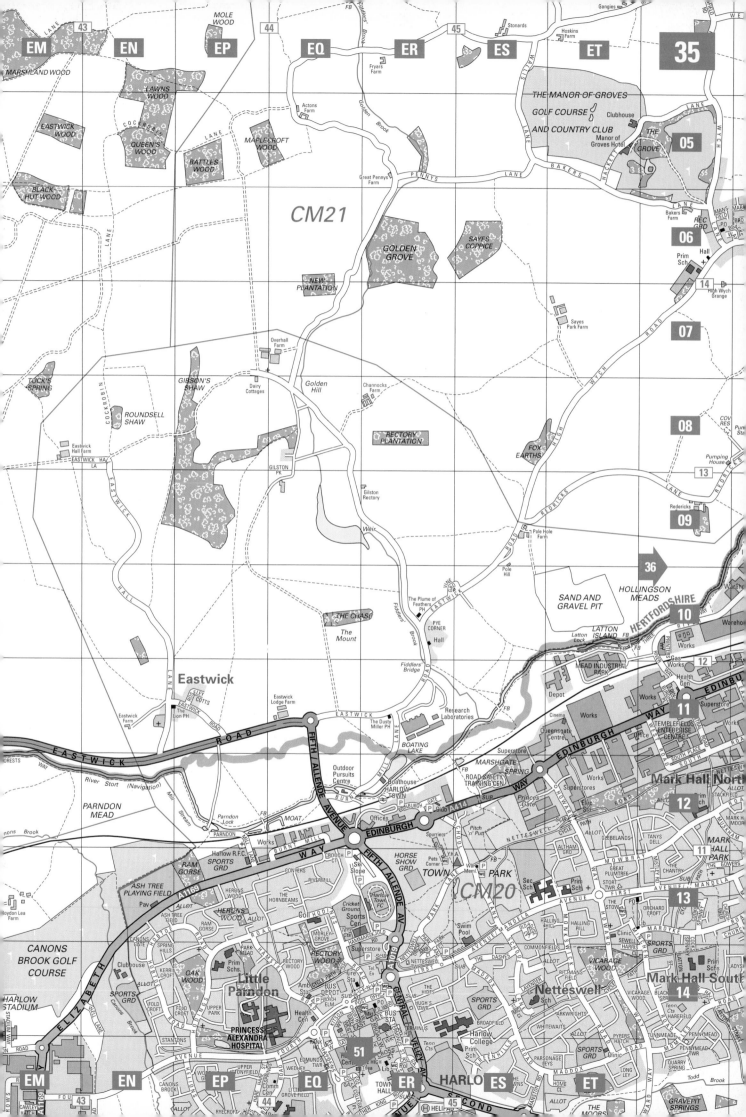

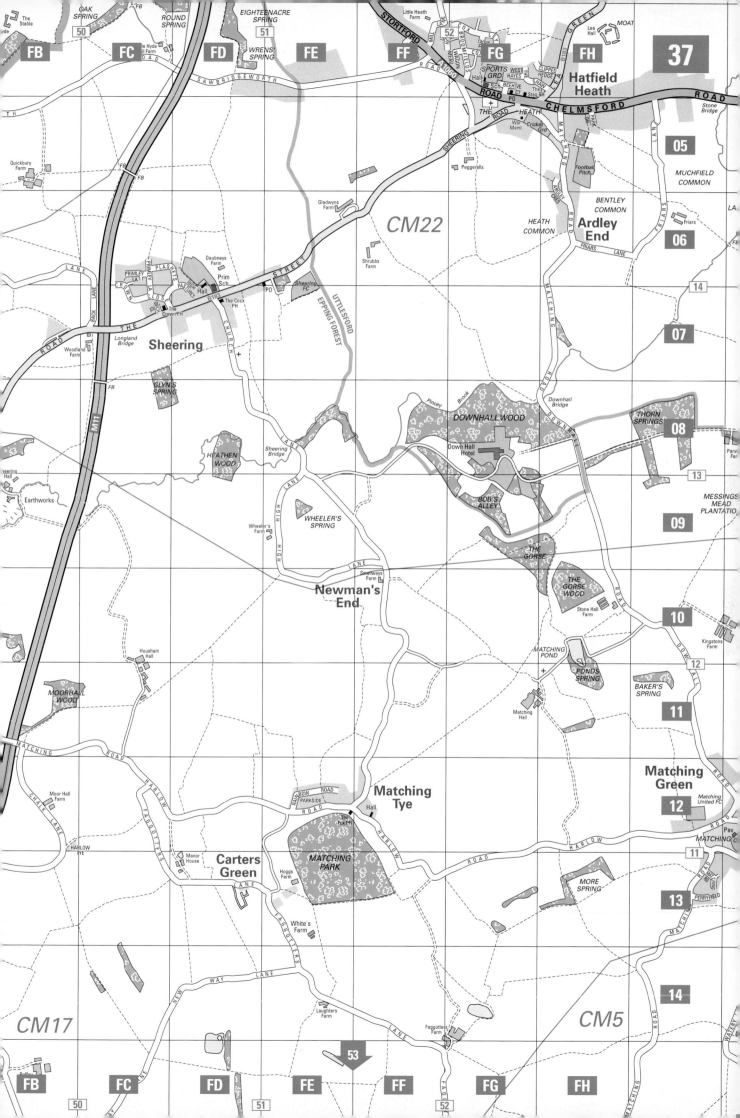

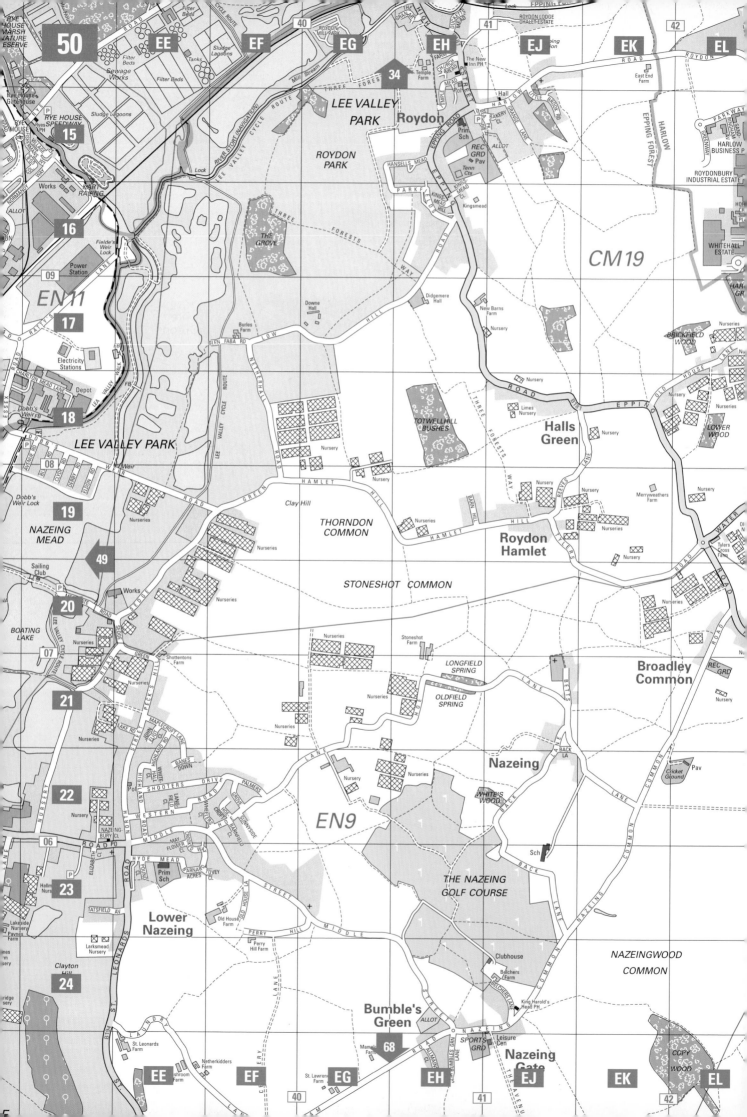

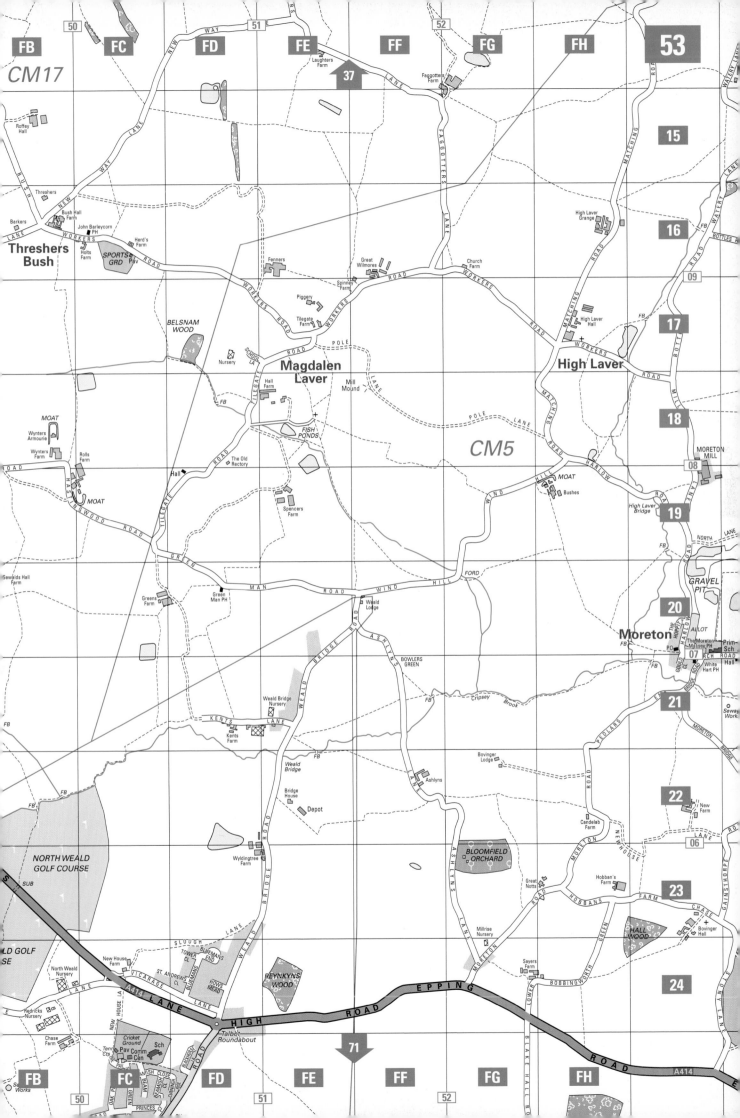

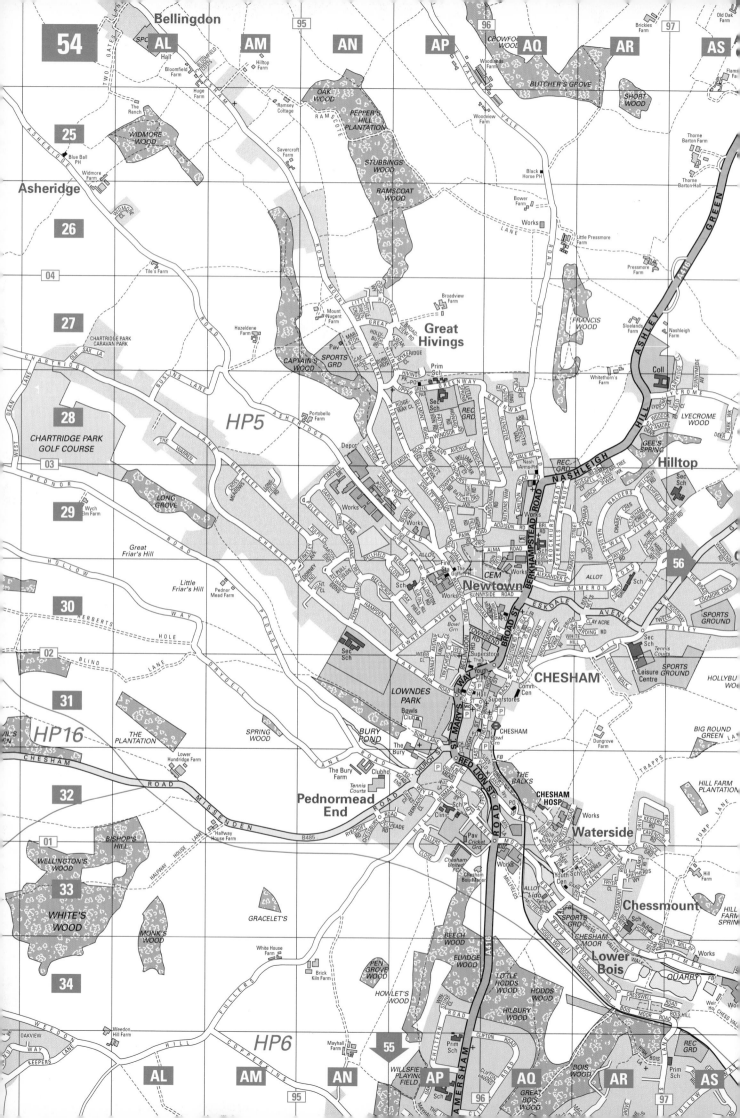

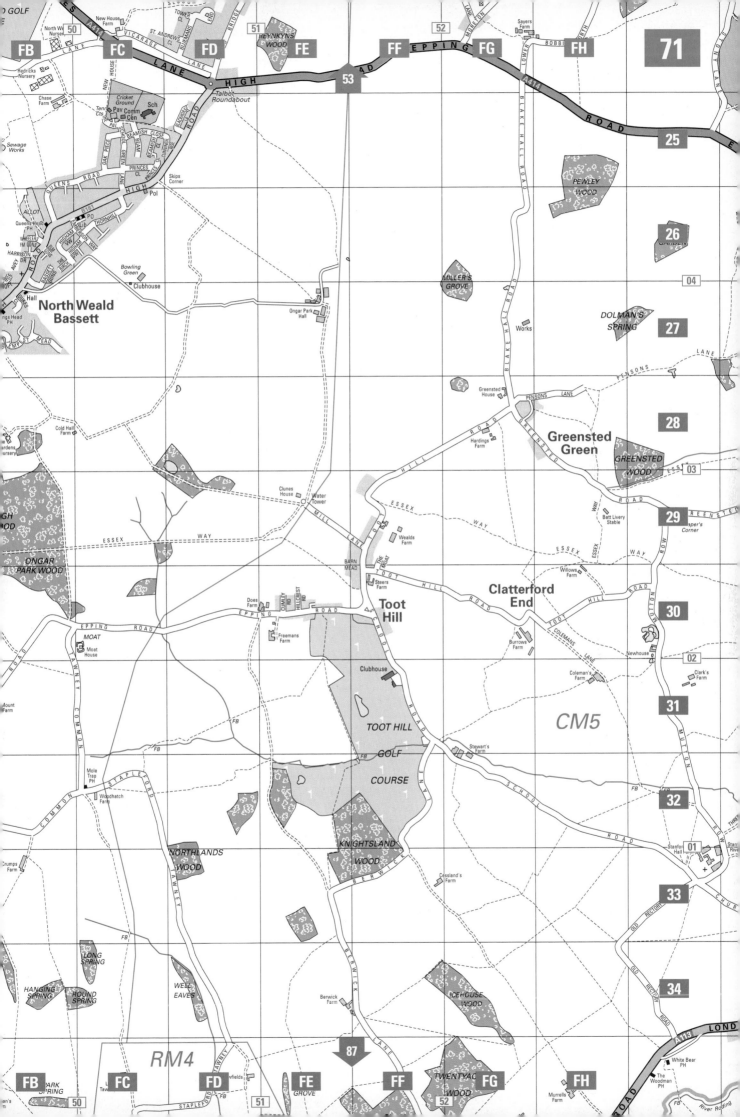

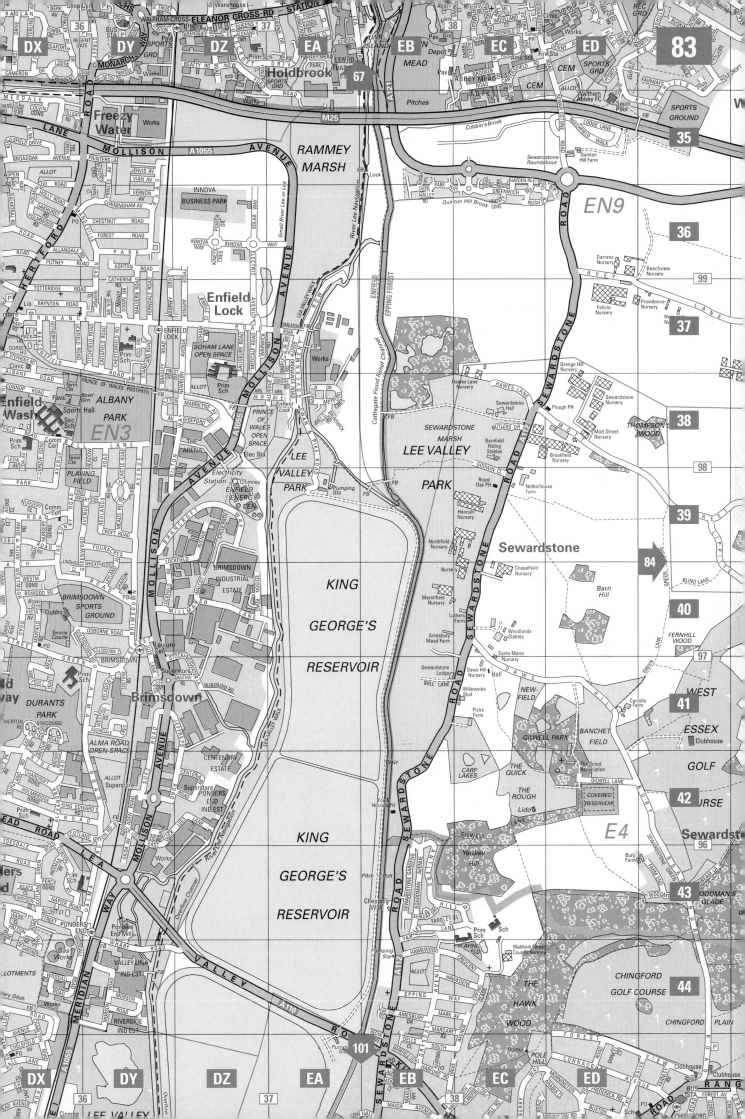

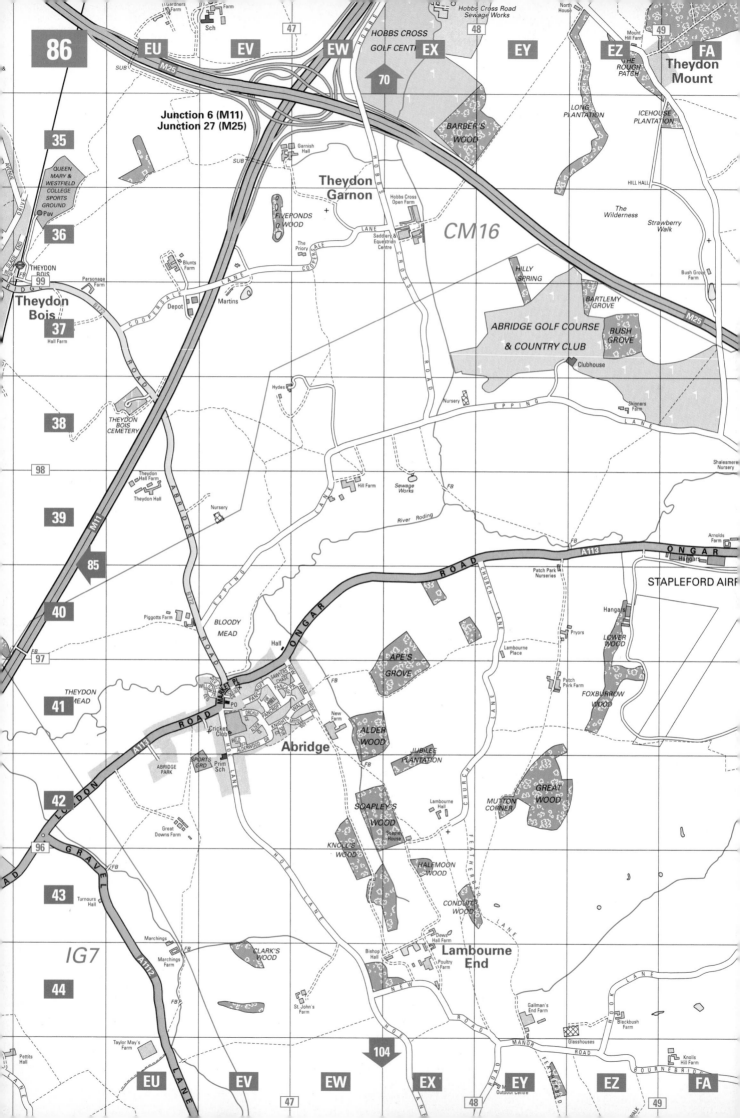

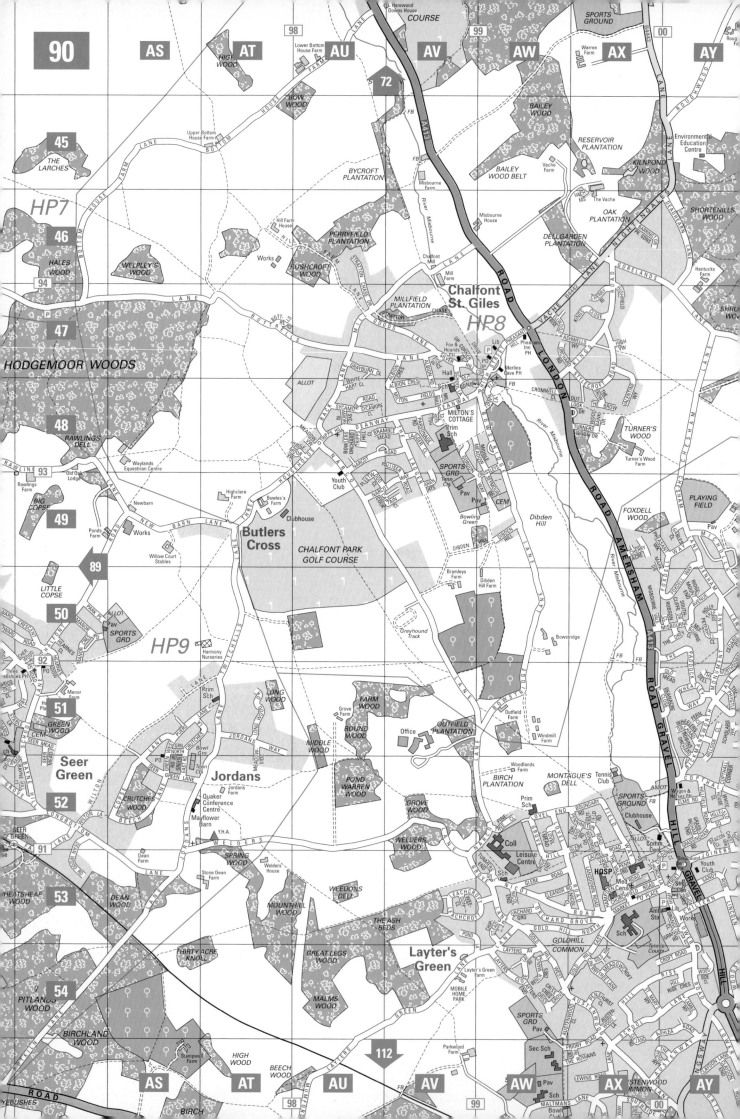

RAINHAM MARSHES
Silt Lagoons

168

FJ **FK** **FL** **FM** **FN** **FP** **FQ**

54 55 56

148

Works

LONDON A1306 ROAD

PURFLEET IND PARK

Nursery

Bowling Green

Clubhouse

SPORTS GROUND

SPORTS GROUND

Fanns Farm

75

WENNINGTON MARSHES

AVELEY MARSHES

RIFLE RANGES

LC

Depot

Mar

Dyke

RM13

RM1

76

COV RES

79

WATER

Works

FANNS RISE

PURFLEET

Prim Sch

PO

TANK

Oil Depot

Works

Channel Tunnel Rd

77

THURROCK

HAVERING

HAVERING
BEXLEY

LONDON

Oil Storage Tanks

PURFLEET

CHALK PIT

Beacon Hill

RM19

78

Crayford Ness

DA8

LANDAU WAY

Works

DAYTON DRIVE

Jetty

Harrisons Wharf

Works

Mill

Mill

HELIPAD
Jetty
Pier

78

The Saltings

Sailing Club

DARENT INDUSTRIAL PARK

MAYPOLE CRESCENT

NESS ROAD

BURNETT

FLOOD BARRIER

Jetty

Mill

Oil Depot

79

Works

Chimney

167

80

SLADE ROAD

CANADA WAY

DURHAM WAY

PIPER RD

LAMB WAY

DARTFORD SALT MARSHES

THURROCK
KENT

Jetty

Jetty

77

HILDEN DR
COMPTON DR
WALLHOUSE RD

HOLLYWOOD WAY

SPORTS

Longreach Sewage
Treatment Works

Jetty

81

HAZEL DRIVE
HAZEL RD

SPORTS GRD

Clubho

MOAT

Howbury Farm

CRAYFORD MARSHES

JOYCE GREEN LANE

DA1

Littlebrook
Power Station

82

RAIL DEPOT

BEXLEY
DARTFORD

River Darent

Joyce Green Farm

76

Chemical Works

Tenn Cts

FB

83

Chemical Works

BEXLEY
DARTFORD

WAY
A206

UNIVERSITY

West Kent Main Sewer

UNIVERSITY

WAY

DARTFORD NORTHERN BYPASS

Toll

CEM

Holiday Inn Express

84

BARNES CRAY

Depot & Civic
Amenity Site

Works

UNIVERSITY ROAD

SWAN BUSINESS PARK

MILLSIDE INDUSTRIAL ESTATE

BURNHAM

DARTFORD FRESH MARSHES

GLAXOWELLCOME

Prim Sch

Prim Sch

Junction 1a

CRAYFORD MARSHES

Farmers Ph

Prim Sch

Mill

Works

188

CROSSWAYS BUS PARK

Hilton

FJ **FK** **FL** **FM** **FN** **FP** **FQ**

54 55 56

REC GRD

VICTORIA INDUSTRIAL EST

Gas Works

VERSIDE IND EST

GlaxoWellc

Youth Cen

A2026

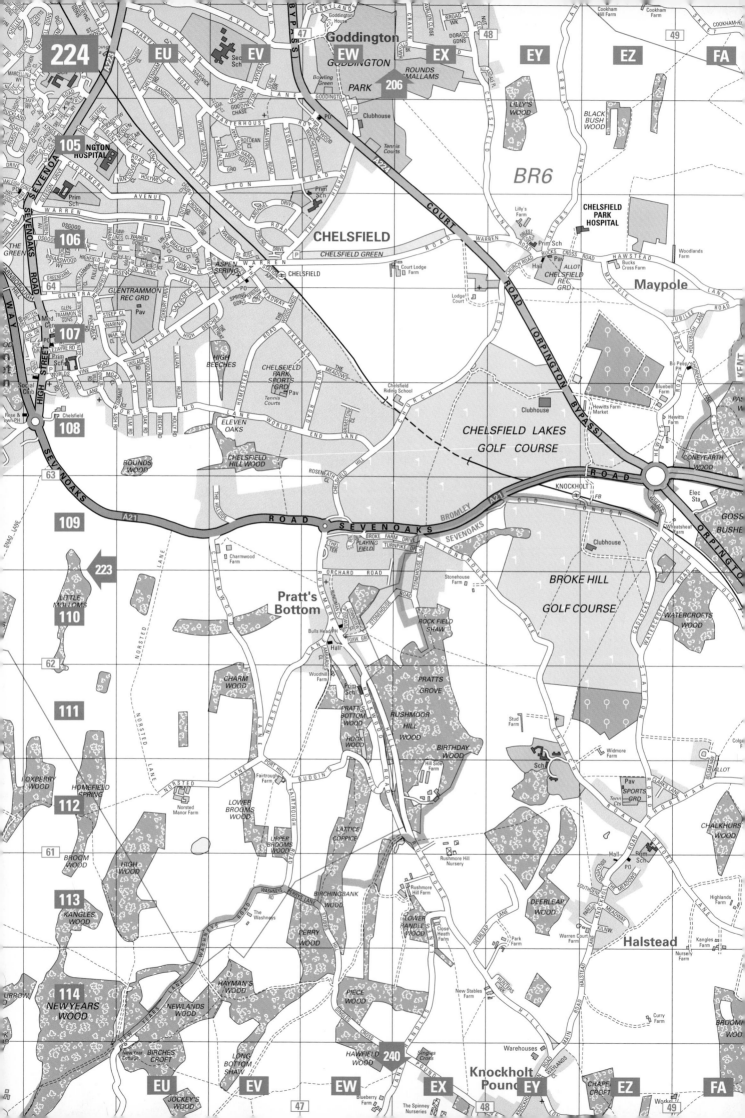

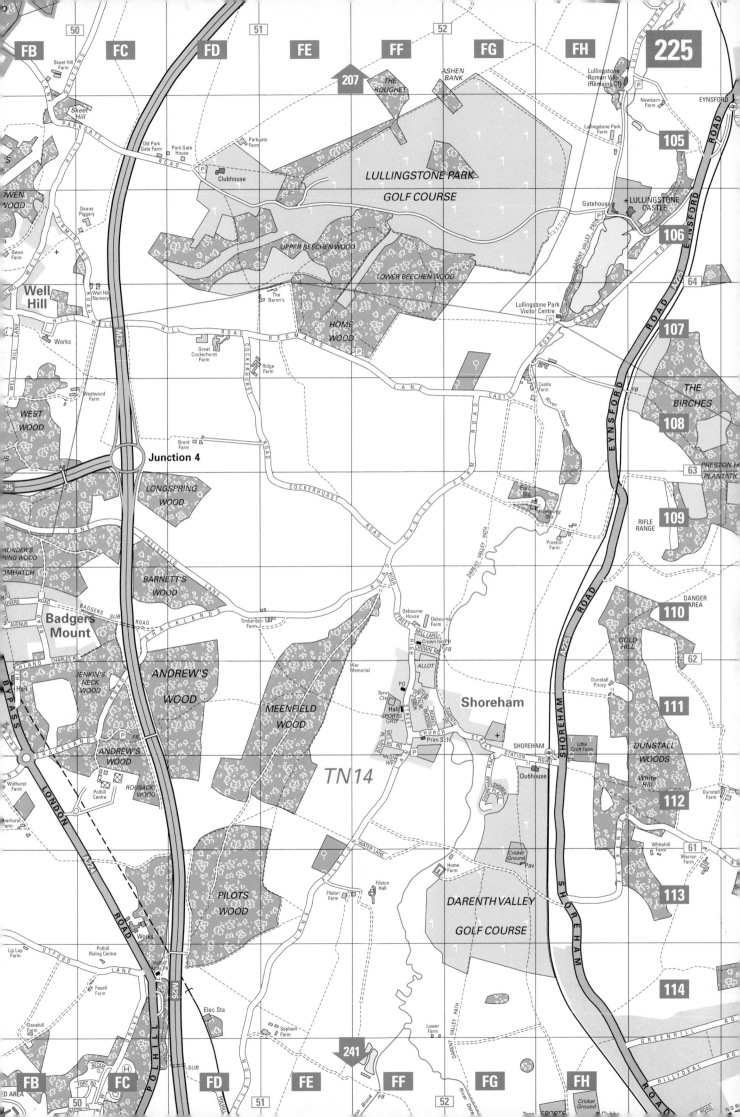

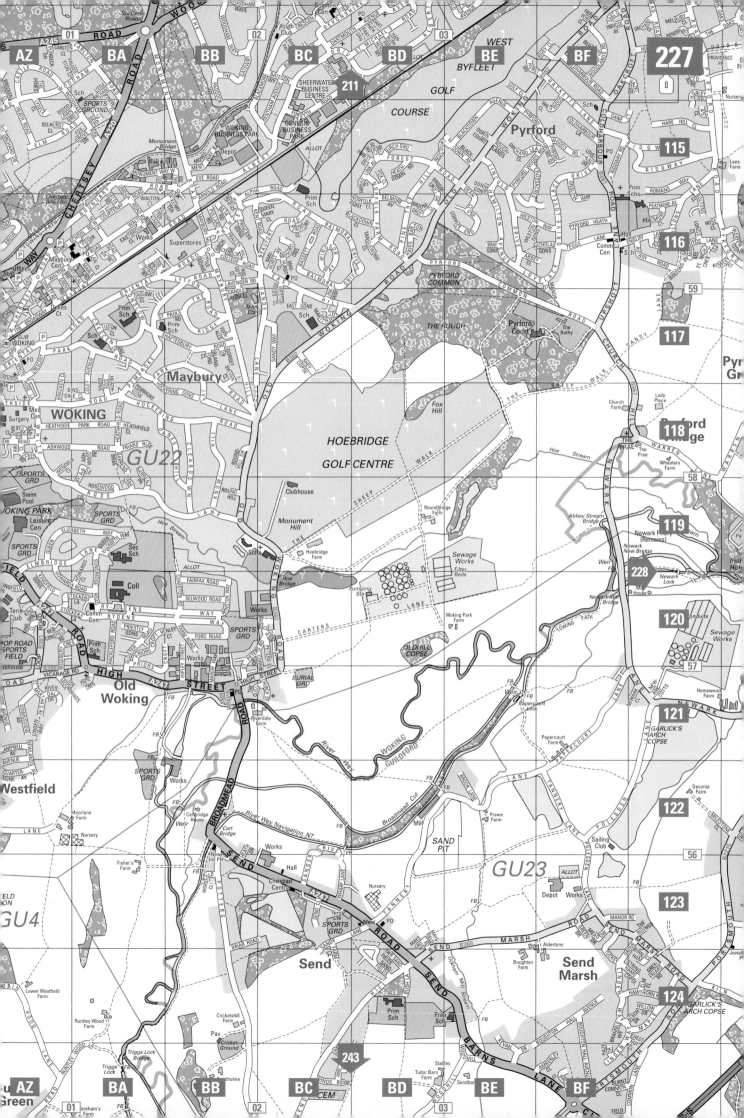

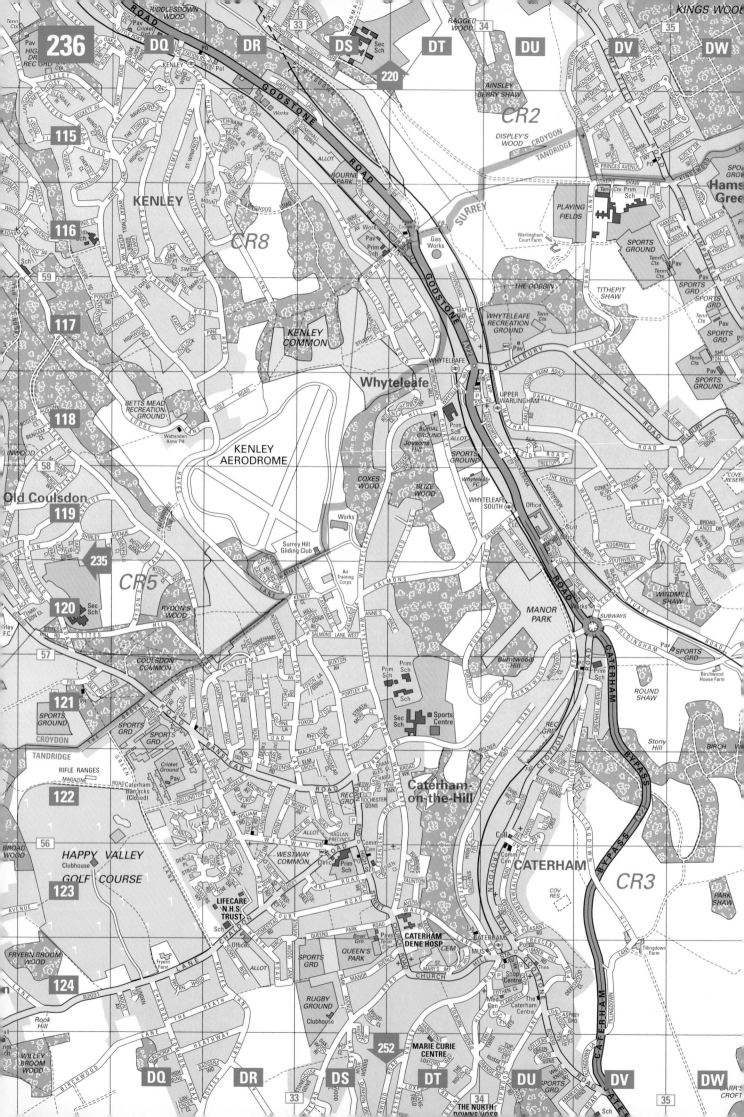

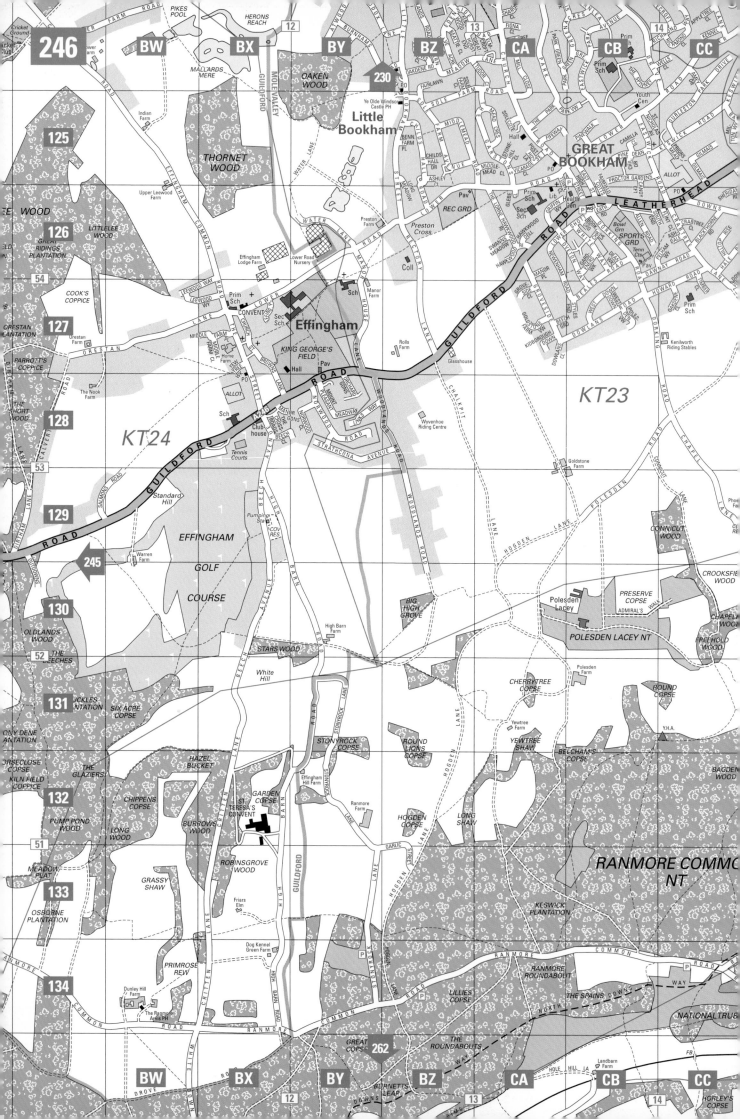

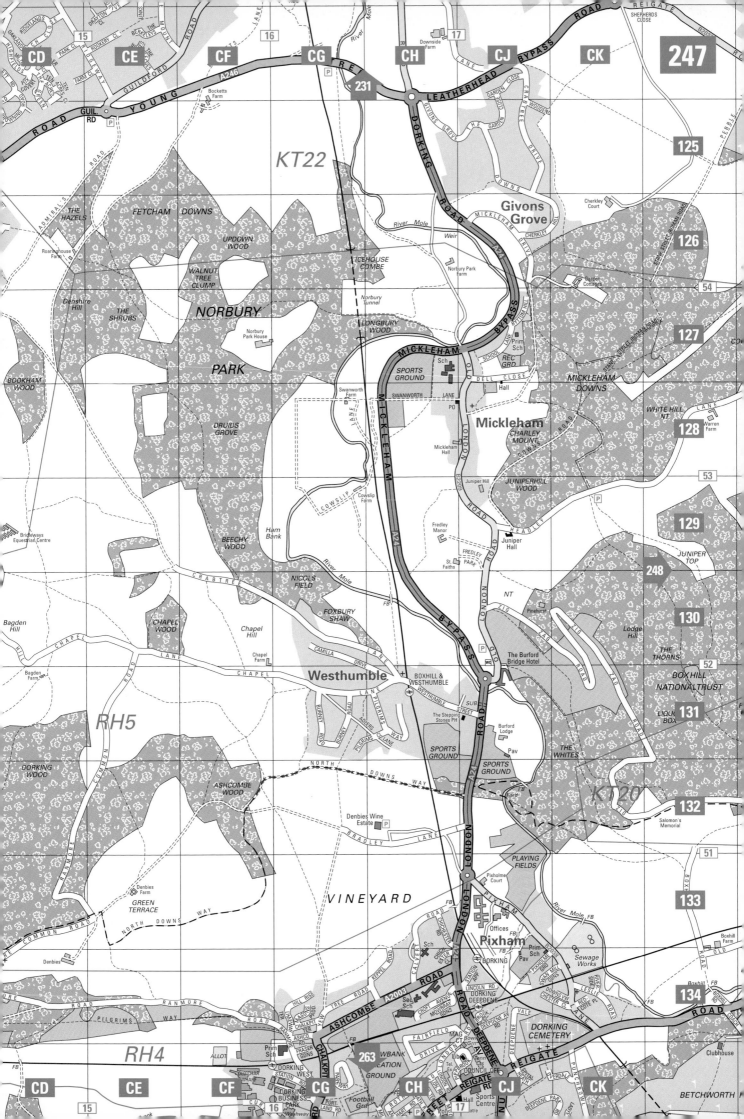

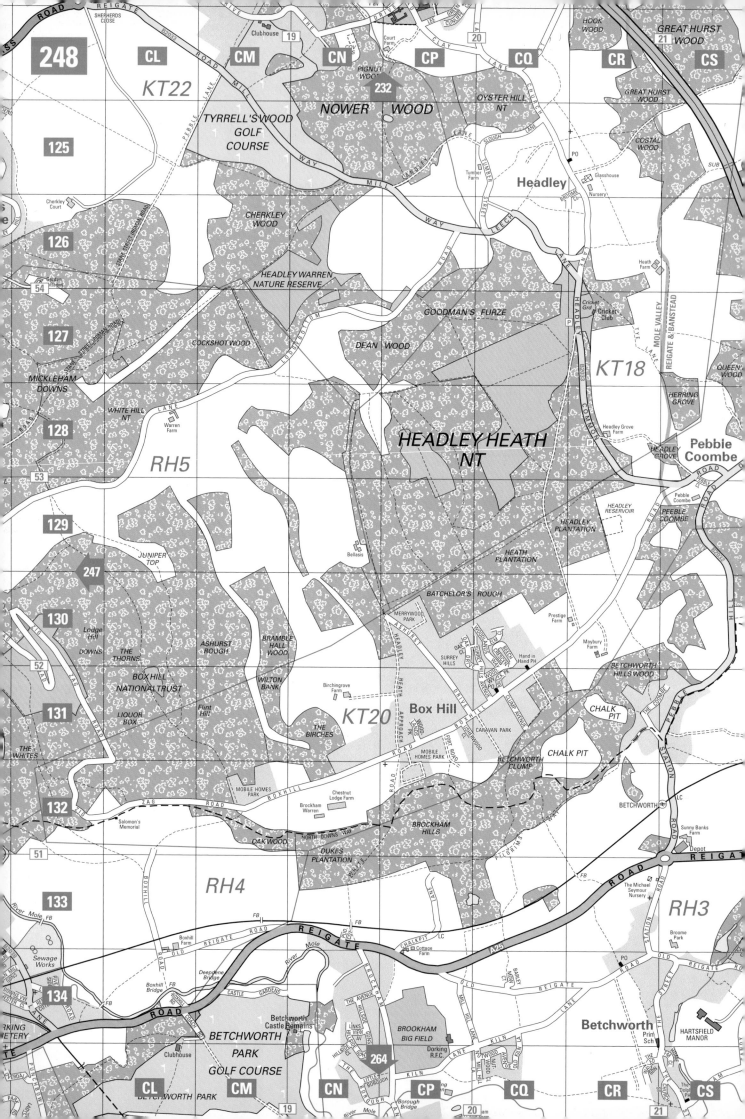

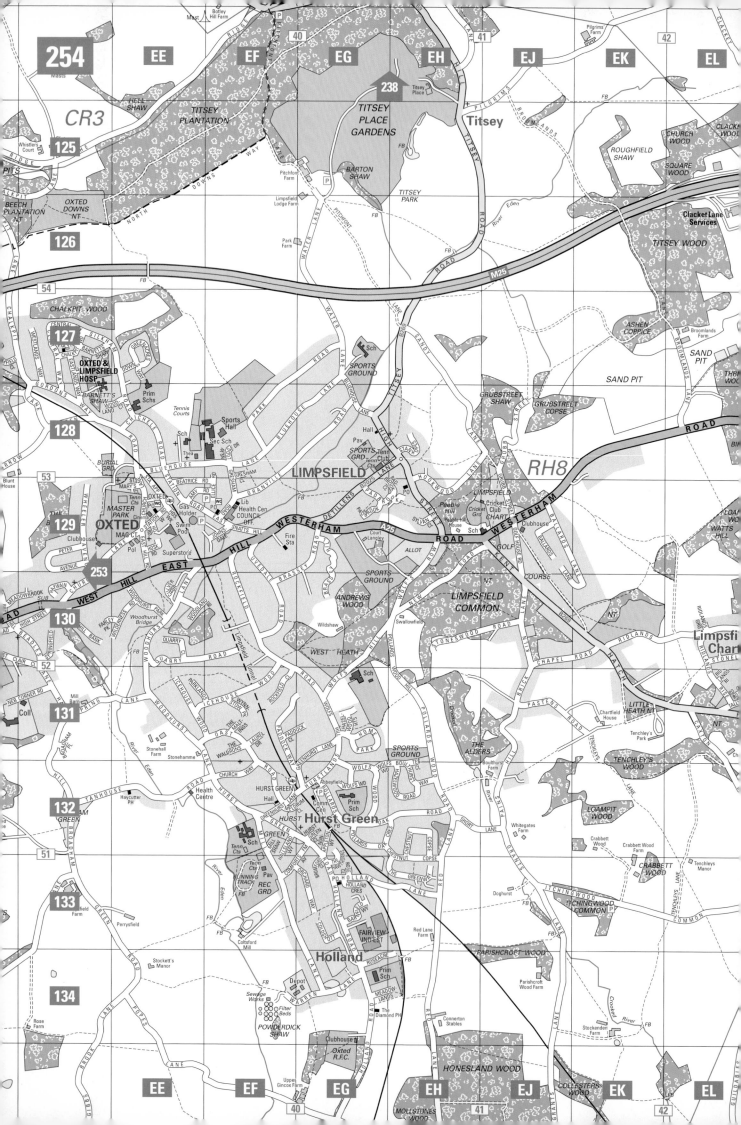

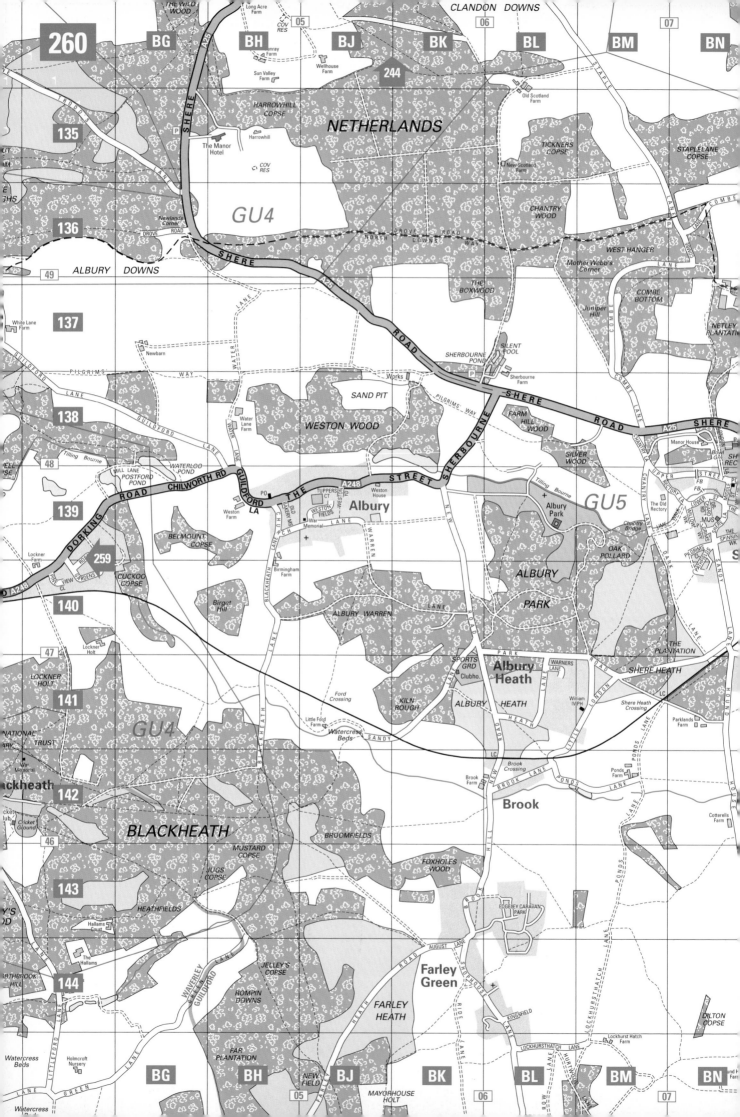

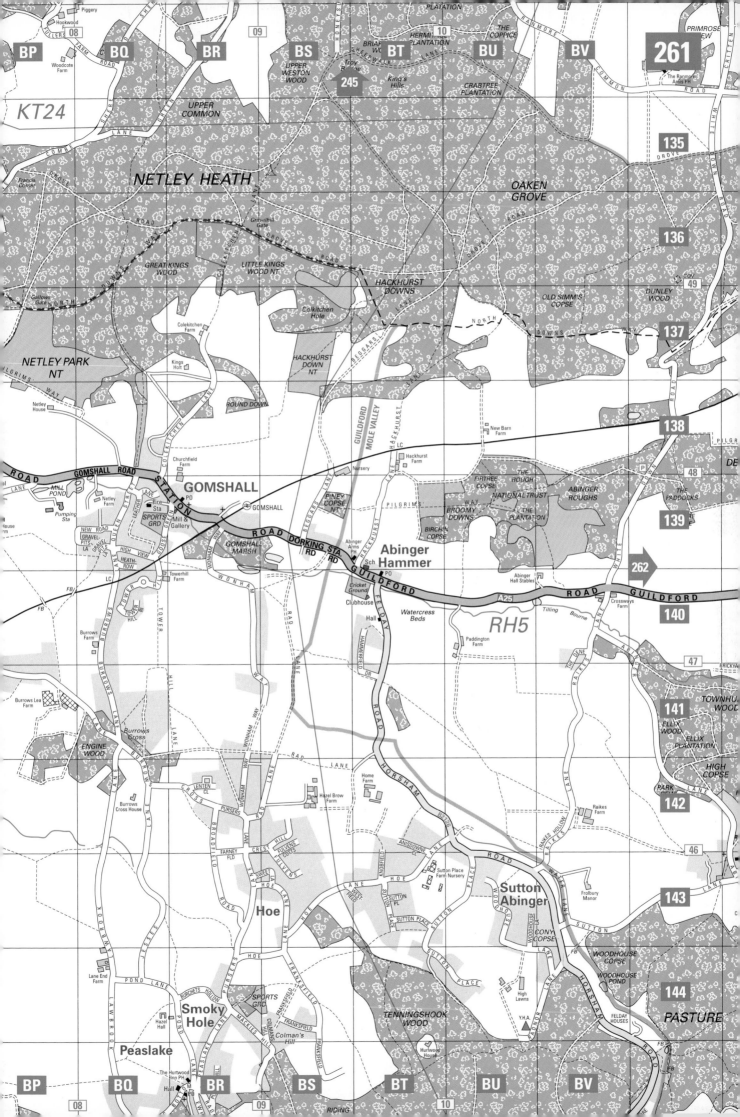

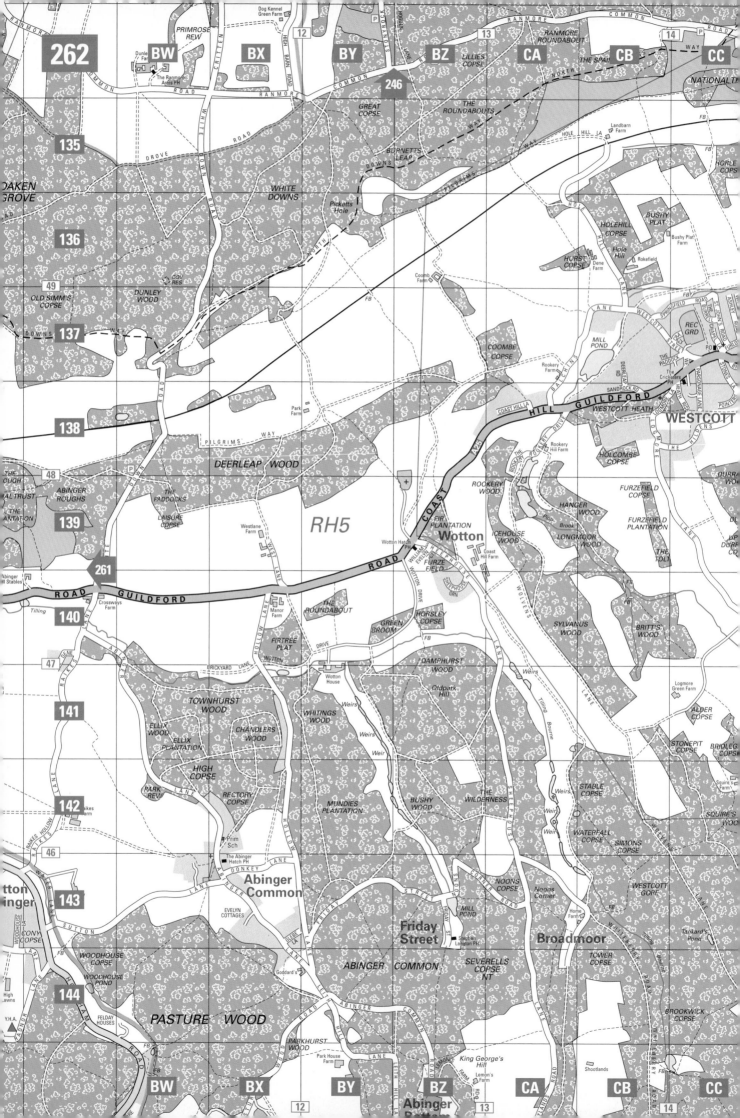

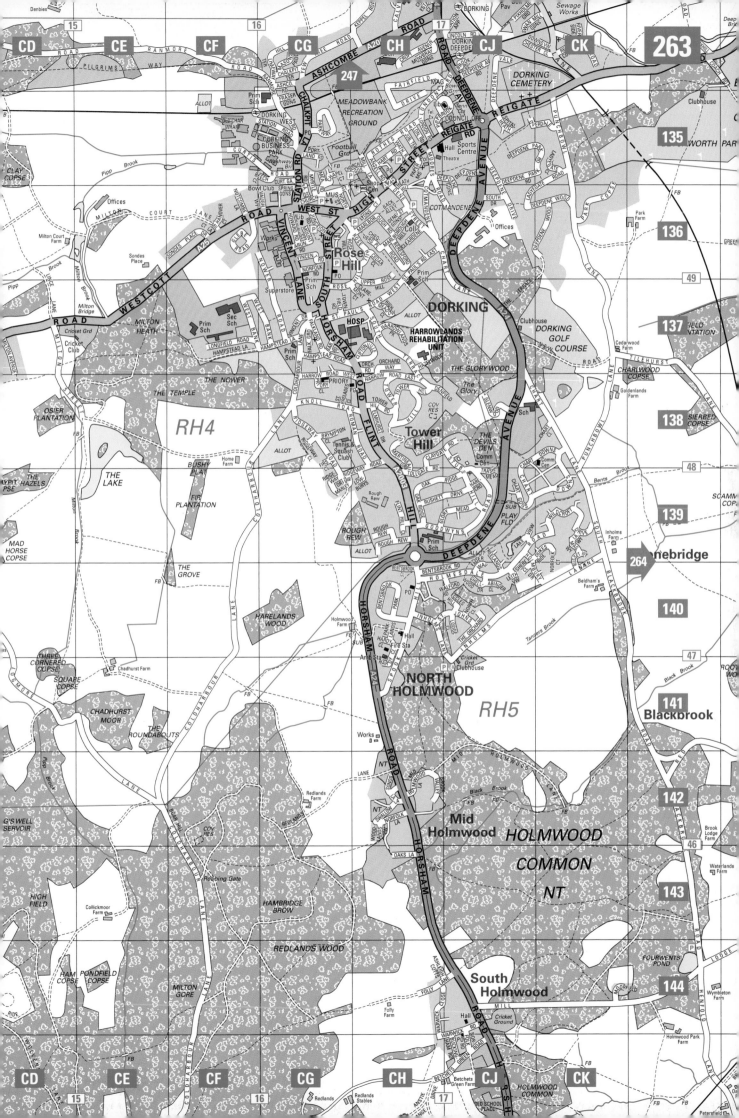

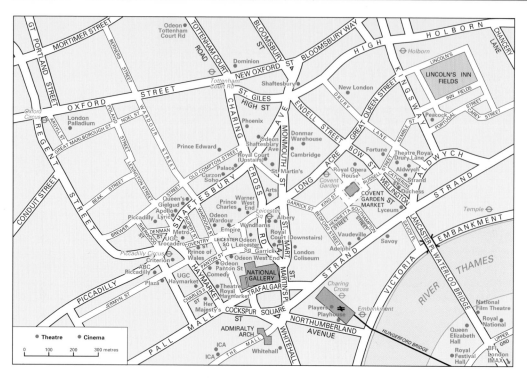

THEATRES

Adelphi 020 7344 0055
Albery 020 7369 1730
Aldwych 08704 000805
Apollo 020 7494 5070
Arts 020 7836 2132
Cambridge 020 7494 5054
Comedy 020 7369 1731
Criterion 020 7839 8811
Dominion 020 7656 1888
Donmar Warehouse 020 7369 1732
Duchess 020 7494 5076
Fortune 020 7369 1747
Garrick 020 7494 5085
Gielgud 020 7494 5065
Her Majesty's 020 7494 5400
ICA 020 7930 3647
London Coliseum 020 7632 8300
London Palladium 020 7494 5020
Lyceum 08702 439000
Lyric 020 7494 5045
New London 020 7405 0072
Palace 020 7434 0909
Peacock 020 7863 8222
Phoenix 020 7369 1733
Piccadilly 020 7369 1744
Players 020 7839 1134
Playhouse 020 7839 4401
Prince Edward 020 7447 5400
Prince of Wales 020 7839 5987
Queen Elizabeth Hall
 020 7960 4242
Queen's 020 7494 5040
Royal Court Theatre Downstairs
 020 7565 5000
Royal Court Theatre Upstairs
 020 7565 5000
Royal Festival Hall
 020 7960 4242
Royal National 020 7452 3000
Royal Opera House
 020 7304 4000
St. Martin's 020 7836 1443
Savoy 020 7836 8888
Shaftesbury 020 7379 5399
Strand 020 7930 8800
Theatre Royal, Drury Lane
 020 7494 5550
Theatre Royal, Haymarket
 020 7930 8800
Vaudeville 020 7836 9987
Whitehall 020 7369 1735
Wyndhams 020 7369 1736

CINEMAS

ABC Piccadilly 020 7437 3561
BFI London IMAX
 020 7902 1220
Curzon Soho 020 7734 2255
Empire 08700 102030
ICA 020 7930 3647
Metro 020 7734 1506
National Film Theatre
 020 7928 3232

Odeon Leicester Sq
 08705 050007
Odeon Panton St
 08705 050007
Odeon Shaftesbury Avenue
 08705 050007
Odeon Tottenham Court Rd
 08705 050007
Odeon Wardour
 08705 050007
Odeon West End 08705 050007

*Plaza 08700 102030
Prince Charles 020 7437 7003
UGC Haymarket 08709 070712
UGC Trocadero 08709 070716
Warner West End 020 7437 4347

*Temporarily closed

WEST END SHOPPING

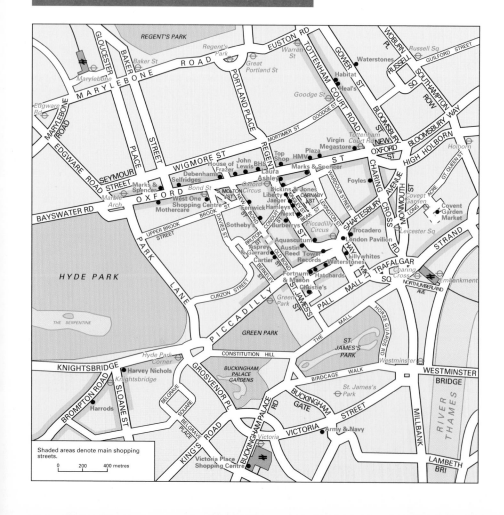

SHOPS

Aquascutum 020 7675 9050
Army & Navy 020 7834 1234
Asprey & Garrard 020 7493 6767
Austin Reed 020 7734 6789
BHS (Oxford St) 020 7629 2011
Cartier 020 7408 5700
Christie's 020 7839 9060
Covent Garden Market 020 7836 9137
Debenhams 020 7580 3000
Dickins & Jones 020 7734 7070
Fenwick 020 7629 9161
Fortnum & Mason 020 7734 8040
Foyles 020 7437 5660
Habitat (Tottenham Court Rd)
 020 7631 3880
Hamleys 020 7734 3161
Harrods 020 7730 1234
Harvey Nichols 020 7235 5000
Hatchards 020 7439 9921
Heal's 020 7636 1666
HMV 020 7631 3423
House of Frazer 020 7529 4700
Jaeger 020 7200 4000
John Lewis 020 7629 7711
Laura Ashley (Regent St) 020 7355 1363
Liberty 020 7734 1234
Lillywhites 020 7930 3181
London Pavilion 020 7437 1838
Marks & Spencer
 (Marble Arch) 020 7935 7954
Marks & Spencer (Oxford St)
 020 7437 7722
Mothercare 020 7629 6621
Next (Regent St) 020 7434 2515
Plaza on Oxford St 020 7637 8811
Selfridges 020 7629 1234
Sotheby's 020 7293 5000
Top Shop & Top Man 020 7636 7700
Tower Records 020 7439 2500
Trocadero 020 7439 1791
Victoria Place Shopping Centre
 020 7931 8811
Virgin Megastore 020 7580 5822
Waterstones 020 7636 1577
Waterstones 020 7851 2400

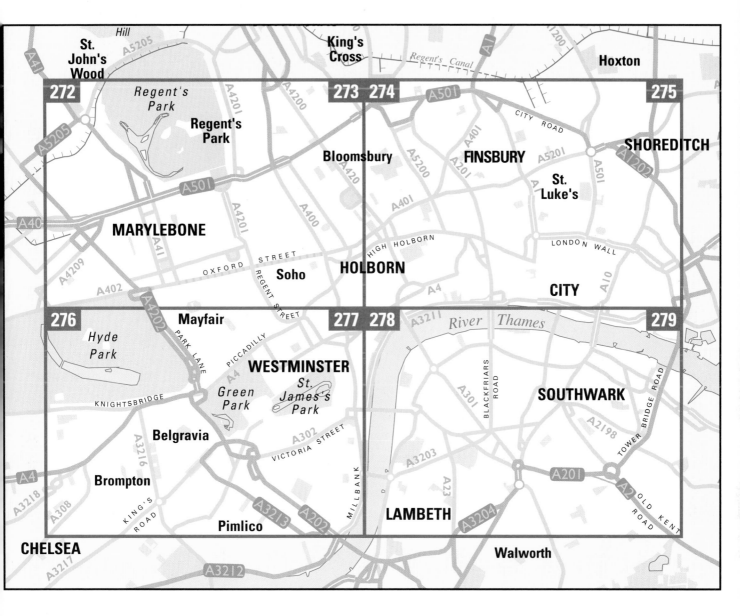

St. John's Wood

Hill A5205

King's Cross

Regent's Canal

Hoxton

272

Regent's Park

Regent's Park

Bloomsbury

273 **274**

A501

FINSBURY

275

SHOREDITCH

A5205

A5200

A5201

A1202

St. Luke's

CITY ROAD

MARYLEBONE

A501

A401

A41

A400

A4201

HIGH HOLBORN

LONDON WALL

OXFORD STREET

REGENT STREET

Soho

HOLBORN

A4

A10

CITY

A4209

A402

A4202

276

Mayfair

277 **278**

River Thames

279

Hyde Park

PARK LANE

PICCADILLY

A3211

BLACKFRIARS ROAD

TOWER BRIDGE ROAD

A4

WESTMINSTER

St. James's Park

A301

SOUTHWARK

KNIGHTSBRIDGE

Green Park

A2198

Belgravia

A3216

VICTORIA STREET

A302

A3203

A201

A2

A308

Brompton

KING'S ROAD

A3213

A202

MILLBANK

A23

LAMBETH

A3204

OLD KENT ROAD

CHELSEA

A4

A3218

Pimlico

Walworth

A3217

A3212

KEY TO MAP SYMBOLS

Dual **A4**	Primary route		Main railway station	Fire Sta	Fire station		Leisure and tourism
Dual **A40**	'A' road		Other railway station	PO	Post office		Shopping
B504	'B' road		London Underground station	Lib	Library		Administration and law
	Other road / One way street	DLR	Docklands Light Railway station	▲	Monument / Statue		Health and welfare
	Street market		Bus / Coach station		Cinema		Education
	Pedestrian street	P	Car park	+	Church		Industry and commerce
	Access restriction	i	Tourist information centre	☾	Mosque		Public open space
	Track / Footpath		Theatre	✡	Synagogue		Park / Garden / Sports ground
	Ferry	⊠	Major hotel	Mormon ■	Other place of worship		Cemetery
CITY	Borough boundary	USA	Embassy	WC	Public toilet		
EC2	Postal district boundary	POL	Police station	□	Tower block		
		10	Grid reference	274	Page continuation number		

Scale
1: 10,000 6.3 inches to 1 mile/10cm to 1 km

0   ¼   ½ mile

0   0.25   0.5   0.75   1 kilometre

The following is a comprehensive listing of the places of interest which appear in this atlas. **Bold** references can be found within the Central London enlarged scale section (pages 272 - 279).

The following is a comprehensive listing of all named places which appear in this atlas. **Bold** references can be found within the Central London enlarged scale section (pages 272 - 279). For an explanation of post town abbreviations please consult page 287.

Place	Page	Ref
Downe, Orp.	223	EM111
Downham, Brom.	184	EF92
Downside, Cob.	229	BV118
Ducks Island, Barn.	79	CX44
Dulwich SE21	182	DS87
Dunton Green, Sev.	241	FC119
Ealing W5	137	CJ73
Earls Court SW5	159	CZ78
Earlsfield SW18	180	DC88
Earlswood, Red.	266	DF136
East Acton W3	138	CR74
East Barnet, Barn.	80	DE44
East Bedfont, Felt.	175	BS88
East Burnham, Slou.	131	AN67
East Clandon, Guil.	244	BL131
East Dulwich SE22	182	DU86
East Ewell, Sutt.	217	CX110
East Finchley N2	120	DD56
East Ham E6	144	EL68
East Horsley, Lthd.	245	BS127
East Molesey, E.Mol.	197	CD98
East Sheen SW14	158	CR84
East Wickham, Well.	166	EU80
Eastbury, Nthwd.	93	BS49
Eastcote, Pnr.	116	BW58
Eastcote Village, Pnr.	115	BV57
Eastwick, Harl.	35	EP11
Eden Park, Beck.	203	EA99
Edgware, Edg.	96	CP50
Edmonton N9	100	DU49
Effingham, Lthd.	246	BY127
Egham, Egh.	173	BA93
Egham Hythe, Stai.	173	BE93
Egham Wick, Egh.	172	AU94
Egypt, Slou.	111	AQ63
Ellenbrook, Hat.	44	CR19
Elm Corner, Wok.	228	BN119
Elm Park, Horn.	127	FH64
Elmers End, Beck.	203	DY97
Elmstead, Chis.	184	EK92
Elstree, Borwd.	77	CK43
Eltham SE9	184	EK86
Emerson Park, Horn.	128	FL58
Enfield, Enf.	82	DT41
Enfield Highway, Enf.	82	DW41
Enfield Lock, Enf.	83	DZ37
Enfield Town, Enf.	82	DR40
Enfield Wash, Enf.	83	DX38
Englefield Green, Egh.	172	AV92
Epping, Epp.	69	ES31
Epping Green, Epp.	51	EN24
Epping Green, Hert.	47	DK21
Epsom, Epsom	216	CQ114
Erith, Erith	167	FD79
Esher, Esher	214	CB105
Essendon, Hat.	46	DE17
Eton, Wind.	151	AQ80
Eton Wick, Wind.	151	AL77
Ewell, Epsom	217	CU110
Eynsford, Dart.	208	FL103
Fairmile, Cob.	214	BZ112
Falconwood, Well.	165	ER83
Farleigh, Warl.	221	DZ114
Farley Green, Guil.	260	BK144
Farnborough, Orp.	223	EP106
Farncombe, Gdmg.	258	AT144
Farnham Common, Slou.	131	AQ65
Farnham Royal, Slou.	131	AQ68
Farningham, Dart.	208	FN100
Fawkham Green, Long.	209	FV104
Felden, Hem.H.	40	BG24
Feltham, Felt.	175	BU89
Felthamhill, Felt.	175	BT92
Fetcham, Lthd.	231	CD123
Fiddlers Hamlet, Epp.	70	EW32
Fifield, Maid.	150	AD81
Finchley N3	98	DB53
Finsbury EC1	**274**	**E2**
Finsbury Park N4	121	DN60
Flamstead End, Wal.Cr.	66	DU28
Flaunden, Hem.H.	57	BB33
Fleetville, St.Alb.	43	CG20
Foots Cray, Sid.	186	EV93
Forest Gate E7	124	EG64
Forest Hill SE23	183	DX88
Forestdale, Croy.	221	EA109
Fortis Green N2	120	DF56
Forty Green, Beac.	88	AH50
Forty Hill, Enf.	82	DS37
Freezy Water, Wal.Cr.	83	DY35
Friday Hill E4	101	ED47
Friday Street, Dor.	262	BZ143
Friern Barnet N11	98	DE49
Froghole, Eden.	255	ER133
Frogmore, St.Alb.	61	CE28
Fulham SW6	159	CY82
Fullwell Cross, Ilf.	103	ER53
Fulmer, Slou.	112	AX63
Furzedown SW17	180	DG92
Gadebridge, Hem.H.	39	BF18
Gants Hill, Ilf.	125	EN57
Ganwick Corner, Barn.	80	DB35
Garston, Wat.	76	BW35
Gatton, Reig.	250	DF128
George Green, Slou.	132	AX72
Gerrards Cross, Ger.Cr.	112	AX58
Gidea Park, Rom.	127	FG55
Givons Grove, Lthd.	247	CJ126
Goathurst Common, Sev.	256	FB130

Place	Page	Ref
Godden Green, Sev.	257	FN125
Goddington, Orp.	206	EW104
Godstone, Gdse.	252	DV131
Goffs Oak, Wal.Cr.	66	DQ29
Golders Green NW11	120	DA59
Goldsworth Park, Wok.	226	AU117
Gomshall, Guil.	261	BR139
Goodley Stock, West.	255	EP130
Goodmayes, Ilf.	126	EV61
Gospel Oak NW5	120	DG63
Grange Hill, Chig.	103	ER51
Grange Park N21	81	DP43
Gravesend, Grav.	191	GJ85
Grays, Grays	170	GA78
Great Amwell, Ware	33	DZ10
Great Bookham, Lthd.	246	CB125
Great Hivings, Chesh.	54	AP27
Great Parndon, Harl.	51	EP17
Great Warley, Brwd.	107	FV53
Green Street, Borwd.	78	CP37
Green Street Green, Dart.	189	FU93
Green Street Green, Orp.	223	ES107
Greenford, Grnf.	136	CB69
Greenhithe, Green.	189	FV85
Greensted Green, Ong.	71	FH28
Greenwich SE10	163	ED79
Grove Park SE12	184	EG89
Grove Park W4	158	CP80
Grovehill, Hem.H.	40	BL16
Guildford, Guil.	258	AU137
Guildford Park, Guil.	258	AV135
Gunnersbury W4	158	CP77
Hackbridge, Wall.	201	DH103
Hackney E8	142	DV65
Hackney Wick E9	123	EA64
Hacton, Rain.	128	FM64
Hadley, Barn.	79	CZ40
Hadley Wood, Barn.	80	DD38
Haggerston E2	142	DT68
Hainault, Ilf.	103	ES52
Hale End E4	101	ED51
Hall Grove, Welw.G.C.	30	DB11
Halls Green, Harl.	50	EJ18
Halstead, Sev.	224	EZ113
Ham, Rich.	177	CK90
Hammerfield, Hem.H.	40	BG20
Hammersmith W6	159	CW78
Hammond Street, Wal.Cr.	66	DR26
Hampstead NW3	120	DD63
Hampstead Garden Suburb N2	120	DC57
Hampton, Hmptn.	196	CB95
Hampton Hill, Hmptn.	176	CC93
Hampton Wick, Kings.T.	197	CH95
Hamsey Green, Warl.	236	DW116
Handside, Welw.G.C.	29	CV10
Hanwell W7	137	CF74
Hanworth, Felt.	176	BX91
Hare Street, Harl.	51	EP16
Harefield, Uxb.	92	BL53
Harlesden NW10	138	CS68
Harlington, Hayes	155	BQ79
Harlow, Harl.	51	ER15
Harmondsworth, West Dr.	154	BK79
Harold Hill, Rom.	106	FL50
Harold Park, Rom.	106	FN51
Harold Wood, Rom.	106	FL54
Harringay N8	121	DN57
Harrow, Har.	117	CD59
Harrow on the Hill, Har.	117	CE61
Harrow Weald, Har.	95	CD53
Hartley Green, Long.	209	FX99
Hastingwood, Harl.	52	EZ19
Hatch End, Pnr.	94	BY51
Hatfield, Hat.	45	CV17
Hatfield Garden Village, Hat.	29	CU14
Hatfield Hyde, Welw.G.C.	29	CZ12
Hatton, Felt.	155	BT84
Havering Park, Rom.	104	FA50
Havering-atte-Bower, Rom.	105	FE48
Hawley, Dart.	188	FM92
Hayes, Brom.	204	EG103
Hayes, Hayes	135	BS72
Hayes End, Hayes	135	BQ71
Hayes Town, Hayes	155	BS75
Hazelwood, Sev.	223	ER111
Headley, Epsom	248	CQ125
Headstone, Har.	116	CC56
Hedgerley, Slou.	111	AR60
Hemel Hempstead, Hem.H.	40	BK21
Hendon NW4	119	CV56
Herne Hill SE24	182	DQ85
Heronsgate, Rick.	91	BD45
Hersham, Walt.	214	BX107
Hertford, Hert.	31	DP10
Hertford Heath, Hert.	32	DW12
Hertingfordbury, Hert.	31	DL10
Heston, Houns.	156	BZ80
Hextable, Swan.	187	FG94
High Barnet, Barn.	79	CX40
High Beach, Loug.	84	EG39
High Laver, Ong.	53	FH17
High Wych, Saw.	36	EV6
Higham Hill E17	101	DY54
Highams Park E4	101	ED50
Highbury N5	121	DP64
Higher Denham, Uxb.	113	BB59
Highfield, Hem.H.	40	BL18
Highgate N6	120	DG61
Highwood Hill NW7	97	CU47

Place	Page	Ref
Hill End, Uxb.	92	BH51
Hillingdon, Uxb.	134	BN69
Hilltop, Chesh.	54	AR28
Hinchley Wood, Esher	197	CF104
Hither Green SE13	184	EE86
Hoddesdon, Hodd.	49	DZ18
Hoe, Guil.	261	BS143
Hogpits Bottom, Hem.H.	57	BA31
Holborn WC2	**274**	**B8**
Holdbrook, Wal.Cr.	67	EA34
Holdens, Welw.G.C.	30	DA6
Holders Hill NW4	97	CX54
Holland, Oxt.	254	EG134
Holloway N7	121	DL63
Holmethorpe, Red.	251	DH132
Holtspur, Beac.	88	AF54
Holyfield, Wal.Abb.	67	ED28
Holyport, Maid.	150	AC78
Holywell, Wat.	75	BS44
Homerton E9	123	DY64
Honor Oak SE23	182	DW86
Honor Oak Park SE4	183	DY86
Hook, Chess.	216	CL105
Hook Green, Dart.	187	FG91
Hook Green, Grav.	190	FZ93
Hook Heath, Wok.	226	AV120
Hookwood, Horl.	268	DC150
Hooley, Couls.	234	DG122
Horley, Horl.	269	DH146
Hornchurch, Horn.	128	FJ61
Horns Green, Sev.	239	ES117
Hornsey N8	121	DM55
Horsell, Wok.	226	AY116
Horton, Epsom	216	CP110
Horton, Slou.	153	BA83
Horton Kirby, Dart.	209	FR98
Hosey Hill, West.	255	ES127
Hounslow, Houns.	156	BZ84
Hounslow West, Houns.	156	BX83
How Wood, St.Alb.	60	CC27
Hoxton N1	**275**	**M1**
Hulberry, Swan.	207	FG103
Hunsdon, Ware	34	EJ6
Hunsdonbury, Ware	34	EJ8
Hunton Bridge, Kings L.	59	BP33
Hurst Green, Oxt.	254	EG132
Hutton, Brwd.	109	GD44
Hutton Mount, Brwd.	109	GB46
Hyde, The NW9	119	CT56
Hythe End, Stai.	173	BB90
Ickenham, Uxb.	115	BQ62
Ilford, Ilf.	125	EQ62
Irons Bottom, Reig.	266	DA142
Isleworth, Islw.	157	CF83
Islington N1	141	DM67
Istead Rise, Grav.	190	GE94
Iver, Iver	133	BF72
Iver Heath, Iver	133	BD69
Ivy Chimneys, Epp.	69	ES32
Jacobs Well, Guil.	242	AY129
Jersey Farm, St.Alb.	43	CJ15
Jordans, Beac.	90	AT52
Joydens Wood, Bex.	187	FC92
Katherines, Harl.	51	EM18
Kenley, Ken.	236	DQ116
Kennington SE11	161	DN79
Kensal Green NW10	139	CW69
Kensal Rise NW6	139	CX68
Kensal Town W10	139	CX70
Kensington W8	159	CZ75
Kent Hatch, Eden.	255	EP131
Kentish Town NW5	141	DJ65
Kenton, Har.	117	CH57
Keston, Brom.	222	EJ106
Kew, Rich.	158	CN79
Kidbrooke SE3	164	EH83
Kilburn NW6	140	DA68
King's Cross N1	141	DK67
Kings Farm, Grav.	191	GJ90
Kings Langley, Kings L.	58	BM30
Kingsbury NW9	118	CP58
Kingsland N1	142	DS65
Kingsmoor, Harl.	51	EQ20
Kingston upon Thames, Kings.T.	198	CL96
Kingston Vale SW15	178	CS91
Kingswood, Tad.	233	CY123
Kingswood, Wat.	59	BV34
Kippington, Sev.	256	FG126
Kitt's End, Barn.	79	CY37
Knockhall, Green.	189	FW85
Knockholt, Sev.	240	EU116
Knockholt Pound, Sev.	240	EX115
Knotty Green, Beac.	88	AJ49
Ladywell SE13	183	EA85
Laleham, Stai.	194	BJ97
Lambeth SE1	**278**	**B6**
Lambourne End, Rom.	86	EX44
Lamorbey, Sid.	185	ET88
Lampton, Houns.	156	CB81
Lane End, Dart.	189	FR92
Langley, Slou.	153	BA76
Langley Vale, Epsom	232	CR120
Langleybury, Kings L.	59	BP34
Latimer, Chesh.	72	AY36
Latton Bush, Harl.	52	EU18
Layter's Green, Ger.Cr.	90	AV54
Lea Bridge E5	123	DX62
Leatherhead, Lthd.	231	CF121
Leatherhead Common, Lthd.	231	CF119

Place	Page	Grid
Leaves Green, Kes.	222	EK109
Leavesden Green, Wat.	59	BT34
Lee SE12	164	EE84
Leigh, Reig.	265	CU141
Lemsford, Welw.G.C.	29	CT10
Lessness Heath, Belv.	167	FB78
Letchmore Heath, Wat.	77	CD38
Letty Green, Hert.	31	DH13
Leverstock Green, Hem.H.	41	BQ21
Lewisham SE13	163	EB84
Leyton E11	123	EB60
Leytonstone E11	123	ED59
Limehouse E14	143	DY73
Limpsfield, Oxt.	254	EG128
Limpsfield Chart, Oxt.	254	EL130
Linford, Stanford le Hope	171	GM75
Lisson Grove NW8	**272**	**A5**
Little Berkhamsted, Hert.	47	DH18
Little Bookham, Lthd.	246	BY125
Little Chalfont, Amer.	72	AW40
Little Chalfont, Ch.St.G.	72	AW40
Little Ealing W5	157	CJ77
Little Ilford E12	124	EL64
Little Parndon, Harl.	35	EP14
Little Thurrock, Grays	170	GD76
Little Woodcote, Cars.	218	DG111
Littleton, Guil.	258	AU140
Littleton, Shep.	195	BP97
London Colney, St.Alb.	62	CL26
Long Ditton, Surb.	197	CJ102
Longcross, Cher.	192	AU104
Longford, Sev.	241	FD120
Longford, West Dr.	154	BH81
Longlands, Chis.	185	EQ90
Loudwater, H.Wyc.	88	AD53
Loudwater, Rick.	74	BK41
Loughton, Loug.	85	EM43
Low Street, Til.	171	GM79
Lower Ashtead, Ash.	231	CJ119
Lower Bois, Chesh.	54	AR34
Lower Clapton E5	123	DX63
Lower Edmonton N9	100	DT46
Lower Feltham, Felt.	175	BS90
Lower Green, Esher	196	CA103
Lower Holloway N7	121	DM64
Lower Kingswood, Tad.	250	DA127
Lower Nazeing, Wal.Abb.	50	EE23
Lower Sydenham SE26	183	DX91
Loxford, Ilf.	125	EQ64
Lye Green, Chesh.	56	AT27
Lyne, Cher.	193	BA102
Magdalen Laver, Ong.	53	FE17
Maida Hill W9	139	CZ70
Maida Vale W9	140	DB70
Malden Rushett, Chess.	215	CH111
Manor Park E12	124	EL63
Manor Park, Slou.	131	AQ70
Maple Cross, Rick.	91	BD49
Margery, Tad.	250	DA129
Mark Hall North, Harl.	36	EU12
Mark Hall South, Harl.	36	EU14
Mark's Gate, Rom.	104	EY54
Marshalswick, St.Alb.	43	CG17
Martyr's Green, Wok.	229	BR120
Marylebone NW1	**272**	**D8**
Matching Tye, Harl.	37	FF12
Maybury, Wok.	227	BB117
Mayfair W1	**277**	**H1**
Mayford, Wok.	226	AW122
Maypole, Orp.	224	EZ106
Mead Vale, Red.	266	DD136
Meath Green, Horl.	268	DD146
Meriden, Wat.	76	BY35
Merrow, Guil.	243	BB133
Merry Hill, Wat.	94	CA46
Merstham, Red.	250	DG128
Merton SW19	200	DA95
Merton Park SW19	200	DA96
Mickleham, Dor.	247	CJ128
Mid Holmwood, Dor.	263	CJ142
Middle Green, Slou.	132	AY73
Mile End E1	143	DX69
Mile End Green, Dart.	209	FW96
Mill End, Rick.	91	BF46
Mill Green, Hat.	45	CY15
Mill Hill NW7	97	CU50
Millwall E14	163	EB76
Milton, Grav.	191	GK86
Mimbridge, Wok.	210	AV113
Mitcham, Mitch.	200	DG97
Mogador, Tad.	249	CY129
Moneyhill, Rick.	92	BH46
Monken Hadley, Barn.	79	CZ39
Monks Orchard, Croy.	203	DZ101
Moor Park, Nthwd.	93	BQ49
Morden, Mord.	200	DA97
Morden Park, Mord.	199	CY99
Moreton, Ong.	53	FH20
Mortlake SW14	158	CQ83
Motspur Park, N.Mal.	199	CU100
Mottingham SE9	184	EJ89
Mount End, Epp.	70	EZ32
Mount Hermon, Wok.	226	AX118
Muckingford, Stanford le Hope	171	GM76
Mugswell, Couls.	250	DB125
Muswell Hill N10	121	DH55
Nalderswood, Reig.	265	CW144
Nazeing, Wal.Abb.	50	EJ22
Nazeing Gate, Wal.Abb.	68	EJ25
Neasden NW2	118	CS62
Netteswell, Harl.	35	ES14
New Addington, Croy.	221	ED109
New Ash Green, Long.	209	FX103
New Barnet, Barn.	80	DB42
New Beckenham, Beck.	183	DZ93
New Charlton SE7	164	EJ77
New Cross SE14	163	DY81
New Cross Gate SE14	163	DX81
New Eltham SE9	185	EN89
New Greens, St.Alb.	42	CC16
New Haw, Add.	212	BK108
New Malden, N.Mal.	198	CR97
New Southgate N11	99	DK49
New Town, Dart.	188	FN86
Newbury Park, Ilf.	125	ER57
Newgate Street, Hert.	47	DK24
Newington SE1	**279**	**H8**
Newman's End, Harl.	37	FE10
Newtown, Chesh.	54	AP30
Newyears Green, Uxb.	114	BN59
Nine Elms SW8	161	DH80
Noak Hill, Rom.	106	FK47
Noel Park N22	99	DN54
Norbiton, Kings.T.	198	CP96
Norbury SW16	201	DN95
Nork, Bans.	233	CY115
North Acton W3	138	CR70
North Beckton E6	144	EL70
North Cheam, Sutt.	199	CW104
North Cray, Sid.	186	FA90
North Finchley N12	98	DD50
North Harrow, Har.	116	CA58
North Hillingdon, Uxb.	135	BQ66
North Holmwood, Dor.	263	CH141
North Hyde, Sthl.	156	BY77
North Kensington W10	139	CW72
North Looe, Epsom	217	CW113
North Ockendon, Upmin.	129	FV64
North Sheen, Rich.	158	CN82
North Watford, Wat.	75	BV37
North Weald Bassett, Epp.	71	FB27
North Wembley, Wem.	117	CH61
North Woolwich E16	164	EL75
Northaw, Pot.B.	64	DF30
Northchurch, Berk.	38	AT17
Northfleet, Grav.	190	GD86
Northfleet Green, Grav.	190	GC92
Northolt, Nthlt.	136	BZ66
Northumberland Heath, Erith	167	FC80
Northwood, Nthwd.	93	BR51
Northwood Hills, Nthwd.	93	BT54
Norwood SE19	182	DS93
Norwood Green, Sthl.	156	CA77
Norwood New Town SE19	182	DQ93
Notting Hill W11	139	CY73
Nunhead SE15	162	DW83
Nuper's Hatch, Rom.	105	FE45
Nutfield, Red.	251	DM133
Oakleigh Park N20	98	DD46
Oakley Green, Wind.	150	AH82
Oakwood N14	81	DK44
Oatlands Park, Wey.	213	BR105
Ockham, Wok.	228	BN121
Old Bexley, Bex.	187	FB87
Old Coulsdon, Couls.	235	DN119
Old Ford E3	143	DZ67
Old Harlow, Harl.	36	EX11
Old Hatfield, Hat.	45	CX17
Old Malden, Wor.Pk.	198	CR102
Old Oak Common NW10	139	CT71
Old Windsor, Wind.	172	AU86
Old Woking, Wok.	227	BA121
Onslow Village, Guil.	258	AS136
Orchard Leigh, Chesh.	56	AV28
Orpington, Orp.	205	ES102
Orsett Heath, Grays	171	GG75
Osidge N14	99	DH46
Osterley, Islw.	156	CC80
Otford, Sev.	241	FG116
Ottershaw, Cher.	211	BC106
Outwood, Red.	267	DP143
Oxhey, Wat.	76	BW44
Oxlease, Hat.	45	CV19
Oxshott, Lthd.	215	CD113
Oxted, Oxt.	253	ED129
Pachesham Park, Lthd.	231	CG116
Paddington W2	140	DB71
Palmers Green N13	99	DN48
Panshanger, Welw.G.C.	30	DB9
Park Barn, Guil.	242	AS133
Park Langley, Beck.	203	EC99
Park Royal NW10	138	CN69
Park Street, St.Alb.	61	CD26
Parrock Farm, Grav.	191	GK91
Parsons Green SW6	160	DA81
Passmores, Harl.	51	ER17
Patchetts Green, Wat.	76	CC39
Peartree, Welw.G.C.	29	CZ9
Peasmarsh, Guil.	258	AW142
Pebble Coombe, Tad.	248	CS128
Peckham SE15	162	DU81
Pednormead End, Chesh.	54	AN32
Penge SE20	182	DW94
Penn, H.Wyc.	88	AE48
Pentonville N1	**274**	**D1**
Perivale, Grnf.	137	CJ67
Perry Street, Grav.	190	GE88
Petersham, Rich.	178	CL88
Petts Wood, Orp.	205	ER99
Piccotts End, Hem.H.	40	BJ16
Pilgrim's Hatch, Brwd.	108	FU42
Pimlico SW1	**277**	**K10**
Pinden, Dart.	209	FW96
Pinnacles, Harl.	51	EN15
Pinner, Pnr.	116	BY56
Pinner Green, Pnr.	94	BW53
Pinnerwood Park, Pnr.	94	BW52
Pitch Place, Guil.	242	AT129
Pixham, Dor.	247	CJ133
Plaistow E13	144	EF69
Plaistow, Brom.	184	EF93
Plumstead SE18	165	ES78
Ponders End, Enf.	82	DW43
Pooley Green, Egh.	173	BC92
Poplar E14	143	EB73
Potten End, Berk.	39	BC16
Potter Street, Harl.	52	EW17
Potters Bar, Pot.B.	64	DA32
Potters Crouch, St.Alb.	60	BX25
Poverest, Orp.	205	ET99
Poyle, Slou.	153	BE81
Pratt's Bottom, Orp.	224	EV110
Preston, Wem.	118	CL59
Primrose Hill NW8	140	DF67
Purfleet, Purf.	168	FP77
Purley, Pur.	219	DM111
Putney SW15	159	CY84
Putney Heath SW15	179	CW86
Putney Vale SW15	179	CT90
Pyrford, Wok.	227	BE115
Pyrford Green, Wok.	228	BH117
Pyrford Village, Wok.	228	BG118
Queensbury, Har.	117	CK55
Radlett, Rad.	77	CH35
Rainham, Rain.	147	FG69
Ramsden, Orp.	206	EW102
Rayners Lane, Har.	116	BZ60
Raynes Park SW20	199	CV97
Redbridge, Ilf.	125	EM58
Redhill, Red.	250	DG134
Redstreet, Grav.	190	GB93
Regent's Park NW1	**272**	**G1**
Reigate, Reig.	250	DA134
Richings Park, Iver	153	BD75
Richmond, Rich.	178	CL86
Rickmansworth, Rick.	92	BL45
Ridge, Pot.B.	62	CS34
Ridge Green, Red.	267	DL137
Ridgehill, Rad.	62	CQ30
Ripley, Wok.	228	BJ122
Ripley Springs, Egh.	172	AY93
Riverhead, Sev.	256	FD122
Riverview Park, Grav.	191	GK92
Roe Green, Hat.	45	CU18
Roehampton SW15	179	CU85
Roestock, St.Alb.	44	CR23
Romford, Rom.	127	FF57
Rose Hill, Dor.	263	CG136
Rosehill, Sutt.	200	DB102
Rosherville, Grav.	191	GF85
Rotherhithe SE16	163	DX76
Round Bush, Wat.	76	CC38
Row Town, Add.	211	BF108
Rowley Green, Barn.	79	CT42
Roxeth, Har.	117	CD61
Roydon, Harl.	50	EH15
Roydon Hamlet, Harl.	50	EJ19
Ruislip, Ruis.	115	BS59
Ruislip Common, Ruis.	115	BR57
Ruislip Gardens, Ruis.	115	BS63
Ruislip Manor, Ruis.	115	BU61
Rush Green, Rom.	127	FC59
Ryde, The, Hat.	45	CW15
Rydens, Walt.	196	BW103
Rydeshill, Guil.	242	AS131
Rye Park, Hodd.	49	EB16
St. Albans, St.Alb.	43	CE20
St. George's Hill, Wey.	213	BQ110
St. Helier, Cars.	200	DD101
St. James's SW1	**277**	**L3**
St. John's SE8	163	EA82
St. John's, Wok.	226	AV118
St. John's Wood NW8	140	DD69
St. Julians, St.Alb.	43	CD23
St. Luke's EC1	**275**	**J4**
St. Margarets, Twick.	177	CG85
St. Margarets, Ware	33	EB10
St. Mary Cray, Orp.	206	EW99
St. Pancras WC1	**273**	**P3**
St. Paul's Cray, Orp.	206	EU96
St. Stephens, St.Alb.	42	CC22
St. Vincent's Hamlet, Brwd.	106	FP46
Salfords, Red.	266	DF142
Sanderstead, S.Croy.	220	DT111
Sands End SW6	160	DC81
Sarratt, Rick.	74	BG35
Sawbridgeworth, Saw.	36	EW5
Seal, Sev.	257	FN121
Seer Green, Beac.	89	AR52
Selhurst SE25	202	DS100
Selsdon, S.Croy.	220	DW110
Send, Wok.	227	BC124
Send Marsh, Wok.	227	BF124
Sendgrove, Wok.	243	BC126
Seven Kings, Ilf.	125	ES59
Sevenoaks, Sev.	257	FJ125
Sevenoaks Common, Sev.	257	FH129

General Abbreviations

All	Alley	Coron	Coroners	Gdns	Gardens	Mt	Mount
Allot	Allotments	Cors	Corners	Govt	Government	Mus	Museum
Amb	Ambulance	Cotts	Cottages	Gra	Grange	N	North
App	Approach	Cov	Covered	Grd	Ground	NT	National Trust
Arc	Arcade	Crem	Crematorium	Grds	Grounds	Nat	National
Av	Avenue	Cres	Crescent	Grn	Green	PH	Public House
Bdy	Broadway	Ct	Court	Grns	Greens	PO	Post Office
Bk	Bank	Cts	Courts	Gro	Grove	Par	Parade
Bldgs	Buildings	Ctyd	Courtyard	Gros	Groves	Pas	Passage
Boul	Boulevard	Dep	Depot	Gt	Great	Pav	Pavilion
Bowl	Bowling	Dev	Development	Ho	House	Pk	Park
Br	Bridge	Dr	Drive	Hos	Houses	Pl	Place
C of E	Church of England	Dws	Dwellings	Hosp	Hospital	Pol	Police
Cath	Cathedral	E	East	Hts	Heights	Prec	Precinct
Cem	Cemetery	Ed	Education	Ind	Industrial	Prim	Primary
Cen	Central, Centre	Elec	Electricity	Int	International	Prom	Promenade
Cft	Croft	Embk	Embankment	Junct	Junction	Pt	Point
Cfts	Crofts	Est	Estate	La	Lane	Quad	Quadrant
Ch	Church	Ex	Exchange	Las	Lanes	RC	Roman Catholic
Chyd	Churchyard	Exhib	Exhibition	Lib	Library	Rd	Road
Cin	Cinema	FB	Footbridge	Lo	Lodge	Rds	Roads
Circ	Circus	FC	Football Club	Lwr	Lower	Rec	Recreation
Cl	Close	Fld	Field	Mag	Magistrates	Res	Reservoir
Co	County	Flds	Fields	Mans	Mansions	Ri	Rise
Coll	College	Fm	Farm	Mem	Memorial	S	South
Comm	Community	Gall	Gallery	Mkt	Market	Sch	School
Conv	Convent	Gar	Garage	Mkts	Markets	Sec	Secondary
Cor	Corner	Gdn	Garden	Ms	Mews	Shop	Shopping
						Sq	Square
						St.	Saint
						St	Street
						Sta	Station
						Sts	Streets
						Sub	Subway
						Swim	Swimming
						TA	Territorial Army
						TH	Town Hall
						Tenn	Tennis
						Ter	Terrace
						Thea	Theatre
						Trd	Trading
						Twr	Tower
						Twrs	Towers
						Uni	University
						Vil	Villa, Villas
						Vw	View
						W	West
						Wd	Wood
						Wds	Woods
						Wf	Wharf
						Wk	Walk
						Wks	Works
						Yd	Yard

Post town Abbreviations

Abb.L.	Abbots Langley	Chig.	Chigwell	Hert.	Hertford	Rad.	Radlett	Twick.	Twickenham
Add.	Addlestone	Chis.	Chislehurst	Hmptn.	Hampton	Rain.	Rainham	S. le. H.	Stanford le Hope
Amer.	Amersham	Cob.	Cobham	Hodd.	Hoddesdon	Red.	Redhill	Upmin.	Upminster
Ash.	Ashtead	Couls.	Coulsdon	Horl.	Horley	Reig.	Reigate	Uxb.	Uxbridge
Ashf.	Ashford	Craw.	Crawley	Horn.	Hornchurch	Rich.	Richmond	Vir.W.	Virginia Water
B.End	Bourne End	Croy.	Croydon	Houns.	Hounslow	Rick.	Rickmansworth	W.Byf.	West Byfleet
B.Stort.	Bishop's Stortford	Dag.	Dagenham	Ilf.	Ilford	Rom.	Romford	W.Mol.	West Molesey
Bans.	Banstead	Dart.	Dartford	Islw.	Isleworth	Ruis.	Ruislip	W.Wick.	West Wickham
Bark.	Barking	Dor.	Dorking	Ken.	Kenley	S.Croy.	South Croydon	Wal.Abb.	Waltham Abbey
Barn.	Barnet	E.Mol.	East Molesey	Kes.	Keston	S.Ock.	South Ockendon	Wal.Cr.	Waltham Cross
Beac.	Beaconsfield	Eden.	Edenbridge	Kings L.	Kings Langley	Saw.	Sawbridgeworth	Wall.	Wallington
Beck.	Beckenham	Edg.	Edgware	Kings.T.	Kingston upon Thames	Sev.	Sevenoaks	Walt.	Walton-on-Thames
Belv.	Belvedere	Egh.	Egham			Shep.	Shepperton	Warl.	Warlingham
Berk.	Berkhamsted	Enf.	Enfield	Long.	Longfield	Sid.	Sidcup	Wat.	Watford
Bet.	Betchworth	Epp.	Epping	Loug.	Loughton	Slou.	Slough	Wdf.Grn.	Woodford Green
Bex.	Bexley	Felt.	Feltham	Lthd.	Leatherhead	St.Alb.	Saint Albans	Well.	Welling
Bexh.	Bexleyheath	Gat.	Gatwick	Maid.	Maidenhead	Stai.	Staines	Welw.	Welwyn
Borwd.	Borehamwood	Gdmg.	Godalming	Mitch.	Mitcham	Stan.	Stanmore	Welw.G.C.	Welwyn Garden City
Brent.	Brentford	Gdse.	Godstone	Mord.	Morden	Sthl.	Southall	Wem.	Wembley
Brom.	Bromley	Ger.Cr.	Gerrards Cross	N.Mal.	New Malden	Sun.	Sunbury-on-Thames	West Dr.	West Drayton
Brox.	Broxbourne	Grav.	Gravesend	Nthlt.	Northolt	Surb.	Surbiton	West.	Westerham
Brwd.	Brentwood	Green.	Greenhithe	Nthwd.	Northwood	Sutt.	Sutton	Wey.	Weybridge
Buck.H.	Buckhurst Hill	Grnf.	Greenford	Ong.	Ongar	Swan.	Swanley	Whyt.	Whyteleafe
Cars.	Carshalton	Guil.	Guildford	Orp.	Orpington	Swans.	Swanscombe	Wind.	Windsor
Cat.	Caterham	H.Wyc.	High Wycombe	Oxt.	Oxted	T.Ditt.	Thames Ditton	Wok.	Woking
Ch.St.G.	Chalfont Saint Giles	Har.	Harrow	Pnr.	Pinner	Tad.	Tadworth	Wor.Pk.	Worcester Park
Cher.	Chertsey	Harl.	Harlow	Pot.B.	Potters Bar	Tedd.	Teddington		
Chesh.	Chesham	Hat.	Hatfield	Pur.	Purley	Th.Hth.	Thornton Heath		
Chess.	Chessington	Hem.H.	Hemel Hempstead	Purf.	Purfleet	Til.	Tilbury		

Notes

A strict word-by-word alphabetical order is followed in the index, for example Abbot St comes before Abbots Av . Also, generic terms such as Avenue, Close, Gardens, etc., although abbreviated, are ordered in their expanded form,

e.g. Abbots Ri comes before Abbots Rd

Street names preceded by a definite article (i.e. The) are indexed from their second word onwards with the article being placed at the end of the name,

e.g. Avenue, The, or Long Walk, The

The alphabetical order extends to include postal information so that where two or more streets have exactly the same name, London post town references are given first in alpha-numeric order and are followed by non-London post town references in alphabetical order,

e.g. Abbey Gdns NW8 is followed by Abbey Gdns W6 and then Abbey Gdns, Chertsey.

In cases where two or more streets of the same name occur in the same postal area, extra information will be given in brackets to aid location. Large non-London post towns also show locational information for streets in district suburbs or villages,

e.g. High St (Ponders End), Enfield
High St, Epsom
High St (Ewell), Epsom

The street name and postal district or post town of an entry is followed by the page number and grid reference on which the name will be found, e.g. Abbey Rd SW19 will be found on page 180 and in square DC94. Likewise, Norfolk Crescent, Sidcup will be found on page 185 and in square ES87 (within postal district DA15).

All streets within the Central London enlarged-scale section (pages 272-279) are shown in **bold type** when named in the index, e.g. **Abbey St SE1** will be found on page **279** and in square **N6**. Certain streets may also be duplicated on parts of pages 140-142 and 160-162. In these cases the Central London section reference is always given first in bold type, followed by the same name in standard type,

e.g. **Abbey Orchard St SW1 277   N6**
Abbey Orchard St SW1 161   DK76

The index also contains some roads for which there is insufficient space to name on the map. The adjoining, or nearest named thoroughfare to such roads is shown in *italics*, and the reference indicates where the unnamed road is located off the named thoroughfare,

e.g. Oyster Catchers Cl E16 is off *Freemasons Rd* and is located off this road on page 144 in square EH72.

02 - Adm

This index reads in the sequence: Street Name / Postal District or Post Town / Map Page Number / Grid Reference

02 Shop Cen NW3 140 DC65
Finchley Rd
A.C. Ct, T.Ditt. 197 CG100
Harvest La
Aaron Hill Rd E6 145 EN71
Abberley Ms SW4 161 DH83
Cedars Rd
Abberton Wk, Rain. 147 FE66
Ongar Way
Abbess Cl E6 144 EL71
Oliver Gdns
Abbess Cl SW2 181 DP88
Abbeville Rd N8 121 DK56
Barrington Rd
Abbeville Rd SW4 181 DJ86
Abbey Av, St.Alb. 42 CA23
Abbey Av, Wem. 138 CL68
Abbey Cl, Hayes 135 BV74
Abbey Cl, Nthlt. 136 BZ69
Invicta Gro
Abbey Cl, Pnr. 115 BV55
Abbey Cl, Rom. 127 FG58
Abbey Cl, Slou. 131 AL73
Abbey Cl, Wok. 227 BE116
Abbey Ct, Wal.Abb. 67 EB34
Abbey Cres, Belv. 166 FA77
Abbey Dr SW17 180 DG92
Church La
Abbey Dr, Abb.L. 59 BU32
Abbey Dr, Stai. 194 BJ98
Abbey Gdns NW8 140 DC68
Abbey Gdns SE16 162 DU77
Monnow Rd
Abbey Gdns W6 159 CY79
Abbey Gdns, Cher. 194 BG100
Abbey Gdns, Chis. 205 EN95
Abbey Gdns, Wal.Abb. 67 EC33
Abbey Grn, Cher. 194 BG100
Abbey Gro SE2 166 EV77
Abbey Ind Est, Mitch. 200 DF99
Abbey Ind Est, Wem. 138 CM67
Abbey La E15 143 EC68
Abbey La, Beck. 183 EA94
Abbey Mead Ind Pk, Wal.Abb. 67 EC34
Abbey Ms E17 123 EA57
Leamington Av
Abbey Mill End, St.Alb. 42 CC21
Abbey Mill La, St.Alb. 42 CC21
Abbey Mills, St.Alb. 42 CC21
Abbey Orchard St SW1 277 N6
Abbey Orchard St SW1 161 DK76
Abbey Par SW19 180 DC94
Merton High St
Abbey Par W5 138 CM69
Hanger La
Abbey Pk, Beck. 183 EA94
Abbey Pk La (Burnham), Slou. 111 AL61
Abbey Pl, Dart. 188 FK85
Priory Rd N
Abbey Retail Pk, Bark. 145 EP67
Abbey Rd E15 144 EE68
Abbey Rd NW6 140 DB66
Abbey Rd NW8 140 DC68
Abbey Rd NW10 138 CP68
Abbey Rd SE2 166 EX77
Abbey Rd SW19 180 DC94
Abbey Rd, Bark. 145 EQ67
Abbey Rd, Belv. 166 EX77
Abbey Rd, Bexh. 166 EY84
Abbey Rd, Cher. 194 BH101
Abbey Rd, Croy. 201 DP104
Abbey Rd, Enf. 82 DS43
Abbey Rd, Grav. 191 GL88
Abbey Rd, Green. 189 FW85
Abbey Rd, Ilf. 125 ER57
Abbey Rd, Shep. 194 BN102
Abbey Rd, S.Croy. 221 DX110
Abbey Rd, Vir.W. 192 AX99
Abbey Rd, Wal.Cr. 67 DY34
Abbey Rd, Wok. 226 AW117
Abbey Rd Est NW8 140 DB67
Abbey St E13 144 EG70
Abbey St SE1 279 N6
Abbey St SE1 162 DS76
Abbey Ter SE2 166 EW77
Abbey Vw NW7 97 CT48
Abbey Vw, Rad. 77 CF35
Abbey Vw, Wal.Abb. 67 EB33
Abbey Vw, Wat. 76 BX36
Abbey Vw Rd, St.Alb. 42 CC20
Abbey Vw Roundabout, Wal.Abb. 67 EB33
Abbey Wk, W.Mol. 196 CB97
Abbey Way SE2 166 EX76
Abbey Wf Ind Est, Bark. 145 ER68
Abbey Wd La, Rain. 148 FK68
Abbey Wd Rd SE2 166 EV77
Abbeydale Cl, Harl. 52 EW16
Abbeydale Rd, Wem. 138 CN67
Abbeyfield Rd SE16 162 DW77
Abbeyfields Cl NW10 138 CN68
Abbeyfields Mobile Home Pk, Cher. 194 BJ101
Abbeyhill Rd, Sid. 186 EW89
Abbot Cl, Stai. 174 BK94
Abbot Cl (Byfleet), W.Byf. 212 BK110
Abbot Rd, Guil. 258 AX136
Abbot St E8 142 DT65
Abbots Av, Epsom 216 CN111
Abbots Av, St.Alb. 43 CE23
Abbots Av W, St.Alb. 43 CD23
Abbots Cl N1 142 DQ65
Alwyne Rd
Abbots Cl, Brwd. 109 GA46
Abbots Cl, Guil. 258 AS137
Abbots Cl, Orp. 205 EQ102
Abbots Cl, Rain. 148 FJ68
Abbots Cl, Ruis. 116 BX62
Abbots Dr, Har. 116 CA61
Abbots Dr, Vir.W. 192 AV99
Abbots Fld, Grav. 191 GJ93
Ruffets Wd
Abbots Gdns N2 120 DD56
Abbots Gdns W8 160 DB76
St. Mary's Pl
Abbots Grn, Croy. 221 DX107
Abbots La SE1 279 N3
Abbots La, Ken. 236 DQ116
Abbots Manor Est SW1 277 H9
Abbots Manor Est SW1 161 DH77
Abbots Pk SW2 181 DN88
Abbots Pk, St.Alb. 43 CF22
Abbot's Pl NW6 140 DB67
Abbots Ri, Kings L. 58 BM26
Abbots Ri, Red. 250 DG132
Abbot's Rd E6 144 EK67
Abbots Rd, Abb.L. 59 BS30
Abbots Rd, Edg. 96 CQ52
Abbots Ter N8 121 DL58
Abbots Vw, Kings L. 58 BM27
Abbots Wk W8 160 DB76
St. Mary's Pl
Abbots Wk, Cat. 236 DU122
Tillingdown Hill
Abbots Wk, Wind. 151 AL82
Abbots Way, Beck. 203 DY99
Abbots Way, Cher. 193 BF101
Abbots Way, Guil. 243 BD133
Abbotsbury Cl E15 143 EC68
Abbotsbury Cl W14 159 CZ75
Abbotsbury Rd
Abbotsbury Gdns, Pnr. 116 BW58
Abbotsbury Ms SE15 162 DW83
Abbotsbury Rd W14 159 CY75
Abbotsbury Rd, Brom. 204 EF103
Abbotsbury Rd, Mord. 200 DB99
Abbotsford Av N15 122 DQ56
Abbotsford Cl, Wok. 227 BA117
Onslow Cres
Abbotsford Gdns, Wdf.Grn. 102 EG52
Abbotsford Lo, Nthwd. 93 BS50
Abbotsford Rd, Ilf. 126 EU61
Abbotshade Rd SE16 143 DX74
Abbotshall Av N14 99 DJ48
Abbotshall Rd SE6 183 ED88
Abbotsleigh Cl, Sutt. 218 DB108
Abbotsleigh Rd SW16 181 DJ91
Abbotsmede Cl, Twick. 177 CF89
Abbotstone Rd SW15 159 CW83
Abbotsweld, Harl. 51 ER18
Abbotswell Rd SE4 183 DZ85
Abbotswood, Guil. 243 AZ131
Abbotswood Cl, Belv. 166 EY76
Coptefield Dr
Abbotswood Cl, Guil. 243 AZ131
Abbotswood Dr, Wey. 213 BR110
Abbotswood Gdns, Ilf. 125 EM55
Abbotswood Rd SE22 162 DS84
Abbotswood Rd SW16 181 DK90
Abbotswood Way, Hayes 135 BV74
Abbott Av SW20 199 CX96
Abbott Cl, Hmptn. 176 BY93
Abbott Cl, Nthlt. 136 BZ65
Abbott Rd E14 143 EC71
Abbotts Cl SE28 146 EW73
Cairns Rd
Abbotts Cl, Rom. 127 FB55
Abbotts Cl, Swan. 207 FG98
Abbotts Cl, Uxb. 134 BK71
Abbotts Cres E4 101 ED49
Abbotts Cres, Enf. 81 DP40
Abbotts Dr, Wal.Abb. 68 EG34
Abbotts Dr, Wem. 117 CH61
Abbotts Pk Rd E10 123 EC59
Abbotts Pl, Chesh. 54 AQ28
Abbotts Ri, Ware 33 ED11
Abbotts Rd, Barn. 80 DB42
Abbotts Rd, Mitch. 201 DJ98
Abbotts Rd, Sthl. 136 BY74
Abbotts Rd, Sutt. 199 CZ104
Abbott's Tilt, Walt. 196 BY104
Abbotts Vale, Chesh. 54 AQ28
Abbotts Wk, Bexh. 166 EX80
Abbotts Way, Slou. 131 AK74
Abbotts Way, Ware 33 ED11
Abbs Cross Gdns, Horn. 128 FJ60
Abbs Cross La, Horn. 128 FJ62
Abchurch La EC4 275 L10
Abchurch La EC4 142 DR73
Abchurch Yd EC4 275 K10
Abdale Rd W12 139 CV74
Abel Cl, Hem.H. 40 BM20
Abenberg Way, Brwd. 109 GB47
Aberavon Rd E3 143 DY69
Abercairn Rd SW16 181 DJ94
Aberconway Rd, Mord. 200 DB97
Abercorn Cl NW7 97 CY52
Abercorn Cl NW8 140 DC69
Abercorn Cl, S.Croy. 221 DX112
Abercorn Cres, Har. 116 CB60
Abercorn Gdns, Har. 117 CK59
Abercorn Gdns, Rom. 126 EV58
Abercorn Gro, Ruis. 115 BR56
Abercorn Pl NW8 140 DC69
Abercorn Rd NW7 97 CY52
Abercorn Rd, Stan. 95 CJ52
Abercorn Way SE1 162 DU78
Abercorn Way, Wok. 226 AU118
Abercrombie Dr, Enf. 82 DU39
Linwood Cres
Abercrombie St SW11 160 DE82
Abercrombie Way, Harl. 51 EQ16
Aberdale Ct SE16 163 DX75
Poolmans St
Aberdale Gdns, Pot.B. 63 CZ33
Aberdare Cl, W.Wick. 203 EC103
Aberdare Gdns NW6 140 DB66
Aberdare Gdns NW7 97 CX52
Aberdare Rd, Enf. 82 DW42
Aberdeen Av, Slou. 131 AN73
Aberdeen La N5 121 DP64
Aberdeen Par N18 100 DV50
Angel Rd
Aberdeen Pk N5 122 DQ64
Aberdeen Pk Ms N5 122 DQ63
Aberdeen Pl NW8 140 DD70
Aberdeen Rd N5 122 DQ63
Aberdeen Rd N18 100 DV50
Aberdeen Rd NW10 119 CT64
Aberdeen Rd, Croy. 220 DQ105
Aberdeen Rd, Har. 95 CF54
Aberdeen Sq E14 143 DZ74
Westferry Circ
Aberdeen Ter SE3 163 ED82
Aberdour Rd, Ilf. 126 EV62
Aberdour St SE1 279 M8
Aberdour St SE1 162 DS77
Aberfeldy St E14 143 EC72
Aberford Gdns SE18 164 EL81
Aberford Rd, Borwd. 78 CN40
Aberfoyle Rd SW16 181 DK93
Abergeldie Rd SE12 184 EH86
Aberglen Ind Est, Hayes 155 BR75
Abernethy Rd SE13 164 EE84
Abersham Rd E8 122 DT64
Abery St SE18 165 ES77
Abigail Ms, Rom. 106 FM54
King Alfred Rd
Abingdon Cl NW1 141 DK65
Camden Sq
Abingdon Cl SE1 162 DT77
Bushwood Dr
Abingdon Cl SW19 180 DC93
Abingdon Cl, Uxb. 134 BM67
Abingdon Cl, Wok. 226 AV118
Abingdon Pl, Pot.B. 64 DB32
Abingdon Rd N3 98 DC54
Abingdon Rd SW16 201 DL96
Abingdon Rd W8 160 DA76
Abingdon St SW1 277 P6
Abingdon St SW1 161 DL76
Abingdon Vil W8 160 DA76
Abingdon Way, Orp. 224 EV105
Abinger Av, Sutt. 217 CW109
Abinger Cl, Bark. 126 EU63
Abinger Cl, Brom. 204 EL97
Abinger Cl, Croy. 221 EC107
Abinger Cl (North Holmwood), Dor. 263 CJ140
Abinger Cl, Wall. 219 DL106
Abinger Common Rd, Dor. 262 BY144
Abinger Dr, Red. 266 DE136
Abinger Gdns, Islw. 157 CE83
Abinger Gro SE8 163 DZ79
Abinger La (Abinger Common), Dor. 261 BV140
Abinger Ms W9 140 DA70
Warlock Rd
Abinger Rd W4 158 CS76
Abinger Way, Guil. 243 BB129
Ablett St SE16 162 DW78
Abney Gdns N16 122 DT61
Stoke Newington High St
Aboyne Dr SW20 199 CU96
Aboyne Est SW17 180 DD90
Aboyne Rd NW10 118 CS62
Aboyne Rd SW17 180 DD90
Abraham Cl, Wat. 93 BV49
Muirfield Rd
Abridge Cl, Wal.Cr. 83 DX35
Abridge Gdns, Rom. 104 FA51
Abridge Pk (Abridge), Rom. 86 EU42
Abridge Rd, Chig. 85 ER44
Abridge Rd, Epp. 85 ES36
Abridge Rd (Abridge), Rom. 86 EU39
Abridge Way, Bark. 146 EV69
Abyssinia Cl SW11 160 DE84
Cairns Rd
Acacia Av N17 100 DR52
Acacia Av, Brent. 157 CH80
Acacia Av, Hayes 135 BT72
Acacia Av, Horn. 127 FF61
Acacia Av, Mitch. 201 DH96
Acacia Rd
Acacia Av, Ruis. 115 BU60
Acacia Av, Shep. 194 BN99
Acacia Av (Wraysbury), Stai. 152 AY84
Acacia Av, Wem. 118 CL64
Acacia Av, West Dr. 134 BM73
Acacia Av, Wok. 226 AX120
Acacia Cl SE8 163 DY77
Acacia Cl SE20 202 DU96
Selby Rd
Acacia Cl (Woodham), Add. 211 BF110
Acacia Cl, Orp. 205 ER99
Acacia Cl, Stan. 95 CE51
Acacia Cl, Wal.Cr. 66 DS27
Acacia Ct, Wal.Abb. 68 EG34
Farthingale La
Acacia Dr (Woodham), Add. 211 BF110
Acacia Dr, Bans. 217 CX114
Acacia Dr, Sutt. 199 CZ102
Acacia Dr, Upmin. 128 FN63
Acacia Gdns NW8 140 DD68
Acacia Rd
Acacia Gdns, Upmin. 129 FT59
Acacia Gdns, W.Wick. 203 EC103
Acacia Gro SE21 182 DR89
Acacia Gro, Berk. 38 AV20
Acacia Gro, N.Mal. 198 CR97
Acacia Ms, West Dr. 154 BK79
Acacia Pl NW8 140 DD68
Acacia Rd E11 124 EE61
Acacia Rd E17 123 DY58
Acacia Rd N22 99 DN53
Acacia Rd NW8 140 DD68
Acacia Rd SW16 201 DL95
Acacia Rd W3 138 CQ73
Acacia Rd, Beck. 203 DZ97
Acacia Rd, Dart. 188 FK88
Acacia Rd, Enf. 82 DR39
Acacia Rd, Green. 189 FS86
Acacia Rd, Guil. 242 AX134
Acacia Rd, Hmptn. 176 CA93
Acacia Rd, Mitch. 201 DH96
Acacia Rd, Stai. 174 BH92
Acacia St, Hat. 45 CU21
Acacia Wk, Swan. 207 FD96
Acacia Way, Sid. 185 ET88
Academy Gdns, Croy. 202 DT102
Academy Gdns, Nthlt. 136 BX68
Academy Pl SE18 165 EM81
Academy Rd SE18 165 EM81
Acanthus Dr SE1 162 DU78
Acanthus Rd SW11 160 DG83
Accommodation La, West Dr. 154 BJ79
Accommodation Rd NW11 119 CZ59
Accommodation Rd (Longcross), Cher. 192 AX104
Acer Av, Hayes 136 BY71
Acer Av, Rain. 148 FK69
Acer Rd (Biggin Hill), West. 238 EK116
Acers (Park St), St.Alb. 60 CC28
Acfold Rd SW6 160 DB81
Achilles Cl SE1 162 DU78
Achilles Cl, Hem.H. 40 BM18
Achilles Pl, Wok. 226 AW117
Achilles Rd NW6 120 DA64
Achilles St SE14 163 DY80
Achilles Way W1 276 G3
Acklam Rd W10 139 CZ71
Acklington Dr NW9 96 CS53
Ackmar Rd SW6 160 DA81
Ackroyd Dr E3 143 DZ71
Ackroyd Rd SE23 183 DX87
Acland Cl SE18 165 ER80
Clothworkers Rd
Acland Cres SE5 162 DR84
Acland Rd NW2 139 CV65
Acme Rd, Wat. 75 BU38
Acock Gro, Nthlt. 116 CB64
Acol Cres, Ruis. 115 BV64
Acol Rd NW6 140 DA66
Aconbury Rd, Dag. 146 EV67
Acorn Cl E4 101 EB50
Acorn Cl, Chis. 185 EQ92
Acorn Cl, Enf. 81 DP39
Acorn Cl, Hmptn. 176 CB93
Acorn Cl, Horl. 269 DJ147
Acorn Cl, Stan. 95 CH52
Acorn Ct, Ilf. 125 ES58
Acorn Gdns SE19 202 DT95
Acorn Gdns W3 138 CR71
Acorn Gro, Hayes 155 BT80
Acorn Gro, Ruis. 115 BT63
Acorn Gro, Tad. 233 CY124
Acorn Gro, Wok. 226 AY121
Old Sch Pl
Acorn Ind Pk, Dart. 187 FG85
Acorn La (Cuffley), Pot.B. 65 DL29
Acorn Ms, Harl. 51 ET17
Acorn Par SE15 162 DV80
Carlton Gro
Acorn Pl, Wat. 75 BU37
Acorn Rd, Dart. 187 FF85
Acorn Rd, Hem.H. 40 BN21
Acorn St, Ware 34 EK08
Acorn Wk SE16 143 DY74
Acorn Way SE23 183 DX90
Acorn Way, Beck. 203 EC99
Acorn Way, Orp. 223 EP105
Acorns, The, Chig. 103 ES49
Acorns, The, Horl. 269 DP148
Acorns Way, Esher 214 CC106
Acre Dr SE22 162 DU84
Acre La SW2 161 DL84
Acre La, Cars. 218 DG105
Acre La, Wall. 218 DG105
Acre Pas, Wind. 151 AR81
Madeira Wk
Acre Path, Nthlt. 136 BY65
Arnold Rd
Acre Rd SW19 180 DD93
Acre Rd, Dag. 147 FB66
Acre Rd, Kings.T. 198 CL95
Acre Vw, Horn. 128 FL56
Acre Way, Nthwd. 93 BT53
Acrefield Rd (Chalfont St. Peter), Ger.Cr. 112 AX55
Acres End, Amer. 55 AS39
Acres Gdns, Tad. 233 CX119
Acrewood, Hem.H. 40 BL20
Acrewood Way, St.Alb. 44 CM20
Acris St SW18 180 DC85
Acton Cl N9 100 DU47
Acton Cl (Cheshunt), Wal.Cr. 67 DY31
Acton Hill Ms W3 138 CP74
Uxbridge Rd
Acton La NW10 138 CS68
Acton La W3 158 CQ75
Acton La W4 158 CR76
Acton Ms E8 142 DT67
Acton Pk Ind Est W3 158 CR75
Acton St WC1 274 B3
Acton St WC1 141 DM69
Acuba Rd SW18 180 DB89
Acworth Cl N9 100 DW45
Turin Rd
Ada Gdns E14 143 ED72
Ada Gdns E15 144 EF67
Ada Pl E2 142 DU67
Ada Rd SE5 162 DS80
Ada Rd, Wem. 117 CK62
Ada St E8 142 DV67
Adair Cl SE25 202 DV97
Adair Rd W10 139 CY70
Adair Twr W10 139 CY70
Appleford Rd
Adam & Eve Ct W1 273 L8
Adam & Eve Ms W8 160 DA76
Adam Cl SE6 183 EA91
Adam Cl, Slou. 131 AN74
Telford Dr
Adam Ct SW7 160 DC77
Gloucester Rd
Adam Pl N16 122 DT61
Stoke Newington High St
Adam Rd E4 101 DZ51
Adam St WC2 278 A1
Adam St WC2 141 DL73
Adam Wk SW6 159 CW80
Adams Cl N3 98 DA52
Falkland Av
Adams Cl NW9 118 CP61
Adams Cl, Surb. 198 CM100
Adams Ct EC2 275 L8
Adams Gdns Est SE16 162 DW75
St. Marychurch St
Adams Pl E14 143 EB74
Canada Sq
Adams Pl N7 121 DM64
George's Rd
Adams Rd N17 100 DS54
Adams Rd, Beck. 203 DY99
Adams Row W1 276 G1
Adams Row W1 140 DG73
Adams Sq, Bexh. 166 EY83
Regency Way
Adams Wk, Kings.T. 198 CL96
Adams Way, Croy. 202 DT100
Adamsfield, Wal.Cr. 66 DU27
Adamson Rd E16 144 EG72
Adamson Rd NW3 140 DD66
Adamsrill Cl, Enf. 82 DR44
Adamsrill Rd SE26 183 DY91
Adare Wk SW16 181 DM90
Adastral Est NW9 96 CS53
Adcock Wk, Orp. 223 ET105
Borkwood Pk
Adderley Gdns SE9 185 EN91
Adderley Gro SW11 180 DG85
Culmstock Rd
Adderley Rd, Har. 95 CF53
Adderley St E14 143 EC72
Addington Border, Croy. 221 DY110
Addington Cl, Wind. 151 AN83
Addington Ct SW14 158 CR83
Addington Dr N12 98 DC51
Addington Gro SE26 183 DY91
Addington Rd E3 143 EA69
Addington Rd E16 144 EE70
Addington Rd N4 121 DN58
Addington Rd, Croy. 201 DN102
Addington Rd, S.Croy. 220 DU111
Addington Rd, W.Wick. 204 EE103
Addington Sq SE5 162 DQ79
Addington St SE1 278 C5
Addington Village Rd, Croy. 221 EA106
Addis Cl, Enf. 83 DX39
Addiscombe Av, Croy. 202 DU101
Addiscombe Cl, Har. 117 CJ57
Addiscombe Ct Rd, Croy. 202 DS102
Addiscombe Gro, Croy. 202 DR103
Addiscombe Rd, Croy. 202 DS103
Addiscombe Rd, Wat. 75 BV42
Addison Av N14 81 DH44
Addison Av W11 139 CY74
Addison Av, Houns. 156 CC81
Addison Br Pl W14 159 CZ77
Addison Cl, Cat. 236 DR122
Addison Cl, Nthwd. 93 BU53
Addison Cl, Orp. 205 EQ100
Addison Ct, Epp. 70 EU31
Centre Dr
Addison Cres W14 159 CY76
Addison Dr SE12 184 EH85
Eltham Rd
Addison Gdns W14 159 CX76
Addison Gdns, Grays 170 GC77
Palmers Dr
Addison Gdns, Surb. 198 CM98
Addison Gro W4 158 CS76
Addison Pl W11 139 CY74
Addison Pl, Sthl. 136 CA73
Longford Av
Addison Rd E11 124 EG58
Addison Rd E17 123 EB57
Addison Rd SE25 202 DU98
Addison Rd W14 159 CZ76
Addison Rd, Brom. 204 EJ99
Addison Rd, Cat. 236 DR121
Addison Rd, Chesh. 54 AQ29
Addison Rd, Enf. 82 DW39
Addison Rd, Guil. 258 AY135
Addison Rd, Ilf. 103 EQ53
Addison Rd, Tedd. 177 CH93
Addison Rd, Wok. 227 AZ117
Chertsey Rd
Addison Way NW11 119 CZ56
Addison Way, Hayes 135 BU72
Addison Way, Nthwd. 93 BT53
Addison's Cl, Croy. 203 DZ103
Addle Hill EC4 274 G10
Addle St EC2 275 J7
Addlestone Moor, Add. 194 BJ103
Addlestone Pk, Add. 212 BH106
Addlestone Rd, Add. 212 BL105
Adecroft Way, W.Mol. 196 CC97
Adela Av, N.Mal. 199 CV99
Adela St W10 139 CY70
Kensal Rd
Adelaide Av SE4 163 DZ84
Adelaide Cl, Enf. 82 DT38
Adelaide Cl, Slou. 151 AN75
Amerden Way
Adelaide Cl, Stan. 95 CG49
Adelaide Cotts W7 157 CF75
Adelaide Gdns, Rom. 126 EY57
Adelaide Gro W12 139 CU74
Adelaide Pl, Wey. 213 BR105
Adelaide Rd E10 123 EC62
Adelaide Rd NW3 140 DD66
Adelaide Rd SW18 180 DA85
Putney Br Rd
Adelaide Rd W13 137 CG74
Adelaide Rd, Ashf. 174 BK92
Adelaide Rd, Chis. 185 EP92
Adelaide Rd, Houns. 156 BY81
Adelaide Rd, Ilf. 125 EP61
Adelaide Rd, Rich. 158 CM84
Adelaide Rd, Sthl. 156 BY77
Adelaide Rd, Surb. 198 CL99
Adelaide Rd, Tedd. 177 CF93
Adelaide Rd, Til. 171 GF81
Adelaide Rd, Walt. 195 BU104
Adelaide Sq, Wind. 151 AR82
Adelaide St WC2 277 P1
Adelaide St, St.Alb. 43 CD19
Adelaide Ter, Brent. 157 CK78
Adelaide Wk SW9 161 DN84
Sussex Wk
Adelina Gro E1 142 DW71
Adelina Ms SW12 181 DK88
King's Av
Adeline Pl WC1 273 N7
Adeline Pl WC1 141 DK71
Adeliza Cl, Bark. 145 EP66
North St
Adelphi Ct SE16 163 DX75
Poolmans St
Adelphi Cres, Hayes 135 BT69
Adelphi Cres, Horn. 127 FG61
Adelphi Gdns, Slou. 152 AS75
Adelphi Rd, Epsom 216 CR113
Adelphi Ter WC2 278 A1
Adelphi Way, Hayes 135 BT69
Aden Gro N16 122 DR63
Aden Rd, Enf. 83 DY42
Aden Rd, Ilf. 125 EP59
Aden Ter N16 122 DR63
Adeney Cl W6 159 CX79
Adenmore Rd SE6 183 EA87
Adeyfield Gdns, Hem.H. 40 BM19
Adeyfield Rd, Hem.H. 40 BM20
Adhern Ct, St.Alb. 43 CJ22
Adie Rd W6 159 CW76
Adine Rd E13 144 EH70
Adler Ind Est, Hayes 155 BR75
Adler St E1 142 DU72
Adlers La (Westhumble), Dor. 247 CG131
Adley St E5 123 DY64
Adlington Cl N18 100 DS50
Admaston Rd SE18 165 EQ80
Admiral Cl, Orp. 206 EX98
Admiral Ct NW4 119 CU57
Barton Cl

Admiral Ho, Tedd. 177 CG91
Twickenham Rd
Admiral Pl SE16 143 DY74
Admiral Seymour Rd SE9 165 EM84
Admiral Sq SW10 160 DD81
Admiral Stirling Ct, Wey. 212 BM105
Admiral St SE8 163 EA81
Admiral St, Hert. 32 DU09
Admiral Wk W9 140 DA71
Admiral Way, Berk. 38 AT17
Admirals Cl E18 124 EH56
Admirals Cl (Colney Heath), St.Alb. 44 CR23
Admirals Ct, Guil. 243 BB133
Admiral's Rd, Lthd. 247 CD126
Admirals Wk NW3 120 DC62
Admirals Wk, Couls. 235 DM120
Admiral's Wk, Dor. 246 CB130
Admirals Wk, Green. 189 FV85
Admirals Wk, Hodd. 49 EA19
Admirals Wk, St.Alb. 43 CG23
Admirals Way E14 163 EA75
Admiralty Cl SE8 163 EA80
Reginald Sq
Admiralty Rd, Tedd. 177 CF93
Adnams Wk, Rain. 147 FF65
Lovell Wk
Adolf St SE6 183 EB91
Adolphus Rd N4 121 DP61
Adolphus St SE8 163 DZ80
Adomar Rd, Dag. 126 EX62
Adpar St W2 140 DD70
Adrian Av NW2 119 CV60
North Circular Rd
Adrian Cl (Harefield), Uxb. 92 BK53
Adrian Ms SW10 160 DB79
Adrian Rd, Abb.L. 59 BS31
Adrienne Av, Sthl. 136 BZ70
Adstock Ms (Chalfont St. Peter), Ger.Cr. 90 AX53
Church La
Adstock Way, Grays 170 FZ77
Advance Rd SE27 182 DQ91
Advent Ct, Wdf.Grn. 102 EF50
Wood La
Advent Way N18 101 DX50
Advice Av, Grays 170 GA75
Adys Rd SE15 162 DT83
Aerodrome Rd NW4 119 CT55
Aerodrome Rd NW9 97 CT54
Aerodrome Way, Houns. 156 BW79
Aeroville NW9 96 CS54
Affleck St N1 274 C1
Afghan Rd SW11 160 DE82
Africa Ho SE16 162 DV76
Afton Dr, S.Ock. 149 FV72
Agamemnon Rd NW6 119 CZ64
Agar Cl, Surb. 198 CM103
Agar Gro NW1 141 DJ66
Agar Gro Est NW1 141 DK66
Agar Pl NW1 141 DJ66
Agar St WC2 277 P1
Agar St WC2 141 DL73
Agars Plough (Datchet), Slou. 152 AU79
Agate Cl E16 144 EK72
Agate Rd W6 159 CW76
Agates La, Ash. 231 CK118
Agatha Cl E1 142 DV74
Prusom St
Agaton Rd SE9 185 EQ89
Agave Rd NW2 119 CW63
Agdon St EC1 274 F4
Agdon St EC1 141 DP70
Agincourt Rd NW3 120 DF63
Agister Rd, Chig. 104 EU50
Agnes Av, Ilf. 125 EP63
Agnes Cl E6 145 EN73
Agnes Gdns, Dag. 126 EX63
Agnes Rd W3 139 CT74
Agnes Scott Ct, Wey. 195 BP104
Palace Dr
Agnes St E14 143 DZ72
Agnesfield Cl N12 98 DE51
Agnew Rd SE23 183 DX87
Agraria Rd, Guil. 258 AV135
Agricola Ct E3 143 DZ67
Parnell Rd
Agricola Pl, Enf. 82 DT43
Aidan Cl, Dag. 126 EY63
Aileen Wk E15 144 EF66
Ailsa Av, Twick. 177 CG85
Ailsa Rd, Twick. 177 CH85
Ailsa St E14 143 EC71
Ainger Ms NW3 140 DF66
Ainger Rd
Ainger Rd NW3 140 DF66
Ainsdale Cl, Orp. 205 ER102
Ainsdale Cres, Pnr. 116 CA55
Ainsdale Dr SE1 162 DU78
Ainsdale Rd W5 137 CK70
Ainsdale Rd, Wat. 94 BW48
Ainsdale Way, Wok. 226 AU118
Ainsley Av, Rom. 127 FB58
Ainsley Cl N9 100 DS46
Ainsley St E2 142 DV69
Ainslie Wk SW12 181 DH87
Ainslie Wd Cres E4 101 EB50
Ainslie Wd Gdns E4 101 EB49
Ainslie Wd Rd E4 101 EA50
Ainsty Est SE16 163 DX75
Ainsworth Cl NW2 119 CU62
Ainsworth Cl SE15 162 DS82
Lyndhurst Gro
Ainsworth Rd E9 142 DW66
Ainsworth Rd, Croy. 201 DP103
Ainsworth Way NW8 140 DC67
Aintree Av E6 144 EL67
Aintree Cl, Grav. 191 GH90
Aintree Cl (Colnbrook), Slou. 153 BE81
Aintree Cl, Uxb. 135 BP72
Craig Dr
Aintree Cres, Ilf. 103 EQ54
Aintree Est SW6 159 CY80
Dawes Rd
Aintree Gro, Upmin. 128 FM62
Aintree Rd, Grnf. 137 CH68
Aintree St SW6 159 CY80
Air Links Ind Est, Houns. 156 BW78
Air Pk Way, Felt. 175 BV89
Air St W1 277 L1
Air St W1 141 DJ73
Aird Ct, Hmptn. 196 BZ95
Oldfield Rd
Airdrie Cl N1 141 DM66
Airdrie Cl, Hayes 136 BY71
Glencoe Rd
Aire Dr, S.Ock. 149 FV70
Airedale, Hem.H. 40 BL17
Wharfedale
Airedale Av W4 159 CT77
Airedale Av S W4 159 CT78
Netheravon Rd S
Airedale Cl, Dart. 188 FQ88
Airedale Rd SW12 180 DF87
Airedale Rd W5 157 CJ76
Airey Neave Ct, Grays 170 GA75
Airfield Way, Horn. 147 FH65
Airlie Gdns W8 160 DA75
Airlie Gdns, Ilf. 125 EP60
Airport Ind Est, West. 222 EK114
Airport Roundabout E16 144 EK74
Connaught Br
Airport Way, Gat. 268 DG151
Airport Way, Stai. 153 BF84
Airthrie Rd, Ilf. 126 EV61
Aisgill Av W14 159 CZ78
Aisher Rd SE28 146 EW73
Aisher Way (Riverhead), Sev. 256 FE121
Aislibie Rd SE12 164 EE84
Aitken Cl E8 142 DU67
Pownall Rd
Aitken Cl, Mitch. 200 DF101
Aitken Rd SE6 183 EB89
Aitken Rd, Barn. 79 CW43
Ajax Av NW9 118 CS55
Ajax Av, Slou. 131 AP73
Ajax Rd NW6 120 DA64
Akabusi Cl, Croy. 202 DU100
Akehurst La, Sev. 257 FJ125
Akehurst St SW15 179 CU86
Akeman Cl, St.Alb. 42 BZ22
Meautys
Akenside Rd NW3 120 DD64
Akerman Rd SW9 161 DP82
Akerman Rd, Surb. 197 CJ100
Akers Way, Rick. 73 BD44
Alabama St SE18 165 ER80
Alacross Rd W5 157 CJ75
Alamein Cl, Brox. 49 DX20
Alamein Gdns, Dart. 189 FR87
Alamein Rd, Swans. 189 FX86
Alan Cl, Dart. 168 FJ84
Alan Dr, Barn. 79 CY44
Alan Gdns, Rom. 126 FA59
Alan Hocken Way E15 144 EE68
Alan Rd SW19 179 CY92
Alan Way (George Grn), Slou. 132 AY72
Alanbrooke, Grav. 191 GJ87
Aland Ct SE16 163 DY76
Finland St
Alandale Dr, Pnr. 93 BV54
Alander Ms E17 123 EC56
Alanthus Cl SE12 184 EF86
Alaska St SE1 278 D3
Alba Cl, Hayes 136 BX70
Ramulis Dr
Alba Gdns NW11 119 CY58
Alba Pl W11 139 CZ72
Portobello Rd
Albacore Cres SE13 183 EB86
Albain Cres, Ashf. 174 BL89
Alban Av, St.Alb. 43 CD18
Alban Cres, Borwd. 78 CP39
Alban Cres (Farningham), Dart. 208 FN102
Alban Highwalk EC2 142 DQ71
London Wall
Alban Ind Pk, St.Alb. 44 CN20
Alban Pk, St.Alb. 44 CM20
Alban Way Cycle Route, Hat. 44 CM20
Alban Way Cycle Route, St.Alb. 43 CH20
Albans Vw, Wat. 59 BV33
Albany W1 277 K1
Albany, The, Wdf.Grn. 102 EF49
Albany Cl N15 121 DP56
Albany Cl SW14 158 CP84
Albany Cl, Bex. 186 EW87
Albany Cl, Bushey 77 CD44
Albany Cl, Esher 214 CA109
Albany Cl, Reig. 250 DA132
Albany Cl, Uxb. 114 BN64
Albany Ct E4 83 EB44
Chelwood Cl
Albany Ct, Epp. 69 ET30
Albany Ctyd W1 277 L1
Albany Cres, Edg. 96 CN52
Albany Cres (Claygate), Esher 215 CE107
Albany Gate, Chesh. 54 AP30
Bellingdon Rd
Albany Mans SW11 160 DE80
Albany Ms N1 141 DN66
Barnsbury Pk
Albany Ms SE5 162 DQ79
Albany Rd
Albany Ms, Brom. 184 EG93
Albany Ms, Kings.T. 177 CK93
Albany Pk Rd
Albany Ms, St.Alb. 60 CA27
North Orbital Rd
Albany Ms, Sutt. 218 DB106
Camden Rd
Albany Ms, Ware 33 DY06
Albany Quay
Albany Pk (Colnbrook), Slou. 153 BD81
Albany Pk Av, Enf. 82 DW39
Albany Pk Rd, Kings.T. 178 CL93
Albany Pk Rd, Lthd. 231 CG119
Albany Pas, Rich. 178 CM85
Albany Pl N7 121 DN63
Benwell Rd
Albany Pl, Brent. 158 CL79
Albany Rd
Albany Pl, Egh. 173 BA91
Albany Quay, Ware 33 DY06
Albany Rd E10 123 EA59
Albany Rd E12 124 EK63
Albany Rd E17 123 DZ58
Albany Rd N4 121 DM58
Albany Rd N18 100 DV50
Albany Rd SE5 162 DR79
Albany Rd SW19 180 DB92
Albany Rd W13 137 CH73
Albany Rd, Belv. 166 EZ79
Albany Rd, Bex. 186 EW87
Albany Rd, Brent. 157 CK79
Albany Rd, Brwd. 108 FV44
Albany Rd, Chis. 185 EP92
Albany Rd, Enf. 83 DX37
Albany Rd, Horn. 127 FG60
Albany Rd, N.Mal. 198 CR98
Albany Rd, Rich. 178 CM85
Albert Rd
Albany Rd, Rom. 126 EZ58
Albany Rd, Walt. 214 BX105
Albany Rd, Wind. 151 AQ82
Albany Rd (Old Windsor), Wind. 172 AU85
Albany St NW1 141 DH68
Albany Ter NW1 141 DH70
Marylebone Rd
Albany Vw, Buck.H. 102 EG46
Albanys, The, Reig. 250 DA131
Albatross Gdns, S.Croy. 221 DX111
Albatross St SE18 165 ES80
Albatross Way SE16 163 DX75
Albemarle SW19 179 CX89
Albemarle App, Ilf. 125 EP58
Albemarle Av, Pot.B. 64 DB33
Albemarle Av, Twick. 176 BZ88
Albemarle Av (Cheshunt), Wal.Cr. 66 DW28
Albemarle Cl, Grays 170 GA75
Albemarle Gdns, Ilf. 125 EP58
Albemarle Gdns, N.Mal. 198 CR98
Albemarle Pk, Stan. 95 CJ50
Marsh La
Albemarle Rd, Barn. 98 DE45
Albemarle Rd, Beck. 203 EB95
Albemarle St W1 277 J1
Albemarle St W1 141 DH73
Albemarle Way EC1 274 F5
Albeny Gate, St.Alb. 43 CD21
Alberon Gdns NW11 119 CZ56
Albert Av E4 101 EA49
Albert Av SW8 161 DM80
Albert Av, Cher. 194 BG97
Albert Br SW3 160 DE79
Albert Br SW11 160 DE79
Albert Br Rd SW11 160 DE80
Albert Carr Gdns SW16 181 DL92
Albert Cl E9 142 DV67
Northiam St
Albert Cl N22 99 DK53
Albert Cl, Grays 170 GC76
Albert Cl, Slou. 152 AT76
Albert St
Albert Ct SW7 160 DD75
Albert Cres E4 101 EA49
Albert Dr SW19 179 CY89
Albert Dr, Wok. 211 BD114
Albert Embk SE1 161 DL78
Albert Gdns E1 143 DX72
Albert Gdns, Harl. 52 EX16
Albert Gate SW1 276 E4
Albert Gate SW1 160 DF75
Albert Gro SW20 199 CX95
Albert Hall Mans SW7 160 DD75
Kensington Gore
Albert Mans SW11 160 DF81
Albert Br Rd
Albert Ms E14 143 DY73
Narrow St
Albert Ms W8 160 DC76
Victoria Gro
Albert Murray Cl, Grav. 191 GJ87
Armoury Dr
Albert Pl N3 98 DA53
Albert Pl N17 122 DT55
High Rd
Albert Pl W8 160 DB75
Albert Pl (Eton Wick), Wind. 151 AN78
Common Rd
Albert Rd E10 123 EC61
Albert Rd E16 144 EL74
Albert Rd E17 123 EA57
Albert Rd E18 124 EH55
Albert Rd N4 121 DM60
Albert Rd N15 122 DS58
Albert Rd N22 99 DJ53
Albert Rd NW4 119 CX56
Albert Rd NW6 139 CZ68
Albert Rd NW7 97 CT50
Albert Rd SE9 184 EL90
Albert Rd SE20 183 DX94
Albert Rd SE25 202 DU98
Albert Rd W5 137 CH70
Albert Rd, Add. 194 BK104
Albert Rd, Ashf. 174 BM92
Albert Rd, Ash. 232 CM118
Albert Rd, Barn. 80 DC42
Albert Rd, Belv. 166 EZ78
Albert Rd, Bex. 186 FA86
Albert Rd, Brom. 204 EK99
Albert Rd, Buck.H. 102 EK47
Albert Rd, Chesh. 54 AQ31
Albert Rd, Dag. 126 FA60
Albert Rd, Dart. 188 FJ90
Albert Rd (Englefield Grn), Egh. 172 AX93
Albert Rd, Epsom 217 CT113
Albert Rd (Hampton Hill), Hmptn. 176 CC92
Albert Rd, Har. 116 CC55
Albert Rd, Hayes 155 BS76
Albert Rd, Horl. 268 DG147
Albert Rd, Houns. 156 CA84
Albert Rd, Ilf. 125 EP62
Albert Rd, Kings.T. 198 CM96
Albert Rd, Mitch. 200 DF97
Albert Rd, N.Mal. 199 CT98
Albert Rd (Chelsfield), Orp. 224 EU106
Albert Rd (St. Mary Cray), Orp. 206 EV100
Albert Rd, Red. 251 DJ129
Albert Rd, Rich. 178 CL85
Albert Rd, Rom. 127 FF57
Albert Rd, Sthl. 156 BX76
Albert Rd, Sutt. 218 DD106
Albert Rd, Swans. 190 FZ86
Albert Rd, Tedd. 177 CF93
Albert Rd, Twick. 177 CF88
Albert Rd, Warl. 237 DZ117
Albert Rd, West Dr. 134 BL74
Albert Rd, Wind. 151 AR84
Albert Rd Est, Belv. 166 EZ78
Albert Rd N, Reig. 249 CZ133
Albert Rd N, Wat. 75 BV41
Albert Rd S, Wat. 75 BV41
Albert Sq E15 124 EE64
Albert Sq SW8 161 DM80
Albert St N12 98 DC50
Albert St NW1 141 DH67
Albert St, Brwd. 108 FW50
Albert St, St.Alb. 43 CD21
Albert St, Slou. 152 AT76
Albert St, Wind. 151 AP81
Albert Ter NW1 140 DG67
Albert Ter NW10 138 CR67
Albert Ter, Buck.H. 102 EK47
Albert Ter Ms NW1 140 DG67
Regents Pk Rd
Albert Way SE15 162 DV80
Alberta Av, Sutt. 217 CY105
Alberta Dr, Horl. 269 DN148
Alberta Est SE17 278 G10
Alberta Est SE17 161 DP78
Alberta Rd, Enf. 82 DT44
Alberta Rd, Erith 167 FC81
Alberta St SE17 278 F10
Alberta St SE17 161 DP78
Albertine Cl, Epsom 233 CV116
Rose Bushes
Albion Av N10 98 DG53
Albion Av SW8 161 DK82
Albion Bldgs EC1 142 DQ71
Bartholomew Cl
Albion Cl W2 272 C10
Albion Cl, Hert. 32 DS09
Albion Cl, Rom. 127 FD58
Albion Cl, Slou. 132 AU74
Albion Cres, Ch.St.G. 90 AV48
Albion Dr E8 142 DT66
Albion Est SE16 163 DX75
Albion Gdns W6 159 CV77
Albion Gro N16 122 DS63
Albion Hill SE13 163 EB82
Albion Hill, Hem.H. 40 BK21
Wolsey Rd
Albion Hill, Loug. 84 EJ43
Albion Ho, Slou. 153 BB78
Albion Ho, Wok. 227 AZ117
Albion Ms N1 141 DN67
Albion Ms NW6 139 CZ66
Kilburn High Rd
Albion Ms W2 272 C9
Albion Ms W2 140 DE72
Albion Ms W6 159 CV77
Galena Rd
Albion Par N16 122 DR63
Albion Rd
Albion Par, Grav. 191 GK86
Albion Pk, Loug. 84 EK43
Albion Pl EC1 274 F6
Albion Pl EC1 141 DP71
Albion Pl SE25 202 DU97
High St
Albion Pl W6 159 CV77
Albion Rd E17 123 EC55
Albion Rd N16 122 DR63
Albion Rd N17 100 DT54
Albion Rd, Bexh. 166 EZ84
Albion Rd, Ch.St.G. 90 AV47
Albion Rd, Grav. 191 GJ87
Albion Rd, Hayes 135 BS72
Albion Rd, Houns. 156 CA84
Albion Rd, Kings.T. 198 CQ95
Albion Rd, Reig. 266 DC135
Albion Rd, St.Alb. 43 CF20
Albion Rd, Sutt. 218 DD107
Albion Rd, Twick. 177 CE88
Albion Sq E8 142 DT66
Albion St SE16 162 DW75
Albion St W2 272 C9
Albion St W2 140 DE72
Albion St, Croy. 201 DP102
Albion Ter E8 142 DT66
Albion Ter, Grav. 191 GJ86
Albion Vil Rd SE26 182 DW90
Albion Way EC1 275 H7
Albion Way SE13 163 EC84
Albion Way, Wem. 118 CP62
North End Rd
Albright Ind Est, Rain. 147 FF71
Albrighton Rd SE22 162 DS83
Albuhera Cl, Enf. 81 DN39
Albury Av, Bexh. 166 EY82
Albury Av, Islw. 157 CF80
Albury Av, Sutt. 217 CW109
Albury Cl (Longcross), Cher. 192 AU104
Albury Cl, Hmptn. 176 CA93
Albury Ct, Sutt. 218 DC105
Ripley Gdns
Albury Dr, Pnr. 94 BX52
Albury Gro Rd (Cheshunt), Wal.Cr. 67 DX30
Albury Heath (Albury), Guil. 260 BL141
Albury Ms E12 124 EJ60
Albury Pk (Albury), Guil. 260 BL140
Albury Ride (Cheshunt), Wal.Cr. 67 DX31
Albury Rd, Chess. 216 CL106
Albury Rd, Guil. 259 AZ135
Albury Rd, Red. 251 DJ129
Albury Rd, Walt. 213 BS107
Albury St SE8 163 EA79
Albury Wk (Cheshunt), Wal.Cr. 67 DX32
Albyfield, Brom. 205 EM97
Albyn Ho, Hem.H. 40 BK19
Alexandra Rd
Albyn Rd SE8 163 EA81
Albyns Cl, Rain. 147 FG66
Albyns La, Rom. 87 FC40
Alcester Cres E5 122 DV61
Alcester Rd, Wall. 219 DH105
Alcock Cl, Wall. 219 DK108
Alcock Rd, Houns. 156 BX80
Alcocks Cl, Tad. 233 CY120
Alcocks La (Kingswood), Tad. 233 CY120
Alconbury, Welw.G.C. 30 DE09
Alconbury Rd E5 122 DU61
Alcorn Cl, Sutt. 200 DA103
Alcott Cl W7 137 CF71
Westcott Cres
Alcuin Ct, Stan. 95 CJ52
Old Ch La
Aldborough Rd, Dag. 147 FC65
Aldborough Rd, Upmin. 128 FM61
Aldborough Rd N, Ilf. 125 ET57
Aldborough Rd S, Ilf. 125 ES60
Aldborough Spur, Slou. 132 AS72
Aldbourne Rd W12 139 CT74
Aldbourne Rd (Burnham), Slou. 130 AH71
Aldbridge St SE17 279 N10
Aldbridge St SE17 162 DS78
Aldburgh Ms W1 272 G8
Aldbury Av, Wem. 138 CP66
Aldbury Cl, St.Alb. 43 CJ15
Sandringham Cres
Aldbury Cl, Wat. 76 BX36
Aldbury Gro, Welw.G.C. 30 DB09
Aldbury Ms N9 100 DR45
Aldbury Rd, Rick. 91 BF45
Aldebert Ter SW8 161 DL80
Aldeburgh Cl E5 122 DV61
Southwold Rd
Aldeburgh Pl, Wdf.Grn. 102 EG49
Aldeburgh St SE10 164 EG78
Alden Av E15 144 EF69
Alden Vw, Wind. 151 AK81
Aldenham Av, Rad. 77 CG36
Aldenham Dr, Uxb. 135 BP70
Aldenham Gro, Rad. 61 CH34
Aldenham Rd, Borwd. 77 CH42
Aldenham Rd, Bushey 76 BZ41
Aldenham Rd, Rad. 77 CG35
Aldenham Rd, Wat. 76 BX44
Aldenham Rd (Letchmore Heath), Wat. 77 CE39
Aldenham St NW1 273 L1
Aldenham St NW1 141 DK68
Aldenholme, Wey. 213 BS107
Aldensley Rd W6 159 CV76
Alder Av, Upmin. 128 FM63
Alder Cl SE15 162 DT79
Alder Cl (Englefield Grn), Egh. 172 AY92
Alder Cl, Hodd. 49 EB15
Alder Cl (Park St), St.Alb. 60 CB28
Alder Cl, Slou. 131 AM74
Alder Dr, S.Ock. 149 FW70
Laburnum Gro
Alder Gro NW2 119 CV61
Alder Ms N19 121 DJ61
Bredgar Rd
Alder Rd SW14 158 CR83
Alder Rd, Iver 133 BC68
Alder Rd, Sid. 185 ET90
Alder Rd (Denham), Uxb. 134 BJ65
Alder Wk, Ilf. 125 EQ64
Alder Wk, Wat. 75 BV35
Aspen Pk Dr
Alder Way, Swan. 207 FD96
Alderbourne La, Iver 113 BA64
Alderbourne La (Fulmer), Slou. 112 AX63
Alderbrook Rd SW12 181 DH86
Alderbury Rd SW13 159 CU79
Alderbury Rd, Slou. 153 AZ75
Alderbury Rd W, Slou. 153 AZ75
Aldercombe La, Cat. 252 DS127
Aldercroft, Couls. 235 DM116
Aldergrove Gdns, Houns. 156 BY82
Bath Rd
Aldergrove Wk, Horn. 148 FJ65
Airfield Way
Alderholt Way SE15 162 DT80
Daniel Gdns
Alderley Ct, Berk. 38 AV20
Alderman Av, Bark. 146 EU69
Alderman Cl, Hat. 45 CW24
Alderman Judge Mall, Kings.T. 198 CL96
Eden St
Aldermanbury EC2 275 J8
Aldermanbury EC2 142 DQ72
Aldermanbury Sq EC2 275 J7
Aldermans Hill N13 99 DL49
Alderman's Wk EC2 275 M7
Aldermary Rd, Brom. 204 EG95
Aldermoor Rd SE6 183 DZ90
Alderney Av, Houns. 156 CB80
Alderney Gdns, Nthlt. 136 BZ66
Alderney Rd E1 143 DX70
Alderney Rd, Erith 167 FG80
Alderney St SW1 277 J10
Alderney St SW1 161 DH77
Alders, The N21 81 DN44
Alders, The, Felt. 176 BY91
Alders, The, Houns. 156 BZ79
Alders, The, W.Byf. 212 BJ112
Alders, The, W.Wick. 203 EB102
Alders Av, Wdf.Grn. 102 EE51
Alders Cl E11 124 EH61
Aldersbrook Rd
Alders Cl W5 157 CK76
Alders Cl, Edg. 96 CQ50
Alders Ct, Welw.G.C. 30 DA09
Alders Gro, E.Mol. 197 CD99
Esher Rd
Alders Rd, Edg. 96 CQ50
Alders Rd, Reig. 250 DB132
Alders Wk, Saw. 36 EY05
Aldersbrook Av, Enf. 82 DS40
Aldersbrook Dr, Kings.T. 178 CM93
Aldersbrook La E12 125 EM62
Aldersbrook Rd E11 124 EH61
Aldersbrook Rd E12 124 EK62
Aldersey Gdns, Bark. 145 ER65
Aldersey Rd, Guil. 243 AZ134
Aldersford Cl SE4 183 DX85
Aldersgate St EC1 275 H8
Aldersgate St EC1 142 DQ71
Aldersgrove, Wal.Abb. 68 EE34
Roundhills
Aldersgrove Av SE9 184 EJ90
Aldershot Rd NW6 139 CZ67
Aldershot Rd, Guil. 242 AT132
Alderside Wk (Englefield Grn), Egh. 172 AY92
Aldersmead Av, Croy. 203 DX100
Aldersmead Rd, Beck. 183 DY94
Alderson Pl, Sthl. 136 CC74
Alderson St W10 139 CY70
Kensal Rd
Alderstead Heath, Red. 235 DK124
Alderstead Heath Caravan Club Site, Red. 235 DL123
Dean La
Alderstead La, Red. 251 DK126
Alderton Cl NW10 118 CR62
Alderton Cl, Brwd. 108 FV43
Alderton Cl, Loug. 85 EN42
Alderton Cres NW4 119 CV57
Alderton Hall La, Loug. 85 EN42
Alderton Hill, Loug. 84 EL43
Alderton Ms, Loug. 85 EN42
Alderton Hall La
Alderton Ri, Loug. 85 EN42
Alderton Rd SE24 162 DQ83
Alderton Rd, Croy. 202 DT101
Alderton Way NW4 119 CV57
Alderton Way, Loug. 85 EM43
Alderville Rd SW6 159 CZ82
Alderwick Dr, Houns. 157 CD83
Alderwood Cl, Cat. 252 DS125
Alderwood Cl, Rom. 86 EV41
Alderwood Dr, Rom. 86 EV41
Alderwood Rd SE9 185 ER86
Aldford St W1 276 F2
Aldford St W1 140 DG74
Aldgate EC3 275 P9
Aldgate EC3 142 DT72
Aldgate Av E1 275 P8
Aldgate Barrs Shop Cen E1 142 DT72
Whitechapel High St
Aldgate High St EC3 275 P9
Aldgate High St EC3 142 DT72
Aldham Dr, S.Ock. 149 FW71
Aldin Av N, Slou. 152 AV75
Aldin Av S, Slou. 152 AU75
Aldine Ct W12 139 CW74
Aldine St
Aldine Pl W12 139 CW74
Uxbridge Rd
Aldine St W12 159 CW75
Aldingham Ct, Horn. 127 FG64
Easedale Dr
Aldingham Gdns, Horn. 127 FG64
Aldington Cl, Dag. 126 EW59
Aldington Rd SE18 164 EK76
Aldis Ms SW17 180 DE92
Aldis St
Aldis St SW17 180 DE92
Aldock, Welw.G.C. 30 DA12
Aldred Rd NW6 120 DA64
Aldren Rd SW17 180 DC90
Aldrich Cres (New Addington), Croy. 221 EC109
Aldrich Gdns, Sutt. 199 CZ104
Aldrich Ter SW18 180 DC89
Lidiard Rd
Aldriche Way E4 101 EC51

Aldridge Av, Edg. 96 CP48
Aldridge Av, Enf. 83 EA38
Aldridge Av, Ruis. 116 BX61
Aldridge Av, Stan. 96 CL53
Aldridge Ri, N.Mal. 198 CS101
Aldridge Rd, Slou. 131 AN70
Aldridge Rd Vil W11 139 CZ71
Aldridge Wk N14 99 DL45
Aldrington Rd SW16 181 DJ92
Aldsworth Cl W9 140 DB70
Aldwick, St.Alb. 43 CH22
Aldwick Cl SE9 185 ER90
Aldwick Rd, Croy. 201 DM104
Aldworth Gro SE13 183 EC86
Aldworth Rd E15 144 EE66
Aldwych WC2 274 B10
Aldwych WC2 141 DM73
Aldwych Av, Ilf. 125 EQ56
Aldwych Cl, Horn. 127 FG61
Aldwych Underpass WC2 141 DM72
Kingsway
Aldykes, Hat. 45 CT18
Alers Rd, Bexh. 186 EX85
Alesia Cl N22 99 DL52
Nightingale Rd
Alestan Beck Rd E16 144 EK72
Alex Ct, Hem.H. 40 BK19
Alexandra Rd
Alexa Ct W8 160 DA77
Lexham Gdns
Alexa Ct, Sutt. 218 DA107
Mulgrave Rd
Alexander Av NW10 139 CV66
Alexander Cl, Barn. 80 DD42
Alexander Cl, Brom. 204 EG102
Alexander Cl, Sid. 185 ES85
Alexander Cl, Sthl. 136 CC74
Alexander Cl, Twick. 177 CF89
Alexander Ct, Wal.Cr. 67 DX30
Alexander Cres, Cat. 236 DQ122
Coulsdon Rd
Alexander Evans Ms SE23 183 DX88
Sunderland Rd
Alexander Godley Cl, Ash. 232 CM119
Alexander La, Brwd. 109 GB44
Alexander Ms W2 140 DB72
Alexander St
Alexander Pl SW7 276 B8
Alexander Pl SW7 160 DE77
Alexander Rd N19 121 DL62
Alexander Rd, Bexh. 166 EX82
Alexander Rd, Chis. 185 EP92
Alexander Rd, Couls. 235 DH115
Alexander Rd, Egh. 173 BB92
Alexander Rd, Green. 189 FW85
Alexander Rd, Hert. 31 DN09
Alexander Rd, Reig. 266 DA137
Alexander Rd (London Colney), St.Alb. 61 CJ25
Alexander Sq SW3 276 B8
Alexander Sq SW3 160 DE77
Alexander St W2 140 DA72
Alexander St, Chesh. 54 AQ30
Alexanders Wk, Cat. 252 DT126
Alexandra Av N22 99 DK53
Alexandra Av SW11 160 DG81
Alexandra Av W4 158 CR80
Alexandra Av, Har. 116 BZ60
Alexandra Av, Sthl. 136 BZ73
Alexandra Av, Sutt. 200 DA104
Alexandra Av, Warl. 237 DZ117
Alexandra Cl, Ashf. 175 BR94
Alexandra Rd
Alexandra Cl, Grays 171 GH75
Alexandra Cl, Har. 116 CA62
Alexandra Av
Alexandra Cl, Stai. 174 BK93
Alexandra Cl, Swan. 207 FE96
Alexandra Cl, Walt. 195 BU103
Alexandra Cotts SE14 163 DZ81
Alexandra Ct N14 81 DJ43
Alexandra Ct N16 122 DT63
Belgrade Rd
Alexandra Ct, Ashf. 175 BR93
Alexandra Rd
Alexandra Ct, Wem. 118 CM63
Alexandra Cres, Brom. 184 EF93
Alexandra Dr SE19 182 DS92
Alexandra Dr, Surb. 198 CN101
Alexandra Gdns N10 121 DH56
Alexandra Gdns W4 158 CR80
Alexandra Gdns, Cars. 218 DG109
Alexandra Gdns, Houns. 156 CB82
Alexandra Gro N4 121 DP60
Alexandra Gro N12 98 DB50
Alexandra Ms N2 120 DF55
Fortis Grn
Alexandra Ms SW19 180 DA93
Alexandra Rd
Alexandra Palace N22 99 DK54
Alexandra Palace Way N22 121 DJ55
Alexandra Pk Rd N10 99 DH54
Alexandra Pk Rd N22 99 DK54
Alexandra Pl NW8 140 DC67
Alexandra Pl SE25 202 DR99
Alexandra Pl, Croy. 202 DS102
Alexandra Rd
Alexandra Pl, Guil. 259 AZ136
Alexandra Rd E6 145 EN69
Alexandra Rd E10 123 EC62
Alexandra Rd E17 123 DZ58
Alexandra Rd E18 124 EH55
Alexandra Rd N8 121 DN55
Alexandra Rd N9 100 DV45
Alexandra Rd N10 99 DH52
Alexandra Rd N15 122 DR57
Alexandra Rd NW4 119 CX56
Alexandra Rd NW8 140 DC66
Alexandra Rd SE26 183 DX93
Alexandra Rd SW14 158 CR83
Alexandra Rd SW19 179 CZ93
Alexandra Rd W4 158 CR75
Alexandra Rd, Add. 212 BK105
Alexandra Rd, Ashf. 175 BR94
Alexandra Rd, Borwd. 78 CR38
Alexandra Rd, Brent. 157 CK79
Alexandra Rd, Brwd. 108 FW48
Alexandra Rd, Croy. 202 DS102
Alexandra Rd (Englefield Grn), Egh. 172 AW93
Alexandra Rd, Enf. 83 DX42
Alexandra Rd, Epsom 217 CT113
Alexandra Rd, Erith 167 FF79
Alexandra Rd, Grav. 191 GL87
Alexandra Rd, Hem.H. 40 BK20
Alexandra Rd, Houns. 156 CB82
Alexandra Rd, Kings L. 58 BN29
Alexandra Rd (Chipperfield), Kings L. 58 BG30
Alexandra Rd, Kings.T. 178 CN94
Alexandra Rd, Mitch. 180 DE94
Alexandra Rd, Rain. 147 FF67
Alexandra Rd, Rich. 158 CM82
Alexandra Rd, Rick. 74 BG36
Alexandra Rd, Rom. 127 FF58
Alexandra Rd (Chadwell Heath), Rom. 126 EX58
Alexandra Rd, St.Alb. 43 CE20
Alexandra Rd, Slou. 151 AR76
Alexandra Rd, T.Ditt. 197 CF99
Alexandra Rd, Til. 171 GF82
Alexandra Rd, Twick. 177 CJ86
Alexandra Rd, Uxb. 134 BK68
Alexandra Rd, Warl. 237 DY117
Alexandra Rd, Wat. 75 BU40
Alexandra Rd (Biggin Hill), West. 238 EH119
Alexandra Rd, Wind. 151 AR82
Alexandra Sq, Mord. 200 DA99
Alexandra St E16 144 EG71
Alexandra St SE14 163 DY80
Alexandra Ter, Guil. 258 AY135
Alexandra Wk SE19 182 DS92
Alexandra Way, Epsom 216 CN111
Alexandra Way, Wal.Cr. 67 DZ34
Alexandria Rd W13 137 CG73
Alexis St SE16 162 DU77
Alfan La, Dart. 187 FD92
Alfearn Rd E5 122 DW63
Alford Cl, Guil. 243 AZ131
Alford Grn (New Addington), Croy. 221 ED107
Alford Pl N1 275 J1
Alford Rd SW8 161 DK81
Alford Rd, Erith 167 FD78
Alfoxton Av N15 121 DP56
Alfred Cl W4 158 CR77
Belmont Rd
Alfred Gdns, Sthl. 136 BY73
Alfred Ms W1 273 M6
Alfred Ms W1 141 DK71
Alfred Pl WC1 273 M6
Alfred Pl WC1 141 DK71
Alfred Pl (Northfleet), Grav. 191 GF88
Alfred Prior Ho E12 125 EN63
Alfred Rd E15 124 EF64
Alfred Rd SE25 202 DU99
Alfred Rd W2 140 DA71
Alfred Rd W3 138 CQ74
Alfred Rd, Belv. 166 EZ78
Alfred Rd, Brwd. 108 FX47
Alfred Rd, Buck.H. 102 EK47
Alfred Rd (Hawley), Dart. 188 FL91
Alfred Rd, Felt. 176 BW89
Alfred Rd, Grav. 191 GH89
Alfred Rd, Kings.T. 198 CL97
Alfred Rd, S.Ock. 148 FQ74
Alfred Rd, Sutt. 218 DC106
Alfred St E3 143 DZ69
Alfred St, Grays 170 GC79
Alfreda St SW11 161 DH81
Alfred's Gdns, Bark. 145 ES68
Alfreds Way, Bark. 145 EQ69
Alfreds Way Ind Est, Bark. 146 EU67
Alfreton Cl SW19 179 CX90
Alfriston Av, Croy. 201 DL101
Alfriston Av, Har. 116 CA58
Alfriston Cl, Surb. 198 CM99
Alfriston Rd SW11 180 DF85
Algar Cl, Islw. 157 CG83
Algar Rd
Algar Cl, Stan. 95 CF50
Algar Rd, Islw. 157 CG83
Algarve Rd SW18 180 DB88
Algernon Rd NW4 119 CU58
Algernon Rd NW6 140 DA67
Algernon Rd SE13 163 EB84
Algers Cl, Loug. 84 EK43
Algers Mead, Loug. 84 EK43
Algers Rd, Loug. 84 EK43
Algiers Rd SE13 163 EA84
Alibon Gdns, Dag. 126 FA64
Alibon Rd, Dag. 126 FA64
Alice Cl, Barn. 80 DC42
Alice Ct SW15 159 CZ84
Deodar Rd
Alice Gilliatt Ct W14 159 CZ79
Alice La E3 143 DZ67
Alice La (Burnham), Slou. 130 AH70
Alice Ms, Tedd. 177 CF92
Luther Rd
Alice Ruston Pl, Wok. 226 AW119
Alice St SE1 279 M7
Alice St SE1 162 DS76
Alice Thompson Cl SE12 184 EJ89
Alice Walker Cl SE24 161 DP84
Shakespeare Rd
Alice Way, Houns. 156 CB84
Alicia Av, Har. 117 CH56
Alicia Cl, Har. 117 CJ56
Alicia Gdns, Har. 117 CJ56
Alie St E1 142 DT72
Alington Cres NW9 118 CQ60
Alington Gro, Wall. 219 DJ109
Alison Cl E6 145 EN72
Alison Cl, Croy. 203 DX102
Shirley Oaks Rd
Alison Cl, Wok. 226 AY115
Aliwal Rd SW11 160 DE84
Alkerden La, Green. 189 FW86
Alkerden La, Swans. 189 FW86
Alkerden Rd W4 158 CS78
Alkham Rd N16 122 DT61
All Hallows Rd N17 100 DS53
All Saints Cl N9 100 DT47
All Saints Cl, Chig. 104 EU48
All Saints Cl, Swans. 190 FZ85
High St
All Saints Cres, Wat. 60 BX33
All Saints Dr SE3 164 EE82
All Saints Dr, S.Croy. 220 DT112
All Saints La, Rick. 74 BN44
All Saints Ms, Har. 95 CE51
All Saints Pas SW18 180 DB85
Wandsworth High St
All Saints Rd SW19 180 DC94
All Saints Rd W3 158 CQ76
All Saints Rd W11 139 CZ71
All Saints Rd (Northfleet), Grav. 191 GF88
All Saints Rd, Sutt. 200 DB104
All Saints St N1 141 DM68
All Saints Twr E10 123 EB59
All Souls Av NW10 139 CV68
All Souls Pl W1 273 J7
Allan Barclay Cl N15 122 DT58
High Rd
Allan Cl, N.Mal. 198 CR99
Allan Way W3 138 CQ71
Allandale, Hem.H. 40 BK18
Allandale, St.Alb. 42 CB23
Allandale Av N3 119 CY55
Allandale Cres, Pot.B. 63 CY32
Allandale Pl, Orp. 206 EX104
Allandale Rd, Enf. 83 DX36
Allandale Rd, Horn. 127 FF59
Allard Cl, Orp. 206 EW101
Allard Cl (Cheshunt), Wal.Cr. 66 DT27
Allard Cres, Bushey 94 CC46
Allard Gdns SW4 181 DK85
Allard Way, Brox. 49 DY21
Allardyce St SW4 161 DM84
Allbrook Cl, Tedd. 177 CE92
Allcot Cl, Felt. 175 BT88
Allcroft Rd NW5 120 DG64
Alldicks Rd, Hem.H. 40 BM22
Allen Cl, Mitch. 201 DH95
Allen Cl, Rad. 62 CL32
Russet Dr
Allen Cl, Sun. 195 BV95
Allen Ct, Dor. 263 CH136
High St
Allen Ct, Grnf. 117 CF64
Allen Ct, Hat. 45 CV20
Drakes Way
Allen Edwards Dr SW8 161 DL81
Allen Ho Pk, Wok. 226 AW120
Allen Pl, Twick. 177 CG88
Church St
Allen Rd E3 143 DZ68
Allen Rd N16 122 DS63
Allen Rd, Beck. 203 DX96
Allen Rd, Croy. 201 DM101
Allen Rd (Bookham), Lthd. 246 CB126
Allen Rd, Rain. 148 FJ68
Allen Rd, Sun. 195 BV95
Allen St W8 160 DA76
Allenby Av, S.Croy. 220 DQ109
Allenby Cl, Grnf. 136 CA69
Allenby Cres, Grays 170 GB78
Allenby Dr, Horn. 128 FL60
Allenby Rd SE23 183 DY90
Allenby Rd, Sthl. 136 CA72
Allenby Rd (Biggin Hill), West. 238 EL117
Allendale Av, Sthl. 136 CA72
Allendale Cl SE5 162 DR81
Daneville Rd
Allendale Cl SE26 183 DX92
Allendale Cl, Dart. 189 FR88
Princes Rd
Allendale Rd, Grnf. 137 CH65
Allende Av, Harl. 35 ER13
Allenford Ho SW15 179 CT86
Tunworth Cres
Allens Rd, Enf. 82 DW43
Allensbury Pl NW1 141 DK66
Allenswood Rd SE9 164 EL83
Allerds Rd (Farnham Royal), Slou. 131 AM67
Allerford Ct, Har. 116 CB57
Allerford Rd SE6 183 EB91
Allerton Cl, Borwd. 78 CM38
Allerton Ct NW4 97 CX54
Holders Hill Rd
Allerton Rd N16 122 DQ61
Allerton Rd, Borwd. 78 CL38
Allerton Wk N7 121 DM61
Durham Rd
Allestree Rd SW6 159 CY80
Alleyn Cres SE21 182 DR89
Alleyn Pk SE21 182 DR89
Alleyn Pk, Sthl. 156 BZ77
Alleyn Rd SE21 182 DR90
Alleyndale Rd, Dag. 126 EW61
Allfarthing La SW18 180 DB86
Allgood Cl, Mord. 199 CX100
Allgood St E2 142 DT68
Hackney Rd
Allhallows La EC4 279 K1
Allhallows Rd E6 144 EL71
Allhusen Gdns (Fulmer), Slou. 112 AY63
Alderbourne La
Alliance Cl, Wem. 117 CK63
Alliance Ct W3 138 CP70
Alliance Rd
Alliance Rd E13 144 EJ70
Alliance Rd SE18 166 EU79
Alliance Rd W3 138 CP70
Allied Way W3 158 CS75
Larden Rd
Allingham Cl W7 137 CF73
Allingham Ct, Gdmg. 258 AT144
Summers Rd
Allingham Ms N1 142 DQ68
Allingham St
Allingham Rd, Reig. 266 DA137
Allingham St N1 142 DQ68
Allington Av N17 100 DS51
Allington Cl SW19 179 CX92
High St Wimbledon
Allington Cl, Grav. 191 GM88
Farley Rd
Allington Cl, Grnf. 136 CC66
Allington Ct, Enf. 83 DX43
Allington Ct, Slou. 132 AT73
Myrtle Cres
Allington Rd NW4 119 CV57
Allington Rd W10 139 CY68
Allington Rd, Har. 116 CC57
Allington Rd, Orp. 205 ER103
Allington St SW1 277 K7
Allington St SW1 161 DH76
Allison Cl SE10 163 EC81
Dartmouth Hill
Allison Cl, Wal.Abb. 68 EG32
Allison Gro SE21 182 DS88
Allison Rd N8 121 DN57
Allison Rd W3 138 CQ72
Allitsen Rd NW8 272 B1
Allitsen Rd NW8 140 DE68
Allmains Cl, Wal.Abb. 68 EH25
Allnutt Way SW4 181 DK85
Allnutts Rd, Epp. 70 EU33
Alloa Rd SE8 163 DX78
Alloa Rd, Ilf. 126 EU61
Allonby Dr, Ruis. 115 BP59
Allonby Gdns, Wem. 117 CJ60
Allotment La, Sev. 257 FJ122
Alloway Cl, Wok. 226 AV118
Inglewood
Alloway Rd E3 143 DY69
Allsop Pl NW1 272 E5
Allsop Pl NW1 140 DF70
Allum Cl, Borwd. 78 CL42
Allum Gro, Tad. 233 CV121
Preston La
Allum La, Borwd. 78 CM42
Allum Way N20 98 DC46
Allwood Cl SE26 183 DX91
Allwood Rd, Wal.Cr. 66 DT27
Allyn Cl, Stai. 173 BF93
Penton Rd
Alma Av E4 101 EC52
Alma Av, Horn. 128 FL63
Alma Cl (Knaphill), Wok. 226 AS118
Alma Cres, Sutt. 217 CY106
Alma Cut, St.Alb. 43 CE21
Alma Gro SE1 162 DT77
Alma Pl NW10 139 CV69
Harrow Rd
Alma Pl SE19 182 DT94
Alma Pl, Th.Hth. 201 DN99
Alma Rd N10 98 DG52
Alma Rd SW18 180 DC85
Alma Rd, Berk. 38 AS17
Alma Rd, Cars. 218 DE106
Alma Rd, Chesh. 54 AQ29
Alma Rd, Enf. 83 DY43
Alma Rd, Esher 197 CE102
Alma Rd, Orp. 206 EX103
Alma Rd, Reig. 250 DB133
Alma Rd, St.Alb. 43 CE21
Alma Rd, Sid. 186 EU90
Alma Rd, Sthl. 136 BY73
Alma Rd, Swans. 190 FZ85
Alma Rd, Wind. 151 AQ81
Alma Rd (Eton Wick), Wind. 151 AM77
Alma Row, Har. 95 CD53
Alma Sq NW8 140 DC69
Alma St E15 143 ED65
Alma St NW5 141 DH65
Alma Ter SW18 180 DD87
Alma Ter W8 160 DA76
Allen St
Almack Rd E5 122 DW63
Almeida St N1 141 DP66
Almer Rd SW20 179 CU94
Almeric Rd SW11 160 DF84
Almington St N4 121 DM60
Almners Rd (Lyne), Cher. 193 BC100
Almond Av W5 158 CL76
Almond Av, Cars. 200 DF103
Almond Av, Uxb. 115 BP62
Almond Av, West Dr. 154 BN76
Almond Av, Wok. 226 AX121
Almond Cl SE15 162 DU82
Almond Cl, Brom. 205 EN101
Almond Cl (Englefield Grn), Egh. 172 AV93
Highfield Rd
Almond Cl, Felt. 175 BU88
Almond Cl, Grays 171 GG76
Almond Cl, Guil. 242 AX130
Almond Cl, Hayes 135 BS73
Almond Cl, Ruis. 115 BT62
Roundways
Almond Cl, Shep. 195 BQ96
Almond Cl, Wind. 151 AP82
Almond Dr, Swan. 207 FD96
Almond Gro, Brent. 157 CH80
Almond Rd N17 100 DU52
Almond Rd SE16 162 DV77
Almond Rd, Dart. 188 FQ87
Almond Rd, Epsom 216 CR111
Almond Rd (Burnham), Slou. 130 AH68
Almond Wk, Hat. 45 CU21
Southdown Rd
Almond Way, Borwd. 78 CP42
Almond Way, Brom. 205 EN101
Almond Way, Har. 94 CB54
Almond Way, Mitch. 201 DK99
Almonds, The, St.Alb. 43 CH24
Almonds Av, Buck.H. 102 EG47
Almons Way, Slou. 132 AV71
Almorah Rd N1 142 DR66
Almorah Rd, Houns. 156 BX81
Alms Heath (Ockham), Wok. 229 BP121
Almshouse La, Chess. 215 CJ109
Almshouse La, Enf. 82 DV37
Almshouses, The, Dor. 263 CH135
Cotmandene
Alnwick Gro, Mord. 200 DB98
Bordesley Rd
Alnwick Rd E16 144 EJ72
Alnwick Rd SE12 184 EH87
Alperton La, Grnf. 137 CK69
Alperton La, Wem. 137 CK69
Alperton St W10 139 CY70
Alpha Business Pk, Hat. 45 CW23
Alpha Cl NW1 272 C3
Alpha Ct, Whyt. 236 DU118
Alpha Gro E14 163 EA75
Alpha Pl NW6 140 DA68
Alpha Pl SW3 160 DE79
Alpha Rd E4 101 EB48
Alpha Rd N18 100 DU51
Alpha Rd SE14 163 DZ81
Alpha Rd, Brwd. 109 GD44
Alpha Rd, Croy. 202 DS102
Alpha Rd, Enf. 83 DY42
Alpha Rd, Surb. 198 CM100
Alpha Rd, Tedd. 177 CD92
Alpha Rd, Uxb. 135 BP70
Alpha Rd, Wok. 227 BB116
Alpha Rd (Chobham), Wok. 210 AT110
Alpha St SE15 162 DU82
Alpha St N, Slou. 152 AU75
Alpha St S, Slou. 152 AT76
Alpha Way, Egh. 193 BC95
Alphabet Gdns, Cars. 200 DD100
Alphabet Sq E3 143 EA71
Hawgood St
Alphea Cl SW19 180 DE94
Courtney Rd
Alpine Av, Surb. 198 CQ103
Alpine Business Cen E6 145 EN71
Alpine Cl, Croy. 202 DS104
Alpine Copse, Brom. 205 EN96
Alpine Gro E9 142 DW66
Alpine Rd SE16 162 DW77
Alpine Rd, Red. 250 DG131
Alpine Rd, Walt. 195 BU101
Alpine Vw, Cars. 218 DE106
Alpine Wk, Stan. 95 CE47
Alpine Way E6 145 EN71
Alresford Rd, Guil. 258 AU135
Alric Av NW10 138 CR66
Alric Av, N.Mal. 198 CS97
Alroy Rd N4 121 DN59
Alsace Rd SE17 279 M10
Alsace Rd SE17 162 DS78
Alscot Rd SE1 162 DT77
Alscot Way SE1 279 P8
Alscot Way SE1 162 DT77
Alsford Wf, Berk. 38 AX19
Alsike Rd SE2 166 EX76
Alsike Rd, Erith 166 EY76
Alsom Av, Wor.Pk. 217 CU105
Alsop Cl (London Colney), St.Alb. 62 CM27
Alston Cl, Surb. 197 CH101
Alston Rd N18 100 DV50
Alston Rd SW17 180 DD91
Alston Rd, Barn. 79 CY41
Alston Rd, Hem.H. 40 BG21
Alt Gro SW19 179 CZ94
St. George's Rd
Altair Cl N17 100 DT51
Altair Way, Nthwd. 93 BT49
Altash Way SE9 185 EM89
Altenburg Av W13 157 CH76
Altenburg Gdns SW11 160 DF84
Alterton Cl, Wok. 226 AU117
Altham Gro, Harl. 35 ET12
Altham Rd, Pnr. 94 BY52
Althea St SW6 160 DB83
Althorne Gdns E18 124 EF56
Althorne Rd, Red. 266 DG136
Althorne Way, Dag. 126 FA61
Althorp Cl, Barn. 97 CU45
Althorp Rd SW17 180 DF88
Althorp Rd, St.Alb. 43 CE19
Althorpe Gro SW11 160 DD81
Westbridge Rd
Althorpe Ms SW11 160 DD81
Westbridge Rd
Althorpe Rd, Har. 116 CC57
Altmore Av E6 145 EM66
Alton Av, Stan. 95 CF52
Alton Cl, Bex. 186 EY88
Alton Cl, Islw. 157 CF82
Alton Ct, Stai. 193 BE95
Alton Gdns, Beck. 183 EA94
Alton Gdns, Twick. 177 CD87
Alton Rd N17 122 DR55
Alton Rd SW15 179 CU88
Alton Rd, Croy. 201 DN104
Alton Rd, Rich. 158 CL84
Alton St E14 143 EB71
Altona Rd (Loudwater), H.Wyc. 88 AC52
Altona Way, Slou. 131 AP72
Altwood Cl, Slou. 131 AL71
Burnham La
Altyre Cl, Beck. 203 DZ99
Altyre Rd, Croy. 202 DR103
Altyre Way, Beck. 203 DZ99
Aluric Cl, Grays 171 GH77
Alva Way, Wat. 94 BX47
Alvanley Gdns NW6 120 DB64
Alverstoke Rd, Rom. 106 FL52
Alverston Gdns SE25 202 DS99
Alverstone Av SW19 180 DA89
Alverstone Av, Barn. 98 DE45
Alverstone Gdns SE9 185 EQ88
Alverstone Rd E12 125 EN63
Alverstone Rd NW2 139 CW66
Alverstone Rd, N.Mal. 199 CT98
Alverstone Rd, Wem. 118 CM60
Alverton, St.Alb. 42 CC17
Green La
Alverton St SE8 163 DZ78
Alveston Av, Har. 117 CH55
Alvey Est SE17 279 M9
Alvey Est SE17 162 DS77
Alvey St SE17 279 M10
Alvey St SE17 162 DS78
Alvia Gdns, Sutt. 218 DC105
Alvington Cres E8 122 DT64
Alvista Av, Maid. 130 AH72
Alway Av, Epsom 216 CQ106
Alwen Gro, S.Ock. 149 FV71
Alwold Cres SE12 184 EH86
Alwyn Av W4 158 CR78
Alwyn Cl, Borwd. 78 CM44
Alwyn Cl (New Addington), Croy. 221 EB108
Alwyn Gdns NW4 119 CU56
Alwyn Gdns W3 138 CP72
Alwyne Av, Brwd. 109 GA44
Alwyne Ct, Wok. 226 AY116
Alwyne La N1 141 DP66
Alwyne Vil
Alwyne Pl N1 142 DQ65
Alwyne Rd N1 142 DQ66
Alwyne Rd SW19 179 CZ93
Alwyne Rd W7 137 CE73
Alwyne Sq N1 142 DQ65
Alwyne Vil N1 141 DP66
Alwyns Cl, Cher. 194 BG100
Alwyns La
Alwyns La, Cher. 193 BF100
Alyngton, Berk. 38 AS16
Alyth Gdns NW11 120 DA58
Alzette Ho E2 143 DX69
Amalgamated Dr, Brent. 157 CG79
Amanda Cl, Chig. 103 ER51
Amanda Ct, Slou. 152 AX76
Amanda Ms, Rom. 127 FC57
Amazon St E1 142 DV72
Hessel St
Ambassador Cl, Houns. 156 BY82
Ambassador Gdns E6 145 EM71
Ambassador Sq E14 163 EB77
Cahir St
Ambassador's Ct SW1 277 L3
Amber Av E17 101 DY53
Amber Ct SW17 180 DG91
Brudenell Rd
Amber Ct, Stai. 173 BF92
Laleham Rd
Amber Gro NW2 119 CX60
Prayle Gro
Amber St E15 143 ED65
Great Eastern Rd
Ambercroft Way, Couls. 235 DP119
Amberden Av N3 120 DA55
Ambergate St SE17 278 G10
Ambergate St SE17 161 DP78
Amberley Cl, Orp. 223 ET106
Warnford Rd
Amberley Cl, Pnr. 116 BZ55
Amberley Cl (Send), Wok. 243 BF125
Amberley Ct, Maid. 130 AC69
Amberley Ct, Sid. 186 EW92
Amberley Dr (Woodham), Add. 211 BF110
Amberley Gdns, Enf. 100 DS45
Amberley Gdns, Epsom 217 CT105
Amberley Gro SE26 182 DV91
Amberley Gro, Croy. 202 DT101
Amberley Rd E10 123 EB59
Amberley Rd N13 99 DM47
Amberley Rd SE2 166 EX79
Amberley Rd W9 140 DA71
Amberley Rd, Buck.H. 102 EJ46
Amberley Rd, Enf. 100 DT45
Amberley Rd, Slou. 131 AL71
Amberley Way, Houns. 176 BW85
Amberley Way, Mord. 199 CZ101
Amberley Way, Rom. 127 FB56
Amberley Way, Uxb. 134 BL69
Amberry Ct, Harl. 35 ER14
Amberside Cl, Islw. 177 CD86
Amberwood Cl, Wall. 219 DL106
The Chase
Amberwood Ri, N.Mal. 198 CS100
Amblecote, Cob. 214 BY111
Amblecote Cl SE12 184 EH90
Amblecote Meadows SE12 184 EH90
Amblecote Rd SE12 184 EH90
Ambler Rd N4 121 DP62
Ambleside, Brom. 183 ED93

Ambleside, Epp. 70 EU31
Ambleside Av SW16 181 DK91
Ambleside Av, Beck. 203 DY99
Ambleside Av, Horn. 127 FH64
Ambleside Av, Walt. 196 BW102
Ambleside Cl E9 122 DW64
Churchill Wk
Ambleside Cl E10 123 EB59
Ambleside Cl, Red. 267 DH139
Ambleside Cres, Enf. 83 DX41
Ambleside Dr, Felt. 175 BT88
Ambleside Gdns SW16 181 DK92
Ambleside Gdns, Ilf. 124 EL56
Ambleside Gdns, S.Croy. 221 DX109
Ambleside Gdns, Sutt. 218 DC107
Ambleside Gdns, Wem. 117 CK60
Ambleside Pt SE15 162 DW80
Ilderton Rd
Ambleside Rd NW10 139 CT66
Ambleside Rd, Bexh. 166 FA82
Ambleside Wk, Uxb. 134 BK67
High St
Ambleside Way, Egh. 173 BB94
Ambrey Way, Wall. 219 DK109
Ambrooke Rd, Belv. 166 FA76
Ambrosden Av SW1 277 L7
Ambrosden Av SW1 161 DJ76
Ambrose Av NW11 119 CY59
Ambrose Cl E6 144 EL71
Lovage App
Ambrose Cl (Crayford), Dart. 167 FF84
Ambrose Cl, Orp. 205 ET104
Stapleton Rd
Ambrose Ms SW11 160 DE82
Ambrose St SE16 162 DV77
Ambrose Wk E3 143 EA68
Malmesbury Rd
Amelia St SE17 278 G10
Amelia St SE17 161 DP78
Amen Cor EC4 274 G9
Amen Cor SW17 180 DF93
Amen Ct EC4 274 G8
Amenity Way, Mord. 199 CW101
Amerden Caravan Pk, Maid. 150 AE75
Amerden Cl, Maid. 130 AD72
Amerden La, Maid. 130 AD74
Amerden Way, Slou. 151 AN75
America Sq EC3 275 P10
America St SE1 279 H3
Amerland Rd SW18 179 CZ86
Amersham Av N18 100 DR51
Amersham Bypass, Amer. 55 AN41
Amersham Cl, Rom. 106 FM51
Amersham Dr, Rom. 106 FL51
Amersham Gro SE14 163 DZ80
Amersham Pl, Amer. 72 AW39
Amersham Rd SE14 163 DZ81
Amersham Rd (Chesham Bois), Amer. 55 AP36
Amersham Rd (Coleshill), Amer. 89 AP46
Amersham Rd (Little Chalfont), Amer. 72 AX39
Amersham Rd, Beac. 89 AM53
Amersham Rd, Ch.St.G. 72 AU43
Amersham Rd, Chesh. 55 AP35
Amersham Rd, Croy. 202 DQ100
Amersham Rd, Ger.Cr. 113 BB59
Amersham Rd (Chalfont St. Peter), Ger.Cr. 112 AY55
Amersham Rd, Rick. 73 BB39
Amersham Rd, Rom. 106 FM51
Amersham Vale SE14 163 DZ80
Amersham Wk, Rom. 106 FM51
Amersham Rd
Amersham Way, Amer. 72 AX39
Amery Gdns NW10 139 CV67
Amery Gdns, Rom. 128 FK55
Amery Rd, Har. 117 CG61
Ames Rd, Swans. 190 FY86
Amesbury, Wal.Abb. 68 EG32
Amesbury Av SW2 181 DL89
Amesbury Cl, Epp. 69 ET31
Amesbury Rd
Amesbury Cl, Wor.Pk. 199 CW102
Amesbury Dr E4 83 EB44
Amesbury Rd, Brom. 204 EK97
Amesbury Rd, Dag. 146 EX66
Amesbury Rd, Epp. 69 ET31
Amesbury Rd, Felt. 176 BX89
Amesbury Twr SW8 161 DJ82
Westbury St
Amethyst Rd E15 123 ED63
Amey Dr (Bookham), Lthd. 230 CC124
Amherst Av W13 137 CJ72
Amherst Cl, Orp. 206 EU98
Amherst Dr, Orp. 205 ET98
Amherst Hill, Sev. 256 FE122
Amherst Rd W13 137 CJ72
Amherst Rd, Sev. 257 FH122
Amhurst Gdns, Islw. 157 CF81
Amhurst Par N16 122 DT59
Amhurst Pk
Amhurst Pk N16 122 DR59
Amhurst Pas E8 122 DU64
Amhurst Rd E8 122 DV64
Amhurst Rd N16 122 DT63
Amhurst Ter E8 122 DU63
Amhurst Wk SE28 146 EU74
Pitfield Cres
Amidas Gdns, Dag. 126 EV63
Amiel St E1 142 DW70
Amies St SW11 160 DF83
Amina Way SE16 162 DU76
Yalding Rd
Amis Av (New Haw), Add. 212 BG111
Amis Av, Epsom 216 CP107
Amis Rd, Wok. 226 AS119
Amity Gro SW20 199 CW95
Amity Rd E15 144 EF67
Ammanford Grn NW9 118 CS58
Ruthin Cl
Amner Rd SW11 180 DG86
Amor Rd W6 159 CW76
Amott Rd SE15 162 DU83
Amoy Pl E14 143 EA72
Ampere Way, Croy. 201 DL101
Ampleforth Rd SE2 166 EV75
Ampthill Sq Est NW1 273 L1
Ampton Pl WC1 274 B3
Ampton St WC1 274 B3
Ampton St WC1 141 DM69
Amroth Cl SE23 182 DV88
Amroth Grn NW9 118 CS58
Fryent Gro
Amstel Way, Wok. 226 AT118
Amsterdam Rd E14 163 EC76
Amundsen Ct E14 163 EA78
Napier Av
Amwell Cl, Enf. 82 DR43
Amwell Cl, Wat. 76 BY35
Phillipers
Amwell Common, Welw.G.C. 30 DB10
Amwell Ct, Hodd. 49 EA16
Amwell Ct, Wal.Abb. 68 EF33
Amwell Ct Est N4 122 DQ60
Amwell End, Ware 33 DX06
Amwell Hill, Ware 33 DZ08
Amwell La, Ware 33 EA09
Amwell Pl, Hert. 32 DW11
Amwell St EC1 274 D2
Amwell St EC1 141 DN69
Amwell St, Hodd. 49 EA17
Amy Cl, Wall. 219 DL108
Mollison Dr
Amy La, Chesh. 54 AP32
Amy Rd, Oxt. 254 EE129
Amy Warne Cl E6 144 EL70
Evelyn Denington Rd
Amyand Cotts, Twick. 177 CH86
Amyand Pk Rd
Amyand La, Twick. 177 CH87
Marble Hill Gdns
Amyand Pk Gdns, Twick. 177 CH87
Amyand Pk Rd
Amyand Pk Rd, Twick. 177 CG87
Amyruth Rd SE4 183 EA85
Anatola Rd N19 121 DH61
Dartmouth Pk Hill
Ancaster Cres, N.Mal. 199 CU100
Ancaster Ms, Beck. 203 DX97
Ancaster Rd, Beck. 203 DX97
Ancaster St SE18 165 ES80
Anchor & Hope La SE7 164 EH76
Anchor Bay Ind Est, Erith 167 FG79
Anchor Boul, Dart. 168 FQ84
Anchor Cl, Bark. 146 EV69
Anchor Cl (Cheshunt), Wal.Cr. 67 DX28
Anchor Dr, Rain. 147 FH69
Anchor La, Hem.H. 40 BH21
Anchor Ms SW12 181 DH86
Hazelbourne Rd
Anchor St SE16 162 DV77
Anchor Ter E1 142 DW70
Cephas Av
Anchor Wf E3 143 EB71
Watts Gro
Anchor Yd EC1 275 J4
Anchorage Cl SW19 180 DA92
Anchorage Pt Ind Est SE7 164 EJ76
Ancill Cl W6 159 CY79
Ancona Rd NW10 139 CU68
Ancona Rd SE18 165 ER78
Andace Pk Gdns, Brom. 204 EJ95
Andalus Rd SW9 161 DL83
Ander Cl, Wem. 117 CK63
Andermans, Wind. 151 AK81
Anderson Cl N21 81 DM43
Anderson Cl W3 138 CR72
Anderson Cl, Epsom 216 CP112
Anderson Cl, Sutt. 200 DA102
Anderson Cl (Harefield), Uxb. 92 BG53
Anderson Dr, Ashf. 175 BQ91
Anderson Ho, Bark. 145 ER68
The Coverdales
Anderson Pl, Houns. 156 CB84
Anderson Rd E9 143 DX65
Anderson Rd, Rad. 62 CN33
Anderson Rd, Wey. 195 BR104
Anderson Rd, Wdf.Grn. 124 EK55
Anderson St SW3 276 D10
Anderson St SW3 160 DF78
Anderson Way, Belv. 167 FB75
Anderton Cl SE5 162 DR83
Andmark Ct, Sthl. 136 BZ74
Herbert Rd
Andover Av E16 144 EK72
King George Av
Andover Cl, Epsom 216 CR111
Andover Cl, Felt. 175 BT88
Andover Cl, Grnf. 136 CB70
Ruislip Rd
Andover Cl, Uxb. 134 BH68
Andover Pl NW6 140 DB68
Andover Rd N7 121 DM61
Andover Rd, Orp. 205 ER102
Andover Rd, Twick. 177 CD88
Andre St E8 122 DU64
Andrea Av, Grays 170 GA75
Andrew Borde St WC2 273 N8
Andrew Cl, Dart. 187 FD85
Andrew Cl, Ilf. 103 ER51
Andrew Cl (Shenley), . Rad 62 CM33
Andrew Hill La (Hedgerley), Slou. 111 AQ61
Andrew Pl SW8 161 DK81
Cowthorpe Rd
Andrew Reed Ho SW18 179 CY87
Linstead Way
Andrew St E14 143 EC72
Andrewes Gdns E6 144 EL72
Andrewes Ho EC2 275 J7
Andrews Cl E6 144 EL72
Linton Gdns
Andrews Cl, Buck.H. 102 EJ47
Andrews Cl, Epsom 217 CT114
Andrews Cl, Har. 117 CD59
Bessborough Rd
Andrews Cl, Hem.H. 40 BK18
Church St
Andrews Cl, Orp. 206 EX96
Andrews Cl, Wor.Pk. 199 CX103
Andrews Crosse WC2 274 D9
Andrews La (Cheshunt), Wal.Cr. 66 DU28
Andrews Pl SE9 185 EP86
Andrew's Rd E8 142 DV67
Andrews Wk SE17 161 DP79
Dale Rd
Andrewsfield, Welw.G.C. 30 DC09
Andwell Cl SE2 166 EV75
Anelle Ri, Hem.H. 40 BM24
Anerley Gro SE19 182 DT94
Anerley Hill SE19 182 DT93
Anerley Pk SE20 182 DU94
Anerley Pk Rd SE20 182 DV94
Anerley Rd SE19 182 DU94
Anerley Rd SE20 182 DU94
Anerley Sta Rd SE20 202 DV95
Anerley St SW11 160 DF82
Anerley Vale SE19 182 DT94
Anfield Cl SW12 181 DJ87
Belthorn Cres
Angas Ct, Wey. 213 BQ106
Angel All E1 142 DU72
Whitechapel Rd
Angel Cl N18 100 DT49
Angel Cor Par N18 100 DU50
Fore St
Angel Ct EC2 275 L8
Angel Ct EC2 142 DR72
Angel Ct SW1 277 L3
Angel Ct SW17 180 DF91
Angel Gate EC1 274 G2
Angel Gate, Guil. 258 AX135
High St
Angel Hill, Sutt. 200 DB104
Sutton Common Rd
Angel Hill Dr, Sutt. 200 DB104
Angel La E15 143 ED65
Angel La, Hayes 135 BR71
Angel Ms E1 142 DU73
Cable St
Angel Ms N1 274 E1
Angel Ms N1 141 DN68
Angel Ms SW15 179 CU87
Roehampton High St
Angel Pas EC4 279 K1
Angel Pl N18 100 DU50
Angel Pl SE1 279 K4
Angel Rd N18 100 DV50
Angel Rd, Har. 117 CE58
Angel Rd, T.Ditt. 197 CG101
Angel Rd Wks N18 100 DW50
Angel Sq EC1 274 E1
Angel St EC1 275 H8
Angel St EC1 142 DQ72
Angel Wk W6 159 CW77
Angel Way, Rom. 127 FE57
Angelfield, Houns. 156 CB84
Angelica Cl, West Dr. 134 BL72
Lovibonds Av
Angelica Dr E6 145 EN71
Angelica Gdns, Croy. 203 DX102
Angelica Rd, Guil. 242 AU130
Angell Pk Gdns SW9 161 DN83
Angell Rd SW9 161 DN83
Angell Town Est SW9 161 DN82
Angerstein La SE3 164 EF80
Angle Cl, Uxb. 134 BN67
Angle Grn, Dag. 126 EW60
Angle Pl, Berk. 38 AU19
Angle Rd, Grays 169 FX79
Anglefield Rd, Berk. 38 AU19
Anglers Cl, Rich. 177 CJ91
Locksmeade Rd
Angler's La NW5 141 DH65
Anglers Reach, Surb. 197 CK99
Angles Rd SW16 181 DL91
Anglesea Av SE18 165 EP77
Anglesea Cen, Grav. 191 GH86
New Rd
Anglesea Pl, Grav. 191 GH86
Clive Rd
Anglesea Rd SE18 165 EP77
Anglesea Rd, Kings.T. 197 CK98
Anglesea Rd, Orp. 206 EW100
Anglesea Ter W6 159 CV76
Wellesley Av
Anglesey Cl, Ashf. 174 BN90
Anglesey Ct Rd, Cars. 218 DG107
Anglesey Dr, Rain. 147 FG71
Anglesey Gdns, Cars. 218 DG107
Anglesey Rd, Enf. 82 DV42
Anglesey Rd, Wat. 94 BW50
Anglesmede Cres, Pnr. 116 CA55
Anglesmede Way, Pnr. 116 BZ55
Anglia Cl N17 100 DV52
Park La
Anglia Ct, Dag. 126 EX60
Spring Cl
Anglia Ho E14 143 DY72
Anglia Wk E6 145 EM67
Anglian Cl, Wat. 76 BW40
Anglian Rd E11 123 ED62
Anglo Rd E3 143 DZ68
Anglo Way, Red. 250 DG132
Angrave Ct E8 142 DT67
Angrave Pas E8 142 DT67
Haggerston Rd
Angus Cl, Chess. 216 CN106
Angus Dr, Ruis. 116 BW63
Angus Gdns NW9 96 CR53
Angus Rd E13 144 EJ69
Angus St SE14 163 DY80
Anhalt Rd SW11 160 DE80
Anisdowne Cl (Abinger Hammer), Dor. 261 BT142
Ankerdine Cres SE18 165 EN80
Ankerwycke Priory (Wraysbury), Stai. 173 AZ89
Anlaby Rd, Tedd. 177 CE92
Anley Rd W14 159 CX75
Anmersh Gro, Stan. 95 CK53
Ann La SW10 160 DD80
Ann Moss Way SE16 162 DW76
Ann St SE18 165 ER77
Anna Cl E8 142 DT67
Anna Neagle Cl E7 124 EG63
Dames Rd
Annabel Cl E14 143 EB72
Annalee Gdns, S.Ock. 149 FV71
Annalee Rd, S.Ock. 149 FV71
Annan Dr, Cars. 218 DG109
Kenny Dr
Annan Way, Rom. 105 FD53
Annandale Gro, Uxb. 115 BQ62
Thorpland Av
Annandale Rd SE10 164 EF79
Annandale Rd W4 158 CS77
Annandale Rd, Croy. 202 DU103
Annandale Rd, Guil. 258 AV136
Annandale Rd, Sid. 185 ES87
Anne Boleyn's Wk, Kings.T. 178 CL92
Anne Boleyn's Wk, Sutt. 217 CX108
Anne Case Ms, N.Mal. 198 CR97
Sycamore Gro
Anne Compton Ms SE12 184 EF87
Anne of Cleves Rd, Dart. 188 FK85
Anne St E13 144 EG70
Anne Taylor Ho E12 125 EN63
Walton Rd
Anne Way, Ilf. 103 EQ51
Anne Way, W.Mol. 196 CB98
Anners Cl, Egh. 193 BC97
Anne's Wk, Cat. 236 DS120
Annesley Av NW9 118 CR55
Annesley Cl NW10 118 CS62
Annesley Dr, Croy. 203 DZ104
Annesley Rd SE3 164 EH81
Annesley Wk N19 121 DJ61
Annett Cl, Shep. 195 BS98
Annett Rd, Walt. 195 BU101
Annette Cl, Har. 95 CE54
Spencer Rd
Annette Cres N1 142 DQ66
Essex Rd
Annette Rd N7 121 DM63
Annie Besant Cl E3 143 DZ67
Annie Brookes Cl, Stai. 173 BD90
Annifer Way, S.Ock. 149 FV71
Anning St EC2 275 N4
Annington Rd N2 120 DF55
Annis Rd E9 143 DY65
Ann's Cl SW1 276 E5
Ann's Pl E1 275 P7
Annsworthy Av, Th.Hth. 202 DR97
Grange Pk Rd
Annsworthy Cres SE25 202 DR96
Grange Rd
Ansculf Rd, Slou. 131 AN69
Ansdell Rd SE15 162 DW82
Ansdell St W8 160 DB76
Ansdell Ter W8 160 DB76
Ansdell St
Ansell Gro, Cars. 200 DG102
Ansell Rd SW17 180 DE90
Ansell Rd, Dor. 263 CH135
Anselm Cl, Croy. 202 DT104
Park Hill Ri
Anselm Rd SW6 160 DA79
Anselm Rd, Pnr. 94 BZ52
Ansford Rd, Brom. 183 EC92
Ansleigh Pl W11 139 CX73
Ansley Cl, S.Croy. 220 DV114
Anslow Gdns, Iver 133 BD68
Anslow Pl, Slou. 130 AJ71
Anson Cl (Bovingdon), Hem.H. 57 AZ27
Anson Cl, Ken. 236 DR120
Anson Cl, Rom. 105 FB54
Anson Cl, St.Alb. 43 CH22
Anson Pl SE28 165 ER75
Princess Alice Way
Anson Rd N7 121 DK63
Anson Rd NW2 119 CX64
Anson Ter, Nthlt. 136 CB65
Anson Wk, Nthwd. 93 BQ49
Anstead Dr, Rain. 147 FG68
Anstey Rd SE15 162 DU83
Anstey Wk N15 121 DP56
Anstice Cl W4 158 CS80
Anston Ct, Guil. 242 AS134
Southway
Anstridge Path SE9 185 ER86
Anstridge Rd SE9 185 ER86
Antelope Av, Grays 170 GA76
Hogg La
Antelope Rd SE18 165 EM76
Anthony Cl NW7 96 CS49
Anthony Cl (Dunton Grn), Sev. 241 FE120
Anthony Cl, Wat. 94 BW46
Anthony La, Swan. 207 FG95
Anthony Rd SE25 202 DU100
Anthony Rd, Borwd. 78 CM40
Anthony Rd, Grnf. 137 CE68
Anthony Rd, Well. 166 EU81
Anthony St E1 142 DV72
Commercial Rd
Anthony Way, Slou. 131 AK73
Anthonys, Wok. 211 BB112
Anthorne Cl, Pot.B. 64 DB31
Anthus Ms, Nthwd. 93 BS52
Antigua Cl SE19 182 DR92
Salters Hill
Antigua Wk SE19 182 DR92
Antill Rd E3 143 DY69
Antill Rd N15 122 DT56
Antill Ter E1 143 DX72
Antlands La, Horl. 269 DK153
Antlands La E, Horl. 269 DL153
Antlands La W, Horl. 269 DL153
Antlers Hill E4 83 EB43
Antoinette Ct, Abb.L. 59 BT29
Dairy Way
Anton Cres, Sutt. 200 DA104
Anton Rd, S.Ock. 149 FV70
Anton St E8 122 DU64
Antoneys Cl, Pnr. 94 BX54
Antonine Gate, St.Alb. 42 CA21
Antrim Gro NW3 140 DF65
Antrim Ho E3 143 DZ67
Antrim Mans NW3 140 DE65
Antrim Rd NW3 140 DF65
Antrobus Cl, Sutt. 217 CZ106
Antrobus Rd W4 158 CQ77
Anugraha Conference Cen, Egh. 172 AU91
Anvil Cl SW16 181 DJ94
Anvil Cl (Bovingdon), Hem.H. 57 BB28
Yew Tree Dr
Anvil Ct (Langley), Slou. 153 BA77
Blacksmith Row
Anvil La, Cob. 213 BU114
Anvil Pl, St.Alb. 60 CA26
Anvil Rd, Sun. 195 BU97
Anworth Cl, Wdf.Grn. 102 EH51
Anyards Rd, Cob. 213 BV113
Apeldoorn Dr, Wall. 219 DL109
Aperdele Rd, Lthd. 231 CG118
Aperfield Rd, Erith 167 FF79
Aperfield Rd (Biggin Hill), West. 238 EL117
Apers Av, Wok. 227 AZ121
Apex Cl, Beck. 203 EB95
Apex Cl, Wey. 195 BR104
Apex Cor NW7 96 CR49
Apex Retail Pk, Felt. 176 BZ90
Apex Twr, N.Mal. 198 CS97
Apley Rd, Reig. 266 DA137
Aplin Way, Islw. 157 CE81
Apollo Av, Brom. 204 EH95
Rodway Rd
Apollo Av, Nthwd. 93 BU50
Apollo Cl, Horn. 127 FH61
Apollo Pl E11 124 EE62
Apollo Pl SW10 160 DD80
Apollo Pl (St. John's), Wok. 226 AU119
Church Rd
Apollo Way SE28 165 ER76
Broadwater Rd
Apollo Way, Hem.H. 40 BM18
Apostle Way, Th.Hth. 201 DP96
Apothecary St EC4 274 F9
Appach Rd SW2 181 DN86
Apperlie Dr, Horl. 269 DJ150
Apple Cotts (Bovingdon), Hem.H. 57 BA27
Apple Garth, Brent. 157 CK77
Apple Gro, Chess. 216 CL105
Apple Gro, Enf. 82 DS41
Apple Mkt, Kings.T. 197 CK96
Eden St
Apple Orchard, Swan. 207 FD98
Apple Orchard, The, Hem.H. 40 BM18
Highfield La
Apple Rd E11 124 EE62
Apple Tree Roundabout, West Dr. 134 BM73
Apple Tree Yd SW1 277 L2
Appleby Cl E4 101 EC51
Appleby Cl N15 122 DR57
Appleby Cl, Twick. 177 CD89
Appleby Dr, Rom. 106 FJ50
Appleby Gdns, Felt. 175 BT88
Appleby Grn, Rom. 106 FJ50
Appleby Dr
Appleby Rd E8 142 DU66
Appleby Rd E16 144 EF72
Appleby St E2 142 DT68
Appleby St (Cheshunt), Wal.Cr. 66 DT26
Applecroft, Berk. 38 AS17
Applecroft (Park St), St.Alb. 60 CB28
Applecroft Rd, Welw.G.C. 29 CV09
Appledore Av, Bexh. 167 FC81
Appledore Av, Ruis. 115 BV62
Appledore Cl SW17 180 DF89
Appledore Cl, Brom. 204 EF99
Appledore Cl, Edg. 96 CN53
Appledore Cl, Rom. 106 FJ53
Appledore Cres, Sid. 185 ES90
Appledown Ri, Couls. 235 DJ115
Applefield, Amer. 72 AW39
Appleford Cl, Hodd. 49 DZ15
Appleford Rd W10 139 CY70
Applegarth (New Addington), Croy. 221 EB108
Applegarth (Claygate), Esher 215 CF106
Applegarth Dr, Dart. 188 FL89
Applegarth Dr, Ilf. 125 ET56
Applegarth Ho, Erith 167 FF82
Lincoln Cl
Applegarth Rd SE28 146 EV74
Applegarth Rd W14 159 CX76
Applegate, Brwd. 108 FT43
Appleshaw Cl, Grav. 191 GG92
Appleton Cl, Amer. 72 AV40
Appleton Cl, Harl. 51 EQ16
Appleton Dr, Dart. 187 FH90
Appleton Gdns, N.Mal. 199 CU100
Appleton Rd SE9 164 EL83
Appleton Rd, Loug. 85 EP41
Appleton Sq, Mitch. 200 DE95
Silbury Av
Appleton Way, Horn. 128 FK60
Appletree Av, Uxb. 134 BM71
Appletree Av, West Dr. 134 BM71
Appletree Cl SE20 202 DV95
Jasmine Gro
Appletree Cl, Lthd. 230 CC124
Appletree Ct, Guil. 243 BD131
Old Merrow St
Appletree Gdns, Barn. 80 DE42
Appletree La, Slou. 152 AW76
Appletree Wk, Chesh. 54 AR34
Cresswell Rd
Appletree Wk, Wat. 59 BV34
Applewood Cl N20 98 DE46
Applewood Cl NW2 119 CV62
Appold St EC2 275 M6
Appold St EC2 142 DS71
Appold St, Erith 167 FF79
Apprentice Way E5 122 DV63
Clarence Rd
Approach, The NW4 119 CX57
Approach, The W3 138 CR72
Approach, The, Enf. 82 DV40
Approach, The, Lthd. 230 BY123
Maddox La
Approach, The, Orp. 205 ET103
Approach, The, Pot.B. 63 CZ32
Approach, The, Upmin. 128 FP62
Approach Cl N16 122 DS64
Cowper Rd
Approach Rd E2 142 DW68
Approach Rd SW20 199 CW96
Approach Rd, Ashf. 175 BQ93
Approach Rd, Barn. 80 DD42
Approach Rd, Maid. 130 AE72
Approach Rd, Pur. 219 DP112
Approach Rd, St.Alb. 43 CE21
Approach Rd, W.Mol. 196 CA99
Appspond La (Potters Crouch), St.Alb. 41 BV23
Aprey Gdns NW4 119 CW56
April Cl W7 137 CE73
April Cl, Ash. 232 CM117
April Cl, Felt. 175 BU90
April Cl, Orp. 223 ET106
Briarswood Way
April Glen SE23 183 DX90
April St E8 122 DT63
Aprilwood Cl (Woodham), Add. 211 BF111
Apsledene, Grav. 191 GK93
Miskin Way
Apsley Cl, Har. 116 CC57
Apsley Gra, Hem.H. 58 BL25
London Rd
Apsley Mills Retail Pk, Hem.H. 40 BL24
Apsley Rd SE25 202 DV98
Apsley Rd, N.Mal. 198 CQ97
Apsley Way NW2 119 CU61
Apsley Way W1 276 G4
Aquarius Business Pk NW2 119 CU60
Aquarius Way, Nthwd. 93 BU50
Aquila Cl, Lthd. 232 CL121
Aquila St NW8 140 DD68
Aquinas St SE1 278 E3
Aquis Ct, St.Alb. 42 CC20
Arabella Dr SW15 158 CS84
Arabia Cl E4 101 ED45
Arabin Rd SE4 163 DY84
Araglen Av, S.Ock. 149 FV71
Aragon Av, Epsom 217 CV109
Aragon Av, T.Ditt. 197 CF99
Aragon Cl, Brom. 205 EM102
Aragon Cl (New Addington), Croy. 222 EE110
Aragon Cl, Enf. 81 DM38
Aragon Cl, Hem.H. 41 BQ15
Aragon Cl, Loug. 84 EL44
Aragon Cl, Rom. 105 FB51
Aragon Cl, Sun. 175 BT94
Aragon Dr, Ilf. 103 EQ52
Aragon Dr, Ruis. 116 BX60
Aragon Rd, Kings.T. 178 CL92
Aragon Rd, Mord. 199 CX100
Aragon Twr SE8 163 DZ77
Aragon Wk (Byfleet), W.Byf. 212 BM113
Aran Ct, Wey. 195 BR103
Mallards Reach
Aran Dr, Stan. 95 CJ49
Aran Hts, Ch.St.G. 90 AV49
Arandora Cres, Rom. 126 EV59
Arbery Rd E3 143 DY69
Arbor Cl, Beck. 203 EB96
Arbor Ct N16 122 DR61
Lordship Rd
Arbor Rd E4 101 ED48
Arborfield Cl SW2 181 DM88
Arborfield Cl, Slou. 152 AS76
Arbour, The, Hert. 32 DR11
Arbour Cl, Brwd. 108 FW50
Arbour Cl (Fetcham), Lthd. 231 CF123
Arbour Rd, Enf. 83 DX42
Arbour Sq E1 143 DX72
Arbour Vw, Amer. 72 AV39
Arbour Way, Horn. 127 FH64
Arbroath Grn, Wat. 93 BU48

Arbroath Rd SE9 164 EL83
Arbrook Chase, Esher 214 CC107
Arbrook Cl, Orp. 206 EU97
Arbrook La, Esher 214 CC107
Arbury Ter SE26 182 DV90
Oaksford Av
Arbuthnot La, Bex. 186 EY86
Arbuthnot Rd SE14 163 DX82
Arbutus Cl, Red. 266 DC136
Arbutus Rd, Red. 266 DC136
Arbutus St E8 142 DS67
Arcade, The EC2 275 M7
Arcade, The, Croy. 202 DQ104
High St
Arcade, The, Hat. 45 CV17
Kennelwood La
Arcade Pl, Rom. 127 FE57
Arcadia Av N3 98 DA53
Arcadia Caravans, Stai. 194 BH95
Arcadia Cl, Cars. 218 DG105
Arcadia Shop Cen W5 137 CK73
Arcadia St E14 143 EA72
Arcadian Av, Bex. 186 EY86
Arcadian Cl, Bex. 186 EY86
Arcadian Gdns N22 99 DM52
Arcadian Rd, Bex. 186 EY86
Arcany Rd, S.Ock. 149 FV70
Arch Rd, Walt. 196 BX104
Arch St SE1 279 H7
Arch St SE1 162 DQ76
Archangel St SE16 163 DX75
Archates Av, Grays 170 GA76
Archbishops Pl SW2 181 DM86
Archdale Pl, N.Mal. 198 CP97
Archdale Rd SE22 182 DT85
Archel Rd W14 159 CZ79
Archer Cl, Kings L. 58 BM29
Archer Cl, Kings.T. 178 CL94
Archer Ho SW11 160 DD81
Vicarage Cres
Archer Ms (Hampton Hill), Hmptn. 176 CC93
Windmill Rd
Archer Rd SE25 202 DV98
Archer Rd, Orp. 206 EU99
Archer Sq SE14 163 DY79
Chubworthy St
Archer St W1 273 M10
Archer Ter, West Dr. 134 BL73
Yew Av
Archer Way, Swan. 207 FF96
Archers, Harl. 51 EP20
Archers Ct, Hert. 32 DQ08
Archers Ct, S.Ock. 149 FV71
Archers Dr, Enf. 82 DW40
Archers Fld, St.Alb. 43 CF18
Archers Ride, Welw.G.C. 30 DB11
Archery Cl W2 272 C9
Archery Cl W2 140 DE72
Archery Cl, Har. 117 CF55
Archery Rd SE9 185 EM85
Arches, The SW6 159 CZ82
Munster Rd
Arches, The WC2 278 A2
Arches, The, Har. 116 CB61
Archfield, Welw.G.C. 29 CY06
Archibald Ms W1 276 G2
Archibald Ms W1 140 DG74
Archibald Rd N7 121 DK63
Archibald Rd, Rom. 106 FN53
Archibald St E3 143 EA69
Archie Cl, West Dr. 154 BN75
Archie St SE1 279 N5
Archway, Rom. 105 FH51
Archway Cl N19 121 DJ61
St. Johns Way
Archway Cl SW19 180 DB91
Archway Cl W10 139 CX71
Archway Cl, Wall. 201 DK104
Archway Mall N19 121 DJ61
Magdala Av
Archway Ms SW15 159 CY84
Putney Br Rd
Archway Ms, Dor. 263 CG135
Chapel Ct
Archway Pl, Dor. 263 CG135
Chapel Ct
Archway Rd N6 120 DG58
Archway Rd N19 121 DJ60
Archway St SW13 158 CS83
Arcola St E8 122 DT64
Arctic St NW5 120 DG64
Gillies St
Arcus Rd, Brom. 184 EE93
Ardbeg Rd SE24 182 DR86
Arden Cl, Bushey 95 CF45
Arden Cl, Har. 117 CD62
Arden Cl (Bovingdon), Hem.H. 57 BA28
Arden Cl, Reig. 266 DB138
Arden Ct Gdns N2 120 DD58
Arden Cres E14 163 EA77
Arden Cres, Dag. 146 EW66
Arden Est N1 275 M1
Arden Est N1 142 DS68
Arden Gro, Orp. 223 EP105
Arden Ho SW9 161 DL82
Grantham Rd
Arden Ms E17 123 EB57
Arden Mhor, Pnr. 115 BV56
Arden Rd N3 119 CY55
Arden Rd W13 137 CJ73
Ardens Way, St.Alb. 43 CK18
Ardent Cl SE25 202 DS97
Ardesley Wd, Wey. 213 BS105
Ardfern Av SW16 201 DN97
Ardfillan Rd SE6 183 ED88
Ardgowan Rd SE6 184 EE87
Ardilaun Rd N5 122 DQ63
Ardingly Cl, Croy. 203 DX104
Ardleigh Cl, Horn. 128 FK55
Ardleigh Ct, Brwd. 109 FZ45
Ardleigh Gdns, Brwd. 109 GE44
Fairview Av
Ardleigh Gdns, Sutt. 200 DA101
Ardleigh Grn Rd, Horn. 128 FK57
Ardleigh Ho, Bark. 145 EQ67
St. Ann's
Ardleigh Ms, Ilf. 125 EP62
Bengal Rd
Ardleigh Rd E17 101 DZ53
Ardleigh Rd N1 142 DR65
Ardleigh Ter E17 101 DZ53
Ardley Cl NW10 118 CS62
Ardley Cl SE6 183 DY90
Ardley Cl, Ruis. 115 BQ59
Ardley Cres (Hatfield Heath), B.Stort. 37 FH05
Ardlui Rd SE27 182 DQ89
Ardmay Gdns, Surb. 198 CL99
Ardmere Rd SE13 183 ED86
Ardmore Av, Guil. 242 AV132
Ardmore La, Buck.H. 102 EH45
Ardmore Pl, Buck.H. 102 EH45
Ardmore Rd, S.Ock. 149 FV70
Ardmore Way, Guil. 242 AV132
Ardoch Rd SE6 183 ED89
Ardra Rd N9 101 DX48
Ardross Av, Nthwd. 93 BS50
Ardrossan Cl, Slou. 131 AQ70
Ardrossan Gdns, Wor.Pk. 199 CU104
Ardshiel Cl SW15 159 CX83
Bemish Rd
Ardshiel Dr, Red. 266 DE136
Ardwell Av, Ilf. 125 EQ57
Ardwell Rd SW2 181 DL89
Ardwick Rd NW2 120 DA63
Arena, The, Enf. 83 DZ38
Arewater Grn, Loug. 85 EM39
Argali Ho, Erith 166 EY76
Kale Rd
Argall Av E10 123 DX59
Argall Way E10 123 DX60
Argent Cl, Egh. 173 BC93
Holbrook Meadow
Argent St SE1 278 G4
Argent St, Grays 170 FY79
Argent Way (Cheshunt), Wal.Cr. 66 DR26
Argenta Way NW10 138 CP66
Argles Cl, Green. 189 FU85
Cowley Av
Argon Ms SW6 160 DA80
Argon Rd N18 100 DW50
Argosy Gdns, Stai. 173 BF93
Argosy La (Stanwell), Stai. 174 BK87
Argus Cl, Rom. 105 FB53
Argus Way W3 158 CP76
Argus Way, Nthlt. 136 BY69
Argyle Av, Houns. 176 CA86
Argyle Cl W13 137 CG70
Argyle Gdns, Upmin. 129 FR61
Argyle Pas N17 100 DT53
Argyle Pl W6 159 CV77
Argyle Rd E1 143 DX70
Argyle Rd E15 124 EE63
Argyle Rd E16 144 EJ72
Argyle Rd N12 98 DA50
Argyle Rd N17 100 DU53
Argyle Rd N18 100 DU49
Argyle Rd W13 137 CG71
Argyle Rd, Barn. 79 CW42
Argyle Rd, Grnf. 137 CF69
Argyle Rd, Har. 116 CB57
Argyle Rd, Houns. 176 CB85
Argyle Rd, Ilf. 125 EN61
Argyle Rd, Sev. 257 FH125
Argyle Rd, Tedd. 177 CE92
Argyle Sq WC1 274 A2
Argyle Sq WC1 141 DL69
Argyle St WC1 273 P2
Argyle St WC1 141 DL69
Argyle Wk WC1 274 A3
Argyle Way SE16 162 DU78
Argyll Av, Slou. 131 AN73
Argyll Av, Sthl. 136 CB74
Argyll Cl SW9 161 DM83
Dalyell Rd
Argyll Gdns, Edg. 96 CP54
Argyll Rd W8 160 DA75
Argyll Rd, Grays 170 GA78
Argyll Rd, Hem.H. 40 BL15
Argyll St W1 273 K9
Argyll St W1 141 DJ72
Arica Rd SE4 163 DY84
Ariel Cl, Grav. 191 GM91
Ariel Rd NW6 140 DA65
Ariel Way W12 139 CW74
Ariel Way, Houns. 155 BV83
Arisdale Av, S.Ock. 149 FV71
Aristotle Rd SW4 161 DK83
Ark Av, Grays 170 GA76
Arkell Gro SE19 181 DP94
Arkindale Rd SE6 183 EC90
Arkley Ct, Hem.H. 41 BP15
Arkley Rd
Arkley Cres E17 123 DZ57
Arkley Dr, Barn. 79 CU42
Arkley La, Barn. 79 CU41
Arkley Pk, Barn. 78 CR44
Arkley Rd E17 123 DZ57
Arkley Rd, Hem.H. 41 BP15
Arkley Vw, Barn. 79 CV42
Arklow Ct, Rick. 73 BC42
Station App
Arklow Ms, Surb. 198 CL103
Vale Rd S
Arklow Rd SE14 163 DZ79
Arkwright Rd NW3 120 DC64
Arkwright Rd (Colnbrook), Slou. 153 BE82
Arkwright Rd, S.Croy. 220 DT110
Arkwright Rd, Til. 171 GG82
Arkwrights, Harl. 35 ET14
Arlesey Cl SW15 179 CY86
Lytton Gro
Arlesford Rd SW9 161 DL83
Arlingford Rd SW2 181 DN85
Arlingham Ms, Wal.Abb. 67 EC33
Sun St
Arlington N12 98 DA48
Arlington Av N1 142 DQ68
Arlington Cl SE13 183 ED85
Arlington Cl, Sid. 185 ES87
Arlington Cl, Sutt. 200 DA103
Arlington Cl, Twick. 177 CJ86
Arlington Ct, Hayes 155 BR78
Shepiston La
Arlington Ct, Reig. 250 DB132
Oakfield Dr
Arlington Cres, Wal.Cr. 67 DY34
Arlington Dr, Cars. 200 DF103
Arlington Dr, Ruis. 115 BR58
Arlington Gdns W4 158 CQ78
Arlington Gdns, Ilf. 125 EN60
Arlington Gdns, Rom. 106 FL53
Arlington Lo SW2 161 DM84
Arlington Lo, Wey. 213 BP105
Arlington Ms, Twick. 177 CH86
Arlington Rd
Arlington Pl SE10 163 EC80
Greenwich S St
Arlington Rd N14 99 DH47
Arlington Rd NW1 141 DH67
Arlington Rd W13 137 CH72
Arlington Rd, Ashf. 174 BM92
Arlington Rd, Rich. 177 CK89
Arlington Rd, Surb. 197 CK100
Arlington Rd, Tedd. 177 CF91
Arlington Rd, Twick. 177 CJ86
Arlington Rd, Wdf.Grn. 102 EG53
Arlington Sq N1 142 DQ67
Arlington St SW1 277 K2
Arlington St SW1 141 DJ74
Arlington Way EC1 274 E2
Arlington Way EC1 141 DN69
Arliss Way, Nthlt. 136 BW67
Arlow Rd N21 99 DN46
Armada Ct SE8 163 EA79
Watergate St
Armada Ct, Grays 170 GA76
Hogg La
Armada St SE8 163 EA79
Armada Way E6 145 EQ73
Armadale Cl N17 122 DV56
Armadale Rd SW6 160 DA80
Armadale Rd, Felt. 175 BU85
Armadale Rd, Wok. 226 AU117
Armagh Rd E3 143 DZ67
Armand Cl, Wat. 75 BT38
Armfield Cl, W.Mol. 196 BZ99
Armfield Cres, Mitch. 200 DF96
Armfield Rd, Enf. 82 DR39
Arminger Rd W12 139 CV74
Armistice Gdns SE25 202 DU97
Penge Rd
Armitage Cl, Rick. 74 BK42
Armitage Rd NW11 119 CZ60
Armitage Rd SE10 164 EF78
Armor Rd, Purf. 169 FR77
Armour Cl N7 141 DM65
Roman Way
Armoury Dr, Grav. 191 GJ87
Armoury Rd SE8 163 EB82
Armoury Way SW18 180 DA85
Armstead Wk, Dag. 146 FA66
Armstrong Av, Wdf.Grn. 102 EE51
Armstrong Cl E6 145 EM72
Porter Rd
Armstrong Cl, Borwd. 78 CQ41
Manor Way
Armstrong Cl, Dag. 126 EX60
Palmer Rd
Armstrong Cl, Pnr. 115 BU58
Armstrong Cl (London Colney), St.Alb. 62 CL27
Willowside
Armstrong Cl (Halstead), Sev. 241 FB115
Armstrong Cl, Walt. 195 BU100
Sunbury La
Armstrong Cres, Barn. 80 DD41
Armstrong Gdns, Rad. 62 CL32
Armstrong Pl, Hem.H. 40 BK19
High St
Armstrong Rd SW7 160 DD76
Armstrong Rd W3 139 CT74
Armstrong Rd (Englefield Grn), Egh. 172 AW93
Armstrong Rd, Felt. 176 BY92
Armstrong Way, Sthl. 156 CB75
Armytage Rd, Houns. 156 BX80
Arnal Cres SW18 179 CY87
Arncliffe Cl N11 98 DG51
Kettlewell Cl
Arncroft Ct, Bark. 146 EV69
Renwick Rd
Arndale Wk SW18 180 DB85
Garratt La
Arndale Way, Egh. 173 BA92
Church Rd
Arne Gro, Horl. 268 DE146
Arne Gro, Orp. 205 ET104
Arne St WC2 274 A9
Arne St WC2 141 DL72
Arne Wk SE3 164 EF84
Arnett Cl, Rick. 74 BG44
Arnett Sq E4 101 DZ51
Burnside Av
Arnett Way, Rick. 74 BG44
Arneway St SW1 277 N7
Arneways Av, Rom. 126 EX55
Arnewood Cl SW15 179 CU88
Arnewood Cl (Oxshott), Lthd. 214 CB113
Arney's La, Mitch. 200 DG100
Arngask Rd SE6 183 ED87
Arnhem Av, S.Ock. 148 FQ74
Arnhem Dr (New Addington), Croy. 221 ED111
Arnhem Pl E14 163 EA76
Arnhem Way SE22 182 DS85
East Dulwich Gro
Arnhem Wf E14 163 EA76
Arnhem Pl
Arnison Rd, E.Mol. 197 CD98
Arnold Av E, Enf. 83 EA38
Arnold Av W, Enf. 83 DZ38
Arnold Circ E2 275 P3
Arnold Circ E2 142 DT69
Arnold Cl, Har. 118 CM59
Arnold Cres, Islw. 177 CD85
Arnold Dr, Chess. 215 CK107
Arnold Est SE1 162 DT75
Arnold Gdns N13 99 DP50
Arnold Pl, Til. 171 GJ81
Kipling Av
Arnold Rd E3 143 EA69
Arnold Rd N15 122 DT55
Arnold Rd SW17 180 DF94
Arnold Rd, Dag. 146 EZ66
Arnold Rd, Grav. 191 GJ89
Arnold Rd, Nthlt. 136 BX65
Arnold Rd, Stai. 174 BJ94
Arnold Rd, Wal.Abb. 83 EC36
Arnold Rd, Wok. 227 BB116
Arnolds Av, Brwd. 109 GC43
Arnolds Cl, Brwd. 109 GC43
Arnolds Fm La, Brwd. 109 GE41
Arnolds La (Sutton at Hone), Dart. 188 FN93
Arnos Gro N14 99 DK49
Arnos Rd N11 99 DJ50
Arnott Cl SE28 146 EW73
Applegarth Rd
Arnott Cl W4 158 CR77
Fishers La
Arnould Av SE5 162 DR84
Arnsberg Way, Bexh. 166 FA84
Arnside Gdns, Wem. 117 CK60
Arnside Rd, Bexh. 166 FA81
Arnside St SE17 162 DQ79
Arnulf St SE6 183 EB91
Arnulls Rd SW16 181 DN93
Arodene Rd SW2 181 DM86
Arosa Rd, Twick. 177 CK86
Arpley Sq SE20 182 DW94
High St
Arragon Gdns SW16 181 DL94
Arragon Gdns, W.Wick. 203 EB104
Arragon Rd E6 144 EK67
Arragon Rd SW18 180 DB88
Arragon Rd, Twick. 177 CG87
Arran Cl, Erith 167 FD79
Arran Cl, Hem.H. 41 BP22
Arran Cl, Wall. 219 DH105
Arran Dr E12 124 EK60
Arran Grn, Wat. 94 BW46
Prestwick Rd
Arran Ms W5 138 CM74
Arran Rd SE6 183 EB89
Arran Wk N1 142 DQ66
Arran Way, Esher 196 CB103
Arranmore Ct, Bushey 76 BY42
Bushey Hall Rd
Arras Av, Mord. 200 DC99
Arretine Cl, St.Alb. 42 BZ22
Arreton Mead (Horsell), Wok. 210 AY114
Arrol Rd, Beck. 202 DW97
Arrow Rd E3 143 EB69
Arrowscout Wk, Nthlt. 136 BY69
Argus Way
Arrowsmith Cl, Chig. 103 ET50
Arrowsmith Path, Chig. 103 ET50
Arrowsmith Rd, Chig. 103 ES50
Arrowsmith Rd, Loug. 84 EL41
Arsenal Rd SE9 165 EM82
Artemis Cl, Grav. 191 GL87
Arterberry Rd SW20 179 CW94
Arterial Av, Rain. 147 FH70
Arterial Rd N Stifford, Grays 170 FY75
Arterial Rd Purfleet, Purf. 168 FN76
Arterial Rd W Thurrock, Grays 169 FU76
Artesian Cl NW10 138 CR66
Artesian Cl, Horn. 127 FF58
Artesian Gro, Barn. 80 DC42
Artesian Rd W2 140 DA72
Artesian Wk E11 124 EE62
Arthingworth St E15 144 EE67
Arthur Ct W2 140 DB72
Queensway
Arthur Gro SE18 165 EQ77
Arthur Henderson Ho SW6 159 CZ82
Arthur Horsley Wk E7 124 EF64
Magpie Cl
Arthur Rd E6 145 EM68
Arthur Rd N7 121 DM63
Arthur Rd N9 100 DT47
Arthur Rd SW19 180 DA90
Arthur Rd, Kings.T. 178 CN94
Arthur Rd, N.Mal. 199 CV99
Arthur Rd, Rom. 126 EW59
Arthur Rd, St.Alb. 43 CH20
Arthur Rd, Slou. 151 AR75
Arthur Rd (Biggin Hill), West. 238 EJ115
Arthur Rd, Wind. 151 AP81
Arthur St EC4 279 L1
Arthur St, Bushey 76 BX42
Arthur St, Erith 167 FF80
Arthur St, Grav. 191 GG87
Arthur St, Grays 170 GC79
Arthur St W, Grav. 191 GG87
Arthur Toft Ho, Grays 170 GB79
New Rd
Arthurdon Rd SE4 183 EA85
Arthur's Br Rd, Wok. 226 AW117
Artichoke Dell, Rick. 73 BE43
Artichoke Hill E1 142 DV73
Pennington St
Artichoke Pl SE5 162 DR81
Camberwell Ch St
Artillery Cl, Ilf. 125 EQ58
Horns Rd
Artillery La E1 275 N7
Artillery La E1 142 DS71
Artillery La W12 139 CU72
Artillery Pas E1 275 N7
Artillery Pl SE18 165 EM77
Artillery Pl SW1 277 M7
Artillery Pl, Har. 94 CC52
Chicheley Rd
Artillery Rd, Guil. 258 AX135
Artillery Row SW1 277 M7
Artillery Row SW1 161 DK76
Artillery Row, Grav. 191 GJ87
Artillery Ter, Guil. 242 AX134
Artington Cl, Orp. 223 EQ105
Artington Wk, Guil. 258 AW137
Artisan Cl E6 145 EP72
Ferndale St
Artisan Cres, St.Alb. 42 CC19
Artizan St E1 275 N8
Arundel Av, Epsom 217 CV110
Arundel Av, Mord. 199 CZ98
Arundel Av, S.Croy. 220 DU110
Arundel Cl E15 124 EE63
Arundel Cl SW11 180 DE85
Chivalry Rd
Arundel Cl, Bex. 186 EZ86
Arundel Cl, Croy. 201 DP104
Arundel Cl (Hampton Hill), Hmptn. 176 CB92
Arundel Cl, Hem.H. 41 BP19
Arundel Cl (Cheshunt), Wal.Cr. 66 DW29
Arundel Ct N12 98 DE51
Arundel Ct, Har. 116 CA63
Arundel Ct, Slou. 152 AX77
Arundel Dr, Borwd. 78 CQ43
Arundel Dr, Har. 116 BZ63
Arundel Dr, Orp. 224 EV106
Arundel Dr, Wdf.Grn. 102 EG52
Arundel Gdns N21 99 DN46
Arundel Gdns W11 139 CZ73
Arundel Gdns, Edg. 96 CR52
Arundel Gdns, Ilf. 126 EU61
Arundel Gt Ct WC2 274 C10
Arundel Gro N16 122 DS64
Arundel Gro, St.Alb. 43 CD15
Arundel Pl N1 141 DN65
Arundel Rd, Abb.L. 59 BU32
Arundel Rd, Barn. 80 DE41
Arundel Rd, Croy. 202 DR100
Arundel Rd, Dart. 168 FJ84
Arundel Rd, Dor. 263 CG136
Arundel Rd, Houns. 156 BW83
Arundel Rd, Kings.T. 198 CP96
Arundel Rd, Rom. 106 FM53
Arundel Rd, Sutt. 217 CZ108
Arundel Rd, Uxb. 134 BH68
Arundel Sq N7 141 DN65
Arundel St WC2 274 C10
Arundel St WC2 141 DM73
Arundel Ter SW13 159 CV79
Arvon Rd N5 121 DN64
Asbaston Ter, Ilf. 125 EQ64
Buttsbury Rd
Ascalon St SW8 161 DJ80
Ascension Rd, Rom. 105 FC51
Ascham Dr E4 101 EB52
Rushcroft Rd
Ascham End E17 101 DY53
Ascham St NW5 121 DJ64
Aschurch Rd, Croy. 202 DT101
Ascot Cl, Borwd. 78 CN43
Ascot Cl, Ilf. 103 ES51
Ascot Cl, Nthlt. 116 CA64
Ascot Gdns, Enf. 82 DW37
Ascot Gdns, Horn. 128 FL63
Ascot Gdns, Sthl. 136 BZ71
Ascot Ms, Wall. 219 DJ109
Ascot Rd E6 145 EM69
Ascot Rd N15 122 DR57
Ascot Rd N18 100 DU49
Ascot Rd SW17 180 DG93
Ascot Rd, Felt. 174 BN88
Ascot Rd, Grav. 191 GH90
Ascot Rd, Orp. 205 ET98
Ascot Rd, Wat. 75 BS43
Ascots La, Welw.G.C. 29 CY14
Ascott Av W5 158 CL75
Ash Cl SE20 202 DW96
Ash Cl, Abb.L. 59 BR32
Ash Cl, Brwd. 108 FT43
Ash Cl, Cars. 200 DF103
Ash Cl, Edg. 96 CQ49
Ash Cl, Hat. 64 DA25
Ash Cl, N.Mal. 198 CR96
Ash Cl, Orp. 205 ER99
Ash Cl, Red. 251 DJ130
Ash Cl, Rom. 105 FB52
Ash Cl, Sid. 186 EV90
Ash Cl, Slou. 153 BB76
Ash Cl, Stan. 95 CG51
Ash Cl, Swan. 207 FC96
Ash Cl (Harefield), Uxb. 92 BK53
Ash Cl, Wat. 75 BV35
Ash Cl, Wok. 226 AY120
Ash Cl (Pyrford), Wok. 228 BG115
Ash Copse (Bricket Wd), St.Alb. 60 BZ31
Ash Ct, Epsom 216 CQ105
Ash Dr, Hat. 45 CU21
Ash Dr, Red. 267 DH136
Ash Grn (Denham), Uxb. 134 BH65
Ash Gro E8 142 DV67
Ash Gro N13 100 DQ48
Ash Gro NW2 119 CX63
Ash Gro SE20 202 DW96
Ash Gro W5 158 CL75
Ash Gro, Amer. 55 AN36
Ash Gro, Enf. 100 DS45
Ash Gro, Felt. 175 BS88
Ash Gro, Guil. 242 AU134
Ash Gro, Hayes 135 BR73
Ash Gro, Hem.H. 40 BM24
Ash Gro, Houns. 156 BX81
Ash Gro (Stoke Poges), Slou. 132 AT66
Ash Gro, Sthl. 136 CA71
Ash Gro, Stai. 174 BJ93
Ash Gro (Harefield), Uxb. 92 BK53
Ash Gro, Wem. 117 CG63
Ash Gro, West Dr. 134 BM73
Ash Gro, W.Wick. 203 EC103
Ash Gros, Saw. 36 FA05
Ash Hill Cl, Bushey 94 CB46
Ash Hill Dr, Pnr. 116 BW55
Ash Ind Est, Harl. 51 EM16
Flex Meadow
Ash Island, E.Mol. 197 CD97
Ash La, Horn. 128 FN56
Southend Arterial Rd
Ash La, Rom. 105 FG51
Ash La, Wind. 151 AK82
Ash Ms, Epsom 216 CS113
Ash Platt, The (Seal), Sev. 257 FL121
Ash Platt Rd (Seal), Sev. 257 FL121
Ash Ride, Enf. 81 DN35
Ash Rd E15 124 EE64
Ash Rd, Croy. 203 EA103
Ash Rd, Dart. 188 FK88
Ash Rd (Hawley), Dart. 188 FM91
Ash Rd, Grav. 191 GJ91
Ash Rd, Orp. 223 ET108
Ash Rd, Shep. 194 BN98
Ash Rd, Sutt. 199 CY101
Ash Rd, West. 255 ER125
Ash Rd, Wok. 226 AX120
Ash Row, Brom. 205 EN101
Ash Tree Cl, Croy. 203 DY100
Ash Tree Cl, Surb. 198 CL102
Ash Tree Dell NW9 118 CQ57
Ash Tree Fld, Harl. 35 EN13
Ash Tree Rd, Wat. 75 BV36
Ash Tree Way, Croy. 203 DY99
Ash Vale, Rick. 91 BD50
Ash Wk SW2 181 DM88
Ash Wk, S.Ock. 149 FX69
Ash Wk, Wem. 117 CJ63
Ashbeam Cl, Brwd. 107 FW51
Canterbury Way
Ashbourne Av E18 124 EH56
Ashbourne Av N20 98 DF47
Ashbourne Av NW11 119 CZ57
Ashbourne Av, Bexh. 166 EY80
Ashbourne Av, Har. 117 CD61
Ashbourne Cl N12 98 DB49
Ashbourne Cl W5 138 CN71
Ashbourne Cl, Couls. 235 DJ118
Ashbourne Ct E5 123 DY63
Daubeney Rd
Ashbourne Gro NW7 96 CR50
Ashbourne Gro SE22 182 DT85
Ashbourne Gro W4 158 CS78
Ashbourne Par W5 138 CM70
Ashbourne Rd
Ashbourne Ri, Orp. 223 ER105
Ashbourne Rd W5 138 CM71
Ashbourne Rd, Brox. 49 DZ21
Ashbourne Rd, Mitch. 180 DG93
Ashbourne Rd, Rom. 106 FJ49
Ashbourne Sq, Nthwd. 93 BS51
Ashbourne Ter SW19 180 DA94
Ashbourne Way NW11 119 CZ57
Ashbourne Av
Ashbridge Rd E11 124 EF59
Ashbridge St NW8 272 B5
Ashbridge St NW8 140 DE70
Ashbrook Rd N19 121 DK60
Ashbrook Rd, Dag. 127 FB62
Ashbrook Rd (Old Windsor), Wind. 172 AV87
Ashburn Gdns SW7 160 DC77
Ashburn Pl SW7 160 DC77
Ashburnham Av, Har. 117 CF58
Ashburnham Cl N2 120 DD55
Ashburnham Cl, Sev. 257 FJ127
Fiennes Way
Ashburnham Cl, Wat. 93 BU48
Ashburnham Dr
Ashburnham Dr, Wat. 93 BU48
Ashburnham Gdns, Har. 117 CF58
Ashburnham Gdns, Upmin. 128 FP60
Ashburnham Gro SE10 163 EB80
Ashburnham Pk, Esher 214 CC105
Ashburnham Pl SE10 163 EB80
Ashburnham Retreat SE10 163 EB80
Ashburnham Rd NW10 139 CW69
Ashburnham Rd SW10 160 DC80
Ashburnham Rd, Belv. 167 FC77
Ashburnham Rd, Rich. 177 CH90
Ashburton Av, Croy. 202 DV102

Ashburton Av, Ilf. 125 ES63
Ashburton Cl, Croy. 202 DU102
Ashburton Ct, Pnr. 116 BX55
Ashburton Gdns, Croy. 202 DU103
Ashburton Gro N7 121 DN63
Ashburton Rd E16 144 EG72
Ashburton Rd, Croy. 202 DU102
Ashburton Rd, Ruis. 115 BU61
Ashburton Ter E13 144 EG68
Grasmere Rd
Ashbury Cl, Hat. 44 CS18
Ashbury Cres, Guil. 243 BC132
Ashbury Dr, Uxb. 115 BP61
Ashbury Gdns, Rom. 126 EX57
Ashbury Pl SW19 180 DC93
Ashbury Rd SW11 160 DF83
Ashby Av, Chess. 216 CN107
Ashby Cl, Horn. 128 FN60
Holme Rd
Ashby Gdns, St.Alb. 43 CD24
Ashby Gro N1 142 DQ66
Ashby Ms SE4 163 DZ82
Ashby Rd N15 122 DU57
Ashby Rd SE4 163 DZ82
Ashby Rd, Wat. 75 BU38
Ashby St EC1 274 G3
Ashby Wk, Croy. 202 DQ100
Ashby Way, West Dr. 154 BN80
Ashchurch Gro W12 159 CU75
Ashchurch Pk Vil W12 159 CU76
Ashchurch Ter W12 159 CU76
Ashcombe, Welw.G.C. 29 CY05
Ashcombe Av, Surb. 197 CK101
Ashcombe Gdns, Edg. 96 CN49
Ashcombe Ho, Enf. 83 DX41
Ashcombe Pk NW2 118 CS62
Ashcombe Rd SW19 180 DA92
Ashcombe Rd, Cars. 218 DG107
Ashcombe Rd, Dor. 247 CG134
Ashcombe Rd, Red. 251 DJ127
Ashcombe Sq, N.Mal. 198 CQ97
Ashcombe St SW6 160 DB82
Ashcombe Ter, Tad. 233 CV120
Ashcroft (Shalford), Guil. 258 AY141
Ashcroft, Pnr. 94 CA51
Ashcroft Av, Sid. 186 EU86
Ashcroft Ct N20 98 DD47
Oakleigh Rd N
Ashcroft Ct, Brox. 49 DZ22
Winford Dr
Ashcroft Ct (Burnham), Slou. 130 AH68
Ashcroft Cres, Sid. 186 EU86
Ashcroft Dr (Denham), Uxb. 113 BF58
Ashcroft Pk, Cob. 214 BY112
Ashcroft Ri, Couls. 235 DL116
Ashcroft Rd E3 143 DY69
Ashcroft Rd, Chess. 198 CM104
Ashcroft Sq W6 159 CW77
King St
Ashdale (Bookham), Lthd. 246 CC126
Ashdale Cl, Stai. 174 BL89
Ashdale Cl, Twick. 176 CC87
Ashdale Gro, Stan. 95 CF51
Ashdale Rd SE12 184 EH88
Ashdale Way, Twick. 176 CC87
Ashdale Cl
Ashdales, St.Alb. 43 CD24
Ashdene SE15 162 DV81
Ashdene, Pnr. 116 BW55
Ashdene Cl, Ashf. 175 BQ94
Ashdon Cl, Brwd. 109 GC44
Poplar Dr
Ashdon Cl, S.Ock. 149 FV72
Afton Dr
Ashdon Cl, Wdf.Grn. 102 EH51
Ashdon Rd NW10 138 CS67
Ashdon Rd, Bushey 76 BX41
Ashdown Cl, Beck. 203 EB96
Ashdown Cl, Bex. 187 FC87
Ashdown Cl, Reig. 266 DB138
Ashdown Cres NW5 120 DG64
Queen's Cres
Ashdown Cres (Cheshunt), Wal.Cr. 67 DY28
Ashdown Dr, Borwd. 78 CL40
Ashdown Est E11 124 EE63
High Rd Leytonstone
Ashdown Gdns, S.Croy. 236 DV115
Ashdown Rd, Enf. 82 DW41
Ashdown Rd, Epsom 217 CT113
Ashdown Rd, Kings.T. 198 CL96
Ashdown Rd, Reig. 266 DB138
Ashdown Rd, Uxb. 134 BN68
Ashdown Wk E14 163 EA77
Ashdown Wk, Rom. 105 FB54
Ashdown Way SW17 180 DG89
Ashdown Way, Amer. 55 AR37
Ashen E6 145 EN72
Downings
Ashen Dr, Dart. 187 FG86
Ashen Gro SW19 180 DA90
Ashen Vale, S.Croy. 221 DX109
Ashenden Rd E5 123 DX64
Ashenden Rd, Guil. 258 AT135
Ashenden Wk (Farnham Common), Slou. 111 AR63
Ashendene Rd, Hert. 47 DL20
Ashentree Ct EC4 274 E9
Asher Loftus Way N11 98 DF51
Asher Way E1 142 DU73
Asheridge Rd, Chesh. 54 AM28
Ashfield Av, Bushey 76 CB44
Ashfield Av, Felt. 175 BV88
Ashfield Cl, Beck. 183 EA94
Ashfield Cl, Rich. 178 CL88
Ashfield La, Chis. 185 EQ93
Ashfield Par N14 99 DK46
Ashfield Rd N4 122 DQ58
Ashfield Rd N14 99 DJ48
Ashfield Rd W3 139 CT74
Ashfield Rd, Chesh. 54 AR29
Ashfield St E1 142 DV71
Ashfield Yd E1 142 DV71
Ashfield St
Ashfields, Loug. 85 EM40
Ashfields, Reig. 250 DB132
Ashfields, Wat. 75 BT35
Ashford Av N8 121 DL56
Ashford Av, Ashf. 175 BP93
Ashford Av, Brwd. 108 FV48
Ashford Av, Hayes 136 BX72
Ashford Cl E17 123 DZ58
Ashford Cl, Ashf. 174 BL91
Ashford Cres, Ashf. 174 BL90
Ashford Cres, Enf. 82 DW40
Ashford Gdns, Cob. 230 BX116
Ashford Grn, Wat. 94 BX50
Ashford Ind Est, Ashf. 175 BQ91
Ashford La, Maid. 150 AG75
Ashford La (Dorney), Wind. 150 AH75
Ashford Ms N17 100 DU53
Vicarage Rd
Ashford Rd E6 145 EN65
Ashford Rd E18 102 EH54
Ashford Rd NW2 119 CX63
Ashford Rd, Ashf. 175 BQ94
Ashford Rd, Felt. 175 BT90
Ashford Rd, Iver 133 BC66
Ashford Rd, Stai. 194 BK95
Ashford St N1 275 M2
Ashgrove Rd, Ashf. 175 BQ92
Ashgrove Rd, Brom. 183 ED93
Ashgrove Rd, Ilf. 125 ET60
Ashgrove Rd, Sev. 256 FG127
Ashingdon Cl E4 101 EC48
Ashington Rd SW6 159 CZ82
Ashlake Rd SW16 181 DL91
Ashland Pl W1 272 F6
Ashland Pl W1 140 DG71
Ashlar Pl SE18 165 EP77
Masons Hill
Ashlea Rd (Chalfont St. Peter), Ger.Cr. 90 AX54
Ashleigh Av, Egh. 173 BC94
Ashleigh Cl, Amer. 55 AS39
Ashleigh Cl, Horl. 268 DF148
Ashleigh Cotts, Dor. 263 CH144
Ashleigh Ct, Wal.Abb. 68 EG34
Lamplighters Cl
Ashleigh Gdns, Sutt. 200 DB103
Ashleigh Gdns, Upmin. 129 FR62
Ashleigh Pt SE23 183 DX90
Dacres Rd
Ashleigh Rd SE20 202 DV97
Ashleigh Rd SW14 158 CS83
Ashley Av, Epsom 216 CR113
Ashley Av, Ilf. 103 EP54
Ashley Av, Mord. 200 DA99
Chalgrove Av
Ashley Cen, Epsom 216 CR113
Ashley Cl NW4 97 CW54
Ashley Cl, Hem.H. 40 BM22
Ashley Cl (Bookham), Lthd. 246 BZ125
Ashley Cl, Pnr. 93 BV54
Ashley Cl, Sev. 257 FH124
Ashley Cl, Walt. 195 BT102
Ashley Cl, Welw.G.C. 29 CW07
Ashley Ct, Epsom 216 CR113
Ashley Ct, Hat. 45 CV17
Ashley Ct, Wok. 226 AT118
Ashley Cres N22 99 DN54
Ashley Cres SW11 160 DG83
Ashley Dr, Bans. 218 DA114
Ashley Dr, Borwd. 78 CQ43
Ashley Dr (Penn), H.Wyc. 88 AC45
Ashley Dr, Islw. 157 CE79
Ashley Dr, Twick. 176 CB87
Ashley Dr, Walt. 195 BU104
Ashley Gdns N13 100 DQ49
Ashley Gdns SW1 277 L7
Ashley Gdns SW1 161 DJ76
Ashley Gdns (Shalford), Guil. 259 AZ141
Ashley Gdns, Orp. 223 ES106
Ashley Gdns, Rich. 177 CK90
Ashley Gdns, Wem. 118 CL61
Ashley Grn Rd, Chesh. 54 AR27
Ashley Gro, Loug. 84 EL41
Staples Rd
Ashley La NW4 97 CW54
Ashley La, Croy. 219 DP105
Ashley Pk Av, Walt. 195 BT103
Ashley Pk Cres, Walt. 195 BT102
Ashley Pk Rd, Walt. 195 BU103
Ashley Pl SW1 277 K7
Ashley Pl SW1 161 DJ76
Ashley Ri, Walt. 213 BU105
Ashley Rd E4 101 EA50
Ashley Rd E7 144 EJ66
Ashley Rd N17 122 DU55
Ashley Rd N19 121 DL60
Ashley Rd SW19 180 DB93
Ashley Rd (Westcott), Dor. 262 CC137
Ashley Rd, Enf. 82 DW40
Ashley Rd, Epsom 216 CR114
Ashley Rd, Hmptn. 196 CA95
Ashley Rd, Hert. 31 DN10
Ashley Rd, Rich. 158 CL83
Jocelyn Rd
Ashley Rd, St.Alb. 43 CJ20
Ashley Rd, Sev. 257 FH123
Ashley Rd, T.Ditt. 197 CF100
Ashley Rd, Th.Hth. 201 DM98
Ashley Rd, Uxb. 134 BH68
Ashley Rd, Walt. 195 BU102
Ashley Rd, Wok. 226 AT118
Ashley Sq, Epsom 216 CR113
Ashley Wk NW7 97 CW52
Ashleys, Rick. 91 BF45
Ashlin Rd E15 123 ED63
Ashling Rd, Croy. 202 DU102
Ashlone Rd SW15 159 CW83
Ashlyn Cl, Bushey 76 BY42
Ashlyn Gro, Horn. 128 FK55
Ashlyns Ct, Berk. 38 AV20
Ashlyns La, Ong. 53 FG23
Ashlyns Pk, Cob. 214 BY113
Ashlyns Rd, Berk. 38 AV20
Ashlyns Rd, Epp. 69 ET30
Ashlyns Way, Chess. 215 CK107
Ashmead N14 81 DJ44
Ashmead Dr (Denham), Uxb. 114 BG61
Ashmead Gate, Brom. 204 EJ95
Ashmead La (Denham), Uxb. 114 BG61
Ashmead Rd SE8 163 EA82
Ashmead Rd, Felt. 175 BU88
Ashmeads Ct (Shenley), Rad. 61 CK33
Porters Pk Dr
Ashmere Av, Beck. 203 ED96
Ashmere Cl, Sutt. 217 CW106
Ashmere Gro SW2 161 DL84
Ashmill St NW1 272 B6
Ashmill St NW1 140 DE71
Ashmole Pl SW8 161 DM79
Ashmole St SW8 161 DM79
Ashmore Ct, Houns. 156 CA79
Wheatlands
Ashmore Gdns (Northfleet), Grav. 190 GD91
Ashmore Gdns, Hem.H. 41 BP21
Ashmore Gro, Well. 165 ER83
Ashmore La, Kes. 222 EH111
Ashmore Rd W9 139 CZ70
Ashmount Est N19 121 DK59
Ashmount Rd
Ashmount Rd N15 122 DT57
Ashmount Rd N19 121 DJ59
Ashmount Ter W5 157 CK77
Murray Rd
Ashmour Gdns, Rom. 105 FD54
Ashneal Gdns, Har. 117 CD62
Ashness Gdns, Grnf. 137 CH65
Ashness Rd SW11 180 DF85
Ashridge Cl, Har. 117 CJ58
Ashridge Cl (Bovingdon), Hem.H. 57 BA28
Ashridge Cres SE18 165 EQ80
Ashridge Dr (Bricket Wd), St.Alb. 60 BY30
Ashridge Dr, Wat. 94 BW50
Ashridge Gdns N13 99 DK50
Ashridge Gdns, Pnr. 116 BY56
Ashridge Ri, Berk. 38 AT18
Ashridge Rd, Chesh. 56 AW31
Ashridge Way, Mord. 199 CZ97
Ashridge Way, Sun. 175 BU93
Ashstead Gap, Lthd. 231 CH116
Ashtead Rd E5 122 DU59
Ashtead Wds Rd, Ash. 231 CJ117
Ashton Cl, Sutt. 218 DA105
Ashton Cl, Walt. 213 BV107
Ashton Gdns, Houns. 156 BZ84
Ashton Gdns, Rom. 126 EY58
Ashton Rd E15 123 ED64
Ashton Rd, Enf. 83 DY36
Ashton Rd, Rom. 106 FK52
Ashton Rd, Wok. 226 AT117
Ashton St E14 143 EC73
Ashtree Av, Mitch. 200 DE96
Ashtree Cl, Orp. 223 EP105
Broadwater Gdns
Ashtree Ct, St.Alb. 43 CF20
Granville Rd
Ashtree Ct, Wal.Abb. 68 EG34
Farthingale La
Ashtree Way, Hem.H. 40 BG21
Ashurst Cl SE20 202 DV95
Ashurst Cl, Dart. 167 FF83
Ashurst Cl, Ken. 236 DR115
Ashurst Cl, Nthwd. 93 BS52
Ashurst Dr, Ilf. 125 EP58
Ashurst Dr, Shep. 194 BL99
Ashurst Dr, Tad. 248 CP130
Ashurst Rd N12 98 DE50
Ashurst Rd, Barn. 80 DF43
Ashurst Rd, Tad. 233 CV121
Ashurst Wk, Croy. 202 DV103
Ashvale Dr, Upmin. 129 FS61
Ashvale Gdns, Rom. 105 FD50
Ashvale Gdns, Upmin. 129 FS61
Ashvale Rd SW17 180 DF92
Ashview Cl, Ashf. 174 BL93
Ashview Gdns, Ashf. 174 BL92
Ashville Rd E11 123 ED61
Ashwater Rd SE12 184 EG88
Ashwell Cl E6 144 EL72
Northumberland Rd
Ashwell St, St.Alb. 43 CD19
Ashwells Rd, Brwd. 108 FS41
Ashwells Way, Ch.St.G. 90 AW47
Ashwick Cl, Cat. 252 DU125
Ashwin St E8 142 DT65
Ashwindham Ct, Wok. 226 AS118
Ashwood, Warl. 236 DW120
Ashwood Av, Rain. 147 FH70
Ashwood Av, Uxb. 134 BN72
Ashwood Gdns (New Addington), Croy. 221 EB107
Ashwood Gdns, Hayes 155 BT77
Cranford Dr
Ashwood Pk (Fetcham), Lthd. 230 CC124
Ashwood Pk, Wok. 227 BA118
Ashwood Pl (Bean), Dart. 189 FV90
Bean La
Ashwood Rd E4 101 ED48
Ashwood Rd (Englefield Grn), Egh. 172 AV93
Ashwood Rd, Pot.B. 64 DB33
Ashwood Rd, Wok. 227 AZ118
Ashworth Cl SE5 162 DR82
Love Wk
Ashworth Pl, Guil. 242 AT134
Ashworth Pl, Harl. 52 EX15
Ashworth Rd W9 140 DB69
Aske St N1 275 M2
Askern Cl, Bexh. 166 EX84
Askew Cres W12 159 CT75
Askew Fm La, Grays 170 FY78
Askew Rd W12 139 CT74
Askew Rd, Nthwd. 93 BR47
Askham Ct W12 139 CU74
Askham Rd W12 139 CU74
Askill Dr SW15 179 CY85
Keswick Rd
Askwith Rd, Rain. 147 FD69
Asland Rd E15 144 EE67
Aslett St SW18 180 DB87
Asmar Cl, Couls. 235 DL115
Asmara Rd NW2 119 CY64
Asmuns Hill NW11 120 DA57
Asmuns Pl NW11 119 CZ57
Asolando Dr SE17 279 J9
Aspasia Cl, St.Alb. 43 CF21
Aspdin Rd (Northfleet), Grav. 190 GD90
Aspen Cl N19 121 DJ61
Hargrave Pk
Aspen Cl W5 158 CM75
Aspen Cl (Stoke D'Abernon), Cob. 230 BY116
Aspen Cl, Guil. 243 BD131
Aspen Cl, Orp. 224 EU106
Aspen Cl (Bricket Wd), St.Alb. 60 BY30
Aspen Cl, Slou. 131 AP71
Birch Gro
Aspen Cl, Stai. 173 BF90
Aspen Cl, Swan. 207 FD95
Aspen Cl, West Dr. 134 BM74
Aspen Copse, Brom. 205 EM96
Aspen Ct, Hayes 155 BS77
Aspen Ct, Vir.W. 192 AY98
Aspen Dr, Wem. 117 CG63
Aspen Gdns W6 159 CV78
Aspen Gdns, Ashf. 175 BQ92
Aspen Gdns, Mitch. 200 DG99
Aspen Grn, Erith 166 EZ76
Aspen Gro, Upmin. 128 FN63
Aspen La, Nthlt. 136 BY69
Aspen Pk Dr, Wat. 75 BV35
Aspen Sq, Wey. 195 BR104
Oatlands Dr
Aspen Vale, Whyt. 236 DT118
Whyteleafe Hill
Aspen Way E14 143 EB73
Aspen Way, Bans. 217 CX114
Aspen Way, Enf. 83 DX35
Aspen Way, Felt. 175 BV90
Aspen Way, S.Ock. 149 FX69
Aspen Way, Welw.G.C. 30 DC10
Aspenlea Rd W6 159 CX79
Aspern Gro NW3 120 DE64
Aspfield Row, Hem.H. 40 BH18
Aspinall Rd SE4 163 DX83
Aspinden Rd SE16 162 DV77
Aspley Rd SW18 180 DB85
Asplins Rd N17 100 DU53
Asprey Gro, Cat. 236 DU124
Asprey Pl, Brom. 204 EK96
Chislehurst Rd
Asquith Cl, Dag. 126 EW60
Ass Ho La, Har. 94 CB49
Assam St E1 142 DU72
White Ch La
Assata Ms N1 141 DP65
St. Paul's Rd
Assembly Pas E1 142 DW71
Assembly Wk, Cars. 200 DE101
Assher Rd, Walt. 196 BY104
Assheton Rd, Beac. 89 AK51
Assurance Cotts, Belv. 166 EZ78
Heron Hill
Astall Cl, Har. 95 CE53
Astbury Rd SE15 162 DW81
Aste St E14 163 EC75
Astell St SW3 276 C10
Astell St SW3 160 DE78
Asters, The, Wal.Cr. 66 DR28
Asteys Row N1 141 DP66
River Pl
Asthall Gdns, Ilf. 125 EQ56
Astle St SW11 160 DG82
Astleham Rd, Shep. 194 BL97
Astley, Grays 170 FZ79
Astley Av NW2 119 CW64
Astley Rd, Hem.H. 40 BJ20
Aston Av, Har. 117 CJ59
Aston Cl, Ash. 231 CJ118
Aston Cl, Bushey 76 CC44
Aston Cl, Sid. 186 EU90
Aston Cl, Wat. 76 BW40
Aston Grn, Houns. 156 BW82
Aston Mead, Wind. 151 AL80
Aston Ms, Rom. 126 EW59
Aston Pl SW16 181 DP93
Averil Gro
Aston Rd SW20 199 CW96
Aston Rd W5 137 CK72
Aston Rd (Claygate), Esher 215 CE106
Aston St E14 143 DY72
Aston Ter SW12 181 DH86
Cathles Rd
Aston Way, Epsom 233 CT116
Aston Way, Pot.B. 64 DD32
Astons Rd, Nthwd. 93 BQ48
Astonville St SW18 180 DA88
Astor Av, Rom. 127 FC58
Astor Cl, Add. 212 BK105
Astor Cl, Kings.T. 178 CP93
Astoria Wk SW9 161 DN83
Astra Cl, Horn. 147 FH65
Astra Dr, Grav. 191 GL92
Astrop Ms W6 159 CW76
Astrop Ter W6 159 CW76
Astwick Av, Hat. 45 CT15
Astwood Ms SW7 160 DB77
Asylum Arch Rd, Red. 266 DF137
Asylum Rd SE15 162 DV80
Atalanta Cl, Pur. 219 DN110
Atalanta St SW6 159 CX81
Atbara Ct, Tedd. 177 CH93
Atbara Rd, Tedd. 177 CH93
Atcham Rd, Houns. 156 CC84
Atcost Rd, Bark. 146 EU71
Atheldene Rd SW18 180 DB88
Athelney St SE6 183 EA90
Athelstan Cl, Rom. 106 FM54
Athelstan Rd
Athelstan Rd, Hem.H. 40 BM23
Athelstan Rd, Kings.T. 198 CM98
Athelstan Rd, Rom. 106 FM53
Athelstan Wk N, Welw.G.C. 29 CY10
Athelstan Wk S, Welw.G.C. 29 CX10
Athelstan Way, Orp. 206 EU95
Athelstane Gro E3 143 DZ68
Athelstane Ms N4 121 DN60
Stroud Grn Rd
Athelstone Rd, Har. 95 CD54
Athena Cl, Har. 117 CE61
Byron Hill Rd
Athena Cl, Kings.T. 198 CM97
Athena Pl, Nthwd. 93 BT53
The Dr
Athenaeum Pl N10 121 DH55
Fortis Grn Rd
Athenaeum Rd N20 98 DC46
Athenia Cl, Wal.Cr. 65 DP29
Cuffley Hill
Athenlay Rd SE15 183 DX85
Athens Gdns W9 140 DA70
Harrow Rd
Atherden Rd E5 122 DW63
Atherfield Rd, Reig. 266 DC137
Atherfold Rd SW9 161 DL83
Atherley Way, Houns. 176 BZ87
Atherstone Ct W2 140 DB71
Delamere Ter
Atherstone Ms SW7 160 DC77
Atherton Cl (Shalford), Guil. 258 AY140
Atherton Cl (Stanwell), Stai. 174 BK86
Atherton Ct (Eton), Wind. 151 AR80
Meadow La
Atherton Dr SW19 179 CX91
Atherton Gdns, Grays 171 GJ77
Atherton Hts, Wem. 137 CJ65
Atherton Ms E7 144 EF65
Atherton Pl, Har. 117 CD55
Atherton Pl, Sthl. 136 CB73
Longford Av
Atherton Rd E7 124 EF64
Atherton Rd SW13 159 CU80
Atherton Rd, Ilf. 102 EL54
Atherton St SW11 160 DE82
Athlon Rd, Wem. 137 CK68
Athlone (Claygate), Esher 215 CE107
Athlone Cl E5 122 DV63
Goulton Rd
Athlone Cl, Rad. 77 CH36
Athlone Rd SW2 181 DM87
Athlone Sq, Wind. 151 AQ81
Alma Rd
Athlone St NW5 140 DG65
Athol Cl, Pnr. 93 BV53
Athol Gdns, Pnr. 93 BV53
Athol Rd, Erith 167 FC78
Athol Sq E14 143 EC72
Athol Way, Uxb. 134 BN69
Atholl Gdns, Enf. 82 DS43
Atholl Rd, Ilf. 126 EU59
Atkins Cl, Wok. 226 AU118
Greythorne Rd
Atkins Dr, W.Wick. 203 ED103
Atkins Rd E10 123 EB58
Atkins Rd SW12 181 DK87
Atkinson Cl, Orp. 224 EU106
Martindale Av
Atkinson Rd E16 144 EJ71
Atlanta Boul, Rom. 127 FE58
Atlantic Rd SW9 161 DN84
Atlantis Cl, Bark. 146 EV69
Atlas Gdns SE7 164 EJ77
Atlas Ms E8 142 DT65
Tyssen St
Atlas Ms N7 141 DM65
Atlas Rd E13 144 EG68
Atlas Rd N11 99 DH51
Atlas Rd NW10 138 CS69
Atlas Rd, Dart. 168 FM83
Cornwall Rd
Atlas Rd, Wem. 118 CQ63
Atley Rd E3 143 EA67
Atlip Rd, Wem. 138 CL67
Atney Rd SW15 159 CY84
Atria Rd, Nthwd. 93 BU50
Attenborough Cl, Wat. 94 BY48
Harrow Way
Atterbury Cl, West. 255 ER126
Atterbury Rd N4 121 DN58
Atterbury St SW1 277 N9
Atterbury St SW1 161 DL77
Attewood Av NW10 118 CS62
Attewood Rd, Nthlt. 136 BY65
Attfield Cl N20 98 DD47
Attimore Cl, Welw.G.C. 29 CV10
Attimore Rd, Welw.G.C. 29 CV10
Attle Cl, Uxb. 134 BN68
Attlee Cl, Hayes 135 BV69
Attlee Cl, Th.Hth. 202 DQ100
Attlee Ct, Grays 170 GA76
Attlee Dr, Dart. 188 FN85
Attlee Rd SE28 146 EV73
Attlee Rd, Hayes 135 BU69
Attlee Ter E17 123 EB56
Attneave St WC1 274 D3
Attwood Cl, S.Croy. 220 DV114
Atwater Cl SW2 181 DN88
Atwell Cl E10 123 EB58
Belmont Pk Rd
Atwell Pl, T.Ditt. 197 CF102
Atwell Rd SE15 162 DU82
Rye La
Atwood (Bookham), Lthd. 230 BY124
Atwood Av, Rich. 158 CN82
Atwood Rd W6 159 CV77
Atwoods All, Rich. 158 CN81
Leyborne Pk
Aubert Pk N5 121 DP63
Aubert Rd N5 121 DP63
Aubretia Cl, Rom. 106 FL53
Aubrey Av (London Colney), St.Alb. 61 CJ26
Aubrey Pl NW8 140 DC68
Violet Hill
Aubrey Rd E17 123 EA55
Aubrey Rd N8 121 DL57
Aubrey Rd W8 139 CZ74
Aubrey Wk W8 139 CZ74
Aubreys Rd, Hem.H. 39 BE21
Auburn Cl SE14 163 DY80
Aubyn Hill SE27 182 DQ91
Aubyn Sq SW15 159 CU84
Auckland Av, Rain. 147 FF69
Auckland Cl SE19 202 DT95
Auckland Cl, Enf. 82 DV37
Auckland Cl, Til. 171 GG82
Auckland Gdns SE19 202 DS95
Auckland Hill SE27 182 DQ91
Auckland Ri SE19 202 DS95
Auckland Rd E10 123 EB62
Auckland Rd SE19 202 DT95
Auckland Rd SW11 160 DE84
Auckland Rd, Cat. 236 DS122
Auckland Rd, Ilf. 125 EP60
Auckland Rd, Kings.T. 198 CM98
Auckland Rd, Pot.B. 63 CY32
Auckland St SE11 161 DM78
Kennington La
Auden Pl NW1 140 DG67
Auden Pl, Sutt. 217 CW105
Wordsworth Dr
Audleigh Pl, Chig. 103 EN51
Audley Cl N10 99 DH52
Audley Cl SW11 160 DG83
Audley Cl, Add. 212 BH106
Audley Cl, Borwd. 78 CN41
Audley Ct E18 124 EF56
Audley Ct, Pnr. 94 BW54
Rickmansworth Rd
Audley Dr E16 144 EH74
Wesley Av
Audley Dr, Warl. 236 DW115
Audley Firs, Walt. 214 BW105
Audley Gdns, Ilf. 125 ET61
Audley Gdns, Loug. 85 EQ40
Audley Gdns, Wal.Abb. 67 EC34
Audley Pl, Sutt. 218 DA108
Audley Rd NW4 119 CV58
Audley Rd W5 138 CM71
Audley Rd, Enf. 81 DP40
Audley Rd, Rich. 178 CM85
Audley Sq W1 276 G2
Audley Wk, Orp. 206 EW100
Audrey Cl, Beck. 203 EB100
Audrey Gdns, Wem. 117 CH61
Audrey Rd, Ilf. 125 EP62
Audrey St E2 142 DU68
Audric Cl, Kings.T. 198 CN95
Audwick Cl (Cheshunt), Wal.Cr. 67 DX28
Augur Cl, Stai. 173 BF92
Augurs La E13 144 EH69
August End (George Grn), Slou. 132 AY72
August La (Albury), Guil. 260 BK144
Augusta Cl, W.Mol. 196 BZ97
Freeman Dr
Augusta Rd, Twick. 176 CC89
Augusta St E14 143 EB72
Augustine Cl (Colnbrook), Slou. 153 BE83
Augustine Ct, Wal.Abb. 67 EB33
Beaulieu Dr
Augustine Rd W14 159 CX76
Augustine Rd, Grav. 191 GJ87
Augustine Rd, Har. 94 CB53
Augustine Rd, Orp. 206 EX97
Augustus Cl, Brent. 157 CJ80
Augustus Cl, St.Alb. 42 CA22
Augustus La, Orp. 206 EU103
Augustus Rd SW19 179 CY88
Augustus St NW1 273 J1
Augustus St NW1 141 DH68
Aulton Pl SE11 161 DN78
Aultone Way, Cars. 200 DF104
Aultone Way, Sutt. 200 DB103
Aurelia Gdns, Croy. 201 DM99
Aurelia Rd, Croy. 201 DL100
Auriel Av, Dag. 147 FD65
Auriga Ms N16 122 DR64
Auriol Cl, Wor.Pk. 198 CS104
Auriol Pk Rd
Auriol Dr, Grnf. 137 CD66

Auriol Dr, Uxb. 134 BN65
Auriol Pk Rd, Wor.Pk. 198 CS104
Auriol Rd W14 159 CY77
Aurum Cl, Horl. 269 DH149
Austell Gdns NW7 96 CS48
Austen Cl SE28 146 EV74
Austen Cl, Green. 189 FW85
Austen Cl, Loug. 85 ER41
Austen Cl, Til. 171 GJ82
Coleridge Rd
Austen Gdns, Dart. 168 FM84
Austen Ho NW6 140 DA69
Austen Rd, Erith 167 FB80
Austen Rd, Guil. 259 AZ135
Austen Rd, Har. 116 CB61
Austenway (Chalfont St. Peter), Ger.Cr. 112 AX55
Austenwood Cl (Chalfont St. Peter), Ger.Cr. 90 AX54
Austenwood La (Chalfont St. Peter), Ger.Cr. 90 AX54
Austin Av, Brom. 204 EL99
Austin Cl SE23 183 DZ87
Austin Cl, Couls. 235 DP118
Austin Cl, Twick. 177 CJ85
Austin Ct E6 144 EJ67
Kings Rd
Austin Friars EC2 275 L8
Austin Friars EC2 142 DR72
Austin Friars Pas EC2 275 L8
Austin Friars Sq EC2 275 L8
Austin Rd SW11 160 DG81
Austin Rd (Northfleet), Grav. 191 GF88
Austin Rd, Hayes 155 BT75
Austin Rd, Orp. 206 EU100
Austin St E2 275 P3
Austin St E2 142 DT69
Austin Waye, Uxb. 134 BJ67
Austin's La, Uxb. 115 BR63
Austins Mead (Bovingdon), Hem.H. 57 BB28
Austins Pl, Hem.H. 40 BK19
St. Mary's Rd
Austral Cl, Sid. 185 ET90
Austral Dr, Horn. 128 FK59
Austral St SE11 278 F8
Austral St SE11 161 DP77
Australia Rd W12 139 CV73
Australia Rd, Slou. 152 AV75
Austyn Gdns, Surb. 198 CP102
Autumn Cl SW19 180 DC93
Autumn Cl, Enf. 82 DU39
Autumn Cl, Slou. 131 AM74
Autumn Dr, Sutt. 218 DB109
Autumn Glades, Hem.H. 41 BQ22
Autumn Gro, Welw.G.C. 30 DB11
Autumn St E3 143 EA67
Auxiliaries Way, Uxb. 113 BF57
Avalon Cl SW20 199 CY96
Avalon Cl W13 137 CG71
Avalon Cl, Enf. 81 DN40
Avalon Cl, Orp. 206 EX104
Avalon Cl, Wat. 60 BY32
Avalon Rd SW6 160 DB81
Avalon Rd W13 137 CG70
Avalon Rd, Orp. 206 EW103
Avard Gdns, Orp. 223 EQ105
Avarn Rd SW17 180 DF93
Ave Maria La EC4 274 G9
Ave Maria La EC4 141 DP72
Avebury, Slou. 131 AN74
Avebury Ct N1 142 DR67
Poole St
Avebury Ct, Hem.H. 40 BN17
Avebury Pk, Surb. 197 CK101
Avebury Rd E11 123 ED60
Southwest Rd
Avebury Rd SW19 199 CZ95
Avebury Rd, Orp. 205 ER104
Avebury St N1 142 DR67
Poole St
Aveley Bypass, S.Ock. 148 FQ73
Aveley Cl, Erith 167 FF79
Aveley Cl, S.Ock. 149 FR74
Aveley Rd, Rom. 127 FD56
Aveley Rd, Upmin. 148 FP65
Aveline St SE11 278 D10
Aveline St SE11 161 DN78
Aveling Cl, Pur. 219 DM113
Aveling Pk Rd E17 101 EA54
Avelon Rd, Rain. 147 FG67
Avelon Rd, Rom. 105 FD51
Avenell Rd N5 121 DP62
Avening Rd SW18 180 DA87
Brathway Rd
Avening Ter SW18 180 DA86
Avenons Rd E13 144 EG70
Avenue, The E4 101 ED51
Avenue, The (Leytonstone) E11 124 EF61
Avenue, The (Wanstead) E11 124 EF61
Avenue, The N3 98 DA54
Avenue, The N8 121 DN55
Avenue, The N10 99 DJ54
Avenue, The N11 99 DH49
Avenue, The N17 100 DS54
Avenue, The NW6 139 CX67
Avenue, The SE7 164 EJ80
Avenue, The SE10 163 ED80
Avenue, The SW4 180 DG85
Avenue, The SW11 180 DE87
Avenue, The SW18 180 DE87
Avenue, The W4 158 CS76
Avenue, The W13 137 CH73
Avenue, The (New Haw), Add. 212 BG110
Avenue, The, Amer. 55 AQ38
Avenue, The, Barn. 79 CY41
Avenue, The, Beck. 203 EB95
Avenue, The (Brockham), Bet. 248 CN134
Avenue, The, Bex. 186 EX87
Avenue, The, Brwd. 107 FX51
Avenue, The, Brom. 204 EK97
Avenue, The, Bushey 76 BZ42
Avenue, The, Cars. 218 DG108
Avenue, The, Couls. 235 DK115
Avenue, The, Croy. 202 DS104
Avenue, The, Egh. 173 BB91
Avenue, The, Epsom 217 CV108
Avenue, The (Claygate), Esher 215 CE107
Avenue, The, Grav. 191 GG88
Avenue, The, Green. 169 FV84
Avenue, The (Worplesdon), Guil. 242 AS127
Avenue, The, Hmptn. 176 BZ93
Avenue, The, Har. 95 CF53
Avenue, The, Hem.H. 39 BE19
Avenue, The, Hert. 31 DP07
Avenue, The, Hodd. 49 DZ19
Avenue, The, Horl. 268 DF149
Avenue, The, Horn. 128 FJ61
Avenue, The, Houns. 176 CB85
Avenue, The (Cranford), Houns. 155 BU81
Avenue, The, Islw. 157 CD79
Avenue, The, Kes. 204 EK104
Avenue, The, Lthd. 215 CF112
Avenue, The, Loug. 84 EK44
Avenue, The, Nthwd. 93 BQ51
Avenue, The, Orp. 205 ET103
Avenue, The (St. Paul's Cray), Orp. 186 EV94
Avenue, The, Pnr. 116 BZ58
Avenue, The (Hatch End), Pnr. 94 CA52
Avenue, The, Pot.B. 63 CZ30
Avenue, The, Rad. 61 CG33
Avenue, The (South Nutfield), Red. 267 DL137
Avenue, The, Rich. 158 CM82
Avenue, The, Rom. 127 FD56
Avenue, The (Datchet), Slou. 152 AV81
Avenue, The (Farnham Common), Slou. 111 AP64
Avenue, The, Stai. 194 BH95
Avenue, The (Wraysbury), Stai. 152 AX83
Avenue, The, Sun. 195 BV95
Avenue, The, Surb. 198 CM100
Avenue, The, Sutt. 217 CZ109
Avenue, The (Cheam), Sutt. 217 CW108
Avenue, The, Tad. 233 CV122
Avenue, The, Twick. 177 CJ85
Avenue, The (Cowley), Uxb. 134 BK70
Avenue, The (Ickenham), Uxb. 114 BN63
Avenue, The, Wal.Abb. 68 EJ25
Avenue, The, Wat. 75 BV40
Avenue, The, Wem. 118 CM61
Avenue, The, West Dr. 154 BL76
Avenue, The, W.Wick. 203 ED101
Avenue, The, West. 239 EP123
Avenue, The, Whyt. 236 DU119
Avenue, The (Old Windsor), Wind. 172 AV85
Avenue, The (Chobham), Wok. 210 AT109
Avenue, The, Wor.Pk. 199 CT103
Avenue App, Kings L. 58 BN30
Avenue Cl N14 81 DJ44
Avenue Cl NW8 140 DE67
Avenue Cl, Houns. 155 BU81
The Av
Avenue Cl, Rom. 106 FM52
Avenue Cl, Tad. 233 CV122
Avenue Cl, West Dr. 154 BK76
Avenue Cres W3 158 CP75
Avenue Cres, Houns. 155 BV80
Avenue Dr, Slou. 133 AZ71
Avenue Elmers, Surb. 198 CL99
Avenue Gdns SE25 202 DU97
Avenue Gdns SW14 158 CS83
Avenue Gdns W3 158 CP75
Avenue Gdns, Horl. 269 DJ149
Avenue Gdns, Houns. 155 BU80
The Av
Avenue Gdns, Tedd. 177 CF94
Avenue Gate, Loug. 84 EJ44
Avenue Ind Est E4 101 DZ51
Avenue Ind Est, Rom. 106 FK54
Avenue Ms N10 121 DH55
Avenue Pk Rd SE27 181 DP89
Avenue Ri, Bushey 76 CA43
Avenue Rd E7 124 EH64
Avenue Rd N6 121 DJ59
Avenue Rd N12 98 DC49
Avenue Rd N14 99 DJ45
Avenue Rd N15 122 DR57
Avenue Rd NW3 140 DD66
Avenue Rd NW8 140 DD67
Avenue Rd NW10 139 CT68
Avenue Rd SE20 202 DW95
Avenue Rd SE25 202 DU96
Avenue Rd SW16 201 DK96
Avenue Rd SW20 199 CV96
Avenue Rd W3 158 CP75
Avenue Rd, Bans. 234 DB115
Avenue Rd, Beck. 202 DW95
Avenue Rd, Belv. 167 FC77
Avenue Rd, Bexh. 166 EY83
Avenue Rd, Brent. 157 CJ78
Avenue Rd, Brwd. 108 FW49
Avenue Rd, Cat. 236 DR122
Avenue Rd, Cob. 230 BX116
Avenue Rd, Epp. 85 ER36
Avenue Rd, Epsom 216 CR114
Avenue Rd, Erith 167 FC80
Avenue Rd, Felt. 175 BT90
Avenue Rd, Hmptn. 196 CB95
Avenue Rd, Hodd. 49 ED19
Avenue Rd, Islw. 157 CF81
Avenue Rd, Kings.T. 198 CL97
Avenue Rd, N.Mal. 198 CS98
Avenue Rd, Pnr. 116 BY55
Avenue Rd (Chadwell Heath), Rom. 126 EV59
Avenue Rd (Harold Wd), Rom. 106 FM52
Avenue Rd, St.Alb. 43 CE19
Avenue Rd, Sev. 257 FJ123
Avenue Rd, Sthl. 156 BZ75
Avenue Rd, Stai. 173 BD92
Avenue Rd, Sutt. 218 DA110
Avenue Rd, Tedd. 177 CG94
Avenue Rd, Wall. 219 DJ108
Avenue Rd, West. 238 EL120
Avenue Rd, Wdf.Grn. 102 EJ51
Avenue S, Surb. 198 CM101
Avenue Ter, N.Mal. 198 CQ97
Kingston Rd
Avenue Ter, Wat. 76 BY44
Averil Ct, Maid. 130 AJ72
Averil Gro SW16 181 DP93
Averill St W6 159 CX79
Avern Gdns, W.Mol. 196 CB98
Avern Rd, W.Mol. 196 CB99
Avery Fm Row SW1 276 G9
Avery Gdns, Ilf. 125 EM57
Avery Hill Rd SE9 185 ER86
Avery Row W1 273 H10
Avery Row W1 141 DH73
Avey La, Loug. 84 EH39
Avey La, Wal.Abb. 83 ED36
Avia Cl, Hem.H. 40 BK24
Aviary Cl E16 144 EF71
Aviary Rd, Wok. 228 BG116
Aviemore Cl, Beck. 203 DZ99
Aviemore Way, Beck. 203 DY99
Avignon Rd SE4 163 DX83
Avington Cl, Guil. 242 AY134
London Rd
Avington Ct SE1 162 DS77
Old Kent Rd
Avington Gro SE20 182 DW94
Avington Way SE15 162 DT80
Daniel Gdns
Avion Cres NW9 97 CU53
Avior Dr, Nthwd. 93 BT49
Avis Gro, Croy. 221 DY110
Avis Sq E1 143 DX72
Avoca Rd SW17 180 DG91
Avocet Ms SE28 165 ER76
Avon Cl, Add. 212 BG107
Avon Cl, Grav. 191 GK89
Avon Cl, Hayes 136 BW70
Avon Cl, Slou. 131 AL73
Avon Cl, Sutt. 218 DC105
Avon Cl, Wat. 60 BW34
Avon Cl, Wor.Pk. 199 CU103
Avon Ct, Grnf. 136 CB70
Braund Av
Avon Grn, S.Ock. 149 FV72
Avon Ms, Pnr. 94 BZ53
Avon Path, S.Croy. 220 DQ107
Avon Pl SE1 279 J5
Avon Rd E17 123 ED55
Avon Rd SE4 163 EA83
Avon Rd, Grnf. 136 CA70
Avon Rd, Sun. 175 BT94
Avon Rd, Upmin. 129 FR58
Avon Sq, Hem.H. 40 BM15
Avon Way E18 124 EG55
Avondale Av N12 98 DB50
Avondale Av NW2 118 CS62
Avondale Av, Barn. 98 DF46
Avondale Av, Esher 197 CG104
Avondale Av, Stai. 173 BF94
Avondale Av, Wor.Pk. 199 CT102
Avondale Cl, Horl. 268 DF146
Avondale Cl, Loug. 103 EM45
Avondale Cl, Walt. 214 BW106
Pleasant Pl
Avondale Ct E11 124 EE60
Avondale Ct E16 144 EE71
Avondale Rd
Avondale Ct E18 102 EH53
Avondale Cres, Enf. 83 DY41
Avondale Cres, Ilf. 124 EK57
Avondale Dr, Hayes 135 BU74
Avondale Dr, Loug. 103 EM45
Avondale Gdns, Houns. 176 BZ85
Avondale Ms, Brom. 184 EG93
Avondale Rd
Avondale Pk Gdns W11 139 CY73
Avondale Pk Rd W11 139 CY73
Avondale Pavement SE1 162 DU78
Avondale Sq
Avondale Ri SE15 162 DT83
Avondale Rd E16 144 EE71
Avondale Rd E17 123 EA59
Avondale Rd N3 98 DC53
Avondale Rd N13 99 DN47
Avondale Rd N15 121 DP57
Avondale Rd SE9 184 EL89
Avondale Rd SW14 158 CR83
Avondale Rd SW19 180 DB92
Avondale Rd, Ashf. 174 BK90
Avondale Rd, Brom. 184 EE93
Avondale Rd, Har. 117 CF55
Avondale Rd, S.Croy. 220 DQ107
Avondale Rd, Well. 166 EW82
Avondale Sq SE1 162 DU78
Avonley Rd SE14 162 DW80
Avonmead, Wok. 226 AW118
Silversmiths Way
Avonmore Av, Guil. 243 AZ133
Avonmore Gdns W14 159 CY77
Avonmore Rd
Avonmore Pl W14 159 CY77
Avonmore Rd
Avonmore Rd W14 159 CZ77
Avonmouth Rd, Dart. 188 FK85
Avonmouth St SE1 279 H6
Avonmouth St SE1 162 DQ76
Avonstowe Cl, Orp. 205 EQ104
Avontar Rd, S.Ock. 149 FV70
Avonwick Rd, Houns. 156 CB82
Avril Way E4 101 EC50
Avro Way, Wall. 219 DL108
Avro Way, Wey. 212 BL110
Awlfield Av N17 100 DR53
Awliscombe Rd, Well. 165 ET82
Axe St, Bark. 145 EQ67
Axes La, Red. 267 DJ141
Axholme Av, Edg. 96 CN53
Axis Pk (Langley), Slou. 153 BB78
Axminster Cres, Well. 166 EW81
Axminster Rd N7 121 DL62
Axtaine Rd, Orp. 206 EX101
Axtane (Southfleet), Grav. 190 FZ94
Axtane Cl (Sutton at Hone), Dart. 208 FQ96
Axwood, Epsom 232 CQ115
Aybrook St W1 272 F7
Aybrook St W1 140 DG71
Aycliffe Cl, Brom. 205 EM98
Aycliffe Dr, Hem.H. 40 BL16
Aycliffe Rd W12 139 CT74
Aycliffe Rd, Borwd. 78 CL39
Aylebridges Av, Egh. 173 BC94
Aylands Cl, Wem. 118 CL61
Preston Rd
Aylands Rd, Enf. 82 DW36
Ayles Rd, Hayes 135 BV69
Aylesbury Cl E7 144 EF65
Atherton Rd
Aylesbury Ct, Sutt. 200 DC104
Benhill Wd Rd
Aylesbury Cres, Slou. 131 AR72
Aylesbury End, Beac. 89 AL54
Aylesbury Est SE17 162 DR78
Villa St
Aylesbury Rd SE17 162 DR78
Aylesbury Rd, Brom. 204 EG97
Aylesbury St EC1 274 F5
Aylesbury St EC1 141 DP70
Aylesbury St NW10 118 CR62
Aylesford Av, Beck. 203 DY99
Aylesford St SW1 277 M10
Aylesford St SW1 161 DK78
Aylesham Cen, The SE15 162 DU81
Aylesham Cl NW7 97 CU52
Aylesham Rd, Orp. 205 ET101
Aylestone Av NW6 139 CX67
Aylesworth Av, Slou. 131 AN69
Doddsfield Rd
Aylesworth Spur (Old Windsor), Wind. 172 AV87
Aylets Fld, Harl. 51 ES19
Aylett Rd SE25 202 DV98
Aylett Rd, Islw. 157 CE82
Aylett Rd, Upmin. 128 FQ61
Ayley Cft, Enf. 82 DU43
Ayliffe Cl, Kings.T. 198 CN96
Cambridge Gdns
Aylmer Cl, Stan. 95 CG49
Aylmer Dr, Stan. 95 CG49
Aylmer Par N2 120 DF57
Aylmer Rd E11 124 EF60
Aylmer Rd N2 120 DE57
Aylmer Rd W12 159 CT75
Aylmer Rd, Dag. 126 EY62
Ayloffe Rd, Dag. 146 EZ65
Ayloffs Cl, Horn. 128 FL57
Ayloffs Wk, Horn. 128 FK57
Aylsham Dr, Uxb. 115 BR61
Aylsham La, Rom. 106 FJ49
Aylsham Rd, Hodd. 49 EC15
Aylton Est SE16 162 DW75
Renforth St
Aylward Gdns, Chesh. 54 AN30
Aylward Rd SE23 183 DX89
Aylward Rd SW20 199 CZ96
Aylward St E1 142 DW72
Aylwards Ri, Stan. 95 CG49
Aylwyn Est SE1 279 P6
Aylwyn Est SE1 162 DS76
Aymer Cl, Stai. 193 BE95
Aymer Dr, Stai. 193 BE95
Aynho St, Wat. 75 BV43
Aynhoe Rd W14 159 CX77
Aynscombe Angle, Orp. 206 EV101
Aynscombe La SW14 158 CQ83
Aynscombe Path SW14 158 CQ82
Thames Bk
Aynsley Gdns, Harl. 52 EW15
Ayot Grn, Welw. 29 CU06
Ayot Greenway, St.Alb. 28 CN06
Ayot Little Grn, Welw. 29 CT06
Ayot Path, Borwd. 78 CN37
Ayr Ct W3 138 CN71
Monks Dr
Ayr Grn, Rom. 105 FE52
Ayr Way, Rom. 105 FE52
Ayres Cl E13 144 EG69
Ayres Cres NW10 138 CR66
Ayres St SE1 279 J4
Ayres St SE1 162 DQ75
Ayron Rd, S.Ock. 149 FV70
Ayrsome Rd N16 122 DS62
Ayrton Rd SW7 160 DD76
Wells Way
Aysgarth Ct, Sutt. 200 DB104
Sutton Common Rd
Aysgarth Rd SE21 182 DS86
Aytoun Pl SW9 161 DM82
Aytoun Rd SW9 161 DM82
Azalea Cl W7 137 CF74
Azalea Cl, Ilf. 125 EP64
Azalea Ct, Wok. 226 AX119
Azalea Ct, Wdf.Grn. 102 EE52
The Bridle Path
Azalea Dr, Swan. 207 FD98
Azalea Wk, Pnr. 115 BV57
Azalea Wk, Sthl. 156 CC75
Navigator Dr
Azalea Way (George Grn), Slou. 132 AY72
Blinco La
Azenby Rd SE15 162 DT82
Azile Everitt Ho SE18 165 EQ78
Vicarage Pk
Azof St SE10 164 EE77

B

B.A.T. Export Ho, Wok. 226 AY117
Baalbec Rd N5 121 DP64
Baas Hill, Brox. 49 DX21
Baas Hill Cl, Brox. 49 DY21
Baas La, Brox. 49 DY21
Babbacombe Cl, Chess. 215 CK106
Babbacombe Gdns, Ilf. 124 EL56
Babbacombe Rd, Brom. 204 EG95
Baber Dr, Felt. 176 BW86
Babington Ri, Wem. 138 CN65
Babington Rd NW4 119 CV56
Babington Rd SW16 181 DK92
Babington Rd, Dag. 126 EW64
Babington Rd, Horn. 127 FH60
Babmaes St SW1 277 L1
Babylon La (Lower Kingswood), Tad. 250 DA127
Bacchus Wk N1 275 M1
Bachelors Acre, Wind. 151 AR81
Bachelor's La, Wok. 228 BN124
Baches St N1 275 L3
Baches St N1 142 DR69
Back, The, Berk. 39 BB16
Back All, Dor. 263 CH136
Back Ch La E1 142 DU73
Back Grn, Walt. 214 BW107
Back Hill EC1 274 D5
Back Hill EC1 141 DN70
Back La N8 121 DL57
Back La NW3 120 DC63
Heath St
Back La, Bex. 186 FA87
Back La (Sheering), B.Stort. 36 FA06
Back La, Brent. 157 CK79
Back La, Ch.St.G. 90 AU48
Back La, Edg. 96 CQ53
Back La, Grays 149 FW74
Back La (East Clandon), Guil. 244 BK130
Back La, Hert. 48 DQ18
Back La, Purf. 169 FS76
Back La, Rich. 177 CJ90
Back La, Rick. 73 BB38
Back La, Rom. 126 EY59
St. Chad's Rd
Back La (Godden Grn), Sev. 257 FN124
Back La (Ide Hill), Sev. 256 FC126
Back La, Wal.Abb. 50 EJ23
Back La, Wat. 77 CE39
Back La, Welw. 30 DD05
Back Path, Red. 252 DQ133
Back Rd, Sid. 186 EU91
Back St, Harl. 36 EW11
Broadway Av
Backhouse Pl SE17 279 N9
Backley Gdns SE25 202 DU100
Backs, The, Chesh. 54 AQ31
Bacon Gro SE1 279 P7
Bacon Gro SE1 162 DT76
Bacon La NW9 118 CP56
Bacon La, Edg. 96 CN53
Bacon Link, Rom. 105 FB51
Bacon St E1 142 DT70
Bacon St E2 142 DT70
Bacon Ter, Dag. 126 EV64
Fitzstephen Rd
Bacons Dr (Cuffley), Pot.B. 65 DL29
Bacons La N6 120 DG60
Bacons Mead (Denham), Uxb. 114 BG61
Bacton NW5 120 DG64
Bacton St E2 142 DW69
Roman Rd
Badburgham Ct, Wal.Abb. 68 EF33
Baddeley Cl, Enf. 83 EA38
Government Row
Baddow Cl, Dag. 146 FA67
Baddow Cl, Wdf.Grn. 102 EK51
Baddow Wk N1 142 DQ67
Baden Cl, Stai. 174 BG94
Baden Dr, Horl. 268 DE147
Baden Pl SE1 279 K4
Baden Powell Cl, Dag. 146 EY67
Baden Powell Cl, Surb. 198 CM103
Baden Powell Rd, Sev. 256 FE121
Baden Rd N8 121 DK56
Baden Rd, Guil. 242 AV132
Baden Rd, Ilf. 125 EP64
Bader Cl, Ken. 236 DR115
Bader Cl, Welw.G.C. 30 DC09
Bader Gdns, Slou. 151 AN75
Bader Wk (Northfleet), Grav. 190 GE90
Bader Way, Rain. 147 FG65
Badger Cl, Felt. 175 BU90
Sycamore Cl
Badger Cl, Guil. 242 AV131
Badger Cl, Houns. 156 BW83
Badger Cl, Ilf. 125 EQ59
Badger Way, Hat. 45 CV20
Badgers Cl, Ashf. 174 BM92
Fordbridge Rd
Badgers Cl, Borwd. 78 CM40
Kingsley Av
Badgers Cl, Enf. 81 DP41
Badgers Cl, Har. 117 CD58
Badgers Cl, Hayes 135 BS73
Badgers Cl, Hert. 32 DV09
Badgers Cl, Wok. 226 AW118
Badgers Copse, Orp. 205 ET103
Badgers Copse, Wor.Pk. 199 CT103
Badgers Cft N20 97 CY46
Badgers Cft SE9 185 EN90
Badgers Cft, Brox. 49 DY21
Badgers Cft, Hem.H. 41 BR21
Badgers Hill, Vir.W. 192 AW99
Badgers Hole, Croy. 221 DX105
Badgers La, Warl. 236 DW120
Badgers Mt, Grays 171 GF75
Badgers Ri (Badgers Mt), Sev. 224 FA110
Badgers Rd (Badgers Mt), Sev. 225 FB110
Badgers Wk, N.Mal. 198 CS96
Badgers Wk, Pur. 219 DK111
Badgers Wk, Rick. 73 BF42
Badgers Wk, Whyt. 236 DT119
Badgers Wd, Cat. 252 DQ125
Badgers Wd (Farnham Common), Slou. 111 AQ64
Badingham Dr (Fetcham), Lthd. 231 CE123
Badlis Rd E17 123 EA55
Badlow Cl, Erith 167 FE80
Badminton Cl, Borwd. 78 CN40
Badminton Cl, Har. 117 CE56
Badminton Cl, Nthlt. 136 CA65
Badminton Ms E16 144 EG74
Hanameel St
Badminton Pl, Brox. 49 DY20
Badminton Rd SW12 180 DG86
Badric Ct SW11 160 DD82
Yelverton Rd
Badsworth Rd SE5 162 DQ80
Baffin Way E14 143 EC73
Prestons Rd
Bagden Hill (Westhumble), Dor. 247 CD130
Bagley Cl, West Dr. 154 BL75
Bagley's La SW6 160 DB81
Bagleys Spring, Rom. 126 EY56
Bagot Cl, Ash. 232 CM116
Bagshot Ct SE18 165 EN81
Prince Imperial Rd
Bagshot Rd (Englefield Grn), Egh. 172 AW94
Bagshot Rd, Enf. 100 DT45
Bagshot St SE17 162 DS78
Bahram Rd, Epsom 216 CR110
Baildon St SE8 163 DZ80
Bailey Cl E4 101 EC49
Bailey Cl N11 99 DK52
Bailey Cl, Purf. 169 FR77
Gabion Av
Bailey Cl, Wind. 151 AN82
Bailey Pl SE26 183 DX93
Bailey Rd (Westcott), Dor. 262 CC137
Baillie Cl, Rain. 147 FH70
Baillie Rd, Guil. 259 AZ135
Baillies Wk W5 157 CK75
Liverpool Rd
Bainbridge Cl, Rich. 178 CL92
Latchmere Cl
Bainbridge Rd, Dag. 126 EZ63
Bainbridge St WC1 273 N8
Bainbridge St WC1 141 DK72
Baines Cl, S.Croy. 220 DQ106
Brighton Rd
Bainton Mead, Wok. 226 AU117
Baird Av, Sthl. 136 CB73
Baird Cl E10 123 EA60
Marconi Rd
Baird Cl NW9 118 CQ58
Baird Cl, Bushey 76 CB44
Ashfield Av
Baird Cl, Slou. 151 AP75
Haig Dr
Baird Gdns SE19 182 DS91
Baird Rd, Enf. 82 DV42
Baird St EC1 275 J4
Bairstow Cl, Borwd. 78 CL39
Baizdon Rd SE3 164 EE82
Bakeham La (Englefield Grn), Egh. 172 AW94
Bakehouse Rd, Horl. 268 DF146
Baker Boy La, Croy. 221 DZ112
Baker Hill Cl (Northfleet), Grav. 191 GF91
Baker La, Mitch. 200 DG96
Baker Pas NW10 138 CS67
Acton La
Baker Rd NW10 138 CS67
Baker Rd SE18 164 EL80
Baker St NW1 272 E5
Baker St NW1 140 DF70
Baker St W1 272 E6
Baker St W1 140 DF71
Baker St, Enf. 82 DR41
Baker St, Hert. 32 DS09
Baker St, Pot.B. 79 CY35
Baker St, Wey. 212 BN105
Bakers Av E17 123 EB58
Bakers Ct SE25 202 DS97
Bakers End SW20 199 CY96
Bakers Fld N7 121 DK63
Crayford Rd
Bakers Gdns, Cars. 200 DE103
Bakers Gro, Welw.G.C. 30 DC08
Bakers Hill E5 122 DW60
Bakers Hill, Barn. 80 DB40

Bakers La N6 120 DF57
Bakers La, Epp. 69 ET30
Bakers La, Saw. 35 ET05
Bakers Mead, Gdse. 252 DW130
Baker's Ms W1 272 F8
Bakers Ms, Orp. 223 ET107
Bakers Orchard (Wooburn Grn), H.Wyc. 110 AE58
Bakers Pas NW3 120 DC63
Heath St
Baker's Rents E2 275 P3
Bakers Rd, Uxb. 134 BK66
Bakers Rd (Cheshunt), Wal.Cr. 66 DV30
Bakers Row E15 144 EE68
Baker's Row EC1 274 D5
Baker's Row EC1 141 DN70
Bakers Wk, Saw. 36 EY05
Bakers Wd (Denham), Uxb. 113 BD60
Baker's Yd EC1 141 DN70
Baker's Row
Baker's Yd, Uxb. 134 BK66
Bakers Rd
Bakery Cl SW9 161 DM81
Bakery Cl, Harl. 50 EJ15
Bakery Path, Edg. 96 CP51
Station Rd
Bakery Pl SW11 160 DF84
Altenburg Gdns
Bakewell Way, N.Mal. 198 CS96
Bala Grn NW9 118 CS58
Snowdon Dr
Balaam St E13 144 EG69
Balaams La N14 99 DK47
Balaclava Rd SE1 162 DT77
Balaclava Rd, Surb. 197 CJ101
Balcary Gdns, Berk. 38 AS20
Balcaskie Rd SE9 185 EM85
Balchen Rd SE3 164 EK82
Balchier Rd SE22 182 DV86
Balchins La (Westcott), Dor. 262 CA138
Balcombe Cl, Bexh. 166 EX84
Balcombe Gdns, Horl. 269 DJ149
Balcombe Rd, Horl. 269 DH147
Balcombe St NW1 272 D5
Balcombe St NW1 140 DF70
Balcon Ct W5 138 CM72
Boileau Rd
Balcon Way, Borwd. 78 CQ39
Balcorne St E9 142 DW66
Balder Ri SE12 184 EH89
Balderton St W1 272 G9
Balderton St W1 140 DG72
Baldock St E3 143 EB68
Baldock St, Ware 33 DX06
Baldock Way, Borwd. 78 CM39
Baldocks Rd, Epp. 85 ES35
Baldry Gdns SW16 181 DL93
Baldwin Cres SE5 162 DQ81
Baldwin Cres, Guil. 243 BC132
Baldwin Gdns, Houns. 156 CC81
Chamberlain Gdns
Baldwin Rd, Beac. 89 AP54
Baldwin Rd (Burnham), Slou. 130 AJ69
Baldwin St EC1 275 K3
Baldwin Ter N1 142 DQ68
Baldwins, Welw.G.C. 30 DB09
Baldwin's Gdns EC1 274 D6
Baldwin's Gdns EC1 141 DN71
Baldwins Hill, Loug. 85 EM40
Baldwins La, Rick. 75 BP42
Baldwins Shore (Eton), Wind. 151 AR79
Baldwyn Gdns W3 138 CR73
Baldwyns Pk, Bex. 187 FD89
Baldwyns Rd, Bex. 187 FD89
Bale Rd E1 143 DY71
Balfe St N1 274 A1
Balfe St N1 141 DL68
Balfern Gro W4 158 CS78
Balfern St SW11 160 DE81
Balfont Cl, S.Croy. 220 DU113
Balfour Av W7 137 CF74
Balfour Av, Wok. 226 AY122
Balfour Business Cen, Sthl. 156 BW76
Balfour Gro N20 98 DF48
Balfour Ho W10 139 CX71
St. Charles Sq
Balfour Ms N9 100 DU48
The Bdy
Balfour Ms W1 276 G2
Balfour Pl SW15 159 CV84
Balfour Pl W1 276 G1
Balfour Rd N5 122 DQ63
Balfour Rd SE25 202 DU98
Balfour Rd SW19 180 DB94
Balfour Rd W3 138 CQ71
Balfour Rd W13 157 CG75
Balfour Rd, Brom. 204 EK99
Balfour Rd, Cars. 218 DF108
Balfour Rd, Grays 170 GC77
Balfour Rd, Har. 117 CD57
Balfour Rd, Houns. 156 CB83
Balfour Rd, Ilf. 125 EP61
Balfour Rd, Sthl. 156 BX76
Balfour Rd, Wey. 212 BN105
Balfour St SE17 279 K8
Balfour St SE17 162 DR77
Balfour St, Hert. 32 DQ08
Balfron Twr E14 143 EC72
Balgonie Rd E4 101 ED46
Balgores Cres, Rom. 127 FH55
Balgores La, Rom. 127 FH55
Balgores Sq, Rom. 127 FH56
Balgowan Cl, N.Mal. 198 CS99
Balgowan Rd, Beck. 203 DY97
Balgowan St SE18 165 ET77
Balham Continental Mkt SW12 181 DH88
Shipka Rd
Balham Gro SW12 180 DG87
Balham High Rd SW12 180 DG88
Balham High Rd SW17 180 DG89
Balham Hill SW12 181 DH87
Balham New Rd SW12 181 DH87
Balham Pk Rd SW12 180 DF88
Balham Rd N9 100 DU47
Balham Sta Rd SW12 181 DH88
Balkan Wk E1 142 DV73
Pennington St
Balladier Wk E14 143 EB71
Ballamore Rd, Brom. 184 EG90
Ballance Rd E9 143 DX65
Ballands N, The, Lthd. 231 CE122
Ballands S, The, Lthd. 231 CE123
Ballantine St SW18 160 DC84
Ballantyne Dr (Kingswood), Tad. 233 CZ121
Ballard Cl, Kings.T. 178 CR94
Ballard Grn, Wind. 151 AL80
Ballards Cl, Dag. 147 FB67
Ballards Fm Rd, Croy. 220 DU107
Ballards Fm Rd, S.Croy. 220 DU107
Ballards Grn, Tad. 233 CY119
Ballards La N3 98 DA53
Ballards La N12 98 DA53
Ballards La, Oxt. 254 EJ129
Ballards Ms, Edg. 96 CN51
Ballards Ri, S.Croy. 220 DU107
Ballards Rd NW2 119 CU61
Ballards Rd, Dag. 147 FB67
Ballards Way, Croy. 220 DV107
Ballards Way, S.Croy. 220 DU107
Ballast Quay SE10 163 ED78
Ballater Cl, Wat. 94 BW49
Ballater Rd SW2 161 DL84
Ballater Rd, S.Croy. 220 DT106
Ballenger Ct, Wat. 75 BV41
Ballina St SE23 183 DX86
Ballingdon Rd SW11 180 DG86
Ballinger Ct, Berk. 38 AV20
Ballinger Pt E3 143 EB69
Bromley High St
Balliol Av E4 101 ED49
Balliol Rd N17 100 DS53
Balliol Rd W10 139 CW72
Balliol Rd, Well. 166 EV82
Balloch Rd SE6 183 ED88
Ballogie Av NW10 118 CS63
Ballow Cl SE5 162 DS80
Harris St
Balls Pk, Hert. 32 DT11
Balls Pond Pl N1 142 DR65
Balls Pond Rd
Balls Pond Rd N1 142 DR65
Balmain Cl W5 137 CK74
Balmer Rd E3 143 DZ68
Balmes Rd N1 142 DR67
Balmoral Av N11 98 DG50
Balmoral Av, Beck. 203 DY98
Balmoral Cl SW15 179 CX86
Westleigh Av
Balmoral Cl (Park St), St.Alb. 60 CC28
Balmoral Cl, Slou. 131 AL72
Balmoral Ct, Wor.Pk. 199 CV103
Balmoral Rd
Balmoral Cres, W.Mol. 196 CA97
Balmoral Dr, Borwd. 78 CR43
Balmoral Dr, Hayes 135 BU71
Balmoral Dr, Sthl. 136 BZ70
Balmoral Dr, Wok. 227 BC116
Balmoral Gdns W13 157 CG76
Balmoral Gdns, Bex. 186 EZ87
Balmoral Gdns, Couls. 220 DR110
Balmoral Gdns, Ilf. 125 ET60
Balmoral Gdns, Wind. 151 AR83
Balmoral Gro N7 141 DM65
Balmoral Ms W12 159 CT75
Balmoral Rd E7 124 EJ63
Balmoral Rd E10 123 EB61
Balmoral Rd NW2 139 CV65
Balmoral Rd, Abb.L. 59 BU32
Balmoral Rd, Brwd. 108 FV44
Balmoral Rd (Sutton at Hone), Dart. 188 FP94
Balmoral Rd, Enf. 83 DX36
Balmoral Rd, Har. 116 CA63
Balmoral Rd, Horn. 128 FK62
Balmoral Rd, Kings.T. 198 CM98
Balmoral Rd, Rom. 127 FH56
Balmoral Rd, Wat. 76 BW38
Balmoral Rd, Wor.Pk. 199 CV104
Balmoral Way, Sutt. 218 DA110
Balmore Cres, Barn. 80 DG43
Balmore St N19 121 DH61
Balmuir Gdns SW15 159 CW84
Balnacraig Av NW10 118 CS63
Balniel Gate SW1 277 N10
Balniel Gate SW1 161 DK78
Balquhain Cl, Ash. 231 CK117
Balsams Cl, Hert. 32 DR11
Baltic Cl SW19 180 DD94
Baltic Ct SE16 163 DX75
Timber Pond Rd
Baltic Pl N1 142 DS67
Kingsland Rd
Baltic St E EC1 275 H5
Baltic St E EC1 142 DQ70
Baltic St W EC1 275 H5
Baltic St W EC1 142 DQ70
Baltimore Pl, Well. 165 ET82
Balvaird Pl SW1 161 DK78
Balvernie Gro SW18 179 CZ87
Bamber Ho, Bark. 145 EQ67
St. Margarets
Bamborough Gdns W12 159 CW75
Bamford Av, Wem. 138 CM67
Bamford Ct E15 123 EB64
Clays La
Bamford Rd, Bark. 145 EQ65
Bamford Rd, Brom. 183 EC92
Bamford Way, Rom. 105 FB50
Bampfylde Cl, Wall. 201 DJ104
Bampton Dr NW7 97 CU52
Bampton Rd SE23 183 DX90
Bampton Rd, Rom. 106 FL53
Bampton Way, Wok. 226 AU118
Banavie Gdns, Beck. 203 EC95
Banbury Av, Slou. 131 AM71
Banbury Cl, Enf. 81 DP39
Holtwhites Hill
Banbury Ct WC2 273 P10
Banbury Ct, Sutt. 218 DA108
Banbury Enterprise Cen, Croy. 201 DP103
Factory La
Banbury Rd E9 143 DX66
Banbury Rd E17 101 DX52
Banbury St SW11 160 DE82
Banbury St, Wat. 75 BV43
Banbury Vil, Grav. 190 FZ93
Banbury Wk, Nthlt. 136 CA68
Brabazon Rd
Banchory Rd SE3 164 EH80
Bancroft Av N2 120 DE57
Bancroft Av, Buck.H. 102 EG47
Bancroft Cl, Ashf. 174 BN92
Feltham Hill Rd
Bancroft Ct, Nthlt. 136 BW67
Bancroft Ct, Reig. 250 DB134
Bancroft Gdns, Har. 94 CC53
Bancroft Gdns, Orp. 205 ET102
Bancroft Rd E1 142 DW69
Bancroft Rd, Har. 94 CC54
Bancroft Rd, Reig. 250 DA134
Band La, Egh. 173 AZ92
Banders Ri, Guil. 243 BC133
Bandon Cl, Uxb. 134 BM67
Bandon Ri, Wall. 219 DK106
Banes Down, Wal.Abb. 50 EE22
Banfield Rd SE15 162 DV83
Bangalore St SW15 159 CW83
Bangor Cl, Nthlt. 116 CB64
Bangors Cl, Iver 133 BE72
Bangors Rd N, Iver 133 BD67
Bangors Rd S, Iver 133 BE71
Banim St W6 159 CV76
Banister Rd W10 139 CX69
Bank, The N6 121 DH60
Cholmeley Pk
Bank Av, Mitch. 200 DD96
Bank Ct, Dart. 188 FL86
High St
Bank Ct, Hem.H. 40 BJ21
Bank End SE1 279 J2
Bank End SE1 142 DQ74
Bank La SW15 178 CS85
Bank La, Kings.T. 178 CL94
Bank Ms, Sutt. 218 DA111
Sutton Ct Rd
Bank Mill, Berk. 38 AY19
Bank Mill La, Berk. 38 AY20
Bank Pl, Brwd. 108 FW47
High St
Bank Rd (Penn), H.Wyc. 88 AC47
Bank St, Grav. 191 GH86
Bank St, Sev. 257 FH125
Bankfoot, Grays 170 FZ77
Bankfoot Rd, Brom. 184 EE91
Bankhurst Rd SE6 183 DZ87
Banks La, Bexh. 166 EZ84
Banks La, Epp. 70 EY32
Bank's La, Lthd. 229 BV122
Banks Rd, Borwd. 78 CQ40
Banks Spur, Slou. 151 AP75
Cooper Way
Banks Way E12 125 EN63
Grantham Rd
Banks Way, Guil. 243 AZ131
Banksia Rd N18 100 DW50
Banksian Wk, Islw. 157 CE81
Bankside SE1 279 H1
Bankside, Enf. 81 DP39
Bankside (Northfleet), Grav. 190 GC86
Bankside (Dunton Grn), Sev. 256 FE121
Bankside, S.Croy. 220 DT107
Bankside, Sthl. 136 BX74
Bankside, Wok. 226 AV118
Wyndham Rd
Bankside Av, Nthlt. 135 BU68
Townson Av
Bankside Cl, Bex. 187 FD91
Bankside Cl, Cars. 218 DE107
Bankside Cl, Islw. 157 CF84
Bankside Cl (Biggin Hill), West. 238 EJ118
Bankside Dr, T.Ditt. 197 CH102
Bankside Rd, Ilf. 125 EQ64
Bankside Way SE19 182 DS93
Lunham Rd
Bankton Rd SW2 161 DN84
Bankwell Rd SE13 164 EE84
Bann Cl, S.Ock. 149 FV73
Banner Cl, Purf. 169 FR77
Brimfield Rd
Banner St EC1 275 J5
Banner St EC1 142 DQ70
Bannerman Ho SW8 161 DM79
Banning St SE10 164 EE78
Bannister Cl SW2 181 DN88
Ewen Cres
Bannister Cl, Grnf. 117 CD64
Bannister Cl, Slou. 152 AY75
Bannister Dr, Brwd. 109 GC44
Bannister Gdns, Orp. 206 EW97
Main Rd
Bannister Ho E9 123 DX64
Homerton High St
Bannister's Rd, Guil. 258 AT136
Bannockburn Rd SE18 165 ES77
Banstead Gdns N9 100 DS48
Banstead Pl, Bans. 234 DC116
Park Rd
Banstead Rd, Bans. 217 CX112
Banstead Rd, Cars. 218 DE107
Banstead Rd, Cat. 236 DR121
Banstead Rd, Epsom 217 CV111
Banstead Rd, Pur. 219 DN111
Banstead Rd S, Sutt. 218 DD110
Banstead St SE15 162 DW83
Banstead Way, Wall. 219 DL106
Banstock Rd, Edg. 96 CP51
Banting Dr N21 81 DM43
Banton Cl, Enf. 82 DV40
Central Av
Bantry St SE5 162 DR80
Banwell Rd, Bex. 186 EX86
Woodside La
Banyard Rd SE16 162 DV76
Southwark Pk Rd
Banyards, Horn. 128 FL56
Bapchild Pl, Orp. 206 EW98
Baptist Gdns NW5 140 DG65
Queen's Cres
Barandon Wk W11 139 CX73
Barb Ms W6 159 CW76
Barbara Brosnan Ct NW8 140 DD68
Grove End Rd
Barbara Cl, Shep. 195 BP99
Barbara Hucklesby Cl N22 99 DP54
The Sandlings
Barbauld Rd N16 122 DS62
Barbel Cl, Wal.Cr. 67 EA34
Barber Cl N21 99 DN45
Barberry Cl, Rom. 106 FJ52
Barberry Rd, Hem.H. 40 BG20
Barber's All E13 144 EH69
Barbers Rd E15 143 EB68
Barbican, The EC2 275 H6
Barbican, The EC2 142 DQ71
Barbican Rd, Grnf. 136 CB72
Barbon Cl WC1 274 B6
Barbot Cl N9 100 DU48
Barchard St SW18 180 DB85
Barchester Cl W7 137 CF74
Barchester Cl, Uxb. 134 BJ70
Barchester Rd, Har. 95 CD54
Barchester Rd, Slou. 153 AZ75
Barchester St E14 143 EB71
Barclay Cl SW6 160 DA80
Barclay Cl, Hert. 32 DV11
Barclay Cl (Fetcham), Lthd. 230 CB123
Barclay Ct, Wat. 75 BU44
Barclay Ct, Hodd. 49 EA18
Barclay Ct, Slou. 151 AQ75
Barclay Oval, Wdf.Grn. 102 EG49
Barclay Path E17 123 EC57
Barclay Rd E11 124 EE60
Barclay Rd E13 144 EJ70
Barclay Rd E17 123 EC57
Barclay Rd N18 100 DR51
Barclay Rd SW6 160 DA80
Barclay Rd, Croy. 202 DR104
Barclay Way SE22 182 DU87
Lordship La
Barclay Way, Grays 169 FT78
Barcombe Av SW2 181 DL89
Barcombe Cl, Orp. 205 ET97
Bard Rd W10 139 CX73
Barden Cl (Harefield), Uxb. 92 BJ52
Barden St SE18 165 ES80
Bardeswell Cl, Brwd. 108 FW47
Bardfield Av, Rom. 126 EX55
Bardney Rd, Mord. 200 DB98
Bardolph Av, Croy. 221 DZ109
Bardolph Rd N7 121 DL63
Bardolph Rd, Rich. 158 CM83
St. Georges Rd
Bardon Wk, Wok. 226 AV117
Bampton Way
Bards Cor, Hem.H. 40 BH19
Laureate Way
Bardsey Pl E1 142 DW71
Mile End Rd
Bardsey Wk N1 142 DQ65
Clephane Rd
Bardsley Cl, Croy. 202 DT104
Bardsley La SE10 163 EC79
Bardwell Ct, St.Alb. 43 CD21
Bardwell Rd, St.Alb. 43 CD21
Barfett St W10 139 CZ70
Barfield (Sutton at Hone), Dart. 208 FP95
Barfield Av N20 98 DE47
Barfield Rd E11 124 EF60
Barfield Rd, Brom. 205 EN97
Barfields, Loug. 85 EN42
Barfields (Bletchingley), Red. 251 DP133
Barfields Gdns, Loug. 85 EN42
Barfields
Barfields Path, Loug. 85 EN42
Barfolds, Hat. 45 CW23
Dixons Hill Rd
Barford Cl NW4 97 CU53
Barford St N1 141 DN67
Barforth Rd SE15 162 DV83
Barfreston Way SE20 202 DV95
Bargate Cl SE18 165 ET78
Bargate Cl, N.Mal. 199 CU100
Bargate Ct, Guil. 242 AS134
Park Barn Dr
Barge Ho Rd E16 145 EP74
Barge Ho St SE1 278 E2
Barge Wk, E.Mol. 197 CK96
Barge Wk, Kings.T. 197 CK95
Barge Wk, Walt. 196 CC96
Bargery Rd SE6 183 EB88
Bargrove Av, Hem.H. 40 BG21
Bargrove Cl SE20 182 DU94
Bargrove Cres SE6 183 DZ89
Elm La
Barham Av, Borwd. 78 CM41
Barham Cl, Brom. 204 EL102
Barham Cl, Chis. 185 EP92
Barham Cl, Grav. 191 GM88
Barham Cl, Rom. 105 FB54
Barham Cl, Wem. 137 CH65
Barham Cl, Wey. 213 BQ105
Barham Rd SW20 179 CU94
Barham Rd, Chis. 185 EP92
Barham Rd, Dart. 188 FN87
Barham Rd, S.Croy. 220 DQ106
Baring Cl SE12 184 EG89
Baring Cres, Beac. 88 AJ52
Baring Rd SE12 184 EG87
Baring Rd, Barn. 80 DD41
Baring Rd, Beac. 88 AJ52
Baring Rd, Croy. 202 DU102
Baring St N1 142 DR67
Bark Burr Rd, Grays 170 FZ75
Bark Hart Rd, Orp. 206 EV102
Bark Pl W2 140 DB73
Barkantine Shop Par, The E14 163 EA75
The Quarterdeck
Barker Cl, N.Mal. 198 CP98
Barker Cl, Nthwd. 93 BT52
Barker Dr NW1 141 DJ66
Barker Ms SW4 161 DH84
Barker Rd, Cher. 193 BE101
Barker St SW10 160 DC79
Barker Wk SW16 181 DK90
Barker Way SE22 182 DU88
Dulwich Common
Barkham Rd N17 100 DR52
Barkham Ter SE1 278 E6
Barking Ind Pk, Bark. 145 ET67
Barking Rd E6 144 EK68
Barking Rd E13 144 EH70
Barking Rd E16 144 EF71
Barkston Gdns SW5 160 DB77
Barkston Path, Borwd. 78 CN38
Barkwood Cl, Rom. 127 FC57
Barkworth Rd SE16 162 DV78
Barlborough St SE14 162 DW80
Barlby Gdns W10 139 CX70
Barlby Rd W10 139 CX71
Barle Gdns, S.Ock. 149 FV72
Barlee Cres, Uxb. 134 BJ71
Barley Brow, Wat. 60 BW31
High Elms La
Barley Cl, Bushey 76 CB43
Barley Cft, Harl. 51 ES19
Barley Cft, Hem.H. 41 BQ20
Barley Cft, Hert. 32 DR07
Barley Flds (Wooburn Grn), H.Wyc. 110 AE55
Barley La, Ilf. 126 EU59
Barley La, Rom. 126 EV58
Barley Mow Caravan Pk, St.Alb. 44 CM22
Barley Mow Ct, Bet. 248 CQ134
Barley Mow La, St.Alb. 44 CL23
Barley Mow Pas EC1 274 G7
Barley Mow Pas W4 158 CR78
Barley Mow Rd (Englefield Grn), Egh. 172 AW92
Barley Mow Way, Shep. 194 BN98
Barley Ponds Cl, Ware 33 DZ06
Barley Ponds Rd, Ware 33 DZ06
Barley Shotts Business Pk W10 139 CZ71
St. Ervans Rd
Barleycorn Way E14 143 DZ73
Barleycorn Way, Horn. 128 FM58
Barleycroft Grn, Welw.G.C. 29 CW09
Barleycroft Rd, Welw.G.C. 29 CW10
Barleyfields Cl, Rom. 126 EV59
Barleymead, Horl. 269 DH147
Oatlands
Barlow Cl, Wall. 219 DL107
Barlow Pl W1 277 J1
Barlow Rd NW6 139 CZ65
Barlow Rd W3 138 CP74
Barlow Rd, Hmptn. 176 CA94
Barlow St SE17 279 L9
Barlow Way, Rain. 147 FD71
Barmeston Rd SE6 183 EB89
Barmor Cl, Har. 94 CB54
Barmouth Av, Grnf. 137 CF68
Barmouth Rd SW18 180 DC86
Barmouth Rd, Croy. 203 DX103
Barn Cl, Ashf. 175 BP92
Barn Cl, Bans. 234 DD115
Barn Cl, Epsom 232 CQ115
Barn Cl, Hem.H. 40 BM23
Barnfield
Barn Cl, Nthlt. 136 BW68
Barn Cl, Rad. 77 CG35
Barn Cl (Farnham Common), Slou. 111 AP63
Barn Cl, Welw.G.C. 29 CW09
Barn Cres, Pur. 220 DR113
Barn Cres, Stan. 95 CJ51
Barn Elms Pk SW15 159 CW82
Barn End Dr, Dart. 188 FJ90
Barn End La, Dart. 188 FJ92
Barn Hill, Harl. 50 EH19
Barn Hill, Wem. 118 CP61
Barn Lea, Rick. 92 BG46
Barn Mead, Epp. 85 ES36
Barn Mead, Harl. 51 ER17
Barn Mead, Ong. 71 FE29
Barn Meadow, Epp. 69 ET25
Upland Rd
Barn Meadow La (Bookham), Lthd. 230 BZ124
Barn Ms, Har. 116 CA62
Barn Ri, Wem. 118 CN60
Barn St N16 122 DS62
Stoke Newington Ch St
Barn Way, Wem. 118 CN60
Barnabas Ct N21 81 DN43
Cheyne Wk
Barnabas Rd E9 123 DX64
Barnaby Cl, Har. 116 CC61
Barnaby Pl SW7 160 DD77
Barnaby Way, Chig. 103 EP48
Barnacre Cl, Uxb. 134 BK72
New Peachey La
Barnacres Rd, Hem.H. 58 BM25
Barnard Acres, Wal.Abb. 50 EE23
Barnard Cl SE18 165 EN77
Barnard Cl, Chis. 205 ER95
Barnard Cl, Sun. 175 BV94
Oak Gro
Barnard Cl, Wall. 219 DK108
Barnard Ct, Wok. 226 AS118
Raglan Rd
Barnard Gdns, Hayes 135 BV70
Barnard Gdns, N.Mal. 199 CU98
Barnard Grn, Welw.G.C. 29 CZ10
Barnard Gro E15 144 EF66
Vicarage La
Barnard Hill N10 98 DG54
Barnard Ms SW11 160 DE84
Barnard Rd SW11 160 DE84
Barnard Rd, Enf. 82 DV40
Barnard Rd, Mitch. 200 DG97
Barnard Rd, Warl. 237 EB119
Barnard Way, Hem.H. 40 BL21
Barnardo Dr, Ilf. 125 EQ56
Barnardo Gdns E1 143 DX73
Devonport St
Barnardo St E1 143 DX72
Devonport St
Barnardos Village, Ilf. 125 EQ55
Barnard's Inn EC1 274 E8
Barnards Pl, S.Croy. 219 DP109
Barnato Cl, W.Byf. 212 BL112
Viscount Gdns
Barnby Sq E15 144 EE67
Barnby St
Barnby St E15 144 EE67
Barnby St NW1 273 L1
Barnby St NW1 141 DJ68
Barncroft Cl, Loug. 85 EN43
Barncroft Cl, Uxb. 135 BP71
Barncroft Grn, Loug. 85 EN43
Barncroft Rd, Berk. 38 AT20
Barncroft Rd, Loug. 85 EN43
Barncroft Way, St.Alb. 43 CG21
Barndicott, Welw.G.C. 30 DC09
Barnehurst Av, Bexh. 167 FC81
Barnehurst Av, Erith 167 FC81
Barnehurst Cl, Erith 167 FC81
Barnehurst Rd, Bexh. 167 FC82
Barnes All, Hmptn. 196 CC96
Hampton Ct Rd
Barnes Av SW13 159 CU80
Barnes Av, Chesh. 54 AQ30
Barnes Av, Sthl. 156 BZ77
Barnes Br SW13 158 CS82
Barnes Br W4 158 CS82
Barnes Cl E12 124 EK63
Barnes Ct E16 144 EJ71
Ridgwell Rd
Barnes Ct, Wdf.Grn. 102 EK50
Barnes Cray Cotts, Dart. 187 FG85
Maiden La
Barnes Cray Rd, Dart. 167 FG84
Barnes End, N.Mal. 199 CU99
Barnes High St SW13 159 CT82
Barnes Ho, Bark. 145 ER67
St. Marys
Barnes La, Kings L. 58 BH27
Barnes Pikle W5 137 CJ73
Barnes Ri, Kings L. 58 BM27
Barnes Rd N18 100 DW49
Barnes Rd, Gdmg. 258 AS143
Barnes Rd, Ilf. 125 EQ64
Barnes St E14 143 DY72
Barnes Ter SE8 163 DZ78
Barnes Wallis Dr, Wey. 212 BL111
Barnes Way, Iver 133 BF73
Barnesbury Ho SW4 181 DK85
Barnesdale Cres, Orp. 206 EU100
Barnet Bypass, Barn. 78 CS41
Barnet Dr, Brom. 204 EL103
Barnet Gate La, Barn. 79 CT44
Barnet Gro E2 142 DU69
Barnet Hill, Barn. 80 DA42
Barnet Ho N20 98 DC47
Barnet La N20 97 CZ46
Barnet La, Barn. 79 CZ44
Barnet La, Borwd. 77 CK44
Barnet Rd (Arkley), Barn. 79 CV43
Barnet Rd, Pot.B. 64 DB34
Barnet Rd (London Colney), St.Alb. 62 CL27
Barnet Trd Est, Barn. 79 CZ41
Barnet Way NW7 96 CR45
Barnet Wd Rd, Brom. 204 EJ103
Barnett Cl, Erith 167 FF82
Barnett Cl (Wonersh), Guil. 259 BC143
Barnett Cl, Lthd. 231 CH119
Barnett La (Wonersh), Guil. 259 BB144
Barnett Row, Guil. 242 AX129
Barnett St E1 142 DV72
Cannon St Rd
Barnett Wd La, Ash. 231 CJ119
Barnett Wd La, Lthd. 231 CH120

Barnetts Shaw, Oxt. 253 ED127
Barney Cl SE7 164 EJ78
Barnfield, Bans. 218 DB114
Barnfield, Epp. 70 EU28
Barnfield, Grav. 191 GG89
Barnfield, Hem.H. 40 BM23
Barnfield, Horl. 268 DG149
Barnfield, Iver 133 BE72
Barnfield, N.Mal. 198 CS100
Barnfield, Slou. 131 AK74
Barnfield Av, Croy. 202 DW103
Barnfield Av, Kings.T. 178 CL92
Barnfield Av, Mitch. 201 DH98
Barnfield Cl N4 121 DL59
Crouch Hill
Barnfield Cl SW17 180 DC90
Barnfield Cl, Couls. 236 DQ119
Barnfield Cl, Green. 189 FT86
Barnfield Cl, Hodd. 49 EA15
Barnfield Cl, Swan. 207 FC101
Barnfield Cl, Wal.Abb. 50 EF22
Barnfield Gdns SE18 165 EP79
Plumstead Common Rd
Barnfield Gdns, Kings.T. 178 CL91
Barnfield Pl E14 163 EA77
Barnfield Rd SE18 165 EP79
Barnfield Rd W5 137 CJ70
Barnfield Rd, Belv. 166 EZ79
Barnfield Rd, Edg. 96 CQ53
Barnfield Rd, Orp. 206 EX97
Barnfield Rd, St.Alb. 43 CJ17
Barnfield Rd, Sev. 256 FD123
Barnfield Rd, S.Croy. 220 DS109
Barnfield Rd, Welw.G.C. 29 CY11
Barnfield Rd (Tatsfield), West. 238 EK120
Barnfield Way, Oxt. 254 EG133
Barnfield Wd Cl, Beck. 203 ED100
Barnfield Wd Rd, Beck. 203 ED100
Barnham Dr SE28 145 ET74
Barnham Rd, Grnf. 136 CC69
Barnham St SE1 279 N4
Barnham St SE1 162 DS75
Barnhill, Pnr. 116 BW57
Barnhill Av, Brom. 204 EF99
Barnhill La, Hayes 135 BV69
Barnhill Rd, Hayes 135 BV69
Barnhill Rd, Wem. 118 CQ62
Barnhurst Path, Wat. 94 BW50
Barningham Way NW9 118 CR58
Barnlea Cl, Felt. 176 BY89
Barnmead (Chobham), Wok. 210 AT110
Barnmead Gdns, Dag. 126 EZ64
Barnmead Rd, Beck. 203 DY95
Barnmead Rd, Dag. 126 EZ64
Barns Ct, Harl. 51 EN20
Barnsbury Cl, N.Mal. 198 CQ98
Barnsbury Cres, Surb. 198 CQ102
Barnsbury Est N1 141 DN67
Barnsbury Rd
Barnsbury Gro N7 141 DM66
Barnsbury La, Surb. 198 CP103
Barnsbury Pk N1 141 DN66
Barnsbury Rd N1 141 DN68
Barnsbury Sq N1 141 DN66
Barnsbury St N1 141 DN66
Barnsbury Ter N1 141 DM66
Barnscroft SW20 199 CV97
Barnsdale Av E14 163 EA77
Barnsdale Cl, Borwd. 78 CM39
Barnsdale Rd W9 139 CZ70
Barnsfield Pl, Uxb. 134 BJ66
Barnside Ct, Welw.G.C. 29 CW09
Barnsley Rd, Rom. 106 FM52
Barnsley St E1 142 DV70
Barnstaple Path, Rom. 106 FJ50
Barnstaple Rd, Rom. 106 FJ50
Barnstaple Rd, Ruis. 116 BW62
Barnston Wk N1 142 DQ67
Popham St
Barnston Way, Brwd. 109 GC43
Barnsway, Kings L. 58 BL28
Barnway (Englefield Grn), Egh. 172 AW92
Barnwell Rd SW2 181 DN85
Barnwell Rd, Dart. 168 FM83
Barnwood Cl W9 140 DB70
Barnwood Cl, Guil. 242 AS132
Barnwood Cl, Ruis. 115 BR61
Lysander Rd
Barnwood Rd, Guil. 242 AS133
Barnyard, The, Tad. 233 CU124
Baron Cl N11 98 DG50
Balmoral Av
Baron Cl, Sutt. 218 DB110
Baron Gdns, Ilf. 125 EQ55
Baron Gro, Mitch. 200 DE98
Baron Rd, Dag. 126 EX60
Baron St N1 141 DN68
Baron Wk E16 144 EF71
Baron Wk, Mitch. 200 DE98
Baroness Rd E2 142 DT69
Diss St
Baronet Gro N17 100 DU53
St. Paul's Rd
Baronet Rd N17 100 DU53
Barons, The, Twick. 177 CH86
Barons Ct, Wall. 201 DK104
Whelan Way
Barons Ct Rd W14 159 CY78
Barons Gate, Barn. 80 DE44
Barons Hurst, Epsom 232 CQ116
Barons Keep W14 159 CY78
Barons Mead, Har. 117 CE56
Barons Pl SE1 278 E5
Barons Pl SE1 161 DN75
Barons Wk, Croy. 203 DY100
Barons Way, Egh. 173 BD93
Barons Way, Reig. 266 DA138
Baronsfield Rd, Twick. 177 CH86
Baronsmead Rd SW13 159 CU81
Baronsmede W5 158 CM75
Baronsmere Rd N2 120 DE56
Barque Ms SE8 163 EA79
Watergate St
Barr Rd, Grav. 191 GM89
Barr Rd, Pot.B. 64 DC33
Barra Cl, Hem.H. 41 BP23
Barra Hall Circ, Hayes 135 BS72
Barra Hall Rd, Hayes 135 BS73
Barrack La, Wind. 151 AR81
Barrack Path, Wok. 226 AT118
Barrack Rd, Guil. 242 AU132
Barrack Rd, Houns. 156 BX84
Barrack Row, Grav. 191 GH86
Barracks, The, Add. 194 BH104
Barracks Hill, Amer. 89 AM45
Barracks La, Barn. 79 CY41
High St
Barrards Way (Seer Grn), Beac. 89 AQ51
Barras Cl, Enf. 83 EA38
Government Row
Barratt Av N22 99 DM54
Barratt Ind Pk, Sthl. 156 CA75
Barratt Way, Har. 117 CD55
Tudor Rd
Barrenger Rd N10 98 DF53
Barrens Brae, Wok. 227 BA118
Barrens Cl, Wok. 227 BA118
Barrens Pk, Wok. 227 BA118
Barrett Cl, Rom. 105 FH52
Barrett Rd E17 123 EC56
Barrett Rd (Fetcham), Lthd. 230 CC124
Barrett St W1 272 G9
Barrett St W1 140 DG72
Barretts Grn Rd NW10 138 CQ68
Barretts Gro N16 122 DS64
Barretts Rd (Dunton Grn), Sev. 241 FD120
Barrhill Rd SW2 181 DL89
Barricane, Wok. 226 AV119
Barrie Cl, Couls. 235 DJ115
Barrie Est W2 140 DD73
Craven Ter
Barrie Ho W3 158 CP75
Barriedale SE14 163 DY82
Barrier App SE7 164 EK76
Barrier Pt Rd E16 144 EJ74
Barringer Sq SW17 180 DG91
Barrington Cl NW5 120 DG64
Barrington Cl, Ilf. 103 EM53
Barrington Cl, Loug. 85 EQ42
Barrington Rd
Barrington Ct, Brwd. 109 GC44
Barrington Ct, Dor. 263 CG137
Barrington Rd
Barrington Dr (Harefield), Uxb. 92 BG52
Barrington Grn, Loug. 85 EQ42
Barrington Lo, Wey. 213 BQ106
Barrington Pk Gdns, Ch.St.G. 90 AX46
Barrington Rd E12 145 EN65
Barrington Rd N8 121 DK57
Barrington Rd SW9 161 DP83
Barrington Rd, Bexh. 166 EX82
Barrington Rd, Dor. 263 CG137
Barrington Rd, Loug. 85 EQ41
Barrington Rd, Pur. 219 DJ112
Barrington Rd, Sutt. 200 DA102
Barrington Vil SE18 165 EN81
Barrow Av, Cars. 218 DF108
Barrow Cl N21 99 DP48
Barrow Grn Rd, Oxt. 253 EC128
Barrow Hedges Cl, Cars. 218 DE108
Barrow Hedges Way, Cars. 218 DE108
Barrow Hill, Wor.Pk. 198 CS103
Barrow Hill Cl, Wor.Pk. 198 CS103
Barrow Hill
Barrow Hill Est NW8 140 DE68
Barrow Hill Rd
Barrow Hill Rd NW8 272 B1
Barrow Hill Rd NW8 140 DE68
Barrow La (Cheshunt), Wal.Cr. 66 DT30
Barrow Pt Av, Pnr. 94 BY54
Barrow Pt La, Pnr. 94 BY54
Barrow Rd SW16 181 DK93
Barrow Rd, Croy. 219 DN106
Barrow Wk, Brent. 157 CJ78
Glenhurst Rd
Barrowdene Cl, Pnr. 94 BY54
Paines La
Barrowell Grn N21 99 DP47
Barrowfield Cl N9 100 DV48
Barrowgate Rd W4 158 CQ78
Barrows Rd, Harl. 51 EM15
Barrowsfield, S.Croy. 220 DT112
Barrs Rd NW10 138 CR66
Barr's Rd, Maid. 130 AH72
Barry Av N15 122 DT58
Craven Pk Rd
Barry Av, Bexh. 166 EY80
Barry Av, Wind. 151 AQ80
Barry Cl, Grays 171 GG75
Barry Cl, Orp. 205 ES104
Barry Cl, St.Alb. 60 CB25
Barry Rd E6 144 EL72
Barry Rd NW10 138 CQ66
Barry Rd SE22 182 DU86
Bars, The, Guil. 258 AX135
Barset Rd SE15 162 DW83
Barson Cl SE20 182 DW94
Barston Rd SE27 182 DQ90
Barstow Cres SW2 181 DM88
Bartel Cl, Hem.H. 41 BR22
Bartelotts Rd, Slou. 131 AK70
Barter St WC1 274 A7
Barter St WC1 141 DL71
Barters Wk, Pnr. 116 BY55
High St
Barth Rd SE18 165 ES77
Bartholomew Cl EC1 275 H7
Bartholomew Cl EC1 142 DQ71
Bartholomew Cl SW18 160 DC84
Bartholomew Ct, Dor. 263 CG137
South St
Bartholomew Dr, Rom. 106 FK54
Bartholomew La EC2 275 L9
Bartholomew Pl EC1 275 H7
Bartholomew Rd NW5 141 DJ65
Bartholomew Sq E1 142 DV70
Coventry Rd
Bartholomew Sq EC1 275 J4
Bartholomew Sq EC1 142 DQ70
Bartholomew St SE1 279 K7
Bartholomew St SE1 162 DR76
Bartholomew Vil NW5 141 DJ65
Bartholomew Way, Swan. 207 FE97
Bartle Av E6 144 EL68
Bartle Rd W11 139 CY72
Bartlett Cl E14 143 EA72
Bartlett Ct EC4 274 E8
Bartlett Rd, Grav. 191 GG88
Bartlett Rd, West. 255 EQ126
Bartlett St, S.Croy. 220 DR106
Bartletts Mead, Hert. 32 DR06
Bartletts Pas EC4 274 E8
Bartlow Gdns, Rom. 105 FD53
Barton, The, Cob. 214 BX112
Barton Av, Rom. 127 FB60
Barton Cl E6 145 EM72
Barton Cl E9 122 DW64
Churchill Wk
Barton Cl NW4 119 CU56
Barton Cl SE15 162 DV83
Kirkwood Rd
Barton Cl, Add. 212 BG107
Barton Cl, Bexh. 186 EY85
Barton Cl, Chig. 103 EQ47
Barton Cl, Shep. 195 BP100
Barton Grn, N.Mal. 198 CR96
Barton Meadows, Ilf. 125 EQ56
Barton Rd W14 159 CY78
Barton Rd (Sutton at Hone), Dart. 208 FP95
Barton Rd (Bramley), Guil. 259 BA144
Barton Rd, Horn. 127 FG60
Barton Rd, Sid. 186 EY93
Barton Rd, Slou. 153 AZ75
Barton St SW1 277 P6
Barton Way, Borwd. 78 CN40
Barton Way, Rick. 75 BP43
Bartons, The, Borwd. 77 CK44
Bartonway NW8 140 DD68
Queen's Ter
Bartram Cl, Uxb. 135 BP70
Lees Rd
Bartram Rd SE4 183 DY85
Bartrams La, Barn. 80 DC38
Bartrop Cl, Wal.Cr. 66 DR28
Poppy Wk
Barts Cl, Beck. 203 EA99
Barville Cl SE4 163 DY84
St. Norbert Rd
Barwell Business Pk, Chess. 215 CK109
Barwick Rd E7 124 EH63
Barwood Av, W.Wick. 203 EB102
Bascombe St SW2 181 DN86
Basden Gro, Felt. 176 CA89
Basedale Rd, Dag. 146 EV66
Baseing Cl E6 145 EN73
Basevi Way SE8 163 EB79
Basford Way, Wind. 151 AK83
Bashley Rd NW10 138 CR70
Basil Av E6 144 EL68
Basil Gdns SE27 182 DQ92
Basil Gdns, Croy. 203 DX102
Primrose La
Basil St SW3 276 D6
Basil St SW3 160 DF76
Basildene Rd, Houns. 156 BX82
Basildon Av, Ilf. 103 EN53
Basildon Cl, Sutt. 218 DB109
Basildon Cl, Wat. 75 BQ44
Basildon Rd SE2 166 EU78
Basildon Sq, Hem.H. 40 BM16
Basilon Rd, Bexh. 166 EY82
Basin App E14 143 DY72
Commercial Rd
Basing Cl, T.Ditt. 197 CF101
Basing Ct SE15 162 DT81
Basing Dr, Bex. 186 EZ86
Basing Hill NW11 119 CZ60
Basing Hill, Wem. 118 CM61
Basing Ho, Bark. 145 ER67
St. Margarets
Basing Ho Yd E2 275 N2
Basing Pl E2 275 N2
Basing Rd, Bans. 217 CZ114
Basing Rd, Rick. 91 BF46
Basing St W11 139 CZ72
Basing Way N3 120 DB55
Basing Way, T.Ditt. 197 CF101
Basingdon Way SE5 162 DR84
Basingfield Rd, T.Ditt. 197 CF101
Basinghall Av EC2 275 K7
Basinghall Av EC2 142 DR71
Basinghall Gdns, Sutt. 218 DB109
Basinghall St EC2 275 K8
Basinghall St EC2 142 DQ71
Basire St N1 142 DQ67
Baskerville Rd SW18 180 DE87
Basket Gdns SE9 184 EL85
Baslow Cl, Har. 95 CD53
Baslow Wk E5 123 DX63
Overbury St
Basnett Rd SW11 160 DG83
Basque Ct SE16 163 DX75
Poolmans St
Bassano St SE22 182 DT85
Bassant Rd SE18 165 ET79
Bassein Pk Rd W12 159 CT75
Basset Cl (New Haw), Add. 212 BH110
Bassett Cl, Sutt. 218 DB109
Bassett Dr, Reig. 250 DA133
Bassett Gdns, Epp. 71 FB26
Bassett Gdns, Islw. 156 CC80
Bassett Ho, Dag. 146 EV67
Bassett Rd W10 139 CX72
Bassett Rd, Uxb. 134 BJ66
New Windsor St
Bassett Rd, Wok. 227 BC116
Bassett St NW5 140 DG65
Bassett Way, Grnf. 136 CB72
Bassett Way, Slou. 131 AL70
Pemberton Rd
Bassetts Cl, Orp. 223 EP105
Bassetts Way, Orp. 223 EP105
Bassil Rd, Hem.H. 40 BK21
Bassingbourne Cl, Brox. 49 DZ20
Bassingburn Wk, Welw.G.C. 29 CZ10
Bassingham Rd SW18 180 DC87
Bassingham Rd, Wem. 137 CK65
Bassishaw Highwalk EC2 142 DQ71
London Wall
Basswood Cl SE15 162 DV83
Linden Gro
Bastable Av, Bark. 145 ES68
Bastion Highwalk EC2 142 DQ71
London Wall
Bastion Ho EC2 142 DQ71
London Wall
Bastion Rd SE2 166 EU78
Baston Manor Rd, Brom. 204 EH104
Baston Rd, Brom. 204 EH102
Bastwick St EC1 275 H4
Bastwick St EC1 141 DP70
Basuto Rd SW6 160 DA81
Bat & Ball Rd, Sev. 257 FJ121
Batavia Cl, Sun. 196 BW95
Batavia Ms SE14 163 DY80
Goodwood Rd
Batavia Rd SE14 163 DY80
Batavia Rd, Sun. 195 BV95
Batchelor St N1 141 DN68
Batchelors Way, Amer. 55 AR39
Batchelors Way, Chesh. 54 AP29
Batchwood Dr, St.Alb. 42 CC17
Batchwood Gdns, St.Alb. 43 CD17
Batchwood Grn, Orp. 206 EU97
Batchwood Vw, St.Alb. 42 CC18
Batchworth Heath Hill, Rick. 92 BN49
Batchworth Hill, Rick. 92 BM48
Batchworth La, Nthwd. 93 BS50
Batchworth Roundabout, Rick. 92 BK46
Bate St E14 143 DZ73
Three Colt St
Bateman Cl, Bark. 145 EQ65
Glenny Rd
Bateman Ho SE17 161 DP79
Otto St
Bateman Rd E4 101 EA51
Bateman Rd, Rick. 74 BN44
Bateman St W1 273 M9
Bateman's Bldgs W1 273 M9
Bateman's Row EC2 275 N4
Bateman's Row EC2 142 DS70
Bates Cl (George Grn), Slou. 132 AY72
Bates Cres SW16 181 DJ94
Bates Cres, Croy. 219 DN106
Bates Ind Est, Rom. 106 FP52
Bates Pt E13 144 EG67
Pelly Rd
Bates Rd, Rom. 106 FN52
Bates Wk, Add. 212 BJ108
Bateson St SE18 165 ES77
Bateson Way, Wok. 211 BC114
Batford Cl, Welw.G.C. 30 DB10
Waterford Grn
Bath Cl SE15 162 DV80
Asylum Rd
Bath Ct EC1 274 D5
Bath Ho Rd, Croy. 201 DL102
Bath Pas, Kings.T. 197 CK96
St. James Rd
Bath Pl EC2 275 M3
Bath Pl, Barn. 79 CZ41
Bath Rd E7 144 EK65
Bath Rd N9 100 DV47
Bath Rd W4 158 CS77
Bath Rd, Dart. 187 FH87
Bath Rd, Hayes 155 BQ81
Bath Rd, Houns. 156 BW81
Bath Rd, Maid. 130 AC72
Bath Rd, Mitch. 200 DD97
Bath Rd, Rom. 126 EY58
Bath Rd, Slou. 131 AP74
Bath Rd (Colnbrook), Slou. 153 BB79
Bath Rd, West Dr. 154 BK81
Bath St EC1 275 J3
Bath St EC1 142 DR69
Bath St, Grav. 191 GH86
Bath Ter SE1 279 H7
Bath Ter SE1 162 DQ76
Bathgate Rd SW19 179 CX90
Baths Rd, Brom. 204 EK98
Bathurst Av SW19 200 DB95
Brisbane Av
Bathurst Cl, Iver 153 BF75
Bathurst Gdns NW10 139 CV68
Bathurst Ms W2 140 DD73
Sussex Pl
Bathurst Rd, Hem.H. 40 BK17
Bathurst Rd, Ilf. 125 EP60
Bathurst St W2 140 DD73
Bathurst Wk, Iver 153 BE75
Bathway SE18 165 EN77
Batley Cl, Mitch. 200 DF101
Batley Pl N16 122 DT62
Batley Rd N16 122 DT62
Stoke Newington High St
Batley Rd, Enf. 82 DQ39
Batman Cl W12 139 CV74
Baton Cl, Purf. 169 FR77
Brimfield Rd
Batoum Gdns W6 159 CW76
Batson St W12 159 CU75
Batsworth Rd, Mitch. 200 DD97
Batten Av, Wok. 226 AS119
Batten Cl E6 145 EM72
Savage Gdns
Batten St SW11 160 DE83
Battenburg Wk SE19 182 DS92
Brabourne Cl
Batterdale, Hat. 45 CW17
Battersby Rd SE6 183 ED89
Battersea Br SW3 160 DD80
Battersea Br SW11 160 DD80
Battersea Br Rd SW11 160 DE80
Battersea Ch Rd SW11 160 DD81
Battersea High St SW11 160 DD81
Battersea Pk SW11 160 DF80
Battersea Pk Rd SW8 161 DH81
Battersea Pk Rd SW11 160 DE82
Battersea Ri SW11 180 DE85
Battersea Sq SW11 160 DD81
Battersea High St
Battery Rd SE28 165 ES75
Battis, The, Rom. 127 FE58
Waterloo Rd
Battishill Gdns N1 141 DP66
Waterloo Ter
Battishill St N1 141 DP66
Waterloo Ter
Battle Br La SE1 279 M3
Battle Br La SE1 142 DS74
Battle Br Rd NW1 273 P1
Battle Br Rd NW1 141 DL68
Battle Cl SW19 180 DC93
North Rd
Battle Rd, Belv. 167 FC77
Battle Rd, Erith 167 FC77
Battlebridge La, Red. 251 DH130
Battledean Rd N5 121 DP64
Battlefield Rd, St.Alb. 43 CF18
Battlemead Cl, Maid. 130 AC68
Battlers Grn Dr, Rad. 77 CE37
Batts Hill, Red. 250 DE132
Batts Hill, Reig. 250 DD132
Batty St E1 142 DU72
Baudwin Rd SE6 184 EE89
Baugh Rd, Sid. 186 EW92
Baulk, The SW18 180 DA87
Bavant Rd SW16 201 DL96
Bavaria Rd N19 121 DL61
Bavdene Ms NW4 119 CV56
The Burroughs
Bavent Rd SE5 162 DQ82
Bawdale Rd SE22 182 DT85
Bawdsey Av, Ilf. 125 ET56
Bawtree Cl, Sutt. 218 DC110
Bawtree Rd SE14 163 DY80
Bawtree Rd, Uxb. 134 BK65
Bawtry Rd N20 98 DF48
Baxendale N20 98 DC47
Baxendale St E2 142 DU69
Baxter Av, Red. 250 DE134
Baxter Cl, Slou. 152 AS76
Kings Rd
Baxter Cl, Sthl. 156 CB75
Baxter Cl, Uxb. 135 BP69
Baxter Gdns, Rom. 106 FJ48
Cummings Hall La
Baxter Rd E16 144 EJ72
Baxter Rd N1 142 DR65
Baxter Rd N18 100 DV49
Baxter Rd NW10 138 CS70
Baxter Rd, Ilf. 125 EP64
Bay Cl, Horl. 268 DE145
Bay Ct W5 158 CL76
Popes La
Bay Manor La, Grays 169 FT79
Bay Tree Av, Lthd. 231 CG120
Bay Tree Cl, Brom. 204 EJ95
Bay Tree Ct (Burnham), Slou. 130 AJ69
Bayards, Warl. 236 DW118
Baycroft Cl, Pnr. 116 BW55
Baydon Ct, Brom. 204 EF97
Bayes Cl SE26 182 DW92
Bayeux, Tad. 233 CX122
Bayfield Rd SE9 164 EK84
Bayfield Rd, Horl. 268 DE147
Bayford Cl, Hem.H. 41 BQ15
Bayford Cl, Hert. 32 DQ11
Bayford Grn, Hert. 47 DN18
Bayford La, Hert. 31 DM14
Bayford Ms E8 142 DV66
Bayford St
Bayford Rd NW10 139 CX69
Bayford St E8 142 DV66
Bayham Pl NW1 141 DJ67
Bayham Rd W4 158 CR76
Bayham Rd W13 137 CH73
Bayham Rd, Mord. 200 DB98
Bayham Rd, Sev. 257 FJ123
Bayham St NW1 141 DJ67
Bayhorne La, Horl. 269 DJ150
Bayhurst Dr, Nthwd. 93 BT51
Bayley Cres (Burnham), Slou. 130 AG71
Bayley St WC1 273 M7
Bayley St WC1 141 DK71
Bayley Wk SE2 166 EY78
Woolwich Rd
Bayleys Mead, Brwd. 109 GC47
Baylie Ct, Hem.H. 40 BL19
Baylie La
Baylie La, Hem.H. 40 BL18
Baylin Rd SW18 180 DB86
Garratt La
Baylis Par, Slou. 132 AS72
Oatlands Dr
Baylis Rd SE1 278 D5
Baylis Rd SE1 161 DN75
Baylis Rd, Slou. 131 AR73
Bayliss Av SE28 146 EX73
Bayliss Cl N21 81 DL43
Bayliss Ct, Guil. 258 AW135
Mary Rd
Bayly Rd, Dart. 188 FN86
Baymans Wd, Brwd. 108 FY47
Bayne Cl E6 145 EM72
Savage Gdns
Bayne Hill, Beac. 89 AR52
Bayne Hill Cl (Seer Grn), Beac. 89 AR52
Baynes Cl, Enf. 82 DU40
Baynes Ms NW3 140 DD65
Belsize La
Baynes St NW1 141 DJ66
Baynham Cl, Bex. 186 EZ86
Bayonne Rd W6 159 CY79
Bayshill Ri, Nthlt. 136 CB65
Bayston Rd N16 122 DT62
Bayswater Rd W2 272 A10
Bayswater Rd W2 140 DD73
Baythorne St E3 143 DZ71
Baytree Cl (Park St), St.Alb. 60 CB27
Baytree Cl, Sid. 185 ET88
Baytree Cl, Wal.Cr. 66 DT27
Baytree Ho E4 101 EB45
Dells Cl
Baytree Rd SW2 161 DM84
Baytree Wk, Wat. 75 BT38
Baywood Sq, Chig. 104 EV49
Bazalgette Cl, N.Mal. 198 CR99
Bazalgette Gdns, N.Mal. 198 CR99
Bazely St E14 143 EC73
Bazile Rd N21 81 DN44
Beach Gro, Felt. 176 CA89
Beacham Cl SE7 164 EK78
Beachborough Rd, Brom. 183 EC91
Beachcroft Rd E11 124 EE62
Beachcroft Way N19 121 DK60
Beachy Rd E3 143 EA66
Beacon Cl, Bans. 233 CX116
Beacon Cl, Beac. 88 AG54
Beacon Cl (Chalfont St. Peter), Ger.Cr. 90 AY52
Beacon Cl, Uxb. 114 BK64
Beacon Dr (Bean), Dart. 189 FV90
Beacon Gate SE14 163 DX83
Beacon Gro, Cars. 218 DG105
Beacon Hill N7 121 DL64
Beacon Hill (Penn), H.Wyc. 88 AD48
Beacon Hill, Purf. 168 FP78
Beacon Hill, Wok. 226 AW118
Beacon Ri, Sev. 256 FG126
Beacon Rd SE13 183 ED86
Beacon Rd, Erith 167 FH80
Beacon Rd (Heathrow Airport), Houns. 174 BN86
Beacon Rd, Ware 33 EA05
Beacon Rd Roundabout (Heathrow Airport), Houns. 175 BP86
Beacon Way, Bans. 233 CX116
Beacon Way, Rick. 92 BG45
Beaconfield Av, Epp. 69 ET29
Beaconfield Rd, Epp. 69 ET29
Beaconfield Way, Epp. 69 ET29
Beaconfields, Sev. 256 FF126
Beacons, The, Hat. 45 CW17
Beaconsfield Cl
Beacons, The, Loug. 85 EN38
Beacons Cl E6 144 EL71
Oliver Gdns
Beaconsfield Cl N11 98 DG49
Beaconsfield Cl SE3 164 EG79
Beaconsfield Cl W4 158 CQ78
Beaconsfield Cl, Hat. 45 CW17
Beaconsfield Common La, Slou. 111 AQ57
Beaconsfield Par SE9 184 EL91
Beaconsfield Rd
Beaconsfield Pl, Epsom 216 CS112
Beaconsfield Rd E10 123 EC61
Beaconsfield Rd E16 144 EF70
Beaconsfield Rd E17 123 DZ58
Beaconsfield Rd N9 100 DU49
Beaconsfield Rd N11 98 DG48
Beaconsfield Rd N15 122 DS56
Beaconsfield Rd NW10 139 CT65
Beaconsfield Rd SE3 164 EF80
Beaconsfield Rd SE9 184 EL89
Beaconsfield Rd SE17 162 DR78
Beaconsfield Rd W4 158 CR76
Beaconsfield Rd W5 157 CJ75
Beaconsfield Rd, Bex. 187 FE88
Beaconsfield Rd, Brom. 204 EK97
Beaconsfield Rd, Croy. 202 DR100
Beaconsfield Rd, Enf. 83 DX37
Beaconsfield Rd, Epsom 232 CR119
Beaconsfield Rd (Claygate), Esher 215 CE108
Beaconsfield Rd, Hat. 45 CW17
Beaconsfield Rd, Hayes 136 BW74
Beaconsfield Rd, N.Mal. 198 CR96
Beaconsfield Rd, St.Alb. 43 CE20
Beaconsfield Rd, Slou. 131 AQ68
Beaconsfield Rd, Sthl. 136 BX74
Beaconsfield Rd, Surb. 198 CM101
Beaconsfield Rd, Twick. 177 CH86
Beaconsfield Rd, Wok. 227 AZ120
Beaconsfield Ter, Rom. 126 EX58

Beaconsfield Ter Rd W14 159 CY76
Beaconsfield Wk E6 145 EN72
East Ham Manor Way
Beaconsfield Wk SW6 159 CZ81
Beacontree Av E17 101 ED53
Beacontree Rd E11 124 EF59
Beadles La, Oxt. 253 ED130
Beadlow Cl, Cars. 200 DD100
Olveston Wk
Beadman Pl SE27 181 DP91
Norwood High St
Beadman St SE27 181 DP91
Beadnell Rd SE23 183 DX88
Beadon Rd W6 159 CW77
Beadon Rd, Brom. 204 EG98
Beads Hall La, Brwd. 108 FV42
Beaford Gro SW20 199 CY97
Beagle Cl, Felt. 175 BV91
Beagle Cl, Rad. 77 CF37
Beagles Cl, Orp. 206 EX103
Beak St W1 273 L10
Beak St W1 141 DJ73
Beal Cl, Well. 166 EU81
Beal Rd, Ilf. 125 EN61
Beale Cl N13 99 DP50
Beale Pl E3 143 DZ68
Beale Rd E3 143 DZ67
Beales La, Wey. 194 BN104
Beales Rd (Bookham), Lthd. 246 CB127
Bealings End, Beac. 89 AK50
Beam Av, Dag. 147 FB67
Beam Way, Dag. 147 FD66
Beaminster Gdns, Ilf. 103 EP54
Beamish Cl, Epp. 71 FC25
Beamish Dr, Bushey 94 CC46
Beamish Rd N9 100 DU46
Beamish Rd, Orp. 206 EW101
Bean La (Bean), Dart. 189 FV89
Bean Rd, Bexh. 166 EX84
Bean Rd, Green. 189 FU88
Beanacre Cl E9 143 DZ65
Beane Rd, Hert. 31 DP09
Beanshaw SE9 185 EN91
Beansland Gro, Rom. 104 EY54
Bear All EC4 274 F8
Bear Cl, Rom. 127 FB58
Bear Gdns SE1 279 H2
Bear Gdns SE1 142 DQ74
Bear La SE1 278 G2
Bear La SE1 141 DP74
Bear Rd, Felt. 176 BX92
Bear St WC2 273 N10
Beard Rd, Kings.T. 178 CM92
Beardell St SE19 182 DT93
Beardow Gro N14 81 DJ44
Beard's Hill, Hmptn. 196 CA95
Beard's Hill Cl, Hmptn. 196 CA95
Beard's Hill
Beards Rd, Ashf. 175 BS93
Beardsfield E13 144 EG67
Valetta Gro
Beardsley Ter, Dag. 126 EV64
Fitzstephen Rd
Beardsley Way W3 158 CR75
Bearfield Rd, Kings.T. 178 CL94
Bearing Cl, Chig. 104 EU49
Bearing Way, Chig. 104 EU49
Bears Den (Kingswood), Tad. 233 CZ122
Bears Rails Pk (Old Windsor), Wind. 172 AT87
Bearstead Ri SE4 183 DZ85
Bearsted Ter, Beck. 203 EA95
Bearswood End, Beac. 89 AL51
Bearwood Cl, Add. 212 BG107
Ongar Pl
Bearwood Cl, Pot.B. 64 DD31
Beasley's Ait La, Sun. 195 BT100
Beasleys Yd, Uxb. 134 BJ66
Warwick Pl
Beaton Cl SE15 162 DT80
Kelly Av
Beaton Cl, Green. 169 FV84
Beatrice Av SW16 201 DM97
Beatrice Av, Wem. 118 CL64
Beatrice Cl E13 144 EG70
Chargeable La
Beatrice Cl, Pnr. 115 BU56
Reid Cl
Beatrice Ct, Buck.H. 102 EK47
Beatrice Gdns (Northfleet), Grav. 190 GE89
Beatrice Pl W8 160 DB76
Beatrice Rd E17 123 EA57
Beatrice Rd N4 121 DN59
Beatrice Rd N9 100 DW45
Beatrice Rd SE1 162 DU77
Beatrice Rd, Oxt. 254 EE129
Beatrice Rd, Rich. 178 CM85
Albert Rd
Beatrice Rd, Sthl. 136 BZ74
Beatson Wk SE16 143 DY74
Beattie Cl, Felt. 175 BT88
Beattie Cl (Bookham), Lthd. 230 BZ124
Beattock Ri N10 121 DH56
Beatty Av, Guil. 243 BA133
Beatty Rd N16 122 DS63
Beatty Rd, Stan. 95 CJ51
Beatty Rd, Wal.Cr. 67 DZ34
Beatty St NW1 141 DJ68
Beattyville Gdns, Ilf. 125 EN55
Beauchamp Cl W4 158 CQ76
Church Path
Beauchamp Ct, Stan. 95 CJ50
Hardwick Cl
Beauchamp Gdns, Rick. 92 BG46
Beauchamp Pl SW3 276 C6
Beauchamp Pl SW3 160 DE76
Beauchamp Rd E7 144 EH66
Beauchamp Rd SE19 202 DR95
Beauchamp Rd SW11 160 DE84
Beauchamp Rd, E.Mol. 196 CB99
Beauchamp Rd, Sutt. 218 DA106
Beauchamp Rd, Twick. 177 CG87
Beauchamp Rd, W.Mol. 196 CB99
Beauchamp St EC1 274 D7
Beauchamp Ter SW15 159 CV83
Dryburgh Rd
Beauclare Cl, Lthd. 231 CK121
Hatherwood
Beauclerc Rd W6 159 CV76
Beauclerk Cl, Felt. 175 BV88
Florence Rd
Beaudesert Ms, West Dr. 154 BL75
Beaufort E6 145 EN71
Newark Knok
Beaufort Av, Har. 117 CG56
Beaufort Cl E4 101 EB51
Higham Sta Av
Beaufort Cl SW15 179 CV87
Beaufort Cl W5 138 CM71
Beaufort Cl, Epp. 70 FA27
Beaufort Cl, Grays 170 FZ76
Clifford Rd
Beaufort Cl, Reig. 249 CZ133
Beaufort Cl, Rom. 127 FC56
Beaufort Cl, Wok. 227 BC116
Beaufort Ct, Rich. 177 CJ91
Beaufort Rd
Beaufort Dr NW11 120 DA56
Beaufort Gdns NW4 119 CW58
Beaufort Gdns SW3 276 C6
Beaufort Gdns SW3 160 DE76
Beaufort Gdns SW16 181 DM94
Beaufort Gdns, Houns. 156 BY81
Beaufort Gdns, Ilf. 125 EN60
Beaufort Ms SW6 159 CZ79
Lillie Rd
Beaufort Pk NW11 120 DA56
Beaufort Pl, Maid. 150 AD75
Beaufort Rd W5 138 CM71
Beaufort Rd, Kings.T. 198 CL98
Beaufort Rd, Reig. 249 CZ133
Beaufort Rd, Rich. 177 CJ91
Beaufort Rd, Ruis. 115 BR61
Lysander Rd
Beaufort Rd, Twick. 177 CJ87
Beaufort Rd, Wok. 227 BC116
Beaufort St SW3 160 DD79
Beaufort Way, Epsom 217 CU108
Beauforts (Englefield Grn), Egh. 172 AW92
Beaufoy Rd N17 100 DS52
Beaufoy Wk SE11 278 C9
Beaufoy Wk SE11 161 DM77
Beaulieu Av E16 144 EH74
Beaulieu Av SE26 182 DV91
Beaulieu Cl NW9 118 CS56
Beaulieu Cl SE5 162 DR83
Beaulieu Cl, Houns. 176 BZ85
Beaulieu Cl, Mitch. 200 DG95
Beaulieu Cl (Datchet), Slou. 152 AV82
Beaulieu Cl, Twick. 177 CK87
Beaulieu Cl, Wat. 94 BW46
Beaulieu Dr, Pnr. 116 BX58
Beaulieu Dr, Wal.Abb. 67 EB32
Beaulieu Gdns N21 100 DQ45
Beaulieu Pl W4 158 CQ76
Rothschild Rd
Beauly Way, Rom. 105 FE53
Beaumanor Gdns SE9 185 EN91
Beaumaris Dr, Wdf.Grn. 102 EK52
Beaumaris Grn NW9 118 CS58
Goldsmith Av
Beaumayes Cl, Hem.H. 40 BH21
Beaumont Av W14 159 CZ78
Beaumont Av, Har. 116 CB58
Beaumont Av, Rich. 158 CM83
Beaumont Av, St.Alb. 43 CH18
Beaumont Av, Wem. 117 CJ64
Beaumont Cl, Kings.T. 178 CN94
Beaumont Cl, Rom. 106 FJ54
Beaumont Cres W14 159 CZ78
Beaumont Cres, Rain. 147 FG65
Beaumont Dr, Ashf. 175 BR92
Beaumont Dr (Northfleet), Grav. 190 GE87
Beaumont Gdns NW3 120 DA62
Beaumont Gdns, Brwd. 109 GC44
Bannister Dr
Beaumont Gate, Rad. 77 CH35
Shenley Hill
Beaumont Gro E1 143 DX70
Beaumont Ms W1 272 G6
Beaumont Pk Dr, Harl. 50 EH15
Beaumont Pl W1 273 L4
Beaumont Pl W1 141 DJ70
Beaumont Pl, Barn. 79 CZ39
Beaumont Pl, Islw. 177 CF85
Beaumont Ri N19 121 DK60
Beaumont Rd E10 123 EB59
Beaumont Rd E13 144 EH69
Beaumont Rd SE19 182 DQ93
Beaumont Rd SW19 179 CY87
Beaumont Rd W4 158 CQ76
Beaumont Rd, Brox. 48 DR24
Beaumont Rd, Orp. 205 ER100
Beaumont Rd, Pur. 219 DN113
Beaumont Rd, Slou. 131 AR70
Beaumont Rd, Wind. 151 AQ82
Beaumont Sq E1 143 DX70
Beaumont St W1 272 G6
Beaumont St W1 140 DG71
Beaumont Vw (Cheshunt), Wal.Cr. 66 DR26
Beaumont Wk NW3 140 DF66
Beaumonts, Red. 266 DF143
Beauvais Ter, Nthlt. 136 BX69
Beauval Rd SE22 182 DT86
Beaver Cl SE20 182 DU94
Lullington Rd
Beaver Cl, Hmptn. 196 CB95
Beaver Gro, Nthlt. 136 BY69
Jetstar Way
Beaver Rd, Ilf. 104 EW50
Beaverbank Rd SE9 185 ER88
Beaverbrook Roundabout, Lthd. 232 CL123
Beavers Cl, Guil. 242 AS133
Beavers Cres, Houns. 156 BW84
Beavers La, Houns. 156 BW83
Beavers La Camp, Houns. 156 BW83
Beavers La
Beaverwood Rd, Chis. 185 ES93
Beavor Gro W6 159 CU77
Beavor La
Beavor La W6 159 CU77
Beazley Cl, Ware 33 DY05
Bebbington Rd SE18 165 ES77
Beblets Cl, Orp. 223 ET106
Bec Cl, Ruis. 116 BX62
Beccles Dr, Bark. 145 ES65
Beccles St E14 143 DZ73
Beck Cl SE13 163 EB81
Beck Ct, Beck. 203 DX97
Beck La, Beck. 203 DX97
Beck River Pk, Beck. 203 EA95
Beck Rd E8 142 DV67
Beck Way, Beck. 203 DZ97
Beckenham Business Cen, Beck. 183 DY93
Beckenham Gdns N9 100 DS48
Beckenham Gro, Brom. 203 ED96
Beckenham Hill Rd SE6 183 EB92
Beckenham Hill Rd, Beck. 183 EB92
Beckenham La, Brom. 204 EE96
Beckenham Pl Pk, Beck. 183 EB94
Beckenham Rd, Beck. 203 DX95
Beckenham Rd, W.Wick. 203 EB101
Beckenshaw Gdns, Bans. 234 DE115
Beckers, The N16 122 DU62
Rectory Rd
Becket Av E6 145 EN69
Becket Cl SE25 202 DU100
Becket Cl, Brwd. 107 FW51
Becket Fold, Har. 117 CF57
Courtfield Cres
Becket Rd N18 100 DW49
Becket St SE1 279 K6
Beckets Sq, Berk. 38 AU17
Bridle Way
Beckett Av, Ken. 235 DP115
Beckett Cl NW10 138 CR65
Beckett Cl SW16 181 DK89
Beckett Cl, Belv. 166 EY76
Tunstock Way
Beckett Wk, Beck. 183 DY93
Becketts, Hert. 31 DN10
Beckett's Av, St.Alb. 42 CC17
Becketts Cl, Felt. 175 BV86
Becketts Cl, Orp. 205 ET104
Becketts Pl, Kings.T. 197 CK95
Beckford Dr, Orp. 205 ER101
Beckford Pl SE17 162 DQ78
Walworth Rd
Beckford Rd, Croy. 202 DT100
Beckingham Rd, Guil. 242 AU132
Beckings Way (Flackwell Heath), H.Wyc. 110 AC56
Becklow Gdns W12 159 CU75
Becklow Rd
Becklow Ms W12 159 CT75
Becklow Rd
Becklow Rd W12 159 CU75
Beckman Cl (Halstead), Sev. 241 FC115
Becks Rd, Sid. 186 EU90
Beckton Pk Roundabout E16 145 EM73
Royal Albert Way
Beckton Retail Pk E6 145 EN71
Beckton Rd E16 144 EF71
Beckton Triangle Retail Pk E6 145 EP70
Beckway Rd SW16 201 DK96
Beckway St SE17 279 L9
Beckway St SE17 162 DR77
Beckwith Rd SE24 182 DR86
Beclands Rd SW17 180 DG93
Becmead Av SW16 181 DK91
Becmead Av, Har. 117 CH57
Becondale Rd SE19 182 DS92
Becontree Av, Dag. 126 EV63
Bective Pl SW15 159 CZ84
Bective Rd
Bective Rd E7 124 EG63
Bective Rd SW15 159 CZ84
Becton Pl, Erith 167 FB80
Bedale Rd, Enf. 82 DQ38
Bedale Rd, Rom. 106 FN50
Bedale St SE1 279 K3
Bedale St SE1 142 DR74
Bedale Wk, Dart. 188 FP88
Beddington Cross, Croy. 201 DL101
Beddington Fm Rd, Croy. 201 DL102
Beddington Gdns, Cars. 218 DG107
Beddington Gdns, Wall. 219 DH107
Beddington Grn, Orp. 205 ET95
Beddington Gro, Wall. 219 DK106
Beddington La, Croy. 201 DJ99
Beddington Path, Orp. 205 ET95
Beddington Rd, Ilf. 125 ET59
Beddington Rd, Orp. 205 ES96
Beddington Trd Pk W, Croy. 201 DL102
Beddlestead La, Warl. 238 EF117
Bede Cl, Pnr. 94 BX53
Bede Rd, Rom. 126 EW58
Bedenham Way SE15 162 DT80
Daniel Gdns
Bedens Rd, Sid. 186 EY93
Bedfont Cl, Felt. 175 BQ86
Bedfont Cl, Mitch. 200 DG96
Bedfont Ct, Stai. 154 BH84
Bedfont Ct Est, Stai. 154 BG83
Bedfont Grn Cl, Felt. 175 BQ88
Bedfont La, Felt. 175 BT87
Bedfont Rd, Felt. 175 BS89
Bedfont Rd (Stanwell), Stai. 174 BL86
Bedford Av WC1 273 N7
Bedford Av WC1 141 DK71
Bedford Av, Amer. 72 AW39
Bedford Av, Barn. 79 CZ43
Bedford Av, Hayes 135 BV72
Bedford Av, Slou. 131 AM72
Bedford Cl N10 98 DG52
Bedford Cl W4 158 CS79
Bedford Cl, Rick. 73 BB38
Bedford Cl, Wok. 226 AW115
Bedford Cor W4 158 CS77
The Av
Bedford Ct WC2 277 P1
Bedford Cres, Enf. 83 DY35
Bedford Dr (Farnham Common), Slou. 111 AP64
Bedford Gdns W8 140 DA74
Bedford Gdns, Horn. 128 FJ61
Bedford Hill SW12 181 DH88
Bedford Hill SW16 181 DH88
Bedford Ho SW4 161 DK84
Bedford Ms N2 120 DE55
Bedford Rd
Bedford Pk, Croy. 202 DQ102
Bedford Pk Cor W4 158 CS77
Bath Rd
Bedford Pk Rd, St.Alb. 43 CE20
Bedford Pas SW6 159 CY80
Dawes Rd
Bedford Pl W1 273 L6
Bedford Pl WC1 273 P6
Bedford Pl WC1 141 DL71
Bedford Pl, Croy. 202 DR102
Bedford Rd E6 145 EN67
Bedford Rd E17 101 EA54
Bedford Rd E18 102 EG54
Bedford Rd N2 120 DE55
Bedford Rd N8 121 DK58
Bedford Rd N9 100 DV45
Bedford Rd N15 122 DS56
Bedford Rd N22 99 DL53
Bedford Rd NW7 96 CS48
Bedford Rd SW4 161 DL83
Bedford Rd W4 158 CR76
Bedford Rd W13 137 CH73
Bedford Rd, Dart. 188 FN87
Bedford Rd (Northfleet), Grav. 191 GF89
Bedford Rd, Grays 170 GB78
Bedford Rd, Guil. 258 AW135
Bedford Rd, Har. 116 CC58
Bedford Rd, Ilf. 125 EP62
Bedford Rd, Nthwd. 93 BQ48
Bedford Rd, Orp. 206 EV103
Bedford Rd, Ruis. 115 BT63
Bedford Rd, St.Alb. 43 CE21
Bedford Rd, Sid. 185 ES90
Bedford Rd, Twick. 177 CD90
Bedford Rd, Wor.Pk. 199 CW103
Bedford Row WC1 274 C6
Bedford Row WC1 141 DM71
Bedford Sq WC1 273 N7
Bedford Sq WC1 141 DK71
Bedford St WC2 273 P10
Bedford St WC2 141 DL73
Bedford St, Berk. 38 AX19
Bedford St, Wat. 75 BV39
Bedford Ter SW2 181 DL85
Lyham Rd
Bedford Way WC1 273 N5
Bedford Way WC1 141 DK70
Bedfordbury WC2 273 P10
Bedgebury Gdns SW19 179 CY89
Bedgebury Rd SE9 164 EK84
Bedivere Rd, Brom. 184 EG90
Bedlow Way, Croy. 219 DM105
Bedmond La, Abb.L. 59 BV25
Bedmond La, St.Alb. 42 BZ21
Bedmond La (Potters Crouch), St.Alb. 42 BW24
Bedmond Rd, Abb.L. 59 BT29
Bedmond Rd, Hem.H. 41 BS23
Bedonwell Rd SE2 166 EY79
Bedonwell Rd, Belv. 166 FA79
Bedonwell Rd, Bexh. 166 FA79
Bedser Cl SE11 161 DM79
Harleyford Rd
Bedser Cl, Th.Hth. 202 DQ97
Bedser Cl, Wok. 227 BA116
Bedser Dr, Grnf. 117 CD64
Bedster Gdns, W.Mol. 196 CB96
Bedwardine Rd SE19 182 DS94
Bedwell Av, Hat. 46 DG18
Bedwell Cl, Welw.G.C. 29 CY10
Bedwell Gdns, Hayes 155 BS78
Bedwell Rd N17 100 DS53
Bedwell Rd, Belv. 166 FA78
Beeby Rd E16 144 EH71
Beech Av N20 98 DE46
Beech Av W3 138 CS74
Beech Av, Brent. 157 CH80
Beech Av, Brwd. 109 FZ48
Beech Av, Buck.H. 102 EH47
Beech Av, Enf. 81 DN35
Beech Av (Effingham), Lthd. 246 BX129
Beech Av, Rad. 61 CG33
Beech Av, Ruis. 115 BV60
Beech Av, Sid. 186 EU87
Beech Av, S.Croy. 220 DR111
Beech Av, Swan. 207 FF98
Beech Av, Upmin. 128 FP62
Beech Av, West. 238 EK119
Beech Bottom, St.Alb. 43 CD17
Beech Cl N9 82 DU44
Beech Cl SE8 163 DZ79
Clyde St
Beech Cl SW15 179 CU87
Beech Cl SW19 179 CW93
Beech Cl, Ashf. 175 BR92
Beech Cl, Cars. 200 DF103
Beech Cl, Cob. 214 CA112
Beech Cl, Dor. 263 CF135
Beech Cl, Hat. 45 CU19
Beech Cl, Horn. 127 FH62
Beech Cl (Effingham), Lthd. 246 BX128
Beech Cl, Loug. 85 EP40
Cedar Dr
Beech Cl (Stanwell), Stai. 174 BK87
St. Mary's Cres
Beech Cl, Sun. 196 BX96
Harfield Rd
Beech Cl, Walt. 214 BW105
Beech Cl, Ware 33 DX08
Beech Cl (Byfleet), W.Byf. 212 BL112
Beech Cl, West Dr. 154 BN76
Beech Cl Ct, Cob. 214 BZ111
Beech Copse, Brom. 205 EM96
Beech Copse, S.Croy. 220 DS106
Beech Ct E17 123 ED55
Beech Ct SE9 184 EL86
Beech Ct, Ilf. 125 EN62
Riverdene Rd
Beech Ct, Surb. 198 CL101
Beech Cres, Tad. 248 CQ130
Beech Dell, Kes. 223 EM105
Beech Dr N2 120 DF55
Beech Dr, Berk. 38 AW20
Beech Dr, Borwd. 78 CM40
Beech Dr, Reig. 250 DD134
Beech Dr, Saw. 36 EW07
Beech Dr (Kingswood), Tad. 233 CZ122
Beech Dr (Ripley), Wok. 228 BG124
Beech Fm Rd, Warl. 237 EC120
Beech Gdns EC2 142 DQ71
Aldersgate St
Beech Gdns W5 158 CL75
Beech Gdns, Dag. 147 FB66
Beech Gdns, Wok. 226 AY115
Beech Gro, Add. 212 BH105
Beech Gro, Amer. 55 AQ39
Beech Gro, Cat. 252 DS126
Beech Gro, Croy. 221 DY110
Beech Gro, Epsom 233 CV117
Beech Gro, Guil. 242 AT134
Beech Gro, Ilf. 103 ES51
Beech Gro (Bookham), Lthd. 246 CA127
Beech Gro, Mitch. 201 DK98
Beech Gro, N.Mal. 198 CR97
Beech Gro, S.Ock. 148 FQ74
Beech Gro (Mayford), Wok. 226 AX123
Beech Hall (Ottershaw), Cher. 211 BC108
Beech Hall Cres E4 101 ED52
Beech Hall Rd E4 101 EC52
Beech Hill, Barn. 80 DD38
Beech Hill, Wok. 226 AX123
Beech Hill Av, Barn. 80 DC39
Beech Hill Ct, Berk. 38 AX18
Beech Hill Gdns, Wal.Abb. 84 EH37
Beech Holt, Lthd. 231 CJ122
Beech Ho, Croy. 221 EB107
Beech Ho Rd, Croy. 202 DR104
Beech Hyde La (Wheathampstead), Guil.St.Alb. 28 CM07
Beech La (Jordans), Beac. 90 AS52
Beech La, Buck.H. 102 EH47
Beech La, Guil. 258 AW137
Beech Lawn, Guil. 259 AZ135
Beech Lawns N12 98 DD50
Beech Lo, Stai. 173 BE92
Farm Cl
Beech Pk, Amer. 72 AV39
Beech Pl, Epp. 69 ET31
Beech Pl, St.Alb. 43 CD17
Beech Rd N11 99 DL51
Beech Rd SW16 201 DL96
Beech Rd, Dart. 188 FK88
Beech Rd, Epsom 233 CT115
Beech Rd, Felt. 175 BS87
Beech Rd, Orp. 224 EU108
Beech Rd, Red. 251 DJ126
Beech Rd, Reig. 250 DA131
Beech Rd, St.Alb. 43 CE17
Beech Rd, Sev. 257 FH125
Victoria Rd
Beech Rd, Slou. 152 AY75
Beech Rd, Wat. 75 BU37
Beech Rd (Biggin Hill), West. 238 EH118
Beech Rd, Wey. 213 BR105
St. Marys Rd
Beech Row, Rich. 178 CL91
Beech St EC2 275 H6
Beech St EC2 142 DQ71
Beech St, Rom. 127 FC56
Beech Tree Cl, Stan. 95 CJ50
Beech Tree Glade E4 102 EF46
Forest Side
Beech Tree La, Stai. 194 BH96
Staines Rd
Beech Tree Pl, Sutt. 218 DB106
St. Nicholas Way
Beech Vale, Wok. 227 AZ118
Hill Vw Rd
Beech Wk NW7 96 CS51
Beech Wk, Dart. 167 FG84
Beech Wk, Epsom 217 CU111
Beech Wk, Hodd. 49 DZ17
Beech Way NW10 138 CR66
Beech Way, Epsom 233 CT115
Beech Way, S.Croy. 221 DX113
Beech Way, Twick. 176 CA90
Beech Waye, Ger.Cr. 113 AZ59
Beechcroft, Ash. 232 CM119
Beechcroft, Chis. 185 EN94
Beechcroft Av NW11 119 CZ59
Beechcroft Av, Bexh. 167 FD81
Beechcroft Av, Har. 116 CA59
Beechcroft Av, Ken. 236 DR115
Beechcroft Av, N.Mal. 198 CQ95
Beechcroft Av, Rick. 75 BQ44
Beechcroft Av, Sthl. 136 BZ74
Beechcroft Cl, Houns. 156 BY80
Beechcroft Cl, Orp. 223 ER105
Beechcroft Gdns, Wem. 118 CM62
Beechcroft Lo, Sutt. 218 DC108
Devonshire Rd
Beechcroft Manor, Wey. 195 BR104
Beechcroft Rd E18 102 EH54
Beechcroft Rd SW14 158 CQ83
Elm Rd
Beechcroft Rd SW17 180 DE89
Beechcroft Rd, Bushey 76 BY43
Beechcroft Rd, Chesh. 54 AN30
Beechcroft Rd, Chess. 198 CM104
Beechcroft Rd, Orp. 223 ER105
Beechdale N21 99 DM47
Beechdale Rd SW2 181 DM86
Beechdene, Tad. 233 CV122
Beechen Cliff Way, Islw. 157 CF81
Henley Cl
Beechen Gro, Pnr. 116 BZ55
Beechen Gro, Wat. 76 BW42
Beechen La, Tad. 249 CZ125
Beechenlea La, Swan. 207 FH97
Beeches, The, Amer. 55 AN36
Woodfield Pk
Beeches, The, Bans. 234 DB116
Beeches, The, Beac. 88 AH54
Beeches, The, Brwd. 108 FV48
Beeches, The (Bramley), Guil. 259 AZ144
Beeches, The, Houns. 156 CB81
Beeches, The (Fetcham), Lthd. 231 CE124
Beeches, The, Rick. 73 BF43
Beeches, The (Park St), St.Alb. 61 CE27
Beeches, The, Til. 171 GH82
Beeches Av, Cars. 218 DE108
Beeches Cl SE20 202 DW95
Genoa Rd
Beeches Cl (Kingswood), Tad. 234 DA123
Beeches Dr (Farnham Common), Slou. 111 AP64
Beeches Pk, Beac. 89 AK53
Beeches Rd SW17 180 DE90
Beeches Rd (Farnham Common), Slou. 111 AP64
Beeches Rd, Sutt. 199 CY102
Beeches Wk, Cars. 218 DD109
Beeches Way, B.End 110 AD61
Beeches Wd, Tad. 234 DA122
Beechfield, Bans. 218 DB113
Beechfield, Hodd. 33 EA13
Beechfield, Kings L. 58 BM30
Beechfield, Saw. 36 EZ05
Beechfield Cl, Borwd. 78 CL40
Beechfield Cotts, Brom. 204 EJ96
Widmore Rd
Beechfield Gdns, Rom. 127 FC59
Beechfield Rd N4 122 DQ58
Beechfield Rd SE6 183 DZ88
Beechfield Rd, Brom. 204 EJ96
Beechfield Rd, Erith 167 FE80
Beechfield Rd, Hem.H. 40 BH21
Beechfield Rd, Ware 33 DZ05
Beechfield Rd, Welw.G.C. 29 CY11
Beechfield Wk, Wal.Abb. 83 ED35
Beechhill Rd SE9 185 EN85
Beechmeads, Cob. 214 BX113
Beechmont Av, Vir.W. 192 AX99
Beechmont Cl, Brom. 184 EE92
Beechmont Rd, Sev. 257 FH129
Beechmore Gdns, Sutt. 199 CX103
Beechmore Rd SW11 160 DF81
Beechmount Av W7 137 CD71
Beecholm Ms, Wal.Cr. 67 DX28
Beecholme, Bans. 217 CY114
Beecholme Av, Mitch. 201 DH95
Beecholme Est E5 122 DV62
Prout Rd
Beechpark Way, Wat. 75 BS37
Beechtree Av (Englefield Grn), Egh. 172 AV93
Beechtree La, St.Alb. 41 BV22
Beechvale Cl N12 98 DE50
Beechway, Bex. 186 EX86
Beechway, Guil. 243 BB133
Beechwood Av N3 119 CZ55
Beechwood Av, Amer. 72 AW38
Beechwood Av, Couls. 235 DH115
Beechwood Av, Grnf. 136 CB69
Beechwood Av, Har. 116 CB62
Beechwood Av, Hayes 135 BR73
Beechwood Av, Orp. 223 ES106
Beechwood Av, Pot.B. 64 DB33
Beechwood Av, Rich. 158 CN81
Beechwood Av, Rick. 73 BB42
Beechwood Av, Ruis. 115 BT61
Beechwood Av, St.Alb. 43 CH18
Beechwood Av, Stai. 174 BH93
Beechwood Av, Sun. 175 BU93
Beechwood Av (Kingswood), Tad. 234 DA121
Beechwood Av, Th.Hth. 201 DP98
Beechwood Av, Uxb. 134 BN72
Beechwood Av, Wey. 213 BS105
Beechwood Circle, Har. 116 CB62
Beechwood Gdns

Beechwood Cl NW7 96 CR50
Beechwood Cl, Amer. 72 AW39
Beechwood Cl, Hert. 32 DT09
Beechwood Cl, Surb. 197 CJ101
Beechwood Cl (Cheshunt), Wal.Cr. 66 DS26
Beechwood Cl, Wey. 213 BS105
Beechwood Cl (Knaphill), Wok. 226 AS117
Beechwood Ct, Cars. 218 DF105
Beechwood Ct, Sun. 175 BU93
Beechwood Cres, Bexh. 166 EX83
Beechwood Dr, Cob. 214 CA111
Beechwood Dr, Kes. 222 EK105
Beechwood Dr, Wdf.Grn. 102 EF50
Beechwood Gdns NW10 138 CM69
 St. Annes Gdns
Beechwood Gdns, Cat. 236 DU122
Beechwood Gdns, Har. 116 CB62
Beechwood Gdns, Ilf. 125 EM57
Beechwood Gdns, Rain. 147 FH71
Beechwood Gdns, Slou. 152 AS75
Beechwood Gro W3 138 CS73
 East Acton La
Beechwood Gro, Surb. 197 CJ101
Beechwood La, Warl. 237 DX119
Beechwood Manor, Wey. 213 BS105
Beechwood Ms N9 100 DU47
Beechwood Pk E18 124 EG55
Beechwood Pk, Hem.H. 39 BF24
Beechwood Pk, Lthd. 231 CJ123
Beechwood Pk (Chorleywood), Rick. 73 BF42
 Rickmansworth Rd
Beechwood Ri, Chis. 185 EP91
Beechwood Ri, Wat. 75 BV36
Beechwood Rd E8 142 DT65
Beechwood Rd N8 121 DK56
Beechwood Rd, Beac. 88 AJ53
Beechwood Rd, Cat. 236 DU122
Beechwood Rd, Slou. 131 AR71
Beechwood Rd, S.Croy. 220 DS109
Beechwood Rd, Vir.W. 192 AU101
Beechwood Rd (Knaphill), Wok. 226 AS117
Beechwood Vil, Red. 266 DG144
Beechwoods Ct SE19 182 DT92
 Crystal Palace Par
Beechworth Cl NW3 120 DA61
Beecot La, Walt. 196 BW103
Beecroft Rd SE4 183 DY85
Beehive Cl E8 142 DT66
Beehive Cl, Borwd. 77 CK44
Beehive Cl, Uxb. 134 BM66
 Honey Hill
Beehive Ct, Rom. 106 FM52
 Arundel Rd
Beehive Grn, Welw.G.C. 30 DA11
Beehive La, Ilf. 125 EM58
Beehive La, Welw.G.C. 30 DA12
Beehive Pas EC3 275 M9
Beehive Pl SW9 161 DN83
Beehive Rd, Stai. 173 BF92
Beehive Rd (Cheshunt), Wal.Cr. 65 DP28
Beehive Way, Reig. 266 DB138
Beeken Dene, Orp. 223 EQ105
 Isabella Dr
Beel Cl, Amer. 72 AW39
Beeleigh Rd, Mord. 200 DB98
Beesfield La (Farningham), Dart. 208 FN101
Beeston Cl E8 122 DU64
 Ferncliff Rd
Beeston Cl, Wat. 94 BX49
Beeston Dr, Wal.Cr. 67 DX27
Beeston Pl SW1 277 J7
Beeston Pl SW1 161 DH76
Beeston Rd, Barn. 80 DD44
Beeston Way, Felt. 176 BW86
Beethoven Rd, Borwd. 77 CK44
Beethoven St W10 139 CY69
Beeton Cl, Pnr. 94 CA52
Begbie Rd SE3 164 EJ81
Beggars Bush La, Wat. 75 BR43
Beggars Hill, Epsom 217 CT108
Beggars Hollow, Enf. 82 DR37
Beggars La (Abinger Hammer), Dor. 261 BT137
Beggars La, West. 255 ER125
Beggars Roost La, Sutt. 218 DA107
Begonia Cl E6 144 EL71
Begonia Pl, Hmptn. 176 CA93
 Gresham Rd
Begonia Wk W12 139 CT72
 Du Cane Rd
Beira St SW12 181 DH87
Beken Ct, Wat. 76 BW35
Bekesbourne St E14 143 DY72
 Ratcliffe La
Bekesbourne Twr, Orp. 206 EY102
Belcher Rd, Hodd. 49 EA16
 Amwell St
Belchers La, Wal.Abb. 50 EJ24
Belcon Ind Est, Hodd. 49 EC17
Belcroft Cl, Brom. 184 EF94
 Hope Pk
Beldam Haw (Halstead), Sev. 224 FA112
Beldham Gdns, W.Mol. 196 CB97
Belfairs Dr, Rom. 126 EW59
Belfairs Grn, Wat. 94 BX50
 Heysham Dr
Belfast Av, Slou. 131 AQ72
Belfast Rd N16 122 DT61
Belfast Rd SE25 202 DV98
Belfield Gdns, Harl. 52 EW16
Belfield Rd, Epsom 216 CR109
Belfont Wk N7 121 DL63
Belford Gro SE18 165 EN77
Belford Rd, Borwd. 78 CM38
Belfort Rd SE15 162 DW82
Belfour Ter N3 98 DB54
Belfry Av (Harefield), Uxb. 92 BG53
Belfry Cl SE16 162 DV78
 Masters Dr
Belfry La, Rick. 92 BJ46
Belfry Shop Cen, The, Red. 250 DF133
Belgrade Rd N16 122 DS63
Belgrade Rd, Hmptn. 196 CB95
Belgrave Av, Rom. 128 FJ55
Belgrave Av, Wat. 75 BT43
Belgrave Cl N14 81 DJ43
 Prince George Av
Belgrave Cl NW7 96 CR50
Belgrave Cl W3 158 CQ75
 Avenue Rd
Belgrave Cl, Orp. 206 EW98
Belgrave Cl, St.Alb. 43 CJ16
Belgrave Cl, Walt. 213 BV105
Belgrave Ct E14 143 EA74
 Westferry Circ
Belgrave Cres, Sun. 195 BV95
Belgrave Dr, Kings L. 59 BQ28
Belgrave Gdns N14 81 DK43
Belgrave Gdns NW8 140 DB67
Belgrave Gdns, Stan. 95 CJ50
 Copley Rd
Belgrave Hts E11 124 EG60
Belgrave Manor, Wok. 226 AY119
Belgrave Ms, Uxb. 134 BK70
Belgrave Ms N SW1 276 F5
Belgrave Ms N SW1 160 DG76
Belgrave Ms S SW1 276 G6
Belgrave Ms S SW1 160 DG76
Belgrave Ms W SW1 276 F6
Belgrave Ms W SW1 160 DG76
Belgrave Pl SW1 276 G6
Belgrave Pl SW1 160 DG76
Belgrave Pl, Slou. 152 AV75
 Clifton Rd
Belgrave Rd E10 123 EC60
Belgrave Rd E11 124 EG61
Belgrave Rd E13 144 EJ70
Belgrave Rd E17 123 EA57
Belgrave Rd SE25 202 DT98
Belgrave Rd SW1 277 K9
Belgrave Rd SW1 161 DH77
Belgrave Rd SW13 159 CT80
Belgrave Rd, Houns. 156 BZ83
Belgrave Rd, Ilf. 125 EM60
Belgrave Rd, Mitch. 200 DD97
Belgrave Rd, Slou. 132 AS73
Belgrave Rd, Sun. 195 BV95
Belgrave Sq SW1 276 F6
Belgrave Sq SW1 160 DG76
Belgrave St E1 143 DX72
Belgrave Ter, Wdf.Grn. 102 EG48
Belgrave Wk, Mitch. 200 DD97
Belgrave Yd SW1 277 H7
Belgravia Cl, Barn. 79 CZ41
Belgravia Gdns, Brom. 184 EE93
Belgravia Ho SW4 181 DL86
Belgravia Ms, Kings.T. 197 CK98
Belgrove St WC1 273 P2
Belgrove St WC1 141 DL69
Belham Rd, Kings L. 58 BM28
Belham Wk SE5 162 DR81
 D'Eynsford Rd
Belhaven Ct, Borwd. 78 CM39
Belhus Pk, S.Ock. 149 FR71
Belinda Rd SW9 161 DP83
Belitha Vil N1 141 DM66
Bell Av, Rom. 105 FH53
Bell Av, West Dr. 154 BM77
Bell Br Rd, Cher. 193 BF102
Bell Cl, Abb.L. 59 BT27
Bell Cl, Beac. 89 AM53
Bell Cl, Green. 189 FT85
Bell Cl, Pnr. 116 BW55
Bell Cl, Ruis. 115 BT62
Bell Cl, Slou. 132 AV71
Bell Common, Epp. 69 ES32
Bell Common Tunnel, Epp. 69 ER33
Bell Ct, Surb. 198 CP103
 Barnsbury La
Bell Cres, Couls. 235 DH121
 Maple Way
Bell Dr SW18 179 CY87
Bell Fm Av, Dag. 127 FC62
Bell Gdns E10 123 EA60
 Church Rd
Bell Gdns E17 123 DZ57
 Markhouse Rd
Bell Gdns, Orp. 206 EW99
Bell Grn SE26 183 DZ90
Bell Grn (Bovingdon), Hem.H. 57 BB27
Bell Grn La SE26 183 DY92
Bell Hill, Croy. 202 DQ104
 Surrey St
Bell Ho Rd, Rom. 127 FC60
Bell Inn Yd EC3 275 L9
Bell La E1 275 P7
Bell La E1 142 DT71
Bell La E16 144 EG74
Bell La NW4 119 CX56
Bell La, Abb.L. 59 BT27
Bell La, Amer. 72 AV39
Bell La, Berk. 38 AS18
Bell La, Brox. 49 DY21
Bell La, Enf. 83 DX38
Bell La, Hat. 64 DA25
Bell La, Hert. 32 DR09
Bell La, Hodd. 49 EA17
Bell La (Fetcham), Lthd. 231 CD123
Bell La (London Colney), St.Alb. 62 CL29
Bell La, Twick. 177 CG88
 The Embk
Bell La, Wem. 117 CK61
 Magnet Rd
Bell La (Eton Wick), Wind. 151 AM77
Bell La Cl (Fetcham), Lthd. 231 CD123
Bell Mead, Saw. 36 EY05
Bell Meadow SE19 182 DS91
 Dulwich Wd Av
Bell Meadow, Gdse. 252 DV132
Bell Par, Wind. 151 AM82
 St. Andrews Av
Bell Rd, E.Mol. 197 CD99
Bell Rd, Enf. 82 DR39
Bell Rd, Houns. 156 CB84
Bell St NW1 272 B6
Bell St NW1 140 DE71
Bell St, Reig. 250 DA134
Bell St, Saw. 36 EY05
Bell Vw, St.Alb. 43 CK20
Bell Vw, Wind. 151 AM83
Bell Vw Cl, Wind. 151 AM82
Bell Water Gate SE18 165 EN76
Bell Weir Cl, Stai. 173 BB89
Bell Wf La EC4 275 J10
Bell Wf La EC4 142 DQ73
Bell Yd WC2 274 D8
Bell Yd WC2 141 DN72
Bellamy Cl E14 163 EA75
 Byng St
Bellamy Cl W14 159 CZ78
 Aisgill Av
Bellamy Cl, Edg. 96 CQ48
Bellamy Cl, Uxb. 114 BN62
Bellamy Cl, Wat. 75 BU39
Bellamy Dr, Stan. 95 CH53
Bellamy Rd E4 101 EB51
Bellamy Rd, Enf. 82 DR40
Bellamy Rd (Cheshunt), Wal.Cr. 67 DY29
Bellamy St SW12 181 DH87
Bellasis Av SW2 181 DL89
Bellclose Rd, West Dr. 154 BL75
Belle Vue, Grnf. 137 CD67
Belle Vue Cl, Stai. 194 BG95
Belle Vue Est NW4 119 CW56
 Bell La
Belle Vue La, Bushey 95 CD46
Belle Vue Pk, Th.Hth. 202 DQ97
Belle Vue Rd E17 101 ED54
Belle Vue Rd NW4 119 CW56
 Bell La
Belle Vue Rd, Orp. 223 EN110
 Standard Rd
Belle Vue Rd, Ware 33 DZ06
Bellefield Rd, Orp. 206 EV99
Bellefields Rd SW9 161 DM83
Bellegrove Cl, Well. 165 ET82
Bellegrove Par, Well. 165 ET83
 Bellegrove Rd
Bellegrove Rd, Well. 165 ER82
Bellenden Rd SE15 162 DT82
Bellestaines Pleasaunce E4 101 EA47
Belleville Rd SW11 180 DF85
Bellevue Ms N11 98 DG50
 Bellevue Rd
Bellevue Par SW17 180 DE88
 Bellevue Rd
Bellevue Pl E1 142 DW70
Bellevue Pl, Slou. 152 AT76
 Albert St
Bellevue Rd N11 98 DG49
Bellevue Rd SW13 159 CU82
Bellevue Rd SW17 180 DE88
Bellevue Rd W13 137 CH70
Bellevue Rd, Bexh. 186 EZ85
Bellevue Rd, Horn. 128 FM60
Bellevue Rd, Kings.T. 198 CL97
Bellevue Rd, Rom. 105 FC51
Bellevue Ter (Harefield), Uxb. 92 BG52
Bellew St SW17 180 DC90
Bellfield, Croy. 221 DY109
Bellfield Av, Har. 95 CD51
Bellfields Ct, Guil. 242 AW130
 Oak Tree Dr
Bellfields Rd, Guil. 242 AX132
Bellflower Cl E6 144 EL71
 Sorrel Gdns
Bellflower Path, Rom. 106 FJ52
Bellgate, Hem.H. 40 BL17
Bellgate Ms NW5 121 DH62
 York Ri
Bellhouse La, Brwd. 108 FS43
Bellingdon Rd, Chesh. 54 AP31
Bellingham Ct, Bark. 146 EV69
 Renwick Rd
Bellingham Grn SE6 183 EA90
Bellingham Rd SE6 183 EB90
Bellmaker Ct E3 143 DZ71
 St. Pauls Way
Bellman Av, Grav. 191 GL88
Bellmarsh Rd, Add. 212 BH105
Bellmount Wd Av, Wat. 75 BS39
Bello Cl SE24 181 DP87
Bellot Gdns SE10 164 EE78
Bellot St SE10 164 EE78
Bellring Cl, Belv. 166 FA79
Bells All SW6 160 DA82
Bells Gdn Est SE15 162 DU80
 Buller Cl
Bells Hill, Barn. 79 CX43
Bell's Hill (Stoke Poges), Slou. 132 AU67
Bells Hill Grn (Stoke Poges), Slou. 132 AU66
Bells La (Horton), Slou. 153 BB83
Bellswood La, Iver 133 BB71
Belltrees Gro SW16 181 DM92
Bellwether La (Outwood), Red. 267 DP143
Bellwood Rd SE15 163 DX84
Belmarsh Rd SE28 165 ES75
 Western Way
Belmont, Slou. 131 AN71
Belmont Av N9 100 DU46
Belmont Av N13 99 DL50
Belmont Av N17 122 DQ55
Belmont Av, Barn. 80 DF43
Belmont Av, Guil. 242 AT131
Belmont Av, N.Mal. 199 CU99
Belmont Av, Sthl. 156 BY76
Belmont Av, Upmin. 128 FM61
Belmont Av, Well. 165 ES83
Belmont Av, Wem. 138 CM67
Belmont Circle, Har. 95 CH53
Belmont Cl E4 101 ED50
Belmont Cl N20 98 DB46
Belmont Cl SW4 161 DJ83
Belmont Cl, Barn. 80 DF42
Belmont Cl, Uxb. 134 BK65
Belmont Cl, Wdf.Grn. 102 EH49
Belmont Cotts (Colnbrook), Slou. 153 BC80
 High St
Belmont Ct NW11 119 CZ57
Belmont Gro SE13 163 ED83
Belmont Gro W4 158 CR77
 Belmont Rd
Belmont Hall Ct SE13 163 ED83
 Belmont Gro
Belmont Hill SE13 163 ED83
Belmont Hill, St.Alb. 43 CD21
Belmont La, Chis. 185 EQ92
Belmont La, Stan. 95 CJ52
Belmont Ms SW19 179 CX89
 Chapman Sq
Belmont Pk SE13 163 ED84
Belmont Pk Cl SE13 163 ED84
 Belmont Pk
Belmont Pk Rd E10 123 EB58
Belmont Ri, Sutt. 217 CZ109
Belmont Rd N15 122 DQ56
Belmont Rd N17 122 DQ56
Belmont Rd SE25 202 DV99
Belmont Rd SW4 161 DJ83
Belmont Rd W4 158 CR77
Belmont Rd, Beck. 203 DZ96
Belmont Rd, Bushey 76 BY43
Belmont Rd, Chesh. 54 AP29
Belmont Rd, Chis. 185 EP92
Belmont Rd, Erith 166 FA80
Belmont Rd, Grays 170 FZ78
Belmont Rd, Har. 117 CF55
Belmont Rd, Hem.H. 40 BL24
Belmont Rd, Horn. 128 FK62
Belmont Rd, Ilf. 125 EQ62
Belmont Rd, Lthd. 231 CG122
Belmont Rd, Reig. 266 DC135
Belmont Rd, Sutt. 218 DA110
Belmont Rd, Twick. 177 CD89
Belmont Rd, Uxb. 134 BK66
Belmont Rd, Wall. 219 DH106
Belmont St NW1 140 DG66
Belmont Ter W4 158 CR77
 Belmont Rd
Belmor, Borwd. 78 CN43
Belmore Av, Hayes 135 BU72
Belmore Av, Wok. 227 BD116
Belmore La N7 121 DK64
Belmore St SW8 161 DK81
Beloe Cl SW15 159 CU83
Belper Ct E5 123 DX63
 Pedro St
Belsham St E9 142 DW65
Belsize Av N13 99 DM51
Belsize Av NW3 140 DE65
Belsize Av W13 157 CH76
Belsize Cl, Hem.H. 40 BN21
Belsize Cl, St.Alb. 43 CJ15
Belsize Ct NW3 120 DE64
 Belsize La
Belsize Cres NW3 120 DD64
Belsize Gdns, Sutt. 218 DB105
Belsize Gro NW3 140 DE65
Belsize La NW3 140 DD65
Belsize Ms NW3 140 DD65
 Belsize La
Belsize Pk NW3 140 DD65
Belsize Pk Gdns NW3 140 DE65
Belsize Pk Ms NW3 140 DD65
 Belsize La
Belsize Pl NW3 140 DD65
 Belsize La
Belsize Rd NW6 140 DC66
Belsize Rd, Har. 95 CD52
Belsize Rd, Hem.H. 40 BN21
Belsize Sq NW3 140 DD65
Belsize Ter NW3 140 DD65
Belson Rd SE18 165 EM77
Belswains Grn, Hem.H. 40 BL23
 Belswains La
Belswains La, Hem.H. 58 BM25
Beltana Dr, Grav. 191 GL91
Beltane Dr SW19 179 CX90
Belthorn Cres SW12 181 DJ87
Beltinge Rd, Rom. 128 FM55
Belton Rd E7 144 EH66
Belton Rd E11 124 EE63
Belton Rd N17 122 DS55
Belton Rd NW2 139 CU65
Belton Rd, Berk. 38 AU18
Belton Rd, Sid. 186 EU91
Belton Way E3 143 EA71
Beltona Gdns (Cheshunt), Wal.Cr. 67 DX27
Beltran Rd SW6 160 DB82
Beltwood Rd, Belv. 167 FC77
Belvedere Av SW19 179 CY92
Belvedere Av, Ilf. 103 EP54
Belvedere Bldgs SE1 278 G5
Belvedere Cl, Esher 214 CB106
Belvedere Cl, Grav. 191 GJ88
Belvedere Cl, Guil. 242 AV132
Belvedere Cl, Tedd. 177 CE92
Belvedere Cl, Wey. 212 BN106
Belvedere Ct N2 120 DD57
Belvedere Dr SW19 179 CY92
Belvedere Gdns, St.Alb. 60 CA27
Belvedere Gdns, W.Mol. 196 BZ99
Belvedere Gro SW19 179 CY92
Belvedere Ho, Felt. 175 BU88
Belvedere Ind Est, Belv. 167 FC76
Belvedere Ms SE15 162 DV83
Belvedere Pl SE1 278 G5
Belvedere Pl SE1 161 DP75
Belvedere Pl SW2 161 DM84
 Acre La
Belvedere Rd E10 123 DY60
Belvedere Rd SE1 278 C4
Belvedere Rd SE1 141 DM74
Belvedere Rd SE2 146 EX74
Belvedere Rd SE19 182 DT94
Belvedere Rd W7 157 CF76
Belvedere Rd, Bexh. 166 EZ83
Belvedere Rd, Brwd. 108 FT48
Belvedere Rd (Biggin Hill), West. 239 EM118
Belvedere Sq SW19 179 CY92
Belvedere Strand NW9 97 CT54
Belvedere Twr, The SW10 160 DC81
Belvedere Way, Har. 118 CL58
Belvoir Cl SE9 184 EL90
Belvoir Rd SE22 182 DU87
Belvue Cl, Nthlt. 136 CA66
Belvue Rd, Nthlt. 136 CA66
Bembridge Cl NW6 139 CY66
Bembridge Ct, Slou. 152 AT76
 Park St
Bembridge Gdns, Ruis. 115 BR61
Bemerton Est N1 141 DM66
Bemerton St N1 141 DM67
Bemish Rd SW15 159 CX83
Bempton Dr, Ruis. 115 BV61
Bemsted Rd E17 123 DZ55
Ben Hale Cl, Stan. 95 CH49
Ben Jonson Rd E1 143 DY71
Ben Smith Way SE16 162 DU76
 Jamaica Rd
Ben Tillet Cl, Bark. 146 EU66
Ben Tillett Cl E16 145 EM74
 Newland St
Benares Rd SE18 165 ET77
Benbow Cl, St.Alb. 43 CH22
Benbow Rd W6 159 CV76
Benbow St SE8 163 EA79
Benbow Waye, Uxb. 134 BJ71
Benbrick Rd, Guil. 258 AU135
Benbury Cl, Brom. 183 EC92
Bence, The, Egh. 193 BB97
Bench Fld, S.Croy. 220 DT107
Bench Manor Cres (Chalfont St. Peter), Ger.Cr. 90 AW54
Benchleys Rd, Hem.H. 39 BF21
Bencombe Rd, Pur. 219 DN114
Bencroft (Cheshunt), Wal.Cr. 66 DU26
Bencroft Rd SW16 181 DJ94
Bencroft Rd, Hem.H. 40 BL20
Bencurtis Pk, W.Wick. 203 ED104
Bendall Ms NW1 272 C6
Bendemeer Rd SW15 159 CX83
Bendish Rd E6 144 EL66
Bendmore Av SE2 166 EU78
Bendon Valley SW18 180 DB87
Bendysh Rd, Bushey 76 BY41
Benedict Cl, Belv. 166 EY76
 Tunstock Way
Benedict Cl, Orp. 205 ES104
Benedict Dr, Felt. 175 BR87
Benedict Rd SW9 161 DM83
Benedict Rd, Mitch. 200 DD97
Benedict Way N2 120 DC55
Benedictine Gate, Wal.Cr. 67 DY27
Benen-Stock Rd, Stai. 173 BF85
Benenden Grn, Brom. 204 EG99
Benets Rd, Horn. 128 FN60
Benett Gdns SW16 201 DL96
Benfleet Cl, Cob. 214 BY112
Benfleet Cl, Sutt. 200 DC104
Benfleet Way N11 98 DG47
Benford Rd, Hodd. 49 DY19
Bengal Ct EC3 142 DR72
 Birchin La
Bengal Rd, Ilf. 125 EP63
Bengarth Dr, Har. 95 CD54
Bengarth Rd, Nthlt. 136 BX67
Bengeo Meadows, Hert. 32 DR06
Bengeo Ms, Hert. 32 DQ06
 Bengeo St
Bengeo St, Hert. 32 DQ08
Bengeworth Rd SE5 162 DQ83
Bengeworth Rd, Har. 117 CG61
Benham Cl SW11 160 DD83
Benham Cl, Chesh. 54 AP29
Benham Cl, Chess. 215 CJ107
 Merritt Gdns
Benham Cl, Couls. 235 DP118
Benham Gdns, Houns. 156 BZ84
Benham Rd W7 137 CE71
Benhams Cl, Horl. 268 DG146
Benhams Dr, Horl. 268 DG146
Benhams Pl NW3 120 DC63
 Holly Wk
Benhill Av, Sutt. 218 DB105
Benhill Rd SE5 162 DR80
Benhill Rd, Sutt. 200 DC104
Benhill Wd Rd, Sutt. 200 DC104
Benhilton Gdns, Sutt. 200 DB104
Benhurst Av, Horn. 127 FH62
Benhurst Cl, S.Croy. 221 DX110
Benhurst Ct SW16 181 DN92
Benhurst Gdns, S.Croy. 220 DW110
Benhurst La SW16 181 DN92
Benin St SE13 183 ED87
Benison Ct, Slou. 152 AT76
 Osborne St
Benjafield Cl N18 100 DV49
 Brettenham Rd
Benjamin Cl E8 142 DU67
Benjamin Cl, Horn. 127 FG58
Benjamin St EC1 274 F6
Benjamin St EC1 141 DP71
Benledi St E14 143 ED72
Benn St E9 143 DY65
Bennelong Cl W12 139 CV73
Bennerley Rd SW11 180 DE85
Bennet's Hill EC4 274 G10
Bennetsfield Rd, Uxb. 135 BP74
Bennett Cl, Cob. 213 BU113
Bennett Cl, Kings.T. 197 CJ95
Bennett Cl, Nthwd. 93 BT52
Bennett Cl, Well. 166 EU82
Bennett Cl, Welw.G.C. 29 CZ13
Bennett Gro SE13 163 EB81
Bennett Pk SE3 164 EF83
Bennett Rd E13 144 EJ70
Bennett Rd N16 122 DS63
Bennett Rd, Rom. 126 EY58
Bennett St SW1 277 K2
Bennett St W4 158 CS79
Bennett Way (Lane End), Dart. 189 FR91
Bennett Way (West Clandon), Guil. 244 BG129
Bennetts, Chesh. 54 AR30
Bennetts Av, Croy. 203 DY103
Bennetts Av, Grnf. 137 CE67
Bennetts Castle La, Dag. 126 EW63
Bennetts Cl N17 100 DT51
Bennetts Cl, Mitch. 201 DH95
Bennetts Cl (Colney Heath), St.Alb. 44 CR23
 Meadway
Bennetts Cl, Slou. 131 AN74
Bennetts Copse, Chis. 184 EL93
Bennetts End Cl, Hem.H. 40 BM21
Bennetts End Rd, Hem.H. 40 BM21
Bennetts Fm Pl (Bookham), Lthd. 246 BZ125
Bennetts Gate, Hem.H. 40 BN23
 Bennetts End Rd
Bennetts Way, Croy. 203 DY103
Bennetts Yd SW1 277 N7
Bennetts Yd, Uxb. 134 BJ66
 High St
Benning Cl, Wind. 151 AK83
Benningholme Rd, Edg. 96 CS51
Bennington Rd N17 100 DS53
Bennington Rd, Wdf.Grn. 102 EE52
Bennions Cl, Horn. 148 FK65
 Franklin Rd
Bennison Dr, Rom. 106 FK54
Benn's Wk, Rich. 158 CL84
 Rosedale Rd
Benrek Cl, Ilf. 103 EQ53
Bensbury Cl SW15 179 CV87
Bensham Cl, Th.Hth. 202 DQ98
Bensham Gro, Th.Hth. 202 DQ96
Bensham La, Croy. 201 DP101
Bensham La, Th.Hth. 201 DP98
Bensham Manor Rd, Th.Hth. 202 DQ98
Bensington Ct, Felt. 175 BR86
Benskin Rd, Wat. 75 BU43
Benskins La (Havering-atte-Bower), Rom. 106 FK46
Bensley Cl N11 98 DF50
Benson Av E6 144 EJ68
Benson Cl, Houns. 156 CA84
Benson Cl, Slou. 132 AU74
Benson Cl, Uxb. 134 BL71
Benson Quay E1 142 DW73
 Garnet St
Benson Rd SE23 182 DW88
Benson Rd, Croy. 201 DN104
Benson Rd, Grays 170 GB79
Bentalls Cen, Kings.T. 197 CK96
Bentfield Gdns SE9 184 EJ90
 Aldersgrove Av
Benthal Rd N16 122 DU61
Benthall Gdns, Ken. 236 DQ116
Bentham Av, Wok. 227 BC115
Bentham Ct N1 142 DQ66
 Rotherfield St
Bentham Rd E9 143 DX65
Bentham Rd SE28 146 EV73
Bentham Wk NW10 118 CQ64
Bentinck Cl, Ger.Cr. 112 AX57
Bentinck Ms W1 272 G8
Bentinck Pl NW8 272 B1
Bentinck Rd, West Dr. 134 BK74
Bentinck St W1 272 G8
Bentinck St W1 140 DG72
Bentley Dr NW2 119 CZ62
Bentley Dr, Harl. 52 EW16
Bentley Dr, Ilf. 125 EQ58
Bentley Dr, Wey. 212 BN109
Bentley Heath La, Barn. 63 CY34
Bentley Ms, Enf. 82 DR44
Bentley Pk (Burnham), Slou. 131 AK68
Bentley Rd N1 142 DS65
 Tottenham Rd
Bentley Rd, Hert. 31 DL08
Bentley Rd, Slou. 131 AN74
Bentley St, Grav. 191 GJ86
Bentley Way, Stan. 95 CG50
Bentley Way, Wdf.Grn. 102 EG47
Benton Rd, Ilf. 125 ER60
Benton Rd, Wat. 94 BX50

Bentons, Harl. 51 ES17
Bentons La SE27 182 DQ91
Bentons Ri SE27 182 DR92
Bentry Cl, Dag. 126 EY61
Bentry Rd, Dag. 126 EY61
Bentsbrook Cl (North Holmwood), Dor. 263 CH140
Bentsbrook Pk (North Holmwood), Dor. 263 CH140
Bentsbrook Rd (North Holmwood), Dor. 263 CH140
Bentsley Cl, St.Alb. 43 CJ16
Bentworth Rd W12 139 CV72
Benwell Ct, Sun. 195 BU95
Benwell Rd N7 121 DN63
Benwick Cl SE16 162 DV76
Benworth St E3 143 DZ69
Benyon Path, S.Ock. 149 FW68
Tyssen Pl
Benyon Rd N1 142 DR67
Southgate Rd
Beomonds Row, Cher. 194 BG101
Heriot Rd
Berber Rd SW11 180 DF85
Berberis Cl, Guil. 242 AW132
Berberis Wk, West Dr. 154 BL77
Berberry Cl, Edg. 96 CQ49
Larkspur Gro
Berceau Wk, Wat. 75 BS39
Bercta Rd SE9 185 EQ89
Bere St E1 143 DX73
Cranford St
Berecroft, Harl. 51 ER20
Beredens La, Brwd. 129 FT55
Berefeld, Hem.H. 40 BK18
Berenger Wk SW10 160 DD80
Blantyre St
Berens Rd NW10 139 CX69
Berens Rd, Orp. 206 EX99
Berens Way, Chis. 205 ET98
Beresford Av N20 98 DF47
Beresford Av W7 137 CD71
Beresford Av, Slou. 132 AW74
Beresford Av, Surb. 198 CP102
Beresford Av, Twick. 177 CJ86
Beresford Av, Wem. 138 CM67
Beresford Dr, Brom. 204 EK97
Beresford Dr, Wdf.Grn. 102 EJ49
Beresford Gdns, Enf. 82 DS42
Beresford Gdns, Houns. 176 BZ85
Beresford Gdns, Rom. 126 EY57
Beresford Rd E4 102 EE46
Beresford Rd E17 101 EB53
Beresford Rd N2 120 DE55
Beresford Rd N5 122 DQ64
Beresford Rd N8 121 DN57
Beresford Rd, Dor. 263 CH136
Beresford Rd (Northfleet), Grav. 190 GE87
Beresford Rd, Har. 117 CD57
Beresford Rd, Kings.T. 198 CM95
Beresford Rd, N.Mal. 198 CQ98
Beresford Rd, Rick. 91 BF46
Beresford Rd, St.Alb. 43 CH21
Beresford Rd, Sthl. 136 BX74
Beresford Rd, Sutt. 217 CZ108
Beresford Sq SE18 165 EP77
Beresford St SE18 165 EP76
Beresford Ter N5 122 DQ64
Berestede Rd W6 159 CT78
Bergen Sq SE16 163 DY76
Norway Gate
Berger Cl, Orp. 205 ER100
Berger Rd E9 143 DX65
Berghem Ms W14 159 CX76
Blythe Rd
Berghers Hill (Wooburn Grn), H.Wyc. 110 AF59
Bergholt Av, Ilf. 124 EL57
Bergholt Cres N16 122 DS59
Bergholt Ms NW1 141 DJ66
Rossendale Way
Berglen Ct E14 143 DY72
Branch Rd
Bericot Way, Welw.G.C. 30 DC09
Bering Sq E14 163 EA78
Napier Av
Bering Wk E16 144 EK72
Berisford Ms SW18 180 DC86
Berkeley Av, Bexh. 166 EX81
Berkeley Av, Chesh. 54 AN30
Berkeley Av, Grnf. 137 CE65
Berkeley Av, Houns. 155 BU82
Berkeley Av, Ilf. 103 EN54
Berkeley Av, Rom. 105 FC52
Berkeley Cl, Abb.L. 59 BT32
Berkeley Cl, Borwd. 78 CN43
Berkeley Cl, Chesh. 54 AN30
Berkeley Av
Berkeley Cl, Horn. 128 FP61
Berkeley Cl, Kings.T. 178 CL94
Berkeley Cl, Orp. 205 ES101
Berkeley Cl, Pot.B. 63 CY32
Berkeley Cl, Ruis. 115 BU62
Berkeley Cl, Stai. 173 BD89
Berkeley Cl, Ware 32 DW05
Berkeley Ct N14 81 DJ44
Berkeley Ct, Rick. 75 BR43
Mayfare
Berkeley Ct, Wall. 201 DJ104
Berkeley Ct, Wey. 195 BR103
Berkeley Cres, Barn. 80 DD43
Berkeley Cres, Dart. 188 FM88
Berkeley Dr, Horn. 128 FN60
Berkeley Dr, W.Mol. 196 BZ97
Berkeley Gdns N21 100 DR45
Berkeley Gdns W8 140 DA74
Brunswick Gdns
Berkeley Gdns (Claygate), Esher 215 CG107
Berkeley Gdns, Walt. 195 BT101
Berkeley Gdns, W.Byf. 211 BF114
Berkeley Ho E3 143 EA70
Berkeley Ms W1 272 E8
Berkeley Pl SW19 179 CX93
Berkeley Pl, Epsom 232 CR115
Berkeley Rd E12 124 EL64
Berkeley Rd N8 121 DK57
Berkeley Rd N15 122 DR58
Berkeley Rd NW9 118 CN56
Berkeley Rd SW13 159 CU81
Berkeley Rd (Loudwater), H.Wyc. 88 AC53
Berkeley Rd, Uxb. 135 BQ66
Berkeley Sq W1 277 J1
Berkeley Sq W1 141 DH73
Berkeley St W1 277 J1
Berkeley St W1 141 DH73
Berkeley Wk N7 121 DM61
Durham Rd
Berkeley Waye, Houns. 156 BX80
Berkeleys, The (Fetcham), Lthd. 231 CE124
Berkhampstead Rd, Belv. 166 FA78
Berkhampstead Rd, Chesh. 54 AQ30
Berkhamsted Av, Wem. 138 CM65
Berkhamsted Bypass, Berk. 38 AV21
Berkhamsted Bypass, Hem.H. 39 BB23
Berkhamsted Hill, Berk. 38 AY17
Berkhamsted La, Hat. 46 DF20
Berkhamsted Pl, Berk. 38 AW17
Berkhamsted Rd, Hem.H. 39 BD17
Berkley Av, Wal.Cr. 67 DX34
Berkley Cl, St.Alb. 43 CJ16
Berkley Ct, Berk. 38 AW19
Mill St
Berkley Ct, Guil. 242 AY134
London Rd
Berkley Cres, Grav. 191 GJ86
Milton Rd
Berkley Gro NW1 140 DF66
Berkley Rd
Berkley Rd NW1 140 DF66
Berkley Rd, Beac. 89 AK49
Berkley Rd, Grav. 191 GH86
Berks Hill, Rick. 73 BC43
Berkshire Av, Slou. 131 AP72
Berkshire Cl, Cat. 236 DR122
Berkshire Gdns N13 99 DN51
Berkshire Gdns N18 100 DV50
Berkshire Rd E9 143 DZ65
Berkshire Sq, Mitch. 201 DL98
Berkshire Way
Berkshire Way, Horn. 128 FN57
Berkshire Way, Mitch. 201 DL98
Bermans Cl, Brwd. 109 GB47
Hanging Hill La
Bermans Way NW10 118 CS63
Bermondsey Sq SE1 279 N6
Bermondsey St SE1 279 M3
Bermondsey St SE1 162 DS75
Bermondsey Wall E SE16 162 DU75
Bermondsey Wall W SE16 162 DU75
Bermuda Rd, Til. 171 GG82
Bernal Cl SE28 146 EX73
Haldane Rd
Bernard Ashley Dr SE7 164 EH78
Bernard Av W13 157 CH76
Bernard Cassidy St E16 144 EF71
Bernard Gdns SW19 179 CZ92
Bernard Gro, Wal.Abb. 67 EB33
Beaulieu Dr
Bernard Rd N15 122 DT57
Bernard Rd, Rom. 127 FC59
Bernard Rd, Wall. 219 DH105
Bernard St WC1 273 P5
Bernard St WC1 141 DL70
Bernard St, Grav. 191 GH86
Bernard St, St.Alb. 43 CD19
Bernards Cl, Ilf. 103 EQ51
Bernato Cl, W.Byf. 212 BL112
Viscount Gdns
Bernays Cl, Stan. 95 CJ51
Bernays Gro SW9 161 DM84
Berne Rd, Th.Hth. 202 DQ99
Bernel Dr, Croy. 203 DZ104
Berners Cl, Slou. 131 AL73
Berners Dr W13 137 CG72
Berners Dr, Brox. 49 DZ23
Berners Way
Berners Dr, St.Alb. 43 CD23
Berners Ms W1 273 L7
Berners Ms W1 141 DJ71
Berners Pl W1 273 L8
Berners Pl W1 141 DJ72
Berners Rd N1 141 DN67
Berners Rd N22 99 DN53
Berners St W1 273 L7
Berners St W1 141 DJ71
Berners Way, Brox. 49 DZ23
Bernersmede SE3 164 EG83
Blackheath Pk
Berney Rd, Croy. 202 DR101
Bernhardt Cres NW8 272 B4
Bernhardt Cres NW8 140 DE70
Bernhart Cl, Edg. 96 CQ52
Bernice Cl, Rain. 148 FJ70
Bernville Way, Har. 118 CM57
Kenton Rd
Bernwell Rd E4 102 EE48
Berridge Grn, Edg. 96 CN52
Berridge Ms NW6 120 DA64
Hillfield Rd
Berridge Rd SE19 182 DR92
Berries, The (Sandridge), St.Alb. 43 CG16
Berriman Rd N7 121 DM62
Berrington Dr (East Horsley), Lthd. 229 BT124
Berriton Rd, Har. 116 BZ60
Berry Av, Wat. 75 BV36
Berry Cl N21 99 DP46
Berry Cl NW10 138 CS66
Berry Cl, Dag. 126 FA64
Berry Cl, Horn. 128 FJ64
Airfield Way
Berry Cl, Rick. 92 BH45
Berry Ct, Houns. 176 BZ85
Berry Fld Pk, Amer. 55 AP37
Berry Gro La, Wat. 76 CA39
Berry Hill, Maid. 130 AD71
Berry Hill, Stan. 95 CK49
Berry Hill Ct, Maid. 130 AD71
Berry La SE21 182 DR91
Berry La, Rick. 92 BH46
Berry La, Walt. 214 BX106
Burwood Rd
Berry Meade, Ash. 232 CM117
Berry Pl EC1 274 G3
Berry St EC1 274 G4
Berry St EC1 141 DP70
Berry Wk, Ash. 232 CM119
Berry Way W5 158 CL76
Berry Way, Rick. 92 BH45
Berrybank Cl E4 101 EC47
Greenbank Cl
Berrydale Rd, Hayes 136 BY70
Berryfield, Slou. 132 AW72
Berryfield Cl E17 123 EB56
Berryfield Cl, Brom. 204 EL95
Berryfield Rd SE17 278 G10
Berryfield Rd SE17 161 DP78
Berryhill SE9 165 EP84
Berryhill Gdns SE9 165 EP84
Berrylands SW20 199 CW97
Berrylands, Orp. 206 EW104
Berrylands, Surb. 198 CN99
Berrylands Rd, Surb. 198 CM100
Berryman Cl, Dag. 126 EW62
Bennetts Castle La
Berrymans La SE26 183 DX91
Berrymead, Hem.H. 40 BM19
Berrymead Gdns W3 138 CQ74
Berrymede Rd W4 158 CR76
Berry's Grn Rd (Berry's Grn), West. 239 EP116
Berry's Hill (Berry's Grn), West. 239 EP115
Berrys La (Byfleet), W.Byf. 212 BK111
Berryscroft Ct, Stai. 174 BJ94
Berryscroft Rd
Berryscroft Rd, Stai. 174 BJ94
Bersham La, Grays 170 FZ77
Bert Rd, Th.Hth. 202 DQ99
Bertal Rd SW17 180 DD91
Berther Rd, Horn. 128 FK59
Berthold Ms, Wal.Abb. 67 EB33
Berthon St SE8 163 EA80
Bertie Rd NW10 139 CU65
Bertie Rd SE26 183 DX93
Bertram Cotts SW19 180 DA94
Hartfield Rd
Bertram Rd NW4 119 CU58
Bertram Rd, Enf. 82 DU42
Bertram Rd, Kings.T. 178 CN94
Bertram St N19 121 DH61
Bertram Way, Enf. 82 DT42
Bertrand St SE13 163 EB83
Bertrand Way SE28 146 EV73
Berwick Av, Hayes 136 BX72
Berwick Av, Slou. 131 AP73
Berwick Cl, Beac. 89 AP54
Berwick Cl, Stan. 95 CF52
Gordon Av
Berwick Cl, Wal.Cr. 67 EA34
Berwick Cres, Sid. 185 ES86
Berwick La, Ong. 87 FF36
Berwick Pond Cl, Rain. 148 FK68
Berwick Pond Rd, Rain. 148 FL68
Berwick Pond Rd, Upmin. 148 FM66
Berwick Rd E16 144 EH72
Berwick Rd N22 99 DP53
Berwick Rd, Borwd. 78 CM38
Berwick Rd, Rain. 148 FK68
Berwick Rd, Well. 166 EV81
Berwick St W1 273 M9
Berwick St W1 141 DK72
Berwick Way, Orp. 206 EU102
Berwick Way, Sev. 257 FH121
Berwyn Av, Houns. 156 CB81
Berwyn Rd SE24 181 DP88
Berwyn Rd, Rich. 158 CP84
Beryl Av E6 144 EL71
Beryl Ho SE18 165 ET78
Spinel Cl
Beryl Rd W6 159 CX78
Berystede, Kings.T. 178 CP94
Besant Ct N1 122 DR64
Newington Grn Rd
Besant Rd NW2 119 CY63
Besant Wk N7 121 DM61
Newington Barrow Way
Besant Way NW10 118 CQ64
Besley St SW16 181 DJ93
Bessant Dr, Rich. 158 CP81
Bessborough Gdns SW1 277 N10
Bessborough Gdns SW1 161 DK78
Bessborough Pl SW1 277 N10
Bessborough Pl SW1 161 DK78
Bessborough Rd SW15 179 CU88
Bessborough Rd, Har. 117 CD60
Bessborough St SW1 277 M10
Bessborough St SW1 161 DK78
Bessels Grn Rd, Sev. 256 FD123
Bessels Meadow, Sev. 256 FD124
Bessels Way, Sev. 256 FC124
Bessemer Rd SE5 162 DQ82
Bessemer Rd, Welw.G.C. 29 CY05
Bessie Lansbury Cl E6 145 EN72
Bessingby Rd, Ruis. 115 BU61
Bessingham Wk SE4 163 DX84
Frendsbury Rd
Besson St SE14 162 DW81
Bessy St E2 142 DW69
Roman Rd
Bestobell Rd, Slou. 131 AQ72
Bestwood St SE8 163 DX77
Beswick Ms NW6 140 DB65
Lymington Rd
Beta Pl SW4 161 DL84
Santley St
Beta Rd, Wok. 227 BB116
Beta Rd (Chobham), Wok. 210 AT110
Beta Way, Egh. 193 BC95
Betam Rd, Hayes 155 BR75
Betchworth Cl, Sutt. 218 DD106
Turnpike La
Betchworth Rd, Ilf. 125 ES61
Betchworth Way (New Addington), Croy. 221 EC109
Betenson Av, Sev. 256 FF122
Betham Rd, Grnf. 137 CD69
Bethany Waye, Felt. 175 BS87
Bethecar Rd, Har. 117 CE57
Bethel Rd, Sev. 257 FJ123
Bethel Rd, Well. 166 EW83
Bethell Av E16 144 EF70
Bethell Av, Ilf. 125 EN59
Bethersden Cl, Beck. 183 DZ94
Bethnal Grn Est E2 142 DW69
Roman Rd
Bethnal Grn Rd E1 275 P4
Bethnal Grn Rd E1 142 DT70
Bethnal Grn Rd E2 275 P4
Bethnal Grn Rd E2 142 DT70
Bethune Av N11 98 DF49
Bethune Rd N16 122 DR59
Bethune Rd NW10 138 CR70
Bethwin Rd SE5 161 DP80
Betjeman Cl, Couls. 235 DM117
Betjeman Cl, Pnr. 116 CA56
Betjeman Cl, Wal.Cr. 66 DU28
Rosedale Way
Betjeman Way, Hem.H. 40 BH18
Betley Ct, Walt. 195 BV104
Betony Cl, Croy. 203 DX102
Primrose La
Betony Rd, Rom. 106 FK51
Cloudberry Rd
Betoyne Av E4 102 EE49
Betsham Rd, Erith 167 FF80
Betsham Rd (Southfleet), Grav. 189 FX92
Betsham Rd, Swans. 190 FY87
Betstyle Rd N11 99 DH49
Betterton Dr, Sid. 186 EY89
Betterton Rd, Rain. 147 FE69
Betterton St WC2 273 P9
Betterton St WC2 141 DL72
Bettles Cl, Uxb. 134 BJ68
Wescott Way
Bettons Pk E15 144 EE67
Bettridge Rd SW6 159 CZ82
Betts Cl, Beck. 203 DY96
Kendall Rd
Betts La, Wal.Abb. 50 EJ21
Betts Ms E17 123 DZ58
Queen's Rd
Betts Rd E16 144 EH73
Victoria Dock Rd
Betts St E1 142 DV73
The Highway
Betts Way SE20 202 DV95
Betts Way, Surb. 197 CH102
Betula Cl, Ken. 236 DR115
Betula Wk, Rain. 148 FK69
Between Sts, Cob. 213 BU114
Beulah Av, Th.Hth. 201 DM98
Beulah Rd
Beulah Cl, Edg. 96 CP48
Beulah Cres, Th.Hth. 202 DQ96
Beulah Gro, Croy. 202 DQ100
Beulah Hill SE19 181 DP93
Beulah Path E17 123 EB57
Addison Rd
Beulah Rd E17 123 EB57
Beulah Rd SW19 179 CZ94
Beulah Rd, Epp. 70 EU29
Beulah Rd, Horn. 128 FJ62
Beulah Rd, Sutt. 218 DA105
Beulah Rd, Th.Hth. 202 DQ97
Beulah Wk (Woldingham), Cat. 237 DY120
Beult Rd, Dart. 167 FG83
Bev Callender Cl SW8 161 DH83
Daley Thompson Way
Bevan Av, Bark. 146 EU66
Bevan Cl, Hem.H. 40 BK22
Bevan Ct, Croy. 219 DN106
Bevan Hill, Chesh. 54 AP29
Bevan Ho, Grays 170 GD75
Laird Av
Bevan Pl, Swan. 207 FF98
Bevan Rd SE2 166 EV78
Bevan Rd, Barn. 80 DF42
Bevan St N1 142 DQ67
Bevan Way, Horn. 128 FM63
Bevans Cl, Green. 189 FW86
Johnsons Way
Bevenden St N1 275 L2
Bevenden St N1 142 DR69
Bevercote Wk, Belv. 166 EZ79
Osborne Rd
Beveridge Rd NW10 138 CS66
Curzon Cres
Beverley Av SW20 199 CT95
Beverley Av, Houns. 156 BZ84
Beverley Av, Sid. 185 ET87
Beverley Cl N21 100 DQ46
Beverley Cl SW11 160 DD84
Maysoule Rd
Beverley Cl SW13 159 CT82
Beverley Cl, Add. 212 BK106
Beverley Cl, Brox. 49 DY21
Beverley Cl, Chess. 215 CJ105
Beverley Cl, Enf. 82 DS42
Beverley Cl, Epsom 217 CW111
Beverley Cl, Horn. 128 FM59
Beverley Cl, Wey. 195 BS103
Beverley Cotts SW15 178 CR91
Kingston Vale
Beverley Ct N14 99 DJ45
Beverley Ct N20 98 DC45
Farnham Cl
Beverley Ct SE4 163 DZ83
Beverley Ct, Slou. 152 AV75
Dolphin Rd
Beverley Cres, Wdf.Grn. 102 EH53
Beverley Dr, Edg. 118 CP55
Beverley Gdns NW11 119 CY59
Beverley Gdns SW13 159 CT83
Beverley Gdns, Horn. 128 FM59
Beverley Gdns, St.Alb. 43 CK16
Beverley Gdns, Stan. 95 CG53
Beverley Gdns (Cheshunt), Wal.Cr. 66 DT30
Beverley Gdns, Welw.G.C. 30 DC09
Beverley Gdns, Wem. 118 CM60
Beverley Gdns, Wor.Pk. 199 CU102
Green La
Beverley Hts, Reig. 250 DB132
Beverley Ho NW8 272 B3
Beverley La SW15 179 CT90
Beverley La, Kings.T. 178 CS94
Beverley Ms E4 101 ED51
Beverley Rd
Beverley Path SW13 159 CT82
Beverley Rd E4 101 ED51
Beverley Rd E6 144 EK69
Beverley Rd SE20 202 DV96
Wadhurst Cl
Beverley Rd SW13 159 CT83
Beverley Rd W4 159 CT78
Beverley Rd, Bexh. 167 FC82
Beverley Rd, Brom. 204 EL103
Beverley Rd, Dag. 126 EY63
Beverley Rd, Kings.T. 197 CJ95
Beverley Rd, Mitch. 201 DK98
Beverley Rd, N.Mal. 199 CU98
Beverley Rd, Ruis. 115 BU61
Beverley Rd, Sthl. 156 BY76
Beverley Rd, Sun. 195 BT95
Beverley Rd, Whyt. 236 DS116
Beverley Rd, Wor.Pk. 199 CW103
Beverley Trd Est, Mord. 199 CX101
Garth Rd
Beverley Way SW20 199 CT95
Beverley Way, N.Mal. 199 CT95
Beversbrook Rd N19 121 DK62
Beverston Ms W1 272 D7
Beverstone Rd SW2 181 DM85
Beverstone Rd, Th.Hth. 201 DN98
Bevil Ct, Hodd. 33 EA14
Molesworth
Bevill Allen Cl SW17 180 DF92
Bevill Cl SE25 202 DU97
Bevin Cl SE16 143 DY74
Stave Yd Rd
Bevin Ct WC1 141 DN69
Holford St
Bevin Rd, Hayes 135 BU69
Bevin Sq SW17 180 DF90
Bevin Way WC1 274 D2
Bevington Rd W10 139 CY71
Bevington Rd, Beck. 203 EB96
Bevington St SE16 162 DU75
Bevis Cl, Dart. 188 FQ87
Bevis Marks EC3 275 N8
Bevis Marks EC3 142 DS72
Bewcastle Gdns, Enf. 81 DL42
Bewdley St N1 141 DN66
Bewick St SW8 161 DH82
Bewley Cl (Cheshunt), Wal.Cr. 67 DX31
Bewley St E1 142 DV73
Dellow St
Bewlys Rd SE27 181 DP92
Bexhill Cl, Felt. 176 BY89
Bexhill Rd N11 99 DK50
Bexhill Rd SE4 183 DZ86
Bexhill Rd SW14 158 CQ83
Bexhill Wk E15 144 EE68
Mitre Rd
Bexley Cl, Dart. 187 FE85
Bexley Gdns N9 100 DR48
Bexley Gdns, Rom. 126 EV57
Bexley High St, Bex. 186 FA87
Bexley La, Dart. 187 FE85
Bexley La, Sid. 186 EW90
Bexley Rd SE9 185 EP85
Bexley Rd, Erith 167 FC80
Bexley St, Wind. 151 AP81
Beyers Gdns, Hodd. 33 EA14
Beyers Prospect, Hodd. 33 EA13
Beyers Ride, Hodd. 33 EA13
Beynon Rd, Cars. 218 DF106
Bianca Ho N1 142 DS68
Crondall St
Bianca Rd SE15 162 DT79
Bibsworth Rd N3 97 CZ54
Bibury Cl SE15 162 DS79
Bicester Rd, Rich. 158 CN83
Bickenhall St W1 272 E6
Bickenhall St W1 140 DF71
Bickersteth Rd SW17 180 DF93
Bickerton Rd N19 121 DJ61
Bickley Cres, Brom. 204 EL98
Bickley Pk Rd, Brom. 204 EL97
Bickley Rd E10 123 EB59
Bickley Rd, Brom. 204 EK96
Bickley St SW17 180 DE92
Bicknell Rd SE5 162 DQ83
Bickney Way (Fetcham), Lthd. 230 CC122
Bicknoller Cl, Sutt. 218 DB110
Bicknoller Rd, Enf. 82 DT39
Bicknor Rd, Orp. 205 ES101
Bidborough Cl, Brom. 204 EF99
Bidborough St WC1 273 P3
Bidborough St WC1 141 DK69
Biddenden Way SE9 185 EN91
Biddenden Way (Istead Ri), Grav. 190 GE94
Biddenham Turn, Wat. 76 BW35
Bidder St E16 144 EE71
Biddestone Rd N7 121 DM63
Biddles Cl, Slou. 151 AL75
Biddulph Rd W9 140 DB69
Biddulph Rd, S.Croy. 220 DQ109
Bideford Av, Grnf. 137 CH68
Bideford Cl, Edg. 96 CN53
Bideford Cl, Felt. 176 BZ90
Bideford Cl, Rom. 106 FJ53
Bideford Gdns, Enf. 100 DS45
Bideford Rd, Brom. 184 EF90
Bideford Rd, Enf. 83 DZ38
Bideford Rd, Ruis. 115 BV62
Bideford Rd, Well. 166 EV80
Bideford Spur, Slou. 131 AP69
Bidhams Cres, Tad. 233 CW121
Bidwell Gdns N11 99 DJ52
Bidwell St SE15 162 DV81
Big Common La (Bletchingley), Red. 251 DP133
Big Hill E5 122 DV60
Bigbury Cl N17 100 DR52
Weir Hall Rd
Bigbury Rd N17 100 DS52
Barkham Rd
Biggerstaff Rd E15 143 EC67
Biggerstaff St N4 121 DN61
Biggin Av, Mitch. 200 DF95
Biggin Hill SE19 181 DP94
Biggin Hill Business Pk, West. 238 EK115
Biggin Hill Cl, Kings.T. 177 CJ92
Biggin La, Grays 171 GH79
Biggin Way SE19 181 DP94
Bigginwood Rd SW16 181 DP94
Biggs Gro Rd (Cheshunt), Wal.Cr. 66 DR26
Biggs Row SW15 159 CX83
Felsham Rd
Bigland St E1 142 DV72
Bignell Rd SE18 165 EP78
Bignold Rd E7 124 EG63
Bigwood Rd NW11 120 DB57
Biko Cl, Uxb. 134 BJ72
Sefton Way
Bill Hamling Cl SE9 185 EM89
Bill Nicholson Way N17 122 DT55
High Rd
Billet Cl, Rom. 126 EX55
Billet La, Berk. 38 AU18
Billet La, Horn. 128 FK60
Billet La, Iver 133 BB69
Billet La, Slou. 133 BB73
Billet Rd E17 101 DX54
Billet Rd, Rom. 126 EV55
Billet Rd, Stai. 174 BG90
Farnell Rd
Billet Wks E17 101 DZ53
Billets Hart Cl W7 157 CE75
Billing Pl SW10 160 DB80
Billing Rd SW10 160 DB80
Billing St SW10 160 DB80
Billingford Cl SE4 163 DX84
Billings Cl, Dag. 146 EW66
Ellerton Rd
Billington Rd SE14 163 DX80
Billiter Sq EC3 275 N10
Billiter St EC3 275 N9
Billiter St EC3 142 DS72
Billockby Cl, Chess. 216 CM107
Billson St E14 163 EC77
Billy Lows La, Pot.B. 64 DA31
Bilsby Gro SE9 184 EK91
Bilton Cl (Poyle), Slou. 153 BE82
Bilton Rd, Erith 167 FG79
Bilton Rd, Grnf. 137 CJ67
Bilton Way, Enf. 83 DY39
Bilton Way, Hayes 155 BV75
Bina Gdns SW5 160 DC77
Bincote Rd, Enf. 81 DM41
Binden Rd W12 159 CT76
Bindon Grn, Mord. 200 DB98
Binfield Rd SW4 161 DL81
Binfield Rd, S.Croy. 220 DT106
Binfield Rd (Byfleet), W.Byf. 212 BL112
Bingfield St N1 141 DL67
Bingham Cl, Hem.H. 39 BF18
Bingham Cl, S.Ock. 149 FV72
Bingham Ct N1 141 DP66
Halton Rd
Bingham Dr, Stai. 174 BK94
Bingham Dr, Wok. 226 AT118
Bingham Pl W1 272 F6
Bingham Pt SE18 165 EP77
Whitworth Pl
Bingham Rd, Croy. 202 DU102
Bingham Rd (Burnham), Slou. 130 AG71
Bingham St N1 142 DR65
Bingley Rd E16 144 EJ72

Bin - Bla This index reads in the sequence: Street Name / Postal District or Post Town / Map Page Number / Grid Reference

Bingley Rd, Grnf. 136 CC71
Bingley Rd, Hodd. 49 EC17
Bingley Rd, Sun. 175 BU94
Binley Ho SW15 179 CU86
Highcliffe Dr
Binney St W1 272 G10
Binney St W1 140 DG72
Binns Rd W4 158 CS78
Binns Ter W4 158 CS78
Binns Rd
Binscombe Cres, Gdmg. 258 AS144
Binsey Wk SE2 146 EW74
Binyon Cres, Stan. 95 CF50
Birbetts Rd SE9 185 EM89
Birch Av N13 100 DQ48
Birch Av, Cat. 236 DR124
Birch Av, Lthd. 231 CF120
Birch Av, West Dr. 134 BM72
Birch Circle, Gdmg. 258 AT143
Birch Cl E16 144 EE71
Birch Cl N19 *Hargrave Pk* 121 DJ61
Birch Cl SE15 162 DU82
Bournemouth Rd
Birch Cl (New Haw), Add. 212 BK109
Birch Cl, Amer. 55 AS37
Birch Cl, Brent. 157 CH80
Birch Cl, Buck.H. 102 EK48
Birch Cl (Eynsford), Dart. 208 FK104
Birch Cl, Houns. 157 CD83
Birch Cl, Iver 133 BD68
Birch Cl, Rom. 127 FB55
Birch Cl, Sev. 257 FH123
Birch Cl, S.Ock. 149 FX69
Birch Cl, Tedd. 177 CG92
Birch Cl, Wok. 226 AW119
Birch Cl (Send Marsh), Wok. 243 BF125
Birch Copse (Bricket Wd), St.Alb. 60 BY30
Birch Ct, Nthwd. 93 BQ51
Rickmansworth Rd
Birch Cres, Horn. 128 FL56
Birch Cres, S.Ock. 149 FX69
Birch Cres, Uxb. 134 BM67
Birch Dr, Hat. 45 CU19
Birch Dr, Rick. 91 BD50
Birch Gdns, Amer. 55 AS39
Birch Gdns, Dag. 127 FC62
Birch Grn NW9 96 CS52
Clayton Fld
Birch Grn, Hem.H. 39 BF19
Birch Grn, Hert. 31 DJ12
Birch Grn, Stai. 174 BG91
Birch Gro E11 124 EE62
Birch Gro SE12 184 EF87
Birch Gro W3 138 CN74
Birch Gro, Cob. 214 BW114
Birch Gro, Pot.B. 64 DA32
Birch Gro, Shep. 195 BS96
Birch Gro, Slou. 131 AP71
Birch Gro, Tad. 233 CY124
Birch Gro, Well. 166 EU84
Birch Gro, Wind. 151 AK81
Birch Gro, Wok. 227 BD115
Birch Hill, Croy. 221 DX106
Birch La (Flaunden), Hem.H. 57 BB33
Birch La, Pur. 219 DL111
Birch Leys, Hem.H. 41 BQ15
Hunters Oak
Birch Mead, Orp. 205 EN103
Birch Pk, Har. 94 CC52
Birch Pl, Green. 189 FS86
Birch Rd, Felt. 176 BX92
Birch Rd, Gdmg. 258 AT143
Birch Rd, Rom. 127 FB55
Birch Row, Brom. 205 EN101
Birch Tree Av, W.Wick. 222 EF106
Birch Tree Gro (Ley Hill), Chesh. 56 AV30
Birch Tree Wk, Wat. 75 BT37
Birch Tree Way, Croy. 202 DV103
Birch Vale, Cob. 214 CA112
Birch Vw, Epp. 70 EV29
Birch Wk, Borwd. 78 CN39
Birch Wk, Erith 167 FC79
Birch Wk, Mitch. 201 DH95
Birch Wk, W.Byf. 212 BG112
Birch Way, Chesh. 54 AR29
Birch Way, Hat. 45 CV16
Crawford Rd
Birch Way (London Colney), St.Alb. 61 CK27
Birch Way, Warl. 237 DY118
Birch Wd, Rad. 62 CN34
Birchall La, Hert. 30 DF12
Birchall Wd, Welw.G.C. 30 DC10
Bircham Path SE4 163 DX84
St. Norbert Rd
Birchanger Rd SE25 202 DU99
Birchcroft Cl, Cat. 252 DQ125
Birchdale, Ger.Cr. 112 AX60
Birchdale Cl, W.Byf. 212 BJ111
Birchdale Gdns, Rom. 126 EX59
Birchdale Rd E7 124 EJ64
Birchdene Dr SE28 166 EU75
Birchen Cl NW9 118 CR61
Birchen Gro NW9 118 CR61
Birchend Cl, S.Croy. 220 DR107
Bircherley Ct, Hert. 32 DR09
Priory St
Bircherley Grn Cen, The, Hert. 32 DR09
Green St
Bircherley St, Hert. 32 DR09
Birches, The N21 81 DM44
Birches, The SE7 164 EH79
Birches, The, Beac. 88 AH53
Birches, The, Brwd. 108 FY48
Birches, The, Bushey 76 CC43
Birches, The, Epp. 71 FB26
Birches, The, Hem.H. 39 BF23
Birches, The (East Horsley), Lthd. 245 BS126
Birches, The, Orp. 223 EN105
Birches, The, Swan. 207 FE96
Birches, The, Wok. 227 AZ118
Heathside Rd
Birches Cl, Epsom 232 CS115
Birches Cl, Mitch. 200 DF97
Birches Cl, Pnr. 116 BY57
Birchfield Cl, Add. 212 BH105
Birchfield Cl, Couls. 235 DM116
Birchfield Gro, Epsom 217 CW110
Birchfield Rd (Cheshunt), Wal.Cr. 66 DV29
Birchfield St E14 143 EA73
Birchgate Ms, Tad. 233 CW121
Bidhams Cres
Birchin La EC3 275 L9
Birchin La EC3 142 DR72
Birchington Cl, Bexh. 167 FB81
Birchington Cl, Orp. 206 EW102
Hart Dyke Rd
Birchington Rd N8 121 DK58
Birchington Rd NW6 140 DA67
Birchington Rd, Surb. 198 CM101
Birchington Rd, Wind. 151 AN82
Birchlands Av SW12 180 DF87
Birchmead, Wat. 75 BT38
Birchmead Av, Pnr. 116 BW56
Birchmead Cl, St.Alb. 43 CD17
Birchmere Row SE3 164 EF82
Birchmore Wk N5 122 DQ62
Birchville Ct, Bushey 95 CE46
Heathbourne Rd
Birchway, Hayes 135 BU74
Birchway, Red. 267 DH136
Birchwood, Wal.Abb. 68 EE34
Roundhills
Birchwood Av N10 120 DG55
Birchwood Av, Beck. 203 DZ98
Birchwood Av, Hat. 45 CU16
Birchwood Av, Sid. 186 EW89
Birchwood Av, Wall. 200 DG104
Birchwood Cl, Brwd. 107 FW51
Canterbury Way
Birchwood Cl, Hat. 45 CU16
Birchwood Cl, Horl. 269 DH147
Birchwood Cl, Mord. 200 DB98
Birchwood Ct N13 99 DP50
Birchwood Ct, Edg. 96 CQ54
Birchwood Dr NW3 120 DB62
Birchwood Dr, Dart. 187 FE91
Birchwood Dr, W.Byf. 212 BG112
Birchwood Gro, Hmptn. 176 CA93
Birchwood La, Cat. 251 DP125
Birchwood La, Esher 215 CD110
Birchwood La, Lthd. 215 CD110
Birchwood La (Knockholt), Sev. 240 EZ115
Birchwood Pk Av, Swan. 207 FE97
Birchwood Rd SW17 181 DH92
Birchwood Rd, Dart. 187 FE92
Birchwood Rd, Orp. 205 ER98
Birchwood Rd, Swan. 207 FC95
Birchwood Rd, W.Byf. 212 BG112
Birchwood Ter, Swan. 207 FC95
Birchwood Rd
Birchwood Way (Park St), St.Alb. 60 CB28
Bird in Bush Rd SE15 162 DU80
Bird La, Brwd. 129 FX55
Bird La, Upmin. 129 FR57
Bird La (Harefield), Uxb. 92 BJ54
Bird St W1 272 G9
Bird Wk, Twick. 176 BZ88
Bird-in-Hand La, Brom. 204 EK96
Bird-in-Hand Pas SE23 182 DW89
Dartmouth Rd
Birdbrook Cl, Brwd. 109 GB44
Birdbrook Cl, Dag. 147 FC66
Birdbrook Rd SE3 164 EJ83
Birdcage Wk SW1 277 L5
Birdcage Wk SW1 161 DJ75
Birdcage Wk, Harl. 35 EQ14
Birdcroft Rd, Welw.G.C. 29 CW09
Birdham Cl, Brom. 204 EL99
Birdhouse La, Orp. 239 EN115
Birdhurst Av, S.Croy. 220 DR105
Birdhurst Gdns, S.Croy. 220 DR105
Birdhurst Ri, S.Croy. 220 DS106
Birdhurst Rd SW18 160 DC84
Birdhurst Rd SW19 180 DE93
Birdhurst Rd, S.Croy. 220 DS106
Birdie Way, Hert. 32 DV08
Birdlip Cl SE15 162 DS79
Birds Cl, Welw.G.C. 30 DB11
Birds Fm Av, Rom. 105 FB53
Birds Hill Dr (Oxshott), Lthd. 215 CD113
Birds Hill Ri (Oxshott), Lthd. 215 CD113
Birds Hill Rd (Oxshott), Lthd. 215 CD112
Birdsfield La E3 143 DZ67
Birdswood Dr, Wok. 226 AS119
Birdwood Cl, S.Croy. 221 DX111
Birdwood Cl, Tedd. 177 CE91
Birfield Rd (Loudwater), H.Wyc. 88 AC53
Birkbeck Av W3 138 CQ73
Birkbeck Av, Grnf. 136 CC67
Birkbeck Gdns, Wdf.Grn. 102 EF47
Birkbeck Gro W3 158 CR75
Birkbeck Hill SE21 181 DP89
Birkbeck Ms E8 122 DT64
Sandringham Rd
Birkbeck Pl SE21 182 DQ88
Birkbeck Rd E8 122 DT64
Birkbeck Rd N8 121 DL56
Birkbeck Rd N12 98 DC50
Birkbeck Rd N17 100 DT53
Birkbeck Rd NW7 97 CT50
Birkbeck Rd SW19 180 DB92
Birkbeck Rd W3 138 CR74
Birkbeck Rd W5 157 CJ77
Birkbeck Rd, Beck. 202 DW96
Birkbeck Rd, Brwd. 109 GD44
Birkbeck Rd, Enf. 82 DR39
Birkbeck Rd, Ilf. 125 ER57
Birkbeck Rd, Rom. 127 FD60
Birkbeck Rd, Sid. 186 EU90
Birkbeck St E2 142 DV69
Birkbeck Way, Grnf. 136 CC67
Birkdale Av, Pnr. 116 CA55
Birkdale Av, Rom. 106 FM52
Birkdale Cl SE16 162 DV78
Masters Dr
Birkdale Cl, Orp. 205 ER101
Birkdale Gdns, Croy. 221 DX105
Birkdale Gdns, Wat. 94 BX48
Birkdale Rd SE2 166 EU77
Birkdale Rd W5 138 CL71
Birken Ms, Nthwd. 93 BP50
Birkenhead Av, Kings.T. 198 CM96
Birkenhead St WC1 274 A2
Birkenhead St WC1 141 DL69
Birkett Way, Ch.St.G. 72 AX41
Birkhall Rd SE6 183 ED88
Birkheads Rd, Reig. 250 DA133
Birklands La, St.Alb. 61 CH25
Birklands Pk, St.Alb. 43 CH24
Birkwood Cl SW12 181 DK87
Birley Rd N20 98 DC47
Birley Rd, Slou. 131 AR72
Birley St SW11 160 DG82
Birling Rd, Erith 167 FD80
Birnam Rd N4 121 DM61
Birnham Cl (Send Marsh), Wok. 228 BG123
Birrell Ho SW9 161 DM82
Stockwell Rd
Birse Cres NW10 118 CS63
Birstall Grn, Wat. 94 BX49
Birstall Rd N15 122 DS57
Birtley Path, Borwd. 78 CL39
Biscay Rd W6 159 CX78
Biscoe Cl, Houns. 156 CA79
Biscoe Way SE13 163 ED83
Bisenden Rd, Croy. 202 DS103
Bisham Cl, Cars. 200 DF102
Bisham Gdns N6 120 DG60
Bishop Butt Cl, Orp. 205 ET104
Stapleton Rd
Bishop Cen (Taplow), Maid. 130 AF72
Bishop Cl W4 158 CQ78
Bishop Duppa's Pk, Shep. 195 BR101
Bishop Fox Way, W.Mol. 196 BZ98
Bishop Ken Rd, Har. 95 CF54
Bishop Kings Rd W14 159 CY77
Bishop Rd N14 99 DH45
Bishop Sq Business Pk, Hat. 44 CS17
Bishop St N1 142 DQ67
Bishop Wk, Brwd. 109 FZ47
Bishop Way NW10 138 CS66
Bishop Wilfred Wd Cl SE15 162 DU82
Moncrieff St
Bishop's Av E13 144 EH67
Bishop's Av SW6 159 CX82
Bishops Av, Borwd. 78 CM43
Bishops Av, Brom. 204 EJ96
Bishops Av, Nthwd. 93 BS49
Bishops Av, Rom. 126 EW58
Bishops Av, The N2 120 DD59
Bishops Br W2 140 DC71
Bishops Br Rd W2 140 DC72
Bishops Cl E17 123 EB56
Bishops Cl N19 121 DJ62
Wyndham Cres
Bishops Cl SE9 185 EQ89
Bishops Cl, Barn. 79 CX44
Bishop's Cl, Couls. 235 DN118
Bishops Cl, Enf. 82 DV40
Central Av
Bishops Cl, Hat. 45 CT18
Bishops Cl, Rich. 177 CK90
Bishops Cl, St.Alb. 43 CG16
Bishop's Cl, Sutt. 200 DA104
Bishops Cl, Uxb. 134 BN68
Bishop's Ct EC4 274 F8
Bishop's Ct WC2 274 D8
Bishops Ct, Green. 189 FS85
Bishops Ct, Wal.Cr. 66 DV30
Churchgate
Bishops Dr, Felt. 175 BR86
Bishops Dr, Nthlt. 136 BY67
Bishops Fm Cl (Oakley Grn), Wind. 150 AH82
Bishops Garth, St.Alb. 43 CG16
Bishops Cl
Bishops Gro N2 120 DD58
Bishops Gro, Hmptn. 176 BZ91
Bishop's Hall, Kings.T. 197 CK96
Bishops Hall Rd, Brwd. 108 FV44
Bishops Hill, Walt. 195 BU101
Bishops Mead, Hem.H. 40 BH22
Bishops Orchard (Farnham Royal), Slou. 131 AP69
Bishop's Pk SW6 159 CX82
Bishop's Pk Rd SW6 159 CX82
Bishops Pk Rd SW16 201 DL95
Bishops Pl, Sutt. 218 DC106
Lind Rd
Bishops Ri, Hat. 45 CT22
Bishops Rd N6 120 DG58
Bishops Rd SW6 159 CZ81
Bishops Rd W7 157 CE75
Bishops Rd, Croy. 201 DP101
Bishops Rd, Hayes 135 BQ71
Bishops Rd, Slou. 152 AU75
Bishops Ter SE11 278 E8
Bishops Ter SE11 161 DN77
Bishops Wk, Chis. 205 EQ95
Bishops Wk, Croy. 221 DX106
Bishops Wk (Wooburn Grn), H.Wyc. 110 AE58
Bishop's Wk, Pnr. 116 BY55
High St
Bishops Way E2 142 DV68
Bishops Way, Egh. 173 BD93
Bishops Wd, Wok. 226 AT117
Bishopsfield, Harl. 51 ES18
Bishopsford Rd, Mord. 200 DC101
Bishopsgate EC2 275 N7
Bishopsgate EC2 142 DS72
Bishopsgate Arc EC2 275 N7
Bishopsgate Chyd EC2 275 M8
Bishopsgate Rd (Englefield Grn), Egh. 172 AT90
Bishopsmead Cl (East Horsley), Lthd. 245 BS128
Ockham Rd S
Bishopsmead Dr (East Horsley), Lthd. 245 BT129
Bishopsmead Par (East Horsley), Lthd. 245 BS129
Ockham Rd S
Bishopsthorpe Rd SE26 183 DX91
Bishopswood Rd N6 120 DF59
Biskra, Wat. 75 BU39
Bisley Cl, Wal.Cr. 67 DX33
Bisley Cl, Wor.Pk. 199 CW102
Bisley Ho SW19 179 CX89
Bispham Rd NW10 138 CM69
Bisson Rd E15 143 EC68
Bisterne Av E17 123 ED55
Bittacy Cl NW7 97 CX51
Bittacy Hill NW7 97 CX51
Bittacy Pk Av NW7 97 CX51
Bittacy Ri NW7 97 CW51
Bittacy Rd NW7 97 CX51
Bittams La, Cher. 211 BE105
Bittern Cl, Hayes 136 BX71
Bittern Cl (Cheshunt), Wal.Cr. 66 DQ25
Bittern St SE1 279 H5
Bitterne Dr, Wok. 226 AT117
Bittoms, The, Kings.T. 197 CK97
Bixley Cl, Sthl. 156 BZ77
Black Acre Cl, Amer. 55 AS39
Black Boy La N15 122 DQ57
Black Boy Wd (Bricket Wd), St.Alb. 60 CA30
Black Cut, St.Alb. 43 CE21
Black Eagle Cl, West. 255 EQ127
Black Fan Cl, Enf. 82 DQ39
Black Fan Rd, Welw.G.C. 30 DB09
Black Friars Ct EC4 274 F10
Black Friars La EC4 274 F10
Black Friars La EC4 141 DP73
Black Gates, Pnr. 116 BZ55
Church La
Black Horse Av, Chesh. 54 AR33
Black Horse Cl, Wind. 151 AK81
Black Horse Ct SE1 279 L6
Black Horse Pl, Uxb. 134 BJ67
Waterloo Rd
Black Lake Cl, Egh. 193 BA95
Black Lion Ct, Harl. 36 EW11
Black Lion Hill, Rad. 62 CL32
Black Lion La W6 159 CU77
Black Lion Ms W6 159 CU77
Black Lion La
Black Pk Rd, Slou. 133 AZ68
Black Path E10 123 DX59
Black Prince Cl (Byfleet), W.Byf. 212 BM114
Black Prince Rd SE1 278 B9
Black Prince Rd SE1 161 DM77
Black Prince Rd SE11 278 C9
Black Prince Rd SE11 161 DM77
Black Rod Cl, Hayes 155 BT76
Black Swan Ct, Ware 33 DX06
Baldock St
Black Swan Yd SE1 279 N4
Blackacre Rd, Epp. 85 ES37
Blackall St EC2 275 M4
Blackberry Cl, Guil. 242 AV131
Blackberry Cl, Shep. 195 BS98
Cherry Way
Blackberry Fm Cl, Houns. 156 BY80
Blackberry Fld, Orp. 206 EU95
Blackbird Hill NW9 118 CQ61
Blackbird Yd E2 142 DT69
Ravenscroft St
Blackbirds La, Wat. 77 CD35
Blackborne Rd, Dag. 146 FA65
Blackborough Cl, Reig. 250 DC134
Blackborough Rd, Reig. 266 DC135
Blackbridge Rd, Wok. 226 AX119
Blackbrook La, Brom. 205 EN97
Blackbrook Rd, Dor. 263 CK140
Blackburn, The, Lthd. 230 BZ124
Little Bookham St
Blackburn Rd NW6 140 DB65
Blackburn Trd Est (Stanwell), Stai. 174 BM86
Blackburnie's Ms W1 272 F10
Blackburnie's Ms W1 140 DG73
Blackbury Cl, Pot.B. 64 DC31
Blackbush Av, Rom. 126 EX57
Blackbush Cl, Sutt. 218 DB108
Blackbush Spring, Harl. 36 EU14
Blackdale (Cheshunt), Wal.Cr. 66 DU27
Blackdown Av, Wok. 227 BE115
Blackdown Cl N2 98 DC54
Blackdown Cl, Wok. 227 BC116
Blackdown Ter SE18 165 EN80
Prince Imperial Rd
Blackett Cl, Stai. 193 BE96
Blackett St SW15 159 CX83
Blacketts Wd Dr, Rick. 73 BB43
Blackfen Rd, Sid. 185 ES85
Blackford Cl, S.Croy. 219 DP109
Blackford Rd, Wat. 94 BX50
Blackford's Path SW15 179 CU87
Roehampton High St
Blackfriars Br EC4 274 F10
Blackfriars Br EC4 141 DP73
Blackfriars Br SE1 274 F10
Blackfriars Br SE1 141 DP73
Blackfriars Pas EC4 274 F10
Blackfriars Rd SE1 278 F5
Blackfriars Rd SE1 141 DP74
Blackhall La, Sev. 257 FK123
Blackhall Pl, Sev. 257 FL124
Blackhall La
Blackheath Av SE10 163 ED80
Blackheath Gro SE3 164 EF82
Blackheath Gro (Wonersh), Guil. 259 BB143
Blackheath Hill SE10 163 EC81
Blackheath La, Guil. 260 BH140
Blackheath Pk SE3 164 EF83
Blackheath Ri SE13 163 EC82
Blackheath Rd SE10 163 EB81
Blackheath Vale SE3 164 EE82
Blackheath Village SE3 164 EF82
Blackhills, Esher 214 CA109
Blackhorse Cl, Amer. 55 AS38
Blackhorse Cres, Amer. 55 AS38
Blackhorse La E17 123 DX56
Blackhorse La, Croy. 202 DU101
Blackhorse La, Epp. 71 FD25
Blackhorse La, Pot.B. 62 CS30
Blackhorse La, Reig. 250 DB129
Blackhorse Ms E17 123 DX55
Blackhorse La
Blackhorse Rd E17 123 DX56
Blackhorse Rd SE8 163 DY78
Blackhorse Rd, Sid. 186 EU91
Blackhorse Rd, Wok. 226 AS122
Blacklands Dr, Hayes 135 BQ70
Blacklands Meadow (Nutfield), Red. 251 DL133
Blacklands Rd SE6 183 EC91
Blacklands Ter SW3 276 D9
Blacklands Ter SW3 160 DF77
Blackley Cl, Wat. 75 BT37
Blackmans Cl, Dart. 188 FJ88
Blackmans La, Warl. 222 EE114
Blackmans Yd E2 142 DU70
Cheshire St
Blackmead (Riverhead), Sev. 256 FE121
Blackmoor La, Wat. 75 BR43
Blackmore Av, Sthl. 137 CD74
Blackmore Cl, Grays 170 GC78
Blackmore Ct, Wal.Abb. 68 EG33
Blackmore Cres, Wok. 227 BB115
Blackmore Rd, Buck.H. 102 EL45
Blackmore Way, Uxb. 134 BK65
Blackmores, Harl. 51 EP15
Blackmores Gro, Tedd. 177 CG93
Blackness La, Kes. 222 EK109
Blackness La, Wok. 226 AY119
Blacknest Rd, Vir.W. 192 AT97
Blackpond La (Farnham Common), Slou. 131 AP66
Blackpool Gdns, Hayes 135 BS70
Blackpool Rd SE15 162 DV82
Blacks Rd W6 159 CW77
Queen Caroline St
Blackshaw Pl N1 142 DS66
Hertford Rd
Blackshaw Rd SW17 180 DC91
Blackshots La, Grays 170 GD75
Blacksmith Cl, Ash. 232 CM119
Rectory La
Blacksmith Cl, Ware 33 DZ08
Blacksmith La (Chilworth), Guil. 259 BC139
Blacksmith Row, Slou. 153 BA77
Blacksmiths Cl, Rom. 126 EW58
Blacksmiths Hill, S.Croy. 220 DU113
Blacksmiths La, Cher. 194 BG101
Blacksmiths La, Orp. 206 EW99
Blacksmiths La, Rain. 147 FF67
Blacksmiths La, St.Alb. 42 CB20
Blacksmiths La, Stai. 194 BH97
Blacksmiths La (Denham), Uxb. 113 BC61
Blacksmiths Way, Saw. 36 EU06
Blackstock Ms N4 121 DP61
Blackstock Rd
Blackstock Rd N4 121 DP61
Blackstock Rd N5 121 DP61
Blackstone Cl, Red. 250 DE134
Blackstone Est E8 142 DV66
Blackstone Hill, Red. 266 DE135
Blackstone Rd NW2 119 CW64
Blackthorn Av, West Dr. 154 BN77
Blackthorn Cl, Reig. 266 DC136
Blackthorn Cl, St.Alb. 43 CJ17
Blackthorn Cl, Wat. 59 BV32
Blackthorn Ct, Houns. 156 BY80
Blackthorn Dell, Slou. 152 AW76
Blackthorn Gro, Bexh. 166 EY83
Blackthorn Rd, Reig. 266 DC136
Blackthorn Rd, Welw.G.C. 30 DA10
Blackthorn St E3 143 EA70
Blackthorn Way, Brwd. 108 FX50
Blackthorne Av, Croy. 202 DW101
Blackthorne Cl, Hat. 45 CT21
Blackthorne Cres (Colnbrook), Slou. 153 BE82
Blackthorne Rd
Blackthorne Dr E4 101 ED49
Blackthorne Rd (Bookham), Lthd. 246 CC126
Blackthorne Rd (Colnbrook), Slou. 153 BE83
Blackthorne Rd (Biggin Hill), West. 238 EK116
Blacktree Ms SW9 161 DN83
Blackwall La SE10 164 EE78
Blackwall Pier E14 144 EE73
Blackwall Trd Est E14 143 ED71
Blackwall Tunnel E14 143 ED74
Blackwall Tunnel App SE10 164 EE75
Blackwall Tunnel Northern App E3 143 EA68
Blackwall Tunnel Northern App E14 143 EA68
Blackwall Way E14 143 EC73
Blackwater Cl E7 124 EF63
Blackwater Cl, Rain. 147 FE71
Blackwater La, Hem.H. 41 BS23
Blackwater Rd, Sutt. 218 DB105
High St
Blackwater St SE22 182 DT85
Blackwell Cl E5 123 DX63
Blackwell Cl, Har. 95 CD52
Blackwell Dr, Wat. 76 BW44
Blackwell Gdns, Edg. 96 CN48
Blackwell Hall La, Chesh. 56 AW33
Blackwell Rd, Kings L. 58 BN29
Blackwood Cl, W.Byf. 212 BJ112
Blackwood Ct, Brox. 67 DZ26
Groom Rd
Blackwood St SE17 279 K10
Blackwood St SE17 162 DR78
Blade Ms SW15 159 CZ84
Deodar Rd
Bladen Cl, Wey. 213 BR107
Blades Cl, Lthd. 231 CK120
Blades Ct SW15 159 CZ84
Deodar Rd
Bladindon Dr, Bex. 186 EW87
Bladon Cl, Guil. 243 BA133
Bladon Gdns, Har. 116 CB58
Blagdens Cl N14 99 DJ47
Blagdens La N14 99 DK47
Blagdon Rd SE13 183 EB86
Blagdon Rd, N.Mal. 199 CT98
Blagdon Wk, Tedd. 177 CJ93
Blagrove Rd W10 139 CY71
Blair Av NW9 118 CS59
Blair Av, Esher 196 CC103
Blair Cl N1 142 DQ65
Blair Cl, Hayes 155 BU77
Blair Cl, Sid. 185 ES85
Blair Dr, Sev. 257 FH123
Blair Rd, Slou. 132 AS74
Blair St E14 143 EC72
Blairderry Rd SW2 181 DL89
Blairhead Dr, Wat. 93 BV48
Blake Av, Bark. 145 ES67
Blake Cl W10 139 CW71
Blake Cl, Cars. 200 DE101
Blake Cl, Rain. 147 FF67
Blake Cl, St.Alb. 43 CG23
Blake Cl, Well. 165 ES81
Blake Gdns SW6 160 DB81
Blake Gdns, Dart. 168 FM84
Blake Hall Cres E11 124 EG60
Blake Hall Rd E11 124 EG59
Blake Hall Rd, Ong. 71 FG25
Blake Ho, Beck. 183 EA93
Blake Rd E16 144 EF70
Blake Rd N11 99 DJ52
Blake Rd, Croy. 202 DS103
Blake Rd, Mitch. 200 DE97
Blake St SE8 163 EA79
Watergate St
Blakeborough Dr, Rom. 106 FL54
Blakeden Dr (Claygate), Esher 215 CF107
Blakehall Rd, Cars. 218 DF107
Blakeley Cotts SE10 163 ED75
Tunnel Av
Blakemere Rd, Welw.G.C. 29 CX07
Blakemore Rd SW16 181 DL90
Blakemore Rd, Th.Hth. 201 DM99
Blakemore Way, Belv. 166 EY76
Blakeney Av, Beck. 203 DZ95
Blakeney Cl E8 122 DU64
Ferncliff Rd
Blakeney Cl N20 98 DC46
Blakeney Cl NW1 141 DK66
Rossendale Way
Blakeney Cl, Epsom 216 CR111
Blakeney Rd, Beck. 183 DZ94
Blakenham Rd SW17 180 DF91
Blaker Ct SE7 164 EJ80
Fairlawn
Blaker Rd E15 143 EC67
Blakes Av, N.Mal. 199 CT99
Blakes Ct, Saw. 36 EY05
Church St
Blake's Grn, W.Wick. 203 EC102
Blakes La (East Clandon), Guil. 244 BL132
Blakes La (West Horsley), Lthd. 244 BM131
Blakes La, N.Mal. 199 CT99
Blakes Rd SE15 162 DS80
Blakes Ter, N.Mal. 199 CU99
Blakes Way, Til. 171 GJ82
Coleridge Rd
Blakesley Av W5 137 CJ72
Blakesley Wk SW20 199 CZ96
Kingston Rd
Blakesware Gdns N9 100 DR45
Blakewood Cl, Felt. 176 BW91
Blanch Cl SE15 162 DW80
Culmore Rd
Blanchard Cl SE9 184 EL90
Blanchard Gro, Enf. 83 EA37
Government Row
Blanchard Way E8 142 DU65
Blanchards Hill, Guil. 242 AY128

Blanche La, Pot.B. 63 CT34
Blanche St E16 144 EF70
Blanchedowne SE5 162 DR84
Blanchland Rd, Mord. 200 DB99
Blanchmans Rd, Warl. 237 DY118
Bland St SE9 164 EK84
Blandfield Rd SW12 180 DG86
Blandford Av, Beck. 203 DY96
Blandford Av, Twick. 176 CB88
Blandford Cl N2 120 DC56
Blandford Cl, Croy. 201 DL104
Blandford Cl, Rom. 127 FB56
Blandford Cl, Slou. 152 AX76
Blandford Cl, Wok. 227 BB117
Blandford Ct, Slou. 152 AX76
Blandford Rd S
Blandford Cres E4 101 EC45
Blandford Rd W4 158 CS76
Blandford Rd W5 157 CK75
Blandford Rd, Beck. 202 DW96
Blandford Rd, St.Alb. 43 CG20
Blandford Rd, Sthl. 156 CA77
Blandford Rd, Tedd. 177 CD92
Blandford Rd N, Slou. 152 AX76
Blandford Rd S, Slou. 152 AX76
Blandford Sq NW1 272 C5
Blandford Sq NW1 140 DE70
Blandford St W1 272 E8
Blandford St W1 140 DG71
Blandford Waye, Hayes 136 BW72
Blaney Cres E6 145 EP69
Blanford Rd, Reig. 266 DC135
Blanmerle Rd SE9 185 EP88
Blann Cl SE9 184 EK86
Blantyre St SW10 160 DD80
Blantyre Wk SW10 160 DD80
Blantyre St
Blashford NW3 140 DF66
Blashford St SE13 183 ED87
Blasker Wk E14 163 EA78
Blattner Cl, Borwd. 78 CL42
Blawith Rd, Har. 117 CE56
Blaxland Ter (Cheshunt), Wal.Cr. 67 DX28
Davison Dr
Blaydon Cl N17 100 DV52
Blaydon Cl, Ruis. 115 BS59
Blaydon Wk N17 100 DV52
Blays Cl (Englefield Grn), Egh. 172 AW93
Blays La (Englefield Grn), Egh. 172 AV94
Bleak Hill La SE18 165 ET79
Blean Gro SE20 182 DW94
Bleasdale Av, Grnf. 137 CG68
Blechynden St W10 139 CX73
Bramley Rd
Bleddyn Cl, Sid. 186 EW86
Bledlow Cl SE28 146 EW73
Bledlow Ri, Grnf. 136 CC68
Bleeding Heart Yd EC1 274 E7
Blegborough Rd SW16 181 DJ93
Blencarn Cl, Wok. 226 AT116
Blendon Dr, Bex. 186 EX86
Blendon Path, Brom. 184 EF94
Blendon Rd, Bex. 186 EX86
Blendon Ter SE18 165 EQ78
Blendworth Pt SW15 179 CV88
Wanborough Dr
Blendworth Way SE15 162 DS80
Daniel Gdns
Blenheim Av, Ilf. 125 EN58
Blenheim Cl N21 100 DQ46
Elm Pk Rd
Blenheim Cl SW20 199 CW97
Blenheim Cl, Dart. 188 FJ86
Blenheim Cl, Grnf. 137 CD68
Leaver Gdns
Blenheim Cl, Rom. 127 FC56
Blenheim Cl, Saw. 36 EW07
Blenheim Cl, Slou. 133 AZ74
Blenheim Cl, Upmin. 129 FS60
Blenheim Cl, Wall. 219 DJ108
Blenheim Cl, Wat. 94 BX45
Blenheim Cl, W.Byf. 211 BF113
Madeira Rd
Blenheim Ct N19 121 DL61
Marlborough Rd
Blenheim Ct, Sid. 185 ER90
Blenheim Ct, Sutt. 218 DC107
Wellesley Rd
Blenheim Ct, Wdf.Grn. 102 EJ52
Navestock Cres
Blenheim Cres W11 139 CY72
Blenheim Cres, Ruis. 115 BR61
Blenheim Cres, S.Croy. 220 DQ108
Blenheim Dr, Well. 165 ET81
Blenheim Gdns NW2 119 CW64
Blenheim Gdns SW2 181 DM86
Blenheim Gdns, Kings.T. 178 CP94
Blenheim Gdns, S.Croy. 220 DU112
Blenheim Gdns, S.Ock. 148 FP74
Blenheim Gdns, Wall. 219 DJ107
Blenheim Gdns, Wem. 118 CL62
Blenheim Gdns, Wok. 226 AV119
Blenheim Gro SE15 162 DU82
Blenheim Pk Rd, S.Croy. 220 DQ109
Blenheim Pas NW8 140 DC68
Blenheim Ter
Blenheim Ri N15 122 DT56
Talbot Rd
Blenheim Rd E6 144 EK69
Blenheim Rd E15 124 EE63
Blenheim Rd E17 123 DX55
Blenheim Rd NW8 140 DC68
Blenheim Rd SE20 182 DW94
Maple Rd
Blenheim Rd SW20 199 CW97
Blenheim Rd W4 158 CS76
Blenheim Rd, Abb.L. 59 BU33
Blenheim Rd, Barn. 79 CX41
Blenheim Rd, Brwd. 108 FU44
Blenheim Rd, Brom. 204 EL98
Blenheim Rd, Dart. 188 FJ86
Blenheim Rd, Epsom 216 CR111
Blenheim Rd, Har. 116 CB58
Blenheim Rd, Nthlt. 136 CB65
Blenheim Rd, Orp. 206 EW103
Blenheim Rd, St.Alb. 43 CF19
Blenheim Rd, Sid. 186 EW88
Blenheim Rd, Slou. 152 AX77
Blenheim Rd, Sutt. 200 DA104
Blenheim Shop Cen SE20 182 DW94
Blenheim St W1 273 H9
Blenheim Ter NW8 140 DC68
Blenheim Way, Epp. 70 FA27
Blenheim Way, Islw. 157 CG81
Blenhiem Ct, Welw.G.C. 29 CZ08
Blenkarne Rd SW11 180 DF86
Blenkin Cl, St.Alb. 42 CC16
Bleriot Rd, Houns. 156 BW80
Blessbury Rd, Edg. 96 CQ53
Blessing Way, Bark. 146 EW69
Blessington Cl SE13 163 ED83
Blessington Rd SE13 163 ED83
Bletchingley Cl, Red. 251 DJ129
Bletchingley Cl, Th.Hth. 201 DP98
Bletchingley Rd, Gdse. 252 DU131
Bletchingley Rd (Bletchingley), Red. 251 DN133
Bletchingley Rd (South Merstham), Red. 251 DJ129
Bletchley Ct N1 275 K1
Bletchley Ct N1 142 DR68
Bletchley St N1 275 J1
Bletchley St N1 142 DQ68
Bletchmore Cl, Hayes 155 BR78
Bletsoe Wk N1 142 DQ68
Cropley St
Blewbury Ho SE2 166 EX75
Yarnton Way
Bligh Rd, Grav. 191 GG86
Blighs Rd, Sev. 257 FH125
Blinco La (George Grn), Slou. 132 AY72
Blincoe Cl SW19 179 CX89
Blind La, Bans. 234 DE115
Blind La, Bet. 264 CQ137
Blind La (High Beach), Loug. 84 EE40
Blind La, Wal.Abb. 68 EJ33
Blindman's La (Cheshunt), Wal.Cr. 67 DX30
Bliss Cres SE13 163 EB82
Coldbath St
Bliss Ms W10 139 CY69
Third Av
Blissett St SE10 163 EC81
Blisworth Cl, Hayes 136 BY70
Braunston Dr
Blithbury Rd, Dag. 146 EV65
Blithdale Rd SE2 166 EU77
Blithfield St W8 160 DB76
Blockhouse Rd, Grays 170 GC79
Blockley Rd, Wem. 117 CH61
Bloemfontein Av W12 139 CV74
Bloemfontein Rd W12 139 CV73
Blomfield Rd W9 140 DC71
Blomfield St EC2 275 L7
Blomfield St EC2 142 DR71
Blomfield Vil W2 140 DB71
Blomville Rd, Dag. 126 EY62
Blondel St SW11 160 DG82
Blondell Cl, West Dr. 154 BK79
Blondin Av W5 157 CJ77
Blondin St E3 143 EA68
Bloom Gro SE27 181 DP90
Bloom Pk Rd SW6 159 CZ80
Bloomburg St SW1 277 L9
Bloomfield Cl (Knaphill), Wok. 226 AS118
Bloomfield Cres, Ilf. 125 EP58
Bloomfield Pl W1 273 J10
Bloomfield Pl W1 141 DH73
Bloomfield Rd N6 120 DG58
Bloomfield Rd SE18 165 EP78
Bloomfield Rd, Brom. 204 EK99
Bloomfield Rd, Kings.T. 198 CL98
Bloomfield Rd (Cheshunt), Wal.Cr. 66 DQ25
Bloomfield Ter SW1 276 G10
Bloomfield Ter SW1 160 DG78
Bloomfield Ter, West. 255 ES125
Bloomhall Rd SE19 182 DR92
Bloomsbury Cl W5 138 CM73
Bloomsbury Cl, Epsom 216 CR110
Bloomsbury Ct WC1 274 A7
Bloomsbury Ct, Guil. 259 AZ135
St. Lukes Sq
Bloomsbury Ct, Pnr. 116 BZ55
Bloomsbury Ho SW4 181 DK86
Bloomsbury Pl SW18 180 DC85
Fullerton Rd
Bloomsbury Pl WC1 274 A6
Bloomsbury Pl WC1 141 DL71
Bloomsbury Sq WC1 274 A7
Bloomsbury Sq WC1 141 DL71
Bloomsbury St WC1 273 N7
Bloomsbury St WC1 141 DK71
Bloomsbury Way WC1 273 P8
Bloomsbury Way WC1 141 DL72
Blore Cl SW8 161 DK81
Thessaly Rd
Blore Ct W1 273 M9
Blossom Cl W5 158 CL75
Almond Av
Blossom Cl, Dag. 146 EZ67
Blossom Cl, S.Croy. 220 DT106
Blossom La, Enf. 82 DQ39
Blossom Pl E1 275 N5
Blossom St E1 275 N6
Blossom St E1 142 DS70
Blossom Way, Uxb. 134 BM66
Blossom Way, West Dr. 154 BN77
Blossom Waye, Houns. 156 BY80
Blount St E14 143 DY71
Bloxam Gdns SE9 184 EL85
Bloxhall Rd E10 123 DZ60
Bloxham Cres, Hmptn. 196 BZ95
Bloxworth Cl, Wall. 201 DJ104
Blucher Rd SE5 162 DQ80
Blucher St, Chesh. 54 AP31
Blue Anchor All, Rich. 158 CL84
Kew Rd
Blue Anchor La SE16 162 DU77
Blue Anchor La, Til. 171 GL77
Blue Anchor Yd E1 142 DU73
Blue Ball La, Egh. 173 AZ92
Blue Ball Yd SW1 277 K3
Blue Barn La, Wey. 212 BN111
Blue Cedars, Bans. 217 CX114
Blue Cedars Pl, Cob. 214 BX112
Blue Ho Hill, St.Alb. 42 CA20
Blue Leaves Av, Couls. 235 DK122
Bluebell Av E12 124 EL64
Bluebell Cl E9 142 DW67
Moulins Rd
Bluebell Cl SE26 182 DT91
Bluebell Cl, Hem.H. 39 BE21
Sundew Rd
Bluebell Cl, Hert. 32 DU09
Bluebell Cl, Orp. 205 EQ103
Bluebell Cl, Rom. 127 FE61
Bluebell Cl, Wall. 201 DH102
Bluebell Ct, Wok. 226 AX119
Bluebell Dr, Abb.L. 59 BT27
Bluebell Dr, Wal.Cr. 66 DR28
Bluebell La (East Horsley), Lthd. 245 BS129
Bluebell Way, Hat. 29 CT14
Great Braitch La
Bluebell Way, Ilf. 145 EP65
Blueberry Cl, St.Alb. 43 CD16
Blueberry Cl, Wdf.Grn. 102 EG51
Blueberry Gdns, Couls. 235 DM116
Blueberry La (Knockholt), Sev. 240 EW116
Bluebird La, Dag. 146 FA66
Bluebird Way, St.Alb. 60 BY30
Bluebridge Av, Hat. 63 CZ27
Bluebridge Rd, Hat. 63 CY26
Bluecoat Ct, Hert. 32 DR09
Railway St
Bluecoat Yd, Ware 33 DX06
Bluecoats Av, Hert. 32 DS09
Bluefield Cl, Hmptn. 176 CA92
Bluegates (Ewell), Epsom 217 CU108
Bluehouse La, Oxt. 254 EG127
Bluehouse Rd E4 102 EE48
Bluelion Pl SE1 279 M6
Bluemans, Epp. 53 FD24
Bluemans End, Epp. 53 FD24
Bluett Rd (London Colney), St.Alb. 61 CK27
Bluewater Ho SW18 160 DB84
Smugglers Way
Bluewater Parkway (Bluewater), Green. 189 FS87
Bluewater Shop Cen, Green. 189 FT88
Blumfield Ct, Slou. 131 AK70
Blumfield Cres, Slou. 131 AK70
Blundel La (Stoke D'Abernon), Cob. 214 CB114
Blundell Av, Horl. 268 DF148
Blundell Cl, St.Alb. 43 CD16
Blundell Rd, Edg. 96 CR53
Blundell St N7 141 DL66
Blunden Cl, Dag. 126 EW60
Blunden Dr, Slou. 153 BB77
Blunesfield, Pot.B. 64 DD31
Blunt Rd, S.Croy. 220 DR106
Blunts Av, West Dr. 154 BN80
Blunts La, St.Alb. 60 BW27
Blunts Rd SE9 185 EN85
Blurton Rd E5 122 DW63
Blyth Cl E14 163 ED77
Manchester Rd
Blyth Cl, Borwd. 78 CM39
Blyth Cl, Twick. 177 CF86
Grimwood Rd
Blyth Rd E17 123 DZ59
Blyth Rd SE28 146 EW73
Blyth Rd, Brom. 204 EF95
Blyth Rd, Hayes 155 BS75
Blyth Wk, Upmin. 129 FS58
Blyth Wd Pk, Brom. 204 EF95
Blyth Rd
Blythe Cl SE6 183 DZ87
Blythe Cl, Iver 133 BF72
Blythe Hill SE6 183 DZ87
Blythe Hill, Orp. 205 ET95
Blythe Hill La SE6 183 DZ87
Blythe Rd W14 159 CX76
Blythe Rd, Hodd. 49 ED19
Blythe St E2 142 DV69
Blythe Vale SE6 183 DZ88
Blyth's Wf E14 143 DY73
Narrow St
Blythswood Rd, Ilf. 126 EU60
Blythway, Welw.G.C. 29 CZ06
Blythwood Rd N4 121 DL59
Blythwood Rd, Pnr. 94 BX53
Blyton Cl, Beac. 89 AK51
Boades Ms NW3 120 DD63
New End
Boadicea Cl, Slou. 131 AL74
Boadicea St N1 141 DM67
Copenhagen St
Boakes Cl NW9 118 CQ56
Boakes Meadow (Shoreham), Sev. 225 FF111
Boar Cl, Chig. 104 EU50
Boar Hill, Dor. 263 CF142
Board Sch Rd, Wok. 227 AZ116
Boardman Av E4 83 EB43
Boardman Cl, Barn. 79 CY43
Boardwalk Pl E14 143 EC74
Boarlands Cl, Slou. 131 AM73
Boarlands Path, Slou. 131 AM73
Brook Path
Boar's Head Yd, Brent. 157 CK80
Brent Way
Boars Rd, Harl. 36 FA14
Boat Lifter Way SE16 163 DY77
Sweden Gate
Boathouse Wk SE15 162 DT80
Boathouse Wk, Rich. 158 CL81
Bob Anker Cl E13 144 EG69
Chesterton Rd
Bob Marley Way SE24 161 DN84
Mayall Rd
Bobbin Cl SW4 161 DJ83
Bobby Moore Way N10 98 DF52
Bobs La, Rom. 105 FG52
Bocketts La, Lthd. 231 CF124
Bockhampton Rd, Kings.T. 178 CM94
Bocking St E8 142 DV67
Boddicott Cl SW19 179 CY89
Bodell Cl, Grays 170 GB76
Bodiam Cl, Enf. 82 DR40
Bodiam Rd SW16 181 DK94
Bodicea Ms, Houns. 176 BZ87
Bodle Av, Swans. 190 FY87
Bodley Cl, Epp. 69 ET30
Bodley Cl, N.Mal. 198 CS99
Bodley Manor Way SW2 181 DN87
Papworth Way
Bodley Rd, N.Mal. 198 CR100
Bodmin Av, Slou. 131 AN71
Bodmin Cl, Har. 116 BZ62
Bodmin Cl, Orp. 206 EW102
Bodmin Gro, Mord. 200 DB99
Bodmin St SW18 180 DA88
Bodnant Gdns SW20 199 CU97
Bodney Rd E8 122 DV64
Bodwell Cl, Hem.H. 39 BF19
Boeing Way, Sthl. 155 BV76
Boevey Path, Belv. 166 EZ79
Bogey La, Orp. 223 EN108
Bognor Gdns, Wat. 94 BW50
Bowring Grn
Bognor Rd, Well. 166 EX81
Bohemia, Hem.H. 40 BL19
Bohemia Pl E8 142 DV65
Bohn Rd E1 143 DY71
Bohun Gro, Barn. 80 DE44
Boileau Par W5 138 CM72
Boileau Rd
Boileau Rd SW13 159 CU80
Boileau Rd W5 138 CM72
Bois Av, Amer. 55 AP36
Bois Hall Rd, Add. 212 BK106
Bois Hill, Chesh. 54 AS34
Bois La, Amer. 55 AR35
Bois Moor Rd, Chesh. 54 AQ33
Boissy Cl, St.Alb. 44 CL21
Bolden St SE8 163 EB82
Bolderwood Way, W.Wick. 203 EB103
Boldmere Rd, Pnr. 116 BW59
Boleyn Av, Enf. 82 DV39
Boleyn Av, Epsom 217 CV110
Boleyn Cl E17 123 EA56
Boleyn Cl, Grays 170 FZ76
Clifford Rd
Boleyn Cl, Hem.H. 41 BQ15
Parr Cres
Boleyn Cl, Loug. 84 EL44
Roding Gdns
Boleyn Cl, Stai. 173 BE92
Chertsey La
Boleyn Ct, Brox. 49 DY21
Boleyn Ct, Buck.H. 102 EG46
Boleyn Dr, Ruis. 116 BX61
Boleyn Dr, St.Alb. 43 CD22
Boleyn Dr, W.Mol. 196 BZ97
Boleyn Gdns, Brwd. 109 GA48
Boleyn Gdns, Dag. 147 FC66
Boleyn Gdns, W.Wick. 203 EB103
Boleyn Gro, W.Wick. 203 EC103
Boleyn Rd E6 144 EK68
Boleyn Rd E7 144 EG66
Boleyn Rd N16 122 DS64
Boleyn Wk, Lthd. 231 CF120
Boleyn Way, Barn. 80 DC41
Boleyn Way, Ilf. 103 EQ51
Boleyn Way, Swans. 190 FY87
Bolina Rd SE16 162 DW78
Bolingbroke Gro SW11 160 DE84
Bolingbroke Rd W14 159 CX76
Bolingbroke Wk SW11 160 DD80
Bolingbroke Way, Hayes 135 BR74
Bolingbrook, St.Alb. 43 CG16
Bolliger Ct NW10 138 CQ70
Park Royal Rd
Bollo Br Rd W3 158 CP76
Bollo La W3 158 CP75
Bollo La W4 158 CQ77
Bolney Gate SW7 276 B5
Bolney St SW8 161 DM80
Bolney Way, Felt. 176 BY90
Bolsover Gro, Red. 251 DL129
Bolsover St W1 273 J5
Bolsover St W1 141 DH70
Bolstead Rd, Mitch. 201 DH95
Bolt Cellar La, Epp. 69 ES29
Bolt Ct EC4 274 E9
Bolters La, Bans. 217 CZ114
Bolters Rd, Horl. 268 DG146
Bolters Rd S, Horl. 268 DF146
Boltmore Cl NW4 119 CX55
Bolton Av, Wind. 151 AQ83
Bolton Cl SE20 202 DU96
Selby Rd
Bolton Cl, Chess. 215 CK107
Bolton Cres SE5 161 DP79
Bolton Cres, Wind. 151 AQ83
Bolton Gdns NW10 139 CX68
Bolton Gdns SW5 160 DB78
Bolton Gdns, Brom. 184 EF93
Bolton Gdns, Tedd. 177 CG93
Bolton Gdns Ms SW10 160 DB78
Bolton Rd E15 144 EF65
Bolton Rd N18 100 DT50
Bolton Rd NW8 140 DB67
Bolton Rd NW10 138 CS67
Bolton Rd W4 158 CQ80
Bolton Rd, Chess. 215 CK107
Bolton Rd, Har. 116 CC56
Bolton Rd, Wind. 151 AQ83
Bolton St W1 277 J2
Bolton St W1 141 DH74
Bolton Wk N7 121 DM61
Durham Rd
Boltons, The SW10 160 DC78
Boltons, The, Wem. 117 CF63
Boltons, The, Wdf.Grn. 102 EG49
Boltons Cl, Wok. 228 BG116
Boltons La, Hayes 155 BQ80
Boltons La, Wok. 228 BG116
Boltons Pl SW5 160 DC78
Bombay St SE16 162 DV77
Bombers La, West. 239 ER119
Bomer Cl, West Dr. 154 BN80
Bomore Rd W11 139 CX73
Bon Marche Ter Ms SE27 182 DS91
Gipsy Rd
Bonar Pl, Chis. 184 EL94
Bonar Rd SE15 162 DU80
Bonaventure Ct, Grav. 191 GM91
Bonchester Cl, Chis. 185 EN94
Bonchurch Cl, Sutt. 218 DB108
Bonchurch Rd W10 139 CY71
Bonchurch Rd W13 137 CH74
Bond Cl (Knockholt), Sev. 240 EX115
Bond Cl, West Dr. 134 BM72
Bond Ct EC4 275 K9
Bond Ct EC4 142 DR72
Bond Gdns, Wall. 219 DJ105
Bond Rd, Mitch. 200 DE96
Bond Rd, Surb. 198 CM103
Bond Rd, Warl. 237 DX118
Bond St E15 124 EE64
Bond St W4 158 CS77
Bond St W5 137 CK73
Bond St (Englefield Grn), Egh. 172 AV92
Bond St, Grays 170 GC79
Bondfield Av, Hayes 135 BU69
Bondfield Rd E6 144 EL71
Lovage App
Bondfield Wk, Dart. 168 FM84
Bonding Yd Wk SE16 163 DY76
Finland St
Bonds La (Mid Holmwood), Dor. 263 CH142
Bondway SW8 161 DL79
Bone Mill La, Gdse. 253 DY134
Eastbourne Rd
Bonehurst Rd, Horl. 266 DG144
Bonehurst Rd (Salfords), Red. 266 DG142
Boneta Rd SE18 165 EM76
Bonfield Rd SE13 163 EC84
Bonham Gdns, Dag. 126 EX61
Bonham Rd SW2 181 DM85
Bonham Rd, Dag. 126 EX61
Bonheur Rd W4 158 CR75
Bonhill St EC2 275 L5
Bonhill St EC2 142 DR70
Boniface Gdns, Har. 94 CB52
Boniface Rd, Uxb. 115 BP62
Boniface Wk, Har. 94 CB52
Bonington Ho, Enf. 82 DU43
Ayley Cft
Bonington Rd, Horn. 128 FK64
Bonks Hill, Saw. 36 EX06
Bonner Hill Rd, Kings.T. 198 CM97
Bonner Rd E2 142 DW68
Bonner St E2 142 DW68
Bonner Wk, Grays 170 FZ76
Clifford Rd
Bonners Cl, Wok. 226 AY122
Bonnersfield Cl, Har. 117 CF58
Bonnersfield La, Har. 117 CG58
Bonnett Ms, Horn. 128 FL60
Bonneville Gdns SW4 181 DJ86
Bonney Gro (Cheshunt), Wal.Cr. 66 DU30
Bonney Way, Swan. 207 FE96
Bonnington Sq SW8 161 DM79
Bonnington Twr, Brom. 204 EL100
Bonningtons, Brwd. 109 GB48
Bonny St NW1 141 DJ66
Bonny's Rd, Reig. 265 CX135
Bonser Rd, Twick. 177 CF89
Bonsey Cl, Wok. 226 AY121
Bonsey La, Wok. 226 AY121
Bonseys La (Chobham), Wok. 211 AZ110
Bonsor Dr, Tad. 233 CY122
Bonsor St SE5 162 DS80
Bonville Gdns NW4 119 CU56
Handowe Cl
Bonville Rd, Brom. 184 EF92
Book Ms WC2 273 N9
Bookbinders' Cotts N20 98 DF48
Manor Dr
Booker Cl E14 143 DZ71
Wallwood St
Booker Rd N18 100 DU50
Bookham Ct, Lthd. 230 BZ123
Church Rd
Bookham Gro (Bookham), Lthd. 246 CB126
Bookham Ind Est (Bookham), Lthd. 230 BZ123
Bookham Rd (Downside), Cob. 230 BW119
Boone Ct N9 100 DW48
Boone St SE13 164 EE84
Boones Rd SE13 164 EE84
Boord St SE10 164 EE76
Boot St N1 275 M3
Boot St N1 142 DS69
Booth Cl E9 142 DV67
Victoria Pk Rd
Booth Cl SE28 146 EV73
Booth Dr, Stai. 174 BK93
Booth Rd NW9 96 CS54
Booth Rd, Croy. 201 DP103
Waddon New Rd
Boothby Rd N19 121 DK61
Booths Cl, Hat. 45 CX24
Booth's Ct (Hutton), Brwd. 109 GC44
Booth's Pl W1 273 L7
Bordars Rd W7 137 CE71
Bordars Wk W7 137 CE71
Borden Av, Enf. 82 DR44
Border Cres SE26 182 DV92
Border Gdns, Croy. 221 EB105
Border Rd SE26 182 DV92
Bordergate, Mitch. 200 DE95
Borders La, Loug. 85 EN42
Borderside, Slou. 132 AU72
Bordesley Rd, Mord. 200 DB98
Bordon Wk SW15 179 CU87
Boreas Wk N1 274 G1
Boreham Av E16 144 EG72
Boreham Cl E11 123 EC60
Hainault Rd
Boreham Holt, Borwd. 78 CM42
Boreham Rd N22 100 DQ54
Borehamwood Ind Pk, Borwd. 78 CR40
Borgard Rd SE18 165 EM77
Borkwood Pk, Orp. 223 ET105
Borkwood Way, Orp. 223 ES105
Borland Cl, Green. 189 FU85
Steele Av
Borland Rd SE15 162 DW84
Borland Rd, Tedd. 177 CH93
Bornedene, Pot.B. 63 CY31
Borneo St SW15 159 CW83
Borough, The (Brockham), Bet. 264 CN135
Borough High St SE1 279 H5
Borough High St SE1 162 DQ75
Borough Hill, Croy. 201 DP104
Borough Rd SE1 278 F6
Borough Rd SE1 161 DP76
Borough Rd, Islw. 157 CE81
Borough Rd, Kings.T. 198 CN95
Borough Rd, Mitch. 200 DE96
Borough Rd (Tatsfield), West. 238 EK121
Borough Sq SE1 279 H5
Borough Way, Pot.B. 63 CY32
Borrell Cl, Brox. 49 DY20
Borrett Cl SE17 162 DQ78
Penrose St
Borrodaile Rd SW18 180 DB86
Borrowdale Av, Har. 95 CG54
Borrowdale Cl, Egh. 173 BB94
Derwent Rd
Borrowdale Cl, Ilf. 124 EL56
Borrowdale Cl, S.Croy. 220 DT113
Borrowdale Ct, Enf. 82 DQ39
Borrowdale Ct, Hem.H. 40 BL17
Borrowdale Dr, S.Croy. 220 DT112
Borthwick Ms E15 124 EE63
Borthwick Rd
Borthwick Rd E15 124 EE63
Borthwick Rd NW9 119 CT58
West Hendon Bdy
Borthwick St SE8 163 EA78
Borwick Av E17 123 DZ55
Bosanquet Cl, Uxb. 134 BK70
Bosanquet Rd, Hodd. 49 EC15
Bosbury Rd SE6 183 EC90
Boscastle Rd NW5 121 DH62
Bosco Cl, Orp. 223 ET105
Strickland Way
Boscobel Pl SW1 276 G8
Boscobel Pl SW1 160 DG77
Boscobel St NW8 272 A5
Boscobel St NW8 140 DD70
Boscombe Av E10 123 ED59
Boscombe Av, Grays 170 GD77
Boscombe Av, Horn. 128 FK60
Boscombe Cl E5 123 DY64
Boscombe Cl, Egh. 193 BC95
Boscombe Gdns SW16 181 DL93
Boscombe Rd SW17 180 DG93
Boscombe Rd SW19 200 DB95
Boscombe Rd W12 139 CU74
Boscombe Rd, Wor.Pk. 199 CW102
Bose Cl N3 97 CY53
Claremont Pk
Bosgrove E4 101 EC46
Boshers Gdns, Egh. 173 AZ93
Boss St SE1 279 P4
Bostal Row, Bexh. 166 EZ83
Harlington Rd
Bostall Heath SE2 166 EW78
Bostall Hill SE2 166 EU78
Bostall La SE2 166 EV78

Bostall Manorway SE2 166 EV77
Bostall Pk Av, Bexh. 166 EY80
Bostall Rd, Orp. 186 EV94
Boston Gdns W4 158 CS79
Boston Gdns W7 157 CG77
Boston Gdns, Brent. 157 CG77
Boston Gro, Ruis. 115 BQ58
Boston Gro, Slou. 131 AQ72
Boston Manor Rd, Brent. 157 CH77
Boston Pk Rd, Brent. 157 CJ78
Boston Pl NW1 272 D5
Boston Pl NW1 140 DF70
Boston Rd E6 144 EL69
Boston Rd E17 123 EA58
Boston Rd W7 137 CE74
Boston Rd, Croy. 201 DM100
Boston Rd, Edg. 96 CQ52
Boston St E2 142 DU68
Audrey St
Boston Vale W7 157 CG77
Bostonthorpe Rd W7 157 CE75
Bosun Cl E14 163 EA75
Byng St
Bosville Av, Sev. 256 FG123
Bosville Dr, Sev. 256 FG123
Bosville Rd, Sev. 256 FG123
Boswell Cl, Orp. 206 EW100
Killewarren Way
Boswell Cl (Shenley), Rad. 62 CL32
Boswell Ct WC1 274 A6
Boswell Path, Hayes 155 BT77
Croyde Av
Boswell Rd, Th.Hth. 202 DQ98
Boswell St WC1 274 A6
Boswell St WC1 141 DL71
Bosworth Cl E17 101 DZ53
Bosworth Cres, Rom. 106 FJ51
Bosworth Rd N11 99 DK51
Bosworth Rd W10 139 CY70
Bosworth Rd, Barn. 80 DA41
Bosworth Rd, Dag. 126 FA63
Botany Bay La, Chis. 205 EQ96
Botany Cl, Barn. 80 DE42
Botany Rd (Northfleet), Grav. 170 GA83
Botany Way, Purf. 168 FP78
Boteley Cl E4 101 ED47
Botery's Cross, Red. 251 DP133
Botha Rd E13 144 EH71
Botham Cl, Edg. 96 CQ52
Pavilion Way
Botham Dr, Slou. 152 AS76
Kings Rd
Bothwell Cl E16 144 EF71
Bothwell Rd (New Addington), Croy. 221 EC110
Bothwell St W6 159 CX79
Delorme St
Botley La, Chesh. 56 AU30
Botley Rd, Chesh. 56 AT30
Botley Rd, Hem.H. 40 BN15
Botolph All EC3 275 M10
Botolph La EC3 275 M10
Botsford Rd SW20 199 CY96
Bott Rd (Hawley), Dart. 188 FM91
Bottom Ho Fm La, Ch.St.G. 90 AT45
Bottom La (Seer Grn), Beac. 89 AP51
Bottom La, Chesh. 56 AT34
Bottom La, Kings L. 74 BH35
Bottrells Cl, Ch.St.G. 90 AT47
Bottrells La (Coleshill), Amer. 89 AP46
Bottrells La, Ch.St.G. 90 AT47
Botts Ms W2 140 DA72
Chepstow Rd
Botts Pas W2 140 DA72
Chepstow Rd
Botwell Common Rd, Hayes 135 BR73
Botwell Cres, Hayes 135 BS72
Botwell La, Hayes 135 BS74
Boucher Cl, Tedd. 177 CF92
Boucher Dr (Northfleet), Grav. 191 GF90
Bouchier Wk, Rain. 147 FG65
Deere Av
Boughton Av, Brom. 204 EF101
Boughton Hall Av (Send), Wok. 227 BF124
Boughton Rd SE28 165 ES76
Boughton Way, Amer. 72 AW38
Boulcott St E1 143 DX72
Boulevard, The SW17 180 DG89
Balham High Rd
Boulevard, The, Pnr. 116 CA56
Pinner Rd
Boulevard, The, Wat. 75 BR43
Boulevard, The, Welw.G.C. 29 CZ07
Boulevard, The, Wdf.Grn. 103 EN52
Boulevard 25 Retail Pk, Borwd. 78 CN41
Boulmer Rd, Uxb. 134 BJ69
Boulogne Rd, Croy. 202 DQ100
Boulter Gdns, Rain. 147 FG65
Boulters Cl, Maid. 130 AC70
Boulters Cl, Slou. 151 AN75
Amerden Way
Boulters Ct, Maid. 130 AC70
Boulters Gdns, Maid. 130 AC70
Boulters La, Maid. 130 AC70
Boulters Lock Island, Maid. 130 AC69
Boulthurst Way, Oxt. 254 EH132
Boulton Ho, Brent. 158 CL78
Green Dragon La
Boulton Rd, Dag. 126 EY62
Boultwood Rd E6 144 EL72
Bounce, The, Hem.H. 40 BK18
Bounce Hill (Navestock), Rom. 87 FH38
Mill La
Bounces La N9 100 DV47
Bounces Rd N9 100 DV46
Boundaries Rd SW12 180 DF89
Boundaries Rd, Felt. 176 BW88
Boundary Av E17 123 DZ59
Boundary Cl SE20 202 DU96
Haysleigh Gdns
Boundary Cl, Barn. 79 CZ39
Boundary Cl, Ilf. 125 ES63
Loxford La
Boundary Cl, Kings.T. 198 CP97
Boundary Cl, Sthl. 156 CA78
Boundary Ct, Welw.G.C. 29 CZ13
Boundary La
Boundary Dr, Brwd. 109 GE45
Boundary Dr, Hert. 32 DR07
Boundary La E13 144 EK69
Boundary La SE17 162 DQ79
Boundary La, Welw.G.C. 29 CY12
Boundary Pas E2 275 P4
Boundary Pl (Wooburn Grn), H.Wyc. 110 AD55
Boundary Rd E13 144 EJ69
Boundary Rd E17 123 DZ59
Boundary Rd N9 82 DW44
Boundary Rd N22 121 DP55
Boundary Rd NW8 140 DB67
Boundary Rd SW19 180 DD93
Boundary Rd, Ashf. 174 BJ92
Boundary Rd, Bark. 145 EQ68
Boundary Rd, Cars. 219 DH107
Boundary Rd (Chalfont St. Peter), Ger.Cr. 90 AX52
Boundary Rd (Loudwater), H.Wyc. 88 AC54
Boundary Rd, Maid. 130 AE70
Boundary Rd, Pnr. 116 BX58
Boundary Rd, Rom. 127 FG58
Boundary Rd, St.Alb. 43 CE18
Boundary Rd, Sid. 185 ES85
Boundary Rd, Upmin. 128 FN62
Boundary Rd, Wall. 219 DH107
Boundary Rd, Wem. 118 CL62
Boundary Rd, Wok. 227 BA116
Boundary Row SE1 278 F4
Boundary St E2 275 P3
Boundary St E2 142 DT70
Boundary St, Erith 167 FF80
Boundary Way, Croy. 221 EA106
Boundary Way, Hem.H. 41 BQ18
Boundary Way, Wat. 59 BV32
Boundary Way, Wok. 227 BA115
Boundary Yd, Wok. 227 BA116
Boundary Rd
Boundfield Rd SE6 184 EE90
Bounds Grn Rd N11 99 DJ51
Bounds Grn Rd N22 99 DJ51
Bourchier Cl, Sev. 257 FH126
Bourchier St W1 273 M10
Bourdon Pl W1 273 J10
Bourdon Rd SE20 202 DW96
Bourdon St W1 277 H1
Bourdon St W1 141 DH73
Bourke Cl NW10 138 CS65
Mayo Rd
Bourke Cl SW4 181 DL86
Bourke Hill, Couls. 234 DF118
Bourlet Cl W1 273 K7
Bourn Av N15 122 DR56
Bourn Av, Barn. 80 DD43
Bourn Av, Uxb. 134 BN70
Bournbrook Rd SE3 164 EK83
Bourne, The N14 99 DK46
Bourne, The (Bovingdon), Hem.H. 57 BA27
Bourne, The, Ware 33 DX05
Bourne Av N14 99 DL47
Bourne Av, Cher. 194 BG97
Bourne Av, Hayes 155 BQ76
Bourne Av, Ruis. 116 BW64
Bourne Av, Wind. 151 AQ84
Bourne Cl, Brox. 49 DZ20
Bourne Cl (Chilworth), Guil. 259 BB140
Bourne Cl, T.Ditt. 197 CF103
Bourne Cl, Ware 33 DX05
Bourne Cl, W.Byf. 212 BH113
Bourne Ct, Ruis. 115 BV64
Bourne Dr, Mitch. 200 DD96
Bourne End, Horn. 128 FN59
Bourne End La, Hem.H. 39 BC22
Bourne End Mills, Hem.H. 39 BB22
Bourne End Rd, Maid. 110 AD62
Bourne End Rd, Nthwd. 93 BS49
Bourne Est EC1 274 D6
Bourne Est EC1 141 DN71
Bourne Gdns E4 101 EB49
Bourne Gro, Ash. 231 CK119
Bourne Hill N13 99 DL46
Bourne Ind Pk, Dart. 187 FE85
Bourne Rd
Bourne La, Cat. 236 DR121
Bourne Mead, Bex. 187 FD85
Bourne Meadow, Egh. 193 BB98
Bourne Pk Cl, Ken. 236 DS115
Bourne Pl W4 158 CR78
Dukes Av
Bourne Rd E7 124 EF62
Bourne Rd N8 121 DL58
Bourne Rd, Berk. 38 AT18
Bourne Rd, Bex. 187 FB86
Bourne Rd, Brom. 204 EK98
Bourne Rd, Bushey 76 CA43
Bourne Rd, Dart. 187 FC86
Bourne Rd, Gdmg. 258 AT143
Bourne Rd, Grav. 191 GM89
Bourne Rd, Red. 251 DJ130
Bourne Rd, Slou. 151 AQ75
Bourne Rd, Vir.W. 192 AX99
Bourne St SW1 276 F9
Bourne St SW1 160 DG77
Bourne St, Croy. 201 DP103
Waddon New Rd
Bourne Ter W2 140 DB71
Bourne Vale, Brom. 204 EG101
Bourne Vw, Grnf. 137 CF65
Bourne Vw, Ken. 236 DR115
Bourne Way, Add. 212 BJ106
Bourne Way, Brom. 204 EF103
Bourne Way, Epsom 216 CQ105
Bourne Way, Sutt. 217 CZ106
Bourne Way, Swan. 207 FC97
Bourne Way, Wok. 226 AX122
Bournebridge Cl, Brwd. 109 GE45
Bournebridge La, Rom. 104 EZ45
Bournefield Rd, Whyt. 236 DT118
Godstone Rd
Bournehall Av, Bushey 76 CA43
Bournehall La, Bushey 76 CA44
Bournehall Rd, Bushey 76 CA44
Bournemead Av, Nthlt. 135 BU68
Bournemead Cl, Nthlt. 135 BU68
Bournemead Way, Nthlt. 135 BV68
Bournemouth Cl SE15 162 DU82
Bournemouth Rd SE15 162 DU82
Bournemouth Rd SW19 200 DA95
Bourneside, Vir.W. 192 AU101
Bourneside Cres N14 99 DK46
Bourneside Gdns SE6 183 EC92
Bourneside Rd, Add. 212 BK105
Bournevale Rd SW16 181 DL91
Bournewood Rd SE18 166 EU80
Bournewood Rd, Orp. 206 EV101
Bournville Rd SE6 183 EA87
Bournwell Cl, Barn. 80 DF41
Bourton Cl, Hayes 135 BU74
Avondale Dr
Bousfield Rd SE14 163 DX82
Bousley Ri (Ottershaw), Cher. 211 BD108
Boutflower Rd SW11 160 DE84
Bouverie Gdns, Har. 117 CK58
Bouverie Gdns, Pur. 219 DL114
Bouverie Ms N16 122 DS61
Bouverie Rd
Bouverie Pl W2 272 A8
Bouverie Pl W2 140 DD72
Bouverie Rd N16 122 DS61
Bouverie Rd, Couls. 234 DG118
Bouverie Rd, Har. 116 CC58
Bouverie St EC4 274 E9
Bouverie St EC4 141 DN72
Bouverie Way, Slou. 152 AY78
Bouvier Rd, Enf. 82 DW38
Boveney Cl, Slou. 151 AN75
Amerden Way
Boveney New Rd (Eton Wick), Wind. 151 AL77
Boveney Rd SE23 183 DX87
Boveney Rd (Dorney), Wind. 150 AJ77
Boveney Wd La (Burnham), Slou. 110 AJ62
Bovey Way, S.Ock. 149 FV71
Bovill Rd SE23 183 DX87
Bovingdon Av, Wem. 138 CN65
Bovingdon Cl N19 121 DJ61
Junction Rd
Bovingdon Cres, Wat. 60 BX34
Bovingdon La NW9 96 CS53
Bovingdon Rd SW6 160 DB81
Bovingdon Sq, Mitch. 201 DL98
Leicester Av
Bow Arrow La, Dart. 188 FN86
Bow Br Est E3 143 EB69
Bow Chyd EC4 275 J9
Bow Common La E3 143 DY70
Bow Ind Pk E15 143 EA66
Bow La EC4 275 J9
Bow La EC4 142 DQ72
Bow La N12 98 DC53
Bow La, Mord. 199 CY100
Bow Rd E3 143 DZ69
Bow St E15 124 EE64
Bow St WC2 274 A9
Bow St WC2 141 DL72
Bowater Cl NW9 118 CR57
Bowater Cl SW2 181 DL86
Bowater Gdns, Sun. 196 BW96
Bowater Pl SE3 164 EH80
Bowater Ridge, Wey. 213 BR110
Bowater Rd SE18 164 EK76
Bowden Cl, Felt. 175 BS88
Bowden Dr, Horn. 128 FL60
Bowden St SE11 161 DN78
Bowditch SE8 163 DZ78
Bowdon Rd E17 123 EA59
Bowen Dr SE21 182 DS90
Bowen Rd, Har. 116 CC59
Bowen St E14 143 EB72
Bowens Wd, Croy. 221 DZ109
Bower Av SE10 164 EE81
Bower Cl, Nthlt. 136 BW68
Bower Cl, Rom. 105 FD52
Bower Ct, Epp. 70 EU32
Bower Ct, Wok. 227 BB116
Princess Rd
Bower Fm Rd (Havering-atte-Bower), Rom. 105 FC48
Bower Hill, Epp. 70 EU32
Bower Hill Cl (South Nutfield), Red. 267 DL137
Bower Hill Ind Est, Epp. 70 EU32
Bower Hill La (South Nutfield), Red. 267 DK135
Bower La (Eynsford), Dart. 208 FL104
Bower Rd, Swan. 187 FG94
Bower St E1 143 DX72
Bower Ter, Epp. 70 EU32
Bower Hill
Bower Vale, Epp. 70 EU32
Bower Way, Slou. 131 AM73
Bowerdean St SW6 160 DB81
Bowerman Av SE14 163 DY79
Bowerman Rd, Grays 171 GG77
Bowers Av (Northfleet), Grav. 191 GF91
Bowers Cl, Guil. 243 BA130
Cotts Wd Dr
Bowers Fm Dr, Guil. 243 BA130
Bowers La, Guil. 243 BA129
Bowers Rd (Shoreham), Sev. 225 FF111
Bowers Wk E6 145 EM72
Bowes Cl, Sid. 186 EV86
Bowes Rd N11 99 DH50
Bowes Rd N13 99 DL50
Bowes Rd W3 138 CS73
Bowes Rd, Dag. 126 EW63
Bowes Rd, Stai. 173 BE92
Bowes Rd, Walt. 195 BV103
Bowes-Lyon Cl, Wind. 151 AQ81
Alma Rd
Bowes-Lyon Ms, St.Alb. 43 CD20
Bowfell Rd W6 159 CW79
Bowford Av, Bexh. 166 EY81
Bowgate, St.Alb. 43 CE19
Bowhay, Brwd. 109 GA47
Bowhill Cl SW9 161 DN80
Bowie Cl SW4 181 DK87
Bowl Ct EC2 275 N5
Bowl Ct EC2 142 DS70
Bowland Rd SW4 161 DK84
Bowland Rd, Wdf.Grn. 102 EJ51
Bowland Yd SW1 276 E5
Bowlers Grn, Ong. 53 FF21
Bowlers Orchard, Ch.St.G. 90 AU48
Bowles Grn, Enf. 82 DV36
Bowles Rd SE1 162 DU79
Old Kent Rd
Bowley Cl SE19 182 DT93
Bowley La SE19 182 DT92
Bowling Cl, Uxb. 134 BM67
Birch Cres
Bowling Ct, Wat. 75 BU42
Bowling Grn Cl SW15 179 CV87
Bowling Grn La EC1 274 E4
Bowling Grn La EC1 141 DN70
Bowling Grn Pl SE1 279 K4
Bowling Grn Pl SE1 162 DR75
Bowling Grn Rd (Chobham), Wok. 210 AS109
Bowling Grn Row SE18 165 EM76
Samuel St
Bowling Grn St SE11 161 DN79
Bowling Grn Wk N1 275 M2
Bowling Rd, Ware 33 DY06
Bowls, The, Chig. 103 ES49
Bowls Cl, Stan. 95 CH50
Bowman Av E16 144 EF73
Bowman Ms SW18 179 CZ88
Bowmans Cl W13 137 CH74
Bowmans Cl, Pot.B. 64 DD32
Bowmans Cl (Burnham), Slou. 130 AH67
Bowmans Ct, Hem.H. 40 BK18
Bowmans Grn, Wat. 76 BX36
Bowmans Lea SE23 182 DW87
Bowmans Meadow, Wall. 201 DH104
Bowmans Ms E1 142 DU72
Hooper St
Bowmans Ms N7 121 DL62
Seven Sisters Rd
Bowmans Pl N7 121 DL62
Holloway Rd
Bowmans Rd, Dart. 187 FF87
Bowman's Trd Est NW9 118 CM55
Westmoreland Rd
Bowmead SE9 185 EM89
Bowmont Cl, Brwd. 109 GB44
Bowmore Wk NW1 141 DK66
St. Paul's Cres
Bown Cl, Til. 171 GH82
Bowness Cl E8 142 DT65
Beechwood Rd
Bowness Cres SW15 178 CS92
Bowness Dr, Houns. 156 BY84
Bowness Rd SE6 183 EB87
Bowness Rd, Bexh. 167 FB82
Bowness Way, Horn. 127 FG64
Bowood Rd SW11 160 DG84
Bowood Rd, Enf. 83 DX40
Bowring Grn, Wat. 94 BW50
Bowrons Av, Wem. 137 CK66
Bowry Dr (Wraysbury), Stai. 173 AZ86
Bowsley Ct, Felt. 175 BU88
Highfield Rd
Bowsprit, The, Cob. 230 BW115
Bowsprit Pt E14 163 EA76
Bowstridge La, Ch.St.G. 90 AW51
Bowyer Cl E6 145 EM71
Bowyer Cres (Denham), Uxb. 113 BF58
Bowyer Dr, Slou. 131 AL74
Bowyer Pl SE5 162 DR80
Bowyer St SE5 162 DQ80
Bowyers, Hem.H. 40 BK18
Bowyers Cl, Ash. 232 CM118
Box La, Bark. 146 EV68
Box La, Hem.H. 39 BE24
Box La, Hodd. 49 DX16
Box Ridge Av, Pur. 219 DM112
Box Tree Cl, Chesh. 54 AR33
Box Wk, Lthd. 245 BS132
Boxall Rd SE21 182 DS86
Boxfield, Welw.G.C. 30 DB12
Boxford Cl, S.Croy. 221 DX112
Boxgrove Av, Guil. 243 BA132
Boxgrove La, Guil. 243 BA133
Boxgrove Rd SE2 166 EW76
Boxgrove Rd, Guil. 243 BA133
Boxhill, Hem.H. 40 BK18
Boxhill Dr, Grays 170 FY79
Boxhill Rd, Dor. 248 CL133
Boxhill Rd, Tad. 248 CP131
Boxhill Way (Strood Grn), Bet. 264 CP138
Boxley Rd, Mord. 200 DC98
Boxley St E16 144 EH74
Boxmoor Rd, Har. 117 CH56
Boxmoor Rd, Rom. 105 FC50
Boxoll Rd, Dag. 126 EZ63
Boxted Cl, Buck.H. 102 EL46
Boxted Rd, Hem.H. 39 BF18
Boxtree La, Har. 94 CC53
Boxtree Rd, Har. 95 CD52
Boxtree Wk, Orp. 206 EX102
Boxwell Rd, Berk. 38 AV19
Boxwood Cl, West Dr. 154 BM75
Hawthorne Cres
Boxwood Way, Warl. 237 DX117
Boxworth Cl N12 98 DD50
Boxworth Gro N1 141 DM67
Richmond Av
Boyard Rd SE18 165 EP78
Boyce Cl, Borwd. 78 CL39
Boyce St SE1 278 C3
Boyce Way E13 144 EG70
Boycroft Av NW9 118 CQ58
Boyd Av, Sthl. 136 BZ74
Boyd Cl, Kings.T. 178 CN94
Crescent Rd
Boyd Rd SW19 180 DD93
Boyd St E1 142 DU72
Boydell Ct NW8 140 DD66
St. John's Wd Pk
Boyfield St SE1 278 G5
Boyfield St SE1 161 DP75
Boyland Rd, Brom. 184 EF92
Boyle Av, Stan. 95 CG51
Boyle Cl, Uxb. 134 BM68
Boyle Fm Island, T.Ditt. 197 CG100
Boyle Fm Rd, T.Ditt. 197 CG100
Boyle St W1 273 K10
Boyne Av NW4 119 CX56
Boyne Rd SE13 163 EC83
Boyne Rd, Dag. 126 FA62
Boyne Ter Ms W11 139 CZ74
Boyseland Ct, Edg. 96 CQ47
Boyson Rd SE17 162 DR79
Boyton Cl E1 143 DX70
Stayner's Rd
Boyton Cl N8 121 DL55
Boyton Rd N8 121 DL55
Brabant Ct EC3 275 M10
Brabant Rd N22 99 DM54
Brabazon Av, Wall. 219 DL108
Brabazon Rd, Houns. 156 BW80
Brabazon Rd, Nthlt. 136 CA68
Brabazon St E14 143 EB72
Brabourn Gro SE15 162 DW82
Brabourne Cl SE19 182 DS92
Brabourne Cres, Bexh. 166 EZ79
Brabourne Hts NW7 96 CS48
Brabourne Ri, Beck. 203 EC99
Brace Cl (Cheshunt), Wal.Cr. 65 DP25
Bracewell Av, Grnf. 117 CF64
Bracewell Rd W10 139 CW71
Bracewood Gdns, Croy. 202 DT104
Bracey Ms N4 121 DL61
Bracey St
Bracey St N4 121 DL61
Bracken, The E4 101 EC47
Hortus Rd
Bracken Av SW12 180 DG86
Bracken Av, Croy. 203 EB104
Bracken Cl E6 145 EM71
Bracken Cl, Borwd. 78 CP39
Bracken Cl (Bookham), Lthd. 230 BZ124
Bracken Cl (Farnham Common), Slou. 111 AR63
Bracken Cl, Sun. 175 BT93
Cavendish Rd
Bracken Cl, Twick. 176 CA87
Hedley Rd
Bracken Cl, Wok. 227 AZ118
Bracken Dr, Chig. 103 EP51
Bracken End, Islw. 177 CD85
Bracken Gdns SW13 159 CU82
Bracken Hill Cl, Brom. 204 EF95
Bracken Hill La
Bracken Hill La, Brom. 204 EF95
Bracken Ind Est, Ilf. 103 ET52
Bracken Ms E4 101 EC47
Hortus Rd
Bracken Ms, Rom. 126 FA58
Bracken Path, Epsom 216 CP113
Bracken Way, Guil. 242 AS132
Bracken Way (Chobham), Wok. 210 AT110
Brackenbridge Dr, Ruis. 116 BX62
Brackenbury Gdns W6 159 CV76
Brackenbury Rd N2 120 DC55
Brackenbury Rd W6 159 CV76
Brackendale N21 99 DM47
Brackendale, Pot.B. 64 DA33
Brackendale Cl, Houns. 156 CB81
Brackendale Gdns, Upmin. 128 FQ63
Brackendene, Dart. 187 FE91
Brackendene (Bricket Wd), St.Alb. 60 BZ30
Brackendene Cl, Wok. 227 BA115
Brackenfield Cl E5 122 DV63
Tiger Way
Brackenforde, Slou. 152 AW75
Brackenhill, Berk. 39 AZ17
Brackenhill, Cob. 214 CA111
Brackens, The, Enf. 100 DS45
Brackens, The, Hem.H. 40 BK19
Heather Way
Brackens, The, Orp. 224 EU106
Brackens Dr, Brwd. 108 FW50
Brackenside, Horl. 269 DH147
Stockfield
Brackenwood, Sun. 195 BU95
Brackley, Wey. 213 BR106
Brackley Cl, Wall. 219 DL108
Brackley Rd W4 158 CS78
Brackley Rd, Beck. 183 DZ94
Brackley Sq, Wdf.Grn. 102 EK52
Brackley St EC1 275 H6
Brackley Ter W4 158 CS78
Bracklyn Cl N1 142 DR68
Parr St
Bracklyn Ct N1 142 DR68
Wimbourne St
Bracklyn St N1 142 DR68
Bracknell Cl N22 99 DN53
Bracknell Gdns NW3 120 DB63
Bracknell Gate NW3 120 DB64
Bracknell Pl, Hem.H. 40 BM16
Bracknell Way NW3 120 DB63
Bracondale, Esher 214 CC107
Bracondale Rd SE2 166 EU77
Brad St SE1 278 E3
Bradbery, Rick. 91 BD50
Bradbourne Pk Rd, Sev. 256 FG123
Bradbourne Rd, Bex. 186 FA87
Bradbourne Rd, Grays 170 GB79
Bradbourne Rd, Sev. 257 FH122
Bradbourne St SW6 160 DA82
Bradbourne Vale Rd, Sev. 256 FF122
Bradbury Cl, Borwd. 78 CP39
Bradbury Cl, Sthl. 156 BZ77
Bradbury Gdns (Fulmer), Slou. 112 AX63
Bradbury Ms N16 122 DS64
Bradbury St
Bradbury St N16 122 DS64
Bradd Cl, S.Ock. 149 FW69
Brandon Gros Av
Braddock Cl, Islw. 157 CF83
Braddon Rd, Rich. 158 CM83
Braddyll St SE10 164 EE78
Braden St W9 140 DB70
Shirland Rd
Bradenham Av, Well. 166 EU84
Bradenham Cl SE17 162 DR79
Bradenham Rd, Har. 117 CH56
Bradenham Rd, Hayes 135 BS69
Bradenhurst Cl, Cat. 252 DT126
Bradfield Cl, Guil. 243 BA131
Bradfield Cl, Wok. 226 AY118
Bradfield Dr, Bark. 126 EU64
Bradfield Rd E16 164 EG75
Bradfield Rd, Ruis. 116 BY64
Bradford Cl N17 100 DS51
Commercial Rd
Bradford Cl SE26 182 DV91
Coombe Rd
Bradford Cl, Brom. 205 EM102
Bradford Dr, Epsom 217 CT107
Bradford Rd W3 158 CS75
Warple Way
Bradford Rd, Ilf. 125 ER60
Bradford Rd, Rick. 91 BC45
Bradford Rd, Slou. 131 AN72
Bradgate (Cuffley), Pot.B. 65 DK27
Bradgate Cl (Cuffley), Pot.B. 65 DK28
Bradgate Rd SE6 183 EA86
Brading Cres E11 124 EH61
Brading Rd SW2 181 DM87
Brading Rd, Croy. 201 DM100
Bradiston Rd W9 139 CZ69
Bradleigh Av, Grays 170 GC77
Bradley Cl N7 141 DM65
Sutterton St
Bradley Cl (Belmont), Sutt. 218 DA110
Station Rd
Bradley Gdns W13 137 CH72
Bradley La, Dor. 247 CG132
Bradley Ms SW17 180 DF88
Bellevue Rd
Bradley Rd N22 99 DM54
Bradley Rd SE19 182 DQ93
Bradley Rd, Enf. 83 DY38
Bradley Rd, Slou. 131 AR73
Bradley Rd, Wal.Abb. 83 EC36
Bradley Stone Rd E6 145 EM71
Bradley's Cl N1 141 DN68
White Lion St
Bradman Row, Edg. 96 CQ52
Pavilion Way
Bradmead SW8 161 DH80
Bradmore Grn, Couls. 235 DM118
Coulsdon Rd
Bradmore Grn, Hat. 63 CY26
Bradmore Ho E1 142 DW71
Bradmore La, Hat. 63 CW26
Bradmore Pk Rd W6 159 CV76
Bradmore Way, Couls. 235 DL117
Bradmore Way, Hat. 63 CY26
Bradshaw Cl SW19 180 DA93
Bradshaw Cl, Wind. 151 AL81
Bradshaw Rd, Wat. 76 BW39
Bradshawe Waye, Uxb. 134 BL71
Bradshaws, Hat. 45 CT22
Bradshaws Cl SE25 202 DU97
Bradstock Rd E9 143 DX65
Bradstock Rd, Epsom 217 CU106
Bradwell Av, Dag. 126 FA61
Bradwell Cl E18 124 EF56
Bradwell Cl, Horn. 147 FH65
Bradwell Grn, Brwd. 109 GC44
Bradwell Ms N18 100 DU49
Lyndhurst Rd
Bradwell Rd, Buck.H. 102 EL46
Bradwell St E1 143 DX69
Brady Av, Loug. 85 EQ40
Brady St E1 142 DV70
Bradymead E6 145 EP72
Braemar Av N22 99 DL53

Braemar Av NW10 118 CR62
Braemar Av SW19 180 DA89
Braemar Av, Bexh. 167 FC84
Braemar Av, S.Croy. 220 DQ109
Braemar Av, Th.Hth. 201 DN97
Braemar Av, Wem. 137 CK66
Braemar Gdns NW9 96 CR53
Braemar Gdns, Horn. 128 FN58
Braemar Gdns, Sid. 185 ER90
Braemar Gdns, Slou. 151 AN75
Braemar Gdns, W.Wick. 203 EC102
Braemar Rd E13 144 EF70
Braemar Rd N15 122 DS57
Braemar Rd, Brent. 158 CL79
Braemar Rd, Wor.Pk. 199 CV104
Braes Mead (South Nutfield), Red. 267 DL135
Braes St N1 141 DP66
Braeside (New Haw), Add. 212 BH111
Braeside, Beck. 183 EA92
Braeside Av SW19 199 CY95
Braeside Av, Sev. 256 FF124
Braeside Cl, Pnr. 94 CA52
The Av
Braeside Cl, Sev. 256 FF123
Braeside Cres, Bexh. 167 FC84
Braeside Rd SW16 181 DJ94
Braesyde Cl, Belv. 166 EZ77
Brafferton Rd, Croy. 220 DQ105
Braganza St SE17 278 F10
Braganza St SE17 161 DP78
Bragg Cl, Dag. 146 EV65
Porters Av
Bragmans La (Flaunden), Hem.H. 57 BB34
Bragmans La, Rick. 57 BE33
Braham St E1 142 DT72
Braid, The, Chesh. 54 AS30
Braid Av W3 138 CS72
Braid Cl, Felt. 176 BZ89
Braidwood Pas EC1 142 DQ71
Aldersgate St
Braidwood Rd SE6 183 ED88
Braidwood St SE1 279 M3
Brailsford Cl, Mitch. 180 DE94
Brailsford Rd SW2 181 DN85
Brain Cl, Hat. 45 CV18
Brainton Av, Felt. 175 BV87
Braintree Av, Ilf. 124 EL56
Braintree Ind Est, Ruis. 115 BV63
Braintree Rd, Dag. 126 FA62
Braintree Rd, Ruis. 115 BV63
Braintree St E2 142 DW69
Braithwaite Av, Rom. 126 FA59
Braithwaite Gdns, Stan. 95 CJ53
Braithwaite Rd, Enf. 83 DZ41
Braithwaite Twr W2 140 DD71
Brakefield Rd (Southfleet), Grav. 190 GB93
Brakey Hill (Bletchingley), Red. 252 DS134
Brakynbery, Berk. 38 AS16
Bramah Grn SW9 161 DN81
Bramalea Cl N6 120 DG58
Bramall Cl E15 124 EF64
Idmiston Rd
Bramber Ct, Brent. 158 CL77
Sterling Pl
Bramber Ct, Slou. 131 AN74
Bramber Rd N12 98 DE50
Bramber Rd W14 159 CZ79
Bramble Av (Bean), Dart. 189 FW90
Bramble Banks, Cars. 218 DG109
Bramble Cl, Beck. 203 EC99
Bramble Cl, Croy. 221 EA105
Bramble Cl, Guil. 242 AS132
Bramble Cl, Red. 266 DG136
Bramble Cl, Shep. 195 BR98
Halliford Cl
Bramble Cl, Stan. 95 CK52
Bramble Cl, Uxb. 134 BM71
Bramble Cl, Wat. 59 BU34
Bramble Cft, Erith 167 FC77
Bramble Gdns W12 139 CT73
Wallflower St
Bramble La, Amer. 55 AS41
Bramble La, Hmptn. 176 BZ93
Bramble La, Hodd. 49 DY17
Bramble La, Sev. 257 FH128
Bramble La, Upmin. 148 FQ67
Bramble Mead, Ch.St.G. 90 AU48
Bramble Ri, Cob. 230 BW115
Bramble Ri, Harl. 35 EQ14
Bramble Rd, Hat. 44 CR18
Bramble Wk, Epsom 216 CP114
Bramble Way (Ripley), Wok. 227 BF124
Brambleacres Cl, Sutt. 218 DA108
Bramblebury Rd SE18 165 EQ78
Brambledene Cl, Wok. 226 AW118
Brambledown, Stai. 194 BG95
Brambledown Cl, W.Wick. 204 EE99
Brambledown Rd, Cars. 218 DG108
Brambledown Rd, S.Croy. 220 DS108
Brambledown Rd, Wall. 219 DH108
Bramblefield Cl, Long. 209 FX97
Brambles, The, Chig. 103 EQ50
Clayside
Brambles, The, St.Alb. 43 CD22
Brambles, The, Wal.Cr. 67 DX31
Brambles, The, West Dr. 154 BL77
Brambles Cl, Cat. 236 DS122
Brambles Cl, Islw. 157 CH80
Brambles Fm Dr, Uxb. 134 BN69
Brambletye Pk Rd, Red. 266 DG135
Bramblewood, Red. 251 DH129
Bramblewood Cl, Cars. 200 DE102
Brambling Cl, Bushey 76 BY42
Brambling Ri, Hem.H. 40 BL17
Bramblings, The E4 101 ED49
Bramcote Av, Mitch. 200 DF98
Bramcote Ct, Mitch. 200 DF98
Bramcote Av
Bramcote Gro SE16 162 DW78
Bramcote Rd SW15 159 CV84
Bramdean Cres SE12 184 EG88
Bramdean Gdns SE12 184 EG88
Bramerton Rd, Beck. 203 DZ97
Bramerton St SW3 160 DE79
Bramfield, Wat. 60 BY34
Garston La
Bramfield Ct N4 122 DQ61
Queens Dr
Bramfield Ct, Hert. 31 DN08
Windsor Dr
Bramfield La, Hert. 31 DL05
Bramfield Rd SW11 180 DE86
Bramfield Rd, Hert. 31 DL06
Bramford Ct N14 99 DK47
Bramford Rd SW18 160 DC84
Bramham Gdns SW5 160 DB78
Bramham Gdns, Chess. 215 CK105
Bramhope La SE7 164 EH79
Bramlands Cl SW11 160 DE83
Bramleas, Wat. 75 BT42
Bramley Av, Couls. 235 DJ115
Bramley Cl E17 101 DY54
Bramley Cl N14 81 DH43
Bramley Cl, Cher. 194 BH102
Bramley Cl (Istead Ri), Grav. 191 GF94
Bramley Cl, Hayes 135 BU73
Orchard Rd
Bramley Cl, Orp. 205 EP102
Bramley Cl, Pnr. 115 BT55
Wiltshire La
Bramley Cl, Red. 266 DE136
Abinger Dr
Bramley Cl, S.Croy. 219 DP106
Bramley Cl, Stai. 174 BJ93
Bramley Cl, Swan. 207 FE98
Bramley Cl, Twick. 176 CC86
Bramley Ct, Wat. 59 BV31
Orchard Av
Bramley Ct, Well. 166 EV81
Bramley Cres SW8 161 DK80
Pascal St
Bramley Cres, Ilf. 125 EN58
Bramley Gdns, Wat. 94 BW50
Bramley Hill, S.Croy. 219 DP106
Bramley Ho SW15 179 CT86
Tunworth Cres
Bramley Pl, Dart. 167 FG84
Bramley Rd N14 81 DH43
Bramley Rd W5 157 CJ76
Bramley Rd W10 139 CX73
Bramley Rd, Sutt. 218 DD106
Bramley Rd (Cheam), Sutt. 217 CX109
Bramley Shaw, Wal.Abb. 68 EF33
Bramley Wk, Horl. 269 DJ148
Carlton Tye
Bramley Way, Ash. 232 CM117
Bramley Way, Houns. 176 BZ85
Bramley Way, St.Alb. 43 CJ21
Bramley Way, W.Wick. 203 EB103
Brammas Cl, Slou. 151 AQ76
Brampton Cl E5 122 DV61
Brampton Cl (Cheshunt), Wal.Cr. 66 DU28
Brampton Gdns N15 122 DQ57
Brampton Rd
Brampton Gdns, Walt. 214 BW106
Brampton Gro NW4 119 CV56
Brampton Gro, Har. 117 CG56
Brampton Gro, Wem. 118 CN60
Brampton La NW4 119 CW56
Brampton Pk Rd N22 121 DN55
Brampton Rd E6 144 EK69
Brampton Rd N15 122 DQ57
Brampton Rd NW9 118 CN56
Brampton Rd SE2 166 EW79
Brampton Rd, Bexh. 166 EX80
Brampton Rd, Croy. 202 DT101
Brampton Rd, St.Alb. 43 CG19
Brampton Rd, Uxb. 135 BP68
Brampton Rd, Wat. 93 BU48
Brampton Ter, Borwd. 78 CN38
Bramshaw Gdns, Wat. 94 BX50
Bramshaw Ri, N.Mal. 198 CS100
Bramshaw Rd E9 143 DX65
Bramshill Cl, Chig. 103 ES50
Tine Rd
Bramshill Gdns NW5 121 DH62
Bramshill Rd NW10 139 CT68
Bramshot Av SE7 164 EG79
Bramshot Way, Wat. 93 BU47
Bramston Cl, Ilf. 103 ET51
Bramston Rd NW10 139 CU68
Bramston Rd SW17 180 DC90
Bramwell Cl, Sun. 196 BX96
Bramwell Ms N1 141 DM67
Brancaster Dr NW7 97 CT52
Brancaster La, Pur. 220 DQ112
Brancaster Pl, Loug. 85 EM41
Brancaster Rd E12 125 EM63
Brancaster Rd SW16 181 DL90
Brancaster Rd, Ilf. 125 ER58
Brancepeth Gdns, Buck.H. 102 EG47
Branch Cl, Hat. 45 CW16
Branch Hill NW3 120 DC62
Branch Pl N1 142 DR67
Branch Rd E14 143 DY73
Branch Rd, Ilf. 104 EV50
Branch Rd, St.Alb. 42 CB19
Branch Rd (Park St), St.Alb. 61 CD27
Branch St SE15 162 DS80
Brancker Cl, Wall. 219 DL108
Brown Cl
Brancker Rd, Har. 117 CK55
Brancroft Way, Enf. 83 DY39
Brand St SE10 163 EC80
Brandesbury Sq, Wdf.Grn. 103 EN52
Brandlehow Rd SW15 159 CZ84
Brandon Cl, Grays 170 FZ75
Brandon Cl (Cheshunt), Wal.Cr. 66 DS26
Brandon Est SE17 161 DP79
Brandon Gros Av, S.Ock. 149 FW69
Brandon Ms EC2 142 DQ71
The Barbican
Brandon Rd E17 123 EC55
Brandon Rd N7 141 DL66
Brandon Rd, Dart. 188 FN87
Brandon Rd, Sthl. 156 BZ78
Brandon Rd, Sutt. 218 DB105
Brandon St SE17 279 J9
Brandon St SE17 162 DQ77
Brandon St, Grav. 191 GH87
Brandram Rd SE13 164 EE83
Brandreth Rd E6 145 EM72
Brandreth Rd SW17 181 DH89
Brandries, The, Wall. 201 DK104
Brands Rd, Slou. 153 BB79
Brandsland, Reig. 266 DB138
Brandville Gdns, Ilf. 125 EP56
Brandville Rd, West Dr. 154 BL75
Brandy Way, Sutt. 218 DA108
Branfill Rd, Upmin. 128 FP61
Brangbourne Rd, Brom. 183 EC92
Brangton Rd SE11 161 DM78
Brangwyn Cres SW19 200 DD95
Branksea St SW6 159 CY80
Branksome Av N18 100 DT50
Branksome Cl, Hem.H. 40 BN19
Branksome Cl, Tedd. 177 CD91
Branksome Cl, Walt. 196 BX103
Branksome Rd SW2 181 DL85
Branksome Rd SW19 200 DA95
Branksome Way, Har. 118 CL58
Branksome Way, N.Mal. 198 CQ95
Bransby Rd, Chess. 216 CL107
Branscombe Gdns N21 99 DN45
Branscombe St SE13 163 EB83
Bransdale Cl NW6 140 DB67
West End La
Bransell Cl, Swan. 207 FC100
Bransgrove Rd, Edg. 96 CM53
Branston Cres, Orp. 205 ER102
Branstone Rd, Rich. 158 CM81
Branton Rd, Green. 189 FT86
Brants Wk W7 137 CE70
Brantwood Av, Erith 167 FC80
Brantwood Av, Islw. 157 CG84
Brantwood Cl E17 123 EB55
Brantwood Cl, W.Byf. 212 BG113
Brantwood Gdns
Brantwood Ct, W.Byf. 211 BF113
Brantwood Dr
Brantwood Dr, W.Byf. 211 BF113
Brantwood Gdns, Enf. 81 DL42
Brantwood Gdns, Ilf. 124 EL56
Brantwood Gdns, W.Byf. 211 BF113
Brantwood Rd N17 100 DU51
Brantwood Rd SE24 182 DQ85
Brantwood Rd, Bexh. 167 FB82
Brantwood Rd, S.Croy. 220 DQ109
Brantwood Way, Orp. 206 EW97
Brasenose Dr SW13 159 CW79
Brasher Cl, Grnf. 117 CD64
Brass Tally All SE16 163 DX75
Middleton Dr
Brassett Pt E15 144 EE67
Brassey Cl, Felt. 175 BU88
Brassey Cl, Oxt. 254 EF129
Westerham Rd
Brassey Hill, Oxt. 254 EG130
Brassey Rd NW6 139 CZ65
Brassey Rd, Oxt. 254 EF130
Brassey Sq SW11 160 DG83
Brassie Av W3 138 CS72
Brasted Cl SE26 182 DW91
Brasted Cl, Bexh. 186 EX85
Brasted Cl, Orp. 206 EU103
Brasted Cl, Sutt. 218 DA110
Brasted Hill (Knockholt), Sev. 240 EU120
Brasted Hill Rd (Brasted), West. 240 EV121
Brasted La (Knockholt), Sev. 240 EU119
Brasted Rd, Erith 167 FE80
Brasted Rd, West. 255 ES126
Brathway Rd SW18 180 DA87
Bratley St E1 142 DU70
Weaver St
Brattle Wd, Sev. 257 FH129
Braund Av, Grnf. 136 CB70
Braundton Av, Sid. 185 ET88
Braunston Dr, Hayes 136 BY70
Bravington Cl, Shep. 194 BM99
Bravington Pl W9 139 CZ70
Bravington Rd
Bravington Rd W9 139 CZ68
Brawlings La (Chalfont St. Peter), Ger.Cr. 91 BA49
Brawne Ho SE17 161 DP79
Hillingdon St
Braxfield Rd SE4 163 DY84
Braxted Pk SW16 181 DM93
Bray NW3 140 DE66
Bray Cl, Borwd. 78 CQ39
Bray Cl, Maid. *Bray Rd* 150 AC75
Bray Ct, Maid. 150 AC77
Bray Cres SE16 163 DX75
Marlow Way
Bray Dr E16 144 EF73
Bray Gdns, Wok. 227 BE116
Bray Pas E16 144 EG73
Bray Pl SW3 276 D9
Bray Pl SW3 160 DF77
Bray Rd NW7 97 CX51
Bray Rd (Stoke D'Abernon), Cob. 230 BY116
Bray Rd, Guil. 258 AV135
Bray Rd, Maid. 150 AC75
Bray Springs, Wal.Abb. 68 EE34
Brayards Rd SE15 162 DV82
Braybank, Maid. 150 AC75
Braybourne Cl, Uxb. 134 BJ65
Braybourne Dr, Islw. 157 CF80
Braybrook St W12 139 CT71
Braybrooke Gdns SE19 182 DT94
Fox Hill
Brayburne Av SW4 161 DJ82
Braycourt Av, Walt. 195 BV101
Braydon Rd N16 122 DU60
Brayfield Rd, Maid. 150 AC75
Brayfield Ter N1 141 DN66
Lofting Rd
Brayford Sq E1 142 DW72
Summercourt Rd
Brays Mead, Harl. 51 ET17
Brayton Gdns, Enf. 81 DK42
Braywood Av, Egh. 173 AZ93
Braywood Rd SE9 165 ER84
Braziers Fld, Hert. 32 DT09
Brazil Cl (Beddington), Croy. 201 DL101
Breach Barn Mobile Home Pk, Wal.Abb. 68 EH29
Breach Barns La, Wal.Abb. 68 EF30
Galley Hill
Breach La, Dag. 146 FA69
Breach La (Little Berkhamsted), Hert. 47 DJ18
Breach Rd, Grays 169 FT79
Bread & Cheese La (Cheshunt), Wal.Cr. 66 DR25
Bread St EC4 275 J9
Bread St EC4 142 DQ73
Breakfield, Couls. 235 DL116
Breakmead, Welw.G.C. 30 DB10
Breakneck Hill, Green. 189 FV85
Breaks Rd, Hat. 45 CV18
Breakspear Av, St.Alb. 43 CF21
Breakspear Ct, Abb.L. 59 BT30
Breakspear Path (Harefield), Uxb. 114 BJ55
Breakspear Rd, Ruis. 115 BP58
Breakspear Rd N (Harefield), Uxb. 114 BN57
Breakspear Rd S (Ickenham), Uxb. 114 BM62
Breakspear Way, Hem.H. 41 BQ20
Breakspeare Cl, Wat. 75 BV38
Breakspeare Rd, Abb.L. 59 BS31
Breakspears Dr, Orp. 206 EU95
Breakspears Ms SE4 163 EA82
Breakspears Rd
Breakspears Rd SE4 163 DZ84
Bream Cl N17 122 DV56
Bream Gdns E6 145 EN69
Bream St E3 143 EA66
Breamore Cl SW15 179 CU88
Breamore Rd, Ilf. 125 ET61
Bream's Bldgs EC4 274 D8
Bream's Bldgs EC4 141 DN72
Breamwater Gdns, Rich. 177 CH90
Brearley Cl, Edg. 96 CQ52
Pavilion Way
Brearley Cl, Uxb. 134 BL65
Breasley Cl SW15 159 CV84
Brechin Pl SW7 160 DC77
Rosary Gdns
Brecken Cl, St.Alb. 43 CG16
Brecknock Rd N7 121 DJ63
Brecknock Rd N19 121 DJ63
Brecknock Rd Est N7 121 DJ63
Breckonmead, Brom. 204 EJ96
Wanstead Rd
Brecon Cl, Mitch. 201 DL97
Brecon Cl, Wor.Pk. 199 CW103
Brecon Grn NW9 118 CS58
Goldsmith Av
Brecon Rd W6 159 CY79
Brecon Rd, Enf. 82 DW42
Brede Cl E6 145 EN69
Bredgar SE13 183 EB85
Bredgar Rd N19 121 DJ61
Bredhurst Cl SE20 182 DW93
Bredon Rd SE5 162 DQ83
Bredon Rd, Croy. 202 DT101
Bredune, Ken. 236 DR115
Bredward Cl (Burnham), Slou. 130 AH69
Breech La, Tad. 233 CU124
Breer St SW6 160 DB83
Breeze Ter (Cheshunt), Wal.Cr. 67 DX28
Collet Cl
Breezers Hill E1 142 DU73
Pennington St
Brember Rd, Har. 116 CC61
Bremer Ms E17 123 EB56
Church La
Bremer Rd, Stai. 174 BG90
Bremner Av, Horl. 268 DF147
Bremner Cl, Swan. 207 FG98
Bremner Rd SW7 160 DC75
Brenchley Av, Grav. 191 GH92
Brenchley Cl, Brom. 204 EF100
Brenchley Cl, Chis. 205 EN95
Brenchley Gdns SE23 182 DW86
Brenchley Rd, Orp. 205 ET95
Brenda Rd SW17 180 DF89
Brenda Ter, Swans. 190 FY87
Manor Rd
Brendans Cl, Horn. 128 FL60
Brende Gdns, W.Mol. 196 CB98
Brendon Av NW10 118 CS63
Brendon Cl, Erith 167 FE81
Brendon Cl, Esher 214 CC107
Brendon Cl, Hayes 155 BQ80
Brendon Ct, Rad. 61 CH34
The Av
Brendon Dr, Esher 214 CC107
Brendon Gdns, Har. 116 CB63
Brendon Gdns, Ilf. 125 ES57
Brendon Gro N2 98 DC54
Brendon Rd SE9 185 ER89
Brendon Rd, Dag. 126 EZ60
Brendon St W1 272 C8
Brendon St W1 140 DE72
Brendon Way, Enf. 100 DS45
Brenley Cl, Mitch. 200 DG97
Brenley Gdns SE9 164 EK84
Brennan Rd, Til. 171 GH82
Brent, The, Dart. 188 FN87
Brent Cl, Bex. 186 EY88
Brent Cl, Dart. 188 FP86
Brent Cres NW10 138 CM68
Brent Cross Gdns NW4 119 CX58
Haley Rd
Brent Cross Shop Cen NW4 119 CW59
Brent Grn NW4 119 CW57
Brent Grn Wk, Wem. 118 CQ62
Brent La, Dart. 188 FM87
Brent Lea, Brent. 157 CJ80
Brent Pk NW10 118 CR64
Brent Pk Rd NW4 119 CV59
Brent Pk Rd NW9 119 CU60
Brent Pl, Barn. 80 DA43
Brent Rd E16 144 EG71
Brent Rd SE18 165 EP80
Brent Rd, Brent. 157 CJ79
Brent Rd, S.Croy. 220 DV109
Brent Rd, Sthl. 156 BW76
Brent Side, Brent. 157 CJ79
Brent St NW4 119 CW56
Brent Ter NW2 119 CW61
Brent Vw Rd NW9 119 CU59
Brent Way N3 98 DA51
Brent Way, Brent. 157 CK80
Brent Way, Dart. 188 FP86
Brent Way, Wem. 138 CP65
Brentcot Cl W13 137 CH70
Brentfield NW10 138 CP66
Brentfield Cl NW10 138 CR65
Normans Mead
Brentfield Gdns NW2 119 CX59
Hendon Way
Brentfield Rd NW10 138 CR65
Brentfield Rd, Dart. 188 FN86
Brentford Business Cen, Brent. 157 CJ80
Brentford Cl, Hayes 136 BX70
Brenthall Twrs, Harl. 52 EW17
Brentham Way W5 137 CK70
Brenthouse Rd E9 142 DV66
Brenthurst Rd NW10 139 CT65
Brentlands Dr, Dart. 188 FN88
Brentmead Cl W7 137 CE73
Brentmead Gdns NW10 138 CM68
Brentmead Pl NW11 119 CX58
North Circular Rd
Brenton St E14 143 DY72
Brentside Cl W13 137 CG70
Brentside Executive Cen, Brent. 157 CH79
Brentvale Av, Sthl. 137 CD74
Brentvale Av, Wem. 138 CM67
Brentwick Gdns, Brent. 158 CL77
Brentwood Bypass, Brwd. 107 FR49
Brentwood Cl SE9 185 EQ88
Brentwood Ct, Add. 212 BH105
Brentwood Ho SE18 164 EK80
Shooter's Hill Rd
Brentwood Pl, Brwd. 108 FX46
Brentwood Rd, Brwd. 109 GA49
Brentwood Rd, Grays 171 GH77
Brentwood Rd, Rom. 127 FF58
Brereton Ct, Hem.H. 40 BL22
Brereton Rd N17 100 DT52
Bressenden Pl SW1 277 J6
Bressenden Pl SW1 161 DH76
Bressey Av, Enf. 82 DU39
Bressey Gro E18 102 EF54
Bretlands Rd, Cher. 193 BE103
Brett Cl N16 122 DS61
Yoakley Rd
Brett Cl, Nthlt. 136 BX69
Broomcroft Av
Brett Ct N9 100 DW47
Brett Cres NW10 138 CR66
Brett Gdns, Dag. 146 EY66
Brett Ho Cl SW15 179 CX86
Putney Heath La
Brett Pas E8 122 DV64
Kenmure Rd
Brett Pl, Wat. 75 BU37
The Harebreaks
Brett Rd E8 122 DV64
Brett Rd, Barn. 79 CW43
Brettell St SE17 162 DR78
Merrow St
Brettenham Av E17 101 EA53
Brettenham Rd E17 101 EA54
Brettenham Rd N18 100 DV49
Brettgrave, Epsom 216 CQ110
Brevet Cl, Purf. 169 FR77
Brew Ho Rd (Strood Grn), Bet. 264 CQ138
Tanners Meadow
Brewer St W1 273 L10
Brewer St W1 141 DJ73
Brewer St (Bletchingley), Red. 252 DQ131
Brewer's Fld, Dart. 188 FJ91
Brewer's Grn SW1 277 M6
Brewers Hall Gdns EC2 275 J7
Brewers La, Rich. 177 CK85
Brewery Cl, Wem. 117 CG64
Brewery La, Sev. 257 FJ125
High St
Brewery La, Twick. 177 CF87
Brewery La (Byfleet), W.Byf. 212 BL113
Brewery Rd N7 141 DL66
Brewery Rd SE18 165 ER78
Brewery Rd, Brom. 204 EL102
Brewery Rd, Hodd. 49 EA17
Brewery Rd, Wok. 226 AX117
Brewery Sq SE1 142 DT74
Horselydown La
Brewery Wk, Rom. 127 FE57
Brewhouse La E1 142 DV74
Brewhouse La, Hert. 32 DQ09
St. Andrew St
Brewhouse Rd SE18 165 EM77
Brewhouse St SW15 159 CY83
Brewhouse Wk SE16 143 DY74
Brewhouse Yd EC1 274 F4
Brewhouse Yd, Grav. 191 GH86
Queen St
Brewood Rd, Dag. 146 EV65
Brewster Gdns W10 139 CW71
Brewster Ho E14 143 DZ73
Brewster Rd E10 123 EB60
Brian Av, S.Croy. 220 DS112
Brian Cl, Horn. 127 FH63
Brian Rd, Rom. 126 EW57
Briane Rd, Epsom 216 CQ110
Briant St SE14 163 DX81
Briants Cl, Pnr. 94 BZ54
Briar Av SW16 181 DM94
Briar Banks, Cars. 218 DG109
Briar Cl N2 120 DB55
Briar Cl N13 100 DQ48
Briar Cl, Berk. 39 BA16
Briar Cl, Buck.H. 102 EK47
Briar Cl, Hmptn. 176 BZ92
Briar Cl, Islw. 177 CF85
Briar Cl, Maid. 130 AH72
Briar Cl (Cheshunt), Wal.Cr. 66 DW29
Briar Cl, W.Byf. 212 BJ111
Briar Ct, Sutt. 217 CW105
Briar Cres, Nthlt. 136 CB65
Briar Gdns, Brom. 204 EF102
Briar Gro, S.Croy. 220 DU113
Briar Hill, Pur. 219 DL111
Briar La, Cars. 218 DG109
Briar La, Croy. 221 EB105
Briar Pas SW16 201 DL97
Briar Pl SW16 201 DM97
Briar Rd NW2 119 CW63
Briar Rd SW16 201 DL97
Briar Rd, Bex. 187 FD90
Briar Rd, Har. 117 CJ57
Briar Rd, Rom. 106 FJ52
Briar Rd, St.Alb. 43 CJ17
Briar Rd, Shep. 194 BM99
Briar Rd, Twick. 177 CE88
Briar Rd, Wat. 59 BU34
Briar Rd (Send), Wok. 227 BB123
Briar Wk SW15 159 CV84
Briar Wk W10 139 CY70
Droop St
Briar Wk, Edg. 96 CQ52
Briar Wk, W.Byf. 212 BG112
Briar Way, Berk. 38 AW20
Briar Way, Guil. 243 BB130
Briar Way, Slou. 131 AP71
Briar Way, West Dr. 154 BN75
Briarbank Rd W13 137 CG72
Briarcliff, Hem.H. 39 BE19
Briardale Gdns NW3 120 DA62
Briarfield Av N3 98 DB54
Briaris Cl N17 100 DV52
Briarleas Gdns, Upmin. 129 FS59
Briarley Cl, Brox. 49 DZ22
Briars, The, Bushey 95 CE45
Briars, The, Harl. 51 ES19
Briars, The, Hert. 32 DU09
Briars, The, Rick. 74 BH36
Briars, The, Slou. 153 AZ78
Briars, The (Cheshunt), Wal.Cr. 67 DY31
Briars Cl, Hat. 45 CU18
Briars Ct, Lthd. 215 CD114
Briars La, Hat. 45 CU18
Briars Wk, Rom. 106 FL54
Briars Wd, Hat. 45 CT18
Briars Wd, Horl. 269 DJ147
Briarswood, Wal.Cr. 66 DR28
Briarswood Way, Orp. 223 ET106
Briarwood, Bans. 234 DA115
High St
Briarwood Cl NW9 118 CQ58
Briarwood Cl, Felt. 175 BS90
Briarwood Dr, Nthwd. 93 BU54
Briarwood Rd SW4 181 DK85
Briarwood Rd, Epsom 217 CU107
Briary Cl NW3 140 DE66
Fellows Rd
Briary Ct, Sid. 186 EV92
Briary Gdns, Brom. 184 EH92
Briary Gro, Edg. 96 CP54
Briary La N9 100 DT48
Brick Ct EC4 274 D9
Brick Ct, Grays 170 GA79
Columbia Wf Rd
Brick Fm Cl, Rich. 158 CP81
Brick Kiln Cl, Wat. 76 BY44
Brick Kiln La, Oxt. 254 EJ131
Brick Knoll Pk, St.Alb. 43 CJ21
Brick La E1 142 DT71
Brick La E2 142 DT69
Brick La, Enf. 82 DV40
Brick La, Stan. 95 CK52
Honeypot La
Brick St W1 277 H3
Brick St W1 141 DH74

Brickcroft, Brox. 67 DY26
Brickenden Ct, Wal.Abb. 68 EF33
Brickendon Grn, Hert. 48 DQ19
Brickendon La, Hert. 48 DQ18
Bricket Rd, St.Alb. 43 CD20
Brickett Cl, Ruis. 115 BQ57
Brickfield, Hat. 45 CU21
Brickfield Av, Hem.H. 41 BP21
Brickfield Cl, Brent. 157 CJ80
Brickfield Cotts SE18 165 ET79
Brickfield Fm Gdns, Orp. 223 EQ105
Brickfield La, Barn. 79 CT44
Brickfield La, Hayes 155 BR79
Brickfield La (Burnham), Slou. 130 AG67
Brickfield Rd SW19 180 DB91
Brickfield Rd, Epp. 70 EX29
Brickfield Rd (Outwood), Red. 267 DN142
Brickfield Rd, Th.Hth. 201 DP95
Brickfields, Har. 117 CD61
Brickfields, The, Ware 32 DV05
Brickfields La, Epp. 70 EX29
Brickfield Rd
Brickfields Way, West Dr. 154 BM76
Bricklayer's Arms Distribution Cen SE1 279 N8
Bricklayer's Arms Distribution Cen SE1 162 DS77
Bricklayer's Arms Roundabout SE1 162 DR76
Old Kent Rd
Brickmakers La, Hem.H. 41 BP21
Brickwall Cl, Welw. 29 CU07
Brickwall La, Ruis. 115 BS60
Brickwood Cl SE26 182 DV90
Brickwood Rd, Croy. 202 DS103
Brickyard La (Wotton), Dor. 262 BW141
Bride Ct EC4 274 F9
Bride La EC4 274 F9
Bride St N7 141 DM65
Brideale Cl SE15 162 DT80
Colegrove Rd
Bridel Ms N1 141 DP67
Colebrooke Row
Bridewain St SE1 162 DT76
Bridewell Pl E1 142 DV74
Brewhouse La
Bridewell Pl EC4 274 F9
Bridford Ms W1 273 J6
Bridge, The, Har. 117 CE55
Bridge App NW1 140 DG66
Bridge Av W6 159 CW78
Bridge Av W7 137 CD71
Bridge Av, Upmin. 128 FN61
Bridge Barn La, Wok. 226 AW117
Bridge Cl W10 139 CX72
Kingsdown Cl
Bridge Cl, Brwd. 109 FZ49
Bridge Cl, Dart. 169 FR83
Bridge Cl, Enf. 82 DV40
Bridge Cl, Rom. 127 FE58
Bridge Cl, Slou. 131 AM73
Bridge Cl, Tedd. 177 CF91
Shacklegate La
Bridge Cl, Walt. 195 BT101
Bridge Cl (Byfleet), W.Byf. 212 BM112
Bridge Cl, Wok. 226 AW117
Bridge Cotts, Upmin. 129 FU64
Bridge Ct, Wok. 226 AX117
Bridge Dr N13 99 DM49
Bridge End E17 101 EC53
Bridge Gdns, Ashf. 175 BQ94
Bridge Gdns, E.Mol. 197 CD98
Bridge Gate N21 100 DQ45
Ridge Av
Bridge Hill, Epp. 69 ET33
Bridge Ho Quay E14 143 EC74
Prestons Rd
Bridge La NW11 119 CY57
Bridge La SW11 160 DE81
Bridge La, Vir.W. 192 AY99
Bridge Meadows SE14 163 DX79
Bridge Ms, Wok. 226 AX117
Bridge Barn La
Bridge Pk SW18 180 DA85
Bridge Pk, Guil. 243 BC131
Bridge Pl SW1 277 J8
Bridge Pl SW1 161 DH77
Bridge Pl, Amer. 72 AT38
Bridge Pl, Croy. 202 DR101
Bridge Pl, Wat. 76 BX43
Bridge Rd E6 145 EM66
Bridge Rd E15 143 ED66
Bridge Rd E17 123 DZ59
Bridge Rd N9 100 DU48
The Bdy
Bridge Rd N22 99 DL53
Bridge Rd NW10 138 CS65
Bridge Rd, Beck. 183 DZ94
Bridge Rd, Bexh. 166 EY82
Bridge Rd, Cher. 194 BH101
Bridge Rd, Chess. 216 CL106
Bridge Rd, E.Mol. 197 CE98
Bridge Rd, Epsom 217 CT112
Bridge Rd, Erith 167 FF81
Bridge Rd, Grays 170 GB78
Bridge Rd, Houns. 157 CD83
Bridge Rd, Islw. 157 CD83
Bridge Rd, Kings L. 59 BQ33
Bridge Rd, Orp. 206 EV100
Bridge Rd, Rain. 147 FF70
Bridge Rd, Sthl. 156 BZ75
Bridge Rd, Sutt. 218 DB107
Bridge Rd, Twick. 177 CH86
Bridge Rd, Uxb. 134 BJ68
Bridge Rd, Wall. 219 DJ106
Bridge Rd, Welw.G.C. 29 CW08
Bridge Rd, Wem. 118 CN62
Bridge Rd, Wey. 212 BM105
Bridge Rd E, Welw.G.C. 29 CY08
Bridge Row, Croy. 202 DR102
Cross Rd
Bridge St SW1 277 P5
Bridge St SW1 161 DL75
Bridge St W4 158 CR77
Bridge St, Berk. 38 AX19
Bridge St, Guil. 258 AW135
Bridge St, Hem.H. 40 BJ21
Bridge St, Lthd. 231 CG122
Bridge St, Pnr. 116 BX55
Bridge St, Rich. 177 CK85
Bridge St (Colnbrook), Slou. 153 BD80
Bridge St, Stai. 173 BE91
Bridge St, Walt. 195 BT102
Bridge Ter E15 143 ED66
Bridge Rd
Bridge Vw W6 159 CW78
Bridge Way N11 99 DJ48
Pymmes Grn Rd
Bridge Way NW11 119 CZ57
Bridge Way, Cob. 213 BT113
Bridge Way, Couls. 234 DE119
Bridge Way, Twick. 176 CC87
Bridge Way, Uxb. 115 BP64
Bridge Wf, Cher. 194 BJ102
Bridge Wf Rd, Islw. 157 CH83
Church St
Bridge Wks, Uxb. 134 BJ70
Bridge Yd SE1 279 L2
Bridgefield Cl, Bans. 233 CW115
Bridgefield Rd, Sutt. 218 DA107
Bridgefields, Welw.G.C. 29 CZ08
Bridgefoot SE1 161 DL78
Bridgefoot, Ware 33 DX06
High St
Bridgefoot La, Pot.B. 63 CX33
Bridgeham Cl, Wey. 212 BN106
Mayfield Rd
Bridgeham Way, Horl. 269 DP148
Bridgehill Cl, Guil. 242 AU133
Bridgeland Rd E16 144 EG73
Bridgeman Dr, Wind. 151 AN82
Bridgeman Rd N1 141 DM66
Bridgeman Rd, Tedd. 177 CG93
Bridgeman St NW8 272 B1
Bridgeman St NW8 140 DE68
Bridgen Rd, Bex. 186 EY86
Bridgend Rd SW18 160 DC84
Bridgend Rd, Enf. 82 DW35
Bridgenhall Rd, Enf. 82 DT39
Bridgeport Pl E1 142 DU74
Kennet St
Bridger Cl, Wat. 60 BX33
Bridges Cl, Horl. 269 DK148
Bridges Ct SW11 160 DD83
Bridges Dr, Dart. 188 FP85
Bridges La, Croy. 219 DL105
Bridges Pl SW6 159 CZ81
Bridges Rd SW19 180 DB93
Bridges Rd, Stan. 95 CF50
Bridges Rd Ms SW19 180 DB93
Bridges Rd
Bridgetown Cl SE19 182 DS92
St. Kitts Ter
Bridgeview Ct, Ilf. 103 ER51
Bridgewater Cl, Chis. 205 ES97
Bridgewater Ct, Slou. 153 BA78
Bridgewater Gdns, Edg. 96 CM54
Bridgewater Hill (Northchurch), Berk. 38 AT16
Bridgewater Rd, Berk. 38 AU17
Bridgewater Rd, Ruis. 115 BU63
Bridgewater Rd, Wem. 137 CJ66
Bridgewater Rd, Wey. 213 BR107
Bridgewater Sq EC2 275 H6
Bridgewater St EC2 275 H6
Bridgewater Ter, Wind. 151 AR81
Bridgewater Way, Bushey 76 CB44
Bridgeway, Bark. 145 ET66
Bridgeway, Wem. 138 CL66
Bridgeway St NW1 273 M1
Bridgeway St NW1 141 DJ68
Bridgewood Cl SE20 182 DV94
Bridgewood Rd SW16 181 DK94
Bridgewood Rd, Wor.Pk. 217 CU105
Bridgford St SW18 180 DC90
Bridgman Rd W4 158 CQ76
Bridgwater Cl, Rom. 106 FK50
Bridgwater Rd E15 143 EC67
Bridgwater Rd, Rom. 106 FJ50
Bridgwater Wk, Rom. 106 FK50
Bridle Cl, Enf. 83 DZ37
Bridle Cl, Epsom 216 CR106
Bridle Cl, Hodd. 33 EA13
Bridle Cl, Kings.T. 197 CK98
Bridle Cl, St.Alb. 43 CE18
Bridle Cl, Sun. 195 BU97
Forge La
Bridle End, Epsom 217 CT114
Bridle La W1 273 L10
Bridle La, Cob. 230 CB115
Bridle La, Lthd. 230 CB115
Bridle La, Rick. 74 BK41
Bridle La, Twick. 177 CH86
Crown Rd
Bridle Path, Croy. 201 DM104
Bridle Path, Wat. 75 BV40
Bridle Path, The, Epsom 217 CV110
Bridle Path, The, Wdf.Grn. 102 EE52
Bridle Rd, Croy. 203 EA104
Bridle Rd, Epsom 217 CT113
Bridle Rd (Claygate), Esher 215 CH107
Bridle Rd, Pnr. 116 BW58
Bridle Rd, The, Pur. 219 DL110
Bridle Way, Berk. 38 AU17
Bridle Way, Croy. 221 EA106
Bridle Way, Hodd. 33 EA14
Bridle Way, Orp. 223 EQ105
Bridle Way, Ware 33 EA09
Bridle Way, The, Croy. 221 DY110
Bridle Way N, Hodd. 33 EA13
Bridle Way S, Hodd. 33 EA14
Bridlepath Way, Felt. 175 BS88
Bridleway, The, Wall. 219 DJ105
Bridleway Cl, Epsom 217 CW110
Bridlington Cl (Biggin Hill), West. 238 EH119
Bridlington Rd N9 100 DV45
Bridlington Rd, Wat. 94 BX48
Bridlington Spur, Slou. 151 AP75
Scarborough Way
Bridport Av, Rom. 127 FB58
Bridport Pl N1 142 DR68
Bridport Rd N18 100 DS50
Bridport Rd, Grnf. 136 CB67
Bridport Rd, Th.Hth. 201 DN97
Bridport Ter SW8 161 DK81
Wandsworth Rd
Bridport Way, Slou. 131 AP69
Bridstow Pl W2 140 DA72
Talbot Rd
Brief St SE5 161 DP81
Brier Lea (Lower Kingswood), Tad. 249 CZ126
Brier Rd, Tad. 233 CV119
Brierley (New Addington), Croy. 221 EB107
Brierley Av N9 100 DW46
Brierley Cl SE25 202 DU98
Brierley Cl, Horn. 128 FJ58
Brierley Rd E11 123 ED63
Brierley Rd SW12 181 DJ89
Brierly Cl, Guil. 242 AU132
Brierly Gdns E2 142 DW68
Royston St
Briery Ct, Hem.H. 40 BN19
Briery Ct, Rick. 74 BG42
Briery Fld, Rick. 74 BG42
Briery Way, Amer. 55 AS37
Briery Way, Hem.H. 40 BN18
Brig Ms SE8 163 EA79
Watergate St
Brigade Cl, Har. 117 CD61
Brigade Pl, Cat. 236 DQ122
Coulsdon Rd
Brigade St SE3 164 EF82
Royal Par
Brigadier Av, Enf. 82 DQ39
Brigadier Hill, Enf. 82 DQ38
Briggeford Cl E5 122 DU61
Geldeston Rd
Briggs Cl, Mitch. 201 DH95
Bright Cl, Belv. 166 EX77
Bright Hill, Guil. 258 AX136
Bright St E14 143 EB72
Brightfield Rd SE12 184 EF85
Brightlands (Northfleet), Grav. 190 GE91
Brightlands Rd, Reig. 250 DC132
Brightling Rd SE4 183 DZ86
Brightlingsea Pl E14 143 DZ73
Brightman Rd SW18 180 DD88
Brighton Av E17 123 DZ57
Brighton Cl, Add. 212 BJ106
Brighton Cl, Uxb. 135 BP66
Brighton Dr, Nthlt. 136 CA65
Brighton Rd E6 145 EN69
Brighton Rd N2 98 DC54
Brighton Rd N16 122 DS63
Brighton Rd, Add. 212 BJ105
Brighton Rd, Bans. 217 CZ114
Brighton Rd, Couls. 235 DJ119
Brighton Rd, Horl. 268 DF149
Brighton Rd, Pur. 220 DQ110
Brighton Rd, Red. 266 DF135
Brighton Rd, S.Croy. 220 DQ106
Brighton Rd, Surb. 197 CJ100
Brighton Rd, Sutt. 218 DB109
Brighton Rd, Tad. 233 CY119
Brighton Rd, Wat. 75 BU38
Brighton Spur, Slou. 131 AP70
Brighton Ter SW9 161 DM84
Brighton Ter, Red. 266 DF135
Hooley La
Brights Av, Rain. 147 FH70
Brightside, The, Enf. 83 DX39
Brightside Av, Stai. 174 BJ94
Brightside Rd SE13 183 ED86
Brightview Cl (Bricket Wd), St.Alb. 60 BY29
Brightwell Cl, Croy. 201 DN102
Sumner Rd
Brightwell Cres SW17 180 DF92
Brightwell Rd, Wat. 75 BU43
Brigstock Rd, Belv. 167 FB77
Brigstock Rd, Couls. 235 DH115
Brigstock Rd, Th.Hth. 201 DN99
Brill Pl NW1 273 N1
Brill Pl NW1 141 DK68
Brim Hill N2 120 DC56
Brimfield Rd, Purf. 169 FR77
Brimpsfield Cl SE2 166 EV76
Brimsdown Av, Enf. 83 DY40
Brimsdown Ind Est, Enf. 83 DZ40
Brimshot La (Chobham), Wok. 210 AS109
Brimstone Cl, Orp. 224 EW108
Brimstone La, Dor. 264 CM143
Brimstone Wk, Berk. 38 AT17
Brindle Gate, Sid. 185 ES88
Brindle La (Forty Grn), Beac. 88 AG51
Brindles, Horn. 128 FL56
Brindles, The, Bans. 233 CZ117
Brindles Cl, Brwd. 109 GC47
Brindley Cl, Bexh. 167 FB83
Brindley Cl, Wem. 137 CK67
Brindley Ho SW2 181 DL87
New Pk Rd
Brindley St SE14 163 DZ81
Brindley Way, Brom. 184 EG92
Brindley Way, Hem.H. 58 BM25
London Rd
Brindley Way, Sthl. 136 CB73
Brindwood Rd E4 101 DZ48
Brinkburn Cl SE2 166 EU77
Brinkburn Cl, Edg. 96 CP54
Brinkburn Gdns, Edg. 118 CN55
Brinkley, Kings.T. 198 CN96
Burritt Rd
Brinkley Rd, Wor.Pk. 199 CV103
Brinklow Ct, St.Alb. 42 CB23
Brinklow Cres SE18 165 EP80
Brinklow Ho W2 140 DB71
Brinkworth Rd, Ilf. 124 EL55
Brinkworth Way E9 143 DZ65
Brinley Cl (Cheshunt), Wal.Cr. 67 DX31
Brinsdale Rd NW4 119 CX56
Brinsley Rd, Har. 95 CD54
Brinsley St E1 142 DV72
Watney St
Brinsmead (Park St), St.Alb. 61 CE27
Brinsmead Rd, Rom. 106 FN54
Brinsworth Cl, Twick. 177 CD89
Brinton Wk SE1 278 F3
Brion Pl E14 143 EC71
Brisbane Av SW19 200 DB95
Brisbane Ct N10 99 DH52
Sydney Rd
Brisbane Ho, Til. 171 GF81
Leicester Rd
Brisbane Rd E10 123 EB61
Brisbane Rd W13 157 CG75
Brisbane Rd, Ilf. 125 EP59
Brisbane St SE5 162 DR80
Briscoe Cl E11 124 EF61
Briscoe Cl, Hodd. 49 DZ15
Briscoe Rd SW19 180 DD93
Briscoe Rd, Hodd. 49 DZ15
Briscoe Rd, Rain. 148 FJ68
Briset Rd SE9 164 EK83
Briset St EC1 274 F6
Briset Way N7 121 DM61
Brisson Cl, Esher 214 BZ107
Bristol Cl (Stanwell), Stai. 174 BL86
Bristol Gdns SW15 179 CW87
Portsmouth Rd
Bristol Gdns W9 140 DB70
Bristol Ms W9 140 DB70
Bristol Gdns
Bristol Pk Rd E17 123 DY56
Bristol Rd E7 144 EJ65
Bristol Rd, Grav. 191 GK90
Bristol Rd, Grnf. 136 CB67
Bristol Rd, Mord. 200 DC99
Bristol Way, Slou. 132 AT74
Briston Gro N8 121 DL58
Briston Ms NW7 97 CU52
Bristow Rd SE19 182 DS92
Bristow Rd, Bexh. 166 EY81
Bristow Rd, Croy. 219 DL105
Bristow Rd, Houns. 156 CC83
Britannia Cl SW4 161 DK84
Bowland Rd
Britannia Cl, Nthlt. 136 BX69
Britannia Dr, Grav. 191 GM92
Britannia Gate E16 144 EG74
Britannia Ind Est (Colnbrook), Slou. 153 BE82
Britannia La, Twick. 176 CC87
Britannia Rd E14 163 EA77
Britannia Rd N12 98 DC48
Britannia Rd SW6 160 DB80
Britannia Rd, Brwd. 108 FW50
Britannia Rd, Chesh. 54 AQ29
Britannia Rd, Ilf. 125 EP62
Britannia Rd, Surb. 198 CM101
Britannia Rd, Wal.Cr. 67 DZ34
Britannia Row N1 141 DP67
Britannia St WC1 274 B2
Britannia St WC1 141 DM69
Britannia Wk N1 275 K2
Britannia Wk N1 142 DR68
Britannia Way NW10 138 CP70
Britannia Way SW6 160 DB81
Britannia Rd
Britannia Way (Stanwell), Stai. 174 BK87
British Gro W4 159 CT78
British Gro Pas W4 159 CT78
British Gro S W4 159 CT78
British Gro Pas
British Legion Rd E4 102 EF47
British St E3 143 DZ69
Briton Cl, S.Croy. 220 DS111
Briton Cres, S.Croy. 220 DS111
Briton Hill Rd, S.Croy. 220 DS110
Brittain Rd, Dag. 126 EY62
Brittain Rd, Walt. 214 BX106
Brittains La, Sev. 256 FF123
Britten Cl NW11 120 DB60
Britten Cl, Borwd. 77 CK44
Rodgers Cl
Britten Dr, Sthl. 136 CA72
Britten St SW3 160 DE78
Brittenden Cl, Orp. 223 ES107
Brittens Cl, Guil. 242 AU129
Britton Av, St.Alb. 43 CD20
Britton Cl SE6 183 ED87
Brownhill Rd
Britton St EC1 274 F5
Britton St EC1 141 DP70
Britwell Est, Slou. 131 AN70
Britwell Rd, Slou. 131 AK69
Brixham Cres, Ruis. 115 BU60
Brixham Gdns, Ilf. 125 ES64
Brixham Rd, Well. 166 EX81
Brixham St E16 145 EN74
Brixton Est, Edg. 96 CP54
Brixton Hill SW2 181 DL87
Brixton Hill Pl SW2 181 DL87
Brixton Hill
Brixton Oval SW2 161 DN84
Brixton Rd SW9 161 DN82
Brixton Rd, Wat. 75 BV39
Brixton Sta Rd SW9 161 DN84
Brixton Water La SW2 181 DM85
Broad Acre (Bricket Wd), St.Alb. 60 BY30
Broad Acres, Gdmg. 258 AS143
Broad Acres, Hat. 45 CT15
Broad Cl, Walt. 196 BX104
Broad Ct WC2 274 A9
Broad Ct, Welw.G.C. 29 CY09
Broad Ditch Rd (Southfleet), Grav. 190 GC94
Broad Grn, Hert. 47 DM15
Broad Grn Av, Croy. 201 DP101
Broad Grn Wd, Hert. 47 DM15
Broad Highway, Cob. 214 BX114
Broad La EC2 275 M6
Broad La EC2 142 DS71
Broad La N8 121 DM57
Tottenham La
Broad La N15 122 DT56
Broad La, Beac. 110 AH55
Broad La, Dart. 187 FG91
Broad La, Hmptn. 176 CA93
Broad La (Wooburn Grn), H.Wyc. 110 AG58
Broad Lawn SE9 185 EN89
Broad Mead, Ash. 232 CM117
Broad Oak, Slou. 131 AQ70
Broad Oak, Sun. 175 BT93
Broad Oak, Wdf.Grn. 102 EH50
Broad Oak Cl E4 101 EA50
Royston Av
Broad Oak Cl, Orp. 206 EU96
Broad Platts, Slou. 152 AX76
Broad Ride, Egh. 192 AU96
Broad Ride, Vir.W. 192 AU96
Broad Rd, Swans. 190 FY86
Broad Sanctuary SW1 277 N5
Broad Sanctuary SW1 161 DK75
Broad St, Chesh. 54 AQ30
Broad St, Dag. 146 FA66
Broad St, Hem.H. 40 BK19
Broad St, Tedd. 177 CF93
Broad St Av EC2 275 M7
Broad St Pl EC2 275 L7
Broad Vw NW9 118 CN58
Broad Wk N21 99 DM47
Broad Wk NW1 273 H3
Broad Wk NW1 141 DH69
Broad Wk SE3 164 EJ82
Broad Wk W1 276 F2
Broad Wk W1 140 DG74
Broad Wk, Cat. 236 DT122
Broad Wk, Couls. 234 DG123
Broad Wk, Croy. 221 DY110
Broad Wk, Epsom 232 CS117
Chalk La
Broad Wk (Burgh Heath), Epsom 233 CX119
Broad Wk, Harl. 35 ER14
Broad Wk, Houns. 156 BX81
Broad Wk, Orp. 206 EX104
Broad Wk, Rich. 158 CM80
Broad Wk, Sev. 257 FL128
Broad Wk, The W8 140 DB74
Broad Wk, The, E.Mol. 197 CF97
Broad Wk La NW11 119 CZ59
Broad Wk N, The, Brwd. 109 GA49
Broad Wk S, The, Brwd. 109 GA49
Broad Water Cres, Wey. 195 BQ104
Churchill Dr
Broad Yd EC1 274 F5
Broadacre, Stai. 174 BG92
Broadacre Cl, Uxb. 115 BP62
Broadacres, Guil. 242 AS132
Broadbent Cl N6 121 DH60
Broadbent St W1 273 H10
Broadberry Ct N18 100 DV50
Broadbridge Cl SE3 164 EG80
Broadbridge La, Horl. 269 DN148
Broadcoombe, S.Croy. 220 DW108
Broadcroft, Hem.H. 40 BK18
Broadcroft Av, Stan. 95 CK54
Broadcroft Rd, Orp. 205 ER101
Broadeaves Cl, S.Croy. 220 DS106
Broadfield, Harl. 35 ES14
Broadfield Cl NW2 119 CW62
Broadfield Cl, Croy. 201 DM103
Progress Way
Broadfield Cl, Rom. 127 FF57
Broadfield Cl, Tad. 233 CW120
Broadfield Ct, Bushey 95 CE47
Broadfield La NW1 141 DL66
Broadfield Pl, Welw.G.C. 29 CV10
Broadfield Rd SE6 184 EE87
Broadfield Rd (Peaslake), Guil. 261 BR142
Broadfield Rd, Hem.H. 40 BM20
Broadfield Sq, Enf. 82 DV40
Broadfield Way, Buck.H. 102 EJ48
Broadfields, E.Mol. 197 CD100
Broadfields, Har. 94 CB54
Broadfields, Saw. 36 EV06
Broadfields (Cheshunt), Wal.Cr. 65 DP29
Broadfields Av N21 99 DN45
Broadfields Av, Edg. 96 CP49
Broadfields Hts, Edg. 96 CP49
Broadfields La, Wat. 93 BV46
Broadfields Way NW10 119 CT64
Broadford La (Chobham), Wok. 210 AT112
Broadford Pk (Shalford), Guil. 258 AX141
Broadford Rd (Peasmarsh), Guil. 258 AW142
Broadgate E13 144 EJ68
Broadgate EC2 142 DS71
Liverpool St
Broadgate, Wal.Abb. 68 EF33
Broadgate Circle EC2 275 M6
Broadgate Rd E16 144 EK72
Broadgates Av, Barn. 80 DB39
Broadgates Rd SW18 180 DD88
Ellerton Rd
Broadgreen Rd (Cheshunt), Wal.Cr. 66 DR26
Broadham Grn Rd, Oxt. 253 ED132
Broadham Pl, Oxt. 253 ED131
Broadhead Strand NW9 97 CT53
Broadheath Dr, Chis. 185 EM92
Broadhinton Rd SW4 161 DH83
Broadhurst, Ash. 232 CL116
Broadhurst Av, Edg. 96 CP49
Broadhurst Av, Ilf. 125 ET63
Broadhurst Cl NW6 140 DC65
Broadhurst Gdns
Broadhurst Cl, Rich. 178 CM85
Lower Gro Rd
Broadhurst Gdns NW6 140 DB65
Broadhurst Gdns, Chig. 103 EQ49
Broadhurst Gdns, Reig. 266 DB137
Broadhurst Gdns, Ruis. 116 BW61
Broadhurst Wk, Rain. 147 FG65
Broadlake Cl (London Colney), St.Alb. 61 CK27
Broadlands, Felt. 176 BZ90
Broadlands, Grays 170 FZ78
Bankfoot
Broadlands, Horl. 269 DJ147
Broadlands Av SW16 181 DL89
Broadlands Av, Chesh. 54 AQ31
Broadlands Av, Enf. 82 DV41
Broadlands Av, Shep. 195 BQ100
Broadlands Cl N6 120 DG59
Broadlands Cl SW16 181 DL89
Broadlands Cl, Enf. 82 DV41
Broadlands Cl, Wal.Cr. 67 DX34
Broadlands Dr, Warl. 236 DW119
Broadlands Rd N6 120 DF59
Broadlands Rd, Brom. 184 EH91
Broadlands Way, N.Mal. 199 CT100
Broadlawns Ct, Har. 95 CF53
Broadleaf Gro, Welw.G.C. 29 CV06
Broadley Gdns (Shenley), Rad. 62 CL32
Queens Way
Broadley Rd, Harl. 51 EM19
Broadley St NW8 272 A6
Broadley St NW8 140 DE71
Broadley Ter NW1 272 C5
Broadley Ter NW1 140 DE70
Broadmark Rd, Slou. 132 AV73
Broadmayne SE17 279 K10
Broadmead SE6 183 EA90
Broadmead, Horl. 269 DJ147
Broadmead Av, Wor.Pk. 199 CU101
Broadmead Cl, Hmptn. 176 CA93
Broadmead Cl, Pnr. 94 BY52
Broadmead Est, Wdf.Grn. 102 EJ52
Broadmead Rd, Hayes 136 BY70
Broadmead Rd, Nthlt. 136 BY70
Broadmead Rd (Old Woking), Wok. 227 BB122
Broadmead Rd, Wdf.Grn. 102 EG51
Broadmeads, Ware 33 DX06
Broadmeads (Send), Wok. 227 BB122
Broadmead Rd
Broadoak Av, Enf. 83 DX35
Broadoak Cl (Sutton at Hone), Dart. 188 FN93
Broadoak Ct, Slou. 131 AQ70
Broadoak Rd, Erith 167 FD80
Broadoaks, Epp. 69 ET31
Broadoaks, Surb. 198 CP102
Broadoaks Cres, W.Byf. 212 BH114
Broadoaks Way, Brom. 204 EF99
Broadstone Pl W1 272 F7
Broadstone Rd, Horn. 127 FG61
Broadstrood, Loug. 85 EN38
Broadview Av, Grays 170 GD75
Broadview Rd SW16 181 DK94
Broadview Rd, Chesh. 54 AP27
Broadwalk E18 124 EF55
Broadwalk, Har. 116 CA57
Broadwalk, The, Nthwd. 93 BQ54
Broadwalk Ct W8 140 DA74
Broadwalk Shop Cen, Edg. 96 CN51
Broadwall SE1 278 E2
Broadwall SE1 141 DN74
Broadwater, Berk. 38 AW18
Broadwater, Pot.B. 64 DB30
Broadwater Cl (Wraysbury), Stai. 173 AZ87
Broadwater Cl, Walt. 213 BU106
Broadwater Cl, Wok. 211 BD112
Broadwater Cres, Welw.G.C. 29 CX10
Broadwater Gdns, Orp. 223 EP105
Broadwater Gdns (Harefield), Uxb. 114 BH56
Broadwater La (Harefield), Uxb. 114 BH56
Broadwater Pk, Maid. 150 AE78
Broadwater Pk (Denham), Uxb. 114 BG58
Broadwater Pl, Wey. 195 BS103
Oatlands Dr
Broadwater Ri, Guil. 243 BA134
Broadwater Rd N17 100 DS53
Broadwater Rd SE28 165 ER76

Broseley Rd, Rom. 106 FL49
Broster Gdns SE25 202 DT97
Brough Cl SW8 161 DL80
Kenchester Cl
Brough Cl, Kings.T. 177 CK92
Brougham Rd E8 142 DU67
Brougham Rd W3 138 CQ72
Brougham St SW11 160 DF82
Broughinge Rd, Borwd. 78 CP40
Broughton Av N3 119 CY55
Broughton Av, Rich. 177 CH90
Broughton Dr SW9 161 DN84
Broughton Gdns N6 121 DJ58
Broughton Rd SW6 160 DB82
Broughton Rd W13 137 CH73
Broughton Rd, Orp. 205 ER103
Broughton Rd (Otford), Sev. 241 FG116
Broughton Rd, Th.Hth. 201 DN100
Broughton Rd App SW6 160 DB82
Wandsworth Br Rd
Broughton St SW8 160 DG82
Broughton Way, Rick. 92 BG45
Brouncker Rd W3 158 CQ75
Brow, The, Ch.St.G. 90 AX48
Brow, The, Red. 266 DG139
Spencer Way
Brow, The, Wat. 59 BV33
Brow Cl, Orp. 206 EX101
Brow Cres
Brow Cres, Orp. 206 EW102
Browells La, Felt. 175 BV89
Brown Cl, Wall. 219 DL108
Brown Hart Gdns W1 272 G10
Brown Hart Gdns W1 140 DG73
Brown Rd, Grav. 191 GL88
Brown St W1 272 D8
Brown St W1 140 DF72
Brownacres Towpath, Wey. 195 BP102
Browne Cl, Brwd. 108 FV46
Browne Cl, Rom. 105 FB50
Bamford Way
Brownfield St E14 143 EB72
Brownfields, Welw.G.C. 29 CZ08
Brownfields Ct, Welw.G.C. 30 DA08
Brownfields
Browngraves Rd, Hayes 155 BQ80
Brownhill Rd SE6 183 EB87
Browning Av W7 137 CF72
Browning Av, Sutt. 218 DE105
Browning Av, Wor.Pk. 199 CV102
Browning Cl E17 123 EC56
Browning Cl W9 140 DC70
Randolph Av
Browning Cl, Hmptn. 176 BZ91
Browning Cl, Rom. 104 EZ52
Browning Cl, Well. 165 ES81
Browning Ho W12 139 CW72
Wood La
Browning Ms W1 273 H7
Browning Rd E11 124 EF59
Browning Rd E12 145 EM65
Browning Rd, Dart. 168 FM84
Browning Rd, Enf. 82 DR38
Browning Rd (Fetcham), Lthd. 247 CD125
Browning St SE17 279 J10
Browning St SE17 162 DQ78
Browning Wk, Til. 171 GJ82
Coleridge Rd
Browning Way, Houns. 156 BX81
Brownlea Gdns, Ilf. 126 EU61
Brownlow Ms WC1 274 C5
Brownlow Ms WC1 141 DM70
Brownlow Rd E7 124 EH63
Woodford Rd
Brownlow Rd E8 142 DT67
Brownlow Rd N3 98 DB52
Brownlow Rd N11 99 DL51
Brownlow Rd NW10 138 CS66
Brownlow Rd W13 137 CG74
Brownlow Rd, Berk. 38 AW18
Brownlow Rd, Borwd. 78 CN42
Brownlow Rd, Croy. 220 DS105
Brownlow Rd, Red. 250 DE134
Brownlow St WC1 274 C7
Brownlow St WC1 141 DM71
Brownrigg Rd, Ashf. 174 BN91
Brown's Bldgs EC3 275 N9
Brown's Bldgs EC3 142 DS72
Browns La NW5 121 DH64
Browns La (Effingham), Lthd. 246 BX127
Browns Rd E17 123 EA55
Browns Rd, Surb. 198 CM101
Browns Spring, Berk. 39 BC16
Brownsea Wk NW7 97 CX51
Sanders La
Brownspring Dr SE9 185 EP91
Brownswell Rd N2 98 DD54
Brownswood Rd N4 121 DP62
Brownswood Rd, Beac. 89 AK51
Brox La (Ottershaw), Cher. 211 BD109
Brox Rd (Ottershaw), Cher. 211 BC107
Broxash Rd SW11 180 DG86
Broxbourne Av E18 124 EH56
Broxbourne Common, Brox. 48 DU19
Broxbourne Rd E7 124 EG62
Broxbourne Rd, Orp. 205 ET101
Broxbournebury Ms, Brox. 48 DW21
White Stubbs La
Broxburn Dr, S.Ock. 149 FV73
Broxburn Par, S.Ock. 149 FV73
Broxburn Dr
Broxhill Rd (Havering-atte-Bower), Rom. 105 FH48
Broxholm Rd SE27 181 DN90
Broxted Ms, Brwd. 109 GC44
Bannister Dr
Broxted Rd SE6 183 DZ89
Broxwood Way NW8 140 DE67
Bruce Av, Horn. 128 FK61
Bruce Av, Shep. 195 BQ100
Bruce Castle Rd N17 100 DT53
Bruce Cl W10 139 CY71
Ladbroke Gro
Bruce Cl, Slou. 131 AN74
Bruce Cl, Well. 166 EV81
Bruce Cl (Byfleet), W.Byf. 212 BK113
Bruce Dr, S.Croy. 221 DX109
Bruce Gdns N20 98 DF48
Balfour Gro
Bruce Gro N17 100 DS53
Bruce Gro, Orp. 206 EU102
Bruce Gro, Wat. 76 BW38
Bruce Hall Ms SW17 180 DG91
Brudenell Rd
Bruce Rd E3 143 EB69
Bruce Rd NW10 138 CR66
Bruce Rd SE25 202 DR98
Bruce Rd, Barn. 79 CY41
St. Albans Rd
Bruce Rd, Har. 95 CE54
Bruce Rd, Mitch. 180 DG94
Bruce Wk, Wind. 151 AK82
Tinkers La
Bruce Way, Wal.Cr. 67 DX33
Bruce's Wf Rd, Grays 170 GA79
Bruckner St W10 139 CZ69
Brudenell, Wind. 151 AM83
Brudenell Rd SW17 180 DF90
Bruffs Meadow, Nthlt. 136 BY65
Bruges Pl NW1 141 DJ66
Randolph St
Brumana Cl, Wey. 213 BP106
Elgin Rd
Brumfield Rd, Epsom 216 CQ106
Brummel Cl, Bexh. 167 FC83
Brune St E1 275 P7
Brune St E1 142 DT71
Brunel Cl SE19 182 DT93
Brunel Cl, Houns. 155 BV80
Brunel Cl, Nthlt. 136 BZ69
Brunel Cl, Rom. 127 FE56
Brunel Cl, Til. 171 GH83
Brunel Est W2 140 DA71
Brunel Pl, Sthl. 136 CB72
Brunel Rd E17 123 DY58
Brunel Rd SE16 162 DW75
Brunel Rd W3 138 CS71
Brunel Rd, Wdf.Grn. 103 EM50
Brunel St E16 144 EF72
Victoria Dock Rd
Brunel Wk N15 122 DS56
Brunel Wk, Twick. 176 CA87
Stephenson Rd
Brunel Way, Slou. 132 AT74
Brunner Cl NW11 120 DC57
Brunner Ct (Ottershaw), Cher. 211 BC106
Brunner Rd E17 123 DZ57
Brunner Rd W5 137 CK70
Bruno Pl NW9 118 CQ61
Brunswick Av N11 98 DG48
Brunswick Av, Upmin. 129 FS59
Brunswick Cen WC1 273 P4
Brunswick Cl, Bexh. 166 EX84
Brunswick Cl, Pnr. 116 BY58
Brunswick Cl, T.Ditt. 197 CF102
Brunswick Cl, Twick. 177 CD90
Brunswick Cl, Walt. 196 BW103
Brunswick Ct EC1 141 DP69
Northampton Sq
Brunswick Ct SE1 279 N5
Brunswick Ct SE1 162 DS75
Brunswick Ct, Barn. 80 DD43
Brunswick Ct, Upmin. 129 FS59
Waycross Rd
Brunswick Cres N11 98 DG48
Brunswick Gdns W5 138 CL69
Brunswick Gdns W8 140 DA74
Brunswick Gdns, Ilf. 103 EQ52
Brunswick Gro N11 98 DG48
Brunswick Gro, Cob. 214 BW113
Brunswick Ind Pk N11 99 DH49
Brunswick Ms SW16 181 DK93
Potters La
Brunswick Ms W1 272 E8
Brunswick Pk SE5 162 DR81
Brunswick Pk Gdns N11 98 DG47
Brunswick Pk Rd N11 98 DG47
Brunswick Pl N1 275 L3
Brunswick Pl N1 142 DR69
Brunswick Pl SE19 182 DU94
Brunswick Quay SE16 163 DX76
Brunswick Rd E10 123 EC60
Brunswick Rd E14 143 EC72
Blackwall Tunnel Northern App
Brunswick Rd N15 122 DS57
Brunswick Rd W5 137 CK70
Brunswick Rd, Bexh. 166 EX84
Brunswick Rd, Enf. 83 EA38
Brunswick Rd, Kings.T. 198 CN95
Brunswick Rd, Sutt. 218 DB105
Brunswick Sq N17 100 DT51
Brunswick Sq WC1 274 A5
Brunswick Sq WC1 141 DL70
Brunswick St E17 123 EC57
Brunswick Vil SE5 162 DS81
Brunswick Wk, Grav. 191 GK87
Brunswick Way N11 99 DH49
Brunton Pl E14 143 DY72
Brushfield St E1 275 N7
Brushfield St E1 142 DS71
Brushrise, Wat. 75 BU36
Brushwood Dr, Rick. 73 BC42
Brushwood Rd, Chesh. 54 AR29
Brussels Rd SW11 160 DD84
Bruton Cl, Chis. 185 EM94
Bruton La W1 277 J1
Bruton La W1 141 DH73
Bruton Pl W1 277 J1
Bruton Pl W1 141 DH73
Bruton Rd, Mord. 200 DC99
Bruton St W1 277 J1
Bruton St W1 141 DH73
Bruton Way W13 137 CG71
Bryan Av NW10 139 CV66
Bryan Cl, Sun. 175 BU94
Bryan Rd SE16 163 DZ75
Bryan's All SW6 160 DB82
Wandsworth Br Rd
Bryanston Av, Twick. 176 CB88
Bryanston Cl, Sthl. 156 BZ77
Bryanston Ms E W1 272 D7
Bryanston Ms W W1 272 D7
Bryanston Pl W1 272 D7
Bryanston Pl W1 140 DF71
Bryanston Rd, Til. 171 GJ82
Bryanston Sq W1 272 D7
Bryanston Sq W1 140 DF71
Bryanston St W1 272 D9
Bryanston St W1 140 DF72
Bryanstone Av, Guil. 242 AU131
Bryanstone Cl, Guil. 242 AT131
Bryanstone Ct, Sutt. 218 DC105
Oakhill Rd
Bryanstone Gro, Guil. 242 AT130
Bryanstone Rd N8 121 DK57
Bryanstone Rd, Wal.Cr. 67 DZ34
Bryant Av, Rom. 106 FK53
Bryant Av, Slou. 132 AS71
Bryant Cl, Barn. 79 CZ43
Bryant Ct E2 142 DT68
Bryant Rd, Nthlt. 136 BW69
Bryant Row, Rom. 106 FJ48
Cummings Hall La
Bryant St E15 143 ED66
Bryantwood Rd N7 121 DN64
Bryce Rd, Dag. 126 EW63
Brycedale Cres N14 99 DK49
Bryden Cl SE26 183 DY92
Brydges Pl WC2 277 P1
Brydges Rd E15 123 ED64
Brydon Wk N1 141 DL67
Outram Pl
Bryer Ct EC2 142 DQ71
Aldersgate St
Bryer Pl, Wind. 151 AK83
Bryett Rd N7 121 DL62
Brymay Cl E3 143 EA68
Brympton Cl, Dor. 263 CG138
Bryn-y-Mawr Rd, Enf. 82 DT42
Brynford Cl, Wok. 226 AY115
Brynmaer Rd SW11 160 DF81
Bryony Cl, Loug. 85 EP42
Bryony Cl, Uxb. 134 BM71
Bryony Rd W12 139 CU73
Bryony Rd, Guil. 243 BB131
Bryony Way, Sun. 175 BT93
Bubblestone Rd (Otford), Sev. 241 FH116
Buccleuch Rd (Datchet), Slou. 152 AU80
Buchan Cl, Uxb. 134 BJ69
Buchan Rd SE15 162 DW83
Buchanan Cl N21 81 DM43
Buchanan Cl, S.Ock. 148 FQ74
Buchanan Ct, Borwd. 78 CQ40
Buchanan Gdns NW10 139 CV68
Bucharest Rd SW18 180 DC87
Buck Hill Wk W2 276 A1
Buck La NW9 118 CR57
Buck St NW1 141 DH66
Buck Wk E17 123 ED56
Wood St
Buckbean Path, Rom. 106 FJ52
Clematis Cl
Buckden Cl N2 120 DF56
Southern Rd
Buckden Cl SE12 184 EF86
Upwood Rd
Buckettsland La, Borwd. 78 CR38
Buckfast Rd, Mord. 200 DB98
Buckfast St E2 142 DU69
Buckham Thorns Rd, West. 255 EQ126
Buckhold Rd SW18 180 DA86
Buckhurst Av, Cars. 200 DE102
Buckhurst Av, Sev. 257 FJ125
Buckhurst Cl, Red. 250 DE132
Buckhurst La, Sev. 257 FJ125
Buckhurst Rd, West. 239 EN121
Buckhurst St E1 142 DV70
Buckhurst Way, Buck.H. 102 EK49
Buckingham Arc WC2 278 A1
Buckingham Av N20 98 DC45
Buckingham Av, Felt. 175 BV86
Buckingham Av, Grnf. 137 CG67
Buckingham Av, Slou. 131 AN72
Buckingham Av, Th.Hth. 201 DN95
Buckingham Av, Well. 165 ES84
Buckingham Av, W.Mol. 196 CB97
Buckingham Av E, Slou. 131 AQ72
Buckingham Cl W5 137 CJ71
Buckingham Cl, Enf. 82 DS40
Buckingham Cl, Guil. 243 AZ133
Buckingham Cl, Hmptn. 176 BZ92
Buckingham Cl, Horn. 128 FK58
Buckingham Cl, Orp. 205 ES101
Buckingham Ct NW4 119 CU55
Buckingham Ct, Loug. 85 EN40
Rectory La
Buckingham Dr, Chis. 185 EP92
Buckingham Gdns, Edg. 96 CM52
Buckingham Gdns, Slou. 152 AT75
Buckingham Gdns, Th.Hth. 201 DN96
Buckingham Gdns, W.Mol. 196 CB96
Buckingham Av
Buckingham Gate SW1 277 K5
Buckingham Gate SW1 161 DJ76
Buckingham Gate, Gat. 269 DJ152
Buckingham Gro, Uxb. 134 BN68
Buckingham La SE23 183 DY87
Buckingham Ms N1 142 DS65
Buckingham Rd
Buckingham Ms NW10 139 CT68
Buckingham Rd
Buckingham Ms SW1 277 K6
Buckingham Palace Rd SW1 277 H9
Buckingham Palace Rd SW1 161 DH77
Buckingham Pl SW1 277 K6
Buckingham Rd E10 123 EB62
Buckingham Rd E11 124 EJ57
Buckingham Rd E15 124 EF64
Buckingham Rd E18 102 EF53
Buckingham Rd N1 142 DS65
Buckingham Rd N22 99 DL53
Buckingham Rd NW10 139 CT68
Buckingham Rd, Borwd. 78 CR42
Buckingham Rd, Edg. 96 CM52
Buckingham Rd, Grav. 190 GD87
Dover Rd
Buckingham Rd, Hmptn. 176 BZ92
Buckingham Rd, Har. 117 CD57
Buckingham Rd, Ilf. 125 ER61
Buckingham Rd, Kings.T. 198 CM98
Buckingham Rd, Mitch. 201 DL99
Buckingham Rd, Rich. 177 CK89
Buckingham Rd, Wat. 76 BW37
Buckingham St WC2 278 A1
Buckingham Way, Wall. 219 DJ109
Buckland Av, Slou. 152 AV77
Buckland Cres NW3 140 DD66
Buckland Cres, Wind. 151 AM81
Buckland La, Bet. 249 CT129
Buckland La, Tad. 249 CT129
Buckland Ri, Pnr. 94 BW53
Buckland Rd E10 123 EC61
Buckland Rd, Chess. 216 CM106
Buckland Rd, Orp. 223 ES105
Buckland Rd, Reig. 249 CX133
Buckland Rd, Sutt. 217 CW110
Buckland Rd (Lower Kingswood), Tad. 249 CZ128
Buckland St N1 275 L1
Buckland St N1 142 DR68
Buckland Wk W3 158 CQ75
Buckland Wk, Mord. 200 DC98
Buckland Way, Wor.Pk. 199 CW102
Bucklands, The, Rick. 92 BG45
Bucklands Rd, Tedd. 177 CJ93
Buckle St E1 142 DT72
Leman St
Bucklebury Cl, Maid. 150 AC78
Buckleigh Av SW20 199 CY97
Buckleigh Rd SW16 181 DK93
Buckleigh Way SE19 202 DT95
Buckler Gdns SE9 185 EM90
Southold Ri
Bucklers All SW6 159 CZ79
Bucklers Cl, Brox. 49 DZ22
Bucklers Ct, Brwd. 108 FW50
Bucklers Way, Cars. 200 DF104
Bucklersbury EC4 275 K9
Bucklersbury EC4 142 DR72
Bucklersbury Pas EC4 275 K9
Buckles Ct, Belv. 166 EX76
Fendyke Rd
Buckles La, S.Ock. 149 FW71
Buckles Way, Bans. 233 CY116
Buckley Cl, Dart. 167 FF82
Buckley Rd NW6 139 CZ66
Buckley St SE1 278 D3
Buckmaster Cl SW9 161 DM83
Stockwell Pk Rd
Buckmaster Rd SW11 160 DE84
Bucknall St WC2 273 N8
Bucknall St WC2 141 DK72
Bucknall Way, Beck. 203 EB98
Bucknalls Cl, Wat. 60 BY32
Bucknalls Dr (Bricket Wd), St.Alb. 60 BZ31
Bucknalls La, Wat. 60 BX32
Bucknell Cl SW2 161 DM84
Buckner Rd SW2 161 DM84
Bucknills Cl, Epsom 216 CP114
Buckrell Rd E4 101 ED47
Bucks All, Hert. 47 DK19
Bucks Av, Wat. 94 BY45
Bucks Cl, W.Byf. 212 BH114
Bucks Cross Rd (Northfleet), Grav. 191 GF90
Bucks Cross Rd, Orp. 224 EY106
Bucks Hill, Kings L. 58 BK34
Buckstone Cl SE23 182 DW86
Buckstone Rd N18 100 DU50
Buckters Rents SE16 143 DY74
Buckthorne Ho, Chig. 104 EV49
Buckthorne Rd SE4 183 DY86
Buckton Rd, Borwd. 78 CM38
Budd Cl N12 98 DB49
Buddcroft, Welw.G.C. 30 DB08
Buddings Circle, Wem. 118 CQ62
Budd's All, Twick. 177 CJ85
Arlington Cl
Bude Cl E17 123 DZ57
Budebury Rd, Stai. 174 BG92
Budge La, Mitch. 200 DF101
Budge Row EC4 275 K10
Budgen Dr, Red. 250 DG131
Budge's Wk W2 140 DC73
Budgin's Hill, Orp. 224 EW112
Budleigh Cres, Well. 166 EW81
Budoch Ct, Ilf. 126 EU61
Budoch Dr, Ilf. 126 EU61
Buer Rd SW6 159 CY82
Buff Av, Bans. 218 DB114
Buffins, Maid. 130 AE69
Bug Hill (Woldingham), Cat. 237 DX120
Bugsby's Way SE7 164 EH77
Bugsby's Way SE10 164 EF77
Bulbourne Cl, Berk. 38 AT17
Bulbourne Cl, Hem.H. 40 BG21
Bulganak Rd, Th.Hth. 202 DQ98
Bulinga St SW1 277 P9
Bulinga St SW1 161 DK77
Bulkeley Av, Wind. 151 AP82
Bulkeley Cl (Englefield Grn), Egh. 172 AW91
Bull All, Well. 166 EV83
Welling High St
Bull Cl, Grays 170 FZ75
Bull Hill (Horton Kirby), Dart. 208 FQ98
Bull Hill, Lthd. 231 CG121
Bull Inn Ct WC2 278 A1
Bull La N18 100 DS50
Bull La, Chis. 185 ER94
Bull La, Dag. 127 FB62
Bull La (Chalfont St. Peter), Ger.Cr. 112 AX55
Bull La (Sutton Grn), Guil. 243 AZ126
Bull Plain, Hert. 32 DR09
Bull Rd E15 144 EF68
Bull Stag Grn, Hat. 45 CW15
Bull Wf La EC4 275 J10
Bull Yd, Grav. 191 GH86
High St
Bullace Cl, Hem.H. 40 BG19
Bullace La, Dart. 188 FL86
High St
Bullace Row SE5 162 DQ81
Bullards Pl E2 143 DX69
Bullbanks Rd, Belv. 167 FC77
Bullbeggars La, Berk. 39 AZ20
Bullbeggars La, Gdse. 252 DW132
Bullbeggars La, Wok. 226 AV116
Bullen St SW11 160 DE82
Bullens Grn La (Colney Heath), St.Alb. 44 CS23
Buller Cl SE15 162 DU80
Buller Rd N17 100 DU54
Buller Rd N22 99 DN54
Buller Rd NW10 139 CX69
Chamberlayne Rd
Buller Rd, Bark. 145 ES66
Buller Rd, Th.Hth. 202 DR96
Bullers Cl, Sid. 186 EY92
Bullers Wd Dr, Chis. 184 EL94
Bullescroft Rd, Edg. 96 CN48
Bullfinch Cl, Horl. 268 DE147
Bullfinch Cl, Sev. 256 FD122
Bullfinch Dene, Sev. 256 FD122
Bullfinch La, Sev. 256 FD122
Bullfinch Rd, S.Croy. 221 DX110
Bullhead Rd, Borwd. 78 CQ41
Bullied Way SW1 277 J9
Bullivant Cl, Green. 189 FU85
Bullivant St E14 143 EC73
Bullocks La, Hert. 32 DQ11
Bullrush Cl, Croy. 202 DS100
Bullrush Cl, Hat. 45 CV19
Bullrush Gro, Uxb. 134 BJ70
Bull's All SW14 158 CR82
Bulls Br Ind Est, Sthl. 155 BV76
Bulls Br Rd, Sthl. 155 BV76
Bulls Cross, Enf. 82 DU37
Bulls Cross Ride, Wal.Cr. 82 DU35
Bulls Gdns SW3 276 C8
Bull's Head Pas EC3 275 M9
Bulls La, Hat. 45 CZ24
Bullsbrook Rd, Hayes 136 BW74
Bullsland Gdns, Rick. 73 BB44
Bullsland La, Ger.Cr. 91 BB45
Bullsland La, Rick. 73 BB44
Bullsmoor Cl, Wal.Cr. 82 DW35
Bullsmoor Gdns, Wal.Cr. 82 DV35
Bullsmoor La, Enf. 82 DW35
Bullsmoor La, Wal.Cr. 82 DU35
Bullsmoor Ride, Wal.Cr. 82 DW35
Bullsmoor Way, Wal.Cr. 82 DV35
Bullwell Cres (Cheshunt), Wal.Cr. 67 DY29
Bulmer Gdns, Har. 117 CK59
Bulmer Ms W11 140 DA73
Ladbroke Rd
Bulmer Pl W11 140 DA74
Bulmer Wk, Rain. 148 FJ68
Bulow Est SW6 160 DB82
Broughton Rd
Bulstrode Av, Houns. 156 BZ82
Bulstrode Ct, Ger.Cr. 112 AX58
Bulstrode Gdns, Houns. 156 BZ83
Bulstrode La (Felden), Hem.H. 58 BG27
Bulstrode La, Kings L. 57 BE29
Bulstrode Pl W1 272 G7
Bulstrode Pl, Slou. 152 AT76
Bulstrode Rd, Houns. 156 CA83
Bulstrode St W1 272 G8
Bulstrode St W1 140 DG72
Bulstrode Way, Ger.Cr. 112 AX57
Bulwer Ct Rd E11 123 ED60
Bulwer Gdns, Barn. 80 DC42
Bulwer Rd
Bulwer Rd E11 123 ED59
Bulwer Rd N18 100 DS49
Bulwer Rd, Barn. 80 DB42
Bulwer St W12 139 CW74
Bumbles Grn La, Wal.Abb. 68 EH25
Bunbury Way, Epsom 233 CV116
Bunby Rd (Stoke Poges), Slou. 132 AT66
Bunce Common Rd (Leigh), Reig. 264 CR141
Bunce Dr, Cat. 236 DR123
Buncefield La, Hem.H. 41 BR20
Bunces Cl (Eton Wick), Wind. 151 AP78
Bunces La, Wdf.Grn. 102 EF52
Bundys Way, Stai. 173 BF93
Bungalow Rd SE25 202 DS98
Bungalow Rd, Wok. 229 BQ124
Bungalows, The SW16 181 DH94
Bungalows, The, Wall. 219 DH106
Bunhill Row EC1 275 K4
Bunhill Row EC1 142 DR70
Bunhouse Pl SW1 276 F10
Bunhouse Pl SW1 160 DG78
Bunkers Hill NW11 120 DC59
Bunkers Hill, Belv. 166 FA77
Bunkers Hill, Sid. 186 EZ90
Bunkers La, Hem.H. 41 BQ24
Bunning Way N7 141 DL66
Bunns La NW7 97 CT51
Bunn's La, Chesh. 56 AU34
Bunnsfield, Welw.G.C. 30 DC08
Bunsen St E3 143 DY68
Kenilworth Rd
Bunten Meade, Slou. 131 AP74
Bunting Cl N9 101 DX46
Dunnock Cl
Bunting Cl, Mitch. 200 DF99
Buntingbridge Rd, Ilf. 125 ER57
Bunton St SE18 165 EN76
Bunyan Ct EC2 142 DQ71
Beech St
Bunyan Rd E17 123 DY55
Bunyard Dr, Wok. 211 BC114
Bunyons Cl, Brwd. 107 FW51
Essex Way
Buonaparte Ms SW1 277 M10
Burbage Cl SE1 279 K7
Burbage Cl SE1 162 DR76
Burbage Cl, Hayes 135 BR72
Burbage Cl (Cheshunt), Wal.Cr. 67 DZ31
Burbage Rd SE21 182 DR86
Burbage Rd SE24 182 DQ86
Burberry Cl, N.Mal. 198 CS96
Burbidge Rd, Shep. 194 BN98
Burbridge Way N17 100 DT54
Burch Rd (Northfleet), Grav. 191 GF86
Burcham St E14 143 EB72
Burcharbro Rd SE2 166 EX79
Burchell Ct, Bushey 94 CC45
Catsey La
Burchell Rd E10 123 EB60
Burchell Rd SE15 162 DV81
Burchets Hollow (Peaslake), Guil. 261 BR144
Burchett Way, Rom. 126 EZ58
Burchetts Way, Shep. 195 BP100
Burchwall Cl, Rom. 105 FC52
Burcote, Wey. 213 BR107
Burcote Rd SW18 180 DD88
Burcott Gdns, Add. 212 BJ107
Burcott Rd, Pur. 219 DN114
Burden Cl, Brent. 157 CJ78
Burden Way E11 124 EH61
Brading Cres
Burden Way, Guil. 242 AV129
Burdenshot Hill (Worplesdon), Guil. 242 AU125
Burdenshott Av, Rich. 158 CP84
Burdenshott Rd (Worplesdon), Guil. 242 AU125
Burdenshott Rd, Wok. 242 AU125
Burder Cl N1 142 DS65
Burder Rd N1 142 DS65
Balls Pond Rd
Burdett Av SW20 199 CU95
Burdett Cl W7 157 CF75
Cherington Rd
Burdett Cl, Sid. 186 EY92
Burdett Ms NW3 140 DD65
Belsize Cres
Burdett Ms W2 140 DB72
Hatherley Gro
Burdett Rd E3 143 DZ70
Burdett Rd E14 143 DZ70
Burdett Rd, Croy. 202 DR100
Burdett Rd, Rich. 158 CM83
Burdett St SE1 278 D6
Burdetts Rd, Dag. 146 EZ67
Burdock Cl, Croy. 203 DX102
Burdock Rd N17 122 DU55
Burdon La, Sutt. 217 CY108
Burdon Pk, Sutt. 217 CZ109
Burfield Cl SW17 180 DD91
Burfield Cl, Hat. 45 CU16
Burfield Dr, Warl. 236 DW119
Burfield Rd, Rick. 73 BB43
Burfield Rd (Old Windsor), Wind. 172 AU86
Burford Cl, Dag. 126 EW62
Burford Cl, Ilf. 125 EQ56
Burford Cl, Uxb. 114 BL63
Burford Gdns N13 99 DM48
Burford Gdns, Hodd. 49 EB16
Burford Gdns, Slou. 130 AJ71
Buttermere Av
Burford La, Epsom 217 CW111
Burford Ms, Hodd. 49 EA16
Burford St
Burford Pl, Hodd. 49 EB16
Burford Rd E6 144 EL69
Burford Rd E15 143 ED66
Burford Rd SE6 183 DZ89
Burford Rd, Brent. 158 CL78
Burford Rd, Brom. 204 EL98
Burford Rd, Sutt. 200 DA103
Burford Rd, Wor.Pk. 199 CT101
Burford St, Hodd. 49 EA17
Burford Wk SW6 160 DB80
Cambria St
Burford Way (New Addington), Croy. 221 EC107
Burgage La, Ware 33 DX06
Burgate Cl, Dart. 167 FF83
Burge St SE1 279 L7

Burge St SE1 162 DR76
Burges Cl, Horn. 128 FM58
Burges Ct E6 145 EN66
Burges Gro SW13 159 CV80
Burges Rd E6 144 EL66
Burges Way, Stai. 174 BG92
Burgess Av NW9 118 CR58
Burgess Cl, Felt. 176 BY91
Burgess Cl (Cheshunt), Wal.Cr. 66 DQ25
Burgess Ct, Borwd. 78 CM38
Belford Rd
Burgess Hill NW2 120 DA63
Burgess Rd E15 124 EE63
Burgess Rd, Sutt. 218 DB105
Burgess St E14 143 EA71
Burgess Wd Gro, Beac. 88 AH53
Burgess Wd Rd, Beac. 88 AH53
Burgess Wd Rd S, Beac. 110 AH55
Cadet Dr
Burgett Rd, Slou. 151 AP76
Burgh Heath Rd, Epsom 216 CS114
Burgh Mt, Bans. 233 CZ115
Burgh St N1 141 DP68
Burgh Wd, Bans. 233 CY115
Burghfield, Epsom 233 CT115
Burghfield Rd (Istead Ri), Grav. 191 GF94
Burghill Rd SE26 183 DY91
Burghley Av, Borwd. 78 CQ43
Burghley Av, N.Mal. 198 CR95
Burghley Hall Cl SW19 179 CY87
Burghley Ho SW19 179 CX90
Burghley Pl, Mitch. 200 DG99
Burghley Rd E11 124 EE60
Burghley Rd N8 121 DN55
Burghley Rd NW5 121 DH64
Burghley Rd SW19 179 CX91
Burghley Rd, Grays 169 FW76
Burghley Twr W3 139 CT73
Burgon St EC4 274 G9
Burgos Cl, Croy. 219 DN107
Burgos Gro SE10 163 EB81
Burgoyne Hatch, Harl. 36 EU14
Momples Rd
Burgoyne Rd N4 121 DP58
Burgoyne Rd SE25 202 DT98
Burgoyne Rd SW9 161 DM83
Burgoyne Rd, Sun. 175 BT93
Burgundy Cft, Welw.G.C. 29 CZ11
Burham Cl SE20 182 DW94
Maple Rd
Burhill Gro, Pnr. 94 BY54
Burhill Rd, Walt. 214 BW107
Burke Cl SW15 158 CS84
Burke St E16 144 EF72
Burkes Cl, Beac. 110 AH55
Burkes Cres, Beac. 89 AK53
Burkes Par, Beac. 89 AK52
Station Rd
Burkes Rd, Beac. 88 AJ54
Burket Cl, Sthl. 156 BZ77
Kingsbridge Rd
Burland Rd SW11 180 DF85
Burland Rd, Brwd. 108 FX46
Burland Rd, Rom. 105 FC51
Burlea Cl, Walt. 213 BV106
Burleigh Av, Sid. 185 ET85
Burleigh Av, Wall. 200 DG104
Burleigh Cl, Add. 212 BH106
Burleigh Gdns N14 99 DJ46
Burleigh Gdns, Ashf. 175 BQ92
Burleigh Ho W10 139 CX71
St. Charles Sq
Burleigh Mead, Hat. 45 CW16
Burleigh Pk, Cob. 214 BY112
Burleigh Pl SW15 179 CX85
Burleigh Rd, Add. 212 BH105
Burleigh Rd, Enf. 82 DS42
Burleigh Rd, Hem.H. 41 BQ21
Burleigh Rd, Hert. 32 DU08
Burleigh Rd, St.Alb. 43 CH20
Burleigh Rd, Sutt. 199 CY102
Burleigh Rd, Uxb. 135 BP67
Burleigh Rd (Cheshunt), Wal.Cr. 67 DY32
Burleigh St WC2 274 B10
Burleigh Wk SE6 183 EC88
Muirkirk Rd
Burleigh Way, Enf. 82 DR41
Church St
Burleigh Way (Cuffley), Pot.B. 65 DL30
Burley Cl E4 101 EA50
Burley Cl SW16 201 DK96
Burley Hill, Harl. 52 EX16
Burley Orchard, Cher. 194 BG100
Burley Rd E16 144 EJ72
Burlingham Cl, Guil. 243 BD132
Gilliat Dr
Burlings La (Knockholt), Sev. 239 ET118
Burlington Arc W1 277 K1
Burlington Arc W1 141 DJ73
Burlington Av, Rich. 158 CN81
Burlington Av, Rom. 127 FB58
Burlington Av, Slou. 152 AS75
Burlington Cl E6 144 EL72
Northumberland Rd
Burlington Cl W9 139 CZ70
Burlington Cl, Felt. 175 BR87
Burlington Cl, Orp. 205 EP103
Burlington Cl, Pnr. 115 BV55
Burlington Gdns W1 277 K1
Burlington Gdns W1 141 DJ73
Burlington Gdns W3 138 CQ74
Burlington Gdns W4 158 CQ78
Burlington Gdns, Rom. 126 EY59
Burlington La W4 158 CS80
Burlington Ms SW15 179 CZ85
Burlington Ms W3 138 CQ74
Burlington Pl SW6 159 CY82
Burlington Rd
Burlington Pl, Reig. 250 DA134
Burlington Pl, Wdf.Grn. 102 EG48
Burlington Ri, Barn. 98 DE46
Burlington Rd N10 98 DG54
Tetherdown
Burlington Rd N17 100 DU53
Burlington Rd SW6 159 CY82
Burlington Rd W4 158 CQ78
Burlington Rd, Enf. 82 DR39
Burlington Rd, Islw. 157 CD81
Burlington Rd, N.Mal. 199 CU98
Burlington Rd, Slou. 152 AS75
Burlington Rd (Burnham), Slou. 130 AH70
Burlington Rd, Th.Hth. 202 DQ96
Burma Rd N16 122 DR63
Burma Rd (Longcross), Cher. 192 AT104
Burman Cl, Dart. 188 FQ87
Burmester Rd SW17 180 DC90
Burn Cl, Add. 212 BK105
Burn Cl (Oxshott), Lthd. 230 CC115
Burn Side N9 100 DW48
Burn Wk (Burnham), Slou. 130 AH70
Burnaby Cres W4 158 CP79
Burnaby Gdns W4 158 CQ79
Burnaby Rd (Northfleet), Grav. 190 GE87
Burnaby St SW10 160 DC80
Burnbrae Cl N12 98 DB51
Burnbury Rd SW12 181 DJ88
Burncroft Av, Enf. 82 DW40
Burne Jones Ho W14 159 CZ77
Burne St NW1 272 B6
Burne St NW1 140 DE71
Burnell Av, Rich. 177 CJ92
Burnell Av, Well. 166 EU82
Burnell Gdns, Stan. 95 CK53
Burnell Rd, Sutt. 218 DB105
Burnell Wk SE1 162 DT78
Cadet Dr
Burnell Wk, Brwd. 107 FW51
Burnels Av E6 145 EN69
Burness Cl N7 141 DM65
Roman Way
Burness Cl, Uxb. 134 BK68
Whitehall Rd
Burnet Av, Guil. 243 BB131
Burnet Cl, Hem.H. 40 BL21
Burnet Gro, Epsom 216 CQ113
Burnett Cl E9 122 DW64
Burnett Pk, Harl. 51 EP20
Burnett Rd, Erith 168 FK79
Burnett Sq, Hert. 31 DM08
Burnetts Rd, Wind. 151 AL81
Burney Av, Surb. 198 CM99
Burney Cl (Fetcham), Lthd. 246 CC125
Burney Dr, Loug. 85 EP40
Burney Rd (Westhumble), Dor. 247 CG131
Burney St SE10 163 EC80
Burnfoot Av SW6 159 CY81
Burnfoot Ct SE22 182 DV88
Burnham NW3 140 DE66
Burnham Av, Beac. 111 AN55
Burnham Av, Uxb. 115 BQ63
Burnham Cl NW7 97 CU52
Burnham Cl SE1 162 DT77
Bushwood Dr
Burnham Cl, Enf. 82 DS38
Burnham Cl (Wealdstone), Har. 117 CG56
Burnham Cl, Wind. 151 AK82
Burnham Ct NW4 119 CW56
Burnham Cres E11 124 EJ56
Burnham Cres, Dart. 168 FJ84
Burnham Dr, Reig. 250 DA133
Burnham Dr, Wor.Pk. 199 CX103
Burnham Gdns, Croy. 202 DT101
Burnham Gdns, Hayes 155 BR76
Burnham Gdns, Houns. 155 BV81
Burnham La, Slou. 131 AL72
Burnham Rd E4 101 DZ50
Burnham Rd, Beac. 111 AL58
Burnham Rd, Dag. 146 EV66
Burnham Rd, Dart. 168 FJ84
Burnham Rd, Mord. 200 DB99
Burnham Rd, Rom. 127 FD55
Burnham Rd, St.Alb. 43 CG20
Burnham Rd, Sid. 186 EY89
Burnham St E2 142 DW69
Burnham St, Kings.T. 198 CN95
Burnham Wk, Slou. 111 AN64
Burnham Way SE26 183 DZ92
Burnham Way W13 157 CH77
Burnhams Rd (Bookham), Lthd. 230 BY124
Burnhill Rd, Beck. 203 EA96
Burnley Cl, Wat. 94 BW50
Burnley Rd NW10 119 CU64
Burnley Rd SW9 161 DM82
Burnley Rd, Grays 169 FT81
Burns Av, Felt. 175 BU86
Burns Av, Rom. 126 EW59
Burns Av, Sid. 186 EV86
Burns Av, Sthl. 136 CA73
Burns Cl E17 123 EC56
Burns Cl SW19 180 DD93
Burns Cl, Cars. 218 DG109
Kenny Dr
Burns Cl, Erith 167 FF81
Burns Cl, Hayes 135 BT71
Burns Cl, Well. 165 ET81
Burns Dr, Bans. 217 CY114
Burns Pl, Til. 171 GH81
Burns Rd NW10 139 CT67
Burns Rd SW11 160 DF82
Burns Rd W13 157 CH75
Burns Rd, Wem. 137 CK68
Burns Way, Brwd. 109 GD45
Burns Way, Houns. 156 BX82
Burnsall St SW3 276 C10
Burnsall St SW3 160 DE78
Burnside, Ash. 232 CM118
Burnside, Hert. 31 DN10
Burnside, Hodd. 49 DZ17
Burnside, St.Alb. 43 CH22
Burnside, Saw. 36 EX05
Burnside Av E4 101 DZ51
Burnside Cl SE16 143 DX74
Burnside Cl, Barn. 80 DA41
Burnside Cl, Hat. 45 CU15
Homestead Rd
Burnside Cl, Twick. 177 CG86
Burnside Cres, Wem. 137 CK67
Burnside Rd, Dag. 126 EW61
Burnside Ter, Harl. 36 EZ12
Burnt Ash Hill SE12 184 EF86
Burnt Ash La, Brom. 184 EG93
Burnt Ash Rd SE12 184 EF85
Burnt Common Cl (Ripley), Wok. 243 BF125
Burnt Common La (Ripley), Wok. 244 BG125
Burnt Fm Ride, Enf. 65 DP34
Burnt Fm Ride, Wal.Cr. 65 DP31
Burnt Ho La (Hawley), Dart. 188 FL91
Burnt Mill, Harl. 35 EQ13
Burnt Mill Cl, Harl. 35 EQ12
Burnt Mill La
Burnt Mill La, Harl. 35 EQ12
Burnt Oak Bdy, Edg. 96 CP52
Burnt Oak Flds, Edg. 96 CQ53
Burnt Oak La, Sid. 186 EU86
Burnthwaite Rd SW6 160 DA80
Burntmill Cor, Harl. 35 EQ11
Eastwick Rd
Burntwood, Brwd. 108 FW48
Burntwood Av, Horn. 128 FK58
Burntwood Cl SW18 180 DD88
Burntwood Cl, Cat. 236 DU121
Burntwood Gra Rd SW18 180 DD88
Burntwood Gro, Sev. 257 FH127
Burntwood La SW17 180 DE89
Burntwood La, Cat. 236 DU121
Burntwood Rd, Sev. 257 FH128
Burntwood Vw SE19 182 DT92
Bowley La
Burnway, Horn. 128 FL59
Buross St E1 142 DV72
Commercial Rd
Burpham La, Guil. 243 BA129
Burr Cl E1 142 DU74
Burr Cl, Bexh. 166 EZ83
Burr Cl (London Colney), St.Alb. 62 CL27
Burr Hill La (Chobham), Wok. 210 AS109
Burr Rd SW18 180 DA87
Burrage Gro SE18 165 EQ77
Burrage Pl SE18 165 EP78
Burrage Rd SE18 165 EQ78
Burrard Rd E16 144 EH72
Burrard Rd NW6 120 DA63
Burrell, The (Westcott), Dor. 262 CC137
Burrell Cl, Croy. 203 DY100
Burrell Cl, Edg. 96 CP47
Burrell Row, Beck. 203 EA96
High St
Burrell St SE1 278 F2
Burrell St SE1 141 DP74
Burrell Twr E10 123 EA59
Burrells Wf Sq E14 163 EB78
Burrfield Dr, Orp. 206 EX99
Burritt Rd, Kings.T. 198 CN96
Burroughs, The NW4 119 CV57
Burroughs Gdns NW4 119 CV56
Burroughs Par NW4 119 CV56
The Burroughs
Burrow Cl, Chig. 103 ET50
Burrow Rd
Burrow Grn, Chig. 103 ET50
Burrow Rd SE22 162 DS84
Burrow Rd, Chig. 103 ET50
Burrow Wk SE21 182 DQ87
Rosendale Rd
Burroway Rd, Slou. 153 BB76
Burrowfield, Welw.G.C. 29 CX11
Burrows Chase, Wal.Abb. 83 EC36
Burrows Cl, Guil. 242 AT133
Burrows Cl (Penn), H.Wyc. 88 AC45
Burrows Cl (Bookham), Lthd. 230 BZ124
Burrows Cross (Gomshall), Guil. 261 BQ141
Burrows Hill Cl (Heathrow Airport), Houns. 154 BJ84
Burrows Hill La (Heathrow Airport), Houns. 154 BH84
Burrows La (Gomshall), Guil. 261 BQ140
Burrows Ms SE1 278 F4
Burrows Rd NW10 139 CW69
Bursdon Cl, Sid. 185 ET89
Burses Way, Brwd. 109 GB45
Bursland Rd, Enf. 83 DX42
Burslem Av, Ilf. 104 EU51
Burslem St E1 142 DU72
Burstead Cl, Cob. 214 BX113
Burstock Rd SW15 159 CY84
Burston Dr (Park St), St.Alb. 60 CC28
Burston Rd SW15 179 CX85
Burston Vil SW15 179 CX85
St. John's Av
Burstow Lo Business Cen, Horl. 269 DP146
Burstow Rd SW20 199 CY95
Burt Rd E16 144 EJ74
Burtenshaw Rd, T.Ditt. 197 CG101
Burtley Cl N4 122 DQ60
Burton Av, Wat. 75 BU42
Burton Cl, Chess. 215 CK108
Burton Cl, Horl. 268 DG149
Burton Cl, Th.Hth. 202 DR97
Burton Ct SW3 160 DF78
Franklin's Row
Burton Dr, Enf. 83 EA37
Government Row
Burton Gdns, Houns. 156 BZ81
Burton Gro SE17 162 DR78
Portland St
Burton La SW9 161 DN82
Burton La (Cheshunt), Wal.Cr. 66 DS29
Burton Ms SW1 276 G9
Burton Pl WC1 273 N3
Burton Rd E18 124 EH55
Burton Rd NW6 139 CZ66
Burton Rd SW9 161 DP82
Burton Rd, Kings.T. 178 CL94
Burton Rd, Loug. 85 EQ42
Burton St WC1 273 N3
Burton St WC1 141 DK69
Burton Way, Wind. 151 AL83
Burtonhole Cl NW7 97 CX49
Burtonhole La NW7 97 CY49
Burtons La, Ch.St.G. 73 AZ43
Burtons La, Rick. 73 AZ43
Burtons Rd (Hampton Hill), Hmptn. 176 CB91
Burtons Way, Ch.St.G. 72 AW40
Burtwell La SE27 182 DR91
Burwash Ct, Orp. 206 EW99
Rookery Gdns
Burwash Ho SE1 279 L5
Burwash Rd SE18 165 ER78
Burway Cres, Cher. 194 BG97
Burwell Av, Grnf. 137 CE65
Burwell Cl E1 142 DV72
Bigland St
Burwell Ind Est E10 123 DY60
Burwell Rd E10 123 DY60
Burwell Wk E3 143 EA70
Burwood Av, Brom. 204 EH103
Burwood Av, Ken. 219 DP114
Burwood Av, Pnr. 116 BW57
Burwood Cl, Guil. 243 BD133
Burwood Cl, Reig. 250 DD134
Burwood Cl, Surb. 198 CN102
Burwood Cl, Walt. 214 BW107
Burwood Gdns, Rain. 147 FF69
Burwood Pk Rd, Walt. 213 BV105
Burwood Pl W2 272 C8
Burwood Pl W2 140 DE72
Burwood Rd, Walt. 213 BV107
Bury Av, Hayes 135 BS68
Bury Av, Ruis. 115 BQ58
Bury Cl SE16 143 DX74
Rotherhithe St
Bury Cl, Wok. 226 AX116
Bury Ct EC3 275 N8
Bury Fm, Amer. 55 AP40
Gore Hill
Bury Flds, Guil. 258 AW136
Bury Grn, Hem.H. 40 BJ19
Bury Grn Rd (Cheshunt), Wal.Cr. 66 DU31
Bury Gro, Mord. 200 DB99
Bury Hill, Hem.H. 40 BH19
Bury Hill Cl, Hem.H. 40 BJ19
Bury La, Chesh. 54 AP31
Bury La, Epp. 69 ES31
Bury La, Rick. 92 BK46
Bury La, Wok. 226 AW116
Bury Meadows, Rick. 92 BK46
Bury Pl WC1 273 P7
Bury Pl WC1 141 DL71
Bury Ri, Hem.H. 57 BD25
Bury Rd E4 84 EE43
Bury Rd N22 121 DN55
Bury Rd, Dag. 127 FB64
Bury Rd, Epp. 69 ES31
Bury Rd, Harl. 36 EW11
Bury Rd, Hat. 45 CW17
Bury Rd, Hem.H. 40 BJ19
Bury St EC3 275 N9
Bury St EC3 142 DS72
Bury St N9 100 DU46
Bury St SW1 277 K2
Bury St SW1 141 DJ74
Bury St, Guil. 258 AW136
Bury St, Ruis. 115 BR57
Bury St W N9 100 DR45
Bury Wk SW3 276 B9
Bury Wk SW3 160 DE78
Burycroft, Welw.G.C. 29 CY06
Burydell La (Park St), St.Alb. 61 CD27
Buryholme, Brox. 49 DZ23
Busbridge Ho E14 143 EA71
Brabazon St
Busby Ms NW5 141 DK65
Torriano Av
Busby Pl NW5 141 DK65
Busby St E2 142 DT70
Chilton St
Bush Cl, Add. 212 BJ106
Bush Cl, Ilf. 125 ER57
Bush Cotts SW18 180 DA85
Putney Br Rd
Bush Ct W12 159 CX75
Shepherds Bush Grn
Bush Elms Rd, Horn. 127 FG59
Bush Fair, Harl. 52 EU17
Tilegate Rd
Bush Gro NW9 118 CQ59
Bush Gro, Stan. 95 CK53
Bush Hall Fm, Harl. 53 FB16
New Way La
Bush Hall La, Hat. 45 CX15
Bush Hill N21 100 DQ45
Bush Hill Rd N21 82 DR44
Bush Hill Rd, Har. 118 CM58
Bush Ind Est NW10 138 CR70
Bush La EC4 275 K10
Bush La (Send), Wok. 227 BD124
Bush Rd E8 142 DV67
Bush Rd E11 124 EF59
Bush Rd SE8 163 DX77
Bush Rd, Buck.H. 102 EK49
Bush Rd, Rich. 158 CM79
Bush Rd, Shep. 194 BM99
Bushbaby Cl SE1 279 M7
Bushbarns (Cheshunt), Wal.Cr. 66 DU29
Bushberry Rd E9 143 DY65
Bushbury La, Bet. 264 CN139
Bushby Av, Brox. 49 DZ22
Bushell Cl SW2 181 DM89
Bushell Grn, Bushey 95 CD47
Bushell St E1 142 DU74
Hermitage Wall
Bushell Way, Chis. 185 EN92
Bushetts Gro, Red. 251 DH129
Bushey Av E18 124 EF55
Bushey Av, Orp. 205 ER101
Bushey Cl E4 101 EC48
Bushey Cl, Ken. 236 DS116
Bushey Cl, Uxb. 115 BP61
Bushey Cl, Welw.G.C. 30 DB10
Bushey Ct SW20 199 CV96
Bushey Cft, Harl. 51 ES17
Bushey Cft, Oxt. 253 EC130
Bushey Down SW12 181 DH89
Bedford Hill
Bushey Grn, Welw.G.C. 30 DB10
Bushey Gro Rd, Bushey 76 BX42
Bushey Hall Dr, Bushey 76 BY42
Bushey Hall Rd, Bushey 76 BX42
Bushey Hill Rd SE5 162 DS81
Bushey La, Sutt. 218 DA105
Bushey Lees, Sid. 185 ET86
Fen Gro
Bushey Ley, Welw.G.C. 30 DB10
Bushey Mill Cres, Wat. 76 BW37
Bushey Mill La, Bushey 76 BZ40
Bushey Mill La, Wat. 76 BW37
Bushey Rd E13 144 EJ68
Bushey Rd N15 122 DS58
Bushey Rd SW20 199 CV97
Bushey Rd, Croy. 203 EA103
Bushey Rd, Hayes 155 BS77
Bushey Rd, Sutt. 218 DB105
Bushey Rd, Uxb. 114 BN61
Bushey Shaw, Ash. 231 CH117
Bushey Vw Wk, Wat. 76 BX40
Bushey Way, Beck. 203 ED100
Bushfield Cl, Edg. 96 CP47
Bushfield Cres, Edg. 96 CP47
Bushfield Dr, Red. 266 DG139
Bushfield Rd (Bovingdon), Hem.H. 57 BC25
Bushfield Wk, Swans. 190 FY86
Bushfields, Loug. 85 EN43
Bushgrove Rd, Dag. 126 EX63
Bushmead Cl N15 122 DT56
Copperfield Dr
Bushmoor Cres SE18 165 EQ80
Bushnell Rd SW17 181 DH89
Bushway, Dag. 126 EX63
Bushwood E11 124 EF60
Bushwood Cl, Hat. 45 CV23
Dellsome La
Bushwood Dr SE1 162 DT77
Bushwood Rd, Rich. 158 CN79
Bushy Hill Dr, Guil. 243 BB132
Bushy Pk (Hampton Hill), Hmptn. 197 CF95
Bushy Pk, Tedd. 197 CF95
Bushy Pk Gdns, Tedd. 177 CD92
Bushy Pk Rd, Tedd. 177 CH94
Bushy Rd (Fetcham), Lthd. 230 CB122
Bushy Rd, Tedd. 177 CF93
Buslins La, Chesh. 54 AL28
Butcher Row E1 143 DX73
Butcher Row E14 143 DX73
Butcher Wk, Swans. 190 FY87
Butchers La, Sev. 209 FX103
Butchers Rd E16 144 EG72
Bute Av, Rich. 178 CL89
Bute Ct, Wall. 219 DJ106
Bute Rd
Bute Gdns W6 159 CX77
Bute Gdns, Wall. 219 DJ106
Bute Gdns W, Wall. 219 DJ106
Bute Rd, Croy. 201 DN102
Bute Rd, Ilf. 125 EP57
Bute Rd, Wall. 219 DJ105
Bute St SW7 160 DD77
Bute Wk N1 142 DR65
Marquess Rd
Butler Av, Har. 117 CD59
Butler Ct, Wem. 117 CG63
Harrow Rd
Butler Ho, Grays 170 GA79
Argent St
Butler Pl SW1 277 M6
Butler Rd NW10 139 CT66
Curzon Cres
Butler Rd, Dag. 126 EV63
Butler Rd, Har. 116 CC59
Butler St E2 142 DW69
Knottisford St
Butler St, Uxb. 135 BP70
Butler Wk, Grays 170 GD77
Palmers Dr
Butlers Cl, Amer. 55 AN37
Butlers Cl, Wind. 151 AK81
Butlers Ct, Wal.Cr. 67 DY32
Trinity La
Butlers Ct Rd, Beac. 89 AK54
Butlers Dene Rd (Woldingham), Cat. 237 DZ120
Butlers Dr E4 83 EC38
Butlers Hill (West Horsley), Lthd. 245 BP130
Butlers Wf SE1 142 DT74
Butt Fld Vw, St.Alb. 42 CC24
Buttell Cl, Grays 170 GD78
Butter Hill, Cars. 200 DG104
Butter Hill, Dor. 263 CG136
South St
Butter Hill, Wall. 200 DG104
Buttercross La, Epp. 70 EU30
Buttercup Cl, Hat. 29 CT14
Great Braitch La
Buttercup Cl, Rom. 106 FK53
Copperfields Way
Buttercup Sq (Stanwell), Stai. 174 BK88
Diamedes Av
Butterfield (Wooburn Grn), H.Wyc. 110 AD59
Butterfield Cl N17 100 DQ51
Devonshire Rd
Butterfield Cl SE16 162 DV75
Wilson Gro
Butterfield Cl, Twick. 177 CF86
Rugby Rd
Butterfield La, St.Alb. 43 CE24
Butterfield Sq E6 145 EM72
Harper Rd
Butterfields E17 123 EC57
Butterfly La SE9 185 EP86
Butterfly La, Borwd. 77 CG41
Butterfly Wk SE5 162 DR81
Denmark Hill
Butterfly Wk, Warl. 236 DW120
Butteridges Cl, Dag. 146 EZ67
Butterly Av, Dart. 188 FM89
Buttermere Av, Slou. 130 AJ71
Buttermere Cl E15 123 ED63
Buttermere Cl SE1 279 P8
Buttermere Cl, Felt. 175 BT88
Buttermere Cl, Mord. 199 CX100
Buttermere Cl, St.Alb. 43 CH21
Buttermere Dr SW15 179 CY85
Buttermere Gdns, Pur. 220 DR113
Buttermere Rd, Orp. 206 EX98
Buttermere Wk E8 142 DT65
Buttermere Way, Egh. 173 BB94
Keswick Rd
Buttersweet Ri, Saw. 36 EY06
Brook Rd
Butterwick W6 159 CW77
Butterwick, Wat. 76 BY36
Butterwick La, St.Alb. 44 CN22
Butterworth Gdns, Wdf.Grn. 102 EG51
Buttesland St N1 275 L2
Buttesland St N1 142 DR69
Buttfield Cl, Dag. 147 FB65
Buttlehide, Rick. 91 BD50
Buttmarsh Cl SE18 165 EP78
Button Rd, Grays 170 FZ77
Button St, Swan. 208 FJ96
Buttondene Cres, Brox. 49 EB22
Butts, The, Brent. 157 CK79
Butts, The, Brox. 49 DY24
Butts, The (Otford), Sev. 241 FH116
Butts, The, Sun. 196 BW97
Elizabeth Gdns
Butts Cotts, Felt. 176 BZ90
Butts Cres, Felt. 176 CA90
Butts End, Hem.H. 40 BG18
Butts Grn Rd, Horn. 128 FK58
Butts Piece, Nthlt. 135 BV68
Longhook Gdns
Butts Rd, Brom. 184 EE92
Butts Rd, Wok. 226 AY117
Buttsbury Rd, Ilf. 125 EQ64
Buttsmead, Nthwd. 93 BQ52
Buxhall Cres E9 143 DZ65
Buxted Rd E8 142 DT66
Buxted Rd N12 98 DE50
Buxted Rd SE22 162 DS84
Buxton Av, Cat. 236 DS121
Buxton Cl, St.Alb. 43 CK17
Buxton Cl, Wdf.Grn. 102 EK51
Buxton Ct N1 275 J2
Buxton Cres, Sutt. 217 CY105
Buxton Dr E11 124 EE56
Buxton Dr, N.Mal. 198 CR96
Buxton Gdns W3 138 CP73
Buxton La, Cat. 236 DR120
Buxton Path, Wat. 94 BW48
Buxton Rd E4 101 ED45
Buxton Rd E6 144 EL69
Buxton Rd E15 124 EE64
Buxton Rd E17 123 DY56
Buxton Rd N19 121 DK60
Buxton Rd NW2 139 CV65
Buxton Rd SW14 158 CS83
Buxton Rd, Ashf. 174 BK92
Buxton Rd, Epp. 85 ES36
Buxton Rd, Erith 167 FD80
Buxton Rd, Grays 170 GE75
Buxton Rd, Ilf. 125 ES58
Buxton Rd, Th.Hth. 201 DP99
Buxton Rd, Wal.Abb. 68 EG32
Buxton St E1 142 DT70
Buzzard Creek Ind Est, Bark. 145 ET71
By the Mt, Welw.G.C. 29 CX10
By the Wd, Wat. 94 BX47
By-Wood End (Chalfont St. Peter), Ger.Cr. 91 AZ50
Byam St SW6 160 DC82
Byards Cft SW16 201 DK95

Byatt Wk, Hmptn. 176 BY93
Victors Dr
Bybend Cl (Farnham Royal), Slou. 131 AP67
Bychurch End, Tedd. 177 CF92
Church Rd
Bycliffe Ter, Grav. 191 GF87
Bycroft Rd, Sthl. 136 CA70
Bycroft St SE20 183 DX94
Parish La
Bycullah Av, Enf. 81 DP41
Bycullah Rd, Enf. 81 DP41
Byde St, Hert. 32 DQ08
Bye, The W3 138 CS72
Bye Way, The, Har. 95 CE53
Byegrove Rd SW19 180 DD93
Byers Cl, Pot.B. 64 DC34
Byewaters, Wat. 75 BQ44
Byeway, The SW14 158 CQ83
Byeway, The, Rick. 92 BL47
Byeways, Twick. 176 CB90
Byeways, The, Ash. 231 CK118
Skinners La
Byeways, The, Surb. 198 CN99
Byfeld Gdns SW13 159 CU81
Byfield, Welw.G.C. 29 CY06
Byfield Cl SE16 163 DY75
Byfield Pas, Islw. 157 CG83
Byfield Rd, Islw. 157 CG83
Byfleet Rd (New Haw), Add. 212 BK108
Byfleet Rd, Cob. 213 BS113
Byfleet Rd (Byfleet), W.Byf. 212 BN112
Byfleet Technical Cen (Byfleet), W.Byf. 212 BK111
Byford Cl E15 144 EE66
Bygrove (New Addington), Croy. 221 EB107
Bygrove St E14 143 EB72
Byland Cl N21 99 DM45
Bylands, Wok. 227 BA119
Bylands Cl SE2 166 EV76
Finchale Rd
Bylands Cl SE16 143 DX74
Rotherhithe St
Byne Rd SE26 182 DW93
Byne Rd, Cars. 200 DE103
Bynes Rd, S.Croy. 220 DR108
Byng Dr, Pot.B. 64 DA31
Byng Pl WC1 273 M5
Byng Pl WC1 141 DK70
Byng Rd, Barn. 79 CX41
Byng St E14 163 EA75
Bynghams, Harl. 51 EM17
Bynon Av, Bexh. 166 EY83
Byre, The N14 81 DH44
Farm La
Byre Rd N14 80 DG44
Farm La
Byrefield Rd, Guil. 242 AT131
Byrne Rd SW12 181 DH88
Byron Av E12 144 EL65
Byron Av E18 124 EF55
Byron Av NW9 118 CP56
Byron Av, Borwd. 78 CN43
Byron Av, Couls. 235 DL115
Byron Av, Houns. 155 BU82
Byron Av, N.Mal. 199 CU99
Byron Av, Sutt. 218 DD105
Byron Av, Wat. 76 BX39
Byron Av E, Sutt. 218 DD105
Byron Cl E8 142 DU67
Byron Cl SE26 183 DY91
Porthcawe Rd
Byron Cl SE28 146 EW74
Byron Cl, Hmptn. 176 BZ91
Byron Cl, Wal.Cr. 66 DT27
Allard Cl
Byron Cl, Walt. 196 BY102
Byron Cl (Knaphill), Wok. 226 AS117
Byron Ct W9 140 DA70
Lanhill Rd
Byron Ct, Enf. 81 DP40
Bycullah Rd
Byron Ct, Har. 117 CE58
Byron Dr N2 120 DD58
Byron Dr, Erith 167 FB80
Byron Gdns, Sutt. 218 DD105
Byron Gdns, Til. 171 GJ81
Byron Hill Rd, Har. 117 CD60
Byron Ho, Beck. 183 EA93
Byron Ho, Slou. 153 BB78
Byron Ms NW3 120 DE64
Byron Ms W9 140 DA70
Shirland Rd
Byron Pl, Lthd. 231 CH122
Byron Rd E10 123 EB60
Byron Rd E17 123 EA55
Byron Rd NW2 119 CV61
Byron Rd NW7 97 CU50
Byron Rd W5 138 CM74
Byron Rd, Add. 212 BL105
Byron Rd, Brwd. 109 GD45
Byron Rd, Dart. 168 FP84
Byron Rd, Har. 117 CE58
Byron Rd (Wealdstone), Har. 95 CF54
Byron Rd, S.Croy. 220 DV110
Byron Rd, Wem. 117 CJ62
Byron St E14 143 EC72
St. Leonards Rd
Byron Ter N9 100 DW45
Byron Way, Hayes 135 BT70
Byron Way, Nthlt. 136 BY69
Byron Way, Rom. 106 FJ53
Byron Way, West Dr. 154 BM77
Bysouth Cl N15 122 DR56
Bysouth Cl, Ilf. 103 EP53
Bythorn St SW9 161 DM83
Byton Rd SW17 180 DF93
Byttom Hill (Mickleham), Dor. 247 CJ127
Byward Av, Felt. 176 BW86
Byward St EC3 279 N1
Byward St EC3 142 DS73
Bywater Pl SE16 143 DY74
Bywater St SW3 276 D10
Bywater St SW3 160 DF78
Byway, The, Epsom 217 CT105
Byway, The, Pot.B. 64 DA33
Byway, The, Sutt. 218 DD109
Byways, Berk. 38 AY18
Byways (Burnham), Slou. 130 AG71
Bywell Pl W1 273 K7
Bywood Av, Croy. 202 DW100
Bywood Cl, Ken. 235 DP115
Byworth Wk N19 121 DK60
Courtauld Rd

C

C.I. Twr, N.Mal. 198 CS97
Cabbell Pl, Add. 212 BJ105
Cabbell St NW1 272 B7
Cabbell St NW1 140 DE71
Cabell Rd, Guil. 242 AS133
Caberfeigh Pl, Red. 250 DE134
Cabinet Way E4 101 DZ51
Cable Pl SE10 163 EC81
Diamond Ter
Cable St E1 142 DU73
Cable Trade Pk SE7 164 EJ77
Cabot Sq E14 143 EA74
Cabot Way E6 144 EK67
Parr Rd
Cabrera Av, Vir.W. 192 AW100
Cabrera Cl, Vir.W. 192 AX100
Cabul Rd SW11 160 DE82
Cacket's Cotts, Sev. 239 ES115
Cackets La
Cackets La (Cudham), Sev. 239 ER115
Cactus Cl SE15 162 DS82
Lyndhurst Gro
Cactus Wk W12 139 CT72
Du Cane Rd
Cadbury Cl, Islw. 157 CG81
Cadbury Cl, Sun. 175 BS94
Cadbury Rd, Sun. 175 BS94
Cadbury Way SE16 162 DU76
Yalding Rd
Caddington Cl, Barn. 80 DE43
Caddington Rd NW2 119 CY62
Caddis Cl, Stan. 95 CF52
Daventer Dr
Caddy Cl, Egh. 173 BA92
Cade La, Sev. 257 FJ128
Cade Rd SE10 163 ED81
Cadell Cl E2 142 DT69
Shipton St
Cader Rd SW18 180 DC86
Cadet Dr SE1 162 DT77
Cadet Pl SE10 164 EE78
Cadiz Ct, Dag. 147 FD66
Rainham Rd S
Cadiz Rd, Dag. 147 FC66
Cadiz St SE17 162 DQ78
Cadley Ter SE23 182 DW89
Cadlocks Hill (Halstead), Sev. 224 EZ110
Cadman Cl SW9 161 DP80
Langton Rd
Cadmer Cl, N.Mal. 198 CS98
Cadmore Ct, Hert. 31 DM07
The Ridgeway
Cadmore La (Cheshunt), Wal.Cr. 67 DX28
Cadmus Cl SW4 161 DK83
Aristotle Rd
Cadnam Pt SW15 179 CV88
Dilton Gdns
Cadogan Av, Dart. 189 FR87
Cadogan Cl E9 143 DZ66
Cadogan Ter
Cadogan Cl, Beck. 203 ED95
Albemarle Rd
Cadogan Cl, Har. 116 CB63
Cadogan Cl, Tedd. 177 CE92
Cadogan Ct, Sutt. 218 DB107
Cadogan Gdns E18 124 EH55
Cadogan Gdns N3 98 DB53
Cadogan Gdns N21 81 DN43
Cadogan Gdns SW3 276 E8
Cadogan Gdns SW3 160 DF77
Cadogan Gate SW1 276 E8
Cadogan Gate SW1 160 DF77
Cadogan La SW1 276 F7
Cadogan La SW1 160 DG76
Cadogan Pl SW1 276 E7
Cadogan Pl SW1 160 DF76
Cadogan Rd, Surb. 197 CK99
Cadogan Sq SW1 276 E7
Cadogan Sq SW1 160 DF76
Cadogan St SW3 276 D9
Cadogan St SW3 160 DF77
Cadogan Ter E9 143 DZ65
Cadoxton Av N15 122 DT58
Cadwallon Rd SE9 185 EP89
Caedmon Rd N7 121 DM63
Caen Wd Rd, Ash. 231 CJ118
Caenshill Rd, Wey. 212 BN108
Caenwood Cl, Wey. 212 BN107
Caerleon Cl, Sid. 186 EW92
Caerleon Ter SE2 166 EV77
Blithdale Rd
Caernarvon Cl, Hem.H. 40 BK20
Caernarvon Cl, Horn. 128 FN60
Caernarvon Cl, Mitch. 201 DL97
Caernarvon Dr, Ilf. 103 EN53
Caesars Wk, Mitch. 200 DF99
Caesars Way, Shep. 195 BR100
Cage Pond Rd, Rad. 62 CM33
Cage Yd, Reig. *High St* 250 DA134
Cages Wd Dr (Farnham Common), Slou. 111 AP63
Cahill St EC1 275 J5
Cahir St E14 163 EB77
Caillard Rd (Byfleet), W.Byf. 212 BL111
Cains La, Felt. 175 BS85
Caird St W10 139 CY69
Cairn Av W5 137 CK74
Cairn Way, Stan. 95 CF51
Cairndale Cl, Brom. 184 EF94
Cairnfield Av NW2 118 CS62
Cairngorm Cl, Tedd. 177 CG92
Vicarage Rd
Cairngorm Pl, Slou. 131 AR70
Cairns Av, Wdf.Grn. 102 EL51
Cairns Cl, Dart. 188 FK85
Cairns Cl, St.Alb. 43 CK21
Cairns Rd SW11 180 DE85
Cairo New Rd, Croy. 201 DP103
Cairo Rd E17 123 EA56
Caishowe Rd, Borwd. 78 CP39
Caister Cl, Hem.H. 40 BL21
Caistor Ms SW12 181 DH87
Caistor Rd
Caistor Pk Rd E15 144 EF67
Caistor Rd SW12 181 DH87
Caithness Gdns, Sid. 185 ET86
Caithness Rd W14 159 CX77
Caithness Rd, Mitch. 181 DH94
Calabria Rd N5 141 DP65
Calais Cl, Wal.Cr. 66 DR26
Argent Way
Calais Gate SE5 161 DP81
Calais St
Calais St SE5 161 DP81
Calbourne Av, Horn. 127 FH64
Calbourne Rd SW12 180 DF87
Calbroke Ct, Slou. 131 AM69
Calbroke Rd
Calbroke Rd, Slou. 131 AM70
Calcott Cl, Brwd. 108 FV46
Calcott Wk SE9 184 EK91
Calcutta Rd, Til. 171 GF82
Caldbeck, Wal.Abb. 67 ED34
Caldbeck Av, Wor.Pk. 199 CU103
Caldecot Av, Wal.Cr. 66 DT29
Caldecot Rd SE5 162 DQ82
Caldecot Way, Brox. 49 DZ22
Caldecote Gdns, Bushey 77 CE44
Caldecote La, Bushey 77 CF44
Caldecott Way E5 123 DX62
Calder Av, Grnf. 137 CF68
Calder Av, Hat. 64 DB26
Calder Cl, Enf. 82 DS41
Calder Ct, Slou. 153 AZ78
Calder Gdns, Edg. 118 CN55
Calder Rd, Mord. 200 DC99
Calder Way (Colnbrook), Slou. 153 BF83
Calderon Pl W10 139 CW71
St. Quintin Gdns
Calderon Rd E11 123 EC63
Caldervale Rd SW4 181 DK85
Calderwood, Grav. 191 GL92
Calderwood St SE18 165 EN77
Caldicot Grn NW9 118 CS58
Snowdon Dr
Caldwell Rd, Wat. 94 BX49
Caldwell St SW9 161 DM80
Caldwell Yd EC4 142 DQ73
Upper Thames St
Caldy Rd, Belv. 167 FB76
Caldy Wk N1 142 DQ65
Clephane Rd
Cale St SW3 276 B10
Cale St SW3 160 DE78
Caleb St SE1 279 H4
Caledon Cl, Beac. 89 AK52
Caledon Pl, Guil. 243 BA131
Darfield Rd
Caledon Rd E6 145 EM67
Caledon Rd, Beac. 89 AL52
Caledon Rd (London Colney), St.Alb. 61 CK26
Caledon Rd, Wall. 218 DG105
Caledonia Rd, Stai. 174 BL88
Caledonia St N1 274 A1
Caledonia St N1 141 DL68
Caledonian Cl, Ilf. 126 EV60
Caledonian Rd N1 274 A1
Caledonian Rd N1 141 DM68
Caledonian Rd N7 121 DM64
Caledonian Way, Gat. 269 DH151
Queen's Gate
Caledonian Wf E14 163 ED77
Caletock Way SE10 164 EF78
Calfstock La (South Darenth), Dart. 208 FL98
Calico Row SW11 160 DC83
York Pl
Calidore Cl SW2 181 DM86
Endymion Rd
California La, Bushey 95 CD46
California Rd, N.Mal. 198 CQ98
Caliph Cl, Grav. 191 GM90
Callaby Ter N1 142 DR65
Wakeham St
Callaghan Cl SE13 164 EE84
Glenton Rd
Callan Gro, S.Ock. 149 FV73
Callander Rd SE6 183 EB89
Callard Av N13 99 DP50
Callcott Rd NW6 139 CZ66
Callcott St W8 140 DA74
Hillgate Pl
Callendar Rd SW7 160 DD76
Calley Down Cres (New Addington), Croy. 221 ED110
Callingham Cl E14 143 DZ71
Wallwood St
Callis Fm Cl (Stanwell), Stai. 174 BL86
Bedfont Rd
Callis Rd E17 123 DZ58
Callisto Ct, Hem.H. 40 BM17
Jupiter Dr
Callow Fld, Pur. 219 DN113
Callow Hill, Vir.W. 192 AW97
Callow St SW3 160 DD79
Callowland Cl, Wat. 75 BV38
Calluna Ct, Wok. 227 AZ118
Heathside Rd
Calmont Rd, Brom. 183 ED93
Calmore Cl, Horn. 128 FJ64
Calne Av, Ilf. 103 EP53
Calonne Rd SW19 179 CX91
Calshot Av, Grays 170 FZ75
Calshot Rd (Heathrow Airport), Houns. 154 BN82
Calshot St N1 141 DM68
Calshot Way, Enf. 81 DP41
Calshot Way (Heathrow Airport), Houns. 155 BP82
Calshot Rd
Calthorpe Gdns, Edg. 96 CL50
Jesmond Way
Calthorpe Gdns, Sutt. 200 DC104
Calthorpe St WC1 274 C4
Calthorpe St WC1 141 DM70
Calton Av SE21 182 DS85
Calton Av, Hert. 31 DM08
Calton Ct, Hert. 31 DM09
Calton Av
Calton Rd, Barn. 80 DC44
Calverley Cl, Beck. 183 EB93
Calverley Cres, Dag. 126 FA61
Calverley Gdns, Har. 117 CK59
Calverley Gro N19 121 DK60
Calverley Rd, Epsom 217 CU107
Calvert Av E2 275 N3
Calvert Av E2 142 DS69
Calvert Cl, Belv. 166 FA77
Calvert Cl, Sid. 186 EY93
Calvert Cres, Dor. 247 CH134
Calvert Rd
Calvert Rd SE10 164 EF78
Calvert Rd, Barn. 79 CX40
Calvert Rd, Dor. 247 CH134
Calvert Rd (Effingham), Lthd. 245 BV128
Calvert St NW1 140 DG67
Chalcot Rd
Calverton SE5 162 DS79
Calverton Rd E6 145 EN67
Calvert's Bldgs SE1 279 K3
Calvin Cl, Orp. 206 EX97
Calvin St E1 275 P5
Calvin St E1 142 DT70
Calydon Rd SE7 164 EH78
Calypso Way SE16 163 DZ76
Cam Grn, S.Ock. 149 FV72
Cam Rd E15 143 ED67
Camac Rd, Twick. 177 CD88
Cambalt Rd SW15 179 CX85
Camberley Av SW20 199 CV96
Camberley Av, Enf. 82 DS42
Camberley Cl, Sutt. 199 CX104
Camberley Rd (Heathrow Airport), Houns. 154 BN83
Cambert Way SE3 164 EH84
Camberwell Ch St SE5 162 DR81
Camberwell Glebe SE5 162 DR81
Camberwell Grn SE5 162 DR81
Camberwell Gro SE5 162 DR81
Camberwell New Rd SE5 161 DN80
Camberwell Pas SE5 162 DQ81
Camberwell Grn
Camberwell Rd SE5 162 DQ79
Camberwell Sta Rd SE5 162 DQ81
Cambeys Rd, Dag. 127 FB64
Camborne Av W13 157 CH75
Camborne Av, Rom. 106 FL52
Camborne Cl (Heathrow Airport), Houns. 154 BN83
Camborne Rd S
Camborne Dr, Hem.H. 40 BL16
Camborne Ms W11 139 CY72
St. Marks Rd
Camborne Rd SW18 180 DA87
Camborne Rd, Croy. 202 DU101
Camborne Rd, Mord. 199 CX99
Camborne Rd, Sid. 186 EW90
Camborne Rd, Sutt. 218 DA108
Camborne Rd, Well. 165 ET82
Camborne Rd N (Heathrow Airport), Houns. 154 BN83
Camborne Rd S
Camborne Rd S (Heathrow Airport), Houns. 154 BN83
Camborne Way, Houns. 156 CA81
Camborne Way (Heathrow Airport), Houns. 154 BN83
Camborne Rd S
Camborne Way, Rom. 106 FL52
Cambourne Av N9 101 DX45
Cambray Rd SW12 181 DJ88
Cambray Rd, Orp. 205 ET101
Cambria Cl, Houns. 156 CA84
Cambria Cl, Sid. 185 ER88
Cambria Ct, Felt. 175 BV87
Hounslow Rd
Cambria Ct, Slou. 152 AW75
Turner Rd
Cambria Cres, Grav. 191 GL91
Cambria Gdns, Stai. 174 BL87
Cambria Rd SE5 162 DQ83
Cambria St SW6 160 DB80
Cambrian Av, Ilf. 125 ES57
Cambrian Cl SE27 181 DP90
Cambrian Grn NW9 118 CS57
Snowdon Dr
Cambrian Gro, Grav. 191 GG87
Cambrian Rd E10 123 EA59
Cambrian Rd, Rich. 178 CM86
Cambrian Way, Hem.H. 40 BL17
Cambridge Av NW6 140 DA68
Cambridge Av, Grnf. 117 CF64
Cambridge Av, N.Mal. 199 CT96
Cambridge Av, Rom. 128 FJ55
Cambridge Av, Slou. 131 AM72
Cambridge Av (Burnham), Slou. 130 AH68
Cambridge Av, Well. 165 ET84
Cambridge Barracks Rd SE18 165 EM77
Cambridge Circ WC2 273 N9
Cambridge Circ WC2 141 DK72
Cambridge Cl E17 123 DZ58
Cambridge Cl N22 99 DN53
Pellatt Gro
Cambridge Cl NW10 118 CQ62
Cambridge Cl SW20 199 CV95
Cambridge Cl, Houns. 156 BY84
Cambridge Cl (Cheshunt), Wal.Cr. 66 DW29
Cambridge Cl, West Dr. 154 BK79
Cambridge Cl, Wok. 226 AT118
Bingham Dr
Cambridge Cotts, Rich. 158 CN79
Cambridge Cres E2 142 DV68
Cambridge Cres, Tedd. 177 CG92
Cambridge Dr SE12 184 EG85
Cambridge Dr, Pot.B. 63 CX31
Cambridge Dr, Ruis. 116 BW61
Cambridge Gdns N10 99 DH53
Cambridge Gdns N13 99 DN50
Cambridge Gdns N17 100 DR52
Great Cambridge Rd
Cambridge Gdns N21 100 DR45
Cambridge Gdns NW6 140 DA68
Cambridge Gdns W10 139 CY72
Cambridge Gdns, Enf. 82 DU40
Cambridge Gdns, Grays 171 GG77
Cambridge Gdns, Kings.T. 198 CN96
Cambridge Gate NW1 273 J3
Cambridge Gate Ms NW1 273 J3
Cambridge Grn SE9 185 EP88
Cambridge Gro SE20 182 DV94
Cambridge Gro W6 159 CV77
Cambridge Gro Rd, Kings.T. 198 CN96
Cambridge Heath Rd E1 142 DV68
Cambridge Heath Rd E2 142 DV68
Cambridge Mans SW11 160 DF81
Cambridge Rd
Cambridge Par, Enf. 82 DU39
Great Cambridge Rd
Cambridge Pk E11 124 EG59
Cambridge Pk, Twick. 177 CK87
Cambridge Pk Rd E11 124 EF59
Cambridge Pk
Cambridge Pl W8 160 DB75
Cambridge Rd E4 101 ED46
Cambridge Rd E11 124 EF58
Cambridge Rd NW6 140 DA69
Cambridge Rd SE20 202 DV97
Cambridge Rd SW11 160 DF81
Cambridge Rd SW13 159 CT82
Cambridge Rd SW20 199 CU95
Cambridge Rd W7 157 CF75
Cambridge Rd, Ashf. 175 BQ94
Cambridge Rd, Bark. 145 EQ66
Cambridge Rd, Beac. 88 AJ53
Cambridge Rd, Brom. 184 EG94
Cambridge Rd, Cars. 218 DE107
Cambridge Rd, Hmptn. 176 BZ94
Cambridge Rd, Harl. 36 EW09
Cambridge Rd, Har. 116 CA57
Cambridge Rd, Houns. 156 BY84
Cambridge Rd, Ilf. 125 ES60
Cambridge Rd, Kings.T. 198 CM96
Cambridge Rd, Mitch. 201 DJ97
Cambridge Rd, N.Mal. 198 CS98
Cambridge Rd, Rich. 158 CN80
Cambridge Rd, St.Alb. 43 CH21
Cambridge Rd, Sid. 185 ES91
Cambridge Rd, Sthl. 136 BZ74
Cambridge Rd, Tedd. 177 CF91
Cambridge Rd, Twick. 177 CK86
Cambridge Rd, Uxb. 134 BK65
Cambridge Rd, Walt. 195 BV100
Cambridge Rd, Wat. 76 BW42
Cambridge Rd, W.Mol. 196 BZ98
Cambridge Rd N W4 158 CP78
Cambridge Rd S W4 158 CP78
Oxford Rd S
Cambridge Row SE18 165 EP78
Cambridge Sq W2 272 B8
Cambridge Sq W2 140 DE72
Cambridge St SW1 277 J9
Cambridge St SW1 161 DH78
Cambridge Ter N13 99 DN50
Cambridge Ter NW1 273 J3
Cambridge Ter, Berk. 38 AX19
Cambridge Ter Ms NW1 273 J3
Cambstone Cl N11 98 DG47
Cambus Cl, Hayes 136 BY71
Cambus Rd E16 144 EG71
Camdale Rd SE18 165 ET80
Camden Av, Felt. 176 BW89
Camden Av, Hayes 136 BW73
Camden Cl, Chis. 185 EQ94
Camden Cl, Grav. 190 GC88
Camden Cl, Grays 171 GH77
Camden Gdns NW1 141 DH66
Kentish Town Rd
Camden Gdns, Sutt. 218 DB106
Camden Gdns, Th.Hth. 201 DP97
Camden Gro, Chis. 185 EP93
Camden High St NW1 141 DH67
Camden Hill Rd SE19 182 DS93
Camden La N7 141 DK65
Rowstock Gdns
Camden Lock Pl NW1 141 DH66
Chalk Fm Rd
Camden Ms NW1 141 DK65
Camden Pk Rd NW1 141 DK65
Camden Pk Rd, Chis. 185 EM94
Camden Pas N1 141 DP67
Camden Rd E11 124 EH58
Camden Rd E17 123 DZ58
Camden Rd N7 121 DK64
Camden Rd NW1 141 DJ66
Camden Rd, Bex. 186 EZ88
Camden Rd, Cars. 218 DF105
Camden Rd, Grays 170 FY76
Camden Rd, Sev. 257 FH122
Camden Rd, Sutt. 218 DA106
Camden Row SE3 164 EE82
Camden Sq NW1 141 DK65
Camden Sq SE15 162 DT81
Watts St
Camden St NW1 141 DJ66
Camden Ter NW1 141 DK65
North Vil
Camden Wk N1 141 DP67
Camden Way, Chis. 185 EM94
Camden Way, Th.Hth. 201 DP97
Camdenhurst St E14 143 DY72
Camel Gro, Kings.T. 177 CK92
Camel Rd E16 144 EK74
Camelford Wk W11 139 CY72
Lancaster Rd
Camellia Cl, Rom. 106 FL53
Columbine Way
Camellia Ct, Wdf.Grn. 102 EE52
The Bridle Path
Camellia Pl, Twick. 176 CB87
Camellia St SW8 161 DL80
Camelot Cl SE28 165 ER75
Camelot Cl SW19 180 DA91
Camelot Cl (Biggin Hill), West. 238 EJ116
Camelot Ho N9 100 DU48
Salisbury Rd
Camelot St SE15 162 DV80
Bird in Bush Rd
Camera Pl SW10 160 DD79
Cameron Cl N18 100 DV49
Cameron Cl N20 98 DE47
Myddelton Pk
Cameron Cl, Bex. 187 FD90
Cameron Cl, Brwd. 108 FW49
Cameron Ct, Ware 33 DX05
Crib St
Cameron Dr, Wal.Cr. 67 DX34
Cameron Pl E1 142 DV72
Varden St
Cameron Rd SE6 183 DZ89
Cameron Rd, Brom. 204 EG98
Cameron Rd, Chesh. 54 AQ30
Cameron Rd, Croy. 201 DP100
Cameron Rd, Ilf. 125 ES60
Cameron Sq, Mitch. 200 DE95
Camerton Cl E8 142 DT65
Buttermere Wk
Camfield, Welw.G.C. 29 CZ13
Camfield Pl, Hat. 46 DD21
Camgate Cen (Stanwell), Stai. 174 BM86
Camilla Cl (Bookham), Lthd. 246 CB125
Camilla Cl, Sun. 175 BS93
Camilla Dr (Westhumble), Dor. 247 CG130
Camilla Rd SE16 162 DV77
Camille Cl SE25 202 DU97
Camlan Rd, Brom. 184 EF91
Camlet St E2 275 P4
Camlet St E2 142 DT70
Camlet Way, Barn. 80 DA40
Camlet Way, St.Alb. 42 CB19
Camley St NW1 141 DK66
Camm Av, Wind. 151 AL83
Camm Gdns, Kings.T. 198 CM96
Church Rd
Camm Gdns, T.Ditt. 197 CE101
Camms Ter, Dag. 127 FC64
Camomile Av, Mitch. 200 DF95
Camomile Rd, Rom. 127 FD61
Camomile St EC3 275 M8
Camomile St EC3 142 DS72
Camomile Way, West Dr. 134 BL72
Camp End Rd, Wey. 213 BR110
Camp Rd SW19 179 CW92
Camp Rd (Woldingham), Cat. 237 DY120
Camp Rd, Ger.Cr. 112 AX59
Camp Rd, St.Alb. 43 CJ21
Camp Vw SW19 179 CV92
Camp Vw Rd, St.Alb. 43 CH21
Campana Rd SW6 160 DA81
Campbell Av, Ilf. 125 EQ56
Campbell Av, Wok. 227 AZ121
Campbell Cl SE18 165 EN81
Moordown
Campbell Cl SW16 181 DK91
Campbell Cl (Havering-atte-Bower), Rom. 105 FE51
Campbell Cl, Ruis. 115 BU58
Campbell Cl, Twick. 177 CD89
Campbell Ct N17 100 DT53
Campbell Cft, Edg. 96 CN50
Campbell Dr, Beac. 88 AJ51
Campbell Gordon Way NW2 119 CV63
Campbell Rd E3 143 EA69
Campbell Rd E6 144 EL67
Campbell Rd E15 124 EF63
Trevelyan Rd
Campbell Rd E17 123 DZ56
Campbell Rd N17 100 DU53
Campbell Rd W7 137 CE73

Campbell Rd, Cat. 236 DR121
Campbell Rd, Croy. 201 DP101
Campbell Rd, E.Mol. 197 CF97
Hampton Ct Rd
Campbell Rd, Grav. 191 GF88
Campbell Rd, Twick. 177 CD89
Campbell Rd, Wey. 212 BN108
Campbell Wk N1 141 DL67
Outram Pl
Campbells Cl, Harl. 52 EV16
Carters Mead
Campdale Rd N7 121 DK62
Campden Cres, Dag. 126 EV63
Campden Cres, Wem. 117 CH61
Campden Gro W8 160 DA75
Campden Hill Gdns W8 140 DA74
Campden Hill Gate W8 160 DA75
Duchess of Bedford's Wk
Campden Hill Pl W11 139 CZ74
Holland Pk Av
Campden Hill Rd W8 140 DA74
Campden Hill Sq W8 139 CZ74
Campden Hill Twrs W11 140 DA74
Notting Hill Gate
Campden Ho Cl W8 160 DA75
Hornton St
Campden Rd, S.Croy. 220 DS106
Campden Rd, Uxb. 114 BM62
Campden St W8 140 DA74
Campen Cl SW19 179 CY89
Queensmere Rd
Camperdown St E1 142 DT72
Leman St
Campfield Rd SE9 184 EK87
Campfield Rd, Hert. 31 DP09
Campfield Rd, St.Alb. 43 CG21
Camphill Ct, W.Byf. 212 BG112
Camphill Ind Est, W.Byf. 212 BH111
Camphill Rd, W.Byf. 212 BG112
Campine Cl (Cheshunt), Wal.Cr. 67 DX28
Welsummer Way
Campion Cl E6 145 EM73
Campion Cl, Croy. 220 DS105
Campion Cl (Northfleet), Grav. 190 GE91
Campion Cl, Har. 118 CM58
Campion Cl, Rom. 127 FD61
Campion Cl (Denham), Uxb. 114 BG62
Lindsey Rd
Campion Cl (Hillingdon), Uxb. 134 BM71
Campion Cl, Wat. 59 BU33
Campion Ct, Grays 170 GD79
Campion Dr, Tad. 233 CV120
Campion Gdns, Wdf.Grn. 102 EG50
Campion Pl SE28 146 EV74
Campion Rd SW15 159 CW84
Campion Rd, Hat. 29 CT14
Great Braitch La
Campion Rd, Hem.H. 39 BE21
Campion Rd, Islw. 157 CF81
Campion Ter NW2 119 CX62
Campion Way, Edg. 96 CQ49
Campions, Epp. 70 EU28
Campions, Loug. 85 EN38
Campions, The, Borwd. 78 CN38
Campions Cl, Borwd. 78 CP37
Campions Ct, Berk. 38 AU20
Cample La, S.Ock. 149 FU73
Camplin Rd, Har. 118 CL57
Camplin St SE14 163 DX80
Campsbourne, The N8 121 DL56
High St
Campsbourne Rd N8 121 DL55
Campsey Gdns, Dag. 146 EV66
Campsey Rd, Dag. 146 EV66
Campsfield Rd N8 121 DL55
Campsbourne Rd
Campshill Pl SE13 183 EC85
Campshill Rd
Campshill Rd SE13 183 EC85
Campus, The, Welw.G.C. 29 CX08
Campus Rd E17 123 DZ58
Campus Way NW4 119 CV55
Greyhound Hill
Camrose Av, Edg. 96 CM53
Camrose Av, Erith 167 FB79
Camrose Av, Felt. 175 BV91
Camrose Cl, Croy. 203 DY101
Camrose Cl, Mord. 200 DA98
Camrose St SE2 166 EU78
Can Hatch, Tad. 233 CY118
Canada Av N18 100 DQ51
Canada Av, Red. 266 DG138
Canada Cres W3 138 CQ71
Canada Dr, Red. 266 DG138
Canada Est SE16 162 DW76
Canada Fm Rd (South Darenth), Dart. 209 FU98
Canada Fm Rd, Long. 209 FU99
Canada Gdns SE13 183 EC85
Canada La, Brox. 67 DY25
Canada Rd W3 138 CQ70
Canada Rd, Cob. 214 BW113
Canada Rd, Erith 167 FH80
Canada Rd, Slou. 152 AV75
Canada Rd (Byfleet), W.Byf. 212 BK111
Canada Sq E14 143 EB74
Canada St SE16 163 DX75
Canada Way W12 139 CV73
Canadas, The, Brox. 67 DY25
Canadian Av SE6 183 EB88
Canadian Mem Av, Egh. 192 AT96
Canal App SE8 163 DY78
Canal Basin, Grav. 191 GK86
Canal Cl E1 143 DY70
Canal Cl W10 139 CX70
Canal Ct, Berk. *George St* 38 AY19
Canal Est (Langley), Slou. 153 BA75
Canal Gro SE15 162 DU79
Canal Path E2 142 DT67
Canal Rd, Grav. 191 GJ86
Canal Side (Harefield), Uxb. 92 BG51
Summerhouse La
Canal St SE5 162 DR79
Canal Wk N1 142 DR67
Canal Wk SE26 182 DW92
Canal Wk, Croy. 202 DS100
Canal Way N1 142 DQ68
Packington Sq
Canal Way NW1 272 A4
Canal Way NW8 272 A4
Canal Way NW10 139 CT70
Canal Way W10 139 CX70
Canal Way Wk W10 139 CX70
Canal Wf, Slou. 153 BA75
Canberra Cl NW4 119 CU55
Canberra Cl, Dag. 147 FD66
Canberra Cl, Horn. 128 FJ63
Canberra Cl, St.Alb. 43 CF16
Canberra Cres, Dag. 147 FD66
Canberra Dr, Hayes 136 BW69
Canberra Dr, Nthlt. 136 BW69
Canberra Rd E6 145 EM67
Barking Rd
Canberra Rd SE7 164 EJ79
Canberra Rd W13 137 CG74
Canberra Rd, Bexh. 166 EX79
Canberra Rd (Heathrow Airport), Houns. 154 BN83
Canberra Sq, Til. 171 GG82
Canbury Av, Kings.T. 198 CM95
Canbury Ms SE26 182 DU90
Wells Pk Rd
Canbury Pk Rd, Kings.T. 198 CL95
Canbury Pas, Kings.T. 197 CK95
Canbury Path, Orp. 206 EU98
Cancell Rd SW9 161 DN81
Candahar Rd SW11 160 DE82
Cander Way, S.Ock. 149 FV73
Candlefield Cl, Hem.H. 40 BN23
Candlefield Rd
Candlefield Rd, Hem.H. 40 BN23
Candlefield Wk, Hem.H. 40 BN23
Candlefield Rd
Candlemas La, Beac. 89 AL53
Candlemas Mead, Beac. 89 AL53
Candler St N15 122 DR58
Candlerush Cl, Wok. 227 BB117
Candlestick La, Wal.Cr. 66 DV27
Park La
Candover Cl, West Dr. 154 BK80
Candover Rd, Horn. 127 FH60
Candover St W1 273 K7
Candy Cft (Bookham), Lthd. 246 CB126
Candy St E3 143 DZ67
Cane Cl, Wall. 219 DL108
Cane Hill, Rom. 106 FK54
Bennison Dr
Caneland Ct, Wal.Abb. 68 EF34
Canes La, Epp. 53 FB23
Canes La, Harl. 52 EX21
Canewdon Cl, Wok. 226 AY119
Guildford Rd
Caney Ms NW2 119 CX61
Claremont Rd
Canfield Dr, Ruis. 115 BV64
Canfield Gdns NW6 140 DC66
Canfield Pl NW6 140 DC65
Canfield Gdns
Canfield Rd, Rain. 147 FF67
Canfield Rd, Wdf.Grn. 102 EL52
Canford Av, Nthlt. 136 BY67
Canford Cl, Enf. 81 DN40
Canford Dr, Add. 194 BH103
Canford Gdns, N.Mal. 198 CR100
Canford Pl, Tedd. 177 CH93
Canford Rd SW11 180 DG85
Cangels Cl, Hem.H. 39 BF22
Canham Rd SE25 202 DS97
Canham Rd W3 158 CS75
Canmore Gdns SW16 181 DJ94
Cann Hall Rd E11 124 EE63
Canning Cres N22 99 DM53
Canning Cross SE5 162 DS82
Canning Pas W8 160 DC76
Canning Pl W8 160 DC76
Canning Pl Ms W8 160 DC76
Canning Pl
Canning Rd E15 144 EE68
Canning Rd E17 123 DY56
Canning Rd N5 121 DP62
Canning Rd, Croy. 202 DT103
Canning Rd, Har. 117 CF55
Cannington Rd, Dag. 146 EW65
Cannizaro Rd SW19 179 CW93
Cannon Cl SW20 199 CW97
Cannon Cl, Hmptn. 176 CB93
Hanworth Rd
Cannon Cres (Chobham), Wok. 210 AS111
Cannon Dr E14 143 EA73
Cannon Gro (Fetcham), Lthd. 231 CE121
Cannon Hill N14 99 DK48
Cannon Hill NW6 120 DA64
Cannon Hill Cl, Maid. 150 AC77
Cannon Hill La SW20 199 CY97
Cannon La NW3 120 DD62
Cannon La, Pnr. 116 BY60
Cannon Ms, Wal.Abb. 67 EB33
Cannon Mill Av, Chesh. 54 AR33
Cannon Pl NW3 120 DD62
Cannon Pl SE7 164 EL78
Cannon Rd N14 99 DL48
Cannon Rd, Bexh. 166 EY81
Cannon Rd, Wat. 76 BW43
Cannon St EC4 275 H9
Cannon St EC4 142 DQ72
Cannon St, St.Alb. 43 CD19
Cannon St Rd E1 142 DV72
Cannon Trd Est, Wem. 118 CP63
Cannon Way (Fetcham), Lthd. 231 CE121
Cannon Way, W.Mol. 196 CA98
Cannon Wf Business Cen SE8 163 DY77
Cannonbury Av, Pnr. 116 BX58
Cannons Meadow, Welw. 30 DE06
Cannonside (Fetcham), Lthd. 231 CE122
Canon Av, Rom. 126 EW57
Canon Beck Rd SE16 162 DW75
Canon Mohan Cl N14 81 DH44
Farm La
Canon Rd, Brom. 204 EJ97
Canon Row SW1 277 P5
Canon Row SW1 161 DL75
Canon St N1 142 DQ67
Canonbie Rd SE23 182 DW87
Canonbury Cres N1 142 DQ66
Canonbury Gro N1 142 DQ66
Canonbury La N1 141 DP66
Canonbury Pk N N1 142 DQ65
Canonbury Pk S N1 142 DQ65
Canonbury Pl N1 141 DP65
Canonbury Rd N1 141 DP65
Canonbury Rd, Enf. 82 DS39
Canonbury Sq N1 141 DP66
Canonbury St N1 142 DQ66
Canonbury Vil N1 141 DP66
Canonbury Yd N1 142 DQ67
New N Rd
Canonbury Yd W N1 141 DP65
Compton Rd
Canons Brook, Harl. 51 EN15
Canons Cl N2 120 DD59
Canons Cl, Edg. 96 CM51
Canons Cl, Rad. 77 CH35
Canons Cl, Reig. 249 CZ133
Canons Cor, Edg. 96 CL49
Canons Dr, Edg. 96 CL51
Canons Gate, Harl. 35 EN13
Canons Gate (Cheshunt), Wal.Cr. 67 DZ26
Canon's Hill, Couls. 235 DN117
Canons La, Tad. 233 CY118
Canons Pk Cl, Edg. 96 CL52
Donnefield Av
Canons Rd, Ware 32 DW05
Canons Wk, Croy. 203 DX104
Canonsleigh Rd, Dag. 146 EV66
Canopus Way, Nthwd. 93 BU49
Canopus Way, Stai. 174 BL87
Canrobert St E2 142 DV69
Cantelowes Rd NW1 141 DK65
Canterbury Av, Ilf. 124 EL59
Canterbury Av, Sid. 186 EW89
Canterbury Av, Slou. 131 AQ70
Canterbury Av, Upmin. 129 FT60
Canterbury Cl E6 145 EM72
Harper Rd
Canterbury Cl, Amer. 55 AS39
Canterbury Cl, Beck. 203 EB95
Canterbury Cl, Chig. 103 ET48
Canterbury Cl, Dart. 188 FN87
Canterbury Cl, Grnf. 136 CB72
Canterbury Cl, Nthwd. 93 BT51
Canterbury Cres SW9 161 DN83
Canterbury Gro SE27 181 DP90
Canterbury Ho, Borwd. 78 CN40
Canterbury Ms (Oxshott), Lthd. 214 CC113
Steels La
Canterbury Par, S.Ock. 149 FW69
Canterbury Pl SE17 278 G9
Canterbury Pl SE17 161 DP77
Canterbury Rd E10 123 EC59
Canterbury Rd NW6 140 DA68
Canterbury Rd, Borwd. 78 CN40
Canterbury Rd, Croy. 201 DM101
Canterbury Rd, Felt. 176 BY89
Canterbury Rd, Grav. 191 GJ89
Canterbury Rd, Guil. 242 AT132
Canterbury Rd, Har. 116 CB57
Canterbury Rd, Mord. 200 DC99
Canterbury Rd, Wat. 75 BV40
Canterbury Ter NW6 140 DA68
Canterbury Way, Brwd. 107 FW51
Canterbury Way, Purf. 169 FS80
Canterbury Way, Rick. 75 BQ41
Cantley Gdns SE19 202 DT95
Cantley Gdns, Ilf. 125 EQ58
Cantley Rd W7 157 CG76
Canton St E14 143 EA72
Cantrell Rd E3 143 DZ70
Cantwell Rd SE18 165 EP80
Canute Gdns SE16 163 DX77
Canvey St SE1 278 G2
Cape Cl, Bark. 145 EQ65
North St
Cape Rd N17 122 DU55
High Cross Rd
Cape Rd, St.Alb. 43 CH20
Cape Yd E1 142 DU74
Asher Way
Capel Av, Wall. 219 DM106
Capel Cl N20 98 DC48
Capel Cl, Brom. 204 EL102
Capel Ct EC2 275 L9
Capel Ct SE20 202 DW95
Melvin Rd
Capel Gdns, Ilf. 125 ET63
Capel Gdns, Pnr. 116 BZ56
Capel Pl, Dart. 188 FJ91
Capel Pt E7 124 EH63
Capel Rd E7 124 EH63
Capel Rd E12 124 EJ63
Capel Rd, Barn. 80 DE44
Capel Rd, Enf. 82 DV36
Capel Rd, Wat. 76 BY44
Capel Vere Wk, Wat. 75 BS39
Capell Av, Rick. 73 BC43
Capell Rd, Rick. 73 BC43
Capell Way, Rick. 73 BD43
Capella Rd, Nthwd. 93 BT50
Capener's Cl SW1 276 F5
Capern Rd SW18 180 DC88
Cargill Rd
Capital Business Cen, Wem. 137 CK68
Capital Ind Est, Mitch. 200 DF99
Willow La
Capital Interchange Way, Brent. 158 CN78
Capital Pl, Harl. 51 EN16
Capitol Ind Pk NW9 118 CQ55
Capitol Way NW9 118 CQ55
Capland St NW8 272 A4
Capland St NW8 140 DD70
Caple Par NW10 138 CS68
Harley Rd
Caple Rd NW10 139 CT68
Capon Cl, Brwd. 108 FV46
Caponfield, Welw.G.C. 30 DB11
Cappell La, Ware 33 ED10
Capper St WC1 273 L5
Capper St WC1 141 DJ70
Caprea Cl, Hayes 136 BX71
Triandra Way
Capri Rd, Croy. 202 DT102
Capstan Cen, Til. 170 GD80
Capstan Cl, Rom. 126 EV58
Capstan Ct, Dart. 168 FQ84
Capstan Ride, Enf. 81 DN40
Capstan Rd SE8 163 DZ77
Capstan Sq E14 163 EC75
Capstan Way SE16 143 DY74
Capstan's Wf (St. John's), Wok. 226 AT118
Capstone Rd, Brom. 184 EF91
Captain Cook Cl, Ch.St.G. 90 AU49
Captains Cl, Chesh. 54 AN27
Captains Wk, Berk. 38 AX20
Capthorne Av, Har. 116 BY60
Capuchin Cl, Stan. 95 CH51
Capulet Ms E16 144 EG74
Hanover Av
Capworth St E10 123 EA60
Caractacus Cottage Vw, Wat. 93 BU45
Caractacus Grn, Wat. 75 BT44
Caradoc Cl W2 140 DA72
Caradoc St SE10 164 EE78
Caradon Cl E11 124 EE61
Brockway Cl
Caradon Cl, Wok. 226 AV118
Caradon Way N15 122 DR56
Caravan La, Rick. 92 BL45
Caravel Cl E14 163 EA76
Tiller Rd
Caravel Cl, Grays 170 FZ76
Caravel Ms SE8 163 EA79
Watergate St
Caravelle Gdns, Nthlt. 136 BX69
Javelin Way
Caraway Cl E13 144 EH71
Caraway Pl, Guil. 242 AU129
Caraway Pl, Wall. 201 DH104
Carberry Rd SE19 182 DS93
Carbery Av W3 158 CM75
Carbis Cl E4 101 ED46
Carbis Rd E14 143 DZ72
Carbone Hill (Newgate St), Hert. 65 DK26
Carbone Hill (Cuffley), Pot.B. 65 DJ27
Carbuncle Pas Way N17 100 DU54
Carburton St W1 273 J6
Carburton St W1 141 DH71
Carbury Cl, Horn. 148 FJ65
Cardale St E14 163 EC76
Plevna St
Cardamom Cl, Guil. 242 AU130
Carde Cl, Hert. 31 DM08
Carden Rd SE15 162 DV83
Cardiff Rd W7 157 CG76
Cardiff Rd, Enf. 82 DV42
Cardiff Rd, Wat. 75 BV44
Cardiff St SE18 165 ES80
Cardiff Way, Abb.L. 59 BU32
Cardigan Cl, Slou. 131 AM73
Cardigan Cl, Wok. 226 AS118
Bingham Dr
Cardigan Gdns, Ilf. 126 EU61
Cardigan Rd E3 143 DZ68
Cardigan Rd SW13 159 CU82
Cardigan Rd SW19 180 DC93
Haydons Rd
Cardigan Rd, Rich. 178 CL86
Cardigan St SE11 278 D10
Cardigan St SE11 161 DN78
Cardigan Wk N1 142 DQ66
Ashby Gro
Cardinal Av, Borwd. 78 CP41
Cardinal Av, Kings.T. 178 CL92
Cardinal Av, Mord. 199 CY100
Cardinal Bourne St SE1 279 L7
Cardinal Bourne St SE1 162 DR76
Cardinal Cl, Chis. 205 ER95
Cardinal Cl, Edg. 96 CR52
Abbots Rd
Cardinal Cl, Mord. 199 CY101
Cardinal Cl, S.Croy. 220 DU113
Cardinal Cl (Cheshunt), Wal.Cr. 66 DT26
Adamsfield
Cardinal Cl, Wor.Pk. 217 CU105
Cardinal Ct, Borwd. 78 CP41
Cardinal Av
Cardinal Cres, N.Mal. 198 CQ96
Cardinal Dr, Ilf. 103 EQ51
Cardinal Dr, Walt. 196 BX102
Cardinal Gro, St.Alb. 42 CB22
Cardinal Pl SW15 159 CX84
Cardinal Rd, Felt. 175 BV88
Cardinal Rd, Ruis. 116 BX60
Cardinal Way, Har. 117 CE55
Wolseley Rd
Cardinal Way, Rain. 148 FK68
Cardinals Wk, Hmptn. 176 CC94
Cardinals Wk, Maid. 130 AJ72
Cardinals Wk, Sun. 175 BS93
Cardinals Way N19 121 DK60
Cardine Ms SE15 162 DV80
Cardingham, Wok. 226 AU117
Cardington Sq, Houns. 156 BX84
Cardington St NW1 273 K2
Cardington St NW1 141 DJ69
Cardinham Rd, Orp. 223 ET105
Cardozo Rd N7 121 DL64
Cardrew Av N12 98 DD50
Cardrew Cl N12 98 DE50
Cardross St W6 159 CV76
Cardwell Rd N7 121 DL63
Cardwells Keep, Guil. 242 AU131
Cardy Rd, Hem.H. 40 BH21
Carew Cl N7 121 DM61
Carew Cl, Couls. 235 DP119
Carew Ct, Sutt. 218 DB109
Carew Rd N17 100 DU54
Carew Rd W13 157 CJ75
Carew Rd, Ashf. 175 BQ93
Carew Rd, Mitch. 200 DG96
Carew Rd, Nthwd. 93 BS51
Carew Rd, Th.Hth. 201 DP97
Carew Rd, Wall. 219 DJ107
Carew St SE5 162 DQ82
Carew Way, Wat. 94 BZ48
Carey Cl, Wind. 151 AP83
Carey Ct, Bexh. 187 FB85
Carey Gdns SW8 161 DJ81
Carey La EC2 275 H8
Carey Pl SW1 277 M9
Carey Rd, Dag. 126 EY63
Carey St WC2 274 C9
Carey St WC2 141 DM72
Carey Way, Wem. 118 CQ63
Careys Cft, Berk. 38 AU16
Careys Wd, Horl. 269 DP148
Carfax Pl SW4 161 DK84
Holwood Pl
Carfax Rd, Hayes 155 BT78
Carfax Rd, Horn. 127 FF63
Carfree Cl N1 141 DN66
Bewdley St
Cargill Rd SW18 180 DB88
Cargo Forecourt Rd, Gat. 268 DD152
Cargo Rd, Gat. 268 DD152
Cargreen Pl SE25 202 DT98
Cargreen Rd
Cargreen Rd SE25 202 DT98
Carholme Rd SE23 183 DZ88
Carisbrook Rd, Brwd. 108 FV44
Carisbrooke Av, Bex. 186 EX88
Carisbrooke Av, Wat. 76 BX39
Carisbrooke Cl, Enf. 82 DT39
Carisbrooke Cl, Horn. 128 FN60
Carisbrooke Cl, Stan. 95 CK54
Carisbrooke Ct, Slou. 132 AT73
Carisbrooke Gdns SE15 162 DT80
Commercial Way
Carisbrooke Rd E17 123 DY56
Carisbrooke Rd, Brom. 204 EJ98
Carisbrooke Rd, Mitch. 201 DK98
Carisbrooke Rd, St.Alb. 60 CB26
Carker's La NW5 121 DH64
Carl Ekman Ho, Grav. 190 GD87
Carlbury Cl, St.Alb. 43 CH21
Carleton Av, Wall. 219 DK109
Carleton Cl, Esher 197 CD102
Carleton Pl (Horton Kirby), Dart. 208 FQ98
Carleton Rd N7 121 DK64
Carleton Rd, Dart. 188 FN87
Carleton Rd (Cheshunt), Wal.Cr. 67 DX28
Carleton Vil NW5 121 DJ64
Leighton Gro
Carlile Cl E3 143 DZ68
Carlina Gdns, Wdf.Grn. 102 EH50
Carlingford Gdns, Mitch. 180 DF94
Carlingford Rd N15 121 DP55
Carlingford Rd NW3 120 DD63
Carlingford Rd, Mord. 199 CX100
Carlisle Av EC3 275 N9
Carlisle Av W3 138 CS72
Carlisle Av, St.Alb. 43 CD18
Carlisle Cl, Kings.T. 198 CN95
Carlisle Cl, Pnr. 116 BY59
Carlisle Gdns, Har. 117 CK59
Carlisle Gdns, Ilf. 124 EL58
Carlisle La SE1 278 C7
Carlisle La SE1 161 DM76
Carlisle Ms NW8 272 A6
Carlisle Ms NW8 140 DD71
Carlisle Pl N11 99 DH49
Carlisle Pl SW1 277 K7
Carlisle Pl SW1 161 DJ76
Carlisle Rd E10 123 EA60
Carlisle Rd N4 121 DN59
Carlisle Rd NW6 139 CY67
Carlisle Rd NW9 118 CQ55
Carlisle Rd, Dart. 188 FN86
Carlisle Rd, Hmptn. 176 CB94
Carlisle Rd, Rom. 127 FG57
Carlisle Rd, Slou. 131 AR73
Carlisle Rd, Sutt. 217 CZ106
Carlisle St W1 273 M9
Carlisle Wk E8 142 DT65
Laurel St
Carlisle Way SW17 180 DG92
Carlos Pl W1 276 G1
Carlos Pl W1 140 DG73
Carlow St NW1 141 DJ68
Arlington Rd
Carlton Av N14 81 DK43
Carlton Av, Felt. 176 BW86
Carlton Av, Green. 189 FS86
Carlton Av, Har. 117 CH57
Carlton Av, Hayes 155 BS77
Carlton Av, S.Croy. 220 DS108
Carlton Av E, Wem. 118 CL60
Carlton Av W, Wem. 117 CH61
Carlton Cl NW3 120 DA61
Carlton Cl, Borwd. 78 CR42
Carlton Cl, Chess. 215 CK107
Carlton Cl, Edg. 96 CN50
Carlton Cl, Nthlt. 116 CC64
Whitton Av W
Carlton Cl, Upmin. 128 FP61
Carlton Cl, Wok. 211 AZ114
Carlton Ct SW9 161 DP81
Carlton Ct, Ilf. 125 ER55
Carlton Ct, Uxb. 134 BK71
Carlton Cres, Sutt. 217 CY105
Carlton Dr SW15 179 CY85
Carlton Dr, Ilf. 125 ER55
Carlton Gdns SW1 277 M3
Carlton Gdns SW1 141 DK74
Carlton Gdns W5 137 CJ72
Carlton Grn, Red. 250 DE131
Carlton Gro SE15 162 DV81
Carlton Hill NW8 140 DB68
Carlton Ho, Felt. 175 BT87
Carlton Ho Ter SW1 277 M3
Carlton Ho Ter SW1 141 DK74
Carlton Par, Orp. 206 EV101
Carlton Par, Sev. 257 FJ122
St. John's Hill
Carlton Pk Av SW20 199 CW96
Carlton Pl, Nthwd. 93 BP50
Carlton Pl, Wey. 213 BP105
Castle Vw Rd
Carlton Rd E11 124 EF60
Carlton Rd E12 124 EK63
Carlton Rd E17 101 DY53
Carlton Rd N4 121 DN59
Carlton Rd N11 98 DG50
Carlton Rd SW14 158 CQ83
Carlton Rd W4 158 CR75
Carlton Rd W5 137 CJ73
Carlton Rd, Erith 167 FB79
Carlton Rd, Grays 171 GF75
Carlton Rd, N.Mal. 198 CS96
Carlton Rd, Red. 250 DF131
Carlton Rd, Reig. 250 DD132
Carlton Rd, Rom. 127 FG57
Carlton Rd, Sid. 185 ET92
Carlton Rd, Slou. 132 AV73
Carlton Rd, S.Croy. 220 DR107
Carlton Rd, Sun. 175 BT94
Carlton Rd, Walt. 195 BV101
Carlton Rd, Well. 166 EV83
Carlton Rd, Wok. 211 BA114
Carlton Sq E1 143 DX70
Argyle Rd
Carlton St SW1 277 M1
Carlton Ter E11 124 EH57
Carlton Ter N18 100 DR48
Carlton Ter SE26 182 DW90
Carlton Twr Pl SW1 276 E6
Carlton Twr Pl SW1 160 DF76
Carlton Tye, Horl. 269 DJ148
Carlton Vale NW6 140 DB68
Carlton Vil SW15 179 CW85
St. John's Av
Carlwell St SW17 180 DE92
Carlyle Av, Brom. 204 EK97
Carlyle Av, Sthl. 136 BZ73
Carlyle Cl N2 120 DC58
Carlyle Cl NW10 138 CR67
Carlyle Cl, W.Mol. 196 CB96
Carlyle Gdns, Sthl. 136 BZ73
Carlyle Lo (New Barnet), Barn. *Richmond Rd* 80 DC43
Carlyle Ms E1 143 DX70
Alderney Rd
Carlyle Pl SW15 159 CX84
Carlyle Rd E12 124 EL63
Carlyle Rd SE28 146 EV73
Carlyle Rd W5 157 CJ78
Carlyle Rd, Croy. 202 DU103
Carlyle Rd, Stai. 173 BF94
Carlyle Sq SW3 160 DD78
Carlyon Av, Har. 116 BZ63
Carlyon Cl, Wem. 138 CL67
Carlyon Rd, Hayes 136 BW72
Carlyon Rd, Wem. 138 CL68
Carmalt Gdns SW15 159 CW84
Carmalt Gdns, Walt. 214 BW106
Carmarthen Grn NW9 118 CS58
Snowdon Dr
Carmarthen Rd, Slou. 132 AS73
Carmel Cl, Wok. 226 AY118
Carmel Ct W8 160 DB75
Holland St
Carmel Ct, Wem. 118 CP61
Carmelite Cl, Har. 94 CC53
Carmelite Rd, Har. 94 CC53
Carmelite St EC4 274 E10
Carmelite St EC4 141 DN73
Carmelite Wk, Har. 94 CC53
Carmelite Way, Har. 94 CC54
Carmen Ct, Borwd. 78 CM38
Belford Rd
Carmen St E14 143 EB72

Car - Cec This index reads in the sequence: Street Name / Postal District or Post Town / Map Page Number / Grid Reference

Carmichael Cl SW11 160 DD83
Darien Rd
Carmichael Cl, Ruis. 115 BU63
Carmichael Ms SW18 180 DD87
Carmichael Rd SE25 202 DU99
Carminia Rd SW17 181 DH89
Carnaby Rd, Brox. 49 DY20
Carnaby St W1 273 K9
Carnaby St W1 141 DJ72
Carnac St SE27 182 DR91
Carnach Grn, S.Ock. 149 FV73
Carnanton Rd E17 101 ED53
Carnarvon Av, Enf. 82 DT41
Carnarvon Dr, Hayes 155 BQ76
Carnarvon Rd E10 123 EC58
Carnarvon Rd E15 144 EF65
Carnarvon Rd E18 102 EF53
Carnarvon Rd, Barn. 79 CY41
Carnation Cl, Rom. 127 FE61
Carnation St SE2 166 EV78
Carnbrook Rd SE3 164 EK83
Carnecke Gdns SE9 184 EL85
Carnegie Cl, Enf. 83 EA37
Government Row
Carnegie Cl, Surb. 198 CM103
Fullers Av
Carnegie Pl SW19 179 CX90
Carnegie Rd, St.Alb. 43 CD16
Carnegie St N1 141 DM67
Carnforth Cl, Epsom 216 CP107
Carnforth Gdns, Horn. 127 FG64
Carnforth Rd SW16 181 DK94
Carnie Lo SW17 181 DH90
Manville Rd
Carnoustie Dr N1 141 DM66
Carnwath Rd SW6 160 DA83
Caro La, Hem.H. 40 BN22
Carol St NW1 141 DJ67
Carolina Cl E15 124 EE64
Carolina Rd, Th.Hth. 201 DP96
Caroline Cl N10 99 DH54
Alexandra Pk Rd
Caroline Cl SW16 181 DM91
Caroline Cl W2 140 DB73
Bayswater Rd
Caroline Cl, Croy. 220 DS105
Brownlow Rd
Caroline Cl, Islw. 157 CD80
Caroline Cl, West Dr. 154 BK75
Caroline Ct, Ashf. 175 BP93
Caroline Ct, Stan. 95 CG51
The Chase
Caroline Gdns SE15 162 DV80
Caroline Pl SW11 160 DG82
Caroline Pl W2 140 DB73
Caroline Pl, Hayes 155 BS80
Caroline Pl, Wat. 76 BY44
Caroline Pl Ms W2 140 DB73
Orme La
Caroline Rd SW19 179 CZ94
Caroline St E1 143 DX72
Caroline Ter SW1 276 F9
Caroline Ter SW1 160 DG77
Caroline Wk W6 159 CY79
Carolyn Cl, Wok. 226 AT119
Carolyn Dr, Orp. 206 EU104
Caroon Dr, Rick. 74 BH36
Carpenders Av, Wat. 94 BY48
Carpenders Pk, Wat. 94 BY47
Carpenter Cl, Epsom 217 CT109
West St
Carpenter Gdns N21 99 DP47
Carpenter Path, Brwd. 109 GD43
Carpenter St W1 277 H1
Carpenter Way, Pot.B. 64 DC33
Carpenters Arms La, Epp. 70 EV25
Carpenters Arms Path SE9 185 EM86
Eltham High St
Carpenters Ct, Twick. 177 CE89
Carpenters Pl SW4 161 DK84
Carpenters Rd E15 143 EB65
Carpenters Rd, Enf. 82 DW36
Carpenters Wd Dr, Rick. 73 BB42
Carr Gro SE18 164 EL77
Carr Rd E17 101 DZ54
Carr Rd, Nthlt. 136 CB65
Carr St E14 143 DY71
Carrara Wk SW9 161 DP84
Carrara Wf SW6 159 CY83
Carriage Dr E SW11 160 DG80
Carriage Dr N SW11 160 DG79
Carriage Dr S SW11 160 DF81
Carriage Dr W SW11 160 DF80
Carriage Ms, Ilf. 125 EQ61
Carriage Pl N16 122 DR62
Carriage Pl SW16 181 DJ92
Eardley Rd
Carriageway, The, West. 240 EX124
Carrick Cl, Islw. 157 CG83
Carrick Dr, Ilf. 103 EQ53
Carrick Dr, Sev. 257 FH123
Carrick Gdns N17 100 DS52
Flexmere Rd
Carrick Gate, Esher 196 CC104
Carrick Ms SE8 163 EA79
Watergate St
Carriden Ct, Hert. 31 DM07
The Ridgeway
Carrill Way, Belv. 166 EX77
Carrington Av, Borwd. 78 CP43
Carrington Av, Houns. 176 CB85
Carrington Cl, Barn. 79 CU43
Carrington Cl, Borwd. 78 CQ43
Carrington Cl, Croy. 203 DY101
Carrington Cl, Kings.T. 178 CQ92
Carrington Cl, Red. 250 DF133
Carrington Gdns E7 124 EH63
Woodford Rd
Carrington Pl, Esher 214 CC105
Carrington Rd, Dart. 188 FM86
Carrington Rd, Rich. 158 CN84
Carrington Rd, Slou. 132 AS73
Carrington Sq, Har. 94 CC52
Carrington St W1 277 H3
Carrol Cl NW5 121 DH63
Carroll Av, Guil. 243 BB134
Carroll Cl E15 124 EF64
Carroll Hill, Loug. 85 EM41
Carron Cl E14 143 EB72
Carronade Pl SE28 165 EQ76
Carroun Rd SW8 161 DM80
Carrow Rd, Dag. 146 EV66
Carrow Rd, Walt. 196 BX104
Kenilworth Dr
Carroway La, Grnf. 137 CD69
Cowgate Rd
Carrs La N21 82 DQ43
Carshalton Gro, Sutt. 218 DD105
Carshalton Pk Rd, Cars. 218 DF106
Carshalton Pl, Cars. 218 DG105
Carshalton Rd, Bans. 218 DF114
Carshalton Rd, Cars. 218 DC106
Carshalton Rd, Mitch. 200 DG98
Carshalton Rd, Sutt. 218 DC106
Carsington Gdns, Dart. 188 FK89
Carslake Rd SW15 179 CW86
Carson Rd E16 144 EG70
Carson Rd SE21 182 DR89
Carson Rd, Barn. 80 DF42
Carstairs Rd SE6 183 EC90
Carston Cl SE12 184 EG85
Carswell Cl, Brwd. 109 GD44
Carswell Cl, Ilf. 124 EK56
Roding La S
Carswell Rd SE6 183 EC87
Cart La E4 101 ED45
Cart Path, Wat. 60 BW33
Cartbridge Cl (Send), Wok. 227 BB123
Send Rd
Cartel Cl, Purf. 169 FR77
Carter Cl, Rom. 105 FB52
Carter Cl, Wall. 219 DK108
Carter Cl, Wind. 151 AN82
Carter Ct EC4 141 DP72
Carter La
Carter Dr, Rom. 105 FB52
Carter La EC4 274 G9
Carter La EC4 141 DP72
Carter Pl SE17 162 DQ78
Carter Rd E13 144 EH67
Carter Rd SW19 180 DD93
Carter St SE17 162 DQ79
Carter Wk (Penn), H.Wyc. 88 AC47
Carteret St SW1 277 M5
Carteret St SW1 161 DK75
Carteret Way SE8 163 DY77
Carterhatch La, Enf. 82 DU40
Carterhatch Rd, Enf. 82 DW40
Carters Cl, Wor.Pk. 199 CX103
Carters Cotts, Red. 266 DE136
Kings Av
Carters Hill (Underriver), Sev. 257 FP127
Carters Hill Cl SE9 184 EJ88
Carters La SE23 183 DY89
Carters La, Epp. 51 EP24
Carters La, Wok. 227 BC120
Carters Mead, Harl. 52 EV17
Carters Rd, Epsom 233 CT115
Carters Row (Northfleet), Grav. 191 GF88
Carters Yd SW18 180 DA85
Wandsworth High St
Cartersfield Rd, Wal.Abb. 67 EC34
Cartersmeade Cl, Horl. 269 DH147
Wheatfield Way
Carthagena Est, Brox. 49 EC20
Carthew Rd W6 159 CV76
Carthew Vil W6 159 CV76
Carthouse La, Wok. 210 AS114
Carthusian St EC1 275 H6
Carthusian St EC1 142 DQ71
Cartier Circle E14 143 EB74
Carting La WC2 278 A1
Carting La WC2 141 DL73
Cartmel Cl N17 100 DV52
Heybourne Rd
Cartmel Cl, Reig. 250 DE133
Cartmel Gdns, Mord. 200 DC99
Cartmel Rd, Bexh. 166 FA81
Carton St W1 272 E8
Cartwright Gdns WC1 273 P3
Cartwright Gdns WC1 141 DL69
Cartwright Rd, Dag. 146 EZ66
Cartwright St E1 142 DT73
Cartwright Way SW13 159 CV80
Carve Ley, Welw.G.C. 30 DB10
Carver Cl W4 158 CQ76
Carver Rd SE24 182 DQ86
Carville Cres, Brent. 158 CL78
Cary Rd E11 124 EE63
Cary Wk, Rad. 61 CH34
Carysfort Rd N8 121 DK57
Carysfort Rd N16 122 DR62
Cascade Av N10 121 DJ56
Cascade Cl, Buck.H. 102 EK47
Cascade Rd
Cascade Cl, Orp. 206 EW97
Cascade Rd, Buck.H. 102 EK47
Cascades, Croy. 221 DZ110
Caselden Cl, Add. 212 BJ106
Casella Rd SE14 163 DX80
Casewick Rd SE27 181 DP91
Casey Cl NW8 272 B3
Casey Cl NW8 140 DE69
Casimir Rd E5 122 DV62
Casino Av SE24 182 DQ85
Caspian St SE5 162 DR80
Caspian Wk E16 144 EK72
Caspian Wf E3 143 EB71
Violet Rd
Cassandra Cl, Nthlt. 117 CD63
Cassandra Gate, Wal.Cr. 67 DZ27
Casselden Rd NW10 138 CR66
Cassidy Rd SW6 160 DA80
Cassilda Rd SE2 166 EU77
Cassilis Rd, Twick. 177 CH85
Cassio Rd, Wat. 75 BV41
Cassiobridge, Wat. 75 BR42
Cassiobridge Rd, Wat. 75 BS42
Cassiobury Av, Felt. 175 BT86
Cassiobury Ct, Wat. 75 BT40
Cassiobury Dr, Wat. 75 BT40
Cassiobury Pk, Wat. 75 BS41
Cassiobury Pk Av, Wat. 75 BS41
Cassiobury Rd E17 123 DX57
Cassis Ct, Loug. 85 EQ42
Cassland Rd E9 142 DW66
Cassland Rd, Th.Hth. 202 DR98
Casslee Rd SE6 183 DZ87
Cassocks Sq, Shep. 195 BR100
Casson St E1 142 DU71
Casstine Cl, Swan. 187 FF94
Castalia Sq E14 163 EC75
Roserton St
Castalia St E14 163 EC75
Plevna St
Castano Ct, Abb.L. 59 BS31
Castell Rd, Loug. 85 EQ39
Castellain Rd W9 140 DB70
Castellan Av, Rom. 127 FH55
Castellane Cl, Stan. 95 CF52
Daventer Dr
Castello Av SW15 179 CW85
Castelnau SW13 159 CV79
Castelnau Gdns SW13 159 CV79
Arundel Ter
Castelnau Pl SW13 159 CV79
Castelnau
Castelnau Row SW13 159 CV79
Lonsdale Rd
Casterbridge NW6 140 DB67
Casterbridge Rd SE3 164 EG83
Casterton St E8 142 DV65
Wilton Way
Castile Rd SE18 165 EN77
Castillon Rd SE6 184 EE89
Castlands Rd SE6 183 DZ89
Castle Av E4 101 ED50
Castle Av, Epsom 217 CU109
Castle Av, Rain. 147 FE66
Castle Av (Datchet), Slou. 152 AU79
Castle Av, West Dr. 134 BL73
Castle Baynard St EC4 274 G10
Castle Cl E9 123 DY64
Swinnerton St
Castle Cl SW19 179 CX90
Castle Cl W3 158 CP75
Castle Cl, Brom. 204 EE97
Castle Cl, Bushey 76 CB44
Castle Cl, Hodd. 33 EC14
Castle Cl (Bletchingley), Red. 252 DQ133
Castle Cl, Reig. 266 DB138
Castle Cl, Rom. 106 FJ48
Castle Cl, Sun. 175 BS94
Mill Fm Av
Castle Ct EC3 275 L9
Castle Ct SE26 183 DY91
Champion Rd
Castle Dr, Horl. 269 DJ150
Castle Dr, Ilf. 124 EL58
Castle Dr, Reig. 266 DA138
Castle Fm Rd (Shoreham), Sev. 225 FF109
Castle Gdns, Dor. 248 CM134
Castle Gateway, Berk. 38 AW17
Castle Grn, Wey. 195 BS104
Castle Gro Rd (Chobham), Wok. 210 AS113
Castle Hill, Berk. 38 AW17
Castle Hill, Guil. 258 AX136
Castle Hill (Fawkham), Long. 209 FX99
Castle Hill, Wind. 151 AR81
Castle Hill Av, Berk. 38 AW18
Castle Hill Av (New Addington), Croy. 221 EB109
Castle Hill Cl, Berk. 38 AV18
Castle Hill Rd, Egh. 172 AV91
Castle La SW1 277 L6
Castle La SW1 161 DJ76
Castle Mead, Hem.H. 40 BH22
Castle Ms N12 98 DC50
Castle Rd
Castle Ms NW1 141 DH65
Castle Rd
Castle Par, Epsom 217 CU108
Ewell Bypass
Castle Pl NW1 141 DH65
Castle Pl W4 158 CS77
Windmill Rd
Castle Pt E13 144 EJ68
Castle Rd N12 98 DC50
Castle Rd NW1 141 DH65
Castle Rd, Couls. 234 DE120
Castle Rd, Dag. 146 EV67
Castle Rd (Eynsford), Dart. 225 FH107
Castle Rd, Enf. 83 DY39
Castle Rd, Epsom 232 CP115
Castle Rd, Grays 170 FZ79
Castle Rd, Hodd. 33 EB14
Castle Rd, Islw. 157 CF82
Castle Rd, Nthlt. 136 CB65
Castle Rd, St.Alb. 43 CH20
Castle Rd (Shoreham), Sev. 225 FG108
Castle Rd, Sthl. 156 BZ76
Castle Rd, Swans. 190 FZ86
Castle Rd, Wey. 195 BS104
Castle Rd, Wok. 211 AZ114
Castle Sq, Guil. 258 AX136
Castle Sq (Bletchingley), Red. 252 DQ133
Castle St E6 144 EJ68
Castle St, Berk. 38 AW19
Castle St, Green. 189 FU85
Castle St, Guil. 258 AX136
Castle St, Hert. 32 DQ10
Castle St, Kings.T. 198 CL96
Castle St (Bletchingley), Red. 251 DP133
Castle St, Slou. 152 AT76
Castle St, Swans. 190 FZ86
Castle Vw, Epsom 216 CP114
Castle Vw Rd, Wey. 213 BP105
Castle Wk, Reig. 250 DA134
High St
Castle Wk, Sun. 196 BW97
Elizabeth Gdns
Castle Way SW19 179 CX90
Castle Way, Epsom 217 CU109
Castle Av
Castle Way, Felt. 176 BW91
Castle Yd N6 120 DG59
North Rd
Castle Yd SE1 278 G2
Castle Yd, Rich. 177 CK85
Hill St
Castlebar Hill W5 137 CH71
Castlebar Ms W5 137 CJ71
Castlebar Pk W5 137 CH71
Castlebar Rd W5 137 CJ71
Castlebrook Cl SE11 278 F8
Castlebrook Cl SE11 161 DP77
Castlecombe Dr SW19 179 CX87
Castlecombe Rd SE9 184 EL91
Castledine Rd SE20 182 DV94
Castlefield Rd, Reig. 250 DA133
Castleford Av SE9 185 EP88
Castleford Cl N17 100 DT51
Castlegate, Rich. 158 CM83
Castlehaven Rd NW1 141 DH66
Castleleigh Ct, Enf. 82 DR43
Castlemaine Av, Epsom 217 CV109
Castlemaine Av, S.Croy. 220 DT106
Castlemaine Twr SW11 160 DF81
Castlereagh St W1 272 D8
Castleton Av, Bexh. 167 FD81
Castleton Av, Wem. 118 CL63
Castleton Cl, Bans. 234 DA115
Castleton Cl, Croy. 203 DY100
Castleton Dr, Bans. 234 DA115
Castleton Gdns, Wem. 118 CL62
Castleton Rd E17 101 ED54
Castleton Rd SE9 184 EK91
Castleton Rd, Ilf. 126 EU60
Castleton Rd, Mitch. 201 DK98
Castleton Rd, Ruis. 116 BX60
Castletown Rd W14 159 CY78
Castleview Cl N4 122 DQ60
Castleview Gdns, Ilf. 124 EL58
Castleview Rd, Slou. 152 AW77
Castlewood Dr SE9 165 EM82
Castlewood Rd N15 122 DU58
Castlewood Rd N16 122 DU59
Castlewood Rd, Barn. 80 DD41
Castor La E14 143 EB73
Cat Hill, Barn. 80 DE44
Catalin Ct, Wal.Abb. 67 ED33
Howard Cl
Catalina Av (Chafford Hundred), Grays 170 FZ75
Catalpa Cl, Guil. 242 AW132
Cedar Way
Cater Gdns, Guil. 242 AT132
Caterham Av, Ilf. 103 EM54
Caterham Bypass, Cat. 236 DV120
Caterham Cl, Cat. 236 DS120
Caterham Ct, Wal.Abb. 68 EF34
Caterham Dr, Couls. 235 DP118
Caterham Rd SE13 163 EC83
Catesby St SE17 279 L9
Catesby St SE17 162 DR77
Catford Bdy SE6 183 EB87
Catford Hill SE6 183 DZ89
Catford Ms SE6 183 EB87
Holbeach Rd
Catford Rd SE6 183 EA87
Cathall Rd E11 123 ED62
Catham Cl, St.Alb. 43 CH22
Cathay St SE16 162 DV75
Cathay Wk, Nthlt. 136 CA68
Brabazon Rd
Cathcart Dr, Orp. 205 ES103
Cathcart Hill N19 121 DJ62
Cathcart Rd SW10 160 DC79
Cathcart St NW5 141 DH65
Cathedral Cl, Guil. 258 AV135
Cathedral Ct, St.Alb. 42 CB22
Cathedral Hill Ind Est, Guil. 242 AU133
Cathedral Piazza SW1 277 K7
Cathedral Pl EC4 275 H8
Cathedral St SE1 279 K2
Cathedral St SE1 142 DR74
Cathedral Vw, Guil. 242 AT134
Catherall Rd N5 122 DQ62
Catherine Cl, Brwd. 108 FU43
Catherine Cl, Grays 170 FZ75
Catherine Cl, Hem.H. 41 BP15
Parr Cres
Catherine Cl, Loug. 85 EM44
Roding Gdns
Catherine Cl (Byfleet), W.Byf. 212 BL114
Catherine Ct N14 81 DJ43
Conisbee Ct
Catherine Dr, Rich. 158 CL84
Catherine Dr, Sun. 175 BT93
Catherine Gdns, Houns. 157 CD84
Catherine Griffiths Ct EC1 274 E4
Catherine Gro SE10 163 EB81
Catherine Howard Ct, Wey. 195 BP104
Old Palace Rd
Catherine Pl SW1 277 K6
Catherine Pl SW1 161 DJ76
Catherine Pl, Har. 117 CF57
Catherine Rd, Enf. 83 DY36
Catherine Rd, Rom. 127 FH57
Catherine Rd, Surb. 197 CK99
Catherine St WC2 274 B10
Catherine St WC2 141 DM73
Catherine St, St.Alb. 43 CD19
Catherine Wheel All E1 275 N7
Catherine Wheel Rd, Brent. 157 CK80
Catherine Wheel Yd SW1 277 K3
Catherine's Cl, West Dr. 154 BK76
Money La
Cathles Rd SW12 181 DH86
Cathnor Rd W12 159 CV75
Catisfield Rd, Enf. 83 DY37
Catkin Cl, Hem.H. 40 BH19
Catlin Cres, Shep. 195 BR99
Catlin Gdns, Gdse. 252 DV130
Catlin St SE16 162 DU78
Catlin St, Hem.H. 40 BH23
Catling Cl SE23 182 DW90
Catlins La, Pnr. 115 BV55
Cato Rd SW4 161 DK83
Cato St W1 272 C7
Cato St W1 140 DE71
Cator Cl (New Addington), Croy. 222 EE111
Cator Cres (New Addington), Croy. 221 ED111
Cator La, Beck. 203 DZ96
Cator Rd SE26 183 DX93
Cator Rd, Cars. 218 DF106
Cator St SE15 162 DT79
Catsey La, Bushey 94 CC45
Catsey Wds, Bushey 94 CC45
Catterick Cl N11 98 DG51
Catterick Way, Borwd. 78 CM39
Cattistock Rd SE9 184 EL92
Cattlegate Hill, Pot.B. 65 DK31
Cattlegate Rd, Enf. 65 DL34
Cattlegate Rd, Pot.B. 65 DK31
Cattley Cl, Barn. 79 CY42
Wood St
Cattlins Cl, Wal.Cr. 66 DT29
Catton St WC1 274 B7
Catton St WC1 141 DM71
Cattsdell, Hem.H. 40 BL18
Caulfield Rd E6 145 EM66
Caulfield Rd SE15 162 DV82
Causeway, The N2 120 DE56
Causeway, The SW18 160 DB84
Causeway, The SW19 179 CX92
Causeway, The, Cars. 200 DG104
Causeway, The, Chess. 216 CL105
Causeway, The (Claygate), Esher 215 CF108
Causeway, The, Felt. 155 BU84
Causeway, The, Maid. 150 AC75
Causeway, The, Pot.B. 64 DC31
Causeway, The, Stai. 173 BC91
Causeway, The, Sutt. 218 DC109
Causeway, The, Tedd. 177 CF93
Broad St
Causeway Cl, Pot.B. 64 DD31
Causeway Ct, Wok. 226 AT118
Bingham Dr
Causeyware Rd N9 100 DV45
Causton Rd N6 121 DH59
Causton Sq, Dag. 146 FA66
Causton St SW1 277 N9
Causton St SW1 161 DK77
Cautherly La, Ware 33 DZ10
Cautley Av SW4 181 DJ85
Cavalier Cl, Rom. 126 EX56
Cavalier Gdns, Hayes 135 BR72
Hanover Circle
Cavalry Barracks, Houns. 156 BX83
Cavalry Cres, Houns. 156 BX84
Cavalry Cres, Wind. 151 AP83
Cavalry Gdns SW15 179 CY85
Cavan Dr, St.Alb. 43 CD15
Cavan Ho E3 143 DZ67
Cavaye Pl SW10 160 DC78
Fulham Rd
Cave Rd E13 144 EH68
Cave Rd, Rich. 177 CJ91
Cave St N1 141 DM68
Carnegie St
Cavell Cres, Dart. 168 FN84
Cavell Cres, Rom. 106 FL54
Cavell Dr, Enf. 81 DN40
Cavell Rd N17 100 DR52
Cavell Rd (Cheshunt), Wal.Cr. 66 DT27
Cavell St E1 142 DV71
Cavell Way, Epsom 216 CN111
Cavendish Av N3 98 DA54
Cavendish Av NW8 272 A1
Cavendish Av NW8 140 DD68
Cavendish Av W13 137 CG71
Cavendish Av, Erith 167 FC79
Cavendish Av, Har. 117 CD63
Cavendish Av, Horn. 147 FH65
Cavendish Av, N.Mal. 199 CV99
Cavendish Av, Ruis. 115 BV64
Cavendish Av, Sev. 256 FG122
Cavendish Av, Sid. 186 EU87
Cavendish Av, Well. 165 ET83
Cavendish Av, Wdf.Grn. 102 EH53
Cavendish Cl N18 100 DV50
Cavendish Cl NW6 139 CZ66
Cavendish Rd
Cavendish Cl NW8 272 A2
Cavendish Cl NW8 140 DD69
Cavendish Cl, Amer. 72 AV39
Cavendish Cl, Hayes 135 BS71
Westacott
Cavendish Cl, Maid. 130 AG72
Cavendish Cl, Sun. 175 BT93
Cavendish Ct EC3 275 N8
Cavendish Ct, Rick. 75 BR43
Mayfare
Cavendish Ct, Sun. 175 BT93
Cavendish Cres, Borwd. 78 CN42
Cavendish Cres, Horn. 147 FH65
Cavendish Dr E11 123 ED60
Cavendish Dr, Edg. 96 CM51
Cavendish Dr (Claygate), Esher 215 CE106
Cavendish Gdns, Bark. 125 ES64
Cavendish Gdns, Ilf. 125 EN60
Cavendish Gdns, Red. 250 DG133
Cavendish Gdns, Rom. 126 EY57
Cavendish Ms N W1 273 J6
Cavendish Ms S W1 273 J7
Cavendish Par, Houns. 156 BY82
Bath Rd
Cavendish Pl W1 273 J8
Cavendish Pl W1 141 DH72
Cavendish Rd E4 101 EC51
Cavendish Rd N4 121 DN58
Cavendish Rd N18 100 DV50
Cavendish Rd NW6 139 CY66
Cavendish Rd SW12 181 DH86
Cavendish Rd SW19 180 DD94
Cavendish Rd W4 158 CQ81
Cavendish Rd, Barn. 79 CW41
Cavendish Rd, Chesh. 54 AR32
Cavendish Rd, Croy. 201 DP102
Cavendish Rd, N.Mal. 199 CT99
Cavendish Rd, Red. 250 DG134
Cavendish Rd, St.Alb. 43 CF20
Cavendish Rd, Sun. 175 BT93
Cavendish Rd, Sutt. 218 DC108
Cavendish Rd, Wey. 213 BQ108
Cavendish Rd, Wok. 226 AX119
Cavendish Sq W1 273 J8
Cavendish Sq W1 141 DH72
Cavendish Sq, Long. 209 FX97
Cavendish St N1 275 K1
Cavendish St N1 142 DR68
Cavendish Ter, Felt. 175 BU89
High St
Cavendish Way, Hat. 45 CT18
Cavendish Way, W.Wick. 203 EB102
Cavenham Cl, Wok. 226 AY119
Cavenham Gdns, Horn. 128 FJ57
Cavenham Gdns, Ilf. 125 ER62
Caverleigh Way, Wor.Pk. 199 CU102
Caversham Av N13 99 DN48
Caversham Av, Sutt. 199 CY103
Caversham Ct N11 98 DG48
Caversham Flats SW3 160 DF79
Caversham St
Caversham Rd N15 122 DQ56
Caversham Rd NW5 141 DJ65
Caversham Rd, Kings.T. 198 CM96
Caversham St SW3 160 DF79
Caverswall St W12 139 CW72
Caveside Cl, Chis. 205 EN95
Cavill's Wk, Chig. 104 EW47
Cavill's Wk, Rom. 104 EX47
Cawcott Dr, Wind. 151 AL81
Cawdor Av, S.Ock. 149 FU73
Cawdor Cres W7 157 CG77
Cawley Hatch, Harl. 51 EM15
Cawnpore St SE19 182 DS92
Cawsey Way, Wok. 226 AY117
Caxton Av, Add. 212 BG107
Caxton Dr, Uxb. 134 BK68
Chiltern Vw Rd
Caxton Gdns, Guil. 242 AV133
Caxton Gro E3 143 EA69
Caxton Hill, Hert. 32 DT09
Caxton Hill Extension Rd, Hert. 32 DT09
Caxton La, Oxt. 254 EL131
Caxton Ms, Brent. 157 CK79
The Butts
Caxton Ri, Red. 250 DG133
Caxton Rd N22 99 DM54
Caxton Rd SW19 180 DC92
Caxton Rd W12 159 CX75
Caxton Rd, Hodd. 33 EB13
Caxton Rd, Sthl. 156 BX76
Caxton St SW1 277 L6
Caxton St SW1 161 DJ76
Caxton St N E16 144 EF73
Victoria Dock Rd
Caxton Way, Rom. 127 FE56
Caxton Way, Wat. 75 BR44
Caxtons Ct, Guil. 243 BA132
Caygill Cl, Brom. 204 EF98
Cayley Cl, Wall. 219 DL108
Cayley Rd, Sthl. 156 CB76
McNair Rd
Cayton Pl EC1 275 K3
Cayton Rd, Couls. 235 DH121
Brighton Rd
Cayton Rd, Grnf. 137 CE68
Cayton St EC1 275 K3
Cazenove Rd E17 101 EA53
Cazenove Rd N16 122 DT61
Cearn Way, Couls. 235 DM115
Cearns Ho E6 144 EK67
Cecil Av, Bark. 145 ER66
Cecil Av, Enf. 82 DT42
Cecil Av, Grays 170 FZ75
Cecil Av, Horn. 128 FL55
Cecil Av, Wem. 118 CM64
Cecil Cl W5 137 CK71
Helena Rd
Cecil Cl, Ashf. 175 BQ93
Cecil Cl, Chess. 215 CK105
Cecil Ct WC2 277 N1

Cecil Ct, Barn. 79 CX41
Cecil Cres, Hat. 45 CV16
Cecil Pk, Pnr. 116 BY56
Cecil Pl, Mitch. 200 DF99
Cecil Rd E11 124 EE62
Cecil Rd E13 144 EG67
Cecil Rd E17 101 EA53
Cecil Rd N10 99 DH54
Cecil Rd N14 99 DJ46
Cecil Rd NW9 118 CS55
Cecil Rd NW10 138 CS67
Cecil Rd SW19 180 DB94
Cecil Rd W3 138 CQ71
Cecil Rd, Ashf. 175 BQ94
Cecil Rd, Croy. 201 DM100
Cecil Rd, Enf. 82 DR42
Cecil Rd, Grav. 191 GF88
Cecil Rd, Har. 117 CE55
Cecil Rd, Hert. 32 DQ12
Cecil Rd, Hodd. 49 EC15
Cecil Rd, Houns. 156 CC82
Cecil Rd, Ilf. 125 EP63
Cecil Rd, Iver 133 BE72
Cecil Rd, Pot.B. 63 CU32
Cecil Rd, Rom. 126 EX59
Cecil Rd, St.Alb. 43 CF20
Cecil Rd, Sutt. 217 CZ107
Cecil Rd (Cheshunt), Wal.Cr. 67 DX32
Cecil St, Wat. 75 BV38
Cecil Way, Brom. 204 EG102
Cecil Way, Slou. 131 AM70
Cecile Pk N8 121 DL58
Cecilia Cl N2 120 DC55
Cecilia Rd E8 122 DU64
Cedar Av, Barn. 98 DE45
Cedar Av, Cob. 230 BW115
Cedar Av, Enf. 82 DW40
Cedar Av, Grav. 191 GJ91
Cedar Av, Hayes 135 BU72
Cedar Av, Rom. 126 EY57
Cedar Av, Ruis. 136 BW65
Cedar Av, Sid. 186 EU87
Cedar Av, Twick. 176 CB86
Cedar Av, Upmin. 128 FN63
Cedar Av, Wal.Cr. 67 DX33
Cedar Av, West Dr. 134 BM74
Cedar Chase, Maid. 130 AD70
Cedar Cl SE21 182 DQ88
Cedar Cl SW15 178 CR91
Cedar Cl, Borwd. 78 CP42
Cedar Cl, Brwd. 109 GD45
Cedar Cl, Brom. 204 EL104
Cedar Cl, Buck.H. 102 EK47
Cedar Cl, Cars. 218 DF107
Cedar Cl, Dor. 263 CH136
Cedar Cl, E.Mol. 197 CE98
Cedar Rd
Cedar Cl, Epsom 217 CT114
Cedar Cl, Esher 214 BZ108
Cedar Cl, Hert. 31 DP09
Cedar Cl, Iver 133 BC66
Thornbridge Rd
Cedar Cl, Pot.B. 64 DA30
Cedar Cl, Reig. 266 DC136
Cedar Cl, Rom. 127 FC56
Cedar Cl, Saw. 36 EY06
Cedar Cl, Stai. 194 BJ97
Cedar Cl, Swan. 207 FC96
Cedar Cl, Ware 33 DX07
Cedar Cl, Warl. 237 DY118
Cedar Copse, Brom. 205 EM96
Cedar Ct E8 142 DT66
Cedar Ct E11 124 EH57
Grosvenor Rd
Cedar Ct N1 142 DQ66
Essex Rd
Cedar Ct SE9 184 EL86
Cedar Ct SW19 179 CX90
Cedar Ct, Egh. 173 BA91
Cedar Ct, Epp. 70 EU31
Cedar Ct, St.Alb. 43 CK20
Cedar Cres, Brom. 204 EL104
Cedar Dr N2 120 DE56
Cedar Dr (Sutton at Hone), Dart. 208 FP96
Cedar Dr (Fetcham), Lthd. 231 CE123
Cedar Dr, Loug. 85 EP40
Cedar Dr, Pnr. 94 CA51
Cedar Gdns, Sutt. 218 DC107
Cedar Gdns, Upmin. 128 FQ62
Cedar Gdns, Wok. 226 AV118
St. John's Rd
Cedar Grn, Hodd. 49 EA18
Cedar Gro W5 158 CL76
Cedar Gro, Amer. 55 AR39
Cedar Gro, Bex. 186 EW86
Cedar Gro, Sthl. 136 CA71
Cedar Gro, Wey. 213 BQ105
Cedar Hts, Rich. 178 CL88
Cedar Hill, Epsom 232 CQ116
Cedar Ho, Croy. 221 EB107
Cedar Ho, Sun. 175 BT94
Cedar Lawn Av, Barn. 79 CY43
Cedar Mt SE9 184 EK88
Cedar Pk, Chig. 103 EP49
High Rd
Cedar Pk Gdns, Rom. 126 EX59
Cedar Pk Rd, Enf. 82 DQ38
Cedar Pl SE7 164 EJ78
Floyd Rd
Cedar Pl, Nthwd. 93 BQ51
Cedar Ri N14 98 DG45
Cedar Ri, S.Ock. 149 FX70
Sycamore Way
Cedar Rd N17 100 DT53
Cedar Rd NW2 119 CW63
Cedar Rd, Berk. 38 AX20
Cedar Rd, Brwd. 109 GD44
Cedar Rd, Brom. 204 EJ96
Cedar Rd, Cob. 213 BV114
Cedar Rd, Croy. 202 DS103
Cedar Rd, Dart. 188 FK88
Cedar Rd, E.Mol. 197 CE98
Cedar Rd, Enf. 81 DP38
Cedar Rd, Erith 167 FG81
Cedar Rd, Felt. 175 BR88
Cedar Rd, Grays 171 GG76
Cedar Rd, Hat. 45 CU19
Cedar Rd, Horn. 128 FJ62
Cedar Rd, Houns. 156 BW82
Cedar Rd, Rom. 127 FC56
Cedar Rd, Sutt. 218 DC107
Cedar Rd, Tedd. 177 CG92
Cedar Rd, Wat. 76 BW44
Cedar Rd, Wey. 212 BN105
Cedar Rd, Wok. 226 AV120
Cedar Ter, Rich. 158 CM84
Cedar Ter Rd, Sev. 257 FJ123
Cedar Tree Gro SE27 181 DP92
Cedar Vista, Rich. 158 CL81
Kew Rd
Cedar Wk (Claygate), Esher 215 CF107
Cedar Wk, Hem.H. 40 BK22
Cedar Wk, Ken. 236 DQ116
Cedar Wk (Kingswood), Tad. 233 CY120
Cedar Wk, Wal.Abb. 67 ED34
Cedar Wk, Welw.G.C. 30 DB10
Cedar Way NW1 141 DK66
Cedar Way, Berk. 38 AX20
Cedar Way, Guil. 242 AW132
Cedar Way, Slou. 152 AY78
Cedar Way, Sun. 175 BS94
Cedar Wd Dr, Wat. 75 BV35
Cedarcroft Rd, Chess. 216 CM105
Cedarhurst, Brom. 184 EE94
Elstree Hill
Cedarhurst Dr SE9 184 EJ85
Cedarne Rd SW6 160 DB80
Cedars, Bans. 218 DF114
Cedars, The E15 144 EF67
Portway
Cedars, The W13 137 CJ72
Heronsforde
Cedars, The, Buck.H. 102 EG46
Cedars, The, Guil. 243 BA131
Cedars, The, Lthd. 232 CL121
Cedars, The, Reig. 250 DD134
Cedars, The, Slou. 131 AM69
Calbroke Rd
Cedars, The, Tedd. 177 CF93
Adelaide Rd
Cedars, The (Byfleet), W.Byf. 212 BM112
Cedars Av E17 123 EA57
Cedars Av, Mitch. 200 DG98
Cedars Av, Rick. 92 BJ46
Cedars Cl NW4 119 CX55
Cedars Cl (Chalfont St. Peter), Ger.Cr. 90 AY50
Cedars Ct N9 100 DS47
Church St
Cedars Dr, Uxb. 134 BM68
Cedars Ms SW4 161 DH84
Cedars Rd
Cedars Rd E15 144 EE65
Cedars Rd N9 100 DU47
Church St
Cedars Rd N21 99 DP47
Cedars Rd SW4 161 DH83
Cedars Rd SW13 159 CT82
Cedars Rd W4 158 CQ78
Cedars Rd, Beck. 203 DY96
Cedars Rd, Croy. 201 DL104
Cedars Rd, Kings.T. 197 CJ95
Cedars Rd, Mord. 200 DA98
Cedars Wk, Rick. 73 BF42
Cedarville Gdns SW16 181 DM93
Cedarwood Dr, St.Alb. 43 CK20
Cedra Ct N16 122 DU60
Cedric Av, Rom. 127 FE55
Cedric Rd SE9 185 EQ90
Celadon Cl, Enf. 83 DY41
Celandine Cl E14 143 EA71
Celandine Cl, S.Ock. 149 FW70
Celandine Dr E8 142 DT66
Richmond Rd
Celandine Dr SE28 146 EV74
Celandine Rd, Walt. 214 BY105
Celandine Way E15 144 EE69
Celbridge Ms W2 140 DB72
Porchester Rd
Celedon Cl, Grays 170 FY75
Celestial Gdns SE13 163 ED84
Celia Cres, Ashf. 174 BK93
Celia Rd N19 121 DJ63
Cell Barnes Cl, St.Alb. 43 CH22
Cell Barnes La
Cell Barnes La, St.Alb. 43 CH23
Cell Fm Av (Old Windsor), Wind. 172 AV85
Celtic Av, Brom. 204 EE97
Celtic Rd (Byfleet), W.Byf. 212 BL114
Celtic St E14 143 EB71
Cement Block Cotts, Grays 170 GC79
Cemetery Hill, Hem.H. 40 BJ21
Cemetery La SE7 164 EL79
Cemetery La, Shep. 195 BP101
Cemetery La, Wal.Abb. 68 EF25
Cemetery Rd E7 124 EF63
Cemetery Rd N17 100 DS52
Cemetery Rd SE2 166 EV80
Cemmaes Ct Rd, Hem.H. 40 BJ20
Cemmaes Meadow, Hem.H. 40 BJ20
Cenacle Cl NW3 120 DA62
Centaur St SE1 278 C6
Centaur St SE1 161 DM76
Centaurs Business Cen, Islw. 157 CG79
Centaury Ct, Grays 170 GD79
Centenary Est, Enf. 83 DZ42
Centenary Rd, Enf. 83 DZ42
Centenary Wk, Loug. 84 EH41
Centenary Way, Amer. 72 AT38
Centennial Av, Borwd. 95 CH45
Centennial Pk, Borwd. 95 CJ45
Central Av E11 123 ED61
Central Av N2 98 DD54
Central Av N9 100 DS48
Central Av SW11 160 DF80
Central Av, Enf. 82 DV40
Central Av, Grav. 191 GH89
Central Av, Grays 169 FT77
Central Av, Harl. 35 ER14
Central Av, Hayes 135 BU73
Central Av, Houns. 156 CC84
Central Av, Pnr. 116 BZ58
Central Av, S.Ock. 168 FQ75
Central Av, Til. 171 GG81
Central Av, Wall. 219 DL106
Central Av, Wal.Cr. 67 DY33
Central Av, Well. 165 ET82
Central Av, W.Mol. 196 BZ98
Central Circ NW4 119 CV57
Hendon Way
Central Dr, Horn. 128 FL62
Central Dr, St.Alb. 43 CJ19
Central Dr, Slou. 131 AM73
Central Dr, Welw.G.C. 29 CZ07
Central Gdns, Mord. 200 DB99
Central Rd
Central Hill SE19 182 DR92
Central Mkts EC1 274 G7
Central Mkts EC1 141 DP71
Central Par (New Addington), Croy. 221 EC110
Central Par, Felt. 176 BW87
Central Par, Grnf. 137 CG69
Central Par, Houns. 156 CA80
Heston Rd
Central Par, Surb. 198 CL100
St. Mark's Hill
Central Pk Av, Dag. 127 FB62
Central Pk Est, Houns. 176 BX85
Central Pk Rd E6 144 EK68
Central Pl SE25 202 DV98
Portland Rd
Central Rd, Dart. 188 FL85
Central Rd, Harl. 36 EU11
Central Rd, Mord. 200 DA99
Central Rd, Wem. 117 CH64
Central Rd, Wor.Pk. 199 CU103
Central Sch Footpath SW14 158 CQ83
Central Sq NW11 120 DB58
Central Sq, Wem. 118 CL64
Station Gro
Central Sq, W.Mol. 196 BZ98
Central St EC1 275 H3
Central St EC1 142 DQ69
Central Way NW10 138 CQ68
Central Way SE28 146 EU73
Central Way, Cars. 218 DE108
Central Way, Felt. 175 BV85
Central Way, Oxt. 253 ED127
Centre, The, Felt. 175 BU89
Centre, The, Walt. 195 BT102
Centre Av W3 138 CR74
Centre Av W10 139 CW69
Harrow Rd
Centre Av, Epp. 69 ET32
Centre Cl, Epp. 69 ET32
Centre Av
Centre Common Rd, Chis. 185 EQ93
Centre Ct Shop Cen SW19 179 CZ93
Centre Dr, Epp. 69 ET32
Centre Grn, Epp. 69 ET32
Centre Av
Centre Rd E7 124 EG61
Centre Rd E11 124 EG61
Centre Rd, Dag. 147 FB68
Centre St E2 142 DV68
Centre Way E17 101 EC52
Centre Way N9 100 DW47
Centrepoint WC1 273 N8
Centrepoint WC1 141 DK72
Centreway, Ilf. 125 EQ61
Centric Cl NW1 141 DH67
Oval Rd
Centurion Cl N7 141 DM66
Centurion Ct, Wall. 201 DH103
Wandle Rd
Centurion La E3 143 DZ68
Libra Rd
Centurion Way, Erith 166 FA76
Centurion Way, Purf. 168 FM77
Century Cl NW4 119 CX57
Century Ct, Wok. 227 AZ116
Victoria Way
Century Ms E5 122 DW63
Lower Clapton Rd
Century Pk, Wat. 76 BX43
Century Rd E17 123 DY55
Century Rd, Hodd. 49 EA16
Century Rd, Stai. 173 BC92
Century Rd, Ware 33 DX05
Cephas Av E1 142 DW70
Cephas St E1 142 DW70
Ceres Rd SE18 165 ET77
Cerise Rd SE15 162 DU81
Cerne Cl, Hayes 136 BX73
Cerne Rd, Grav. 191 GL91
Cerne Rd, Mord. 200 DC100
Cerney Ms W2 140 DD73
Gloucester Ter
Cerotus Pl, Cher. 193 BF101
Cervantes Ct W2 140 DB72
Inverness Ter
Cervantes Ct, Nthwd. 93 BT52
Green La
Cervia Way, Grav. 191 GM90
Cester St E2 142 DU67
Whiston Rd
Cestreham Cres, Chesh. 54 AR29
Ceylon Rd W14 159 CX76
Chace Av, Pot.B. 64 DD32
Chacombe Pl, Beac. 89 AK50
Chadacre Av, Ilf. 125 EM55
Chadacre Rd, Epsom 217 CV107
Chadbourn St E14 143 EB71
Chadd Dr, Brom. 204 EL97
Chadd Grn E13 144 EG67
Chadfields, Til. 171 GG80
Chadhurst Cl (North Holmwood), Dor. 263 CK139
Wildcroft Dr
Chadview Ct, Rom. 126 EX59
Chadville Gdns, Rom. 126 EX57
Chadway, Dag. 126 EW60
Chadwell, Ware 32 DW07
Chadwell Av, Rom. 126 EV59
Chadwell Av (Cheshunt), Wal.Cr. 66 DW28
Chadwell Bypass, Grays 171 GF78
Chadwell Heath La, Rom. 126 EV57
Chadwell Hill, Grays 171 GH78
Chadwell Ri, Ware 32 DW07
Chadwell Rd, Grays 170 GC77
Chadwell St EC1 274 E2
Chadwell St EC1 141 DN69
Chadwick Av E4 101 ED49
Chadwick Av N21 81 DM43
Chadwick Av SW19 180 DA93
Chadwick Cl SW15 179 CT87
Chadwick Cl W7 137 CF71
Westcott Cres
Chadwick Cl (Northfleet), Grav. 190 GE89
Chadwick Cl, Tedd. 177 CG93
Chadwick Dr, Rom. 106 FK54
Chadwick Pl, Surb. 197 CJ101
Chadwick Rd E11 124 EE59
Chadwick Rd NW10 139 CT67
Chadwick Rd SE15 162 DT82
Chadwick Rd, Ilf. 125 EP62
Chadwick St SW1 277 N7
Chadwick St SW1 161 DK76
Chadwick Way SE28 146 EX73
Chadwin Rd E13 144 EH71
Chadworth Way (Claygate), Esher 215 CD106
Chaffers Mead, Ash. 232 CM116
Chaffinch Av, Croy. 203 DX100
Chaffinch Cl N9 101 DX46
Chaffinch Cl, Croy. 203 DX100
Chaffinch Cl, Surb. 198 CN104
Chaffinch La, Wat. 93 BT45
Chaffinch Rd, Beck. 203 DY95
Chaffinch Way, Horl. 268 DE147
Chaffinches Grn, Hem.H. 40 BN24
Chafford Wk, Rain. 148 FJ68
Chafford Way, Rom. 126 EW56
Chagford St NW1 272 D5
Chagford St NW1 140 DF70
Chailey Av, Enf. 82 DT40
Chailey Cl, Houns. 156 BX81
Springwell Rd
Chailey Pl, Walt. 214 BY105
Chailey St E5 122 DW62
Chairmans Av (Denham), Uxb. 113 BF58
Chalbury Wk N1 141 DM68
Chalcombe Rd SE2 166 EV76
Chalcot Cl, Sutt. 218 DA108
Chalcot Cres NW1 140 DF67
Chalcot Gdns NW3 140 DF65
Chalcot Ms SW16 181 DL90
Chalcot Rd NW1 140 DG66
Chalcot Sq NW1 140 DG66
Chalcott Gdns, Surb. 197 CJ102
Chalcroft Rd SE13 184 EE85
Chaldon Cl, Red. 266 DE136
Chaldon Common Rd, Cat. 236 DQ124
Chaldon Path, Th.Hth. 201 DP98
Chaldon Rd SW6 159 CY80
Chaldon Rd, Cat. 236 DR124
Chaldon Way, Couls. 235 DL117
Chale Rd SW2 181 DL86
Chale Wk, Sutt. 218 DB109
Hulverston Cl
Chalet Cl, Berk. 38 AT19
Chalet Cl, Bex. 187 FD91
Chalet Est NW7 97 CU49
Chalfont Av, Amer. 72 AX39
Chalfont Av, Wem. 138 CP65
Chalfont Cl, Hem.H. 41 BP15
Chalfont Ct NW9 119 CT55
Chalfont Grn N9 100 DS48
Chalfont La, Ger.Cr. 91 BC51
Chalfont La, Rick. 73 BB43
Chalfont La (Maple Cross), Rick. 91 BC51
Chalfont Pk (Chalfont St. Peter), Ger.Cr. 113 AZ55
Chalfont Rd N9 100 DT48
Chalfont Rd SE25 202 DT97
Chalfont Rd (Seer Grn), Beac. 89 AR50
Chalfont Rd, Ger.Cr. 91 BB48
Chalfont Rd, Hayes 155 BU75
Chalfont Rd, Rick. 91 BD49
Chalfont Sta Rd, Amer. 72 AW40
Chalfont Wk, Pnr. 94 BW54
Willows Cl
Chalfont Way W13 157 CH76
Chalford Cl, W.Mol. 196 CA98
Chalford Flats (Wooburn Grn), H.Wyc. 110 AE57
Chalford Rd SE21 182 DR91
Chalford Wk, Wdf.Grn. 102 EK53
Chalforde Gdns, Rom. 127 FH56
Chalgrove, Welw.G.C. 30 DD08
Chalgrove Av, Mord. 200 DA99
Chalgrove Cres, Ilf. 102 EL54
Chalgrove Gdns N3 119 CY55
Chalgrove Rd N17 100 DV53
Chalgrove Rd, Sutt. 218 DD108
Chalice Cl, Wall. 219 DK107
Lavender Vale
Chalice Way, Green. 189 FS85
Chalk Fm Rd NW1 140 DG66
Chalk Hill (Coleshill), Amer. 89 AM45
Chalk Hill, Chesh. 54 AP29
Chalk Hill, Wat. 76 BX44
Chalk Hill Rd W6 159 CX77
Shortlands
Chalk La, Ash. 232 CM119
Chalk La, Barn. 80 DF42
Chalk La, Epsom 232 CR115
Chalk La, Harl. 36 FA14
Chalk La (East Horsley), Lthd. 245 BT130
Chalk Paddock, Epsom 232 CR115
Chalk Pit Av, Orp. 206 EW97
Chalk Pit La (Burnham), Slou. 130 AH66
Chalk Pit Rd, Bans. 234 DA117
Chalk Pit Rd, Epsom 232 CQ119
Chalk Pit Way, Sutt. 218 DC106
Chalk Rd E13 144 EJ71
Chalkdale, Welw.G.C. 30 DB08
Chalkdell Flds, St.Alb. 43 CG16
Chalkdell Hill, Hem.H. 40 BL20
Chalkenden Cl SE20 182 DV94
Chalkhill Rd, Wem. 118 CP62
Chalklands, Wem. 118 CQ62
Chalkley Cl, Mitch. 200 DF96
Chalkmill Dr, Enf. 82 DV41
Chalkpit La, Bet. 248 CP133
Chalkpit La, Dor. 263 CG135
Chalkpit La (Great Bookham), Lthd. 246 BZ128
Chalkpit La, Oxt. 253 EC125
Chalkpit Ter, Dor. 247 CG134
Chalkpit Wd, Oxt. 253 ED127
Chalkpits Caravan Pk (Wooburn Grn), H.Wyc. 110 AE57
Chalkstone Cl, Well. 166 EU81
Chalkwell Pk Av, Enf. 82 DS42
Chalky Bk, Grav. 191 GG91
Chalky La, Chess. 215 CK109
Challacombe Cl, Brwd. 109 GB46
Challenge Cl, Grav. 191 GM91
Challenge Rd, Ashf. 175 BQ90
Challice Way SW2 181 DM88
Challin St SE20 202 DW95
Challinor, Harl. 52 EY15
Challis Rd, Brent. 157 CK78
Challock Cl (Biggin Hill), West. 238 EJ116
Challoner Cl N2 98 DD54
Challoner Cres W14 159 CZ78
Challoner St
Challoner St W14 159 CZ78
Challoners Cl, E.Mol. 197 CD98
Chalmers Ct, Rick. 74 BM44
Chalmers Rd, Ashf. 175 BP91
Chalmers Rd, Bans. 234 DD115
Chalmers Rd E, Ashf. 175 BP91
Chalmers Wk SE17 161 DP79
Hillingdon St
Chalmers Way, Felt. 175 BU85
Chaloner Ct SE1 279 K4
Chalsey Rd SE4 163 DZ84
Chalton Dr N2 120 DC58
Chalton St NW1 273 N2
Chalton St NW1 141 DK68
Chalvey Gdns, Slou. 152 AS75
Chalvey Gro, Slou. 151 AP75
Chalvey Pk, Slou. 152 AS75
Chalvey Rd E, Slou. 152 AS75
Chalvey Rd W, Slou. 151 AR75
Chamber St E1 142 DT73
Chamberlain Cl SE28 165 ER76
Broadwater Rd
Chamberlain Cl, Harl. 52 EW15
Chamberlain Cotts SE5 162 DR81
Camberwell Gro
Chamberlain Cres, W.Wick. 203 EB102
Chamberlain Gdns, Houns. 156 CC81
Chamberlain La, Pnr. 115 BU56
Chamberlain Pl E17 123 DY55
Chamberlain Rd N2 98 DC54
Chamberlain Rd N9 100 DU48
Chamberlain Rd W13 157 CG75
Midhurst Rd
Chamberlain St NW1 140 DF66
Regents Pk Rd
Chamberlain Wk, Felt. 176 BY91
Burgess Cl
Chamberlain Way, Pnr. 115 BV55
Chamberlain Way, Surb. 198 CL101
Chamberlayne Av, Wem. 118 CL61
Chamberlayne Rd NW10 139 CX69
Chambers Cl, Green. 189 FU85
Chambers Gdns N2 98 DD53
Chambers La NW10 139 CV66
Chambers Pl, S.Croy. 220 DR108
Rolleston Rd
Chambers Rd N7 121 DL63
Chambers St SE16 162 DU75
Chambers St, Hert. 32 DQ09
Chambersbury La, Hem.H. 58 BN25
Chambord St E2 142 DT69
Champion Cres SE26 183 DY91
Champion Gro SE5 162 DR83
Champion Hill SE5 162 DR83
Champion Hill Est SE5 162 DS83
Champion Pk SE5 162 DR82
Champion Pk Est SE5 162 DR83
Denmark Hill
Champion Rd SE26 183 DY91
Champion Rd, Upmin. 128 FP61
Champions Grn, Hodd. 33 EA14
Champions Way, Hodd. 33 EA14
Champness Cl SE27 182 DR91
Rommany Rd
Champness Rd, Bark. 145 ET66
Champneys Cl, Sutt. 217 CZ108
Chance Cl, Grays 170 FZ76
Chance St E1 275 P4
Chance St E1 142 DT70
Chance St E2 275 P4
Chance St E2 142 DT70
Chancel St SE1 278 F2
Chancel St SE1 141 DP74
Chancellor Gdns, S.Croy. 219 DP109
Chancellor Gro SE21 182 DQ89
Chancellor Pas E14 143 DZ74
South Colonnade
Chancellor Pl NW9 97 CT54
Chancellor Way, Sev. 256 FG122
Chancellors Rd W6 159 CW78
Chancellors St W6 159 CW78
Chancelot Rd SE2 166 EV77
Chancery Cl, St.Alb. 43 CK15
Chancery Ct, Dart. 188 FN87
Downs Av
Chancery La WC2 274 D8
Chancery La WC2 141 DN71
Chancery La, Beck. 203 EB96
Chancery Ms SW17 180 DE89
Chanctonbury Chase, Red. 251 DH134
Chanctonbury Cl SE9 185 EP90
Chanctonbury Gdns, Sutt. 218 DB108
Chanctonbury Way N12 97 CZ49
Chandler Av E16 144 EG71
Chandler Cl, Hmptn. 196 CA95
Chandler Rd, Loug. 85 EP39
Chandler St E1 142 DV74
Wapping La
Chandler Way SE15 162 DT80
Chandlers Cl, Felt. 175 BT87
Chandlers Dr, Erith 167 FD77
Chandler's La, Rick. 74 BL37
Chandlers Ms E14 163 EA75
Chandlers Rd, St.Alb. 43 CJ17
Chandlers Way SW2 181 DN87
Chandlers Way, Hert. 31 DN09
Chandlers Way, Rom. 127 FE57
Chandon Lo, Sutt. 218 DC108
Devonshire Rd
Chandos Av E17 101 EA54
Chandos Av N14 99 DJ48
Chandos Av N20 98 DC46
Chandos Av W5 157 CJ77
Chandos Cl, Amer. 72 AW38
Chandos Cl, Buck.H. 102 EH47
Chandos Cres, Edg. 96 CM52
Chandos Mall, Slou. 152 AT75
High St
Chandos Par, Edg. 96 CM52
Chandos Cres
Chandos Pl WC2 277 P1
Chandos Pl WC2 141 DL73
Chandos Rd E15 123 ED64
Chandos Rd N2 98 DD54
Chandos Rd N17 100 DS54
Chandos Rd NW2 119 CW64
Chandos Rd NW10 138 CS70
Chandos Rd, Borwd. 78 CM40
Chandos Rd, Har. 116 CC57
Chandos Rd, Pnr. 116 BW59
Chandos Rd, Stai. 173 BD92
Chandos St W1 273 J7
Chandos St W1 141 DH71
Chandos Way NW11 120 DB60
Change All EC3 275 L9
Chanlock Path, S.Ock. 149 FV73
Carnach Grn
Channel Cl, Houns. 156 CA81
Channel Gate Rd NW10 139 CT69
Old Oak La
Channelsea Rd E15 143 ED67
Channing Cl, Horn. 128 FM59
Channings (Horsell), Wok. 226 AY115
Chant Sq E15 143 ED66
Chant St E15 143 ED66
Chanton Dr, Epsom 217 CW110
Chanton Dr, Sutt. 217 CW110
Chantress Cl, Dag. 147 FC67
Chantrey Cl, Ash. 231 CJ119
Chantrey Rd SW9 161 DM83
Chantreywood, Brwd. 109 GA48
Chantry, The, Harl. 36 EU13
Chantry, The, Uxb. 134 BM69
Chantry Cl NW7 79 CT44
Hendon Wd La
Chantry Cl W9 139 CZ70
Elgin Av
Chantry Cl, Enf. 82 DQ38
Bedale Rd
Chantry Cl, Har. 118 CM57
Chantry Cl, Horl. 268 DF147
Chantry Cl, Kings L. 58 BN29
Chantry Cl, Sid. 186 EY92
Ellenborough Rd
Chantry Cl, Sun. 175 BU94
Chantry Cl, West Dr. 134 BK73
Chantry Cl, Wind. 151 AN81
Chantry Cotts (Chilworth), Guil. 259 BB140
Chantry Ct, Cars. 200 DE104
Chantry Ct, Hat. 45 CU19
Chantry Ho, Rain. 147 FD68
Chantry Way
Chantry Hurst, Epsom 232 CR115
Chantry La, Brom. 204 EK99
Bromley Common
Chantry La (Shere), Guil. 260 BM138

Chantry La, Hat. 45 CT19
Chantry La (London Colney), St.Alb. 61 CK26
Chantry Pl, Har. 94 CB53
Chantry Rd, Cher. 194 BJ101
Chantry Rd, Chess. 216 CM106
Chantry Rd (Chilworth), Guil. 259 BB140
Chantry Rd, Har. 94 CB53
Chantry Sq W8 160 DB76 *St. Mary's Pl*
Chantry St N1 141 DP67
Chantry Vw Rd, Guil. 258 AX137
Chantry Way, Mitch. 200 DD97
Chantry Way, Rain. 147 FD68
Chapel Av, Add. 212 BH105
Chapel Cl, Dart. 187 FE85
Chapel Cl, Grays 169 FV79
Chapel Cl, Hat. 64 DD27
Chapel Cl, Wat. 59 BT34
Chapel Cotts, Hem.H. 40 BK18
Chapel Ct N2 120 DE55
Chapel Ct SE1 279 K4
Chapel Ct, Dor. 263 CG135
Chapel Cft, Kings L. 58 BG31
Chapel Cfts, Berk. 38 AS17
Chapel End (Chalfont St. Peter), Ger.Cr. 90 AX54 *Austenwood La*
Chapel End, Hodd. 49 EA18
Chapel Fm Rd SE9 185 EM90
Chapel Flds, Harl. 52 EW18
Chapel Gro, Add. 212 BH105
Chapel Gro, Epsom 233 CW119
Chapel High Shop Prec, Brwd. 108 FW47
Chapel Hill, Dart. 187 FE85
Chapel Hill (Effingham), Lthd. *The St* 246 BX127
Chapel Ho St E14 163 EB78
Chapel La, Chig. 103 ET48
Chapel La (Westcott), Dor. 262 CC137
Chapel La (Westhumble), Dor. 247 CD130
Chapel La, Harl. 52 EW17
Chapel La, Hert. 31 DH13
Chapel La (Great Bookham), Lthd. 246 CC128
Chapel La, Pnr. 116 BX55
Chapel La, Rom. 126 EX59
Chapel La (Stoke Poges), Slou. 132 AV66
Chapel La, Uxb. 134 BN72
Chapel Mkt N1 141 DN68
Chapel Ms, Wdf.Grn. 103 EN51
Chapel Pk Rd, Add. 212 BH105
Chapel Path E11 124 EG58
Chapel Pl EC2 275 M3
Chapel Pl N1 141 DN68 *Chapel Mkt*
Chapel Pl N17 100 DT52 *White Hart La*
Chapel Pl W1 273 H9
Chapel Pl W1 141 DH72
Chapel Rd SE27 181 DP91
Chapel Rd W13 137 CH74
Chapel Rd, Bexh. 166 FA84
Chapel Rd, Epp. 69 ET30
Chapel Rd (Smallfield), Horl. 269 DP148
Chapel Rd, Houns. 156 CB83
Chapel Rd, Ilf. 125 EN62
Chapel Rd, Oxt. 254 EJ130
Chapel Rd, Red. 250 DF134
Chapel Rd, Tad. 233 CW123
Chapel Rd, Twick. 177 CH87
Chapel Rd, Warl. 237 DX118
Chapel Row (Harefield), Uxb. 92 BJ53
Chapel Side W2 140 DB73
Chapel Sq, Vir.W. 192 AY98
Chapel Stones N17 100 DT53
Chapel St NW1 272 B7
Chapel St NW1 140 DE71
Chapel St SW1 276 G6
Chapel St SW1 160 DG76
Chapel St, Berk. 38 AW19
Chapel St, Enf. 82 DQ41
Chapel St, Guil. 258 AX136 *Castle St*
Chapel St, Hem.H. 40 BK19
Chapel St, Slou. 152 AT75
Chapel St, Uxb. 134 BJ67 *Trumper Way*
Chapel St, Wok. 227 AZ117
Chapel Ter, Loug. 84 EL42 *Forest Rd*
Chapel Vw, S.Croy. 220 DV107
Chapel Wk NW4 119 CV56
Chapel Wk, Croy. 202 DQ103 *Wellesley Rd*
Chapel Way N7 121 DM62 *Sussex Way*
Chapel Way, Abb.L. 59 BT27
Chapel Way, Epsom 233 CW119
Chapel Yd SW18 180 DA85 *Wandsworth High St*
Chapelfields, Ware 33 ED10
Chapelhouse Cl, Guil. 242 AS134 *Park Barn Dr*
Chapelmount Rd, Wdf.Grn. 103 EM51
Chapels Cl, Slou. 131 AL74
Chaplaincy Gdns, Horn. 128 FL60
Chaplin Cl SE1 278 E4
Chaplin Cl SE1 161 DN75
Chaplin Cres, Sun. 175 BS93
Chaplin Rd E15 144 EE68
Chaplin Rd N17 122 DT55
Chaplin Rd NW2 139 CU65
Chaplin Rd, Dag. 146 EY66
Chaplin Rd, Wem. 137 CJ65
Chaplin Sq N12 98 DD52
Chapman Cl, West Dr. 154 BM76
Chapman Cres, Har. 118 CL57
Chapman Pk Ind Est NW10 139 CT65
Chapman Pl N4 121 DP61
Chapman Rd E9 143 DZ65
Chapman Rd, Belv. 166 FA78
Chapman Rd, Croy. 201 DN102
Chapman Sq SW19 179 CX89
Chapman St E1 142 DV73
Chapmans Cres, Chesh. 54 AN29
Chapman's La SE2 166 EW77
Chapman's La, Belv. 166 EX77
Chapmans La, Orp. 206 EX96
Chapmans Rd (Sundridge), Sev. 240 EY124
Chapmans Yd, Wat. 76 BW42 *New Rd*
Chapone Pl W1 273 M9
Chapter Cl W4 158 CQ76 *Beaumont Rd*
Chapter Cl, Uxb. 134 BM66
Chapter Ho Ct EC4 275 H9
Chapter Rd NW2 119 CU64
Chapter Rd SE17 161 DP78
Chapter St SW1 277 M9
Chapter St SW1 161 DK77
Chapter Way, Hmptn. 176 CA91
Chaptree Ms, Wind. 151 AR80
Chara Pl W4 158 CR79
Charcot Ho SW15 179 CT86 *Highcliffe Dr*
Charcroft Gdns, Enf. 83 DX42
Chard Rd (Heathrow Airport), Houns. 154 BN83 *Heathrow Tunnel App*
Chardin Rd W4 158 CS77 *Elliott Rd*
Chardins Cl, Hem.H. 39 BF19
Chardmore Rd N16 122 DU60
Chardwell Cl E6 144 EL72 *Northumberland Rd*
Charecroft Way W12 159 CX75
Charfield Ct W9 140 DB70 *Shirland Rd*
Charford Rd E16 144 EG71
Chargate Cl, Walt. 213 BT107
Chargeable La E13 144 EF70
Chargeable St E16 144 EF70
Chargrove Cl SE16 163 DX75 *Marlow Way*
Charing Cl, Orp. 223 ET105
Charing Cross SW1 277 P2
Charing Cross Rd WC2 273 N8
Charing Cross Rd WC2 141 DK72
Chariotts Pl, Wind. 151 AR81 *Victoria St*
Charlbert St NW8 140 DE68
Charlbury Av, Stan. 95 CK50
Charlbury Cl, Rom. 106 FJ51
Charlbury Cres, Rom. 106 FJ51
Charlbury Gdns, Ilf. 125 ET61
Charlbury Gro W5 137 CJ72
Charlbury Rd, Uxb. 114 BM62
Charldane Rd SE9 185 EP90
Charlecote Gro SE26 182 DV90
Charlecote Rd, Dag. 126 EY62
Charlemont Rd E6 145 EM69
Charles Babbage Cl, Chess. 215 CJ108
Charles Barry Cl SW4 161 DJ83
Charles Burton Ct E5 123 DY64 *Ashenden Rd*
Charles Cl, Sid. 186 EV91
Charles Cobb Gdns, Croy. 219 DN106
Charles Coveney Rd SE15 162 DT81
Charles Cres, Har. 117 CD59
Charles Dickens Ho E2 142 DV69
Charles Dickens Ter SE20 182 DW94 *Maple Rd*
Charles Flemwell Ms E16 144 EG74 *Hanameel St*
Charles Gdns, Slou. 132 AV72
Charles Grinling Wk SE18 165 EN77
Charles Haller St SW2 181 DN87 *Tulse Hill*
Charles Ho N17 100 DT52 *Love La*
Charles Ho, Wind. 151 AQ81 *Alma Rd*
Charles La NW8 272 A1
Charles Pl NW1 273 L3
Charles Rd E7 144 EJ66 *Lens Rd*
Charles Rd SW19 200 DA95
Charles Rd W13 137 CG71
Charles Rd, Dag. 147 FD65
Charles Rd, Rom. 126 EX59
Charles Rd (Badgers Mt), Sev. 225 FB110
Charles Rd, Stai. 174 BK93
Charles II Pl SW3 160 DF78 *King's Rd*
Charles II St SW1 277 M2
Charles II St SW1 141 DK74
Charles Sevright Dr NW7 97 CX50
Charles Sq N1 275 L3
Charles Sq N1 142 DR69
Charles Sq Est N1 142 DR69 *Pitfield St*
Charles St E16 144 EK74
Charles St SW13 158 CS82
Charles St W1 277 H2
Charles St W1 141 DH74
Charles St, Berk. 38 AV19
Charles St, Cher. 193 BF102
Charles St, Croy. 202 DQ104
Charles St, Enf. 82 DT43
Charles St, Epp. 70 EU28
Charles St, Grays 170 GB79
Charles St, Green. 189 FT85
Charles St, Hem.H. 40 BJ21
Charles St, Houns. 156 BZ82
Charles St, Uxb. 135 BP70
Charles St, Wind. 151 AQ81
Charles Townsend Ho EC1 274 E3
Charles Whincup Rd E16 144 EH74
Charlesfield SE9 184 EJ90
Charlesfield Rd, Horl. 268 DF147
Charleston Cl, Felt. 175 BU90 *Vineyard Rd*
Charleston St SE17 279 J9
Charleston St SE17 162 DQ77
Charlesworth Cl, Hem.H. 40 BK22
Charleville Circ SE26 182 DU92
Charleville Rd W14 159 CY78
Charlie Chaplin Wk SE1 141 DN74 *Waterloo Rd*
Charlieville Rd, Erith 167 FC80 *Northumberland Pk*
Charlmont Rd SW17 180 DF93
Charlock Way, Guil. 243 BB131
Charlock Way, Wat. 75 BT44
Charlotte Av, Slou. 132 AT72
Charlotte Cl, Bexh. 186 EY85
Charlotte Cl, Ilf. 103 EQ53 *Connor Cl*
Charlotte Despard Av SW11 160 DG81
Charlotte Gdns, Rom. 105 FB51
Charlotte Gro, Horl. 269 DN147
Charlotte Ms W1 273 L6
Charlotte Ms W10 139 CX72
Charlotte Ms W14 159 CY77 *Munden St*
Charlotte Pl NW9 118 CQ57 *Uphill Dr*
Charlotte Pl SW1 277 K9
Charlotte Pl W1 273 L7
Charlotte Pl, Grays 169 FV79
Charlotte Rd EC2 275 M4
Charlotte Rd EC2 142 DS70
Charlotte Rd SW13 159 CT81
Charlotte Rd, Dag. 147 FB65
Charlotte Rd, Wall. 219 DJ107
Charlotte Row SW4 161 DJ83
Charlotte Sq, Rich. 178 CM86 *Greville Rd*
Charlotte St W1 273 L7
Charlotte St W1 141 DJ71
Charlotte Ter N1 141 DM67
Charlow Cl SW6 160 DC82 *Townmead Rd*
Charlton Av, Walt. 213 BV105
Charlton Ch La SE7 164 EJ78
Charlton Cl, Hodd. 49 EA17
Charlton Cl, Slou. 151 AP75 *Haig Dr*
Charlton Cl, Uxb. 115 BP61
Charlton Cres, Bark. 145 ET68
Charlton Dene SE7 164 EJ80
Charlton Dr (Biggin Hill), West. 238 EK117
Charlton Gdns, Couls. 235 DJ118
Charlton Kings, Wey. 195 BS104
Charlton Kings Rd NW5 121 DK64
Charlton La SE7 164 EK78
Charlton La, Shep. 195 BS98
Charlton Mead La, Hodd. 49 EC18
Charlton Mead La S, Hodd. 49 ED18 *Charlton Mead La*
Charlton Pk La SE7 164 EK80
Charlton Pk Rd SE7 164 EK79
Charlton Pl N1 141 DP68
Charlton Pl, Wind. 150 AJ82 *Charlton Row*
Charlton Rd N9 101 DX46
Charlton Rd NW10 138 CS67
Charlton Rd SE3 164 EG80
Charlton Rd SE7 164 EH79
Charlton Rd, Har. 117 CK56
Charlton Rd, Shep. 195 BQ97
Charlton Rd, Wem. 118 CM60
Charlton Row, Wind. 150 AJ82
Charlton Sq, Wind. 150 AJ82 *Charlton Row*
Charlton St, Grays 169 FX79
Charlton Wk, Wind. 150 AJ82 *Charlton Row*
Charlton Way SE3 164 EE81
Charlton Way, Hodd. 49 EA17
Charlton Way, Wind. 150 AJ82
Charlwood, Croy. 221 DZ109
Charlwood Cl, Har. 95 CE52 *Kelvin Cres*
Charlwood Dr (Oxshott), Lthd. 231 CD115
Charlwood Pl SW1 277 L9
Charlwood Pl SW1 161 DJ77
Charlwood Rd SW15 159 CX83
Charlwood Rd (Lowfield Heath), Horl. 268 DB152
Charlwood Sq, Mitch. 200 DD97
Charlwood St SW1 277 L9
Charlwood St SW1 161 DJ78
Charlwood Ter SW15 159 CX84 *Cardinal Pl*
Charm Cl, Horl. 268 DE147
Charman Rd, Red. 250 DE134
Charmans La, Reig. 264 CS141
Charmian Av, Stan. 117 CK55
Charminster Av SW19 200 DB96
Charminster Ct, Surb. 197 CK101
Charminster Rd SE9 184 EK91
Charminster Rd, Wor.Pk. 199 CX102
Charmouth Ct, St.Alb. 43 CG17
Charmouth Rd, St.Alb. 43 CG18
Charmouth Rd, Well. 166 EW81
Charmwood La, Orp. 224 EV109
Charne, The (Otford), Sev. 241 FG117
Charnock, Swan. 207 FE98
Charnock Rd E5 122 DV62
Charnwood Av SW19 200 DA96
Charnwood Cl, N.Mal. 198 CS98
Charnwood Dr E18 124 EH55
Charnwood Gdns E14 163 EA77
Charnwood Pl N20 98 DC48
Charnwood Rd SE25 202 DR99
Charnwood Rd, Enf. 82 DV36
Charnwood Rd, Uxb. 134 BN68
Charnwood St E5 122 DU61
Charrington Rd, Croy. 201 DP103 *Drayton Rd*
Charrington St NW1 141 DK68
Charsley Cl, Amer. 72 AW39
Charsley Rd SE6 183 EB89
Chart Cl, Brom. 204 EE95
Chart Cl, Croy. 202 DW100 *Stockbury Rd*
Chart Cl, Dor. 263 CK138
Chart Downs, Dor. 263 CJ139
Chart Gdns, Dor. 263 CJ139
Chart Hills Cl SE28 146 EY72 *Fairway Dr*
Chart La, Dor. 263 CH136
Chart La, Reig. 250 DB134
Chart La S, Dor. 263 CJ138
Chart St N1 275 L2
Chart St N1 142 DR69
Charta Rd, Egh. 173 BC92
Charter Av, Ilf. 125 ER60
Charter Cl, St.Alb. 43 CE20 *Bricket Rd*
Charter Cl, Slou. 152 AT76 *Osborne St*
Charter Ct, N.Mal. 198 CS97
Charter Cres, Houns. 156 BY84
Charter Dr, Amer. 72 AT38
Charter Dr, Bex. 186 EY87
Charter Pl, Stai. 173 BF93
Charter Pl, Uxb. 134 BK66
Charter Pl, Wat. 76 BW41
Charter Rd, Kings.T. 198 CP97
Charter Rd, Slou. 131 AL73
Charter Rd, The, Wdf.Grn. 102 EE51
Charter Sq, Kings.T. 198 CP96
Charter Way N3 119 CZ56
Charter Way N14 81 DJ44
Charterhouse Av, Wem. 117 CJ63
Charterhouse Bldgs EC1 274 G5
Charterhouse Dr, Sev. 256 FG123
Charterhouse Ms EC1 274 G6
Charterhouse Rd, Orp. 206 EU104
Charterhouse Sq EC1 274 G6
Charterhouse Sq EC1 141 DP71
Charterhouse St EC1 274 E7
Charterhouse St EC1 141 DP71
Charteris Rd N4 121 DN60
Charteris Rd NW6 139 CZ67
Charteris Rd, Wdf.Grn. 102 EH52
Charters Cl SE19 182 DS92
Charters Cross, Harl. 51 ER18
Chartfield Av SW15 179 CV85
Chartfield Pl, Wey. 213 BP106 *Hanger Hill*
Chartfield Rd, Reig. 266 DC135
Chartfield Sq SW15 179 CX85
Chartham Gro SE27 181 DN90 *Royal Circ*
Chartham Rd SE25 202 DV97
Chartley Av NW2 118 CS62
Chartley Av, Stan. 95 CF51
Charton Cl, Belv. 166 EZ79 *Nuxley Rd*
Chartridge Cl, Barn. 79 CU43
Chartridge Cl, Bushey 76 CC44
Chartridge La, Chesh. 54 AM29
Chartridge Way, Hem.H. 41 BQ20
Chartway, Reig. 250 DB133
Chartway, Sev. 257 FJ124
Chartwell Cl SE9 185 EQ89
Chartwell Cl, Croy. 202 DR102
Chartwell Cl, Grnf. 136 CB67
Chartwell Cl, Wal.Abb. 68 EE33
Chartwell Dr, Orp. 223 ER106
Chartwell Gdns, Sutt. 217 CY105
Chartwell Gate, Beac. 89 AK53
Chartwell Pl, Epsom 216 CS114
Chartwell Pl, Har. 117 CD61
Chartwell Pl, Sutt. 217 CZ105
Chartwell Rd, Nthwd. 93 BT51
Chartwell Way SE20 202 DV95
Charville La, Hayes 135 BS68
Charville La W, Uxb. 135 BP69
Charwood SW16 181 DN91
Charwood Cl (Shenley), Rad. 62 CL33
Chasden Rd, Hem.H. 39 BF17
Chase, The E12 124 EK63
Chase, The SW4 161 DH83
Chase, The SW16 181 DM94
Chase, The SW20 199 CY95
Chase, The, Ash. 231 CJ118
Chase, The, Bexh. 167 FB83
Chase, The (Cromwell Rd), Brwd. 108 FV49
Chase, The (Ingrave), Brwd. 109 GC50
Chase, The (Seven Arches Rd), Brwd. 108 FX48
Chase, The (Woodman Rd), Brwd. 108 FX50
Chase, The, Brom. 204 EH97
Chase, The, Chesh. 54 AP29 *Chalk Hill*
Chase, The, Chig. 103 EQ49
Chase, The, Couls. 219 DJ114
Chase, The, Edg. 96 CP53
Chase, The, Grays 169 FX79
Chase, The, Guil. 258 AU135
Chase, The, Hem.H. 40 BL21 *Turners Hill*
Chase, The (Penn), H.Wyc. 88 AC46
Chase, The (Wooburn Grn), H.Wyc. 110 AF59
Chase, The, Horn. 127 FE62
Chase, The (East Horsley), Lthd. 245 BT126
Chase, The (Oxshott), Lthd. 230 CC115
Chase, The, Loug. 102 EJ45
Chase, The, Pnr. 116 BZ56
Chase, The (Eastcote), Pnr. 116 BW58
Chase, The, Rad. 77 CF35
Chase, The, Reig. 266 DD135
Chase, The, Rom. 127 FE55
Chase, The (Chadwell Heath), Rom. 126 EY58
Chase, The (Rush Grn), Rom. 127 FD62
Chase, The, Stan. 95 CG50
Chase, The, Sun. 195 BV95
Chase, The (Kingswood), Tad. 234 DA122
Chase, The, Upmin. 129 FS62
Chase, The, Uxb. 114 BN64
Chase, The, Wall. 219 DL106
Chase, The (Cheshunt), Wal.Cr. 65 DP28
Chase, The, Ware 33 EA09
Chase, The, Wat. 75 BS42
Chase Cl (Coleshill), Amer. 55 AN43
Chase Cl (Penn), H.Wyc. 88 AC46
Chase Ct Gdns, Enf. 82 DQ41
Chase Cross Rd, Rom. 105 FC52
Chase End, Epsom 216 CR112
Chase Gdns E4 101 EA49
Chase Gdns, Twick. 177 CD86
Chase Grn, Enf. 82 DQ41
Chase Grn Av, Enf. 81 DP40
Chase Hill, Enf. 82 DQ41
Chase Ho Gdns, Horn. 128 FM57 *Great Nelmes Chase*
Chase La, Chig. 104 EU48
Chase La, Ilf. 125 ER57
Chase Ridings, Enf. 81 DN40
Chase Rd N14 81 DK44
Chase Rd NW10 138 CR70
Chase Rd W3 138 CR70
Chase Rd, Brwd. 108 FW48
Chase Rd, Epsom 216 CR112
Chase Side N14 80 DG44
Chase Side, Enf. 82 DQ41
Chase Side Av SW20 199 CY95
Chase Side Av, Enf. 82 DQ40
Chase Side Cres, Enf. 82 DQ39
Chase Side Pl, Enf. 82 DQ40 *Chase Side*
Chase Sq, Grav. 191 GH86 *High St*
Chase Way N14 99 DH47
Chasefield Cl, Guil. 243 BA131
Chasefield Rd SW17 180 DF91
Chaseley Dr W4 158 CP81 *Wellesley Rd*
Chaseley Dr, S.Croy. 220 DR110
Chaseley St E14 143 DY72
Chasemore Cl, Mitch. 200 DF101
Chasemore Gdns, Croy. 219 DP106 *Thorneloe Gdns*
Chaseside Cl, Rom. 105 FE51
Chaseside Gdns, Cher. 194 BH101
Chaseville Pk Rd N21 81 DL43
Chaseways, Saw. 36 EW07
Chasewood Av, Enf. 81 DP40
Chasewood Pk, Har. 117 CF62
Chastilian Rd, Dart. 187 FF87
Chatelet Cl, Horl. 269 DH147
Chatfield, Slou. 131 AN71
Chatfield Ct, Cat. 236 DR122 *Yorke Gate Rd*
Chatfield Dr, Guil. 243 BC132 *Kingfisher Dr*
Chatfield Rd SW11 160 DC83
Chatfield Rd, Croy. 201 DP102
Chatham Av, Brom. 204 EF101
Chatham Cl NW11 120 DA57
Chatham Cl, Sutt. 199 CZ101
Chatham Hill Rd, Sev. 257 FJ121
Chatham Pl E9 142 DW65
Chatham Rd E17 123 DY55
Chatham Rd E18 102 EF54 *Grove Hill*
Chatham Rd SW11 180 DF86
Chatham Rd, Kings.T. 198 CN96
Chatham Rd, Orp. 223 EQ106
Chatham St SE17 279 K8
Chatham St SE17 162 DR77
Chatsfield, Epsom 217 CU110
Chatsfield Pl W5 138 CL72
Chatsworth Av NW4 97 CW54
Chatsworth Av SW20 199 CY95
Chatsworth Av, Brom. 184 EH91
Chatsworth Av, Sid. 186 EU88
Chatsworth Av, Wem. 118 CM64
Chatsworth Cl NW4 97 CW54
Chatsworth Cl, Borwd. 78 CN41
Chatsworth Cl, W.Wick. 204 EF103
Chatsworth Ct W8 160 DA77
Chatsworth Ct, Stan. 95 CJ50 *Marsh La*
Chatsworth Cres, Houns. 157 CD84
Chatsworth Dr, Enf. 100 DU45
Chatsworth Est E5 123 DX63 *Elderfield Rd*
Chatsworth Gdns W3 138 CP73
Chatsworth Gdns, Har. 116 CB60
Chatsworth Gdns, N.Mal. 199 CT99
Chatsworth Par, Orp. 205 EQ99 *Queensway*
Chatsworth Pl (Oxshott), Lthd. 215 CD112
Chatsworth Pl, Mitch. 200 DF97
Chatsworth Pl, Tedd. 177 CG91
Chatsworth Ri W5 138 CM70
Chatsworth Rd E5 122 DW62
Chatsworth Rd E15 124 EF64
Chatsworth Rd NW2 139 CX65
Chatsworth Rd W4 158 CQ79
Chatsworth Rd W5 138 CM70
Chatsworth Rd, Croy. 220 DR105
Chatsworth Rd, Dart. 188 FJ85
Chatsworth Rd, Hayes 135 BV70
Chatsworth Rd, Sutt. 217 CX106
Chatsworth Way SE27 181 DP90
Chatteris Av, Rom. 106 FJ51
Chattern Hill, Ashf. 175 BP91
Chattern Rd, Ashf. 175 BQ91
Chatterton Rd N4 121 DP62
Chatterton Rd, Brom. 204 EK98
Chatto Rd SW11 180 DF85
Chaucer Av, Hayes 135 BU71
Chaucer Av, Houns. 155 BV82
Chaucer Av, Rich. 158 CN82
Chaucer Av, Wey. 212 BN108
Chaucer Cl N11 99 DJ50
Chaucer Cl, Bans. 217 CY114
Chaucer Cl, Berk. 38 AT18
Chaucer Cl, Til. 171 GJ82
Chaucer Ct N16 122 DS63
Chaucer Ct, Guil. 258 AW137 *Lawn Rd*
Chaucer Dr SE1 162 DT77
Chaucer Gdns, Sutt. 200 DA104
Chaucer Grn, Croy. 202 DV101
Chaucer Ho, Sutt. 200 DA104
Chaucer Pk, Dart. 188 FM87
Chaucer Rd E7 144 EG65
Chaucer Rd E11 124 EG58
Chaucer Rd E17 101 EC54
Chaucer Rd SE24 181 DN85
Chaucer Rd W3 138 CQ74
Chaucer Rd, Ashf. 174 BL91
Chaucer Rd (Northfleet), Grav. 190 GD90
Chaucer Rd, Rom. 105 FH52
Chaucer Rd, Sid. 186 EW88
Chaucer Rd, Sutt. 218 DA105
Chaucer Rd, Well. 165 ES81
Chaucer Way SW19 180 DD93
Chaucer Way, Add. 212 BG107
Chaucer Way, Dart. 168 FN84
Chaucer Way, Hodd. 33 EA13
Chaulden Ho Gdns, Hem.H. 39 BF21
Chaulden La, Hem.H. 39 BD22
Chaulden Ter, Hem.H. 39 BF21
Chauncey Cl N9 100 DU48
Chauncy Av, Pot.B. 64 DC33
Chauncy Ct, Hert. 32 DR09 *Bluecoats Av*
Chaundrye Cl SE9 184 EL86
Chauntler Cl E16 144 EH72
Chauntry Cl, Maid. 130 AC72
Chave Rd, Dart. 188 FL90
Chavecroft Ter, Epsom 233 CW119
Chaworth Rd (Ottershaw), Cher. 211 BC107
Cheam Cl, Tad. 233 CV121 *Waterfield*
Cheam Common Rd, Wor.Pk. 199 CV103
Cheam Mans, Sutt. 217 CY108
Cheam Pk Way, Sutt. 217 CY107
Cheam Rd, Epsom 217 CU109
Cheam Rd, Sutt. 217 CZ107
Cheam Rd (East Ewell), Sutt. 217 CX110
Cheam St SE15 162 DV83 *Evelina Rd*
Cheapside EC2 275 J9
Cheapside EC2 142 DQ72
Cheapside N13 100 DQ49 *Taplow Rd*
Cheapside, Wok. 210 AX114
Cheapside La (Denham), Uxb. 113 BF61
Chedburgh, Welw.G.C. 30 DD08
Cheddar Cl N11 98 DG51 *Martock Gdns*
Cheddar Rd (Heathrow Airport), Houns. 154 BN82 *Cromer Rd*
Cheddar Waye, Hayes 135 BV72
Cheddington Rd N18 100 DS48
Chedworth Cl E16 144 EF72 *Hallsville Rd*
Cheelson Rd, S.Ock. 149 FW68
Cheeseman Cl, Hmptn. 176 BY93
Cheesemans Ter W14 159 CZ78
Cheffins Rd, Hodd. 33 DZ14
Chelford Rd, Brom. 183 ED92
Chelmer Cres, Bark. 146 EV68
Chelmer Dr, Brwd. 109 GE44
Chelmer Dr, S.Ock. 149 FW73
Chelmer Rd E9 123 DX64
Chelmer Rd, Grays 171 GG78
Chelmer Rd, Upmin. 129 FR58
Chelmsford Av, Rom. 105 FD52
Chelmsford Cl E6 145 EM72 *Guildford Rd*
Chelmsford Cl W6 159 CX79
Chelmsford Cl, Sutt. 218 DA109
Chelmsford Dr, Upmin. 128 FM62
Chelmsford Gdns, Ilf. 124 EL59
Chelmsford Rd E11 123 ED60
Chelmsford Rd E17 123 EA58
Chelmsford Rd E18 102 EF53
Chelmsford Rd N14 99 DJ45
Chelmsford Rd (Hatfield Heath), B.Stort. 37 FH05
Chelmsford Rd, Brwd. 109 FZ44

Chelmsford Rd, Hert. 31 DN10
Chelmsford Sq NW10 139 CW67
Chelsea Br SW1 161 DH79
Chelsea Br SW8 161 DH79
Chelsea Br Rd SW1 276 F10
Chelsea Br Rd SW1 160 DG78
Chelsea Cloisters SW3 160 DE77
Lucan Pl
Chelsea Cl NW10 138 CR67
Winchelsea Rd
Chelsea Cl, Edg. 96 CN54
Chelsea Cl (Hampton Hill), Hmptn. 176 CC92
Chelsea Cl, Wor.Pk. 199 CU101
Chelsea Embk SW3 160 DE79
Chelsea Flds, Hodd. 33 EB13
Chelsea Gdns W13 137 CF71
Hathaway Gdns
Chelsea Gdns, Harl. 52 EY16
Chelsea Gdns, Sutt. 217 CY105
Chelsea Harbour SW10 160 DD81
Chelsea Harbour Dr SW10 160 DC81
Chelsea Manor Gdns SW3 160 DE79
Chelsea Manor St SW3 160 DE78
Chelsea Ms, Horn. 127 FH60
St. Leonards Way
Chelsea Pk Gdns SW3 160 DD79
Chelsea Sq SW3 276 A10
Chelsea Sq SW3 160 DD78
Chelsea Wf SW10 160 DD80
Chelsfield Av N9 101 DX45
Chelsfield Gdns SE26 182 DW90
Chelsfield Grn N9 101 DX45
Chelsfield Av
Chelsfield Hill, Orp. 224 EW109
Chelsfield La, Orp. 206 EX101
Chelsfield La (Maypole), Orp. 224 FA108
Chelsfield La, Sev. 225 FC109
Chelsfield Rd, Orp. 206 EW100
Chelsham Cl, Warl. 237 DY118
Chelsham Common Rd, Warl. 237 EA116
Chelsham Ct Rd, Warl. 237 ED118
Chelsham Rd SW4 161 DK83
Chelsham Rd, S.Croy. 220 DR107
Chelsham Rd, Warl. 237 EA117
Chelsing Ri, Hem.H. 41 BQ21
Chelston App, Ruis. 115 BU61
Chelston Rd, Ruis. 115 BU60
Chelsworth Cl, Rom. 106 FM53
Chelsworth Dr
Chelsworth Dr SE18 165 ER79
Chelsworth Dr, Rom. 106 FL53
Cheltenham Av, Twick. 177 CG87
Cheltenham Cl, Grav. 191 GJ92
Cheltenham Cl, N.Mal. 198 CQ97
Northcote Rd
Cheltenham Cl, Nthlt. 136 CB65
Cheltenham Gdns E6 144 EL68
Cheltenham Gdns, Loug. 84 EL44
Cheltenham Pl W3 138 CP74
Cheltenham Pl, Har. 118 CL56
Cheltenham Rd E10 123 EC58
Cheltenham Rd SE15 162 DW84
Cheltenham Rd, Orp. 206 EU104
Cheltenham Ter SW3 276 E10
Cheltenham Ter SW3 160 DF78
Cheltenham Vil, Stai. 173 BF86
Chelverton Rd SW15 159 CX84
Chelveston, Welw.G.C. 30 DD08
Chelwood N20 98 DD47
Oakleigh Rd N
Chelwood Av, Hat. 45 CU16
Chelwood Cl E4 83 EB44
Chelwood Cl, Epsom 217 CT112
Chelwood Cl, Nthwd. 93 BQ52
Chelwood Gdns, Rich. 158 CN82
Chelwood Gdns Pas, Rich. 158 CN82
Chelwood Gdns
Chelwood Wk SE4 163 DY84
Chenappa Cl E13 144 EG69
Chenduit Way, Stan. 95 CF50
Chene Dr, St.Alb. 43 CD18
Cheney Rd NW1 273 P1
Cheney Rd NW1 141 DL68
Cheney Row E17 101 DZ53
Cheney St, Pnr. 116 BW57
Cheneys Rd E11 124 EE62
Chenies, The, Dart. 187 FE91
Chenies, The, Orp. 205 ES100
Chenies Av, Amer. 72 AW39
Chenies Ct, Hem.H. 41 BP15
Datchet Cl
Chenies Hill (Flaunden), Hem.H. 57 BB34
Chenies Ms WC1 273 M5
Chenies Par, Amer. 72 AW40
Chenies Pl NW1 141 DK68
Chenies Rd, Rick. 73 BD40
Chenies St WC1 273 M6
Chenies St WC1 141 DK71
Chenies Way, Wat. 93 BS45
Cheniston Cl, W.Byf. 212 BG113
Cheniston Gdns W8 160 DB76
Chennells, Hat. 45 CT19
Chepstow Av, Horn. 128 FL62
Chepstow Cl SW15 179 CY86
Lytton Gro
Chepstow Cres W11 140 DA73
Chepstow Cres, Ilf. 125 ES58
Chepstow Gdns, Sthl. 136 BZ72
Chepstow Pl W2 140 DA72
Chepstow Ri, Croy. 202 DS104
Chepstow Rd W2 140 DA72
Chepstow Rd W7 157 CG76
Chepstow Rd, Croy. 202 DS104
Chepstow Vil W11 139 CZ73
Chepstow Way SE15 162 DT81
Chequer St EC1 275 J5
Chequer St, St.Alb. 43 CD20
Chequer Tree Cl (Knaphill), Wok. 226 AS116
Chequers, Buck.H. 102 EH46
Hills Rd
Chequers, Hat. 29 CX13
Chequers, Welw.G.C. 29 CX11
Chequers Cl NW9 118 CS55
Chequers Cl, Horl. 268 DG147
Chequers Cl, Orp. 205 ET98
Chequers Cl, Tad. 249 CU125
Chequers Dr, Horl. 268 DG147
Chequers Fld, Welw.G.C. 29 CX12
Chequers Gdns N13 99 DP50
Chequers Hill, Amer. 55 AR40
Chequers La, Dag. 146 EZ70
Chequers La, Tad. 249 CU125
Chequers La, Wat. 60 BW30
Chequers Orchard, Iver 133 BF72
Chequers Par SE9 185 EM86
Eltham High St
Chequers Pl, Dor. 263 CH136
Chequers Rd, Brwd. 106 FM46
Chequers Rd, Loug. 85 EN43
Chequers Rd, Rom. 106 FL47
Chequers Sq, Uxb. 134 BJ66
High St
Chequers Wk, Wal.Abb. 68 EF33
Chequers Way N13 100 DQ50
Chequers Yd, Dor. 263 CH136
Chequers Pl
Cherbury Cl SE28 146 EX72
Cherbury Ct N1 142 DR68
Cherbury St N1 275 L1
Cherbury St N1 142 DR68
Cherchefelle Ms, Stan. 95 CH50
Cherimoya Gdns, W.Mol. 196 CB97
Kelvinbrook
Cherington Rd W7 137 CF74
Cheriton Av, Brom. 204 EF99
Cheriton Av, Ilf. 103 EM54
Cheriton Cl W5 137 CJ71
Cheriton Cl, Barn. 80 DF41
Cheriton Cl, St.Alb. 43 CK16
Cheriton Ct, Walt. 196 BW102
St. Johns Dr
Cheriton Dr SE18 165 ER80
Cheriton Sq SW17 180 DG89
Cherkley Hill, Lthd. 247 CJ126
Cherries, The, Slou. 132 AV72
Cherry Acre (Chalfont St. Peter), Ger.Cr. 90 AX49
Cherry Av, Brwd. 109 FZ48
Cherry Av, Slou. 152 AX75
Cherry Av, Sthl. 136 BX74
Cherry Av, Swan. 207 FD98
Cherry Blossom Cl N13 99 DP50
Cherry Bounce, Hem.H. 40 BK18
Cherry Cl E17 123 EB56
Eden Rd
Cherry Cl SW2 181 DN87
Tulse Hill
Cherry Cl W5 157 CK76
Cherry Cl, Bans. 217 CX114
Cherry Cl, Cars. 200 DF103
Cherry Cl, Mord. 199 CY98
Cherry Cl, Ruis. 115 BT62
Roundways
Cherry Cres, Brent. 157 CH80
Cherry Cft, Rick. 74 BN44
Cherry Cft, Welw.G.C. 29 CX05
Cherry Dr (Forty Grn), Beac. 88 AH51
Cherry Gdn St SE16 162 DV75
Cherry Gdns, Dag. 126 EZ64
Cherry Gdns, Nthlt. 136 CB66
Cherry Garth, Brent. 157 CK77
Cherry Grn Cl, Red. 267 DH136
Cherry Gro, Hayes 135 BV74
Cherry Gro, Uxb. 135 BP71
Cherry Hill, Barn. 80 DB44
Cherry Hill, Har. 95 CE51
Cherry Hill, Rick. 74 BH41
Cherry Hill, St.Alb. 60 CA25
Cherry Hill Gdns, Croy. 219 DM105
Cherry Hills, Wat. 94 BY50
Cherry Hollow, Abb.L. 59 BT31
Cherry La, Amer. 55 AN40
Cherry La, West Dr. 154 BM77
Cherry La Roundabout, West Dr. 155 BP77
Cherry Laurel Wk SW2 181 DM86
Beechdale Rd
Cherry Orchard, Amer. 55 AS37
Cherry Orchard, Ash. 232 CP118
Cherry Orchard, Hem.H. 40 BG18
Cherry Orchard (Stoke Poges), Slou. 132 AV66
Cherry Orchard, Stai. 174 BG92
Cherry Orchard, West Dr. 154 BL75
Cherry Orchard Cl, Orp. 206 EW99
Cherry Orchard Gdns, Croy. 202 DR103
Oval Rd
Cherry Orchard Gdns, W.Mol. 196 BZ97
Cherry Orchard Rd, Brom. 204 EL103
Cherry Orchard Rd, Croy. 202 DR103
Cherry Orchard Rd, W.Mol. 196 CA97
Cherry Ri, Ch.St.G. 90 AX47
Cherry Rd, Enf. 82 DW38
Cherry St, Rom. 127 FD57
Cherry St, Wok. 226 AY118
Cherry Tree Av, Guil. 242 AT134
Cherry Tree Av (London Colney), St.Alb. 61 CK26
Cherry Tree Av, Stai. 174 BH93
Cherry Tree Av, West Dr. 134 BM72
Cherry Tree Cl E9 142 DW67
Moulins Rd
Cherry Tree Cl, Grays 170 GC79
Cherry Tree Cl, Rain. 147 FG68
Cherry Tree Cl, Wem. 117 CF63
Cherry Tree Ct NW9 118 CQ56
Cherry Tree Ct, Couls. 235 DM117
Cherry Tree Dr SW16 181 DL90
Cherry Tree Dr, S.Ock. 149 FX70
Cherry Tree Grn, Hert. 31 DM07
Cherry Tree Grn, S.Croy. 220 DV114
Cherry Tree La, Dart. 187 FF90
Cherry Tree La, Epsom 216 CN112
Christ Ch Rd
Cherry Tree La, Hem.H. 41 BQ17
Cherry Tree La, Iver 134 BG67
Cherry Tree La, Pot.B. 64 DB34
Cherry Tree La, Rain. 147 FE69
Cherry Tree La, Rick. 91 BC46
Cherry Tree La (Fulmer), Slou. 133 AZ65
Cherry Tree Ri, Buck.H. 102 EJ49
Cherry Tree Rd E15 124 EE63
Wingfield Rd
Cherry Tree Rd N2 120 DF56
Cherry Tree Rd, Beac. 88 AH54
Cherry Tree Rd, Hodd. 49 EA16
Cherry Tree Rd (Farnham Royal), Slou. 131 AQ66
Cherry Tree Rd, Wat. 75 BV36
Cherry Tree Wk EC1 275 J5
Cherry Tree Wk, Beck. 203 DZ98
Cherry Tree Wk, Chesh. 54 AR29
Cherry Tree Wk, W.Wick. 222 EF105
Cherry Tree Way (Penn), H.Wyc. 88 AC46
Cherry Tree Way, Stan. 95 CH51
Cherry Wk, Brom. 204 EG102
Cherry Wk, Grays 171 GG76
Cherry Wk, Rain. 147 FF68
Cherry Wk, Rick. 74 BJ40
Cherry Way, Epsom 216 CR107
Cherry Way, Hat. 45 CU21
Cherry Way, Shep. 195 BR98
Cherry Way (Horton), Slou. 153 BC83
Cherry Wd Cl (Seer Grn), Beac. 89 AR50
Cherry Wd Way W5 138 CN71
Hanger Vale La
Cherrycot Hill, Orp. 223 ER105
Cherrycot Ri, Orp. 223 EQ105
Cherrycroft Gdns, Pnr. 94 BZ52
Westfield Pk
Cherrydale, Wat. 75 BT42
Cherrydown Av E4 101 DZ48
Cherrydown Cl E4 101 DZ48
Cherrydown Rd, Sid. 186 EX89
Cherrydown Wk, Rom. 105 FB54
Cherrytree La (Chalfont St. Peter), Ger.Cr. 90 AX54
Cherrywood Av (Englefield Grn), Egh. 172 AV93
Cherrywood Cl E3 143 DY69
Cherrywood Cl, Kings.T. 178 CN94
Cherrywood Dr SW15 179 CX85
Cherrywood Dr (Northfleet), Grav. 190 GE90
Cherrywood La, Mord. 199 CY98
Cherston Gdns, Loug. 85 EN42
Cherston Rd
Cherston Rd, Loug. 85 EN42
Chertsey Br Rd, Cher. 194 BK101
Chertsey Cl, Ken. 235 DP115
Chertsey Cres (New Addington), Croy. 221 EC110
Chertsey Dr, Sutt. 199 CY103
Chertsey La, Cher. 193 BE95
Chertsey La, Epsom 216 CN112
Chertsey La, Stai. 173 BE92
Chertsey Rd E11 123 ED61
Chertsey Rd, Add. 194 BH103
Chertsey Rd, Ashf. 175 BR94
Chertsey Rd, Felt. 175 BS92
Chertsey Rd, Ilf. 125 ER63
Chertsey Rd, Shep. 194 BN101
Chertsey Rd, Sun. 175 BR94
Chertsey Rd, Twick. 177 CF86
Chertsey Rd (Byfleet), W.Byf. 212 BK111
Chertsey Rd, Wok. 211 BA113
Chertsey Rd (Chobham), Wok. 210 AY110
Chertsey St SW17 180 DG92
Chertsey St, Guil. 258 AX135
Cherubs, The (Farnham Common), Slou. 131 AQ65
Chervil Cl, Felt. 175 BU90
Chervil Ms SE28 146 EV74
Cherwell Cl, Rick. 74 BN43
Cherwell Cl, Slou. 153 BB79
Tweed Rd
Cherwell Ct, Epsom 216 CQ105
Cherwell Gro, S.Ock. 149 FV73
Cherwell Way, Ruis. 115 BQ58
Cheryls Cl SW6 160 DB81
Cheselden Rd, Guil. 258 AY135
Cheseman St SE26 182 DV90
Chesfield Rd, Kings.T. 178 CL94
Chesham Av, Orp. 205 EP100
Chesham Cl SW1 276 F7
Chesham Cl, Rom. 127 FD56
Chesham Cl, Sutt. 217 CY110
Chesham Ct, Nthwd. 93 BT51
Frithwood Av
Chesham Cres SE20 202 DW96
Chesham La, Ch.St.G. 90 AY48
Chesham La (Chalfont St. Peter), Ger.Cr. 90 AY49
Chesham Ms SW1 276 F6
Chesham Ms SW1 160 DG76
Chesham Ms, Guil. 259 AZ135
Chesham Rd
Chesham Pl SW1 276 F7
Chesham Pl SW1 160 DG76
Chesham Rd SE20 202 DW96
Chesham Rd SW19 180 DD92
Chesham Rd, Amer. 55 AQ38
Chesham Rd, Berk. 38 AV21
Chesham Rd (Ashley Grn), Chesh. 38 AT24
Chesham Rd, Guil. 258 AY135
Chesham Rd (Bovingdon), Hem.H. 56 AY27
Chesham Rd, Kings.T. 198 CN95
Chesham St NW10 118 CR62
Chesham St SW1 276 F7
Chesham St SW1 160 DG76
Chesham Ter W13 157 CH75
Chesham Way, Wat. 75 BS44
Cheshire Cl E17 101 EB53
Cheshire Cl SE4 163 DZ82
Cheshire Cl (Ottershaw), Cher. 211 BC107
Cheshire Cl, Horn. 128 FN57
Cheshire Cl, Mitch. 201 DL97
Cheshire Ct EC4 274 E9
Cheshire Ct, Slou. 152 AV75
Clements Cl
Cheshire Gdns, Chess. 215 CK107
Cheshire Ho N18 100 DV50
Cameron Cl
Cheshire Rd N22 99 DM52
Cheshire St E2 142 DT70
Chesholm Rd N16 122 DS62
Cheshunt Link Rd (Cheshunt), Wal.Cr. 66 DW33
Cheshunt Pk (Cheshunt), Wal.Cr. 66 DV26
Cheshunt Rd E7 144 EH65
Cheshunt Rd, Belv. 166 FA78
Cheshunt Wash (Cheshunt), Wal.Cr. 67 DY27
Chesil Ct E2 142 DV68
Chesil Way, Hayes 135 BT69
Chesilton Rd SW6 159 CZ81
Chesley Gdns E6 144 EK68
Cheslyn Gdns, Wat. 75 BT37
Chesney Cres (New Addington), Croy. 221 EC108
Chesney St SW11 160 DG81
Chesnut Est N17 122 DT55
Chesnut Gro N17 122 DT55
Chesnut Rd
Chesnut Rd N17 122 DT55
Chess Cl (Latimer), Chesh. 72 AX36
Chess Cl, Rick. 74 BK42
Chess Hill, Rick. 74 BK42
Chess La, Rick. 74 BK42
Chess Vale Ri, Rick. 74 BM44
Chess Valley Wk, Chesh. 72 AU35
Chess Valley Wk, Rick. 74 BL44
Chess Way, Rick. 74 BG41
Chessbury Cl, Chesh. 54 AP32
Missenden Rd
Chessbury Rd, Chesh. 54 AN32
Chessfield Pk, Amer. 72 AY39
Chessholme Ct, Sun. 175 BS94
Scotts Av
Chessholme Rd, Ashf. 175 BQ93
Chessington Av N3 119 CY55
Chessington Av, Bexh. 166 EY80
Chessington Cl, Epsom 216 CQ107
Chessington Ct, Pnr. 116 BZ56
Chessington Hall Gdns, Chess. 215 CK108
Chessington Hill Pk, Chess. 216 CN106
Chessington Lo N3 119 CZ55
Chessington Rd, Epsom 217 CT109
Chessington Way, W.Wick. 203 EB103
Chessmount Ri, Chesh. 54 AR33
Chesson Rd W14 159 CZ79
Chesswood Way, Pnr. 94 BX54
Chester Av, Rich. 178 CM85
Chester Av, Twick. 176 BZ88
Chester Av, Upmin. 129 FS61
Chester Cl SW1 276 G5
Chester Cl SW1 160 DG75
Chester Cl SW13 159 CV83
Chester Cl, Ashf. 175 BR92
Chester Cl, Dor. 247 CJ134
Chester Cl, Guil. 242 AT132
Chester Cl, Loug. 85 EQ39
Chester Cl, Pot.B. 64 DB29
Chester Cl, Sutt. 200 DA103
Chester Cl, Uxb. 135 BP72
Dawley Av
Chester Cl N NW1 273 J2
Chester Cl S NW1 273 J3
Chester Cotts SW1 276 F9
Chester Ct NW1 273 J2
Chester Ct SE5 162 DR80
Chester Cres E8 142 DT65
Ridley Rd
Chester Dr, Har. 116 BZ58
Chester Gdns W13 137 CG72
Chester Gdns, Enf. 82 DV44
Chester Gdns, Mord. 200 DC100
Chester Gate NW1 273 H3
Chester Gate NW1 141 DH69
Chester Gibbons Grn, St.Alb. 61 CK26
High St
Chester Grn, Loug. 85 EQ39
Chester Ms SW1 277 H6
Chester Ms SW1 161 DH76
Chester Path, Loug. 85 EQ39
Chester Pl NW1 273 J2
Chester Rd E7 144 EK66
Chester Rd E11 124 EH58
Chester Rd E16 144 EE70
Chester Rd E17 123 DX57
Chester Rd N9 100 DV46
Chester Rd N17 122 DR55
Chester Rd N19 121 DH61
Chester Rd NW1 272 G3
Chester Rd NW1 140 DG69
Chester Rd SW19 179 CW93
Chester Rd, Borwd. 78 CQ41
Chester Rd, Chig. 103 EN48
Chester Rd, Houns. 155 BV83
Chester Rd (Heathrow Airport), Houns. 154 BN83
Chester Rd, Ilf. 125 ET60
Chester Rd (Effingham), Lthd. 245 BV129
Dirtham La
Chester Rd, Loug. 85 EP40
Chester Rd, Nthwd. 93 BS52
Chester Rd, Sid. 185 ES85
Chester Rd, Slou. 131 AR72
Chester Rd, Wat. 75 BU43
Chester Row SW1 276 F9
Chester Row SW1 160 DG77
Chester Sq SW1 277 H8
Chester Sq SW1 161 DH76
Chester Sq Ms SW1 277 H7
Chester St E2 142 DU70
Chester St SW1 276 G6
Chester St SW1 160 DG76
Chester Ter NW1 273 H2
Chester Way SE11 278 E9
Chester Way SE11 161 DN77
Chesterfield Cl, Orp. 206 EX98
Chesterfield Dr, Dart. 187 FH85
Chesterfield Dr, Esher 197 CG103
Chesterfield Dr, Sev. 256 FD122
Chesterfield Gdns N4 121 DP57
Chesterfield Gdns SE10 163 ED80
Crooms Hill
Chesterfield Gdns W1 277 H2
Chesterfield Gdns W1 141 DH74
Chesterfield Gro SE22 182 DT85
Chesterfield Hill W1 277 H1
Chesterfield Hill W1 141 DH73
Chesterfield Ms N4 121 DP57
Chesterfield Gdns
Chesterfield Ms, Ashf. 174 BL91
Chesterfield Rd
Chesterfield Rd E10 123 EC58
Chesterfield Rd N3 98 DA51
Chesterfield Rd W4 158 CQ79
Chesterfield Rd, Ashf. 174 BL91
Chesterfield Rd, Barn. 79 CX43
Chesterfield Rd, Enf. 83 DY37
Chesterfield Rd, Epsom 216 CR108
Chesterfield St W1 277 H2
Chesterfield St W1 141 DH74
Chesterfield Wk SE10 163 ED81
Chesterfield Way SE15 162 DW80
Chesterfield Way, Hayes 155 BU75
Chesterford Gdns NW3 120 DB63
Chesterford Ho SE18 164 EK80
Shooter's Hill Rd
Chesterford Rd E12 125 EM64
Chesters, Horl. 268 DE146
Chesters, The, N.Mal. 198 CS95
Chesterton Cl SW18 180 DA85
Ericcson Cl
Chesterton Cl, Chesh. 54 AP29
Milton Rd
Chesterton Cl, Grnf. 136 CB68
Chesterton Dr, Red. 251 DL128
Chesterton Dr, Stai. 174 BM88
Chesterton Grn, Beac. 89 AL52
Chesterton Rd E13 144 EG69
Chesterton Rd W10 139 CX71
Chesterton Sq W8 159 CZ77
Pembroke Rd
Chesterton Ter E13 144 EG69
Chesterton Ter, Kings.T. 198 CN96
Chesterton Way, Til. 171 GJ82
Chesthunte Rd N17 100 DQ53
Chestnut All SW6 159 CZ79
Lillie Rd
Chestnut Av E7 124 EH63
Chestnut Av N8 121 DL57
Chestnut Av SW14 158 CR83
Thornton Rd
Chestnut Av, Brent. 157 CK77
Chestnut Av, Brwd. 108 FS45
Chestnut Av, Buck.H. 102 EK48
Chestnut Av, Chesh. 54 AR29
Chestnut Av, E.Mol. 197 CF97
Chestnut Av, Edg. 96 CL51
Chestnut Av, Epsom 216 CS105
Chestnut Av, Esher 197 CD101
Chestnut Av, Grays 170 GB75
Chestnut Av (Bluewater), Green. 189 FT87
Chestnut Av, Guil. 258 AW138
Chestnut Av, Hmptn. 176 CA94
Chestnut Av, Horn. 127 FF61
Chestnut Av, Nthwd. 93 BT54
Chestnut Av, Rick. 74 BG43
Chestnut Av, Slou. 152 AX75
Chestnut Av, Tedd. 197 CF96
Chestnut Av, Vir.W. 192 AT98
Chestnut Av, Walt. 213 BS109
Chestnut Av, Wem. 117 CH64
Chestnut Av, West Dr. 134 BM73
Chestnut Av, W.Wick. 222 EE106
Chestnut Av, West. 238 EK122
Chestnut Av, Wey. 213 BQ108
Chestnut Av N E17 123 EC56
Chestnut Av S E17 123 EC56
Chestnut Cl N14 81 DJ43
Chestnut Cl N16 122 DR61
Lordship Gro
Chestnut Cl SE6 183 EC92
Chestnut Cl SE14 163 DZ83
Shardeloes Rd
Chestnut Cl SW16 181 DN91
Chestnut Cl, Add. 212 BK106
Chestnut Cl, Amer. 55 AR37
Chestnut Cl, Ashf. 175 BP91
Chestnut Cl, Berk. 39 BB17
Chestnut Cl, Buck.H. 102 EK47
Chestnut Cl, Cars. 200 DF102
Chestnut Cl (Englefield Grn), Egh. 172 AW93
Chestnut Cl (Chalfont St. Peter), Ger.Cr. 91 AZ52
Chestnut Cl (Northfleet), Grav. 191 GF86
Burch Rd
Chestnut Cl, Hayes 135 BS73
Chestnut Cl, Horn. 128 FJ63
Lancaster Dr
Chestnut Cl, Orp. 224 EU106
Chestnut Cl, Red. 267 DH136
Haigh Cres
Chestnut Cl, Sid. 186 EU88
Chestnut Cl, Sun. 175 BT93
Chestnut Cl, Tad. 234 DA123
Chestnut Cl, Ware 34 EK06
Chestnut Cl, West Dr. 155 BP80
Chestnut Cl (Ripley), Wok. 228 BG124
Chestnut Copse, Oxt. 254 EG132
Chestnut Ct SW6 159 CZ79
North End Rd
Chestnut Ct, Amer. 55 AS36
Chestnut Ct, Surb. 198 CL101
Penners Gdns
Chestnut Cres, Walt. 213 BS109
Chestnut Av
Chestnut Dr E11 124 EG58
Chestnut Dr, Berk. 38 AX20
Chestnut Dr, Bexh. 166 EX83
Chestnut Dr (Englefield Grn), Egh. 172 AX93
Chestnut Dr, Har. 95 CF52
Chestnut Dr, Pnr. 116 BX58
Chestnut Dr, St.Alb. 43 CH18
Chestnut Dr, Wind. 151 AL84
Chestnut Glen, Horn. 127 FF61
Chestnut Gro SE20 182 DW94
Chestnut Gro SW12 180 DG87
Chestnut Gro W5 157 CK76
Chestnut Gro, Barn. 80 DF43
Chestnut Gro, Brwd. 108 FW47
Chestnut Gro, Dart. 187 FD91
Chestnut Gro, Ilf. 103 ES51
Chestnut Gro, Islw. 157 CG84
Chestnut Gro, Mitch. 201 DK98
Chestnut Gro, N.Mal. 198 CR97
Chestnut Gro, S.Croy. 220 DV108
Chestnut Gro, Stai. 174 BJ93
Chestnut Gro, Wem. 117 CH64
Chestnut Gro, Wok. 226 AY120
Chestnut La N20 97 CY46
Chestnut La, Amer. 55 AR36
Chestnut La, Sev. 257 FH124
Chestnut La, Wey. 213 BP106
Chestnut Manor Cl, Stai. 174 BH92
Chestnut Mead, Red. 250 DE133
Oxford Rd
Chestnut Pl, Ash. 232 CL119
Chestnut Pl, Epsom 217 CU111
Chestnut Ri SE18 165 ER79
Chestnut Ri, Bushey 94 CB45
Chestnut Rd SE27 181 DP90
Chestnut Rd SW20 199 CX96
Chestnut Rd, Ashf. 175 BP91
Chestnut Rd, Beac. 88 AH54
Chestnut Rd, Dart. 188 FK88
Chestnut Rd, Enf. 83 DY36
Chestnut Rd, Guil. 242 AX134
Chestnut Rd, Horl. 268 DG146
Chestnut Rd, Kings.T. 178 CL94
Chestnut Rd, Twick. 177 CE89
Chestnut Row N3 98 DA52
Nether St
Chestnut Wk, Epp. 51 EP24
Epping Rd
Chestnut Wk (Chalfont St. Peter), Ger.Cr. 90 AY52
Chestnut Wk, Sev. 257 FL129
Chestnut Wk, Shep. 195 BS99
Chestnut Wk, Walt. 213 BS109
Octagon Rd
Chestnut Wk, Wat. 75 BU37
Chestnut Wk (Byfleet), W.Byf. 212 BL112
Royston Rd
Chestnut Wk, Wdf.Grn. 102 EG50
Chestnut Way, Felt. 175 BV90
Chestnuts, Brwd. 109 GB46
Chestnuts, The SE14 163 DZ81
Chestnuts, The, Hem.H. 39 BF24
Chestnuts, The, Hert. 32 DR10
Chestnuts, The, Horl. 269 DH146
Chestnuts, The, Rom. 86 EV41
Chestnuts, The, Walt. 195 BU102
Cheston Av, Croy. 203 DY103
Chestwood Gro, Uxb. 134 BM66
Cheswick Cl, Dart. 167 FF84
Chesworth Cl, Erith 167 FE81
Chettle Cl SE1 279 K6
Chettle Ct N8 121 DN58
Chetwode Dr, Epsom 233 CX118
Chetwode Rd SW17 180 DF90
Chetwode Rd, Tad. 233 CW119
Chetwood Wk E6 144 EL72
Chetwynd Av, Barn. 98 DF46
Chetwynd Dr, Uxb. 134 BM68
Chetwynd Rd NW5 121 DH63
Cheval Pl SW7 276 C6
Cheval Pl SW7 160 DE76
Cheval St E14 163 EA76
Chevalier Cl, Stan. 96 CL49
Cheveley Cl, Rom. 106 FM53
Chelsworth Dr
Cheveley Gdns (Burnham), Slou. 130 AJ68

Chevely Cl, Epp. 70 EX29
Cheveney Wk, Brom. 204 EG97
Marina Cl
Chevening La (Knockholt), Sev. 240 EY115
Chevening Rd NW6 139 CX68
Chevening Rd SE10 164 EF78
Chevening Rd SE19 182 DR93
Chevening Rd (Chevening), Sev. 240 EZ119
Chevening Rd (Sundridge), Sev. 240 EY123
Chevenings, The, Sid. 186 EW90
Cheverton Rd N19 121 DK60
Chevet St E9 123 DY64
Kenworthy Rd
Chevington Way, Horn. 128 FK63
Cheviot Cl, Bans. 234 DB115
Cheviot Cl, Bexh. 167 FE82
Cheviot Cl, Bushey 76 CC44
Cheviot Cl, Enf. 82 DR40
Cheviot Cl, Hayes 155 BR80
Cheviot Cl, Sutt. 218 DD109
Cheviot Gdns NW2 119 CX61
Cheviot Gdns SE27 181 DP91
Cheviot Gate NW2 119 CY61
Cheviot Rd SE27 181 DN92
Cheviot Rd, Horn. 127 FG60
Cheviot Rd, Slou. 153 BA78
Cheviot Way, Ilf. 125 ES56
Cheviots, Hat. 45 CU21
Cheviots, Hem.H. 40 BM17
Chevron Cl E16 144 EG72
Chevy Rd, Sthl. 156 CC75
Chewton Rd E17 123 DY56
Cheyham Gdns, Sutt. 217 CX110
Cheyham Way, Sutt. 217 CY110
Cheyne Av E18 124 EF55
Cheyne Av, Twick. 176 BZ88
Cheyne Cl NW4 119 CW57
Cheyne Cl, Amer. 55 AR36
Cheyne Cl, Brom. 204 EL104
Cedar Cres
Cheyne Cl, Ger.Cr. 112 AY60
Cheyne Cl, Ware 33 DX05
Cheyne Ct SW3 160 DF79
Flood St
Cheyne Ct, Bans. 234 DB115
Park Rd
Cheyne Gdns SW3 160 DE79
Cheyne Hill, Surb. 198 CM98
Cheyne Ms SW3 160 DE79
Cheyne Path W7 137 CF72
Copley Cl
Cheyne Pl SW3 160 DF79
Cheyne Rd, Ashf. 175 BR93
Cheyne Row SW3 160 DE79
Cheyne Wk N21 81 DP43
Cheyne Wk NW4 119 CW58
Cheyne Wk SW3 160 DE79
Cheyne Wk SW10 160 DD80
Cheyne Wk, Chesh. 54 AR31
Cheyne Wk, Croy. 202 DU103
Cheyne Wk, Horl. 268 DG149
Cheyne Wk, Long. 209 FX97
Cavendish Sq
Cheyneys Av, Edg. 95 CK51
Chichele Gdns, Croy. 220 DT105
Brownlow Rd
Chichele Rd NW2 119 CX64
Chichele Rd, Oxt. 254 EE128
Chicheley Gdns, Har. 94 CC52
Chicheley Rd, Har. 94 CC52
Chicheley St SE1 278 C4
Chicheley St SE1 161 DM75
Chichester Av, Ruis. 115 BR61
Chichester Cl E6 144 EL72
Chichester Cl SE3 164 EJ81
Chichester Cl, Dor. 247 CH134
Chichester Cl, Hmptn. 176 BZ93
Maple Cl
Chichester Cl, S.Ock. 148 FQ74
Chichester Ct, Epsom 217 CT109
Chichester Ct, Slou. 152 AU75
Chichester Ct, Stan. 118 CL55
Chichester Dr, Pur. 219 DM112
Chichester Dr, Sev. 256 FF125
Chichester Gdns, Ilf. 124 EL59
Chichester Ms SE27 181 DN91
Chichester Rents WC2 274 D8
Chichester Ri, Grav. 191 GK91
Chichester Rd E11 124 EE62
Chichester Rd N9 100 DU46
Chichester Rd NW6 140 DA68
Chichester Rd W2 140 DB71
Chichester Rd, Croy. 202 DS104
Chichester Rd, Dor. 247 CH133
Chichester Rd, Green. 189 FT85
Chichester Row, Amer. 55 AR38
Chichester St SW1 161 DJ78
Chichester Way E14 163 ED77
Chichester Way, Felt. 175 BV87
Chichester Way, Wat. 60 BY33
Chicksand St E1 142 DT71
Chiddingfold N12 98 DA48
Chiddingstone Av, Bexh. 166 EZ80
Chiddingstone Cl, Sutt. 218 DA110
Chiddingstone St SW6 160 DA82
Chieftan Dr, Purf. 168 FM77
Chieveley Rd, Bexh. 167 FB84
Chiffinch Gdns (Northfleet), Grav. 190 GE90
Chignell Pl W13 137 CG74
Broadway
Chigwell Hill E1 142 DV73
Pennington St
Chigwell Hurst Ct, Pnr. 116 BX55
Chigwell La, Loug. 85 EQ43
Chigwell Pk, Chig. 103 EP49
Chigwell Pk Dr, Chig. 103 EN48
Chigwell Ri, Chig. 103 EN47
Chigwell Rd E18 124 EH55
Chigwell Rd, Wdf.Grn. 102 EJ54
Chigwell Vw, Rom. 104 FA51
Lodge La
Chilberton Dr, Red. 251 DJ130
Chilbrook Rd (Downside), Cob. 229 BU118
Chilcombe Ho SW15 179 CU87
Fontley Way
Chilcot Cl E14 *Grundy St* 143 EB72
Chilcote La (Little Chalfont), Amer. 72 AV39
Chilcott Rd, Wat. 75 BS36
Childebert Rd SW17 181 DH89
Childeric Rd SE14 163 DY80
Childerley, Kings.T. 198 CN97
Burritt Rd
Childerley St SW6 159 CX81
Fulham Palace Rd
Childers, The, Wdf.Grn. 103 EM50
Childers St SE8 163 DY79
Childs Av (Harefield), Uxb. 92 BJ54
Childs Cl, Horn. 128 FJ58
Childs Cres, Swans. 189 FX86
Childs Hall Cl (Bookham), Lthd. 246 BZ125
Childs Hall Rd
Childs Hall Dr (Bookham), Lthd. 246 BZ125
Childs Hall Rd (Bookham), Lthd. 246 BZ125
Childs Hill Wk NW2 119 CZ62
Childs La SE19 182 DS93
Westow St
Child's Ms SW5 160 DA77
Child's Pl
Child's Pl SW5 160 DA77
Child's St SW5 160 DA77
Child's Wk SW5 160 DA77
Child's St
Childs Way NW11 119 CZ57
Childwick Ct, Hem.H. 40 BN23
Rumballs Rd
Chilham Cl, Bex. 186 EZ87
Chilham Cl, Grnf. 137 CG68
Chilham Cl, Hem.H. 40 BL21
Chilham Rd SE9 184 EL91
Chilham Way, Brom. 204 EG101
Chillerton Rd SW17 180 DG92
Chillingworth Gdns, Twick. 177 CF90
Tower Rd
Chillingworth Rd N7 121 DM64
Chilmans Dr (Bookham), Lthd. 246 CB125
Chilmark Gdns, N.Mal. 199 CT101
Chilmark Gdns, Red. 251 DL129
Chilmark Rd SW16 201 DK96
Chilmead La (Nutfield), Red. 251 DK132
Chilsey Grn Rd, Cher. 193 BE100
Chiltern Av, Amer. 55 AR38
Chiltern Av, Bushey 76 CC44
Chiltern Av, Twick. 176 CA88
Chiltern Business Village, Uxb. 134 BH68
Chiltern Cl, Berk. 38 AT18
Chiltern Cl, Bexh. 167 FE81
Cumbrian Av
Chiltern Cl, Borwd. 78 CM40
Chiltern Cl, Bushey 76 CB44
Chiltern Cl, Croy. 202 DS104
Chiltern Cl (Ickenham), Uxb. 115 BP61
Chiltern Cl (Cheshunt), Wal.Cr. 65 DP27
Chiltern Cl, Wok. 226 AW122
Chiltern Cl, Wor.Pk. 199 CW103
Cotswold Way
Chiltern Cor, Berk. 38 AU18
Durrants Rd
Chiltern Dene, Enf. 81 DM42
Chiltern Dr, Rick. 91 BF45
Chiltern Dr, Surb. 198 CP99
Chiltern Gdns NW2 119 CX62
Chiltern Gdns, Brom. 204 EF98
Chiltern Gdns, Horn. 128 FJ62
Chiltern Hill (Chalfont St. Peter), Ger.Cr. 90 AY53
Chiltern Hills Rd, Beac. 88 AJ53
Chiltern Par, Amer. 55 AQ37
Chiltern Pk Av, Berk. 38 AU17
Chiltern Rd E3 143 EA70
Chiltern Rd, Amer. 55 AP35
Chiltern Rd (Northfleet), Grav. 190 GE90
Chiltern Rd, Ilf. 125 ES56
Chiltern Rd, Pnr. 116 BW57
Chiltern Rd, St.Alb. 43 CJ15
Chiltern Rd (Burnham), Slou. 130 AH71
Chiltern Rd, Sutt. 218 DB109
Chiltern St W1 272 F6
Chiltern St W1 140 DG71
Chiltern Vw Rd, Uxb. 134 BJ68
Chiltern Way, Wdf.Grn. 102 EG48
Chilterns, Berk. 38 AT17
Chilterns, Hat. 45 CU21
Chilterns, Hem.H. 40 BL18
Chilterns, The, Sutt. 218 DB109
Gatton Cl
Chilthorne Cl SE6 183 DZ87
Ravensbourne Pk Cres
Chilton Av W5 157 CK77
Chilton Cl (Penn), H.Wyc. 88 AC45
Chilton Ct, Hert. 31 DM07
The Ridgeway
Chilton Ct, Walt. 213 BU105
Chilton Grn, Welw.G.C. 30 DC09
Chilton Gro SE8 163 DX77
Chilton Rd, Chesh. 54 AQ29
Chilton Rd, Edg. 96 CN51
Manor Pk Cres
Chilton Rd, Grays 171 GG76
Chilton Rd, Rich. 158 CN83
Chilton St E2 142 DT70
Chiltonian Ind Est SE12 184 EF86
Chiltons, The E18 102 EG54
Grove Hill
Chiltons Cl, Bans. 234 DB115
High St
Chilver St SE10 164 EF78
Chilwell Gdns, Wat. 94 BW49
Chilwick Rd, Slou. 131 AM69
Chilworth Ct SW19 179 CX88
Windlesham Gro
Chilworth Gdns, Sutt. 200 DC104
Chilworth Ms W2 140 DC72
Chilworth Rd (Albury), Guil. 260 BG139
Chilworth St W2 140 DC72
Chimes Av N13 99 DN50
Chimes Shop Cen, The, Uxb. 134 BK66
China Ms SW2 181 DM87
Craster Rd
Chinbrook Cres SE12 184 EH90
Chinbrook Est SE9 184 EK90
Chinbrook Rd SE12 184 EH90
Chinchilla Dr, Houns. 156 BW82
Chindit Cl, Brox. 49 DY20
Chindits La, Brwd. 108 FW50
Chine, The N10 121 DJ56
Chine, The N21 81 DP44
Chine, The, Dor. 263 CH135
High St
Ching, The, Wem. 117 CH64
Ching Ct WC2 273 P9
Ching Way E4 101 DZ51
Chingdale Rd E4 102 EE48
Chingford Av E4 101 EB48
Chingford Ind Cen E4 101 DY50
Chingford La, Wdf.Grn. 102 EE49
Chingford Mt Rd E4 101 EA49
Chingford Rd E4 101 EA51
Chingford Rd E17 101 EB53
Chingley Cl, Brom. 184 EE93
Chinnery Cl, Enf. 82 DT39
Garnault Rd
Chinnor Cres, Grnf. 136 CB68
Chinthurst La, Guil. 258 AY141
Chinthurst Pk (Shalford), Guil. 258 AY142
Chip St SW4 161 DK84
Chipka St E14 163 EC75
Chipley St SE14 163 DY79
Chipmunk Gro, Nthlt. 136 BY69
Argus Way
Chippendale All, Uxb. 134 BK66
Chippendale Waye
Chippendale St E5 123 DX62
Chippendale Waye, Uxb. 134 BK66
Chippenham Av, Wem. 118 CP64
Chippenham Cl, Pnr. 115 BT56
Chippenham Cl, Rom. 106 FK50
Chippenham Rd
Chippenham Gdns NW6 140 DA69
Chippenham Gdns, Rom. 106 FK50
Chippenham Ms W9 140 DA70
Chippenham Rd W9 140 DA70
Chippenham Rd, Rom. 106 FK51
Chippenham Wk, Rom. 106 FK51
Chippenham Rd
Chipperfield Cl, Upmin. 129 FS60
Chipperfield Rd, Hem.H. 40 BJ24
Chipperfield Rd (Bovingdon), Hem.H. 57 BB27
Chipperfield Rd, Kings L. 58 BK29
Chipperfield Rd, Orp. 206 EU95
Chipping Cl, Barn. 79 CY41
St. Albans Rd
Chippingfield, Harl. 36 EW12
Chipstead (Chalfont St. Peter), Ger.Cr. 90 AW53
Chipstead Av, Th.Hth. 201 DP98
Chipstead Cl SE19 182 DT94
Chipstead Cl, Couls. 234 DG116
Chipstead Cl, Red. 266 DF136
Chipstead Cl, Sutt. 218 DB109
Chipstead Ct (Knaphill), Wok. 226 AS117
Creston Av
Chipstead Gdns NW2 119 CV61
Chipstead Gate, Couls. 235 DJ119
Woodfield Cl
Chipstead La, Couls. 234 DB124
Chipstead La, Sev. 256 FC122
Chipstead La, Tad. 249 CZ125
Chipstead Pk, Sev. 256 FD122
Chipstead Pk Cl, Sev. 256 FC122
Chipstead Pl Gdns, Sev. 256 FC122
Chipstead Rd, Bans. 233 CZ117
Chipstead Rd, Erith 167 FE80
Chipstead Sta Par (Chipstead), Couls. 234 DF118
Station App
Chipstead St SW6 160 DA81
Chipstead Valley Rd, Couls. 235 DH116
Chipstead Way, Bans. 234 DF115
Chirk Cl, Hayes 136 BY70
Braunston Dr
Chirton Wk, Wok. 226 AU118
Shilburn Way
Chisenhale Rd E3 143 DY68
Chisholm Rd, Croy. 202 DS103
Chisholm Rd, Rich. 178 CM86
Chisledon Wk E9 143 DZ65
Osborne Rd
Chislehurst Av N12 98 DC52
Chislehurst Rd, Brom. 204 EK96
Chislehurst Rd, Chis. 204 EK96
Chislehurst Rd, Orp. 205 ES98
Chislehurst Rd, Rich. 178 CL86
Chislehurst Rd, Sid. 186 EU92
Chislet Cl, Beck. 183 EA94
Abbey La
Chisley Rd N15 122 DS58
Chiswell Ct, Wat. 76 BW38
Chiswell Grn La, St.Alb. 60 BX25
Chiswell Sq SE3 164 EH82
Brook La
Chiswell St EC1 275 J6
Chiswell St EC1 142 DQ71
Chiswick Br SW14 158 CQ82
Chiswick Br W4 158 CQ82
Chiswick Cl, Croy. 201 DM104
Chiswick Common Rd W4 158 CR77
Chiswick Ct, Pnr. 116 BZ55
Chiswick Grn Studios W4 158 CQ77
Evershed Wk
Chiswick High Rd W4 158 CR77
Chiswick High Rd, Brent. 158 CM78
Chiswick Ho Grds W4 158 CR79
Chiswick La W4 158 CS78
Chiswick La S W4 159 CT78
Chiswick Mall W4 159 CT79
Chiswick Mall W6 159 CT79
Chiswick Quay W4 158 CQ81
Chiswick Rd N9 100 DU47
Chiswick Rd W4 158 CQ77
Chiswick Roundabout W4 158 CN78
Chiswick High Rd
Chiswick Sq W4 158 CS79
Hogarth Roundabout
Chiswick Staithe W4 158 CQ81
Chiswick Ter W4 158 CQ77
Acton La
Chiswick Village W4 158 CP78
Chiswick Wf W4 159 CT79
Chittenden Cl, Hodd. 33 EB14
Founders Rd
Chittenden Cotts (Wisley), Wok. 228 BL116
Chitterfield Gate, West Dr. 154 BN80
Chitty St W1 273 L6
Chitty St W1 141 DJ71
Chitty's Common, Guil. 242 AT130
Chitty's La, Dag. 126 EX61
Chittys Wk, Guil. 242 AT130
Chivalry Rd SW11 180 DE85
Chivenor Gro, Kings.T. 177 CK92
Chivenor Pl, St.Alb. 43 CJ22
Chivers Rd E4 101 EB48
Choats Manor Way, Bark. 146 EW70
Choats Rd, Bark. 146 EW68
Choats Rd, Dag. 146 EY69
Chobham Cl (Ottershaw), Cher. 211 BB107
Chobham Gdns SW19 179 CX89
Chobham La (Longcross), Cher. 192 AV102
Chobham Pk La (Chobham), Wok. 210 AU110
Chobham Rd E15 123 ED64
Chobham Rd (Ottershaw), Cher. 211 BA108
Chobham Rd, Wok. 226 AY116
Chobham Rd (Horsell), Wok. 210 AW113
Choir Grn (Knaphill), Wok. 226 AS117
Semper Cl
Cholmeley Cres N6 121 DH59
Cholmeley Pk N6 121 DH60
Cholmley Gdns NW6 120 DA64
Fortune Grn Rd
Cholmley Rd, T.Ditt. 197 CH100
Cholmondeley Av NW10 139 CU68
Cholmondeley Wk, Rich. 177 CJ85
Choppins Ct E1 142 DV74
Wapping La
Chopwell Cl E15 143 ED66
Bryant St
Chorleywood Bottom, Rick. 73 BD43
Chorleywood Cl, Rick. 92 BK45
Nightingale Rd
Chorleywood Common, Rick. 73 BE42
Chorleywood Cres, Orp. 205 ET96
Chorleywood Ho Dr, Rick. 73 BE41
Chorleywood Lo La, Rick. 73 BF41
Rickmansworth Rd
Chorleywood Rd, Rick. 74 BG42
Choumert Gro SE15 162 DU82
Choumert Rd SE15 162 DT83
Choumert Sq SE15 162 DU82
Chow Sq E8 122 DT64
Arcola St
Chrislaine Cl (Stanwell), Stai. 174 BK86
High St
Chrisp St E14 143 EB71
Christ Ch Mt, Epsom 216 CP112
Christ Ch Pas EC1 274 G8
Christ Ch Path, Hayes 155 BQ76
Christ Ch Rd, Beck. 203 EA96
Fairfield Rd
Christ Ch Rd, Epsom 216 CL112
Christ Ch Rd, Surb. 198 CM100
Christchurch Av N12 98 DC51
Christchurch Av NW6 139 CY66
Christchurch Av, Erith 167 FD79
Christchurch Av, Har. 117 CH56
Christchurch Av, Rain. 147 FF68
Christchurch Av, Tedd. 177 CG92
Christchurch Av, Wem. 138 CL65
Christchurch Cl SW19 180 DD94
Christchurch Cl, Enf. 82 DQ40
Christchurch Cl, St.Alb. 42 CC19
Christchurch Ct NW6 139 CY66
Christchurch Cres, Grav. 191 GJ87
Christchurch Rd
Christchurch Cres, Rad. 77 CG36
Christchurch Gdns, Epsom 216 CP111
Christchurch Gdns, Har. 117 CG56
Christchurch Grn, Wem. 138 CL65
Christchurch Hill NW3 120 DD62
Christchurch La, Barn. 79 CY40
Christchurch Pk, Sutt. 218 DC108
Christchurch Pas NW3 120 DC62
Christchurch Pas, Barn. 79 CY41
Christchurch Pl, Epsom 216 CP111
Christchurch Rd N8 121 DL58
Christchurch Rd SW2 181 DM88
Christchurch Rd SW14 178 CP85
Christchurch Rd SW19 180 DD94
Christchurch Rd, Dart. 188 FJ87
Christchurch Rd, Grav. 191 GJ88
Christchurch Rd, Hem.H. 40 BK19
Christchurch Rd (Heathrow Airport), Houns. 154 BN83
Courtney Rd
Christchurch Rd, Ilf. 125 EP60
Christchurch Rd, Pur. 219 DP110
Christchurch Rd, Sid. 185 ET91
Christchurch Rd, Til. 171 GG81
Christchurch Rd, Vir.W. 192 AU97
Christchurch Sq E9 142 DW67
Victoria Pk Rd
Christchurch St SW3 160 DF79
Christchurch Ter SW3 160 DF79
Christchurch St
Christchurch Way SE10 164 EE77
Christchurch Way, Wok. 227 AZ117
Church St E
Christian Ct SE16 143 DZ74
Christian Flds SW16 181 DN94
Christian Flds Av, Grav. 191 GJ91
Christian Sq, Wind. 151 AQ81
Alma Rd
Christian St E1 142 DU72
Christie Cl, Brox. 49 DZ21
Christie Cl, Guil. 242 AX131
Christie Dr, Croy. 202 DU99
Christie Gdns, Rom. 126 EV58
Christie Rd E9 143 DY65
Christie Rd, Wal.Abb. 83 EB36
Deer Pk Way
Christie Wk, Cat. 236 DR122
Hambledon Rd
Christies Av (Badgers Mt), Sev. 224 FA110
Christina Sq N4 121 DP60
Adolphus Rd
Christina St EC2 275 M4
Christine Worsley Cl N21 99 DP47
Highfield Rd
Christmas Hill, Guil. 259 AZ141
Christmas La (Farnham Common), Slou. 111 AQ62
Christopher Av W7 157 CG76
Christopher Cl SE16 163 DX75
Christopher Cl, Horn. 128 FK63
Chevington Way
Christopher Cl, Sid. 185 ET85
Christopher Ct, Hem.H. 40 BK23
Seaton Rd
Christopher Ct, Tad. 233 CW123
High St
Christopher Gdns, Dag. 126 EX64
Wren Rd
Christopher Pl NW1 273 N3
Christopher Pl, St.Alb. 43 CD20
Market Pl
Christopher Rd, Sthl. 155 BV77
Christopher St EC2 275 L5
Christopher St EC2 142 DR70
Christopher's Ms W11 139 CY74
Penzance St
Christy Rd (Biggin Hill), West. 238 EJ115
Chryssell Rd SW9 161 DN80
Chrystie La (Bookham), Lthd. 246 CB126
Chubworthy St SE14 163 DY79
Chucks La, Tad. 233 CV124
Chudleigh Cres, Ilf. 125 ES63
Chudleigh Gdns, Sutt. 200 DC104
Chudleigh Rd NW6 139 CX66
Chudleigh Rd SE4 183 DZ85
Chudleigh Rd, Rom. 106 FL49
Chudleigh Rd, Twick. 177 CF87
Chudleigh St E1 143 DX72
Chudleigh Way, Ruis. 115 BU60
Chulsa Rd SE26 182 DV92
Chumleigh St SE5 162 DS79
Chumleigh Wk, Surb. 198 CM98
Church All, Croy. 201 DN102
Church All, Grav. 191 GH86
High St
Church All, Wat. 76 CC38
Church App SE21 182 DR90
Church App, Egh. 193 BC97
Church App (Cudham), Sev. 239 EQ115
Cudham La S
Church App (Stanwell), Stai. 174 BK86
Church Av E4 101 ED51
Church Av NW1 141 DH65
Kentish Town Rd
Church Av SW14 158 CR83
Church Av, Beck. 203 EA95
Church Av, Nthlt. 136 BZ66
Church Av, Pnr. 116 BY58
Church Av, Ruis. 115 BR60
Church Av, Sid. 186 EU92
Church Av, Sthl. 156 BY76
Church Cl N20 98 DE48
Church Cl W8 160 DB75
Kensington Ch St
Church Cl, Add. 212 BH105
Church Cl, Edg. 96 CQ50
Church Cl, Hayes 135 BR71
Church Cl, Hert. 47 DJ19
Goddards Cl
Church Cl (Fetcham), Lthd. 231 CD124
Church Cl, Loug. 85 EM40
Church Cl, Nthwd. 93 BT52
Church Cl (Cuffley), Pot.B. 65 DL29
Church Cl, Rad. 77 CG36
Church Cl, Stai. 194 BJ97
The Bdy
Church Cl, Tad. 249 CZ127
Buckland Rd
Church Cl, Uxb. 134 BH68
Church Cl, West Dr. 154 BL76
Church Cl (Eton), Wind. 151 AR79
Church Cl (Horsell), Wok. 226 AX116
Church Ct, Reig. 250 DB134
Church Ct, Rich. 177 CK85
George St
Church Cres E9 143 DX66
Church Cres N3 97 CZ53
Church Cres N10 121 DH56
Church Cres N20 98 DE48
Church Cres, St.Alb. 42 CC19
Church Cres, Saw. 36 EZ05
Church Cres, S.Ock. 149 FW69
Church Cft, St.Alb. 43 CJ22
Church Dr NW9 118 CR60
Church Dr, Har. 116 BZ58
Church Dr, Maid. 150 AC75
Church Dr, W.Wick. 204 EE104
Church Elm La, Dag. 146 FA65
Church End E17 123 EB56
Church End NW4 119 CV55
Church End, Harl. 51 EN17
Church Entry EC4 274 G9
Church Fm Cl, Swan. 207 FC100
Church Fm La, Sutt. 217 CY107
Church Fm Way, Wat. 76 CB38
Church Fld, Dart. 188 FK89
Church Fld, Epp. 70 EU29
Church Fld, Rad. 77 CG36
Church Fld, Sev. 256 FE122
Church Gdns W5 157 CK75
Church Gdns, Dor. 263 CG135
Church Gdns, Wem. 117 CG63
Church Gate SW6 159 CY83
Church Grn, Hayes 135 BT72
Church Grn, St.Alb. 43 CD19
Hatfield Rd
Church Grn, Walt. 214 BW107
Church Gro SE13 163 EB84
Church Gro, Amer. 72 AY39
Church Gro, Kings.T. 197 CJ95
Church Gro (Wexham), Slou. 132 AW71
Church Hill E17 123 EA56
Church Hill N21 99 DM45
Church Hill SE18 165 EM76
Church Hill SW19 179 CZ92
Church Hill, Abb.L. 59 BT26
Church Hill, Cars. 218 DF106
Church Hill, Cat. 236 DT124
Church Hill, Dart. 188 FK90
Church Hill (Crayford), Dart. 167 FE84
Church Hill, Epp. 70 EU29
Church Hill, Green. 189 FS85
Church Hill (Shere), Guil. 260 BN139
Church Hill, Har. 117 CE60
Church Hill, Hert. 32 DV11
Church Hill, Loug. 84 EL41
Church Hill, Orp. 206 EU101
Church Hill, Pur. 219 DL110
Church Hill (Merstham), Red. 251 DH126
Church Hill (Nutfield), Red. 251 DM133
Church Hill (Plaxtol), Sev. 239 EQ115
Church Hill (Harefield), Uxb. 114 BJ55
Church Hill, Welw.G.C. 29 CU10
Church Hill (Tatsfield), West. 238 EK122
Church Hill (Horsell), Wok. 226 AX116
Church Hill (Pyrford), Wok. 227 BF117
Church Hill Rd E17 123 EB56
Church Hill Rd, Barn. 98 DF45
Church Hill Rd, Surb. 198 CL99
Church Hill Rd, Sutt. 217 CX105
Church Hill Wd, Orp. 205 ET99
Church Hollow, Purf. 168 FN78
Church Hyde SE18 165 ES79
Old Mill Rd
Church Island, Stai. 173 BD91
Church La E11 124 EE60
Church La E17 123 EB56
Church La N2 120 DD55
Church La N8 121 DM56
Church La N9 100 DU47
Church La N17 100 DS53
Church La NW9 118 CQ61
Church La SW17 181 DH91
Church La SW19 199 CZ95
Church La W5 157 CJ75
Church La (Nork), Bans. 233 CX117
Church La, Berk. 38 AW19
Church La (Sheering), B.Stort. 37 FD07
Church La (Great Warley), Brwd. 129 FW58
Church La (Hutton), Brwd. 109 GE46
Church La, Brom. 204 EL102
Church La, Brox. 48 DW22
Church La, Cat. 235 DN123
Church La, Chess. 216 CM107
Church La, Chis. 205 EQ95
Church La, Couls. 234 DG122
Church La, Dag. 147 FB65
Church La, Enf. 82 DR41
Church La, Epp. 71 FB26
Church La (Headley), Epsom 232 CQ124
Church La (Chalfont St. Peter), Ger.Cr. 90 AX53
Church La, Gdse. 253 DX132
Church La (Albury), Guil. 260 BH139

Clive Rd, Twick. 177 CF91
Clive Way, Enf. 82 DU42
Clive Way, Wat. 76 BW39
Cliveden Cl N12 98 DC49
Woodside Av
Cliveden Cl, Brwd. 109 FZ45
Cliveden Est, Maid. 110 AE64
Cliveden Pl SW1 276 F8
Cliveden Pl SW1 160 DG77
Cliveden Pl, Shep. 195 BP100
Cliveden Rd SW19 199 CZ95
Cliveden Rd, Maid. 130 AE65
Cliveden Rd (Burnham), Slou. 130 AE65
Clivedon Ct W13 137 CH71
Clivedon Rd E4 102 EE50
Clivesdale Dr, Hayes 135 BV74
Cloak La EC4 275 J10
Cloak La EC4 142 DQ73
Clock Ho Cl (Byfleet), W.Byf. 212 BM112
Clock Ho La, Sev. 256 FG123
Clock Ho Mead (Oxshott), Lthd. 214 CB114
Clock Ho Rd, Beck. 203 DY97
Clock Twr Ms N1 142 DQ67
Arlington Av
Clock Twr Ms SE28 146 EV73
Clock Twr Pl N7 141 DL65
Clock Twr Rd, Islw. 157 CF83
Clockhouse Av, Bark. 145 EQ67
Clockhouse Cl SW19 179 CW90
Clockhouse La, Ashf. 174 BN91
Clockhouse La, Felt. 175 BP89
Clockhouse La, Grays 149 FX74
Clockhouse La, Rom. 105 FB52
Clockhouse La E, Egh. 173 BB94
Clockhouse La W, Egh. 173 BA94
Clockhouse Ms, Rick. 73 BD41
Chorleywood Ho Dr
Clockhouse Pl SW15 179 CY85
Clockhouse Pl, Felt. 175 BQ88
Clockhouse Roundabout, Felt. 175 BP88
Cloister Cl, Rain. 147 FH70
Cloister Cl, Tedd. 177 CH92
Cloister Gdns SE25 202 DV100
Cloister Gdns, Edg. 96 CQ50
Cloister Garth, Berk. 38 AW19
Cloister Garth, St.Alb. 43 CE24
Cloister Rd NW2 119 CZ62
Cloister Rd W3 138 CQ71
Cloister Wk, Hem.H. 40 BK18
Townsend
Cloisters, The, Bushey 76 CB44
Cloisters, The, Rick. 92 BL45
Cloisters, The, Welw.G.C. 29 CX09
Cloisters, The, Wok. 227 BB121
Cloisters Av, Brom. 205 EM99
Cloisters Mall, Kings.T. 197 CK96
Union St
Clonard Way, Pnr. 94 CA51
Clonbrock Rd N16 122 DS63
Cloncurry St SW6 159 CX82
Clonmel Cl, Har. 117 CD60
Clonmel Rd SW6 159 CZ80
Clonmel Rd, Tedd. 177 CD91
Clonmel Way (Burnham), Slou. 130 AH69
Clonmell Rd N17 122 DR55
Clonmore St SW18 179 CZ88
Cloonmore Av, Orp. 223 ET105
Clorane Gdns NW3 120 DA62
Close, The E4 101 EC52
Beech Hall Rd
Close, The N14 99 DK47
Close, The N20 97 CZ47
Close, The SE3 163 ED82
Heath La
Close, The, Barn. 80 DF44
Close, The, Beck. 203 DY98
Close, The (Strood Grn), Bet. 264 CP138
Close, The, Bex. 186 FA86
Close, The, Brwd. 108 FW48
Close, The, Bushey 76 CB43
Close, The, Cars. 218 DE109
Close, The, Dart. 188 FJ90
Close, The, Grays 170 GC75
Close, The (Wonersh), Guil. 259 BB144
Close, The, Har. 94 CC54
Close, The, Hat. 63 CY26
Close, The, Horl. 269 DJ150
Close, The, Islw. 157 CD82
Close, The, Iver 133 BC69
Close, The, Mitch. 200 DF98
Close, The, N.Mal. 198 CQ96
Close, The, Orp. 205 ES100
Close, The (Eastcote), Pnr. 116 BW59
Close, The (Rayners La), Pnr. 116 BZ59
Close, The, Pot.B. 64 DA32
Close, The (Pampisford Rd), Pur. 219 DP110
Close, The (Russell Hill), Pur. 219 DM110
Close, The, Rad. 61 CF33
Close, The, Reig. 266 DB135
Close, The, Rich. 158 CP83
Close, The, Rick. 92 BJ46
Close, The, Rom. 126 EY58
Close, The, Sev. 256 FE124
Close, The, Sid. 186 EV92
Close, The, Slou. 131 AK73
St. George's Cres
Close, The, Sutt. 199 CZ101
Close, The, Uxb. 134 BL66
Close, The (Hillingdon), Uxb. 134 BN67
Close, The, Vir.W. 192 AW99
Close, The, Ware 33 DY06
Close, The (Barnhill Rd), Wem. 118 CQ62
Close, The (Lyon Pk Av), Wem. 138 CL65
Close, The, W.Byf. 212 BG113
Closemead Cl, Nthwd. 93 BQ51
Cloth Ct EC1 274 G7
Cloth Fair EC1 274 G7
Cloth Fair EC1 141 DP71
Cloth St EC1 275 H6
Clothier St E1 275 N8
Clothworkers Rd SE18 165 ER80
Cloudberry Rd, Rom. 106 FK51
Cloudesdale Rd SW17 181 DH89
Cloudesley Pl N1 141 DN67
Cloudesley Rd N1 141 DN67
Cloudesley Rd, Bexh. 166 EZ81
Cloudesley Rd, Erith 167 FF81
Cloudesley Sq N1 141 DN67
Cloudesley St N1 141 DN67
Clouston Cl, Wall. 219 DL106
Clova Rd E7 144 EF65
Clove Cres E14 143 ED73
Clove Hitch Quay SW11 160 DC83
Clove St E13 144 EG70
Barking Rd
Clovelly Av NW9 119 CT56
Clovelly Av, Uxb. 115 BQ63
Clovelly Av, Warl. 236 DV118
Clovelly Cl, Pnr. 115 BV55
Clovelly Cl, Uxb. 115 BQ63
Clovelly Ct, Horn. 128 FN61
Clovelly Gdns SE19 202 DT95
Clovelly Gdns, Enf. 100 DS45
Clovelly Gdns, Rom. 105 FB53
Clovelly Rd N8 121 DK56
Clovelly Rd W4 158 CQ75
Clovelly Rd W5 157 CJ75
Clovelly Rd, Bexh. 166 EY79
Clovelly Rd, Houns. 156 CA82
Clovelly Way E1 142 DW72
Jamaica St
Clovelly Way, Har. 116 BZ61
Clovelly Way, Orp. 205 ET100
Clover Cl E11 123 ED61
Norman Rd
Clover Ct, Grays 170 GD79
Churchill Rd
Clover Ct, Wok. 226 AX118
Clover Fld, Harl. 52 EU18
Clover Fld, The, Bushey 76 BZ44
Clover Hill, Couls. 235 DH121
Clover Lea, Gdmg. 258 AS143
Clover Leas, Epp. 69 ET30
Clover Ms SW3 160 DF79
Dilke St
Clover Rd, Guil. 242 AS132
Clover Way, Hem.H. 40 BH19
Clover Way, Wall. 200 DG102
Cloverdale Gdns, Sid. 185 ET86
Cloverfield, Welw.G.C. 29 CZ06
Cloverfields, Horl. 269 DH147
Cloverland, Hat. 45 CT21
Cloverleys, Loug. 84 EK43
Clovers, The (Northfleet), Grav. 190 GE91
Clowders Rd SE6 183 DZ90
Clowser Cl, Sutt. 218 DC106
Turnpike La
Cloyster Wd, Edg. 95 CK52
Cloysters Grn E1 142 DU74
Club Gdns Rd, Brom. 204 EG101
Club Row E1 275 P4
Club Row E1 142 DT70
Club Row E2 275 P4
Club Row E2 142 DT70
Clump, The, Rick. 74 BG43
Clump Av, Tad. 248 CQ131
Clumps, The, Ashf. 175 BR91
Clunas Gdns, Rom. 128 FK55
Clunbury Av, Sthl. 156 BZ78
Clunbury St N1 275 L1
Cluny Est SE1 279 M6
Cluny Ms SW5 160 DA77
Cluny Pl SE1 279 M6
Cluse Ct N1 142 DQ68
Dame St
Clutterbucks, Rick. 74 BG36
Clutton St E14 143 EB71
Clydach Rd, Enf. 82 DT42
Clyde Av, S.Croy. 236 DV115
Clyde Circ N15 122 DS56
Clyde Cl, Red. 250 DG133
Clyde Ct, Red. 250 DG133
Clyde Cl
Clyde Cres, Upmin. 129 FS58
Clyde Pl E10 123 EB59
Clyde Rd N15 122 DS56
Clyde Rd N22 99 DK53
Clyde Rd, Croy. 202 DT102
Clyde Rd, Hodd. 49 ED19
Clyde Rd (Stanwell), Stai. 174 BK88
Clyde Rd, Sutt. 218 DA106
Clyde Rd, Wall. 219 DJ106
Clyde Sq, Hem.H. 40 BM15
Clyde St SE8 163 DZ79
Clyde Ter SE23 182 DW89
Clyde Ter, Hert. 32 DU09
Clyde Vale SE23 182 DW89
Clyde Way, Rom. 105 FE53
Clydesdale, Enf. 83 DX42
Clydesdale Av, Stan. 117 CK55
Clydesdale Cl, Borwd. 78 CR43
Clydesdale Cl, Islw. 157 CF83
Clydesdale Gdns, Rich. 158 CP84
Clydesdale Ho, Erith 166 EY75
Kale Rd
Clydesdale Rd W11 139 CZ72
Clydesdale Rd, Horn. 127 FF59
Clydesdale Wk, Brox. 67 DZ25
Tarpan Way
Clydon Cl, Erith 167 FE79
Clyfford Rd, Ruis. 115 BT63
Clyfton Cl, Brox. 49 DZ23
Clymping Dene, Felt. 175 BV87
Clyston Rd, Wat. 75 BT44
Clyston St SW8 161 DJ82
Clyve Way, Stai. 193 BE95
Coach All (Wooburn Grn), H.Wyc. 110 AF60
Coach & Horses Yd W1 273 J10
Coach Ho La N5 121 DP63
Highbury Hill
Coach Ho La SW19 179 CX91
Coach Ho Ms SE14 163 DX82
Waller Rd
Coach Ho Ms SE23 183 DX86
Coach Ho Ms, Red. 266 DF135
Mill St
Coach Ho Yd SW18 160 DB84
Ebner St
Coach Rd (Brockham), Bet. 248 CL134
Coach Rd (Ottershaw), Cher. 211 BC107
Coach Yd Ms N19 121 DL60
Trinder Rd
Coachhouse Ms SE20 182 DV94
Coachlads Av, Guil. 242 AT134
Coachmaker Ms SW4 161 DL83
Fenwick Pl
Coal Ct, Grays 170 GA79
Columbia Wf Rd
Coal Rd, Til. 171 GL77
Coal Wf Rd W12 159 CX75
Sterne St
Coaldale Wk SE21 182 DQ87
Lairdale Cl
Coalecroft Rd SW15 159 CW84
Coalmans Way (Burnham), Slou. 130 AG72
Coalport Cl, Harl. 52 EW16
Coast Hill (Westcott), Dor. 262 BZ139
Coast Hill La (Westcott), Dor. 262 CA138
Coat Wicks (Seer Grn), Beac. 89 AQ51
Coate St E2 142 DU68
Coates Av SW18 180 DD86
Coates Dell, Wat. 60 BY33
Coates Hill Rd, Brom. 205 EN96
Coates Rd, Borwd. 95 CK45
Coates Wk, Brent. 158 CL78
Coates Way, Wat. 60 BX33
Cob Mead, Hat. 45 CV16
Cobb Cl, Borwd. 78 CQ43
Cobb Cl (Datchet), Slou. 152 AX81
Cobb Grn, Wat. 59 BV32
Cobb Rd, Berk. 38 AT19
Cobb St E1 275 P7
Cobb St E1 142 DT71
Cobbett Cl, Enf. 82 DW36
Cobbett Rd SE9 164 EL83
Cobbett Rd, Guil. 242 AS133
Cobbett Rd, Twick. 176 CA88
Cobbett St SW8 161 DM80
Cobbetts Av, Ilf. 124 EK57
Cobbetts Cl, Wok. 226 AV117
Cobbetts Hill, Wey. 213 BP107
Cobbins, The, Wal.Abb. 68 EE33
Cobbins Way, Harl. 36 EY11
Cobbinsend Rd, Wal.Abb. 68 EK29
Cobble La N1 141 DP66
Edwards Ms
Cobblers Cl (Farnham Royal), Slou. 131 AP68
Cobblers Wk, E.Mol. 197 CG95
Cobblers Wk, Hmptn. 176 CC94
Cobblers Wk, Kings.T. 197 CG95
Cobblers Wk, Tedd. 177 CD94
Cobbles, The, Brwd. 108 FY47
Cobbles, The, Upmin. 129 FT59
Cobblestone Pl, Croy. 202 DQ102
Oakfield Rd
Cobbold Est NW10 139 CT65
Cobbold Ms W12 159 CT75
Cobbold Rd
Cobbold Rd E11 124 EF62
Cobbold Rd NW10 139 CT65
Cobbold Rd W12 159 CT75
Cobb's Ct EC4 141 DP72
Carter La
Cobb's Rd, Houns. 156 BZ84
Cobden Cl, Uxb. 134 BJ67
Cobden Hill, Rad. 77 CH36
Cobden Rd E11 124 EE62
Cobden Rd SE25 202 DU99
Cobden Rd, Orp. 223 ER105
Cobden Rd, Sev. 257 FJ123
Cobham, Grays 170 GB75
Cobham Av, N.Mal. 199 CU99
Cobham Cl SW11 180 DE86
Cobham Cl, Brom. 204 EL101
Cobham Cl, Edg. 96 CP54
Cobham Cl, Enf. 82 DU41
Cobham Cl, Sid. 186 EV86
Park Mead
Cobham Cl, Slou. 151 AM75
Cobham Cl, Wall. 219 DL107
Cobham Gate, Cob. 213 BV114
Cobham Ho, Bark. 145 EQ67
St. Margarets
Cobham Ms NW1 141 DK66
Agar Gro
Cobham Pk Rd, Cob. 229 BV117
Cobham Pl, Bexh. 186 EX85
Cobham Rd E17 101 EC53
Cobham Rd N22 121 DP55
Cobham Rd (Stoke D'Abernon), Cob. 230 CA118
Cobham Rd, Houns. 156 BW80
Cobham Rd, Ilf. 125 ES61
Cobham Rd, Kings.T. 198 CN95
Cobham Rd (Fetcham), Lthd. 231 CE122
Cobham Rd, Ware 33 DZ05
Cobham St, Grav. 191 GG87
Cobham Way (East Horsley), Lthd. 245 BS126
Cobill Cl, Horn. 128 FJ56
Cobland Rd SE12 184 EJ91
Coborn Rd E3 143 DZ69
Coborn St E3 143 DZ69
Cobourg Rd SE5 162 DT79
Cobourg St NW1 273 L3
Cobourg St NW1 141 DJ69
Cobs Way (New Haw), Add. 212 BJ110
Cobsdene, Grav. 191 GK93
Coburg Cl SW1 277 L8
Coburg Cres SW2 181 DM88
Coburg Gdns, Ilf. 102 EK54
Coburg Rd N22 121 DM55
Cochrane Ms NW8 272 A1
Cochrane Rd SW19 179 CZ94
Cochrane St NW8 272 A1
Cochrane St NW8 140 DD68
Cock Grn, Harl. 51 EP17
Cock Hill E1 275 N7
Cock La EC1 274 F7
Cock La EC1 141 DP71
Cock La, Brox. 48 DU20
Cock La, Hodd. 49 DY19
Cock La (Fetcham), Lthd. 230 CC122
Cockayne Way SE8 163 DY78
Cockbush Av, Hert. 32 DU08
Cocker Rd, Enf. 82 DV36
Cockerell Rd E17 123 DY58
Cockerhurst Rd (Shoreham), Sev. 225 FD107
Cockett Rd, Slou. 152 AY76
Cockfosters Rd, Barn. 80 DF40
Cockle Way, Rad. 62 CL33
Cockmannings La, Orp. 206 EX102
Cockmannings Rd, Orp. 206 EX101
Cockpit Steps SW1 277 N5
Cockpit Yd WC1 274 C6
Cockrobin La, Harl. 35 EN08
Cockrobin La, Ware 35 EN05
Cocks Cres, N.Mal. 199 CT98
Cock's Yd, Uxb. 134 BJ66
Bakers Rd
Cocksett Av, Orp. 223 ES107
Cockshot Hill, Reig. 266 DB136
Cockshot Rd, Reig. 266 DB135
Cockspur Ct SW1 277 N2
Cockspur St SW1 277 N2
Cockspur St SW1 141 DK74
Cocksure La, Sid. 186 FA90
Code St E1 142 DT70
Codham Hall La, Brwd. 129 FV56
Codicote Dr, Wat. 60 BX34
Codicote Rd, Welw. 28 CL05
Codicote Row, Hem.H. 40 BN15
Codicote Ter N4 122 DQ61
Green Las
Codling Cl E1 142 DU74
Torrington Pl
Codling Way, Wem. 117 CK63
Codmore Cres, Chesh. 54 AS30
Codmore Wd Rd, Chesh. 56 AW33
Codrington Ct, Wok. 226 AS118
Raglan Rd
Codrington Cres, Grav. 191 GJ92
Codrington Gdns, Grav. 191 GK92
Codrington Hill SE23 183 DY87
Codrington Ms W11 139 CY72
Blenheim Cres
Cody Cl, Har. 117 CK55
Cody Cl, Wall. 219 DK108
Alcock Cl
Cody Rd E16 143 ED70
Cody Rd Business Cen E16 143 ED70
Coe Av SE25 202 DU100
Coe Spur, Slou. 151 AP75
Coe's All, Barn. 79 CY42
Wood St
Coffers Circle, Wem. 118 CP62
Coftards, Slou. 132 AW72
Cogan Av E17 101 DY53
Cohen Cl, Wal.Cr. 67 DY31
Coin St SE1 278 D2
Coin St SE1 141 DN74
Coity Rd NW5 140 DG65
Coke St E1 142 DU72
Cokers La SE21 182 DR88
Perifield
Coke's Fm La, Ch.St.G. 72 AV41
Coke's La, Amer. 72 AW41
Coke's La, Ch.St.G. 72 AU42
Colas Ms NW6 140 DA67
Birchington Rd
Colbeck Ms SW7 160 DB77
Colbeck Rd, Har. 116 CC59
Colberg Pl N16 122 DS59
Colborne Way, Wor.Pk. 199 CW104
Colbrook Av, Hayes 155 BR76
Colbrook Cl, Hayes 155 BR76
Colburn Av, Cat. 236 DT124
Colburn Av, Pnr. 94 BY51
Colburn Cres, Guil. 243 BA131
Sutherland Dr
Colburn Way, Sutt. 200 DD104
Colby Ms SE19 182 DS92
Gipsy Hill
Colby Rd SE19 182 DS92
Colby Rd, Walt. 195 BU102
Winchester Rd
Colchester Av E12 125 EM62
Colchester Dr, Pnr. 116 BX57
Colchester Rd E10 123 EC59
Colchester Rd E17 123 EA58
Colchester Rd, Edg. 96 CQ52
Colchester Rd, Nthwd. 93 BU54
Colchester Rd, Rom. 106 FP51
Colchester St E1 142 DT72
Braham St
Colcokes Rd, Bans. 234 DA116
Cold Arbor Rd, Sev. 256 FD124
Cold Blow Cres, Bex. 187 FD88
Cold Blow La SE14 163 DX80
Cold Blows, Mitch. 200 DG97
Cold Harbour E14 163 EC75
Coldbath Sq EC1 274 D4
Coldbath St SE13 163 EB81
Coldershaw Rd W13 137 CG74
Coldfall Av N10 98 DF54
Coldham Gro, Enf. 83 DY37
Coldharbour Cl, Egh. 193 BC97
Coldharbour Crest SE9 185 EN90
Great Harry Dr
Coldharbour La SE5 161 DN84
Coldharbour La SW9 161 DN84
Coldharbour La, Bushey 76 CB44
Coldharbour La, Dor. 263 CG138
Coldharbour La, Egh. 193 BC97
Coldharbour La, Hayes 135 BU73
Coldharbour La, Pur. 219 DN110
Coldharbour La, Rain. 147 FE72
Coldharbour La (Bletchingley), Red. 252 DT134
Coldharbour La, Wok. 227 BF115
Coldharbour Pl SE5 162 DQ82
Denmark Hill
Coldharbour Rd, Croy. 219 DN106
Coldharbour Rd (Northfleet), Grav. 190 GE89
Coldharbour Rd, Harl. 51 EM16
Coldharbour Rd, W.Byf. 211 BF114
Coldharbour Rd, Wok. 227 BF115
Coldharbour Way, Croy. 219 DN106
Coldmoreham Yd, Amer. 55 AM39
Coldshott, Oxt. 254 EG133
Coldstream Gdns SW18 179 CZ86
Coldstream Rd, Cat. 236 DQ122
Coulsdon Rd
Cole Av, Grays 171 GJ77
Cole Cl SE28 146 EV74
Cole Gdns, Houns. 155 BU80
Cole Grn Bypass, Hert. 30 DF13
Cole Grn La, Welw.G.C. 30 DB11
Cole Grn Way, Hert. 31 DK12
Cole Pk Gdns, Twick. 177 CG86
Cole Pk Rd, Twick. 177 CG86
Cole Pk Vw, Twick. 177 CG86
Hill Vw Rd
Cole Rd, Twick. 177 CG86
Cole Rd, Wat. 75 BV39
Stamford Rd
Cole St SE1 279 J5
Cole St SE1 162 DQ75
Colebeck Ms N1 141 DP65
Colebert Av E1 142 DW70
Colebrook (Ottershaw), Cher. 211 BD107
Colebrook Cl SW15 179 CX87
West Hill
Colebrook Gdns, Loug. 85 EP40
Colebrook Ho E14 143 EB72
Brabazon St
Colebrook La, Loug. 85 EP40
Colebrook Path, Loug. 85 EP40
Colebrook Pl (Ottershaw), Cher. 211 BB108
Colebrook Rd SW16 201 DL95
Colebrook Way N11 99 DH50
Colebrooke Av W13 137 CH72
Colebrooke Dr E11 124 EH59
Colebrooke Pl N1 141 DP67
St. Peters St
Colebrooke Ri, Brom. 204 EE96
Colebrooke Rd, Red. 250 DE132
Colebrooke Row N1 274 F1
Colebrooke Row N1 141 DP68
Coleby Path SE5 162 DR80
Harris St
Coledale Dr, Stan. 95 CJ53
Coleford Rd SW18 180 DC85
Colegrave Rd E15 123 ED64
Colegrove Rd SE15 162 DT80
Coleherne Ct SW5 160 DB78
Coleherne Ms SW10 160 DB78
Coleherne Rd SW10 160 DB78
Colehill Gdns SW6 159 CY82
Fulham Palace Rd
Colehill La SW6 159 CY81
Colekitchen La (Gomshall), Guil. 261 BR136
Coleman Cl SE25 202 DU96
Warminster Rd
Coleman Flds N1 142 DQ67
Coleman Grn (Wheathampstead), St.Alb. 28 CM10
Coleman Grn La (Wheathampstead), St.Alb. 28 CM10
Coleman Rd SE5 162 DS80
Coleman Rd, Belv. 166 FA77
Coleman Rd, Dag. 146 EY65
Coleman St EC2 275 K8
Coleman St EC2 142 DR72
Colemans Heath SE9 185 EP90
Colemans La, Ong. 71 FH30
Coleman's La, Wal.Abb. 67 ED26
Colenorton Cres (Eton Wick), Wind. 151 AL77
Colenso Dr NW7 97 CU52
Colenso Rd E5 122 DW63
Colenso Rd, Ilf. 125 ES60
Colepits Wd Rd SE9 185 EQ85
Coleraine Rd N8 121 DN55
Coleraine Rd SE3 164 EF79
Coleridge Av E12 144 EL65
Coleridge Av, Sutt. 218 DE105
Coleridge Cl SW8 161 DH82
Coleridge Cl (Cheshunt), Wal.Cr. 66 DT27
Peakes La
Coleridge Cres (Colnbrook), Slou. 153 BE81
Coleridge Gdns NW6 140 DC66
Fairhazel Gdns
Coleridge La N8 121 DL58
Coleridge Rd
Coleridge Rd E17 123 DZ56
Coleridge Rd N4 121 DN61
Coleridge Rd N8 121 DK58
Coleridge Rd N12 98 DC50
Coleridge Rd, Ashf. 174 BL91
Coleridge Rd, Croy. 202 DW101
Coleridge Rd, Dart. 168 FN84
Coleridge Rd, Rom. 105 FH52
Coleridge Rd, Til. 171 GJ82
Coleridge Sq W13 137 CG72
Berners Dr
Coleridge Wk NW11 120 DA56
Coleridge Wk, Brwd. 109 GC45
Coleridge Way, Hayes 135 BU72
Coleridge Way, Orp. 206 EU100
Coleridge Way, West Dr. 154 BM77
Coles Cres, Har. 116 CB61
Coles Grn, Bushey 94 CC46
Coles Grn, Loug. 85 EN39
Coles Grn Ct NW2 119 CU61
Coles Grn Rd NW2 119 CU60
Coles Hill, Hem.H. 40 BG18
Coles La (Brasted), West. 240 EW123
Colesburg Rd, Beck. 203 DZ97
Colescroft Hill, Pur. 235 DN115
Colesdale (Cuffley), Pot.B. 65 DL30
Coleshill La (Coleshill), Amer. 88 AJ45
Coleshill Rd, Tedd. 177 CE93
Colesmead Rd, Red. 250 DF131
Colestown St SW11 160 DE82
Colet Cl N13 99 DP51
Colet Gdns W14 159 CX77
Colet Rd, Brwd. 109 GC43
Colets Orchard (Otford), Sev. 241 FH116
Coley Av, Wok. 227 BA118
Coley St WC1 274 C5
Coley St WC1 141 DM70
Colfe Rd SE23 183 DY88
Colgate Pl, Enf. 83 EA38
Government Row
Colgrove, Welw.G.C. 29 CW10
Colham Av, West Dr. 134 BL74
Colham Grn Rd, Uxb. 134 BN71
Colham Mill Rd, West Dr. 154 BK75
Colham Rd, Uxb. 134 BM70
Colham Roundabout, Uxb. 134 BN73
Colin Cl NW9 118 CS56
Colin Cl, Croy. 203 DZ104
Colin Cl, Dart. 188 FP86
Colin Cl, W.Wick. 204 EF104
Colin Cres NW9 119 CT56
Colin Dr NW9 119 CT57
Colin Gdns NW9 119 CT57
Colin Par NW9 118 CS56
Edgware Rd
Colin Pk Rd NW9 118 CS56
Colin Rd NW10 139 CU65
Colin Rd, Cat. 236 DU123
Colin Way, Slou. 151 AP76
Colina Ms N15 121 DP57
Harringay Rd
Colina Rd N15 121 DP57
Colindale Av NW9 118 CR55
Colindale Av, St.Alb. 43 CF22
Colindale Business Pk NW9 118 CQ55
Colindeep Gdns NW4 119 CU57
Colindeep La NW4 118 CS55
Colindeep La NW9 118 CS55
Colinette Rd SW15 159 CW84
Colinton Rd, Ilf. 126 EV61
Coliston Pas SW18 180 DA87
Coliston Rd
Coliston Rd SW18 180 DA87
Collamore Av SW18 180 DE88
Collapit Cl, Har. 116 CB57
Collard Av, Loug. 85 EQ40
Collard Grn, Loug. 85 EQ40
Collard Av
College App SE10 163 EC79
College Av, Egh. 173 BB93
College Av, Epsom 217 CT114
College Av, Grays 170 GB77
College Av, Har. 95 CE53
College Av, Slou. 152 AS76
College Cl E9 122 DW64
Median Rd
College Cl N18 100 DT50
College Cl, Add. 194 BK104
College Cl, Grays 170 GC77
College Cl, Har. 95 CE52
College Cl, Twick. 177 CD88
Meadway
College Cl, Ware 33 DX07
College Ct (Cheshunt), Wal.Cr. 66 DW30
College Cres NW3 140 DD65
College Cres, Red. 250 DG131
College Cres, Wind. 151 AP82
College Cross N1 141 DN66
College Dr, Ruis. 115 BU59
College Dr, T.Ditt. 197 CE101
College Gdns E4 101 EB45
College Gdns N18 100 DT50
College Gdns SE21 182 DS88
College Gdns SW17 180 DE89

College Gdns, Enf. 82 DR39
College Gdns, Ilf. 124 EL57
College Gdns, N.Mal. 199 CT99
College Gate, Harl. 51 EQ15
College Grn SE19 182 DS94
College Gro NW1 141 DK67
St. Pancras Way
College Hill EC4 275 J10
College Hill Rd, Har. 95 CF53
College La NW5 121 DH63
College La, Hat. 44 CS20
College La, Wok. 226 AW119
College Ms SW1 277 P6
College Ms SW18 180 DB85
St. Ann's Hill
College Pk Cl SE13 163 ED84
College Pk Rd N17 100 DT51
College Rd
College Pl E17 124 EE56
College Pl NW1 141 DJ67
College Pl SW10 160 DC80
Hortensia Rd
College Pl, Harl. 51 ER15
College Pl, St.Alb. 42 CC20
College Pt E15 144 EF65
College Rd E17 123 EC57
College Rd N17 100 DT51
College Rd N21 99 DN47
College Rd NW10 139 CW68
College Rd SE19 182 DT92
College Rd SE21 182 DS87
College Rd SW19 180 DD93
College Rd W13 137 CH72
College Rd, Abb.L. 59 BT31
College Rd, Brom. 184 EG94
College Rd, Croy. 202 DR103
College Rd, Enf. 82 DR40
College Rd, Epsom 217 CU114
College Rd (Northfleet), Grav. 190 GB85
College Rd, Grays 170 GC77
College Rd, Guil. 258 AX135
College Rd (Harrow on the Hill), Har. 117 CE58
College Rd (Harrow Weald), Har. 95 CE53
College Rd, Hert. 32 DW13
College Rd, Hodd. 49 DZ15
College Rd, Islw. 157 CF81
College Rd, St.Alb. 43 CH21
College Rd, Slou. 131 AM74
College Rd, Swan. 207 FE95
College Rd (Cheshunt), Wal.Cr. 66 DV30
College Rd, Wem. 117 CK60
College Rd, Wok. 227 BB116
College Row E9 123 DX64
College Slip, Brom. 204 EG95
College Sq, Harl. 51 EQ15
College Gate
College St EC4 275 K10
College St, St.Alb. 43 CD20
College Ter E3 143 DZ69
College Ter N3 97 CZ54
Hendon La
College Vw SE9 184 EK88
College Wk, Kings.T. 198 CL96
Grange Rd
College Way, Ashf. 174 BM91
College Way, Hayes 135 BU73
College Way, Nthwd. 93 BR51
College Way, Welw.G.C. 29 CX08
College Yd NW5 121 DH63
College La
Collent St E9 142 DW65
Coller Cres (Lane End), Dart. 189 FS91
Colless Rd N15 122 DT57
Collet Cl (Cheshunt), Wal.Cr. 67 DX28
Collet Gdns (Cheshunt), Wal.Cr. 67 DX28
Collet Cl
Collett Rd SE16 162 DU76
Collett Rd, Hem.H. 40 BJ20
Collett Rd, Ware 33 DX05
Collett Way, Sthl. 136 CB74
Colley Hill La (Hedgerley), Slou. 112 AT62
Colley La, Reig. 249 CY132
Colley Manor Dr, Reig. 249 CX133
Colley Way, Reig. 249 CY131
Colleyland, Rick. 73 BD42
Collier Cl E6 145 EP72
Trader Rd
Collier Cl, Epsom 216 CN107
Collier Dr, Edg. 96 CN54
Collier Row La, Rom. 105 FB52
Collier Row Rd, Rom. 104 EZ53
Collier St N1 274 B1
Collier St N1 141 DM68
Collier Way, Guil. 243 BD132
Colliers, Cat. 252 DU125
Colliers Cl, Wok. 226 AV117
Colliers Shaw, Kes. 222 EK105
Colliers Water La, Th.Hth. 201 DN99
Collindale Av, Erith 167 FB79
Collindale Av, Sid. 186 EU88
Collingbourne Rd W12 139 CV74
Collingham Gdns SW5 160 DB77
Collingham Pl SW5 160 DB77
Collingham Rd SW5 160 DB77
Collings Cl N22 99 DM51
Whittington Rd
Collington Cl (Northfleet), Grav. 190 GE87
Beresford Rd
Collingtree Rd SE26 182 DW91
Collingwood Av N10 120 DG55
Collingwood Av, Surb. 198 CQ102
Collingwood Cl SE20 202 DV95
Collingwood Cl, Horl. 269 DH147
Collingwood Cl, Twick. 176 CA86
Collingwood Cres, Guil. 243 BA133
Collingwood Dr (London Colney), St.Alb. 61 CK25
Collingwood Pl, Walt. 195 BU104
Collingwood Rd E17 123 EA58
Collingwood Rd N15 122 DS56
Collingwood Rd, Mitch. 200 DE96
Collingwood Rd, Sutt. 200 DA104
Collingwood Rd, Uxb. 135 BP70
Collingwood St E1 142 DV70
Collins Av, Stan. 96 CL54
Collins Dr, Ruis. 116 BW61
Collins Meadow, Harl. 51 EP15
Collins Rd N5 122 DQ63
Collins Sq SE3 164 EF82
Tranquil Vale
Collins St SE3 164 EE82
Collins Way, Brwd. 109 GE43
Collin's Yd N1 141 DP67
Islington Grn
Collinson St SE1 279 H5
Collinson Wk SE1 279 H5
Collinswood Rd (Farnham Common), Slou. 111 AN60
Collinwood Av, Enf. 82 DW41
Collinwood Gdns, Ilf. 125 EM57
Collis All, Twick. 177 CE88
The Grn
Colls Rd SE15 162 DW81
Collum Grn Rd, Slou. 111 AR62
Collyer Av, Croy. 219 DL105
Collyer Pl SE15 162 DU81
Peckham High St
Collyer Rd, Croy. 219 DL105
Collyer Rd (London Colney), St.Alb. 61 CJ27
Colman Cl, Epsom 233 CW117
Colman Rd E16 144 EJ71
Colman Way, Red. 250 DE132
Colmans Hill (Peaslake), Guil. 261 BS144
Colmar Cl E1 143 DX70
Alderney Rd
Colmer Pl, Har. 95 CD52
Colmer Rd SW16 201 DL95
Colmore Ms SE15 162 DV81
Colmore Rd, Enf. 82 DW42
Colnbridge Cl, Stai. 173 BE91
Clarence St
Colnbrook Bypass, Slou. 153 BF80
Colnbrook Bypass, West Dr. 154 BH80
Colnbrook Cl (London Colney), St.Alb. 62 CL28
Colnbrook Ct, Slou. 153 BF81
Colnbrook St SE1 278 F7
Colnbrook St SE1 161 DP76
Colndale Rd (Colnbrook), Slou. 153 BE82
Colne Av, Rick. 92 BG47
Colne Av, Wat. 75 BV44
Colne Av, West Dr. 154 BJ75
Colne Bk (Horton), Slou. 153 BC83
Colne Br Retail Pk, Wat. 76 BX44
Lower High St
Colne Cl, S.Ock. 149 FW73
Colne Ct, Epsom 216 CQ105
Colne Dr, Rom. 106 FM51
Colne Dr, Walt. 196 BX104
Colne Gdns (London Colney), St.Alb. 62 CL27
Colne Ho, Bark. 145 EP65
Colne Mead, Rick. 92 BG47
Uxbridge Rd
Colne Orchard, Iver 133 BF72
Colne Pk Caravan Site, West Dr. 154 BJ77
Colne Reach, Stai. 173 BF85
Colne Rd E5 123 DY63
Colne Rd N21 100 DR45
Colne Rd, Twick. 177 CE88
Colne St E13 144 EG69
Grange Rd
Colne Valley, Upmin. 129 FS58
Colne Way, Hem.H. 40 BM15
Colne Way, Stai. 173 BB90
Colne Way, Wat. 76 BY37
Colnedale Rd, Uxb. 114 BK64
Colney Hatch La N10 99 DH54
Colney Hatch La N11 98 DF51
Colney Heath La, St.Alb. 44 CL20
Colney Rd, Dart. 188 FM86
Cologne Rd SW11 160 DD84
Colomb St SE10 164 EE78
Colombo Rd, Ilf. 125 EQ60
Colombo St SE1 278 F3
Colombo St SE1 141 DP74
Colonels La, Cher. 194 BG100
Colonels Wk, Enf. 81 DP41
Colonial Av, Twick. 176 CC85
Colonial Rd, Felt. 175 BS87
Colonial Rd, Slou. 152 AU75
Colonial Way, Wat. 76 BX39
Colonnade WC1 273 P5
Colonnade WC1 141 DL70
Colonnade Wk SW1 277 H9
Colonnade Wk SW1 161 DH77
Colonnades, The W2 140 DB72
Colonsay, Hem.H. 41 BQ22
Colosseum Ter NW1 141 DH70
Albany St
Colson Gdns, Loug. 85 EP42
Colson Rd
Colson Path, Loug. 85 EN42
Colson Rd, Croy. 202 DS103
Colson Rd, Loug. 85 EP42
Colson Way SW16 181 DJ91
Colsterworth Rd N15 122 DT56
Colston Av, Cars. 218 DE105
Colston Cl, Cars. 218 DF105
West St
Colston Cres (Cheshunt), Wal.Cr. 65 DP27
Colston Rd E7 144 EK65
Colston Rd SW14 158 CQ84
Colt Hatch, Harl. 35 EP14
Hobtoe Rd
Colthurst Cres N4 122 DQ61
Colthurst Dr N9 100 DV48
Plevna Rd
Colthurst Gdns, Hodd. 49 ED15
Coltishall Rd, Horn. 148 FJ65
Coltness Cres SE2 166 EV78
Colton Gdns N17 122 DQ55
Colton Rd, Har. 117 CE57
Coltsfoot, Welw.G.C. 30 DB11
Coltsfoot, The, Hem.H. 39 BE21
Coltsfoot Ct, Grays 170 GD79
Coltsfoot Dr, Guil. 243 BA131
Coltsfoot Dr, West Dr. 134 BL72
Coltsfoot Path, Rom. 106 FJ52
Columbia Av, Edg. 96 CP53
Columbia Av, Ruis. 115 BV60
Columbia Av, Wor.Pk. 199 CT101
Columbia Rd E2 275 P2
Columbia Rd E2 142 DT69
Columbia Rd E13 144 EF70
Columbia Sq SW14 158 CQ84
Upper Richmond Rd W
Columbia Wf Rd, Grays 170 GA79
Columbine Av E6 144 EL71
Columbine Av, S.Croy. 219 DP108
Columbine Way SE13 163 EC82
Columbine Way, Rom. 106 FL53
Columbus Ct SE16 142 DW74
Rotherhithe St
Columbus Ctyd E14 143 EA74
West India Av
Columbus Gdns, Nthwd. 93 BU53
Columbus Sq, Erith 167 FF79
Colva Wk N19 121 DH61
Chester Rd
Colvestone Cres E8 122 DT64
Colview Ct SE9 184 EK88
Mottingham La
Colville Est N1 142 DS67
Colville Gdns W11 139 CZ72
Colville Hos W11 139 CZ72
Colville Ms W11 139 CZ72
Lonsdale Rd
Colville Pl W1 273 L7
Colville Rd E11 123 EC62
Colville Rd E17 101 DY54
Colville Rd N9 100 DV46
Colville Rd W3 158 CP76
Colville Rd W11 139 CZ72
Colville Sq W11 139 CZ72
Colville Sq Ms W11 139 CZ72
Portobello Rd
Colville Ter W11 139 CZ72
Colvin Cl SE26 182 DW92
Colvin Gdns E4 101 EC48
Colvin Gdns E11 124 EH56
Colvin Gdns, Ilf. 103 EQ53
Colvin Gdns, Wal.Cr. 83 DX35
Colvin Rd E6 144 EL66
Colvin Rd, Th.Hth. 201 DN99
Colwall Gdns, Wdf.Grn. 102 EG50
Colwell Rd SE22 182 DT85
Colwick Cl N6 121 DK59
Colwith Rd W6 159 CW79
Colwood Gdns SW19 180 DD94
Colworth Gro SE17 279 J9
Colworth Rd E11 124 EE58
Colworth Rd, Croy. 202 DU102
Colwyn Av, Grnf. 137 CF68
Colwyn Cl SW16 181 DJ92
Colwyn Cres, Houns. 156 CC81
Colwyn Grn NW9 118 CS58
Snowdon Dr
Colwyn Rd NW2 119 CV62
Colyer Cl N1 141 DM68
Colyer Cl SE9 185 EP89
Colyer Rd (Northfleet), Grav. 190 GC89
Colyers Cl, Erith 167 FD81
Colyers La, Erith 167 FC81
Colyers Wk, Erith 167 FE81
Colyers La
Colyton Cl, Well. 166 EX81
Colyton Cl, Wem. 137 CJ65
Bridgewater Rd
Colyton Cl, Wok. 226 AW118
Colyton Rd SE22 182 DV85
Colyton Way N18 100 DU50
Combe Av SE3 164 EF80
Combe Bk Dr (Sundridge), Sev. 240 EY122
Combe Bottom, Guil. 260 BM137
Combe La, Guil. 261 BP135
Combe La, Walt. 213 BT109
Combe Lo SE7 164 EJ79
Elliscombe Rd
Combe Martin, Kings.T. 178 CQ92
Combe Ms SE3 164 EF80
Combe Rd, Gdmg. 258 AS143
Combe Rd, Wat. 75 BT44
Combe St, Hem.H. 40 BJ20
Combedale Rd SE10 164 EG78
Combemartin Rd SW18 179 CY87
Comber Cl NW2 119 CV62
Comber Gro SE5 162 DQ81
Combermere Rd SW9 161 DM83
Combermere Rd, Mord. 200 DB100
Comberton Rd E5 122 DV61
Combeside SE18 165 ET80
Combwell Cres SE2 166 EU76
Comely Bk Rd E17 123 EC57
Comer Cres, Sthl. 156 CC75
Windmill Av
Comeragh Cl, Wok. 226 AU120
Comeragh Ms W14 159 CY78
Comeragh Rd W14 159 CY78
Comerford Rd SE4 163 DY84
Comet Cl E12 124 EK63
Comet Cl, Purf. 168 FN77
Comet Cl, Wat. 59 BT34
Comet Pl SE8 163 EA80
Comet Rd, Hat. 45 CT18
Comet Rd (Stanwell), Stai. 174 BK87
Comet St SE8 163 EA80
Comet Way, Hat. 44 CS19
Comfort St SE15 162 DT79
St. Georges Way
Comforts Fm Av, Oxt. 254 EF133
Comfrey Ct, Grays 170 GD79
Commerce Rd N22 99 DM53
Commerce Rd, Brent. 157 CJ80
Commerce Way, Croy. 201 DM103
Commercial Pl, Grav. 191 GJ86
Commercial Rd E1 142 DU72
Commercial Rd E14 142 DW72
Commercial Rd N17 100 DS51
Commercial Rd N18 100 DS50
Commercial Rd, Guil. 258 AX135
Commercial Rd, Stai. 174 BG93
Commercial St E1 275 P5
Commercial St E1 142 DT70
Commercial Way NW10 138 CP68
Commercial Way SE15 162 DT80
Commercial Way, Wok. 227 AZ117
Commerell St SE10 164 EE78
Commodity Quay E1 142 DT73
East Smithfield
Commodore St E1 143 DY70
Common, The W5 138 CL73
Common, The, Berk. 39 AZ17
Common, The (Shalford), Guil. 258 AY141
Common, The (Wonersh), Guil. 259 BB143
Common, The, Hat. 45 CU17
Common, The, Kings L. 58 BG32
Common, The, Rich. 177 CK90
Common, The, Sthl. 156 BW77
Common, The, Stan. 95 CE47
Common, The, West Dr. 154 BJ77
Common Cl, Wok. 210 AX114
Common Gdns, Berk. 39 BB17
Common Gate Rd, Rick. 73 BD43
Common La (New Haw), Add. 212 BJ109
Common La, Dart. 187 FG89
Common La (Claygate), Esher 215 CG108
Common La, Kings L. 58 BM28
Common La, Rad. 77 CE39
Common La (Burnham), Slou. 111 AK62
Common La, Wat. 77 CE39
Common La (Eton), Wind. 151 AQ78
Common Rd SW13 159 CU83
Common Rd, Brwd. 109 GC50
Common Rd (Claygate), Esher 215 CG107
Common Rd, Lthd. 230 BY121
Common Rd, Red. 266 DF136
Common Rd, Rick. 73 BD42
Common Rd (Langley), Slou. 153 BA77
Common Rd, Stan. 95 CD49
Common Rd, Wal.Abb. 50 EK22
Common Rd (Dorney), Wind. 150 AJ77
Common Rd (Eton Wick), Wind. 151 AM78
Common Wd (Farnham Common), Slou. 111 AQ63
Common Wd La (Penn), H.Wyc. 88 AD46
Commondale SW15 159 CW83
Commonfield La SW17 180 DE92
Tooting Gro
Commonfield Rd, Bans. 218 DA114
Commonfields, Harl. 35 ES14
Commonmeadow La, Wat. 60 CB33
Commons, The, Welw.G.C. 30 DA12
Commons La, Hem.H. 40 BL19
Commons Wd Caravan Club Site, Welw.G.C. 30 DA13
Ascots La
Commonside, Epsom 232 CN115
Commonside, Harl. 51 ES19
Fern Hill La
Commonside, Kes. 222 EJ105
Commonside (Bookham), Lthd. 230 CA122
Commonside Cl, Couls. 235 DP120
Coulsdon Rd
Commonside Cl, Sutt. 218 DB111
Commonside E, Mitch. 200 DF97
Commonside Rd, Harl. 51 ES19
Commonside W, Mitch. 200 DF97
Commonwealth Av W12 139 CV73
Commonwealth Av, Hayes 135 BR72
Commonwealth Rd N17 100 DU52
Commonwealth Rd, Cat. 236 DU123
Commonwealth Way SE2 166 EV78
Commonwood La, Kings L. 74 BH35
Community Cl, Houns. 155 BV81
Community Cl, Uxb. 115 BQ62
Community La N7 121 DK64
Community Rd E15 123 ED64
Community Rd, Grnf. 136 CC67
Community Wk, Esher 214 CC105
High St
Community Way, Rick. 75 BP43
Barton Way
Como Rd SE23 183 DY89
Como St, Rom. 127 FD57
Compass Hill, Rich. 177 CK86
Compass Ho SW18 160 DB84
Smugglers Way
Compass Pt, Berk. 38 AS17
Admiral Way
Compayne Gdns NW6 140 DB66
Comport Grn (New Addington), Croy. 222 EE112
Compton Av E6 144 EK68
Compton Av N1 141 DP65
Compton Av N6 120 DE59
Compton Av, Brwd. 109 GC46
Compton Av, Rom. 127 FH55
Compton Cl E3 143 EA71
Compton Cl NW1 273 J3
Compton Cl NW11 119 CX62
The Vale
Compton Cl W13 137 CG72
Compton Cl, Edg. 96 CQ52
Pavilion Way
Compton Cl, Esher 214 CC106
Compton Ct SE19 182 DS92
Victoria Cres
Compton Ct, Slou. 131 AL72
Brook Cres
Compton Cres N17 100 DQ52
Compton Cres W4 158 CQ79
Compton Cres, Chess. 216 CL107
Compton Cres, Nthlt. 136 BX67
Compton Gdns, Add. 212 BH106
Monks Cres
Compton Gdns, St.Alb. 60 CB26
Compton Pas EC1 274 G4
Compton Pl WC1 273 P4
Compton Pl, Erith 167 FF79
Compton Pl, Wat. 94 BY48
Compton Ri, Pnr. 116 BY57
Compton Rd N1 141 DP65
Compton Rd N21 99 DN46
Compton Rd NW10 139 CX69
Compton Rd SW19 179 CZ93
Compton Rd, Croy. 202 DV102
Compton Rd, Hayes 135 BS73
Compton St EC1 274 F4
Compton St EC1 141 DP70
Compton Ter N1 141 DP65
Computer Ho, Brent. 157 CJ79
Comreddy Cl, Enf. 81 DP39
Comus Pl SE17 279 M9
Comus Pl SE17 162 DS77
Comyn Rd SW11 160 DE84
Comyne Rd, Wat. 75 BT36
Comyns, The, Bushey 94 CC46
Comyns Cl E16 144 EF71
Comyns Rd, Dag. 146 FA66
Conant Ms E1 142 DU73
Back Ch La
Conaways Cl, Epsom 217 CU110
Concanon Rd SW2 161 DM84
Concert Hall App SE1 278 C3
Concert Hall App SE1 141 DM74
Concord Cl, Nthlt. 136 BX69
Britannia Cl
Concord Rd W3 138 CP70
Concord Rd, Enf. 82 DW43
Concorde Cl, Houns. 156 CB82
Lampton Rd
Concorde Cl, Uxb. 134 BL68
Concorde Dr E6 145 EM71
Concorde Dr, Hem.H. 40 BK20
Concorde Way, Slou. 151 AQ75
Concourse, The N9 100 DU47
New Rd
Concourse, The NW9 97 CT53
Concrete Cotts (Wisley), Wok. 228 BL116
Wisley La
Condell Rd SW8 161 DJ81
Conder St E14 143 DY72
Salmon La
Conderton Rd SE5 162 DQ83
Condor Ct, Guil. 258 AW136
Millmead Ter
Condor Path, Nthlt. 136 CA68
Brabazon Rd
Condor Rd, Stai. 194 BH97
Condor Wk, Horn. 147 FH66
Heron Flight Av
Condover Cres SE18 165 EP80
Condray Pl SW11 160 DE80
Conduit, The (Bletchingley), Red. 252 DS129
Conduit Av SE10 163 ED81
Crooms Hill
Conduit Ct WC2 273 P10
Conduit La N18 100 DW50
Conduit La, Croy. 220 DU106
Conduit La, Enf. 83 DY44
Morson Rd
Conduit La, S.Croy. 220 DU106
Conduit La E, Hodd. 49 EB17
Conduit La W, Hodd. 49 EA17
Conduit Ms W2 140 DD72
Conduit Pas W2 140 DD72
Conduit Pl
Conduit Pl W2 140 DD72
Conduit Rd SE18 165 EP78
Conduit Rd, Slou. 152 AY78
Conduit St W1 273 J10
Conduit St W1 141 DH73
Conduit Way NW10 138 CQ66
Conegar Ct, Slou. 132 AS74
Conewood St N5 121 DP62
Coney Acre SE21 182 DQ88
Coney Burrows E4 102 EE47
Wyemead Cres
Coney Cl, Hat. 45 CV19
Coney Gro, Uxb. 134 BN69
Coney Hill Rd, W.Wick. 204 EE103
Coney Way SW8 161 DM79
Coneyberry, Reig. 266 DC138
Coneybury (Bletchingley), Red. 252 DS134
Coneybury Cl, Warl. 236 DV119
Coneydale, Welw.G.C. 29 CX07
Coneygrove Path, Nthlt. 136 BY65
Arnold Rd
Conference Cl E4 101 EC47
Greenbank Cl
Conference Rd SE2 166 EW77
Conford Dr (Shalford), Guil. 258 AY141
Congleton Gro SE18 165 EQ78
Congo Rd SE18 165 ER78
Congress Rd SE2 166 EW77
Congreve Rd SE9 165 EM83
Congreve Rd, Wal.Abb. 68 EE33
Congreve St SE17 279 M8
Congreve St SE17 162 DS77
Congreve Wk E16 144 EK71
Conical Cor, Enf. 82 DQ40
Coniers Way, Guil. 243 BB131
Conifer Av, Rom. 105 FB50
Conifer Cl, Orp. 223 ER105
Conifer Cl, Reig. 250 DA132
Conifer Cl, Wal.Cr. 66 DT29
Conifer Dr, Brwd. 108 FX50
Conifer Gdns SW16 181 DL90
Conifer Gdns, Enf. 82 DS44
Conifer Gdns, Sutt. 200 DB103
Conifer La, Egh. 173 BC92
Conifer Way, Hayes 135 BU73
Longmead Rd
Conifer Way, Swan. 207 FC95
Conifer Way, Wem. 117 CJ62
Conifers, Wey. 213 BS105
Conifers, The, Hem.H. 39 BF23
Conifers, The, Wat. 76 BW35
Conifers Cl, Tedd. 177 CH94
Coniger Rd SW6 160 DA82
Coningesby Dr, Wat. 75 BS39
Coningham Ms W12 139 CU74
Percy Rd
Coningham Rd W12 139 CV74
Coningsby Bk, St.Alb. 42 CC24
Coningsby Cl, Hat. 45 CX24
Coningsby Cotts W5 157 CK75
Coningsby Rd
Coningsby Dr, Pot.B. 64 DD33
Coningsby Gdns E4 101 EB51
Coningsby La, Maid. 150 AC81
Coningsby Rd N4 121 DP59
Coningsby Rd W5 157 CJ75
Coningsby Rd, S.Croy. 220 DQ109
Conington Rd SE13 163 EB82
Conisbee Ct N14 81 DJ43
Conisborough Cres SE6 183 EC90
Coniscliffe Cl, Chis. 205 EN95
Coniscliffe Rd N13 100 DQ48
Conista Ct, Wok. 226 AT116
Roundthorn Way
Coniston Av, Bark. 145 ES66
Coniston Av, Grnf. 137 CH69
Coniston Av, Upmin. 128 FQ63
Coniston Av, Well. 165 ES83
Coniston Cl N20 98 DC48
Coniston Cl SW13 159 CT80
Lonsdale Rd
Coniston Cl SW20 199 CX100
Coniston Cl W4 158 CQ81
Coniston Cl, Bark. 145 ES66
Coniston Av
Coniston Cl, Bexh. 167 FC81
Coniston Cl, Dart. 187 FH88
Coniston Cl, Erith 167 FE80
Coniston Cl, Hem.H. 41 BQ21
Coniston Cres, Slou. 130 AJ71
Coniston Gdns N9 100 DW46
Coniston Gdns NW9 118 CR57
Coniston Gdns, Ilf. 124 EL56
Coniston Gdns, Pnr. 115 BU56
Coniston Gdns, Sutt. 218 DD107
Coniston Gdns, Wem. 117 CJ60
Coniston Ho SE5 162 DQ80
Coniston Rd N10 99 DH54
Coniston Rd N17 100 DU51
Coniston Rd, Bexh. 167 FC81
Coniston Rd, Brom. 184 EE93
Coniston Rd, Couls. 235 DJ116
Coniston Rd, Croy. 202 DU101
Coniston Rd, Kings L. 58 BM28
Coniston Rd, Twick. 176 CB86
Coniston Rd, Wok. 227 BB120
Coniston Wk E9 122 DW64
Clifden Rd
Coniston Way, Chess. 198 CL104
Coniston Way, Egh. 173 BB94
Coniston Way, Horn. 127 FG64
Coniston Way, Reig. 250 DE133
Conistone Way N7 141 DL66
Conlan St W10 139 CY70
Conley Rd NW10 138 CS65
Conley St SE10 164 EE78
Pelton Rd
Connaught Av E4 101 ED45
Connaught Av SW14 158 CQ83
Connaught Av, Ashf. 174 BL91
Connaught Av, Barn. 98 DF46
Connaught Av, Enf. 82 DS40
Connaught Av, Grays 170 GB75
Connaught Av, Houns. 176 BY85
Connaught Av, Loug. 84 EK42
Connaught Br E16 144 EK73
Connaught Business Cen, Mitch. 200 DF99
Wandle Way
Connaught Cl E10 123 DY61
Connaught Cl W2 272 B9
Connaught Cl, Enf. 82 DS40
Connaught Cl, Hem.H. 40 BN18

Connaught Cl, Sutt. 200 DD103
Connaught Cl, Uxb. 135 BQ70
New Rd
Connaught Ct E17 123 EB56
Orford Rd
Connaught Ct, Buck.H. 102 EH46
Connaught Dr NW11 120 DA56
Connaught Dr, Wey. 212 BN111
Connaught Gdns N10 121 DH57
Connaught Gdns N13 99 DP49
Connaught Gdns, Berk. 38 AT16
Connaught Gdns, Mord. 200 DC98
Connaught Hill, Loug. 84 EK42
Connaught La, Ilf. 125 ER61
Connaught Rd
Connaught Ms SE18 165 EN78
Connaught Ms, Ilf. 125 ER61
Connaught Rd
Connaught Pl W2 272 D10
Connaught Pl W2 140 DF73
Connaught Rd E4 102 EE45
Connaught Rd E11 123 ED60
Connaught Rd E16 144 EK74
Connaught Rd E17 123 EA57
Connaught Rd N4 121 DN59
Connaught Rd NW10 138 CS67
Connaught Rd SE18 165 EN78
Connaught Rd W13 137 CH73
Connaught Rd, Barn. 79 CX44
Connaught Rd, Har. 95 CF53
Connaught Rd, Horn. 128 FK62
Connaught Rd, Ilf. 125 ER61
Connaught Rd, N.Mal. 198 CS98
Connaught Rd, Rich. 178 CM85
Albert Rd
Connaught Rd, St.Alb. 42 CC17
Connaught Rd, Slou. 152 AV75
Connaught Rd, Sutt. 200 DD103
Connaught Rd, Tedd. 177 CD92
Connaught Roundabout E16 144 EK73
Connaught Br
Connaught Sq W2 272 D9
Connaught Sq W2 140 DF72
Connaught St W2 272 B9
Connaught St W2 140 DE72
Connaught Way N13 99 DP49
Connell Cres W5 138 CM70
Connemara Cl, Borwd. 78 CR44
Percheron Rd
Connicut La, Lthd. 246 CB128
Connington Cres E4 101 ED48
Connop Rd, Enf. 83 DX38
Connor Cl E11 124 EE59
Connor Cl, Ilf. 103 EQ53
Connor Rd, Dag. 126 EZ63
Connor St E9 143 DX67
Lauriston Rd
Conolly Rd W7 137 CE74
Conquerors Hill (Wheathampstead), St.Alb. 28 CL07
Conquest Rd, Add. 212 BG106
Conrad Cl, Grays 170 GB75
Conrad Dr, Wor.Pk. 199 CW102
Conrad Gdns, Grays 170 GA75
Conrad Ho N16 122 DS64
Cons St SE1 278 E4
Consfield Av, N.Mal. 199 CU98
Consort Cl, Brwd. 108 FW50
Consort Ms, Islw. 177 CD85
Consort Rd SE15 162 DV81
Consort Way, Horl. 268 DG148
Consort Way (Denham), Uxb. 113 BF58
Knowland Way
Consort Way E, Horl. 269 DH149
Constable Av E16 144 EH74
Wesley Av
Constable Cl NW11 120 DB58
Constable Cl, Hayes 135 BQ69
Charville La
Constable Cres N15 122 DU57
Constable Gdns, Edg. 96 CN53
Constable Gdns, Islw. 177 CD85
Constable Ms, Dag. 126 EV63
Stonard Rd
Constable Rd (Northfleet), Grav. 190 GE90
Constable Wk SE21 182 DT90
Constance Cres, Brom. 204 EF101
Constance Rd, Croy. 201 DP101
Constance Rd, Enf. 82 DS44
Constance Rd, Sutt. 218 DC105
Constance Rd, Twick. 176 CB87
Constance St E16 144 EL74
Albert Rd
Constantine Pl (Hillingdon), Uxb. 134 BM67
Constantine Rd NW3 120 DE63
Constitution Hill SW1 277 H4
Constitution Hill SW1 161 DH75
Constitution Hill, Grav. 191 GJ88
Constitution Hill, Wok. 226 AY119
Constitution Ri SE18 165 EN81
Consul Av, Dag. 147 FC69
Consul Gdns, Swan. 187 FG93
Content St SE17 279 J9
Content St SE17 162 DR77
Contessa Cl, Orp. 223 ES106
Control Twr Rd, Gat. 268 DD153
Control Twr Rd (Heathrow Airport), Houns. 154 BN83
Convair Wk, Nthlt. 136 BX69
Kittiwake Rd
Convent Cl, Beck. 183 EC94
Convent Gdns W5 157 CJ77
Convent Gdns W11 139 CZ72
Kensington Pk Rd
Convent Hill SE19 182 DQ93
Convent La, Cob. 213 BS111
Seven Hills Rd
Convent Rd, Ashf. 174 BN92
Convent Rd, Wind. 151 AN82
Convent Way, Sthl. 156 BW77
Conway Cl (Loudwater), H.Wyc. 88 AC53
Conway Cl, Rain. 147 FG66
Conway Cl, Stan. 95 CG51
Conway Cres, Grnf. 137 CE68
Conway Cres, Rom. 126 EW59
Conway Dr, Ashf. 175 BQ93
Conway Dr, Hayes 155 BQ76
Conway Dr, Sutt. 218 DB107
Conway Gdns, Enf. 82 DS38
Conway Gdns, Grays 170 GB80
Conway Gdns, Mitch. 201 DK98
Conway Gdns, Wem. 117 CJ59
Conway Gro W3 138 CR71
Conway Ms W1 273 K5
Conway Rd N14 99 DL48
Conway Rd N15 121 DP57
Conway Rd NW2 119 CW61
Conway Rd SE18 165 ER77
Conway Rd SW20 199 CW95
Conway Rd, Felt. 176 BX92
Conway Rd, Houns. 176 BZ87
Conway Rd (Heathrow Airport), Houns. 155 BP83
Inner Ring E
Conway Rd, Maid. 130 AH72
Conway St E13 144 EG70
Conway St W1 273 K5
Conway St W1 141 DJ71
Conway Wk, Hmptn. 176 BZ93
Fearnley Cres
Cony Cl (Cheshunt), Wal.Cr. 66 DS26
Conybeare NW3 140 DE66
King Henry's Rd
Conybury Cl, Wal.Abb. 68 EG32
Conyer St E3 143 DY68
Conyers, Harl. 35 EQ13
Conyers Cl, Walt. 214 BX106
Conyers Cl, Wdf.Grn. 102 EE51
Conyers Rd SW16 181 DK92
Conyers Way, Loug. 85 EP41
Cooden Cl, Brom. 184 EH94
Plaistow La
Cook Ct SE16 142 DW74
Rotherhithe St
Cook Rd, Dag. 146 EY67
Cook Sq, Erith 167 FF80
Cooke Cl E14 143 EA74
Cabot Sq
Cookes Cl E11 124 EF61
Cookes La, Sutt. 217 CY107
Cookham Cl, Sthl. 156 CB75
Cookham Cres SE16 163 DX75
Marlow Way
Cookham Dene Cl, Chis. 205 ER95
Cookham Hill, Orp. 206 FA104
Cookham Rd, Sid. 186 FA94
Cookham Rd, Swan. 206 FA95
Cookhill Rd SE2 166 EV75
Cooks Cl, Rom. 105 FC53
Cook's Hole Rd, Enf. 81 DP38
Cooks Mead, Bushey 76 CB44
Cook's Rd E15 143 EB68
Cooks Rd SE17 161 DP79
Cooks Spinney, Harl. 36 EU13
Cooks Vennel, Hem.H. 40 BG18
Cooks Way, Hat. 45 CV20
Cookson Gro, Erith 167 FB80
Cool Oak La NW9 118 CS59
Coolfin Rd E16 144 EG72
Coolgardie Av E4 101 EC50
Coolgardie Av, Chig. 103 EN48
Coolgardie Rd, Ashf. 175 BQ92
Coolhurst Rd N8 121 DK58
Coomassie Rd W9 139 CZ70
Bravington Rd
Coombe, The, Bet. 248 CR131
Coombe Av, Croy. 220 DS105
Coombe Av, Sev. 241 FH120
Coombe Bk, Kings.T. 198 CS95
Coombe Cl, Edg. 96 CM54
Coombe Cl, Houns. 156 CA84
Coombe Cor N21 99 DP46
Coombe Cres, Hmptn. 176 BY94
Coombe Dr, Add. 211 BF107
Coombe Dr, Kings.T. 178 CR94
Coombe Dr, Ruis. 115 BV60
Coombe End, Kings.T. 178 CR94
Coombe Gdns SW20 199 CU96
Coombe Gdns, Berk. 38 AT18
Coombe Gdns, N.Mal. 199 CT98
Coombe Hts, Kings.T. 178 CS94
Coombe Hill Ct, Wind. 151 AL83
Coombe Hill Glade, Kings.T. 178 CS94
Coombe Hill Rd, Kings.T. 178 CS94
Coombe Hill Rd, Rick. 92 BG45
Coombe Ho Chase, N.Mal. 198 CR95
Coombe La SW20 199 CV96
Coombe La, Croy. 220 DV106
Coombe La W, Kings.T. 199 CU95
Coombe Lea, Brom. 204 EL97
Coombe Neville, Kings.T. 178 CR94
Coombe Pk, Kings.T. 178 CR92
Coombe Ridings, Kings.T. 178 CQ92
Coombe Ri, Brwd. 109 FZ46
Coombe Ri, Kings.T. 198 CQ95
Coombe Rd N22 99 DN53
Coombe Rd NW10 118 CR62
Coombe Rd SE26 182 DV91
Coombe Rd W4 158 CS78
Coombe Rd W13 157 CH76
Northcroft Rd
Coombe Rd, Bushey 94 CC45
Coombe Rd, Croy. 220 DR105
Coombe Rd, Grav. 191 GJ89
Coombe Rd, Hmptn. 176 BZ93
Coombe Rd, Kings.T. 198 CN95
Coombe Rd, N.Mal. 198 CS96
Coombe Rd, Rom. 128 FM55
Coombe Vale, Ger.Cr. 112 AY60
Coombe Wk, Sutt. 200 DB104
Coombe Way (Byfleet), W.Byf. 212 BM112
Coombe Wd Hill, Pur. 220 DQ112
Coombe Wd Rd, Kings.T. 178 CQ92
Coombefield Cl, N.Mal. 198 CS99
Coombehurst Cl, Barn. 80 DF40
Coombelands La, Add. 212 BG107
Coomber Way, Croy. 201 DK101
Coombermere Cl, Wind. 151 AP82
Coombes Rd, Dag. 146 EZ67
Coombes Rd (London Colney), St.Alb. 61 CH26
Coombewood Dr, Rom. 126 EZ58
Coombfield Dr (Lane End), Dart. 189 FR91
Coombs St N1 274 G1
Coombs St N1 141 DP68
Coomer Ms SW6 159 CZ79
Coomer Pl
Coomer Pl SW6 159 CZ79
Coomer Rd SW6 159 CZ79
Coomer Pl
Cooms Wk, Edg. 96 CQ53
East Rd
Cooper Av E17 101 DX53
Cooper Cl SE1 278 E5
Cooper Cl, Green. 189 FT85
Cooper Cl, Horl. 269 DN148
Cooper Ct E15 123 EB64
Clays La
Cooper Cres, Cars. 200 DF104
Cooper Rd NW4 119 CX58
Cooper Rd NW10 119 CU64
Cooper Rd, Croy. 219 DN105
Cooper Rd, Guil. 258 AY136
Cooper St E16 144 EF71
Lawrence St
Cooper Way, Berk. 38 AW19
High St
Cooper Way, Slou. 151 AP76
Cooperage Cl N17 100 DT51
Brantwood Rd
Coopers Cl E1 142 DW70
Coopers Cl, Chig. 104 EV47
Coopers Cl, Dag. 147 FB65
Coopers Cl (South Darenth), Dart. 208 FQ95
Coopers Cl, Stai. 173 BE92
Cooper's Ct, Ware 33 DY06
Crane Mead
Coopers Cres, Borwd. 78 CQ39
Coopers Grn La, Hat. 28 CS13
Coopers Grn La, St.Alb. 44 CL17
Coopers Grn La, Welw.G.C. 28 CQ14
Coopers Hill La, Egh. 172 AY91
Coopers Hill Rd (Nutfield), Red. 251 DM133
Coopers La E10 123 EB60
Coopers La NW1 141 DK68
Cooper's La SE12 184 EH89
Coopers La, Pot.B. 64 DD31
Coopers La Rd, Pot.B. 64 DE31
Coopers Rd SE1 162 DT78
Coopers Rd (Northfleet), Grav. 190 GE88
Coopers Rd, Pot.B. 64 DC30
Cooper's Row EC3 275 P10
Coopers Row, Iver 133 BC70
Coopers Shaw Rd, Til. 171 GK80
Coopers Wk E15 123 ED64
Maryland St
Coopers Wk (Cheshunt), Wal.Cr. 67 DX28
Cooper's Yd SE19 182 DS93
Westow Hill
Coopersale Common, Epp. 70 EX28
Coopersale La, Epp. 86 EU37
Coopersale Rd E9 123 DX64
Coopersale St, Epp. 70 EW32
Coopersall Cl, Wdf.Grn. 102 EJ52
Navestock Cres
Coote Gdns, Dag. 126 EZ62
Coote Rd, Bexh. 166 EZ81
Coote Rd, Dag. 126 EZ62
Cope Pl W8 160 DA76
Cope St SE16 163 DX77
Copeland Dr E14 163 EA77
Copeland Rd E17 123 EB57
Copeland Rd SE15 162 DU82
Copeman Cl SE26 182 DW92
Copeman Rd, Brwd. 109 GD45
Copenhagen Gdns W4 158 CQ75
Copenhagen Pl E14 143 DZ72
Copenhagen St N1 141 DL67
Copenhagen Way, Walt. 195 BV104
Copers Cope Rd, Beck. 183 DZ93
Copford Cl, Wdf.Grn. 102 EL51
Copford Wk N1 142 DQ67
Popham St
Copgate Path SW16 181 DM93
Copinger Wk, Edg. 96 CP53
North Rd
Copland Av, Wem. 117 CK64
Copland Cl, Wem. 117 CJ64
Copland Ms, Wem. 138 CL65
Copland Rd
Copland Rd, Wem. 138 CL65
Copleigh Dr, Tad. 233 CY120
Copleston Ms SE15 162 DT82
Copleston Rd
Copleston Pas SE15 162 DT83
Copleston Rd SE15 162 DT83
Copley Cl SE17 161 DP79
Hillingdon St
Copley Cl W7 137 CF71
Copley Cl, Red. 250 DE132
Copley Cl, Wok. 226 AS119
Copley Dene, Brom. 204 EK95
Copley Pk SW16 181 DM93
Copley Rd, Stan. 95 CJ50
Copley St E1 143 DX71
Copley Way, Tad. 233 CX120
Copmans Wick, Rick. 73 BD43
Copnor Way SE15 162 DS80
Diamond St
Coppard Gdns, Chess. 215 CJ107
Copped Hall SE21 182 DR89
Glazebrook Cl
Coppelia Rd SE3 164 EF84
Coppen Rd, Dag. 126 EZ59
Copper Beech Cl NW3 140 DD65
Daleham Ms
Copper Beech Cl, Grav. 191 GK87
Copper Beech Cl, Hem.H. 39 BF23
Copper Beech Cl, Ilf. 103 EN53
Copper Beech Cl, Orp. 206 EW99
Rookery Gdns
Copper Beech Cl, Wind. 151 AK81
Copper Beech Cl, Wok. 226 AV121
Copper Beech Ct, Loug. 85 EN39
Copper Beech Rd, S.Ock. 149 FW69
Copper Beeches, Islw. 157 CD81
Eversley Cres
Copper Cl SE19 182 DT94
Auckland Rd
Copper Ct, Saw. 36 EX06
Brook Rd
Copper Mead Cl NW2 119 CW62
Copper Mill Dr, Islw. 157 CF82
Copper Mill La SW17 180 DC91
Copper Ridge (Chalfont St. Peter), Ger.Cr. 91 AZ50
Copper Row SE1 279 P3
Copper Row SE1 142 DT74
Copperas St SE8 163 EB79
Copperbeech Cl NW3 120 DD64
Akenside Rd
Copperdale Rd, Hayes 155 BU75
Copperfield, Chig. 103 ER51
Copperfield App, Chig. 103 ER51
Copperfield Av, Uxb. 134 BN71
Copperfield Cl, S.Croy. 220 DQ111
Copperfield Ct, Lthd. 231 CG121
Kingston Rd
Copperfield Ct, Pnr. 116 BZ56
Copperfield Way
Copperfield Dr N15 122 DT56
Copperfield Gdns, Brwd. 108 FV46
Copperfield Ms N18 100 DS50
Copperfield Ri, Add. 211 BF106
Copperfield Rd E3 143 DY70
Copperfield Rd SE28 146 EW72
Copperfield St SE1 278 G4
Copperfield St SE1 161 DP75
Copperfield Ter, Slou. 132 AV73
Mirador Cres
Copperfield Way, Chis. 185 EQ93
Copperfield Way, Pnr. 116 BZ56
Copperfields, Beac. 89 AL50
Copperfields, Dart. 188 FL86
Spital St
Copperfields (Fetcham), Lthd. 230 CC122
Copperfields, Welw.G.C. 30 DC10
Forresters Dr
Copperfields Way, Rom. 106 FK53
Coppergate Cl, Brom. 204 EH95
Coppergate Ct, Wal.Abb. 68 EG34
Farthingale La
Copperkins Gro, Amer. 55 AP36
Copperkins La, Amer. 55 AM35
Coppermill La E17 122 DW58
Coppermill La, Rick. 91 BE52
Coppermill La (Harefield), Uxb. 91 BE52
Coppermill Rd (Wraysbury), Stai. 173 BA86
Copperwood, Hert. 32 DT09
Coppetts Cl N12 98 DE52
Coppetts Rd N10 98 DG54
Coppice, The, Ashf. 175 BP93
School Rd
Coppice, The, Beac. 89 AR51
School La
Coppice, The, Enf. 81 DP42
Coppice, The, Hem.H. 41 BP19
Coppice, The, Wat. 76 BW44
Coppice, The, West Dr. 134 BL72
Coppice Cl SW20 199 CW97
Coppice Cl, Beck. 203 EB98
Coppice Cl, Hat. 45 CT22
Coppice Cl, Ruis. 115 BR58
Coppice Cl, Stan. 95 CF51
Coppice Dr SW15 179 CV86
Coppice Dr (Wraysbury), Stai. 172 AX87
Coppice End, Wok. 227 BE116
Coppice Fm Rd (Penn), H.Wyc. 88 AC45
Coppice Hatch, Harl. 51 ER17
Coppice La, Reig. 249 CZ132
Coppice Path, Chig. 104 EV49
Coppice Row, Epp. 85 EM36
Coppice Wk N20 98 DA48
Coppice Way E18 124 EF56
Coppice Way (Hedgerley), Slou. 111 AR60
Coppies Gro N11 98 DG49
Copping Cl, Croy. 220 DS105
Tipton Dr
Coppings, The, Hodd. 33 EA14
Danemead
Coppins, The (New Addington), Croy. 221 EB107
Coppins, The, Har. 95 CE51
Coppins, The, Welw.G.C. 29 CU11
Coppins Cl, Berk. 38 AS19
Coppins La, Iver 133 BF71
Coppock Cl SW11 160 DE82
Coppsfield, W.Mol. 196 CA97
Hurst Rd
Copse, The E4 102 EF46
Copse, The, Amer. 55 AQ38
Copse, The, Beac. 88 AJ51
Copse, The, Cat. 252 DU126
Tupwood La
Copse, The, Hem.H. 39 BE18
Copse, The, Hert. 32 DU09
Copse, The (Fetcham), Lthd. 230 CB123
Copse, The (South Nutfield), Red. 267 DL136
Copse Av, W.Wick. 203 EB104
Copse Cl SE7 164 EH79
Copse Cl (Chilworth), Guil. 259 BC140
Copse Cl, Nthwd. 93 BQ54
Copse Cl, Slou. 131 AM74
Copse Cl, West Dr. 154 BK76
Copse Edge Av, Epsom 217 CT113
Copse Glade, Surb. 197 CK102
Copse Hill SW20 179 CV94
Copse Hill, Harl. 51 EP18
Copse Hill, Pur. 219 DL113
Copse Hill, Sutt. 218 DB108
Copse La (Jordans), Beac. 90 AS52
Copse La, Horl. 269 DJ147
Copse Rd, Cob. 213 BV113
Copse Rd, Red. 266 DC136
Copse Rd, Wok. 226 AT118
Copse Vw, S.Croy. 221 DX109
Copse Way, Chesh. 54 AN27
Copse Wd, Iver 133 BD67
Copse Wd Ct, Reig. 250 DE132
Green La
Copse Wd Way, Nthwd. 93 BQ52
Copsem Dr, Esher 214 CB107
Copsem La, Esher 214 CC107
Copsem La (Oxshott), Lthd. 214 CC111
Copsem Way, Esher 214 CC107
Copsen Wd, Lthd. 214 CC111
Copsewood Cl, Sid. 185 ES86
Copsewood Rd, Wat. 75 BV39
Copshall Cl, Harl. 51 ES19
Copsleigh Av, Red. 266 DG141
Copsleigh Cl (Salfords), Red. 266 DG140
Copsleigh Way, Red. 266 DG140
Copt Hill La, Tad. 233 CY120
Coptefield Dr, Belv. 166 EX76
Coptfold Rd, Brwd. 108 FW47
Copthall Av EC2 275 L8
Copthall Av EC2 142 DR72
Copthall Bldgs EC2 275 K8
Copthall Cl EC2 275 K8
Copthall Cl (Chalfont St. Peter), Ger.Cr. 91 AZ52
Copthall Cor (Chalfont St. Peter), Ger.Cr. 90 AY52
Copthall Ct EC2 142 DR72
Copthall Dr NW7 97 CU52
Copthall Gdns NW7 97 CU52
Copthall Gdns, Twick. 177 CF88
Copthall La (Chalfont St. Peter), Ger.Cr. 90 AY52
Copthall Rd E, Uxb. 114 BN61
Copthall Rd W, Uxb. 114 BN61
Copthall Way (New Haw), Add. 211 BF110
Copthorn Av, Brox. 49 DZ21
Copthorne Av SW12 181 DK87
Copthorne Av, Brom. 205 EM103
Copthorne Av, Ilf. 103 EP51
Copthorne Chase, Ashf. 174 BM91
Ford Rd
Copthorne Cl, Rick. 74 BM43
Copthorne Cl, Shep. 195 BQ100
Copthorne Gdns, Horn. 128 FN57
Copthorne Ms, Hayes 155 BS77
Copthorne Ri, S.Croy. 220 DR113
Copthorne Rd, Lthd. 231 CH120
Copthorne Rd, Rick. 74 BM44
Coptic St WC1 273 P7
Coptic St WC1 141 DL71
Copwood Cl N12 98 DD49
Coral Cl, Rom. 126 EW55
Coral Gdns, Hem.H. 40 BM19
Coral Row SW11 160 DC83
Gartons Way
Coral St SE1 278 E5
Coral St SE1 161 DN75
Coraline Cl, Sthl. 136 BZ69
Coralline Wk SE2 166 EW75
Corals Mead, Welw.G.C. 29 CX10
Coram Cl, Berk. 38 AW20
Coram Grn, Brwd. 109 GD44
Coram St WC1 273 P5
Coram St WC1 141 DL70
Coran Cl N9 101 DX45
Corban Rd, Houns. 156 CA83
Corbar Cl, Barn. 80 DD38
Corbden Cl SE15 162 DT81
Corbet Cl, Wall. 200 DG102
Corbet Ct EC3 275 L9
Corbet Pl E1 275 P6
Corbet Rd, Epsom 216 CS110
Corbets Av, Upmin. 128 FP64
Corbets Tey Rd, Upmin. 128 FP63
Corbett Cl, Croy. 221 ED112
Corbett Gro N22 99 DL52
Corbett Ho, Wat. 94 BW48
Corbett Rd E11 124 EJ58
Corbett Rd E17 123 EC55
Corbetts La SE16 162 DW77
Rotherhithe New Rd
Corbetts Pas SE16 162 DW77
Rotherhithe New Rd
Corbicum E11 124 EE59
Corbiere Ct SW19 179 CX93
Thornton Rd
Corbiere Ho N1 142 DS67
Corbins La, Har. 116 CB62
Corbridge Cres E2 142 DV68
Corby Cl (Englefield Grn), Egh. 172 AW93
Corby Cl, St.Alb. 60 CA25
Corby Cres, Enf. 81 DL42
Corby Dr (Englefield Grn), Egh. 172 AV93
Corby Rd NW10 138 CR68
Corby Way E3 143 EA70
Knapp Rd
Corbylands Rd, Sid. 185 ES87
Corbyn St N4 121 DL60
Corcorans, Brwd. 108 FV44
Cord Way E14 163 EA76
Mellish St
Cordelia Cl SE24 161 DP84
Cordelia Gdns, Stai. 174 BL87
Cordelia Rd, Stai. 174 BL87
Cordelia St E14 143 EB72
Cordell Cl (Cheshunt), Wal.Cr. 67 DY28
Cordell Ho N15 122 DT57
Newton Rd
Corder Cl, St.Alb. 42 CA23
Corderoy Pl, Cher. 193 BE100
Cording St E14 143 EB71
Chrisp St
Cordingley Rd, Ruis. 115 BR61
Cordons Cl (Chalfont St. Peter), Ger.Cr. 90 AX53
Cordova Rd E3 143 DY69
Cordrey Gdns, Couls. 235 DL115
Cordwainers Wk E13 144 EG68
Clegg St
Cordwell Rd SE13 184 EE85
Corefield Cl N11 98 DG47
Benfleet Way
Corelli Rd SE3 164 EL82
Corfe Av, Har. 116 CA63
Corfe Cl, Ash. 231 CJ118
Corfe Cl, Borwd. 78 CR41
Chester Rd
Corfe Cl, Hayes 136 BW72
Corfe Cl, Hem.H. 40 BL21
Corfe Gdns, Slou. 131 AN73
Avebury
Corfe Twr W3 158 CP75
Corfield Rd N21 81 DM43
Corfield St E2 142 DV69
Corfton Rd W5 138 CL72
Coriander Av E14 143 ED72
Coriander Cres, Guil. 242 AU129
Cories Cl, Dag. 126 EX61
Corinium Cl, Wem. 118 CM63
Corinium Gate, St.Alb. 42 CA22
Corinium Ind Est, Amer. 72 AT38
Raans Rd
Corinne Rd N19 121 DJ63
Corinthian Manorway, Erith 167 FD77
Corinthian Rd, Erith 167 FD77
Corinthian Way (Stanwell), Stai. 174 BK87
Clare Rd
Cork Sq E1 142 DV74
Smeaton St
Cork St W1 277 K1
Cork St W1 141 DJ73
Cork St Ms W1 277 K1
Cork Tree Way E4 101 DY50
Corker Wk N7 121 DM61
Corkran Rd, Surb. 197 CK101
Corkscrew Hill, W.Wick. 203 ED103
Corlett St NW1 272 B6
Corlett St NW1 140 DE71
Cormongers La (Nutfield), Red. 251 DK131
Cormont Rd SE5 161 DP81
Cormorant Cl E17 101 DX53
Banbury Rd
Cormorant Ho, Enf. 83 DX43
Alma Rd
Cormorant Pl, Sutt. 217 CZ106
Sandpiper Rd
Cormorant Rd E7 124 EF64
Cormorant Wk, Horn. 147 FH65
Heron Flight Av
Corn Mead, Welw.G.C. 29 CW06
Corn Mill Dr, Orp. 205 ET101
Corn Way E11 123 ED62
Cornbury Rd, Edg. 95 CK52
Corncroft, Hat. 45 CV16
Cornelia Pl, Erith 167 FE79
Queen St
Cornelia St N7 141 DM65
Cornell Cl, Sid. 186 EY93
Cornell Way, Rom. 104 FA50
Corner, The, W.Byf. 212 BG113
Corner Fm Cl, Tad. 233 CW122
Corner Grn SE3 164 EG82
Corner Hall, Hem.H. 40 BJ22
Corner Hall Av, Hem.H. 40 BK22
Corner Ho St WC2 277 P2
Corner Mead NW9 97 CT52
Corner Meadow, Harl. 52 EU19
Corner Vw, Hat. 45 CW24
Cornerfield, Hat. 45 CV15
Corners, Welw.G.C. 30 DA07
Cornerside, Ashf. 175 BQ94
Corney Reach Way W4 158 CS80
Corney Rd W4 158 CS79
Cornfield Cl, Uxb. 134 BK68
The Greenway
Cornfield Rd, Bushey 76 CB42
Cornfield Rd, Reig. 266 DC135

Cornfields, Gdmg. 258 AT143
Cornfields, Hem.H. 40 BH21
Cornflower La, Croy. 203 DX102
Cornflower Ter SE22 182 DV86
Cornflower Way, Rom. 106 FL53
Cornford Cl, Brom. 204 EG99
Cornford Gro SW12 181 DH89
Cornhill EC3 275 L9
Cornhill EC3 142 DR72
Cornhill Cl, Add. 194 BH103
Cornhill Dr, Enf. 83 DY37
Ordnance Rd
Cornish Ct N9 100 DV45
Cornish Gro SE20 182 DV94
Cornish Ho SE17 161 DP79
Otto St
Cornish Ho, Brent. 158 CM78
Green Dragon La
Cornmill, Wal.Abb. 67 EB33
Cornmill La SE13 163 EB83
Cornmill Ms, Wal.Abb. 67 EB33
Highbridge St
Cornmow Dr NW10 119 CT64
Cornshaw Rd, Dag. 126 EX60
Cornsland, Brwd. 108 FX48
Cornsland Ct, Brwd. 108 FW48
Cornthwaite Rd E5 122 DW62
Cornwall Av E2 142 DW69
Cornwall Av N3 98 DA52
Cornwall Av N22 99 DL53
Cornwall Av (Claygate), Esher 215 CF108
The Causeway
Cornwall Av, Slou. 131 AQ70
Cornwall Av, Sthl. 136 BZ71
Cornwall Av, Well. 165 ES83
Cornwall Av (Byfleet), W.Byf. 212 BM114
Cornwall Cl, Bark. 145 ET65
Cornwall Cl, Horn. 128 FN56
Cornwall Cl, Wal.Cr. 67 DY33
Cornwall Cl (Eton Wick), Wind. 151 AL78
Cornwall Cres W11 139 CY73
Cornwall Dr, Orp. 186 EW94
Cornwall Gdns NW10 139 CV65
Cornwall Gdns SW7 160 DC76
Cornwall Gdns Wk SW7 160 DB76
Cornwall Gdns
Cornwall Gate, Purf. 168 FN77
Fanns Ri
Cornwall Gro W4 158 CS78
Cornwall Ms S SW7 160 DC76
Cornwall Ms W SW7 160 DB76
Cornwall Gdns
Cornwall Rd N4 121 DN59
Cornwall Rd N15 122 DR57
Cornwall Rd N18 100 DU50
Fairfield Rd
Cornwall Rd SE1 278 D2
Cornwall Rd SE1 141 DN74
Cornwall Rd, Brwd. 108 FV43
Cornwall Rd, Croy. 201 DP103
Cornwall Rd, Dart. 168 FM83
Cornwall Rd (Claygate), Esher 215 CG108
Cornwall Rd, Har. 116 CC58
Cornwall Rd, Pnr. 94 BZ52
Cornwall Rd, Ruis. 115 BT62
Cornwall Rd, St.Alb. 43 CE22
Cornwall Rd, Sutt. 217 CZ108
Cornwall Rd, Twick. 177 CG88
Cornwall Rd, Uxb. 134 BK65
Cornwall Rd, Wind. 172 AU86
Cornwall St E1 142 DV73
Watney St
Cornwall Ter NW1 272 E5
Cornwall Ter Ms NW1 272 E5
Cornwall Way, Stai. 173 BE93
Cornwallis Av N9 100 DV47
Cornwallis Av SE9 185 ER89
Cornwallis Cl, Cat. 236 DQ122
Drake Av
Cornwallis Cl, Erith 167 FF79
Cornwallis Gro N9 100 DV47
Cornwallis Rd E17 123 DX56
Cornwallis Rd N9 100 DV47
Cornwallis Rd N19 121 DL61
Cornwallis Rd, Dag. 126 EX63
Cornwallis Sq N19 121 DL61
Cornwallis Wk SE9 165 EM83
Cornwell Av, Grav. 191 GJ90
Cornwood Cl N2 120 DD57
Cornwood Dr E1 142 DW72
Cornworthy Rd, Dag. 126 EW64
Corona Rd SE12 184 EG87
Coronation Av N16 122 DT62
Victorian Rd
Coronation Av (George Grn), Slou. 132 AY72
Coronation Av, Wind. 152 AT81
Coronation Cl, Bex. 186 EX86
Coronation Cl, Ilf. 125 EQ56
Coronation Dr, Horn. 127 FH63
Coronation Hill, Epp. 69 ET30
Coronation Rd E13 144 EJ69
Coronation Rd NW10 138 CM69
Coronation Rd, Hayes 155 BT77
Coronation Rd, Ware 33 DX05
Coronation Wk, Twick. 176 BZ88
Coronet, The, Horl. 269 DJ150
Coronet St N1 275 M3
Coronet St N1 142 DS69
Corporation Av, Houns. 156 BY84
Corporation Row EC1 274 E4
Corporation Row EC1 141 DN70
Corporation St E15 144 EE68
Corporation St N7 121 DL64
Corran Way, S.Ock. 149 FV73
Corrance Rd SW2 161 DL84
Corri Av N14 99 DK49
Corrib Dr, Sutt. 218 DE106
Corrie Gdns, Vir.W. 192 AW101
Corrie Rd, Add. 212 BK105
Corrie Rd, Wok. 227 BC120
Corrigan Av, Couls. 218 DG114
Corringham Ct NW11 120 DB59
Corringham Rd
Corringham Ct, St.Alb. 43 CF19
Lemsford Rd
Corringham Rd NW11 120 DA59
Corringham Rd, Wem. 118 CN61
Corringway NW11 120 DB59
Corringway W5 138 CN70
Corris Grn NW9 118 CS58
Snowdon Dr
Corsair Cl, Stai. 174 BK87
Corsair Rd, Stai. 174 BL87
Corscombe Cl, Kings.T. 178 CQ92
Corsehill St SW16 181 DJ93
Corsham St N1 275 L3
Corsham St N1 142 DR69
Corsica St N5 141 DP65
Corsley Way E9 143 DZ65
Osborne Rd
Cortayne Rd SW6 159 CZ82
Cortis Rd SW15 179 CV86
Cortis Ter SW15 179 CV86
Corunna Rd SW8 161 DJ81
Corunna Ter SW8 161 DJ81
Corve La, S.Ock. 149 FV73
Corvette Sq SE10 163 ED79
Feathers Pl
Corwell Gdns, Uxb. 135 BQ72
Corwell La, Uxb. 135 BQ72
Cory Dr, Brwd. 109 GB45
Cory Wright Way (Wheathampstead), St.Alb. 28 CL06
Coryton Path W9 139 CZ70
Ashmore Rd
Cosbycote Av SE24 182 DQ85
Cosdach Av, Wall. 219 DK108
Cosedge Cres, Croy. 219 DN106
Cosgrove Cl N21 100 DQ47
Cosgrove Cl, Hayes 136 BY70
Kingsash Dr
Cosmo Pl WC1 274 A6
Cosmur Cl W12 159 CT76
Cossall Wk SE15 162 DV81
Cossar Ms SW2 181 DN86
Tulse Hill
Cosser St SE1 278 D6
Cosser St SE1 161 DN76
Costa St SE15 162 DU82
Costead Manor Rd, Brwd. 108 FV46
Costell's Meadow, West. 255 ER126
Costins Wk, Berk. 38 AW19
High St
Coston Wk SE4 163 DX84
Frendsbury Rd
Costons Av, Grnf. 137 CD69
Costons La, Grnf. 137 CD69
Cosway St NW1 272 C6
Cosway St NW1 140 DE71
Cotall St E14 143 EA72
Coteford Cl, Loug. 85 EP40
Coteford Cl, Pnr. 115 BU57
Coteford St SW17 180 DF91
Cotelands, Croy. 202 DS104
Cotesbach Rd E5 122 DW62
Cotesmore Gdns, Dag. 126 EW63
Cotesmore Rd, Hem.H. 39 BE21
Cotford Rd, Th.Hth. 202 DQ98
Cotham St SE17 279 J9
Cotherstone, Epsom 216 CR110
Cotherstone Rd SW2 181 DM88
Cotland Acres, Red. 266 DD136
Cotlandswick (London Colney), St.Alb. 61 CJ26
Cotleigh Av, Bex. 186 EX89
Cotleigh Rd NW6 140 DA66
Cotleigh Rd, Rom. 127 FD58
Cotman Cl NW11 120 DC58
Cotman Cl SW15 179 CX86
Westleigh Av
Cotman Gdns, Edg. 96 CN54
Cotman Ms, Dag. 126 EW64
Highgrove Rd
Cotmandene, Dor. 263 CH136
Cotmandene Cres, Orp. 206 EU96
Cotmans Cl, Hayes 135 BU74
Coton Rd, Well. 166 EU83
Cotsford Av, N.Mal. 198 CQ99
Cotswold, Hem.H. 40 BL17
Mendip Way
Cotswold Av, Bushey 76 CC44
Cotswold Cl, Bexh. 167 FE82
Cotswold Cl, Esher 197 CF104
Cotswold Cl, Kings.T. 178 CP93
Cotswold Cl, St.Alb. 43 CJ15
Chiltern Rd
Cotswold Cl, Slou. 151 AP76
Cotswold Cl, Stai. 174 BG92
Cotswold Cl, Uxb. 134 BJ67
Cotswold Ct EC1 275 H4
Cotswold Ct N11 98 DG49
Cotswold Gdns E6 144 EK69
Cotswold Gdns NW2 119 CX61
Cotswold Gdns, Brwd. 109 GE45
Cotswold Gdns, Ilf. 125 ER59
Cotswold Gate NW2 119 CY60
Cotswold Gdns
Cotswold Grn, Enf. 81 DM42
Cotswold Way
Cotswold Ms SW11 160 DD81
Battersea High St
Cotswold Ri, Orp. 205 ET100
Cotswold Rd (Northfleet), Grav. 190 GE90
Cotswold Rd, Hmptn. 176 CA93
Cotswold Rd, Rom. 106 FM54
Cotswold Rd, Sutt. 218 DB110
Cotswold St SE27 181 DP91
Norwood High St
Cotswold Way, Enf. 81 DM42
Cotswold Way, Wor.Pk. 199 CW103
Cotswolds, Hat. 45 CU20
Cottage Av, Brom. 204 EL102
Cottage Cl (Ottershaw), Cher. 211 BC107
Cottage Cl, Rick. 74 BM44
Scots Hill
Cottage Cl, Ruis. 115 BR60
Cottage Cl, Wat. 75 BT40
Cottage Fm Way, Egh. 193 BC97
Green Rd
Cottage Fld Cl, Sid. 186 EW88
Cottage Gdns, Wal.Cr. 66 DW29
Cottage Grn SE5 162 DR80
Cottage Gro SW9 161 DL83
Cottage Gro, Surb. 197 CK100
Cottage Homes NW7 97 CU49
Cottage Pk Rd (Hedgerley), Slou. 111 AR61
Cottage Pl SW3 276 B6
Cottage Pl SW3 160 DE76
Cottage Rd, Epsom 216 CR108
Cottage St E14 143 EB73
Cottage Wk N16 122 DT62
Smalley Cl
Cottenham Dr NW9 119 CT55
Cottenham Dr SW20 179 CV94
Cottenham Par SW20 199 CV96
Durham Rd
Cottenham Pk Rd SW20 179 CV94
Cottenham Pl SW20 179 CV94
Cottenham Rd E17 123 DZ56
Cotterells, Hem.H. 40 BJ21
Cotterells Hill, Hem.H. 40 BJ20
Cotterill Rd, Surb. 198 CL103
Cottesbrook St SE14 163 DY80
Nynehead St
Cottesbrooke Cl (Colnbrook), Slou. 153 BD81
Cottesloe Ms SE1 278 E6
Cottesmore Av, Ilf. 103 EN54
Cottesmore Gdns W8 160 DB76
Cottimore Av, Walt. 195 BV102
Cottimore Cres, Walt. 195 BV101
Cottimore La, Walt. 196 BW102
Cottimore Ter, Walt. 195 BV101
Cottingham Chase, Ruis. 115 BU62
Cottingham Rd SE20 183 DX94
Cottingham Rd SW8 161 DM80
Cottington Rd, Felt. 176 BX91
Cottington St SE11 278 E10
Cottle Way SE16 162 DW75
St. Marychurch St
Cotton Av W3 138 CR72
Cotton Cl, Dag. 146 EW66
Flamstead Rd
Cotton Dr, Hert. 32 DV08
Cotton Fld, Hat. 45 CV16
Cotton Hill, Brom. 183 ED91
Cotton La, Dart. 188 FQ86
Cotton La, Green. 188 FQ85
Cotton Rd, Pot.B. 64 DC31
Cotton Row SW11 160 DC83
Cotton St E14 143 EC73
Cottongrass Cl, Croy. 203 DX102
Cornflower La
Cottonmill Cres, St.Alb. 43 CD21
Cottonmill La, St.Alb. 43 CE23
Cottons App, Rom. 127 FD57
Cottons Ct, Rom. 127 FD57
Cottons Gdns E2 275 N2
Cottons La SE1 279 L2
Cotts Cl W7 137 CF71
Westcott Cres
Cotts Wd Dr, Guil. 243 BA129
Couchmore Av, Esher 197 CE103
Couchmore Av, Ilf. 103 EM54
Coulgate St SE4 163 DY83
Coulsdon Common, Cat. 236 DQ121
Coulsdon Ct Rd, Couls. 235 DM116
Coulsdon La, Couls. 234 DF119
Coulsdon Pl, Cat. 236 DR122
Coulsdon Ri, Couls. 235 DL117
Coulsdon Rd, Cat. 236 DQ122
Coulsdon Rd, Couls. 235 DM115
Coulser Cl, Hem.H. 40 BG17
Coulson Cl, Dag. 126 EW59
Coulson St SW3 276 D10
Coulson St SW3 160 DF77
Coulson Way (Burnham), Slou. 130 AH72
Coulter Cl, Hayes 136 BY70
Coulter Cl (Cuffley), Pot.B. 65 DK27
Coulter Rd W6 159 CV76
Coulton Av (Northfleet), Grav. 190 GE87
Council Av (Northfleet), Grav. 190 GC86
Council Cotts (Wisley), Wok. 228 BK115
Councillor St SE5 162 DQ80
Counter Ct SE1 142 DR74
Southwark St
Counter St SE1 279 M3
Counters Cl, Hem.H. 40 BG20
Countess Cl (Harefield), Uxb. 92 BJ54
Countess Rd NW5 121 DJ64
Countisbury Av, Enf. 100 DT45
Countisbury Gdns, Add. 212 BH106
Addlestone Pk
Country Way, Felt. 175 BV93
Country Way, Sun. 175 BV93
County Gate SE9 185 EQ90
County Gate, Barn. 80 DB44
County Gro SE5 162 DQ81
County Rd E6 145 EP71
County Rd, Th.Hth. 201 DP96
County St SE1 279 J7
County St SE1 162 DR76
Coupland Pl SE18 165 EQ78
Courage Cl, Horn. 128 FJ58
Courage Wk, Brwd. 109 GD44
Courcy Rd N8 121 DN55
Courier Rd, Dag. 147 FC70
Courland Gro SW8 161 DK81
Courland Rd, Add. 194 BH104
Courland St SW8 161 DK81
Course, The SE9 185 EN90
Coursers Rd (Colney Heath), St.Alb. 62 CN27
Court, The, Ruis. 116 BY63
Court, The, Warl. 237 DY118
Court Av, Belv. 166 EZ78
Court Av, Couls. 235 DN118
Court Av, Rom. 106 FN52
Court Bushes Rd, Whyt. 236 DU120
Court Cl, Har. 118 CL55
Court Cl, Maid. 150 AC77
Court Cl, Twick. 176 CB90
Court Cl, Wall. 219 DK108
Court Cl Av, Twick. 176 CB90
Court Cres, Chess. 215 CK106
Court Cres, Slou. 131 AR72
Court Cres, Swan. 207 FE98
Court Downs Rd, Beck. 203 EB96
Court Dr, Croy. 219 DM105
Court Dr, Maid. 130 AC68
Court Dr, Stan. 96 CL49
Court Dr, Sutt. 218 DE105
Court Dr, Uxb. 134 BM67
Court Fm Av, Epsom 216 CR106
Court Fm Rd SE9 184 EK89
Court Fm Rd, Nthlt. 136 CA66
Court Fm Rd, Warl. 236 DU118
Court Gdns N7 141 DN65
Court Grn Hts, Wok. 226 AW120
Court Haw, Bans. 234 DE115
Court Hill, Couls. 234 DE118
Court Hill, S.Croy. 220 DS112
Court Ho Gdns N3 98 DA51
Court La SE21 182 DS86
Court La, Epsom 216 CQ113
Court La, Iver 134 BG74
Court La (Burnham), Slou. 131 AK69
Court La (Dorney), Wind. 150 AG76
Court La Gdns SE21 182 DS87
Court Lawns (Penn), H.Wyc. 88 AC46
Court Lo Rd, Horl. 268 DE147
Court Mead, Nthlt. 136 BZ69
Court Par, Wem. 117 CH62
Court Rd SE9 184 EL89
Court Rd SE25 202 DT96
Court Rd, Bans. 234 DA116
Court Rd, Cat. 236 DR123
Court Rd (Lane End), Dart. 189 FS92
Court Rd, Gdse. 252 DW131
Court Rd, Maid. 130 AC69
Court Rd, Orp. 206 EV101
Court Rd, Sthl. 156 BZ77
Court Rd, Uxb. 115 BP64
Court St E1 142 DV71
Durward St
Court St, Brom. 204 EG96
Court Way NW9 118 CS56
Court Way W3 138 CQ71
Court Way, Ilf. 125 EQ55
Court Way, Rom. 106 FL54
Court Way, Twick. 177 CF87
Court Wd Dr, Sev. 256 FG124
Court Wd Gro, Croy. 221 DZ111
Court Wd La, Croy. 221 DZ111
Court Yd SE9 184 EL86
Courtauld Cl SE28 146 EU74
Pitfield Cres
Courtauld Rd N19 121 DK60
Courtaulds, Kings L. 58 BH30
Courtenay Av N6 120 DE59
Courtenay Av, Har. 94 CC53
Courtenay Av, Sutt. 218 DA109
Courtenay Dr, Beck. 203 ED96
Courtenay Dr, Grays 170 FZ76
Clifford Rd
Courtenay Gdns, Har. 94 CC54
Courtenay Gdns, Upmin. 128 FQ60
Courtenay Ms E17 123 DY57
Cranbrook Ms
Courtenay Pl E17 123 DY57
Courtenay Rd E11 124 EF62
Courtenay Rd E17 123 DX56
Courtenay Rd SE20 183 DX94
Courtenay Rd, Wem. 117 CK62
Courtenay Rd, Wok. 227 BA116
Courtenay Rd, Wor.Pk. 199 CW104
Courtenay Sq SE11 161 DN78
Courtenay St
Courtenay St SE11 278 D10
Courtenay St SE11 161 DN78
Courtens Ms, Stan. 95 CJ52
Courtfield W5 137 CJ71
Castlebar Hill
Courtfield Av, Har. 117 CF57
Courtfield Cl, Brox. 49 EA20
Courtfield Cres, Har. 117 CF57
Courtfield Gdns SW5 160 DB77
Courtfield Gdns W13 137 CG72
Courtfield Gdns, Ruis. 115 BT61
Courtfield Gdns (Denham), Uxb. 114 BG62
Courtfield Ms SW5 160 DB77
Courtfield Gdns
Courtfield Ri, W.Wick. 203 ED104
Courtfield Rd SW7 160 DB77
Courtfield Rd, Ashf. 175 BP93
Courthill Rd SE13 163 EC84
Courthope Rd NW3 120 DF63
Courthope Rd SW19 179 CY92
Courthope Rd, Grnf. 137 CD68
Courthope Vil SW19 179 CY94
Courthouse Rd N12 98 DB51
Courtland Av E4 102 EF47
Courtland Av NW7 96 CR48
Courtland Av SW16 181 DM94
Courtland Av, Ilf. 125 EM61
Courtland Dr, Chig. 103 EP48
Courtland Gro SE28 146 EX73
Courtland Rd E6 144 EL67
Harrow Rd
Courtlands, Rich. 158 CN84
Courtlands Av SE12 184 EH85
Courtlands Av, Brom. 204 EF102
Courtlands Av, Esher 214 BZ107
Courtlands Av, Hmptn. 176 BZ93
Courtlands Av, Rich. 158 CP82
Courtlands Av, Slou. 152 AX77
Courtlands Cl, Ruis. 115 BT59
Courtlands Cl, S.Croy. 220 DT110
Courtlands Cl, Wat. 75 BS35
Courtlands Cres, Bans. 234 DA116
Courtlands Dr, Epsom 216 CS107
Courtlands Dr, Wat. 75 BS37
Courtlands Rd, Surb. 198 CN101
Courtleas, Cob. 214 CA113
Courtleet Dr, Erith 167 FB81
Courtleigh Av, Barn. 80 DD38
Courtleigh Gdns NW11 119 CY56
Courtman Rd N17 100 DQ52
Courtmead Cl SE24 182 DQ86
Courtnell St W2 140 DA72
Courtney Cl SE19 182 DS93
Courtney Cres, Cars. 218 DF108
Courtney Pl, Cob. 214 BZ112
Courtney Pl, Croy. 201 DN104
Courtney Rd N7 121 DN64
Bryantwood Rd
Courtney Rd SW19 180 DE94
Courtney Rd, Croy. 201 DN104
Courtney Rd, Grays 171 GJ75
Courtney Rd (Heathrow Airport), Houns. 154 BN83
Courtney Way (Heathrow Airport), Houns. 154 BN82
Courtrai Rd SE23 183 DY86
Courtside N8 121 DK58
Courtway, Wdf.Grn. 102 EJ50
Courtway, The, Wat. 94 BY47
Courtyard, The N1 141 DM66
Courtyards, The, Slou. 153 BA75
Waterside Dr
Cousin La EC4 279 K1
Cousins Cl, West Dr. 134 BL73
Couthurst Rd SE3 164 EH79
Coutts Av, Chess. 216 CL106
Coutts Cres NW5 120 DG62
Coval Gdns SW14 158 CP84
Coval La SW14 158 CP84
Coval Rd SW14 158 CP84
Coveham Cres, Cob. 213 BU113
Covelees Wall E6 145 EN72
Covell Ct SE8 163 EA80
Reginald Sq
Covenbrook, Brwd. 109 GB48
Covent Gdn WC2 274 A10
Covent Gdn WC2 141 DL73
Coventry Cl E6 145 EM72
Harper Rd
Coventry Cl NW6 140 DA67
Kilburn High Rd
Coventry Cross E3 143 EC70
Gillender St
Coventry Rd E1 142 DV70
Coventry Rd E2 142 DV70
Coventry Rd SE25 202 DU98
Coventry Rd, Ilf. 125 EP60
Coventry St W1 277 M1
Coventry St W1 141 DK73
Coverack Cl N14 81 DJ44
Coverack Cl, Croy. 203 DY101
Coverdale, Hem.H. 40 BL17
Wharfedale
Coverdale Cl, Stan. 95 CH50
Coverdale Ct, Enf. 83 DY37
Raynton Rd
Coverdale Gdns, Croy. 202 DT104
Park Hill Ri
Coverdale Rd N11 98 DG51
Coverdale Rd NW2 139 CX66
Coverdale Rd W12 139 CV74
Coverdale Way, Slou. 131 AL70
Coverdales, The, Bark. 145 ER68
Coverley Cl E1 142 DU71
Coverley Cl, Brwd. 107 FW51
Wilmot Grn
Covert, The, Nthwd. 93 BQ53
Covert, The, Orp. 205 ES100
Covert Rd, Ilf. 103 ET51
Covert Way, Barn. 80 DC40
Coverton Rd SW17 180 DE92
Coverts, The, Brwd. 109 GA46
Coverts Rd (Claygate), Esher 215 CF109
Covet Wd Cl, Orp. 205 ET100
Lockesley Dr
Covey Cl SW19 200 DB96
Covington Gdns SW16 181 DP94
Covington Way SW16 181 DM93
Cow La, Grnf. 137 CD68
Cow La, Wat. 76 BW36
Cow Leaze E6 145 EN72
Cowan Cl E6 144 EL71
Oliver Gdns
Cowbridge, Hert. 32 DQ09
Cowbridge La, Bark. 145 EP66
Cowbridge Rd, Har. 118 CM56
Cowcross St EC1 274 F6
Cowcross St EC1 141 DP71
Cowden Rd, Orp. 205 ET101
Cowden St SE6 183 EA91
Cowdenbeath Path N1 141 DM67
Cowdray Rd, Uxb. 135 BQ67
Cowdray Way, Horn. 127 FF63
Cowdrey Cl, Enf. 82 DS40
Cowdrey Ct, Dart. 187 FH87
Cowdrey Rd SW19 180 DB92
Cowdry Rd E9 143 DY65
Wick Rd
Cowen Av, Har. 116 CC61
Cowgate Rd, Grnf. 137 CD68
Cowick Rd SW17 180 DF91
Cowings Mead, Nthlt. 136 BY66
Cowland Av, Enf. 82 DW42
Cowleaze Rd, Kings.T. 198 CL95
Cowles (Cheshunt), Wal.Cr. 66 DT27
Cowley Av, Cher. 193 BF101
Cowley Av, Green. 189 FT85
Cowley Business Pk, Uxb. 134 BJ69
Cowley Cl, S.Croy. 220 DW109
Cowley Cres, Uxb. 134 BJ71
Cowley Cres, Walt. 214 BW105
Cowley Hill, Borwd. 78 CP37
Cowley La E11 124 EE62
Cathall Rd
Cowley La, Cher. 193 BF101
Cowley Mill Rd, Uxb. 134 BH68
Cowley Pl NW4 119 CW57
Cowley Rd E11 124 EH57
Cowley Rd SW9 161 DN81
Cowley Rd SW14 158 CS83
Cowley Rd W3 139 CT74
Cowley Rd, Ilf. 125 EM59
Cowley Rd, Rom. 105 FH52
Cowley Rd, Uxb. 134 BJ68
Cowley St SW1 277 P6
Cowling Cl W11 139 CY74
Wilsham St
Cowlins, Harl. 36 EX11
New Rd
Cowper Av E6 144 EL66
Cowper Av, Sutt. 218 DD105
Cowper Av, Til. 171 GH81
Cowper Cl, Brom. 204 EK98
Cowper Cl, Cher. 193 BF100
Cowper Cl, Well. 186 EU85
Cowper Ct, Wat. 75 BU37
Cowper Cres, Hert. 31 DP07
Cowper Gdns N14 81 DJ44
Cowper Gdns, Wall. 219 DJ107
Cowper Rd N14 99 DH46
Cowper Rd N16 122 DS64
Cowper Rd N18 100 DU50
Cowper Rd SW19 180 DC93
Cowper Rd W3 138 CR74
Cowper Rd W7 137 CF73
Cowper Rd, Belv. 166 FA77
Cowper Rd, Berk. 38 AV19
Cowper Rd, Brom. 204 EK98
Cowper Rd, Chesh. 54 AP29
Cowper Rd, Hem.H. 40 BH21
Cowper Rd, Kings.T. 178 CM92
Cowper Rd, Rain. 147 FG70
Cowper Rd, Slou. 131 AN70
Cowper Rd, Welw.G.C. 29 CZ11
Cowper St EC2 275 L4
Cowper St EC2 142 DR70
Cowper Ter W10 139 CX71
St. Marks Rd
Cowslip Cl, Uxb. 134 BL66
Cowslip La (Mickleham), Dor. 247 CG129
Cowslip La, Wok. 226 AV115
Cowslip Rd E18 102 EH54
Cowslips, Welw.G.C. 30 DC10
Cowthorpe Rd SW8 161 DK81
Cox Cl, Rad. 62 CM32
Cox La, Chess. 216 CM105
Cox La, Epsom 216 CP106
Coxdean, Epsom 233 CW119
Coxe Pl (Wealdstone), Har. 117 CG56
Coxfield Cl, Hem.H. 40 BL21
Coxley Ri, Pur. 220 DQ113
Coxmount Rd SE7 164 EK78
Cox's Wk SE21 182 DU88
Coxson Way SE1 279 P5
Coxwell Rd SE18 165 ER78
Coxwell Rd SE19 182 DS94
Coxwold Path, Chess. 216 CL108
Garrison La
Cozens La E, Brox. 49 DZ23
Cozens La W, Brox. 49 DY22
Cozens Rd, Ware 33 DZ06
Crab Hill, Beck. 183 ED94
Crab Hill La, Red. 267 DM138
Crab La, Wat. 76 CB35
Crabbe Cres, Chesh. 54 AR29
Crabbs Cft Cl, Orp. 223 EQ106
Ladycroft Way
Crabtree Av, Rom. 126 EX56
Crabtree Av, Wem. 138 CL68
Crabtree Cl E2 275 P1
Crabtree Cl E2 142 DT68
Crabtree Cl, Beac. 88 AH54
Crabtree Cl, Bushey 76 CB43
Crabtree Cl, Hem.H. 40 BK22
Crabtree Cl (Bookham), Lthd. 246 CC126
Crabtree Ct E15 123 EB64
Clays La
Crabtree Ct, Hem.H. 40 BL22
Crabtree La
Crabtree Dr, Lthd. 231 CJ124
Crabtree Hill, Rom. 104 EZ45
Crabtree La SW6 159 CX80
Crabtree La (Westhumble), Dor. 247 CF130

This index reads in the sequence: Street Name / Postal District or Post Town / Map Page Number / Grid Reference **Cra - Cro**

Crabtree La, Hem.H. 40 BK22
Crabtree La (Bookham), Lthd. 246 CC126
Crabtree Manorway Ind Est, Belv. 167 FB76
Crabtree Manorway N, Belv. 167 FC75
Crabtree Manorway S, Belv. 167 FC76
Crabtree Rd, Egh. 193 BC96
Crace St NW1 273 M2
Crackley Meadow, Hem.H. 41 BP15
Craddock Rd, Enf. 82 DT41
Craddock St NW5 140 DG65
Prince of Wales Rd
Craddocks Av, Ash. 232 CL117
Craddocks Par, Ash. 232 CL117
Cradhurst Cl (Westcott), Dor. 262 CC137
Cradley Rd SE9 185 ER88
Cragg Av, Rad. 77 CF36
Craig Dr, Uxb. 135 BP72
Craig Gdns E18 102 EF54
Craig Mt, Rad. 77 CH35
Craig Pk Rd N18 100 DV50
Craig Rd, Rich. 177 CJ91
Craigavon Rd, Hem.H. 40 BM16
Craigdale Rd, Horn. 127 FF58
Craigen Av, Croy. 202 DV102
Craigerne Rd SE3 164 EH80
Craigholm SE18 165 EN82
Craiglands, St.Alb. 43 CK16
Craigmore Twr, Wok. 226 AY119
Guildford Rd
Craigmuir Pk, Wem. 138 CM67
Craignair Rd SW2 181 DN87
Craignish Av SW16 201 DM96
Craigs Ct SW1 277 P2
Craigs Wk (Cheshunt), Wal.Cr. 67 DX28
Davison Dr
Craigton Rd SE9 165 EM84
Craigweil Av, Rad. 77 CH35
Craigweil Cl, Stan. 95 CK50
Craigweil Dr, Stan. 95 CK50
Craigwell Av, Felt. 175 BU90
Craigwell Cl, Stai. 193 BE95
Craik Ct NW6 139 CZ68
Carlton Vale
Crail Row SE17 279 L9
Crakell Rd, Reig. 266 DC135
Cramer Ct, N.Mal. 198 CQ97
Warwick Rd
Cramer St W1 272 G7
Crammerville Wk, Rain. 147 FH70
Crammond Pk, Harl. 51 EN16
Cramond Cl W6 159 CY79
Cramond Ct, Felt. 175 BR88
Kilross Rd
Crampshaw La, Ash. 232 CM119
Crampton Rd SE20 182 DW93
Crampton St SE17 279 H9
Crampton St SE17 162 DQ77
Cramptons Rd, Sev. 241 FH120
Cranberry Cl, Nthlt. 136 BX68
Parkfield Av
Cranberry La E16 144 EE70
Cranborne Av, Sthl. 156 CA77
Cranborne Av, Surb. 198 CN104
Cranborne Cl, Hert. 32 DQ12
Cranborne Cl, Pot.B. 63 CY31
Cranborne Cres, Pot.B. 63 CY31
Cranborne Gdns, Upmin. 128 FP61
Cranborne Gdns, Welw.G.C. 29 CZ10
Cranborne Ind Est, Pot.B. 63 CY30
Cranborne Rd, Bark. 145 ER67
Cranborne Rd, Hat. 45 CV17
Cranborne Rd, Hodd. 49 EB16
Cranborne Rd, Pot.B. 63 CY30
Cranborne Rd (Cheshunt), Wal.Cr. 67 DX32
Cranborne Waye, Hayes 136 BW73
Cranbourn All WC2 273 N10
Cranbourn Pas SE16 162 DV75
Marigold St
Cranbourn St WC2 273 N10
Cranbourn St WC2 141 DK73
Cranbourne Av E11 124 EH56
Cranbourne Av, Wind. 151 AM82
Cranbourne Cl SW16 201 DL97
Cranbourne Cl, Horl. 269 DH146
Cranbourne Cl, Slou. 131 AQ74
Cranbourne Dr, Hodd. 33 EB13
Cranbourne Dr, Pnr. 116 BX57
Cranbourne Gdns NW11 119 CY57
Cranbourne Gdns, Ilf. 125 EQ55
Cranbourne Rd E12 124 EL64
High St N
Cranbourne Rd E15 123 EC63
Cranbourne Rd N10 99 DH54
Cranbourne Rd, Nthwd. 115 BT55
Cranbourne Rd, Slou. 131 AQ74
Cranbrook Cl, Brom. 204 EG100
Cranbrook Dr, Esher 196 CC102
Cranbrook Dr, Rom. 127 FH56
Cranbrook Dr, St.Alb. 44 CL20
Cranbrook Dr, Twick. 176 CB88
Cranbrook Ms E17 123 DZ57
Cranbrook Pk N22 99 DM53
Cranbrook Ri, Ilf. 125 EM59
Cranbrook Rd SE8 163 EA81
Cranbrook Rd SW19 179 CY94
Cranbrook Rd W4 158 CS78
Cranbrook Rd, Barn. 80 DD44
Cranbrook Rd, Bexh. 166 EZ81
Cranbrook Rd, Houns. 156 BZ84
Cranbrook Rd, Ilf. 125 EN60
Cranbrook Rd, Th.Hth. 202 DQ96
Cranbrook St E2 143 DX68
Mace St
Cranbury Rd SW6 160 DB82
Crane Av W3 138 CQ73
Crane Av, Islw. 177 CG85
Crane Cl, Dag. 146 FA65
Crane Cl, Har. 116 CC62
Crane Ct EC4 274 E9
Crane Ct, Epsom 216 CQ105
Crane Gdns, Hayes 155 BT77
Crane Gro N7 141 DN65
Crane Lo Rd, Houns. 155 BV79
Crane Mead SE16 163 DX77
Crane Mead, Ware 33 DY06
Crane Pk Rd, Twick. 176 CB89
Crane Rd, Twick. 177 CE88
Crane St SE10 163 ED78
Crane St SE15 162 DT81
Crane Way, Twick. 176 CC87
Cranebrook, Twick. 176 CC89
Manor Rd
Cranefield Dr, Wat. 60 BY32
Craneford Cl, Twick. 177 CF87
Craneford Way, Twick. 177 CE87
Cranell Grn, S.Ock. 149 FV74
Cranes Dr, Surb. 198 CL98
Cranes Pk, Surb. 198 CL98
Cranes Pk Av, Surb. 198 CL98
Cranes Pk Cres, Surb. 198 CM98
Cranes Way, Borwd. 78 CQ43
Cranesbill Cl NW9 118 CR55
Colindale Av
Craneswater, Hayes 155 BT80
Craneswater Pk, Sthl. 156 BZ78
Cranfield Cl SE27 182 DQ90
Dunelm Gro
Cranfield Ct, Wok. 226 AU118
Martindale Rd
Cranfield Cres (Cuffley), Pot.B. 65 DL29
Cranfield Dr NW9 96 CS52
Cranfield Rd SE4 163 DZ83
Cranfield Rd E, Cars. 218 DG109
Cranfield Rd W, Cars. 218 DF109
Cranfield Row SE1 278 E6
Cranford Av N13 99 DL50
Cranford Av, Stai. 174 BL87
Cranford Cl SW20 199 CV95
Cranford Cl, Pur. 220 DQ113
Cranford Cl, Stai. 174 BL87
Canopus Way
Cranford Cotts E1 143 DX73
Cranford St
Cranford Ct, Hert. 31 DM07
The Ridgeway
Cranford Dr, Hayes 155 BT77
Cranford La, Hayes 155 BR79
Cranford La (Heathrow Airport), Houns. 155 BT83
Cranford La (Heathrow Airport N), Houns. 155 BT81
Cranford La (Heston), Houns. 156 BX80
Cranford Pk Rd, Hayes 155 BT77
Cranford Ri, Esher 214 CC106
Cranford Rd, Dart. 188 FL88
Cranford St E1 143 DX73
Cranford Way N8 121 DM57
Cranham Gdns, Upmin. 129 FS60
Cranham Rd, Horn. 127 FH58
Cranhurst Rd NW2 119 CW64
Cranleigh Cl SE20 202 DV96
Cranleigh Cl, Bex. 187 FB86
Cranleigh Cl, Orp. 206 EU104
Cranleigh Cl, S.Croy. 220 DU112
Cranleigh Cl (Cheshunt), Wal.Cr. 66 DU28
Cranleigh Dr, Swan. 207 FE98
Cranleigh Gdns N21 81 DN43
Cranleigh Gdns SE25 202 DS97
Cranleigh Gdns, Bark. 145 ER66
Cranleigh Gdns, Har. 118 CL57
Cranleigh Gdns, Kings.T. 178 CM93
Cranleigh Gdns, Loug. 85 EM44
Cranleigh Gdns, S.Croy. 220 DU112
Cranleigh Gdns, Sthl. 136 BZ72
Cranleigh Gdns, Sutt. 200 DB103
Cranleigh Gdns Ind Est, Sthl. 136 BZ72
Cranleigh Ms SW11 160 DE82
Cranleigh Rd N15 122 DQ57
Cranleigh Rd SW19 200 DA97
Cranleigh Rd, Esher 196 CC102
Cranleigh Rd, Felt. 175 BT91
Cranleigh Rd (Wonersh), Guil. 259 BB144
Cranleigh St NW1 273 L1
Cranleigh St NW1 141 DJ68
Cranley Cl, Guil. 243 BA134
Cranley Dene Ct N10 121 DH56
Cranley Dr, Ilf. 125 EQ59
Cranley Dr, Ruis. 115 BT61
Cranley Gdns N10 121 DJ56
Cranley Gdns N13 99 DM48
Cranley Gdns SW7 160 DC78
Cranley Gdns, Wall. 219 DJ108
Cranley Ms SW7 160 DC78
Cranley Par SE9 184 EL91
Beaconsfield Rd
Cranley Pl SW7 160 DD77
Cranley Rd E13 144 EH71
Cranley Rd, Guil. 243 AZ134
Cranley Rd, Ilf. 125 EQ58
Cranley Rd, Walt. 213 BS106
Cranmer Av W13 157 CH76
Cranmer Cl, Mord. 199 CX100
Cranmer Cl, Pot.B. 64 DB30
Cranmer Cl, Ruis. 116 BX60
Cranmer Cl, Stan. 95 CJ52
Cranmer Cl, Warl. 237 DY117
Cranmer Cl, Wey. 212 BN108
Cranmer Ct SW3 276 C9
Cranmer Ct SW4 161 DK83
Cranmer Ct (Hampton Hill), Hmptn. 176 CB92
Cranmer Rd
Cranmer Fm Cl, Mitch. 200 DF98
Cranmer Gdns, Dag. 127 FC63
Cranmer Gdns, Warl. 237 DY117
Cranmer Rd E7 124 EH63
Cranmer Rd SW9 161 DN80
Cranmer Rd, Croy. 201 DP104
Cranmer Rd, Edg. 96 CP48
Cranmer Rd (Hampton Hill), Hmptn. 176 CB92
Cranmer Rd, Hayes 135 BR72
Cranmer Rd, Kings.T. 178 CL92
Cranmer Rd, Mitch. 200 DF98
Cranmer Rd, Sev. 256 FE123
Cranmer Ter SW17 180 DD92
Cranmore Av, Islw. 156 CC80
Cranmore Cotts, Lthd. 245 BP129
Cranmore Ct, St.Alb. 43 CF19
Cranmore La (West Horsley), Lthd. 245 BP129
Cranmore Rd, Brom. 184 EE90
Cranmore Rd, Chis. 185 EM92
Cranmore Way N10 121 DJ56
Cranston Cl, Houns. 156 BY82
Cranston Cl, Reig. 266 DB135
Cranston Cl, Uxb. 115 BR61
Cranston Est N1 275 L1
Cranston Est N1 142 DR68
Cranston Gdns E4 101 EB50
Cranston Pk Av, Upmin. 128 FQ63
Cranston Rd SE23 183 DY88
Cranstoun Cl, Guil. 242 AT130
Cranswick Rd SE16 162 DV78
Crantock Rd SE6 183 EB89
Cranwell Cl E3 143 EB70
Cranwell Cl, St.Alb. 43 CJ22
Cranwell Gro, Shep. 194 BM98
Cranwich Av N21 100 DR45
Cranwich Rd N16 122 DR59
Cranwood St EC1 275 K3
Cranwood St EC1 142 DR69
Cranworth Cres E4 101 ED46
Cranworth Gdns SW9 161 DN81
Craster Rd SW2 181 DM87
Crathie Rd SE12 184 EH86
Cravan Av, Felt. 175 BU89
Craven Av W5 137 CJ73
Craven Av, Sthl. 136 BZ71
Craven Cl, Hayes 135 BU72
Craven Gdns SW19 180 DA92
Craven Gdns, Bark. 145 ES68
Craven Gdns, Ilf. 103 ER54
Craven Gdns (Collier Row), Rom. 104 FA50
Craven Gdns (Harold Wd), Rom. 106 FQ51
Craven Hill W2 140 DC73
Craven Hill Gdns W2 140 DC73
Craven Hill Ms W2 140 DC73
Craven Ms SW11 160 DG83
Taybridge Rd
Craven Pk NW10 138 CS67
Craven Pk Ms NW10 138 CS67
Craven Pk Rd N15 122 DT58
Craven Pk Rd NW10 138 CS67
Craven Pas WC2 277 P2
Craven Pas WC2 141 DL74
Craven Rd NW10 138 CR67
Craven Rd W2 140 DC73
Craven Rd W5 137 CJ73
Craven Rd, Croy. 202 DV102
Craven Rd, Kings.T. 198 CM95
Craven Rd, Orp. 206 EX104
Craven St WC2 277 P2
Craven St WC2 141 DL74
Craven Ter W2 140 DC73
Craven Wk N16 122 DU59
Cravens, The, Horl. 269 DN148
Crawford Av, Wem. 117 CK64
Crawford Cl, Islw. 157 CE82
Crawford Compton Cl, Horn. 148 FJ65
Crawford Est SE5 162 DQ82
Crawford Gdns N13 99 DP48
Crawford Gdns, Nthlt. 136 BZ69
Crawford Ms W1 272 D7
Crawford Pas EC1 274 D5
Crawford Pl W1 272 C8
Crawford Pl W1 140 DE72
Crawford Rd SE5 162 DQ81
Crawford Rd, Hat. 45 CU16
Crawford St W1 272 D7
Crawford St W1 140 DF71
Crawfords, Swan. 187 FE94
Crawley Dr, Hem.H. 40 BM16
Crawley Rd E10 123 EB60
Crawley Rd N22 100 DQ54
Crawley Rd, Enf. 100 DS45
Crawshaw Rd (Ottershaw), Cher. 211 BD107
Crawshay Cl, Sev. 256 FG123
Crawshay Ct SW9 161 DN81
Eythorne Rd
Crawthew Gro SE22 162 DT84
Cray Av, Ash. 232 CL116
Cray Av, Orp. 206 EV99
Cray Cl, Dart. 167 FG84
Cray Riverway, Dart. 187 FG85
Cray Rd, Belv. 166 FA79
Cray Rd, Sid. 186 EW94
Cray Rd, Swan. 207 FB100
Cray Valley Rd, Orp. 206 EU99
Craybrooke Rd, Sid. 186 EV91
Crayburne (Southfleet), Grav. 190 FZ92
Craybury End SE9 185 EQ89
Craydene Rd, Erith 167 FF81
Crayfield Ind Pk, Orp. 206 EW96
Crayford Cl E6 144 EL71
Neatscourt Rd
Crayford High St, Dart. 167 FE84
Crayford Rd N7 121 DK63
Crayford Rd, Dart. 187 FF85
Crayford Way, Dart. 187 FF85
Crayke Hill, Chess. 216 CL108
Craylands, Orp. 206 EW97
Craylands La, Swans. 189 FX85
Craylands Sq, Swans. 189 FX85
Crayle St, Slou. 131 AN69
Craymill Sq, Dart. 167 FF82
Crayonne Cl, Sun. 195 BS95
Crayside Ind Est, Dart. 167 FH84
Thames Rd
Crealock Gro, Wdf.Grn. 102 EF50
Crealock St SW18 180 DB86
Creasey Cl, Horn. 127 FH61
Creasy Cl, Abb.L. 59 BT31
Creasy Est SE1 279 M7
Creasy Est SE1 162 DS76
Crebor St SE22 182 DU86
Credenhall Dr, Brom. 205 EM102
Credenhill St SW16 181 DJ93
Crediton Hill NW6 120 DB64
Crediton Rd E16 144 EG72
Pacific Rd
Crediton Rd NW10 139 CX67
Crediton Way (Claygate), Esher 215 CG106
Credo Way, Grays 169 FV79
Credon Rd E13 144 EJ68
Credon Rd SE16 162 DV78
Cree Way, Rom. 105 FE52
Creechurch La EC3 275 N9
Creechurch La EC3 142 DS72
Creechurch Pl EC3 275 N9
Creed Ct EC4 141 DP72
Ludgate Hill
Creed La EC4 274 G9
Creek, The, Grav. 190 GB85
Creek, The, Sun. 195 BU99
Creek Rd SE8 163 EA79
Creek Rd SE10 163 EA79
Creek Rd, Bark. 145 ET69
Creek Rd, E.Mol. 197 CE98
Creekside SE8 163 EB80
Creekside, Rain. 147 FE70
Creeland Gro SE6 183 DZ88
Catford Hill
Crefeld Cl W6 159 CX79
Creffield Rd W3 138 CM73
Creffield Rd W5 138 CM73
Creighton Av E6 144 EK68
Creighton Av N2 120 DE55
Creighton Av N10 120 DE55
Creighton Av, St.Alb. 43 CD24
Creighton Cl W12 139 CV73
Bloemfontein Rd
Creighton Rd N17 100 DS52
Creighton Rd NW6 139 CX68
Creighton Rd W5 157 CK76
Cremer St E2 275 P1
Cremer St E2 142 DT68
Cremorne Est SW10 160 DD79
Milman's St
Cremorne Gdns, Epsom 216 CR109
Cremorne Rd SW10 160 DC80
Cremorne Rd (Northfleet), Grav. 191 GF87
Crescent EC3 275 P10
Crescent, The E17 123 DY57
Crescent, The N11 98 DF49
Crescent, The NW2 119 CV62
Crescent, The SW13 159 CT82
Crescent, The SW19 180 DA90
Crescent, The W3 138 CS72
Crescent, The, Abb.L. 59 BT30
Crescent, The, Ashf. 174 BM92
Crescent, The, Barn. 80 DB41
Crescent, The, Beck. 203 EA95
Crescent, The, Bex. 186 EW87
Crescent, The, Cat. 237 EA123
Crescent, The, Cher. 194 BG97
Western Av
Crescent, The, Croy. 202 DR99
Crescent, The, Egh. 172 AY93
Crescent, The, Epp. 69 ET32
Crescent, The, Epsom 216 CN114
Crescent, The (Northfleet), Grav. 191 GF89
Crescent, The, Green. 189 FW85
Crescent, The, Guil. 242 AU132
Crescent, The, Harl. 36 EW09
Crescent, The, Har. 117 CD60
Crescent, The, Hayes 155 BQ80
Crescent, The, Horl. 269 DH150
Crescent, The, Ilf. 125 EN58
Crescent, The, Lthd. 231 CH122
Crescent, The, Loug. 84 EK43
Crescent, The, N.Mal. 198 CQ96
Crescent, The, Reig. 250 DB134
Chartway
Crescent, The, Rick. 75 BP44
Crescent, The (Bricket Wd), St.Alb. 60 CA30
Crescent, The, Sev. 257 FK121
Crescent, The, Shep. 195 BT101
Crescent, The, Sid. 185 ET91
Crescent, The, Slou. 152 AS75
Crescent, The, Sthl. 156 BZ75
Crescent, The, Surb. 198 CL99
Crescent, The, Sutt. 218 DD105
Crescent, The (Belmont), Sutt. 218 DA111
Crescent, The, Upmin. 129 FS59
Crescent, The, Wat. 76 BW42
Crescent, The (Aldenham), Wat. 76 CB37
Crescent, The, Wem. 117 CH61
Crescent, The, W.Mol. 196 CA98
Crescent, The, W.Wick. 204 EE100
Crescent, The, Wey. 194 BN104
Crescent Av, Grays 170 GD78
Crescent Av, Horn. 127 FF61
Crescent Cotts, Sev. 241 FE120
Crescent Ct, Surb. 197 CK99
Crescent Dr, Brwd. 108 FY46
Crescent Dr, Orp. 205 EP100
Crescent E, Barn. 80 DC38
Crescent Gdns SW19 180 DA90
Crescent Gdns, Ruis. 115 BV58
Crescent Gdns, Swan. 207 FC96
Crescent Gro SW4 161 DJ84
Crescent Gro, Mitch. 200 DE98
Crescent Ho SE13 163 EB82
Ravensbourne Pl
Crescent La SW4 181 DK85
Crescent Ms N22 99 DL53
Palace Gates Rd
Crescent Pl SW3 276 B8
Crescent Pl SW3 160 DE77
Crescent Ri N22 99 DK53
Crescent Ri, Barn. 80 DE43
Crescent Rd E4 102 EE45
Crescent Rd E6 144 EJ67
Crescent Rd E10 123 EB61
Crescent Rd E13 144 EG67
Crescent Rd E18 102 EJ54
Crescent Rd N3 97 CZ53
Crescent Rd N8 121 DK59
Crescent Rd N9 100 DU46
Crescent Rd N11 98 DF49
Crescent Rd N15 121 DP55
Carlingford Rd
Crescent Rd N22 99 DK53
Crescent Rd SE18 165 EP78
Crescent Rd SW20 199 CX95
Crescent Rd, Barn. 80 DE43
Crescent Rd, Beck. 203 EB96
Crescent Rd, Brwd. 108 FV49
Crescent Rd, Brom. 184 EG94
Crescent Rd, Cat. 236 DU124
Crescent Rd, Dag. 127 FB63
Crescent Rd, Enf. 81 DP41
Crescent Rd, Erith 167 FF79
Crescent Rd, Hem.H. 40 BK20
Crescent Rd, Kings.T. 178 CN94
Crescent Rd (Bletchingley), Red. 252 DQ133
Crescent Rd, Reig. 266 DA136
Crescent Rd, Shep. 195 BQ99
Crescent Rd, Sid. 185 ET90
Crescent Rd, S.Ock. 168 FQ75
Crescent Row EC1 275 H5
Crescent Stables SW15 159 CY84
Upper Richmond Rd
Crescent St N1 141 DM66
Crescent Vw, Loug. 84 EK44
Crescent Wk, S.Ock. 168 FQ75
Crescent Way N12 98 DE51
Crescent Way SE4 163 EA83
Crescent Way SW16 181 DM94
Crescent Way, Horl. 268 DG150
Crescent Way, Orp. 223 ES106
Crescent Way, S.Ock. 149 FR74
Crescent W, Barn. 80 DC38
Crescent Wd Rd SE26 182 DU90
Cresford Rd SW6 160 DB81
Crespigny Rd NW4 119 CV58
Cress End, Rick. 92 BG46
Springwell Av
Cress Rd, Slou. 151 AP75
Cressage Cl, Sthl. 136 CA70
Cressall Cl, Lthd. 231 CH120
Cressall Mead, Lthd. 231 CH120
Cresset Cl, Ware 33 EC12
Cresset Rd E9 142 DW65
Cresset St SW4 161 DK83
Cressfield Cl NW5 120 DG64
Cressida Rd N19 121 DJ60
Cressingham Gro, Sutt. 218 DC105
Cressingham Rd SE13 163 EC83
Cressingham Rd, Edg. 96 CR51
Cressington Cl N16 122 DS64
Wordsworth Rd
Cresswell Gdns SW5 160 DC78
Cresswell Pk SE3 164 EF83
Cresswell Pl SW10 160 DC78
Cresswell Rd SE25 202 DU98
Cresswell Rd, Chesh. 54 AR34
Cresswell Rd, Felt. 176 BY91
Cresswell Rd, Twick. 177 CK86
Cresswell Way N21 99 DN45
Cressy Ct E1 142 DW71
Cressy Pl
Cressy Ct W6 159 CV76
Cressy Pl E1 142 DW71
Cressy Rd NW3 120 DF63
Crest, The N13 99 DN49
Crest, The NW4 119 CW57
Crest, The, Beac. 88 AG54
Crest, The, Saw. 36 EX05
Crest, The, Surb. 198 CN99
Crest, The (Cheshunt), Wal.Cr. 65 DP27
Orchard Way
Crest Av, Grays 170 GB80
Crest Cl (Badgers Mt), Sev. 225 FB111
Crest Dr, Enf. 82 DW38
Crest Gdns, Ruis. 116 BW62
Crest Hill (Peaslake), Guil. 261 BR142
Crest Pk, Hem.H. 41 BQ19
Crest Rd NW2 119 CT62
Crest Rd, Brom. 204 EF101
Crest Rd, S.Croy. 220 DV108
Crest Vw, Green. 169 FU84
Woodland Way
Crest Vw, Pnr. 116 BX56
Crest Vw Dr, Orp. 205 EP99
Cresta Dr (Woodham), Add. 211 BF110
Crestbrook Av N13 99 DP48
Crestbrook Pl N13 99 DP48
Crestfield St WC1 274 A2
Crestfield St WC1 141 DL69
Cresthill Av, Grays 170 GC77
Creston Av (Knaphill), Wok. 226 AS116
Creston Way, Wor.Pk. 199 CX102
Crestway SW15 179 CV86
Crestwood Way, Houns. 176 BZ85
Creswick Ct, Welw.G.C. 29 CX10
Creswick Rd W3 138 CP73
Creswick Wk E3 143 EA69
Malmesbury Rd
Creswick Wk NW11 119 CZ56
Crete Hall Rd, Grav. 190 GD86
Creton St SE18 165 EN76
Crewdson Rd SW9 161 DN80
Crewdson Rd, Horl. 269 DH148
Crewe Curve, Berk. 38 AT16
Crewe Pl NW10 139 CT69
Crewe's Av, Warl. 236 DW116
Crewe's Cl, Warl. 236 DW116
Crewe's Fm La, Warl. 237 DX116
Crewe's La, Warl. 237 DX116
Crews St E14 163 EA77
Crewys Rd NW2 119 CZ61
Crewys Rd SE15 162 DV82
Crib St, Ware 33 DX05
Crichton Av, Wall. 219 DK106
Crichton Rd, Cars. 218 DF107
Cricket Fld Rd, Uxb. 134 BK67
Cricket Grn, Mitch. 200 DF97
Cricket Grd Rd, Chis. 205 EP95
Cricket Hill (South Nutfield), Red. 267 DM136
Cricket La, Beck. 183 DY93
Cricket Way, Wey. 195 BS103
Cricketers Arms Rd, Enf. 82 DQ40
Cricketers Cl N14 99 DJ45
Cricketers Cl, Chess. 215 CK105
Cricketers Cl, Erith 167 FE78
Cricketers Cl, St.Alb. 43 CE19
Stonecross
Cricketers Ct SE11 278 F9
Cricketers Ct SE11 161 DP77
Cricketers Ms SW18 180 DB85
East Hill
Cricketers Ter, Cars. 200 DE104
Wrythe La
Cricketfield Rd E5 122 DV63
Cricketfield Rd, West Dr. 154 BJ77
Cricklade Av SW2 181 DL89
Cricklade Av, Rom. 106 FK51
Cricklewood Bdy NW2 119 CX62
Cricklewood La NW2 119 CX63
Cricklewood Trd Est NW2 119 CY62
Cridland St E15 144 EF67
Church St
Crieff Ct, Tedd. 177 CJ94
Crieff Rd SW18 180 DC86
Criffel Av SW2 181 DK89
Crimp Hill Rd, Egh. 172 AU90
Crimp Hill Rd (Old Windsor), Wind. 172 AT87
Crimscott St SE1 279 N7
Crimscott St SE1 162 DS76
Crimsworth Rd SW8 161 DK81
Crinan St N1 141 DL68
Cringle St SW8 161 DJ80
Cripplegate St EC2 275 H6
Cripps Grn, Hayes 135 BV70
Stratford Rd
Crisp Rd W6 159 CW78
Crispe Ho, Bark. 145 ER68
Dovehouse Mead
Crispen Rd, Felt. 176 BY91
Crispian Cl NW10 118 CS63
Crispin Cl, Ash. 232 CM118
Crispin Cl, Beac. 88 AJ51
Crispin Cl, Croy. 201 DL103
Harrington Cl
Crispin Cres, Croy. 201 DK104
Crispin Rd, Edg. 96 CQ51
Crispin St E1 275 P7
Crispin St E1 142 DT71
Crispin Way (Farnham Common), Slou. 111 AR63
Criss Cres, Ger.Cr. 90 AW54
Criss Gro (Chalfont St. Peter), Ger.Cr. 90 AW54
Cristowe Rd SW6 159 CZ82
Criterion Ms N19 121 DK61
Crittall's Cor, Sid. 186 EW94
Critten La, Dor. 246 BX132
Crockenhall Way (Istead Ri), Grav. 190 GE94
Crockenhill La (Eynsford), Dart. 208 FJ102
Crockenhill La, Swan. 207 FG101
Crockenhill Rd, Orp. 206 EX99
Crockenhill Rd, Swan. 206 EZ100
Crockerton Rd SW17 180 DF89
Crockery La (East Clandon), Guil. 244 BL129
Crockford Cl, Add. 212 BJ105
Crockford Pk Rd, Add. 212 BJ106
Crockham Way SE9 185 EN91
Crocknorth Rd (East Horsley), Lthd. 245 BT132
Crocus Cl, Croy. 203 DX102
Cornflower La
Crocus Fld, Barn. 79 CZ44
Croffets, Tad. 233 CX121
Croft, The E4 102 EE47
Croft, The NW10 139 CT68
Croft, The W5 138 CL71
Croft, The, Barn. 79 CX42
Croft, The, Brox. 49 DY23
Croft, The, Houns. 156 BY79
Croft, The, Loug. 85 EN40

Croft, The, Pnr. 116 BZ59
Rayners La
Croft, The, Ruis. 116 BW63
Croft, The, St.Alb. 60 CA25
Croft, The, Swan. 207 FC97
Croft, The, Welw.G.C. 29 CZ12
Croft, The, Wem. 117 CJ64
Croft Av, Dor. 247 CH134
Croft Av, W.Wick. 203 EC102
Croft Cl NW7 96 CS48
Croft Cl, Belv. 166 EZ78
Croft Cl, Chis. 185 EM91
Croft Cl, Hayes 155 BQ80
Croft Cl, Kings L. 58 BG30
Croft Cl, Uxb. 134 BN66
Croft Ct, Borwd. 78 CR41
Kensington Way
Croft End Cl, Chess. 198 CM104
Ashcroft Rd
Croft End Rd, Kings L. 58 BG30
Croft Fld, Hat. 45 CU18
Croft Fld, Kings L. 58 BG30
Croft Gdns W7 157 CG75
Croft Gdns, Ruis. 115 BT60
Croft La, Kings L. 58 BG30
Croft Lo Cl, Wdf.Grn. 102 EH51
Croft Meadow, Kings L. 58 BG30
Croft Ms N12 98 DC48
Croft Rd SW16 201 DN95
Croft Rd SW19 180 DC94
Croft Rd, Brom. 184 EG93
Croft Rd (Woldingham), Cat. 237 DZ122
Croft Rd, Enf. 83 DY39
Croft Rd (Chalfont St. Peter), Ger.Cr. 90 AY54
Croft Rd, Sutt. 218 DE106
Croft Rd, Ware 32 DW05
Croft Rd, West. 255 EP126
Croft St SE8 163 DY77
Croft Wk, Brox. 49 DY23
Croft Way, Sev. 256 FF125
Croft Way, Sid. 185 ES90
Croftdown Rd NW5 120 DG62
Crofters, The, Wind. 172 AU86
Crofters Cl, Islw. 177 CD85
Ploughmans End
Crofters Ct SE8 163 DY77
Croft St
Crofters Mead, Croy. 221 DZ109
Crofters Rd, Nthwd. 93 BS49
Crofters Way NW1 141 DK67
Crofthill Rd, Slou. 131 AP70
Croftleigh Av, Pur. 235 DN116
Crofton, Ash. 232 CL118
Crofton Av W4 158 CR80
Crofton Av, Bex. 186 EX87
Crofton Av, Orp. 205 EQ103
Crofton Av, Walt. 196 BW104
Crofton Cl (Ottershaw), Cher. 211 BC108
Crofton Gro E4 101 ED49
Crofton La, Orp. 205 ES101
Crofton Pk Rd SE4 183 DZ86
Crofton Rd E13 144 EH70
Crofton Rd SE5 162 DS81
Crofton Rd, Grays 170 GE76
Crofton Rd, Orp. 205 EN104
Crofton Ter E5 123 DY64
Studley Cl
Crofton Ter, Rich. 158 CM84
Crofton Way, Barn. 80 DB44
Wycherley Cres
Crofton Way, Enf. 81 DN40
Croftongate Way SE4 183 DY85
Crofts, The, Hem.H. 41 BP21
Crofts, The, Shep. 195 BS98
Crofts La N22 99 DN52
Glendale Av
Crofts Path, Hem.H. 41 BP22
Crofts Rd, Har. 117 CG58
Crofts St E1 142 DU73
Croftside SE25 202 DU97
Sunny Bk
Croftway NW3 120 DA63
Croftway, Rich. 177 CH90
Crogsland Rd NW1 140 DG66
Croham Cl, S.Croy. 220 DS107
Croham Manor Rd, S.Croy. 220 DS108
Croham Mt, S.Croy. 220 DS108
Croham Pk Av, S.Croy. 220 DT106
Croham Rd, S.Croy. 220 DS106
Croham Valley Rd, S.Croy. 220 DT107
Croindene Rd SW16 201 DL95
Cromartie Rd N19 121 DK59
Cromarty Rd, Edg. 96 CP47
Crombie Cl, Ilf. 125 EM57
Crombie Rd, Sid. 185 ER88
Cromer Cl, Uxb. 135 BQ72
Dawley Av
Cromer Hyde La, Welw.G.C. 28 CR11
Cromer Pl, Orp. 205 ER102
Andover Rd
Cromer Rd E10 123 ED58
James La
Cromer Rd N17 100 DU54
Cromer Rd SE25 202 DV97
Cromer Rd SW17 180 DG93
Cromer Rd, Barn. 80 DC42
Cromer Rd, Horn. 128 FK59
Cromer Rd (Heathrow Airport), Houns. 154 BN83
Cromer Rd, Rom. 127 FC58
Cromer Rd (Chadwell Heath), Rom. 126 EY58
Cromer Rd, Wat. 76 BW38
Cromer Rd, Wdf.Grn. 102 EG49
Cromer Rd W (Heathrow Airport), Houns. 154 BN83
Cromer St WC1 274 A3
Cromer St WC1 141 DL69
Cromer Ter E8 122 DU64
Ferncliff Rd
Cromer Vil Rd SW18 179 CZ86
Cromford Cl, Orp. 205 ES104
Cromford Path E5 123 DX63
Overbury St
Cromford Rd SW18 180 DA85
Cromford Way, N.Mal. 198 CR95
Cromlix Cl, Chis. 205 EP96
Crompton Pl, Enf. 83 EA37
Government Row
Crompton St W2 140 DD70
Cromwell Av N6 121 DH60
Cromwell Av W6 159 CV78
Cromwell Av, Brom. 204 EH98
Cromwell Av, N.Mal. 199 CT99
Cromwell Av (Cheshunt), Wal.Cr. 66 DU30
Cromwell Cl E1 142 DU74
Vaughan Way
Cromwell Cl N2 120 DD56
Cromwell Cl W3 *High St* 138 CQ74
Cromwell Cl, Brom. 204 EH98
Cromwell Cl, Ch.St.G. 90 AW48
Cromwell Cl, St.Alb. 43 CK15
Cromwell Cl, Walt. 195 BV102
Cromwell Cres SW5 160 DA77
Cromwell Gdns SW7 276 A7
Cromwell Gdns SW7 160 DD76
Cromwell Gro W6 159 CW76
Cromwell Gro, Cat. 236 DQ121
Cromwell Highwalk EC2 142 DQ71
Beech St
Cromwell Ind Est E10 123 DY60
Cromwell Ms SW7 276 A8
Cromwell Ms SW7 160 DD77
Cromwell Pl N6 121 DH60
Cromwell Pl SW7 276 A8
Cromwell Pl SW7 160 DD77
Cromwell Pl SW14 158 CQ83
Cromwell Pl W3 138 CQ74
Grove Pl
Cromwell Rd E7 144 EJ66
Cromwell Rd E17 123 EC57
Cromwell Rd N3 98 DC53
Cromwell Rd N10 98 DG52
Cromwell Rd SW5 160 DB77
Cromwell Rd SW7 160 DB77
Cromwell Rd SW9 161 DP81
Cromwell Rd SW19 180 DA92
Cromwell Rd, Beck. 203 DY96
Cromwell Rd, Borwd. 78 CL39
Cromwell Rd, Brwd. 108 FV49
Cromwell Rd, Cat. 236 DQ121
Cromwell Rd, Croy. 202 DR101
Cromwell Rd, Felt. 175 BV88
Cromwell Rd, Grays 170 GA77
Cromwell Rd, Hayes 135 BR72
Cromwell Rd, Hert. 32 DT08
Cromwell Rd, Houns. 156 CA84
Cromwell Rd, Kings.T. 198 CL95
Cromwell Rd, Red. 250 DF133
Cromwell Rd, Tedd. 177 CG93
Cromwell Rd (Cheshunt), Wal.Cr. 66 DV28
Cromwell Rd, Walt. 195 BV102
Cromwell Rd, Ware 33 DZ06
Cromwell Rd, Wem. 138 CL68
Cromwell Rd, Wor.Pk. 198 CR104
Cromwell St, Houns. 156 CA84
Cromwell Twr EC2 275 J6
Cromwell Twr EC2 142 DQ71
Cromwell Wk, Red. 250 DF134
Cromwells Mere, Rom. 105 FD51
Havering Rd
Crondace Rd SW6 160 DA81
Crondall Ct N1 275 M1
Crondall Ct N1 142 DR68
Crondall Ho SW15 179 CU88
Fontley Way
Crondall St N1 275 L1
Crondall St N1 142 DR68
Cronin St SE15 162 DT80
Cronks Hill, Red. 266 DC135
Cronks Hill, Reig. 266 DC135
Cronks Hill Cl, Red. 266 DD136
Cronks Hill Rd, Red. 266 DD136
Crook Log, Bexh. 166 EX83
Crooke Rd SE8 163 DY78
Crooked Billet SW19 179 CW93
Woodhayes Rd
Crooked Billet Roundabout E17 101 EA52
Crooked Billet Roundabout, Stai. 174 BG91
Crooked Billet Yd E2 142 DS69
Kingsland Rd
Crooked La, Grav. 191 GH86
Crooked Mile, Wal.Abb. 67 EC33
Crooked Mile Roundabout, Wal.Abb. 67 EC33
Crooked Usage N3 119 CY55
Crooked Way, Wal.Abb. 50 EE22
Crookham Rd SW6 159 CZ81
Crookhams, Welw.G.C. 30 DA07
Crookston Rd SE9 165 EN83
Croombs Rd E16 144 EJ71
Crooms Hill SE10 163 ED80
Crooms Hill Gro SE10 163 EC80
Crop Common, Hat. 45 CV16
Cropley Ct N1 142 DR68
Cropley St N1 142 DR68
Croppath Rd, Dag. 126 FA63
Cropthorne Ct W9 140 DC69
Maida Vale
Crosby Cl, Beac. 111 AM55
Crosby Cl, Felt. 176 BY91
Crosby Cl, St.Alb. 43 CJ23
Crosby Ct SE1 279 K4
Crosby Rd E7 144 EG65
Crosby Rd, Dag. 147 FB68
Crosby Row SE1 279 K5
Crosby Row SE1 162 DR75
Crosby Sq EC3 275 M9
Crosby Wk E8 142 DT65
Laurel St
Crosby Wk SW2 181 DN87
Crosier Rd (Ickenham), Uxb. 115 BQ63
Crosier Way, Ruis. 115 BS62
Crosland Pl SW11 160 DG83
Taybridge Rd
Cross Av SE10 163 ED79
Cross Cl SE15 162 DV81
Gordon Rd
Cross Deep, Twick. 177 CF89
Cross Deep Gdns, Twick. 177 CF89
Cross Keys Cl N9 100 DU47
Balham Rd
Cross Keys Cl W1 272 G7
Cross Keys Cl, Sev. 256 FG127
Cross Keys Sq EC1 275 H7
Cross Lances Rd, Houns. 156 CB84
Cross La EC3 279 M1
Cross La N8 121 DM56
Cross La, Beac. 111 AM55
Cross La, Bex. 186 EZ87
Cross La (Ottershaw), Cher. 211 BB107
Cross La, Hert. 31 DP09
Cross La E, Grav. 191 GH89
Cross La W, Grav. 191 GH89
Cross Las (Chalfont St. Peter), Ger.Cr. 90 AY50
Cross Las, Guil. 259 AZ135
Cross Las Cl (Chalfont St. Peter), Ger.Cr. 91 AZ50
Cross Las
Cross Meadow, Chesh. 54 AM29
Cross Oak, Wind. 151 AN82
Cross Oak Rd, Berk. 38 AU20
Cross Rd E4 102 EE46
Cross Rd N11 99 DH50
Cross Rd N22 99 DN52
Cross Rd SE5 162 DS82
Cross Rd SW19 180 DA94
Cross Rd, Brom. 204 EL103
Cross Rd, Croy. 202 DR102
Cross Rd, Dart. 188 FJ86
Cross Rd (Hawley), Dart. 188 FM91
Cross Rd, Enf. 82 DS42
Cross Rd, Felt. 176 BY91
Cross Rd (Northfleet), Grav. 191 GF86
Cross Rd, Har. 117 CD56
Cross Rd (South Harrow), Har. 116 CB62
Cross Rd (Wealdstone), Har. 95 CG54
Cross Rd, Hert. 32 DQ08
Cross Rd, Kings.T. 178 CM94
Cross Rd, Orp. 206 EV99
Cross Rd, Pur. 219 DP113
Cross Rd, Rom. 126 FA55
Cross Rd (Chadwell Heath), Rom. 126 EW59
Cross Rd, Sid. 186 EV91
Sidcup Hill
Cross Rd, Sutt. 218 DD106
Cross Rd (Belmont), Sutt. 218 DA110
Cross Rd, Tad. 233 CW122
Cross Rd, Uxb. 134 BJ66
New Windsor St
Cross Rd, Wal.Cr. 67 DY33
Cross Rd, Wat. 76 BY44
Cross Rd, Wey. 195 BR104
Cross Rd, Wdf.Grn. 103 EM51
Cross Rds (High Beach), Loug. 84 EH40
Cross St N1 141 DP67
Cross St SW13 158 CS82
Cross St, Erith 167 FE78
Bexley Rd
Cross St (Hampton Hill), Hmptn. 176 CC92
Cross St, Harl. 51 ER15
Cross St, St.Alb. 43 CD20
Spencer St
Cross St, Uxb. 134 BJ66
Cross St, Ware 33 DY06
Cross St, Wat. 76 BW41
Cross Ter, Wal.Abb. 68 EE34
Stonyshotts
Cross Way, The, Har. 95 CE54
Crossacres, Wok. 227 BE115
Crossbow Rd, Chig. 103 ET50
Crossbrook, Hat. 44 CS19
Crossbrook Rd SE3 164 EL82
Crossbrook St (Cheshunt), Wal.Cr. 67 DX31
Crossett Grn, Hem.H. 41 BQ22
Crossfell Rd, Hem.H. 41 BQ22
Crossfield Cl, Berk. 38 AT19
Crossfield Pl, Wey. 213 BP108
Crossfield Rd N17 122 DQ55
Crossfield Rd NW3 140 DD66
Crossfield Rd, Hodd. 49 EB15
Crossfield St SE8 163 EA80
Crossfields, Loug. 85 EP43
Crossfields, St.Alb. 42 CB23
Crossford St SW9 161 DM82
Crossgate, Edg. 96 CN48
Crossgate, Grnf. 137 CH65
Crossing Rd, Epp. 70 EU32
Crossland Rd, Red. 250 DG134
Crossland Rd, Th.Hth. 201 DP100
Crosslands, Cher. 193 BE104
Crosslands Av W5 138 CM74
Crosslands Av, Sthl. 156 BZ78
Crosslands Rd, Epsom 216 CR107
Crosslet St SE17 279 L8
Crosslet Vale SE10 163 EB81
Crossley Cl (Biggin Hill), West. 238 EK115
Crossley St N7 141 DN65
Crossleys, Ch.St.G. 90 AW49
Crossmead SE9 185 EM88
Crossmead, Wat. 75 BV44
Crossmead Av, Grnf. 136 CA69
Crossmount Ho SE5 162 DQ80
Crossness La SE28 146 EX73
Crossness Rd, Bark. 145 ET69
Crossoak La, Red. 267 DH144
Crossoaks La, Borwd. 78 CR35
Crossoaks La (South Mimms), Pot.B. 62 CS34
Crosspath, The, Rad. 77 CG35
Crossroads, The (Effingham), Lthd. 246 BX128
Crossthwaite Av SE5 162 DR84
Crosswall EC3 275 P10
Crosswall EC3 142 DT73
Crossway N12 98 DD51
Crossway N16 122 DS64
Crossway NW9 119 CT56
Crossway SE28 146 EW72
Crossway SW20 199 CW98
Crossway W13 137 CG70
Crossway, Chesh. 54 AS30
Crossway, Dag. 126 EW62
Crossway, Enf. 100 DS45
Crossway, Hayes 135 BU74
Crossway, Orp. 205 ER98
Crossway, Pnr. 93 BV54
Crossway, Ruis. 116 BW63
Crossway, Walt. 195 BV103
Crossway, Welw.G.C. 29 CW05
Crossway, Wdf.Grn. 102 EJ49
Crossway, The N22 99 DP52
Crossway, The SE9 184 EK89
Crossway, The, Uxb. 134 BM68
Crossways N21 82 DQ44
Crossways, Beac. 89 AM54
Crossways, Berk. 38 AT20
Crossways, Brwd. 109 GA44
Crossways, Egh. 173 BD93
Crossways, Hem.H. 41 BP20
Crossways, Lthd. 246 BX127
The St
Crossways, Rom. 127 FH55
Crossways, S.Croy. 221 DY108
Crossways, Sun. 175 BT94
Crossways, Sutt. 218 DD109
Crossways (Tatsfield), West. 238 EJ120
Crossways, The, Couls. 235 DM119
Crossways, The, Guil. 258 AU135
Crossways, The, Houns. 156 BZ80
Crossways, The, Red. 251 DJ130
Crossways, The, Wem. 118 CN61
Crossways Boul, Dart. 168 FQ84
Crossways Boul, Green. 169 FT84
Crossways Business Pk, Dart. 168 FQ84
Crossways La, Reig. 250 DC128
Crossways Rd, Beck. 203 EA98
Crossways Rd, Mitch. 201 DH97
Crosswell Cl, Shep. 195 BQ96
Crossthwaite Way, Slou. 131 AK71
Croston St E8 142 DU67
Crothall Cl N13 99 DM48
Crouch Av, Bark. 146 EV68
Crouch Cl, Beck. 183 EA93
Abbey La
Crouch Ct, Harl. 35 EQ13
Crouch Cft SE9 185 EN90
Crouch End Hill N8 121 DK59
Crouch Hall Rd N8 121 DK58
Crouch Hill N4 121 DL58
Crouch Hill N8 121 DL58
Crouch La (Cheshunt), Wal.Cr. 66 DQ28
Crouch Oak La, Add. 212 BJ105
Crouch Rd NW10 138 CR66
Crouch Rd, Grays 171 GG78
Crouch Valley, Upmin. 129 FS59
Crouchfield, Hem.H. 40 BH21
Crouchfield, Hert. 32 DQ06
Crouchman's Cl SE26 182 DT90
Crow Dr (Halstead), Sev. 241 FC115
Crow Grn La, Brwd. 108 FU43
Crow Grn Rd, Brwd. 108 FT43
Crow La, Rom. 126 EZ59
Crow Piece La, Slou. 131 AM68
Crowborough Cl, Warl. 237 DY117
Crowborough Dr, Warl. 237 DY118
Crowborough Path, Wat. 94 BX49
Prestwick Rd
Crowborough Rd SW17 180 DG93
Crowden Way SE28 146 EW73
Crowder St E1 142 DV73
Crowfoot Cl E9 123 DZ64
Lee Conservancy Rd
Crowhurst Cl SW9 161 DN82
Crowhurst Mead, Gdse. 252 DW130
Crowhurst Way, Orp. 206 EW99
Crowland Av, Hayes 155 BS77
Crowland Gdns N14 99 DL45
Crowland Rd N15 122 DT57
Crowland Rd, Th.Hth. 202 DR98
Crowland Ter N1 142 DR66
Crowland Wk, Mord. 200 DB100
Crowlands Av, Rom. 127 FB58
Crowley Cres, Croy. 219 DN106
Crowline Wk N1 142 DR65
Clephane Rd
Crowmarsh Gdns SE23 182 DW87
Tyson Rd
Crown Arc, Kings.T. 197 CK96
Union St
Crown Ash Hill, West. 222 EH114
Crown Ash La, Warl. 238 EG116
Crown Ash La, West. 238 EG116
Crown Cl E3 143 EA67
Crown Cl NW6 140 DB65
Crown Cl NW7 97 CT47
Crown Cl (Sheering), B.Stort. 37 FC07
Crown Cl, Hayes 155 BT75
Crown Cl, Orp. 224 EU105
Crown Cl (Colnbrook), Slou. 153 BC80
Crown Cl, Walt. 196 BW101
Crown Ct EC2 275 J9
Crown Ct SE12 184 EH86
Crown Ct WC2 274 A9
Crown Ct, Brom. 204 EK99
Victoria Rd
Crown Dale SE19 181 DP93
Crown Gate, Harl. 51 ER15
Crown Hts, Guil. 258 AY137
Crown Hill, Croy. 202 DQ103
Church St
Crown Hill, Epp. 69 EM33
Crown Hill, Wal.Abb. 69 EM33
Crown La N14 99 DJ46
Crown La SW16 181 DN92
Crown La, Brom. 204 EK99
Crown La, Chis. 205 EQ95
Crown La, H.Wyc. 88 AF48
Crown La, Mord. 200 DB97
Crown La (Farnham Royal), Slou. 131 AN68
Crown La, Vir.W. 192 AX100
Crown La Gdns SW16 181 DN92
Crown La
Crown La Spur, Brom. 204 EK100
Crown Meadow (Colnbrook), Slou. 153 BB80
Crown Ms E13 144 EJ67
Waghorn Rd
Crown Ms W6 159 CU77
Crown Office Row EC4 274 D10
Crown Pas SW1 277 L3
Crown Pas SW1 141 DJ74
Crown Pas, Kings.T. 197 CK96
Church St
Crown Pas, Wat. 76 BW42
The Cres
Crown Pl EC2 275 M6
Crown Pl EC2 142 DS71
Crown Pl NW5 141 DH65
Kentish Town Rd
Crown Pt Par SE19 181 DP93
Beulah Hill
Crown Ri, Cher. 193 BF102
Crown Ri, Wat. 60 BW34
Crown Rd N10 98 DG52
Crown Rd, Borwd. 78 CN39
Crown Rd, Enf. 82 DV42
Crown Rd, Grays 170 GA79
Crown Rd, Ilf. 125 ER56
Crown Rd, Mord. 200 DB98
Crown Rd, N.Mal. 198 CQ95
Crown Rd, Orp. 224 EU106
Crown Rd, Ruis. 116 BX64
Crown Rd (Shoreham), Sev. 225 FF110
Crown Rd, Sutt. 218 DB105
Crown Rd, Twick. 177 CH86
Crown Rd, Vir.W. 192 AW100
Crown Sq, Wok. 227 AZ117
Commercial Way
Crown St SE5 162 DQ80
Crown St W3 138 CP74
Crown St, Brwd. 108 FW47
Crown St, Dag. 147 FC65
Crown St, Egh. 173 BA92
Crown St, Har. 117 CD60
Crown Ter, Rich. 158 CM84
Crown Wk, Uxb. 134 BJ66
Oxford Rd
Crown Wk, Wem. 118 CM62
Crown Way, West Dr. 134 BM74
Crown Wds La SE9 165 EP82
Crown Wds La SE18 165 EP82
Crown Wds Way SE9 185 ER85
Crown Wks E2 142 DV68
Temple St
Crown Yd, Houns. 156 CC83
High St
Crowndale Rd NW1 141 DJ68
Crownfield, Brox. 49 EA21
Crownfield Av, Ilf. 125 ES57
Crownfield Rd E15 123 ED64
Crownfields, Sev. 257 FH125
Crownhill Rd NW10 139 CT67
Crownhill Rd, Wdf.Grn. 102 EL52
Crownmead Way, Rom. 127 FB56
Crownstone Rd SW2 181 DN85
Crowntree Cl, Islw. 157 CF79
Crows Rd E15 143 ED69
Crows Rd, Bark. 145 EP65
Crows Rd, Epp. 69 ET30
Crowshott Av, Stan. 95 CJ53
Crowstone Rd, Grays 170 GC75
Crowther Av, Brent. 158 CL77
Crowther Rd SE25 202 DU98
Crowthorne Cl SW18 179 CZ88
Crowthorne Rd W10 139 CX72
Croxdale Rd, Borwd. 78 CM40
Croxden Cl, Edg. 118 CM55
Croxden Wk, Mord. 200 DC100
Croxford Gdns N22 99 DP52
Croxford Way, Rom. 127 FD60
Horace Av
Croxley Business Pk, Wat. 75 BR43
Croxley Cl, Orp. 206 EV96
Croxley Grn, Orp. 206 EV95
Croxley Rd W9 139 CZ69
Croxley Vw, Wat. 75 BS44
Croxted Cl SE21 182 DQ87
Croxted Rd SE21 182 DQ87
Croxted Rd SE24 182 DQ87
Croyde Av, Grnf. 136 CC69
Croyde Av, Hayes 155 BS77
Croyde Cl, Sid. 185 ER87
Croydon Flyover, Croy. 219 DP105
Croydon Gro, Croy. 201 DP102
Croydon La, Bans. 218 DB114
Croydon La S, Bans. 218 DB114
Croydon Rd E13 144 EF70
Croydon Rd SE20 202 DV96
Croydon Rd, Beck. 203 DY98
Croydon Rd, Brom. 204 EF104
Croydon Rd, Cat. 236 DU122
Croydon Rd (Beddington), Croy. 219 DH105
Croydon Rd (Heathrow Airport), Houns. 155 BP82
Croydon Rd, Kes. 204 EJ104
Croydon Rd, Mitch. 200 DG98
Croydon Rd, Reig. 250 DB134
Croydon Rd, Wall. 219 DH105
Croydon Rd, Warl. 237 ED122
Croydon Rd, W.Wick. 204 EE104
Croydon Rd, West. 239 EM123
Croyland Rd N9 100 DU46
Croylands Dr, Surb. 198 CL101
Croysdale Av, Sun. 195 BU97
Crozier Dr, S.Croy. 220 DV110
Crozier Ho SE3 164 EH83
Ebdon Way
Crozier Ter E9 123 DX64
Crucible Cl, Rom. 126 EV58
Crucifix La SE1 279 M4
Crucifix La SE1 162 DS75
Cruden Ho SE17 161 DP79
Hillingdon St
Cruden Rd, Grav. 191 GM90
Cruden St N1 141 DP67
Cruick Av, S.Ock. 149 FW73
Cruikshank Rd E15 124 EE63
Cruikshank St WC1 274 D2
Cruikshank St WC1 141 DN69
Crummock Cl, Slou. 130 AJ72
Crummock Gdns NW9 118 CS57
Crumpsall St SE2 166 EW77
Crundal Twr, Orp. 206 EW102
Crundale Av NW9 118 CN57
Crunden Rd, S.Croy. 220 DR108
Crusader Cl, Purf. 168 FN77
Centurion Way
Crusader Gdns, Croy. 202 DS104
Cotelands
Crusader Way, Wat. 75 BT44
Crushes Cl, Brwd. 109 GE44
Crusoe Ms N16 122 DR61
Crusoe Rd, Erith 167 FD78
Crusoe Rd, Mitch. 180 DF94
Crutched Friars EC3 275 N10
Crutched Friars EC3 142 DS73
Crutches La (Jordans), Beac. 90 AS51
Crutchfield La, Horl. 268 DA145
Crutchfield La, Walt. 195 BV103
Crutchley Rd SE6 184 EE89
Crystal Av, Horn. 128 FL63
Crystal Ct SE19 182 DT92
College Rd
Crystal Ho SE18 165 ET78
Spinel Cl
Crystal Palace Par SE19 182 DT93
Crystal Palace Pk Rd SE26 182 DU92
Crystal Palace Rd SE22 162 DU84
Crystal Palace Sta Rd SE19 182 DU93
Anerley Hill
Crystal Ter SE19 182 DR93
Crystal Vw Ct, Brom. 183 ED91
Winlaton Rd
Crystal Way, Dag. 126 EW60
Crystal Way, Har. 117 CF57
Cuba Dr, Enf. 82 DW40
Cuba St E14 163 EA75
Cubitt Sq, Sthl. 136 CC74
Windmill Av
Cubitt Steps E14 143 DZ74
Cabot Sq
Cubitt St WC1 274 B3
Cubitt St WC1 141 DM69
Cubitt St, Croy. 219 DM106
Cubitt Ter SW4 161 DJ83
Cubitts Yd WC2 274 A10
Cublands, Hert. 32 DV09
Cuckmans Dr, St.Alb. 60 CA25
Cuckoo Av W7 137 CE70
Cuckoo Dene W7 137 CD71
Cuckoo Hall La N9 100 DW45
Cuckoo Hill, Pnr. 116 BW55
Cuckoo Hill Dr, Pnr. 116 BW55
Cuckoo Hill Rd, Pnr. 116 BW56
Cuckoo La W7 137 CE73
Cuckoo Pound, Shep. 195 BS99
Cucumber La, Hat. 46 DF20
Cucumber La, Hert. 46 DF20
Cudas Cl, Epsom 217 CT105
Cuddington Av, Wor.Pk. 199 CT104
Cuddington Cl, Tad. 233 CW120
Cuddington Pk Cl, Bans. 217 CZ113
Cuddington Way, Sutt. 217 CX112
Cudham Cl (Belmont), Sutt. 218 DA110
Cudham Dr (New Addington), Croy. 221 EC110
Cudham La N, Orp. 223 ES110
Cudham La N (Cudham), Sev. 223 ER112
Cudham La S (Cudham), Sev. 239 EQ115
Cudham Pk Rd (Cudham), Sev. 223 ES110
Cudham Rd, Orp. 223 EN111
Cudham Rd (Tatsfield), West. 238 EL120
Cudham St SE6 183 EC87
Cudworth St E1 142 DV70
Cuff Cres SE9 184 EK86

Cuff Pt E2 275 P2
Cuff Pt E2 142 DT69
Cuffley Av, Wat. 60 BX34
Cuffley Ct, Hem.H. 41 BQ15
Cuffley Hill (Cheshunt), Wal.Cr. 65 DN29
Cugley Rd, Dart. 188 FQ87
Culford Gdns SW3 276 E9
Culford Gdns SW3 160 DF77
Culford Gro N1 142 DS65
Culford Ms N1 142 DS65
Culford Rd
Culford Rd N1 142 DS66
Culford Rd, Grays 170 GC75
Culgaith Gdns, Enf. 81 DL42
Cullen Sq, S.Ock. 149 FW73
Cullen Way NW10 138 CQ70
Cullera Cl, Nthwd. 93 BT51
Cullerne Cl (Ewell), Epsom 217 CT110
Cullesden Rd, Ken. 235 DP115
Culling Rd SE16 162 DW76
Lower Rd
Cullings Ct, Wal.Abb. 68 EF33
Cullington Cl, Har. 117 CG56
Cullingworth Rd NW10 119 CU64
Culloden Cl SE16 162 DU78
Culloden Rd, Enf. 81 DP40
Culloden St E14 143 EC72
Cullum St EC3 275 M10
Culmington Rd W13 157 CJ75
Culmington Rd, S.Croy. 220 DQ109
Culmore Cross SW12 181 DH88
Culmore Rd SE15 162 DV80
Culmstock Rd SW11 180 DG85
Culpeper Cl, Ilf. 103 EP51
Culross Cl N15 122 DQ56
Culross St W1 276 F1
Culross St W1 140 DG73
Culsac Rd, Surb. 198 CL103
Culver Dr, Oxt. 254 EE130
Culver Gro, Stan. 95 CJ54
Culver Rd, St.Alb. 43 CE19
Culverden Rd SW12 181 DJ89
Culverden Rd, Wat. 93 BV48
Culverhay, Ash. 232 CL116
Culverhouse Gdns SW16 181 DM90
Culverlands Cl, Stan. 95 CH49
Culverley Rd SE6 183 EB88
Culvers Av, Cars. 200 DF103
Culvers Cft (Seer Grn), Beac. 89 AQ51
Culvers Retreat, Cars. 200 DF102
Culvers Way, Cars. 200 DF103
Culverstone Cl, Brom. 204 EF100
Culvert La, Uxb. 134 BH68
Culvert Pl SW11 160 DG82
Culvert Rd N15 122 DS57
Culvert Rd SW11 160 DF82
Culworth St NW8 272 B1
Cum Cum Hill, Hat. 46 DD21
Cumberland Av NW10 138 CP69
Cumberland Av, Grav. 191 GJ87
Cumberland Av, Guil. 242 AU129
Cumberland Av, Horn. 128 FL62
Cumberland Av, Slou. 131 AQ70
Cumberland Av, Well. 165 ES83
Cumberland Cl E8 142 DT65
Cumberland Cl SW20 179 CX94
Lansdowne Rd
Cumberland Cl, Amer. 72 AV39
Cumberland Cl, Epsom 216 CS110
Cumberland Cl, Hem.H. 41 BS24
Cumberland Cl, Hert. 32 DQ06
Cumberland Cl, Horn. 128 FL62
Cumberland Cl, Ilf. 103 EQ53
Carrick Dr
Cumberland Cl, Twick. 177 CH86
Westmorland Cl
Cumberland Cres W14 159 CY77
Cumberland Dr, Bexh. 166 EY80
Cumberland Dr, Chess. 198 CM104
Cumberland Dr, Dart. 188 FM87
Cumberland Dr, Esher 197 CG103
Cumberland Gdns NW4 97 CY54
Cumberland Gdns WC1 274 C2
Cumberland Gate W1 272 D10
Cumberland Gate W1 140 DF73
Cumberland Mkt NW1 273 J2
Cumberland Mkt NW1 141 DH69
Cumberland Mkt Est NW1 273 J2
Cumberland Mills Sq E14 163 ED78
Saunders Ness Rd
Cumberland Pk NW10 139 CU69
Cumberland Pk W3 138 CQ73
Cumberland Pl NW1 273 H2
Cumberland Pl SE6 184 EF88
Cumberland Pl, Sun. 195 BU98
Cumberland Rd E12 124 EK63
Cumberland Rd E13 144 EH71
Cumberland Rd E17 101 DY54
Cumberland Rd N9 100 DW46
Cumberland Rd N22 99 DM54
Cumberland Rd SE25 202 DV100
Cumberland Rd SW13 159 CT81
Cumberland Rd W3 138 CQ73
Cumberland Rd W7 157 CF75
Cumberland Rd, Ashf. 174 BK90
Cumberland Rd, Brom. 204 EE98
Cumberland Rd, Grays 170 FY75
Cumberland Rd, Har. 116 CB57
Cumberland Rd, Rich. 158 CN80
Cumberland Rd, Stan. 118 CM55
Cumberland St SW1 277 J10
Cumberland St SW1 161 DH78
Cumberland St, Stai. 173 BD92
Cumberland Ter NW1 273 H2
Cumberland Ter Ms NW1 273 H1
Cumberland Vil W3 138 CQ73
Cumberland Rd
Cumberlands, Ken. 236 DR115
Cumberlow Av SE25 202 DT97
Cumberlow Pl, Hem.H. 41 BQ21
Cumbernauld Gdns, Sun. 175 BT92
Cumberton Rd N17 100 DR53
Cumbrae Cl, Slou. 132 AU74
St. Pauls Av
Cumbrae Gdns, Surb. 197 CJ102
Cumbria Ho SE26 182 DU91
High Level Dr
Cumbrian Av, Bexh. 167 FE81
Cumbrian Gdns NW2 119 CX61
Cumbrian Way, Uxb. 134 BK66
Chippendale Waye
Cumley Rd, Ong. 71 FE30
Cumming St N1 274 B1
Cumming St N1 141 DM68
Cummings Hall La, Rom. 106 FJ48
Cumnor Gdns, Epsom 217 CU107
Cumnor Ri, Ken. 236 DQ117
Cumnor Rd, Sutt. 218 DC107
Cunard Cres N21 82 DR44
Cunard Pl EC3 275 N9
Cunard Rd NW10 138 CR69
Cunard St SE5 162 DS79
Albany Rd
Cunard Wk SE16 163 DY77
Cundalls Rd, Ware 33 DY05
Cundy Rd E16 144 EJ72
Cundy St SW1 276 G9
Cundy St SW1 160 DG77
Cundy St Est SW1 276 G9
Cunliffe Cl (Headley), Epsom 232 CP124
Cunliffe Rd, Epsom 217 CT105
Cunliffe St SW16 181 DJ93
Cunningham Av, Enf. 83 DY36
Cunningham Av, Guil. 243 BA133
Cunningham Av, St.Alb. 43 CF22
Cunningham Cl, Rom. 126 EW57
Cunningham Cl, W.Wick. 203 EB103
Cunningham Hill Rd, St.Alb. 43 CF22
Cunningham Pk, Har. 116 CC57
Cunningham Pl NW8 140 DD70
Cunningham Ri, Epp. 71 FC25
Cunningham Rd N15 122 DU56
Cunningham Rd, Bans. 234 DD115
Cunningham Rd (Cheshunt), Wal.Cr. 67 DY27
Cunnington St W4 158 CQ76
Cupar Rd SW11 160 DG81
Cupid Grn La, Hem.H. 40 BN15
Cupola Cl, Brom. 184 EH92
Curates Wk, Dart. 188 FK90
Cureton St SW1 277 N9
Cureton St SW1 161 DK77
Curfew Bell Rd, Cher. 193 BF101
Curfew Ho, Bark. 145 EQ67
St. Ann's
Curfew Yd, Wind. 151 AR80
Thames St
Curie Gdns NW9 96 CS54
Pasteur Cl
Curlew Cl SE28 146 EX73
Curlew Cl, Berk. 38 AW20
Curlew Cl, S.Croy. 221 DX111
Curlew Ct, Brox. 49 DZ23
Curlew Ct, Surb. 198 CM104
Curlew Gdns, Guil. 243 BD132
Curlew Ho, Enf. 83 DX43
Allington Ct
Curlew St SE1 279 P4
Curlew St SE1 162 DT75
Curlew Ter, Ilf. 125 EN55
Tiptree Cres
Curlew Way, Hayes 136 BX71
Curlews, The, Grav. 191 GK89
Curling Cl, Couls. 235 DM120
Curling La, Grays 170 FZ78
Curling Vale, Guil. 258 AU136
Curnick's La SE27 182 DQ91
Chapel Rd
Curnock Est NW1 141 DJ67
Plender St
Curran Av, Sid. 185 ET85
Curran Av, Wall. 200 DG104
Curran Cl, Uxb. 134 BJ70
Currey Rd, Grnf. 137 CD65
Curricle St W3 138 CS74
Currie Hill Cl SW19 179 CZ91
Currie St, Hert. 32 DS09
Curries La, Slou. 111 AK64
Curry Ri NW7 97 CX51
Cursitor St EC4 274 D8
Cursitor St EC4 141 DN72
Curtain Pl EC2 142 DS69
Curtain Rd
Curtain Rd EC2 275 M5
Curtain Rd EC2 142 DS70
Curteys, Harl. 36 EX10
Curthwaite Gdns, Enf. 81 DK42
Curtis Cl, Rick. 92 BG46
Curtis Dr W3 138 CR72
Curtis Fld Rd SW16 181 DM91
Curtis Gdns, Dor. 263 CG135
Curtis La, Wem. 138 CL65
Montrose Cres
Curtis Mill Grn, Rom. 87 FF42
Curtis Mill La, Rom. 87 FF42
Curtis Rd, Dor. 263 CF135
Curtis Rd, Epsom 216 CQ105
Curtis Rd, Hem.H. 41 BQ21
Curtis Rd, Horn. 128 FM60
Curtis Rd, Houns. 176 BZ87
Curtis St SE1 279 P8
Curtis St SE1 162 DT77
Curtis Way SE1 279 P8
Curtis Way SE1 162 DT77
Curtis Way SE28 146 EV73
Tawney Rd
Curtis Way, Berk. 38 AX20
Curtismill Cl, Orp. 206 EV97
Curtismill Way, Orp. 206 EV97
Curvan Cl, Epsom 217 CT110
Curve, The W12 139 CU73
Curwen Av E7 124 EH63
Woodford Rd
Curwen Rd W12 159 CU75
Curzon Av, Beac. 89 AK51
Curzon Av, Enf. 83 DX43
Curzon Av (Hazlemere), H.Wyc. 88 AC45
Curzon Av, Stan. 95 CG53
Curzon Cl (Hazlemere), H.Wyc. 88 AC45
Curzon Cl, Orp. 223 ER105
Curzon Cl, Wey. 212 BN105
Curzon Rd
Curzon Cres NW10 139 CT66
Curzon Cres, Bark. 145 ET68
Curzon Dr, Grays 170 GC80
Curzon Gate W1 276 G3
Curzon Gate W1 140 DG74
Curzon Mall, Slou. 152 AT75
High St
Curzon Pl W1 276 G3
Curzon Pl, Pnr. 116 BW57
Curzon Rd N10 99 DH54
Curzon Rd W5 137 CH70
Curzon Rd, Th.Hth. 201 DN100
Curzon Rd, Wey. 212 BN105
Curzon St W1 276 G3
Curzon St W1 140 DG74
Cusack Cl, Twick. 177 CF91
Waldegrave Rd
Cussons Cl (Cheshunt), Wal.Cr. 66 DU29
Custom Ho Quay EC3 142 DS73
Lower Thames St
Custom Ho Reach SE16 163 DZ75
Custom Ho Wk EC3 279 M1
Custom Ho Wk EC3 142 DS73
Cut, The SE1 278 E4
Cut, The SE1 161 DN75
Cut, The, Slou. 131 AN70
Cut Hills, Egh. 192 AV95
Cut Hills, Vir.W. 192 AV95
Cutcombe Rd SE5 162 DQ82
Cuthberga Cl, Bark. 145 EQ66
George St
Cuthbert Gdns SE25 202 DS97
Cuthbert Rd E17 123 EC55
Cuthbert Rd N18 100 DU50
Fairfield Rd
Cuthbert Rd, Croy. 201 DP103
Cuthbert St W2 140 DD70
Cuthberts Cl, Wal.Cr. 66 DT29
Cuthill Wk SE5 162 DR81
Kerfield Pl
Cutler St E1 275 N8
Cutler St E1 142 DS72
Cutlers Gdns E1 275 N8
Cutlers Gdns Arc EC2 142 DS72
Cutler St
Cutlers Sq E14 163 EA77
Britannia Rd
Cutlers Ter N1 142 DR65
Balls Pond Rd
Cutmore Dr (Colney Heath), St.Alb. 44 CP22
Cutmore St, Grav. 191 GH87
Cutthroat All, Rich. 177 CJ89
Ham St
Cutthroat La, Hodd. 49 DZ15
Cutting, The, Red. 266 DF136
Cuttsfield Ter, Hem.H. 39 BF21
Cutty Sark Ct, Green. 189 FU85
Low Cl
Cutty Sark Gdns SE10 163 EC79
King William Wk
Cuxton Cl, Bexh. 186 EY85
Cwmbran Ct, Hem.H. 40 BM16
Cyclamen Cl, Hmptn. 176 CA93
Gresham Rd
Cyclamen Rd, Swan. 207 FD98
Cyclamen Way, Epsom 216 CP106
Cyclops Ms E14 163 EA77
Cygnet Av, Felt. 176 BW87
Cygnet Cl NW10 118 CR64
Cygnet Cl, Borwd. 78 CQ39
Cygnet Cl, Nthwd. 93 BQ52
Cygnet Cl, Wok. 226 AV116
Cygnet Gdns (Northfleet), Grav. 191 GF89
Cygnet St E1 142 DT70
Sclater St
Cygnet Vw, Grays 169 FT77
Cygnet Way, Harl. 34 EG14
Roydon Mill Pk
Cygnet Way, Hayes 136 BX71
Cygnets, The, Felt. 176 BY91
Cygnets, The, Stai. 173 BF92
Edgell Rd
Cygnets Cl, Red. 250 DG132
Cygnus Business Cen NW10 139 CT65
Cymbeline Ct, Har. 117 CF58
Cynthia St N1 274 C1
Cynthia St N1 141 DM68
Cyntra Pl E8 142 DV66
Cypress Av, Enf. 81 DN35
Cypress Av, Twick. 176 CC87
Cypress Av, Welw.G.C. 30 DC10
Cypress Cl, Wal.Abb. 67 ED34
Cypress Ct, Vir.W. 192 AY98
Cypress Gro, Ilf. 103 ES51
Cypress Path, Rom. 106 FK52
Cypress Pl W1 273 L5
Cypress Rd SE25 202 DS96
Cypress Rd, Guil. 242 AW132
Cypress Rd, Har. 95 CD54
Cypress Tree Cl, Sid. 185 ET87
White Oak Gdns
Cypress Wk (Englefield Grn), Egh. 172 AV93
Cypress Wk, Wat. 75 BV35
Cedar Wd Dr
Cypress Way, Bans. 217 CX114
Cyprus Av N3 97 CY54
Cyprus Cl N4 121 DP58
Atterbury Rd
Cyprus Gdns N3 97 CY54
Cyprus Pl E2 142 DW68
Cyprus Pl E6 145 EN73
Cyprus Rd N3 97 CZ54
Cyprus Rd N9 100 DT47
Cyprus Roundabout E16 145 EN73
Royal Albert Way
Cyprus St E2 142 DW68
Cyrena Rd SE22 182 DT86
Cyril Mans SW11 160 DF81
Cyril Rd, Bexh. 166 EY82
Cyril Rd, Orp. 206 EU101
Cyrils Way, St.Alb. 43 CD23
Maynard Dr
Cyrus St EC1 274 G4
Cyrus St EC1 141 DP70
Czar St SE8 163 EA79

D

Dabbling Cl, Erith 167 FH80
Dabbs Hill La, Nthlt. 116 CB64
D'Abernon Cl, Esher 214 CA105
D'Abernon Dr (Stoke D'Abernon), Cob. 230 BY116
Dabin Cres SE10 163 EC81
Dacca St SE8 163 DZ79
Dace Rd E3 143 EA66
Dacorum Way, Hem.H. 40 BJ20
Dacre Av, Ilf. 103 EN54
Dacre Av, S.Ock. 149 FR74
Dacre Cl, Chig. 103 EQ49
Dacre Cl, Grnf. 136 CB68
Dacre Cres, S.Ock. 149 FR74
Dacre Gdns SE13 164 EE84
Dacre Gdns, Borwd. 78 CR43
Dacre Gdns, Chig. 103 EQ49
Dacre Pk SE13 164 EE83
Dacre Pl SE13 164 EE83
Dacre Rd E11 124 EF60
Dacre Rd E13 144 EH67
Dacre Rd, Croy. 201 DL101
Dacre St SW1 277 M6
Dacre St SW1 161 DK76
Dacres Rd SE23 183 DX90
Dade Way, Sthl. 156 BZ78
Dad's Wd, Harl. 51 EQ15
Haydens Rd
Daerwood Cl, Brom. 205 EM102
Daffodil Av, Brwd. 108 FV43
Daffodil Cl, Croy. 203 DX102
Primrose La
Daffodil Cl, Hat. 29 CT14
Great Braitch La
Daffodil Gdns, Ilf. 125 EP64
Daffodil Pl, Hmptn. 176 CA93
Gresham Rd
Daffodil St W12 139 CT73
Dafforne Rd SW17 180 DG90
Dagden Rd (Shalford), Guil. 258 AY140
Dagenham Av, Dag. 146 EY67
Dagenham Rd E10 123 DZ60
Dagenham Rd, Dag. 127 FC63
Dagenham Rd, Rain. 147 FD66
Dagenham Rd, Rom. 127 FD62
Dagger La, Borwd. 77 CG44
Daggs Dell Rd, Hem.H. 39 BE18
Dagley Fm Pk Homes (Shalford), Guil. 258 AX140
Dagley La (Shalford), Guil. 258 AX140
Dagmar Av, Wem. 118 CM63
Dagmar Gdns NW10 139 CX68
Dagmar Ms, Sthl. 156 BY76
Dagmar Rd
Dagmar Pas N1 141 DP67
Cross St
Dagmar Rd N4 121 DN59
Dagmar Rd N15 122 DR56
Cornwall Rd
Dagmar Rd N22 99 DK53
Dagmar Rd SE5 162 DS81
Dagmar Rd SE25 202 DS99
Dagmar Rd, Dag. 147 FC66
Dagmar Rd, Kings.T. 198 CM95
Dagmar Rd, Sthl. 156 BY76
Dagmar Rd, Wind. 151 AR82
Dagmar Ter N1 141 DP67
Dagnall Cres, Uxb. 134 BJ71
Dagnall Pk SE25 202 DS100
Dagnall Rd SE25 202 DS99
Dagnall St SW11 160 DF82
Dagnam Pk Cl, Rom. 106 FN50
Dagnam Pk Dr, Rom. 106 FL50
Dagnam Pk Gdns, Rom. 106 FN51
Dagnam Pk Sq, Rom. 106 FP51
Dagnan Rd SW12 181 DH87
Dagonet Gdns, Brom. 184 EG90
Dagonet Rd, Brom. 184 EG90
Dahlia Cl (Cheshunt), Wal.Cr. 66 DQ25
Dahlia Dr, Swan. 207 FF96
Dahlia Gdns, Ilf. 145 EP65
Dahlia Gdns, Mitch. 201 DK98
Dahlia Rd SE2 166 EV77
Dahomey Rd SW16 181 DJ93
Daiglen Dr, S.Ock. 149 FU73
Daimler Way, Wall. 219 DL108
Daines Cl E12 125 EM62
Colchester Av
Daines Cl, S.Ock. 149 FU70
Dainford Cl, Brom. 183 ED92
Dainton Cl, Brom. 204 EH95
Daintry Cl, Har. 117 CG56
Daintry Lo, Nthwd. 93 BT52
Dairsie Rd SE9 165 EN83
Dairy Cl NW10 139 CU67
Dairy Cl (Sutton at Hone), Dart. 188 FP94
Dairy Cl, Th.Hth. 202 DQ96
Dairy La SE18 165 EM77
Dairy La, Eden. 255 EN134
Dairy Ms SW9 161 DL83
Dairy Wk SW19 179 CY91
Dairy Way, Abb.L. 59 BT29
Dairyglen Av, Wal.Cr. 67 DY31
Dairyman Cl NW2 119 CY62
Claremont Rd
Dairyman's Wk, Guil. 243 BB129
Daisy Cl, Croy. 203 DX102
Primrose La
Daisy Dobbins Wk N19 121 DL59
Hillrise Rd
Daisy La SW6 160 DA83
Daisy Rd E16 144 EE70
Cranberry La
Daisy Rd E18 102 EH54
Dakota Cl, Wall. 219 DM108
Handley Page Rd
Dakota Gdns E6 144 EL70
Dakota Gdns, Nthlt. 136 BY69
Argus Way
Dalberg Rd SW2 181 DN85
Dalberg Way SE2 166 EX76
Lanridge Rd
Dalby Rd SW18 160 DC84
Dalby St NW5 141 DH65
Dalcross Rd, Houns. 156 BY82
Dale, The, Kes. 222 EK105
Dale, The, Wal.Abb. 68 EE34
Dale Av, Edg. 96 CM53
Dale Av, Houns. 156 BY83
Dale Cl SE3 164 EG83
Dale Cl, Add. 212 BH106
Dale Cl, Barn. 80 DB44
Dale Cl, Dart. 187 FF86
Dale Cl, Pnr. 93 BV53
Dale Cl, S.Ock. 149 FU72
Dale Ct, Saw. 36 EX06
The Crest
Dale Ct, Slou. 151 AQ75
Tuns La
Dale Dr, Hayes 135 BT70
Dale End, Dart. 187 FF86
Dale Rd
Dale Gdns, Wdf.Grn. 102 EH49
Dale Grn Rd N11 99 DH48
Dale Gro N12 98 DC50
Dale Pk Av, Cars. 200 DF103
Dale Pk Rd SE19 202 DQ95
Dale Rd NW5 120 DG64
Grafton Rd
Dale Rd SE17 161 DP79
Dale Rd, Dart. 187 FF86
Dale Rd (Southfleet), Grav. 190 GA91
Dale Rd, Grnf. 136 CB71
Dale Rd, Pur. 219 DN112
Dale Rd, Sun. 175 BT94
Dale Rd, Sutt. 217 CZ105
Dale Rd, Swan. 207 FC96
Dale Rd, Walt. 195 BT101
Dale Row W11 139 CY72
St. Marks Rd
Dale St W4 158 CS78
Dale Vw (Headley), Epsom 232 CP123
Dale Vw, Erith 167 FF82
Dale Vw, Wok. 226 AU118
Dale Vw Av E4 101 EC47
Dale Vw Cres E4 101 EC47
Dale Vw Gdns E4 101 ED48
Dale Wk, Dart. 188 FQ88
Dale Wd Rd, Orp. 205 ES101
Dalebury Rd SW17 180 DE89
Dalegarth Gdns, Pur. 220 DR113
Daleham Av, Egh. 173 BA93
Daleham Dr, Uxb. 135 BP72
Daleham Gdns NW3 120 DD64
Daleham Ms NW3 140 DD65
Dalehead NW1 273 K1
Dalehead NW1 141 DJ68
Dalemain Ms E16 144 EG74
Hanover Av
Dales Path, Borwd. 78 CR43
Farriers Way
Dales Rd, Borwd. 78 CR43
Daleside, Ger.Cr. 112 AY60
Daleside, Orp. 224 EU106
Daleside Cl, Orp. 224 EU107
Daleside Dr, Pot.B. 63 CZ32
Daleside Gdns, Chig. 103 EQ48
Daleside Rd SW16 181 DH92
Daleside Rd, Epsom 216 CR107
Dalestone Ms, Rom. 105 FH51
Daleview Rd N15 122 DS58
Dalewood, Welw.G.C. 30 DD10
Dalewood Cl, Horn. 128 FM59
Dalewood Gdns, Wor.Pk. 199 CV103
Daley St E9 143 DX65
Daley Thompson Way SW8 161 DH82
Dalgarno Gdns W10 139 CW71
Dalgarno Way W10 139 CW70
Dalgleish St E14 143 DY72
Daling Way E3 143 DY67
Dalkeith Gro, Stan. 95 CK50
Dalkeith Rd SE21 182 DQ88
Dalkeith Rd, Ilf. 125 EQ62
Dallas Rd NW4 119 CU59
Dallas Rd SE26 182 DV91
Dallas Rd W5 138 CM71
Dallas Rd, Sutt. 217 CY107
Dallas Ter, Hayes 155 BT76
Dallega Cl, Hayes 135 BR73
Dawley Rd
Dallin Rd SE18 165 EP80
Dallin Rd, Bexh. 166 EX84
Dalling Rd W6 159 CV76
Dallinger Rd SE12 184 EF86
Dallington Cl, Walt. 214 BW107
Dallington Sq EC1 141 DP70
Dallington St
Dallington St EC1 274 G4
Dallington St EC1 141 DP70
Dalmain Rd SE23 183 DX88
Dalmally Rd, Croy. 202 DT101
Dalmeny Av N7 121 DK63
Dalmeny Av SW16 201 DN96
Dalmeny Cl, Wem. 137 CJ65
Dalmeny Cres, Houns. 157 CD84
Dalmeny Rd N7 121 DK62
Dalmeny Rd, Barn. 80 DC44
Dalmeny Rd, Cars. 218 DG108
Dalmeny Rd, Erith 167 FB81
Dalmeny Rd, Wor.Pk. 199 CV104
Dalmeyer Rd NW10 139 CT65
Dalmore Av (Claygate), Esher 215 CF107
Dalmore Rd SE21 182 DQ89
Dalroy Cl, S.Ock. 149 FU72
Dalrymple Cl N14 99 DK45
Dalrymple Rd SE4 163 DY84
Dalston Cross Shop Cen E8 142 DT65
Dalston Gdns, Stan. 96 CL53
Dalston La E8 142 DT65
Dalton Av, Mitch. 200 DE96
Dalton Cl, Hayes 135 BR70
Dalton Cl, Orp. 205 ES104
Dalton Cl, Pur. 220 DQ112
Dalton Rd (Harrow Weald), Har. 95 CD54
Dalton St SE27 181 DP89
Dalton St, St.Alb. 43 CD19
Dalton Way, Wat. 76 BX43
Daltons Rd, Orp. 207 FB104
Daltons Rd, Swan. 207 FC102
Dalwood St SE5 162 DS81
Daly Ct E15 123 EC64
Clays La
Dalyell Rd SW9 161 DM83
Damascene Wk SE21 182 DQ88
Lovelace Rd
Damask Cres E16 144 EE70
Cranberry La
Damask Grn, Hem.H. 39 BE21
Dame St N1 142 DQ68
Damer Ter SW10 160 DC80
Tadema Rd
Dames Rd E7 124 EG62
Dameswick Vw, St.Alb. 60 CA27
Damien St E1 142 DV72
Damigos Rd, Grav. 191 GM88
Damon Cl, Sid. 186 EV90
Damphurst La, Dor. 262 BZ139
Sheephouse La
Damson Ct, Swan. 207 FD98
Damson Dr, Hayes 135 BU73
Damson Gro, Slou. 151 AQ75
Damson Way, Cars. 218 DF110
Damson Way, St.Alb. 43 CJ18
Damsonwood Rd, Sthl. 156 CA76
Dan Leno Wk SW6 160 DB80
Britannia Rd
Danbrook Rd SW16 201 DL95
Danbury Cl, Brwd. 108 FT43
Danbury Cl, Rom. 126 EX55
Danbury Cres, S.Ock. 149 FV72
Danbury Ms, Wall. 219 DH105
Danbury Rd, Loug. 102 EL45
Danbury Rd, Rain. 147 FF67
Danbury St N1 141 DP68
Danbury Way, Wdf.Grn. 102 EJ51
Danby St SE15 162 DT83
Dancer Rd SW6 159 CZ81
Dancer Rd, Rich. 158 CN83
Dancers Hill Rd, Barn. 79 CY36
Dancers La, Barn. 79 CW35
Dandelion Cl, Rom. 127 FE61
Dando Cres SE3 164 EH83
Dandridge Cl SE10 164 EF78
Dandridge Cl, Slou. 152 AX76
Dandridge Dr, B.End 110 AC60
Millside
Dane Cl, Amer. 72 AT41
Dane Cl, Bex. 186 FA87
Dane Cl, Orp. 223 ER106
Dane Ct, Wok. 227 BF115
Dane Pl E3 143 DY68
Roman Rd
Dane Rd N18 100 DW48
Dane Rd SW19 200 DC95
Dane Rd W13 137 CJ74
Dane Rd, Ashf. 175 BQ93
Dane Rd, Ilf. 125 EQ64
Dane Rd (Otford), Sev. 241 FE117
Dane Rd, Sthl. 136 BY73
Dane Rd, Warl. 237 DX117
Dane St WC1 274 B7
Danebury (New Addington), Croy. 221 EB107
Danebury Av SW15 178 CS86
Daneby Rd SE6 183 EB90
Danecourt Gdns, Croy. 202 DT104
Danecroft Rd SE24 182 DQ85
Danehill Wk, Sid. 186 EU90
Hatherley Rd
Danehurst Gdns, Ilf. 124 EL57
Danehurst St SW6 159 CY81
Daneland, Barn. 80 DF44
Danemead, Hodd. 33 EA14

Danemead Gro, Nthlt. 116 CB64
Danemere St SW15 159 CW83
Danes, The (Park St), St.Alb. 60 CC28
Danes Cl (Northfleet), Grav. 190 GC90
Danes Cl (Oxshott), Lthd. 214 CC114
Danes Ct, Wem. 118 CP62
Danes Gate, Har. 117 CE55
Danes Hill, Wok. 227 BA118
Danes Rd, Rom. 127 FC59
Danes Way, Brwd. 108 FU43
Danes Way (Oxshott), Lthd. 215 CD114
Danesbury Pk, Hert. 32 DR08
Danesbury Rd, Felt. 175 BV88
Danescombe SE12 184 EG88
Winn Rd
Danescourt Cres, Sutt. 200 DC103
Danescroft NW4 119 CX57
Danescroft Av NW4 119 CX57
Danescroft Gdns NW4 119 CX57
Danesdale Rd E9 143 DY65
Danesfield SE5 162 DS79
Albany Rd
Danesfield Cl, Walt. 195 BV104
Daneshill, Red. 250 DE133
Daneshill Cl, Red. 250 DE133
Danesrood, Guil. 259 AZ135
Lower Edgeborough Rd
Daneswood Av SE6 183 EC90
Daneswood Cl, Wey. 213 BP106
Danethorpe Rd, Wem. 137 CK65
Danetree Cl, Epsom 216 CQ108
Danetree Rd, Epsom 216 CQ108
Danette Gdns, Dag. 126 EZ61
Daneville Rd SE5 162 DR81
Dangan Rd E11 124 EG58
Daniel Bolt Cl E14 143 EB71
Uamvar St
Daniel Cl N18 100 DW49
Daniel Cl SW17 180 DE93
Daniel Cl, Grays 171 GH76
Daniel Cl (Chafford Hundred), Grays 170 FY75
Daniel Cl, Houns. 176 BZ87
Harvey Rd
Daniel Gdns SE15 162 DT80
Daniel Pl NW4 119 CV59
Daniel Rd W5 138 CM73
Daniel Way, Bans. 218 DB114
Daniell Way, Croy. 201 DL102
Daniells, Welw.G.C. 30 DA08
Daniels La, Warl. 237 DZ116
Daniels Ms SE4 163 DZ84
Daniels Rd SE15 162 DW83
Danses Cl, Guil. 243 BD132
Dansey Pl W1 273 M10
Dansington Rd, Well. 166 EU84
Danson Cres, Well. 166 EV83
Danson La, Well. 166 EV84
Danson Mead, Well. 166 EW83
Danson Pk, Bexh. 166 EW84
Danson Rd, Bex. 186 EX85
Danson Rd, Bexh. 186 EX85
Danson Underpass, Sid. 186 EW86
Danson Rd
Dante Pl SE11 278 G8
Dante Rd SE11 278 F8
Dante Rd SE11 161 DP77
Danube St SW3 276 C10
Danvers Rd N8 121 DK56
Danvers St SW3 160 DD79
Danvers Way, Cat. 236 DQ123
Danyon Cl, Rain. 148 FJ68
Danziger Way, Borwd. 78 CQ39
Dapdune Ct, Guil. 242 AW134
Dapdune Rd, Guil. 242 AW134
Dapdune Wf, Guil. 242 AW134
Daphne Gdns E4 101 EC48
Gunners Gro
Daphne St SW18 180 DC86
Daplyn St E1 142 DU71
Hanbury St
Darblay Cl (Sandridge), St.Alb. 28 CM10
D'Arblay St W1 273 L9
D'Arblay St W1 141 DJ72
Darby Cl, Cat. 236 DQ122
Fairbourne La
Darby Cres, Sun. 196 BW96
Darby Dr, Wal.Abb. 67 EC33
Darby Gdns, Sun. 196 BW96
Darcy Av, Wall. 219 DJ105
Darcy Cl N20 98 DD47
D'Arcy Cl, Brwd. 109 GB45
Darcy Cl, Couls. 235 DP119
Darcy Cl (Cheshunt), Wal.Cr. 67 DY31
D'Arcy Dr, Har. 117 CK56
Darcy Gdns, Dag. 146 EZ67
D'Arcy Gdns, Har. 118 CL56
D'Arcy Pl, Ash. 232 CM117
D'Arcy Pl, Brom. 204 EG98
Darcy Rd SW16 201 DL96
D'Arcy Rd, Ash. 232 CM117
Darcy Rd, Islw. 157 CG81
London Rd
D'Arcy Rd, Sutt. 217 CX105
Dare Gdns, Dag. 126 EY62
Grafton Rd
Darell Rd, Rich. 158 CN83
Darent Ind Pk, Erith 168 FJ79
Darent Mead (Sutton at Hone), Dart. 208 FP95
Darent Valley Path, Dart. 188 FM89
Darent Valley Path, Sev. 241 FG115
Darenth Cl, Sev. 256 FC122
Darenth Gdns, West. 255 ER126
Quebec Av
Darenth Hill (Darenth), Dart. 188 FQ92
Darenth La (Dunton Grn), Sev. 256 FE121
Darenth La, S.Ock. 149 FU72
Darenth Pk Av, Dart. 189 FR89
Darenth Rd N16 122 DT59
Darenth Rd, Dart. 188 FM87
Darenth Rd (Darenth), Dart. 188 FP91
Darenth Rd, Well. 166 EU81
Darenth Way, Horl. 268 DF145
Darenth Way (Shoreham), Sev. 225 FG111
Darenth Wd Rd, Dart. 189 FS89
Darfield Rd SE4 183 DZ85
Darfield Rd, Guil. 243 BA131
Darfield Way W10 139 CX72
Darfur St SW15 159 CX83
Dargate Cl SE19 182 DT94
Chipstead Cl
Darien Rd SW11 160 DD83
Dark Ho Wk EC3 142 DS73
King William St
Dark La, Brwd. 107 FU52
Dark La (Puttenham), Guil. 260 BM139
Dark La (Cheshunt), Wal.Cr. 66 DU31
Dark La (Musley La), Ware 33 DY05
Darkes La, Pot.B. 64 DA32
Darkhole Ride, Wind. 150 AH84
Darlan Rd SW6 159 CZ80
Darlands Dr, Barn. 79 CX43
Darlaston Rd SW19 179 CX94
Darley Cl, Add. 212 BJ106
Darley Cl, Croy. 203 DY100
Darley Cft, St.Alb. 60 CB28
Darley Dr, N.Mal. 198 CR96
Darley Gdns, Mord. 200 DB100
Darley Rd N9 100 DT46
Darley Rd SW11 180 DF86
Darling Rd SE4 163 EA83
Darling Row E1 142 DV70
Darlington Cl, Amer. 55 AR38
King George V Rd
Darlington Gdns, Rom. 106 FK50
Darlington Path, Rom. 106 FK50
Darlington Gdns
Darlington Rd SE27 181 DP92
Darlton Cl, Dart. 167 FF83
Darmaine Cl, S.Croy. 220 DQ108
Churchill Rd
Darndale Cl E17 101 DZ54
Darnets Fld (Otford), Sev. 241 FF117
Darnhills, Rad. 77 CG35
Darnicle Hill (Cheshunt), Wal.Cr. 65 DM25
Darnley Ho E14 143 DY72
Darnley Pk, Wey. 195 BP104
Darnley Rd E9 142 DV65
Darnley Rd, Grav. 191 GG88
Darnley Rd, Grays 170 GB79
Stanley Rd
Darnley Rd, Wdf.Grn. 102 EG53
Darnley St, Grav. 191 GG87
Darnley Ter W11 139 CY74
St. James's Gdns
Darns Hill, Swan. 207 FC101
Darrell Cl, Slou. 153 AZ77
Darrell Rd SE22 182 DU85
Darren Cl N4 121 DM59
Darrick Wd Rd, Orp. 205 ER103
Darrington Rd, Borwd. 78 CL39
Darris Cl, Hayes 136 BY70
Darsley Dr SW8 161 DL81
Dart, The, Hem.H. 40 BN15
Dart Cl, Slou. 153 BB78
Dart Cl, Upmin. 129 FR58
Dart Grn, S.Ock. 149 FV71
Dart St W10 139 CY69
Dartfields, Rom. 106 FK51
Dartford Av N9 82 DW44
Dartford Bypass, Dart. 187 FE88
Dartford Gdns, Rom. 126 EV58
Heathfield Pk Dr
Dartford Northern Bypass, Dart. 168 FN83
Dartford Rd, Bex. 187 FC88
Dartford Rd, Dart. 187 FG86
Dartford Rd (Farningham), Dart. 208 FP95
Dartford Rd, Sev. 257 FJ124
Dartford St SE17 162 DQ79
Dartford Trade Pk, Dart. 188 FL89
Dartford Tunnel, Dart. 169 FR83
Dartford Tunnel, Purf. 169 FR83
Dartford Tunnel App Rd, Dart. 188 FN86
Dartmoor Wk E14 163 EA77
Charnwood Gdns
Dartmouth Av, Wok. 211 BC114
Dartmouth Cl W11 139 CZ72
Dartmouth Grn, Wok. 211 BD114
Dartmouth Gro SE10 163 EC81
Dartmouth Hill SE10 163 EC81
Dartmouth Pk Av NW5 121 DH62
Dartmouth Pk Hill N19 121 DH60
Dartmouth Pk Hill NW5 121 DH60
Dartmouth Pk Rd NW5 121 DH63
Dartmouth Path, Wok. 211 BD114
Dartmouth Pl SE23 182 DW89
Dartmouth Rd
Dartmouth Pl W4 158 CS79
Dartmouth Rd E16 144 EG72
Fords Pk Rd
Dartmouth Rd NW2 139 CX65
Dartmouth Rd NW4 119 CU58
Dartmouth Rd SE23 182 DW90
Dartmouth Rd SE26 182 DW90
Dartmouth Rd, Brom. 204 EG101
Dartmouth Rd, Ruis. 115 BU62
Dartmouth Row SE10 163 EC81
Dartmouth St SW1 277 M5
Dartmouth St SW1 161 DK75
Dartmouth Ter SE10 163 ED81
Dartnell Av, W.Byf. 212 BH112
Dartnell Cl, W.Byf. 212 BH112
Dartnell Ct, W.Byf. 212 BJ112
Dartnell Cres, W.Byf. 212 BH112
Dartnell Pk Rd, W.Byf. 212 BJ111
Dartnell Pl, W.Byf. 212 BH112
Dartnell Rd, Croy. 202 DT101
Dartrey Wk SW10 160 DD80
World's End Est
Dartview Cl, Grays 170 GE77
Darvel Cl, Wok. 226 AU116
Darvell Dr, Chesh. 54 AN29
Darville Rd N16 122 DT62
Darvills La, Slou. 151 AR75
Darwell Cl E6 145 EN68
Darwin Cl N11 99 DH48
Darwin Cl, Orp. 223 ER106
Darwin Cl, St.Alb. 43 CE16
Darwin Ct, Guil. 242 AX130
Darwin Dr, Sthl. 136 CB72
Darwin Gdns, Wat. 94 BW50
Barnhurst Path
Darwin Rd N22 99 DP53
Darwin Rd W5 157 CJ78
Darwin Rd, Slou. 153 AZ75
Darwin Rd, Til. 171 GF81
Darwin Rd, Well. 165 ET83
Darwin St SE17 279 L8
Darwin St SE17 162 DR77
Daryngton Dr, Grnf. 137 CD68
Daryngton Dr, Guil. 243 BB134
Dashes, The, Harl. 35 ES14
Dashwood Cl, Bexh. 186 FA85
Dashwood Cl, Slou. 152 AW77
Dashwood Cl, W.Byf. 212 BJ112
Dashwood Rd N8 121 DM58
Dashwood Rd, Grav. 191 GG89
Dassett Rd SE27 181 DP92
Datchelor Pl SE5 162 DR81
Datchet Cl, Hem.H. 41 BP15
Datchet Pl (Datchet), Slou. 152 AV81
Datchet Rd SE6 183 DZ90
Datchet Rd, Slou. 152 AT76
Datchet Rd (Horton), Slou. 153 AZ83
Datchet Rd, Wind. 151 AR80
Datchet Rd (Old Windsor), Wind. 172 AU84
Datchworth Ct N4 122 DQ62
Queens Dr
Datchworth Turn, Hem.H. 41 BQ20
Date St SE17 162 DQ78
Daubeney Gdns N17 100 DQ52
Daubeney Rd E5 123 DY63
Daubeney Rd N17 100 DQ52
Daubeney Twr SE8 163 DZ77
Dault Rd SW18 180 DC86
Davall Ho, Grays 170 GA79
Argent St
Davema Cl, Chis. 205 EN95
Brenchley Cl
Davenant Rd N19 121 DK61
Davenant Rd, Croy. 219 DP105
Duppas Hill Rd
Davenant St E1 142 DU71
Davenham Av, Nthwd. 93 BT50
Davenport (Church Langley), Harl. 52 EY16
Davenport Cl, Tedd. 177 CG93
Davenport Rd SE6 183 EB86
Davenport Rd, Sid. 186 EX89
Daventer Dr, Stan. 95 CF52
Daventry Av E17 123 EA57
Daventry Cl (Colnbrook), Slou. 153 BF81
Daventry Gdns, Rom. 106 FJ50
Daventry Grn, Rom. 106 FJ50
Hailsham Rd
Daventry Rd, Rom. 106 FJ50
Daventry St NW1 272 B6
Daventry St NW1 140 DE71
Davern Cl SE10 164 EF77
Davey Cl N7 141 DM65
Davey Rd E9 143 EA66
Davey St SE15 162 DT79
David Av, Grnf. 137 CE69
David Cl, Hayes 155 BR80
David Dr, Rom. 106 FN51
David Lee Pt E15 144 EE67
David Ms W1 272 E6
David Rd, Dag. 126 EY61
David Rd (Colnbrook), Slou. 153 BF82
David St E15 143 ED65
David Twigg Cl, Kings.T. 198 CL95
Davidge St SE1 278 F5
Davidge St SE1 161 DP75
Davids Rd SE23 182 DW88
David's Way, Ilf. 103 ES52
Davidson Gdns SW8 161 DL80
Davidson La, Har. 117 CF59
Grove Hill
Davidson Rd, Croy. 202 DT100
Davidson Way, Rom. 127 FE58
Davies Cl, Croy. 202 DU100
Davies Cl, Rain. 148 FJ69
Davies La E11 124 EE61
Davies Ms W1 273 H10
Davies St W1 273 H10
Davies St W1 141 DH73
Davies St, Hert. 32 DS09
Davies Way (Loudwater), H.Wyc. 88 AC54
Davington Gdns, Dag. 126 EV64
Davington Rd, Dag. 146 EV65
Davinia Cl, Wdf.Grn. 103 EM51
Deacon Way
Davis Av (Northfleet), Grav. 190 GE88
Davis Cl, Sev. 257 FJ122
Davis Rd W3 139 CT74
Davis Rd, Chess. 216 CN105
Davis Rd, Grays 170 FZ76
Davis Rd, S.Ock. 149 FR74
Davis Rd, Wey. 212 BM110
Davis St E13 144 EH68
Davison Cl, Wal.Cr. 67 DX28
Davison Dr (Cheshunt), Wal.Cr. 67 DX28
Davisville Rd W12 159 CU75
Davos Cl, Wok. 226 AY119
Davys Cl (Wheathampstead), St.Alb. 28 CL08
Davys Pl, Grav. 191 GL93
Dawell Dr (Biggin Hill), West. 238 EJ117
Dawes Av, Horn. 128 FK62
Dawes Av, Islw. 177 CG85
Dawes Cl, Chesh. 54 AP32
Dawes Cl, Green. 189 FT85
Dawes Ct, Esher 214 CB105
Dawes E Rd (Burnham), Slou. 130 AJ69
Dawes Ho SE17 279 L9
Dawes La, Rick. 73 BE37
Dawes Moor Cl, Slou. 132 AW72
Dawes Rd SW6 159 CY80
Dawes Rd, Uxb. 134 BL68
Dawes St SE17 279 L10
Dawes St SE17 162 DR78
Dawley, Welw.G.C. 29 CZ06
Dawley Av, Uxb. 135 BQ71
Dawley Ct, Hem.H. 40 BM16
Dawley Grn, S.Ock. 149 FU72
Dawley Par, Hayes 135 BQ73
Dawley Rd
Dawley Ride (Colnbrook), Slou. 153 BE81
Dawley Rd, Hayes 155 BS76
Dawlish Av N13 99 DL49
Dawlish Av SW18 180 DB89
Dawlish Av, Grnf. 137 CG68
Dawlish Dr, Ilf. 125 ES63
Dawlish Dr, Pnr. 116 BY57
Dawlish Dr, Ruis. 115 BU61
Dawlish Rd E10 123 EC61
Dawlish Rd N17 122 DU55
Dawlish Rd NW2 139 CX65
Dawlish Wk, Rom. 106 FJ53
Dawn Cl, Houns. 156 BY83
Dawn Cres E15 143 ED67
Bridge Rd
Dawn Redwood Cl (Horton), Slou. 153 BA83
Dawnay Gdns SW18 180 DD89
Dawnay Rd SW18 180 DC89
Dawnay Rd (Bookham), Lthd. 246 CB126
Dawpool Rd NW2 119 CT61
Daws Hill E4 83 EC41
Daws La NW7 97 CT50
Dawson Av, Bark. 145 ET66
Dawson Av, Orp. 206 EV96
Dawson Cl SE18 165 EQ77
Dawson Cl, Hayes 135 BR71
Dawson Cl, Wind. 151 AN82
Dawson Dr, Rain. 147 FH66
Dawson Dr, Swan. 187 FE94
Dawson Gdns, Bark. 145 ET66
Dawson Av
Dawson Hts Est SE22 182 DU87
Dawson Pl W2 140 DA73
Dawson Rd NW2 119 CW64
Dawson Rd, Kings.T. 198 CM97
Dawson Rd (Byfleet), W.Byf. 212 BK111
Dawson St E2 142 DT68
Dax Ct, Sun. 196 BW97
Thames St
Daybrook Rd SW19 200 DB96
Daye Mead, Welw.G.C. 30 DB12
Daylesford Av SW15 159 CU84
Daylop Dr, Chig. 104 EV48
Daymer Gdns, Pnr. 115 BV56
Daymerslea Ridge, Lthd. 231 CJ121
Days Acre, S.Croy. 220 DT110
Days Cl, Hat. 45 CT18
Days La, Brwd. 108 FU42
Days La, Sid. 185 ES87
Days Mead, Hat. 45 CT18
Daysbrook Rd SW2 181 DM88
Dayseys Hill (Outwood), Red. 267 DN143
Dayspring, Guil. 242 AV130
Dayton Dr, Erith 168 FK78
Dayton Gro SE15 162 DW81
De Barowe Ms N5 121 DP63
Leigh Rd
De Beauvoir Cres N1 142 DS67
De Beauvoir Est N1 142 DR67
De Beauvoir Rd N1 142 DS67
De Beauvoir Sq N1 142 DS66
De Bohun Av N14 81 DH44
De Brome Rd, Felt. 176 BW88
De Burgh Pk, Bans. 234 DB115
De Crespigny Pk SE5 162 DR82
De Frene Rd SE26 183 DX91
De Gama Pl E14 163 EA78
Maritime Quay
De Havilland Av, Hat. 44 CS17
De Havilland Cl, Hat. 45 CT17
De Havilland Ct, Rad. 62 CL32
Armstrong Gdns
De Havilland Dr, Wey. 212 BL111
De Havilland Rd, Edg. 96 CP54
De Havilland Rd, Houns. 156 BW80
De Havilland Rd, Wall. 219 DL108
De Havilland Way, Abb.L. 59 BT32
De Havilland Way (Stanwell), Stai. 174 BK86
De Lapre Cl, Orp. 206 EX101
De Lara Way, Wok. 226 AX118
De Laune St SE17 161 DP78
De Luci Rd, Erith 167 FC78
De Lucy St SE2 166 EV77
De Mandeville Gate, Enf. 82 DU42
Southbury Rd
De Mel Cl, Epsom 216 CN112
Abbots Av
De Montfort Par SW16 181 DL90
Streatham High Rd
De Montfort Rd SW16 181 DL90
De Morgan Rd SW6 160 DB83
De Quincey Ms E16 144 EG74
Wesley Av
De Quincey Rd N17 100 DR53
De Ros Pl, Egh. 173 BA93
De Salis Rd, Uxb. 135 BQ70
De Tany Ct, St.Alb. 43 CD21
De Vere Cotts W8 160 DC76
Canning Pl
De Vere Gdns W8 160 DC75
De Vere Gdns, Ilf. 125 EM61
De Vere Ms W8 160 DC76
Canning Pl
De Vere Wk, Wat. 75 BS40
De Walden St W1 272 G7
Deacon Cl (Downside), Cob. 229 BV119
Deacon Cl, Pur. 219 DL109
Deacon Cl, St.Alb. 43 CD24
Creighton Av
Deacon Fld, Guil. 242 AV133
Midleton Rd
Deacon Ms N1 142 DR66
Deacon Pl, Cat. 236 DQ123
Deacon Rd NW2 119 CU64
Deacon Rd, Kings.T. 198 CM95
Deacon Way SE17 279 H8
Deacon Way SE17 162 DQ77
Deacon Way, Wdf.Grn. 103 EM52
Deacons Cl, Borwd. 78 CN42
Deacons Cl, Pnr. 93 BV54
Deacons Hill, Wat. 76 BW44
Deacon's Hill Rd, Borwd. 78 CM42
Deacons Leas, Orp. 223 ER105
Deacons Ri N2 120 DD57
Deacons Wk, Hmptn. 176 BZ91
Bishops Gro
Deaconsfield Rd, Hem.H. 40 BK23
Deadfield La, Hert. 30 DF13
Deadhearn La, Ch.St.G. 90 AY46
Deadman's Ash La, Rick. 74 BH36
Deakin Cl, Wat. 93 BS45
Chenies Way
Deal Av, Slou. 131 AM72
Deal Ms W5 157 CK77
Darwin Rd
Deal Porters Way SE16 162 DW76
Deal Rd SW17 180 DG93
Deal St E1 142 DU71
Deal Wk SW9 161 DN80
Mandela St
Deal's Gateway SE10 163 EB81
Blackheath Rd
Dealtry Rd SW15 159 CW84
Dean Av, Hodd. 49 DX17
Dean Bradley St SW1 277 P7
Dean Bradley St SW1 161 DL76
Dean Cl E9 122 DW64
Churchill Wk
Dean Cl SE16 143 DX74
Surrey Water Rd
Dean Cl, Uxb. 134 BM66
Dean Cl, Wind. 151 AK83
Dean Cl, Wok. 227 BE115
Dean Ct, Wem. 117 CH62
Dean Dr, Stan. 96 CL54
Dean Farrar St SW1 277 M6
Dean Farrar St SW1 161 DK76
Dean Fld (Bovingdon), Hem.H. 57 BA27
Dean Gdns E17 123 ED56
Dean Gdns W13 137 CH74
Northfield Av
Dean La, Red. 235 DH123
Dean Moore Cl, St.Alb. 43 CD21
Dean Oak La (Leigh), Reig. 265 CW144
Dean Rd NW2 139 CW65
Dean Rd SE28 146 EU73
Dean Rd, Croy. 220 DR105
Dean Rd, Hmptn. 176 CA92
Dean Rd, Houns. 176 CB85
Dean Ryle St SW1 277 P8
Dean Ryle St SW1 161 DL77
Dean Stanley St SW1 277 P7
Dean Stanley St SW1 161 DL76
Dean St E7 124 EG64
Dean St W1 273 M8
Dean St W1 141 DK72
Dean Trench St SW1 277 P7
Dean Trench St SW1 161 DL76
Dean Wk, Edg. 96 CQ51
Deansbrook Rd
Dean Wk, Lthd. 246 CB126
Dean Way, Sthl. 156 CB75
Dean Wd Rd (Jordans), Beac. 89 AR52
Deanacre Cl (Chalfont St. Peter), Ger.Cr. 90 AY51
Deancroft Rd (Chalfont St. Peter), Ger.Cr. 90 AY51
Deancross St E1 142 DW72
Deane Av, Ruis. 116 BW64
Deane Cft Rd, Pnr. 116 BW58
Deane Way, Ruis. 115 BV58
Deanery Cl N2 120 DE56
Deanery Ms W1 276 G2
Deanery Rd E15 144 EE65
Deanery Rd, Eden. 255 EQ134
Deanery St W1 276 G2
Deanery St W1 140 DG74
Deanhill Rd SW14 158 CP84
Deans Bldgs SE17 279 K9
Deans Bldgs SE17 162 DR77
Deans Cl W4 158 CP79
Deans Cl, Abb.L. 59 BR32
Deans Cl, Amer. 72 AT37
Dean's Cl, Croy. 202 DT104
Deans Cl, Edg. 96 CQ51
Deans Cl (Stoke Poges), Slou. 132 AV67
Deans Cl, Tad. 233 CV124
Deans La
Deans Ct EC4 274 G9
Deans Dr N13 99 DP51
Deans Dr, Edg. 96 CR50
Deans Gdns, St.Alb. 43 CG16
Dean's Gate Cl SE23 183 DX90
Deans La W4 158 CP79
Deans La, Edg. 96 CQ51
Deans La (Nutfield), Red. 251 DN133
Deans La, Tad. 233 CV124
Deans Ms W1 273 J8
Dean's Pl SW1 277 M10
Dean's Pl SW1 161 DK78
Deans Rd W7 137 CF74
Deans Rd, Brwd. 108 FV49
Deans Rd, Red. 251 DJ130
Deans Rd, Sutt. 200 DB104
Deans Wk, Couls. 235 DN118
Deans Way, Edg. 96 CQ50
Dean's Yd SW1 277 N6
Deansbrook Cl, Edg. 96 CQ52
Deansbrook Rd, Edg. 96 CQ51
Deanscroft Av NW9 118 CQ61
Deansfield, Cat. 252 DT125
Deansway N2 120 DD56
Deansway N9 100 DS48
Deansway, Chesh. 54 AP29
Deansway, Hem.H. 40 BM23
Deanway, Ch.St.G. 90 AU48
De'Arn Gdns, Mitch. 200 DE97
Dearne Cl, Stan. 95 CG50
Dearsley Ho, Rain. 147 FD68
Dearsley Rd, Enf. 82 DU41
Deason St E15 143 EC67
High St
Debden Cl, Kings.T. 177 CK92
Debden Cl, Wdf.Grn. 102 EJ52
Debden Grn, Loug. 85 EP38
Debden La, Loug. 85 EP38
Debden Rd, Loug. 85 EP38
Debden Wk, Horn. 147 FH65
Debenham Rd (Cheshunt), Wal.Cr. 66 DV27
Debnams Rd SE16 162 DW77
Rotherhithe New Rd
Deborah Cl, Islw. 157 CE81
Deborah Cres, Ruis. 115 BR59
Debrabant Cl, Erith 167 FD79
Deburgh Rd SW19 180 DC94
Decies Way (Stoke Poges), Slou. 132 AU67
Decima St SE1 279 M6
Decima St SE1 162 DS76
Deck Cl SE16 163 DX75
Thame Rd
Decoy Av NW11 119 CY57
Dedswell Dr (West Clandon), Guil. 244 BG128
Dedworth Dr, Wind. 151 AL81
Dedworth Rd, Wind. 151 AL82
Dee, The, Hem.H. 40 BM15
Dee Cl, Upmin. 129 FS58
Dee Rd, Rich. 158 CM84
Dee St E14 143 EC72
Dee Way, Epsom 216 CS110
Dee Way, Rom. 105 FE53
Deeley Rd SW8 161 DK81
Deena Cl W3 138 CM72
Deena Cl, Slou. 131 AL73
Deep Acres, Amer. 55 AN36
Deep Fld (Datchet), Slou. 152 AV80
Deep Pool La (Chobham), Wok. 210 AV114
Deepdale SW19 179 CX91
Deepdale Av, Brom. 204 EF98
Deepdale Cl N11 98 DG51
Ribblesdale Av
Deepdene W5 138 CM70
Deepdene, Pot.B. 63 CX31
Deepdene Av, Croy. 202 DT104
Deepdene Av, Dor. 263 CJ135
Deepdene Av Rd, Dor. 247 CJ134
Deepdene Cl E11 124 EG56
Deepdene Ct N21 81 DP44
Deepdene Dr, Dor. 263 CJ135
Deepdene Gdns SW2 181 DM87
Deepdene Gdns, Dor. 263 CH135
Deepdene Pk Rd, Dor. 263 CJ135
Deepdene Path, Loug. 85 EN42
Deepdene Pt SE23 183 DX90
Dacres Rd
Deepdene Rd SE5 162 DR84
Deepdene Rd, Loug. 85 EN42
Deepdene Rd, Well. 166 EU83
Deepdene Vale, Dor. 263 CJ135
Deepdene Wd, Dor. 263 CJ136
Deepfield Way, Couls. 235 DL116
Deepfields, Horl. 268 DF146
Deeprose Cl, Guil. 242 AV130
Deepwell Cl, Islw. 157 CG81
Deepwood La, Grnf. 137 CD69
Cowgate Rd
Deer Cl, Hert. 32 DT09
Deer Pk, Harl. 51 EN18
Deer Pk Cl, Kings.T. 178 CP94
Deer Pk Gdns, Mitch. 200 DD97
Deer Pk Rd SW19 200 DB96
Deer Pk Wk, Chesh. 54 AS28
Deer Pk Way, Wal.Abb. 83 EB36
Deer Pk Way, W.Wick. 204 EF103
Deerbarn Rd, Guil. 242 AV133

Deerbrook Rd SE24 181 DP88
Deerdale Rd SE24 162 DQ84
Deere Av, Rain. 147 FG65
Deerfield Cl, Ware 33 DX05
Deerhurst Cl, Felt. 175 BU91
Deerhurst Cres (Hampton Hill), Hmptn. 176 CC92
Deerhurst Rd NW2 139 CX65
Deerhurst Rd SW16 181 DM92
Deerings Dr, Pnr. 115 BU57
Deerings Rd, Reig. 250 DB134
Deerleap Gro E4 83 EB43
Deerleap La, Sev. 224 EX113
Deerleap Rd (Westcott), Dor. 262 CB137
Deers Fm Cl (Wisley), Wok. 228 BL116
Deerswood Av, Hat. 45 CV20
Deerswood Cl, Cat. 236 DU124
Deeside Rd SW17 180 DD90
Deeves Hall La, Pot.B. 62 CS33
Defiance Wk SE18 165 EM76
Defiant Way, Wall. 219 DL108
Defoe Av, Rich. 158 CN80
Defoe Cl SE16 163 DZ75
Vaughan St
Defoe Cl SW17 180 DE93
Defoe Cl, Erith 167 FE81
Selkirk Dr
Defoe Ho EC2 275 J6
Defoe Par, Grays 171 GH76
Defoe Pl EC2 142 DQ71
Beech St
Defoe Pl SW17 180 DF91
Lessingham Av
Defoe Rd N16 122 DS61
Defoe Way, Rom. 105 FB51
Degema Rd, Chis. 185 EP92
Dehar Cres NW9 119 CT59
Dehavilland Cl, Nthlt. 136 BX69
Deimos Dr, Hem.H. 40 BN17
Dekker Rd SE21 182 DS86
Delabole Rd, Red. 251 DL129
Delacourt Rd SE3 164 EH80
Old Dover Rd
Delafield Rd SE7 164 EH78
Delafield Rd, Grays 170 GD78
Delaford Cl, Iver 133 BF72
Delaford Rd SE16 162 DV78
Delaford St SW6 159 CY80
Delagarde Rd, West. 255 EQ126
Delahay Ri, Berk. 38 AV17
Delamare Cres, Croy. 202 DW100
Delamare Rd (Cheshunt), Wal.Cr. 67 DZ30
Delamere Gdns NW7 96 CR51
Delamere Rd SW20 199 CX95
Delamere Rd W5 138 CL74
Delamere Rd, Borwd. 78 CP39
Delamere Rd, Hayes 136 BX73
Delamere Rd, Reig. 266 DB138
Delamere Ter W2 140 DB71
Delancey Pas NW1 141 DH67
Delancey St
Delancey St NW1 141 DH67
Delaporte Cl, Epsom 216 CS112
Delargy Cl, Grays 171 GH76
Delaware Rd W9 140 DB70
Delawyk Cres SE24 182 DQ86
Delcombe Av, Wor.Pk. 199 CW102
Delderfield, Lthd. 231 CK120
Delfcroft, Ware 32 DW05
Delft Way SE22 182 DS85
East Dulwich Gro
Delhi Rd, Enf. 100 DT45
Delhi St N1 141 DL67
Delia St SW18 180 DB87
Delisle Rd SE28 145 ES74
Delius Cl, Borwd. 77 CJ44
Delius Gro E15 143 ED68
Dell, The SE2 166 EU78
Dell, The SE19 202 DT95
Dell, The, Bex. 187 FE88
Dell, The, Brent. 157 CJ79
Dell, The, Brwd. 107 FV51
Dell, The, Felt. 175 BV87
Harlington Rd W
Dell, The (Chalfont St. Peter), Ger.Cr. 90 AY51
Dell, The, Hert. 32 DQ12
Dell, The (Penn), H.Wyc. 88 AC46
Dell, The, Horl. 269 DH147
Dell, The, Nthwd. 93 BS47
Dell, The, Pnr. 94 BX54
Dell, The, Rad. 77 CG36
Dell, The, Reig. 250 DA133
Dell, The, St.Alb. 43 CG18
Dell, The, Tad. 233 CW121
Dell, The, Wal.Abb. 83 EC36
Greenwich Way
Dell, The, Wem. 117 CH64
Dell, The, Wok. 226 AW118
Dell, The, Wdf.Grn. 102 EH48
Dell Cl E15 143 ED67
Dell Cl (Mickleham), Dor. 247 CJ127
Dell Cl (Fetcham), Lthd. 231 CE123
Dell Cl (Farnham Common), Slou. 111 AQ64
Dell Cl, Wall. 219 DK105
Dell Cl, Wdf.Grn. 102 EH48
Dell Fm Rd, Ruis. 115 BR57
Dell La, Epsom 217 CU106
Dell Lees (Seer Grn), Beac. 89 AQ51
Dell Meadow, Hem.H. 40 BL24
Belswains La
Dell Ri (Park St), St.Alb. 60 CB26
Dell Rd, Enf. 82 DW38
Dell Rd, Epsom 217 CU107
Dell Rd, Grays 170 GB77
Dell Rd, Wat. 75 BU37
Dell Rd, West Dr. 154 BM76
Dell Side, Wat. 75 BU37
The Harebreaks
Dell Wk, N.Mal. 198 CS96
Dell Way W13 137 CJ72
Della Path E5 122 DV62
Napoleon Rd
Dellbow Rd, Felt. 175 BV85
Central Way
Dellcott Cl, Welw.G.C. 29 CV08
Dellcut Rd, Hem.H. 40 BN18
Dellfield, Chesh. 54 AN29
Dellfield, St.Alb. 43 CF21
Dellfield Av, Berk. 38 AV17
Dellfield Cl, Beck. 183 EC94
Foxgrove Rd
Dellfield Cl, Berk. 38 AU17
Dellfield Cl, Rad. 77 CE35
Dellfield Cl, Wat. 75 BU40
Dellfield Cres, Uxb. 134 BJ70
Dellfield Par (Cowley), Uxb. 134 BJ70
High St
Dellfield Rd, Hat. 45 CU18
Dellmeadow, Abb.L. 59 BS30
Dellors Cl, Barn. 79 CX43
Dellow Cl, Ilf. 125 ER59
Dellow St E1 142 DV73
Dells, The, Hem.H. 41 BP21
Dells Cl E4 101 EB45
Dells Cl, Tedd. 177 CF93
Middle La
Dell's Ms SW1 277 L9
Dells Wd Cl, Hodd. 33 DZ14
Dellside (Harefield), Uxb. 114 BJ57
Dellsome La, Hat. 45 CV23
Dellsome La (Colney Heath), St.Alb. 44 CS23
Dellswood Cl, Hert. 32 DS10
Hagsdell Rd
Dellwood, Rick. 92 BH46
Dellwood Gdns, Ilf. 125 EN55
Delmar Av, Hem.H. 41 BR21
Delmare Cl SW9 161 DM84
Brighton Ter
Delme Cres SE3 164 EH82
Delmeade Rd, Chesh. 54 AN32
Delmey Cl, Croy. 202 DT104
Radcliffe Rd
Deloraine St SE8 163 EA81
Delorme St W6 159 CX79
Delta Bungalows, Horl. 268 DG150
Michael Cres
Delta Cl (Chobham), Wok. 210 AT110
Delta Cl, Wor.Pk. 199 CT104
Delta Ct NW2 119 CU61
Delta Dr, Horl. 268 DG150
Cheyne Wk
Delta Gain, Wat. 94 BX47
Delta Gro, Nthlt. 136 BX69
Delta Rd, Brwd. 109 GD44
Delta Rd, Wok. 227 BA116
Delta Rd (Chobham), Wok. 210 AT110
Delta Rd, Wor.Pk. 198 CS104
Delta St E2 142 DU69
Wellington Row
Delta Way, Egh. 193 BC95
Delvan Cl SE18 165 EN80
Ordnance Rd
Delvers Mead, Dag. 127 FC63
Delverton Rd SE17 161 DP78
Delves, Tad. 233 CX121
Heathcote
Delvino Rd SW6 160 DA81
Demesne Rd, Wall. 219 DK106
Demeta Cl, Wem. 118 CQ62
Dempster Cl, Surb. 197 CJ102
Dempster Rd SW18 180 DC85
Den Cl, Beck. 203 ED97
Den Rd, Brom. 203 ED97
Denbar Par, Rom. 127 FC56
Mawney Rd
Denberry Dr, Sid. 186 EV90
Denbigh Cl NW10 138 CS66
Denbigh Cl W11 139 CZ73
Denbigh Cl, Chis. 185 EM93
Denbigh Cl, Hem.H. 40 BL21
Denbigh Cl, Horn. 128 FN56
Denbigh Cl, Ruis. 115 BT61
Denbigh Cl, Sthl. 136 BZ72
Denbigh Cl, Sutt. 217 CZ106
Denbigh Dr, Hayes 155 BQ75
Denbigh Gdns, Rich. 178 CM85
Denbigh Ms SW1 277 K9
Denbigh Pl SW1 277 K10
Denbigh Pl SW1 161 DJ78
Denbigh Rd E6 144 EK69
Denbigh Rd W11 139 CZ73
Denbigh Rd W13 137 CH73
Denbigh Rd, Houns. 156 CB82
Denbigh Rd, Sthl. 136 BZ72
Denbigh St SW1 277 K9
Denbigh St SW1 161 DJ77
Denbigh Ter W11 139 CZ73
Denbridge Rd, Brom. 205 EM96
Denby Gra, Harl. 52 EY15
Denby Rd, Cob. 214 BW113
Dendridge Cl, Enf. 82 DV37
Dene, The W13 137 CH71
Dene, The, Croy. 221 DX105
Dene, The (Abinger Hammer), Dor. 261 BV141
Dene, The, Sev. 257 FH126
Dene, The, Sutt. 217 CZ111
Dene, The, Wem. 118 CL63
Dene, The, W.Mol. 196 BZ99
Dene Av, Houns. 156 BZ83
Dene Av, Sid. 186 EV87
Dene Cl SE4 163 DY83
Dene Cl, Brom. 204 EF102
Dene Cl, Couls. 234 DE119
Dene Cl, Dart. 187 FE91
Dene Cl, Guil. 243 BB132
Dene Cl, Horl. 268 DE146
Dene Cl, Wor.Pk. 199 CT103
Dene Ct, Stan. 95 CJ50
Marsh La
Dene Dr, Orp. 206 EV104
Dene Gdns, Stan. 95 CJ50
Dene Gdns, T.Ditt. 197 CG103
Dene Holm Rd (Northfleet), Grav. 190 GD90
Dene Path, S.Ock. 149 FU72
Dene Pl, Wok. 226 AV118
Dene Rd N11 98 DF46
Dene Rd, Ash. 232 CM119
Dene Rd, Buck.H. 102 EK46
Dene Rd, Dart. 188 FM87
Dene Rd, Guil. 258 AY135
Dene Rd, Nthwd. 93 BS51
Dene St, Dor. 263 CH136
Dene St Gdns, Dor. 263 CH136
Denecroft Cres, Uxb. 135 BP67
Denecroft Gdns, Grays 170 GD76
Denefield Dr, Ken. 236 DR115
Denehurst Gdns NW4 119 CW58
Denehurst Gdns W3 138 CP74
Denehurst Gdns, Rich. 158 CN84
Denehurst Gdns, Twick. 177 CD87
Denehurst Gdns, Wdf.Grn. 102 EH49
Denes, The, Hem.H. 40 BM24
Barnacres Rd
Denewood, Barn. 80 DC43
Denewood Cl, Wat. 75 BT37
Denewood Rd N6 120 DF58
Denfield, Dor. 263 CH138
Dengie Wk N1 142 DQ67
Basire St
Denham Av (Denham), Uxb. 113 BF61
Denham Cl, Hem.H. 40 BN15
Denham Cl (Denham), Uxb. 114 BG62
Denham Cl, Well. 166 EW83
Park Vw Rd
Denham Ct Dr (Denham), Uxb. 114 BH63
Denham Cres, Mitch. 200 DF98
Denham Dr, Ilf. 125 EQ58
Denham Gdn Village, Uxb. 113 BF58
Denham Grn La
Denham Grn Cl (Denham), Uxb. 114 BG59
Denham Grn La (Denham), Uxb. 113 BE57
Denham La (Chalfont St. Peter), Ger.Cr. 91 BA53
Denham Lo, Uxb. 134 BJ65
Denham Rd N20 98 DF48
Denham Rd, Egh. 173 BA91
Denham Rd, Epsom 217 CT112
Denham Rd, Felt. 176 BW86
Denham Rd, Iver 133 BE65
Denham Rd (Denham), Uxb. 133 BE65
Denham St SE10 164 EG78
Denham Wk (Chalfont St. Peter), Ger.Cr. 91 AZ51
Denham Way, Bark. 145 ES67
Denham Way, Borwd. 78 CR39
Denham Way, Rick. 91 BE52
Denham Way (Denham), Uxb. 114 BG62
Denholm Gdns, Guil. 243 BA131
Denholme Rd W9 139 CZ69
Denholme Wk, Rain. 147 FF65
Ryder Gdns
Denison Cl N2 120 DC55
Denison Rd SW19 180 DD93
Denison Rd W5 137 CJ70
Denison Rd, Felt. 175 BT91
Deniston Av, Bex. 186 EY88
Denleigh Gdns N21 99 DN46
Denleigh Gdns, T.Ditt. 197 CE100
Denman Dr NW11 120 DA57
Denman Dr, Ashf. 175 BP93
Denman Dr (Claygate), Esher 215 CG106
Denman Dr N NW11 120 DA57
Denman Dr S NW11 120 DA57
Denman Rd SE15 162 DT81
Denman St W1 277 M1
Denmark Av SW19 179 CY94
Denmark Ct, Mord. 200 DA99
Denmark Gdns, Cars. 200 DG104
Denmark Gro N1 141 DN68
Denmark Hill SE5 162 DR81
Denmark Hill Dr NW9 119 CT56
Denmark Hill Est SE5 162 DR84
Denmark Pl WC2 273 N8
Denmark Rd N8 121 DM56
Denmark Rd NW6 139 CZ68
Denmark Rd SE5 162 DQ81
Denmark Rd SE25 202 DU99
Denmark Rd SW19 179 CX93
Denmark Rd W13 137 CH73
Denmark Rd, Brom. 204 EH95
Denmark Rd, Cars. 200 DF104
Denmark Rd, Guil. 258 AY135
Denmark Rd, Kings.T. 198 CL97
Denmark Rd, Twick. 177 CD90
Denmark St E11 124 EE62
High Rd Leytonstone
Denmark St E13 144 EH71
Denmark St N17 100 DV53
Denmark St WC2 273 N9
Denmark St WC2 141 DK72
Denmark St, Wat. 75 BV40
Denmark Wk SE27 182 DQ91
Denmead Cl, Ger.Cr. 112 AY59
Denmead Ho SW15 179 CT86
Highcliffe Dr
Denmead Rd, Croy. 201 DP102
Denmead Way SE15 162 DT80
Pentridge St
Dennan Rd, Surb. 198 CM102
Dennard Way, Orp. 223 EP105
Denne Ter E8 142 DT67
Denner Rd E4 101 EA47
Dennett Rd, Croy. 201 DN102
Dennetts Gro SE14 163 DX82
Dennetts Rd
Dennetts Rd SE14 162 DW81
Dennettsland Rd, Eden. 255 EQ134
Denning Av, Croy. 219 DN105
Denning Cl NW8 140 DC69
Denning Cl, Hmptn. 176 BZ93
Denning Rd NW3 120 DD63
Dennington Cl E5 122 DV61
Detmold Rd
Dennington Pk Rd NW6 140 DA65
Denningtons, The, Wor.Pk. 198 CS103
Dennis Av, Wem. 118 CM64
Dennis Cl, Ashf. 175 BR93
Dennis Cl, Red. 250 DE132
Dennis Gdns, Stan. 95 CJ50
Dennis La, Stan. 95 CH48
Dennis Pk Cres SW20 199 CY95
Dennis Reeve Cl, Mitch. 200 DF95
Dennis Rd, E.Mol. 196 CC98
Dennis Rd, Grav. 191 GG90
Dennis Rd, S.Ock. 149 FU66
Dennis Way SW4 161 DK83
Gauden Rd
Dennis Way, Guil. 242 AY129
Dennis Way, Slou. 131 AK73
Dennises La, Upmin. 149 FS67
Dennison Pt E15 143 EC66
Denny Av, Wal.Abb. 67 ED34
Denny Cl E6 144 EL71
Linton Gdns
Denny Cres SE11 278 E9
Denny Gdns, Dag. 146 EV66
Canonsleigh Rd
Denny Gate, Wal.Cr. 67 DZ27
Denny Rd N9 100 DV46
Denny Rd, Slou. 153 AZ77
Denny St SE11 278 E10
Denny St SE11 161 DN78
Dennys La, Berk. 38 AT21
Densham Dr, Pur. 219 DN114
Densham Rd E15 144 EE67
Densley Cl, Welw.G.C. 29 CX07
Densole Cl, Beck. 203 DY95
Kings Hall Rd
Densworth Gro N9 100 DW47
Dent Cl, S.Ock. 149 FU72
Denton Cl, Barn. 79 CW43
Denton Cl, Red. 266 DG139
Denton Ct Rd, Grav. 191 GL87
Denton Gro, Walt. 196 BX103
Denton Rd N8 121 DM57
Denton Rd N18 100 DS49
Denton Rd, Bex. 187 FE89
Denton Rd, Dart. 187 FE89
Denton Rd, Twick. 177 CK86
Denton Rd, Well. 166 EW80
Denton St SW18 180 DB86
Denton St, Grav. 191 GL87
Denton Ter, Bex. 187 FE89
Denton Rd
Denton Way E5 123 DX62
Denton Way, Wok. 226 AT118
Dents Gro, Tad. 249 CZ128
Dents Rd SW11 180 DF86
Denvale Wk, Wok. 226 AU118
Denver Cl, Orp. 205 ES100
Denver Ind Est, Rain. 147 FF71
Denver Rd N16 122 DS59
Denver Rd, Dart. 187 FG87
Denyer St SW3 276 C9
Denyer St SW3 160 DE77
Denzil Rd NW10 119 CT64
Denzil Rd, Guil. 258 AV135
Denziloe Av, Uxb. 135 BP69
Deodar Rd SW15 159 CY84
Deodara Cl N20 98 DE48
Depot Rd, Epsom 216 CS113
Depot Rd, Houns. 157 CD83
Deptford Br SE8 163 EA81
Deptford Bdy SE8 163 EA81
Deptford Ch St SE8 163 EA79
Deptford Ferry Rd E14 163 EA77
Deptford Grn SE8 163 EA79
Deptford High St SE8 163 EA79
Deptford Strand SE8 163 DZ77
Deptford Wf SE8 163 DZ77
Derby Arms Rd, Epsom 233 CT117
Derby Av N12 98 DC50
Derby Av, Har. 95 CD53
Derby Av, Rom. 127 FC58
Derby Av, Upmin. 128 FM62
Derby Cl, Epsom 233 CV119
Derby Ct E5 123 DX63
Overbury St
Derby Gate SW1 277 P4
Derby Hill SE23 182 DW89
Derby Hill Cres SE23 182 DW89
Derby Rd E7 144 EJ66
Derby Rd E9 143 DX67
Derby Rd E18 102 EF53
Derby Rd N18 100 DW50
Derby Rd SW14 158 CP84
Derby Rd SW19 180 DA94
Russell Rd
Derby Rd, Croy. 201 DP103
Derby Rd, Enf. 82 DV43
Derby Rd, Grays 170 GB78
Derby Rd, Grnf. 136 CB67
Derby Rd, Guil. 242 AS134
Derby Rd, Hodd. 49 ED19
Derby Rd, Houns. 156 CB84
Derby Rd, Surb. 198 CN102
Derby Rd, Sutt. 217 CZ107
Derby Rd, Uxb. 134 BJ68
Derby Rd, Wat. 76 BW41
Derby Rd Br, Grays 170 GB79
Derby Stables Rd, Epsom 232 CS117
Derby St W1 276 G3
Derbyshire St E2 142 DU69
Dereham Pl EC2 275 N3
Dereham Pl, Rom. 105 FB51
Dereham Rd, Bark. 145 ET65
Derehams Av (Loudwater), H.Wyc. 88 AC52
Derehams La (Loudwater), H.Wyc. 88 AC53
Derek Av, Epsom 216 CN106
Derek Av, Wall. 219 DH105
Derek Av, Wem. 138 CP66
Derek Cl (Ewell), Epsom 216 CP106
Derek Walcott Cl SE24 181 DP85
Shakespeare Rd
Derham Gdns, Upmin. 128 FQ62
Deri Av, Rain. 147 FH70
Dericote St E8 142 DU67
Deridene Cl (Stanwell), Stai. 174 BL86
Bedfont Rd
Derifall Cl E6 145 EM71
Dering Pl, Croy. 220 DQ105
Dering Rd, Croy. 220 DQ105
Dering St W1 273 H9
Dering St W1 141 DH72
Dering Way, Grav. 191 GM88
Derinton Rd SW17 180 DF91
Derley Rd, Sthl. 156 BW76
Dermody Gdns SE13 183 ED85
Dermody Rd SE13 183 ED85
Deronda Rd SE24 181 DP88
Deroy Cl, Cars. 218 DF107
Derrick Av, S.Croy. 220 DQ110
Derrick Gdns SE7 164 EJ77
Anchor & Hope La
Derrick Rd, Beck. 203 DZ97
Derry Av, S.Ock. 149 FU72
Derry Downs, Orp. 206 EW100
Derry Rd, Croy. 201 DL104
Derry St W8 160 DB75
Derrydown, Wok. 226 AW121
Dersingham Av E12 125 EN64
Dersingham Rd NW2 119 CY62
Derwent Av N18 100 DR50
Derwent Av NW7 96 CR50
Derwent Av SW15 178 CS91
Derwent Av, Barn. 98 DF46
Derwent Av, Pnr. 94 BY51
Derwent Av, Uxb. 114 BN62
Derwent Cl, Add. 212 BK106
Derwent Cl, Amer. 72 AV39
Derwent Cl, Dart. 187 FH88
Derwent Cl (Claygate), Esher 215 CE107
Derwent Cl, Felt. 175 BT88
Derwent Cres N20 98 DC48
Derwent Cres, Bexh. 166 FA82
Derwent Cres, Stan. 95 CJ54
Derwent Dr NW9 118 CS57
Derwent Dr, Hayes 135 BS71
Derwent Dr, Orp. 205 ER101
Derwent Dr, Pur. 220 DR113
Derwent Dr, Slou. 130 AJ71
Derwent Gdns, Ilf. 124 EL56
Derwent Gdns, Wem. 117 CJ59
Derwent Gro SE22 162 DT84
Derwent Par, S.Ock. 149 FV72
Derwent Ri NW9 118 CS58
Derwent Rd N13 99 DM49
Derwent Rd SE20 202 DU96
Derwent Rd SW20 199 CX100
Derwent Rd W5 157 CJ76
Derwent Rd, Egh. 173 BB94
Derwent Rd, Hem.H. 40 BQ21
Derwent Rd, Sthl. 136 CA72
Derwent Rd, Twick. 176 CB86
Derwent St SE10 164 EE78
Derwent Wk, Wall. 219 DH108
Derwent Way, Horn. 127 FH64
Derwent Yd W5 157 CJ76
Northfield Av
Derwentwater Rd W3 138 CQ74
Desborough Cl W2 140 DB71
Desborough Cl, Hert. 31 DP06
Desborough Cl, Shep. 194 BN101
Desborough St W2 140 DB71
Cirencester St
Desenfans Rd SE21 182 DS86
Desford Ct, Ashf. 174 BM89
Desford Way
Desford Ms E16 144 EE70
Desford Rd
Desford Rd E16 144 EE70
Desford Way, Ashf. 174 BM89
Desmond Rd, Wat. 75 BT36
Desmond St SE14 163 DY79
Despard Rd N19 121 DJ60
Detillens La, Oxt. 254 EG129
Detling Cl, Horn. 128 FJ64
Detling Rd, Brom. 184 EG92
Detling Rd, Erith 167 FD80
Detling Rd (Northfleet), Grav. 190 GD88
Detmold Rd E5 122 DW61
Deva Cl, St.Alb. 42 CA22
Devalls Cl E6 145 EN73
Devana End, Cars. 200 DF104
Devas Rd SW20 199 CW95
Devas St E3 143 EB70
Devenay Rd E15 144 EF66
Devenish Rd SE2 166 EU75
Deventer Cres SE22 182 DS85
Deverell St SE1 279 K7
Deverell St SE1 162 DR76
Devereux Ct WC2 274 D9
Devereux Dr, Wat. 75 BS38
Devereux La SW13 159 CV80
Devereux Rd SW11 180 DF86
Devereux Rd, Grays 170 FZ76
Devereux Rd, Wind. 151 AR82
Deverill Ct SE20 202 DW95
Deverills Way, Slou. 153 BC77
Deveron Gdns, S.Ock. 149 FU72
Deveron Way, Rom. 105 FE53
Devey Cl, Kings.T. 178 CS94
Devils La, Egh. 173 BD94
Devil's La, Hert. 47 DP21
Devitt Cl, Ash. 232 CN116
Devizes St N1 142 DR67
Poole St
Devoil Cl, Guil. 243 BB130
Devoke Way, Walt. 196 BX103
Devon Av, Slou. 131 AQ72
Devon Av, Twick. 176 CC88
Devon Bk, Guil. 258 AW137
Portsmouth Rd
Devon Cl N17 122 DT55
Devon Cl, Buck.H. 102 EH47
Devon Cl, Grnf. 137 CJ67
Devon Cl, Ken. 236 DT116
Devon Ct, Buck.H. 102 EH46
Devon Ct (Sutton at Hone), Dart. 208 FP95
Devon Ct, St.Alb. 43 CE21
Devon Cres, Red. 250 DD134
Devon Gdns N4 121 DP58
Devon Ri N2 120 DD56
Devon Rd, Bark. 145 ES67
Devon Rd (Sutton at Hone), Dart. 208 FP95
Devon Rd, Red. 251 DJ130
Devon Rd, Sutt. 217 CY109
Devon Rd, Walt. 214 BW105
Devon Rd, Wat. 76 BX39
Devon St SE15 162 DV79
Devon Way, Chess. 215 CJ106
Devon Way, Epsom 216 CP106
Devon Way, Uxb. 134 BM68
Devon Waye, Houns. 156 BZ80
Devoncroft Gdns, Twick. 177 CG87
Devonhurst Pl W4 158 CR78
Heathfield Ter
Devonia Gdns N18 100 DQ51
Devonia Rd N1 141 DP68
Devonport Gdns, Ilf. 125 EM58
Devonport Ms W12 139 CV74
Devonport Rd
Devonport Rd W12 159 CV75
Devonport St E1 142 DW72
Devons Est E3 143 EB69
Devons Rd E3 143 EA71
Devonshire Av, Amer. 55 AP37
Devonshire Av, Dart. 187 FH86
Devonshire Av, Sutt. 218 DC108
Devonshire Av, Wok. 211 BC114
Devonshire Cl E15 124 EE63
Devonshire Cl N13 99 DN49
Devonshire Cl W1 273 H6
Devonshire Cl W1 141 DH71
Devonshire Cl, Amer. 55 AQ37
Devonshire Cl (Farnham Royal), Slou. 131 AP68
Devonshire Cres NW7 97 CX52
Devonshire Dr SE10 163 EB80
Devonshire Dr, Surb. 197 CK102
Devonshire Gdns N17 100 DQ51
Devonshire Gdns N21 100 DQ45
Devonshire Gdns W4 158 CQ80
Devonshire Grn (Farnham Royal), Slou. 131 AP68
Devonshire Gro SE15 162 DV79
Devonshire Hill La N17 100 DQ51
Devonshire Ho, Sutt. 218 DC108
Devonshire Av
Devonshire Ms W4 158 CS78
Glebe St
Devonshire Ms N W1 273 H6
Devonshire Ms S W1 273 H6
Devonshire Ms S W1 141 DH71
Devonshire Ms W W1 273 H5
Devonshire Ms W W1 141 DH71
Devonshire Pas W4 158 CS78
Devonshire Pl NW2 120 DA62
Devonshire Pl W1 272 G5
Devonshire Pl W1 140 DG70
Devonshire Pl W4 158 CS78
Devonshire Pl W8 160 DB76
St. Mary's Pl
Devonshire Pl Ms W1 272 G5
Devonshire Rd E15 124 EE63
Janson Rd
Devonshire Rd E16 144 EH72
Devonshire Rd E17 123 EA58
Devonshire Rd N9 100 DW46
Devonshire Rd N13 99 DM49
Devonshire Rd N17 100 DQ51
Devonshire Rd NW7 97 CX52
Devonshire Rd SE9 184 EL89
Devonshire Rd SE23 182 DW88
Devonshire Rd SW19 180 DE94
Devonshire Rd W4 158 CS78
Devonshire Rd W5 157 CJ76
Devonshire Rd, Bexh. 166 EY84
Devonshire Rd, Cars. 218 DG105
Devonshire Rd, Croy. 202 DR101
Devonshire Rd, Felt. 176 BY90
Devonshire Rd, Grav. 191 GH88
Devonshire Rd, Grays 170 FY77
Devonshire Rd, Har. 117 CD58
Devonshire Rd, Horn. 128 FJ61
Devonshire Rd, Ilf. 125 ES59
Devonshire Rd, Orp. 206 EU101
Devonshire Rd (Eastcote), Pnr. 116 BW58
Devonshire Rd (Hatch End), Pnr. 94 BZ53
Devonshire Rd, Sthl. 136 CA71
Devonshire Rd, Sutt. 218 DC108
Devonshire Rd, Wey. 212 BN105

Dev - Dou This index reads in the sequence: Street Name / Postal District or Post Town / Map Page Number / Grid Reference

Devonshire Row EC2 275 N7
Devonshire Row Ms W1 273 J5
Devonshire Sq EC2 275 N8
Devonshire Sq, Brom. 204 EH98
Devonshire St W1 272 G6
Devonshire St W1 141 DH71
Devonshire St W4 158 CS78
Devonshire Ter W2 140 DC72
Devonshire Way, Croy. 203 DY103
Devonshire Way, Hayes 135 BV72
Dewar St SE15 162 DU83
Dewberry Gdns E6 144 EL71
Dewberry St E14 143 EC71
Dewey Path, Horn. 148 FJ65
Dewey Rd N1 141 DN68
Dewey Rd, Dag. 147 FB65
Dewey St SW17 180 DF92
Dewgrass Gro, Wal.Cr. 83 DX35
Dewhurst Rd W14 159 CX76
Dewhurst Rd (Cheshunt), Wal.Cr. 66 DW29
Dewlands, Gdse. 252 DW131
Dewlands Av, Dart. 188 FP87
Dewlands Ct NW4 97 CX54
Holders Hill Rd
Dewsbury Cl, Pnr. 116 BZ58
Dewsbury Cl, Rom. 106 FL51
Dewsbury Ct W4 158 CQ77
Chiswick Rd
Dewsbury Gdns, Rom. 106 FK51
Dewsbury Gdns, Wor.Pk. 199 CU104
Dewsbury Rd NW10 119 CU64
Dewsbury Rd, Rom. 106 FK51
Dewsbury Ter NW1 141 DH67
Camden High St
Dexter Cl, Grays 170 GA76
Dexter Cl, St.Alb. 43 CG21
Camp Rd
Dexter Ho, Erith 166 EY76
Kale Rd
Dexter Rd, Barn. 79 CX44
Dexter Rd (Harefield), Uxb. 92 BJ54
Deyncourt Gdns, Upmin. 128 FQ61
Deyncourt Rd N17 100 DQ53
Deynecourt Gdns E11 124 EJ56
D'Eynsford Rd SE5 162 DR81
Diadem Ct W1 273 M9
Dial Cl, Green. 189 FX85
Knockhall Rd
Dial Wk, The W8 160 DB75
Dialmead, Pot.B. 63 CT34
Crossbrooks La
Diamedes Av (Stanwell), Stai. 174 BK87
Diameter Rd, Orp. 205 EP101
Diamond Cl, Dag. 126 EW60
Diamond Cl, Grays 170 FZ76
Diamond Rd, Ruis. 116 BX63
Diamond Rd, Slou. 152 AU75
Diamond Rd, Wat. 75 BU38
Diamond St SE15 162 DS80
Diamond Ter SE10 163 EC81
Diamond Way SE8 163 EA80
Deptford High St
Diana Cl E18 102 EH53
Diana Cl, Grays 170 FZ76
Diana Cl (George Grn), Slou. 132 AY72
Diana Gdns, Surb. 198 CM103
Diana Ho SW13 159 CT81
Diana Pl NW1 273 J4
Diana Pl NW1 141 DH70
Diana Rd E17 123 DZ55
Diana Wk, Horl. 269 DH148
High St
Dianne Way, Barn. 80 DE43
Dianthus Cl SE2 166 EV78
Carnation St
Dianthus Cl, Cher. 193 BE101
Dianthus Ct, Wok. 226 AX118
Diban Av, Horn. 127 FH63
Dibden Hill, Ch.St.G. 90 AW49
Dibden La (Ide Hill), Sev. 256 FE126
Dibden Row SE1 161 DN76
Gerridge St
Dibden St N1 142 DQ67
Dibdin Cl, Sutt. 200 DA104
Dibdin Rd, Sutt. 200 DA104
Diceland Rd, Bans. 233 CZ116
Dicey Av NW2 119 CW64
Dick Turpin Way, Felt. 155 BT84
Dickens Av N3 98 DC53
Dickens Av, Dart. 168 FN84
Dickens Av, Til. 171 GH81
Dickens Av, Uxb. 135 BP72
Dickens Cl, Erith 167 FB80
Dickens Cl, Hayes 155 BS77
Croyde Av
Dickens Cl, Rich. 178 CL89
Dickens Cl, St.Alb. 43 CD19
Dickens Cl, Wal.Cr. 66 DU26
Dickens Ct, Hat. 45 CV16
Dickens Dr, Add. 211 BF107
Dickens Dr, Chis. 185 EQ93
Dickens Est SE1 162 DU75
Dickens Est SE16 162 DU75
Dickens Ho NW6 140 DA69
Dickens La N18 100 DS50
Dickens Ri, Chig. 103 EN48
Dickens Rd E6 144 EK68
Dickens Rd, Grav. 191 GL88
Dickens Sq SE1 279 J6
Dickens Sq SE1 162 DQ76
Dickens St SW8 161 DH82
Dickens Way, Rom. 127 FE56
Dickenson Cl N9 100 DU46
Croyland Rd
Dickenson Rd N8 121 DL59
Dickenson Rd, Felt. 176 BW92
Dickenson St NW5 141 DH65
Dalby St
Dickensons La SE25 202 DU99
Dickensons Pl SE25 202 DU100
Dickenswood Cl SE19 181 DP94
Dicker Mill Ind Pk, Hert. 32 DS08
Dickerage La, N.Mal. 198 CQ97
Dickerage Rd, Kings.T. 198 CQ95
Dickerage Rd, N.Mal. 198 CQ95
Dickinson Av, Rick. 74 BN44
Dickinson Sq, Rick. 74 BN44
Dickson (Cheshunt), Wal.Cr. 66 DT27
Dickson Fold, Pnr. 116 BX56
Dickson Rd SE9 164 EL83
Didsbury Cl E6 145 EM67
Barking Rd
Dig Dag Hill (Cheshunt), Wal.Cr. 66 DT27
Digby Cres N4 122 DQ61
Digby Gdns, Dag. 146 FA67
Digby Pl, Croy. 202 DT104
Digby Rd E9 143 DX65
Digby Rd, Bark. 145 ET66
Digby St E2 142 DW69
Digby Wk, Horn. 148 FJ65
Pembrey Way
Digby Way (Byfleet), W.Byf. 212 BM112
High Rd
Digdens Ri, Epsom 232 CQ115
Diggon St E1 143 DX71
Stepney Way
Dighton Ct SE5 162 DQ79
Dighton Rd SW18 180 DC85
Digswell Cl, Borwd. 78 CN38
Digswell Hill, Welw. 29 CV05
Digswell Ho, Welw.G.C. 29 CX05
Digswell Ho Ms, Welw.G.C. 29 CX05
Digswell La, Welw.G.C. 29 CZ05
Digswell Pl, Welw.G.C. 29 CW06
Digswell Ri, Welw.G.C. 29 CX07
Digswell Rd, Welw.G.C. 29 CY06
Digswell St N7 141 DN65
Holloway Rd
Dilhorne Cl SE12 184 EH90
Dilke St SW3 160 DF79
Dilloway Yd, Sthl. 156 BY75
The Grn
Dillwyn Cl SE26 183 DY91
Dilston Cl, Nthlt. 136 BW69
Yeading La
Dilston Gro SE16 162 DW77
Abbeyfield Rd
Dilston Rd, Lthd. 231 CG119
Dilton Gdns SW15 179 CU88
Dilwyn Ct E17 123 DY55
Hillyfield
Dimes Pl W6 159 CV77
King St
Dimmock Dr, Grnf. 117 CD64
Dimmocks La, Rick. 74 BH36
Dimond Cl E7 124 EG63
Dimsdale Dr NW9 118 CQ60
Dimsdale Dr, Enf. 82 DU44
Dimsdale Dr, Slou. 111 AM63
Dimsdale St, Hert. 32 DQ09
Dimsdale Wk E13 144 EG67
Stratford Rd
Dimson Cres E3 143 EA70
Dinant Link Rd, Hodd. 49 DY16
Dingle, The, Uxb. 135 BP68
Dingle Cl, Barn. 79 CT44
Dingle Gdns E14 143 EA73
Dingle Rd, Ashf. 175 BP92
Dingley La SW16 181 DK89
Dingley Pl EC1 275 J3
Dingley Pl EC1 142 DQ69
Dingley Rd EC1 275 H3
Dingley Rd EC1 142 DQ69
Dingwall Av, Croy. 202 DQ103
Dingwall Gdns NW11 120 DA58
Dingwall Rd SW18 180 DC87
Dingwall Rd, Cars. 218 DF109
Dingwall Rd, Croy. 202 DR103
Dinmont St E2 142 DV68
Coate St
Dinmore (Bovingdon), Hem.H. 57 AZ28
Dinsdale Cl, Wok. 227 BA118
Dinsdale Gdns SE25 202 DS99
Dinsdale Gdns, Barn. 80 DB43
Dinsdale Rd SE3 164 EF79
Dinsmore Rd SW12 181 DH87
Dinton Rd SW19 180 DD93
Dinton Rd, Kings.T. 178 CM94
Dione Rd, Hem.H. 40 BM17
Saturn Way
Diploma Av N2 120 DE56
Diploma Ct N2 120 DE56
Diploma Av
Dirdene Cl, Epsom 217 CT112
Dirdene Gdns, Epsom 217 CT112
Dirdene Gro, Epsom 216 CS112
Dirleton Rd E15 144 EF67
Dirtham La (Effingham), Lthd. 245 BU127
Disbrowe Rd W6 159 CY79
Discovery Wk E1 142 DV74
Dishforth La NW9 96 CS53
Disney Ms N4 121 DP57
Chesterfield Gdns
Disney Pl SE1 279 J4
Disney St SE1 279 J4
Dison Cl, Enf. 83 DX39
Disraeli Cl SE28 146 EW74
Disraeli Cl W4 158 CR77
Acton La
Disraeli Ct, Slou. 153 BB79
Sutton Pl
Disraeli Gdns SW15 159 CZ84
Fawe Pk Rd
Disraeli Pk, Beac. 89 AK50
Disraeli Rd E7 144 EG65
Disraeli Rd NW10 138 CQ68
Disraeli Rd SW15 159 CY84
Disraeli Rd W5 137 CK74
Diss St E2 275 P2
Diss St E2 142 DT69
Distaff La EC4 275 H10
Distaff La EC4 142 DQ73
Distillery La W6 159 CW78
Fulham Palace Rd
Distillery Rd W6 159 CW78
Distillery Wk, Brent. 158 CL79
Distin St SE11 278 D9
Distin St SE11 161 DN77
District Rd, Wem. 117 CH64
Ditch All SE10 163 EB81
Ditchburn St E14 143 EC73
Ditches La, Couls. 235 DL120
Ditches Ride, The, Loug. 85 EN37
Ditchfield Rd, Hayes 136 BY70
Ditchfield Rd, Hodd. 33 EA14
Dittisham Rd SE9 184 EL91
Ditton Cl, T.Ditt. 197 CG101
Ditton Gra Cl, Surb. 197 CK102
Ditton Gra Dr, Surb. 197 CK102
Ditton Hill, Surb. 197 CJ102
Ditton Hill Rd, Surb. 197 CJ102
Ditton Lawn, T.Ditt. 197 CG102
Ditton Pk, Slou. 152 AX78
Ditton Pk Rd, Slou. 152 AY79
Ditton Pl SE20 202 DV95
Ditton Reach, T.Ditt. 197 CH100
Ditton Rd, Bexh. 186 EX85
Ditton Rd, Slou. 153 AZ79
Ditton Rd (Datchet), Slou. 152 AX81
Ditton Rd, Sthl. 156 BZ77
Ditton Rd, Surb. 198 CL102
Dittoncroft Cl, Croy. 220 DS105
Divis Way SW15 179 CV86
Divot Pl, Hert. 32 DV08
Dixon Clark Ct N1 141 DP65
Canonbury Rd
Dixon Cl E6 145 EM72
Brandreth Rd
Dixon Dr, Wey. 212 BM110
Dixon Ho W10 139 CX72
Dixon Pl, W.Wick. 203 EB102
Dixon Rd SE14 163 DY81
Dixon Rd SE25 202 DS97
Dixon's All SE16 162 DV75
Dixon's Ct, Ware 33 DY06
Crane Mead
Dixons Hill Cl, Hat. 63 CV25
Dixons Hill Rd, Hat. 63 CU25
Dobbin Cl, Har. 95 CG54
Dobb's Weir, Hodd. 49 ED18
Dobb's Weir Caravan Pk, Hodd. 49 EC19
Dobb's Weir Rd, Hodd. 49 ED18
Dobell Rd SE9 185 EM85
Dobree Av NW10 139 CV66
Dobson Cl NW6 140 DD66
Dobson Rd, Grav. 191 GL92
Dock Hill Av SE16 163 DX75
Dock Rd E16 144 EF73
Dock Rd, Brent. 157 CK80
Dock Rd, Grays 170 GD79
Dock Rd, Til. 171 GF82
Dock St E1 142 DU73
Dockers Tanner Rd E14 163 EA76
Dockett Eddy La, Shep. 194 BM102
Dockhead SE1 162 DT75
Dockland St E16 145 EN74
Dockley Rd SE16 162 DU76
Dockwell Cl, Felt. 155 BU84
Dockyard Ind Est SE18 164 EL76
Woolwich Ch St
Doctor Johnson Av SW17 181 DH90
Doctors Cl SE26 182 DW92
Doctors Commons Rd, Berk. 38 AV20
Doctors La, Cat. 235 DN123
Docwra's Bldgs N1 142 DS65
Dod St E14 143 EA72
Dodbrooke Rd SE27 181 DN90
Doddinghurst Rd, Brwd. 108 FW45
Doddington Gro SE17 161 DP79
Doddington Pl SE17 161 DP79
Dodd's Cres, W.Byf. 212 BH114
Dodds La, Ch.St.G. 90 AU47
Dodds La, Hem.H. 40 BJ16
Dodd's La, Wok. 212 BG114
Dodds Pk (Brockham), Bet. 264 CP136
Doddsfield Rd, Slou. 131 AN69
Dodsley Pl N9 100 DV48
Dodson St SE1 278 E5
Dodson St SE1 161 DN75
Dodwood, Welw.G.C. 30 DB10
Doebury Wk SE18 166 EU79
Prestwood Cl
Doel Cl SW19 180 DC94
Dog Kennel Hill SE22 162 DS83
Dog Kennel Hill Est SE22 162 DS83
Dog Kennel La, Hat. 45 CU17
Dog Kennel La, Rick. 73 BF42
Dog La NW10 118 CS63
Doggets Ct, Barn. 80 DE43
Doggett Rd SE6 183 EA87
Doggetts Fm Rd (Denham), Uxb. 113 BC59
Doggetts Way, St.Alb. 42 CC22
Doggetts Wd Cl, Ch.St.G. 72 AV42
Doggetts Wd La, Ch.St.G. 72 AV41
Doghurst Av, Hayes 155 BP80
Doghurst Dr, West Dr. 155 BP80
Doghurst La, Couls. 234 DF120
Dognell Grn, Welw.G.C. 29 CV08
Dogwood Cl (Northfleet), Grav. 190 GE91
Doherty Rd E13 144 EG70
Dokal Ind Est, Sthl. 156 BY75
Dolben St SE1 278 F3
Dolben St SE1 141 DP74
Dolby Ct EC4 275 J10
Dolby Rd SW6 159 CZ82
Dolland St SE11 161 DM78
Dollis Av N3 97 CZ53
Dollis Brook Wk, Barn. 79 CY44
Dollis Cres, Ruis. 116 BW60
Dollis Hill Av NW2 119 CV62
Dollis Hill Est NW2 119 CU62
Dollis Hill La NW2 119 CV62
Dollis Ms N3 97 CZ53
Dollis Pk
Dollis Pk N3 97 CZ53
Dollis Rd N3 97 CY52
Dollis Rd NW7 97 CY52
Dollis Valley Grn Wk N20 98 DC47
Totteridge La
Dollis Valley Grn Wk, Barn. 79 CY44
Dollis Valley Way, Barn. 79 CZ44
Dolman Cl N3 98 DC54
Avondale Rd
Dolman Rd W4 158 CR77
Dolman St SW4 161 DM84
Dolphin App, Rom. 127 FF56
Dolphin Cl SE16 163 DX75
Kinburn St
Dolphin Cl SE28 146 EX72
Dolphin Cl, Surb. 197 CK100
Dolphin Ct NW11 119 CY58
Dolphin Ct, Slou. 152 AV75
Dolphin Rd
Dolphin Ct, Stai. 174 BG90
Bremer Rd
Dolphin Ct N, Stai. 174 BG90
Bremer Rd
Dolphin Est, Sun. 195 BS95
Dolphin Ho SW18 160 DB84
Smugglers Way
Dolphin La E14 143 EB73
Dolphin Rd, Nthlt. 136 BZ68
Dolphin Rd, Slou. 152 AV75
Dolphin Rd, Sun. 195 BS95
Dolphin Rd N, Sun. 195 BS95
Dolphin Rd S, Sun. 195 BR95
Dolphin Rd W, Sun. 195 BR95
Dolphin Sq SW1 161 DJ78
Dolphin Sq W4 158 CS80
Dolphin St, Kings.T. 198 CL95
Dolphin Twr SE8 163 DZ79
Abinger Gro
Dolphin Way, Purf. 169 FS78
Dolphin Yd, St.Alb. 43 CD20
Dolphin Yd, Ware 33 DX06
East St
Dombey St WC1 274 B6
Dombey St WC1 141 DM71
Dome Hill, Cat. 252 DS127
Dome Hill Pk SE26 182 DT91
Dome Hill Peak, Cat. 252 DS126
Dome Way, Red. 250 DF133
Domett Cl SE5 162 DR84
Domfe Pl E5 122 DW63
Rushmore Rd
Domingo St EC1 275 H4
Dominic Ct, Wal.Abb. 67 EB33
Dominica Cl E13 144 EJ68
Dominion Dr, Rom. 105 FB51
Dominion Rd, Croy. 202 DT101
Dominion Rd, Sthl. 156 BY76
Dominion St EC2 275 L6
Dominion Way, Rain. 147 FG69
Domonic Dr SE9 185 EP91
Domville Cl N20 98 DD47
Don Phelan Cl SE5 162 DR81
Don Way, Rom. 105 FE52
Donald Biggs Dr, Grav. 191 GK87
Donald Dr, Rom. 126 EW57
Donald Rd E13 144 EH67
Donald Rd, Croy. 201 DM100
Donald Wds Gdns, Surb. 198 CP103
Donaldson Rd NW6 139 CZ67
Donaldson Rd SE18 165 EN81
Doncaster Dr, Nthlt. 116 BZ64
Doncaster Gdns N4 122 DQ58
Stanhope Gdns
Doncaster Gdns, Nthlt. 116 BZ64
Doncaster Grn, Wat. 94 BW50
Doncaster Rd N9 100 DV45
Doncaster Way, Upmin. 128 FM62
Doncel Ct E4 101 ED45
Donegal St N1 274 C1
Donegal St N1 141 DM68
Doneraile St SW6 159 CX82
Dongola Rd E1 143 DY71
Dongola Rd E13 144 EH69
Dongola Rd N17 122 DS55
Dongola Rd W E13 144 EH69
Balaam St
Donington Av, Ilf. 125 EQ57
Donkey All SE22 182 DU87
Donkey La (Farningham), Dart. 208 FP103
Donkey La (Abinger Common), Dor. 262 BX143
Donkey La, Enf. 82 DU40
Donkey La, Horl. 269 DK152
Donkey La, West Dr. 154 BJ77
Donnay Cl, Ger.Cr. 112 AX58
Donne Ct SE24 182 DQ86
Donne Gdns, Wok. 227 BE115
Donne Pl SW3 276 C8
Donne Pl SW3 160 DE77
Donne Pl, Mitch. 201 DH98
Donne Rd, Dag. 126 EW61
Donnefield Av, Edg. 96 CL52
Donnington Rd NW10 139 CV66
Donnington Rd, Har. 117 CK57
Donnington Rd (Dunton Grn), Sev. 241 FD120
Donnington Rd, Wor.Pk. 199 CU103
Donnybrook Rd SW16 181 DJ94
Donovan Av N10 99 DH54
Donovan Cl, Epsom 216 CR110
Nimbus Rd
Doods Pk Rd, Reig. 250 DC133
Doods Rd, Reig. 250 DC133
Doods Way, Reig. 250 DD133
Doon St SE1 278 D3
Doone Cl, Tedd. 177 CG93
Dora Rd SW19 180 DA92
Dora St E14 143 DZ72
Dorado Gdns, Orp. 206 EX104
Doral Way, Cars. 218 DF106
Doran Dr, Red. 250 DD134
Doran Gdns, Red. 250 DD134
Doran Gro SE18 165 ES80
Doran Wk E15 143 EC66
Dorando Cl W12 139 CV73
Dorcas Ct, St.Alb. 43 CE21
Dorchester Av N13 100 DQ49
Dorchester Av, Bex. 186 EX88
Dorchester Av, Har. 116 CC58
Dorchester Av, Hodd. 49 EA15
Dorchester Cl, Dart. 188 FM87
Dorchester Cl, Nthlt. 116 CB64
Dorchester Cl, Orp. 186 EU94
Grovelands Rd
Dorchester Ct N14 99 DH45
Dorchester Ct SE24 182 DQ85
Dorchester Ct, Rick. 75 BR43
Mayfare
Dorchester Ct, Wok. 227 BA116
Dorchester Dr SE24 182 DQ85
Dorchester Dr, Felt. 175 BS86
Dorchester Gdns E4 101 EA49
Dorchester Gdns NW11 120 DA56
Dorchester Gro W4 158 CS78
Dorchester Ms, N.Mal. 198 CR98
Elm Rd
Dorchester Ms, Twick. 177 CJ87
Dorchester Rd, Grav. 191 GK90
Dorchester Rd, Mord. 200 DB101
Dorchester Rd, Nthlt. 116 CB64
Dorchester Rd, Wey. 195 BP104
Dorchester Rd, Wor.Pk. 199 CW102
Dorchester Way, Har. 118 CM58
Dorchester Waye, Hayes 136 BW72
Dorcis Av, Bexh. 166 EY82
Dordrecht Rd W3 138 CS74
Dore Av E12 125 EN64
Dore Gdns, Mord. 200 DB101
Doreen Av NW9 118 CR60
Dorell Cl, Sthl. 136 BZ71
Doria Dr, Grav. 191 GL90
Doria Rd SW6 159 CZ82
Dorian Rd, Horn. 127 FG60
Doric Dr, Tad. 233 CZ120
Doric Way NW1 273 M2
Doric Way NW1 141 DK69
Dorien Rd SW20 199 CX96
Dorincourt, Wok. 227 BE115
Doris Av, Erith 167 FC81
Doris Rd E7 144 EG66
Doris Rd, Ashf. 175 BR93
Dorking Business Pk, Dor. 263 CG135
Dorking Cl SE8 163 DZ79
Dorking Cl, Wor.Pk. 199 CX103
Dorking Gdns, Rom. 106 FK50
Dorking Glen, Rom. 106 FK49
Dorking Ri, Rom. 106 FK49
Dorking Rd (Abinger Hammer), Dor. 261 BS139
Dorking Rd, Epsom 232 CN116
Dorking Rd, Guil. 259 BF139
Dorking Rd, Lthd. 231 CH122
Dorking Rd (Great Bookham), Lthd. 246 CB126
Dorking Rd, Rom. 106 FK49
Dorking Rd, Tad. 233 CX123
Dorking Wk, Rom. 106 FK49
Dorkins Way, Upmin. 129 FS59
Dorlcote Rd SW18 180 DE87
Dorling Dr, Epsom 217 CT112
Dorly Cl, Shep. 195 BS99
Dorma Trd Pk E10 123 DX60
Dorman Pl N9 100 DU47
Balham Rd
Dorman Wk NW10 118 CR64
Garden Way
Dorman Way NW8 140 DD67
Dormans Cl, Nthwd. 93 BR52
Dormay St SW18 180 DB85
Dormer Cl E15 144 EF65
Dormer Cl, Barn. 79 CX43
Dormers Av, Sthl. 136 CA72
Dormers Ri, Sthl. 136 CB72
Dormers Wells La, Sthl. 136 CA72
Dormie Cl, St.Alb. 42 CC18
Dormywood, Ruis. 115 BT57
Dornberg Cl SE3 164 EG80
Dornberg Rd SE3 164 EH80
Banchory Rd
Dorncliffe Rd SW6 159 CY82
Dornels, Slou. 132 AW72
Dorney NW3 140 DE66
Dorney End, Chesh. 54 AN30
Dorney Gro, Wey. 195 BP103
Dorney Reach Rd, Maid. 150 AF76
Dorney Ri, Orp. 205 ET98
Dorney Way, Houns. 176 BY85
Dorney Wd Rd (Burnham), Slou. 111 AK63
Dornfell St NW6 119 CZ64
Dornford Gdns, Couls. 236 DQ119
Dornton Rd SW12 181 DH89
Dornton Rd, S.Croy. 220 DR106
Dorothy Av, Wem. 138 CL66
Dorothy Evans Cl, Bexh. 167 FB84
Dorothy Gdns, Dag. 126 EV63
Dorothy Rd SW11 160 DF83
Dorrell Pl SW9 161 DN84
Brixton Rd
Dorrien Wk SW16 181 DK89
Dorriens Cft, Berk. 38 AT16
Dorrington Ct SE25 202 DS96
Dorrington Gdns, Horn. 128 FK60
Dorrington Pt E3 143 EB69
Bromley High St
Dorrington St EC1 274 D6
Dorrington St EC1 141 DN71
Dorrit Cres, Guil. 242 AS132
Dorrit Ms N18 100 DS49
Dorrit Way, Chis. 185 EQ93
Dorrofield Cl, Rick. 75 BQ43
Dors Cl NW9 118 CR60
Dorset Av, Hayes 135 BS69
Dorset Av, Rom. 127 FD55
Dorset Av, Sthl. 156 CA77
Dorset Av, Well. 165 ET84
Dorset Bldgs EC4 274 F9
Dorset Cl NW1 272 D6
Dorset Cl, Berk. 38 AT18
Dorset Cl, Hayes 135 BS69
Dorset Cres, Grav. 191 GL91
Dorset Dr, Edg. 96 CM51
Dorset Dr, Wok. 227 BB117
Dorset Est E2 142 DT69
Dorset Gdns, Mitch. 201 DM98
Dorset Ho, Enf. 83 DX37
Dorset Ms N3 98 DA53
Dorset Ms SW1 277 H6
Dorset Pl E15 143 ED65
Dorset Pl SW1 277 M10
Dorset Ri EC4 274 F9
Dorset Ri EC4 141 DP72
Dorset Rd E7 144 EJ66
Dorset Rd N15 122 DR56
Dorset Rd N22 99 DL53
Dorset Rd SE9 184 EL89
Dorset Rd SW8 161 DM80
Dorset Rd SW19 200 DA95
Dorset Rd W5 157 CJ76
Dorset Rd, Ashf. 174 BK90
Dorset Rd, Beck. 203 DX97
Dorset Rd, Har. 116 CC58
Dorset Rd, Mitch. 200 DE96
Dorset Rd, Sutt. 218 DA110
Dorset Rd, Wind. 151 AQ82
Dorset Sq NW1 272 D5
Dorset Sq NW1 140 DF70
Dorset Sq, Epsom 216 CR110
Dorset St W1 272 E7
Dorset St W1 140 DG71
Dorset St, Sev. 257 FH125
High St
Dorset Way, Twick. 177 CD88
Dorset Way, Uxb. 134 BM68
Dorset Way (Byfleet), W.Byf 212 BK110
Dorset Waye, Houns. 156 BZ80
Dorton Cl SE15 162 DT80
Chandler Way
Dorton Dr, Sev. 257 FM122
Dorton Way (Ripley), Wok. 228 BH121
Dorville Cres W6 159 CV76
Dorville Rd SE12 184 EF85
Dothill Rd SE18 165 ER80
Douai Gro, Hmptn. 196 CC95
Doubleday Rd, Loug. 85 EQ41
Doug Siddons Ct, Grays 170 GC79
Elm Rd
Doughty Ms WC1 274 B5
Doughty Ms WC1 141 DM70
Doughty St WC1 274 B4
Doughty St WC1 141 DM70
Douglas Av E17 101 EA53
Douglas Av, N.Mal. 199 CV98
Douglas Av, Rom. 106 FL54
Douglas Av, Wat. 76 BX37
Douglas Av, Wem. 138 CL66
Douglas Cl, Grays 170 FY76
Douglas Cl, Guil. 242 AX128
Douglas Cl, Stan. 95 CG50
Douglas Cl, Wall. 219 DL108
Douglas Ct, Cat. 236 DQ122
Fairbourne La
Douglas Ct, West. 238 EL117
Douglas Cres, Hayes 136 BW70
Douglas Dr, Croy. 203 EA104
Douglas Est N1 142 DQ65
Douglas Gdns, Berk. 38 AT18
Douglas La (Wraysbury), Stai. 173 AZ85
Douglas Ms NW2 119 CY62
Douglas Ms, Bans. 233 CZ116
North Acre
Douglas Rd E4 102 EE45
Douglas Rd E16 144 EG71
Douglas Rd N1 142 DQ66
Douglas Rd N22 99 DN53
Douglas Rd NW6 139 CZ67
Douglas Rd, Add. 194 BH104
Douglas Rd, Esher 196 CB103
Douglas Rd, Horn. 127 FF58
Douglas Rd, Houns. 156 CB83
Douglas Rd, Ilf. 126 EU58
Douglas Rd, Kings.T. 198 CP96
Douglas Rd, Reig. 250 DA133
Douglas Rd, Slou. 131 AR71
Douglas Rd (Stanwell), Stai. 174 BK86
Douglas Rd, Surb. 198 CM103
Douglas Rd, Well. 166 EV81
Douglas Sq, Mord. 200 DA100
Douglas St SW1 277 M9
Douglas St SW1 161 DK77
Douglas Ter E17 101 EA53
Douglas Av
Douglas Way SE8 163 DZ80

Douglas Way, Welw.G.C. 30 DC09
Doulton Cl, Harl. 52 EY16
Doulton Ms NW6 140 DB65
Lymington Rd
Doultons, The, Stai. 174 BG94
Dounesforth Gdns SW18 180 DB88
Dounsell Ct, Brwd. 108 FU44
Ongar Rd
Douro Pl W8 160 DB76
Douro St E3 143 EA68
Douthwaite Sq E1 142 DU74
Torrington Pl
Dove App E6 144 EL71
Dove Cl NW7 97 CT52
Dove Cl, Nthlt. 136 BX70
Wayfarer Rd
Dove Cl, S.Croy. 221 DX111
Dove Cl, Wall. 219 DM108
Hurricane Rd
Dove Ct EC2 275 K9
Dove Ct, Beac. 89 AK52
Dove Ct, Hat. 45 CU19
Dove Ho Cres, Slou. 131 AL69
Dove Ho Gdns E4 101 EA47
Dove La, Pot.B. 64 DB34
Dove Ms SW5 160 DC77
Dove Pk, Pnr. 94 CA52
Dove Pk, Rick. 73 BB44
Dove Rd N1 142 DR65
Dove Row E2 142 DU67
Dove Wk SW1 276 F10
Dove Wk, Horn. 147 FH65
Heron Flight Av
Dovecot Cl, Pnr. 115 BV57
Dovecote Av N22 121 DN55
Dovecote Cl, Wey. 195 BP104
Dovecote Gdns SW14 158 CR83
Avondale Rd
Dovedale Av, Har. 117 CJ58
Dovedale Av, Ilf. 103 EN54
Dovedale Cl, Guil. 243 BA131
Weylea Av
Dovedale Cl (Harefield), Uxb. 92 BJ54
Dovedale Cl, Well. 166 EU82
Dovedale Ri, Mitch. 180 DF94
Dovedale Rd SE22 182 DV85
Dovedale Rd, Dart. 188 FQ88
Dovedon Cl N14 99 DL47
Dovehouse Cft, Harl. 36 EU13
Mistley Rd
Dovehouse Grn, Wey. 213 BR105
Rosslyn Pk
Dovehouse Mead, Bark. 145 ER68
Dovehouse St SW3 276 B10
Dovehouse St SW3 160 DD78
Doveney Cl, Orp. 206 EW97
Dover Cl NW2 119 CX61
Brent Ter
Dover Cl, Rom. 105 FC54
Dover Flats SE1 162 DS77
Old Kent Rd
Dover Gdns, Cars. 200 DF104
Dover Ho Rd SW15 159 CU84
Dover Pk Dr SW15 179 CV86
Dover Patrol SE3 164 EH82
Kidbrooke Way
Dover Rd E12 124 EJ61
Dover Rd N9 100 DW47
Dover Rd SE19 182 DR93
Dover Rd (Northfleet), Grav. 190 GD87
Dover Rd, Rom. 126 EY58
Dover Rd, Slou. 131 AM72
Dover Rd E, Grav. 190 GE87
Dover St W1 277 J1
Dover St W1 141 DH73
Dover Way, Rick. 75 BQ42
Dover Yd W1 277 K2
Dovercourt Av, Th.Hth. 201 DN98
Dovercourt Est N1 142 DR65
Dovercourt Gdns, Stan. 96 CL50
Dovercourt La, Sutt. 200 DC104
Dovercourt Rd SE22 182 DS86
Doverfield, Wal.Cr. 66 DQ29
Doverfield Rd SW2 181 DL86
Doverfield Rd, Guil. 243 BA131
Doveridge Gdns N13 99 DP49
Dovers Grn Rd, Reig. 266 DB139
Doversmead (Knaphill), Wok. 226 AS116
Doves Cl, Brom. 204 EL103
Doves Yd N1 141 DN67
Doveton Rd, S.Croy. 220 DR106
Doveton St E1 142 DW70
Malcolm Rd
Dowanhill Rd SE6 183 ED88
Dowdeswell Cl SW15 158 CS84
Dowding Pl, Stan. 95 CG51
Dowding Rd, Uxb. 134 BM66
Dowding Rd (Biggin Hill), West. 238 EK115
Dowding Wk (Northfleet), Grav. 190 GE90
Dowding Way, Horn. 147 FH66
Dowdney Cl NW5 121 DJ64
Dower Av, Wall. 219 DH109
Dower Cl (Knotty Grn), Beac. 88 AJ50
Dower Pk, Wind. 151 AL84
Dowgate Hill EC4 275 K10
Dowgate Hill EC4 142 DR73
Dowland St W10 139 CY68
Dowlans Cl (Bookham), Lthd. 246 CA127
Dowlans Rd (Bookham), Lthd. 246 CB127
Dowlas Est SE5 162 DS80
Dowlas St
Dowlas St SE5 162 DS80
Dowlerville Rd, Orp. 223 ET107
Dowling Ct, Hem.H. 40 BK23
Dowman Cl SW19 200 DB95
Nelson Gro Rd
Down Cl, Nthlt. 135 BV68
Down Hall Rd, Kings.T. 197 CK95
Down Pl W6 159 CV77
Down Pl (Water Oakley), Wind. 150 AG79
Down Rd, Guil. 243 BB134
Down Rd, Tedd. 177 CH93
Down St W1 277 H3
Down St W1 141 DH74
Down St, W.Mol. 196 CA99
Down St Ms W1 277 H3
Down Way, Nthlt. 135 BV69
Downage NW4 119 CW55
Downage, The, Grav. 191 GG89
Downalong, Bushey 95 CD46
Downbank Av, Bexh. 167 FD81
Downbarns Rd, Ruis. 116 BX62
Downbury Ms SW18 180 DA86
Merton Rd
Downderry Rd, Brom. 183 ED90
Downe Av (Cudham), Sev. 223 EQ112
Downe Cl, Horl. 268 DE146
Downe Cl, Well. 166 EW80
Downe Rd, Kes. 222 EL109
Downe Rd, Mitch. 200 DF96
Downe Rd (Cudham), Sev. 223 EQ114
Downedge, St.Alb. 42 CB19
Downend SE18 165 EP80
Moordown
Downer Dr, Rick. 74 BG36
Downer Meadow, Gdmg. 258 AS143
Downers Cotts SW4 161 DJ84
The Pavement
Downes Cl, Twick. 177 CH86
St. Margarets Rd
Downes Ct N21 99 DN46
Downes Rd, St.Alb. 43 CH16
Downfield, Wor.Pk. 199 CT102
Downfield Cl W9 140 DB70
Downfield Cl, Hert. 32 DW11
Downfield Rd, Hert. 32 DW09
Downfield Rd (Cheshunt), Wal.Cr. 67 DY31
Downfields, Welw.G.C. 29 CV11
Downhall Rd (Hatfield Heath), B.Stort. 37 FH08
Downham Cl, Rom. 104 FA52
Downham La, Brom. 183 ED92
Downham Way
Downham Rd N1 142 DR66
Downham Way, Brom. 183 ED92
Downhills Av N17 122 DR55
Downhills Pk Rd N17 122 DQ55
Downhills Way N17 122 DQ55
Downhurst Av NW7 96 CR50
Downing Av, Guil. 258 AT135
Downing Cl, Har. 116 CC55
Downing Dr, Grnf. 137 CD67
Downing Path, Slou. 131 AL70
Downing Rd, Dag. 146 EZ67
Downing St SW1 277 P4
Downing St SW1 161 DL75
Downings E6 145 EN72
Downings Wd, Rick. 91 BD50
Downland Cl N20 98 DC46
Downland Cl, Couls. 219 DH114
Downland Cl, Epsom 233 CV118
Downland Gdns, Epsom 233 CV118
Downland Way, Epsom 233 CV118
Downlands, Wal.Abb. 68 EE34
Downlands Rd, Pur. 219 DL113
Downleys Cl SE9 184 EL89
Downman Rd SE9 164 EL83
Downs, The SW20 179 CX94
Downs, The, Harl. 51 ES15
Downs, The, Hat. 45 CU20
Downs, The, Lthd. 247 CJ125
Downs Av, Chis. 185 EM92
Downs Av, Dart. 188 FN87
Downs Av, Epsom 216 CS114
Downs Av, Pnr. 116 BZ58
Downs Br Rd, Beck. 203 ED95
Downs Ct, Sutt. 218 DB111
Downs Ct Rd, Pur. 219 DP112
Downs Hill, Beck. 203 ED95
Downs Hill (Southfleet), Grav. 190 GC94
Downs Hill Rd, Epsom 216 CS114
Downs Ho Rd, Epsom 233 CT118
Downs La E5 122 DV63
Downs Rd
Downs La, Hat. 45 CU20
Downs La, Lthd. 231 CH123
Downs Pk Rd E5 122 DU64
Downs Pk Rd E8 122 DT64
Downs Rd E5 122 DU63
Downs Rd, Beck. 203 EB96
Downs Rd, Couls. 235 DK118
Downs Rd, Dor. 247 CJ128
Downs Rd, Enf. 82 DS42
Downs Rd, Epsom 232 CS115
Downs Rd (Istead Ri), Grav. 190 GD91
Downs Rd, Pur. 219 DP111
Downs Rd, Slou. 152 AX75
Downs Rd, Sutt. 218 DB110
Downs Rd, Th.Hth. 202 DQ95
Downs Side, Sutt. 217 CZ111
Downs Vw, Dor. 247 CJ134
Downs Vw, Islw. 157 CF80
Downs Vw, Tad. 233 CV121
Downs Vw Rd (Bookham), Lthd. 246 CC126
Downs Way, Epsom 233 CT116
Downs Way (Bookham), Lthd. 246 CC126
Downs Way, Oxt. 254 EE127
Downs Way, Tad. 233 CV121
Downs Way Cl, Tad. 233 CU121
Downs Wd, Epsom 233 CV117
Downsbury Ms SW18 180 DA85
Merton Rd
Downsell Rd E15 123 EC63
Downsfield, Hat. 45 CV21
Sandifield
Downsfield Rd E17 123 DY58
Downshall Av, Ilf. 125 ES58
Downshire Hill NW3 120 DD63
Downside, Cher. 193 BF102
Downside, Epsom 216 CS114
Downside, Hem.H. 40 BL19
Downside, Sun. 195 BU95
Downside, Twick. 177 CF90
Downside Br Rd, Cob. 229 BV115
Downside Cl SW19 180 DC93
Downside Common (Downside), Cob. 229 BV118
Downside Common Rd (Downside), Cob. 229 BV118
Downside Cres NW3 120 DE64
Downside Cres W13 137 CG70
Downside Orchard, Wok. 227 BA117
Park Rd
Downside Rd (Downside), Cob. 229 BV116
Downside Rd, Guil. 259 BB135
Downside Rd, Sutt. 218 DD107
Downside Wk, Nthlt. 136 BZ69
Downsland Dr, Brwd. 108 FW48
Downsview Av, Wok. 227 AZ121
Downsview Cl, Orp. 224 EW110
Downsview Cl, Swan. 207 FF97
Downsview Ct, Guil. 242 AW130
Hazel Av
Downsview Gdns SE19 181 DP94
Downsview Gdns, Dor. 263 CH137
South Ter
Downsview Rd SE19 182 DQ94
Downsview Rd, Sev. 256 FF125
Downsway, Guil. 243 BD134
Downsway, Orp. 223 ES106
Downsway, S.Croy. 220 DS111
Downsway, Whyt. 236 DT116
Downsway, The, Sutt. 218 DC109
Downswood, Reig. 250 DE131
Downton Av SW2 181 DL89
Downtown Rd SE16 163 DY75
Downview Cl, Cob. 229 BV119
Downway N12 98 DE52
Dowrey St N1 141 DN67
Richmond Av
Dowry Wk, Wat. 75 BT38
Dowsett Rd N17 100 DT54
Dowson Cl SE5 162 DR84
Doyce St SE1 279 H4
Doyle Cl, Erith 167 FE81
Doyle Gdns NW10 139 CU67
Doyle Rd SE25 202 DU98
Doyle Way, Til. 171 GJ82
Coleridge Rd
D'Oyley St SW1 276 F8
D'Oyley St SW1 160 DG77
D'Oyly Carte Island, Wey. 195 BP102
Doynton St N19 121 DH61
Draco St SE17 162 DQ79
Dragon La, Wey. 212 BN110
Dragon Rd SE15 162 DS79
Dragon Rd, Hat. 45 CT16
Dragonfly Cl E13 144 EH69
Hollybush St
Dragoon Rd SE8 163 DZ78
Dragor Rd NW10 138 CQ70
Drake Av, Cat. 236 DQ122
Drake Av, Slou. 152 AX77
Drake Av, Stai. 173 BF92
Drake Cl SE16 163 DX75
Middleton Dr
Drake Cl, Brwd. 108 FX50
Drake Ct SE19 182 DT92
Drake Ct W12 159 CW75
Drake Ct, Har. 116 BZ60
Drake Cres SE28 146 EW72
Drake Ms, Horn. 147 FG66
Fulmar Rd
Drake Rd SE4 163 EA83
Drake Rd, Chess. 216 CN106
Drake Rd, Croy. 201 DM101
Drake Rd, Grays 170 FY75
Drake Rd, Har. 116 BZ61
Drake Rd, Horl. 268 DE148
Drake Rd, Mitch. 200 DG100
Drake St WC1 274 B7
Drake St, Enf. 82 DR39
Drakefell Rd SE4 163 DX82
Drakefell Rd SE14 163 DX82
Drakefield Rd SW17 180 DG90
Drakeley Ct N5 121 DP63
Highbury Hill
Drakes Cl, Esher 214 CA106
Drakes Cl (Cheshunt), Wal.Cr. 67 DX28
Drakes Ctyd NW6 139 CZ66
Drakes Dr, Nthwd. 93 BP53
Drakes Dr, St.Alb. 43 CH23
Drakes Rd, Amer. 55 AR39
Drakes Wk E6 145 EM67
Drakes Way, Hat. 45 CV20
Drakes Way, Wok. 226 AX122
Drakewood Rd SW16 181 DK94
Draper Cl, Belv. 166 EZ77
Draper Cl, Islw. 157 CD82
Draper Pl N1 141 DP67
Dagmar Ter
Drapers Gdns EC2 142 DR72
Copthall Av
Drapers Rd E15 123 ED63
Drapers Rd N17 122 DT55
Drapers Rd, Enf. 81 DP40
Drappers Way SE16 162 DU77
St. James's Rd
Draven Cl, Brom. 204 EF101
Drawdock Rd SE10 143 ED74
Drawell Cl SE18 165 ES78
Drax Av SW20 179 CU94
Draxmont SW19 179 CY93
Dray Ct, Guil. 258 AV135
The Chase
Dray Gdns SW2 181 DM85
Draycot Rd E11 124 EH58
Draycot Rd, Surb. 198 CN102
Draycott Av SW3 276 C8
Draycott Av SW3 160 DE77
Draycott Av, Har. 117 CH58
Draycott Cl, Har. 117 CH58
Draycott Ms SW6 159 CZ82
New Kings Rd
Draycott Pl SW3 276 D9
Draycott Pl SW3 160 DF77
Draycott Ter SW3 276 E8
Draycott Ter SW3 160 DF77
Drayford Cl W9 139 CZ70
Draymans Way, Islw. 157 CF83
Drayside Ms, Sthl. 156 BZ75
Kingston Rd
Drayson Cl, Wal.Abb. 68 EE32
Drayson Ms W8 160 DA75
Drayton Av W13 137 CG73
Drayton Av, Loug. 85 EM44
Drayton Av, Orp. 205 EP102
Drayton Av, Pot.B. 63 CY32
Drayton Br Rd W7 137 CF73
Drayton Br Rd W13 137 CF73
Drayton Cl, Houns. 176 BZ85
Bramley Way
Drayton Cl, Ilf. 125 ER60
Drayton Cl (Fetcham), Lthd. 231 CE124
Drayton Ford, Rick. 92 BG48
Drayton Gdns N21 99 DP45
Drayton Gdns SW10 160 DC78
Drayton Gdns W13 137 CG73
Drayton Gdns, West Dr. 154 BL75
Drayton Grn W13 137 CG73
Drayton Grn Rd W13 137 CH73
Drayton Gro W13 137 CG73
Drayton Pk N5 121 DN64
Drayton Pk Ms N5 121 DN64
Drayton Pk
Drayton Rd E11 123 ED60
Drayton Rd N17 100 DS54
Drayton Rd NW10 139 CT67
Drayton Rd W13 137 CG73
Drayton Rd, Borwd. 78 CN42
Drayton Rd, Croy. 201 DP103
Drayton Waye, Har. 117 CH58
Drenon Sq, Hayes 135 BT73
Dresden Cl NW6 140 DB65
Dresden Rd N19 121 DK60
Dresden Way, Wey. 213 BQ106
Dressington Av SE4 183 EA86
Drew Av NW7 97 CY51
Drew Gdns, Grnf. 137 CF65
Drew Meadow (Farnham Common), Slou. 111 AQ63
Drew Pl, Cat. 236 DR123
Drew Rd E16 144 EL74
Drews Pk (Knotty Grn), Beac. 88 AH49
Drewstead Rd SW16 181 DK89
Drey, The (Chalfont St. Peter), Ger.Cr. 90 AY50
Driffield Rd E3 143 DY68
Drift, The, Brom. 204 EK104
Drift La, Cob. 230 BZ117
Drift Rd, Lthd. 229 BT124
Drift Rd, Wind. 150 AD84
Drift Way, Rich. 178 CM88
Drift Way (Colnbrook), Slou. 153 BC81
Driftway, The, Bans. 233 CW115
Driftway, The, Hem.H. 40 BM20
Driftway, The, Lthd. 231 CH123
Downs La
Driftway, The, Mitch. 200 DG95
Driftwood Av, St.Alb. 60 CA26
Driftwood Dr, Ken. 235 DP117
Drill Hall Rd, Cher. 194 BG101
Drinkwater Rd, Har. 116 CB61
Drive, The E4 101 ED45
Drive, The E17 123 EB56
Drive, The E18 124 EG56
Drive, The N3 98 DA52
Drive, The N6 120 DF57
Fordington Rd
Drive, The N11 99 DJ51
Drive, The NW10 139 CT67
Longstone Av
Drive, The NW11 119 CY59
Drive, The SW6 159 CY82
Fulham Rd
Drive, The SW16 201 DM97
Drive, The SW20 179 CW94
Drive, The W3 138 CQ72
Drive, The, Amer. 55 AR38
Drive, The, Ashf. 175 BR94
Drive, The, Bans. 233 CY117
Drive, The, Bark. 145 ET66
Drive, The, Barn. 79 CY41
Drive, The (New Barnet), Barn. 80 DC44
Drive, The, Beck. 203 EA96
Drive, The, Bex. 186 EW86
Drive, The, Brwd. 108 FW50
Drive, The, Buck.H. 102 EJ45
Drive, The, Chis. 205 ET97
Drive, The (Scadbury Pk), Chis. 205 ES95
Drive, The, Cob. 214 BY114
Drive, The, Couls. 219 DL114
Drive, The, Edg. 96 CN50
Drive, The, Enf. 82 DR39
Drive, The, Epsom 217 CT107
Drive, The (Headley), Epsom 232 CN124
Drive, The, Erith 167 FB80
Drive, The, Esher 196 CC102
Drive, The, Felt. 176 BW87
Drive, The (Chalfont St. Peter), Ger.Cr. 90 AY52
Drive, The, Grav. 191 GK91
Drive, The, Guil. 242 AT134
Beech Gro
Drive, The (Artington), Guil. 258 AV138
Drive, The (Onslow Village), Guil. 258 AT136
Drive, The, Harl. 35 ES14
Drive, The, Har. 116 CA59
Drive, The, Hat. 64 DA25
Drive, The, Hert. 32 DQ07
Drive, The (Newgate St), Hert. 47 DL24
Drive, The, Hodd. 49 EA15
Drive, The, Horl. 269 DH149
Drive, The, Houns. 157 CD82
Drive, The, Ilf. 125 EM60
Drive, The, Islw. 157 CD82
Drive, The, Kings.T. 178 CQ94
Drive, The (Fetcham), Lthd. 231 CE122
Drive, The (Tyrrell's Wd), Lthd. 232 CN124
Drive, The, Loug. 84 EL41
Drive, The, Mord. 200 DD99
Drive, The, Nthwd. 93 BS54
Drive, The, Orp. 205 ET103
Drive, The, Pot.B. 63 CZ33
Drive, The, Rad. 61 CG34
Drive, The, Rick. 74 BJ44
Drive, The (Collier Row), Rom. 105 FC53
Drive, The (Harold Wd), Rom. 106 FL53
Drive, The (Wheathampstead), St.Alb. 61 CG26
Drive, The, Saw. 36 EY05
Drive, The, Sev. 257 FH124
Drive, The, Sid. 186 EV90
Drive, The, Slou. 152 AY75
Drive, The (Datchet), Slou. 152 AV81
Drive, The (Wraysbury), Stai. 172 AX85
Drive, The, Surb. 198 CL101
Drive, The, Sutt. 217 CZ112
Drive, The, Th.Hth. 202 DR98
Drive, The, Uxb. 114 BL63
Drive, The, Vir.W. 193 AZ99
Drive, The, Wall. 219 DJ110
Drive, The (Cheshunt), Wal.Cr. 65 DP28
Drive, The, Wat. 75 BR37
Drive, The, Wem. 118 CQ61
Drive, The, W.Wick. 203 ED101
Drive, The, Wok. 226 AV120
Drive Mead, Couls. 219 DL114
Drive Rd, Couls. 235 DM119
Drive Spur, Tad. 234 DB121
Driveway, The E17 123 EB58
Hoe St
Driveway, The (Cuffley), Pot.B. 65 DL28
Drodges Cl (Bramley), Guil. 259 AZ143
Droitwich Cl SE26 182 DU90
Dromey Gdns, Har. 95 CF52
Dromore Rd SW15 179 CY86
Dronfield Gdns, Dag. 126 EW64
Droop St W10 139 CY70
Drop La (Bricket Wd), St.Alb. 60 CB30
Dropmore Rd (Burnham), Slou. 130 AJ67
Drove Rd, Dor. 261 BP135
Drove Rd, Guil. 260 BG136
Drove Way, The (Istead Ri), Grav. 190 GE94
Drover La SE15 162 DV80
Drovers Pl SE15 162 DV80
Drovers Rd, S.Croy. 220 DR106
Drovers Way (Seer Grn), Beac. 89 AQ51
Drovers Way, Hat. 45 CV15
Drovers Way, St.Alb. 43 CD20
Droveway, Loug. 85 EP40
Druce Rd SE21 182 DS86
Drudgeon Way (Bean), Dart. 189 FV90
Druid St SE1 279 N4
Druid St SE1 162 DS75
Druids Cl, Ash. 232 CM120
Druids Way, Brom. 203 ED98
Drum St E1 142 DT72
Whitechapel High St
Drumaline Ridge, Wor.Pk. 198 CS103
Drummond Av, Rom. 127 FD56
Drummond Cen, Croy. 202 DQ103
Drummond Cl, Erith 167 FE81
Drummond Cres NW1 273 M2
Drummond Cres NW1 141 DK69
Drummond Dr, Stan. 95 CF52
Drummond Gdns, Epsom 216 CP111
Drummond Gate SW1 277 N10
Drummond Gate SW1 161 DK78
Drummond Ho, Wind. 151 AR83
Balmoral Gdns
Drummond Pl, Rich. 158 CL84
Drummond Pl, Twick. 177 CH86
Drummond Rd E11 124 EJ58
Drummond Rd SE16 162 DV76
Drummond Rd, Croy. 202 DQ103
Drummond Rd, Guil. 242 AX134
Drummond Rd, Rom. 127 FD56
Drummond St NW1 273 K4
Drummond St NW1 141 DJ70
Drummonds, The, Buck.H. 102 EH47
Drummonds, The, Epp. 70 EU30
Drury Cres, Croy. 201 DN103
Drury La WC2 274 A9
Drury La WC2 141 DL72
Drury La, Ware 34 EK06
Drury Rd, Har. 116 CC59
Drury Way NW10 118 CR64
Drury Way Ind Est NW10 118 CQ64
Dryad St SW15 159 CX83
Dryburgh Gdns NW9 118 CN55
Dryburgh Rd SW15 159 CV83
Drycroft, Welw.G.C. 29 CY13
Drydell La, Chesh. 54 AM31
Dryden Av W7 137 CF72
Dryden Cl, Ilf. 103 ET51
Dryden Ct SE11 278 E9
Dryden Ct SE11 161 DN77
Dryden Pl, Til. 171 GH81
Fielding Av
Dryden Rd SW19 180 DC93
Dryden Rd, Enf. 82 DS44
Dryden Rd, Har. 95 CF53
Dryden Rd, Well. 165 ES81
Dryden St WC2 274 A9
Dryden Twrs, Rom. 105 FH52
Dryden Way, Orp. 206 EU102
Dryfield Cl NW10 138 CQ65
Dryfield Rd, Edg. 96 CQ51
Dryfield Wk SE8 163 EA79
New King St
Dryhill La (Sundridge), Sev. 256 FB123
Dryhill Rd, Belv. 166 EZ79
Dryland Av, Orp. 223 ET105
Drylands Rd N8 121 DL58
Drynham Pk, Wey. 195 BS104
Drysdale Av E4 101 EB45
Drysdale Cl, Nthwd. 93 BS52
Northbrook Dr
Drysdale Pl N1 275 N2
Drysdale St N1 275 N2
Drysdale St N1 142 DS69
Du Burstow Ter W7 157 CE75
Du Cane Cl W12 139 CW72
Du Cane Ct SW17 180 DG88
Du Cane Rd W12 139 CT72
Du Cros Dr, Stan. 95 CJ51
Du Cros Rd W3 138 CS74
The Vale
Du Pre Wk (Wooburn Grn), H.Wyc. 110 AD59
Stratford Dr
Duarte Pl, Grays 170 FZ76
Dublin Av E8 142 DU67
Dubrae Cl, St.Alb. 42 CA22
Ducal St E2 142 DT69
Brick La
Duchess Cl N11 99 DH50
Duchess Cl, Sutt. 218 DC105
Duchess Gro, Buck.H. 102 EH47
Duchess Ms W1 273 J7
Duchess of Bedford's Wk W8 160 DA75
Duchess St W1 273 J7
Duchess St W1 141 DH71
Duchess St, Slou. 131 AL74
Duchess Wk, Sev. 257 FL125
Duchy Rd, Barn. 80 DD38
Duchy St SE1 278 E2
Duchy St SE1 141 DN74
Ducie St SW4 161 DM84
Duck La W1 273 M9
Duck La, Epp. 70 EW26
Duck Lees La, Enf. 83 DY42
Duckett Ms N4 121 DP58
Duckett Rd
Duckett Rd N4 121 DP58
Duckett St E1 143 DX71
Ducketts Mead, Harl. 34 EH14
Ducketts Rd, Dart. 187 FF85
Ducking Stool Ct, Rom. 127 FE56
Duckling La, Saw. 36 EY05
Vantorts Rd
Ducks Hill, Nthwd. 93 BP54
Ducks Hill Rd, Nthwd. 93 BP54
Ducks Hill Rd, Ruis. 93 BP54
Ducks Wk, Twick. 177 CJ85
Dudden Hill La NW10 119 CT63
Duddington Cl SE9 184 EK91
Dudley Av, Har. 117 CJ55
Dudley Av, Wal.Cr. 67 DX32
Dudley Cl, Add. 194 BJ104
Dudley Cl, Grays 170 FY75
Dudley Cl (Bovingdon), Hem.H. 57 BA27
Dudley Ct NW11 119 CZ56
Dudley Ct, Slou. 152 AU76
Upton Rd
Dudley Dr, Mord. 199 CY101
Dudley Dr, Ruis. 115 BV64
Dudley Gdns W13 157 CH75
Dudley Gdns, Har. 117 CD60
Dudley Gdns, Rom. 106 FK51
Dudley Rd
Dudley Gro, Epsom 216 CQ114
Dudley Ms SW2 181 DN86
Bascombe St
Dudley Rd E17 101 EA54
Dudley Rd N3 98 DB54
Dudley Rd NW6 139 CY68
Dudley Rd SW19 180 DA93
Dudley Rd, Ashf. 174 BM92
Dudley Rd, Felt. 175 BQ88
Dudley Rd (Northfleet), Grav. 190 GE87
Dudley Rd, Har. 116 CC61
Dudley Rd, Ilf. 125 EP63
Dudley Rd, Kings.T. 198 CM97
Dudley Rd, Rich. 158 CM82

Dudley Rd, Rom. 106 FK51
Dudley Rd, Sthl. 156 BX75
Dudley Rd, Walt. 195 BU100
Dudley St W2 140 DD71
Dudlington Rd E5 122 DW61
Dudmaston Ms SW3 276 A10
Dudsbury Rd, Dart. 187 FG86
Dudsbury Rd, Sid. 186 EV93
Dudset La, Houns. 155 BU81
Duff St E14 143 EB72
Dufferin Av EC1 275 K5
Dufferin St EC1 275 J5
Dufferin St EC1 142 DQ70
Duffield Cl (Daniel Cl), Grays 170 FY75
Duffield Cl (Davis Rd), Grays 170 FZ76
Duffield Cl, Har. 117 CF57
Duffield Dr N15 122 DT56
Copperfield Dr
Duffield La (Stoke Poges), Slou. 132 AT65
Duffield Pk (Stoke Poges), Slou. 132 AT69
Duffield Rd, Tad. 233 CV124
Duffins Orchard (Ottershaw), Cher. 211 BC108
Dufour's Pl W1 273 L9
Dugard Way SE11 278 F8
Dugard Way SE11 161 DP77
Dugdale Hill La, Pot.B. 63 CY33
Dugdales, Rick. 74 BN42
Duke Gdns, Ilf. 125 ER56
Duke Rd
Duke Humphrey Rd SE3 164 EE81
Duke of Cambridge Cl, Twick. 177 CD86
Duke of Edinburgh Rd, Sutt. 200 DD103
Duke of Wellington Pl SW1 276 G4
Duke of Wellington Pl SW1 160 DG75
Duke of York St SW1 277 L2
Duke of York St SW1 141 DJ74
Duke Rd W4 158 CR78
Duke Rd, Ilf. 125 ES56
Duke Shore Pl E14 143 DZ73
Narrow St
Duke Shore Wf E14 143 DZ73
Narrow St
Duke St SW1 277 L2
Duke St SW1 141 DJ74
Duke St W1 272 G8
Duke St W1 140 DG72
Duke St, Hodd. 49 EA16
Duke St, Rich. 157 CK84
Duke St, Sutt. 218 DD105
Duke St, Wat. 76 BW41
Duke St, Wind. 151 AP80
Duke St, Wok. 227 AZ117
Duke St Hill SE1 279 L2
Dukes Av N3 98 DB53
Dukes Av N10 121 DJ55
Dukes Av W4 158 CR78
Dukes Av, Edg. 96 CM51
Dukes Av, Epp. 85 ES35
Dukes Av, Grays 170 GA75
Dukes Av, Har. 117 CE56
Dukes Av (North Harrow), Har. 116 BZ58
Dukes Av, Houns. 156 BY84
Dukes Av, Kings.T. 177 CJ91
Dukes Av, N.Mal. 199 CT97
Dukes Av, Nthlt. 136 BY66
Dukes Av, Rich. 177 CJ91
Dukes Cl, Ashf. 175 BQ91
Dukes Cl, Epp. 71 FB27
Dukes Cl, Ger.Cr. 112 AX60
Dukes Cl, Hmptn. 176 BZ92
Dukes Ct E6 145 EN67
Dukes Ct, Wok. 227 AZ117
Dukes Dr, Slou. 111 AM64
Dukes Grn Av, Felt. 175 BU85
Dukes Head Yd N6 121 DH60
Highgate High St
Dukes Hill (Woldingham), Cat. 237 DY120
Dukes Kiln Dr, Ger.Cr. 112 AW60
Dukes La W8 160 DA75
Dukes La, Ger.Cr. 112 AY59
Dukes Lo, Nthwd. 93 BS50
Eastbury Av
Duke's Meadows W4 158 CQ82
Great Chertsey Rd
Dukes Ms N10 121 DH55
Dukes Av
Duke's Ms W1 272 G8
Dukes Orchard, Bex. 187 FC88
Duke's Pas E17 123 EC56
Dukes Pl EC3 275 N9
Dukes Pl EC3 142 DS72
Dukes Ride (North Holmwood), Dor. 263 CK139
Dukes Ride, Ger.Cr. 112 AY60
Dukes Ride, Uxb. 114 BL63
Dukes Rd E6 145 EN67
Dukes Rd W3 138 CN71
Duke's Rd WC1 273 N3
Duke's Rd WC1 141 DK69
Dukes Rd, Walt. 214 BX106
Dukes Valley, Ger.Cr. 112 AV61
Dukes Way, Berk. 38 AU17
Dukes Way, Uxb. 134 BJ67
Waterloo Rd
Dukes Way, W.Wick. 204 EE104
Dukes Wd Av, Ger.Cr. 112 AY60
Dukes Wd Dr, Ger.Cr. 112 AW60
Duke's Yd W1 272 G10
Dukesthorpe Rd SE26 183 DX91
Dulas St N4 121 DM60
Everleigh St
Dulford St W11 139 CY73
Dulka Rd SW11 180 DF85
Dulverton Rd SE9 185 EQ89
Dulverton Rd, Rom. 106 FK51
Dulverton Rd, Ruis. 115 BU60
Dulverton Rd, S.Croy. 220 DW110
Dulwich Common SE21 182 DS88
Dulwich Common SE22 182 DS88
Dulwich Lawn Cl SE22 182 DT85
Colwell Rd
Dulwich Oaks, The SE21 182 DS90
Dulwich Rd SE24 181 DN85
Dulwich Village SE21 182 DS86
Dulwich Way, Rick. 74 BN43
Dulwich Wd Av SE19 182 DS91
Dulwich Wd Pk SE19 182 DS91
Dumbarton Av, Wal.Cr. 67 DX34
Dumbarton Rd SW2 181 DL86
Dumbleton Cl, Kings.T. 198 CP95
Gloucester Rd
Dumbreck Rd SE9 165 EN84
Dumfries Cl, Wat. 93 BT48
Dumont Rd N16 122 DS62
Dumpton Pl NW1 140 DG66
Gloucester Av
Dumville Dr, Gdse. 252 DV131
Dunally Pk, Shep. 195 BR101
Dunbar Av SW16 201 DN96
Dunbar Av, Beck. 203 DY98
Dunbar Av, Dag. 126 FA62
Dunbar Cl, Hayes 135 BU71
Dunbar Cl, Slou. 132 AU72
Dunbar Ct, Sutt. 218 DD106
Dunbar Ct, Walt. 196 BW103
Dunbar Gdns, Dag. 126 FA64
Dunbar Rd E7 144 EG65
Dunbar Rd N22 99 DN53
Dunbar Rd, N.Mal. 198 CQ98
Dunbar St SE27 182 DQ90
Dunblane Cl, Edg. 96 CP47
Tayside Dr
Dunblane Rd SE9 164 EL83
Dunboe Pl, Shep. 195 BQ101
Dunboyne Rd NW3 120 DF64
Dunbridge Ho SW15 179 CT86
Highcliffe Dr
Dunbridge St E2 142 DU70
Duncan Cl, Barn. 80 DC42
Duncan Cl, Welw.G.C. 29 CY10
Duncan Dr, Guil. 243 BA133
Duncan Gdns, Stai. 174 BG92
Burges Way
Duncan Gro W3 138 CS72
Duncan Rd E8 142 DV67
Duncan Rd, Rich. 158 CL84
Duncan Rd, Tad. 233 CY119
Duncan St N1 141 DP68
Duncan Ter N1 274 F1
Duncan Ter N1 141 DP68
Duncan Way, Bushey 76 BZ40
Duncannon Cres, Wind. 151 AK83
Duncannon St WC2 277 P1
Duncannon St WC2 141 DL73
Dunch St E1 142 DV72
Watney St
Duncombe Cl, Amer. 55 AS38
Duncombe Cl, Hert. 32 DQ07
Duncombe Ct, Stai. 173 BF94
Duncombe Hill SE23 183 DY87
Duncombe Rd N19 121 DK60
Duncombe Rd, Berk. 38 AS17
Duncombe Rd, Hert. 32 DQ08
Duncrievie Rd SE13 183 ED86
Duncroft SE18 165 ES80
Duncroft, Wind. 151 AM83
Duncroft Cl, Reig. 249 CZ133
Dundalk Rd SE4 163 DY83
Dundas Gdns, W.Mol. 196 CB97
Dundas Ms, Enf. 83 EA37
Government Row
Dundas Rd SE15 162 DW82
Dundee Rd E13 144 EH68
Dundee Rd SE25 202 DV99
Dundee Rd, Slou. 131 AM72
Dundee St E1 142 DV74
Dundee Way, Enf. 83 DY41
Dundela Gdns, Wor.Pk. 217 CV105
Dundonald Cl E6 144 EL72
Northumberland Rd
Dundonald Rd NW10 139 CX67
Dundonald Rd SW19 179 CY94
Dundrey Cres, Red. 251 DL129
Dunedin Dr, Cat. 252 DS125
Dunedin Ho E16 145 EM74
Manwood St
Dunedin Rd E10 123 EB62
Dunedin Rd, Ilf. 125 EQ60
Dunedin Rd, Rain. 147 FF69
Dunedin Way, Hayes 136 BW70
Dunelm Gro SE27 182 DQ91
Dunelm St E1 143 DX72
Dunfee Way, W.Byf. 212 BL112
Dunfield Gdns SE6 183 EB91
Dunfield Rd SE6 183 EB92
Dunford Rd N7 121 DM63
Dungarvan Av SW15 159 CU84
Dungates La (Buckland), Bet. 249 CU133
Dunheved Cl, Th.Hth. 201 DN100
Dunheved Rd N, Th.Hth. 201 DN100
Dunheved Rd S, Th.Hth. 201 DN100
Dunheved Rd W, Th.Hth. 201 DN100
Dunhill Pt SW15 179 CV88
Dilton Gdns
Dunholme Grn N9 100 DT48
Dunholme La N9 100 DT48
Dunholme Rd
Dunholme Rd N9 100 DT48
Dunkeld Rd SE25 202 DR98
Dunkeld Rd, Dag. 126 EV61
Dunkellin Gro, S.Ock. 149 FU72
Dunkellin Way
Dunkellin Way, S.Ock. 149 FU72
Dunkery Rd SE9 184 EK91
Dunkin Rd, Dart. 168 FN84
Dunkirk Cl, Grav. 191 GJ92
Dunkirk St SE27 182 DQ91
Waring St
Dunkirks Ms, Hert. 32 DR11
Queens Rd
Dunlace Rd E5 122 DW63
Dunleary Cl, Houns. 176 BZ87
Dunley Dr (New Addington), Croy. 221 EB108
Dunlin Cl, Red. 266 DE139
Dunlin Ho W13 137 CF70
Dunlin Ri, Guil. 243 BD132
Dunlin Rd, Hem.H. 40 BL15
Dunloe Av N17 122 DR55
Dunloe St E2 275 P1
Dunloe St E2 142 DT68
Dunlop Pl SE16 162 DT76
Spa Rd
Dunlop Rd, Til. 171 GF81
Dunmail Dr, Pur. 220 DS114
Dunmore Pt E2 275 P3
Dunmore Rd NW6 139 CY67
Dunmore Rd SW20 199 CW95
Dunmow Cl, Felt. 176 BY91
Dunmow Cl, Loug. 84 EL44
Dunmow Cl, Rom. 126 EW57
Dunmow Dr, Rain. 147 FF67
Dunmow Ho, Dag. 146 EV67
Dunmow Rd E15 123 ED63
Dunmow Wk N1 142 DQ67
Popham St
Dunn Mead NW9 97 CT52
Field Mead
Dunn St E8 122 DT64
Dunnage Cres SE16 163 DY77
Plough Way
Dunnets (Knaphill), Wok. 226 AS117
Dunning Cl, S.Ock. 149 FU72
Dent Cl
Dunningford Cl, Horn. 127 FF64
Dunnock Cl N9 101 DX46
Dunnock Cl, Borwd. 78 CN42
Dunnock Rd E6 144 EL72
Dunns Pas WC1 274 A8
Dunny La, Kings L. 57 BE32
Dunnymans Rd, Bans. 233 CZ115
Dunollie Pl NW5 121 DJ64
Dunollie Rd
Dunollie Rd NW5 121 DJ64
Dunoon Rd SE23 182 DW87
Dunottar Cl, Red. 266 DD136
Dunraven Dr, Enf. 81 DN40
Dunraven Rd W12 139 CU74
Dunraven St W1 272 E10
Dunsany Rd W14 159 CX76
Dunsborough Pk (Ripley), Wok. 228 BJ120
Dunsbury Cl, Sutt. 218 DB109
Nettlecombe Cl
Dunsdon Av, Guil. 258 AV135
Dunsfold Ri, Couls. 219 DK113
Dunsfold Way (New Addington), Croy. 221 EB108
Dunsford Way SW15 179 CV86
Dover Pk Dr
Dunsmore Cl, Bushey 77 CD44
Dunsmore Cl, Hayes 136 BY70
Kingsash Dr
Dunsmore Rd, Walt. 195 BV100
Dunsmore Way, Bushey 77 CD44
Dunsmure Rd N16 122 DS60
Dunspring La, Ilf. 103 EP54
Dunstable Cl, Rom. 106 FK51
Dunstable Rd
Dunstable Ms W1 272 G6
Dunstable Rd, Rich. 158 CL84
Dunstable Rd, Rom. 106 FK51
Dunstable Rd, W.Mol. 196 BZ98
Dunstall Grn (Chobham), Wok. 210 AW109
Dunstall Rd SW20 179 CV93
Dunstall Way, W.Mol. 196 CB97
Dunstalls, Harl. 51 EN19
Dunstan Cl N2 120 DC55
Thomas More Way
Dunstan Rd NW11 119 CZ60
Dunstan Rd, Couls. 235 DK117
Dunstans Gro SE22 182 DV86
Dunstans Rd SE22 182 DU87
Dunster Av, Mord. 199 CX102
Dunster Cl, Barn. 79 CX42
Dunster Cl, Rom. 105 FC54
Dunster Cl (Harefield), Uxb. 92 BH53
Dunster Ct EC3 275 N10
Dunster Ct, Borwd. 78 CR41
Kensington Way
Dunster Cres, Horn. 128 FN61
Dunster Dr NW9 118 CQ60
Dunster Gdns NW6 139 CZ66
Dunster Gdns, Slou. 131 AN73
Avebury
Dunster Way, Har. 116 BY62
Dunsters Mead, Welw.G.C. 30 DA11
Dunsterville Way SE1 279 L5
Dunston Rd E8 142 DT67
Dunston Rd SW11 160 DG82
Dunston St E8 142 DT67
Dunton Cl, Surb. 198 CL102
Dunton Rd E10 123 EB59
Dunton Rd SE1 279 P10
Dunton Rd SE1 162 DT78
Dunton Rd, Rom. 127 FE56
Duntshill Rd SW18 180 DB88
Dunvegan Cl, W.Mol. 196 CB98
Dunvegan Rd SE9 165 EM84
Dunwich Rd, Bexh. 166 EZ81
Dunworth Ms W11 139 CZ72
Portobello Rd
Duplex Ride SW1 276 E5
Dupont Rd SW20 199 CX96
Dupont St E14 143 DY71
Maroon St
Duppas Av, Croy. 219 DP105
Violet La
Duppas Cl, Shep. 195 BR99
Green La
Duppas Hill La, Croy. 219 DP105
Duppas Hill Rd
Duppas Hill Rd, Croy. 219 DP105
Duppas Hill Ter, Croy. 201 DP104
Duppas Rd, Croy. 201 DN104
Dupre Cl, Grays 170 FY76
Dupre Cl, Slou. 151 AL75
Eltham Av
Dupre Cres, Beac. 89 AP54
Dupree Rd SE7 164 EH78
Dura Den Cl, Beck. 183 EB94
Durand Cl, Cars. 200 DF102
Durand Gdns SW9 161 DM81
Durand Way NW10 138 CQ66
Durands Wk SE16 163 DZ75
Durant Rd, Swan. 187 FG93
Durant St E2 142 DU69
Durants Pk Av, Enf. 83 DX42
Durants Rd, Enf. 82 DW42
Durban Gdns, Dag. 147 FC66
Durban Rd E15 144 EE69
Durban Rd E17 101 DZ53
Durban Rd N17 100 DS51
Durban Rd SE27 182 DQ91
Durban Rd, Beck. 203 DZ96
Durban Rd, Ilf. 125 ES60
Durban Rd E, Wat. 75 BU42
Durban Rd W, Wat. 75 BU42
Durbin Rd, Chess. 216 CL105
Durdans Rd, Sthl. 136 BZ72
Durell Gdns, Dag. 126 EX64
Durell Rd, Dag. 126 EX64
Durfold Dr, Reig. 250 DC134
Durford Cres SW15 179 CV88
Durham Av, Brom. 204 EF98
Durham Av, Houns. 156 BZ78
Durham Av, Rom. 128 FJ56
Durham Av, Slou. 131 AN72
Durham Av, Wdf.Grn. 102 EK50
Durham Cl SW20 199 CV96
Durham Rd
Durham Cl, Guil. 242 AT132
Durham Cl, Saw. 36 EW06
Durham Cl, Ware 33 EB10
Durham Hill, Brom. 184 EF91
Durham Ho St WC2 278 A1
Durham Pl SW3 160 DF78
Smith St
Durham Pl, Ilf. 125 EQ63
Eton Rd
Durham Ri SE18 165 EQ78
Durham Rd E12 124 EK63
Durham Rd E16 144 EE70
Durham Rd N2 120 DE55
Durham Rd N7 121 DM61
Durham Rd N9 100 DU47
Durham Rd SW20 199 CV95
Durham Rd W5 157 CK76
Durham Rd, Borwd. 78 CQ41
Durham Rd, Brom. 204 EF97
Durham Rd, Dag. 127 FC64
Durham Rd, Felt. 176 BW87
Durham Rd, Har. 116 CB57
Durham Rd, Sid. 186 EV92
Durham Row E1 143 DY71
Durham St SE11 161 DM78
Durham Ter W2 140 DB72
Durham Wf, Brent. 157 CJ80
London Rd
Durham Yd E2 142 DV69
Teesdale St
Duriun Way, Erith 167 FH80
Durleston Pk Dr (Bookham), Lthd. 246 CC125
Durley Av, Pnr. 116 BY59
Durley Gdns, Orp. 224 EV105
Durley Rd N16 122 DS59
Durlston Rd E5 122 DU61
Durlston Rd, Kings.T. 178 CL93
Durndale La (Northfleet), Grav. 191 GF91
Durnell Way, Loug. 85 EN41
Durnford St N15 122 DS57
Durnford St SE10 163 EC79
Greenwich Ch St
Durning Rd SE19 182 DR92
Durnsford Av SW19 180 DA89
Durnsford Rd N11 99 DK53
Durnsford Rd SW19 180 DA89
Durrant Path, Chesh. 54 AN27
Durrant Way, Orp. 223 ER106
Durrant Way, Swans. 190 FY87
Durrants Cl, Rain. 148 FJ68
Durrants Dr, Rick. 75 BQ42
Durrants Hill Rd, Hem.H. 40 BK23
Durrants La, Berk. 38 AT18
Durrants Rd, Berk. 38 AT18
Durrell Rd SW6 159 CZ81
Durrell Way, Shep. 195 BR100
Durrington Av SW20 199 CW95
Durrington Pk Rd SW20 179 CW94
Durrington Rd E5 123 DY63
Durrington Twr SW8 161 DJ82
Westbury St
Dursley Cl SE3 164 EJ82
Dursley Gdns SE3 164 EK81
Dursley Rd SE3 164 EJ82
Durward St E1 142 DV71
Durweston Ms W1 272 E6
Durweston St W1 272 E6
Durweston St W1 140 DF71
Dury Falls Cl, Horn. 128 FM60
Dury Rd, Barn. 79 CZ39
Dutch Barn Cl (Stanwell), Stai. 174 BK86
Dutch Elm Av, Wind. 152 AT80
Dutch Gdns, Kings.T. 178 CP93
Windmill Ri
Dutch Yd SW18 180 DA85
Wandsworth High St
Duthie St E14 143 EC73
Prestons Rd
Dutton St SE10 163 EC81
Dutton Way, Iver 133 BE72
Duxberry Cl, Brom. 204 EL99
Southborough La
Duxford Cl, Horn. 147 FH65
Duxford Ho SE2 166 EX75
Wolvercote Rd
Duxhurst La, Reig. 266 DB144
Duxons Turn, Hem.H. 41 BP19
Maylands Av
Dwight Ct SW6 159 CY82
Burlington Rd
Dwight Rd, Wat. 93 BR45
Dye Ho La E3 143 EA67
Dyer's Bldgs EC1 274 D7
Dyers Fld, Horl. 269 DP148
Dyers Hall Rd E11 124 EE60
Dyers La SW15 159 CV84
Dyers Way, Rom. 105 FH52
Dyke Dr, Orp. 206 EW102
Dykes Path, Wok. 227 BC115
Bentham Av
Dykes Way, Brom. 204 EF97
Dykewood Cl, Bex. 187 FE90
Dylan Cl, Borwd. 95 CK45
Coates Rd
Dylan Rd SE24 161 DP84
Dylan Rd, Belv. 166 FA76
Dylan Thomas Ho N8 121 DM56
Dylways SE5 162 DR84
Dymchurch Cl, Ilf. 103 EN54
Dymchurch Cl, Orp. 223 ES105
Dymes Path SW19 179 CX89
Queensmere Rd
Dymock St SW6 160 DB83
Dymoke Grn, St.Alb. 43 CG16
Dymoke Rd, Horn. 127 FF59
Dymokes Way, Hodd. 33 EA14
Dymond Est SW17 180 DE90
Glenburnie Rd
Dyne Rd NW6 139 CZ66
Dyneley Rd SE12 184 EJ91
Dynevor Rd N16 122 DS62
Dynevor Rd, Rich. 178 CL85
Dynham Rd NW6 140 DA66
Dyott St WC1 273 P8
Dyott St WC1 141 DK72
Dyrham La, Barn. 79 CU36
Dysart Av, Kings.T. 177 CJ92
Dysart St EC2 275 M5
Dyson Cl, Wind. 151 AP83
Dyson Rd E11 124 EE58
Dyson Rd E15 144 EF65
Dysons Cl, Wal.Cr. 67 DX33
Dysons Rd N18 100 DV50

E

Eade Rd N4 122 DQ59
Eagans Cl N2 120 DE55
Market Pl
Eagle Av, Rom. 126 EY58
Eagle Cl SE16 162 DW78
Varcoe Rd
Eagle Cl, Amer. 72 AT37
Eagle Cl, Enf. 82 DW42
Eagle Cl, Horn. 147 FH65
Eagle Cl, Wall. 219 DL107
Eagle Cl, Wal.Abb. 68 EG34
Eagle Ct EC1 274 F6
Eagle Ct EC1 141 DP71
Eagle Ct, Hert. 32 DV08
Eagle Dr NW9 96 CS54
Eagle Hill SE19 182 DR93
Eagle La E11 124 EG56
Eagle Ms N1 142 DS65
Tottenham Rd
Eagle Pl SW1 277 L1
Eagle Pl SW7 160 DC78
Old Brompton Rd
Eagle Rd, Guil. 258 AX135
Eagle Rd, Wem. 137 CK66
Eagle St WC1 274 B7
Eagle St WC1 141 DM71
Eagle Ter, Wdf.Grn. 102 EH52
Eagle Trd Est, Mitch. 200 DF100
Eagle Way, Brwd. 107 FV51
Eagle Way (Northfleet), Grav. 190 GA85
Eagle Way, Hat. 45 CU20
Eagle Wf E14 143 EB71
Broomfield St
Eagle Wf Rd N1 142 DQ68
Eagles Dr (Tatsfield), West. 238 EK118
Eagles Rd, Green. 169 FV84
Eaglesfield Rd SE18 165 EP80
Ealdham Sq SE9 164 EJ84
Ealing Bdy Shop Cen W5 137 CK73
Ealing Cl, Borwd. 78 CR39
Ealing Downs Ct, Grnf. 137 CG69
Perivale La
Ealing Grn W5 137 CK74
Ealing Pk Gdns W5 157 CJ77
Ealing Rd, Brent. 157 CK78
Ealing Rd, Nthlt. 136 CA66
Ealing Rd, Wem. 138 CL67
Ealing Village W5 138 CL72
Eamont Cl, Ruis. 115 BP59
Allonby Dr
Eamont St NW8 140 DE68
Eardemont Cl, Dart. 167 FF84
Eardley Cres SW5 160 DA78
Eardley Pt SE18 165 EP77
Wilmount St
Eardley Rd SW16 181 DJ92
Eardley Rd, Belv. 166 FA78
Eardley Rd, Sev. 257 FH124
Earl Cl N11 99 DH50
Earl Ri SE18 165 ER77
Earl Rd SW14 158 CQ84
Elm Rd
Earl Rd (Northfleet), Grav. 190 GE89
Earl St EC2 275 M6
Earl St EC2 142 DR71
Earl St, Wat. 76 BW41
Earldom Rd SW15 159 CW84
Earle Gdns, Kings.T. 178 CL93
Earleswood, Cob. 214 BX112
Earlham Gro E7 124 EF64
Earlham Gro N22 99 DM52
Earlham St WC2 273 N9
Earlham St WC2 141 DK72
Earls Ct Gdns SW5 160 DB77
Earls Ct Rd SW5 160 DA77
Earls Ct Rd W8 160 DA76
Earls Ct Sq SW5 160 DB78
Earls Cres, Har. 117 CE56
Earls La, Pot.B. 62 CS32
Earls La, Slou. 131 AL74
Earl's Path, Loug. 84 EJ40
Earls Ter W8 159 CZ76
Earls Wk W8 160 DA76
Earls Wk, Dag. 126 EV63
Earls Way, Orp. 205 ET103
Station Rd
Earlsbrook Rd, Red. 266 DF136
Earlsdown Ho, Bark. 145 ER68
Wheelers Cross
Earlsferry Way N1 141 DM67
Earlsfield, Maid. 150 AC77
Earlsfield Rd SW18 180 DC88
Earlshall Rd SE9 165 EM84
Earlsmead, Har. 116 BZ63
Earlsmead Rd N15 122 DT57
Earlsmead Rd NW10 139 CW68
Earlsthorpe Ms SW12 180 DG86
Earlsthorpe Rd SE26 183 DX91
Earlstoke St EC1 274 F2
Earlston Gro E9 142 DV67
Earlswood Av, Th.Hth. 201 DN99
Earlswood Cl SE10 164 EE78
Earlswood St
Earlswood Gdns, Ilf. 125 EN55
Earlswood Rd, Red. 266 DF135
Earlswood St SE10 164 EE78
Early Ms NW1 141 DH67
Arlington Rd
Earnshaw St WC2 273 N8
Earnshaw St WC2 141 DK72
Earsby St W14 159 CY77
Easby Cres, Mord. 200 DB100
Easebourne Rd, Dag. 126 EW64
Easedale Dr, Horn. 127 FG64
Easedale Ho, Islw. 177 CF85
Summerwood Rd
Eashing Pt SW15 179 CV88
Wanborough Dr
Easington Pl, Guil. 259 AZ135
Maori Rd
Easington Way, S.Ock. 149 FU71
Easley's Ms W1 272 G8
East Acton La W3 138 CS74
East Arbour St E1 143 DX72
East Av E12 144 EL66
East Av E17 123 EB56
East Av, Hayes 155 BT75
East Av, Sthl. 136 BZ73
East Av, Wall. 219 DM106
East Av, Walt. 213 BT110
Octagon Rd
East Bk N16 122 DS59
East Barnet Rd, Barn. 80 DE44
East Burnham La (Farnham Royal), Slou. 131 AN67
East Burrowfield, Welw.G.C. 29 CX11
East Churchfield Rd W3 138 CR74
East Cl W5 138 CN70
East Cl, Barn. 80 DG42
East Cl, Grnf. 136 CC68
East Cl, Rain. 147 FH70
East Cl, St.Alb. 60 CB25
East Common, Ger.Cr. 112 AY59
East Ct, Wem. 117 CJ61
East Cres N11 98 DF49
East Cres, Enf. 82 DT43
East Cres, Wind. 151 AM81
East Cres Rd, Grav. 191 GJ86
East Cross Cen E15 143 EA65
East Cross Route E3 143 EA67
East Dene Dr, Rom. 106 FK50
East Dr, Cars. 218 DE109
East Dr, Nthwd. 93 BS47
East Dr, Orp. 206 EV100
East Dr (Oaklands), St.Alb. 44 CL19
East Dr, Saw. 36 EY06
East Dr (Stoke Poges), Slou. 132 AS69
East Dr, Vir.W. 192 AU101
East Dr, Wat. 75 BV35
East Duck Lees La, Enf. 83 DY42
East Dulwich Gro SE22 182 DS86
East Dulwich Rd SE15 162 DT84
East Dulwich Rd SE22 162 DT84
East End Rd N2 120 DC55
East End Rd N3 98 DA54
East End Way, Pnr. 116 BY55

East Entrance, Dag. 147 FB68
East Ferry Rd E14 163 EB76
East Flint, Hem.H. 39 BF19
East Gdns SW17 180 DE93
East Gdns, Wok. 227 BC117
East Gate, Harl. 35 EQ14
East Gorse, Croy. 221 DY112
East Grn, Hem.H. 58 BM25
East Hall La (Wennington), Rain. 148 FK72
East Hall Rd, Orp. 206 EY101
East Ham Ind Est E6 144 EL70
East Ham Manor Way E6 145 EN72
East Ham Shop Hall E6 144 EL67
Myrtle Rd
East Harding St EC4 274 E8
East Heath Rd NW3 120 DD62
East Hill SW18 180 DB85
East Hill, Dart. 188 FM87
East Hill (South Darenth), Dart. 208 FQ95
East Hill, Oxt. 254 EE129
East Hill, S.Croy. 220 DS110
East Hill, Wem. 118 CN61
East Hill (Biggin Hill), West. 238 EH118
East Hill, Wok. 227 BC116
East Hill Dr, Dart. 188 FM87
East Hill Rd, Oxt. 254 EE129
East Holme, Erith 167 FD81
East India Dock Rd E14 143 ED72
East Kent Av (Northfleet), Grav. 190 GC86
East La SE16 162 DU75
East La, Abb.L. 59 BU29
East La (South Darenth), Dart. 209 FR96
East La, Kings.T. 197 CK97
High St
East La (West Horsley), Lthd. 245 BQ125
East La, Wem. 117 CK62
East Lo La, Enf. 81 DK36
East Mascalls SE7 164 EJ79
Mascalls Rd
East Mead, Ruis. 116 BX62
East Mead, Welw.G.C. 30 DB12
East Meads, Guil. 258 AT135
East Mill, Grav. 191 GF86
East Milton Rd, Grav. 191 GK87
East Mimms, Hem.H. 40 BL19
East Mt St E1 142 DV71
East Pk, Harl. 36 EV12
East Pk, Saw. 36 EY06
East Pk Cl, Rom. 126 EX57
East Parkside SE10 164 EE75
East Pas EC1 274 G6
East Pier E1 142 DV74
Wapping High St
East Pl SE27 182 DQ91
Pilgrim Hill
East Poultry Av EC1 274 F7
East Ramp (Heathrow Airport), Houns. 155 BP81
East Ridgeway (Cuffley), Pot.B. 65 DL29
East Rd E15 144 EG67
East Rd N1 275 K3
East Rd N1 142 DR69
East Rd SW19 180 DC93
East Rd, Barn. 98 DG46
East Rd, Edg. 96 CP53
East Rd, Enf. 82 DW38
East Rd, Felt. 175 BR87
East Rd, Harl. 36 EV11
East Rd, Kings.T. 198 CL95
East Rd, Reig. 249 CZ133
East Rd (Chadwell Heath), Rom. 126 EY57
East Rd (Rush Grn), Rom. 127 FD59
East Rd, Well. 166 EV82
East Rd, West Dr. 154 BM77
East Rd, Wey. 213 BR108
East Rochester Way SE9 165 ES84
East Rochester Way, Bex. 187 FC87
East Rochester Way, Sid. 165 ES84
East Row E11 124 EG58
East Row W10 139 CY70
East Shalford La, Guil. 258 AY139
East Sheen Av SW14 158 CR84
East Smithfield E1 142 DT73
East St SE17 279 J10
East St SE17 162 DQ78
East St, Bark. 145 EQ66
East St, Bexh. 166 FA84
East St, Brent. 157 CJ80
East St, Brom. 204 EG96
East St, Cher. 194 BG101
East St, Chesh. 54 AP32
East St, Epsom 216 CS112
East St, Grays 170 GC79
East St (South Stifford), Grays 170 FY79
East St, Hem.H. 40 BK20
East St (Bookham), Lthd. 246 CB125
East St, Ware 33 DX06
East Surrey Gro SE15 162 DT80
East Tenter St E1 142 DT72
East Ter, Grav. 191 GJ86
East Thurrock Rd, Grays 170 GB79
East Twrs, Pnr. 116 BX57
East Vw E4 101 EC50
East Vw, Barn. 79 CZ41
East Vw, Hat. 46 DF17
East Wk, Barn. 98 DG45
East Wk, Harl. 35 ER14
East Wk, Hayes 135 BU74
East Wk, Reig. 250 DB134
East Way E11 124 EH57
East Way, Beac. 88 AG54
East Way, Brom. 204 EG101
East Way, Croy. 203 DY103
East Way, Guil. 242 AT134
East Way, Hayes 135 BU74
East Way, Ruis. 115 BU60
East Woodside, Bex. 186 EY88
Eastbank Rd (Hampton Hill), Hmptn. 176 CC92
Eastbourne Av W3 138 CR72
Eastbourne Gdns SW14 158 CQ83
Eastbourne Ms W2 140 DC72
Eastbourne Rd E6 145 EN69
Eastbourne Rd E15 144 EE67
Eastbourne Rd N15 122 DS58
Eastbourne Rd SW17 180 DG93
Eastbourne Rd W4 158 CQ79
Eastbourne Rd, Brent. 157 CJ78
Eastbourne Rd, Felt. 176 BX89
Eastbourne Rd, Gdse. 252 DW132
Eastbourne Rd, Slou. 131 AM72
Eastbourne Ter W2 140 DC72
Eastbournia Av N9 100 DV48
Eastbridge, Slou. 132 AV74
Victoria Rd
Eastbrook Av N9 100 DW45
Eastbrook Av, Dag. 127 FC63
Eastbrook Cl, Wok. 227 BA116
Eastbrook Dr, Rom. 127 FE62
Eastbrook Rd SE3 164 EH80
Eastbrook Rd, Wal.Abb. 68 EE33
Eastbrook Way, Hem.H. 40 BL20
Eastbury Av, Bark. 145 ES67
Eastbury Av, Enf. 82 DS39
Eastbury Av, Nthwd. 93 BS50
Eastbury Ct, Bark. 145 ES67
Eastbury Ct, St.Alb. 43 CF19
Eastbury Gro W4 158 CS78
Eastbury Ho, Bark. 145 ET67
Eastbury Pl, Nthwd. 93 BT50
Eastbury Av
Eastbury Rd E6 145 EN70
Eastbury Rd, Kings.T. 178 CL94
Eastbury Rd, Nthwd. 93 BS51
Eastbury Rd, Orp. 205 ER100
Eastbury Rd, Rom. 127 FD58
Eastbury Rd, Wat. 93 BV45
Eastbury Sq, Bark. 145 ET67
Eastbury Ter E1 143 DX70
Eastcastle St W1 273 K8
Eastcastle St W1 141 DJ72
Eastcheap EC3 275 L10
Eastcheap EC3 142 DR73
Eastchurch Rd (Heathrow Airport), Houns. 155 BS82
Eastcombe Av SE7 164 EH79
Eastcote, Orp. 205 ET102
Eastcote Av, Grnf. 117 CG64
Eastcote Av, Har. 116 CB61
Eastcote Av, W.Mol. 196 BZ99
Eastcote La, Har. 116 CA62
Eastcote La, Nthlt. 136 CA66
Eastcote La N, Nthlt. 136 BZ65
Eastcote Pl, Pnr. 115 BV58
Eastcote Rd, Har. 116 CC62
Eastcote Rd, Pnr. 116 BX57
Eastcote Rd (Eastcote Village), Pnr. 115 BU58
Eastcote Rd, Ruis. 115 BS59
Eastcote Rd, Well. 165 ER82
Eastcote St SW9 161 DM82
Eastcote Vw, Pnr. 116 BW56
Eastcourt, Sun. 196 BW96
Eastcroft, Slou. 131 AP70
Eastcroft Rd, Epsom 216 CS108
Eastdean Av, Epsom 216 CP113
Eastdown Pk SE13 163 ED84
Eastergate, Beac. 88 AJ51
Eastern Av E11 124 EJ58
Eastern Av, Cher. 194 BG97
Eastern Av, Grays 169 FT78
Eastern Av, Ilf. 124 EL58
Eastern Av, Pnr. 116 BX59
Eastern Av, Rom. 126 EW56
Eastern Av, S.Ock. 148 FQ74
Eastern Av, Wal.Cr. 67 DY33
Eastern Av E, Rom. 127 FD55
Eastern Av W, Rom. 126 EY56
Eastern Dr, B.End 110 AC59
Eastern Ind Est, Erith 166 FA75
Eastern Pathway, Horn. 148 FJ67
Eastern Perimeter Rd (Heathrow Airport), Houns. 155 BT83
Eastern Rd E13 144 EH68
Eastern Rd E17 123 EC57
Eastern Rd N2 120 DF55
Eastern Rd N22 99 DL53
Eastern Rd SE4 163 EA84
Eastern Rd, Grays 170 GD77
Eastern Rd, Rom. 127 FE57
Eastern Vw (Biggin Hill), West. 238 EJ117
Eastern Way SE2 146 EX74
Eastern Way SE28 166 EU75
Eastern Way, Belv. 167 FB75
Eastern Way, Erith 146 EX74
Eastern Way, Grays 170 GA79
Easternville Gdns, Ilf. 125 EQ58
Eastfield Av, Wat. 76 BX39
Eastfield Cl, Slou. 152 AU76
St. Laurence Way
Eastfield Cotts, Hayes 155 BS78
Eastfield Ct, St.Alb. 43 CK17
Southfield Way
Eastfield Gdns, Dag. 126 FA63
Eastfield Par, Pot.B. 64 DD32
Eastfield Rd E17 123 EA56
Eastfield Rd N8 121 DL55
Eastfield Rd, Brwd. 108 FX47
Eastfield Rd, Dag. 126 FA63
Eastfield Rd, Enf. 83 DX38
Eastfield Rd, Red. 267 DJ135
Eastfield Rd (Burnham), Slou. 130 AG71
Eastfield Rd, Wal.Cr. 67 DY32
Eastfields, Pnr. 116 BW57
Eastfields Rd W3 138 CQ71
Eastfields Rd, Mitch. 200 DG96
Eastgate, Bans. 217 CY114
Eastgate Cl SE28 146 EX72
Eastgate Gdns, Guil. 258 AY135
Eastglade, Nthwd. 93 BS50
Eastglade, Pnr. 116 BY55
Eastham Cl, Barn. 79 CY43
Eastham Cres, Brwd. 109 GA49
Eastholm NW11 120 DB56
Eastholme, Hayes 135 BU74
Eastlake Rd SE5 161 DP82
Eastlands Cl, Oxt. 253 ED127
Eastlands Way
Eastlands Cres SE21 182 DT86
Eastlands Way, Oxt. 253 ED127
Eastlea Av, Wat. 76 BY37
Eastlea Ms E16 144 EE70
Desford Rd
Eastleigh Av, Har. 116 CB61
Eastleigh Cl NW2 118 CS62
Eastleigh Cl, Sutt. 218 DB108
Eastleigh Rd E17 101 DZ54
Eastleigh Rd, Bexh. 167 FC82
Eastleigh Rd (Heathrow Airport), Houns. 155 BT83
Cranford La
Eastleigh Wk SW15 179 CU87
Eastleigh Way, Felt. 175 BU88
Eastman Rd W3 138 CR74
Eastman Way, Hem.H. 40 BN17
Eastmead, Wok. 226 AV117
Eastmead Av, Grnf. 136 CB69
Eastmead Cl, Brom. 204 EL96
Eastmearn Rd SE21 182 DQ89
Eastmont Rd, Esher 197 CE103
Eastmoor Pl SE7 164 EK76
Eastmoor St
Eastmoor St SE7 164 EK76
Eastney Rd, Croy. 201 DP102
Eastney St SE10 163 ED78
Eastnor (Bovingdon), Hem.H. 57 BA28
Eastnor Cl, Reig. 265 CZ137
Eastnor Rd SE9 185 EQ88
Eastnor Rd, Reig. 266 DA136
Easton Gdns, Borwd. 78 CR42
Easton St WC1 274 D3
Eastor, Welw.G.C. 30 DA06
Eastry Av, Brom. 204 EF100
Eastry Rd, Erith 166 FA80
Eastside Rd NW11 119 CZ56
Eastview Av SE18 165 ES80
Eastville Av NW11 119 CZ58
Eastway E9 143 DZ65
Eastway E10 123 EC63
Eastway E15 123 EA64
Eastway, Epsom 216 CQ112
Eastway, Gat. 269 DH152
Eastway, Mord. 199 CX99
Eastway, Wall. 219 DJ105
Eastway Commercial Cen E9 123 EA64
Eastwell Cl, Beck. 203 DY95
Eastwick Ct SW19 179 CX88
Victoria Dr
Eastwick Cres, Rick. 91 BF47
Eastwick Dr (Bookham), Lthd. 230 CA123
Eastwick Hall La, Harl. 35 EN09
Eastwick Pk Av (Bookham), Lthd. 230 CB124
Eastwick Rd, Harl. 35 EM11
Eastwick Rd (Bookham), Lthd. 246 CB125
Eastwick Rd, Walt. 213 BV106
Eastwick Rd (Hunsdonbury), Ware 34 EK08
Eastwick Rd (Stanstead Abbotts), Ware 34 EF12
Eastwick Row, Hem.H. 40 BN21
Eastwood Cl E18 102 EG54
George La
Eastwood Cl N17 100 DV52
Northumberland Gro
Eastwood Ct, Hem.H. 40 BN19
Eastwood Dr, Rain. 147 FH72
Eastwood Rd E18 102 EG54
Eastwood Rd N10 98 DG54
Eastwood Rd (Bramley), Guil. 259 AZ144
Eastwood Rd, Ilf. 126 EU59
Eastwood Rd, West Dr. 154 BN75
Eastwood St SW16 181 DJ93
Eastworth Rd, Cher. 194 BG102
Eatington Rd E10 123 ED57
Eaton Cl SW1 276 F9
Eaton Cl SW1 160 DG77
Eaton Cl, Stan. 95 CH49
Eaton Ct, Guil. 243 BA132
Eaton Dr SW9 161 DP84
Eaton Dr, Kings.T. 178 CN94
Eaton Dr, Rom. 105 FB52
Eaton Gdns, Dag. 146 EY66
Eaton Gate SW1 276 F8
Eaton Gate SW1 160 DG77
Eaton Gate, Nthwd. 93 BQ51
Eaton Ho E14 143 EA74
Westferry Circ
Eaton La SW1 277 J7
Eaton La SW1 161 DH76
Eaton Ms N SW1 276 F8
Eaton Ms N SW1 160 DG76
Eaton Ms S SW1 276 G8
Eaton Ms S SW1 161 DH76
Eaton Ms W SW1 276 G8
Eaton Ms W SW1 160 DG77
Eaton Pk, Cob. 214 BY114
Eaton Pk Rd N13 99 DN47
Eaton Pk Rd, Cob. 214 BY114
Eaton Pl SW1 276 F7
Eaton Pl SW1 160 DG76
Eaton Ri E11 124 EJ57
Eaton Ri W5 137 CK72
Eaton Rd NW4 119 CW57
Eaton Rd, Enf. 82 DS41
Eaton Rd, Hem.H. 41 BP17
Eaton Rd, Houns. 157 CD84
Eaton Rd, St.Alb. 43 CH20
Eaton Rd, Sid. 186 EX89
Eaton Rd, Sutt. 218 DD107
Eaton Rd, Upmin. 129 FS61
Eaton Row SW1 277 H7
Eaton Row SW1 161 DH76
Eaton Sq SW1 277 H6
Eaton Sq SW1 160 DG77
Eaton Sq, Long. 209 FX97
Bramblefield Cl
Eaton Ter SW1 276 F8
Eaton Ter SW1 160 DG77
Eaton Ter Ms SW1 276 F8
Eatons Mead E4 101 EA47
Eatonville Rd SW17 180 DF89
Eatonville Vil SW17 180 DF89
Eatonville Rd
Ebbas Way, Epsom 232 CP115
Ebberns Rd, Hem.H. 40 BK23
Ebbisham Cl, Dor. 263 CG136
Nower Rd
Ebbisham Dr SW8 161 DM79
Ebbisham La, Tad. 233 CT121
Ebbisham Rd, Epsom 216 CP114
Ebbisham Rd, Wor.Pk. 199 CW103
Ebbsfleet Ind Est (Northfleet), Grav. 190 GA85
Ebbsfleet Rd NW2 119 CY63
Ebbsfleet Wk (Northfleet), Grav. 190 GB86
Ebdon Way SE3 164 EH83
Ebenezer St N1 275 K2
Ebenezer St N1 142 DR69
Ebenezer Wk SW16 201 DJ95
Ebley Cl SE15 162 DT79
Ebner St SW18 180 DB85
Ebor St E1 275 P4
Ebor St E1 142 DT70
Ebrington Rd, Har. 117 CK58
Ebsworth Cl, Maid. 130 AC68
Ebsworth St SE23 183 DX87
Eburne Rd N7 121 DL62
Ebury Br SW1 277 H10
Ebury Br SW1 161 DH78
Ebury Br Est SW1 277 H10
Ebury Br Est SW1 161 DH78
Ebury Br Rd SW1 160 DG78
Ebury Cl, Kes. 204 EL104
Ebury Cl, Nthwd. 93 BQ50
Ebury Ms SE27 181 DP90
Ebury Ms SW1 277 H8
Ebury Ms SW1 161 DH77
Ebury Ms E SW1 277 H8
Ebury Rd, Rick. 92 BK46
Ebury Rd, Wat. 76 BW41
Ebury Sq SW1 276 G9
Ebury Sq SW1 160 DG77
Ebury St SW1 277 H8
Ebury St SW1 160 DG77
Ebury Way Cycle Path, The, Rick. 93 BP45
Ebury Way Cycle Path, The, Wat. 93 BP45
Eccles Hill (North Holmwood), Dor. 263 CJ140
Eccles Rd SW11 160 DF84
Ecclesbourne Cl N13 99 DN50
Ecclesbourne Gdns N13 99 DN50
Ecclesbourne Rd N1 142 DQ66
Ecclesbourne Rd, Th.Hth. 202 DQ99
Eccleston Br SW1 277 J8
Eccleston Br SW1 161 DH77
Eccleston Cl, Barn. 80 DF42
Eccleston Cl, Orp. 205 ER102
Eccleston Cres, Rom. 126 EU59
Eccleston Ms SW1 276 G7
Eccleston Ms SW1 160 DG76
Eccleston Pl SW1 277 H8
Eccleston Pl SW1 161 DH77
Eccleston Rd W13 137 CG73
Eccleston Sq SW1 277 J9
Eccleston Sq SW1 161 DH77
Eccleston Sq Ms SW1 277 K9
Eccleston St SW1 277 H7
Eccleston St SW1 160 DG76
Ecclestone Ct, Wem. 118 CL64
St. John's Rd
Ecclestone Pl, Wem. 118 CM64
Echelforde Dr, Ashf. 174 BN91
Echo Hts E4 101 EB46
Mount Echo Dr
Echo Pit Rd, Guil. 258 AY138
Echo Sq, Grav. 191 GJ89
Old Rd E
Eckersley St E1 142 DU70
Buxton St
Eckford St N1 141 DN68
Eckington Ho N15 122 DR58
Fladbury Rd
Eckstein Rd SW11 160 DE84
Eclipse Rd E13 144 EH71
Ecob Cl, Guil. 242 AT130
Ecton Rd, Add. 212 BH105
Ector Rd SE6 184 EE89
Edbrooke Rd W9 140 DA70
Eddiscombe Rd SW6 159 CZ82
Eddy Cl, Rom. 127 FB58
Eddy St, Berk. 38 AU18
Eddystone Rd SE4 183 DY85
Eddystone Twr SE8 163 DY78
Eddystone Wk, Stai. 174 BL87
Ede Cl, Houns. 156 BZ83
Eden Cl NW3 120 DA61
Eden Cl W8 160 DA76
Adam & Eve Ms
Eden Cl (New Haw), Add. 212 BH110
Eden Cl, Bex. 187 FD91
Eden Cl, Enf. 83 EA38
Government Row
Eden Cl, Slou. 153 BA78
Eden Cl, Wem. 137 CK67
Eden Dr, Enf. 83 EA37
Government Row
Eden Grn, S.Ock. 149 FV71
Bovey Way
Eden Gro E17 123 EB57
Eden Gro N7 121 DM64
Eden Gro Rd (Byfleet), W.Byf. 212 BL113
Eden Ms SW17 180 DC90
Huntspill St
Eden Pk Av, Beck. 203 DY98
Eden Pl, Grav. 191 GH87
Lord St
Eden Rd E17 123 EB57
Eden Rd SE27 181 DP92
Eden Rd, Beck. 203 DY98
Eden Rd, Bex. 187 FC91
Eden Rd, Croy. 220 DR105
Eden St, Kings.T. 197 CK96
Eden Wk, Kings.T. 198 CL96
Eden St
Eden Wk Shop Cen, Kings.T. 198 CL96
Eden Way, Beck. 203 DZ99
Eden Way, Warl. 237 DY118
Edenbridge Cl SE16 162 DV78
Masters Dr
Edenbridge Cl, Orp. 206 EX98
Edenbridge Rd E9 143 DX66
Edenbridge Rd, Enf. 82 DS44
Edencourt Rd SW16 181 DH93
Edencroft (Bramley), Guil. 259 AZ144
Edendale Rd, Bexh. 167 FD81
Edenfield Gdns, Wor.Pk. 199 CT104
Edenhall Cl, Hem.H. 41 BR21
Edenhall Cl, Rom. 106 FJ50
Edenhall Glen, Rom. 106 FJ50
Edenhall Rd, Rom. 106 FJ50
Edenham Way W10 139 CZ71
Elkstone Rd
Edenhurst Av SW6 159 CZ83
Edenside Rd (Bookham), Lthd. 230 BZ124
Edensor Gdns W4 158 CS80
Edensor Rd W4 158 CS80
Edenvale Cl, Mitch. 180 DG94
Edenvale Rd
Edenvale Rd, Mitch. 180 DG94
Edenvale St SW6 160 DB82
Ederline Av SW16 201 DM97
Edes Flds, Reig. 265 CY136
Edgar Cl, Swan. 207 FF97
Edgar Kail Way SE22 162 DS84
Edgar Rd E3 143 EB69
Edgar Rd, Houns. 176 BZ87
Edgar Rd, Rom. 126 EX59
Edgar Rd, S.Croy. 220 DR109
Edgar Rd, West Dr. 134 BL73
Edgar Rd (Tatsfield), West. 238 EK121
Edgarley Ter SW6 159 CY81
Edgars Ct, Welw.G.C. 29 CY10
Edgbaston Dr, Rad. 62 CL32
Edgbaston Rd, Wat. 93 BV48
Edge Cl, Wey. 212 BN108
Edge Hill SE18 165 EP79
Edge Hill SW19 179 CX94
Edge Hill Av N3 120 DA55
Edge Hill Ct SW19 179 CX94
Edge St W8 140 DA74
Kensington Ch St
Edgeborough Way, Brom. 184 EK94
Edgebury, Chis. 185 EP91
Edgebury Wk, Chis. 185 EQ91
Edgecombe Ho SW19 179 CY88
Edgecoombe, S.Croy. 220 DW108
Edgecoombe Cl, Kings.T. 178 CR94
Edgecot Gro N15 122 DR57
Oulton Rd
Edgecote Cl W3 138 CQ74
Cheltenham Pl
Edgefield Av, Bark. 145 ET66
Edgefield Cl, Dart. 188 FP88
Edgefield Cl, Red. 266 DG139
Edgehill Ct, Walt. 196 BW102
St. Johns Dr
Edgehill Gdns, Dag. 126 FA63
Edgehill Rd W13 137 CJ71
Edgehill Rd, Chis. 185 EQ90
Edgehill Rd, Mitch. 201 DH95
Edgehill Rd, Pur. 219 DN110
Edgel St SW18 160 DB84
Ferrier St
Edgeley (Bookham), Lthd. 230 BY124
Edgeley Caravan Pk (Farley Grn), Guil. 260 BL143
Edgeley La SW4 161 DK83
Edgeley Rd
Edgeley Rd SW4 161 DK83
Edgell Cl, Vir.W. 193 AZ97
Edgell Rd, Stai. 173 BF92
Edgepoint Cl SE27 181 DP92
Knights Hill
Edgewood Dr, Orp. 223 ET106
Edgewood Grn, Croy. 203 DX102
Edgeworth Av NW4 119 CU57
Edgeworth Cl NW4 119 CU57
Edgeworth Cl, Whyt. 236 DU118
Edgeworth Cres NW4 119 CU57
Edgeworth Rd SE9 164 EJ84
Edgeworth Rd, Barn. 80 DE42
Edgington Rd SW16 181 DK93
Edgington Way, Sid. 186 EW94
Edgware Ct, Edg. 96 CN51
Cavendish Dr
Edgware Rd NW2 119 CV60
Edgware Rd NW9 118 CR55
Edgware Rd W2 272 C8
Edgware Rd W2 140 DE72
Edgware Rd Sub W2 140 DE71
Edgware Rd
Edgware Way, Edg. 96 CM49
Edgwarebury Gdns, Edg. 96 CN50
Edgwarebury La, Borwd. 96 CL45
Edgwarebury La, Edg. 96 CN49
Edinburgh Av, Rick. 74 BG44
Edinburgh Av, Slou. 131 AN71
Edinburgh Cl E2 142 DW68
Russia La
Edinburgh Cl, Pnr. 116 BX59
Edinburgh Cl, Uxb. 115 BP63
Edinburgh Ct SW20 199 CX99
Edinburgh Cres, Wal.Cr. 67 DY33
Edinburgh Dr, Abb.L. 59 BU32
Edinburgh Dr, Rom. 127 FC56
Eastern Av W
Edinburgh Dr, Stai. 174 BK93
Edinburgh Dr (Denham), Uxb. 113 BF58
Edinburgh Dr (Ickenham), Uxb. 115 BP63
Edinburgh Gdns, Wind. 151 AR83
Edinburgh Gate SW1 276 D4
Edinburgh Gate SW1 160 DF75
Edinburgh Gate, Harl. 35 ER12
Edinburgh Ho W9 140 DC69
Edinburgh Ms, Til. 171 GH82
Edinburgh Pl, Harl. 36 EU11
Edinburgh Rd E13 144 EH68
Edinburgh Rd E17 123 EA57
Edinburgh Rd N18 100 DU50
Edinburgh Rd W7 157 CF75
Edinburgh Rd, Sutt. 200 DC103
Edinburgh Way, Harl. 35 ER12
Edington Rd SE2 166 EV76
Edington Rd, Enf. 82 DW40
Edis St NW1 140 DG67
Edison Av, Horn. 127 FF61
Edison Cl E17 123 EA57
Exeter Rd
Edison Cl, Horn. 127 FF60
Edison Av
Edison Cl, St.Alb. 43 CJ21
Edison Dr, Sthl. 136 CB72
Edison Dr, Wem. 118 CL61
Edison Gro SE18 165 ET80
Edison Rd N8 121 DK58
Edison Rd, Brom. 204 EG96
Edison Rd, Enf. 83 DZ40
Edison Rd, Well. 165 ET81
Edith Cavell Cl N19 121 DK59
Hornsey Ri Gdns
Edith Gdns, Surb. 198 CP101
Edith Gro SW10 160 DC79
Edith Rd E6 144 EK66
Edith Rd E15 123 ED64
Chandos Rd
Edith Rd N11 99 DK52
Edith Rd SE25 202 DR99
Edith Rd SW19 180 DB93
Edith Rd W14 159 CY77
Edith Rd, Orp. 224 EU106
Edith Rd, Rom. 126 EX58
Edith Row SW6 160 DB81
Edith St E2 142 DU68
Edith Summerskill Ho SW6 159 CZ80
Clem Attlee Ct
Edith Ter SW10 160 DC80
Edith Vil SW15 159 CY84
Bective Rd
Edith Vil W14 159 CZ77
Edith Yd SW10 160 DC80
World's End Est
Edithna St SW9 161 DL83
Edlyn Cl, Berk. 38 AT18
Edmansons Cl N17 100 DS53
Bruce Gro
Edmeston Cl E9 143 DY65
Edmond Beaufort Dr, St.Alb. 43 CD18
Edmond Halley Way SE10 164 EE75
Edmonds Ct, W.Mol. 196 CB98
Avern Rd
Edmonton Grn N9 100 DV47
Hertford Rd
Edmund Gro, Felt. 176 BZ89
Edmund Hurst Dr E6 145 EP71
Edmund Rd (Chafford Hundred), Grays 169 FX75
Edmund Rd, Mitch. 200 DE97
Edmund Rd, Orp. 206 EW100
Edmund Rd, Rain. 147 FE68
Edmund Rd, Well. 166 EU83
Edmund St SE5 162 DR80
Edmunds Av, Orp. 206 EX97
Edmunds Cl, Hayes 136 BW71
Edmunds Rd, Hert. 31 DM08
Edmunds Twr, Harl. 51 EQ15
Edmunds Wk N2 120 DD56
Edmunds Way, Slou. 132 AV71
Edna Rd SW20 199 CX96
Edna St SW11 160 DE81
Edric Rd SE14 163 DX80
Edrich Ho SW4 161 DL81
Edrick Rd, Edg. 96 CQ51
Edrick Wk, Edg. 96 CQ51
Edridge Cl, Bushey 76 CC43
Edridge Cl, Horn. 128 FK64

Edridge Rd, Croy. 202 DQ104
Edulf Rd, Borwd. 78 CP39
Edward Amey Cl, Wat. 76 BW36
Edward Av E4 101 EB51
Edward Av, Mord. 200 DD99
Edward Cl N9 100 DT45
Edward Cl, Abb.L. 59 BT32
Edward Cl (Chafford Hundred), Grays 169 FX76
Edward Cl (Hampton Hill), Hmptn. 176 CC92
Edward Rd
Edward Cl, Nthlt. 136 BW68
Edward Cl, Rom. 128 FJ55
Edward Cl, St.Alb. 43 CF21
Edward Ct E16 144 EG71
Alexandra St
Edward Ct, Hem.H. 40 BK24
King Edward St
Edward Ct, Stai. 174 BJ93
Elizabeth Av
Edward Ct, Wal.Abb. 68 EF33
Edward Gro, Barn. 80 DD43
Edward Ms NW1 273 J1
Edward Pauling Ho, Felt. 175 BT87
Westmacott Dr
Edward Pl SE8 163 DZ79
Edward Rd E17 123 DX56
Edward Rd SE20 183 DX94
Edward Rd, Barn. 80 DD43
Edward Rd, Brom. 184 EH94
Edward Rd, Chis. 185 EP92
Edward Rd, Couls. 235 DK115
Edward Rd, Croy. 202 DS101
Edward Rd, Felt. 175 BR85
Edward Rd (Hampton Hill), Hmptn. 176 CC92
Edward Rd, Har. 116 CC55
Edward Rd, Nthlt. 136 BW68
Edward Rd, Rom. 126 EY58
Edward Rd (Biggin Hill), West. 238 EL118
Edward II Av (Byfleet), W.Byf. 212 BM114
Edward Sq N1 141 DM67
Caledonian Rd
Edward Sq SE16 143 DY74
Rotherhithe St
Edward St E16 144 EG70
Edward St SE8 163 DZ79
Edward St SE14 163 DY80
Edward Temme Av E15 144 EF66
Edward Tyler Rd SE12 184 EH89
Edward Way, Ashf. 174 BM89
Edwardes Pl W8 159 CZ76
Edwardes Sq
Edwardes Sq W8 160 DA76
Edward's Av, Ruis. 135 BV65
Edwards Cl, Brwd. 109 GE44
Edwards Cl, Wor.Pk. 199 CX103
Edwards Cotts N1 141 DP65
Compton Av
Edwards Ct, Slou. 152 AS75
Edwards Ct, Wal.Cr. 67 DX31
Turners Hill
Edwards Dr N11 99 DK52
Gordon Rd
Edwards Gdns, Swan. 207 FD98
Ladds Way
Edwards La N16 122 DR61
Edwards Ms N1 141 DN66
Edwards Ms W1 272 F9
Edwards Ms W1 140 DG72
Edwards Rd, Belv. 166 FA77
Edwards Way, Brwd. 109 GE44
Edwards Yd, Wem. 138 CL67
Mount Pleasant
Edwin Av E6 145 EN68
Edwin Cl, Bexh. 166 EZ79
Edwin Cl (West Horsley), Lthd. 245 BR125
Edwin Cl, Rain. 147 FF69
Edwin Pl, Croy. 202 DR102
Cross Rd
Edwin Rd, Dart. 187 FH90
Edwin Rd, Edg. 96 CR51
Edwin Rd (West Horsley), Lthd. 245 BQ125
Edwin Rd, Twick. 177 CF88
Edwin St E1 142 DW70
Edwin St E16 144 EG71
Edwin St, Grav. 191 GH87
Edwina Gdns, Ilf. 124 EL57
Edwin's Mead E9 123 DY63
Lindisfarne Way
Edwyn Cl, Barn. 79 CW44
Eel Brook Studios SW6 160 DA80
Moore Pk Rd
Eel Pie Island, Twick. 177 CH88
Effie Pl SW6 160 DA80
Effie Rd SW6 160 DA80
Effingham Cl, Sutt. 218 DB108
Effingham Common (Effingham), Lthd. 229 BU123
Effingham Common Rd (Effingham), Lthd. 229 BU123
Effingham Ct, Wok. 226 AY118
Constitution Hill
Effingham Hill, Dor. 246 BX132
Critten La
Effingham Pl (Effingham), Lthd. 246 BX127
Effingham Rd N8 121 DN57
Effingham Rd SE12 184 EE85
Effingham Rd, Croy. 201 DM101
Effingham Rd, Reig. 266 DB135
Effingham Rd, Surb. 197 CH101
Effort St SW17 180 DE92
Effra Par SW2 181 DN85
Effra Rd SW2 161 DN84
Effra Rd SW19 180 DB93
Egan Way, Hayes 135 BS73
Egbert St NW1 140 DG67
Egbury Ho SW15 179 CT86
Tangley Gro
Egdean Wk, Sev. 257 FJ123
Egerton Av, Swan. 187 FF94
Egerton Cl, Dart. 187 FH88
Egerton Cl, Pnr. 115 BU56
Egerton Ct, Guil. 242 AS134
Egerton Rd
Egerton Cres SW3 276 C8
Egerton Cres SW3 160 DE77
Egerton Dr SE10 163 EB81
Egerton Gdns NW4 119 CV56
Egerton Gdns NW10 139 CW67
Egerton Gdns SW3 276 B7
Egerton Gdns SW3 160 DE76
Egerton Gdns W13 137 CH72
Egerton Gdns, Ilf. 125 ET62
Egerton Gdns Ms SW3 276 C7
Egerton Gdns Ms SW3 160 DE76
Egerton Pl SW3 276 C7
Egerton Pl SW3 160 DE76
Egerton Pl, Wey. 213 BQ107
Egerton Rd N16 122 DT59
Egerton Rd SE25 202 DS97
Egerton Rd, Berk. 38 AU17
Egerton Rd, Guil. 242 AS134
Egerton Rd, N.Mal. 199 CT98
Egerton Rd, Slou. 131 AL70
Egerton Rd, Twick. 177 CE87
Egerton Rd, Wem. 138 CM66
Egerton Rd, Wey. 213 BQ107
Egerton Ter SW3 276 C7
Egerton Ter SW3 160 DE76
Egerton Way, Hayes 155 BP80
Egg Hall, Epp. 70 EU29
Eggardon Ct, Nthlt. 136 CC65
Lancaster Rd
Egham Bypass, Egh. 173 AZ92
Egham Cl SW19 179 CY89
Winterfold Cl
Egham Cl, Sutt. 199 CY103
Egham Cres, Sutt. 199 CX104
Egham Hill, Egh. 172 AX93
Egham Rd E13 144 EH71
Eghams Cl (Knotty Grn), Beac. 88 AJ51
Eghams Wd Rd, Beac. 88 AH51
Eglantine La (Horton Kirby), Dart. 208 FN101
Eglantine Rd SW18 180 DC85
Egleston Rd, Mord. 200 DB100
Egley Dr, Wok. 226 AX122
Egley Rd, Wok. 226 AX122
Eglington Ct SE17 162 DQ79
Carter St
Eglington Rd E4 101 ED45
Eglinton Hill SE18 165 EP79
Eglinton Rd SE18 165 EN79
Eglinton Rd, Swans. 190 FZ86
Eglise Rd, Warl. 237 DY117
Egliston Ms SW15 159 CW83
Egliston Rd SW15 159 CW83
Eglon Ms NW1 140 DF66
Berkley Rd
Egmont Av, Surb. 198 CM102
Egmont Pk Rd, Tad. 249 CU125
Egmont Rd, N.Mal. 199 CT98
Egmont Rd, Surb. 198 CM102
Egmont Rd, Sutt. 218 DC108
Egmont Rd, Walt. 195 BV101
Egmont St SE14 163 DX80
Egmont Way, Tad. 233 CY119
Oatlands Rd
Egremont Gdns, Slou. 131 AN74
Egremont Ho SE13 163 EB82
Conington Rd
Egremont Rd SE27 181 DN90
Egret Way, Hayes 136 BX71
Egypt La (Farnham Common), Slou. 111 AP61
Eider Cl E7 124 EF64
Eider Cl, Hayes 136 BX71
Cygnet Way
Eight Acres (Burnham), Slou. 130 AH70
Eighteenth Rd, Mitch. 201 DL98
Eighth Av E12 125 EM63
Eighth Av, Hayes 135 BU74
Eileen Rd SE25 202 DR99
Eindhoven Cl, Cars. 200 DG102
Eisenhower Dr E6 144 EL71
Elaine Gro NW5 120 DG64
Elam Cl SE5 161 DP82
Elam St SE5 161 DP82
Elan Rd, S.Ock. 149 FU71
Eland Pl, Croy. 201 DP104
Eland Rd
Eland Rd SW11 160 DF83
Eland Rd, Croy. 201 DP104
Elba Pl SE17 279 J8
Elbe St SW6 160 DC82
Elberon Av, Croy. 201 DJ100
Elborough Rd SE25 202 DU99
Elborough St SW18 180 DA88
Elbow La, Hert. 48 DV17
Elbow Meadow (Colnbrook), Slou. 153 BF81
Elbury Dr E16 144 EG72
Elcho St SW11 160 DE80
Elcot Av SE15 162 DV80
Elder Av N8 121 DL57
Elder Cl N20 98 DB47
Elder Cl, Guil. 243 BA131
Elder Cl, Sid. 185 ET88
Elder Cl, West Dr. 134 BL73
Yew Av
Elder Ct, Bushey 95 CE47
Elder Gdns SE27 182 DQ91
Gladstone Ter
Elder Oak Cl SE20 202 DV95
Elder Rd SE27 182 DQ92
Elder St E1 275 P5
Elder St E1 142 DT71
Elder Wk N1 141 DP67
Essex Rd
Elder Way (North Holmwood), Dor. 263 CJ140
Elder Way, Rain. 148 FK69
Elder Way (Langley), Slou. 153 AZ75
Elderbek Cl, Wal.Cr. 66 DU28
Elderberry Gro SE27 182 DQ92
Linton Gro
Elderberry Rd W5 158 CL75
Elderberry Way, Wat. 75 BV35
Elderfield, Harl. 36 EX11
Elderfield Pl SW17 181 DH91
Elderfield Rd E5 122 DW63
Elderfield Rd (Stoke Poges), Slou. 132 AT65
Elderfield Wk E11 124 EH57
Elderflower Way E15 144 EE66
Eldersley Cl, Red. 250 DF132
Elderslie Cl, Beck. 203 EB99
Elderslie Rd SE9 185 EN85
Elderton Rd SE26 183 DY91
Eldertree Pl, Mitch. 201 DJ95
Eldertree Way
Eldertree Way, Mitch. 201 DH95
Elderwood Pl SE27 182 DQ92
Elder Rd
Eldon Av, Borwd. 78 CN40
Eldon Av, Croy. 202 DW103
Eldon Av, Houns. 156 CA80
Eldon Gro NW3 120 DD64
Eldon Pk SE25 202 DV98
Eldon Rd E17 123 DZ56
Eldon Rd N9 100 DW47
Eldon Rd N22 99 DP53
Eldon Rd W8 160 DB76
Eldon Rd, Cat. 236 DR121
Eldon Rd, Hodd. 49 ED19
Eldon St EC2 275 L7
Eldon St EC2 142 DR71
Eldon Way NW10 138 CP68
Eldred Dr, Orp. 206 EW103
Eldred Gdns, Upmin. 129 FS59
Eldred Rd, Bark. 145 ES67
Eldrick Ct, Felt. 175 BR88
Kilross Rd
Eldridge Cl, Felt. 175 BU88
Eleanor Av, Epsom 216 CR110
Eleanor Av, St.Alb. 43 CD18
Eleanor Cl N15 122 DT55
Arnold Rd
Eleanor Cl SE16 163 DX75
Eleanor Cres NW7 97 CX49
Eleanor Cross Rd, Wal.Cr. 67 DY34
Eleanor Gdns, Barn. 79 CX43
Eleanor Gdns, Dag. 126 EZ62
Eleanor Gro SW13 158 CS83
Eleanor Gro (Ickenham), Uxb. 115 BP62
Eleanor Rd E8 142 DV66
Eleanor Rd E15 144 EF65
Eleanor Rd N11 99 DL51
Eleanor Rd (Chalfont St. Peter), Ger.Cr. 90 AW53
Eleanor Rd, Hert. 32 DQ08
Eleanor Rd, Wal.Cr. 67 DY33
Eleanor St E3 143 EA69
Eleanor Wk SE18 165 EM77
Samuel St
Eleanor Way, Brwd. 108 FX50
Eleanor Way, Wal.Cr. 67 DZ33
Electric Av SW9 161 DN84
Electric Av, Enf. 83 DZ36
Electric La SW9 161 DN84
Electric Par E18 102 EG54
George La
Electric Par, Surb. 197 CK100
Elephant & Castle SE1 278 G7
Elephant & Castle SE1 161 DP77
Elephant & Castle Shop Cen SE1 162 DQ77
Elephant & Castle
Elephant La SE16 162 DW75
Elephant Rd SE17 279 H8
Elephant Rd SE17 162 DQ77
Elers Rd W13 157 CJ75
Elers Rd, Hayes 155 BR77
Eleven Acre Ri, Loug. 85 EM41
Eley Est N18 100 DW50
Eley Rd N18 101 DX50
Elf Row E1 142 DW73
Elfin Gro, Tedd. 177 CF92
Broad St
Elfindale Rd SE24 182 DQ85
Elford Cl SE3 164 EH84
Elfort Rd N5 121 DN63
Elfrida Cres SE6 183 EA91
Elfrida Rd, Wat. 76 BW43
Elfwine Rd W7 137 CE71
Elgal Cl, Orp. 223 EP106
Orchard Rd
Elgar Av NW10 138 CR65
Mitchellbrook Way
Elgar Av SW16 201 DL97
Elgar Av W5 158 CL75
Elgar Av, Surb. 198 CP101
Elgar Cl E13 144 EJ68
Bushey Rd
Elgar Cl SE8 163 EA80
Comet St
Elgar Cl, Borwd. 95 CK45
Elgar Cl, Buck.H. 102 EK47
Elgar Cl, Uxb. 114 BN61
Elgar Gdns, Til. 171 GH81
Elgar St SE16 163 DY76
Elgin Av W9 140 DB69
Elgin Av, Ashf. 175 BQ93
Elgin Av, Har. 95 CH54
Elgin Av, Rom. 106 FP52
Elgin Cres W11 139 CZ72
Elgin Cres, Cat. 236 DU122
Elgin Cres (Heathrow Airport), Houns. 155 BS82
Eastern Perimeter Rd
Elgin Dr, Nthwd. 93 BS52
Elgin Gdns, Guil. 243 BA133
Elgin Ms W11 139 CY72
Ladbroke Gro
Elgin Ms N W9 140 DB69
Randolph Av
Elgin Ms S W9 140 DB69
Randolph Av
Elgin Rd N22 99 DJ54
Elgin Rd, Brox. 49 DZ24
Elgin Rd, Croy. 202 DT102
Elgin Rd, Ilf. 125 ES60
Elgin Rd, Sutt. 200 DC104
Elgin Rd, Wall. 219 DJ107
Elgin Rd (Cheshunt), Wal.Cr. 66 DW30
Elgin Rd, Wey. 212 BN106
Elgiva La, Chesh. 54 AP31
Elgood Av, Nthwd. 93 BU51
Elgood Cl W11 139 CY73
Avondale Pk Rd
Elham Cl, Brom. 184 EK94
Elia Ms N1 274 F1
Elia Ms N1 141 DP68
Elia St N1 274 F1
Elia St N1 141 DP68
Elias Pl SW8 161 DN79
Elibank Rd SE9 165 EN84
Elim Est SE1 279 M6
Elim Est SE1 162 DS76
Elim Way E13 144 EF69
Eliot Bk SE23 182 DV89
Eliot Cotts SE3 164 EE82
Eliot Pl
Eliot Ct N15 122 DT56
Tynemouth Rd
Eliot Dr, Har. 116 CB61
Eliot Gdns SW15 159 CU84
Eliot Hill SE13 163 EC82
Eliot Ms NW8 140 DC68
Eliot Pk SE13 163 EC83
Eliot Pl SE3 164 EE82
Eliot Rd, Dag. 126 EX63
Eliot Rd, Dart. 188 FP85
Eliot Vale SE3 163 ED82
Elizabeth Av N1 142 DQ66
Elizabeth Av, Amer. 72 AV39
Elizabeth Av, Enf. 81 DP41
Elizabeth Av, Ilf. 125 ER61
Elizabeth Av, Stai. 174 BJ93
Elizabeth Blackwell Ho N22 99 DN53
Progress Way
Elizabeth Br SW1 277 H9
Elizabeth Br SW1 161 DH77
Elizabeth Cl E14 143 EB72
Grundy St
Elizabeth Cl W9 140 DC70
Randolph Av
Elizabeth Cl, Barn. 79 CX41
Elizabeth Cl, Rom. 105 FB53
Elizabeth Cl, Sutt. 217 CZ105
Elizabeth Cl, Til. 171 GH82
Elizabeth Cl, Wal.Abb. 49 ED23
Elizabeth Cl, Welw.G.C. 30 DC09
Elizabeth Clyde Cl N15 122 DS56
Elizabeth Cotts, Rich. 158 CM81
Elizabeth Ct SW1 277 N7
Elizabeth Ct, Gdmg. 258 AS144
Elizabeth Ct, Grav. 191 GG86
St. James's Rd
Elizabeth Ct, Horl. 268 DG148
Arnold Rd
Elizabeth Ct, St.Alb. 43 CK17
Villiers Cres
Elizabeth Ct, Wat. 75 BT38
Elizabeth Ct, Wdf.Grn. 102 EJ52
Navestock Cres
Elizabeth Dr, Epp. 85 ES36
Elizabeth Est SE17 162 DR79
Elizabeth Fry Rd E8 142 DV66
Lamb La
Elizabeth Gdns W3 139 CT74
Elizabeth Gdns, Stan. 95 CJ51
Elizabeth Gdns, Sun. 196 BW97
Elizabeth Huggins Cotts, Grav. 191 GG89
Elizabeth Ms NW3 140 DE65
Elizabeth Pl N15 122 DR56
Elizabeth Ride N9 100 DV45
Elizabeth Rd E6 144 EK67
Elizabeth Rd N15 122 DS57
Elizabeth Rd, Brwd. 108 FV44
Elizabeth Rd, Gdmg. 258 AS144
Elizabeth Rd, Grays 170 FZ76
Elizabeth Rd, Rain. 147 FH71
Elizabeth Sq SE16 143 DY73
Rotherhithe St
Elizabeth St SW1 276 G8
Elizabeth St SW1 160 DG77
Elizabeth St, Green. 189 FS85
Elizabeth Ter SE9 185 EM86
Elizabeth Way SE19 182 DR94
Elizabeth Way, Felt. 176 BW91
Elizabeth Way, Harl. 51 EM16
Elizabeth Way, Orp. 206 EW99
Elizabeth Way (Stoke Poges), Slou. 132 AT67
Elizabethan Cl (Stanwell), Stai. 174 BK87
Elizabethan Way
Elizabethan Way (Stanwell), Stai. 174 BK87
Elkanette Ms N20 98 DC47
Ridgeview Rd
Elkington Rd E13 144 EH70
Elkins, The, Rom. 105 FE54
Elkins Gdns, Guil. 243 BA131
Elkins Rd (Hedgerley), Slou. 112 AS61
Elkstone Rd W10 139 CZ71
Ella Rd N8 121 DL59
Ellaline Rd W6 159 CX79
Ellanby Cres N18 100 DV50
Elland Rd SE15 162 DW84
Elland Rd, Walt. 196 BX103
Ellement Cl, Pnr. 116 BX57
Ellen Cl, Brom. 204 EK97
Ellen Cl, Hem.H. 40 BM19
Ellen Ct N9 100 DW47
Densworth Gro
Ellen St E1 142 DU72
Ellen Webb Dr (Wealdstone), Har. 117 CE55
Ellenborough Pl SW15 159 CU84
Ellenborough Rd N22 100 DQ53
Ellenborough Rd, Sid. 186 EX92
Ellenbridge Way, S.Croy. 220 DS109
Ellenbrook Cl, Wat. 75 BV39
Hatfield Rd
Ellenbrook Cres, Hat. 44 CR18
Ellenbrook La
Ellenbrook La, Hat. 44 CR18
Elleray Rd, Tedd. 177 CF93
Ellerby St SW6 159 CX81
Ellerdale Cl NW3 120 DC63
Ellerdale Rd
Ellerdale Rd NW3 120 DC64
Ellerdale St SE13 163 EB84
Ellerdine Rd, Houns. 156 CC84
Ellerker Gdns, Rich. 178 CL86
Ellerman Av, Twick. 176 BZ88
Ellerman Rd, Til. 171 GF82
Ellerslie, Grav. 191 GK87
Ellerslie Gdns NW10 139 CU67
Ellerslie Rd W12 139 CV74
Ellerslie Sq Ind Est SW2 181 DL85
Ellerton Gdns, Dag. 146 EW66
Ellerton Rd SW13 159 CU81
Ellerton Rd SW18 180 DD88
Ellerton Rd SW20 179 CU94
Ellerton Rd, Dag. 146 EW66
Ellerton Rd, Surb. 198 CM103
Ellery Rd SE19 182 DR94
Ellery St SE15 162 DV82
Elles Av, Guil. 243 BB134
Ellesborough Cl, Wat. 94 BW50
Ellesmere Av NW7 96 CR48
Ellesmere Av, Beck. 203 EB96
Ellesmere Cl E11 124 EF57
Ellesmere Cl, Ruis. 115 BQ59
Ellesmere Dr, S.Croy. 220 DV114
Ellesmere Gdns, Ilf. 124 EL57
Ellesmere Gro, Barn. 79 CZ43
Ellesmere Pl, Walt. 213 BS106
Ellesmere Rd E3 143 DY68
Ellesmere Rd NW10 119 CU64
Ellesmere Rd W4 158 CR79
Ellesmere Rd, Berk. 38 AX19
Ellesmere Rd, Grnf. 136 CC70
Ellesmere Rd, Twick. 177 CJ86
Ellesmere Rd, Wey. 213 BR107
Ellesmere St E14 143 EB72
Ellice Rd, Oxt. 254 EF129
Elliman Av, Slou. 132 AS73
Ellingfort Rd E8 142 DV66
Ellingham Cl, Hem.H. 40 BN18
Ellingham Rd E15 123 ED63
Ellingham Rd W12 159 CU75
Ellingham Rd, Chess. 215 CK107
Ellingham Rd, Hem.H. 40 BM19
Ellington Ct, Maid. 130 AC72
Ellington Rd
Ellington Gdns, Maid. 130 AC72
Ellington Rd N10 121 DH56
Ellington Rd, Felt. 175 BT91
Ellington Rd, Houns. 156 CB82
Ellington Rd, Maid. 130 AC72
Ellington St N7 141 DN65
Ellington Way, Epsom 233 CV117
Elliot Cl E15 144 EE66
Elliot Cl, Welw.G.C. 29 CX12
Elliot Rd NW4 119 CV58
Elliot Rd, Stan. 95 CG51
Elliott Av, Ruis. 115 BV61
Elliott Cl, Wem. 118 CM62
Elliott Gdns, Rom. 105 FH53
Elliott Gdns, Shep. 194 BN98
Elliott Rd SW9 161 DP80
Elliott Rd W4 158 CS77
Elliott Rd, Brom. 204 EK98
Elliott Rd, Th.Hth. 201 DP98
Elliott Sq NW3 140 DE66
Elliott St, Grav. 191 GK87
Elliotts Cl (Cowley), Uxb. 134 BJ71
Elliotts La (Brasted), West. 240 EW124
Elliott's Pl N1 141 DP67
St. Peters St
Elliotts Row SE11 278 F8
Elliotts Row SE11 161 DP77
Ellis Av (Chalfont St. Peter), Ger.Cr. 91 AZ53
Ellis Av (Onslow Village), Guil. 258 AT136
Ellis Av, Rain. 147 FG71
Ellis Av, Slou. 152 AS75
Ellis Cl NW10 139 CV65
High Rd
Ellis Cl SE9 185 EQ89
Ellis Cl, Couls. 235 DM120
Ellis Ct W7 137 CF71
Ellis Fm Cl, Wok. 226 AX122
Ellis Ms SE7 164 EJ79
Ellis Rd, Couls. 235 DM120
Ellis Rd, Mitch. 200 DF100
Ellis Rd, Sthl. 136 CC74
Ellis St SW1 276 E8
Ellis St SW1 160 DF77
Ellis Way, Dart. 188 FM89
Elliscombe Rd SE7 164 EJ78
Ellisfield Dr SW15 179 CT87
Ellison Cl, Wind. 151 AM83
Ellison Gdns, Sthl. 156 BZ77
Ellison Ho SE13 163 EC82
Lewisham Rd
Ellison Rd SW13 159 CT82
Ellison Rd SW16 181 DK94
Ellison Rd, Sid. 185 ER88
Elliston Ho SE18 165 EN77
Ellmore Cl, Rom. 105 FH53
Ellora Rd SW16 181 DK92
Ellsworth St E2 142 DV69
Ellwood Ct W9 140 DB70
Clearwell Dr
Ellwood Gdns, Wat. 59 BV34
Ellwood Ri, Ch.St.G. 90 AW47
Ellwood Rd, Beac. 88 AH54
Elm Av W5 138 CL74
Elm Av, Cars. 218 DF110
Elm Av, Ruis. 115 BU60
Elm Av, Upmin. 128 FP62
Elm Av, Wat. 94 BY45
Elm Bk, Brom. 204 EK96
Elm Bk Gdns SW13 158 CS82
Elm Cl E11 124 EH58
Elm Cl N19 121 DJ61
Hargrave Pk
Elm Cl NW4 119 CX57
Elm Cl SW20 199 CW98
Grand Dr
Elm Cl, Amer. 55 AQ38
Elm Cl, Buck.H. 102 EK47
Elm Cl, Cars. 200 DF102
Elm Cl, Dart. 188 FJ88
Elm Cl, Epp. 51 EP24
Elm Cl, Har. 116 CB58
Elm Cl, Hayes 135 BU72
Elm Cl, Lthd. 231 CH122
Elm Cl, Rom. 105 FB54
Elm Cl (Farnham Common), Slou. 131 AQ65
Elm Cl, S.Croy. 220 DS107
Elm Cl (Stanwell), Stai. 174 BK88
Elm Cl, Surb. 198 CQ101
Elm Cl, Tad. 248 CQ130
Elm Cl, Twick. 176 CB89
Elm Cl, Wal.Abb. 67 ED34
Elm Cl, Warl. 237 DX117
Elm Cl, Wok. 226 AX115
Elm Cl (Send Marsh), Wok. 228 BG124
Elm Ct EC4 274 D10
Elm Ct, Mitch. 200 DF96
Armfield Cres
Elm Ct, Sun. 175 BT94
Elm Cres W5 138 CL74
Elm Cres, Kings.T. 198 CL95
Elm Cft (Datchet), Slou. 152 AW81
Elm Dr, Har. 116 CB58
Elm Dr, Hat. 45 CU19
Elm Dr, Lthd. 231 CH122
Elm Dr, St.Alb. 43 CJ20
Elm Dr, Sun. 196 BW96
Elm Dr, Swan. 207 FD96
Elm Dr (Cheshunt), Wal.Cr. 67 DY28
Elm Dr (Chobham), Wok. 210 AT110
Elm Fm Caravan Pk (Lyne), Cher. 193 BC101
Elm Friars Wk NW1 141 DK66
Elm Gdns N2 120 DC55
Elm Gdns, Enf. 82 DR38
Elm Gdns, Epp. 71 FB26
Elm Gdns, Epsom 233 CW119
Elm Gdns (Claygate), Esher 215 CF107
Elm Gdns, Mitch. 201 DK98
Elm Gdns, Welw.G.C. 29 CV09
Elm Grn W3 138 CS72
Elm Grn, Hem.H. 39 BE18
Elm Gro N8 121 DL58
Elm Gro NW2 119 CX63
Elm Gro SE15 162 DT82
Elm Gro SW19 179 CY94
Elm Gro, Berk. 38 AV19
Elm Gro, Cat. 236 DS122
Elm Gro, Epsom 216 CQ114
Elm Gro, Erith 167 FD80
Elm Gro, Har. 116 CA59
Elm Gro, Horn. 128 FL58
Elm Gro, Kings.T. 198 CL95
Elm Gro, Orp. 205 ET102
Elm Gro, Sutt. 218 DB105
Elm Gro, Wat. 75 BU37
Elm Gro, West Dr. 134 BM73
Willow Av
Elm Gro, Wdf.Grn. 102 EF50
Elm Gro Par, Wall. 200 DG104
Butter Hill
Elm Gro Rd SW13 159 CU82
Elm Gro Rd W5 158 CL75
Elm Gro Rd, Cob. 230 BX116
Elm Hall Gdns E11 124 EH57
Elm Hatch, Harl. 51 ES16
Elm La SE6 183 DZ89
Elm La, Wok. 229 BP118
Elm Lawn Cl, Uxb. 134 BL66
Park Rd
Elm Ms, Rich. 178 CM86
Grove Rd
Elm Par, Horn. 127 FH63
St. Nicholas Av
Elm Pk SW2 181 DM86
Elm Pk, Stan. 95 CH50
Elm Pk Av N15 122 DT57
Elm Pk Av, Horn. 127 FG63
Elm Pk Ct, Pnr. 116 BW55
Elm Pk Gdns NW4 119 CX57
Elm Pk Gdns SW10 160 DD78

Epping Rd, Harl. 50 EK18
Epping Rd, Ong. 53 FF24
Epping Rd (Toot Hill), Ong. 71 FC30
Epping Rd, Wal.Abb. 50 EK18
Epping Way E4 83 EB44
Epple Rd SW6 159 CZ81
Epsom Cl, Bexh. 167 FB83
Epsom Cl, Nthlt. 116 BZ64
Epsom Downs, Epsom 233 CU118
Epsom Downs Metro Cen, Tad. 233 CV120
Waterfield
Epsom Gap, Lthd. 231 CH115
Epsom La N, Epsom 233 CV118
Epsom La N, Tad. 233 CV118
Epsom La S, Tad. 233 CW121
Epsom Rd E10 123 EC58
Epsom Rd, Ash. 232 CM118
Epsom Rd, Croy. 219 DN105
Epsom Rd, Epsom 217 CT110
Epsom Rd, Guil. 243 BD133
Epsom Rd (East Clandon), Guil. 244 BM131
Epsom Rd, Ilf. 125 ET58
Epsom Rd, Lthd. 231 CH121
Epsom Rd (West Horsley), Lthd. 245 BP130
Epsom Rd, Mord. 199 CZ100
Epsom Rd, Sutt. 199 CZ101
Epsom Sq (Heathrow Airport), Houns. 155 BT82
Eastern Perimeter Rd
Epsom Way, Horn. 128 FM63
Epstein Rd SE28 146 EU74
Epworth Rd, Islw. 157 CH80
Epworth St EC2 275 L5
Epworth St EC2 142 DR70
Equity Sq E2 142 DT69
Shacklewell St
Erasmus St SW1 277 N9
Erasmus St SW1 161 DK77
Erconwald St W12 139 CT72
Eresby Dr, Beck. 203 EA102
Eresby Pl NW6 140 DA66
Eric Clarke La, Bark. 145 EP70
Eric Cl E7 124 EG63
Eric Rd E7 124 EG63
Eric Rd NW10 139 CT65
Church Rd
Eric Rd, Rom. 126 EX59
Eric Steele Ho, St.Alb. 60 CB27
Eric St E3 143 DZ70
Erica Cl, Slou. 131 AL73
Erica Ct, Swan. 207 FE98
Azalea Dr
Erica Ct, Wok. 226 AX118
Erica Gdns, Croy. 221 EB105
Erica St W12 139 CU73
Ericcson Cl SW18 180 DA85
Eridge Grn Cl, Orp. 206 EW102
Petten Gro
Eridge Rd W4 158 CR76
Erin Cl, Brom. 184 EE94
Erin Cl, Ilf. 126 EU58
Erindale SE18 165 ER79
Erindale Ter SE18 165 ER79
Eriswell Cres, Walt. 213 BS107
Eriswell Rd, Walt. 213 BT105
Erith Ct, Purf. 168 FN77
Thamley
Erith Cres, Rom. 105 FC53
Erith High St, Erith 167 FE78
Erith Rd, Belv. 166 FA78
Erith Rd, Bexh. 167 FB84
Erith Rd, Erith 167 FB84
Erkenwald Cl, Cher. 193 BE101
Erlanger Rd SE14 163 DX81
Erlesmere Gdns W13 157 CG76
Ermine Cl, Houns. 156 BW82
Ermine Cl, St.Alb. 42 CA21
Ermine Cl (Cheshunt), Wal.Cr. 66 DV31
Ermine Ho N17 100 DT52
Moselle St
Ermine Rd N15 122 DT58
Ermine Rd SE13 163 EB83
Ermine Side, Enf. 82 DU43
Ermington Rd SE9 185 EQ89
Ermyn Cl, Lthd. 231 CK121
Ermyn Way, Lthd. 231 CK121
Ernald Av E6 144 EL68
Ernan Cl, S.Ock. 149 FU71
Ernan Rd, S.Ock. 149 FU71
Erncroft Way, Twick. 177 CF86
Ernest Av SE27 181 DP91
Ernest Cl, Beck. 203 EA99
Ernest Gdns W4 158 CP79
Ernest Gro, Beck. 203 DZ99
Ernest Rd, Horn. 128 FL58
Ernest Rd, Kings.T. 198 CP96
Ernest Sq, Kings.T. 198 CP96
Ernest St E1 143 DX70
Ernle Rd SW20 179 CV94
Ernshaw Pl SW15 179 CY85
Carlton Dr
Erpingham Rd SW15 159 CW83
Erridge Rd SW19 200 DA96
Erriff Dr, S.Ock. 149 FT71
Errington Cl, Grays 171 GH76
Cedar Rd
Errington Dr, Wind. 151 AN81
Errington Rd W9 139 CZ70
Errol Gdns, Hayes 135 BV70
Errol Gdns, N.Mal. 199 CU98
Errol St EC1 275 J5
Errol St EC1 142 DQ70
Erroll Rd, Rom. 127 FF56
Erskine Cl, Sutt. 200 DE104
Erskine Cres N17 122 DV56
Erskine Hill NW11 120 DA57
Erskine Ms NW3 140 DF66
Erskine Rd
Erskine Rd E17 123 DZ56
Erskine Rd NW3 140 DF66
Erskine Rd, Sutt. 218 DD105
Erskine Rd, Wat. 94 BW48
Erwood Rd SE7 164 EL78
Esam Way SW16 181 DN92
Escombe Dr, Guil. 242 AV129
Escot Way, Barn. 79 CW43
Escott Gdns SE9 184 EL91
Escott Pl (Ottershaw), Cher. 211 BC107
Escreet Gro SE18 165 EN77
Esdaile Gdns, Upmin. 129 FR59
Esdaile La, Hodd. 49 EA18
Esher Av, Rom. 127 FC58
Esher Av, Sutt. 199 CX104
Esher Av, Walt. 195 BU101
Esher Bypass, Chess. 215 CJ105
Esher Bypass, Cob. 215 CH108
Esher Bypass, Esher 214 CA110
Esher Cl, Bex. 186 EY88
Esher Cl, Esher 214 CB106
Esher Cres (Heathrow Airport), Houns. 155 BS82
Eastern Perimeter Rd
Esher Gdns SW19 179 CX89
Esher Grn, Esher 214 CB105
Esher Ms, Mitch. 200 DF97
Esher Pk Av, Esher 214 CC105
Esher Pl Av, Esher 214 CB105
Esher Rd, E.Mol. 197 CD100
Esher Rd, Ilf. 125 ES62
Esher Rd, Walt. 214 BX106
Esk Rd E13 144 EG70
Esk Way, Rom. 105 FD52
Eskdale (London Colney), St.Alb. 62 CM27
Eskdale Av, Chesh. 54 AQ30
Eskdale Av, Nthlt. 136 BZ67
Eskdale Cl, Dart. 188 FQ89
Eskdale Cl, Wem. 117 CK61
Eskdale Ct, Hem.H. 40 BL17
Lonsdale
Eskdale Gdns, Pur. 220 DR114
Eskdale Rd, Bexh. 166 FA82
Eskdale Rd, Uxb. 134 BH68
Eskley Gdns, S.Ock. 149 FV70
Eskmont Ridge SE19 182 DS94
Esmar Cres NW9 119 CU59
Esme Ho SW15 159 CT84
Esmeralda Rd SE1 162 DU77
Esmond Cl, Rain. 147 FH66
Dawson Dr
Esmond Rd NW6 139 CZ67
Esmond Rd W4 158 CR77
Esmond St SW15 159 CY84
Esparto St SW18 180 DB87
Essenden Rd, Belv. 166 FA78
Essenden Rd, S.Croy. 220 DS108
Essendene Cl, Cat. 236 DS123
Essendene Rd, Cat. 236 DS123
Essendine Rd W9 140 DA70
Essendon Gdns, Welw.G.C. 29 CZ09
Essendon Hill, Hat. 46 DE17
Essendon Rd, Hert. 46 DG15
Essex Av, Islw. 157 CE83
Essex Av, Slou. 131 AQ71
Essex Cl E17 123 DY56
Essex Cl, Add. 212 BJ105
Essex Cl, Mord. 199 CX101
Essex Cl, Rom. 127 FB56
Essex Cl, Ruis. 116 BX60
Essex Ct EC4 274 D9
Essex Ct SW13 159 CT82
Essex Gdns N4 121 DP58
Essex Gdns, Horn. 128 FN57
Essex Gro SE19 182 DR93
Essex Ho E14 143 EB72
Giraud St
Essex La, Kings L. 59 BS33
Essex Pk N3 98 DB51
Essex Pk Ms W3 138 CS74
Essex Pl W4 158 CQ77
Essex Pl Sq W4 158 CR77
Chiswick High Rd
Essex Rd E4 102 EE46
Essex Rd E10 123 EC58
Essex Rd E12 124 EL64
Essex Rd E17 123 DY58
Essex Rd E18 102 EH54
Essex Rd N1 141 DP67
Essex Rd NW10 138 CS66
Essex Rd W3 138 CQ73
Essex Rd W4 158 CR77
Belmont Rd
Essex Rd, Bark. 145 ER66
Essex Rd, Borwd. 78 CN41
Essex Rd, Chesh. 54 AQ29
Essex Rd, Dag. 127 FC64
Essex Rd, Dart. 188 FK86
Essex Rd, Enf. 82 DR42
Essex Rd, Grav. 191 GG88
Essex Rd, Grays 169 FU79
Essex Rd, Hodd. 49 EC18
Essex Rd, Long. 209 FX96
Essex Rd, Rom. 127 FB56
Essex Rd (Chadwell Heath), Rom. 126 EW59
Essex Rd, Wat. 75 BU40
Essex Rd S E11 123 ED59
Essex St E7 124 EG64
Essex St WC2 274 D10
Essex St, St.Alb. 43 CE19
Essex Twr SE20 202 DV95
Essex Vil W8 160 DA75
Essex Way, Brwd. 107 FW51
Essex Way, Epp. 70 EV32
Essex Way, Ong. 71 FF29
Essex Wf E5 123 DX61
Essian St E1 143 DY71
Essoldo Way, Edg. 118 CM55
Estate Way E10 123 DZ60
Estcourt Rd SE25 202 DV100
Estcourt Rd SW6 159 CZ80
Estcourt Rd, Wat. 76 BW41
Este Rd SW11 160 DE83
Estella Av, N.Mal. 199 CV98
Estelle Rd NW3 120 DF63
Esterbrooke St SW1 277 M9
Esterbrooke St SW1 161 DK77
Estfeld Cl, Hodd. 33 EB14
Esther Cl N21 99 DN45
Esther Rd E11 124 EE59
Estoria Cl SW2 181 DN87
Estreham Rd SW16 181 DK93
Estridge Cl, Houns. 156 CA84
Estuary Cl, Bark. 146 EV69
Eswyn Rd SW17 180 DF91
Etchingham Pk Rd N3 98 DB52
Etchingham Rd E15 123 EC63
Eternit Wk SW6 159 CW81
Etfield Gro, Sid. 186 EV92
Ethel Bailey Cl, Epsom 216 CN112
Ethel Rd E16 144 EH72
Ethel Rd, Ashf. 174 BL92
Ethel St SE17 279 H9
Ethel Ter, Orp. 224 EW109
Ethelbert Cl, Brom. 204 EG97
Ethelbert Gdns, Ilf. 125 EM57
Ethelbert Rd SW20 199 CX95
Ethelbert Rd, Brom. 204 EG97
Ethelbert Rd (Hawley), Dart. 188 FL91
Ethelbert Rd, Erith 167 FC80
Ethelbert Rd, Orp. 206 EX97
Ethelbert St SW12 181 DH88
Fernlea Rd
Ethelburga Rd, Rom. 106 FM53
Ethelburga St SW11 160 DE81
Ethelden Rd W12 139 CV74
Etheldene Av N10 121 DJ56
Ethelred Cl, Welw.G.C. 29 CZ10
Ethelwine Pl, Abb.L. 59 BT30
The Cres
Etheridge Grn, Loug. 85 EQ41
Etheridge Rd
Etheridge Rd NW2 119 CW59
Etheridge Rd, Loug. 85 EP40
Etherley Rd N15 122 DQ57
Etherow St SE22 182 DU86
Etherstone Grn SW16 181 DN91
Etherstone Rd
Etherstone Rd SW16 181 DN91
Ethnard Rd SE15 162 DV79
Ethorpe Cl, Ger.Cr. 112 AY57
Ethorpe Cres, Ger.Cr. 112 AY57
Ethronvi Rd, Bexh. 166 EY83
Etloe Rd E10 123 EA61
Etna Rd, St.Alb. 43 CD19
Eton Av N12 98 DC52
Eton Av NW3 140 DD66
Eton Av, Barn. 80 DE44
Eton Av, Houns. 156 BZ79
Eton Av, N.Mal. 198 CR99
Eton Av, Wem. 117 CH63
Eton Cl SW18 180 DB87
Eton Cl (Datchet), Slou. 152 AU79
Eton Coll, Wind. 151 AR79
Eton Coll Rd NW3 140 DF65
Eton Ct NW3 140 DD66
Eton Av
Eton Ct, Stai. 173 BF92
Richmond Rd
Eton Ct, Wem. 117 CJ63
Eton Av
Eton Ct (Eton), Wind. 151 AR80
Eton Garages NW3 140 DE65
Lambolle Pl
Eton Gro NW9 118 CN55
Eton Gro SE13 164 EE83
Eton Hall NW3 140 DF65
Eton Coll Rd
Eton Pl NW3 140 DG66
Haverstock Hill
Eton Ri NW3 140 DF65
Eton Coll Rd
Eton Rd NW3 140 DF66
Eton Rd, Hayes 155 BT80
Eton Rd, Ilf. 125 EQ64
Eton Rd, Orp. 224 EV105
Eton Rd (Datchet), Slou. 152 AT78
Eton Sq (Eton), Wind. 151 AR80
Eton St, Rich. 178 CL85
Eton Vil NW3 140 DF65
Eton Way, Dart. 168 FJ84
Eton Wick Rd (Eton Wick), Wind. 151 AL77
Etta St SE8 163 DY79
Etton Cl, Horn. 128 FL61
Ettrick St E14 143 EC72
Etwell Pl, Surb. 198 CM100
Euclid Way, Grays 169 FU77
Euesden Cl N9 100 DV48
Plevna Rd
Eugene Cl, Rom. 128 FJ56
Eugenia Rd SE16 162 DW77
Eunice Gro, Chesh. 54 AR32
Eureka Rd, Kings.T. 198 CN96
Washington Rd
Europa Pk Rd, Guil. 242 AW133
Europa Pl EC1 275 H3
Europa Rd, Hem.H. 40 BM17
Jupiter Dr
Europa Trd Est, Erith 167 FD78
Europe Rd SE18 165 EM76
Eustace Rd E6 144 EL69
Eustace Rd SW6 160 DA80
Eustace Rd, Guil. 243 BD132
Eustace Rd, Rom. 126 EX59
Euston Av, Wat. 75 BT43
Euston Cen NW1 141 DJ70
Triton Sq
Euston Gro NW1 273 M3
Euston Gro NW1 141 DK69
Euston Rd N1 273 P2
Euston Rd N1 141 DK70
Euston Rd NW1 273 J5
Euston Rd NW1 141 DH70
Euston Rd, Croy. 201 DN102
Euston Sq NW1 273 M3
Euston Sq NW1 141 DK69
Euston Sta Colonnade NW1 273 M3
Euston St NW1 273 L4
Euston St NW1 141 DJ69
Euston Twr NW1 141 DJ70
Eva Rd, Rom. 126 EW59
Evandale Rd SW9 161 DN82
Evangelist Rd NW5 121 DH63
Evans Av, Wat. 75 BT35
Evans Cl E8 142 DT65
Buttermere Wk
Evans Cl, Green. 189 FU85
Evans Cl, Rick. 74 BN43
New Rd
Evans Gro, Felt. 176 CA89
Evans Gro, St.Alb. 43 CJ16
Evans Rd SE6 184 EE89
Evansdale, Rain. 147 FF69
New Zealand Way
Evanston Av E4 101 EC52
Evanston Gdns, Ilf. 124 EL58
Eve Rd E11 124 EE63
Eve Rd E15 144 EE68
Eve Rd N17 122 DS55
Eve Rd, Islw. 157 CG84
Eve Rd, Wok. 227 BB115
Evelina Rd SE15 162 DW83
Evelina Rd SE20 183 DX94
Eveline Lowe Est SE16 162 DU76
Eveline Rd, Mitch. 200 DF95
Evelyn Av NW9 118 CR56
Evelyn Av, Ruis. 115 BT58
Evelyn Cl, Twick. 176 CB87
Evelyn Cl, Wok. 226 AX120
Evelyn Cotts, Dor. 262 BX143
Evelyn Ct N1 275 K1
Evelyn Cres, Sun. 195 BT95
Evelyn Denington Rd E6 144 EL70
Evelyn Dr, Pnr. 94 BX52
Evelyn Fox Ct W10 139 CW71
Evelyn Gdns SW7 160 DD78
Evelyn Gdns, Gdse. 252 DW130
Evelyn Gdns, Rich. 158 CL84
Kew Rd
Evelyn Gro W5 138 CM74
Evelyn Gro, Sthl. 136 BZ72
Evelyn Rd E16 144 EH74
Evelyn Rd E17 123 EC56
Evelyn Rd SW19 180 DB92
Evelyn Rd W4 158 CR76
Evelyn Rd, Barn. 80 DF42
Evelyn Rd, Rich. 158 CL83
Evelyn Rd (Ham), Rich. 177 CJ90
Evelyn Sharp Cl, Rom. 128 FK55
Amery Gdns
Evelyn St SE8 163 DY78
Evelyn Ter, Rich. 158 CL83
Evelyn Wk N1 275 K1
Evelyn Wk N1 142 DR68
Evelyn Wk, Brwd. 107 FW51
Evelyn Way (Stoke D'Abernon), Cob. 230 BZ116
Evelyn Way, Epsom 216 CN111
Queen Alexandra's Way
Evelyn Way, Sun. 195 BT95
Evelyn Way, Wall. 219 DK105
Evelyn Yd W1 273 M8
Evelyns Cl, Uxb. 134 BN72
Evening Hill, Beck. 183 EC94
Evensyde, Wat. 75 BR44
Evenwood Cl SW15 179 CY85
Everard Av, Brom. 204 EG102
Everard Av, Slou. 152 AS75
Everard Cl, St.Alb. 43 CD22
Everard La, Cat. 236 DU122
Tillingdown Hill
Everard Way, Wem. 118 CL62
Everatt Cl SW18 179 CZ86
Amerland Rd
Everdon Rd SW13 159 CU79
Everest Cl (Northfleet), Grav. 190 GE90
Everest Ct, Wok. 226 AS116
Langmans Way
Everest Pl E14 143 EC71
Everest Pl, Swan. 207 FD98
Everest Rd SE9 185 EM85
Everest Rd (Stanwell), Stai. 174 BK87
Everest Way, Hem.H. 40 BN19
Everett Cl, Bushey 95 CE46
Everett Cl, Pnr. 115 BT55
Everett Cl (Cheshunt), Wal.Cr. 66 DQ26
Everett Wk, Belv. 166 EZ78
Osborne Rd
Everglade (Biggin Hill), West. 238 EK118
Everglade Strand NW9 97 CT53
Evergreen Ct (Stanwell), Stai. 174 BK87
Evergreen Way
Evergreen Oak Av, Wind. 152 AU83
Evergreen Wk, Hem.H. 40 BL22
Evergreen Way, Hayes 135 BT73
Evergreen Way (Stanwell), Stai. 174 BK87
Everilda St N1 141 DM67
Evering Rd E5 122 DT62
Evering Rd N16 122 DT62
Everington Rd N10 98 DF54
Everington St W6 159 CX79
Everitt Rd NW10 138 CR69
Everlands Cl, Wok. 226 AY118
Everlasting La, St.Alb. 42 CC19
Everleigh St N4 121 DM60
Eversfield Gdns NW7 96 CS52
Eversfield Rd, Reig. 250 DB134
Eversfield Rd, Rich. 158 CM82
Evershed Wk W4 158 CR77
Eversholt St NW1 141 DJ68
Evershot Rd N4 121 DM60
Eversleigh Gdns, Upmin. 129 FR60
Eversleigh Rd E6 144 EK67
Eversleigh Rd N3 97 CZ52
Eversleigh Rd SW11 160 DG82
Eversleigh Rd, Barn. 80 DC43
Eversley Av, Bexh. 167 FD82
Eversley Av, Wem. 118 CN61
Eversley Cl N21 81 DM44
Eversley Cl, Loug. 85 EQ41
The Bdy
Eversley Cres N21 81 DM44
Eversley Cres, Islw. 157 CD81
Eversley Cres, Ruis. 115 BS61
Eversley Cross, Bexh. 167 FE82
Eversley Mt N21 81 DM44
Eversley Pk SW19 179 CV92
Eversley Pk Rd N21 81 DM44
Eversley Rd SE7 164 EH79
Eversley Rd SE19 182 DR94
Eversley Rd, Surb. 198 CM98
Eversley Way, Croy. 221 EA105
Eversley Way, Egh. 193 BC96
Everthorpe Rd SE15 162 DT83
Everton Bldgs NW1 273 K3
Everton Dr, Stan. 118 CM55
Everton Rd, Croy. 202 DU102
Evesham Av E17 101 EA54
Evesham Cl, Grnf. 136 CB68
Evesham Cl, Reig. 249 CZ133
Evesham Cl, Sutt. 218 DA108
Evesham Grn, Mord. 200 DB100
Evesham Rd E15 144 EF67
Evesham Rd N11 99 DJ50
Evesham Rd, Grav. 191 GK89
Evesham Rd, Mord. 200 DB100
Evesham Rd, Reig. 249 CZ134
Evesham Rd N, Reig. 249 CZ133
Evesham St W11 139 CX73
Evesham Wk SE5 162 DR82
Love Wk
Evesham Wk SW9 161 DN82
Evesham Way SW11 160 DG83
Evesham Way, Ilf. 125 EN55
Evreham Rd, Iver 133 BE72
Evron Pl, Hert. 32 DR09
Fore St
Evry Rd, Sid. 186 EW93
Ewald Rd SW6 159 CZ82
Ewan Rd, Rom. 106 FK54
Ewanrigg Ter, Wdf.Grn. 102 EJ50
Ewart Gro N22 99 DN53
Ewart Pl E3 143 DZ68
Roman Rd
Ewart Rd SE23 183 DX87
Ewe Cl N7 141 DL65
Ewelands, Horl. 269 DJ147
Ewell Bypass, Epsom 217 CU108
Ewell Ct Av, Epsom 216 CS106
Ewell Downs Rd, Epsom 217 CU111
Ewell Ho Gro, Epsom 217 CT110
Ewell Pk Gdns, Epsom 217 CU108
Ewell Pk Way (Ewell), Epsom 217 CU107
Ewell Rd, Surb. 198 CL100
Ewell Rd (Long Ditton), Surb. 197 CH101
Ewell Rd, Sutt. 217 CY107
Ewellhurst Rd, Ilf. 102 EL54
Ewelme Rd SE23 182 DW88
Ewen Cres SW2 181 DN88
Ewer St SE1 279 H3
Ewer St SE1 142 DQ74
Ewhurst Av, S.Croy. 220 DT109
Ewhurst Cl, Sutt. 217 CW109
Ewhurst Ho E1 142 DW71
Ewhurst Rd SE4 183 DZ86
Exbury Rd SE6 183 EA89
Excel Ct WC2 277 N1
Excelsior Cl, Kings.T. 198 CN96
Washington Rd
Excelsior Gdns SE13 163 EC82
Exchange Arc EC2 275 N6
Exchange Bldgs E1 142 DS72
Cutler St
Exchange Cl N11 98 DG47
Benfleet Way
Exchange Ct WC2 278 A1
Exchange Pl EC2 275 M6
Exchange Rd, Wat. 75 BV42
Exchange Sq EC2 275 M6
Exchange Sq EC2 142 DS71
Exchange St, Rom. 127 FE57
Exchange Ill Shop Cen, The, Ilf. 125 EP61
Exchequer Ct EC3 142 DS72
St. Mary Axe
Exeforde Av, Ashf. 174 BN91
Exeter Cl E6 145 EM72
Harper Rd
Exeter Cl, Wat. 76 BW40
Exeter Gdns, Ilf. 124 EL60
Exeter Ho SW15 179 CW86
Putney Heath
Exeter Ms NW6 140 DB65
West Hampstead Ms
Exeter Pl, Guil. 242 AT132
Exeter Rd E16 144 EG71
Exeter Rd E17 123 EA57
Exeter Rd N9 100 DW47
Exeter Rd N14 99 DH46
Exeter Rd NW2 119 CY64
Exeter Rd, Croy. 202 DS101
Exeter Rd, Dag. 147 FB65
Exeter Rd, Enf. 83 DX41
Exeter Rd, Felt. 176 BZ90
Exeter Rd, Grav. 191 GK90
Exeter Rd, Har. 116 BY61
Exeter Rd (Heathrow Airport), Houns. 155 BS82
Exeter Rd, Well. 165 ET82
Exeter St WC2 274 A10
Exeter St WC2 141 DL73
Exeter Way SE14 163 DZ80
Exeter Way (Heathrow Airport), Houns. 155 BS83
Exford Gdns SE12 184 EH88
Exford Rd SE12 184 EH89
Exhibition Cl W12 139 CW73
Exhibition Rd SW7 276 A5
Exhibition Rd SW7 160 DD75
Exmoor Cl, Ilf. 103 EQ53
Exmoor St W10 139 CX70
Exmouth Mkt EC1 274 D4
Exmouth Mkt EC1 141 DN70
Exmouth Ms NW1 273 L3
Exmouth Pl E8 142 DV66
Exmouth Rd E17 123 DZ57
Exmouth Rd, Brom. 204 EH97
Exmouth Rd, Grays 170 GB79
Exmouth Rd, Hayes 135 BS69
Exmouth Rd, Ruis. 116 BW62
Exmouth Rd, Well. 166 EW81
Exmouth St E1 142 DW72
Commercial Rd
Exning Rd E16 144 EF70
Exon St SE17 279 M10
Exon St SE17 162 DS78
Explorer Av, Stai. 174 BL88
Explorer Dr, Wat. 75 BT44
Express Dr, Ilf. 126 EV60
Exton Cres NW10 138 CQ66
Exton Gdns, Dag. 126 EW64
Exton St SE1 278 D3
Exton St SE1 141 DN74
Eyebright Cl, Croy. 203 DX102
Primrose La
Eyhurst Av, Horn. 127 FG62
Eyhurst Cl NW2 119 CU61
Eyhurst Cl (Kingswood), Tad. 233 CZ123
Eyhurst Pk, Tad. 234 DC123
Eyhurst Spur, Tad. 233 CZ124
Eylewood Rd SE27 182 DQ92
Eynella Rd SE22 182 DT87
Eynham Rd W12 139 CW72
Eynsford Cl, Orp. 205 EQ101
Eynsford Cres, Bex. 186 EW88
Eynsford Rd, Green. 189 FW85
Eynsford Rd, Ilf. 125 ES61
Eynsford Rd, Sev. 225 FH108
Eynsford Rd, Swan. 207 FD100
Eynsham Dr SE2 166 EU77
Eynswood Dr, Sid. 186 EV92
Eyot Gdns W6 159 CT78
Eyot Grn W4 159 CT79
Chiswick Mall
Eyre Cl, Rom. 127 FH56
Eyre Ct NW8 140 DD68
Finchley Rd
Eyre Grn, Slou. 131 AN69
Eyre St Hill EC1 274 D5
Eyston Dr, Wey. 212 BN110
Eythorne Rd SW9 161 DN81
Eywood Rd, St.Alb. 42 CC22
Ezra St E2 142 DT69

F

Faber Gdns NW4 119 CU57
Fabian Rd SW6 159 CZ80
Fabian St E6 145 EM70
Fackenden La (Shoreham), Sev. 225 FH113
Factory La N17 100 DT54
Factory La, Croy. 201 DN102
Factory Rd E16 144 EL74
Factory Rd (Northfleet), Grav. 190 GC86
Factory Sq SW16 181 DL93
Factory Yd W7 137 CE74
Uxbridge Rd
Faesten Way, Bex. 187 FE90
Faggotters La, Harl. 37 FE13
Faggotters La, Ong. 53 FF15
Faggotts Cl, Rad. 77 CJ35
Faggs Rd, Felt. 175 BU85
Fagnall La (Winchmore Hill), Amer. 88 AJ45
Fagus Av, Rain. 148 FK69
Faints Cl, Wal.Cr. 66 DT29
Fair Acres, Brom. 204 EG99
Fair Cl, Bushey 94 CB45
Claybury
Fair Grn, Saw. 36 EY05
The Sq
Fair La, Couls. 250 DC125
Fair Leas, Chesh. 54 AN29
Fair St SE1 279 N4
Fair St, Houns. 156 CC83
High St
Fairacre, Hem.H. 40 BM24
Fairacre, N.Mal. 198 CS97
Fairacres SW15 159 CU84
Fairacres, Cob. 214 BX112
Fairacres, Croy. 221 DZ109

Fairacres, Red. 267 DJ142
Fairacres, Ruis. 115 BX62
Fairacres, Tad. 233 CW121
Fairacres, Wind. 151 AK82
Fairacres Cl, Pot.B. 63 CZ33
Fairbairn Cl, Pur. 219 DN113
Fairbairn Grn SW9 161 DN81
Fairbank Av, Orp. 205 EP103
Fairbank Est N1 142 DR68
East Rd
Fairbanks Rd N17 122 DT55
Fairborne Way, Guil. 242 AU131
Fairbourne, Cob. 214 BX113
Fairbourne Cl, Wok. 226 AU118
Abercorn Way
Fairbourne La, Cat. 236 DQ122
Fairbourne Rd N17 122 DS55
Fairbridge Rd N19 121 DK61
Fairbrook Cl N13 99 DN50
Fairbrook Rd N13 99 DN51
Fairburn Cl, Borwd. 78 CN39
Fairburn Ct SW15 179 CY85
Mercier Rd
Fairby Rd SE12 184 EH85
Faircharm Trd Est SE8 163 EB80
Fairchild Cl SW11 160 DD82
Wye St
Fairchild Pl EC2 275 N5
Fairchild St EC2 275 N5
Fairchildes Av (New Addington), Croy. 221 ED112
Fairchildes La, Warl. 221 ED114
Fairclough St E1 142 DU72
Faircroft, Slou. 131 AP70
Faircross Av, Bark. 145 EQ65
Faircross Av, Rom. 105 FD52
Faircross Way, St.Alb. 43 CG18
Fairdale Gdns SW15 159 CV84
Fairdale Gdns, Hayes 135 BU74
Fairdene Rd, Couls. 235 DK117
Fairey Av, Hayes 155 BT77
Fairfax Av, Epsom 217 CV109
Fairfax Av, Red. 250 DE133
Fairfax Cl, Walt. 195 BV102
Fairfax Gdns SE3 164 EK81
Fairfax Ms E16 144 EH74
Wesley Av
Fairfax Ms SW15 159 CW84
Fairfax Ms, Amer. 55 AN40
Fairfax Pl NW6 140 DC66
Fairfax Rd N8 121 DN56
Fairfax Rd NW6 140 DC66
Fairfax Rd W4 158 CS76
Fairfax Rd, Grays 170 GB78
Fairfax Rd, Hert. 32 DT08
Fairfax Rd, Tedd. 177 CG93
Fairfax Rd, Til. 171 GF81
Fairfax Rd, Wok. 227 BB120
Fairfax Way N10 98 DG52
Cromwell Rd
Fairfield App (Wraysbury), Stai. 172 AX86
Fairfield Av NW4 119 CV58
Fairfield Av, Edg. 96 CP51
Fairfield Av, Horl. 268 DG149
Fairfield Av, Ruis. 115 BQ59
Fairfield Av (Datchet), Slou. 152 AW80
Fairfield Av, Stai. 173 BF91
Fairfield Av, Twick. 176 CB88
Fairfield Av, Upmin. 128 FQ62
Fairfield Av, Wat. 94 BW48
Fairfield Cl N12 98 DC49
Fairfield Cl, Dor. 247 CH134
Fairfield Dr
Fairfield Cl, Enf. 83 DY42
Scotland Grn Rd N
Fairfield Cl (Ewell), Epsom 216 CS106
Fairfield Cl, Hat. 45 CW15
Fairfield Cl, Horn. 127 FG60
Fairfield Cl, Mitch. 180 DE94
Fairfield Cl, Nthwd. 93 BP50
Thirlmere Gdns
Fairfield Cl, Rad. 77 CE37
Fairfield Cl, Sid. 185 ET86
Fairfield Cl (Datchet), Slou. 152 AX80
Fairfield Cotts, Lthd. 246 CB125
Fairfield Ct NW10 139 CU67
Fairfield Ct, Nthwd. 93 BU54
Windsor Cl
Fairfield Cres, Edg. 96 CP51
Fairfield Dr SW18 180 DB85
Fairfield Dr, Brox. 49 DZ24
Fairfield Dr, Dor. 247 CH134
Fairfield Dr, Grnf. 137 CJ67
Fairfield Dr, Har. 116 CC55
Fairfield E, Kings.T. 198 CL96
Fairfield Gdns N8 121 DL57
Elder Av
Fairfield Gro SE7 164 EK78
Fairfield Ind Est, Kings.T. 198 CM97
Fairfield La (Farnham Royal), Slou. 131 AP68
Fairfield N, Kings.T. 198 CL96
Fairfield Pk, Cob. 214 BX114
Fairfield Path, Croy. 202 DR104
Fairfield Pathway, Horn. 148 FJ66
Fairfield Pl, Kings.T. 198 CL97
Fairfield Ri, Guil. 242 AT133
Fairfield Rd E3 143 EA68
Fairfield Rd E17 101 DY54
Fairfield Rd N8 121 DL57
Fairfield Rd N18 100 DU49
Fairfield Rd W7 157 CG76
Fairfield Rd, Beck. 203 EA96
Fairfield Rd, Bexh. 166 EZ82
Fairfield Rd, Brwd. 108 FW48
Fairfield Rd, Brom. 184 EG94
Fairfield Rd, Croy. 202 DS104
Fairfield Rd, Epp. 70 EV29
Fairfield Rd, Hodd. 49 EA15
Fairfield Rd, Ilf. 145 EP65
Fairfield Rd, Kings.T. 198 CL96
Fairfield Rd, Lthd. 231 CH121
Fairfield Rd, Orp. 205 ER100
Fairfield Rd (Burnham), Slou. 130 AJ69
Fairfield Rd, Sthl. 136 BZ72
Fairfield Rd (Wraysbury), Stai. 172 AX86
Fairfield Rd, Uxb. 134 BK65
Fairfield Rd, West Dr. 134 BL74
Fairfield Rd, Wdf.Grn. 102 EG51
Fairfield S, Kings.T. 198 CL96
Fairfield St SW18 180 DB85
Fairfield Wk, Lthd. 231 CH121
Fairfield Rd
Fairfield Wk (Cheshunt), Wal.Cr. 67 DY28
Fairfield Way, Barn. 80 DA43
Fairfield Way, Couls. 219 DK114
Fairfield Way, Epsom 216 CS106
Fairfield W, Kings.T. 198 CL96
Fairfields, Cher. 194 BG102
Fairfields, Grav. 191 GL92
Fairfields Cl NW9 118 CQ57
Fairfields Cres NW9 118 CQ56
Fairfields Rd, Houns. 156 CC83
Fairfolds, Wat. 76 BY36
Fairfoot Rd E3 143 EA70
Fairford Av, Bexh. 167 FD81
Fairford Av, Croy. 203 DX99
Fairford Cl, Croy. 203 DY99
Fairford Cl, Reig. 250 DC132
Fairford Cl, Rom. 106 FP51
Fairford Way
Fairford Cl, W.Byf. 211 BF114
Fairford Ct, Sutt. 218 DB108
Grange Rd
Fairford Gdns, Wor.Pk. 199 CT103
Fairford Way, Rom. 106 FP51
Fairgreen, Barn. 80 DF41
Fairgreen E, Barn. 80 DF41
Fairgreen Par, Mitch. 200 DF97
London Rd
Fairgreen Rd, Th.Hth. 201 DP99
Fairham Av, S.Ock. 149 FU73
Fairhaven, Egh. 173 AZ92
Fairhaven Av, Croy. 203 DX100
Fairhaven Cres, Wat. 93 BU48
Fairhaven Rd, Red. 250 DG130
Fairhazel Gdns NW6 140 DB65
Fairhill, Hem.H. 40 BM24
Fairholme, Felt. 175 BR87
Fairholme Av, Rom. 127 FG57
Fairholme Cl N3 119 CY56
Fairholme Cres, Ash. 231 CJ117
Fairholme Cres, Hayes 135 BT70
Fairholme Gdns N3 119 CY55
Fairholme Gdns, Upmin. 129 FT59
Fairholme Rd W14 159 CY78
Fairholme Rd, Ashf. 174 BL92
Fairholme Rd, Croy. 201 DN101
Fairholme Rd, Har. 117 CF57
Fairholme Rd, Ilf. 125 EM59
Fairholme Rd, Sutt. 217 CZ107
Fairholt Cl N16 122 DS60
Fairholt Rd N16 122 DR60
Fairholt St SW7 276 C6
Fairkytes Av, Horn. 128 FK60
Fairland Rd E15 144 EF65
Fairlands Av, Buck.H. 102 EG47
Fairlands Av, Sutt. 200 DA103
Fairlands Av, Th.Hth. 201 DM98
Fairlands Ct SE9 185 EN86
North Pk
Fairlawn SE7 164 EJ79
Fairlawn (Bookham), Lthd. 230 BZ124
Fairlawn Av N2 120 DE56
Fairlawn Av W4 158 CQ77
Fairlawn Av, Bexh. 166 EX82
Fairlawn Cl N14 81 DJ44
Fairlawn Cl (Claygate), Esher 215 CF107
Fairlawn Cl, Felt. 176 BZ91
Fairlawn Cl, Kings.T. 178 CQ93
Fairlawn Dr, Red. 266 DE136
Fairlawn Dr, Wdf.Grn. 102 EG52
Fairlawn Gdns, Sthl. 136 BZ73
Fairlawn Gro W4 158 CQ77
Fairlawn Gro, Bans. 218 DD113
Fairlawn Pk SE26 183 DY92
Fairlawn Pk, Wind. 151 AL84
Fairlawn Pk, Wok. 210 AY114
Fairlawn Rd SW19 179 CZ94
Fairlawn Rd, Bans. 218 DD112
Fairlawn Rd, Cars. 218 DC111
Fairlawnes, Wall. 219 DH106
Maldon Rd
Fairlawns (Woodham), Add. 211 BF111
Fairlawns, Brwd. 108 FU48
Fairlawns, Horl. 269 DH149
Fairlawns, Pnr. 94 BW54
Fairlawns, Sun. 195 BU97
Fairlawns, Twick. 177 CJ86
Fairlawns, Wat. 75 BT38
Langley Rd
Fairlawns, Wey. 213 BS106
Fairlawns Cl, Horn. 128 FM59
Fairlawns Cl, Stai. 174 BH93
Fairlea Pl W5 137 CK70
Fairley Way (Cheshunt), Wal.Cr. 66 DV28
Fairlie Gdns SE23 182 DW87
Fairlie Rd, Slou. 131 AN72
Fairlight Av E4 101 ED47
Fairlight Av NW10 138 CS68
Fairlight Av, Wind. 151 AR82
Fairlight Av, Wdf.Grn. 102 EG51
Fairlight Cl E4 101 ED47
Fairlight Cl, Wor.Pk. 217 CW105
Fairlight Dr, Uxb. 134 BK65
Fairlight Rd SW17 180 DD91
Fairlop Cl, Horn. 147 FH65
Fairlop Gdns, Ilf. 103 EQ52
Fairlop Rd E11 123 ED59
Fairlop Rd, Ilf. 103 EQ54
Fairmark Dr, Uxb. 134 BN65
Fairmead, Brom. 205 EM98
Fairmead, Surb. 198 CP102
Fairmead, Wok. 226 AW118
Fairmead Cl, Brom. 205 EM98
Fairmead Cl, Houns. 156 BX80
Fairmead Cl, N.Mal. 198 CR97
Fairmead Cres, Edg. 96 CQ48
Fairmead Gdns, Ilf. 124 EL57
Fairmead Rd N19 121 DK62
Fairmead Rd, Croy. 201 DM102
Fairmead Rd, Loug. 84 EH42
Fairmead Side, Loug. 84 EJ43
Fairmeads, Cob. 214 BZ113
Fairmeads, Loug. 85 EP40
Fairmile Av SW16 181 DK92
Fairmile Av, Cob. 214 BY114
Fairmile Ho, Tedd. 177 CG91
Twickenham Rd
Fairmile La, Cob. 214 BX112
Fairmile Pk Copse, Cob. 214 BZ112
Fairmile Pk Rd, Cob. 214 BZ113
Fairmont Cl, Belv. 166 EZ78
Lullingstone Rd
Fairmount Rd SW2 181 DM86
Fairoak Cl, Ken. 235 DP115
Fairoak Cl (Oxshott), Lthd. 215 CD112
Fairoak Cl, Orp. 205 EP101
Fairoak Dr SE9 185 ER85
Fairoak Gdns, Rom. 105 FE54
Fairoak La, Chess. 214 CC112
Fairoak La (Oxshott), Lthd. 215 CF111
Fairs Rd, Lthd. 231 CG119
Fairseat Cl, Bushey 95 CE47
Hive Rd
Fairstead Wk N1 142 DQ67
Popham Rd
Fairstone Ct, Horl. 269 DH147
Tanyard Way
Fairthorn Rd SE7 164 EG78
Fairtrough Rd, Orp. 224 EV112
Fairview, Epsom 217 CW111
Fairview, Erith 167 FF80
Guild Rd
Fairview, Pot.B. 64 DB29
Hawkshead Rd
Fairview Av, Brwd. 109 GE45
Fairview Av, Rain. 148 FK68
Fairview Av, Wem. 137 CK65
Fairview Av, Wok. 226 AY118
Fairview Cl E17 101 DY53
Fairview Cl, Chig. 103 ES49
Fairview Cl, Wok. 227 AZ118
Fairview Av
Fairview Ct, Ashf. 174 BN92
Fairview Cres, Har. 116 CA60
Fairview Dr, Chig. 103 ES49
Fairview Dr, Orp. 223 ER105
Fairview Dr, Shep. 194 BM99
Fairview Dr, Wat. 75 BS36
Fairview Gdns, Wdf.Grn. 102 EH53
Fairview Ind Est, Oxt. 254 EG133
Fairview Ind Pk, Rain. 147 FE71
Fairview Pl SW2 181 DM87
Fairview Rd N15 122 DT57
Fairview Rd SW16 201 DM95
Fairview Rd, Chig. 103 ES49
Fairview Rd, Enf. 81 DN39
Fairview Rd, Epsom 217 CT111
Fairview Rd (Istead Ri), Grav. 190 GD94
Fairview Rd, Maid. 130 AG72
Fairview Rd, Slou. 131 AM70
Fairview Rd, Sutt. 218 DD106
Fairview Way, Edg. 96 CN49
Fairwater Av, Well. 166 EU84
Fairwater Dr (New Haw), Add. 212 BK109
Fairway SW20 199 CW97
Fairway, Bexh. 186 EY85
Fairway, Cars. 218 DC111
Fairway, Cher. 194 BH102
Fairway, Guil. 243 BD133
Fairway, Hem.H. 40 BM24
Fairway, Orp. 205 ER99
Fairway, Saw. 36 EY05
Fairway, Vir.W. 192 AV100
Fairway, Ware 32 DW07
Fairway, Wdf.Grn. 102 EJ50
Fairway, The N13 100 DQ48
Fairway, The N14 81 DH44
Fairway, The NW7 96 CR48
Fairway, The W3 138 CS72
Fairway, The, Abb.L. 59 BR32
Fairway, The, Barn. 80 DB44
Fairway, The, Brom. 205 EM99
Fairway, The, Grav. 191 GG89
Fairway, The, Harl. 51 ET17
Fairway, The (Flackwell Heath), H.Wyc. 110 AC56
Fairway, The, Lthd. 231 CG118
Fairway, The, N.Mal. 198 CR95
Fairway, The, Nthlt. 136 CC65
Fairway, The, Nthwd. 93 BS49
Fairway, The, Ruis. 116 BX62
Fairway, The (Burnham), Slou. 130 AJ68
Fairway, The, Upmin. 128 FQ59
Fairway, The, Uxb. 134 BM68
Fairway, The, Wem. 117 CH62
Fairway, The, W.Mol. 196 CB97
Fairway, The, Wey. 212 BN111
Fairway Av NW9 118 CP55
Fairway Av, Borwd. 78 CP40
Fairway Av, West Dr. 134 BJ74
Fairway Cl NW11 120 DC59
Fairway Cl, Croy. 203 DY99
Fairway Cl, Epsom 216 CQ105
Fairway Cl, Houns. 176 BW85
Fairway Cl (Park St), St.Alb. 60 CC27
Fairway Cl, West Dr. 134 BK74
Fairway Av
Fairway Cl, Wok. 226 AU119
Fairway Ct NW7 96 CR48
The Fairway
Fairway Ct, Hem.H. 40 BM24
Fairway
Fairway Dr SE28 146 EX72
Fairway Dr, Dart. 188 FP87
Fairway Dr, Grnf. 136 CB66
Fairway Gdns, Beck. 203 ED100
Fairway Gdns, Ilf. 125 EQ64
Fairways, Ashf. 175 BP93
Fairways, Ken. 236 DQ117
Fairways, Stan. 96 CL54
Fairways, Tedd. 177 CK94
Fairways, Wal.Abb. 68 EE34
Fairways, Wal.Cr. 67 DX26
Fairways, The, Red. 266 DD137
Fairweather Cl N15 122 DS56
Fairweather Rd N16 122 DU58
Fairwell La (West Horsley), Lthd. 245 BP128
Fairwyn Rd SE26 183 DY91
Fakenham Cl NW7 97 CU52
Fakenham Cl, Nthlt. 136 CA65
Goodwood Dr
Fakruddin St E1 142 DU70
Falaise, Egh. 172 AY92
Falcon Av, Brom. 204 EL98
Falcon Av, Grays 170 GB79
Falcon Cl SE1 278 G2
Falcon Cl W4 158 CQ79
Sutton La S
Falcon Cl, Dart. 188 FM85
Falcon Cl, Hat. 45 CU20
Falcon Cl, Nthwd. 93 BS52
Falcon Cl, Saw. 36 EW06
Falcon Cl, Wal.Abb. 68 EG34
Kestrel Rd
Falcon Ct EC4 274 D9
Falcon Ct EC4 141 DN72
Falcon Ct, Wok. 211 BC114
Blackmore Cres
Falcon Cres, Enf. 83 DX43
Falcon Dr (Stanwell), Stai. 174 BK86
Falcon Gro SW11 160 DE83
Falcon Ho W13 137 CF70
Falcon La SW11 160 DE83
Falcon Ms, Grav. 190 GE88
Falcon Pk Ind Est NW10 119 CT64
Falcon Ridge, Berk. 38 AW20
Falcon Rd SW11 160 DE82
Falcon Rd, Enf. 83 DX43
Falcon Rd, Guil. 242 AX134
Falcon Rd, Hmptn. 176 BZ94
Falcon St E13 144 EG70
Falcon Ter SW11 160 DE83
Falcon Way E11 124 EG56
Falcon Way E14 163 EB77
Falcon Way NW9 96 CS54
Falcon Way, Felt. 175 BV85
Falcon Way, Har. 118 CL57
Falcon Way, Horn. 147 FG66
Falcon Way, Sun. 195 BS96
Falcon Way, Wat. 60 BY34
Falcon Way, Welw.G.C. 29 CY07
Falconberg Ct W1 273 N8
Falconberg Ms W1 273 M8
Falconer Rd, Bushey 76 BZ44
Falconer Rd, Ilf. 104 EV50
Falconer Wk N7 121 DM61
Newington Barrow Way
Falconers Pk, Saw. 36 EX06
Falconhurst (Oxshott), Lthd. 231 CD115
Falcons Cl (Biggin Hill), West. 238 EK117
Falcons Cft, H.Wyc. 110 AE55
Falconwood, Egh. 172 AY92
Falconwood (East Horsley), Lthd. 231 CF120
Falconwood Av, Well. 165 ER82
Falconwood Par, Well. 165 ES84
Falconwood Rd, Croy. 221 EA108
Falcourt Cl, Sutt. 218 DB106
Falkirk Cl, Horn. 128 FN60
Falkirk Gdns, Wat. 94 BX50
Blackford Rd
Falkirk Ho W9 140 DB69
Falkirk St N1 275 N1
Falkirk St N1 142 DS68
Falkland Av N3 98 DA52
Falkland Av N11 98 DG49
Falkland Gdns, Dor. 263 CG137
Harrow Rd W
Falkland Gro, Dor. 263 CG137
Falkland Pk Av SE25 202 DS97
Falkland Pl NW5 121 DJ64
Falkland Rd
Falkland Rd N8 121 DN56
Falkland Rd NW5 121 DJ64
Falkland Rd, Barn. 79 CY40
Falkland Rd, Dor. 263 CG137
Fallaize Av, Ilf. 125 EP63
Riverdene Rd
Falling La, West Dr. 134 BL73
Falloden Way NW11 120 DA56
Fallow Cl, Chig. 103 ET50
Fallow Ct SE16 162 DU78
Argyle Way
Fallow Ct Av N12 98 DC52
Fallow Flds, Loug. 102 EJ45
Fallow Ri, Hert. 32 DS09
Fallowfield (Bean), Dart. 189 FV90
Fallowfield, Stan. 95 CG48
Fallowfield, Welw.G.C. 29 CZ06
Fallowfield Cl (Harefield), Uxb. 92 BJ53
Fallowfield Ct, Stan. 95 CG48
Fallowfield Wk, Hem.H. 40 BG17
Tollpit End
Fallowfield Way, Horl. 269 DH147
Fallowfields Dr N12 98 DE51
Fallows Cl N2 98 DC54
Fallsbrook Rd SW16 181 DJ94
Falman Cl N9 100 DU46
Croyland Rd
Falmer Rd E17 123 EB55
Falmer Rd N15 122 DQ57
Falmer Rd, Enf. 82 DS42
Falmouth Av E4 101 ED50
Falmouth Cl N22 99 DM52
Truro Rd
Falmouth Cl SE12 184 EF85
Falmouth Gdns, Ilf. 124 EL57
Falmouth Rd SE1 279 J6
Falmouth Rd SE1 162 DQ76
Falmouth Rd, Slou. 131 AN72
Falmouth Rd, Walt. 214 BW105
Falmouth St E15 123 ED64
Falmouth Way E17 123 DZ57
Gosport Rd
Falstaff Gdns, St.Alb. 42 CB23
Falstaff Ms (Hampton Hill), Hmptn. 177 CD92
Hampton Rd
Falstone, Wok. 226 AV118
Fambridge Cl SE26 183 DZ91
Fambridge Rd, Dag. 126 FA60
Famet Av, Pur. 220 DQ113
Famet Cl, Pur. 220 DQ113
Famet Wk, Pur. 220 DQ113
Fane St W14 159 CZ79
North End Rd
Fangrove Caravan Pk (Lyne), Cher. 193 BB102
Fanhams Rd, Ware 33 DY05
Fann St EC1 275 H5
Fann St EC1 142 DQ70
Fann St EC2 275 H5
Fann St EC2 142 DQ70
Fanns Ri, Purf. 168 FN77
Fanshaw St N1 275 M2
Fanshaw St N1 142 DS69
Fanshawe Av, Bark. 145 EQ65
Fanshawe Ct, Hert. 32 DQ08
Byde St
Fanshawe Cres, Dag. 126 EY64
Fanshawe Cres, Horn. 128 FK58
Fanshawe Cres, Ware 32 DW05
Fanshawe Rd, Grays 171 GG76
Fanshawe Rd, Rich. 177 CJ91
Fanshawe St, Hert. 31 DP08
Fanshaws La, Hert. 48 DQ18
Fanthorpe St SW15 159 CW83
Far End, Hat. 45 CV21
Faraday Av, Sid. 186 EU89
Faraday Cl N7 141 DM65
Bride St
Faraday Cl, Slou. 131 AP71
Faraday Cl, Wat. 75 BR44
Faraday Rd E15 144 EF65
Faraday Rd SW19 180 DA93
Faraday Rd W3 138 CQ73
Faraday Rd W10 139 CY71
Faraday Rd, Slou. 131 AP71
Faraday Rd, Sthl. 136 CB73
Faraday Rd, Well. 166 EU83
Faraday Rd, W.Mol. 196 CA98
Faraday Way SE18 164 EK76
Faraday Way, Croy. 201 DM102
Ampere Way
Faraday Way, Orp. 206 EV98
Fareham Rd, Felt. 176 BW87
Fareham St W1 273 M8
Farewell Pl, Mitch. 200 DE95
Faringdon Av, Brom. 205 EP100
Faringdon Av, Rom. 106 FJ53
Faringford Cl, Pot.B. 64 DD31
Faringford Rd E15 144 EE66
Farington Acres, Wey. 195 BR104
Faris Barn Dr (Woodham), Add. 211 BF112
Faris La (Woodham), Add. 211 BF111
Farjeon Rd SE3 164 EK81
Farland Rd, Hem.H. 40 BN21
Farleigh Av, Brom. 204 EF100
Farleigh Border, Croy. 221 DY112
Farleigh Ct, Guil. 242 AS134
Park Barn Dr
Farleigh Ct Rd, Warl. 221 DZ114
Farleigh Dean Cres, Croy. 221 EB111
Farleigh Pl N16 122 DT63
Farleigh Rd
Farleigh Rd N16 122 DT63
Farleigh Rd (New Haw), Add. 212 BG111
Farleigh Rd, Warl. 237 DX118
Farleton Cl, Wey. 213 BR107
Farley Common, West. 255 EP126
Farley Dr, Ilf. 125 ES60
Farley Heath (Albury), Guil. 260 BJ144
Farley La, West. 255 EP127
Farley Ms SE6 183 EC87
Farley Nursery, West. 255 EQ127
Farley Pk, Oxt. 253 ED130
Farley Pl SE25 202 DU98
Farley Rd SE6 183 EB87
Farley Rd, Grav. 191 GM88
Farley Rd, S.Croy. 220 DV108
Farleycroft, West. 255 EQ126
Farleys Cl (West Horsley), Lthd. 245 BQ126
Farlington Pl SW15 179 CV87
Roehampton La
Farlow Cl (Northfleet), Grav. 191 GF90
Farlow Rd SW15 159 CX83
Farlton Rd SW18 180 DB87
Farm Av NW2 119 CY62
Farm Av SW16 181 DL91
Farm Av, Har. 116 BZ59
Farm Av, Swan. 207 FC97
Farm Av, Wem. 137 CJ65
Farm Cl, Amer. 72 AX39
Farm Cl, Barn. 79 CW43
Farm Cl, Borwd. 77 CK38
Farm Cl, Brwd. 109 GC45
Farm Cl, Buck.H. 102 EJ48
Farm Cl (Lyne), Cher. 193 BA100
Farm Cl, Couls. 234 DF120
Farm Cl, Dag. 147 FC66
Farm Cl, Guil. 242 AX131
Christie Cl
Farm Cl, Harl. 34 EH14
Farm Cl, Hert. 31 DN09
Farm Cl (East Horsley), Lthd. 245 BT128
Farm Cl (Fetcham), Lthd. 231 CD124
Farm Cl, Maid. 150 AC78
Farm Cl (Cuffley), Pot.B. 65 DK27
Farm Cl, Rad. 62 CL30
Farm Cl, Shep. 194 BN101
Farm Cl, Sthl. 136 CB73
Farm Cl, Stai. 173 BE92
Farm Cl, Sutt. 218 DD108
Farm Cl, Uxb. 115 BP61
Farm Cl, Wall. 219 DJ110
Farm Cl (Cheshunt), Wal.Cr. 66 DW30
Farm Cl, Welw.G.C. 29 CW09
Farm Cl (Byfleet), W.Byf. 212 BM112
Farm Cl, W.Wick. 204 EE104
Farm Ct NW4 119 CU55
Farm Cres, Slou. 132 AV71
Farm Dr, Croy. 203 DZ103
Farm Dr, Pur. 219 DK112
Farm End E4 84 EE43
Farm End, Nthwd. 93 BP53
Drakes Dr
Farm Fld, Wat. 75 BS38
Farm Flds, S.Croy. 220 DS111
Farm Gro (Knotty Grn), Beac. 88 AJ50
Farm Hill Rd, Wal.Abb. 67 EC34
Farm Ho Cl, Brox. 67 DZ25
Farm La N14 80 DG44
Farm La SW6 160 DA79
Farm La, Add. 212 BG107
Farm La, Ash. 232 CN116
Farm La (Jordans), Beac. 89 AR52
Farm La, Cars. 218 DF110
Farm La, Croy. 203 DZ103
Farm La, Epsom 232 CP119
Farm La (East Horsley), Lthd. 245 BT128
Farm La, Pur. 219 DJ110
Farm La, Rick. 74 BH41
Farm La, Slou. 131 AR73
Farm La (Send), Wok. 227 BC124
Farm Lea (Wooburn Grn), H.Wyc. 110 AF56
Farm Pl W8 140 DA74
Uxbridge St
Farm Pl, Berk. 38 AT18
Farm Pl, Dart. 167 FG84
Farm Rd N21 100 DQ46
Farm Rd NW10 138 CR67
Mordaunt Rd
Farm Rd, Edg. 96 CP51
Farm Rd, Esher 196 CB102
Farm Rd, Grays 171 GF75
Farm Rd, Hodd. 49 EC16
Farm Rd, Houns. 176 BY88
Farm Rd, Maid. 130 AG73
Farm Rd, Mord. 200 DB99
Farm Rd, Nthwd. 93 BQ50
Farm Rd, Rain. 148 FJ69
Farm Rd, Rick. 73 BA42
Farm Rd, St.Alb. 43 CH19
Farm Rd, Sev. 257 FJ121
Farm Rd, Stai. 174 BH93
Farm Rd, Sutt. 218 DD108
Farm Rd, Warl. 237 DY119
Farm Rd, Wok. 227 BB120
Farm St W1 277 H1
Farm St W1 141 DH73
Farm Vale, Bex. 187 FB86
Farm Vw (Lower Kingswood), Tad. 249 CZ127
Farm Wk NW11 119 CZ57
Farm Wk, Guil. 258 AT136
Wilderness Rd
Farm Wk, Horl. 268 DF148
Court Lo Rd
Farm Way, Buck.H. 102 EJ49
Farm Way, Bushey 76 CB42
Farm Way, Hat. 45 CV15
Farm Way, Horn. 127 FH63
Farm Way, Nthwd. 93 BS49
Farm Way, Stai. 173 BF86
Farm Way, Wor.Pk. 199 CW104
Farm Yd, Wind. 151 AR80
Farman Gro, Nthlt. 136 BX69
Wayfarer Rd
Farmborough Cl, Har. 117 CD59
Pool Rd
Farmcote Rd SE12 184 EG88
Farmcroft, Grav. 191 GG89
Farmdale Rd SE10 164 EG78
Farmdale Rd, Cars. 218 DE108
Farmer Rd E10 123 EB60
Farmer St W8 140 DA74
Uxbridge St
Farmers Cl, Wat. 59 BV33

Farmers Ct, Wal.Abb. 68 EG33
Winters Way
Farmers Rd SE5 161 DP80
Farmers Rd, Stai. 173 BE92
Farmers Way (Seer Grn), Beac. 89 AQ51
Farmfield Dr, Horl. 268 DB150
Farmfield Rd, Brom. 184 EE92
Farmhouse Cl, Wok. 227 BD115
Farmhouse La, Hem.H. 40 BN18
Farmhouse Rd SW16 181 DJ94
Farmilo Rd E17 123 DZ59
Farmington Av, Sutt. 200 DD104
Farmland Wk, Chis. 185 EP92
Farmlands, Enf. 81 DN39
Farmlands, Pnr. 115 BU56
Farmlands, The, Nthlt. 136 BZ65
Farmleigh N14 99 DJ45
Farmleigh Gro, Walt. 213 BT106
Farmstead Rd SE6 183 EB91
Farmstead Rd, Har. 95 CD53
Farmview, Cob. 230 BX116
Farmway, Dag. 126 EW63
Farnaby Dr, Sev. 256 FF126
Farnaby Rd SE9 164 EJ84
Farnaby Rd, Brom. 183 ED94
Farnan Av E17 101 EA54
Farnan Rd SW16 181 DL92
Farnborough Av E17 123 DY55
Farnborough Av, S.Croy. 221 DX108
Farnborough Cl, Wem. 118 CP61
Chalkhill Rd
Farnborough Common, Orp. 205 EM104
Farnborough Cres, Brom. 204 EF102
Saville Row
Farnborough Cres, S.Croy. 221 DY109
Farnborough Hill, Orp. 223 ER106
Farnborough Ho SW15 179 CU88
Fontley Way
Farnborough Way SE15 162 DT80
Chandler Way
Farnborough Way, Orp. 223 EQ105
Farnburn Av, Slou. 131 AP71
Farncombe St SE16 162 DU75
Farncombe St, Gdmg. 258 AS144
Farndale Av N13 99 DP48
Farndale Cres, Grnf. 136 CC69
Farnell Ms SW5 160 DB78
Earls Ct Sq
Farnell Pt E5 122 DU63
Tiger Way
Farnell Rd, Islw. 157 CD83
Farnell Rd, Stai. 174 BG90
Farnes Dr, Rom. 106 FJ54
Farney Fld (Peaslake), Guil. 261 BR142
Farnham Cl N20 98 DC45
Farnham Cl (Bovingdon), Hem.H. 57 BA28
Farnham Cl, Saw. 36 EW06
Farnham Gdns SW20 199 CV96
Farnham La, Slou. 131 AN68
Farnham Pk La (Farnham Royal), Slou. 131 AQ66
Farnham Pl SE1 278 G3
Farnham Rd, Guil. 258 AS137
Farnham Rd, Ilf. 125 ET59
Farnham Rd, Rom. 106 FK50
Farnham Rd, Slou. 131 AQ71
Farnham Rd, Well. 166 EW82
Farnham Royal SE11 161 DM78
Farningham Cres, Cat. 236 DU123
Commonwealth Rd
Farningham Hill Rd (Farningham), Dart. 208 FJ99
Farningham Rd N17 100 DU52
Farningham Rd, Cat. 236 DU123
Farnley, Wok. 226 AT117
Farnley Rd E4 102 EE45
Farnley Rd SE25 202 DR98
Farnol Rd, Dart. 168 FN84
Faro Cl, Brom. 205 EN96
Faroe Rd W14 159 CX76
Farorna Wk, Enf. 81 DN39
Farquhar Rd SE19 182 DT92
Farquhar Rd SW19 180 DA90
Farquhar St, Hert. 32 DQ08
Farquharson Rd, Croy. 202 DQ102
Farr Av, Bark. 146 EU68
Farr Rd, Enf. 82 DR39
Farraline Rd, Wat. 75 BV42
Farrance Rd, Rom. 126 EY58
Farrance St E14 143 DZ72
Farrans Ct, Har. 117 CH59
Farrant Av N22 99 DN54
Farrant Cl, Orp. 224 EU108
Farrant Way, Borwd. 78 CL39
Farrell Ho E1 142 DW72
Farren Rd SE23 183 DY89
Farrer Ms N8 121 DJ56
Farrer Rd
Farrer Rd N8 121 DJ56
Farrer Rd, Har. 118 CL57
Farrer's Pl, Croy. 221 DX105
Farriday Cl, St.Alb. 43 CE16
Farrier Cl, Sun. 195 BU98
Farrier Cl, Uxb. 134 BN72
Horseshoe Dr
Farrier Rd, Nthlt. 136 CA68
Farrier St NW1 141 DH66
Farrier Wk SW10 160 DC79
Farriers, Ware 33 EA09
Farriers Cl, Epsom 216 CS112
Farriers Cl, Grav. 191 GM88
Farriers Cl (Bovingdon), Hem.H. 57 BB28
Chipperfield Rd
Farriers Ct, Sutt. 217 CY108
Forge La
Farriers Ct, Wat. 59 BV32
Farriers End, Brox. 67 DZ26
Farriers Rd, Epsom 216 CS112
Farriers Way, Borwd. 78 CQ44
Farringdon La EC1 274 E5
Farringdon La EC1 141 DN70
Farringdon Rd EC1 274 D4
Farringdon Rd EC1 141 DN70
Farringdon St EC4 274 F8
Farringdon St EC4 141 DP71
Farringford Cl, St.Alb. 60 CA26
Farrington Av, Orp. 206 EV97
Farrington Pl, Chis. 185 ER94
Farrington Pl, Nthwd. 93 BT49
Farrins Rents SE16 143 DY74
Farrow La SE14 162 DW80
Farrow Pl SE16 163 DY76
Ropemaker Rd
Farthing All SE1 162 DU75
Wolseley St
Farthing Cl, Dart. 168 FM84
Farthing Flds E1 142 DV74
Raine St
Farthing Grn La (Stoke Poges), Slou. 132 AU68
Farthing St, Orp. 223 EM108
Farthingale Ct, Wal.Abb. 68 EG34
Farthingale La, Wal.Abb. 68 EG34
Farthingale Wk E15 143 ED66
Farthings (Knaphill), Wok. 226 AS116
Farthings, The, Amer. 55 AR36
Milton Lawns
Farthings, The, Hem.H. 40 BH20
Farthings, The, Kings.T. 198 CN95
Brunswick Rd
Farthings Cl E4 102 EE48
Farthings Cl, Pnr. 115 BV58
Farwell Rd, Sid. 186 EV90
Farwig La, Brom. 204 EF95
Fashion St E1 275 P7
Fashion St E1 142 DT71
Fashoda Rd, Brom. 204 EK98
Fassett Rd E8 142 DU65
Fassett Rd, Kings.T. 198 CL98
Fassett Sq E8 142 DU65
Fassnidge Way, Uxb. 134 BJ66
Oxford Rd
Fauconberg Rd W4 158 CQ79
Faulkner Cl, Dag. 126 EX59
Faulkner St SE14 162 DW81
Faulkner's All EC1 274 F6
Faulkners Rd, Walt. 214 BW106
Fauna Cl, Rom. 126 EW59
Faunce St SE17 161 DP78
Harmsworth St
Favart Rd SW6 160 DA81
Faverolle Grn, Wal.Cr. 67 DX28
Faversham Av E4 102 EE46
Faversham Av, Enf. 82 DR44
Faversham Cl, Chig. 104 EV47
Faversham Rd SE6 183 DZ87
Faversham Rd, Beck. 203 DZ96
Faversham Rd, Mord. 200 DB100
Fawcett Cl SW11 160 DD82
Fawcett Cl SW16 181 DN91
Fawcett Est E5 122 DU60
Fawcett Rd NW10 139 CT67
Fawcett Rd, Croy. 201 DP104
Fawcett Rd, Wind. 151 AP81
Fawcett St SW10 160 DC79
Fawcus Cl (Claygate), Esher 215 CF107
Dalmore Av
Fawe Pk Rd SW15 159 CZ84
Fawe St E14 143 EB71
Fawke Common (Underriver), Sev. 257 FP127
Fawke Common Rd, Sev. 257 FP126
Fawkes Av, Dart. 188 FM89
Fawkham Grn Rd (Fawkham Grn), Long. 209 FV104
Fawkham Rd, Long. 209 FX97
Fawkon Wk, Hodd. 49 EA17
Taverners Way
Fawley Rd NW6 120 DB64
Fawn Ct, Hat. 45 CW16
Fawn Rd E13 144 EJ68
Fawn Rd, Chig. 103 ET50
Fawnbrake Av SE24 181 DP85
Fawns Manor Cl, Felt. 175 BQ88
Fawns Manor Rd, Felt. 175 BR88
Fawood Av NW10 138 CR66
Fawsley Cl (Colnbrook), Slou. 153 BE80
Fawters Cl, Brwd. 109 GD44
Fay Grn, Abb.L. 59 BR33
Fayerfield, Pot.B. 64 DD31
Faygate Cres, Bexh. 186 FA85
Faygate Rd SW2 181 DM89
Fayland Av SW16 181 DJ92
Faymore Gdns, S.Ock. 149 FU72
Feacey Down, Hem.H. 40 BG18
Fearn Cl (East Horsley), Lthd. 245 BS129
Fearney Mead, Rick. 92 BG46
Fearnley Cres, Hmptn. 176 BZ92
Fearnley Rd, Welw.G.C. 29 CW10
Fearnley St, Wat. 75 BV42
Fearns Mead, Brwd. 108 FW50
Bucklers Ct
Fearon St SE10 164 EG78
Feather Dell, Hat. 45 CT18
Featherbed La, Abb.L. 59 BV26
Sergehill La
Featherbed La, Croy. 221 DZ108
Featherbed La, Hem.H. 40 BJ24
Featherbed La, Rom. 104 EY45
Featherbed La, Warl. 221 ED113
Feathers La (Wraysbury), Stai. 173 BA89
Feathers Pl SE10 163 ED79
Featherstone Av SE23 182 DV89
Featherstone Gdns, Borwd. 78 CQ42
Featherstone Ind Est, Sthl. 156 BY75
Featherstone Rd NW7 97 CV51
Featherstone Rd, Sthl. 156 BY76
Featherstone St EC1 275 K4
Featherstone St EC1 142 DR70
Featherstone Ter, Sthl. 156 BY76
Featley Rd SW9 161 DP83
Federal Rd, Grnf. 137 CJ68
Federal Way, Wat. 76 BW38
Federation Rd SE2 166 EV77
Fee Fm Rd (Claygate), Esher 215 CF108
Feenan Highway, Til. 171 GH80
Felbridge Av, Stan. 95 CG53
Felbridge Cl SW16 181 DN91
Felbridge Cl, Sutt. 218 DC109
Felbrigge Rd, Ilf. 125 ET61
Felcott Cl, Walt. 196 BW104
Felcott Rd, Walt. 196 BW104
Felday Hos (Holmbury St. Mary), Dor. 261 BV144
Felday Rd SE13 183 EB86
Felday Rd (Abinger Hammer), Dor. 261 BT140
Felden Cl, Pnr. 94 BY52
Felden Cl, Wat. 60 BX34
Felden Dr (Felden), Hem.H. 40 BG24
Felden La (Felden), Hem.H. 40 BG24
Felden St SW6 159 CZ81
Feldman Cl N16 122 DU60
Felgate Ms W6 159 CV77
Felhampton Rd SE9 185 EP89
Felhurst Cres, Dag. 127 FB63
Felicia Way, Grays 171 GH77
Felipe Rd, Grays 169 FW76
Felix Av N8 121 DL58
Felix Dr (West Clandon), Guil. 244 BG128
Felix La, Shep. 195 BS100
Felix Rd W13 137 CG73
Felix Rd, Walt. 195 BU100
Felix St E2 142 DV68
Hackney Rd
Felixstowe Ct E16 165 EP75
Fishguard Way
Felixstowe Rd N9 100 DU49
Felixstowe Rd N17 122 DT55
Felixstowe Rd NW10 139 CV69
Felixstowe Rd SE2 166 EV76
Fell Rd, Croy. 202 DQ104
Fell Wk, Edg. 96 CP53
East Rd
Felland Way, Reig. 266 DC138
Fellbrigg Rd SE22 182 DT85
Fellbrigg St E1 142 DV70
Headlam St
Fellbrook, Rich. 177 CH90
Fellmongers Path SE1 279 N5
Fellmongers Yd, Croy. 202 DQ103
Surrey St
Fellowes Cl, Hayes 136 BX70
Paddington Cl
Fellowes La (Colney Heath), St.Alb. 44 CS23
Fellowes Rd, Cars. 200 DE104
Fellows Ct E2 275 P1
Fellows Ct E2 142 DT68
Fellows Rd NW3 140 DD66
Felltram Way SE7 164 EG78
Woolwich Rd
Felmersham Cl SW4 161 DK84
Haselrigge Rd
Felmingham Rd SE20 202 DW96
Felmongers, Harl. 36 EV13
Felnex Trd Est, Wall. 200 DG103
Fels Cl, Dag. 127 FB62
Fels Fm Av, Dag. 127 FC62
Felsberg Rd SW2 181 DL86
Felsham Rd SW15 159 CX83
Felspar Cl SE18 165 ET78
Felstead Av, Ilf. 103 EN53
Felstead Cl, Brwd. 109 GC44
Felstead Gdns E14 163 EC78
Ferry St
Felstead Rd E11 124 EG59
Felstead Rd, Epsom 216 CR111
Felstead Rd, Loug. 102 EL45
Felstead Rd, Orp. 206 EU103
Felstead Rd, Rom. 105 FC51
Felstead Rd, Wal.Cr. 67 DY32
Felstead St E9 143 DZ65
Felsted Rd E16 144 EK72
Feltham Av, E.Mol. 197 CE98
Feltham Business Complex, Felt. 175 BV89
Feltham Hill Rd, Ashf. 175 BP92
Feltham Hill Rd, Felt. 175 BU91
Feltham Rd, Ashf. 175 BP91
Feltham Rd, Mitch. 200 DF96
Feltham Rd, Red. 266 DF139
Feltham Wk, Red. 266 DF139
Felthambrook Way, Felt. 175 BV90
Felton Cl, Borwd. 78 CL38
Felton Cl, Brox. 67 DZ25
Felton Cl, Orp. 205 EP100
Felton Gdns, Bark. 145 ES67
Sutton Rd
Felton Ho SE3 164 EH84
Ryan Cl
Felton Lea, Sid. 185 ET92
Felton Rd W13 157 CJ75
Camborne Av
Felton Rd, Bark. 145 ES68
Sutton Rd
Felton St N1 142 DR67
Fen Cl, Brwd. 109 GC42
Fen Ct EC3 275 M10
Fen Gro, Sid. 185 ET86
Fen La, Upmin. 129 FW64
Fen St E16 144 EF73
Victoria Dock Rd
Fencepiece Rd, Chig. 103 EQ50
Fencepiece Rd, Ilf. 103 EQ50
Fenchurch Av EC3 275 M9
Fenchurch Av EC3 142 DS72
Fenchurch Bldgs EC3 275 N9
Fenchurch Pl EC3 275 N10
Fenchurch St EC3 275 M10
Fenchurch St EC3 142 DS73
Fendall Rd, Epsom 216 CQ106
Fendall St SE1 279 N7
Fendall St SE1 162 DS76
Fendt Cl E16 144 EF73
Bowman Av
Fendyke Rd, Belv. 166 EX76
Fenelon Pl W14 159 CZ77
Fengates Rd, Red. 250 DE134
Fenham Rd SE15 162 DU80
Fenman Ct N17 100 DV53
Shelbourne Rd
Fenman Gdns, Ilf. 126 EV60
Fenn Cl, Brom. 184 EG93
Fenn St E9 122 DW64
Fennel Cl E16 144 EE70
Cranberry La
Fennel Cl, Croy. 203 DX102
Primrose La
Fennel Cl, Guil. 243 BB131
Fennel St SE18 165 EN79
Fennells, Harl. 51 EQ20
Fennells Mead, Epsom 217 CT109
Fenner Cl SE16 162 DV77
Layard Rd
Fenner Ho, Walt. 213 BU105
Fenner Rd, Grays 169 FW77
Fenner Sq SW11 160 DD83
Thomas Baines Rd
Fenning St SE1 279 M4
Fennings, The, Amer. 55 AR36
Fenns Way, Wok. 226 AY115
Fennycroft Rd, Hem.H. 40 BG17
Fens Way, Swan. 187 FG93
Fensomes All, Hem.H. 40 BK19
Fenstanton Av N12 98 DD50
Fenswood Cl, Bex. 186 FA85
Fentiman Rd SW8 161 DL79
Fentiman Way, Horn. 128 FL60
Fenton Av, Stai. 174 BJ93
Fenton Cl E8 142 DT65
Laurel St
Fenton Cl SW9 161 DM82
Fenton Cl, Chis. 185 EM92
Fenton Cl, Red. 250 DG134
Fenton Gra, Harl. 52 EW16
Fenton Rd N17 100 DQ52
Fenton Rd, Grays 170 FY75
Fenton Rd, Red. 250 DG134
Fentons Av E13 144 EH68
Fentum Rd, Guil. 242 AU132
Fenwick Cl SE18 165 EN79
Ritter St
Fenwick Cl, Wok. 226 AV118
Fenwick Gro SE15 162 DU83
Fenwick Path, Borwd. 78 CM38
Fenwick Pl SW9 161 DL83
Fenwick Pl, S.Croy. 219 DP108
Columbine Av
Fenwick Rd SE15 162 DU83
Ferdinand Pl NW1 140 DG66
Ferdinand St
Ferdinand St NW1 140 DG65
Fergus Rd N5 121 DP64
Calabria Rd
Ferguson Av, Grav. 191 GJ91
Ferguson Av, Rom. 106 FJ54
Ferguson Av, Surb. 198 CM99
Ferguson Cl E14 163 EA77
Ferguson Cl, Brom. 203 EC97
Ferguson Ct, Rom. 106 FK54
Ferguson Dr W3 138 CR72
Ferme Pk Rd N4 121 DL57
Ferme Pk Rd N8 121 DL57
Fermor Rd SE23 183 DY88
Fermoy Rd W9 139 CZ70
Fermoy Rd, Grnf. 136 CB70
Fern Av, Mitch. 201 DK98
Fern Cl, Brox. 49 DZ23
Fern Cl, Erith 167 FH81
Hollywood Way
Fern Cl, Warl. 237 DY118
Fern Dells, Hat. 45 CT19
Fern Dene W13 137 CH71
Templewood
Fern Dr, Hem.H. 40 BL21
Fern Dr, Maid. 130 AH72
Fern Gro, Felt. 175 BV87
Fern Gro, Welw.G.C. 29 CX05
Fern Hill La, Harl. 51 ES19
Fern La, Houns. 156 BZ78
Fern Leys, St.Alb. 43 CJ17
Fern St E3 143 EA70
Fern Twrs, Cat. 252 DU125
Fern Wk SE16 162 DU78
Argyle Way
Fern Wk, Ashf. 174 BK92
Ferndale Rd
Fern Way, Wat. 75 BU35
Fernbank, Buck.H. 102 EH46
Fernbank Av, Horn. 128 FJ63
Fernbank Av, Walt. 196 BY101
Fernbank Av, Wem. 117 CF63
Fernbank Ms SW12 181 DJ86
Fernbank Rd, Add. 212 BG106
Fernbrook Av, Sid. 185 ES85
Blackfen Rd
Fernbrook Cres SE13 184 EE86
Fernbrook Dr, Har. 116 CB59
Fernbrook Rd SE13 184 EE86
Ferncliff Rd E8 122 DU64
Ferncroft Av N12 98 DE51
Ferncroft Av NW3 120 DA62
Ferncroft Av, Ruis. 116 BW61
Ferndale, Brom. 204 EJ96
Ferndale, Guil. 242 AS132
Ferndale Av E17 123 ED57
Ferndale Av, Cher. 193 BE104
Ferndale Av, Houns. 156 BY83
Ferndale Cl, Bexh. 166 EY81
Ferndale Ct SE3 164 EF80
Ferndale Cres, Uxb. 134 BJ69
Ferndale Rd E7 144 EH66
Ferndale Rd E11 124 EE61
Ferndale Rd N15 122 DT58
Ferndale Rd SE25 202 DV99
Ferndale Rd SW4 161 DL84
Ferndale Rd SW9 161 DM83
Ferndale Rd, Ashf. 174 BK92
Ferndale Rd, Bans. 233 CZ116
Ferndale Rd, Enf. 83 DY37
Ferndale Rd, Grav. 191 GH89
Ferndale Rd, Rom. 105 FC54
Ferndale Rd, Wok. 227 AZ116
Ferndale St E6 145 EP73
Ferndale Ter, Har. 117 CF56
Ferndale Way, Orp. 223 ER106
Ferndell Av, Bex. 187 FD90
Fernden Ri, Gdmg. 258 AS144
Fernden Way, Rom. 127 FB58
Ferndene (Bricket Wd), St.Alb. 60 BZ31
Ferndene Rd SE24 162 DQ84
Ferndown, Horl. 268 DF146
Ferndown, Horn. 128 FM58
Ferndown, Nthwd. 93 BU54
Ferndown Av, Orp. 205 ER102
Ferndown Cl, Guil. 259 BA135
Ferndown Cl, Pnr. 94 BY52
Ferndown Cl, Sutt. 218 DD107
Ferndown Ct, Guil. 242 AW133
Ferndown Gdns, Cob. 214 BW113
Ferndown Rd SE9 184 EK87
Ferndown Rd, Wat. 94 BW48
Fernecroft, St.Alb. 43 CD23
Fernery, The, Stai. 173 BE92
Fernes Cl, Uxb. 134 BJ72
Ferney Ct (Byfleet), W.Byf. 212 BK112
Ferney Rd
Ferney Meade Way, Islw. 157 CG82
Ferney Rd, Barn. 98 DG45
Ferney Rd (Cheshunt), Wal.Cr. 66 DR26
Ferney Rd (Byfleet), W.Byf. 212 BK112
Fernhall Dr, Ilf. 124 EK57
Fernhall La, Wal.Abb. 68 EK31
Fernham Rd, Th.Hth. 202 DQ97
Fernhead Rd W9 139 CZ70
Fernheath Way, Dart. 187 FD92
Fernhill, Harl. 51 ES18
Fernhill (Oxshott), Lthd. 215 CD114
Fernhill Cl, Wok. 226 AW120
Fernhill Ct E17 101 ED54
Fernhill Gdns, Kings.T. 177 CK92
Fernhill La, Wok. 226 AW120
Fernhill Pk, Wok. 226 AW120
Fernhill Rd, Horl. 269 DK152
Fernhill St E16 145 EM74
Fernhills, Kings L. 59 BR33
Fernholme Rd SE15 183 DX85
Fernhurst Cl, Beac. 89 AM53
Fernhurst Gdns, Edg. 96 CN51
Fernhurst Rd SW6 159 CY81
Fernhurst Rd, Ashf. 175 BQ91
Fernhurst Rd, Croy. 202 DU101
Fernie Cl, Chig. 104 EU50
Fernihough Cl, Wey. 212 BN111
Fernlands Cl, Cher. 193 BE104
Fernlea (Bookham), Lthd. 230 CB123
Fernlea Rd SW12 181 DH88
Fernlea Rd, Mitch. 200 DG96
Fernleigh Cl W9 139 CZ69
Fernleigh Cl, Croy. 219 DN105
Stafford Rd
Fernleigh Cl, Walt. 195 BV104
Fernleigh Ct, Har. 94 CB54
Fernleigh Ct, Wem. 118 CL61
Fernleigh Rd N21 99 DN47
Ferns, The, Beac. 89 AM54
Ferns Cl, Enf. 83 DY36
Ferns Cl, S.Croy. 220 DV110
Ferns Rd E15 144 EF65
Fernsbury St WC1 274 D3
Fernshaw Rd SW10 160 DC79
Fernside NW11 120 DA61
Finchley Rd
Fernside, Buck.H. 102 EH46
Fernside Av NW7 96 CR48
Fernside Av, Felt. 175 BV91
Fernside La, Sev. 257 FJ129
Fernside Rd SW12 180 DF88
Fernsleigh Cl (Chalfont St. Peter), Ger.Cr. 90 AY51
Fernthorpe Rd SW16 181 DJ93
Ferntower Rd N5 122 DR64
Fernville La, Hem.H. 40 BK20
Midland Rd
Fernways, Ilf. 125 EP63
Cecil Rd
Fernwood Av SW16 181 DK91
Fernwood Av, Wem. 117 CJ64
Bridgewater Rd
Fernwood Cl, Brom. 204 EJ96
Fernwood Cres N20 98 DF48
Ferny Hill, Barn. 80 DF38
Ferranti Cl SE18 164 EK76
Ferraro Cl, Houns. 156 CA79
Ferrers Av, Wall. 219 DK105
Ferrers Av, West Dr. 154 BK75
Ferrers Cl, Slou. 131 AL74
Ferrers Rd SW16 181 DK92
Ferrestone Rd N8 121 DM56
Ferriby Cl N1 141 DN66
Bewdley St
Ferrier Pt E16 144 EH71
Forty Acre La
Ferrier St SW18 160 DB84
Ferriers Way, Epsom 233 CW119
Ferring Cl, Har. 116 CC60
Ferrings SE21 182 DS89
Ferris Av, Croy. 203 DZ104
Ferris Rd SE22 162 DU84
Ferro Rd, Rain. 147 FG70
Ferron Rd E5 122 DV62
Ferrour Ct N2 120 DD55
Ferry Av, Stai. 173 BE94
Ferry La N17 122 DV56
Ferry La SW13 159 CT79
Ferry La, Brent. 158 CL79
Ferry La, Cher. 194 BH98
Ferry La, Guil. 258 AW138
Portsmouth Rd
Ferry La, Rain. 147 FE72
Ferry La, Rich. 158 CM79
Ferry La, Shep. 194 BN102
Ferry La (Laleham), Stai. 194 BJ97
Ferry La (Wraysbury), Stai. 173 BB89
Ferry Pl SE18 165 EN76
Woolwich High St
Ferry Rd SW13 159 CU80
Ferry Rd, Maid. 150 AC75
Ferry Rd, Tedd. 177 CH92
Ferry Rd, T.Ditt. 197 CH100
Ferry Rd, Til. 171 GG83
Ferry Rd, Twick. 177 CH88
Ferry Rd, W.Mol. 196 CA97
Ferry Sq, Brent. 157 CK79
Ferry Sq, Shep. 195 BP101
Ferry St E14 163 EC78
Ferryhills Cl, Wat. 94 BW48
Ferrymead Av, Grnf. 136 CA69
Ferrymead Dr, Grnf. 136 CA68
Ferrymead Gdns, Grnf. 136 CC68
Ferrymoor, Rich. 177 CH90
Feryby Rd, Grays 171 GH76
Feryngs Cl, Harl. 36 EX11
Watlington Rd
Fesants Cft, Harl. 36 EV12
Festing Rd SW15 159 CX83
Festival Cl, Bex. 186 EX88
Festival Cl, Erith 167 FF80
Betsham Rd
Festival Cl, Uxb. 135 BP67
Festival Path, Wok. 226 AT119
Festival Wk, Cars. 218 DF106
Fetcham Common La (Fetcham), Lthd. 230 CB121
Fetcham Downs (Fetcham), Lthd. 247 CE126
Fetcham Pk Dr (Fetcham), Lthd. 231 CE123
Fetherstone Cl, Pot.B. 64 DD32
Fetter La EC4 274 E9
Fetter La EC4 141 DN72
Ffinch St SE8 163 EA80
Fiddicroft Av, Bans. 218 DB114
Fiddlebridge La, Hat. 45 CT17
Fiddlers Cl, Green. 169 FV84
Fidler Pl, Bushey 76 CB44
Ashfield Av
Field Cl E4 101 EB51
Field Cl, Brom. 204 EJ96
Field Cl, Buck.H. 102 EJ48
Field Cl, Chesh. 54 AS28
Field Cl, Chess. 215 CJ106
Field Cl, Guil. 243 BD132
Field Cl, Hayes 155 BQ80
Field Cl, Houns. 155 BV81
Field Cl, Rom. 86 EV41
Field Cl, Ruis. 115 BQ60
Field Way
Field Cl (Sandridge), St.Alb. 43 CG16
Field Cl, S.Croy. 220 DV114
Field Cl, W.Mol. 196 CB99
Field Ct WC1 274 C7
Field Ct, Oxt. 254 EE127
Silkham Rd
Field End, Barn. 79 CV42
Field End, Couls. 219 DK114
Field End, Nthlt. 136 BX65
Field End, Ruis. 136 BW65
Field End, Twick. 177 CF91
Field End Cl, Wat. 94 BY45
Field End Rd, Pnr. 115 BV58
Field End Rd, Ruis. 116 BY63
Field La, Brent. 157 CJ80
Field La, Gdmg. 258 AT144
The Oval
Field La, Tedd. 177 CG92
Field Mead NW7 96 CS52
Field Mead NW9 96 CS52
Field Pl, Gdmg. 258 AS144
Field Pl, N.Mal. 199 CT100
Field Rd E7 124 EG63
Field Rd N17 122 DR55
Field Rd W6 159 CY78
Field Rd, Felt. 175 BV86
Field Rd, Hem.H. 40 BN21
Field Rd, S.Ock. 148 FQ74
Field Rd (Denham), Uxb. 113 BE63
Field Rd, Wat. 76 BY44
Field St WC1 274 B2
Field St WC1 141 DM69
Field Vw, Egh. 173 BC92
Field Vw, Felt. 175 BR91
Field Vw Ri (Bricket Wd), St.Alb. 60 BY29
Field Vw Rd, Pot.B. 64 DA33
Field Way NW10 138 CQ66
Twybridge Way
Field Way, Berk. 38 AY21
Field Way, Croy. 221 EB107

Field Way (Chalfont St. Peter), Ger.Cr. 90 AX52
Field Way, Grnf. 136 CB67
Field Way (Bovingdon), Hem.H. 57 BA27
Field Way, Hodd. 33 EC13
Field Way, Rick. 92 BH46
Field Way, Ruis. 115 BQ60
Field Way, Uxb. 134 BK70
Field Way (Ripley), Wok. 243 BF125
Fieldcommon La, Walt. 196 BZ101
Fieldend Rd SW16 201 DJ95
Fielders Cl, Enf. 82 DS42
Woodfield Cl
Fielders Cl, Har. 116 CC60
Fielders Grn, Guil. 243 AZ134
Fielders Way (Shenley), Rad. 62 CL33
Fieldfare Rd SE28 146 EW73
Fieldgate La, Mitch. 200 DE97
Fieldgate St E1 142 DU71
Fieldhouse Cl E18 102 EG53
Fieldhouse Rd SW12 181 DJ88
Fieldhurst, Slou. 153 AZ78
Fieldhurst Cl, Add. 212 BH106
Fielding Av, Til. 171 GH81
Fielding Av, Twick. 176 CC90
Fielding Gdns, Slou. 152 AW75
Fielding Ho NW6 140 DA69
Fielding Ms SW13 159 CV79
Castelnau
Fielding Rd W4 158 CR76
Fielding Rd W14 159 CX76
Fielding St SE17 162 DQ79
Fielding Wk W13 157 CH76
Fielding Way, Brwd. 109 GC44
Fieldings, The SE23 182 DW88
Fieldings, The, Horl. 269 DH147
Fieldings, The, Wok. 226 AT116
Fieldings Rd (Cheshunt), Wal.Cr. 67 DZ29
Fields, The, Slou. 151 AR75
Fields Ct, Pot.B. 64 DD33
Fields End La, Hem.H. 39 BE18
Fields Est E8 142 DU66
Fields Pk Cres, Rom. 126 EX57
Fieldsend Rd, Sutt. 217 CY106
Fieldside Cl, Orp. 223 EQ105
State Fm Av
Fieldside Rd, Brom. 183 ED92
Fieldview SW18 180 DD88
Fieldview, Horl. 269 DH147
Stockfield
Fieldview Ct, Stai. 174 BG93
Burges Way
Fieldway, Amer. 55 AP41
Fieldway, Dag. 126 EV63
Fieldway, Orp. 205 ER100
Fieldway, Ware 33 EB11
Fieldway Cres N5 121 DN64
Fiennes Cl, Dag. 126 EW60
Fiennes Way, Sev. 257 FJ127
Fiesta Dr, Dag. 147 FC70
Fife Rd E16 144 EG71
Fife Rd N22 99 DP52
Fife Rd SW14 178 CQ85
Fife Rd, Kings.T. 198 CL96
Fife Ter N1 141 DM68
Fifehead Cl, Ashf. 174 BL93
Fifeway, Lthd. 246 CA125
Fifield La, Wind. 150 AD84
Fifield Path SE23 183 DX90
Bampton Rd
Fifield Rd, Maid. 150 AD80
Fifth Av E12 125 EM63
Fifth Av W10 139 CY69
Fifth Av, Grays 169 FU79
Fifth Av, Harl. 35 ER13
Fifth Av, Hayes 135 BT74
Fifth Av, Wat. 76 BX35
Fifth Cross Rd, Twick. 177 CD89
Fifth Way, Wem. 118 CP63
Fig St, Sev. 256 FF129
Fig Tree Cl NW10 138 CS67
Craven Pk
Fig Tree Hill, Hem.H. 40 BK19
Figges Rd, Mitch. 180 DG94
Filby Rd, Chess. 216 CM107
Filey Av N16 122 DU60
Filey Cl, Sutt. 218 DC108
Filey Cl (Biggin Hill), West. 238 EH119
Filey Spur, Slou. 151 AP75
Filey Waye, Ruis. 115 BU61
Filigree Ct SE16 143 DZ74
Silver Wk
Fillebrook Av, Enf. 82 DS40
Fillebrook Rd E11 123 ED60
Filmer La, Sev. 257 FL121
Filmer Rd SW6 159 CY81
Filmer Rd, Wind. 151 AK82
Filston La, Sev. 225 FE113
Filston Rd, Erith 167 FB78
Riverdale Rd
Finborough Rd SW10 160 DB78
Finborough Rd SW17 180 DF93
Finch Av SE27 182 DR91
Finch Cl NW10 118 CR64
Finch Cl, Barn. 80 DA43
Finch Cl, Hat. 45 CU20
Eagle Way
Finch Dr, Felt. 176 BX87
Finch End (Penn), H.Wyc. 88 AC47
Finch Gdns E4 101 EA50
Finch Grn, Rick. 73 BF42
Finch La EC3 275 L9
Finch La, Amer. 72 AV40
Finch La (Knotty Grn), Beac. 88 AJ50
Finch La, Bushey 76 CA43
Finch Ms SE15 162 DT80
Finch Rd, Berk. 38 AU19
Finch Rd, Guil. 242 AX134
Finchale Rd SE2 166 EU76
Fincham Cl, Uxb. 115 BQ61
Aylsham Dr
Finchdale, Hem.H. 40 BG20
Finchdean Ho SW15 179 CT87
Tangley Gro
Finches, The, Hert. 32 DV09
Finches Ri, Guil. 243 BC132
Finchingfield Av, Wdf.Grn. 102 EJ52
Finchley Cl, Dart. 188 FN86
Finchley Ct N3 98 DB51
Finchley La NW4 119 CW56
Finchley Pk N12 98 DC49
Finchley Pl NW8 140 DD68
Finchley Rd NW2 120 DA62
Finchley Rd NW3 140 DC65
Finchley Rd NW8 140 DD67
Finchley Rd NW11 119 CZ58
Finchley Rd, Grays 170 GB79
Finchley Way N3 98 DA52
Finchmoor, Harl. 51 ER18
Finck St SE1 278 C5
Finden Rd E7 124 EH64
Findhorn Av, Hayes 135 BV71
Findhorn St E14 143 EC72
Findlay Dr, Guil. 242 AT130
Findon Cl SW18 180 DA86
Wimbledon Pk Rd
Findon Cl, Har. 116 CB62
Findon Gdns, Rain. 147 FG71
Findon Rd N9 100 DV46
Findon Rd W12 159 CU75
Fine Bush La (Harefield), Uxb. 115 BP58
Fingal St SE10 164 EF78
Finglesham Cl, Orp. 206 EX102
Westwell Cl
Finians Cl, Uxb. 134 BM66
Finland Quay SE16 163 DY76
Finland Rd SE4 163 DY83
Finland St SE16 163 DY76
Finlay Gdns, Add. 212 BJ105
Finlay St SW6 159 CX81
Finlays Cl, Chess. 216 CN106
Finnart Cl, Wey. 213 BQ105
Finnart Ho Dr, Wey. 213 BQ105
Vaillant Rd
Finney La, Islw. 157 CG81
Finnis St E2 142 DV69
Finnymore Rd, Dag. 146 EY66
Finsbury Av EC2 275 L7
Finsbury Circ EC2 275 L7
Finsbury Circ EC2 142 DR71
Finsbury Cotts N22 99 DL52
Clarence Rd
Finsbury Ct, Wal.Cr. 67 DY34
Parkside
Finsbury Est EC1 274 F3
Finsbury Est EC1 141 DN69
Finsbury Ho N22 99 DL53
Finsbury Mkt EC2 275 M5
Finsbury Mkt EC2 142 DS70
Finsbury Pk Av N4 122 DQ58
Finsbury Pk Rd N4 121 DP62
Finsbury Pavement EC2 275 L6
Finsbury Pavement EC2 142 DR71
Finsbury Rd N22 99 DM53
Finsbury Sq EC2 275 L6
Finsbury Sq EC2 142 DR71
Finsbury St EC2 275 K6
Finsbury St EC2 142 DR71
Finsbury Twr EC1 275 K5
Finsbury Way, Bex. 186 EZ86
Finsen Rd SE5 162 DQ83
Finstock Rd W10 139 CX72
Finucane Dr, Orp. 206 EW101
Finucane Gdns, Rain. 147 FG65
Finucane Ri, Bushey 94 CC47
Finway Ct, Wat. 75 BT43
Whippendell Rd
Finway Rd, Hem.H. 41 BP16
Fiona Cl (Bookham), Lthd. 230 CA124
Fir Cl, Walt. 195 BU101
Fir Dene, Orp. 205 EM104
Fir Gra Av, Wey. 213 BP106
Fir Gro, N.Mal. 199 CT100
Fir Gro, Wok. 226 AU119
Fir Pk, Harl. 51 EP18
Fir Rd, Felt. 176 BX92
Fir Rd, Sutt. 199 CZ102
Fir Tree Av, Mitch. 200 DG96
Fir Tree Av (Stoke Poges), Slou. 132 AT70
Fir Tree Av, West Dr. 154 BN76
Fir Tree Cl SW16 181 DJ92
Fir Tree Cl W5 138 CL72
Fir Tree Cl, Epsom 233 CW115
Fir Tree Cl (Ewell), Epsom 217 CT105
Fir Tree Cl, Esher 214 CC106
Fir Tree Cl, Grays 170 GD79
Fir Tree Cl, Hem.H. 40 BN21
Fir Tree Cl, Lthd. 231 CJ123
Fir Tree Cl, Orp. 223 ET106
Highfield Av
Fir Tree Cl, Rom. 127 FD55
Fir Tree Gdns, Croy. 221 EA105
Fir Tree Gro, Cars. 218 DF108
Fir Tree Hill, Rick. 74 BM38
Fir Tree Pl, Ashf. 174 BN92
Percy Av
Fir Tree Rd, Bans. 217 CW114
Fir Tree Rd, Epsom 233 CV116
Fir Tree Rd, Guil. 242 AX131
Fir Tree Rd, Houns. 156 BY84
Fir Tree Rd, Lthd. 231 CJ123
Fir Tree Wk, Dag. 127 FC62
Wheel Fm Dr
Fir Tree Wk, Enf. 82 DR41
Fir Tree Wk, Reig. 250 DD134
Fir Trees, Rom. 86 EV41
Fir Trees Cl SE16 143 DY74
Firbank Cl E16 144 EK71
Firbank Cl, Enf. 82 DQ42
Gladbeck Way
Firbank Dr, Wat. 94 BY45
Firbank Dr, Wok. 226 AV119
Firbank La, Wok. 226 AV119
Firbank Pl (Englefield Grn), Egh. 172 AV93
Firbank Rd SE15 162 DV82
Firbank Rd, Rom. 105 FB50
Firbank Rd, St.Alb. 43 CF16
Fircroft Cl (Stoke Poges), Slou. 132 AU65
Fircroft Cl, Wok. 227 AZ118
Fircroft Ct, Wok. 227 AZ118
Fircroft Cl
Fircroft Gdns, Har. 117 CE62
Fircroft Rd SW17 180 DF89
Fircroft Rd, Chess. 216 CM105
Firdene, Surb. 198 CQ102
Fire Bell All, Surb. 198 CL100
Fire Sta All, Barn. 79 CZ40
Christchurch La
Firecrest Dr NW3 120 DB62
Firefly Cl, Wall. 219 DL108
Firefly Gdns E6 144 EL70
Jack Dash Way
Firethorn Cl, Edg. 96 CQ49
Larkspur Gro
Firfield Rd, Add. 212 BG105
Firfields, Wey. 213 BP107
Firham Pk Av, Rom. 106 FN52
Firhill Rd SE6 183 EA91
Firlands, Horl. 269 DH147
Stockfield
Firlands, Wey. 213 BS107
Firmin Rd, Dart. 188 FJ85
Firmingers Rd, Orp. 225 FB106
Firs, The E17 123 DY57
Leucha Rd
Firs, The N20 98 DD46
Firs, The W5 137 CK71
Firs, The, Bex. 187 FD88
Dartford Rd
Firs, The, Brwd. 108 FU44
Firs, The, Cat. 236 DR122
Yorke Gate Rd
Firs, The (Artington), Guil. 258 AV138
Firs, The, St.Alb. 43 CH24
Firs, The, Tad. 249 CZ126
Brighton Rd
Firs, The, Wal.Cr. 66 DS27
Firs, The, Welw.G.C. 29 CW05
Firs Av N10 120 DG55
Firs Av N11 98 DG51
Firs Av SW14 158 CQ84
Firs Av, Wind. 151 AM83
Firs Cl N10 120 DG55
Firs Av
Firs Cl SE23 183 DX87
Firs Cl, Dor. 263 CG138
Firs Cl (Claygate), Esher 215 CE107
Firs Cl, Hat. 45 CV19
Firs Cl, Iver 133 BC67
Thornbridge Rd
Firs Cl, Mitch. 201 DH96
Firs Dr, Houns. 155 BV80
Firs Dr, Loug. 85 EN39
Firs Dr, Slou. 133 AZ74
Firs End (Chalfont St. Peter), Ger.Cr. 112 AY55
Firs La N13 100 DQ48
Firs La N21 100 DQ47
Firs La, Pot.B. 64 DB33
Firs Pk Av N21 100 DR46
Firs Pk Gdns N21 100 DQ46
Firs Rd, Ken. 235 DP115
Firs Wk, Nthwd. 93 BR51
Firs Wk, Wdf.Grn. 102 EG50
Firs Wd Cl, Pot.B. 64 DF32
Firsby Av, Croy. 203 DX102
Firsby Rd N16 122 DT60
Firscroft N13 100 DQ48
Firsdene Cl (Ottershaw), Cher. 211 BD107
Slade Rd
Firsgrove Cres, Brwd. 108 FV49
Firsgrove Rd, Brwd. 108 FV49
Firside Gro, Sid. 185 ET88
First Av E12 124 EL63
First Av E13 144 EG69
First Av E17 123 EA57
First Av N18 100 DW49
First Av NW4 119 CW56
First Av SW14 158 CS83
First Av W3 139 CT74
First Av W10 139 CZ70
First Av, Amer. 55 AQ40
First Av, Bexh. 166 EW80
First Av, Dag. 147 FB68
First Av, Enf. 82 DT44
First Av, Epsom 216 CS109
First Av (Northfleet), Grav. 190 GE88
First Av, Grays 169 FU79
First Av, Grnf. 137 CD66
First Av, Harl. 36 EV12
First Av, Hayes 135 BT74
First Av, Rom. 126 EW57
First Av, Wal.Abb. 68 EH30
Breach Barn Mobile Home Pk
First Av, Walt. 195 BV100
First Av, Wat. 76 BW35
First Av, Wem. 117 CK61
First Av, W.Mol. 196 BZ98
First Cl, W.Mol. 196 CC97
First Cres, Slou. 131 AQ71
First Cross Rd, Twick. 177 CE89
First Dr NW10 138 CQ66
First Slip, Lthd. 231 CG118
First St SW3 276 C8
First St SW3 160 DE77
First Way, Wem. 118 CP63
Firstway SW20 199 CW96
Firsway, Guil. 242 AT133
Firswood Av, Epsom 217 CT106
Firth Gdns SW6 159 CY81
Firtree Ct, Borwd. 78 CM42
Highfield Rd
Firwood Av, St.Alb. 44 CL20
Firwood Cl, Wok. 226 AS119
Firwood Rd, Vir.W. 192 AS100
Fish St Hill EC3 275 L10
Fish St Hill EC3 142 DR73
Fisher Cl, Croy. 202 DT102
Grant Rd
Fisher Cl, Enf. 83 EA37
Government Row
Fisher Cl, Grnf. 136 CA69
Gosling Cl
Fisher Cl, Kings L. 58 BN29
Fisher Cl, Walt. 213 BV105
Fisher Rd, Har. 95 CF54
Fisher St E16 144 EG71
Fisher St WC1 274 B7
Fisher St WC1 141 DM71
Fisherman Cl, Rich. 177 CJ91
Locksmeade Rd
Fishermans Dr SE16 163 DX75
Fishermans Hill, Grav. 190 GB85
Fisherman's Wk E14 143 EA74
Fishermans Wk SE28 165 ES75
Tugboat St
Fishermans Way, Hodd. 49 ED15
Fishers, Horl. 269 DJ147
Ewelands
Fishers Cl SW16 181 DK90
Garrad's Rd
Fishers Cl, Bushey 76 BY41
Fishers Cl, Wal.Cr. 67 EA34
Fishers Ct SE14 163 DX81
Besson St
Fishers Grn La, Wal.Abb. 67 EB29
Fishers Hatch, Harl. 35 ES14
School La
Fishers La W4 158 CR77
Fishers La, Epp. 69 ES32
Fishers Way, Belv. 147 FC74
Fishersdene (Claygate), Esher 215 CG108
Fisherton St NW8 140 DD70
Fishery Pas, Hem.H. 40 BG22
Fishery Rd
Fishery Rd, Hem.H. 40 BG22
Fishery Rd, Maid. 130 AC74
Fishguard Spur, Slou. 152 AV75
Fishguard Way E16 165 EP75
Fishing Temple, Stai. 193 BF95
Fishponds Rd SW17 180 DE91
Fishponds Rd, Kes. 222 EK106
Fishpool St, St.Alb. 42 CB20
Fitzalan Rd N3 119 CY55
Fitzalan Rd (Claygate), Esher 215 CE108
Fitzalan St SE11 278 C8
Fitzalan St SE11 161 DM77
Fitzgeorge Av W14 159 CY77
Fitzgeorge Av, N.Mal. 198 CR95
Fitzgerald Av SW14 158 CS83
Fitzgerald Cl E11 124 EG57
Fitzgerald Rd
Fitzgerald Ho E14 143 EB72
Fitzgerald Ho, Hayes 135 BV74
Fitzgerald Rd E11 124 EG57
Fitzgerald Rd SW14 158 CR83
Fitzgerald Rd, T.Ditt. 197 CG100
Fitzhardinge St W1 272 F8
Fitzhardinge St W1 140 DG72
Fitzherbert Ho, Rich. 178 CM86
Kingsmead
Fitzhugh Gro SW18 180 DD86
Fitzilian Av, Rom. 106 FM53
Fitzjames Av W14 159 CY77
Fitzjames Av, Croy. 202 DU103
Fitzjohn Av, Barn. 79 CY43
Fitzjohn Cl, Guil. 243 BC131
Fitzjohn's Av NW3 120 DD64
Fitzmaurice Pl W1 277 J2
Fitzmaurice Pl W1 141 DH73
Fitzneal St W12 139 CT72
Fitzrobert Pl, Egh. 173 BA93
Fitzroy Cl N6 120 DF60
Fitzroy Ct W1 273 L5
Fitzroy Cres W4 158 CR80
Fitzroy Gdns SE19 182 DS94
Fitzroy Ms W1 273 K5
Fitzroy Pk N6 120 DF60
Fitzroy Rd NW1 140 DG67
Fitzroy Sq W1 273 K5
Fitzroy Sq W1 141 DJ70
Fitzroy St W1 273 K5
Fitzroy St W1 141 DJ70
Fitzroy Yd NW1 140 DG67
Fitzroy Rd
Fitzstephen Rd, Dag. 126 EV64
Fitzwarren Gdns N19 121 DJ60
Fitzwilliam Av, Rich. 158 CM82
Fitzwilliam Ct, Harl. 36 EY11
Fitzwilliam Ms E16 144 EG74
Hanover Av
Fitzwilliam Rd SW4 161 DJ83
Fitzwygram Cl (Hampton Hill), Hmptn. 176 CC92
Five Acre NW9 97 CT53
Five Acres, Chesh. 54 AR33
Five Acres, Harl. 51 ES18
Five Acres (Wooburn Grn), H.Wyc. 110 AF56
Five Acres, Kings L. 58 BM29
Five Acres (London Colney), St.Alb. 61 CK25
Five Acres Av (Bricket Wd), St.Alb. 60 BZ29
Five Bell All E14 143 DZ73
Three Colt St
Five Elms Rd, Brom. 204 EH104
Five Elms Rd, Dag. 126 EZ62
Five Flds Cl, Wat. 94 BZ48
Five Oaks, Add. 211 BF107
Five Oaks La, Chig. 104 EY51
Five Points, Iver 133 BC69
Five Ways Cor NW4 97 CV53
Five Wents, Swan. 207 FG96
Fiveacre Cl, Th.Hth. 201 DN100
Fiveash Rd, Grav. 191 GF87
Fives Ct SE11 278 F8
Fiveways Rd SW9 161 DP82
Fladbury Rd N15 122 DR58
Fladgate Rd E11 124 EE58
Flag Cl, Croy. 203 DX102
Flag Wk, Pnr. 115 BU58
Eastcote Rd
Flags, The, Hem.H. 41 BP20
Flagstaff Cl, Wal.Abb. 67 EB33
Flagstaff Rd, Wal.Abb. 67 EB33
Flambard Rd, Har. 117 CG58
Flamborough Cl (Biggin Hill), West. 238 EH119
Flamborough Rd, Ruis. 115 BU62
Flamborough Spur, Slou. 151 AN75
Flamborough St E14 143 DY72
Flamborough Wk E14 143 DY72
Flamborough St
Flamingo Gdns, Nthlt. 136 BY69
Jetstar Way
Flamingo Wk, Horn. 147 FG65
Flamstead End Rd (Cheshunt), Wal.Cr. 66 DV28
Flamstead Gdns, Dag. 146 EW66
Flamstead Rd
Flamstead Rd, Dag. 146 EW66
Flamsted Av, Wem. 138 CN65
Flamsteed Rd SE7 164 EL78
Flanchford Rd W12 159 CT76
Flanchford Rd, Reig. 249 CX134
Flanders Ct, Egh. 173 BC92
Flanders Cres SW17 180 DF94
Flanders Rd E6 145 EM68
Flanders Rd W4 158 CS77
Flanders Way E9 143 DX65
Flank St E1 142 DU73
Dock St
Flash La, Enf. 81 DP37
Flask Cotts NW3 120 DD63
New End Sq
Flask Wk NW3 120 DD63
Flat Iron Sq SE1 142 DQ74
Union St
Flatfield Rd, Hem.H. 40 BN22
Flaunden Bottom, Chesh. 72 AY36
Flaunden Bottom (Flaunden), Hem.H. 72 AY35
Flaunden Hill (Flaunden), Hem.H. 57 AZ33
Flaunden La (Bovingdon), Hem.H. 57 BB32
Flaunden La, Rick. 57 BD33
Flaunden Pk (Flaunden), Hem.H. 57 BA32
Flavell Ms SE10 164 EE78
Flavian Cl, St.Alb. 42 BZ22
Flaxen Cl E4 101 EB48
Flaxen Rd
Flaxen Rd E4 101 EB48
Flaxley Rd, Mord. 200 DB100
Flaxman Ct W1 273 M9
Flaxman Rd SE5 161 DP82
Flaxman Ter WC1 273 N3
Flaxman Ter WC1 141 DK69
Flaxton Rd SE18 165 ER81
Flecker Cl, Stan. 95 CF50
Fleece Dr N9 100 DU49
Fleece Rd, Surb. 197 CJ102
Fleece Wk N7 141 DL65
Manger Rd
Fleeming Cl E17 101 DZ54
Pennant Ter
Fleeming Rd E17 101 DZ54
Fleet Av, Dart. 188 FQ88
Fleet Av, Upmin. 129 FR58
Fleet Cl, Ruis. 115 BQ58
Fleet Cl, Upmin. 129 FR58
Fleet Cl, W.Mol. 196 BZ99
Fleet La, W.Mol. 196 BZ100
Fleet Pl EC4 141 DN72
Farringdon St
Fleet Rd NW3 120 DE64
Fleet Rd, Dart. 188 FQ88
Fleet Rd (Northfleet), Grav. 190 GC90
Fleet Sq WC1 274 B3
Fleet St EC4 274 D9
Fleet St EC4 141 DN72
Fleet St Hill E1 142 DU70
Weaver St
Fleetdale Par, Dart. 188 FQ88
Fleet Av
Fleetside, W.Mol. 196 BZ100
Fleetway, Egh. 193 BC97
Fleetway Business Pk, Grnf. 137 CH68
Fleetwood Cl E16 144 EK71
Fleetwood Cl, Ch.St.G. 90 AU49
Fleetwood Cl, Chess. 215 CK108
Fleetwood Cl, Croy. 202 DS104
Fleetwood Cl, Tad. 233 CW120
Fleetwood Ct E6 145 EM71
Evelyn Denington Rd
Fleetwood Ct, W.Byf. 212 BG113
Fleetwood Gro W3 138 CS73
East Acton La
Fleetwood Rd NW10 119 CU64
Fleetwood Rd, Kings.T. 198 CP97
Fleetwood Rd, Slou. 132 AT74
Fleetwood Sq, Kings.T. 198 CP97
Fleetwood St N16 122 DS61
Stoke Newington Ch St
Fleetwood Way, Wat. 94 BW49
Fleming Cl W9 140 DA70
Chippenham Rd
Fleming Cl (Cheshunt), Wal.Cr. 66 DU26
Fleming Ct W2 140 DD71
St. Marys Ter
Fleming Ct, Croy. 219 DN106
Fleming Cres, Hert. 31 DN09
Windsor Dr
Fleming Dr N21 81 DM43
Fleming Gdns, Rom. 106 FK54
Bartholomew Dr
Fleming Gdns, Til. 171 GJ81
Fielding Av
Fleming Mead, Mitch. 180 DE94
Fleming Rd SE17 161 DP79
Fleming Rd, Grays 169 FW77
Fleming Rd, Sthl. 136 CB72
Fleming Wk NW9 96 CS54
Pasteur Cl
Fleming Way SE28 146 EX73
Fleming Way, Islw. 157 CF83
Flemings, Brwd. 107 FW51
Flemish Flds, Cher. 194 BG101
Flemming Av, Ruis. 115 BV60
Flempton Rd E10 123 DY60
Fletcher Cl E6 145 EP72
Trader Rd
Fletcher Cl (Ottershaw), Cher. 211 BE107
Fletcher La E10 123 EC59
Fletcher Path SE8 163 EA80
New Butt La
Fletcher Rd W4 158 CQ76
Fletcher Rd (Ottershaw), Cher. 211 BD107
Fletcher Rd, Chig. 103 ET50
Fletcher St E1 142 DU73
Fletcher Way, Hem.H. 40 BJ18
Fletchers Cl, Brom. 204 EH98
Fletching Rd E5 122 DW62
Fletching Rd SE7 164 EJ79
Fletton Rd N11 99 DL52
Fleur de Lis St E1 275 N5
Fleur de Lis St E1 142 DS70
Fleur Gates SW19 179 CX87
Princes Way
Flex Meadow, Harl. 50 EL16
Flexley Wd, Welw.G.C. 29 CZ06
Flexmere Gdns N17 100 DR53
Flexmere Rd
Flexmere Rd N17 100 DR53
Flight App NW9 97 CT54
Flimwell Cl, Brom. 184 EE92
Flinders Cl, St.Alb. 43 CG22
Flint Cl, Bans. 218 DB114
Flint Cl (Bookham), Lthd. 246 CC126
Flint Cl, Red. 250 DF133
Flint Down Cl, Orp. 206 EU95
Flint Hill, Dor. 263 CH138
Flint Hill Cl, Dor. 263 CH139
Flint St SE17 279 L9
Flint St SE17 162 DR77
Flint St, Grays 169 FV79
Flint Way, St.Alb. 42 CC15
Flintlock Cl, Stai. 154 BG84
Flintmill Cres SE3 164 EL82
Flinton St SE17 279 N10
Flinton St SE17 162 DS78
Flitcroft St WC2 273 N8
Floats, The (Riverhead), Sev. 256 FE121
Flock Mill Pl SW18 180 DB88
Flockton St SE16 162 DU75
George Row
Flodden Rd SE5 162 DQ81
Flood La, Twick. 177 CG88
Church La
Flood Pas SE18 165 EM77
Samuel St
Flood St SW3 160 DE78
Flood Wk SW3 160 DE79
Flora Cl E14 143 EB72
Flora Gdns W6 159 CV77
Ravenscourt Rd
Flora Gdns, Croy. 221 EC111
Flora Gdns, Rom. 126 EW58
Flora Gro, St.Alb. 43 CF21
Flora St, Belv. 166 EZ78
Victoria St
Floral Ct, Ash. 231 CJ118
Rosedale
Floral Dr (London Colney), St.Alb. 61 CK26
Floral St WC2 273 P10
Floral St WC2 141 DL73
Florence Av (New Haw), Add. 212 BG111
Florence Av, Enf. 82 DQ41
Florence Av, Mord. 200 DC99
Florence Cantwell Wk N19 121 DL59
Hillrise Rd
Florence Cl, Grays 170 FY79
Florence Cl, Harl. 52 EW17
Florence Cl, Horn. 128 FL61
Florence Cl, Walt. 195 BV101
Florence Rd
Florence Cl, Wat. 75 BU35
Florence Dr, Enf. 82 DQ41
Florence Elson Cl E12 125 EN63
Grantham Rd
Florence Gdns W4 158 CQ79
Florence Gdns, Rom. 126 EW59
Roxy Av
Florence Gdns, Stai. 174 BH94

Florence Nightingale Ho N1 *Clephane Rd*	142	DR65
Florence Rd E6	144	EJ67
Florence Rd E13	144	EF68
Florence Rd N4	121	DN60
Florence Rd SE2	166	EW76
Florence Rd SE14	163	DZ81
Florence Rd SW19	180	DB93
Florence Rd W4	158	CR76
Florence Rd W5	138	CL73
Florence Rd, Beck.	203	DX96
Florence Rd, Brom.	204	EG95
Florence Rd, Felt.	175	BV88
Florence Rd, Kings.T.	178	CM94
Florence Rd, S.Croy.	220	DR109
Florence Rd, Sthl.	156	BX77
Florence Rd, Walt.	195	BV101
Florence St E16	144	EF70
Florence St N1	141	DP66
Florence St NW4	119	CW56
Florence Ter SE14	163	DZ81
Florence Way SW12	180	DF88
Florence Way, Uxb. *Wyvern Way*	134	BJ67
Florfield Pas E8 *Reading La*	142	DV65
Florfield Rd E8 *Reading La*	142	DV65
Florian Av, Sutt.	218	DD105
Florian Rd SW15	159	CY84
Florida Cl, Bushey	95	CD47
Florida Rd (Shalford), Guil.	258	AY140
Florida Rd, Th.Hth.	201	DP95
Florida St E2	142	DU69
Floris Pl SW4 *Fitzwilliam Rd*	161	DJ83
Floriston Av, Uxb.	135	BQ66
Floriston Cl, Stan.	95	CH53
Floriston Ct, Nthlt.	116	CB64
Floriston Gdns, Stan.	95	CH53
Floss St SW15	159	CW82
Flower & Dean Wk E1 *Thrawl St*	142	DT71
Flower Cres (Ottershaw), Cher.	211	BB107
Flower La NW7	97	CT50
Flower La, Gdse.	253	DY128
Flower Ms NW11 *Russell Gdns*	119	CY58
Flower Pot Cl N15 *St. Ann's Rd*	122	DT58
Flower Wk, Guil.	258	AW137
Flower Wk, The SW7	160	DC75
Flowerfield (Otford), Sev.	241	FF117
Flowerhill Way (Istead Ri), Grav.	190	GE94
Flowers Ms N19 *Archway Rd*	121	DJ61
Flowersmead SW17	180	DG89
Floyd Rd SE7	164	EJ78
Floyds La, Wok.	228	BG116
Fludyer St SE13	164	EE84
Flux's La, Epp.	70	EU33
Flyer's Way, The, West.	255	ER126
Fogerty Cl, Enf. *Government Row*	83	EA37
Fold Cft, Harl.	35	EN14
Foley Cl, Beac.	88	AJ51
Foley Ms (Claygate), Esher	215	CE108
Foley Rd (Claygate), Esher	215	CE108
Foley Rd (Biggin Hill), West.	238	EK118
Foley St W1	**273**	**K7**
Foley St W1	141	DJ71
Folgate St E1	**275**	**N6**
Folgate St E1	142	DS71
Foliot St W12	139	CT72
Folkes La, Upmin.	129	FT57
Folkestone Ct, Slou.	153	BA78
Folkestone Rd E6	145	EN68
Folkestone Rd E17	123	EB56
Folkestone Rd N18	100	DU49
Folkingham La NW9	96	CR53
Folkington Cor N12	97	CZ50
Follet Dr, Abb.L.	59	BT31
Follett Cl (Old Windsor), Wind.	172	AV86
Follett St E14	143	EC72
Folly, The, Hert.	32	DR09
Folly Av, St.Alb.	42	CC19
Folly Cl, Rad.	77	CF36
Folly La E4	101	DZ52
Folly La E17	101	DY53
Folly La (Holmwood), Dor.	263	CH144
Folly La, St.Alb.	42	CC19
Folly Ms W11 *Portobello Rd*	139	CZ72
Folly Pathway, Rad.	77	CF35
Folly Vw, Ware	33	EB10
Folly Wall E14	163	EC75
Follyfield Rd, Bans.	218	DA114
Font Hills N2	98	DC54
Fontaine Rd SW16	181	DM94
Fontarabia Rd SW11	160	DG84
Fontayne Av, Chig.	103	EQ49
Fontayne Av, Rain.	147	FE66
Fontayne Av, Rom.	105	FE54
Fontenoy Rd SW12	181	DH89
Fonteyne Gdns, Wdf.Grn. *Lechmere Av*	102	EK54
Fonthill Cl SE20 *Selby Rd*	202	DU96
Fonthill Ms N4 *Lennox Rd*	121	DN61
Fonthill Rd N4	121	DM60
Fontigarry Fm Business Pk, Reig.	266	DC143
Fontley Way SW15	179	CU87
Fontmell Cl, Ashf.	174	BN92
Fontmell Cl, St.Alb.	43	CE18
Fontmell Pk, Ashf.	174	BM92
Fontwell Cl, Har.	95	CE52
Fontwell Cl, Nthlt.	136	CA65
Fontwell Dr, Brom.	205	EN99
Fontwell Pk Gdns, Horn.	128	FL63
Foord Cl, Dart.	189	FS89
Football La, Har.	117	CE60
Footbury Hill Rd, Orp.	206	EU101
Footpath, The SW15	179	CU85
Foots Cray High St, Sid.	186	EW93
Foots Cray La, Sid.	186	EW88
Footscray Rd SE9	185	EN86
Footway, The SE9	185	EQ87
Forbench Cl (Ripley), Wok.	228	BH122
Forbes Av, Pot.B.	64	DD33
Forbes Cl NW2	119	CU62
Forbes Cl, Horn. *St. Leonards Way*	127	FH60
Forbes Ct SE19	182	DS92
Forbe's Ride, Wind.	150	AG84
Forbes St E1 *Ellen St*	142	DU72
Forbes Way, Ruis.	115	BV61
Forburg Rd N16	122	DU60
Force Grn La, West.	239	ER124
Ford Cl E3 *Roman Rd*	143	DY68
Ford Cl, Ashf.	174	BL93
Ford Cl, Bushey	76	CC42
Ford Cl, Har.	117	CD59
Ford Cl, Rain.	147	FF66
Ford Cl, Shep.	194	BN98
Ford Cl, Th.Hth.	201	DP100
Ford End (Denham), Uxb.	113	BF61
Ford End, Wdf.Grn.	102	EH51
Ford La, Iver	134	BG72
Ford La, Rain.	147	FF66
Ford Rd E3	143	DY67
Ford Rd, Ashf.	174	BM91
Ford Rd, Cher.	194	BH102
Ford Rd, Dag.	146	EZ66
Ford Rd (Northfleet), Grav.	190	GB85
Ford Rd (Old Woking), Wok.	227	BB120
Ford Sq E1	142	DV71
Ford St E3	143	DY67
Ford St E16	144	EF72
Fordbridge Cl, Cher.	194	BH102
Fordbridge Rd, Ashf.	174	BL93
Fordbridge Rd, Shep.	195	BS100
Fordbridge Rd, Sun.	195	BS100
Fordcroft Rd, Orp.	206	EV99
Forde Av, Brom.	204	EJ97
Fordel Rd SE6	183	ED88
Fordham Cl, Barn.	80	DE41
Fordham Cl, Horn.	128	FN59
Fordham Rd, Barn.	80	DD41
Fordham St E1	142	DU72
Fordhook Av W5	138	CM73
Fordingley Rd W9	139	CZ69
Fordington Rd N6	120	DF57
Fordmill Rd SE6	183	EA89
Fords Gro N21	100	DQ46
Fords Pk Rd E16	144	EG72
Fordwater Rd, Cher.	194	BH102
Fordwater Trd Est, Cher.	194	BJ102
Fordwich Cl, Hert.	31	DN09
Fordwich Cl, Orp.	205	ET101
Fordwich Hill, Hert.	31	DN09
Fordwich Ri, Hert.	31	DN09
Fordwich Rd, Welw.G.C.	29	CW10
Fordwych Rd NW2	119	CY64
Fordyce Cl, Horn.	128	FM59
Fordyce Ho SW16 *Colson Way*	181	DJ91
Fordyce Rd SE13	183	EC86
Fordyke Rd, Dag.	126	EZ61
Fore St EC2	**275**	**J7**
Fore St EC2	142	DQ71
Fore St N9	100	DU50
Fore St N18	100	DT51
Fore St, Harl.	36	EW11
Fore St, Hat.	45	CW17
Fore St, Hert.	32	DR09
Fore St, Pnr.	115	BU57
Fore St Av EC2	**275**	**K7**
Forebury, The, Saw.	36	EY05
Forebury Av, Saw.	36	EZ05
Forebury Cres, Saw.	36	EZ05
Forefield, St.Alb.	60	CA27
Foreland Ct NW4	97	CY53
Foreland St SE18 *Plumstead Rd*	165	ER77
Forelands Way, Chesh.	54	AQ32
Foreman Ct W6 *Hammersmith Bdy*	159	CW77
Foremark Cl, Ilf.	103	ET50
Foreshore SE8	163	DZ77
Forest, The E11	124	EE56
Forest App E4	102	EE45
Forest App, Wdf.Grn.	102	EF52
Forest Av E4	102	EE45
Forest Av, Chig.	103	EN50
Forest Av, Hem.H.	40	BK22
Forest Business Pk E17	123	DX59
Forest Cl E11	124	EF57
Forest Cl, Chis.	205	EN95
Forest Cl (East Horsley), Lthd.	245	BT125
Forest Cl, Wal.Abb.	84	EH37
Forest Cl, Wok.	227	BD115
Forest Cl, Wdf.Grn.	102	EH48
Forest Ct E4	102	EF46
Forest Ct E11	124	EE56
Forest Cres, Ash.	232	CN116
Forest Cft SE23	182	DV89
Forest Dr E12	124	EK62
Forest Dr, Epp.	85	ES36
Forest Dr, Kes.	222	EL105
Forest Dr, Sun.	175	BT94
Forest Dr (Kingswood), Tad.	233	CZ121
Forest Dr, Wdf.Grn.	101	ED52
Forest Dr E E11	123	ED59
Forest Dr W E11	123	EC59
Forest Edge, Buck.H.	102	EJ49
Forest Gdns N17	100	DT54
Forest Gate NW9	118	CS57
Forest Glade E4	102	EE49
Forest Glade E11	124	EE58
Forest Glade, Epp.	70	EY27
Forest Grn Rd, Maid.	150	AD82
Forest Grn Rd, Wind.	150	AE82
Forest Gro E8	142	DT66
Forest Hts, Buck.H.	102	EG47
Forest Hill Business Cen SE23	182	DW89
Forest Hill Ind Est SE23 *Perry Vale*	182	DW89
Forest Hill Rd SE22	182	DV85
Forest Hill Rd SE23	182	DV85
Forest Ind Pk, Ilf.	103	ES53
Forest La E7	124	EE64
Forest La E15	124	EE64
Forest La, Chig.	103	EN50
Forest La (East Horsley), Lthd.	229	BT124
Forest Mt Rd, Wdf.Grn.	101	ED52
Forest Ridge, Beck.	203	EA97
Forest Ridge, Kes.	222	EL105
Forest Ri E17	123	ED57
Forest Rd E7	124	EG63
Forest Rd E8	142	DT65
Forest Rd E11	123	ED59
Forest Rd E17	122	DW56
Forest Rd N9	100	DV46
Forest Rd N17	122	DW56
Forest Rd, Enf.	83	DY36
Forest Rd, Erith	167	FG81
Forest Rd, Felt.	176	BW89
Forest Rd, Ilf.	103	ES53
Forest Rd (East Horsley), Lthd.	229	BU123
Forest Rd, Loug.	84	EK41
Forest Rd, Rich.	158	CN80
Forest Rd, Rom.	127	FB55
Forest Rd, Sutt.	200	DA102
Forest Rd (Cheshunt), Wal.Cr.	67	DX29
Forest Rd, Wat.	59	BV33
Forest Rd, Wind.	151	AK82
Forest Rd, Wok.	227	BD115
Forest Rd, Wdf.Grn.	123	EB55
Forest Side E4	102	EF45
Forest Side E7 *Capel Rd*	124	EH63
Forest Side, Buck.H.	102	EJ46
Forest Side, Epp.	69	ER33
Forest Side, Wal.Abb.	84	EJ36
Forest Side, Wor.Pk.	199	CT102
Forest St E7	124	EG64
Forest Vw E4	101	ED45
Forest Vw E11 *High Rd Leytonstone*	124	EF59
Forest Vw Av E10	123	ED57
Forest Vw Rd E12	124	EL63
Forest Vw Rd E17	101	EC53
Forest Vw Rd, Loug.	84	EK42
Forest Wk, Bushey *Millbrook Rd*	76	BZ39
Forest Way N19 *Hargrave Pk*	121	DJ61
Forest Way, Ash.	232	CM117
Forest Way, Loug.	84	EK35
Forest Way, Orp.	205	ET99
Forest Way, Sid.	185	ER87
Forest Way, Wal.Abb.	84	EK35
Forest Way, Wdf.Grn.	102	EH49
Forestdale N14	99	DK49
Forester Rd SE15	162	DV84
Foresters Cl, Wall.	219	DK108
Foresters Cl, Wal.Cr.	66	DS27
Foresters Cl, Wok.	226	AT118
Foresters Cres, Bexh.	167	FB84
Foresters Dr E17	123	ED56
Foresters Dr, Wall.	219	DK108
Forestholme Cl SE23	182	DW89
Forfar Rd N22	99	DP53
Forfar Rd SW11	160	DG81
Forge Av, Couls.	235	DN120
Forge Br La, Couls.	235	DH121
Forge Cl, Brom.	204	EG102
Forge Cl, Hayes *High St*	155	BR79
Forge Cl, Kings L.	58	BG31
Forge Cotts W5 *Ealing Grn*	137	CK74
Forge Dr (Claygate), Esher	215	CG108
Forge Dr (Farnham Common), Slou.	131	AQ65
Forge End, Amer.	55	AP40
Forge End, St.Alb.	60	CA26
Forge End, Wok.	226	AY117
Forge La (Horton Kirby), Dart.	208	FQ98
Forge La, Felt.	176	BY92
Forge La, Grav.	191	GM89
Forge La, Nthwd.	93	BS52
Forge La, Sun.	195	BU97
Forge La, Sutt.	217	CY108
Forge Ms, Sun. *Forge La*	195	BU97
Forge Pl NW1 *Malden Cres*	140	DG65
Forge Way (Shoreham), Sev.	225	FF111
Forgefield (Biggin Hill), West. *Main Rd*	238	EK116
Forlong Path, Nthlt. *Arnold Rd*	136	BY65
Forman Pl N16 *Farleigh Rd*	122	DT63
Formby Av, Stan.	117	CJ55
Formby Cl, Slou.	153	BC77
Formosa St W9	140	DB70
Formunt Cl E16 *Vincent St*	144	EF71
Forres Cl, Hodd.	49	EA15
Forres Gdns NW11	120	DA58
Forrest Gdns SW16	201	DM97
Forrester Path SE26	183	DX91
Forresters Dr, Welw.G.C.	30	DC10
Forris Av, Hayes	135	BT74
Forset St W1	**272**	**C8**
Forset St W1	140	DE72
Forstal Cl, Brom. *Ridley Rd*	204	EG97
Forster Cl E17	101	ED52
Forster Rd E17	123	DY58
Forster Rd N17	122	DT55
Forster Rd SW2	181	DL87
Forster Rd, Beck.	203	DY97
Forster Rd, Croy. *Windmill Rd*	202	DQ101
Forsters Cl, Rom.	126	EZ58
Forster's Way SW18	180	DB88
Forsters Way, Hayes	135	BV72
Forston St N1 *Cropley St*	142	DR68
Forsyte Cres SE19	202	DS95
Forsyth Gdns SE17	161	DP79
Forsyth Path, Wok.	211	BD113
Forsyth Pl, Enf.	82	DS43
Forsyth Rd, Wok.	211	BC114
Forsythia Cl, Ilf.	125	EP64
Forsythia Gdns, Slou.	152	AY76
Forsythia Pl, Guil. *Larch Av*	242	AW132
Fort La, Reig.	250	DB130
Fort Rd SE1	162	DT77
Fort Rd, Guil.	258	AY137
Fort Rd, Nthlt.	136	CA66
Fort Rd (Halstead), Sev.	241	FC115
Fort Rd, Tad.	248	CP131
Fort Rd, Til.	171	GH84
Fort St E1	**275**	**N7**
Fort St E16	144	EH74
Forterie Gdns, Ilf.	126	EU62
Fortescue Av E8 *Mentmore Ter*	142	DV66
Fortescue Av, Twick.	176	CC90
Fortescue Rd SW19	180	DD94
Fortescue Rd, Edg.	96	CR53
Fortescue Rd, Wey.	212	BM105
Fortess Gro NW5 *Fortess Rd*	121	DH64
Fortess Rd NW5	121	DH64
Fortess Wk NW5 *Fortess Rd*	121	DH64
Forth Rd, Upmin.	129	FR58
Forthbridge Rd SW11	160	DG84
Fortin Cl, S.Ock.	149	FU73
Fortin Path, S.Ock.	149	FU73
Fortin Way, S.Ock.	149	FU73
Fortis Cl E16	144	EJ72
Fortis Grn N2	120	DE56
Fortis Grn N10	120	DE56
Fortis Grn Av N2	120	DF55
Fortis Grn Rd N10	120	DG55
Fortismere Av N10	120	DG55
Fortnam Rd N19	121	DK61
Fortnums Acre, Stan.	95	CF51
Fortress Distribution Pk, Til.	171	GG84
Fortrose Gdns SW2 *New Pk Rd*	181	DK88
Fortrye Cl (Northfleet), Grav.	190	GE89
Fortuna Cl N7 *Vulcan Way*	141	DM65
Fortune Gate Rd NW10	138	CS67
Fortune Grn Rd NW6	120	DA63
Fortune La, Borwd.	77	CK44
Fortune St EC1	**275**	**J5**
Fortune St EC1	142	DQ70
Fortune Wk SE28 *Broadwater Rd*	165	ER76
Fortune Way NW10	139	CU69
Fortunes, The, Harl.	51	ET17
Fortunes Mead, Nthlt.	136	BY65
Forty Acre La E16	144	EG71
Forty Av, Wem.	118	CM62
Forty Cl, Wem.	118	CM61
Forty Footpath SW14	158	CQ83
Forty Grn Rd (Knotty Grn), Beac.	88	AH51
Forty Hill, Enf.	82	DT38
Forty La, Wem.	118	CP61
Fortyfoot Rd, Lthd.	231	CJ121
Forum, The, W.Mol.	196	CB98
Forum Magnum Sq SE1	**278**	**B4**
Forum Pl, Hat.	45	CU17
Forum Way, Edg. *High St*	96	CN51
Forumside, Edg. *High St*	96	CN51
Forval Cl, Mitch.	200	DF99
Forward Dr, Har.	117	CF56
Fosbury Ms W2 *Inverness Ter*	140	DB73
Foscote Ms W9 *Amberley Rd*	140	DA71
Foscote Rd NW4	119	CV58
Foskett Rd SW6	159	CZ82
Foss Av, Croy.	219	DN106
Foss Rd SW17	180	DD91
Fossdene Rd SE7	164	EH78
Fossdyke Cl, Hayes	136	BY71
Fosse Way W13	137	CG71
Fosse Way, W.Byf. *Brantwood Dr*	211	BF113
Fossil Rd SE13	163	EA83
Fossington Rd, Belv.	166	EX77
Fossway, Dag.	126	EW61
Foster Av, Wind.	151	AL83
Foster Cl (Cheshunt), Wal.Cr.	67	DX30
Foster La EC2	**275**	**H8**
Foster La EC2	142	DQ72
Foster Rd E13	144	EG70
Foster Rd W3	138	CS73
Foster Rd W4	158	CR78
Foster Rd, Hem.H.	40	BG22
Foster St NW4	119	CW56
Foster St, Harl.	52	EY17
Foster Wk NW4 *New Brent St*	119	CW56
Fosterdown, Gdse.	252	DV129
Fosters Cl E18	102	EH53
Fosters Cl, Chis.	185	EM92
Fosters Path, Slou. *Vermont Rd*	131	AM70
Fothergill Cl E13	144	EG68
Fothergill Dr N21	81	DM43
Fotheringay Gdns, Slou.	131	AN73
Fotheringham Rd, Enf.	82	DT42
Fotherley Rd, Rick.	91	BF47
Foubert's Pl W1	**273**	**K9**
Foubert's Pl W1	141	DJ72
Foulden Rd N16	122	DT63
Foulden Ter N16 *Foulden Rd*	122	DT63
Foulis Ter SW7	**276**	**A10**
Foulis Ter SW7	160	DD78
Foulser Rd SW17	180	DF90
Foulsham Rd, Th.Hth.	202	DQ97
Founder Cl E6 *Trader Rd*	145	EP72
Founders Ct EC2	**275**	**K8**
Founders Dr (Denham), Uxb.	113	BF58
Founders Gdns SE19	182	DQ94
Founders Rd, Hodd.	33	EB14
Foundry Cl SE16	143	DY74
Foundry La (Horton), Slou.	153	BB83
Foundry Ms NW1	**273**	**L4**
Fount St SW8	161	DK80
Fountain Cl, Uxb. *New Rd*	135	BQ71
Fountain Ct EC4	**274**	**D10**
Fountain Dr SE19	182	DT91
Fountain Dr, Cars.	218	DF109
Fountain Dr, Hert. *Merchant Dr*	32	DT08
Fountain Fm, Harl.	51	ET17
Fountain Gdns, Wind.	151	AR83
Fountain Grn Sq SE16 *Bermondsey Wall E*	162	DU75
Fountain La, Sev.	257	FP122
Fountain Ms N5 *Kelross Rd*	122	DQ63
Fountain Pl SW9	161	DN81
Fountain Pl, Wal.Abb.	67	EC34
Fountain Rd SW17	180	DD92
Fountain Rd, Red.	266	DE136
Fountain Rd, Th.Hth.	202	DQ96
Fountain Sq SW1	**277**	**H8**
Fountain Sq SW1	161	DH77
Fountain St E2 *Columbia Rd*	142	DT69
Fountain Wk (Northfleet), Grav.	190	GE86
Fountains, The, Loug. *Fallow Flds*	102	EK45
Fountains Av, Felt.	176	BZ90
Fountains Cl, Felt.	176	BZ89
Fountains Cres N14	99	DL45
Fountayne Rd N15	122	DU56
Fountayne Rd N16	122	DU61
Four Acres, Cob.	214	BY113
Four Acres, Guil.	243	BC132
Four Acres, Welw.G.C.	29	CZ11
Four Acres, The, Saw.	36	EZ06
Four Acres Wk, Hem.H.	40	BM22
Four Seasons Cl E3	143	EA68
Four Trees, St.Alb. *North Cl*	42	CB24
Four Tubs, The, Bushey	95	CD45
Four Wents, Cob.	213	BV113
Four Wents, The E4 *Kings Rd*	101	ED47
Fouracres SW12 *Little Dimocks*	181	DH89
Fouracres, Enf.	83	DY39
Fouracres Dr, Hem.H.	40	BM22
Fourland Wk, Edg.	96	CQ51
Fournier St E1	**275**	**P6**
Fournier St E1	142	DT71
Fourth Av E12	125	EM63
Fourth Av W10	139	CY70
Fourth Av, Grays	169	FU79
Fourth Av, Harl.	51	EM15
Fourth Av, Hayes	135	BT74
Fourth Av, Rom.	127	FD60
Fourth Av, Wat.	76	BX35
Fourth Cross Rd, Twick.	177	CD89
Fourth Dr, Couls.	235	DK116
Fourth Way, Wem.	118	CQ63
Fourways, St.Alb. *Hatfield Rd*	44	CM20
Fowey Av, Ilf.	124	EK57
Fowey Cl E1 *Kennet St*	142	DV74
Fowler Cl SW11	160	DD83
Fowler Rd E7	124	EG63
Fowler Rd N1 *Halton Rd*	141	DP66
Fowler Rd, Ilf.	104	EV51
Fowler Rd, Mitch.	200	DG96
Fowlers Cl, Sid. *Thursland Rd*	186	EY92
Fowlers Mead (Chobham), Wok. *Windsor Rd*	210	AS109
Fowlers Wk W5	137	CK70
Fowley Cl, Wal.Cr.	67	DZ34
Fowley Mead Pk, Wal.Cr.	67	EA34
Fownes St SW11	160	DE83
Fox & Knot St EC1	**274**	**G6**
Fox Cl E1	142	DW70
Fox Cl E16	144	EG71
Fox Cl, Borwd. *Rodgers Cl*	77	CK44
Fox Cl, Bushey	76	CB42
Fox Cl, Orp.	224	EU106
Fox Cl, Rom.	105	FB50
Fox Cl, Wey.	213	BR106
Fox Cl, Wok.	227	BD115
Fox Covert (Fetcham), Lthd.	231	CD124
Fox Gro, Walt.	195	BV101
Fox Hill SE19	182	DT94
Fox Hill, Kes.	222	EJ106
Fox Hill Gdns SE19	182	DT94
Fox Hollow Cl SE18	165	ES78
Fox Hollow Dr, Bexh.	166	EX83
Fox Ho Rd, Belv.	167	FB77
Fox La N13	99	DM48
Fox La W5	138	CL70
Fox La, Cat.	235	DP121
Fox La, Kes.	222	EH106
Fox La (Bookham), Lthd.	230	BY124
Fox La, Reig.	250	DB131
Fox La N, Cher.	193	BF102
Fox La S, Cher. *Guildford St*	193	BF102
Fox Manor Way, Grays	169	FV79
Fox Rd E16	144	EF71
Fox Rd, Slou.	152	AX77
Foxacre, Cat. *Town End Cl*	236	DS122
Foxberry Rd SE4	163	DY83
Foxberry Wk (Northfleet), Grav. *Rowmarsh Cl*	190	GD91
Foxborough Cl, Slou.	153	AZ78
Foxborough Gdns SE4	183	EA85
Foxbourne Rd SW17	180	DG89
Foxburrow Rd, Chig.	104	EX50
Foxburrows Av, Guil.	242	AT134
Foxbury Av, Chis.	185	ER93
Foxbury Cl, Brom.	184	EH93
Foxbury Cl, Orp. *Foxbury Dr*	224	EU106
Foxbury Dr, Orp.	224	EU107
Foxbury Rd, Brom.	184	EG93
Foxcombe (New Addington), Croy.	221	EB107
Foxcombe Cl E6 *Boleyn Rd*	144	EK68
Foxcombe Rd SW15 *Alton Rd*	179	CU88
Foxcote SE5	162	DS78
Foxcroft, St.Alb.	43	CG22
Foxcroft Rd SE18	165	EP81
Foxdell, Nthwd.	93	BR51
Foxdell Way (Chalfont St. Peter), Ger.Cr.	90	AY50
Foxdells, Hert.	31	DJ12
Foxearth Cl (Biggin Hill), West.	238	EL118
Foxearth Rd, S.Croy.	220	DW110
Foxearth Spur, S.Croy.	220	DW109
Foxenden Rd, Guil.	258	AY135
Foxes Cl, Hert.	32	DV09
Foxes Dale SE3	164	EG83
Foxes Dale, Brom.	203	ED97
Foxes Dr, Wal.Cr.	66	DU29
Foxes Grn, Grays	171	GG75
Foxes La, Hat.	45	CY23
Foxes La (Cuffley), Pot.B.	65	DL28
Foxes Path (Sutton Grn), Guil.	243	AZ126
Foxfield Cl, Nthwd.	93	BT51
Foxfield Rd, Orp.	205	ER103
Foxglove Cl, Hat.	45	CV19
Foxglove Cl, Hodd. *Castle Cl*	33	EC14
Foxglove Cl, Sthl.	136	BY73
Foxglove Cl (Stanwell), Stai.	174	BK88
Foxglove Gdns E11	124	EJ56
Foxglove Gdns, Guil.	243	BC132
Foxglove Gdns, Pur.	219	DL111
Foxglove La, Chess.	216	CN105
Foxglove Rd, Rom.	127	FE61
Foxglove Rd, S.Ock.	149	FW71
Foxglove St W12	139	CT73
Foxglove Way, Wall.	201	DH102
Foxgloves, The, Hem.H.	39	BE21
Foxgrove N14	99	DL48
Foxgrove Av, Beck.	183	EB94
Foxgrove Dr, Wok.	227	BA115
Foxgrove Path, Wat.	94	BX50
Foxgrove Rd, Beck.	183	EB94
Foxhall Rd, Upmin.	128	FQ64
Foxham Rd N19	121	DK62
Foxhanger Gdns, Wok. *Oriental Rd*	227	BA116
Foxherne, Slou.	152	AW75
Foxhill, Wat.	75	BU36
Foxhills, Wok.	226	AW117
Foxhills Cl (Ottershaw), Cher.	211	BB107
Foxhills Rd (Ottershaw), Cher.	211	BA105
Foxhole Rd SE9	184	EL85
Foxholes, Wey.	213	BR106
Foxholes Av, Hert.	32	DT09
Foxholes Business Pk, Hert.	32	DT09
Foxhollow Dr (Farnham Common), Slou.	111	AQ64
Foxhollows, Hat.	45	CV16

Foxholt Gdns NW10 138 CQ66
Foxhome Cl, Chis. 185 EN93
Foxhounds La, Grav. 190 GA90
Foxlake Rd (Byfleet), W.Byf. 212 BM112
Foxlands Cl, Wat. 59 BU34
Foxlands Cres, Dag. 127 FC64
Foxlands La, Dag. 127 FC64
Foxlands Rd, Dag. 127 FC64
Foxlees, Wem. 117 CG63
Foxley Cl E8 122 DU64
Ferncliff Rd
Foxley Cl, Loug. 85 EP40
Foxley Cl, Red. 266 DG139
Foxley Ct, Sutt. 218 DC108
Foxley Gdns, Pur. 219 DP113
Foxley Hill Rd, Pur. 219 DN112
Foxley La, Pur. 219 DK111
Foxley Rd SW9 161 DN80
Foxley Rd, Ken. 219 DP114
Foxley Rd, Th.Hth. 201 DP98
Foxley Sq SW9 161 DP80
Cancell Rd
Foxleys, Wat. 94 BY48
Foxmead Cl, Enf. 81 DM41
Foxmoor Ct (Denham), Uxb. 114 BG58
North Orbital Rd
Foxmore St SW11 160 DF81
Foxon Cl, Cat. 236 DS121
Foxon La, Cat. 236 DR121
Foxon La Gdns, Cat. 236 DS121
Fox's Path, Mitch. 200 DE96
Foxton Gro, Mitch. 200 DD96
Foxton Rd, Grays 169 FX79
Foxton Rd, Hodd. 49 DZ17
Foxwarren (Claygate), Esher 215 CF109
Foxwell Ms SE4 163 DY83
Foxwell St
Foxwell St SE4 163 DY83
Foxwood Chase, Wal.Abb. 83 EC40
Foxwood Cl NW7 96 CS49
Foxwood Cl, Felt. 175 BV90
Foxwood Grn Cl, Enf. 82 DS44
Foxwood Gro (Northfleet), Grav. 190 GE88
Foxwood Gro, Orp. 224 EW110
Foxwood Rd SE3 164 EF84
Foxwood Rd (Bean), Dart. 189 FV90
Foyle Dr, S.Ock. 149 FU71
Foyle Rd N17 100 DU53
Foyle Rd SE3 164 EF79
Frailey Cl, Wok. 227 BB116
Frailey Hill, Wok. 227 BB116
Framewood Rd, Slou. 132 AW66
Framfield Cl N12 98 DA48
Framfield Ct, Enf. 82 DS44
Framfield Rd N5 121 DP64
Framfield Rd W7 137 CE72
Framfield Rd, Mitch. 180 DG94
Framlingham Cl E5 122 DW61
Detmold Rd
Framlingham Cres SE9 184 EL91
Frampton Cl, Sutt. 218 DA108
Frampton Pk Rd E9 142 DW65
Frampton Rd, Epp. 70 EU28
Frampton Rd, Houns. 176 BY85
Frampton Rd, Pot.B. 64 DC30
Frampton St NW8 140 DD70
Frampton St, Hert. 32 DR09
Francemary Rd SE4 183 EA85
Frances Av (Chafford Hundred), Grays 169 FW77
Frances Av, Maid. 130 AC70
Frances Gdns, S.Ock. 149 FT72
Frances Rd E4 101 EA51
Frances Rd, Wind. 151 AR82
Frances St SE18 165 EM77
Frances St, Chesh. 54 AQ30
Franche Ct Rd SW17 180 DC90
Franchise St, Chesh. 54 AQ30
Francis Av, Bexh. 166 FA82
Francis Av, Felt. 175 BU90
Francis Av, Ilf. 125 ER61
Francis Av, St.Alb. 42 CC17
Francis Barber Cl SW16 181 DM91
Well Cl
Francis Chichester Way SW11 160 DG81
Francis Cl E14 163 ED77
Saunders Ness Rd
Francis Cl, Epsom 216 CR105
Francis Cl, Shep. 194 BN98
Francis Gro SW19 179 CZ93
Francis Rd E10 123 EC60
Francis Rd N2 120 DF56
Lynmouth Rd
Francis Rd, Cat. 236 DR122
Francis Rd, Croy. 201 DP101
Francis Rd, Dart. 188 FK85
Francis Rd, Grnf. 137 CJ67
Francis Rd, Har. 117 CG57
Francis Rd, Houns. 156 BX82
Francis Rd, Ilf. 125 ER61
Francis Rd, Orp. 206 EX97
Francis Rd, Pnr. 116 BW57
Francis Rd, Wall. 219 DJ107
Francis Rd, Ware 33 DX05
Francis Rd, Wat. 75 BV42
Francis St E15 124 EE64
Francis St SW1 277 K8
Francis St SW1 161 DJ77
Francis St, Ilf. 125 ER61
Francis Ter N19 121 DJ62
Junction Rd
Francis Wk N1 141 DM67
Bingfield St
Francis Way, Slou. 131 AK73
Franciscan Rd SW17 180 DF92
Francisco Cl (Chafford Hundred), Grays 169 FW76
Francklyn Gdns, Edg. 96 CN48
Francombe Gdns, Rom. 127 FG58
Franconia Rd SW4 181 DJ85
Frank Bailey Wk E12 125 EN64
Gainsborough Av
Frank Burton Cl SE7 164 EH78
Victoria Way
Frank Dixon Cl SE21 182 DS88
Frank Dixon Way SE21 182 DS88
Frank Lunnon Cl, B.End 110 AC60
Frank Martin Ct, Wal.Cr. 66 DU30
Frank St E13 144 EG70
Frank Towell Ct, Felt. 175 BU88
Frankfurt Rd SE24 182 DQ85
Frankham St SE8 163 EA80
Frankland Cl SE16 162 DW77
Frankland Cl, Rick. 92 BN45
Frankland Cl, Wdf.Grn. 102 EJ50
Frankland Rd E4 101 EA50
Frankland Rd SW7 160 DD76
Armstrong Rd
Frankland Rd, Rick. 75 BP44
Franklands Dr, Add. 211 BF108
Franklin Av, Slou. 131 AP71
Franklin Av (Cheshunt), Wal.Cr. 66 DV30
Franklin Cl N20 98 DC45
Franklin Cl SE13 163 EB81
Franklin Cl SE27 181 DP90
Franklin Cl, Hem.H. 40 BL23
Franklin Cl, Kings.T. 198 CN97
Franklin Cl (Colney Heath), St.Alb. 44 CS22
Franklin Cres, Mitch. 201 DJ98
Franklin Ho NW9 119 CT59
Franklin Pas SE9 164 EL83
Franklin Rd SE20 182 DW94
Franklin Rd, Bexh. 166 EY81
Franklin Rd, Grav. 191 GK92
Franklin Rd, Horn. 148 FJ65
Franklin Rd, Wat. 75 BV40
Franklin Sq W14 159 CZ78
Marchbank Rd
Franklin St E3 143 EB69
St. Leonards St
Franklin St N15 122 DS58
Franklin Way, Croy. 201 DL101
Franklins Ms, Har. 116 CC61
Franklin's Row SW3 276 E10
Franklin's Row SW3 160 DF78
Franklyn Ct, Guil. 242 AT134
Humbolt Cl
Franklyn Cres, Wind. 151 AK83
Franklyn Gdns, Ilf. 103 ER51
Franklyn Rd NW10 139 CT66
Franklyn Rd, Walt. 195 BU100
Franks Av, N.Mal. 198 CQ98
Franks La (Horton Kirby), Dart. 208 FN98
Franks Rd, Guil. 242 AU132
Franksfield (Peaslake), Guil. 261 BS144
Frankswood Av, Orp. 205 EP99
Frankswood Av, West Dr. 134 BM72
Franlaw Cres N13 100 DQ49
Franmil Rd, Horn. 127 FG60
Fransfield Gro SE26 182 DV90
Frant Cl SE20 182 DW94
Frant Rd, Th.Hth. 201 DP99
Franthorne Way SE6 183 EB89
Fraser Cl E6 144 EL72
Linton Gdns
Fraser Cl, Bex. 187 FC88
Dartford Rd
Fraser Gdns, Dor. 263 CG135
Fraser Ho, Brent. 158 CM78
Green Dragon La
Fraser Rd E17 123 EB57
Fraser Rd N9 100 DV48
Fraser Rd, Erith 167 FC78
Fraser Rd, Grnf. 137 CH67
Fraser Rd (Cheshunt), Wal.Cr. 67 DY28
Fraser St W4 158 CS78
Frating Cres, Wdf.Grn. 102 EG51
Frays Av, West Dr. 154 BK75
Frays Cl, West Dr. 154 BK76
Frays Lea, Uxb. 134 BJ68
Frays Waye, Uxb. 134 BJ67
Frazer Av, Ruis. 116 BW64
Frazer Cl, Rom. 127 FF59
Frazier St SE1 278 D5
Frazier St SE1 161 DN75
Frean St SE16 162 DU76
Fred Wigg Twr E11 124 EF61
Freda Corbett Cl SE15 162 DU80
Bird in Bush Rd
Frederic Ms SW1 276 E5
Frederic St E17 123 DY57
Frederica Rd E4 101 ED45
Frederica St N7 141 DM66
Caledonian Rd
Frederick Andrews Ct, Grays 170 GD79
Frederick Cl W2 272 D10
Frederick Cl W2 140 DE73
Frederick Cl, Sutt. 217 CZ105
Frederick Ct NW2 119 CY62
Douglas Ms
Frederick Cres SW9 161 DP80
Frederick Cres, Enf. 82 DW40
Frederick Gdns, Sutt. 217 CZ106
Frederick Pl SE18 165 EP78
Frederick Rd SE17 161 DP78
Chapter Rd
Frederick Rd, Rain. 147 FD68
Frederick Rd, Sutt. 217 CZ106
Frederick Sq SE16 143 DY73
Rotherhithe St
Frederick St WC1 274 B3
Frederick St WC1 141 DM69
Frederick Ter E8 142 DT67
Haggerston Rd
Frederick Vil W7 137 CE74
Lower Boston Rd
Frederick's Pl EC2 275 K9
Fredericks Pl N12 98 DC49
Frederick's Row EC1 274 F2
Fredley Pk (Mickleham), Dor. 247 CJ129
Fredora Av, Hayes 135 BT70
Free Prae Rd, Cher. 194 BG102
Free Trade Wf E1 142 DU73
The Highway
Freeborne Gdns, Rain. 147 FG65
Mungo Pk Rd
Freedom Cl E17 123 DY56
Freedom Rd N17 100 DR54
Freedom St SW11 160 DF82
Freedown La, Sutt. 218 DC113
Freegrove Rd N7 121 DL64
Freeland Pk NW4 97 CY54
Freeland Rd W5 138 CM73
Freeland Way, Erith 167 FG81
Slade Grn Rd
Freelands Av, S.Croy. 221 DX109
Freelands Gro, Brom. 204 EH95
Freelands Rd, Brom. 204 EH95
Freelands Rd, Cob. 213 BV114
Freeling St N1 141 DM66
Caledonian Rd
Freeman Cl, Nthlt. 136 BY66
Freeman Cl, Shep. 195 BS98
Freeman Ct N7 121 DL62
Tollington Way
Freeman Ct, Chesh. 54 AQ30
Barnes Av
Freeman Dr, W.Mol. 196 BZ97
Freeman Rd, Grav. 191 GL90
Freeman Rd, Mord. 200 DD99
Freeman Way, Horn. 128 FL58
Freemans Cl (Stoke Poges), Slou. 132 AT65
Freemans La, Hayes 135 BS73
Freemantle Av, Enf. 83 DX43
Freemantle St SE17 279 M10
Freemantle St SE17 162 DS78
Freemasons Rd E16 144 EH71
Freemasons Rd, Croy. 202 DS102
Freesia Cl, Orp. 223 ET106
Briarswood Way
Freethorpe Cl SE19 202 DR95
Freezeland Way, Uxb. 134 BN65
Western Av
Freightmaster Est, Rain. 167 FG76
Freke Rd SW11 160 DG83
Fremantle Ho, Til. 171 GF81
Leicester Rd
Fremantle Rd, Belv. 166 FA77
Fremantle Rd, Ilf. 103 EQ54
Fremont St E9 142 DW67
French Apartments, The, Pur. 219 DN112
Lansdowne Rd
French Gdns, Cob. 214 BW114
French Horn La, Hat. 45 CV17
French Ordinary Ct EC3 275 N10
French Pl E1 275 N3
French Row, St.Alb. 43 CD20
Market Pl
French St, Sun. 196 BW96
French St, West. 255 ES128
Frenchaye, Add. 212 BJ106
Frenches, The, Red. 250 DG132
Frenches Ct, Red. 250 DG132
Frenches Rd
Frenches Dr, Red. 250 DG132
The Frenches
Frenches Rd, Red. 250 DG132
Frenchlands Hatch (East Horsley), Lthd. 245 BS127
French's Cl, Ware 33 EB11
French's Wells, Wok. 226 AV117
Frenchum Gdns, Slou. 131 AL73
Frendsbury Rd SE4 163 DY84
Frensham (Cheshunt), Wal.Cr. 66 DT27
Frensham Cl, Sthl. 136 BZ70
Frensham Ct, Mitch. 200 DD97
Phipps Br Rd
Frensham Dr SW15 179 CU89
Frensham Dr (New Addington), Croy. 221 EC108
Frensham Rd SE9 185 ER89
Frensham Rd, Ken. 219 DP114
Frensham St SE15 162 DU79
Frensham Wk (Farnham Common), Slou. 111 AQ64
Frensham Way, Epsom 233 CW116
Frere St SW11 160 DE82
Fresh Wf Rd, Bark. 145 EP67
Freshborough Ct, Guil. 259 AZ135
Lower Edgeborough Rd
Freshfield Av E8 142 DT66
Freshfield Cl SE13 163 ED84
Marischal Rd
Freshfield Dr N14 99 DH45
Freshfields, Croy. 203 DZ101
Freshfields Av, Upmin. 128 FP64
Freshford St SW18 180 DC90
Freshmount Gdns, Epsom 216 CP111
Freshwater Cl SW17 180 DG93
Freshwater Rd SW17 180 DG93
Freshwater Rd, Dag. 126 EX60
Freshwaters, Harl. 35 ES14
School La
Freshwell Av, Rom. 126 EW56
Freshwood Cl, Beck. 203 EB95
Freshwood Way, Wall. 219 DH109
Freston Gdns, Barn. 80 DG43
Freston Pk N3 97 CZ54
Freston Rd W10 139 CX73
Freston Rd W11 139 CX73
Freta Rd, Bexh. 186 EZ85
Fretherne Rd, Welw.G.C. 29 CX09
Frewin Rd SW18 180 DD88
Friar Ms SE27 *Prioress Rd* 181 DP90
Friar Rd, Hayes 136 BX70
Friar Rd, Orp. 206 EU99
Friar St EC4 274 G9
Friars, The, Chig. 103 ES49
Friars, The, Harl. 51 EN17
Friars Av N20 98 DE48
Friars Av SW15 179 CT90
Friars Av, Brwd. 109 GA46
Friars Cl E4 101 EC48
Friars Cl N2 120 DD56
Friars Cl, Brwd. 109 FZ45
Friars Cl, Nthlt. 136 BX69
Broomcroft Av
Friars Fld, Berk. 38 AS16
Herons Elm
Friars Gdns W3 138 CR72
St. Dunstans Av
Friars Gate, Guil. 258 AU136
Friars Gate Cl, Wdf.Grn. 102 EG49
Friars La (Hatfield Heath), B.Stort. 37 FH06
Friars La, Rich. 177 CK85
Friars Mead E14 163 EC76
Friars Ms SE9 185 EN85
Friars Orchard (Fetcham), Lthd. 231 CD121
Friars Pl La W3 138 CR73
Friars Ri, Wok. 227 BA118
Friars Rd E6 144 EK67
Friars Rd, Vir.W. 192 AX98
Friars Stile Pl, Rich. 178 CL86
Friars Stile Rd
Friars Stile Rd, Rich. 178 CL86
Friars Wk N14 99 DH46
Friars Wk SE2 166 EX78
Friars Way W3 138 CR72
Friars Way, Bushey 76 BZ39
Friars Way, Cher. 194 BG100
Friars Way, Kings L. 58 BN30
Friars Wd, Croy. 221 DY109
Friarscroft, Brox. 49 EA20
Friary, The (Old Windsor), Wind. 172 AV86
Friary Br, Guil. 258 AW135
Friary Cl N12 98 DE50
Friary Ct SW1 277 L3
Friary Ct, Wok. 226 AT118
Friary Est SE15 162 DU79
Friary Island (Wraysbury), Stai. 172 AW86
Friary La, Wdf.Grn. 102 EG49
Friary Pas, Guil. 258 AW136
Friary St
Friary Rd N12 98 DD49
Friary Rd SE15 162 DU80
Friary Rd W3 138 CQ72
Friary Rd (Wraysbury), Stai. 172 AW86
Friary Shop Cen, The, Guil. 258 AW135
Onslow St
Friary St, Guil. 258 AW136
Friary Way N12 98 DE49
Friday Hill E4 102 EE47
Friday Hill E E4 102 EE48
Friday Hill W E4 102 EE47
Friday Rd, Erith 167 FD78
Friday Rd, Mitch. 180 DF94
Friday St EC4 275 H9
Friday St EC4 142 DQ72
Friday St (Abinger Common), Dor. 262 BZ143
Frideswide Pl NW5 121 DJ64
Islip St
Friend St EC1 274 F2
Friend St EC1 141 DP69
Friendly Pl SE13 163 EB81
Lewisham Rd
Friendly St SE8 163 EA81
Friendly St Ms SE8 163 EA82
Friendly St
Friends Av, Wal.Cr. 67 DX31
Friends Rd, Croy. 202 DR104
Friends Rd, Pur. 219 DP112
Friends Wk, Stai. 173 BF92
Friends Wk, Uxb. 134 BK66
Bakers Rd
Friendship Wk, Nthlt. 136 BX69
Wayfarer Rd
Friern Barnet La N11 98 DE49
Friern Barnet La N20 98 DE49
Friern Barnet Rd N11 98 DF50
Friern Br Retail Pk N11 99 DH51
Friern Ct N20 98 DD48
Friern Mt Dr N20 98 DC45
Friern Pk N12 98 DC50
Friern Rd SE22 182 DU86
Friern Watch Av N12 98 DC49
Frigate Ms SE8 163 EA79
Watergate St
Frimley Av, Horn. 128 FN60
Frimley Av, Wall. 219 DL106
Frimley Cl SW19 179 CY89
Frimley Cl (New Addington), Croy. 221 EC108
Frimley Ct, Sid. 186 EV92
Frimley Cres (New Addington), Croy. 221 EC108
Frimley Gdns, Mitch. 200 DE97
Frimley Rd, Chess. 216 CL106
Frimley Rd, Hem.H. 39 BE19
Frimley Rd, Ilf. 125 ES62
Frimley Vw, Wind. 151 AK81
Frimley Way E1 143 DX70
Fringewood Cl, Nthwd. 93 BP53
Frinstead Ho W10 139 CX73
Frinsted Cl, Orp. 206 EX98
Frinsted Rd, Erith 167 FD80
Frinton Cl, Wat. 93 BV47
Frinton Dr, Wdf.Grn. 101 ED52
Frinton Ms, Ilf. 125 EN58
Bramley Cres
Frinton Rd E6 144 EK69
Frinton Rd N15 122 DS58
Frinton Rd SW17 180 DG93
Frinton Rd, Rom. 104 EZ52
Frinton Rd, Sid. 186 EY89
Friston Path, Chig. 103 ES50
Friston St SW6 160 DB82
Friswell Pl, Bexh. 166 FA84
Frith Ct NW7 97 CY52
Frith Knowle, Walt. 213 BV106
Frith La NW7 97 CY52
Frith Rd E11 123 EC63
Frith Rd, Croy. 202 DQ103
Frith St W1 273 M9
Frith St W1 141 DK72
Fritham Cl, N.Mal. 198 CS100
Frithe, The, Slou. 132 AV72
Friths Dr, Reig. 250 DB131
Frithsden Copse, Berk. 39 AZ15
Frithsden Rd, Berk. 38 AY17
Frithville Gdns W12 139 CW74
Frithwald Rd, Cher. 193 BF101
Frithwood Av, Nthwd. 93 BS51
Frizlands La, Dag. 127 FB63
Frobisher Cl, Bushey 76 CA44
Frobisher Cl, Ken. 236 DR117
Hayes La
Frobisher Cl, Pnr. 116 BX59
Frobisher Cres EC2 142 DQ71
Beech St
Frobisher Cres, Stai. 174 BL87
Frobisher Gdns, Guil. 243 BA133
Frobisher Gdns, Stai. 174 BL87
Frobisher Pas E14 143 DZ74
North Colonnade
Frobisher Rd E6 145 EM72
Frobisher Rd N8 121 DN56
Frobisher Rd, Erith 167 FF80
Frobisher Rd, St.Alb. 43 CJ22
Frobisher St SE10 164 EE79
Frobisher Way, Grav. 191 GL92
Frobisher Way, Green. 169 FV84
Frobisher Way, Hat. 44 CR15
Frog La (Sutton Grn), Guil. 242 AY125
Froggy La (Denham), Uxb. 113 BD62
Froghall La, Chig. 103 ER49
Froghole La, Eden. 255 ER132
Frogley Rd SE22 162 DT84
Frogmoor La, Rick. 92 BK47
Frogmore SW18 180 DA85
Frogmore, St.Alb. 61 CD27
Frogmore Av, Hayes 135 BS70
Frogmore Cl, Slou. 151 AN75
Frogmore Cl, Sutt. 199 CX104
Frogmore Dr, Wind. 152 AS81
Frogmore Est, Ruis. 116 BX64
Frogmore Gdns, Hayes 135 BS70
Frogmore Gdns, Sutt. 217 CY105
Frogmore Home Pk, St.Alb. 61 CD28
Frogmore Ind Est NW10 138 CQ69
Frogmore Rd, Hem.H. 40 BK23
Frognal NW3 120 DC64
Frognal Av, Har. 117 CF56
Frognal Av, Sid. 186 EU93
Frognal Cl NW3 120 DC64
Frognal Ct NW3 140 DC65
Frognal Gdns NW3 120 DC63
Frognal La NW3 120 DB64
Frognal Par NW3 140 DC65
Frognal Ct
Frognal Pl, Sid. 186 EU93
Frognal Ri NW3 120 DC63
Frognal Way NW3 120 DC63
Froissart Rd SE9 184 EK85
Frome Rd N22 121 DP55
Westbury Av
Frome Sq, Hem.H. 40 BN15
Waveney
Frome St N1 142 DQ68
Fromer Rd (Wooburn Grn), H.Wyc. 110 AD59
Fromondes Rd, Sutt. 217 CY106
Front, The, Berk. 39 BB16
Front La, Upmin. 129 FS59
Frostic Wk E1 142 DT71
Froude St SW8 161 DH82
Frowick Cl, Hat. 45 CW23
Frowyke Cres, Pot.B. 63 CU32
Fruen Rd, Felt. 175 BT87
Fruiterers Pas EC4 142 DQ73
Southwark Br
Fry Cl, Rom. 104 FA50
Fry Rd E6 144 EK66
Fry Rd NW10 139 CT67
Fryatt Rd N17 100 DR52
Fryent Cl NW9 118 CN58
Fryent Cres NW9 118 CS58
Fryent Flds NW9 118 CS58
Fryent Gro NW9 118 CS58
Fryent Way NW9 118 CN58
Fryer Cl, Chesh. 54 AR33
Fryern Wd, Cat. 236 DQ124
Frye's Bldgs N1 141 DN68
Upper St
Frying Pan All E1 275 P7
Fryston Av, Couls. 219 DH114
Fryston Av, Croy. 202 DU103
Fryth Mead, St.Alb. 42 CB19
Frythe, The, Welw. 29 CU05
Fuchsia Cl, Rom. 127 FE61
Fuchsia St SE2 166 EV78
Fulbeck Dr NW9 96 CS53
Fulbeck Wk, Edg. 96 CP47
Knightswood Cl
Fulbeck Way, Har. 94 CC54
Fulbourne Cl, Red. 250 DE132
Dennis Cl
Fulbourne Rd E17 101 EC53
Fulbourne St E1 142 DV71
Durward St
Fulbrook Av (New Haw), Add. 212 BG111
Fulbrook La, S.Ock. 149 FT73
Fulbrook Rd N19 121 DJ63
Junction Rd
Fulford Gro, Wat. 93 BV47
Fulford Rd, Cat. 236 DR121
Fulford Rd, Epsom 216 CR108
Fulford St SE16 162 DV75
Fulham Bdy SW6 160 DA80
Fulham Cl, Uxb. 135 BQ70
Uxbridge Rd
Fulham Ct SW6 160 DA80
Shottendane Rd
Fulham High St SW6 159 CY82
Fulham Palace Rd SW6 159 CX80
Fulham Palace Rd W6 159 CW78
Fulham Pk Gdns SW6 159 CZ82
Fulham Pk Rd SW6 159 CZ82
Fulham Rd SW3 160 DC79
Fulham Rd SW6 159 CY82
Fulham Rd SW10 160 DB80
Fulkes Cotts, Lthd. 245 BP128
Fullarton Cres, S.Ock. 149 FT72
Fullbrooks Av, Wor.Pk. 199 CT102
Fuller Cl E2 142 DU70
St. Matthew's Row
Fuller Cl, Orp. 223 ET106
Fuller Gdns, Wat. 75 BV37
Fuller Rd
Fuller Rd, Dag. 126 EV62
Fuller Rd, Wat. 75 BV37
Fuller St NW4 119 CW56
Fuller Ter, Ilf. 125 EQ64
Oaktree Gro
Fuller Way, Hayes 155 BT78
Fuller Way, Rick. 74 BN43
Fullers Av, Surb. 198 CM103
Fullers Av, Wdf.Grn. 102 EF52
Fullers Cl, Chesh. 54 AP32
Fullers Cl, Rom. 105 FC52
Fullers Cl, Wal.Abb. 68 EG33
Fullers Fm Rd (West Horsley), Lthd. 245 BP134
Fullers Hill (Hyde Heath), Amer. 54 AM34
Fullers Hill, Chesh. 54 AM34
Fullers Hill, West. 255 ER126
High St
Fullers La, Rom. 105 FC52
Fullers Mead, Harl. 52 EW16
Fullers Rd E18 102 EF53
Fullers Way N, Surb. 198 CM104
Fullers Way S, Chess. 216 CL105
Fullers Wd, Croy. 221 EA106
Fullers Wd La (South Nutfield), Red. 251 DJ134
Fullerton Cl (Byfleet), W.Byf. 212 BM114
Fullerton Dr (Byfleet), W.Byf. 212 BL114
Fullerton Rd SW18 180 DC85
Fullerton Rd, Cars. 218 DE109
Fullerton Rd, Croy. 202 DT101
Fullerton Rd (Byfleet), W.Byf. 212 BM114
Fullerton Way (Byfleet), W.Byf. 212 BL114
Fullmer Way (Woodham), Add. 211 BF110
Fullwell Av, Ilf. 103 EM53
Fullwell Cross Roundabout, Ilf. 103 ER54
Fencepiece Rd
Fullwoods Ms N1 275 L2
Fulmar Cl, Surb. 198 CM100
Fulmar Cres, Hem.H. 40 BG21
Fulmar Rd, Horn. 147 FG66
Fulmead St SW6 160 DB81
Fulmer Cl, Hmptn. 176 BY92
Fulmer Common Rd, Iver 133 AZ65
Fulmer Common Rd (Fulmer), Slou. 133 AZ65
Fulmer Dr, Ger.Cr. 112 AW60
Fulmer La, Ger.Cr. 113 BB60
Fulmer La (Fulmer), Slou. 112 AY62
Fulmer Ri Est, Slou. 133 AZ65
Fulmer Rd E16 144 EK71
Fulmer Rd, Ger.Cr. 112 AY62
Fulmer Rd (Fulmer), Slou. 112 AY63
Fulmer Way W13 157 CH76
Fulmer Way, Ger.Cr. 112 AY58
Fulready Rd E10 123 ED57
Fulstone Cl, Houns. 156 BZ84
Fulthorp Rd SE3 164 EF82
Fulton Ms W2 140 DC73
Porchester Ter
Fulton Rd, Wem. 118 CN62
Fulvens (Peaslake), Guil. 261 BS143
Fulvens Cotts (Peaslake), Guil. 261 BS142
Fulwell Pk Av, Twick. 176 CB89
Fulwell Rd, Tedd. 177 CD91
Fulwich Rd, Dart. 188 FM86
Fulwood Av, Wem. 138 CM67
Fulwood Cl, Hayes 135 BT72
Fulwood Gdns, Twick. 177 CF86
Fulwood Pl WC1 274 C7
Fulwood Pl WC1 141 DM71
Fulwood Wk SW19 179 CY88
Furber St W6 159 CV76
Furham Feild, Pnr. 94 CA52
Furley Rd SE15 162 DU80
Furlong Cl, Wall. 200 DG102

Furlong Rd N7 141 DN65
Furlong Rd (Westcott), Dor. 262 CC137
Furlong Way, Ware 33 DZ09
Furlongs, Hem.H. 40 BG19
Furlough, The, Wok. 227 BA117
Pembroke Rd
Furmage St SW18 180 DB87
Furneaux Av SE27 181 DP92
Furner Cl, Dart. 167 FF83
Furness Cl, Grays 171 GH78
Furness Pl, Wind. 150 AJ82
Furness Row
Furness Rd NW10 139 CU68
Furness Rd SW6 160 DB82
Furness Rd, Har. 116 CB59
Furness Rd, Mord. 200 DB101
Furness Row, Wind. 150 AJ82
Furness Sq, Wind. 150 AJ82
Furness Row
Furness Wk, Wind. 150 AJ82
Furness Row
Furness Way, Horn. 127 FG64
Furness Way, Wind. 150 AJ82
Furnival Av, Slou. 131 AP71
Furnival Cl, Vir.W. 192 AX100
Furnival St EC4 274 D8
Furnival St EC4 141 DN72
Furrow La E9 122 DW64
Furrowfield, Hat. 45 CV16
Cob Mead
Furrows, The (Harefield), Uxb. 114 BJ57
Furrows, The, Walt. 196 BW103
Furrows Pl, Cat. 236 DT123
Fursby Av N3 98 DA51
Furse Av, St.Alb. 43 CG17
Further Acre NW9 97 CT54
Further Grn Rd SE6 184 EE87
Furtherfield, Abb.L. 59 BS32
Furtherfield Cl, Croy. 201 DN100
Furtherground, Hem.H. 40 BL21
Furze Cl, Horl. 269 DK148
Jennings Way
Furze Cl, Red. 250 DF133
Furze Cl, Wat. 94 BW50
Furze Fm Cl, Rom. 104 EY54
Furze Fld (Oxshott), Lthd. 215 CD113
Furze Gro, Tad. 233 CZ121
Furze Hill, Pur. 219 DL111
Furze Hill, Red. 250 DE133
Linkfield La
Furze Hill (Kingswood), Tad. 233 CZ120
Furze La, Gdmg. 258 AT143
Furze La, Pur. 219 DL111
Furze Rd, Add. 211 BF107
Furze Rd, Hem.H. 39 BE21
Furze Rd, Th.Hth. 202 DQ97
Furze St E3 143 EA71
Furze Vw, Rick. 73 BC44
Furzebushes La, St.Alb. 60 BY25
Furzedown Dr SW17 181 DH92
Furzedown Rd SW17 181 DH92
Furzedown Rd, Sutt. 218 DC111
Furzefield (Cheshunt), Wal.Cr. 66 DV28
Furzefield Cl, Chis. 185 EP93
Furzefield Cres, Reig. 266 DC136
Furzefield Rd SE3 164 EH79
Furzefield Rd, Beac. 88 AJ53
Furzefield Rd, Reig. 266 DC136
Furzefield Rd, Welw.G.C. 29 CY10
Furzeground Way, Uxb. 135 BQ74
Furzeham Rd, West Dr. 154 BL75
Furzehill Rd, Borwd. 78 CN42
Furzehill Sq (St. Mary Cray), Orp. 206 EV98
Furzen Cl, Slou. 131 AN69
Furzen Cres, Hat. 45 CT21
Furzewood, Sun. 195 BU95
Fuschia Ct, Wdf.Grn. 102 EE52
The Bridle Path
Fusedale Way, S.Ock. 149 FT73
Fuzzens Wk, Wind. 151 AL82
Fyfe Way, Brom. 204 EG96
Widmore Rd
Fyfield Cl, Brom. 203 ED98
Fyfield Ct E7 144 EG65
Fyfield Rd E17 123 ED55
Fyfield Rd SW9 161 DN83
Fyfield Rd, Enf. 82 DS41
Fyfield Rd, Rain. 147 FF67
Fyfield Rd, Wdf.Grn. 102 EJ52
Fynes St SW1 277 M8
Fynes St SW1 161 DK77

G

G.E.C. Est, Wem. 117 CK62
Gabion Av, Purf. 169 FR77
Gable Cl, Abb.L. 59 BS32
Gable Cl, Dart. 187 FG85
Gable Cl, Pnr. 94 CA52
Gable Ct SE26 182 DV92
Lawrie Pk Av
Gables, The, Bans. 233 CZ117
Gables, The, Hem.H. 40 BK19
Chapel St
Gables, The (Oxshott), Lthd. 214 CC112
Gables, The, Wem. 118 CM63
Gables Av, Ashf. 174 BM92
Gables Av, Borwd. 78 CM41
Gables Cl SE5 162 DS81
Gables Cl SE12 184 EG88
Gables Cl (Chalfont St. Peter), Ger.Cr. 90 AY49
Gables Cl (Datchet), Slou. 152 AU79
Gables Cl (Kingfield), Wok. 227 AZ120
Kingfield Rd
Gables Ct (Kingfield), Wok. 227 AZ120
Kingfield Rd
Gabriel Cl, Felt. 176 BX91
Gabriel Cl (Chafford Hundred), Grays 169 FW76
Gabriel Cl, Rom. 105 FC52
Gabriel Spring Rd (Fawkham Grn), Long. 209 FR103
Gabriel Spring Rd (East) (Fawkham Grn), Long. 209 FS103
Gabriel St SE23 183 DX87
Gabrielle Cl, Wem. 118 CM62
Gabrielle Ct NW3 140 DD65
Gabriels Gdns, Grav. 191 GL92
Gabriel's Wf SE1 278 D2
Gad Cl E13 144 EH69
Gadbrook Rd, Bet. 264 CS139
Gaddesden Av, Wem. 138 CM65
Gaddesden Cres, Wat. 60 BX34
Gaddesden Gro, Welw.G.C. 30 DC09
Widford Rd
Gade Av, Wat. 75 BS42
Gade Bk, Rick. 75 BR42
Gade Cl, Hayes 135 BV74
Gade Cl, Hem.H. 40 BH17
Gade Cl, Wat. 75 BS42
Gade Twr, Hem.H. 58 BN25
Gade Valley Cl, Kings L. 58 BN28
Gade Vw Gdns, Kings L. 59 BQ32
Gadebridge La, Hem.H. 40 BJ18
Gadebridge Rd, Hem.H. 40 BG18
Gadesden Rd, Epsom 216 CQ107
Gadeview Rd, Hem.H. 40 BK24
Gadsbury Cl NW9 119 CT58
Gadsden Cl, Upmin. 129 FS58
Gadswell Cl, Wat. 76 BX36
Gadwall Cl E16 144 EH72
Freemasons Rd
Gadwall Way SE28 165 ER75
Gage Rd E16 144 EE71
Malmesbury Rd
Gage St WC1 274 A6
Gainford St N1 141 DN67
Richmond Av
Gainsboro Gdns, Grnf. 117 CE64
Gainsborough Av E12 125 EN64
Gainsborough Av, Dart. 188 FJ85
Gainsborough Av, St.Alb. 43 CF19
Gainsborough Av, Til. 171 GG81
Gainsborough Cl, Beck. 183 EA94
Gainsborough Cl, Esher 197 CE102
Lime Tree Av
Gainsborough Ct N12 98 DB50
Gainsborough Ct W12 159 CW75
Lime Gro
Gainsborough Ct, Walt. 213 BU105
Gainsborough Dr (Northfleet), Grav. 190 GD90
Gainsborough Dr, S.Croy. 220 DU113
Gainsborough Gdns NW3 120 DD62
Gainsborough Gdns NW11 119 CZ59
Gainsborough Gdns, Edg. 96 CM54
Gainsborough Gdns, Islw. 177 CD85
Gainsborough Ho, Enf. 82 DU43
Ayley Cft
Gainsborough Ms SE26 182 DV90
Panmure Rd
Gainsborough Pl, Chig. 103 ET48
Gainsborough Rd E11 124 EE59
Gainsborough Rd E15 144 EE69
Gainsborough Rd N12 98 DB50
Gainsborough Rd W4 159 CT77
Gainsborough Rd, Dag. 126 EV63
Gainsborough Rd, Epsom 216 CQ110
Gainsborough Rd, Hayes 135 BQ68
Gainsborough Rd, N.Mal. 198 CR101
Gainsborough Rd, Rain. 147 FG67
Gainsborough Rd, Rich. 158 CM83
Gainsborough Rd, Wdf.Grn. 102 EL51
Gainsborough Sq, Bexh. 166 EX83
Regency Way
Gainsford Rd E17 123 DZ56
Gainsford St SE1 279 P4
Gainsford St SE1 162 DT75
Gainswood, Welw.G.C. 29 CY10
Mill Grn Rd
Gairloch Rd SE5 162 DS82
Gaisford St NW5 141 DJ65
Gaist Av, Cat. 236 DU122
Gaitskell Ct SW11 160 DE82
Gaitskell Rd SE9 185 EQ88
Galahad Cl, Slou. 151 AN75
Mitchell Cl
Galahad Rd, Brom. 184 EG90
Galata Rd SW13 159 CU80
Galatea Sq SE15 162 DV83
Scylla Rd
Galbraith St E14 163 EC76
Galdana Av, Barn. 80 DC41
Gale Cl, Hmptn. 176 BY93
Stewart Cl
Gale Cl, Mitch. 200 DD97
Gale Cres, Bans. 234 DA117
Gale St E3 143 EA71
Gale St, Dag. 146 EX67
Galeborough Av, Wdf. Grn. 101 ED52
Galen Cl, Epsom 216 CN111
Williams Evans Rd
Galen Pl WC1 274 A7
Galena Ho SE18 165 ET78
Grosmont Rd
Galena Rd W6 159 CV77
Gales Cl, Guil. 243 BD132
Gilliat Dr
Gales Gdns E2 142 DV69
Gales Way, Wdf.Grn. 102 EL52
Galesbury Rd SW18 180 DC86
Galey Grn, S.Ock. 149 FV71
Bovey Way
Galgate Cl SW19 179 CY88
Gallants Fm Rd, Barn. 98 DE45
Galleon Boul, Dart. 169 FR84
Galleon Cl SE16 163 DX75
Kinburn St
Galleon Cl, Erith 167 FD77
Galleon Rd, Grays 169 FW77
Galleons Dr, Bark. 145 ES69
Galleons La (George Grn), Slou. 132 AX71
Gallery Gdns, Nthlt. 136 BX68
Gallery Rd SE21 182 DR88
Galley Grn, Hert. 33 EA13
Galley Hill, Hem.H. 39 BF18
Galley Hill, Wal.Abb. 68 EF30
Galley Hill Rd (Northfleet), Grav. 190 FZ85
Galley Hill Rd, Swans. 190 FZ85
Galley La, Barn. 79 CV41
Galleymead Rd (Colnbrook), Slou. 153 BF81
Galleywall Rd SE16 162 DV77
Galleywood Cres, Rom. 105 FD51
Gallia Rd N5 121 DP64
Galliard Cl N9 82 DW44
Galliard Rd N9 100 DU46
Gallions Cl, Bark. 146 EU69
Gallions Rd SE7 164 EH77
Gallions Roundabout E16 145 EP73
Gallions Vw Rd SE28 165 ES75
Goldfinch Rd
Gallon Cl SE7 164 EJ77
Gallop, The, S.Croy. 220 DV108
Gallop, The, Sutt. 218 DC108
Gallops, The, Tad. 249 CV126
Gallosson Rd SE18 165 ES77
Galloway Chase, Slou. 132 AU73
Galloway Cl, Brox. 67 DZ26
Galloway Path, Croy. 220 DR105
Galloway Rd W12 139 CU74
Gallows Cor, Rom. 106 FK53
Gallows Hill, Kings L. 59 BQ31
Gallows Hill La, Abb.L. 59 BQ32
Gallus Cl N21 81 DM44
Gallus Sq SE3 164 EH83
Gallys Rd, Wind. 151 AK82
Galpins Rd, Th.Hth. 201 DM98
Galsworthy Av, Rom. 126 EV59
Galsworthy Cl SE28 146 EV74
Galsworthy Cres SE3 164 EJ81
Merriman Rd
Galsworthy Rd NW2 119 CY63
Galsworthy Rd, Cher. 194 BG101
Galsworthy Rd, Kings.T. 178 CP94
Galsworthy Rd, Til. 171 GJ81
Galsworthy Ter N16 122 DS62
Hawksley Rd
Galton St W10 139 CY70
Galva Cl, Barn. 80 DG42
Galvani Way, Croy. 201 DM102
Ampere Way
Galveston Rd SW15 179 CZ85
Galvin Rd, Slou. 131 AQ74
Galvins Cl, Guil. 242 AU131
Galway Cl SE16 162 DV78
Masters Dr
Galway St EC1 275 J3
Galway St EC1 142 DQ69
Gambetta St SW8 161 DH82
Gambia St SE1 278 G3
Gambles La (Ripley), Wok. 228 BJ124
Gambole Rd SW17 180 DE91
Games Rd, Barn. 80 DF41
Gamlen Rd SW15 159 CX84
Gammon Cl, Hem.H. 40 BN21
Gammons Fm Cl, Wat. 75 BT36
Gammons La, Brox. 66 DT25
Gammons La, Wat. 75 BV38
Gamuel Cl E17 123 EA58
Gander Grn Cres, Hmptn. 196 CA95
Gander Grn La, Sutt. 199 CY103
Ganders Ash, Wat. 59 BU33
Gandhi Cl E17 123 EA58
Gandolfi St SE15 162 DS79
St. Georges Way
Gangers Hill (Woldingham), Cat. 253 EA127
Gangers Hill, Gdse. 253 EA127
Ganghill, Guil. 243 BA132
Gant Ct, Wal.Abb. 68 EF34
Ganton St W1 273 K10
Ganton Wk, Wat. 94 BY49
Woodhall La
Gants Hill, Ilf. 125 EN58
Eastern Av
Gantshill Cres, Ilf. 125 EN57
Ganymede Pl, Hem.H. 40 BM18
Jupiter Dr
Gap Rd SW19 180 DA92
Garage Rd W3 138 CN72
Garbrand Wk, Epsom 217 CT109
Garbutt Pl W1 272 G6
Garbutt Rd, Upmin. 128 FQ61
Gard St EC1 274 G2
Garden Av, Bexh. 166 FA83
Garden Av, Hat. 45 CU22
Garden Av, Mitch. 181 DH94
Garden City, Edg. 96 CN51
Garden Cl E4 101 EA50
Garden Cl SE12 184 EH90
Garden Cl SW15 179 CV87
Garden Cl, Add. 212 BK105
Garden Cl, Ashf. 175 BQ93
Garden Cl, Bans. 234 DA115
Garden Cl, Barn. 79 CW42
Garden Cl, Hmptn. 176 BZ92
Garden Cl, Lthd. 231 CJ124
Garden Cl, Nthlt. 136 BY67
Garden Cl, Ruis. 115 BS61
Garden Cl, St.Alb. 43 CH19
Garden Cl, Wall. 219 DL106
Garden Cl, Wat. 75 BT40
Garden Cotts, Orp. 206 EW96
Main Rd
Garden Ct EC4 274 D10
Garden Ct N12 98 DB50
Holden Rd
Garden Ct, Rich. 158 CM81
Lichfield Rd
Garden Ct, Stan. 95 CJ50
Marsh La
Garden Ct, Welw.G.C. 29 CY08
Garden Ct, W.Mol. 196 CB98
Avern Rd
Garden End, Amer. 55 AS37
Garden Fld La, Berk. 39 AZ21
Garden La SW2 181 DM88
Christchurch Rd
Garden La, Brom. 184 EH93
Garden Ms W2 140 DA73
Linden Gdns
Garden Ms, Slou. 132 AT74
Littledown Rd
Garden Pl, Dart. 188 FK90
Garden Reach, Ch.St.G. 72 AX41
Garden Rd NW8 140 DC69
Garden Rd SE20 202 DW95
Garden Rd, Abb.L. 59 BS31
Garden Rd, Brom. 184 EH94
Garden Rd, Rich. 158 CN83
Garden Rd, Sev. 257 FK122
Garden Rd, Walt. 195 BV100
Garden Row SE1 278 F7
Garden Row SE1 161 DP76
Garden Row (Northfleet), Grav. 191 GF90
Garden St E1 143 DX71
Garden Ter SW1 277 M10
Garden Ter Rd, Harl. 36 EW11
Garden Wk EC2 275 M3
Garden Wk, Beck. 203 DZ95
Hayne Rd
Garden Wk, Couls. 235 DH123
Garden Way NW10 138 CQ65
Garden Way, Loug. 85 EN38
Gardeners Cl N11 98 DG47
Gardeners Rd, Croy. 201 DP102
Gardeners Wk (Bookham), Lthd. 246 CB126
Gardenia Rd, Enf. 82 DS44
Gardenia Way, Wdf. Grn 102 EG50
Gardens, The SE22 162 DU84
Gardens, The, Beck. 203 EC96
Gardens, The, Esher 214 CA105
Gardens, The, Felt. 175 BR85
Gardens, The, Har. 116 CC58
Gardens, The, Hat. 63 CY27
Gardens, The, Pnr. 116 BZ58
Gardens, The, Wat. 75 BT40
Gardiner Av NW2 119 CW64
Gardiner Cl, Dag. 126 EX63
Gardiner Cl, Enf. 83 DX44
Gardiner Cl, Orp. 206 EW96
Gardiners, The, Harl. 52 EV16
Gardner Cl E11 124 EH58
Gardner Gro, Felt. 176 BZ89
Gardner Pl, Felt. 175 BV86
Gardner Rd E13 144 EH70
Gardner Rd, Guil. 242 AW134
Gardners La EC4 275 H10
Gardnor Rd NW3 120 DD63
Flask Wk
Garendon Gdns, Mord. 200 DB101
Garendon Rd, Mord. 200 DB101
Gareth Cl, Wor.Pk. 199 CX103
Burnham Dr
Gareth Gro, Brom. 184 EG91
Garfield Ms SW11 160 DG83
Garfield Rd
Garfield Pl, Wind. 151 AR82
Albany Rd
Garfield Rd E4 101 ED46
Garfield Rd E13 144 EF70
Garfield Rd SW11 160 DG83
Garfield Rd SW19 180 DC92
Garfield Rd, Add. 212 BJ106
Garfield Rd, Enf. 82 DW42
Garfield Rd, Twick. 177 CG88
Garfield St, Wat. 75 BV38
Garford St E14 143 EA73
Garganey Wk SE28 146 EX73
Garibaldi Rd, Red. 266 DF135
Garibaldi St SE18 165 ES77
Garland Cl, Hem.H. 40 BK19
Garland Cl, Wal.Cr. 67 DY31
Garland Rd SE18 165 ER80
Garland Rd, Stan. 96 CL53
Garland Rd, Ware 33 DY06
Garland Way, Cat. 236 DR122
Garland Way, Horn. 128 FL56
Garlands Ct, Croy. 220 DR105
Chatsworth Rd
Garlands Rd, Lthd. 231 CH121
Garlands Rd, Red. 266 DF135
Garlic St, Dor. 246 BZ133
Garlichill Rd, Epsom 233 CV117
Garlick Hill EC4 275 J10
Garlick Hill EC4 142 DQ73
Garlies Rd SE23 183 DY90
Garlinge Rd NW2 139 CZ65
Garman Cl N18 100 DR50
Garman Rd N17 100 DW52
Garnault Ms EC1 274 E3
Garnault Pl EC1 274 E3
Garnault Rd, Enf. 82 DT38
Garner Cl, Dag. 126 EX60
Garner Dr, Brox. 67 DY26
Garner Rd E17 101 EC53
Garner St E2 142 DU68
Coate St
Garners Cl (Chalfont St. Peter), Ger.Cr. 90 AY51
Garners End (Chalfont St. Peter), Ger.Cr. 90 AY51
Garners Rd (Chalfont St. Peter), Ger.Cr. 90 AY51
Garnet Cl, Slou. 151 AN75
Mitchell Cl
Garnet Rd NW10 138 CS65
Garnet Rd, Th.Hth. 202 DR98
Garnet St E1 142 DW73
Garnet Wk E6 144 EL71
Kingfisher St
Garnett Cl SE9 165 EM83
Garnett Cl, Wat. 76 BX37
Garnett Dr (Bricket Wd), St.Alb. 60 BZ29
Garnett Rd NW3 120 DF64
Garnett Way E17 101 DY53
McEntee Av
Garnham Cl N16 122 DT61
Garnham St
Garnham St N16 122 DT61
Garnies Cl SE15 162 DT80
Garnon Mead, Epp. 70 EX28
Garrad's Rd SW16 181 DK90
Garrard Cl, Bexh. 166 FA83
Garrard Cl, Chis. 185 EP92
Garrard Rd, Bans. 234 DA116
Garrard Rd, Slou. 131 AL70
Garrard Wk NW10 138 CS65
Garnet Rd
Garratt Cl, Croy. 219 DL105
Garratt La SW17 180 DD91
Garratt La SW18 180 DB85
Garratt Rd, Edg. 96 CN52
Garratt Ter SW17 180 DE91
Garratts La, Bans. 233 CZ116
Garratts Rd, Bushey 94 CC45
Garrett Cl W3 138 CR71
Jenner Av
Garrett Cl, Chesh. 54 AQ33
Garrett St EC1 275 J4
Garrick Av NW11 119 CY58
Garrick Cl SW18 160 DC84
Garrick Cl W5 138 CL70
Garrick Cl, Rich. 177 CK85
The Grn
Garrick Cl, Stai. 174 BG94
Garrick Cl, Walt. 213 BV105
Garrick Cres, Croy. 202 DS103
Garrick Dr NW4 97 CW54
Garrick Dr SE28 165 ER76
Broadwater Rd
Garrick Gdns, W.Mol. 196 CA97
Garrick Pk NW4 97 CX54
Garrick Rd NW9 119 CT58
Garrick Rd, Grnf. 136 CB70
Garrick Rd, Rich. 158 CN82
Garrick St WC2 273 P10
Garrick St WC2 141 DL73
Garrick St, Grav. 191 GH86
Barrack Row
Garrick Way NW4 119 CX56
Garrison Cl SE18 165 EN80
Red Lion La
Garrison Cl, Houns. 176 BZ85
Garrison La, Chess. 215 CK108
Garrison Par, Purf. 168 FN77
Comet Cl
Garrolds Cl, Swan. 207 FD96
Garron La, S.Ock. 149 FT72
Garry Cl, Rom. 105 FE52
Garry Way, Rom. 105 FE52
Garsdale Cl N11 98 DG51
Garside Cl SE28 165 ER76
Goosander Way
Garside Cl, Hmptn. 176 CB93
Garsington Ms SE4 163 DZ83
Garsmouth Way, Wat. 76 BX36
Garson Cl, Esher 214 BZ107
Garson Rd
Garson Gro, Chesh. 54 AN29
Garson La (Wraysbury), Stai. 172 AX87
Garson Mead, Esher 214 BZ106
Garson Rd, Esher 214 BZ107
Garston Cres, Wat. 60 BW34
Garston Dr, Wat. 60 BW34
Garston Gdns, Ken. 236 DR115
Godstone Rd
Garston La, Ken. 220 DR114
Garston La, Wat. 60 BX34
Garston Pk Par, Wat. 60 BX34
Garstons, The (Bookham), Lthd. 246 CA125
Garter Way SE16 163 DX75
Poolmans St
Garth, The N12 98 DB50
Holden Rd
Garth, The, Abb.L. 59 BR33
Garth, The, Cob. 214 BY113
Garth, The (Hampton Hill), Hmptn. 176 CB93
Uxbridge Rd
Garth, The, Har. 118 CM58
Garth Cl W4 158 CR78
Garth Cl, Kings.T. 178 CM92
Garth Cl, Mord. 199 CX101
Garth Cl, Ruis. 116 BX60
Garth Ct W4 158 CR78
Garth Rd
Garth Ms W5 138 CL70
Greystoke Gdns
Garth Rd NW2 119 CZ61
Garth Rd W4 158 CR79
Garth Rd, Kings.T. 178 CM92
Garth Rd, Mord. 199 CW100
Garth Rd, Sev. 257 FJ128
Garth Rd, S.Ock. 149 FW70
Garth Rd Ind Cen, Mord. 199 CX101
Garthland Dr, Barn. 79 CV43
Garthorne Rd SE23 183 DX87
Garthside, Rich. 178 CL92
Garthway N12 98 DE51
Gartlett Rd, Wat. 76 BW41
Gartmoor Gdns SW19 179 CZ88
Gartmore Rd, Ilf. 125 ET60
Garton Pl SW18 180 DC86
Gartons Cl, Enf. 82 DW43
Gartons Way SW11 160 DC83
Garvary Rd E16 144 EH72
Garvin Av, Beac. 89 AL52
Garvock Dr, Sev. 256 FG126
Garway Rd W2 140 DB72
Gas Wks La, Brox. 49 EA19
Gascoigne Gdns, Wdf.Grn. 102 EE52
Gascoigne Pl E2 275 P3
Gascoigne Pl E2 142 DT69
Gascoigne Rd, Bark. 145 EQ67
Gascoigne Rd (New Addington), Croy. 221 EC110
Gascoigne Rd, Wey. 195 BP104
Gascons Gro, Slou. 131 AN70
Gascony Av NW6 140 DA66
Gascoyne Cl, Pot.B. 63 CU32
Gascoyne Cl, Rom. 106 FK52
Gascoyne Dr, Dart. 167 FF82
Gascoyne Rd E9 143 DX66
Gascoyne Way, Hert. 32 DQ09
Gaselee St E14 143 EC73
Gasholder Pl SE11 161 DM78
Kennington La
Gaskarth Rd SW12 181 DH86
Gaskarth Rd, Edg. 96 CQ53
Gaskell Rd N6 120 DF58
Gaskell St SW4 161 DL82
Gaskin St N1 141 DP67
Gaspar Cl SW5 160 DB77
Courtfield Gdns
Gaspar Ms SW5 160 DB77
Courtfield Gdns
Gassiot Rd SW17 180 DF91
Gassiot Way, Sutt. 200 DD104
Gasson Rd, Swans. 190 FY86
Gastein Rd W6 159 CX79
Gaston Bell Cl, Rich. 158 CM83
Gaston Br Rd, Shep. 195 BS99
Gaston Rd, Mitch. 200 DG97
Gaston Way, Shep. 195 BR99
Gataker St SE16 162 DV76
Gatcombe Rd E16 144 EG74
Gatcombe Rd N19 121 DK62
Gatcombe Way, Barn. 80 DF41
Gate Cl, Borwd. 78 CQ39
Gate End, Nthwd. 93 BU52
Gate Ms SW7 276 C5
Gate Ms SW7 160 DE75
Gate St WC2 274 B8
Gatecroft, Hem.H. 40 BM22
Gateforth St NW8 272 B5
Gateforth St NW8 140 DE70
Gatehill Rd, Nthwd. 93 BT52
Gatehope Dr, S.Ock. 149 FT72
Gatehouse Cl, Kings.T. 178 CQ94
Gatehouse Sq SE1 142 DQ74
Southwark Br Rd
Gateley Rd SW9 161 DM83
Gater Dr, Enf. 82 DR39
Gates Grn Rd, Kes. 222 EG105
Gates Grn Rd, W.Wick. 204 EF104
Gatesborough St EC2 275 M4
Gatesden Cl (Fetcham), Lthd. 230 CC123
Gatesden Rd (Fetcham), Lthd. 230 CC123
Gateshead Rd, Borwd. 78 CM39
Gateside Rd SW17 180 DF90
Gatestone Rd SE19 182 DS93
Gateway SE17 162 DQ79
Gateway, Wey. 195 BP104
Palace Dr
Gateway, The, Wok. 211 BB114
Gateway Arc N1 141 DP68
Islington High St
Gateway Cl, Nthwd. 93 BQ51
Gateway Ho, Bark. 145 EQ67
St. Ann's
Gateway Ind Est NW10 139 CT69
Gateway Ms E8 122 DT64
Shacklewell La
Gateway Retail Pk E6 145 EP70
Gateway Rd E10 123 EB62
Gateways, Guil. 243 BA134
Gateways, The SW3 276 C9
Gateways, The SW3 160 DF77
Gateways, The, Wal.Cr. 66 DR28
Gatewick Cl, Slou. 132 AS74
Gatfield Gro, Felt. 176 CA89
Gathorne Rd N22 99 DN54
Gathorne St E2 143 DX68
Mace St
Gatley Av, Epsom 216 CP106
Gatley Dr, Guil. 243 AZ131
Gatliff Rd SW1 161 DH78
Gatling Rd SE2 166 EU78
Gatonby St SE15 162 DT80
Kelly Av
Gatting Cl, Edg. 96 CQ52
Pavilion Way
Gatting Way, Uxb. 134 BL65
Gatton Bottom, Red. 251 DH127
Gatton Bottom, Reig. 250 DE128
Gatton Cl, Reig. 250 DC131
Gatton Cl, Sutt. 218 DB109
Gatton Pk, Reig. 250 DF129
Gatton Pk Rd, Red. 250 DD132
Gatton Pk Rd, Reig. 250 DD132

Gatton Rd SW17 180 DE91
Gatton Rd, Reig. 250 DC131
Gattons Way, Sid. 186 EZ91
Gatward Cl N21 81 DP44
Gatward Grn N9 100 DS47
Gatwick Gate, Craw. 268 DD154
Gatwick Gate Ind Est, Craw. 268 DE154
Gatwick Metro Cen, Horl. 269 DH147
Gatwick Rd SW18 179 CZ87
Gatwick Rd, Gat. 268 DG154
Gatwick Rd, Grav. 191 GH90
Gatwick Way, Gat. 268 DF151
Gatwick Way, Horn. 128 FM63
Haydock Cl
Gauden Cl SW4 161 DK83
Gauden Rd SW4 161 DK82
Gaumont App, Wat. 75 BV41
Gaumont Ter W12 159 CW75
Lime Gro
Gaunt St SE1 279 H6
Gauntlet Cl, Nthlt. 136 BY66
Gauntlet Cres, Ken. 236 DR120
Gauntlett Ct, Wem. 117 CH64
Gauntlett Rd, Sutt. 218 DD106
Gautrey Rd SE15 162 DW82
Gautrey Sq E6 145 EM72
Gavel St SE17 279 L8
Gavell Rd, Cob. 213 BU113
Gavenny Path, S.Ock. 149 FT72
Gaveston Cl (Byfleet), W.Byf. 212 BM113
Gaveston Dr, Berk. 38 AV17
Gaveston Rd, Lthd. 231 CG120
Gaveston Rd, Slou. 131 AL69
Gavestone Cres SE12 184 EH87
Gavestone Rd SE12 184 EH87
Gaviller Pl E5 122 DV63
Clarence Rd
Gavin St SE18 165 ES77
Gavina Cl, Mord. 200 DE99
Gaviots Cl, Ger.Cr. 113 AZ60
Gaviots Grn, Ger.Cr. 112 AY60
Gaviots Way, Ger.Cr. 112 AY59
Gawber St E2 142 DW69
Gawsworth Cl E15 124 EE64
Ash Rd
Gawthorne Av NW7 97 CY50
Lane App
Gawthorne Ct E3 143 EA68
Mostyn Gro
Gay Cl NW2 119 CV64
Gay Gdns, Dag. 127 FC63
Gay Rd E15 143 ED68
Gay St SW15 159 CX83
Gaydon Ho W2 140 DB71
Gaydon La NW9 96 CS53
Gayfere Rd, Epsom 217 CU106
Gayfere Rd, Ilf. 125 EM55
Gayfere St SW1 277 P7
Gayfere St SW1 161 DL76
Gayford Rd W12 159 CT75
Gayhurst SE17 162 DR79
Hopwood Rd
Gayhurst Rd E8 142 DU66
Gayler Cl (Bletchingley), Red. 252 DT133
Gaylor Rd, Nthlt. 116 BZ64
Gaylor Rd, Til. 170 GE81
Gaynes Ct, Upmin. 128 FP63
Gaynes Hill Rd, Wdf.Grn. 102 EL51
Gaynes Pk, Epp. 70 EY31
Gaynes Pk Rd, Upmin. 128 FN63
Gaynes Rd, Upmin. 128 FP61
Gaynesford Rd SE23 183 DX89
Gaynesford Rd, Cars. 218 DF108
Gaysham Av, Ilf. 125 EN57
Gaysham Hall, Ilf. 125 EP55
Gayton Cl, Amer. 55 AS35
Gayton Cl, Ash. 232 CL118
Gayton Ct, Har. 117 CF58
Gayton Cres NW3 120 DD63
Gayton Rd NW3 120 DD63
Gayton Rd SE2 166 EW76
Florence Rd
Gayton Rd, Har. 117 CF58
Gayville Rd SW11 180 DF86
Gaywood Av (Cheshunt), Wal.Cr. 67 DX30
Gaywood Cl SW2 181 DM88
Gaywood Est SE1 278 G7
Gaywood Est SE1 161 DP76
Gaywood Rd E17 123 EA55
Gaywood Rd, Ash. 232 CM118
Gaywood St SE1 278 G7
Gaza St SE17 161 DP78
Braganza St
Gazelle Glade, Grav. 191 GM92
Geariesville Gdns, Ilf. 125 EP56
Geary Cl, Horl. 269 DP150
Geary Dr, Brwd. 108 FW46
Geary Rd NW10 119 CU64
Geary St N7 121 DM64
Geddes Pl, Bexh. 166 FA84
Market Pl
Geddes Rd, Bushey 76 CC42
Geddings Rd, Hodd. 49 EB17
Gedeney Rd N17 100 DQ53
Gedling Pl SE1 162 DT75
Gee St EC1 275 H4
Gee St EC1 142 DQ70
Geere Rd E15 144 EF67
Gees Ct W1 272 G9
Geffrye Ct N1 275 N1
Geffrye Est N1 142 DS68
Stanway St
Geffrye St E2 142 DT68
Geisthorp Ct, Wal.Abb. 68 EG33
Winters Way
Geldart Rd SE15 162 DV80
Geldeston Rd E5 122 DU61
Gell Cl, Uxb. 114 BM62
Gellatly Rd SE14 162 DW82
Gelsthorpe Rd, Rom. 105 FB52
Gemini Gro, Nthlt. 136 BY69
Javelin Way
General Gordon Pl SE18 165 EP77
General Wolfe Rd SE10 163 ED81
Generals Wk, The, Enf. 83 DY37
Genesis Business Pk, Wok. 227 BC115
Genesis Cl (Stanwell), Stai. 174 BM88
Genesta Rd SE18 165 EP79
Geneva Cl, Shep. 195 BS96
Geneva Dr SW9 161 DN84
Geneva Gdns, Rom. 126 EY57
Geneva Rd, Kings.T. 198 CL98
Geneva Rd, Th.Hth. 202 DQ99
Genever Cl E4 101 EA50
Genista Rd N18 100 DV50
Genoa Av SW15 179 CW85
Genoa Rd SE20 202 DW95
Genotin Rd, Enf. 82 DR41
Genotin Ter, Enf. 82 DR41
Genotin Rd
Gentian Row SE13 163 EC81
Sparta St
Gentlemans Row, Enf. 82 DQ41
Gentry Gdns E13 144 EG70
Whitwell Rd
Genyn Rd, Guil. 258 AV136
Geoffrey Av, Rom. 106 FN51
Geoffrey Cl SE5 162 DQ82
Geoffrey Gdns E6 144 EL68
Geoffrey Rd SE4 163 DZ83
Geoffrey Avey Cft, Epp. 71 FB26
George Beard Rd SE8 163 DZ77
George Comberton Wk E12 125 EN64
Gainsborough Av
George Ct WC2 278 A1
George Cres N10 98 DG52
George Crook's Ho, Grays 170 GB79
New Rd
George Downing Est N16 122 DT61
Cazenove Rd
George V Av, Pnr. 116 CA55
George V Cl, Pnr. 116 CA55
George V Av
George V Way, Grnf. 137 CH67
George V Way, Rick. 74 BG36
George Gange Way (Wealdstone), Har. 117 CE55
George Grn Dr (George Grn), Slou. 133 AZ71
George Grn Rd (George Grn), Slou. 132 AX72
George Gro Rd SE20 202 DU95
George Inn Yd SE1 279 K3
George La E18 102 EG54
George La SE13 183 EC86
George La, Brom. 204 EH102
George Lansbury Ho N22 99 DN53
Progress Way
George Loveless Ho E2 142 DT69
Diss St
George Lovell Dr, Enf. 83 EA37
Government Row
George Lowe Ct W2 140 DB71
Bourne Ter
George Mathers Rd SE11 278 F8
George Mathers Rd SE11 161 DP77
George Ms NW1 273 K3
George Ms, Enf. 82 DR41
Sydney Rd
George Pl N17 122 DS55
Dongola Rd
George Rd E4 101 EA51
George Rd, Gdmg. 258 AS144
George Rd, Guil. 242 AX134
George Rd, Kings.T. 178 CP94
George Rd, N.Mal. 199 CT98
George Row SE16 162 DU75
George Sq SW19 199 CZ97
Mostyn Rd
George St E16 144 EF72
George St W1 272 E8
George St W1 140 DG72
George St W7 137 CE74
The Bdy
George St, Bark. 145 EQ66
George St, Berk. 38 AY19
George St, Chesh. 54 AQ30
Berkhampstead Rd
George St, Croy. 202 DR103
George St, Grays 170 GA79
George St, Hem.H. 40 BK19
George St, Hert. 32 DQ09
George St, Houns. 156 BZ82
George St, Rich. 177 CK85
George St, Rom. 127 FF58
George St, St.Alb. 42 CC20
George St, Sthl. 156 BY77
George St, Stai. 173 BF91
George St, Uxb. 134 BK66
George St, Wat. 76 BW42
George Tilbury Ho, Grays 171 GH75
George Wyver Cl SW19 179 CY87
Beaumont Rd
George Yd EC3 275 L9
George Yd W1 272 G10
George Yd W1 140 DG73
Georgelands (Ripley), Wok. 228 BH121
Georges Cl, Orp. 206 EW97
Georges Dr, Brwd. 108 FT43
Georges Dr (Flackwell Heath), H.Wyc. 110 AC56
Georges Mead, Borwd. 77 CK44
George's Rd N7 121 DM64
Georges Rd (Tatsfield), West. 238 EK120
Georges Sq SW6 159 CZ79
North End Rd
Georges Ter, Cat. 236 DQ122
Coulsdon Rd
George's Wd Rd, Hat. 64 DA26
Georgetown Cl SE19 182 DR92
St. Kitts Ter
Georgette Pl SE10 163 EC80
King George St
Georgeville Gdns, Ilf. 125 EP56
Georgewood Rd, Hem.H. 58 BM25
Georgia Rd, N.Mal. 198 CQ98
Georgia Rd, Th.Hth. 201 DP95
Georgian Cl, Brom. 204 EH101
Georgian Cl, Stai. 174 BH91
Georgian Cl, Stan. 95 CG52
Georgian Cl, Uxb. 114 BL63
Georgian Ct SW16 181 DL91
Gleneldon Rd
Georgian Ct, Wem. 138 CN65
Georgian Way, Har. 117 CD61
Georgiana St NW1 141 DJ67
Georgina Gdns E2 142 DT69
Columbia Rd
Geraint Rd, Brom. 184 EG91
Gerald Ms SW1 276 G8
Gerald Rd E16 144 EF70
Gerald Rd SW1 276 G8
Gerald Rd SW1 160 DG77
Gerald Rd, Dag. 126 EZ61
Gerald Rd, Grav. 191 GL87
Geraldine Rd SW18 180 DC85
Geraldine Rd W4 158 CN79
Geraldine St SE11 278 F7
Geraldine St SE11 161 DP76
Geralds Gro, Bans. 217 CX114
Gerard Av, Houns. 176 CA87
Redfern Av
Gerard Gdns, Rain. 147 FE68
Gerard Rd SW13 159 CT81
Gerard Rd, Har. 117 CG58
Gerards Cl SE16 162 DW78
Gerda Rd SE9 185 EQ89
Gerdview Dr, Dart. 188 FJ91
Germain St, Chesh. 54 AP32
Germains Cl, Chesh. 54 AP32
Germander Way E15 144 EE69
Gernigan Ho SW18 180 DD86
Fitzhugh Gro
Gernon Cl, Rain. 148 FK68
Jordans Way
Gernon Rd E3 143 DY68
Geron Way NW2 119 CV60
Gerpins La, Upmin. 148 FM68
Gerrard Cres, Brwd. 108 FV48
Gerrard Gdns, Pnr. 115 BU57
Gerrard Pl W1 273 N10
Gerrard Rd N1 141 DP68
Gerrard St W1 273 M10
Gerrard St W1 141 DK73
Gerrards Cl N14 81 DJ43
Gerrards Cross Rd (Stoke Poges), Slou. 132 AU66
Gerrards Mead, Bans. 233 CZ117
Garratts La
Gerridge St SE1 278 E5
Gerridge St SE1 161 DN76
Gerry Raffles Sq E15 143 ED65
Great Eastern Rd
Gertrude Rd, Belv. 166 FA77
Gertrude St SW10 160 DC79
Gervaise Cl, Slou. 131 AM74
Gervase Cl, Wem. 118 CQ62
Gervase Rd, Edg. 96 CQ53
Gervase St SE15 162 DV80
Gews Cor (Cheshunt), Wal.Cr. 67 DX29
Ghent St SE6 183 EA89
Ghent Way E8 142 DT65
Tyssen St
Giant Arches Rd SE24 182 DQ87
Giant Tree Hill, Bushey 95 CD46
Gibb Cft, Harl. 51 ES19
Gibbard Ms SW19 179 CX92
Gibbfield Cl, Rom. 126 EY55
Gibbins Rd E15 143 EC66
Gibbon Rd SE15 162 DW82
Gibbon Rd W3 138 CS73
Gibbon Rd, Kings.T. 198 CL95
Gibbon Wk SW15 159 CU84
Swinburne Rd
Gibbons Cl, Borwd. 78 CL39
Gibbons Rd NW10 138 CR65
Gibbs Av SE19 182 DR92
Gibbs Cl SE19 182 DR92
Gibbs Cl (Cheshunt), Wal.Cr. 67 DX29
Gibbs Couch, Wat. 94 BX48
Gibbs Grn W14 159 CZ78
Gibbs Grn, Edg. 96 CQ50
Gibbs Rd N18 100 DW49
Gibbs Sq SE19 182 DR92
Gibraltar Cl, Brwd. 107 FW51
Essex Way
Gibraltar Cres, Epsom 216 CS110
Gibraltar Ho, Brwd. 107 FW51
Gibraltar Wk E2 142 DT69
Gibson Cl E1 142 DW70
Colebert Av
Gibson Cl N21 81 DN44
Gibson Cl, Chess. 215 CJ107
Gibson Cl, Epp. 71 FC25
Beamish Cl
Gibson Cl (Northfleet), Grav. 191 GF90
Gibson Cl, Islw. 157 CD83
Gibson Ct, Slou. 153 AZ78
Gibson Gdns N16 122 DT61
Northwold Rd
Gibson Pl (Stanwell), Stai. 174 BJ86
Gibson Rd SE11 278 C9
Gibson Rd SE11 161 DM77
Gibson Rd, Dag. 126 EW60
Gibson Rd, Sutt. 218 DB106
Gibson Rd, Uxb. 114 BM63
Gibson Sq N1 141 DN67
Gibson St SE10 164 EE78
Gibson's Hill SW16 181 DN93
Gidd Hill, Couls. 234 DG116
Gidea Av, Rom. 127 FG55
Gidea Cl, Rom. 127 FG55
Gidea Cl, S.Ock. 149 FW69
Tyssen Pl
Gideon Cl, Belv. 167 FB77
Gideon Ms W5 157 CK75
Gideon Rd SW11 160 DG83
Gidian Ct, St.Alb. 61 CD27
Giesbach Rd N19 121 DJ61
Giffard Rd N18 100 DS50
Giffard Way, Guil. 242 AU131
Giffin St SE8 163 EA80
Gifford Gdns W7 137 CD71
Gifford Pl, Brwd. 108 FX50
Blackthorn Way
Gifford St N1 141 DL66
Giffordside, Grays 171 GH78
Gift La E15 144 EE67
Giggs Hill, Orp. 206 EU96
Giggs Hill Gdns, T.Ditt. 197 CG102
Giggs Hill Rd, T.Ditt. 197 CG101
Gilbert Cl SE18 165 EM81
Gilbert Cl, Swans. 189 FX86
Gilbert Gro, Edg. 96 CR53
Gilbert Ho EC2 142 DQ71
The Barbican
Gilbert Ho SE8 163 EA79
McMillan St
Gilbert Pl WC1 273 P7
Gilbert Rd SE11 278 E9
Gilbert Rd SE11 161 DN77
Gilbert Rd SW19 180 DC94
Gilbert Rd, Belv. 166 FA76
Gilbert Rd, Brom. 184 EG94
Gilbert Rd, Grays 169 FW76
Gilbert Rd, Pnr. 116 BX56
Gilbert Rd, Rom. 127 FF56
Gilbert Rd (Harefield), Uxb. 92 BK54
Gilbert St E15 124 EE63
Gilbert St W1 272 G10
Gilbert St W1 140 DG72
Gilbert St, Houns. 156 CC83
High St
Gilbert Way, Berk. 38 AU19
Gilbert Way, Croy. 201 DL102
Beddington Fm Rd
Gilbey Cl, Uxb. 115 BP63
Gilbey Rd SW17 180 DE91
Gilbey Wk (Wooburn Grn), H.Wyc. 110 AD59
Stratford Dr
Gilbeys Yd NW1 140 DG66
Gilbourne Rd SE18 165 ET79
Gilda Av, Enf. 83 DY43
Gilda Cres N16 122 DU60
Gildea Cl, Pnr. 94 CA52
Gildea St W1 273 J7
Gilden Cl, Harl. 36 EY11
Gilden Cres NW5 120 DG64
Gilden Way, Harl. 36 EW12
Gildenhill Rd, Swan. 188 FJ94
Gilders, Saw. 36 EX05
Gilders Rd, Chess. 216 CM107
Gildersome St SE18 165 EN79
Nightingale Vale
Giles Cl, Rain. 148 FK68
Giles Coppice SE19 182 DT91
Giles Travers Cl, Egh. 193 BC97
Gilfrid Cl, Uxb. 135 BP72
Craig Dr
Gilhams Av, Bans. 217 CY112
Gilkes Cres SE21 182 DS86
Gilkes Pl SE21 182 DS86
Gill Av E16 144 EG72
Gill Av, Guil. 258 AS135
Gill Cl, Wat. 75 BQ44
Gill Cres (Northfleet), Grav. 191 GF90
Gill St E14 143 DZ72
Gillam Way, Rain. 147 FG65
Gillan Grn, Bushey 94 CC47
Gillards Ms E17 123 EA56
Gillards Way
Gillards Way E17 123 EA56
Gillender St E3 143 EC70
Gillender St E14 143 EC70
Gillespie Rd N5 121 DN62
Gillett Av E6 144 EL68
Gillett Pl N16 122 DS64
Gillett St
Gillett Rd, Th.Hth. 202 DR98
Gillett St N16 122 DS64
Gillette Cor, Islw. 157 CG80
Gillfoot NW1 273 L1
Gillfoot NW1 141 DJ68
Gillham Ter N17 100 DU51
Gilliam Gro, Pur. 219 DN110
Gillian Av, St.Alb. 42 CC24
Gillian Cres, Rom. 106 FJ54
Gillian Pk Rd, Sutt. 199 CZ102
Gillian St SE13 183 EB85
Gilliat Cl, Iver 133 BE72
Dutton Way
Gilliat Dr, Guil. 243 BD132
Gilliat Rd, Slou. 132 AS73
Gilliat's Grn, Rick. 73 BD42
Gillies St NW5 120 DG64
Gilling Ct NW3 140 DE65
Gillingham Ms SW1 277 K8
Gillingham Rd NW2 119 CY62
Gillingham Row SW1 277 K8
Gillingham St SW1 277 K8
Gillingham St SW1 161 DH77
Gillison Wk SE16 162 DU76
Tranton Rd
Gillman Dr E15 144 EF67
Gillmans Rd, Orp. 206 EV102
Gills Hill, Rad. 77 CF35
Gills Hill La, Rad. 77 CF36
Gills Hollow, Rad. 77 CF36
Gill's Rd (South Darenth), Dart. 209 FS95
Gillum Cl, Barn. 98 DF46
Gilmais (Bookham), Lthd. 246 CC125
Gilman Cres, Wind. 151 AK83
Gilmore Cl, Slou. 152 AW75
Gilmore Cl, Uxb. 114 BN62
Gilmore Cres, Ashf. 174 BN92
Gilmore Rd SE13 163 ED84
Gilmour Cl, Wal.Cr. 82 DU35
Gilpin Av SW14 158 CR84
Gilpin Cl W2 140 DC71
Porteus Rd
Gilpin Cl, Mitch. 200 DE96
Gilpin Cres N18 100 DT50
Gilpin Cres, Twick. 176 CB87
Gilpin Rd E5 123 DY63
Gilpin Rd, Ware 33 DY07
Gilpin Way, Hayes 155 BR80
Gilpin's Gallop, Ware 33 EB11
Gilpins Ride, Berk. 38 AX18
Gilroy Cl, Rain. 147 FF65
Gilroy Way, Orp. 206 EV101
Gilsland, Wal.Abb. 84 EE35
Gilsland Rd, Th.Hth. 202 DR98
Gilstead Ho, Bark. 146 EV68
Gilstead Rd SW6 160 DB82
Gilston Pk, Harl. 35 EQ08
Gilston Rd SW10 160 DC78
Gilton Rd SE6 184 EE90
Giltspur St EC1 274 G8
Giltspur St EC1 141 DP72
Gilwell Cl E4 83 EB42
Antlers Hill
Gilwell La E4 83 EC42
Gilwell Pk E4 83 EC41
Gimcrack Hill, Lthd. 231 CH123
Dorking Rd
Gippeswyck Cl, Pnr. 94 BX53
Uxbridge Rd
Gipsy Hill SE19 182 DS92
Gipsy La SW15 159 CU83
Gipsy La, Grays 170 GC79
Gipsy Rd SE27 182 DQ91
Gipsy Rd, Well. 166 EX81
Gipsy Rd Gdns SE27 182 DQ91
Giralda Cl E16 144 EK71
Fulmer Rd
Giraud St E14 143 EB72
Girdlers Rd W14 159 CX77
Girdlestone Wk N19 121 DJ61
Girdwood Rd SW18 179 CY87
Girling Way, Felt. 155 BU83
Girona Cl (Chafford Hundred), Grays 169 FW76
Gironde Rd SW6 159 CZ80
Girtin Rd, Bushey 76 CB43
Girton Av NW9 118 CN55
Girton Cl, Nthlt. 136 CC65
Girton Ct, Wal.Cr. 67 DY30
Girton Gdns, Croy. 203 EA104
Girton Rd SE26 183 DX92
Girton Rd, Nthlt. 136 CC65
Girton Vil W10 139 CX72
Girton Way, Rick. 75 BQ43
Gisborne Gdns, Rain. 147 FF69
Gisborne Cl, Wall. 201 DK104
Gisburn Rd N8 121 DM56
Gisburne Way, Wat. 75 BU37
Gissing Wk N1 141 DN66
Lofting Rd
Gittens Cl, Brom. 184 EF91
Given Wilson Wk E13 144 EF68
Givons Gro, Lthd. 247 CH125
Glacier Way, Wem. 137 CK68
Gladbeck Way, Enf. 81 DP42
Gladding Rd E12 124 EK63
Gladding Rd (Cheshunt), Wal.Cr. 65 DP25
Glade, The N21 81 DM44
Glade, The SE7 164 EJ80
Glade, The, Brwd. 109 GA46
Glade, The, Brom. 204 EK96
Glade, The, Couls. 235 DN119
Glade, The, Croy. 203 DX99
Glade, The, Enf. 81 DN41
Glade, The, Epsom 217 CU106
Glade, The, Ger.Cr. 112 AX60
Glade, The (Penn), H.Wyc. 88 AC46
Glade, The, Ilf. 103 EM53
Glade, The (Fetcham), Lthd. 230 CA122
Glade, The, Sev. 257 FH123
Glade, The, Stai. 174 BH94
Glade, The, Sutt. 217 CY109
Glade, The, Tad. 234 DA121
Glade, The, Upmin. 128 FQ64
Glade, The, Welw.G.C. 29 CW07
Glade, The, W.Byf. 211 BE113
Glade, The, W.Wick. 203 EB104
Glade, The, Wdf.Grn. 102 EH48
Glade Cl, Surb. 197 CK103
Glade Ct, Ilf. 103 EM53
The Glade
Glade Gdns, Croy. 203 DY101
Glade La, Sthl. 156 CB75
Glade Spur, Tad. 234 DB121
Glades, The, Grav. 191 GK93
Glades, The, Hem.H. 39 BE19
Glades Shop Cen, The, Brom. 204 EG96
Gladeside N21 81 DM44
Gladeside, Croy. 203 DX100
Gladeside, St.Alb. 43 CK17
Gladeside Cl, Chess. 215 CK108
Leatherhead Rd
Gladeside Ct, Warl. 236 DV120
Gladesmore Rd N15 122 DT58
Gladeswood Rd, Belv. 167 FB77
Gladeway, The, Wal.Abb. 67 ED33
Gladiator St SE23 183 DY86
Glading Ter N16 122 DT62
Gladioli Cl, Hmptn. 176 CA93
Gresham Rd
Gladsdale Dr, Pnr. 115 BU56
Gladsmuir Cl, Walt. 196 BW103
Gladsmuir Rd N19 121 DJ60
Gladsmuir Rd, Barn. 79 CY40
Gladstone Av E12 144 EL66
Gladstone Av N22 99 DN54
Gladstone Av, Felt. 175 BU86
Gladstone Av, Twick. 177 CD87
Gladstone Ct SW19 180 DA94
Gladstone Rd
Gladstone Gdns, Houns. 156 CC81
Palmerston Rd
Gladstone Ms N22 99 DN54
Pelham Rd
Gladstone Ms NW6 139 CZ66
Cavendish Rd
Gladstone Ms SE20 182 DW94
Gladstone Par NW2 119 CV60
Edgware Rd
Gladstone Pk Gdns NW2 119 CV62
Gladstone Pl E3 143 DZ68
Roman Rd
Gladstone Pl, Barn. 79 CX42
Gladstone Rd SW19 180 DA94
Gladstone Rd W4 *Acton La* 158 CR76
Gladstone Rd, Ash. 231 CK118
Gladstone Rd, Buck.H. 102 EH46
Gladstone Rd, Chesh. 54 AQ31
Gladstone Rd, Croy. 202 DR101
Gladstone Rd, Dart. 188 FM86
Gladstone Rd, Hodd. 49 EB16
Gladstone Rd, Kings.T. 198 CN97
Gladstone Rd, Orp. 223 EQ106
Gladstone Rd, Sthl. 156 BY76
Gladstone Rd, Surb. 197 CK103
Gladstone Rd, Ware 32 DW05
Gladstone Rd, Wat. 76 BW41
Gladstone St SE1 278 F6
Gladstone St SE1 161 DP76
Gladstone Ter SE27 182 DQ91
Gladstone Ter SW8 161 DH81
Gladstone Way (Wealdstone), Har. 117 CE55
Gladstone Way, Slou. 151 AN75
Gladwell Rd N8 121 DM58
Gladwell Rd, Brom. 184 EG93
Gladwyn Rd SW15 159 CX83
Gladys Rd NW6 140 DA66
Glaisher St SE8 163 EB79
Glaisyer Way, Iver 133 BC68
Glamis Cl (Cheshunt), Wal.Cr. 66 DU29
Glamis Cres, Hayes 155 BQ76
Glamis Dr, Horn. 128 FL60
Glamis Pl E1 142 DW73
Glamis Rd E1 142 DW73
Glamis Way, Nthlt. 136 CC65
Glamorgan Cl, Mitch. 201 DL97
Glamorgan Rd, Kings.T. 177 CJ94
Glanfield, Hem.H. 40 BL17
Bathurst Rd
Glanfield Rd, Beck. 203 DZ98
Glanleam Rd, Stan. 95 CK49
Glanmead, Brwd. 108 FY46
Glanmor Rd, Slou. 132 AV73
Glanthams Cl, Brwd. 108 FY47
Glanthams Rd, Brwd. 109 FZ47
Glanty, The, Egh. 173 BB91
Glanville Dr, Horn. 128 FM60
Glanville Rd SW2 181 DL85
Glanville Rd, Brom. 204 EH97
Glasbrook Av, Twick. 176 BZ88
Glasbrook Rd SE9 184 EK87
Glaserton Rd N16 122 DS59
Glasford St SW17 180 DF93
Glasgow Ho W9 140 DB68
Glasgow Rd E13 144 EH68
Glasgow Rd N18 100 DV50
Aberdeen Rd
Glasgow Rd, Slou. 131 AN72
Glasgow Ter SW1 161 DJ78
Glass St E2 142 DV70
Coventry Rd
Glass Yd SE18 165 EN76
Woolwich High St
Glasse Cl W13 137 CG73
Glasshill St SE1 278 G4
Glasshill St SE1 161 DP75
Glasshouse Flds E1 143 DX73
Glasshouse St W1 277 L1
Glasshouse St W1 141 DJ73
Glasshouse Wk SE11 278 A10
Glasshouse Wk SE11 161 DL78
Glasshouse Yd EC1 275 H6
Glasslyn Rd N8 121 DK57
Glassmill La, Brom. 204 EF96
Glastonbury Av, Wdf.Grn. 102 EK52
Glastonbury Cl, Orp. 206 EW102
Glastonbury Pl E1 142 DW72
Sutton St
Glastonbury Rd N9 100 DT46
Glastonbury Rd, Mord. 200 DA101
Glastonbury St NW6 119 CZ64
Glaucus St E3 143 EB71
Glazbury Rd W14 159 CY77
Glazebrook Cl SE21 182 DR89
Glazebrook Rd, Tedd. 177 CF94
Glean Wk, Hat. 45 CU21
Southdown Rd

Gleave Cl, St.Alb. 43 CH19
Glebe, The SE3 164 EE83
Glebe, The SW16 181 DK91
Glebe, The, Chis. 205 EQ95
Glebe, The, Harl. 35 ET13
Halling Hill
Glebe, The, Horl. 268 DF148
Glebe, The, Kings L. 58 BN29
Glebe, The (Leigh), Reig. 265 CU141
Glebe, The, Wat. 60 BW33
Glebe, The, West Dr. 154 BM77
Glebe, The, Wor.Pk. 199 CT102
Glebe Av, Enf. 81 DP41
Glebe Av, Har. 118 CL55
Glebe Av, Mitch. 200 DE96
Glebe Av, Ruis. 135 BV65
Glebe Av, Uxb. 115 BQ63
Glebe Av, Wdf.Grn. 102 EG51
Glebe Cl W4 158 CS78
Glebe St
Glebe Cl (Chalfont St. Peter), Ger.Cr. 90 AX52
Glebe Cl, Hat. 46 DF17
Glebe Cl, Hem.H. 40 BL24
Glebe Cl (Bookham), Lthd. 246 CA126
Glebe Cl, Maid. 150 AF75
Glebe Cl, S.Croy. 220 DT111
Glebe Cl, Uxb. 115 BQ63
Glebe Cotts (West Clandon), Guil. 244 BH132
Glebe Cotts, Hat. 46 DF17
Glebe Cotts, Sutt. 218 DB105
Vale Rd
Glebe Cotts, West. 240 EV123
Glebe Ct W7 137 CD73
Glebe Ct, Guil. 243 AZ134
Glebe Ct, Mitch. 200 DF97
Glebe Ct, Sev. 257 FH126
Oak La
Glebe Ct, Stan. 95 CJ50
Glebe Rd
Glebe Cres NW4 119 CW56
Glebe Cres, Har. 118 CL55
Glebe Gdns, N.Mal. 198 CS101
Glebe Gdns (Byfleet), W.Byf. 212 BK114
Glebe Ho Dr, Brom. 204 EH102
Glebe Hyrst SE19 182 DT91
Giles Coppice
Glebe Hyrst, S.Croy. 220 DT112
Glebe La, Barn. 79 CU43
Glebe La (Abinger Common), Dor. 262 BX143
Glebe La, Har. 118 CL56
Glebe La, Sev. 257 FH126
Glebe Path, Mitch. 200 DE97
Glebe Pl SW3 160 DE79
Glebe Pl (Horton Kirby), Dart. 208 FQ98
Glebe Rd E8 142 DT66
Middleton Rd
Glebe Rd N3 98 DC53
Glebe Rd N8 121 DM56
Glebe Rd NW10 139 CT65
Glebe Rd SW13 159 CU82
Glebe Rd, Ash. 231 CK118
Glebe Rd, Brom. 204 EG95
Glebe Rd, Cars. 218 DF107
Glebe Rd, Dag. 147 FB65
Glebe Rd, Dor. 263 CF136
Glebe Rd, Egh. 173 BC93
Glebe Rd (Chalfont St. Peter), Ger.Cr. 90 AW53
Glebe Rd, Grav. 191 GF88
Glebe Rd, Hayes 135 BT74
Glebe Rd, Hert. 32 DR07
Glebe Rd, Rain. 148 FJ69
Glebe Rd, Red. 235 DH124
Glebe Rd, Stai. 174 BH93
Glebe Rd, Stan. 95 CJ50
Glebe Rd, Sutt. 217 CY109
Glebe Rd, Uxb. 134 BJ68
Glebe Rd, Warl. 237 DX117
Glebe Rd (Old Windsor), Wind. 172 AV85
Glebe Side, Twick. 177 CF86
Glebe St W4 158 CS78
Glebe Ter E3 143 EA69
Bow Rd
Glebe Way, Amer. 55 AR36
Glebe Way, Erith 167 FE79
Glebe Way, Felt. 176 CA90
Glebe Way, Horn. 128 FL59
Glebe Way, S.Croy. 220 DT111
Glebe Way, W.Wick. 203 EC103
Glebefield, The, Sev. 256 FF123
Glebeland, Hat. 45 CW18
St. Ethelredas Dr
Glebeland Gdns, Shep. 195 BQ100
Glebelands, Chig. 104 EV48
Glebelands, Dart. 167 FF84
Glebelands (Claygate), Esher 215 CF109
Glebelands, Harl. 35 ET12
Glebelands (Penn), H.Wyc. 88 AC47
Glebelands, W.Mol. 196 CB99
Glebelands Av E18 102 EG54
Glebelands Av, Ilf. 125 ER59
Glebelands Cl SE5 162 DS83
Grove Hill Rd
Glebelands Rd, Felt. 175 BU87
Glebeway, Wdf.Grn. 102 EJ50
Gledhow Gdns SW5 160 DC77
Gledhow Wd, Tad. 234 DB121
Gledstanes Rd W14 159 CY78
Gledwood Av, Hayes 135 BT71
Gledwood Cres, Hayes 135 BT71
Gledwood Dr, Hayes 135 BT71
Gledwood Gdns, Hayes 135 BT71
Gleed Av, Bushey 95 CD47
Gleeson Dr, Orp. 223 ET106
Gleeson Ms, Add. 212 BJ105
Glegg Pl SW15 159 CX84
Glen, The, Add. 211 BF106
Glen, The, Brom. 204 EE96
Glen, The, Croy. 203 DX103
Glen, The, Enf. 81 DP42
Glen, The, Hem.H. 40 BM15
Glen, The, Nthwd. 93 BR52
Glen, The, Orp. 205 EM104
Glen, The, Pnr. 116 BY59
Glen, The (Eastcote), Pnr. 115 BV57
Glen, The, Rain. 148 FJ70
Glen, The, Slou. 152 AW77
Glen, The, Sthl. 156 BZ78
Glen, The, Wem. 117 CK63
Glen Albyn Rd SW19 179 CX89
Glen Av, Ashf. 174 BN91
Glen Cl, Shep. 194 BN98
Glen Cl (Kingswood), Tad. 233 CY123
Glen Cres, Wdf.Grn. 102 EH51
Glen Faba Rd, Harl. 50 EF17
Glen Gdns, Croy. 201 DN104
Glen Ri, Wdf.Grn. 102 EH51
Glen Rd E13 144 EJ70
Glen Rd E17 123 DZ57
Glen Rd, Chess. 198 CL104
Glen Rd End, Wall. 219 DH109
Glen Ter E14 163 EC75
Manchester Rd
Glen Vw, Grav. 191 GJ88
Glen Wk, Islw. 177 CD85
Glen Way, Wat. 75 BS38
Glena Mt, Sutt. 218 DC105
Glenaffric Av E14 163 ED77
Glenalla Rd, Ruis. 115 BT59
Glenalmond Rd, Har. 118 CL56
Glenalvon Way SE18 164 EL77
Glenarm Rd E5 122 DW64
Glenavon Cl (Claygate), Esher 215 CG108
Glenavon Gdns, Slou. 152 AW77
Glenavon Rd E15 144 EE66
Glenbarr Cl SE9 165 EP83
Dumbreck Rd
Glenbow Rd, Brom. 184 EE93
Glenbrook N, Enf. 81 DM42
Glenbrook Rd NW6 120 DA64
Glenbrook S, Enf. 81 DM42
Glenbuck Ct, Surb. 197 CK100
Glenbuck Rd
Glenbuck Rd, Surb. 197 CK100
Glenburnie Rd SW17 180 DF90
Glencairn Dr W5 137 CJ70
Glencairn Rd SW16 181 DL94
Glencairne Cl E16 144 EK71
Glencoe Av, Ilf. 125 ER59
Glencoe Dr, Dag. 126 FA63
Glencoe Rd, Bushey 76 CA44
Glencoe Rd, Hayes 136 BX71
Glencoe Rd, Wey. 194 BN104
Glencorse Grn, Wat. 94 BX49
Caldwell Rd
Glendale, Hem.H. 40 BH20
Glendale, Swan. 207 FF99
Glendale Av N22 99 DN52
Glendale Av, Edg. 96 CM49
Glendale Av, Rom. 126 EW59
Glendale Cl SE9 165 EN83
Dumbreck Rd
Glendale Cl, Brwd. 108 FY45
Glendale Cl, Wok. 226 AW118
Glendale Dr SW19 179 CZ92
Glendale Dr, Guil. 243 BB130
Glendale Gdns, Wem. 117 CK60
Glendale Ms, Beck. 203 EB95
Glendale Ri, Ken. 235 DP115
Glendale Rd, Erith 167 FC77
Glendale Rd (Northfleet), Grav. 190 GE91
Glendale Wk (Cheshunt), Wal.Cr. 67 DY30
Glendale Way SE28 146 EW73
Glendall St SW9 161 DM84
Glendarvon St SW15 159 CX83
Glendene Av (East Horsley), Lthd. 245 BS126
Glendevon Cl, Edg. 96 CP48
Tayside Dr
Glendish Rd N17 100 DV53
Glendor Gdns NW7 96 CR49
Glendower Cres, Orp. 206 EU100
Glendower Gdns SW14 158 CR83
Glendower Rd
Glendower Pl SW7 160 DD77
Glendower Rd E4 101 ED46
Glendower Rd SW14 158 CR83
Glendown Rd SE2 166 EU78
Glendun Rd W3 138 CS73
Gleneagle Ms SW16 181 DK92
Ambleside Av
Gleneagle Rd SW16 181 DK92
Gleneagles, Stan. 95 CH51
Gleneagles Cl SE16 162 DV78
Ryder Dr
Gleneagles Cl, Orp. 205 ER102
Gleneagles Cl, Rom. 106 FM52
Gleneagles Cl (Stanwell), Stai. 174 BK86
Gleneagles Cl, Wat. 94 BX49
Gleneagles Grn, Orp. 205 ER102
Tandridge Dr
Gleneagles Twr, Sthl. 136 CC72
Gleneldon Ms SW16 181 DL91
Gleneldon Rd SW16 181 DL91
Glenelg Rd SW2 181 DL85
Glenesk Rd SE9 165 EN83
Glenester Cl, Hodd. 33 EA14
Glenfarg Rd SE6 183 ED88
Glenferrie Rd, St.Alb. 43 CG20
Glenfield Cl (Brockham), Bet. 264 CP138
Glenfield Cres, Ruis. 115 BR59
Glenfield Rd SW12 181 DJ88
Glenfield Rd W13 157 CH75
Glenfield Rd, Ashf. 175 BP93
Glenfield Rd, Bans. 234 DB115
Glenfield Rd (Brockham), Bet. 264 CP138
Glenfield Ter W13 157 CH75
Glenfinlas Way SE5 161 DP80
Glenforth St SE10 164 EF78
Glengall Causeway E14 163 EA76
Glengall Gro E14 163 EC76
Glengall Rd NW6 139 CZ67
Glengall Rd SE15 162 DT79
Glengall Rd, Bexh. 166 EY83
Glengall Rd, Edg. 96 CP48
Glengall Rd, Wdf.Grn. 102 EG51
Glengall Ter SE15 162 DT79
Glengarnock Av E14 163 EC77
Glengarry Rd SE22 182 DS85
Glenham Dr, Ilf. 125 EP57
Glenhaven Av, Borwd. 78 CN41
Glenhead Cl SE9 165 EP83
Dumbreck Rd
Glenheadon Cl, Lthd. 231 CK123
Glenheadon Ri
Glenheadon Ri, Lthd. 231 CK123
Glenhill Cl N3 98 DA54
Glenhouse Rd SE9 185 EN85
Glenhurst Av NW5 120 DG63
Glenhurst Av, Bex. 186 EZ88
Glenhurst Av, Ruis. 115 BQ59
Glenhurst Ct SE19 182 DT92
Glenhurst Ri SE19 182 DQ94
Glenhurst Rd N12 98 DD50
Glenhurst Rd, Brent. 157 CJ79
Glenilla Rd NW3 140 DE65
Glenister Ho, Hayes 135 BV74
Glenister Pk Rd SW16 181 DK94
Glenister Rd SE10 164 EF78
Glenister Rd, Chesh. 54 AQ28
Glenister St E16 145 EN74
Glenkerry Ho E14 143 EC72
Glenlea Rd SE9 185 EM85
Glenlion Ct, Wey. 195 BS104
Glenloch Rd NW3 140 DE65
Glenloch Rd, Enf. 82 DW40
Glenluce Rd SE3 164 EG79
Glenlyn Av, St.Alb. 43 CH21
Glenlyon Rd SE9 185 EN85
Glenmere Av NW7 97 CU52
Glenmill, Hmptn. 176 BZ92
Glenmire Ter, Ware 33 ED11
Glenmore Cl, Add. 194 BH104
Glenmore Gdns, Abb.L. 59 BU32
Stewart Cl
Glenmore Rd NW3 140 DE65
Glenmore Rd, Well. 165 ET81
Glenmore Way, Bark. 146 EU68
Glenmount Path SE18 165 EQ78
Raglan Rd
Glenn Av, Pur. 219 DP111
Glennie Rd SE27 181 DN90
Glenny Rd, Bark. 145 EQ65
Glenorchy Cl, Hayes 136 BY71
Glenparke Rd E7 144 EH65
Glenrosa Gdns, Grav. 191 GM92
Glenrosa St SW6 160 DC82
Glenrose Ct, Sid. 186 EV92
Glenroy St W12 139 CW72
Glensdale Rd SE4 163 DZ83
Glenshee Cl, Nthwd. 93 BQ51
Rickmansworth Rd
Glenshiel Rd SE9 185 EN85
Glenside, Chig. 103 EP51
Glenside Cotts, Slou. 152 AT76
Glentanner Way SW17 180 DD90
Aboyne Rd
Glentham Gdns SW13 159 CV79
Glentham Rd
Glentham Rd SW13 159 CU79
Glenthorne Av, Croy. 202 DV102
Glenthorne Cl, Sutt. 200 DA102
Glenthorne Cl, Uxb. 134 BN69
Uxbridge Rd
Glenthorne Gdns, Ilf. 125 EN55
Glenthorne Gdns, Sutt. 200 DA102
Glenthorne Ms W6 159 CV77
Glenthorne Rd
Glenthorne Rd E17 123 DY57
Glenthorne Rd N11 98 DF50
Glenthorne Rd W6 159 CW77
Glenthorne Rd, Kings.T. 198 CM98
Glenthorpe Rd, Mord. 199 CX99
Glenton Cl, Rom. 105 FE51
Glenton Rd SE13 164 EE84
Glenton Way, Rom. 105 FE52
Glentrammon Av, Orp. 223 ET107
Glentrammon Cl, Orp. 223 ET107
Glentrammon Gdns, Orp. 223 ET107
Glentrammon Rd, Orp. 223 ET107
Glentworth Pl, Slou. 131 AQ74
Glentworth St NW1 272 E5
Glentworth St NW1 140 DF70
Glenure Rd SE9 185 EN85
Glenview SE2 166 EX79
Glenview Gdns, Hem.H. 40 BH20
Glenview Rd
Glenview Rd, Brom. 204 EK96
Glenview Rd, Hem.H. 40 BH20
Glenville Av, Enf. 82 DQ38
Glenville Ct SE19 182 DT92
Lymer Av
Glenville Gro SE8 163 DZ80
Glenville Ms SW18 180 DB87
Glenville Rd, Kings.T. 198 CN95
Glenwood, Brox. 49 DZ19
Glenwood, Dor. 263 CJ138
Glenwood, Welw.G.C. 30 DD10
Glenwood Av NW9 118 CS60
Glenwood Av, Rain. 147 FH70
Glenwood Cl, Har. 117 CF57
Glenwood Dr, Rom. 127 FG56
Glenwood Gdns, Ilf. 125 EN57
Glenwood Gro NW9 118 CQ60
Glenwood Rd N15 121 DP57
Glenwood Rd NW7 96 CS48
Glenwood Rd SE6 183 DZ88
Glenwood Rd, Epsom 217 CU107
Glenwood Rd, Houns. 157 CD83
Glenwood Way, Croy. 203 DX100
Glenworth Av E14 163 ED77
Glevum Cl, St.Alb. 42 BZ22
Gliddon Rd W14 159 CY77
Glimpsing Grn, Erith 166 EY76
Glisson Rd, Uxb. 134 BN68
Gload Cres, Orp. 206 EX103
Global App E3 143 EB68
Hancock Rd
Globe Ct, Hert. 32 DQ07
Grove Wk
Globe Ind Estates, Grays 170 GC78
Globe Pond Rd SE16 143 DY74
Globe Rd E1 142 DW69
Globe Rd E2 142 DW69
Globe Rd E15 124 EF64
Globe Rd, Horn. 127 FG58
Globe Rd, Wdf.Grn. 102 EJ51
Globe Rope Wk E14 163 EC77
Globe St SE1 279 J6
Globe St SE1 162 DR76
Globe Ter E2 142 DW69
Globe Rd
Globe Yd W1 273 H9
Glory Cl (Wooburn Grn), H.Wyc. 110 AF56
Glory Hill La, Beac. 110 AF55
Glory Mead, Dor. 263 CH139
Glory Mill La (Wooburn Grn), H.Wyc. 110 AE56
Glossop Rd, S.Croy. 220 DR109
Gloster Rd, N.Mal. 198 CS98
Gloster Rd, Wok. 227 BA120
Gloucester Arc SW7 160 DC77
Gloucester Rd
Gloucester Av NW1 140 DG66
Gloucester Av, Grays 170 GC75
Gloucester Av, Horn. 128 FN56
Gloucester Av, Sid. 185 ES89
Gloucester Av, Slou. 131 AQ71
Gloucester Av, Wal.Cr. 67 DY33
Gloucester Av, Well. 165 ET84
Gloucester Circ SE10 163 EC80
Gloucester Cl NW10 138 CR66
Gloucester Cl, T.Ditt. 197 CG102
Gloucester Ct EC3 279 N1
Gloucester Ct, Rich. 158 CN80
Gloucester Ct, Til. 171 GF82
Dock Rd
Gloucester Ct (Denham), Uxb. 114 BG58
Moorfield Rd
Gloucester Cres NW1 141 DH67
Gloucester Cres, Stai. 174 BK93
Gloucester Dr N4 121 DP61
Gloucester Dr NW11 120 DA56
Gloucester Dr, Stai. 173 BC90
Gloucester Gdns NW11 119 CZ59
Gloucester Gdns W2 140 DC72
Bishops Br Rd
Gloucester Gdns, Barn. 80 DG42
Gloucester Gdns, Ilf. 124 EL59
Gloucester Gdns, Sutt. 200 DB103
Gloucester Gate NW1 141 DH68
Gloucester Gate Ms NW1 141 DH68
Gloucester Gate
Gloucester Gro, Edg. 96 CR53
Gloucester Gro Est SE15 162 DS79
Gloucester Ho N7 121 DL62
Gloucester Ho NW6 140 DA68
Gloucester Ms E10 123 EA59
Gloucester Rd
Gloucester Ms W2 140 DC72
Gloucester Ms W W2 140 DC72
Cleveland Ter
Gloucester Par, Sid. 186 EU85
Gloucester Pl NW1 272 D4
Gloucester Pl NW1 140 DF70
Gloucester Pl W1 272 E6
Gloucester Pl W1 140 DF71
Gloucester Pl, Enf. 82 DQ40
Chase Side
Gloucester Pl, Wind. 151 AR82
Gloucester Pl Ms W1 272 E7
Gloucester Rd E10 123 EA59
Gloucester Rd E11 124 EH57
Gloucester Rd E12 125 EM62
Gloucester Rd E17 101 DX54
Gloucester Rd N17 100 DR54
Gloucester Rd N18 100 DT50
Gloucester Rd SW7 160 DC77
Gloucester Rd W3 158 CQ75
Gloucester Rd W5 157 CJ75
Gloucester Rd, Barn. 80 DC43
Gloucester Rd, Belv. 166 EZ78
Gloucester Rd, Brwd. 108 FV43
Gloucester Rd, Croy. 202 DR100
Gloucester Rd, Dart. 187 FH87
Gloucester Rd, Enf. 82 DQ38
Gloucester Rd, Felt. 176 BW88
Gloucester Rd, Grav. 191 GJ91
Gloucester Rd, Guil. 242 AT132
Gloucester Rd, Hmptn. 176 CB94
Gloucester Rd, Har. 116 CB57
Gloucester Rd, Houns. 156 BY84
Gloucester Rd, Kings.T. 198 CP96
Gloucester Rd, Red. 250 DF133
Gloucester Rd, Rich. 158 CN80
Gloucester Rd, Rom. 127 FE58
Gloucester Rd, Tedd. 177 CE92
Gloucester Rd, Twick. 176 CC88
Gloucester Sq E2 142 DU67
Whiston Rd
Gloucester Sq W2 272 A9
Gloucester Sq W2 140 DD72
Gloucester Sq, Wok. 226 AY117
Church St E
Gloucester St SW1 161 DJ78
Gloucester Ter W2 140 DD73
Gloucester Wk W8 160 DA75
Gloucester Wk, Wok. 227 AZ117
Gloucester Way EC1 274 E3
Gloucester Way EC1 141 DN69
Glover Cl SE2 166 EW77
Glover Cl, Wal.Cr. 66 DT27
Allwood Rd
Glover Dr N18 100 DW51
Glover Rd, Pnr. 116 BX58
Glovers Cl, Hert. 32 DQ11
Glovers Gro, Ruis. 115 BP59
Glovers La, Harl. 52 EY20
Glovers Rd, Reig. 266 DB135
Gloxinia Rd (Southfleet), Grav. 190 GB93
Gloxinia Wk, Hmptn. 176 CA93
Glycena Rd SW11 160 DF83
Glyn Av, Barn. 80 DD42
Glyn Cl SE25 202 DS96
Glyn Cl, Epsom 217 CU109
Glyn Ct SW16 181 DN90
Glyn Davies Cl (Dunton Grn), Sev. 241 FE120
Glyn Dr, Sid. 186 EV91
Glyn Rd E5 123 DX63
Glyn Rd, Enf. 82 DW42
Glyn Rd, Wor.Pk. 199 CX103
Glyn St SE11 161 DM78
Kennington La
Glynde Ms SW3 276 C7
Glynde Rd, Bexh. 166 EX83
Glynde St SE4 183 DZ86
Glyndebourne Pk, Orp. 205 EP103
Glyndon Rd SE18 165 EQ77
Glynfield Rd NW10 138 CS66
Glynne Rd N22 99 DN54
Glynswood (Chalfont St. Peter), Ger.Cr. 91 AZ52
Glynwood Ct SE23 182 DW89
Goat La, Enf. 82 DT38
Goat La, Surb. 197 CJ103
Goat Rd, Mitch. 200 DG101
Goat St SE1 279 P4
Goat Wf, Brent. 158 CL79
Goaters All SW6 159 CZ80
Goatsfield Rd (Tatsfield), West. 238 EJ120
Goatswood La, Rom. 105 FH45
Gobions Av, Rom. 105 FD52
Gobions Way, Pot.B. 64 DB28
Swanley Bar La
Goblins Grn, Welw.G.C. 29 CX10
Godalming Av, Wall. 219 DL106
Godalming Rd E14 143 EB71
Godbold Rd E15 144 EE69
Goddard Cl, Shep. 194 BM97
Magdalene Rd
Goddard Pl N19 121 DJ62
Goddard Rd, Beck. 203 DX98
Goddards Cl, Hert. 47 DJ19
Goddards Way, Ilf. 125 ER60
Goddington Chase, Orp. 224 EV105
Goddington La, Orp. 206 EU104
Godfrey Av, Nthlt. 136 BY67
Godfrey Av, Twick. 177 CD87
Godfrey Hill SE18 164 EL77
Godfrey Rd SE18 165 EM77
Godfrey St E15 143 EC68
Godfrey St SW3 276 C10
Godfrey St SW3 160 DE78
Godfrey Way, Houns. 176 BZ87
Goding St SE11 161 DL78
Godley Rd SW18 180 DD88
Godley Rd (Byfleet), W.Byf. 212 BM113
Godliman St EC4 275 H9
Godliman St EC4 142 DQ72
Godman Rd SE15 162 DV82
Godman Rd, Grays 171 GG76
Godolphin Cl N13 99 DP51
Godolphin Cl, Sutt. 217 CZ111
Godolphin Pl W3 138 CR73
Vyner Rd
Godolphin Rd W12 159 CV75
Godolphin Rd (Seer Grn), Beac. 89 AQ51
Godolphin Rd, Slou. 131 AR73
Godolphin Rd, Wey. 213 BR107
Godric Cres (New Addington), Croy. 221 ED110
Godson Rd, Croy. 201 DN104
Godson St N1 141 DN68
Godstone Bypass, Gdse. 252 DW129
Godstone Grn, Gdse. 252 DV131
Godstone Grn Rd, Gdse. 252 DV131
Godstone Hill, Gdse. 252 DV127
Godstone Rd, Cat. 236 DU124
Godstone Rd, Ken. 219 DN112
Godstone Rd, Oxt. 253 EA131
Godstone Rd, Pur. 219 DN112
Godstone Rd (Bletchingley), Red. 252 DR133
Godstone Rd, Sutt. 218 DC105
Godstone Rd, Twick. 177 CH86
Godstone Rd, Whyt. 236 DT116
Godstow Rd SE2 166 EW75
Godwin Cl E4 83 EC38
Godwin Cl N1 142 DQ68
Napier Gro
Godwin Cl, Epsom 216 CQ107
Godwin Ct NW1 141 DJ68
Crowndale Rd
Godwin Rd E7 124 EH63
Godwin Rd, Brom. 204 EJ97
Goffers Rd SE3 163 ED81
Goffs Cres (Cheshunt), Wal.Cr. 65 DP29
Goffs La (Cheshunt), Wal.Cr. 66 DR29
Goffs Oak Av (Cheshunt), Wal.Cr. 65 DP28
Goffs Rd, Ashf. 175 BR93
Gogmore Fm Cl, Cher. 193 BF101
Gogmore La, Cher. 194 BG101
Goidel Cl, Wall. 219 DK105
Golborne Gdns W10 139 CZ70
Golborne Rd
Golborne Ms W10 139 CY71
Portobello Rd
Golborne Rd W10 139 CY71
Gold Cl, Brox. 49 DY20
Gold Hill, Edg. 96 CR51
Gold Hill E (Chalfont St. Peter), Ger.Cr. 90 AX54
Gold Hill N (Chalfont St. Peter), Ger.Cr. 90 AW53
Gold Hill W (Chalfont St. Peter), Ger.Cr. 90 AW53
Gold La, Edg. 96 CR51
Golda Cl, Barn. 79 CX44
Goldace, Grays 170 FZ79
Goldbeaters Gro, Edg. 96 CS51
Goldcliff Cl, Mord. 200 DA100
Goldcrest Cl E16 144 EK71
Sheerwater Rd
Goldcrest Cl SE28 146 EW73
Goldcrest Cl, Horl. 268 DE147
Wither Dale
Goldcrest Ms W5 137 CK71
Montpelier Av
Goldcrest Way, Bushey 94 CC46
Goldcrest Way (New Addington), Croy. 221 ED109
Goldcrest Way, Pur. 219 DK110
Goldcroft, Hem.H. 40 BN22
Golden Ct, Rich. 177 CK85
George St
Golden Cres, Hayes 135 BT74
Golden Cross Ms W11 139 CZ72
Basing St
Golden Dell, Welw.G.C. 29 CZ13
Golden La EC1 275 H5
Golden La EC1 142 DQ70
Golden La Est EC1 275 H5
Golden Manor W7 137 CE73
Golden Oak Cl (Farnham Common), Slou. 131 AQ65
Golden Plover Cl E16 144 EH72
Maplin Rd
Golden Sq W1 273 L10
Golden Sq W1 141 DJ73
Golden Yd NW3 120 DC63
Heath St
Golders Cl, Edg. 96 CP50
Golders Gdns NW11 119 CY59
Golders Grn Cres NW11 119 CZ59
Golders Grn Rd NW11 119 CY58
Golders Manor Dr NW11 119 CX58
Golders Pk Cl NW11 120 DB60
Golders Ri NW4 119 CX57
Golders Way NW11 119 CZ59
Goldfinch Cl, Orp. 224 EU106
Goldfinch Gdns, Guil. 243 BD133
Goldfinch Rd SE28 165 ER76
Goldfinch Rd, S.Croy. 221 DY110
Goldfinch Way, Borwd. 78 CN42
Goldfort Wk, Wok. 226 AS116
Langmans Way
Goldhawk Ms W12 159 CV75
Devonport Rd
Goldhawk Rd W6 159 CT77
Goldhawk Rd W12 159 CU76
Goldhaze Cl, Wdf.Grn. 102 EK52
Goldhurst Ter NW6 140 DB66
Golding Cl, Chess. 215 CJ107
Coppard Gdns
Golding Rd, Sev. 257 FJ122
Golding St E1 142 DU72
Golding Ter SW11 160 DG82
Longhedge St
Goldingham Av, Loug. 85 EQ40
Goldings, The, Wok. 226 AT116
Goldings Cres, Hat. 45 CV17
Goldings Hill, Loug. 85 EN39
Goldings La, Hert. 31 DN06
Goldings Ri, Loug. 85 EN39
Goldings Rd, Loug. 85 EN39
Goldington Cl, Hodd. 33 DZ14
Goldington Cres NW1 141 DK68
Goldington St NW1 141 DK68
Goldman Cl E2 142 DU70
Goldmark Ho SE3 164 EH83
Lebrun Sq
Goldney Rd W9 140 DA70
Goldrill Dr N11 98 DG47
Goldrings Rd (Oxshott), Lthd. 214 CC113
Goldsboro Rd SW8 161 DK81
Goldsborough Cres E4 101 EB47
Goldsdown Cl, Enf. 83 DY40
Goldsdown Rd, Enf. 83 DX40
Goldsel Rd, Swan. 207 FD99
Goldsmid St SE18 165 ES78
Sladedale Rd
Goldsmith, Grays 170 FZ79
Goldsmith Av E12 144 EL65
Goldsmith Av NW9 119 CT58
Goldsmith Av W3 138 CR73
Goldsmith Av, Rom. 126 FA59
Goldsmith Cl W3 138 CS74
East Acton La

Goldsmith Cl, Har. 116 CB60
Goldsmith La NW9 118 CP56
Goldsmith Rd E10 123 EA60
Goldsmith Rd E17 101 DX54
Goldsmith Rd N11 98 DF50
Goldsmith Rd SE15 162 DU81
Goldsmith Rd W3 138 CR74
Goldsmith St EC2 275 J8
Goldsmiths Bottom, Sev. 256 FE127
Goldsmiths Cl, Wok. 226 AW118
Goldsmith's Row E2 142 DU68
Goldsmith's Sq E2 142 DU68
Goldstone Cl, Ware 33 DX05
High Oak Rd
Goldstone Fm Vw, Lthd. 246 CA127
Goldsworth Orchard, Wok. 226 AU118
St. John's Rd
Goldsworth Pk Trd Est, Wok. 226 AV116
Goldsworth Rd, Wok. 226 AW118
Goldsworthy Gdns SE16 162 DW77
Goldsworthy Way, Slou. 130 AJ72
Goldwell Rd, Th.Hth. 201 DM98
Goldwin Cl SE14 162 DW81
Goldwing Cl E16 144 EG72
Golf Cl, Bushey 76 BX41
Golf Cl, Stan. 95 CJ52
Golf Cl, Th.Hth. 201 DN95
Kensington Av
Golf Cl, Wok. 211 BE114
Golf Club Dr, Kings.T. 178 CR94
Golf Club Rd, Hat. 64 DA26
Golf Club Rd, Wey. 213 BP109
Golf Club Rd, Wok. 226 AU120
Golf Ho Rd, Oxt. 254 EJ129
Golf Links Av, Grav. 191 GH92
Golf Ride, Enf. 81 DN35
Golf Rd W5 138 CM72
Boileau Rd
Golf Rd, Brom. 205 EN97
Golf Rd, Ken. 236 DR118
Golf Side, Sutt. 217 CY111
Golf Side, Twick. 177 CD90
Golfe Rd, Ilf. 125 ER62
Golfside Cl N20 98 DE48
Golfside Cl, N.Mal. 198 CS96
Goliath Cl, Wall. 219 DL108
Gollogly Ter SE7 164 EJ78
Gombards, St.Alb. 43 CD19
Gombards All, St.Alb. 43 CD19
Worley Rd
Gomer Gdns, Tedd. 177 CG93
Gomer Pl, Tedd. 177 CG93
Gomm Rd SE16 162 DW76
Gomms Wd Cl (Forty Grn), Beac. 88 AH51
Gomshall Av, Wall. 219 DL106
Gomshall Gdns, Ken. 236 DS115
Gomshall La (Shere), Guil. 260 BN139
Gomshall Rd (Gomshall), Guil. 261 BP138
Gomshall Rd, Sutt. 217 CW110
Gondar Gdns NW6 119 CZ64
Gonnerston, St.Alb. 42 CB19
Kings Rd
Gonson Pl SE8 163 EA79
Gonson St SE8 163 EB79
Gonston Cl SW19 179 CY89
Boddicott Cl
Gonville Av, Rick. 75 BP44
Gonville Cres, Nthlt. 136 CB65
Gonville Rd, Th.Hth. 201 DM99
Gonville St SW6 159 CY83
Putney Br App
Goodall Rd E11 123 EC62
Gooden Ct, Har. 117 CE62
Goodenough Cl, Couls. 235 DN120
Goodenough Rd SW19 179 CZ94
Goodenough Way, Couls. 235 DM120
Gooderham Ho, Grays 171 GH75
Goodge Pl W1 273 L7
Goodge St W1 273 L7
Goodge St W1 141 DJ71
Goodhall St NW10 138 CS69
Goodhart Pl E14 143 DY73
Goodhart Way, W.Wick. 204 EE101
Goodhew Rd, Croy. 202 DU100
Gooding Cl, N.Mal. 198 CQ98
Goodinge Cl N7 141 DL65
Goodlake Ct (Denham), Uxb. 113 BF59
Goodley Stock, West. 255 EP129
Goodley Stock Rd, Eden. 255 EP131
Goodley Stock Rd, West. 255 EP128
Goodman Cres SW2 181 DK89
Goodman Pk, Slou. 132 AW74
Goodman Pl, Stai. 173 BF91
Goodman Rd E10 123 EC59
Goodmans Ct E1 275 P10
Goodmans Ct, Wem. 117 CK63
Goodman's Stile E1 142 DU72
Goodmans Yd E1 275 P10
Goodmans Yd E1 142 DT73
Goodmayes Av, Ilf. 126 EU60
Goodmayes La, Ilf. 126 EU63
Goodmayes Rd, Ilf. 126 EU60
Goodmead Rd, Orp. 206 EU101
Goodrich Cl, Wat. 75 BU35
Goodrich Rd SE22 182 DT86
Goods Way NW1 141 DL68
Goodson Rd NW10 138 CS66
Goodway Gdns E14 143 ED72
Goodwin Cl SE16 162 DU76
Goodwin Cl, Mitch. 200 DD97
Goodwin Ct, Barn. 80 DE44
Goodwin Ct, Wal.Cr. 67 DY28
Goodwin Dr, Sid. 186 EX90
Goodwin Gdns, Croy. 219 DP107
Goodwin Meadows (Wooburn Grn), H.Wyc. 110 AE57
Goodwin Rd N9 100 DW46
Goodwin Rd W12 159 CU75
Goodwin Rd, Croy. 219 DP106
Goodwin Rd, Slou. 131 AM69
Goodwin St N4 121 DN61
Fonthill Rd
Goodwins Ct WC2 273 P10
Goodwood Av, Brwd. 109 GE44
Goodwood Av, Enf. 82 DW37
Goodwood Av, Horn. 128 FL63
Goodwood Av, Wat. 75 BS35
Goodwood Cl, Hodd. 49 DZ16
Goodwood Cl, Mord. 200 DA98
Goodwood Cl, Stan. 95 CJ50
Goodwood Cres, Grav. 191 GJ93
Goodwood Dr, Nthlt. 136 CA65
Goodwood Path, Borwd. 78 CN41
Stratfield Rd
Goodwood Rd SE14 163 DY80
Goodwood Rd, Red. 250 DF132
Goodwyn Av NW7 96 CS50
Goodwyns Rd, Dor. 263 CH139
Goodwyns Vale N10 98 DG53
Goodyers Av, Rad. 61 CF33
Goodyers Gdns NW4 119 CX57
Goosander Way SE28 165 ER76
Goose Acre, Chesh. 56 AT30
Goose Grn, Cob. 229 BU119
Goose Grn (Gomshall), Guil. 261 BQ139
Goose Grn, Hodd. 49 DY17
Lord St
Goose Grn (Farnham Royal), Slou. 131 AP68
Goose Grn Cl, Orp. 206 EU96
Goose La, Wok. 226 AV122
Goose Rye Rd (Worplesdon), Guil. 242 AT125
Goose Sq E6 145 EM72
Harper Rd
Gooseacre, Welw.G.C. 29 CZ11
Gooseacre La, Har. 117 CK57
Goosecroft, Hem.H. 39 BF19
Goosefields, Rick. 74 BJ44
Gooseley La E6 145 EN69
Goosens Cl, Sutt. 218 DC106
Turnpike La
Gooshays Dr, Rom. 106 FL50
Gooshays Gdns, Rom. 106 FL51
Gophir La EC4 275 K10
Gopsall St N1 142 DR67
Goral Mead, Rick. 92 BK46
Gordon Av E4 102 EE51
Gordon Av SW14 158 CS84
Gordon Av, Horn. 127 FF61
Gordon Av, S.Croy. 220 DQ110
Gordon Av, Stan. 95 CH51
Gordon Av, Twick. 177 CG85
Gordon Cl E17 123 EA58
Gordon Cl N19 121 DJ60
Highgate Hill
Gordon Cl, Cher. 193 BE104
Gordon Cl, St.Alb. 43 CH21
Kitchener Cl
Gordon Cl, Stai. 174 BH93
Gordon Ct W12 139 CW72
Gordon Cres, Croy. 202 DS102
Gordon Cres, Hayes 155 BU76
Gordon Dr, Cher. 193 BE104
Gordon Dr, Shep. 195 BR100
Gordon Gdns, Edg. 96 CP54
Gordon Gro SE5 161 DP82
Gordon Hill, Enf. 82 DQ39
Gordon Ho E1 142 DW73
Gordon Ho Rd NW5 120 DG63
Gordon Pl W8 160 DA75
Gordon Pl, Grav. 191 GJ86
East Ter
Gordon Prom, Grav. 191 GJ86
Gordon Prom E, Grav. 191 GJ86
Gordon Rd E4 102 EE45
Gordon Rd E11 124 EG58
Gordon Rd E15 123 EC63
Gordon Rd E18 102 EH53
Gordon Rd N3 97 CZ52
Gordon Rd N9 100 DV47
Gordon Rd N11 99 DK52
Gordon Rd SE15 162 DV82
Gordon Rd W4 158 CP79
Gordon Rd W5 137 CJ73
Gordon Rd W13 137 CH73
Gordon Rd, Ashf. 174 BL90
Gordon Rd, Bark. 145 ES67
Gordon Rd, Beck. 203 DZ97
Gordon Rd, Belv. 167 FC77
Gordon Rd, Brwd. 109 GA46
Gordon Rd, Cars. 218 DF107
Gordon Rd, Cat. 236 DR121
Gordon Rd, Chesh. 54 AQ32
Gordon Rd, Dart. 188 FK87
Gordon Rd, Enf. 82 DQ39
Gordon Rd (Claygate), Esher 215 CE107
Gordon Rd (Northfleet), Grav. 190 GE87
Gordon Rd, Grays 171 GF75
Gordon Rd, Har. 117 CE55
Gordon Rd, Houns. 156 CC84
Gordon Rd, Ilf. 125 ER62
Gordon Rd, Kings.T. 198 CM95
Gordon Rd, Red. 250 DG131
Gordon Rd, Rich. 158 CM82
Gordon Rd, Rom. 126 EZ58
Gordon Rd, Sev. 257 FH125
Gordon Rd, Shep. 195 BR100
Gordon Rd, Sid. 185 ES85
Gordon Rd, Sthl. 156 BY77
Gordon Rd, Stai. 173 BC91
Gordon Rd, Surb. 198 CM101
Gordon Rd, Wal.Abb. 67 EA34
Gordon Rd, West Dr. 134 BL73
Gordon Rd, Wind. 151 AM82
Gordon Sq WC1 273 N5
Gordon Sq WC1 141 DK70
Gordon St E13 144 EG69
Grange Rd
Gordon St WC1 273 M4
Gordon St WC1 141 DK70
Gordon Way, Barn. 79 CZ42
Gordon Way, Brom. 204 EG95
Gordon Way, Ch.St.G. 90 AW48
Gordonbrock Rd SE4 183 EA85
Gordondale Rd SW19 180 DA89
Gordons Way, Oxt. 253 ED128
Gore, The (Burnham), Slou. 130 AG69
Gore Ct (Harefield), Uxb. 114 BH56
Gore Ct NW9 118 CN57
Gore Hill, Amer. 55 AP43
Gore Rd E9 142 DW67
Gore Rd SW20 199 CW96
Gore Rd, Dart. 188 FQ89
Gore Rd (Burnham), Slou. 130 AH69
Gore St SW7 160 DC76
Gorefield Pl NW6 140 DA68
Gorelands La, Ch.St.G. 91 AZ47
Gorell Rd, Beac. 89 AP54
Goresbrook Rd, Dag. 146 EV67
Goresbrook Village, Dag. 146 EV67
Goresbrook Rd
Gorham Dr, St.Alb. 43 CE23
Gorham Pl W11 139 CY73
Mary Pl
Gorhambury Dr, St.Alb. 42 BW19
Goring Cl, Rom. 105 FC53
Goring Gdns, Dag. 126 EW63
Goring Rd N11 99 DL51
Goring Rd, Dag. 147 FD65
Goring Rd, Stai. 173 BD92
Goring St EC3 275 N8
Goring St EC3 142 DS72
Goring Way, Grnf. 136 CC68
Gorings Sq, Stai. 173 BE91
Gorle Cl, Wat. 59 BU34
Gorleston Rd N15 122 DR57
Gorleston St W14 159 CY77
Gorman Rd SE18 165 EM77
Gorringe Av (South Darenth), Dart. 209 FR96
Gorringe Pk Av, Mitch. 180 DF94
Gorse Cl E16 144 EG72
Gorse Cl, Hat. 45 CT21
Gorse Cl, Tad. 233 CV120
Gorse Ct, Guil. 243 BC132
Kingfisher Dr
Gorse Hill (Farningham), Dart. 208 FL100
Gorse Hill La, Vir.W. 192 AX98
Gorse Hill Rd, Vir.W. 192 AX98
Gorse La (Chobham), Wok. 210 AS108
Gorse Meade, Slou. 131 AP74
Gorse Ri SW17 180 DG92
Gorse Rd, Croy. 221 EA105
Gorse Rd, Orp. 206 FA103
Gorse Wk, West Dr. 134 BL72
Gorselands Cl, W.Byf. 212 BJ111
Gorseway, Rom. 127 FE61
Gorst Rd NW10 138 CQ70
Gorst Rd SW11 180 DF86
Gorsuch Pl E2 275 P2
Gorsuch St E2 275 P2
Gorsuch St E2 142 DT69
Gosberton Rd SW12 180 DG88
Gosbury Hill, Chess. 216 CL105
Gosden Cl (Bramley), Guil. 258 AY143
Gosden Common (Bramley), Guil. 258 AY143
Gosden Hill Rd, Guil. 243 BC130
Gosfield Rd, Dag. 126 FA61
Gosfield Rd, Epsom 216 CR112
Gosfield St W1 273 K6
Gosfield St W1 141 DJ71
Gosford Gdns, Ilf. 125 EM57
Gosforth La, Wat. 94 BW48
Gosforth Path, Wat. 93 BU48
Goshawk Gdns, Hayes 135 BS69
Goslar Way, Wind. 151 AP82
Goslett Ct, Bushey 76 CA43
Bournehall Av
Goslett Yd WC2 273 N9
Gosling Cl, Grnf. 136 CA69
Gosling Grn, Slou. 152 AY76
Gosling Rd, Slou. 152 AY76
Gosling Way SW9 161 DN81
Gospatrick Rd N17 100 DQ53
Gospel Oak Est NW5 120 DF64
Gosport Dr, Horn. 148 FJ65
Gosport Rd E17 123 DZ57
Gosport Wk N17 122 DV57
Yarmouth Cres
Gosport Way SE15 162 DT80
Pentridge St
Goss Hill, Dart. 188 FJ93
Goss Hill, Swan. 188 FJ93
Gossage Rd SE18 165 ER78
Ancona Rd
Gossage Rd, Uxb. 134 BM66
Gossamers, The, Wat. 76 BY36
Gosselin Rd, Hert. 32 DQ07
Gosset St E2 142 DT69
Gosshill Rd, Chis. 205 EN96
Gossington Cl, Chis. 185 EP91
Beechwood Ri
Gossoms End, Berk. 38 AU18
Gossoms Ryde, Berk. 38 AU18
Gosterwood St SE8 163 DY79
Gostling Rd, Twick. 176 CA88
Goston Gdns, Th.Hth. 201 DN97
Goswell Hill, Wind. 151 AR81
Goswell Rd EC1 275 H5
Goswell Rd EC1 141 DP69
Goswell Rd, Wind. 151 AR81
Gothic Cl, Dart. 188 FK90
Gothic Ct, Hayes 155 BR79
Sipson La
Gothic Rd, Twick. 177 CD89
Gottfried Ms NW5 121 DJ63
Fortess Rd
Gouch Ho E5 122 DV62
Goudhurst Rd, Brom. 184 EE92
Gouge Av (Northfleet), Grav. 190 GE88
Gough Rd E15 124 EF63
Gough Rd, Enf. 82 DV40
Gough Sq EC4 274 E8
Gough Sq EC4 141 DN72
Gough St WC1 274 C4
Gough St WC1 141 DM70
Gough Wk E14 143 EA72
Saracen St
Gould Cl, Hat. 45 CV24
Gould Ct SE19 182 DT92
Gould Ct, Guil. 243 BD132
Eustace Rd
Gould Rd, Felt. 175 BS87
Gould Rd, Twick. 177 CE88
Gould Ter E8 122 DV64
Kenmure Rd
Goulden Ho App SW11 160 DE82
Goulding Gdns, Th.Hth. 201 DP96
Goulds Grn, Uxb. 135 BP72
Goulston St E1 275 P8
Goulston St E1 142 DT72
Goulton Rd E5 122 DV63
Gourley Pl N15 122 DS57
Gourley St
Gourley St N15 122 DS57
Gourock Rd SE9 185 EN85
Govan St E2 142 DU67
Whiston Rd
Government Row, Enf. 83 EA38
Governors Av (Denham), Uxb. 113 BF57
Governors Cl, Amer. 72 AT37
Govett Av, Shep. 195 BQ99
Govier Cl E15 144 EE66
Gowan Av SW6 159 CY81
Gowan Rd NW10 139 CV65
Gowar Fld, Pot.B. 63 CU32
Gower, The, Egh. 193 BB97
Gower Cl SW4 181 DJ86
Gower Ct WC1 273 M4
Gower Ms WC1 273 M7
Gower Ms WC1 141 DK71
Gower Pl WC1 273 L4
Gower Pl WC1 141 DJ70
Gower Rd E7 144 EG65
Gower Rd, Horl. 268 DE148
Gower Rd, Islw. 157 CF79
Gower Rd, Wey. 213 BR107
Gower St WC1 273 M5
Gower St WC1 141 DJ70
Gowers, The, Amer. 55 AS36
Gowers, The, Harl. 36 EU13
Gowers La, Grays 171 GF75
Gower's Wk E1 142 DU72
Gowings Grn, Slou. 151 AL75
Eltham Av
Gowland Pl, Beck. 203 DZ96
Gowlett Rd SE15 162 DU83
Gowrie Pl, Cat. 236 DQ122
Coulsdon Rd
Gowrie Rd SW11 160 DG83
Graburn Way, E.Mol. 197 CD97
Grace Av, Bexh. 166 EZ82
Grace Av (Shenley), Rad. 61 CK33
Grace Business Cen, Mitch. 200 DF100
Grace Cl SE9 184 EK90
Grace Cl, Borwd. 78 CR39
Grace Cl, Edg. 96 CQ52
Pavilion Way
Grace Cl, Ilf. 103 ET51
Grace Ct, Slou. 131 AQ74
Grace Jones Cl E8 142 DU65
Parkholme Rd
Grace Path SE26 182 DW91
Grace Pl E3 143 EB69
St. Leonards St
Grace Rd, Croy. 202 DQ100
Grace St E3 143 EB69
Gracechurch St EC3 275 L10
Gracechurch St EC3 142 DR73
Gracedale Rd SW16 181 DH92
Gracefield Gdns SW16 181 DL90
Grace's All E1 142 DU73
Graces Ms SE5 162 DS82
Graces Rd SE5 162 DS82
Gracious La, Sev. 256 FG130
Gracious La End, Sev. 256 FF130
Gracious Pond Rd (Chobham), Wok. 210 AT108
Gradient, The SE26 182 DU91
Graduate Pl SE1 162 DS76
Long La
Graeme Rd, Enf. 82 DR40
Graemesdyke Av SW14 158 CP84
Graemesdyke Rd, Berk. 38 AU20
Grafton Cl W13 137 CG72
Grafton Cl, Houns. 176 BY88
Grafton Cl, St.Alb. 43 CK21
Princess Diana Dr
Grafton Cl (George Grn), Slou. 132 AY72
Grafton Cl, W.Byf. 211 BF113
Madeira Rd
Grafton Cl, Wor.Pk. 198 CS104
Grafton Ct, Felt. 175 BR88
Loxwood Cl
Grafton Cres NW1 141 DH65
Grafton Gdns N4 122 DQ58
Grafton Gdns, Dag. 126 EY61
Grafton Ho E3 143 EA69
Grafton Ms W1 273 K5
Grafton Pk Rd, Wor.Pk. 198 CS103
Grafton Pl NW1 273 M3
Grafton Pl NW1 141 DK69
Grafton Rd NW5 120 DG64
Grafton Rd W3 138 CQ73
Grafton Rd, Croy. 201 DN102
Grafton Rd, Dag. 126 EY61
Grafton Rd, Enf. 81 DM41
Grafton Rd, Har. 116 CC57
Grafton Rd, N.Mal. 198 CS97
Grafton Rd, Wor.Pk. 198 CR104
Grafton Sq SW4 161 DJ83
Grafton St W1 277 J1
Grafton St W1 141 DH73
Grafton Ter NW5 120 DF64
Grafton Way W1 273 K5
Grafton Way W1 141 DJ70
Grafton Way WC1 273 K5
Grafton Way WC1 141 DJ70
Grafton Way, W.Mol. 196 BZ98
Grafton Yd NW5 141 DH65
Prince of Wales Rd
Graftons, The NW2 120 DA62
Hermitage La
Graham Av W13 157 CH75
Graham Av, Brox. 49 DY20
Graham Av, Mitch. 200 DG95
Graham Cl, Brwd. 109 GC43
Graham Cl, Croy. 203 EA103
Graham Cl, St.Alb. 43 CD23
Graham Gdns, Surb. 198 CL102
Graham Rd E8 142 DU65
Graham Rd E13 144 EG70
Graham Rd N15 121 DP55
Graham Rd NW4 119 CV58
Graham Rd SW19 179 CZ94
Graham Rd W4 158 CR76
Graham Rd, Bexh. 166 FA84
Graham Rd, Hmptn. 176 CA91
Graham Rd, Har. 117 CE55
Graham Rd, Mitch. 200 DG95
Graham Rd, Pur. 219 DN113
Graham St N1 274 G1
Graham St N1 141 DP68
Graham Ter SW1 276 F9
Graham Ter SW1 160 DG77
Grahame Pk Est NW9 97 CT53
Grahame Pk Way NW7 97 CT52
Grahame Pk Way NW9 97 CT54
Grainger Cl, Nthlt. 116 CC64
Lancaster Rd
Grainger Rd N22 100 DQ53
Grainger Rd, Islw. 157 CF82
Grainge's Yd, Uxb. 134 BJ66
Cross St
Gramer Cl E11 123 ED61
Norman Rd
Grampian Cl, Hayes 155 BR80
Grampian Cl, Orp. 205 ET100
Cotswold Ri
Grampian Cl, Sutt. 218 DC108
Devonshire Rd
Grampian Gdns NW2 119 CY60
Grampian Ho N9 100 DV47
Plevna Rd
Grampian Way, Slou. 153 BA78
Granard Av SW15 179 CV85
Granard Rd SW12 180 DF87
Granaries, The, Wal.Abb. 68 EE34
Granary, The, Harl. 34 EH14
Granary Cl N9 100 DW45
Turin Rd
Granary Cl, Horl. 268 DG146
Waterside
Granary Rd E1 142 DV70
Granary St NW1 141 DK67
Granby Pk Rd (Cheshunt), Wal.Cr. 66 DT28
Granby Pl SE1 278 D5
Granby Rd SE9 165 EM82
Granby Rd, Grav. 190 GD86
Granby St E2 142 DT70
Granby Ter NW1 273 K1
Granby Ter NW1 141 DJ68
Grand Arc N12 98 DC50
Ballards La
Grand Av EC1 274 G6
Grand Av N10 120 DG56
Grand Av, Surb. 198 CP99
Grand Av, Wem. 118 CN64
Grand Av E, Wem. 118 CP64
Grand Dep Rd SE18 165 EN78
Grand Dr SW20 199 CW96
Grand Dr, Sthl. 156 CC75
Grand Junct Wf N1 275 H1
Grand Junct Wf N1 142 DQ68
Grand Par Ms SW15 179 CY85
Upper Richmond Rd
Grand Stand Rd, Epsom 233 CT117
Grand Union Canal Wk W7 157 CE76
Grand Union Cl W9 139 CZ71
Woodfield Rd
Grand Union Cres E8 142 DU66
Grand Union Ind Est NW10 138 CP68
Grand Union Wk NW1 141 DH66
Grand Vw Av (Biggin Hill), West. 238 EJ117
Grand Wk E1 143 DY70
Solebay St
Granden Rd SW16 201 DL96
Grandfield Av, Wat. 75 BT39
Grandis Cotts (Ripley), Wok. 228 BH122
Grandison Rd SW11 180 DF85
Grandison Rd, Wor.Pk. 199 CW103
Granfield St SW11 160 DD81
Grange, The N2 98 DD54
Central Av
Grange, The N20 98 DC46
Grange, The SE1 279 P6
Grange, The SE1 162 DT76
Grange, The SW19 179 CX93
Grange, The, Croy. 203 DZ103
Grange, The (South Darenth), Dart. 209 FR95
Grange, The, Walt. 195 BV103
Grange, The, Wem. 138 CN66
Grange, The (Old Windsor), Wind. 172 AV85
Grange, The (Chobham), Wok. 210 AS110
Grange, The, Wor.Pk. 198 CR104
Grange Av N12 98 DC50
Grange Av N20 97 CY45
Grange Av SE25 202 DS96
Grange Av, Barn. 98 DE46
Grange Av, Stan. 95 CH54
Grange Av, Twick. 177 CE89
Grange Av, Wdf.Grn. 102 EG51
Grange Cl, Brwd. 109 GC50
Grange Cl, Edg. 96 CQ50
Grange Cl (Chalfont St. Peter), Ger.Cr. 90 AY53
Grange Cl, Guil. 242 AV130
Grange Cl, Hayes 135 BS71
Grange Cl, Hem.H. 40 BN21
Grange Cl, Hert. 31 DP09
Grange Cl, Houns. 156 BZ79
Grange Cl, Lthd. 231 CK120
Grange Cl (Bletchingley), Red. 252 DR133
Grange Cl (Merstham), Red. 251 DH128
Grange Cl, Sid. 186 EU90
Grange Cl (Wraysbury), Stai. 172 AY86
Grange Cl, Wat. 75 BU39
Grange Cl, W.Mol. 196 CB98
Grange Cl, West. 255 EQ126
Grange Cl, Wdf.Grn. 102 EG52
Grange Ct E8 142 DT66
Grange Ct WC2 274 C9
Grange Ct, Chig. 103 EQ47
Grange Ct, Loug. 84 EK43
Grange Ct, Nthlt. 136 BW68
Grange Ct, Stai. 174 BG92
Grange Ct, Wal.Abb. 67 EC34
Grange Ct, Walt. 195 BU103
Grange Cres SE28 146 EW72
Grange Cres, Chig. 103 ER50
Grange Cres, Dart. 188 FP86
Grange Dr, Chis. 184 EL93
Grange Dr (Wooburn Grn), H.Wyc. 110 AD60
Grange Dr, Orp. 224 EW109
Rushmore Hill
Grange Dr (Merstham), Red. 251 DH128
London Rd S
Grange Dr, Wok. 210 AY114
Grange End, Horl. 269 DN148
Grange Fm Cl, Har. 116 CC61
Grange Flds (Chalfont St. Peter), Ger.Cr. 90 AY53
Lower Rd
Grange Gdns N14 99 DK46
Grange Gdns NW3 120 DB62
Grange Gdns SE25 202 DS96
Grange Gdns, Bans. 218 DB113
Grange Gdns, Pnr. 116 BZ56
Grange Gdns (Farnham Common), Slou. 111 AR64
Grange Gdns, Ware 33 DY07
Grange Gro N1 142 DQ65
Grange Hill SE25 202 DS96
Grange Hill, Edg. 96 CQ50
Grange Ho, Bark. 145 ER67
St. Margarets
Grange Ho, Erith 167 FG82
Sun Ct
Grange La SE21 182 DT89
Grange La, Harl. 50 EJ15
Grange La, Wat. 77 CD39
Grange Mans, Epsom 217 CT108
Grange Meadow, Bans. 218 DB113
Grange Ms SE10 163 ED80
Crooms Hill
Grange Pk W5 138 CL74
Grange Pk, Wok. 226 AY115
Grange Pk Av N21 81 DP44
Grange Pk Pl SW20 179 CV94
Grange Pk Rd E10 123 EB60
Grange Pk Rd, Th.Hth. 202 DR98
Grange Pl NW6 140 DA66
Grange Pl, Stai. 194 BJ96
Grange Pl, Walt. 195 BU103
Grange Rd E10 123 EA60
Grange Rd E13 144 EF69
Grange Rd E17 123 DY57
Grange Rd N6 120 DG58
Grange Rd N17 100 DU51
Grange Rd N18 100 DU51
Grange Rd NW10 139 CV65
Grange Rd SE1 279 N7
Grange Rd SE1 162 DS76
Grange Rd SE19 202 DR98
Grange Rd SE25 202 DR98
Grange Rd SW13 159 CU81
Grange Rd W4 158 CP78
Grange Rd W5 137 CK74
Grange Rd (New Haw), Add. 212 BG110
Grange Rd, Borwd. 78 CM43
Grange Rd, Bushey 76 BY43
Grange Rd, Cat. 252 DU125
Grange Rd, Chess. 216 CL105
Grange Rd, Edg. 96 CR51
Grange Rd, Egh. 173 AZ92
Grange Rd (Chalfont St. Peter), Ger.Cr. 90 AY53
Grange Rd, Grav. 191 GG87
Grange Rd, Grays 170 GB79
Grange Rd, Guil. 242 AV129

Gra - Gre This index reads in the sequence: Street Name / Postal District or Post Town / Map Page Number / Grid Reference

Grange Rd, Har. 117 CG58
Grange Rd (South Harrow), Har. 117 CD61
Grange Rd, Hayes 135 BS72
Grange Rd, Ilf. 125 EP63
Grange Rd, Kings.T. 198 CL97
Grange Rd, Lthd. 231 CK120
Grange Rd, Orp. 205 EQ103
Grange Rd, Rom. 105 FH51
Grange Rd, Sev. 256 FG127
Grange Rd, S.Croy. 220 DQ110
Grange Rd, S.Ock. 148 FQ74
Grange Rd, Sthl. 156 BY75
Grange Rd, Sutt. 218 DA108
Grange Rd, Th.Hth. 202 DR98
Grange Rd, Walt. 214 BY105
Grange Rd, W.Mol. 196 CB98
Grange Rd, Wok. 210 AY114
Grange St N1 142 DR67
Grange St, St.Alb. 43 CD19
Grange Vale, Sutt. 218 DB108
Grange Vw Rd N20 98 DC46
Grange Wk SE1 279 N6
Grange Wk SE1 162 DS76
Grange Way, Erith 167 FH80
Grange Way, Iver 133 BF72
Grange Yd SE1 279 P7
Grange Yd SE1 162 DT76
Grangecliffe Gdns SE25 202 DS96
Grangecourt Rd N16 122 DS60
Grangedale Cl, Nthwd. 93 BS53
Grangefields Rd, Guil. 242 AX128
Grangehill Pl SE9 165 EM83
Westmount Rd
Grangehill Rd SE9 165 EM83
Grangemill Rd SE6 183 EA90
Grangemill Way SE6 183 EA89
Grangemount, Lthd. 231 CK120
Granger Way, Rom. 127 FG58
Grangeway N12 98 DB49
Grangeway NW6 140 DA66
Messina Av
Grangeway, Horl. 269 DN148
Grangeway, Wdf.Grn. 102 EJ49
Grangeway, The N21 81 DP44
Grangeway Gdns, Ilf. 124 EL57
Grangeways Cl (Northfleet), Grav. 191 GF91
Grangewood, Bex. 186 EZ88
Hurst Rd
Grangewood, Pot.B. 64 DB30
Grangewood (Wexham), Slou. 132 AW71
Grangewood Av, Grays 170 GE76
Grangewood Av, Rain. 148 FJ70
Grangewood Cl, Brwd. 109 GA48
Knight's Way
Grangewood Cl, Pnr. 115 BU57
Grangewood Dr, Sun. 175 BT94
Forest Dr
Grangewood La, Beck. 183 DZ93
Grangewood St E6 144 EJ67
Grangewood Ter SE25 202 DR97
Grange Rd
Granham Gdns N9 100 DT47
Granite St SE18 165 ET78
Granleigh Rd E11 124 EE61
Gransden Av E8 142 DV66
Gransden Rd W12 159 CT75
Wendell Rd
Grant Av, Slou. 132 AS72
Grant Cl N14 99 DJ45
Grant Cl, Shep. 195 BP100
Grant Pl, Croy. 202 DT102
Grant Rd SW11 160 DD84
Grant Rd, Croy. 202 DT102
Grant Rd, Har. 117 CF55
Grant St E13 144 EG69
Grant St N1 141 DN68
Chapel Mkt
Grant Way, Islw. 157 CG79
Grantbridge St N1 141 DP68
Grantchester Cl, Har. 117 CF62
Grantham Cl, Edg. 96 CL48
Grantham Gdns, Rom. 126 EZ58
Grantham Gdns, Ware 33 DY05
Grantham Grn, Borwd. 78 CQ43
Grantham Pl W1 277 H3
Grantham Rd E12 125 EN63
Grantham Rd SW9 161 DL82
Grantham Rd W4 158 CS80
Grantley Cl (Shalford), Guil. 258 AY141
Grantley Gdns, Guil. 242 AU133
Grantley Pl, Esher 214 CB106
Grantley Rd, Guil. 242 AU133
Grantley Rd, Houns. 156 BW82
Grantley St E1 143 DX69
Grantock Rd E17 101 ED53
Granton Av, Upmin. 128 FM61
Granton Rd SW16 201 DJ95
Granton Rd, Ilf. 126 EU60
Granton Rd, Sid. 186 EW93
Grants Cl NW7 97 CW52
Grants La, Oxt. 254 EJ132
Grant's Quay Wf EC3 279 L1
Grantully Rd W9 140 DB69
Grantwood Cl, Red. 267 DH139
Bushfield Dr
Granville Av N9 100 DW48
Granville Av, Felt. 175 BU89
Granville Av, Houns. 176 CA85
Granville Av, Slou. 131 AR71
Granville Cl, Croy. 202 DS103
Granville Cl (Byfleet), W.Byf. 212 BM113
Church Rd
Granville Cl, Wey. 213 BQ107
Granville Ct N1 142 DR67
Granville Dene (Bovingdon), Hem.H. 57 BA27
Granville Gdns SW16 201 DM95
Granville Gdns W5 138 CM74
Granville Gdns, Hodd. 33 EA13
Granville Gro SE13 163 EC83
Granville Ms, Sid. 186 EU91
Granville Pk SE13 163 EC83
Granville Pl (North Finchley) N12 98 DC52
High Rd
Granville Pl W1 272 F9
Granville Pl W1 140 DG72
Granville Pl, Pnr. 116 BX55
Granville Rd E17 123 EB58
Granville Rd E18 102 EH54
Granville Rd N4 121 DM58
Granville Rd N12 98 DB52
Granville Rd N13 99 DM51
Russell Rd
Granville Rd N22 99 DP53
Granville Rd NW2 119 CZ61
Granville Rd NW6 140 DA68
Granville Rd SW18 180 DA87
Granville Rd SW19 180 DA94
Russell Rd
Granville Rd, Barn. 79 CW42
Granville Rd, Berk. 38 AS17
Granville Rd, Epp. 70 EV29
Granville Rd, Grav. 191 GF87
Granville Rd, Hayes 155 BT77
Granville Rd, Ilf. 125 EP60
Granville Rd, Oxt. 254 EF129
Granville Rd, St.Alb. 43 CF20
Granville Rd, Sev. 256 FG124
Granville Rd, Sid. 186 EU91
Granville Rd, Uxb. 135 BP65
Granville Rd, Wat. 76 BW42
Granville Rd, Well. 166 EW83
Granville Rd, West. 255 EQ126
Granville Rd, Wey. 213 BQ107
Granville Rd, Wok. 227 AZ120
Granville Sq SE15 162 DS80
Granville Sq WC1 274 C3
Granville Sq WC1 141 DM69
Granville St WC1 274 C3
Grape St WC2 273 P8
Graphite Sq SE11 278 B10
Grapsome Cl, Chess. 215 CJ108
Nigel Fisher Way
Grasdene Rd SE18 166 EU80
Grasholm Way, Slou. 153 BC77
Grasmere Av SW15 178 CR91
Grasmere Av SW19 200 DA97
Grasmere Av W3 138 CQ73
Grasmere Av, Houns. 176 CB86
Grasmere Av, Orp. 205 EP104
Grasmere Av, Ruis. 115 BQ59
Grasmere Av, Slou. 132 AU73
Grasmere Av, Wem. 117 CK59
Grasmere Cl, Egh. 173 BB94
Keswick Rd
Grasmere Cl, Felt. 175 BT88
Grasmere Cl, Guil. 243 BB133
Grasmere Cl, Hem.H. 41 BP22
Grasmere Cl, Loug. 85 EM40
Grasmere Cl, Wat. 59 BV32
Grasmere Ct N22 99 DM51
Palmerston Rd
Grasmere Gdns, Har. 95 CG54
Grasmere Gdns, Ilf. 125 EM57
Grasmere Gdns, Orp. 205 EP104
Grasmere Pt SE15 162 DW80
Ilderton Rd
Grasmere Rd E13 144 EG68
Grasmere Rd N10 99 DH53
Grasmere Rd N17 100 DU51
Grasmere Rd SE25 202 DV100
Grasmere Rd SW16 181 DM92
Grasmere Rd, Bexh. 167 FC81
Grasmere Rd, Brom. 204 EF95
Grasmere Rd, Orp. 205 EP104
Grasmere Rd, Pur. 219 DP111
Grasmere Rd, St.Alb. 43 CH22
Grasmere Way (Byfleet), W.Byf. 212 BM112
Grass Pk N3 97 CZ53
Grass Warren, Welw. 30 DE06
Grassfield Cl, Couls. 235 DH119
Grasshaven Way SE28 145 ET74
Grassingham End (Chalfont St. Peter), Ger.Cr. 90 AY52
Grassingham Rd (Chalfont St. Peter), Ger.Cr. 90 AY52
Grassington Cl N11 98 DG51
Ribblesdale Av
Grassington Cl (Bricket Wd), St.Alb. 60 CA30
Grassington Rd, Sid. 186 EU91
Grasslands, Horl. 269 DN148
Grassmere, Horl. 269 DH147
Grassmere Rd, Horn. 128 FM56
Grassmount SE23 182 DV89
Grassmount, Pur. 219 DJ110
Grassway, Wall. 219 DJ105
Grassy Cl, Hem.H. 40 BG19
Grassy La, Sev. 257 FH126
Grasvenor Av, Barn. 80 DA44
Grately Way SE15 162 DT80
Daniel Gdns
Gratton Dr, Wind. 151 AL84
Gratton Rd W14 159 CY76
Gratton Ter NW2 119 CX62
Gravel Cl, Chig. 104 EU47
Gravel Hill N3 97 CZ54
Gravel Hill, Bexh. 187 FB85
Gravel Hill, Croy. 221 DX107
Gravel Hill (Chalfont St. Peter), Ger.Cr. 90 AY53
Gravel Hill, Hem.H. 40 BH20
Gravel Hill, Lthd. 231 CH121
North St
Gravel Hill (High Beach), Loug. 84 EG38
Gravel Hill, Uxb. 114 BK64
Gravel Hill Cl, Bexh. 187 FB85
Gravel Hill Ter, Hem.H. 40 BG21
Gravel La E1 275 P8
Gravel La, Chig. 104 EU46
Gravel La, Hem.H. 40 BG21
Gravel Path, Berk. 38 AX19
Gravel Path, Hem.H. 40 BG20
Gravel Pit La SE9 185 EQ85
Gravel Pit Way, Orp. 206 EU103
Gravel Rd, Brom. 204 EL103
Gravel Rd (Sutton at Hone), Dart. 188 FP94
Gravel Rd, Twick. 177 CE88
Graveley, Kings.T. 198 CN96
Willingham Way
Graveley Av, Borwd. 78 CQ42
Graveley Ct, Hem.H. 41 BQ21
Graveley Dell, Welw.G.C. 30 DB10
Waterford Grn
Gravelly Hill, Cat. 252 DS128
Gravelly Ride SW19 179 CV91
Gravelpits La (Gomshall), Guil. 261 BQ139
Gravelwood Cl, Chis. 185 EQ90
Gravely Way (Penn), H.Wyc. 88 AF45
Graveney Gro SE20 182 DW94
Graveney Rd SW17 180 DE91
Gravesend Rd W12 139 CU73
Gravesham Ct, Grav. 191 GH87
Clarence Row
Gravetts La, Guil. 242 AS130
Gray Av, Dag. 126 EZ60
Gray Gdns, Rain. 147 FG65
Gray Pl (Ottershaw), Cher. 211 BC107
Clarendon Gate
Gray St SE1 278 E5
Grayburn Cl, Ch.St.G. 90 AU47
Grayham Cres, N.Mal. 198 CR98
Grayham Rd, N.Mal. 198 CR98
Grayland Cl, Brom. 204 EK95
Graylands, Epp. 85 ER37
Graylands, Wok. 226 AY116
Graylands Cl, Wok. 226 AY116
Grayling Cl E16 144 EE70
Cranberry La
Grayling Ct, Berk. 38 AT17
Tortoiseshell Way
Grayling Rd N16 122 DR61
Grayling Sq E2 142 DU69
Graylings, The, Abb.L. 59 BR33
Grays End Cl, Grays 170 GA76
Grays Fm Rd, Orp. 206 EV95
Gray's Inn WC1 274 C6
Gray's Inn WC1 141 DN71
Gray's Inn Pl WC1 274 C7
Gray's Inn Rd WC1 274 B3
Gray's Inn Rd WC1 141 DM69
Gray's Inn Sq WC1 274 C6
Grays La, Ashf. 175 BP91
Gray's La, Ash. 232 CM119
Gray's La, Epsom 232 CP121
Shepherds' Wk
Grays Pk Rd (Stoke Poges), Slou. 132 AU68
Grays Pl, Slou. 132 AT74
Grays Rd, Gdmg. 258 AT144
Grays Rd, Slou. 132 AT74
Grays Rd, Uxb. 134 BL67
Grays Rd, West. 239 EP121
Grays Wk, Brwd. 109 GD45
Grays Wk, Chesh. 54 AP29
Grays Wd, Horl. 269 DJ148
Gray's Yd W1 272 G9
Grayscroft Rd SW16 181 DK94
Graysfield, Welw.G.C. 30 DA12
Grayshott Rd SW11 160 DG82
Grayswood Gdns SW20 199 CV96
Farnham Gdns
Grayswood Pt SW15 179 CU88
Norley Vale
Graywood Ct N12 98 DC52
Grazebrook Rd N16 122 DR61
Grazeley Cl, Bexh. 187 FC85
Grazeley Ct SE19 182 DS91
Gipsy Hill
Grazings, The, Hem.H. 40 BM18
Great Acre Ct SW4 161 DK84
St. Alphonsus Rd
Great Bell All EC2 275 K8
Great Benty, West Dr. 154 BL77
Great Bois Wd, Amer. 55 AP35
Bois Av
Great Braitch La, Hat. 28 CS13
Great Brays, Harl. 52 EU16
Great Break, Welw.G.C. 30 DB10
Great Brownings SE21 182 DT91
Great Bushey Dr N20 98 DB46
Great Cambridge Rd N9 100 DT46
Great Cambridge Rd N17 100 DR50
Great Cambridge Rd N18 100 DR50
Great Cambridge Rd, Brox. 67 DY26
Great Cambridge Rd, Enf. 82 DU42
Great Cambridge Rd (Cheshunt), Wal.Cr. 66 DW34
Great Castle St W1 273 J8
Great Castle St W1 141 DJ72
Great Cen Av, Ruis. 116 BW64
Great Cen St NW1 272 D6
Great Cen St NW1 140 DF71
Great Cen Way NW10 118 CS64
Great Cen Way, Wem. 118 CQ63
Great Chapel St W1 273 M8
Great Chapel St W1 141 DK72
Great Chertsey Rd W4 158 CQ82
Great Chertsey Rd, Felt. 176 CA90
Great Ch La W6 159 CX78
Great Coll St SW1 277 P6
Great Coll St SW1 161 DL76
Great Conduit, Welw.G.C. 30 DC08
Great Cross Av SE10 164 EE80
Great Cullings, Rom. 127 FE61
Great Cumberland Ms W1 272 D9
Great Cumberland Pl W1 272 D8
Great Cumberland Pl W1 140 DF72
Great Dell, Welw.G.C. 29 CX07
Great Dover St SE1 279 J5
Great Dover St SE1 162 DR75
Great Eastern Rd E15 143 ED66
Great Eastern Rd, Brwd. 108 FW49
Great Eastern St EC2 275 M3
Great Eastern St EC2 142 DS69
Great Eastern Wk EC2 275 N7
Great Ellshams, Bans. 234 DA116
Great Elms Rd, Brom. 204 EJ98
Great Elms Rd, Hem.H. 40 BM24
Great Fld NW9 96 CS53
Great Fleete Way, Bark. 146 EW68
Great Galley Cl, Bark. 146 EV69
Great Ganett, Welw.G.C. 30 DB11
Great Gdns Rd, Horn. 127 FH58
Great Gatton Cl, Croy. 203 DY101
Great George St SW1 277 N5
Great George St SW1 161 DK75
Great Goodwin Dr, Guil. 243 BB132
Great Gregories La, Epp. 69 ES33
Great Gro, Bushey 76 CB42
Great Gros, Wal.Cr. 66 DS28
Great Guildford St SE1 279 H2
Great Guildford St SE1 142 DQ74
Great Harry Dr SE9 185 EN90
Great Heart, Hem.H. 40 BL18
Great Heath, Hat. 45 CV15
Great Hivings, Chesh. 54 AN27
Great James St WC1 274 B5
Great James St WC1 141 DM71
Great Julians, Rick. 74 BN42
Grove Cres
Great Lake Ct, Horl. 269 DH147
Tanyard Way
Great Ley, Welw.G.C. 29 CY11
Great Leylands, Harl. 52 EU16
Great Marlborough St W1 273 K9
Great Marlborough St W1 141 DJ72
Great Maze Pond SE1 279 L4
Great Maze Pond SE1 162 DR75
Great Meadow, Brox. 49 EB22
Great Molewood, Hert. 31 DP06
Great Nelmes Chase, Horn. 128 FM57
Great New St EC4 274 E8
Great Newport St WC2 141 DK73
Cranbourn St
Great N Rd N2 120 DE56
Great N Rd N6 120 DE56
Great N Rd, Barn. 79 CZ38
Great N Rd (New Barnet), Barn. 80 DA43
Great N Rd, Hat. 45 CZ23
Great N Rd, Pot.B. 64 DB27
Great N Rd, Welw.G.C. 29 CV13
Great N Way NW4 97 CW54
Great Oaks, Brwd. 109 GB44
Great Oaks, Chig. 103 EQ49
Great Oaks Pk, Guil. 243 BB129
Great Ormond St WC1 274 A6
Great Ormond St WC1 141 DL71
Great Owl Rd, Chig. 103 EN48
Great Palmers, Hem.H. 40 BM15
Great Pk, Kings L. 58 BM30
Great Percy St WC1 274 C2
Great Percy St WC1 141 DM69
Great Peter St SW1 277 M7
Great Peter St SW1 161 DK76
Great Pettits Ct, Rom. 105 FE54
Great Plumtree, Harl. 35 ET13
Great Portland St W1 273 J6
Great Portland St W1 141 DH71
Great Pulteney St W1 273 L10
Great Pulteney St W1 141 DJ73
Great Quarry, Guil. 258 AX137
Great Queen St WC2 274 A9
Great Queen St WC2 141 DL72
Great Queen St, Dart. 188 FM87
Great Rd, Hem.H. 40 BM19
Great Ropers La, Brwd. 107 FU51
Great Russell St WC1 273 N8
Great Russell St WC1 141 DL71
Great St. Helens EC3 275 M8
Great St. Helens EC3 142 DS72
Great St. Thomas Apostle EC4 275 J10
Great Scotland Yd SW1 277 P3
Great Scotland Yd SW1 141 DL74
Great Slades, Pot.B. 63 CZ33
Great Smith St SW1 277 N6
Great Smith St SW1 161 DK76
Great South-West Rd, Felt. 175 BQ87
Great South-West Rd, Houns. 155 BT84
Great Spilmans SE22 182 DS85
Great Stockwood Rd (Cheshunt), Wal.Cr. 66 DR26
Great Strand NW9 97 CT53
Great Sturgess Rd, Hem.H. 39 BF20
Great Suffolk St SE1 278 G3
Great Suffolk St SE1 161 DP75
Great Sutton St EC1 274 G5
Great Sutton St EC1 141 DP70
Great Swan All EC2 275 K8
Great Tattenhams, Epsom 233 CV118
Great Thrift, Orp. 205 EQ98
Great Till Cl (Otford), Sev. 241 FE116
Great Titchfield St W1 273 K8
Great Titchfield St W1 141 DJ72
Great Twr St EC3 275 M10
Great Twr St EC3 142 DS73
Great Trinity La EC4 275 J10
Great Turnstile WC1 274 C7
Great Warley St, Brwd. 107 FU53
Great W Rd W4 158 CP78
Great W Rd W6 159 CT78
Great W Rd, Brent. 158 CP78
Great W Rd, Houns. 156 BX82
Great W Rd, Islw. 157 CF80
Great Western Rd W2 139 CZ71
Great Western Rd W9 139 CZ71
Great Western Rd W11 139 CZ71
Great Wf Rd E14 143 EB74
Churchill Pl
Great Whites Rd, Hem.H. 40 BM22
Great Winchester St EC2 275 L8
Great Winchester St EC2 142 DR72
Great Windmill St W1 273 M10
Great Windmill St W1 141 DK73
Great Woodcote Dr, Pur. 219 DK110
Great Woodcote Pk, Pur. 219 DK110
Great Yd SE1 279 N4
Greatdown Rd W7 137 CF70
Greatfield Av E6 145 EM70
Greatfield Cl N19 121 DJ63
Warrender Rd
Greatfield Cl SE4 163 EA84
Greatfields Dr, Uxb. 134 BN71
Greatfields Rd, Bark. 145 ER67
Greatford Dr, Guil. 243 BD134
Greatham Rd, Bushey 76 BX41
Greatham Wk SW15 179 CU88
Greathurst End (Bookham), Lthd. 230 BZ124
Greatness La, Sev. 257 FJ121
Greatness Rd, Sev. 257 FJ121
Greatorex St E1 142 DU71
Greatwood, Chis. 185 EN94
Greatwood Cl (Ottershaw), Cher. 211 BC109
Greaves Cl, Bark. 145 ES66
Norfolk Rd
Greaves Pl SW17 180 DE91
Grebe Av, Hayes 136 BX72
Cygnet Way
Grebe Cl E7 124 EF64
Cormorant Rd
Grebe Cl E17 101 DY52
Grebe Cl, Bark. 145 ES69
Grebe Ct, Sutt. 217 CZ106
Grebe Crest, Grays 169 FU77
Grecian Cres SE19 181 DP93
Greding Wk, Brwd. 109 GB47
Gredo Ho, Bark. 146 EV69
Greek Ct W1 273 N9
Greek St W1 273 N9
Greek St W1 141 DK72
Greek Yd WC2 273 P10
Green, The E4 101 EC46
Green, The E11 124 EH58
Green, The E15 144 EE65
Green, The N9 100 DU47
Green, The N14 99 DK48
Green, The N21 99 DN45
Green, The SW14 158 CQ83
Green, The SW19 179 CX92
Green, The W3 138 CS72
Green, The W5 137 CK74
High St
Green, The, Amer. 55 AR38
Green, The, Berk. 39 BB17
Green, The, Bexh. 166 FA81
Green, The, Brom. 204 EG101
Green, The, Cars. 218 DG105
Green, The (Woldingham), Cat. 237 EA123
Green, The, Ch.St.G. 90 AW47
High St
Green, The, Croy. 221 DZ109
Green, The, Dart. 189 FR89
Green, The, Epp. 85 ES37
Green, The, Epsom 217 CU111
Green, The (Claygate), Esher 215 CF107
Green, The, Felt. 175 BV89
Green, The, Hayes 135 BS72
Wood End
Green, The (Bovingdon), Hem.H. 57 BA29
Green, The (Wooburn Grn), H.Wyc. 110 AE58
Green, The, Houns. 156 CA79
Heston Rd
Green, The (Fetcham), Lthd. 231 CD124
Green, The, Mord. 199 CY98
Green, The, N.Mal. 198 CQ97
Green, The (Pratt's Bottom), Orp. 224 EW110
Rushmore Hill
Green, The (St. Paul's Cray), Orp. 186 EV94
The Av
Green, The (Wennington), Rain. 148 FL73
Green, The, Rich. 177 CK85
Green, The (Croxley Grn), Rick. 74 BN44
Green, The (Sarratt), Rick. 74 BG35
Green, The, Rom. 105 FE48
Green, The, Sev. 257 FK122
Green, The, Shep. 195 BS98
Green, The, Sid. 186 EU91
Green, The, Slou. 130 AH70
Green, The (Chalvey), Slou. 151 AR75
Green, The (Datchet), Slou. 152 AV80
Green, The, S.Ock. 149 FW69
Green, The, Sthl. 156 BY76
Green, The (Wraysbury), Stai. 172 AY86
Green, The, Sutt. 200 DB104
Green, The (Burgh Heath), Tad. 233 CY119
Green, The, Til. 171 GL79
Green, The, Twick. 177 CE88
Green, The (Harefield), Uxb. 92 BJ53
Green, The (Ickenham), Uxb. 115 BQ61
Green, The, Wal.Abb. 67 EC34
Sewardstone Rd
Green, The (Cheshunt), Wal.Cr. 66 DW28
Green, The, Walt. 213 BS110
Octagon Rd
Green, The, Warl. 237 DX117
Green, The, Wat. 77 CE39
Green, The, Well. 165 ES84
Green, The, Welw.G.C. 30 DA11
Green, The, Wem. 117 CG61
Green, The, West Dr. 154 BK76
Green, The, West. 255 ER126
Green, The (Ripley), Wok. 228 BH121
Green, The, Wdf.Grn. 102 EG50
Green Acres, Croy. 202 DT104
Green Acres, Hem.H. 41 BR22
Green Acres, Welw.G.C. 29 CZ12
Green Arbour Ct EC1 274 F8
Green Av NW7 96 CR49
Green Av W13 157 CH76
Green Bk E1 142 DV74
Green Bk N12 98 DB49
Green Cl NW9 118 CQ58
Green Cl NW11 120 DC59
Green Cl, Brom. 204 EE97
Green Cl, Cars. 200 DF103
Green Cl, Epp. 51 EP24
Green Cl, Felt. 176 BY92
Green Cl, Hat. 63 CY26
Station Rd
Green Cl, Maid. 130 AG72
Green Cl (Cheshunt), Wal.Cr. 67 DY32
Green Common La (Wooburn Grn), H.Wyc. 110 AG59
Green Ct Rd, Swan. 207 FD99
Green Cres (Flackwell Heath), H.Wyc. 110 AC56
Green Cft, Edg. 96 CQ50
Deans La
Green Cft, Hat. 45 CU15
Talbot Rd
Green Curve, Bans. 217 CZ114
Green Dale SE5 162 DR84
Green Dale SE22 182 DS85
Green Dale Cl SE22 182 DS85
Green Dale
Green Dell Way, Hem.H. 41 BP20
Green Dene (East Horsley), Lthd. 245 BT131
Green Dragon Ct SE1 279 K2
Green Dragon La N21 81 DP44
Green Dragon La, Brent. 158 CL78
Green Dragon Yd E1 142 DU71
Old Montague St
Green Dr, Maid. 130 AE65
Green Dr, Slou. 152 AY77
Green Dr, Sthl. 136 CA74
Green Dr (Ripley), Wok. 227 BF123
Green E Rd (Jordans), Beac. 90 AS52
Green Edge, Wat. 75 BU35
Clarke Grn
Green End N21 99 DP47
Green End, Chess. 216 CL105
Green End Gdns, Hem.H. 40 BG21
Green End La, Hem.H. 39 BF20
Green End Rd, Hem.H. 40 BG21
Green Gdns, Orp. 223 EQ106
Green Glade, Epp. 85 ES37
Green Glades, Horn. 128 FM58
Green Hill, Buck.H. 102 EJ46
Green Hill, Orp. 222 EL112
Green Hill La, Warl. 237 DY117
Green Hundred Rd SE15 162 DU79
Green La E4 84 EE41
Green La NW4 119 CX57
Green La SE9 185 EN89
Green La SE20 183 DX94
Green La SW16 181 DM94
Green La W7 157 CE75
Green La, Add. 194 BG104
Green La, Amer. 55 AS38
Green La (Chesham Bois), Amer. 55 AR35
Green La, Ash. 231 CJ117
Green La (Pilgrim's Hatch), Brwd. 108 FV43
Green La (Warley), Brwd. 107 FU52
Green La, Brox. 49 EB23
Green La, Cat. 236 DQ122
Green La, Cher. 193 BE103
Green La, Chesh. 56 AV33
Green La, Chess. 216 CL109
Green La, Chig. 103 ER47
Green La, Chis. 185 EP91
Green La, Cob. 214 BY112
Green La, Couls. 250 DA125
Green La, Dag. 126 EX61
Green La, Edg. 96 CN50
Green La, Egh. 173 BB91
Green La (Thorpe), Egh. 193 BD95
Green La, Felt. 176 BY92
Green La, Gdmg. 258 AS142
Green La, Guil. 243 BB134
Green La (Shamley Grn), Guil. 260 BG144
Green La (West Clandon), Guil. 244 BG127
Green La, Harl. 52 FA16
Green La, Har. 117 CE62
Green La, Hem.H. 41 BQ21
Green La (Bovingdon), Hem.H. 57 AZ28
Green La, Horl. 269 DM152
Green La, Houns. 155 BV83

Green La, Ilf. 125 EQ61
Green La, Lthd. 231 CK121
Green La (Fifield), Maid. 150 AC81
Green La, Mord. 200 DB100
Green La, N.Mal. 198 CQ99
Green La, Nthwd. 93 BT52
Green La, Pur. 219 DJ111
Green La, Red. 250 DE132
Green La (Bletchingley), Red. 252 DS131
Green La (Outwood), Red. 267 DL141
Green La (White Bushes), Red. 266 DG139
Green La, Reig. 249 CZ134
Green La, Rick. 74 BM43
Green La, St.Alb. 43 CD16
Green La, Shep. 195 BQ100
Green La (Burnham), Slou. 131 AK66
Green La (Datchet), Slou. 152 AV81
Green La (Farnham Common), Slou. 111 AP64
Green La, S.Ock. 149 FR69
Green La, Stai. 193 BE95
Green La, Stan. 95 CH49
Green La, Sun. 175 BT94
Green La, Tad. 249 CZ126
Green La, Th.Hth. 201 DN95
Green La, Upmin. 149 FR68
Green La, Uxb. 135 BQ71
Green La, Wal.Abb. 68 EJ34
Green La, Walt. 213 BV107
Green La, Warl. 237 DY116
Green La, Wat. 94 BW46
Green La (Panshanger), Welw.G.C. 30 DD10
Green La (Byfleet), W.Byf. 212 BM112
Green La, W.Mol. 196 CB99
Green La, Wind. 151 AP82
Green La (Chobham), Wok. 210 AT110
Green La (Mayford), Wok. 226 AV121
Copper Beech Cl
Green La (Ockham), Wok. 229 BP124
Green La, Wor.Pk. 199 CU102
Green La Av, Walt. 214 BW106
Green La Caravan Pk, Red. 267 DL141
Green La Cl, Amer. 55 AR36
Green La Cl, Cher. 193 BE103
Green La Cl (Byfleet), W.Byf. 212 BM112
Green La Gdns, Th.Hth. 202 DQ96
Green La W, Wok. 244 BN125
Green Las N4 122 DQ60
Green Las N8 121 DP55
Green Las N13 99 DM51
Green Las N15 121 DP55
Green Las N16 122 DQ62
Green Las N21 99 DP46
Green Las, Epsom 216 CS109
Green Las, Hat. 29 CT13
Green Las, Welw.G.C. 29 CT11
Green Lawns, Ruis. 116 BW60
Green Leaf Av, Wall. 219 DK105
Green Leas, Sun. 175 BT93
Green Leas, Wal.Abb. 67 ED34
Roundhills
Green Leas Cl, Sun. 175 BT93
Green Leas
Green Man Gdns W13 137 CG73
Green Man La W13 137 CG74
Green Man La, Felt. 155 BU84
Green Man Pas W13 137 CG73
Green Man Rd, Ong. 53 FD19
Green Man Roundabout E11 124 EF59
Green Manor Way, Grav. 170 FZ84
Green Mead, Esher 214 BZ107
Winterdown Gdns
Green Meadow, Pot.B. 64 DA30
Green Moor Link N21 99 DP45
Green N Rd (Jordans), Beac. 90 AS51
Green Pk, Stai. 173 BE90
Green Pk Way, Grnf. 137 CE67
Green Pl, Dart. 187 FE85
Green Pt E15 144 EE65
Green Pond Cl E17 123 DZ55
Green Pond Rd E17 123 DY55
Green Ride, Epp. 85 EP35
Green Ride, Loug. 84 EG43
Green Rd N14 81 DH44
Green Rd N20 98 DC48
Green Rd (Thorpe), Egh. 193 BB98
Green Sand Rd, Red. 250 DG133
Noke Dr
Green Slip Rd, Barn. 79 CZ40
Green St E7 144 EH65
Green St E13 144 EJ67
Green St W1 272 F10
Green St W1 140 DG73
Green St, Borwd. 78 CN36
Green St, Enf. 82 DW40
Green St, Hat. 45 CZ21
Green St, Hert. 32 DR09
Green St, Rad. 78 CN36
Green St, Rick. 73 BC40
Green St, Sun. 195 BU95
Green St Grn Rd, Dart. 188 FP88
Green Ter EC1 274 E3
Green Tiles La (Denham), Uxb. 113 BF58
Green Vale W5 138 CM72
Green Vale, Bexh. 186 EX85
Green Valley (Wooburn Grn), H.Wyc. 88 AE54
Green Verges, Stan. 95 CK52
Green Vw, Chess. 216 CM108
Green Vw Cl (Bovingdon), Hem.H. 57 BA29
Green Wk NW4 119 CX57
Green Wk SE1 279 M7
Green Wk, Buck.H. 102 EL45
Green Wk, Dart. 167 FF84
Green Wk, Hmptn. 176 BZ93
Orpwood Cl
Green Wk, Ruis. 115 BT60
Green Wk, Sthl. 156 CA78
Green Wk, Wdf.Grn. 102 EL51
Green Wk, The E4 101 EC46
Green Way SE9 184 EK85
Green Way, Brom. 204 EL100
Green Way, Red. 250 DE132
Green Way, Slou. 130 AH69
Green Way, Sun. 195 BU98
Green W Rd (Jordans), Beac. 90 AS52
Green Wrythe Cres, Cars. 200 DE102
Green Wrythe La, Cars. 200 DD100
Greenacre, Dart. 188 FL89
Oakfield La
Greenacre, Wind. 151 AL82
Greenacre (Knaphill), Wok. 226 AS116
Mead Ct
Greenacre Cl, Barn. 79 CZ38
Greenacre Cl, Nthlt. 116 BZ64
Greenacre Cl, Swan. 207 FE98
Greenacre Ct (Englefield Grn), Egh. 172 AW93
Greenacre Gdns E17 123 EC56
Greenacre Pl (Hackbridge), Wall. 201 DH103
Park Rd
Greenacre Sq SE16 163 DX75
Fishermans Dr
Greenacre Wk N14 99 DL48
Greenacres N3 97 CY54
Greenacres SE9 185 EN86
Greenacres, Bushey 95 CD47
Greenacres, Epp. 69 ET29
Greenacres (Bookham), Lthd. 230 CB124
Greenacres, Oxt. 254 EE127
Greenacres Av, Uxb. 114 BM62
Greenacres Cl, Orp. 223 EQ105
Greenacres Cl, Rain. 148 FL69
Greenacres Dr, Stan. 95 CH52
Greenall Cl (Cheshunt), Wal.Cr. 67 DY30
Greenaway Gdns NW3 120 DB63
Greenbank (Cheshunt), Wal.Cr. 66 DV28
Greenbank Av, Wem. 117 CG64
Greenbank Cl E4 101 EC47
Greenbank Cl, Rom. 106 FK48
Greenbank Cres NW4 119 CY56
Greenbank Rd, Wat. 75 BR36
Greenbanks, Dart. 188 FL89
Greenbanks, St.Alb. 43 CF22
Colindale Av
Greenbanks, Upmin. 129 FS60
Greenbay Rd SE7 164 EK80
Greenberry St NW8 272 B1
Greenberry St NW8 140 DE68
Greenbrook Av, Barn. 80 DC39
Greenbury Cl, Rick. 73 BC41
Green St
Greencoat Pl SW1 277 L8
Greencoat Pl SW1 161 DJ77
Greencoat Row SW1 277 L7
Greencoates, Hert. 32 DS10
Greencourt Av, Croy. 202 DV103
Greencourt Av, Edg. 96 CP53
Greencourt Gdns, Croy. 202 DV102
Greencourt Rd, Orp. 205 ER99
Greencrest Pl NW2 119 CV62
Dollis Hill La
Greencroft, Guil. 243 BB134
Greencroft Av, Ruis. 116 BW61
Greencroft Cl E6 144 EL71
Neatscourt Rd
Greencroft Gdns NW6 140 DB66
Greencroft Gdns, Enf. 82 DS41
Greencroft Rd, Houns. 156 BZ81
Greendale Ms, Slou. 132 AU73
Greendale Wk (Northfleet), Grav. 190 GE90
Greene Fld Rd, Berk. 38 AW19
Greene Fielde End, Stai. 174 BK94
Greene Wk, Berk. 38 AX20
Greenend Rd W4 158 CS75
Greenes Ct, Berk. 38 AW18
Lower Kings Rd
Greenfarm Cl, Orp. 223 ET106
Greenfern Av, Slou. 130 AJ72
Greenfield, Hat. 45 CX15
Greenfield, Welw.G.C. 29 CX06
Greenfield Av, Surb. 198 CP101
Greenfield Av, Wat. 94 BX47
Greenfield End (Chalfont St. Peter), Ger.Cr. 90 AY51
Greenfield Gdns NW2 119 CY61
Greenfield Gdns, Dag. 146 EX67
Greenfield Gdns, Orp. 205 ER101
Greenfield Link, Couls. 235 DL115
Greenfield Rd E1 142 DU71
Greenfield Rd N15 122 DS57
Greenfield Rd, Dag. 146 EW67
Greenfield Rd, Dart. 187 FD92
Greenfield St, Wal.Abb. 67 EC34
Greenfield Way, Har. 116 CB55
Greenfields, Loug. 85 EN42
Greenfields (Cuffley), Pot.B. 65 DL30
South Dr
Greenfields Cl, Brwd. 107 FW51
Essex Way
Greenfields Cl, Horl. 268 DE146
Greenfields Cl, Loug. 85 EN42
Greenfields Rd, Horl. 268 DE146
Greenford Av W7 137 CE70
Greenford Av, Sthl. 136 BZ73
Greenford Gdns, Grnf. 136 CB69
Greenford Rd, Grnf. 136 CC71
Greenford Rd, Har. 137 CD68
Greenford Rd, Sthl. 136 CC74
Greenford Rd, Sutt. 218 DB105
Greengate, Grnf. 137 CH65
Greengate St E13 144 EH68
Greenhalgh Wk N2 120 DC56
Greenham Cl SE1 278 D5
Greenham Cl SE1 161 DN75
Greenham Cres E4 101 DZ51
Greenham Rd N10 98 DG54
Greenham Wk, Wok. 226 AW118
Greenhaven Dr SE28 146 EV72
Greenhayes Av, Bans. 218 DA114
Greenhayes Cl, Reig. 250 DC134
Greenhayes Gdns, Bans. 234 DA115
Greenheys Cl, Nthwd. 93 BS53
Greenheys Dr E18 124 EF55
Greenheys Pl, Wok. 227 AZ118
White Rose La
Greenhill NW3 120 DD63
Hampstead High St
Greenhill SE18 165 EM78
Greenhill, Sutt. 200 DC103
Greenhill, Wem. 118 CP61
Greenhill Av, Cat. 236 DV121
Greenhill Cres, Wat. 75 BS44
Greenhill Gdns, Guil. 243 BC131
Greenhill Gdns, Nthlt. 136 BZ68
Greenhill Gro E12 124 EL63
Greenhill Pk NW10 138 CS67
Greenhill Pk, Barn. 80 DB43
Greenhill Rd NW10 138 CS67
Greenhill Rd (Northfleet), Grav. 191 GF89
Greenhill Rd, Har. 117 CE58
Greenhill Ter SE18 165 EM78
Greenhill Ter, Nthlt. 136 BZ68
Greenhill Way, Croy. 221 DX111
Greenhill Way, Har. 117 CE58
Greenhill Way, Wem. 118 CP61
Greenhills, Harl. 51 ES15
Greenhills Cl, Rick. 74 BH43
Greenhill's Rents EC1 274 G6
Greenhills Ter N1 142 DR65
Baxter Rd
Greenhithe Cl, Sid. 185 ES87
Greenholm Rd SE9 185 EP85
Greenhurst La, Oxt. 254 EG132
Greenhurst Rd SE27 181 DN92
Greening St SE2 166 EW77
Greenlake Ter, Stai. 174 BG94
Greenland Cres, Sthl. 156 BW76
Greenland Ms SE8 163 DX78
Trundleys Rd
Greenland Pl NW1 141 DH67
Greenland Rd
Greenland Quay SE16 163 DX77
Greenland Rd NW1 141 DJ67
Greenland Rd, Barn. 79 CW44
Greenland St NW1 141 DH67
Camden High St
Greenlands Rd, Stai. 174 BG91
Greenlands Rd, Wey. 195 BP104
Greenlaw Gdns, N.Mal. 199 CT101
Greenlaw St SE18 165 EN76
Greenlea Pk SW19 200 DD95
Greenleaf Cl SW2 181 DN87
Tulse Hill
Greenleaf Rd E6 144 EJ67
Redclyffe Rd
Greenleaf Rd E17 123 DZ55
Greenleafe Dr, Ilf. 125 EP56
Greenleaves Ct, Ashf. 175 BP93
Redleaves Av
Greenleigh Av, Orp. 206 EV98
Greenman St N1 142 DQ66
Greenmead Cl SE25 202 DU99
Greenmeads, Wok. 226 AY122
Greenmoor Rd, Enf. 82 DW40
Greeno Cres, Shep. 194 BN99
Greenoak Pl, Barn. 80 DF41
Greenoak Ri (Biggin Hill), West. 238 EJ118
Greenoak Way SW19 179 CX91
Greenock Rd SW16 201 DK95
Greenock Rd W3 158 CP76
Greenock Rd, Slou. 131 AN72
Greenock Way, Rom. 105 FE51
Greenpark Ct, Wem. 137 CJ66
Greens Cl, The, Loug. 85 EN40
Green's Ct W1 273 M10
Green's End SE18 165 EP77
Greensand Cl (South Merstham), Red. 251 DK128
Greensand Rd, Red. 250 DG133
Greensand Way, Bet. 264 CM136
Old Sch La
Greensand Way, Dor. 264 CM136
Greensand Way, Gdse. 267 DP135
Greenshank Cl E17 101 DY52
Banbury Rd
Greenshaw, Brwd. 108 FV46
Greenshields Ind Est E16 144 EG74
Greenside, Bex. 186 EY88
Greenside, Borwd. 78 CN38
Greenside, Dag. 126 EW60
Greenside, Slou. 131 AN71
Greenside, Swan. 207 FD96
Greenside Cl N20 98 DD47
Greenside Cl SE6 183 ED89
Greenside Cl, Guil. 243 BC132
Foxglove Gdns
Greenside Rd W12 159 CU76
Greenside Rd, Croy. 201 DN101
Greenside Rd, Wey. 195 BP104
Greenside Wk (Biggin Hill), West. 238 EH118
Kings Rd
Greenslade Av, Ash. 232 CP119
Greenslade Rd, Bark. 145 ER66
Greensleeves Cl, St.Alb. 43 CJ21
Greenstead, Saw. 36 EY06
Greenstead Av, Wdf.Grn. 102 EJ52
Greenstead Cl, Brwd. 109 GE45
Greenstead Cl, Wdf.Grn. 102 EJ51
Greenstead Gdns
Greenstead Gdns SW15 179 CU85
Greenstead Gdns, Wdf.Grn. 102 EJ51
Greensted Rd, Loug. 102 EL45
Greensted Rd, Ong. 71 FG28
Greenstone Ms E11 124 EG58
Greensward, Bushey 76 CB44
Greentrees, Epp. 70 EU31
Greenvale, Welw.G.C. 30 DA10
Greenvale Rd SE9 165 EM84
Greenview Av, Beck. 203 DY100
Greenview Av, Croy. 203 DY100
Greenview Ct, Ashf. 174 BM91
Village Way
Greenway N14 99 DL47
Greenway N20 98 DA47
Greenway SW20 199 CW98
Greenway, Berk. 38 AU19
Greenway, Brwd. 109 GA45
Greenway, Chesh. 54 AP28
Greenway, Chis. 185 EN92
Greenway, Dag. 126 EW61
Greenway, Harl. 50 EL15
Greenway, Har. 118 CL57
Greenway, Hayes 135 BV70
Greenway, Hem.H. 41 BP20
Greenway, Lthd. 230 CB123
Greenway, Pnr. 93 BV54
Greenway, Rom. 106 FP51
Greenway, Wall. 219 DJ105
Greenway (Tatsfield), West. 238 EJ120
Greenway, Wdf.Grn. 102 EJ50
Greenway, The NW9 96 CR54
Greenway, The, Enf. 83 DX35
Greenway, The, Epsom 232 CN115
Greenway, The (Chalfont St. Peter), Ger.Cr. 112 AX55
Greenway, The, Har. 95 CE53
Greenway, The, Houns. 156 BZ84
Greenway, The, Orp. 206 EV100
Greenway, The, Oxt. 254 EH133
Greenway, The, Pnr. 116 BZ58
Greenway, The, Pot.B. 64 DA33
Greenway, The, Rick. 92 BG45
Greenway, The, Slou. 131 AK74
Greenway, The, Uxb. 134 BJ68
Greenway, The (Ickenham), Uxb. 115 BQ61
Greenway Av E17 123 ED56
Greenway Cl N4 122 DQ61
Greenway Cl N11 98 DG51
Greenway Cl N15 122 DT56
Copperfield Dr
Greenway Cl N20 98 DA47
Greenway Cl NW9 96 CR54
Greenway Cl, W.Byf. 212 BG113
Greenway Dr, Stai. 194 BK95
Greenway Gdns NW9 96 CR54
Greenway Gdns, Croy. 203 DZ104
Greenway Gdns, Grnf. 136 CA69
Greenway Gdns, Har. 95 CE53
Greenway Par, Chesh. 54 AP28
Greenways, Abb.L. 59 BS32
Greenways, Beck. 203 EA96
Greenways, Egh. 172 AY93
Greenways, Esher 215 CE105
Greenways, Hert. 31 DN09
Greenways, Tad. 249 CV125
Greenways (Cheshunt), Wal.Cr. 65 DP29
Greenways, Wok. 227 BA117
Pembroke Rd
Greenways, The, Twick. 177 CG86
South Western Rd
Greenwell Cl, Gdse. 252 DV130
Greenwell St W1 273 J5
Greenwell St W1 141 DH70
Greenwich Ch St SE10 163 EC79
Greenwich Ct, Wal.Cr. 67 DY34
Parkside
Greenwich Cres E6 144 EL71
Swan App
Greenwich Foot Tunnel E14 163 EC78
Greenwich Foot Tunnel SE10 163 EC78
Greenwich High Rd SE10 163 EB81
Greenwich Ind Est SE7 164 EH77
Greenwich Mkt SE10 163 EC79
King William Wk
Greenwich Pk SE10 164 EE80
Greenwich Pk St SE10 163 ED78
Greenwich S St SE10 163 EB81
Greenwich Vw Pl E14 163 EB76
Greenwich Way, Wal.Abb. 83 EC36
Greenwood, The, Guil. 243 BA134
Greenwood Av, Dag. 127 FB63
Greenwood Av, Enf. 83 DY40
Greenwood Av (Cheshunt), Wal.Cr. 66 DV31
Greenwood Cl (Woodham), Add. 211 BF111
Greenwood Cl, Amer. 55 AS37
Greenwood Cl (Seer Grn), Beac. 89 AQ51
Farmers Way
Greenwood Cl, Bushey 95 CE45
Langmead Dr
Greenwood Cl, Mord. 199 CY98
Greenwood Cl, Orp. 205 ES100
Greenwood Cl, Sid. 186 EU89
Hurst Rd
Greenwood Cl, T.Ditt. 197 CG102
Greenwood Cl (Cheshunt), Wal.Cr. 66 DV31
Greenwood Av
Greenwood Ct E18 124 EG55
Woodford Rd
Greenwood Ct SW1 277 K10
Greenwood Ct SW1 161 DJ78
Greenwood Dr E4 101 EC50
Avril Way
Greenwood Dr, Red. 266 DG139
Greenwood Dr, Wat. 59 BV34
Greenwood Gdns N13 99 DP48
Greenwood Gdns, Cat. 252 DU125
Greenwood Gdns, Ilf. 103 EQ52
Greenwood Gdns (Shenley), Rad. 62 CL33
Greenwood Ho, Grays 170 GA79
Argent St
Greenwood La (Hampton Hill), Hmptn. 176 CB92
Greenwood Pk, Kings.T. 178 CS94
Greenwood Pl NW5 121 DH64
Highgate Rd
Greenwood Rd E8 142 DU65
Greenwood Rd E13 144 EF68
Maud Rd
Greenwood Rd, Bex. 187 FD91
Greenwood Rd, Chig. 104 EV49
Greenwood Rd, Croy. 201 DP101
Greenwood Rd, Islw. 157 CE83
Greenwood Rd, Mitch. 201 DK97
Greenwood Rd, T.Ditt. 197 CG102
Greenwood Rd, Wok. 226 AS120
Greenwood Ter NW10 138 CR67
Greenwood Way, Sev. 256 FF125
Greenwoods, The (South Harrow), Har. 116 CC61
Greenyard, Wal.Abb. 67 EC33
Greer Rd, Har. 94 CC53
Greet St SE1 278 E3
Greet St SE1 141 DN74
Greg Cl E10 123 EC58
Gregor Ms SE3 164 EG80
Gregories Fm La, Beac. 89 AK53
Gregories Rd, Beac. 88 AH53
Gregory Av, Pot.B. 64 DC33
Gregory Cl, Wok. 226 AW117
Gregory Cres SE9 184 EK87
Gregory Dr (Old Windsor), Wind. 172 AV86
Gregory Ms, Wal.Abb. 67 EB33
Beaulieu Dr
Gregory Pl W8 160 DB75
Gregory Rd, Rom. 126 EX56
Gregory Rd (Hedgerley), Slou. 111 AR61
Gregory Rd, Sthl. 156 CA76
Gregson Cl, Borwd. 78 CQ39
Gregson's Ride, Loug. 85 EN38
Greig Cl N8 121 DL57
Greig Ter SE17 161 DP79
Lorrimore Sq
Grena Gdns, Rich. 158 CM84
Grena Rd, Rich. 158 CM84
Grenaby Av, Croy. 202 DR101
Grenaby Rd, Croy. 202 DR101
Grenada Rd SE7 164 EJ80
Grenade St E14 143 DZ73
Grenadier Cl, St.Alb. 43 CJ21
Grenadier Pl, Cat. 236 DQ122
Coulsdon Rd
Grenadier St E16 145 EN74
Grenadine Cl, Wal.Cr. 66 DT27
Allwood Rd
Grendon Cl, Horl. 268 DF146
Grendon Gdns, Wem. 118 CN61
Grendon St NW8 272 B4
Grendon St NW8 140 DE70
Grenfell Av, Horn. 127 FF60
Grenfell Cl, Borwd. 78 CQ39
Grenfell Gdns, Har. 118 CL59
Grenfell Rd W11 139 CX73
Grenfell Rd, Beac. 89 AL52
Grenfell Rd, Mitch. 180 DF93
Grenfell Twr W11 139 CX73
Grenfell Wk W11 139 CX73
Grennell Cl, Sutt. 200 DD103
Grennell Rd, Sutt. 200 DC103
Grenoble Gdns N13 99 DN51
Grenville Av, Brox. 49 DZ21
Grenville Cl N3 97 CZ53
Grenville Cl, Cob. 214 BX113
Grenville Cl (Burnham), Slou. 130 AH68
Grenville Cl, Surb. 198 CQ102
Grenville Cl, Wal.Cr. 67 DX32
Grenville Gdns, Wdf.Grn. 102 EJ53
Grenville Ms SW7 160 DC77
Grenville Ms, Hmptn. 176 CB92
Grenville Pl NW7 96 CR50
Grenville Pl SW7 160 DC76
Grenville Rd N19 121 DL60
Grenville Rd (New Addington), Croy. 221 EC109
Grenville Rd, Grays 169 FV77
Grenville St WC1 274 A5
Grenville St WC1 141 DL70
Gresford Cl, St.Alb. 43 CK20
Gresham Av N20 98 DF49
Gresham Av, Warl. 237 DY118
Gresham Cl, Bex. 186 EY86
Gresham Cl, Brwd. 108 FW48
Gresham Cl, Enf. 82 DQ41
Gresham Cl, Oxt. 254 EF128
Gresham Ct, Berk. 38 AV20
Gresham Dr, Rom. 126 EV57
Gresham Gdns NW11 119 CY60
Gresham Rd E6 145 EM68
Gresham Rd E16 144 EH72
Gresham Rd NW10 118 CR64
Gresham Rd SE25 202 DU98
Gresham Rd SW9 161 DN83
Gresham Rd, Beck. 203 DY96
Gresham Rd, Brwd. 108 FW48
Gresham Rd, Edg. 96 CM51
Gresham Rd, Hmptn. 176 CA93
Gresham Rd, Houns. 156 CC81
Gresham Rd, Oxt. 254 EF128
Gresham Rd, Slou. 131 AN72
Gresham Rd, Stai. 173 BF92
Gresham Rd, Uxb. 134 BN68
Gresham St EC2 275 H8
Gresham St EC2 142 DQ72
Gresham Way SW19 180 DA90
Gresley Cl E17 123 DY58
Gresley Cl N15 122 DR56
Clinton Rd
Gresley Cl, Welw.G.C. 29 CY08
Gresley Ct, Pot.B. 64 DC29
Gresley Rd N19 121 DJ60
Gresse St W1 273 M7
Gresse St W1 141 DK71
Gressenhall Rd SW18 179 CZ86
Gresswell Cl, Sid. 186 EU90
Greswell St SW6 159 CX81
Greta Bk (West Horsley), Lthd. 245 BQ126
Gretton Rd N17 100 DS52
Greville Av, S.Croy. 221 DX110
Greville Cl, Ash. 232 CL119
Greville Cl, Guil. 242 AT134
Greville Cl, Hat. 45 CV24
Greville Cl, Twick. 177 CH87
Greville Ct (Bookham), Lthd. 246 CC125
Keswick Rd
Greville Hall NW6 140 DB68
Greville Ms NW6 140 DB68
Greville Rd
Greville Pk Av, Ash. 232 CL118
Greville Pk Rd, Ash. 232 CL118
Greville Pl NW6 140 DB68
Greville Rd E17 123 EC56
Greville Rd NW6 140 DB67
Greville Rd, Rich. 178 CM86
Greville St EC1 274 E7
Greville St EC1 141 DN71
Grey Alders, Bans. 217 CW114
High Beeches
Grey Cl NW11 120 DC58
Grey Eagle St E1 275 P6
Grey Eagle St E1 142 DT71
Grey Twrs Av, Horn. 128 FK60
Grey Twrs Gdns, Horn. 128 FK60
Grey Twrs Av
Greycaine Rd, Wat. 76 BX37
Greycoat Pl SW1 277 M7
Greycoat Pl SW1 161 DK76
Greycoat St SW1 277 M7
Greycoat St SW1 161 DK76
Greycot Rd, Beck. 183 EA92
Greyfell Cl, Stan. 95 CH50
Coverdale Cl
Greyfields Cl, Pur. 219 DP113
Greyfriars, Brwd. 109 GB45
Greyfriars Pas EC1 274 G8
Greyfriars Rd (Ripley), Wok. 228 BG124
Greygoose Pk, Harl. 51 EN18
Greyhound Hill NW4 119 CU55
Greyhound La SW16 181 DK93
Greyhound La, Grays 171 GG75
Greyhound La, Pot.B. 63 CU33
Greyhound Rd N17 122 DS55
Greyhound Rd NW10 139 CV69
Greyhound Rd W6 159 CX79
Greyhound Rd W14 159 CX79
Greyhound Rd, Sutt. 218 DC106
Greyhound Ter SW16 201 DJ95
Greyhound Way, Dart. 187 FE86
Greys Pk Cl, Kes. 222 EJ106
Greystead Rd SE23 182 DW87
Greystoke Av, Pnr. 116 CA55
Greystoke Cl, Berk. 38 AU20
Greystoke Dr, Ruis. 115 BP58
Greystoke Gdns W5 138 CL70
Greystoke Gdns, Enf. 81 DK42
Greystoke Pk Ter W5 137 CK69
Greystoke Pl EC4 274 D8
Greystoke Rd, Slou. 131 AM71
Greystone Cl, S.Croy. 220 DW111
Greystone Gdns, Har. 117 CJ58
Greystone Gdns, Ilf. 103 EQ54
Greystone Path E11 124 EF59
Grove Rd
Greystones Cl, Red. 266 DD136
Hardwick Rd
Greystones Dr, Reig. 250 DC132
Greyswood St SW16 181 DH93
Greythorne Rd, Wok. 226 AU118
Grice Av (Biggin Hill), West. 222 EH113
Gridiron Pl, Upmin. 128 FP62
Grierson Rd SE23 183 DX87
Grieves Rd (Northfleet), Grav. 191 GF90
Griffetts Yd, Chesh. 54 AP30
Bellingdon Rd
Griffin Av, Upmin. 129 FS58
Griffin Cen, The, Felt. 175 BV85
Griffin Cl NW10 119 CV64
Griffin Cl, Slou. 151 AQ75
Griffin Ct, Lthd. 246 CA126
Griffin Way
Griffin Manor Way SE28 165 ER76
Griffin Rd N17 100 DS54
Griffin Rd SE18 165 ER78
Griffin Wk, Green. 189 FT85
Church Rd
Griffin Way (Bookham), Lthd. 246 CA126
Griffin Way, Sun. 195 BU96
Griffins, The, Grays 170 GB75
Griffith Cl, Dag. 126 EW60
Gibson Rd
Griffiths Cl, Wor.Pk. 199 CV103
Griffiths Rd SW19 180 DA94
Griffiths Way, St.Alb. 42 CC22
Grifon Rd, Grays 169 FW76

Griggs App, Ilf. 125 EQ61
Griggs Gdns, Horn. 128 FJ64
Tylers Cres
Griggs Pl SE1 279 N7
Griggs Rd E10 123 EC58
Grilse Cl N9 100 DV49
Grimsby Gro E16 165 EP75
Grimsby St E2 142 DU70
Cheshire St
Grimsdells La, Amer. 55 AR37
Grimsdyke Cres, Barn. 79 CW41
Grimsdyke Rd, Pnr. 94 BY52
Grimsel Path SE5 161 DP80
Laxley Cl
Grimshaw Cl N6 120 DG59
Grimshaw Way, Rom. 127 FF57
Grimston Rd SW6 159 CZ82
Grimston Rd, St.Alb. 43 CF21
Grimstone Cl, Rom. 105 FB51
Grimthorpe Cl, St.Alb. 43 CD17
Grimwade Av, Croy. 202 DU104
Grimwade Cl SE15 162 DW83
Grimwood Rd, Twick. 177 CF87
Grindal St SE1 278 D5
Grindall Cl, Croy. 219 DP105
Hillside Rd
Grindcobbe, St.Alb. 43 CD23
Grindleford Av N11 98 DG47
Grindley Gdns, Croy. 202 DT100
Grinling Pl SE8 163 EA79
Grinstead Rd SE8 163 DY78
Grisedale Cl, Pur. 220 DS114
Grisedale Gdns, Pur. 220 DS114
Grittleton Av, Wem. 138 CP65
Grittleton Rd W9 140 DA70
Grizedale Ter SE23 182 DV89
Grobars Av, Wok. 226 AW115
Grocer's Hall Ct EC2 275 K9
Grogan Cl, Hmptn. 176 BZ93
Groom Cl, Brom. 204 EH98
Groom Cres SW18 180 DD87
Groom Pl SW1 276 G6
Groom Pl SW1 160 DG76
Groom Rd, Brox. 67 DZ26
Groom Wk, Guil. 242 AY131
Groombridge Cl, Walt. 213 BV106
Groombridge Cl, Well. 186 EU85
Groombridge Rd E9 143 DX66
Groomfield Cl SW17 180 DG91
Grooms Cotts, Chesh. 56 AV30
Grooms Dr, Pnr. 115 BU57
Grosmont Rd SE18 165 ET78
Grosse Way SW15 179 CV86
Grosvenor Av N5 122 DQ64
Grosvenor Av SW14 158 CS83
Grosvenor Av, Cars. 218 DF107
Grosvenor Av, Har. 116 CB58
Grosvenor Av, Hayes 135 BS68
Grosvenor Av, Kings L. 59 BQ28
Grosvenor Av, Rich. 178 CL85
Grosvenor Rd
Grosvenor Cl, Iver 133 BD69
Grosvenor Cl, Loug. 85 EP39
Grosvenor Cotts SW1 276 F8
Grosvenor Ct N14 99 DJ45
Grosvenor Ct NW6 139 CX67
Christchurch Av
Grosvenor Ct, Guil. 243 BA132
London Rd
Grosvenor Ct, Rick. 75 BR43
Mayfare
Grosvenor Ct, Slou. 132 AS72
Stoke Poges La
Grosvenor Cres NW9 118 CN56
Grosvenor Cres SW1 276 G5
Grosvenor Cres SW1 160 DG75
Grosvenor Cres, Dart. 188 FK85
Grosvenor Cres, Uxb. 135 BP66
Grosvenor Cres Ms SW1 276 F5
Grosvenor Cres Ms SW1 160 DG75
Grosvenor Dr, Horn. 128 FJ60
Grosvenor Dr, Loug. 85 EP39
Grosvenor Dr, Maid. 130 AC71
Grosvenor Est SW1 277 N8
Grosvenor Est SW1 161 DK77
Grosvenor Gdns E6 144 EK69
Grosvenor Gdns N10 121 DJ55
Grosvenor Gdns N14 81 DK43
Grosvenor Gdns NW2 119 CW64
Grosvenor Gdns NW11 119 CZ58
Grosvenor Gdns SW1 277 H6
Grosvenor Gdns SW1 161 DH76
Grosvenor Gdns SW14 158 CS83
Grosvenor Gdns, Kings.T. 177 CK93
Grosvenor Gdns, Upmin. 129 FR60
Grosvenor Gdns, Wall. 219 DJ108
Grosvenor Gdns, Wdf.Grn. 102 EG51
Grosvenor Gdns Ms E SW1 277 J6
Grosvenor Gdns Ms N SW1 277 H7
Grosvenor Gdns Ms S SW1 277 J7
Grosvenor Gate W1 276 E1
Grosvenor Gate W1 140 DF73
Grosvenor Hill SW19 179 CY93
Grosvenor Hill W1 273 H10
Grosvenor Hill W1 141 DH73
Grosvenor Ms, Reig. 266 DB137
Grosvenor Pk SE5 162 DQ79
Grosvenor Pk Rd E17 123 EA57
Grosvenor Path, Loug. 85 EP39
Grosvenor Pl SW1 276 G5
Grosvenor Pl SW1 160 DG75
Grosvenor Pl, Wey. 195 BR104
Vale Rd
Grosvenor Ri E E17 123 EB57
Grosvenor Rd E6 144 EK67
Grosvenor Rd E7 144 EH65
Grosvenor Rd E10 123 EC60
Grosvenor Rd E11 124 EG57
Grosvenor Rd N3 97 CZ52
Grosvenor Rd N9 100 DV46
Grosvenor Rd N10 99 DH53
Grosvenor Rd SE25 202 DU98
Grosvenor Rd SW1 161 DH79
Grosvenor Rd W4 158 CP78
Grosvenor Rd W7 137 CG74
Grosvenor Rd, Belv. 166 FA79
Grosvenor Rd, Bexh. 186 EX85
Grosvenor Rd, Borwd. 78 CN41
Grosvenor Rd, Brent. 157 CK79
Grosvenor Rd, Brox. 49 DZ20
Grosvenor Rd, Dag. 126 EZ60
Grosvenor Rd, Epsom 232 CR119
Grosvenor Rd, Houns. 156 BZ83
Grosvenor Rd, Ilf. 125 EQ62
Grosvenor Rd, Nthwd. 93 BT50
Grosvenor Rd, Orp. 205 ES100
Grosvenor Rd, Rich. 178 CL85
Grosvenor Rd, Rom. 127 FD59
Grosvenor Rd, St.Alb. 43 CE21
Grosvenor Rd, Sthl. 156 BZ76
Grosvenor Rd, Stai. 174 BG94
Grosvenor Rd, Twick. 177 CG87
Grosvenor Rd, Wall. 219 DH107
Grosvenor Rd, Wat. 76 BW42
Grosvenor Rd, W.Wick. 203 EB102
Grosvenor Sq W1 272 G10
Grosvenor Sq W1 140 DG73
Grosvenor Sq, Kings L. 59 BQ28
Grosvenor Av
Grosvenor St W1 273 H10
Grosvenor St W1 141 DH73
Grosvenor Ter SE5 161 DP80
Grosvenor Ter, Hem.H. 40 BG21
Grosvenor Vale, Ruis. 115 BT61
Grosvenor Way E5 122 DW61
Grosvenor Wf Rd E14 163 ED77
Grote's Bldgs SE3 164 EE82
Grote's Pl SE3 164 EE82
Groton Rd SW18 180 DB89
Grotto, The, Ware 33 DX07
Grotto Pas W1 272 G6
Grotto Rd, Twick. 177 CF89
Grotto Rd, Wey. 195 BP104
Ground La, Hat. 45 CV16
Grove, The E15 144 EE65
Grove, The N3 98 DA53
Grove, The N4 121 DM59
Grove, The N6 120 DG60
Grove, The N8 121 DK57
Grove, The N13 99 DN49
Grove, The N14 81 DJ43
Grove, The NW9 118 CR57
Grove, The NW11 119 CY59
Grove, The W5 137 CK74
Grove, The, Add. 212 BH106
Grove, The, Amer. 55 AR36
Grove, The, Bexh. 166 EX84
Grove, The, Brwd. 108 FT49
Grove, The, Cat. 235 DP121
Grove, The, Chesh. 72 AX36
Grove, The, Couls. 235 DK115
Grove, The, Edg. 96 CP49
Grove, The, Egh. 173 BA92
Grove, The, Enf. 81 DN40
Grove, The, Epsom 216 CS113
Grove, The (Ewell), Epsom 217 CT110
Grove, The, Esher 196 CB102
Grove, The, Grav. 191 GH87
Grove, The, Grnf. 136 CC72
Grove, The, Hat. 64 DA27
Grove, The, Horl. 269 DH149
Grove, The, Islw. 157 CE81
Grove, The, Pot.B. 64 DC32
Grove, The, Rad. 61 CG34
Grove, The, Sid. 186 EY91
Grove, The, Slou. 152 AU75
Grove, The, Stan. 95 CG47
Grove, The, Swan. 207 FF97
Grove, The, Swans. 190 FZ85
Grove, The, Tedd. 177 CG91
Grove, The, Twick. 177 CH86
Bridge Rd
Grove, The, Upmin. 128 FP63
Grove, The, Uxb. 114 BN64
Grove, The, Walt. 195 BV101
Grove, The, Wat. 75 BQ37
Grove, The, W.Wick. 203 EB104
Grove, The (Biggin Hill), West. 238 EK118
Grove, The, Wok. 227 AZ116
Grove Av N3 98 DA52
Grove Av N10 99 DJ54
Grove Av W7 137 CE72
Grove Av, Epsom 216 CS113
Grove Av, Pnr. 116 BY56
Grove Av, Sutt. 218 DA107
Grove Av, Twick. 177 CF88
Grove Bk, Wat. 94 BX46
Grove Cl N14 99 DH45
Avenue Rd
Grove Cl SE23 183 DX88
Grove Cl, Brom. 204 EG103
Grove Cl, Felt. 176 BY91
Grove Cl (Chalfont St. Peter), Ger.Cr. 90 AW53
Grove La
Grove Cl, Kings.T. 198 CM98
Grove Cl, Slou. 152 AU76
Alpha St S
Grove Cl, Uxb. 114 BN64
Grove Cl (Old Windsor), Wind. 172 AV87
Grove Cor (Bookham), Lthd. 246 CA126
Lower Shott
Grove Cotts SW3 160 DE79
Grove Ct SE3 164 EG81
Grove Ct, Barn. 79 CZ41
High St
Grove Ct, Beac. 89 AK53
Station Rd
Grove Ct, E.Mol. 197 CD99
Walton Rd
Grove Ct, Wal.Abb. 67 EB33
Highbridge St
Grove Cres E18 102 EF54
Grove Cres NW9 118 CQ56
Grove Cres SE5 162 DS82
Grove Cres, Felt. 176 BY91
Grove Cres, Kings.T. 198 CL97
Grove Cres, Rick. 74 BN42
Grove Cres, Walt. 195 BV101
Grove Cres Rd E15 143 ED65
Grove End E18 102 EF54
Grove Hill
Grove End NW5 121 DH63
Chetwynd Rd
Grove End (Chalfont St. Peter), Ger.Cr. 90 AW53
Grove End Gdns NW8 140 DD68
Grove End Rd
Grove End La, Esher 197 CD102
Grove End Rd NW8 140 DD69
Grove Fm Ct, Mitch. 200 DF98
Brookfields Av
Grove Fm Pk, Nthwd. 93 BR50
Grove Footpath, Surb. 198 CL98
Grove Gdns NW4 119 CU56
Grove Gdns NW8 272 C3
Grove Gdns, Dag. 127 FC62
Grove Gdns, Enf. 83 DX39
Grove Gdns, Tedd. 177 CG91
Grove Grn Rd E11 123 EC62
Grove Hall Ct NW8 140 DC69
Hall Rd
Grove Hall Rd, Bushey 76 BY42
Grove Heath (Ripley), Wok. 228 BJ124
Grove Heath Ct (Ripley), Wok. 228 BJ124
Grove Heath N (Ripley), Wok. 228 BH122
Grove Heath Rd (Ripley), Wok. 228 BJ123
Grove Hill E18 102 EF54
Grove Hill (Chalfont St. Peter), Ger.Cr. 90 AW52
Grove Hill, Har. 117 CE59
Grove Hill Rd SE5 162 DS83
Grove Hill Rd, Har. 117 CE59
Grove Ho Rd N8 121 DL56
Grove La SE5 162 DR81
Grove La, Chesh. 56 AV27
Grove La, Chig. 103 ET48
Grove La, Couls. 218 DG113
Grove La, Epp. 70 EU30
High St
Grove La (Chalfont St. Peter), Ger.Cr. 90 AW53
Grove La, Kings.T. 198 CL98
Grove La, Uxb. 134 BM70
Grove La Ter SE5 162 DS83
Grove La
Grove Lea, Hat. 45 CU21
Grove Mkt Pl SE9 185 EM86
Grove Mead, Hat. 45 CT18
Grove Meadow, Welw.G.C. 30 DC09
Grove Ms W6 159 CW76
Grove Ms W11 139 CZ72
Portobello Rd
Grove Mill La, Wat. 75 BP37
Grove Mill Pl, Cars. 200 DG104
Grove Pk E11 124 EH58
Grove Pk NW9 118 CQ56
Grove Pk SE5 162 DS82
Grove Pk Av E4 101 EB52
Grove Pk Br W4 158 CQ80
Grove Pk Gdns W4 158 CP79
Grove Pk Ms W4 158 CQ80
Grove Pk Rd N15 122 DS56
Grove Pk Rd SE9 184 EJ90
Grove Pk Rd W4 158 CP80
Grove Pk Rd, Rain. 147 FG67
Grove Pk Ter W4 158 CP79
Grove Pas E2 142 DV68
Grove Pas, Tedd. 177 CG92
Grove Path (Cheshunt), Wal.Cr. 66 DU31
Grove Pl NW3 120 DD63
Christchurch Hill
Grove Pl SW12 181 DH86
Cathles Rd
Grove Pl W3 138 CQ74
Grove Pl W5 137 CK74
The Gro
Grove Pl, Bans. 218 DF112
Grove Pl, Bark. 145 EQ67
Clockhouse Av
Grove Pl, Hat. 45 CW24
Dixons Hill Rd
Grove Pl, Wat. 76 CB39
Hartspring La
Grove Pl, Wey. 213 BQ106
Princes Rd
Grove Rd E3 143 DX67
Grove Rd E4 101 EB49
Grove Rd E11 124 EF59
Grove Rd E17 123 EB57
Grove Rd E18 102 EF54
Grove Rd N11 99 DH50
Grove Rd N12 98 DD50
Grove Rd N15 122 DS57
Grove Rd NW2 139 CW65
Grove Rd SW13 159 CT82
Grove Rd SW19 180 DC94
Grove Rd W3 138 CQ74
Grove Rd W5 137 CK73
Grove Rd, Amer. 72 AT37
Grove Rd, Ash. 232 CM118
Grove Rd, Barn. 80 DE41
Grove Rd, Beac. 89 AK53
Grove Rd, Belv. 166 EZ79
Grove Rd, Bexh. 167 FC84
Grove Rd, Borwd. 78 CN39
Grove Rd, Brent. 157 CJ78
Grove Rd, Cher. 193 BF100
Grove Rd, E.Mol. 197 CD98
Grove Rd, Edg. 96 CN51
Grove Rd, Epsom 216 CS113
Grove Rd (Northfleet), Grav. 190 GB85
Grove Rd, Grays 170 GC79
Grove Rd, Guil. 243 BC134
Grove Rd, Hem.H. 40 BG22
Grove Rd, Horl. 268 DE147
Grove Rd, Houns. 156 CA84
Grove Rd, Islw. 157 CE81
Grove Rd, Mitch. 201 DH96
Grove Rd, Nthwd. 93 BR50
Grove Rd, Oxt. 253 EC134
Southlands La
Grove Rd, Pnr. 116 BZ57
Grove Rd, Rich. 178 CM86
Grove Rd, Rick. 92 BG47
Grove Rd, Rom. 126 EV59
Grove Rd, St.Alb. 43 CD21
Grove Rd, Sev. 257 FJ121
Grove Rd (Seal), Sev. 257 FN122
Grove Rd, Shep. 195 BQ100
Grove Rd (Burnham), Slou. 131 AL67
Grove Rd, Surb. 197 CK99
Grove Rd, Sutt. 218 DB107
Grove Rd, Th.Hth. 201 DN98
Grove Rd, Twick. 177 CD90
Grove Rd, Uxb. 134 BK66
Grove Rd, Ware 33 DZ05
Grove Rd (Tatsfield), West. 238 EJ120
Grove Rd, Wind. 151 AQ82
Grove Rd, Wok. 227 AZ116
Grove Rd W, Enf. 82 DW37
Grove Shaw (Kingswood), Tad. 233 CY124
Grove St N18 100 DT51
Grove St SE8 163 DZ77
Grove Ter NW5 121 DH62
Grove Ter, Tedd. 177 CG91
Grove Ter Ms NW5 121 DH62
Grove Ter
Grove Vale SE22 162 DT84
Grove Vale, Chis. 185 EN93
Grove Vil E14 143 EB73
Grove Wk, Hert. 32 DQ07
Grove Way, Esher 196 CC101
Grove Way, Rick. 73 BB42
Grove Way, Uxb. 134 BK66
Grove Way, Wem. 118 CP64
Grove Wd Hill, Couls. 219 DK114
Grovebarns, Stai. 174 BG93
Grovebury Cl, Erith 167 FD79
Grovebury Gdns (Park St), St.Alb. 60 CC27
Grovebury Rd SE2 166 EV75
Grovedale Cl (Cheshunt), Wal.Cr. 66 DT30
Grovedale Rd N19 121 DK61
Groveherst Rd, Dart. 168 FM83
Grovehill Rd, Red. 250 DE134
Groveland Av SW16 181 DM94
Groveland Ct EC4 275 J9
Groveland Rd, Beck. 203 DZ97
Groveland Way, N.Mal. 198 CQ99
Grovelands, Hem.H. 41 BQ18
Grovelands (Park St), St.Alb. 60 CB27
Grovelands, W.Mol. 196 CA98
Grovelands Cl SE5 162 DS82
Grovelands Cl, Har. 116 CB62
Grovelands Ct N14 99 DK45
Grovelands Rd N13 99 DM49
Grovelands Rd N15 122 DU58
Grovelands Rd, Orp. 186 EU94
Grovelands Rd, Pur. 219 DL112
Grovelands Way, Grays 170 FZ78
Groveley Rd, Sun. 175 BT92
Grover Cl, Hem.H. 40 BK19
Grover Rd, Wat. 94 BX45
Groves Cl, B.End 110 AC60
Groveside (Bookham), Lthd. 246 CA127
Groveside Cl W3 138 CN72
Groveside Cl, Cars. 200 DE103
Groveside Cl (Bookham), Lthd. 246 CA127
Groveside Rd E4 102 EE47
Grovestile Waye, Felt. 175 BR87
Groveway SW9 161 DM81
Groveway, Dag. 126 EX63
Grovewood, Rich. 158 CN81
Sandycombe Rd
Grovewood Cl, Rick. 73 BB43
Grovewood Pl, Wdf.Grn. 103 EM51
Grubb St, Oxt. 254 EJ128
Grubbs La, Hat. 46 DA22
Grummant Rd SE15 162 DT81
Grundy St E14 143 EB72
Gruneisen Rd N3 98 DB52
Gryphon Ind Pk, The (Porters Wd), St.Alb. 43 CF15
Guardian Cl, Horn. 127 FH60
Guards Av, Cat. 236 DQ122
Coulsdon Rd
Guards Club Rd, Maid. 130 AC72
Guards Rd, Wind. 150 AJ82
Guards Wk, Wind. 150 AJ82
Guards Rd
Guardsman Cl, Brwd. 108 FX50
Gubbins La, Rom. 106 FM52
Gubyon Av SE24 181 DP85
Guerin Sq E3 143 DZ69
Guernsey Cl, Guil. 243 BA129
Cotts Wd Dr
Guernsey Cl, Houns. 156 CA81
Guernsey Fm Dr, Wok. 226 AX115
Guernsey Gro SE24 182 DQ87
Guernsey Ho, Enf. 83 DX38
Eastfield Rd
Guernsey Rd E11 123 ED60
Guessens Ct, Welw.G.C. 29 CW09
Guessens Gro, Welw.G.C. 29 CW09
Guessens Rd, Welw.G.C. 29 CW09
Guessens Wk, Welw.G.C. 29 CW08
Guibal Rd SE12 184 EH87
Guild Rd SE7 164 EK78
Guild Rd, Erith 167 FF80
Guildcroft, Guil. 243 BA134
Guildersfield Rd SW16 181 DL94
Guildford & Godalming Bypass, Guil. 258 AS137
Guildford Av, Felt. 175 BT89
Guildford Business Pk, Guil. 242 AV133
Guildford Bypass, Guil. 243 AZ131
Guildford Gdns, Rom. 106 FL51
Guildford Gro SE10 163 EB81
Guildford La (Albury), Guil. 260 BH139
Guildford La, Wok. 226 AX120
Guildford Lo Dr (East Horsley), Lthd. 245 BT129
Guildford Pk Av, Guil. 258 AV135
Guildford Pk Rd, Guil. 258 AV135
Guildford Rd E6 144 EL72
Guildford Rd E17 101 EC53
Guildford Rd SW8 161 DL81
Guildford Rd, Cher. 193 BE102
Guildford Rd, Croy. 202 DR100
Guildford Rd (Abinger Hammer), Dor. 262 BW140
Guildford Rd (Westcott), Dor. 262 CA138
Guildford Rd, Gdmg. 258 AU144
Guildford Rd (Normandy), Guil. 242 AX127
Guildford Rd, Ilf. 125 ES61
Guildford Rd (East Horsley), Lthd. 246 BW129
Guildford Rd (Fetcham), Lthd. 231 CG122
Guildford Rd (Great Bookham), Lthd. 246 BZ127
Guildford Rd, Rom. 106 FL51
Guildford Rd, St.Alb. 43 CH21
Guildford Rd, Wok. 226 AY119
Guildford Rd (Mayford), Wok. 226 AX122
Guildford St, Cher. 194 BG101
Guildford St, Stai. 174 BG93
Guildford Way, Wall. 219 DL106
Guildhall Bldgs EC2 142 DR72
Basinghall St
Guildhall Yd EC2 275 K8
Guildhouse St SW1 277 K8
Guildhouse St SW1 161 DJ77
Guildown Av N12 98 DB49
Guildown Av, Guil. 258 AV137
Guildown Rd, Guil. 258 AV137
Guildsway E17 101 DZ53
Guileshill La (Ockham), Wok. 228 BL123
Guilford Av, Surb. 198 CM99
Guilford Pl WC1 274 B5
Guilford Pl WC1 141 DM70
Guilford St WC1 273 P5
Guilford St WC1 141 DL70
Guilford Vil, Surb. 198 CM100
Alpha Rd
Guilfords, Harl. 36 EX10
Guilsborough Cl NW10 138 CS66
Guinevere Gdns, Wal.Cr. 67 DY31
Guinness Cl E9 143 DY66
Guinness Cl, Hayes 155 BR76
Guinness Ct, Wok. 226 AT118
Iveagh Rd
Guinness Sq SE1 279 M8
Guinness Trust Bldgs SE1 162 DS75
Snowsfields
Guinness Trust Bldgs SE11 278 G10
Guinness Trust Bldgs SE11 161 DP78
Guinness Trust Bldgs SW3 276 D9
Guinness Trust Bldgs SW9 161 DP84
Guinness Trust Est N16 122 DS60
Holmleigh Rd
Guion Rd SW6 159 CZ82
Gull Cl, Wall. 219 DL108
Gull Wk, Horn. 147 FH66
Heron Flight Av
Gulland Cl, Bushey 76 CC43
Gulland Wk N1 142 DQ65
Clephane Rd
Gullbrook, Hem.H. 40 BG20
Gullet Wd Rd, Wat. 75 BU35
Gulliver Cl, Nthlt. 136 BZ67
Gulliver Rd, Sid. 185 ES89
Gulliver St SE16 163 DZ76
Gulphs, The, Hert. 32 DR10
Gulston Wk SW3 276 E9
Gulston Wk W11 139 CZ72
Basing St
Gumleigh Rd W5 157 CJ77
Gumley Gdns, Islw. 157 CG83
Gumley Rd, Grays 169 FX79
Gumping Rd, Orp. 205 EQ103
Gun Hill, Til. 171 GK79
Gun St E1 275 P7
Gun St E1 142 DT71
Gundulph Rd, Brom. 204 EJ97
Gunfleet Cl, Grav. 191 GL87
Gunmakers La E3 143 DY67
Gunn Rd, Swans. 190 FY86
Gunnell Cl SE26 182 DU92
Gunnell Cl, Croy. 202 DU100
Gunner Dr, Enf. 83 EA37
Government Row
Gunner La SE18 165 EN78
Gunners Gro E4 101 EC48
Gunners Rd SW18 180 DD89
Gunnersbury Av W3 158 CN76
Gunnersbury Av W4 158 CN76
Gunnersbury Av W5 138 CM74
Gunnersbury Cl W4 158 CP78
Grange Rd
Gunnersbury Ct W3 158 CP75
Bollo La
Gunnersbury Cres W3 158 CN75
Gunnersbury Dr W5 158 CM75
Gunnersbury Gdns W3 158 CN75
Gunnersbury La W3 158 CN76
Gunnersbury Ms W4 158 CP78
Chiswick High Rd
Gunnersbury Pk W3 158 CM77
Gunnersbury Pk W5 158 CM77
Gunning Rd, Grays 170 GD78
Gunning St SE18 165 ES77
Gunpowder Sq EC4 274 E8
Gunstor Rd N16 122 DS63
Gunter Gro SW10 160 DC79
Gunter Gro, Edg. 96 CR53
Gunterstone Rd W14 159 CY77
Gunthorpe St E1 142 DT72
Gunton Rd E5 122 DV62
Gunton Rd SW17 180 DG93
Gunwhale Cl SE16 143 DX74
Gurdon Rd SE7 164 EG78
Gurnard Cl, West Dr. 134 BK73
Trout Rd
Gurnell Gro W13 137 CF70
Gurnells Rd (Seer Grn), Beac. 89 AQ51
Gurney Cl E15 124 EE64
Gurney Rd
Gurney Cl E17 101 DX53
Gurney Cl, Bark. 145 EP65
Gurney Cl, Beac. 88 AJ53
Gurney Ct Rd, St.Alb. 43 CF18
Gurney Cres, Croy. 201 DM102
Gurney Dr N2 120 DC57
Gurney Rd E15 124 EE64
Gurney Rd, Cars. 218 DG105
Gurney Rd, Nthlt. 135 BV69
Gurney's Cl, Red. 266 DF135
Guthrie St SW3 276 B10
Gutter La EC2 275 J8
Gutter La EC2 142 DQ72
Gutteridge La, Rom. 87 FC44
Guy Barnett Gro SE3 164 EG83
Casterbridge Rd
Guy Rd, Wall. 201 DK104
Guy St SE1 279 L4
Guy St SE1 162 DR75
Guyatt Gdns, Mitch. 200 DG96
Ormerod Gdns
Guyscliff Rd SE13 183 EC85
Guysfield Cl, Rain. 147 FG67
Guysfield Dr, Rain. 147 FG67
Gwalior Rd SW15 159 CX83
Felsham Rd
Gwendolen Av SW15 179 CX85
Gwendolen Cl SW15 179 CX85
Gwendoline Av E13 144 EH67
Gwendwr Rd W14 159 CY78
Gwent Cl, Wat. 60 BX34
Gwillim Cl, Sid. 186 EU85
Gwydor Rd, Beck. 203 DX98
Gwydyr Rd, Brom. 204 EF97
Gwyn Cl SW6 160 DC80
Gwynn Rd (Northfleet), Grav. 190 GC89
Gwynne Av, Croy. 203 DX101
Gwynne Cl W4 159 CT79
Pumping Sta Rd
Gwynne Cl, Wind. 151 AL81
Gwynne Pk Av, Wdf.Grn. 103 EM51
Gwynne Pl WC1 274 C3
Gwynne Rd SW11 160 DD82
Gwynne Rd, Cat. 236 DR123
Gwynne Vaughan Av, Guil. 242 AU130
Gwynns Wk, Hert. 32 DR09
Gyfford Wk, Wal.Cr. 66 DV31
Gylcote Cl SE5 162 DR84
Gyles Pk, Stan. 95 CJ53
Gyllyngdune Gdns, Ilf. 125 ET61
Gypsy Cl, Ware 33 DZ11
Gypsy La, Kings L. 75 BR35
Gypsy La (Stoke Poges), Slou. 112 AS63
Gypsy La, Ware 33 DZ11
Gypsy La, Welw.G.C. 29 CZ13

H

Ha-Ha Rd SE18 165 EM79
Haarlem Rd W14 159 CX76
Haberdasher Est N1 142 DR69
Haberdasher St
Haberdasher Pl N1 275 L2
Haberdasher St N1 275 L2
Haberdasher St N1 142 DR69
Habgood Rd, Loug. 84 EL41
Haccombe Rd SW19 180 DC93
Haydons Rd
Hackbridge Grn, Wall. 200 DG103
Hackbridge Pk Gdns, Cars. 200 DG103
Hackbridge Rd, Wall. 200 DG103
Hackett La, Saw. 35 ET05
Hacketts La, Wok. 211 BF114
Hackford Rd SW9 161 DM81
Hackforth Cl, Barn. 79 CV43
Hackhurst La (Abinger Hammer), Dor. 261 BT138
Hackington Cres, Beck. 183 EA93
Hackney Cl, Borwd. 78 CR43
Hackney Gro E8 142 DV65
Reading La
Hackney Rd E2 275 P3

Hackney Rd E2 142 DT69
Hackworth Pt E3 143 EB69
Rainhill Way
Hacton Dr, Horn. 128 FK63
Hacton La, Horn. 128 FM64
Hacton La, Upmin. 128 FM64
Hadden Rd SE28 165 ES76
Hadden Way, Grnf. 137 CD65
Haddestoke Gate (Cheshunt), Wal.Cr. 67 DZ26
Haddington Rd, Brom. 183 ED90
Haddo St SE10 163 EB79
Haddon Cl, Borwd. 78 CN41
Haddon Cl, Enf. 82 DU44
Haddon Cl, Hem.H. 40 BN21
Haddon Cl, N.Mal. 199 CT99
Haddon Cl, Wey. 195 BR104
Haddon Gro, Sid. 186 EU87
Haddon Rd, Orp. 206 EW99
Haddon Rd, Rick. 73 BC43
Haddon Rd, Sutt. 218 DB105
Haddonfield SE8 163 DX77
Hadfield Cl, Sthl. 136 BZ69
Adrienne Av
Hadfield Rd (Stanwell), Stai. 174 BK86
Hadlands Cl (Bovingdon), Hem.H. 57 AZ26
Hadleigh Cl E1 142 DW70
Mantus Rd
Hadleigh Cl SW20 199 CZ96
Hadleigh Ct, Brox. 49 DZ22
Hadleigh Dr, Sutt. 218 DA109
Hadleigh Rd N9 100 DV45
Hadleigh St E2 142 DW70
Hadleigh Wk E6 144 EL72
Hadley Cl N21 81 DN44
Hadley Cl, Borwd. 78 CM44
Hadley Common, Barn. 80 DA40
Hadley Gdns W4 158 CR78
Hadley Gdns, Sthl. 156 BZ78
Hadley Gra, Harl. 52 EW16
Hadley Grn, Barn. 79 CZ40
Hadley Grn Rd, Barn. 79 CZ40
Hadley Grn W, Barn. 79 CZ40
Hadley Gro, Barn. 79 CY40
Hadley Highstone, Barn. 79 CZ39
Hadley Pl, Wey. 212 BN108
Hadley Ridge, Barn. 79 CZ41
Hadley Rd (Hadley Wd), Barn. 81 DH38
Hadley Rd (New Barnet), Barn. 80 DB42
Hadley Rd, Belv. 166 EZ77
Hadley Rd, Enf. 81 DL38
Hadley Rd, Mitch. 201 DK98
Hadley St NW1 141 DH65
Hadley Way N21 81 DN44
Hadley Wd Ri, Ken. 235 DP115
Hadlow Ct, Slou. 131 AQ73
Hadlow Pl SE19 182 DU94
Hadlow Rd, Sid. 186 EU91
Hadlow Rd, Well. 166 EW80
Hadlow Way (Istead Ri), Grav. 190 GE94
Hadrian Cl, St.Alb. 42 BZ22
Hadrian Cl, Stai. 174 BL88
Hadrian Way
Hadrian Cl, Wall. 219 DL108
Hadrian Ct, Sutt. 218 DB108
Stanley Rd
Hadrian Est E2 142 DU68
Hadrian St SE10 164 EE78
Hadrian Way (Stanwell), Stai. 174 BL87
Hadrians Ride, Enf. 82 DT43
Hadyn Pk Rd W12 159 CU75
Hafer Rd SW11 160 DF84
Hafton Rd SE6 184 EE88
Hag Hill La, Maid. 130 AG72
Hag Hill Ri, Maid. 130 AG72
Hagden La, Wat. 75 BT43
Haggard Rd, Twick. 177 CH87
Haggerston Rd E8 142 DT66
Haggerston Rd, Borwd. 78 CL38
Hagsdell La, Hert. 32 DR10
Hagsdell Rd, Hert. 32 DR10
Hague St E2 142 DU69
Derbyshire St
Haig Cl, St.Alb. 43 CH21
Kitchener Cl
Haig Dr, Slou. 151 AP75
Haig Gdns, Grav. 191 GJ87
Haig Pl, Mord. 200 DA100
Green La
Haig Rd, Grays 171 GG76
Haig Rd, Stan. 95 CJ50
Haig Rd, Uxb. 135 BP71
Haig Rd (Biggin Hill), West. 238 EL117
Haig Rd E E13 144 EJ69
Haig Rd W E13 144 EJ69
Haigh Cres, Red. 267 DH136
Haigville Gdns, Ilf. 125 EP56
Hailes Cl SW19 180 DC93
North Rd
Hailey Av, Hodd. 33 EA13
Hailey Cl, Hert. 33 DY13
Hailey La, Hert. 33 DX14
Hailey Rd, Erith 166 FA75
Haileybury Av, Enf. 82 DT44
Haileybury Rd, Orp. 224 EU105
Hailsham Av SW2 181 DM89
Hailsham Cl, Rom. 106 FJ50
Hailsham Cl, Surb. 197 CK101
Hailsham Dr, Har. 117 CD55
Hailsham Gdns, Rom. 106 FJ50
Hailsham Rd SW17 180 DG93
Hailsham Rd, Rom. 106 FJ50
Hailsham Ter N18 100 DQ50
Haimo Rd SE9 184 EK85
Hainault Ct E17 123 ED56
Hainault Gore, Rom. 126 EY57
Hainault Gro, Chig. 103 EQ49
Hainault Ind Est, Ilf. 104 EW50
Hainault Rd E11 123 EC60
Hainault Rd, Chig. 103 EP48
Hainault Rd, Rom. 105 FC54
Hainault Rd (Chadwell Heath), Rom. 126 EZ58
Hainault Rd (Hainault), Rom. 126 EV55
Hainault St SE9 185 EP88
Hainault St, Ilf. 125 EP61
Haines Ct, Wey. 213 BR106
St. George's Lo
Haines Wk, Mord. 200 DB101
Dorchester Rd
Haines Way, Wat. 59 BU34
Hainford Cl SE4 163 DX84
Haining Cl W4 158 CN78
Wellesley Rd
Hainthorpe Rd SE27 181 DP90
Hainton Cl E1 142 DV72
Halberd Ms E5 122 DV61
Knightland Rd
Halbutt Gdns, Dag. 126 EZ62
Halbutt St, Dag. 126 EZ63
Halcomb St N1 142 DS67
Halcot Av, Bexh. 187 FB85
Halcrow St E1 142 DV71
Newark St
Halcyon Ct, Wem. 118 CP62
Coffers Circle
Halcyon Way, Horn. 128 FM60
Haldan Rd E4 101 EC51
Haldane Cl N10 99 DH52
Haldane Cl, Enf. 83 EA37
Government Row
Haldane Gdns, Grav. 190 GC88
Haldane Pl SW18 180 DB88
Haldane Rd E6 144 EK69
Haldane Rd SE28 146 EX73
Haldane Rd SW6 159 CZ80
Haldane Rd, Sthl. 136 CC72
Haldens, Welw.G.C. 29 CZ06
Haldon Cl, Chig. 103 ES50
Arrowsmith Rd
Haldon Rd SW18 179 CZ85
Hale, The E4 101 ED52
Hale, The N17 122 DU56
Hale Cl E4 101 EC48
Hale Cl, Edg. 96 CQ50
Hale Cl, Orp. 223 EQ105
Hale Dr NW7 96 CQ51
Hale End, Rom. 105 FH51
Hale End, Wok. 226 AV121
Hale End Cl, Ruis. 115 BU58
Hale End Rd E4 101 ED51
Hale End Rd E17 101 ED53
Hale End Rd, Wdf.Grn. 101 ED52
Hale Gdns N17 122 DU55
Hale Gdns W3 138 CN74
Hale Gro Gdns NW7 96 CR50
Hale La NW7 96 CR50
Hale La, Edg. 96 CP50
Hale La (Otford), Sev. 241 FE117
Hale Path SE27 181 DP91
Hale Pit Rd (Bookham), Lthd. 246 CC126
Hale Rd E6 144 EL70
Hale Rd N17 122 DU55
Hale Rd, Hert. 32 DR10
Hale St E14 143 EB73
Hale St, Stai. 173 BE91
Hale Wk W7 137 CE71
Halefield Rd N17 100 DU53
Hales Oak (Bookham), Lthd. 246 CC126
Hales Pk, Hem.H. 41 BQ19
Hales Pk Cl, Hem.H. 41 BQ19
Hales St SE8 163 EA80
Deptford High St
Halesowen Rd, Mord. 200 DB101
Haleswood, Cob. 213 BV114
Haleswood Rd, Hem.H. 40 BN19
Halesworth Cl E5 122 DW61
Theydon Rd
Halesworth Cl, Rom. 106 FL52
Halesworth Rd SE13 163 EB83
Halesworth Rd, Rom. 106 FL51
Haley Rd NW4 119 CW58
Half Acre, Brent. 157 CK79
Half Acre Rd W7 137 CE74
Half Moon Ct EC1 275 H7
Half Moon Cres N1 141 DM68
Half Moon La SE24 182 DQ86
Half Moon La, Epp. 69 ET31
Half Moon Meadow, Hem.H. 41 BQ15
Half Moon Ms, St.Alb. 43 CD20
London Rd
Half Moon Pas E1 142 DT72
Braham St
Half Moon St W1 277 J2
Half Moon St W1 141 DH74
Half Moon Yd, St.Alb. 43 CD20
Chequer St
Halfacre Hill (Chalfont St. Peter), Ger.Cr. 90 AY53
Halfhide La (Cheshunt), Wal.Cr. 67 DX27
Halfhides, Wal.Abb. 67 ED33
Halford Cl, Edg. 96 CP54
Halford Rd E10 123 ED57
Halford Rd SW6 160 DA79
Halford Rd, Rich. 178 CL85
Halford Rd, Uxb. 114 BN64
Halfpenny Cl (Chilworth), Guil. 259 BD140
Halfpenny La, Guil. 259 BC136
Halfway Ct, Purf. 168 FN77
Thamley
Halfway Grn, Walt. 195 BV104
Halfway Ho La, Amer. 54 AL33
Halfway St, Sid. 185 ER87
Haliburton Rd, Twick. 177 CG85
Haliday Wk N1 142 DR65
Balls Pond Rd
Halidon Cl E9 122 DW64
Urswick Rd
Halidon Ri, Rom. 106 FP51
Halifax Cl, St.Alb. 60 BZ31
Halifax Rd, Enf. 82 DQ40
Halifax Rd, Grnf. 136 CB67
Halifax Rd, Rick. 91 BC45
Halifax St SE26 182 DV91
Halifax Way, Welw.G.C. 30 DE09
Halifield Dr, Belv. 166 EY76
Haling Down Pas, S.Croy. 220 DQ109
Haling Gro, S.Croy. 220 DQ108
Haling Pk, S.Croy. 220 DQ107
Haling Pk Gdns, S.Croy. 219 DP107
Haling Pk Rd, S.Croy. 219 DP106
Haling Rd, S.Croy. 220 DR107
Halings La (Denham), Uxb. 113 BE56
Halkin Arc SW1 276 F6
Halkin Arc SW1 160 DG76
Halkin Ms SW1 276 F6
Halkin Pl SW1 276 F6
Halkin Pl SW1 160 DG76
Halkin St SW1 276 G5
Halkin St SW1 160 DG75
Halkingcroft, Slou. 152 AW75
Hall, The SE3 164 EG83
Hall Av N18 100 DR51
Weir Hall Av
Hall Av, S.Ock. 148 FQ74
Hall Cl W5 138 CL71
Hall Cl, Gdmg. 258 AS144
Hall Cl, Rick. 92 BG46
Hall Ct (Datchet), Slou. 152 AV80
Hall Ct, Tedd. 177 CF92
Teddington Pk
Hall Cres, S.Ock. 168 FQ75
Hall Dene Cl, Guil. 243 BC133
Hall Dr SE26 182 DW92
Hall Dr W7 137 CE72
Hall Dr (Harefield), Uxb. 92 BJ53
Hall Fm Cl, Stan. 95 CH49
Hall Fm Dr, Twick. 177 CD87
Hall Gdns E4 101 DZ49
Hall Gdns (Colney Heath), St.Alb. 44 CR23
Hall Gate NW8 140 DC69
Hall Rd
Hall Grn La, Brwd. 109 GC45
Hall Gro, Welw.G.C. 30 DB11
Hall Heath Cl, St.Alb. 43 CH18
Hall Hill, Oxt. 253 ED131
Hall Hill (Seal), Sev. 257 FP123
Hall La E4 101 DY50
Hall La NW4 97 CU53
Hall La (Shenfield), Brwd. 109 FZ44
Hall La, Hayes 155 BR80
Hall La, S.Ock. 149 FX68
Hall La, Upmin. 128 FQ60
Hall Meadow, Slou. 130 AJ68
Hall Oak Wk NW6 139 CZ65
Barlow Rd
Hall Pk, Berk. 38 AY20
Hall Pk Gate, Berk. 38 AY21
Hall Pk Hill, Berk. 38 AY21
Hall Pk Rd, Upmin. 128 FQ64
Hall Pl W2 140 DD70
Hall Pl, Wok. 227 BA116
Hall Pl Cl, St.Alb. 43 CE19
Hall Pl Cres, Bex. 187 FC85
Hall Pl Dr, Wey. 213 BS106
Hall Pl Gdns, St.Alb. 43 CE19
Hall Rd E6 145 EM67
Hall Rd E15 123 ED63
Hall Rd NW8 140 DC69
Hall Rd, Dart. 168 FM84
Hall Rd (Northfleet), Grav. 190 GC90
Hall Rd, Hem.H. 41 BP18
Hall Rd, Islw. 177 CD85
Hall Rd (Chadwell Heath), Rom. 126 EW58
Hall Rd (Gidea Pk), Rom. 127 FH55
Hall Rd, S.Ock. 168 FQ75
Hall Rd, Wall. 219 DH109
Hall St EC1 274 G2
Hall St EC1 141 DP69
Hall St N12 98 DC50
Hall Ter, Rom. 106 FN52
Hall Ter, S.Ock. 169 FR75
Hall Twr W2 272 A6
Hall Twr W2 140 DD71
Hall Vw SE9 184 EK89
Hall Way, Pur. 219 DP113
Hallam Cl, Chis. 185 EM92
Hallam Cl, Wat. 76 BW40
Hallam Gdns, Pnr. 94 BY52
Hallam Ms W1 273 J6
Hallam Rd N15 121 DP56
Hallam Rd SW13 159 CV83
Hallam St W1 273 J5
Hallam St W1 141 DH71
Halland Way, Nthwd. 93 BR51
Halley Gdns SE13 163 ED84
Halley Rd E7 144 EJ65
Halley Rd E12 144 EK65
Halley Rd, Wal.Abb. 83 EB36
Halley St E14 143 DY71
Halleys App, Wok. 226 AU118
Halleys Ct, Wok. 226 AU118
Halleys App
Halleys Ridge, Hert. 31 DN10
Halleys Wk, Add. 212 BK108
Hallfield Est W2 140 DC72
Hallford Way, Dart. 188 FJ85
Halliards, The, Walt. 195 BU100
Felix Rd
Halliday Cl (Shenley), Rad. 62 CL32
Halliday Sq, Sthl. 137 CD74
Halliford Cl, Shep. 195 BR98
Halliford Rd, Shep. 195 BS99
Halliford Rd, Sun. 195 BS99
Halliford St N1 142 DQ66
Halling Hill, Harl. 35 ET13
Hallingbury Ct E17 123 EB55
Hallington Cl, Wok. 226 AV117
Halliwell Rd SW2 181 DM86
Halliwick Rd N10 98 DG53
Hallmark Trd Est NW10 118 CQ63
Great Cen Way
Hallmead Rd, Sutt. 200 DB104
Hallmores, Brox. 49 EA19
Hallowell Av, Croy. 219 DL105
Hallowell Cl, Mitch. 200 DG97
Hallowell Rd, Nthwd. 93 BS52
Hallowes Cres, Wat. 93 BU48
Hayling Rd
Hallowfield Way, Mitch. 200 DE97
Hallside Rd, Enf. 82 DT38
Hallsland Way, Oxt. 254 EF133
Hallsville Rd E16 144 EF72
Hallswelle Rd NW11 119 CZ57
Hallwood Cres, Brwd. 108 FY45
Hallywell Cres E6 145 EM71
Halons Rd SE9 185 EN87
Halpin Pl SE17 279 L9
Halsbrook Rd SE3 164 EK83
Halsbury Cl, Stan. 95 CH49
Halsbury Rd W12 139 CV74
Halsbury Rd E, Nthlt. 116 CC63
Halsbury Rd W, Nthlt. 116 CB64
Halse Dr, Slou. 111 AM64
Halsend, Hayes 135 BV74
Halsey Dr, Hem.H. 39 BF18
Halsey Ms SW3 276 D8
Halsey Pk (London Colney), St.Alb. 62 CM27
Halsey Pl, Wat. 75 BV38
Halsey Rd, Wat. 75 BV41
Halsey St SW3 276 D8
Halsey St SW3 160 DF77
Halsham Cres, Bark. 145 ET65
Halsmere Rd SE5 161 DP81
Halstead Cl, Croy. 202 DQ104
Charles St
Halstead Ct N1 275 L1
Halstead Gdns N21 100 DR46
Halstead Hill (Cheshunt), Wal.Cr. 66 DS29
Halstead La (Knockholt), Sev. 224 EZ114
Halstead Rd E11 124 EG57
Halstead Rd N21 100 DQ46
Halstead Rd, Enf. 82 DS42
Halstead Rd, Erith 167 FE81
Halstead Way, Brwd. 109 GC44
Halston Cl SW11 180 DF86
Halstow Rd NW10 139 CX69
Halstow Rd SE10 164 EG78
Halsway, Hayes 135 BU74
Halt Robin La, Belv. 167 FB77
Halt Robin Rd
Halt Robin Rd, Belv. 166 FA77
Halter Cl, Borwd. 78 CR43
Clydesdale Cl
Halton Cl N11 98 DF51
Colney Hatch La
Halton Cross St N1 141 DP67
Halton Pl N1 142 DQ67
Dibden St
Halton Rd N1 141 DP66
Halton Rd, Grays 171 GJ76
Haltside, Hat. 44 CS19
Halwick Cl, Hem.H. 40 BH21
Ham, The, Brent. 157 CJ80
Ham Cl, Rich. 177 CJ90
Ham Common, Rich. 178 CM91
Ham Fm Rd, Rich. 177 CK91
Ham Gate Av, Rich. 177 CK90
Ham Island (Old Windsor), Wind. 152 AX84
Ham La (Englefield Grn), Egh. 172 AV91
Ham La (Old Windsor), Wind. 152 AX84
Ham Pk Rd E7 144 EF66
Ham Pk Rd E15 144 EF66
Ham Ridings, Rich. 178 CM92
Ham St, Rich. 177 CJ89
Ham Vw, Croy. 203 DY100
Ham Yd W1 273 M10
Hambalt Rd SW4 181 DJ85
Hamble Cl, Ruis. 115 BS61
Chichester Av
Hamble Cl, Wok. 226 AU117
Hamble Ct, Kings.T. 177 CK94
Hamble La, S.Ock. 149 FT71
Hamble St SW6 160 DB83
Hamble Wk, Nthlt. 136 CA68
Brabazon Rd
Hamble Wk, Wok. 226 AU118
Hambledon Cl, Uxb. 135 BP71
Aldenham Dr
Hambledon Gdns SE25 202 DT97
Hambledon Hill, Epsom 232 CQ116
Hambledon Pl SE21 182 DS88
Hambledon Rd SW18 179 CZ87
Hambledon Rd, Cat. 236 DR123
Hambledon Vale, Epsom 232 CQ116
Hambledown Rd, Sid. 185 ER87
Hambleton Cl, Wor.Pk. 199 CW103
Cotswold Way
Hamblings Cl, Rad. 61 CK33
Hambridge Way SW2 181 DN87
Hambro Av, Brom. 204 EG102
Hambro Rd SW16 181 DK93
Hambro Rd, Brwd. 108 FX47
Hambrook Rd SE25 202 DV97
Hambrough Rd, Sthl. 136 BY74
Hamburgh Ct, Wal.Cr. 67 DX28
Hamden Cres, Dag. 127 FB62
Hamel Cl, Har. 117 CK55
Hamelin St E14 143 EC72
St. Leonards Rd
Hamels Dr, Hert. 32 DV08
Hamer Cl (Bovingdon), Hem.H. 57 BA28
Hamerton Rd (Northfleet), Grav. 190 GB85
Hameway E6 145 EN70
Hamfield Cl, Oxt. 253 EC127
Hamfrith Rd E15 144 EF65
Hamhaugh Island, Shep. 194 BN103
Hamilton Av N9 100 DU45
Hamilton Av, Cob. 213 BU113
Hamilton Av, Hodd. 49 EA15
Hamilton Av, Ilf. 125 EP56
Hamilton Av, Rom. 105 FD54
Hamilton Av, Surb. 198 CP102
Hamilton Av, Sutt. 199 CY103
Hamilton Av, Wok. 227 BE115
Hamilton Cl N17 122 DT55
Hamilton Cl NW8 140 DD69
Hamilton Cl SE16 163 DY75
Somerford Way
Hamilton Cl, Barn. 80 DE42
Hamilton Cl, Cher. 193 BF102
Hamilton Cl, Epsom 216 CQ112
Hamilton Cl, Felt. 175 BT92
Hamilton Cl, Guil. 242 AU129
Hamilton Cl, Pot.B. 63 CU33
Hamilton Cl, Pur. 219 DP112
Hamilton Cl (Bricket Wd), St.Alb. 60 CA30
Hamilton Cl, Stan. 95 CF47
Hamilton Ct W5 138 CM73
Hamilton Ct W9 140 DC69
Maida Vale
Hamilton Ct, Hat. 45 CV20
Cooks Way
Hamilton Ct, Lthd. 246 CB125
Eastwick Pk Av
Hamilton Cres N13 99 DN49
Hamilton Cres, Brwd. 108 FW49
Hamilton Cres, Har. 116 BZ62
Hamilton Cres, Houns. 176 CB85
Hamilton Dr, Guil. 242 AU129
Hamilton Dr, Rom. 106 FL54
Hamilton Gdns NW8 140 DC69
Hamilton Gdns (Burnham), Slou. 130 AH69
Hamilton Gordon Ct, Guil. 242 AW133
Langley Cl
Hamilton La N5 121 DP63
Hamilton Pk
Hamilton Mead (Bovingdon), Hem.H. 57 BA27
Hamilton Ms SW18 180 DA88
Merton Rd
Hamilton Ms W1 277 H4
Hamilton Pk N5 121 DP63
Hamilton Pk W N5 121 DP63
Hamilton Pl N19 121 DK62
Wedmore St
Hamilton Pl W1 276 G3
Hamilton Pl W1 140 DG74
Hamilton Pl, Guil. 242 AU129
Hamilton Pl, Sun. 175 BV94
Hamilton Pl (Kingswood), Tad. 233 CZ122
Hamilton Rd E15 144 EE69
Hamilton Rd E17 101 DY54
Hamilton Rd N2 120 DC55
Hamilton Rd N9 100 DU45
Hamilton Rd NW10 119 CU64
Hamilton Rd NW11 119 CX59
Hamilton Rd SE27 182 DR91
Hamilton Rd SW19 180 DB94
Hamilton Rd W4 158 CS75
Hamilton Rd W5 138 CL73
Hamilton Rd, Barn. 80 DE42
Hamilton Rd, Berk. 38 AV19
Hamilton Rd, Bexh. 166 EY82
Hamilton Rd, Brent. 157 CK79
Hamilton Rd, Felt. 175 BT91
Hamilton Rd, Har. 117 CE57
Hamilton Rd, Hayes 135 BV73
Hamilton Rd, Ilf. 125 EP63
Hamilton Rd, Kings L. 59 BQ33
Hamilton Rd, Rom. 127 FH57
Hamilton Rd, St.Alb. 43 CG19
Hamilton Rd, Sid. 186 EU91
Hamilton Rd, Slou. 131 AN72
Hamilton Rd, Sthl. 136 BZ74
Hamilton Rd, Th.Hth. 202 DR97
Hamilton Rd, Twick. 177 CE88
Hamilton Rd, Uxb. 134 BK71
Hamilton Rd, Wat. 93 BV48
Hamilton Rd Ind Est SE27 182 DR91
Hamilton Sq N12 98 DD51
Sandringham Gdns
Hamilton Sq SE1 279 L4
Hamilton St SE8 163 EA79
Deptford High St
Hamilton St, Wat. 76 BW43
Hamilton Ter NW8 140 DB68
Hamilton Wk, Erith 167 FF80
Hamilton Way N3 98 DA51
Hamilton Way N13 99 DP49
Hamilton Way, Wall. 219 DK109
Hamlea Cl SE12 184 EF85
Hamlet, The SE5 162 DR83
Hamlet, The, Berk. 39 BA16
Hamlet Cl SE13 164 EE84
Old Rd
Hamlet Cl, Rom. 104 FA52
Hamlet Cl, St.Alb. 60 BZ30
Hamlet Gdns W6 159 CU77
Hamlet Hill, Harl. 50 EG19
Hamlet Rd SE19 182 DT94
Hamlet Rd, Rom. 104 FA52
Hamlet Sq NW2 119 CY62
Hamlet Way SE1 279 L4
Hamlets Way E3 143 DZ70
Hamlin Cres, Pnr. 116 BW57
Hamlin Rd, Sev. 256 FE121
Hamlyn Cl, Edg. 96 CL48
Hamlyn Gdns SE19 182 DS94
Hamm Ct, Wey. 194 BL103
Hamm Moor La, Add. 212 BL106
Hammarskjold Rd, Harl. 35 EQ14
Hammelton Grn SW9 161 DP81
Cromwell Rd
Hammelton Rd, Brom. 204 EF95
Hammer La, Hem.H. 40 BH19
Hammer Par, Wat. 59 BU33
Hammerfield Dr (Abinger Hammer), Dor. 261 BT140
Hammers Gate, St.Alb. 60 CA25
Hammers La NW7 97 CU50
Hammersmith Br SW13 159 CV78
Hammersmith Br W6 159 CV78
Hammersmith Br Rd W6 159 CW78
Hammersmith Bdy W6 159 CW77
Hammersmith Flyover W6 159 CW78
Hammersmith Gro W6 159 CW76
Hammersmith Rd W6 159 CX77
Hammersmith Rd W14 159 CX77
Hammersmith Ter W6 159 CU78
Hammet Cl, Hayes 136 BX71
Willow Tree La
Hammett St EC3 275 P10
Hammond Av, Mitch. 201 DH96
Hammond Cl, Barn. 79 CY43
Hammond Cl, Grnf. 117 CD64
Lilian Board Way
Hammond Cl, Hmptn. 196 CA95
Hammond Cl (Cheshunt), Wal.Cr. 66 DS26
Hammond Cl, Wok. 226 AW115
Hammond End (Farnham Common), Slou. 111 AP63
Hammond Rd, Enf. 82 DV40
Hammond Rd, Sthl. 156 BY76
Hammond Rd, Wok. 226 AW115
Hammond St NW5 141 DJ65
Hammond Way SE28 146 EV73
Oriole Way
Hammonds Cl, Dag. 126 EW62
Hammonds La, Brwd. 107 FV51
Hammond's La, Hat. 28 CQ13
Hammond's La (Sandridge), St.Alb. 28 CN12
Hammondstreet Rd (Cheshunt), Wal.Cr. 66 DR26
Hamond Cl, S.Croy. 219 DP109
Hamonde Cl, Edg. 96 CP47
Hampden Av, Beck. 203 DY96
Hampden Av, Chesh. 54 AN30
Hampden Cl NW1 273 N1
Hampden Cl, Epp. 70 FA27
Hampden Cl (Stoke Poges), Slou. 132 AU69
Hampden Cres, Brwd. 108 FW49
Hampden Cres (Cheshunt), Wal.Cr. 66 DV31
Hampden Gurney St W1 272 D9
Hampden Hill, Beac. 88 AH53
Hampden Hill, Ware 33 DZ06
Hampden Hill Cl, Ware 33 DZ05
Hampden La N17 100 DT53
Hampden Pl (Frogmore), St.Alb. 61 CE29
Hampden Rd N8 121 DN56
Hampden Rd N10 98 DG52
Hampden Rd N17 100 DU53
Hampden Rd N19 121 DK61
Holloway Rd
Hampden Rd, Beck. 203 DY96
Hampden Rd (Chalfont St. Peter), Ger.Cr. 90 AX53
Hampden Rd, Grays 170 GB78
Hampden Rd, Har. 94 CC53
Hampden Rd, Kings.T. 198 CN97
Hampden Rd, Rom. 105 FB52
Hampden Rd, Slou. 153 AZ76
Hampden Sq N14 99 DH46
Osidge La
Hampden Way N14 99 DH47
Hampden Way, Wat. 75 BS36
Hampermill La, Wat. 93 BT47
Hampshire Av, Slou. 131 AQ71
Hampshire Cl N18 100 DV50
Berkshire Gdns
Hampshire Hog La W6 159 CV77
King St
Hampshire Rd N22 99 DM52
Hampshire Rd, Horn. 128 FN56
Hampshire St NW5 141 DK65
Torriano Av
Hampson Way SW8 161 DM81
Hampstead Cl SE28 146 EV74
Hampstead Gdns NW11 120 DA58
Hampstead Gdns, Rom. 126 EV57
Hampstead Grn NW3 120 DE64
Hampstead Gro NW3 120 DC62
Hampstead Hts N2 120 DC56
Hampstead High St NW3 120 DC63
Hampstead Hill Gdns NW3 120 DD63
Hampstead La N6 120 DD59
Hampstead La NW3 120 DD59
Hampstead La, Dor. 263 CG137
Hampstead Rd NW1 273 K1
Hampstead Rd NW1 141 DJ68
Hampstead Rd, Dor. 263 CG137
Hampstead Sq NW3 120 DC62

Hampstead Wk E3 143 DZ67
Parnell Rd
Hampstead Way NW11 120 DC60
Hampton Cl N11 99 DH50
Balmoral Av
Hampton Cl NW6 140 DA69
Hampton Cl SW20 179 CW94
Hampton Ct N1 141 DP65
Upper St
Hampton Ct Av, E.Mol. 197 CD99
Hampton Ct Cres, E.Mol. 197 CD97
Hampton Ct Palace, E.Mol. 197 CF97
Hampton Ct Par, E.Mol. 197 CE98
Creek Rd
Hampton Ct Rd, E.Mol. 197 CF97
Hampton Ct Rd, Hmptn. 196 CC96
Hampton Ct Rd, Kings.T. 197 CF97
Hampton Ct Way, E.Mol. 197 CE100
Hampton Ct Way, T.Ditt. 197 CE103
Hampton Cres, Grav. 191 GL89
Hampton Fm Ind Est, Felt. 176 BZ90
Hampton Gdns, Saw. 36 EV08
Hampton Gro, Epsom 217 CT111
Hampton Hill Business Pk, Hmptn. 176 CC92
Wellington Rd
Hampton La, Felt. 176 BY91
Hampton Mead, Loug. 85 EP41
Hampton Ms NW10 138 CR69
Minerva Rd
Hampton Ri, Har. 118 CL58
Hampton Rd E4 101 DZ50
Hampton Rd E7 124 EH64
Hampton Rd E11 123 ED60
Hampton Rd, Croy. 202 DQ100
Hampton Rd (Hampton Hill), Hmptn. 177 CD92
Hampton Rd, Ilf. 125 EP63
Hampton Rd, Red. 266 DF139
Hampton Rd, Tedd. 177 CD92
Hampton Rd, Twick. 177 CD90
Hampton Rd, Wor.Pk. 199 CU103
Hampton Rd E, Felt. 176 BZ90
Hampton Rd W, Felt. 176 BY89
Hampton St SE1 278 G9
Hampton St SE1 161 DP77
Hampton St SE17 278 G9
Hampton St SE17 161 DP77
Hamsey Grn Gdns, Warl. 236 DV116
Hamsey Way, S.Croy. 236 DV115
Hamshades Cl, Sid. 185 ET90
Hamstel Rd, Harl. 35 EP14
Hanah Ct SW19 179 CX94
Hanameel St E16 144 EH74
Hanbury Cl NW4 119 CW55
Parson St
Hanbury Cl (Burnham), Slou. 130 AG71
Hanbury Cl (Cheshunt), Wal.Cr. 67 DX29
Hanbury Cl, Ware 33 DY06
Hanbury Dr N21 81 DM43
Hanbury Dr (Biggin Hill), West. 222 EH113
Hanbury La, Hat. 46 DE17
Hanbury Ms N1 142 DQ67
Mary St
Hanbury Path, Wok. 211 BD114
Hanbury Rd N17 100 DV54
Hanbury Rd W3 158 CP75
Hanbury St E1 275 P6
Hanbury St E1 142 DT71
Hanbury Wk, Bex. 187 FE90
Hancock Ct, Borwd. 78 CQ39
Hancock Rd E3 143 EC69
Hancock Rd SE19 182 DR93
Hancroft Rd, Hem.H. 40 BM22
Hand Ct WC1 274 C7
Hand Ct WC1 141 DM71
Hand La, Saw. 36 EW06
Handa Cl, Hem.H. 41 BP23
Handa Wk N1 142 DR65
Clephane Rd
Handcroft Rd, Croy. 201 DP101
Handel Cl, Edg. 96 CM51
Handel Cres, Til. 171 GG80
Handel Pl NW10 138 CR65
Mitchellbrook Way
Handel St WC1 273 P4
Handel St WC1 141 DL70
Handel Way, Edg. 96 CN52
Handen Rd SE12 184 EE85
Handforth Rd SW9 161 DN80
Handforth Rd, Ilf. 125 EP62
Winston Way
Handley Page Rd, Wall. 219 DM108
Handley Rd E9 142 DW66
Handowe Cl NW4 119 CU56
Handpost Hill, Pot.B. 65 DH28
Hands Wk E16 144 EG72
Handside Cl, Welw.G.C. 29 CW09
Handside Cl, Wor.Pk. 199 CX102
Carters Cl
Handside Grn, Welw.G.C. 29 CW08
Handside La, Welw.G.C. 29 CV11
Handsworth Av E4 101 ED51
Handsworth Rd N17 122 DR55
Handsworth Way, Wat. 93 BU48
Hayling Rd
Handtrough Way, Bark. 145 EP68
Fresh Wf Rd
Hanford Cl SW18 180 DA88
Hanford Rd, S.Ock. 148 FQ74
Hanford Row SW19 179 CW93
Hangar Ruding, Wat. 94 BZ48
Hanger Cl, Hem.H. 40 BH21
Hanger Grn W5 138 CN70
Hanger Hill, Wey. 213 BP107
Hanger La W5 138 CM70
Hanger Vale La W5 138 CM72
Hanger Vw Way W3 138 CN72
Hanging Hill La, Brwd. 109 GB48
Hangrove Hill, Orp. 223 EP113
Hankey Pl SE1 279 L5
Hankey Pl SE1 162 DR75
Hankins La NW7 96 CS48
Hanley Cl, Wind. 151 AK81
Hanley Pl, Beck. 183 EA94
Hanley Rd N4 121 DL60
Hanmer Wk N7 121 DM62
Newington Barrow Way
Hannah Cl NW10 118 CQ63
Hannah Cl, Beck. 203 EC97
Hannah Mary Way SE1 162 DU77
Simms Rd
Hannah Ms, Wall. 219 DJ108
Hannards Way, Ilf. 104 EV50
Hannay La N8 121 DK59
Hannay Wk SW16 181 DK89
Hannell Rd SW6 159 CY80
Hannen Rd SE27 181 DP90
Norwood High St
Hannibal Rd E1 142 DW71
Hannibal Rd (Stanwell), Stai. 174 BK87
Hannibal Way, Croy. 219 DM106
Hannington Rd SW4 161 DH83
Hanover Av E16 144 EG74
Hanover Av, Felt. 175 BU88
Hanover Circle, Hayes 135 BQ72
Hanover Cl (Englefield Grn), Egh. 172 AV93
Hanover Cl, Red. 251 DJ128
Hanover Cl, Rich. 158 CN80
Hanover Cl, Slou. 152 AU76
Hanover Cl, Sutt. 217 CZ105
Hanover Cl, Wind. 151 AM81
Hanover Way
Hanover Ct SE19 182 DU94
Anerley Rd
Hanover Ct W12 139 CU74
Uxbridge Rd
Hanover Ct, Dor. 263 CF136
Hanover Ct, Guil. 242 AX132
Riverside
Hanover Ct, Hodd. 49 EA16
Jersey Cl
Hanover Ct, Wok. 226 AY119
Midhope Rd
Hanover Dr, Chis. 185 EQ91
Hanover Gdns SE11 161 DN79
Hanover Gdns, Abb.L. 59 BT30
Hanover Gdns, Ilf. 103 EQ52
Hanover Gate NW1 272 C3
Hanover Gate NW1 140 DE69
Hanover Gate Mans NW1 272 C4
Hanover Grn, Hem.H. 40 BG22
Hanover Ho, Surb. 198 CN102
Lenelby Rd
Hanover Mead, Maid. 150 AC76
Hanover Pk SE15 162 DU81
Hanover Pl E3 143 DZ69
Brokesley St
Hanover Pl WC2 274 A9
Hanover Rd N15 122 DT56
Hanover Rd NW10 139 CW66
Hanover Rd SW19 180 DC94
Hanover Sq W1 273 J9
Hanover Sq W1 141 DH72
Hanover St W1 273 J9
Hanover St W1 141 DH72
Hanover St, Croy. 201 DP104
Abbey Rd
Hanover Ter NW1 272 D3
Hanover Ter NW1 140 DE69
Hanover Ter Ms NW1 272 C3
Hanover Wk, Hat. 45 CT21
Hanover Wk, Wey. 195 BS104
Hanover Way, Bexh. 166 EX83
Hanover Way, Wind. 151 AM82
Hanover W Ind Est NW10 138 CR68
Hanover Yd N1 141 DP68
Noel Rd
Hans Cres SW1 276 D6
Hans Cres SW1 160 DF76
Hans Pl SW1 276 E6
Hans Pl SW1 160 DF76
Hans Rd SW3 276 D6
Hans Rd SW3 160 DF76
Hans St SW1 276 E7
Hansard Ms W14 159 CX75
Holland Rd
Hansart Way, Enf. 81 DN39
The Ridgeway
Hanselin Cl, Stan. 95 CF50
Chenduit Way
Hansells Mead, Harl. 50 EG15
Hansen Dr N21 81 DM43
Hansha Dr, Edg. 96 CR53
Hansler Gro, E.Mol. 197 CD98
Hansler Rd SE22 182 DT85
Hansol Rd, Bexh. 186 EY85
Hanson Cl SW12 181 DH87
Hanson Cl SW14 158 CQ83
Hanson Cl, Beck. 183 EB93
Hanson Cl, Guil. 243 AZ131
Hanson Cl, Loug. 85 EQ40
Hanson Dr
Hanson Cl, West Dr. 154 BM76
Hanson Dr, Loug. 85 EQ40
Hanson Gdns, Sthl. 156 BY75
Hanson Grn, Loug. 85 EQ40
Hanson Dr
Hanson St W1 273 K6
Hanson St W1 141 DJ71
Hanway Pl W1 273 M8
Hanway Rd W7 137 CD72
Hanway St W1 273 M8
Hanway St W1 141 DK72
Hanworth La, Cher. 193 BF102
Hanworth Rd, Felt. 175 BV88
Hanworth Rd, Hmptn. 176 CB93
Hanworth Rd, Houns. 156 CB83
Hanworth Rd, Red. 266 DF139
Hanworth Rd, Sun. 175 BU94
Hanworth Ter, Houns. 156 CB84
Hanworth Trd Est, Felt. 176 BY90
Hanyards End (Cuffley), Pot.B. 65 DL28
Hanyards La (Cuffley), Pot.B. 65 DK28
Hapgood Cl, Grnf. 117 CD64
Harads Pl E1 142 DU73
Ensign St
Harben Rd NW6 140 DC66
Harberson Rd E15 144 EF67
Harberson Rd SW12 181 DH88
Harberton Rd N19 121 DJ60
Harberts Rd, Harl. 51 EP16
Harbet Rd E4 101 DX50
Harbet Rd N18 101 DX50
Harbet Rd W2 272 A7
Harbet Rd W2 140 DD71
Harbex Cl, Bex. 187 FB87
Harbinger Rd E14 163 EB77
Harbledown Pl, Orp. 206 EW98
Harbledown Rd SW6 160 DA81
Harbledown Rd, S.Croy. 220 DU111
Harbord Cl SE5 162 DR82
De Crespigny Pk
Harbord St SW6 159 CX81
Harborne Cl, Wat. 94 BW50
Harborough Av, Sid. 185 ES87
Harborough Cl, Slou. 131 AK74
West Pt
Harborough Rd SW16 181 DM91
Harbour Av SW10 160 DC81
Harbour Ex Sq E14 163 EB75
Harbour Rd SE5 162 DQ83
Harbourer Cl, Ilf. 104 EV50
Harbourer Rd, Ilf. 104 EV50
Harbourfield Rd, Bans. 234 DB115
Harbridge Av SW15 179 CT87
Harbury Rd, Cars. 218 DE109
Harbut Rd SW11 160 DD84
Harcamlow Way, Harl. 34 EH10
Harcamlow Way, Ware 33 EC05
Harcombe Rd N16 122 DS62
Harcourt Av E12 125 EM63
Harcourt Av, Edg. 96 CQ48
Harcourt Av, Sid. 186 EW86
Harcourt Av, Wall. 219 DH105
Harcourt Cl, Egh. 173 BC93
Harcourt Cl, Islw. 157 CG83
Harcourt Cl, Maid. 150 AF76
Harcourt Fld, Wall. 219 DH105
Harcourt Lo, Wall. 219 DH105
Croydon Rd
Harcourt Ms, Rom. 127 FF57
Harcourt Rd E15 144 EF68
Harcourt Rd N22 99 DK53
Harcourt Rd SE4 163 DY84
Harcourt Rd SW19 180 DA94
Russell Rd
Harcourt Rd, Bexh. 166 EY84
Harcourt Rd, Bushey 76 CC43
Harcourt Rd, Maid. 150 AF76
Harcourt Rd, Th.Hth. 201 DM100
Harcourt Rd, Wall. 219 DH105
Harcourt Rd, Wind. 151 AL81
Harcourt St W1 272 C7
Harcourt St W1 140 DE71
Harcourt Ter SW10 160 DB78
Hardcastle Cl, Croy. 202 DU100
Hardcourts Cl, W.Wick. 203 EB104
Hardel Ri SW2 181 DP89
Hardel Wk SW2 181 DN87
Papworth Way
Hardell Cl, Egh. 173 BA92
Harden Fm Cl, Couls. 235 DK122
Netherne La
Harden Rd (Northfleet), Grav. 191 GF90
Hardens Manorway SE7 164 EK76
Harders Rd SE15 162 DV82
Hardess St SE24 162 DQ83
Herne Hill Rd
Hardie Cl NW10 118 CR64
Hardie Rd, Dag. 127 FC62
Harding Cl SE17 162 DQ79
Hillingdon St
Harding Cl, Croy. 202 DT104
Harding Cl, Wat. 60 BW33
Harding Ho, Hayes 135 BV72
Harding Rd, Bexh. 166 EZ82
Harding Rd, Chesh. 54 AR30
Harding Rd, Epsom 232 CS119
Harding Rd, Grays 171 GG76
Hardinge Cl, Uxb. 135 BP72
Dawley Av
Hardinge La E1 142 DW72
Hardinge St
Hardinge Rd N18 100 DS50
Hardinge Rd NW10 139 CV67
Hardinge St E1 142 DW72
Hardings, Welw.G.C. 30 DC08
Hardings Cl, Iver 133 BD69
Harding's Cl, Kings.T. 198 CM95
Hardings La SE20 183 DX93
Hardings Row, Iver 133 BC69
Hardley Cres, Horn. 128 FK56
Hardman Rd SE7 164 EH78
Hardman Rd, Kings.T. 198 CL96
Hardwick Cl (Oxshott), Lthd. 230 CC115
Hardwick Cl, Stan. 95 CJ50
Hardwick Cres, Dart. 188 FP86
Hardwick Grn W13 137 CH71
Hardwick La (Lyne), Cher. 193 BC101
Hardwick Rd, Red. 266 DD136
Hardwick St EC1 274 E3
Hardwick St EC1 141 DN69
Hardwicke Av, Houns. 156 CA81
Hardwicke Gdns, Amer. 55 AS38
Hardwicke Pl (London Colney), St.Alb. 61 CK27
Hardwicke Rd N13 99 DL51
Hardwicke Rd W4 158 CR77
Hardwicke Rd, Reig. 250 DA133
Hardwicke Rd, Rich. 177 CJ91
Hardwicke St, Bark. 145 EQ67
Hardwicks Way SW18 180 DA85
Buckhold Rd
Hardwidge St SE1 279 M4
Hardy Av E16 144 EG74
Wesley Av
Hardy Av (Northfleet), Grav. 190 GE89
Hardy Av, Ruis. 115 BV64
Hardy Cl SE16 163 DX75
Middleton Dr
Hardy Cl, Barn. 79 CY44
Hardy Cl (North Holmwood), Dor. 263 CH141
Hardy Cl, Horl. 268 DE148
Hardy Cl, Pnr. 116 BX59
Hardy Cl, Slou. 131 AN74
Hardy Gro, Dart. 168 FN84
Hardy Rd E4 101 DZ51
Hardy Rd SE3 164 EF80
Hardy Rd SW19 180 DB94
Hardy Rd, Hem.H. 40 BM19
Hardy Way, Enf. 81 DN39
Hare & Billet Rd SE3 163 ED81
Hare Ct EC4 274 D9
Hare Cres, Wat. 59 BU32
Hare Hall La, Rom. 127 FH56
Hare Hill, Add. 211 BF107
Hare Hill Cl (Pyrford), Wok. 228 BG115
Hare La (Claygate), Esher 215 CE107
Hare La, Hat. 45 CU20
Hare Marsh E2 142 DU70
Cheshire St
Hare Pl EC4 274 E9
Hare Row E2 142 DV68
Hare St SE18 165 EN76
Hare St, Harl. 51 EP15
Hare St Springs, Harl. 51 EP15
Hare Ter, Grays 169 FX78
Mill La
Hare Wk N1 275 N1
Hare Wk N1 142 DS68
Harebell, Welw.G.C. 29 CY13
Harebell Cl, Hert. 32 DV09
Harebell Dr E6 145 EN71
Harebell Hill, Cob. 214 BX114
Harebell Way, Rom. 106 FK52
Harebreaks, The, Wat. 75 BV38
Harecastle Cl, Hayes 136 BY70
Braunston Dr
Harecourt Rd N1 142 DQ65
Harecroft, Dor. 263 CJ139
Harecroft (Fetcham), Lthd. 230 CB123
Haredale Rd SE24 162 DQ84
Haredon Cl SE23 182 DW87
Harefield, Esher 215 CE105
Harefield, Harl. 36 EU14
Harefield Av, Sutt. 217 CY109
Harefield Cl, Enf. 81 DN39
Harefield Ms SE4 163 DZ83
Harefield Pl, St.Alb. 43 CK17
Harefield Rd N8 121 DK57
Harefield Rd SE4 163 DZ83
Harefield Rd SW16 181 DM94
Harefield Rd, Rick. 92 BK50
Harefield Rd, Sid. 186 EX89
Harefield Rd, Uxb. 134 BK65
Harefield Rd Ind Est, Rick. 92 BL49
Harehatch La, Slou. 111 AL60
Harelands Cl, Wok. 226 AW117
Harelands La, Wok. 226 AW117
Harendon, Tad. 233 CW121
Harepark Cl, Hem.H. 39 BF19
Hares Bk (New Addington), Croy. 221 ED110
Haresfield Rd, Dag. 146 FA65
Harestone Dr, Cat. 236 DT124
Harestone Hill, Cat. 252 DT126
Harestone La, Cat. 252 DS125
Harestone Valley Rd, Cat. 252 DT126
Hareward Rd, Guil. 243 BC132
Harewood, Rick. 74 BH43
Harewood Av NW1 272 C5
Harewood Av NW1 140 DE70
Harewood Av, Nthlt. 136 BY66
Harewood Cl, Nthlt. 136 BZ66
Harewood Cl, Reig. 250 DC132
Harewood Dr, Ilf. 103 EM54
Harewood Gdns, S.Croy. 236 DV115
Harewood Hill, Epp. 85 ES35
Harewood Pl W1 273 J9
Harewood Pl, Slou. 152 AU76
Harewood Rd SW19 180 DE93
Harewood Rd, Brwd. 108 FV44
Harewood Rd, Ch.St.G. 72 AW41
Harewood Rd, Islw. 157 CF80
Harewood Rd, S.Croy. 220 DS107
Harewood Rd, Wat. 93 BV48
Harewood Row NW1 272 C6
Harewood Ter, Sthl. 156 BZ77
Harfield Gdns SE5 162 DS83
Harfield Rd, Sun. 196 BX96
Harford Cl E4 101 EB45
Harford Dr, Wat. 75 BS38
Harford Rd E4 101 EB45
Harford St E1 143 DY70
Harford Wk N2 120 DD57
Harfst Way, Swan. 207 FC95
Hargood Cl, Har. 118 CL58
Hargood Rd SE3 164 EJ81
Hargrave Pk N19 121 DJ61
Hargrave Pl N7 121 DK64
Brecknock Rd
Hargrave Rd N19 121 DJ61
Hargreaves Av (Cheshunt), Wal.Cr. 66 DV30
Hargreaves Cl (Cheshunt), Wal.Cr. 66 DV31
Hargwyne St SW9 161 DM83
Haringey Pk N8 121 DL58
Haringey Pas N4 121 DP58
Haringey Pas N8 121 DN56
Haringey Rd N8 121 DL56
Harington Ter N9 100 DR48
Harington Ter N18 100 DR48
Harkett Cl, Har. 95 CF54
Byron Rd
Harkett Ct, Har. 95 CF54
Harkness (Cheshunt), Wal.Cr. 66 DU29
Harkness Cl, Epsom 233 CW116
Harkness Cl, Rom. 106 FM50
Harkness Rd (Burnham), Slou. 130 AH71
Harland Av, Croy. 202 DT104
Harland Av, Sid. 185 ER90
Harland Cl SW19 200 DB97
Harland Rd SE12 184 EG88
Harlands Gro, Orp. 223 EP105
Pinecrest Gdns
Harlech Gdns, Houns. 156 BW79
Harlech Gdns, Pnr. 116 BX59
Harlech Rd N14 99 DL48
Harlech Rd, Abb.L. 59 BU31
Harlech Twr W3 158 CP75
Harlequin Av, Brent. 157 CG79
Harlequin Cen, Wat. 76 BW42
Harlequin Cl, Hayes 136 BX71
Cygnet Way
Harlequin Cl, Islw. 177 CE85
Harlequin Ho, Erith 166 EY76
Kale Rd
Harlequin Rd, Tedd. 177 CH94
Harlescott Rd SE15 163 DX84
Harlesden Cl, Rom. 106 FM52
Harlesden Gdns NW10 139 CT67
Harlesden La NW10 139 CU67
Harlesden Rd NW10 139 CU67
Harlesden Rd, Rom. 106 FM51
Harlesden Rd, St.Alb. 43 CG20
Harlesden Wk, Rom. 106 FM52
Harlesden Rd
Harleston Cl E5 122 DW61
Theydon Rd
Harley Cl, Wem. 137 CK65
Harley Ct E11 124 EG59
Blake Hall Rd
Harley Ct, St.Alb. 43 CK16
Villiers Cres
Harley Cres, Har. 117 CD56
Harley Gdns SW10 160 DC78
Harley Gdns, Orp. 223 ES105
Harley Gro E3 143 DZ69
Harley Pl W1 273 H7
Harley Pl W1 141 DH71
Harley Rd NW3 140 DD66
Harley Rd NW10 138 CS68
Harley Rd, Har. 117 CD56
Harley St W1 273 H7
Harley St W1 141 DH70
Harleyford, Brom. 204 EH95
Harleyford Rd SE11 161 DM79
Harleyford St SE11 161 DN79
Harlinger St SE18 164 EL76
Harlings, Hert. 32 DW13
Harlington Cl, Hayes 155 BQ80
New Rd
Harlington Rd, Bexh. 166 EY83
Harlington Rd (Heathrow Airport), Houns. 155 BT84
Harlington Rd, Uxb. 135 BP71
Harlington Rd E, Felt. 175 BV87
Harlington Rd W, Felt. 175 BV86
Harlow Business Pk, Harl. 50 EL15
Harlow Common, Harl. 52 EW18
Harlow Ct, Hem.H. 40 BM16
Harlow Gdns, Rom. 105 FC51
Harlow Potter St Bypass, Harl. 52 EV15
Harlow Rd N13 100 DR48
Harlow Rd (Sheering), B.Stort. 36 FA09
Harlow Rd (Matching Tye), Harl. 37 FC12
Harlow Rd (Old Harlow), Harl. 36 FA09
Harlow Rd (Roydon), Harl. 50 EJ15
Harlow Rd, Ong. 53 FH18
Harlow Rd, Rain. 147 FF67
Harlow Rd, Saw. 36 EW08
Harlow Tye, Harl. 37 FC12
Harlton Ct, Wal.Abb. 68 EF34
Harlyn Dr, Pnr. 115 BV55
Harman Av, Grav. 191 GH92
Harman Av, Wdf.Grn. 102 EF52
Harman Cl E4 101 ED49
Harman Cl NW2 119 CY62
Harman Dr NW2 119 CY62
Harman Dr, Sid. 185 ET86
Harman Pl, Pur. 219 DP111
Harman Rd, Enf. 82 DT43
Harmer Rd, Swans. 190 FZ86
Harmer St, Grav. 191 GJ86
Harmondsworth La, West Dr. 154 BL79
Harmondsworth Rd, West Dr. 154 BL78
Harmony Cl NW11 119 CY57
Harmony Cl, Hat. 45 CU16
Harmony Cl, Wall. 219 DL109
Harmony Way NW4 119 CW56
Victoria Rd
Harmood Gro NW1 141 DH66
Clarence Way
Harmood Pl NW1 141 DH66
Harmood St
Harmood St NW1 141 DH66
Harms Gro, Guil. 243 BC131
Harmsworth Ms SE11 278 F7
Harmsworth St SE17 161 DP78
Harmsworth Way N20 97 CZ46
Harness Rd SE28 166 EU75
Harness Way, St.Alb. 43 CK17
Harnetts Cl, Swan. 207 FD100
Harold Av, Belv. 166 EZ78
Harold Av, Hayes 155 BT76
Harold Ct Rd, Rom. 106 FP51
Harold Cres, Wal.Abb. 67 EC32
Harold Est SE1 279 N7
Harold Est SE1 162 DS76
Harold Gibbons Ct SE7 164 EJ79
Victoria Way
Harold Hill Ind Est, Rom. 106 FK52
Harold Laski Ho EC1 274 F3
Harold Pl SE11 161 DN78
Harold Rd E4 101 EC49
Harold Rd E11 124 EE60
Harold Rd E13 144 EH67
Harold Rd N8 121 DM57
Harold Rd N15 122 DT57
Harold Rd NW10 138 CR69
Harold Rd SE19 182 DR94
Harold Rd (Hawley), Dart. 188 FM91
Harold Rd, Sutt. 218 DD105
Harold Rd, Wdf.Grn. 102 EG53
Harold Vw, Rom. 106 FM54
Harolds Cl, Harl. 51 EM16
Harolds Rd, Harl. 50 EL16
Haroldslea, Horl. 269 DK150
Haroldslea Cl, Horl. 269 DJ150
Haroldslea Dr, Horl. 269 DJ150
Haroldstone Rd E17 123 DX57
Harp All EC4 274 F8
Harp Island Cl NW10 118 CR61
Harp La EC3 279 M1
Harp Rd W7 137 CF70
Harpenden Rd E12 124 EJ61
Harpenden Rd SE27 181 DP90
Harpenden Rd, St.Alb. 43 CD17
Harpenmead Pt NW2 119 CZ61
Granville Rd
Harper Cl N14 81 DJ43
Alexandra Ct
Harper La, Rad. 61 CG32
Harper Ms SW17 180 DC90
Harper Rd E6 145 EM72
Harper Rd SE1 279 H6
Harper Rd SE1 162 DQ76
Harpers Yd N17 100 DT53
Ruskin Rd
Harpesford Av, Vir.W. 192 AV99
Harpley Sq E1 142 DW69
Harpour Rd, Bark. 145 EQ65
Harps Oak La, Red. 250 DF125
Harpsden St SW11 160 DG81
Harpsfield Bdy, Hat. 45 CT17
Harptree Way, St.Alb. 43 CG18
Harpur Ms WC1 274 B6
Harpur St WC1 274 B6
Harpur St WC1 141 DM71
Harpurs, Tad. 233 CX122
Harraden Rd SE3 164 EJ81
Harrap Chase, Grays 170 FZ78
Harrap St E14 143 EC73
Harrier Av E11 124 EH58
Eastern Av
Harrier Cl, Horn. 147 FH65
Harrier Ms SE28 165 ER76
Harrier Rd NW9 96 CS54
Harrier Way E6 145 EM71
Harrier Way, Wal.Abb. 68 EG34
Harriers Cl W5 138 CL73
Harries Cl, Chesh. 54 AP30
Deansway
Harries Rd, Hayes 136 BW70
Harriescourt, Wal.Abb. 68 EG32
Harriet Cl E8 142 DU67
Harriet Gdns, Croy. 202 DU103
Harriet St SW1 276 E5
Harriet Tubman Cl SW2 181 DN87
Harriet Wk SW1 276 E5
Harriet Wk SW1 160 DF75
Harriet Way, Bushey 95 CD45
Harringay Gdns N8 121 DP56
Harringay Rd N15 121 DP57
Harrington Cl NW10 118 CR62
Harrington Cl, Croy. 201 DL103
Harrington Cl (Leigh), Reig. 265 CU141
Harrington Cl, Wind. 151 AM84
Harrington Ct W10 139 CZ69
Dart St
Harrington Ct, Hert. 32 DW12
Trinity Rd
Harrington Gdns SW7 160 DB77
Harrington Hill E5 122 DV60
Harrington Rd E11 124 EE60
Harrington Rd SE25 202 DV98
Harrington Rd SW7 160 DD77
Harrington Sq NW1 273 K1
Harrington Sq NW1 141 DJ68
Harrington St NW1 273 K2
Harrington St NW1 141 DJ69
Harrington Way SE18 164 EK76
Harriott Cl SE10 164 EF77
Harriotts Cl, Ash. 231 CJ120
Harriotts La
Harriotts La, Ash. 231 CJ119
Harris Cl, Enf. 81 DP39
Harris Cl (Northfleet), Grav. 190 GE90
Harris Cl, Houns. 156 CA81
Harris Cl, Rom. 106 FL52
Harris Gdns, Slou. 151 AQ75
Harris La, Rad. 62 CN34

Harris Rd, Bexh. 166 EY81
Harris Rd, Dag. 126 EZ64
Harris Rd, Wat. 75 BU35
Harris St E17 123 DZ59
Harris St SE5 162 DR80
Harris Way, Sun. 195 BS95
Harrison Cl N20 98 DE46
Harrison Cl, Brwd. 109 GD43
Harrison Cl, Nthwd. 93 BQ51
Harrison Cl, Reig. 266 DB135
Harrison Ct, Shep. 195 BP99
Greeno Cres
Harrison Dr, Epp. 71 FB26
Harrison Rd, Dag. 147 FB65
Harrison St WC1 274 A3
Harrison St WC1 141 DL69
Harrison Wk (Cheshunt), Wal.Cr. 67 DX30
Harrison Way, Sev. 256 FG122
Harrison Way, Slou. 131 AK74
Harrison Way, Wal.Abb. 83 EC36
Greenwich Way
Harrisons Ri, Croy. 201 DP104
Harrisons Wf, Purf. 168 FN78
Harris's La, Ware 32 DW05
Harrogate Ct N11 98 DG51
Coverdale Rd
Harrogate Ct, Slou. 153 BA78
Harrogate Rd, Wat. 94 BW48
Harrold Rd, Dag. 126 EV64
Harrow Av, Enf. 82 DT44
Harrow Bottom Rd, Vir.W. 193 AZ100
Harrow Cl, Add. 194 BH103
Harrow Cl, Chess. 215 CK108
Harrow Cl, Dor. 263 CG137
Harrow Rd W
Harrow Cres, Rom. 105 FH52
Harrow Dr N9 100 DT46
Harrow Dr, Horn. 127 FH59
Harrow Flds Gdns, Har. 117 CE62
Harrow Gdns, Orp. 224 EV105
Harrow Gdns, Warl. 237 DZ115
Harrow Gate Gdns, Dor. 263 CH138
Horsham Rd
Harrow Grn E11 124 EE62
Harrow Rd
Harrow La E14 143 EC73
Harrow La, Gdmg. 258 AS144
Harrow Manorway SE2 146 EW74
Harrow Mkt, Slou. 153 BA76
Harrow Pk, Har. 117 CE61
Harrow Pas, Kings.T. 197 CK96
Market Pl
Harrow Pl E1 275 N8
Harrow Pl E1 142 DS72
Harrow Rd E6 144 EL67
Harrow Rd E11 124 EE62
Harrow Rd NW10 139 CV69
Harrow Rd W2 139 CZ70
Harrow Rd W9 139 CZ70
Harrow Rd W10 139 CX70
Harrow Rd, Bark. 145 ES67
Harrow Rd, Cars. 218 DE106
Harrow Rd, Felt. 174 BN88
Harrow Rd, Ilf. 125 EQ63
Harrow Rd (Knockholt), Sev. 240 EY115
Harrow Rd, Slou. 153 AZ76
Harrow Rd, Warl. 237 DZ115
Harrow Rd, Wem. 117 CJ64
Harrow Rd (Tokyngton), Wem. 138 CP65
Harrow Rd E, Dor. 263 CH138
Harrow Rd W, Dor. 263 CG138
Harrow Vw, Har. 117 CD56
Harrow Vw, Hayes 135 BU72
Harrow Vw, Uxb. 135 BQ69
Harrow Vw Rd W5 137 CH70
Harrow Way, Shep. 195 BQ96
Harrow Way, Wat. 94 BY48
Harrow Weald Pk, Har. 95 CD51
Harroway Rd SW11 160 DD82
Harrowby Gdns (Northfleet), Grav. 190 GE89
Harrowby St W1 272 C8
Harrowby St W1 140 DE72
Harrowdene Cl, Wem. 117 CK63
Harrowdene Gdns, Tedd. 177 CG93
Harrowdene Rd, Wem. 117 CK62
Harrowes Meade, Edg. 96 CN48
Harrowgate Rd E9 143 DY65
Harrowlands Pk, Dor. 263 CH137
Harrowsley Ct, Horl. 269 DH147
Tanyard Way
Harrowsley Grn La, Horl. 269 DJ149
Harston Dr, Enf. 83 EA38
Hart Cl (Bletchingley), Red. 252 DT134
Hart Cor, Grays 169 FX78
Hart Cres, Chig. 103 ET50
Hart Dyke Cres, Swan. 207 FD97
Hart Dyke Rd
Hart Dyke Rd, Orp. 206 EW102
Hart Dyke Rd, Swan. 207 FD97
Hart Gdns, Dor. 263 CH135
Hart Rd
Hart Gro W5 138 CN74
Hart Gro, Sthl. 136 CA71
Hart Rd, Dor. 263 CH135
Hart Rd, Harl. 36 EW10
Hart Rd, St.Alb. 43 CD21
Hart Rd (Byfleet), W.Byf. 212 BL113
Hart St EC3 275 N10
Hart St, Brwd. 108 FW47
Harte Rd, Houns. 156 BZ82
Hartfield Av, Borwd. 78 CN43
Hartfield Av, Nthlt. 135 BV68
Hartfield Cl, Borwd. 78 CN43
Hartfield Ct, Ware 33 DX05
Hartfield Cres SW19 179 CZ94
Hartfield Cres, W.Wick. 204 EG104
Hartfield Gro SE20 202 DV95
Hartfield Pl (Northfleet), Grav. 190 GD87
Hartfield Rd SW19 179 CZ94
Hartfield Rd, Chess. 215 CK106
Hartfield Rd, W.Wick. 222 EG105
Hartfield Ter E3 143 EA68
Hartford Av, Har. 117 CG55
Hartford Rd, Bex. 186 FA86
Hartford Rd, Epsom 216 CN107
Hartforde Rd, Borwd. 78 CN40
Harthall La, Hem.H. 59 BS26
Harthall La, Kings L. 59 BP28
Hartham Cl N7 121 DL64
Hartham Cl, Islw. 157 CG81
Hartham La, Hert. 32 DQ09
Hartham Rd N7 121 DL64
Hartham Rd N17 100 DT54
Hartham Rd, Islw. 157 CF81
Harting Rd SE9 184 EL91
Hartington Cl, Har. 117 CE63
Hartington Ct W4 158 CP80
Hartington Pl, Reig. 250 DA132
Hartington Rd E16 144 EH72
Hartington Rd E17 123 DY58
Hartington Rd SW8 161 DL81
Hartington Rd W4 158 CP80
Hartington Rd W13 137 CH73
Hartington Rd, Sthl. 156 BY75
Hartington Rd, Twick. 177 CH87
Hartismere Rd SW6 159 CZ80
Hartlake Rd E9 143 DX65
Hartland Cl N21 82 DQ44
Elmscott Gdns
Hartland Cl (New Haw), Add. 212 BJ110
Hartland Cl, Edg. 96 CN47
Hartland Cl, Slou. 131 AR74
Hartland Dr, Edg. 96 CN47
Hartland Dr, Ruis. 115 BV62
Hartland Rd E15 144 EF66
Hartland Rd N11 98 DF50
Hartland Rd NW1 141 DH66
Hartland Rd NW6 139 CZ68
Hartland Rd, Add. 212 BG108
Hartland Rd, Epp. 70 EU31
Hartland Rd (Hampton Hill), Hmptn. 176 CB91
Hartland Rd, Horn. 127 FG61
Hartland Rd, Islw. 157 CG83
Hartland Rd, Mord. 200 DA101
Hartland Rd (Cheshunt), Wal.Cr. 67 DX30
Hartland Way, Croy. 203 DY103
Hartland Way, Mord. 199 CZ101
Hartlands Cl, Bex. 186 EZ86
Hartlepool Ct E16 165 EP75
Fishguard Way
Hartley Av E6 144 EL67
Hartley Av NW7 97 CT50
Hartley Cl NW7 97 CT50
Hartley Cl, Brom. 205 EM96
Hartley Cl (Stoke Poges), Slou. 132 AW67
Hartley Copse (Old Windsor), Wind. 172 AU86
Hartley Down, Pur. 219 DM113
Hartley Fm Est, Pur. 235 DM115
Hartley Hill, Pur. 235 DM115
Hartley Old Rd, Pur. 219 DM114
Hartley Rd E11 124 EF60
Hartley Rd, Croy. 201 DP101
Hartley Rd, Well. 166 EW80
Hartley Rd, West. 255 ER125
Hartley St E2 142 DW69
Hartley Way, Pur. 235 DM115
Hartmann Rd E16 144 EK74
Hartmoor Ms, Enf. 83 DX37
Hartnoll St N7 121 DM64
Eden Gro
Harton Cl, Brom. 204 EK95
Harton Rd N9 100 DV47
Harton St SE8 163 EA81
Harts Cl, Bushey 76 CA40
Harts Gdns, Guil. 242 AV131
Harts Gro, Wdf.Grn. 102 EG50
Harts La SE14 163 DY80
Harts La, Bark. 145 EP65
Hartsbourne Av, Bushey 94 CC47
Hartsbourne Cl, Bushey 95 CD47
Hartsbourne Rd, Bushey 95 CD47
Hartsbourne Way, Hem.H. 41 BQ21
Hartscroft, Croy. 221 DY109
Hartshill Cl, Uxb. 134 BN65
Hartshill Rd (Northfleet), Grav. 191 GF89
Hartshill Wk, Wok. 226 AV116
Hartshorn All EC3 275 N9
Hartshorn Gdns E6 145 EN70
Hartslands Rd, Sev. 257 FJ123
Hartslock Dr SE2 166 EX75
Hartsmead Rd SE9 185 EM89
Hartspiece Rd, Red. 266 DG136
Hartspring La, Bushey 76 CA39
Hartspring La, Wat. 76 CA39
Hartsway, Enf. 82 DW42
Hartswood (North Holmwood), Dor. 263 CK139
Wildcroft Dr
Hartswood Av, Reig. 266 DA138
Hartswood Cl, Brwd. 108 FY49
Hartswood Gdns W12 159 CT76
Hartswood Grn, Bushey 95 CD47
Hartswood Rd W12 159 CT75
Hartswood Rd, Brwd. 108 FY49
Hartsworth Cl E13 144 EF68
Hartville Rd SE18 165 ES77
Hartwell Cl (Penn), H.Wyc. 88 AC45
Hartwell Dr E4 101 EC51
Hartwell Dr, Beac. 89 AK52
Hartwell St E8 142 DT65
Dalston La
Harvard Hill W4 158 CP79
Harvard La W4 158 CP78
Harvard Rd SE13 183 EC85
Harvard Rd W4 158 CP78
Harvard Rd, Islw. 157 CE81
Harvard Wk, Horn. 127 FG63
Harvel Cl, Orp. 206 EU97
Harvel Cres SE2 166 EX78
Harvest Bk Rd, W.Wick. 204 EF104
Harvest Ct, St.Alb. 43 CK16
Harvesters
Harvest Ct, Shep. 194 BN98
Harvest End, Wat. 76 BX36
Harvest Hill, B.End 110 AD61
Harvest La, Loug. 102 EJ45
Harvest La, T.Ditt. 197 CG100
Harvest Mead, Hat. 45 CV16
Harvest Rd, Bushey 76 CB42
Harvest Rd (Englefield Grn), Egh. 172 AX92
Harvest Rd, Felt. 175 BU91
Harvest Way, Swan. 207 FD101
Harvester Rd, Epsom 216 CR110
Harvesters, St.Alb. 43 CK16
Harvesters Cl, Islw. 177 CD85
Harvestside, Horl. 269 DJ147
Harvey, Grays 170 GB75
Harvey Cen, Harl. 51 EQ15
Harvey Dr, Hmptn. 196 CB95
Harvey Gdns E11 124 EF60
Harvey Rd
Harvey Gdns SE7 164 EK77
Harvey Gdns, Loug. 85 EP41
Harvey Ho, Brent. 158 CL78
Green Dragon La
Harvey Orchard, Beac. 88 AJ52
Harvey Pt E16 144 EH71
Fife Rd
Harvey Rd E11 124 EF60
Harvey Rd N8 121 DM57
Harvey Rd SE5 162 DR81
Harvey Rd, Guil. 258 AY136
Harvey Rd, Houns. 176 BZ87
Harvey Rd, Ilf. 125 EP64
Harvey Rd, Nthlt. 136 BW66
Harvey Rd, Rick. 74 BN44
Harvey Rd (London Colney), St.Alb. 61 CJ26
Harvey Rd, Slou. 153 BB76
Harvey Rd, Uxb. 134 BN68
Harvey Rd, Walt. 195 BU101
Harvey St N1 142 DR67
Harveyfields, Wal.Abb. 67 EC34
Harveys La, Rom. 127 FD61
Harvil Rd (Harefield), Uxb. 114 BK58
Harvil Rd (Ickenham), Uxb. 114 BL60
Harvill Rd, Sid. 186 EX92
Harvington Wk E8 142 DU66
Wilman Gro
Harvist Est N7 121 DN63
Harvist Rd NW6 139 CX68
Harwater Dr, Loug. 85 EM40
Harwell Cl, Ruis. 115 BR60
Harwell Pas N2 120 DF56
Harwich La EC2 275 N6
Harwich La EC2 142 DS71
Harwich Rd, Slou. 131 AN72
Harwood Av, Brom. 204 EH96
Harwood Av, Horn. 128 FL55
Harwood Av, Mitch. 200 DE97
Harwood Cl N12 98 DE51
Summerfields Av
Harwood Cl, Welw. 30 DE05
Harwood Cl, Welw.G.C. 29 CY05
Harwood Cl, Wem. 117 CK63
Harrowdene Rd
Harwood Dr, Uxb. 134 BM67
Harwood Gdns (Old Windsor), Wind. 172 AV87
Harwood Hall La, Upmin. 148 FP65
Harwood Hill, Welw.G.C. 29 CY06
Harwood Pk, Red. 266 DG143
Harwood Rd SW6 160 DA80
Harwood Ter SW6 160 DB81
Harwoods Rd, Wat. 75 BU42
Harwoods Yd N21 99 DN45
Wades Hill
Hascombe Ter SE5 162 DR82
Love Wk
Hasedines Rd, Hem.H. 40 BG19
Haselbury Rd N9 100 DS49
Haselbury Rd N18 100 DS49
Haseldine Meadows, Hat. 45 CT19
Haseldine Rd (London Colney), St.Alb. 61 CK26
Haseley End SE23 182 DW87
Tyson Rd
Haselrigge Rd SW4 161 DK84
Haseltine Rd SE26 183 DZ91
Haselwood Dr, Enf. 81 DP42
Haskard Rd, Dag. 126 EX63
Haskell Ho NW10 138 CR67
Hasker St SW3 276 C8
Hasker St SW3 160 DE77
Haslam Av, Sutt. 199 CY102
Haslam Cl N1 141 DN66
Haslam Cl, Uxb. 115 BQ61
Haslam St SE15 162 DT80
Haslemere Av NW4 119 CX58
Haslemere Av SW18 180 DB89
Haslemere Av W7 157 CG76
Haslemere Av W13 157 CG76
Haslemere Av, Barn. 98 DF46
Haslemere Av, Houns. 156 BW82
Haslemere Av, Mitch. 200 DD96
Haslemere Cl, Hmptn. 176 BZ92
Haslemere Cl, Wall. 219 DL106
Stafford Rd
Haslemere Gdns N3 119 CZ55
Haslemere Heathrow Est, Houns. 155 BV82
Haslemere Ind Est, Harl. 51 EN16
Haslemere Rd N8 121 DK59
Haslemere Rd N21 99 DP47
Haslemere Rd, Bexh. 166 EZ82
Haslemere Rd, Ilf. 125 ET61
Haslemere Rd, Th.Hth. 201 DP99
Haslemere Rd, Wind. 151 AN81
Hasler Cl SE28 146 EV73
Haslett Rd, Shep. 195 BS96
Haslewood Av, Hodd. 49 EA17
Hasluck Gdns, Barn. 80 DC44
Hassard St E2 142 DT68
Hackney Rd
Hassendean Rd SE3 164 EH79
Hassett Rd E9 143 DX65
Hassock Wd, Kes. 222 EK105
Hassocks Cl SE26 182 DV90
Hassocks Rd SW16 201 DK95
Hassop Rd NW2 119 CX63
Hassop Wk SE9 184 EL91
Hasted Cl, Green. 189 FW86
Hasted Rd SE7 164 EK78
Hastings Av, Ilf. 125 EQ56
Hastings Cl SE15 162 DU80
Hastings Cl, Barn. 80 DC42
Leicester Rd
Hastings Cl, Grays 170 FY79
Hastings Cl, Maid. 150 AC77
Hastings Dr, Surb. 197 CJ100
Hastings Ho SE18 165 EM77
Hastings Rd N11 99 DJ50
Hastings Rd N17 122 DR55
Hastings Rd W13 137 CH73
Hastings Rd, Brom. 204 EL102
Hastings Rd, Croy. 202 DT102
Hastings Rd, Rom. 127 FH57
Hastings St WC1 273 P3
Hastings St WC1 141 DL69
Hastings Way, Bushey 76 BY42
Hastings Way, Rick. 75 BP42
Hastingwood Rd, Harl. 52 EX20
Hastingwood Trd Est N18 101 DX51
Hastoe Cl, Hayes 136 BY70
Kingsash Dr
Hat and Mitre Ct EC1 274 G5
Hatch, The, Enf. 83 DX39
Hatch, The, Wind. 150 AJ80
Hatch Cl, Add. 194 BH104
Hatch Gdns, Tad. 233 CX120
Hatch Gro, Rom. 126 EY56
Hatch La E4 101 ED49
Hatch La, Cob. 229 BP119
Hatch La, Couls. 234 DG115
Hatch La, Red. 267 DM142
Hatch La, West Dr. 154 BK80
Hatch La, Wind. 151 AN83
Hatch La (Ockham), Wok. 229 BP120
Hatch Pl, Kings.T. 178 CM92
Hatch Rd SW16 201 DL96
Hatch Rd, Brwd. 108 FU43
Hatch Side, Chig. 103 EN50
Hatcham Pk Ms SE14 163 DX81
Hatcham Pk Rd
Hatcham Pk Rd SE14 163 DX81
Hatcham Rd SE15 162 DW79
Hatchard Rd N19 121 DK61
Hatchcroft NW4 119 CV55
Hatchett Rd, Felt. 175 BQ88
Hatchgate, Horl. 268 DF149
Hatchgate Gdns (Burnham), Slou. 131 AK69
Hatchlands Rd, Red. 250 DE134
Hatchwood Cl, Wdf.Grn. 102 EF49
Sunset Av
Hatcliffe Cl SE3 164 EF83
Hatcliffe St SE10 164 EF78
Woolwich Rd
Hatfield Av, Hat. 44 CS15
Hatfield Business Pk, Hat. 44 CS15
Hatfield Cl SE14 163 DX80
Reaston St
Hatfield Cl, Brwd. 109 GD45
Hatfield Cl, Horn. 128 FK64
Hatfield Cl, Ilf. 125 EP55
Hatfield Cl, Mitch. 200 DD98
Hatfield Cl, Sutt. 218 DA109
Hatfield Cl, W.Byf. 212 BH112
Hatfield Cres, Hem.H. 40 BM16
Hatfield Ho, Hat. 45 CX18
Hatfield Mead, Mord. 200 DA99
Central Rd
Hatfield Pk, Hat. 45 CX18
Hatfield Rd E15 124 EE64
Hatfield Rd W4 158 CR75
Hatfield Rd W13 137 CG74
Hatfield Rd, Ash. 232 CM119
Hatfield Rd, Dag. 146 EY66
Hatfield Rd, Grays 169 FW78
Hatfield Rd, Hat. 30 DE14
Hatfield Rd, Hert. 30 DG11
Hatfield Rd, Pot.B. 64 DC30
Hatfield Rd, St.Alb. 43 CK20
Hatfield Rd, Slou. 152 AU75
Hatfield Rd, Wat. 75 BV39
Hatfield Tunnel, Hat. 45 CT17
Hatfields SE1 278 E2
Hatfields SE1 141 DP74
Hatfields, Loug. 85 EP41
Hathaway Cl, Brom. 205 EM102
Hathaway Cl, Ruis. 115 BT63
Stafford Rd
Hathaway Cl, Stan. 95 CG50
Hathaway Ct, St.Alb. 44 CL20
Hathaway Cres E12 145 EM65
Hathaway Gdns W13 137 CF71
Hathaway Gdns, Grays 170 GB76
Hathaway Rd
Hathaway Gdns, Rom. 126 EX57
Hathaway Rd, Croy. 201 DP101
Hathaway Rd, Grays 170 GB77
Hatherleigh Cl, Chess. 215 CK106
Hatherleigh Cl, Mord. 200 DA98
Hatherleigh Gdns, Pot.B. 64 DD32
Hatherleigh Rd, Ruis. 115 BU61
Hatherleigh Way, Rom. 106 FK53
Hatherley Cres, Sid. 186 EU89
Hatherley Gdns E6 144 EK69
Hatherley Gdns N8 121 DL58
Hatherley Gro W2 140 DB72
Hatherley Ms E17 123 EA56
Hatherley Rd E17 123 DZ56
Hatherley Rd, Rich. 158 CM82
Hatherley Rd, Sid. 186 EU91
Hatherley St SW1 277 L8
Hathern Gdns SE9 185 EN91
Hatherop Rd, Hmptn. 176 BZ94
Hathersham Cl, Horl. 269 DN147
Hathersham La, Horl. 267 DK144
Hatherwood, Lthd. 231 CK121
Hathorne Cl SE15 162 DV82
Hathway St SE15 162 DW82
Gibbon Rd
Hathway Ter SE14 162 DW82
Kitto Rd
Hatley Av, Ilf. 125 EQ56
Hatley Cl N11 98 DF50
Hatley Rd N4 121 DM61
Hatteraick St SE16 162 DW75
Brunel Rd
Hatters La, Wat. 75 BR44
Hattersfield Cl, Belv. 166 EZ77
Hatton Av, Slou. 131 AR70
Hatton Cl SE18 165 ER80
Hatton Cl (Northfleet), Grav. 190 GE90
Hatton Cl (Chafford Hundred), Grays 169 FX76
Hatton Ct E5 123 DY63
Gilpin Rd
Hatton Gdn EC1 274 E6
Hatton Gdn EC1 141 DN71
Hatton Gdns, Mitch. 200 DF99
Hatton Grn, Felt. 155 BU84
Hatton Gro, West Dr. 154 BK75
Hatton Ho E1 142 DU73
Wellclose Sq
Hatton Pl EC1 274 E5
Hatton Pl EC1 141 DN70
Hatton Rd, Croy. 201 DN102
Hatton Rd, Felt. 175 BS85
Hatton Rd (Cheshunt), Wal.Cr. 67 DX29
Hatton Row NW8 272 A5
Hatton St NW8 272 A5
Hatton Wall EC1 274 D6
Hatton Wall EC1 141 DN71
Haunch of Venison Yd W1 273 H9
Havana Cl, Rom. 127 FE57
South St
Havana Rd SW19 180 DA89
Havannah St E14 163 EA75
Havant Rd E17 123 EC55
Havant Way SE15 162 DT80
Daniel Gdns
Havelock Pl, Har. 117 CE58
Havelock Rd N17 100 DU54
Havelock Rd SW19 180 DC92
Havelock Rd, Belv. 166 EZ77
Havelock Rd, Brom. 204 EJ98
Havelock Rd, Croy. 202 DT102
Havelock Rd, Dart. 187 FH87
Havelock Rd, Grav. 191 GF88
Havelock Rd, Har. 117 CE55
Havelock Rd, Kings L. 58 BN28
Havelock Rd, Sthl. 156 BZ76
Havelock St N1 141 DL67
Havelock St, Ilf. 125 EP61
Havelock Ter SW8 161 DH80
Havelock Wk SE23 182 DW88
Haven, The SE26 182 DV92
Springfield Rd
Haven, The, Grays 171 GF78
Haven, The, Rich. 158 CN83
Haven, The, Sun. 175 BU94
Haven Cl SE9 185 EM90
Haven Cl SW19 179 CX90
Haven Cl (Istead Ri), Grav. 191 GF94
Haven Cl, Hat. 45 CT17
Haven Cl, Hayes 135 BS71
Haven Cl, Sid. 186 EV93
Haven Cl, Swan. 207 FF96
Haven Grn W5 137 CK72
Haven Grn Ct W5 137 CK72
Haven Grn
Haven La W5 138 CL72
Haven Ms E3 143 DZ71
St. Pauls Way
Haven Pl W5 137 CK73
The Bdy
Haven Pl, Grays 170 GC75
Haven Rd, Ashf. 175 BP91
Haven St NW1 141 DH66
Castlehaven Rd
Haven Ter W5 137 CK73
The Bdy
Havenbury Ind Est, Dor. 263 CG135
Station Rd
Havengore Av, Grav. 191 GL87
Havenhurst Ri, Enf. 81 DN40
Havensfield, Kings L. 58 BH31
Havenwood, Wem. 118 CP62
Havenwood Cl, Brwd. 107 FW51
Wilmot Grn
Havercroft Cl, St.Alb. 42 CB22
King Harry La
Haverfield Gdns, Rich. 158 CN80
Haverfield Rd E3 143 DY69
Haverford Way, Edg. 96 CM53
Haverhill Rd E4 101 EC46
Haverhill Rd SW12 181 DJ88
Havering Dr, Rom. 127 FE56
Havering Gdns, Rom. 126 EW57
Havering Rd, Rom. 127 FD55
Havering St E1 143 DX72
Devonport St
Havering Way, Bark. 146 EV69
Havers Av, Walt. 214 BX106
Haversfield Est, Brent. 158 CL78
Haversham Cl, Twick. 177 CK86
Haversham Pl N6 120 DF61
Haverstock Ct, Orp. 206 EU96
Haverstock Hill NW3 120 DE64
Haverstock Pl N1 141 DP68
Haverstock St
Haverstock Rd NW5 120 DG64
Haverstock St N1 274 G1
Haverstock St N1 141 DP68
Haverthwaite Rd, Orp. 205 ER103
Havil St SE5 162 DS80
Havisham Pl SE19 181 DP93
Haward Rd, Hodd. 49 EC15
Hawarden Gro SE24 182 DQ87
Hawarden Hill NW2 119 CU62
Hawarden Rd E17 123 DX56
Hawarden Rd, Cat. 236 DQ121
Hawbridge Rd E11 123 ED60
Hawes Cl, Nthwd. 93 BT52
Hawes La E4 83 EC38
Hawes La, W.Wick. 203 ED102
Hawes Rd N18 100 DV51
Hawes Rd, Brom. 204 EH95
Hawes Rd, Tad. 233 CX120
Hatch Gdns
Hawes St N1 141 DP66
Haweswater Dr, Wat. 60 BW33
Haweswater Ho, Islw. 177 CF85
Summerwood Rd
Hawfield Bk, Orp. 206 EX104
Hawfield Gdns (Park St), St.Alb. 61 CD26
Hawgood St E3 143 EA71
Hawk Cl, Wal.Abb. 68 EG34
Hawk Ter, Ilf. 125 EN55
Tiptree Cres
Hawkdene E4 83 EB44
Hawke Pk Rd N22 121 DP55
Hawke Pl SE16 163 DX75
Middleton Dr
Hawke Rd SE19 182 DS93
Hawke Twr SE14 163 DY79
Hawkenbury, Harl. 51 EP17
Hawker Cl, Wall. 219 DL108
Hawkes Cl, Grays 170 GB79
New Rd
Hawke's Pl, Sev. 256 FG127
Hawkes Rd, Felt. 175 BU87
Hawkes Rd, Mitch. 200 DE95
Hawkesbury Rd SW15 179 CV85
Hawkesfield Rd SE23 183 DY89
Hawkesley Cl, Twick. 177 CG91
Hawkesworth Cl, Nthwd. 93 BS52
Hawkewood Rd, Sun. 195 BU97
Hawkhirst Rd, Ken. 236 DR115
Hawkhurst, Cob. 214 CA114
Hawkhurst Gdns, Chess. 216 CL105
Hawkhurst Gdns, Rom. 105 FD51
Hawkhurst Rd SW16 201 DK95
Hawkhurst Way, N.Mal. 198 CR99
Hawkhurst Way, W.Wick. 203 EB103
Hawkinge Wk, Orp. 206 EV97
Hawkinge Way, Horn. 148 FJ65
Hawkins Av, Grav. 191 GJ91
Hawkins Cl NW7 96 CR50
Hale La
Hawkins Cl, Borwd. 78 CQ40
Banks Rd
Hawkins Cl, Har. 117 CD59
Hawkins Dr, Grays 169 FX75
Hawkins Rd, Tedd. 177 CH93
Hawkins Way SE6 183 EA91
Hawkins Way (Bovingdon), Hem.H. 57 BA26
Hawkley Gdns SE27 181 DP89
Hawkridge Cl, Rom. 126 EW59
Hawkridge Dr, Grays 170 GD78
Hawks Hill, B.End 110 AC61
Hawks Hill, Epp. 70 FA27
Hawk's Hill, Lthd. 231 CF123
Hawks Hill Cl (Fetcham), Lthd. 231 CF122
Hawks Ms SE10 163 EC80
Luton Pl
Hawks Rd, Kings.T. 198 CM96
Hawksbrook La, Beck. 203 EB100
Hawkshaw Cl SW2 181 DL87
Tierney Rd
Hawkshead Cl, Brom. 184 EE94
Hawkshead La, Hat. 63 CW28
Hawkshead Rd NW10 139 CT66
Hawkshead Rd W4 158 CS75
Hawkshead Rd, Pot.B. 64 DB29
Hawkshill, St.Alb. 43 CG21
Hawkshill Cl, Esher 214 CA107
Hawkshill Dr (Felden), Hem.H. 39 BE23
Hawkshill Rd, Slou. 131 AN69
Hawkshill Way, Esher 214 BZ107
Hawkslade Rd SE15 183 DX85
Hawksley Rd N16 122 DS62
Hawksmead Cl, Enf. 83 DX35
Hawksmoor, Rad. 62 CN33
Hawksmoor Cl E6 144 EL72
Allhallows Rd
Hawksmoor Cl SE18 165 ES78
Hawksmoor Grn, Brwd. 109 GD43
Hawksmoor Ms E1 142 DV73
Cable St
Hawksmoor St W6 159 CX79

Hawksmouth E4 101 EB45
Hawkstone Rd SE16 162 DW77
Hawksview, Cob. 214 CA113
Hawksway, Stai. 173 BF90
Hawkswell Cl, Wok. 226 AT117
Hawkswell Wk, Wok. 226 AS117
Lockfield Dr
Hawkswood Gro (Fulmer), Slou. 133 AZ65
Hawkswood La, Ger.Cr. 113 AZ64
Hawkwell Ct E4 101 EC48
Colvin Gdns
Hawkwell Ho, Dag. 126 FA60
Hawkwell Wk N1 142 DQ67
Basire St
Hawkwood Cres E4 83 EB44
Hawkwood Dell (Bookham), Lthd. 246 CA126
Hawkwood La, Chis. 205 EQ95
Hawkwood Mt E5 122 DV60
Hawkwood Ri (Bookham), Lthd. 246 CA126
Hawlands Dr, Pnr. 116 BY59
Hawley Cl, Hmptn. 176 BZ93
Hawley Cres NW1 141 DH66
Hawley Ms NW1 141 DH66
Hawley St
Hawley Mill, Dart. 188 FN91
Hawley Rd N18 101 DX50
Hawley Rd NW1 141 DH66
Hawley Rd, Dart. 188 FL89
Hawley St NW1 141 DH66
Hawley Ter, Dart. 188 FN92
Hawley Rd
Hawley Vale, Dart. 188 FN92
Hawley Way, Ashf. 174 BN92
Haws La, Stai. 174 BG86
Hawstead La, Orp. 224 EZ106
Hawstead Rd SE6 183 EB86
Hawsted, Buck.H. 102 EH45
Hawthorn Av E3 143 DZ67
Hawthorn Av N13 99 DL50
Hawthorn Av, Brwd. 109 FZ48
Hawthorn Av, Cars. 218 DG108
Hawthorn Av, Rain. 147 FH70
Hawthorn Av, Rich. 158 CL82
Kew Rd
Hawthorn Av, Th.Hth. 201 DP95
Hawthorn Cen, Har. 117 CF56
Hawthorn Cl, Abb.L. 59 BU32
Hawthorn Cl, Bans. 217 CY114
Hawthorn Cl, Grav. 191 GH91
Hawthorn Cl, Hmptn. 176 CA92
Hawthorn Cl, Hert. 31 DN08
Hawthorn Cl, Houns. 155 BV80
Hawthorn Cl, Iver 133 BD68
Hawthorn Cl, Orp. 205 ER100
Hawthorn Cl, Red. 266 DG139
Bushfield Dr
Hawthorn Cl, Wat. 75 BT38
Hawthorn Cl, Wok. 226 AY120
Hawthorn Cotts, Well. 166 EU83
Hook La
Hawthorn Ct, Rich. 158 CP81
West Hall Rd
Hawthorn Cres SW17 180 DG92
Hawthorn Cres, S.Croy. 220 DW111
Hawthorn Dr, Har. 116 BZ58
Hawthorn Dr (Denham), Uxb. 134 BJ65
Hawthorn Dr, W.Wick. 222 EE105
Hawthorn Gdns W5 157 CK76
Hawthorn Gro SE20 182 DV94
Hawthorn Gro, Barn. 79 CT44
Hawthorn Gro, Enf. 82 DR38
Hawthorn Hatch, Brent. 157 CH80
Hawthorn La, Sev. 256 FF122
Hawthorn La (Farnham Common), Slou. 131 AP65
Hawthorn Ms NW7 97 CY53
Holders Hill Rd
Hawthorn Pl, Erith 167 FC78
Hawthorn Pl (Penn), H.Wyc. 88 AC47
Hawthorn Rd N8 121 DK55
Hawthorn Rd N18 100 DT50
Hawthorn Rd NW10 139 CU66
Hawthorn Rd, Bexh. 166 EZ84
Hawthorn Rd, Brent. 157 CH80
Hawthorn Rd, Buck.H. 102 EK49
Hawthorn Rd, Dart. 188 FK88
Hawthorn Rd, Hodd. 49 EB15
Hawthorn Rd, Sutt. 218 DE107
Hawthorn Rd, Wall. 219 DH108
Hawthorn Rd, Wok. 226 AX120
Hawthorn Rd (Send Marsh), Wok. 228 BG124
Hawthorn Wk W10 139 CY70
Droop St
Hawthorn Way (New Haw), Add. 212 BJ110
Hawthorn Way, Chesh. 54 AR29
Hawthorn Way, Red. 267 DH136
Hawthorn Way, St.Alb. 42 CA24
Hawthorn Way, Shep. 195 BR98
Hawthornden Cl N12 98 DE51
Fallowfields Dr
Hawthorndene Cl, Brom. 204 EG103
Hawthorndene Rd, Brom. 204 EF103
Hawthorne Av, Har. 117 CG58
Hawthorne Av, Mitch. 200 DD96
Hawthorne Av, Ruis. 115 BV58
Hawthorne Av (Cheshunt), Wal.Cr. 66 DV31
Hawthorne Av (Biggin Hill), West. 238 EK115
Hawthorne Cl N1 142 DS65
Hawthorne Cl, Brom. 205 EM97
Hawthorne Cl, Sutt. 200 DB103
Aultone Way
Hawthorne Cl (Cheshunt), Wal.Cr. 66 DV31
Hawthorne Ct, Nthwd. 93 BU54
Ryefield Cres
Hawthorne Ct, Walt. 196 BX103
Ambleside Av
Hawthorne Cres, Slou. 132 AS71
Hawthorne Cres, West Dr. 154 BM75
Hawthorne Fm Av, Nthlt. 136 BY67
Hawthorne Gro NW9 118 CQ59
Hawthorne La, Hem.H. 39 BF19
Hawthorne Ms, Grnf. 136 CC72
Greenford Rd
Hawthorne Pl, Epsom 216 CS112
Hawthorne Pl, Hayes 135 BT73
Hawthorne Rd E17 123 EA55
Hawthorne Rd, Brom. 205 EM97
Hawthorne Rd, Rad. 61 CG34
Hawthorne Rd, Stai. 173 BC92
Hawthorne Way N9 100 DS47
Hawthorne Way, Guil. 243 BB130
Hawthorne Way (Stanwell), Stai. 174 BK87
Hawthornes, Hat. 45 CT20
Hazel Gro
Hawthorns, Harl. 51 ET19
Hawthorns, Welw.G.C. 29 CX07
Hawthorns, Wdf.Grn. 102 EG48
Hawthorns, The, Berk. 38 AU18
Hawthorns, The, Ch.St.G. 72 AW40
Hawthorns, The, Epsom 217 CT107
Ewell Bypass
Hawthorns, The, Hem.H. 39 BF24
Hawthorns, The, Loug. 85 EN42
Hawthorns, The, Oxt. 254 EG133
Hawthorns, The, Rick. 91 BD50
Hawthorns, The (Colnbrook), Slou. 153 BF81
Hawtrees, Rad. 77 CF35
Hawtrey Av, Nthlt. 136 BX68
Hawtrey Cl, Slou. 152 AV75
Hawtrey Dr, Ruis. 115 BU59
Hawtrey Rd NW3 140 DE66
Hawtrey Rd, Wind. 151 AQ82
Haxted Rd, Brom. 204 EH95
North Rd
Hay Cl E15 144 EE66
Hay Cl, Borwd. 78 CQ40
Hay Currie St E14 143 EB72
Hay Hill W1 277 J1
Hay Hill W1 141 DH73
Hay La NW9 118 CR56
Hay La (Fulmer), Slou. 112 AX63
Hay St E2 142 DU67
Haybourn Mead, Hem.H. 40 BH21
Hayburn Way, Horn. 127 FF60
Haycroft Cl, Couls. 235 DP118
Caterham Dr
Haycroft Gdns NW10 139 CU67
Haycroft Rd SW2 181 DL85
Haycroft Rd, Surb. 198 CL104
Hayday Rd E16 144 EG71
Hayden Ct (New Haw), Add. 212 BH111
Hayden Rd, Wal.Abb. 83 EC36
Hayden Way, Rom. 105 FC54
Haydens Cl, Orp. 206 EV100
Haydens Pl W11 139 CZ72
Portobello Rd
Haydens Rd, Harl. 51 EQ15
Haydn Av, Pur. 219 DN114
Haydns Ms W3 138 CQ72
Emanuel Av
Haydock Av, Nthlt. 136 CA65
Haydock Cl, Horn. 128 FM63
Haydock Grn, Nthlt. 136 CA65
Haydock Av
Haydon Cl NW9 118 CQ56
Haydon Cl, Enf. 82 DS44
Mortimer Dr
Haydon Dr, Pnr. 115 BU56
Haydon Pk Rd SW19 180 DB92
Haydon Pl, Guil. 258 AX135
Haydon Rd, Dag. 126 EW61
Haydon Rd, Wat. 76 BY44
Haydon St EC3 275 P10
Haydon Wk E1 142 DT73
Mansell St
Haydon Way SW11 160 DD84
St. John's Hill
Haydons Rd SW19 180 DB92
Hayes, The, Epsom 232 CR119
Hayes Barton, Wok. 227 BD116
Hayes Bypass, Hayes 136 BX70
Hayes Chase, W.Wick. 204 EE99
Hayes Cl, Brom. 204 EG103
Hayes Cl, Grays 169 FW79
Hayes Ct SW2 181 DL88
Hayes Cres NW11 119 CZ57
Hayes Cres, Sutt. 217 CX105
Hayes Dr, Rain. 147 FH66
Hayes End Cl, Hayes 135 BR70
Hayes End Dr, Hayes 135 BR70
Hayes End Rd, Hayes 135 BR70
Hayes Gdn, Brom. 204 EG103
Hayes Hill, Brom. 204 EE102
Hayes Hill Rd, Brom. 204 EF102
Hayes La, Beck. 203 EC97
Hayes La, Brom. 204 EG99
Hayes La, Ken. 220 DQ114
Hayes Mead Rd, Brom. 204 EE102
Hayes Metro Cen, Hayes 136 BW73
Hayes Pk, Hayes 135 BS70
Hayes Pl NW1 272 C5
Hayes Rd, Brom. 204 EG98
Hayes Rd, Green. 189 FS87
Hayes Rd, Sthl. 155 BV77
Hayes St, Brom. 204 EH102
Hayes Wk, Brox. 67 DZ25
Landau Way
Hayes Wk, Horl. 269 DN147
Hayes Wk, Pot.B. 64 DB33
Hyde Av
Hayes Way, Beck. 203 EC98
Hayes Wd Av, Brom. 204 EH102
Hayesford Pk Dr, Brom. 204 EF99
Hayfield Cl, Bushey 76 CB42
Hayfield Pas E1 142 DW70
Stepney Grn
Hayfield Rd, Orp. 206 EU99
Hayfield Yd E1 142 DW70
Mile End Rd
Hayfields, Horl. 269 DJ147
Ryelands
Haygarth Pl SW19 179 CX92
Haygreen Cl, Kings.T. 178 CP93
Hayland Cl NW9 118 CR56
Hayles St SE11 278 F8
Hayles St SE11 161 DP77
Haylett Gdns, Kings.T. 197 CK98
Anglesea Rd
Hayling Av, Felt. 175 BU90
Hayling Cl N16 122 DS64
Pellerin Rd
Hayling Rd, Wat. 93 BV47
Haymaker Cl, Uxb. 134 BM66
Honey Hill
Hayman Cres, Hayes 135 BR68
Hayman St N1 141 DP66
Cross St
Haymarket SW1 277 M1
Haymarket SW1 141 DK73
Haymarket Arc SW1 277 M1
Haymeads, Welw.G.C. 29 CY06
Haymeads Dr, Esher 214 CC107
Haymer Gdns, Wor.Pk. 199 CU104
Haymerle Rd SE15 162 DU79
Haymill Cl, Grnf. 137 CF69
Haymill Rd, Slou. 131 AK70
Hayne Rd, Beck. 203 DZ96
Hayne St EC1 274 G6
Haynes Cl N11 98 DG48
Haynes Cl N17 100 DV52
Haynes Cl SE3 164 EE83
Haynes Cl, Slou. 153 AZ78
Haynes Cl, Welw.G.C. 30 DA10
Haynes Cl (Ripley), Wok. 228 BH122
Haynes Dr N9 100 DV48
Plevna Rd
Haynes La SE19 182 DS93
Haynes Mead, Berk. 38 AU17
Haynes Rd (Northfleet), Grav. 191 GF90
Haynes Rd, Horn. 128 FK57
Haynes Rd, Wem. 138 CL66
Haynt Wk SW20 199 CY97
Hay's La SE1 279 M3
Hay's Ms W1 277 H1
Hay's Ms W1 141 DH73
Hays Wk, Sutt. 217 CX110
Hayse Hill, Wind. 151 AK81
Haysleigh Gdns SE20 202 DU96
Haysoms Cl, Rom. 127 FE56
Haystall Cl, Hayes 135 BS68
Hayter Ct E11 124 EH61
Hayter Rd SW2 181 DL85
Hayton Cl E8 142 DT65
Buttermere Wk
Haywain, Oxt. 253 ED130
Hayward Cl SW19 200 DB95
Hayward Cl, Dart. 187 FD85
Hayward Dr, Dart. 188 FM89
Hayward Gdns SW15 179 CW86
Hayward Rd N20 98 DC47
Hayward Rd, T.Ditt. 197 CG102
Haywards Cl, Brwd. 109 GE44
Haywards Cl, Rom. 126 EV57
Haywards Mead (Eton Wick), Wind. 151 AM78
Hayward's Pl EC1 274 F4
Haywood Cl, Pnr. 94 BX54
Haywood Ct, Wal.Abb. 68 EF34
Haywood Dr, Hem.H. 39 BF23
Haywood Pk, Rick. 73 BF43
Haywood Ri, Orp. 223 ES105
Haywood Rd, Brom. 204 EK98
Hayworth Cl, Enf. 83 DY40
Green St
Hazel Av, Guil. 242 AW130
Hazel Av, West Dr. 154 BN76
Hazel Cl N13 100 DR48
Hazel Cl N19 121 DJ61
Hargrave Pk
Hazel Cl SE15 162 DU82
Hazel Cl, Brent. 157 CH80
Hazel Cl, Croy. 203 DX101
Hazel Cl (Englefield Grn), Egh. 172 AV93
Hazel Cl, Horn. 127 FH62
Hazel Cl, Mitch. 201 DK98
Hazel Cl, Reig. 266 DC136
Hazel Cl, Twick. 176 CC87
Hazel Cl, Wal.Cr. 66 DS26
The Laurels
Hazel Dr, Erith 167 FH81
Hazel Dr, S.Ock. 149 FX69
Hazel Dr (Ripley), Wok. 243 BF125
Hazel End, Swan. 207 FE99
Hazel Gdns, Edg. 96 CP49
Hazel Gdns, Grays 170 GE76
Hazel Gdns, Saw. 36 EZ06
Sun St
Hazel Gro SE26 183 DX91
Hazel Gro, Enf. 82 DU44
Dimsdale Dr
Hazel Gro, Hat. 45 CT21
Hazel Gro, Orp. 205 EP103
Hazel Gro, Rom. 126 EY55
Hazel Gro, Stai. 174 BH93
Hazel Gro, Wat. 75 BV35
Cedar Wd Dr
Hazel Gro, Welw.G.C. 30 DB08
Hazel Gro, Wem. 138 CL67
Carlyon Rd
Hazel Gro Est SE26 183 DX91
Hazel La, Rich. 178 CL89
Hazel Mead, Barn. 79 CV43
Hazel Mead, Epsom 217 CU110
Hazel Ri, Horn. 128 FJ58
Hazel Rd E15 124 EE64
Wingfield Rd
Hazel Rd NW10 139 CW69
Hazel Rd, Berk. 38 AX20
Hazel Rd, Dart. 188 FK89
Hazel Rd, Erith 167 FG81
Hazel Rd, Reig. 266 DC136
Hazel Rd (Park St), St.Alb. 60 CB28
Hazel Rd, W.Byf. 212 BG114
Hazel Tree Rd, Wat. 75 BV37
Hazel Wk, Brom. 205 EN100
Hazel Wk (North Holmwood), Dor. 263 CJ139
Lake Vw
Hazel Way E4 101 DZ51
Hazel Way SE1 279 P8
Hazel Way, Couls. 234 DF119
Hazel Way (Fetcham), Lthd. 230 CC122
Hazelbank, Surb. 198 CQ102
Hazelbank Ct, Cher. 194 BJ102
Hazelbank Rd SE6 183 ED89
Hazelbank Rd, Cher. 194 BJ102
Hazelbourne Rd SW12 181 DH86
Hazelbrouck Gdns, Ilf. 103 ER52
Hazelbury Av, Abb.L. 59 BQ32
Hazelbury Cl SW19 200 DA96
Hazelbury Grn N9 100 DS48
Hazelbury La N9 100 DS48
Hazelcroft, Pnr. 94 CA51
Hazelcroft Cl, Uxb. 134 BM66
Hazeldean Rd NW10 138 CR66
Hazeldell Link, Hem.H. 39 BF21
Hazeldell Rd, Hem.H. 39 BE21
Hazeldene, Add. 212 BJ106
Hazeldene, Wal.Cr. 67 DY32
Hazeldene Ct, Ken. 236 DR115
Hazeldene Dr, Pnr. 116 BW55
Hazeldene Gdns, Uxb. 135 BQ67
Hazeldene Rd, Ilf. 126 EV61
Hazeldene Rd, Well. 166 EW82
Hazeldon Rd SE4 183 DY85
Hazeleigh, Brwd. 109 GB48
Hazeleigh Gdns, Wdf.Grn. 102 EL50
Hazelgreen Cl N21 99 DP46
Hazelhurst, Beck. 203 ED95
Hazelhurst, Horl. 269 DJ146
Hazelhurst Cl, Guil. 243 BB129
Weybrook Dr
Hazelhurst Rd SW17 180 DC91
Hazelhurst Rd, Slou. 130 AJ68
Hazell Cres, Rom. 105 FB53
Hazell Pk, Amer. 55 AR39
Hazell Way (Stoke Poges), Slou. 132 AT65
Hazells Rd, Grav. 190 GD92
Hazellville Rd N19 121 DK59
Hazelmere Cl, Felt. 175 BR86
Hazelmere Cl, Lthd. 231 CH119
Hazelmere Cl, Nthlt. 136 BZ68
Hazelmere Dr, Nthlt. 136 BZ68
Hazelmere Gdns, Horn. 127 FH57
Hazelmere Rd NW6 140 DA67
Hazelmere Rd, Nthlt. 136 BZ68
Hazelmere Rd, Orp. 205 EQ98
Hazelmere Rd, St.Alb. 43 CJ17
Hazelmere Wk, Nthlt. 136 BZ68
Hazelmere Way, Brom. 204 EG100
Hazels, The, Welw. 30 DE05
Hazeltree La, Nthlt. 136 BY69
Hazelwood, Dor. 263 CH137
Hazelwood, Loug. 84 EK43
Hazelwood Av, Mord. 200 DB98
Hazelwood Cl W5 158 CL75
Hazelwood Cl, Chesh. 54 AR29
Hazelwood Cl, Har. 116 CB56
Hazelwood Ct NW10 118 CS62
Neasden La N
Hazelwood Cres N13 99 DN49
Hazelwood Cft, Surb. 198 CL100
Hazelwood Dr, Pnr. 93 BV54
Hazelwood Dr, St.Alb. 43 CJ19
Hazelwood Gdns, Brwd. 108 FU44
Hazelwood Gro, S.Croy. 220 DV113
Hazelwood Hts, Oxt. 254 EG131
Hazelwood La N13 99 DN49
Hazelwood La, Abb.L. 59 BQ32
Hazelwood La, Couls. 234 DF119
Hazelwood Pk Cl, Chig. 103 ES50
Hazelwood Rd E17 123 DY57
Hazelwood Rd, Enf. 82 DT44
Hazelwood Rd, Oxt. 254 EH132
Hazelwood Rd, Rick. 75 BQ44
Hazelwood Rd (Cudham), Sev. 223 ER112
Hazelwood Rd (Knaphill), Wok. 226 AS118
Hazlebury Rd SW6 160 DB82
Hazledean Rd, Croy. 202 DR103
Hazledene Rd W4 158 CQ79
Hazlemere Gdns, Wor.Pk. 199 CV102
Hazlemere Rd (Penn), H.Wyc. 88 AC45
Hazlemere Rd, Slou. 132 AW74
Hazlewell Rd SW15 179 CW85
Hazlewood Cl E5 123 DY62
Mandeville St
Hazlewood Cres W10 139 CY70
Hazlitt Cl, Felt. 176 BY91
Hazlitt Ms W14 159 CY76
Hazlitt Rd
Hazlitt Rd W14 159 CY76
Hazon Way, Epsom 216 CR112
Heacham Av, Uxb. 115 BQ62
Head St E1 143 DX72
Headcorn Pl, Th.Hth. 201 DM98
Headcorn Rd
Headcorn Rd N17 100 DT52
Headcorn Rd, Brom. 184 EF92
Headcorn Rd, Th.Hth. 201 DM98
Headfort Pl SW1 276 G5
Headfort Pl SW1 160 DG75
Headingley Cl, Ilf. 103 ET51
Headingley Cl, Rad. 62 CL32
Headingley Cl (Cheshunt), Wal.Cr. 66 DT26
Headington Rd SW18 180 DC89
Headlam Rd SW4 181 DK86
Headlam St E1 142 DV70
Headley App, Ilf. 125 EN57
Headley Av, Wall. 219 DM106
Headley Chase, Brwd. 108 FW49
Headley Cl, Epsom 216 CN107
Headley Common, Brwd. 107 FV52
Warley Gap
Headley Common Rd (Headley), Epsom 248 CR127
Headley Common Rd, Tad. 248 CR127
Headley Ct SE26 182 DV92
Headley Dr (New Addington), Croy. 221 EB108
Headley Dr, Epsom 233 CV119
Headley Dr, Ilf. 125 EP58
Headley Gro, Tad. 233 CV120
Headley Heath App (Mickleham), Dor. 248 CP130
Ashurst Dr
Headley Heath App, Tad. 248 CP130
Headley La (Mickleham), Dor. 247 CJ129
Headley Rd (Tyrrell's Wd), Epsom 232 CN123
Headley Rd (Woodcote), Epsom 232 CP118
Headley Rd, Lthd. 231 CK123
Head's Ms W11 140 DA72
Artesian Rd
Headstone Dr, Har. 117 CE55
Headstone Gdns, Har. 116 CC56
Headstone La, Har. 116 CB56
Headstone Rd, Har. 117 CE57
Headway, The, Epsom 217 CT109
Headway Cl, Rich. 177 CJ91
Locksmeade Rd
Heald St SE14 163 DZ81
Healey Dr, Orp. 223 ET105
Healey Rd, Wat. 75 BT44
Healey St NW1 141 DH65
Heanor Ct E5 123 DX62
Pedro St
Heards La, Brwd. 109 FZ41
Hearn Ri, Nthlt. 136 BX67
Hearn Rd, Rom. 127 FF58
Hearn St EC2 275 N5
Hearn St EC2 142 DS70
Hearne Ct, Ch.St.G. 90 AV48
Gordon Way
Hearne Rd W4 158 CN79
Hearnes Cl (Seer Grn), Beac. 89 AR50
Hearnes Meadow (Seer Grn), Beac. 89 AR50
Hearn's Bldgs SE17 279 L9
Hearn's Rd, Orp. 206 EW98
Hearnville Rd SW12 180 DG88
Heath, The W7 137 CE74
Lower Boston Rd
Heath, The (Hatfield Heath), B.Stort. 37 FG05
Heath, The, Cat. 236 DQ124
Heath, The, Rad. 61 CG33
Heath Av, Bexh. 166 EX79
Heath Av, St.Alb. 43 CD18
Heath Brow NW3 120 DC62
North End Way
Heath Brow, Hem.H. 40 BJ22
Heath Cl NW11 120 DB59
Heath Cl W5 138 CM70
Heath Cl, Bans. 218 DB114
Heath Cl, Hayes 155 BR80
Heath Cl, Hem.H. 40 BJ21
Heath Cl, Orp. 206 EW100
Sussex Rd
Heath Cl, Pot.B. 64 DB30
Heath Cl, Rom. 127 FG55
Heath Cl (Stanwell), Stai. 174 BJ86
Heath Cl, Vir.W. 192 AX98
Heath Cotts, Pot.B. 64 DB30
Heath Rd
Heath Ct, Hert. 31 DM08
The Ridgeway
Heath Ct, Houns. 156 BZ84
Heath Ct, Uxb. 134 BL66
Heath Dr NW3 120 DB63
Heath Dr SW20 199 CW98
Heath Dr, Epp. 85 ES35
Heath Dr, Pot.B. 64 DA30
Heath Dr, Rom. 105 FG53
Heath Dr, Sutt. 218 DC109
Heath Dr, Tad. 249 CU125
Heath Dr (Send), Wok. 227 BB122
Heath End Rd, Bex. 187 FE88
Heath Fm Ct, Wat. 75 BR37
Grove Mill La
Heath Fm La, St.Alb. 43 CE18
Heath Gdns, Twick. 177 CF88
Heath Gro SE20 182 DW94
Maple Rd
Heath Gro, Sun. 175 BT94
Heath Hill, Dor. 263 CH136
Heath Hurst Rd NW3 120 DE63
Heath La SE3 163 ED82
Heath La (Lower), Dart. 188 FJ88
Heath La (Upper), Dart. 187 FG89
Heath La (Albury), Guil. 260 BL141
Heath La, Hem.H. 40 BJ22
Heath La, Hert. 32 DW13
Heath Mead SW19 179 CX90
Heath Pk Ct, Rom. 127 FG57
Heath Pk Rd
Heath Pk Dr, Brom. 204 EL97
Heath Pk Rd, Rom. 127 FG57
Heath Pas NW3 120 DB61
Heath Ridge Grn, Cob. 214 CA113
Heath Ri SW15 179 CX86
Heath Ri, Brom. 204 EF100
Heath Ri (Westcott), Dor. 262 CC138
Heath Ri, Vir.W. 192 AX98
Heath Ri (Ripley), Wok. 228 BH123
Heath Rd SW8 161 DH82
Heath Rd, Beac. 110 AG55
Heath Rd, Bex. 187 FC88
Heath Rd, Cat. 236 DR123
Heath Rd, Dart. 187 FF86
Heath Rd, Grays 171 GG75
Heath Rd, Har. 116 CC59
Heath Rd, Houns. 156 CB84
Heath Rd (Oxshott), Lthd. 214 CC112
Heath Rd, Pot.B. 64 DA30
Heath Rd, Rom. 126 EX59
Heath Rd, St.Alb. 43 CE19
Heath Rd, Th.Hth. 202 DQ97
Heath Rd, Twick. 177 CF88
Heath Rd, Uxb. 135 BQ70
Heath Rd, Wat. 94 BX45
Heath Rd, Wey. 212 BN106
Heath Rd, Wok. 227 AZ115
Heath Side NW3 120 DD63
Heath Side, Orp. 205 EQ102
Heath St NW3 120 DC63
Heath St, Dart. 188 FK87
Heath Vw N2 120 DC56
Heath Vw (East Horsley), Lthd. 245 BT125
Heath Vw Cl N2 120 DC56
Heath Vw Gdns, Grays 170 GC75
Heath Vw Rd, Grays 170 GC75
Heath Vil SE18 165 ET78
Heath Vil SW18 180 DC88
Cargill Rd
Heath Way, Erith 167 FC81
Heathacre (Colnbrook), Slou. 153 BE81
Park St
Heatham Pk, Twick. 177 CF87
Heathbourne Rd, Bushey 95 CE47
Heathbourne Rd, Stan. 95 CE47
Heathbridge, Wey. 212 BN108
Heathclose Av, Dart. 187 FH87
Heathclose Rd, Dart. 187 FG88
Heathcock Ct WC2 141 DL73
Strand
Heathcote, Tad. 233 CX121
Heathcote Av, Hat. 45 CU16
Heathcote Av, Ilf. 103 EM54
Heathcote Ct, Ilf. 103 EM54
Heathcote Av
Heathcote Gdns, Harl. 52 EY15
Heathcote Gro E4 101 EC48
Heathcote Pt E9 143 DX65
Wick Rd
Heathcote Rd, Epsom 216 CR114
Heathcote Rd, Twick. 177 CH86
Heathcote St WC1 274 B4
Heathcote St WC1 141 DM70
Heathcote Way, West Dr. 134 BK74
Tavistock Rd
Heathcroft NW11 120 DB60
Heathcroft W5 138 CM70
Heathcroft, Welw.G.C. 30 DC09
Heathcroft Av, Sun. 175 BT94
Heathcroft Gdns E17 101 ED53
Heathdale Av, Houns. 156 BY83
Heathdene, Tad. 233 CY119
Canons La
Heathdene Dr, Belv. 167 FB77
Heathdene Rd SW16 181 DM94
Heathdene Rd, Wall. 219 DH108
Heathdown Rd, Wok. 227 BD115
Heathedge SE26 182 DV89
Heather Av, Rom. 105 FD54
Heather Cl E6 145 EP72
Heather Cl N7 121 DM62
Newington Barrow Way
Heather Cl SE13 183 ED87
Heather Cl SW8 161 DH83
Heather Cl, Abb.L. 59 BU32
Heather Cl (New Haw), Add. 212 BH110
Heather Cl, Brwd. 108 FV43
Heather Cl, Guil. 242 AV132
Heather Cl, Hmptn. 196 BZ95
Heather Cl, Islw. 177 CD85
Harvesters Cl
Heather Cl, Red. 251 DH130
Heather Cl, Rom. 105 FD53
Heather Cl, Tad. 233 CY122
Heather Cl, Uxb. 134 BM71
Violet Av
Heather Cl, Wok. 226 AW115
Heather Dr, Dart. 187 FG87
Heather Dr, Enf. 81 DP40
Chasewood Av
Heather Dr, Rom. 105 FD54
Heather End, Swan. 207 FD98
Heather Gdns NW11 119 CY58
Heather Gdns, Rom. 105 FD54
Heather Gdns, Sutt. 218 DA107
Heather Gdns, Wal.Abb. 83 EC36
Heather Glen, Rom. 105 FD54
Heather La, Wat. 75 BT35
Heather La, West Dr. 134 BL72
Heather Pk Dr, Wem. 138 CN66
Heather Pl, Esher 214 CB105
Park Rd

Heather Ri, Bushey 76 BZ40
Heather Rd E4 101 DZ51
Heather Rd NW2 119 CT61
Heather Rd SE12 184 EG89
Heather Rd, Welw.G.C. 29 CW11
Heather Wk W10 139 CY70
Droop St
Heather Wk, Edg. 96 CP50
Heather Wk, Twick. 176 CA87
Stephenson Rd
Heather Wk, Walt. 213 BT110
Octagon Rd
Heather Way, Hem.H. 40 BK19
Heather Way, Pot.B. 63 CZ32
Heather Way, Rom. 105 FD54
Heather Way, S.Croy. 221 DX109
Heather Way, Stan. 95 CF51
Heather Way (Chobham), Wok. 210 AS108
Heatherbank SE9 165 EM82
Heatherbank, Chis. 205 EN96
Heatherbank Cl, Dart. 187 FE86
Heatherdale Cl, Kings.T. 178 CN93
Heatherden Grn, Iver 133 BC67
Heatherdene (West Horsley), Lthd. 245 BR125
Heatherdene Cl N12 98 DC53
Bow La
Heatherdene Cl, Mitch. 200 DE98
Heatherfields (New Haw), Add. 212 BH110
Heatherfold Way, Pnr. 115 BT55
Heatherlands, Horl. 269 DH147
Stockfield
Heatherlands, Sun. 175 BU93
Heatherley Dr, Ilf. 124 EL55
Heathers, The, Stai. 174 BM87
Heatherset Cl, Esher 214 CC106
Heatherset Gdns SW16 181 DM94
Heatherside Cl, Lthd. 246 BZ125
Little Bookham St
Heatherside Dr, Vir.W. 192 AU100
Heatherside Gdns (Farnham Common), Slou. 111 AR62
Heatherside Rd, Epsom 216 CR108
Heatherside Rd, Sid. 186 EX90
Wren Rd
Heathersland, Dor. 263 CJ139
Goodwyns Rd
Heatherton Pk, Amer. 55 AP36
Heatherton Ter N3 98 DB54
Heathervale Caravan Pk (New Haw), Add. 212 BJ110
Heathervale Rd (New Haw), Add. 212 BH110
Heatherwood Cl E12 124 EJ61
Heatherwood Dr, Hayes 135 BR68
Charville La
Heathfield E4 101 EC48
Heathfield, Chis. 185 EQ93
Heathfield, Cob. 214 CA114
Heathfield Av SW18 180 DD87
Heathfield Rd
Heathfield Av, S.Croy. 221 DY109
Heathfield Cl E16 144 EK71
Heathfield Cl, Kes. 222 EJ106
Heathfield Cl, Pot.B. 64 DB30
Heathfield Cl, Wat. 94 BW45
Heathfield Cl, Wok. 227 BA118
Heathfield Ct, St.Alb. 43 CE19
Avenue Rd
Heathfield Dr, Mitch. 200 DE95
Heathfield Dr, Red. 266 DE139
Heathfield Gdns NW11 119 CX58
Heathfield Gdns SW18 180 DD86
Heathfield Rd
Heathfield Gdns W4 158 CQ78
Heathfield Gdns, Croy. 220 DR105
Coombe Rd
Heathfield La, Chis. 185 EP93
Heathfield N, Twick. 177 CF87
Heathfield Pk NW2 139 CW65
Heathfield Pk Dr, Rom. 126 EV57
Heathfield Ri, Ruis. 115 BQ59
Heathfield Rd SW18 180 DC86
Heathfield Rd W3 158 CP75
Heathfield Rd, Bexh. 166 EZ84
Heathfield Rd, Brom. 184 EF94
Heathfield Rd, Bushey 76 BY42
Heathfield Rd, Croy. 220 DR105
Heathfield Rd, Kes. 222 EJ106
Heathfield Rd, Sev. 256 FF122
Heathfield Rd (Burnham), Slou. 110 AG62
Heathfield Rd, Walt. 214 BY105
Heathfield Rd, Wok. 227 BA118
Heathfield S, Twick. 177 CF87
Heathfield Sq SW18 180 DD87
Heathfield St W11 139 CY73
Portland Rd
Heathfield Ter SE18 165 ET79
Heathfield Ter W4 158 CQ78
Heathfield Vale, S.Croy. 221 DX109
Heathfields Ct, Houns. 176 BY85
Frampton Rd
Heathgate NW11 120 DB58
Heathgate, Hert. 32 DV13
Heathgate Pl NW3 120 DF64
Agincourt Rd
Heathhurst Rd, S.Croy. 220 DS109
Heathland Rd N16 122 DS60
Heathlands, Tad. 233 CX122
Heathlands Cl, Sun. 195 BU96
Heathlands Cl, Twick. 177 CF89
Heathlands Cl, Wok. 210 AY114
Heathlands Dr, St.Alb. 43 CE18
Heathlands Ri, Dart. 187 FH86
Heathlands Way, Houns. 176 BY85
Heathlee Rd SE3 164 EF84
Heathlee Rd, Dart. 187 FE86
Heathley End, Chis. 185 EQ93
Heathmans Rd SW6 159 CZ81
Heathrow (Gomshall), Guil. 261 BQ139
Heathrow Cl, West Dr. 154 BH81
Heathrow Interchange, Hayes 136 BW74
Heathrow Int Trd Est, Houns. 155 BV83
Heathrow Tunnel App (Heathrow Airport), Houns. 155 BP83
Heathrow Vehicle Tunnel (Heathrow Airport), Houns. 155 BP81
Heaths Cl, Enf. 82 DS40
Heathside, Esher 197 CE104
Heathside, Houns. 176 BZ87
Heathside, St.Alb. 43 CE18
Heathside (Colney Heath), St.Alb. 44 CP23
Heathside, Wey. 213 BP106
Heathside Av, Bexh. 166 EY81
Heathside Cl, Esher 197 CE104
Heathside Cl, Nthwd. 93 BR50
Heathside Ct, Tad. 233 CV123
Heathside Cres, Wok. 227 AZ117
Heathside Gdns, Wok. 227 BA117
Heathside Pk Rd, Wok. 227 AZ118
Heathside Pl, Epsom 233 CX118
Heathside Rd, Nthwd. 93 BR49
Heathside Rd, Wok. 227 AZ118
Heathstan Rd W12 139 CU72
Heathview Av, Dart. 187 FE86
Heathview Ct SW19 179 CX89
Heathview Cres, Dart. 187 FG88
Heathview Dr SE2 166 EX79
Heathview Gdns SW15 179 CW87
Heathview Rd, Th.Hth. 201 DN98
Heathville Rd N19 121 DL59
Heathwall St SW11 160 DF83
Heathway SE3 164 EF80
Heathway, Cat. 252 DQ125
Heathway, Croy. 203 DZ104
Heathway, Dag. 146 FA66
Heathway, Iver 133 BD68
Heathway (East Horsley), Lthd. 229 BT124
Heathway, Wdf.Grn. 102 EJ49
Heathway Ind Est, Dag. 127 FB63
Manchester Way
Heathwood Gdns SE7 164 EL77
Heathwood Gdns, Swan. 207 FC96
Heathwood Pt SE23 183 DX90
Dacres Rd
Heathwood Wk, Bex. 187 FE88
Heaton Av, Rom. 105 FH52
Heaton Cl E4 101 EC48
Heaton Cl, Rom. 106 FJ52
Heaton Ct, Wal.Cr. 67 DX29
Heaton Gra Rd, Rom. 105 FF54
Heaton Rd SE15 162 DU83
Heaton Rd, Mitch. 180 DG94
Heaton Way, Rom. 106 FJ52
Heavens Lea, B.End 110 AC61
Heaver Rd SW11 *Wye St* 160 DD83
Heavitree Cl SE18 165 ER78
Heavitree Rd SE18 165 ER78
Heayfield, Welw.G.C. 30 DC08
Hebden Ct E2 142 DT67
Laburnum St
Hebden Ter N17 100 DS51
Commercial Rd
Hebdon Rd SW17 180 DE90
Heber Rd NW2 119 CX64
Heber Rd SE22 182 DT86
Hebron Rd W6 159 CV76
Hecham Cl E17 101 DY54
Heckfield Pl SW6 160 DA80
Fulham Rd
Heckford Cl, Wat. 75 BQ44
Heckford St E1 143 DX73
The Highway
Hector St SE18 165 ES77
Heddington Gro N7 121 DM64
Heddon Cl, Islw. 157 CG84
Heddon Ct Av, Barn. 80 DF43
Heddon Rd, Barn. 80 DF43
Heddon St W1 273 K10
Heddon St W1 141 DJ73
Hedge Hill, Enf. 81 DP39
Hedge La N13 99 DP48
Hedge Lea (Wooburn Grn), H.Wyc. 110 AD55
Hedge Pl Rd, Green. 189 FT86
Hedge Row, Hem.H. 40 BG18
Hedge Wk SE6 183 EB91
Hedgebrooms, Welw.G.C. 30 DC08
Hedgeley, Ilf. 125 EM56
Hedgemans Rd, Dag. 146 EX66
Hedgemans Way, Dag. 146 EY65
Hedger St SE11 278 F8
Hedgerley Ct, Wok. 226 AW117
Hedgerley Gdns, Grnf. 136 CC68
Hedgerley Grn (Hedgerley), Slou. 112 AT58
Hedgerley Hill (Hedgerley), Slou. 111 AR62
Hedgerley La, Beac. 111 AN56
Hedgerley La, Ger.Cr. 112 AV59
Hedgerley La, Slou. 112 AS58
Hedgerow (Chalfont St. Peter), Ger.Cr. 90 AY51
Hedgerow La, Barn. 79 CV43
Hedgerow Wk, Wal.Cr. 67 DX30
Hedgerows, Saw. 36 EZ05
Hedgerows, The (Northfleet), Grav. 190 GE89
Hedgers Cl, Loug. 85 EN42
Newmans La
Hedgers Gro E9 143 DY65
Hedges, The, St.Alb. 42 CC16
Hedges Cl, Hat. 45 CV17
Hedgeside, Berk. 39 BA16
Hedgeside Rd, Nthwd. 93 BQ50
Hedgeway, Guil. 258 AU136
Hedgewood Gdns, Ilf. 125 EN57
Hedgley St SE12 184 EF85
Hedingham Cl N1 142 DQ66
Popham Rd
Hedingham Cl, Horl. 269 DJ147
Hedingham Rd, Dag. 126 EV64
Hedingham Rd, Grays 169 FW78
Hedingham Rd, Horn. 128 FN60
Hedley Av, Grays 169 FW80
Hedley Cl, Rom. 127 FE57
High St
Hedley Rd, St.Alb. 43 CH20
Hedley Rd, Twick. 176 CA87
Hedley Row N5 122 DR64
Poets Rd
Hedley Vw (Loudwater), H.Wyc. 88 AD54
Hedsor Hill, B.End 110 AC62
Hedsor La (Wooburn Grn), H.Wyc. 110 AG61
Hedsor La (Burnham), Slou. 110 AG61
Hedsor Pk, B.End 110 AE63
Hedworth Av, Wal.Cr. 67 DX33
Heenan Cl, Bark. 145 EQ65
Glenny Rd
Heene Rd, Enf. 82 DR39
Heideck Gdns, Brwd. 109 GB47
Victors Cres
Heidegger Cres SW13 159 CV79
Trinity Ch Rd
Heigham Rd E6 144 EK66
Heighams, Harl. 51 EM18
Heighton Gdns, Croy. 219 DP106
Heights, The SE7 164 EJ78
Heights, The, Beck. 183 EC94
Heights, The, Hem.H. 40 BM18
Saturn Way
Heights, The, Loug. 85 EM40
Heights, The, Nthlt. 116 BZ64
Heights, The, Wal.Abb. 68 EH25
Heights, The, Wey. 212 BN110
Heights Cl SW20 179 CV94
Heights Cl, Bans. 233 CY116
Heiron St SE17 161 DP79
Helby Rd SW4 181 DK86
Helder Gro SE12 184 EF87
Helder St, S.Croy. 220 DR107
Heldmann Cl, Houns. 157 CD84
Helegon Cl, Orp. 223 ET105
Helen Av, Felt. 175 BV87
Helen Cl N2 120 DC55
Thomas More Way
Helen Cl, Dart. 187 FH87
Helen Cl, W.Mol. 196 CB98
Helen Rd, Horn. 128 FK55
Helen St SE18 165 EP77
Wilmount St
Helena Cl, Barn. 80 DD38
Helena Cl, Wall. 219 DL108
Helena Pl E9 142 DW67
Fremont St
Helena Rd E13 144 EF68
Helena Rd E17 123 EA57
Helena Rd NW10 119 CV64
Helena Rd W5 137 CK71
Helena Rd, Wind. 151 AR82
Helena Sq SE16 143 DY73
Rotherhithe St
Helens Gate, Wal.Cr. 67 DZ26
Helen's Pl E2 142 DW69
Roman Rd
Helenslea Av NW11 119 CZ60
Helford Cl, Ruis. 115 BS61
Chichester Av
Helford Wk, Wok. 226 AU118
Helford Way, Upmin. 129 FR58
Helgiford Gdns, Sun. 175 BS94
Helions Rd, Harl. 51 EP15
Helix Gdns SW2 181 DM86
Helix Rd
Helix Rd SW2 181 DM86
Helleborine, Grays 170 FZ78
Hellings St E1 142 DU74
Wapping High St
Hellyer Way, B.End 110 AC60
Helm Cl, Epsom 216 CN112
Helme Cl SW19 179 CZ92
Helmet Row EC1 275 J4
Helmet Row EC1 142 DQ70
Helmore Rd, Bark. 145 ET66
Helmsdale, Wok. 226 AV118
Winnington Way
Helmsdale Cl, Hayes 136 BY70
Helmsdale Cl, Rom. 105 FE52
Helmsdale Rd SW16 201 DJ95
Helmsdale Rd, Rom. 105 FE52
Helmsley Pl E8 142 DV66
Helsinki Sq SE16 163 DY76
Helston Cl, Pnr. 94 BZ52
Helston Gro, Hem.H. 40 BK16
Helston La, Wind. 151 AN81
Helston Pl, Abb.L. 59 BT32
Shirley Rd
Helvellyn Cl, Egh. 173 BB94
Helvetia St SE6 183 DZ89
Hemans St SW8 161 DK80
Hemberton Rd SW9 161 DL83
Hemel Hempstead Ind Est, Hem.H. 41 BP17
Hemel Hempstead Rd, Hem.H. 41 BR22
Hemel Hempstead Rd, St.Alb. 42 CA21
Hemel Hempstead Rd (Redbourn), St.Alb. 41 BQ15
Hemery Rd, Grnf. 117 CD64
Heming Rd, Edg. 96 CP52
Hemingford Cl N12 98 DD50
Hemingford Rd N1 141 DM67
Hemingford Rd, Sutt. 217 CW105
Hemingford Rd, Wat. 75 BS36
Hemington Av N11 98 DF50
Hemlock Cl (Kingswood), Tad. 233 CY123
Hemlock Rd W12 139 CT73
Hemmen La, Hayes 135 BT72
Hemming Cl, Hmptn. 196 CA95
Chandler Cl
Hemming St E1 142 DU70
Hemming Way, Slou. 131 AP69
Hemming Way, Wat. 75 BU35
Hemmings, The, Berk. 38 AT20
Hemmings Cl, Sid. 186 EV89
Hemnall St, Epp. 69 ET31
Hemp Wk SE17 279 L8
Hemp Wk SE17 162 DR77
Hempshaw Av, Bans. 234 DF116
Hempson Av, Slou. 152 AW76
Hempstall, Welw.G.C. 30 DB11
Linces Way
Hempstead Cl, Buck.H. 102 EG47
Hempstead La, Berk. 39 BC17
Hempstead Rd E17 101 ED54
Hempstead Rd, Hem.H. 57 BA27
Hempstead Rd, Kings L. 58 BM26
Hempstead Rd, Wat. 75 BT39
Hemsby Rd, Chess. 216 CM107
Hemstal Rd NW6 140 DA66
Hemsted Rd, Erith 167 FE80
Hemswell Dr NW9 96 CS53
Hemsworth Ct N1 142 DS68
Hemsworth St
Hemsworth St N1 142 DS68
Hemus Pl SW3 160 DE78
Chelsea Manor St
Hemwood Rd, Wind. 151 AK83
Hen & Chicken Ct EC4 141 DN72
Fleet St
Henbane Path, Rom. 106 FK52
Clematis Cl
Henbit Cl, Tad. 233 CV119
Henbury Way, Wat. 94 BX48
Henchley Dene, Guil. 243 BD131
Henchman St W12 139 CT72
Hencroft St N, Slou. 152 AT75
Hencroft St S, Slou. 152 AT76
Hendale Av NW4 119 CU55
Henderson Av, Guil. 242 AV129
Henderson Cl NW10 138 CQ65
Henderson Cl, Horn. 127 FH61
Henderson Cl, St.Alb. 42 CC16
Henderson Dr NW8 140 DD70
Cunningham Pl
Henderson Dr, Dart. 168 FM84
Henderson Pl, Abb.L. 59 BT27
Henderson Rd E7 144 EJ65
Henderson Rd N9 100 DV46
Henderson Rd SW18 180 DE87
Henderson Rd, Croy. 202 DR100
Henderson Rd, Hayes 135 BU69
Henderson Rd (Biggin Hill), West. 222 EJ112
Hendham Rd SW17 180 DE89
Hendon Av N3 97 CY53
Hendon Gdns, Rom. 105 FC51
Hendon Hall Ct NW4 119 CX55
Parson St
Hendon La N3 119 CY55
Hendon Pk Row NW11 119 CZ58
Hendon Rd N9 100 DU47
Hendon Way NW2 119 CZ62
Hendon Way NW4 119 CV58
Hendon Way (Stanwell), Stai. 174 BK86
Hendon Wd La NW7 79 CT44
Hendre Rd SE1 279 N9
Hendren Cl, Grnf. 117 CD64
Dimmock Dr
Hendrick Av SW12 180 DF87
Heneage Cres (New Addington), Croy. 221 EC110
Heneage La EC3 275 N9
Heneage St E1 142 DT71
Henfield Cl N19 121 DJ60
Henfield Cl, Bex. 186 FA86
Henfield Rd SW19 199 CZ95
Henfold La, Dor. 264 CL144
Hengelo Gdns, Mitch. 200 DD98
Hengist Rd SE12 184 EH87
Hengist Rd, Erith 167 FB80
Hengist Way, Brom. 204 EE98
Hengrave Rd SE23 183 DX87
Hengrove Ct, Bex. 186 EY88
Hurst Rd
Hengrove Cres, Ashf. 174 BK90
Henhurst Rd (Cobham), Grav. 191 GK94
Henley Av, Sutt. 199 CY104
Henley Bk, Guil. 258 AU136
Henley Cl, Grnf. 136 CC68
Henley Cl, Islw. 157 CF81
Henley Ct N14 99 DJ45
Henley Ct, Wok. 227 BB120
Henley Cross SE3 164 EH83
Henley Deane (Northfleet), Grav. 190 GE91
Henley Dr SE1 162 DT77
Henley Dr, Kings.T. 179 CT94
Henley Gdns, Pnr. 115 BV55
Henley Gdns, Rom. 126 EY57
Henley Rd E16 165 EM75
Henley Rd N18 100 DS49
Henley Rd NW10 139 CW67
Henley Rd, Ilf. 125 EQ63
Henley Rd, Slou. 131 AL72
Henley St SW11 160 DG82
Henley Way, Felt. 176 BX92
Henlow Pl, Rich. 177 CK89
Sandpits Rd
Hennel Cl SE23 182 DW90
Hennessy Ct, Wok. 211 BC113
Henniker Gdns E6 144 EK69
Henniker Ms SW3 160 DD79
Callow St
Henniker Pt E15 124 EE64
Henniker Rd E15 123 ED64
Henning St SW11 160 DE81
Henningham Rd N17 100 DR53
Henrietta Cl SE8 163 EA79
Henrietta Ms WC1 274 A4
Henrietta Pl W1 273 H9
Henrietta Pl W1 141 DH72
Henrietta St E15 123 EC64
Henrietta St WC2 274 A10
Henrietta St WC2 141 DL73
Henriques St E1 142 DU72
Henry Addlington Cl E6 145 EN71
Henry Cl, Enf. 82 DS38
Henry Cooper Way SE9 184 EK90
Henry Darlot Dr NW7 97 CX50
Henry De Gray Cl, Grays 170 FZ77
Henry Dickens Ct W11 139 CX74
Henry Doulton Dr SW17 181 DH91
Henry Jackson Rd SW15 159 CX83
Henry Macaulay Av, Kings.T. 197 CK95
Henry Rd E6 144 EL68
Henry Rd N4 122 DQ60
Henry Rd, Barn. 80 DD43
Henry Rd, Slou. 151 AR75
Henry St, Brom. 204 EH95
Henry St, Grays 170 GC79
East Thurrock Rd
Henry St, Hem.H. 40 BK24
Henry Wells Sq, Hem.H. 40 BL16
Aycliffe Dr
Henry's Av, Wdf.Grn. 102 EF50
Henry's Wk, Ilf. 103 ER52
Henryson Rd SE4 183 EA85
Hensford Gdns SE26 182 DV91
Wells Pk Rd
Henshall St N1 142 DR65
Henshaw St SE17 279 K8
Henshaw St SE17 162 DR77
Henshawe Rd, Dag. 126 EX62
Henshill Pt E3 143 EB69
Bromley High St
Hensley Pt E9 143 DX65
Wick Rd
Henslow Way, Wok. 211 BD114
Henslowe Rd SE22 182 DU85
Henson Av NW2 119 CW64
Henson Cl, Orp. 205 EP103
Henson Path, Har. 117 CK55
Henson Pl, Nthlt. 136 BW67
Henstridge Pl NW8 140 DE68
Hensworth Rd, Ashf. 174 BK93
Henty Cl SW11 160 DE80
Henty Wk SW15 179 CV85
Henville Rd, Brom. 204 EH95
Henwick Rd SE9 164 EK83
Henwood Side, Wdf.Grn. 103 EM51
Love La
Hepburn Cl (Chafford Hundred), Grays 169 FW77
Hepburn Gdns, Brom. 204 EE102
Hepburn Ms SW11 180 DF85
Webbs Rd
Hepple Cl, Islw. 157 CH82
Hepplestone Cl SW15 179 CV86
Dover Pk Dr
Hepscott Rd E9 143 EA66
Hepworth Ct, Bark. 126 EU64
Hepworth Gdns, Bark. 126 EU64
Hepworth Rd SW16 181 DL94
Hepworth Wk NW3 120 DE64
Haverstock Hill
Hepworth Way, Walt. 195 BT102
Heracles Cl, Wall. 219 DL108
Herald Gdns, Wall. 201 DH104
Herald St E2 *Three Colts La* 142 DV70
Herald Wk, Dart. 188 FM85
Temple Hill Sq
Herald's Ct SE11 278 F9
Herald's Pl SE11 278 E8
Herbal Hill EC1 274 E5
Herbal Hill EC1 141 DN70
Herbert Cres SW1 276 E6
Herbert Cres (Knaphill), Wok. 226 AS117
Herbert Gdns NW10 139 CV68
Herbert Gdns W4 158 CP79
Magnolia Rd
Herbert Gdns, Rom. 126 EX59
Herbert Gdns, St.Alb. 60 CB29
Herbert Ms SW2 181 DN86
Bascombe St
Herbert Morrison Ho SW6 159 CZ79
Clem Attlee Ct
Herbert Pl SE18 165 EP79
Plumstead Common Rd
Herbert Rd E12 124 EL63
Herbert Rd E17 123 DZ59
Herbert Rd N11 99 DL52
Herbert Rd N15 122 DT57
Herbert Rd NW9 119 CU58
Herbert Rd SE18 165 EN80
Herbert Rd SW19 179 CZ94
Herbert Rd, Bexh. 166 EY82
Herbert Rd, Brom. 204 EK99
Herbert Rd, Horn. 128 FL59
Herbert Rd, Ilf. 125 ES61
Herbert Rd, Kings.T. 198 CM97
Herbert Rd, Sthl. 136 BZ74
Herbert Rd, Swan. 187 FH93
Herbert Rd, Swans. 190 FZ86
Herbert St E13 144 EG68
Herbert St NW5 140 DG65
Herbert St, Hem.H. 40 BK19
St. Mary's Rd
Herbert Ter SE18 165 EP79
Herbert Rd
Herbrand St WC1 273 P4
Herbrand St WC1 141 DL70
Hercies Rd, Uxb. 134 BM66
Hercules Pl N7 121 DL62
Hercules St
Hercules Rd SE1 278 C7
Hercules Rd SE1 161 DM76
Hercules St N7 121 DL62
Hereford Av, Barn. 98 DF46
Hereford Cl, Epsom 216 CR113
Hereford Cl, Guil. 242 AT132
Hereford Cl, Stai. 194 BH95
Hereford Copse, Wok. 226 AV119
Hereford Ct, Sutt. 218 DA108
Worcester Rd
Hereford Gdns SE13 184 EE85
Longhurst Rd
Hereford Gdns, Ilf. 124 EL59
Hereford Gdns, Pnr. 116 BY57
Hereford Gdns, Twick. 176 CC88
Hereford Ho NW6 140 DA68
Hereford Ms W2 140 DA72
Hereford Rd
Hereford Pl SE14 163 DZ80
Hereford Retreat SE15 162 DU80
Bird in Bush Rd
Hereford Rd E11 124 EH57
Hereford Rd W2 140 DA72
Hereford Rd W3 138 CP73
Hereford Rd W5 157 CJ76
Hereford Rd, Felt. 176 BW88
Hereford Sq SW7 160 DC77
Hereford St E2 142 DU70
Hereford Way, Chess. 215 CJ106
Herent Dr, Ilf. 125 EM55
Hereward Av, Pur. 219 DN111
Hereward Cl, Wal.Abb. 67 ED32
Hereward Gdns N13 99 DN50
Hereward Grn, Loug. 85 EQ39
Hereward Rd SW17 180 DF91
Herga Ct, Har. 117 CE62
Herga Ct, Wat. 75 BU40
Herga Rd, Har. 117 CF56
Herington Gro, Brwd. 109 GA45
Heriot Av E4 101 EA47
Heriot Rd NW4 119 CW57
Heriot Rd, Cher. 194 BG101
Heriots Cl, Stan. 95 CG49
Heritage Cl SW9 161 DP83
Heritage Cl, Uxb. 134 BJ70
Heritage Hill, Kes. 222 EJ106
Heritage Lawn, Horl. 269 DJ147
Heritage Pl SW18 180 DC88
Earlsfield Rd
Heritage Vw, Har. 117 CF62
Heritage Wk, Rick. 73 BE41
Chenies Rd
Herkomer Cl, Bushey 76 CB44
Herkomer Rd, Bushey 76 CA43
Herlwyn Av, Ruis. 115 BS62
Herlwyn Gdns SW17 180 DF91
Herm Ho, Enf. 83 DX38
Eastfield Rd
Hermes Cl W9 140 DA70
Chippenham Rd
Hermes St N1 274 D1
Hermes Wk, Nthlt. 136 CA68
Hotspur Rd
Hermes Way, Wall. 219 DK108
Hermiston Av N8 121 DL57
Hermit Pl NW6 140 DB67
Belsize Rd
Hermit Rd E16 144 EF71
Hermit St EC1 274 F2
Hermit St EC1 141 DP69
Hermitage, The SE23 182 DW88
Hermitage, The SW13 159 CT81
Hermitage, The, Felt. 175 BT90
Hermitage, The, Rich. 177 CK85
Hermitage, The, Uxb. 134 BL65
Hermitage Cl E18 124 EF56
Hermitage Cl, Enf. 81 DP40
Hermitage Cl (Claygate), Esher 215 CG107
Hermitage Cl, Shep. 194 BN98
Hermitage Cl, Slou. 152 AW76
Hermitage Ct E18 124 EG56
Hermitage Ct NW2 120 DA62
Hermitage La
Hermitage Ct, Pot.B. 64 DC33
Southgate Rd
Hermitage Gdns NW2 120 DA62
Hermitage Gdns SE19 182 DQ93
Hermitage La N18 100 DR50
Hermitage La NW2 120 DA62
Hermitage La SE25 202 DU100
Hermitage La SW16 181 DM94
Hermitage La, Croy. 202 DU100
Hermitage La, Wind. 151 AN83
Hermitage Path SW16 201 DL95
Hermitage Rd N4 121 DP59
Hermitage Rd N15 121 DP59
Hermitage Rd SE19 182 DQ94
Hermitage Rd, Ken. 236 DQ116
Hermitage Rd, Wok. 226 AT119
Hermitage Row E8 122 DU64
Hermitage St W2 140 DD71
Hermitage Wk E18 124 EF56
Hermitage Wall E1 142 DU74
Hermitage Way, Stan. 95 CG53
Hermitage Wds Cres, Wok. 226 AS119
Hermon Gro, Hayes 135 BU74
Hermon Hill E11 124 EG57
Hermon Hill E18 124 EG57
Herndon Cl, Egh. 173 BA91

Herndon Rd SW18 180 DC85
Herne Cl NW10 118 CR64
North Circular Rd
Herne Hill SE24 182 DQ86
Herne Hill Ho SE24 181 DP86
Railton Rd
Herne Hill Rd SE24 162 DQ83
Herne Ms N18 100 DU49
Lyndhurst Rd
Herne Pl SE24 181 DP85
Herne Rd, Bushey 76 CB44
Herne Rd, Surb. 197 CK103
Herneshaw, Hat. 45 CT20
Hazel Gro
Herns La, Welw.G.C. 30 DB09
Herns Way, Welw.G.C. 30 DA07
Heron Cl E17 101 DZ54
Heron Cl NW10 138 CS65
Heron Cl, Buck.H. 102 EG46
Heron Cl, Guil. 242 AV131
Heron Cl, Rick. 92 BK47
Heron Cl, Saw. 36 EX06
Heron Cl, Sutt. 217 CZ106
Sandpiper Rd
Heron Cl, Uxb. 134 BK65
Heron Ct, Brom. 204 EJ98
Heron Cres, Sid. 185 ES90
Heron Dale, Add. 212 BK106
Heron Dr N4 122 DQ61
Heron Dr, Slou. 153 BB77
Heron Dr, Ware 33 EC12
Heron Flight Av, Horn. 147 FG66
Heron Hill, Belv. 166 EZ77
Heron Ms, Ilf. 125 EP61
Balfour Rd
Heron Pl SE16 143 DY74
Heron Quay E14 143 EA74
Heron Rd SE24 162 DQ84
Heron Rd, Croy. 202 DS103
Tunstall Rd
Heron Rd, Twick. 157 CG84
Heron Sq, Rich. 177 CK85
Bridge St
Heron Trd Est W3 138 CP70
Alliance Rd
Heron Wk, Nthwd. 93 BS49
Heron Wk, Wok. 211 BC114
Blackmore Cres
Heron Way, Felt. 155 BU84
The Causeway
Heron Way, Grays 169 FV78
Heron Way, Harl. 34 EG14
Roydon Mill Pk
Heron Way, Hat. 45 CU19
Heron Way, Upmin. 129 FS60
Herondale, S.Croy. 221 DX109
Herondale Av SW18 180 DD88
Heronfield (Englefield Grn), Egh. 172 AV93
Heronfield, Pot.B. 64 DC30
Herongate Rd E12 124 EJ61
Herongate Rd, Swan. 187 FE93
Herongate Rd (Cheshunt), Wal.Cr. 67 DY27
Heronry, The, Walt. 213 BU107
Herons, The E11 124 EF58
Herons Cft, Wey. 213 BR107
Herons Elm, Berk. 38 AS16
Heron's Pl, Islw. 157 CH83
Herons Ri, Barn. 80 DE42
Herons Way, St.Alb. 43 CG24
Herons Wd, Harl. 35 EP13
Herons Wd Ct, Horl. 269 DH147
Tanyard Way
Heronsforde W13 137 CJ72
Heronsgate, Edg. 96 CN50
Heronsgate Rd, Rick. 73 BB44
Heronslea, Wat. 76 BW36
Heronslea Dr, Stan. 96 CL50
Heronswood, Wal.Abb. 68 EE34
Roundhills
Heronswood Pl, Welw.G.C. 30 DA10
Heronswood Rd, Welw.G.C. 30 DA09
Heronway, Brwd. 109 GA46
Heronway, Wdf.Grn. 102 EJ49
Herrick Rd N5 122 DQ62
Herrick St SW1 277 N8
Herrick St SW1 161 DK77
Herries St W10 139 CY68
Herringham Rd SE7 164 EJ76
Herrings La, Cher. 194 BG100
Herrongate Cl, Enf. 82 DT40
Hersant Cl NW10 139 CU67
Herschel Pk Dr, Slou. 152 AT75
Herschel St, Slou. 152 AT75
Herschell Rd SE23 183 DY87
Hersham Bypass, Walt. 213 BV106
Hersham Cl SW15 179 CU87
Hersham Gdns, Walt. 214 BW105
Hersham Rd, Walt. 214 BW105
Hertford Av SW14 178 CS85
Hertford Cl, Barn. 80 DD41
Hertford Pl W1 273 K5
Hertford Rd N1 142 DS67
Hertford Rd N2 120 DE55
Hertford Rd N9 100 DV47
Hertford Rd, Bark. 145 EP66
Hertford Rd, Barn. 80 DC41
Hertford Rd, Enf. 82 DW41
Hertford Rd, Hat. 45 CW16
Hertford Rd, Hert. 30 DB06
Hertford Rd (Hertford Heath), Hert. 32 DW13
Hertford Rd (Marden Hill), Hert. 30 DG06
Hertford Rd, Hodd. 49 DY15
Hertford Rd, Ilf. 125 ES58
Hertford Rd, Wal.Cr. 83 DX36
Hertford Rd, Ware 32 DW07
Hertford Rd (Great Amwell), Ware 33 DZ11
Hertford Rd, Welw. 30 DB06
Hertford Rd (Tewin), Welw. 30 DE05
Hertford Sq, Mitch. 201 DL98
Hertford Way
Hertford St W1 277 H2
Hertford St W1 141 DH74
Hertford Wk, Belv. 166 FA78
Hoddesdon Rd
Hertford Way, Mitch. 201 DL98
Hertingfordbury Rd, Hert. 31 DL11
Hertslet Rd N7 121 DM62
Hertsmere Rd E14 143 EA73
Hervey Cl N3 98 DA53
Hervey Pk Rd E17 123 DY56
Hervey Rd SE3 164 EH81
Hervines Ct, Amer. 55 AQ37
Hervines Rd, Amer. 55 AP37
Hesa Rd, Hayes 135 BU72
Hesewall Cl SW4 161 DJ82
Brayburne Av
Hesiers Hill, Warl. 238 EE117
Hesiers Rd, Warl. 238 EE117
Hesketh Av, Dart. 188 FP88
Hesketh Pl W11 139 CY73
Hesketh Rd E7 124 EG62
Heslop Rd SW12 180 DF88
Hesper Ms SW5 160 DB78
Hesperus Cres E14 163 EB77
Hessel Rd W13 157 CG75
Hessel St E1 142 DV72
Hesselyn Dr, Rain. 147 FH66
Hessle Gro, Epsom 217 CT111
Hester Rd N18 100 DU50
Hester Rd SW11 160 DE80
Hester Ter, Rich. 158 CN83
Chilton Rd
Hestercombe Av SW6 159 CY82
Hesterman Way, Croy. 201 DM102
Heston Av, Houns. 156 BY80
Heston Gra La, Houns. 156 BZ79
Heston Ind Mall, Houns. 156 BZ80
Heston Rd, Houns. 156 CA80
Heston Rd, Red. 266 DF138
Heston St SE14 163 DZ81
Heston Wk, Red. 266 DF138
Heswell Grn, Wat. 93 BU48
Fairhaven Cres
Hetchleys, Hem.H. 40 BG17
Hetherington Cl, Slou. 131 AM69
Hetherington Rd SW4 161 DL84
Hetherington Rd, Shep. 195 BQ96
Hetherington Way, Uxb. 114 BL63
Hethersett Cl, Reig. 250 DC131
Hetley Gdns SE19 182 DT94
Fox Hill
Hetley Rd W12 139 CV74
Heton Gdns NW4 119 CU56
Heusden Way, Ger.Cr. 113 AZ60
Hevelius Cl SE10 164 EF78
Hever Ct Rd, Grav. 191 GK93
Hever Cft SE9 185 EN91
Hever Gdns, Brom. 205 EN97
Heverham Rd SE18 165 ES77
Hevers Av, Horl. 268 DF147
Heversham Rd, Bexh. 166 FA82
Hewens Rd, Hayes 135 BQ70
Hewens Rd, Uxb. 135 BQ70
Hewer St W10 139 CX71
Hewers Way, Tad. 233 CV120
Hewett Cl, Stan. 95 CH49
Hewett Pl, Swan. 207 FD98
Hewett Rd, Dag. 126 EX63
Hewett St EC2 275 N5
Hewins Cl, Wal.Abb. 68 EE33
Broomstick Hall Rd
Hewish Rd N18 100 DS49
Hewison St E3 143 DZ68
Hewitt Av N22 99 DP54
Hewitt Cl, Croy. 203 EA104
Hewitt Rd N8 121 DN57
Hewitts Rd, Orp. 224 EZ108
Hewlett Rd E3 143 DY68
Hexagon, The N6 120 DF60
Hexal Rd SE6 184 EE90
Hexham Gdns, Islw. 157 CG80
Hexham Rd SE27 182 DQ89
Hexham Rd, Barn. 80 DB42
Hexham Rd, Mord. 200 DB102
Hextalls La (Bletchingley), Red. 252 DR128
Heybourne Rd N17 100 DV52
Heybridge Av SW16 181 DL94
Heybridge Ct, Hert. 31 DM08
The Ridgeway
Heybridge Dr, Ilf. 125 ER55
Heybridge Way E10 123 DY59
Heydons Cl, St.Alb. 43 CD18
Heyford Av SW8 161 DL80
Heyford Av SW20 199 CZ97
Heyford Rd, Mitch. 200 DE96
Heyford Rd, Rad. 77 CF37
Heyford Ter SW8 161 DL80
Heyford Av
Heyford Way, Hat. 45 CW16
Heygate St SE17 279 H9
Heygate St SE17 162 DQ77
Heylyn Sq E3 143 DZ69
Malmesbury Rd
Heymede, Lthd. 231 CJ123
Heynes Rd, Dag. 126 EW63
Heysham Dr, Wat. 94 BW50
Heysham La NW3 120 DB62
Heysham Rd N15 122 DR58
Heythorp Cl, Wok. 226 AT117
Heythorp St SW18 179 CZ88
Heythrop Dr (Ickenham), Uxb. 114 BM63
Heywood Av NW9 96 CS53
Heyworth Rd E5 122 DV63
Heyworth Rd E15 124 EF64
Hibbert Av, Wat. 76 BX38
Hibbert Lo, Ger.Cr. 90 AX54
Gold Hill E
Hibbert Rd E17 123 DZ59
Hibbert Rd, Har. 95 CF54
Hibbert St SW11 160 DD83
Hibberts All, Wind. 151 AR81
Bachelors Acre
Hibberts Way, Ger.Cr. 112 AY56
North Pk
Hibbs Cl, Swan. 207 FD96
Hibernia Dr, Grav. 191 GM90
Hibernia Gdns, Houns. 156 CA84
Hibernia Pt SE2 166 EX75
Wolvercote Rd
Hibernia Rd, Houns. 156 CA84
Hibiscus Cl, Edg. 96 CQ49
Campion Way
Hichisson Rd SE15 182 DW85
Hickin Cl SE7 164 EK77
Hickin St E14 *Plevna St* 163 EC76
Hickling Rd, Ilf. 125 EP64
Hickman Av E4 101 EC51
Hickman Cl E16 144 EK71
Hickman Cl, Brox. 49 DX20
Hickman Rd, Rom. 126 EW59
Hickmans Cl, Gdse. 252 DW132
Hickmore Wk SW4 161 DJ83
Hickory Cl N9 100 DU45
Hicks Av, Grnf. 137 CD69
Hicks Cl SW11 160 DE83
Hicks St SE8 163 DY78
Hidalgo Ct, Hem.H. 40 BM18
Hidcote Cl, Wok. 227 BB116
Hidcote Gdns SW20 199 CV97
Hide E6 145 EN72
Downings
Hide Pl SW1 277 M9
Hide Pl SW1 161 DK77
Hide Rd, Har. 117 CD56
Hide Twr SW1 277 M9
Hide Twr SW1 161 DK77
Hideaway, The, Abb.L. 59 BU31
Hides, The, Harl. 35 ER14
Hides St N7 141 DM65
Sheringham Rd
Higgins Rd (Cheshunt), Wal.Cr. 66 DR26
Higgins Wk, Hmptn. 176 BY93
Abbott Cl
High, The, Harl. 51 ER15
High Acres, Abb.L. 59 BR32
High Acres, Enf. 81 DP41
Old Pk Vw
High Barn Rd, Dor. 246 BX133
High Barn Rd (Effingham), Lthd. 246 BX129
High Beech, S.Croy. 220 DS108
High Beech Rd, Loug. 84 EK42
High Beeches, Bans. 217 CX114
High Beeches, Ger.Cr. 112 AX60
High Beeches, Orp. 224 EU107
High Beeches, Sid. 186 EY92
High Beeches Cl, Pur. 219 DK110
High Bois La, Amer. 55 AR35
High Br SE10 163 ED78
High Br Wf SE10 163 ED78
High Broom Cres, W.Wick. 203 EB101
High Canons, Borwd. 78 CQ37
High Cedar Dr SW20 179 CV94
High Clandon (East Clandon), Guil. 244 BL133
High Cl, Rick. 74 BJ43
High Coombe Pl, Kings.T. 178 CR93
High Coppice, Amer. 55 AQ39
High Cross, Wat. 77 CD37
High Cross Cen N15 122 DU56
High Cross Rd N17 122 DU55
High Dells, Hat. 45 CT19
High Dr (Woldingham), Cat. 237 DZ122
High Dr (Oxshott), Lthd. 215 CD114
High Dr, N.Mal. 198 CQ95
High Elms, Chig. 103 ES49
High Elms, Upmin. 129 FS60
High Elms, Wdf.Grn. 102 EG50
High Elms Cl, Nthwd. 93 BR51
High Elms La, Wat. 59 BV31
High Elms Rd, Orp. 223 EP110
High Firs, Rad. 77 CF35
High Firs, Swan. 207 FE98
High Foleys (Claygate), Esher 215 CH108
High Gables, Loug. 84 EK43
High Garth, Esher 214 CC107
High Gro SE18 165 ER80
High Gro, Brom. 204 EJ95
High Gro, St.Alb. 43 CD18
High Gro, Welw.G.C. 29 CW08
High Hill Est E5 122 DV60
Mount Pleasant La
High Hill Ferry E5 122 DV60
High Hill Rd, Warl. 237 EC115
High Holborn WC1 274 A8
High Holborn WC1 141 DL72
High Ho La, Til. 171 GJ75
High La W7 137 CD72
High La (Sheering), B.Stort. 37 FE09
High La, Cat. 237 DZ119
High La, Warl. 237 DZ118
High Lawns, Har. 117 CE62
High Level Dr SE26 182 DU91
High Mead, Chig. 103 EQ47
High Mead, Har. 117 CE57
High Mead, W.Wick. 203 ED103
High Meadow Cl, Dor. 263 CH137
High Meadow Cl, Pnr. 115 BV56
Daymer Gdns
High Meadow Cres NW9 118 CR57
High Meadow Pl, Cher. 193 BF100
High Meadows, Chig. 103 ER50
High Meads Rd E16 144 EK72
High Mt NW4 119 CU58
High Oak Rd, Ware 33 DX05
High Oaks, Enf. 81 DM38
High Oaks, St.Alb. 42 CC15
High Oaks Rd, Welw.G.C. 29 CV08
High Pk Av (East Horsley), Lthd. 245 BT126
High Pk Av, Rich. 158 CN81
High Pk Rd, Rich. 158 CN81
High Pastures (Sheering), B.Stort. 37 FD06
High Path SW19 200 DB95
High Path Rd, Guil. 243 BC134
High Pewley, Guil. 258 AY136
High Pine Cl, Wey. 213 BQ106
High Pines, Warl. 236 DW119
High Pt N6 120 DG59
High Pt SE9 185 EP90
High Pt, Wey. 212 BN106
High Ridge (Cuffley), Pot.B. 65 DL27
High Ridge Cl, Hem.H. 58 BK25
High Ridge Rd, Hem.H. 58 BK25
High Rd N2 98 DD54
High Rd N11 99 DH50
High Rd N12 98 DC51
High Rd N15 122 DT58
High Rd N17 100 DT53
High Rd N20 98 DC45
High Rd N22 121 DN55
High Rd (Willesden) NW10 139 CT65
High Rd, Brox. 49 DZ20
High Rd, Buck.H. 102 EH47
High Rd, Bushey 95 CD46
High Rd, Chig. 103 EM50
High Rd, Couls. 234 DF121
High Rd (Wilmington), Dart. 188 FJ90
High Rd, Epp. 69 ER32
High Rd (North Weald Bassett), Epp. 71 FB27
High Rd (Thornwood), Epp. 70 EV28
High Rd (Harrow Weald), Har. 95 CE52
High Rd, Hat. 46 DE17
High Rd, Ilf. 125 EP62
High Rd (Seven Kings), Ilf. 125 ET60
High Rd, Loug. 102 EJ45
High Rd, Pnr. 115 BV56
High Rd, Reig. 250 DD126
High Rd (Chadwell Heath), Rom. 126 EV60
High Rd, Uxb. 134 BJ71
High Rd, Wat. 75 BT35
High Rd, Wem. 117 CK64
High Rd (Byfleet), W.Byf. 212 BM112
High Rd Ickenham, Uxb. 115 BP62
High Rd Leyton E10 123 EB60
High Rd Leyton E15 123 EC62
High Rd Leytonstone E11 124 EE63
High Rd Leytonstone E15 124 EE63
High Rd Turnford, Brox. 67 DY25
High Rd Woodford Grn E18 102 EG54
High Rd Woodford Grn, Wdf.Grn. 102 EF52
High Rd Wormley (Turnford), Brox. 49 DY24
High Silver, Loug. 84 EK42
High Standing, Cat. 252 DQ125
High St E11 124 EG57
High St E13 144 EG68
High St E15 143 EC68
High St E17 123 DZ57
High St N8 121 DL56
High St N14 99 DK46
High St NW7 97 CV49
High St (Harlesden) NW10 139 CT68
High St SE20 182 DV93
High St (South Norwood) SE25 202 DT98
High St W3 138 CP74
High St W5 137 CK73
High St, Abb.L. 58 BN29
High St (Bedmond), Abb.L. 59 BS31
High St, Add. 212 BH105
High St, Amer. 55 AM38
High St, Bans. 234 DA115
High St, Barn. 79 CY41
High St, Beck. 203 EA95
High St, Berk. 38 AW19
High St (Elstree), Borwd. 77 CK44
High St, Brent. 157 CK79
High St, Brwd. 108 FW47
High St, Brom. 204 EG96
High St, Bushey 76 CA44
High St, Cars. 218 DG105
High St, Cat. 236 DS123
High St, Ch.St.G. 90 AW48
High St, Chesh. 54 AQ31
High St, Chis. 185 EP93
High St, Cob. 213 BV114
High St, Croy. 202 DQ103
High St, Dart. 188 FL86
High St (Bean), Dart. 189 FV90
High St (Eynsford), Dart. 208 FL103
High St (Farningham), Dart. 208 FM100
High St, Dor. 263 CH136
High St, Edg. 96 CN51
High St, Egh. 173 BA92
High St (Ponders End), Enf. 82 DW42
High St, Epp. 69 ET31
High St, Epsom 216 CR113
High St (Ewell), Epsom 217 CT110
High St, Esher 214 CB105
High St (Claygate), Esher 215 CF107
High St, Felt. 175 BU90
High St (Chalfont St. Peter), Ger.Cr. 90 AY53
High St, Gdse. 252 DV131
High St, Grav. 191 GH86
High St (Northfleet), Grav. 190 GB86
High St, Grays 170 GA79
High St, Green. 169 FV84
High St, Guil. 258 AX135
High St, Hmptn. 176 CC93
High St, Harl. 36 EW11
High St (Roydon), Harl. 34 EH14
High St, Har. 117 CE60
High St (Wealdstone), Har. 117 CE55
High St, Hayes 155 BS78
High St, Hem.H. 40 BJ18
High St (Bovingdon), Hem.H. 57 BA27
High St, Hodd. 49 EA19
High St, Horl. 269 DH148
High St, Horn. 128 FK60
High St, Houns. 156 CC83
High St (Cranford), Houns. 155 BU81
High St (Barkingside), Ilf. 103 EQ54
High St, Iver 133 BE72
High St, Kings L. 59 BT27
High St, Kings.T. 197 CK96
High St (Hampton Wick), Kings.T. 197 CJ95
High St, Lthd. 231 CH122
High St (Great Bookham), Lthd. 246 CB125
High St (Oxshott), Lthd. 215 CD113
High St (Bray), Maid. 150 AC75
High St (Taplow), Maid. 130 AE70
High St, N.Mal. 198 CS97
High St, Nthwd. 93 BT53
High St, Orp. 206 EU102
High St (Downe), Orp. 223 EN111
High St (Farnborough), Orp. 223 EP106
High St (Green St Grn), Orp. 223 ET108
High St (St. Mary Cray), Orp. 206 EW98
High St, Oxt. 253 ED130
High St (Limpsfield), Oxt. 254 EG128
High St, Pnr. 116 BY55
High St, Pot.B. 64 DC33
High St, Purf. 168 FN78
London Rd Purfleet
High St, Pur. 219 DN111
High St, Red. 250 DF134
High St (Bletchingley), Red. 252 DQ133
High St (Merstham), Red. 251 DH128
High St (Nutfield), Red. 251 DM133
High St, Reig. 250 DA134
High St, Rick. 92 BK46
High St, Rom. 127 FE57
High St, Ruis. 115 BS59
High St, St.Alb. 43 CD20
High St (Colney Heath), St.Alb. 44 CP22
High St (London Colney), St.Alb. 61 CJ25
High St, Sev. 257 FJ125
High St (Chipstead), Sev. 256 FC122
High St (Kemsing), Sev. 257 FL121
High St (Otford), Sev. 241 FF116
High St (Seal), Sev. 257 FL121
High St (Shoreham), Sev. 225 FF110
High St, Shep. 195 BP100
High St, Slou. 152 AU75
High St (Burnham), Slou. 130 AJ69
High St (Chalvey), Slou. 151 AQ76
High St (Colnbrook), Slou. 153 BC80
High St (Datchet), Slou. 152 AV81
High St (Langley), Slou. 153 AZ78
High St, S.Ock. 149 FR74
High St, Sthl. 136 BZ74
High St, Stai. 173 BF91
High St (Stanwell), Stai. 174 BK86
High St (Wraysbury), Stai. 172 AY86
High St, Sutt. 218 DB105
High St (Cheam), Sutt. 217 CY107
High St, Swan. 207 FF98
High St, Swans. 190 FZ85
High St, Tad. 233 CW123
High St, Tedd. 177 CG92
High St, T.Ditt. 197 CG101
High St, Th.Hth. 202 DQ98
High St (Whitton), Twick. 176 CC87
High St, Uxb. 134 BK67
High St (Cowley), Uxb. 134 BJ70
High St (Harefield), Uxb. 92 BJ54
High St, Wal.Cr. 67 DY34
High St (Cheshunt), Wal.Cr. 67 DX29
High St, Walt. 195 BU102
High St, Ware 33 DX06
High St (Hunsdon), Ware 34 EK06
High St (Stanstead Abbotts), Ware 33 EC11
High St, Wat. 75 BV42
High St, Wem. 118 CM63
High St (Harmondsworth), West Dr. 154 BK79
High St (Yiewsley), West Dr. 134 BK74
High St, W.Mol. 196 CA98
High St, W.Wick. 203 EB102
High St, West. 255 EQ127
High St (Brasted), West. 240 EV124
High St, Wey. 212 BN105
High St, Wind. 151 AR81
High St (Eton), Wind. 151 AR79
High St, Wok. 226 AY117
High St (Chobham), Wok. 210 AS111
High St (Horsell), Wok. 226 AV115
High St (Old Woking), Wok. 227 BB121
High St (Ripley), Wok. 228 BJ121
High St Colliers Wd SW19 180 DD94
High St Grn, Hem.H. 40 BN18
High St Ms SW19 179 CY92
High St N E6 144 EL67
High St N E12 124 EL64
High St S E6 145 EM68
High St Wimbledon SW19 179 CX92
High Timber St EC4 275 H10
High Timber St EC4 142 DQ73
High Tor Cl, Brom. 184 EH94
Babbacombe Rd
High Tree Cl, Add. 211 BF106
High Tree Cl, Saw. 36 EX06
High Tree Ct W7 137 CE73
High Trees SW2 181 DN88
High Trees, Barn. 80 DE43
High Trees, Croy. 203 DY102
High Trees Cl, Cat. 236 DT123
High Trees Ct, Brwd. 108 FW49
Warley Mt
High Trees Rd, Reig. 266 DD135
High Vw, Ch.St.G. 90 AX47
High Vw (Gomshall), Guil. 261 BQ139
High Vw, Hat. 45 CT20
High Vw, Pnr. 116 BW56
High Vw, Rick. 74 BG42
High Vw, Sutt. 217 CZ111
High Vw, Wat. 75 BT44
High Vw Av, Grays 170 GC78
High Vw Caravan Pk, Kings L. 59 BR28
High Vw Cl SE19 202 DT96
High Vw Cl, Loug. 84 EJ43
High Vw Gdns, Grays 170 GC78
High Vw Rd E18 124 EF55
High Vw Rd, Guil. 258 AS137
High Wickfield, Welw.G.C. 30 DC10
Amwell Common
High Wd Rd, Hodd. 49 DZ15
High Worple, Har. 116 BZ59
High Wych La, Saw. 36 EU05
High Wych Rd, Saw. 36 EV06
Higham Hill Rd E17 101 DY54
Higham Mead, Chesh. 54 AQ30
Higham Pl E17 123 DY55
Higham Rd N17 122 DR55
Higham Rd, Chesh. 54 AP30
Higham Rd, Wdf.Grn. 102 EG51
Higham Sta Av E4 101 EB51
Higham St E17 123 DY55
Higham Vw, Epp. 71 FB26
Highams Ct E4 101 ED48
Friars Cl
Highams Lo Business Cen E17 123 DY55
Highams Pk Ind Est E4 101 EC51
Highbank Way N8 121 DN58
Highbanks Cl, Well. 166 EV80
Highbanks Rd, Pnr. 94 CB50
Highbarns, Hem.H. 58 BN25
Highbarrow Rd, Croy. 202 DU101
Highbridge Ind Est, Uxb. 134 BJ66
Highbridge Rd, Bark. 145 EP67
Highbridge St, Wal.Abb. 67 EA33
Highbrook Rd SE3 164 EK83
Highbury Av, Hodd. 49 EA15
Highbury Av, Th.Hth. 201 DN96
Highbury Cl, N.Mal. 198 CQ98
Highbury Cl, W.Wick. 203 EB103
Highbury Cor N5 141 DN65
Highbury Cres N5 121 DN64
Highbury Est N5 122 DQ64
Highbury Gdns, Ilf. 125 ES61
Highbury Gra N5 121 DP63
Highbury Gro N5 141 DP65
Highbury Hill N5 121 DN62
Highbury Ms N7 141 DN65
Holloway Rd
Highbury New Pk N5 122 DQ64
Highbury Pk N5 121 DP62
Highbury Pk Ms N5 122 DQ63
Highbury Gra
Highbury Pl N5 141 DP65
Highbury Quad N5 122 DQ62
Highbury Rd SW19 179 CY92
Highbury Sta Rd N1 141 DN65
Highbury Ter N5 121 DP64
Highbury Ter Ms N5 121 DP64
Highclere, Guil. 243 BA132
Highclere Cl, Ken. 236 DQ115
Highclere Ct, St.Alb. 43 CE19
Avenue Rd
Highclere Dr, Hem.H. 41 BP24
Highclere Rd, N.Mal. 198 CR97
Highclere St SE26 183 DY91
Highcliffe Dr SW15 179 CT86
Highcliffe Gdns, Ilf. 124 EL57
Highcombe SE7 164 EH79
Highcombe Cl SE9 184 EK88
Highcotts La, Guil. 243 BF126
Highcotts La (Send Marsh), Wok. 243 BF125
Highcroft NW9 118 CR57
Highcroft Av, Wem. 138 CN67
Highcroft Ct (Bookham), Lthd. 230 CA123
Highcroft Gdns NW11 119 CZ58
Highcroft Rd N19 121 DL59
Highcroft Rd (Felden), Hem.H. 58 BG25
Highcross Rd (Southfleet), Grav. 189 FX92
Highcross Way SW15 179 CU88
Highdaun Dr SW16 201 DM98
Highdown, Wor.Pk. 199 CT103
Highdown La, Sutt. 218 DB111
Highdown Rd SW15 179 CV86
Higher Dr, Bans. 217 CX112
Higher Dr, Lthd. 245 BS127
Higher Dr, Pur. 219 DN113
Higher Grn, Epsom 217 CU113
Highfield, Bans. 234 DE117
Highfield, Ch.St.G. 90 AX47
Highfield, Felt. 175 BU88
Highfield (Shalford), Guil. 258 AY142
Highfield, Harl. 52 EU16
Highfield, Kings L. 58 BL28
Highfield, Wat. 94 BZ48

Highfield Av NW9 118 CQ57
Highfield Av NW11 119 CX59
Highfield Av, Erith 167 FB79
Highfield Av, Grnf. 117 CE64
Highfield Av, Orp. 223 ET106
Highfield Av, Pnr. 116 BZ57
Highfield Av, Wem. 118 CM62
Highfield Cl N22 99 DN53
Highfield Cl NW9 118 CQ57
Highfield Cl SE13 183 ED87
Highfield Cl, Amer. 55 AR37
Highfield Cl (Englefield Grn), Egh. 172 AW93
Highfield Cl (Oxshott), Lthd. 215 CD111
Highfield Cl, Nthwd. 93 BS53
Highfield Cl, Rom. 105 FC51
Highfield Cl, Surb. 197 CJ102
Highfield Cl, W.Byf. 212 BG113
Highfield Ct N14 81 DJ44
Highfield Cres, Horn. 128 FM61
Highfield Cres, Nthwd. 93 BS53
Highfield Dr, Brom. 204 EE98
Highfield Dr, Brox. 49 DY21
Highfield Dr, Cat. 236 DU122
Highfield Dr, Epsom 217 CT108
Highfield Dr (Ickenham), Uxb. 114 BL63
Highfield Dr, W.Wick. 203 EB103
Highfield Gdns NW11 119 CY58
Highfield Gdns, Grays 170 GD75
Highfield Grn, Epp. 69 ES31
Highfield Hill SE19 182 DR94
Highfield La, Hem.H. 40 BM18
Highfield La (Tyttenhanger), St.Alb. 44 CL23
Highfield Link, Rom. 105 FC51
Highfield Pk Dr, St.Alb. 43 CH23
Highfield Pl, Epp. 69 ES31
Highfield Rd N21 99 DP47
Highfield Rd NW11 119 CY58
Highfield Rd W3 138 CP71
Highfield Rd, Berk. 38 AX20
Highfield Rd, Bexh. 186 EZ85
Highfield Rd, Brom. 205 EM98
Highfield Rd, Bushey 76 BY43
Highfield Rd, Cat. 236 DU122
Highfield Rd, Cher. 194 BG102
Highfield Rd, Chesh. 54 AP29
Highfield Rd, Chis. 205 ET97
Highfield Rd, Dart. 188 FK87
Highfield Rd, Felt. 175 BU89
Highfield Rd, Hert. 32 DR11
Highfield Rd, Horn. 128 FM61
Highfield Rd, Islw. 157 CF81
Highfield Rd, Nthwd. 93 BS53
Highfield Rd, Pur. 219 DM110
Highfield Rd, Rom. 105 FC52
Highfield Rd, Sun. 195 BT98
Highfield Rd, Surb. 198 CQ101
Highfield Rd, Sutt. 218 DE106
Highfield Rd (Cheshunt), Wal.Cr. 66 DS26
Highfield Rd, Walt. 195 BU102
Highfield Rd, W.Byf. 212 BG113
Highfield Rd (Biggin Hill), West. 238 EJ117
Highfield Rd, Wind. 151 AM83
Highfield Rd, Wdf.Grn. 102 EL52
Highfield Rd S, Dart. 188 FK87
Highfield Twr, Rom. 105 FD50
Highfield Way, Horn. 128 FM61
Highfield Way, Pot.B. 64 DB32
Highfield Way, Rick. 74 BH44
Highfields, Ash. 231 CK119
Highfields (East Horsley), Lthd. 245 BS128
Highfields (Fetcham), Lthd. 231 CD124
Highfields (Cuffley), Pot.B. 65 DL28
Highfields, Rad. 77 CF35
Highfields Gro N6 120 DF60
Highgate Av N6 121 DH58
Highgate Cl N6 120 DG59
Highgate Gro, Saw. 36 EX05
Highgate High St N6 120 DG60
Highgate Hill N6 121 DH60
Highgate Hill N19 121 DH60
Highgate Rd NW5 121 DH63
Highgate Wk SE23 182 DW89
Highgate W Hill N6 120 DG61
Highgrove, Brwd. 108 FV44
Highgrove Cl N11 98 DG50
Balmoral Av
Highgrove Cl, Chis. 204 EL95
Highgrove Ms, Cars. 200 DF104
Highgrove Ms, Grays 170 GC78
Highgrove Rd, Dag. 126 EW64
Highgrove Way, Ruis. 115 BU58
Highland Av W7 137 CE72
Highland Av, Brwd. 108 FW46
Highland Av, Dag. 127 FC62
Highland Av, Loug. 84 EL44
Highland Cotts, Wall. 219 DH105
Highland Ct E18 102 EH53
Highland Cft, Beck. 183 EB92
Highland Dr, Bushey 94 CC45
Highland Dr, Hem.H. 41 BP20
Highland Pk, Felt. 175 BT91
Highland Rd SE19 182 DS93
Highland Rd, Amer. 55 AR39
Highland Rd, Bexh. 186 FA85
Highland Rd, Brom. 204 EF95
Highland Rd, Nthwd. 93 BT54
Highland Rd, Pur. 219 DN114
Highland Rd (Badgers Mt), Sev. 225 FB111
Highland Rd, Wal.Abb. 50 EE22
Highlands, Ash. 231 CJ119
Highlands, Hat. 45 CW15
Highlands (Farnham Common), Slou. 111 AP64
Highlands, Wat. 94 BW46
Highlands, The, Edg. 96 CP54
Highlands, The (East Horsley), Lthd. 245 BS125
Highlands, The, Pot.B. 80 DB43
Highlands, The, Rick. 92 BH45
Highlands Av N21 81 DM43
Highlands Av W3 138 CQ73
Highlands Av, Lthd. 231 CJ122
Highlands Cl N4 121 DL59
Mount Vw Rd
Highlands Cl (Chalfont St. Peter), Ger.Cr. 91 AZ52
Highlands Cl, Houns. 156 CB81
Highlands Cl, Lthd. 231 CH122
Highlands End (Chalfont St. Peter), Ger.Cr. 90 AY52
Highlands Gdns, Ilf. 125 EM60
Highlands Heath SW15 179 CW87
Highlands Hill, Swan. 207 FG96
Highlands La (Chalfont St. Peter), Ger.Cr. 91 AZ51
Highlands La, Wok. 226 AY122
Highlands Pk, Lthd. 231 CK123
Highlands Pk (Seal), Sev. 257 FL121
Highlands Rd, Barn. 80 DA43
Highlands Rd (Seer Grn), Beac. 89 AQ50
Highlands Rd, Lthd. 231 CH122
Highlands Rd, Orp. 206 EV101
Highlands Rd, Reig. 250 DD133
Highlea Cl NW9 96 CS53
Highlever Rd W10 139 CW71
Highmead SE18 165 ET80
Highmead Cres, Wem. 138 CM66
Highmoor, Amer. 55 AR39
Highmore Rd SE3 164 EE79
Highover Pk, Amer. 55 AR40
Highridge Cl, Epsom 232 CS115
Highridge La, Bet. 264 CP140
Highshore Rd SE15 162 DT82
Highstead Cres, Erith 167 FE81
Highstone Av E11 124 EG58
Highview, Cat. 236 DS124
Highview, Nthlt. 136 BY69
Highview (Knaphill), Wok. 226 AS117
Mulgrave Way
Highview Av, Edg. 96 CQ49
Highview Av, Wall. 219 DM106
Highview Cl, Pot.B. 64 DC33
Highview Cres, Brwd. 109 GC44
Highview Gdns N3 119 CY55
Highview Gdns N11 99 DJ50
Highview Gdns, Edg. 96 CQ49
Highview Gdns, Pot.B. 64 DC33
Highview Gdns, St.Alb. 43 CJ15
Highview Gdns, Upmin. 128 FP61
Highview Ho, Rom. 126 EY56
Highview Path, Bans. 234 DA115
Highview Rd SE19 182 DR93
Highview Rd W13 137 CG71
Highview Rd, Sid. 186 EV91
Highway, The E1 142 DV73
Highway, The E14 142 DV73
Highway, The, Beac. 89 AK52
Station Rd
Highway, The, Orp. 224 EW106
Highway, The, Stan. 95 CF53
Highway, The, Sutt. 218 DC109
Highway Ct, Beac. 89 AK52
Station Rd
Highwold, Couls. 234 DG118
Highwood, Brom. 204 EE97
Highwood Av N12 98 DC49
Highwood Av, Bushey 76 BZ39
Highwood Cl, Brwd. 108 FV45
Highwood Cl, Ken. 236 DQ117
Highwood Cl, Orp. 205 EQ103
Highwood Dr, Orp. 205 EQ103
Highwood Gdns, Ilf. 125 EM57
Highwood Gro NW7 96 CR50
Highwood Hall La, Hem.H. 59 BQ25
Highwood Hill NW7 97 CT48
Highwood La, Loug. 85 EN43
Highwood Rd N19 121 DL62
Highwoods, Cat. 252 DS125
Highwoods, Lthd. 231 CJ121
Highworth Rd N11 99 DK51
Hilary Av, Mitch. 200 DG97
Hilary Cl SW6 160 DB80
Hilary Cl, Erith 167 FC81
Hilary Cl, Horn. 128 FK64
Hilary Rd W12 139 CT72
Hilary Rd, Slou. 152 AY76
Hilbert Rd, Sutt. 199 CX104
Hilborough Way, Orp. 223 ER106
Hilbury Cl, Amer. 55 AQ35
Hilda May Av, Swan. 207 FE97
Hilda Rd E6 144 EK66
Hilda Rd E16 144 EE70
Hilda Ter SW9 161 DN82
Hilda Vale Cl, Orp. 223 EP105
Hilda Vale Rd, Orp. 223 EN105
Hilden Dr, Erith 167 FH80
Hildenborough Gdns, Brom. 184 EE93
Hildenlea Pl, Brom. 204 EE96
Hildenley Cl, Red. 251 DK128
Malmstone Av
Hildens, The (Westcott), Dor. 262 CB138
Hilders, The, Ash. 232 CP117
Hildreth St SW12 181 DH88
Hildyard Rd SW6 160 DA79
Hiley Rd NW10 139 CW69
Hilfield La, Wat. 77 CD41
Hilfield La S, Bushey 77 CF44
Hilgay, Guil. 243 AZ134
Hilgay Cl, Guil. 243 AZ134
Hilgrove Rd NW6 140 DC66
Hiliary Gdns, Stan. 95 CJ54
Hiljon Cres (Chalfont St. Peter), Ger.Cr. 90 AY53
Hill, The, Cat. 236 DT124
Hill, The (Northfleet), Grav. 190 GC86
Hill, The, Harl. 36 EW11
Hill Av, Amer. 55 AQ38
Hill Barn, S.Croy. 220 DS111
Hill Brow, Brom. 204 EK95
Hill Brow, Dart. 187 FF86
Hill Cl NW2 119 CV62
Hill Cl NW11 120 DA58
Hill Cl, Barn. 79 CW43
Hill Cl, Chis. 185 EP92
Hill Cl, Cob. 214 CA112
Hill Cl (Istead Ri), Grav. 190 GE94
Hill Cl, Har. 117 CE62
Hill Cl (Wooburn Grn), H.Wyc. 110 AF56
Hill Cl, Pur. 220 DQ113
Hill Cl, Stan. 95 CH49
Hill Cl, Wok. 226 AX115
Hill Common, Hem.H. 40 BN24
Hill Ct, Gdmg. 258 AS144
Hill Ct, Nthlt. 116 CA64
Hill Cres N20 98 DB47
Hill Cres, Bex. 187 FC88
Hill Cres, Har. 117 CG57
Hill Cres, Horn. 128 FJ58
Hill Cres, Surb. 198 CM99
Hill Cres, Wor.Pk. 199 CW103
Hill Crest, Pot.B. 64 DC34
Hill Crest, Sev. 256 FG122
Hill Crest, Sid. 186 EU87
Hill Dr NW9 118 CQ60
Hill Dr SW16 201 DM97
Hill End, Orp. 205 ET103
The App
Hill End La, St.Alb. 43 CJ23
Hill End Rd (Harefield), Uxb. 92 BH51
Hill Fm App (Wooburn Grn), H.Wyc. 110 AE55
Hill Fm Av, Wat. 59 BU33
Hill Fm Cl, Wat. 59 BU33
Hill Fm Ind Est, Wat. 59 BT33
Hill Fm La, Ch.St.G. 90 AT46
Hill Fm Rd W10 139 CW71
Hill Fm Rd, Chesh. 54 AR34
Hill Fm Rd (Chalfont St. Peter), Ger.Cr. 90 AY52
Hill Fm Rd, Maid. 130 AE68
Hill Fm Rd, Uxb. 115 BR63
Austin's La
Hill Gro, Felt. 176 BZ89
Watermill Way
Hill Gro, Rom. 127 FE55
Hill Hall, Epp. 86 EZ35
Hill Ho Av, Stan. 95 CF52
Hill Ho Cl N21 99 DN45
Hill Ho Cl (Chalfont St. Peter), Ger.Cr. 90 AY52
Rickmansworth La
Hill Ho Dr, Hmptn. 196 CA95
Hill Ho Dr, Wey. 212 BN111
Hill Ho Rd SW16 181 DM92
Hill La, Ruis. 115 BQ60
Hill La (Kingswood), Tad. 233 CY121
Hill Ley, Hat. 45 CT18
Hill Leys (Cuffley), Pot.B. 65 DL28
Hill Meadow (Coleshill), Amer. 55 AM43
Hill Pk Dr, Lthd. 231 CF119
Hill Path SW16 181 DM92
Valley Rd
Hill Pl (Farnham Common), Slou. 131 AP66
Hill Ri N9 82 DV44
Hill Ri NW11 120 DB56
Hill Ri SE23 182 DV88
London Rd
Hill Ri (Lane End), Dart. 189 FR92
Hill Ri, Dor. 247 CG134
Hill Ri, Esher 197 CH103
Hill Ri (Chalfont St. Peter), Ger.Cr. 90 AX54
Hill Ri, Grnf. 136 CC66
Hill Ri, Pot.B. 64 DC34
Hill Ri (Cuffley), Pot.B. 65 DK27
Hill Ri, Rich. 177 CK85
Hill Ri, Rick. 74 BH44
Hill Ri, Ruis. 115 BQ60
Hill Ri, Slou. 153 BA79
Hill Ri, Upmin. 128 FN61
Hill Ri Cres (Chalfont St. Peter), Ger.Cr. 90 AY54
Hill Rd N10 98 DF53
Hill Rd NW8 140 DC68
Hill Rd, Brwd. 108 FU48
Hill Rd, Cars. 218 DE107
Hill Rd, Dart. 188 FL89
Hill Rd, Epp. 85 ES37
Hill Rd, Har. 117 CG57
Hill Rd (Fetcham), Lthd. 230 CB122
Hill Rd, Mitch. 201 DH95
Hill Rd, Nthwd. 93 BR51
Hill Rd, Pnr. 116 BY57
Hill Rd, Pur. 219 DM112
Hill Rd, Sutt. 218 DB106
Hill Rd, Wem. 117 CH62
Hill St W1 276 G2
Hill St W1 141 DH74
Hill St, Rich. 177 CK85
Hill St, St.Alb. 42 CC20
Hill Top NW11 120 DB56
Hill Top, Loug. 85 EN40
Hill Top, Mord. 200 DA100
Hill Top, Sutt. 199 CZ101
Hill Top Cl, Loug. 85 EN41
Hill Top Pl, Loug. 85 EN41
Hill Top Vw, Wdf.Grn. 103 EM51
Hill Vw, Berk. 38 AU17
Hill Vw Cl, Tad. 233 CW121
Shelvers Way
Hill Vw Cres, Orp. 205 ET102
Hill Vw Dr, Well. 165 ES82
Hill Vw Gdns NW9 118 CR57
Hill Vw Rd (Claygate), Esher 215 CG108
Hill Vw Rd, Orp. 205 ET102
Hill Vw Rd (Wraysbury), Stai. 172 AX86
Hill Vw Rd, Twick. 177 CG86
Hill Vw Rd, Wok. 227 AZ118
Hill Waye, Ger.Cr. 113 AZ58
Hillars Heath Rd, Couls. 235 DL115
Hillary Av (Northfleet), Grav. 190 GE90
Hillary Cres, Walt. 196 BW102
Hillary Dr, Islw. 157 CF84
Hillary Ri, Barn. 80 DA42
Hillary Rd, Hem.H. 40 BN19
Hillary Rd, Sthl. 156 CA76
Hillbeck Cl SE15 162 DW80
Hillbeck Way, Grnf. 137 CD67
Hillborne Cl, Hayes 155 BU78
Hillborough Av, Sev. 257 FK122
Hillborough Cl SW19 180 DC94
Hillbrook Gdns, Wey. 212 BN108
Hillbrook Rd SW17 180 DF90
Hillbrow, N.Mal. 199 CT97
Hillbrow Cl, Bex. 187 FD91
Hillbrow Cotts, Gdse. 252 DW132
Hillbrow Ct, Gdse. 252 DW132
Hillbrow Rd, Brom. 184 EE94
Hillbrow Rd, Esher 214 CC105
Hillbury, Hat. 45 CT19
Hillbury Av, Har. 117 CH57
Hillbury Cl, Warl. 236 DV118
Hillbury Gdns, Warl. 236 DW118
Hillbury Rd SW17 181 DH90
Hillbury Rd, Warl. 236 DU117
Hillbury Rd, Whyt. 236 DU117
Hillcote Av SW16 181 DN94
Hillcourt Av N12 98 DB51
Hillcourt Est N16 122 DR60
Hillcourt Rd SE22 182 DV86
Hillcrest N6 120 DG59
Hillcrest N21 99 DP45
Hillcrest, Hat. 45 CU18
Hillcrest, St.Alb. 42 CB22
Hillcrest, Wey. 213 BP105
Hillcrest Av NW11 119 CY57
Hillcrest Av, Cher. 211 BE105
Hillcrest Av, Edg. 96 CP49
Hillcrest Av, Grays 169 FU79
Hillcrest Av, Pnr. 116 BX56
Hillcrest Cl SE26 182 DU91
Hillcrest Cl, Beck. 203 DZ99
Hillcrest Cl, Epsom 233 CT115
Hillcrest Ct, Sutt. 218 DD107
Eaton Rd
Hillcrest Dr, Green. 189 FV85
Riverview Rd
Hillcrest Gdns N3 119 CY56
Hillcrest Gdns NW2 119 CU62
Hillcrest Gdns, Esher 197 CF104
Hillcrest Par, Couls. 219 DH114
Hillcrest Rd E17 101 ED54
Hillcrest Rd E18 102 EF54
Hillcrest Rd W3 138 CN74
Hillcrest Rd W5 138 CL71
Hillcrest Rd, Brom. 184 EG92
Hillcrest Rd, Dart. 187 FF87
Hillcrest Rd, Guil. 242 AT133
Hillcrest Rd, Horn. 127 FG59
Hillcrest Rd, Loug. 84 EK44
Hillcrest Rd, Ong. 71 FE30
Hillcrest Rd, Orp. 206 EU103
Hillcrest Rd, Pur. 219 DM110
Hillcrest Rd, Rad. 62 CN33
Hillcrest Rd (Biggin Hill), West. 238 EK116
Hillcrest Rd, Whyt. 236 DT117
Hillcrest Vw, Beck. 203 DZ100
Hillcrest Way, Epp. 70 EU31
Hillcrest Waye, Ger.Cr. 113 AZ59
Hillcroft, Loug. 85 EN40
Hillcroft Av, Pnr. 116 BZ58
Hillcroft Av, Pur. 219 DJ113
Hillcroft Cres W5 138 CL72
Hillcroft Cres, Ruis. 116 BX62
Hillcroft Cres, Wat. 93 BV46
Hillcroft Cres, Wem. 118 CM63
Hillcroft Rd E6 145 EP71
Hillcroft Rd, Chesh. 54 AR29
Hillcroft Rd (Penn), H.Wyc. 88 AC46
Hillcroome Rd, Sutt. 218 DD107
Hillcross Av, Mord. 199 CZ99
Hilldale Rd, Sutt. 217 CZ105
Hilldeane Rd, Pur. 219 DN109
Hilldene Av, Rom. 106 FJ51
Hilldene Cl, Rom. 106 FK50
Hilldown Rd SW16 181 DL94
Hilldown Rd, Brom. 204 EE102
Hilldown Rd, Hem.H. 40 BG18
Hilldrop Cres N7 121 DK64
Hilldrop Est N7 121 DK64
Hilldrop La N7 121 DK64
Hilldrop Rd N7 121 DK64
Hilldrop Rd, Brom. 184 EG93
Hillend SE18 165 EN81
Hillersdon, Slou. 132 AV71
Hillersdon Av SW13 159 CU82
Hillersdon Av, Edg. 96 CM50
Hillery Cl SE17 279 L9
Hilley Fld La (Fetcham), Lthd. 230 CC122
Hillfield, Hat. 45 CV15
Hillfield Av N8 121 DL57
Hillfield Av NW9 118 CS57
Hillfield Av, Wem. 138 CL66
Hillfield Cl, Guil. 243 BC132
Hillfield Cl, Har. 116 CC56
Hillfield Cl, Red. 250 DG134
Hillfield Ct NW3 120 DE64
Hillfield Ct, Hem.H. 40 BL20
Hillfield Par, Mord. 200 DE100
Hillfield Pk N10 121 DH56
Hillfield Pk N21 99 DN47
Hillfield Pk Ms N10 121 DH56
Hillfield Rd NW6 119 CZ64
Hillfield Rd (Chalfont St. Peter), Ger.Cr. 90 AY52
Hillfield Rd, Hmptn. 176 BZ94
Hillfield Rd, Hem.H. 40 BK20
Hillfield Rd, Red. 250 DG134
Hillfield Rd (Dunton Grn), Sev. 241 FE120
Hillfield Sq (Chalfont St. Peter), Ger.Cr. 90 AY52
Hillfoot Av, Rom. 105 FC53
Hillfoot Rd, Rom. 105 FC53
Hillford Pl, Red. 266 DG140
Hillgate Pl SW12 181 DH87
Hillgate Pl W8 140 DA74
Hillgate St W8 140 DA74
Hillgrove (Chalfont St. Peter), Ger.Cr. 91 AZ53
Hillgrove Business Pk, Wal.Abb. 49 EC22
Hillhouse, Wal.Abb. 68 EF33
Hillhouse Dr, Reig. 266 DB136
Hillhouse Rd, Dart. 188 FQ87
Hillhurst Gdns, Cat. 236 DS120
Hilliard Rd, Nthwd. 93 BT53
Hilliards Ct E1 142 DV74
Wapping High St
Hilliards Rd, Uxb. 134 BK72
Hillier Cl, Barn. 80 DB44
Hillier Gdns, Croy. 219 DN106
Crowley Cres
Hillier Pl, Chess. 215 CJ107
Hillier Rd SW11 180 DF86
Hillier Rd, Guil. 243 BA134
Hilliers Av, Uxb. 134 BN69
Harlington Rd
Hilliers La, Croy. 201 DL104
Hillingdale (Biggin Hill), West. 238 EH118
Hillingdon Av, Sev. 257 FJ121
Hillingdon Av, Stai. 174 BL88
Hillingdon Hill, Uxb. 134 BL69
Hillingdon Ri, Sev. 257 FK122
Hillingdon Rd, Bexh. 167 FC82
Hillingdon Rd, Grav. 191 GG89
Hillingdon Rd, Uxb. 134 BL67
Hillingdon Rd, Wat. 59 BU34
Hillingdon St SE5 161 DP79
Hillingdon St SE17 161 DP79
Hillington Gdns, Wdf.Grn. 102 EK54
Hillman Cl, Horn. 128 FK55
Hillman Cl, Uxb. 114 BL64
Hillman Dr W10 139 CW70
Hillman St E8 142 DV65
Hillmarton Rd N7 121 DL64
Hillmead, Berk. 38 AU20
Hillmead Ct, Maid. 130 AF71
Hillmead Dr SW9 161 DP84
Hillmont Rd, Esher 197 CE104
Hillmore Gro SE26 183 DX92
Hillmount, Wok. 226 AY119
Constitution Hill
Hillpoint, Rick. 74 BJ43
Hillreach SE18 165 EM78
Hillrise, Walt. 195 BT101
Hillrise Av, Wat. 76 BX38
Hillrise Rd N19 121 DL59
Hillrise Rd, Rom. 105 FC51
Hills Chace, Brwd. 108 FW49
Hills La, Nthwd. 93 BS53
Hills Ms W5 138 CL73
Hills Pl W1 273 K9
Hills Rd, Buck.H. 102 EH46
Hillsborough Grn, Wat. 93 BU48
Ashburnham Dr
Hillsborough Rd SE22 182 DS85
Hillsgrove, Well. 166 EW80
Hillside NW9 118 CR56
Hillside NW10 138 CQ67
Hillside SW19 179 CX93
Hillside, Bans. 233 CY115
Hillside, Barn. 80 DC43
Hillside, Chesh. 54 AN28
Hillside (Farningham), Dart. 208 FM101
Hillside (Lane End), Dart. 189 FS92
Hillside, Erith 167 FD77
Hillside, Grays 170 GD77
Hillside, Harl. 52 EW17
Hillside, Hat. 45 CU18
Hillside, Hodd. 49 DZ16
Hillside, Slou. 152 AS75
Hillside (Harefield), Uxb. 114 BJ57
Hillside, Vir.W. 192 AW100
Hillside, Ware 32 DW07
Hillside, Welw.G.C. 30 DB12
Hillside, Wok. 226 AX120
Hillside, The, Orp. 224 EV109
Hillside Av N11 98 DF51
Hillside Av, Borwd. 78 CP42
Hillside Av, Grav. 191 GK89
Hillside Av, Pur. 219 DP113
Hillside Av (Cheshunt), Wal.Cr. 67 DX31
Hillside Av, Wem. 118 CM63
Hillside Av, Wdf.Grn. 102 EJ50
Hillside Cl NW8 140 DB68
Hillside Cl, Abb.L. 59 BS32
Hillside Cl, Bans. 233 CY116
Hillside Cl (Brockham), Bet. 264 CN135
Hillside Cl, Ch.St.G. 90 AV48
Hillside Cl (Chalfont St. Peter), Ger.Cr. 90 AY51
Hillside Cl, Mord. 199 CY98
Hillside Cl, Wdf.Grn. 102 EJ50
Hillside Ct, St.Alb. 43 CE19
Hillside Rd
Hillside Ct, Swan. 207 FG98
Hillside Cres, Enf. 82 DR38
Hillside Cres, Har. 116 CC60
Hillside Cres, Nthwd. 93 BU53
Hillside Cres (Cheshunt), Wal.Cr. 67 DX31
Hillside Cres, Ware 33 EB11
Hillside Cres, Wat. 76 BY44
Hillside Dr, Edg. 96 CN51
Hillside Dr, Grav. 191 GK89
Hillside Est N15 122 DT58
Hillside Gdns E17 123 ED55
Hillside Gdns N6 120 DG58
Hillside Gdns SW2 181 DN89
Hillside Gdns, Add. 211 BF107
Hillside Gdns, Barn. 79 CY42
Hillside Gdns, Berk. 38 AX20
Hillside Gdns (Brockham), Bet. 248 CN134
Hillside Gdns, Edg. 96 CM49
Hillside Gdns, Har. 118 CL59
Hillside Gdns, Nthwd. 93 BU52
Hillside Gdns, Wall. 219 DJ108
Hillside Gate, St.Alb. 43 CE19
Hillside Gro N14 99 DK45
Hillside Gro NW7 97 CU52
Hillside La, Brom. 204 EG103
Hillside La, Ware 33 EA10
Hillside Pas SW2 181 DM89
Hillside Ri, Nthwd. 93 BU52
Hillside Rd N15 122 DS59
Hillside Rd SW2 181 DN89
Hillside Rd W5 138 CL71
Hillside Rd, Ash. 232 CM117
Hillside Rd, Brom. 204 EF97
Hillside Rd, Bushey 76 BY43
Hillside Rd, Couls. 235 DM118
Hillside Rd, Croy. 219 DP106
Hillside Rd, Dart. 187 FG86
Hillside Rd, Epsom 217 CW110
Hillside Rd, Nthwd. 93 BU52
Hillside Rd, Pnr. 93 BV52
Hillside Rd, Rad. 77 CH35
Hillside Rd, Rick. 73 BC43
Hillside Rd, St.Alb. 43 CE19
Hillside Rd, Sev. 257 FK123
Hillside Rd, Sthl. 136 CA70
Hillside Rd, Surb. 198 CM99
Hillside Rd, Sutt. 217 CZ108
Hillside Rd (Tatsfield), West. 238 EL119
Hillside Rd, Whyt. 236 DU118
Hillside Ter, Hert. 32 DQ11
Hillside Wk, Brwd. 108 FU48
Hillsleigh Rd W8 139 CZ74
Hillsmead Way, S.Croy. 220 DU113
Hillspur Cl, Guil. 242 AT133
Hillspur Rd, Guil. 242 AT133
Hillstowe St E5 122 DW61
Hilltop Cl, Guil. 242 AT130
Hilltop Cl, Lthd. 231 CJ123
Hilltop Cl (Cheshunt), Wal.Cr. 66 DT26
Hilltop Gdns NW4 97 CV54
Hilltop Gdns, Dart. 188 FM85
Hilltop Gdns, Orp. 205 ES103
Hilltop La, Cat. 251 DN126
Hilltop La, Red. 251 DN126
Hilltop Ri (Bookham), Lthd. 246 CC126
Hilltop Rd NW6 140 DA66
Hilltop Rd, Berk. 38 AW20
Hilltop Rd, Grays 169 FV79
Hilltop Rd, Kings L. 59 BR27
Hilltop Rd, Reig. 266 DB136
Hilltop Rd, Whyt. 236 DS117
Hilltop Wk, Cat. 237 DY120
Hilltop Way, Stan. 95 CG48
Hillview SW20 179 CV94
Hillview, Mitch. 201 DL98
Hillview Av, Har. 118 CL57
Hillview Av, Horn. 128 FJ58
Hillview Cl, Pnr. 94 BZ51
Hillview Cl, Pur. 219 DP111
Hillview Ct, Wok. 227 AZ118
Hillview Cres, Guil. 242 AT132
Hillview Cres, Ilf. 125 EM58
Hillview Dr, Red. 266 DG135
Philanthropic Rd
Hillview Gdns NW4 119 CX56
Hillview Gdns, Har. 116 CA55
Hillview Gdns (Cheshunt), Wal.Cr. 67 DX27
Hillview Rd NW7 97 CX49
Hillview Rd, Chis. 185 EN92
Hillview Rd, Pnr. 94 BZ52
Hillview Rd, Sutt. 200 DC104
Hillway N6 120 DG61
Hillway NW9 118 CS60
Hillway, Amer. 55 AP41
Hillwood Cl, Brwd. 109 GB46
Hillwood Gro, Brwd. 109 GB46
Hillworth Rd SW2 181 DN87
Hilly Fld, Harl. 51 ET19
Hilly Flds Cres SE4 163 EA83
Hillyard Rd W7 137 CE71
Hillyard St SW9 161 DN81
Hillyfield E17 123 DY55
Hillyfields, Loug. 85 EN40
Hillyfields, Welw.G.C. 30 DC08
Hilmay Dr, Hem.H. 40 BH21
Hilperton Rd, Slou. 152 AS75
Hilsea Pt SW15 179 CV88
Wanborough Dr
Hilsea St E5 122 DW63
Hilton Av N12 98 DD50
Hilton Cl, Uxb. 134 BH68

Hilton Ct, Horl. 269 DK147
Clarence Way
Hilton Way, S.Croy. 236 DV115
Hilversum Cres SE22 182 DS85
East Dulwich Gro
Himalayan Way, Wat. 75 BT44
Himley Rd SW17 180 DE92
Hinchcliffe Cl, Wall. 219 DM108
Hinchley Cl, Esher 197 CF104
Hinchley Dr, Esher 197 CF104
Hinchley Way, Esher 197 CG104
Hinckley Rd SE15 162 DU84
Hind Cl, Chig. 103 ET50
Hind Ct EC4 274 E9
Hind Cres, Erith 167 FD79
Hind Gro E14 143 EA72
Hind Ho N7 121 DN63
Harvist Est
Hind Ter, Grays 169 FX78
Mill La
Hinde Ms W1 140 DG72
Marylebone La
Hinde St W1 272 G8
Hinde St W1 140 DG72
Hindes Rd, Har. 117 CD57
Hindhead Cl N16 122 DS60
Hindhead Cl, Uxb. 135 BP71
Aldenham Dr
Hindhead Gdns, Nthlt. 136 BY67
Hindhead Grn, Wat. 94 BW50
Hindhead Pt SW15 179 CV88
Wanborough Dr
Hindhead Way, Wall. 219 DL106
Hindmans Rd SE22 182 DU85
Hindmans Way, Dag. 146 EZ70
Hindmarsh Cl E1 142 DU73
Cable St
Hindrey Rd E5 122 DV64
Hindsley's Pl SE23 182 DW89
Hine Cl, Couls. 235 DH121
Brighton Rd
Hinkler Cl, Wall. 219 DL108
Hinkler Rd, Har. 117 CK55
Hinkley Cl (Harefield), Uxb. 114 BJ56
Hinksey Cl, Slou. 153 BB76
Hinksey Path SE2 166 EX76
Hinstock Rd SE18 165 EQ79
Hinton Av, Houns. 156 BX84
Hinton Cl SE9 184 EL88
Hinton Rd N18 100 DS49
Hinton Rd SE24 161 DP83
Hinton Rd, Slou. 131 AL73
Hinton Rd, Uxb. 134 BJ67
Hinton Rd, Wall. 219 DJ107
Hintons, Harl. 51 EM19
Hipkins Pl, Brox. 49 DY21
Baas La
Hipley Ct, Guil. 259 BA135
Warren Rd
Hipley St, Wok. 227 BB121
Hippodrome Ms W11 139 CY73
Portland Rd
Hippodrome Pl W11 139 CY73
Hiscocks Ho NW10 138 CQ66
Hitcham La, Maid. 130 AG69
Hitcham La (Burnham), Slou. 130 AG69
Hitcham Rd E17 123 DZ59
Hitcham Rd, Maid. 130 AF72
Hitcham Rd (Burnham), Slou. 130 AF70
Hitchcock Cl, Shep. 194 BM97
Hitchen Hatch La, Sev. 256 FG124
Hitchens Cl, Hem.H. 39 BF19
Hitchin Cl, Rom. 106 FJ49
Hitchin Sq E3 143 DY68
Hitchings Way, Reig. 266 DA138
Hither Fm Rd SE3 164 EJ83
Hither Grn La SE13 183 EC85
Hither Meadow (Chalfont St. Peter), Ger.Cr. 90 AY53
Lower Rd
Hitherbaulk, Welw.G.C. 29 CY11
Hitherbroom Rd, Hayes 135 BU74
Hitherbury Cl, Guil. 258 AW137
Hitherfield Rd SW16 181 DM89
Hitherfield Rd, Dag. 126 EY61
Hitherlands SW12 181 DH89
Hithermoor Rd, Stai. 174 BG85
Hitherway, Welw.G.C. 29 CY05
Hitherwell Dr, Har. 95 CD53
Hitherwood Cl, Horn. 128 FK63
Swanbourne Dr
Hitherwood Cl, Reig. 250 DD132
Hitherwood Dr SE19 182 DT91
Hive, The (Northfleet), Grav. 190 GB85
Fishermans Hill
Hive Cl, Brwd. 108 FU47
Hive Cl, Bushey 95 CD47
Hive La (Northfleet), Grav. 190 GB86
Hive Rd, Bushey 95 CD47
Hivings Hill, Chesh. 54 AN28
Hivings Pk, Chesh. 54 AP28
Hixberry La, St.Alb. 43 CK21
Hoadly Rd SW16 181 DK90
Hobart Cl N20 98 DE47
Oakleigh Rd N
Hobart Cl, Hayes 136 BX70
Hobart Dr, Hayes 136 BX70
Hobart Gdns, Th.Hth. 202 DR97
Hobart La, Hayes 136 BX70
Hobart Pl SW1 277 H6
Hobart Pl SW1 161 DH76
Hobart Pl, Rich. 178 CM86
Chisholm Rd
Hobart Rd, Dag. 126 EX63
Hobart Rd, Hayes 136 BX70
Hobart Rd, Ilf. 103 EQ54
Hobart Rd, Til. 171 GG81
Hobart Rd, Wor.Pk. 199 CV104
Hobart Wk, St.Alb. 43 CF16
Valley Rd
Hobarts Dr (Denham), Uxb. 113 BF58
Hobbans Fm Chase, Ong. 53 FH23
Hobbayne Rd W7 137 CD72
Hobbes Wk SW15 179 CV85
Hobbs Cl, St.Alb. 44 CL21
Hobbs Cl (Cheshunt), Wal.Cr. 67 DX29
Hobbs Cl, W.Byf. 212 BH113
Hobbs Cross Rd, Epp. 86 EW35
Hobbs Cross Rd, Harl. 36 EY12
Hobbs Grn N2 120 DC55
Hobbs Hill Rd, Hem.H. 40 BL24
Hobbs Ms, Ilf. 125 ET61
Ripley Rd
Hobbs Pl Est N1 142 DS67
Pitfield St
Hobbs Rd SE27 182 DQ91
Hobbs Way, Welw.G.C. 29 CW10
Hobby Horse Cl (Cheshunt), Wal.Cr. 66 DR26
Great Stockwood Rd
Hobday St E14 143 EB71
Hobill Wk, Surb. 198 CM100
Hoblands End, Chis. 185 ES93
Hobletts Rd, Hem.H. 40 BM19
Hobsons Cl, Hodd. 33 DZ14
Hobsons Pl E1 142 DU71
Hanbury St
Hobtoe Rd, Harl. 35 EN14
Hobury St SW10 160 DC79
Hockenden La, Swan. 207 FB96
Hocker St E2 275 P3
Hockeridge Bottom, Berk. 38 AT21
Hockering Gdns, Wok. 227 BA117
Hockering Rd, Wok. 227 BA118
Hockett Cl SE8 163 DZ77
Grove St
Hocklands, Welw.G.C. 30 DC08
Hockley Av E6 144 EL68
Hockley Ct E18 102 EG53
Churchfields
Hockley Dr, Rom. 105 FH54
Hockley La (Stoke Poges), Slou. 132 AV67
Hockley Ms, Bark. 145 ES68
Hocroft Av NW2 119 CZ62
Hocroft Rd NW2 119 CZ63
Hocroft Wk NW2 119 CZ62
Hodder Dr, Grnf. 137 CF68
Hoddesdon Bypass, Brox. 33 DY14
Hoddesdon Bypass, Hert. 33 DY14
Hoddesdon Bypass, Hodd. 33 DY14
Hoddesdon Ind Cen, Hodd. 49 EC16
Hoddesdon Rd, Belv. 166 FA78
Hoddesdon Rd, Brox. 67 DX27
Hoddesdon Rd, Ware 33 EC11
Hodds Wd Rd, Chesh. 54 AQ33
Hodford Rd NW11 119 CZ61
Hodgemoor Vw, Ch.St.G. 90 AT48
Hodges Way, Wat. 75 BU44
Hodgkin Cl SE28 146 EX73
Fleming Way
Hodgson Gdns, Guil. 243 AZ131
Sutherland Dr
Hodings Rd, Harl. 35 EP14
Hodister Cl SE5 162 DQ80
Badsworth Rd
Hodnet Gro SE16 163 DX77
Hodsoll Ct, Orp. 206 EX100
Hodson Cl, Har. 116 BZ62
Hodson Cres, Orp. 206 EX100
Hodson Pl, Enf. 83 EA37
Government Row
Hoe, The, Wat. 94 BX47
Hoe La (Abinger Hammer), Dor. 261 BT143
Hoe La, Enf. 82 DU38
Hoe La (Peaslake), Guil. 261 BR144
Hoe La, Rom. 86 EV43
Hoe La, Wal.Abb. 50 EF22
Hoe La, Ware 33 DX09
Hoe Meadow, Beac. 88 AJ51
Hoe St E17 123 EA56
Hoebrook Cl, Wok. 226 AX121
Hoechst, Houns. 156 BW82
Hoecroft, Wal.Abb. 50 EF22
Hoestock Rd, Saw. 36 EX05
Hofland Rd W14 159 CX76
Hog Hill Rd, Rom. 104 EZ52
Hog Pits (Flaunden), Hem.H. 57 BB32
Hogan Ms W2 140 DD71
Porteus Rd
Hogan Way E5 122 DU61
Geldeston Rd
Hogarth Av, Ashf. 175 BQ93
Hogarth Av, Brwd. 108 FY48
Hogarth Business Pk W4 158 CS79
Hogarth La
Hogarth Cl E16 144 EK71
Hogarth Cl W5 138 CL71
Hogarth Cl, Slou. 131 AL73
Hogarth Ct EC3 275 N10
Hogarth Ct SE19 182 DT91
Fountain Dr
Hogarth Ct, Bushey 94 CB45
Steeplands
Hogarth Cres SW19 200 DD95
Hogarth Cres, Croy. 202 DQ101
Hogarth Gdns, Houns. 156 CA80
Hogarth Hill NW11 119 CZ56
Hogarth La W4 158 CS79
Hogarth Pl SW5 160 DB77
Hogarth Rd
Hogarth Reach, Loug. 85 EM43
Hogarth Rd SW5 160 DB77
Hogarth Rd, Dag. 126 EV64
Hogarth Rd, Edg. 96 CN54
Hogarth Roundabout W4 158 CS79
Hogarth Roundabout Flyover W4 158 CS79
Burlington La
Hogarth Way, Hmptn. 196 CC95
Hogback Wd Rd, Beac. 88 AH51
Hogden La (Ranmore Common), Dor. 246 BZ132
Hogden La, Lthd. 246 CA129
Hogfair La (Burnham), Slou. 130 AJ69
Hogg End La, Hem.H. 41 BR17
Hogg End La, St.Alb. 41 BT17
Hogg La, Borwd. 77 CG42
Hogg La, Grays 170 GA76
Hogg La Roundabout, Grays 170 FZ75
Hogges Cl, Hodd. 49 EA17
Conduit La W
Hogpits Bottom (Flaunden), Hem.H. 57 BA32
Hogs Back, Guil. 258 AS137
Hogs La, Grav. 190 GD90
Hogs Orchard, Swan. 207 FH95
Hogscross La, Couls. 234 DF123
Hogsdell La, Hert. 32 DV11
Hogshead Pas E1 142 DV73
Pennington St
Hogshill La, Cob. 214 BX112
Hogsmill Way, Epsom 216 CQ106
Hogtrough Hill (Brasted), West. 239 ET120
Hogtrough La, Gdse. 253 EA128
Hogtrough La, Oxt. 253 EB128
Hogtrough La, Red. 267 DJ135
Holbeach Gdns, Sid. 185 ES86
Holbeach Ms SW12 181 DH88
Harberson Rd
Holbeach Rd SE6 183 EA87
Holbeck La (Cheshunt), Wal.Cr. 66 DT26
Holbeck Row SE15 162 DU80
Holbein Gate, Nthwd. 93 BS50
Holbein Ms SW1 276 F10
Holbein Ms SW1 160 DG78
Holbein Pl SW1 276 F9
Holbein Pl SW1 160 DG77
Holbein Ter, Dag. 126 EV63
Marlborough Rd
Holberton Gdns NW10 139 CV69
Holborn EC1 274 D7
Holborn EC1 141 DN71
Holborn Circ EC1 274 E7
Holborn Cl, St.Alb. 43 CK15
Holborn Pl WC1 274 B7
Holborn Rd E13 144 EH70
Holborn Viaduct EC1 274 E7
Holborn Viaduct EC1 141 DN71
Holborn Way, Mitch. 200 DF96
Holbreck Pl, Wok. 227 AZ118
Heathside Rd
Holbrook Cl N19 121 DH60
Dartmouth Pk Hill
Holbrook Cl, Enf. 82 DT39
Holbrook La, Chis. 185 ER94
Holbrook Meadow, Egh. 173 BC93
Holbrook Rd E15 144 EF68
Holbrook Way, Brom. 205 EM100
Holbrooke Ct N7 121 DL63
Holbrooke Pl, Rich. 177 CK85
Hill Ri
Holburne Cl SE3 164 EJ81
Holburne Gdns SE3 164 EK81
Holburne Rd SE3 164 EJ81
Holcombe Hill NW7 97 CU48
Highwood Hill
Holcombe Rd N17 122 DT55
Holcombe Rd, Ilf. 125 EN59
Holcombe St W6 159 CV77
Holcon Ct, Red. 250 DG131
Holcote Cl, Belv. 166 EY76
Blakemore Way
Holcroft Rd E9 142 DW66
Holdbrook N, Wal.Cr. 67 DZ34
Eleanor Way
Holdbrook S, Wal.Cr. 67 DZ34
Queens Way
Holdbrook Way, Rom. 106 FM54
Holden Av N12 98 DB50
Holden Av NW9 118 CQ60
Holden Cl, Dag. 126 EV62
Holden Cl, Hert. 32 DS09
Holden Gdns, Brwd. 108 FX50
Holden Pl, Cob. 213 BV114
Holden Pt E15 143 ED65
Waddington Rd
Holden Rd N12 98 DB50
Holden St SW11 160 DG82
Holden Way, Upmin. 129 FR59
Holdenby Rd SE4 183 DY85
Holdenhurst Av N12 98 DB52
Holder Cl N3 98 DB52
Holderness Way SE27 181 DP92
Holdernesse Cl, Islw. 157 CG81
Holdernesse Rd SW17 180 DF90
Holders Hill Av NW4 97 CX54
Holders Hill Circ NW7 97 CY52
Dollis Rd
Holders Hill Cres NW4 97 CX54
Holders Hill Dr NW4 119 CX55
Holders Hill Gdns NW4 97 CY54
Holders Hill Rd NW4 97 CX54
Holders Hill Rd NW7 97 CY53
Holdgate St SE7 164 EK76
Westmoor St
Holdings, The, Hat. 45 CW16
Hole Fm La, Brwd. 107 FU54
Hole Hill La, Dor. 262 CA135
Holecroft, Wal.Abb. 68 EE34
Holford Pl WC1 274 C2
Holford Rd NW3 120 DC62
Holford Rd, Grays 171 GK76
Holford Rd, Guil. 243 BC134
Holford Rd, S.le H. 171 GL75
Holford Rd, Til. 171 GK76
Holford St WC1 274 D2
Holford St WC1 141 DN69
Holgate Av SW11 160 DD83
Holgate Gdns, Dag. 126 FA64
Holgate Rd, Dag. 126 FA64
Holland Av SW20 199 CT95
Holland Av, Sutt. 218 DA109
Holland Cl, Barn. 98 DD45
Holland Cl, Brom. 204 EF103
Holland Cl, Red. 250 DF134
Holland Cl, Rom. 127 FC57
Holland Cl, Stan. 95 CH50
Holland Ct E17 123 EC56
Evelyn Rd
Holland Ct NW7 97 CU51
Page St
Holland Cres, Oxt. 254 EG133
Holland Dr SE23 183 DY90
Holland Gdns W14 159 CY76
Holland Gdns, Egh. 193 BF96
Holland Gdns, Wat. 76 BW35
Holland Gro SW9 161 DN80
Holland La, Oxt. 254 EG133
Holland Pk W8 159 CZ75
Holland Pk W11 159 CZ75
Holland Pk Av W11 159 CY75
Holland Pk Av, Ilf. 125 ES58
Holland Pk Gdns W14 139 CY74
Holland Pk Ms W11 139 CY74
Holland Pk Rd W14 159 CZ76
Holland Pas N1 142 DQ67
Basire St
Holland Pl W8 160 DB75
Kensington Ch St
Holland Rd E6 145 EM67
Holland Rd E15 144 EE69
Holland Rd NW10 139 CU67
Holland Rd SE25 202 DU99
Holland Rd W14 159 CX75
Holland Rd, Oxt. 254 EG133
Holland Rd, Wem. 137 CK65
Holland St SE1 278 G2
Holland St SE1 141 DP74
Holland St W8 160 DA75
Holland Vil Rd W14 159 CY75
Holland Wk N19 121 DK60
Duncombe Rd
Holland Wk W8 159 CZ75
Holland Wk, Stan. 95 CG50
Holland Way, Brom. 204 EF103
Hollands, The, Felt. 176 BX91
Hollands, The, Wok. 226 AY118
Montgomery Rd
Hollands, The, Wor.Pk. 199 CT102
Hollands Cft, Ware 34 EK06
Hollar Rd N16 122 DT62
Stoke Newington High St
Hollen St W1 273 M8
Hollen St W1 141 DJ72
Holles Cl, Hmptn. 176 CA93
Holles St W1 273 J8
Holles St W1 141 DH72
Holley Rd W3 158 CS75
Hollickwood Av N12 98 DF51
Holliday Sq SW11 160 DD83
Fowler Cl
Holliday St, Berk. 38 AX19
Hollidge Way, Dag. 147 FB65
Hollier Ct, Hat. 45 CV17
Cranborne Rd
Holliers Way, Hat. 45 CU18
Hollies, The E11 124 EG57
Hollies, The N20 98 DD46
Oakleigh Pk N
Hollies, The, Grav. 191 GK93
Hollies, The, Har. 117 CG56
Hollies, The (Bovingdon), Hem.H. 57 BA29
Hollies, The, Welw.G.C. 29 CV13
Hollies Av, Sid. 185 ET89
Hollies Av, W.Byf. 211 BF113
Hollies Cl SW16 181 DN93
Hollies Cl, Twick. 177 CF89
Hollies Ct, Add. 212 BJ106
Hollies End NW7 97 CV50
Hollies Rd W5 157 CJ77
Hollies Way SW12 180 DG87
Bracken Av
Hollies Way, Pot.B. 64 DC31
Holligrave Rd, Brom. 204 EG95
Hollingbourne Av, Bexh. 166 EZ80
Hollingbourne Gdns W13 137 CH71
Hollingbourne Rd SE24 182 DQ85
Hollingbourne Twr, Orp. 206 EX102
Hollingsworth Rd, Croy. 220 DV107
Hollington Cres, N.Mal. 199 CT100
Hollington Rd E6 145 EM69
Hollington Rd N17 100 DU54
Hollingworth Cl, W.Mol. 196 BZ98
Hollingworth Rd, Orp. 205 EP100
Hollingworth Way, West. 255 ER126
Hollis Pl, Grays 170 GA77
Ward Av
Hollman Gdns SW16 181 DP93
Hollow, The, Wdf.Grn. 102 EF49
Hollow Cl, Guil. 258 AV135
Lynwood
Hollow Cotts, Purf. 168 FN78
Hollow Hill La, Iver 133 BB73
Hollow La (Wotton), Dor. 262 BX140
Hollow La, Vir.W. 192 AY97
Hollow Wk, Rich. 158 CL80
Kew Rd
Hollow Way La, Amer. 55 AS35
Hollow Way La, Chesh. 55 AS35
Holloway Cl, West Dr. 154 BL78
Holloway Dr, Vir.W. 192 AY98
Holloway Hill, Cher. 193 BC104
Holloway La, Rick. 73 BD36
Holloway La, West Dr. 154 BL79
Holloway Rd E6 145 EM69
Holloway Rd E11 124 EE62
Holloway Rd N7 141 DN65
Holloway Rd N19 121 DK61
Holloway St, Houns. 156 CB83
Holloways La, Hat. 45 CX23
Hollowfield Av, Grays 170 GD77
Hollowfield Wk, Nthlt. 136 BY65
Hollows, The, Brent. 158 CM79
Kew Br Rd
Holly Av (New Haw), Add. 212 BG110
Holly Av, Stan. 96 CL54
Holly Av, Walt. 196 BX102
Holly Bk Rd, Wok. 226 AV121
Holly Bush Hill NW3 120 DC63
Holly Bush La, Hmptn. 176 BZ94
Holly Bush La, Sev. 257 FJ123
Holly Bush Steps NW3 120 DC63
Heath St
Holly Bush Vale NW3 120 DC63
Heath St
Holly Cl NW10 138 CS66
Holly Cl, Beck. 203 EC98
Holly Cl, Buck.H. 102 EK48
Holly Cl (Longcross), Cher. 192 AU104
Holly Cl (Englefield Grn), Egh. 172 AV93
Holly Cl, Felt. 176 BY92
Holly Cl, Hat. 45 CT19
Holly Cl (Farnham Common), Slou. 111 AQ63
Holly Cl, Wall. 219 DH108
Holly Cl, Wok. 226 AV119
Holly Cottage Ms, Uxb. 134 BN71
Pield Heath Rd
Holly Ct, Sutt. 218 DA108
Worcester Rd
Holly Cres, Beck. 203 DZ99
Holly Cres, Wind. 151 AK82
Holly Cres, Wdf.Grn. 101 ED52
Holly Cft, Hert. 31 DN08
Holly Cross Rd, Ware 33 DZ07
Holly Dr E4 101 EB45
Holly Dr, Berk. 38 AX20
Holly Dr, Brent. 157 CG79
Holly Dr, Pot.B. 64 DB33
Holly Dr, S.Ock. 149 FX70
Holly Dr, Wind. 172 AS85
Holly Fm Rd, Sthl. 156 BY78
Holly Fld, Harl. 51 EQ18
Holly Gdns, West Dr. 154 BM75
Holly Grn, Wey. 195 BR104
Holly Gro NW9 118 CQ59
Holly Gro SE15 162 DT82
Holly Gro, Bushey 95 CD45
Holly Gro, Pnr. 94 BY53
Holly Gro Rd, Hert. 31 DH07
Holly Hedge Ter SE13 183 ED85
Holly Hedges La (Bovingdon), Hem.H. 57 BC30
Holly Hedges La, Rick. 57 BC30
Holly Hill N21 81 DM44
Holly Hill NW3 120 DC63
Holly Hill Dr, Bans. 234 DA116
Holly Hill Rd, Belv. 167 FB78
Holly Hill Rd, Erith 167 FB78
Holly Ho, Brwd. 108 FX46
Sawyers Hall La
Holly La, Bans. 234 DA116
Holly La E, Bans. 234 DA116
Holly La W, Bans. 234 DA117
Holly Lea, Guil. 242 AX128
Holly Lo, Tad. 249 CY126
Holly Lo Gdns N6 120 DG61
Holly Ms SW10 160 DC78
Drayton Gdns
Holly Mt NW3 120 DC63
Holly Bush Hill
Holly Pk N3 119 CZ55
Holly Pk N4 121 DM59
Holly Pk Est N4 121 DM59
Blythwood Rd
Holly Pk Gdns N3 120 DA55
Holly Pk Rd N11 98 DG50
Holly Pk Rd W7 137 CF74
Holly Pl NW3 120 DC63
Holly Wk
Holly Rd E11 124 EF59
Holly Rd W4 158 CR77
Dolman Rd
Holly Rd, Dart. 188 FK88
Holly Rd, Enf. 83 DX36
Holly Rd (Hampton Hill), Hmptn. 176 CC93
Holly Rd, Houns. 156 CB84
Holly Rd, Orp. 224 EU108
Holly Rd, Reig. 266 DB136
Holly Rd, Twick. 177 CG88
Holly St E8 142 DT65
Holly St Est E8 142 DT66
Holly Ter N6 120 DG60
Highgate W Hill
Holly Ter N20 98 DC47
Swan La
Holly Tree Av, Swan. 207 FE96
Holly Tree Cl (Ley Hill), Chesh. 56 AV31
Holly Tree Rd, Cat. 236 DS122
Elm Gro
Holly Vw Cl NW4 119 CU58
Holly Village N6 121 DH61
Swains La
Holly Wk NW3 120 DC63
Holly Wk, Enf. 82 DR41
Holly Wk, Rich. 158 CL82
Holly Wk, Welw.G.C. 29 CW05
Holly Way, Mitch. 201 DK98
Hollybank Cl, Hmptn. 176 CA92
Hollybank Rd, W.Byf. 212 BG114
Hollyberry La NW3 120 DC63
Holly Wk
Hollybrake Cl, Chis. 185 ER94
Hollybush Av, St.Alb. 42 CA24
Hollybush Cl E11 124 EG57
Hollybush Cl, Berk. 39 BD16
Hollybush Cl, Har. 95 CE53
Hollybush Cl, Sev. 257 FJ124
Hollybush Cl, Wat. 94 BW45
Hollybush Ct, Sev. 257 FJ124
Hollybush Gdns E2 142 DV69
Hollybush Hill E11 124 EF58
Hollybush Hill (Stoke Poges), Slou. 132 AU66
Hollybush La, Amer. 55 AR37
Hollybush La, Hem.H. 39 BF19
Hollybush La, Iver 133 BB72
Hollybush La, Orp. 224 FA107
Hollybush La (Denham), Uxb. 113 BE63
Hollybush La, Welw.G.C. 29 CZ13
Hollybush La (Ripley), Wok. 228 BK119
Hollybush Pl E2 142 DV69
Bethnal Grn Rd
Hollybush Rd, Chesh. 54 AN27
Hollybush Rd, Grav. 191 GJ89
Hollybush Rd, Kings.T. 178 CL92
Hollybush St E13 144 EH69
Hollybush Wk SW9 161 DP84
Hollybush Way, Wal.Cr. 66 DU28
Hollycombe (Englefield Grn), Egh. 172 AW91
Hollycroft Av NW3 120 DA62
Hollycroft Av, Wem. 118 CM61
Hollycroft Cl, S.Croy. 220 DS106
Hollycroft Cl, West Dr. 154 BN79
Hollycroft Gdns, West Dr. 154 BN79
Hollydale Cl, Nthlt. 116 CB63
Dorchester Rd
Hollydale Dr, Brom. 205 EM104
Hollydale Rd SE15 162 DW81
Hollydell, Hert. 32 DQ11
Hollydene SE15 162 DV81
Hollydown Way E11 123 ED62
Hollyfield, Hat. 45 CU21
Hollyfield Av N11 98 DF50
Hollyfield Rd, Surb. 198 CM101
Hollyfields, Brox. 67 DY26
Hollyhedge Rd, Cob. 213 BV114
Hollyhock Cl, Hem.H. 39 BE18
Hollymead, Cars. 200 DF104
Hollymead Rd, Couls. 234 DG118
Hollymeoak Rd, Couls. 235 DH119
Hollymoor La, Epsom 216 CR110
Hollymount Cl SE10 163 EC81
Hollytree Cl SW19 179 CX88
Hollytree Cl (Chalfont St. Peter), Ger.Cr. 90 AY50
Hollywood Ct, Borwd. 78 CM42
Deacon's Hill Rd
Hollywood Gdns, Hayes 135 BV72
Hollywood Ms SW10 160 DC79
Hollywood Rd
Hollywood Rd E4 101 DY50
Hollywood Rd SW10 160 DC79
Hollywood Way, Erith 167 FH81
Hollywood Way, Wdf.Grn. 101 ED52
Hollywoods, Croy. 221 DZ109
Holm Cl (Woodham), Add. 211 BE112
Holm Gro, Uxb. 134 BN66
Holm Oak Cl SW15 179 CZ86
West Hill
Holm Oak Ms SW4 181 DL85
King's Av
Holm Wk SE3 164 EG82
Blackheath Pk
Holman Rd SW11 160 DD82
Holman Rd, Epsom 216 CQ106
Holmbank Dr, Shep. 195 BS98
Holmbridge Gdns, Enf. 83 DX42
Holmbrook Dr NW4 119 CX57
Holmbury Ct SW17 180 DF90
Holmbury Ct SW19 180 DE94
Cavendish Rd
Holmbury Dr (North Holmwood), Dor. 263 CJ139
Holmbury Gdns, Hayes 135 BT74
Church Rd
Holmbury Gro, Croy. 221 DZ108
Holmbury Pk, Brom. 184 EL94
Holmbury Vw E5 122 DV60
Holmbush Rd SW15 179 CY86
Holmcote Gdns N5 122 DQ64
Holmcroft, Tad. 249 CV125
Holmcroft Way, Brom. 205 EM99
Holmdale Cl, Borwd. 78 CM40
Holmdale Gdns NW4 119 CX57
Holmdale Rd NW6 120 DA64
Holmdale Rd, Chis. 185 EQ92
Holmdale Ter N15 122 DS59
Holmdene Av NW7 97 CU51
Holmdene Av SE24 182 DQ85
Holmdene Av, Har. 116 CB55
Holmdene Cl, Beck. 203 EC96
Holme Chase, Wey. 213 BQ107
Holme Cl, Hat. 45 CT15
Holme Cl (Cheshunt), Wal.Cr. 67 DY31
Holme Lacey Rd SE12 184 EF86
Holme Lea, Wat. 60 BW34
Kingsway
Holme Pk, Borwd. 78 CM40
Holme Pl, Hem.H. 41 BQ19
Crest Pk
Holme Rd E6 144 EL67
Holme Rd, Hat. 45 CT15
Holme Rd, Horn. 128 FN60
Holme Way, Stan. 95 CF51
Holmead Rd SW6 160 DB80
Holmebury Cl, Bushey 95 CE47

Holmedale, Slou. 132 AW73
Holmefield Ct NW3 140 DE65
Holmes Av E17 123 DZ55
Holmes Av NW7 97 CY50
Holmes Cl, Wok. 227 AZ121
Holmes Meadow, Harl. 51 EP21
Holmes Pl SW10 160 DC79
Fulham Rd
Holmes Rd NW5 121 DH64
Holmes Rd SW19 180 DC94
Holmes Rd, Twick. 177 CF89
Holmes Ter SE1 278 D4
Holmes Ter SE1 161 DN75
Holmesdale, Wal.Cr. 83 DX35
Holmesdale Av SW14 158 CP83
Holmesdale Cl SE25 202 DT97
Holmesdale Cl, Guil. 243 BB133
Holmesdale Hill (South Darenth), Dart. 208 FQ95
Holmesdale Rd N6 121 DH59
Holmesdale Rd SE25 202 DR99
Holmesdale Rd, Bexh. 166 EX82
Holmesdale Rd, Croy. 202 DR99
Holmesdale Rd (South Darenth), Dart. 208 FQ95
Holmesdale Rd (North Holmwood), Dor. 263 CH140
Holmesdale Rd (South Nutfield), Red. 267 DM136
Holmesdale Rd, Reig. 250 DA133
Holmesdale Rd, Rich. 158 CM81
Holmesdale Rd, Sev. 257 FJ123
Holmesdale Rd, Tedd. 177 CJ93
Holmesdale Ter (North Holmwood), Dor. 263 CH140
Holmesdale Rd
Holmesley Rd SE23 183 DY86
Holmethorpe Av, Red. 251 DH131
Holmethorpe Ind Est, Red. 251 DH131
Holmethorpe Av
Holmewood Gdns SW2 181 DM87
Holmewood Rd SE25 202 DS97
Holmewood Rd SW2 181 DL87
Holmfield Av NW4 119 CX57
Holmhurst Rd, Belv. 167 FB78
Holmlea Rd (Datchet), Slou. 152 AX81
Holmlea Wk (Datchet), Slou. 152 AW81
Holmleigh Av, Dart. 168 FJ84
Holmleigh Rd N16 122 DS60
Holmleigh Rd Est N16 122 DT60
Holmleigh Rd
Holms St E2 142 DU68
Holmsdale Cl, Iver 133 BF72
Holmsdale Gro, Bexh. 167 FE82
Holmshaw Cl SE26 183 DY91
Holmshill La, Borwd. 78 CS36
Holmside Ri, Wat. 93 BV48
Holmside Rd SW12 180 DG86
Holmsley Cl, N.Mal. 199 CT100
Holmsley Ho SW15 179 CT87
Tangley Gro
Holmstall Av, Edg. 118 CQ55
Holmwood Av, Brwd. 109 GA44
Holmwood Av, S.Croy. 220 DT113
Holmwood Cl, Add. 212 BG106
Holmwood Cl, Har. 116 CC55
Holmwood Cl (East Horsley), Lthd. 245 BS128
Holmwood Cl, Nthlt. 136 CB65
Holmwood Cl, Sutt. 217 CX109
Holmwood Gdns N3 98 DA54
Holmwood Gdns, Wall. 219 DH107
Holmwood Gro NW7 96 CR50
Holmwood Rd, Chess. 215 CK106
Holmwood Rd, Enf. 83 DX36
Holmwood Rd, Ilf. 125 ES61
Holmwood Rd, Sutt. 217 CW110
Holmwood Vw Rd (Mid Holmwood), Dor. 263 CH142
Horsham Rd
Holmwood Vil SE7 164 EG78
Woolwich Rd
Holne Chase N2 120 DC58
Holne Chase, Mord. 199 CZ100
Holness Rd E15 144 EF65
Holroyd Cl (Claygate), Esher 215 CF109
Holroyd Rd SW15 159 CW84
Holroyd Rd (Claygate), Esher 215 CF109
Holstein Av, Wey. 212 BN105
Holstein Way, Erith 166 EY76
Holstock Rd, Ilf. 125 EQ62
Holsworth Cl, Har. 116 CC57
Holsworthy Sq WC1 274 C5
Holsworthy Way, Chess. 215 CJ106
Holt, The, Hem.H. 40 BL21
Turners Hill
Holt, The, Ilf. 103 EQ51
Holt, The, Wall. 219 DJ105
Holt, The, Welw.G.C. 30 DD10
Holt Cl N10 120 DG56
Holt Cl SE28 146 EV73
Holt Cl, Borwd. 78 CM42
Holt Cl, Chig. 103 ET50
Holt Ct E15 123 EC64
Clays La
Holt Rd E16 144 EL74
Holt Rd, Rom. 106 FL52
Holt Rd, Wem. 117 CH62
Holt Way, Chig. 103 ET50
Holton St E1 143 DX70
Holtsmere Cl, Wat. 76 BW35
Holtspur Av (Wooburn Grn), H.Wyc. 110 AE56
Holtspur Cl, Beac. 88 AG54
Holtspur La (Wooburn Grn), H.Wyc. 110 AE57
Holtspur Top La, Beac. 88 AG54
Holtspur Way, Beac. 88 AG54
Holtwhite Av, Enf. 82 DQ40
Holtwhites Hill, Enf. 81 DP39
Holtwood Rd (Oxshott), Lthd. 214 CC113
Holwell Caravan Site, Hat. 30 DE14
Holwell Hyde, Welw.G.C. 30 DC11
Holwell Hyde La, Welw.G.C. 30 DC12
Holwell La, Hat. 30 DE14
Holwell Pl, Pnr. 116 BY56
Holwell Rd, Welw.G.C. 29 CY10
Holwood Cl, Walt. 196 BW103
Holwood Pk Av, Orp. 223 EM105
Holwood Pl SW4 161 DK84
Holy Acre, Harl. 34 EG14
Roydon Mill Pk
Holy Cross Hill, Brox. 48 DU24
Holy Wk, Brox. 49 EA19
St. Catherines Rd
Holy Wk, Hodd. 49 EA18
High St
Holybourne Av SW15 179 CU87
Holyfield Rd, Wal.Abb. 67 EC29
Holyhead Cl E3 143 EA69
Holyhead Cl E6 145 EM71
Valiant Way
Holyoak Rd SE11 278 F8
Holyoake Av, Wok. 226 AW117
Holyoake Ct SE16 163 DZ75
Bryan Rd
Holyoake Cres, Wok. 226 AW117
Holyoake Ter, Sev. 256 FG124
Holyoake Wk N2 120 DC55
Holyoake Wk W5 137 CJ70
Holyport Rd SW6 159 CW80
Holyrood Av, Har. 116 BY63
Holyrood Cres, St.Alb. 43 CD24
Holyrood Gdns, Edg. 118 CP55
Holyrood Gdns, Grays 171 GJ77
Holyrood Ms E16 144 EG74
Wesley Av
Holyrood Rd, Barn. 80 DC44
Holyrood St SE1 279 M3
Holywell Cl SE3 164 EG79
Holywell Cl SE16 162 DV78
Masters Dr
Holywell Cl, Orp. 224 EU105
Holywell Cl, Stai. 174 BL88
Holywell Hill, St.Alb. 42 CC21
Holywell Ind Est, Wat. 75 BR44
Holywell La EC2 275 N4
Holywell La EC2 142 DS70
Holywell Rd, Wat. 75 BU43
Holywell Row EC2 275 M5
Holywell Row EC2 142 DS70
Holywell Way, Stai. 174 BL88
Home Barn Ct, Lthd. 246 BX127
The St
Home Cl, Brox. 49 DZ24
Home Cl, Cars. 200 DF103
Home Cl, Harl. 51 ET15
Home Cl (Fetcham), Lthd. 231 CD121
Home Cl, Nthlt. 136 BZ69
Home Ct, Felt. 175 BU88
Home Fm Cl, Bet. 264 CS135
Home Fm Cl (Ottershaw), Cher. 211 BA108
Home Fm Cl, Esher 214 CB107
Home Fm Cl, Shep. 195 BS98
Home Fm Cl, Tad. 233 CX117
Home Fm Cl, T.Ditt. 197 CF101
Home Fm Gdns, Walt. 196 BW103
Home Fm Ind Est (Stanstead Abbotts), Ware 34 EF10
Home Fm Rd, Rick. 92 BN49
Home Fm Way (Stoke Poges), Slou. 132 AW67
Home Fld, Berk. 39 BB16
Home Gdns, Dag. 127 FC62
Home Gdns, Dart. 188 FL86
Home Hill, Swan. 187 FF94
Home Lea, Orp. 223 ET106
Home Ley, Welw.G.C. 29 CY10
Home Mead, Stan. 95 CJ53
Home Mead Cl, Grav. 191 GH87
Home Meadow, Bans. 234 DA116
Home Meadow (Farnham Royal), Slou. 131 AQ68
Home Meadow, Welw.G.C. 29 CZ09
Home Orchard, Dart. 188 FL86
Home Pk, Oxt. 254 EG131
Home Pk Mill Link Rd, Kings L. 59 BP31
Home Pk Rd SW19 180 DA90
Home Pk Wk, Kings.T. 197 CK98
Home Rd SW11 160 DE82
Home Way, Rick. 91 BF46
Homecroft Gdns, Loug. 85 EP42
Homecroft Rd N22 100 DQ53
Homecroft Rd SE26 182 DW92
Homedean Rd (Chipstead), Sev. 256 FC122
Homefarm Rd W7 137 CE72
Homefield (Bovingdon), Hem.H. 57 BB28
Homefield, Wal.Abb. 68 EG32
Homefield, Walt. 214 BX105
Homefield Av, Ilf. 125 ES57
Homefield Cl NW10 138 CQ65
Homefield Cl (Woodham), Add. 211 BE112
Homefield Cl, Epp. 70 EU30
Homefield Cl, Hayes 136 BW70
Homefield Cl, Horl. 269 DH147
Tanyard Way
Homefield Cl, Lthd. 231 CJ121
Homefield Cl, Orp. 206 EV98
Homefield Cl, Swan. 207 FF97
Homefield Fm Rd (Sutton at Hone), Dart. 208 FM96
Homefield Gdns N2 120 DD55
Homefield Gdns, Mitch. 200 DC96
Homefield Gdns, Tad. 233 CW120
Homefield Ms, Beck. 203 EA95
Homefield Pk, Sutt. 218 DB107
Homefield Ri, Orp. 206 EU102
Homefield Rd SW19 179 CX93
Homefield Rd W4 159 CT77
Homefield Rd, Brom. 204 EJ95
Homefield Rd, Bushey 76 CA43
Homefield Rd, Couls. 235 DP119
Homefield Rd, Edg. 96 CR51
Homefield Rd, Hem.H. 40 BN20
Homefield Rd, Rad. 77 CF37
Homefield Rd, Rick. 73 BC42
Green St
Homefield Rd, Sev. 256 FE122
Homefield Rd, Walt. 196 BY101
Homefield Rd, Ware 33 DY05
Homefield Rd, Warl. 236 DW119
Homefield Rd, Wem. 117 CG63
Homefield St N1 275 M1
Homefield St N1 142 DS68
Homeland Dr, Sutt. 218 DB109
Homelands, Lthd. 231 CJ121
Homelands Dr SE19 182 DS94
Homeleigh Ct, Wal.Cr. 66 DV29
Homeleigh Rd SE15 183 DX85
Homemead SW12 181 DJ89
Homemead, Grav. 191 GH87
Home Mead Cl
Homemead Rd, Brom. 205 EM99
Homemead Rd, Croy. 201 DJ100
Homer Cl, Bexh. 167 FC81
Homer Dr E14 163 EA77
Homer Rd E9 143 DY65
Homer Rd, Croy. 203 DX100
Homer Row W1 272 C7
Homer Row W1 140 DE71
Homer St W1 272 C7
Homer St W1 140 DE71
Homerfield, Welw.G.C. 29 CW08
Homers Rd, Wind. 151 AK81
Homersham Rd, Kings.T. 198 CN96
Homerswood La, Welw. 29 CU05
Homerton Gro E9 123 DX64
Homerton High St E9 122 DW64
Homerton Rd E9 123 DY64
Homerton Row E9 122 DW64
Homerton Ter E9 142 DW65
Morning La
Homesdale Cl E11 124 EG57
Homesdale Rd, Brom. 204 EJ98
Homesdale Rd, Cat. 236 DR123
Homesdale Rd, Orp. 205 ES101
Homesfield NW11 120 DA57
Homestall Rd SE22 182 DW85
Homestead, The N11 99 DH49
Homestead, The, Dart. 188 FJ86
Homestead Cl (Park St), St.Alb. 60 CC27
Homestead Ct, Welw.G.C. 29 CZ11
Homestead Gdns (Claygate), Esher 215 CE106
Homestead La, Welw.G.C. 29 CZ12
Homestead Paddock N14 81 DH43
Homestead Pk NW2 119 CT62
Homestead Rd SW6 159 CZ80
Homestead Rd, Cat. 236 DR123
Homestead Rd, Dag. 126 EZ61
Homestead Rd, Hat. 45 CU15
Homestead Rd, Orp. 224 EV108
Homestead Rd, Rick. 92 BK45
Park Rd
Homestead Rd, Stai. 174 BH93
Homestead Way (New Addington), Croy. 221 EC111
Homesteads, The, Ware 34 EK07
Hunsdon Rd
Homewaters Av, Sun. 195 BT95
Homeway, Rom. 106 FP51
Homewillow Cl N21 81 DP44
Homewood (George Grn), Slou. 132 AX72
Homewood Av (Cuffley), Pot.B. 65 DL27
Homewood Cl, Hmptn. 176 BZ93
Fearnley Cres
Homewood Cres, Chis. 185 ES93
Homewood La, Pot.B. 65 DJ27
Homewood Pk, Cher. 211 BC105
Homewood Rd, St.Alb. 43 CH17
Honduras St EC1 275 H4
Honey Brook, Wal.Abb. 68 EE33
Honey Cl, Dag. 147 FB65
Honey Hill, Uxb. 134 BM66
Honey La EC2 275 J9
Honey La, Hert. 32 DR09
Fore St
Honey La, Wal.Abb. 84 EG35
Honeybourne Rd NW6 120 DB64
Honeybourne Way, Orp. 205 ER102
Honeybrook Rd SW12 181 DJ87
Honeycrock La, Red. 266 DG141
Honeycroft, Loug. 85 EN42
Honeycroft, Welw.G.C. 29 CW10
Honeycroft Dr, St.Alb. 43 CJ22
Honeycroft Hill, Uxb. 134 BL66
Honeycross Rd, Hem.H. 39 BE21
Honeyden Rd, Sid. 186 EY93
Honeyman Cl NW6 139 CX66
Honeymeade, Saw. 36 EW08
Honeypot Cl NW9 118 CM56
Honeypot La NW9 118 CM55
Honeypot La, Brwd. 108 FU48
Honeypot La, Stan. 118 CM55
Honeypots Rd, Wok. 226 AX122
Honeysett Rd N17 100 DT54
Reform Row
Honeysuckle Bottom (East Horsley), Lthd. 245 BS134
Honeysuckle Cl, Brwd. 108 FV43
Honeysuckle Cl, Hert. 32 DU09
Honeysuckle Cl, Horl. 269 DJ147
Briars Wd
Honeysuckle Cl, Iver 133 BC72
Honeysuckle Cl, Rom. 106 FK51
Cloudberry Rd
Honeysuckle Cl, Sthl. 136 BY73
Honeysuckle Fld, Chesh. 54 AQ30
Honeysuckle Gdns, Croy. 203 DX102
Primrose La
Honeysuckle Gdns, Hat. 45 CV19
Honeysuckle La (North Holmwood), Dor. 263 CJ139
Treelands
Honeywell Rd SW11 180 DF86
Honeywood Cl, Pot.B. 64 DE33
Honeywood Rd NW10 139 CT68
Honeywood Rd, Islw. 157 CG84
Honeywood Wk, Cars. 218 DF105
Honister Cl, Stan. 95 CH53
Honister Gdns, Stan. 95 CH52
Honister Hts, Pur. 220 DR114
Honister Pl, Stan. 95 CH53
Honiton Rd NW6 139 CZ68
Honiton Rd, Rom. 127 FD58
Honiton Rd, Well. 165 ET82
Honley Rd SE6 183 EB87
Honnor Gdns, Islw. 157 CD82
Honnor Rd, Stai. 174 BK94
Honor Oak Pk SE23 182 DW86
Honor Oak Ri SE23 182 DW86
Honor Oak Rd SE23 182 DW88
Hoo, The, Harl. 36 EW10
Hood Av N14 81 DH44
Hood Av SW14 178 CQ85
Hood Av, Orp. 206 EV99
Hood Cl, Croy. 201 DP102
Parson's Mead
Hood Ct EC4 274 E9
Hood Rd SW20 179 CT94
Hood Rd, Rain. 147 FE67
Hood Wk, Rom. 105 FB53
Hoodcote Gdns N21 99 DP45
Hook, The, Barn. 80 DD44
Hook Fm Rd, Brom. 204 EK99
Hook Gate, Enf. 82 DV36
Hook Grn La, Dart. 187 FF90
Hook Grn Rd (Southfleet), Grav. 190 FY94
Hook Heath Av, Wok. 226 AV119
Hook Heath Gdns, Wok. 226 AT121
Hook Heath Rd, Wok. 226 AW121
Hook Hill, S.Croy. 220 DS110
Hook Hill La, Wok. 226 AV121
Hook Hill Pk, Wok. 226 AV121
Hook La (Shere), Guil. 260 BN140
Hook La, Pot.B. 64 DF32
Hook La, Rom. 86 EZ44
Hook La, Well. 185 ET85
Hook Ri N, Surb. 198 CN104
Hook Ri S, Surb. 198 CN104
Hook Ri S Ind Pk, Surb. 198 CN104
Hook Rd, Chess. 215 CK106
Hook Rd, Epsom 216 CR111
Hook Rd, Surb. 198 CL104
Hook Wk, Edg. 96 CQ51
Hooke Rd (East Horsley), Lthd. 245 BT125
Hookers Rd E17 123 DX55
Hookfield, Epsom 216 CQ113
Hookfield, Harl. 51 ET17
Hookfields (Northfleet), Grav. 190 GE90
Hooking Grn, Har. 116 CB57
Hooks Cl SE15 162 DV81
Woods Rd
Hooks Hall Dr, Dag. 127 FC62
Hooks Way SE22 182 DU88
Dulwich Common
Hookstone Way, Wdf.Grn. 102 EK52
Hookwood Cor, Oxt. 254 EH128
Hookwood La
Hookwood La, Oxt. 254 EH128
Hookwood Rd, Orp. 224 EW111
Hooley La, Red. 266 DF135
Hoop La NW11 119 CZ59
Hooper Rd E16 144 EG72
Hooper Sq E1 142 DU73
Hooper St
Hooper St E1 142 DU72
Hooper's Ct SW3 276 D5
Hoopers Yd, Sev. 257 FJ126
Hop Gdn Way, Wat. 60 BW31
High Elms La
Hop Gdns WC2 277 P1
Hope Cl N1 142 DQ65
Wallace Rd
Hope Cl SE12 184 EH90
Hope Cl, Brent. 158 CL78
Burford Rd
Hope Cl, Rom. 126 EX56
Hope Cl, Sutt. 218 DC106
Hope Cl, Wdf.Grn. 102 EJ51
West Gro
Hope Grn, Wat. 59 BU33
Hope Pk, Brom. 184 EF94
Hope Rd, Swans. 190 FZ86
Hope St SW11 160 DD83
Hope Ter, Grays 169 FX78
Hope Wf SE16 162 DW75
St. Marychurch St
Hopedale Rd SE7 164 EH79
Hopefield Av NW6 139 CY68
Hopes Cl, Houns. 156 CA79
Old Cote Dr
Hopetown St E1 142 DT71
Brick La
Hopewell Dr, Grav. 191 GM92
Hopewell St SE5 162 DR80
Hopewell Yd SE5 162 DR80
Hopewell St
Hopfield (Horsell), Wok. 226 AY116
Hopfield Av (Byfleet), W.Byf. 212 BL112
Hopgarden La, Sev. 256 FG128
Hopgood St W12 139 CW74
Macfarlane Rd
Hopground Cl, St.Alb. 43 CG22
Hopkins Cl N10 98 DG52
Hopkins Cl, Rom. 128 FJ55
Hopkins Ms E15 144 EF67
West Rd
Hopkins St W1 273 L9
Hopkinsons Pl NW1 140 DG67
Fitzroy Rd
Hoppers Rd N13 99 DN47
Hoppers Rd N21 99 DN47
Hoppett Rd E4 102 EE48
Hoppety, The, Tad. 233 CX122
Hopping La N1 141 DP65
St. Mary's Gro
Hoppingwood Av, N.Mal. 198 CS97
Hoppit Rd, Wal.Abb. 67 EB32
Hoppner Rd, Hayes 135 BQ68
Hopton Ct, Guil. 242 AS134
Park Barn Dr
Hopton Gdns SE1 278 G2
Hopton Gdns SE1 141 DP74
Hopton Gdns, N.Mal. 199 CU100
Hopton Rd SW16 181 DL92
Hopton St SE1 278 G2
Hopton St SE1 141 DP74
Hopwood Cl SW17 180 DC90
Hopwood Cl, Wat. 75 BR36
Hopwood Rd SE17 162 DR79
Hopwood Wk E8 142 DU66
Wilman Gro
Horace Av, Rom. 127 FC60
Horace Rd E7 124 EH63
Horace Rd, Ilf. 125 EQ55
Horace Rd, Kings.T. 198 CM97
Horatio Ct SE16 142 DW74
Rotherhithe St
Horatio Pl E14 163 EC75
Cold Harbour
Horatio Pl SW19 180 DA94
Kingston Rd
Horatio St E2 142 DT68
Horatius Way, Croy. 219 DM106
Horbury Cres W11 140 DA73
Horbury Ms W11 139 CZ73
Ladbroke Rd
Horder Rd SW6 159 CY81
Hordle Gdns, St.Alb. 43 CF22
Hordle Prom E SE15 162 DT80
Daniel Gdns
Hordle Prom N SE15 162 DT80
Daniel Gdns
Hordle Prom S SE15 162 DT80
Pentridge St
Hordle Prom W SE15 162 DS80
Diamond St
Horizon Way SE7 164 EH77
Horksley Gdns, Brwd. 109 GC44
Bannister Dr
Horle Wk SE5 161 DP82
Lilford Rd
Horley Cl, Bexh. 186 FA85
Horley Lo La, Red. 266 DF143
Horley Rd SE9 184 EL91
Horley Rd, Red. 266 DF136
Horley Row, Horl. 268 DF147
Hormead Rd W9 139 CZ70
Horn La SE10 164 EG77
Horn La W3 138 CQ73
Horn La, Wdf.Grn. 102 EG51
Horn Link Way SE10 164 EG77
Horn Pk Cl SE12 184 EH85
Horn Pk La SE12 184 EH85
Hornbeam Av, Upmin. 128 FN63
Hornbeam Chase, S.Ock. 149 FX69
Hornbeam Cl NW7 97 CT48
Hornbeam Cl SE11 278 D8
Hornbeam Cl, Borwd. 78 CN39
Hornbeam Cl, Brwd. 109 GB48
Hornbeam Cl, Buck.H. 102 EK48
Hornbeam Rd
Hornbeam Cl, Epp. 85 ES37
Hornbeam Cl, Hert. 31 DP08
Hornbeam Cl, Ilf. 125 ER64
Hornbeam Cl, Nthlt. 116 BZ64
Hornbeam Cres, Brent. 157 CH80
Hornbeam Gdns, Slou. 152 AU76
Upton Rd
Hornbeam Gro E4 102 EE48
Hornbeam La E4 84 EE43
Hornbeam La, Bexh. 167 FC82
Hornbeam La, Hat. 46 DE22
Hornbeam Rd, Buck.H. 102 EK48
Hornbeam Rd, Epp. 85 ER37
Hornbeam Rd, Guil. 242 AW131
Hornbeam Rd, Hayes 136 BW71
Hornbeam Rd, Reig. 266 DB137
Hornbeam Ter, Cars. 200 DE102
Hornbeam Twr E11 123 ED62
Hollydown Way
Hornbeam Wk, Rich. 178 CM90
Hornbeam Wk, Walt. 213 BT109
Octagon Rd
Hornbeam Way, Brom. 205 EN100
Hornbeam Way, Wal.Cr. 66 DT29
Hornbeams (Bricket Wd), St.Alb. 60 BZ30
Hornbeams, The, Harl. 35 EQ13
Hornbeams Av, Enf. 82 DW35
Hornbeams Ri N11 98 DG51
Hornbill Cl, Uxb. 134 BK72
Hornblower Cl SE16 163 DY77
Greenland Quay
Hornbuckle Cl, Har. 117 CD61
Hornby Cl NW3 140 DD66
Horncastle Cl SE12 184 EG87
Horncastle Rd SE12 184 EG87
Hornchurch Cl, Kings.T. 177 CK91
Hornchurch Hill, Whyt. 236 DT117
Hornchurch Rd, Horn. 127 FG60
Horndean Cl SW15 179 CU88
Bessborough Rd
Horndon Cl, Rom. 105 FC53
Horndon Grn, Rom. 105 FC53
Horndon Rd, Rom. 105 FC54
Horne Rd, Shep. 194 BN98
Horne Way SW15 159 CW82
Horner La, Mitch. 200 DD96
Hornets, The, Wat. 75 BV42
Hornfair Rd SE7 164 EJ79
Hornford Way, Rom. 127 FE59
Hornhatch (Chilworth), Guil. 259 BB140
Hornhatch Cl (Chilworth), Guil. 259 BB140
Hornhatch La, Guil. 259 BA140
Hornhill Rd, Ger.Cr. 91 BB50
Hornhill Rd, Rick. 91 BD50
Horniman Dr SE23 182 DV88
Horning Cl SE9 184 EL91
Hornminster Glen, Horn. 128 FN61
Horns Cl, Hert. 32 DQ11
Horns End Pl, Pnr. 116 BW56
Horns Mill Rd, Hert. 32 DQ12
Horns Rd, Hert. 32 DQ10
Horns Rd, Ilf. 125 EQ58
Hornsby La, Grays 171 GG75
Hornsey La N6 121 DH60
Hornsey La N19 121 DJ59
Hornsey La Est N19 121 DK59
Hornsey La
Hornsey La Gdns N6 121 DJ59
Hornsey Pk Rd N8 121 DM55
Hornsey Ri N19 121 DK59
Hornsey Ri Gdns N19 121 DK59
Hornsey Rd N7 121 DL61
Hornsey Rd N19 121 DL61
Hornsey St N7 121 DM64
Hornsfield, Welw.G.C. 30 DC08
Hornshay St SE15 162 DW79
Hornton Pl W8 160 DA75
Hornton St W8 160 DA75
Horsa Cl, Wall. 219 DL108
Horsa Rd SE12 184 EJ87
Horsa Rd, Erith 167 FC80
Horse & Dolphin Yd W1 273 N10
Horse Fair, Kings.T. 197 CK96
Horse Guards Av SW1 277 P3
Horse Guards Av SW1 141 DL74
Horse Guards Rd SW1 277 N3
Horse Guards Rd SW1 141 DK74
Horse Hill, Chesh. 56 AX32
Horse Leaze E6 145 EN72
Horse Ride SW1 277 M3
Horse Ride SW1 141 DJ74
Horse Ride, Dor. 263 CD144
Horse Ride, Lthd. 245 BR130
Horse Ride, Tad. 249 CY125
Horse Rd E7 124 EH62
Centre Rd
Horse Shoe Cres, Nthlt. 136 CA68
Horse Shoe Grn, Sutt. 200 DB103
Aultone Way
Horse Yd N1 141 DP67
Essex Rd
Horsebridge Cl, Dag. 146 EY67
Horsecroft, Bans. 233 CZ117
Lyme Regis Rd
Horsecroft Cl, Orp. 206 EV102
Horsecroft Pl, Harl. 50 EL16
Horsecroft Rd, Edg. 96 CR52
Horsecroft Rd, Harl. 50 EL16
Horsecroft Rd, Hem.H. 40 BG22
Horseferry Pl SE10 163 EC79
Horseferry Rd E14 143 DY73
Horseferry Rd SW1 277 M7
Horseferry Rd SW1 161 DK77
Horsehill, Horl. 268 DA146
Horselers, Hem.H. 40 BN23
Horsell Birch, Wok. 226 AV115
Horsell Common, Wok. 210 AX114
Horsell Common Rd, Wok. 210 AW114
Horsell Ct, Cher. 194 BH101
Stepgates
Horsell Moor, Wok. 226 AX117
Horsell Pk, Wok. 226 AX116
Horsell Pk Cl, Wok. 226 AX116
Horsell Ri, Wok. 226 AX115
Horsell Ri Cl, Wok. 226 AX115
Horsell Rd N5 121 DN64
Horsell Rd, Orp. 206 EV95
Horsell Vale, Wok. 226 AY115
Horsell Way, Wok. 226 AW116
Horselydown La SE1 279 P4
Horselydown La SE1 162 DT75
Horselydown Old Stairs SE1 279 P3
Horseman Side, Brwd. 105 FH45
Horsemans Ride, St.Alb. 60 CA26
Horsemoor Cl, Slou. 153 BA77
Parlaunt Rd
Horsenden Av, Grnf. 117 CE64
Horsenden Cres, Grnf. 117 CF64
Horsenden La N, Grnf. 137 CF65
Horsenden La S, Grnf. 137 CG68
Horseshoe, The, Bans. 233 CZ115
Horseshoe, The, Hem.H. 41 BQ22
Horseshoe Cl E14 163 EC78
Horseshoe Cl NW2 119 CV61
Horseshoe Cl, Wal.Abb. 68 EG34
Horseshoe Cres, Beac. 89 AL54
Horseshoe Dr, Uxb. 134 BN72
Horseshoe Hill (Burnham), Slou. 110 AJ63

Horseshoe Hill, Wal.Abb. 68 EJ33
Horseshoe La N20 97 CX46
Horseshoe La, Enf. 82 DQ41
Chase Side
Horseshoe La, Wat. 59 BV32
Horseshoe La E, Guil. 243 BB133
Horseshoe La W, Guil. 243 BB133
Horseshoe Ridge, Wey. 213 BQ111
Horsfeld Gdns SE9 184 EL85
Horsfeld Rd SE9 184 EK85
Horsfield Cl, Dart. 188 FQ87
Horsford Rd SW2 181 DM85
Horsham Av N12 98 DE50
Horsham Rd, Bexh. 186 FA85
Horsham Rd, Dor. 263 CG137
Horsham Rd (North Holmwood), Dor. 263 CH140
Horsham Rd (Sutton Abinger), Dor. 261 BT142
Horsham Rd, Felt. 175 BQ86
Horsham Rd, Guil. 258 AY142
Horsley Cl, Epsom 216 CR113
Horsley Dr (New Addington), Croy. 221 EC108
Horsley Dr, Kings.T. 177 CK92
Horsley Rd E4 101 EC47
Horsley Rd, Brom. 204 EH95
Palace Rd
Horsley Rd, Cob. 229 BV119
Horsley St SE17 162 DR79
Horsleys, Rick. 91 BD50
Horsmonden Cl, Orp. 205 ES101
Horsmonden Rd SE4 183 DZ85
Hortensia Rd SW10 160 DC80
Horticultural Pl W4 158 CR78
Heathfield Ter
Horton Av NW2 119 CY63
Horton Br Rd, West Dr. 134 BM74
Horton Cl, Maid. 130 AC70
Horton Cl, West Dr. 134 BM74
Horton Footpath, Epsom 216 CQ111
Horton Gdns, Epsom 216 CQ111
Horton Hill
Horton Hill, Epsom 216 CQ111
Horton Ind Pk, West Dr. 134 BM74
Horton La, Epsom 216 CP110
Horton Rd E8 142 DV65
Horton Rd (Horton Kirby), Dart. 208 FQ97
Horton Rd (Colnbrook), Slou. 153 BA81
Horton Rd (Datchet), Slou. 152 AW81
Horton Rd (Poyle), Slou. 153 BE83
Horton Rd, Stai. 174 BG85
Horton Rd, West Dr. 134 BN74
Horton St SE13 163 EB83
Horton Way, Croy. 203 DX99
Horton Way (Farningham), Dart. 208 FM101
Hortons Way, West. 255 ER126
Hortus Rd E4 101 EC47
Hortus Rd, Sthl. 156 BZ75
Horvath Cl, Wey. 213 BR105
Horwood Cl, Rick. 92 BG45
Thellusson Way
Horwood Ct, Wat. 76 BX37
Hosack Rd SW17 180 DF89
Hoser Av SE12 184 EG89
Hosey Common La, West. 255 ES130
Hosey Common Rd, Eden. 255 EQ133
Hosey Common Rd, West. 255 ER130
Hosey Hill, West. 255 ER127
Hosier La EC1 274 F7
Hosier La EC1 141 DP71
Hoskins Cl E16 144 EJ72
Hoskins Cl, Hayes 155 BT78
Cranford Dr
Hoskins Rd, Oxt. 254 EE129
Hoskins St SE10 163 ED78
Hoskins Wk, Oxt. 254 EE129
Hospital Br Rd, Twick. 176 CB87
Hospital Hill, Chesh. 54 AQ32
Hospital Rd E9 123 DX64
Homerton Row
Hospital Rd, Houns. 156 CA83
Hospital Rd, Sev. 257 FJ121
Hotham Cl (Sutton at Hone), Dart. 188 FP94
Hotham Cl, Swan. 207 FH95
Hotham Cl, W.Mol. 196 CA97
Garrick Gdns
Hotham Rd SW15 159 CW83
Hotham Rd SW19 180 DC94
Hotham Rd Ms SW19 180 DC94
Haydons Rd
Hotham St E15 144 EE67
Hothfield Pl SE16 162 DW76
Lower Rd
Hotspur Rd, Nthlt. 136 CA68
Hotspur St SE11 278 D10
Hotspur St SE11 161 DN78
Houblon Rd, Rich. 178 CL85
Houblons Hill, Epp. 70 EW31
Houghton Cl E8 142 DT65
Buttermere Wk
Houghton Cl, Hmptn. 176 BY93
Houghton Rd N15 122 DT57
West Grn Rd
Houghton St WC2 274 C9
Houlder Cres, Croy. 219 DP107
Hound Ho Rd (Shere), Guil. 260 BN141
Houndsden Rd N21 81 DM44
Houndsditch EC3 275 N8
Houndsditch EC3 142 DS72
Houndsfield Rd N9 100 DV45
Hounslow Av, Houns. 176 CB85
Hounslow Business Pk, Houns. 156 CB84
Alice Way
Hounslow Gdns, Houns. 176 CB85
Hounslow Rd (Feltham), Felt. 175 BV88
Hounslow Rd (Hanworth), Felt. 176 BX91
Hounslow Rd, Twick. 176 CC86
House La (Sandridge), St.Alb. 43 CK16
Housefield Way, St.Alb. 43 CJ22
Houseman Way SE5 162 DR80
Hopewell St
Housewood End, Hem.H. 40 BH17
Houston Pl, Esher 197 CE102
Lime Tree Av
Houston Rd SE23 183 DY89
Houston Rd, Surb. 197 CH100
Hove Av E17 123 DZ57
Hove Cl, Brwd. 109 GC47
Hove Cl, Grays 170 GA79
Argent St
Hove Gdns, Sutt. 200 DB102
Hoveden Rd NW2 119 CY64
Hoveton Rd SE28 146 EW72
How La, Couls. 234 DG117
How Wd (Park St), St.Alb. 60 CB28
Howard Agne Cl (Bovingdon), Hem.H. 57 BA27
Howard Av, Bex. 186 EW88
Howard Av, Epsom 217 CU110
Howard Av, Slou. 131 AR71
Howard Business Pk, Wal.Abb. 67 ED33
Howard Cl
Howard Cl N11 98 DG47
Howard Cl NW2 119 CY63
Howard Cl W3 138 CP72
Howard Cl, Ash. 232 CM118
Howard Cl, Bushey 95 CE45
Howard Cl, Hmptn. 176 CC93
Howard Cl, Lthd. 231 CJ123
Windmill Dr
Howard Cl (West Horsley), Lthd. 245 BR125
Howard Cl, Loug. 84 EL44
Howard Cl, St.Alb. 43 CJ22
Howard Cl, Sun. 175 BT93
Catherine Dr
Howard Cl, Tad. 249 CT125
Howard Cl, Wal.Abb. 67 ED34
Howard Cl, Wat. 75 BU37
Howard Ct, Reig. 250 DC133
Howard Cres (Seer Grn), Beac. 89 AQ50
Howard Dr, Borwd. 78 CR42
Howard Gdns, Guil. 243 BA133
Howard Ms N5 121 DP63
Hamilton Pk
Howard Pl SW1 277 K7
Howard Pl, Reig. 250 DA132
Howard Ridge (Burpham), Guil. 243 BA130
Howard Rd E6 145 EM68
Howard Rd E11 124 EE62
Howard Rd E17 123 EA55
Howard Rd N15 122 DS58
Howard Rd N16 122 DR63
Howard Rd NW2 119 CX63
Howard Rd SE20 202 DW95
Howard Rd SE25 202 DU99
Howard Rd, Bark. 145 ER67
Howard Rd (Seer Grn), Beac. 89 AQ50
Howard Rd, Brom. 184 EG94
Howard Rd, Chesh. 54 AP28
Howard Rd, Couls. 235 DJ115
Howard Rd, Dart. 188 FN86
Howard Rd, Dor. 263 CG136
Howard Rd (North Holmwood), Dor. 263 CJ140
Holmesdale Rd
Howard Rd, Grays 169 FW76
Howard Rd, Ilf. 125 EP63
Howard Rd, Islw. 157 CF83
Howard Rd (Effingham Junct), Lthd. 229 BU122
Howard Rd (Great Bookham), Lthd. 246 CB127
Howard Rd, N.Mal. 198 CS97
Howard Rd, Reig. 266 DB135
Howard Rd, Sthl. 136 CB72
Howard Rd, Surb. 198 CM100
Howard Rd, Upmin. 128 FQ61
Howard St, T.Ditt. 197 CH101
Howard Wk N2 120 DC56
Howard Way, Barn. 79 CX43
Howard Way, Harl. 52 EU15
Howards Cl, Pnr. 93 BV54
Howards Cl, Wok. 227 BA120
Howards Crest Cl, Beck. 203 EC96
Howards Dr, Hem.H. 39 BF17
Howards La SW15 159 CV84
Howards La, Add. 211 BE107
Howards Rd E13 144 EG69
Howards Rd, Wok. 227 AZ120
Howards Thicket, Ger.Cr. 112 AW61
Howards Wd Dr, Ger.Cr. 112 AX61
Howardsgate, Welw.G.C. 29 CX08
Howarth Ct E15 123 EC64
Clays La
Howarth Rd SE2 166 EU78
Howberry Cl, Edg. 95 CK51
Howberry Rd, Edg. 95 CK51
Howberry Rd, Stan. 95 CK51
Howberry Rd, Th.Hth. 202 DR95
Howbury La, Erith 167 FG82
Howbury Rd SE15 162 DW83
Howcroft Cres N3 98 DA52
Howcroft La, Grnf. 137 CD69
Cowgate Rd
Howden Cl SE28 146 EX73
Howden Rd SE25 202 DT96
Howden St SE15 162 DU83
Howe Cl, Rad. 62 CL32
Howe Cl, Rom. 104 FA53
Howe Dell, Hat. 45 CV18
Howe Dr, Beac. 89 AK50
Howe Dr, Cat. 236 DR122
Yorke Gate Rd
Howe Rd, Hem.H. 40 BN22
Howell Cl, Rom. 126 EX57
Howell Hill Cl, Epsom 217 CW111
Howell Hill Gro, Epsom 217 CW110
Howell Wk SE1 278 G9
Howes Cl N3 120 DA55
Howfield Grn, Hodd. 33 DZ14
Howfield Pl N17 122 DT55
Howgate Rd SW14 158 CR83
Howick Pl SW1 277 L7
Howick Pl SW1 161 DJ76
Howicks Grn, Welw.G.C. 30 DA12
Howie St SW11 160 DE80
Howitt Cl NW3 140 DE65
Howitt Rd
Howitt Rd NW3 140 DE65
Howitts Cl, Esher 214 CA107
Howland Est SE16 162 DW76
Howland Garth, St.Alb. 42 CC24
Howland Ms E W1 273 L6
Howland St W1 273 K6
Howland St W1 141 DJ71
Howland Way SE16 163 DY75
Howlands, Welw.G.C. 30 DB12
Howletts La, Ruis. 115 BQ57
Howletts Rd SE24 182 DQ86
Howley Pl W2 140 DC71
Howley Rd, Croy. 201 DP104
Hows Cl, Uxb. 134 BJ67
Hows Rd
Hows Mead, Epp. 53 FD24
Hows Rd, Uxb. 134 BJ67
Hows St E2 142 DT68
Howse Rd, Wal.Abb. 83 EB35
Deer Pk Way
Howsman Rd SW13 159 CU79
Howson Rd SE4 163 DY84
Howson Ter, Rich. 178 CL86
Howton Pl, Bushey 95 CD46
Hoxton Mkt N1 275 M3
Hoxton Sq N1 275 M3
Hoxton Sq N1 142 DS69
Hoxton St N1 275 N3
Hoxton St N1 142 DS67
Hoy St E16 144 EF72
Hoy Ter, Grays 169 FX78
Hoylake Cl, Slou. 151 AL75
Eltham Av
Hoylake Cres (Ickenham), Uxb. 115 BP61
Hoylake Gdns, Mitch. 201 DJ97
Hoylake Gdns, Rom. 106 FN53
Hoylake Gdns, Ruis. 115 BV60
Hoylake Gdns, Wat. 94 BX49
Hoylake Rd W3 138 CS72
Hoyland Cl SE15 162 DV80
Commercial Way
Hoyle Rd SW17 180 DE92
Hubbard Dr, Chess. 215 CJ107
Hubbard Rd SE27 182 DQ91
Hubbard St E15 144 EE67
Hubbards Chase, Horn. 128 FN57
Hubbards Cl, Horn. 128 FN57
Hubbards Cl, Uxb. 135 BP72
Hubbard's Hill (Sevenoaks Weald), Sev. 257 FH130
Hubbards Rd, Rick. 73 BD43
Hubbinet Ind Est, Rom. 127 FC55
Hubert Day Cl, Beac. 89 AK52
Seeleys Rd
Hubert Gro SW9 161 DL83
Hubert Rd E6 144 EK69
Hubert Rd, Brwd. 108 FV48
Hubert Rd, Rain. 147 FF69
Hubert Rd, Slou. 152 AX76
Hucknall Cl, Rom. 106 FM51
Huddart St E3 143 EA71
Huddleston Cl E2 142 DW68
Huddleston Rd N7 121 DK63
Huddlestone Cres, Red. 251 DK128
Huddlestone Rd E7 124 EF63
Huddlestone Rd NW2 139 CV65
Hudons Cl, Grays 169 FT78
Hudson Av (Denham), Uxb. 113 BF58
Hudson Cl, St.Alb. 43 CD23
Hudson Cl, Wat. 75 BT36
Hudson Ct E14 163 EA78
Maritime Quay
Hudson Ct SW19 180 DB94
Hudson Ct, Guil. 242 AT133
Cobbett Rd
Hudson Gdns, Orp. 223 ET107
Superior Dr
Hudson Pl SE18 165 EQ78
Hudson Rd, Bexh. 166 EZ82
Hudson Rd, Hayes 155 BR79
Hudsons, Tad. 233 CX121
Hudson's Pl SW1 277 J8
Huggin Ct EC4 275 J10
Huggin Hill EC4 275 J10
Huggins La, Hat. 45 CV23
Huggins Pl SW2 181 DM88
Roupell Rd
Hugh Dalton Av SW6 159 CZ79
Hugh Gaitskell Cl SW6 159 CZ79
Hugh Ms SW1 277 J9
Hugh Pl SW1 277 M8
Hugh St SW1 277 J9
Hugh St SW1 161 DH77
Hughan Rd E15 123 ED64
Hughenden Av, Har. 117 CH57
Hughenden Gdns, Nthlt. 136 BW69
Hughenden Rd, St.Alb. 43 CH17
Hughenden Rd, Slou. 131 AR72
Hughenden Rd, Wor.Pk. 199 CU101
Hughendon Ter E15 123 EC63
Westdown Rd
Hughes Cl N12 98 DC50
Coleridge Rd
Hughes Rd, Ashf. 175 BQ94
Hughes Rd, Grays 171 GG76
Hughes Rd, Hayes 135 BV73
Hughes Wk, Croy. 202 DQ101
St. Saviours Rd
Hugh's Twr, Harl. 35 ER14
Hugo Gdns, Rain. 147 FG65
Hugo Gryn Way, Rad. 62 CL31
Farm Cl
Hugo Rd N19 121 DJ63
Hugon Rd SW6 160 DB83
Huguenot Pl E1 142 DT71
Huguenot Pl SW18 180 DC85
Huguenot Sq SE15 162 DV83
Scylla Rd
Hull Cl SE16 163 DX75
Hull Cl, Slou. 151 AQ75
Hull Cl, Sutt. 218 DB110
Yarbridge Cl
Hull Cl (Cheshunt), Wal.Cr. 66 DR26
Hull Gro, Harl. 51 EN20
Hull Pl E16 165 EP75
Fishguard Way
Hull St EC1 275 H3
Hullbridge Ms N1 142 DR67
Sherborne St
Hulletts La, Brwd. 108 FS41
Hulse Av, Bark. 145 ER65
Hulse Av, Rom. 105 FB53
Hulse Ter, Ilf. 125 EQ64
Buttsbury Rd
Hulsewood Cl, Dart. 187 FH90
Hulton Cl, Lthd. 231 CJ123
Windmill Dr
Hulverston Cl, Sutt. 218 DB110
Humber Av, S.Ock. 149 FT72
Humber Cl, West Dr. 134 BK74
Humber Dr W10 139 CX70
Humber Dr, Upmin. 129 FR58
Humber Rd NW2 119 CV61
Humber Rd SE3 164 EF79
Humber Rd, Dart. 188 FK85
Humber Way, Slou. 153 BA77
Humberstone Rd E13 144 EJ69
Humberton Cl E9 123 DY64
Marsh Hill
Humbolt Cl, Guil. 242 AS134
Humbolt Rd W6 159 CY79
Hume Av, Til. 171 GG83
Hume Ter E16 144 EJ72
Prince Regent La
Hume Way, Ruis. 115 BU58
Humes Av W7 157 CE76
Hummer Rd, Egh. 173 BA91
Humphrey Cl, Ilf. 103 EM53
Humphrey Cl (Fetcham), Lthd. 230 CC122
Humphrey St SE1 279 P10
Humphrey St SE1 162 DT78
Humphries Cl, Dag. 126 EZ63
Hundred Acre NW9 97 CT54
Hundred Acres La, Amer. 55 AR40
Hungerdown E4 101 EC46
Hungerford Av, Slou. 132 AS71
Hungerford Br SE1 278 A2
Hungerford Br SE1 141 DL74
Hungerford Br WC2 278 A2
Hungerford Br WC2 141 DL74
Hungerford La WC2 277 P2
Hungerford Rd N7 121 DL64
Hungerford Sq, Wey. 213 BR105
Rosslyn Pk
Hungerford St E1 142 DV72
Commercial Rd
Hungry Hill (Ripley), Wok. 228 BK124
Hungry Hill La
Hungry Hill La (Send), Wok. 228 BK124
Hunsdon, Welw.G.C. 30 DD09
Hunsdon Cl, Dag. 146 EY65
Hunsdon Dr, Sev. 257 FH123
Hunsdon Rd SE14 163 DX79
Hunsdon Rd (Stanstead Abbotts), Ware 34 EE11
Hunslett St E2 142 DW68
Royston St
Hunstanton Cl (Colnbrook), Slou. 153 BC80
Hunston Rd, Mord. 200 DB102
Hunt Cl, St.Alb. 43 CK17
Villiers Cres
Hunt Rd (Northfleet), Grav. 190 GE90
Hunt Rd, Sthl. 156 CA76
Hunt Way SE22 182 DU88
Dulwich Common
Hunter Av, Brwd. 109 GA44
Hunter Cl SE1 279 L7
Hunter Cl SW12 180 DG88
Balham Pk Rd
Hunter Cl, Borwd. 78 CQ43
Hunter Cl, Pot.B. 64 DB33
Hunter Dr, Horn. 128 FJ63
Hunter Ho, Felt. 175 BU88
Hunter Rd SW20 199 CW95
Hunter Rd, Guil. 258 AY135
Hunter Rd, Ilf. 125 EP64
Hunter Rd, Th.Hth. 202 DR97
Hunter St WC1 274 A4
Hunter St WC1 141 DL70
Hunter Wk E13 144 EG68
Hunter Wk, Borwd. 78 CQ43
Hunter Cl
Huntercombe Cl, Maid. 130 AH72
Huntercombe La N, Maid. 130 AJ71
Huntercombe La N, Slou. 130 AJ71
Huntercombe La S, Maid. 130 AH74
Huntercombe Spur, Slou. 130 AJ73
Huntercrombe Gdns, Wat. 94 BW49
Hunters, The, Beck. 203 EC95
Hunters Cl, Bex. 187 FE90
Hunters Cl, Chesh. 54 AN30
Hunters Cl, Epsom 216 CQ113
Marshalls Cl
Hunters Cl (Bovingdon), Hem.H. 57 BA29
Hunters Ct, Rich. 177 CK85
Friars La
Hunters Gate, Wat. 59 BU33
Hunters La
Hunters Gro, Har. 117 CJ56
Hunters Gro, Hayes 135 BU74
Hunters Gro, Orp. 223 EP105
Hunters Gro, Rom. 105 FB50
Hunters Hall Rd, Dag. 126 FA63
Hunters Hill, Ruis. 116 BW62
Hunters La, Wat. 59 BT33
Hunters Meadow SE19 182 DS91
Dulwich Wd Av
Hunters Oak, Hem.H. 41 BP15
Hunters Pk, Berk. 38 AY18
Hunters Reach, Wal.Cr. 66 DT29
Hunters Ride (Bricket Wd), St.Alb. 60 CA31
Hunters Rd, Chess. 198 CL104
Hunters Sq, Dag. 126 FA63
Hunters Wk (Knockholt), Sev. 224 EY114
Hunters Way, Croy. 220 DS105
Brownlow Rd
Hunters Way, Enf. 81 DN39
Hunters Way, Slou. 131 AL74
Hunters Way, Welw.G.C. 29 CZ12
Huntersfield Cl, Reig. 250 DB131
Hunting Cl, Esher 214 CA105
Hunting Gate, Hem.H. 40 BL16
Hunting Gate Cl, Enf. 81 DN41
Hunting Gate Dr, Chess. 216 CL108
Hunting Gate Ms, Sutt. 200 DB104
Hunting Gate Ms, Twick. 177 CE88
Colne Rd
Huntingdon Cl, Brox. 49 DY24
Huntingdon Cl, Mitch. 201 DL97
Huntingdon Gdns W4 158 CQ80
Huntingdon Gdns, Wor.Pk. 199 CW104
Huntingdon Rd N2 120 DE55
Huntingdon Rd N9 100 DW46
Huntingdon Rd, Red. 250 DF134
Huntingdon Rd, Wok. 226 AT117
Huntingdon St E16 144 EF72
Huntingdon St N1 141 DM66
Huntingfield, Croy. 221 DZ108
Huntingfield Rd SW15 179 CU85
Huntingfield Way, Egh. 173 BD94
Huntings Rd, Dag. 146 FA65
Huntland Cl, Rain. 147 FH71
Huntley Av (Northfleet), Grav. 190 GB86
Huntley Cl (Stanwell), Stai. 174 BL87
Cambria Gdns
Huntley Dr N3 98 DA51
Huntley St WC1 273 L5
Huntley St WC1 141 DJ70
Huntley Way SW20 199 CU96
Huntly Rd SE25 202 DS98
Hunton Br Hill, Kings L. 59 BQ33
Hunton St E1 142 DU70
Hunt's Cl SE3 164 EG82
Hunt's Ct WC2 277 N1
Hunts La E15 143 EC68
Hunts La, Maid. 130 AE68
Hunts Mead, Enf. 83 DX41
Hunts Mead Cl, Chis. 185 EM94
Hunts Slip Rd SE21 182 DS90
Huntsman Cl, Warl. 236 DW119
Huntsman Rd, Ilf. 104 EU51
Huntsman St SE17 279 L9
Huntsman St SE17 162 DR77
Huntsmans Cl, Felt. 175 BV91
Huntsmans Cl (Fetcham), Lthd. 231 CD124
The Grn
Huntsmans Dr, Upmin. 128 FQ64
Huntsmill Rd, Hem.H. 39 BE21
Huntsmoor Rd, Epsom 216 CR106
Huntspill St SW17 180 DC90
Huntswood La, Maid. 130 AE66
Huntswood La, Slou. 130 AE66
Huntsworth Ms NW1 272 D5
Hurdwick Pl NW1 141 DJ68
Harrington Sq
Hurley Cl, Walt. 195 BV103
Hurley Cres SE16 163 DX75
Marlow Way
Hurley Gdns, Guil. 243 AZ130
Hurley Rd SE11 278 E9
Hurley Rd SE11 161 DN77
Hurley Rd, Grnf. 136 CB72
Hurlfield, Dart. 188 FJ90
Hurlford, Wok. 226 AU117
Hurlingham Ct SW6 159 CZ83
Hurlingham Gdns SW6 159 CZ83
Hurlingham Rd SW6 159 CZ82
Hurlingham Rd, Bexh. 166 EZ80
Hurlingham Sq SW6 160 DB83
Peterborough Rd
Hurlock St N5 121 DP62
Hurlstone Rd SE25 202 DR99
Hurn Ct Rd, Houns. 156 BX82
Renfrew Rd
Hurnford Cl, S.Croy. 220 DS110
Huron Cl, Orp. 223 ET107
Winnipeg Dr
Huron Rd SW17 180 DG89
Hurren Cl SE3 164 EE83
Hurricane Rd, Wall. 219 DM108
Hurricane Way, Abb.L. 59 BU32
Abbey Dr
Hurricane Way, Epp. 70 EZ27
Hurricane Way, Slou. 153 BB79
Sutton La
Hurry Cl E15 144 EE66
Hursley Rd, Chig. 103 ET50
Tufter Rd
Hurst Av E4 101 EA49
Hurst Av N6 121 DJ58
Hurst Cl E4 101 EA48
Hurst Cl NW11 120 DB58
Hurst Cl, Brom. 204 EF102
Hurst Cl, Chess. 216 CN106
Hurst Cl, Nthlt. 116 BZ64
Hurst Cl, Welw.G.C. 30 DC10
Hurst Cl, Wok. 226 AW120
Hurst Cft, Guil. 258 AY137
Hurst Dr, Tad. 249 CU126
Hurst Dr, Wal.Cr. 67 DX34
Hurst Est SE2 166 EX78
Hurst Grn Cl, Oxt. 254 EG132
Hurst Grn Rd, Oxt. 254 EF132
Hurst Gro, Walt. 195 BT102
Hurst La SE2 166 EX78
Hurst La, E.Mol. 196 CC98
Hurst La, Egh. 193 BA96
Hurst La (Headley), Epsom 232 CQ124
Hurst Pk Av, Horn. 128 FL63
Newmarket Way
Hurst Pl, Nthwd. 93 BP53
Hurst Ri, Barn. 80 DA41
Hurst Rd E17 123 EB55
Hurst Rd N21 99 DN46
Hurst Rd, Bex. 186 EX88
Hurst Rd, Buck.H. 102 EK46
Hurst Rd, Croy. 220 DR106
Hurst Rd, E.Mol. 196 CB97
Hurst Rd, Epsom 216 CR111
Hurst Rd (Headley), Epsom 232 CR123
Hurst Rd, Erith 167 FC80
Hurst Rd, Horl. 268 DE147
Hurst Rd, Sid. 186 EU89
Hurst Rd, Slou. 131 AK71
Hurst Rd, Tad. 232 CR123
Hurst Rd, Walt. 196 BW99
Hurst Rd, W.Mol. 196 BY97
Hurst Springs, Bex. 186 EY88
Hurst St SE24 181 DP86
Hurst Vw Rd, S.Croy. 220 DS108
Hurst Way, Sev. 257 FJ127
Hurst Way, S.Croy. 220 DS107
Hurst Way (Pyrford), Wok. 211 BE114
Hurstbourne (Claygate), Esher 215 CF107
Hurstbourne Gdns, Bark. 145 ES65
Hurstbourne Ho SW15 179 CT86
Tangley Gro
Hurstbourne Rd SE23 183 DY88
Hurstcourt Rd, Sutt. 200 DB103
Hurstdene Av, Brom. 204 EF102
Hurstdene Av, Stai. 174 BH93
Hurstdene Gdns N15 122 DS59
Hurstfield, Brom. 204 EG99
Hurstfield Cres, Hayes 135 BS70
Hurstfield Dr, Maid. 130 AH72
Hurstfield Rd, W.Mol. 196 CA97
Hurstlands, Oxt. 254 EG132
Hurstlands Cl, Horn. 128 FJ59
Hurstleigh Cl, Red. 250 DF132
Hurstleigh Dr, Red. 250 DF132
Hurstleigh Gdns, Ilf. 103 EM53
Hurstlings, Welw.G.C. 30 DB10
Hurstmead Ct, Edg. 96 CP49
Hurstway Wk W11 139 CX73
Hurstwood Av E18 124 EH56
Hurstwood Av, Bex. 186 EY88
Hurstwood Av, Bexh. 167 FE81
Hurstwood Av, Brwd. 108 FV45
Ongar Rd
Hurstwood Av, Erith 167 FE81
Hurstwood Ct, Upmin. 128 FQ60
Hurstwood Dr, Brom. 205 EM97
Hurstwood Rd NW11 119 CY56
Hurtwood Rd, Walt. 196 BZ101
Hurworth Rd, Slou. 152 AW76
Huson Cl NW3 140 DE66
Hussars Cl, Houns. 156 BY83
Husseywell Cres, Brom. 204 EG102
Hutchings Rd, Beac. 89 AK50
Hutchings St E14 163 EA75
Hutchings Wk NW11 120 DB56
Hutchingsons Rd (New Addington), Croy. 221 EC111
Hutchins Cl E15 143 EC66
Gibbins Rd
Hutchins Cl, Horn. 128 FL62
Hutchins Rd SE28 146 EU73
Hutchins Way, Horl. 268 DF146
Hutchinson Ter, Wem. 117 CK62
Hutson Ter, Dart. 169 FR78
Hutton Cl, Grnf. 117 CD64
Mary Peters Dr
Hutton Cl, Hert. 31 DN09
Hutton Cl, Wdf.Grn. 102 EH51
Hutton Dr, Brwd. 109 GD45
Hutton Gdns, Har. 94 CC52
Hutton Gate, Brwd. 109 GB45
Hutton Gro N12 98 DB50
Hutton La, Har. 94 CC52
Hutton Rd, Brwd. 109 FZ45
Hutton Row, Edg. 96 CQ52
Pavilion Way
Hutton St EC4 274 E9
Hutton Village, Brwd. 109 GE45
Hutton Wk, Har. 94 CC52
Huxbear St SE4 183 DZ85
Huxley Cl, Nthlt. 136 BY67
Huxley Cl, Uxb. 134 BK70
Huxley Dr, Rom. 126 EV59

Huxley Gdns NW10 138 CM69
Huxley Par N18 100 DR50
Huxley Pl N13 99 DP49
Huxley Rd E10 123 EC61
Huxley Rd N18 100 DR49
Huxley Rd (Surrey Research Pk), Guil. 258 AS135
Huxley Rd, Well. 165 ET83
Huxley Sayze N18 100 DR50
Huxley St W10 139 CY69
Hyacinth Cl, Hmptn. 176 CA93
Gresham Rd
Hyacinth Cl, Ilf. 145 EP65
Hyacinth Ct, Pnr. 116 BW55
Tulip Ct
Hyacinth Dr, Uxb. 134 BL66
Hyacinth Rd SW15 179 CU88
Hyburn Cl, Hem.H. 41 BP21
Hyburn Cl (Bricket Wd), St.Alb. 60 BZ30
Hycliffe Gdns, Chig. 103 EQ49
Hyde, The NW9 118 CS57
Hyde, The, Ware 32 DV05
Hyde Av, Pot.B. 64 DB33
Hyde Cl E13 144 EG68
Hyde Cl, Ashf. 175 BS93
Hyde Ter
Hyde Cl, Barn. 79 CZ41
Hyde Cl (Chafford Hundred), Grays 169 FX76
Hyde Ct N20 98 DD48
Hyde Ct, Wal.Cr. 67 DY34
Parkside
Hyde Cres NW9 118 CS57
Hyde Dr, Orp. 206 EV98
Hyde Est Rd NW9 119 CT57
Hyde Fm Ms SW12 181 DK88
Telferscot Rd
Hyde Grn, Beac. 89 AM52
Hyde Ho NW9 118 CS57
Hyde La SW11 160 DE81
Battersea Br Rd
Hyde La, Hem.H. 59 BR26
Hyde La (Bovingdon), Hem.H. 57 BA27
Hyde La (Frogmore), St.Alb. 61 CE28
Hyde La (Ockham), Wok. 228 BN120
Hyde Mead, Wal.Abb. 50 EE23
Hyde Meadows (Bovingdon), Hem.H. 57 BA28
Hyde Pk SW7 276 B2
Hyde Pk SW7 140 DF74
Hyde Pk W1 276 B2
Hyde Pk W1 140 DF74
Hyde Pk W2 276 B2
Hyde Pk W2 140 DF74
Hyde Pk Av N21 100 DQ47
Hyde Pk Cor W1 276 G4
Hyde Pk Cor W1 160 DG75
Hyde Pk Cres W2 272 B9
Hyde Pk Cres W2 140 DE72
Hyde Pk Gdns N21 100 DQ46
Hyde Pk Gdns W2 272 A10
Hyde Pk Gdns W2 140 DD73
Hyde Pk Gdns Ms W2 272 A10
Hyde Pk Gate SW7 160 DC75
Hyde Pk Gate Ms SW7 160 DC75
Hyde Pk Gate
Hyde Pk Pl W2 272 C10
Hyde Pk Pl W2 140 DE73
Hyde Pk Sq W2 272 B9
Hyde Pk Sq W2 140 DE72
Hyde Pk Sq Ms W2 272 B9
Hyde Pk St W2 272 B9
Hyde Pk St W2 140 DE72
Hyde Rd N1 142 DR67
Hyde Rd, Bexh. 166 EZ82
Hyde Rd, Rich. 178 CM85
Albert Rd
Hyde Rd, S.Croy. 220 DS113
Hyde Rd, Wat. 75 BU40
Hyde St SE8 163 EA79
Deptford High St
Hyde Ter, Ashf. 175 BS93
Hyde Vale SE10 163 EC80
Hyde Valley, Welw.G.C. 29 CZ11
Hyde Wk, Mord. 200 DA101
Hyde Way N9 100 DT47
Hyde Way, Hayes 155 BT77
Hyde Way, Welw.G.C. 29 CY09
Hydefield Cl N21 100 DR46
Hydefield Ct N9 100 DS47
Hyder Rd, Grays 171 GJ76
Hyderabad Way E15 144 EE66
Hydes Pl N1 141 DP66
Compton Av
Hydeside Gdns N9 100 DT47
Hydethorpe Av N9 100 DT47
Hydethorpe Rd SW12 181 DJ88
Hyland Cl, Horn. 127 FH59
Hyland Way, Horn. 127 FH59
Hylands Cl, Epsom 232 CQ115
Hylands Ms, Epsom 232 CQ115
Hylands Rd E17 101 ED54
Hylands Rd, Epsom 232 CQ115
Hylle Cl, Wind. 151 AL81
Hylton St SE18 165 ET77
Hyndewood SE23 183 DX90
Hyndman St SE15 162 DV79
Hynton Rd, Dag. 126 EW61
Hyperion Ct, Hem.H. 40 BM17
Hyperion Pl, Epsom 216 CR109
Hyperion Wk, Horl. 269 DH150
Hyrons Cl, Amer. 55 AS38
Hyrons La, Amer. 55 AR38
Hyrstdene, S.Croy. 219 DP105
Hyson Rd SE16 162 DV77
Galleywall Rd
Hythe, The, Stai. 173 BE92
Hythe Av, Bexh. 166 EZ80
Hythe Cl N18 100 DU49
Hythe Cl, Orp. 206 EW98
Sandway Rd
Hythe End Rd (Wraysbury), Stai. 173 BA89
Hythe Fld Av, Egh. 173 BD93
Hythe Pk Rd, Egh. 173 BC92
Hythe Path, Th.Hth. 202 DR97
Hythe Rd NW10 139 CU70
Hythe Rd, Stai. 173 BD92
Hythe Rd, Th.Hth. 202 DR96
Hythe St, Dart. 188 FL86
Hythe St Lwr, Dart. 188 FL85
Hyver Hill NW7 78 CR44

I

Ian Sq, Enf. 83 DX39
Lansbury Rd
Ibbetson Path, Loug. 85 EP41
Ibbotson Av E16 144 EF72
Ibbott St E1 142 DW70
Mantus Rd
Iberian Av, Wall. 219 DK105
Ibis La W4 158 CQ81
Ibis Way, Hayes 136 BX72
Cygnet Way
Ibscott Cl, Dag. 147 FC65
Ibsley Gdns SW15 179 CU88
Ibsley Way, Barn. 80 DE43
Ice Wf Marina N1 141 DL68
New Wf Rd
Icehouse Wd, Oxt. 254 EE131
Iceland Rd E3 143 EA67
Iceni Ct E3 143 DZ67
Roman Rd
Ickburgh Est E5 122 DV62
Ickburgh Rd
Ickburgh Rd E5 122 DV62
Ickenham Cl, Ruis. 115 BR61
Ickenham Rd, Ruis. 115 BR60
Ickenham Rd (Ickenham), Uxb. 115 BQ61
Ickleton Rd SE9 184 EL91
Icklingham Gate, Cob. 214 BW112
Icklingham Rd, Cob. 214 BW112
Icknield Cl, St.Alb. 42 BZ22
Icknield Dr, Ilf. 125 EP57
Ickworth Pk Rd E17 123 DY56
Ida Rd N15 122 DR57
Ida St E14 143 EC72
Iden Cl, Brom. 204 EE97
Idlecombe Rd SW17 180 DG93
Idmiston Rd E15 124 EF64
Idmiston Rd SE27 182 DQ90
Idmiston Rd, Wor.Pk. 199 CT101
Idmiston Sq, Wor.Pk. 199 CT101
Idol La EC3 279 M1
Idonia St SE8 163 DZ80
Iffley Cl, Uxb. 134 BK66
Iffley Rd W6 159 CV76
Ifield Cl, Red. 266 DE137
Ifield Rd SW10 160 DB79
Ifield Way, Grav. 191 GK93
Ifold Rd, Red. 266 DG136
Ifor Evans Pl E1 143 DX70
Mile End Rd
Ightham Rd, Erith 166 FA80
Ikea Twr NW10 118 CR64
Ikona Ct, Wey. 213 BQ106
Ilbert St W10 139 CX69
Ilchester Gdns W2 140 DB73
Ilchester Pl W14 159 CZ76
Ilchester Rd, Dag. 126 EV64
Ildersly Gro SE21 182 DR89
Ilderton Rd SE15 162 DW80
Ilderton Rd SE16 162 DV78
Ilex Cl (Englefield Grn), Egh. 172 AV94
Ilex Cl, Sun. 196 BW96
Oakington Dr
Ilex Ct, Berk. 38 AV19
Ilex Ho N4 121 DM59
Ilex Rd NW10 139 CT65
Ilex Way SW16 181 DN92
Ilford Hill, Ilf. 125 EN62
Ilford La, Ilf. 125 EP62
Ilfracombe Cres, Horn. 128 FJ63
Ilfracombe Gdns, Rom. 126 EV59
Ilfracombe Rd, Brom. 184 EF90
Iliffe St SE17 278 G10
Iliffe St SE17 161 DP78
Iliffe Yd SE17 278 G10
Ilkeston Ct E5 123 DX63
Overbury St
Ilkley Cl SE19 182 DR93
Ilkley Rd E16 144 EJ71
Ilkley Rd, Wat. 94 BX50
Illingworth, Wind. 151 AL84
Illingworth Cl, Mitch. 200 DD97
Illingworth Way, Enf. 82 DS42
Ilmington Rd, Har. 117 CK58
Ilminster Gdns SW11 160 DE84
Imber Cl N14 99 DJ45
Imber Cl, Esher 197 CD102
Ember La
Imber Ct Trd Est, E.Mol. 197 CD100
Imber Gro, Esher 197 CD101
Imber Pk Rd, Esher 197 CD102
Imber St N1 142 DR67
Imer Pl, T.Ditt. 197 CF101
Imperial Av N16 122 DT62
Victorian Rd
Imperial Business Est, Grav. 191 GF86
Imperial Cl, Har. 116 CA58
Imperial Coll Rd SW7 160 DD76
Imperial Cres, Wey. 195 BQ104
Churchill Dr
Imperial Dr, Grav. 191 GM92
Imperial Dr, Har. 116 CA59
Imperial Gdns, Mitch. 201 DH97
Imperial Ms E6 144 EJ68
Central Pk Rd
Imperial Pk, Wat. 76 BW39
Imperial Way
Imperial Retail Pk, Grav. 191 GG86
Imperial Rd N22 99 DL53
Imperial Rd SW6 160 DC81
Imperial Rd, Felt. 175 BS87
Imperial Rd, Wind. 151 AN83
Imperial Sq SW6 160 DB81
Imperial St E3 143 EC69
Imperial Way, Chis. 185 EQ90
Imperial Way, Croy. 219 DM107
Imperial Way, Har. 118 CL58
Imperial Way, Wat. 76 BW39
Imprimo Pk, Loug. 85 ER42
Lenthall Rd
Imre Cl W12 139 CV74
Ellerslie Rd
Inca Dr SE9 185 EP87
Ince Rd, Walt. 213 BS107
Inchmery Rd SE6 183 EB89
Inchwood, Croy. 221 EB105
Indells, Hat. 45 CT19
Independent Pl E8 122 DT64
Downs Pk Rd
Independents Rd SE3 164 EF83
Blackheath Village
Inderwick Rd N8 121 DM57
Indescon Ct E14 163 EB75
India Pl WC2 274 B10
India Rd, Slou. 152 AV75
India St EC3 275 P9
India Way W12 139 CV73
Indigo Ms E14 143 EC73
Ashton St
Indigo Ms N16 122 DR62
Indus Rd SE7 164 EJ80
Industry Ter SW9 161 DN83
Canterbury Cres
Ingal Rd E13 144 EG70
Ingate Pl SW8 161 DH81
Ingatestone Rd E12 124 EJ60
Ingatestone Rd SE25 202 DV98
Ingatestone Rd, Wdf.Grn. 102 EG52
Ingelow Rd SW8 161 DH82
Ingels Mead, Epp. 69 ET29
Ingersoll Rd W12 139 CV74
Ingersoll Rd, Enf. 82 DW38
Ingestre Pl W1 273 L9
Ingestre Rd E7 124 EG63
Ingestre Rd NW5 121 DH63
Ingham Cl, S.Croy. 221 DX109
Ingham Rd NW6 120 DA63
Ingham Rd, S.Croy. 220 DW109
Ingle Cl, Pnr. 116 BY55
Inglebert St EC1 274 D2
Ingleboro Dr, Pur. 220 DR113
Ingleborough St SW9 161 DN82
Ingleby Dr, Har. 117 CD62
Ingleby Gdns, Chig. 104 EV48
Ingleby Rd, Dag. 147 FB65
Ingleby Rd, Grays 171 GH76
Ingleby Rd, Ilf. 125 EP60
Ingleby Way, Chis. 185 EN92
Ingleby Way, Wall. 219 DK109
Ingledew Rd SE18 165 ER78
Inglefield, Pot.B. 64 DA30
Ingleglen, Horn. 128 FN59
Ingleglen (Farnham Common), Slou. 111 AP64
Inglehurst (New Haw), Add. 212 BH110
Inglehurst Gdns, Ilf. 125 EM57
Inglemere Rd SE23 183 DX90
Inglemere Rd, Mitch. 180 DF94
Ingles, Welw.G.C. 29 CX06
Inglesham Wk E9 143 DZ65
Ingleside (Colnbrook), Slou. 153 BE81
Ingleside Cl, Beck. 183 EA94
Ingleside Gro SE3 164 EF79
Inglethorpe St SW6 159 CX81
Ingleton Av, Well. 186 EU85
Ingleton Rd N18 100 DU51
Ingleton Rd, Cars. 218 DE109
Ingleton St SW9 161 DN82
Ingleway N12 98 DD51
Inglewood, Cher. 193 BF104
Inglewood, Croy. 221 DY109
Inglewood, Wok. 226 AV118
Inglewood Cl E14 163 EA77
Inglewood Cl, Horn. 128 FK63
Inglewood Cl, Ilf. 103 ET51
Inglewood Copse, Brom. 204 EL96
Inglewood Rd NW6 120 DA64
Inglewood Rd, Bexh. 167 FD84
Inglis Barracks NW7 97 CY51
Inglis Rd W5 138 CM73
Inglis Rd, Croy. 202 DT102
Inglis St SE5 161 DP81
Ingoldsby Rd, Grav. 191 GL88
Ingram Av NW11 120 DC59
Ingram Cl SE11 278 C8
Ingram Cl, Stan. 95 CJ50
Ingram Rd N2 120 DE56
Ingram Rd, Dart. 188 FL88
Ingram Rd, Grays 170 GD77
Ingram Rd, Th.Hth. 202 DQ95
Ingram Way, Grnf. 137 CD67
Ingrams Cl, Walt. 214 BW106
Ingrave Ho, Dag. 146 EV67
Ingrave Rd, Brwd. 108 FX47
Ingrave Rd, Rom. 127 FD56
Ingrave St SW11 160 DD83
Ingrebourne Gdns, Upmin. 128 FQ60
Ingrebourne Rd, Rain. 147 FH70
Ingrebourne Valley Grn Way, Horn. 128 FK64
Ingress Gdns, Green. 189 FX85
Ingress St W4 158 CS78
Devonshire Rd
Ingreway, Rom. 106 FP52
Inholms La, Dor. 263 CH140
Inigo Jones Rd SE7 164 EL80
Inigo Pl WC2 273 P10
Inkerman Rd NW5 141 DH65
Inkerman Rd, St.Alb. 43 CE21
Inkerman Rd (Eton Wick), Wind. 151 AM77
Inkerman Rd (Knaphill), Wok. 226 AS118
Inkerman Ter W8 160 DA76
Allen St
Inkerman Ter, Chesh. 54 AQ33
Inkerman Way, Wok. 226 AS118
Inks Grn E4 101 EC50
Inman Rd NW10 138 CS67
Inman Rd SW18 180 DC87
Inmans Row, Wdf.Grn. 102 EG49
Inner Circle NW1 272 F2
Inner Circle NW1 140 DG69
Inner Pk Rd SW19 179 CX88
Inner Ring E (Heathrow Airport), Houns. 155 BP83
Inner Ring W (Heathrow Airport), Houns. 154 BN83
Inner Temple La EC4 274 D9
Innes Cl SW20 199 CY96
Innes Ct, Hem.H. 40 BK22
Innes Gdns SW15 179 CV86
Innes Yd, Croy. 202 DQ104
Whitgift St
Inniskilling Rd E13 144 EJ68
Innova Pk, Enf. 83 DZ36
Innova Way, Enf. 83 DZ36
Innovation Cl, Wem. 138 CL67
Inskip Cl E10 123 EB61
Inskip Dr, Horn. 128 FL60
Inskip Rd, Dag. 126 EX60
Institute Pl E8 122 DV64
Amhurst Rd
Institute Rd (Westcott), Dor. 262 CC137
Guildford Rd
Institute Rd, Epp. 70 EX29
Institute Rd, Maid. 130 AF72
Instone Cl, Wall. 219 DL108
Instone Rd, Dart. 188 FK87
Integer Gdns E11 123 ED59
Forest Rd
Interchange E Ind Est E5 122 DW60
Theydon Rd
International Av, Houns. 156 BW78
International Trd Est, Sthl. 155 BV76
Inver Cl E5 122 DW61
Theydon Rd
Inver Ct W2 140 DB72
Inverness Ter
Inveraray Pl SE18 165 ER79
Old Mill Rd
Inverclyde Gdns, Rom. 126 EX56
Inveresk Gdns, Wor.Pk. 199 CT104
Inverforth Cl NW3 120 DC61
North End Way
Inverforth Rd N11 99 DH50
Inverine Rd SE7 164 EH78
Invermore Pl SE18 165 EQ77
Inverness Av, Enf. 82 DS39
Inverness Dr, Ilf. 103 ES51
Inverness Gdns W8 140 DB74
Vicarage Gate
Inverness Ms E16 165 EP75
Inverness Ms W2 140 DB73
Inverness Ter
Inverness Pl W2 140 DB73
Inverness Rd N18 100 DV50
Aberdeen Rd
Inverness Rd, Houns. 156 BZ84
Inverness Rd, Sthl. 156 BY77
Inverness Rd, Wor.Pk. 199 CX102
Inverness St NW1 141 DH67
Inverness Ter W2 140 DB73
Inverton Rd SE15 163 DX84
Invicta Cl, Chis. 185 EN92
Invicta Cl, Felt. 175 BT88
Westmacott Dr
Invicta Gro, Nthlt. 136 BZ69
Invicta Plaza SE1 278 F2
Invicta Rd SE3 164 EG80
Invicta Rd, Dart. 188 FP86
Inville Rd SE17 162 DR78
Inwen Ct SE8 163 DY78
Inwood Av, Couls. 235 DN120
Inwood Av, Houns. 156 CC83
Inwood Cl, Croy. 203 DY103
Inwood Ct, Walt. 196 BW103
Elliman Av
Inwood Rd, Houns. 156 CB84
Inworth St SW11 160 DE82
Inworth Wk N1 142 DQ67
Popham St
Ion Sq E2 142 DU68
Hackney Rd
Iona Cl SE6 183 EA87
Iona Cl, Mord. 200 DB101
Iona Cres, Slou. 131 AL72
Ionian Way, Hem.H. 40 BM18
Jupiter Dr
Ipswich Rd SW17 180 DG93
Ipswich Rd, Slou. 131 AN73
Ireland Cl E6 145 EM71
Bradley Stone Rd
Ireland Pl N22 99 DL52
Whittington Rd
Ireland Yd EC4 274 G9
Ireland Yd EC4 141 DP72
Irene Rd SW6 160 DA81
Irene Rd (Stoke D'Abernon), Cob. 214 CA114
Irene Rd, Orp. 205 ET101
Ireton Av, Walt. 195 BS103
Ireton Cl N10 98 DG52
Ireton Pl, Grays 170 GA77
Russell Rd
Ireton St E3 143 EA70
Tidworth Rd
Iris Av, Bex. 186 EY85
Iris Cl E6 144 EL70
Iris Cl, Brwd. 108 FV43
Iris Cl, Croy. 203 DX102
Iris Cl, Surb. 198 CM101
Iris Ct, Pnr. 116 BW55
Iris Cres, Bexh. 166 EZ79
Iris Path, Rom. 106 FJ52
Clematis Cl
Iris Rd (West Ewell), Epsom 216 CP106
Iris Wk, Edg. 96 CQ49
Ash Cl
Iris Way E4 101 DZ51
Irkdale Av, Enf. 82 DT39
Iron Br Cl NW10 118 CS64
Iron Br Cl, Sthl. 136 CC74
Iron Br Rd, Uxb. 154 BN75
Iron Br Rd, West Dr. 154 BN75
Iron Dr, Hert. 32 DV08
Iron Mill La, Dart. 167 FE84
Iron Mill Pl SW18 180 DB86
Garratt La
Iron Mill Pl, Dart. 167 FF84
Iron Mill Rd SW18 180 DB86
Ironmonger La EC2 275 K9
Ironmonger Pas EC1 275 J4
Ironmonger Row EC1 275 J4
Ironmonger Row EC1 142 DQ69
Ironmongers Pl E14 163 EA77
Spindrift Av
Irons Way, Rom. 105 FC52
Ironsbottom, Horl. 268 DA146
Ironsbottom (Sidlow), Reig. 266 DB141
Ironside Cl SE16 163 DX75
Kinburn St
Irvine Av, Har. 117 CG55
Irvine Cl N20 98 DE47
Irvine Gdns, S.Ock. 149 FT72
Irvine Pl, Vir.W. 192 AY99
Irvine Way, Orp. 205 ET101
Irving Av, Nthlt. 136 BX67
Irving Gro SW9 161 DM82
Irving Ms N1 142 DQ65
Alwyne Rd
Irving Rd W14 159 CX76
Irving St WC2 273 N10
Irving St WC2 141 DK73
Irving Wk, Swans. 190 FY87
Irving Way NW9 119 CT57
Irving Way, Swan. 207 FD96
Irwin Av SE18 165 ES80
Irwin Cl, Uxb. 114 BN62
Irwin Gdns NW10 139 CV67
Irwin Rd, Guil. 258 AU135
Isabel Gate (Cheshunt), Wal.Cr. 67 DZ26
Isabel Hill Cl, Hmptn. 196 CB95
Upper Sunbury Rd
Isabel St SW9 161 DM81
Isabella Cl N14 99 DJ45
Isabella Ct, Rich. 178 CM86
Grove Rd
Isabella Dr, Orp. 223 EQ105
Isabella Rd E9 122 DW64
Isabella St SE1 278 F3
Isabella St SE1 141 DP74
Isabelle Cl, Wal.Cr. 66 DQ29
Isambard Cl, Uxb. 134 BK69
Isambard Ms E14 163 EC76
Isambard Pl SE16 142 DW74
Rotherhithe St
Isbell Gdns, Rom. 105 FE52
Isbells Dr, Reig. 266 DB135
Isel Way SE22 182 DS85
East Dulwich Gro
Isenburg Way, Hem.H. 40 BK15
Isham Rd SW16 201 DL96
Isis Cl SW15 159 CW84
Isis Cl, Ruis. 115 BQ58
Isis Dr, Upmin. 129 FS58
Isis St SW18 180 DC89
Isla Rd SE18 165 EQ79
Island, The (Wraysbury), Stai. 173 BA90
Island, The, West Dr. 154 BH81
Island Cl, Stai. 173 BE91
Island Fm Av, W.Mol. 196 BZ99
Island Fm Rd, W.Mol. 196 BZ99
Island Rd, Mitch. 180 DF94
Island Row E14 143 DZ72
Islay Gdns, Houns. 176 BX85
Islay Wk N1 142 DQ66
Douglas Rd
Isledon Rd N7 121 DN62
Islehurst Cl, Chis. 205 EN95
Islet Pk Dr, Maid. 130 AC68
Islet Pk Rd, Maid. 130 AC68
Isleworth Business Complex, Islw. 157 CF82
St. John's Rd
Isleworth Prom, Twick. 157 CH84
Islington Grn N1 141 DP67
Islington High St N1 274 E1
Islington High St N1 141 DP68
Islington Pk Ms N1 141 DN66
Islington Pk St
Islington Pk St N1 141 DN66
Islip Gdns, Edg. 96 CR52
Islip Gdns, Nthlt. 136 BY66
Islip Manor Rd, Nthlt. 136 BY66
Islip St NW5 121 DJ64
Ismailia Rd E7 144 EH66
Ismay Ct, Slou. 132 AS73
Elliman Av
Isom Cl E13 144 EJ70
Belgrave Rd
Istead Ri, Grav. 191 GF94
Itchingwood Common Rd, Oxt. 254 EJ133
Ivanhoe Cl, Uxb. 134 BK71
Ivanhoe Dr, Har. 117 CG55
Ivanhoe Rd SE5 162 DT83
Ivanhoe Rd, Houns. 156 BX83
Ivatt Pl W14 159 CZ78
Ivatt Way N17 121 DP55
Ive Fm Cl E10 123 EA61
Ive Fm La E10 123 EA61
Iveagh Av NW10 138 CN68
Iveagh Cl E9 143 DX67
Iveagh Cl NW10 138 CN68
Iveagh Cl, Nthwd. 93 BP53
Iveagh Ct, Hem.H. 40 BK19
Iveagh Rd, Guil. 258 AV135
Iveagh Rd, Wok. 226 AT118
Iveagh Ter NW10 138 CN68
Iveagh Av
Ivedon Rd, Well. 166 EW82
Iveley Rd SW4 161 DJ82
Iver La, Iver 134 BH71
Iver La, Uxb. 134 BH71
Iver Rd, Brwd. 108 FV44
Iver Rd, Iver 134 BG72
Iverdale Cl, Iver 133 BC73
Ivere Dr, Barn. 80 DB44
Iverhurst Cl, Bexh. 186 EX85
Iverna Ct W8 160 DA76
Iverna Gdns W8 160 DA76
Iverna Gdns, Felt. 175 BR85
Ivers Way (New Addington), Croy. 221 EB108
Iverson Rd NW6 139 CZ65
Ives Gdns, Rom. 127 FF56
Sims Cl
Ives Rd E16 144 EE71
Ives Rd, Hert. 31 DP08
Ives Rd, Slou. 153 AZ76
Ives St SW3 276 C8
Ives St SW3 160 DE77
Ivestor Ter SE23 182 DW87
Ivimey St E2 142 DU69
Ivinghoe Cl, Enf. 82 DS40
Ivinghoe Cl, St.Alb. 43 CJ15
Highview Gdns
Ivinghoe Cl, Wat. 76 BX35
Ivinghoe Rd, Bushey 95 CD45
Ivinghoe Rd, Dag. 126 EV64
Ivinghoe Rd, Rick. 92 BG45
Ivins Rd, Beac. 88 AG54
Ivor Cl, Guil. 259 AZ135
Ivor Gro SE9 185 EP88
Ivor Pl NW1 272 D5
Ivor Pl NW1 140 DF70
Ivor St NW1 141 DJ66
Ivory Cl, St.Alb. 43 CJ22
Ivory Ct, Hem.H. 40 BL23
Ivory Sq SW11 160 DC83
Gartons Way
Ivorydown, Brom. 184 EG91
Ivy Bower Cl, Green. 189 FV85
Riverview Rd
Ivy Chimneys Rd, Epp. 69 ES32
Ivy Cl, Dart. 188 FN87
Ivy Cl, Grav. 191 GJ90
Ivy Cl, Har. 116 BZ63
Ivy Cl, Pnr. 116 BW59
Ivy Cl, Sun. 196 BW96
Ivy Cotts E14 143 EB73
Grove Vil
Ivy Ct SE16 162 DU78
Argyle Way
Ivy Cres W4 158 CQ77
Ivy Cres, Slou. 131 AM73
Ivy Gdns N8 121 DL58
Ivy Gdns, Mitch. 201 DK97
Ivy Ho La, Berk. 38 AY19
Ivy Ho La, Sev. 241 FD118
Ivy Ho Rd, Uxb. 115 BP62
Ivy La, Houns. 156 BZ84
Ivy La (Knockholt), Sev. 240 EY116
Ivy La, Wok. 227 BB118
Ivy Lea, Rick. 92 BG46
Springwell Av
Ivy Lo La, Rom. 106 FP53
Ivy Mill Cl, Gdse. 252 DV132
Ivy Mill La, Gdse. 252 DU132
Ivy Pl, Surb. 198 CM100
Alpha Rd
Ivy Rd E16 144 EG72
Pacific Rd
Ivy Rd E17 123 EA58
Ivy Rd N14 99 DJ45
Ivy Rd NW2 119 CW63
Ivy Rd SE4 163 DZ84
Ivy Rd SW17 180 DE92
Tooting High St
Ivy Rd, Houns. 156 CB84
Ivy Rd, Surb. 198 CN102
Ivy St N1 142 DS68
Ivy Ter, Hodd. 49 EC15
Ivy Wk, Dag. 146 EY65
Ivybridge, Brox. 49 EA19
Ivybridge Cl, Twick. 177 CG86
Ivybridge Cl, Uxb. 134 BL69
Ivybridge Est, Islw. 177 CF85
Ivybridge La WC2 278 A1
Ivychurch Cl SE20 182 DW94
Ivychurch La SE17 279 P10
Ivydale Rd SE15 163 DX83
Ivydale Rd, Cars. 200 DF103
Ivyday Gro SW16 181 DM90
Ivydene, W.Mol. 196 BZ99
Ivydene Cl, Red. 267 DH139
Ivydene Cl, Sutt. 218 DC105
Ivyhouse Rd, Dag. 146 EX65

Ivy - Jun This index reads in the sequence: Street Name / Postal District or Post Town / Map Page Number / Grid Reference

Ivymount Rd SE27 181 DN90
Ixworth Pl SW3 276 B10
Ixworth Pl SW3 160 DE78
Izane Rd, Bexh. 166 EZ84

J

Jacaranda Cl, N.Mal. 198 CS97
Jacaranda Gro E8 142 DT66
Queensbridge Rd
Jack Barnett Way N22 99 DM54
Jack Clow Rd E15 144 EE68
Jack Cornwell St E12 125 EN63
Jack Dash Way E6 144 EL70
Jack Goodchild Way, Kings.T. 198 CP97
Kingston Rd
Jack Stevens Cl, Harl. 52 EW17
Hillside
Jack Walker Ct N5 121 DP63
Jackass La, Kes. 222 EH107
Jackass La (Tandridge), Oxt. 253 DZ131
Jackdaws, Welw.G.C. 30 DC09
Jackets La, Nthwd. 93 BP53
Jackets La (Harefield), Uxb. 92 BN52
Jacketts Fld, Abb.L. 59 BT31
Jacklin Grn, Wdf.Grn. 102 EG49
Jackman Ms NW10 118 CS62
Jackman St E8 142 DV67
Jackmans La, Wok. 226 AU119
Jacks La (Harefield), Uxb. 92 BG53
Jackson Cl E9 142 DW66
Jackson Cl, Epsom 216 CR114
Jackson Cl, Green. 189 FU85
Cowley Av
Jackson Cl, Horn. 128 FM56
Jackson Cl, Uxb. 134 BL66
Jackson Rd
Jackson Ct E11 124 EG60
Brading Cres
Jackson Rd N7 121 DM63
Jackson Rd, Bark. 145 ER67
Jackson Rd, Barn. 80 DE44
Jackson Rd, Brom. 204 EL103
Jackson Rd, Uxb. 134 BL66
Jackson St SE18 165 EN79
Jackson Way, Sthl. 156 CB75
Jacksons Dr, Wal.Cr. 66 DU28
Jacksons La N6 120 DG59
Jacksons Pl, Croy. 202 DR102
Cross Rd
Jacksons Way, Croy. 203 EA104
Jacob Ho, Erith 166 EX75
Kale Rd
Jacob St SE1 162 DU75
Jacobs Av, Rom. 106 FL54
Jacobs Cl, Dag. 127 FB63
Jacobs Cl, Wind. 151 AL81
Jacobs Ho E13 144 EJ69
Jacobs Ladder, Hat. 45 CW18
The Bdy
Jacobs La (Horton Kirby), Dart. 208 FQ97
Jacob's Well Ms W1 272 G8
Jacob's Well Rd, Guil. 242 AX129
Jacqueline Cl, Nthlt. 136 BZ67
Canford Av
Jade Cl E16 144 EK72
Jade Cl NW2 119 CX59
Marble Dr
Jade Cl, Dag. 126 EW60
Jaffe Rd, Ilf. 125 EQ60
Jaffray Pl SE27 181 DP91
Chapel Rd
Jaffray Rd, Brom. 204 EK98
Jaggard Way SW12 180 DF87
Jagger Cl, Dart. 188 FQ87
Jago Cl SE18 165 EQ79
Jago Wk SE5 162 DR80
Jail La (Biggin Hill), West. 238 EK116
Jamaica Rd SE1 162 DU75
Jamaica Rd SE16 162 DV75
Jamaica Rd, Th.Hth. 201 DP100
Jamaica St E1 142 DW72
James Av NW2 119 CW64
James Av, Dag. 126 EZ60
James Bedford Cl, Pnr. 94 BW54
James Boswell Cl SW16 181 DN91
Curtis Fld Rd
James Cl E13 144 EG68
Richmond St
James Cl NW11 119 CY58
Woodlands
James Cl, Bushey 76 BY43
Aldenham Rd
James Cl, Rom. 127 FG57
James Collins Cl W9 139 CZ70
Fermoy Rd
James Ct N1 142 DQ66
Morton Rd
James Dudson Ct NW10 138 CQ66
James Gdns N22 99 DP52
James Hammett Ho E2 142 DT69
Ravenscroft St
James Joyce Wk SE24 161 DP84
Shakespeare Rd
James La E10 123 ED59
James La E11 123 ED58
James Lee Sq, Enf. 83 EA37
Government Row
James Martin Cl (Denham), Uxb. 114 BG58
James Newman Ct SE9 185 EN90
Great Harry Dr
James Pl N17 100 DT53
James Rd, Dart. 187 FG87
James Rd (Peasmarsh), Guil. 258 AW142
James Sinclair Pt E13 144 EJ67
James St W1 272 G8
James St W1 140 DG72
James St WC2 274 A10
James St, Bark. 145 EQ66
James St, Enf. 82 DT43
James St, Epp. 69 ET28
James St, Houns. 157 CD83
James St, Wind. 151 AR81
James Ter SW14 158 CR83
Mullins Path
James Watt Way, Erith 167 FE79
James Yd E4 101 ED51
Jameson Cl W3 158 CQ75
Acton La
Jameson Ct E2 142 DW68
Russia La
Jameson Ct, St.Alb. 43 CF19
Avenue Rd
Jameson St W8 140 DA74
Jameson Wk, Wdf.Grn. 102 EK51
Baddow Cl
James's Cotts, Rich. 158 CN80
Kew Rd
Jamestown Rd NW1 141 DH67
Jamestown Way E14 143 ED73
Jamieson Ho, Houns. 176 BZ87
Jamnagar Cl, Stai. 173 BF93
Jane Cl, Hem.H. 41 BP15
Jane St E1 142 DV72
Commercial Rd
Janet St E14 163 EA76
Janeway Pl SE16 162 DV75
Janeway St
Janeway St SE16 162 DU75
Janice Ms, Ilf. 125 EP62
Oakfield Rd
Janmead, Brwd. 109 GB45
Janoway Hill La, Wok. 226 AW119
Jansen Wk SW11 160 DD84
Hope St
Janson Cl E15 124 EE64
Janson Rd
Janson Cl NW10 118 CR62
Janson Rd E15 124 EE64
Jansons Rd N15 122 DS55
Japan Cres N4 121 DM59
Japan Rd, Rom. 126 EX58
Japonica Cl, Wok. 226 AW118
Jardine Rd E1 143 DX73
Jarman Cl, Hem.H. 40 BL22
Jarmans Pk, Hem.H. 40 BM21
Jarmans Way, Hem.H. 40 BM21
Jarrah Cotts, Purf. 169 FR79
London Rd Purfleet
Jarrett Cl SW2 181 DP88
Jarrow Cl, Mord. 200 DB99
Jarrow Rd N17 122 DV56
Jarrow Rd SE16 162 DW77
Jarrow Rd, Rom. 126 EW58
Jarrow Way E9 123 DY63
Jarvis Cleys (Cheshunt), Wal.Cr. 66 DT26
Jarvis Cl, Bark. 145 ER67
Westbury Rd
Jarvis Cl, Barn. 79 CX43
Jarvis Rd SE22 162 DS84
Melbourne Gro
Jarvis Rd, S.Croy. 220 DR107
Jarvis Way, Rom. 106 FL54
Jasmin Cl, Nthwd. 93 BT53
Jasmin Rd, Epsom 216 CP106
Jasmin Way, Hem.H. 39 BE19
Larkspur Cl
Jasmine Cl, Ilf. 125 EP64
Jasmine Cl, Orp. 205 EP103
Jasmine Cl, Red. 266 DG139
Spencer Way
Jasmine Cl, Sthl. 136 BY73
Jasmine Cl, Wok. 226 AT116
Jasmine Dr, Hert. 32 DU09
Jasmine Gdns, Croy. 203 EB104
Jasmine Gdns, Har. 116 CA61
Jasmine Gdns, Hat. 45 CU16
Jasmine Gro SE20 202 DV95
Jasmine Rd, Rom. 127 FE61
Jasmine Ter, West Dr. 154 BN75
Jasmine Way, E.Mol. 197 CE98
Hampton Ct Way
Jason Cl, Brwd. 108 FT49
Jason Cl, Red. 266 DE139
Jason Cl, Wey. 213 BQ106
Jason Ct W1 140 DG72
Marylebone La
Jason Wk SE9 185 EN91
Jasons Dr, Guil. 243 BC131
Jasons Hill, Chesh. 56 AV30
Jasper Cl, Enf. 82 DW38
Jasper Pas SE19 182 DT93
Jasper Rd E16 144 EK72
Jasper Rd SE19 182 DT92
Jasper Wk N1 275 K2
Javelin Way, Nthlt. 136 BX69
Jay Gdns, Chis. 185 EM91
Jay Ms SW7 160 DC75
Jaycroft, Enf. 81 DN39
The Ridgeway
Jays Covert, Couls. 234 DG119
Jean Batten Cl, Wall. 219 DM108
Lancastrian Rd
Jebb Av SW2 181 DL86
Jebb St E3 143 EA68
Jedburgh Rd E13 144 EJ69
Jedburgh St SW11 160 DG84
Jeddo Rd W12 159 CT75
Jefferson Cl W13 157 CH76
Jefferson Cl, Ilf. 125 EP57
Jefferson Cl, Slou. 153 BA77
Jefferson Wk SE18 165 EN79
Kempt St
Jeffreys Pl NW1 141 DJ66
Jeffreys St
Jeffreys Rd SW4 161 DL82
Jeffreys Rd, Enf. 83 DZ41
Jeffreys St NW1 141 DH66
Jeffreys Wk SW4 161 DL82
Jeffries Ho NW10 138 CR67
Jeffries Pas, Guil. 258 AX135
High St
Jeffries Rd (West Horsley), Lthd. 245 BQ130
Jeffries Rd, Ware 33 DY06
Jeffs Cl, Hmptn. 176 CB93
Uxbridge Rd
Jeffs Rd, Sutt. 217 CZ105
Jeger Av E2 142 DT67
Jeken Rd SE9 164 EJ84
Jelf Rd SW2 181 DN85
Jellicoe Av, Grav. 191 GJ90
Jellicoe Av W, Grav. 191 GJ90
Kitchener Av
Jellicoe Cl, Slou. 151 AP75
Jellicoe Gdns, Stan. 95 CF51
Jellicoe Rd E13 144 EG70
Jutland Rd
Jellicoe Rd N17 100 DR52
Jellicoe Rd, Wat. 75 BU44
Jemmett Cl, Kings.T. 198 CP95
Jengar Cl, Sutt. 218 DB105
Jenkins Av (Bricket Wd), St.Alb. 60 BY30
Jenkins La E6 145 EN68
Jenkins La, Bark. 145 EP68
Jenkins Rd E13 144 EH70
Jenner Av W3 138 CR71
Jenner Ho SE3 164 EE79
Jenner Pl SW13 159 CV79
Jenner Rd N16 122 DT61
Jenner Rd, Guil. 258 AY135
Jennery La (Burnham), Slou. 130 AJ69
Jennett Rd, Croy. 201 DN104
Jennifer Rd, Brom. 184 EF90
Jennings Cl (New Haw), Add. 212 BJ109
Woodham La
Jennings Cl, Surb. 197 CJ101
Jennings Fld (Flackwell Heath), H.Wyc. 110 AC56
Jennings Rd SE22 182 DT86
Jennings Rd, St.Alb. 43 CJ19
Jennings Way, Barn. 79 CW41
Jennings Way, Hem.H. 40 BL22
Jennings Way, Horl. 269 DK148
Jenningtree Rd, Erith 167 FH80
Jenningtree Way, Belv. 167 FC75
Jenny Hammond Cl E11 124 EF62
Newcomen Rd
Jenny Path, Rom. 106 FK52
Jennys Way, Couls. 235 DH121
Brighton Rd
Jenson Way SE19 182 DT94
Jenton Av, Bexh. 166 EY81
Jephson Rd E7 144 EJ66
Jephson St SE5 162 DR81
Grove La
Jephtha Rd SW18 180 DA86
Jeppos La, Mitch. 200 DF98
Jepps Cl, Wal.Cr. 66 DS27
Little Gro Av
Jerdan Pl SW6 160 DA80
Jeremiah St E14 143 EB72
Jeremys Grn N18 100 DV49
Jermyn St SW1 277 K2
Jermyn St SW1 141 DK73
Jerningham Av, Ilf. 103 EP54
Jerningham Rd SE14 163 DY82
Jerome Cres NW8 272 B4
Jerome Cres NW8 140 DE70
Jerome Dr, St.Alb. 42 CA22
Jerome Pl, Kings.T. 197 CK96
Wadbrook St
Jerome St E1 275 P6
Jerounds, Harl. 51 EP17
Jerrard St N1 275 N1
Jerrard St SE13 163 EB83
Jersey Av, Stan. 95 CH54
Jersey Cl, Cher. 193 BF104
Jersey Cl, Guil. 243 BB129
Weybrook Dr
Jersey Cl, Hodd. 49 EA16
Jersey Dr, Orp. 205 ER100
Jersey Ho, Enf. 83 DX38
Eastfield Rd
Jersey La, St.Alb. 43 CH18
Jersey Par, Houns. 156 CB81
Jersey Rd E11 123 ED60
Jersey Rd E16 144 EJ72
Prince Regent La
Jersey Rd SW17 181 DH93
Jersey Rd W7 157 CG75
Jersey Rd, Houns. 156 CB81
Jersey Rd, Ilf. 125 EP63
Jersey Rd, Islw. 157 CE79
Jersey Rd, Rain. 147 FG66
Jersey St E2 142 DV69
Bethnal Grn Rd
Jerusalem Pas EC1 274 F5
Jervis Av, Enf. 83 DY35
Jervis Ct W1 273 J9
Jerviston Gdns SW16 181 DN93
Jesmond Av, Wem. 138 CM65
Jesmond Cl, Mitch. 201 DH97
Jesmond Rd, Croy. 202 DT101
Jesmond Way, Stan. 96 CL50
Jessam Av E5 122 DV60
Jessamine Pl, Dart. 188 FQ87
Jessamine Rd W7 137 CE74
Jessamine Ter, Swan. 207 FC95
Birchwood Rd
Jessamy Rd, Wey. 195 BP103
Jesse Rd E10 123 EC60
Jessel Dr, Loug. 85 EQ39
Jesses La (Peaslake), Guil. 261 BQ144
Jessett Cl, Erith 167 FD77
West St
Jessica Rd SW18 180 DC86
Jessie Blythe La N19 121 DL59
Jessiman Ter, Shep. 194 BN99
Jessop Av, Sthl. 156 BZ77
Jessop Rd SE24 161 DP84
Milkwood Rd
Jessop Sq E14 143 EA74
Heron Quay
Jessops Way, Croy. 201 DJ100
Jessup Cl SE18 165 EQ77
Jetstar Way, Nthlt. 136 BY69
Jetty Wk, Grays 170 GA79
Jevington Way SE12 184 EH88
Jewel Rd E17 123 EA55
Jewels Hill (Biggin Hill), West. 222 EG112
Jewry St EC3 275 P9
Jewry St EC3 142 DT72
Jew's Row SW18 160 DC84
Jews Wk SE26 182 DV91
Jeymer Av NW2 119 CV64
Jeymer Dr, Grnf. 136 CC67
Jeypore Pas SW18 180 DC86
Jeypore Rd
Jeypore Rd SW18 180 DC87
Jillian Cl, Hmptn. 176 CA94
Jim Bradley Cl SE18 165 EN77
John Wilson St
Jim Desormeaux Bungalows, Harl. 35 ES13
School La
Jim Griffiths Ho SW6 159 CZ79
Clem Attlee Ct
Jinnings, The, Welw.G.C. 30 DA12
Joan Cres SE9 184 EK87
Joan Gdns, Dag. 126 EY61
Joan Rd, Dag. 126 EY61
Joan St SE1 278 F3
Joan St SE1 141 DP74
Jocelyn Rd, Rich. 158 CL83
Jocelyn St SE15 162 DU81
Jocelyns, Harl. 36 EW11
Jocketts Hill, Hem.H. 39 BF20
Jocketts Rd, Hem.H. 39 BF21
Jockey's Flds WC1 274 C6
Jockey's Flds WC1 141 DM71
Jodane St SE8 163 DZ77
Jodies Ct, St.Alb. 43 CJ18
Jodrell Cl, Islw. 157 CG81
Jodrell Rd E3 143 DZ67
Jodrell Way, Grays 169 FT78
Joel St, Nthwd. 115 BU55
Joel St, Pnr. 115 BU55
Johanna St SE1 278 D5
John Adam St WC2 278 A1
John Adam St WC2 141 DL73
John Aird Ct W2 140 DC71
John Archer Way SW18 180 DD86
John Ashby Cl SW2 181 DL86
John Austin Cl, Kings.T. 198 CM95
Queen Elizabeth Rd
John Barnes Wk E15 144 EF65
John Bradshaw Rd N14 99 DK46
High St
John Burns Dr, Bark. 145 ES66
John Campbell Rd N16 122 DS64
John Carpenter St EC4 274 F10
John Carpenter St EC4 141 DP73
John Cobb Rd, Wey. 212 BN108
John Cornwell VC Ho E12 125 EN63
John Ct, Hodd. 33 EA14
Molesworth
John Eliot Cl, Wal.Abb. 50 EE21
John Felton Rd SE16 162 DU75
John Fisher St E1 142 DU73
John Gooch Dr, Enf. 81 DP39
John Harrison Way SE10 164 EF76
John Horner Ms N1 142 DQ68
Frome St
John Islip St SW1 277 P9
John Islip St SW1 161 DL77
John Keats Ho N22 99 DM52
John Maurice Cl SE17 279 K8
John Maurice Cl SE17 162 DR77
John McKenna Wk SE16 162 DU76
Tranton Rd
John Newton Ct, Well. 166 EV83
Danson La
John Parker Cl, Dag. 147 FB66
John Parker Sq SW11 160 DD83
Thomas Baines Rd
John Penn St SE13 163 EB81
John Perrin Pl, Har. 118 CL59
John Princes St W1 273 J8
John Princes St W1 141 DH72
John Rennie Wk E1 142 DV74
Wine Cl
John Roll Way SE16 162 DU76
John Ruskin St SE5 161 DP80
John Russell Cl, Guil. 242 AU131
John Silkin La SE8 163 DX77
John Smith Av SW6 159 CZ80
John Spencer Sq N1 141 DP65
John St E15 144 EF67
John St SE25 202 DU98
John St WC1 274 C5
John St WC1 141 DM70
John St, Enf. 82 DT43
John St, Grays 170 GC79
John St, Houns. 156 BY82
John Tate Rd, Hert. 32 DT10
John Taylor Ct, Slou. 131 AQ74
John Trundle Ct EC2 142 DQ71
The Barbican
John Walsh Twr E11 124 EF61
John Williams Cl SE14 163 DX79
John Williams Cl, Kings.T. 197 CK95
Henry Macaulay Av
John Wilson St SE18 165 EN76
John Woolley Cl SE13 164 EE84
Johnby Cl, Enf. 83 DY37
Manly Dixon Dr
Johns Av NW4 119 CW56
Johns Cl, Ashf. 175 BQ91
Johns Ct, Sutt. 218 DB107
Mulgrave Rd
Johns La, Mord. 200 DC99
John's Ms WC1 274 C5
John's Ms WC1 141 DM70
John's Pl E1 142 DV72
Damien St
Johns Rd (Tatsfield), West. 238 EK120
John's Ter, Croy. 202 DR102
John's Ter, Rom. 106 FP51
Johns Wk, Whyt. 236 DU119
Johnsdale, Oxt. 254 EF129
Johnson Cl E8 142 DU67
Johnson Cl (Northfleet), Grav. 190 GD90
Johnson Ct, Hem.H. 40 BL22
Johnson Rd NW10 138 CR67
Milton Av
Johnson Rd, Brom. 204 EK99
Johnson Rd, Croy. 202 DR101
Johnson Rd, Houns. 156 BW80
Johnson St E1 142 DW73
Cable St
Johnson St, Sthl. 156 BW76
Johnsons Av (Badgers Mt), Sev. 225 FB110
Johnsons Cl, Cars. 200 DF104
Johnson's Ct EC4 141 DN72
Fleet St
Johnsons Ct (Seal), Sev. 257 FM121
School La
Johnsons Dr, Hmptn. 196 CC95
Johnson's Pl SW1 161 DJ78
Johnsons Way NW10 138 CP70
Johnsons Way, Green. 189 FW86
Johnsons Yd, Uxb. 134 BJ66
Redford Way
Johnston Cl SW9 161 DM81
Hackford Rd
Johnston Grn, Guil. 242 AU130
Johnston Rd, Wdf.Grn. 102 EG50
Johnston Ter NW2 119 CX62
Campion Ter
Johnston Wk, Guil. 242 AU130
Johnstone Rd E6 145 EM69
Joiner St SE1 279 L3
Joiner's Arms Yd SE5 162 DR81
Denmark Hill
Joiners Cl (Ley Hill), Chesh. 56 AV30
Joiners Cl (Chalfont St. Peter), Ger.Cr. 91 AZ52
Joiners La (Chalfont St. Peter), Ger.Cr. 90 AY53
Joiners Pl N5 122 DR63
Leconfield Rd
Joiners Way (Chalfont St. Peter), Ger.Cr. 90 AY52
Joinville Pl, Add. 212 BK105
Jolliffe Rd, Red. 251 DJ126
Jollys La, Har. 117 CD60
Jollys La, Hayes 136 BX71
Jonathan Ct W4 158 CS77
Windmill Rd
Jonathan St SE11 278 B10
Jonathan St SE11 161 DM78
Jones Rd E13 144 EH70
Holborn Rd
Jones Rd (Cheshunt), Wal.Cr. 65 DP30
Jones St W1 277 H1
Jones Wk, Rich. 178 CM86
Pyrland Rd
Jones Way (Hedgerley), Slou. 111 AR61
Jonquil Cl, Welw.G.C. 30 DB11
Jonquil Gdns, Hmptn. 176 BZ93
Partridge Rd
Jonson Cl, Hayes 135 BU71
Jonson Cl, Mitch. 201 DH98
Jordan Cl, Dag. 127 FB63
Muggeridge Rd
Jordan Cl, Har. 116 BZ62
Hamilton Cres
Jordan Cl, S.Croy. 220 DT111
Jordan Cl, Wat. 75 BT35
Jordan Rd, Grnf. 137 CH67
Jordans Cl, Guil. 243 BA133
Beatty Av
Jordans Cl, Islw. 157 CE81
Jordans Cl, Red. 266 DG139
Spencer Way
Jordans Cl (Stanwell), Stai. 174 BJ87
Jordans La (Jordans), Beac. 90 AS53
Jordans Rd, Rick. 92 BG45
Jordans Way (Jordans), Beac. 90 AT51
Jordans Way, Rain. 148 FK68
Jordans Way (Bricket Wd), St.Alb. 60 BZ30
Joseph Av W3 138 CR72
Joseph Locke Way, Esher 196 CA103
Mill Rd
Joseph Powell Cl SW12 181 DH86
Hazelbourne Rd
Joseph Ray Rd E11 124 EE61
Joseph St E3 143 DZ70
Joseph Trotter Cl EC1 141 DN69
Myddelton St
Josephine Av SW2 181 DM85
Josephine Av, Tad. 249 CZ126
Josephine Cl, Tad. 249 CZ127
Joseph's Rd, Guil. 242 AW133
Joshua Cl N10 99 DH52
Roman Rd
Joshua St E14 143 EC72
St. Leonards Rd
Joshua Wk, Wal.Cr. 67 EA34
Longcroft Dr
Joslin Rd, Purf. 168 FQ78
Josling Cl, Grays 170 FZ79
Joslyn Cl, Enf. 83 EA38
Joubert St SW11 160 DF82
Journeys End (Stoke Poges), Slou. 132 AS71
Jowett St SE15 162 DT80
Joy Rd, Grav. 191 GJ88
Joyce Av N18 100 DT50
Joyce Ct, Wal.Abb. 67 ED34
Joyce Dawson Way SE28 146 EU73
Thamesmere Dr
Joyce Grn La, Dart. 168 FL81
Joyce Grn Wk, Dart. 168 FM84
Joyce Page Cl SE7 164 EK79
Lansdowne La
Joyce Wk SW2 181 DN86
Joydens Wd Rd, Bex. 187 FD91
Joydon Dr, Rom. 126 EV58
Joyes Cl, Rom. 106 FK49
Joyners Cl, Dag. 126 EZ63
Joyners Fld, Harl. 51 EQ19
Jubb Powell Ho N15 122 DS58
Jubilee Av E4 101 EC51
Jubilee Av, Rom. 127 FB57
Jubilee Av (London Colney), St.Alb. 61 CK26
Jubilee Av, Twick. 176 CC88
Jubilee Av, Ware 33 DZ05
Jubilee Cl NW9 118 CR58
Jubilee Cl, Green. 189 FW86
Jubilee Cl, Pnr. 94 BW54
Jubilee Cl, Rom. 127 FB57
Jubilee Cl (Stanwell), Stai. 174 BJ87
Jubilee Ct, Hat. 45 CV15
Jubilee Ct, Stai. 174 BG92
Leacroft
Jubilee Ct, Wal.Abb. 68 EF33
Jubilee Cres E14 163 EC76
Jubilee Cres N9 100 DU46
Jubilee Cres, Add. 212 BK106
Jubilee Cres, Grav. 191 GL89
Jubilee Dr, Ruis. 116 BX63
Jubilee Gdns, Sthl. 136 CA72
Jubilee Pl SW3 276 C10
Jubilee Pl SW3 160 DE78
Jubilee Ri (Seal), Sev. 257 FM121
Jubilee Rd, Grays 169 FV79
Jubilee Rd, Grnf. 137 CH67
Jubilee Rd, Orp. 224 FA107
Jubilee Rd, Sutt. 217 CX108
Jubilee Rd, Wat. 75 BU38
Jubilee St E1 142 DW72
Jubilee Ter, Bet. 264 CQ138
Jubilee Ter, Dor. 263 CH135
Jubilee Wk, Wat. 93 BV49
Jubilee Way SW19 200 DB95
Jubilee Way, Chess. 216 CN105
Jubilee Way, Felt. 175 BT88
Jubilee Way, Sid. 186 EU89
Judd St WC1 273 P3
Judd St WC1 141 DL69
Jude St E16 144 EF72
Judeth Gdns, Grav. 191 GL92
Judge Heath La, Hayes 135 BQ72
Judge Heath La, Uxb. 135 BQ72
Judge St, Wat. 75 BV38
Judge Wk (Claygate), Esher 215 CE107
Judges Hill, Pot.B. 64 DE29
Judith Av, Rom. 105 FB51
Juer St SW11 160 DE80
Jug Hill, West. 238 EK116
Hillcrest Rd
Juglans Rd, Orp. 206 EU102
Jules Thorn Av, Enf. 82 DU42
Julia Gdns, Bark. 146 EX68
Julia Garfield Ms E16 144 EH74
Wesley Av
Julia St NW5 120 DG63
Oak Village
Julian Av W3 138 CP73
Julian Cl, Barn. 80 DB41
Julian Cl, Wok. 226 AW118
Julian Hill, Har. 117 CE61
Julian Hill, Wey. 212 BN108
Julian Pl E14 163 EB78
Julian Rd, Orp. 224 EU107
Juliana Cl N2 120 DC55
Julians Cl, Sev. 256 FG127
Julians Way, Sev. 256 FG127
Julien Rd W5 157 CJ76
Julien Rd, Couls. 235 DK115
Juliette Rd E13 144 EF68
Juliette Way, S.Ock. 168 FM75
Julius Nyerere Cl N1 141 DN70
Copenhagen St
Junction App SE13 163 EC83
Junction App SW11 160 DE83
Junction Av W10 139 CW69
Harrow Rd
Junction Ms W2 272 B8
Junction Pk, Kings L. 59 BQ33
Junction Pl W2 272 B8
Junction Rd E13 144 EH68
Junction Rd N9 100 DU46
Junction Rd N17 122 DU55
Junction Rd N19 121 DJ63
Junction Rd W5 157 CK77
Junction Rd, Ashf. 175 BQ92
Junction Rd, Brent. 157 CK77
Junction Rd, Brwd. 108 FW49

Junction Rd, Dart. 188 FK86
Junction Rd, Dor. 263 CG136
Junction Rd, Har. 117 CE58
Junction Rd, Rom. 127 FF56
Junction Rd, S.Croy. 220 DR106
Junction Rd E, Rom. 126 EY59
Kenneth Rd
Junction Rd W, Rom. 126 EY59
Junction Shop Cen, The SW11 160 DE84
St. John's Hill
June Cl, Couls. 219 DH114
June La, Red. 267 DH141
Junewood Cl (Woodham), Add. 211 BF111
Juniper Av (Bricket Wd), St.Alb. 60 CA31
Juniper Cl, Barn. 79 CX43
Juniper Cl, Brox. 67 DZ25
Juniper Cl, Chess. 216 CM107
Juniper Cl, Guil. 242 AV129
Juniper Cl, Reig. 266 DC136
Juniper Cl, Rick. 92 BK48
Juniper Cl, Wem. 118 CM64
Juniper Cl (Biggin Hill), West. 238 EL117
Juniper Ct, Slou. 152 AU75
Nixey Cl
Juniper Cres NW1 140 DG66
Juniper Gdns SW16 201 DJ95
Leonard Rd
Juniper Gdns (Shenley), Rad. 62 CL33
Juniper Gdns, Sun. 175 BT93
Juniper Gate, Rick. 92 BK47
Juniper Grn, Hem.H. 39 BE20
Juniper Gro, Wat. 75 BU38
Juniper La E6 144 EL71
Juniper La (Wooburn Grn), H.Wyc. 110 AD56
Juniper Pl (Shalford), Guil. 258 AX141
Juniper Rd, Ilf. 125 EN63
Juniper Rd, Reig. 266 DC136
Juniper St E1 142 DW73
Juniper Ter (Shalford), Guil. 258 AX141
Juniper Wk (Brockham), Bet. 264 CQ136
Juniper Wk, Swan. 207 FD96
Juniper Way, Hayes 135 BR73
Juniper Way, Rom. 106 FL53
Juno Rd, Hem.H. 40 BM17
Saturn Way
Juno Way SE14 163 DX79
Jupiter Dr, Hem.H. 40 BM18
Jupiter Way N7 141 DM65
Jupp Rd E15 143 ED66
Jupp Rd W E15 143 EC67
Jurgens Rd, Purf. 169 FR79
London Rd Purfleet
Jury St, Grav. 191 GH86
Princes St
Justice Wk SW3 160 DE79
Lawrence St
Justin Cl, Brent. 157 CK80
Justin Rd E4 101 DZ51
Jute La, Enf. 83 DY40
Jutland Cl N19 121 DL60
Sussex Way
Jutland Gdns, Couls. 235 DL120
Goodenough Way
Jutland Pl, Egh. 173 BC92
Mullens Rd
Jutland Rd E13 144 EG70
Jutland Rd SE6 183 EC87
Jutsums Av, Rom. 127 FB58
Jutsums La, Rom. 127 FB58
Juxon Cl, Har. 94 CB53
Augustine Rd
Juxon St SE11 278 C8
Juxon St SE11 161 DM77

K

Kaduna Cl, Pnr. 115 BU57
Kale Rd, Erith 166 EY75
Kambala Rd SW11 160 DD83
Kandlewood, Brwd. 109 GB45
Kangley Br Rd SE26 183 DZ92
Kaplan Dr N21 81 DM43
Kara Way NW2 119 CX63
Karen Cl, Brwd. 108 FW45
Karen Cl, Rain. 147 FE68
Karen Ct SE4 163 DZ82
Wickham Rd
Karen Ct, Brom. 204 EF95
Blyth Rd
Karen Ter E11 124 EF61
Montague Rd
Karenza Ct, Wem. 117 CJ59
Lulworth Av
Karina Cl, Chig. 103 ES50
Karoline Gdns, Grnf. 137 CD68
Oldfield La N
Kashgar Rd SE18 165 ET77
Kashmir Cl (New Haw), Add. 212 BK109
Kashmir Rd SE7 164 EK80
Kassala Rd SW11 160 DF81
Katella Trd Est, Bark. 145 ES69
Kates Cl, Barn. 79 CU43
Katescroft, Welw.G.C. 29 CY13
Katharine St, Croy. 202 DQ104
Katherine Cl SE16 143 DX74
Rotherhithe St
Katherine Cl, Add. 212 BG107
Katherine Cl, Hem.H. 40 BL23
Katherine Cl (Penn), H.Wyc. 88 AC47
Katherine Gdns SE9 164 EK84
Katherine Gdns, Ilf. 103 EQ52
Katherine Rd E6 144 EK66
Katherine Rd E7 124 EJ64
Katherine Rd, Twick. 177 CG88
London Rd
Katherine Sq W11 139 CY74
Wilsham St
Katherines Hatch, Harl. 51 EN17
Brookside
Katherines Way, Harl. 51 EN18
Kathleen Av W3 138 CQ71
Kathleen Av, Wem. 138 CL66
Kathleen Rd SW11 160 DF83
Katrine Sq, Hem.H. 40 BK16
Kavanaghs Rd, Brwd. 108 FU48
Kavanaghs Ter, Brwd. 108 FV48
Kavanaghs Rd
Kay Rd SW9 161 DL82
Kay St E2 142 DU68
Kay St, Well. 166 EV81
Kay Wk, St.Alb. 43 CK19
Kay Way SE10 163 EB80
Greenwich High Rd
Kaye Ct, Guil. 242 AW131
Kaye Don Way, Wey. 212 BN110
Kayemoor Rd, Sutt. 218 DE108
Kays Ter E18 102 EF53
Walpole Rd
Kaywood Cl, Slou. 152 AW76
Kean St WC2 274 B9
Kean St WC2 141 DM72
Kearton Cl, Ken. 236 DQ117
Keary Rd, Swans. 190 FZ87
Keatley Grn E4 101 DZ51
Keats Av E16 144 EH74
Wesley Av
Keats Av, Red. 250 DG132
Keats Av, Rom. 105 FH52
Keats Cl E11 124 EH57
Nightingale La
Keats Cl NW3 120 DE63
Keats Gro
Keats Cl SE1 279 P9
Keats Cl SW19 180 DD93
North Rd
Keats Cl, Chig. 103 EQ51
Keats Cl, Enf. 83 DX43
Keats Cl, Hayes 135 BU71
Keats Gdns, Til. 171 GH82
Keats Gro NW3 120 DD63
Keats Ho, Beck. 183 EA93
Keats La, Wind. 151 AR79
Keats Pl EC2 275 K7
Keats Rd, Belv. 167 FC76
Keats Rd, Well. 165 ES81
Keats Wk, Brwd. 109 GD45
Byron Rd
Keats Way, Croy. 202 DW100
Keats Way, Grnf. 136 CB71
Keats Way, West Dr. 154 BM77
Keble Cl, Nthlt. 116 CC64
Keble Cl, Wor.Pk. 199 CT102
Keble Pl SW13 159 CV79
Somerville Av
Keble St SW17 180 DC91
Keble Ter, Abb.L. 59 BT32
Kechill Gdns, Brom. 204 EG101
Kedelston Ct E5 123 DX63
Redwald Rd
Kedeston Ct, Sutt. 200 DB102
Hurstcourt Rd
Kedleston Dr, Orp. 205 ET100
Kedleston Wk E2 142 DV69
Middleton St
Keedonwood Rd, Brom. 184 EE92
Keefield, Harl. 51 EP20
Keel Cl SE16 143 DX74
Keel Cl, Bark. 146 EY69
Choats Rd
Keel Dr, Slou. 151 AQ75
Keele Cl, Wat. 76 BW40
Keeler Cl, Wind. 151 AL83
Keeley Rd, Croy. 202 DQ103
Keeley St WC2 274 B9
Keeley St WC2 141 DM72
Keeling Rd SE9 184 EK85
Keely Cl, Barn. 80 DE43
Keemor Cl SE18 165 EN80
Llanover Rd
Keens Cl SW16 181 DK92
Keens La, Guil. 242 AT130
Keens Pk Rd, Guil. 242 AT130
Keens Rd, Croy. 220 DQ105
Keens Yd N1 141 DP65
St. Paul's Rd
Keensacre, Iver 133 BD68
Keep, The SE3 164 EG82
Keep, The, Kings.T. 178 CM93
Keep La N11 98 DG47
Gardeners Cl
Keepers Cl, Guil. 243 BD131
Keepers Fm Cl, Wind. 151 AL83
Keepers Ms, Tedd. 177 CJ93
Keepers Wk, Vir.W. 192 AX99
Keesey St SE17 162 DR79
Keetons Rd SE16 162 DV76
Keevil Dr SW19 179 CX87
Keighley Cl N7 121 DL64
Penn Rd
Keighley Rd, Rom. 106 FL52
Keightley Dr SE9 185 EQ88
Keilder Cl, Uxb. 134 BN68
Charnwood Rd
Keildon Rd SW11 160 DF84
Keir, The SW19 179 CW92
West Side Common
Keir Hardie Est E5 122 DV60
Springfield
Keir Hardie Ho W6 159 CW79
Lochaline St
Keir Hardie Way, Bark. 146 EU66
Keir Hardie Way, Hayes 135 BU69
Keith Av (Sutton at Hone), Dart. 188 FP93
Keith Connor Cl SW8 161 DH83
Daley Thompson Way
Keith Gro W12 159 CU75
Keith Pk Cres (Biggin Hill), West. 222 EH112
Keith Pk Rd, Uxb. 134 BM66
Keith Rd E17 101 DZ53
Keith Rd, Bark. 145 ER68
Keith Rd, Hayes 155 BS76
Keith Way, Horn. 128 FL59
Keiths Rd, Hem.H. 40 BN21
Kelbrook Rd SE3 164 EL83
Kelburn Way, Rain. 147 FG69
Dominion Way
Kelby Path SE9 185 EP90
Kelbys, Welw.G.C. 30 DC08
Kelceda Cl NW2 119 CU61
Kelf Gro, Hayes 135 BT72
Kelfield Gdns W10 139 CW72
Kelfield Ms W10 139 CX72
Kelfield Gdns
Kell St SE1 278 G6
Kelland Cl N8 121 DK57
Palace Rd
Kelland Rd E13 144 EG70
Kellaway Rd SE3 164 EJ82
Keller Cres E12 124 EK63
Kellerton Rd SE13 184 EE85
Kellett Rd SW2 161 DN84
Kelling Gdns, Croy. 201 DP101
Kellino St SW17 180 DF91
Kellner Rd SE28 165 ET76
Kelly Av SE15 162 DT80
Kelly Cl NW10 118 CR62
Kelly Cl, Shep. 195 BS96
Kelly Ct, Borwd. 78 CQ40
Kelly Ms W9 139 CZ71
Woodfield Rd
Kelly Rd NW7 97 CY51
Kelly St NW1 141 DH65
Kelly Way, Rom. 126 EY57
Kelman Cl SW4 161 DK82
Kelman Cl, Wal.Cr. 67 DX31
Kelmore Gro SE22 162 DU84
Kelmscott Cl E17 101 DZ54
Kelmscott Cl, Wat. 75 BU43
Kelmscott Cres, Wat. 75 BU43
Kelmscott Gdns W12 159 CU76
Kelmscott Rd SW11 180 DF85
Kelpatrick Rd, Slou. 131 AK72
Kelross Pas N5 122 DQ63
Kelross Rd
Kelross Rd N5 122 DQ63
Kelsall Cl SE3 164 EH82
Kelsey Cl, Horl. 268 DF148
Court Lo Rd
Kelsey Gate, Beck. 203 EB96
Kelsey La, Beck. 203 EA96
Kelsey Pk Av, Beck. 203 EB96
Kelsey Pk Rd, Beck. 203 EA96
Kelsey Rd, Orp. 206 EV96
Kelsey Sq, Beck. 203 EA96
Kelsey St E2 142 DV70
Kelsey Way, Beck. 203 EA97
Kelshall, Wat. 76 BY36
Kelshall Ct N4 122 DQ61
Brownswood Rd
Kelsie Way, Ilf. 103 ES52
Kelso Dr, Grav. 191 GM91
Kelso Pl W8 160 DB76
Kelso Rd, Cars. 200 DC101
Kelson Ho E14 163 EC76
Kelston Rd, Ilf. 103 EP54
Kelvedon Av, Walt. 213 BS108
Kelvedon Cl, Brwd. 109 GE44
Kelvedon Cl, Kings.T. 178 CM93
Kelvedon Ho SW8 161 DL81
Kelvedon Rd SW6 159 CZ80
Kelvedon Wk, Rain. 147 FE67
Ongar Way
Kelvedon Way, Wdf.Grn. 103 EM51
Kelvin Av N13 99 DM51
Kelvin Av, Lthd. 231 CF119
Kelvin Av, Tedd. 177 CE93
Kelvin Cl, Epsom 216 CN107
Kelvin Cres, Har. 95 CE52
Kelvin Dr, Twick. 177 CH86
Kelvin Gdns, Croy. 201 DL101
Kelvin Gdns, Sthl. 136 CA72
Kelvin Gro SE26 182 DV90
Kelvin Gro, Chess. 198 CL104
Kelvin Ind Est, Grnf. 136 CB66
Kelvin Par, Orp. 205 ES102
Kelvin Rd N5 122 DQ63
Kelvin Rd, Til. 171 GG82
Kelvin Rd, Well. 166 EU83
Kelvinbrook, W.Mol. 196 CB97
Kelvington Cl, Croy. 203 DY101
Kelvington Rd SE15 183 DX85
Kember St N1 141 DM66
Carnoustie Dr
Kemble Cl, Pot.B. 64 DD33
Kemble Cl, Wey. 213 BR105
Kemble Cotts, Add. 194 BG104
Emley Rd
Kemble Dr, Brom. 204 EL104
Kemble Par, Pot.B. 64 DC32
High St
Kemble Rd N17 100 DU53
Kemble Rd SE23 183 DX88
Kemble Rd, Croy. 201 DN104
Kemble St WC2 274 B9
Kemble St WC2 141 DM72
Kembleside Rd (Biggin Hill), West. 238 EJ118
Kemerton Rd SE5 162 DQ83
Kemerton Rd, Beck. 203 EB96
Kemerton Rd, Croy. 202 DT101
Kemeys St E9 123 DY64
Kemishford, Wok. 226 AU123
Kemnal Rd, Chis. 185 ER91
Kemp Gdns, Croy. 202 DQ100
St. Saviours Rd
Kemp Pl, Bushey 76 CA44
Kemp Rd, Dag. 126 EX60
Kempe Cl, St.Alb. 42 CC24
Kempe Cl, Slou. 153 BC77
Kempe Rd NW6 139 CX68
Kempe Rd, Enf. 82 DV36
Kempis Way SE22 182 DS85
East Dulwich Gro
Kemplay Rd NW3 120 DD63
Kemprow, Wat. 77 CD36
Kemp's Ct W1 273 L9
Kemps Dr E14 143 EA73
Morant St
Kemps Dr, Nthwd. 93 BT52
Kemps Gdns SE13 183 EC85
Thornford Rd
Kempsford Gdns SW5 160 DA78
Kempsford Rd SE11 278 F8
Kempsford Rd SE11 161 DN77
Kempshott Rd SW16 181 DK94
Kempson Rd SW6 160 DA81
Kempt St SE18 165 EN79
Kempthorne Rd SE8 163 DY77
Kempton Av, Horn. 128 FM63
Kempton Av, Nthlt. 136 CA65
Kempton Av, Sun. 195 BV95
Kempton Cl, Erith 167 FC79
Kempton Cl, Uxb. 115 BQ63
Kempton Ct E1 142 DV71
Durward St
Kempton Ct, Sun. 195 BV95
Kempton Rd E6 145 EM67
Kempton Rd, Hmptn. 196 BZ96
Kempton Wk, Croy. 203 DY100
Kemsing Cl, Bex. 186 EY87
Kemsing Cl, Brom. 204 EF103
Kemsing Cl, Th.Hth. 202 DQ98
Kemsing Rd SE10 164 EG78
Kemsley SE13 183 EB85
Kemsley Chase (Farnham Royal), Slou. 131 AR67
Kemsley Cl (Northfleet), Grav. 191 GF91
Kemsley Cl, Green. 189 FV86
Kemsley Rd (Tatsfield), West. 238 EK119
Ken Way, Wem. 118 CQ61
Kenbury Cl, Uxb. 114 BN62
Kenbury Gdns SE5 162 DQ82
Kenbury St
Kenbury St SE5 162 DQ82
Kenchester Cl SW8 161 DL80
Kencot Cl, Erith 166 EZ75
Kendal Av N18 100 DR49
Kendal Av W3 138 CN71
Kendal Av, Bark. 145 ES66
Kendal Av, Epp. 70 EU31
Kendal Cl SW9 161 DP80
Kendal Cl, Felt. 175 BT88
Ambleside Dr
Kendal Cl, Hayes 135 BS68
Kendal Cl, Reig. 250 DD133
Kendal Cl, Slou. 132 AU73
Kendal Cl, Wdf.Grn. 102 EF47
Kendal Cft, Horn. 127 FG64
Kendal Dr, Slou. 132 AU73
Kendal Gdns N18 100 DR49
Kendal Gdns, Sutt. 200 DC103
Kendal Par N18 100 DR49
Great Cambridge Rd
Kendal Pl SW15 179 CZ85
Kendal Rd NW10 119 CU63
Kendal Rd, Wal.Abb. 83 EC36
Deer Pk Way
Kendal St W2 272 C9
Kendal St W2 140 DE72
Kendale, Grays 171 GH76
Kendale, Hem.H. 41 BP21
Kendale Rd, Brom. 184 EE92
Kendall Av, Beck. 203 DY96
Kendall Av, S.Croy. 220 DR109
Kendall Av S, S.Croy. 220 DQ110
Kendall Cl, Welw.G.C. 29 CY13
Kendall Ct SW19 180 DD93
Byegrove Rd
Kendall Ct, Borwd. 78 CQ39
Gregson Cl
Kendall Pl W1 272 F7
Kendall Rd, Beck. 203 DY96
Kendall Rd, Islw. 157 CG82
Kendalmere Cl N10 99 DH53
Kendals Cl, Rad. 77 CE36
Kender St SE14 162 DW80
Kendoa Rd SW4 161 DK84
Kendon Cl E11 124 EH57
The Av
Kendor Av, Epsom 216 CQ111
Kendra Hall Rd, S.Croy. 219 DP108
Kendrey Gdns, Twick. 177 CE86
Kendrick Ms SW7 160 DD77
Reece Ms
Kendrick Pl SW7 160 DD77
Kendrick Rd, Slou. 152 AV76
Kenelm Cl, Har. 117 CG62
Kenerne Dr, Barn. 79 CY43
Kenford Cl, Wat. 59 BV32
Kenia Wk, Grav. 191 GM90
Kenilford Rd SW12 181 DH87
Kenilworth Av E17 101 EA54
Kenilworth Av SW19 180 DA92
Kenilworth Av (Stoke D'Abernon), Cob. 214 CB114
Kenilworth Av, Har. 116 BZ63
Kenilworth Av, Rom. 106 FP50
Kenilworth Cl, Bans. 234 DB116
Kenilworth Cl, Borwd. 78 CQ41
Kenilworth Cl, Hem.H. 40 BL21
Kenilworth Cl, Slou. 152 AT76
Kenilworth Ct SW15 159 CX83
Lower Richmond Rd
Kenilworth Ct, Wat. 75 BU39
Hempstead Rd
Kenilworth Cres, Enf. 82 DS39
Kenilworth Dr, Borwd. 78 CQ41
Kenilworth Dr, Rick. 75 BP42
Kenilworth Dr, Walt. 196 BX104
Kenilworth Gdns SE18 165 EP82
Kenilworth Gdns, Hayes 135 BT71
Kenilworth Gdns, Horn. 128 FJ62
Kenilworth Gdns, Ilf. 125 ET61
Kenilworth Gdns, Loug. 85 EM44
Kenilworth Gdns, Sthl. 136 BZ69
Kenilworth Gdns, Stai. 174 BJ92
Kenilworth Gdns, Wat. 94 BW50
Kenilworth Rd E3 143 DY68
Kenilworth Rd NW6 139 CZ67
Kenilworth Rd SE20 203 DX95
Kenilworth Rd W5 138 CL74
Kenilworth Rd, Ashf. 174 BK90
Kenilworth Rd, Edg. 96 CQ48
Kenilworth Rd, Epsom 217 CU107
Kenilworth Rd, Orp. 205 EQ100
Kenley Av NW9 96 CS53
Kenley Cl, Barn. 80 DE42
Kenley Cl, Bex. 186 FA87
Kenley Cl, Cat. 236 DR120
Kenley Cl, Chis. 205 ES97
Kenley Gdns, Horn. 128 FM61
Kenley Gdns, Th.Hth. 201 DP98
Kenley La, Ken. 220 DQ114
Kenley Rd SW19 199 CZ96
Kenley Rd, Kings.T. 198 CP96
Kenley Rd, Twick. 177 CG86
Kenley Wk W11 139 CY73
Kenley Wk, Sutt. 217 CX105
Kenlor Rd SW17 180 DD92
Kenmare Dr, Mitch. 180 DF94
Kenmare Gdns N13 99 DP49
Kenmare Rd, Th.Hth. 201 DN100
Kenmere Gdns, Wem. 138 CN67
Kenmere Rd, Well. 166 EW82
Kenmont Gdns NW10 139 CV69
Kenmore Av, Har. 117 CG56
Kenmore Cl, Rich. 158 CN80
Kent Rd
Kenmore Cres, Hayes 135 BT69
Kenmore Gdns, Edg. 96 CP54
Kenmore Rd, Har. 117 CK55
Kenmore Rd, Ken. 219 DP114
Kenmure Rd E8 122 DV64
Kenmure Yd E8 122 DV64
Kenmure Rd
Kennacraig Cl E16 144 EG74
Hanameel St
Kennard Rd E15 143 ED66
Kennard Rd N11 98 DF50
Kennard St E16 145 EM74
Kennard St SW11 160 DG82
Kenneally Cl, Wind. 150 AJ82
Kenneally Row
Kenneally Pl, Wind. 150 AJ82
Kenneally Row
Kenneally Rd, Wind. 150 AJ82
Kenneally Row
Kenneally Row, Wind. 150 AJ82
Kenneally Wk, Wind. 150 AJ82
Kenneally Row
Kennedy Av, Enf. 82 DW44
Kennedy Av, Hodd. 49 DZ17
Kennedy Cl E13 144 EG68
Kennedy Cl, Mitch. 200 DG96
Kennedy Cl, Orp. 205 ER102
Kennedy Cl, Pnr. 94 BZ51
Kennedy Cl (Farnham Common), Slou. 131 AQ65
Kennedy Cl (Cheshunt), Wal.Cr. 67 DX28
Kennedy Gdns, Sev. 257 FJ123
Kennedy Path W7 137 CF70
Harp Rd
Kennedy Rd W7 137 CE71
Kennedy Rd, Bark. 145 ES67
Kennedy Wk SE17 162 DR77
Flint St
Kennel Cl (Fetcham), Lthd. 230 CC124
Kennel La, Horl. 268 DD149
Kennel La (Fetcham), Lthd. 230 CC122
Kennelwood Cres (New Addington), Croy. 221 ED111
Kennelwood La, Hat. 45 CV17
Kenners La, Wal.Abb. 50 EL20
Kennet Cl SW11 160 DD84
Maysoule Rd
Kennet Cl, Upmin. 129 FS58
Kennet Grn, S.Ock. 149 FV73
Kennet Rd W9 139 CZ70
Kennet Rd, Dart. 167 FG83
Kennet Rd, Islw. 157 CF83
Kennet Sq, Mitch. 200 DE95
Kennet St E1 142 DU74
Kennet Wf La EC4 275 J10
Kenneth Av, Ilf. 125 EP63
Kenneth Cres NW2 119 CV64
Kenneth Gdns, Stan. 95 CG51
Kenneth More Rd, Ilf. 125 EP62
Oakfield Rd
Kenneth Rd, Bans. 234 DD115
Kenneth Rd, Rom. 126 EX59
Kenneth Robbins Ho N17 100 DV52
Kennett Ct, Swan. 207 FE97
Kennett Dr, Hayes 136 BY71
Kennett Rd, Slou. 153 BB76
Kenning Rd, Hodd. 49 EB15
Kenning St SE16 162 DW75
Railway Av
Kenning Ter N1 142 DS67
Kenninghall Rd E5 122 DU62
Kenninghall Rd N18 100 DW50
Kennings Way SE11 278 F10
Kennings Way SE11 161 DN78
Kennington Grn SE11 161 DN78
Montford Pl
Kennington Gro SE11 161 DM79
Oval Way
Kennington La SE11 278 E10
Kennington La SE11 161 DM78
Kennington Oval SE11 161 DM79
Kennington Pk Est SE11 161 DN79
Harleyford St
Kennington Pk Gdns SE11 161 DP79
Kennington Pk Pl SE11 161 DN79
Kennington Pk Rd SE11 161 DN79
Kennington Rd SE1 278 D6
Kennington Rd SE1 161 DN76
Kennington Rd SE11 278 D7
Kennington Rd SE11 161 DN77
Kenny Dr, Cars. 218 DF109
Kenny Rd NW7 97 CY50
Kenrick Pl W1 272 F6
Kenrick Sq (Bletchingley), Red. 252 DS133
Kensal Rd W10 139 CY70
Kensington Av E12 144 EL65
Kensington Av, Th.Hth. 201 DN95
Kensington Av, Wat. 75 BT42
Kensington Ch Ct W8 160 DB75
Kensington Ch St W8 140 DA74
Kensington Ch Wk W8 160 DB75
Kensington Cl N11 98 DG51
Kensington Cl, St.Alb. 43 CG22
Kensington Ct NW7 96 CR50
Grenville Pl
Kensington Ct W8 160 DB75
Kensington Ct Gdns W8 160 DB76
Kensington Ct Pl
Kensington Ct Ms W8 160 DB75
Kensington Ct Pl
Kensington Ct Pl W8 160 DB76
Kensington Dr, Wdf.Grn. 102 EK53
Kensington Gdns W2 140 DC74
Kensington Gdns, Ilf. 125 EM60
Kensington Gdns, Kings.T. 197 CK97
Portsmouth Rd
Kensington Gdns Sq W2 140 DB72
Kensington Gate W8 160 DC76
Kensington Gore SW7 160 DD75
Kensington Hall Gdns W14 159 CZ78
Beaumont Av
Kensington High St W8 160 DA76
Kensington High St W14 159 CY77
Kensington Mall W8 140 DA74
Kensington Palace Gdns W8 140 DB74
Kensington Pk Gdns W11 139 CZ73
Kensington Pk Ms W11 139 CZ72
Kensington Pk Rd
Kensington Pk Rd W11 139 CZ73
Kensington Pl W8 140 DA74
Kensington Rd SW7 276 A5
Kensington Rd SW7 160 DD75
Kensington Rd W8 160 DB75
Kensington Rd, Brwd. 108 FU44
Kensington Rd, Nthlt. 136 CA69
Kensington Rd, Rom. 127 FC58
Kensington Sq W8 160 DB75
Kensington Ter, S.Croy. 220 DR108
Sanderstead Rd
Kensington Way, Borwd. 78 CR41
Kent Av W13 137 CH71
Kent Av, Dag. 146 FA70
Kent Av, Slou. 131 AQ71
Kent Av, Well. 185 ET85
Kent Cl, Borwd. 78 CR38
Kent Cl, Mitch. 201 DL98
Kent Cl, Orp. 223 ES107
Kent Cl, Stai. 174 BK93
Kent Cl, Uxb. 134 BJ65
Kent Dr, Barn. 80 DG42
Kent Dr, Horn. 128 FK63
Kent Dr, Tedd. 177 CE92
Kent Gdns W13 137 CH71
Kent Gdns, Ruis. 115 BV58
Kent Gate Way, Croy. 221 EA106
Kent Hatch Rd, Eden. 255 EM131
Kent Hatch Rd, Oxt. 254 EJ129
Kent Ho La, Beck. 183 DY92
Kent Ho Rd SE26 203 DX95
Kent Ho Rd, Beck. 183 DY92
Kent Pas NW1 272 D4
Kent Pas NW1 140 DF69
Kent Rd N21 100 DR46
Kent Rd W4 158 CQ76
Kent Rd, Dag. 127 FB64
Kent Rd, Dart. 188 FK86
Kent Rd, E.Mol. 196 CC98
Kent Rd, Grav. 191 GG88
Kent Rd, Grays 170 GC79
Kent Rd, Kings.T. 197 CK97
The Bittoms
Kent Rd, Long. 209 FX96
Kent Rd, Orp. 206 EV100
Kent Rd, Rich. 158 CN80
Kent Rd, W.Wick. 203 EB102
Kent Rd, Wok. 227 BB116
Kent St E2 142 DT68
Kent St E13 144 EJ69
Kent Ter NW1 272 C3
Kent Ter NW1 140 DE69
Kent Twr SE20 182 DV94
Kent Vw, S.Ock. 168 FQ75
Kent Vw Gdns, Ilf. 125 ES61
Kent Wk SW9 161 DP84
Moorland Rd
Kent Way, Surb. 198 CL104
Kent Yd SW7 276 C5

Kentford Way, Nthlt. 136 BY67
Kentish Bldgs SE1 279 K3
Kentish La, Hat. 64 DC25
Kentish Rd, Belv. 166 FA77
Kentish Town Rd NW1 141 DH66
Kentish Town Rd NW5 141 DH66
Kentish Way, Brom. 204 EG96
Kentlea Rd SE28 165 ES75
Kentmere Rd SE18 165 ES77
Kenton Av, Har. 117 CF59
Kenton Av, Sthl. 136 CA73
Kenton Av, Sun. 196 BY96
Kenton Ct W14 159 CZ76
Kensington High St
Kenton Gdns, Har. 117 CJ57
Kenton Gdns, St.Alb. 43 CF21
Kenton La, Har. 117 CJ55
Kenton Pk Av, Har. 117 CK56
Kenton Pk Cl, Har. 117 CJ56
Kenton Pk Cres, Har. 117 CK56
Kenton Pk Rd, Har. 117 CJ56
Kenton Rd E9 143 DX65
Kenton Rd, Har. 117 CK57
Kenton St WC1 273 P4
Kenton St WC1 141 DL70
Kenton Way, Hayes 135 BS69
Exmouth Rd
Kenton Way, Wok. 226 AT117
Kentons La, Wind. 151 AL82
Kents Av, Hem.H. 40 BK24
Kents La, Epp. 53 FD21
Kents Pas, Hmptn. 196 BZ95
Kentwode Grn SW13 159 CU80
Kentwyns Ri (South Nutfield), Red. 267 DM135
Kenver Av N12 98 DD51
Kenward Rd SE9 184 EJ85
Kenway, Rain. 148 FJ69
Kenway, Rom. 105 FC54
Kenway Cl, Rain. 148 FJ69
Kenway
Kenway Dr, Amer. 72 AV39
Kenway Rd SW5 160 DB77
Kenway Wk, Rain. 148 FK69
Kenway
Kenwood Av N14 81 DK43
Kenwood Av SE14 163 DX81
Besson St
Kenwood Cl NW3 120 DD60
Kenwood Cl, West Dr. 154 BN79
Kenwood Dr, Beck. 203 EC97
Kenwood Dr, Rick. 91 BF47
Kenwood Dr, Walt. 213 BV107
Kenwood Gdns E18 124 EH55
Kenwood Gdns, Ilf. 125 EN56
Kenwood Pk, Wey. 213 BR107
Kenwood Ridge, Ken. 235 DP117
Kenwood Rd N6 120 DF58
Kenwood Rd N9 100 DU46
Kenworth Cl, Wal.Cr. 67 DX33
Kenworthy Rd E9 123 DY64
Kenwyn Dr NW2 118 CS62
Kenwyn Rd SW4 161 DK84
Kenwyn Rd SW20 199 CW95
Kenwyn Rd, Dart. 188 FK85
Kenya Rd SE7 164 EK80
Kenyngton Dr, Sun. 175 BU92
Kenyngton Pl, Har. 117 CJ57
Kenyon St SW6 159 CX81
Kenyons (West Horsley), Lthd. 245 BP128
Keogh Rd E15 144 EE65
Kepler Rd SW4 161 DL84
Keppel Rd E6 145 EM66
Keppel Rd, Dag. 126 EY63
Keppel Rd, Dor. 247 CH134
Keppel Row SE1 279 H3
Keppel Spur (Old Windsor), Wind. 172 AV87
Keppel St WC1 273 N6
Keppel St WC1 141 DK71
Keppel St, Wind. 151 AR82
Kerbela St E2 142 DU70
Cheshire St
Kerbey St E14 143 EB72
Kerdistone Cl, Pot.B. 64 DB30
Kerfield Cres SE5 162 DR81
Kerfield Pl SE5 162 DR81
Kernow Cl, Horn. 128 FL61
Kerri Cl, Barn. 79 CW42
Kerridge Ct N1 142 DS65
Kerril Cft, Harl. 35 EN14
Kerrill Av, Couls. 235 DN119
Kerrison Pl W5 137 CK74
Kerrison Rd E15 143 ED67
Kerrison Rd SW11 160 DE83
Kerrison Rd W5 137 CK74
Kerrison Vil W5 137 CK74
Kerrison Pl
Kerry Av, S.Ock. 168 FM75
Kerry Av, Stan. 95 CK49
Kerry Cl E16 144 EH72
Kerry Cl N13 99 DM47
Kerry Cl, Upmin. 129 FT59
Kerry Ct, Stan. 95 CK49
Kerry Dr, Upmin. 129 FT59
Kerry Path SE14 163 DZ79
Kerry Rd
Kerry Rd SE14 163 DZ79
Kerry Ter, Wok. 227 BB116
Kersey Dr, S.Croy. 220 DW112
Kersey Gdns SE9 184 EL91
Kersey Gdns, Rom. 106 FL53
Kersfield Rd SW15 179 CX86
Kershaw Cl SW18 180 DD86
Westover Rd
Kershaw Cl (Chafford Hundred), Grays 169 FW77
Kershaw Cl, Horn. 128 FL59
Kershaw Rd, Dag. 126 FA62
Kersley Ms SW11 160 DF82
Kersley Rd N16 122 DS62
Kersley St SW11 160 DF82
Kerstin Cl, Hayes 135 BT73
St. Mary's Rd
Keswell Cl N15 122 DS57
Kerwick Cl N7 141 DM66
Sutterton St
Keslake Rd NW6 139 CX68
Kessock Cl N17 122 DV57
Kesters Rd, Chesh. 54 AR32
Kesteven Cl, Ilf. 103 ET51
Kestlake Rd, Bex. 186 EW86
East Rochester Way
Keston Av (New Haw), Add. 212 BG111
Keston Av, Couls. 235 DN119
Keston Av, Kes. 222 EJ106
Keston Cl N18 100 DR48
Keston Cl, Well. 166 EW80
Keston Gdns, Kes. 222 EJ105
Keston Ms, Wat. 75 BV40
Nascot Rd
Keston Pk Cl, Kes. 205 EM104
Keston Rd N17 122 DR55
Keston Rd SE15 162 DU83
Keston Rd, Th.Hth. 201 DN100
Kestral Ct, Wall. 219 DJ106
Carew Rd
Kestrel Av E6 144 EL71
Swan App
Kestrel Av SE24 181 DP85
Kestrel Av, Stai. 173 BF90
Kestrel Cl NW9 96 CS54
Kestrel Cl NW10 118 CR64
Kestrel Cl, Berk. 38 AW20
Kestrel Cl, Epsom 216 CN111
Abbots Av
Kestrel Cl, Guil. 243 BD132
Kestrel Cl, Horn. 147 FH66
Kestrel Cl, Ilf. 104 EW49
Kestrel Cl, Kings.T. 177 CK91
Kestrel Cl, Wat. 60 BY34
Kestrel Grn, Hat. 45 CU19
Kestrel Ho EC1 275 H2
Kestrel Ho EC1 141 DP69
Kestrel Ho W13 137 CF70
Kestrel Ho, Enf. 83 DX43
Alma Rd
Kestrel Path, Slou. 131 AL70
Kestrel Pl SE14 163 DY79
Milton Ct Rd
Kestrel Rd, Wal.Abb. 68 EG34
Kestrel Way (New Addington), Croy. 221 ED109
Kestrel Way, Hayes 155 BR75
Betam Rd
Kestrel Way, Welw.G.C. 29 CZ07
Kestrels, The, St.Alb. 60 BZ31
Bucknalls Dr
Keswick Av SW15 178 CS92
Keswick Av SW19 200 DA96
Keswick Av, Horn. 128 FK60
Keswick Bdy SW15 179 CY85
Upper Richmond Rd
Keswick Cl, St.Alb. 43 CH21
Keswick Cl, Sutt. 218 DC105
Keswick Ct, Slou. 132 AT73
Stoke Rd
Keswick Dr, Enf. 82 DW36
Keswick Gdns, Ilf. 124 EL57
Keswick Gdns, Ruis. 115 BR58
Keswick Gdns, Wem. 118 CL63
Keswick Ms W5 138 CL74
Keswick Rd SW15 179 CY85
Keswick Rd, Bexh. 166 FA82
Keswick Rd, Egh. 173 BB94
Keswick Rd (Fetcham), Lthd. 246 CC125
Keswick Rd, Orp. 205 ET102
Keswick Rd, Twick. 176 CC86
Keswick Rd, W.Wick. 204 EE103
Kett Gdns SW2 181 DM85
Kettering Rd, Enf. 83 DX37
Beaconsfield Rd
Kettering Rd, Rom. 106 FL52
Kettering St SW16 181 DJ93
Kettlebaston Rd E10 123 DZ60
Kettlewell Cl N11 98 DG51
Kettlewell Cl, Wok. 210 AX114
Kettlewell Ct, Swan. 207 FF96
Kettlewell Dr, Wok. 210 AY114
Kettlewell Hill, Wok. 210 AY114
Ketton Grn, Red. 251 DK128
Malmstone Av
Kevan Dr (Send), Wok. 227 BE124
Kevan Ho SE5 162 DQ80
Kevelioc Rd N17 100 DQ53
Kevin Cl, Houns. 156 BX82
Kevington Cl, Orp. 205 ET98
Kevington Dr, Chis. 205 ET98
Kevington Dr, Orp. 205 ET98
Kew Br, Brent. 158 CM79
Kew Br, Rich. 158 CM79
Kew Br Arches, Rich. 158 CM79
Kew Br
Kew Br Ct W4 158 CN78
Kew Br Rd, Brent. 158 CM79
Kew Cres, Sutt. 199 CY104
Kew Foot Rd, Rich. 158 CL84
Kew Gdns Rd, Rich. 158 CM80
Kew Grn, Rich. 158 CN79
Kew Meadow Path, Rich. 158 CN81
Kew Palace, Rich. 158 CL80
Kew Rd, Rich. 158 CL83
Kewferry Dr, Nthwd. 93 BP50
Kewferry Rd, Nthwd. 93 BQ51
Key Cl E1 142 DV70
Keybridge Ho SW8 161 DL79
Keyes Rd NW2 119 CX64
Keyes Rd, Dart. 168 FM84
Keyfield Ter, St.Alb. 43 CD21
Keymer Cl (Biggin Hill), West. 238 EK116
Keymer Rd SW2 181 DM89
Keynes Cl N2 120 DF55
Keynsham Av, Wdf.Grn. 102 EE49
Keynsham Gdns SE9 184 EL85
Keynsham Rd SE9 184 EK85
Keynsham Rd, Mord. 200 DB102
Keynsham Wk, Mord. 200 DB102
Keynton Cl, Hert. 31 DM08
Keys, The, Brwd. 107 FW51
Eagle Way
Keys Ho, Enf. 83 DX37
Beaconsfield Rd
Keyse Rd SE1 279 P7
Keysers Est, Brox. 49 EB21
Keysers Rd, Brox. 49 EA22
Keysham Av, Houns. 155 BU81
The Av
Keystone Cres N1 274 A1
Keywood Dr, Sun. 175 BU93
Keyworth Cl E5 123 DY63
Keyworth St SE1 278 G6
Keyworth St SE1 161 DP76
Kezia St SE8 163 DY78
Trundleys Rd
Khalsa Av, Grav. 191 GJ87
Khalsa Ct N22 99 DP53
Acacia Rd
Khama Rd SW17 180 DE91
Khartoum Pl, Grav. 191 GJ86
Khartoum Rd E13 144 EH69
Khartoum Rd SW17 180 DD91
Khartoum Rd, Ilf. 125 EP64
Khyber Rd SW11 160 DE82
Kibes La, Ware 33 DX06
Kibworth St SW8 161 DM80
Kidborough Down (Bookham), Lthd. 246 CA127
Kidbrooke Gdns SE3 164 EG82
Kidbrooke Gro SE3 164 EG81
Kidbrooke La SE9 164 EL84
Kidbrooke Pk Cl SE3 164 EH81
Kidbrooke Pk Rd SE3 164 EH81
Kidbrooke Way SE3 164 EH82
Kidd Pl SE7 164 EL78
Kidderminster Pl, Croy. 201 DP102
Kidderminster Rd
Kidderminster Rd, Croy. 201 DP102
Kidderminster Rd, Slou. 131 AN69
Kidderpore Av NW3 120 DA63
Kidderpore Gdns NW3 120 DA63
Kidlington Way NW9 96 CS54
Kidworth Cl, Horl. 268 DF146
Kielder Cl, Ilf. 103 ET51
Kiffen St EC2 275 L4
Kilberry Cl, Islw. 157 CD81
Kilbride Ct, Hem.H. 40 BL16
Aycliffe Dr
Kilburn Br NW6 139 CZ66
Kilburn High Rd
Kilburn Gate NW6 140 DB68
Kilburn Priory
Kilburn High Rd NW6 139 CZ66
Kilburn La W9 139 CX69
Kilburn La W10 139 CX69
Kilburn Pk Rd NW6 140 DA69
Kilburn Pl NW6 140 DA67
Kilburn Priory NW6 140 DB67
Kilburn Sq NW6 140 DA67
Kilburn High Rd
Kilburn Vale NW6 140 DB67
Belsize Rd
Kilby Cl, Wat. 76 BX35
Kilby Ter, Wdf.Grn. 102 EK51
Baddow Cl
Kilcorral Cl, Epsom 217 CU114
Kildare Cl, Ruis. 116 BW60
Kildare Gdns W2 140 DA72
Kildare Rd E16 144 EG71
Kildare Ter W2 140 DA72
Kildare Wk E14 143 EA72
Farrance St
Kildonan Cl, Wat. 75 BT39
Kildoran Rd SW2 181 DL85
Kildowan Rd, Ilf. 126 EU60
Kilfillan Gdns, Berk. 38 AU20
Kilgour Rd SE23 183 DY86
Kilkie St SW6 160 DC82
Killarney Rd SW18 180 DC86
Killasser Ct, Tad. 233 CW123
Killburns Mill Cl, Wall. 219 DH105
London Rd
Killearn Rd SE6 183 ED88
Killester Gdns, Wor.Pk. 217 CV105
Killewarren Way, Orp. 206 EW100
Killick Cl (Dunton Grn), Sev. 256 FE121
Killick St N1 141 DM68
Killieser Av SW2 181 DL89
Killip Cl E16 144 EF72
Killowen Av, Nthlt. 116 CC64
Killowen Rd E9 143 DX65
Killy Hill (Chobham), Wok. 210 AS108
Killyon Rd SW8 161 DJ82
Killyon Ter SW8 161 DJ82
Kilmaine Rd SW6 159 CY80
Kilmarnock Gdns, Dag. 126 EW62
Lindsey Rd
Kilmarnock Pk, Reig. 250 DB133
Kilmarnock Rd, Wat. 94 BX49
Kilmarsh Rd W6 159 CW77
Kilmartin Av SW16 201 DM97
Kilmartin Rd, Ilf. 126 EU61
Kilmartin Way, Horn. 127 FH64
Kilmeston Way SE15 162 DT80
Daniel Gdns
Kilmington Cl, Brwd. 109 GB47
Kilmington Rd SW13 159 CU79
Kilmiston Av, Shep. 195 BQ100
Kilmorey Gdns, Twick. 177 CH85
Kilmorey Rd, Twick. 157 CH84
Kilmorie Rd SE23 183 DY88
Kiln Av, Amer. 72 AW38
Kiln Cl, Hayes 155 BR79
Brickfield La
Kiln Ct, Beac. 110 AH55
Kiln Flds (Wooburn Grn), H.Wyc. 110 AE61
Kiln Grd, Hem.H. 40 BN22
Kiln Ho Cl, Ware 33 DY05
Kiln La (Brockham), Bet. 264 CP135
Kiln La, B.End 110 AC60
Kiln La (Ley Hill), Chesh. 56 AV31
Kiln La, Epsom 216 CS111
Kiln La, Harl. 52 EW16
Kiln La (Wooburn Grn), H.Wyc. 110 AC60
Kiln La, Horl. 268 DG146
Kiln La (Hedgerley), Slou. 111 AQ60
Kiln La (Ripley), Wok. 228 BH124
Kiln Ms SW17 180 DD92
Kiln Pl NW5 120 DG64
Kiln Rd, Epp. 70 FA27
Kiln Wk, Red. 267 DH139
Bushfield Dr
Kiln Way, Grays 170 FZ78
Kiln Way, Nthwd. 93 BS51
Kiln Wd La, Rom. 105 FD50
Kilncroft, Hem.H. 41 BP22
Kilndown, Grav. 191 GK93
Kilner St E14 143 EA71
Kilnfield, Welw.G.C. 29 CZ06
Kilnside (Claygate), Esher 215 CG108
Kilnwood (Halstead), Sev. 224 EZ113
Kilpatrick Way, Hayes 136 BY71
Kilravock St W10 139 CY69
Kilross Rd, Felt. 175 BR88
Kilrue La, Walt. 213 BT105
Kilrush Ter, Wok. 227 BA116
Kilsby Wk, Dag. 146 EV65
Rugby Rd
Kilsha Rd, Walt. 195 BV100
Kilsmore La, Wal.Cr. 67 DX28
Kilvinton Dr, Enf. 82 DR38
Kilworth Av, Brwd. 109 GA44
Kilworth Cl, Welw.G.C. 30 DB11
Kimbell Gdns SW6 159 CY81
Kimbell Pl SE3 164 EJ84
Tudway Rd
Kimber Cl, Wind. 151 AM83
Kimber Ct, Guil. 243 BD132
Gilliat Dr
Kimber Rd SW18 180 DA87
Kimberley Av E6 144 EL68
Kimberley Av SE15 162 DV82
Kimberley Av, Ilf. 125 ER59
Kimberley Av, Rom. 127 FC58
Kimberley Cl, Horl. 268 DE148
Kimberley Cl, Slou. 153 AZ77
Kimberley Dr, Sid. 186 EX89
Kimberley Gdns N4 121 DP57
Kimberley Gdns, Enf. 82 DT41
Kimberley Gate, Brom. 184 EF94
Oaklands Rd
Kimberley Ind Est E17 101 DZ53
Kimberley Pl, Pur. 219 DN111
Brighton Rd
Kimberley Ride, Cob. 214 CB113
Kimberley Rd E4 102 EE46
Kimberley Rd E11 123 ED61
Kimberley Rd E16 144 EF70
Kimberley Rd E17 101 DZ53
Kimberley Rd N17 100 DU54
Kimberley Rd N18 100 DV51
Kimberley Rd NW6 139 CY67
Kimberley Rd SW9 161 DL82
Kimberley Rd, Beck. 203 DX96
Kimberley Rd, Croy. 201 DP100
Kimberley Rd, St.Alb. 42 CC19
Kimberley Way E4 102 EE46
Kimbers Dr (Burnham), Slou. 131 AK69
Kimble Cl, Wat. 75 BS44
Kimble Cres, Bushey 94 CC45
Kimble Rd SW19 180 DD93
Kimbolton Cl SE12 184 EF86
Kimbolton Grn, Borwd. 78 CQ42
Kimbolton Row SW3 276 B9
Kimmeridge Gdns SE9 184 EL91
Kimmeridge Rd SE9 184 EL91
Kimps Way, Hem.H. 40 BN23
Kimpton Av, Brwd. 108 FV45
Kimpton Cl, Hem.H. 41 BP15
Kimpton Ho SW15 179 CU87
Fontley Way
Kimpton Pl, Wat. 60 BX34
Kimpton Rd SE5 162 DR81
Kimpton Rd, Sutt. 199 CZ103
Kimpton Trade Business Cen, Sutt. 199 CZ103
Kimptons Cl, Pot.B. 63 CX33
Kimptons Mead, Pot.B. 63 CX32
Kinburn Dr, Egh. 172 AY92
Kinburn St SE16 163 DX75
Kincaid Rd SE15 162 DV80
Kincardine Gdns W9 139 CZ70
Harrow Rd
Kinch Gro, Wem. 118 CM59
Kincraig Dr, Sev. 256 FG124
Kinder Cl SE28 146 EX73
Kinder St E1 142 DV72
Cannon St Rd
Kinderscout, Hem.H. 40 BN22
Kindersley Way, Abb.L. 59 BQ31
Kinetic Cres, Enf. 83 DZ36
Kinfauns Av, Horn. 128 FJ58
Kinfauns Rd SW2 181 DN89
Kinfauns Rd, Ilf. 126 EU60
King Acre Ct, Stai. 173 BE90
Victoria Rd
King Alfred Av SE6 183 EA90
King Alfred Rd, Rom. 106 FM54
King & Queen Cl SE9 184 EL91
St. Keverne Rd
King & Queen St SE17 279 J9
King & Queen St SE17 162 DQ78
King Arthur Cl SE15 162 DW80
King Arthur Ct, Wal.Cr. 67 DX31
King Charles Cres, Surb. 198 CM101
King Charles Rd, Rad. 62 CL32
King Charles Rd, Surb. 198 CM99
King Charles St SW1 277 N4
King Charles St SW1 161 DK75
King Charles Ter E1 142 DV73
Sovereign Cl
King Charles Wk SW19 179 CY88
Princes Way
King David La E1 142 DW73
King Edward Av, Dart. 188 FK86
King Edward Av, Rain. 148 FK68
King Edward Ct, Wind. 151 AR81
King Edward Dr, Chess. 198 CL104
Kelvin Gro
King Edward Dr, Grays 170 GE75
King Edward Ms SW13 159 CU81
King Edward Rd E10 123 EC60
King Edward Rd E17 123 DY55
King Edward Rd, Barn. 80 DA42
King Edward Rd, Brwd. 108 FW48
King Edward Rd, Green. 189 FU85
King Edward Rd, Rad. 62 CM33
King Edward Rd, Rom. 127 FF58
King Edward Rd, Wal.Cr. 67 DY33
King Edward Rd, Wat. 76 BY44
King Edward VII Av, Wind. 152 AS80
King Edward St EC1 275 H8
King Edward St EC1 142 DQ72
King Edward St, Hem.H. 40 BJ24
King Edward St, Slou. 151 AR75
King Edward III Ms SE16 162 DV75
Paradise St
King Edward Wk SE1 278 E6
King Edward Wk SE1 161 DN76
King Edward's Gdns W3 138 CN74
King Edwards Gro, Tedd. 177 CH93
King Edward's Pl W3 138 CN74
King Edward's Gdns
King Edwards Rd E9 142 DV67
King Edwards Rd N9 100 DV45
King Edwards Rd, Bark. 145 ER67
King Edward's Rd, Enf. 83 DX42
King Edwards Rd, Ruis. 115 BR60
King Edwards Rd, Ware 33 DY05
King Frederik IX Twr SE16 163 DZ76
King Gdns, Croy. 219 DP106
King George Av E16 144 EK72
King George Av, Bushey 76 CB44
King George Av, Ilf. 125 ER57
King George Av, Walt. 196 BX102
King George Cl, Rom. 127 FC55
King George Cl, Sun. 175 BT92
King George V Rd, Amer. 55 AR38
King George Rd, Wal.Abb. 67 EC34
King George Rd, Ware 33 DY05
King George VI Av, Mitch. 200 DF98
King George VI Av, West. 238 EK116
King George Sq, Rich. 178 CM86
King George St SE10 163 EC80
King Georges Av, Wat. 75 BS43
King Georges Dr (New Haw), Add. 212 BG110
King Georges Dr, Sthl. 136 BZ71
King Georges Rd, Brwd. 108 FV44
King George's Trd Est, Chess. 216 CN105
King Harolds Way, Bexh. 166 EX80
King Harry La, St.Alb. 42 CA21
King Harry St, Hem.H. 40 BK21
King Henry Ms, Orp. 223 ET106
Osgood Av
King Henry St N16 122 DS64
King Henry Ter E1 142 DV73
Sovereign Cl
King Henry's Ct, Wal.Abb. 83 EC36
Deer Pk Way
King Henry's Dr (New Addington), Croy. 221 EC109
King Henry's Ms, Enf. 83 EA37
King Henry's Reach W6 159 CW79
King Henry's Rd NW3 140 DE66
King Henry's Rd, Kings.T. 198 CP97
King Henry's Wk N1 142 DS65
King James Av (Cuffley), Pot.B. 65 DL29
King James Ct SE1 161 DP75
Borough Rd
King James St SE1 278 G5
King James St SE1 161 DP75
King John Ct EC2 275 N4
King John St E1 143 DX71
King John's Cl (Wraysbury), Stai. 172 AW86
King Johns Wk SE9 184 EK88
King Sq EC1 275 H3
King Stable Ct, Wind. 151 AR80
King Stable St
King Stable St (Eton), Wind. 151 AR80
King Stairs Cl SE16 162 DV75
Elephant La
King St E13 144 EG70
King St EC2 275 J9
King St EC2 142 DQ72
King St N2 120 DD55
King St N17 100 DT53
King St SW1 277 L3
King St SW1 141 DJ74
King St W3 138 CP74
King St W6 159 CU77
King St WC2 273 P10
King St WC2 141 DL73
King St, Cher. 194 BG102
King St, Chesh. 54 AP32
King St, Grav. 191 GH86
King St, Rich. 177 CK85
King St, Sthl. 156 BY76
King St, Twick. 177 CG88
King St, Wat. 76 BW42
King William Ct, Wal.Abb. 83 EC40
Sewardstone Rd
King William IV Gdns SE20 182 DW93
St. John's Rd
King William La SE10 164 EE78
Orlop St
King William St EC4 279 L1
King William St EC4 142 DR73
King William Wk SE10 163 EC79
Kingaby Gdns, Rain. 147 FG66
Kingcup Cl, Croy. 203 DX102
Primrose La
Kingdon Rd NW6 140 DA65
Kingfield Cl, Wok. 227 AZ120
Kingfield Dr, Wok. 227 AZ120
Kingfield Gdns, Wok. 227 AZ120
Kingfield Grn, Wok. 227 AZ120
Kingfield Rd W5 137 CK70
Kingfield Rd, Wok. 226 AY120
Kingfield St E14 163 EC77
Kingfisher Av E11 124 EH58
Eastern Av
Kingfisher Cl SE28 146 EW73
Kingfisher Cl, Brwd. 109 GA45
Kingfisher Cl (Harrow Weald), Har. 95 CF52
Kingfisher Cl, Nthwd. 93 BP53
Kingfisher Cl, Orp. 206 EX98
Kingfisher Cl, Walt. 214 BY106
Old Esher Rd
Kingfisher Cl, Ware 33 EC12
Lawrence Av
Kingfisher Ct SW19 179 CY89
Queensmere Rd
Kingfisher Ct, Enf. 81 DM38
Mount Vw
Kingfisher Ct, Surb. 198 CM101
Ewell Rd
Kingfisher Ct, Sutt. 217 CZ106
Sandpiper Rd
Kingfisher Ct, Wok. 226 AY117
Vale Fm Rd
Kingfisher Ct (Sheerwater), Wok. 211 BC114
Blackmore Cres
Kingfisher Dr, Guil. 243 BC132
Kingfisher Dr, Red. 250 DG131
Kingfisher Dr, Rich. 177 CH91
Kingfisher Dr, Stai. 173 BF91
Kingfisher Gdns, S.Croy. 221 DX111
Kingfisher Lure, Kings L. 59 BP29
Kingfisher Lure, Rick. 74 BH42
Kingfisher Rd, Upmin. 129 FT60
Kingfisher Sq SE8 163 DZ79
Abinger Gro
Kingfisher St E6 144 EL71
Kingfisher Wk NW9 96 CS54
Eagle Dr
Kingfisher Way NW10 118 CR64
Kingfisher Way, Beck. 203 DX99
Kingfisher Way, Harl. 34 EG14
Roydon Mill Pk
Kingham Cl SW18 180 DC87
Kingham Cl W11 159 CY75
Kinghorn St EC1 275 H7
Kinglake Ct, Wok. 226 AS118
Raglan Rd
Kinglake Est SE17 279 N10
Kinglake St SE17 162 DS78
Kingly Ct W1 273 K10
Kingly St W1 273 K9
Kingly St W1 141 DJ72
Kings Arbour, Sthl. 156 BY78
Kings Arms Ct E1 142 DU71
Old Montague St
Kings Arms Yd EC2 275 K8
Kings Av N10 120 DG55
Kings Av N21 99 DP46
King's Av SW4 181 DK87
King's Av SW12 181 DK88
Kings Av W5 137 CK72
Kings Av, Brom. 184 EF93
Kings Av, Buck.H. 102 EK47
Kings Av, Cars. 218 DE108
Kings Av, Grnf. 136 CB72
Kings Av, Hem.H. 40 BM24
Kings Av, Houns. 156 CB81
Kings Av, N.Mal. 198 CS98
Kings Av, Red. 266 DE136
Kings Av, Rom. 126 EZ58
Kings Av, Sun. 175 BT92
Kings Av, Wat. 75 BT42
Kings Av (Byfleet), W.Byf. 212 BK112
Kings Av, Wdf.Grn. 102 EH50
Kings Bench St SE1 278 G4
Kings Bench Wk EC4 274 E9
Kings Chace Vw, Enf. 81 DN40
Crofton Way
Kings Chase, Brwd. 108 FW48
Kings Chase, E.Mol. 196 CC97
Kings Cl E10 123 EB59
Kings Cl NW4 119 CX56
Kings Cl, Beac. 110 AG55
Kings Cl, Ch.St.G. 90 AX47
Kings Cl, Dart. 167 FE84
Kings Cl, Kings L. 58 BH31
Kings Cl, Nthwd. 93 BT51
Kings Cl, Stai. 174 BK94
Kings Cl, T.Ditt. 197 CG100
Kings Cl, Walt. 195 BV102
King's Cl, Wat. 75 BV42
Lady's Cl
Kings Coll Rd NW3 140 DE66

Kings Coll Rd, Ruis. 115 BT58
Kings Ct E13 144 EH67
Kings Ct W6 159 CU77
King St
Kings Ct, Berk. 38 AW18
Lower Kings Rd
Kings Ct, Tad. 233 CW122
Kings Ct, Wem. 118 CP61
Kings Ct S SW3 160 DE78
Chelsea Manor Gdns
Kings Cres N4 122 DQ62
Kings Cres Est N4 122 DQ61
King's Cross Br N1 274 A2
Kings Cross La (South Nutfield), Red. 267 DL136
King's Cross Rd WC1 274 C2
King's Cross Rd WC1 141 DM69
Kings Dr, Edg. 96 CM49
Kings Dr, Grav. 191 GH90
Kings Dr, Surb. 198 CN101
Kings Dr, Tedd. 177 CD92
Kings Dr, T.Ditt. 197 CH100
Kings Dr, Wem. 118 CP61
Kings Dr, The, Walt. 213 BT109
Kings Fm Av, Rich. 158 CN84
Kings Fm Rd, Rick. 73 BD44
Kings Gdns NW6 140 DA66
West End La
Kings Gdns, Ilf. 125 ER60
Kings Gdns, Upmin. 129 FS59
King's Garth Ms SE23 182 DW89
London Rd
Kings Grn, Loug. 84 EL41
Kings Gro SE15 162 DV80
Kings Gro, Rom. 127 FG57
Kings Hall Rd, Beck. 183 DY94
Kings Head Hill E4 101 EB45
Kings Head La (Byfleet), W.Byf. 212 BK111
Kings Head Yd SE1 279 K3
Kings Highway SE18 165 ES79
Kings Hill, Loug. 84 EL40
Kings Keep, Kings.T. 198 CL98
Beaufort Rd
Kings La (Englefield Grn), Egh. 172 AU92
Kings La, Kings L. 58 BG31
Kings La, Sutt. 218 DD107
Kings Langley Bypass, Hem.H. 40 BG23
Kings Langley Bypass, Kings L. 58 BK28
Kings Lynn Cl, Rom. 106 FK51
Kings Lynn Dr
Kings Lynn Dr, Rom. 106 FK51
Kings Lynn Path, Rom. 106 FK51
Kings Lynn Dr
Kings Mall Shop Cen W6 159 CW77
Kings Mead, Horl. 269 DP148
Kings Mead (South Nutfield), Red. 267 DL136
Kings Mead Pk (Claygate), Esher 215 CE108
Kings Meadow, Kings L. 58 BN28
Kings Ms SW4 181 DL85
King's Av
King's Ms WC1 274 C5
King's Ms WC1 141 DM71
Kings Ms, Chig. 103 EQ47
Kings Mill La, Red. 267 DK138
Kings Oak, Rom. 126 FA55
King's Orchard SE9 184 EL86
Kings Paddock, Hmptn. 196 CC95
Kings Par, Cars. 200 DE104
Wrythe La
King's Pas E11 124 EE59
Kings Pas, Kings.T. 197 CK96
Kings Pl SE1 279 H5
Kings Pl W4 158 CQ78
Kings Pl, Buck.H. 102 EJ47
Kings Pl, Loug. 102 EK45
King's Reach Twr SE1 278 E2
Kings Reach Twr SE1 141 DN74
Kings Ride Gate, Rich. 158 CN84
Kings Rd E4 101 ED46
Kings Rd E6 144 EJ67
Kings Rd E11 124 EE59
King's Rd N17 100 DT53
Kings Rd N18 100 DU50
Kings Rd N22 99 DM53
Kings Rd NW10 139 CV66
Kings Rd SE25 202 DU97
King's Rd SW1 276 C10
King's Rd SW1 160 DF78
King's Rd SW3 276 C10
King's Rd SW3 160 DF78
King's Rd SW6 160 DB81
King's Rd SW10 160 DB81
Kings Rd SW14 158 CR83
Kings Rd SW19 180 DA93
Kings Rd W5 137 CK71
Kings Rd (New Haw), Add. 212 BH110
Kings Rd, Bark. 145 EQ66
North St
Kings Rd, Barn. 79 CW41
Kings Rd, Berk. 38 AU20
Kings Rd, Brwd. 108 FW48
Kings Rd, Ch.St.G. 90 AX47
Kings Rd, Egh. 173 BA91
Kings Rd, Felt. 176 BW88
Kings Rd, Guil. 242 AX134
Kings Rd (Shalford), Guil. 258 AY141
Kings Rd, Har. 116 BZ61
King's Rd, Hert. 32 DU08
Kings Rd, Horl. 268 DG148
Kings Rd, Kings.T. 178 CL94
Kings Rd, Mitch. 200 DG97
Kings Rd, Orp. 223 ET105
Kings Rd, Rich. 178 CM85
Kings Rd, Rom. 127 FG57
Kings Rd, St.Alb. 42 CB19
Kings Rd (London Colney), St.Alb. 61 CJ26
Kings Rd, Slou. 152 AS76
Kings Rd, Surb. 197 CJ102
Kings Rd, Sutt. 218 DA110
Kings Rd, Tedd. 177 CD92
Kings Rd, Twick. 177 CH86
King's Rd, Uxb. 134 BK68
Kings Rd, Wal.Cr. 67 DY34
Kings Rd, Walt. 195 BV103
Kings Rd, West Dr. 154 BM75
Kings Rd (Biggin Hill), West. 238 EJ116
King's Rd, Wind. 151 AR82
Kings Rd, Wok. 227 BA116
Kings Rd Bungalows, Har. 116 BZ62
Kings Rd
King's Scholars' Pas SW1 277 K8
King's Ter NW1 141 DJ67
Plender St
Kings Ter, Islw. 157 CG83
Worple Rd
Kings Wk, Grays 170 GA79
King's Wk, Kings.T. 197 CK95
Kings Wk, S.Croy. 220 DV114
Kings Wk Shop Mall SW3 160 DF78
King's Rd
Kings Warren (Oxshott), Lthd. 214 CC111
Kings Way, Har. 117 CE56
King's Yd SW15 159 CW83
Stanbridge Rd
Kingsand Rd SE12 184 EG89
Kingsash Dr, Hayes 136 BY70
Kingsbridge Av W3 158 CM75
Kingsbridge Circ, Rom. 106 FL51
Kingsbridge Cl, Rom. 106 FL51
Kingsbridge Ct E14 163 EA77
Dockers Tanner Rd
Kingsbridge Cres, Sthl. 136 BZ71
Kingsbridge Rd W10 139 CW72
Kingsbridge Rd, Bark. 145 ER68
Kingsbridge Rd, Mord. 199 CX101
Kingsbridge Rd, Rom. 106 FL51
Kingsbridge Rd, Sthl. 156 BZ77
Kingsbridge Rd, Walt. 195 BV101
Kingsbridge Way, Hayes 135 BS69
Kingsbrook, Lthd. 231 CG118
Ryebrook Rd
Kingsbury Av, St.Alb. 42 CC19
Kingsbury Circle NW9 118 CN57
Kingsbury Cres, Stai. 173 BD91
Kingsbury Dr (Old Windsor), Wind. 172 AV86
Kingsbury Rd N1 142 DS65
Kingsbury Rd NW9 118 CP57
Kingsbury Ter N1 142 DS65
Kingsbury Trd Est NW9 118 CR58
Kingsclere Cl SW15 179 CU87
Kingsclere Ct, Barn. 80 DC43
Gloucester Rd
Kingsclere Pl, Enf. 82 DQ40
Chase Side
Kingscliffe Gdns SW19 179 CZ88
Kingscote Rd W4 158 CR76
Kingscote Rd, Croy. 202 DV101
Kingscote Rd, N.Mal. 198 CR97
Kingscote St EC4 274 F10
Kingscourt Rd SW16 181 DK90
Kingscroft, Welw.G.C. 30 DB08
Kingscroft Rd NW2 139 CZ65
Kingscroft Rd, Bans. 234 DD115
Kingscroft Rd, Lthd. 231 CH120
Kingsdale Ct, Wal.Abb. 68 EG34
Lamplighters Cl
Kingsdale Gdns W11 139 CX74
Kingsdale Rd SE18 165 ET80
Kingsdale Rd SE20 183 DX94
Kingsdale Rd, Berk. 38 AU20
Kingsdene, Tad. 233 CV121
Kingsdon La, Harl. 52 EW16
Kingsdown Av W3 138 CS73
Kingsdown Av W13 157 CH75
Kingsdown Av, S.Croy. 219 DP109
Kingsdown Cl SE16 162 DV78
Masters Dr
Kingsdown Cl W10 139 CX72
Kingsdown Cl, Grav. 191 GM88
Farley Rd
Kingsdown Rd E11 124 EE62
Kingsdown Rd N19 121 DL61
Kingsdown Rd, Epsom 217 CU113
Kingsdown Rd, Sutt. 217 CY106
Kingsdown Way, Brom. 204 EG101
Kingsdowne Rd, Surb. 198 CL101
Kingsend, Ruis. 115 BR60
Kingsfield (Albury), Guil. 260 BL144
Kingsfield, Hodd. 49 EA15
Kingsfield, Wind. 151 AK81
Kingsfield Av, Har. 116 CB56
Kingsfield Ct, Wat. 94 BX45
Kingsfield Dr, Enf. 83 DX35
Kingsfield Ho SE9 184 EK90
Kingsfield Rd, Har. 117 CD59
Kingsfield Rd, Wat. 94 BX45
Kingsfield Ter, Dart. 188 FK86
Priory Rd S
Kingsfield Way, Enf. 83 DX35
Kingsford Av, Wall. 219 DL108
Kingsford St NW5 120 DF64
Kingsford Way E6 145 EM71
Kingsgate, Wem. 118 CQ62
Kingsgate Av N3 120 DA55
Kingsgate Cl, Bexh. 166 EY81
Kingsgate Cl, Orp. 206 EW97
Main Rd
Kingsgate Pl NW6 140 DA66
Kingsgate Rd NW6 140 DA66
Kingsgate Rd, Kings.T. 198 CL95
Kingsground SE9 184 EL87
Kingshall Ms SE13 163 EC83
Lewisham Rd
Kingshill Av, Har. 117 CH56
Kingshill Av, Hayes 135 BS69
Kingshill Av, Nthlt. 135 BU69
Kingshill Av, Rom. 105 FC51
Kingshill Av, St.Alb. 43 CG17
Kingshill Av, Wor.Pk. 199 CU101
Kingshill Dr, Har. 117 CH55
Kingshill Way, Berk. 38 AU21
Kingshold Rd E9 142 DW66
Kingsholm Gdns SE9 164 EK84
Kingshurst Rd SE12 184 EG87
Kingsland NW8 140 DE67
Broxwood Way
Kingsland, Harl. 51 EQ17
Kingsland, Pot.B. 63 CZ33
Kingsland Grn E8 142 DS65
Kingsland High St E8 122 DT64
Kingsland Pas E8 142 DS65
Kingsland Grn
Kingsland Rd E2 275 N2
Kingsland Rd E2 142 DS68
Kingsland Rd E8 142 DS68
Kingsland Rd E13 144 EJ69
Kingsland Rd, Hem.H. 40 BG22
Kingslawn Cl SW15 179 CV85
Howards La
Kingslea, Lthd. 231 CG120
Kingsleigh Pl, Mitch. 200 DF97
Chatsworth Pl
Kingsleigh Wk, Brom. 204 EF98
Stamford Dr
Kingsley Av W13 137 CG72
Kingsley Av, Bans. 234 DA115
Kingsley Av, Borwd. 78 CM40
Kingsley Av, Dart. 188 FN85
Kingsley Av (Englefield Grn), Egh. 172 AV93
Kingsley Av, Houns. 156 CC82
Kingsley Av, Sthl. 136 CA73
Kingsley Av, Sutt. 218 DD105
Kingsley Av (Cheshunt), Wal.Cr. 66 DV29
Kingsley Cl N2 120 DC57
Kingsley Cl, Dag. 127 FB63
Kingsley Cl, Horl. 268 DF146
Kingsley Rd
Kingsley Ct, Edg. 96 CP47
Kingsley Ct, Welw.G.C. 29 CZ13
Kingsley Dr, Wor.Pk. 199 CT103
Badgers Copse
Kingsley Flats SE1 162 DS77
Old Kent Rd
Kingsley Gdns E4 101 EA50
Kingsley Gdns, Horn. 128 FK56
Kingsley Gro, Reig. 266 DA137
Kingsley Ms E1 142 DV73
Wapping La
Kingsley Ms W8 160 DB76
Stanford Rd
Kingsley Ms, Chis. 185 EP93
Kingsley Path, Slou. 131 AK70
Wordsworth Rd
Kingsley Pl N6 120 DG59
Kingsley Rd E7 144 EG66
Kingsley Rd E11 101 EC54
Kingsley Rd N13 99 DN49
Kingsley Rd NW6 139 CZ67
Kingsley Rd SW19 180 DB92
Kingsley Rd, Brwd. 109 GD45
Kingsley Rd, Croy. 201 DN102
Kingsley Rd, Har. 116 CC63
Kingsley Rd, Horl. 268 DF146
Kingsley Rd, Houns. 156 CC82
Kingsley Rd, Ilf. 103 EQ53
Kingsley Rd, Loug. 85 ER41
Kingsley Rd, Orp. 223 ET108
Kingsley Rd, Pnr. 116 BZ56
Kingsley St SW11 160 DF83
Kingsley Wk, Grays 171 GG77
Kingsley Way N2 120 DC58
Kingsley Wd Dr SE9 185 EM90
Kingslyn Cres SE19 202 DS95
Kingsman Par SE18 165 EM76
Woolwich Ch St
Kingsman St SE18 165 EM76
Kingsmead, Barn. 80 DA42
Kingsmead (Cuffley), Pot.B. 65 DL28
Kingsmead, Rich. 178 CM86
Kingsmead, St.Alb. 43 CK17
Kingsmead, Saw. 36 EY06
Kingsmead, Wal.Cr. 67 DX28
Kingsmead (Biggin Hill), West. 238 EK116
Kingsmead Av N9 100 DV46
Kingsmead Av NW9 118 CR59
Kingsmead Av, Mitch. 201 DJ97
Kingsmead Av, Rom. 127 FE58
Kingsmead Av, Sun. 196 BW97
Kingsmead Av, Surb. 198 CN103
Kingsmead Av, Wor.Pk. 199 CV104
Kingsmead Cl, Epsom 216 CR108
Kingsmead Cl, Harl. 50 EH16
Kingsmead Cl, Sid. 186 EU89
Kingsmead Cl, Tedd. 177 CG93
Kingsmead Dr, Nthlt. 136 BZ66
Kingsmead Est E9 123 DY63
Kingsmead Way
Kingsmead Hill, Harl. 50 EH16
Kingsmead Rd SW2 181 DN89
Kingsmead Way E9 123 DY63
Kingsmere Cl SW15 159 CY83
Felsham Rd
Kingsmere Pk NW9 118 CP60
Kingsmere Rd SW19 179 CX89
Kingsmill Ct, Hat. 45 CV20
Drakes Way
Kingsmill Gdns, Dag. 126 EZ64
Kingsmill Rd, Dag. 126 EZ64
Kingsmill Ter NW8 140 DD68
Kingsmoor Rd, Harl. 51 EP18
Kingsnympton Pk, Kings.T. 178 CP93
Kingspark Ct E18 124 EG55
Kingsridge SW19 179 CY89
Kingsridge Gdns, Dart. 188 FK86
Kingsthorpe Rd SE26 183 DX91
Kingston Av, Felt. 175 BS86
Kingston Av, Lthd. 231 CH121
Kingston Av (East Horsley), Lthd. 245 BS126
Kingston Av, Sutt. 199 CY104
Kingston Av, West Dr. 134 BM73
Kingston Br, Kings.T. 197 CK96
Kingston Bypass SW15 178 CS91
Kingston Bypass SW20 178 CS91
Kingston Bypass, Esher 197 CG104
Kingston Bypass, N.Mal. 199 CT95
Kingston Bypass, Surb. 198 CL104
Kingston Cl, Nthlt. 136 BZ67
Kingston Cl, Rom. 126 EY55
Kingston Cl, Tedd. 177 CH93
Kingston Ct N4 122 DQ58
Wiltshire Gdns
Kingston Ct (Northfleet), Grav. 190 GB85
Kingston Cres, Ashf. 174 BJ92
Kingston Cres, Beck. 203 DZ95
Kingston Gdns, Croy. 201 DL104
Wandle Rd
Kingston Hall Rd, Kings.T. 197 CK97
Kingston Hill, Kings.T. 178 CQ93
Kingston Hill Av, Rom. 126 EY55
Kingston Hill Pl, Kings.T. 178 CQ91
Kingston Ho Gdns, Lthd. 231 CG121
Upper Fairfield Rd
Kingston La, Lthd. 244 BM127
Kingston La, Tedd. 177 CG92
Kingston La, Uxb. 134 BL69
Kingston La, West Dr. 154 BM75
Kingston Pk Est, Kings.T. 178 CP93
Kingston Pl, Har. 95 CF52
Richmond Gdns
Kingston Ri (New Haw), Add. 212 BG110
Kingston Rd N9 100 DU47
Kingston Rd SW15 179 CU88
Kingston Rd SW19 199 CZ95
Kingston Rd SW20 199 CX96
Kingston Rd, Ashf. 174 BM93
Kingston Rd, Barn. 80 DD43
Kingston Rd, Epsom 216 CS106
Kingston Rd, Ilf. 125 EP63
Kingston Rd, Kings.T. 198 CP97
Kingston Rd, Lthd. 231 CG117
Kingston Rd, N.Mal. 198 CR98
Kingston Rd, Rom. 127 FF56
Kingston Rd, Sthl. 156 BZ75
Kingston Rd, Stai. 174 BH93
Kingston Rd, Surb. 198 CP103
Kingston Rd, Tedd. 177 CH92
Kingston Rd, Wor.Pk. 198 CP103
Kingston Sq SE19 182 DR92
Kingston Vale SW15 178 CR91
Kingstown St NW1 140 DG67
Kingswater Pl SW11 160 DE80
Battersea Ch Rd
Kingsway N12 98 DC51
Kingsway SW14 158 CP83
Kingsway WC2 274 B8
Kingsway WC2 141 DM72
Kingsway, Croy. 219 DM106
Kingsway, Enf. 82 DV43
Kingsway (Chalfont St. Peter), Ger.Cr. 112 AY55
Kingsway, Hayes 135 BQ71
Kingsway, Iver 133 BE72
High St
Kingsway, N.Mal. 199 CW98
Kingsway, Orp. 205 ES99
Kingsway (Cuffley), Pot.B. 65 DL30
Kingsway (Farnham Common), Slou. 131 AP65
Kingsway, Stai. 174 BK88
Kingsway, Wat. 60 BW34
Kingsway, Wem. 118 CL63
Kingsway, W.Wick. 204 EE104
Kingsway, Wok. 226 AX118
Kingsway, Wdf.Grn. 102 EJ50
Kingsway, The, Epsom 217 CT111
Kingsway Av, S.Croy. 220 DW109
Kingsway Av, Wok. 226 AX118
Kingsway Business Pk, Hmptn. 196 BZ95
Kingsway Cres, Har. 116 CC56
Kingsway Pl EC1 274 E4
Kingsway Rd, Sutt. 217 CY108
Kingsway Shop Cen NW3 120 DC63
Hampstead High St
Kingswear Rd NW5 121 DH62
Kingswear Rd, Ruis. 115 BU61
Kingswell Ride (Cuffley), Pot.B. 65 DL30
Kingswood Av NW6 139 CY67
Kingswood Av, Belv. 166 EZ77
Kingswood Av, Brom. 204 EE97
Kingswood Av, Hmptn. 176 CB93
Kingswood Av, Houns. 156 BZ81
Kingswood Av, S.Croy. 236 DV115
Kingswood Av, Swan. 207 FF98
Kingswood Av, Th.Hth. 201 DN99
Kingswood Cl N20 80 DC44
Kingswood Cl SW8 161 DL80
Kingswood Cl, Dart. 188 FJ86
Kingswood Cl (Englefield Grn), Egh. 172 AX91
Kingswood Cl, Enf. 82 DS43
Kingswood Cl, Guil. 243 BC133
Kingswood Cl, N.Mal. 199 CT100
Motspur Pk
Kingswood Cl, Orp. 205 ER101
Kingswood Cl, Surb. 198 CL101
Kingswood Cl, Wey. 213 BP108
Kingswood Creek (Wraysbury), Stai. 172 AX85
Kingswood Dr SE19 182 DS91
Kingswood Dr, Cars. 200 DF102
Kingswood Dr, Sutt. 218 DB109
Kingswood Est SE21 182 DS91
Bowen Dr
Kingswood La, S.Croy. 220 DW113
Kingswood La, Warl. 236 DW115
Kingswood Pk N3 97 CZ54
Kingswood Pl SE13 164 EE84
Kingswood Ri (Englefield Grn), Egh. 172 AX92
Kingswood Rd E11 123 ED61
Grove Grn Rd
Kingswood Rd SE20 182 DW93
Kingswood Rd SW2 181 DL86
Kingswood Rd SW19 179 CZ94
Kingswood Rd W4 158 CQ76
Kingswood Rd, Brom. 203 ED98
Kingswood Rd, Ilf. 126 EU60
Kingswood Rd (Dunton Grn), Sev. 241 FE120
Kingswood Rd, Tad. 233 CV121
Kingswood Rd, Wat. 59 BV34
Kingswood Rd, Wem. 118 CN62
Kingswood Ter W4 158 CQ76
Kingswood Rd
Kingswood Way, S.Croy. 220 DW113
Kingswood Way, Wall. 219 DL106
Kingsworth Cl, Beck. 203 DY99
Kingsworthy Cl, Kings.T. 198 CM97
Kingthorpe Rd NW10 138 CR66
Kingthorpe Ter NW10 138 CR65
Kingwell Rd, Barn. 80 DD38
Kingwood Rd SW6 159 CY81
Kinlet Rd SE18 165 EQ81
Kinloch Dr NW9 118 CS59
Kinloch St N7 121 DM62
Hornsey Rd
Kinloss Ct N3 119 CZ56
Haslemere Gdns
Kinloss Gdns N3 119 CZ56
Kinloss Rd, Cars. 200 DC101
Kinnaird Av W4 158 CQ80
Kinnaird Av, Brom. 184 EF93
Kinnaird Cl, Brom. 184 EF93
Kinnaird Cl, Slou. 130 AJ72
Kinnaird Way, Wdf.Grn. 103 EM51
Kinnear Rd W12 159 CT75
Kinnersley Manor, Reig. 266 DC142
Kinnersley Wk, Reig. 266 DB139
Castle Dr
Kinnerton Pl N SW1 276 E5
Kinnerton Pl S SW1 276 E5
Kinnerton St SW1 276 F5
Kinnerton St SW1 160 DG75
Kinnerton Yd SW1 276 E5
Kinnoul Rd W6 159 CY79
Kinross Av, Wor.Pk. 199 CU103
Kinross Cl, Edg. 96 CP47
Tayside Dr
Kinross Cl, Har. 118 CM57
Kinross Cl, Sun. 175 BT92
Kinross Dr, Sun. 175 BT92
Kinross Ter E17 101 DZ54
Kinsale Rd SE15 162 DU83
Kintore Way SE1 279 P8
Kintyre Cl SW16 201 DM97
Kinveachy Gdns SE7 164 EL78
Kinver Rd SE26 182 DW91
Kipings, Tad. 233 CX122
Kipling Av, Til. 171 GH81
Kipling Dr SW19 180 DD93
Kipling Est SE1 279 L5
Kipling Est SE1 162 DR75
Kipling Pl, Stan. 95 CF51
Uxbridge Rd
Kipling Rd, Bexh. 166 EY81
Kipling Rd, Dart. 188 FP85
Kipling St SE1 279 L5
Kipling St SE1 162 DR75
Kipling Ter N9 100 DR48
Kipling Twrs, Rom. 105 FH52
Kippington Cl, Sev. 256 FF124
Kippington Dr SE9 184 EK88
Kippington Ho, Sev. 256 FG126
Kippington Rd
Kippington Rd, Sev. 256 FG124
Kirby Cl, Epsom 217 CT106
Kirby Cl, Ilf. 103 ES51
Kirby Cl, Loug. 102 EL45
Kirby Cl, Nthwd. 93 BT51
Kirby Cl, Rom. 106 FN50
Kirby Est SE16 162 DV76
Kirby Gro SE1 279 M4
Kirby Gro SE1 162 DS75
Kirby Rd, Dart. 188 FQ87
Kirby Rd, Wok. 226 AW117
Kirby St EC1 274 E6
Kirby Way, Walt. 196 BW100
Kirchen Rd W13 137 CH73
Kirk Ct, Sev. 256 FG123
Kirk La SE18 165 EQ79
Kirk Ri, Sutt. 200 DB104
Kirk Rd E17 123 DZ58
Kirkby Cl N11 98 DG51
Coverdale Rd
Kirkcaldy Grn, Wat. 94 BW48
Trevose Way
Kirkdale SE26 182 DV89
Kirkdale Rd E11 124 EE60
Kirkfields, Guil. 242 AU131
Kirkfield Cl W13 137 CH74
Broomfield Rd
Kirkham Rd E6 144 EL72
Kirkham St SE18 165 ES79
Kirkland Av, Ilf. 103 EN54
Kirkland Av, Wok. 226 AS116
Kirkland Cl, Sid. 185 ES86
Kirkland Dr, Enf. 82 DQ39
Kirkland Wk E8 142 DT65
Kirklands, Welw.G.C. 29 CX05
Kirkleas Rd, Surb. 198 CL102
Kirklees Rd, Dag. 126 EW64
Kirklees Rd, Th.Hth. 201 DN99
Kirkley Rd SW19 200 DA95
Kirkly Cl, S.Croy. 220 DS109
Kirkman Pl W1 273 M7
Kirkmichael Rd E14 143 EC72
Dee St
Kirks Pl E14 143 DZ71
Rhodeswell Rd
Kirkside Rd SE3 164 EG79
Kirkstall Av N17 122 DR56
Kirkstall Gdns SW2 181 DL88
Kirkstall Rd SW2 181 DK88
Kirkstead Ct E5 123 DY62
Mandeville St
Kirksted Rd, Mord. 200 DB102
Kirkstone Way, Brom. 184 EE94
Kirkton Rd N15 122 DS56
Kirkwall Pl E2 142 DW69
Kirkwall Spur, Slou. 132 AS71
Kirkwood Rd SE15 162 DV82
Kirn Rd W13 137 CH73
Kirchen Rd
Kirrane Cl, N.Mal. 199 CT99
Kirtle Rd, Chesh. 54 AQ31
Kirtley Rd SE26 183 DY91
Kirtling St SW8 161 DJ80
Kirton Cl W4 158 CR77
Dolman Rd
Kirton Cl, Horn. 148 FJ65
Kirton Gdns E2 142 DT69
Chambord St
Kirton Rd E13 144 EJ68
Kirton Wk, Edg. 96 CQ52
Kirwyn Way SE5 161 DP80
Kitcat Ter E3 143 EA69
Kitchener Av, Grav. 191 GJ90
Kitchener Cl, St.Alb. 43 CH21
Kitchener Rd E7 144 EH65
Kitchener Rd E17 101 EB53
Kitchener Rd N2 120 DE55
Kitchener Rd N17 122 DR55
Kitchener Rd, Dag. 147 FB65
Kitchener Rd, Th.Hth. 202 DR97
Kitcheners Mead, St.Alb. 42 CC20
Kite Fld, Berk. 38 AS16
Kite Pl E2 142 DU69
Nelson Gdns
Kite Yd SW11 160 DF81
Cambridge Rd
Kitley Gdns SE19 202 DT95
Kitsbury Rd, Berk. 38 AV19
Kitsbury Ter, Berk. 38 AV19
Kitsmead La (Longcross), Cher. 192 AX103
Kitson Rd SE5 162 DR80
Kitson Rd SW13 159 CU81
Kitson Way, Harl. 35 EQ14
Kitswell Way, Rad. 61 CF33
Kitten La, Ware 34 EE11
Kitters Grn, Abb.L. 59 BS31
High St
Kittiwake Cl, S.Croy. 221 DY110
Kittiwake Pl, Sutt. 217 CZ106
Sandpiper Rd
Kittiwake Rd, Nthlt. 136 BX69
Kittiwake Way, Hayes 136 BX71
Kitto Rd SE14 163 DX82
Kitt's End Rd, Barn. 79 CX36
Kitts Riding, Harl. 52 EX15
Kiver Rd N19 121 DK61
Kiwi Cl, Twick. 177 CH86
Crown Rd
Klea Av SW4 181 DJ86
Knapdale Cl SE23 182 DV89
Knapmill Rd SE6 183 EA89
Knapmill Way SE6 183 EB89
Knapp Cl NW10 138 CS65
Knapp Rd E3 143 EA70
Knapp Rd, Ashf. 174 BM91
Knapton Ms SW17 180 DG93
Seely Rd
Knaresborough Dr SW18 180 DB88
Knaresborough Pl SW5 160 DB77
Knatchbull Rd NW10 138 CR67
Knatchbull Rd SE5 162 DQ81
Knaves Beech (Loudwater), H.Wyc. 88 AD53
Knaves Beech Business Cen (Loudwater), H.Wyc. 88 AC54
Knaves Beech Way (Loudwater), H.Wyc. 88 AC54
Knaves Hollow, H.Wyc. 88 AD54
Knebworth Av E17 101 EA53
Knebworth Path, Borwd. 78 CR42
Knebworth Rd N16 122 DS63
Nevill Rd
Knee Hill SE2 166 EW77
Knee Hill Cres SE2 166 EW77
Knella Grn, Welw.G.C. 30 DA09
Knella Rd, Welw.G.C. 29 CY10
Kneller Gdns, Islw. 177 CD85
Kneller Rd SE4 163 DY84
Kneller Rd, N.Mal. 198 CS101
Kneller Rd, Twick. 176 CC86
Knight St, Saw. 36 EY05
Knighten St E1 142 DU74
Knighthead Pt E14 163 EA75
Knightland Rd E5 122 DV61
Knighton Cl, Rom. 127 FD58
Knighton Cl, S.Croy. 219 DP108
Knighton Cl, Wdf.Grn. 102 EH49

Knighton Dr, Wdf.Grn. 102 EG49
Knighton Grn, Buck.H. 102 EH47
High Rd
Knighton La, Buck.H. 102 EH47
Knighton Pk Rd SE26 183 DX92
Knighton Rd E7 124 EG62
Knighton Rd, Red. 266 DG136
Knighton Rd, Rom. 127 FC58
Knighton Rd (Otford), Sev. 241 FF116
Knighton Way La (Denham), Uxb. 134 BH65
Knightrider Ct EC4 275 H10
Knightrider St EC4 142 DQ73
Godliman St
Knights Arc SW1 276 D5
Knights Av W5 158 CL75
Knights Cl E9 122 DW64
Churchill Wk
Knights Cl, Egh. 173 BD93
Knights Cl, Wind. 151 AK81
Knights Ct, Kings.T. 198 CL97
Knights Ct, Rom. 126 EY58
Knights Hill SE27 181 DP92
Knights Hill Sq SE27 181 DP91
Knights Hill
Knights La N9 100 DU48
Knights Manor Way, Dart. 188 FM86
Knights Ms, Sutt. 218 DA108
York Rd
Knights Orchard, Hem.H. 39 BF18
Knights Pk, Kings.T. 198 CL97
Knights Pl, Red. 250 DG133
Noke Dr
Knights Pl, Wind. 151 AQ83
Frances Rd
Knights Ridge, Orp. 224 EV106
Stirling Dr
Knights Rd E16 164 EG75
Knights Rd, Stan. 95 CJ49
Knights Wk SE11 278 F9
Knights Wk, Rom. 86 EV41
Knight's Way, Brwd. 109 GA48
Knights Way, Ilf. 103 EQ51
Knightsbridge SW1 276 E5
Knightsbridge SW1 160 DF75
Knightsbridge SW7 276 C5
Knightsbridge SW7 160 DE75
Knightsbridge Cres, Stai. 174 BH93
Knightsbridge Gdns, Rom. 127 FD57
Knightsbridge Grn SW1 276 D5
Knightsbridge Grn SW1 160 DF75
Knightsbridge Way, Hem.H. 40 BL20
Knightsfield, Welw.G.C. 29 CY06
Knightswood, Wok. 226 AT118
Knightswood Cl, Edg. 96 CQ47
Knightwood Cl, Reig. 266 DA136
Knightwood Cres, N.Mal. 198 CS100
Knipp Hill, Cob. 214 BZ113
Knivet Rd SW6 160 DA79
Knobfield, Dor. 261 BT143
Knobs Hill Rd E15 143 EB67
Knockhall Chase, Green. 189 FV85
Knockhall Rd, Green. 189 FW86
Knockholt Cl, Sutt. 218 DB110
Knockholt Main Rd (Knockholt), Sev. 240 EY115
Knockholt Rd SE9 184 EK85
Knockholt Rd (Halstead), Sev. 224 EZ113
Knole, The SE9 185 EN91
Knole, The (Istead Ri), Grav. 190 GE94
Knole Cl, Croy. 202 DW100
Stockbury Rd
Knole Gate, Sid. 185 ES90
Woodside Cres
Knole La, Sev. 257 FJ126
Knole Rd, Dart. 187 FG87
Knole Rd, Sev. 257 FK123
Knole Way, Sev. 257 FJ125
Knoll, The W13 137 CJ71
Knoll, The, Beck. 203 EB95
Knoll, The, Brom. 204 EG103
Knoll, The, Cher. 193 BF102
Knoll, The, Cob. 214 CA113
Knoll, The, Hert. 32 DV08
Knoll, The, Lthd. 231 CJ120
Knoll Ct SE19 182 DT92
Knoll Cres, Nthwd. 93 BS53
Knoll Dr N14 98 DG45
Knoll Pk Rd, Cher. 193 BF102
Knoll Ri, Orp. 205 ET102
Knoll Rd SW18 180 DC85
Knoll Rd, Bex. 186 FA87
Knoll Rd, Dor. 263 CG138
Knoll Rd, Sid. 186 EV92
Knolles Cres, Hat. 45 CV24
Knollmead, Surb. 198 CQ102
Knolls, The, Epsom 233 CW116
Knolls Cl, Wor.Pk. 199 CV104
Knollys Cl SW16 181 DN90
Knollys Rd SW16 181 DN90
Knolton Way, Slou. 132 AW72
Knottisford St E2 142 DW69
Knottocks Cl, Beac. 88 AJ50
Knottocks Dr, Beac. 88 AJ50
Knottocks End, Beac. 89 AK50
Knotts Grn Ms E10 123 EB58
Knotts Grn Rd E10 123 EB58
Knotts Pl, Sev. 256 FG124
Knowl Hill, Wok. 227 BB119
Knowl Pk, Borwd. 78 CL43
Knowl Way, Borwd. 78 CM42
Knowland Way (Denham), Uxb. 113 BF58
Knowle, The, Hodd. 49 EA18
Knowle, The, Tad. 233 CW121
Knowle Av, Bexh. 166 EY80
Knowle Cl SW9 161 DN83
Knowle Gdns, W.Byf. 211 BF113
Madeira Rd
Knowle Grn, Stai. 174 BG92
Knowle Gro, Vir.W. 192 AW101
Knowle Gro Cl, Vir.W. 192 AW101
Knowle Hill, Vir.W. 192 AV101
Knowle Pk, Cob. 230 BY115
Knowle Pk Av, Stai. 174 BH93
Knowle Rd, Brom. 204 EL103
Knowle Rd, Twick. 177 CE88
Knowles Cl, West Dr. 134 BL74
Knowles Hill Cres SE13 183 ED85
Knowles Wk SW4 161 DJ83
Knowlton Grn, Brom. 204 EF99
Knowsley Av, Sthl. 136 CA74
Knowsley Rd SW11 160 DF82
Knox Rd E7 144 EF65
Knox Rd, Guil. 242 AV130
Knox St W1 272 D6
Knox St W1 140 DF71
Knoxfield Caravan Pk, Dart. 189 FS90
Knoyle St SE14 163 DY79
Chubworthy St
Knutsford Av, Wat. 76 BX38
Kodak Ho, Hem.H. 40 BJ22
Koh-i-noor Av, Bushey 76 CA44
Kohat Rd SW19 180 DB92
Koonowla Cl (Biggin Hill), West. 238 EK115
Kooringa, Warl. 236 DV119
Korda Cl, Shep. 194 BM97
Kossuth St SE10 164 EE78
Kotree Way SE1 162 DU77
Beatrice Rd
Kramer Ms SW5 160 DA78
Kempsford Gdns
Kreedman Wk E8 122 DU64
Kreisel Wk, Rich. 158 CM79
Kuala Gdns SW16 201 DM95
Kuhn Way E7 124 EG64
Forest La
Kydbrook Cl, Orp. 205 ER101
Kylemore Cl E6 144 EK68
Parr Rd
Kylemore Rd NW6 140 DA66
Kymberley Rd, Har. 117 CE58
Kyme Rd, Horn. 127 FF58
Kynance Cl, Rom. 106 FJ48
Kynance Gdns, Stan. 95 CJ53
Kynance Ms SW7 160 DB76
Kynance Pl SW7 160 DC76
Kynaston Av N16 122 DT62
Dynevor Rd
Kynaston Av, Th.Hth. 202 DQ99
Kynaston Cl, Har. 95 CD52
Kynaston Cres, Th.Hth. 202 DQ99
Kynaston Rd N16 122 DS62
Kynaston Rd, Brom. 184 EG92
Kynaston Rd, Enf. 82 DR39
Kynaston Rd, Orp. 206 EV101
Kynaston Rd, Th.Hth. 202 DQ99
Kynaston Wd, Har. 95 CD52
Kynersley Cl, Cars. 200 DF104
William St
Kynock Rd N18 100 DW49
Kyrle Rd SW11 180 DG85
Kytes Dr, Wat. 60 BX33
Kytes Est, Wat. 60 BX33
Kyverdale Rd N16 122 DT61

L

La Plata Gro, Brwd. 108 FV48
La Roche Cl, Slou. 152 AW76
La Tourne Gdns, Orp. 205 EQ104
Laburnham Cl, Upmin. 129 FU59
Laburnham Gdns, Upmin. 129 FT59
Laburnum Av N9 100 DS47
Laburnum Av N17 100 DR52
Laburnum Av, Dart. 188 FJ88
Laburnum Av, Horn. 127 FF62
Laburnum Av, Sutt. 200 DE104
Laburnum Av, Swan. 207 FC97
Laburnum Av, West Dr. 134 BM73
Laburnum Cl E4 101 DZ51
Laburnum Cl N11 98 DG51
Laburnum Cl SE15 162 DW80
Clifton Way
Laburnum Cl, Guil. 242 AW131
Laburnum Cl (Cheshunt), Wal.Cr. 67 DX31
Laburnum Ct E2 142 DT67
Laburnum St
Laburnum Ct, Stan. 95 CJ49
Laburnum Cres, Sun. 195 BV95
Batavia Rd
Laburnum Gdns N21 100 DQ47
Laburnum Gdns, Croy. 203 DX101
Laburnum Gro N21 100 DQ47
Laburnum Gro NW9 118 CQ59
Laburnum Gro (Northfleet), Grav. 190 GD87
Laburnum Gro, Houns. 156 BZ84
Laburnum Gro, N.Mal. 198 CR96
Laburnum Gro, Ruis. 115 BR58
Laburnum Gro, St.Alb. 60 CB25
Laburnum Gro, Slou. 153 BB79
Laburnum Gro, S.Ock. 149 FW69
Laburnum Gro, Sthl. 136 BZ70
Laburnum Ho, Dag. 126 FA61
Bradwell Av
Laburnum Pl (Englefield Grn), Egh. 172 AV93
Laburnum Rd SW19 180 DC94
Laburnum Rd, Cher. 194 BG102
Laburnum Rd, Epp. 70 EW29
Laburnum Rd, Epsom 216 CS113
Laburnum Rd, Hayes 155 BT77
Laburnum Rd, Hodd. 49 EB15
Laburnum Rd, Mitch. 200 DG96
Laburnum Rd, Wok. 226 AX120
Laburnum St E2 142 DT67
Laburnum Wk, Horn. 128 FJ64
Laburnum Way, Brom. 205 EN101
Laburnum Way, Stai. 174 BM88
Laburnum Way (Cheshunt), Wal.Cr. 65 DP28
Millcrest Rd
Lacebark Cl, Sid. 185 ET87
Lacey Av, Couls. 235 DN120
Lacey Cl N9 100 DU47
Lacey Cl, Egh. 173 BD94
Lacey Dr, Couls. 235 DN120
Lacey Dr, Dag. 126 EV63
Lacey Dr, Edg. 96 CL49
Lacey Dr, Hmptn. 196 BZ95
Lacey Grn, Couls. 235 DN120
Lacey Wk E3 143 EA68
Lackford Rd, Couls. 234 DF118
Lackington St EC2 275 L6
Lackington St EC2 142 DR71
Lackmore Rd, Enf. 82 DW35
Lacock Cl SW19 180 DC93
Lacon Rd SE22 162 DU84
Lacy Rd SW15 159 CX84
Ladas Rd SE27 182 DQ91
Ladbroke Ct, Red. 250 DG132
Ladbroke Rd
Ladbroke Cres W11 139 CY72
Ladbroke Gro
Ladbroke Gdns W11 139 CZ73
Ladbroke Gro W10 139 CX70
Ladbroke Gro W11 139 CY72
Ladbroke Gro, Red. 250 DG133
Ladbroke Ms W11 139 CY74
Ladbroke Rd
Ladbroke Rd W11 139 CZ74
Ladbroke Rd, Enf. 82 DT44
Ladbroke Rd, Epsom 216 CR114
Ladbroke Rd, Horl. 268 DG146
Ladbroke Rd, Red. 250 DG133
Ladbroke Sq W11 139 CZ73
Ladbroke Ter W11 139 CZ73
Ladbroke Wk W11 139 CZ74
Ladbrook Cl, Pnr. 116 BZ57
Ladbrook Rd SE25 202 DR97
Ladbrooke Cl, Pot.B. 64 DA32
Strafford Gate
Ladbrooke Cres, Sid. 186 EX90
Ladbrooke Dr, Pot.B. 64 DA32
Ladbrooke Rd, Slou. 151 AQ76
Ladderstile Ride, Kings.T. 178 CP92
Ladderswood Way N11 99 DJ50
Ladds Way, Swan. 207 FD98
Ladies Gro, St.Alb. 42 CB18
Lady Booth Rd, Kings.T. 198 CL96
Lady Dock Path SE16 163 DY75
Salter Rd
Lady Gro, Welw.G.C. 29 CY12
Lady Hay, Wor.Pk. 199 CT103
Lady Margaret Rd N19 121 DJ63
Lady Margaret Rd NW5 121 DJ64
Lady Margaret Rd, Sthl. 136 BZ71
Lady Somerset Rd NW5 121 DH63
Ladybower Ct E5 123 DY63
Gilpin Rd
Ladycroft Gdns, Orp. 223 EQ106
Ladycroft Rd SE13 163 EB83
Ladycroft Wk, Stan. 95 CK53
Ladycroft Way, Orp. 223 EQ106
Ladyday Pl, Slou. 131 AQ74
Glentworth Pl
Ladyegate Cl, Dor. 263 CK135
Ladyegate Rd, Dor. 263 CJ136
Ladyfield Cl, Loug. 85 EP42
Ladyfields (Northfleet), Grav. 191 GF91
Ladyfields, Loug. 85 EP42
Ladygate La, Ruis. 115 BP58
Ladygrove, Croy. 221 DY109
Ladygrove Dr, Guil. 243 BA129
Ladymead, Guil. 242 AW133
Ladymeadow, Kings L. 58 BK27
Lady's Cl, Wat. 75 BV42
Ladyshot, Harl. 36 EU14
Ladysmith Av E6 144 EL68
Ladysmith Av, Ilf. 125 ER59
Ladysmith Cl NW7 97 CU52
Colenso Dr
Ladysmith Rd E16 144 EF69
Ladysmith Rd N17 100 DU54
Ladysmith Rd N18 100 DV50
Ladysmith Rd SE9 185 EN86
Ladysmith Rd, Enf. 82 DS41
Ladysmith Rd, Har. 95 CE54
Ladysmith Rd, St.Alb. 43 CD19
Ladythorpe Cl, Add. 212 BH105
Church Rd
Ladywalk, Rick. 91 BE50
Ladywell Cl SE4 163 DZ84
Adelaide Av
Ladywell Hts SE4 183 DZ86
Ladywell Prospect, Saw. 36 FA06
Ladywell Rd SE13 183 EA85
Ladywell St E15 144 EF67
Plaistow Gro
Ladywood Av, Orp. 205 ES99
Ladywood Cl, Rick. 74 BH41
Ladywood Rd (Lane End), Dart. 189 FS92
Ladywood Rd, Hert. 31 DM09
Ladywood Rd, Surb. 198 CN103
Lafone Av, Felt. 176 BW88
Alfred Rd
Lafone St SE1 279 P4
Lafone St SE1 162 DT75
Lagado Ms SE16 143 DX74
Lagger, The, Ch.St.G. 90 AV48
Lagger Cl, Ch.St.G. 90 AV48
Laglands Cl, Reig. 250 DC132
Lagonda Av, Ilf. 103 ET51
Lagonda Way, Dart. 168 FJ84
Lagoon Rd, Orp. 206 EV99
Laidlaw Dr N21 81 DM43
Laidon Sq, Hem.H. 40 BK16
Laing Cl, Ilf. 103 ER51
Laing Dean, Nthlt. 136 BW67
Laings Av, Mitch. 200 DF96
Lainlock Pl, Houns. 156 CB81
Spring Gro Rd
Lainson St SW18 180 DA87
Laird Av, Grays 170 GD75
Laird Ho SE5 162 DQ80
Lairdale Cl SE21 182 DQ88
Lairs Cl N7 141 DL65
Manger Rd
Laitwood Rd SW12 181 DH88
Lake, The, Bushey 94 CC46
Lake Av, Brom. 184 EG93
Lake Av, Rain. 148 FK68
Lake Av, Slou. 131 AR73
Lake Cl SW19 179 CZ92
Lake Rd
Lake Cl (Byfleet), W.Byf. 212 BK112
Lake Dr, Bushey 94 CC47
Lake End Ct, Maid. 130 AH72
Taplow Rd
Lake End Rd, Maid. 130 AH73
Lake End Rd (Dorney), Wind. 150 AH76
Lake Gdns, Dag. 126 FA64
Lake Gdns, Rich. 177 CH89
Lake Gdns, Wall. 201 DH104
Lake Ho Rd E11 124 EG62
Lake La, Horl. 267 DJ144
Lake Ri, Grays 169 FU77
Lake Ri, Rom. 127 FF55
Lake Rd SW19 179 CZ92
Lake Rd, Croy. 203 DZ103
Lake Rd, Rom. 126 EX56
Lake Rd, Vir.W. 192 AV98
Lake Rd, Wal.Abb. 50 EE21
Lake Vw (North Holmwood), Dor. 263 CJ139
Lake Vw, Edg. 96 CM50
Lake Vw, Pot.B. 64 DC33
Lake Vw Rd, Sev. 256 FG122
Lakedale Rd SE18 165 ES79
Lakefield Cl SE20 182 DV94
Limes Av
Lakefield Rd N22 99 DP54
Lakefields Cl, Rain. 148 FK68
Lakehall Gdns, Th.Hth. 201 DP99
Lakehall Rd, Th.Hth. 201 DP99
Lakehurst Rd, Epsom 216 CS106
Lakeland Cl, Chig. 104 EV49
Lakeland Cl, Har. 95 CD51
Lakenheath N14 81 DK44
Laker Pl SW15 179 CZ86
Lakers Ri, Bans. 234 DE116
Lakes Cl (Chilworth), Guil. 259 BB140
Lakes La, Beac. 89 AM54
Lakes Rd, Kes. 222 EJ106
Lakeside N3 98 DB54
Lakeside W13 137 CJ72
Edgehill Rd
Lakeside, Beck. 203 EB97
Lakeside, Enf. 81 DK42
Lakeside, Rain. 148 FL68
Lakeside, Red. 250 DG132
Lakeside, Wall. 201 DH104
Derek Av
Lakeside, Wey. 195 BS103
Lakeside, Wok. 226 AS119
Lakeside Av SE28 146 EU74
Lakeside Av, Ilf. 124 EK56
Lakeside Cl SE25 202 DU96
Lakeside Cl, Chig. 103 ET49
Lakeside Cl, Ruis. 115 BR56
Lakeside Cl, Sid. 186 EW85
Lakeside Cl, Wok. 226 AS119
Lakeside Ct N4 121 DP61
Lakeside Ct, Borwd. 78 CN43
Cavendish Cres
Lakeside Cres, Barn. 80 DF43
Lakeside Cres, Brwd. 108 FX48
Lakeside Cres, Wey. 195 BQ104
Churchill Dr
Lakeside Dr, Brom. 204 EL104
Lakeside Dr, Esher 214 CC107
Lakeside Dr (Stoke Poges), Slou. 132 AS67
Lakeside Gra, Wey. 195 BQ104
Lakeside Pl (London Colney), St.Alb. 61 CK27
Lakeside Rd N13 99 DM49
Lakeside Rd W14 159 CX76
Lakeside Rd, Slou. 153 BF80
Lakeside Rd (Cheshunt), Wal.Cr. 66 DW28
Lakeside Way, Wem. 118 CN63
Lakeswood Rd, Orp. 205 EP100
Lakeview Ct SW19 179 CY89
Victoria Dr
Lakeview Rd SE27 181 DN92
Lakeview Rd, Well. 166 EV84
Lakis Cl NW3 120 DC63
Flask Wk
Laleham Av NW7 96 CR48
Laleham Cl, Stai. 194 BH95
Worple Rd
Laleham Ct, Wok. 226 AY116
Laleham Pk, Stai. 194 BJ98
Laleham Reach, Cher. 194 BH96
Laleham Rd SE6 183 EC86
Laleham Rd, Shep. 194 BM98
Laleham Rd, Stai. 173 BF92
Lalor St SW6 159 CY82
Lamb Cl, Hat. 45 CV19
Lamb Cl, Til. 171 GJ82
Coleridge Rd
Lamb Cl, Wat. 60 BW34
Lamb La E8 142 DV66
Lamb St E1 275 P6
Lamb St E1 142 DT71
Lamb Wk SE1 279 M5
Lamb Yd, Wat. 76 BX43
Lambarde Av SE9 185 EN91
Lambarde Dr, Sev. 256 FG123
Lambarde Rd, Sev. 256 FG122
Lambardes Cl, Orp. 224 EW110
Lamberhurst Cl, Orp. 206 EX102
Lamberhurst Rd SE27 181 DN91
Lamberhurst Rd, Dag. 126 EZ60
Lambert Av, Rich. 158 CP83
Lambert Av, Slou. 152 AY75
Lambert Cl (Biggin Hill), West. 238 EK116
Lambert Ct, Bushey 76 BX42
Lambert Jones Ms EC2 142 DQ71
The Barbican
Lambert Rd E16 144 EH72
Lambert Rd N12 98 DD50
Lambert Rd SW2 181 DL85
Lambert Rd, Bans. 218 DA114
Lambert St N1 141 DN66
Lambert Wk, Wem. 117 CK62
Lambert Way N12 98 DC50
Woodhouse Rd
Lamberts Pl, Croy. 202 DR102
Lamberts Rd, Surb. 198 CL99
Lambeth Br SE1 278 A8
Lambeth Br SE1 161 DL77
Lambeth Br SW1 278 A8
Lambeth Br SW1 161 DL77
Lambeth High St SE1 278 B9
Lambeth High St SE1 161 DM77
Lambeth Hill EC4 275 H10
Lambeth Hill EC4 142 DQ73
Lambeth Palace Rd SE1 278 B7
Lambeth Palace Rd SE1 161 DM76
Lambeth Rd SE1 278 C7
Lambeth Rd SE1 161 DM77
Lambeth Rd SE11 278 C7
Lambeth Rd SE11 161 DM77
Lambeth Rd, Croy. 201 DN101
Lambeth Wk SE11 278 C8
Lambeth Wk SE11 161 DM77
Lamble St NW5 120 DG64
Lambley Rd, Dag. 146 EV65
Lambly Hill, Vir.W. 192 AY97
Lambolle Pl NW3 140 DE65
Lambolle Rd NW3 140 DE65
Lambourn Chase, Rad. 77 CF36
Lambourn Cl W7 157 CF75
Lambourn Rd SW4 161 DH83
Lambourne Av SW19 179 CZ91
Lambourne Cl, Chig. 104 EV47
Lambourne Rd
Lambourne Ct, Wdf.Grn. 102 EJ52
Navestock Cres
Lambourne Cres, Chig. 104 EV47
Lambourne Cres, Wok. 211 BD113
Lambourne Dr, Brwd. 109 GE45
Lambourne Dr, Cob. 230 BX115
Lambourne Gdns E4 101 EA47
Lambourne Gdns, Bark. 145 ET66
Lambourne Rd
Lambourne Gdns, Enf. 82 DT40
Lambourne Gdns, Horn. 128 FK61
Lambourne Gro, Kings.T. 198 CP96
Kenley Rd
Lambourne Pl SE3 164 EH81
Shooter's Hill Rd
Lambourne Rd E11 123 EC59
Lambourne Rd, Bark. 145 ES66
Lambourne Rd, Chig. 103 ES49
Lambourne Rd, Ilf. 125 ES61
Lambrook Ter SW6 159 CY81
Lamb's Bldgs EC1 275 K5
Lambs Cl (Cuffley), Pot.B. 65 DM29
Lambs Conduit Pas WC1 274 B6
Lamb's Conduit St WC1 274 B5
Lamb's Conduit St WC1 141 DM70
Lambs La N, Rain. 148 FJ70
Lambs La S, Rain. 147 FH71
Lambs Meadow, Wdf.Grn. 102 EK54
Lambs Ms N1 141 DP67
Colebrooke Row
Lamb's Pas EC1 275 K5
Lamb's Pas EC1 142 DR71
Lambs Ter N9 100 DR47
Lambs Wk, Enf. 82 DQ40
Lambscroft Av SE9 184 EJ90
Lambscroft Way (Chalfont St. Peter), Ger.Cr. 90 AY54
Lambton Av, Wal.Cr. 67 DX32
Lambton Pl W11 139 CZ72
Westbourne Gro
Lambton Rd N19 121 DL60
Lambton Rd SW20 199 CW95
Lambyn Cft, Horl. 269 DJ147
Lamerock Rd, Brom. 184 EF91
Lamerton Rd, Ilf. 103 EP54
Lamerton St SE8 163 EA79
Lamford Cl N17 100 DR52
Lamington St W6 159 CV77
Lamlash St SE11 278 F8
Lammas Av, Mitch. 200 DG96
Lammas Cl, Stai. 173 BE90
Lammas Ct, Stai. 173 BD89
Lammas Ct, Wind. 151 AQ82
Lammas Dr, Stai. 173 BD90
Lammas Grn SE26 182 DV90
Lammas La, Esher 214 CA106
Lammas Pk W5 157 CJ75
Lammas Pk Gdns W5 157 CJ75
Lammas Pk Rd W5 137 CJ74
Lammas Rd E9 143 DX66
Lammas Rd E10 123 DY61
Lammas Rd, Rich. 177 CJ91
Lammas Rd, Slou. 131 AK71
Lammas Rd, Wat. 76 BW43
Lammas Way (Loudwater), H.Wyc. 88 AC54
Lammasmead, Brox. 49 DZ23
Lammermoor Rd SW12 181 DH87
Lamont Rd SW10 160 DC79
Lamont Rd Pas SW10 160 DD79
Lamont Rd
Lamorbey Cl, Sid. 185 ET88
Lamorna Av, Grav. 191 GJ90
Lamorna Cl E17 101 EC53
Lamorna Cl, Orp. 206 EU101
Lamorna Cl, Rad. 61 CH34
Lamorna Gro, Stan. 95 CK53
Lamp Office Ct WC1 274 B5
Lampard Gro N16 122 DT60
Lampern Sq E2 142 DU69
Nelson Gdns
Lampeter Cl NW9 118 CS58
Lampeter Cl, Wok. 226 AY118
Lampeter Sq W6 159 CY79
Humbolt Rd
Lampits, Hodd. 49 EB17
Lamplighter Cl E1 142 DW70
Cleveland Way
Lamplighters Cl, Dart. 188 FM86
Lamplighters Cl, Wal.Abb. 68 EG34
Lampmead Rd SE12 184 EE85
Lamport Cl SE18 165 EM77
Lampton Av, Houns. 156 CB81
Lampton Ho Cl SW19 179 CX91
Lampton Pk Rd, Houns. 156 CB82
Lampton Rd, Houns. 156 CB82
Lamsey Rd, Hem.H. 40 BK22
Lamson Rd, Rain. 147 FF70
Lanacre Av NW9 97 CT53
Lanark Cl W5 137 CJ71
Lanark Ms W9 140 DC69
Lanark Rd
Lanark Pl W9 140 DC70
Lanark Rd W9 140 DB68
Lanark Sq E14 163 EB76
Lanata Wk, Hayes 136 BX70
Ramulis Dr
Lanbury Rd SE15 163 DX84
Lancashire Ct W1 273 J10
Lancaster Av E18 124 EH56
Lancaster Av SE27 181 DP89
Lancaster Av SW19 179 CX92
Lancaster Av, Bark. 145 ES66
Lancaster Av, Barn. 80 DD38
Lancaster Av, Mitch. 201 DL99
Lancaster Av, Slou. 131 AQ70
Lancaster Cl N1 142 DS66
Hertford Rd
Lancaster Cl N17 100 DU52
Park La
Lancaster Cl NW9 97 CT52
Lancaster Cl, Brwd. 108 FU43
Lancaster Cl, Brom. 204 EF98
Lancaster Cl, Egh. 172 AX92
Lancaster Cl, Kings.T. 177 CK92
Lancaster Cl (Stanwell), Stai. 174 BL86
Lancaster Cl, Wok. 227 BA116
Lancaster Cotts, Rich. 178 CL86
Lancaster Pk
Lancaster Ct SE27 181 DP89
Lancaster Ct SW6 159 CZ80
Lancaster Ct W2 140 DC73
Lancaster Gate
Lancaster Ct, Bans. 217 CZ114
Lancaster Ct, Walt. 195 BU101
Lancaster Dr E14 143 EC74
Prestons Rd
Lancaster Dr NW3 140 DE65
Lancaster Dr (Bovingdon), Hem.H. 57 AZ27
Lancaster Dr, Horn. 127 FH64
Lancaster Dr, Loug. 84 EL44
Lancaster Gdns SW19 179 CY92
Lancaster Gdns W13 157 CH75
Lancaster Gdns, Brom. 204 EL99
Southborough Rd
Lancaster Gdns, Kings.T. 177 CK92
Lancaster Gate W2 140 DC73
Lancaster Gro NW3 140 DD65
Lancaster Ms SW18 180 DB85
East Hill
Lancaster Ms W2 140 DC73
Lancaster Ms, Rich. 178 CL86
Richmond Hill
Lancaster Pk, Rich. 178 CL85
Lancaster Pl SW19 179 CX92
Lancaster Rd
Lancaster Pl WC2 274 B10
Lancaster Pl WC2 141 DM73
Lancaster Pl, Houns. 156 BW82
Lancaster Pl, Ilf. 125 EQ64
Staines Rd
Lancaster Pl, Twick. 177 CG86
Lancaster Rd E7 144 EG66
Lancaster Rd E11 124 EE61
Lancaster Rd E17 101 DX54
Lancaster Rd N4 121 DN59
Lancaster Rd N11 99 DK51
Lancaster Rd N18 100 DT50
Lancaster Rd NW10 119 CU64
Lancaster Rd SE25 202 DT96
Lancaster Rd SW19 179 CX92
Lancaster Rd W11 139 CY72
Lancaster Rd, Barn. 80 DD43
Lancaster Rd, Enf. 82 DR39
Lancaster Rd, Epp. 70 FA26
Lancaster Rd, Grays 169 FX78
Lancaster Rd, Har. 116 CA57
Lancaster Rd, Nthlt. 136 CC65
Lancaster Rd, St.Alb. 43 CF18

Lancaster Rd, Sthl. 136 BY73
Lancaster Rd, Uxb. 134 BK65
Lancaster St SE1 278 G5
Lancaster St SE1 161 DP75
Lancaster Ter W2 140 DD73
Lancaster Wk W2 140 DC74
Lancaster Wk, Hayes 135 BQ72
Lancaster Way, Abb.L. 59 BT31
Lancaster W W11 139 CX73
Grenfell Rd
Lancastrian Rd, Wall. 219 DL108
Lance Rd, Har. 116 CC59
Lancefield St W10 139 CZ69
Lancell St N16 122 DS61
Stoke Newington Ch St
Lancelot Av, Wem. 117 CK63
Lancelot Cl, Slou. 151 AN75
Mitchell Cl
Lancelot Cres, Wem. 117 CK63
Lancelot Gdns, Barn. 98 DG45
Lancelot Ho N9 100 DU48
Barbot Cl
Lancelot Pl SW7 276 D5
Lancelot Pl SW7 160 DF75
Lancelot Rd, Ilf. 103 ES51
Lancelot Rd, Well. 166 EU84
Lancelot Rd, Wem. 117 CK64
Lancer Sq W8 160 DB75
Old Ct Pl
Lancey Cl SE7 164 EK77
Cleveley Cl
Lanchester Rd N6 120 DF57
Lancing Gdns N9 100 DT46
Lancing Rd W13 137 CH73
Drayton Grn Rd
Lancing Rd, Croy. 201 DM100
Lancing Rd, Felt. 175 BT89
Lancing Rd, Ilf. 125 ER58
Lancing Rd, Orp. 206 EU103
Lancing Rd, Rom. 106 FL52
Lancing St NW1 273 M3
Lancing Way, Rick. 75 BP43
Lancresse Cl, Uxb. 134 BK65
Lancresse Ct N1 142 DS67
Landale Gdns, Dart. 188 FJ87
Landau Way, Brox. 67 DZ26
Landau Way, Erith 168 FK78
Landcroft Rd SE22 182 DT86
Landells Rd SE22 182 DT86
Landen Pk, Horl. 268 DE146
Lander Rd, Grays 170 GD78
Landford Cl, Rick. 92 BL47
Landford Rd SW15 159 CW83
Landgrove Rd SW19 180 DA92
Landmann Way SE14 163 DX78
Landmead Rd (Cheshunt), Wal.Cr. 67 DY29
Landon Pl SW1 276 D6
Landon Pl SW1 160 DF76
Landon Wk E14 143 EB73
Cottage St
Landon Way, Ashf. 175 BP93
Courtfield Rd
Landons Cl E14 143 EC74
Landor Rd SW9 161 DL83
Landor Wk W12 159 CU75
Landport Way SE15 162 DT80
Daniel Gdns
Landra Gdns N21 81 DP44
Landridge Dr, Enf. 82 DV38
Landridge Rd SW6 159 CZ82
Landrock Rd N8 121 DL58
Lands End, Borwd. 77 CK44
Landscape Rd, Warl. 236 DV119
Landscape Rd, Wdf.Grn. 102 EH52
Landseer Av E12 125 EN64
Landseer Av (Northfleet), Grav. 190 GD90
Landseer Cl SW19 200 DC95
Brangwyn Cres
Landseer Cl, Edg. 96 CN54
Landseer Cl, Horn. 127 FH60
Landseer Rd N19 121 DL62
Landseer Rd, Enf. 82 DU43
Landseer Rd, N.Mal. 198 CR101
Landseer Rd, Sutt. 218 DA107
Landstead Rd SE18 165 ER80
Landway, The, Orp. 206 EW97
Lane, The NW8 140 DC68
Marlborough Pl
Lane, The SE3 164 EG83
Lane, The, Cher. 194 BG97
Lane, The, Vir.W. 192 AY97
Lane App NW7 97 CY50
Lane Av, Green. 189 FW86
Lane Cl NW2 119 CV62
Lane Cl, Add. 212 BG106
Lane End, Berk. 38 AT19
Lane End, Bexh. 167 FB83
Lane End, Epsom 216 CP114
Lane End, Harl. 52 EY15
Lane End, Hat. 45 CT21
Lane Gdns, Bushey 95 CE45
Lane Ms E12 125 EM62
Colchester Av
Lane Wd Cl, Amer. 72 AT39
Lanefield Wk, Welw.G.C. 29 CW09
Lanercost Cl SW2 181 DN89
Lanercost Gdns N14 99 DL45
Lanercost Rd SW2 181 DN89
Lanes Av (Northfleet), Grav. 191 GG90
Lanesborough Pl SW1 276 F4
Laneside, Chis. 185 EP92
Laneside, Edg. 96 CQ50
Laneside Av, Dag. 126 EZ59
Laneway SW15 179 CV85
Lanfranc Rd E3 143 DY68
Lanfrey Pl W14 159 CZ78
North End Rd
Lang Cl (Fetcham), Lthd. 230 CB123
Lang St E1 142 DW70
Langaller La, Lthd. 230 CB122
Langbourne Av N6 120 DG61
Langbourne Pl E14 163 EB78
Langbourne Way (Claygate), Esher 215 CG107
Langbrook Rd SE3 164 EK83
Langcroft Cl, Cars. 200 DF104
Langdale Av, Mitch. 200 DF97
Langdale Cl SE17 162 DQ79
Langdale Cl SW14 158 CP84
Langdale Cl, Dag. 126 EW60
Langdale Cl, Orp. 205 EP104
Grasmere Rd
Langdale Cl, Wok. 226 AW116
Langdale Ct, Hem.H. 40 BL17
Wharfedale
Langdale Cres, Bexh. 166 FA80
Langdale Dr, Hayes 135 BS68
Langdale Gdns, Grnf. 137 CH69
Langdale Gdns, Horn. 127 FG64
Langdale Gdns, Wal.Cr. 83 DX35
Langdale Rd SE10 163 EC80
Langdale Rd, Th.Hth. 201 DN98
Langdale St E1 142 DV72
Burslem St
Langdale Wk (Northfleet), Grav. 190 GE90
Landseer Av
Langdon Ct NW10 138 CS67
Langdon Cres E6 145 EN68
Langdon Dr NW9 118 CQ60
Langdon Pk Rd N6 121 DJ59
Langdon Pl SW14 158 CQ83
Rosemary La
Langdon Rd E6 145 EN67
Langdon Rd, Brom. 204 EH97
Langdon Rd, Mord. 200 DC99
Langdon Shaw, Sid. 185 ET92
Langdon Wk, Mord. 200 DC99
Langdon Way SE1 162 DU77
Simms Rd
Langdons Ct, Sthl. 156 CA76
Langfield Cl, Wal.Abb. 50 EE22
Langford Cl E8 122 DU64
Langford Cl N15 122 DS58
Langford Cl NW8 140 DC68
Langford Pl
Langford Cl W3 158 CP75
Langford Ct NW8 140 DC68
Langford Cres, Barn. 80 DF42
Langford Grn SE5 162 DS83
Langford Grn, Brwd. 109 GC44
Langford Pl NW8 140 DC68
Langford Pl, Sid. 186 EU90
Langford Rd SW6 160 DB82
Langford Rd, Barn. 80 DE42
Langford Rd, Wdf.Grn. 102 EJ51
Langfords, Buck.H. 102 EK47
Langfords Way, Croy. 221 DY111
Langham Cl N15 121 DP55
Langham Rd
Langham Cl, St.Alb. 43 CK15
Langham Ct, Horn. 128 FK59
Langham Dene, Ken. 235 DP115
Langham Dr, Rom. 126 EV58
Langham Gdns N21 81 DN43
Langham Gdns W13 137 CH73
Langham Gdns, Edg. 96 CQ52
Langham Gdns, Rich. 177 CJ91
Langham Gdns, Wem. 117 CJ61
Langham Ho Cl, Rich. 177 CK91
Langham Pk Pl, Brom. 204 EF98
Langham Pl N15 121 DP55
Langham Pl W1 273 J7
Langham Pl W1 141 DH71
Langham Pl W4 158 CS79
Hogarth Roundabout
Langham Pl, Egh. 173 AZ92
Langham Rd N15 121 DP55
Langham Rd SW20 199 CW95
Langham Rd, Edg. 96 CQ51
Langham Rd, Tedd. 177 CH92
Langham St W1 273 J7
Langham St W1 141 DH71
Langhedge Cl N18 100 DT51
Langhedge La
Langhedge La N18 100 DT50
Langhedge La Ind Est N18 100 DT51
Langholm Cl SW12 181 DK87
King's Av
Langholme, Bushey 94 CC46
Langhorn Dr, Twick. 177 CE87
Langhorne Rd, Dag. 146 FA66
Langland Ct, Nthwd. 93 BQ52
Langland Cres, Stan. 118 CL55
Langland Dr, Pnr. 94 BY52
Langland Gdns NW3 120 DB64
Langland Gdns, Croy. 203 DZ103
Langlands Dr (Lane End), Dart. 189 FS92
Langlands Ri, Epsom 216 CQ113
Burnet Gro
Langler Rd NW10 139 CW68
Langley Av, Hem.H. 40 BL23
Langley Av, Ruis. 115 BV60
Langley Av, Surb. 197 CK102
Langley Av, Wor.Pk. 199 CX103
Langley Broom, Slou. 153 AZ78
Langley Business Cen (Langley), Slou. 153 BA75
Langley Cl, Epsom 232 CR119
Langley Cl, Guil. 242 AW133
Langley Cl, Rom. 106 FK52
Langley Ct SE9 185 EN86
Langley Ct WC2 273 P10
Langley Ct, Beck. 203 EB99
Langley Cres E11 124 EJ59
Langley Cres, Dag. 146 EW66
Langley Cres, Edg. 96 CQ48
Langley Cres, Hayes 155 BT80
Langley Cres, Kings L. 58 BN30
Langley Cres, St.Alb. 42 CC18
Langley Dr E11 124 EH59
Langley Dr W3 158 CP75
Langley Dr, Brwd. 108 FU48
Langley Gdns, Brom. 204 EJ98
Langley Gdns, Dag. 146 EX66
Langley Gdns, Orp. 205 EP100
Langley Gro, N.Mal. 198 CS96
Langley Hill, Kings L. 58 BM29
Langley Hill Cl, Kings L. 58 BN29
Langley La SW8 161 DM79
Langley La, Abb.L. 59 BT31
Langley La (Headley), Epsom 248 CP125
Langley Lo La, Kings L. 58 BN31
Langley Meadow, Loug. 85 ER40
Langley Oaks Av, S.Croy. 220 DU110
Langley Pk NW7 96 CS51
Langley Pk Rd, Iver 133 BC72
Langley Pk Rd, Slou. 153 BA75
Langley Pk Rd, Sutt. 218 DC106
Langley Quay (Langley), Slou. 153 BA75
Langley Rd SW19 199 CZ95
Langley Rd, Abb.L. 59 BS31
Langley Rd, Beck. 203 DY98
Langley Rd, Islw. 157 CF82
Langley Rd, Kings L. 58 BH30
Langley Rd, Slou. 152 AW75
Langley Rd, S.Croy. 221 DX109
Langley Rd, Stai. 173 BF93
Langley Rd, Surb. 198 CL101
Langley Rd, Wat. 75 BU39
Langley Rd, Well. 166 EW79
Langley Row, Barn. 79 CZ39
Langley St WC2 273 P9
Langley St WC2 141 DL72
Langley Vale Rd, Epsom 232 CR118
Langley Wk, Wok. 226 AY119
Midhope Rd
Langley Way, Wat. 75 BT39
Langley Way, W.Wick. 203 ED102
Langleybury La, Kings L. 75 BP37
Langmans La, Wok. 226 AV118
Langmans Way, Wok. 226 AS116
Langmead Dr, Bushey 95 CD46
Langmead St SE27 181 DP91
Beadman St
Langmore Ct, Bexh. 166 EX83
Regency Way
Langport Ct, Walt. 196 BW102
Langridge Ms, Hmptn. 176 BZ93
Oak Av
Langroyd Rd SW17 180 DF89
Langshott, Horl. 269 DH146
Langshott Cl (Woodham), Add. 211 BE111
Langshott La, Horl. 269 DH148
Langside Av SW15 159 CU84
Langside Cres N14 99 DK48
Langston Hughes Cl SE24 161 DP84
Shakespeare Rd
Langston Rd, Loug. 85 EQ43
Langthorn Ct EC2 275 K8
Langthorne Cres, Grays 170 GC77
Langthorne Rd E11 123 EC62
Langthorne St SW6 159 CX80
Langton Av E6 145 EN69
Langton Av N20 98 DC45
Langton Av, Epsom 217 CT111
Langton Cl WC1 274 C3
Langton Cl, Add. 194 BH104
Langton Cl, Slou. 131 AK74
Langton Cl, Wok. 226 AT117
Langton Gro, Nthwd. 93 BQ50
Langton Ho SW16 181 DJ91
Colson Way
Langton Pl SW18 180 DA88
Merton Rd
Langton Ri SE23 182 DV87
Langton Rd NW2 119 CW62
Langton Rd SW9 161 DP80
Langton Rd, Har. 94 CC52
Langton Rd, Hodd. 49 DZ17
Langton Rd, W.Mol. 196 CC98
Langton St SW10 160 DC79
Langton Way SE3 164 EF81
Langton Way, Croy. 220 DS105
Langton Way, Egh. 173 BC93
Langton Way, Grays 171 GJ77
Langton's Meadow (Farnham Common), Slou. 131 AQ65
Langtry Rd NW8 140 DB67
Langtry Rd, Nthlt. 136 BX68
Langtry Wk NW8 140 DC66
Alexandra Pl
Langwood Chase, Tedd. 177 CJ93
Langwood Cl, Ash. 232 CN117
Langwood Gdns, Wat. 75 BU39
Langworth Cl, Dart. 188 FK90
Langworth Dr, Hayes 135 BU72
Lanhill Rd W9 140 DA70
Lanier Rd SE13 183 EC86
Lanigan Dr, Houns. 176 CB85
Lankaster Gdns N2 98 DD53
Lankers Dr, Har. 116 BZ58
Lankton Cl, Beck. 203 EC95
Lannock Rd, Hayes 135 BS74
Lannoy Rd SE9 185 EQ88
Lanrick Copse, Berk. 38 AY18
Lanrick Rd E14 143 ED72
Lanridge Rd SE2 166 EX76
Lansbury Av N18 100 DR50
Lansbury Av, Bark. 146 EU66
Lansbury Av, Felt. 175 BV86
Lansbury Av, Rom. 126 EY57
Lansbury Cl NW10 118 CQ64
Lansbury Cres, Dart. 188 FN85
Lansbury Dr, Hayes 135 BT71
Lansbury Est E14 143 EB72
Lansbury Gdns E14 143 ED72
Lansbury Gdns, Til. 171 GG81
Lansbury Rd, Enf. 83 DX39
Lansbury Way N18 100 DS50
Lanscombe Wk SW8 161 DL81
Lansdell Rd, Mitch. 200 DG96
Lansdown, Guil. 243 BA134
Lansdown Cl, Walt. 196 BW102
St. Johns Dr
Lansdown Cl, Wok. 226 AT119
Lansdown Pl (Northfleet), Grav. 191 GF88
Lansdown Rd E7 144 EJ66
Lansdown Rd (Chalfont St. Peter), Ger.Cr. 90 AX53
Lansdown Rd, Sid. 186 EV90
Lansdowne Av, Bexh. 166 EX80
Lansdowne Av, Orp. 205 EP102
Lansdowne Av, Slou. 132 AS74
Lansdowne Cl SW20 179 CX94
Lansdowne Cl, Surb. 198 CP103
Kingston Rd
Lansdowne Cl, Twick. 177 CF88
Lion Rd
Lansdowne Cl, Wat. 60 BX34
Lansdowne Copse, Wor.Pk. 199 CU103
The Av
Lansdowne Ct, Pur. 219 DP110
Lansdowne Ct, Slou. 132 AS74
Lansdowne Ct, Wor.Pk. 199 CU103
The Av
Lansdowne Cres W11 139 CY73
Lansdowne Dr E8 142 DU65
Lansdowne Gdns SW8 161 DL81
Lansdowne Grn SW8 161 DL81
Hartington Rd
Lansdowne Gro NW10 118 CS63
Lansdowne Hill SE27 181 DP90
Lansdowne La SE7 164 EK79
Lansdowne Ms SE7 164 EK78
Lansdowne Ms W11 139 CZ74
Lansdowne Rd
Lansdowne Pl SE1 279 L7
Lansdowne Pl SE19 182 DT94
Lansdowne Ri W11 139 CY73
Lansdowne Rd E4 101 EA47
Lansdowne Rd E11 124 EF61
Lansdowne Rd E17 123 EA57
Lansdowne Rd E18 124 EG55
Lansdowne Rd N3 97 CZ52
Lansdowne Rd N10 99 DJ54
Lansdowne Rd N17 100 DT53
Lansdowne Rd SW20 179 CW94
Lansdowne Rd W11 139 CY73
Lansdowne Rd, Brom. 184 EG94
Lansdowne Rd, Chesh. 54 AQ29
Lansdowne Rd, Croy. 202 DR103
Lansdowne Rd, Epsom 216 CQ108
Lansdowne Rd, Har. 117 CE59
Lansdowne Rd, Houns. 156 CB83
Lansdowne Rd, Ilf. 125 ET60
Lansdowne Rd, Pur. 219 DN112
Lansdowne Rd, Sev. 257 FK122
Lansdowne Rd, Stai. 174 BH94
Lansdowne Rd, Stan. 95 CJ51
Lansdowne Rd, Til. 171 GF82
Lansdowne Rd, Uxb. 135 BP72
Lansdowne Row W1 277 J2
Lansdowne Sq (Northfleet), Grav. 191 GF86
Lansdowne Ter WC1 274 A5
Lansdowne Ter WC1 141 DL70
Lansdowne Wk W11 139 CY74
Lansdowne Way SW8 161 DL81
Lansdowne Wd Cl SE27 181 DP90
Lansfield Av N18 100 DU49
Lant St SE1 279 H4
Lant St SE1 162 DQ75
Lantern Cl SW15 159 CU84
Lantern Cl, Wem. 117 CK64
Lantern Way, West Dr. 154 BL75
Lanterns Ct E14 163 EA75
Lanvanor Rd SE15 162 DW82
Lapford Cl W9 139 CZ70
Lapponum Wk, Hayes 136 BX71
Lochan Cl
Lapse Wd Wk SE23 182 DV88
Lapstone Gdns, Har. 117 CJ58
Lapwing Cl, Erith 167 FH80
Lapwing Cl, Hem.H. 40 BL16
Lapwing Cl, S.Croy. 221 DY110
Lapwing Ct, Surb. 198 CN104
Chaffinch Cl
Lapwing Gro, Guil. 243 BD132
Lapwing Twr SE8 163 DZ79
Abinger Gro
Lapwing Way, Abb.L. 59 BU31
Lapwing Way, Hayes 136 BX72
Lapwings, The, Grav. 191 GK89
Lapworth Cl, Orp. 206 EW103
Lara Cl SE13 183 EC86
Lara Cl, Chess. 216 CL108
Larbert Rd SW16 201 DJ95
Larby Pl, Epsom 216 CS110
Larch Av W3 138 CS74
Larch Av, Guil. 242 AW132
Larch Av (Bricket Wd), St.Alb. 60 BY30
Larch Cl E13 144 EH70
Larch Cl N11 98 DG52
Larch Cl N19 121 DJ61
Bredgar Rd
Larch Cl SE8 163 DZ79
Clyde St
Larch Cl SW12 181 DH89
Larch Cl (Penn), H.Wyc. 88 AC45
Larch Cl, Red. 266 DC136
Larch Cl, Slou. 131 AP71
Larch Cl, Tad. 234 DC121
Larch Cl, Wal.Cr. 66 DS27
The Firs
Larch Cl, Warl. 237 DY119
Larch Cres, Epsom 216 CP107
Larch Cres, Hayes 136 BW70
Larch Dr W4 158 CN78
Gunnersbury Av
Larch Grn NW9 96 CS53
Clayton Fld
Larch Gro, Sid. 185 ET88
Larch Ri, Berk. 38 AU18
Larch Rd E10 123 EA61
Walnut Rd
Larch Rd NW2 119 CW63
Larch Rd, Dart. 188 FK87
Larch Tree Way, Croy. 203 EA104
Larch Wk, Swan. 207 FD96
Larch Way, Brom. 205 EN101
Larchdene, Orp. 205 EN103
Larches, The N13 100 DQ48
Larches, The, Amer. 72 AV38
Larches, The, Bushey 76 BY43
Larches, The, Nthwd. 93 BQ51
Rickmansworth Rd
Larches, The, St.Alb. 43 CK16
Larches, The, Uxb. 135 BP69
Larches, The, Wok. 226 AY116
Larches Av SW14 158 CR84
Larches Av, Enf. 82 DW35
Larchlands, The (Penn), H.Wyc. 88 AD46
Larchwood Av, Rom. 105 FB51
Larchwood Cl, Bans. 233 CY116
Larchwood Cl, Rom. 105 FC51
Larchwood Dr (Englefield Grn), Egh. 172 AV93
Larchwood Gdns, Brwd. 108 FU44
Larchwood Rd SE9 185 EP89
Larchwood Rd, Hem.H. 40 BM18
Larcom St SE17 279 J9
Larcom St SE17 162 DQ77
Larcombe Cl, Croy. 220 DT105
Larden Rd W3 138 CS74
Largewood Av, Surb. 198 CN103
Largo Wk, Erith 167 FE81
Selkirk Dr
Larissa St SE17 279 L10
Lark Av, Stai. 173 BF90
Kestrel Av
Lark Ri, Hat. 45 CU20
Lark Ri (East Horsley), Lthd. 245 BS131
Lark Row E2 142 DW67
Lark Way, Cars. 200 DE101
Larkbere Rd SE26 183 DY91
Larken Cl, Bushey 94 CC46
Larken Dr
Larken Dr, Bushey 94 CC46
Larkfield, Cob. 213 BU113
Larkfield Av, Har. 117 CH55
Larkfield Cl, Brom. 204 EF103
Larkfield Ct, Horl. 269 DN148
Cooper Cl
Larkfield Rd, Rich. 158 CL84
Larkfield Rd, Sev. 256 FC123
Larkfield Rd, Sid. 185 ET90
Larkfields (Northfleet), Grav. 190 GE90
Larkhall Cl, Walt. 214 BW107
Larkhall La SW4 161 DK82
Larkhall Ri SW4 161 DJ83
Larkham Cl, Felt. 175 BS90
Larkhill Ter SE18 165 EN80
Larkin Cl, Brwd. 109 GC45
Larkin Cl, Couls. 235 DM117
Larkings La (Stoke Poges), Slou. 132 AV67
Larkins Rd, Gat. 268 DD152
Larks Gro, Bark. 145 ES66
Larks Ri, Chesh. 54 AR33
Larksfield (Englefield Grn), Egh. 172 AW94
Larksfield, Horl. 269 DH147
Larksfield Gro, Enf. 82 DV39
Larkshall Ct, Rom. 105 FC54
Larkshall Cres E4 101 EC49
Larkshall Rd E4 101 EC50
Larkspur Cl E6 144 EL71
Larkspur Cl N17 100 DR52
Fryatt Rd
Larkspur Cl NW9 118 CP57
Larkspur Cl, Hem.H. 39 BE19
Larkspur Cl, Orp. 206 EW103
Larkspur Cl, Ruis. 115 BQ59
Larkspur Cl, S.Ock. 149 FW69
Larkspur Gro, Edg. 96 CQ49
Larkspur Way (North Holmwood), Dor. 263 CK139
Larkspur Way, Epsom 216 CQ106
Larkswood, Harl. 52 EW17
Larkswood Cl, Erith 167 FG81
Larkswood Ct E4 101 ED50
Larkswood Ri, Pnr. 116 BW56
Larkswood Ri, St.Alb. 43 CJ15
Larkswood Rd E4 101 EA49
Larkway Cl NW9 118 CR56
Larmans Rd, Enf. 82 DW36
Larnach Rd W6 159 CX79
Larne Rd, Ruis. 115 BT59
Larner Rd, Erith 167 FE80
Larpent Av SW15 179 CW85
Larsen Dr, Wal.Abb. 67 ED34
Larwood Cl, Grnf. 117 CD64
Las Palmas Est, Shep. 195 BQ101
Lascelles Av, Har. 117 CD59
Lascelles Cl E11 123 ED61
Lascelles Cl, Brwd. 108 FU43
Lascelles Rd, Slou. 152 AV76
Lascotts Rd N22 99 DM51
Lassa Rd SE9 184 EL85
Lassell St SE10 163 ED78
Lasseter Pl SE3 164 EF79
Vanbrugh Hill
Lasswade Rd, Cher. 193 BF101
Latchett Rd E18 102 EH53
Latchford Pl, Chig. 104 EV49
Manford Way
Latching Cl, Rom. 106 FK49
Troopers Dr
Latchingdon Ct E17 123 DX56
Latchingdon Gdns, Wdf.Grn. 102 EL51
Latchmere Cl, Rich. 178 CL92
Latchmere La, Kings.T. 178 CM93
Latchmere Pas SW11 160 DE82
Cabul Rd
Latchmere Rd SW11 160 DF82
Latchmere Rd, Kings.T. 178 CL94
Latchmere St SW11 160 DF82
Latchmoor Av (Chalfont St. Peter), Ger.Cr. 112 AX56
Latchmoor Gro (Chalfont St. Peter), Ger.Cr. 112 AX56
Latchmoor Way (Chalfont St. Peter), Ger.Cr. 112 AX56
Lateward Rd, Brent. 157 CK79
Latham Cl E6 144 EL72
Oliver Gdns
Latham Cl, Dart. 189 FS89
Latham Cl, Twick. 177 CG87
Latham Cl (Biggin Hill), West. 238 EJ116
Latham Ho E1 143 DX72
Latham Rd, Bexh. 186 FA85
Latham Rd, Twick. 177 CF87
Lathams Way, Croy. 201 DM102
Lathkill Cl, Enf. 100 DU45
Lathom Rd E6 145 EM66
Latimer SE17 162 DS78
Latimer Av E6 145 EM67
Latimer Cl, Amer. 72 AW39
Latimer Cl, Hem.H. 40 BN15
Latimer Cl, Pnr. 94 BW53
Latimer Cl, Wat. 93 BS45
Latimer Cl, Wok. 227 BB116
Latimer Cl, Wor.Pk. 217 CV105
Latimer Dr, Horn. 128 FK62
Latimer Gdns, Pnr. 94 BW53
Latimer Gdns, Welw.G.C. 30 DB09
Latimer Pl W10 139 CW72
Latimer Rd E7 124 EH63
Latimer Rd N15 122 DS58
Latimer Rd SW19 180 DB93
Latimer Rd W10 139 CW72
Latimer Rd, Barn. 80 DB41
Latimer Rd, Chesh. 72 AU36
Latimer Rd, Croy. 201 DP104
Abbey Rd
Latimer Rd, Rick. 73 BB38
Latimer Rd, Tedd. 177 CF92
Latimer Way (Knotty Grn), Beac. 88 AJ49
Latium Cl, St.Alb. 43 CD21
Latona Dr, Grav. 191 GM92
Latona Rd SE15 162 DU79
Lattimer Pl W4 158 CS79
Lattimore Rd, St.Alb. 43 CE21
Latton Cl, Esher 214 CB105
Latton Cl, Walt. 196 BY101
Latton Common, Harl. 52 EV18
Latton Common Rd, Harl. 52 EU18
Latton Grn, Harl. 51 ET19
Latton Hall Cl, Harl. 36 EU14
Latton St, Harl. 36 EU14
Latymer Cl, Wey. 213 BQ105
Latymer Ct W6 159 CX77
Latymer Rd N9 100 DT46
Latymer Way N9 100 DR47
Laud St SE11 278 B10
Laud St, Croy. 202 DQ104
Lauder Cl, Nthlt. 136 BX68
Lauderdale Dr, Rich. 177 CK90
Lauderdale Pl EC2 142 DQ71
Beech St
Lauderdale Rd W9 140 DB69
Lauderdale Rd, Kings L. 59 BQ33
Lauderdale Twr EC2 275 H6
Lauderdale Twr EC2 142 DQ71
Laughton Ct, Borwd. 78 CR40
Banks Rd
Laughton Rd, Nthlt. 136 BX67
Launcelot Rd, Brom. 184 EG91
Launcelot St SE1 278 D5
Launceston Cl, Rom. 106 FJ53
Launceston Gdns, Grnf. 137 CJ67
Launceston Pl W8 160 DC76
Launceston Rd, Grnf. 137 CJ67
Launch St E14 163 EC76
Launders La, Rain. 148 FM69
Laundress La N16 122 DU62
Laundry La N1 142 DQ67
Greenman St
Laundry La, Wal.Abb. 68 EE25
Laundry Rd W6 159 CY79
Laundry Rd, Guil. 258 AW135
Laura Cl E11 124 EJ57
Laura Cl, Enf. 82 DS43
Laura Dr, Swan. 187 FG94
Laura Pl E5 122 DW63
Lauradale Rd N2 120 DF56
Laureate Way, Hem.H. 40 BG18
Laurel Av (Englefield Grn), Egh. 172 AV92
Laurel Av, Grav. 191 GJ89
Laurel Av, Pot.B. 63 CZ32
Laurel Av, Slou. 152 AY75
Laurel Av, Twick. 177 CF88
Laurel Bk (Felden), Hem.H. 39 BF23
Laurel Bk Gdns SW6 159 CZ82
New Kings Rd
Laurel Bk Rd, Enf. 82 DQ39

Laurel Bk Vil W7 137 CE74
Lower Boston Rd
Laurel Cl N19 121 DJ61
Hargrave Pk
Laurel Cl SW17 180 DE92
Laurel Cl, Brwd. 109 GB43
Laurel Cl, Dart. 188 FJ88
Willow Rd
Laurel Cl, Hem.H. 40 BM19
Laurel Cl, Ilf. 103 EQ51
Laurel Cl, Sid. 186 EU90
Laurel Cl (Colnbrook), Slou. 153 BE80
Laurel Cl, Wok. 211 BD113
Laurel Ct (Cuffley), Pot.B. 65 DM29
Station Rd
Laurel Cres, Croy. 203 EA104
Laurel Cres, Rom. 127 FE60
Laurel Cres, Wok. 211 BC113
Laurel Dr N21 99 DN45
Laurel Dr, Oxt. 254 EF131
Laurel Dr, S.Ock. 149 FX70
Laurel Flds, Pot.B. 63 CZ31
Laurel Gdns E4 101 EB45
Laurel Gdns NW7 96 CR48
Laurel Gdns W7 137 CE74
Laurel Gdns (New Haw), Add. 212 BH110
Laurel Gdns, Houns. 156 BY84
Laurel Gro SE20 182 DV94
Laurel Gro SE26 183 DX91
Laurel La, Horn. 128 FL61
Station La
Laurel La, West Dr. 154 BL77
Laurel Lo La, Barn. 79 CW36
Laurel Manor, Sutt. 218 DC108
Devonshire Rd
Laurel Pk, Har. 95 CF52
Laurel Rd SW13 159 CU82
Laurel Rd SW20 199 CV95
Laurel Rd (Chalfont St. Peter), Ger.Cr. 90 AX53
Laurel Rd (Hampton Hill), Hmptn. 177 CD92
Laurel Rd, St.Alb. 43 CF20
Laurel St E8 142 DT65
Laurel Vw N12 98 DB48
Laurel Way E18 124 EF56
Laurel Way N20 98 DA48
Laurels, The, Bans. 233 CZ117
Laurels, The, Berk. 39 BB17
Laurels, The, Cob. 230 BY115
Laurels, The, Dart. 188 FJ90
Laurels, The, Wal.Cr. 66 DS27
Laurels, The, Wey. 195 BR104
Laurels Rd, Iver 133 BD68
Laurelsfield, St.Alb. 42 CB23
Laurence Ms W12 159 CU75
Askew Rd
Laurence Pountney Hill EC4 275 K10
Laurence Pountney La EC4 275 K10
Laurie Gro SE14 163 DY81
Laurie Rd W7 137 CE71
Laurie Wk, Rom. 127 FE57
Laurier Rd NW5 121 DH62
Laurier Rd, Croy. 202 DT101
Lauries Cl, Hem.H. 39 BB22
Laurimel Cl, Stan. 95 CH51
September Way
Laurino Pl, Bushey 94 CC47
Lauriston Rd E9 143 DX67
Lauriston Rd SW19 179 CX93
Lausanne Rd N8 121 DN56
Lausanne Rd SE15 162 DW81
Lauser Rd (Stanwell), Stai. 174 BJ87
Laustan Cl, Guil. 243 BC134
Lavell St N16 122 DR63
Lavender Av NW9 118 CQ60
Lavender Av, Brwd. 108 FV43
Lavender Av, Mitch. 200 DE95
Lavender Av, Wor.Pk. 199 CW104
Lavender Cl SW3 160 DD79
Danvers St
Lavender Cl, Brom. 204 EL100
Lavender Cl, Cars. 218 DG105
Lavender Cl, Cat. 252 DQ125
Lavender Cl, Couls. 235 DJ119
Lavender Cl, Harl. 35 ES14
Lavender Cl, Red. 267 DH139
Lavender Cl, Rom. 106 FK52
Lavender Cl, S.Ock. 149 FX70
Lavender Cl (Cheshunt), Wal.Cr. 66 DT27
Lavender Ct, W.Mol. 196 CB97
Molesham Way
Lavender Dr, Uxb. 134 BM71
Lavender Gdns SW11 160 DF84
Lavender Gdns, Enf. 81 DP39
Lavender Gdns, Har. 95 CE51
Uxbridge Rd
Lavender Gate, Lthd. 214 CB114
Lavender Gro E8 142 DT66
Lavender Gro, Mitch. 200 DE95
Lavender Hill SW11 160 DE84
Lavender Hill, Enf. 81 DN39
Lavender Hill, Swan. 207 FD97
Lavender Pk Rd, W.Byf. 212 BG112
Lavender Pl, Ilf. 125 EP64
Lavender Ri, West Dr. 154 BN75
Lavender Rd SE16 143 DY74
Lavender Rd SW11 160 DD83
Lavender Rd, Cars. 218 DG105
Lavender Rd, Croy. 201 DM100
Lavender Rd, Enf. 82 DR39
Lavender Rd, Epsom 216 CP106
Lavender Rd, Sutt. 218 DD105
Lavender Rd, Uxb. 134 BM71
Lavender Rd, Wok. 227 BB116
Lavender Sq E11 123 ED62
Anglian Rd
Lavender St E15 144 EE65
Manbey Gro
Lavender Sweep SW11 160 DF84
Lavender Ter SW11 160 DE83
Falcon Rd
Lavender Vale, Wall. 219 DK107
Lavender Wk SW11 160 DF84
Lavender Wk, Hem.H. 40 BK18
Lavender Wk, Mitch. 200 DG97
Lavender Way, Croy. 203 DX100
Lavengro Rd SE27 182 DQ89
Lavenham Rd SW18 179 CZ89
Lavernock Rd, Bexh. 166 FA82
Lavers Rd N16 122 DS62
Laverstoke Gdns SW15 179 CU87
Laverton Ms SW5 160 DB77
Laverton Pl
Laverton Pl SW5 160 DB77
Lavidge Rd SE9 184 EL89
Lavina Gro N1 141 DM68
Wharfdale Rd
Lavington Rd W13 137 CH74
Lavington Rd, Croy. 201 DM104
Lavington St SE1 278 G3
Lavington St SE1 141 DP74
Lavinia Av, Wat. 60 BX34
Lavinia Rd, Dart. 188 FM86
Lavrock La, Rick. 92 BM45
Law Ho, Bark. 146 EU68
Law St SE1 279 L6
Law St SE1 162 DR76
Lawbrook La (Peaslake), Guil. 261 BQ144
Lawdons Gdns, Croy. 219 DP105
Lawford Av, Rick. 73 BC44
Lawford Cl, Horn. 128 FJ63
Lawford Cl, Rick. 73 BC44
Lawford Cl, Wall. 219 DL109
Lawford Gdns, Dart. 188 FJ85
Lawford Gdns, Ken. 236 DQ116
Lawford Rd N1 142 DS66
Lawford Rd NW5 141 DJ65
Lawford Rd W4 158 CQ80
Lawkland (Farnham Royal), Slou. 131 AQ69
Lawless St E14 143 EB73
Lawley Rd N14 99 DH45
Lawley St E5 122 DW63
Lawn, The, Harl. 36 EV12
Lawn, The, Sthl. 156 CA78
Lawn Av, West Dr. 154 BJ75
Lawn Cl N9 100 DT45
Lawn Cl, Brom. 184 EH93
Lawn Cl, N.Mal. 198 CS96
Lawn Cl, Ruis. 115 BT62
Lawn Cl (Datchet), Slou. 152 AW80
Lawn Cl, Swan. 207 FC96
Lawn Cres, Rich. 158 CN82
Lawn Fm Gro, Rom. 126 EY56
Lawn Gdns W7 137 CE74
Lawn Ho Cl E14 163 EC75
Lawn La SW8 161 DL79
Lawn La, Hem.H. 40 BK22
Lawn Pk, Sev. 257 FH127
Lawn Rd NW3 120 DF64
Lawn Rd, Beck. 183 DZ94
Lawn Rd, Grav. 190 GC86
Lawn Rd, Guil. 258 AW137
Lawn Rd, Uxb. 134 BJ66
New Windsor St
Lawn Ter SE3 164 EE83
Lawn Vale, Pnr. 94 BX54
Lawnfield NW2 139 CX66
Coverdale Rd
Lawns, The E4 101 EA50
Lawns, The SE3 164 EE83
Lee Ter
Lawns, The SE19 202 DR95
Lawns, The, Hem.H. 39 BE19
Lawns, The, Pnr. 94 CB52
Lawns, The (Shenley), Rad. 62 CL33
Lawns, The, St.Alb. 42 CC19
Lawns, The, Sid. 186 EV91
Lawns, The, Sutt. 217 CY108
Lawns, The, Welw.G.C. 29 CX06
Lawns Ct, Wem. 118 CM61
The Av
Lawns Cres, Grays 170 GD79
Lawns Dr, The, Brox. 49 DZ21
Lawns Way, Rom. 105 FC52
Lawnside SE3 164 EF84
Lawrance Gdns (Cheshunt), Wal.Cr. 67 DX28
Lawrance Rd, St.Alb. 42 CC16
Lawrence Av E12 125 EN63
Lawrence Av E17 101 DX53
Lawrence Av N13 99 DP49
Lawrence Av NW7 96 CS49
Lawrence Av, N.Mal. 198 CR100
Lawrence Av, Ware 33 EC11
Lawrence Bldgs N16 122 DT62
Lawrence Campe Cl N20 98 DD48
Friern Barnet La
Lawrence Cl E3 143 EA68
Lawrence Cl N15 122 DS55
Lawrence Rd
Lawrence Cl, Guil. 243 BB129
Ladygrove Dr
Lawrence Cl, Hert. 31 DL08
Lawrence Ct NW7 96 CS50
Lawrence Ct, Wdf.Grn. 102 EJ51
Baddow Cl
Lawrence Cres, Dag. 127 FB62
Lawrence Cres, Edg. 96 CN54
Lawrence Dr, Uxb. 115 BQ63
Lawrence Gdns NW7 97 CT48
Lawrence Gdns, Til. 171 GH80
Lawrence Hill E4 101 EA47
Lawrence Hill Gdns, Dart. 188 FJ86
Lawrence Hill Rd, Dart. 188 FJ86
Lawrence La EC2 275 J9
Lawrence La (Buckland), Bet. 249 CV131
Lawrence Moorings, Saw. 36 EZ06
Lawrence Pl N1 141 DL67
Outram Pl
Lawrence Rd E6 144 EK67
Lawrence Rd E13 144 EH67
Lawrence Rd N15 122 DS56
Lawrence Rd N18 100 DV49
Lawrence Rd SE25 202 DT98
Lawrence Rd W5 157 CK77
Lawrence Rd, Erith 167 FB80
Lawrence Rd, Hmptn. 176 BZ94
Lawrence Rd, Hayes 135 BQ68
Lawrence Rd, Houns. 156 BW84
Lawrence Rd, Pnr. 116 BX57
Lawrence Rd, Rich. 177 CJ91
Lawrence Rd, Rom. 127 FH57
Lawrence Rd, W.Wick. 222 EG105
Lawrence Sq, Grav. 191 GF90
Haynes Rd
Lawrence St E16 144 EF71
Lawrence St NW7 97 CT49
Lawrence St SW3 160 DE79
Lawrence Way NW10 118 CQ63
Lawrence Way, Slou. 131 AK71
Lawrence Weaver Cl, Mord. 200 DB100
Green La
Lawrie Pk Av SE26 182 DV92
Lawrie Pk Cres SE26 182 DV92
Lawrie Pk Gdns SE26 182 DV91
Lawrie Pk Rd SE26 182 DV93
Lawson Cl E16 144 EJ71
Lawson Cl SW19 179 CX90
Lawson Est SE1 279 K7
Lawson Est SE1 162 DR76
Lawson Gdns, Dart. 188 FK85
Lawson Gdns, Pnr. 115 BV55
Lawson Rd, Dart. 168 FK84
Lawson Rd, Enf. 82 DW39
Lawson Rd, Sthl. 136 BZ70
Lawson Wk, Cars. 218 DF110
Lawton Rd E3 143 DY69
Lawton Rd E10 123 EC60
Lawton Rd, Barn. 80 DD41
Lawton Rd, Loug. 85 EP41
Laxcon Cl NW10 118 CQ64
Laxey Rd, Orp. 223 ET107
Laxley Cl SE5 161 DP80
Laxton Gdns (Shenley), Rad. 62 CL32
Porters Pk Dr
Laxton Gdns, Red. 251 DK128
Laxton Pl NW1 273 J4
Layard Rd SE16 162 DV77
Layard Rd, Enf. 82 DT39
Layard Rd, Th.Hth. 202 DR96
Layard Sq SE16 162 DV77
Layborne Av, Rom. 106 FJ48
Cummings Hall La
Laybrook, St.Alb. 43 CG16
Layburn Cres, Slou. 153 BB79
Laycock St N1 141 DN65
Layer Gdns W3 138 CN73
Layfield Cl NW4 119 CV59
Layfield Cres NW4 119 CV59
Layfield Rd NW4 119 CV59
Layhams Rd, Kes. 222 EF106
Layhams Rd, W.Wick. 203 ED104
Layhill, Hem.H. 40 BK18
Laymarsh Cl, Belv. 166 EZ76
Laymead Cl, Nthlt. 136 BY65
Laystall St EC1 274 D5
Laystall St EC1 141 DN70
Layters Av (Chalfont St. Peter), Ger.Cr. 90 AW54
Layters Av S (Chalfont St. Peter), Ger.Cr. 90 AW54
Layters Cl (Chalfont St. Peter), Ger.Cr. 90 AW54
Layters End (Chalfont St. Peter), Ger.Cr. 90 AW54
Layters Grn La (Chalfont St. Peter), Ger.Cr. 112 AU55
Layters Way, Ger.Cr. 112 AX56
Layton Ct, Wey. 213 BP105
Castle Vw Rd
Layton Cres, Croy. 219 DN106
Layton Pl, Rich. 158 CN81
Station Av
Layton Rd N1 141 DN68
Parkfield St
Layton Rd, Brent. 157 CK78
Layton Rd, Houns. 156 CB84
Laytons Bldgs SE1 279 J4
Laytons La, Sun. 195 BT96
Layzell Wk SE9 184 EK88
Mottingham La
Lazar Wk N7 121 DM61
Briset Way
Le Corte Cl, Kings L. 58 BM29
Le May Av SE12 184 EH90
Le May Cl, Horl. 268 DG147
Le Personne Rd, Cat. 236 DR122
Lea, The, Egh. 193 BB95
Lea Br Business Cen E10 123 DY60
Burwell Rd
Lea Br Rd E5 122 DW62
Lea Br Rd E10 123 DY60
Lea Br Rd E17 123 ED56
Lea Bushes, Wat. 76 BY35
Lea Cl, Bushey 76 CB43
Lea Cl, Twick. 176 BZ87
Lea Cres, Ruis. 115 BT63
Lea Gdns, Wem. 118 CL63
Lea Hall Rd E10 123 EA60
Lea Mt, Wal.Cr. 66 DS28
Lea Rd, Beck. 203 EA96
Fairfield Rd
Lea Rd, Enf. 82 DR39
Lea Rd, Grays 171 GG78
Lea Rd, Hodd. 49 EC15
Lea Rd, Sev. 257 FJ127
Lea Rd, Sthl. 156 BY77
Lea Rd, Wal.Abb. 67 EA34
Lea Vale, Dart. 167 FD84
Lea Valley Rd E4 83 DX43
Lea Valley Rd, Enf. 83 DX43
Lea Valley Trd Est N18 101 DX50
Lea Valley Viaduct E4 101 DX50
Lea Valley Viaduct N18 101 DX50
Lea Valley Wk E3 143 EC70
Lea Valley Wk E5 122 DW61
Lea Valley Wk E9 123 DZ64
Lea Valley Wk E10 122 DW59
Lea Valley Wk E14 143 EB71
Lea Valley Wk E15 143 EC69
Lea Valley Wk E17 122 DW59
Lea Valley Wk N9 101 DY46
Lea Valley Wk N15 122 DU58
Lea Valley Wk N16 122 DU58
Lea Valley Wk N17 100 DW53
Lea Valley Wk N18 100 DW53
Lea Valley Wk, Brox. 49 EB21
Lea Valley Wk, Enf. 83 DZ41
Lea Valley Wk, Hat. 46 DA15
Lea Valley Wk, Hert. 31 DP11
Lea Valley Wk, Hodd. 49 ED18
Lea Valley Wk, Wal.Abb. 67 DZ30
Lea Valley Wk, Wal.Cr. 67 DZ30
Lea Valley Wk, Ware 32 DW06
Lea Valley Wk, Welw.G.C. 29 CW13
Lea Vw Hos E5 122 DV60
Springfield
Leabank Cl, Har. 117 CE62
Leabank Sq E9 143 EA65
Leabank Vw N15 122 DU58
Leabourne Rd N16 122 DU58
Leach Gro, Lthd. 231 CJ122
Leachcroft (Chalfont St. Peter), Ger.Cr. 90 AV53
Leacroft, Stai. 174 BH91
Leacroft Av SW12 180 DF87
Leacroft Cl, Ken. 236 DQ116
Leacroft Cl, Stai. 174 BH91
Leacroft Cl, West Dr. 134 BL72
Leacroft Rd, Iver 133 BD72
Leadale Av E4 101 EA47
Leadale Rd N15 122 DU58
Leadale Rd N16 122 DU58
Leadbeaters Cl N11 98 DF50
Goldsmith Rd
Leadenhall Mkt EC3 275 M9
Leadenhall Pl EC3 275 M9
Leadenhall St EC3 275 M9
Leadenhall St EC3 142 DS72
Leader Av E12 125 EN64
Leadings, The, Wem. 118 CQ62
Leaf Cl, Nthwd. 93 BR52
Leaf Cl, T.Ditt. 197 CE99
Leaf Gro SE27 181 DN92
Leafield Cl SW16 181 DP93
Leafield Cl, Wok. 226 AV118
Winnington Way
Leafield La, Sid. 186 EZ91
Leafield Rd SW20 199 CZ97
Leafield Rd, Sutt. 200 DA103
Leaford Cres, Wat. 75 BT37
Leaforis Rd, Wal.Cr. 66 DU28
Leafy Gro, Croy. 221 DY111
Leafy Gro, Kes. 222 EJ106
Leafy Oak Rd SE12 184 EJ90
Leafy Way, Brwd. 109 GD46
Leafy Way, Croy. 202 DT103
Leagrave St E5 122 DW62
Leahoe Gdns, Hert. 32 DQ10
Leaholme Gdns, Slou. 130 AJ71
Leaholme Way, Ruis. 115 BP58
Leahurst Rd SE13 183 ED85
Leake St SE1 278 C4
Leake St SE1 161 DM75
Lealand Rd N15 122 DT58
Leamington Av E17 123 EA57
Leamington Av, Brom. 184 EJ92
Leamington Av, Mord. 199 CZ98
Leamington Av, Orp. 223 ES105
Leamington Cl E12 124 EL64
Leamington Cl, Brom. 184 EJ92
Leamington Cl, Houns. 176 CC85
Leamington Cl, Rom. 106 FM51
Leamington Cres, Har. 116 BY62
Leamington Gdns, Ilf. 125 ET61
Leamington Pk W3 138 CR71
Leamington Pl, Hayes 135 BT70
Leamington Rd, Rom. 106 FN50
Leamington Rd, Sthl. 156 BX77
Leamington Rd Vil W11 139 CZ71
Leamore St W6 159 CV77
Leamouth Rd E6 144 EL72
Remington Rd
Leamouth Rd E14 143 ED72
Leander Ct SE8 163 EA81
Leander Dr, Grav. 191 GM91
Leander Gdns, Wat. 76 BY37
Leander Rd SW2 181 DM86
Leander Rd, Nthlt. 136 CA68
Leander Rd, Th.Hth. 201 DM98
Leapale La, Guil. 258 AX135
Leapale Rd, Guil. 258 AX135
Learner Dr, Har. 116 CA61
Learoyd Gdns E6 145 EN73
Leas, The, Bushey 76 BZ39
Leas, The, Hem.H. 40 BN24
Leas, The, Stai. 174 BG91
Raleigh Ct
Leas, The, Upmin. 129 FR59
Leas Cl, Chess. 216 CM108
Leas Dale SE9 185 EN90
Leas Dr, Iver 133 BE72
Leas Grn, Chis. 185 ET93
Leas La, Warl. 237 DX118
Leas Rd, Guil. 258 AW135
Leas Rd, Warl. 237 DX118
Leaside, Hem.H. 41 BQ21
Leaside (Bookham), Lthd. 230 CA123
Leaside Av N10 120 DG55
Leaside Ct, Uxb. 135 BP69
The Larches
Leaside Rd E5 122 DW60
Leaside Wk, Ware 33 DX06
East St
Leasowes Rd E10 123 EA60
Leasway, Brwd. 108 FX48
Leasway, Upmin. 128 FQ62
Leathart Cl, Horn. 147 FH66
Dowding Way
Leather Bottle La, Belv. 166 EY77
Leather Cl, Mitch. 200 DG96
Leather Gdns E15 144 EE67
Abbey Rd
Leather La EC1 274 E7
Leather La EC1 141 DN71
Leather La (Gomshall), Guil. 261 BQ139
Leather La, Horn. 128 FK60
North St
Leatherbottle Grn, Erith 166 EZ76
Leatherdale St E1 142 DW70
Portelet Rd
Leatherhead Bypass Rd, Lthd. 231 CH120
Leatherhead Cl N16 122 DT60
Leatherhead Rd, Ash. 231 CK121
Leatherhead Rd, Chess. 215 CJ110
Leatherhead Rd, Lthd. 231 CK121
Leatherhead Rd (Great Bookham), Lthd. 246 CB126
Leatherhead Rd (Oxshott), Lthd. 215 CD114
Leathermarket Ct SE1 279 M5
Leathermarket Ct SE1 162 DS75
Leathermarket St SE1 279 M5
Leathermarket St SE1 162 DS75
Leathersellers Cl, Barn. 79 CY42
The Av
Leathsail Rd, Har. 116 CB62
Leathwaite Rd SW11 160 DF84
Leathwell Rd SE8 163 EB82
Leaveland Cl, Beck. 203 EA98
Leaver Gdns, Grnf. 137 CD68
Leaves Grn Cres, Kes. 222 EJ111
Leaves Grn Rd, Kes. 222 EK111
Leavesden Rd, Stan. 95 CG51
Leavesden Rd, Wat. 75 BV38
Leavesden Rd, Wey. 213 BP106
Leaview, Wal.Abb. 67 EB33
Leaway E10 123 DX60
Leazes Av, Cat. 235 DN123
Leazes La, Cat. 235 DN123
Lebanon Av, Felt. 176 BX92
Lebanon Cl, Wat. 75 BR36
Lebanon Ct, Twick. 177 CH87
Lebanon Dr, Cob. 214 CA113
Lebanon Gdns SW18 180 DA86
Lebanon Gdns (Biggin Hill), West. 238 EK117
Lebanon Pk, Twick. 177 CH87
Lebanon Rd SW18 180 DA85
Lebanon Rd, Croy. 202 DS102
Lebrun Sq SE3 164 EH83
Lechford Rd, Horl. 268 DG149
Lechmere App, Wdf.Grn. 102 EJ54
Lechmere Av, Chig. 103 EQ49
Lechmere Av, Wdf.Grn. 102 EK54
Lechmere Rd NW2 139 CV65
Leckford Rd SW18 180 DC89
Leckwith Av, Bexh. 166 EY79
Lecky St SW7 160 DD78
Leclair Ho SE3 164 EH83
Gallus Sq
Leconfield Av SW13 159 CT83
Leconfield Rd N5 122 DR63
Leconfield Wk, Horn. 148 FJ65
Airfield Way
Lectern La, St.Alb. 43 CD24
Leda Av, Enf. 83 DX39
Leda Rd SE18 165 EM76
Ledborough La, Beac. 89 AK52
Ledborough Wd, Beac. 89 AL51
Ledbury Est SE15 162 DV80
Ledbury Ms N W11 140 DA73
Ledbury Rd
Ledbury Ms W W11 140 DA73
Ledbury Rd
Ledbury Pl, Croy. 220 DQ105
Ledbury Rd
Ledbury Rd W11 139 CZ72
Ledbury Rd, Croy. 220 DQ105
Ledbury Rd, Reig. 249 CZ133
Ledbury St SE15 162 DU80
Ledger Cl, Guil. 243 BB132
Ledger Dr, Add. 211 BF106
Ledger La, Maid. 150 AD82
Ledgers Rd, Slou. 151 AR75
Ledgers Rd, Warl. 237 EB117
Ledrington Rd SE19 182 DU93
Anerley Hill
Ledway Dr, Wem. 118 CM59
Lee, The, Nthwd. 93 BT50
Lee Av, Rom. 126 EY58
Lee Br SE13 163 EC83
Lee Ch St SE13 164 EE84
Lee Cl E17 101 DX53
Lee Cl, Barn. 80 DC42
Lee Cl, Hert. 32 DQ11
Lee Cl, Ware 33 EC11
Lee Conservancy Rd E9 123 DZ64
Lee Fm Cl, Chesh. 56 AU30
Lee Gdns Av, Horn. 128 FN60
Lee Grn SE12 184 EF85
Lee Grn, Orp. 206 EU99
Lee Grn La, Epsom 232 CP124
Lee Gro, Chig. 103 EN47
Lee High Rd SE12 163 ED83
Lee High Rd SE13 163 ED83
Lee Pk SE3 164 EF84
Lee Pk Way N9 101 DX49
Lee Pk Way N18 101 DX49
Lee Rd NW7 97 CX52
Lee Rd SE3 164 EF83
Lee Rd SW19 200 DB95
Lee Rd, Enf. 82 DU44
Lee Rd, Grnf. 137 CJ67
Lee St E8 142 DT67
Lee St, Horl. 268 DE148
Lee Ter SE3 164 EE83
Lee Ter SE13 164 EE83
Lee Valley Cycle Route, Brox. 49 ED20
Lee Valley Cycle Route, Harl. 50 EF18
Lee Valley Cycle Route, Hodd. 34 EE13
Lee Valley Cycle Route, Wal.Abb. 67 EC26
Lee Valley Cycle Route, Ware 33 EB09
Lee Valley Pathway E9 123 EA64
Lee Valley Pathway E10 123 DX61
Lee Valley Pathway E17 122 DW58
Lee Valley Pathway, Wal.Abb. 67 EB28
Lee Valley Technopark N17 122 DU55
Lee Vw, Enf. 81 DP39
Leech La (Headley), Epsom 248 CQ126
Leech La, Lthd. 248 CQ126
Leechcroft Av, Sid. 185 ET85
Leechcroft Av, Swan. 207 FF97
Leechcroft Rd, Wall. 200 DG104
Leecroft Rd, Barn. 79 CY43
Leeds Cl, Orp. 206 EX103
Leeds Pl N4 121 DM61
Tollington Pk
Leeds Rd, Ilf. 125 ER60
Leeds Rd, Slou. 132 AS73
Leeds St N18 100 DU50
Leefe Way, Pot.B. 65 DK28
Leefern Rd W12 159 CU75
Leegate SE12 184 EF85
Leegate Cl, Wok. 226 AV116
Sythwood
Leeke St WC1 274 B2
Leeke St WC1 141 DM69
Leeland Rd W13 137 CG74
Leeland Ter W13 137 CG74
Leeland Way NW10 119 CT63
Leeming Rd, Borwd. 78 CM39
Leerdam Dr E14 163 EC76
Lees, The, Croy. 203 DZ103
Lees Av, Nthwd. 93 BT53
Lees Pl W1 272 F10
Lees Pl W1 140 DG73
Lees Rd, Uxb. 135 BP70
Leeside, Barn. 79 CY43
Leeside, Pot.B. 64 DD31
Wayside
Leeside Ct SE16 143 DX74
Rotherhithe St
Leeside Cres NW11 119 CZ58
Leeside Rd N17 100 DV51
Leeson Gdns (Eton Wick), Wind. 151 AL77
Victoria Rd
Leeson Rd SE24 161 DN84
Leesons Hill, Chis. 205 ET97
Leesons Hill, Orp. 206 EU97
Leesons Way, Orp. 205 ET96
Leeward Gdns SW19 179 CZ93
Leeway SE8 163 DZ78
Leeway Cl, Pnr. 94 BZ52
Leewood Cl SE12 184 EF86
Upwood Rd
Leewood Pl, Swan. 207 FD98
Leewood Way (Effingham), Lthd. 246 BW127
Lefevre Wk E3 143 EA67
Lefroy Rd W12 159 CT75
Legard Rd N5 121 DP62
Legatt Rd SE9 184 EK85
Leggatt Rd E15 143 EC68
Leggatts Cl, Wat. 75 BT36
Leggatts Ri, Wat. 75 BU35
Leggatts Way, Wat. 75 BT36
Leggatts Wd Av, Wat. 75 BV36
Legge St SE13 183 EC85
Leggfield Ter, Hem.H. 39 BF20
Leghorn Rd NW10 139 CT68
Leghorn Rd SE18 165 ER78
Legion Cl N1 141 DN65
Legion Ct, Mord. 200 DA100
Legion Rd, Grnf. 136 CC67
Legion Ter E3 143 DZ67
Lefevre Wk
Legion Way N12 98 DE52
Legon Av, Rom. 127 FC60
Legra Av, Hodd. 49 EA17
Legrace Av, Houns. 156 BX82
Leicester Av, Mitch. 201 DL98
Leicester Cl, Wor.Pk. 217 CW105
Leicester Ct WC2 273 N10
Leicester Gdns, Ilf. 125 ES59
Leicester Pl WC2 273 N10
Leicester Rd E11 124 EH57
Leicester Rd N2 120 DE55
Leicester Rd NW10 138 CR66
Leicester Rd, Barn. 80 DB43
Leicester Rd, Croy. 202 DS101
Leicester Rd, Til. 171 GF81
Leicester Sq WC2 277 N1
Leicester Sq WC2 141 DK73
Leicester St WC2 273 N10

Leigh Av, Ilf. 124 EK56
Leigh Cl, Add. 211 BF108
Leigh Cl, N.Mal. 198 CR98
Leigh Common, Welw.G.C. 29 CY11
Leigh Cor, Cob. 214 BW114
Leigh Hill Rd
Leigh Ct SE4 163 EA82
Lewisham Way
Leigh Ct, Borwd. 78 CR40
Banks Rd
Leigh Ct, Har. 117 CE60
Leigh Ct Cl, Cob. 214 BW114
Leigh Cres (New Addington), Croy. 221 EB108
Leigh Dr, Rom. 106 FK49
Leigh Gdns NW10 139 CW68
Leigh Hill Rd, Cob. 214 BW114
Leigh Hunt Dr N14 99 DK46
Leigh Hunt St SE1 279 H4
Leigh Orchard Cl SW16 181 DM90
Leigh Pk (Datchet), Slou. 152 AV80
Leigh Pl EC1 274 D6
Leigh Pl, Cob. 230 BW115
Leigh Pl, Dart. 188 FN92
Hawley Rd
Leigh Pl, Well. 166 EU82
Leigh Pl La, Gdse. 253 DY132
Leigh Pl Rd, Reig. 265 CU140
Leigh Rd E6 145 EN65
Leigh Rd E10 123 EC59
Leigh Rd N5 121 DP63
Leigh Rd, Bet. 264 CQ140
Leigh Rd, Cob. 213 BV113
Leigh Rd, Grav. 191 GH89
Leigh Rd, Houns. 157 CD84
Leigh Rd, Slou. 131 AP73
Leigh Rodd, Wat. 94 BZ48
Leigh Sq, Wind. 151 AK82
Leigh St WC1 273 P4
Leigh St WC1 141 DL70
Leigh Ter, Orp. 206 EV97
Saxville Rd
Leigham Av SW16 181 DL90
Leigham Ct, Wall. 219 DJ107
Stafford Rd
Leigham Ct Rd SW16 181 DL89
Leigham Dr, Islw. 157 CE80
Leigham Vale SW2 181 DM90
Leigham Vale SW16 181 DM90
Leighton Av E12 125 EN64
Leighton Av, Pnr. 116 BY55
Leighton Buzzard Rd, Hem.H. 40 BJ19
Leighton Cl, Edg. 96 CN54
Leighton Cres NW5 121 DJ64
Leighton Gro
Leighton Gdns NW10 139 CV68
Leighton Gdns, S.Croy. 220 DV113
Leighton Gdns, Til. 171 GG80
Leighton Gro NW5 121 DJ64
Leighton Pl NW5 121 DJ64
Leighton Rd NW5 121 DK64
Leighton Rd W13 157 CG75
Leighton Rd, Enf. 82 DT43
Leighton Rd (Harrow Weald), Har. 95 CD54
Leighton St, Croy. 201 DP102
Leighton Way, Epsom 216 CR114
Leila Parnell Pl SE7 164 EJ79
Leinster Av SW14 158 CQ83
Leinster Gdns W2 140 DC72
Leinster Ms W2 140 DC73
Leinster Pl W2 140 DC72
Leinster Rd N10 121 DH56
Leinster Sq W2 140 DA72
Leinster Ter W2 140 DC73
Leiston Spur, Slou. 132 AS72
Leisure La, W.Byf. 212 BH112
Leisure Way N12 98 DD52
Leith Cl NW9 118 CR60
Leith Cl, Slou. 132 AU74
Leith Hill, Orp. 206 EU95
Leith Hill Grn, Orp. 206 EU95
Leith Hill
Leith Hill La (Holmbury St. Mary), Dor. 262 BY144
Leith Pk Rd, Grav. 191 GH88
Leith Rd N22 99 DP53
Leith Rd, Epsom 216 CS112
Leith Vw (North Holmwood), Dor. 263 CJ140
Leith Yd NW6 140 DA67
Quex Rd
Leithcote Gdns SW16 181 DM91
Leithcote Path SW16 181 DM90
Lela Av, Houns. 156 BW82
Lelitia Cl E8 142 DU67
Pownall Rd
Leman St E1 142 DT72
Lemark Cl, Stan. 95 CJ50
Lemmon Rd SE10 164 EE79
Lemna Rd E11 124 EE59
Lemonfield Dr, Wat. 60 BY32
Lemonwell Ct SE9 185 EQ85
Lemonwell Dr
Lemonwell Dr SE9 185 EQ85
Lemsford Cl N15 122 DU57
Lemsford Ct N4 122 DQ61
Brownswood Rd
Lemsford Ct, Borwd. 78 CQ42
Lemsford La, Welw.G.C. 29 CV10
Lemsford Rd, Hat. 45 CT17
Lemsford Rd, St.Alb. 43 CF20
Lemsford Rd, Welw.G.C. 29 CT10
Lemsford Village, Welw.G.C. 29 CU10
Lemuel St SW18 180 DB86
Len Freeman Pl SW6 159 CZ80
John Smith Av
Lena Gdns W6 159 CW76
Lena Kennedy Cl E4 101 EB51
Lenanton Steps E14 163 EA75
Manilla St
Lendal Ter SW4 161 DK83
Lenelby Rd, Surb. 198 CN102
Lenham Rd SE12 164 EF84
Lenham Rd, Bexh. 166 EZ79
Lenham Rd, Sutt. 218 DB105
Lenham Rd, Th.Hth. 202 DR96
Lenmore Av, Grays 170 GC76
Lennard Av, W.Wick. 204 EE103
Lennard Cl, W.Wick. 204 EE103
Lennard Rd SE20 182 DW93
Lennard Rd, Beck. 183 DX93
Lennard Rd, Brom. 205 EM102
Lennard Rd, Croy. 202 DQ102
Lennard Rd (Dunton Grn), Sev. 241 FE120
Lennard Row, S.Ock. 149 FR74
Lennon Rd NW2 119 CW64
Lennox Av, Grav. 191 GF86
Lennox Cl, Grays 169 FW77
Lennox Cl, Rom. 127 FF58
Lennox Gdns NW10 119 CT63
Lennox Gdns SW1 276 D7
Lennox Gdns SW1 160 DF76
Lennox Gdns, Croy. 219 DP105
Lennox Gdns, Ilf. 125 EM60
Lennox Gdns Ms SW1 276 D7
Lennox Gdns Ms SW1 160 DF76
Lennox Rd E17 123 DZ58
Lennox Rd N4 121 DM61
Lennox Rd, Grav. 191 GF86
Lennox Rd E, Grav. 191 GG87
Lenor Cl, Bexh. 166 EY84
Lens Rd E7 144 EJ66
Lensbury Cl (Cheshunt), Wal.Cr. 67 DY28
Ashdown Cres
Lensbury Way SE2 166 EW76
Lent Grn (Burnham), Slou. 130 AH70
Lent Grn La (Burnham), Slou. 130 AH70
Lent Ri Rd, Maid. 130 AH72
Lent Ri Rd (Burnham), Slou. 130 AH72
Lenten Cl (Peaslake), Guil. 261 BR142
Lenthall Av, Grays 170 GA75
Lenthall Rd E8 142 DU66
Lenthall Rd, Loug. 85 ER42
Lenthorp Rd SE10 164 EF77
Lentmead Rd, Brom. 184 EF90
Lenton Path SE18 165 ER79
Lenton Ri, Rich. 158 CL83
Evelyn Ter
Lenton St SE18 165 ER77
Leo St SE15 162 DV80
Leo Yd EC1 274 G5
Leof Cres SE6 183 EB92
Leominster Rd, Mord. 200 DC100
Leominster Wk, Mord. 200 DC100
Leonard Av, Mord. 200 DC99
Leonard Av, Rom. 127 FD60
Leonard Av (Otford), Sev. 241 FH116
Leonard Av, Swans. 190 FY87
Leonard Rd E4 101 EA51
Leonard Rd E7 124 EG63
Leonard Rd N9 100 DT48
Leonard Rd SW16 201 DJ95
Leonard Rd, Sthl. 156 BX76
Leonard Robbins Path SE28 146 EV73
Tawney Rd
Leonard St E16 144 EL74
Leonard St EC2 275 L4
Leonard St EC2 142 DR70
Leonard Way, Brwd. 108 FS49
Leontine Cl SE15 162 DU80
Leopards Ct EC1 274 D6
Leopold Av SW19 179 CZ92
Leopold Ms E9 142 DW67
Fremont St
Leopold Rd E17 123 EA57
Leopold Rd N2 120 DD55
Leopold Rd N18 100 DV50
Leopold Rd NW10 138 CS66
Leopold Rd SW19 179 CZ91
Leopold Rd W5 138 CM74
Leopold St E3 143 DZ71
Leopold Ter SW19 180 DA92
Dora Rd
Leppoc Rd SW4 181 DK85
Leret Way, Lthd. 231 CH121
Leroy St SE1 279 M8
Leroy St SE1 162 DS77
Lerwick Dr, Slou. 132 AS71
Lesbourne Rd, Reig. 266 DB135
Lescombe Cl SE23 183 DY90
Lescombe Rd SE23 183 DY90
Lesley Cl, Bex. 187 FB87
Lesley Cl (Istead Ri), Grav. 191 GF94
Lesley Cl, Swan. 207 FD97
Leslie Gdns, Sutt. 218 DA108
Leslie Gro, Croy. 202 DS102
Leslie Gro Pl, Croy. 202 DR102
Leslie Gro
Leslie Pk Rd, Croy. 202 DS102
Leslie Rd E11 123 EC63
Leslie Rd E16 144 EH72
Leslie Rd N2 120 DD55
Leslie Rd, Dor. 247 CK134
Leslie Rd (Chobham), Wok. 210 AS110
Leslie Smith Sq SE18 165 EN79
Nightingale Vale
Lesney Fm Est, Erith 167 FD80
Lesney Pk, Erith 167 FD79
Lesney Pk Rd, Erith 167 FD79
Lessar Av SW4 181 DJ85
Lessing St SE23 183 DY87
Lessingham Av SW17 180 DF91
Lessingham Av, Ilf. 125 EN55
Lessington Av, Rom. 127 FC58
Lessness Av, Bexh. 166 EX80
Lessness Pk, Belv. 166 EZ78
Lessness Rd, Belv. 166 FA78
Stapley Rd
Lessness Rd, Mord. 200 DC100
Lester Av E15 144 EE69
Leston Cl, Rain. 147 FG69
Leswin Pl N16 122 DT62
Leswin Rd
Leswin Rd N16 122 DT62
Letchfield (Ley Hill), Chesh. 56 AV31
Letchford Gdns NW10 139 CU69
Letchford Ms NW10 139 CU69
Letchford Gdns
Letchford Ter, Har. 94 CB53
Letchmore Rd, Rad. 77 CG36
Letchworth Av, Felt. 175 BT87
Letchworth Cl, Brom. 204 EG99
Letchworth Cl, Wat. 94 BX50
Letchworth Dr, Brom. 204 EG99
Letchworth St SW17 180 DF91
Lethbridge Cl SE13 163 EC81
Lett Rd E15 143 ED66
Letter Box La, Sev. 257 FJ129
Letterstone Rd SW6 159 CZ80
Varna Rd
Lettice St SW6 159 CZ81
Lettsom St SE5 162 DS82
Lettsom Wk E13 144 EG68
Leucha Rd E17 123 DY57
Levana Cl SW19 179 CY88
Levehurst Way SW4 161 DL82
Leven Cl, Wal.Cr. 67 DX33
Leven Cl, Wat. 94 BX50
Leven Dr, Wal.Cr. 67 DX33
Leven Rd E14 143 EC71
Leven Way, Hayes 135 BS72
Leven Way, Hem.H. 40 BK16
Levendale Rd SE23 183 DY89
Lever Sq, Grays 171 GG77
Lever St EC1 274 G3
Lever St EC1 141 DP69
Leverett Cl (New Addington), Croy. 221 ED111
Leverett St SW3 276 C8
Leverholme Gdns SE9 185 EN90
Leverson St SW16 181 DJ93
Leverstock Grn Rd, Hem.H. 41 BQ21
Leverstock Grn Way, Hem.H. 41 BQ20
Leverton Pl NW5 121 DJ64
Leverton St
Leverton St NW5 121 DJ64
Leverton Way, Wal.Abb. 67 EC33
Leveson Rd, Grays 171 GH76
Levett Gdns, Ilf. 125 ET63
Levett Rd, Bark. 145 ES65
Levett Rd, Lthd. 231 CH120
Levine Gdns, Bark. 146 EX68
Levison Way N19 121 DK61
Grovedale Rd
Levylsdene, Guil. 243 BD134
Lewes Cl, Grays 170 GA79
Lewes Cl, Nthlt. 136 CA65
Lewes Rd N12 98 DE50
Lewes Rd, Brom. 204 EK96
Lewes Rd, Rom. 106 FJ49
Lewes Way, Rick. 75 BQ42
Lewesdon Cl SW19 179 CX88
Leweston Pl N16 122 DT59
Lewey Ho E3 143 DZ70
Lewgars Av NW9 118 CQ58
Lewin Rd SW14 158 CR83
Lewin Rd SW16 181 DK93
Lewin Rd, Bexh. 166 EY84
Lewins Rd, Epsom 216 CP114
Lewins Rd (Chalfont St. Peter), Ger.Cr. 112 AX55
Lewins Way, Slou. 131 AM73
Lewis Av E17 101 EA53
Lewis Cl N14 99 DJ45
Orchid Rd
Lewis Cl, Add. 212 BJ105
Lewis Cl, Brwd. 109 FZ45
Lewis Cl (Harefield), Uxb. 92 BJ54
Lewis Cres NW10 118 CQ64
Lewis Gdns N2 98 DD54
Lewis Gro SE13 163 EC83
Lewis La (Chalfont St. Peter), Ger.Cr. 90 AY53
Lewis Pl E8 122 DU64
Lewis Rd, Horn. 128 FJ58
Lewis Rd, Mitch. 200 DD96
Lewis Rd, Rich. 177 CK85
Red Lion St
Lewis Rd, Sid. 186 EW90
Lewis Rd, Sthl. 156 BY75
Lewis Rd, Sutt. 218 DB105
Lewis Rd, Swans. 190 FY86
Lewis Rd, Well. 166 EW83
Lewis St NW1 141 DH66
Lewis Way, Dag. 147 FB65
Lewisham Cen SE13 163 EC83
Lewisham High St SE13 163 EC83
Lewisham Hill SE13 163 EC82
Lewisham Pk SE13 183 EB86
Lewisham Rd SE13 163 EB81
Lewisham St SW1 277 N5
Lewisham Way SE4 163 DZ81
Lewisham Way SE14 163 DZ81
Lexden Dr, Rom. 126 EV58
Lexden Rd W3 138 CP73
Lexden Rd, Mitch. 201 DK98
Lexham Ct, Grnf. 137 CD67
Lexham Gdns W8 160 DB76
Lexham Gdns, Amer. 55 AQ37
Lexham Gdns Ms W8 160 DB76
Lexham Ho, Bark. 145 ER67
St. Margarets
Lexham Ms W8 160 DA77
Lexham Wk W8 160 DB76
Lexham Gdns
Lexington, The EC1 275 K4
Lexington, The EC1 142 DR70
Lexington Cl, Borwd. 78 CM41
Lexington Ct, Pur. 220 DQ110
Lexington St W1 273 L9
Lexington St W1 141 DJ72
Lexington Way, Barn. 79 CX42
Lexington Way, Upmin. 129 FT58
Lexton Gdns SW12 181 DK88
Ley Hill Rd (Bovingdon), Hem.H. 56 AX30
Ley St, Ilf. 125 EP61
Ley Wk, Welw.G.C. 30 DC09
Leyborne Av W13 157 CH75
Leyborne Pk, Rich. 158 CN81
Leybourne Av (Byfleet), W.Byf. 212 BM113
Leybourne Cl, Brom. 204 EG100
Leybourne Cl (Byfleet), W.Byf. 212 BM113
Leybourne Av
Leybourne Rd E11 124 EF60
Leybourne Rd NW1 141 DH66
Leybourne Rd NW9 118 CN57
Leybourne Rd, Uxb. 135 BQ67
Leybourne St NW1 141 DH66
Hawley St
Leybridge Ct SE12 184 EG85
Leyburn Cl E17 123 EB56
Church La
Leyburn Cres, Rom. 106 FL52
Leyburn Gdns, Croy. 202 DS103
Leyburn Gro N18 100 DU51
Leyburn Rd N18 100 DU51
Leyburn Rd, Rom. 106 FL52
Leycroft Cl, Loug. 85 EN43
Leycroft Gdns, Erith 167 FH81
Leyden St E1 275 P7
Leydenhatch La, Swan. 207 FC95
Leydon Cl SE16 143 DX74
Lagado Ms
Leyfield, Wor.Pk. 198 CS102
Leyhill Cl, Swan. 207 FE99
Leyland Av, Enf. 83 DY40
Leyland Av, St.Alb. 43 CD22
Leyland Cl (Cheshunt), Wal.Cr. 66 DW28
Leyland Gdns, Wdf.Grn. 102 EJ50
Leyland Rd SE12 184 EG85
Leylands La, Stai. 173 BF85
Leylang Rd SE14 163 DX80
Leys, The N2 120 DC56
Leys, The, Amer. 55 AP35
Leys, The, Har. 118 CM58
Leys, The, St.Alb. 43 CK17
Leys Av, Dag. 147 FC66
Leys Cl, Dag. 147 FC66
Leys Cl, Har. 117 CD57
Leys Cl (Harefield), Uxb. 92 BK53
Leys Gdns, Barn. 80 DG43
Leys Rd, Hem.H. 40 BL22
Leys Rd (Oxshott), Lthd. 215 CD112
Leys Rd E, Enf. 83 DY39
Leys Rd W, Enf. 83 DY39
Leysdown, Welw.G.C. 30 DD09
Leysdown Av, Bexh. 167 FC84
Leysdown Rd SE9 184 EL89
Leysfield Rd W12 159 CU75
Leyspring Rd E11 124 EF60
Leyswood Dr, Ilf. 125 ES57
Leythe Rd W3 158 CQ75
Leyton Business Cen E10 123 EA61
Leyton Cross Rd, Dart. 187 FF90
Leyton Gra E10 123 EB60
Goldsmith Rd
Leyton Gra Est E10 123 EB60
Leyton Grn Rd E10 123 EC58
Leyton Ind Village E10 123 DX59
Leyton Pk Rd E10 123 EC62
Leyton Rd E15 123 ED64
Leyton Rd SW19 180 DC94
Leyton Way E11 124 EE59
Leytonstone Rd E15 124 EE64
Leywick St E15 144 EE68
Leywood Cl, Amer. 55 AS40
Lezayre Rd, Orp. 223 ET107
Liardet St SE14 163 DY79
Liberia Rd N5 141 DP65
Liberty, The, Rom. 127 FE57
Liberty Av SW19 200 DD95
Liberty Cl, Hert. 32 DQ11
Liberty Hall Rd, Add. 212 BG106
Liberty La, Add. 212 BG106
Liberty Ms SW12 181 DH86
Liberty Ri, Add. 212 BG107
Liberty St SW9 161 DM81
Libra Rd E3 143 DZ67
Libra Rd E13 144 EG68
Library Hill, Brwd. 108 FX47
Coptfold Rd
Library Pl E1 142 DV73
Cable St
Library St SE1 278 F5
Library St SE1 161 DP75
Library Way, Twick. 176 CC87
Nelson Rd
Licenced Victuallers Nat Homes (Denham), Uxb. 113 BF58
Denham Grn La
Lichfield Cl, Barn. 80 DF41
Lichfield Ct, Rich. 158 CL84
Sheen Rd
Lichfield Gdns, Rich. 158 CL84
Lichfield Gro N3 98 DB54
Lichfield Rd E3 143 DY69
Lichfield Rd E6 144 EK69
Lichfield Rd N9 100 DU47
Winchester Rd
Lichfield Rd NW2 119 CY63
Lichfield Rd, Dag. 126 EV63
Lichfield Rd, Houns. 156 BW83
Lichfield Rd, Nthwd. 115 BU55
Lichfield Rd, Rich. 158 CM81
Lichfield Rd, Wdf.Grn. 102 EE49
Lichfield Ter, Upmin. 129 FS61
Lichfield Way, Brox. 49 DZ22
Lichfield Way, S.Croy. 221 DX110
Lichlade Cl, Orp. 223 ET105
Lidbury Rd NW7 97 CY51
Lidcote Gdns SW9 161 DN82
Liddall Way, West Dr. 134 BM74
Liddell Cl, Har. 117 CK55
Liddell Gdns NW10 139 CW68
Liddell Pl, Wind. 150 AJ83
Liddell Way
Liddell Rd NW6 140 DA65
Liddell Sq, Wind. 150 AJ83
Liddell Way
Liddell Way, Wind. 150 AJ83
Lidding Rd, Har. 117 CK57
Liddington Hall Dr (Rydeshill), Guil. 242 AS131
Liddington New Rd (Rydeshill), Guil. 242 AS131
Liddington Rd E15 144 EF67
Liddon Rd E13 144 EH69
Liddon Rd, Brom. 204 EJ97
Liden Cl E17 123 DZ60
Hitcham Rd
Lidfield Rd N16 122 DR63
Lidgate Rd SE15 162 DT80
Chandler Way
Lidiard Rd SW18 180 DC89
Lidlington Pl NW1 273 L1
Lidlington Pl NW1 141 DJ68
Lido Sq N17 100 DR54
Lidstone Cl, Wok. 226 AV117
Lidyard Rd N19 121 DJ60
Lieutenant Ellis Way, Wal.Cr. 66 DT31
Liffler Rd SE18 165 ES78
Lifford St SW15 159 CX84
Liffords Pl SW13 159 CT82
Lightcliffe Rd N13 99 DN49
Lighter Cl SE16 163 DY77
Lighterman Ms E1 143 DX72
Lightermans Rd E14 163 EA75
Lightfoot Rd N8 121 DL57
Lightley Cl, Wem. 138 CM66
Stanley Av
Lightswood Cl (Cheshunt), Wal.Cr. 66 DR26
Ligonier St E2 275 P4
Lila Pl, Swan. 207 FE98
Lilac Av, Enf. 82 DW36
Lilac Av, Wok. 226 AX120
Lilac Cl E4 101 DZ51
Lilac Cl, Brwd. 108 FV43
Magnolia Way
Lilac Cl, Guil. 242 AW130
Lilac Cl (Cheshunt), Wal.Cr. 66 DV31
Greenwood Av
Lilac Gdns W5 157 CK76
Lilac Gdns, Croy. 203 EA104
Lilac Gdns, Hayes 135 BS72
Lilac Gdns, Rom. 127 FE60
Lilac Gdns, Swan. 207 FD97
Lilac Pl SE11 278 B9
Lilac Pl SE11 161 DM77
Lilac Pl, West Dr. 134 BM73
Cedar Av
Lilac Rd, Hodd. 49 EB15
Lilac St W12 139 CU73
Lilbourne Dr, Hert. 32 DT08
Stanstead Rd
Lilburne Gdns SE9 184 EL85
Lilburne Rd SE9 184 EL85
Lilburne Wk NW10 138 CQ65
Lile Cres W7 137 CE71
Lilestone Est NW8 140 DD70
Fisherton St
Lilestone St NW8 272 B4
Lilestone St NW8 140 DE70
Lilford Rd SE5 161 DP82
Lilian Barker Cl SE12 184 EG85
Lilian Board Way, Grnf. 117 CD64
Lilian Cl N16 122 DS62
Barbauld Rd
Lilian Cres, Brwd. 109 GC47
Lilian Gdns, Wdf.Grn. 102 EH53
Lilian Rd SW16 201 DJ95
Lillechurch Rd, Dag. 146 EV65
Lilleshall Rd, Mord. 200 DD100
Lilley Cl E1 142 DU74
Hermitage Wall
Lilley Cl, Brwd. 108 FT49
Lilley Dr (Kingswood), Tad. 234 DB122
Lilley La NW7 96 CR50
Lilley Way, Slou. 131 AL74
Lillian Av W3 158 CN75
Lillian Rd SW13 159 CU79
Lilliards Cl, Hodd. 33 EB13
Lillie Rd SW6 159 CY80
Lillie Rd (Biggin Hill), West. 238 EK118
Lillie Yd SW6 160 DA79
Lillieshall Rd SW4 161 DH83
Lillington Gdns Est SW1 277 L9
Lillington Ho N7 121 DN63
Harvist Est
Lilliots La, Lthd. 231 CG119
Kingston Rd
Lilliput Av, Nthlt. 136 BZ67
Lilliput Rd, Rom. 127 FD59
Lilly La, Hem.H. 41 BR16
Lily Cl W14 159 CY77
Lily Dr, West Dr. 154 BK76
Lily Gdns, Wem. 137 CJ68
Lily Pl EC1 274 E6
Lily Pl EC1 141 DN71
Lily Rd E17 123 EA58
Lilyville Rd SW6 159 CZ81
Limbourne Av, Dag. 126 EZ59
Limburg Rd SW11 160 DF84
Lime Av, Brwd. 109 FZ48
Lime Av (Northfleet), Grav. 190 GD87
Lime Av, Upmin. 128 FN63
Lime Av, West Dr. 134 BM73
Lime Av, Wind. 152 AT80
Lime Cl E1 142 DU74
Lime Cl, Brom. 204 EL98
Lime Cl, Buck.H. 102 EK48
Lime Cl, Cars. 200 DF103
Lime Cl (West Clandon), Guil. 244 BH128
Lime Cl, Har. 95 CG54
Lime Cl, Pnr. 115 BT55
Lime Cl, Reig. 266 DB137
Lime Cl, Rom. 127 FC56
Lime Cl, S.Ock. 149 FW69
Lime Cl, Ware 33 DY05
Lime Cl, Wat. 94 BX45
Lime Ct, Mitch. 200 DD96
Lewis Rd
Lime Cres, Sun. 196 BW96
Lime Gro N20 97 CZ46
Lime Gro W12 159 CW75
Lime Gro, Add. 212 BG105
Lime Gro, Guil. 242 AV130
Lime Gro (West Clandon), Guil. 244 BG128
Lime Gro, Hayes 135 BR73
Lime Gro, Ilf. 103 ET51
Lime Gro, N.Mal. 198 CR97
Lime Gro, Orp. 205 EP103
Lime Gro, Ruis. 115 BV59
Lime Gro, Sid. 185 ET86
Lime Gro, Twick. 177 CF86
Lime Gro, Warl. 237 DY118
Lime Gro, Wok. 226 AY121
Lime Meadow Av, S.Croy. 220 DU113
Lime Pit La, Sev. 241 FC117
Lime Rd, Epp. 69 ET31
Lime Rd, Rich. 158 CM84
St. Mary's Gro
Lime Rd, Swan. 207 FD97
Lime Row, Erith 166 EZ76
Northwood Pl
Lime St E17 123 DY56
Lime St EC3 275 M10
Lime St EC3 142 DS73
Lime St Pas EC3 275 M9
Lime Ter W7 137 CE73
Manor Ct Rd
Lime Tree Av, Esher 197 CD102
Lime Tree Av (Bluewater), Green. 189 FU88
Lime Tree Av, T.Ditt. 197 CD102
Lime Tree Cl (Bookham), Lthd. 230 CA124
Lime Tree Gro, Croy. 203 DZ104
Lime Tree Pl, Mitch. 201 DH95
Lime Tree Pl, St.Alb. 43 CF21
Lime Tree Rd, Houns. 156 CB81
Lime Tree Ter SE6 183 DZ88
Winterstoke Rd
Lime Tree Wk, Amer. 72 AT39
Lime Tree Wk, Bushey 95 CE46
Lime Tree Wk, Enf. 82 DQ38
Lime Tree Wk, Rick. 74 BH43
Lime Tree Wk, Sev. 257 FH125
Lime Tree Wk, Vir.W. 192 AY98
Lime Tree Wk, W.Wick. 222 EF105
Lime Wk E15 144 EE67
Church St N
Lime Wk (Shere), Guil. 260 BM139
Lime Wk, Hem.H. 40 BM22
Lime Wk (Denham), Uxb. 114 BJ64
Lime Wks Rd (Merstham), Red. 251 DJ126
Limeburner La EC4 274 F9
Limeburner La EC4 141 DP72
Limebush Cl (New Haw), Add. 212 BJ109
Limecroft Cl, Epsom 216 CR108
Limedene Cl, Pnr. 94 BX53
Limeharbour E14 163 EB76
Limehouse Causeway E14 143 DZ73
Limehouse Flds Est E14 143 DY71
Limehouse Link E14 143 DY73
Limekiln Dr SE7 164 EH79
Limekiln Pl SE19 182 DT94
Limerick Cl SW12 181 DJ87
Limerick Gdns, Upmin. 129 FT59
Limerston St SW10 160 DC79
Limes, The W2 140 DA73
Linden Gdns
Limes, The, Amer. 55 AP35
Limes, The, Brwd. 109 FZ48
Limes, The, Brom. 204 EL103
Limes, The, Purf. 168 FN78
Tank Hill Rd
Limes, The, St.Alb. 43 CE18
Limes, The, Welw.G.C. 30 DA11
Limes, The, Wok. 226 AX115
Limes Av E11 124 EH56
Limes Av N12 98 DC49
Limes Av NW7 96 CS51
Limes Av NW11 119 CY59
Limes Av SE20 182 DV94
Limes Av SW13 159 CT82
Limes Av, Cars. 200 DF102
Limes Av, Chig. 103 ER51
Limes Av, Croy. 201 DN104
Limes Av, Horl. 269 DH150
Limes Av, The N11 99 DH50
Limes Cl, Ashf. 174 BN92

Limes Ct, Brwd. 108 FX46
Sawyers Hall La
Limes Ct, Hodd. 49 EA17
Charlton Way
Limes Fld Rd SW14 158 CS83
White Hart La
Limes Gdns SW18 180 DA86
Limes Gro SE13 163 EC84
Limes Pl, Croy. 202 DR101
Limes Rd, Beck. 203 EB96
Limes Rd, Croy. 202 DR100
Limes Rd, Egh. 173 AZ92
Limes Rd (Cheshunt), Wal.Cr. 67 DX32
Limes Rd, Wey. 212 BN105
Limes Row, Orp. 223 EP106
Orchard Rd
Limes Wk SE15 162 DV84
Limes Wk W5 157 CK75
Chestnut Gro
Limesdale Gdns, Edg. 96 CQ54
Limesford Rd SE15 163 DX84
Limestone Wk, Erith 166 EX76
Limetree Cl SW2 181 DM88
Limetree Ter, Well. 166 EU83
Hook La
Limetree Wk SW17 180 DG92
Church La
Limeway Ter, Dor. 247 CG134
Limewood Cl E17 123 DZ56
Limewood Cl W13 137 CH72
St. Stephens Rd
Limewood Cl, Beck. 203 EC99
Limewood Ct, Ilf. 125 EM57
Limewood Rd, Erith 167 FC80
Limpsfield Av SW19 179 CX89
Limpsfield Av, Th.Hth. 201 DM99
Limpsfield Rd, S.Croy. 220 DU112
Limpsfield Rd, Warl. 236 DW116
Linacre Ct W6 159 CX78
Linacre Rd NW2 139 CV65
Linberry Wk SE8 163 DZ77
Lince La (Westcott), Dor. 263 CD136
Linces Way, Welw.G.C. 30 DB11
Linchfield Rd (Datchet), Slou. 152 AW81
Linchmere Rd SE12 184 EF87
Lincoln Av N14 99 DJ48
Lincoln Av SW19 179 CX90
Lincoln Av, Rom. 127 FD60
Lincoln Av, Twick. 176 CC89
Lincoln Cl SE25 202 DU100
Woodside Grn
Lincoln Cl, Erith 167 FF82
Lincoln Cl, Grnf. 136 CC67
Lincoln Cl, Har. 116 BZ57
Lincoln Cl, Horl. 268 DG149
Lincoln Cl, Horn. 128 FN57
Lincoln Cl, Welw.G.C. 30 DD08
Lincoln Ct N16 122 DR59
Lincoln Ct, Berk. 38 AV19
Lincoln Ct, Borwd. 78 CR43
Lincoln Cres, Enf. 82 DS43
Lincoln Dr, Rick. 75 BP42
Lincoln Dr, Wat. 94 BW48
Lincoln Dr, Wok. 227 BE115
Lincoln Gdns, Ilf. 124 EL59
Lincoln Grn Rd, Orp. 205 ET99
Lincoln Hatch La (Burnham), Slou. 130 AJ70
Lincoln Ms NW6 139 CZ67
Willesden La
Lincoln Ms SE21 182 DR88
Lincoln Pk, Amer. 55 AS39
Lincoln Rd E7 144 EK65
Lincoln Rd E13 144 EH70
Lincoln Rd E18 102 EG53
Grove Rd
Lincoln Rd N2 120 DE55
Lincoln Rd SE25 202 DV97
Lincoln Rd, Dor. 247 CJ134
Lincoln Rd, Enf. 82 DU43
Lincoln Rd, Erith 167 FF82
Lincoln Rd, Felt. 176 BZ90
Lincoln Rd (Chalfont St. Peter), Ger.Cr. 90 AY53
Lincoln Rd, Guil. 242 AT132
Lincoln Rd, Har. 116 BZ57
Lincoln Rd, Mitch. 201 DL99
Lincoln Rd, N.Mal. 198 CQ97
Lincoln Rd, Nthwd. 115 BT55
Lincoln Rd, Sid. 186 EV92
Lincoln Rd, Wem. 137 CK65
Lincoln Rd, Wor.Pk. 199 CV102
Lincoln St E11 124 EE61
Lincoln St SW3 276 D9
Lincoln St SW3 160 DF77
Lincoln Wk, Epsom 216 CR110
Hollymoor La
Lincoln Way, Enf. 82 DV43
Lincoln Way, Rick. 75 BP42
Lincoln Way, Slou. 131 AK73
Lincoln Way, Sun. 195 BS95
Lincolns, The NW7 97 CT48
Lincolns Cl, St.Alb. 43 CJ15
Lincolns Flds, Epp. 69 ET29
Lincoln's Inn WC2 274 C8
Lincoln's Inn WC2 141 DN72
Lincoln's Inn Flds WC2 274 B8
Lincoln's Inn Flds WC2 141 DM72
Lincolnshott (Southfleet), Grav. 190 GB92
Lincombe Rd, Brom. 184 EF90
Lind Rd, Sutt. 218 DC106
Lind St SE8 163 EB82
Lindal Cres, Enf. 81 DL42
Lindal Rd SE4 183 DZ85
Lindale Cl, Vir.W. 192 AT98
Lindales, The N17 100 DT51
Brantwood Rd
Lindbergh, Welw.G.C. 30 DC09
Lindbergh Rd, Wall. 219 DL109
Linden Av NW10 139 CX68
Linden Av, Couls. 235 DH116
Linden Av, Dart. 188 FJ88
Linden Av, Enf. 82 DU39
Linden Av, Houns. 176 CB85
Linden Av, Ruis. 115 BU60
Linden Av, Th.Hth. 201 DP98
Linden Av, Wem. 118 CM64
Linden Chase Rd, Sev. 257 FH122
Linden Cl N14 81 DJ44
Linden Cl (New Haw), Add. 212 BG111
Linden Cl, Orp. 224 EU106
Linden Cl, Purf. 168 FQ79
Linden Cl, Ruis. 115 BU60
Linden Cl, Stan. 95 CH50
Linden Cl, Tad. 233 CX120
Linden Cl, T.Ditt. 197 CF101
Linden Cl, Wal.Cr. 66 DV30
Linden Ct W12 139 CW74
Linden Ct (Englefield Grn), Egh. 172 AV93
Linden Ct, Lthd. 231 CH121
Linden Cres, Grnf. 137 CF65
Linden Cres, Kings.T. 198 CM96
Linden Cres, St.Alb. 43 CJ20
Linden Cres, Wdf.Grn. 102 EH51
Linden Dr, Cat. 236 DQ124
Linden Dr (Chalfont St. Peter), Ger.Cr. 90 AY54
Woodside Hill
Linden Dr (Farnham Royal), Slou. 131 AQ66
Linden Gdns W2 140 DA73
Linden Gdns W4 158 CR78
Linden Gdns, Enf. 82 DU39
Linden Gdns, Lthd. 231 CJ121
Linden Glade, Hem.H. 40 BG21
Linden Gro SE15 162 DW83
Linden Gro SE26 182 DW93
Linden Gro, N.Mal. 198 CS97
Linden Gro, Tedd. 177 CF92
Waldegrave Rd
Linden Gro, Walt. 195 BT103
Linden Gro, Warl. 237 DY118
Linden Ho, Slou. 153 BB78
Linden Lawns, Wem. 118 CM63
Linden Lea N2 120 DC57
Linden Lea, Wat. 59 BU33
Linden Leas, W.Wick. 203 ED103
Linden Ms N1 122 DR64
Mildmay Gro N
Linden Ms W2 140 DA73
Linden Gdns
Linden Pas W4 158 CR78
Linden Gdns
Linden Pit Path, Lthd. 231 CH121
Linden Pl, Epsom 216 CS112
East St
Linden Pl, Lthd. 245 BS126
Station App
Linden Pl, Mitch. 200 DE98
Linden Ri, Brwd. 108 FX50
Linden Rd E17 123 DZ57
High St
Linden Rd N10 121 DH56
Linden Rd N11 98 DF47
Linden Rd N15 122 DQ56
Linden Rd, Guil. 242 AX134
Linden Rd, Hmptn. 176 CA94
Linden Rd, Lthd. 231 CH121
Linden Rd, Wey. 213 BQ109
Linden Sq, Sev. 256 FE122
London Rd
Linden St, Rom. 127 FD56
Linden Wk N19 121 DJ61
Hargrave Pk
Linden Way N14 81 DJ44
Linden Way, Pur. 219 DJ110
Linden Way, Shep. 195 BQ99
Linden Way, Wok. 227 AZ121
Linden Way (Send Marsh), Wok. 227 BF124
Lindenfield, Chis. 205 EP96
Lindens, The N12 98 DD50
Lindens, The W4 158 CQ81
Hartington Rd
Lindens, The (New Addington), Croy. 221 EC107
Lindens, The, Hem.H. 39 BF23
Lindens, The, Loug. 85 EM43
Lindens Cl (Effingham), Lthd. 246 BY128
Mount Pleasant
Lindeth Cl, Stan. 95 CJ51
Old Ch La
Lindfield Gdns NW3 120 DB64
Lindfield Gdns, Guil. 243 AZ133
Lindfield Rd W5 137 CJ70
Lindfield Rd, Croy. 202 DT100
Lindfield Rd, Rom. 106 FL50
Lindfield St E14 143 EA72
Lindhill Cl, Enf. 83 DX39
Lindisfarne Cl, Grav. 191 GL89
St. Benedict's Av
Lindisfarne Rd SW20 179 CU94
Lindisfarne Rd, Dag. 126 EW62
Lindisfarne Way E9 123 DY63
Lindley Est SE15 162 DU80
Bird in Bush Rd
Lindley Pl, Rich. 158 CN81
Lindley Rd E10 123 EB61
Lindley Rd, Gdse. 252 DW130
Lindley Rd, Walt. 196 BX104
Lindley St E1 142 DW71
Lindlings, Hem.H. 39 BE21
Lindo Cl, Chesh. 54 AP30
Lindo St SE15 162 DW82
Selden Rd
Lindore Rd SW11 160 DF84
Lindores Rd, Cars. 200 DC101
Lindrop St SW6 160 DC82
Lindsay Cl, Chess. 216 CL108
Lindsay Cl, Epsom 216 CQ113
Lindsay Cl (Stanwell), Stai. 174 BK85
Lindsay Dr, Har. 118 CL58
Lindsay Dr, Shep. 195 BR100
Lindsay Pl, Wal.Cr. 66 DV30
Lindsay Rd (New Haw), Add. 212 BG110
Lindsay Rd (Hampton Hill), Hmptn. 176 CB91
Lindsay Rd, Wor.Pk. 199 CV103
Lindsay Sq SW1 277 N10
Lindsay Sq SW1 161 DK78
Lindsell St SE10 163 EC81
Lindsey Cl, Brwd. 108 FU49
Lindsey Cl, Brom. 204 EK97
Lindsey Cl, Mitch. 201 DL98
Lindsey Gdns, Felt. 175 BR87
Lindsey Ms N1 142 DQ66
Lindsey Rd, Dag. 126 EW63
Lindsey Rd (Denham), Uxb. 114 BG62
Lindsey St EC1 274 G6
Lindsey St EC1 141 DP71
Lindsey St, Epp. 69 ER28
Lindsey Way, Horn. 128 FJ57
Lindum Pl, St.Alb. 42 BZ22
Lindum Rd, Tedd. 177 CJ94
Lindvale, Wok. 226 AY115
Lindway SE27 181 DP92
Lindwood Cl E6 144 EL71
Northumberland Rd
Linfield Cl NW4 119 CW55
Linfield Cl, Walt. 213 BV106
Linfield Ct, Hert. 31 DM08
The Ridgeway
Linfields, Amer. 72 AW40
Linford Cl, Harl. 51 EP17
Linford End, Harl. 51 EQ17
Linford Rd E17 123 EC55
Linford Rd, Grays 171 GH78
Linford St SW8 161 DJ81
Ling Rd E16 144 EG71
Ling Rd, Erith 167 FC79
Lingards Rd SE13 163 EC84
Lingey Cl, Sid. 185 ET89
Lingfield Av, Dart. 188 FP87
Lingfield Av, Kings.T. 198 CL98
Lingfield Av, Upmin. 128 FM62
Lingfield Cl, Enf. 82 DS44
Lingfield Cl, Nthwd. 93 BS52
Lingfield Cres SE9 165 ER84
Lingfield Gdns N9 100 DV45
Lingfield Gdns, Couls. 235 DP119
Lingfield Rd SW19 179 CX92
Lingfield Rd, Grav. 191 GH89
Lingfield Rd, Wor.Pk. 199 CW104
Lingfield Way, Wat. 75 BT38
Lingham St SW9 161 DL82
Lingholm Way, Barn. 79 CX43
Lingmere Cl, Chig. 103 EQ47
Lingmoor Dr, Wat. 60 BW33
Lingrove Gdns, Buck.H. 102 EH47
Beech La
Lings Coppice SE21 182 DR89
Lingwell Rd SW17 180 DE90
Lingwood Gdns, Islw. 157 CE80
Lingwood Rd E5 122 DU59
Linhope St NW1 272 D4
Linhope St NW1 140 DF70
Linington Av, Chesh. 56 AU30
Link, The SE9 185 EN90
Link, The W3 138 CP72
Link, The, Enf. 83 DY39
Link, The, Nthlt. 116 BZ64
Eastcote La
Link, The, Pnr. 116 BW59
Link, The, Slou. 132 AV72
Link, The, Wem. 117 CJ60
Nathans Rd
Link Av, Wok. 227 BD115
Link Cl, Hat. 45 CV18
Link Dr, Hat. 45 CV18
Link La, Wall. 219 DK107
Link Rd N11 98 DG49
Link Rd, Add. 212 BL105
Weybridge Rd
Link Rd, Dag. 147 FB68
Link Rd, Felt. 175 BT87
Link Rd, Hem.H. 40 BJ17
Link Rd (Datchet), Slou. 152 AW80
Link Rd, Wall. 200 DG102
Link Rd, Wat. 76 BX40
Link St E9 142 DW65
Link Wk, Hat. 45 CV17
Link Way, Brom. 204 EL101
Link Way, Horn. 128 FL60
Link Way, Pnr. 94 BX53
Link Way, Stai. 174 BH93
Link Way (Denham), Uxb. 114 BG58
Link Way Rd, Brwd. 108 FT48
Linkfield, Brom. 204 EG100
Linkfield, Welw.G.C. 29 CY13
Linkfield, W.Mol. 196 CA97
Linkfield Cor, Red. 250 DE133
Hatchlands Rd
Linkfield Gdns, Red. 250 DE134
Hatchlands Rd
Linkfield La, Red. 250 DE133
Linkfield Rd, Islw. 157 CF82
Linkfield St, Red. 250 DE134
Linklea Cl NW9 96 CS52
Links, The E17 123 DY56
Links, The (Cheshunt), Wal.Cr. 67 DX26
Links, The, Walt. 195 BU103
Links, The, Welw.G.C. 29 CV09
Applecroft Rd
Links Av, Hert. 32 DV08
Links Av, Mord. 200 DA98
Links Av, Rom. 105 FH54
Links Brow (Fetcham), Lthd. 231 CE124
Links Cl, Ash. 231 CJ117
Links Dr N20 98 DA46
Links Dr, Borwd. 78 CM41
Links Dr, Rad. 61 CF33
Links Gdns SW16 181 DN94
Links Grn Way, Cob. 214 CA114
Links Pl, Ash. 231 CK117
Links Rd NW2 119 CT61
Links Rd SW17 180 DG93
Links Rd W3 138 CN72
Links Rd, Ashf. 174 BL92
Links Rd, Ash. 231 CJ118
Links Rd, Epsom 217 CU113
Links Rd (Bramley), Guil. 258 AY144
Links Rd (Flackwell Heath), H.Wyc. 110 AC56
Links Rd, W.Wick. 203 EC102
Links Rd, Wdf.Grn. 102 EG50
Links Side, Enf. 81 DN41
Links Vw N3 97 CZ52
Links Vw, Dart. 188 FJ88
Links Vw, St.Alb. 42 CB18
Links Vw Av (Brockham), Bet. 248 CN134
Links Vw Cl, Stan. 95 CG51
Links Vw Rd, Croy. 203 EA104
Links Vw Rd (Hampton Hill), Hmptn. 176 CC92
Links Way, Beck. 203 EA100
Links Way (Bookham), Lthd. 246 BY128
Links Way, Rick. 75 BQ41
Links Yd E1 142 DU71
Spelman St
Linkscroft Av, Ashf. 175 BP93
Linkside N12 97 CZ51
Linkside, Chig. 103 EQ50
Linkside, N.Mal. 198 CS96
Linkside Cl, Enf. 81 DM41
Linkside Gdns, Enf. 81 DM41
Linksway NW4 97 CX54
Linksway, Nthwd. 93 BQ53
Linkswood Rd (Burnham), Slou. 130 AJ68
Linkway N4 122 DQ59
Linkway SW20 199 CV97
Linkway, Dag. 126 EW63
Linkway, Guil. 242 AT133
Linkway, Rich. 177 CH89
Linkway, Wok. 227 BC117
Linkway, The, Barn. 80 DB44
Linkway, The, Sutt. 218 DD109
Linkwood Wk NW1 141 DK66
Maiden La
Linley Cres, Rom. 127 FB55
Linley Rd N17 100 DS54
Linnell Cl NW11 120 DB58
Linnell Dr NW11 120 DB58
Linnell Rd N18 100 DU50
Fairfield Rd
Linnell Rd SE5 162 DS82
Linnell Rd, Red. 266 DG135
Linnet Cl N9 101 DX46
Linnet Cl SE28 146 EW73
Linnet Cl, Bushey 94 CC45
Linnet Cl, S.Croy. 221 DX110
Linnet Gro, Guil. 243 BD132
Partridge Way
Linnet Ms SW12 180 DG87
Linnet Rd, Abb.L. 59 BU31
Linnet Ter, Ilf. 125 EN55
Tiptree Cres
Linnet Wk, Hat. 45 CU20
Lark Ri
Linnet Way, Purf. 168 FP78
Linnett Cl E4 101 EC49
Linom Rd SW4 161 DL84
Linscott Rd E5 122 DW63
Linsdell Rd, Bark. 145 EQ67
Linsey Cl, Hem.H. 40 BN24
Linsey St SE16 162 DU77
Linslade Cl, Houns. 176 BY85
Frampton Rd
Linslade Cl, Pnr. 115 BV55
Linslade Rd, Orp. 224 EU107
Linstead Ct SE9 185 ES86
Linstead St NW6 140 DA66
Linstead Way SW18 179 CY87
Linster Gro, Borwd. 78 CQ43
Lintaine Cl W6 159 CY79
Moylan Rd
Linthorpe Av, Wem. 137 CJ65
Linthorpe Rd N16 122 DS59
Linthorpe Rd, Barn. 80 DE41
Linton Av, Borwd. 78 CM39
Linton Cl, Mitch. 200 DF101
Linton Cl, Well. 166 EV81
Anthony Rd
Linton Gdns E6 144 EL72
Linton Glade, Croy. 221 DY109
Linton Gro SE27 181 DP92
Linton Rd, Bark. 145 EQ66
Linton St N1 142 DQ67
Lintons, The, Bark. 145 EQ66
Lintons La, Epsom 216 CS112
Lintott Ct (Stanwell), Stai. 174 BK86
Linver Rd SW6 160 DA82
Linwood, Saw. 36 EY05
Linwood Cl SE5 162 DT82
Linwood Cres, Enf. 82 DU39
Linwood Way SE15 162 DT80
Daniel Gdns
Linzee Rd N8 121 DL56
Lion Av, Twick. 177 CF88
Lion Rd
Lion Cl SE4 183 EA86
Lion Cl, Shep. 194 BL97
Lion Ct, Borwd. 78 CQ39
Lion Gate Gdns, Rich. 158 CM83
Lion Grn Rd, Couls. 235 DK115
Lion La, Red. 250 DF133
Lion Pk Av, Chess. 216 CN105
Lion Plaza EC2 142 DR72
Threadneedle St
Lion Rd E6 145 EM71
Lion Rd N9 100 DU47
Lion Rd, Bexh. 166 EZ84
Lion Rd, Croy. 202 DQ99
Lion Rd, Twick. 177 CF88
Lion Way, Brent. 157 CK80
Lion Wf Rd, Islw. 157 CH83
Lion Yd SW4 161 DK84
Tremadoc Rd
Lionel Gdns SE9 184 EK85
Lionel Ms W10 139 CY71
Telford Rd
Lionel Oxley Ho, Grays 170 GB79
New Rd
Lionel Rd SE9 184 EK85
Lionel Rd N, Brent. 158 CM78
Lionel Rd S, Brent. 158 CM78
Lions Cl SE9 184 EJ90
Liphook Cl, Horn. 127 FF63
Petworth Way
Liphook Cres SE23 182 DW87
Liphook Rd, Wat. 94 BX49
Lippitts Hill (High Beach), Loug. 84 EE39
Lipsham Cl, Bans. 218 DD113
Lipton Cl SE28 146 EW73
Aisher Rd
Lipton Rd E1 143 DX72
Bower St
Lisbon Av, Twick. 176 CC89
Lisbon Cl E17 101 DZ54
Lisburne Rd NW3 120 DF63
Lisford St SE15 162 DT81
Lisgar Ter W14 159 CZ77
Liskeard Cl, Chis. 185 EQ93
Liskeard Gdns SE3 164 EG81
Liskeard Lo, Cat. 252 DU126
Lisle Cl SW17 181 DH91
Lisle Pl, Grays 170 GA76
Lisle St WC2 273 N10
Lisle St WC2 141 DK73
Lismore, Hem.H. 41 BQ22
Lismore Circ NW5 120 DG64
Lismore Cl, Islw. 157 CG82
Lismore Pk, Slou. 132 AT72
Lismore Rd N17 122 DR55
Lismore Rd, S.Croy. 220 DS107
Lismore Wk N1 142 DQ65
Clephane Rd
Liss Way SE15 162 DT80
Pentridge St
Lissenden Gdns NW5 120 DG63
Lissoms Rd, Couls. 234 DG118
Lisson Grn Est NW8 272 B3
Lisson Grn Est NW8 140 DE69
Lisson Gro NW1 272 B5
Lisson Gro NW1 140 DE70
Lisson Gro NW8 272 A3
Lisson Gro NW8 140 DD69
Lisson St NW1 272 B6
Lisson St NW1 140 DE71
Lister Av, Rom. 106 FK54
Lister Cl W3 138 CR71
Lister Cl, Mitch. 200 DE95
Lister Ct NW9 96 CS54
Pasteur Cl
Lister Gdns N18 100 DQ50
Lister Ho SE3 164 EE79
Lister Rd E11 124 EE60
Lister Rd, Til. 171 GG82
Lister Wk SE28 146 EX73
Haldane Rd
Liston Ct, Wdf.Grn. 102 EJ52
Navestock Cres
Liston Rd N17 100 DU53
Liston Rd SW4 161 DJ83
Liston Way, Wdf.Grn. 102 EJ52
Listowel Cl SW9 161 DN80
Mandela St
Listowel Rd, Dag. 126 FA62
Listria Pk N16 122 DS61
Litcham Spur, Slou. 131 AR72
Litchfield Av E15 144 EE65
Litchfield Av, Mord. 199 CZ101
Litchfield Gdns NW10 139 CU65
Litchfield Rd, Sutt. 218 DC105
Litchfield St WC2 273 N10
Litchfield St WC2 141 DK73
Litchfield Way NW11 120 DB57
Litchfield Way, Guil. 258 AT136
Lithos Rd NW3 140 DB65
Little Acre, Beck. 203 EA97
Little Acre, St.Alb. 43 CD17
Little Acres, Ware 33 DX07
Little Albany St NW1 273 J4
Little Argyll St W1 273 K9
Little Aston Rd, Rom. 106 FM52
Little Belhus Cl, S.Ock. 149 FU70
Little Benty, West Dr. 154 BK78
Little Berkhamsted La, Hert. 47 DH20
Little Birch Cl (New Haw), Add. 212 BK109
Little Birches, Sid. 185 ES89
Little Boltons, The SW5 160 DB78
Little Boltons, The SW10 160 DB78
Little Bookham Common (Bookham), Lthd. 230 BY122
Little Bookham St (Bookham), Lthd. 230 BZ124
Little Bornes SE21 182 DS91
Little Borough (Brockham), Bet. 264 CN135
Little Brays, Harl. 52 EU16
Little Br Rd, Berk. 38 AX19
Little Britain EC1 274 G7
Little Britain EC1 141 DP71
Little Brook Rd, Harl. 50 EJ15
Little Brownings SE23 182 DV89
Little Buntings, Wind. 151 AM83
Little Burrow, Welw.G.C. 29 CX11
Little Bury St N9 100 DR46
Little Bushey La, Bushey 77 CD44
Little Bushey La Footpath, Bushey 95 CD45
Little Bushey La
Little Catherells, Hem.H. 39 BE18
Little Cattins, Harl. 51 EM19
Little Cedars N12 98 DC49
Woodside Av
Little Chapels Way, Slou. 131 AN74
Little Chester St SW1 276 G6
Little Chester St SW1 161 DH76
Little Cloisters SW1 161 DK76
Tufton St
Little Coll La EC4 142 DR73
Garlick Hill
Little Coll St SW1 277 P6
Little Collins, Red. 267 DP144
Little Common, Stan. 95 CG48
Little Common La (Bletchingley), Red. 251 DP132
Little Ct, W.Wick. 204 EE103
Little Cranmore La (West Horsley), Lthd. 245 BP128
Little Dean's Yd SW1 277 P6
Little Dell, Welw.G.C. 29 CX07
Little Dimocks SW12 181 DH89
Little Dormers, Ger.Cr. 113 AZ56
Little Dorrit Ct SE1 279 J4
Little Dorrit Ct SE1 162 DQ75
Little Dragons, Loug. 84 EK42
Little Ealing La W5 157 CJ77
Little Edward St NW1 273 J2
Little Elms, Hayes 155 BR80
Little Essex St WC2 274 D10
Little Ferry Rd, Twick. 177 CH88
Ferry Rd
Little Friday Rd E4 102 EE47
Little Ganett, Welw.G.C. 30 DB11
Little Gaynes Gdns, Upmin. 128 FP63
Little Gaynes La, Upmin. 128 FM63
Little Gearies, Ilf. 125 EP56
Little George St SW1 277 P5
Little Gerpins La, Upmin. 148 FM67
Little Gra, Grnf. 137 CG69
Perivale La
Little Graylings, Abb.L. 59 BS33
Little Grn, Rich. 157 CK84
Little Grn La, Cher. 193 BE104
Little Grn La, Rick. 75 BP41
Little Grn St NW5 121 DH63
College La
Little Greencroft, Chesh. 54 AN27
Little Gregories La, Epp. 85 ER35
Little Gro, Bushey 76 CB42
Little Gro Av (Cheshunt), Wal.Cr. 66 DS27
Little Gro Fld, Harl. 51 EQ15
Little Halliards, Walt. 195 BU100
Felix Rd
Little Hardings, Welw.G.C. 30 DC08
Little Hayes, Kings L. 58 BN29
Little Heath SE7 164 EL79
Little Heath, Rom. 126 EV56
Little Heath La, Berk. 39 BB21
Little Heath La (Chobham), Wok. 210 AS109
Little Heath Rd, Bexh. 166 EZ81
Little Heath Rd (Chobham), Wok. 210 AS109
Little Henleys, Ware 34 EK06
Little Hide, Guil. 243 BB132
Little Hill, Rick. 73 BC44
Little Hivings, Chesh. 54 AN27
Little How Cft, Abb.L. 59 BQ31
Little Ilford La E12 125 EM63
Little Julians Hill, Sev. 256 FG128
Little Kiln, Gdmg. 258 AS143
Little Lake, Welw.G.C. 30 DB12
Little Ley, Welw.G.C. 29 CY12
Little London (Albury), Guil. 260 BL141
Little Marlborough St W1 273 K9
Little Martins, Bushey 76 CB43
Little Mead, Hat. 45 CV15
Little Mead, Wok. 226 AT116
Little Mimms, Hem.H. 40 BK19
Little Moreton Cl, W.Byf. 212 BH112
Little Moss La, Pnr. 94 BY54
Little Mundells, Welw.G.C. 29 CZ07
Little New St EC4 274 E8
Little Newport St WC2 273 N10
Little Newport St WC2 141 DK73
Little Orchard (Woodham), Add. 211 BF111
Little Orchard, Hem.H. 40 BN18
Little Orchard, Wok. 211 BA114
Little Orchard Cl, Abb.L. 59 BR32
Little Orchard Cl, Pnr. 94 BY54
Barrow Pt La
Little Orchard Way (Shalford), Guil. 258 AY141
Little Oxhey La, Wat. 94 BX50
Little Pk (Bovingdon), Hem.H. 57 BA28
Little Pk Dr, Felt. 176 BX89
Little Pk Gdns, Enf. 82 DQ41
Little Pipers Cl (Cheshunt), Wal.Cr. 65 DP29
Little Plucketts Way, Buck.H. 102 EJ46
Little Portland St W1 273 K8
Little Portland St W1 141 DH72
Little Potters, Bushey 95 CD45

Little Pynchons, Harl. 52 EU18
Little Queen St, Dart. 188 FM87
Little Queens Rd, Tedd. 177 CF93
Little Redlands, Brom. 204 EL96
Little Reeves Av, Amer. 72 AT39
Little Ridge, Welw.G.C. 30 DA09
Little Riding, Wok. 227 BB116
Little Rivers, Welw.G.C. 30 DA08
Little Rd, Croy. 202 DS102
Lower Addiscombe Rd
Little Rd, Hayes 155 BT75
Little Rd, Hem.H. 40 BM19
Little Roke Av, Ken. 219 DP114
Little Roke Rd, Ken. 220 DQ114
Little Russell St WC1 273 P7
Little Russell St WC1 141 DL71
Little Russets, Brwd. 109 GE45
Hutton Village
Little St. James's St SW1 277 K3
Little St. James's St SW1 141 DJ74
Little St. Leonards SW14 158 CQ83
Little Sanctuary SW1 277 N5
Little Shardeloes, Amer. 55 AN39
Little Smith St SW1 277 N6
Little Somerset St E1 275 P9
Little Spring, Chesh. 54 AP28
Little Strand NW9 97 CT54
Little Stream Cl, Nthwd. 93 BS50
Little St, Guil. 242 AV130
Little St, Wal.Abb. 83 EB36
Greenwich Way
Little Sutton La, Slou. 153 BC78
Little Thistle, Welw.G.C. 30 DC12
Little Thrift, Orp. 205 EQ98
Little Titchfield St W1 273 K7
Little Trinity La EC4 275 J10
Little Turnstile WC1 274 B7
Little Wade, Welw.G.C. 29 CZ12
Little Wk, Harl. 51 EQ15
Little Warren Cl, Guil. 259 BB136
Little Widbury, Ware 33 DZ06
Little Widbury La, Ware 33 DZ06
Little Windmill Hill, Kings L. 57 BE32
Little Wd Cl, Orp. 206 EU95
Little Woodcote Est, Cars. 218 DG111
Woodmansterne La
Little Woodcote Est, Wall. 218 DG111
Woodmansterne La
Little Woodcote La, Cars. 219 DH112
Little Woodcote La, Pur. 219 DH112
Little Woodcote La, Wall. 219 DH112
Little Woodlands, Wind. 151 AM83
Little Youngs, Welw.G.C. 29 CW09
Littlebrook Av, Slou. 131 AL70
Littlebrook Cl, Croy. 203 DX100
Littlebrook Gdns (Cheshunt), Wal.Cr. 66 DW30
Littlebrook Manor Way, Dart. 188 FN85
Littlebury Rd SW4 161 DK83
Littlecombe SE7 164 EH79
Littlecombe Cl SW15 179 CX86
Littlecote Cl SW19 179 CX87
Littlecote Pl, Pnr. 94 BY53
Littlecourt Rd, Sev. 256 FG124
Littlecroft SE9 165 EN83
Littlecroft (Istead Ri), Grav. 190 GE94
Littlecroft Rd, Egh. 173 AZ92
Littledale SE2 166 EU79
Littledale, Dart. 188 FQ90
Littledown Rd, Slou. 132 AT74
Littlefield Cl N19 121 DJ63
Tufnell Pk Rd
Littlefield Cl, Kings.T. 198 CL96
Fairfield W
Littlefield Rd, Edg. 96 CQ52
Littleford La, Guil. 259 BE142
Littlegrove, Barn. 80 DE44
Littleheath La, Cob. 214 CA114
Littleheath Rd, S.Croy. 220 DV108
Littlehorse La, Ware 33 DX05
Littlejohn Rd W7 137 CF72
Littlejohn Rd, Orp. 206 EU100
Littlemead, Esher 215 CD105
Littlemede SE9 185 EM90
Littlemoor Rd, Ilf. 125 ER62
Littlemore Rd SE2 166 EU75
Littleport Spur, Slou. 132 AS72
Littlers Cl SW19 200 DD95
Runnymede
Littlestock Rd (Cheshunt), Wal.Cr. 66 DR26
Littlestone Cl, Beck. 183 EA93
Abbey La
Littleton Av E4 102 EF46
Littleton Cres, Har. 117 CF61
Littleton La (Littleton), Guil. 258 AU139
Littleton La, Reig. 265 CX136
Littleton La, Shep. 194 BK101
Littleton Rd, Ashf. 175 BQ94
Littleton Rd, Har. 117 CF61
Littleton St SW18 180 DC89
Littlewick Rd, Wok. 210 AW114
Littlewood SE13 183 EC85
Littlewood, Sev. 257 FJ122
Littlewood Cl W13 157 CH76
Littleworth Av, Esher 215 CD106
Littleworth Common Rd, Esher 197 CD104
Littleworth La, Esher 215 CD105
Littleworth Pl, Esher 215 CD105
Littleworth Rd, Esher 215 CE105
Littleworth Rd (Burnham), Slou. 111 AK61
Litton Ct (Loudwater), H.Wyc. 88 AC53
Livermere Rd E8 142 DT67
Liverpool Gro SE17 162 DR78
Liverpool Rd E10 123 EC58
Liverpool Rd E16 144 EE71
Liverpool Rd N1 141 DN68
Liverpool Rd N7 121 DN64
Liverpool Rd W5 157 CK75
Liverpool Rd, Kings.T. 178 CN94
Liverpool Rd, St.Alb. 43 CE20
Liverpool Rd, Slou. 131 AP72
Liverpool Rd, Th.Hth. 202 DQ97
Liverpool Rd, Wat. 75 BV43
Liverpool St EC2 275 M7
Liverpool St EC2 142 DS71
Livesey Cl, Kings.T. 198 CM97
Livesey Pl SE15 162 DU79
Peckham Pk Rd
Livingston Coll Twrs E10 123 EC58
Essex Rd
Livingstone Ct E10 123 EC58
Matlock Rd
Livingstone Ct, Barn. 79 CY40
Christchurch La
Livingstone Gdns, Grav. 191 GK92
Livingstone Pl E14 163 EC78
Ferry St
Livingstone Rd E15 143 EC67
Livingstone Rd E17 123 EB58
Livingstone Rd N13 99 DL51
Livingstone Rd SW11 160 DD83
Winstanley Rd
Livingstone Rd, Cat. 236 DR122
Livingstone Rd, Grav. 191 GK92
Livingstone Rd, Houns. 156 CC84
Livingstone Rd, Sthl. 136 BX73
Livingstone Rd, Th.Hth. 202 DQ96
Livingstone Ter, Rain. 147 FE67
Livingstone Wk SW11 160 DD83
Livingstone Wk, Hem.H. 40 BM16
Livonia St W1 273 L9
Lizard St EC1 275 J3
Lizard St EC1 142 DQ69
Lizban St SE3 164 EH80
Llanbury Cl (Chalfont St. Peter), Ger.Cr. 90 AY52
Llanelly Rd NW2 119 CZ61
Llanover Rd SE18 165 EN79
Llanover Rd, Wem. 117 CK62
Llanthony Rd, Mord. 200 DD100
Llanvanor Rd NW2 119 CZ61
Llewellyn St SE16 162 DU75
Chambers St
Lloyd Av SW16 201 DL95
Lloyd Av, Couls. 218 DG114
Lloyd Baker St WC1 274 C3
Lloyd Baker St WC1 141 DM69
Lloyd Ct, Pnr. 116 BX57
Lloyd Ms, Enf. 83 EA37
Government Row
Lloyd Pk Av, Croy. 220 DT105
Lloyd Rd E6 145 EM67
Lloyd Rd E17 123 DX56
Lloyd Rd, Dag. 146 EZ65
Lloyd Rd, Wor.Pk. 199 CW104
Lloyd Sq WC1 274 D2
Lloyd Sq WC1 141 DN69
Lloyd St WC1 274 D2
Lloyd St WC1 141 DN69
Lloyd's Av EC3 275 N9
Lloyd's Av EC3 142 DS72
Lloyds Pl SE3 164 EE82
Lloyd's Row EC1 274 E3
Lloyds Way, Beck. 203 DY99
Loampit Hill SE13 163 EA82
Loampit Vale SE13 163 EB83
Loanda Cl E8 142 DT67
Clarissa St
Loates La, Wat. 76 BW41
Loats Rd SW2 181 DL86
Lobelia Cl E6 144 EL71
Sorrel Gdns
Local Board Rd, Wat. 76 BW43
Locarno Rd W3 138 CQ74
High St
Locarno Rd, Grnf. 136 CC70
Lochaber Rd SE13 164 EE84
Lochaline St W6 159 CW79
Lochan Cl, Hayes 136 BY70
Lochinvar Cl, Slou. 151 AP75
Haig Dr
Lochinvar St SW12 181 DH87
Lochmere Cl, Erith 167 FB79
Lochnagar St E14 143 EC71
Lochnell Rd, Berk. 38 AT17
Lock Av, Maid. 130 AC69
Lock Chase SE3 164 EF83
Lock Cl (Woodham), Add. 211 BE113
Lock Cl, Sthl. 156 CC75
Navigator Dr
Lock Island, Shep. 194 BN103
Lock La, Wok. 228 BH116
Lock Mead, Maid. 130 AC69
Lock Path (Dorney), Wind. 151 AL79
Lock Rd, Guil. 242 AX131
Lock Rd, Rich. 177 CJ91
Locke Cl, Rain. 147 FF65
Locke Gdns, Slou. 152 AW75
Locke King Cl, Wey. 212 BN108
Locke King Rd, Wey. 212 BN108
Locke Way, Wok. 227 AZ117
The Bdy
Lockers Pk La, Hem.H. 40 BH20
Lockesfield Pl E14 163 EB78
Lockesley Dr, Orp. 205 ET100
Lockesley Sq, Surb. 197 CK100
Locket Rd, Har. 117 CE55
Lockets Cl, Wind. 151 AK81
Lockfield Av, Enf. 83 DY40
Lockfield Dr, Wok. 226 AT118
Lockgate Cl E9 123 DZ64
Lee Conservancy Rd
Lockhart Cl N7 141 DM65
Lockhart Cl, Enf. 82 DV43
Derby Rd
Lockhart Rd, Cob. 214 BW113
Lockhart St E3 143 DZ70
Lockhurst St E5 123 DX63
Lockhurstshatch La (Farley Grn), Guil. 260 BM144
Lockie Pl SE25 202 DU97
Lockier Wk, Wem. 117 CK62
Lockington Rd SW8 161 DH81
Lockley Cres, Hat. 45 CV16
Lockmead Rd N15 122 DU58
Lockmead Rd SE13 163 EC83
Lockner Holt (Chilworth), Guil. 259 BF141
Locks La, Mitch. 200 DF95
Locksley Dr, Wok. 226 AT118
Robin Hood Rd
Locksley Est E14 143 DZ72
Locksley St E14 143 DZ71
Locksmeade Rd, Rich. 177 CJ91
Lockswood Cl, Barn. 80 DF42
Lockwood Cl SE26 183 DX91
Lockwood Ind Pk N17 122 DV55
Lockwood Path, Wok. 211 BD113
Lockwood Sq SE16 162 DV76
Lockwood Wk, Rom. 127 FE57
Lockwood Way E17 101 DX54
Lockwood Way, Chess. 216 CN106
Lockyer Est SE1 279 L4
Lockyer Rd, Purf. 168 FQ79
Lockyer St SE1 279 L5
Loddiges Rd E9 142 DW66
Loddon Spur, Slou. 132 AS73
Loder Cl, Wok. 211 BD113
Loder St SE15 162 DW81
Lodge Av SW14 158 CS83
Lodge Av, Borwd. 78 CM43
Lodge Av, Croy. 201 DN104
Lodge Av, Dag. 146 EU67
Lodge Av, Dart. 188 FJ86
Lodge Av, Har. 118 CL56
Lodge Av, Rom. 127 FG56
Lodge Cl N18 100 DQ50
Lodge Cl, Brwd. 109 GE45
Lodge Cl, Chig. 104 EU48
Lodge Cl (Stoke D'Abernon), Cob. 230 BZ115
Lodge Cl (North Holmwood), Dor. 263 CJ140
Lodge Cl, Edg. 96 CM51
Lodge Cl (Englefield Grn), Egh. 172 AX92
Lodge Cl, Epsom 217 CW110
Howell Hill Gro
Lodge Cl, Hert. 32 DQ07
Lodge Cl, Islw. 157 CH81
Lodge Cl (Fetcham), Lthd. 231 CD122
Lodge Cl, Orp. 206 EV102
Lodge Cl, Slou. 151 AQ75
Lodge Cl, Uxb. 134 BJ70
Lodge Cl, Wall. 200 DG102
Lodge Ct, Horn. 128 FL61
Lodge Ct, Wem. 118 CL64
Lodge Cres, Orp. 206 EV102
Lodge Cres, Wal.Cr. 67 DX34
Lodge Dr N13 99 DN49
Lodge Dr, Hat. 45 CX15
Lodge Dr, Rick. 74 BJ42
Lodge End, Rad. 61 CH34
Lodge End, Rick. 75 BR42
Lodge Gdns, Beck. 203 DZ99
Lodge Hall, Harl. 51 ES19
Lodge Hill SE2 166 EV80
Lodge Hill, Ilf. 124 EL56
Lodge Hill, Pur. 235 DN115
Lodge Hill, Well. 166 EV80
Lodge La N12 98 DC50
Lodge La, Bex. 186 EX86
Lodge La, Ch.St.G. 73 AZ41
Lodge La (New Addington), Croy. 221 EA107
Lodge La (Holmwood), Dor. 264 CL144
Lodge La, Grays 170 GA75
Lodge La, Red. 266 DE143
Lodge La, Rom. 104 FA52
Lodge La, Wal.Abb. 83 ED35
Lodge La, West. 255 EQ127
Lodge Pl, Sutt. 218 DB106
Lodge Rd NW4 119 CW56
Lodge Rd NW8 272 A3
Lodge Rd NW8 140 DD69
Lodge Rd, Brom. 184 EH94
Lodge Rd, Croy. 201 DP100
Lodge Rd (Fetcham), Lthd. 230 CC122
Lodge Rd, Sutt. 218 DB106
Throwley Way
Lodge Rd, Wall. 219 DH106
Lodge Vil, Wdf.Grn. 102 EF52
Lodge Way, Ashf. 174 BL89
Lodge Way, Shep. 195 BQ96
Lodge Way, Wind. 151 AL83
Lodgebottom Rd, Lthd. 248 CM127
Lodgefield, Welw.G.C. 29 CY06
Lodgehill Pk Cl, Har. 116 CB61
Lodore Gdns NW9 118 CS57
Lodore Grn, Uxb. 114 BL62
Lodore St E14 143 EC72
Loewen Rd, Grays 171 GG76
Lofthouse Pl, Chess. 215 CJ107
Loftie St SE16 162 DU75
Lofting Rd N1 141 DM66
Loftus Rd W12 139 CV74
Logan Cl, Enf. 83 DX39
Logan Cl, Houns. 156 BZ83
Logan Ct, Rom. 127 FE57
Logan Ms
Logan Ms W8 160 DA77
Logan Ms, Rom. 127 FE57
Logan Pl W8 160 DA77
Logan Rd N9 100 DV47
Logan Rd, Wem. 118 CL61
Loggetts, The SE21 182 DS89
Logmore La, Dor. 262 CB138
Logs Hill, Brom. 184 EL94
Logs Hill, Chis. 184 EL94
Logs Hill Cl, Chis. 204 EL95
Lois Dr, Shep. 195 BP99
Lolesworth Cl E1 142 DT71
Commercial St
Lollard St SE11 278 C8
Lollard St SE11 161 DM77
Lollards Cl, Amer. 55 AQ37
Lollesworth La (West Horsley), Lthd. 245 BQ126
Loman Path, S.Ock. 149 FT72
Loman St SE1 278 G4
Loman St SE1 161 DP75
Lomas Cl, Croy. 221 EC108
Lomas Ct E8 142 DT66
Lomas St E1 142 DU71
Lombard Av, Enf. 82 DW39
Lombard Av, Ilf. 125 ES60
Lombard Business Pk SW19 200 DC96
Lombard Ct EC3 275 L10
Lombard Ct W3 138 CP74
Crown St
Lombard La EC4 274 E9
Lombard Rd N11 99 DH50
Lombard Rd SW11 160 DD82
Lombard Rd SW19 200 DB96
Lombard St EC3 275 L9
Lombard St EC3 142 DR72
Lombard St (Horton Kirby), Dart. 208 FQ99
Lombard Wall SE7 164 EH76
Lombards, The, Horn. 128 FM59
Lombardy Cl, Hem.H. 41 BR21
Lombardy Cl, Wok. 226 AT117
Nethercote Av
Lombardy Dr, Berk. 38 AX20
Lombardy Pl W2 140 DB73
Bark Pl
Lombardy Retail Pk, Hayes 135 BV73
Lombardy Way, Borwd. 78 CL39
Lomond Cl N15 122 DS56
Lomond Cl, Wem. 138 CM66
Lomond Gdns, S.Croy. 221 DY108
Lomond Gro SE5 162 DR80
Lomond Rd, Hem.H. 40 BK16
Loncin Mead Av (New Haw), Add. 212 BJ109
Loncroft Rd SE5 162 DS79
Londesborough Rd N16 122 DS63
London Br EC4 279 L2
London Br EC4 142 DR74
London Br SE1 279 L2
London Br SE1 142 DR74
London Br St SE1 279 K3
London Br St SE1 142 DR74
London Br Wk SE1 279 L2
London Br Wk SE1 142 DS74
London City Airport E16 145 EM74
London Colney Bypass, St.Alb. 61 CK25
London End, Beac. 89 AM54
London Flds E8 142 DV66
London Flds E Side E8 142 DV66
London Flds W Side E8 142 DU66
London La E8 142 DV66
London La, Brom. 184 EF94
London La (Shere), Guil. 260 BN138
London La, Lthd. 245 BU131
London Ms W2 272 A9
London Rd E13 144 EG68
London Rd SE1 278 F6
London Rd SE1 161 DP76
London Rd SE23 182 DU88
London Rd SW16 201 DM95
London Rd SW17 200 DF96
London Rd, Amer. 55 AQ40
London Rd, Ashf. 174 BH90
London Rd, Bark. 145 EP66
London Rd, Beac. 89 AM54
London Rd, Berk. 38 AY20
London Rd, Borwd. 62 CN34
London Rd, Brent. 157 CJ80
London Rd, Brwd. 108 FT49
London Rd, Brom. 184 EF94
London Rd, Bushey 76 BY44
London Rd, Cat. 236 DR123
London Rd, Ch.St.G. 90 AW47
London Rd, Croy. 201 DP101
London Rd (Crayford), Dart. 187 FD85
London Rd (Farningham), Dart. 208 FL100
London Rd (Stone), Dart. 188 FP87
London Rd, Dor. 247 CJ133
London Rd (Englefield Grn), Egh. 192 AV95
London Rd, Enf. 82 DR41
London Rd, Epp. 52 EV23
London Rd, Epsom 217 CT109
London Rd, Felt. 174 BH90
London Rd, Gat. 268 DF150
London Rd (Northfleet), Grav. 190 GD86
London Rd, Grays 169 FW79
London Rd, Green. 189 FS86
London Rd, Guil. 243 BB129
London Rd (Old Harlow), Harl. 52 EV16
London Rd (Potter St), Harl. 52 EW18
London Rd (Thornwood), Harl. 52 EV23
London Rd, Har. 117 CE61
London Rd, Hem.H. 40 BK24
London Rd, Hert. 32 DT10
London Rd, H.Wyc. 88 AD54
London Rd, Houns. 157 CD83
London Rd, Islw. 157 CF82
London Rd, Kings.T. 198 CM96
London Rd, Mitch. 200 DF96
London Rd (Beddington Cor), Mitch. 200 DG101
London Rd, Mord. 200 DA99
London Rd, Ong. 87 FH36
London Rd, Rad. 62 CM33
London Rd, Red. 250 DG132
London Rd, Reig. 250 DA134
London Rd, Rick. 92 BM47
London Rd, Rom. 126 FA58
London Rd (Abridge), Rom. 85 ET42
London Rd (Stapleford Tawney), Rom. 87 FC40
London Rd, St.Alb. 43 CH24
London Rd, Saw. 52 EW15
London Rd, Sev. 256 FF123
London Rd (Halstead), Sev. 225 FB112
London Rd (Longford), Sev. 241 FD117
London Rd, Slou. 153 AZ78
London Rd (Datchet), Slou. 152 AX80
London Rd, S.Ock. 148 FM74
London Rd, Stai. 173 BF91
London Rd, Stan. 95 CJ50
London Rd, Sutt. 199 CX104
London Rd, Swan. 207 FC96
London Rd, Swans. 189 FV85
London Rd, Th.Hth. 201 DN99
London Rd, Til. 171 GH82
London Rd, Twick. 177 CG85
London Rd, Vir.W. 192 AV95
London Rd, Wall. 219 DH105
London Rd, Ware 33 DY07
London Rd, Wem. 138 CL65
London Rd, West. 255 ER125
London Rd (Send), Wok. 243 BC128
London Rd E, Amer. 72 AT42
London Rd N (Merstham), Red. 251 DH125
London Rd Purfleet, Purf. 168 FN78
London Rd S (Merstham), Red. 250 DG130
London Rd W, Amer. 55 AQ40
London Rd W Thurrock, Grays 169 FS79
London Sq, Guil. 242 AY134
London Stile W4 158 CN78
Wellesley Rd
London St EC3 275 N10
London St W2 272 A9
London St W2 140 DD72
London St, Cher. 194 BG101
London Wall EC2 275 J7
London Wall EC2 142 DQ71
London Wall Bldgs EC2 275 L7
Londons Cl, Upmin. 128 FQ64
Londrina Ter, Berk. 38 AX19
Lone Oak, Horl. 269 DP150
Lonesome La, Reig. 266 DB138
Lonesome Way SW16 201 DH95
Long Acre WC2 273 P10
Long Acre WC2 141 DL73
Long Acre, Orp. 206 EX103
Long Arrotts, Hem.H. 40 BH18
Long Banks, Harl. 51 ER19
Long Barn Cl, Wat. 59 BV32
Long Chaulden, Hem.H. 39 BE20
Long Cl (Farnham Common), Slou. 131 AP66
Long Copse Cl (Bookham), Lthd. 230 CB123
Long Ct, Purf. 168 FN77
Thamley
Long Deacon Rd E4 102 EE46
Long Dr W3 138 CS72
Long Dr, Grnf. 136 CB67
Long Dr, Ruis. 116 BX63
Long Dr (Burnham), Slou. 130 AJ69
Long Dyke, Guil. 243 BB132
Long Elms, Har. 94 CB53
Long Elms, Abb.L. 59 BR33
Long Elms Cl, Abb.L. 59 BR33
Long Elms
Long Fallow, St.Alb. 60 CA27
Long Fld NW9 96 CS52
Long Furlong Dr, Slou. 131 AN70
Long Gore, Gdmg. 258 AS142
Long Grn, Chig. 103 ES49
Long Gro (Seer Grn), Beac. 89 AQ51
Long Gro, Rom. 106 FL54
Long Gro Rd, Epsom 216 CP110
Long Hedges, Houns. 156 CA81
Long Hill (Woldingham), Cat. 237 DX121
Long John, Hem.H. 40 BM22
Long La EC1 274 G6
Long La EC1 141 DP71
Long La N2 98 DC54
Long La N3 98 DC54
Long La SE1 279 K5
Long La SE1 162 DR75
Long La, Bexh. 166 EX80
Long La, Croy. 202 DW99
Long La, Grays 170 GA75
Long La (Bovingdon), Hem.H. 57 AZ31
Long La, Rick. 91 BF47
Long La (Heronsgate), Rick. 73 BC44
Long La (Stanwell), Stai. 174 BM89
Long La, Uxb. 134 BN69
Long Ley, Harl. 51 ET15
Long Ley, Welw.G.C. 30 DC09
Long Leys E4 101 EB51
Long Lo Dr, Walt. 196 BW104
Long Mark Rd E16 144 EK71
Fulmer Rd
Long Mead NW9 97 CT53
Long Meadow NW5 121 DK64
Torriano Av
Long Meadow, Brwd. 109 GC47
Long Meadow, Chesh. 54 AQ28
Long Meadow, Lthd. 246 BZ125
Long Meadow, Rom. 106 FJ48
Long Meadow (Riverhead), Sev. 256 FD121
Long Meadow Cl, W.Wick. 203 EC101
Long Mimms, Hem.H. 40 BL19
Long Orchard Dr (Penn), H.Wyc. 88 AC47
Long Pk, Amer. 55 AQ36
Long Pk Cl, Amer. 55 AQ36
Long Pk Way, Amer. 55 AQ35
Long Pond Rd SE3 164 EE81
Long Reach (West Horsley), Lthd. 245 BP125
Long Reach (Ockham), Wok. 228 BN123
Long Reach Ct, Bark. 145 ER68
Long Readings La, Slou. 131 AP70
Long Ride, The, Hat. 45 CZ18
Long Ridings Av, Brwd. 109 GB43
Long Rd SW4 161 DJ84
Long Shaw, Lthd. 231 CG119
Long Spring (Porters Wd), St.Alb. 43 CF16
Long St E2 275 P2
Long St E2 142 DT69
Long St, Wal.Abb. 68 EL32
Long Vw, Berk. 38 AU17
Long Wk SE1 279 N6
Long Wk SE18 165 EP79
Long Wk SW13 158 CS82
Long Wk, Ch.St.G. 72 AX41
Long Wk, Epsom 233 CX119
Long Wk, Lthd. 244 BN128
Long Wk, N.Mal. 198 CQ97
Long Wk, Wal.Abb. 67 EA30
Long Wk, W.Byf. 212 BJ114
Long Wk, The, Wind. 151 AR83
Long Wd Dr (Jordans), Beac. 90 AT51
Long Yd WC1 274 B5
Long Yd WC1 141 DM70
Longacre, Harl. 36 EV11
Longacre Pl, Cars. 218 DG107
Beddington Gdns
Longacre Rd E17 101 ED53
Longacres, St.Alb. 43 CK20
Longaford Way, Brwd. 109 GB46
Longbeach Rd SW11 160 DF83
Longberrys NW2 119 CZ62
Longboat Row, Sthl. 136 BZ72
Longbottom La, Beac. 89 AR52
Longbourn, Wind. 151 AN83
Imperial Rd
Longbourne Grn, Gdmg. 258 AS143
Barnes Rd
Longbourne Way, Cher. 193 BF100
Longboyds, Cob. 213 BV114
Longbridge Rd, Bark. 145 EQ66
Longbridge Rd, Dag. 126 EU63
Longbridge Rd, Gat. 268 DF150
Longbridge Rd, Horl. 268 DF150
Longbridge Roundabout, Horl. 268 DF149
Longbridge Wk, Horl. 268 DF150
Longbridge Way SE13 183 EC85
Longbridge Way, Uxb. 134 BH68
Longbury Cl, Orp. 206 EV97
Longbury Dr, Orp. 206 EV97
Longchamp Cl, Horl. 269 DJ148
Carlton Tye
Longcliffe Path, Wat. 93 BU48
Gosforth La
Longcroft SE9 185 EM90
Longcroft, Wat. 93 BV45
Longcroft Av, Bans. 218 DC114
Longcroft Dr, Wal.Cr. 67 DZ34
Longcroft Gdns, Welw.G.C. 29 CX10
Longcroft Grn, Welw.G.C. 29 CX11
Longcroft La (Bovingdon), Hem.H. 57 BC28
Longcroft La, Welw.G.C. 29 CX10
Longcroft Ri, Loug. 85 EN43
Longcroft Rd, Rick. 91 BD50
Longcrofte Rd, Edg. 95 CK52
Longcrofts, Wal.Abb. 68 EE34
Roundhills
Longcross Rd (Longcross), Cher. 192 AY104
Longdean Pk, Hem.H. 40 BN24
Longdon Wd, Kes. 222 EL105
Longdown La N, Epsom 217 CU114
Longdown La S, Epsom 217 CU114
Longdown Rd SE6 183 EA91
Longdown Rd, Epsom 217 CU114
Longdown Rd, Guil. 259 BB137
Longfellow Dr, Brwd. 109 GC45
Longfellow Rd E17 123 DZ58
Longfellow Rd, Wor.Pk. 199 CU103
Longfellow Way SE1 162 DT77
Chaucer Dr
Longfield, Brom. 204 EF95
Longfield, Harl. 52 EU17
Longfield, Hem.H. 41 BP22
Longfield, Loug. 84 EJ43
Longfield (Hedgerley), Slou. 111 AR61
Longfield Av E17 123 DY56
Longfield Av NW7 97 CU52
Longfield Av W5 137 CJ73
Longfield Av, Enf. 82 DW37
Longfield Av, Horn. 127 FF59
Longfield Av, Wall. 200 DG102
Longfield Av, Wem. 118 CL60
Longfield Cres SE26 182 DW90
Longfield Cres, Tad. 233 CW120
Longfield Dr SW14 178 CP85
Longfield Dr, Amer. 55 AP38
Longfield Dr, Mitch. 180 DE94
Longfield Est SE1 162 DT77
Longfield La (Cheshunt), Wal.Cr. 66 DU27

Longfield Rd W5 137 CJ73
Longfield Rd, Chesh. 54 AM29
Longfield Rd, Dor. 263 CF137
Longfield St SW18 180 DA87
Longfield Wk W5 137 CJ72
Longford Av, Felt. 175 BS86
Longford Av, Sthl. 136 CA73
Longford Av, Stai. 174 BL88
Longford Cl (Hampton Hill), Hmptn. 176 CA91
Longford Cl, Hayes 136 BX73
Longford Gdns
Longford Ct E5 123 DX63
Pedro St
Longford Ct NW4 119 CX56
Longford Ct, Epsom 216 CQ105
Longford Gdns, Hayes 136 BX73
Longford Gdns, Sutt. 200 DC104
Longford Rd, Twick. 176 CA88
Longford Roundabout, West Dr. 154 BH81
Longford St NW1 273 J4
Longford St NW1 141 DH70
Longford Wk SW2 181 DN87
Longford Way, Stai. 174 BL88
Longhayes Av, Rom. 126 EX56
Longhayes Ct, Rom. 126 EX56
Longhayes Av
Longheath Gdns, Croy. 202 DW99
Longhedge Ho SE26 182 DT91
Longhedge St SW11 160 DG82
Longhill Rd SE6 183 ED89
Longhook Gdns, Nthlt. 135 BU68
Longhope Cl SE15 162 DS79
Longhouse Rd, Grays 171 GH76
Longhurst Rd SE13 183 ED85
Longhurst Rd, Croy. 202 DV100
Longhurst Rd (East Horsley), Lthd. 245 BS129
Longland Br (Sheering), B.Stort. 37 FC07
Longland Ct SE1 162 DU78
Rolls Rd
Longland Dr N20 98 DB48
Longlands, Hem.H. 40 BN20
Longlands Av, Couls. 218 DG114
Longlands Cl (Cheshunt), Wal.Cr. 67 DX32
Longlands Ct W11 139 CZ73
Portobello Rd
Longlands Ct, Mitch. 200 DG95
Summerhill Way
Longlands Pk Cres, Sid. 185 ES90
Longlands Rd, Sid. 185 ES90
Longlands Rd, Welw.G.C. 29 CY11
Longleat Ms, Orp. 206 EW98
High St
Longleat Rd, Enf. 82 DS43
Longleat Way, Felt. 175 BR87
Longlees, Rick. 91 BC50
Longleigh La SE2 166 EW79
Longleigh La, Bexh. 166 EW79
Longlents Ho NW10 138 CR67
Longley Av, Wem. 138 CM67
Longley Rd SW17 180 DE93
Longley Rd, Croy. 201 DP101
Longley Rd, Har. 116 CC57
Longley St SE1 162 DU77
Longley Way NW2 119 CW62
Longmans Cl, Wat. 75 BQ44
Byewaters
Longmarsh Vw (Sutton at Hone), Dart. 208 FP95
Longmead, Chis. 205 EN96
Longmead, Epsom 216 CR110
Longmead, Guil. 243 BC134
Longmead, Hat. 45 CV15
Longmead, Wind. 151 AL81
Longmead Business Pk, Epsom 216 CR111
Longmead Cl, Brwd. 108 FY46
Longmead Cl, Cat. 236 DS122
Longmead Dr, Sid. 186 EX89
Longmead La, Slou. 131 AK66
Longmead Rd SW17 180 DF92
Longmead Rd, Epsom 216 CR111
Longmead Rd, Hayes 135 BT73
Longmead Rd, T.Ditt. 197 CE101
Longmeadow Rd, Sid. 185 ES88
Longmere Gdns, Tad. 233 CW119
Longmoor, Wal.Cr. 67 DY29
Longmoor Pt SW15 179 CV88
Norley Vale
Longmoore St SW1 277 K9
Longmoore St SW1 161 DJ77
Longmore Av, Barn. 80 DC44
Longmore Cl, Rick. 91 BF49
Longmore Gdns, Welw.G.C. 29 CZ09
Longmore Rd, Walt. 214 BY105
Longnor Rd E1 143 DX69
Longport Cl, Ilf. 104 EU51
Longreach Rd, Bark. 145 ET70
Longreach Rd, Erith 167 FH80
Longridge Gro, Wok. 211 BE114
Old Woking Rd
Longridge La, Sthl. 136 CB73
Longridge Rd SW5 160 DA77
Longs Cl, Wok. 228 BG116
Long's Ct WC2 273 M10
Long's Ct WC2 141 DK73
Longs Ct, Rich. 158 CM84
Crown Ter
Longsdon Way, Cat. 236 DU124
Longshaw Rd E4 101 ED48
Longshore SE8 163 DZ77
Longside Cl, Egh. 193 BC95
Longspring, Wat. 75 BV38
Longspring Wd, Sev. 256 FF130
Longstaff Cres SW18 180 DA86
Longstaff Rd SW18 180 DA86
Longstone Av NW10 139 CT66
Longstone Rd SW17 181 DH92
Longstone Rd, Iver 133 BC68
Longthornton Rd SW16 201 DJ96
Longton Av SE26 182 DU91
Longton Gro SE26 182 DV91
Longtown Cl, Rom. 106 FJ50
Longtown Rd, Rom. 106 FJ50
Longview, Beac. 110 AF55
Longview Way, Rom. 105 FD53
Longville Rd SE11 278 F8
Longwalk Rd, Uxb. 135 BP74
Longwood, Harl. 51 ER20
Longwood Business Pk, Sun. 195 BT99
Longwood Cl, Upmin. 128 FQ64
Longwood Dr SW15 179 CU86
Longwood Gdns, Ilf. 125 EM56
Longwood La, Amer. 55 AR39
Longwood Rd, Hert. 31 DM08
Longwood Rd, Ken. 236 DR116
Longworth Cl SE28 146 EX72
Longworth Dr, Maid. 130 AC70
Loning, The NW9 118 CS56
Loning, The, Enf. 82 DW38
Lonsdale, Hem.H. 40 BL17
Lonsdale Av E6 144 EK70
Lonsdale Av, Brwd. 109 GD44
Lonsdale Av, Rom. 127 FC58
Lonsdale Av, Wem. 118 CL64
Lonsdale Cl E6 144 EL70
Lonsdale Av
Lonsdale Cl SE9 184 EK90
Lonsdale Cl, Edg. 96 CM50
Orchard Dr
Lonsdale Cl, Pnr. 94 BY52
Lonsdale Cl, Uxb. 135 BQ71
Dawley Av
Lonsdale Cres, Dart. 188 FQ88
Lonsdale Cres, Ilf. 125 EP58
Lonsdale Dr, Enf. 81 DL43
Lonsdale Gdns, Th.Hth. 201 DM98
Lonsdale Ms, Rich. 158 CN81
Elizabeth Cotts
Lonsdale Pl N1 141 DN66
Barnsbury St
Lonsdale Rd E11 124 EF59
Lonsdale Rd NW6 139 CZ68
Lonsdale Rd SE25 202 DV98
Lonsdale Rd SW13 159 CU79
Lonsdale Rd W4 159 CT77
Lonsdale Rd W11 139 CZ72
Lonsdale Rd, Bexh. 166 EZ82
Lonsdale Rd, Dor. 263 CH135
Lonsdale Rd, Sthl. 156 BX76
Lonsdale Rd, Wey. 212 BN108
Lonsdale Sq N1 141 DN66
Lonsdale Way, Maid. 150 AC78
Loobert Rd N15 122 DS55
Looe Gdns, Ilf. 125 EP55
Loom Ct E1 275 N5
Loom La, Rad. 77 CG37
Loom Pl, Rad. 77 CG36
Loop Rd, Chis. 185 EQ93
Loop Rd, Epsom 232 CQ116
Woodcote Side
Loop Rd, Wal.Abb. 67 EB32
Loop Rd, Wok. 227 AZ121
Lopen Rd N18 100 DS49
Loraine Cl, Enf. 82 DW43
Loraine Gdns, Ash. 232 CL117
Loraine Rd N7 121 DM63
Loraine Rd W4 158 CP79
Lorane Ct, Wat. 75 BU40
Lord Amory Way E14 163 EC75
Lord Av, Ilf. 125 EM56
Lord Chancellor Wk, Kings.T. 198 CQ95
Lord Chatham's Ride, Sev. 240 EX117
Lord Gdns, Ilf. 124 EL56
Lord Hills Br W2 140 DB71
Porchester Rd
Lord Hills Rd W2 140 DB71
Lord Holland La SW9 161 DN81
St. Lawrence Way
Lord Knyvett Cl (Stanwell), Stai. 174 BK86
Lord Mayors Dr (Farnham Common), Slou. 111 AN64
Lord Napier Pl W6 159 CU78
Upper Mall
Lord N St SW1 277 P7
Lord N St SW1 161 DL76
Lord Roberts Ms SW6 160 DB80
Moore Pk Rd
Lord Roberts Ter SE18 165 EN78
Lord St E16 144 EL74
Lord St, Grav. 191 GH87
Lord St, Hodd. 48 DV17
Lord St, Wat. 76 BW41
Lord Warwick St SE18 165 EM76
Lordell Pl SW19 179 CW93
Lorden Wk E2 142 DU69
Lord's Cl SE21 182 DQ89
Lords Cl, Felt. 176 BY89
Lords Cl, Rad. 62 CL32
Lord's Vw NW8 272 A3
Lords Wd, Welw.G.C. 30 DC09
Lords Wd Ho, Couls. 235 DK122
Netherne La
Lordsbury Fld, Wall. 219 DJ110
Lordsgrove Cl, Tad. 233 CV120
Whitegate Way
Lordship Cl, Brwd. 109 GD46
Lordship Gro N16 122 DR61
Lordship La N17 100 DQ53
Lordship La N22 99 DN54
Lordship La SE22 182 DT86
Lordship La Est SE22 182 DU88
Lordship Pk N16 122 DQ61
Lordship Pk Ms N16 122 DQ61
Allerton Rd
Lordship Pl SW3 160 DE79
Cheyne Row
Lordship Rd N16 122 DR61
Lordship Rd, Nthlt. 136 BY66
Lordship Rd (Cheshunt), Wal.Cr. 66 DV30
Lordship Ter N16 122 DR61
Lordsmead Rd N17 100 DS53
Lordswood Cl (Lane End), Dart. 189 FS91
Lorenzo St WC1 274 B2
Lorenzo St WC1 141 DM69
Loretto Gdns, Har. 118 CL56
Lorian Cl N12 98 DB49
Lorian Dr, Reig. 250 DC133
Loriners Cl, Cob. 213 BU114
Between Sts
Loring Rd N20 98 DE47
Loring Rd, Berk. 38 AW20
Loring Rd, Islw. 157 CF82
Loring Rd, Wind. 151 AM81
Loris Rd W6 159 CW76
Lorn Ct SW9 161 DN82
Lorn Rd SW9 161 DM82
Lorne, The (Bookham), Lthd. 246 CA126
Lorne Av, Croy. 203 DX101
Lorne Cl NW8 272 C3
Lorne Cl, Slou. 151 AP76
Lorne Gdns E11 124 EJ56
Lorne Gdns W11 159 CX75
Lorne Gdns, Croy. 203 DY101
Lorne Rd E7 124 EH63
Lorne Rd E17 123 EA57
Lorne Rd N4 121 DM60
Lorne Rd, Brwd. 108 FW49
Lorne Rd, Har. 95 CF54
Lorne Rd, Rich. 178 CM85
Albert Rd
Lorraine Chase, S.Ock. 168 FM75
Lorraine Pk, Har. 95 CE52
Lorrimore Rd SE17 161 DP79
Lorrimore Sq SE17 161 DP79
Lorton Cl, Grav. 191 GL89
Loseberry Rd (Claygate), Esher 215 CD106
Loseley Pk (Littleton), Guil. 258 AT140
Loseley Rd, Gdmg. 258 AS143
Losfield Rd, Wind. 151 AL81
Lossie Dr, Iver 133 BB73
Lothair Rd W5 157 CK75
Lothair Rd N N4 121 DP58
Lothair Rd S N4 121 DN59
Lothbury EC2 275 K8
Lothbury EC2 142 DR72
Lothian Av, Hayes 135 BV71
Lothian Cl, Wem. 117 CG63
Lothian Rd SW9 161 DP81
Lothian Wd, Tad. 233 CV122
Lothrop St W10 139 CY69
Lots Rd SW10 160 DC80
Lotus Cl SE21 182 DQ90
Lotus Rd (Biggin Hill), West. 239 EM118
Loubet St SW17 180 DF93
Loudhams Rd, Amer. 72 AW39
Loudhams Wd La, Ch.St.G. 72 AX40
Loudoun Av, Ilf. 125 EP57
Loudoun Rd NW8 140 DC66
Loudoun Rd Ms NW8 140 DC67
Loudoun Rd
Loudwater Cl, Sun. 195 BU98
Loudwater Dr, Rick. 74 BJ42
Loudwater Hts, Rick. 74 BH41
Loudwater La, Rick. 74 BK42
Loudwater Ridge, Rick. 74 BJ42
Loudwater Rd, Sun. 195 BU98
Lough Rd N7 141 DM65
Loughborough Est SW9 161 DP82
Loughborough Rd
Loughborough Pk SW9 161 DP84
Loughborough Rd SW9 161 DN82
Loughborough St SE11 278 C10
Loughborough St SE11 161 DM78
Loughton Ct, Wal.Abb. 68 EH33
Loughton La, Epp. 85 ER38
Loughton Way, Buck.H. 102 EK46
Louis Ms N10 99 DH53
Louisa Gdns E1 143 DX70
Louisa St
Louisa Ho SW15 158 CS84
Louisa St E1 143 DX70
Louise Aumonier Wk N19 121 DL59
Hillrise Rd
Louise Bennett Cl SE24 161 DP84
Shakespeare Rd
Louise Ct E11 124 EH57
Grosvenor Rd
Louise Gdns, Rain. 147 FE69
Louise Rd E15 144 EE65
Louise Wk (Bovingdon), Hem.H. 57 BA28
Louisville Rd SW17 180 DG90
Louvain Rd, Green. 189 FS87
Louvain Way, Wat. 59 BV32
Louvaine Rd SW11 160 DD84
Lovage App E6 144 EL71
Lovat Cl NW2 119 CT62
Lovat La EC3 279 M1
Lovat Wk, Houns. 156 BY80
Cranford La
Lovatt Cl, Edg. 96 CP51
Lovatt Dr, Ruis. 115 BU57
Lovatts, Rick. 74 BN42
Love Grn La, Iver 133 BD71
Love Hill La, Slou. 133 BA73
Love La EC2 275 J8
Love La EC2 142 DQ72
Love La N17 100 DT52
Love La SE18 165 EP77
Love La SE25 202 DV97
Love La, Abb.L. 59 BT30
Love La, Bex. 186 EZ86
Love La, Gdse. 252 DW132
Love La, Grav. 191 GJ87
Love La, Iver 133 BD72
Love La, Kings L. 58 BL29
Love La, Mitch. 200 DE97
Love La, Mord. 200 DA101
Love La, Pnr. 116 BY55
Love La, S.Ock. 168 FQ75
Love La, Surb. 197 CK103
Love La, Sutt. 217 CY106
Love La, Tad. 249 CT126
Love La, Wdf.Grn. 103 EM51
Love Wk SE5 162 DR82
Loveday Rd W13 137 CH74
Lovegrove Dr, Slou. 131 AM70
Lovegrove St SE1 162 DU78
Lovegrove Wk E14 143 EC74
Lovejoy La, Wind. 151 AK82
Lovekyn Cl, Kings.T. 198 CM96
Queen Elizabeth Rd
Lovel Av, Well. 166 EU82
Lovel Cl, Hem.H. 40 BG20
Lovel End (Chalfont St. Peter), Ger.Cr. 90 AW52
Lovel Mead (Chalfont St. Peter), Ger.Cr. 90 AW52
Lovel Rd (Chalfont St. Peter), Ger.Cr. 90 AW52
Lovelace Av, Brom. 205 EN100
Lovelace Cl (Effingham Junct), Lthd. 229 BU123
Lovelace Dr, Wok. 227 BF115
Lovelace Gdns, Bark. 126 EU63
Lovelace Gdns, Surb. 197 CK101
Lovelace Gdns, Walt. 214 BW106
Lovelace Grn SE9 165 EM83
Lovelace Rd SE21 182 DQ89
Lovelace Rd, Barn. 98 DE45
Lovelace Rd, Surb. 197 CJ101
Lovelands La, Tad. 250 DB127
Lovelinch Cl SE15 162 DW79
Lovell Ho E8 142 DU67
Lovell Pl SE16 163 DY76
Ropemaker Rd
Lovell Rd, Enf. 82 DV35
Lovell Rd, Rich. 177 CJ90
Lovell Rd, Sthl. 136 CB72
Lovell Wk, Rain. 147 FG65
Lovelock Cl, Ken. 236 DQ117
Loveridge Ms NW6 139 CZ65
Loveridge Rd
Loveridge Rd NW6 139 CZ65
Lovering Rd (Cheshunt), Wal.Cr. 66 DQ26
Lovers La, Green. 169 FX84
Lovers Wk N3 98 DA52
Lovers Wk NW7 97 CZ51
Lovers Wk SE10 164 EE79
Lover's Wk W1 276 F2
Lover's Wk W1 140 DG74
Lovet Rd, Harl. 51 EN16
Lovett Dr, Cars. 200 DC101
Lovett Gdns, Maid. 130 AC68
Lovett Rd, Stai. 173 BB91
Lovett Rd (Harefield), Uxb. 114 BJ55
Lovett Way NW10 118 CQ64
Lovett's Pl SW18 160 DB84
Old York Rd
Lovibonds Av, Orp. 205 EP104
Lovibonds Av, West Dr. 134 BM72
Low Cl, Green. 189 FU85
Low Cross Wd La SE21 182 DT90
Low Hall Cl E4 101 EA45
Low Hall La E17 123 DY58
Low Hill Rd, Harl. 50 EF17
Low Rd, Hat. 46 DF15
Low St La, Til. 171 GM78
Lowbell La (London Colney), St.Alb. 62 CL27
Lowbrook Rd, Ilf. 125 EP64
Lowburys, Dor. 263 CH139
Lowdell Cl, West Dr. 134 BL72
Lowden Rd N9 100 DV46
Lowden Rd SE24 161 DP84
Lowden Rd, Sthl. 136 BY73
Lowe, The, Chig. 104 EU50
Lowe Av E16 144 EG71
Lowe Cl, Chig. 104 EU50
Lowell St E14 143 DY72
Lowen Rd, Rain. 147 FD68
Lower Aberdeen Wf E14 143 DZ74
Lower Addiscombe Rd, Croy. 202 DS102
Lower Addison Gdns W14 159 CY75
Lower Adeyfield Rd, Hem.H. 40 BK19
Lower Alderton Hall La, Loug. 85 EN43
Lower Barn, Hem.H. 40 BM23
Lower Barn Rd, Pur. 220 DR112
Lower Bedfords Rd, Rom. 105 FE51
Lower Belgrave St SW1 277 H7
Lower Belgrave St SW1 161 DH76
Lower Bobbingworth Grn, Ong. 53 FG24
Lower Boston Rd W7 137 CE74
Lower Br Rd, Red. 250 DF134
Lower Britwell Rd, Slou. 131 AK70
Lower Broad St, Dag. 146 FA67
Lower Bury La, Epp. 69 ES31
Lower Camden, Chis. 185 EM94
Lower Ch Hill, Green. 189 FS85
Lower Ch St, Croy. 201 DP103
Waddon New Rd
Lower Cippenham La, Slou. 131 AL74
Lower Clabdens, Ware 33 DZ06
Lower Clapton Rd E5 122 DV64
Lower Clarendon Wk W11 139 CY72
Lancaster Rd
Lower Common S SW15 159 CV83
Lower Coombe St, Croy. 220 DQ105
Lower Ct Rd, Epsom 216 CQ111
Lower Cft, Swan. 207 FF98
Lower Dagnall St, St.Alb. 42 CC20
Lower Downs Rd SW20 199 CX95
Lower Drayton Pl, Croy. 201 DP103
Drayton Rd
Lower Dr, Beac. 89 AK50
Lower Dunnymans, Bans. 217 CZ114
Basing Rd
Lower Edgeborough Rd, Guil. 259 AZ135
Lower Emms, Hem.H. 41 BQ15
Hunters Oak
Lower Fm Rd (Effingham), Lthd. 229 BV124
Lower George St, Rich. 177 CK85
George St
Lower Gravel Rd, Brom. 204 EL102
Lower Grn, Welw. 30 DE05
Lower Grn Rd, Esher 196 CB103
Lower Grn W, Mitch. 200 DE97
Lower Grosvenor Pl SW1 277 H6
Lower Grosvenor Pl SW1 161 DH76
Lower Gro Rd, Rich. 178 CM86
Lower Guild Hall (Bluewater), Green. 189 FU88
Bluewater Parkway
Lower Hall La E4 101 DY50
Lower Ham Rd, Kings.T. 177 CK93
Lower Hampton Rd, Sun. 196 BW97
Lower Hatfield Rd, Hert. 47 DK15
Lower High St, Wat. 76 BX43
Lower Higham Rd, Grav. 191 GM88
Lower Hill Rd, Epsom 216 CP112
Lower James St W1 273 L10
Lower John St W1 273 L10
Lower Kenwood Av, Enf. 81 DK43
Lower Kings Rd, Berk. 38 AW19
Lower Lea Crossing E14 144 EE73
Lower Lea Crossing E16 144 EE73
Lower Lees Rd, Slou. 131 AN69
Lower Maidstone Rd N11 99 DJ51
Telford Rd
Lower Mall W6 159 CV78
Lower Mardyke Av, Rain. 147 FC68
Lower Marsh SE1 278 D5
Lower Marsh SE1 161 DN75
Lower Marsh La, Kings.T. 198 CM98
Lower Mead, Iver 133 BD69
Lower Meadow, Harl. 51 ES19
Lower Meadow, Wal.Cr. 67 DX27
Lower Merton Ri NW3 140 DE66
Lower Morden La, Mord. 199 CW100
Lower Mortlake Rd, Rich. 158 CL84
Lower Noke Cl, Brwd. 106 FL47
Lower Northfield, Bans. 217 CZ114
Lower Paddock Rd, Wat. 76 BY44
Lower Pk Rd N11 99 DJ50
Lower Pk Rd, Belv. 166 FA76
Lower Pk Rd, Couls. 234 DE118
Lower Pk Rd, Loug. 84 EK43
Lower Paxton Rd, St.Alb. 43 CE21
Lower Peryers (East Horsley), Lthd. 245 BS128
Lower Pillory Down, Cars. 218 DG113
Lower Plantation, Rick. 74 BJ41
Lower Queens Rd, Buck.H. 102 EK47
Lower Range Rd, Grav. 191 GL87
Lower Richmond Rd SW14 158 CP83
Lower Richmond Rd SW15 159 CW83
Lower Richmond Rd, Rich. 158 CN83
Lower Riding, Beac. 88 AH53
Lower Rd SE8 162 DW76
Lower Rd SE16 162 DW76
Lower Rd, Belv. 167 FB76
Lower Rd, Brwd. 109 GD41
Lower Rd, Erith 167 FD77
Lower Rd, Ger.Cr. 90 AY53
Lower Rd (Northfleet), Grav. 170 FY84
Lower Rd, Har. 117 CD60
Lower Rd, Hem.H. 58 BN25
Lower Rd, Ken. 219 DP113
Lower Rd (Fetcham), Lthd. 231 CD123
Lower Rd, Loug. 85 EN40
Lower Rd, Orp. 206 EV100
Lower Rd, Red. 266 DD136
Lower Rd, Rick. 73 BC42
Lower Rd, Sutt. 218 DC105
Lower Rd, Swan. 187 FF94
Lower Rd, Til. 171 GG84
Lower Rd (Denham), Uxb. 113 BC59
Lower Rd, Ware 33 DZ08
Lower Robert St WC2 141 DL73
John Adam St
Lower Rose Gall (Bluewater), Green. 189 FU88
Bluewater Parkway
Lower Sales, Hem.H. 39 BF21
Lower Sand Hills, T.Ditt. 197 CK101
Lower Sandfields (Send), Wok. 227 BD124
Lower Sawley Wd, Bans. 217 CZ114
Upper Sawley Wd
Lower Shott (Bookham), Lthd. 246 CA126
Lower Shott (Cheshunt), Wal.Cr. 66 DT26
Lower Sloane St SW1 276 F9
Lower Sloane St SW1 160 DG77
Lower Sq, Islw. 157 CH83
Lower Sta Rd (Crayford), Dart. 187 FE86
Lower Strand NW9 97 CT54
Lower St (Shere), Guil. 260 BN139
Lower Sunbury Rd, Hmptn. 196 BZ96
Lower Swaines, Epp. 69 ES30
Lower Sydenham Ind Est SE26 183 DZ92
Lower Tail, Wat. 94 BY48
Lower Talbot Wk W11 139 CY72
Lancaster Rd
Lower Teddington Rd, Kings.T. 197 CK95
Lower Ter NW3 120 DC62
Lower Thames St EC3 279 L1
Lower Thames St EC3 142 DR73
Lower Thames Wk (Bluewater), Green. 189 FU88
Bluewater Parkway
Lower Tub, Bushey 95 CD45
Lower Wd Rd (Claygate), Esher 215 CG107
Lower Woodside, Hat. 45 CZ22
Lower Yott, Hem.H. 40 BM21
Lowerfield, Welw.G.C. 30 DA10
Lowestoft Cl E5 122 DW61
Theydon Rd
Lowestoft Dr, Slou. 130 AJ72
Lowestoft Ms E16 165 EP75
Lowestoft Rd, Wat. 75 BV39
Loweswater Cl, Wat. 60 BW33
Loweswater Cl, Wem. 117 CK61
Lowfield, Saw. 36 EX06
Lowfield La, Hodd. 49 EA17
Lowfield Rd NW6 140 DA66
Lowfield Rd W3 138 CQ72
Lowfield St, Dart. 188 FL88
Lowick Rd, Har. 117 CE56
Lowlands, Hat. 45 CW15
Lowlands Dr (Stanwell), Stai. 174 BK85
Lowlands Gdns, Rom. 127 FB58
Lowlands Rd, Har. 117 CE59
Lowlands Rd, Pnr. 116 BW59
Lowlands Rd, S.Ock. 148 FP74
Lowman Rd N7 121 DM63
Lowndes Av, Chesh. 54 AP30
Lowndes Cl SW1 276 G7
Lowndes Cl SW1 160 DG76
Lowndes Ct W1 273 K9
Lowndes Ct, Brom. 204 EG96
Queens Rd
Lowndes Pl SW1 276 F7
Lowndes Pl SW1 160 DG76
Lowndes Sq SW1 276 E5
Lowndes Sq SW1 160 DF75
Lowndes St SW1 276 E6
Lowndes St SW1 160 DG76
Lowood Ct SE19 182 DT92
Lowood St E1 142 DV73
Dellow St
Lowry Cl, Erith 167 FD77
Lowry Cres, Mitch. 200 DE96
Lowry Rd, Dag. 126 EV63
Lowshoe La, Rom. 105 FB53
Lowson Gro, Wat. 94 BY45
Lowswood Cl, Nthwd. 93 BQ53
Lowth Rd SE5 162 DQ82
Lowther Cl, Borwd. 78 CM43
Lowther Dr, Enf. 81 DL42
Lowther Gdns SW7 276 A5
Lowther Gdns SW7 160 DD75
Lowther Hill SE23 183 DY87
Lowther Rd E17 101 DY54
Lowther Rd N7 121 DN64
Mackenzie Rd
Lowther Rd SW13 159 CT81
Lowther Rd, Kings.T. 198 CM95
Lowther Rd, Stan. 118 CM55
Lowthorpe, Wok. 226 AU118
Shilburn Way
Loxford Av E6 144 EK68
Loxford La, Ilf. 125 EQ64
Loxford Rd, Bark. 145 EP65
Loxford Rd, Cat. 252 DT125
Loxford Ter, Bark. 145 EQ65
Fanshawe Av
Loxford Way, Cat. 252 DT125
Loxham Rd E4 101 EA52
Loxham St WC1 274 A3
Loxley Cl SE26 183 DX92
Loxley Cl, Ware 33 DY06
Crane Mead
Loxley Rd SW18 180 DD88
Loxley Rd, Berk. 38 AS17
Loxley Rd, Hmptn. 176 BZ91
Loxton Rd SE23 183 DX88
Loxwood Cl, Felt. 175 BR88
Loxwood Cl, Orp. 206 EX103
Loxwood Rd N17 122 DS55
Lubbock Rd, Chis. 185 EM94
Lubbock St SE14 162 DW80
Lucan Dr, Stai. 174 BK94
Lucan Pl SW3 276 B9
Lucan Pl SW3 160 DE77
Lucan Rd, Barn. 79 CY41
Lucas Av E13 144 EH67
Lucas Av, Har. 116 CA61
Lucas Cl NW10 139 CU66
Pound La
Lucas Ct, Har. 116 CA60
Lucas Ct, Wal.Abb. 68 EF33
Lucas Gdns N2 98 DC54
Lucas Rd SE20 182 DW93
Lucas Rd, Grays 170 GA76
Lucas Sq NW11 120 DA58
Hampstead Way
Lucas St SE8 163 EA81
Lucern Cl (Cheshunt), Wal.Cr. 66 DS27
Lucerne Cl N13 99 DL49
Lucerne Cl, Wok. 226 AY119
Claremont Av
Lucerne Ct, Erith 166 EY76
Middle Way

Lucerne Gro E17 123 ED56
Lucerne Ms W8 140 DA74
Kensington Mall
Lucerne Rd N5 121 DP63
Lucerne Rd, Orp. 205 ET102
Lucerne Rd, Th.Hth. 201 DP99
Lucerne Way, Rom. 106 FK51
Lucey Rd SE16 162 DU76
Lucey Way SE16 162 DU76
Linsey St
Lucie Av, Ashf. 175 BP93
Lucien Rd SW17 180 DG91
Lucien Rd SW19 180 DB89
Lucknow St SE18 165 ES80
Lucks Hill, Hem.H. 39 BE20
Lucorn Cl SE12 184 EF86
Lucton Ms, Loug. 85 EP42
Luctons Av, Buck.H. 102 EJ46
Lucy Cres W3 138 CQ71
Lucy Gdns, Dag. 126 EY62
Grafton Rd
Luddesdon Rd, Erith 166 FA80
Luddington Av, Vir.W. 193 AZ96
Ludford Cl NW9 96 CS54
Ludford Cl, Croy. 219 DP105
Warrington Rd
Ludgate Bdy EC4 274 F9
Ludgate Circ EC4 274 F9
Ludgate Hill EC4 274 F9
Ludgate Hill EC4 141 DP72
Ludgate Sq EC4 274 G9
Ludham Cl SE28 146 EW72
Rollesby Way
Ludlow Cl, Brom. 204 EG97
Aylesbury Rd
Ludlow Cl, Har. 116 BZ63
Ludlow Mead, Wat. 93 BV48
Ludlow Pl, Grays 170 GB76
Ludlow Rd W5 137 CJ70
Ludlow Rd, Felt. 175 BU91
Ludlow Rd, Guil. 258 AV135
Ludlow St EC1 275 H4
Ludlow Way N2 120 DC56
Ludlow Way, Rick. 75 BQ42
Ludovick Wk SW15 158 CS84
Ludwick Cl, Welw.G.C. 29 CZ11
Ludwick Grn, Welw.G.C. 29 CZ10
Ludwick Ms SE14 163 DY80
Ludwick Way, Welw.G.C. 29 CZ09
Luff Cl, Wind. 151 AL83
Luffield Rd SE2 166 EV76
Luffman Rd SE12 184 EH90
Lugard Rd SE15 162 DV82
Lugg App E12 125 EN62
Luke Ho E1 142 DV72
Luke St EC2 275 M4
Luke St EC2 142 DS70
Lukin Cres E4 101 ED48
Lukin St E1 142 DW72
Lukintone Cl, Loug. 84 EL44
Lullarook Cl (Biggin Hill), West. 238 EJ116
Lullingstone Av, Swan. 207 FF97
Lullingstone Cl, Orp. 186 EV94
Lullingstone Cres
Lullingstone Cres, Orp. 186 EU94
Lullingstone La SE13 183 ED87
Lullingstone La (Eynsford), Dart. 208 FJ104
Lullingstone Rd, Belv. 166 EZ79
Lullington Garth N12 97 CZ50
Lullington Garth, Borwd. 78 CP43
Lullington Garth, Brom. 184 EE94
Lullington Rd SE20 182 DU94
Lullington Rd, Dag. 146 EY66
Lulot Gdns N19 121 DH61
Lulworth SE17 279 K10
Lulworth Av, Houns. 156 CB80
Lulworth Av (Cheshunt), Wal.Cr. 65 DP29
Lulworth Av, Wem. 117 CJ59
Lulworth Cl, Har. 116 BZ62
Lulworth Cres, Mitch. 200 DE96
Lulworth Dr, Pnr. 116 BX58
Lulworth Dr, Rom. 105 FB50
Lulworth Gdns, Har. 116 BY61
Lulworth Rd SE9 184 EL89
Lulworth Rd SE15 162 DV82
Lulworth Rd, Well. 165 ET82
Lulworth Waye, Hayes 136 BW72
Lumbards, Welw.G.C. 30 DA06
Lumen Rd, Wem. 117 CK61
Lumley Cl, Belv. 166 FA79
Lumley Ct WC2 278 A1
Lumley Ct, Horl. 268 DG147
Lumley Gdns, Sutt. 217 CY106
Lumley Rd, Horl. 268 DG147
Lumley Rd, Sutt. 217 CY107
Lumley St W1 272 G9
Luna Rd, Th.Hth. 202 DQ97
Lunar Cl (Biggin Hill), West. 238 EK116
Lundin Wk, Wat. 94 BX49
Woodhall La
Lundy Dr, Hayes 155 BS77
Lundy Wk N1 142 DQ65
Clephane Rd
Lunedale Rd, Dart. 188 FQ88
Lunedale Wk, Dart. 188 FP88
Lunedale Rd
Lunghurst Rd (Woldingham), Cat. 237 DZ120
Lunham Rd SE19 182 DS93
Lupin Cl SW2 181 DP89
Palace Rd
Lupin Cl, Croy. 203 DX102
Primrose La
Lupin Cl, Rom. 127 FD61
Lupin Cl, West Dr. 154 BK78
Magnolia St
Lupin Cres, Ilf. 125 EP64
Bluebell Way
Luppit Cl, Brwd. 109 GA46
Lupton Cl SE12 184 EH90
Lupton St NW5 121 DJ63
Lupus St SW1 277 L10
Lupus St SW1 161 DH79
Luralda Gdns E14 163 EC78
Saunders Ness Rd
Lurgan Av W6 159 CX79
Lurline Gdns SW11 160 DG81
Luscombe Ct, Brom. 204 EE96
Luscombe Way SW8 161 DL80
Lushes Ct, Loug. 85 EP43
Lushes Rd
Lushes Rd, Loug. 85 EP43
Lushington Dr, Cob. 213 BV114
Lushington Rd NW10 139 CV68
Lushington Rd SE6 183 EB92
Lushington Ter E8 122 DU64
Wayland Av
Lusted Hall La (Tatsfield), West. 238 EJ120
Lusted Rd, Sev. 241 FE120
Lusteds Cl, Dor. 263 CJ139
Glory Mead
Luther Cl, Edg. 96 CQ47
Luther King Cl E17 123 DY58
Luther King Rd, Harl. 51 EQ15
Luther Rd, Tedd. 177 CF92
Luton Pl SE10 163 EC80
Luton Rd E17 123 DZ55
Luton Rd, Sid. 186 EW90
Luton St NW8 272 A5
Luton St NW8 140 DD70
Lutton Ter NW3 120 DD63
Flask Wk
Luttrell Av SW15 179 CV85
Lutwyche Rd SE6 183 DZ89
Luxborough La, Chig. 102 EL48
Luxborough St W1 272 F6
Luxborough St W1 140 DG70
Luxemburg Gdns W6 159 CX77
Luxfield Rd SE9 184 EL88
Luxford Pl, Saw. 36 EZ06
Luxford St SE16 163 DX77
Luxmore St SE4 163 DZ81
Luxor St SE5 162 DQ83
Luxted Rd, Orp. 223 EN112
Lyal Rd E3 143 DY68
Lyall Av SE21 182 DS90
Lyall Ms SW1 276 F7
Lyall Ms SW1 160 DG76
Lyall Ms W SW1 276 F7
Lyall St SW1 276 F7
Lyall St SW1 160 DG76
Lycaste Cl, St.Alb. 43 CG21
Lycett Pl W12 159 CU75
Becklow Rd
Lych Gate, Wat. 60 BX33
Lych Gate Rd, Orp. 206 EU102
Lych Gate Wk, Hayes 135 BT73
Lych Way, Wok. 226 AX116
Lyconby Gdns, Croy. 203 DY101
Lycrome La, Chesh. 54 AR28
Lycrome Rd, Chesh. 54 AR28
Lydd Cl, Sid. 185 ES90
Lydd Rd, Bexh. 166 EZ80
Lydden Ct SE9 185 ES86
Lydden Gro SW18 180 DB87
Lydden Rd SW18 180 DB87
Lydeard Rd E6 145 EM66
Lydele Cl, Wok. 227 AZ115
Lydford Av, Slou. 131 AR71
Lydford Cl N16 122 DS64
Pellerin Rd
Lydford Rd N15 122 DR57
Lydford Rd NW2 139 CX65
Lydford Rd W9 139 CZ70
Lydhurst Av SW2 181 DM89
Lydia Ms, Hat. 45 CW24
Lydia Rd, Erith 167 FF79
Lydney Cl SE15 162 DS80
Lydney Cl SW19 179 CY89
Princes Way
Lydon Rd SW4 161 DJ83
Lydsey Cl, Slou. 131 AN69
Lydstep Rd, Chis. 185 EN91
Lye, The, Tad. 233 CW122
Lye Grn Rd, Chesh. 54 AR30
Lye La (Bricket Wd), St.Alb. 60 CA30
Lyell Pl E, Wind. 150 AJ83
Lyell Pl W, Wind. 150 AJ83
Lyell Pl E
Lyell Wk E, Wind. 150 AJ83
Lyell Pl E
Lyell Wk W, Wind. 150 AJ83
Lyell Pl E
Lyfield (Oxshott), Lthd. 214 CB114
Lyford Rd SW18 180 DD87
Lygean Av, Ware 33 DY06
Lygon Pl SW1 277 H7
Lyham Cl SW2 181 DL86
Lyham Rd SW2 181 DL85
Lyle Cl, Mitch. 200 DG101
Lyle Pk, Sev. 257 FH123
Lymbourne Cl, Sutt. 218 DA110
Lymden Gdns, Reig. 266 DB135
Lyme Fm Rd SE12 164 EG84
Lyme Gro E9 142 DW66
St. Thomas's Sq
Lyme Regis Rd, Bans. 233 CZ117
Lyme Rd, Well. 166 EV81
Lyme St NW1 141 DJ66
Lyme Ter NW1 141 DJ66
Royal Coll St
Lymer Av SE19 182 DT92
Lymescote Gdns, Sutt. 200 DA103
Lyminge Cl, Sid. 185 ET91
Lyminge Gdns SW18 180 DE88
Lymington Av N22 99 DN54
Lymington Cl E6 145 EM71
Valiant Way
Lymington Cl SW16 201 DK96
Lymington Dr, Ruis. 115 BR61
Lymington Gdns, Epsom 217 CT106
Lymington Rd NW6 140 DB65
Lymington Rd, Dag. 126 EX60
Lympstone Gdns SE15 162 DU80
Lyn Ms E3 143 DZ69
Tredegar Sq
Lynbridge Gdns N13 99 DP49
Lynbrook Cl SE15 162 DS80
Blakes Rd
Lynbrook Cl, Rain. 147 FD68
Lynceley Gra, Epp. 70 EU29
Lynch, The, Hodd. 49 EB17
Lynch, The, Uxb. 134 BJ67
New Windsor St
Lynch Cl, Uxb. 134 BJ66
New Windsor St
Lynch Hill La, Slou. 131 AL70
Lynch Wk SE8 163 DZ79
Prince St
Lynchen Cl, Houns. 155 BU81
The Av
Lyncott Cres SW4 161 DH84
Lyncroft Av, Pnr. 116 BY57
Lyncroft Gdns NW6 120 DA64
Lyncroft Gdns W13 157 CJ75
Lyncroft Gdns, Epsom 217 CT109
Lyncroft Gdns, Houns. 156 CC84
Lyndale NW2 119 CZ63
Lyndale Av NW2 119 CZ62
Lyndale Cl SE3 164 EF79
Lyndale Ct, W.Byf. 212 BG113
Parvis Rd
Lyndale Est, Grays 169 FV79
Lyndale Rd, Red. 250 DF131
Lynden Way, Swan. 207 FC97
Lyndhurst Av N12 98 DF51
Lyndhurst Av NW7 96 CS51
Lyndhurst Av SW16 201 DK96
Lyndhurst Av, Pnr. 93 BV53
Lyndhurst Av, Sthl. 136 CB74
Lyndhurst Av, Sun. 195 BU97
Lyndhurst Av, Surb. 198 CP102
Lyndhurst Av, Twick. 176 BZ88
Lyndhurst Cl NW10 118 CR62
Lyndhurst Cl, Bexh. 167 FB83
Lyndhurst Cl, Croy. 202 DT104
Lyndhurst Cl, Orp. 223 EP105
Lyndhurst Cl, Wok. 226 AX115
Lyndhurst Ct E18 102 EG53
Churchfields
Lyndhurst Ct, Sutt. 218 DA108
Overton Rd
Lyndhurst Dr E10 123 EC59
Lyndhurst Dr, Horn. 128 FJ60
Lyndhurst Dr, N.Mal. 198 CS100
Lyndhurst Dr, Sev. 256 FE124
Lyndhurst Gdns N3 97 CY53
Lyndhurst Gdns NW3 120 DD64
Lyndhurst Gdns, Bark. 145 ES65
Lyndhurst Gdns, Enf. 82 DS42
Lyndhurst Gdns, Ilf. 125 ER58
Lyndhurst Gdns, Pnr. 93 BV53
Lyndhurst Gro SE15 162 DS82
Lyndhurst Ho SW15 179 CU87
Ellisfield Dr
Lyndhurst Ri, Chig. 103 EN49
Lyndhurst Rd E4 101 EC52
Lyndhurst Rd N18 100 DU49
Lyndhurst Rd N22 99 DM51
Lyndhurst Rd NW3 120 DD64
Lyndhurst Rd, Bexh. 167 FB83
Lyndhurst Rd, Chesh. 54 AP28
Lyndhurst Rd, Couls. 234 DG116
Lyndhurst Rd, Grnf. 136 CB70
Lyndhurst Rd, Reig. 266 DA137
Lyndhurst Rd, Th.Hth. 201 DN98
Lyndhurst Sq SE15 162 DT81
Lyndhurst Ter NW3 120 DD64
Lyndhurst Way SE15 162 DT81
Lyndhurst Way, Brwd. 109 GC45
Lyndhurst Way, Cher. 193 BE104
Lyndhurst Way, Sutt. 218 DA108
Lyndon Av, Pnr. 94 BY51
Lyndon Av, Sid. 185 ET85
Lyndon Av, Wall. 200 DG104
Lyndon Rd, Belv. 166 FA77
Lyndwood Dr (Old Windsor), Wind. 172 AU86
Lyne Cl, Vir.W. 193 AZ100
Lyne Cres E17 101 DZ53
Lyne Crossing Rd (Lyne), Cher. 193 BA100
Lyne La (Lyne), Cher. 193 BA100
Lyne La, Egh. 193 BA99
Lyne La, Vir.W. 193 BA100
Lyne Rd, Vir.W. 192 AX100
Lyne Way, Hem.H. 39 BF18
Lynegrove Av, Ashf. 175 BQ92
Lyneham Wk E5 123 DY64
Lyneham Wk, Pnr. 115 BT55
Lynett Rd, Dag. 126 EX61
Lynette Av SW4 181 DH86
Lynford Cl, Barn. 79 CT43
Rowley La
Lynford Cl, Edg. 96 CQ52
Lynford Gdns, Edg. 96 CP48
Lynford Gdns, Ilf. 125 ET61
Lynhurst Cres, Uxb. 135 BQ66
Lynhurst Rd, Uxb. 135 BQ66
Lynmere Rd, Well. 166 EV82
Lynmouth Av, Enf. 82 DT44
Lynmouth Av, Mord. 199 CX101
Lynmouth Dr, Ruis. 115 BV61
Lynmouth Gdns, Grnf. 137 CH67
Lynmouth Gdns, Houns. 156 BX81
Lynmouth Ri, Orp. 206 EV98
Lynmouth Rd E17 123 DY58
Lynmouth Rd N2 120 DF55
Lynmouth Rd N16 122 DT60
Lynmouth Rd, Grnf. 137 CH67
Lynmouth Rd, Welw.G.C. 29 CZ09
Lynn Cl, Ashf. 175 BR92
Goffs Rd
Lynn Cl, Har. 95 CD54
Lynn Ms E11 124 EE61
Lynn Rd
Lynn Rd E11 124 EE61
Lynn Rd SW12 181 DH87
Lynn Rd, Ilf. 125 ER59
Lynn St, Enf. 82 DR39
Lynn Wk, Reig. 266 DB137
Lynne Cl, Orp. 223 ET107
Lynne Cl, S.Croy. 220 DW111
Lynne Wk, Esher 214 CC106
Lynne Way NW10 138 CS65
Lynne Way, Nthlt. 136 BX68
Lynross Cl, Rom. 106 FM54
Lynscott Way, S.Croy. 219 DP109
Lynsted Cl, Bexh. 187 FB85
Lynsted Cl, Brom. 204 EJ96
Lynsted Ct, Beck. 203 DY96
Churchfields Rd
Lynsted Gdns SE9 164 EK83
Lynton Av N12 98 DD49
Lynton Av NW9 119 CT56
Lynton Av W13 137 CG72
Lynton Av, Orp. 206 EV98
Lynton Av, Rom. 104 FA53
Lynton Av, St.Alb. 43 CJ21
Lynton Cl NW10 118 CS64
Lynton Cl, Chess. 216 CL105
Lynton Cl, Islw. 157 CF84
Lynton Cres, Ilf. 125 EP58
Lynton Crest, Pot.B. 64 DA32
Strafford Gate
Lynton Est SE1 162 DU77
Lynton Rd
Lynton Gdns N11 99 DK51
Lynton Gdns, Enf. 100 DS45
Lynton Mead N20 98 DA48
Lynton Par, Wal.Cr. 67 DX30
Turners Hill
Lynton Rd E4 101 EB50
Lynton Rd N8 121 DK57
Lynton Rd NW6 139 CZ67
Lynton Rd SE1 162 DT77
Lynton Rd W3 138 CN73
Lynton Rd, Chesh. 54 AP28
Lynton Rd, Croy. 201 DN100
Lynton Rd, Grav. 191 GG88
Lynton Rd, Har. 116 BY61
Lynton Rd, N.Mal. 198 CR99
Lynton Rd S, Grav. 191 GG88
Lynton Ter W3 138 CQ72
Lynton Rd
Lynton Wk, Hayes 135 BS69
Lynwood, Guil. 258 AV135
Lynwood Av, Couls. 235 DH115
Lynwood Av, Egh. 172 AY93
Lynwood Av, Epsom 217 CT114
Lynwood Av, Slou. 152 AX76
Lynwood Cl E18 102 EJ53
Lynwood Cl, Har. 116 BY62
Lynwood Cl, Rom. 105 FB51
Lynwood Cl, Wok. 211 BD113
Lynwood Dr, Nthwd. 93 BT53
Lynwood Dr, Rom. 105 FB51
Lynwood Dr, Wor.Pk. 199 CU103
Lynwood Gdns, Croy. 219 DM105
Lynwood Gdns, Sthl. 136 BZ72
Lynwood Gro N21 99 DN46
Lynwood Gro, Orp. 205 ES101
Lynwood Hts, Rick. 74 BH43
Lynwood Rd SW17 180 DF90
Lynwood Rd W5 138 CL70
Lynwood Rd, Epsom 217 CT114
Lynwood Rd, Red. 250 DG132
Lynwood Rd, T.Ditt. 197 CF103
Lynx Hill (East Horsley), Lthd. 245 BS128
Lyon Business Pk, Bark. 145 ES68
Lyon Meade, Stan. 95 CJ53
Lyon Pk Av, Wem. 138 CL65
Lyon Rd SW19 200 DC95
Lyon Rd, Har. 117 CF58
Lyon Rd, Rom. 127 FF59
Lyon Rd, Walt. 196 BY103
Lyon St N1 141 DM66
Caledonian Rd
Lyon Way, Grnf. 137 CE67
Lyon Way, St.Alb. 44 CN20
Lyons Ct, Dor. 263 CH136
Lyons Dr, Guil. 242 AU129
Lyons Pl NW8 140 DD70
Lyons Wk W14 159 CY77
Lyonsdene, Tad. 249 CZ127
Lyonsdown Av, Barn. 80 DC44
Lyonsdown Rd, Barn. 80 DC44
Lyoth Rd, Orp. 205 EQ103
Lyric Dr, Grnf. 136 CB70
Lyric Ms SE26 182 DW91
Lyric Rd SW13 159 CT81
Lyrical Way, Hem.H. 40 BH18
Lys Hill Gdns, Hert. 31 DP07
Lysander Cl (Bovingdon), Hem.H. 57 AZ27
Lysander Gdns, Surb. 198 CM100
Ewell Rd
Lysander Gro N19 121 DK60
Lysander Rd, Croy. 219 DM107
Lysander Rd, Ruis. 115 BR61
Lysander Way, Abb.L. 59 BU32
Lysander Way, Orp. 205 EQ104
Lysander Way, Welw.G.C. 30 DD08
Lysia St SW6 159 CX80
Lysias Rd SW12 180 DG86
Lysley Pl, Hat. 64 DC27
Lysons Wk SW15 179 CU85
Swinburne Rd
Lyster Ms, Cob. 213 BV113
Lytchet Rd, Brom. 184 EH94
Lytchet Way, Enf. 82 DW39
Lytchgate Cl, S.Croy. 220 DS108
Lytcott Dr, W.Mol. 196 BZ97
Freeman Dr
Lytcott Gro SE22 182 DT85
Lyte St E2 142 DW68
Bishops Way
Lytham Av, Wat. 94 BX50
Lytham Cl SE28 146 EY72
Lytham Gro W5 138 CL69
Lytham St SE17 162 DR78
Lyttelton Cl NW3 140 DE66
Lyttelton Rd E10 123 EB62
Lyttelton Rd N2 120 DC57
Lyttleton Rd N8 121 DN55
Lytton Av N13 99 DN47
Lytton Av, Enf. 83 DY38
Lytton Cl N2 120 DD57
Lytton Cl, Loug. 85 ER41
Lytton Cl, Nthlt. 136 BZ66
Lytton Gdns, Wall. 219 DK105
Lytton Gdns, Welw.G.C. 29 CX09
Lytton Gro SW15 179 CX85
Lytton Pk, Cob. 214 BZ112
Lytton Rd E11 124 EE59
Lytton Rd, Barn. 80 DC42
Lytton Rd, Grays 171 GG77
Lytton Rd, Pnr. 94 BY52
Lytton Rd, Rom. 127 FH57
Lytton Rd, Wok. 227 BB116
Lytton Strachey Path SE28 146 EV73
Titmuss Av
Lyttons Way, Hodd. 33 EA14
Lyveden Rd SE3 164 EH80
Lyveden Rd SW17 180 DE93
Lywood Cl, Tad. 233 CW122

M

Mabbotts, Tad. 233 CX121
Mabbutt Cl (Bricket Wd), St.Alb. 60 BY30
Mabel Rd, Swan. 187 FG93
Mabel St, Wok. 226 AX117
Maberley Cres SE19 182 DU94
Maberley Rd SE19 202 DT95
Maberley Rd, Beck. 203 DX97
Mabeys Wk, Saw. 36 EU06
Mabledon Pl WC1 273 N3
Mabledon Pl WC1 141 DK69
Mablethorpe Rd SW6 159 CY80
Mabley St E9 143 DY65
Macaret Cl N20 98 DB45
MacArthur Cl E7 144 EG65
MacArthur Ter SE7 164 EL79
Macaulay Av, Esher 197 CF103
Macaulay Ct SW4 161 DH83
Macaulay Rd E6 144 EK68
Macaulay Rd SW4 161 DH83
Macaulay Rd, Cat. 236 DS122
Macaulay Sq SW4 161 DH84
Macaulay Way SE28 146 EV73
Booth Cl
Macauley Ms SE13 163 EC82
Macbean St SE18 165 EN76
Macbeth St W6 159 CV78
Macclesfield Br NW1 140 DE68
Macclesfield Rd EC1 275 H2
Macclesfield Rd EC1 142 DQ69
Macclesfield Rd SE25 202 DV99
Macclesfield St W1 273 N10
Macclesfield St W1 141 DK73
Macdonald Av, Dag. 127 FB62
Macdonald Av, Horn. 128 FL56
Macdonald Cl, Amer. 55 AR35
Macdonald Rd E7 124 EG63
Macdonald Rd E17 101 EC54
Macdonald Rd N11 98 DF50
Macdonald Rd N19 121 DJ61
Macdonald Way, Horn. 128 FL56
Macdonnell Gdns, Wat. 75 BT35
High Rd
Macduff Rd SW11 160 DG81
Mace Cl E1 142 DV74
Kennet St
Mace Ct, Grays 170 GE79
Mace Gateway E16 144 EG73
Mace La (Cudham), Sev. 223 ER113
Mace St E2 143 DX68
Macers Ct, Brox. 49 DZ24
Macers La, Brox. 49 DZ24
MacFarlane La, Islw. 157 CF79
Macfarlane Rd W12 139 CW74
Macfarren Pl NW1 272 G5
Macgregor Rd E16 144 EJ71
Machell Rd SE15 162 DW83
Macintosh Cl, Wal.Cr. 66 DR26
Mackay Rd SW4 161 DH83
Mackennal St NW8 272 C1
Mackennal St NW8 140 DE68
Mackenzie Mall, Slou. 152 AT75
High St
Mackenzie Rd N7 141 DM65
Mackenzie Rd, Beck. 202 DW96
Mackenzie St, Slou. 132 AT74
Mackenzie Wk E14 143 EA74
Mackenzie Way, Grav. 191 GK93
Mackeson Rd NW3 120 DF63
Mackie Rd SW2 181 DN87
Mackies Hill (Peaslake), Guil. 261 BR144
Mackintosh La E9 123 DX64
Homerton High St
Macklin St WC2 274 A8
Macklin St WC2 141 DL72
Mackrells, Red. 266 DC137
Mackrow Wk E14 143 EC73
Robin Hood La
Macks Rd SE16 162 DU77
Mackworth St NW1 273 K2
Mackworth St NW1 141 DJ69
Maclaren Ms SW15 159 CW84
Clarendon Dr
Maclean Rd SE23 183 DY86
Maclennan Av, Rain. 148 FK69
Macleod Cl, Grays 170 GD77
Macleod Rd N21 81 DL43
Macleod St SE17 162 DQ78
Maclise Rd W14 159 CY76
Macmillan Gdns, Dart. 168 FN84
Macmillan Way SW17 181 DH91
Church La
Macoma Rd SE18 165 ER79
Macoma Ter SE18 165 ER79
Macon Way, Upmin. 129 FT59
Maconochies Rd E14 163 EB78
Macquarie Way E14 163 EB77
Macroom Rd W9 139 CZ69
Mada Rd, Orp. 205 EP104
Madan Rd, West. 255 ER125
Madans Wk, Epsom 216 CR114
Maddams St E3 143 EB70
Madden Cl, Swans. 189 FX86
Maddison Cl, Tedd. 177 CF93
Maddock Way SE17 161 DP79
Maddocks Cl, Sid. 186 EY92
Maddox La (Bookham), Lthd. 230 BY123
Maddox Pk (Bookham), Lthd. 230 BY123
Maddox Rd, Harl. 35 ES14
Maddox Rd, Hem.H. 41 BP20
Maddox St W1 273 J10
Maddox St W1 141 DH73
Madeira Av, Brom. 184 EE94
Madeira Cl, W.Byf. 212 BG113
Brantwood Gdns
Madeira Cres, W.Byf. 212 BG113
Brantwood Gdns
Madeira Gro, Wdf.Grn. 102 EJ51
Madeira Rd E11 123 ED60
Madeira Rd N13 99 DP49
Madeira Rd SW16 181 DL92
Madeira Rd, Mitch. 200 DF98
Madeira Rd, W.Byf. 211 BF113
Madeira Wk, Brwd. 108 FY48
Madeira Wk, Reig. 250 DD133
Madeira Wk, Wind. 151 AR81
Madeley Cl, Amer. 55 AR36
Madeley Rd W5 138 CL72
Madeline Gro, Ilf. 125 ER64
Madeline Rd SE20 202 DU95
Madells, Epp. 69 ET31
Madge Gill Way E6 144 EL67
Ron Leighton Way
Madgeways Cl, Ware 33 DZ09
Madgeways La, Ware 33 DZ10
Madinah Rd E8 142 DU65
Madingley, Kings.T. 198 CN96
St. Peters Rd
Madison Cres, Bexh. 166 EW80
Madison Gdns, Bexh. 166 EW80
Madison Gdns, Brom. 204 EF97
Madison Way, Sev. 256 FF123
Madras Pl N7 141 DN65
Madras Rd, Ilf. 125 EP63
Madresfield Ct, Rad. 62 CL32
Russet Dr
Madrid Rd SW13 159 CU81
Madrid Rd, Guil. 258 AV135
Madrigal La SE5 161 DP80
Madron St SE17 279 N10
Madron St SE17 162 DS78
Maesmaur Rd (Tatsfield), West. 238 EK121
Mafeking Av E6 144 EK68
Mafeking Av, Brent. 158 CL79
Mafeking Av, Ilf. 125 ER59
Mafeking Rd E16 144 EF70
Mafeking Rd N17 100 DU54
Mafeking Rd, Enf. 82 DT41
Mafeking Rd (Wraysbury), Stai. 173 BB89
Magazine Pl, Lthd. 231 CH122
Magazine Rd, Cat. 235 DP122
Magdala Av N19 121 DH61
Magdala Rd, Islw. 157 CG83
Magdala Rd, S.Croy. 220 DR108
Napier Rd
Magdalen Cl (Byfleet), W.Byf. 212 BL114
Magdalen Cres (Byfleet), W.Byf. 212 BL114
Magdalen Gdns, Brwd. 109 GE44
Magdalen Gro, Orp. 224 EV105
Magdalen Pas E1 142 DT73
Prescot St
Magdalen Rd SW18 180 DC88
Magdalen St SE1 279 M3
Magdalen St SE1 142 DS74
Magdalene Cl SE15 162 DV82
Heaton Rd
Magdalene Gdns E6 145 EN70
Magdalene Rd, Shep. 194 BM98
Magee St SE11 161 DN79
Magellan Pl E14 163 EA78
Maritime Quay
Maggie Blake's Cause SE1 279 P3
Magna Carta La (Wraysbury), Stai. 172 AX88
Magna Rd (Englefield Grn), Egh. 172 AV93
Magnaville Rd, Bushey 95 CE45

Magnet Est, Grays 169 FW78
Magnet Rd, Grays 169 FW79
Magnet Rd, Wem. 117 CK61
Magnin Cl E8 142 DU67
Wilde Cl
Magnolia Av, Abb.L. 59 BU32
Magnolia Cl E10 123 EA61
Magnolia Cl, Hert. 32 DU09
Magnolia Cl, Kings.T. 178 CQ93
Magnolia Cl (Park St), St.Alb. 61 CD27
Magnolia Ct, Har. 118 CM59
Magnolia Ct, Horl. 268 DG148
Magnolia Ct, Rich. 158 CP81
West Hall Rd
Magnolia Ct, Wall. 219 DH106
Parkgate Rd
Magnolia Dr (Biggin Hill), West. 238 EK116
Magnolia Gdns, Edg. 96 CQ49
Magnolia Gdns, Slou. 152 AW76
Magnolia Pl SW4 181 DL85
Magnolia Pl W5 138 CL71
Montpelier Rd
Magnolia Rd W4 158 CP79
Magnolia St, West Dr. 154 BK77
Magnolia Way, Brwd. 108 FV43
Magnolia Way (North Holmwood), Dor. 263 CK139
Magnolia Way, Epsom 216 CQ106
Magnum Cl, Rain. 148 FJ70
Magpie All EC4 274 E9
Magpie Cl E7 124 EF64
Magpie Cl NW9 96 CS54
Eagle Dr
Magpie Cl, Couls. 235 DJ118
Ashbourne Cl
Magpie Cl, Enf. 82 DU39
Magpie Hall Cl, Brom. 204 EL100
Magpie Hall La, Brom. 205 EM99
Magpie Hall Rd, Bushey 95 CE47
Magpie La (Coleshill), Amer. 89 AM45
Magpie La, Brwd. 107 FW54
Magpie Pl SE14 163 DY79
Milton Ct Rd
Magpie Wk, Hat. 45 CU20
Lark Ri
Magpie Way, Slou. 131 AL70
Pemberton Rd
Magpies, The, Epp. 51 EN24
Magri Wk E1 142 DW71
Ashfield St
Maguire Dr, Rich. 177 CJ91
Maguire St SE1 162 DT75
Mahatma Gandhi Ho, Wem. 118 CN64
Mahlon Av, Ruis. 115 BV64
Mahogany Cl SE16 143 DY74
Mahon Cl, Enf. 82 DT39
Maida Av E4 101 EB45
Maida Av W2 140 DC71
Maida Rd, Belv. 166 FA76
Maida Vale W9 140 DB68
Maida Vale Rd, Dart. 187 FG85
Maida Way E4 101 EB45
Maiden Erlegh Av, Bex. 186 EY88
Maiden La NW1 141 DK66
Maiden La SE1 279 J2
Maiden La WC2 278 A1
Maiden La WC2 141 DL73
Maiden La, Dart. 167 FG83
Maiden Rd E15 144 EE66
Maidenhead Rd, Wind. 151 AP81
Maidenhead St, Hert. 32 DR09
Maidenshaw Rd, Epsom 216 CR112
Maidenstone Hill SE10 163 EC81
Maids of Honour Row, Rich. 177 CK85
The Grn
Maidstone Av, Rom. 105 FC54
Maidstone Bldgs SE1 279 J3
Maidstone Ho E14 143 EB72
Carmen St
Maidstone Rd N11 99 DK51
Maidstone Rd, Grays 170 GA79
Maidstone Rd, Sev. 256 FE122
Maidstone Rd (Seal), Sev. 257 FN121
Maidstone Rd, Sid. 186 EX93
Maidstone Rd, Swan. 207 FB95
Maidstone St E2 142 DU68
Audrey St
Main Av, Enf. 82 DT43
Main Av, Nthwd. 93 BQ48
Main Dr, Ger.Cr. 112 AW57
Main Dr, Iver 153 BE77
Main Dr, Wem. 117 CK62
Main Par, Rick. 73 BC42
Whitelands Av
Main Par Flats, Rick. 73 BC42
Whitelands Av
Main Ride, Egh. 172 AS93
Main Rd (Farningham), Dart. 208 FL100
Main Rd (Sutton at Hone), Dart. 188 FP93
Main Rd, Eden. 255 EQ134
Main Rd, Long. 209 FX96
Main Rd, Orp. 206 EW95
Main Rd, Rom. 127 FF56
Main Rd (Knockholt), Sev. 239 ET119
Main Rd (Sundridge), Sev. 240 EX124
Main Rd, Sid. 185 ES90
Main Rd (Crockenhill), Swan. 207 FD100
Main Rd (Hextable), Swan. 187 FF94
Main Rd, West. 222 EJ113
Main St, Felt. 176 BX92
Mainridge Rd, Chis. 185 EN91
Maisemore St SE15 162 DU80
Peckham Pk Rd
Maisie Webster Cl (Stanwell), Stai. 174 BK87
Lauser Rd
Maitland Cl SE10 163 EB80
Maitland Cl, Houns. 156 BZ83
Maitland Cl, Walt. 196 BY103
Maitland Cl, W.Byf. 212 BG113
Maitland Pk Est NW3 140 DF65
Maitland Pk Rd NW3 140 DF65
Maitland Pk Vil NW3 140 DF65
Maitland Pl E5 122 DV63
Clarence Rd
Maitland Rd E15 144 EF65
Maitland Rd SE26 183 DX93
Maize Cft, Horl. 269 DJ147
Maizey Ct, Brwd. 108 FU43
Danes Way
Majendie Rd SE18 165 ER78
Majestic Way, Mitch. 200 DF96
Major Rd E15 123 ED64
Major Rd SE16 162 DU76
Jamaica Rd
Majors Fm Rd, Slou. 152 AX80
Makepeace Av N6 120 DG61
Makepeace Rd E11 124 EG56
Makepeace Rd, Nthlt. 136 BY68
Makins St SW3 276 C9
Makins St SW3 160 DE77
Malabar St E14 163 EA75
Malacca Fm (West Clandon), Guil. 244 BH127
Malam Gdns E14 143 EB73
Wades Pl
Malan Cl (Biggin Hill), West. 238 EL117
Malan Sq, Rain. 147 FH65
Malbrook Rd SW15 159 CV84
Malcolm Ct, Stan. 95 CJ50
Malcolm Cres NW4 119 CU58
Malcolm Dr, Surb. 198 CL102
Malcolm Gdns, Horl. 268 DD150
Malcolm Pl E2 142 DW70
Malcolm Rd E1 142 DW70
Malcolm Rd SE20 182 DW94
Malcolm Rd SE25 202 DU100
Malcolm Rd SW19 179 CY93
Malcolm Rd, Couls. 235 DK115
Malcolm Rd, Uxb. 114 BM63
Malcolm Way E11 124 EG57
Malcolms Way N14 81 DJ43
Malden Av SE25 202 DV98
Malden Av, Grnf. 117 CE64
Malden Cl, Amer. 72 AT38
Malden Cres NW1 140 DG65
Malden Grn Av, Wor.Pk. 199 CT102
Malden Hill, N.Mal. 199 CT97
Malden Hill Gdns, N.Mal. 199 CT97
Malden Pk, N.Mal. 199 CT100
Malden Pl NW5 120 DG64
Grafton Ter
Malden Rd NW5 120 DG64
Malden Rd, Borwd. 78 CN41
Malden Rd, N.Mal. 198 CS99
Malden Rd, Sutt. 217 CX105
Malden Rd, Wat. 75 BV40
Malden Rd, Wor.Pk. 199 CT101
Malden Way, N.Mal. 199 CT99
Maldon Cl E15 123 ED64
David St
Maldon Cl N1 142 DQ67
Maldon Cl SE5 162 DS83
Maldon Ct, Wall. 219 DJ106
Maldon Rd
Maldon Rd N9 100 DT48
Maldon Rd W3 138 CQ73
Maldon Rd, Rom. 127 FC59
Maldon Rd, Wall. 219 DH106
Maldon Wk, Wdf.Grn. 102 EJ51
Malet Cl, Egh. 173 BD93
Malet Pl WC1 273 M5
Malet Pl WC1 141 DK70
Malet St WC1 273 M5
Malet St WC1 141 DK70
Maley Av SE27 181 DP89
Malford Ct E18 102 EG54
Malford Gro E18 124 EF56
Malfort Rd SE5 162 DS83
Malham Cl N11 98 DG51
Catterick Cl
Malham Rd SE23 183 DX88
Malins Cl, Barn. 79 CV43
Malkin Dr, Beac. 88 AJ52
Mall, The E15 143 ED66
Mall, The N14 99 DL48
Mall, The SW1 277 L4
Mall, The SW1 161 DJ75
Mall, The SW14 178 CQ85
Mall, The W5 138 CL73
Mall, The, Croy. 202 DQ103
Mall, The, Har. 118 CM58
Mall, The, Horn. 127 FH60
Mall, The (Park St), St.Alb. 60 CC27
Mall, The, Surb. 197 CK99
Mall Rd W6 159 CV78
Mallams Ms SW9 161 DP83
St. James's Cres
Mallard Cl E9 143 DZ65
Mallard Cl NW6 140 DA68
Mallard Cl W7 157 CE75
Mallard Cl, Barn. 80 DD44
The Hook
Mallard Cl, Dart. 188 FM85
Mallard Cl, Horl. 268 DG146
Mallard Cl, Red. 250 DG131
Mallard Cl, Twick. 176 CA87
Stephenson Rd
Mallard Cl, Upmin. 129 FT59
Mallard Dr, Slou. 131 AM73
Mallard Path SE28 165 ER76
Mallard Pl, Twick. 177 CG90
Mallard Pt E3 143 EB69
Rainhill Way
Mallard Rd, Abb.L. 59 BU31
Mallard Rd, S.Croy. 221 DX110
Mallard Wk, Beck. 203 DX99
Mallard Wk, Sid. 186 EW92
Mallard Way NW9 118 CQ59
Mallard Way, Brwd. 109 GB45
Mallard Way, Harl. 34 EG14
Roydon Mill Pk
Mallard Way, Nthwd. 93 BQ52
Mallard Way, Wall. 219 DJ109
Mallard Way, Wat. 76 BY37
Mallards, The, Stai. 194 BH96
Thames Side
Mallards Reach, Wey. 195 BR103
Mallards Ri, Harl. 52 EX15
Mallards Rd, Bark. 145 ES69
Mallards Rd, Wdf.Grn. 102 EH52
Mallet Dr, Nthlt. 116 BZ64
Mallet Rd SE13 183 ED86
Malling SE13 183 EB85
Malling Cl, Croy. 202 DW100
Malling Gdns, Mord. 200 DC100
Malling Way, Brom. 204 EF101
Mallinson Cl, Horn. 128 FJ64
Mallinson Rd SW11 180 DE85
Mallinson Rd, Croy. 201 DK104
Mallion Ct, Wal.Abb. 68 EF33
Mallord St SW3 160 DD79
Mallory Cl SE4 163 DY84
Mallory Gdns, Barn. 98 DG45
Mallory St NW8 272 C4
Mallory St NW8 140 DE70
Mallow Cl, Croy. 203 DX102
Marigold Way
Mallow Cl (Northfleet), Grav. 190 GE91
Mallow Cl, Tad. 233 CV119
Mallow Ct, Grays 170 GD79
Mallow Cres, Guil. 243 BB131
Mallow Cft, Hat. 45 CV19
Oxlease Dr
Mallow Mead NW7 97 CY52
Mallow St EC1 275 K4
Mallow Wk, Wal.Cr. 66 DR28
Mallows, The, Uxb. 115 BP62
Mallows Grn, Harl. 51 EN20
Mallys Pl (South Darenth), Dart. 208 FQ95
Malm Cl, Rick. 92 BK47
Malmains Cl, Beck. 203 ED99
Malmains Way, Beck. 203 EC98
Malmesbury Cl, Pnr. 115 BT56
Malmesbury Rd E3 143 DZ69
Malmesbury Rd E16 144 EE71
Malmesbury Rd E18 102 EF53
Malmesbury Rd, Mord. 200 DC101
Malmesbury Ter E16 144 EF71
Malmescroft, Hem.H. 41 BQ22
Malmsdale, Welw.G.C. 29 CX05
Malmstone Av, Red. 251 DJ128
Malpas Dr, Pnr. 116 BX57
Malpas Rd E8 142 DV65
Malpas Rd SE4 163 DZ82
Malpas Rd, Dag. 146 EX65
Malpas Rd, Grays 171 GJ76
Malpas Rd, Slou. 132 AV73
Malt Hill, Egh. 172 AY92
Malt Ho Cl (Old Windsor), Wind. 172 AV87
Malt La, Rad. 77 CG35
Malt St SE1 162 DU79
Malta Rd E10 123 EA60
Malta Rd, Til. 171 GF82
Malta St EC1 274 G4
Maltby Cl, Orp. 206 EU102
Vinson Cl
Maltby Dr, Enf. 82 DV38
Maltby Rd, Chess. 216 CN107
Maltby St SE1 279 P5
Maltby St SE1 162 DT75
Malthouse Dr W4 158 CS79
Malthouse Dr, Felt. 176 BX92
Malthouse Pas SW13 158 CS82
The Ter
Malthouse Pl, Rad. 61 CG34
Malthouse Sq, Beac. 111 AM55
Malthus Path SE28 146 EW74
Owen Cl
Malting Ho E14 143 DZ73
Malting Way, Islw. 157 CF83
Maltings, The, Harl. 36 EW11
Maltings, The, Kings L. 59 BQ33
Maltings, The, Orp. 205 ET102
Maltings, The, Oxt. 254 EF131
Maltings, The, Rom. 127 FF59
Maltings, The, St.Alb. 43 CD20
Maltings, The, Saw. 36 FA05
Maltings, The, Stai. 173 BE91
Church St
Maltings, The (Byfleet), W.Byf. 212 BM113
Maltings Cl SW13 158 CS82
Cleveland Gdns
Maltings Dr, Epp. 70 EU29
Palmers Hill
Maltings La, Epp. 70 EU29
Maltings Ms, Amer. 55 AP40
Maltings Ms, Sid. 186 EU90
Station Rd
Maltings Pl SW6 160 DC81
Maltmans La (Chalfont St. Peter), Ger.Cr. 112 AW55
Malton Av, Slou. 131 AP72
Malton Ms SE18 165 ES79
Malton St
Malton Ms W10 139 CY72
Cambridge Gdns
Malton Rd W10 139 CY72
St. Marks Rd
Malton St SE18 165 ES79
Maltravers St WC2 274 C10
Malus Cl, Add. 211 BF108
Malus Cl, Hem.H. 40 BN19
Malus Dr, Add. 211 BF108
Malva Cl SW18 180 DB85
St. Ann's Hill
Malvern Av E4 101 ED52
Malvern Av, Bexh. 166 EY80
Malvern Av, Har. 116 BY62
Malvern Cl SE20 202 DU96
Derwent Rd
Malvern Cl W10 139 CZ71
Malvern Cl, Bushey 76 CC44
Malvern Cl (Ottershaw), Cher. 211 BC107
Malvern Cl, Hat. 45 CT17
Malvern Cl, Mitch. 201 DJ97
Malvern Cl, St.Alb. 43 CH16
Malvern Cl, Surb. 198 CL102
Malvern Cl, Uxb. 115 BP61
Malvern Ct SE14 162 DW80
Avonley Rd
Malvern Ct SW7 276 A9
Malvern Ct SW7 160 DD77
Malvern Ct, Slou. 153 BA79
Hill Ri
Malvern Ct, Sutt. 218 DA108
Overton Rd
Malvern Dr, Felt. 176 BX92
Malvern Dr, Ilf. 125 ET63
Malvern Dr, Wdf.Grn. 102 EJ50
Malvern Gdns NW2 119 CY61
Malvern Gdns NW6 139 CZ68
Carlton Vale
Malvern Gdns, Har. 118 CL55
Malvern Gdns, Loug. 85 EM44
Malvern Ms NW6 140 DA69
Malvern Rd
Malvern Pl NW6 139 CZ69
Malvern Rd E6 144 EL67
Malvern Rd E8 142 DU66
Malvern Rd E11 124 EE61
Malvern Rd N8 121 DM55
Malvern Rd N17 122 DU55
Malvern Rd NW6 140 DA69
Malvern Rd, Enf. 83 DY37
Malvern Rd, Grays 170 GD77
Malvern Rd, Hmptn. 176 CA94
Malvern Rd, Hayes 155 BS80
Malvern Rd, Horn. 127 FG58
Malvern Rd, Orp. 224 EV105
Malvern Rd, Surb. 198 CL103
Malvern Rd, Th.Hth. 201 DN98
Malvern Ter N1 141 DN67
Malvern Ter N9 100 DT46
Latymer Rd
Malvern Way W13 137 CH71
Templewood
Malvern Way, Hem.H. 40 BM18
Malvern Way, Rick. 75 BP43
Malvina Av, Grav. 191 GH89
Malwood Rd SW12 181 DH86
Malyons, The, Shep. 195 BR100
Gordon Rd
Malyons Rd SE13 183 EB85
Malyons Rd, Swan. 187 FF94
Malyons Ter SE13 183 EB85
Managers St E14 143 EC74
Prestons Rd
Manan Cl, Hem.H. 41 BQ22
Manatee Pl, Wall. 201 DK104
Croydon Rd
Manaton Cl SE15 162 DV83
Manaton Cres, Sthl. 136 CA72
Manbey Gro E15 144 EE65
Manbey Pk Rd E15 144 EE65
Manbey Rd E15 144 EE65
Manbey St E15 144 EE65
Manbre Rd W6 159 CW79
Manbrough Av E6 145 EM69
Manchester Dr W10 139 CY70
Manchester Gro E14 163 EC78
Manchester Ms W1 272 F7
Manchester Rd E14 163 EC78
Manchester Rd N15 122 DR58
Manchester Rd, Th.Hth. 202 DQ97
Manchester Sq W1 272 F8
Manchester Sq W1 140 DG72
Manchester St W1 272 F7
Manchester St W1 140 DG71
Manchester Way, Dag. 127 FB63
Manchuria Rd SW11 180 DG86
Manciple St SE1 279 K5
Manciple St SE1 162 DR76
Mandalay Rd SW4 181 DJ85
Mandarin St E14 143 EA73
Salter St
Mandarin Way, Hayes 136 BX71
Mandela Av, Harl. 35 ES13
Mandela Cl NW10 138 CQ66
Mandela Rd E16 144 EG72
Mandela St NW1 141 DJ67
Mandela St SW9 161 DN80
Mandela Way SE1 279 N8
Mandela Way SE1 162 DS77
Mandelyns, Berk. 38 AS16
Mandeville Cl SE3 164 EF80
Vanbrugh Pk
Mandeville Cl SW20 199 CY95
Mandeville Cl, Brox. 49 DZ20
Mandeville Cl, Guil. 242 AU131
Mandeville Cl, Harl. 52 EW17
Mandeville Cl, Hert. 32 DQ12
Mandeville Cl, Wat. 75 BT38
Mandeville Ct E4 101 DY49
Mandeville Ct, Egh. 173 BA91
Mandeville Dr, St.Alb. 43 CD23
Mandeville Dr, Surb. 197 CK102
Mandeville Pl W1 272 G8
Mandeville Pl W1 140 DG72
Mandeville Ri, Welw.G.C. 29 CX07
Mandeville Rd N14 99 DH47
Mandeville Rd, Enf. 83 DX36
Mandeville Rd, Hert. 32 DQ12
Mandeville Rd, Islw. 157 CG82
Mandeville Rd, Nthlt. 136 CA66
Mandeville Rd, Pot.B. 64 DC32
Mandeville Rd, Shep. 194 BN99
Mandeville St E5 123 DY62
Mandeville Wk, Brwd. 109 GE44
Mandrake Rd SW17 180 DF90
Mandrake Way E15 144 EE66
Mandrell Rd SW2 181 DL85
Manette St W1 273 N9
Manette St W1 141 DK72
Manfield Cl, Slou. 131 AN69
Manford Cl, Chig. 104 EU49
Manford Cross, Chig. 104 EU50
Manford Ind Est, Erith 167 FG79
Manford Way, Chig. 103 ES50
Manfred Rd SW15 179 CZ85
Manger Rd N7 141 DL65
Mangles Rd, Guil. 242 AX132
Mangold Way, Erith 166 EY76
Mangrove Dr, Hert. 32 DS11
Mangrove La, Hert. 48 DT16
Mangrove Rd, Hert. 32 DS10
Manhattan Wf E16 164 EG75
Manilla St E14 163 EA75
Manister Rd SE2 166 EU76
Manitoba Ct SE16 162 DW75
Renforth St
Manitoba Gdns, Orp. 223 ET107
Superior Dr
Manley Ct N16 122 DT62
Stoke Newington High St
Manley Rd, Hem.H. 40 BL19
Knightsbridge Way
Manley St NW1 140 DG67
Manly Dixon Dr, Enf. 83 DY37
Mann Cl, Croy. 202 DQ104
Salem Pl
Mannamead, Epsom 232 CS119
Mannamead Cl, Epsom 232 CS119
Mannamead
Mannicotts, Welw.G.C. 29 CV09
Mannin Rd, Rom. 126 EV59
Manning Gdns, Har. 117 CK59
Manning Pl, Rich. 178 CM86
Grove Rd
Manning Rd E17 123 DY57
Southcote Rd
Manning Rd, Dag. 146 FA65
Manning Rd, Orp. 206 EX99
Manning St, S.Ock. 148 FQ74
Manningford Cl EC1 274 F2
Manningtree Cl SW19 179 CY88
Manningtree Rd, Ruis. 115 BV63
Manningtree St E1 142 DU72
White Ch La
Mannock Dr, Loug. 85 EQ40
Mannock Rd N22 121 DP55
Mannock Rd, Dart. 168 FM83
Barnwell Rd
Manns Cl, Islw. 177 CF85
Manns Rd, Edg. 96 CN51
Manoel Rd, Twick. 176 CC89
Manor Av SE4 163 DZ82
Manor Av, Cat. 236 DS124
Manor Av, Hem.H. 40 BK23
Manor Av, Horn. 128 FJ57
Manor Av, Houns. 156 BX83
Manor Av, Nthlt. 136 BZ66
Manor Chase, Wey. 213 BP106
Manor Cl E17 101 DY54
Manor Rd
Manor Cl NW7 96 CR50
Manor Dr
Manor Cl NW9 118 CP57
Manor Cl SE28 146 EW73
Manor Cl, Barn. 79 CY42
Manor Cl, Berk. 38 AW19
Manor Cl, Dag. 147 FD65
Manor Cl (Crayford), Dart. 167 FD84
Manor Cl (Wilmington), Dart. 187 FG90
Manor Cl, Hat. 45 CT15
Manor Cl, Hert. 32 DR07
Manor Cl, Horl. 268 DF148
Manor Cl (East Horsley), Lthd. 245 BS128
Manor Cl, Rom. 127 FG57
Manor Rd
Manor Cl, Ruis. 115 BT60
Manor Cl, S.Ock. 148 FQ74
Manor Cl, Warl. 237 DY117
Manor Cl, Wok. 227 BF116
Manor Cl, Wor.Pk. 198 CS102
Manor Cl S, S.Ock. 148 FQ74
Manor Cotts, Nthwd. 93 BT53
Manor Cotts App N2 98 DC54
Manor Ct E10 123 EB60
Grange Pk Rd
Manor Ct N2 120 DF57
Manor Ct SW6 160 DB81
Bagley's La
Manor Ct, Enf. 82 DV36
Manor Ct, Rad. 77 CF38
Manor Ct, Slou. 131 AM74
Richards Way
Manor Ct, Twick. 176 CC89
Manor Ct, Wem. 118 CL64
Manor Ct, Wey. 213 BP105
Manor Ct Rd W7 137 CE73
Manor Cres (Seer Grn), Beac. 89 AR51
Manor Cres, Epsom 216 CN112
Abbots Av
Manor Cres, Guil. 242 AV132
Manor Cres, Horn. 128 FJ57
Manor Cres, Surb. 198 CN100
Manor Cres (Byfleet), W.Byf. 212 BM113
Manor Dr N14 99 DH45
Manor Dr N20 98 DE48
Manor Dr NW7 96 CR50
Manor Dr (New Haw), Add. 212 BG110
Manor Dr, Amer. 55 AP36
Manor Dr, Epsom 216 CS107
Manor Dr, Esher 197 CF103
Manor Dr, Felt. 176 BX92
Lebanon Av
Manor Dr, Horl. 268 DF148
Manor Dr, St.Alb. 60 CA27
Manor Dr, Sun. 195 BU96
Manor Dr, Surb. 198 CM100
Manor Dr, Wem. 118 CM63
Manor Dr, The, Wor.Pk. 198 CS102
Manor Dr N, N.Mal. 198 CR101
Manor Dr N, Wor.Pk. 198 CS102
Manor Est SE16 162 DV77
Manor Fm (Farningham), Dart. 208 FM101
Manor Fm Av, Shep. 195 BP100
Manor Fm Cl, Wind. 151 AM83
Manor Fm Cl, Wor.Pk. 198 CS102
Manor Fm Dr E4 102 EE48
Manor Fm Est (Wraysbury), Stai. 172 AX86
Manor Fm La, Egh. 173 BA92
Manor Fm Rd, Enf. 82 DV35
Manor Fm Rd, Th.Hth. 201 DN96
Manor Fm Rd, Wem. 137 CK68
Manor Fm Way (Seer Grn), Beac. 89 AR51
Orchard Rd
Manor Flds SW15 179 CX86
Manor Gdns N7 121 DL62
Manor Gdns SW20 199 CZ96
Manor Gdns W3 158 CN77
Manor Gdns W4 158 CS78
Devonshire Rd
Manor Gdns, Gdmg. 258 AS144
Farncombe St
Manor Gdns, Guil. 242 AV132
Manor Gdns, Hmptn. 176 CB94
Manor Gdns (Wooburn Grn), H.Wyc. 110 AE58
Manor Gdns (Effingham), Lthd. 246 BX128
Manor Gdns, Rich. 158 CM84
Manor Gdns, Ruis. 116 BW64
Manor Gdns, S.Croy. 220 DT107
Manor Gdns, Sun. 195 BU96
Manor Gate, Nthlt. 136 BY66
Manor Grn Rd, Epsom 216 CP113
Manor Gro SE15 162 DW79
Manor Gro, Beck. 203 EB96
Manor Gro, Maid. 150 AD80
Manor Gro, Rich. 158 CN84
Manor Hall Av NW4 97 CW54
Manor Hall Dr NW4 97 CX54
Manor Hatch Cl, Harl. 52 EV16
Manor Ho Ct, Epsom 216 CQ113
Manor Ho Ct, Shep. 195 BP101
Manor Ho Dr NW6 139 CX66
Manor Ho Dr, Nthwd. 93 BP52
Manor Ho Dr, Walt. 213 BT106
Manor Ho Est, Stan. 95 CH51
Old Ch La
Manor Ho Gdns, Abb.L. 59 BR31
Manor Ho La (Bookham), Lthd. 246 BY126
Manor Ho La (Datchet), Slou. 152 AV80
Horton Rd
Manor Ho Way, Islw. 157 CH83
Manor La SE12 184 EE86
Manor La SE13 164 EE84
Manor La, Felt. 175 BU89
Manor La, Ger.Cr. 112 AX59
Manor La, Hayes 155 BR79
Manor La (Fawkham Grn), Long. 209 FW101
Manor La, Sev. 209 FW103
Manor La, Sun. 195 BU96
Manor La, Sutt. 218 DC106
Manor La, Tad. 250 DA129
Manor La Ter SE13 164 EE84
Manor Leaze, Egh. 173 BB92
Manor Lo, Guil. 242 AV132
Manor Ms NW6 140 DA68
Cambridge Av
Manor Ms SE4 163 EA82
Manor Mt SE23 182 DW88
Manor Par NW10 139 CT68
Station Rd
Manor Par, Hat. 45 CT15
Manor Pk SE13 163 ED84
Manor Pk, Chis. 205 ER96
Manor Pk, Rich. 158 CM84
Manor Pk, Stai. 173 BD90
Manor Pk Cl, W.Wick. 203 EB102
Manor Pk Cres, Edg. 96 CN51
Manor Pk Dr, Har. 116 CB55
Manor Pk Gdns, Edg. 96 CN50
Manor Pk Par SE13 163 ED84
Lee High Rd
Manor Pk Rd E12 124 EK63
Manor Pk Rd N2 120 DD55
Manor Pk Rd NW10 139 CT67
Manor Pk Rd, Chis. 205 EQ95
Manor Pk Rd, Sutt. 218 DC106
Manor Pk Rd, W.Wick. 203 EB102
Manor Pl SE17 161 DP78
Manor Pl, Chis. 205 ER95
Manor Pl, Dart. 188 FL88
Highfield Rd S
Manor Pl, Felt. 175 BU88
Manor Pl (Bookham), Lthd. 246 CA126
Manor Pl, Mitch. 201 DJ97
Manor Pl, Stai. 174 BH92

Manor Pl, Sutt. 218 DB105
Manor Pl, Walt. 195 BT101
Manor Rd
Manor Rd E10 123 EA59
Manor Rd E15 144 EE68
Manor Rd E16 144 EE69
Manor Rd E17 101 DY54
Manor Rd N16 122 DR60
Manor Rd N17 100 DU53
Manor Rd N22 99 DL51
Manor Rd SE25 202 DU98
Manor Rd SW20 199 CZ96
Manor Rd W13 137 CG73
Manor Rd, Ashf. 174 BM92
Manor Rd, Bark. 145 ET65
Manor Rd, Barn. 79 CY43
Manor Rd (Seer Grn), Beac. 89 AR50
Manor Rd, Beck. 203 EB96
Manor Rd, Bex. 187 FB88
Manor Rd, Chesh. 54 AP29
Lansdowne Rd
Manor Rd, Chig. 103 EP50
Manor Rd, Dag. 147 FC65
Manor Rd, Dart. 167 FE84
Manor Rd, E.Mol. 197 CD98
Manor Rd, Enf. 82 DR40
Manor Rd, Erith 167 FF79
Manor Rd, Grav. 191 GH86
Manor Rd, Grays 170 GC79
Manor Rd (West Thurrock), Grays 169 FW79
Manor Rd, Guil. 242 AV132
Manor Rd, Harl. 36 EW10
Manor Rd, Har. 117 CG58
Manor Rd, Hat. 45 CT15
Manor Rd, Hayes 135 BU72
Manor Rd, Hodd. 49 EA16
Manor Rd, Loug. 84 EH44
Manor Rd (High Beach), Loug. 84 EH38
Manor Rd, Mitch. 201 DJ98
Manor Rd, Pot.B. 63 CZ31
Manor Rd, Red. 251 DJ129
Manor Rd, Reig. 249 CZ132
Manor Rd, Rich. 158 CM83
Manor Rd, Rom. 127 FG57
Manor Rd (Chadwell Heath), Rom. 126 EX58
Manor Rd (Lambourne End), Rom. 104 EW47
Manor Rd, Ruis. 115 BR60
Manor Rd, St.Alb. 43 CE19
Manor Rd (London Colney), St.Alb. 61 CJ26
Manor Rd (Sundridge), Sev. 240 EX124
Manor Rd, Sid. 185 ET90
Manor Rd, Sutt. 217 CZ108
Manor Rd, Swans. 189 FX86
Manor Rd, Tedd. 177 CH92
Manor Rd, Til. 171 GG82
Manor Rd, Twick. 176 CC89
Manor Rd, Wall. 219 DH105
Manor Rd, Wal.Abb. 67 ED33
Manor Rd, Walt. 195 BT101
Manor Rd, Wat. 75 BV39
Manor Rd, W.Wick. 203 EB103
Manor Rd (Tatsfield), West. 238 EL120
Manor Rd, Wind. 151 AL82
Manor Rd, Wok. 226 AW116
Manor Rd (Send Marsh), Wok. 227 BF123
Manor Rd, Wdf.Grn. 103 EM51
Manor Rd N, Esher 197 CF104
Manor Rd N, T.Ditt. 197 CG103
Manor Rd N, Wall. 219 DH105
Manor Rd S, Esher 215 CE105
Manor Sq, Dag. 126 EX61
Manor St, Berk. 38 AX19
Manor Vale, Brent. 157 CJ78
Manor Vw N3 98 DB54
Manor Wk, Wey. 213 BP106
Manor Way E4 101 ED49
Manor Way NW9 118 CS55
Manor Way SE3 164 EF84
Manor Way SE28 146 EW74
Manor Way (Coleshill), Amer. 55 AM44
Manor Way, Bans. 234 DF116
Manor Way, Beck. 203 EA96
Manor Way, Bex. 186 FA88
Manor Way, Bexh. 167 FD83
Manor Way, Borwd. 78 CQ42
Manor Way, Brwd. 108 FU48
Manor Way, Brom. 204 EL100
Manor Way, Chesh. 54 AR30
Manor Way, Egh. 173 AZ93
Manor Way, Grays 170 GB80
Manor Way, Guil. 258 AS137
Manor Way, Har. 116 CB56
Manor Way (Oxshott), Lthd. 230 CC116
Manor Way, Mitch. 201 DJ97
Manor Way, Orp. 205 EQ98
Manor Way, Pot.B. 64 DA30
Manor Way, Pur. 219 DL112
Manor Way, Rain. 147 FF71
Manor Way, Rick. 74 BN42
Manor Way, Ruis. 115 BS59
Manor Way, S.Croy. 220 DS107
Manor Way, Sthl. 156 BX77
Manor Way, Swans. 169 FX84
Manor Way (Cheshunt), Wal.Cr. 67 DY31
Russells Ride
Manor Way, Wok. 227 BB121
Manor Way, Wor.Pk. 198 CS102
Manor Way, The, Wall. 219 DH105
Manor Way Ind Est, Grays 170 GC80
Manor Waye, Uxb. 134 BK67
Manor Wd Rd, Pur. 219 DL113
Manorbrook SE3 164 EG84
Manorcrofts Rd, Egh. 173 BA93
Manordene Cl, T.Ditt. 197 CG102
Manordene Rd SE28 146 EW72
Manorfield Cl N19 121 DJ63
Junction Rd
Manorfields Cl, Chis. 205 ET97
Manorgate Rd, Kings.T. 198 CN95
Manorhall Gdns E10 123 EA60
Manorside, Barn. 79 CY42
Manorside Cl SE2 166 EW77
Manorville Rd, Hem.H. 40 BJ24
Manorway, Enf. 100 DS45
Manorway, Wdf.Grn. 102 EJ50
Manpreet Ct E12 125 EM64
Morris Av
Manresa Rd SW3 160 DE78
Mansard Beeches SW17 180 DG92
Mansard Cl, Horn. 127 FG61
Mansard Cl, Pnr. 116 BX55
Mansards, The, St.Alb. 43 CE19
Avenue Rd
Manscroft Rd, Hem.H. 40 BH17
Manse Cl, Hayes 155 BR79
Manse Rd N16 122 DT62
Manse Way, Swan. 207 FG98
Mansel Cl, Guil. 242 AV129
Mansel Cl, Slou. 132 AV71
Mansel Gro E17 101 EA53
Mansel Rd SW19 179 CY93
Mansell Cl, Wind. 151 AL81
Mansell Rd W3 158 CR75
Mansell Rd, Grnf. 136 CB71
Mansell St E1 142 DT72
Mansell Way, Cat. 236 DR122
Manser Rd, Rain. 147 FE69
Mansergh Cl SE18 164 EL80
Mansfield, Saw. 36 EU06
Mansfield Av N15 122 DR56
Mansfield Av, Barn. 80 DF44
Mansfield Av, Ruis. 115 BV60
Mansfield Cl N9 82 DU44
Mansfield Cl, Orp. 206 EX101
Mansfield Cl, Wey. 213 BP106
Mansfield Dr, Hayes 135 BS70
Mansfield Dr, Red. 251 DK128
Mansfield Gdns, Hert. 32 DQ07
Mansfield Gdns, Horn. 128 FK61
Mansfield Hill E4 101 EB46
Mansfield Ms W1 273 H7
Mansfield Pl NW3 120 DC63
New End
Mansfield Rd E11 124 EH58
Mansfield Rd E17 123 DZ56
Mansfield Rd NW3 120 DF64
Mansfield Rd W3 138 CP70
Mansfield Rd, Chess. 215 CJ106
Mansfield Rd, Ilf. 125 EN61
Mansfield Rd, S.Croy. 220 DR107
Mansfield Rd, Swan. 187 FE93
Mansfield St W1 273 H7
Mansfield St W1 141 DH71
Mansford St E2 142 DU68
Manship Rd, Mitch. 180 DG94
Mansion, The, Guil. 260 BL139
Albury Rd
Mansion Cl SW9 161 DN81
Cowley Rd
Mansion Gdns NW3 120 DB62
Mansion Ho EC4 275 K9
Mansion Ho EC4 142 DR72
Mansion Ho Pl EC4 275 K9
Mansion Ho St EC4 275 K9
Mansion La, Iver 133 BC74
Manson Ms SW7 160 DC77
Manson Pl SW7 160 DD77
Manstead Gdns, Rain. 147 FH72
Mansted Gdns, Rom. 126 EW59
Manston Av, Sthl. 156 CA77
Manston Cl SE20 202 DW95
Garden Rd
Manston Cl (Cheshunt), Wal.Cr. 66 DW30
Manston Gro, Kings.T. 177 CK92
Manston Rd, Guil. 243 BA130
Manston Rd, Harl. 51 ES15
Manston Way, Horn. 147 FH65
Manston Way, St.Alb. 43 CK21
Manstone Rd NW2 119 CY64
Manthorp Rd SE18 165 EQ78
Mantilla Rd SW17 180 DG91
Mantle Rd SE4 163 DY83
Mantle Way E15 144 EE66
Romford Rd
Mantlet Cl SW16 181 DJ94
Manton Av W7 157 CF75
Manton Cl, Hayes 135 BS73
Manton Rd SE2 166 EU77
Manton Rd, Enf. 83 EA37
Government Row
Mantua St SW11 160 DD83
Mantus Cl E1 142 DW70
Mantus Rd
Mantus Rd E1 142 DW70
Manus Way N20 98 DC47
Blakeney Cl
Manville Gdns SW17 181 DH89
Manville Rd SW17 180 DG89
Manwood Rd SE4 183 DZ85
Manwood St E16 145 EM74
Manygate La, Shep. 195 BQ101
Manygates SW12 181 DH89
Maori Rd, Guil. 243 AZ134
Mape St E2 142 DV70
Mapesbury Rd NW2 139 CY65
Mapeshill Pl NW2 139 CW65
Maple Av E4 101 DZ50
Maple Av W3 138 CS74
Maple Av, Har. 116 CB61
Maple Av, St.Alb. 42 CC16
Maple Av, Upmin. 128 FP62
Maple Av, West Dr. 134 BL73
Maple Cl N3 98 DA51
Maple Cl N16 122 DU58
Maple Cl SW4 181 DK86
Maple Cl, Brwd. 109 FZ48
Cherry Av
Maple Cl, Buck.H. 102 EK48
Maple Cl, Bushey 76 BY40
Maple Cl, Epp. 85 ER37
Loughton La
Maple Cl, Hmptn. 176 BZ93
Maple Cl, Hat. 45 CU19
Elm Dr
Maple Cl, Hayes 136 BX69
Maple Cl, Horn. 127 FH62
Maple Cl, Ilf. 103 ES50
Maple Cl, Mitch. 201 DH95
Maple Cl, Orp. 205 ER99
Maple Cl, Ruis. 115 BV58
Maple Cl, Swan. 207 FE96
Maple Cl, Whyt. 236 DT117
Maple Ct (Englefield Grn), Egh. 172 AV93
Ashwood Rd
Maple Ct, N.Mal. 198 CS97
Maple Ct, Ware 33 ED11
Maple Cres, Sid. 186 EU86
Maple Cres, Slou. 132 AV73
Maple Cross Ind Est, Rick. 91 BF49
Maple Dr, S.Ock. 149 FX70
Maple Gdns, Edg. 96 CS52
Maple Gdns, Stai. 174 BL89
Maple Gate, Loug. 85 EN40
Maple Grn, Hem.H. 39 BE18
Maple Gro NW9 118 CQ59
Maple Gro W5 157 CK76
Maple Gro, Brent. 157 CH80
Maple Gro, Guil. 242 AX132
Maple Gro, Sthl. 136 BZ71
Maple Gro, Wat. 75 BU39
Maple Gro, Welw.G.C. 29 CZ06
Maple Gro, Wok. 226 AY121
Maple Hill (Bovingdon), Hem.H. 56 AX30
Ley Hill Rd
Maple Ind Est, Felt. 175 BU90
Maple Way
Maple Leaf Cl, Abb.L. 59 BU32
Maple Leaf Cl, Ware 33 ED12
Maple Leaf Cl (Biggin Hill), West. 238 EK116
Main Rd
Maple Leaf Dr, Sid. 185 ET88
Maple Leaf Sq SE16 163 DX75
St. Elmos Rd
Maple Lo Cl, Rick. 91 BE49
Maple Ms NW6 140 DB68
Kilburn Pk Rd
Maple Ms SW16 181 DM92
Maple Pl W1 273 L5
Maple Pl, Bans. 217 CX114
Maple Pl, West Dr. 134 BM73
Maple Av
Maple River Ind Est, Harl. 36 EV09
Maple Rd E11 124 EE58
Maple Rd SE20 202 DV95
Maple Rd, Ash. 231 CK119
Maple Rd, Dart. 188 FJ88
Maple Rd, Grav. 191 GJ91
Maple Rd, Grays 170 GC79
Maple Rd, Hayes 136 BW69
Maple Rd, Red. 266 DF138
Maple Rd, Surb. 198 CL99
Maple Rd, Whyt. 236 DT117
Maple Rd (Ripley), Wok. 228 BG124
Maple Springs, Wal.Abb. 68 EG33
Maple St W1 273 K6
Maple St W1 141 DJ71
Maple St, Rom. 127 FC56
Maple Wk W10 139 CX70
Droop St
Maple Wk, Sutt. 218 DB110
Maple Way, Couls. 235 DH121
Maple Way, Felt. 175 BV90
Maple Way, Wal.Abb. 68 EH30
Breach Barn Mobile Home Pk
Maplecourt Wk, Wind. 151 AN77
Common Rd
Maplecroft Cl E6 144 EL72
Allhallows Rd
Maplecroft La, Wal.Abb. 50 EE21
Mapledale Av, Croy. 202 DU103
Mapledene, Chis. 185 EQ92
Kemnal Rd
Mapledene Rd E8 142 DT66
Maplefield (Park St), St.Alb. 60 CB29
Maplefield La, Ch.St.G. 72 AV41
Maplehurst, Lthd. 231 CD123
Maplehurst Cl, Kings.T. 198 CL98
Mapleleaf Cl, S.Croy. 221 DX111
Mapleleafe Gdns, Ilf. 125 EP55
Maples, The, Bans. 218 DB114
Maples, The (Ottershaw), Cher. 211 BB107
Maples, The (Claygate), Esher 215 CG108
Maples, The, Harl. 51 EP20
Maples, The, Wal.Cr. 66 DS28
Maples Pl E1 142 DV71
Raven Row
Maplescombe La (Farningham), Dart. 208 FN104
Maplestead Rd SW2 181 DM87
Maplestead Rd, Dag. 146 EV67
Maplethorpe Rd, Th.Hth. 201 DP98
Mapleton Cl, Brom. 204 EG100
Mapleton Cres SW18 180 DB86
Mapleton Cres, Enf. 82 DW38
Mapleton Rd E4 101 EC48
Mapleton Rd SW18 180 DB86
Mapleton Rd, Eden. 255 ET133
Mapleton Rd, Enf. 82 DV40
Mapleton Rd, West. 255 ES130
Maplin Cl N21 81 DM44
Maplin Ho SE2 166 EX75
Wolvercote Rd
Maplin Pk, Slou. 153 BC75
Maplin Rd E16 144 EG72
Maplin St E3 143 DZ69
Mapperley Dr, Wdf.Grn. 102 EE52
Forest Dr
Mar Rd, S.Ock. 149 FW70
Maran Way, Erith 166 EX75
Marban Rd W9 139 CZ69
Marbeck Cl, Wind. 151 AK81
Marble Arch W1 272 E10
Marble Arch W1 140 DF73
Marble Cl W3 138 CP74
Marble Dr NW2 119 CX59
Marble Hill Cl, Twick. 177 CH87
Marble Hill Gdns, Twick. 177 CH87
Marble Ho SE18 165 ET78
Felspar Cl
Marble Quay E1 142 DU74
Marbles Way, Tad. 233 CX119
Marbrook Ct SE12 184 EJ90
Marcellina Way, Orp. 205 ES104
Marcet Rd, Dart. 188 FJ85
March Rd, Twick. 177 CG87
March Rd, Wey. 212 BN106
Marchant Rd E11 123 ED61
Marchant St SE14 163 DY79
Sanford St
Marchbank Rd W14 159 CZ79
Marchmant Cl, Horn. 128 FJ62
Marchmont Gdns, Rich. 178 CM85
Marchmont Rd
Marchmont Grn, Hem.H. 40 BK18
Paston Rd
Marchmont Rd, Rich. 178 CM85
Marchmont Rd, Wall. 219 DJ108
Marchmont St WC1 273 P4
Marchmont St WC1 141 DL70
Marchside Cl, Houns. 156 BX81
Springwell Rd
Marchwood Cl SE5 162 DS80
Marchwood Cres W5 137 CJ72
Marcia Ct, Slou. 131 AM74
Richards Way
Marcia Rd SE1 279 N9
Marcia Rd SE1 162 DS77
Marcilly Rd SW18 180 DD85
Marco Rd W6 159 CW76
Marcon Pl E8 142 DV65
Marconi Rd E10 123 EA60
Marconi Rd (Northfleet), Grav. 190 GD90
Marconi Way, Sthl. 136 CB72
Marcourt Lawns W5 138 CL70
Marcus Ct E15 144 EE67
Marcus Garvey Ms SE22 182 DV85
St. Aidan's Rd
Marcus Garvey Way SE24 161 DN84
Marcus Rd, Dart. 187 FG87
Marcus St E15 144 EF67
Marcus St SW18 180 DB86
Marcus Ter SW18 180 DB86
Marcuse Rd, Cat. 236 DR123
Mardale Dr NW9 118 CR57
Mardell Rd, Croy. 203 DX99
Marden Av, Brom. 204 EG100
Marden Cl, Chig. 104 EV47
Marden Cres, Bex. 187 FC85
Marden Cres, Croy. 201 DM100
Marden Pk (Woldingham), Cat. 253 DZ125
Marden Rd N17 122 DS55
Marden Rd, Croy. 201 DM100
Marden Rd, Rom. 127 FE58
Marden Sq SE16 162 DV76
Marder Rd W13 157 CG75
Mardyke Ho, Rain. 147 FD68
Lower Mardyke Av
Mardyke Rd, Harl. 36 EU13
Mare St E8 142 DV67
Marechal Niel Av, Sid. 185 ER90
Mareschal Rd, Guil. 258 AW136
Marescroft Rd, Slou. 131 AL70
Maresfield, Croy. 202 DS104
Maresfield Gdns NW3 120 DC64
Marfleet Cl, Cars. 200 DE103
Marford Rd (Wheathampstead), St.Alb. 28 CN07
Marford Rd, Welw.G.C. 28 CS10
Margaret Av E4 83 EB44
Margaret Av, Brwd. 109 FZ45
Margaret Av, St.Alb. 43 CD18
Margaret Bondfield Av, Bark. 146 EU66
Margaret Bldgs N16 122 DT60
Margaret Rd
Margaret Cl, Abb.L. 59 BT32
Margaret Cl, Epp. 70 EU29
Margaret Rd
Margaret Cl, Pot.B. 64 DC33
Margaret Cl, Rom. 127 FH57
Margaret Rd
Margaret Cl, Stai. 174 BK93
Charles Rd
Margaret Cl, Wal.Abb. 67 ED33
Margaret Ct W1 273 K8
Margaret Dr, Horn. 128 FM60
Margaret Gardner Dr SE9 185 EM89
Margaret Ingram Cl SW6 159 CZ79
John Smith Av
Margaret Lockwood Cl, Kings.T. 198 CM98
Margaret Rd N16 122 DT60
Margaret Rd, Barn. 80 DD42
Margaret Rd, Bex. 186 EX86
Margaret Rd, Epp. 70 EU29
Margaret Rd, Guil. 258 AW135
Margaret Rd, Rom. 127 FH57
Margaret Sq, Uxb. 134 BJ67
Margaret St W1 273 J8
Margaret St W1 141 DH72
Margaret Way, Couls. 235 DP118
Margaret Way, Ilf. 124 EL58
Margaretta Ter SW3 160 DE79
Margaretting Rd E12 124 EJ60
Margate Rd SW2 181 DL85
Margeholes, Wat. 94 BY47
Margery Gro, Tad. 249 CY129
Margery La, Tad. 249 CZ129
Margery Pk Rd E7 144 EG65
Margery Rd, Dag. 126 EX62
Margery St WC1 274 D3
Margery St WC1 141 DN69
Margery Wd, Welw.G.C. 30 DA06
Margery Wd La, Tad. 249 CZ129
Margery La
Margherita Pl, Wal.Abb. 68 EF34
Margherita Rd, Wal.Abb. 68 EG34
Margin Dr SW19 179 CX92
Margravine Gdns W6 159 CX78
Margravine Rd W6 159 CX79
Marham Gdns SW18 180 DE88
Marham Gdns, Mord. 200 DC100
Maria Cl SE1 162 DU77
Beatrice Rd
Maria Ter E1 143 DX70
Maria Theresa Cl, N.Mal. 198 CR99
Mariam Gdns, Horn. 128 FM61
Marian Cl, Hayes 136 BX70
Marian Ct, Sutt. 218 DB106
Marian Pl E2 142 DV68
Marian Rd SW16 201 DJ95
Marian Sq E2 142 DU68
Pritchard's Rd
Marian St E2 142 DV68
Hackney Rd
Marian Way NW10 139 CT66
Maricas Av, Har. 95 CD53
Marie Lloyd Gdns N19 121 DL59
Hornsey Ri Gdns
Marie Lloyd Wk E8 142 DU65
Forest Rd
Mariette Way, Wall. 219 DL109
Marigold All SE1 278 F1
Marigold Cl, Sthl. 136 BY73
Lancaster Rd
Marigold Pl, Harl. 36 EV11
Broadway Av
Marigold Rd N17 100 DW52
Marigold St SE16 162 DV75
Marigold Way E4 101 DZ51
Silver Birch Av
Marigold Way, Croy. 203 DX102
Marina App, Hayes 136 BY71
Marina Av, N.Mal. 199 CV99
Marina Cl, Brom. 204 EG97
Marina Cl, Cher. 194 BH102
Marina Dr, Dart. 188 FN88
Marina Dr (Northfleet), Grav. 191 GF87
Marina Dr, Well. 165 ES82
Marina Gdns, Rom. 127 FC58
Marina Gdns (Cheshunt), Wal.Cr. 66 DW30
Marina Way, Iver 133 BF73
Marina Way, Slou. 131 AK73
Marina Way, Tedd. 177 CK94
Fairways
Marine Dr SE18 165 EM77
Marine Dr, Bark. 145 ES69
Marine St SE16 162 DU76
Enid St
Marine Twr SE8 163 DZ79
Abinger Gro
Marinefield Rd SW6 160 DB82
Mariner Gdns, Rich. 177 CJ90
Mariner Rd E12 125 EM63
Dersingham Av
Mariner Way, Hem.H. 40 BN21
Mariners Ct, Green. 169 FV84
High St
Mariners Ms E14 163 ED77
Mariners Wk, Erith 167 FF79
Frobisher Rd
Marion Av, Shep. 195 BP99
Marion Cl, Bushey 76 BZ39
Marion Cl, Ilf. 103 ER52
Marion Cres, Orp. 206 EU99
Marion Gro, Wdf.Grn. 102 EE50
Marion Rd NW7 97 CU50
Marion Rd, Th.Hth. 202 DQ99
Marion Wk, Hem.H. 40 BM15
Washington Av
Marischal Rd SE13 163 ED83
Marisco Cl, Grays 171 GH77
Marish La (Denham), Uxb. 113 BC56
Marish Wf (Middlegreen), Slou. 152 AY75
Maritime Cl, Green. 189 FV85
Maritime Quay E14 163 EA78
Maritime St E3 143 DZ70
Marius Pas SW17 180 DG89
Marius Rd
Marius Rd SW17 180 DG89
Marjoram Cl, Guil. 242 AU130
Marjorams Av, Loug. 85 EM40
Marjorie Gro SW11 160 DF84
Marjorie Ms E1 143 DX72
Arbour Sq
Mark Av E4 83 EB44
Mark Cl, Bexh. 166 EY81
Mark Cl, Sthl. 136 CB74
Longford Av
Mark Dr (Chalfont St. Peter), Ger.Cr. 90 AX49
Mark Hall Moors, Harl. 36 EV12
Mark La EC3 275 N10
Mark La EC3 142 DS73
Mark La, Grav. 191 GL86
Mark Oak La, Lthd. 230 CA122
Mark Rd N22 99 DP54
Mark Rd, Hem.H. 40 BN18
Mark Sq EC2 275 M4
Mark St E15 144 EE66
Mark St EC2 275 M4
Mark St, Reig. 250 DB133
Mark Way, Swan. 207 FG99
Markab Rd, Nthwd. 93 BT50
Marke Cl, Kes. 222 EL105
Markedge La, Couls. 234 DE124
Markedge La, Red. 250 DF126
Markenfield Rd, Guil. 242 AX134
Markeston Grn, Wat. 94 BX49
Market Ct W1 273 K8
Market Est N7 141 DL65
Market Hill SE18 165 EN76
Market La, Edg. 96 CQ53
Market La, Iver 153 BC75
Market La, Slou. 153 BC75
Market Link, Rom. 127 FE56
Market Meadow, Orp. 206 EW98
Market Ms W1 277 H3
Market Ms W1 141 DH74
Market Oak La, Hem.H. 40 BN24
Market Pl N2 120 DE55
Market Pl NW11 120 DC56
Market Pl SE16 162 DU77
Southwark Pk Rd
Market Pl W1 273 K8
Market Pl W1 141 DJ72
Market Pl W3 138 CQ74
Market Pl, Bexh. 166 FA84
Market Pl, Brent. 157 CJ80
Market Pl, Dart. 188 FL87
Market St
Market Pl, Enf. 82 DR41
The Town
Market Pl (Chalfont St. Peter), Ger.Cr. 90 AX53
Market Pl, Hat. 45 CU17
Dog Kennel La
Market Pl, Hert. 32 DR09
Fore St
Market Pl, Kings.T. 197 CK96
Market Pl, Rom. 127 FE57
Market Pl (Abridge), Rom. 86 EV41
Market Pl, St.Alb. 43 CD20
Market Pl, Til. 171 GF82
Market Rd N7 141 DL65
Market Rd, Rich. 158 CN83
Market Row SW9 161 DN84
Atlantic Rd
Market Sq E2 275 P2
Market Sq E14 143 EB72
Chrisp St
Market Sq N9 100 DU47
New Rd
Market Sq, Amer. 55 AP40
High St
Market Sq, Brom. 204 EG96
Market Sq, Chesh. 54 AP32
High St
Market Sq, Harl. 35 ER14
East Gate
Market Sq, Stai. 173 BE91
Clarence St
Market Sq, Uxb. 134 BJ66
High St
Market Sq, Wal.Abb. 67 EC33
Leverton Way
Market Sq, West. 255 EQ127
Market Sq, Wok. 226 AY117
Cawsey Way
Market St E6 145 EM68
Market St SE18 165 EN77
Market St, Dart. 188 FL87
Market St, Guil. 258 AX135
Market St, Harl. 36 EW11
Market St, Hert. 32 DR09
Market St, Wat. 75 BV42
Market St, Wind. 151 AR81
Market Way E14 143 EB72
Kerbey St
Market Way, Wem. 118 CL64
Turton Rd
Market Way, West. 255 ER126
Costell's Meadow
Marketfield Rd, Red. 250 DF134
Marketfield Way, Red. 250 DF134
Markfield, Croy. 221 DZ110
Markfield Gdns E4 101 EB45
Markfield Rd N15 122 DU56
Markfield Rd, Cat. 252 DV126
Markham Pl SW3 276 D10
Markham Rd (Cheshunt), Wal.Cr. 66 DQ26
Markham Sq SW3 276 D10
Markham Sq SW3 160 DF78
Markham St SW3 276 C10
Markham St SW3 160 DE78
Markhole Cl, Hmptn. 176 BZ94
Priory Rd
Markhouse Av E17 123 DY58
Markhouse Rd E17 123 DZ57
Markland Ho W10 139 CX73
Markmanor Av E17 123 DY59
Marks Rd, Rom. 127 FC57
Marks Rd, Warl. 237 DY118
Marks Sq (Northfleet), Grav. 191 GF91
Marksbury Av, Rich. 158 CN83
Markville Gdns, Cat. 252 DU125
Markway, Sun. 196 BW96

Markwell Cl SE26 182 DV91
Longton Gro
Markwell Wd, Harl. 51 EP21
Markyate Rd, Dag. 126 EV64
Marl Rd SW18 160 DB84
Marl St SW18 160 DC84
Marl Rd
Marlands Rd, Ilf. 124 EL55
Marlborough Av E8 142 DU67
Marlborough Av N14 99 DJ48
Marlborough Av, Edg. 96 CP48
Marlborough Av, Ruis. 115 BQ58
Marlborough Bldgs SW3 276 C8
Marlborough Bldgs SW3 160 DE77
Marlborough Cl N20 98 DF48
Marlborough Gdns
Marlborough Cl SE17 278 G9
Marlborough Cl SW19 180 DE93
Marlborough Cl, Grays 170 GC75
Marlborough Cl, Orp. 205 ET101
Aylesham Rd
Marlborough Cl, Upmin. 129 FS60
Marlborough Cl, Walt. 196 BX104
Arch Rd
Marlborough Ct W1 273 K9
Marlborough Ct W8 160 DA77
Marlborough Ct, Dor. 263 CH136
Marlborough Rd
Marlborough Ct, Wall. 219 DJ108
Cranley Gdns
Marlborough Cres W4 158 CR76
Marlborough Cres, Sev. 256 FE124
Marlborough Dr, Ilf. 124 EL55
Marlborough Dr, Wey. 195 BQ104
Marlborough Gdns N20 98 DF48
Marlborough Gdns, Upmin. 129 FR60
Marlborough Gate, St.Alb. 43 CE20
Marlborough Gate Ho W2 140 DD73
Elms Ms
Marlborough Gro SE1 162 DU78
Marlborough Hill NW8 140 DC67
Marlborough Hill, Dor. 263 CH136
Marlborough Hill, Har. 117 CF56
Marlborough La SE7 164 EJ79
Marlborough Pk Av, Sid. 186 EU87
Marlborough Pl NW8 140 DC68
Marlborough Ri, Hem.H. 40 BL17
Marlborough Rd E4 101 EA51
Marlborough Rd E7 144 EJ66
Marlborough Rd E15 124 EE63
Borthwick Rd
Marlborough Rd E18 124 EG55
Marlborough Rd N9 100 DT46
Marlborough Rd N19 121 DK61
Marlborough Rd N22 99 DL52
Marlborough Rd SW1 277 L3
Marlborough Rd SW1 141 DJ74
Marlborough Rd SW19 180 DD93
Marlborough Rd W4 158 CQ78
Marlborough Rd W5 157 CK75
Marlborough Rd, Ashf. 174 BK92
Marlborough Rd, Bexh. 166 EX83
Marlborough Rd, Brwd. 108 FU44
Marlborough Rd, Brom. 204 EJ98
Marlborough Rd, Dag. 126 EV63
Marlborough Rd, Dart. 188 FJ86
Marlborough Rd, Dor. 263 CH136
Marlborough Rd, Felt. 176 BX89
Marlborough Rd, Hmptn. 176 CA93
Marlborough Rd, Islw. 157 CH81
Marlborough Rd, Rich. 178 CL86
Marlborough Rd, Rom. 126 FA56
Marlborough Rd, St.Alb. 43 CE20
Marlborough Rd, Slou. 152 AX77
Marlborough Rd, S.Croy. 220 DQ108
Marlborough Rd, Sthl. 156 BW76
Marlborough Rd, Sutt. 200 DA104
Marlborough Rd, Uxb. 135 BP70
Marlborough Rd, Wat. 75 BV42
Marlborough Rd, Wok. 227 BA116
Marlborough St SW3 276 B9
Marlborough St SW3 160 DE77
Marlborough Yd N19 121 DK61
Marlborough Rd
Marld, The, Ash. 232 CM118
Marle Gdns, Wal.Abb. 67 EC32
Marler Rd SE23 183 DY88
Marlescroft Way, Loug. 85 EP43
Marley Av, Bexh. 166 EX79
Marley Cl N15 121 DP56
Stanmore Rd
Marley Cl, Add. 211 BF107
Marley Cl, Grnf. 136 CA69
Marley Ct, Brox. 49 DZ23
Marley Ri, Dor. 263 CG139
Marley Rd, Welw.G.C. 30 DA11
Marley Wk NW2 119 CW64
Lennon Rd
Marlin Cl, Berk. 38 AT18
Marlin Cl, Sun. 175 BT93
Marlin Copse, Berk. 38 AU20
Marlin End, Berk. 38 AT20
Marlin Sq, Abb.L. 59 BT31
Marling Way, Grav. 191 GL92
Marlingdene Cl, Hmptn. 176 CA93
Marlings Cl, Chis. 205 ES98
Marlings Cl, Whyt. 236 DS117
Marlings Pk Av, Chis. 205 ES98
Marlins, The, Nthwd. 93 BT51
Marlins Cl, Rick. 73 BE40
Marlins Cl, Sutt. 218 DC106
Turnpike La
Marlins Meadow, Wat. 75 BR44
Marlins Turn, Hem.H. 40 BH17
Marloes Cl, Wem. 117 CK63
Marloes Rd W8 160 DB76
Marlow Av, Purf. 168 FN77
Marlow Cl SE20 202 DV97
Marlow Ct NW6 139 CX66
Marlow Ct NW9 119 CT55
Marlow Cres, Twick. 177 CF86
Marlow Dr, Sutt. 199 CX103
Marlow Gdns, Hayes 155 BR76
Marlow Rd E6 145 EM69
Marlow Rd SE20 202 DV97
Marlow Rd, Sthl. 156 BZ76
Marlow Way SE16 163 DX75
Marlowe Cl, Chis. 185 ER93
Marlowe Cl, Ilf. 103 EQ53
Marlowe Ct SE19 182 DT92
Lymer Av
Marlowe Gdns SE9 185 EN86
Marlowe Gdns, Rom. 106 FJ53
Shenstone Gdns
Marlowe Rd E17 123 EC56
Marlowe Sq, Mitch. 201 DJ98
Marlowe Way, Croy. 201 DL103
Marlowes, Hem.H. 40 BK21
Marlowes, The NW8 140 DD67
Marlowes, The, Dart. 167 FD84
Marlpit Av, Couls. 235 DL117
Marlpit La, Couls. 235 DK116
Marlton St SE10 164 EF78
Woolwich Rd
Marlwood Cl, Sid. 185 ES89
Marlyns Cl, Guil. 243 BA130
Marlyns Dr, Guil. 243 BA130
Marlyon Rd, Ilf. 104 EV50
Marmadon Rd SE18 165 ET77
Marmion App E4 101 EA49
Marmion Av E4 101 DZ49
Marmion Cl E4 101 DZ49
Marmion Ms SW11 160 DG83
Taybridge Rd
Marmion Rd SW11 160 DG84
Marmont Rd SE15 162 DU81
Marmora Rd SE22 182 DW86
Marmot Rd, Houns. 156 BX83
Marne Av N11 99 DH49
Marne Av, Well. 166 EU83
Marne St W10 139 CY69
Marnell Way, Houns. 156 BX83
Marney Rd SW11 160 DG84
Marneys Cl, Epsom 232 CN115
Marnfield Cres SW2 181 DM87
Marnham Av NW2 119 CY63
Marnham Cres, Grnf. 136 CB69
Marnham Ri, Hem.H. 40 BG18
Marnock Rd SE4 183 DY85
Maroon St E14 143 DY71
Maroons Way SE6 183 EA92
Marquess Rd N1 142 DR65
Marquis Cl, Wem. 138 CM66
Marquis Rd N4 121 DM60
Marquis Rd N22 99 DM51
Marquis Rd NW1 141 DK65
Marrabon Cl, Sid. 186 EU88
Marram Ct, Grays 170 GE79
Medlar Rd
Marrick Cl SW15 159 CU84
Marrilyne Av, Enf. 83 DZ38
Marriot Ter, Rick. 73 BF42
Marriots Cl NW9 119 CT58
Marriott Cl, Felt. 175 BR86
Marriott Lo Cl, Add. 212 BJ105
Marriott Rd E15 144 EE67
Marriott Rd N4 121 DM60
Marriott Rd N10 98 DF53
Marriott Rd, Barn. 79 CX41
Marriott Rd, Dart. 188 FN87
Marriotts, Harl. 36 EW10
Old Rd
Marriotts Way, Hem.H. 40 BK22
Marrods Bottom, Beac. 88 AJ47
Marrowells, Wey. 195 BT104
Marryat Pl SW19 179 CY91
Marryat Rd SW19 179 CX92
Marryat Rd, Enf. 82 DV35
Marryat Sq SW6 159 CY81
Marsala Rd SE13 163 EB84
Marsden Cl, Welw.G.C. 29 CV11
Marsden Grn, Welw.G.C. 29 CV10
Marsden Rd N9 100 DV47
Marsden Rd SE15 162 DT83
Marsden Rd, Welw.G.C. 29 CV10
Marsden St NW5 140 DG65
Marsden Way, Orp. 223 ET105
Marsh Av, Epsom 216 CS110
Marsh Av, Mitch. 200 DG96
Marsh Cl NW7 97 CT48
Marsh Cl, Wal.Cr. 67 DZ33
Marsh Ct SW19 200 DC95
Marsh Dr NW9 119 CT58
Marsh Fm Rd, Twick. 177 CF88
Marsh Grn Rd, Dag. 146 FA67
Marsh Hill E9 123 DY64
Marsh La E10 123 EA61
Marsh La N17 100 DV52
Marsh La NW7 96 CS49
Marsh La, Add. 212 BH105
Marsh La, Harl. 36 EY10
Marsh La, Maid. 150 AF75
Marsh La, Stan. 95 CJ50
Marsh La, Ware 33 DY07
Marsh La (Stanstead Abbotts), Ware 33 ED12
Marsh La (Dorney), Wind. 150 AF75
Marsh Rd, Pnr. 116 BY56
Marsh Rd, Wem. 137 CK68
Marsh St E14 163 EB77
Harbinger Rd
Marsh St, Dart. 168 FN82
Marsh Ter, Orp. 206 EX98
Buttermere Rd
Marsh Wall E14 143 EA74
Marsh Way, Rain. 147 FD72
Marshall Av, St.Alb. 43 CE17
Marshall Cl SW18 180 DC86
Allfarthing La
Marshall Cl, Har. 117 CD59
Bowen Rd
Marshall Cl, Houns. 176 BZ85
Marshall Cl, S.Croy. 220 DU113
Marshall Dr, Hayes 135 BT71
Marshall Path SE28 146 EV73
Attlee Rd
Marshall Pl (New Haw), Add. 212 BJ109
Marshall Rd E10 123 EB62
Marshall Rd N17 100 DR53
Marshall St W1 273 L9
Marshall St W1 141 DJ72
Marshalls Cl N11 99 DH49
Marshalls Cl, Epsom 216 CQ113
Marshalls Dr, Rom. 127 FE55
Marshall's Gro SE18 164 EL77
Marshalls Pl SE16 162 DT76
Spa Rd
Marshalls Rd, Rom. 127 FD56
Marshall's Rd, Sutt. 218 DB105
Marshals Dr, St.Alb. 43 CG17
Marshalsea Rd SE1 279 J4
Marshalsea Rd SE1 162 DQ75
Marshalswick La, St.Alb. 43 CH17
Marsham Cl, Chis. 185 EP92
Marsham La, Ger.Cr. 112 AY58
Marsham Lo, Ger.Cr. 112 AY58
Marsham St SW1 277 N7
Marsham St SW1 161 DK76
Marsham Way, Ger.Cr. 112 AY57
Marshbrook Cl SE3 164 EK83
Marshcroft Dr (Cheshunt), Wal.Cr. 67 DY30
Marshe Cl, Pot.B. 64 DD32
Marshfield (Datchet), Slou. 152 AW81
Marshfield St E14 163 EC76
Marshfoot Rd, Grays 170 GE78
Marshgate, Harl. 35 ES12
School La
Marshgate Dr, Hert. 32 DS08
Marshgate La E15 143 EB67
Marshgate Path SE28 165 EQ77
Tom Cribb Rd
Marshgate Sidings E15 143 EB66
Marshgate La
Marshgate Trd Est, Maid. 130 AG72
Marshmoor Cres, Hat. 45 CW22
Marshmoor La, Hat. 45 CW22
Marshside Cl N9 100 DW46
Marsland Cl SE17 161 DP78
Marston, Epsom 216 CQ111
Marston Av, Chess. 216 CL107
Marston Av, Dag. 126 FA61
Marston Cl NW6 140 DC66
Fairfax Rd
Marston Cl, Chesh. 54 AN27
Marston Cl, Dag. 126 FA62
Marston Cl, Hem.H. 40 BN21
Marston Ct, Walt. 196 BW102
St. Johns Dr
Marston Dr, Warl. 237 DY118
Marston Ho, Grays 170 GA79
Marston Rd, Hodd. 49 EB16
Marston Rd, Ilf. 102 EL53
Marston Rd, Tedd. 177 CH92
Marston Rd, Wok. 226 AV117
Marston Way SE19 181 DP94
Marsworth Av, Pnr. 94 BX53
Marsworth Cl, Hayes 136 BY71
Marsworth Cl, Wat. 75 BS44
Mart St WC2 274 A9
Martaban Rd N16 122 DS61
Martel Pl E8 142 DT65
Dalston La
Martell Rd SE21 182 DR90
Martello St E8 142 DV66
Martello Ter E8 142 DV66
Marten Gate, St.Alb. 43 CG16
Marten Rd E17 101 EA54
Martens Av, Bexh. 167 FC84
Martens Cl, Bexh. 167 FC84
Martha Ct E2 142 DV68
Martha Rd E4 101 DZ51
Martha Rd E15 144 EE65
Martha St E1 142 DV72
Martham Cl SE28 146 EX73
Martha's Bldgs EC1 275 K4
Marthorne Cres, Har. 95 CD54
Martian Av, Hem.H. 40 BM17
Martin Bowes Rd SE9 165 EM83
Martin Cl N9 101 DX46
Martin Cl, Hat. 45 CU20
Martin Cl, S.Croy. 221 DX111
Martin Cl, Uxb. 134 BL68
Valley Rd
Martin Cl, Warl. 236 DV116
Martin Cl, Wind. 150 AJ81
Martin Cres, Croy. 201 DN102
Martin Dene, Bexh. 186 EZ85
Martin Dr (Stone), Dart. 188 FQ86
Martin Dr, Nthlt. 116 BZ64
Martin Dr, Rain. 147 FH70
Martin Gdns, Dag. 126 EW63
Martin Gro, Mord. 200 DA97
Martin La EC4 275 L10
Martin Ri, Bexh. 186 EZ85
Martin Rd, Dag. 126 EW63
Martin Rd, Dart. 188 FJ90
Martin Rd, Guil. 242 AU132
Martin Rd, Slou. 152 AS76
Martin Rd, S.Ock. 149 FR73
Martin St SE28 145 ES74
Martin Way SW20 199 CY97
Martin Way, Mord. 199 CY97
Martin Way, Wok. 226 AU118
Martina Ter, Chig. 103 ET50
Manford Way
Martinbridge Trd Est, Enf. 82 DU43
Martindale SW14 178 CQ85
Martindale, Iver 133 BD70
Martindale Av E16 144 EG73
Martindale Av, Orp. 224 EU106
Martindale Cl, Guil. 243 BD132
Gilliat Dr
Martindale Rd SW12 181 DH87
Martindale Rd, Hem.H. 39 BF19
Martindale Rd, Houns. 156 BY83
Martindale Rd, Wok. 226 AT118
Martineau Cl, Esher 215 CD105
Martineau Dr, Dor. 263 CH138
Martineau Ms N5 121 DP63
Martineau Rd
Martineau Rd N5 121 DP63
Martineau St E1 142 DW73
Martinfield, Welw.G.C. 29 CZ08
Martingale Cl, Sun. 195 BU98
Martingales Cl, Rich. 177 CK90
Martini Dr, Enf. 83 EA37
Government Row
Martins Cl, Guil. 243 BC133
Martins Cl, Orp. 206 EX97
Martins Cl, Rad. 77 CE36
Martins Cl, W.Wick. 203 ED102
Martins Ct, St.Alb. 43 CH23
Cell Barnes La
Martins Dr, Hert. 32 DV09
Martins Dr (Cheshunt), Wal.Cr. 67 DY28
Martins Mt, Barn. 80 DA42
Martin's Plain, Slou. 132 AS69
Martins Rd, Brom. 204 EE96
Martins Shaw (Chipstead), Sev. 256 FC122
Martins Wk N10 98 DG53
Martins Wk, Borwd. 78 CN42
Siskin Cl
Martinsfield Cl, Chig. 103 ES49
Martinstown Cl, Horn. 128 FN58
Martinsyde, Wok. 227 BC117
Martlesham, Welw.G.C. 30 DE09
Martlesham Cl, Horn. 128 FJ64
Martlet Gro, Nthlt. 136 BX69
Javelin Way
Martlett Ct WC2 274 A9
Martley Dr, Ilf. 125 EP57
Martock Cl, Har. 117 CG56
Martock Gdns N11 98 DF50
Marton Cl SE6 183 EA90
Marton Rd N16 122 DS61
Martyr Cl, St.Alb. 43 CD24
Creighton Av
Martyr Rd, Guil. 258 AX135
Martyrs La, Wok. 211 BB112
Martys Yd NW3 120 DD63
Hampstead High St
Marunden Grn, Slou. 131 AM69
Marvell Av, Hayes 135 BU71
Marvels Cl SE12 184 EH89
Marvels La SE12 184 EH89
Marville Rd SW6 159 CZ80
Marvin St E8 142 DV65
Sylvester Rd
Marwell, West. 255 EP126
Marwell Cl, Rom. 127 FG57
Marwell Cl, W.Wick. 204 EF103
Deer Pk Way
Marwood Cl, Kings L. 58 BN29
Marwood Cl, Well. 166 EV83
Mary Adelaide Cl SW15 178 CS91
Mary Ann Gdns SE8 163 EA79
Mary Cl, Stan. 118 CM56
Mary Datchelor Cl SE5 162 DR81
Mary Grn NW8 140 DB67
Mary Lawrenson Pl SE3 164 EF80
Mary Macarthur Ho W6 159 CY79
Field Rd
Mary Morgan Ct, Slou. 131 AR71
Douglas Rd
Mary Peters Dr, Grnf. 117 CD64
Mary Pl W11 139 CY73
Mary Rd, Guil. 258 AW135
Mary Rose Cl, Grays 169 FW77
Mary Rose Cl, Hmptn. 196 CA95
Ashley Rd
Mary Rose Mall E6 145 EN71
Frobisher Rd
Mary Seacole Cl E8 142 DT67
Clarissa St
Mary St E16 144 EF71
Barking Rd
Mary St N1 142 DQ67
Mary Ter NW1 141 DH67
Maryatt Av, Har. 116 CB61
Marybank SE18 165 EM77
Maryfield Cl, Bex. 187 FE90
Marygold Wk, Amer. 72 AV39
Maryhill Cl, Ken. 236 DQ117
Maryland, Hat. 45 CT19
Maryland Conv, St.Alb. 43 CD18
Maryland Ind Est E15 123 ED64
Maryland Rd
Maryland Pk E15 124 EE64
Maryland Pt E15 144 EE65
Leytonstone Rd
Maryland Rd E15 123 ED64
Maryland Rd N22 99 DM51
Maryland Rd, Th.Hth. 201 DP95
Maryland Sq E15 124 EE64
Maryland St E15 123 ED64
Maryland Wk N1 142 DQ67
Popham St
Maryland Way, Sun. 195 BU96
Marylands Rd W9 140 DA70
Marylebone Flyover NW1 272 A7
Marylebone Flyover W2 272 A7
Marylebone High St W1 272 G6
Marylebone High St W1 140 DG71
Marylebone La W1 273 H9
Marylebone La W1 140 DG72
Marylebone Ms W1 273 H7
Marylebone Ms W1 141 DH71
Marylebone Pas W1 273 L8
Marylebone Rd NW1 272 C6
Marylebone Rd NW1 140 DE71
Marylebone St W1 272 G7
Marylebone St W1 140 DG71
Marylee Way SE11 278 C10
Marylee Way SE11 161 DM77
Maryon Gro SE7 164 EL77
Maryon Ms NW3 120 DE63
South End Rd
Maryon Rd SE7 164 EL77
Maryon Rd SE18 164 EL77
Maryrose Way N20 98 DD46
Mary's Ter, Twick. 177 CG87
Maryside, Slou. 152 AY75
Masbro Rd W14 159 CX76
Mascalls Ct SE7 164 EJ79
Victoria Way
Mascalls Gdns, Brwd. 108 FT49
Mascalls La, Brwd. 108 FT49
Mascalls Rd SE7 164 EJ79
Mascoll Path, Slou. 131 AM69
Mascotte Rd SW15 159 CX84
Mascotts Cl NW2 119 CV62
Masefield Av, Borwd. 78 CP43
Masefield Av, Sthl. 136 CA73
Masefield Av, Stan. 95 CF50
Masefield Cl, Chesh. 54 AP28
Masefield Cl, Erith 167 FF81
Masefield Cl, Rom. 106 FJ53
Masefield Ct, Brwd. 108 FW49
Masefield Cres N14 81 DJ44
Masefield Cres, Rom. 106 FJ53
Masefield Dr, Upmin. 128 FQ59
Masefield Gdns E6 145 EN70
Masefield La, Hayes 135 BV70
Masefield Rd, Dart. 188 FP85
Masefield Rd (Northfleet), Grav. 190 GD90
Masefield Rd, Grays 170 GE75
Masefield Rd, Hmptn. 176 BZ91
Wordsworth Rd
Masefield Vw, Orp. 205 EQ104
Masefield Way, Stai. 174 BM88
Masham Ho, Erith 166 EX75
Kale Rd
Mashie Rd W3 138 CS72
Mashiters Hill, Rom. 105 FD53
Mashiters Wk, Rom. 127 FE55
Maskall Cl SW2 181 DN88
Maskani Wk SW16 181 DJ94
Bates Cres
Maskell Rd SW17 180 DC90
Maskelyne Cl SW11 160 DE81
Maslen Rd, St.Alb. 43 CJ23
Mason Bradbear Ct N1 142 DR65
St. Paul's Rd
Mason Cl E16 144 EG73
Mason Cl SE16 162 DU78
Stevenson Cres
Mason Cl SW20 199 CX95
Mason Cl, Bexh. 167 FB83
Mason Cl, Borwd. 78 CQ40
Mason Cl, Hmptn. 196 BZ95
Mason Dr, Rom. 106 FL54
Whitmore Av
Mason Rd, Sutt. 218 DB106
Manor Pl
Mason Rd, Wdf.Grn. 102 EE49
Mason St SE17 279 L8
Mason St SE17 162 DR77
Mason Way, Wal.Abb. 68 EF34
Masonic Hall Rd, Cher. 193 BF100
Masons Arms Ms W1 273 J9
Masons Av EC2 275 K8
Masons Av, Croy. 202 DQ104
Masons Av, Har. 117 CF56
Masons Br Rd, Red. 267 DH139
Masons Ct, Slou. 131 AL73
Masons Ct, Wem. 118 CN61
Mayfields
Masons Grn La W3 138 CN71
Masons Hill SE18 165 EP77
Masons Hill, Brom. 204 EG97
Masons Paddock, Dor. 247 CG134
Mason's Pl EC1 274 G2
Mason's Pl EC1 141 DP69
Masons Pl, Mitch. 200 DF95
Masons Rd, Enf. 82 DW36
Masons Rd, Hem.H. 41 BP19
Masons Rd, Slou. 131 AL73
Mason's Yd SW1 277 L2
Mason's Yd SW19 179 CX92
High St Wimbledon
Massetts Rd, Horl. 268 DF149
Massey Cl N11 99 DH50
Grove Rd
Massey Ct E6 144 EJ67
Massie Rd E8 142 DU65
Graham Rd
Massingberd Way SW17 181 DH91
Massinger St SE17 279 M9
Massingham St E1 143 DX70
Masson Av, Ruis. 136 BW65
Mast Ho Ter E14 163 EA77
Mast Leisure Pk SE16 163 DX76
Master Cl, Oxt. 254 EE129
Church La
Master Gunner Pl SE18 164 EL80
Masterman Ho SE5 162 DR80
Masterman Rd E6 144 EL69
Masters Cl SW16 181 DJ93
Blegborough Rd
Masters Dr SE16 162 DV78
Masters St E1 143 DX71
Masthead Cl, Dart. 168 FQ84
Mastmaker Rd E14 163 EA75
Maswell Pk Cres, Houns. 176 CC85
Maswell Pk Rd, Houns. 176 CB85
Matcham Rd E11 124 EE62
Matching Rd (Hatfield Heath), B.Stort. 37 FH06
Matching Rd (Old Harlow), Harl. 37 FB11
Matching Rd, Ong. 53 FH18
Matchless Dr SE18 165 EN80
Matfield Cl, Brom. 204 EG99
Matfield Rd, Belv. 166 FA79
Matham Gro SE22 162 DT84
Matham Rd, E.Mol. 197 CD99
Matheson Rd W14 159 CZ77
Mathews Av E6 145 EN68
Mathews Pk Av E15 144 EF65
Mathias Cl, Epsom 216 CQ113
Mathisen Way (Colnbrook), Slou. 153 BE81
Mathon Ct, Guil. 243 AZ134
Cross Las
Matilda Cl SE19 182 DR94
Elizabeth Way
Matilda St N1 141 DM67
Matlock Cl SE24 162 DQ84
Matlock Cl, Barn. 79 CX44
Matlock Ct SE5 162 DR84
Denmark Hill Est
Matlock Cres, Sutt. 217 CY105
Matlock Cres, Wat. 94 BW48
Matlock Gdns, Horn. 128 FL62
Matlock Gdns, Sutt. 217 CY105
Matlock Pl, Sutt. 217 CY105
Matlock Rd E10 123 EC58
Matlock Rd, Cat. 236 DS121
Matlock St E14 143 DY72
Matlock Way, N.Mal. 198 CR95
Matrimony Pl SW8 161 DJ82
Matson Ct, Wdf.Grn. 102 EE52
The Bridle Path
Matthew Arnold Cl, Cob. 213 BU114
Matthew Arnold Cl, Stai. 174 BJ93
Elizabeth Av
Matthew Cl W10 139 CX70
Matthew Ct, Mitch. 201 DK99
Matthew Parker St SW1 277 N5
Matthew Parker St SW1 161 DK75
Matthews Cl (Havering-atte-Bower), Rom. 106 FM53
Oak Rd
Matthews Gdns (New Addington), Croy. 221 ED111
Matthews Rd, Grnf. 117 CD64
Matthews St SW11 160 DF82
Matthews St, Reig. 266 DA138
Matthews Yd WC2 273 P9
Matthias Rd N16 122 DR64
Mattingley Way SE15 162 DT80
Daniel Gdns
Mattison Rd N4 121 DN58
Mattock La W5 137 CH74
Mattock La W13 137 CH74
Maud Cashmore Way SE18 165 EM76
Maud Gdns E13 144 EF67
Maud Gdns, Bark. 145 ET68
Maud Rd E10 123 EC62
Maud Rd E13 144 EF68
Maud St E16 144 EF71
Maud Wilkes Cl NW5 121 DJ64
Maude Cres, Wat. 75 BV37
Maude Rd E17 123 DY57
Maude Rd SE5 162 DS81
Maude Rd, Beac. 89 AN54
Maude Rd, Swan. 187 FG93
Maude Ter E17 123 DY56
Maudesville Cotts W7 137 CE74
The Bdy
Maudlin's Grn E1 142 DU74
Marble Quay
Maudslay Rd SE9 165 EM83
Maudsley Ho, Brent. 158 CL78
Green Dragon La
Mauleverer Rd SW2 181 DL85
Maundeby Wk NW10 138 CS65
Neasden La
Maunder Rd W7 137 CF74
Maunds Hatch, Harl. 51 ER19
Maunsel St SW1 277 M8
Maunsel St SW1 161 DK77
Maurice Av N22 99 DP54
Maurice Av, Cat. 236 DR122
Maurice Brown Cl NW7 97 CX50
Maurice St W12 139 CV72
Maurice Wk NW11 120 DC56
Maurier Cl, Nthlt. 136 BW67
Mauritius Rd SE10 164 EE77
Maury Rd N16 122 DU61
Mavelstone Cl, Brom. 204 EL95
Mavelstone Rd, Brom. 204 EL95
Maverton Rd E3 143 EA67
Mavis Av, Epsom 216 CS106
Mavis Cl, Epsom 216 CS106
Mavis Gro, Horn. 128 FL61
Mavis Wk E6 144 EL71
Mawbey Est SE1 162 DU78
Mawbey Pl SE1 162 DT78
Mawbey Rd SE1 162 DT78
Old Kent Rd
Mawbey Rd (Ottershaw), Cher. 211 BD107
Mawbey St SW8 161 DL80
Mawney Cl, Rom. 105 FB54
Mawney Rd, Rom. 127 FC56
Mawson Cl SW20 199 CY96
Mawson La W4 159 CT79
Great W Rd
Maxey Gdns, Dag. 126 EY63
Maxey Rd SE18 165 EQ77
Maxey Rd, Dag. 126 EY63
Maxfield Cl N20 98 DC45

372

Middle Rd, Wal.Abb. 67 EB32
Middle Row W10 139 CY70
Middle St EC1 275 H6
Middle St, Bet. 264 CP136
Middle St, Croy. 202 DQ104
Surrey St
Middle St (Shere), Guil. 260 BN139
Middle St, Wal.Abb. 50 EG23
Middle Temple EC4 274 D10
Middle Temple La EC4 274 D9
Middle Temple La EC4 141 DN72
Middle Wk (Burnham), Slou. 130 AH69
Middle Wk, Wok. 226 AY117
Commercial Way
Middle Way SW16 201 DK96
Middle Way, Erith 166 EY76
Middle Way, Hayes 136 BW70
Middle Way, Wat. 75 BV37
Middle Way, The, Har. 95 CF54
Middle Yd SE1 279 L2
Middlefield, Hat. 45 CU17
Middlefield, Horl. 269 DJ147
Middlefield, Welw.G.C. 29 CY13
Middlefield Av, Hodd. 49 EA15
Middlefield Cl, Hodd. 49 EA15
Middlefield Cl, St.Alb. 43 CJ17
Middlefield Gdns, Ilf. 125 EP58
Middlefield Rd, Hodd. 49 EA15
Middlefielde W13 137 CH71
Middlefields, Croy. 221 DY109
Middlegreen Rd, Slou. 132 AX74
Middleham Gdns N18 100 DU51
Middleham Rd N18 100 DU51
Middleknights Hill, Hem.H. 40 BG17
Middlemead Cl (Bookham), Lthd. 246 CA125
Middlemead Rd (Bookham), Lthd. 246 BZ125
Middlesborough Rd N18 100 DU51
Middlesex Business Cen, Sthl. 156 CA75
Middlesex Ct W4 159 CT77
British Gro
Middlesex Ho, Wem. 137 CK67
Middlesex Pas EC1 274 G7
Middlesex Rd, Mitch. 201 DL99
Middlesex St E1 275 N7
Middlesex St E1 142 DS71
Middlesex Wf E5 122 DW61
Middleton Av E4 101 DZ49
Middleton Av, Grnf. 137 CD68
Middleton Av, Sid. 186 EW93
Middleton Cl E4 101 DZ48
Middleton Dr SE16 163 DX75
Middleton Dr, Pnr. 115 BU55
Middleton Gdns, Ilf. 125 EP58
Middleton Gro N7 121 DL64
Middleton Hall La, Brwd. 108 FY47
Middleton Ms N7 121 DL64
Middleton Gro
Middleton Pl W1 273 K7
Middleton Rd E8 142 DT66
Middleton Rd NW11 120 DA59
Middleton Rd, Brwd. 108 FY46
Middleton Rd, Cars. 200 DE101
Middleton Rd (Downside), Cob. 229 BV119
Middleton Rd, Epsom 216 CR110
Middleton Rd, Hayes 135 BR71
Middleton Rd, Mord. 200 DC100
Middleton Rd, Rick. 92 BG46
Middleton St E2 142 DV69
Middleton Way SE13 163 ED84
Middleway NW11 120 DB57
Middlings, The, Sev. 256 FF125
Middlings Ri, Sev. 256 FF126
Middlings Wd, Sev. 256 FF125
Midfield Av, Bexh. 167 FC83
Midfield Av, Swan. 187 FH93
Midfield Par, Bexh. 167 FC83
Midfield Way, Orp. 206 EU95
Midford Pl W1 273 L5
Midgarth Cl (Oxshott), Lthd. 214 CC114
Midholm NW11 120 DB56
Midholm, Wem. 118 CN60
Midholm Cl NW11 120 DB56
Midholm Rd, Croy. 203 DY103
Midhope Cl, Wok. 226 AY119
Midhope Gdns, Wok. 226 AY119
Midhope Rd
Midhope Rd, Wok. 226 AY119
Midhope St WC1 274 A3
Midhurst Av N10 120 DG55
Midhurst Av, Croy. 201 DN101
Midhurst Cl, Horn. 127 FG63
Midhurst Gdns, Uxb. 135 BQ66
Midhurst Hill, Bexh. 186 FA86
Midhurst Rd W13 157 CG75
Midland Cres NW3 140 DC65
Finchley Rd
Midland Pl E14 163 EC78
Ferry St
Midland Rd E10 123 EC59
Midland Rd NW1 273 N1
Midland Rd NW1 141 DK68
Midland Rd, Hem.H. 40 BK20
Midland Ter NW2 119 CX62
Kara Way
Midland Ter NW10 138 CS70
Midleton Ind Est, Guil. 242 AV133
Midleton Ind Est Rd, Guil. 242 AV133
Midleton Rd, Guil. 242 AV133
Midleton Rd, N.Mal. 198 CQ97
Midlothian Rd E3 143 DZ71
Midmoor Rd SW12 181 DJ88
Midmoor Rd SW19 199 CX95
Midship Cl SE16 143 DX74
Surrey Water Rd
Midship Pt E14 163 EA75
Midstrath Rd NW10 118 CS63
Midsummer Av, Houns. 156 BZ84
Midway, St.Alb. 42 CB23
Midway, Sutt. 199 CZ101
Midway, Walt. 195 BV103
Midway Av, Cher. 194 BG97
Midway Av, Egh. 193 BB97
Midway Cl, Stai. 174 BH90
Midwinter Cl, Well. 166 EU83
Hook La
Midwood Cl NW2 119 CV62
Miena Way, Ash. 231 CK117
Miers Cl E6 145 EN67
Mighell Av, Ilf. 124 EK57
Mike Spring Ct, Grav. 191 GK91
Milan Rd, Sthl. 156 BZ75
Milborne Gro SW10 160 DC78
Milborne St E9 142 DW65
Milborough Cres SE12 184 EE86
Milbourne La, Esher 214 CC107
Milbrook, Esher 214 CC107
Milburn Dr, West Dr. 134 BL73
Milburn Wk, Epsom 232 CS115
Milcombe Cl, Wok. 226 AV118
Inglewood
Milcote St SE1 278 F5
Milcote St SE1 161 DP75
Mildenhall Rd E5 122 DW63
Mildenhall Rd, Slou. 132 AS72
Mildmay Av N1 142 DR65
Mildmay Gro N N1 122 DR64
Mildmay Gro S N1 122 DR64
Mildmay Pk N1 122 DR64
Mildmay Pl N16 122 DS64
Boleyn Rd
Mildmay Pl (Shoreham), Sev. 225 FF111
Mildmay Rd N1 122 DS64
Mildmay Rd, Ilf. 125 EP62
Winston Way
Mildmay Rd, Rom. 127 FC57
Mildmay St N1 142 DR65
Mildred Av, Borwd. 78 CN42
Mildred Av, Hayes 155 BR77
Mildred Av, Nthlt. 116 CB64
Mildred Av, Wat. 75 BT42
Mildred Cl, Dart. 188 FN86
Mildred Rd, Erith 167 FE78
Mile Cl, Wal.Abb. 67 EC33
Mile End, The E17 101 DX53
Mile End Pl E1 143 DX70
Mile End Rd E1 142 DW71
Mile End Rd E3 142 DW71
Mile Ho Cl, St.Alb. 43 CG23
Mile Ho La, St.Alb. 43 CG23
Mile Path, Wok. 226 AV120
Mile Rd, Wall. 201 DJ102
Miles Cl, Harl. 51 EP16
Miles Dr SE28 145 ER74
Miles La, Cob. 214 BY113
Miles Pl NW1 272 A6
Miles Pl, Surb. 198 CM98
Villiers Av
Miles Rd N8 121 DL55
Miles Rd, Epsom 216 CR112
Miles Rd, Mitch. 200 DE97
Miles St SW8 161 DL79
Miles Way N20 98 DE47
Milespit Hill NW7 97 CV50
Milestone Cl N9 100 DU47
Chichester Rd
Milestone Cl, Sutt. 218 DD107
Milestone Cl (Ripley), Wok. 228 BG122
Milestone Rd SE19 182 DT93
Milestone Rd, Dart. 188 FP86
Milfoil St W12 139 CU73
Milford Cl SE2 166 EY79
Milford Cl, St.Alb. 43 CK16
Milford Gdns, Croy. 203 DX99
Tannery Cl
Milford Gdns, Edg. 96 CN52
Milford Gdns, Wem. 117 CK64
Milford Gro, Sutt. 218 DC105
Milford La WC2 274 C10
Milford La WC2 141 DM73
Milford Ms SW16 181 DM90
Milford Rd W13 137 CH74
Milford Rd, Sthl. 136 CA73
Milk St E16 145 EP74
Milk St EC2 275 J9
Milk St, Brom. 184 EH93
Milk Yd E1 142 DW73
Milkhouse Gate, Guil. 258 AX136
High St
Milking La, Kes. 222 EK111
Milking La, Orp. 222 EL112
Milkwell Gdns, Wdf.Grn. 102 EH52
Milkwell Yd SE5 162 DQ81
Milkwood Rd SE24 181 DP85
Mill Av, Uxb. 134 BJ68
Mill Br Pl, Uxb. 134 BJ68
Mill Brook Rd, Orp. 206 EW98
Mill Cl, Cars. 200 DG103
Mill Cl, Chesh. 54 AS34
Mill Cl, Hem.H. 58 BN25
Mill Cl (Piccotts End), Hem.H. 40 BH16
Mill Cl, Horl. 268 DE147
Mill Cl (Bookham), Lthd. 230 CA124
Mill Cl, Ware 33 DX06
Mill Cl, Welw.G.C. 29 CU10
Mill Cl, West Dr. 154 BK76
Mill Cor, Barn. 79 CZ39
Mill Ct E10 123 EC62
Mill Fm Av, Sun. 175 BS94
Mill Fm Cl, Pnr. 94 BW54
Mill Fm Cres, Houns. 176 BY88
Mill Fld, Harl. 36 EW11
Mill Gdns SE26 182 DV91
Mill Grn, Mitch. 200 DG101
London Rd
Mill Grn Business Pk, Mitch. 200 DG101
Mill Grn Rd
Mill Grn La, Hat. 45 CY15
Mill Grn Rd, Mitch. 200 DF101
Mill Grn Rd, Welw.G.C. 29 CY10
Mill Hill SW13 159 CU82
Mill Hill Rd
Mill Hill, Brwd. 108 FY45
Mill Hill Circ NW7 97 CT50
Watford Way
Mill Hill Gro W3 138 CP74
Mill Hill Rd
Mill Hill La (Brockham), Bet. 248 CP134
Mill Hill Rd SW13 159 CU82
Mill Hill Rd W3 158 CP75
Mill Ho Cl (Eynsford), Dart. 208 FL102
Mill La
Mill Ho La, Cher. 193 BB98
Mill Ho La, Egh. 193 BB98
Mill La E4 83 EB41
Mill La NW6 119 CZ64
Mill La SE18 165 EN78
Mill La, Amer. 55 AN39
Mill La, Beac. 89 AL54
Mill La, Brox. 49 DZ21
Mill La, Cars. 218 DF105
Mill La, Ch.St.G. 90 AU47
Mill La, Croy. 201 DM104
Mill La (Eynsford), Dart. 208 FL102
Mill La, Dor. 263 CH135
Mill La, Egh. 193 BC98
Mill La, Epsom 217 CT109
Mill La, Ger.Cr. 113 AZ58
Mill La, Grays 169 FX78
Mill La, Guil. 258 AX136
Quarry St
Mill La (Chilworth), Guil. 259 BF139
Mill La (Peasmarsh), Guil. 258 AV142
Mill La, Harl. 36 EY11
Mill La, Horl. 268 DD148
Mill La, Kings L. 58 BN29
Mill La (Fetcham), Lthd. 231 CG122
Mill La (Taplow), Maid. 130 AC71
Mill La (Toot Hill), Ong. 71 FE29
Mill La (Downe), Orp. 223 EN110
Mill La, Oxt. 254 EF132
Mill La (Limpsfield Chart), Oxt. 255 EM131
Mill La, Red. 251 DJ131
Mill La, Rick. 75 BQ44
Mill La (Chadwell Heath), Rom. 126 EY58
Mill La (Navestock), Rom. 87 FH40
Mill La, Sev. 257 FJ121
Mill La (Shoreham), Sev. 225 FF110
Mill La (Horton), Slou. 153 BB83
Mill La, Wal.Cr. 67 DY28
Mill La (Byfleet), W.Byf. 212 BM113
Mill La, West. 255 EQ127
Mill La, Wind. 151 AN80
Mill La (Ripley), Wok. 228 BK119
Mill La, Wdf.Grn. 102 EF50
Mill La Cl, Brox. 49 DZ21
Mill La Trd Est, Croy. 201 DM104
Mill Mead, Stai. 173 BF91
Mill Mead Rd N17 122 DV55
Mill Pk Av, Horn. 128 FL61
Mill Pl E14 143 DZ72
East India Dock Rd
Mill Pl, Chis. 205 EP95
Mill Pl, Dart. 167 FG84
Mill Pl, Kings.T. 198 CM97
Mill Pl (Datchet), Slou. 152 AX82
Mill Pl Caravan Pk (Datchet), Slou. 152 AW82
Mill Plat, Islw. 157 CG82
Mill Plat Av, Islw. 157 CG82
Mill Pond Cl SW8 161 DK80
Crimsworth Rd
Mill Pond Cl, Sev. 257 FK121
Mill Pond Rd, Dart. 188 FL86
Mill Race, Ware 33 ED11
Mill Ridge, Edg. 96 CM50
Mill Rd E16 144 EH74
Mill Rd SE13 163 EC83
Loampit Vale
Mill Rd SW19 180 DC94
Mill Rd, Cob. 230 BW115
Mill Rd (Hawley), Dart. 188 FM91
Mill Rd (Holmwood), Dor. 263 CJ144
Mill Rd, Epsom 217 CT112
Mill Rd, Erith 167 FC80
Mill Rd, Esher 196 CA103
Mill Rd (Northfleet), Grav. 190 GE87
Mill Rd, Hert. 32 DR08
Mill Rd, Ilf. 125 EN62
Mill Rd, Purf. 168 FP79
Mill Rd (Dunton Grn), Sev. 256 FE121
Mill Rd, S.Ock. 148 FQ73
Mill Rd, Tad. 233 CX123
Mill Rd, Twick. 176 CC89
Mill Rd, West Dr. 154 BJ76
Mill Row N1 142 DS67
Mill Shaw, Oxt. 254 EF132
Mill Shot Cl SW6 159 CW80
Mill St SE1 162 DT75
Mill St W1 273 K10
Mill St W1 141 DJ73
Mill St, Berk. 38 AW19
Mill St, Harl. 52 EY17
Mill St, Hem.H. 40 BK24
Mill St, Kings.T. 198 CL97
Mill St, Red. 266 DE135
Mill St, Slou. 132 AT74
Mill St (Colnbrook), Slou. 153 BD80
Mill St, West. 255 ER127
Mill Vale, Brom. 204 EF96
Mill Vw (Park St), St.Alb. 61 CD27
Park St
Mill Vw Cl (Ewell), Epsom 217 CT108
Mill Vw Gdns, Croy. 203 DX104
Mill Way, Bushey 76 BY40
Mill Way, Felt. 175 BV85
Mill Way, Lthd. 232 CM124
Mill Way, Rick. 91 BF46
Mill Yd E1 *Cable St* 142 DU73
Millacres, Ware 33 DX06
Station Rd
Millais Av E12 125 EN64
Millais Gdns, Edg. 96 CN54
Millais Pl, Til. 171 GG80
Millais Rd E11 123 EC63
Millais Rd, Enf. 82 DT43
Millais Rd, N.Mal. 198 CS100
Millais Way, Epsom 216 CQ105
Millan Cl (New Haw), Add. 212 BH110
Milland Ct, Borwd. 78 CR39
Millard Cl N16 122 DS64
Boleyn Rd
Millard Ter, Dag. 146 FA65
Church Elm La
Millbank SW1 277 P7
Millbank SW1 161 DL76
Millbank, Hem.H. 40 BK24
Millbank, Stai. 174 BH92
Millbank Twr SW1 277 P9
Millbank Twr SW1 161 DL77
Millbank Way SE12 184 EG85
Millbourne Rd, Felt. 176 BY91
Millbridge, Hert. 32 DQ09
Millbridge Ms, Hert. 32 DQ09
Millbridge
Millbro, Swan. 187 FG94
Millbrook, Guil. 258 AX136
Millbrook, Wey. 213 BS105
Millbrook Av, Well. 165 ER84
Millbrook Gdns (Chadwell Heath), Rom. 126 EZ58
Millbrook Gdns (Gidea Pk), Rom. 105 FE54
Millbrook Pl NW1 141 DJ68
Hampstead Rd
Millbrook Rd N9 100 DV46
Millbrook Rd SW9 161 DP83
Millbrook Rd, Bushey 76 BZ39
Millbrook Way (Colnbrook), Slou. 153 BE82
Millcrest Rd (Cheshunt), Wal.Cr. 65 DP28
Millcroft Ho SE6 183 EB91
Millender Wk SE16 162 DW77
Millennium Cl E16 144 EG72
Russell Rd
Millennium Cl, Uxb. 134 BJ67
Millennium Dr E14 163 ED77
Millennium Pl E2 142 DV68
Millennium Pt E14 163 EA75
Millennium Sq SE1 162 DT75
Tooley St
Millennium Way SE10 164 EE75
Miller Av, Enf. 83 EA37
Government Row
Miller Cl, Mitch. 200 DF101
Miller Cl, Pnr. 94 BW54
Miller Pl, Ger.Cr. 112 AX57
Miller Rd SW19 180 DD93
Miller Rd, Croy. 201 DM102
Miller Rd, Guil. 243 BC131
Miller St NW1 141 DJ68
Miller Wk SE1 278 E3
Miller Wk SE1 141 DN74
Miller's Av E8 122 DT64
Millers Cl NW7 97 CU49
Millers Cl, Chig. 104 EV47
Millers Cl, Rick. 73 BE41
Millers Cl, Stai. 174 BH92
Millers Copse, Epsom 232 CR119
Millers Copse, Red. 267 DP144
Millers Ct W4 159 CT78
Chiswick Mall
Millers Ct, Hert. 32 DR10
Parliament Sq
Millers Grn Cl, Enf. 81 DP41
Miller's La, Chig. 104 EV46
Millers La (Outwood), Red. 267 DP144
Millers La, Ware 33 EC11
Millers La, Wind. 172 AT86
Millers Meadow Cl SE3 184 EF85
Meadowcourt Rd
Millers Ri, St.Alb. 43 CE21
Miller's Ter E8 122 DT64
Millers Way W6 159 CW75
Millersdale, Harl. 51 EP19
Millet Rd, Grnf. 136 CB69
Millfield, Berk. 38 AX18
Millfield, Sun. 195 BR95
Millfield, Welw.G.C. 30 DC08
Millfield Av E17 101 DY53
Millfield Dr (Northfleet), Grav. 190 GE89
Millfield La N6 120 DF61
Millfield La, Tad. 249 CZ125
Millfield Pl N6 120 DG61
Millfield Rd, Edg. 96 CQ54
Millfield Rd, Houns. 176 BY88
Millfield Wk, Hem.H. 40 BN22
Millfields, Chesh. 54 AQ33
Millfields Cl, Orp. 206 EV97
Millfields Cotts, Orp. 206 EV98
Millfields Cl
Millfields Est E5 123 DX62
Denton Way
Millfields Rd E5 122 DW63
Millford, Wok. 226 AV117
Millgrove St SW11 160 DG82
Millharbour E14 163 EB76
Millhaven Cl, Rom. 126 EV58
Millhedge Cl, Cob. 230 BY116
Millhoo Ct, Wal.Abb. 68 EF34
Millhouse La, Abb.L. 59 BT27
Millhouse Pl SE27 181 DP91
Millhurst Ms, Harl. 36 EY11
Sheering Rd
Millicent Rd E10 123 DZ60
Milligan St E14 143 DZ73
Milliners Ct, Loug. 85 EN40
The Cft
Milling Rd, Edg. 96 CR52
Millington Rd, Hayes 155 BS76
Millman Ms WC1 274 B5
Millman Ms WC1 141 DM70
Millman Pl WC1 141 DM70
Millman St
Millman St WC1 274 B5
Millman St WC1 141 DM70
Millmark Gro SE14 163 DY82
Millmarsh La, Enf. 83 DZ40
Millmead, Guil. 258 AW136
Millmead (Byfleet), W.Byf. 212 BM112
Millmead Ter, Guil. 258 AW136
Millmead Way, Hert. 31 DP08
Millpond Ct, Add. 212 BL106
Millpond Est SE16 162 DV75
West La
Mills Cl, Uxb. 134 BN68
Mills Ct EC2 275 N3
Mills Gro E14 143 EC71
Dewberry St
Mills Gro NW4 119 CX55
Mills Rd, Walt. 214 BW106
Mills Row W4 158 CR77
Mills Spur (Old Windsor), Wind. 172 AV87
Mills Way, Brwd. 109 GC46
Millshot Dr, Amer. 55 AR40
Millside, B.End 110 AC60
Millside, Cars. 200 DF103
Millside Ct, Iver 154 BH75
Millside Ind Est, Dart. 168 FK84
Millside Pl, Islw. 157 CH82
Millsmead Way, Loug. 85 EM40
Millson Cl N20 98 DD47
Millstead Cl, Tad. 233 CV122
Millstone Cl (South Darenth), Dart. 208 FQ96
Millstone Ms (South Darenth), Dart. 208 FQ95
Millstream Cl N13 99 DN50
Millstream Cl, Hert. 31 DP09
Millstream La, Slou. 131 AL74
Millstream Rd SE1 279 P5
Millstream Rd SE1 162 DT75
Millstream Way, H.Wyc. 110 AD55
Millthorne Cl, Rick. 74 BM43
Millview Cl, Reig. 250 DD132
Millwall Dock Rd E14 163 EA76
Millwards, Hat. 45 CV21
Millway NW7 96 CS50
Millway, Reig. 250 DD134
Millway Gdns, Nthlt. 136 BZ65
Millwell Cres, Chig. 103 ER50
Millwood Rd, Houns. 176 CC85
Millwood Rd, Orp. 206 EW97
Millwood St W10 139 CY71
St. Charles Sq
Milman Cl, Pnr. 116 BX55
Milman Rd NW6 139 CY68
Milman's St SW10 160 DD79
Milmead Ind Cen N17 100 DV54
Milne Ct E18 102 EG53
Churchfields
Milne Feild, Pnr. 94 CA52
Milne Gdns SE9 184 EL85
Milne Pk E (New Addington), Croy. 221 ED111
Milne Pk W (New Addington), Croy. 221 ED111
Milne Way (Harefield), Uxb. 92 BH53
Milner App, Cat. 236 DU121
Milner Cl, Cat. 236 DT121
Milner Cl, Wat. 59 BV34
Milner Ct, Bushey 76 CB44
Milner Dr, Cob. 214 BZ112
Milner Dr, Twick. 177 CD87
Milner Pl N1 141 DN67
Milner Pl, Cars. 218 DG105
High St
Milner Rd E15 144 EE69
Milner Rd SW19 200 DB95
Milner Rd, Cat. 236 DU122
Milner Rd, Dag. 126 EW61
Milner Rd, Kings.T. 197 CK97
Milner Rd, Mord. 200 DD99
Milner Rd (Burnham), Slou. 130 AG71
Milner Rd, Th.Hth. 202 DR97
Milner Sq N1 141 DP66
Milner St SW3 276 D8
Milner St SW3 160 DF77
Milner Wk SE9 185 ER88
Milnthorpe Rd W4 158 CR79
Milo Rd SE22 182 DT86
Milroy Av (Northfleet), Grav. 190 GE89
Milroy Wk SE1 278 F2
Milson Rd W14 159 CY76
Milton Av E6 144 EK66
Milton Av N6 121 DJ59
Milton Av NW9 118 CQ55
Milton Av NW10 138 CQ67
Milton Av, Barn. 79 CZ43
Milton Av, Croy. 202 DR101
Milton Av (Westcott), Dor. 263 CD137
Milton Av (Chalfont St. Peter), Ger.Cr. 112 AX56
Milton Av, Grav. 191 GJ88
Milton Av, Horn. 127 FF61
Milton Av (Badgers Mt), Sev. 225 FB110
Milton Av, Sutt. 200 DD104
Milton Cl N2 120 DC57
Milton Cl SE1 279 P9
Milton Cl SE1 162 DT77
Milton Cl, Hayes 135 BU72
Milton Cl (Horton), Slou. 153 BA83
Milton Cl, Sutt. 200 DD104
Milton Ct EC2 275 K6
Milton Ct, Rom. 126 EW59
Cross Rd
Milton Ct, Uxb. 115 BP62
Milton Ct, Wal.Abb. 67 EC34
Milton Ct La, Dor. 263 CF136
Milton Ct Rd SE14 163 DY79
Milton Cres, Ilf. 125 EQ59
Milton Dene, Hem.H. 41 BP15
Milton Dr, Borwd. 78 CP43
Milton Dr, Shep. 194 BL98
Milton Flds, Ch.St.G. 90 AV48
Milton Gdn Est N16 122 DS63
Milton Gro
Milton Gdns, Epsom 216 CS114
Milton Gdns, Stai. 174 BM88
Chesterton Dr
Milton Gdns, Til. 171 GH81
Milton Gro N11 99 DJ50
Milton Gro N16 122 DR63
Milton Hall Rd, Grav. 191 GK88
Milton Hill, Ch.St.G. 90 AV48
Milton Lawns, Amer. 55 AR36
Milton Pk N6 121 DJ59
Milton Pl N7 121 DN64
George's Rd
Milton Pl, Grav. 191 GJ86
Milton Rd E17 123 EA56
Milton Rd N6 121 DJ59
Milton Rd N15 121 DP56
Milton Rd NW7 97 CU50
Milton Rd NW9 119 CU59
West Hendon Bdy
Milton Rd SE24 181 DP86
Milton Rd SW14 158 CR83
Milton Rd SW19 180 DC93
Milton Rd W3 138 CR74
Milton Rd W7 137 CF73
Milton Rd, Add. 212 BG107
Milton Rd, Belv. 166 FA77
Milton Rd, Brwd. 108 FV49
Milton Rd, Cat. 236 DR121
Milton Rd, Chesh. 54 AP29
Milton Rd, Croy. 202 DR102
Milton Rd, Egh. 173 AZ92
Milton Rd, Grav. 191 GJ86
Milton Rd, Grays 170 GB78
Milton Rd, Hmptn. 176 CA94
Milton Rd, Har. 117 CE56
Milton Rd, Mitch. 180 DG94
Milton Rd, Rom. 127 FG58
Milton Rd (Dunton Grn), Sev. 256 FE121
Milton Rd, Slou. 131 AR70
Milton Rd, Sutt. 200 DA104
Milton Rd, Swans. 190 FY86
Milton Rd, Uxb. 115 BP63
Milton Rd, Wall. 219 DJ107
Milton Rd, Walt. 196 BX104
Milton Rd, Ware 33 DX05
Milton Rd, Well. 165 ET81
Milton St EC2 275 K6
Milton St EC2 142 DR71
Milton St (Westcott), Dor. 263 CD137
Milton St, Swans. 189 FX86
Milton St, Wal.Abb. 67 EC34
Milton St, Wat. 75 BV38
Milton Way (Fetcham), Lthd. 246 CC125
Milton Way, West Dr. 154 BM77
Milverton Dr, Uxb. 115 BQ63
Milverton Gdns, Ilf. 125 ET61
Milverton Ho SE23 183 DY90
Milverton Rd NW6 139 CW66
Milverton St SE11 161 DN78
Milverton Way SE9 185 EN91
Milward St E1 142 DV71
Stepney Way
Milward Wk SE18 165 EN79
Spearman St
Milwards, Harl. 51 EP19
Mimas Rd, Hem.H. 40 BM17
Saturn Way
Mimms Hall Rd, Pot.B. 63 CX31
Mimms La, Pot.B. 62 CQ33
Mimms La, Rad. 62 CN33
Mimosa Cl, Brwd. 108 FV43
Mimosa Cl, Orp. 206 EW104
Berrylands
Mimosa Cl, Rom. 106 FJ52
Mimosa Rd, Hayes 136 BW71
Mimosa St SW6 159 CZ81
Mimram Rd, Hert. 31 DP10
Mina Av, Slou. 152 AX75
Mina Rd SE17 162 DS78
Mina Rd SW19 200 DA95
Minard Rd SE6 184 EE87
Minchen Rd, Harl. 35 ET13
Minchenden Cres N14 99 DJ48
Minchin Cl, Lthd. 231 CG122
Mincing La EC3 275 M10
Mincing La EC3 142 DS73
Mincing La (Chobham), Wok. 210 AT108
Minden Rd SE20 202 DV95
Minden Rd, Sutt. 199 CZ103
Minehead Rd SW16 181 DM92
Minehead Rd, Har. 116 CA62
Minera Ms SW1 276 G8
Minera Ms SW1 160 DG77
Mineral La, Chesh. 54 AQ32
Mineral St SE18 165 ES77
Minerva Cl SW9 161 DN80
Minerva Cl, Sid. 185 ES90
Minerva Cl, Stai. 174 BG85
Minerva Dr, Wat. 75 BS36
Minerva Rd E4 101 EB52

Minerva Rd NW10 138 CQ69
Minerva Rd, Kings.T. 198 CM96
Minerva St E2 142 DV68
Minerva Way, Beac. 89 AP54
Minet Av NW10 138 CS68
Minet Dr, Hayes 135 BU74
Minet Gdns NW10 138 CS68
Minet Gdns, Hayes 135 BU74
Minet Rd SW9 161 DP82
Minford Gdns W14 159 CX75
Ming St E14 143 EA73
Mingard Wk N7 121 DM61
Hornsey Rd
Minims, The, Hat. 45 CU17
Ministers Gdns, St.Alb. 61 CE28
Frogmore
Ministry Way SE9 185 EM89
Miniver Pl EC4 142 DQ73
Garlick Hill
Mink Ct, Houns. 156 BW83
Minniecroft Rd (Burnham), Slou. 130 AH69
Minniedale, Surb. 198 CM99
Minnow St SE17 162 DS77
East St
Minnow Wk SE17 279 N9
Minorca Rd, Wey. 212 BN105
Minories EC3 275 P10
Minories EC3 142 DT72
Minshull Pl, Beck. 183 EA94
Minshull St SW8 161 DK81
Wandsworth Rd
Minson Rd E9 143 DX67
Minstead Gdns SW15 179 CT87
Minstead Way, N.Mal. 198 CS100
Minster Av, Sutt. 200 DA103
Leafield Rd
Minster Cl, Hat. 45 CU20
Minster Ct EC3 142 DR73
Mincing La
Minster Ct, Horn. 128 FN61
Minster Ct (Frogmore), St.Alb. 61 CE28
Minster Dr, Croy. 220 DS105
Minster Gdns, W.Mol. 196 BZ99
Molesey Av
Minster Pavement EC3 142 DR73
Mincing La
Minster Rd NW2 119 CY64
Minster Rd, Brom. 184 EH94
Minster Wk N8 121 DL56
Lightfoot Rd
Minster Way, Horn. 128 FM60
Minster Way, Slou. 153 AZ75
Minsterley Av, Shep. 195 BS98
Minstrel Cl, Hem.H. 40 BH19
Minstrel Gdns, Surb. 198 CM98
Mint Business Pk E16 144 EG71
Mint Cl (Hillingdon), Uxb. 135 BP69
Mint Gdns, Dor. 263 CG135
Church St
Mint La (Lower Kingswood), Tad. 250 DA129
Mint Rd, Bans. 234 DC116
Mint Rd, Wall. 219 DH105
Mint St SE1 279 H4
Mint Wk, Croy. 202 DQ104
High St
Mint Wk, Warl. 237 DX118
Mint Wk (Knaphill), Wok. 226 AS117
Mintern Cl N13 99 DP48
Mintern St N1 142 DR68
Minterne Av, Sthl. 156 CA77
Minterne Rd, Har. 118 CM57
Minterne Waye, Hayes 136 BW72
Minton La, Harl. 52 EW15
Minton Ms NW6 140 DB65
Lymington Rd
Minton Ri, Maid. 130 AH72
Mirabel Rd SW6 159 CZ80
Mirador Cres, Slou. 132 AV73
Miramar Way, Horn. 128 FK64
Miranda Cl E1 142 DW71
Sidney St
Miranda Ct W3 138 CM72
Queens Dr
Miranda Rd N19 121 DJ60
Mirfield St SE7 164 EK77
Miriam Rd SE18 165 ES78
Mirravale Trd Est, Dag. 126 EZ59
Mirren Cl, Har. 116 BZ63
Mirrie La (Denham), Uxb. 113 BC57
Mirror Path SE9 184 EJ90
Lambscroft Av
Misbourne Av (Chalfont St. Peter), Ger.Cr. 90 AY50
Misbourne Cl (Chalfont St. Peter), Ger.Cr. 90 AY50
Misbourne Ct, Slou. 153 BA77
High St
Misbourne Meadows (Denham), Uxb. 113 BC60
Misbourne Rd, Uxb. 134 BN67
Misbourne Vale (Chalfont St. Peter), Ger.Cr. 90 AX50
Miskin Rd, Dart. 188 FJ87
Miskin Way, Grav. 191 GK93
Missden Dr, Hem.H. 41 BQ22
Missenden Cl, Felt. 175 BT88
Missenden Gdns, Mord. 200 DC100
Missenden Gdns (Burnham), Slou. 130 AH72
Missenden Rd, Chesh. 54 AL32
Mission Gro E17 123 DY57
Mission Pl SE15 162 DU81
Mission Sq, Brent. 158 CL79
Mistletoe Cl, Croy. 203 DX102
Marigold Way
Mistley Rd, Harl. 36 EU13
Misty's Fld, Walt. 196 BW102
Mitali Pas E1 142 DU72
Back Ch La
Mitcham Gdn Village, Mitch. 200 DG99
Mitcham Ind Est, Mitch. 200 DG95
Mitcham La SW16 181 DJ93
Mitcham Pk, Mitch. 200 DF98
Mitcham Rd E6 144 EL69
Mitcham Rd SW17 180 DF92
Mitcham Rd, Croy. 201 DL100
Mitcham Rd, Ilf. 125 ET59
Mitchell Av (Northfleet), Grav. 190 GD89
Mitchell Cl SE2 166 EW77
Mitchell Cl, Abb.L. 59 BU32
Mitchell Cl, Belv. 167 FC76
Mitchell Cl, Dart. 188 FL89
Mitchell Cl (Bovingdon), Hem.H. 57 AZ27
Mitchell Cl, Rain. 148 FJ68
Mitchell Cl, St.Alb. 43 CD24
Mitchell Cl, Slou. 151 AN75
Mitchell Cl, Welw.G.C. 30 DC09
Mitchell Rd N13 99 DP50
Mitchell Rd, Orp. 223 ET105
Mitchell St EC1 275 H4
Mitchell St EC1 142 DQ70
Mitchell Wk E6 144 EL71
Mitchell Wk, Amer. 55 AS38
Mitchell Wk, Swans. 190 FY87
Mitchell Way NW10 138 CQ65
Mitchell Way, Brom. 204 EG95
Mitchellbrook Way NW10 138 CR65
Mitchells Cl (Shalford), Guil. 258 AY140
Station Rd
Mitchell's Pl SE21 182 DS87
Dulwich Village
Mitchells Row (Shalford), Guil. 258 AY141
Mitchison Rd N1 142 DR65
Mitchley Av, Pur. 220 DQ113
Mitchley Av, S.Croy. 220 DQ113
Mitchley Gro, S.Croy. 220 DU113
Mitchley Hill, S.Croy. 220 DT113
Mitchley Rd N17 122 DU55
Mitchley Vw, S.Croy. 220 DU113
Mitford Cl, Chess. 215 CJ107
Merritt Gdns
Mitford Rd N19 121 DL61
Mitre, The E14 143 DZ73
Three Colt St
Mitre Av E17 123 DZ55
Greenleaf Rd
Mitre Cl, Brom. 204 EF96
Beckenham La
Mitre Cl, Shep. 195 BR100
Gordon Dr
Mitre Cl, Sutt. 218 DC108
Mitre Ct EC2 275 J8
Mitre Ct EC4 274 E9
Mitre Rd E15 144 EE68
Mitre Rd SE1 278 E4
Mitre Rd SE1 161 DN75
Mitre Sq EC3 275 N9
Mitre St EC3 275 N9
Mitre St EC3 142 DS72
Mitre Way W10 139 CV70
Mixbury Gro, Wey. 213 BR107
Mixnams La, Cher. 194 BG97
Mizen Cl, Cob. 214 BX114
Mizen Way, Cob. 230 BW115
Moat, The, N.Mal. 198 CS95
Moat, The, Ong. 71 FF29
Moat Cl, Bushey 76 CB43
Moat Cl, Orp. 223 ET107
Moat Cl (Chipstead), Sev. 256 FB123
Moat Ct, Ash. 232 CL117
Moat Cres N3 120 DB55
Moat Cft, Well. 166 EW83
Moat Dr E13 144 EJ68
Boundary Rd
Moat Dr, Har. 116 CC56
Moat Dr, Ruis. 115 BS59
Moat Dr, Slou. 132 AW71
Moat Fm Rd, Nthlt. 136 BZ65
Moat La, Erith 167 FG81
Moat Pl SW9 161 DM83
Moat Pl W3 138 CP72
Moat Pl (Denham), Uxb. 114 BH63
Moated Fm Dr, Add. 212 BJ108
Moatfield Rd, Bushey 76 CB43
Moats La (South Nutfield), Red. 267 DN140
Moatside, Enf. 83 DX42
Moatside, Felt. 176 BW91
Moatview Ct, Bushey 76 CB43
Moatwood Grn, Welw.G.C. 29 CY10
Moberley Rd SW4 181 DK87
Modbury Gdns NW5 140 DG65
Queen's Cres
Modder Pl SW15 159 CX84
Model Cotts SW14 158 CQ84
Upper Richmond Rd W
Model Fm Cl SE9 184 EL90
Modling Ho E2 143 DX68
Moelwyn Hughes Ct N7 121 DK64
Hilldrop Cres
Moelyn Ms, Har. 117 CG57
Moffat Rd N13 99 DL51
Moffat Rd SW17 180 DE91
Moffat Rd, Th.Hth. 202 DQ96
Moffats Cl, Hat. 64 DA26
Moffats La, Hat. 63 CZ26
Mogador Cotts, Tad. 249 CX128
Mogador Rd
Mogador Rd (Lower Kingswood), Tad. 249 CX128
Mogden La, Islw. 177 CE85
Mohmmad Khan Rd E11 124 EF60
Harvey Rd
Moir Cl, S.Croy. 220 DU109
Moira Cl N17 100 DS54
Moira Rd SE9 165 EM84
Moland Mead SE16 163 DX78
Crane Mead
Molash Rd, Orp. 206 EX98
Molasses Row SW11 160 DC83
Cinnamon Row
Mole Abbey Gdns, W.Mol. 196 CA97
New Rd
Mole Business Pk, Lthd. 231 CG121
Mole Ct, Epsom 216 CQ105
Mole Rd (Fetcham), Lthd. 231 CD121
Mole Rd, Walt. 214 BX106
Mole Valley Pl, Ash. 231 CK119
Molember Ct, E.Mol. 197 CE99
Molember Rd, E.Mol. 197 CE99
Moles Hill (Oxshott), Lthd. 215 CD111
Molescroft SE9 185 EQ90
Molesey Av, W.Mol. 196 BZ98
Molesey Cl, Walt. 214 BY105
Molesey Dr, Sutt. 199 CY103
Molesey Pk Av, W.Mol. 196 CB99
Molesey Pk Cl, E.Mol. 196 CC99
Molesey Pk Rd, E.Mol. 197 CD99
Molesey Pk Rd, W.Mol. 196 CB99
Molesey Rd, Walt. 214 BX106
Molesey Rd, W.Mol. 196 BY99
Molesford Rd SW6 160 DA81
Molesham Cl, W.Mol. 196 CB97
Molesham Way, W.Mol. 196 CB97
Molesworth, Hodd. 33 EA13
Molesworth Rd, Cob. 213 BU113
Molesworth St SE13 163 EC83
Molewood Rd, Hert. 31 DP08
Mollands La, S.Ock. 149 FW70
Mollison Av, Enf. 83 DY40
Mollison Dr, Wall. 219 DL107
Mollison Ri, Grav. 191 GL92
Mollison Way, Edg. 96 CN54
Molloy Ct, Wok. 227 BA116
Courtenay Rd
Molly Huggins Cl SW12 181 DJ87
Molteno Rd, Wat. 75 BU39
Molyneaux Av (Bovingdon), Hem.H. 57 AZ27
Molyneux Dr SW17 181 DH91
Molyneux Rd, Gdmg. 258 AT144
Molyneux Rd, Wey. 212 BN106
Molyneux St W1 272 C7
Molyneux St W1 140 DE71
Molyns Ms, Slou. 131 AL74
Moor Furlong
Momples Rd, Harl. 36 EV13
Mona Rd SE15 162 DW82
Mona St E16 144 EF71
Monahan Av, Pur. 219 DM112
Monarch Cl, Felt. 175 BS87
Monarch Cl, Til. 171 GH82
Monarch Cl, W.Wick. 222 EF105
Monarch Dr E16 144 EK71
Monarch Ms E17 123 EB57
Monarch Ms SW16 181 DN92
Monarch Par, Mitch. 200 DF96
London Rd
Monarch Pl, Buck.H. 102 EJ47
Monarch Rd, Belv. 166 FA76
Monarchs Ct NW7 96 CR50
Grenville Pl
Monarchs Way, Ruis. 115 BR60
Monarchs Way, Wal.Cr. 67 DY34
Monastery Gdns, Enf. 82 DR40
Monaveen Gdns, W.Mol. 196 CA97
Monck St SW1 277 N7
Monck St SW1 161 DK76
Monclar Rd SE5 162 DR84
Moncorvo Cl SW7 276 B5
Moncrieff Cl E6 144 EL72
Linton Gdns
Moncrieff Pl SE15 162 DU82
Rye La
Moncrieff St SE15 162 DU82
Mondial Way, Hayes 155 BQ80
Monega Rd E7 144 EJ65
Monega Rd E12 144 EK65
Money Av, Cat. 236 DR122
Money Hill Rd, Rick. 92 BJ46
Money Hole La, Welw.G.C. 30 DE08
Money La, West Dr. 154 BK76
Money Rd, Cat. 236 DR122
Moneyhill Par, Rick. 92 BH46
Uxbridge Rd
Mongers La, Epsom 217 CT110
Monica Cl, Wat. 76 BW40
Monier Rd E3 143 EA66
Monivea Rd, Beck. 183 DZ94
Monk Dr E16 144 EG72
Monk Pas E16 144 EG73
Monk Dr
Monk St SE18 165 EN77
Monkchester Cl, Loug. 85 EN39
Monkey Island La, Maid. 150 AE77
Monkfrith Av N14 81 DH44
Monkfrith Cl N14 99 DH45
Monkfrith Way N14 98 DG45
Monkhams Av, Wdf.Grn. 102 EG50
Monkhams Dr, Wdf.Grn. 102 EH49
Monkhams La, Buck.H. 102 EH48
Monkhams La, Wdf.Grn. 102 EG50
Monkleigh Rd, Mord. 199 CY97
Monks Av, Barn. 80 DC44
Monks Av, W.Mol. 196 BZ99
Monks Chase, Brwd. 109 GC50
Monks Cl SE2 166 EX77
Monks Cl, Brox. 49 EA20
Monks Cl, Enf. 82 DQ40
Monks Cl, Har. 116 CB61
Monks Cl, Ruis. 116 BX63
Monks Cl, St.Alb. 43 CE22
Monks Cres, Add. 212 BH106
Monks Cres, Walt. 195 BV102
Monks Dr W3 138 CN71
Monks Grn (Fetcham), Lthd. 230 CC121
Monks Horton Way, St.Alb. 43 CH18
Monks Orchard, Dart. 188 FJ89
Monks Orchard Rd, Beck. 203 EA102
Monks Pk, Wem. 138 CQ65
Monks Pk Gdns, Wem. 138 CP65
Monks Pl, Cat. 236 DU122
Tillingdown Hill
Monk's Ridge N20 97 CV47
Monks Ri, Welw.G.C. 29 CX05
Monks Rd, Bans. 234 DA116
Monks Rd, Enf. 82 DQ40
Monks Rd, Vir.W. 192 AX98
Monks Rd, Wind. 151 AK82
Monks Wk, Cher. 193 BE98
Monks Wk (Southfleet), Grav. 190 GA93
Monk's Wk, Reig. 250 DB134
Monks Way NW11 119 CZ56
Hurstwood Rd
Monks Way, Beck. 203 EA99
Monks Way, Orp. 205 EQ102
Monks Way, Stai. 174 BK94
Monks Way, West Dr. 154 BL79
Harmondsworth La
Monksbury, Harl. 52 EU18
Monksdene Gdns, Sutt. 200 DB104
Monksfield Way, Slou. 131 AN69
Monksgrove, Loug. 85 EN43
Monksmead, Borwd. 78 CQ42
Monkswell Ct N10 98 DG53
Pembroke Rd
Monkswell La, Couls. 234 DB124
Monkswick Rd, Harl. 35 ET13
Monkswood, Welw.G.C. 29 CW05
Monkswood Av, Wal.Abb. 67 ED33
Monkswood Gdns, Borwd. 78 CR42
Monkswood Gdns, Ilf. 125 EN55
Monkton Rd, Well. 165 ET82
Monkton St SE11 278 E8
Monkton St SE11 161 DN77
Monkville Av NW11 119 CZ56
Monkwell Sq EC2 275 J7
Monkwood Cl, Rom. 127 FG57
Monmouth Av E18 124 EH55
Monmouth Av, Kings.T. 177 CJ94
Monmouth Cl W4 158 CR76
Beaumont Rd
Monmouth Cl, Mitch. 201 DL98
Recreation Way
Monmouth Cl, Well. 166 EU84
Monmouth Gro, Brent. 158 CL77
Sterling Pl
Monmouth Pl W2 140 DA72
Monmouth Rd
Monmouth Rd E6 145 EM69
Monmouth Rd N9 100 DV47
Monmouth Rd W2 140 DB72
Monmouth Rd, Dag. 126 EZ64
Monmouth Rd, Hayes 155 BS77
Monmouth Rd, Wat. 75 BV41
Monmouth St WC2 273 P9
Monmouth St WC2 141 DL73
Monnery Rd N19 121 DJ62
Monnow Grn, S.Ock. 148 FQ73
Monnow Rd
Monnow Rd SE1 162 DU77
Monnow Rd, S.Ock. 148 FQ73
Mono La, Felt. 175 BV89
Monoux Gro E17 101 EA53
Monro Dr, Guil. 242 AU131
Monro Gdns, Har. 95 CE52
Monroe Cres, Enf. 82 DV39
Monroe Dr SW14 178 CP85
Mons Wk, Egh. 173 BC92
Mons Way, Brom. 204 EL100
Monsal Ct E5 123 DX63
Redwald Rd
Monsell Ct N4 121 DP62
Monsell Rd
Monsell Gdns, Stai. 173 BE92
Monsell Rd N4 121 DP62
Monson Rd NW10 139 CU68
Monson Rd SE14 163 DX80
Monson Rd, Brox. 49 DZ20
Monson Rd, Red. 250 DF130
Montacute Rd SE6 183 DZ87
Montacute Rd, Bushey 95 CE45
Montacute Rd (New Addington), Croy. 221 EC109
Montacute Rd, Mord. 200 DD100
Montagu Cres N18 100 DV49
Montagu Gdns N18 100 DV49
Montagu Gdns, Wall. 219 DJ105
Montagu Mans W1 272 E6
Montagu Ms N W1 272 E7
Montagu Ms N W1 140 DF71
Montagu Ms S W1 272 E8
Montagu Ms W W1 272 E8
Montagu Pl W1 272 D7
Montagu Pl W1 140 DF71
Montagu Rd N9 100 DW48
Montagu Rd N18 100 DV50
Montagu Rd NW4 119 CU58
Montagu Rd Ind Est N18 100 DW49
Montagu Row W1 272 E7
Montagu Sq W1 272 E7
Montagu Sq W1 140 DF71
Montagu St W1 272 E8
Montagu St W1 140 DF72
Montague Av SE4 163 DZ84
Montague Av W7 137 CF74
Montague Av, S.Croy. 220 DS112
Montague Cl SE1 279 K2
Montague Cl SE1 142 DR74
Montague Cl, Walt. 195 BU101
Montague Dr, Cat. 236 DQ122
Drake Av
Montague Gdns W3 138 CN73
Montague Hall Pl, Bushey 76 CA44
Montague Pl WC1 273 N6
Montague Pl WC1 141 DK71
Montague Rd E8 122 DU64
Montague Rd E11 124 EF61
Montague Rd N8 121 DM57
Montague Rd N15 122 DU56
Montague Rd SW19 180 DB94
Montague Rd W7 137 CF74
Montague Rd W13 137 CH72
Montague Rd, Berk. 38 AV19
Montague Rd, Croy. 201 DP102
Montague Rd, Houns. 156 CB83
Montague Rd, Rich. 178 CL86
Montague Rd, Slou. 132 AT73
Montague Rd (Datchet), Slou. 152 AV81
Montague Rd, Sthl. 156 BY77
Montague Rd, Uxb. 134 BK66
Montague Sq SE15 162 DW80
Clifton Way
Montague St EC1 275 H7
Montague St EC1 142 DQ71
Montague St WC1 273 P6
Montague St WC1 141 DL71
Montague Waye, Sthl. 156 BY76
Montalt Rd, Wdf.Grn. 102 EF50
Montana Cl, S.Croy. 220 DR110
Montana Gdns SE26 183 DZ91
Montana Gdns, Sutt. 218 DC106
Lind Rd
Montana Rd SW17 180 DG91
Montana Rd SW20 199 CW95
Montayne Rd (Cheshunt), Wal.Cr. 67 DX32
Montbelle Rd SE9 185 EP90
Montbretia Cl, Orp. 206 EW98
Montcalm Cl, Brom. 204 EG100
Montcalm Cl, Hayes 135 BV69
Ayles Rd
Montcalm Rd SE7 164 EK80
Montclare St E2 275 P3
Monteagle Av, Bark. 145 EQ65
Monteagle Way E5 122 DU62
Rendlesham Rd
Monteagle Way SE15 162 DV83
Montefiore St SW8 161 DH82
Montego Cl SE24 161 DN84
Railton Rd
Montem La, Slou. 131 AR74
Montem Rd SE23 183 DZ87
Montem Rd, N.Mal. 198 CS98
Montem St N4 121 DM60
Thorpedale Rd
Montenotte Rd N8 121 DJ57
Monterey Cl, Bex. 187 FC89
Montesole Ct, Pnr. 94 BW54
Montevetro SW11 160 DD81
Montford Pl SE11 161 DN78
Montford Rd, Sun. 195 BU98
Montfort Gdns, Ilf. 103 EQ51
Montfort Pl SW19 179 CX88
Montfort Ri, Red. 266 DF142
Montgolfier Wk, Nthlt. 136 BY69
Jetstar Way
Montgomerie Cl, Berk. 38 AU17
Mortain Dr
Montgomerie Dr, Guil. 242 AU129
Montgomery Av, Esher 197 CE104
Montgomery Av, Hem.H. 40 BN19
Montgomery Cl, Grays 170 GC75
Montgomery Cl, Mitch. 201 DL98
Montgomery Cl, Sid. 185 ET86
Montgomery Cres, Rom. 106 FJ50
Montgomery Dr (Cheshunt), Wal.Cr. 67 DY28
Montgomery Rd W4 158 CQ77
Montgomery Rd (South Darenth), Dart. 209 FR95
Montgomery Rd, Edg. 96 CM51
Montgomery Rd, Wok. 226 AY118
Montholme Rd SW11 180 DF86
Monthope Rd E1 142 DU71
Casson St
Montolieu Gdns SW15 179 CV85
Montpelier Av W5 137 CJ71
Montpelier Av, Bex. 186 EX87
Montpelier Cl, Uxb. 134 BN67
Montpelier Ct, Wind. 151 AQ82
St. Leonards Rd
Montpelier Gdns E6 144 EK69
Montpelier Gdns, Rom. 126 EW59
Montpelier Gro NW5 121 DJ64
Montpelier Ms SW7 276 C6
Montpelier Pl E1 142 DW72
Montpelier Pl SW7 276 C6
Montpelier Pl SW7 160 DE76
Montpelier Ri NW11 119 CY59
Montpelier Ri, Wem. 117 CK60
Montpelier Rd N3 98 DC53
Montpelier Rd SE15 162 DV81
Montpelier Rd W5 137 CK71
Montpelier Rd, Pur. 219 DP110
Montpelier Rd, Sutt. 218 DC105
Montpelier Row SE3 164 EF82
Montpelier Row, Twick. 177 CJ87
Montpelier Sq SW7 276 C5
Montpelier Sq SW7 160 DE75
Montpelier St SW7 276 C5
Montpelier St SW7 160 DE75
Montpelier Ter SW7 276 C5
Montpelier Vale SE3 164 EF82
Montpelier Wk SW7 276 C6
Montpelier Wk SW7 160 DE76
Montpelier Way NW11 119 CY59
Montrave Rd SE20 182 DW93
Montreal Pl WC2 274 B10
Montreal Rd, Ilf. 125 EQ59
Montreal Rd, Sev. 256 FE123
Montreal Rd, Til. 171 GG82
Montrell Rd SW2 181 DL88
Montrose Av NW6 139 CY68
Montrose Av, Edg. 96 CQ54
Montrose Av, Rom. 106 FJ54
Montrose Av, Sid. 186 EU87
Montrose Av, Slou. 131 AP72
Montrose Av (Datchet), Slou. 152 AW80
Montrose Av, Twick. 176 CB87
Montrose Av, Well. 165 ES83
Montrose Cl, Ashf. 175 BQ93
Montrose Cl, Well. 165 ET83
Montrose Cl, Wdf.Grn. 102 EG49
Montrose Ct SW7 276 A5
Montrose Ct SW7 160 DD75
Montrose Cres N12 98 DC51
Montrose Cres, Wem. 138 CL65
Montrose Gdns (Oxshott), Lthd. 215 CD112
Montrose Gdns, Mitch. 200 DF97
Montrose Gdns, Sutt. 200 DB103
Montrose Pl SW1 276 G5
Montrose Pl SW1 160 DG75
Montrose Rd, Felt. 175 BR86
Montrose Rd, Har. 95 CE54
Montrose Wk, Wey. 195 BP104
Montrose Way SE23 183 DX88
Montrose Way (Datchet), Slou. 152 AX81
Montrouge Cres, Epsom 233 CW116
Montserrat Av, Wdf.Grn. 101 ED52
Montserrat Cl SE19 182 DR92
Montserrat Rd SW15 159 CY84
Monument Gdns SE13 183 EC85
Monument Grn, Wey. 195 BP104
Monument Hill, Wey. 213 BP105
Monument La (Chalfont St. Peter), Ger.Cr. 90 AY51
Monument Rd, Wey. 213 BP105
Monument Rd, Wok. 211 BA114
Monument St EC3 275 L10
Monument St EC3 142 DR73
Monument Way N17 122 DT55
Monument Way E, Wok. 227 BB115
Monument Way W, Wok. 227 BA115
Monza St E1 142 DW73
Moodkee St SE16 162 DW76
Moody Rd SE15 162 DT81
Moody St E1 143 DX69
Moon La, Barn. 79 CZ41
Moon St N1 141 DP67
Moor End, Maid. 150 AC78
Moor End Rd, Hem.H. 40 BJ21
Moor Furlong, Slou. 131 AL74
Moor Hall Rd, Harl. 36 EZ11
Moor La EC2 275 K7
Moor La EC2 142 DR71
Moor La, Chess. 216 CL105
Moor La, Rick. 92 BM47
Moor La (Sarratt), Rick. 73 BE36
Moor La, Stai. 173 BE90
Moor La, Upmin. 129 FS60
Moor La, West Dr. 154 BJ79
Moor La, Wok. 226 AY122
Moor La Crossing, Wat. 93 BQ46
Moor Mead Rd, Twick. 177 CG86
Moor Mill La (Colney St), St.Alb. 61 CE29
Moor Pk Est, Nthwd. 93 BQ49
Moor Pk Gdns, Kings.T. 178 CS94
Moor Pk Ind Est, Wat. 93 BQ45
Moor Pk Mansion, Rick. 92 BN48
Moor Pk Rd, Nthwd. 93 BR50
Moor Pl EC2 275 K7
Moor Rd, Chesh. 54 AQ32
Moor Rd, The, Sev. 241 FH120
Moor St W1 273 N9
Moor Twr, Harl. 51 ET16
Moor Vw, Wat. 93 BU45
Moorcroft Gdns, Brom. 204 EL99
Southborough Rd
Moorcroft La, Uxb. 134 BN71
Moorcroft Rd SW16 181 DL90
Moorcroft Way, Pnr. 116 BY57
Moordown SE18 165 EN81
Moore Av, Grays 170 FY78
Moore Av, Til. 171 GH82
Moore Cl SW14 158 CQ83
Little St. Leonards
Moore Cl, Add. 212 BH106
Moore Cl, Dart. 189 FR89
Moore Cl, Mitch. 201 DH96
Moore Cl, Slou. 151 AP75
Moore Cl, Wall. 219 DL109
Brabazon Av
Moore Cres, Dag. 146 EV67
Moore Gro Cres, Egh. 172 AY94
Moore Pk Rd SW6 160 DB80
Moore Rd SE19 182 DQ93
Moore Rd, Berk. 38 AT17
Moore Rd, Swans. 190 FY86
Moore St SW3 276 D8
Moore St SW3 160 DF77
Moore Wk E7 124 EG63
Stracey Rd
Moore Way SE22 182 DU88
Lordship La
Moore Way, Sutt. 218 DA109
Moorefield Rd N17 100 DT54
Moorehead Way SE3 164 EH83
Mooreland Rd, Brom. 184 EF94
Moorend, Welw.G.C. 30 DA12
Moores La (Eton Wick), Wind. 151 AM77
Moores Pl, Brwd. 108 FX47
Moores Rd, Dor. 263 CH135
Moorey Cl E15 144 EF67
Stephen's Rd

Moorfield (Holmwood), Dor. 263 CK144
Moorfield, Harl. 51 EQ20
Moorfield Av W5 137 CK70
Moorfield Rd, Chess. 216 CL106
Moorfield Rd, Enf. 82 DW39
Moorfield Rd, Guil. 242 AX130
Moorfield Rd, Orp. 206 EU101
Moorfield Rd, Uxb. 134 BK72
Moorfield Rd (Harefield), Uxb. 114 BG59
Moorfields EC2 275 K7
Moorfields EC2 142 DR71
Moorfields Cl, Stai. 193 BE95
Moorfields Highwalk EC2 142 DR71
Fore St
Moorgate EC2 275 K8
Moorgate EC2 142 DR72
Moorgate Pl EC2 275 K8
Moorhall Rd (Harefield), Uxb. 114 BH58
Moorhayes Dr, Stai. 194 BJ97
Moorhen Cl, Erith 167 FH80
Moorhen Way, Harl. 34 EG14
Roydon Mill Pk
Moorholme, Wok. 226 AY119
Oakbank
Moorhouse Rd W2 140 DA72
Moorhouse Rd, Har. 117 CK55
Moorhouse Rd, Oxt. 255 EM131
Moorhouse Rd, West. 255 EM128
Moorhurst Av (Cheshunt), Wal.Cr. 65 DN29
Moorings SE28 146 EV73
Moorings, The (Bookham), Lthd. 246 CA125
Church Rd
Moorings, The, Wind. 172 AW87
Straight Rd
Moorland Cl, Rom. 105 FB52
Moorland Cl, Twick. 176 CA87
Telford Rd
Moorland Rd SW9 161 DP84
Moorland Rd, Hem.H. 40 BG22
Moorland Rd, West Dr. 154 BJ79
Moorlands (Frogmore), St.Alb. 61 CE28
Frogmore
Moorlands, Welw.G.C. 30 DA12
Moorlands, The, Wok. 227 AZ121
Moorlands Av NW7 97 CV51
Moorlands Est SW9 161 DN84
Moorlands Reach, Saw. 36 EZ06
Moormead Dr, Epsom 216 CS106
Moormede Cres, Stai. 173 BF91
Moors, The, Welw.G.C. 30 DA08
Moors Wk, Welw.G.C. 30 DC09
Moorside, Hem.H. 40 BH23
Stratford Way
Moorside (Wooburn Grn), H.Wyc. 110 AE55
Moorside, Welw.G.C. 30 DA12
Moorside Rd, Brom. 184 EE90
Moorsom Way, Couls. 235 DK117
Moorstown Ct, Slou. 152 AS75
Moortown Rd, Wat. 94 BW49
Moot Ct NW9 118 CN57
Mora Rd NW2 119 CW63
Mora St EC1 275 J3
Mora St EC1 142 DQ69
Moran Cl (Bricket Wd), St.Alb. 60 BZ31
Morant Gdns, Rom. 105 FB50
Morant Pl N22 99 DM53
Commerce Rd
Morant Rd, Grays 171 GH76
Morant St E14 143 EA73
Morants Ct Rd (Dunton Grn), Sev. 241 FC118
Morat St SW9 161 DM81
Moravian Pl SW10 160 DD79
Milman's St
Moravian St E2 142 DW69
Moray Av, Hayes 135 BT74
Moray Cl, Edg. 96 CP47
Pentland Av
Moray Cl, Rom. 105 FE52
Moray Dr, Slou. 132 AU72
Moray Ms N7 121 DM61
Durham Rd
Moray Rd N4 121 DM61
Moray Way, Rom. 105 FD52
Morcote Cl (Shalford), Guil. 258 AY141
Mordaunt Gdns, Dag. 146 EY66
Mordaunt Ho NW10 138 CR67
Mordaunt Rd NW10 138 CR67
Mordaunt St SW9 161 DM83
Morden Cl SE13 163 EC82
Morden Cl, Tad. 233 CX120
Marbles Way
Morden Ct, Mord. 200 DB98
Morden Gdns, Grnf. 117 CF64
Morden Gdns, Mitch. 200 DD98
Morden Hall Rd, Mord. 200 DB97
Morden Hill SE13 163 EC82
Morden La SE13 163 EC81
Morden Rd SE3 164 EG82
Morden Rd SW19 200 DB95
Morden Rd, Mitch. 200 DC98
Morden Rd, Rom. 126 EY59
Morden Rd Ms SE3 164 EG82
Morden St SE13 163 EB81
Morden Way, Sutt. 200 DA101
Morden Wf Rd SE10 164 EE76
Mordon Rd, Ilf. 125 ET59
Mordred Rd SE6 184 EE89
More Circle, Gdmg. 258 AS144
More Cl E16 144 EF72
More Cl W14 159 CY77
More Cl, Pur. 219 DN111
More La, Esher 196 CB103
More Rd, Gdmg. 258 AS144
Moreau Wk (George Grn), Slou. 132 AY72
Alan Way
Morecambe Cl E1 143 DX71
Morecambe Cl, Horn. 127 FH64
Morecambe Gdns, Stan. 95 CK49
Morecambe St SE17 279 J9
Morecambe St SE17 162 DQ77
Morecambe Ter N18 100 DR49
Morecoombe Cl, Kings.T. 178 CP94
Moree Way N18 100 DU49
Morel Ct, Sev. 257 FH122
Moreland Av, Grays 170 GC75
Moreland Av (Colnbrook), Slou. 153 BC80
Moreland Cl (Colnbrook), Slou. 153 BC80
Moreland Av
Moreland Dr, Ger.Cr. 113 AZ59
Moreland St EC1 274 G2
Moreland St EC1 141 DP69
Moreland Way E4 101 EB48
Morell Cl, Barn. 80 DC41
Galdana Av
Morella Cl, Vir.W. 192 AW98
Morella Rd SW12 180 DF87
Morello Av, Uxb. 135 BP71
Morello Cl, Swan. 207 FD98
Morello Dr, Slou. 133 AZ74
Moremead, Wal.Abb. 67 ED33
Moremead Rd SE6 183 DZ91
Morena St SE6 183 EB87
Moresby Av, Surb. 198 CP101
Moresby Rd E5 122 DV60
Moresby Wk SW8 161 DJ82
Moretaine Rd, Ashf. 174 BK90
Hengrove Cres
Moreton Av, Islw. 157 CE81
Moreton Cl E5 122 DW61
Moreton Cl N15 122 DR58
Moreton Cl NW7 97 CW51
Moreton Cl SW1 277 L10
Moreton Cl, Swan. 207 FE96
Bonney Way
Moreton Cl (Cheshunt), Wal.Cr. 66 DV27
Moreton Gdns, Wdf.Grn. 102 EL50
Moreton Ind Est, Swan. 207 FH98
Moreton Pl SW1 277 L10
Moreton Pl SW1 161 DJ78
Moreton Rd N15 122 DR58
Moreton Rd, Ong. 53 FG24
Moreton Rd, S.Croy. 220 DR106
Moreton Rd, Wor.Pk. 199 CU103
Moreton St SW1 277 L10
Moreton St SW1 161 DK78
Moreton Ter SW1 277 L10
Moreton Ter SW1 161 DJ78
Moreton Ter Ms N SW1 277 L10
Moreton Ter Ms S SW1 277 L10
Moreton Twr W3 138 CP74
Moreton Way, Slou. 131 AK74
Morewood Cl, Sev. 256 FF123
Morewood Cl Ind Pk, Sev. 256 FF123
Morewood Cl
Morford Cl, Ruis. 115 BV59
Morford Way, Ruis. 115 BV59
Morgan Av E17 123 ED56
Morgan Cl, Dag. 146 FA66
Morgan Cl, Nthwd. 93 BT51
Morgan Cres, Epp. 85 ER36
Morgan Dr, Green. 189 FS87
Morgan Gdns, Wat. 76 CB38
Morgan Rd N7 121 DN64
Morgan Rd W10 139 CZ71
Morgan Rd, Brom. 184 EG94
Morgan St E3 143 DY69
Morgan St E16 144 EF71
Morgan Way, Rain. 148 FJ69
Morgan Way, Wdf.Grn. 102 EL51
Morgans Cl, Hert. 32 DR11
Morgans La SE1 279 M3
Morgans La SE1 142 DS74
Morgans La, Hayes 135 BR71
Morgans Rd, Hert. 32 DR11
Morgans Wk, Hert. 32 DR12
Moriatry Cl N7 121 DL63
Morice Rd, Hodd. 49 DZ15
Morie St SW18 180 DB85
Morieux Rd E10 123 DZ60
Moring Rd SW17 180 DG91
Morkyns Wk SE21 182 DS90
Morland Av, Croy. 202 DS102
Morland Av, Dart. 187 FH85
Morland Cl NW11 120 DB60
Morland Cl, Hmptn. 176 BZ92
Morland Cl, Mitch. 200 DE97
Morland Gdns NW10 138 CR66
Morland Gdns, Sthl. 136 CB74
Morland Ms N1 141 DN66
Lofting Rd
Morland Rd E17 123 DX57
Morland Rd SE20 183 DX93
Morland Rd, Croy. 202 DS102
Morland Rd, Dag. 146 FA66
Morland Rd, Har. 118 CL57
Morland Rd, Ilf. 125 EP61
Morland Rd, Sutt. 218 DC106
Morland Way (Cheshunt), Wal.Cr. 67 DY28
Morley Av E4 101 ED52
Morley Av N18 100 DU49
Morley Av N22 99 DN54
Morley Cl, Orp. 205 EP103
Morley Cl, Slou. 153 AZ75
Morley Cres, Edg. 96 CQ47
Morley Cres, Ruis. 116 BW61
Morley Cres E, Stan. 95 CJ54
Morley Cres W, Stan. 95 CJ54
Morley Gro, Harl. 35 EQ13
Morley Hill, Enf. 82 DR38
Morley Rd E10 123 EC60
Morley Rd E15 144 EF68
Morley Rd SE13 163 EC84
Morley Rd, Bark. 145 ER67
Morley Rd, Chis. 205 EQ95
Morley Rd, Rom. 126 EY57
Morley Rd, S.Croy. 220 DT110
Morley Rd, Sutt. 199 CZ102
Morley Rd, Twick. 177 CK86
Morley Sq, Grays 171 GG77
Morley St SE1 278 E6
Morley St SE1 161 DN75
Morna Rd SE5 162 DQ82
Morning La E9 142 DW65
Morning Ri, Rick. 74 BK41
Morningside Rd, Wor.Pk. 199 CV103
Mornington Av W14 159 CZ77
Mornington Av, Brom. 204 EJ97
Mornington Av, Ilf. 125 EN59
Mornington Cl (Biggin Hill), West. 238 EK117
Mornington Cl, Wdf.Grn. 102 EG49
Mornington Ct, Bex. 187 FC88
Mornington Cres NW1 141 DJ68
Mornington Cres, Houns. 155 BV81
Mornington Gro E3 143 EA69
Mornington Ms SE5 162 DQ81
Mornington Pl NW1 141 DH68
Mornington Ter
Mornington Rd E4 101 ED45
Mornington Rd E11 124 EF60
Mornington Rd SE8 163 DZ80
Mornington Rd, Ashf. 175 BQ92
Mornington Rd, Grnf. 136 CB71
Mornington Rd, Loug. 85 EQ41
Mornington Rd, Rad. 61 CG34
Mornington Rd, Wdf.Grn. 102 EF49
Mornington St NW1 141 DH68
Mornington Ter NW1 141 DH67
Mornington Wk, Rich. 177 CK91
Morningtons, Harl. 51 EQ20
Morocco St SE1 279 M5
Morocco St SE1 162 DS75
Morpeth Av, Borwd. 78 CM38
Morpeth Cl, Hem.H. 40 BL21
York Way
Morpeth Gro E9 143 DX67
Morpeth Rd E9 142 DW67
Morpeth St E2 143 DX69
Morpeth Ter SW1 277 K7
Morpeth Ter SW1 161 DJ76
Morpeth Wk N17 100 DV52
West Rd
Morrab Gdns, Ilf. 125 ET62
Morrell Ct, Welw.G.C. 29 CZ08
Morrice Cl, Slou. 153 AZ77
Morris Av E12 125 EM64
Morris Cl, Croy. 203 DY100
Morris Cl (Chalfont St. Peter), Ger.Cr. 91 AZ53
Morris Cl, Orp. 205 ES104
Morris Ct E4 101 EB48
Flaxen Rd
Morris Ct, Wal.Abb. 68 EF34
Morris Gdns SW18 180 DA87
Morris Gdns, Dart. 188 FN85
Morris Pl N4 121 DN61
Morris Rd E14 143 EB71
Morris Rd E15 124 EE63
Morris Rd, Dag. 126 EZ61
Morris Rd, Islw. 157 CF83
Morris Rd (South Nutfield), Red. 267 DL136
Morris Rd, Rom. 105 FH52
Morris St E1 142 DV72
Morris Way (London Colney), St.Alb. 61 CK26
Morrish Rd SW2 181 DL87
Morrison Av N17 122 DS55
Morrison Rd, Bark. 146 EY68
Morrison Rd, Hayes 135 BV69
Morrison St SW11 160 DG83
Morriston Cl, Wat. 94 BW50
Morse Cl E13 144 EG69
Morse Cl (Harefield), Uxb. 92 BJ54
Morshead Rd W9 140 DA69
Morson Rd, Enf. 83 DY44
Morston Cl, Tad. 233 CV120
Waterfield
Morston Gdns SE9 185 EM91
Mortain Dr, Berk. 38 AT17
Morten Cl SW4 181 DK86
Morten Gdns (Denham), Uxb. 114 BG59
Mortens Wd, Amer. 55 AR40
Morteyne Rd N17 100 DR53
Mortgramit Sq SE18 165 EN76
Powis St
Mortham St E15 144 EE67
Mortimer Cl NW2 119 CZ62
Mortimer Cl SW16 181 DK89
Mortimer Cl, Bushey 76 CB44
Mortimer Cres NW6 140 DB67
Mortimer Cres, Wor.Pk. 198 CR104
Mortimer Dr, Enf. 82 DS43
Mortimer Est NW6 140 DB67
Mortimer Gate, Wal.Cr. 67 DZ27
Mortimer Mkt WC1 273 L5
Mortimer Pl NW6 140 DB67
Mortimer Rd E6 145 EM69
Mortimer Rd N1 142 DS66
Mortimer Rd NW10 139 CW69
Mortimer Rd W13 137 CJ72
Mortimer Rd, Erith 167 FD79
Mortimer Rd, Mitch. 200 DF95
Mortimer Rd, Orp. 206 EU103
Mortimer Rd, Slou. 152 AX76
Mortimer Rd (Biggin Hill), West. 222 EJ112
Mortimer Sq W11 139 CX73
St. Anns Rd
Mortimer St W1 273 K7
Mortimer St W1 141 DJ72
Mortimer Ter NW5 121 DH63
Gordon Ho Rd
Mortlake Cl, Croy. 201 DL104
Richmond Rd
Mortlake Dr, Mitch. 200 DE95
Mortlake High St SW14 158 CR83
Mortlake Rd E16 144 EH72
Mortlake Rd, Ilf. 125 EQ63
Mortlake Rd, Rich. 158 CN80
Mortlake Ter, Rich. 158 CN80
Kew Rd
Mortlock Cl SE15 162 DV81
Cossall Wk
Morton, Tad. 233 CX121
Hudsons
Morton Cl, Wall. 219 DM108
Lancastrian Rd
Morton Cl, Wok. 226 AW115
Morton Ct, Nthlt. 116 CC64
Morton Cres N14 99 DK49
Morton Dr, Slou. 111 AL64
Morton Gdns, Wall. 219 DJ106
Morton Ms SW5 160 DB77
Earls Ct Gdns
Morton Pl SE1 278 D7
Morton Rd E15 144 EF66
Morton Rd N1 142 DQ66
Morton Rd, Mord. 200 DD99
Morton Rd, Wok. 226 AW115
Morton Way N14 99 DJ48
Morval Rd SW2 181 DN85
Morvale Cl, Belv. 166 EZ77
Morven Cl, Pot.B. 64 DC31
Morven Rd SW17 180 DF90
Morville Ho SW18 180 DD86
Fitzhugh Gro
Morville St E3 143 EA68
Morwell St WC1 273 N7
Mosbach Gdns, Brwd. 109 GB47
Moscow Pl W2 140 DB73
Moscow Rd
Moscow Rd W2 140 DA73
Moselle Av N22 99 DN54
Moselle Cl N8 121 DM55
Miles Rd
Moselle Ho N17 100 DT52
William St
Moselle Pl N17 100 DT52
High Rd
Moselle Rd (Biggin Hill), West. 238 EL118
Moselle St N17 100 DT52
Mosford Cl, Horl. 268 DF146
Mospey Cres, Epsom 233 CT115
Moss Bk, Grays 170 FZ78
Moss Cl E1 142 DU71
Old Montague St
Moss Cl, Pnr. 94 BZ54
Moss Cl, Rick. 92 BK47
Moss Gdns, Felt. 175 BU89
Moss Gdns, S.Croy. 221 DX108
Warren Av
Moss Grn, Welw.G.C. 29 CY11
Moss Hall Ct N12 98 DB51
Moss Hall Cres N12 98 DB51
Moss Hall Gro N12 98 DB51
Moss La, Pnr. 116 BZ55
Moss La, Rom. 127 FF58
Wheatsheaf Rd
Moss Rd, Dag. 146 FA66
Moss Rd, S.Ock. 149 FW71
Moss Rd, Wat. 59 BV34
Moss Side (Bricket Wd), St.Alb. 60 BZ30
Moss Way, Beac. 88 AJ51
Moss Way (Lane End), Dart. 189 FR91
Mossborough Cl N12 98 DB51
Mossbury Rd SW11 160 DE83
Mossdown Cl, Belv. 166 FA77
Mossendew Cl (Harefield), Uxb. 92 BK53
Mossfield, Cob. 213 BU113
Mossford Ct, Ilf. 125 EP55
Mossford Grn, Ilf. 125 EP55
Mossford La, Ilf. 103 EP54
Mossford St E3 143 DZ70
Mossington Gdns SE16 162 DW77
Abbeyfield Rd
Mosslea Rd SE20 182 DW93
Mosslea Rd, Brom. 204 EK99
Mosslea Rd, Orp. 205 EQ104
Mosslea Rd, Whyt. 236 DT116
Mossop St SW3 276 C8
Mossop St SW3 160 DE77
Mossville Gdns, Mord. 199 CZ97
Moston Cl, Hayes 155 BT78
Fuller Way
Mostyn Av, Wem. 118 CM64
Mostyn Gdns NW10 139 CX68
Mostyn Gro E3 143 DZ68
Mostyn Rd SW9 161 DN81
Mostyn Rd SW19 199 CZ95
Mostyn Rd, Bushey 76 CC43
Mostyn Rd, Edg. 96 CR52
Mostyn Ter, Red. 266 DG135
Mosul Way, Brom. 204 EL100
Mosyer Dr, Orp. 206 EX103
Motcomb St SW1 276 E6
Motcomb St SW1 160 DG76
Moth Cl, Wall. 219 DL108
Lancastrian Rd
Mothers' Sq E5 122 DV63
Motherwell Way, Grays 169 FU78
Motley Av EC2 142 DS70
Scrutton St
Motley St SW8 161 DJ82
St. Rule St
Motspur Pk, N.Mal. 199 CT100
Mott St E4 83 ED38
Mott St (High Beach), Loug. 84 EF39
Mottingham Gdns SE9 184 EK88
Mottingham La SE9 184 EJ88
Mottingham La SE12 184 EJ88
Mottingham Rd N9 83 DX44
Mottingham Rd SE9 184 EL89
Mottisfont Rd SE2 166 EU76
Motts Hill La, Tad. 233 CU123
Mouchotte Cl (Biggin Hill), West. 222 EH112
Moulins Rd E9 142 DW67
Moulsford Ho N7 121 DK64
Moultain Hill, Swan. 207 FG98
Moulton Av, Houns. 156 BY82
Moultrie Way, Upmin. 129 FS59
Mound, The SE9 185 EN90
Moundfield Rd N16 122 DU58
Mount, The N20 98 DC47
Mount, The NW3 120 DC63
Heath St
Mount, The W3 138 CP74
Mount, The, Brwd. 108 FW48
Mount, The, Couls. 234 DG115
Mount, The (Ewell), Epsom 217 CT110
Mount, The, Esher 214 CA107
Mount, The, Guil. 258 AV137
Mount, The (Fetcham), Lthd. 231 CE123
Mount, The, N.Mal. 199 CT97
Mount, The, Pot.B. 64 DB30
Mount, The, Rick. 74 BJ44
Mount, The, Rom. 106 FJ48
Mount, The, Tad. 249 CZ126
Mount, The, Vir.W. 192 AX100
Mount, The (Cheshunt), Wal.Cr. 66 DR26
Mount, The, Warl. 236 DU119
Mount, The, Wem. 118 CP61
Mount, The, Wey. 195 BS103
Mount, The, Wok. 226 AX118
Mount, The (St. John's), Wok. 226 AU119
Mount, The, Wor.Pk. 217 CV105
Mount Adon Pk SE22 182 DU87
Mount Angelus Rd SW15 179 CT87
Mount Ararat Rd, Rich. 178 CL85
Mount Ash Rd SE26 182 DV90
Mount Av E4 101 EA48
Mount Av W5 137 CK71
Mount Av, Brwd. 109 GB45
Mount Av, Cat. 236 DQ124
Mount Av, Rom. 106 FQ51
Mount Av, Sthl. 136 CA72
Mount Cl W5 137 CJ71
Mount Cl, Barn. 80 DG42
Mount Cl, Brom. 204 EL95
Mount Cl, Cars. 218 DG109
Mount Cl, Hem.H. 39 BF20
Mount Cl, Ken. 236 DQ116
Mount Cl (Fetcham), Lthd. 231 CE123
Mount Cl, Sev. 256 FF123
Mount Cl (Farnham Common), Slou. 111 AQ63
Mount Cl, Wok. 226 AV121
Mount Cl, The, Vir.W. 192 AX100
Mount Cor, Felt. 176 BX89
Mount Ct SW15 159 CY83
Weimar St
Mount Ct, W.Wick. 204 EE103
Mount Cres, Brwd. 108 FX49
Mount Culver Av, Sid. 186 EX93
Mount Dr, Bexh. 186 EY85
Mount Dr, Har. 116 BZ57
Mount Dr (Park St), St.Alb. 61 CD25
Mount Dr, Wem. 118 CQ61
Mount Dr, The, Reig. 250 DC132
Mount Echo Av E4 101 EB47
Mount Echo Dr E4 101 EB46
Mount Ephraim La SW16 181 DK90
Mount Ephraim Rd SW16 181 DK90
Mount Est, The E5 122 DV61
Mount Pleasant La
Mount Felix, Walt. 195 BT102
Mount Gdns SE26 182 DV90
Mount Grace Rd, Pot.B. 64 DA31
Mount Gro, Edg. 96 CQ48
Mount Harry Rd, Sev. 256 FG123
Mount Hermon Cl, Wok. 226 AX118
Mount Hermon Rd, Wok. 226 AX119
Mount Hill La, Ger.Cr. 112 AV60
Mount La (Denham), Uxb. 113 BD61
Mount Lee, Egh. 172 AY92
Mount Ms, Hmptn. 196 CB95
Mount Mills EC1 274 G3
Mount Nod Rd SW16 181 DM90
Mount Nugent, Chesh. 54 AN27
Mount Pk, Cars. 218 DG109
Mount Pk Av, Har. 117 CD61
Mount Pk Av, S.Croy. 219 DP109
Mount Pk Cres W5 137 CK72
Mount Pk Rd W5 137 CK71
Mount Pk Rd, Har. 117 CD62
Mount Pk Rd, Pnr. 115 BU57
Mount Pl W3 138 CP74
High St
Mount Pl, Guil. 258 AW136
The Mt
Mount Pleasant SE27 182 DQ91
Mount Pleasant WC1 274 C5
Mount Pleasant WC1 141 DN70
Mount Pleasant, Barn. 80 DE42
Mount Pleasant, Epsom 217 CT110
Mount Pleasant, Guil. 258 AW136
Mount Pleasant, Hert. 32 DW11
Mount Pleasant (Effingham), Lthd. 246 BY128
Mount Pleasant (West Horsley), Lthd. 245 BP129
Mount Pleasant, Ruis. 116 BW61
Mount Pleasant, St.Alb. 42 CB19
Mount Pleasant (Harefield), Uxb. 92 BG53
Mount Pleasant, Wem. 138 CL67
Mount Pleasant (Biggin Hill), West. 238 EK117
Mount Pleasant, Wey. 194 BN104
Mount Pleasant Av, Brwd. 109 GE44
Mount Pleasant Cl, Hat. 45 CW15
Mount Pleasant Cres N4 121 DM59
Mount Pleasant Hill E5 122 DW61
Mount Pleasant La E5 122 DV61
Mount Pleasant La, Hat. 29 CW14
Mount Pleasant La (Bricket Wd), St.Alb. 60 BY30
Mount Pleasant Pl SE18 165 ER77
Orchard Rd
Mount Pleasant Rd E17 101 DY54
Mount Pleasant Rd N17 100 DS54
Mount Pleasant Rd NW10 139 CW66
Mount Pleasant Rd SE13 183 EB86
Mount Pleasant Rd W5 137 CJ70
Mount Pleasant Rd, Cat. 236 DU123
Mount Pleasant Rd, Chig. 103 ER49
Mount Pleasant Rd, Dart. 188 FM86
Mount Pleasant Rd, N.Mal. 198 CQ97
Mount Pleasant Rd, Rom. 105 FD51
Mount Pleasant Vil N4 121 DM59
Mount Pleasant Wk, Bex. 187 FC85
Mount Ri, Red. 266 DD136
Mount Rd NW2 119 CV62
Mount Rd NW4 119 CU58
Mount Rd SE19 182 DR93
Mount Rd SW19 180 DA89
Mount Rd, Barn. 80 DE43
Mount Rd, Bexh. 186 EX85
Mount Rd, Chess. 216 CM106
Mount Rd, Dag. 126 EZ60
Mount Rd, Dart. 187 FF86
Mount Rd, Epp. 70 EW32
Mount Rd, Felt. 176 BY90
Mount Rd, Hayes 155 BU75
Mount Rd, Hert. 31 DN10
Mount Rd, Ilf. 125 EP64
Mount Rd, Mitch. 200 DE96
Mount Rd, N.Mal. 198 CR97
Mount Rd, Wok. 226 AV121
Mount Rd (Chobham), Wok. 210 AV112
Mount Row W1 277 H1
Mount Row W1 141 DH73
Mount Sq, The NW3 120 DC62
Heath St
Mount Stewart Av, Har. 117 CK58
Mount St W1 276 G1
Mount St W1 140 DG73
Mount St, Dor. 263 CG136
Mount Ter E1 142 DV71
New Rd
Mount Vernon NW3 120 DC63
Mount Vw NW7 96 CR48
Mount Vw W5 137 CK70
Mount Vw, Enf. 81 DM38
Mount Vw, Rick. 92 BH46
Mount Vw, St.Alb. 62 CL27
Mount Vw Rd E4 101 EC45
Mount Vw Rd N4 121 DL59
Mount Vw Rd NW9 118 CR56
Mount Vil SE27 181 DP90
Mount Way, Cars. 218 DG109
Mountacre Cl SE26 182 DT91
Mountague Pl E14 143 EC73
Mountain Ct (Eynsford), Dart. 208 FL103
Pollyhaugh
Mountbatten Cl SE18 165 ES79
Mountbatten Cl SE19 182 DS92
Mountbatten Cl, St.Alb. 43 CH23
Mountbatten Cl, Slou. 152 AU76
Mountbatten Ct SE16 142 DW74
Rotherhithe St
Mountbatten Ct, Buck.H. 102 EK47
Mountbatten Gdns, Beck. 203 DY98
Balmoral Av
Mountbatten Ms SW18 180 DC88
Inman Rd
Mountbatten Sq, Wind. 151 AQ81
Alma Rd
Mountbel Rd, Stan. 95 CG53
Mountcombe Cl, Surb. 198 CL101
Mountearl Gdns SW16 181 DM90
Mountfield Cl SE6 183 ED87
Mountfield Rd E6 145 EN68
Mountfield Rd N3 120 DA55
Mountfield Rd W5 137 CK72
Mountfield Rd, Hem.H. 40 BL20
Mountfield Way, Orp. 206 EW98
Mountford St E1 142 DU72
Adler St
Mountfort Cres N1 141 DN66
Barnsbury Sq
Mountfort Ter N1 141 DN66
Barnsbury Sq
Mountgrove Rd N5 121 DP62
Mounthurst Rd, Brom. 204 EF101
Mountington Pk Cl, Har. 117 CK58
Mountjoy Cl SE2 166 EV75
Mountjoy Ho EC2 142 DQ71
The Barbican
Mountnessing Bypass, Brwd. 109 GD41
Mounts Pond Rd SE3 163 ED82
Mounts Rd, Green. 189 FV85
Mountsfield Cl, Stai. 174 BG86
Mountsfield Ct SE13 183 EE86
Mountside, Felt. 176 BY90

Mou - Nel This index reads in the sequence: Street Name / Postal District or Post Town / Map Page Number / Grid Reference

Mountside, Guil. 258 AV136
Mountside, Stan. 95 CF53
Mountsorrel, Hert. 32 DT08
Mountview, Nthwd. 93 BT51
Mountview Cl, Red. 266 DE136
Mountview Ct N8 121 DP56
Green Las
Mountview Dr, Red. 266 DD136
Mountview Rd (Claygate), Esher 215 CH108
Mountview Rd, Orp. 206 EU101
Mountview Rd (Cheshunt), Wal.Cr. 66 DS26
Mountway, Pot.B. 64 DA30
Mountway, Welw.G.C. 29 CZ12
Mountway Cl, Welw.G.C. 29 CZ12
Mountwood, W.Mol. 196 CA97
Mountwood Cl, S.Croy. 220 DV110
Movers La, Bark. 145 ES68
Mowat Ind Est, Wat. 76 BW38
Mowatt Cl N19 121 DK60
Mowbray Av (Byfleet), W.Byf. 212 BL113
Mowbray Cres, Egh. 173 BA92
Mowbray Gdns, Dor. 247 CH134
Mowbray Rd NW6 139 CY66
Mowbray Rd SE19 202 DT95
Mowbray Rd, Barn. 80 DC42
Mowbray Rd, Edg. 96 CN49
Mowbray Rd, Harl. 35 ET13
Mowbray Rd, Rich. 177 CJ90
Mowbrays Cl, Rom. 105 FC53
Mowbrays Rd, Rom. 105 FC54
Mowbrey Gdns, Loug. 85 EQ40
Mowlem St E2 142 DV68
Mowlem Trd Est N17 100 DW52
Mowll St SW9 161 DN80
Moxom Av (Cheshunt), Wal.Cr. 67 DY30
Moxon Cl E13 144 EF68
Whitelegg Rd
Moxon St W1 272 F7
Moxon St W1 140 DG71
Moxon St, Barn. 79 CZ41
Moye Cl E2 142 DU67
Dove Row
Moyers Rd E10 123 EC59
Moylan Rd W6 159 CY79
Moyne Ct, Wok. 226 AT118
Iveagh Rd
Moyne Pl NW10 138 CN68
Moynihan Dr N21 81 DL43
Moys Cl, Croy. 201 DL100
Moyser Rd SW16 181 DH92
Mozart St W10 139 CZ69
Mozart Ter SW1 276 G9
Mozart Ter SW1 160 DG77
Muchelney Rd, Mord. 200 DC100
Muckhatch La, Egh. 193 BB97
Muckingford Rd, S.le H. 171 GM77
Muckingford Rd, Til. 171 GL77
Mud La W5 137 CK71
Muddy La, Slou. 132 AS71
Muggeridge Cl, S.Croy. 220 DR106
Muggeridge Rd, Dag. 127 FB63
Muir Dr SW18 180 DD86
Muir Rd E5 122 DU63
Muir St E16 145 EM74
Newland St
Muirdown Av SW14 158 CR84
Muirfield W3 138 CS72
Muirfield Cl SE16 162 DV78
Ryder Dr
Muirfield Cl, Wat. 94 BW49
Muirfield Cres E14 163 EB76
Millharbour
Muirfield Grn, Wat. 94 BW49
Muirfield Rd, Wat. 94 BX49
Muirfield Rd, Wok. 226 AU118
Muirkirk Rd SE6 183 EC88
Mulberry Av, Stai. 174 BL88
Mulberry Av, Wind. 152 AT83
Mulberry Business Cen SE16 163 DX75
Quebec Way
Mulberry Cl E4 101 EA47
Mulberry Cl N8 121 DL57
Mulberry Cl NW3 120 DD63
Hampstead High St
Mulberry Cl NW4 119 CW55
Mulberry Cl SE7 164 EK79
Mulberry Cl SE22 182 DU85
Mulberry Cl SW3 160 DD79
Beaufort St
Mulberry Cl SW16 181 DJ91
Mulberry Cl, Amer. 72 AT39
Mulberry Cl, Barn. 80 DD42
Mulberry Cl, Brox. 49 DZ24
Mulberry Cl, Nthlt. 136 BY68
Parkfield Av
Mulberry Cl, Rom. 127 FH56
Mulberry Cl (Park St), St.Alb. 60 CB28
Mulberry Cl, Wey. 195 BP104
Mulberry Cl, Wok. 210 AY114
Mulberry Ct, Bark. 145 ET66
Westrow Dr
Mulberry Ct, Beac. 111 AM55
Mulberry Ct, Guil. 243 BD131
Gilliat Dr
Mulberry Cres, Brent. 157 CH80
Mulberry Cres, West Dr. 154 BN75
Mulberry Dr, Purf. 168 FM77
Mulberry Dr, Slou. 152 AY78
Mulberry Gdns (Shenley), Rad. 62 CL33
Mulberry Grn, Harl. 36 EX11
Mulberry Hill, Brwd. 109 FZ45
Mulberry La, Croy. 202 DT102
Mulberry Ms, Wall. 219 DJ107
Ross Rd
Mulberry Par, West Dr. 154 BN76
Mulberry Pl W6 159 CU78
Chiswick Mall
Mulberry Rd E8 142 DT66
Mulberry Rd (Northfleet), Grav. 190 GE90
Mulberry St E1 142 DU72
Adler St
Mulberry Trees, Shep. 195 BQ101
Mulberry Wk SW3 160 DD79
Mulberry Way E18 102 EH54
Mulberry Way, Belv. 167 FC75
Mulberry Way, Ilf. 125 EQ56
Mulgrave Rd NW10 119 CT63
Mulgrave Rd SE18 165 EM77
Mulgrave Rd SW6 159 CZ79
Mulgrave Rd W5 137 CK69
Mulgrave Rd, Croy. 202 DR104
Mulgrave Rd, Har. 117 CG61
Mulgrave Rd, Sutt. 218 DA107
Mulgrave Way (Knaphill), Wok. 226 AS118
Mulholland Cl, Mitch. 201 DH96
Mulkern Rd N19 121 DK60
Mull Wk N1 142 DQ65
Clephane Rd
Mullards Cl, Mitch. 200 DF102
Mullein Ct, Grays 170 GD79
Mullens Rd, Egh. 173 BB92
Muller Rd SW4 181 DK86
Mullet Gdns E2 142 DU68
St. Peter's Cl
Mullins Path SW14 158 CR83
Mullion Cl, Har. 94 CB53
Mullion Wk, Wat. 94 BX49
Ormskirk Rd
Mulready St NW8 272 B5
Multi Way W3 158 CS75
Valetta Rd
Multon Rd SW18 180 DD87
Mulvaney Way SE1 279 L5
Mulvaney Way SE1 162 DR75
Mumford Ct EC2 275 J8
Mumford Rd SE24 181 DP85
Railton Rd
Mumfords La (Chalfont St. Peter), Ger.Cr. 112 AU55
Muncaster Cl, Ashf. 174 BN91
Muncaster Rd SW11 180 DF85
Muncaster Rd, Ashf. 175 BP92
Muncies Ms SE6 183 EC89
Mund St W14 159 CZ78
Mundania Rd SE22 182 DV86
Munday Rd E16 144 EG72
Mundells, Wal.Cr. 66 DU27
Mundells, Welw.G.C. 29 CZ07
Mundells Cl, Welw.G.C. 29 CZ07
Munden Dr, Wat. 76 BY37
Munden Gro, Wat. 76 BW38
Munden St W14 159 CY77
Munden Vw, Wat. 76 BX36
Mundesley Cl, Wat. 94 BW49
Mundesley Spur, Slou. 132 AS72
Mundford Rd E5 122 DW61
Mundon Gdns, Ilf. 125 ER60
Mundy St N1 275 M2
Mundy St N1 142 DS69
Munford Dr, Swans. 190 FY87
Mungo Pk Cl, Bushey 94 CC47
Mungo Pk Rd, Grav. 191 GK92
Mungo Pk Rd, Rain. 147 FG65
Mungo Pk Way, Orp. 206 EW101
Munnery Way, Orp. 205 EN104
Munnings Gdns, Islw. 177 CD85
Munro Dr N11 99 DJ51
Munro Ms W10 139 CY71
Munro Rd, Bushey 76 CB43
Munro Ter SW10 160 DD80
Munslow Gdns, Sutt. 218 DD105
Munstead Vw (Artington), Guil. 258 AV138
Munster Av, Houns. 156 BZ84
Munster Ct, Tedd. 177 CJ93
Munster Gdns N13 99 DP49
Munster Ms SW6 159 CY80
Munster Rd
Munster Rd SW6 159 CZ81
Munster Rd, Tedd. 177 CJ93
Munster Sq NW1 273 J4
Munster Sq NW1 141 DH69
Munton Rd SE17 279 J8
Munton Rd SE17 162 DQ77
Murchison Av, Bex. 186 EX88
Murchison Rd E10 123 EC61
Murchison Rd, Hodd. 33 EB14
Murdoch Cl, Stai. 174 BG92
Murdock Cl E16 144 EF72
Rogers Rd
Murdock St SE15 162 DV79
Murfett Cl SW19 179 CY89
Murfitt Way, Upmin. 128 FN63
Muriel Av, Wat. 76 BW43
Muriel St N1 141 DM68
Murillo Rd SE13 163 ED84
Murphy St SE1 278 D5
Murphy St SE1 161 DN75
Murray Av, Brom. 204 EH96
Murray Av, Houns. 176 CB85
Murray Business Cen, Orp. 206 EV97
Murray Cres, Pnr. 94 BX53
Murray Grn, Wok. 211 BC114
Bunyard Dr
Murray Gro N1 275 K1
Murray Gro N1 142 DQ68
Murray Ms NW1 141 DK66
Murray Rd SW19 179 CX93
Murray Rd W5 157 CJ77
Murray Rd, Berk. 38 AV18
Murray Rd (Ottershaw), Cher. 211 BC107
Murray Rd, Nthwd. 93 BS53
Murray Rd, Orp. 206 EV97
Murray Rd, Rich. 177 CH89
Murray Sq E16 144 EG72
Murray St NW1 141 DK66
Murray Ter NW3 120 DD63
Flask Wk
Murray Ter W5 157 CK77
Murray Rd
Murrays La (Byfleet), W.Byf. 212 BK114
Murrells Wk (Bookham), Lthd. 230 CA123
Murreys, The, Ash. 231 CK118
Mursell Est SW8 161 DM81
Murthering La, Rom. 87 FG43
Murton Ct, St.Alb. 43 CE19
Murtwell Dr, Chig. 103 EQ51
Musard Rd W6 159 CY79
Musard Rd W14 159 CY79
Musbury St E1 142 DW72
Muscal W6 159 CY79
Muscatel Pl SE5 162 DS81
Dalwood St
Muschamp Rd SE15 162 DT83
Muschamp Rd, Cars. 200 DE103
Muscovy Ho, Erith 166 EY75
Kale Rd
Muscovy St EC3 279 N1
Museum La SW7 160 DD76
Exhibition Rd
Museum Pas E2 142 DV69
Victoria Pk Sq
Museum St WC1 273 P7
Museum St WC1 141 DL72
Musgrave Cl, Barn. 80 DC39
Musgrave Cl, Wal.Cr. 66 DT27
Allwood Rd
Musgrave Cres SW6 160 DA81
Musgrave Rd, Islw. 157 CF81
Musgrove Rd SE14 163 DX81
Musjid Rd SW11 160 DD82
Kambala Rd
Musk Hill, Hem.H. 39 BE21
Muskalls Cl (Cheshunt), Wal.Cr. 66 DU27
Musket Cl, Barn. 80 DD43
East Barnet Rd
Muskham Rd, Harl. 36 EU12
Musleigh Manor, Ware 33 DZ06
Musley Hill, Ware 33 DY05
Musley La, Ware 33 DY05
Musquash Way, Houns. 156 BW82
Mussenden La (Horton Kirby), Dart. 208 FQ99
Mussenden La (Fawkham Grn), Long. 209 FS101
Muston Rd E5 122 DV61
Mustow Pl SW6 159 CZ82
Munster Rd
Muswell Av N10 99 DH54
Muswell Hill N10 121 DH55
Muswell Hill Bdy N10 121 DH55
Muswell Hill Pl N10 121 DH56
Muswell Hill Rd N6 120 DG58
Muswell Hill Rd N10 120 DG56
Muswell Ms N10 121 DH55
Muswell Rd
Muswell Rd N10 121 DH55
Mutchetts Cl, Wat. 60 BY33
Mutrix Rd NW6 140 DA67
Mutton La, Pot.B. 63 CY31
Mutton Pl NW1 141 DH65
Harmood St
Muybridge Rd, N.Mal. 198 CQ96
Myatt Rd SW9 161 DP81
Myatt's Flds N SW9 161 DN81
Eythorne Rd
Myatt's Flds S SW9 161 DN82
Loughborough Rd
Mycenae Rd SE3 164 EG80
Myddelton Av, Enf. 82 DS38
Myddelton Cl, Enf. 82 DT39
Myddelton Gdns N21 99 DP45
Myddelton Pk N20 98 DD48
Myddelton Pas EC1 274 E2
Myddelton Rd N8 121 DL56
Myddelton Sq EC1 274 E2
Myddelton Sq EC1 141 DN69
Myddelton St EC1 274 E3
Myddelton St EC1 141 DN69
Myddleton Av N4 122 DQ61
Myddleton Ms N22 99 DL52
Myddleton Path (Cheshunt), Wal.Cr. 66 DV31
Myddleton Rd N22 99 DL52
Myddleton Rd, Uxb. 134 BJ67
Myddleton Rd, Ware 33 DX07
Myers Dr, Slou. 111 AP64
Myers La SE14 163 DX79
Mygrove Cl, Rain. 148 FK68
Mygrove Gdns, Rain. 148 FK68
Mygrove Rd, Rain. 148 FK68
Myles Ct, Wal.Cr. 66 DQ29
Mylis Cl SE26 182 DV91
Mylius Cl SE14 162 DW81
Kender St
Mylne Cl, Wal.Cr. 66 DW27
Mylne St EC1 274 D1
Mylne St EC1 141 DN69
Mylner Ct, Hodd. 49 EA15
Ditchfield Rd
Mylor Cl, Wok. 210 AY114
Mymms Dr, Hat. 64 DA26
Mynchen Cl, Beac. 89 AK49
Mynchen End, Beac. 89 AK49
Mynchen Rd, Beac. 89 AK50
Mynns Cl, Epsom 216 CP114
Mynterne Ct SW19 179 CX88
Swanton Gdns
Myra St SE2 166 EU77
Myrdle St E1 142 DU71
Myrke, The (Datchet), Slou. 152 AT77
Myrna Cl SW19 180 DE94
Myron Pl SE13 163 EC83
Myrtle Av, Felt. 155 BS84
Myrtle Av, Ruis. 115 BU59
Myrtle Cl, Barn. 98 DF46
Myrtle Cl, Erith 167 FE80
Myrtle Cl (Colnbrook), Slou. 153 BE81
Myrtle Cl, Uxb. 134 BM71
Violet Av
Myrtle Cl, West Dr. 154 BM76
Myrtle Cres, Slou. 132 AT73
Myrtle Gdns W7 137 CE74
Myrtle Grn, Hem.H. 39 BE20
Newlands Rd
Myrtle Gro, Enf. 82 DR38
Myrtle Gro, N.Mal. 198 CQ96
Myrtle Gro, S.Ock. 168 FQ75
Myrtle Pl, Dart. 189 FR87
Myrtle Rd E6 144 EL67
Myrtle Rd E17 123 DY58
Myrtle Rd N13 100 DQ48
Myrtle Rd W3 138 CQ74
Myrtle Rd, Brwd. 108 FW48
Myrtle Rd, Croy. 203 EA104
Myrtle Rd, Dart. 188 FK88
Myrtle Rd, Dor. 263 CG135
Myrtle Rd (Hampton Hill), Hmptn. 176 CC93
Myrtle Rd, Houns. 156 CC82
Myrtle Rd, Ilf. 125 EP61
Myrtle Rd, Rom. 106 FJ51
Myrtle Rd, Sutt. 218 DC106
Myrtle Wk N1 275 M1
Myrtle Wk N1 142 DS68
Myrtleberry Cl E8 142 DT65
Beechwood Rd
Myrtledene Rd SE2 166 EU78
Myrtleside Cl, Nthwd. 93 BR52
Mysore Rd SW11 160 DF83
Myton Rd SE21 182 DR90

N

N.L.A. Twr, Croy. 202 DR103
Nadine Ct, Wall. 219 DJ109
Woodcote Rd
Nadine St SE7 164 EJ78
Nafferton Ri, Loug. 84 EK43
Nagle Cl E17 101 ED54
Nags Head Cl, Hert. 32 DV08
Nag's Head Ct EC1 275 H5
Nags Head La, Brwd. 107 FR51
Nags Head La, Upmin. 106 FQ53
Nags Head La, Well. 166 EV83
Nags Head Rd, Enf. 82 DW42
Nags Head Shop Cen N7 121 DM63
Nailsworth Cres, Red. 251 DK129
Nailzee Cl, Ger.Cr. 112 AY59
Nairn Ct, Til. 171 GF82
Dock Rd
Nairn Grn, Wat. 93 BU48
Nairn Rd, Ruis. 136 BW65
Nairn St E14 143 EC71
Nairne Gro SE24 182 DR85
Naish Ct N1 141 DL67
Nalders Rd, Chesh. 54 AR29
Nallhead Rd, Felt. 176 BW92
Namba Roy Cl SW16 181 DM91
Namton Dr, Th.Hth. 201 DM98
Nan Clark's La NW7 97 CT47
Nancy Downs, Wat. 94 BW45
Nankin St E14 143 EA72
Nansen Rd SW11 160 DG84
Nansen Rd, Grav. 191 GK91
Nansen Village N12 98 DC49
Nant Rd NW2 119 CZ61
Nant St E2 142 DV69
Cambridge Heath Rd
Nantes Cl SW18 160 DC84
Nantes Pas E1 275 P6
Naoroji St WC1 274 D3
Nap, The, Kings L. 58 BN29
Napier Av E14 163 EA78
Napier Av SW6 159 CZ83
Napier Cl SE8 163 DZ80
Amersham Vale
Napier Cl W14 159 CZ76
Napier Rd
Napier Cl, Horn. 127 FH60
Napier Cl (London Colney), St.Alb. 61 CK25
Napier Cl, West Dr. 154 BM76
Napier Ct SW6 159 CZ83
Ranelagh Gdns
Napier Ct (Cheshunt), Wal.Cr. 66 DV28
Flamstead End Rd
Napier Dr, Bushey 76 BY42
Napier Gdns, Guil. 243 BB133
Napier Gro N1 275 J1
Napier Gro N1 142 DQ68
Napier Ho, Rain. 147 FF69
Napier Pl W14 159 CZ76
Napier Rd E6 145 EN67
Napier Rd E11 124 EE63
Napier Rd E15 144 EE68
Napier Rd N17 122 DS55
Napier Rd NW10 139 CV69
Napier Rd SE25 202 DV98
Napier Rd W14 159 CZ76
Napier Rd, Ashf. 175 BR94
Napier Rd, Belv. 166 EZ77
Napier Rd, Brom. 204 EH98
Napier Rd, Enf. 83 DX43
Napier Rd (Northfleet), Grav. 191 GF88
Napier Rd (Heathrow Airport), Houns. 154 BK81
Napier Rd, Islw. 157 CG84
Napier Rd, S.Croy. 220 DR108
Napier Rd, Wem. 117 CK64
Napier Ter N1 141 DP66
Napoleon Rd E5 122 DV62
Napoleon Rd, Twick. 177 CH87
Napsbury Av (London Colney), St.Alb. 61 CJ26
Napsbury La, St.Alb. 43 CG23
Napton Cl, Hayes 136 BY70
Kingsash Dr
Narbonne Av SW4 181 DJ85
Narboro Ct, Rom. 127 FG57
Manor Rd
Narborough Cl, Uxb. 115 BQ61
Aylsham Dr
Narborough St SW6 160 DB82
Narcissus Rd NW6 120 DA64
Narcot La, Ch.St.G. 90 AU48
Narcot La (Chalfont St. Peter), Ger.Cr. 90 AV52
Narcot Rd, Ch.St.G. 90 AU48
Narcot Way, Ch.St.G. 90 AU49
Nare Rd, S.Ock. 148 FQ73
Naresby Fold, Stan. 95 CJ51
Bernays Cl
Narford Rd E5 122 DU62
Narrow La, Warl. 236 DV119
Narrow St E14 143 DY73
Narrow Way, Brom. 204 EL100
Nascot Pl, Wat. 75 BV39
Nascot Rd, Wat. 75 BV40
Nascot St W12 139 CW72
Nascot St, Wat. 75 BV40
Nascot Wd Rd, Wat. 75 BT37
Naseberry Ct E4 101 EC50
Merriam Cl
Naseby Cl NW6 140 DC66
Fairfax Rd
Naseby Cl, Islw. 157 CE81
Naseby Ct, Walt. 196 BW103
Clements Rd
Naseby Rd SE19 182 DR93
Naseby Rd, Dag. 126 FA62
Naseby Rd, Ilf. 103 EM53
Nash Cl, Borwd. 78 CM42
Nash Cl, Hat. 45 CX23
Nash Cl, Sutt. 200 DD104
Nash Ct E14 143 EB74
South Colonnade
Nash Cft (Northfleet), Grav. 190 GE91
Nash Dr, Red. 250 DF132
Nash Gdns, Red. 250 DF132
Nash Grn, Brom. 184 EG93
Nash Grn, Hem.H. 58 BM25
Nash La, Kes. 222 EG106
Nash Mills La, Hem.H. 58 BM26
Nash Rd N9 100 DW47
Nash Rd SE4 163 DY84
Nash Rd, Rom. 126 EX56
Nash Rd, Slou. 153 AZ77
Nash St NW1 273 J3
Nash Way, Har. 117 CH58
Nashdom La (Burnham), Slou. 130 AG66
Nashleigh Hill, Chesh. 54 AQ29
Nash's Yd, Uxb. 134 BK66
Bakers Rd
Nasmyth St W6 159 CV76
Nassau Path SE28 146 EW74
Disraeli Cl
Nassau Rd SW13 159 CT81
Nassau St W1 273 K7
Nassau St W1 141 DJ71
Nassington Rd NW3 120 DE63
Natal Rd N11 99 DL51
Natal Rd SW16 181 DK93
Natal Rd, Ilf. 125 EP63
Natal Rd, Th.Hth. 202 DR97
Natalie Cl, Felt. 175 BR87
Natalie Ms, Twick. 177 CD90
Sixth Cross Rd
Nathan Cl, Upmin. 129 FS60
Nathan Way SE28 165 ES77
Nathaniel Cl E1 142 DT71
Thrawl St
Nathans Rd, Wem. 117 CJ60
Nation Way E4 101 EC46
Natwoke Cl, Beac. 89 AK50
Naunton Way, Horn. 128 FK62
Naval Row E14 143 EC73
Naval Wk, Brom. 204 EG97
High St
Navarino Gro E8 142 DU65
Navarino Rd E8 142 DU65
Navarre Gdns, Rom. 105 FB51
Navarre Rd E6 144 EL68
Navarre St E2 275 P4
Navarre St E2 142 DT70
Navenby Wk E3 143 EA70
Rounton Rd
Navestock Cl E4 101 EC48
Mapleton Rd
Navestock Cres, Wdf.Grn. 102 EJ53
Navestock Ho, Bark. 146 EV68
Navigator Dr, Sthl. 156 CC75
Navy St SW4 161 DK83
Naylor Gro, Enf. 83 DX43
South St
Naylor Rd N20 98 DC47
Naylor Rd SE15 162 DV80
Naylor Ter (Colnbrook), Slou. 153 BC80
Vicarage Way
Nazareth Gdns SE15 162 DV82
Nazeing Common, Wal.Abb. 50 EH24
Nazeing New Rd, Brox. 49 EA21
Nazeing Rd, Wal.Abb. 49 EC22
Nazeing Wk, Rain. 147 FE67
Ongar Way
Nazeingbury Cl, Wal.Abb. 49 ED22
Nazeingbury Par, Wal.Abb. 49 ED22
Nazeing Rd
Nazrul St E2 275 P2
Nazrul St E2 142 DT69
Neagle Cl, Borwd. 78 CQ39
Balcon Way
Neal Av, Sthl. 136 BZ70
Neal Cl, Ger.Cr. 113 BB60
Neal Cl, Nthwd. 93 BU53
Neal Ct, Hert. 32 DQ09
Neal Ct, Wal.Abb. 68 EF33
Neal St WC2 273 P9
Neal St WC2 141 DL72
Neal St, Wat. 76 BW43
Nealden St SW9 161 DM83
Neale Cl N2 120 DC55
Neal's Yd WC2 273 P9
Near Acre NW9 97 CT53
Neasden Cl NW10 118 CS64
Neasden La NW10 118 CS63
Neasden La N NW10 118 CR62
Neasham Rd, Dag. 126 EV64
Neate St SE5 162 DT79
Neath Gdns, Mord. 200 DC100
Neathouse Pl SW1 277 K8
Neats Acre, Ruis. 115 BR59
Neatscourt Rd E6 144 EK71
Neave Cres, Rom. 106 FJ53
Neb Cor Rd, Oxt. 253 EC131
Nebraska St SE1 279 K5
Nebraska St SE1 162 DR75
Neckinger SE16 162 DT76
Neckinger Est SE16 162 DT76
Neckinger St SE1 162 DT75
Nectarine Way SE13 163 EB82
Necton Rd (Wheathampstead), St.Alb. 28 CL07
Needham Cl, Wind. 151 AL81
Needham Rd W11 140 DA72
Westbourne Gro
Needham Ter NW2 119 CX62
Needleman St SE16 163 DX75
Needles Bk, Gdse. 252 DV131
Neela Cl, Uxb. 115 BP63
Neeld Cres NW4 119 CV57
Neeld Cres, Wem. 118 CN64
Neeld Par, Wem. 118 CN64
Harrow Rd
Neil Cl, Ashf. 175 BQ92
Neil Wates Cres SW2 181 DN88
Nelgarde Rd SE6 183 EA87
Nell Gwynn Cl, Rad. 62 CL32
Nell Gwynne Av, Shep. 195 BR100
Nell Gwynne Cl, Epsom 216 CN111
Ripley Way
Nella Rd W6 159 CX79
Nelldale Rd SE16 162 DW77
Nellgrove Rd, Uxb. 135 BP70
Nello James Gdns SE27 182 DR91
Nelmes Cl, Horn. 128 FM57
Nelmes Cres, Horn. 128 FL57
Nelmes Rd, Horn. 128 FL59
Nelmes Way, Horn. 128 FL56
Nelson Av, St.Alb. 43 CH23
Nelson Cl NW6 140 DA68
Nelson Cl, Brwd. 108 FX50
Nelson Cl, Croy. 201 DP102
Nelson Cl, Felt. 175 BT88
Nelson Cl, Rom. 105 FB53
Nelson Cl, Slou. 152 AX77
Nelson Cl, Uxb. 135 BP69
Nelson Cl, Walt. 195 BV102
Nelson Cl (Biggin Hill), West. 238 EL117
Nelson Ct SE16 142 DW74
Brunel Rd
Nelson Gdns E2 142 DU69
Nelson Gdns, Guil. 243 BA133
Nelson Gdns, Houns. 176 CA86
Nelson Gro Rd SW19 200 DB95
Nelson La, Uxb. 135 BP69
Nelson Rd
Nelson Mandela Cl N10 98 DG54
Nelson Mandela Rd SE3 164 EJ83
Nelson Pas EC1 275 J3
Nelson Pl N1 274 G1
Nelson Pl N1 141 DP68
Nelson Pl, Sid. 186 EU91
Nelson Rd E4 101 EB51
Nelson Rd E11 124 EG56
Nelson Rd N8 121 DM57
Nelson Rd N9 100 DV47
Nelson Rd N15 122 DS56
Nelson Rd SE10 163 EC79
Nelson Rd SW19 180 DB94
Nelson Rd, Ashf. 174 BL92
Nelson Rd, Belv. 166 EZ78
Nelson Rd, Brom. 204 EJ98
Nelson Rd, Cat. 236 DR123
Nelson Rd, Dart. 188 FJ86
Nelson Rd, Enf. 83 DX44
Nelson Rd (Northfleet), Grav. 191 GF89
Nelson Rd, Har. 117 CD60
Nelson Rd, Houns. 176 CC87
Nelson Rd (Heathrow Airport), Houns. 154 BM81
Nelson Rd, N.Mal. 198 CR99
Nelson Rd, Rain. 147 FF68
Nelson Rd, Sid. 186 EU91
Nelson Rd, S.Ock. 149 FW68
Nelson Rd, Stan. 95 CJ51
Nelson Rd, Twick. 176 CC86
Nelson Rd, Uxb. 135 BP69
Nelson Rd, Wind. 151 AM83
Nelson Sq SE1 278 F4
Nelson Sq SE1 161 DP75

Nelson St E1 142 DV72
Nelson St E6 145 EM68
Nelson St E16 144 EF73
Huntingdon St
Nelson St, Hert. 31 DP08
Nelson Ter N1 274 G1
Nelson Ter N1 141 DP68
Nelson Trd Est SW19 200 DB95
Nelson Wk SE16 143 DY74
Rotherhithe St
Nelson's Row SW4 161 DK84
Nelsons Yd NW1 141 DJ68
Mornington Cres
Nelwyn Av, Horn. 128 FM57
Nemoure Rd W3 138 CQ73
Nene Gdns, Felt. 176 BZ89
Nene Rd (Heathrow Airport), Houns. 155 BP81
Nepaul Rd SW11 160 DE82
Nepean St SW15 179 CU86
Neptune Ct, Borwd. 78 CN41
Clarendon Rd
Neptune Dr, Hem.H. 40 BL18
Neptune Rd, Har. 117 CD58
Neptune Rd (Heathrow Airport), Houns. 155 BR81
Neptune St SE16 162 DW76
Neptune Wk, Erith 167 FD77
Neptune Way, Slou. 131 AL74
Moor Furlong
Nesbit Rd SE9 164 EK84
Nesbitt Cl SE3 164 EE83
Hurren Cl
Nesbitt Sq SE19 182 DS94
Coxwell Rd
Nesbitts All, Barn. 79 CZ41
Bath Pl
Nesham St E1 142 DU74
Ness Rd, Erith 168 FK79
Ness St SE16 162 DU76
Spa Rd
Nesta Rd, Wdf.Grn. 102 EE51
Nestles Av, Hayes 155 BT76
Neston Rd, Wat. 76 BW37
Nestor Av N21 81 DP44
Nethan Dr, S.Ock. 148 FQ73
Nether Cl N3 98 DA52
Nether Mt, Guil. 258 AV136
Nether St N3 98 DA53
Nether St N12 98 DA52
Netheravon Rd W4 159 CT77
Netheravon Rd W7 137 CF74
Netheravon Rd S W4 159 CT78
Netherbury Rd W5 157 CK76
Netherby Gdns, Enf. 81 DL42
Netherby Pk, Wey. 213 BS106
Netherby Rd SE23 182 DW87
Nethercote Av, Wok. 226 AT117
Nethercourt Av N3 98 DA51
Netherfield Gdns, Bark. 145 ER65
Netherfield La, Ware 34 EE12
Netherfield Rd N12 98 DB50
Netherfield Rd SW17 180 DG90
Netherford Rd SW4 161 DJ82
Netherhall Gdns NW3 140 DC65
Netherhall Rd, Harl. 50 EF17
Netherhall Way NW3 120 DC64
Netherhall Gdns
Netherlands, The, Couls. 235 DJ119
Netherlands Rd, Barn. 80 DD44
Netherleigh Cl N6 121 DH60
Netherleigh Pk, Red. 267 DL137
Nethern Ct Rd (Woldingham), Cat. 237 EA123
Netherne Dr, Couls. 235 DH121
Brighton Rd
Netherne La, Couls. 235 DK121
Netherne La, Red. 235 DJ123
Netherpark Dr, Rom. 105 FF54
Netherton Gro SW10 160 DC79
Netherton Rd N15 122 DR58
Netherton Rd, Twick. 177 CH85
Netherway, St.Alb. 42 CA23
Netherwood N2 98 DD54
Netherwood Pl W14 159 CX76
Netherwood Rd
Netherwood Rd W14 159 CX76
Netherwood Rd, Beac. 89 AK50
Netherwood St NW6 139 CZ66
Netherwood St Est NW6 139 CZ66
Netley Cl (New Addington), Croy. 221 EC108
Netley Cl, Sutt. 217 CX106
Netley Dr, Walt. 196 BZ101
Netley Gdns, Mord. 200 DC101
Netley Rd E17 123 DZ57
Netley Rd, Brent. 158 CL79
Netley Rd (Heathrow Airport), Houns. 155 BR81
Netley Rd, Ilf. 125 ER57
Netley Rd, Mord. 200 DC101
Netley St NW1 273 K3
Netteswell Orchard, Harl. 35 ER14
Netteswell Rd, Harl. 35 ES12
Netteswell Twr, Harl. 35 ER14
Nettlecombe Cl, Sutt. 218 DB109
Nettlecroft, Hem.H. 40 BH21
Nettlecroft, Welw.G.C. 30 DB08
Nettleden Av, Wem. 138 CN65
Nettleden Rd, Berk. 39 BB15
Nettlefold Pl SE27 181 DP90
Nettles Ter, Guil. 242 AX134
Nettlestead Cl, Beck. 183 DZ94
Copers Cope Rd
Nettleton Rd SE14 163 DX81
Nettleton Rd (Heathrow Airport), Houns. 155 BP81
Nettleton Rd, Uxb. 114 BM63
Nettlewood Rd SW16 181 DK94
Neuchatel Rd SE6 183 DZ89
Nevada Cl, N.Mal. 198 CQ98
Georgia Rd
Nevada St SE10 163 EC79
Nevell Rd, Grays 171 GH76
Nevern Pl SW5 160 DA77
Nevern Rd SW5 160 DA77
Nevern Sq SW5 160 DA78
Nevil Cl, Nthwd. 93 BQ50
Nevill Gro, Wat. 75 BV39
Nevill Rd N16 122 DS63
Nevill Way, Loug. 102 EL45
Valley Hill
Neville Av, N.Mal. 198 CR95
Neville Cl E11 124 EF62
Neville Cl NW1 273 N1
Neville Cl NW6 139 CZ68
Neville Cl SE15 162 DU80
Neville Cl W3 158 CQ75
Acton La
Neville Cl, Bans. 218 DB114
Neville Cl, Esher 214 BZ107
Neville Cl, Houns. 156 CB82
Neville Cl, Pot.B. 63 CZ31
Neville Cl, Sid. 185 ET91
Neville Cl (Stoke Poges), Slou. 132 AT65
Neville Ct, Slou. 130 AJ69
Dropmore Rd
Neville Dr N2 120 DC58
Neville Gdns, Dag. 126 EX62
Neville Gill Cl SW18 180 DA86
Neville Pl N22 99 DM53
Neville Rd E7 144 EG66
Neville Rd NW6 139 CZ68
Neville Rd W5 137 CK70
Neville Rd, Croy. 202 DR101
Neville Rd, Dag. 126 EX61
Neville Rd, Ilf. 103 EQ53
Neville Rd, Kings.T. 198 CN96
Neville Rd, Rich. 177 CJ90
Neville St SW7 160 DD78
Neville Ter SW7 160 DD78
Neville Wk, Cars. 200 DE101
Green Wrythe La
Nevilles Ct NW2 119 CU62
Nevin Dr E4 101 EB46
Nevinson Cl SW18 180 DD86
Nevis Cl, Rom. 105 FE51
Nevis Rd SW17 180 DG89
New Arc, Uxb. *High St* 134 BK67
New Ash Cl N2 120 DD55
Oakridge Dr
New Atlas Wf E14 163 DZ76
Arnhem Pl
New Barn Cl, Wall. 219 DM107
Merlin Cl
New Barn La, Beac. 90 AS49
New Barn La (Cudham), Sev. 239 EQ116
New Barn La, West. 239 EQ118
New Barn La, Whyt. 236 DS117
New Barn Rd (Southfleet), Grav. 190 GC92
New Barn Rd, Swan. 207 FE95
New Barn St E13 144 EG70
New Barnes Av, St.Alb. 43 CG23
New Barns Av, Mitch. 201 DK98
New Barns Way, Chig. 103 EP48
New Battlebridge La, Red. 251 DH130
New Berry La, Walt. 214 BX106
New Bond St W1 273 J10
New Bond St W1 141 DH73
New Brent St NW4 119 CW57
New Br St EC4 274 F9
New Br St EC4 141 DP72
New Broad St EC2 275 M7
New Broad St EC2 142 DS71
New Bdy W5 137 CK73
New Bdy (Hampton Hill), Hmptn. 177 CD92
Hampton Rd
New Burlington Ms W1 273 K10
New Burlington Pl W1 273 K10
New Burlington St W1 273 K10
New Burlington St W1 141 DJ73
New Butt La SE8 163 EA80
New Butt La N SE8 163 EA80
Reginald Rd
New Caledonian Wf SE16 163 DZ76
New Causeway, Reig. 266 DB137
New Cavendish St W1 273 J6
New Cavendish St W1 140 DG71
New Change EC4 275 H9
New Change EC4 142 DQ72
New Chapel Sq, Felt. 175 BV88
New Charles St EC1 274 G2
New Ch Ct SE19 182 DU94
Waldegrave Rd
New Ch Rd SE5 162 DQ80
New City Rd E13 144 EJ69
New Cl SW19 200 DC97
New Cl, Felt. 176 BY92
New Coll Ct NW3 140 DC66
College Cres
New Coll Ms N1 141 DN66
Islington Pk St
New Coll Par NW3 140 DD65
College Cres
New Compton St WC2 273 N9
New Compton St WC2 141 DK72
New Coppice, Wok. 226 AS119
New Cotts (Wennington), Rain. 148 FJ72
New Ct EC4 274 D10
New Ct, Add. 194 BJ104
New Covent Gdn Mkt SW8 161 DK80
New Coventry St W1 277 N1
New Crane Pl E1 142 DW74
Garnet St
New Cross Rd SE14 162 DW80
New Cross Rd, Guil. 242 AU132
New Cut, Slou. 130 AG70
New End NW3 120 DC63
New End Sq NW3 120 DD63
New England St, St.Alb. 42 CC20
New Era Est N1 142 DS67
Phillipp St
New Fm Av, Brom. 204 EG98
New Fm Dr, Rom. 86 EV41
New Fm La, Nthwd. 93 BS53
New Ferry App SE18 165 EN76
New Fetter La EC4 274 E8
New Fetter La EC4 141 DN72
New Ford Rd, Wal.Cr. 67 DZ34
New Forest La, Chig. 103 EN51
New Frontiers Science Pk, Harl. 51 EN16
New Gdn Dr, West Dr. 154 BL75
Drayton Gdns
New Globe Wk SE1 279 H2
New Globe Wk SE1 142 DQ74
New Goulston St E1 275 P8
New Grn Pl SE19 182 DS93
Hawke Rd
New Grns Av, St.Alb. 43 CD15
New Hall Cl (Bovingdon), Hem.H. 57 BA27
New Hall Dr, Rom. 106 FL53
New Haw Rd, Add. 212 BJ106
New Heston Rd, Houns. 156 BZ80
New Horizons Ct, Brent. 157 CG79
Shield Dr
New Ho La, Epp. 53 FC24
New Ho La, Grav. 191 GF90
New Ho La, Red. 267 DK142
New Ho Pk, St.Alb. 43 CG23
New Inn Bdy EC2 275 N4
New Inn La, Guil. 243 BB130
New Inn Pas WC2 274 C9
New Inn St EC2 275 N4
New Inn Yd EC2 275 N4
New Inn Yd EC2 142 DS70
New James Ct SE15 162 DV83
Nunhead La
New Jersey Ter SE15 162 DV83
Nunhead La
New Jubilee Ct, Wdf.Grn. 102 EG52
Grange Av
New Kent Rd SE1 279 H7
New Kent Rd SE1 162 DQ76
New Kent Rd, St.Alb. 43 CD20
New King St SE8 163 EA79
New Kings Rd SW6 159 CZ82
New La (Sutton Grn), Guil. 226 AY122
New La Dr, Oxt. 254 EF128
New London St EC3 275 N10
New Lydenburg St SE7 164 EJ76
New Mill Rd, Orp. 206 EW95
New Mt St E15 143 ED66
Bridge Rd
New N Pl EC2 275 M5
New N Rd N1 275 L1
New N Rd N1 142 DR68
New N Rd, Ilf. 103 ER52
New N Rd, Reig. 265 CZ137
New N St WC1 274 B6
New N St WC1 141 DM71
New Oak Rd N2 98 DC54
New Orleans Wk N19 121 DK59
New Oxford St WC1 273 N8
New Oxford St WC1 141 DK72
New Par, Ashf. 174 BM91
Church Rd
New Par, Rick. 73 BC42
Whitelands Av
New Par Flats, Rick. 73 BC42
Whitelands Av
New Pk Av N13 100 DQ48
New Pk Cl, Nthlt. 136 BY65
New Pk Ct SW2 181 DL87
New Pk Dr, Hem.H. 41 BP19
New Pk Par SW2 181 DL86
Doverfield Rd
New Pk Rd SW2 181 DK88
New Pk Rd, Ashf. 175 BQ92
New Pk Rd, Hert. 47 DK24
New Pk Rd (Harefield), Uxb. 92 BJ53
New Peachey La, Uxb. 134 BK72
New Pl Gdns, Upmin. 129 FR61
New Pl Sq SE16 162 DV76
New Plaistow Rd E15 144 EE67
New Printing Ho Sq WC1 141 DM70
Gray's Inn Rd
New Priory Ct NW6 140 DA66
Mazenod Av
New Quebec St W1 272 E9
New Quebec St W1 140 DF72
New Ride SW7 276 D4
New Ride SW7 160 DE75
New River Av, Ware 33 EB11
New River Cl, Hodd. 49 EB16
New River Ct (Cheshunt), Wal.Cr. 66 DV30
Pengelly Cl
New River Cres N13 99 DP49
New River Head EC1 274 E2
New River Trd Est (Cheshunt), Wal.Cr. 67 DX26
New River Wk N1 142 DQ65
New River Way N4 122 DR59
New Rd E1 142 DV71
New Rd E4 101 EB49
New Rd N8 121 DL57
New Rd N9 100 DU48
New Rd N17 100 DT53
New Rd N22 100 DQ53
New Rd NW7 97 CY52
New Rd (Barnet Gate) NW7 97 CT45
New Rd SE2 166 EX77
New Rd, Amer. 55 AS37
New Rd (Coleshill), Amer. 55 AM42
New Rd, Berk. 38 AX18
New Rd (Northchurch), Berk. 38 AS17
New Rd, Borwd. 77 CK44
New Rd, Brent. 157 CK79
New Rd, Brwd. 108 FX47
New Rd, Brox. 49 DZ19
New Rd, Ch.St.G. 72 AY41
New Rd, Cher. 193 BF101
New Rd, Dag. 146 FA67
New Rd (South Darenth), Dart. 208 FQ96
New Rd (Forest Grn), Dor. 263 CK137
New Rd, Epp. 70 FA32
New Rd, Esher 196 CC104
New Rd (Claygate), Esher 215 CF110
New Rd, Felt. 175 BR86
New Rd (East Bedfont), Felt. 175 BV88
New Rd (Hanworth), Felt. 176 BY92
New Rd, Grav. 191 GH86
New Rd, Grays 170 GA79
New Rd (Manor Way), Grays 170 GB79
New Rd (Albury), Guil. 260 BK139
New Rd (Chilworth), Guil. 259 BB141
New Rd (East Clandon), Guil. 244 BL131
New Rd (Gomshall), Guil. 261 BQ139
New Rd (Wonersh), Guil. 259 BB143
New Rd, Harl. 36 EX11
New Rd, Har. 117 CF63
New Rd, Hayes 155 BQ80
New Rd, Hert. 32 DQ07
New Rd, Horl. 269 DP148
New Rd, Houns. 156 CB84
Station Rd
New Rd, Ilf. 125 ES61
New Rd, Kings L. 57 BF30
New Rd, Kings.T. 178 CN94
New Rd, Lthd. 215 CF110
New Rd, Mitch. 200 DF102
New Rd, Orp. 206 EU101
New Rd (Limpsfield), Oxt. 254 EH130
New Rd, Pot.B. 63 CU33
New Rd, Rad. 77 CE36
New Rd (Shenley), Rad. 62 CN34
New Rd, Rain. 147 FG69
New Rd, Rich. 177 CJ91
New Rd, Rick. 74 BN43
New Rd (Church End), Rick. 73 BF39
New Rd, Rom. 86 EX44
New Rd (Sundridge), Sev. 240 EX124
New Rd, Shep. 195 BP97
New Rd (Datchet), Slou. 152 AX81
New Rd (Langley), Slou. 153 BA76
New Rd, Stai. 173 BC92
New Rd, Swan. 207 FF97
New Rd (Hextable), Swan. 187 FF94
New Rd, Tad. 233 CW123
New Rd, Uxb. 135 BQ70
New Rd, Ware 33 DX06
New Rd, Wat. 76 BW42
New Rd (Letchmore Heath), Wat. 77 CE39
New Rd, Well. 166 EV82
New Rd (Stanborough), Welw.G.C. 29 CU12
New Rd, W.Mol. 196 CA97
New Rd, Wey. 213 BQ106
New Rd Hill, Kes. 222 EL109
New Rd Hill, Orp. 222 EL109
New Row WC2 273 P10
New Row WC2 141 DL73
New Spring Gdns Wk SE11 161 DL78
Goding St
New Sq WC2 274 C8
New Sq WC2 141 DM72
New Sq, Felt. 175 BQ88
New Sq, Slou. 152 AT75
New Sq Pas WC2 141 DM72
New Sq
New St EC2 275 N7
New St EC2 142 DS71
New St, Berk. 38 AX19
New St, Stai. 174 BG91
New St, Wat. 76 BW42
New St, West. 255 EQ127
New St Hill, Brom. 184 EH92
New St Sq EC4 274 E8
New Swan Yd, Grav. 191 GH86
Bank St
New Trinity Rd N2 120 DD55
New Turnstile WC1 274 B7
New Union Cl E14 163 EC76
New Union St EC2 275 K7
New Union St EC2 142 DR71
New Wanstead E11 124 EF58
New Way La, Harl. 37 FD14
New Way Rd NW9 118 CS56
New Wf Rd N1 141 DL68
New Wickham La, Egh. 173 BA94
New Windsor St, Uxb. 134 BJ67
New Wd, Welw.G.C. 30 DC08
New Years Grn La (Harefield), Uxb. 114 BL58
New Years La, Orp. 224 EU114
New Years La (Knockholt), Sev. 239 ET116
New Zealand Av, Walt. 195 BT102
New Zealand Way W12 139 CV73
New Zealand Way, Rain. 147 FF69
Newacres Rd SE28 145 ES74
Newall Rd (Heathrow Airport), Houns. 155 BQ81
Newark Cl, Guil. 243 BB129
Dairyman's Wk
Newark Cl (Ripley), Wok. 228 BG121
Newark Cotts (Ripley), Wok. 228 BG121
Newark Ct, Walt. 196 BW102
St. Johns Dr
Newark Cres NW10 138 CR69
Newark Grn, Borwd. 78 CR41
Newark Knok E6 145 EN72
Newark La (Ripley), Wok. 227 BF118
Newark Par NW4 119 CU55
Greyhound Hill
Newark Rd, S.Croy. 220 DR107
Newark St E1 142 DV71
Newark Way NW4 119 CU56
Newberries Av, Rad. 77 CJ35
Newberry Cres, Wind. 151 AK82
Newbery Rd, Erith 167 FF81
Newbery Way, Slou. 151 AR75
Newbiggin Path, Wat. 94 BW49
Newbolt Av, Sutt. 217 CW106
Newbolt Rd, Stan. 95 CF51
Newborough Grn, N.Mal. 198 CR98
Newbridge Pt SE23 183 DX90
Windrush La
Newburgh Rd W3 138 CQ74
Newburgh Rd, Grays 170 GD78
Newburgh St W1 273 K9
Newburgh St W1 141 DJ72
Newburn St SE11 278 C10
Newburn St SE11 161 DM78
Newbury Av, Enf. 83 DZ38
Newbury Cl, Nthlt. 136 BZ65
Newbury Cl, Rom. 106 FK51
Newbury Gdns, Epsom 217 CT105
Newbury Gdns, Rom. 106 FK51
Newbury Gdns, Upmin. 128 FM62
Newbury Ho N22 99 DL53
Newbury Ms NW5 140 DG65
Malden Rd
Newbury Rd E4 101 EC51
Newbury Rd, Brom. 204 EG97
Newbury Rd (Heathrow Airport), Houns. 154 BM81
Newbury Rd, Ilf. 125 ES58
Newbury Rd, Rom. 106 FK50
Newbury St EC1 275 H7
Newbury Wk, Rom. 106 FK50
Newbury Way, Nthlt. 136 BY65
Newby Cl, Enf. 82 DS40
Newby Pl E14 143 EC73
Newby St SW8 161 DH83
Newcastle Av, Ilf. 104 EU51
Newcastle Cl EC4 274 F8
Newcastle Pl W2 272 A7
Newcastle Pl W2 140 DD71
Newcastle Row EC1 274 E4
Newchurch Rd, Slou. 131 AM71
Newcombe Gdns SW16 181 DL91
Newcombe Pk NW7 96 CS50
Newcombe Pk, Wem. 138 CM67
Newcombe Ri, West Dr. 134 BL72
Newcombe St W8 140 DA74
Kensington Pl
Newcome Path (Shenley), Rad. 62 CN34
Newcome Rd
Newcome Rd, Rad. 62 CN34
Newcomen Rd E11 124 EF62
Newcomen Rd SW11 160 DD83
Newcomen St SE1 279 K4
Newcomen St SE1 162 DR75
Newcourt, Uxb. 134 BJ71
Newcourt St NW8 272 B1
Newcourt St NW8 140 DE68
Newcroft Cl, Uxb. 134 BM71
Newdales Cl N9 100 DU47
Balham Rd
Newdene Av, Nthlt. 136 BX68
Newdigate Grn (Harefield), Uxb. 92 BK53
Newdigate Rd (Harefield), Uxb. 92 BJ53
Newdigate Rd E (Harefield), Uxb. 92 BK53
Newell Ri, Hem.H. 40 BL23
Newell Rd, Hem.H. 40 BL23
Newell St E14 143 DZ72
Newenham Rd (Bookham), Lthd. 246 CA126
Newent Cl SE15 162 DS80
Newent Cl, Cars. 200 DF102
Newfield Cl, Hmptn. 196 CA95
Percy Rd
Newfield La, Hem.H. 40 BL20
Newfield Ri NW2 119 CV62
Newfield Way, St.Alb. 43 CK22
Newfields, Welw.G.C. 29 CV10
Newford Cl, Hem.H. 41 BP19
Newgale Gdns, Edg. 96 CM53
Newgate, Croy. 202 DQ102
Newgate Cl, Felt. 176 BY89
Newgate Cl, St.Alb. 43 CK17
Newgate St E4 102 EF48
Newgate St EC1 274 G8
Newgate St EC1 141 DP72
Newgate St, Hert. 47 DK22
Newgate St Village, Hert. 65 DL25
Newgatestreet Rd (Cheshunt), Wal.Cr. 65 DP27
Newhall Ct, Wal.Abb. 68 EF33
Newhall Gdns, Walt. 196 BW103
Rodney Rd
Newham Way E6 144 EJ71
Newham Way E16 144 EF71
Newhams Row SE1 279 N5
Newhaven Cl, Hayes 155 BT77
Newhaven Cres, Ashf. 175 BR92
Newhaven Gdns SE9 164 EK84
Newhaven La E16 144 EF70
Newhaven Rd SE25 202 DR99
Newhaven Spur, Slou. 131 AP70
Newhouse Av, Rom. 126 EX55
Newhouse Cl, N.Mal. 198 CS101
Newhouse Cres, Wat. 59 BV32
Newhouse La, Ong. 53 FH22
Newhouse Rd (Bovingdon), Hem.H. 57 BA26
Newhouse Wk, Mord. 200 DC101
Newick Cl, Bex. 187 FB86
Newick Rd E5 122 DV62
Newing Grn, Brom. 184 EK94
Newington Barrow Way N7 121 DM62
Newington Butts SE1 278 G9
Newington Butts SE1 161 DP77
Newington Butts SE11 278 G9
Newington Butts SE11 161 DP77
Newington Causeway SE1 278 G7
Newington Causeway SE1 161 DP76
Newington Grn N1 122 DR64
Newington Grn N16 122 DR64
Newington Grn Rd N1 142 DR65
Newland Cl, Pnr. 94 BY51
Newland Cl, St.Alb. 43 CG23
Newland Ct, Wem. 118 CN61
Forty Av
Newland Dr, Enf. 82 DV39
Newland Gdns W13 157 CG75
Newland Rd N8 121 DL55
Newland St E16 144 EL74
Newlands, Abb.L. 59 BT26
Newlands, Hat. 45 CW16
Newlands, The, Wall. 219 DJ108
Newlands Av, Rad. 61 CF34
Newlands Av, T.Ditt. 197 CE102
Newlands Av, Wok. 227 AZ121
Newlands Cl, Brwd. 109 GD45
Newlands Cl, Edg. 96 CL48
Newlands Cl, Horl. 268 DF146
Newlands Cl, Sthl. 156 BY78
Newlands Cl, Walt. 214 BY105
Newlands Cl, Wem. 137 CJ65
Newlands Cor, Guil. 260 BG136
Newlands Ct SE9 185 EN86
Newlands Dr (Colnbrook), Slou. 153 BE83
Newlands Pk SE26 183 DX92
Newlands Pl, Barn. 79 CX43
Newlands Quay E1 142 DW73
Newlands Rd SW16 201 DL96
Newlands Rd, Hem.H. 39 BE19
Newlands Rd, Wdf.Grn. 102 EF47
Newlands Wk, Wat. 60 BX33
Trevellance Way
Newlands Way, Chess. 215 CJ106
Newlands Way, Pot.B. 64 DB30
Newlands Wd, Croy. 221 DZ109
Newling Cl E6 145 EM72
Porter Rd
Newlyn Cl, Orp. 223 ET105
Newlyn Cl (Bricket Wd), St.Alb. 60 BY30
Newlyn Cl, Uxb. 134 BN71
Newlyn Gdns, Har. 116 BZ59
Newlyn Rd N17 100 DT53
Newlyn Rd NW2 119 CW60
Tilling Rd
Newlyn Rd, Barn. 79 CZ42
Newlyn Rd, Well. 165 ET82
Newman Cl, Horn. 128 FL57
Newman Pas W1 273 L7
Newman Rd E13 144 EH69
Newman Rd E17 123 DX57
Southcote Rd
Newman Rd, Brom. 204 EG95
Newman Rd, Croy. 201 DM102
Newman Rd, Hayes 135 BV73
Newman St W1 273 L7
Newman St W1 141 DJ71
Newman Yd W1 273 M8
Newmans Cl, Loug. 85 EP41
Newman's Ct EC3 275 L9
Newmans Dr, Brwd. 109 GC45
Newmans La, Loug. 85 EN41
Newmans La, Surb. 197 CK100
Newmans Rd (Northfleet), Grav. 191 GF89
Newman's Row WC2 274 C7
Newmans Way, Barn. 80 DC39
Newmarket Av, Nthlt. 116 CA64
Newmarket Grn SE9 184 EK87
Middle Pk Av
Newmarket Way, Horn. 128 FL63
Newmarsh Rd SE28 145 ET74
Newminster Rd, Mord. 200 DC100
Newnes Path SW15 159 CV84
Putney Pk La
Newnham Av, Ruis. 116 BW60
Newnham Cl, Loug. 84 EK44
Newnham Cl, Nthlt. 116 CC64
Newnham Cl, Slou. 132 AU74
Newnham Cl, Th.Hth. 202 DQ96
Newnham Gdns, Nthlt. 116 CC64
Newnham Ms N22 99 DM53
Newnham Rd
Newnham Pl, Grays 171 GG77
Newnham Rd N22 99 DM53
Newnham Ter SE1 278 D6
Newnham Way, Har. 118 CL57
Newnhams Cl, Brom. 205 EM97
Newnton Cl N4 122 DR59
Newpiece, Loug. 85 EP41
Newport Av E13 144 EH70
Newport Av E14 143 ED73
Newport Cl, Enf. 83 DY37
Newport Ct WC2 273 N10
Newport Mead, Wat. 94 BX49
Kilmarnock Rd
Newport Pl WC2 273 N10
Newport Pl WC2 141 DK73
Newport Rd E10 123 EC61
Newport Rd E17 123 DY56
Newport Rd SW13 159 CU81
Newport Rd, Hayes 135 BR71
Newport Rd (Heathrow Airport), Houns. 154 BN81

Newport Rd, Slou. 131 AL70
Newport St SE11 278 B9
Newport St SE11 161 DM77
Newports, Saw. 36 EW06
Newports, Swan. 207 FD101
Newquay Cres, Har. 116 BY61
Newquay Gdns, Wat. 93 BV47
Fulford Gro
Newquay Rd SE6 183 EB89
Newry Rd, Twick. 157 CG84
Newsam Av N15 122 DR57
Newsham Rd, Wok. 226 AT117
Newsholme Dr N21 81 DM43
Newstead, Hat. 45 CT21
Newstead Av, Orp. 205 ER104
Newstead Ri, Cat. 252 DV126
Newstead Rd SE12 184 EE87
Newstead Wk, Cars. 200 DC101
Newstead Way SW19 179 CX91
Newteswell Dr, Wal.Abb. 67 ED32
Newton Abbot Rd (Northfleet), Grav. 191 GF89
Newton Av N10 98 DG53
Newton Av W3 158 CQ75
Newton Cl E17 123 DY58
Newton Cl, Har. 116 CA61
Newton Cl, Hodd. 33 EB13
Newton Cl, Slou. 153 AZ75
Newton Ct (Old Windsor), Wind. 172 AU86
Newton Cres, Borwd. 78 CQ42
Newton Dr, Saw. 36 EX06
Newton Gro W4 158 CS77
Newton La (Old Windsor), Wind. 172 AV86
Newton Rd E15 123 ED64
Newton Rd N15 122 DT57
Newton Rd NW2 119 CW62
Newton Rd SW19 179 CY94
Newton Rd W2 140 DA72
Newton Rd, Chig. 104 EV50
Newton Rd, Har. 95 CE54
Newton Rd, Islw. 157 CF82
Newton Rd, Pur. 219 DJ112
Newton Rd, Til. 171 GG82
Newton Rd, Well. 166 EU83
Newton Rd, Wem. 138 CM66
Newton St WC2 274 A8
Newton St WC2 141 DL72
Newton Wk, Edg. 96 CP53
North Rd
Newton Way N18 100 DQ50
Newton Wd, Ash. 216 CL114
Newton Wd Rd, Ash. 232 CM116
Newtons Cl, Rain. 147 FF66
Newtons Ct, Dart. 169 FR84
Newtons Yd SW18 180 DB85
Wandsworth High St
Newtonside Orchard, Wind. 172 AU86
Newtown Rd (Denham), Uxb. 134 BH65
Newtown St SW11 161 DH81
Strasburg Rd
Niagara Av W5 157 CJ77
Niagara Cl N1 142 DR68
Cropley St
Niagara Cl (Cheshunt), Wal.Cr. 67 DX29
Nibthwaite Rd, Har. 117 CE57
Nichol Cl N14 99 DK46
Nichol La, Brom. 184 EG94
Nicholas Cl, Grnf. 136 CB68
Nicholas Cl, St.Alb. 43 CD17
Nicholas Cl, S.Ock. 149 FW69
Nicholas Cl, Wat. 75 BV37
Nicholas Ct E13 144 EH69
Tunmarsh La
Nicholas Gdns W5 157 CK75
Nicholas Gdns, Slou. 131 AL74
Nicholas Gdns, Wok. 227 BE116
Nicholas La EC4 275 L10
Nicholas La, Hert. 32 DQ09
Old Cross
Nicholas Pas EC4 275 L10
Nicholas Rd E1 142 DW70
Nicholas Rd, Borwd. 78 CM44
Nicholas Rd, Croy. 219 DL105
Nicholas Rd, Dag. 126 EZ61
Nicholas Wk, Grays 171 GH75
Godman Rd
Nicholas Way, Hem.H. 40 BM18
Nicholas Way, Nthwd. 93 BQ53
Nicholay Rd N19 121 DK60
Nicholes Rd, Houns. 156 CA84
Nicholl Rd, Epp. 69 ET31
Nicholl St E2 142 DU67
Nicholls Av, Uxb. 134 BN70
Nicholls Fld, Harl. 52 EV16
Nicholls Pt E15 144 EG67
Park Gro
Nicholls Twr, Harl. 52 EU16
Nicholls Wk, Wind. 150 AJ83
Nichollsfield Wk N7 121 DM64
Hillmarton Rd
Nichols Cl N4 121 DN60
Osborne Rd
Nichols Cl, Chess. 215 CJ107
Merritt Gdns
Nichols Grn W5 138 CL71
Montpelier Rd
Nicholson Ms, Egh. 173 BA92
Nicholson Wk
Nicholson Rd, Croy. 202 DT102
Nicholson St SE1 278 F3
Nicholson St SE1 141 DP74
Nicholson Wk, Egh. 173 BA92
Nicholson Way, Sev. 257 FK122
Nickelby Cl SE28 146 EW72
Nickelby Cl, Uxb. 135 BP72
Dickens Av
Nicol Cl (Chalfont St. Peter), Ger.Cr. 90 AX53
Nicol Cl, Twick. 177 CH86
Cassilis Rd
Nicol End (Chalfont St. Peter), Ger.Cr. 90 AW53
Nicol Rd (Chalfont St. Peter), Ger.Cr. 90 AW53
Nicola Cl, Har. 95 CD54
Nicola Cl, S.Croy. 220 DQ107
Nicola Ms, Ilf. 103 EP52
Nicoll Pl NW4 119 CV58
Nicoll Rd NW10 138 CS67
Nicoll Way, Borwd. 78 CR43
Nicolson Dr, Bushey 94 CC46
Nicolson Rd, Orp. 206 EX101
Nicosia Rd SW18 180 DE87
Nidderdale, Hem.H. 40 BM17
Wharfedale
Niederwald Rd SE26 183 DY91
Nield Rd, Hayes 155 BT75
Nigel Cl, Nthlt. 136 BY67
Church Rd
Nigel Fisher Way, Chess. 215 CK107
Nigel Ms, Ilf. 125 EP63
Nigel Playfair Av W6 159 CV77
King St
Nigel Rd E7 124 EJ64
Nigel Rd SE15 162 DU83
Nigeria Rd SE7 164 EJ80
Nightingale Av E4 102 EE50
Nightingale Av, Har. 117 CH59
Nightingale Av (West Horsley), Lthd. 229 BR124
Nightingale Av, Upmin. 129 FT60
Nightingale Cl E4 102 EE49
Nightingale Cl W4 158 CQ79
Grove Pk Ter
Nightingale Cl, Abb.L. 59 BU31
Nightingale Cl, Cars. 200 DG103
Nightingale Cl, Cob. 214 BX111
Nightingale Cl, Epsom 216 CN112
Nightingale Cl (Northfleet), Grav. 190 GE91
Nightingale Cl, Pnr. 116 BW57
Nightingale Cl, Rad. 77 CF36
Nightingale Ct E11 124 EH57
Nightingale La
Nightingale Ct, Hert. 32 DQ09
Nightingale Ct, Slou. 152 AU76
St. Laurence Way
Nightingale Cres (West Horsley), Lthd. 229 BQ124
Nightingale Dr, Epsom 216 CP107
Nightingale Est E5 122 DU62
Nightingale Gro SE13 183 ED85
Nightingale Gro, Dart. 168 FN84
Nightingale La E11 124 EH57
Nightingale La N6 120 DE60
Nightingale La N8 121 DL56
Nightingale La SW4 180 DF87
Nightingale La SW12 180 DF87
Nightingale La, Brom. 204 EJ96
Nightingale La, Rich. 178 CL87
Nightingale La, St.Alb. 43 CJ24
Nightingale La (Ide Hill), Sev. 256 FB130
Nightingale Ms E3 143 DY68
Chisenhale Rd
Nightingale Ms, Kings.T. 197 CK97
South La
Nightingale Pk (Farnham Common), Slou. 131 AM66
Nightingale Pl SE18 165 EN79
Nightingale Pl SW10 160 DC79
Fulham Rd
Nightingale Pl, Rick. 92 BK45
Nightingale Rd
Nightingale Rd E5 122 DV62
Nightingale Rd N9 82 DW44
Nightingale Rd N22 99 DL53
Nightingale Rd NW10 139 CT68
Nightingale Rd W7 137 CF74
Nightingale Rd, Bushey 76 CA43
Nightingale Rd, Cars. 200 DF104
Nightingale Rd, Chesh. 54 AP29
Nightingale Rd, Esher 214 BZ106
Nightingale Rd, Guil. 242 AX134
Nightingale Rd, Hmptn. 176 CA92
Nightingale Rd (East Horsley), Lthd. 245 BT125
Nightingale Rd, Orp. 205 EQ100
Nightingale Rd, Rick. 92 BJ46
Nightingale Rd, S.Croy. 221 DX111
Nightingale Rd (Cheshunt), Wal.Cr. 66 DQ25
Nightingale Rd, Walt. 195 BV101
Nightingale Rd, W.Mol. 196 CB99
Nightingale Shott, Egh. 172 AY93
Nobles Way
Nightingale Sq SW12 180 DG87
Nightingale Vale SE18 165 EN79
Nightingale Wk SW4 181 DH86
Nightingale Wk, Wind. 151 AQ83
Nightingale Way E6 144 EL71
Nightingale Way (Bletchingley), Red. 252 DS134
Nightingale Way, Swan. 207 FE97
Nightingale Way (Denham), Uxb. 113 BF59
Nightingales, Wal.Abb. 68 EE34
Roundhills
Nightingales, The, Stai. 174 BM87
Nightingales Cor, Amer. 72 AW40
Chalfont Sta Rd
Nightingales La, Ch.St.G. 90 AX46
Nile Path SE18 165 EN79
Jackson St
Nile Rd E13 144 EJ68
Nile St N1 275 J2
Nile St N1 142 DR69
Nile Ter SE15 162 DT78
Nimbus Rd, Epsom 216 CR110
Nimegen Way SE22 182 DS85
Nimmo Dr, Bushey 95 CD45
Nimrod Cl, Nthlt. 136 BX69
Britannia Cl
Nimrod Cl, St.Alb. 43 CJ18
Nimrod Pas N1 142 DS65
Tottenham Rd
Nimrod Rd SW16 181 DH93
Nina Mackay Cl E15 144 EE67
Arthingworth St
Nine Acres, Slou. 131 AM74
Nine Acres Cl E12 124 EL64
Nine Ashes, Ware 34 EK08
Acorn St
Nine Elms Av, Uxb. 134 BK71
Nine Elms Cl, Felt. 175 BT88
Nine Elms Cl, Uxb. 134 BK72
Nine Elms Gro, Grav. 191 GG87
Nine Elms La SW8 161 DJ79
Nine Stiles Cl (Denham), Uxb. 134 BH65
Nineacres Way, Couls. 235 DL116
Ninefields, Wal.Abb. 68 EF33
Ninehams Cl, Cat. 236 DR120
Ninehams Gdns, Cat. 236 DR120
Ninehams Rd, Cat. 236 DR121
Ninehams Rd (Tatsfield), West. 238 EJ121
Nineteenth Rd, Mitch. 201 DL98
Ninhams Wd, Orp. 223 EN105
Ninian Rd, Hem.H. 40 BL15
Ninnings Rd (Chalfont St. Peter), Ger.Cr. 91 AZ52
Ninnings Way (Chalfont St. Peter), Ger.Cr. 91 AZ52
Ninth Av, Hayes 135 BU73
Nisbet Ho E9 123 DX64
Homerton High St
Nita Rd, Brwd. 108 FW50
Nithdale Rd SE18 165 EP80
Nithsdale Gro, Uxb. 115 BQ62
Tweeddale Gro
Niton Cl, Barn. 79 CX44
Niton Rd, Rich. 158 CN83
Niton St SW6 159 CX80
Niven Cl, Borwd. 78 CQ39
Nixey Cl, Slou. 152 AU75
Noak Hill Rd, Rom. 106 FJ49
Nobel Dr, Hayes 155 BR80
Nobel Rd N18 100 DW50
Noble St EC2 275 H8
Noble St EC2 142 DQ72
Noble St, Walt. 195 BV104
Nobles Way, Egh. 172 AY93
Noel Pk Rd N22 99 DN54
Noel Rd E6 144 EL70
Noel Rd N1 141 DP68
Noel Rd W3 138 CP72
Noel Sq, Dag. 126 EW63
Noel St W1 273 L9
Noel St W1 141 DJ72
Noel Ter SE23 182 DW89
Dartmouth Rd
Noke Dr, Red. 250 DG133
Noke La, St.Alb. 60 BY26
Noke Side, St.Alb. 60 CA27
Nokes, The, Hem.H. 40 BG18
Nolan Way E5 122 DU63
Nolton Pl, Edg. 96 CM53
Nonsuch Cl, Ilf. 103 EP51
Nonsuch Ct Av, Epsom 217 CV110
Nonsuch Ind Est, Epsom 216 CS111
Nonsuch Wk, Sutt. 217 CW110
Nook, The (Stanstead Abbotts), Ware 33 EB11
Noons Cor Rd, Dor. 262 BZ143
Nora Gdns NW4 119 CX56
Norbiton Av, Kings.T. 198 CN96
Norbiton Common Rd, Kings.T. 198 CP97
Norbiton Rd E14 143 DZ72
Norbreck Gdns NW10 138 CM69
Lytham Gro
Norbreck Par NW10 138 CM69
Lytham Gro
Norbroke St W12 139 CT73
Norburn St W10 139 CY71
Chesterton Rd
Norbury Av SW16 201 DM95
Norbury Av, Houns. 177 CD85
Norbury Av, Th.Hth. 201 DN96
Norbury Av, Wat. 76 BW39
Norbury Cl SW16 201 DN95
Norbury Ct Rd SW16 201 DL96
Norbury Cres SW16 201 DM95
Norbury Cross SW16 201 DL97
Norbury Gdns, Rom. 126 EX57
Norbury Gro NW7 96 CS48
Norbury Hill SW16 181 DN94
Norbury Pk (Mickleham), Dor. 247 CF127
Norbury Ri SW16 201 DL97
Norbury Rd E4 101 EA50
Norbury Rd, Reig. 249 CZ134
Norbury Rd, Th.Hth. 202 DQ96
Norbury Way (Bookham), Lthd. 246 CC125
Norcombe Gdns, Har. 117 CJ58
Norcott Cl, Hayes 136 BW70
Willow Tree La
Norcott Rd N16 122 DU61
Norcroft Gdns SE22 182 DU87
Norcutt Rd, Twick. 177 CE88
Nordenfeldt Rd, Erith 167 FD78
Nordmann Pl, S.Ock. 149 FX70
Norelands Dr (Burnham), Slou. 130 AJ68
Norfield Rd, Dart. 187 FC91
Norfolk Av N13 99 DP51
Norfolk Av N15 122 DT58
Norfolk Av, Slou. 131 AQ71
Norfolk Av, S.Croy. 220 DU110
Norfolk Av, Wat. 76 BW38
Norfolk Cl N2 120 DE55
Park Rd
Norfolk Cl N13 99 DP51
Norfolk Cl, Barn. 80 DG42
Norfolk Cl, Dart. 188 FN86
Norfolk Cl, Horl. 268 DF149
Norfolk Cl, Twick. 177 CH86
Cassilis Rd
Norfolk Ct, Dor. 263 CK139
Norfolk Cres W2 272 C8
Norfolk Cres W2 140 DE72
Norfolk Cres, Sid. 185 ES87
Norfolk Fm Cl, Wok. 227 BD116
Norfolk Fm Rd, Wok. 227 BD115
Norfolk Gdns, Bexh. 166 EZ81
Norfolk Gdns, Borwd. 78 CR42
Norfolk Ho SE3 164 EE79
Norfolk Ho Rd SW16 181 DK90
Norfolk La (Mid Holmwood), Dor. 263 CH142
Norfolk Ms W10 139 CZ71
Blagrove Rd
Norfolk Pl W2 272 A8
Norfolk Pl W2 140 DD72
Norfolk Pl, Well. 166 EU82
Norfolk Rd E6 145 EM67
Norfolk Rd E17 101 DX54
Norfolk Rd NW8 140 DD67
Norfolk Rd NW10 138 CS66
Norfolk Rd SW19 180 DE94
Norfolk Rd, Bark. 145 ES66
Norfolk Rd, Barn. 80 DA41
Norfolk Rd, Dag. 127 FB64
Norfolk Rd, Dor. 263 CG136
Norfolk Rd (South Holmwood), Dor. 263 CJ144
Norfolk Rd, Enf. 82 DV44
Norfolk Rd (Claygate), Esher 215 CE106
Norfolk Rd, Felt. 176 BW88
Norfolk Rd, Grav. 191 GK86
Norfolk Rd, Har. 116 CB57
Norfolk Rd, Ilf. 125 ES60
Norfolk Rd, Rick. 92 BL46
Norfolk Rd, Rom. 127 FC58
Norfolk Rd, Th.Hth. 202 DQ97
Norfolk Rd, Upmin. 128 FN62
Norfolk Rd, Uxb. 134 BK65
Norfolk Row SE1 278 B8
Norfolk Sq W2 272 A9
Norfolk Sq W2 140 DD72
Norfolk Sq Ms W2 272 A9
Norfolk St E7 124 EG63
Norfolk Ter W6 159 CY78
Field Rd
Norgrove Pk, Ger.Cr. 112 AY56
Norgrove St SW12 180 DG87
Norheads La, Warl. 238 EG119
Norheads La (Biggin Hill), West. 238 EJ116
Norhyrst Av SE25 202 DT97
Nork Gdns, Bans. 217 CY114
Nork Ri, Bans. 233 CX116
Nork Way, Bans. 233 CY115
Norland Ho W11 139 CX74
Norland Pl W11 139 CY74
Norland Rd W11 139 CX74
Norland Sq W11 139 CY74
Norlands Cres, Chis. 205 EP95
Norlands Gate, Chis. 205 EP95
Norlands La, Egh. 193 BE97
Norley Vale SW15 179 CU88
Norlington Rd E10 123 EC60
Norlington Rd E11 123 EC60
Norman Av N22 99 DP53
Norman Av, Epsom 217 CT112
Norman Av, Felt. 176 BY89
Norman Av, S.Croy. 220 DQ110
Norman Av, Sthl. 136 BY73
Norman Av, Twick. 177 CH87
Norman Cl, Epsom 233 CW119
Merland Ri
Norman Cl, Orp. 205 EQ104
Norman Cl, Rom. 105 FB54
Norman Cl, Wal.Abb. 67 ED33
Norman Ct, Ilf. 125 ER59
Norman Ct, Pot.B. 64 DC30
Norman Ct, Wdf.Grn. 102 EH50
Monkhams Av
Norman Cres, Brwd. 109 GA48
Norman Cres, Houns. 156 BX81
Norman Cres, Pnr. 94 BW53
Norman Gro E3 143 DY68
Norman Rd E6 145 EM70
Norman Rd E11 123 ED61
Norman Rd N15 122 DT57
Norman Rd SE10 163 EB80
Norman Rd SW19 180 DC94
Norman Rd, Ashf. 175 BR93
Norman Rd, Belv. 167 FB76
Norman Rd, Dart. 188 FL88
Norman Rd, Horn. 127 FG59
Norman Rd, Ilf. 125 EP64
Norman Rd, Sutt. 218 DA106
Norman Rd, Th.Hth. 201 DP99
Norman St EC1 275 H3
Norman Way N14 99 DL47
Norman Way W3 138 CP71
Normanby Cl SW15 179 CZ85
Manfred Rd
Normanby Rd NW10 119 CT63
Normand Gdns W14 159 CY79
Greyhound Rd
Normand Ms W14 159 CY79
Normand Rd
Normand Rd W14 159 CZ79
Normandy Av, Barn. 79 CZ43
Normandy Cl SE26 183 DY90
Normandy Ct, Hem.H. 40 BK19
Normandy Dr, Berk. 38 AV17
Normandy Dr, Hayes 135 BQ72
Normandy Rd SW9 161 DN81
Normandy Rd, St.Alb. 43 CD18
Normandy Ter E16 144 EH72
Normandy Wk, Egh. 173 BC92
Mullens Rd
Normandy Way, Erith 167 FE81
Normandy Way, Hodd. 49 EC16
Normanhurst, Ashf. 174 BN92
Normanhurst, Brwd. 109 GC44
Normanhurst Av, Bexh. 166 EX81
Normanhurst Dr, Twick. 177 CH85
St. Margarets Rd
Normanhurst Rd SW2 181 DM89
Normanhurst Rd, Orp. 206 EV96
Normanhurst Rd, Walt. 196 BX103
Normans, The, Slou. 132 AV72
Norman's Bldgs EC1 142 DQ69
Ironmonger Row
Normans Cl NW10 138 CR65
Normans Cl, Grav. 191 GG87
Normans Cl, Uxb. 134 BL71
Normans Mead NW10 138 CR65
Normansfield Av, Tedd. 177 CJ94
Normansfield Cl, Bushey 94 CB45
Normanshire Av E4 101 EC49
Normanshire Dr E4 101 EA49
Normanton Av SW19 180 DA89
Normanton Pk E4 102 EE48
Normanton Rd, S.Croy. 220 DS107
Normanton St SE23 183 DX89
Normington Cl SW16 181 DN92
Norrels Dr (East Horsley), Lthd. 245 BT126
Norrels Ride (East Horsley), Lthd. 245 BT125
Norrice Lea N2 120 DD57
Norris Gro, Brox. 49 DY20
Norris La, Hodd. 49 EA16
Norris Ri, Hodd. 49 DZ16
Norris Rd, Hodd. 49 EA17
Norris Rd, Stai. 173 BF91
Norris St SW1 277 M1
Norris Way, Dart. 167 FF83
Norroy Rd SW15 159 CX84
Norrys Cl, Barn. 80 DF43
Norrys Rd, Barn. 80 DF42
Norseman Cl, Ilf. 126 EV60
Norseman Way, Grnf. 136 CB67
Olympic Way
Norstead Pl SW15 179 CU89
Norsted La, Orp. 224 EU110
North Access Rd E17 123 DX58
North Acre NW9 96 CS53
North Acre, Bans. 233 CZ116
North Acton Rd NW10 138 CR68
North App, Nthwd. 93 BQ47
North App, Wat. 75 BU35
North Arc, Croy. 202 DQ103
North End
North Audley St W1 272 F9
North Audley St W1 140 DG72
North Av N18 100 DU49
North Av W13 137 CH72
North Av, Brwd. 107 FR45
North Av, Cars. 218 DF108
North Av, Har. 116 CB58
North Av, Hayes 135 BU73
North Av, Rad. 62 CL32
North Av, Rich. 158 CN81
Sandycombe Rd
North Av, Sthl. 136 BZ73
North Av, Walt. 213 BS109
North Bk NW8 272 B3
North Bk NW8 140 DE69
North Barn, Brox. 49 EA21
North Birkbeck Rd E11 123 ED62
North Branch Av W10 139 CW69
Harrow Rd
North Burnham Cl (Burnham), Slou. 130 AH68
Wyndham Cres
North Carriage Dr W2 272 B10
North Carriage Dr W2 140 DD73
North Circular Rd E4 101 DZ52
North Circular Rd E18 102 EJ54
North Circular Rd N3 120 DB55
North Circular Rd N12 98 DD53
North Circular Rd N13 99 DN50
North Circular Rd NW2 118 CS62
North Circular Rd NW10 138 CQ66
North Circular Rd NW11 119 CY56
North Cl, Barn. 79 CW43
North Cl, Bexh. 166 EX84
North Cl, Chig. 104 EU50
North Cl, Dag. 146 FA67
North Cl (North Holmwood), Dor. 263 CJ140
North Cl, Felt. 175 BR86
North Rd
North Cl, Mord. 199 CY98
North Cl, St.Alb. 60 CB25
North Cl, Wind. 151 AM81
North Colonnade E14 143 EA74
North Common, Wey. 213 BP105
North Common Rd W5 138 CL73
North Common Rd, Uxb. 114 BK64
North Cotts (London Colney), St.Alb. 61 CG25
North Countess Rd E17 101 DZ53
North Ct W1 273 L6
North Cray Rd, Bex. 186 EZ90
North Cray Rd, Sid. 186 EY93
North Cres E16 143 ED70
North Cres N3 97 CZ54
North Cres WC1 273 M6
North Cres WC1 141 DK71
North Cross Rd SE22 182 DT85
North Cross Rd, Ilf. 125 EQ56
North Dene NW7 96 CR48
North Dene, Houns. 156 CB81
North Down, S.Croy. 220 DS111
North Downs Cres (New Addington), Croy. 221 EB110
North Downs Rd (New Addington), Croy. 221 EB110
North Downs Way, Bet. 249 CU130
North Downs Way, Cat. 251 DN126
North Downs Way, Dor. 247 CE133
North Downs Way, Gdse. 253 DY128
North Downs Way, Guil. 258 AT138
North Downs Way, Oxt. 254 EE126
North Downs Way, Red. 250 DG128
North Downs Way, Reig. 250 DD130
North Downs Way, Sev. 241 FD118
North Downs Way, Tad. 249 CX130
North Downs Way, West. 239 ER121
North Dr SW16 181 DJ91
North Dr, Beac. 110 AG55
North Dr, Houns. 156 CC82
North Dr, Orp. 223 ES105
North Dr, Rom. 128 FJ55
North Dr, Ruis. 115 BS59
North Dr (Oaklands), St.Alb. 44 CL18
North Dr, Slou. 132 AS69
North Dr, Vir.W. 192 AS100
North End NW3 120 DC61
North End, Buck.H. 102 EJ45
North End, Croy. 202 DQ103
North End, Rom. 106 FJ47
North End Av NW3 120 DC61
North End Cres W14 159 CZ77
North End Ho W14 159 CY77
North End La, Orp. 223 EN110
North End Par W14 159 CY77
North End Rd
North End Rd NW11 120 DA60
North End Rd SW6 159 CZ79
North End Rd W14 159 CY77
North End Rd, Wem. 118 CN62
North End Way NW3 120 DC61
North Eyot Gdns W6 159 CU78
North Flockton St SE16 162 DU75
Chambers St
North Gdn E14 143 DZ74
Westferry Circ
North Gdns SW19 180 DD94
North Gate, Harl. 35 EQ14
North Glade, The, Bex. 186 EZ87
North Gower St NW1 273 L3
North Gower St NW1 141 DJ69
North Grn NW9 96 CS52
Clayton Fld
North Grn, Slou. 132 AS73
North Gro N6 120 DG59
North Gro N15 122 DR57
North Gro, Cher. 193 BF100
North Gro, Harl. 52 EU16
North Hatton Rd (Heathrow Airport), Houns. 155 BR81
North Hill N6 120 DF58
North Hill, Rick. 73 BE40
North Hill Av N6 120 DG58
North Hill Dr, Rom. 106 FK48
North Hill Grn, Rom. 106 FK49
North Ho, Harl. 51 ET17
Tilegate Rd
North Hyde Gdns, Hayes 155 BU77
North Hyde La, Houns. 156 BY78
North Hyde La, Sthl. 156 BY78
North Hyde Rd, Hayes 155 BT76
North Kent Av (Northfleet), Grav. 190 GC86
North La, Tedd. 177 CF93
North Lo Cl SW15 179 CX85
Westleigh Av
North Mall N9 100 DV47
St. Martins Rd
North Mead, Red. 250 DF131
North Ms WC1 274 C5
North Ms WC1 141 DM70
North Moors, Guil. 242 AY130
North Mymms Pk, Hat. 63 CT25
North Orbital Rd, Hat. 29 CV14
North Orbital Rd, Rick. 91 BE50
North Orbital Rd, St.Alb. 61 CK25
North Orbital Rd (Denham), Uxb. 113 BF55
North Orbital Rd, Wat. 59 BU34
North Orbital Trd Est, St.Alb. 43 CG24
North Par, Chess. 216 CL106
North Pk SE9 185 EM86
North Pk, Ger.Cr. 112 AY56
North Pk, Iver 153 BC76
North Pk La, Gdse. 252 DU129
North Pas SW18 160 DA84
North Peckham Est SE15 162 DT80
North Perimeter Rd, Uxb. 134 BL69
Kingston La
North Pl, Guil. 258 AX135
North Pl, Mitch. 180 DF94
North Pl, Tedd. 177 CF93
North Pl, Wal.Abb. 67 EB33
Highbridge St
North Pole La, Kes. 222 EF107
North Pole Rd W10 139 CW71
North Ride W2 276 B1
North Ride W2 140 DE73
North Riding (Bricket Wd), St.Alb. 60 CA30
North Rd N6 120 DG59
North Rd N7 141 DL65

North Rd N9 100 DV46
North Rd SE18 165 ES77
North Rd SW19 180 DC93
North Rd W5 157 CK76
North Rd (Chesham Bois), Amer. 55 AQ36
North Rd, Belv. 167 FB76
North Rd, Berk. 38 AV19
North Rd, Brent. 158 CL79
North Rd, Brwd. 108 FW46
North Rd, Brom. 204 EH95
North Rd, Dart. 187 FF86
North Rd, Edg. 96 CP53
North Rd, Felt. 175 BR86
North Rd, Guil. 242 AV131
North Rd, Hayes 135 BR71
North Rd, Hert. 32 DQ09
North Rd, Hodd. 49 EA16
North Rd, Ilf. 125 ES61
North Rd, Purf. 169 FR77
North Rd, Reig. 265 CZ137
North Rd, Rich. 158 CN83
North Rd, Rick. 73 BD43
North Rd, Rom. 126 EY57
North Rd (Havering-atte-Bower), Rom. 105 FE48
North Rd, S.Ock. 149 FW68
North Rd, Sthl. 136 CA73
North Rd, Surb. 197 CK100
North Rd, Wal.Cr. 67 DY33
North Rd, Walt. 214 BW106
North Rd, West Dr. 154 BM76
North Rd, W.Wick. 203 EB102
North Rd, Wok. 227 BA116
North Rd Av, Brwd. 108 FW46
North Rd Av, Hert. 31 DN08
North Rd Gdns, Hert. 31 DP09
North Row W1 272 E10
North Row W1 140 DF73
North Service Rd, Brwd. 108 FW47
North Several SE3 163 ED82
Orchard Rd
North Side Wandsworth Common SW18 180 DD85
North Sq N9 100 DV47
St. Martins Rd
North Sq NW11 120 DA57
North Sta App (South Nutfield), Red. 267 DM136
North St E13 144 EH68
North St NW4 119 CW57
North St SW4 161 DJ83
North St, Bark. 145 EP65
North St, Bexh. 166 FA84
North St, Brom. 204 EG95
North St, Cars. 200 DF104
North St, Dart. 188 FK87
North St, Dor. 263 CG136
North St (Westcott), Dor. 262 CC137
Guildford Rd
North St, Egh. 173 AZ92
North St, Gdmg. 258 AT144
Station Rd
North St, Grav. 191 GH87
South St
North St, Guil. 258 AX135
North St, Horn. 128 FK59
North St, Islw. 157 CG83
North St, Lthd. 231 CG121
North St, Red. 250 DF133
North St, Rom. 127 FD55
North St, Wal.Abb. 50 EE22
North St Pas E13 144 EH68
North Tenter St E1 142 DT72
North Ter SW3 276 B7
North Ter SW3 160 DE76
North Ter, Wind. 151 AR80
The Long Wk
North Verbena Gdns W6 159 CU78
St. Peter's Sq
North Vw SW19 179 CV92
North Vw W5 137 CJ70
North Vw, Ilf. 104 EU52
North Vw, Pnr. 116 BW59
North Vw Av, Til. 171 GG81
North Vw Cres, Epsom 233 CV117
North Vw Dr, Wdf.Grn. 102 EK54
North Vw Rd N8 121 DK55
North Vw Rd, Sev. 257 FJ121
Seal Rd
North Vil NW1 141 DK65
North Wk W2 140 DC73
Bayswater Rd
North Wk (New Addington), Croy. 221 EB106
North Way N9 100 DW47
North Way N11 99 DJ51
North Way NW9 118 CP55
North Way, Pnr. 116 BW55
North Way, Uxb. 134 BL66
North Weald Airfield, Epp. 70 EZ26
North Western Av, Wat. 76 BW36
North Wf Rd W2 140 DD71
North Wd Ct SE25 202 DU97
Regina Rd
North Woolwich Rd E16 144 EG74
North Woolwich Roundabout E16 144 EK74
North Woolwich Rd
North Worple Way SW14 158 CR83
Northall Rd, Bexh. 167 FC82
Northallerton Way, Rom. 106 FK50
Northampton Av, Slou. 131 AQ72
Northampton Gro N1 122 DR64
Northampton Pk N1 142 DQ65
Northampton Rd EC1 274 E4
Northampton Rd EC1 141 DN70
Northampton Rd, Croy. 202 DU103
Northampton Rd, Enf. 83 DY42
Northampton Sq EC1 274 F3
Northampton Sq EC1 141 DP69
Northampton St N1 142 DQ66
Northanger Rd SW16 181 DL93
Northaw Cl, Hem.H. 41 BP15
Northaw Pl, Pot.B. 64 DD30
Northaw Rd E (Cuffley), Pot.B. 65 DK31
Northaw Rd W, Pot.B. 64 DG30
Northbank Rd E17 101 EC54
Northborough Rd SW16 201 DK97
Northborough Rd, Slou. 131 AN70
Northbourne, Brom. 204 EG101
Northbourne, Gdmg. 258 AT143
Northbourne Rd SW4 161 DK84
Northbridge Rd, Berk. 38 AT17
Northbrook Dr, Nthwd. 93 BS53
Northbrook Rd N22 99 DL52
Northbrook Rd SE13 183 ED85
Northbrook Rd, Barn. 79 CY44
Northbrook Rd, Croy. 202 DR99
Northbrook Rd, Ilf. 125 EN61
Northbrooks, Harl. 51 EQ15
Northburgh St EC1 274 G4
Northburgh St EC1 141 DP70
Northchurch SE17 279 L10
Northchurch Common, Berk. 38 AT16
Northchurch Rd N1 142 DR66
Northchurch Rd, Wem. 138 CM65
Northchurch Ter N1 142 DS66
Northcliffe Cl, Wor.Pk. 198 CS104
Northcliffe Dr N20 97 CZ46
Northcote, Add. 212 BK105
Northcote (Oxshott), Lthd. 214 CC114
Northcote, Pnr. 94 BW54
Northcote Av W5 138 CL73
Northcote Av, Islw. 177 CG85
Northcote Av, Sthl. 136 BY73
Northcote Av, Surb. 198 CN101
Northcote Cl (West Horsley), Lthd. 245 BQ125
Northcote Cres (West Horsley), Lthd. 245 BQ125
Northcote Rd E17 123 DY56
Northcote Rd NW10 138 CS66
Northcote Rd SW11 160 DE84
Northcote Rd, Croy. 202 DR100
Northcote Rd, Grav. 191 GF88
Northcote Rd (West Horsley), Lthd. 245 BQ125
Northcote Rd, N.Mal. 198 CQ97
Northcote Rd, Sid. 185 ES91
Northcote Rd, Twick. 177 CG85
Northcott Av N22 99 DL53
Northcotts, Abb.L. 59 BR33
Long Elms
Northcotts, Hat. 45 CW17
Northcourt, Rick. 92 BG46
Springwell Av
Northcroft (Wooburn Grn), H.Wyc. 110 AE56
Northcroft, Slou. 131 AP70
Northcroft Cl (Englefield Grn), Egh. 172 AV92
Northcroft Gdns (Englefield Grn), Egh. 172 AV92
Northcroft Rd W13 157 CH75
Northcroft Rd (Englefield Grn), Egh. 172 AV92
Northcroft Rd, Epsom 216 CR108
Northcroft Ter W13 157 CH75
Northcroft Rd
Northcroft Vil (Englefield Grn), Egh. 172 AV92
Northdene, Chig. 103 ER50
Northdene Gdns N15 122 DT58
Northdown Cl, Ruis. 115 BT62
Northdown Gdns, Ilf. 125 ES57
Northdown La, Guil. 258 AY137
Northdown Rd (Woldingham), Cat. 237 EA123
Northdown Rd (Chalfont St. Peter), Ger.Cr. 90 AY51
Northdown Rd, Hat. 45 CU21
Northdown Rd, Horn. 127 FH59
Northdown Rd, Long. 209 FX96
Northdown Rd, Sutt. 218 DA110
Northdown Rd, Well. 166 EV82
Northdown St N1 141 DM68
Northend, Brwd. 108 FW50
Northend, Hem.H. 41 BP22
Northend Cl (Flackwell Heath), H.Wyc. 110 AC56
Northend Rd, Dart. 167 FF81
Northend Rd, Erith 167 FF80
Northend Trd Est, Erith 167 FE81
Northern Av N9 100 DT47
Northern Perimeter Rd (Heathrow Airport), Houns. 155 BQ81
Northern Perimeter Rd W (Heathrow Airport), Houns. 154 BK81
Northern Relief Rd, Bark. 145 EP66
Northern Rd E13 144 EH67
Northern Rd, Slou. 131 AQ70
Northern Service Rd, Barn. 79 CY41
Northern Wds (Flackwell Heath), H.Wyc. 110 AC56
Northernhay Wk, Mord. 199 CY98
Northey Av, Sutt. 217 CZ110
Northey St E14 143 DY73
Northfield (Shalford), Guil. 258 AY142
Northfield, Hat. 45 CV15
Longmead
Northfield, Loug. 84 EK42
Northfield Av W5 157 CH75
Northfield Av W13 157 CH75
Northfield Av, Orp. 206 EW100
Northfield Av, Pnr. 116 BX56
Northfield Cl, Brom. 204 EL95
Northfield Cl, Hayes 155 BT76
Northfield Ct, Stai. 194 BH95
Northfield Cres, Sutt. 217 CY105
Northfield Gdns, Dag. 126 EZ63
Northfield Rd
Northfield Gdns, Wat. 76 BW37
Northfield Ind Est NW10 138 CN69
Northfield Pk, Hayes 155 BT76
Northfield Path, Dag. 126 EZ62
Northfield Pl, Wey. 213 BP108
Northfield Rd E6 145 EM66
Northfield Rd N16 122 DS59
Northfield Rd W13 157 CH75
Northfield Rd, Barn. 80 DE41
Northfield Rd, Borwd. 78 CP39
Northfield Rd, Cob. 213 BU113
Northfield Rd, Dag. 126 EZ63
Northfield Rd, Enf. 82 DV43
Northfield Rd, Houns. 156 BX79
Northfield Rd, Stai. 194 BH95
Northfield Rd, Wal.Cr. 67 DY32
Northfield Rd (Eton Wick), Wind. 151 AM77
Northfields SW18 160 DA84
Northfields, Ash. 232 CL119
Northfields, Grays 170 GC77
Northfields Ind Est, Wem. 138 CN67
Northfields Rd W3 138 CP71
Northfleet Grn Rd, Grav. 190 GC93
Northfleet Ind Est, Grav. 170 FZ84
Northgate, Gat. 268 DF151
Northgate, Nthwd. 93 BQ52
Northgate Dr NW9 118 CS58
Northgate Ind Pk, Rom. 104 FA53
Northgate Path, Borwd. 78 CM39
Northiam N12 98 DA48
Northiam St E9 142 DV67
Northington St WC1 274 C5
Northington St WC1 141 DM70
Northlands, Pot.B. 64 DD31
Northlands Av, Orp. 223 ES105
Northlands St SE5 162 DQ82
Northmead Rd, Slou. 131 AM70
Northolm, Edg. 96 CR49
Northolme Cl, Grays 170 GC76
Premier Av
Northolme Gdns, Edg. 96 CN53
Northolme Ri, Orp. 205 ES103
Northolme Rd N5 122 DQ63
Northolt Av, Ruis. 115 BV64
Northolt Gdns, Grnf. 117 CF64
Northolt Rd, Har. 116 CB63
Northolt Rd (Heathrow Airport), Houns. 154 BK81
Northolt Way, Horn. 148 FJ65
Northover, Brom. 184 EF90
Northport St N1 142 DR67
Northridge Rd, Grav. 191 GJ90
Northridge Way, Hem.H. 39 BF21
Northrop Rd (Heathrow Airport), Houns. 155 BS81
Northside Rd, Brom. 204 EG95
Mitchell Way
Northspur Rd, Sutt. 200 DA104
Northstead Rd SW2 181 DN89
Northumberland All EC3 275 N9
Northumberland All EC3 142 DS72
Northumberland Av E12 124 EJ60
Northumberland Av WC2 277 P2
Northumberland Av WC2 141 DL74
Northumberland Av, Enf. 82 DV39
Northumberland Av, Horn. 128 FJ57
Northumberland Av, Islw. 157 CF81
Northumberland Av, Well. 165 ES84
Northumberland Cl, Erith 167 FC80
Northumberland Cl (Stanwell), Stai. 174 BL86
Northumberland Cres, Felt. 175 BS86
Northumberland Gdns N9 100 DT48
Northumberland Gdns, Brom. 205 EN98
Northumberland Gdns, Islw. 157 CG80
Northumberland Gdns, Mitch. 201 DK99
Northumberland Gro N17 100 DV52
Northumberland Pk N17 100 DT52
Northumberland Pk, Erith 167 FC80
Northumberland Pl W2 140 DA72
Northumberland Pl, Rich. 177 CK85
Northumberland Rd E6 144 EL72
Northumberland Rd E17 123 EA59
Northumberland Rd, Barn. 80 DC44
Northumberland Rd (Istead Ri), Grav. 191 GF94
Northumberland Rd, Har. 116 BZ57
Northumberland Rd, S.le H. 171 GM75
Northumberland Row, Twick. 177 CE88
Colne Rd
Northumberland St WC2 277 P2
Northumberland St WC2 141 DL74
Northumberland Way, Erith 167 FC81
Northumbria St E14 143 EA72
Northview N7 121 DL62
Northview, Hem.H. 39 BD22
Winkwell
Northview, Swan. 207 FE96
Northview Cres NW10 119 CT63
Northway NW11 120 DB57
Northway, Guil. 242 AU132
Northway, Mord. 199 CY97
Northway, Rick. 92 BK45
Northway, Wall. 219 DJ105
Northway, Welw.G.C. 29 CZ06
Nursery Hill
Northway Circ NW7 96 CR49
Northway Cres NW7 96 CR49
Northway Ho N20 98 DC46
Northway Rd SE5 162 DQ83
Northway Rd, Croy. 202 DT100
Northways Par NW3 140 DD66
College Cres
Northweald La, Kings.T. 177 CK92
Northwest Pl N1 141 DN68
Chapel Mkt
Northwick Av, Har. 117 CG58
Northwick Circle, Har. 117 CJ58
Northwick Cl NW8 140 DD70
Northwick Ter
Northwick Cl, Har. 117 CH59
Nightingale Av
Northwick Pk Rd, Har. 117 CF58
Northwick Rd, Wat. 94 BW49
Northwick Rd, Wem. 137 CK67
Northwick Ter NW8 140 DD70
Northwick Wk, Har. 117 CF59
Northwold Dr, Pnr. 116 BW55
Cuckoo Hill
Northwold Est E5 122 DU61
Northwold Rd E5 122 DT61
Northwold Rd N16 122 DT61
Northwood, Grays 171 GH75
Northwood, Welw.G.C. 30 DD09
Northwood Av, Horn. 127 FG63
Northwood Av, Pur. 219 DN113
Northwood Cl, Wal.Cr. 66 DT27
Northwood Gdns N12 98 DD50
Northwood Gdns, Grnf. 117 CF64
Northwood Gdns, Ilf. 125 EN56
Northwood Hall N6 121 DJ59
Northwood Ho SE27 182 DR91
Northwood Pl, Erith 166 EZ76
Northwood Rd N6 121 DH59
Northwood Rd SE23 183 DZ88
Northwood Rd, Cars. 218 DG107
Northwood Rd (Heathrow Airport), Houns. 154 BK81
Northwood Rd, Th.Hth. 201 DP96
Northwood Rd (Harefield), Uxb. 92 BJ53
Northwood Twr E17 123 EC56
Northwood Way SE19 182 DR93
Roman Ri
Northwood Way, Nthwd. 93 BU52
Northwood Way (Harefield), Uxb. 92 BK53
Nortoft Rd (Chalfont St. Peter), Ger.Cr. 91 AZ51
Norton Av, Surb. 198 CP101
Norton Cl E4 101 EA50
Norton Cl, Borwd. 78 CN39
Norton Cl, Enf. 82 DV40
Brick La
Norton Folgate E1 275 N6
Norton Folgate E1 142 DS71
Norton Gdns SW16 201 DL96
Norton La, Cob. 229 BT119
Norton Rd E10 123 DZ60
Norton Rd, Dag. 147 FD65
Norton Rd, Uxb. 134 BK69
Norton Rd, Wem. 137 CK65
Norval Rd, Wem. 117 CH61
Norway Dr, Slou. 132 AV71
Norway Gate SE16 163 DY76
Norway Pl E14 143 DZ72
East India Dock Rd
Norway St SE10 163 EB79
Norway Wk, Rain. 148 FJ70
The Glen
Norwich Ho E14 143 EB72
Cordelia St
Norwich Ms, Ilf. 126 EU60
Ashgrove Rd
Norwich Pl, Bexh. 166 FA84
Norwich Rd E7 124 EG64
Norwich Rd, Dag. 146 FA68
Norwich Rd, Grnf. 136 CB67
Norwich Rd, Nthwd. 115 BT55
Norwich Rd, Th.Hth. 202 DQ97
Norwich St EC4 274 D8
Norwich St EC4 141 DN72
Norwich Wk, Edg. 96 CQ52
Norwich Way, Rick. 75 BP41
Norwood Av, Rom. 127 FE59
Norwood Av, Wem. 138 CM67
Norwood Cl, Hert. 31 DM08
Norwood Cl (Effingham), Lthd. 246 BY128
Norwood Cl, Sthl. 156 CA77
Norwood Cl, Twick. 177 CD89
Fourth Cross Rd
Norwood Ct, Amer. 55 AP40
Norwood Cres (Heathrow Airport), Houns. 155 BQ81
Norwood Dr, Har. 116 BZ58
Norwood Fm La, Cob. 213 BU111
Norwood Gdns, Hayes 136 BW70
Norwood Gdns, Sthl. 156 BZ77
Norwood Grn Rd, Sthl. 156 CA77
Norwood High St SE27 181 DP90
Norwood La, Iver 133 BD70
Norwood Pk Rd SE27 182 DQ92
Norwood Rd SE24 181 DP88
Norwood Rd SE27 181 DP89
Norwood Rd (Effingham), Lthd. 246 BY128
Norwood Rd, Sthl. 156 BZ77
Norwood Rd (Cheshunt), Wal.Cr. 67 DY30
Norwood Ter, Sthl. 156 CB77
Tentelow La
Notley End (Englefield Grn), Egh. 172 AW93
Notley St SE5 162 DR80
Notre Dame Est SW4 161 DJ84
Notson Rd SE25 202 DV98
Notting Barn Rd W10 139 CX70
Notting Hill Gate W11 140 DA74
Nottingdale Sq W11 139 CY74
Wilsham St
Nottingham Av E16 144 EJ71
Nottingham Cl, Wat. 59 BU33
Nottingham Cl, Wok. 226 AT118
Nottingham Ct WC2 273 P9
Nottingham Ct, Wok. 226 AT118
Nottingham Cl
Nottingham Pl W1 272 F5
Nottingham Pl W1 140 DG70
Nottingham Rd E10 123 EC58
Nottingham Rd SW17 180 DF88
Nottingham Rd, Islw. 157 CF82
Nottingham Rd, Rick. 91 BC45
Nottingham Rd, S.Croy. 220 DQ105
Nottingham St W1 272 F6
Nottingham St W1 140 DG71
Nottingham Ter NW1 272 F5
Nova Ms, Sutt. 199 CY102
Nova Rd, Croy. 201 DP101
Novar Cl, Orp. 205 ET101
Novar Rd SE9 185 EQ88
Novello St SW6 160 DA81
Novello Way, Borwd. 78 CR39
Nowell Rd SW13 159 CU79
Nower, The, Sev. 239 ET119
Nower Hill, Pnr. 116 BZ56
Nower Rd, Dor. 263 CG136
Noyna Rd SW17 180 DF90
Nuding Cl SE13 163 EA83
Nuffield Rd, Swan. 187 FG93
Nugent Ind Pk, Orp. 206 EW99
Nugent Rd N19 121 DL60
Nugent Rd SE25 202 DT97
Nugent Ter NW8 140 DC68
Nugents Ct, Pnr. 94 BY53
St. Thomas' Dr
Nugents Pk, Pnr. 94 BY53
Nun Ct EC2 275 K8
Nunappleton Way, Oxt. 254 EG132
Nuneaton Rd, Dag. 146 EX66
Nunfield, Kings L. 58 BH31
Nunhead Cres SE15 162 DV83
Nunhead Est SE15 162 DV83
Nunhead Grn SE15 162 DV83
Nunhead Grn (Denham), Uxb. 113 BF58
Nunhead Gro SE15 162 DV83
Nunhead La SE15 162 DV83
Nunhead Pas SE15 162 DU83
Peckham Rye
Nunnery Cl, St.Alb. 43 CD22
Nunnery Stables, St.Alb. 43 CD22
Nunnington Cl SE9 184 EL90
Nunns Rd, Enf. 82 DQ40
Nunns Way, Grays 170 GD77
Nuns La, St.Alb. 43 CE24
Nuns Wk, Vir.W. 192 AX99
Nunsbury Dr, Brox. 67 DY25
Nupton Dr, Barn. 79 CW44
Nurseries Rd (Wheathampstead), St.Alb. 28 CL08
Nursery, The, Erith 167 FF80
Nursery Av N3 98 DC54
Nursery Av, Bexh. 166 EZ83
Nursery Av, Croy. 203 DX103
Nursery Cl SE4 163 DZ82
Nursery Cl SW15 159 CX84
Nursery Cl (Woodham), Add. 211 BF110
Nursery Cl, Amer. 55 AS39
Nursery Cl, Croy. 203 DX103
Nursery Cl, Dart. 188 FQ87
Nursery Cl, Enf. 83 DX39
Nursery Cl, Epsom 216 CS110
Nursery Cl, Felt. 175 BV87
Nursery Cl (Penn), H.Wyc. 88 AC47
Nursery Cl, Orp. 206 EU101
Nursery Cl, Rom. 126 EX58
Nursery Cl, Sev. 257 FJ122
Nursery Cl, S.Ock. 149 FW70
Nursery Cl, Swan. 207 FC96
Nursery Cl, Tad. 249 CU125
Nursery Cl, Wok. 226 AW116
Nursery Cl, Wdf.Grn. 102 EH50
Nursery Ct N17 100 DT52
Nursery St
Nursery Flds, Saw. 36 EX05
Nursery Gdns, Chis. 185 EP93
Nursery Gdns, Enf. 83 DX39
Nursery Gdns (Chilworth), Guil. 259 BB140
Nursery Gdns, Houns. 176 BZ85
Nursery Gdns, Stai. 174 BH94
Nursery Gdns, Sun. 195 BT96
Nursery Gdns, Wal.Cr. 66 DR28
Nursery Gdns, Ware 33 DY06
Nursery Gdns, Welw.G.C. 29 CY06
Nursery Hill, Welw.G.C. 29 CY06
Nursery La E2 142 DT67
Nursery La E7 144 EG65
Nursery La W10 139 CW71
Nursery La (Penn), H.Wyc. 88 AC47
Nursery La, Horl. 268 DD149
Nursery La, Slou. 132 AW74
Nursery La, Uxb. 134 BK70
Nursery Pl, Sev. 256 FD122
Nursery Rd E9 142 DW65
Morning La
Nursery Rd N2 98 DD53
Nursery Rd N14 99 DJ45
Nursery Rd SW9 161 DM84
Nursery Rd, Brox. 67 DY25
Nursery Rd, Gdmg. 258 AT144
Nursery Rd, Hodd. 33 EB14
Nursery Rd, Loug. 84 EJ43
Nursery Rd (High Beach), Loug. 84 EH39
Nursery Rd, Maid. 130 AH72
Nursery Rd, Pnr. 116 BW55
Nursery Rd, Sun. 195 BS96
Nursery Rd, Sutt. 218 DC105
Nursery Rd, Tad. 249 CU125
Nursery Rd, Th.Hth. 202 DR98
Nursery Rd, Wal.Abb. 49 ED22
Nursery Rd Merton SW19 200 DB96
Nursery Rd Mitcham, Mitch. 200 DE97
Nursery Rd Wimbledon SW19 179 CY94
Worple Rd
Nursery Row SE17 279 K9
Nursery Row SE17 162 DR77
Nursery Row, Barn. 79 CY41
St. Albans Rd
Nursery St N17 100 DT52
Nursery Ter, Berk. 39 BB16
The Front
Nursery Wk NW4 119 CV55
Nursery Wk, Rom. 127 FD59
Nursery Way (Wraysbury), Stai. 172 AX86
Nursery Waye, Uxb. 134 BK67
Nurserymans Rd N11 98 DG47
Nurstead Rd, Erith 166 FA80
Nut Gro, Welw.G.C. 29 CX06
Nut Tree Cl, Orp. 206 EX104
Nutberry Av, Grays 170 GA75
Nutberry Cl, Grays 170 GA75
Long La
Nutbourne St W10 139 CY69
Nutbrook St SE15 162 DU83
Nutbrowne Rd, Dag. 146 EZ67
Nutcombe La, Dor. 263 CF136
Nutcroft Gro (Fetcham), Lthd. 231 CE121
Nutcroft Rd SE15 162 DV80
Nutfield, Welw.G.C. 30 DA06
Nutfield Cl N18 100 DU51
Nutfield Cl, Cars. 200 DE104
Nutfield Gdns, Ilf. 125 ET61
Nutfield Gdns, Nthlt. 136 BW68
Nutfield Marsh Rd (Nutfield), Red. 251 DJ130
Nutfield Rd E15 123 EC63
Nutfield Rd NW2 119 CU61
Nutfield Rd SE22 182 DT85
Nutfield Rd, Couls. 234 DG116
Nutfield Rd, Red. 250 DG134
Nutfield Rd (South Merstham), Red. 251 DJ129
Nutfield Rd, Th.Hth. 201 DP98
Nutfield Way, Orp. 205 EN103
Nutford Pl W1 272 C8
Nutford Pl W1 140 DF72
Nuthatch Cl, Stai. 174 BM88
Nuthatch Gdns SE28 165 ER75
Nuthatch Gdns, Reig. 266 DC138
Nuthurst Av SW2 181 DM89
Nutkin Wk, Uxb. 134 BL66
Nutkins Way, Chesh. 54 AQ29
Nutley Cl, Swan. 207 FF95
Nutley Ct, Reig. 249 CZ134
Nutley La
Nutley La, Reig. 249 CZ133
Nutley Ter NW3 140 DC65
Nutmead Cl, Bex. 187 FC88
Nutmeg Cl E16 144 EE70
Cranberry La
Nutmeg La E14 143 ED72
Nutt Gro, Edg. 95 CK47
Nutt St SE15 162 DT80
Nuttall St N1 142 DS68
Nutter La E11 124 EJ58
Nuttfield Cl, Rick. 75 BP44
Nutty La, Shep. 195 BQ98
Nutwell St SW17 180 DE92
Nutwood Av (Brockham), Bet. 264 CQ135
Nutwood Cl (Brockham), Bet. 264 CQ135
Nutwood Gdns (Cheshunt), Wal.Cr. 66 DS26
Great Stockwood Rd
Nuxley Rd, Belv. 166 EZ79
Nyanza St SE18 165 ER79
Nye Bevan Est E5 123 DX62
Nye Way (Bovingdon), Hem.H. 57 BA28
Nyefield Pk, Tad. 249 CU126
Nylands Av, Rich. 158 CN81
Nymans Gdns SW20 199 CV97
Hidcote Gdns
Nynehead St SE14 163 DY80
Nyon Gro SE6 183 DZ89
Nyssa Cl, Wdf.Grn. 103 EM51
Gwynne Pk Av
Nyth Cl, Upmin. 129 FR58
Nyton Cl N19 121 DL60
Courtauld Rd

O

Oak Apple Ct SE12 184 EG89
Oak Av N8 121 DL56
Oak Av N10 99 DH52
Oak Av N17 100 DR52
Oak Av, Croy. 203 EA103
Oak Av, Egh. 173 BC94
Oak Av, Enf. 81 DM38
Oak Av, Hmptn. 176 BY92
Oak Av, Houns. 156 BX80
Oak Av (Bricket Wd), St.Alb. 60 CA30
Oak Av, Sev. 257 FH128
Oak Av, Upmin. 128 FP62
Oak Av, Uxb. 115 BP61
Oak Av, West Dr. 154 BN76
Oak Bk (New Addington), Croy. 221 EC107
Oak Cl N14 99 DH45
Oak Cl, Dart. 167 FE84
Oak Cl, Gdmg. 258 AS143
Oak Cl, Hem.H. 40 BM24

Oak Cl, Sutt. 200 DC103
Oak Cl, Tad. 248 CP130
Oak Cl, Wal.Abb. 67 ED34
Oak Cottage Cl SE6 184 EF88
Oak Cres E16 144 EE71
Oak Dene W13 137 CH71
The Dene
Oak Dr, Berk. 38 AX20
Oak Dr, Saw. 36 EW07
Oak Dr, Tad. 248 CP130
Oak End, Harl. 51 ET17
Oak End Dr, Iver 133 BC68
Oak End Way (Woodham), Add. 211 BE112
Oak End Way, Ger.Cr. 112 AY57
Oak Fm, Borwd. 78 CQ43
Oak Fld, Chesh. 54 AP30
Oak Gdns, Croy. 203 EA103
Oak Gdns, Edg. 96 CQ54
Oak Glade, Epp. 70 EX29
Coopersale Common
Oak Glade, Epsom 216 CN112
Christ Ch Rd
Oak Glade, Nthwd. 93 BP53
Oak Glen, Horn. 128 FL55
Oak Gra Rd (West Clandon), Guil. 244 BH128
Oak Grn, Abb.L. 59 BS32
Oak Grn Way, Abb.L. 59 BS32
Oak Gro NW2 119 CY63
Oak Gro, Hat. 45 CT18
Oak Gro, Hert. 32 DS11
Oak Gro, Ruis. 115 BV60
Oak Gro, Sun. 175 BV94
Oak Gro, W.Wick. 203 EC103
Oak Gro Rd SE20 202 DW95
Oak Hall Rd E11 124 EH58
Oak Hill, Epsom 232 CR116
Oak Hill (Burpham), Guil. 243 BC129
Oak Hill, Surb. 198 CL101
Oak Hill, Wdf.Grn. 101 ED52
Oak Hill Cl, Wdf.Grn. 101 ED52
Oak Hill Cres, Surb. 198 CL101
Oak Hill Cres, Wdf.Grn. 101 ED52
Oak Hill Gdns, Wdf.Grn. 102 EE53
Oak Hill Gro, Surb. 198 CL100
Oak Hill Pk NW3 120 DB63
Oak Hill Pk Ms NW3 120 DC63
Oak Hill Rd, Rom. 105 FD45
Oak Hill Rd, Sev. 256 FG124
Oak Hill Rd, Surb. 198 CL100
Oak Hill Way NW3 120 DC63
Oak La E14 143 DZ73
Oak La N2 98 DD54
Oak La N11 99 DK51
Oak La (Englefield Grn), Egh. 172 AW90
Oak La, Islw. 157 CE84
Oak La (Cuffley), Pot.B. 65 DM28
Oak La, Sev. 256 FG127
Oak La, Twick. 177 CG87
Oak La, Wind. 151 AN81
Oak La, Wok. 227 BC116
Beaufort Rd
Oak La, Wdf.Grn. 102 EF49
Oak Leaf Cl, Epsom 216 CQ112
Oak Lo Av, Chig. 103 ER50
Oak Lo Cl, Stan. 95 CJ50
Dennis La
Oak Lo Cl, Walt. 214 BW106
Oak Lo Dr, Red. 266 DG142
Oak Lo Dr, W.Wick. 203 EB101
Oak Lo La, West. 255 ER125
Oak Manor Dr, Wem. 118 CM64
Oakington Manor Dr
Oak Pk, W.Byf. 211 BE113
Oak Pk Gdns SW19 179 CX87
Oak Path, Bushey 76 CB44
Ashfield Av
Oak Piece, Epp. 71 FC25
Oak Pl SW18 180 DB85
East Hill
Oak Ridge, Dor. 263 CH139
Oak Ri, Buck.H. 102 EK48
Oak Rd W5 137 CK73
The Bdy
Oak Rd, Cat. 236 DS122
Oak Rd, Cob. 230 BX115
Oak Rd, Epp. 69 ET30
Oak Rd (Northumberland Heath), Erith 167 FC80
Oak Rd (Slade Grn), Erith 167 FG81
Oak Rd, Grav. 191 GJ90
Oak Rd, Grays 170 GC79
Oak Rd, Green. 189 FS86
Oak Rd, Lthd. 231 CG118
Oak Rd, N.Mal. 198 CR96
Oak Rd, Orp. 224 EU108
Oak Rd, Reig. 250 DB133
Oak Rd, Rom. 106 FM53
Oak Rd, West. 255 ER125
Oak Row SW16 201 DJ96
Oak Sq, Sev. 257 FJ126
High St
Oak St, Hem.H. 40 BM24
Oak St, Rom. 127 FC57
Oak Stubbs La, Maid. 150 AF75
Oak Tree Av (Bluewater), Green. 189 FT87
Oak Tree Cl W5 137 CJ72
Pinewood Gro
Oak Tree Cl, Abb.L. 59 BR32
Oak Tree Cl (Burpham), Guil. 243 BB129
Oak Tree Cl (Jacobs Well), Guil. 242 AW128
Oak Tree Cl, Hat. 45 CU17
Oak Tree Cl, Hert. 32 DW12
Oak Tree Cl, Loug. 85 EQ39
Oak Tree Cl, Stan. 95 CJ52
Oak Tree Cl, Vir.W. 192 AX101
Oak Tree Ct, Borwd. 77 CK44
Barnet La
Oak Tree Dell NW9 118 CQ57
Oak Tree Dr N20 98 DB46
Oak Tree Dr (Englefield Grn), Egh. 172 AW92
Oak Tree Dr, Guil. 242 AW130
Oak Tree Gdns, Brom. 184 EH92
Oak Tree Rd NW8 272 A3
Oak Tree Rd NW8 140 DE69
Oak Village NW5 120 DG63
Oak Wk, Saw. 36 EX07
Oak Way N14 99 DH45
Oak Way W3 138 CS74
Oak Way, Ash. 232 CN116
Oak Way, Croy. 203 DX100
Oak Way, Felt. 175 BS88
Oak Way, Reig. 266 DD135
Oakapple Cl, S.Croy. 220 DV114
Oakbank, Brwd. 109 GE43
Oakbank (Fetcham), Lthd. 230 CC123
Oakbank, Wok. 226 AY119
Oakbank Av, Walt. 196 BZ101
Oakbank Gro SE24 162 DQ84
Oakbrook Cl, Brom. 184 EH91
Oakbury Rd SW6 160 DB82
Oakcombe Cl, N.Mal. 198 CS95
Traps La
Oakcroft Cl, Pnr. 93 BV54
Oakcroft Cl, W.Byf. 211 BF114
Oakcroft Rd SE13 163 ED82
Oakcroft Rd, Chess. 216 CM105
Oakcroft Rd, W.Byf. 211 BF114
Oakcroft Vil, Chess. 216 CM105
Oakdale N14 99 DH46
Oakdale, Welw.G.C. 29 CW05
Oakdale Av, Har. 118 CL57
Oakdale Av, Nthwd. 93 BU54
Oakdale Cl, Wat. 94 BW49
Oakdale Gdns E4 101 EC50
Oakdale La, Eden. 255 EP133
Oakdale Rd E7 144 EH66
Oakdale Rd E11 123 ED61
Oakdale Rd E18 102 EH54
Oakdale Rd N4 122 DQ58
Oakdale Rd SE15 162 DW83
Oakdale Rd SW16 181 DL92
Oakdale Rd, Epsom 216 CR109
Oakdale Rd, Wat. 94 BW48
Oakdale Rd, Wey. 194 BN104
Oakdale Way, Mitch. 200 DG101
Wolseley Rd
Oakden St SE11 278 E8
Oakden St SE11 161 DN77
Oakdene SE15 162 DV81
Carlton Gro
Oakdene, Beac. 89 AL52
Oakdene, Rom. 106 FM54
Oakdene, Tad. 233 CY120
Oakdene (Cheshunt), Wal.Cr. 67 DY30
Oakdene (Chobham), Wok. 210 AT110
Oakdene Av, Chis. 185 EN92
Oakdene Av, Erith 167 FC79
Oakdene Av, T.Ditt. 197 CG102
Oakdene Cl (Brockham), Bet. 264 CQ136
Oakdene Cl, Horn. 127 FH58
Oakdene Cl (Bookham), Lthd. 246 CC127
Oakdene Cl, Pnr. 94 BZ52
Oakdene Dr, Surb. 198 CQ101
Oakdene Ms, Sutt. 199 CZ102
Oakdene Par, Cob. 213 BV114
Anyards Rd
Oakdene Pk N3 97 CZ52
Oakdene Rd (Brockham), Bet. 264 CQ136
Oakdene Rd, Cob. 213 BV114
Oakdene Rd (Peasmarsh), Guil. 258 AW142
Oakdene Rd, Hem.H. 40 BM24
Oakdene Rd (Bookham), Lthd. 230 BZ124
Oakdene Rd, Orp. 205 ET99
Oakdene Rd, Red. 250 DE134
Oakdene Rd, Sev. 256 FG122
Oakdene Rd, Uxb. 135 BP68
Oakdene Rd, Wat. 75 BV36
Oakdene Way, St.Alb. 43 CJ20
Oake Ct SW15 179 CY85
Oaken Coppice, Ash. 232 CN119
Oaken Dr (Claygate), Esher 215 CF107
Oaken Gro, Welw.G.C. 29 CY11
Oaken La (Claygate), Esher 215 CE106
Oakenholt Ho SE2 166 EX75
Hartslock Dr
Oakenshaw Cl, Surb. 198 CL101
Oakes Cl E6 145 EM72
Savage Gdns
Oakeshott Av N6 120 DG61
Oakey La SE1 278 D6
Oakey La SE1 161 DN76
Oakfield E4 101 EB50
Oakfield, Rick. 91 BF45
Oakfield, Wok. 226 AS116
Oakfield Av, Har. 117 CH55
Oakfield Av, Slou. 131 AP74
Oakfield Cl, Amer. 55 AQ37
Oakfield Cl, N.Mal. 199 CT99
Blakes La
Oakfield Cl, Pot.B. 63 CZ31
Oakfield Cl, Ruis. 115 BT58
Oakfield Cl, Wey. 213 BQ105
Oakfield Ct N8 121 DL59
Oakfield Ct NW2 119 CX59
Hendon Way
Oakfield Ct, Borwd. 78 CP41
Oakfield Dr, Reig. 250 DA132
Oakfield Gdns N18 100 DS49
Oakfield Gdns SE19 182 DS92
Oakfield Gdns, Beck. 203 EA99
Oakfield Gdns, Cars. 200 DE102
Oakfield Gdns, Grnf. 137 CD70
Oakfield Glade, Wey. 213 BQ105
Oakfield La, Bex. 187 FE89
Oakfield La, Dart. 187 FG89
Oakfield La, Kes. 222 EJ105
Oakfield Pk Rd, Dart. 188 FK89
Oakfield Pl, Dart. 188 FK89
Oakfield Rd E6 144 EL67
Oakfield Rd E17 101 DY54
Oakfield Rd N3 98 DB53
Oakfield Rd N4 121 DN58
Oakfield Rd N14 99 DL48
Oakfield Rd SE20 182 DV94
Oakfield Rd SW19 179 CX90
Oakfield Rd, Ashf. 175 BP92
Oakfield Rd, Ash. 231 CK117
Oakfield Rd, Cob. 213 BV113
Oakfield Rd, Croy. 202 DQ102
Oakfield Rd, Ilf. 125 EP61
Oakfield Rd, Orp. 206 EU101
Goodmead Rd
Oakfield St SW10 160 DC79
Oakfields, Guil. 242 AS132
Oakfields, Sev. 257 FH126
Oakfields, Walt. 195 BU102
Oakfields, W.Byf. 212 BH114
Oakfields Rd NW11 119 CY58
Oakford Rd NW5 121 DJ63
Oakhall Ct E11 124 EH58
Oakhall Dr, Sun. 175 BT92
Oakham Cl SE6 183 DZ89
Rutland Wk
Oakham Cl, Barn. 80 DF41
Oakham Dr, Brom. 204 EF98
Oakhampton Rd NW7 97 CX52
Oakhill (Claygate), Esher 215 CG107
Oakhill Av NW3 120 DB63
Oakhill Av, Pnr. 94 BY54
Oakhill Cl, Ash. 231 CJ118
Oakhill Cl, Rick. 91 BE49
Oakhill Ct SW19 179 CX94
Oakhill Dr, Surb. 198 CL101
Oakhill Gdns, Wey. 195 BS103
Oakhill Path, Surb. 198 CL100
Oakhill Pl SW15 180 DA85
Oakhill Rd
Oakhill Rd SW15 179 CZ85
Oakhill Rd SW16 201 DL95
Oakhill Rd, Add. 211 BF107
Oakhill Rd, Ash. 231 CJ118
Oakhill Rd, Beck. 203 EC96
Oakhill Rd, Orp. 205 ET102
Oakhill Rd, Purf. 168 FP78
Oakhill Rd, Reig. 266 DB135
Oakhill Rd, Rick. 91 BD49
Oakhill Rd, Sutt. 200 DB104
Oakhouse Rd, Bexh. 186 FA85
Oakhurst (Chobham), Wok. 210 AS109
Oakhurst Av, Barn. 98 DE45
Oakhurst Av, Bexh. 166 EY80
Oakhurst Cl E17 124 EE56
Oakhurst Cl, Chis. 205 EM95
Oakhurst Cl, Ilf. 103 EQ53
Oakhurst Cl, Tedd. 177 CE92
Oakhurst Gdns E4 102 EF46
Oakhurst Gdns E17 124 EE56
Oakhurst Gdns, Bexh. 166 EY80
Oakhurst Gro SE22 162 DU84
Oakhurst Pl, Wat. 75 BT42
Cherrydale
Oakhurst Ri, Cars. 218 DE110
Oakhurst Rd, Enf. 83 DX36
Oakhurst Rd, Epsom 216 CQ107
Oakington, Welw.G.C. 30 DD08
Oakington Av, Amer. 72 AY39
Oakington Av, Har. 116 CA59
Oakington Av, Hayes 155 BR77
Oakington Av, Wem. 118 CM62
Oakington Dr, Sun. 196 BW96
Oakington Manor Dr, Wem. 118 CN64
Oakington Rd W9 140 DA70
Oakington Way N8 121 DL58
Oakland Gdns, Brwd. 109 GC43
Oakland Pl, Buck.H. 102 EG47
Oakland Rd E15 123 ED63
Oakland Way, Epsom 216 CR107
Oaklands N21 99 DM47
Oaklands, Berk. 38 AU19
Oaklands, Horl. 269 DJ148
Oaklands, Ken. 220 DQ114
Oaklands (Fetcham), Lthd. 231 CD124
Oaklands, Twick. 176 CC87
Oaklands Av N9 82 DV44
Oaklands Av, Esher 197 CD102
Oaklands Av, Hat. 63 CY27
Oaklands Av, Islw. 157 CF79
Oaklands Av, Rom. 127 FE55
Oaklands Av, Sid. 185 ET87
Oaklands Av, Th.Hth. 201 DN98
Oaklands Av, Wat. 93 BV46
Oaklands Av, W.Wick. 203 EB104
Oaklands Cl, Bexh. 186 EZ85
Oaklands Cl, Chess. 215 CJ105
Oaklands Cl (Shalford), Guil. 258 AY142
Oaklands Cl, Orp. 205 ES100
Oaklands Ct, Add. 194 BH104
Oaklands Ct, Wat. 75 BU39
Oaklands Ct, Wem. 117 CK64
Oaklands Dr, Harl. 52 EW16
Oaklands Dr, Red. 267 DH136
Oaklands Dr, S.Ock. 149 FW71
Oaklands Est SW4 181 DJ86
Oaklands Gdns, Ken. 220 DQ114
Oaklands Gate, Nthwd. 93 BS51
Green La
Oaklands Gro W12 139 CU74
Oaklands Gro, Brox. 49 DY24
Oaklands La, Barn. 79 CV42
Oaklands La (Smallford), St.Alb. 44 CL18
Oaklands La (Biggin Hill), West. 222 EH113
Oaklands Pk Av, Ilf. 125 ER61
High Rd
Oaklands Pl SW4 161 DJ84
St. Alphonsus Rd
Oaklands Rd N20 97 CZ45
Oaklands Rd NW2 119 CX63
Oaklands Rd SW14 158 CR83
Oaklands Rd W7 157 CF75
Oaklands Rd, Bexh. 166 EZ84
Oaklands Rd, Brom. 184 EE94
Oaklands Rd, Dart. 188 FP88
Oaklands Rd (Northfleet), Grav. 191 GF91
Oaklands Rd (Cheshunt), Wal.Cr. 66 DS26
Oaklands Way, Tad. 233 CW122
Oaklands Way, Wall. 219 DK108
Oaklands Wd, Hat. 45 CU20
Woods Av
Oaklawn Rd, Lthd. 231 CE118
Oaklea Pas, Kings.T. 197 CK97
Oakleafe Gdns, Ilf. 125 EP55
Oakleigh Av N20 98 DD47
Oakleigh Av, Edg. 96 CP54
Oakleigh Av, Surb. 198 CN102
Oakleigh Cl N20 98 DF48
Oakleigh Cl, Swan. 207 FE97
Oakleigh Ct, Barn. 80 DE44
Church Hill Rd
Oakleigh Ct, Edg. 96 CQ54
Oakleigh Cres N20 98 DE48
Oakleigh Dr, Rick. 75 BQ44
Oakleigh Gdns N20 98 DC46
Oakleigh Gdns, Edg. 96 CM50
Oakleigh Gdns, Orp. 223 ES105
Oakleigh Ms N20 98 DC47
Oakleigh Rd N
Oakleigh Pk Av, Chis. 205 EN95
Oakleigh Pk N N20 98 DD46
Oakleigh Pk S N20 98 DE47
Oakleigh Ri, Epp. 70 EU32
Bower Hill
Oakleigh Rd, Pnr. 94 BZ51
Oakleigh Rd, Uxb. 135 BQ66
Oakleigh Rd N N20 98 DD47
Oakleigh Rd S N11 98 DG48
Oakleigh Way, Mitch. 201 DH95
Oakleigh Way, Surb. 198 CN102
Oakley Av W5 138 CN73
Oakley Av, Bark. 145 ET66
Oakley Av, Croy. 219 DL105
Oakley Cl E4 101 EC48
Oakley Cl E6 144 EL72
Northumberland Rd
Oakley Cl W7 137 CE73
Oakley Cl, Add. 212 BK105
Oakley Cl, Grays 169 FW79
Oakley Cl, Islw. 157 CD81
Oakley Ct, Loug. 85 EN40
Hillyfields
Oakley Ct, Mitch. 200 DG102
London Rd
Oakley Cres EC1 274 G1
Oakley Cres, Slou. 132 AS73
Oakley Dell, Guil. 243 BC132
Oakley Dr SE9 185 ER88
Oakley Dr SE13 183 EC85
Hither Grn La
Oakley Dr, Brom. 204 EL104
Oakley Dr, Rom. 106 FN50
Oakley Gdns N8 121 DM57
Oakley Gdns SW3 160 DE79
Oakley Gdns, Bans. 234 DB115
Oakley Grn Rd (Oakley Grn), Wind. 150 AG82
Oakley Pk, Bex. 186 EW87
Oakley Pl SE1 162 DT78
Oakley Rd N1 142 DR66
Oakley Rd SE25 202 DV99
Oakley Rd, Brom. 204 EL104
Oakley Rd, Har. 117 CE58
Oakley Rd, Warl. 236 DU118
Oakley Sq NW1 141 DJ68
Oakley St SW3 160 DE79
Oakley Wk W6 159 CX79
Oakley Yd E2 142 DT70
Bacon St
Oakmead Av, Brom. 204 EG100
Oakmead Gdns, Edg. 96 CR49
Oakmead Grn, Epsom 232 CP115
Oakmead Pl, Mitch. 200 DE95
Oakmead Rd SW12 180 DG88
Oakmead Rd, Croy. 201 DK100
Oakmeade, Pnr. 94 CA51
Oakmere Av, Pot.B. 64 DC33
Oakmere Cl, Pot.B. 64 DD31
Oakmere La, Pot.B. 64 DC32
Oakmere Rd SE2 166 EU79
Oakmoor Way, Chig. 103 ES50
Oakmount Pl, Orp. 205 ER102
Oakridge (Bricket Wd), St.Alb. 60 BZ29
Oakridge Av, Rad. 61 CF34
Oakridge Dr N2 120 DD55
Oakridge La, Brom. 183 ED92
Downham Way
Oakridge La, Rad. 61 CF33
Oakridge La, Wat. 77 CD35
Oakridge Rd, Brom. 183 ED91
Oakroyd Av, Pot.B. 63 CZ33
Oakroyd Cl, Pot.B. 63 CZ34
Oaks, The N12 98 DB49
Oaks, The SE18 165 EQ78
Oaks, The, Berk. 38 AU19
Oaks, The, Epsom 217 CT114
Oaks, The, Hayes 135 BQ68
Charville La
Oaks, The, Ruis. 115 BS59
Oaks, The, Stai. 173 BF91
Moormede Cres
Oaks, The, Swan. 207 FE96
Oaks, The, Tad. 233 CW123
Oaks, The, Wat. 94 BW46
Oaks, The, W.Byf. 212 BG113
Oaks, The, Wdf.Grn. 102 EE51
Oaks Av SE19 182 DS92
Oaks Av, Felt. 176 BY89
Oaks Av, Rom. 105 FC54
Oaks Av, Wor.Pk. 199 CV104
Oaks Cl, Lthd. 231 CG121
Oaks Cl, Rad. 77 CF35
Oaks Gro E4 102 EE47
Oaks La, Croy. 202 DW104
Oaks La (Mid Holmwood), Dor. 263 CH143
Oaks La, Ilf. 125 ES57
Oaks Rd, Croy. 220 DV106
Oaks Rd, Ken. 219 DP114
Oaks Rd, Reig. 250 DC133
Oaks Rd (Stanwell), Stai. 174 BK86
Oaks Rd, Wok. 226 AY117
Oaks Track, Cars. 218 DF111
Oaks Track, Wall. 219 DH110
Oaks Way, Cars. 218 DF108
Oaks Way, Epsom 233 CV119
Epsom La N
Oaks Way, Ken. 220 DQ114
Oaks Way, Surb. 197 CK103
Oaksford Av SE26 182 DV90
Oakshade Rd, Brom. 183 ED91
Oakshade Rd (Oxshott), Lthd. 214 CC114
Oakshaw, Oxt. 253 ED127
Oakshaw Rd SW18 180 DB87
Oakside (Denham), Uxb. 134 BH65
Oakside Ct, Horl. 269 DJ147
Oakside La
Oakside La, Horl. 269 DJ147
Oakthorpe Rd N13 99 DN50
Oaktree Av N13 99 DP48
Oaktree Cl, Brwd. 109 FZ49
Hawthorn Av
Oaktree Cl, Wal.Cr. 65 DP28
Oaktree Garth, Welw.G.C. 29 CY10
Oaktree Gro, Ilf. 125 ER64
Oakview Cl, Wal.Cr. 66 DV28
Oakview Gdns N2 120 DD56
Oakview Gro, Croy. 203 DY102
Oakview Rd SE6 183 EB92
Oakway SW20 199 CW98
Oakway, Amer. 55 AP35
Oakway, Brom. 203 ED96
Oakway, Wok. 226 AS119
Oakway Cl, Bex. 186 EY86
Oakway Pl, Rad. 61 CG34
Watling St
Oakways SE9 185 EP86
Oakwell Dr, Pot.B. 65 DH32
Oakwood, Berk. 38 AT20
Oakwood, Guil. 242 AU129
Oakwood, Wall. 219 DH109
Oakwood, Wal.Abb. 83 ED35
Roundhills
Oakwood Av N14 99 DK45
Oakwood Av, Beck. 203 EC96
Oakwood Av, Borwd. 78 CP42
Oakwood Av, Brwd. 109 GE44
Oakwood Av, Brom. 204 EH97
Oakwood Av, Mitch. 200 DD96
Oakwood Av, Pur. 219 DP112
Oakwood Av, Sthl. 136 CA73
Oakwood Chase, Horn. 128 FM58
Oakwood Cl N14 81 DJ44
Oakwood Cl, Chis. 185 EM93
Oakwood Cl, Dart. 188 FP88
Oakwood Cl (East Horsley), Lthd. 245 BS127
Oakwood Cl, Red. 250 DG134
Oakwood Cl (South Nutfield), Red. 267 DM136
The Av
Oakwood Cl, Wdf.Grn. 102 EL51
Green Wk
Oakwood Ct W14 159 CZ76
Oakwood Cres N21 81 DL44
Oakwood Cres, Grnf. 137 CG65
Oakwood Dr SE19 182 DR93
Oakwood Dr, Bexh. 167 FD84
Oakwood Dr, Edg. 96 CQ51
Oakwood Dr (East Horsley), Lthd. 245 BS127
Oakwood Dr, St.Alb. 43 CJ19
Oakwood Dr, Sev. 257 FH123
Oakwood Gdns, Ilf. 125 ET61
Oakwood Gdns, Orp. 205 EQ103
Oakwood Gdns, Sutt. 200 DA103
Oakwood Hill, Loug. 85 EM44
Oakwood Hill Ind Est, Loug. 85 EQ43
Oakwood La W14 159 CZ76
Oakwood Pk Rd N14 99 DK45
Oakwood Pl, Croy. 201 DN100
Oakwood Ri, Cat. 252 DS125
Oakwood Rd NW11 120 DB57
Oakwood Rd SW20 199 CU95
Oakwood Rd, Croy. 201 DN100
Oakwood Rd, Horl. 268 DG147
Oakwood Rd, Orp. 205 EQ103
Oakwood Rd, Pnr. 93 BV54
Oakwood Rd (Merstham), Red. 251 DN129
Oakwood Rd (Bricket Wd), St.Alb. 60 BZ29
Oakwood Rd, Vir.W. 192 AW99
Oakwood Rd, Wok. 226 AS119
Oakwood Vw N14 81 DK44
Oakworth Rd W10 139 CW71
Oarsman Pl, E.Mol. 197 CE98
Oast Ho Cl (Wraysbury), Stai. 172 AY87
Oast Rd, Oxt. 254 EF131
Oasthouse Way, Orp. 206 EV98
Oat La EC2 275 H8
Oat La EC2 142 DQ72
Oates Cl, Brom. 203 ED97
Oates Rd, Rom. 105 FB50
Oatfield Ho N15 122 DS58
Bushey Rd
Oatfield Rd, Orp. 205 ET102
Oatfield Rd, Tad. 233 CV120
Oatland Ri E17 101 DY54
Oatlands, Horl. 269 DH147
Oatlands Av, Wey. 213 BR106
Oatlands Chase, Wey. 195 BS104
Oatlands Cl, Wey. 213 BQ105
Oatlands Dr, Slou. 131 AR72
Oatlands Dr, Wey. 195 BR104
Oatlands Grn, Wey. 195 BR104
Oatlands Dr
Oatlands Mere, Wey. 195 BR104
Oatlands Rd, Enf. 82 DW39
Oatlands Rd, Tad. 233 CY119
Oban Cl E13 144 EJ70
Oban Ct, Slou. 151 AR75
Montem La
Oban Ho, Bark. 145 ER68
Wheelers Cross
Oban Rd E13 144 EJ69
Oban Rd SE25 202 DR98
Oban St E14 143 ED72
Obelisk Ride, Egh. 172 AS93
Oberon Cl, Borwd. 78 CQ39
Oberon Way, Shep. 194 BL97
Oberstein Rd SW11 160 DD84
Oborne Cl SE24 181 DP85
Observatory Gdns W8 160 DA75
Observatory Ms E14 163 ED77
Storers Quay
Observatory Rd SW14 158 CQ84
Observatory Wk, Red. 250 DF134
Lower Br Rd
Occupation La SE18 165 EP81
Occupation La W5 157 CK77
Occupation Rd SE17 279 H10
Occupation Rd SE17 162 DQ78
Occupation Rd W13 157 CH75
Occupation Rd, Wat. 75 BV43
Ocean Est E1 143 DX70
Ocean St E1 143 DX71
Ocean Wf E14 163 EA75
Ockenden Cl, Wok. 227 AZ118
Ockenden Rd
Ockenden Gdns, Wok. 227 AZ118
Ockenden Rd
Ockenden Rd, Wok. 227 AZ118
Ockendon Ms N1 142 DR65
Ockendon Rd
Ockendon Rd N1 142 DR65
Ockendon Rd, Upmin. 128 FQ64
Ockham Dr (West Horsley), Lthd. 229 BR124
Ockham Dr, Orp. 186 EU94
Ockham La, Cob. 229 BT118
Ockham La (Ockham), Wok. 229 BP120
Ockham Rd N, Lthd. 229 BQ124
Ockham Rd N (Ockham), Wok. 228 BN121
Ockham Rd S (East Horsley), Lthd. 245 BS126
Ockley Ct, Guil. 243 BB129
Cotts Wd Dr
Ockley Ct, Sutt. 218 DC105
Oakhill Rd
Ockley Rd SW16 181 DL90
Ockley Rd, Croy. 201 DM101
Ockleys Mead, Gdse. 252 DW129
Octagon Arc EC2 275 M7
Octagon Rd, Walt. 213 BS109
Octavia Cl, Mitch. 200 DE99
Octavia Rd, Islw. 157 CF82
Octavia St SW11 160 DE81
Octavia Way SE28 146 EV73
Booth Cl
Octavia Way, Stai. 174 BG93
Octavius St SE8 163 EA80
Odard Rd, W.Mol. 196 CA98
Down St
Oddesey Rd, Borwd. 78 CP39
Odell Cl, Bark. 145 ET66
Odencroft Rd, Slou. 131 AN69
Odessa Rd E7 124 EF63
Odessa Rd NW10 139 CU68
Odessa St SE16 163 DZ75
Odger St SW11 160 DF82
Odhams Wk WC2 273 P9
Odyssey Business Pk, Ruis. 115 BV64
Offa Rd, St.Alb. 42 CC20
Offa's Mead E9 123 DY63
Lindisfarne Way
Offenbach Ho E2 143 DX68
Offenham Rd SE9 185 EM91
Offers Ct, Kings.T. 198 CM97
Winery La
Offerton Rd SW4 161 DJ83
Offham Slope N12 97 CZ50
Offley Pl, Islw. 157 CD82
Offley Rd SW9 161 DN80
Offord Cl N17 100 DU52
Offord Rd N1 141 DM66
Offord St N1 141 DM66
Ogard Rd, Hodd. 49 EC15
Ogilby St SE18 165 EM77
Oglander Rd SE15 162 DT84
Ogle St W1 273 K6
Ogle St W1 141 DJ71
Oglethorpe Rd, Dag. 126 EZ62
Ohio Rd E13 144 EF70

Oil Mill La W6 159 CU78
Okeburn Rd SW17 180 DG92
Okehampton Cl N12 98 DD50
Okehampton Cres, Well. 166 EV81
Okehampton Rd NW10 139 CW67
Okehampton Rd, Rom. 106 FJ51
Okehampton Sq, Rom. 106 FJ51
Okemore Gdns, Orp. 206 EW98
Olaf St W11 139 CX73
Old Acre, Wok. 212 BG114
Old Amersham Rd, Ger.Cr. 113 BB60
Old Av, W.Byf. 211 BE113
Old Av, Wey. 213 BR107
Old Av Cl, W.Byf. 211 BE113
Old Bailey EC4 274 G9
Old Bailey EC4 141 DP72
Old Bakery Ms (Albury), Guil. 260 BH139
Old Barge Ho All SE1 141 DN74
Upper Grd
Old Barn Cl, Sutt. 217 CY108
Old Barn La, Ken. 236 DT116
Old Barn La, Rick. 74 BM43
Old Barn Rd, Epsom 232 CQ117
Old Barn Way, Bexh. 167 FD83
Old Barrack Yd SW1 276 F5
Old Barrowfield E15 144 EE67
New Plaistow Rd
Old Bath Rd (Colnbrook), Slou. 153 BE81
Old Beaconsfield Rd (Farnham Common), Slou. 131 AQ65
Old Bell Ct, Hem.H. 40 BK19
George St
Old Bellgate Wf E14 163 EA76
Old Bethnal Grn Rd E2 142 DU69
Old Bexley La, Bex. 187 FD89
Old Bexley La, Dart. 187 FF88
Old Billingsgate Wk EC3 142 DS72
Lower Thames St
Old Bond St W1 277 K1
Old Bond St W1 141 DJ73
Old Brewers Yd WC2 273 P9
Old Brewery Ms NW3 120 DD63
Hampstead High St
Old Br Cl, Nthlt. 136 CA68
Old Br St, Kings.T. 197 CK96
Old Broad St EC2 275 L9
Old Broad St EC2 142 DR72
Old Bromley Rd, Brom. 183 ED92
Old Brompton Rd SW5 160 DA78
Old Brompton Rd SW7 160 DA78
Old Bldgs WC2 274 D8
Old Burlington St W1 273 K10
Old Burlington St W1 141 DJ73
Old Carriageway, The, Sev. 256 FC123
Old Castle St E1 275 P8
Old Castle St E1 142 DT72
Old Cavendish St W1 273 H8
Old Cavendish St W1 141 DH72
Old Change Ct EC4 142 DQ72
Carter La
Old Chapel Rd, Swan. 207 FC101
Old Char Wf, Dor. 263 CF135
Old Charlton Rd, Shep. 195 BQ99
Old Chelsea Ms SW3 160 DD79
Danvers St
Old Chertsey Rd (Chobham), Wok. 210 AV110
Old Chestnut Av, Esher 214 CA107
Old Chorleywood Rd, Rick. 74 BK44
Chorleywood Rd
Old Ch La NW9 118 CQ61
Old Ch La, Brwd. 109 GE42
Old Ch La, Grnf. 137 CG69
Perivale La
Old Ch La, Stan. 95 CJ52
Old Ch Path, Esher 214 CB105
High St
Old Ch Rd E1 143 DX72
Old Ch Rd E4 101 EA49
Old Ch St SW3 160 DD78
Old Claygate La (Claygate), Esher 215 CG107
Old Clem Sq SE18 165 EN79
Kempt St
Old Coach Rd, Cher. 193 BD99
Old Coach Rd, The, Hert. 30 DF12
Old Common Rd, Cob. 213 BU112
Old Compton St W1 273 M10
Old Compton St W1 141 DK73
Old Cote Dr, Houns. 156 CA79
Old Ct, Ash. 232 CL119
Old Ct Grn, Berk. 39 BC17
Hempstead La
Old Ct Pl W8 160 DB75
Old Ct Rd, Guil. 258 AU135
Old Crabtree La, Hem.H. 40 BL21
Old Cross, Hert. 32 DQ09
Old Dairy Ms SW12 180 DG87
Chestnut Gro
Old Dartford Rd (Farningham), Dart. 208 FM100
Old Dean (Bovingdon), Hem.H. 57 BA27
Old Deer Pk Gdns, Rich. 158 CL83
Old Devonshire Rd SW12 181 DH87
Old Dock App Rd, Grays 170 GE77
Old Dock Cl, Rich. 158 CN79
Watcombe Cotts
Old Dover Rd SE3 164 EH80
Old Dr, The, Welw.G.C. 29 CV10
Old Epsom Rd (East Clandon), Guil. 244 BK131
Old Esher Cl, Walt. 214 BX106
Old Esher Rd
Old Esher Rd, Walt. 214 BX106
Old Farleigh Rd, S.Croy. 220 DW110
Old Farleigh Rd, Warl. 221 DY113
Old Fm Av N14 99 DJ45
Old Fm Av, Sid. 185 ER88
Old Fm Cl (Knotty Grn), Beac. 88 AJ50
Old Fm Cl, Houns. 156 BZ84
Old Fm Gdns, Swan. 207 FF97
Old Fm Pas, Hmptn. 196 CC95
Old Fm Rd N2 98 DD53
Old Fm Rd, Guil. 242 AX131
Old Fm Rd, Hmptn. 176 BZ93
Old Fm Rd, West Dr. 154 BK75
Old Fm Rd E, Sid. 186 EU89
Old Fm Rd W, Sid. 185 ET89
Old Farmhouse Dr (Oxshott), Lthd. 231 CD115
Old Ferry Dr (Wraysbury), Stai. 172 AW86
Old Fld Cl, Amer. 72 AY39
Old Fish St Hill EC4 275 H10
Old Fishery La, Hem.H. 39 BF22
Old Fives Ct (Burnham), Slou. 130 AH69
Old Fleet La EC4 274 F8
Old Fold Cl, Barn. 79 CZ39
Old Fold La
Old Fold La, Barn. 79 CZ39
Old Fold Vw, Barn. 79 CW41
Old Ford Rd E2 142 DW68
Old Ford Rd E3 143 DY68
Old Forge Cl, Stan. 95 CG49
Old Forge Cl, Wat. 59 BU33
Old Forge Cl, Welw.G.C. 29 CZ05
Old Forge Cres, Shep. 195 BP100
Old Forge Ms W12 159 CV75
Goodwin Rd
Old Forge Rd, Enf. 82 DT38
Old Forge Rd (Loudwater), H.Wyc. 88 AC53
Old Forge Way, Sid. 186 EV91
Old Fox Cl, Cat. 235 DP121
Old Fox Footpath, S.Croy. 220 DS108
Essenden Rd
Old French Horn La, Hat. 45 CW17
Old Gannon Cl, Nthwd. 93 BQ50
Old Gdn, The, Sev. 256 FD123
Old Gdn Ct, St.Alb. 42 CC20
Old Gloucester St WC1 274 A6
Old Gloucester St WC1 141 DL71
Old Gro Cl (Cheshunt), Wal.Cr. 66 DR26
Old Hall Cl, Pnr. 94 BY53
Old Hall Dr, Pnr. 94 BY53
Old Hall Ri, Harl. 52 EY15
Old Hall St, Hert. 32 DR09
Old Harpenden Rd, St.Alb. 43 CE17
Old Harrow La, West. 239 EQ119
Old Hatch Manor, Ruis. 115 BT59
Old Herns La, Welw.G.C. 30 DC07
Herns La
Old Hertford Rd, Hat. 45 CW16
Old Highway, Hodd. 33 EB14
Old Hill, Chis. 205 EN95
Old Hill, Orp. 223 ER107
Old Hill, Wok. 226 AX120
Old Homesdale Rd, Brom. 204 EJ98
Old Hosp Cl SW12 180 DF88
Old Ho Cl SW19 179 CY92
Old Ho Cl, Epsom 217 CT110
Old Ho Ct, Hem.H. 40 BM20
Old Ho Gdns, Twick. 177 CJ85
Old Ho La, Harl. 50 EK18
Old Ho La, Kings L. 74 BL35
Old Ho La, Wal.Abb. 50 EF23
Old Ho Rd, Hem.H. 40 BM20
Old Howlett's La, Ruis. 115 BQ58
Old Jamaica Rd SE16 162 DU76
Old James St SE15 162 DV83
Old Jewry EC2 275 K9
Old Jewry EC2 142 DR72
Old Kent Rd SE1 279 M8
Old Kent Rd SE1 162 DS77
Old Kent Rd SE15 162 DS77
Old Kenton La NW9 118 CP57
Old Kiln La (Brockham), Bet. 264 CQ135
Old Kiln Rd (Penn), H.Wyc. 88 AC45
Old Kingston Rd, Wor.Pk. 198 CQ104
Old La, Cob. 229 BP117
Old La (Tatsfield), West. 238 EK121
Old La Gdns, Cob. 229 BT122
Old Leys, Hat. 45 CU22
Old Lo Dr, Beac. 89 AL54
Old Lo La, Ken. 235 DN115
Old Lo La, Pur. 219 DM114
Old Lo Pl, Twick. 177 CH86
St. Margarets Rd
Old Lo Way, Stan. 95 CG50
Old London Rd (Mickleham), Dor. 247 CJ127
Old London Rd, Epsom 233 CU118
Old London Rd, Hert. 32 DS09
Old London Rd, Lthd. 245 BU126
Old London Rd, St.Alb. 43 CD21
Old London Rd (Badgers Mt), Sev. 224 FA110
Old London Rd (Knockholt Pound), Sev. 240 EY115
Old Long Gro, Beac. 89 AQ51
Old Maidstone Rd, Sid. 186 EZ94
Old Malden La, Wor.Pk. 198 CR103
Old Malt Way, Wok. 226 AX117
Old Manor Dr, Grav. 191 GJ88
Old Manor Dr, Islw. 176 CC86
Old Manor Gdns (Chilworth), Guil. 259 BD140
Old Manor Ho Ms, Shep. 194 BN97
Squires Br Rd
Old Manor La (Chilworth), Guil. 259 BC140
Old Manor Rd, Sthl. 156 BW77
Old Manor Way, Bexh. 167 FD82
Old Manor Way, Chis. 185 EM92
Old Manor Yd SW5 160 DB77
Earls Ct Rd
Old Mkt Sq E2 142 DT69
Diss St
Old Marsh La, Maid. 150 AF75
Old Marylebone Rd NW1 272 C7
Old Marylebone Rd NW1 140 DE71
Old Mead (Chalfont St. Peter), Ger.Cr. 90 AY51
Old Meadow Cl, Berk. 38 AU21
Old Merrow St, Guil. 243 BC131
Old Ms, Har. 117 CE57
Hindes Rd
Old Mill Cl (Eynsford), Dart. 208 FL102
Old Mill Ct E18 124 EJ55
Old Mill Gdns, Berk. 38 AX20
London Rd
Old Mill La, Maid. 150 AC76
Old Mill La, Red. 251 DH128
Old Mill La, Uxb. 134 BH72
Old Mill Pl, Rom. 127 FD58
Old Mill Rd SE18 165 ER79
Old Mill Rd, Kings L. 59 BQ33
Old Mill Rd (Denham), Uxb. 114 BG62
Old Mitre Ct EC4 141 DN72
Fleet St
Old Montague St E1 142 DU71
Old Moor La, H.Wyc. 110 AE55
Old Nazeing Rd, Brox. 49 EA21
Old Nichol St E2 275 P4
Old Nichol St E2 142 DT70
Old N St WC1 274 B6
Old Nursery Ct (Hedgerley), Slou. 111 AQ61
Old Oak Av, Couls. 234 DE119
Old Oak Cl, Chess. 216 CM105
Old Oak Common La NW10 138 CS70
Old Oak Common La W3 138 CS71
Old Oak La NW10 138 CS69
Old Oak Rd W3 139 CT73
Old Oaks, Wal.Abb. 68 EE32
Old Orchard, Harl. 51 ER17
Old Orchard (Park St), St.Alb. 60 CC26
Old Orchard, Sun. 196 BW96
Old Orchard (Byfleet), W.Byf. 212 BM112
Old Orchard, The NW3 120 DF63
Nassington Rd
Old Orchard Cl, Barn. 80 DD38
Old Orchard Cl, Uxb. 134 BN72
Old Orchard Ms, Berk. 38 AW20
Old Otford Rd, Sev. 241 FH117
Old Palace, The, Hat. 45 CX18
Old Palace La, Rich. 177 CJ85
Old Palace Rd, Croy. 201 DP104
Old Palace Rd, Guil. 258 AU135
Old Palace Rd, Wey. 195 BP104
Old Palace Ter, Rich. 177 CK85
King St
Old Palace Yd SW1 277 P6
Old Palace Yd SW1 161 DL76
Old Palace Yd, Rich. 177 CJ85
Old Paradise St SE11 278 B8
Old Paradise St SE11 161 DM77
Old Pk Av SW12 180 DG86
Old Pk Av, Enf. 82 DQ42
Old Pk Gro, Enf. 82 DQ42
Old Pk La W1 276 G3
Old Pk La W1 140 DG74
Old Pk Ms, Houns. 156 BZ80
Old Pk Ride, Wal.Cr. 66 DT33
Old Pk Ridings N21 81 DP44
Old Pk Rd N13 99 DM49
Old Pk Rd SE2 166 EU78
Old Pk Rd, Enf. 81 DP41
Old Pk Rd S, Enf. 81 DP42
Old Pk Vw, Enf. 81 DN41
Old Parkbury La (Colney St), St.Alb. 61 CF30
Old Parvis Rd, W.Byf. 212 BK112
Old Perry St, Chis. 185 ES94
Old Perry St (Northfleet), Grav. 190 GE89
Old Polhill, Sev. 241 FD115
Old Portsmouth Rd, Gdmg. 258 AV142
Old Portsmouth Rd, Guil. 258 AV142
Old Pottery Cl, Reig. 266 DB136
Old Pound Cl, Islw. 157 CG81
Old Priory (Harefield), Uxb. 115 BP59
Old Pye St SW1 277 M6
Old Pye St SW1 161 DK76
Old Quebec St W1 272 E9
Old Quebec St W1 140 DF72
Old Queen St SW1 277 N5
Old Queen St SW1 161 DK75
Old Rectory Cl, Tad. 233 CU124
Old Rectory Dr, Hat. 45 CV18
Old Rectory Gdns, Edg. 96 CN51
Old Rectory La (East Horsley), Lthd. 245 BS126
Old Rectory La (Denham), Uxb. 113 BE59
Old Rectory Rd, Ong. 71 FH34
Old Redding, Har. 94 CC49
Old Redstone Dr, Red. 266 DG135
Philanthropic Rd
Old Reigate Rd, Bet. 248 CP134
Old Reigate Rd, Dor. 248 CL134
Old Rd SE13 164 EE84
Old Rd, Add. 211 BF108
Old Rd (Buckland), Bet. 248 CR134
Old Rd, Dart. 167 FD84
Old Rd, Enf. 82 DW39
Old Rd, Harl. 36 EX11
Old Rd E, Grav. 191 GH88
Old Rd W, Grav. 191 GF88
Old Rope Wk, Sun. 195 BV97
The Av
Old Royal Free Pl N1 141 DN67
Liverpool Rd
Old Royal Free Sq N1 141 DN67
Old Ruislip Rd, Nthlt. 136 BX68
Old St. Mary's (West Horsley), Lthd. 245 BP129
Ripley La
Old Savill's Cotts, Chig. 103 EQ49
The Chase
Old Sch Cl SW19 200 DA96
Old Sch Cl, Beck. 203 DX96
Old Sch Ct (Wraysbury), Stai. 172 AY87
Old Sch Cres E7 144 EF65
Old Sch La (Brockham), Bet. 264 CN138
Old Sch Ms, Wey. 213 BR105
Old Sch Pl, Wok. 226 AY121
Old Sch Rd, Uxb. 134 BM70
Old Sch Sq E14 143 EA72
Pelling St
Old Sch Sq, T.Ditt. 197 CF100
Old Schools La, Epsom 217 CT109
Old Seacoal La EC4 274 F8
Old Shire La, Ger.Cr. 91 BA46
Old Shire La, Rick. 73 BB44
Old Shire La, Wal.Abb. 84 EG35
Old Slade La, Iver 153 BE76
Old Solesbridge La, Rick. 74 BG41
Old Sopwell Gdns, St.Alb. 43 CE22
Old S Cl, Pnr. 94 BX53
Old S Lambeth Rd SW8 161 DL80
Old Spitalfields Mkt E1 275 P6
Old Spitalfields Mkt E1 142 DT71
Old Sq WC2 274 C8
Old Sq WC2 141 DM72
Old Sta App, Lthd. 231 CG121
Old Sta Rd, Hayes 155 BT76
Old Sta Rd, Loug. 84 EL43
Old Sta Way (Wooburn Grn), H.Wyc. 110 AE58
Old Sta Yd, Brom. 204 EF102
Bourne Way
Old Stockley Rd, West Dr. 155 BP75
Old St E13 144 EH68
Old St EC1 275 H4
Old St EC1 142 DQ70
Old Swan Yd, Cars. 218 DF105
Old Tilburstow Rd, Gdse. 252 DW134
Old Town SW4 161 DJ83
Old Town, Croy. 201 DP104
Old Town Cl, Beac. 89 AL54
Old Tram Yd SE18 165 ES77
Lakedale Rd
Old Tye Av (Biggin Hill), West. 238 EL116
Old Uxbridge Rd, Rick. 91 BE53
Old Vicarage Way (Wooburn Grn), H.Wyc. 110 AE59
Old Wk, The (Otford), Sev. 241 FH117
Old Watery La (Wooburn Grn), H.Wyc. 110 AE55
Old Watford Rd (Bricket Wd), St.Alb. 60 BY30
Old Watling St, Grav. 191 GG92
Old Westhall Cl, Warl. 236 DW119
Old Wf Way, Wey. 212 BM105
Weybridge Rd
Old Windsor Lock (Old Windsor), Wind. 172 AW85
Old Woking Rd, W.Byf. 211 BF113
Old Woking Rd, Wok. 227 BE116
Old Woolwich Rd SE10 163 ED79
Old York Rd SW18 180 DB85
Oldacre Ms SW12 181 DH87
Balham Gro
Oldberry Rd, Edg. 96 CR51
Oldborough Rd, Wem. 117 CJ61
Oldbury Cl, Cher. 193 BE101
Oldbury Rd
Oldbury Cl, Orp. 206 EX98
Oldbury Gro, Beac. 89 AK50
Oldbury Pl W1 272 G6
Oldbury Pl W1 140 DG70
Oldbury Rd, Cher. 193 BE101
Oldbury Rd, Enf. 82 DU40
Oldchurch Gdns, Rom. 127 FD59
Oldchurch Ri, Rom. 127 FD59
Oldchurch Rd, Rom. 127 FD59
Olden La, Pur. 219 DN112
Oldfield Cl, Brom. 205 EM98
Oldfield Cl, Grnf. 117 CE64
Oldfield Cl, Horl. 268 DF150
Oldfield Rd
Oldfield Cl, Stan. 95 CG50
Oldfield Cl (Cheshunt), Wal.Cr. 67 DY28
Oldfield Dr (Cheshunt), Wal.Cr. 67 DY28
Oldfield Fm Gdns, Grnf. 137 CD67
Oldfield Gdns, Ash. 231 CK119
Oldfield Gro SE16 163 DX77
Oldfield La N, Grnf. 137 CE65
Oldfield La S, Grnf. 136 CC70
Oldfield Ms N6 121 DJ59
Oldfield Rd N16 122 DS62
Oldfield Rd NW10 139 CT66
Oldfield Rd SW19 179 CY93
Oldfield Rd W3 159 CT75
Valetta Rd
Oldfield Rd, Bexh. 166 EY82
Oldfield Rd, Brom. 205 EM98
Oldfield Rd, Hmptn. 196 BZ95
Oldfield Rd, Hem.H. 39 BE21
Oldfield Rd, Horl. 268 DF150
Oldfield Rd (London Colney), St.Alb. 61 CK25
Oldfield Wd, Wok. 227 BB117
Maybury Hill
Oldfields Circ, Nthlt. 136 CC65
Oldfields Rd, Sutt. 199 CZ104
Oldfields Trd Est, Sutt. 200 DA104
Oldham Ter W3 138 CQ74
Oldhill St N16 122 DU60
Oldhouse Cft, Harl. 35 ES13
Oldridge Rd SW12 180 DG87
Olds App, Wat. 93 BP46
Olds Cl, Wat. 93 BP46
Oldstead Rd, Brom. 183 ED91
Oldway La, Slou. 151 AK75
Oleander Cl, Orp. 223 ER106
O'Leary Sq E1 142 DW71
Olga St E3 143 DY68
Olinda Rd N16 122 DT58
Oliphant St W10 139 CX69
Olive Rd E13 144 EJ69
Olive Rd NW2 119 CW63
Olive Rd SW19 180 DC94
Norman Rd
Olive Rd W5 157 CK76
Olive Rd, Dart. 188 FK88
Olive St, Rom. 127 FD57
Oliver Av SE25 202 DT97
Oliver Cl E10 123 EB61
Oliver Rd
Oliver Cl W4 158 CP79
Oliver Cl, Add. 212 BG105
Oliver Cl, Grays 169 FT80
Oliver Cl, Hem.H. 40 BL24
Oliver Cl, Hodd. 49 EB15
Oliver Cl (Park St), St.Alb. 61 CD27
Oliver Cres (Farningham), Dart. 208 FM101
Oliver Gdns E6 144 EL72
Oliver Gro SE25 202 DT98
Oliver Ri, Hem.H. 40 BL24
Oliver Rd E10 123 EB61
Oliver Rd E17 123 EC57
Oliver Rd NW10 138 CQ68
Oliver Rd, Brwd. 109 GA43
Oliver Rd, Grays 169 FT81
Oliver Rd, Hem.H. 40 BL24
Oliver Rd, N.Mal. 198 CQ96
Oliver Rd, Rain. 147 FF67
Oliver Rd, Sutt. 218 DD105
Oliver Rd, Swan. 207 FD97
Oliver-Goldsmith Est SE15 162 DU81
Olivers Cl, Berk. 39 BC16
Olivers Yd EC1 275 L4
Olivette St SW15 159 CX84
Olivia Gdns (Harefield), Uxb. 92 BJ53
Ollards Gro, Loug. 84 EK42
Olleberrie La, Rick. 57 BD32
Ollerton Grn E3 143 DZ67
Ollerton Rd N11 99 DK50
Olley Cl, Wall. 219 DL108
Ollgar Cl W12 139 CT74
Olliffe St E14 163 EC76
Olmar St SE1 162 DU79
Olney Rd SE17 161 DP79
Olron Cres, Bexh. 186 EX85
Olven Rd SE18 165 EQ80
Olveston Wk, Cars. 200 DD100
Olwen Ms, Pnr. 94 BX54
Olyffe Av, Well. 166 EU82
Olyffe Dr, Beck. 203 EC95
Olympia Ms W2 140 DB73
Queensway
Olympia Way W14 159 CY76
Olympic Retail Pk, Wem. 118 CP63
Olympic Way, Grnf. 136 CB67
Olympic Way, Wem. 118 CN63
Olympus Sq E5 122 DU63
Nolan Way
Oman Av NW2 119 CW63
O'Meara St SE1 279 J3
O'Meara St SE1 142 DQ74
Omega Cl E14 163 EB76
Tiller Rd
Omega Ct, Ware 33 DX06
Crib St
Omega Pl N1 274 A1
Omega Rd, Wok. 227 BA115
Omega St SE14 163 EA81
Omega Way, Egh. 193 BC95
Ommaney Rd SE14 163 DX81
Omnibus Way E17 101 EA54
On The Hill, Wat. 94 BY47
Ondine Rd SE15 162 DT84
One Pin La (Farnham Common), Slou. 111 AQ63
One Tree Cl SE23 182 DW86
One Tree Hill Rd, Guil. 259 BB135
One Tree La, Beac. 89 AL52
Onega Gate SE16 163 DY76
O'Neill Path SE18 165 EN79
Kempt St
Ongar Cl, Add. 211 BF107
Ongar Cl, Rom. 126 EW57
Ongar Hill, Add. 212 BG107
Ongar Pl, Add. 212 BG107
Ongar Rd SW6 160 DA79
Ongar Rd, Add. 212 BG106
Ongar Rd, Brwd. 108 FV45
Ongar Rd (Pilgrim's Hatch), Brwd. 108 FS42
Ongar Rd, Rom. 86 EW40
Ongar Way, Rain. 147 FE67
Onra Rd E17 123 EA59
Onslow Av, Rich. 178 CL85
Onslow Av, Sutt. 217 CZ110
Onslow Cl E4 101 EC47
Onslow Cl, Hat. 45 CV18
Onslow Cl, T.Ditt. 197 CE102
Onslow Cl, Wok. 227 BA117
Onslow Cres, Chis. 205 EP95
Onslow Cres, Wok. 227 BA117
Onslow Dr, Sid. 186 EX89
Onslow Gdns E18 124 EH55
Onslow Gdns N10 121 DH57
Onslow Gdns N21 81 DN43
Onslow Gdns SW7 160 DD78
Onslow Gdns, S.Croy. 220 DU112
Onslow Gdns, T.Ditt. 197 CE102
Onslow Gdns, Wall. 219 DJ107
Onslow Ms, Cher. 194 BG100
Onslow Ms E SW7 160 DD77
Cranley Pl
Onslow Ms W SW7 160 DD77
Cranley Pl
Onslow Rd, Croy. 201 DM101
Onslow Rd, Guil. 242 AX134
Onslow Rd, N.Mal. 199 CU98
Onslow Rd, Rich. 178 CL85
Onslow Rd, Walt. 213 BT105
Onslow Sq SW7 276 A8
Onslow Sq SW7 160 DD77
Onslow St EC1 274 E5
Onslow St, Guil. 258 AW135
Onslow Way, T.Ditt. 197 CE102
Onslow Way, Wok. 227 BF115
Ontario Cl, Horl. 269 DN149
Ontario St SE1 278 G7
Ontario St SE1 161 DP76
Ontario Way E14 143 EA73
Opal Cl E16 144 EK72
Opal Ct (Wexham), Slou. 132 AV70
Wexham St
Opal Ms NW6 139 CZ67
Priory Pk Rd
Opal Ms, Ilf. 125 EP61
Ley St
Opal St SE11 278 F9
Opal St SE11 161 DP77
Opendale Rd (Burnham), Slou. 130 AH71
Openshaw Rd SE2 166 EV77
Openview SW18 180 DC88
Ophelia Gdns NW2 119 CY62
The Vale
Ophir Ter SE15 162 DU81
Opossum Way, Houns. 156 BW82
Oppenheim Rd SE13 163 EC82
Oppidans Ms NW3 140 DF66
Meadowbank
Oppidans Rd NW3 140 DF66
Optima Business Pk, Hodd. 49 EC16
Pindar Rd
Oram Pl, Hem.H. 40 BK23
Orange Ct E1 142 DU74
Hermitage Wall
Orange Ct La, Orp. 223 EN109
Orange Gro E11 124 EE62
Orange Gro, Chig. 103 EQ51
Orange Hill Rd, Edg. 96 CQ52
Orange Pl SE16 162 DW76
Lower Rd
Orange St WC2 277 M1
Orange St WC2 141 DK73
Orange Tree Hill (Havering-atte-Bower), Rom. 105 FD50
Orange Yd W1 273 N9
Orangery, The, Rich. 177 CJ89
Orangery La SE9 185 EM85
Oratory La SW3 276 A10
Orb St SE17 279 K9
Orb St SE17 162 DR77
Orbain Rd SW6 159 CY80
Orbel St SW11 160 DE81
Orbital Cres, Wat. 75 BT35
Orbital One, Dart. 188 FP89
Orchard, The N14 81 DH43
Orchard, The N21 82 DR44
Orchard, The NW11 120 DA57
Orchard, The SE3 163 ED82
Orchard, The W4 158 CR77
Orchard, The W5 137 CK71
Orchard, The, Bans. 234 DA116
Orchard, The (North Holmwood), Dor. 263 CJ140
Orchard, The, Epsom 217 CT108
Orchard, The (Ewell), Epsom 217 CT110
Tayles Hill Dr
Orchard, The, Hert. 32 DQ06
Orchard, The, Houns. 156 CC82
Orchard, The, Kings L. 58 BN29
Orchard, The, Rick. 74 BM43
Green La
Orchard, The (Dunton Grn), Sev. 241 FE120
Orchard, The, Swan. 207 FD96
Orchard, The, Vir.W. 192 AY99
Orchard, The, Welw.G.C. 29 CX07
Orchard, The, Wey. 213 BP105
Orchard, The, Wok. 226 AY122
Orchard Av N3 120 DA55
Orchard Av N14 81 DJ44
Orchard Av N20 98 DD47
Orchard Av (Woodham), Add. 211 BF111
Orchard Av, Ashf. 175 BQ93
Orchard Av, Belv. 166 EY79
Orchard Av, Berk. 38 AU19
Orchard Av, Brwd. 109 FZ48
Orchard Av, Croy. 203 DY101
Orchard Av, Dart. 187 FH87
Orchard Av, Felt. 175 BR85
Orchard Av, Grav. 191 GH92
Orchard Av, Houns. 156 BY80
Orchard Av, Mitch. 200 DG102
Orchard Av, N.Mal. 198 CS96
Orchard Av, Rain. 148 FJ70
Orchard Av, Slou. 131 AK71
Orchard Av, Sthl. 136 BY74
Orchard Av, T.Ditt. 197 CG102
Orchard Av, Wat. 59 BV32
Orchard Av, Wind. 151 AN81
Orchard Bungalow Caravan Site, Slou. 131 AM66
Orchard Cl E4 101 EA49
Chingford Mt Rd

Orchard Cl E11 124 EH56
Orchard Cl N1 142 DQ66
Morton Rd
Orchard Cl NW2 119 CU62
Orchard Cl SE23 182 DW86
Brenchley Gdns
Orchard Cl SW20 199 CW98
Grand Dr
Orchard Cl W10 139 CY71
Orchard Cl, Ashf. 175 BQ93
Orchard Cl, Bans. 218 DB114
Orchard Cl, Beac. 89 AK52
Seeleys Rd
Orchard Cl, Bexh. 166 EY81
Orchard Cl (Sheering), B.Stort. 37 FC07
Orchard Cl, Borwd. 78 CM42
Orchard Cl, Bushey 95 CD46
Orchard Cl, Edg. 96 CL51
Orchard Cl, Egh. 173 BB92
Orchard Cl (West Ewell), Epsom 216 CP107
Orchard Cl, Guil. 243 BB134
Orchard Cl, Hem.H. 40 BM18
Orchard Cl, Hert. 47 DJ19
Orchard Cl, Horl. 268 DF147
Orchard Cl, Lthd. 231 CF119
Orchard Cl (East Horsley), Lthd. 229 BT124
Orchard Cl (Fetcham), Lthd. 231 CD122
Orchard Cl, Nthlt. 116 CC64
Orchard Cl (Cuffley), Pot.B. 65 DL28
Orchard Cl, Rad. 77 CE37
Orchard Cl, Rick. 73 BD42
Orchard Cl, Ruis. 115 BQ59
Orchard Cl, St.Alb. 43 CF21
Orchard Cl, S.Ock. 149 FW70
Orchard Cl, Surb. 197 CH101
Orchard Cl (Denham), Uxb. 134 BH65
Orchard Cl, Walt. 195 BV101
Garden Rd
Orchard Cl, Ware 33 DX05
Orchard Cl (Stanstead Abbotts), Ware 33 EC11
Orchard Cl, Wat. 75 BT40
Orchard Cl, Wem. 138 CL67
Orchard Cl, Wok. 227 BB116
Orchard Ct (Bovingdon), Hem.H. 57 BA27
Orchard Ct, Islw. 157 CD81
Thornbury Av
Orchard Ct, Twick. 177 CD89
Orchard Ct, Wall. 219 DH106
Parkgate Rd
Orchard Ct, Wor.Pk. 199 CU102
The Av
Orchard Cres, Edg. 96 CQ50
Orchard Cres, Enf. 82 DT39
Orchard Cft, Harl. 36 EU13
Orchard Dr SE3 164 EE82
Orchard Rd
Orchard Dr, Ash. 231 CK120
Orchard Dr, Edg. 96 CM50
Orchard Dr, Epp. 85 ES36
Orchard Dr, Grays 170 GA75
Orchard Dr (Wooburn Grn), H.Wyc. 110 AD59
Orchard Dr, Rick. 73 BC41
Orchard Dr (Park St), St.Alb. 60 CB27
Orchard Dr, Uxb. 134 BK70
Orchard Dr, Wat. 75 BT39
Orchard Dr, Wok. 227 AZ115
Orchard End, Cat. 236 DS122
Orchard End (Fetcham), Lthd. 230 CC124
Orchard End, Wey. 195 BS103
Orchard End Av, Amer. 72 AT39
Orchard Fld Rd, Gdmg. 258 AT144
Orchard Gdns, Chess. 216 CL105
Orchard Gdns, Epsom 216 CQ114
Orchard Gdns (Effingham), Lthd. 246 BY128
Orchard Gdns, Sutt. 218 DA106
Orchard Gdns, Wal.Abb. 67 EC34
Orchard Gate NW9 118 CS56
Orchard Gate, Esher 197 CD102
Orchard Gate, Grnf. 137 CH65
Orchard Gate (Farnham Common), Slou. 111 AQ64
Orchard Grn, Orp. 205 ES103
Orchard Gro SE20 182 DU94
Orchard Gro, Croy. 203 DY101
Orchard Gro, Edg. 96 CN53
Orchard Gro (Chalfont St. Peter), Ger.Cr. 90 AW53
Orchard Gro, Har. 118 CM57
Orchard Gro, Orp. 205 ET103
Orchard Hill SE13 163 EB82
Coldbath St
Orchard Hill, Cars. 218 DF106
Orchard Hill, Dart. 187 FE85
Orchard Ho, Erith 167 FF81
Northend Rd
Orchard La SW20 199 CV95
Orchard La, Amer. 55 AR38
Orchard La, Brwd. 108 FT43
Orchard La, E.Mol. 197 CD100
Orchard La, Harl. 36 EY11
Orchard La, Wdf.Grn. 102 EJ49
Orchard Lea Cl, Wok. 227 BE115
Orchard Leigh, Chesh. 56 AU28
Orchard Mains, Wok. 226 AW119
Orchard Mead, Hat. 45 CT18
Days Mead
Orchard Ms N1 142 DR66
Southgate Gro
Orchard Ms (Seer Grn), Beac. 89 AQ50
Orchard Rd
Orchard Path, Slou. 133 BA72
Orchard Pl E14 144 EE73
Orchard Pl N17 100 DT52
Orchard Pl, Kes. 222 EK109
Orchard Pl (Sundridge), Sev. 240 EY124
Orchard Pl (Cheshunt), Wal.Cr. 67 DX30
Turners Hill
Orchard Ri, Croy. 203 DY102
Orchard Ri, Kings.T. 198 CQ95
Orchard Ri, Pnr. 115 BT55
Orchard Ri, Rich. 158 CP84
Orchard Ri E, Sid. 185 ET85
Orchard Ri W, Sid. 185 ES85
Orchard Rd N6 121 DH59
Orchard Rd SE3 164 EE82
Orchard Rd SE18 165 ER77
Orchard Rd, Barn. 79 CZ42
Orchard Rd, Beac. 89 AM54
Orchard Rd (Seer Grn), Beac. 89 AQ50
Orchard Rd, Belv. 166 FA77
Orchard Rd, Brent. 157 CJ79
Orchard Rd, Brom. 204 EJ95
Orchard Rd, Ch.St.G. 90 AW47
Orchard Rd, Chess. 216 CL105
Orchard Rd, Dag. 146 FA67
Orchard Rd, Dor. 263 CH137
Orchard Rd, Enf. 82 DW43
Orchard Rd (Northfleet), Grav. 190 GC89
Orchard Rd (Burpham), Guil. 243 BB130
Orchard Rd (Onslow Village), Guil. 258 AT136
Orchard Rd (Shalford), Guil. 258 AY140
Orchard Rd (Shere), Guil. 260 BN139
Orchard Rd, Hmptn. 176 BZ94
Orchard Rd, Hayes 135 BT73
Orchard Rd, Houns. 176 BZ85
Orchard Rd, Kings.T. 198 CL96
Orchard Rd, Mitch. 200 DG102
Orchard Rd (Farnborough), Orp. 223 EP106
Orchard Rd (Pratt's Bottom), Orp. 224 EW110
Orchard Rd, Reig. 250 DB134
Orchard Rd, Rich. 158 CN83
Orchard Rd, Rom. 105 FB53
Orchard Rd (Otford), Sev. 241 FF116
Orchard Rd (Riverhead), Sev. 256 FE122
Orchard Rd, Sid. 185 ES91
Orchard Rd, S.Croy. 220 DV114
Orchard Rd, S.Ock. 149 FW70
Orchard Rd, Sun. 175 BV94
Hanworth Rd
Orchard Rd, Sutt. 218 DA106
Orchard Rd, Swans. 190 FY85
Orchard Rd, Twick. 177 CG85
Orchard Rd, Well. 166 EV83
Orchard Rd (Old Windsor), Wind. 172 AV86
Orchard Sq W14 159 CZ78
Sun Rd
Orchard Sq, Brox. 49 DZ24
Orchard St E17 123 DY56
Orchard St W1 272 F9
Orchard St W1 140 DG72
Orchard St, Dart. 188 FL86
Orchard St, Hem.H. 40 BK24
Orchard St, St.Alb. 42 CC21
Orchard Ter, Enf. 82 DU44
Great Cambridge Rd
Orchard Vw, Uxb. 134 BK70
Orchard Vil, Sid. 186 EW93
Orchard Way, Add. 212 BH106
Orchard Way, Ashf. 174 BM89
Orchard Way, Beck. 203 DY99
Orchard Way, Chig. 104 EU48
Orchard Way, Croy. 203 DY101
Orchard Way, Dart. 188 FK90
Orchard Way, Dor. 263 CH137
Orchard Way, Enf. 82 DS41
Orchard Way, Esher 214 CC107
Orchard Way (Bovingdon), Hem.H. 57 BA28
Orchard Way, Oxt. 254 EG133
Orchard Way, Pot.B. 64 DB28
Orchard Way, Reig. 266 DB138
Orchard Way, Rick. 92 BG45
Orchard Way, Slou. 132 AY74
Orchard Way, Sutt. 218 DD105
Orchard Way, Tad. 249 CZ126
Orchard Way (Cheshunt), Wal.Cr. 65 DP27
Orchard Way (Send), Wok. 243 BC125
Orchard Waye, Uxb. 134 BK68
Orchardleigh, Lthd. 231 CH122
Orchardleigh Av, Enf. 82 DW40
Orchardmede N21 82 DR44
Orchards, The, Epp. 70 EU32
Orchards, The, Saw. 36 EY05
Orchards Business Cen, Red. 267 DH143
Orchards Cl, W.Byf. 212 BG114
Orchards Residential Pk, The, Slou. 133 AZ74
Orchards Shop Cen, Dart. 188 FL86
Orchardson St NW8 140 DD70
Orchardville (Burnham), Slou. 130 AH70
Orchehill Av, Ger.Cr. 112 AX56
Orchehill Ct, Ger.Cr. 112 AY56
Orchehill Ri, Ger.Cr. 112 AY57
Orchid Cl E6 144 EL71
Orchid Cl, Chess. 215 CJ108
Orchid Cl, Hat. 29 CT14
Great Braitch La
Orchid Cl, Rom. 86 EV41
Orchid Cl, Sthl. 136 BY72
Orchid Ct, Egh. 173 BB91
Orchid Ct, Rom. 127 FE61
Orchid Rd N14 99 DJ45
Orchid St W12 139 CU73
Orchis Gro, Grays 170 FZ78
Orchis Way, Rom. 106 FM51
Orde Hall St WC1 274 B5
Orde Hall St WC1 141 DM70
Ordell Rd E3 143 DZ68
Ordnance Cl, Felt. 175 BU90
Ordnance Cres SE10 163 ED75
Ordnance Hill NW8 140 DD67
Ordnance Ms NW8 140 DD68
St. Ann's Ter
Ordnance Rd E16 144 EF71
Ordnance Rd SE18 165 EN79
Ordnance Rd, Enf. 83 DX37
Ordnance Rd, Grav. 191 GJ86
Oregano Cl, West Dr. 134 BM72
Camomile Way
Oregano Dr E14 143 ED72
Oregano Way, Guil. 242 AU129
Oregon Av E12 125 EM63
Oregon Cl, N.Mal. 198 CQ98
Georgia Rd
Oregon Sq, Orp. 205 ER102
Orestan La (Effingham), Lthd. 245 BV127
Orestes Ms NW6 120 DA64
Aldred Rd
Oreston Rd, Rain. 148 FK69
Orewell Gdns, Reig. 266 DB136
Orford Ct SE27 181 DP89
Orford Gdns, Twick. 177 CF89
Orford Rd E17 123 EA57
Orford Rd E18 124 EH55
Orford Rd SE6 183 EB90
Organ Hall Rd, Borwd. 78 CL39
Organ La E4 101 EC47
Oriel Cl, Mitch. 201 DK98
Oriel Ct NW3 120 DC63
Heath St
Oriel Dr SW13 159 CV79
Oriel Gdns, Ilf. 125 EM55
Oriel Pl NW3 120 DC63
Heath St
Oriel Rd E9 143 DX65
Oriel Way, Nthlt. 136 CB66
Orient Cl, St.Alb. 43 CE22
Orient Ind Pk E10 123 EA61
Orient St SE11 278 F8
Orient Way E5 123 DX62
Orient Way E10 123 DY61
Oriental Cl, Wok. 227 BA117
Oriental Rd
Oriental Rd E16 144 EK74
Oriental Rd, Wok. 227 BA117
Oriental St E14 143 EA73
Morant St
Oriole Cl, Abb.L. 59 BU31
Oriole Way SE28 146 EV73
Orion Rd N11 99 DH51
Orion Way, Nthwd. 93 BT49
Orissa Rd SE18 165 ES78
Orkney Ct, Maid. 130 AE66
Orkney St SW11 160 DG82
Orlando Gdns, Epsom 216 CR110
Orlando Rd SW4 161 DJ83
Orleans Cl, Esher 197 CD103
Orleans Rd SE19 182 DR93
Orleans Rd, Twick. 177 CH87
Orleston Ms N7 141 DN65
Orleston Rd N7 141 DN65
Orlestone Gdns, Orp. 224 EY106
Orley Fm Rd, Har. 117 CE62
Orlop St SE10 164 EE78
Ormanton Rd SE26 182 DU91
Orme Ct W2 140 DB73
Orme Ct Ms W2 140 DB73
Orme La
Orme La W2 140 DB73
Orme Rd, Kings.T. 198 CP96
Orme Rd, Sutt. 218 DB107
Grove Rd
Orme Sq W2 140 DB73
Bayswater Rd
Ormeley Rd SW12 181 DH88
Ormerod Gdns, Mitch. 200 DG96
Ormesby Cl SE28 146 EX73
Wroxham Rd
Ormesby Dr, Pot.B. 63 CX32
Ormesby Way, Har. 118 CM58
Ormiston Gro W12 139 CV74
Ormiston Rd SE10 164 EG78
Ormond Av, Hmptn. 196 CB95
Ormond Av, Rich. 177 CK85
Ormond Rd
Ormond Cl WC1 274 A6
Ormond Cl, Rom. 106 FK54
Chadwick Dr
Ormond Cres, Hmptn. 196 CB95
Ormond Dr, Hmptn. 176 CB94
Ormond Ms WC1 274 A5
Ormond Rd N19 121 DL60
Ormond Rd, Rich. 177 CK85
Ormond Yd SW1 277 L2
Ormonde Av, Epsom 216 CR109
Ormonde Av, Orp. 205 EQ103
Ormonde Gate SW3 160 DF78
Ormonde Pl SW1 276 F9
Ormonde Ri, Buck.H. 102 EJ46
Ormonde Rd SW14 158 CP83
Ormonde Rd, Nthwd. 93 BR49
Ormonde Rd, Wok. 226 AW116
Ormonde Ter NW8 140 DF67
Ormsby, Sutt. 218 DB108
Grange Rd
Ormsby Gdns, Grnf. 136 CC68
Ormsby Pl N16 122 DT62
Victorian Gro
Ormsby Pt SE18 165 EP77
Troy Ct
Ormsby St E2 142 DT68
Ormside St SE15 162 DW79
Ormside Way, Red. 251 DH130
Ormskirk Rd, Wat. 94 BX49
Ornan Rd NW3 120 DE64
Oronsay, Hem.H. 41 BP22
Northend
Oronsay Wk N1 142 DQ65
Clephane Rd
Orpen Wk N16 122 DS62
Orphanage Rd, Wat. 76 BW40
Orpheus St SE5 162 DR81
Orpin Rd, Red. 251 DH130
Orpington Bypass, Orp. 206 EV103
Orpington Bypass, Sev. 224 FA109
Orpington Gdns N18 100 DS48
Orpington Rd N21 99 DP46
Orpington Rd, Chis. 205 ES97
Orpwood Cl, Hmptn. 176 BZ92
Orsett Heath Cres, Grays 171 GG76
Orsett Rd, Grays 170 GA78
Orsett St SE11 278 C10
Orsett St SE11 161 DM78
Orsett Ter W2 140 DC72
Orsett Ter, Wdf.Grn. 102 EJ53
Orsman Rd N1 142 DS67
Orton Cl, St.Alb. 43 CG16
Orton St E1 142 DU74
Hermitage Wall
Orville Rd SW11 160 DD82
Orwell Cl, Hayes 135 BS73
Orwell Cl, Rain. 147 FD71
Orwell Cl, Wind. 151 AR83
Orwell Ct N5 122 DQ63
Orwell Rd E13 144 EJ68
Osbaldeston Rd N16 122 DU61
Osbert St SW1 277 M9
Osberton Rd SE12 184 EG85
Osborn Cl E8 142 DU67
Osborn Gdns NW7 97 CX52
Osborn La SE23 183 DY87
Osborn St E1 142 DT71
Osborn Ter SE3 164 EF84
Lee Rd
Osborn Way, Welw.G.C. 29 CX10
Osborn Way Tunnel, Welw.G.C. 29 CX09
Osborn Way
Osborne Av, Stai. 174 BL88
Osborne Cl, Barn. 80 DF41
Osborne Cl, Beck. 203 DY98
Osborne Cl, Felt. 176 BX92
Osborne Cl, Horn. 127 FH58
Osborne Ct, Pot.B. 64 DB29
Osborne Ct, Wind. 151 AQ82
Osborne Rd
Osborne Gdns, Pot.B. 64 DB30
Osborne Gdns, Th.Hth. 202 DQ96
Osborne Gro E17 123 DZ56
Osborne Gro N4 121 DN60
Osborne Ms E17 123 DZ56
Osborne Gro
Osborne Ms, Wind. 151 AQ82
Osborne Pl, Sutt. 218 DD106
Osborne Rd E7 124 EH64
Osborne Rd E9 143 DZ65
Osborne Rd E10 123 EB62
Osborne Rd N4 121 DN60
Osborne Rd N13 99 DN48
Osborne Rd NW2 139 CV65
Osborne Rd W3 158 CP76
Osborne Rd, Belv. 166 EZ78
Osborne Rd, Brwd. 108 FU44
Osborne Rd, Brox. 49 EA19
Osborne Rd, Buck.H. 102 EH46
Osborne Rd, Dag. 126 EZ64
Osborne Rd, Egh. 173 AZ93
Osborne Rd, Enf. 83 DY40
Osborne Rd, Horn. 127 FH58
Osborne Rd, Houns. 156 BZ83
Osborne Rd, Kings.T. 178 CL94
Osborne Rd, Pot.B. 64 DB30
Osborne Rd, Red. 250 DG131
Osborne Rd, Sthl. 136 CC72
Osborne Rd, Th.Hth. 202 DQ96
Osborne Rd, Uxb. 134 BJ66
Oxford Rd
Osborne Rd, Wal.Cr. 67 DY27
Osborne Rd, Walt. 195 BU102
Osborne Rd, Wat. 76 BW38
Osborne Rd, Wind. 151 AQ82
Osborne Sq, Dag. 126 EZ63
Osborne St, Slou. 152 AT75
Osborne Ter SW17 180 DG92
Church La
Osbourne Av, Kings L. 58 BM28
Osbourne Rd, Dart. 188 FP86
Oscar St SE8 163 EA81
Oseney Cres NW5 141 DJ65
Osgood Av, Orp. 223 ET106
Osgood Gdns, Orp. 223 ET106
Osidge La N14 98 DG46
Osier Cres N10 98 DF53
Osier Ms W4 159 CT79
Osier Pl, Egh. 173 BC93
Osier St E1 142 DW70
Osier Way E10 123 EB62
Osier Way, Bans. 217 CY114
Osier Way, Mitch. 200 DE99
Osiers Rd SW18 160 DA84
Oslac Rd SE6 183 EB92
Oslo Ct NW8 272 B1
Oslo Sq SE16 163 DY76
Osman Cl N15 122 DR58
Tewkesbury Rd
Osman Rd N9 100 DU48
Osman Rd W6 159 CW76
Batoum Gdns
Osmond Cl, Har. 116 CC61
Osmond Gdns, Wall. 219 DJ106
Osmund St W12 139 CT72
Braybrook St
Osnaburgh St NW1 273 J5
Osnaburgh St NW1 141 DH70
Osnaburgh Ter NW1 273 J4
Osney Ho SE2 166 EX75
Hartslock Dr
Osney Wk, Cars. 200 DD100
Osney Way, Grav. 191 GM89
Osprey Cl E6 144 EL71
Dove App
Osprey Cl E11 124 EG56
Osprey Cl E17 101 DY52
Osprey Cl, Lthd. 230 CC122
Oswald Cl
Osprey Cl, Sutt. 217 CZ106
Sandpiper Rd
Osprey Cl, Wat. 60 BY34
Osprey Cl, West Dr. 154 BL75
Osprey Ct, Wal.Abb. 68 EG34
Osprey Gdns, S.Croy. 221 DX110
Osprey Ms, Enf. 82 DV43
Osprey Rd, Wal.Abb. 68 EG34
Ospringe Cl SE20 182 DW94
Ospringe Ct SE9 185 ER86
Alderwood Rd
Ospringe Rd NW5 121 DJ63
Osram Ct W6 159 CW76
Lena Gdns
Osram Rd, Wem. 117 CK62
Osric Path N1 275 M1
Osric Path N1 142 DS68
Ossian Ms N4 121 DM59
Ossian Rd N4 121 DM59
Ossington Bldgs W1 272 F6
Ossington Cl W2 140 DB73
Ossington St
Ossington St W2 140 DB73
Ossory Rd SE1 162 DU78
Ossulston St NW1 273 M1
Ossulston St NW1 141 DK69
Ossulton Pl N2 120 DC55
East End Rd
Ossulton Way N2 120 DC56
Ostade Rd SW2 181 DM87
Ostell Cres, Enf. 83 EA37
Government Row
Osten Ms SW7 160 DB76
Emperor's Gate
Oster St, St.Alb. 42 CC19
Oster Ter E17 123 DX57
Southcote Rd
Osterberg Rd, Dart. 168 FM84
Osterley Av, Islw. 157 CD80
Osterley Cl, Orp. 206 EU95
Leith Hill
Osterley Ct, Islw. 157 CD81
Osterley Cres, Islw. 157 CE81
Osterley Gdns, Th.Hth. 202 DQ96
Osterley Ho E14 143 EB72
Giraud St
Osterley La, Islw. 157 CE78
Osterley La, Sthl. 156 CA78
Osterley Pk, Islw. 157 CD78
Osterley Pk Rd, Sthl. 156 BZ76
Osterley Pk Vw Rd W7 157 CE75
Osterley Rd N16 122 DS63
Osterley Rd, Islw. 157 CE80
Osterley Views, Sthl. 136 CC74
West Pk Rd
Ostliffe Rd N13 99 DP50
Oswald Cl (Fetcham), Lthd. 230 CC122
Oswald Rd (Fetcham), Lthd. 230 CC122
Oswald Rd, St.Alb. 43 CE21
Oswald Rd, Sthl. 136 BY74
Oswald St E5 123 DX62
Oswald Ter NW2 119 CW62
Temple Rd
Oswald's Mead E9 123 DY63
Lindisfarne Way
Osward, Croy. 221 DZ109
Osward Pl N9 100 DV47
Osward Rd SW17 180 DF89
Oswell Ho E1 142 DV74
Oswin St SE11 278 G8
Oswin St SE11 161 DP77
Oswyth Rd SE5 162 DS82
Otford Cl SE20 202 DW95
Otford Cl, Bex. 187 FB86
Southwold Rd
Otford Cl, Brom. 205 EN97
Otford Cres SE4 183 DZ86
Otford La (Halstead), Sev. 224 EZ112
Otford Rd, Sev. 241 FH118
Othello Cl SE11 278 F10
Otis St E3 143 EC69
Otley App, Ilf. 125 EP58
Otley Dr, Ilf. 125 EP57
Otley Rd E16 144 EJ72
Otley Ter E5 123 DX61
Otley Way, Wat. 94 BW48
Otlinge Cl, Orp. 206 EX98
Ottawa Gdns, Dag. 147 FD66
Ottawa Rd, Til. 171 GG82
Ottaway St E5 122 DU62
Stellman Cl
Ottenden Cl, Orp. 223 ES105
Southfleet Rd
Otter Cl (Ottershaw), Cher. 211 BB107
Otter Gdns, Hat. 45 CV19
Otter Meadow, Lthd. 231 CF119
Otter Rd, Grnf. 136 CC70
Otterbourne Rd E4 101 ED48
Otterbourne Rd, Croy. 202 DQ103
Otterburn Gdns, Islw. 157 CG80
Otterburn Ho SE5 162 DQ80
Otterburn St SW17 180 DF93
Otterden St SE6 183 EA91
Otterfield Rd, West Dr. 134 BL73
Ottermead La (Ottershaw), Cher. 211 BC107
Otters Cl, Orp. 206 EX98
Otterspool La, Wat. 76 BY38
Otterspool Service Rd, Wat. 76 BZ39
Otterspool Way, Wat. 76 BY37
Otto Cl SE26 182 DV90
Otto St SE17 161 DP79
Ottoman Ter, Wat. 76 BW41
Ebury Rd
Ottways Av, Ash. 231 CK119
Ottways La, Ash. 231 CK120
Otway Gdns, Bushey 95 CE45
Otways Cl, Pot.B. 64 DB32
Oulton Cl E5 122 DW61
Mundford Rd
Oulton Cl SE28 146 EW72
Rollesby Way
Oulton Cres, Bark. 145 ET65
Oulton Cres, Pot.B. 63 CX32
Oulton Rd N15 122 DR57
Oulton Way, Wat. 94 BY49
Oundle Av, Bushey 76 CC44
Ousden Cl (Cheshunt), Wal.Cr. 67 DY30
Ousden Dr (Cheshunt), Wal.Cr. 67 DY30
Ouseley Rd SW12 180 DF88
Ouseley Rd (Wraysbury), Stai. 172 AW87
Ouseley Rd (Old Windsor), Wind. 172 AW87
Outdowns (Effingham), Lthd. 245 BV129
Outer Circle NW1 272 F5
Outer Circle NW1 141 DH68
Outfield Rd (Chalfont St. Peter), Ger.Cr. 90 AX52
Outgate Rd NW10 139 CT66
Outlook Dr, Ch.St.G. 90 AX48
Outram Pl N1 141 DL67
Outram Pl, Wey. 213 BQ106
Outram Rd E6 144 EL67
Outram Rd N22 99 DK53
Outram Rd, Croy. 202 DT102
Outwich St EC3 275 N8
Outwood La, Couls. 234 DF118
Outwood La (Bletchingley), Red. 252 DR134
Outwood La (Kingswood), Tad. 234 DB122
Oval, The E2 142 DV68
Oval, The, Bans. 218 DA114
Oval, The, Brox. 67 DY25
Oval, The, Gdmg. 258 AT144
Oval, The, Guil. 258 AU135
Oval, The, Sid. 186 EU87
Oval Gdns, Grays 170 GC76
Oval Pl SW8 161 DM80
Oval Rd NW1 141 DH67
Oval Rd, Croy. 202 DS102
Oval Rd N, Dag. 147 FB67
Oval Rd S, Dag. 147 FB68
Oval Way SE11 161 DM78
Oval Way, Ger.Cr. 112 AY56
Ovenden Rd (Sundridge), Sev. 240 EX120
Over The Misbourne, Ger.Cr. 113 BA58
Over The Misbourne (Denham), Uxb. 113 BC58
Overbrae, Beck. 183 EA93
Overbrook (West Horsley), Lthd. 245 BP129
Overbrook Wk, Edg. 96 CN52
Overbury Av, Beck. 203 EB97
Overbury Cres (New Addington), Croy. 221 EC110
Overbury Rd N15 122 DR58
Overbury St E5 123 DX63
Overcliff Rd SE13 163 EA83
Overcliff Rd, Grays 170 GD78
Overcliffe, Grav. 191 GG86
Overcourt Cl, Sid. 186 EV86
Overdale, Ash. 232 CL115
Overdale, Dor. 263 CJ135
Overdale (Bletchingley), Red. 252 DQ133
Overdale Av, N.Mal. 198 CQ96
Overdale Rd W5 157 CJ76
Overdale Rd, Chesh. 54 AP28
Overdown Rd SE6 183 EA91
Overhill, Warl. 236 DW119
Overhill Rd SE22 182 DU87
Overhill Rd, Pur. 219 DN109
Overhill Way, Beck. 203 ED99
Overlea Rd E5 122 DU59
Overlord Cl, Brox. 49 DY20
Overmead, Sid. 185 ER87
Overmead, Swan. 207 FE99
Oversley Ho W2 140 DA71
Overstand Cl, Beck. 203 EA99
Overstone Gdns, Croy. 203 DZ101
Overstone Rd W6 159 CW76
Overstream, Rick. 74 BH42
Overthorpe Cl (Knaphill), Wok. 226 AS117
Overton Cl NW10 138 CQ65
Overton Cl, Islw. 157 CF81
Avenue Rd
Overton Ct E11 124 EG59
Overton Dr E11 124 EH59
Overton Dr, Rom. 126 EW59
Overton Ho SW15 179 CT87
Tangley Gro
Overton Rd E10 123 DY60
Overton Rd N14 81 DL43

Overton Rd SE2 166 EW76
Overton Rd SW9 161 DN82
Overton Rd, Sutt. 218 DA107
Overton Rd E SE2 166 EX76
Overtons Yd, Croy. 202 DQ104
Overy St, Dart. 188 FL86
Ovesdon Av, Har. 116 BZ60
Oveton Way (Bookham), Lthd. 246 CA126
Ovett Cl SE19 182 DS93
Ovex Cl E14 163 EC75
Ovington Ct, Wok. 226 AT116
Roundthorn Way
Ovington Gdns SW3 276 C7
Ovington Gdns SW3 160 DE76
Ovington Ms SW3 276 C7
Ovington Ms SW3 160 DE76
Ovington Sq SW3 276 C7
Ovington Sq SW3 160 DE76
Ovington St SW3 276 C7
Ovington St SW3 160 DE76
Owen Cl SE28 146 EW74
Owen Cl, Croy. 202 DR100
Owen Cl, Hayes 135 BV69
Owen Cl, Rom. 105 FB51
Owen Gdns, Wdf.Grn. 102 EL51
Owen Pl, Lthd. 231 CH122
Church Rd
Owen Rd N13 100 DQ50
Owen Rd, Hayes 135 BV69
Owen St EC1 274 F1
Owen Wk SE20 182 DU94
Sycamore Gro
Owen Waters Ho, Ilf. 103 EM53
Owen Way NW10 138 CQ65
Owenite St SE2 166 EV77
Owen's Ct EC1 274 F2
Owen's Row EC1 274 F2
Owens Way SE23 183 DY87
Owens Way, Rick. 74 BN43
Owgan Cl SE5 162 DR80
Benhill Rd
Owl Cl, S.Croy. 221 DX110
Owl Pk (High Beach), Loug. 84 EF40
Owlets Hall Cl, Horn. 128 FM55
Prospect Rd
Owlsears Cl, Beac. 89 AK51
Ownstead Gdns, S.Croy. 220 DT111
Ownsted Hill (New Addington), Croy. 221 EC110
Ox La, Epsom 217 CU109
Church St
Oxberry Av SW6 159 CY82
Oxdowne Cl (Stoke D'Abernon), Cob. 214 CB114
Oxenden Dr, Hodd. 49 EA18
Oxenden Wd Rd, Orp. 224 EV107
Oxendon St SW1 277 M1
Oxendon St SW1 141 DK73
Oxenford St SE15 162 DT83
Oxenholme NW1 273 L1
Oxenholme NW1 141 DJ68
Oxenpark Av, Wem. 118 CL59
Oxestalls Rd SE8 163 DY78
Oxfield Cl, Berk. 38 AU20
Oxford Av SW20 199 CY96
Oxford Av, Grays 171 GG77
Oxford Av, Hayes 155 BT80
Oxford Av, Horn. 128 FN56
Oxford Av, Houns. 156 CA78
Oxford Av, St.Alb. 43 CJ21
Oxford Av, Slou. 131 AM71
Oxford Av (Burnham), Slou. 130 AG68
Oxford Circ Av W1 273 K9
Oxford Cl N9 100 DV47
Oxford Cl, Ashf. 175 BQ94
Oxford Cl, Grav. 191 GM89
Oxford Cl, Mitch. 201 DJ97
Oxford Cl, Nthwd. 93 BQ49
Oxford Cl (Cheshunt), Wal.Cr. 67 DX29
Oxford Ct EC4 275 K10
Oxford Ct W3 138 CN72
Oxford Ct (Warley), Brwd. 108 FX49
Oxford Ct, Felt. 176 BX91
Oxford Way
Oxford Cres, N.Mal. 198 CR100
Oxford Dr, Ruis. 116 BW61
Oxford Gdns N20 98 DD46
Oxford Gdns N21 100 DQ45
Oxford Gdns W4 158 CN78
Oxford Gdns W10 139 CY72
Oxford Gdns (Denham), Uxb. 113 BF62
Oxford Gate W6 159 CX77
Oxford Ms, Bex. 186 FA87
Bexley High St
Oxford Pl NW10 118 CR62
Neasden La N
Oxford Rd E15 143 ED65
Oxford Rd N4 121 DN60
Oxford Rd N9 100 DV47
Oxford Rd NW6 140 DA68
Oxford Rd SE19 182 DR93
Oxford Rd SW15 159 CY84
Oxford Rd W5 137 CK73
Oxford Rd, Beac. 111 AP55
Oxford Rd (Holtspur), Beac. 110 AF55
Oxford Rd, Cars. 218 DE107
Oxford Rd, Enf. 82 DV43
Oxford Rd, Ger.Cr. 113 BA60
Oxford Rd, Guil. 258 AX136
Oxford Rd, Har. 116 CC58
Oxford Rd (Wealdstone), Har. 117 CF55
Oxford Rd, H.Wyc. 88 AE54
Oxford Rd, Ilf. 125 EQ63
Oxford Rd, Red. 250 DE133
Oxford Rd, Rom. 106 FM51
Oxford Rd, Sid. 186 EV92
Oxford Rd, Tedd. 177 CD92
Oxford Rd, Uxb. 134 BJ66
Oxford Rd, Wall. 219 DJ106
Oxford Rd, Wind. 151 AP81
Oxford Rd, Wdf.Grn. 102 EJ50
Oxford Rd E, Wind. 151 AQ81
Oxford Rd N W4 158 CP78
Oxford Rd S W4 158 CN78
Oxford Sq W2 272 C9
Oxford Sq W2 140 DE72
Oxford St W1 272 F9
Oxford St W1 141 DH72
Oxford St, Wat. 75 BV43
Oxford Ter, Guil. 258 AX136
Pewley Hill
Oxford Wk, Sthl. 136 BZ74
Oxford Way, Felt. 176 BX91
Oxgate Gdns NW2 119 CV62
Oxgate La NW2 119 CV61
Oxhawth Cres, Brom. 205 EN99
Oxhey Av, Wat. 94 BX45
Oxhey Dr, Nthwd. 93 BV50
Oxhey Dr, Wat. 94 BW48
Oxhey Dr S, Nthwd. 93 BV50
Oxhey La, Har. 94 CB50
Oxhey La, Pnr. 94 CB50
Oxhey La, Wat. 94 BZ48
Oxhey Ridge Cl, Nthwd. 93 BU50
Oxhey Rd, Wat. 94 BW45
Oxleas E6 145 EP72
Oxleas Cl, Well. 165 ER82
Oxlease Dr, Hat. 45 CV19
Oxleay Ct, Har. 116 CA60
Oxleay Rd, Har. 116 CA60
Oxleigh Cl, N.Mal. 198 CS99
Oxley Cl SE1 162 DT78
Oxley Cl, Rom. 106 FJ54
Oxleys, The, Harl. 36 EY11
Oxleys Rd NW2 119 CV62
Oxleys Rd, Wal.Abb. 68 EG32
Oxlip Cl, Croy. 203 DX102
Marigold Way
Oxlow La, Dag. 126 FA63
Oxo Twr Wf SE1 278 E1
Oxo Twr Wf SE1 141 DN73
Oxonian St SE22 162 DT84
Oxshott Ri, Cob. 214 BX113
Oxshott Rd, Lthd. 231 CE115
Oxshott Way, Cob. 230 BY115
Oxted Cl, Mitch. 200 DD97
Oxted Rd, Gdse. 252 DW130
Oxtoby Way SW16 201 DK96
Oyster Catcher Ter, Ilf. 125 EN55
Tiptree Cres
Oyster Catchers Cl E16 144 EH72
Freemasons Rd
Oyster La (Byfleet), W.Byf. 212 BK110
Oyster Row E1 142 DW72
Lukin St
Oysterfields, St.Alb. 42 CB19
Ozolins Way E16 144 EG72

P

Pablo Neruda Cl SE24 161 DP84
Shakespeare Rd
Pace Pl E1 142 DV72
Bigland St
Paceheath Cl, Rom. 105 FD51
Pachesham Dr, Lthd. 231 CF116
Oxshott Rd
Pachesham Pk, Lthd. 231 CG117
Pacific Cl, Felt. 175 BT88
Pacific Rd E16 144 EG72
Packet Boat La, Uxb. 134 BH72
Packham Cl, Orp. 206 EW104
Berrylands
Packham Ct, Wor.Pk. 199 CW104
Lavender Av
Packham Rd (Northfleet), Grav. 191 GF90
Packhorse Cl, St.Alb. 43 CJ17
Packhorse La, Borwd. 78 CS37
Packhorse La, Pot.B. 62 CR31
Packhorse Rd (Chalfont St. Peter), Ger.Cr. 112 AY58
Packhorse Rd, Sev. 256 FC123
Packington Rd W3 158 CQ76
Packington Sq N1 142 DQ67
Packington St N1 141 DP67
Packmores Rd SE9 185 ER85
Padbrook, Oxt. 254 EG129
Padbrook Cl, Oxt. 254 EH128
Padbury SE17 162 DS78
Padbury Cl, Felt. 175 BR88
Padbury Ct E2 142 DT69
Padcroft Rd, West Dr. 134 BK74
Paddenswick Rd W6 159 CU76
Paddick Cl, Hodd. 49 DZ16
Paddington Cl, Hayes 136 BX70
Paddington Grn W2 272 A6
Paddington Grn W2 140 DD71
Paddington St W1 272 F6
Paddington St W1 140 DG71
Paddock, The, Brox. 49 EA20
Paddock, The (Westcott), Dor. 262 CB137
Paddock, The (Chalfont St. Peter), Ger.Cr. 90 AY50
Paddock, The, Guil. 243 BD133
Paddock, The, Hat. 45 CU16
Paddock, The (Datchet), Slou. 152 AV81
Paddock, The (Ickenham), Uxb. 115 BP63
Paddock, The, West. 255 EQ126
Paddock Cl SE3 164 EG82
Paddock Cl SE26 183 DX91
Paddock Cl (South Darenth), Dart. 208 FQ95
Paddock Cl, Nthlt. 136 CA68
Paddock Cl, Orp. 223 EP105
State Fm Av
Paddock Cl, Oxt. 254 EF131
Paddock Cl, Ware 34 EK06
Paddock Cl, Wat. 76 BY44
Paddock Cl, Wor.Pk. 198 CS102
Paddock Gdns SE19 182 DS93
Westow St
Paddock Mead, Harl. 51 EQ20
Paddock Rd NW2 119 CU62
Paddock Rd, Bexh. 166 EY84
Paddock Rd, Ruis. 116 BX62
Paddock Wk, Warl. 236 DV119
Paddock Way, Chis. 185 ER94
Paddock Way, Hem.H. 39 BE20
Paddock Way, Oxt. 254 EF131
Paddock Way, Wok. 211 BB114
Paddocks, The NW7 97 CY51
Paddocks, The (New Haw), Add. 212 BH110
Paddocks, The, Barn. 80 DF41
Paddocks, The, Hert. 32 DV12
Paddocks, The (Bookham), Lthd. 246 CB126
Leatherhead Rd
Paddocks, The, Rick. 73 BF42
Paddocks, The, Rom. 87 FF44
Paddocks, The, Sev. 257 FK124
Paddocks, The, Vir.W. 192 AY100
Paddocks, The, Welw.G.C. 30 DB08
Paddocks, The, Wem. 118 CP61
Paddocks, The, Wey. 195 BS104
Paddocks Cl, Ash. 232 CL118
Paddocks Cl, Cob. 214 BW114
Paddocks Cl, Har. 116 CB63
Paddocks Cl, Orp. 206 EX103
Paddocks Mead, Wok. 226 AS116
Paddocks Retail Pk, Wey. 212 BL111
Paddocks Rd, Guil. 243 BA130
Paddocks Way, Ash. 232 CL118
Paddocks Way, Cher. 194 BH102
Padfield Rd SE5 162 DQ83
Padgets, The, Wal.Abb. 67 ED34
Padley Cl, Chess. 216 CM106
Moor La
Padnall Ct, Rom. 126 EX55
Padnall Rd
Padnall Rd, Rom. 126 EX56
Padstow Cl, Orp. 223 ET105
Padstow Cl, Slou. 152 AY76
Padstow Rd, Enf. 81 DP40
Padstow Wk, Felt. 175 BT88
Padua Rd SE20 202 DW95
Pagden St SW8 161 DH81
Page Cl, Dag. 126 EY64
Page Cl (Bean), Dart. 189 FW90
Page Cl, Hmptn. 176 BY93
Page Cl, Har. 118 CM58
Page Cres, Croy. 219 DN106
Page Cres, Erith 167 FF80
Page Grn Rd N15 122 DU57
Page Grn Ter N15 122 DT57
Page Heath La, Brom. 204 EK97
Page Heath Vil, Brom. 204 EK97
Page Hill, Ware 32 DV05
Page Meadow NW7 97 CU52
Page Rd, Felt. 175 BR86
Page Rd, Hert. 32 DU09
Page St NW7 97 CU53
Page St SW1 277 N8
Page St SW1 161 DL77
Pageant Av NW9 96 CR53
Pageant Cl, Til. 171 GJ81
Pageant Cres SE16 143 DY74
Rotherhithe St
Pageant Rd, St.Alb. 43 CD21
Pageant Wk, Croy. 202 DS104
Pageantmaster Ct EC4 274 F9
Pagehurst Rd, Croy. 202 DV101
Pages Cft, Berk. 38 AU17
Pages Hill N10 98 DG54
Pages La N10 98 DG54
Pages La, Rom. 106 FP54
Pages La, Uxb. 134 BJ65
Pages Wk SE1 279 M8
Pages Wk SE1 162 DS77
Pages Yd W4 158 CS79
Church St
Paget Av, Sutt. 200 DD104
Paget Cl, Hmptn. 177 CD91
Paget Gdns, Chis. 205 EP95
Paget La, Islw. 157 CD83
Paget Pl, Kings.T. 178 CQ93
Paget Pl, T.Ditt. 197 CG102
Brooklands Rd
Paget Ri SE18 165 EN80
Paget Rd N16 122 DR60
Paget Rd, Ilf. 125 EP63
Paget Rd, Slou. 153 AZ77
Paget Rd, Uxb. 135 BQ70
Paget St EC1 274 F2
Paget Ter SE18 165 EN79
Pagette Way, Grays 170 GA77
Pagitts Gro, Barn. 80 DB39
Paglesfield, Brwd. 109 GC44
Pagnell St SE14 163 DZ80
Pagoda Av, Rich. 158 CM83
Pagoda Gdns SE3 163 ED82
Pagoda Vista, Rich. 158 CM82
Paignton Rd N15 122 DS58
Paignton Rd, Ruis. 115 BU62
Paines Brook Rd, Rom. 106 FM51
Paines Brook Way
Paines Brook Way, Rom. 106 FM51
Paines Cl, Pnr. 116 BY55
Paines La, Pnr. 94 BY53
Pains Cl, Mitch. 201 DH96
Pains Hill, Oxt. 254 EJ132
Painsthorpe Rd N16 122 DS62
Oldfield Rd
Painters Ash La (Northfleet), Grav. 190 GD90
Painters La, Enf. 83 DY35
Painters Rd, Ilf. 125 ET55
Paisley Rd N22 99 DP53
Paisley Rd, Cars. 200 DD102
Pakeman St N7 121 DM62
Pakenham Cl SW12 180 DG88
Balham Pk Rd
Pakenham St WC1 274 C4
Pakenham St WC1 141 DM69
Pakes Way, Epp. 85 ES37
Palace Av W8 140 DB74
Palace Cl, Kings L. 58 BM30
Palace Cl, Slou. 131 AM74
Palace Ct NW3 120 DB64
Palace Ct W2 140 DB73
Palace Ct, Brom. 204 EH95
Palace Gro
Palace Ct, Har. 118 CL58
Palace Ct Gdns N10 121 DJ55
Palace Dr, Wey. 195 BP104
Palace Gdns, Buck.H. 102 EK46
Palace Gdns, Enf. 82 DR41
Palace Gdns Ms W8 140 DA74
Palace Gdns Prec, Enf. 82 DR41
Palace Gdns Ter W8 140 DA74
Palace Gate W8 160 DC75
Palace Gates Rd N22 99 DK53
Palace Grn W8 160 DB75
Palace Grn, Croy. 221 DZ108
Palace Gro SE19 182 DT94
Palace Gro, Brom. 204 EH95
Palace Ms E17 123 DZ56
Palace Ms SW1 276 G9
Palace Ms SW6 159 CZ80
Hartismere Rd
Palace of Industry, Wem. 118 CN63
Palace Par E17 123 EA56
High St
Palace Pl SW1 277 K6
Palace Rd N8 121 DK57
Palace Rd N11 99 DL52
Palace Rd SE19 182 DT94
Palace Rd SW2 181 DM88
Palace Rd, Brom. 204 EH95
Palace Rd, E.Mol. 197 CD97
Palace Rd, Kings.T. 197 CK98
Palace Rd, Ruis. 116 BY63
Palace Rd, West. 239 EN121
Chestnut Av
Palace Rd Est SW2 181 DM88
Palace Sq SE19 182 DT94
Palace St SW1 277 K6
Palace St SW1 161 DJ76
Palace Vw SE12 184 EG89
Palace Vw, Brom. 204 EG97
Palace Vw, Croy. 221 DZ105
Palace Vw Rd E4 101 EB50
Palace Way, Wey. 195 BP104
Palace Dr
Palamos Rd E10 123 EA60
Palatine Av N16 122 DT63
Stoke Newington Rd
Palatine Rd N16 122 DS63
Palermo Rd NW10 139 CU68
Palestine Gro SW19 200 DD95
Palewell Cl, Orp. 206 EV96
Palewell Common Dr SW14 178 CR85
Palewell Pk SW14 178 CR85
Paley Gdns, Loug. 85 EQ41
Palfrey Cl, St.Alb. 43 CD18
Palfrey Pl SW8 161 DM80
Palgrave Av, Sthl. 136 CA73
Palgrave Gdns NW1 272 C4
Palgrave Gdns NW1 140 DE70
Palgrave Rd W12 159 CT76
Palissy St E2 275 P3
Pall Mall SW1 277 L3
Pall Mall SW1 141 DJ74
Pall Mall E SW1 277 N2
Pall Mall E SW1 141 DK74
Pall Mall Pl SW1 277 L3
Pall Mall Pl SW1 141 DJ74
Palladino Ho SW17 180 DE92
Laurel Cl
Pallant Way, Orp. 205 EN104
Pallas Rd, Hem.H. 40 BM18
Pallet Way SE18 164 EL81
Palliser Dr, Rain. 147 FG71
Palliser Rd W14 159 CY78
Palliser Rd, Ch.St.G. 90 AU48
Palm Av, Sid. 186 EX93
Palm Cl E10 123 EB62
Palm Gro W5 158 CL76
Palm Gro, Guil. 242 AW129
Palm Rd, Rom. 127 FC57
Palmar Cres, Bexh. 166 FA83
Palmar Rd, Bexh. 166 FA82
Palmarsh Cl, Orp. 206 EX98
Wotton Grn
Palmeira Rd, Bexh. 166 EX83
Palmer Av, Bushey 76 CB43
Palmer Av, Grav. 191 GK91
Palmer Av, Sutt. 217 CW105
Palmer Cl, Hert. 32 DQ07
Palmer Cl, Horl. 268 DF145
Palmer Cl, Houns. 156 CA81
Palmer Cl, Red. 266 DG135
Palmer Cl, W.Wick. 203 ED104
Palmer Cres (Ottershaw), Cher. 211 BD107
Palmer Cres, Kings.T. 198 CL97
Palmer Gdns, Barn. 79 CX43
Palmer Pl N7 121 DN64
Palmer Rd E13 144 EH70
Palmer Rd, Dag. 126 EX60
Palmer Rd, Hert. 32 DR07
Palmer St SW1 277 M5
Palmer St SW1 161 DK76
Palmers Av, Grays 170 GC78
Palmers Dr, Grays 170 GC77
Palmers Gro, Wal.Abb. 50 EF22
Palmers Gro, W.Mol. 196 CA98
Palmers Hill, Epp. 70 EU29
Palmers La, Enf. 82 DV39
Palmer's Lo, Guil. 258 AU135
Old Palace Rd
Palmers Moor La, Iver 134 BG70
Palmers Orchard (Shoreham), Sev. 225 FF111
Palmers Pas SW14 158 CQ83
Palmers Rd
Palmers Rd E2 143 DX68
Palmers Rd N11 99 DJ50
Palmers Rd SW14 158 CQ83
Palmers Rd SW16 201 DM96
Palmers Rd, Borwd. 78 CP39
Palmers Way (Cheshunt), Wal.Cr. 67 DY29
Palmersfield Rd, Bans. 218 DA114
Palmerston Av, Slou. 152 AV76
Palmerston Cl, Welw.G.C. 29 CW09
Palmerston Cl, Wok. 211 AZ114
Palmerston Cres N13 99 DM50
Palmerston Cres SE18 165 EQ79
Palmerston Gdns, Grays 169 FX78
Palmerston Gro SW19 180 DA94
Palmerston Rd E7 124 EH64
Palmerston Rd E17 123 DZ56
Palmerston Rd N22 99 DM52
Palmerston Rd NW6 140 DA66
Palmerston Rd SW14 158 CQ84
Palmerston Rd SW19 180 DA94
Palmerston Rd W3 158 CQ76
Palmerston Rd, Buck.H. 102 EH47
Palmerston Rd, Cars. 218 DF105
Palmerston Rd, Croy. 202 DR99
Palmerston Rd, Grays 169 FX78
Palmerston Rd, Har. 117 CF55
Palmerston Rd, Houns. 156 CC81
Palmerston Rd, Orp. 223 EQ105
Palmerston Rd, Rain. 148 FJ68
Palmerston Rd, Sutt. 218 DC106
Vernon Rd
Palmerston Rd, Twick. 177 CF86
Palmerston Way SW8 161 DH80
Bradmead
Palmerstone Ct, Vir.W. 192 AY99
Sandhills La
Pamela Av, Hem.H. 40 BM23
Pamela Gdns, Pnr. 115 BV57
Pamela Wk E8 142 DU67
Marlborough Av
Pampisford Rd, Pur. 219 DN111
Pampisford Rd, S.Croy. 219 DP108
Pams Way, Epsom 216 CR106
Pancake La, Hem.H. 41 BR21
Pancras La EC4 275 J9
Pancras Rd NW1 141 DK68
Pancroft, Rom. 86 EV41
Pandora Rd NW6 140 DA65
Panfield Ms, Ilf. 125 EN58
Cranbrook Rd
Panfield Rd SE2 166 EU76
Pangbourne Av W10 139 CW71
Pangbourne Dr, Stan. 95 CK50
Pangbourne Ho N7 121 DL64
Panhard Pl, Sthl. 136 CB73
Pank Av, Barn. 80 DC43
Pankhurst Cl SE14 163 DX80
Briant St
Pankhurst Cl, Islw. 157 CF83
Pankhurst Rd, Walt. 196 BW101
Panmuir Rd SW20 199 CV95
Panmure Cl N5 121 DP63
Panmure Rd SE26 182 DV90
Pannells Cl, Cher. 193 BF102
Pannells Ct, Guil. 258 AX135
Panshanger Dr, Welw.G.C. 30 DB09
Panshanger La, Hert. 30 DF10
Pansy Gdns W12 139 CU73
Panters, Swan. 187 FF94
Panther Dr NW10 118 CR64
Pantile Rd, Wey. 213 BR105
Pantile Row, Slou. 153 BA77
Pantile Wk, Uxb. 134 BJ66
High St
Pantiles, The NW11 119 CZ57
Willifield Way
Pantiles, The, Bexh. 166 EZ80
Pantiles, The, Brom. 204 EL97
Pantiles, The, Bushey 95 CD45
Pantiles Cl N13 99 DP50
Pantiles Cl, Wok. 226 AV118
Panton St SW1 277 M1
Panxworth Rd, Hem.H. 40 BL22
Panyer All EC4 275 H8
Paper Ms, Dor. 263 CH135
Papercourt La (Ripley), Wok. 227 BF122
Papermill Cl, Cars. 218 DG105
Papillons Wk SE3 164 EG82
Papworth Gdns N7 121 DM64
Liverpool Rd
Papworth Way SW2 181 DN87
Parade, The SW11 160 DF80
Parade, The, Brwd. 108 FW48
Kings Rd
Parade, The, Dart. 187 FF85
Crayford Way
Parade, The, Epsom 216 CR113
Parade, The (Claygate), Esher 215 CE107
Parade, The, Hmptn. 177 CD92
Hampton Rd
Parade, The, Rom. 106 FP51
Parade, The, S.Ock. 168 FQ75
Parade, The, Sun. 175 BT94
Parade, The, Vir.W. 192 AX100
Parade, The, Wat. 75 BV41
Parade, The (Carpenders Pk), Wat. 94 BY48
Parade, The (South Oxhey), Wat. 94 BX48
Prestwick Rd
Parade, The, Wind. 151 AK81
Parade Ms SE27 181 DP89
Norwood Rd
Paradise, Hem.H. 40 BK21
Paradise Cl (Cheshunt), Wal.Cr. 66 DV28
Paradise Pas N7 121 DN64
Paradise Pl SE18 164 EL77
Woodhill
Paradise Rd SW4 161 DL82
Paradise Rd, Rich. 177 CK85
Paradise Rd, Wal.Abb. 67 EC34
Paradise Row E2 142 DV69
Bethnal Grn Rd
Paradise St SE16 162 DV75
Paradise Wk SW3 160 DF79
Paragon, The SE3 164 EF82
Paragon Cl E16 144 EG72
Paragon Gro, Surb. 198 CM100
Paragon Ms SE1 279 L8
Paragon Pl SE3 164 EF82
Paragon Pl, Surb. 198 CM100
Berrylands Rd
Paragon Rd E9 142 DV65
Parbury Ri, Chess. 216 CL107
Parbury Rd SE23 183 DY86
Parchment Cl, Amer. 55 AS37
Parchmore Rd, Th.Hth. 201 DP96
Parchmore Way, Th.Hth. 201 DP96
Pardon St EC1 274 G4
Pardoner St SE1 279 L6
Pardoner St SE1 162 DR76
Pares Cl, Wok. 226 AX116
Parfett St E1 142 DU71
Parfitt Cl NW3 120 DC61
North End
Parfour Dr, Ken. 236 DQ116
Parfrey St W6 159 CW79
Parham Dr, Ilf. 125 EP58
Parham Way N10 99 DJ54
Paringdon Rd, Harl. 51 EP19
Paris Gdn SE1 278 F2
Paris Gdn SE1 141 DP74
Parish Cl, Horn. 127 FH61
Parish Cl, Wat. 60 BX34
Crown Ri
Parish Gate Dr, Sid. 185 ES86
Parish La SE20 183 DX93
Parish La (Farnham Common), Slou. 111 AP61
Parish Ms SE20 183 DX94
Parish Wf Pl SE18 164 EL77
Woodhill
Park, The N6 120 DG58
Park, The NW11 120 DB60
Park, The SE19 182 DS94
Park, The SE23 182 DV88
Park Hill
Park, The W5 137 CK74
Park, The, Cars. 218 DF106
Park, The (Bookham), Lthd. 230 CA123
Park, The, St.Alb. 43 CG18
Park, The, Sid. 185 ET92
Park App, Well. 166 EV84
Park Av E6 145 EN67
Park Av E15 144 EE65
Park Av N3 98 DB53
Park Av N13 99 DN48
Park Av N18 100 DU49
Park Av N22 99 DL54
Park Av NW2 139 CV65
Park Av NW10 138 CM69
Park Av NW11 120 DB60
Park Av SW14 158 CR84
Park Av, Bark. 145 EQ65
Park Av, Brwd. 109 GC46
Park Av, Brom. 184 EF93
Park Av, Bushey 76 BZ40
Park Av, Cars. 218 DG107
Park Av, Cat. 236 DS124
Park Av, Egh. 173 BC93
Park Av, Enf. 82 DS44
Park Av, Grav. 191 GJ88
Park Av (Perry St), Grav. 190 GE88
Park Av, Grays 169 FU79
Park Av, Harl. 52 EW18
Park Av, Houns. 176 CB86
Park Av, Ilf. 125 EN60
Park Av, Mitch. 181 DH94
Park Av, Orp. 206 EU103
Park Av (Farnborough), Orp. 205 EM104
Park Av, Pot.B. 64 DC34
Park Av, Rad. 61 CH33
Park Av, Red. 266 DF142
Park Av, Rick. 74 BG43
Park Av, Ruis. 115 BR58
Park Av, St.Alb. 43 CG19
Park Av, Sthl. 136 CA74
Park Av, Stai. 173 BF93
Park Av (Wraysbury), Stai. 172 AX85
Park Av, Upmin. 129 FS59
Park Av, Wat. 75 BU42
Park Av, W.Wick. 203 EC103
Park Av, Wdf.Grn. 102 EH50
Park Av E, Epsom 217 CU107
Park Av Ms, Mitch. 181 DH94
Park Av
Park Av N N8 121 DK55
Park Av N NW10 119 CV64
Park Av Rd N17 100 DV52
Park Av S N8 121 DK56
Park Av W, Epsom 217 CU107
Park Barn Dr, Guil. 242 AS132

Park Barn E, Guil. 242 AT133
Park Boul, Rom. 105 FF53
Park Chase, Guil. 242 AY134
Park Chase, Wem. 118 CM63
Park Cl E9 142 DW67
Park Cl NW2 119 CV62
Park Cl NW10 138 CM69
Park Cl SW1 276 D5
Park Cl SW1 160 DF75
Park Cl W4 158 CR78
Park Cl W14 159 CZ76
Park Cl (New Haw), Add. 212 BH110
Park Cl (Strood Grn), Bet. 264 CP139
Park Cl, Bushey 76 BX41
Park Cl, Cars. 218 DF107
Park Cl, Epp. 70 FA27
Park Cl, Esher 214 CA107
Park Cl, Hmptn. 196 CC95
Park Cl, Har. 95 CE53
Park Cl, Hat. 45 CW17
Park Cl (Brookmans Pk), Hat. 63 CZ26
Park Cl, Houns. 176 CC85
Park Cl, Kings.T. 198 CN95
Park Cl (Fetcham), Lthd. 231 CD124
Park Cl, Rick. 93 BP49
Park Cl, Walt. 195 BT103
Park Cl, Wind. 151 AR82
Park Copse, Dor. 263 CK136
Park Cor (Colney Heath), St.Alb. 44 CP23
Park Cor, Wind. 151 AL83
Park Cor Dr (East Horsley), Lthd. 245 BS128
Park Cor Rd (Southfleet), Grav. 190 FZ91
Park Ct SE26 182 DV93
Park Ct, Harl. 35 ER14
Park Ct, Kings.T. 197 CJ95
Park Ct, Lthd. 246 CA125
Church Rd
Park Ct, N.Mal. 198 CR98
Park Ct, Wem. 118 CL64
Park Ct, W.Byf. 212 BG113
Park Ct, Wok. 227 AZ118
Park Dr
Park Cres N3 98 DB52
Park Cres W1 273 H5
Park Cres W1 141 DH70
Park Cres, Borwd. 78 CM41
Park Cres, Enf. 82 DR42
Park Cres, Erith 167 FD79
Park Cres, Har. 95 CE53
Park Cres, Horn. 127 FG59
Park Cres, Twick. 177 CD88
Park Cres Ms E W1 273 J5
Park Cres Ms W W1 273 H6
Park Cres Rd, Erith 167 FD79
Park Cft, Edg. 96 CQ53
Park Dale N11 99 DK51
Park Dr N21 82 DQ44
Park Dr NW11 120 DB60
Park Dr SE7 164 EL79
Park Dr SW14 158 CR84
Park Dr W3 158 CN76
Park Dr, Ash. 232 CN118
Park Dr (Hatfield Heath), B.Stort. 37 FH05
Park Dr, Dag. 127 FC62
Park Dr (Harrow Weald), Har. 95 CE51
Park Dr (North Harrow), Har. 116 CA59
Park Dr, Pot.B. 64 DA31
Park Dr, Rom. 127 FD56
Park Dr, Upmin. 128 FQ63
Park Dr, Wey. 213 BP106
Park Dr, Wok. 227 AZ118
Park Dr Cl SE7 164 EL78
Park End NW3 120 DE63
South Hill Pk
Park End, Brom. 204 EF95
Park End Rd, Rom. 127 FE56
Park Fm Cl N2 120 DC55
Park Fm Cl, Pnr. 115 BV57
Field End Rd
Park Fm Rd, Brom. 204 EK95
Park Fm Rd, Kings.T. 178 CL94
Park Fm Rd, Upmin. 128 FM64
Park Gdns NW9 118 CP55
Park Gdns, Erith 167 FD77
Valley Rd
Park Gdns, Kings.T. 178 CN92
Park Gate N2 120 DD55
Park Gate N21 99 DM45
Park Gate W5 137 CK71
Mount Av
Park Gates, Har. 116 CA63
Park Gra Gdns, Sev. 257 FJ127
Solefields Rd
Park Grn (Bookham), Lthd. 230 CA124
Park Gro E15 144 EG67
Park Gro N11 99 DK52
Park Gro, Bexh. 167 FC84
Park Gro, Brom. 204 EH95
Park Gro, Ch.St.G. 72 AX41
Park Gro, Edg. 96 CM50
Park Gro Rd E11 124 EE61
Park Hall Rd N2 120 DE56
Park Hall Rd SE21 182 DQ90
Park Hall Rd, Reig. 250 DA132
Park Hill SE23 182 DV89
Park Hill SW4 181 DK85
Park Hill W5 137 CK71
Park Hill, Brom. 204 EL98
Park Hill, Cars. 218 DE107
Park Hill, Harl. 36 EV12
Park Hill, Loug. 84 EK43
Park Hill, Rich. 178 CM86
Park Hill Cl, Cars. 218 DE106
Park Hill Ct SW17 180 DF90
Beeches Rd
Park Hill Ri, Croy. 202 DS103
Park Hill Rd, Brom. 204 EE96
Park Hill Rd, Croy. 220 DS105
Park Hill Rd, Epsom 217 CT111
Park Hill Rd, Wall. 219 DH108
Park Horsley (East Horsley), Lthd. 245 BU129
Park Ho N21 99 DM45
Park Ho Dr, Reig. 265 CZ136
Park Ho Gdns, Twick. 177 CJ86
Park Ind Est (Frogmore), St.Alb. 61 CE27
Park La E15 143 ED67
High St
Park La N9 100 DT48
Park La N17 100 DU52
Park La W1 276 G3
Park La W1 140 DG73
Park La, Ash. 232 CM118
Park La, Bans. 234 DD118
Park La, Beac. 89 AM54
Park La, Brox. 49 DY19
Park La (Wormley), Brox. 48 DV22
Park La, Cars. 218 DG105
Park La, Couls. 235 DK121
Park La, Croy. 202 DR104
Park La, Guil. 243 BC131
Park La, Harl. 35 ER13
Park La, Har. 116 CB62
Park La, Hayes 135 BS71
Park La, Hem.H. 40 BK21
Park La, Horn. 127 FG58
Park La (Elm Pk), Horn. 147 FH65
Park La, Houns. 155 BU80
Park La, Reig. 265 CY135
Park La, Rich. 157 CK84
Park La (Chadwell Heath), Rom. 126 EX58
Park La (Colney Heath), St.Alb. 44 CP23
Park La, Sev. 257 FJ124
Park La (Seal), Sev. 257 FN121
Park La, Slou. 152 AV76
Park La (Burnham), Slou. 111 AL64
Park La (Horton), Slou. 153 BA83
Park La, S.Ock. 149 FR74
Park La, Stan. 95 CG48
Park La, Sutt. 217 CY107
Park La, Swan. 208 FJ96
Park La, Tedd. 177 CF93
Park La (Harefield), Uxb. 92 BG53
Park La, Wall. 218 DG105
Park La, Wal.Cr. 66 DW33
Park La (Cheshunt), Wal.Cr. 66 DU26
Park La, Wem. 118 CL64
Park La Cl N17 100 DU52
Park La E, Reig. 266 DA136
Park La Paradise (Cheshunt), Wal.Cr. 48 DU24
Park Lawn (Farnham Royal), Slou. 131 AQ69
Park Lawn Rd, Wey. 213 BQ105
Park Lawns, Wem. 118 CM63
Park Ley Rd (Woldingham), Cat. 237 DX120
Park Mead, Harl. 35 EP14
Park Mead, Har. 116 CB62
Park Mead, Sid. 186 EV85
Park Meadow, Hat. 45 CW17
Park Ms SE24 182 DQ86
Croxted Rd
Park Ms, Chis. 185 EP93
Park Ms, E.Mol. 196 CC98
Park Ms (Hampton Hill), Hmptn. 176 CC92
Park Rd
Park Ms, Hat. 45 CW16
Park Ms, Rain. 147 FG65
Sowrey Av
Park Nook Gdns, Enf. 82 DR37
Park Par NW10 139 CT68
Park Pl E14 143 EA74
Park Pl SW1 277 K3
Park Pl SW1 141 DJ74
Park Pl W3 158 CN77
Park Pl W5 137 CK74
Park Pl, Amer. 72 AT38
Park Pl (Seer Grn), Beac. 89 AR50
Park Pl, Grav. 191 GJ86
Park Pl (Hampton Hill), Hmptn. 176 CC93
Park Pl (Park St), St.Alb. 61 CD27
Park Pl, Sev. 256 FD123
Park Pl, Wem. 118 CM63
Park Pl, Wok. 227 AZ118
Park Dr
Park Pl Vil W2 140 DC71
Park Ridings N8 121 DN55
Park Ri SE23 183 DY88
Park Ri, Berk. 38 AS17
Park Ri, Har. 95 CE53
Park Ri, Lthd. 231 CH121
Park Ri Cl, Lthd. 231 CH121
Park Ri Rd SE23 183 DY88
Park Rd E6 144 EJ67
Park Rd E10 123 EA60
Park Rd E12 124 EH60
Park Rd E15 144 EG67
Park Rd E17 123 DZ57
Park Rd N2 120 DD55
Park Rd N8 121 DJ56
Park Rd N11 99 DK52
Park Rd N14 99 DK45
Park Rd N15 121 DP56
Park Rd N18 100 DT49
Park Rd NW1 272 B2
Park Rd NW1 140 DE69
Park Rd NW4 119 CU59
Park Rd NW8 272 B2
Park Rd NW8 140 DE69
Park Rd NW9 118 CR59
Park Rd NW10 138 CS67
Park Rd SE25 202 DS98
Park Rd SW19 180 DD93
Park Rd W4 158 CQ80
Park Rd W7 137 CF73
Park Rd, Amer. 72 AT37
Park Rd, Ashf. 175 BP92
Park Rd, Ash. 232 CL118
Park Rd, Bans. 234 DB115
Park Rd, Barn. 79 CZ42
Park Rd (New Barnet), Barn. 80 DE42
Park Rd, Beck. 183 DZ94
Park Rd, Brwd. 108 FV46
Park Rd, Brom. 204 EH95
Park Rd, Bushey 76 CA44
Park Rd, Cat. 236 DS123
Park Rd, Chesh. 54 AP31
Park Rd, Chis. 185 EP93
Park Rd, Dart. 188 FN87
Park Rd, E.Mol. 196 CC98
Park Rd, Egh. 173 BA91
Park Rd, Enf. 83 DY36
Park Rd, Esher 214 CB105
Park Rd, Felt. 176 BX91
Park Rd, Grav. 191 GH88
Park Rd, Grays 170 GB78
Park Rd, Guil. 242 AX134
Park Rd (Albury), Guil. 260 BL140
Park Rd (Hampton Hill), Hmptn. 176 CB91
Park Rd, Hayes 135 BS71
Park Rd, Hem.H. 40 BJ22
Park Rd, Hert. 32 DS09
Park Rd, Hodd. 49 EA17
Park Rd, Houns. 156 CC84
Park Rd, Ilf. 125 ER62
Park Rd, Islw. 157 CH81
Park Rd, Ken. 235 DP115
Park Rd, Kings.T. 178 CM92
Park Rd (Hampton Wick), Kings.T. 177 CF93
Park Rd, N.Mal. 198 CR98
Park Rd, Orp. 206 EW99
Park Rd, Oxt. 254 EF128
Park Rd, Pot.B. 64 DG30
Park Rd, Rad. 77 CG35
Park Rd, Red. 250 DF132
Park Rd, Rich. 178 CM86
Park Rd, Rick. 92 BK45
Park Rd, Shep. 194 BN102
Park Rd, Slou. 131 AQ68
Park Rd (Stanwell), Stai. 174 BH86
Park Rd, Sun. 175 BV94
Park Rd, Surb. 198 CM99
Park Rd, Sutt. 217 CY107
Park Rd, Swan. 207 FF97
Park Rd, Swans. 190 FY86
Park Rd, Tedd. 197 CJ95
Park Rd, Twick. 177 CJ86
Park Rd, Uxb. 134 BL66
Park Rd, Wall. 219 DH106
Park Rd (Hackbridge), Wall. 201 DH103
Park Rd, Wal.Cr. 67 DX33
Park Rd, Ware 32 DV05
Park Rd, Warl. 222 EE114
Park Rd, Wat. 75 BU39
Park Rd, Wem. 138 CL65
Park Rd, Wok. 227 BA117
Park Rd E W3 158 CP75
Park Rd E, Uxb. 134 BK68
Hillingdon Rd
Park Rd N W3 158 CP75
Park Rd N W4 158 CR78
Park Row SE10 163 ED79
Park Royal Rd NW10 138 CQ69
Park Royal Rd W3 138 CQ69
Park Sq, Esher 214 CB105
Park Rd
Park Sq E NW1 273 H4
Park Sq E NW1 141 DH70
Park Sq Ms NW1 273 H4
Park Sq Ms NW1 141 DH70
Park Sq W NW1 273 H4
Park Sq W NW1 141 DH70
Park St SE1 279 H2
Park St SE1 142 DQ74
Park St W1 272 F10
Park St W1 140 DG73
Park St, Berk. 38 AV18
Park St, Croy. 202 DQ103
Park St, Guil. 258 AW136
Park St, Hat. 45 CW17
Park St, St.Alb. 61 CD26
Park St, Slou. 152 AT76
Park St (Colnbrook), Slou. 153 BD80
Park St, Tedd. 177 CE93
Park St, Wind. 151 AR81
Park St La (Park St), St.Alb. 60 CB30
Park Ter, Green. 189 FV85
Park Ter (Sundridge), Sev. 240 EX124
Main Rd
Park Ter, Wor.Pk. 199 CU102
Park Vw N21 99 DM45
Park Vw W3 138 CQ71
Park Vw, Hat. 45 CW16
Park Vw, Hodd. 49 EA18
Park Vw, Horl. 268 DG148
Brighton Rd
Park Vw (Bookham), Lthd. 246 CA125
Park Vw, N.Mal. 199 CT97
Park Vw, Pnr. 94 BZ53
Park Vw, Pot.B. 64 DC33
Park Vw, S.Ock. 149 FR74
Park Vw, Wem. 118 CP64
Park Vw Cl, St.Alb. 43 CG21
Park Vw Ct, Ilf. 125 ES58
Brancaster Rd
Park Vw Ct, Wok. 226 AY119
Park Vw Cres N11 99 DH49
Park Vw Est E2 143 DX68
Park Vw Gdns NW4 119 CW57
Park Vw Gdns, Grays 170 GB78
Park Vw Gdns, Ilf. 125 EM56
Park Vw Ho SE24 181 DP86
Hurst St
Park Vw Rd N3 98 DB53
Park Vw Rd N17 122 DU55
Park Vw Rd NW10 119 CT63
Park Vw Rd W5 138 CL71
Park Vw Rd, Berk. 38 AV19
Park Vw Rd (Woldingham), Cat. 237 DY122
Park Vw Rd, Pnr. 93 BV52
Park Vw Rd, Red. 266 DG141
Park Vw Rd, Sthl. 136 CA74
Park Vw Rd, Uxb. 134 BN72
Park Vw Rd, Well. 166 EW83
Park Village E NW1 141 DH68
Park Village W NW1 141 DH68
Park Vil, Rom. 126 EX58
Park Vista SE10 163 ED79
Park Wk N6 120 DG59
North Rd
Park Wk SE10 163 ED80
Crooms Hill
Park Wk SW10 160 DC79
Park Wk, Ash. 232 CM119
Rectory La
Park Way N20 98 DF49
Park Way NW11 119 CY57
Park Way, Bex. 187 FE90
Park Way, Brwd. 109 FZ46
Park Way, Edg. 96 CP53
Park Way, Enf. 81 DN40
Park Way, Felt. 175 BV87
Park Way, Horl. 268 DG148
Park Way (Bookham), Lthd. 230 CA123
Park Way, Rick. 92 BJ46
Park Way, Ruis. 115 BU60
Park Way, W.Mol. 196 CB97
Park W W2 272 C9
Park W Pl W2 272 C8
Park Wks Rd, Red. 251 DM133
Parkcroft Rd SE12 184 EF87
Parkdale Cres, Wor.Pk. 198 CR104
Parkdale Rd SE18 165 ES78
Parke Rd SW13 159 CU81
Parke Rd, Sun. 195 BU98
Parker Av, Hert. 32 DR07
Parker Av, Til. 171 GJ81
Parker Cl E16 144 EL74
Parker Ms WC2 274 A8
Parker Rd, Croy. 220 DQ105
Parker Rd, Grays 170 FZ78
Parker St E16 144 EL74
Parker St WC2 274 A8
Parker St WC2 141 DL72
Parker St, Wat. 75 BV39
Parkers Cl, Ash. 232 CL119
Parkers Hill, Ash. 232 CL119
Parkers La, Ash. 232 CL119
Parkers Row SE1 162 DT75
Jamaica Rd
Parkes Rd, Chig. 103 ES50
Parkfield, Rick. 73 BF42
Parkfield, Sev. 257 FM123
Parkfield Av SW14 158 CS84
Parkfield Av, Amer. 55 AR37
Parkfield Av, Felt. 175 BU90
Parkfield Av, Har. 94 CC54
Parkfield Av, Nthlt. 136 BX68
Parkfield Av (Hillingdon), Uxb. 135 BP69
Parkfield Cl, Edg. 96 CP51
Parkfield Cl, Nthlt. 136 BY68
Parkfield Cres, Felt. 175 BU90
Parkfield Cres, Har. 94 CC54
Parkfield Cres, Ruis. 116 BY62
Parkfield Dr, Nthlt. 136 BX68
Parkfield Gdns, Har. 116 CB55
Parkfield Rd NW10 139 CU66
Parkfield Rd SE14 163 DZ81
Parkfield Rd, Felt. 175 BU90
Parkfield Rd, Har. 116 CC62
Parkfield Rd, Nthlt. 136 BY68
Parkfield Rd (Ickenham), Uxb. 115 BP61
Parkfield St N1 141 DN68
Parkfield Vw, Pot.B. 64 DB32
Parkfield Way, Brom. 205 EM100
Parkfields SW15 159 CW84
Parkfields, Croy. 203 DZ102
Parkfields, Harl. 50 EH16
Parkfields (Oxshott), Lthd. 215 CD111
Parkfields, Welw.G.C. 29 CX09
Parkfields Av NW9 118 CR60
Parkfields Av SW20 199 CV95
Parkfields Cl, Cars. 218 DG105
Devonshire Rd
Parkfields Rd, Kings.T. 178 CM92
Parkgate SE3 164 EF83
Parkgate (Burnham), Slou. 130 AJ70
Parkgate Av, Barn. 80 DC39
Parkgate Cl, Kings.T. 178 CP93
Warboys App
Parkgate Cres, Barn. 80 DC40
Parkgate Gdns SW14 178 CR85
Parkgate Ms N6 121 DJ59
Stanhope Rd
Parkgate Rd SW11 160 DE80
Parkgate Rd, Orp. 225 FB105
Parkgate Rd, Reig. 266 DB135
Parkgate Rd, Wall. 218 DG106
Parkgate Rd, Wat. 76 BW37
Parkham Ct, Brom. 204 EE96
Parkham St SW11 160 DE81
Parkhill Cl, Horn. 128 FJ62
Parkhill Rd E4 101 EC46
Parkhill Rd NW3 120 DF64
Parkhill Rd, Bex. 186 EZ87
Parkhill Rd, Hem.H. 40 BH20
Parkhill Rd, Sid. 185 ER90
Parkhill Wk NW3 120 DF64
Parkholme Rd E8 142 DT65
Parkhouse St SE5 162 DR80
Parkhurst, Epsom 216 CQ110
Parkhurst Av E16 144 EH74
Wesley Av
Parkhurst Gdns, Bex. 186 FA87
Parkhurst Gro, Horl. 268 DE147
Parkhurst Rd E12 125 EN63
Parkhurst Rd E17 123 DY56
Parkhurst Rd N7 121 DL63
Parkhurst Rd N11 98 DG49
Parkhurst Rd N17 100 DU54
Parkhurst Rd N22 99 DM52
Parkhurst Rd, Bex. 186 FA87
Parkhurst Rd, Guil. 242 AU133
Parkhurst Rd, Hert. 31 DP08
Parkhurst Rd, Horl. 268 DE147
Parkhurst Rd, Sutt. 218 DD105
Parkland Av, Rom. 127 FE55
Parkland Av, Slou. 152 AX77
Parkland Av, Upmin. 128 FP64
Parkland Cl, Chig. 103 EQ48
Parkland Cl, Hodd. 33 EB14
Parkland Cl, Sev. 257 FJ129
Parkland Dr, St.Alb. 42 CA21
Parkland Gdns SW19 179 CX88
Parkland Gro, Ashf. 174 BN91
Parkland Rd N22 99 DM54
Parkland Rd, Ashf. 174 BN91
Parkland Rd, Wdf.Grn. 102 EG52
Parkland Wk N4 121 DM59
Parkland Wk N6 121 DK59
Parkland Wk N10 121 DH56
Parklands N6 121 DH59
Parklands, Add. 212 BJ106
Parklands, Chig. 103 EQ48
Parklands (North Holmwood), Dor. 263 CH140
Parklands, Epp. 70 EX29
Parklands, Hem.H. 39 BF18
Parklands (Bookham), Lthd. 230 CA123
Parklands, Oxt. 254 EE131
Parklands, Surb. 198 CM99
Parklands, Wal.Abb. 67 ED32
Parklands Cl SW14 178 CQ85
Parklands Cl, Barn. 80 DD38
Parklands Ct, Houns. 156 BX82
Parklands Dr N3 119 CY55
Parklands Pl, Guil. 243 BB134
Parklands Rd SW16 181 DH92
Parklands Way, Wor.Pk. 198 CS104
Parklawn Av, Epsom 216 CP113
Parklawn Av, Horl. 268 DF146
Parklea Cl NW9 96 CS53
Parkleigh Rd SW19 200 DB96
Parkleys, Rich. 177 CK91
Parkmead SW15 179 CV86
Parkmead, Loug. 85 EN43
Parkmead Gdns NW7 97 CT51
Parkmore Cl, Wdf.Grn. 102 EG49
Parkpale La, Bet. 264 CN139
Parkshot, Rich. 158 CL84
Parkside N3 98 DB53
Parkside NW2 119 CV62
Parkside NW7 97 CU51
Parkside SE3 164 EF80
Parkside SW19 179 CX91
Parkside (New Haw), Add. 212 BH110
Parkside, Buck.H. 102 EH47
Parkside (Chalfont St. Peter), Ger.Cr. 113 AZ56
Lower Rd
Parkside, Grays 170 GE76
Parkside (Hampton Hill), Hmptn. 177 CD92
Parkside (Matching Tye), Harl. 37 FE12
Parkside, Pot.B. 64 DC32
High St
Parkside (Halstead), Sev. 224 EZ113
Parkside, Sid. 186 EV89
Parkside, Sutt. 217 CY107
Parkside, Wal.Cr. 67 DY34
Parkside, Wat. 76 BW44
Parkside Av SW19 179 CX92
Parkside Av, Bexh. 167 FD82
Parkside Av, Brom. 204 EL98
Parkside Av, Rom. 127 FD55
Parkside Av, Til. 171 GH82
Parkside Business Est SE8 163 DY79
Rolt St
Parkside Cl SE20 182 DW94
Parkside Cl (East Horsley), Lthd. 245 BT125
Parkside Ct, Wey. 212 BN105
Parkside Cres N7 121 DN62
Parkside Cres, Surb. 198 CQ100
Parkside Cross, Bexh. 167 FE82
Parkside Dr, Edg. 96 CN48
Parkside Dr, Wat. 75 BS40
Parkside Est E9 142 DW67
Rutland Rd
Parkside Gdns SW19 179 CX91
Parkside Gdns, Barn. 98 DF46
Parkside Gdns, Couls. 235 DH117
Parkside Ho, Dag. 127 FC62
Parkside Pl (East Horsley), Lthd. 245 BS125
Parkside Rd SW11 160 DG81
Parkside Rd, Belv. 167 FC77
Parkside Rd, Houns. 176 CB85
Parkside Rd, Nthwd. 93 BT50
Parkside Ter N18 100 DR49
Great Cambridge Rd
Parkside Wk SE10 164 EE78
Parkside Wk, Slou. 152 AU76
Parkside Way, Har. 116 CB56
Parkstead Rd SW15 179 CU85
Parkstone Av N18 100 DT50
Parkstone Av, Horn. 128 FL58
Parkstone Rd E17 123 EC55
Parkstone Rd SE15 162 DU82
Rye La
Parkthorne Cl, Har. 116 CB58
Parkthorne Dr, Har. 116 CA58
Parkthorne Rd SW12 181 DK87
Parkview, St.Alb. 43 CG21
Parkview Chase, Slou. 131 AL72
Parkview Ct SW18 180 DA86
Broomhill Rd
Parkview Dr, Mitch. 200 DD96
Parkview Rd SE9 185 EP89
Parkview Rd, Croy. 202 DU102
Parkview Vale, Guil. 243 BC132
Foxglove Gdns
Parkville Rd SW6 159 CZ80
Parkway N14 99 DL47
Parkway NW1 141 DH67
Parkway SW20 199 CX98
Parkway (New Addington), Croy. 221 EC109
Parkway, Dor. 263 CG135
Parkway, Erith 166 EY76
Parkway, Guil. 242 AY133
Parkway, Harl. 50 EL15
Parkway, Ilf. 125 ET62
Parkway, Rain. 147 FG70
Upminster Rd S
Parkway, Rom. 127 FF55
Parkway, Saw. 36 EY06
Parkway, Uxb. 134 BN66
Parkway, Welw.G.C. 29 CW11
Parkway, Wey. 213 BR105
Parkway, Wdf.Grn. 102 EJ50
Parkway, The, Hayes 136 BW72
Parkway, The (Cranford), Houns. 155 BV82
Parkway, The, Iver 133 BC68
Parkway, The, Nthlt. 136 BX69
Parkway, The, Sthl. 155 BU78
Parkway Cl, Welw.G.C. 29 CW09
Parkway Ct, St.Alb. 43 CH23
Parkway Gdns, Welw.G.C. 29 CW10
Parkway Trd Est, Houns. 156 BW79
Parkwood N20 98 DF48
Parkwood, Beck. 203 EA95
Parkwood Av, Esher 196 CC102
Parkwood Cl, Bans. 233 CX115
Parkwood Cl, Brox. 49 DY19
Parkwood Dr, Hem.H. 39 BF20
Parkwood Gro, Sun. 195 BU97
Parkwood Ms N6 121 DH58
Parkwood Rd SW19 179 CZ92
Parkwood Rd, Bans. 233 CX115
Parkwood Rd, Bex. 186 EZ87
Parkwood Rd, Islw. 157 CF81
Parkwood Rd (Nutfield), Red. 251 DL133
Parkwood Rd (Tatsfield), West. 238 EL121
Parkwood Vw, Bans. 233 CW116
Parlaunt Rd, Slou. 153 BA77
Parley Dr, Wok. 226 AW117
Parliament Ct E1 142 DS71
Sandy's Row
Parliament Hill NW3 120 DE63
Parliament La (Burnham), Slou. 130 AF66
Parliament Ms SW14 158 CQ82
Thames Bk
Parliament Sq SW1 277 P5
Parliament Sq SW1 161 DL75
Parliament Sq, Hert. 32 DR09
Parliament St SW1 277 P5
Parliament St SW1 161 DL75
Parliament Vw Apartments SE1 278 B8
Parliament Vw Apartments SE1 161 DM77
Parma Cres SW11 160 DF84
Parmiter St E2 142 DV68
Parmoor Ct EC1 275 H4
Parnall Rd, Harl. 51 ER18
Parndon Mill La, Harl. 35 EP12
Parndon Wd Rd, Harl. 51 EQ20
Parnel Rd, Ware 33 DZ05
Parnell Cl, Abb.L. 59 BT30
Parnell Cl, Edg. 96 CP49
Parnell Cl, Grays 169 FW78
Parnell Gdns, Wey. 212 BN111
Parnell Rd E3 143 DZ67
Parnham St E14 143 DY72
Blount St
Parolles Rd N19 121 DJ60
Paroma Rd, Belv. 166 FA76
Parr Av, Epsom 217 CV109
Parr Cl N9 100 DV49
Parr Cl N18 100 DV49
Parr Cl, Grays 169 FW77
Parr Cl, Lthd. 231 CF120
Parr Ct N1 142 DR68
Parr Ct, Felt. 176 BW91
Parr Cres, Hem.H. 41 BP15
Parr Pl W4 159 CT77
Chiswick High Rd
Parr Rd E6 144 EK67
Parr Rd, Stan. 95 CK53
Parr St N1 142 DR68
Parris Cft, Dor. 263 CJ139
Goodwyns Rd
Parrock, The, Grav. 191 GJ88
Parrock Av, Grav. 191 GJ88
Parrock Rd, Grav. 191 GJ88
Parrock St, Grav. 191 GH87
Parrotts Cl, Rick. 74 BN42

Parrotts Fld, Hodd. 49 EB16
Parrs Cl, S.Croy. 220 DR109
Florence Rd
Parrs Pl, Hmptn. 176 CA94
Parry Av E6 145 EM72
Parry Cl, Epsom 217 CU108
Parry Dr, Wey. 212 BN110
Parry Grn N, Slou. 153 AZ77
Parry Grn S, Slou. 153 BA77
Parry Pl SE18 165 EP77
Parry Rd SE25 202 DS97
Parry Rd W10 139 CY69
Parry St SW8 161 DL79
Parsifal Rd NW6 120 DA64
Parsley Gdns, Croy. 203 DX102
Primrose La
Parsloe Rd, Epp. 51 EN21
Parsloe Rd, Harl. 51 EP20
Parsloes Av, Dag. 126 EX63
Parson St NW4 119 CW56
Parsonage Cl, Abb.L. 59 BS30
Parsonage Cl (Westcott), Dor. 262 CC138
Parsonage La
Parsonage Cl, Hayes 135 BT72
Parsonage Cl, Warl. 237 DY116
Parsonage Gdns, Enf. 82 DQ40
Parsonage La (South Darenth), Dart. 188 FP93
Parsonage La (Westcott), Dor. 262 CC137
Parsonage La, Enf. 82 DR40
Parsonage La, Hat. 45 CV23
Parsonage La, Sid. 186 EZ91
Parsonage La (Farnham Common), Slou. 131 AQ68
Parsonage La, Wind. 151 AN81
Parsonage Leys, Harl. 51 ET15
Parsonage Manorway, Belv. 166 FA79
Parsonage Rd, Ch.St.G. 90 AV48
Parsonage Rd (Englefield Grn), Egh. 172 AX92
Parsonage Rd, Grays 169 FW79
Parsonage Rd, Hat. 45 CV23
Parsonage Rd, Rain. 148 FJ68
Parsonage Rd, Rick. 92 BK45
Parsonage Sq, Dor. 263 CG135
Parsonage St E14 163 EC77
Parsons Cl, Horl. 268 DE147
Baden Dr
Parsons Cres, Edg. 96 CN48
Parsons Grn SW6 160 DA81
Parsons Grn, Guil. 242 AX132
Bellfields Rd
Parsons Grn Ct, Guil. 242 AX132
Bellfields Rd
Parsons Grn La SW6 160 DA81
Parsons Gro, Edg. 96 CN48
Parsons Hill SE18 165 EN76
Powis St
Parsons Ho SW2 181 DL87
New Pk Rd
Parson's Ho W2 140 DD70
Parsons La, Dart. 187 FH90
Parson's Mead, Croy. 201 DP102
Parsons Mead, E.Mol. 196 CC97
Parsons Pightle, Couls. 235 DN120
Coulsdon Rd
Parsons Rd E13 144 EJ68
Old St
Parsons Wd (Farnham Common), Slou. 131 AQ65
Parsonsfield Cl, Bans. 233 CX115
Parsonsfield Rd, Bans. 233 CX116
Parthenia Rd SW6 160 DA81
Parthia Cl, Tad. 233 CV119
Partingdale La NW7 97 CX50
Partington Cl N19 121 DK60
Partridge Cl E16 144 EK71
Fulmer Rd
Partridge Cl, Barn. 79 CW44
Partridge Cl, Bushey 94 CB46
Partridge Cl, Chesh. 54 AS28
Partridge Cl, Stan. 96 CL49
Partridge Ct EC1 141 DP70
Percival St
Partridge Dr, Orp. 205 EQ104
Partridge Grn SE9 185 EN90
Partridge Knoll, Pur. 219 DP112
Partridge Mead, Bans. 233 CW116
Partridge Rd, Hmptn. 176 BZ93
Partridge Rd, Harl. 51 ER17
Partridge Rd, St.Alb. 43 CD16
Partridge Rd, Sid. 185 ES90
Partridge Sq E6 144 EL71
Nightingale Way
Partridge Way N22 99 DL53
Partridge Way, Guil. 243 BD132
Parvills, Wal.Abb. 67 ED32
Parvin St SW8 161 DK81
Parvis Rd, W.Byf. 212 BH113
Pasadena Cl, Hayes 155 BV75
Pasadena Cl Trd Est, Hayes 155 BV75
Pasadena Cl
Pascal St SW8 161 DK80
Pascoe Rd SE13 183 ED85
Pasfield, Wal.Abb. 67 ED33
Pasley Cl SE17 162 DQ78
Penrose St
Pasquier Rd E17 123 DY55
Passey Pl SE9 185 EM86
Passfield Dr E14 143 EB71
Uamvar St
Passfield Path SE28 146 EV73
Booth Cl
Passing All EC1 274 G5
Passmore Gdns N11 99 DK51
Passmore St SW1 276 F9
Passmore St SW1 160 DG77
Pastens Rd, Oxt. 254 EJ131
Pasteur Cl NW9 96 CS54
Pasteur Dr, Rom. 106 FK54
Pasteur Gdns N18 99 DP50
Paston Cl E5 123 DX62
Caldecott Way
Paston Cl, Wall. 201 DJ104
Paston Cres SE12 184 EH87
Paston Rd, Hem.H. 40 BK18
Pastor St SE11 278 G8
Pastor St SE11 161 DP77
Pasture Cl, Bushey 94 CC45
Pasture Cl, Wem. 117 CH62
Pasture Rd SE6 184 EF88
Pasture Rd, Dag. 126 EZ63
Pasture Rd, Wem. 117 CH61
Pastures, The N20 97 CZ46
Pastures, The, Hat. 45 CV19
Pastures, The, Hem.H. 39 BE19
Pastures, The, St.Alb. 42 CA24
Pastures, The, Wat. 94 BW45
Pastures, The, Welw.G.C. 30 DB11
Pastures Mead, Uxb. 134 BN65
Patch, The, Sev. 256 FE122
Patch Cl, Uxb. 134 BM67
Patcham Ct, Sutt. 218 DC109
Patcham Ter SW8 161 DH81
Pater St W8 160 DA76
Paternoster Cl, Wal.Abb. 68 EF33
Paternoster Hill, Wal.Abb. 68 EF32
Paternoster Row EC4 275 H9
Paternoster Row (Havering-atte-Bower), Rom. 106 FJ47
Paternoster Sq EC4 274 G8
Paterson Rd, Ashf. 174 BK92
Pates Manor Dr, Felt. 175 BR87
Path, The SW19 200 DB95
Pathfield Rd SW16 181 DK93
Pathfields (Shere), Guil. 260 BN140
Pathway, The, Rad. 77 CF36
Pathway, The, Wat. 94 BX46
Anthony Cl
Pathway, The (Send), Wok. 243 BF125
Patience Rd SW11 160 DE82
Patio Cl SW4 181 DK86
Patmore Est SW8 161 DJ81
Patmore La, Walt. 213 BT107
Patmore Link Rd, Hem.H. 41 BQ20
Patmore Rd, Wal.Abb. 68 EE34
Patmore St SW8 161 DJ81
Patmore Way, Rom. 105 FB50
Patmos Rd SW9 161 DP80
Paton Cl E3 143 EA69
Paton St EC1 275 H3
Patricia Cl, Slou. 131 AL73
Patricia Ct, Chis. 205 ER95
Manor Pk Rd
Patricia Ct, Well. 166 EV80
Patricia Dr, Horn. 128 FL60
Patricia Gdns, Sutt. 218 DA111
The Cres
Patrick Connolly Gdns E3 143 EB69
Talwin St
Patrick Gro, Wal.Abb. 67 EB33
Beaulieu Dr
Patrick Rd E13 144 EJ69
Patrington Cl, Uxb. 134 BJ69
Boulmer Rd
Patriot Sq E2 142 DV68
Patrol Pl SE6 183 EB86
Patrons Dr (Denham), Uxb. 113 BF58
Patshull Pl NW5 141 DJ65
Patshull Rd
Patshull Rd NW5 141 DJ65
Patten All, Rich. 177 CK85
The Hermitage
Patten Rd SW18 180 DE87
Pattenden Rd SE6 183 DZ88
Patterdale Cl, Brom. 184 EF93
Patterdale Rd SE15 162 DW80
Patterdale Rd, Dart. 189 FR88
Patterson Ct SE19 182 DT94
Patterson Ct, Dart. 188 FN85
Patterson Rd SE19 182 DT93
Patterson Rd, Chesh. 54 AP28
Pattina Wk SE16 143 DZ74
Pattison Pt E16 144 EG71
Fife Rd
Pattison Rd NW2 120 DA62
Pattison Wk SE18 165 EQ78
Paul Cl E15 144 EE66
Paul Gdns, Croy. 202 DT103
Paul Julius Cl E14 143 ED73
Paul Robeson Cl E6 145 EN69
Eastbourne Rd
Paul St E15 143 ED67
Paul St EC2 275 L5
Paul St EC2 142 DR70
Paulet Rd SE5 161 DP82
Paulhan Rd, Har. 117 CK56
Paulin Dr N21 99 DN45
Pauline Cres, Twick. 176 CC88
Paulinus Cl, Orp. 206 EW96
Pauls Grn, Wal.Cr. 67 DY33
Eleanor Rd
Pauls Hill (Penn), H.Wyc. 88 AF48
Pauls La, Hodd. 49 EA17
Taverners Way
Paul's Pl, Ash. 232 CP119
Paul's Wk EC4 274 G10
Paul's Wk EC4 142 DQ73
Paultons Sq SW3 160 DD79
Paultons St SW3 160 DD79
Pauntley St N19 121 DJ60
Paved Ct, Rich. 177 CK85
Paveley Dr SW11 160 DE80
Paveley St NW8 272 C4
Paveley St NW8 140 DE70
Pavement, The SW4 161 DJ84
Pavement, The W5 158 CL76
Popes La
Pavement Ms, Rom. 126 EX59
Clarissa Rd
Pavement Sq, Croy. 202 DU102
Pavet Cl, Dag. 147 FB65
Pavilion Gdns, Stai. 174 BH94
Pavilion Ms N3 98 DA54
Windermere Av
Pavilion Rd SW1 276 E7
Pavilion Rd SW1 160 DF75
Pavilion Rd, Ilf. 125 EM59
Pavilion Shop Cen, The, Wal.Cr. 67 DY34
Pavilion St SW1 276 E7
Pavilion Ter, E.Mol. 197 CF98
Pavilion Ter, Ilf. 125 ES57
Southdown Cres
Pavilion Way, Amer. 72 AW39
Pavilion Way, Edg. 96 CP52
Pavilion Way, Ruis. 116 BW61
Pavilions, The, Epp. 71 FC25
Pavilions, The, Uxb. 134 BJ66
Pawleyne Cl SE20 182 DW94
Pawsey Cl E13 144 EG67
Plashet Rd
Pawson's Rd, Croy. 202 DQ100
Paxford Rd, Wem. 117 CH61
Paxton Av, Slou. 151 AQ76
Paxton Cl, Rich. 158 CM82
Paxton Cl, Walt. 196 BW101
Paxton Gdns, Wok. 211 BE112
Paxton Pl SE27 182 DS91
Paxton Rd N17 100 DT52
Paxton Rd SE23 183 DY90
Paxton Rd W4 158 CS79
Paxton Rd, Berk. 38 AX19
Paxton Rd, Brom. 184 EG94
Paxton Rd, St.Alb. 43 CE21
Paxton Ter SW1 161 DH79
Paycock Rd, Harl. 51 EN17
Payne Cl, Bark. 145 ES66
Payne Rd E3 143 EB68
Payne St SE8 163 DZ79
Paynell Ct SE3 164 EE83
Lawn Ter
Paynes La, Wal.Abb. 49 EC24
Paynes Wk W6 159 CY79
Paynesfield Av SW14 158 CR83
Paynesfield Rd, Bushey 95 CF45
Paynesfield Rd (Tatsfield), West. 238 EJ121
Pea La, Upmin. 149 FU66
Peabody Av SW1 277 H10
Peabody Cl SE10 163 EB81
Devonshire Dr
Peabody Cl SW1 161 DH79
Lupus St
Peabody Cl, Croy. 202 DW102
Shirley Rd
Peabody Ct, Enf. 83 EA37
Government Row
Peabody Dws WC1 273 P4
Peabody Est EC1 275 J5
Peabody Est N17 100 DS53
Peabody Est SE1 278 E3
Peabody Est SE24 182 DQ87
Peabody Est SW3 160 DE79
Margaretta Ter
Peabody Est W6 159 CW78
The Sq
Peabody Est W10 139 CW71
Peabody Hill SE21 181 DP88
Peabody Hill Est SE21 181 DP87
Peabody Sq N1 141 DP67
Essex Rd
Peabody Sq SE1 278 F5
Peabody Sq SE1 161 DP75
Peabody Twr EC1 142 DQ70
Peabody Trust SE1 279 H3
Peabody Trust SE1 142 DQ74
Peabody Yd N1 142 DQ67
Greenman St
Peace Cl N14 81 DH43
Peace Cl SE25 202 DS98
Peace Cl, Wal.Cr. 66 DU29
Goffs La
Peace Dr, Wat. 75 BU41
Peace Gro, Wem. 118 CP62
Peace Prospect, Wat. 75 BU41
Peace Rd, Iver 133 BA68
Peace Rd, Slou. 133 BA68
Peace St SE18 165 EP79
Nightingale Vale
Peach Cft (Northfleet), Grav. 190 GE90
Peach Rd W10 139 CX69
Peach Tree Av, West Dr. 134 BM72
Pear Tree Av
Peaches Cl, Sutt. 217 CY108
Peachey Cl, Uxb. 134 BK72
Peachey La, Uxb. 134 BK71
Peachum Rd SE3 164 EF79
Peacock Av, Felt. 175 BR88
Peacock Cl, Horn. 128 FL56
Peacock Gdns, S.Croy. 221 DY110
Peacock St SE17 278 G9
Peacock St, Grav. 191 GJ87
Peacock Wk E16 144 EH72
Peacock Wk, Abb.L. 59 BU31
Peacock Wk, Dor. 263 CG137
Rose Hill
Peacock Yd SE17 278 G9
Peacocks, Harl. 51 EM17
Peacocks Cen, The, Wok. 226 AY117
Peacocks Cl, Berk. 38 AT17
Tortoiseshell Way
Peak, The SE26 182 DW90
Peak Hill SE26 182 DW91
Peak Hill Av SE26 182 DW91
Peak Hill Gdns SE26 182 DW91
Peak Rd, Guil. 242 AU131
Peakes La (Cheshunt), Wal.Cr. 66 DT27
Peakes Way (Cheshunt), Wal.Cr. 66 DT27
Peaketon Av, Ilf. 124 EK56
Peaks Hill, Pur. 219 DK110
Peaks Hill Ri, Pur. 219 DL110
Peal Gdns W13 137 CG70
Ruislip Rd E
Peall Rd, Croy. 201 DM100
Pear Cl NW9 118 CR56
Pear Cl SE14 163 DY80
Southerngate Way
Pear Pl SE1 278 D4
Pear Rd E11 123 ED62
Pear Tree Av, West Dr. 134 BM72
Pear Tree Cl E2 142 DT67
Pear Tree Cl, Add. 212 BG106
Pear Tree Rd
Pear Tree Cl, Amer. 72 AT39
Orchard End Av
Pear Tree Cl (Seer Grn), Beac. 89 AQ51
Pear Tree Cl, Chess. 216 CN106
Pear Tree Cl, Mitch. 200 DE96
Pear Tree Cl, Slou. 131 AM74
Pear Tree Cl, Swan. 207 FD96
Pear Tree Ct EC1 274 E4
Pear Tree Ct EC1 141 DN70
Pear Tree Hill, Red. 266 DG143
Pear Tree Mead, Harl. 52 EU18
Pear Tree Rd, Add. 212 BG106
Pear Tree Rd, Ashf. 175 BQ92
Pear Tree St EC1 274 G4
Pear Tree St EC1 141 DP70
Pear Tree Wk (Cheshunt), Wal.Cr. 66 DR26
Pearce Cl, Mitch. 200 DG96
Pearce Rd, Chesh. 54 AP29
Pearce Rd, W.Mol. 196 CB97
Pearcefield Av SE23 182 DW88
Pearces Wk, St.Alb. 43 CD21
Albert St
Pearcroft Rd E11 123 ED61
Pearcy Cl, Rom. 106 FL52
Peardon St SW8 161 DH82
Peareswood Gdns, Stan. 95 CK53
Peareswood Rd, Erith 167 FF81
Pearfield Rd SE23 183 DY90
Pearl Cl E6 145 EN72
Pearl Cl NW2 119 CX59
Marble Dr
Pearl Ct, Wok. 226 AS116
Langmans Way
Pearl Gdns, Slou. 131 AP74
Pearl Rd E17 123 EA55
Pearl St E1 142 DV74
Penang St
Pearmain Cl, Shep. 195 BP99
Pearman St SE1 278 E6
Pearman St SE1 161 DN75
Pears Rd, Houns. 156 CC83
Pearscroft Ct SW6 160 DB81
Pearscroft Rd SW6 160 DB81
Pearse St SE15 162 DS79
Dragon Rd
Pearson Av, Hert. 32 DQ11
Pearson Cl, Hert. 32 DQ11
Pearson Av
Pearson Ms SW4 161 DK83
Edgeley Rd
Pearson St E2 142 DT68
Pearson Way, Dart. 188 FM89
Pearsons Av SE14 163 EA81
Tanners Hill
Peartree Av SW17 180 DC90
Peartree Cl, Erith 167 FD81
Peartree Cl, Hem.H. 40 BG19
Peartree Cl, S.Croy. 220 DV114
Peartree Cl, S.Ock. 149 FW68
Peartree Cl, Welw.G.C. 29 CY09
Peartree Ct E18 102 EH53
Churchfields
Peartree Ct, Welw.G.C. 29 CY10
Peartree Fm, Welw.G.C. 29 CY09
Peartree Gdns, Dag. 126 EV63
Peartree Gdns, Rom. 105 FB54
Peartree La E1 142 DW73
Glamis Rd
Peartree La, Welw.G.C. 29 CY10
Peartree Rd, Enf. 82 DS41
Peartree Rd, Hem.H. 40 BG19
Peartree Way SE10 164 EG77
Peary Pl E2 142 DW69
Kirkwall Pl
Peascod Pl, Wind. 151 AR81
Peascod St
Peascod St, Wind. 151 AR81
Peascroft Rd, Hem.H. 40 BN23
Pease Cl, Horn. 147 FH66
Dowding Way
Peatfield Cl, Sid. 185 ES90
Woodside Rd
Peatmore Av, Wok. 228 BG116
Peatmore Cl, Wok. 228 BG116
Pebble Cl, Tad. 248 CS128
Pebble Hill, Lthd. 245 BQ133
Pebble Hill Rd, Bet. 248 CS131
Pebble Hill Rd, Tad. 248 CS131
Pebble La, Epsom 232 CN121
Pebble La, Lthd. 248 CL125
Pebble Way W3 138 CP74
Pebworth Rd, Har. 117 CG61
Peckarmans Wd SE26 182 DU90
Peckett Sq N5 122 DQ63
Highbury Gra
Peckford Pl SW9 161 DN82
Peckham Gro SE15 162 DS80
Peckham High St SE15 162 DU81
Peckham Hill St SE15 162 DU80
Peckham Pk Rd SE15 162 DU80
Peckham Rd SE5 162 DS81
Peckham Rd SE15 162 DS81
Peckham Rye SE15 162 DU83
Peckham Rye SE22 162 DU84
Pecks Hill, Wal.Abb. 50 EE21
Pecks Yd E1 275 P6
Peckwater St NW5 121 DJ64
Pedham Pl Ind Est, Swan. 207 FG99
Pedlars End, Ong. 53 FH21
Pedlars Wk N7 141 DL65
Pedley Rd, Dag. 126 EW60
Pedley St E1 142 DT70
Pednor Rd, Chesh. 54 AM30
Pednormead End, Chesh. 54 AP32
Pedro St E5 123 DX62
Pedworth Gdns SE16 162 DW77
Rotherhithe New Rd
Peek Cres SW19 179 CX92
Peeks Brook La, Horl. 269 DM150
Peel Cl E4 101 EB47
Peel Cl N9 100 DU48
Plevna Rd
Peel Cl, Wind. 151 AP83
Peel Ct, Slou. 131 AQ71
Farnburn Av
Peel Cres, Hert. 31 DP07
Peel Dr NW9 119 CT55
Peel Dr, Ilf. 124 EL55
Peel Gro E2 142 DW68
Peel Pas W8 140 DA74
Peel St
Peel Pl, Ilf. 102 EL54
Peel Prec NW6 140 DA68
Peel Rd E18 102 EF53
Peel Rd NW6 139 CZ69
Peel Rd (Wealdstone), Har. 117 CF55
Peel Rd, Orp. 223 EQ106
Peel Rd, Wem. 117 CK62
Peel St W8 140 DA74
Peel Way, Rom. 106 FM54
Peel Way, Uxb. 134 BL71
Peerage Way, Horn. 128 FL59
Peerless Dr (Harefield), Uxb. 114 BJ57
Peerless St EC1 275 K3
Peerless St EC1 142 DR69
Pegamoid Rd N18 100 DW48
Pegasus Cl N16 122 DR63
Green Las
Pegasus Ct, Abb.L. 59 BT32
Furtherfield
Pegasus Ct, Grav. 191 GJ90
Pegasus Pl SE11 161 DN79
Clayton St
Pegasus Rd, Croy. 219 DN107
Pegasus Way N11 99 DH51
Pegelm Gdns, Horn. 128 FM59
Pegg Rd, Houns. 156 BX80
Peggotty Way, Uxb. 135 BP72
Dickens Av
Pegley Gdns SE12 184 EG89
Pegmire La, Wat. 76 CC39
Pegrams Rd, Harl. 51 EQ18
Pegs La, Hert. 32 DR11
Pegwell St SE18 165 ES80
Peket Cl, Stai. 193 BE95
Pekin Cl E14 143 EA72
Pekin St
Pekin St E14 143 EA72
Peldon Ct, Rich. 158 CM84
Peldon Pas, Rich. 158 CM84
Worple Way
Peldon Rd, Harl. 51 EN17
Peldon Wk N1 141 DP67
Britannia Row
Pelham Av, Bark. 145 ET67
Pelham Cl SE5 162 DS82
Pelham Ct, Hem.H. 41 BQ20
Pelham Ct, Welw.G.C. 30 DC10
Amwell Common
Pelham Cres SW7 276 B9
Pelham Cres SW7 160 DE77
Pelham Pl SW7 276 B9
Pelham Pl SW7 160 DE77
Pelham Rd E18 124 EH55
Pelham Rd N15 122 DT56
Pelham Rd N22 99 DN54
Pelham Rd SW19 180 DA94
Pelham Rd, Beck. 202 DW96
Pelham Rd, Bexh. 166 FA83
Pelham Rd, Grav. 191 GF87
Pelham Rd, Ilf. 125 ER61
Pelham Rd S, Grav. 191 GF88
Pelham St SW7 276 A8
Pelham St SW7 160 DE77
Pelham Ter, Grav. 191 GF87
Campbell Rd
Pelham Way (Bookham), Lthd. 246 CB126
Pelhams, The, Wat. 76 BX35
Pelhams Cl, Esher 214 CA105
Pelhams Wk, Esher 196 CA104
Pelican Est SE15 162 DT81
Pelican Pas E1 142 DW70
Cambridge Heath Rd
Pelican Wk SW9 161 DP84
Loughborough Pk
Pelier St SE17 162 DQ79
Langdale Cl
Pelinore Rd SE6 184 EE89
Pellant Rd SW6 159 CY80
Pellatt Gro N22 99 DN53
Pellatt Rd SE22 182 DT85
Pellatt Rd, Wem. 117 CK61
Pellerin Rd N16 122 DS64
Pelling Hill (Old Windsor), Wind. 172 AV87
Pelling St E14 143 EA72
Pellipar Cl N13 99 DN48
Pellipar Gdns SE18 165 EM78
Pelly Ct, Epp. 69 ET31
Pelly Rd E13 144 EG68
Pelter St E2 275 P2
Pelter St E2 142 DT69
Pelton Av, Sutt. 218 DB110
Pelton Rd SE10 164 EE78
Pembar Av E17 123 DY55
Pember Rd NW10 139 CX69
Pemberley Chase (West Ewell), Epsom 216 CP106
Pemberley Cl (West Ewell), Epsom 216 CP106
Pemberton Av, Rom. 127 FH55
Pemberton Cl, St.Alb. 43 CD23
Pemberton Gdns N19 121 DJ62
Pemberton Gdns, Rom. 126 EY57
Pemberton Gdns, Swan. 207 FE97
Pemberton Ho SE26 182 DU91
High Level Dr
Pemberton Pl E8 142 DV66
Mare St
Pemberton Pl, Esher 196 CC104
Carrick Gate
Pemberton Rd N4 121 DN57
Pemberton Rd, E.Mol. 196 CC98
Pemberton Rd, Slou. 131 AL70
Pemberton Row EC4 274 E8
Pemberton Ter N19 121 DJ62
Pembrey Way, Horn. 148 FJ65
Pembridge Av, Twick. 176 BZ88
Pembridge Chase (Bovingdon), Hem.H. 57 BA28
Pembridge Cl
Pembridge Cl (Bovingdon), Hem.H. 57 AZ28
Pembridge Cres W11 140 DA73
Pembridge Gdns W2 140 DA73
Pembridge La, Brox. 48 DR21
Pembridge La, Hert. 48 DQ19
Pembridge Ms W11 140 DA73
Pembridge Pl SW15 180 DA85
Pembridge Pl W2 140 DA73
Pembridge Rd W11 140 DA73
Pembridge Rd (Bovingdon), Hem.H. 57 BA28
Pembridge Sq W2 140 DA73
Pembridge Vil W2 140 DA73
Pembridge Vil W11 140 DA73
Pembroke Av, Enf. 82 DV38
Pembroke Av, Har. 117 CG55
Pembroke Av, Pnr. 116 BX60
Pembroke Av, Surb. 198 CP99
Pembroke Av, Walt. 214 BX105
Pembroke Cl SW1 276 G5
Pembroke Cl SW1 160 DG75
Pembroke Cl, Bans. 234 DB117
Pembroke Cl, Brox. 49 DY23
Pembroke Cl, Erith 167 FD77
Pembroke Rd
Pembroke Cl, Horn. 128 FM56
Pembroke Cotts W8 160 DA76
Pembroke Sq
Pembroke Dr (Cheshunt), Wal.Cr. 65 DP29
Pembroke Gdns W8 159 CZ77
Pembroke Gdns, Dag. 127 FB62
Pembroke Gdns, Wok. 227 BA118
Pembroke Gdns Cl W8 160 DA76
Pembroke Ms E3 143 DY69
Morgan St
Pembroke Ms N10 98 DG53
Pembroke Rd
Pembroke Ms W8 160 DA76
Earls Wk
Pembroke Ms, Sev. 257 FH125
Pembroke Rd
Pembroke Pl W8 160 DA76
Pembroke Pl (Sutton at Hone), Dart. 208 FP95
Pembroke Pl, Edg. 96 CN52
Pembroke Pl, Islw. 157 CE82
Thornbury Rd
Pembroke Rd E6 145 EM71
Pembroke Rd E17 123 EB57
Pembroke Rd N8 121 DL56
Pembroke Rd N10 98 DG53
Pembroke Rd N13 100 DQ48
Pembroke Rd N15 122 DT57
Pembroke Rd SE25 202 DS98
Pembroke Rd W8 160 DA77
Pembroke Rd, Brom. 204 EJ96
Pembroke Rd, Erith 167 FC78
Pembroke Rd, Grnf. 136 CB70
Pembroke Rd, Ilf. 125 ET60
Pembroke Rd, Mitch. 200 DG96
Pembroke Rd, Nthwd. 93 BQ48
Pembroke Rd, Ruis. 115 BT60
Pembroke Rd, Sev. 257 FH125
Pembroke Rd, Wem. 117 CK62
Pembroke Rd, Wok. 227 BA118
Pembroke Sq W8 160 DA76
Pembroke St N1 141 DL66
Pembroke Studios W8 159 CZ76
Pembroke Vil W8 160 DA77
Pembroke Vil, Rich. 157 CK84
Pembroke Wk W8 160 DA77
Pembroke Way, Hayes 155 BQ76
Pembry Cl SW9 161 DN81
Pembury Av, Wor.Pk. 199 CU101
Pembury Cl, Brom. 204 EF101
Pembury Cl, Couls. 218 DG114
Pembury Ct, Hayes 155 BR79
Pembury Cres, Sid. 186 EY89
Pembury Pl E5 122 DV64
Pembury Rd E5 122 DV64
Pembury Rd N17 100 DT54
Pembury Rd SE25 202 DU98
Pembury Rd, Bexh. 166 EY80
Pemdevon Rd, Croy. 201 DN101
Pemell Cl E1 142 DW70
Colebert Av

Pemerich Cl, Hayes 155 BT78
Pempath Pl, Wem. 117 CK61
Pemsel Ct, Hem.H. 40 BK22
Crabtree La
Penally Pl N1 142 DR67
Shepperton Rd
Penang St E1 142 DV74
Penard Rd, Sthl. 156 CA76
Penarth St SE15 162 DW79
Penates, Esher 215 CD105
Penberth Rd SE6 183 EC88
Penbury Rd, Sthl. 156 BZ77
Pencombe Ms W11 139 CZ73
Denbigh Rd
Pencraig Way SE15 162 DV79
Pencroft Dr, Dart. 188 FJ87
Shepherds La
Penda Rd, Erith 167 FB80
Pendall Cl, Barn. 80 DE42
Pendarves Rd SW20 199 CW95
Penda's Mead E9 123 DY63
Lindisfarne Way
Pendell Av, Hayes 155 BT80
Pendell Rd (Bletchingley), Red. 251 DP131
Pendennis Cl, W.Byf. 212 BG114
Pendennis Rd N17 122 DR55
Pendennis Rd SW16 181 DL91
Pendennis Rd, Orp. 206 EW103
Pendennis Rd, Sev. 257 FH123
Penderel Rd, Houns. 176 CA85
Penderry Ri SE6 183 ED89
Penderyn Way N7 121 DK63
Pendle Rd SW16 181 DH93
Pendlestone Rd E17 123 EB57
Pendleton Cl, Red. 266 DF136
Pendleton Rd, Red. 266 DE136
Pendleton Rd, Reig. 266 DC137
Pendragon Ho N9 100 DU48
Salisbury Rd
Pendragon Rd, Brom. 184 EF90
Pendragon Wk NW9 118 CS58
Pendrell Rd SE4 163 DY82
Pendrell St SE18 165 ER80
Pendula Dr, Hayes 136 BX70
Pendulum Ms E8 122 DT64
Birkbeck Rd
Penerley Rd SE6 183 EB88
Penerley Rd, Rain. 147 FH71
Penfold Cl, Croy. 201 DN104
Epsom Rd
Penfold La, Bex. 186 EX89
Penfold Pl NW1 272 B6
Penfold Pl NW1 140 DE71
Penfold Rd N9 101 DX46
Penfold St NW1 272 A5
Penfold St NW1 140 DD70
Penfold St NW8 272 A5
Penfold St NW8 140 DD70
Penford Gdns SE9 164 EK83
Penford St SE5 161 DP82
Pengarth Rd, Bex. 186 EX85
Penge Ho SW11 160 DD83
Wye St
Penge La SE20 182 DW94
Penge Rd E13 144 EJ66
Penge Rd SE20 202 DU97
Penge Rd SE25 202 DU97
Pengelly Cl (Cheshunt), Wal.Cr. 66 DV30
Penhale Cl, Orp. 224 EU105
Penhall Rd SE7 164 EK77
Penhill Rd, Bex. 186 EW87
Penhurst, Wok. 211 AZ114
Penhurst Rd, Ilf. 103 EP52
Penifather La, Grnf. 137 CD69
Peninsular Cl, Felt. 175 BR86
Peninsular Pk Rd SE7 164 EG77
Penistone Rd SW16 181 DL94
Penistone Wk, Rom. 106 FJ51
Okehampton Rd
Penketh Dr, Har. 117 CD62
Penlow Rd, Harl. 51 EQ18
Penman Cl, St.Alb. 60 CA27
Penman's Grn, Kings L. 58 BG32
Penmon Rd SE2 166 EU76
Penn Av, Chesh. 54 AN30
Penn Bottom (Penn), H.Wyc. 88 AG47
Penn Cl, Grnf. 136 CB68
Penn Cl, Har. 117 CJ56
Penn Cl, Rick. 73 BD44
Penn Cl, Uxb. 134 BK70
Penn Dr (Denham), Uxb. 113 BF58
Penn Gdns, Chis. 205 EP96
Penn Gdns, Rom. 104 FA52
Penn Gaskell La (Chalfont St. Peter), Ger.Cr. 91 AZ50
Penn Grn, Beac. 89 AK51
Penn La, Bex. 186 EX85
Penn Meadow (Stoke Poges), Slou. 132 AT67
Penn Pl, Rick. 92 BK45
Northway
Penn Rd N7 121 DL64
Penn Rd, Beac. 88 AJ48
Penn Rd (Chalfont St. Peter), Ger.Cr. 90 AX53
Penn Rd, Rick. 91 BF46
Penn Rd (Park St), St.Alb. 60 CC27
Penn Rd, Slou. 131 AR70
Penn Rd (Datchet), Slou. 152 AX81
Penn Rd, Wat. 75 BV39
Penn St N1 142 DR67
Penn Way, Rick. 73 BD44
Pennack Rd SE15 162 DT79
Pennant Ms W8 160 DB77
Pennant Ter E17 101 DZ54
Pennard Rd W12 159 CW75
Pennards, The, Sun. 196 BW96
Penne Cl, Rad. 61 CF34
Penner Cl SW19 179 CY89
Victoria Dr
Penners Gdns, Surb. 198 CL101
Pennethorne Cl E9 142 DW67
Victoria Pk Rd
Pennethorne Rd SE15 162 DV80
Penney Cl, Dart. 188 FK87
Pennine Dr NW2 119 CY61
Pennine Ho N9 100 DU48
Plevna Rd
Pennine La NW2 119 CY61
Pennine Dr
Pennine Rd, Slou. 131 AN71
Pennine Way, Bexh. 167 FE81
Pennine Way (Northfleet), Grav. 190 GE90
Pennine Way, Hayes 155 BR80
Pennine Way, Hem.H. 40 BM17
Pennings Av, Guil. 242 AT132
Pennington Cl SE27 182 DR91
Hamilton Rd
Pennington Cl, Rom. 104 FA50
Pennington Dr N21 81 DL43
Pennington Dr, Wey. 195 BS104
Pennington Rd, Beac. 110 AH55
Pennington Rd (Chalfont St. Peter), Ger.Cr. 90 AX52
Pennington St E1 142 DU73
Pennington Way SE12 184 EH89
Penningtons, The, Amer. 55 AS37
Pennis La (Fawkham Grn), Long. 209 FX100
Penniston Cl N17 100 DQ54
Penny Cl, Rain. 147 FH69
Penny La, Shep. 195 BS101
Penny Ms SW12 181 DH87
Caistor Rd
Penny Rd NW10 138 CP69
Pennycroft, Croy. 221 DY109
Pennyfather La, Enf. 82 DQ41
Pennyfield, Cob. 213 BU113
Pennyfields E14 143 EA73
Pennyfields, Brwd. 108 FW49
Pennylets Grn (Stoke Poges), Slou. 132 AT66
Pennymead, Harl. 36 EU14
Pennymead Dr (East Horsley), Lthd. 245 BT127
Pennymead Ri (East Horsley), Lthd. 245 BT127
Pennymead Twr, Harl. 52 EU15
Pennymead
Pennymoor Wk W9 139 CZ69
Ashmore Rd
Pennyroyal Av E6 145 EN72
Pennys La, Saw. 35 ER05
Penpoll Rd E8 142 DV65
Penpool La, Well. 166 EV83
Penrhyn Av E17 101 DZ53
Penrhyn Cres E17 101 EA53
Penrhyn Cres SW14 158 CQ84
Penrhyn Gdns, Kings.T. 197 CK98
Surbiton Rd
Penrhyn Gro E17 101 EA53
Penrhyn Rd, Kings.T. 198 CL97
Penrith Cl SW15 179 CY85
Penrith Cl, Beck. 203 EB95
Albemarle Rd
Penrith Cl, Reig. 250 DE133
Penrith Cl, Uxb. 134 BK66
Chippendale Waye
Penrith Cres, Rain. 127 FG64
Penrith Pl SE27 181 DP89
Harpenden Rd
Penrith Rd N15 122 DR57
Penrith Rd, Ilf. 103 ET51
Penrith Rd, N.Mal. 198 CR98
Penrith Rd, Rom. 106 FN51
Penrith Rd, Th.Hth. 202 DQ96
Penrith St SW16 181 DJ93
Penrose Av, Wat. 94 BX47
Penrose Ct, Hem.H. 40 BL16
Penrose Dr, Epsom 216 CN111
Churchill Rd
Penrose Gro SE17 162 DQ78
Penrose Ho SE17 162 DQ78
Penrose Rd (Fetcham), Lthd. 230 CC122
Penrose St SE17 162 DQ78
Penry St SE1 279 N9
Penryn St NW1 141 DK68
Pensbury Pl SW8 161 DJ82
Pensbury St SW8 161 DJ82
Penscroft Gdns, Borwd. 78 CR42
Pensford Av, Rich. 158 CN82
Penshurst, Harl. 36 EV12
Penshurst Av, Sid. 186 EU86
Penshurst Cl (Chalfont St. Peter), Ger.Cr. 90 AX54
Penshurst Gdns, Edg. 96 CP50
Penshurst Grn, Brom. 204 EF99
Penshurst Rd E9 143 DX66
Penshurst Rd N17 100 DT52
Penshurst Rd, Bexh. 166 EZ81
Penshurst Rd, Pot.B. 64 DD31
Penshurst Rd, Th.Hth. 201 DP99
Penshurst Wk, Brom. 204 EF99
Hayesford Pk Dr
Penshurst Way, Orp. 206 EW98
Star La
Penshurst Way, Sutt. 218 DA108
Pensilver Cl, Barn. 80 DE42
Pensons La, Ong. 71 FG28
Penstemon Cl N3 98 DA52
Penstock Footpath N22 121 DL55
Pentavia Retail Pk NW7 97 CT52
Bunns La
Pentelow Gdns, Felt. 175 BU86
Pentire Cl, Upmin. 129 FS58
Pentire Rd E17 101 ED53
Pentland, Hem.H. 40 BM17
Mendip Way
Pentland Av, Edg. 96 CP47
Pentland Av, Shep. 194 BN99
Pentland Cl NW11 119 CY61
Pentland Gdns SW18 180 DC86
St. Ann's Hill
Pentland Pl, Nthlt. 136 BY67
Pentland Rd, Bushey 76 CC44
Pentland Rd, Slou. 131 AN71
Pentland St SW18 180 DC86
Pentland Way, Uxb. 115 BQ62
Pentlands Cl, Mitch. 201 DH97
Pentley Cl, Welw.G.C. 29 CX06
Pentley Pk, Welw.G.C. 29 CX06
Pentlow St SW15 159 CW83
Pentlow Way, Buck.H. 102 EL45
Pentney Rd E4 101 ED46
Pentney Rd SW12 181 DJ88
Pentney Rd SW19 199 CY95
Midmoor Rd
Penton Av, Stai. 173 BF94
Penton Dr (Cheshunt), Wal.Cr. 67 DX29
Penton Gro N1 274 D1
Penton Hall Dr, Stai. 194 BG95
Penton Hook Rd, Stai. 174 BG94
Penton Ho SE2 166 EX75
Hartslock Dr
Penton Pk, Cher. 194 BG97
Penton Pl SE17 278 G10
Penton Pl SE17 161 DP78
Penton Ri WC1 274 C2
Penton Ri WC1 141 DM69
Penton Rd, Stai. 173 BF94
Penton St N1 141 DN68
Pentonville Rd N1 274 B1
Pentonville Rd N1 141 DM68
Pentreath Av, Guil. 258 AT135
Pentrich Av, Enf. 82 DU38
Pentridge St SE15 162 DT80
Pentyre Av N18 100 DR50
Penwerris Av, Islw. 156 CC80
Penwith Rd SW18 180 DB89
Penwith Wk, Wok. 226 AX119
Wych Hill Pk
Penwood End, Wok. 226 AV121
Penwood Ho SW15 179 CT86
Tunworth Cres
Penwortham Rd SW16 181 DH93
Penwortham Rd, S.Croy. 220 DQ110
Penylan Pl, Edg. 96 CN52
Penywern Rd SW5 160 DA78
Penzance Cl (Harefield), Uxb. 92 BK53
Penzance Gdns, Rom. 106 FN51
Penzance Pl W11 139 CY74
Penzance Rd, Rom. 106 FN51
Penzance Spur, Slou. 131 AP70
Penzance St W11 139 CY74
Peony Cl, Brwd. 108 FV44
Peony Ct, Wdf.Grn. 102 EE52
The Bridle Path
Peony Gdns W12 139 CU73
Peplins Cl, Hat. 63 CY26
Peplins Way, Hat. 63 CY25
Peploe Rd NW6 139 CX68
Peplow Cl, West Dr. 134 BK74
Tavistock Rd
Pepper All (High Beach), Loug. 84 EG39
Pepper Cl E6 145 EM71
Pepper Cl, Cat. 252 DS125
Pepper Hill (Northfleet), Grav. 190 GC90
Pepper Hill, Ware 33 DZ10
Pepper St E14 163 EB76
Pepper St SE1 279 H4
Peppercorn Cl, Th.Hth. 202 DR96
Pepperhill La (Northfleet), Grav. 190 GC90
Peppermead Sq SE13 183 EA85
Peppermint Cl, Croy. 201 DL101
Peppermint Pl E11 124 EE62
Birch Gro
Peppie Cl N16 122 DS61
Bouverie Rd
Pepys Cl, Ash. 232 CN117
Pepys Cl, Dart. 168 FN84
Pepys Cl (Northfleet), Grav. 190 GD90
Pepys Cl, Slou. 153 BB79
Pepys Cl, Til. 171 GJ81
Pepys Cl, Uxb. 115 BP63
Pepys Cres E16 144 EG74
Britannia Gate
Pepys Cres, Barn. 79 CW43
Pepys Ri, Orp. 205 ET102
Pepys Rd SE14 163 DX81
Pepys Rd SW20 199 CW95
Pepys St EC3 275 N10
Pepys St EC3 142 DS73
Perceval Av NW3 120 DE64
Perch St E8 122 DT63
Percheron Cl, Islw. 157 CG83
Percheron Rd, Borwd. 78 CR44
Percival Cl, Lthd. 214 CB111
Percival Ct N17 100 DT52
High Rd
Percival Ct, Nthlt. 116 CA64
Percival Gdns, Rom. 126 EW58
Percival Rd SW14 158 CQ84
Percival Rd, Enf. 82 DT42
Percival Rd, Felt. 175 BT89
Percival Rd, Horn. 128 FJ58
Percival Rd, Orp. 205 EP103
Percival St EC1 274 F4
Percival St EC1 141 DP70
Percival Way, Epsom 216 CQ105
Percy Av, Ashf. 174 BN92
Percy Bryant Rd, Sun. 175 BS94
Percy Bush Rd, West Dr. 154 BM76
Percy Circ WC1 274 C2
Percy Circ WC1 141 DM69
Percy Gdns, Enf. 83 DX43
Percy Gdns, Hayes 135 BS69
Percy Gdns, Islw. 157 CG82
Percy Gdns, Wor.Pk. 198 CS102
Percy Ms W1 273 M7
Percy Pas W1 273 L7
Percy Pl (Datchet), Slou. 152 AV81
Percy Rd E11 124 EE59
Percy Rd E16 144 EE71
Percy Rd N12 98 DC50
Percy Rd N21 100 DQ45
Percy Rd SE20 203 DX95
Percy Rd SE25 202 DU99
Percy Rd W12 159 CU75
Percy Rd, Bexh. 166 EY82
Percy Rd, Guil. 242 AV132
Percy Rd, Hmptn. 176 CA94
Percy Rd, Ilf. 126 EU59
Percy Rd, Islw. 157 CG84
Percy Rd, Mitch. 200 DG101
Percy Rd, Rom. 127 FB55
Percy Rd, Twick. 176 CB88
Percy Rd, Wat. 75 BV42
Percy St W1 273 M7
Percy St W1 141 DK71
Percy St, Grays 170 GC79
Percy Ter, Ch.St.G. 90 AU48
Sycamore Rd
Percy Way, Twick. 176 CC88
Percy Yd WC1 274 C2
Peregrine Cl NW10 118 CR64
Peregrine Cl, Wat. 60 BY34
Peregrine Ct SW16 181 DM91
Leithcote Gdns
Peregrine Ct, Well. 165 ET81
Peregrine Gdns, Croy. 203 DY103
Peregrine Ho EC1 274 G2
Peregrine Ho EC1 141 DP69
Peregrine Rd, Ilf. 104 EV50
Peregrine Rd, Sun. 195 BT96
Peregrine Rd, Wal.Abb. 68 EG34
Peregrine Wk, Horn. 147 FH65
Heron Flight Av
Peregrine Way SW19 179 CW94
Perham Rd W14 159 CY78
Perham Way (London Colney), St.Alb. 61 CK26
Peridot St E6 144 EL71
Perifield SE21 182 DQ88
Perimeade Rd, Grnf. 137 CJ68
Perimeter Rd E, Gat. 268 DG154
Perimeter Rd N, Gat. 268 DF151
Perimeter Rd S, Gat. 268 DC154
Periton Rd SE9 164 EK84
Perivale Gdns W13 137 CH70
Bellevue Rd
Perivale Gdns, Wat. 59 BV34
Perivale Gra, Grnf. 137 CG69
Perivale Ind Pk, Grnf. 137 CH68
Perivale La, Grnf. 137 CG69
Perivale New Business Cen, Grnf. 137 CH68
Perkin Cl, Wem. 117 CH64
Perkins Cl, Green. 189 FT85
Perkins Ct, Ashf. 174 BM92
Perkin's Rents SW1 277 M6
Perkin's Rents SW1 161 DK76
Perkins Rd, Ilf. 125 ER57
Perkins Sq SE1 279 J2
Perks Cl SE3 164 EE83
Hurren Cl
Perleybrooke La, Wok. 226 AU117
Bampton Way
Permain Cl (Shenley), Rad. 61 CK33
Perpins Rd SE9 185 ES86
Perram Cl, Brox. 67 DY26
Perran Rd SW2 181 DP89
Christchurch Rd
Perran Wk, Brent. 158 CL78
Perren St NW5 141 DH65
Ryland Rd
Perrers Rd W6 159 CV77
Perrin Cl, Ashf. 174 BM92
Fordbridge Rd
Perrin Ct, Wok. 227 BB115
Blackmore Cres
Perrin Rd, Wem. 117 CG63
Perrins Ct NW3 120 DC63
Hampstead High St
Perrins La NW3 120 DC63
Perrin's Wk NW3 120 DC63
Perrior Rd, Gdmg. 258 AS144
Perriors Cl (Cheshunt), Wal.Cr. 66 DU27
Perrott St SE18 165 EQ77
Perry Av W3 138 CR72
Perry Cl, Rain. 147 FD68
Lowen Rd
Perry Cl, Uxb. 135 BQ72
Harlington Rd
Perry Ct E14 163 EA78
Napier Av
Perry Ct N15 122 DS58
Albert Rd
Perry Cft, Wind. 151 AL83
Perry Gdns N9 100 DS48
Deansway
Perry Garth, Nthlt. 136 BW67
Perry Gro, Dart. 168 FN84
Perry Hall Cl, Orp. 206 EU101
Perry Hall Rd, Orp. 205 ET100
Perry Hill SE6 183 DZ90
Perry Hill (Worplesdon), Guil. 242 AS128
Perry Hill, Wal.Abb. 50 EF23
Perry Ho SW2 181 DL87
Tierney Rd
Perry Ho, Rain. 147 FD68
Lowen Rd
Perry How, Wor.Pk. 199 CT102
Perry Mead, Bushey 94 CB45
Perry Mead, Enf. 81 DP40
Perry Oaks Dr (Heathrow Airport), Houns. 154 BH82
Perry Oaks Dr, West Dr. 154 BH82
Perry Ri SE23 183 DY90
Perry Rd, Dag. 146 EZ70
Perry Rd, Harl. 51 EQ18
Perry Spring, Harl. 52 EX17
Perry St, Chis. 185 ER93
Perry St, Dart. 167 FE84
Perry St (Northfleet), Grav. 190 GE88
Perry St Gdns, Chis. 185 ES93
Old Perry St
Perry Vale SE23 182 DW89
Perry Way, S.Ock. 148 FQ73
Perryfield Way NW9 119 CT58
Perryfield Way, Rich. 177 CH89
Perryfields Way (Burnham), Slou. 130 AH70
Perrylands La, Horl. 269 DM149
Perryman Ho, Bark. 145 EQ67
The Shaftesburys
Perryman Way, Slou. 131 AM69
Perrymans Fm Rd, Ilf. 125 ER58
Perrymead St SW6 160 DA81
Perryn Rd SE16 162 DV76
Drummond Rd
Perryn Rd W3 138 CR73
Perrys La (Knockholt), Sev. 224 EV113
Perrys Pl W1 273 M8
Perrysfield Rd (Cheshunt), Wal.Cr. 67 DY27
Perrywood Business Pk, Red. 267 DH142
Persant Rd SE6 184 EE89
Perseverance Cotts (Ripley), Wok. 228 BJ121
Perseverance Pl SW9 161 DN80
Perseverance Pl, Rich. 158 CL83
Shaftesbury Rd
Persfield Cl, Epsom 217 CU110
Pershore Cl, Ilf. 125 EP57
Pershore Gro, Cars. 200 DD100
Pert Cl N10 99 DH52
Perth Av NW9 118 CR59
Perth Av, Hayes 136 BW70
Perth Av, Slou. 131 AP72
Perth Cl SW20 199 CU96
Huntley Way
Perth Rd E10 123 DY60
Perth Rd E13 144 EH68
Perth Rd N4 121 DN60
Perth Rd N22 99 DP53
Perth Rd, Bark. 145 ER68
Perth Rd, Beck. 203 EC96
Perth Rd, Ilf. 125 EN58
Perth Ter, Ilf. 125 EQ59
Perwell Av, Har. 116 BZ60
Perwell Ct, Har. 116 BZ60
Pescot Hill, Hem.H. 40 BH18
Peter Av NW10 139 CV66
Peter Av, Oxt. 253 ED129
Peter James Business Cen, Hayes 155 BU75
Peter St W1 273 L10
Peter St W1 141 DK73
Peter St, Grav. 191 GH87
Peterboat Cl SE10 164 EE77
Tunnel Av
Peterborough Av, Upmin. 129 FS60
Peterborough Gdns, Ilf. 124 EL59
Peterborough Ms SW6 160 DA82
Peterborough Rd E10 123 EC57
Peterborough Rd SW6 160 DA82
Peterborough Rd, Cars. 200 DE100
Peterborough Rd, Guil. 242 AT132
Peterborough Rd, Har. 117 CE60
Peterborough Vil SW6 160 DB81
Peterchurch Ho SE15 162 DV79
Commercial Way
Petergate SW11 160 DC84
Peterhead Ms, Slou. 153 BA78
Grampian Way
Peterhill Cl (Chalfont St. Peter), Ger.Cr. 90 AY50
Peterlee Ct, Hem.H. 40 BM16
Peters Av (London Colney), St.Alb. 61 CJ26
Peters Cl, Dag. 126 EX60
Peters Cl, Stan. 95 CK51
Peters Cl, Well. 165 ES82
Peters Hill EC4 275 H10
Peter's La EC1 274 G6
Peters Path SE26 182 DV91
Peters Pl, Berk. 38 AS17
Peters Wd Hill, Ware 33 DX07
Petersfield Av, Rom. 106 FL51
Petersfield Av, Slou. 132 AU74
Petersfield Av, Stai. 174 BJ92
Petersfield Cl N18 100 DQ50
Petersfield Cl, Rom. 106 FN51
Petersfield Cres, Couls. 235 DL115
Petersfield Ri SW15 179 CV88
Petersfield Rd W3 158 CQ75
Petersfield Rd, Stai. 174 BJ92
Petersham Av (Byfleet), W.Byf. 212 BL112
Petersham Cl, Rich. 177 CK89
Petersham Cl, Sutt. 218 DA106
Petersham Cl (Byfleet), W.Byf. 212 BL112
Petersham Dr, Orp. 205 ET96
Petersham Gdns, Orp. 205 ET96
Petersham La SW7 160 DC76
Petersham Ms SW7 160 DC76
Petersham Pl SW7 160 DC76
Petersham Rd, Rich. 178 CL86
Petersham Ter, Croy. 201 DL104
Richmond Grn
Peterslea, Kings L. 59 BP29
Petersmead Cl, Tad. 233 CW123
The Av
Peterstone Rd SE2 166 EV76
Peterstow Cl SW19 179 CY89
Peterswood, Harl. 51 ER19
Peterwood Way, Croy. 201 DM103
Petherton Rd N5 122 DQ64
Petley Rd W6 159 CW79
Peto Pl NW1 273 J4
Peto Pl NW1 141 DH70
Peto St N E16 144 EF73
Victoria Dock Rd
Petridge Rd, Red. 266 DF139
Petridgewood Common, Red. 266 DF140
Petrie Cl NW2 139 CY65
Pett Cl, Horn. 127 FH61
Pett St SE18 164 EL77
Petten Cl, Orp. 206 EX102
Petten Gro, Orp. 206 EW102
Petters Rd, Ash. 232 CM116
Petticoat La E1 275 N7
Petticoat La E1 142 DS71
Petticoat Sq E1 275 P8
Petticoat Sq E1 142 DT72
Pettits Boul, Rom. 105 FE53
Pettits Cl, Rom. 105 FE54
Pettits La, Rom. 105 FE54
Pettits La N, Rom. 105 FD53
Pettits Pl, Dag. 126 FA64
Pettits Rd, Dag. 126 FA64
Pettiward Cl SW15 159 CW84
Pettley Gdns, Rom. 127 FD57
Pettman Cres SE28 165 ER76
Petts Hill, Nthlt. 116 CB64
Petts La, Shep. 194 BN98
Petts Wd Rd, Orp. 205 EQ99
Pettsgrove Av, Wem. 117 CJ64
Petty France SW1 277 L6
Petty France SW1 161 DJ76
Pettys Cl (Cheshunt), Wal.Cr. 67 DX28
Petworth Cl, Couls. 235 DJ119
Petworth Cl, Nthlt. 136 BZ66
Petworth Ct, Wind. 151 AP81
Petworth Gdns SW20 199 CV97
Hidcote Gdns
Petworth Gdns, Uxb. 135 BQ67
Petworth Rd N12 98 DE50
Petworth Rd, Bexh. 186 FA85
Petworth St SW11 160 DE81
Petworth Way, Horn. 127 FF63
Petyt Pl SW3 160 DE79
Old Ch St
Petyward SW3 276 C9
Petyward SW3 160 DE77
Pevensey Av N11 99 DK50
Pevensey Av, Enf. 82 DR40
Pevensey Cl, Islw. 156 CC80
Pevensey Rd E7 124 EF63
Pevensey Rd SW17 180 DD91
Pevensey Rd, Felt. 176 BY88
Pevensey Rd, Slou. 131 AN71
Peverel E6 145 EN72
Downings
Peverel Ho, Dag. 126 FA61
Peveret Cl N11 99 DH50
Woodland Rd
Peveril Dr, Tedd. 177 CD92
Pewley Bk, Guil. 258 AY136
Pewley Hill, Guil. 258 AX136
Pewley Pt, Guil. 258 AY136
Pewley Way, Guil. 258 AY136
Pewsey Cl E4 101 EA50
Peyton Pl SE10 163 EC80
Peyton's Cotts, Red. 251 DM132
Pharaoh Cl, Mitch. 200 DF101
Pharaoh's Island, Shep. 194 BM103
Pheasant Cl E16 144 EG72
Maplin Rd
Pheasant Cl, Berk. 38 AW20
Pheasant Cl, Pur. 219 DP113
Partridge Knoll
Pheasant Hill, Ch.St.G. 90 AW47
Pheasant Ri, Chesh. 54 AR33
Pheasant Wk (Chalfont St. Peter), Ger.Cr. 90 AX49
Pheasants Way, Rick. 92 BH45
Phelips Rd, Harl. 51 EN20
Phelp St SE17 162 DR79
Phelps Way, Hayes 155 BT77
Phene St SW3 160 DE79
Phil Brown Pl SW8 161 DH82
Heath Rd
Philan Way, Rom. 105 FD51
Philanthropic Rd, Red. 266 DG135
Philbeach Gdns SW5 160 DA78
Philbye Ms, Slou. 151 AL75
Eltham Av
Philchurch Pl E1 142 DU72
Ellen St
Philimore Cl SE18 165 ES78
Philip Av, Rom. 127 FD60
Philip Av, Swan. 207 FD98
Philip Cl, Brwd. 108 FV44
Philip Cl, Rom. 127 FD60
Philip Av
Philip Dr (Flackwell Heath), H.Wyc. 110 AC56
Philip Gdns, Croy. 203 DZ103
Philip La N15 122 DR56
Philip Rd, Rain. 147 FE69
Philip Rd, Stai. 174 BK93
Philip St E13 144 EG70

Philip Sydney Rd, Grays 169 FX78
Philip Wk SE15 162 DU83
Philipot Path SE9 185 EM86
Philippa Gdns SE9 184 EK85
Philippa Way, Grays 171 GH77
Philips Cl, Cars. 200 DG102
Phillida Rd, Rom. 106 FN54
Phillimore Gdns NW10 139 CW67
Phillimore Gdns W8 160 DA75
Phillimore Gdns Cl W8 160 DA76
Phillimore Gdns
Phillimore Pl W8 160 DA75
Phillimore Pl, Rad. 77 CE36
Phillimore Wk W8 160 DA76
Phillipers, Wat. 76 BY35
Phillipp St N1 142 DS67
Phillips Cl, Dart. 187 FH86
Phillips Hatch (Wonersh), Guil. 259 BC143
Philpot La EC3 275 M10
Philpot La (Chobham), Wok. 210 AV113
Philpot Path, Ilf. 125 EQ62
Sunnyside Rd
Philpot Sq SW6 160 DB83
Peterborough Rd
Philpot St E1 142 DV72
Philpots Cl, West Dr. 134 BK73
Phineas Pett Rd SE9 164 EL83
Phipp St EC2 275 M4
Phipp St EC2 142 DS70
Phipps Br Rd SW19 200 DC96
Phipps Br Rd, Mitch. 200 DC96
Phipps Hatch La, Enf. 82 DQ38
Phipp's Ms SW1 277 H7
Phipps Rd, Slou. 131 AK71
Phoebe Rd, Hem.H. 40 BM17
Phoebeth Rd SE4 183 EA85
Phoenix Cl E8 142 DT67
Stean St
Phoenix Cl E17 101 DZ54
Phoenix Cl, Epsom 216 CN112
Queen Alexandra's Way
Phoenix Cl, Nthwd. 93 BT49
Phoenix Cl, W.Wick. 204 EE103
Phoenix Ct, Guil. 258 AX136
High St
Phoenix Dr, Kes. 204 EK104
Phoenix Pk, Brent. 157 CK78
Phoenix Pl WC1 274 C4
Phoenix Pl WC1 141 DM70
Phoenix Pl, Dart. 188 FK87
Phoenix Rd NW1 273 M2
Phoenix Rd NW1 141 DK69
Phoenix Rd SE20 182 DW93
Phoenix St WC2 273 N9
Phoenix Way, Houns. 156 BW79
Phoenix Wf SE10 164 EF75
Phoenix Wf Rd SE1 162 DT75
Druid St
Phygtle, The (Chalfont St. Peter), Ger.Cr. 90 AY51
Phyllis Av, N.Mal. 199 CV99
Physic Pl SW3 160 DF79
Royal Hosp Rd
Piazza, The WC2 141 DL73
Covent Gdn
Picardy Manorway, Belv. 167 FB76
Picardy Rd, Belv. 166 FA77
Picardy St, Belv. 166 FA76
Piccadilly W1 277 J3
Piccadilly W1 141 DH74
Piccadilly Arc SW1 277 K2
Piccadilly Circ W1 277 M1
Piccadilly Circ W1 141 DK73
Piccadilly Pl W1 277 L1
Piccards, The, Guil. 258 AW138
Chestnut Av
Piccotts End La, Hem.H. 40 BJ17
Piccotts End Rd, Hem.H. 40 BJ18
Pick Hill, Wal.Abb. 68 EF32
Pickard St EC1 274 G2
Pickering Av E6 145 EN68
Pickering Cl E9 143 DX66
Cassland Rd
Pickering Gdns N11 98 DG51
Pickering Gdns, Croy. 202 DT100
Pickering Ms W2 140 DB72
Bishops Br Rd
Pickering Pl SW1 277 L3
Pickering St N1 141 DP67
Essex Rd
Pickets Cl, Bushey 95 CD46
Pickets St SW12 181 DH87
Pickett Cft, Stan. 95 CK53
Picketts, Welw.G.C. 29 CX06
Picketts La, Red. 267 DJ144
Picketts Lock La N9 100 DW47
Pickford Cl, Bexh. 166 EY82
Pickford Dr, Slou. 133 AZ74
Pickford La, Bexh. 166 EY82
Pickford Rd, Bexh. 166 EY83
Pickford Rd, St.Alb. 43 CH20
Pickfords Wf N1 275 H1
Pickfords Wf N1 142 DQ68
Pickhurst Grn, Brom. 204 EF101
Pickhurst La, Brom. 204 EF102
Pickhurst La, W.Wick. 204 EE100
Pickhurst Mead, Brom. 204 EF101
Pickhurst Pk, Brom. 204 EE99
Pickhurst Ri, W.Wick. 203 EC101
Pickins Piece (Horton), Slou. 153 BA82
Pickle Herring St SE1 142 DS74
Tooley St
Pickmoss La (Otford), Sev. 241 FH116
Pickwick Cl, Houns. 176 BY85
Dorney Way
Pickwick Ct SE9 184 EL88
West Pk
Pickwick Gdns (Northfleet), Grav. 190 GD90
Pickwick Ms N18 100 DS50
Pickwick Pl, Har. 117 CE59
Pickwick Rd SE21 182 DR87
Pickwick St SE1 279 H5
Pickwick Ter, Slou. 132 AV73
Maple Cres
Pickwick Way, Chis. 185 EQ93
Pickworth Cl SW8 161 DL80
Kenchester Cl
Picquets Way, Bans. 233 CY116
Picton Pl W1 272 G9
Picton Pl, Surb. 198 CN102
Picton St SE5 162 DR80
Piedmont Rd SE18 165 ER78
Pield Heath Av, Uxb. 134 BN70
Pield Heath Rd, Uxb. 134 BM71
Pier Head E1 142 DV74
Wapping High St
Pier Par E16 165 EN75
Pier Rd
Pier Rd E16 165 EM75
Pier Rd, Erith 167 FE79
Pier Rd, Felt. 175 BV85
Pier Rd (Northfleet), Grav. 191 GF86
Pier Rd, Green. 169 FV84
Pier St E14 163 EC77
Pier Ter SW18 160 DC84
Jew's Row
Pier Wk, Grays 170 GA80
Pier Way SE28 165 ER76
Piercing Hill, Epp. 85 ER35
Pierian Spring, Hem.H. 40 BH18
Piermont Grn SE22 182 DV85
Piermont Pl, Brom. 204 EL96
Piermont Rd SE22 182 DV85
Pierrepoint Arc N1 141 DP68
Islington High St
Pierrepoint Rd W3 138 CP73
Pierrepoint Row N1 141 DP68
Islington High St
Pierson Rd, Wind. 151 AK82
Pigeon La, Hmptn. 176 CA91
Pigeonhouse La, Couls. 250 DC125
Piggotts End, Amer. 55 AP40
Piggotts Orchard, Amer. 55 AP40
Piggs Cor, Grays 170 GC76
Piggy La, Rick. 73 BB44
Pigott St E14 143 EA72
Pike Cl, Brom. 184 EH92
Pike Cl, Uxb. 134 BM67
Pike La, Upmin. 129 FT64
Pike Rd NW7 96 CR49
Ellesmere Av
Pike Way, Epp. 70 FA27
Pikes End, Pnr. 115 BV56
Pikes Hill, Epsom 216 CS113
Pikestone Cl, Hayes 136 BY70
Berrydale Rd
Pilgrim Cl, Mord. 200 DB101
Pilgrim Cl (Park St), St.Alb. 60 CC27
Pilgrim Hill SE27 182 DQ91
Pilgrim Hill, Orp. 206 EY96
Pilgrim St EC4 274 F9
Pilgrimage St SE1 279 K5
Pilgrimage St SE1 162 DR75
Pilgrims Cl N13 99 DM49
Pilgrims Cl, Brwd. 108 FT43
Pilgrims Cl (Westhumble), Dor. 247 CG131
Pilgrims Cl (Shere), Guil. 260 BN139
Pilgrims Cl, Nthlt. 116 CC64
Pilgrims Cl, Wat. 60 BX33
Kytes Dr
Pilgrims Ct SE3 164 EG81
Pilgrims Ct, Dart. 188 FN85
Pilgrim's La NW3 120 DD63
Pilgrims La, Cat. 251 DM125
Pilgrims La, Grays 149 FW74
Pilgrims La (Titsey), Oxt. 254 EH125
Pilgrims La, West. 238 EL123
Pilgrims Ms E14 143 EC73
Blackwall Way
Pilgrims Pl NW3 120 DD63
Hampstead High St
Pilgrims Pl, Reig. 250 DA132
Pilgrims Ri, Barn. 80 DE43
Pilgrims Rd, Swans. 170 FY84
Pilgrims Vw, Green. 189 FW86
Pilgrims Way E6 144 EL67
High St N
Pilgrims Way N19 121 DK60
Pilgrims' Way, Bet. 249 CY131
Pilgrims' Way, Cat. 251 DN126
Pilgrims' Way, Dart. 188 FN88
Pilgrims' Way, Dor. 247 CE134
Pilgrims Way (Westhumble), Dor. 247 CH131
Pilgrims Way, Guil. 258 AX138
Pilgrims' Way (Albury), Guil. 260 BK138
Pilgrims Way (Shere), Guil. 260 BN139
Pilgrims' Way, Red. 251 DJ127
Pilgrims Way, Reig. 250 DA131
Pilgrims Way (Chevening), Sev. 240 EV121
Pilgrims Way, S.Croy. 220 DT106
Pilgrim's Way, Wem. 118 CP60
Pilgrims Way, West. 239 EM123
Pilgrims Way W (Otford), Sev. 241 FD116
Pilkington Rd SE15 162 DV82
Pilkington Rd, Orp. 205 EQ103
Pilkingtons, Harl. 52 EX16
Kitts Riding
Pillions La, Hayes 135 BR70
Pilot Cl SE8 163 DZ79
Pilots Pl, Grav. 191 GJ86
Pilsdon Cl SW19 179 CX88
Inner Pk Rd
Piltdown Rd, Wat. 94 BX49
Pilton Est, The (Pitlake), Croy. 201 DP103
Pitlake
Pilton Pl SE17 279 J10
Pilton Pl SE17 162 DQ78
Pimento Ct W5 157 CK76
Olive Rd
Pimlico Rd SW1 276 F10
Pimlico Rd SW1 160 DG78
Pimlico Wk N1 275 M2
Pimms Cl, Guil. 243 BA130
Pimpernel Way, Rom. 106 FK51
Pinceybrook Rd, Harl. 51 EQ19
Pinchbeck Rd, Orp. 223 ET107
Pinchfield, Rick. 91 BE50
Pinchin St E1 142 DU73
Pincott La, Lthd. 245 BP129
Pincott Pl SE4 163 DX83
Pincott Rd SW19 200 DC95
Pincott Rd, Bexh. 186 FA85
Pindar Rd, Hodd. 49 EC16
Pindar St EC2 275 M6
Pindar St EC2 142 DS71
Pindock Ms W9 140 DB70
Warwick Av
Pine Av E15 123 ED64
Pine Av, Grav. 191 GK88
Pine Av, W.Wick. 203 EB102
Pine Cl E10 123 EB61
Walnut Rd
Pine Cl N14 99 DJ45
Pine Cl N19 121 DJ61
Hargrave Pk
Pine Cl SE20 202 DW95
Pine Cl (New Haw), Add. 212 BH111
Pine Cl, Berk. 38 AV19
Pine Cl, Ken. 236 DR117
Pine Cl, Stan. 95 CH49
Pine Cl, Swan. 207 FF98
Pine Cl (Cheshunt), Wal.Cr. 67 DX28
Pine Cl, Wok. 226 AW117
Pine Coombe, Croy. 221 DX105
Pine Ct, Upmin. 128 FN63
Pine Cres, Brwd. 109 GD43
Pine Cres, Cars. 218 DD111
Pine Dean (Bookham), Lthd. 246 CB125
Pine Gdns, Horl. 268 DF149
Pine Gdns, Ruis. 115 BV60
Pine Gdns, Surb. 198 CN100
Pine Glade, Orp. 223 EM105
Pine Gro N4 121 DL61
Pine Gro N20 97 CZ46
Pine Gro SW19 179 CZ92
Pine Gro, Bushey 76 BZ40
Pine Gro, Hat. 64 DB25
Pine Gro (Bricket Wd), St.Alb. 60 BZ30
Pine Gro, Wey. 213 BP106
Pine Gro Ms, Wey. 213 BQ106
Pine Hill, Epsom 232 CR115
Pine Ms NW10 139 CX68
Clifford Gdns
Pine Pl, Bans. 217 CX114
Pine Pl, Hayes 135 BT70
Pine Ridge, Cars. 218 DG109
Pine Rd N11 98 DG47
Pine Rd NW2 119 CW63
Pine Rd, Wok. 226 AW120
Pine St EC1 274 D4
Pine St EC1 141 DN70
Pine Tree Cl, Hem.H. 40 BK19
Christchurch Rd
Pine Tree Cl, Houns. 155 BV81
Pine Tree Hill, Wok. 227 BD116
Pine Trees Dr, Uxb. 114 BL63
Pine Vw Cl (Chilworth), Guil. 259 BF140
Pine Vw Manor, Epp. 70 EU30
Pine Wk, Bans. 234 DF117
Pine Wk, Brom. 204 EJ95
Pine Wk, Cars. 218 DD110
Pine Wk, Cat. 236 DT122
Pine Wk, Cob. 214 BX114
Pine Wk (East Horsley), Lthd. 245 BT128
Pine Wk, Surb. 198 CN100
Pine Way (Englefield Grn), Egh. 172 AV93
Ashwood Rd
Pine Wd, Sun. 195 BU95
Pineapple Ct SW1 277 K6
Pineapple Rd, Amer. 72 AT39
Pinecrest Gdns, Orp. 223 EP105
Pinecroft, Brwd. 109 GB45
Pinecroft, Hem.H. 40 BM24
Pinecroft, Rom. 128 FJ56
Pinecroft Cres, Barn. 79 CY42
Hillside Gdns
Pinedene SE15 162 DV81
Meeting Ho La
Pinefield Cl E14 143 EA73
Pinehurst, Sev. 257 FL121
Pinehurst Cl, Abb.L. 59 BS32
Pinehurst Cl (Kingswood), Tad. 234 DA122
Pinehurst Wk, Orp. 205 ES102
Pinel Cl, Vir.W. 192 AY98
Pinelands Cl SE3 164 EF80
St. John's Pk
Pinemartin Cl NW2 119 CW62
Pineneedle La, Sev. 257 FH123
Pines, The N14 81 DJ43
Pines, The, Borwd. 78 CM40
Anthony Rd
Pines, The, Couls. 235 DH118
Pines, The, Dor. 263 CH137
South Ter
Pines, The, Hem.H. 39 BF24
Pines, The, Pur. 219 DP113
Pines, The, Sun. 195 BU97
Pines, The, Wok. 211 AZ114
Pines, The, Wdf.Grn. 102 EG48
Pines Av, Enf. 82 DV36
Pines Cl, Amer. 55 AP36
Pines Cl, Nthwd. 93 BS51
Pines Rd, Brom. 204 EL96
Pinetree Cl (Chalfont St. Peter), Ger.Cr. 90 AW52
Pinetree Gdns, Hem.H. 40 BL22
Pinewalk (Great Bookham), Lthd. 246 CB125
Pinewood, Welw.G.C. 29 CY11
Pinewood Av (New Haw), Add. 212 BJ109
Pinewood Av, Pnr. 94 CB51
Pinewood Av, Rain. 147 FH70
Pinewood Av, Sev. 257 FK121
Pinewood Av, Sid. 185 ES88
Pinewood Av, Uxb. 134 BM72
Pinewood Cl, Borwd. 78 CR39
Pinewood Cl, Croy. 203 DY104
Pinewood Cl, Ger.Cr. 112 AY59
Dukes Wd Av
Pinewood Cl, Harl. 52 EW16
Pinewood Cl, Iver 133 BC66
Pinewood Cl, Nthwd. 93 BV50
Pinewood Cl, Orp. 205 ER102
Pinewood Cl, Pnr. 94 CB51
Pinewood Cl, St.Alb. 43 CJ20
Pinewood Cl, Wat. 75 BU39
Pinewood Cl, Wok. 211 BA114
Pinewood Dr, Orp. 223 ES106
Pinewood Dr, Pot.B. 63 CZ31
Pinewood Dr, Stai. 174 BG92
Cotswold Cl
Pinewood Gdns, Hem.H. 40 BH20
Pinewood Grn, Iver 133 BC66
Pinewood Gro W5 137 CJ72
Pinewood Gro (New Haw), Add. 212 BH110
Pinewood Ms (Stanwell), Stai. 174 BK86
Oaks Rd
Pinewood Pk (New Haw), Add. 212 BH111
Pinewood Ride, Iver 133 BA68
Pinewood Ride, Slou. 133 BA65
Fulmer Common Rd
Pinewood Rd SE2 166 EX79
Pinewood Rd, Brom. 204 EG98
Pinewood Rd, Felt. 175 BV90
Pinewood Rd, Iver 133 BB65
Pinewood Rd (Havering-atte-Bower), Rom. 105 FC49
Pinewood Rd, Vir.W. 192 AU98
Pinewood Way, Brwd. 109 GD43
Pinfold Rd SW16 181 DL91
Pinfold Rd, Bushey 76 BZ40
Pinglestone Cl, West Dr. 154 BL80
Pink La (Burnham), Slou. 130 AH68
Pinkcoat Cl, Felt. 175 BV90
Tanglewood Way
Pinkerton Pl SW16 181 DK91
Riggindale Rd
Pinkham Way N11 98 DG52
Pinkneys Ct, Maid. 130 AG72
Pinks Hill, Swan. 207 FE99
Pinkwell Av, Hayes 155 BR77
Pinkwell La, Hayes 155 BQ77
Pinley Gdns, Dag. 146 EV67
Stamford Rd
Pinn Cl, Uxb. 134 BK72
High Rd
Pinn Way, Ruis. 115 BS59
Pinnacle Hill, Bexh. 167 FB84
Pinnacle Hill N, Bexh. 167 FB83
Pinnacles, Wal.Abb. 68 EE34
Pinnate Pl, Welw.G.C. 29 CY13
Pinnell Rd SE9 164 EK84
Pinner Ct, Pnr. 116 CA56
Pinner Grn, Pnr. 94 BW54
Pinner Gro, Pnr. 116 BY56
Pinner Hill, Pnr. 94 BW53
Pinner Hill Rd, Pnr. 94 BW54
Pinner Pk, Pnr. 94 CA53
Pinner Pk Av, Har. 116 CB55
Pinner Pk Gdns, Har. 94 CC54
Pinner Rd, Har. 116 CB57
Pinner Rd, Nthwd. 93 BT53
Pinner Rd, Pnr. 116 BZ56
Pinner Rd, Wat. 76 BX44
Pinner Vw, Har. 116 CC58
Pinnocks Av, Grav. 191 GH88
Pinstone Way, Ger.Cr. 113 BB61
Pintail Cl E6 144 EL71
Swan App
Pintail Rd, Wdf.Grn. 102 EH52
Pintail Way, Hayes 136 BX71
Pinter Ho SW9 161 DL82
Grantham Rd
Pinto Cl, Borwd. 78 CR44
Percheron Rd
Pinto Way SE3 164 EH84
Pioneer Pl, Croy. 221 EA109
Featherbed La
Pioneer St SE15 162 DU81
Pioneer Way W12 139 CV72
Du Cane Rd
Pioneer Way, Swan. 207 FE97
Pioneer Way, Wat. 75 BT44
Pioneers Ind Pk, Croy. 201 DL102
Piper Cl N7 121 DM64
Piper Rd, Kings.T. 198 CN97
Pipers Cl, Cob. 230 BX115
Pipers Cl (Burnham), Slou. 130 AJ69
Pipers End, Hert. 31 DJ13
Pipers End, Vir.W. 192 AX97
Piper's Gdns, Croy. 203 DY101
Pipers Grn NW9 118 CQ57
Pipers Grn La, Edg. 96 CL48
Pipewell Rd, Cars. 200 DE100
Pippbrook, Dor. 263 CH135
Pippbrook Gdns, Dor. 263 CH135
London Rd
Pippens, Welw.G.C. 29 CY06
Pippin Cl NW2 119 CV62
Pippin Cl, Croy. 203 DZ102
Pippin Cl (Shenley), Rad. 61 CK33
Pippins, The, Slou. 133 AZ74
Pickford Dr
Pippins, The, Wat. 60 BW34
Garston Dr
Pippins Cl, West Dr. 154 BK76
Pippins Ct, Ashf. 175 BP93
Piquet Rd SE20 202 DW96
Pirbright Cres (New Addington), Croy. 221 EC107
Pirbright Rd SW18 179 CZ88
Pirie Cl SE5 162 DR83
Denmark Hill
Pirie St E16 144 EH74
Pirrip Cl, Grav. 191 GM89
Pirton Cl, St.Alb. 43 CJ15
Pishiobury Dr, Saw. 36 EW07
Pishiobury Ms, Saw. 36 EX08
Pit Fm Rd, Guil. 243 BA134
Pitcairn Cl, Rom. 126 FA56
Pitcairn Rd, Mitch. 180 DF94
Pitcairn's Path, Har. 116 CC62
Eastcote Rd
Pitch Pond Cl (Knotty Grn), Beac. 88 AH50
Pitchfont La, Oxt. 238 EF124
Pitchford St E15 143 ED66
Pitfield Cres SE28 146 EU74
Pitfield Est N1 275 L2
Pitfield Est N1 142 DR69
Pitfield St N1 275 M2
Pitfield St N1 142 DS69
Pitfield Way NW10 138 CQ65
Pitfield Way, Enf. 82 DW39
Pitfold Cl SE12 184 EG86
Pitfold Rd SE12 184 EG86
Pitlake, Croy. 201 DP103
Pitman St SE5 162 DQ80
Pitmaston Ho SE13 163 EC82
Lewisham Rd
Pitsea Pl E1 143 DX72
Pitsea St
Pitsea St E1 143 DX72
Pitsfield, Welw.G.C. 29 CX06
Pitshanger La W5 137 CH70
Pitshanger Pk W13 137 CJ69
Pitson Cl, Add. 212 BK105
Pitstone Cl, St.Alb. 43 CJ15
Highview Gdns
Pitt Cres SW19 180 DB91
Pitt Dr, St.Alb. 43 CJ23
Pitt Pl, Epsom 216 CS114
Pitt Rd, Croy. 202 DQ99
Pitt Rd, Epsom 216 CS114
Pitt Rd, Orp. 223 EQ105
Pitt Rd, Th.Hth. 202 DQ99
Pitt St W8 160 DA75
Pittman Cl, Brwd. 109 GC50
Pittman Gdns, Ilf. 125 EQ64
Pittmans Fld, Harl. 35 ET14
Pitt's Head Ms W1 276 G3
Pitt's Head Ms W1 140 DG74
Pitts Rd, Slou. 131 AQ74
Pittsmead Av, Brom. 204 EG101
Pittville Gdns SE25 202 DU97
Pittwood, Brwd. 109 GA46
Pitwood Grn, Tad. 233 CW120
Pitwood Pk Ind Est, Tad. 233 CV120
Waterfield
Pix Fm La, Hem.H. 39 BB21
Pixfield Ct, Brom. 204 EF96
Beckenham La
Pixham La, Dor. 247 CJ133
Pixholme Gro, Dor. 247 CJ134
Pixies Hill Cres, Hem.H. 39 BF22
Pixies Hill Rd, Hem.H. 39 BF21
Pixley St E14 143 DZ72
Pixton Way, Croy. 221 DY109
Place Fm Av, Orp. 205 ER102
Place Fm Rd (Bletchingley), Red. 252 DR130
Placehouse La, Couls. 235 DM119
Plackett Way, Slou. 131 AK74
Plain, The, Epp. 70 EV29
Plaines Cl, Slou. 131 AM74
Plaistow Gro E15 144 EF67
Plaistow Gro, Brom. 184 EH94
Plaistow La, Brom. 184 EH94
Plaistow Pk Rd E13 144 EH68
Plaistow Rd E13 144 EF67
Plaistow Rd E15 144 EF67
Plaitford Cl, Rick. 92 BL47
Plane Av (Northfleet), Grav. 190 GD87
Plane St SE26 182 DV90
Plane Tree Cres, Felt. 175 BV90
Plane Tree Wk SE19 182 DS93
Central Hill
Planes, The, Cher. 194 BJ101
Plantaganet Pl, Wal.Abb. 67 EB33
Plantagenet Cl, Wor.Pk. 216 CR105
Plantagenet Gdns, Rom. 126 EX59
Plantagenet Pl, Rom. 126 EX59
Broomfield Rd
Plantagenet Rd, Barn. 80 DC42
Plantain Gdns E11 123 ED62
Hollydown Way
Plantain Pl SE1 279 K4
Plantation, The SE3 164 EG82
Plantation Cl, Green. 189 FT86
Plantation Dr, Orp. 206 EX102
Plantation La, Warl. 237 DY119
Plantation Rd, Amer. 55 AS37
Plantation Rd, Erith 167 FG81
Plantation Rd, Swan. 187 FG94
Plantation Wk, Hem.H. 40 BG17
Plantation Way, Amer. 55 AS37
Plantation Wf SW11 160 DC83
Plasel Ct E13 144 EG67
Plashet Rd
Plashet Gdns, Brwd. 109 GA49
Plashet Gro E6 144 EJ67
Plashet Rd E13 144 EG67
Plashets (Sheering), B.Stort. 37 FC06
Plassy Rd SE6 183 EB87
Platford Grn, Horn. 128 FL56
Platina St EC2 275 L4
Plato Rd SW2 161 DL84
Platt, The SW15 159 CX83
Platt, The, Amer. 55 AP40
Platt Meadow, Guil. 243 BD131
Eustace Rd
Platt St NW1 141 DK68
Platts Av, Wat. 75 BV41
Platt's Eyot, Hmptn. 196 CA96
Platt's La NW3 120 DA63
Platts Rd, Enf. 82 DW39
Plawsfield Rd, Beck. 203 DX95
Plaxtol Cl, Brom. 204 EJ95
Plaxtol Rd, Erith 166 FA80
Plaxton Ct E11 124 EF62
Woodhouse Rd
Playfair St W6 159 CW78
Winslow Rd
Playfield Av, Rom. 105 FC53
Playfield Cres SE22 182 DT85
Playfield Rd, Edg. 96 CQ54
Playford Rd N4 121 DM61
Playgreen Way SE6 183 EA91
Playground Cl, Beck. 203 DX96
Churchfields Rd
Playhouse Yd EC4 274 F9
Plaza Par NW6 140 DB68
Kilburn High Rd
Plaza Shop Cen, The W1 141 DJ72
Plaza Wk, Houns. 156 CB81
Pleasance, The SW15 159 CV84
Pleasance Rd SW15 179 CV85
Pleasance Rd, Orp. 206 EV96
Pleasant Gro, Croy. 203 DZ104
Pleasant Pl N1 141 DP66
Pleasant Pl, Rick. 91 BE52
Pleasant Pl, Walt. 214 BW107
Pleasant Ri, Hat. 45 CW15
Pleasant Row NW1 141 DH67
Pleasant Vw, Erith 167 FE78
Pleasant Vw Pl, Orp. 223 EP106
High St
Pleasant Way, Wem. 137 CJ68
Pleasure Pit Rd, Ash. 232 CP118
Plender St NW1 141 DJ67
Pleshey Rd N7 121 DK63
Plesman Way, Wall. 219 DL109
Plevna Cres N15 122 DS58
Plevna Rd N9 100 DU48
Plevna Rd, Hmptn. 196 CB95
Plevna Rd Shop Cen N9 100 DV47
Plevna Rd
Plevna St E14 163 EC76
Pleydell Av SE19 182 DT94
Pleydell Av W6 159 CT77
Pleydell Ct EC4 274 E9
Pleydell Est EC1 142 DQ69
Radnor St
Pleydell St EC4 274 E9
Plimsoll Cl E14 143 EB72
Grundy St
Plimsoll Rd N4 121 DN62
Plough Ct EC3 275 L10
Plough Fm Cl, Ruis. 115 BR58
Plough Hill (Cuffley), Pot.B. 65 DL28
Plough Ind Est, Lthd. 231 CH119
Plough La SE22 182 DT86
Plough La SW17 180 DB92
Plough La SW19 180 DB92
Plough La, Berk. 39 BB16
Plough La (Downside), Cob. 229 BU116
Plough La, Pur. 219 DL109
Plough La, Rick. 57 BF33
Plough La (Stoke Poges), Slou. 132 AV67
Plough La, Tedd. 177 CG92
Plough La (Harefield), Uxb. 92 BJ51
Plough La, Wall. 219 DL105
Plough La Cl, Wall. 219 DL106
Plough Ms SW11 160 DD84
Plough Ter
Plough Pl EC4 274 E8
Plough Ri, Upmin. 129 FS59
Plough Rd SW11 160 DD83
Plough Rd, Epsom 216 CR109
Plough Rd, Horl. 269 DP148
Plough St E1 142 DT72
Leman St
Plough Ter SW11 160 DD84
Plough Way SE16 163 DX77
Plough Yd EC2 275 N5
Plough Yd EC2 142 DS70
Ploughlees La, Slou. 132 AS73
Ploughmans Cl NW1 141 DK67
Crofters Way
Ploughmans End, Islw. 177 CD85
Ploughmans End, Welw.G.C. 30 DC10
Ploughmans Wk N2 98 DC54
Long La
Plover Cl, Berk. 38 AW20
Plover Cl, Stai. 173 BF90
Waters Dr
Plover Gdns, Upmin. 129 FT60
Plover Way SE16 163 DY76
Plover Way, Hayes 136 BX72
Plowden Bldgs EC4 141 DN72
Middle Temple La
Plowman Cl N18 100 DR50

Plowman Way, Dag. 126 EW60
Ployters Rd, Harl. 51 EQ18
Plum Cl, Felt. 175 BU88
Highfield Rd
Plum Garth, Brent. 157 CK77
Plum La SE18 165 EP80
Plumbers Row E1 142 DU71
Plumbridge St SE10 163 EC81
Blackheath Hill
Plummer La, Mitch. 200 DF96
Plummer Rd SW4 181 DK87
Plummers Cft (Dunton Grn), Sev. 256 FE121
Plumpton Av, Horn. 128 FL63
Plumpton Cl, Nthlt. 136 CA65
Plumpton Rd, Hodd. 49 EC15
Plumpton Way, Cars. 200 DE104
Plumstead Common Rd SE18 165 EP79
Plumstead High St SE18 165 ES77
Plumstead Rd SE18 165 EP77
Plumtree Cl, Dag. 147 FB65
Plumtree Cl, Wall. 219 DK108
Plumtree Ct EC4 274 E8
Plumtree Mead, Loug. 85 EN41
Pluto Ri, Hem.H. 40 BL18
Pluto Way, Slou. 131 AL74
Moor Furlong
Plymouth Dr, Sev. 257 FJ124
Plymouth Ho, Rain. 147 FF69
Plymouth Pk, Sev. 257 FJ124
Plymouth Rd E16 144 EG71
Plymouth Rd, Brom. 204 EH95
Plymouth Rd, Grays 169 FW77
Plymouth Rd, Slou. 131 AL71
Plymouth Wf E14 163 ED77
Plympton Av NW6 139 CZ66
Plympton Cl, Belv. 166 EY76
Halifield Dr
Plympton Pl NW8 272 B5
Plympton Rd NW6 139 CZ66
Plympton St NW8 272 B5
Plympton St NW8 140 DE70
Plymstock Rd, Well. 166 EW80
Pocketsdell La (Bovingdon), Hem.H. 56 AX28
Pocklington Cl NW9 96 CS54
Pocock Av, West Dr. 154 BM76
Pocock St SE1 278 F4
Pocock St SE1 161 DP75
Pococks La (Eton), Wind. 152 AS78
Podmore Rd SW18 160 DC84
Poets Chase, Hem.H. 40 BH18
Laureate Way
Poets Gate, Wal.Cr. 66 DS28
Poets Rd N5 122 DR64
Poets Way, Har. 117 CE56
Blawith Rd
Point, The, Ruis. 115 BU63
Bedford Rd
Point Cl SE10 163 EC81
Point Hill
Point Hill SE10 163 EC80
Point of Thomas Path E1 142 DW73
Glamis Rd
Point Pl, Wem. 138 CP66
Point Pleasant SW18 160 DA84
Pointalls Cl N3 98 DC54
Pointer Cl SE28 146 EX72
Pointers, The, Ash. 232 CL120
Pointers Cl E14 163 EB78
Pointers Hill (Westcott), Dor. 262 CC138
Pointers Rd, Cob. 229 BQ116
Poland Ho E15 143 ED67
Poland St W1 273 L9
Poland St W1 141 DJ72
Polayn Garth, Welw.G.C. 29 CW08
Pole Cat All, Brom. 204 EF103
Pole Hill Rd E4 101 EC45
Pole Hill Rd, Hayes 135 BQ69
Pole Hill Rd, Uxb. 135 BQ69
Pole La, Ong. 53 FE17
Polebrook Rd SE3 164 EJ83
Polecroft La SE6 183 DZ89
Polehamptons, The, Hmptn. 176 CC94
High St
Polehanger La, Hem.H. 39 BE18
Poles Hill, Chesh. 54 AN29
Poles Hill, Rick. 57 BE33
Polesden Gdns SW20 199 CV96
Polesden Lacey, Dor. 246 CA130
Polesden La (Send Marsh), Wok. 227 BF122
Polesden Rd (Bookham), Lthd. 246 CB129
Polesden Vw (Bookham), Lthd. 246 CB127
Polesteeple Hill (Biggin Hill), West. 238 EK117
Polesworth Ho W2 140 DA71
Polesworth Rd, Dag. 146 EX66
Polhill (Halstead), Sev. 241 FC115
Police Sta La, Bushey 94 CB45
Sparrows Herne
Police Sta Rd, Walt. 214 BW107
Pollard Av (Denham), Uxb. 113 BF58
Pollard Cl E16 144 EG73
Pollard Cl N7 121 DM63
Pollard Cl, Chig. 104 EU50
Pollard Cl (Old Windsor), Wind. 172 AV85
Pollard Hatch, Harl. 51 EP18
Pollard Rd N20 98 DE47
Pollard Rd, Mord. 200 DD99
Pollard Rd, Wok. 227 BB116
Pollard Row E2 142 DU69
Pollard St E2 142 DU69
Pollard Wk, Sid. 186 EW93
Pollards, Rick. 91 BD50
Pollards Cl, Loug. 84 EJ43
Pollards Cl (Cheshunt), Wal.Cr. 66 DQ29
Pollards Cres SW16 201 DL97
Pollards Hill E SW16 201 DM97
Pollards Hill N SW16 201 DL97
Pollards Hill S SW16 201 DL97
Pollards Hill W SW16 201 DL97
Pollards Oak Cres, Oxt. 254 EG132
Pollards Oak Rd, Oxt. 254 EG132
Pollards Wd Hill, Oxt. 254 EH130
Pollards Wd Rd SW16 201 DL96
Pollards Wd Rd, Oxt. 254 EH131
Pollen St W1 273 J9
Pollicott Cl, St.Alb. 43 CJ15
Pollitt Dr NW8 140 DD70
Cunningham Pl
Pollyhaugh (Eynsford), Dart. 208 FL104
Polperro Cl, Orp. 205 ET100
Cotswold Ri
Polsted Rd SE6 183 DZ87
Polsten Ms, Enf. 83 EA37
Government Row
Polthorne Est SE18 165 ER77
Polthorne Gro SE18 165 EQ77
Poltimore Rd, Guil. 258 AU136
Polworth Rd SW16 181 DL92
Polygon, The SW4 161 DJ84
Old Town
Polygon Rd NW1 273 M1
Polygon Rd NW1 141 DK68
Polytechnic St SE18 165 EN77
Pomell Way E1 142 DT72
Commercial St
Pomeroy Cl, Amer. 55 AR40
Pomeroy Cres, Wat. 75 BV36
Pomeroy St SE14 162 DW81
Pomfret Rd SE5 161 DP83
Flaxman Rd
Pomoja La N19 121 DK61
Pompadour Cl, Brwd. 108 FW50
Queen St
Pond Cl N12 98 DE51
Summerfields Av
Pond Cl SE3 164 EF82
Pond Cl, Ash. 232 CL117
Pond Cl (Harefield), Uxb. 92 BJ54
Pond Cl, Walt. 213 BU107
Pond Cottage La, W.Wick. 203 EA102
Pond Cotts SE21 182 DS88
Pond Cft, Hat. 45 CT18
Pond Fm Cl, Tad. 233 CU124
Pond Fld, Welw.G.C. 30 DA06
Pond Fld End, Loug. 102 EJ45
Pond Grn, Ruis. 115 BS61
Pond Hill Gdns, Sutt. 217 CY107
Pond La (Chalfont St. Peter), Ger.Cr. 90 AV53
Pond La (Peaslake), Guil. 261 BQ144
Pond Lees Cl, Dag. 147 FD66
Leys Av
Pond Mead SE21 182 DR86
Pond Meadow, Guil. 242 AS134
Pond Pk Rd, Chesh. 54 AP29
Pond Path, Chis. 185 EP93
Heathfield La
Pond Piece (Oxshott), Lthd. 214 CB114
Pond Pl SW3 276 B9
Pond Pl SW3 160 DE77
Pond Rd E15 144 EE68
Pond Rd SE3 164 EF82
Pond Rd, Egh. 173 BC93
Pond Rd, Hem.H. 58 BN25
Pond Rd, Wok. 226 AU120
Pond Sq N6 120 DG60
South Gro
Pond St NW3 120 DE64
Pond Wk, Upmin. 129 FS61
Pond Way, Tedd. 177 CJ93
Holmesdale Rd
Pondcroft, Welw.G.C. 29 CY10
Ponder St N7 141 DM66
Ponders End Ind Est, Enf. 83 DZ42
Pondfield Cres, St.Alb. 43 CH16
Pondfield La, Brwd. 109 GA49
Pondfield Rd, Brom. 204 EE102
Pondfield Rd, Dag. 127 FB64
Pondfield Rd, Gdmg. 258 AT144
Pondfield Rd, Ken. 235 DP116
Pondfield Rd, Orp. 205 EP104
Ponds, The, Wey. 213 BS107
Ellesmere Rd
Ponds La (Albury Heath), Guil. 260 BL142
Pondside Cl, Hayes 155 BR80
Providence La
Pondwicks, Amer. 55 AP39
Pondwicks Cl, St.Alb. 42 CC21
Pondwood Ri, Orp. 205 ES101
Ponler St E1 142 DV72
Ponsard Rd NW10 139 CV69
Ponsbourne Pk, Hert. 47 DL23
Ponsford St E9 142 DW65
Ponsonby Pl SW1 277 N10
Ponsonby Pl SW1 161 DK78
Ponsonby Rd SW15 179 CV87
Ponsonby Ter SW1 277 N10
Ponsonby Ter SW1 161 DK78
Pont St SW1 276 D7
Pont St SW1 160 DF76
Pont St Ms SW1 276 D7
Pont St Ms SW1 160 DF76
Pontefract Rd, Brom. 184 EF92
Pontoise Cl, Sev. 256 FF122
Ponton Rd SW8 161 DK79
Pontypool Pl SE1 278 F4
Pontypool Wk, Rom. 106 FJ51
Saddleworth Rd
Pony Chase, Cob. 214 BZ113
Pool Cl, Beck. 183 EA92
Pool Cl, W.Mol. 196 BZ99
Pool Ct SE6 183 EA89
Pool End Cl, Shep. 194 BN99
Pool Gro, Croy. 221 DY112
Pool La, Slou. 132 AS73
Pool Rd, Har. 117 CD59
Pool Rd, W.Mol. 196 BZ99
Poole Cl, Ruis. 115 BS61
Chichester Av
Poole Ct Rd, Houns. 156 BY82
Vicarage Fm Rd
Poole Ho, Grays 171 GJ75
Poole Rd E9 143 DX65
Poole Rd, Epsom 216 CR107
Poole Rd, Horn. 128 FM59
Poole Rd, Wok. 226 AY117
Poole St N1 142 DR67
Poole Way, Hayes 135 BR69
Pooles Bldgs EC1 274 D5
Pooles La SW10 160 DC80
Lots Rd
Pooles La, Dag. 146 EY68
Pooles Pk N4 121 DN61
Seven Sisters Rd
Pooley Av, Egh. 173 BB92
Pooley Grn Cl, Egh. 173 BB92
Pooley Grn Rd, Egh. 173 BB92
Pooleys La, Hat. 45 CV23
Poolmans Rd, Wind. 151 AK83
Poolmans St SE16 163 DX75
Poolsford Rd NW9 118 CS56
Poonah St E1 142 DW72
Hardinge St
Pootings Rd, Eden. 255 ER134
Pope Cl SW19 180 DD93
Pope Cl, Felt. 175 BT88
Pope Rd, Brom. 204 EK99
Pope St SE1 279 N5
Pope St SE1 162 DS75
Popes Av, Twick. 177 CE89
Popes Cl, Amer. 72 AT37
Popes Cl (Colnbrook), Slou. 153 BB80
Popes Dr N3 98 DA53
Popes Gro, Croy. 203 DZ104
Popes Gro, Twick. 177 CF89
Pope's Head All EC3 142 DR72
Cornhill
Popes La W5 157 CK76
Popes La, Oxt. 254 EE134
Popes La, Wat. 75 BV37
Popes Rd SW9 161 DN83
Popes Rd, Abb.L. 59 BS31
Popham Cl, Felt. 176 BZ90
Popham Gdns, Rich. 158 CN83
Lower Richmond Rd
Popham Rd N1 142 DQ67
Popham St N1 141 DP67
Poplar Av, Amer. 72 AT39
Poplar Av, Grav. 191 GJ91
Poplar Av, Lthd. 231 CH122
Poplar Av, Mitch. 200 DF95
Poplar Av, Orp. 205 EP103
Poplar Av, Sthl. 156 CB76
Poplar Av, West Dr. 134 BM73
Poplar Bath St E14 143 EB73
Lawless St
Poplar Business Pk E14 143 EC73
Poplar Cl E9 123 DZ64
Lee Conservancy Rd
Poplar Cl, Chesh. 54 AQ28
Poplar Cl, Pnr. 94 BX53
Poplar Cl (Colnbrook), Slou. 153 BE81
Poplar Cl, S.Ock. 149 FX70
Poplar Ct SW19 180 DA92
Poplar Cres, Epsom 216 CQ107
Poplar Dr, Bans. 217 CX114
Poplar Dr, Brwd. 109 GC44
Poplar Fm Cl, Epsom 216 CQ107
Poplar Gdns, N.Mal. 198 CR96
Poplar Gro N11 98 DG51
Poplar Gro W6 159 CW75
Poplar Gro, N.Mal. 198 CR97
Poplar Gro, Wem. 118 CQ62
Poplar Gro, Wok. 226 AY119
Poplar High St E14 143 EA73
Poplar Mt, Belv. 167 FB77
Poplar Pl SE28 146 EW73
Poplar Pl W2 140 DB73
Poplar Pl, Hayes 135 BU73
Central Av
Poplar Rd SE24 162 DQ84
Poplar Rd SW19 200 DA96
Poplar Rd, Ashf. 175 BQ92
Poplar Rd (Shalford), Guil. 258 AY141
Poplar Rd, Lthd. 231 CH122
Poplar Rd, Sutt. 199 CZ102
Poplar Rd (Denham), Uxb. 114 BJ64
Poplar Rd S SW19 200 DA97
Poplar Row, Epp. 85 ES37
Poplar Shaw, Wal.Abb. 68 EF33
Poplar St, Rom. 127 FC56
Poplar Vw, Wem. 117 CK61
Magnet Rd
Poplar Wk SE24 162 DQ84
Poplar Wk, Cat. 236 DS123
Poplar Wk, Croy. 202 DQ103
Poplar Way, Felt. 175 BU90
Poplar Way, Ilf. 125 EQ56
Poplars, Welw.G.C. 30 DB08
Poplars, The N14 81 DH43
Poplars, The, Grav. 191 GL87
Poplars, The, Hem.H. 40 BH21
Poplars, The, Rom. 86 EV41
Hoe La
Poplars, The, St.Alb. 43 CH24
Poplars, The, Wal.Cr. 66 DS26
Poplars Av NW10 139 CW65
Poplars Av, Hat. 44 CR18
Poplars Cl, Hat. 44 CQ18
Poplars Cl, Ruis. 115 BS60
Poplars Cl, Wat. 59 BV32
Poplars Rd E17 123 EB58
Poppins Ct EC4 274 F9
Poppleton Rd E11 124 EE58
Poppy Cl, Brwd. 108 FV43
Poppy Cl, Hem.H. 39 BE19
Poppy Cl, Wall. 200 DG102
Poppy La, Croy. 202 DW101
Poppy Wk, Wal.Cr. 66 DR28
Poppyfields, Welw.G.C. 30 DC09
Porch Way N20 98 DF48
Porchester Cl SE5 162 DQ84
Porchester Cl, Horn. 128 FL58
Porchester Gdns W2 140 DB73
Porchester Gdns Ms W2 140 DB72
Porchester Gdns
Porchester Mead, Beck. 183 EB93
Porchester Ms W2 140 DB72
Porchester Pl W2 272 C9
Porchester Pl W2 140 DE72
Porchester Rd W2 140 DB72
Porchester Rd, Kings.T. 198 CP96
Porchester Sq W2 140 DB72
Porchester Ter W2 140 DC73
Porchester Ter N W2 140 DB72
Porchfield Cl, Grav. 191 GJ89
Porchfield Cl, Sutt. 218 DB110
Porcupine Cl SE9 184 EL89
Porden Rd SW2 161 DM84
Porlock Av, Har. 116 CC60
Porlock Rd W10 139 CX70
Ladbroke Gro
Porlock Rd, Enf. 100 DT45
Porlock St SE1 279 K4
Porlock St SE1 162 DR75
Porridge Pot All, Guil. 258 AW136
Bury Flds
Porrington Cl, Chis. 205 EM95
Port Av, Green. 189 FV86
Port Cres E13 144 EH70
Jenkins Rd
Port Hill, Hert. 32 DQ09
Port Hill, Orp. 224 EV112
Port Vale, Hert. 31 DP08
Portal Cl SE27 181 DN90
Portal Cl, Ruis. 115 BU63
Portal Cl, Uxb. 134 BL66
Portbury Cl SE15 162 DU81
Clayton Rd
Portcullis Lo Rd, Enf. 82 DR41
Portelet Ct N1 142 DS67
De Beauvoir Est
Portelet Rd E1 143 DX69
Porten Rd W14 159 CY76
Porter Cl, Grays 169 FW79
Porter Rd E6 145 EM72
Porter Sq N19 121 DL60
Hornsey Rd
Porter St SE1 279 J2
Porter St W1 272 E6
Porters Av, Dag. 146 EV65
Porters Cl, Brwd. 108 FU46
Porters Pk Dr, Rad. 61 CK33
Porters Wk E1 142 DV73
Pennington St
Porters Way, West Dr. 154 BM76
Porters Wd, St.Alb. 43 CE16
Portersfield Rd, Enf. 82 DS42
Porteus Rd W2 140 DC71
Portgate Cl W9 139 CZ70
Porthallow Cl, Orp. 223 ET105
Sevenoaks Rd
Porthcawe Rd SE26 183 DY91
Porthkerry Av, Well. 166 EU84
Portia Way E3 143 DZ70
Portinscale Rd SW15 179 CY85
Portland Av N16 122 DT59
Portland Av, Grav. 191 GH89
Portland Av, N.Mal. 199 CT101
Portland Av, Sid. 186 EU86
Portland Cl, Rom. 126 EY57
Portland Cl, Slou. 131 AK70
Portland Cres SE9 184 EL89
Portland Cres, Felt. 175 BR91
Portland Cres, Grnf. 136 CB70
Portland Cres, Stan. 95 CK54
Portland Dr, Enf. 82 DS38
Portland Dr, Red. 251 DK129
Portland Dr (Cheshunt), Wal.Cr. 66 DU31
Portland Gdns N4 121 DP58
Portland Gdns, Rom. 126 EX57
Portland Gro SW8 161 DM81
Portland Hts, Nthwd. 93 BT49
Portland Ho, Red. 251 DK129
Portland Ms W1 273 L9
Portland Pk, Ger.Cr. 112 AX58
Portland Pl W1 273 H5
Portland Pl W1 141 DH71
Portland Pl, Epsom 216 CS112
Portland Pl, Hert. 32 DW11
Portland Ri N4 121 DP60
Portland Ri Est N4 122 DQ60
Portland Rd N15 122 DT56
Portland Rd SE9 184 EL89
Portland Rd SE25 202 DU98
Portland Rd W11 139 CY74
Portland Rd, Ashf. 174 BL90
Portland Rd, Brom. 184 EJ91
Portland Rd, Dor. 263 CG135
Portland Rd, Grav. 191 GH88
Portland Rd, Hayes 135 BS69
Portland Rd, Kings.T. 198 CL97
Portland Rd, Mitch. 200 DE96
Portland Rd, Sthl. 156 BZ76
Portland Sq E1 142 DV74
Watts St
Portland St SE17 279 K10
Portland St SE17 162 DR78
Portland St, St.Alb. 42 CC20
Portland Ter, Rich. 157 CK84
Portland Wk SE17 162 DR79
Portland St
Portley La, Cat. 236 DS121
Portley Wd Rd, Whyt. 236 DT120
Portman Av SW14 158 CR83
Portman Cl W1 272 E8
Portman Cl W1 140 DF72
Portman Cl, Bex. 187 FE88
Portman Cl, Bexh. 166 EX83
Queen Anne's Gate
Portman Cl, St.Alb. 43 CJ15
Portman Dr, Wdf.Grn. 102 EK54
Portman Gdns NW9 96 CR54
Portman Gdns, Uxb. 134 BN66
Portman Gate NW1 272 C5
Portman Ho, St.Alb. 43 CD17
Portman Ms S W1 272 F9
Portman Ms S W1 140 DG72
Portman Pl E2 142 DW69
Portman Rd, Kings.T. 198 CM96
Portman Sq W1 272 F8
Portman Sq W1 140 DF72
Portman St W1 272 F9
Portman St W1 140 DG72
Portmeadow Wk SE2 166 EX75
Portmeers Cl E17 123 DZ58
Lennox Rd
Portmore Gdns, Rom. 104 FA50
Portmore Pk Rd, Wey. 212 BN105
Portmore Quays, Wey. 212 BM105
Weybridge Rd
Portmore Way, Wey. 194 BN104
Portnall Dr, Vir.W. 192 AT98
Portnall Ri, Vir.W. 192 AT99
Portnall Rd W9 139 CZ69
Portnall Rd, Vir.W. 192 AT99
Portnalls Cl, Couls. 235 DH116
Portnalls Ri, Couls. 235 DH116
Portnalls Rd, Couls. 235 DH118
Portnoi Cl, Rom. 105 FD54
Portobello Cl, Chesh. 54 AN29
Portobello Ct W11 139 CZ73
Westbourne Gro
Portobello Ms W11 140 DA73
Portobello Rd
Portobello Rd W10 139 CZ72
Portobello Rd W11 139 CZ72
Porton Ct, Surb. 197 CJ100
Portpool La EC1 274 D6
Portpool La EC1 141 DN71
Portree Cl N22 99 DM52
Nightingale Rd
Portree St E14 143 ED72
Portsdown, Edg. 96 CN50
Rectory La
Portsdown Av NW11 119 CZ58
Portsdown Ms NW11 119 CZ58
Portsea Ms W2 272 C9
Portsea Pl W2 272 C9
Portsea Rd, Til. 171 GJ81
Portslade Rd SW8 161 DJ82
Portsmouth Av, T.Ditt. 197 CG101
Portsmouth Ct, Slou. 132 AS73
Portsmouth Ms E16 144 EH74
Wesley Av
Portsmouth Rd SW15 179 CV87
Portsmouth Rd, Cob. 213 BU114
Portsmouth Rd, Esher 214 CC105
Portsmouth Rd, Guil. 258 AW138
Portsmouth Rd, Kings.T. 197 CJ99
Portsmouth Rd, Surb. 197 CJ99
Portsmouth Rd, T.Ditt. 197 CE103
Portsmouth Rd (Ripley), Wok. 228 BM119
Portsmouth St WC2 274 B9
Portsoken St E1 275 P10
Portsoken St E1 142 DT73
Portugal Gdns, Twick. 176 CC89
Fulwell Pk Av
Portugal Rd, Wok. 227 BA116
Portugal St WC2 274 B9
Portugal St WC2 141 DM72
Portway E15 144 EF67
Portway, Epsom 217 CU110
Portway Cres, Epsom 217 CU109
Portway Gdns SE18 164 EK80
Shooter's Hill Rd
Post Ho La (Bookham), Lthd. 246 CA125
Post La, Twick. 177 CD88
Post Meadow, Iver 133 BD68
Post Office App E7 124 EH64
Post Office Ct EC3 275 L9
Post Office La, Beac. 89 AK52
Post Office La (George Grn), Slou. 132 AX72
Post Office Rd, Harl. 35 EQ14
Post Office Row, Oxt. 254 EL131
Post Office Wk, Harl. 35 ER14
Post Office Way SW8 161 DK80
Post Rd, Sthl. 156 CB76
Post Wd Rd, Ware 33 DY08
Postern Grn, Enf. 81 DN40
Postfield, Welw.G.C. 30 DA06
Postmill Cl, Croy. 203 DX104
Postway Ms, Ilf. 125 EP62
Clements Rd
Postwood Grn, Hert. 32 DW12
Potier St SE1 279 L7
Potier St SE1 162 DR76
Potkiln La (Jordans), Beac. 111 AQ55
Pott St E2 142 DV69
Potten End Hill, Berk. 39 BD16
Potten End Hill, Hem.H. 39 BD16
Potter Cl, Mitch. 201 DH96
Potter St, Harl. 52 EW16
Potter St, Nthwd. 93 BU53
Potter St, Pnr. 93 BV53
Potter St Hill, Pnr. 93 BV51
Potterells (North Mymms), Hat. 63 CX25
Potterne Cl SW19 179 CX87
Potters Cl, Croy. 203 DY102
Potters Cl, Loug. 84 EL40
Potters Cross, Iver 133 BD69
Potters Fld, Harl. 52 EX17
Potters Fld, St.Alb. 43 CE16
Potters Flds SE1 142 DS74
Tooley St
Potters Gro, N.Mal. 198 CQ98
Potters Hts Cl, Pnr. 93 BV52
Potters La SW16 181 DK93
Potters La, Barn. 80 DA42
Potters La, Borwd. 78 CQ39
Potters La (Send), Wok. 227 BB123
Potters Ms, Borwd. 77 CK44
Elstree Hill N
Potters Rd SW6 160 DC82
Potters Rd, Barn. 80 DB42
Potters Way, Reig. 266 DC138
Pottery La W11 139 CY73
Portland Rd
Pottery Rd, Bex. 187 FC89
Pottery Rd, Brent. 158 CL79
Pottery St SE16 162 DV75
Pouchen End La, Hem.H. 39 BD21
Poulcott (Wraysbury), Stai. 172 AY86
Poulett Gdns, Twick. 177 CG88
Poulett Rd E6 145 EM68
Poulner Way SE15 162 DT80
Daniel Gdns
Poulters Wd, Kes. 222 EK106
Poultney Cl, Rad. 62 CM32
Poulton Av, Sutt. 200 DD104
Poulton Cl E8 122 DV64
Spurstowe Ter
Poultry EC2 275 K9
Poultry EC2 142 DR72
Pound, The (Burnham), Slou. 130 AJ70
Hogfair La
Pound Cl, Orp. 205 ER103
Pound Cl, Surb. 197 CJ102
Pound Cl, Wal.Abb. 50 EE23
Pound Ct, Ash. 232 CM118
Pound Ct Dr, Orp. 205 ER103
Pound Cres (Fetcham), Lthd. 231 CD121
Pound Fld, Guil. 242 AX133
Pound La NW10 139 CU65
Pound La, Epsom 216 CR112
Pound La, Rad. 62 CM33
Pound La, Sev. 240 EX115
Pound La (Knockholt Pound), Sev. 257 FH124
Pound Pk Rd SE7 164 EK77
Pound Pl SE9 185 EN86
Pound Pl (Shalford), Guil. 259 AZ140
Pound Pl Cl (Shalford), Guil. 259 AZ140
Pound Rd, Bans. 233 CZ117
Pound Rd, Cher. 194 BH101
Pound St, Cars. 218 DF106
Pound Way, Chis. 185 EQ94
Royal Par
Poundfield, Wat. 75 BT35
Ashfields
Poundfield Ct, Wok. 227 BC121
High St
Poundfield Gdns, Wok. 227 BC120
Poundfield Rd, Loug. 85 EN43
Poundwell, Welw.G.C. 30 DA10
Pounsley Rd (Dunton Grn), Sev. 256 FE121
Pountney Rd SW11 160 DG83
Poverest Rd, Orp. 205 ET99
Povey Cross Rd, Horl. 268 DD150
Powder Mill La, Dart. 188 FL89
Powder Mill La, Twick. 176 BZ88
Powdermill La, Wal.Abb. 67 EB33
Powdermill Ms, Wal.Abb. 67 EB33
Powdermill La
Powdermill Way, Wal.Abb. 67 EB32
Powell Cl, Chess. 215 CK106
Coppard Gdns
Powell Cl, Dart. 189 FS89
Powell Cl, Edg. 96 CM51
Powell Cl, Guil. 258 AT136
Powell Cl, Horl. 268 DE147
Baden Dr
Powell Cl, Wall. 219 DK108
Powell Gdns, Dag. 126 FA63
Powell Rd E5 122 DV62
Powell Rd, Buck.H. 102 EJ45
Powells Cl, Dor. 263 CJ139
Goodwyns Rd
Powell's Wk W4 158 CS79
Power Dr, Enf. 83 DZ36
Power Ind Est, Erith 167 FG81
Power Rd W4 158 CN77
Powers Ct, Twick. 177 CK87
Powerscroft Rd E5 122 DW63
Powerscroft Rd, Sid. 186 EW93
Powis Ct, Pot.B. 64 DC34
Powis Gdns NW11 119 CZ59
Powis Gdns W11 139 CZ72
Powis Ms W11 139 CZ72
Westbourne Pk Rd
Powis Pl WC1 274 A5
Powis Pl WC1 141 DL70
Powis Rd E3 143 EB69
Powis Sq W11 139 CZ72
Powis St SE18 165 EN76
Powis Ter W11 139 CZ72
Powle Ter, Ilf. 125 EQ64
Oaktree Gro
Powlett Pl NW1 141 DH65
Harmood St
Pownall Gdns, Houns. 156 CB84
Pownall Rd E8 142 DT67
Pownall Rd, Houns. 156 CB84
Pownsett Ter, Ilf. 125 EQ64
Buttsbury Rd

Providence Pl N1 141 DP67
Upper St
Providence Pl, Epsom 216 CS112
Providence Pl, Rom. 104 EZ54
Providence Pl, Wok. 212 BG114
Providence Rd, West Dr. 134 BL74
Providence Row N1 274 B1
Providence Row Cl E2 142 DV69
Ainsley St
Providence Sq SE1 162 DT75
Mill St
Providence St N1 142 DQ68
St. Peters St
Providence St, Green. 189 FU85
Providence Yd E2 142 DU69
Ezra St
Provident Ind Est, Hayes 155 BU75
Provost Est N1 275 K2
Provost Est N1 142 DR68
Provost Rd NW3 140 DF66
Provost St N1 275 K3
Provost St N1 142 DR69
Prowse Av, Bushey 94 CC47
Prowse Pl NW1 141 DH66
Bonny St
Pruden Cl N14 99 DJ47
Prudent Pas EC2 275 J8
Prune Hill (Englefield Grn), Egh. 172 AX94
Prusom St E1 142 DV74
Pryor Cl, Abb.L. 59 BT32
Pryors, The NW3 120 DD62
Puck La, Wal.Abb. 67 ED29
Puddenhole Cotts, Bet. 248 CN133
Pudding La EC3 279 L1
Pudding La EC3 142 DR73
Pudding La, Chig. 103 ET46
Pudding La, Hem.H. 40 BG18
Pudding La (Seal), Sev. 257 FN121
Church St
Pudding Mill La E15 143 EB67
Puddingstone Dr, St.Alb. 43 CJ22
Puddle Dock EC4 274 G10
Puddledock La, Dart. 187 FE92
Puddledock La, West. 255 ET133
Puers La (Jordans), Beac. 90 AS51
Puffin Cl, Bark. 146 EV69
Puffin Cl, Beck. 203 DX99
Puffin Ter, Ilf. 125 EN55
Tiptree Cres
Pulborough Rd SW18 179 CZ87
Pulborough Way, Houns. 156 BW84
Pulford Rd N15 122 DR58
Pulham Av N2 120 DC56
Pulham Av, Brox. 49 DX21
Puller Rd, Barn. 79 CY40
Puller Rd, Hem.H. 40 BG21
Pulleyns Av E6 144 EL69
Pulleys Cl, Hem.H. 39 BF19
Pulleys La, Hem.H. 39 BF19
Pullfields, Chesh. 54 AN30
Pullman Cl, St.Alb. 43 CE22
Ramsbury Rd
Pullman Ct SW2 181 DL88
Pullman Gdns SW15 179 CW86
Pullman Pl SE9 184 EL85
Pullmans Pl, Stai. 174 BG92
Pulpit Cl, Chesh. 54 AN29
Pulross Rd SW9 161 DM83
Pulteney Cl E3 143 DZ67
Pulteney Gdns E18 124 EH55
Pulteney Rd
Pulteney Rd E18 124 EH55
Pulteney Ter N1 141 DM67
Pulton Pl SW6 160 DA80
Puma Ct E1 275 P6
Pump All, Brent. 157 CK80
Pump Cl, Nthlt. 136 CA68
Union Rd
Pump Ct EC4 274 D9
Pump Hill, Loug. 85 EM40
Pump Ho Cl, Brom. 204 EF96
Pump La SE14 162 DW80
Pump La, Chesh. 54 AS32
Pump La, Epp. 51 EP24
Pump La, Hayes 155 BU75
Pump La, Orp. 225 FB106
Pump Pail N, Croy. 202 DQ104
Old Town
Pump Pail S, Croy. 202 DQ104
Southbridge Rd
Pumphandle Path N2 98 DC54
Tarling Rd
Pumping Sta Rd W4 158 CS80
Pumpkin Hill (Burnham), Slou. 131 AL65
Punch Bowl La, Chesh. 54 AQ32
Red Lion St
Punch Bowl La, Hem.H. 41 BR17
Punch Bowl La, St.Alb. 41 BT16
Punchbowl La, Dor. 263 CK135
Pundersons Gdns E2 142 DV69
Punjab La, Sthl. 136 BZ74
Herbert Rd
Purbeck Av, N.Mal. 199 CT100
Purbeck Cl, Red. 251 DK128
Purbeck Ct, Guil. 242 AS134
Egerton Rd
Purbeck Dr NW2 119 CY61
Purbeck Dr, Wok. 211 AZ114
Purbeck Rd, Horn. 127 FG60
Purberry Gro, Epsom 217 CT110
Purbrock Av, Wat. 76 BW36
Purbrook Est SE1 279 N5
Purbrook St SE1 279 N6
Purbrook St SE1 162 DS76
Purcell Cl, Borwd. 77 CK39
Purcell Cl, Ken. 220 DR114
Purcell Cres SW6 159 CY80
Purcell Ms NW10 138 CS66
Suffolk Rd
Purcell Rd, Grnf. 136 CB71
Purcell St N1 142 DS68
Purcells Av, Edg. 96 CN50
Purcells Cl, Ash. 232 CM118
Albert Rd
Purchese St NW1 141 DK68
Purdy St E3 143 EB70
Purelake Ms SE13 163 ED83
Purfleet Bypass, Purf. 168 FP77
Purfleet Ind Pk, S.Ock. 168 FM75
Purfleet Rd, S.Ock. 168 FN75
Purfleet Thames Terminal, Purf. 168 FQ80
Purford Grn, Harl. 52 EU16
Purkiss Rd, Hert. 32 DQ12
Purland Cl, Dag. 126 EZ60
Purland Rd SE28 165 ET75
Purleigh Av, Wdf.Grn. 102 EL51
Purley Av NW2 119 CY62
Purley Bury Av, Pur. 220 DQ110
Purley Bury Cl, Pur. 220 DQ111
Purley Cl, Ilf. 103 EN54
Purley Downs Rd, Pur. 220 DQ110
Purley Downs Rd, S.Croy. 220 DR111
Purley Hill, Pur. 219 DP112
Purley Knoll, Pur. 219 DM111
Purley Oaks Rd, S.Croy. 220 DR109
Purley Par, Pur. 219 DN111
High St
Purley Pk Rd, Pur. 219 DP110
Purley Pl N1 141 DP66
Islington Pk St
Purley Ri, Pur. 219 DM112
Purley Rd N9 100 DR48
Purley Rd, Pur. 219 DN111
Purley Rd, S.Croy. 220 DR108
Purley Vale, Pur. 219 DP113
Purley Way, Croy. 201 DM101
Purley Way, Pur. 219 DN108
Purley Way Cres, Croy. 201 DM101
Purley Way
Purlieu Way, Epp. 85 ES35
Purlings Rd, Bushey 76 CB43
Purneys Rd SE9 164 EK84
Purrett Rd SE18 165 ET78
Purser's Cross Rd SW6 159 CZ81
Pursers La (Peaslake), Guil. 261 BR142
Pursewardens Cl W13 137 CJ74
Pursley Gdns, Borwd. 78 CN38
Pursley Rd NW7 97 CV52
Purton Ct (Farnham Royal), Slou. 131 AQ66
Purton La (Farnham Royal), Slou. 131 AQ66
Purves Rd NW10 139 CW68
Puteaux Ho E2 143 DX68
Putney Br SW6 159 CY83
Putney Br SW15 159 CY83
Putney Br App SW6 159 CY83
Putney Br Rd SW15 159 CY84
Putney Br Rd SW18 180 DA85
Putney Common SW15 159 CW83
Putney Ex Shop Cen SW15 159 CY84
Putney Gdns, Rom. 126 EV58
Heathfield Pk Dr
Putney Heath SW15 179 CW86
Putney Heath La SW15 179 CX86
Putney High St SW15 159 CX84
Putney Hill SW15 179 CX86
Putney Pk Av SW15 159 CU84
Putney Pk La SW15 159 CV84
Putney Rd, Enf. 83 DX36
Puttenham Cl, Wat. 94 BW48
Putters Cft, Hem.H. 40 BM15
Puttocks Cl, Hat. 45 CW23
Puttocks Dr, Hat. 45 CW23
Pycroft Way N9 100 DT49
Pye Cl, Cat. 236 DR123
St. Lawrence Way
Pye Cor, Harl. 35 ER10
Pyebush La, Beac. 111 AN56
Pyecombe Cor N12 97 CZ49
Pyenest Rd, Harl. 51 ER18
Pyghtle, The (Denham), Uxb. 114 BG60
Pylbrook Rd, Sutt. 200 DA104
Pyle Hill, Wok. 226 AX124
Pylon Way, Croy. 201 DL102
Pym Cl, Barn. 80 DD43
Pym Orchard (Brasted), West. 240 EW124
Pym Pl, Grays 170 GA77
Pymers Mead SE21 182 DQ88
Pymmes Cl N13 99 DM50
Pymmes Cl N17 100 DV53
Pymmes Gdns N N9 100 DT48
Pymmes Gdns S N9 100 DT48
Pymmes Grn Rd N11 99 DH49
Pymmes Rd N13 99 DL51
Pymms Brook Dr, Barn. 80 DE42
Pynchester Cl, Uxb. 114 BN61
Pyne Rd, Surb. 198 CN102
Pyne Ter SW19 179 CX88
Windlesham Gro
Pynest Grn La, Wal.Abb. 84 EG38
Pynfolds SE16 162 DV75
Paradise St
Pynham Cl SE2 166 EU76
Pynnacles Cl, Stan. 95 CH50
Pypers Hatch, Harl. 35 ET14
Pyrcroft La, Wey. 213 BP106
Pyrcroft Rd, Cher. 193 BF101
Pyrford Common Rd, Wok. 227 BD116
Pyrford Ct, Wok. 227 BE117
Pyrford Heath, Wok. 227 BF116
Pyrford Lock (Wisley), Wok. 228 BJ116
Pyrford Rd, W.Byf. 212 BG113
Pyrford Rd, Wok. 212 BG114
Pyrford Wds Cl, Wok. 227 BF115
Pyrford Wds Rd, Wok. 227 BE115
Pyrland Rd N5 122 DR64
Pyrland Rd, Rich. 178 CM86
Pyrles Grn, Loug. 85 EP39
Pyrles La, Loug. 85 EP40
Pyrmont Gro SE27 181 DP90
Pyrmont Rd W4 158 CN79
Pyrmont Rd, Ilf. 125 EQ61
High Rd
Pytchley Cres SE19 182 DQ93
Pytchley Rd SE22 162 DS83
Pytt Fld, Harl. 52 EV16

Q

Quad Rd, Wem. 117 CK62
Courtenay Rd
Quadrangle, The W2 272 B8
Quadrangle, The, Guil. 258 AU135
The Oval
Quadrangle, The, Welw.G.C. 29 CW08
Quadrangle Ms, Stan. 95 CJ52
Quadrant, The SE24 182 DQ85
Herne Hill
Quadrant, The SW20 199 CY95
Quadrant, The, Bexh. 166 EX80
Quadrant, The, Epsom 216 CS113
Quadrant, The, Purf. 168 FQ77
Quadrant, The, Rich. 158 CL84
Quadrant, The, St.Alb. 43 CH17
Quadrant, The, Sutt. 218 DC107
Quadrant Arc W1 277 L1
Quadrant Arc, Rom. 127 FE57
Quadrant Cl NW4 119 CV57
The Burroughs
Quadrant Gro NW5 120 DF64
Quadrant Ho, Sutt. 218 DC107
Quadrant Rd, Rich. 157 CK84
Quadrant Rd, Th.Hth. 201 DP98
Quadrant Way, Wey. 212 BM105
Weybridge Rd
Quaggy Wk SE3 164 EG84
Quail Gdns, S.Croy. 221 DY110
Quainton St NW10 118 CR62
Quaker Cl, Sev. 257 FK123
Quaker Ct E1 275 P5
Quaker La, Sthl. 156 CA76
Quaker La, Wal.Abb. 67 EC34
Quaker Rd, Ware 33 DY05
Quaker St E1 275 P5
Quaker St E1 142 DT70
Quakers Course NW9 97 CT53
Quakers Hall La, Sev. 257 FJ122
Quakers La, Islw. 157 CG81
Quakers La, Pot.B. 64 DB30
Quaker's Pl E7 124 EK64
Quakers Wk N21 82 DR44
Quality Ct WC2 274 D8
Quality Ct WC2 141 DN72
Quality St, Red. 251 DH128
Quantock Cl, Hayes 155 BR80
Quantock Cl, St.Alb. 43 CJ16
Quantock Cl, Slou. 153 BA78
Quantock Dr, Wor.Pk. 199 CW103
Quantock Gdns NW2 119 CX61
Quantock Rd, Bexh. 167 FE82
Cumbrian Av
Quantocks, Hem.H. 40 BM17
Quarles Cl, Rom. 104 FA52
Quarley Way SE15 162 DT80
Daniel Gdns
Quarr Rd, Cars. 200 DD100
Quarrendon Rd, Amer. 55 AR40
Quarrendon St SW6 160 DA82
Quarry, The, Bet. 248 CS132
Station Rd
Quarry Cl, Lthd. 231 CK121
Quarry Cl, Oxt. 254 EE130
Quarry Cotts, Sev. 256 FG123
Quarry Gdns, Lthd. 231 CK121
Quarry Hill, Grays 170 GA78
Quarry Hill, Sev. 257 FK123
Quarry Hill Pk, Reig. 250 DC131
Quarry Ms, Purf. 168 FN77
Fanns Ri
Quarry Pk Rd, Sutt. 217 CZ107
Quarry Ri, Sutt. 217 CZ107
Quarry Rd SW18 180 DC86
Quarry Rd, Gdse. 252 DW128
Quarry Rd, Oxt. 254 EE130
Quarry Spring, Harl. 52 EU15
Quarry St, Guil. 258 AX136
Quarryside Business Pk, Red. 251 DH130
Quarter Mile La E10 123 EB63
Quarterdeck, The E14 163 EA75
Quartermaine Av, Wok. 227 AZ122
Quartermass Cl, Hem.H. 40 BG19
Quartermass Rd
Quartermass Rd, Hem.H. 40 BG19
Quaves Rd, Slou. 152 AV76
Quay La, Green. 169 FV84
Quay W, Tedd. 177 CH92
Quayside Wk, Kings.T. 197 CK96
Bishop's Hall
Quebec Av, West. 255 ER126
Quebec Cl, Horl. 269 DN148
Alberta Dr
Quebec Ms W1 272 E9
Quebec Rd, Hayes 136 BW73
Quebec Rd, Ilf. 125 EP59
Quebec Rd, Til. 171 GG82
Quebec Sq, West. 255 ER126
Quebec Way SE16 163 DX75
Queen Adelaide Rd SE20 182 DW93
Queen Alexandra's Ct SW19 179 CZ92
Queen Alexandra's Way, Epsom 216 CN112
Queen Anne Av N15 122 DT57
Suffield Rd
Queen Anne Av, Brom. 204 EF97
Queen Anne Dr (Claygate), Esher 215 CE108
Queen Anne Ms W1 273 J7
Queen Anne Rd E9 143 DX65
Queen Anne St W1 273 H8
Queen Anne St W1 141 DH72
Queen Anne Ter E1 142 DV73
Sovereign Cl
Queen Anne's Cl, Twick. 177 CD90
Queen Anne's Gdns W4 158 CS76
Queen Annes Gdns W5 158 CL75
Queen Annes Gdns, Enf. 82 DS44
Queen Annes Gdns, Lthd. 231 CH121
Upper Fairfield Rd
Queen Anne's Gdns, Mitch. 200 DF97
Queen Anne's Gate SW1 277 M5
Queen Anne's Gate SW1 161 DK75
Queen Anne's Gate, Bexh. 166 EX83
Queen Anne's Gro W4 158 CS76
Queen Annes Gro W5 158 CL75
Queen Annes Gro, Enf. 100 DR45
Queen Anne's Ms, Lthd. 231 CH121
Fairfield Rd
Queen Annes Pl, Enf. 82 DS44
Queen Annes Rd, Wind. 151 AQ84
Queen Annes Ter, Lthd. 231 CH121
Upper Fairfield Rd
Queen Anne's Wk WC1 141 DL70
Guilford St
Queen Caroline Est W6 159 CW78
Queen Caroline St W6 159 CW77
Queen Charlotte St, Wind. 151 AR81
High St
Queen Eleanor's Rd, Guil. 258 AT135
Queen Elizabeth Ct, Brox. 67 DZ26
Groom Rd
Queen Elizabeth Ct, Wal.Abb. 83 EC36
Greenwich Way
Queen Elizabeth Gdns, Mord. 200 DA98
Queen Elizabeth Pl, Til. 171 GG84
Queen Elizabeth Rd E17 123 DY55
Queen Elizabeth Rd, Kings.T. 198 CM95
Queen Elizabeth II Br, Dart. 169 FR82
Queen Elizabeth II Br, Purf. 169 FR82
Queen Elizabeth St SE1 279 N4
Queen Elizabeth St SE1 162 DT75
Queen Elizabeth Wk SW13 159 CV81
Queen Elizabeth Wk, Wind. 152 AS82
Queen Elizabeth Way, Wok. 227 AZ119
Queen Elizabeths Cl N16 122 DR61
Queen Elizabeths Dr N14 99 DL46
Queen Elizabeth's Dr (New Addington), Croy. 221 ED110
Queen Elizabeth's Gdns (New Addington), Croy. 221 ED110
Queen Elizabeth's Dr
Queen Elizabeths Wk N16 122 DR61
Queen Elizabeth's Wk, Wall. 219 DK105
Queen Margaret's Gro N1 122 DS64
Queen Mary Av, Mord. 199 CX99
Queen Mary Cl, Rom. 127 FF58
Queen Mary Cl, Surb. 198 CN104
Queen Mary Cl, Wok. 227 BC116
Queen Mary Rd SE19 181 DP93
Queen Mary Rd, Shep. 195 BQ96
Queen Mary's Av, Cars. 218 DF108
Queen Marys Av, Wat. 75 BS42
Queen Marys Ct, Wal.Abb. 83 EC35
Greenwich Way
Queen Marys Dr (New Haw), Add. 211 BF110
Queen Mother's Dr (Denham), Uxb. 113 BF58
Queen of Denmark Ct SE16 163 DZ76
Queen Sq WC1 274 A5
Queen Sq WC1 141 DL70
Queen Sq Pl WC1 274 A5
Queen St EC4 275 J10
Queen St EC4 142 DQ73
Queen St N17 100 DS51
Queen St W1 277 H2
Queen St W1 141 DH74
Queen St, Bexh. 166 EZ83
Queen St, Brwd. 108 FW50
Queen St, Cher. 194 BG102
Queen St, Croy. 202 DQ104
Church Rd
Queen St, Erith 167 FE79
Queen St, Grav. 191 GH86
Queen St (Gomshall), Guil. 261 BQ139
Queen St, Kings L. 58 BG32
Queen St, Rom. 127 FD58
Queen St, St.Alb. 42 CC20
Queen St Pl EC4 279 J1
Queen Victoria Av, Wem. 137 CK66
Queen Victoria St EC4 274 G10
Queen Victoria St EC4 141 DP73
Queen Victoria Ter E1 142 DV73
Sovereign Cl
Queen Victoria's Wk, Wind. 152 AS81
Queenborough Gdns, Chis. 185 ER93
Queenborough Gdns, Ilf. 125 EN56
Queendale Ct, Wok. 226 AT116
Roundthorn Way
Queenhill Rd, S.Croy. 220 DV110
Queenhithe EC4 275 J10
Queenhithe EC4 142 DQ73
Queenhythe Rd, Guil. 242 AX128
Queens Acre, Sutt. 217 CX108
Queens Acre, Wind. 151 AR84
Queens All, Epp. 69 ET31
Queens Av N3 98 DC52
Queens Av N10 120 DG55
Queens Av N20 98 DD47
Queen's Av N21 99 DP46
Queens Av, Felt. 176 BW91
Queens Av, Grnf. 136 CB72
Queens Av, Stan. 117 CJ55
Queens Av, Wat. 75 BT42
Queens Av (Byfleet), W.Byf. 212 BK112
Queens Av, Wdf.Grn. 102 EH50
Queen's Circ SW8 161 DH80
Queenstown Rd
Queen's Circ SW11 161 DH80
Queenstown Rd
Queens Cl, Edg. 96 CN50
Queens Cl, Tad. 233 CU124
Queens Cl, Wall. 219 DH106
Queens Rd
Queens Cl (Old Windsor), Wind. 172 AU85
Queens Club Gdns W14 159 CY79
Queens Ct SE23 182 DW88
Queens Ct, Brox. 49 DZ24
Queens Ct, Hert. 32 DR10
Queens Rd
Queens Ct, Rich. 178 CM86
Queens Ct, St.Alb. 43 CH20
Hatfield Rd
Queens Ct, Slou. 132 AT73
Queens Ct, Wey. 213 BR106
Queens Ct, Wok. 227 AZ118
Hill Vw Rd
Queens Ct Ride, Cob. 213 BU113
Queen's Cres NW5 140 DG65
Queens Cres, Rich. 178 CM85
Queens Cres, St.Alb. 43 CH17
Queens Dr E10 123 EA59
Queens Dr N4 121 DP61
Queens Dr W3 138 CM72
Queens Dr W5 138 CM72
Queens Dr, Abb.L. 59 BT32
Queens Dr, Guil. 242 AU131
Queens Dr (Oxshott), Lthd. 214 CC111
Queen's Dr, Slou. 133 AZ66
Queens Dr, Surb. 198 CN101
Queens Dr, T.Ditt. 197 CG101
Queens Dr, Wal.Cr. 67 EA34
Queens Dr, The, Rick. 91 BF45
Queens Elm Par SW3 160 DD78
Old Ch St
Queen's Elm Sq SW3 160 DD78
Old Ch St
Queens Gdns NW4 119 CW57
Queens Gdns W2 140 DC73
Queens Gdns W5 137 CJ70
Queens Gdns, Dart. 188 FP88
Queen's Gdns, Houns. 156 BY81
Queens Gdns, Rain. 147 FD68
Queens Gdns, Upmin. 129 FT58
Queen's Gate SW7 160 DC76
Queen's Gate, Gat. 268 DG152
Queen's Gate Gdns SW7 160 DC76
Queens Gate Gdns SW15 159 CV84
Upper Richmond Rd
Queen's Gate Ms SW7 160 DC75
Queen's Gate Pl SW7 160 DC76
Queen's Gate Pl Ms SW7 160 DC76
Queen's Gate Ter SW7 160 DC76
Queen's Gro NW8 140 DD67
Queen's Gro Ms NW8 140 DD67
Queens Gro Rd E4 101 ED46
Queen's Head St N1 141 DP67
Queens Head Wk, Brox. 49 DY23
High Rd Wormley
Queens Head Yd SE1 279 K3
Queens Ho, Tedd. 177 CF93
Queens La N10 121 DH55
Queens La, Ashf. 174 BM91
Clarendon Rd
Queens Mkt E13 144 EJ67
Green St
Queens Ms W2 140 DB73
Queens Par N11 98 DF50
Colney Hatch La
Queens Par W5 138 CM72
Queens Par Cl N11 98 DF50
Colney Hatch La
Queens Pk Ct W10 139 CX69
Queens Pk Gdns, Felt. 175 BU90
Vernon Rd
Queens Pk Rd, Cat. 236 DS123
Queens Pk Rd, Rom. 106 FM53
Queens Pas, Chis. 185 EP93
High St
Queens Pl, Mord. 200 DA98
Queens Pl, Wat. 76 BW41
Queen's Prom, Kings.T. 197 CK97
Portsmouth Rd
Queens Reach, E.Mol. 197 CE98
Queens Ride SW13 159 CU83
Queens Ride SW15 159 CU83
Queen's Ride, Rich. 178 CP88
Queens Ri, Rich. 178 CM86
Queens Rd E11 123 ED59
Queens Rd E13 144 EH67
Queen's Rd E17 123 DZ58
Queens Rd N3 98 DC53
Queens Rd N9 100 DV48
Queen's Rd N11 99 DL52
Queens Rd NW4 119 CW57
Queens Rd SE14 162 DV81
Queens Rd SE15 162 DV81
Queens Rd SW14 158 CR83
Queens Rd SW19 179 CZ93
Queens Rd W5 138 CL72
Queens Rd, Bark. 145 EQ65
Queens Rd, Barn. 79 CX41
Queen's Rd, Beck. 203 DY96
Queens Rd, Berk. 38 AU18
Queens Rd, Brwd. 108 FW48
Queens Rd, Brom. 204 EG96
Queens Rd, Buck.H. 102 EH47
Queens Rd, Chesh. 54 AQ30
Queens Rd, Chis. 185 EP93
Queen's Rd, Croy. 201 DP100
Queens Rd, Egh. 173 AZ93
Queens Rd, Enf. 82 DS42
Queens Rd, Epp. 71 FB26
Queen's Rd, Erith 167 FE79
Queens Rd, Felt. 175 BV88
Queens Rd, Grav. 191 GJ90
Queens Rd, Guil. 242 AX134
Queens Rd (Hampton Hill), Hmptn. 176 CB91
Queens Rd, Hayes 135 BS72
Queens Rd, Hert. 32 DR11
Queens Rd, Horl. 268 DG148
Queen's Rd, Houns. 156 CB83
Queens Rd, Kings.T. 178 CN94
Queens Rd, Loug. 84 EL41
Queens Rd, Mitch. 200 DD97
Queens Rd, Mord. 200 DA98
Queens Rd, N.Mal. 199 CT98
Queens Rd, Rich. 178 CL87
Queen's Rd, Slou. 132 AT73
Queens Rd (Datchet), Slou. 152 AU81
Queens Rd, Sthl. 156 BX75
Queens Rd, Sutt. 218 DA110
Queen's Rd, Tedd. 177 CF93
Queen's Rd, T.Ditt. 197 CF99
Queens Rd, Twick. 177 CF88
Queen's Rd, Uxb. 134 BJ69
Queens Rd, Wall. 219 DH106
Queens Rd, Wal.Cr. 67 DY34
Queens Rd, Walt. 213 BV106
Queens Rd, Ware 33 DZ05
Queens Rd, Wat. 76 BW42
Queen's Rd, Well. 166 EV82
Queens Rd, West Dr. 154 BM75
Queens Rd, Wey. 213 BQ105
Queens Rd, Wind. 151 AQ82
Queens Rd (Eton Wick), Wind. 151 AL78
Queens Rd W E13 144 EG68
Queen's Row SE17 162 DR79
Queen's Sq, The, Hem.H. 40 BM20
Queens Ter E13 144 EH67
Queen's Ter NW8 140 DD68
Queens Ter, Islw. 157 CG84
Queens Ter Cotts W7 157 CE75
Boston Rd
Queens Wk E4 101 ED46
The Grn Wk
Queens Wk NW9 118 CQ61
Queen's Wk SE1 279 N2
Queen's Wk SE1 142 DS74
Queen's Wk SW1 277 K3
Queen's Wk SW1 141 DJ74
Queens Wk W5 137 CJ70
Queens Wk, Ashf. 174 BK91
Queens Wk, Har. 117 CE56
Queens Wk, Ruis. 116 BX62
Queens Way NW4 119 CW57
Queens Way, Croy. 219 DM107
Queens Way, Felt. 176 BW91
Queens Way, Rad. 62 CL32
Queens Way, Wal.Cr. 67 DZ34
Queens Well Av N20 98 DE48
Queen's Wd Rd N10 121 DH58
Queens Yd WC1 273 L5
Queensberry Ms W SW7 160 DD77
Queen's Gate
Queensberry Pl SW7 160 DD77
Queensberry Pl, Rich. 177 CK85
Friars La
Queensberry Way SW7 160 DD77
Harrington Rd
Queensborough Ms W2 140 DC73
Porchester Ter
Queensborough Pas W2 140 DC73
Porchester Ter
Queensborough S Bldgs W2 140 DC73
Porchester Ter
Queensborough Studios W2 140 DC73
Porchester Ter
Queensborough Ter W2 140 DB73
Queensbridge Pk, Islw. 177 CE85
Queensbridge Rd E2 142 DT67
Queensbridge Rd E8 142 DT66
Queensbury Circle Par, Har. 118 CL55
Streatfield Rd
Queensbury Circle Par, Stan. 118 CL55
Streatfield Rd
Queensbury Rd NW9 118 CR59
Queensbury Rd, Wem. 138 CM68
Queensbury Sta Par, Edg. 118 CM55
Queensbury St N1 142 DQ66
Queenscourt, Wem. 118 CL63
Queenscroft Rd SE9 184 EK85
Queensdale Cres W11 139 CX74
Queensdale Pl W11 139 CY74
Queensdale Rd W11 139 CX74
Queensdale Wk W11 139 CY74
Queensdown Rd E5 122 DV63
Queensferry Wk N17 122 DV56
Jarrow Rd
Queensgate, Cob. 214 BX112
Queensgate, Wal.Cr. 67 DZ34
Queensgate Cen, Harl. 35 ET11
Queensgate Gdns, Chis. 205 ER95
Queensgate Pl NW6 140 DA66
Queensland Av N18 100 DQ51
Queensland Av SW19 200 DB95
Queensland Cl E17 101 DZ54
Queensland Ho E16 145 EN74
Rymill St
Queensland Pl N7 121 DN63
Queensland Rd
Queensland Rd N7 121 DN63
Queensmead NW8 140 DD67
Queensmead, Lthd. 214 CC111
Queensmead (Datchet), Slou. 152 AV81

Queensmead Av, Epsom 217 CV110
Queensmead Rd, Brom. 204 EF96
Queensmead Rd (Loudwater), H.Wyc. 88 AC53
Queensmere Cl SW19 179 CX89
Queensmere Rd SW19 179 CX89
Queensmere Rd, Slou. 152 AU75
Wellington St
Queensmere Shop Cen, Slou. 152 AT75
Queensmill Rd SW6 159 CX80
Queensthorpe Rd SE26 183 DX91
Queenstown Gdns, Rain. 147 FF69
Queenstown Ms SW8 161 DH82
Queenstown Rd
Queenstown Rd SW8 161 DH79
Queensville Rd SW12 181 DK87
Queensway W2 140 DB72
Queensway, Enf. 82 DV42
Queensway, Hat. 45 CU18
Queensway, Hem.H. 40 BM18
Queensway, Orp. 205 EQ99
Queensway, Red. 250 DF133
Queensway, Sun. 195 BV96
Queensway, W.Wick. 204 EE104
Queensway, The (Chalfont St. Peter), Ger.Cr. 112 AX55
Queensway N, Walt. 214 BW105
Robinsway
Queensway S, Walt. 214 BW106
Trenchard Cl
Queenswood Av E17 101 EC53
Queenswood Av, Brwd. 109 GD43
Queenswood Av, Hmptn. 176 CB93
Queenswood Av, Houns. 156 BZ82
Queenswood Av, Th.Hth. 201 DN99
Queenswood Av, Wall. 219 DK105
Queenswood Cres, Wat. 59 BU33
Queenswood Gdns E11 124 EH60
Queenswood Pk N3 97 CY54
Queenswood Rd SE23 183 DX90
Queenswood Rd, Sid. 185 ET85
Quemerford Rd N7 121 DM64
Quendell Wk, Hem.H. 40 BL20
Quendon Dr, Wal.Abb. 67 ED33
Quennel Way, Brwd. 109 GC45
Quennell Cl, Ash. 232 CL119
Parkers La
Quentin Pl SE13 164 EE83
Quentin Rd SE13 164 EE83
Quentin Way, Vir.W. 192 AV98
Quernmore Cl, Brom. 184 EG93
Quernmore Rd N4 121 DN58
Quernmore Rd, Brom. 184 EG93
Querrin St SW6 160 DC82
Quex Ms NW6 140 DA67
Quex Rd
Quex Rd NW6 140 DA67
Quick Pl N1 141 DP67
Quick Rd W4 158 CS78
Quick St N1 274 G1
Quick St N1 141 DP68
Quick St Ms N1 274 F1
Quickbeams, Welw.G.C. 30 DA06
Quickberry Pl, Amer. 55 AR39
Quickley La, Rick. 73 BB44
Quickley Ri, Rick. 73 BC44
Quickmoor La, Kings L. 58 BH33
Quicks Rd SW19 180 DB94
Quickswood NW3 140 DE66
King Henry's Rd
Quickwood Cl, Rick. 74 BG44
Quiet Cl, Add. 212 BG105
Quiet Nook, Brom. 204 EK104
Croydon Rd
Quill Hall La, Amer. 72 AT37
Quill La SW15 159 CX84
Quill St N4 121 DN62
Quill St W5 138 CL69
Quillot, The, Walt. 213 BT106
Quilp St SE1 279 H4
Quilter Gdns, Orp. 206 EW102
Quilter Rd, Orp. 206 EW102
Quilter St E2 142 DU69
Quilter St SE18 165 ET78
Quilting Ct SE16 163 DX75
Poolmans St
Quinbrookes, Slou. 132 AW72
Quince Tree Cl, S.Ock. 149 FW70
Quinces Cft, Hem.H. 40 BG18
Quincy Rd, Egh. 173 BA92
Quinta Dr, Barn. 79 CV43
Quintin Av SW20 199 CZ95
Quintin Cl, Pnr. 115 BV57
High Rd
Quinton Cl, Beck. 203 EC97
Quinton Cl, Houns. 155 BV80
Quinton Cl, Wall. 219 DH105
Quinton Rd, T.Ditt. 197 CG102
Quinton St SW18 180 DC89
Quintrell Cl, Wok. 226 AV117
Quixley St E14 143 ED73
Quorn Rd SE22 162 DS84

R

Raans Rd, Amer. 72 AT38
Rabbit La, Walt. 213 BU108
Rabbit Row W8 140 DA74
Kensington Mall
Rabbits Rd E12 124 EL63
Rabbits Rd (South Darenth), Dart. 209 FR96
Rabbs Mill Ho, Uxb. 134 BJ68
Rabies Heath Rd, Gdse. 252 DU134
Rabies Heath Rd (Bletchingley), Red. 252 DS133
Rabournmead Dr, Nthlt. 116 BY64
Raby Rd, N.Mal. 198 CR98
Raby St E14 143 DY72
Salmon La
Raccoon Way, Houns. 156 BW82
Racecourse Way, Gat. 268 DF151
Rachel Cl, Ilf. 125 ER55
Rachel Pt E5 122 DU63
Muir Rd
Rachels Way, Chesh. 54 AR34
Cresswell Rd
Rackham Cl, Well. 166 EV82
Rackham Ms SW16 181 DJ93
Westcote Rd
Racks Ct, Guil. 258 AX136
Racton Rd SW6 160 DA79
Rad La (Abinger Hammer), Dor. 261 BS142
Horsham Rd
Rad La (Peaslake), Guil. 261 BS140
Radbourne Av W5 157 CJ77
Radbourne Cl E5 123 DX63
Overbury St
Radbourne Cres E17 101 ED54
Radbourne Rd SW12 181 DJ87
Radburn Cl, Harl. 52 EU19
Radcliffe Av NW10 139 CU68
Radcliffe Av, Enf. 82 DQ39
Radcliffe Gdns, Cars. 218 DE108
Radcliffe Ms (Hampton Hill), Hmptn. 176 CC92
Taylor Cl
Radcliffe Path SW8 161 DJ82
St. Rule St
Radcliffe Rd N21 99 DP46
Radcliffe Rd SE1 279 N6
Radcliffe Rd, Croy. 202 DT103
Radcliffe Rd, Har. 95 CG54
Radcliffe Sq SW15 179 CX86
Radcliffe Way, Nthlt. 136 BX69
Radcot Av, Slou. 153 BB76
Radcot Pt SE23 183 DX90
Radcot St SE11 161 DN78
Raddington Rd W10 139 CY71
Radfield Way, Sid. 185 ER87
Radford Rd SE13 183 EC86
Radford Way, Bark. 145 ET69
Radipole Rd SW6 159 CZ81
Radius Pk, Felt. 155 BT84
Radland Rd E16 144 EF72
Radlet Av SE26 182 DV90
Radlett Cl E7 144 EF65
Radlett La, Rad. 77 CK35
Radlett Pk Rd, Rad. 61 CG34
Radlett Pl NW8 140 DE67
Radlett Rd, St.Alb. 61 CE28
Radlett Rd, Wat. 76 BW41
Radlett Rd (Aldenham), Wat. 77 CD36
Radley Av, Ilf. 125 ET63
Radley Cl, Felt. 175 BT88
Radley Ct SE16 163 DX75
Thame Rd
Radley Gdns, Har. 118 CL56
Radley Ho SE2 166 EX75
Wolvercote Rd
Radley Ms W8 160 DA76
Radley Rd N17 100 DS54
Radley's La E18 102 EG54
Radleys Mead, Dag. 147 FB65
Radlix Rd E10 123 EA60
Radnor Av, Har. 117 CE57
Radnor Av, Well. 186 EV85
Radnor Cl, Chis. 185 ES93
Homewood Cres
Radnor Cl, Mitch. 201 DL98
Radnor Cres SE18 166 EU80
Radnor Cres, Ilf. 125 EM57
Radnor Gdns, Enf. 82 DS39
Radnor Gdns, Twick. 177 CF89
Radnor Gro, Uxb. 134 BN68
Charnwood Rd
Radnor La (Holmbury St. Mary), Dor. 261 BU144
Radnor Ms W2 272 A9
Radnor Pl W2 272 B9
Radnor Pl W2 140 DE72
Radnor Rd NW6 139 CY67
Radnor Rd SE15 162 DU80
Radnor Rd, Har. 117 CD57
Radnor Rd, Twick. 177 CF89
Radnor Rd, Wey. 194 BN104
Radnor St EC1 275 J3
Radnor St EC1 142 DQ69
Radnor Ter W14 159 CZ77
Radnor Wk E14 163 EA77
Copeland Dr
Radnor Wk SW3 160 DE78
Radnor Wk, Croy. 203 DZ100
Radnor Way NW10 138 CP70
Radnor Way, Slou. 152 AY77
Radolphs, Tad. 233 CX122
Heathcote
Radstock Av, Har. 117 CG55
Radstock Cl N11 98 DG51
Martock Gdns
Radstock St SW11 160 DE80
Radstock Way, Red. 251 DK128
Radstone Ct, Wok. 227 AZ118
Radwell Path, Borwd. 78 CL39
Cromwell Rd
Raebarn Gdns, Barn. 79 CV43
Raeburn Av, Dart. 187 FH85
Raeburn Av, Surb. 198 CP100
Raeburn Cl NW11 120 DC58
Raeburn Cl, Kings.T. 177 CK94
Raeburn Ct, Wok. 226 AU118
Martin Way
Raeburn Rd, Edg. 96 CN53
Raeburn Rd, Hayes 135 BR68
Raeburn Rd, Sid. 185 ES86
Raeburn St SW2 161 DL84
Raeside Cl (Seer Grn), Beac. 89 AQ51
Rafford Way, Brom. 204 EH96
Raft Rd SW18 160 DA84
North Pas
Rag Hill Cl (Tatsfield), West. 238 EL121
Rag Hill Rd (Tatsfield), West. 238 EK121
Ragged Hall La, St.Alb. 42 BZ24
Raggleswood, Chis. 205 EN95
Raglan Av, Wal.Cr. 67 DX34
Raglan Cl, Houns. 176 BY85
Vickers Way
Raglan Cl, Reig. 250 DC132
Raglan Ct SE12 184 EG85
Raglan Ct, S.Croy. 219 DP106
Raglan Ct, Wem. 118 CM63
Raglan Gdns, Wat. 93 BV46
Raglan Prec, Cat. 236 DS122
Raglan Rd E17 123 EC57
Raglan Rd SE18 165 EQ78
Raglan Rd, Belv. 166 EZ77
Raglan Rd, Brom. 204 EJ98
Raglan Rd, Enf. 100 DS45
Raglan Rd, Reig. 250 DB131
Raglan Rd (Knaphill), Wok. 226 AS118
Raglan St NW5 141 DH65
Raglan Ter, Har. 116 CB63
Raglan Way, Nthlt. 136 CC65
Ragley Cl W3 158 CQ75
Church Rd
Rags La (Cheshunt), Wal.Cr. 66 DS27
Ragstone Rd, Slou. 151 AR76
Rahn Rd, Epp. 70 EU31
Raider Cl, Rom. 104 FA53
Raikes Hollow (Abinger Hammer), Dor. 261 BV142
Raikes La (Abinger Hammer), Dor. 261 BV141
Railey Ms NW5 121 DJ64
Railpit La, Warl. 238 EE115
Railshead Rd, Islw. 157 CH84
Railton Rd SE24 181 DN85
Railway App N4 121 DN58
Wightman Rd
Railway App SE1 279 L2
Railway App SE1 142 DR74
Railway App, Har. 117 CF56
Railway App, Hert. 32 DQ09
Railway App, Twick. 177 CG87
Railway App, Wall. 219 DH107
Railway Av SE16 162 DW75
Railway Cotts, Hat. 44 CS19
Ellenbrook La
Railway Cotts, Rad. 77 CH35
Shenley Hill
Railway Cotts, Wat. 75 BV39
Railway Ms E3 143 EA69
Wellington Way
Railway Ms W10 139 CY72
Ladbroke Gro
Railway Pas, Tedd. 177 CG93
Victoria Rd
Railway Pl SW19 179 CZ93
Hartfield Rd
Railway Pl, Belv. 166 FA76
Railway Pl, Grav. 191 GH87
Windmill St
Railway Pl, Hert. 32 DS09
Railway Ri SE22 162 DS84
Grove Vale
Railway Rd, Tedd. 177 CF91
Railway Rd, Wal.Cr. 67 DY33
Railway Side SW13 158 CS83
Railway Sq, Brwd. 108 FW48
Fairfield Rd
Railway St N1 274 A1
Railway St N1 141 DL68
Railway St (Northfleet), Grav. 190 GA85
Railway St, Hert. 32 DR09
Railway St, Rom. 126 EW60
Railway Ter SE13 183 EB85
Ladywell Rd
Railway Ter, Felt. 175 BU88
Railway Ter, Kings L. 58 BN27
Railway Ter, Slou. 132 AT74
Railway Ter, Stai. 173 BD92
Railway Ter, West. 255 ER125
Rainborough Cl NW10 138 CQ65
Rainbow Av E14 163 EB78
Rainbow Ct, Wat. 76 BW44
Oxhey Rd
Rainbow Ct, Wok. 226 AS116
Langmans Way
Rainbow Ind Est, West Dr. 134 BK73
Rainbow Quay SE16 163 DY76
Rainbow Rd, Grays 169 FW77
Rainbow Rd, Harl. 37 FE12
Rainbow St SE5 162 DS80
Raine St E1 142 DV74
Rainer Cl (Cheshunt), Wal.Cr. 67 DX29
Rainham Cl SE9 185 ER86
Rainham Cl SW11 180 DE86
Rainham Rd NW10 139 CW69
Rainham Rd, Rain. 147 FF66
Rainham Rd N, Dag. 127 FB61
Rainham Rd S, Dag. 127 FB63
Rainhill Way E3 143 EA69
Rainsborough Av SE8 163 DY77
Rainsford Cl, Stan. 95 CJ50
Coverdale Cl
Rainsford Rd NW10 138 CP69
Rainsford St W2 272 B8
Rainsford Way, Horn. 127 FG60
Rainton Rd SE7 164 EG78
Rainville Rd W6 159 CW79
Raisins Hill, Pnr. 116 BW55
Raith Av N14 99 DK48
Raleana Rd E14 143 EC74
Raleigh Av, Hayes 135 BV71
Raleigh Av, Wall. 219 DK105
Raleigh Cl NW4 119 CW57
Raleigh Cl, Erith 167 FF79
Raleigh Cl, Pnr. 116 BX59
Raleigh Cl, Ruis. 115 BT61
Raleigh Cl, Slou. 131 AN74
Raleigh Ct SE16 143 DX74
Rotherhithe St
Raleigh Ct SE19 182 DT92
Lymer Av
Raleigh Ct, Beck. 203 EB95
Raleigh Ct, Stai. 174 BG91
Raleigh Ct, Wall. 219 DH107
Raleigh Dr N20 98 DE48
Raleigh Dr (Claygate), Esher 215 CD106
Raleigh Dr, Horl. 269 DN148
Raleigh Dr, Surb. 198 CQ102
Raleigh Gdns SW2 181 DM86
Brixton Hill
Raleigh Gdns, Mitch. 200 DF96
Raleigh Ms N1 141 DP67
Queen's Head St
Raleigh Ms, Orp. 223 ET106
Osgood Av
Raleigh Rd N8 121 DN56
Raleigh Rd SE20 183 DX94
Raleigh Rd, Enf. 82 DR42
Raleigh Rd, Felt. 175 BT89
Raleigh Rd, Rich. 158 CM83
Raleigh Rd, Sthl. 156 BY78
Raleigh St N1 141 DP67
Raleigh Way N14 99 DK46
Raleigh Way, Felt. 176 BW92
Ralliwood Rd, Ash. 232 CN119
Ralph Ct W2 140 DB72
Queensway
Ralph Perring Ct, Beck. 203 EA98
Ralston St SW3 160 DF78
Tedworth Sq
Ralston Way, Wat. 94 BX47
Ram Gorse, Harl. 35 EP13
Ram Pas, Kings.T. 197 CK96
High St
Ram Pl E9 142 DW65
Chatham Pl
Ram St SW18 180 DB85
Rama Cl SW16 181 DK94
Rama Ct, Har. 117 CE61
Rama La SE19 182 DT94
Ramac Way SE7 164 EH77
Rambler Cl SW16 181 DJ91
Rambler Cl, Maid. 130 AH72
Rambler La, Slou. 152 AW76
Ramblers Way, Welw.G.C. 30 DB10
Rambling Way, Berk. 39 BC17
Rame Cl SW17 180 DG92
Ramilles Cl SW2 181 DL86
Ramillies Pl W1 273 K9
Ramillies Pl W1 141 DJ72
Ramillies Rd NW7 96 CS47
Ramillies Rd W4 158 CR77
Ramillies Rd, Sid. 186 EV86
Ramillies St W1 273 K9
Ramin Ct, Guil. 242 AW131
Rowan Cl
Ramney Dr, Enf. 83 DY37
Ramornie Cl, Walt. 214 BZ106
Rampart St E1 142 DV72
Commercial Rd
Ramparts, The, St.Alb. 42 CB21
Rampayne St SW1 277 M10
Rampayne St SW1 161 DK78
Rampton Cl E4 101 EA48
Rams Gro, Rom. 126 EY56
Ramsay Cl, Brox. 49 DY21
Ramsay Gdns, Rom. 106 FJ53
Ramsay Ms SW3 160 DE79
King's Rd
Ramsay Pl, Har. 117 CE60
Ramsay Rd E7 124 EE63
Ramsay Rd W3 158 CQ76
Ramsbury Rd, St.Alb. 43 CE21
Ramscote La (Bellingdon), Chesh. 54 AN25
Ramscroft Cl N9 100 DS45
Ramsdale Rd SW17 180 DG92
Ramsden Cl, Orp. 206 EW102
Ramsden Dr, Rom. 104 FA52
Ramsden Rd N11 98 DF50
Ramsden Rd SW12 180 DG86
Ramsden Rd, Erith 167 FD80
Ramsden Rd, Orp. 206 EV101
Ramsey Cl NW9 119 CT58
Ramsey Cl, Grnf. 116 CC64
Ramsey Cl, Hat. 64 DD27
Ramsey Cl, Horl. 268 DF148
Ramsey Cl, St.Alb. 43 CG22
Ramsey Ct, Slou. 131 AK70
Lower Britwell Rd
Ramsey Ho, Wem. 138 CL65
Ramsey Lo Ct, St.Alb. 43 CE19
Hillside Rd
Ramsey Ms N4 121 DP62
Monsell Rd
Ramsey Rd, Th.Hth. 201 DM100
Ramsey St E2 142 DU70
Ramsey Wk N1 142 DR65
Clephane Rd
Ramsey Way N14 99 DJ45
Ramsgate Cl E16 144 EH74
Hanameel St
Ramsgate St E8 142 DT65
Dalston La
Ramsgill App, Ilf. 125 ET56
Ramsgill Dr, Ilf. 125 ET57
Ramson Ri, Hem.H. 39 BE21
Ramulis Dr, Hayes 136 BX70
Ramus Wd Av, Orp. 223 ES106
Rancliffe Gdns SE9 164 EL84
Rancliffe Rd E6 144 EL68
Randal Cres, Reig. 266 DA136
Randall Av NW2 119 CT62
Randall Cl SW11 160 DE81
Randall Cl, Erith 167 FC79
Randall Cl, Slou. 153 AZ78
Randall Ct NW7 97 CU52
Page St
Randall Dr, Horn. 128 FJ63
Randall Pl SE10 163 EC80
Randall Rd SE11 278 B10
Randall Rd SE11 161 DM77
Randall Row SE11 278 B9
Randalls Cres, Lthd. 231 CG120
Randalls Dr, Brwd. 109 GE44
Randalls Pk Av, Lthd. 231 CG120
Randalls Pk Dr, Lthd. 231 CG121
Randalls Rd
Randalls Ride, Hem.H. 40 BK18
Randalls Rd, Lthd. 231 CE119
Randall's Wk, St.Alb. 60 BZ30
Randalls Way, Lthd. 231 CG121
Randell's Rd N1 141 DL67
Randle Rd, Rich. 177 CJ91
Randles La (Knockholt), Sev. 240 EX115
Randlesdown Rd SE6 183 EA91
Randolph App E16 144 EK72
Randolph Av W9 140 DC70
Randolph Cl, Bexh. 167 FC83
Randolph Cl (Stoke D'Abernon), Cob. 230 CA115
Randolph Cl, Kings.T. 178 CQ92
Randolph Cl (Knaphill), Wok. 226 AS117
Creston Av
Randolph Cres W9 140 DC70
Randolph Gdns NW6 140 DB68
Randolph Gro, Rom. 126 EW57
Donald Dr
Randolph Ho, Croy. 202 DQ102
Randolph Ms W9 140 DC70
Randolph Rd E17 123 EB57
Randolph Rd W9 140 DC70
Randolph Rd, Brom. 205 EM102
Randolph Rd, Epsom 217 CT114
Randolph Rd, Slou. 152 AY76
Randolph Rd, Sthl. 156 BZ75
Randolph St NW1 141 DJ66
Randolph's La, West. 255 EP126
Randon Cl, Har. 94 CB54
Ranelagh Av SW6 159 CZ83
Ranelagh Av SW13 159 CU82
Ranelagh Br W2 140 DB71
Gloucester Ter
Ranelagh Cl, Edg. 96 CN49
Ranelagh Dr, Edg. 96 CN49
Ranelagh Dr, Twick. 177 CH85
Ranelagh Gdns E11 124 EJ57
Ranelagh Gdns SW6 159 CZ83
Ranelagh Gdns W4 158 CQ80
Grove Pk Gdns
Ranelagh Gdns W6 159 CT76
Ranelagh Gdns (Northfleet), Grav. 191 GF87
Ranelagh Gdns, Ilf. 125 EN60
Ranelagh Gro SW1 276 G10
Ranelagh Gro SW1 160 DG78
Ranelagh Ms W5 157 CK75
Ranelagh Rd
Ranelagh Pl, N.Mal. 198 CS99
Rodney Rd
Ranelagh Rd E6 145 EN67
Ranelagh Rd E11 124 EE63
Ranelagh Rd E15 144 EE67
Ranelagh Rd N17 122 DS55
Ranelagh Rd N22 99 DM53
Ranelagh Rd NW10 139 CT68
Ranelagh Rd SW1 161 DJ78
Lupus St
Ranelagh Rd W5 157 CK75
Ranelagh Rd, Hem.H. 41 BP20
Ranelagh Rd, Red. 250 DE134
Ranelagh Rd, Sthl. 136 BX74
Ranelagh Rd, Wem. 117 CK64
Ranfurly Rd, Sutt. 200 DA103
Range Rd, Grav. 191 GL87
Range Way, Shep. 194 BN101
Rangefield Rd, Brom. 184 EE92
Rangemoor Rd N15 122 DT57
Ranger Wk, Add. 212 BH106
Monks Cres
Rangers Rd E4 102 EE45
Rangers Rd, Loug. 102 EE45
Rangers Sq SE10 163 ED81
Rangeworth Pl, Sid. 185 ET90
Priestlands Pk Rd
Rangoon St EC3 142 DT72
Northumberland All
Rank Ho, Harl. 51 EQ15
Rankin Cl NW9 118 CS55
Ranleigh Gdns, Bexh. 166 EZ80
Ranmere St SW12 181 DH88
Ormeley Rd
Ranmoor Cl, Har. 117 CD56
Ranmoor Gdns, Har. 117 CD56
Ranmore Av, Croy. 202 DT104
Ranmore Cl, Red. 250 DG131
Ranmore Common, Dor. 246 CC133
Ranmore Common Rd (Westhumble), Dor. 247 CD133
Ranmore Common Rd, Lthd. 245 BU134
Ranmore Path, Orp. 206 EU98
Ranmore Rd, Dor. 246 CC134
Ranmore Rd, Sutt. 217 CX109
Rannoch Cl, Edg. 96 CP47
Rannoch Rd W6 159 CW79
Rannoch Wk, Hem.H. 40 BK16
Rannock Av NW9 118 CS59
Ranskill Rd, Borwd. 78 CN39
Ransom Cl, Wat. 94 BW45
Ransom Rd SE7 164 EJ78
Harvey Gdns
Ransom Wk SE7 164 EJ78
Woolwich Rd
Ranston Cl (Denham), Uxb. 113 BF58
Nightingale Way
Ranston St NW1 272 B6
Rant Meadow, Hem.H. 40 BN22
Ranulf Cl, Harl. 36 EW09
Ranulf Rd NW2 119 CZ63
Ranwell Cl E3 143 DZ67
Beale Rd
Ranwell St E3 143 DZ67
Ranworth Av, Hodd. 33 EB13
Ranworth Cl, Erith 167 FE82
Ranworth Cl, Hem.H. 40 BK22
Panxworth Rd
Ranworth Rd N9 100 DW47
Ranyard Cl, Chess. 198 CM104
Raphael Av, Rom. 127 FF55
Raphael Av, Til. 171 GG80
Raphael Cl, Rad. 62 CL32
Raphael Dr, T.Ditt. 197 CF101
Raphael Dr, Wat. 76 BX40
Raphael Rd, Grav. 191 GK87
Raphael St SW7 276 D5
Raphael St SW7 160 DF75
Rapier Cl, Purf. 168 FN77
Rasehill Cl, Rick. 74 BJ43
Rashleigh St SW8 161 DH82
Peardon St
Rashleigh Way (Horton Kirby), Dart. 208 FQ98
Rasper Rd N20 98 DC47
Rastell Av SW2 181 DK89
Ratcliff Rd E7 124 EJ64
Ratcliffe Cl SE12 184 EG87
Ratcliffe Cl, Uxb. 134 BK69
Ratcliffe Cross St E1 143 DX72
Ratcliffe La E14 143 DY72
Ratcliffe Orchard E1 143 DX73
Rathbone Mkt E16 144 EF71
Barking Rd
Rathbone Pl W1 273 M8
Rathbone Pl W1 141 DK72
Rathbone Pt E5 122 DU63
Nolan Way
Rathbone St E16 144 EF71
Rathbone St W1 273 L7
Rathbone St W1 141 DJ71
Rathcoole Av N8 121 DM56
Rathcoole Gdns N8 121 DM57
Rathfern Rd SE6 183 DZ88
Rathgar Av W13 137 CH74
Rathgar Cl N3 97 CZ54
Rathgar Cl, Red. 266 DG139
Rathgar Rd SW9 161 DP83
Coldharbour La
Rathlin, Hem.H. 41 BP22
Rathlin Wk N1 142 DQ65
Clephane Rd
Rathmell Dr SW4 181 DK86
Rathmore Rd SE7 164 EH78
Rathmore Rd, Grav. 191 GH87
Rathwell Path, Borwd. 78 CL39
Rats La (High Beach), Loug. 84 EH38
Rattray Rd SW2 161 DN84
Ratty's La, Hodd. 49 ED17
Raul Rd SE15 162 DU81
Raveley Gdns, S.Ock. 148 FQ72
Ravel Rd, S.Ock. 148 FQ72
Raveley St NW5 121 DJ63
Raven Cl NW9 96 CS54
Eagle Dr
Raven Cl, Rick. 92 BJ45
Raven Ct E5 122 DU62
Stellman Cl
Raven Ct, Hat. 45 CU19
Raven Rd E18 102 EJ54
Raven Row E1 142 DV71
Ravencroft, Grays 171 GH75
Alexandra Cl
Ravendale Rd, Sun. 195 BT96
Ravenet St SW11 161 DH81
Strasburg Rd
Ravenfield (Englefield Grn), Egh. 172 AW93
Ravenfield Rd SW17 180 DF90
Ravenhill Rd, Welw.G.C. 29 CZ09
Ravenhill Rd E13 144 EJ68
Ravenna Rd SW15 179 CX85
Ravenoak Way, Chig. 103 ES50
Ravenor Pk Rd, Grnf. 136 CB69
Ravens Cl, Brom. 204 EF96
Ravens Cl, Chess. 197 CK100
Ravens Cl, Enf. 82 DS40
Ravens Cl, Red. 250 DF132
Ravens La, Berk. 38 AX19
Ravens Ms SE12 184 EG85
Ravens Way
Ravens Way SE12 184 EG85
Ravens Wf, Berk. 38 AX19
Ravensbourne Av, Beck. 183 ED94
Ravensbourne Av, Brom. 183 ED94
Ravensbourne Av, Stai. 174 BL88
Ravensbourne Cres, Rom. 128 FM55
Ravensbourne Gdns W13 137 CH71
Ravensbourne Gdns, Ilf. 103 EN53
Ravensbourne Pk SE6 183 EA87
Ravensbourne Pk Cres SE6 183 DZ87
Ravensbourne Pl SE13 163 EB82
Ravensbourne Rd SE6 183 DZ87
Ravensbourne Rd, Brom. 204 EG97
Ravensbourne Rd, Dart. 167 FG83
Ravensbourne Rd, Twick. 177 CJ86
Ravensbury Av, Mord. 200 DC99
Ravensbury Ct, Mitch. 200 DD98
Ravensbury Gro
Ravensbury Gro, Mitch. 200 DD98

Rav - Reg This index reads in the sequence: Street Name / Postal District or Post Town / Map Page Number / Grid Reference

Ravensbury La, Mitch. 200 DD98
Ravensbury Path, Mitch. 200 DD98
Ravensbury Rd SW18 180 DA89
Ravensbury Rd, Orp. 205 ET98
Ravensbury Ter SW18 180 DB88
Ravenscar Rd, Brom. 184 EE91
Ravenscar Rd, Surb. 198 CM103
Ravenscourt, Sun. 195 BT95
Ravenscourt Av W6 159 CU77
Ravenscourt Cl, Horn. 128 FL62
Ravenscourt Dr
Ravenscourt Cl, Ruis. 115 BQ59
Ravenscourt Dr, Horn. 128 FL62
Ravenscourt Gdns W6 159 CU77
Ravenscourt Gro, Horn. 128 FL61
Ravenscourt Pk W6 159 CU76
Ravenscourt Pl W6 159 CV77
Ravenscourt Rd W6 159 CV77
Ravenscourt Rd, Orp. 206 EU97
Ravenscourt Sq W6 159 CU76
Ravenscraig Rd N11 99 DH49
Ravenscroft, Wat. 60 BY34
Ravenscroft Av NW11 119 CZ59
Ravenscroft Av, Wem. 118 CM60
Ravenscroft Cl E16 144 EG71
Ravenscroft Cres SE9 185 EM90
Ravenscroft Pk, Barn. 79 CX42
Ravenscroft Pt E9 143 DX65
Kenton Rd
Ravenscroft Rd E16 144 EG71
Ravenscroft Rd W4 158 CQ77
Ravenscroft Rd, Beck. 202 DW96
Ravenscroft Rd, Wey. 213 BQ111
Ravenscroft St E2 142 DT68
Ravensdale Av N12 98 DC49
Ravensdale Gdns SE19 182 DR94
Ravensdale Gdns, Houns. 156 BY83
Ravensdale Ms, Stai. 174 BH93
Worple Rd
Ravensdale Rd N16 122 DT59
Ravensdale Rd, Houns. 156 BY83
Ravensdell, Hem.H. 39 BF19
Ravensdon St SE11 161 DN78
Ravensfield, Slou. 152 AX75
Ravensfield Cl, Dag. 126 EX63
Ravensfield Gdns, Epsom 216 CS106
Ravenshaw St NW6 119 CZ64
Ravenshead Cl, S.Croy. 220 DW111
Ravenshill, Chis. 205 EP95
Ravenshurst Av NW4 119 CW56
Ravenside Cl N18 101 DX51
Ravenside Retail Pk N18 101 DX50
Ravenslea Rd SW12 180 DF87
Ravensmead (Chalfont St. Peter), Ger.Cr. 91 AZ50
Ravensmead Rd, Brom. 183 ED94
Ravensmede Way W4 159 CT77
Ravensmere, Epp. 70 EU31
Ravenstone SE17 162 DS78
Ravenstone Rd N8 121 DN55
Ravenstone Rd NW9 119 CT58
West Hendon Bdy
Ravenstone St SW12 180 DG88
Ravenswold, Ken. 236 DQ115
Ravenswood, Bex. 186 EY88
Ravenswood Av, Surb. 198 CM103
Ravenswood Av, W.Wick. 203 EC102
Ravenswood Cl, Cob. 230 BX115
Ravenswood Cl, Rom. 105 FB50
Ravenswood Ct, Kings.T. 178 CP93
Ravenswood Ct, Wok. 227 AZ118
Ravenswood Cres, Har. 116 BZ61
Ravenswood Cres, W.Wick. 203 EC102
Ravenswood Gdns, Islw. 157 CE81
Ravenswood Pk, Nthwd. 93 BU51
Ravenswood Rd E17 123 EB56
Ravenswood Rd SW12 181 DH87
Ravenswood Rd, Croy. 201 DP104
Ravensworth Rd NW10 139 CV69
Ravensworth Rd SE9 185 EM91
Ravensworth Rd, Slou. 131 AN69
Wentworth Av
Ravent Rd SE11 278 C9
Ravent Rd SE11 161 DM77
Ravey St EC2 275 M4
Ravine Gro SE18 165 ES79
Rawdon Dr, Hodd. 49 EA18
Rawlings Cl, Orp. 224 EU106
Rawlings La (Seer Grn), Beac. 89 AQ48
Rawlings St SW3 276 D8
Rawlings St SW3 160 DF77
Rawlins Cl N3 119 CY55
Rawlins Cl, S.Croy. 221 DY108
Rawnsley Av, Mitch. 200 DD99
Rawreth Wk N1 142 DQ67
Basire St
Rawson St SW11 160 DG81
Strasburg Rd
Rawsthorne Cl E16 145 EM74
Kennard St
Rawstone Wk E13 144 EG68
Rawstorne Pl EC1 274 F2
Rawstorne St EC1 274 F2
Rawstorne St EC1 141 DP69
Ray Cl, Chess. 215 CJ107
Merritt Gdns
Ray Gdns, Bark. 146 EU68
Ray Gdns, Stan. 95 CH50
Ray Lamb Way, Erith 167 FH79
Ray Lo Rd, Wdf.Grn. 102 EJ51
Ray Massey Way E6 144 EL67
Ron Leighton Way
Ray Mead Ct, Maid. 130 AC70
Boulters La
Ray Mead Rd, Maid. 130 AC72
Ray Rd, Rom. 105 FB50
Ray Rd, W.Mol. 196 CB99
Ray St EC1 274 E5
Ray St EC1 141 DN70
Ray St Br EC1 274 E5
Ray Wk N7 121 DM61
Andover Rd
Raybarn Rd, Hem.H. 40 BG18
Rayburn Rd, Horn. 128 FN59
Raydean Rd, Barn. 80 DB43
Raydon Rd (Cheshunt), Wal.Cr. 67 DX32
Raydon St N19 121 DH61
Raydons Gdns, Dag. 126 EY64
Raydons Rd, Dag. 126 EY64
Rayfield, Epp. 70 EU30
Rayfield, Welw.G.C. 29 CX06
Rayfield Cl, Brom. 204 EL100
Rayford Av SE12 184 EF87
Rayford Cl, Dart. 188 FJ85
Raylands Mead, Ger.Cr. 112 AW57
Bull La
Rayleas Cl SE18 165 EP81
Rayleigh Av, Tedd. 177 CE93
Rayleigh Cl N13 100 DR48
Rayleigh Rd
Rayleigh Cl, Brwd. 109 GC44
Rayleigh Ct, Kings.T. 198 CM96
Rayleigh Ri, S.Croy. 220 DS107
Rayleigh Rd E16 144 EH74
Wesley Av
Rayleigh Rd N13 100 DQ48
Rayleigh Rd SW19 199 CZ95
Rayleigh Rd, Brwd. 109 GC44
Rayleigh Rd, Wdf.Grn. 102 EJ51
Rayley La, Epp. 52 FA24
Raymead NW4 119 CW56
Tenterden Gro
Raymead Av, Th.Hth. 201 DN99
Raymead Cl (Fetcham), Lthd. 231 CE122
Raymead Way (Fetcham), Lthd. 231 CE122
Raymer Cl, St.Alb. 43 CE19
Raymer Wk, Horl. 269 DJ147
Raymere Gdns SE18 165 ER80
Raymond Av E18 124 EF55
Raymond Av W13 157 CG76
Raymond Bldgs WC1 274 C6
Raymond Cl SE26 182 DW92
Raymond Cl, Abb.L. 59 BR32
Raymond Cl (Colnbrook), Slou. 153 BE81
Raymond Ct N10 98 DG52
Pembroke Rd
Raymond Ct, Pot.B. 64 DC34
St. Francis Cl
Raymond Ct, Sutt. 218 DB107
Mulgrave Rd
Raymond Cres, Guil. 258 AT135
Raymond Gdns, Chig. 104 EV48
Raymond Rd E13 144 EJ66
Raymond Rd SW19 179 CY93
Raymond Rd, Beck. 203 DY98
Raymond Rd, Ilf. 125 ER59
Raymond Rd, Slou. 153 BA76
Raymond Way (Claygate), Esher 215 CG107
Raymonds Cl, Welw.G.C. 29 CY11
Raymonds Plain, Welw.G.C. 29 CY11
Raymouth Rd SE16 162 DV77
Rayne Ct E18 124 EF56
Rayner Twr E10 123 EA59
Rayners Cl (Loudwater), H.Wyc. 88 AC52
Rayners Cl (Colnbrook), Slou. 153 BC80
Rayners Cl, Wem. 117 CK64
Rayners Ct, Grav. 190 GB86
Rayners Ct, Har. 116 CA60
Rayners Cres, Nthlt. 135 BV69
Rayners Gdns, Nthlt. 135 BV68
Rayners La, Har. 116 CB61
Rayners La, Pnr. 116 BZ58
Rayners Rd SW15 179 CY85
Raynes Av E11 124 EJ59
Raynham Av N18 100 DU51
Raynham Rd N18 100 DU50
Raynham Rd W6 159 CV77
Raynham St, Hert. 32 DS08
Raynham Ter N18 100 DU50
Raynor Cl, Sthl. 136 BZ74
Raynor Pl N1 142 DQ67
Elizabeth Av
Raynsford Rd, Ware 33 DY06
Raynton Cl, Har. 116 BY60
Raynton Cl, Hayes 135 BT70
Raynton Dr, Hayes 135 BT70
Raynton Rd, Enf. 83 DX37
Rays Av N18 100 DW49
Rays Av, Wind. 151 AM80
Rays Hill (Horton Kirby), Dart. 208 FQ98
Rays La (Penn), H.Wyc. 88 AC47
Rays Rd N18 100 DW49
Rays Rd, W.Wick. 203 EC101
Raywood Cl, Hayes 155 BQ80
Reachview Cl NW1 141 DJ66
Baynes St
Read Cl, T.Ditt. 197 CG101
Read Ct, Wal.Abb. 68 EG33
Read Rd, Ash. 231 CK117
Read Way, Grav. 191 GK92
Reade Ct, Slou. 132 AV72
Victoria Rd
Reade Wk NW10 138 CS66
Denbigh Cl
Readens, The, Bans. 234 DF116
Reading Arch Rd, Red. 250 DF134
Reading La E8 142 DV65
Reading Rd, Nthlt. 116 CB64
Reading Rd, Sutt. 218 DC106
Reading Way NW7 97 CX50
Readings, The, Harl. 51 ET18
Readings, The, Rick. 73 BF41
Reads Cl, Ilf. 125 EP62
Chapel Rd
Reads Rest La, Tad. 233 CZ119
Reapers Cl NW1 141 DK67
Crofters Way
Reapers Way, Islw. 177 CD85
Hall Rd
Reardon Ct N21 100 DQ47
Cosgrove Cl
Reardon Path E1 142 DV74
Reardon St E1 142 DV74
Reaston St SE14 163 DX80
Reckitt Rd W4 158 CS78
Record St SE15 162 DW79
Recovery St SW17 180 DE92
Recreation Av, Rom. 127 FC57
Recreation Av (Harold Wd), Rom. 106 FM54
Recreation Rd SE26 183 DX91
Recreation Rd, Brom. 204 EF96
Recreation Rd, Guil. 242 AW134
Recreation Rd, Sid. 185 ES90
Woodside Rd
Recreation Rd, Sthl. 156 BY77
Recreation Way, Mitch. 201 DK97
Rector St N1 142 DQ67
Rectory Chase (Little Warley), Brwd. 129 FX56
Rectory Cl E4 101 EA48
Rectory Cl N3 97 CZ53
Rectory Cl SW20 199 CW97
Rectory Cl, Ash. 232 CM119
Rectory Cl, Dart. 167 FE84
Rectory Cl, Guil. 243 BD132
Rectory Cl, Hat. 46 DF17
Rectory Cl, Shep. 194 BN97
Rectory Cl, Sid. 186 EV91
Rectory Cl (Farnham Royal), Slou. 131 AQ69
Rectory Cl, Stan. 95 CH51
Rectory Cl, Surb. 197 CJ102
Rectory Cl, Ware 34 EK07
Rectory Cl (Byfleet), W.Byf. 212 BL113
Rectory Cl, Wind. 151 AN81
Rectory Cres E11 124 EJ58
Rectory Fm Rd, Enf. 81 DM38
Rectory Fld, Harl. 51 EP17
Rectory Fld Cres SE7 164 EJ80
Rectory Gdns N8 121 DL56
Rectory Gdns SW4 161 DJ83
Fitzwilliam Rd
Rectory Gdns, Ch.St.G. 90 AV48
Rectory Gdns, Hat. 45 CV18
Rectory Gdns, Nthlt. 136 BZ67
Rectory Gdns, Upmin. 129 FR61
Rectory Grn, Beck. 203 DZ95
Rectory Gro SW4 161 DJ83
Rectory Gro, Croy. 201 DP103
Rectory Gro, Hmptn. 176 BZ91
Rectory Hill, Amer. 55 AP39
Rectory La SW17 180 DG93
Rectory La, Ash. 232 CM118
Rectory La, Bans. 218 DF114
Rectory La, Berk. 38 AW19
Rectory La (Buckland), Bet. 249 CT131
Rectory La, Edg. 96 CN51
Rectory La (Shere), Guil. 260 BM139
Rectory La, Harl. 51 EP17
Rectory La, Kings L. 58 BN28
Rectory La (Bookham), Lthd. 246 BZ126
Rectory La, Loug. 85 EN40
Rectory La, Rad. 62 CN33
Rectory La, Rick. 92 BK46
Rectory La, Sev. 257 FJ126
Rectory La, Sid. 186 EV91
Rectory La, Stan. 95 CH50
Rectory La, Surb. 197 CJ102
Rectory La, Wall. 219 DJ105
Rectory La (Byfleet), W.Byf. 212 BL113
Rectory La, West. 238 EL123
Rectory La (Brasted), West. 240 EW123
Rectory Meadow (Southfleet), Grav. 190 GA93
Rectory Orchard SW19 179 CY91
Rectory Pk, S.Croy. 220 DS113
Rectory Pk Av, Nthlt. 136 BZ69
Rectory Pl SE18 165 EN77
Rectory Rd E12 125 EM64
Rectory Rd E17 123 EB55
Rectory Rd N16 122 DT62
Rectory Rd SW13 159 CU82
Rectory Rd W3 138 CP74
Rectory Rd, Beck. 203 EA95
Rectory Rd, Couls. 250 DD125
Rectory Rd, Dag. 146 FA66
Rectory Rd, Grays 170 GD76
Rectory Rd, Hayes 135 BU72
Rectory Rd, Houns. 155 BV81
Rectory Rd, Kes. 222 EK108
Rectory Rd, Maid. 130 AD70
Rectory Rd, Rick. 92 BK46
Rectory Rd, Sthl. 156 BZ76
Rectory Rd, Sutt. 200 DA104
Rectory Rd, Swans. 190 FY87
Rectory Rd, Til. 171 GK79
Rectory Rd, Welw.G.C. 29 CV06
Rectory Sq E1 143 DX71
Rectory Way, Amer. 55 AP39
Rectory Way, Uxb. 115 BP62
Rectory Wd, Harl. 35 EQ14
Reculver Ms N18 100 DU49
Lyndhurst Rd
Reculver Rd SE16 163 DX78
Red Anchor Cl SW3 160 DE79
Old Ch St
Red Barracks Rd SE18 165 EM77
Red Cedars Rd, Orp. 205 ES101
Red Cottage Ms, Slou. 152 AW76
Red Ct, Slou. 132 AS74
Red Hill, Chis. 185 EN92
Red Hill (Denham), Uxb. 113 BD61
Red Hills, Hodd. 48 DV19
Red Ho Cl (Knotty Grn), Beac. 88 AH51
Red Ho Cl, Ware 33 DY07
Red Ho La, Bexh. 166 EX84
Red Ho La, Walt. 195 BU103
Red Ho Sq N1 142 DQ65
Clephane Rd
Red La, Dor. 264 CL142
Red La (Claygate), Esher 215 CG107
Red La, Oxt. 254 EH133
Red Leaf Cl, Slou. 133 AZ74
Pickford Dr
Red Leys, Uxb. 134 BL66
Park Rd
Red Lion Cl SE17 162 DQ79
Red Lion Row
Red Lion Cl, Orp. 206 EW100
Red Lion Ct EC4 274 E8
Red Lion Cres, Harl. 52 EW17
Red Lion Hill N2 98 DD54
Red Lion La SE18 165 EN80
Red Lion La, Harl. 52 EW17
Red Lion La, Hem.H. 58 BM26
Red Lion La, Rick. 74 BG35
Red Lion La (Chobham), Wok. 210 AS109
Red Lion Pl SE18 165 EN81
Shooter's Hill Rd
Red Lion Rd, Surb. 198 CM103
Red Lion Rd (Chobham), Wok. 210 AS109
Red Lion Row SE17 162 DQ79
Red Lion Sq SW18 180 DA85
Wandsworth High St
Red Lion Sq WC1 274 B7
Red Lion Sq WC1 141 DM71
Red Lion St WC1 274 B6
Red Lion St WC1 141 DM71
Red Lion St, Chesh. 54 AP32
Red Lion St, Rich. 177 CK85
Red Lion Way (Wooburn Grn), H.Wyc. 110 AE57
Red Lion Yd W1 276 G2
Red Lion Yd, Wat. 76 BW42
High St
Red Lo Cres, Bex. 187 FD90
Red Lo Gdns, Berk. 38 AU20
Red Lo Rd, Bex. 187 FD90
Red Lo Rd, W.Wick. 203 ED100
Red Oak Cl, Orp. 205 EP104
Red Oaks Mead, Epp. 85 ER37
Red Path E9 143 DZ65
Red Pl W1 272 F10
Red Post Hill SE21 182 DR85
Red Post Hill SE24 162 DR84
Red Rd, Borwd. 78 CM41
Red Rd, Brwd. 108 FV49
Red St (Southfleet), Grav. 190 GA93
Red Willow, Harl. 51 EM18
Redan Pl W2 140 DB72
Redan St W14 159 CX76
Redan Ter SE5 162 DQ82
Flaxman Rd
Redbarn Cl, Pur. 219 DP111
Whytecliffe Rd S
Redberry Gro SE26 182 DW90
Redbourn Rd, Hem.H. 40 BN16
Redbourn Rd, St.Alb. 42 CA18
Redbourne Av N3 98 DA53
Redbourne Dr SE28 146 EX72
Redbridge Enterprise Cen, Ilf. 125 EQ61
Redbridge Gdns SE5 162 DS80
Redbridge La E, Ilf. 124 EK58
Redbridge La W E11 124 EH58
Redburn St SW3 160 DF79
Redbury Cl, Rain. 147 FH70
Deri Av
Redcar Cl, Nthlt. 116 CB64
Redcar Rd, Rom. 106 FM50
Redcar St SE5 162 DQ80
Redcastle Cl E1 142 DW73
Redchurch St E2 275 P4
Redchurch St E2 142 DT70
Redcliffe Cl SW5 160 DB78
Warwick Rd
Redcliffe Gdns SW5 160 DB78
Redcliffe Gdns SW10 160 DB78
Redcliffe Gdns W4 158 CP80
Redcliffe Gdns, Ilf. 125 EN60
Redcliffe Ms SW10 160 DB78
Redcliffe Pl SW10 160 DC79
Redcliffe Rd SW10 160 DC78
Redcliffe Sq SW10 160 DB78
Redcliffe St SW10 160 DB79
Redclose Av, Mord. 200 DA99
Chalgrove Av
Redclyffe Rd E6 144 EJ67
Redcote Pl, Dor. 247 CK134
Redcourt, Wok. 227 BD115
Redcroft Rd, Sthl. 136 CC73
Redcross Way SE1 279 J4
Redcross Way SE1 162 DQ75
Redden Ct Rd, Rom. 128 FL55
Redding Cl, Dart. 189 FS89
Redding Dr, Amer. 55 AN37
Reddings, Hem.H. 40 BM22
Reddings, Welw.G.C. 29 CW08
Reddings, The NW7 97 CT48
Reddings, The, Borwd. 78 CM41
Reddings Av, Bushey 76 CB43
Reddings Cl NW7 97 CT49
Reddington Cl, S.Croy. 220 DR109
Reddington Dr, Slou. 152 AY76
Reddins Rd SE15 162 DU79
Redditch Ct, Hem.H. 40 BM16
Reddons Rd, Beck. 183 DY94
Reddown Rd, Couls. 235 DK118
Reddy Rd, Erith 167 FF79
Rede Ct, Wey. 195 BP104
Old Palace Rd
Rede Pl W2 140 DA72
Chepstow Pl
Redehall Rd, Horl. 269 DP148
Redenham Ho SW15 179 CT87
Tangley Gro
Redesdale Gdns, Islw. 157 CG80
Redesdale St SW3 160 DF79
Redfern Av, Houns. 176 CA87
Redfern Cl, Uxb. 134 BJ67
Redfern Gdns, Rom. 106 FK54
Redfern Rd NW10 138 CS66
Redfern Rd SE6 183 EC87
Redfield La SW5 160 DA77
Redfield Ms SW5 160 DA77
Redfield La
Redford Av, Couls. 219 DH114
Redford Av, Th.Hth. 201 DM98
Redford Av, Wall. 219 DL107
Redford Cl, Felt. 175 BT89
Redford Rd, Wind. 151 AK81
Redford Wk N1 141 DP67
Britannia Row
Redford Way, Uxb. 134 BJ66
Redgate Dr, Brom. 204 EH103
Redgate Ter SW15 179 CX86
Lytton Gro
Redgrave Cl, Croy. 202 DT100
Redgrave Rd SW15 159 CX83
Redhall Cl, Hat. 45 CT21
Redhall Ct, Cat. 236 DR123
Redhall Dr, Hat. 45 CT22
Redhall La, Rick. 74 BL39
Redheath Cl, Wat. 75 BT35
Redhill Common, Red. 266 DE135
Redhill Dr, Edg. 96 CQ54
Redhill Rd, Cob. 213 BP113
Redhill St NW1 273 J2
Redhill St NW1 141 DH68
Redhouse Rd, Croy. 201 DK100
Redhouse Rd (Tatsfield), West. 238 EJ120
Redington Gdns NW3 120 DB63
Redington Rd NW3 120 DB63
Redland Gdns, W.Mol. 196 BZ98
Dunstable Rd
Redlands, Couls. 235 DL116
Redlands Ct, Brom. 184 EF94
Redlands La, Dor. 263 CG142
Redlands Rd, Enf. 83 DY39
Redlands Rd, Sev. 256 FF124
Redlands Way SW2 181 DM87
Redleaf Cl, Belv. 166 FA79
Redleaves Av, Ashf. 175 BP93
Redlees Cl, Islw. 157 CG84
Redman Cl, Nthlt. 136 BW68
Redmans La (Shoreham), Sev. 225 FE107
Redman's Rd E1 142 DW71
Redmead La E1 142 DU74
Wapping High St
Redmead Rd, Hayes 155 BS77
Redmore Rd W6 159 CV77
Redpoll Way, Erith 166 EX76
Redricks La, Saw. 35 ES09
Redriff Est SE16 163 DZ76
Redriff Rd SE16 163 DX77
Redriff Rd, Rom. 105 FB54
Redriffe Rd E13 144 EF67
Redroofs Cl, Beck. 203 EB95
Redruth Cl N22 99 DM52
Palmerston Rd
Redruth Gdns, Rom. 106 FM50
Redruth Rd E9 143 DX67
Redruth Rd, Rom. 106 FM50
Redruth Wk, Rom. 106 FN50
Redstart Cl E6 144 EL71
Columbine Av
Redstart Cl SE14 163 DY80
Southerngate Way
Redstart Cl (New Addington), Croy. 221 ED110
Redston Rd N8 121 DK56
Redstone Hill, Red. 250 DG134
Redstone Hollow, Red. 266 DG135
Redstone Manor, Red. 250 DG134
Redstone Pk, Red. 250 DG134
Redstone Rd, Red. 266 DG135
Redvers Rd N22 99 DN54
Redvers Rd, Warl. 236 DW118
Redvers St N1 275 N1
Redwald Rd E5 123 DX63
Redway Dr, Twick. 176 CC87
Redwing Cl, S.Croy. 221 DX111
Redwing Gdns, W.Byf. 212 BH112
Redwing Gro, Abb.L. 59 BU31
Redwing Path SE28 165 ER75
Redwing Ri, Guil. 243 BD132
Redwing Rd, Wall. 219 DM108
Redwood, Egh. 193 BE96
Redwood (Burnham), Slou. 130 AG68
Redwood Chase, S.Ock. 149 FW70
Redwood Cl N14 99 DK45
The Vale
Redwood Cl SE16 143 DY74
Redwood Cl, Buck.H. 102 EH47
Beech La
Redwood Cl, Ken. 220 DQ114
Redwood Cl, Sid. 186 EU87
Redwood Cl, Uxb. 135 BP68
The Larches
Redwood Cl, Wat. 94 BW49
Redwood Ct NW6 139 CY66
The Av
Redwood Dr, Hem.H. 40 BL22
Redwood Est, Houns. 155 BV79
Redwood Gdns E4 83 EB44
Redwood Gdns, Chig. 104 EU50
Redwood Gdns, Slou. 131 AR73
Godolphin Rd
Redwood Gro (Chilworth), Guil. 259 BC140
Redwood Ms SW4 161 DH83
Hannington Rd
Redwood Mt, Reig. 250 DA131
Redwood Ri, Borwd. 78 CN37
Redwood Twr E11 123 ED62
Hollydown Way
Redwood Wk, Surb. 197 CK102
Redwood Way, Barn. 79 CX43
Redwoods SW15 179 CU88
Redwoods, Add. 212 BG107
Redwoods, Hert. 32 DQ08
Ree La Cotts, Loug. 85 EN40
Englands La
Reece Ms SW7 160 DD77
Reed Av, Orp. 205 ES104
Reed Cl E16 144 EG71
Reed Cl SE12 184 EG85
Reed Cl, Iver 133 BE72
Reed Cl (London Colney), St.Alb. 62 CL27
Reed Dr, Red. 266 DG137
Reed Pl, Shep. 194 BM102
Reed Pl, W.Byf. 211 BE113
Reed Pond Wk, Rom. 105 FF54
Reed Rd N17 100 DT54
Reede Gdns, Dag. 127 FB64
Reede Rd, Dag. 146 FA65
Reede Way, Dag. 147 FB65
Reedham Cl N17 122 DV56
Reedham Cl (Bricket Wd), St.Alb. 60 CA29
Reedham Dr, Pur. 219 DN113
Reedham Pk Av, Pur. 235 DN116
Reedham St SE15 162 DU82
Reedholm Vil N16 122 DR63
Winston Rd
Reeds, The, Welw.G.C. 29 CX10
Reeds Cres, Wat. 76 BW40
Reeds Pl NW1 141 DJ66
Royal Coll St
Reeds Wk, Wat. 76 BW40
Reedsfield Cl, Ashf. 175 BP91
The Yews
Reedsfield Rd, Ashf. 175 BP91
Reedworth St SE11 278 E9
Reedworth St SE11 161 DN77
Reenglass Rd, Stan. 95 CK49
Rees Dr, Stan. 96 CL49
Rees Gdns, Croy. 202 DT100
Rees St N1 142 DQ67
Reesland Cl E12 125 EN64
Reets Fm Cl NW9 118 CS58
Reeve Rd, Reig. 266 DC138
Reeves Av NW9 118 CR59
Reeves Cor, Croy. 201 DP103
Roman Way
Reeves Cres, Swan. 207 FD97
Reeves La, Harl. 50 EJ19
Reeves Ms W1 276 F1
Reeves Ms W1 140 DG73
Reeves Rd E3 143 EB70
Reeves Rd SE18 165 EP79
Reform Row N17 100 DT54
Reform St SW11 160 DF82
Regal Cl E1 142 DU71
Old Montague St
Regal Cl W5 137 CK71
Regal Ct N18 100 DT50
College Cl
Regal Cres, Wall. 201 DH104
Regal Dr N11 99 DH50
Regal La NW1 140 DG67
Regents Pk Rd
Regal Pl E3 143 DZ69
Coborn St
Regal Pl SW6 160 DB80
Maxwell Rd
Regal Row SE15 162 DW81
Queens Rd
Regal Way, Har. 118 CL58
Regal Way, Wat. 76 BW38
Regalfield Cl, Guil. 242 AU130
Regan Cl, Guil. 242 AV129
Regan Way N1 275 M1
Regan Way N1 142 DS68
Regarder Rd, Chig. 104 EU50
Regarth Av, Rom. 127 FE58
Regatta Ho, Tedd. 177 CG91
Twickenham Rd
Regency Cl W5 138 CL72
Regency Cl, Chig. 103 EQ50
Regency Cl, Hmptn. 176 BZ92
Regency Ct, Brwd. 108 FW47
Regency Ct, Brox. 49 DZ23
Berners Way
Regency Ct, Harl. 52 EU18
Regency Ct, Hem.H. 40 BK20
Alexandra Rd
Regency Ct, Sutt. 218 DB105
Brunswick Rd
Regency Cres NW4 97 CX54
Regency Dr, Ruis. 115 BS60
Regency Dr, W.Byf. 211 BF113
Regency Gdns, Horn. 128 FJ59
Regency Gdns, Walt. 196 BW102
Regency Lo, Buck.H. 102 EK47
Regency Ms NW10 139 CU65
High Rd
Regency Ms, Beck. 203 EC95
Regency Ms, Islw. 177 CE85
Queensbridge Pk
Regency Pl SW1 277 N8
Regency Pl, Wdf.Grn. 103 EN51
Regency St SW1 277 N8

Regency St SW1 161 DK77
Regency Ter SW7 160 DD78
Fulham Rd
Regency Wk, Croy. 203 DY100
Regency Wk, Rich. 178 CL86
Friars Stile Rd
Regency Way, Bexh. 166 EX83
Regency Way, Wok. 227 BD115
Regent Av, Uxb. 135 BP66
Regent Cl N12 98 DC50
Nether St
Regent Cl (New Haw), Add. 212 BK109
Regent Cl, Grays 170 GC75
Regent Cl, Har. 118 CL58
Regent Cl, Houns. 155 BV81
Regent Cl, Red. 251 DJ129
Regent Cl, St.Alb. 43 CJ16
Regent Ct, Slou. 132 AS72
Stoke Poges La
Regent Ct, Wind. 151 AR81
Regent Cres, Red. 250 DF132
Regent Gdns, Ilf. 126 EU58
Regent Gate, Wal.Cr. 67 DY34
Regent Pk, Lthd. 231 CG118
Regent Pl SW19 180 DB92
Haydons Rd
Regent Pl W1 273 L10
Regent Pl, Croy. 202 DT102
Grant Rd
Regent Rd SE24 181 DP86
Regent Rd, Epp. 69 ET30
Regent Rd, Surb. 198 CM99
Regent Sq E3 143 EB69
Regent Sq WC1 274 A3
Regent Sq WC1 141 DL69
Regent Sq, Belv. 167 FB77
Regent St NW10 139 CX69
Wellington Rd
Regent St SW1 277 M1
Regent St SW1 141 DK73
Regent St W1 273 J8
Regent St W1 141 DH72
Regent St W4 158 CN78
Regent St, Wat. 75 BV38
Regents Av N13 99 DM50
Regents Br Gdns SW8 161 DL80
Regents Cl, Hayes 135 BS71
Park Rd
Regents Cl, Rad. 61 CG34
Regents Cl, S.Croy. 220 DS107
Regents Cl, Whyt. 236 DS118
Regents Dr, Kes. 222 EK106
Regents Ms NW8 140 DC68
Langford Pl
Regent's Pk NW1 272 E1
Regent's Pk NW1 140 DG68
Regent's Pk Est NW1 273 K3
Regents Pk Rd N3 119 CZ55
Regents Pk Rd NW1 140 DF67
Regents Pk Ter NW1 141 DH67
Oval Rd
Regent's Pl NW1 273 K4
Regent's Pl NW1 141 DJ70
Regent's Pl SE3 164 EG82
Regents Pl, Loug. 102 EJ45
Regents Row E8 142 DU67
Regina Cl, Barn. 79 CX41
Regina Rd N4 121 DM60
Regina Rd SE25 202 DU97
Regina Rd W13 137 CG74
Regina Rd, Sthl. 156 BY77
Regina Ter W13 137 CH74
Reginald Rd E7 144 EG66
Reginald Rd SE8 163 EA80
Reginald Rd, Nthwd. 93 BT53
Reginald Rd, Rom. 106 FN53
Reginald Sq SE8 163 EA80
Regis Pl SW2 161 DM84
Regis Rd NW5 121 DH64
Regius Ct (Penn), H.Wyc. 88 AD47
Regnart Bldgs NW1 273 L4
Reid Av, Cat. 236 DR121
Reid Cl, Couls. 235 DH116
Reid Cl, Pnr. 115 BU56
Reidhaven Rd SE18 165 ES77
Reigate Av, Sutt. 200 DA102
Reigate Business Ms, Reig. 249 CZ133
Albert Rd N
Reigate Heath, Reig. 265 CX135
Reigate Hill, Reig. 250 DB130
Reigate Hill Cl, Reig. 250 DA131
Reigate Rd, Bet. 248 CS132
Reigate Rd, Brom. 184 EF90
Reigate Rd, Dor. 263 CJ135
Reigate Rd, Epsom 217 CT110
Reigate Rd, Horl. 268 DC146
Reigate Rd, Ilf. 125 ET61
Reigate Rd, Lthd. 231 CJ122
Reigate Rd, Red. 250 DB134
Reigate Rd, Reig. 250 DB134
Reigate Rd (Sidlow), Reig. 266 DB141
Reigate Rd, Tad. 233 CX117
Reigate Way, Wall. 219 DL106
Reighton Rd E5 122 DU62
Reindorp Cl, Guil. 258 AU135
Old Ct Rd
Relay Rd W12 139 CW73
Relf Rd SE15 162 DU83
Relko Ct, Epsom 216 CR110
Relko Gdns, Sutt. 218 DD106
Relton Ms SW7 276 C6
Rembrandt Cl E14 163 ED76
Rembrandt Cl SW1 276 F9
Rembrandt Ct, Epsom 217 CT107
Rembrandt Dr (Northfleet), Grav. 190 GD90
Rembrandt Rd SE13 164 EE84
Rembrandt Rd, Edg. 96 CN54
Rembrandt Way, Walt. 195 BV104
Remington Rd E6 144 EL72
Remington Rd N15 122 DR58
Remington St N1 274 G1
Remington St N1 141 DP68
Remnant St WC2 274 B8
Rempstone Ms N1 142 DR68
Mintern St
Remus Rd E3 143 EA66
Monier Rd
Rendle Cl, Croy. 202 DT99
Rendlesham Av, Rad. 77 CF37
Rendlesham Cl, Ware 32 DV05
Rendlesham Rd E5 122 DU63
Rendlesham Rd, Enf. 81 DP39
Rendlesham Way, Rick. 73 BC44
Renforth St SE16 162 DW75
Renfree Way, Shep. 194 BM101
Renfrew Cl E6 145 EN73
Renfrew Rd SE11 278 F8
Renfrew Rd SE11 161 DP77
Renfrew Rd, Houns. 156 BX82
Renfrew Rd, Kings.T. 178 CP94
Renmans, The, Ash. 232 CM116
Renmuir St SW17 180 DF93
Rennell St SE13 163 EC83
Rennels Way, Islw. 157 CE82
St. John's Rd
Renness Rd E17 123 DY55
Rennets Cl SE9 185 ES85
Rennets Wd Rd SE9 185 ER85
Rennie Cl, Ashf. 174 BK90
Rennie Est SE16 162 DV77
Rennie St SE1 278 F2
Rennie St SE1 141 DP74
Rennie Ter, Red. 266 DG135
Renninson Cl, Wal.Cr. 66 DT27
Allwood Rd
Renown Cl, Croy. 201 DP102
Renown Cl, Rom. 104 FA53
Rensburg Rd E17 123 DX57
Renshaw Cl, Belv. 166 EZ79
Grove Rd
Renters Av NW4 119 CW58
Renton Dr, Orp. 206 EX101
Renwick Ind Est, Bark. 146 EV67
Renwick Rd, Bark. 146 EV70
Repens Way, Hayes 136 BX70
Stipularis Dr
Rephidim St SE1 279 M7
Replingham Rd SW18 179 CZ88
Reporton Rd SW6 159 CY81
Repository Rd SE18 165 EM79
Repton Av, Hayes 155 BR77
Repton Av, Rom. 127 FG55
Repton Av, Wem. 117 CJ63
Repton Cl, Cars. 218 DE106
Repton Ct, Beck. 203 EB95
Repton Ct, Ilf. 103 EM53
Repton Gro
Repton Dr, Rom. 127 FG56
Repton Gdns, Rom. 127 FG55
Repton Grn, St.Alb. 43 CD16
Repton Gro, Ilf. 103 EM53
Repton Pl, Amer. 72 AU39
Repton Rd, Har. 118 CM56
Repton Rd, Orp. 206 EU104
Repton St E14 143 DY72
Repton Way, Rick. 74 BN43
Repulse Cl, Rom. 105 FB53
Reservoir Cl, Th.Hth. 202 DR98
Reservoir Rd N14 81 DJ43
Reservoir Rd SE4 163 DY82
Reservoir Rd, Ruis. 115 BQ56
Resolution Wk SE18 165 EM76
Reson Way, Hem.H. 40 BH21
Restavon Pk, West. 239 EP116
Restell Cl SE3 164 EE79
Restmor Way, Wall. 200 DG103
Reston Cl, Borwd. 78 CN38
Reston Path, Borwd. 78 CN38
Reston Pl SW7 160 DC75
Hyde Pk Gate
Restons Cres SE9 185 ER86
Restormel Cl, Houns. 176 CA85
Retcar Cl N19 121 DH61
Dartmouth Pk Hill
Retcar Pl N19 121 DH61
Retford Cl, Borwd. 78 CN38
The Campions
Retford Cl, Rom. 106 FN51
Retford Path, Rom. 106 FN51
Retford Rd, Rom. 106 FN51
Retford St N1 275 N1
Retingham Way E4 101 EB47
Retreat, The NW9 118 CR57
Retreat, The SW14 158 CS83
South Worple Way
Retreat, The, Abb.L. 59 BQ31
Abbots Rd
Retreat, The, Add. 212 BK106
Retreat, The, Amer. 72 AY39
Retreat, The, Brwd. 108 FV46
Costead Manor Rd
Retreat, The (Hutton), Brwd. 109 GB44
Retreat, The, Egh. 172 AX92
Retreat, The, Grays 170 GB79
Retreat, The, Har. 116 CA59
Retreat, The, Kings L. 59 BQ31
Retreat, The, Maid. 150 AD80
Retreat, The, Orp. 224 EV107
Retreat, The, Surb. 198 CM100
Retreat, The, Th.Hth. 202 DR98
Retreat, The, Wor.Pk. 199 CV103
Retreat Cl, Har. 117 CJ57
Retreat Pl E9 142 DW65
Retreat Rd, Rich. 177 CK85
Retreat Way, Chig. 104 EV48
Reubens Rd, Brwd. 109 GB44
Reunion Row E1 142 DV73
Pennington St
Revel Rd (Wooburn Grn), H.Wyc. 110 AD55
Reveley Sq SE16 163 DY75
Howland Way
Revell Cl (Fetcham), Lthd. 230 CB122
Revell Dr (Fetcham), Lthd. 230 CB122
Revell Ri SE18 165 ET79
Revell Rd, Kings.T. 198 CP95
Revell Rd, Sutt. 217 CZ107
Revelon Rd SE4 163 DY84
Revels Cl, Hert. 32 DR07
Revels Rd, Hert. 32 DR07
Revelstoke Rd SW18 179 CZ89
Reventlow Rd SE9 185 EQ88
Reverdy Rd SE1 162 DU77
Reverend Cl, Har. 116 CB62
Revesby Rd, Cars. 200 DD100
Review Rd NW2 119 CT61
Review Rd, Dag. 147 FB67
Rewell St SW6 160 DC80
Rewley Rd, Cars. 200 DD100
Rex Av, Ashf. 174 BN92
Rex Cl, Rom. 105 FB52
Rex Pl W1 276 G1
Reydon Av E11 124 EJ58
Reynard Cl SE4 163 DY83
Foxwell St
Reynard Cl, Brom. 205 EM97
Reynard Dr SE19 182 DT94
Reynard Pl SE14 163 DY79
Milton Ct Rd
Reynard Way, Hert. 32 DU09
Reynards Way (Bricket Wd), St.Alb. 60 BZ29
Reynardson Rd N17 100 DQ52
Reynolah Gdns SE7 164 EH78
Rathmore Rd
Reynolds Av E12 125 EN64
Reynolds Av, Chess. 216 CL108
Reynolds Av, Rom. 126 EW59
Reynolds Cl NW11 120 DB59
Reynolds Cl SW19 200 DD95
Reynolds Cl, Cars. 200 DF102
Reynolds Cl, Hem.H. 40 BG19
Reynolds Ct E11 124 EF62
Cobbold Rd
Reynolds Ct, Rom. 126 EX55
Reynolds Cres (Sandridge), St.Alb. 43 CH15
Reynolds Dr, Edg. 118 CM55
Reynolds Pl SE3 164 EH80
Reynolds Pl, Rich. 178 CM86
Cambrian Rd
Reynolds Rd SE15 182 DW85
Reynolds Rd W4 158 CQ76
Reynolds Rd, Beac. 88 AJ52
Reynolds Rd, Hayes 136 BW70
Reynolds Rd, N.Mal. 198 CR101
Reynolds Wk, Chesh. 54 AN27
Great Hivings
Reynolds Way, Croy. 220 DS105
Rheidol Ms N1 142 DQ68
Rheidol Ter
Rheidol Ter N1 141 DP68
Rheingold Way, Wall. 219 DL109
Rheola Cl N17 100 DT53
Rhoda St E2 142 DT70
Brick La
Rhodes Av N22 99 DJ53
Rhodes Cl, Egh. 173 BC92
Mullens Rd
Rhodes Moorhouse Ct, Mord. 200 DA100
Rhodes St N7 121 DM64
Mackenzie Rd
Rhodes Way, Wat. 76 BX40
Rhodesia Rd E11 123 ED61
Rhodesia Rd SW9 161 DL82
Rhodeswell Rd E14 143 DZ72
Rhododendron Ride, Egh. 172 AT94
Rhododendron Ride, Slou. 133 AZ69
Rhodrons Av, Chess. 216 CL106
Rhondda Gro E3 143 DY69
Rhyl Rd, Grnf. 137 CF68
Rhyl St NW5 140 DG65
Rhymes, The, Hem.H. 40 BH18
Rhys Av N11 99 DK52
Rialto Rd, Mitch. 200 DG96
Rib Vale, Hert. 32 DR06
Ribble Cl, Wdf.Grn. 102 EJ51
Prospect Rd
Ribbledale (London Colney), St.Alb. 62 CM27
Ribblesdale, Dor. 263 CH138
Roman Rd
Ribblesdale, Hem.H. 40 BL17
Ribblesdale Av N11 98 DG51
Ribblesdale Av, Nthlt. 136 CB65
Ribblesdale Rd N8 121 DM56
Ribblesdale Rd SW16 181 DH93
Ribblesdale Rd, Dart. 188 FQ88
Ribchester Av, Grnf. 137 CF69
Ribston Cl, Brom. 205 EM102
Ribston Cl, Rad. 61 CK33
Wayside
Ricardo Path SE28 146 EW74
Byron Cl
Ricardo Rd (Old Windsor), Wind. 172 AV86
Meadow Way
Ricardo St E14 143 EB72
Ricards Rd SW19 179 CZ92
Rice Cl, Hem.H. 40 BM19
Ricebridge La, Reig. 265 CV137
Rices Cor (Shalford), Guil. 259 BA141
Rich La SW5 160 DB78
Warwick Rd
Rich St E14 143 DZ73
Richard Cl SE18 164 EL77
Richard Fell Ho E12 125 EN63
Walton Rd
Richard Foster Cl E17 123 DZ59
Richard Ho Dr E16 144 EK72
Richard Stagg Cl, St.Alb. 43 CJ22
Richard St E1 142 DV72
Commercial Rd
Richards Av, Rom. 127 FC57
Richards Cl, Bushey 95 CD45
Richards Cl, Har. 117 CG57
Richards Cl, Hayes 155 BR79
Richards Cl, Uxb. 134 BN67
Richards Fld, Epsom 216 CR109
Richards Pl E17 123 EA55
Richards Pl SW3 276 C8
Richards Rd (Stoke D'Abernon), Cob. 214 CB114
Richards Way, Slou. 131 AN74
Richardson Cl E8 142 DT67
Clarissa St
Richardson Cl, Green. 189 FU85
Steele Av
Richardson Cl (London Colney), St.Alb. 62 CL27
Richardson Cres (Cheshunt), Wal.Cr. 65 DP26
Richardson Pl (Colney Heath), St.Alb. 44 CP22
Richardson Rd E15 144 EE68
Richardson's Ms W1 273 K5
Richbell Cl, Ash. 231 CK118
Richbell Pl WC1 274 B6
Richborne Ter SW8 161 DM80
Richborough Cl, Orp. 206 EX98
Richborough Rd NW2 119 CX63
Richens Cl, Houns. 157 CD82
Riches Rd, Ilf. 125 EQ61
Richfield Rd, Bushey 94 CC45
Richford Rd E15 144 EF67
Richford St W6 159 CW75
Richings Way, Iver 153 BF76
Richland Av, Couls. 218 DG114
Richlands Av, Epsom 217 CU105
Richmer Rd, Erith 167 FG80
Richmond Av E4 101 ED50
Richmond Av N1 141 DM67
Richmond Av NW10 139 CW65
Richmond Av SW20 199 CY95
Richmond Av, Felt. 175 BS86
Richmond Av, Uxb. 135 BP65
Richmond Br, Rich. 177 CK86
Richmond Br, Twick. 177 CK86
Richmond Bldgs W1 273 M9
Richmond Cl E17 123 DZ58
Richmond Cl, Amer. 72 AT38
Richmond Cl, Borwd. 78 CR43
Richmond Cl, Epsom 216 CS114
Richmond Cl (Fetcham), Lthd. 230 CC124
Richmond Cl (Cheshunt), Wal.Cr. 66 DW29
Richmond Cl (Biggin Hill), West. 238 EH119
Richmond Ct, Brox. 49 DZ20
Richmond Ct, Hat. 45 CV20
Cooks Way
Richmond Ct, Pot.B. 64 DC31
Richmond Cres E4 101 ED50
Richmond Cres N1 141 DM67
Richmond Cres N9 100 DU46
Richmond Cres, Slou. 132 AU74
Richmond Cres, Stai. 173 BF92
Richmond Dr, Grav. 191 GL89
Richmond Dr, Shep. 195 BQ100
Richmond Dr, Wat. 75 BS39
Richmond Gdns NW4 119 CU57
Richmond Gdns, Har. 95 CF51
Richmond Grn, Croy. 201 DL104
Richmond Gro N1 141 DP66
Richmond Gro, Surb. 198 CM100
Richmond Hill, Rich. 178 CL86
Richmond Hill Ct, Rich. 178 CL86
Richmond Ms W1 273 M9
Richmond Ms, Tedd. 177 CF93
Broad St
Richmond Pk, Kings.T. 178 CQ87
Richmond Pk, Loug. 102 EJ45
Fallow Flds
Richmond Pk, Rich. 178 CQ87
Richmond Pk Rd SW14 178 CQ85
Richmond Pk Rd, Kings.T. 178 CL94
Richmond Pl SE18 165 EQ77
Richmond Rd E4 101 ED46
Richmond Rd E7 124 EH64
Richmond Rd E8 142 DT66
Richmond Rd E11 123 ED61
Richmond Rd N2 98 DC54
Richmond Rd N11 99 DL51
Richmond Rd N15 122 DS58
Richmond Rd SW20 199 CV95
Richmond Rd W5 158 CL75
Richmond Rd, Barn. 80 DB43
Richmond Rd, Couls. 235 DH115
Richmond Rd, Croy. 201 DL104
Richmond Rd, Grays 170 GC79
Richmond Rd, Ilf. 125 EQ62
Richmond Rd, Islw. 157 CG83
Richmond Rd, Kings.T. 177 CK92
Richmond Rd, Pot.B. 64 DC31
Richmond Rd, Rom. 127 FF58
Richmond Rd, Stai. 173 BF92
Richmond Rd, Th.Hth. 201 DP97
Richmond Rd, Twick. 177 CJ86
Richmond St E13 144 EG68
Richmond Ter SW1 277 P4
Richmond Ter SW1 161 DL75
Richmond Ter Ms SW1 161 DL75
Parliament St
Richmond Wk, St.Alb. 43 CK16
Richmond Way E11 124 EG61
Richmond Way W12 159 CX75
Richmond Way W14 159 CX76
Richmond Way (Fetcham), Lthd. 230 CB123
Richmond Way, Rick. 75 BQ42
Richmount Gdns SE3 164 EG83
Rick Roberts Way E15 143 EC67
Rickard Cl NW4 119 CV56
Rickard Cl SW2 181 DM88
Rickard Cl, West Dr. 154 BK76
Rickards Cl, Surb. 198 CL102
Rickett St SW6 160 DA79
Ricketts Hill Rd (Tatsfield), West. 238 EK118
Rickfield Cl, Hat. 45 CU20
Rickman Cres, Add. 194 BH104
Rickman Hill, Couls. 235 DH118
Rickman Hill Rd, Couls. 235 DH118
Rickman St E1 142 DW69
Mantus Rd
Rickmans La (Stoke Poges), Slou. 112 AS64
Rickmansworth La (Chalfont St. Peter), Ger.Cr. 91 AZ50
Rickmansworth Pk, Rick. 92 BK45
Rickmansworth Rd, Amer. 55 AQ37
Rickmansworth Rd, Nthwd. 93 BR52
Rickmansworth Rd, Pnr. 93 BV54
Rickmansworth Rd, Rick. 73 BE41
Rickmansworth Rd (Harefield), Uxb. 92 BJ53
Rickmansworth Rd, Wat. 75 BS42
Ricksons La (West Horsley), Lthd. 245 BP127
Rickthorne Rd N19 121 DL61
Landseer Rd
Rickwood, Horl. 269 DH147
Woodhayes
Rickyard Path SE9 164 EL84
Ridding La, Grnf. 117 CF64
Riddings, The, Cat. 252 DT125
Riddings La, Harl. 51 ET19
Riddlesdown Av, Pur. 220 DQ112
Riddlesdown Rd, Pur. 220 DQ111
Riddons Rd SE12 184 EJ90
Ride, The, Brent. 157 CH78
Ride, The, Enf. 82 DW41
Ride La (Farley Grn), Guil. 260 BK144
Rideout St SE18 165 EM77
Rider Cl, Sid. 185 ES86
Riders Way, Gdse. 252 DW131
Ridgdale St E3 143 EB68
Ridge, The, Bex. 186 EZ87
Ridge, The (Woldingham), Cat. 253 EB126
Ridge, The, Couls. 219 DL114
Ridge, The, Epsom 232 CP117
Ridge, The (Fetcham), Lthd. 231 CD124
Ridge, The, Orp. 205 ER103
Ridge, The, Pur. 219 DJ110
Ridge, The, Surb. 198 CN99
Ridge, The, Twick. 177 CD87
Ridge, The, Wok. 227 BB117
Ridge Av N21 100 DQ45
Ridge Av, Dart. 187 FF86
Ridge Cl NW4 97 CX54
Ridge Cl NW9 118 CR56
Ridge Cl SE28 165 ER75
Ridge Cl (Strood Grn), Bet. 264 CP138
Ridge Cl, Wok. 226 AV121
Ridge Crest, Enf. 81 DM39
Ridge Grn (South Nutfield), Red. 267 DL137
Ridge Grn Cl (South Nutfield), Red. 267 DL137
Ridge Hill NW11 119 CY60
Ridge La, Wat. 75 BS36
Ridge Langley, S.Croy. 220 DU110
Ridge Lea, Hem.H. 39 BF20
Ridge Pk, Pur. 219 DK110
Ridge Rd N8 121 DM58
Ridge Rd N21 100 DQ46
Ridge Rd NW2 119 CZ62
Ridge Rd, Mitch. 181 DH94
Ridge Rd, Sutt. 199 CY102
Ridge St, Wat. 75 BV38
Ridge Way SE19 182 DS93
Central Hill
Ridge Way (Crayford), Dart. 187 FF86
Ridge Way, Felt. 176 BY90
Ridge Way, Iver 133 BE74
Ridgebank, Slou. 131 AM73
Ridgebrook Rd SE3 164 EJ83
Ridgecroft Cl, Bex. 187 FC88
Ridgefield, Wat. 75 BS37
Ridgegate Cl, Reig. 250 DD132
Ridgehurst Av, Wat. 59 BT34
Ridgelands (Fetcham), Lthd. 231 CD124
Ridgemead Rd (Englefield Grn), Egh. 172 AU90
Ridgemont Gdns, Edg. 96 CQ49
Ridgemount, Guil. 258 AV135
Ridgemount, Wey. 195 BS103
Oatlands Dr
Ridgemount Av, Couls. 235 DH117
Ridgemount Av, Croy. 203 DX102
Ridgemount Cl SE20 182 DV94
Anerley Pk
Ridgemount End (Chalfont St. Peter), Ger.Cr. 90 AY50
Ridgemount Gdns, Enf. 81 DP40
Ridgemount Way, Red. 266 DE136
Ridges, The (Artington), Guil. 258 AW139
Ridgeview Cl, Barn. 79 CX44
Ridgeview Lo (London Colney), St.Alb. 62 CM28
Ridgeview Rd N20 98 DB48
Ridgeway SE28 165 ER77
Pettman Cres
Ridgeway, Berk. 38 AT19
Ridgeway, Brwd. 109 GB46
Ridgeway, Brom. 204 EG103
Ridgeway (Lane End), Dart. 189 FS92
Ridgeway, Epsom 216 CQ112
Ridgeway, Grays 170 GE77
Ridgeway, Rick. 92 BH45
Ridgeway, Vir.W. 192 AY99
Ridgeway, Welw.G.C. 30 DA09
Ridgeway (Horsell), Wok. 226 AX115
Ridgeway, Wdf.Grn. 102 EJ49
Ridgeway, The E4 101 EB47
Ridgeway, The N3 98 DB52
Ridgeway, The N11 98 DF49
Ridgeway, The N14 99 DL47
Ridgeway, The NW7 97 CV49
Ridgeway, The NW9 118 CS56
Ridgeway, The NW11 119 CZ60
Ridgeway, The W3 158 CN76
Ridgeway, The, Amer. 55 AR40
Ridgeway, The, Croy. 201 DM104
Ridgeway, The, Enf. 81 DN39
Ridgeway, The (Chalfont St. Peter), Ger.Cr. 112 AX55
Ridgeway, The, Guil. 259 BA135
Ridgeway, The (Kenton), Har. 117 CJ58
Ridgeway, The (North Harrow), Har. 116 BZ57
Ridgeway, The, Hert. 31 DM08
Ridgeway, The, Horl. 268 DG150
Ridgeway, The (Fetcham), Lthd. 231 CD123
Ridgeway, The (Oxshott), Lthd. 214 CC114
Ridgeway, The, Pot.B. 64 DD34
Ridgeway, The (Cuffley), Pot.B. 64 DE28
Ridgeway, The, Rad. 77 CF37
Ridgeway, The (Gidea Pk), Rom. 127 FG56
Ridgeway, The (Harold Wd), Rom. 106 FL53
Ridgeway, The, Ruis. 116 CA58
Ridgeway, The, St.Alb. 43 CH17
Ridgeway, The, S.Croy. 220 DS110
Ridgeway, The, Stan. 95 CJ51
Ridgeway, The, Walt. 195 BT102
Ridgeway, The, Wat. 75 BS37
Ridgeway Av, Barn. 80 DF44
Ridgeway Av, Grav. 191 GH90
Ridgeway Cl, Chesh. 54 AP28
Ridgeway Cl, Dor. 263 CG138
Ridgeway Cl, Hem.H. 58 BM26
London Rd
Ridgeway Cl (Oxshott), Lthd. 214 CC114
Ridgeway Cl, Wok. 226 AX116
Ridgeway Ct, Red. 250 DF134
Ridgeway Rd
Ridgeway Cres, Orp. 205 ES104
Ridgeway Cres Gdns, Orp. 205 ES103
Ridgeway Dr, Brom. 184 EH91
Ridgeway Dr, Dor. 263 CG139
Ridgeway E, Sid. 185 ET85
Ridgeway Est, The, Iver 133 BF74
Ridgeway Gdns N6 121 DJ59
Ridgeway Gdns, Ilf. 124 EL57
Ridgeway Gdns, Wok. 226 AX115
Ridgeway Rd SW9 161 DP83
Ridgeway Rd, Chesh. 54 AN28
Ridgeway Rd, Dor. 263 CG139
Ridgeway Rd, Islw. 157 CE80
Ridgeway Rd, Red. 250 DE134
Ridgeway Rd N, Islw. 157 CE79
Ridgeway Wk, Nthlt. 136 BY65
Fortunes Mead
Ridgeway W, Sid. 185 ES85
Ridgeways, Harl. 52 EY15
Ridgewell Cl N1 142 DQ67
Basire St
Ridgewell Cl SE26 183 DZ91
Ridgewell Cl, Dag. 147 FB67
Ridgmont Rd, St.Alb. 43 CE21
Ridgmount Gdns WC1 273 M5
Ridgmount Pl WC1 273 M6
Ridgmount Rd SW18 180 DB85
Ridgmount St WC1 273 M6
Ridgway SW19 179 CX93
Ridgway (Pyrford), Wok. 228 BG115
Ridgway, The, Sutt. 218 DD108
Ridgway Gdns SW19 179 CX94
Ridgway Pl SW19 179 CY93
Ridgway Rd (Pyrford), Wok. 227 BF115
Ridgwell Rd E16 144 EJ71
Riding, The NW11 119 CZ59
Golders Grn Rd
Riding, The, Wok. 211 BB114
Riding Ct Rd (Datchet), Slou. 152 AW80
Riding Hill, S.Croy. 220 DU113
Riding Ho St W1 273 K7
Riding Ho St W1 141 DH71
Riding La, Beac. 88 AF53
Ridings, The E11 124 EG57
Malcolm Way
Ridings, The W5 138 CM70
Ridings, The, Add. 211 BF107
Ridings, The, Amer. 55 AR35
Ridings, The, Ash. 231 CK117
Ridings, The, Chesh. 72 AX36
Ridings, The, Chig. 104 EV49
Manford Way
Ridings, The, Cob. 214 CA112
Ridings, The, Epsom 232 CS115
Ridings, The (Ewell), Epsom 217 CT109
Ridings, The, Hert. 31 DN10
Ridings, The, Iver 153 BF77
Ridings, The (East Horsley), Lthd. 245 BC125
Ridings, The, Reig. 250 DD131
Ridings, The, Sun. 195 BU95

Rockwell Gdns SE19 182 DS92
Rockwell Rd, Dag. 127 FB64
Rockwood Pl W12 159 CW75
Rocky La, Reig. 250 DF128
Rocliffe St N1 274 G1
Rocombe Cres SE23 182 DW87
Rocque La SE3 164 EF83
Rodborough Rd NW11 120 DA60
Roden Cl, Harl. 36 EZ11
Roden Ct N6 121 DK59
Hornsey La
Roden Gdns, Croy. 202 DS100
Roden St N7 121 DM62
Roden St, Ilf. 125 EN62
Rodenhurst Rd SW4 181 DJ86
Rodeo Cl, Erith 167 FH81
Roderick Rd NW3 120 DF63
Rodgers Cl, Borwd. 77 CK44
Roding Av, Wdf.Grn. 102 EL51
Roding Gdns, Loug. 84 EL44
Roding La, Buck.H. 102 EL46
Roding La, Chig. 103 EN46
Roding La N, Wdf.Grn. 102 EK54
Roding La S, Ilf. 124 EK56
Roding La S, Wdf.Grn. 124 EK56
Roding Ms E1 142 DU74
Kennet St
Roding Rd E5 123 DX63
Roding Rd E6 145 EP71
Roding Rd, Loug. 84 EL43
Roding Trd Est, Bark. 145 EP66
Roding Vw, Buck.H. 102 EK46
Roding Way, Rain. 148 FK68
Rodings, The, Upmin. 129 FR58
Rodings, The, Wdf.Grn. 102 EJ51
Rodings Row, Barn. 79 CY43
Leecroft Rd
Rodmarton St W1 272 E7
Rodmarton St W1 140 DF71
Rodmell Cl, Hayes 136 BY70
Rodmell Slope N12 97 CZ50
Rodmere St SE10 164 EE78
Trafalgar Rd
Rodmill La SW2 181 DL87
Rodney Av, St.Alb. 43 CG22
Rodney Cl, Croy. 201 DP102
Rodney Cl, N.Mal. 198 CS99
Rodney Cl, Pnr. 116 BY59
Rodney Cl, Walt. 196 BW102
Rodney Rd
Rodney Ct W9 140 DC70
Maida Vale
Rodney Cres, Hodd. 49 EA15
Rodney Gdns, Pnr. 115 BV57
Rodney Gdns, W.Wick. 222 EG105
Rodney Grn, Walt. 196 BW103
Rodney Pl E17 101 DY54
Rodney Pl SE17 279 J8
Rodney Pl SE17 162 DQ77
Rodney Pl SW19 200 DC95
Rodney Rd E11 124 EH56
Rodney Rd SE17 279 J8
Rodney Rd SE17 162 DR77
Rodney Rd, Mitch. 200 DE96
Rodney Rd, N.Mal. 198 CS99
Rodney Rd, Twick. 176 CA86
Rodney Rd, Walt. 196 BW103
Rodney St N1 141 DM68
Rodney Way, Guil. 243 BA133
Rodney Way, Rom. 104 FA53
Rodney Way (Colnbrook), Slou. 153 BE81
Rodona Rd, Wey. 213 BR111
Rodway Rd SW15 179 CU87
Rodway Rd, Brom. 204 EH95
Rodwell Cl, Ruis. 116 BW59
Rodwell Ct, Add. 212 BJ105
Garfield Rd
Rodwell Pl, Edg. 96 CN51
Whitchurch La
Rodwell Rd SE22 182 DT86
Roe End NW9 118 CQ56
Roe Grn NW9 118 CQ57
Roe Grn Cl, Hat. 44 CS19
Roe Grn La, Hat. 45 CT18
Roe Hill Cl, Hat. 45 CT19
Roe La NW9 118 CP56
Roe Way, Wall. 219 DL108
Roebourne Way E16 165 EN75
Roebuck Cl, Ash. 232 CL120
Roebuck Cl, Felt. 175 BV91
Roebuck Cl, Hert. 32 DU09
Roebuck Cl, Reig. 250 DB134
Roebuck Grn, Slou. 131 AL74
Roebuck La N17 100 DT51
High Rd
Roebuck La, Buck.H. 102 EJ45
Roebuck Rd, Chess. 216 CN106
Roebuck Rd, Ilf. 104 EV50
Roedean Av, Enf. 82 DW39
Roedean Cl, Enf. 82 DW39
Roedean Cl, Orp. 224 EV105
Roedean Cres SW15 178 CS86
Roedean Dr, Rom. 127 FE56
Roefields Cl (Felden), Hem.H. 40 BG24
Roehampton Cl SW15 159 CU84
Roehampton Cl, Grav. 191 GL87
Roehampton Dr, Chis. 185 EQ93
Roehampton Gate SW15 178 CS86
Roehampton High St SW15 179 CV87
Roehampton La SW15 159 CU84
Roehampton Vale SW15 178 CS90
Roehyde Way, Hat. 44 CS20
Roestock Gdns (Colney Heath), St.Alb. 44 CS22
Roestock La (Colney Heath), St.Alb. 44 CR23
Rofant Rd, Nthwd. 93 BS51
Roffes La, Cat. 236 DR124
Roffey Cl, Horl. 268 DF148
Court Lo Rd
Roffey Cl, Pur. 235 DP116
Roffey St E14 163 EC75
Roffords, Wok. 226 AV117
Rogate Ho E5 122 DU62
Muir Rd
Roger Dowley Ct E2 142 DW68
Russia La
Roger St WC1 274 C5
Roger St WC1 141 DM70
Rogers Cl, Cat. 236 DV122
Tillingdown Hill
Rogers Cl, Couls. 235 DP118
Rogers Cl (Cheshunt), Wal.Cr. 66 DR27
Rogers Ct, Swan. 207 FG98
Rogers Gdns, Dag. 126 FA64
Rogers La (Stoke Poges), Slou. 132 AT67
Rogers La, Warl. 237 DZ118
Rogers Mead, Gdse. 252 DV132
Ivy Mill La
Rogers Rd E16 144 EF72
Rogers Rd SW17 180 DD91
Rogers Rd, Dag. 126 FA64
Rogers Rd, Grays 170 GC77
Rogers Ruff, Nthwd. 93 BQ53
Rogers Wk N12 98 DB48
Brook Meadow
Rojack Rd SE23 183 DX88
Roke Cl, Ken. 220 DQ114
Roke Lo Rd, Ken. 219 DP113
Roke Rd, Ken. 236 DQ115
Rokeby Ct, Wok. 226 AT117
Rokeby Gdns, Wdf.Grn. 102 EG53
Rokeby Pl SW20 179 CV94
Rokeby Rd SE4 163 DZ82
Rokeby St E15 144 EE67
Rokefield, Dor. 262 CB136
Westcott St
Roker Pk Av, Uxb. 114 BL63
Rokesby Cl, Well. 165 ER82
Rokesby Pl, Wem. 117 CK64
Rokesby Rd, Slou. 131 AM69
Rokesly Av N8 121 DL57
Rokewood Ms, Ware 33 DX05
Roland Gdns SW7 160 DC78
Roland Gdns, Felt. 176 BZ90
Roland Ms E1 143 DX71
Stepney Grn
Roland Rd E17 123 ED56
Roland St, St.Alb. 43 CG20
Roland Way SE17 162 DR78
Roland Way SW7 160 DC78
Roland Gdns
Roland Way, Wor.Pk. 199 CT103
Roles Gro, Rom. 126 EX56
Rolfe Cl, Barn. 80 DE42
Rolfe Cl, Beac. 89 AL54
Rolinsden Way, Kes. 222 EK105
Roll Gdns, Ilf. 125 EN57
Rollesby Rd, Chess. 216 CN107
Rollesby Way SE28 146 EW73
Rolleston Av, Orp. 205 EP100
Rolleston Cl, Orp. 205 EP101
Rolleston Rd, S.Croy. 220 DR108
Rollins St SE15 162 DW79
Rollit Cres, Houns. 176 CA85
Rollit St N7 121 DM64
Hornsey Rd
Rollo Rd, Swan. 187 FF94
Rolls Bldgs EC4 274 D8
Rolls Pk Av E4 101 EA51
Rolls Pk Rd E4 101 EB50
Rolls Pas EC4 274 D8
Rolls Rd SE1 162 DT78
Rollscourt Av SE24 182 DQ85
Rollswood, Welw.G.C. 29 CY12
Rolt St SE8 163 DY79
Rolvenden Gdns, Brom. 184 EK94
Rolvenden Pl N17 100 DU53
Manor Rd
Rom Cres, Rom. 127 FF59
Rom Valley Way, Rom. 127 FE59
Roma Read Cl SW15 179 CV87
Bessborough Rd
Roma Rd E17 123 DY55
Roman Cl W3 158 CP75
Avenue Gdns
Roman Cl, Felt. 176 BW85
Roman Cl, Rain. 147 FD68
Roman Cl (Harefield), Uxb. 92 BH53
Roman Gdns, Kings L. 59 BP30
Roman Ho, Rain. 147 FD68
Roman Cl
Roman Ind Est, Croy. 202 DS101
Roman Ms, Hodd. 49 EA16
North Rd
Roman Ri SE19 182 DR93
Roman Ri, Saw. 36 EX05
Roman Rd E2 142 DW69
Roman Rd E3 143 DY68
Roman Rd E6 144 EL70
Roman Rd N10 99 DH52
Roman Rd NW2 119 CW62
Roman Rd W4 159 CT77
Roman Rd, Brwd. 109 GC41
Roman Rd, Dor. 263 CG138
Roman Rd (Northfleet), Grav. 190 GC90
Roman Rd, Ilf. 145 EP65
Roman Sq SE28 146 EU74
Roman St, Hodd. 49 EA16
Roman Vale, Harl. 36 EW10
Roman Vil Rd (South Darenth), Dart. 188 FQ92
Roman Way N7 141 DM65
Roman Way SE15 162 DW80
Clifton Way
Roman Way, Cars. 218 DF109
Roman Way, Croy. 201 DP103
Roman Way, Dart. 187 FE85
Roman Way, Enf. 82 DT43
Roman Way, Wal.Abb. 83 EB36
Roman Way Ind Est N1 141 DM66
Offord St
Romanby Ct, Red. 266 DF135
Mill St
Romanfield Rd SW2 181 DM87
Romanhurst Av, Brom. 204 EE98
Romanhurst Gdns, Brom. 204 EE98
Romans End, St.Alb. 42 CC22
Romans Way, Wok. 228 BG115
Romany Ct, Hem.H. 41 BQ19
Wood End Cl
Romany Gdns E17 101 DY53
McEntee Av
Romany Gdns, Sutt. 200 DA101
Romany Ri, Orp. 205 EQ102
Romberg Rd SW17 180 DG90
Romborough Gdns SE13 183 EC85
Romborough Way SE13 183 EC85
Romeland, Borwd. 77 CK44
Romeland, St.Alb. 42 CC20
Romeland, Wal.Abb. 67 EC33
Romeland Hill, St.Alb. 42 CC20
Romero Cl SW9 161 DM83
Stockwell Rd
Romero Sq SE3 164 EJ84
Romeyn Rd SW16 181 DM90
Romford Rd E7 124 EH64
Romford Rd E12 124 EL63
Romford Rd E15 144 EE66
Romford Rd, Chig. 104 EU48
Romford Rd, Rom. 104 EY52
Romford Rd, S.Ock. 148 FQ73
Romford St E1 142 DU71
Romilly Dr, Wat. 94 BY48
Romilly Rd N4 121 DP61
Romilly St W1 273 M10
Romilly St W1 141 DK73
Rommany Rd SE27 182 DR91
Romney Chase, Horn. 128 FM58
Romney Cl N17 100 DV53
Romney Cl NW11 120 DC60
Romney Cl SE14 162 DW80
Kender St
Romney Cl, Ashf. 175 BQ92
Romney Cl, Chess. 216 CL105
Romney Cl, Har. 116 CA59
Romney Dr, Brom. 184 EK94
Romney Dr, Har. 116 CA59
Romney Gdns, Bexh. 166 EZ81
Romney Lock, Wind. 152 AS79
Romney Lock Rd, Wind. 151 AR80
Romney Ms W1 272 F6
Romney Par, Hayes 135 BR68
Romney Rd
Romney Rd SE10 163 EC79
Romney Rd (Northfleet), Grav. 190 GE90
Romney Rd, Hayes 135 BR68
Romney Rd, N.Mal. 198 CR100
Romney Row NW2 119 CX61
Brent Ter
Romney St SW1 277 N7
Romney St SW1 161 DL76
Romola Rd SE24 181 DP88
Romsey Cl, Orp. 223 EP105
Romsey Cl, Slou. 153 AZ76
Romsey Dr (Farnham Common), Slou. 111 AR62
Romsey Gdns, Dag. 146 EX67
Romsey Rd W13 137 CG73
Romsey Rd, Dag. 146 EX67
Ron Leighton Way E6 144 EL67
Rona Rd NW3 120 DG63
Rona Wk N1 142 DR65
Clephane Rd
Ronald Av E15 144 EE69
Ronald Cl, Beck. 203 DZ98
Ronald Ct, St.Alb. 60 BY29
Ronald Ho SE3 164 EJ84
Cambert Way
Ronald Rd, Beac. 89 AM53
Ronald Rd, Rom. 106 FN53
Ronald St E1 142 DW72
Devonport St
Ronalds Rd N5 121 DN64
Ronalds Rd, Brom. 204 EG95
Ronaldsay Spur, Slou. 132 AS71
Ronaldstone Rd, Sid. 185 ES86
Ronart St (Wealdstone), Har. 117 CF55
Stuart Rd
Rondu Rd NW2 119 CY64
Ronelean Rd, Surb. 198 CM104
Roneo Cor, Horn. 127 FF60
Roneo Link, Horn. 127 FF60
Ronfearn Av, Orp. 206 EX99
Ronneby Cl, Wey. 195 BS104
Ronson Way, Lthd. 231 CG121
Randalls Rd
Ronsons Way, St.Alb. 43 CF17
Ronver Rd SE12 184 EF87
Rood La EC3 275 M10
Rood La EC3 142 DS73
Rook Cl, Horn. 147 FG66
Rook La, Cat. 235 DM124
Rook Rd (Wooburn Grn), H.Wyc. 110 AD59
Rook Wk E6 144 EL72
Allhallows Rd
Rookby Ct N21 99 DP47
Carpenter Gdns
Rookdean (Chipstead), Sev. 256 FC122
Rooke Way SE10 164 EF78
Rookeries Cl, Felt. 175 BV90
Rookery, The (Westcott), Dor. 262 CA138
Rookery, The, Grays 169 FU79
Rookery Cl NW9 119 CT57
Rookery Cl (Fetcham), Lthd. 231 CE124
Rookery Ct, Grays 169 FU79
Rookery Cres, Dag. 147 FB66
Rookery Dr, Chis. 205 EN95
Rookery Dr (Westcott), Dor. 262 CA138
Rookery Gdns, Orp. 206 EW99
Rookery Hill, Ash. 232 CN118
Rookery Hill (Outwood), Red. 269 DN145
Rookery La, Brom. 204 EK100
Rookery La, Grays 170 GD78
Rookery La, Horl. 269 DN146
Rookery Rd SW4 161 DJ84
Rookery Rd, Orp. 223 EM110
Rookery Rd, Stai. 174 BH92
Rookery Vw, Grays 170 GD78
Rookery Way NW9 119 CT57
Rookery Way (Lower Kingswood), Tad. 249 CZ127
Rookes All, Hert. 32 DR09
Mangrove Rd
Rookesley Rd, Orp. 206 EX101
Rookfield Av N10 121 DJ56
Rookfield Cl N10 121 DJ56
Cranmore Way
Rookley Cl, Sutt. 218 DB110
Rooks Cl, Welw.G.C. 29 CX10
Rooks Hill, Rick. 74 BK42
Rooks Hill, Welw.G.C. 29 CW10
Rooksmead Rd, Sun. 195 BT96
Rookstone Rd SW17 180 DF92
Rookwood Av, Loug. 85 EQ41
Rookwood Av, N.Mal. 199 CU98
Rookwood Av, Wall. 219 DK105
Rookwood Cl, Grays 170 GB77
Rookwood Cl, Red. 251 DH129
Rookwood Ct, Guil. 258 AW137
Rookwood Gdns E4 102 EF46
Whitehall Rd
Rookwood Gdns, Loug. 85 EQ41
Rookwood Ho, Bark. 145 ER68
St. Marys
Rookwood Rd N16 122 DT59
Roosevelt Way, Dag. 147 FD65
Rootes Dr W10 139 CX70
Roothill La, Bet. 264 CN140
Rope St SE16 163 DY77
Rope Wk, Sun. 196 BW97
Rope Wk Gdns E1 142 DU72
Commercial Rd
Rope Yd Rails SE18 165 EP76
Ropemaker Rd SE16 163 DY76
Ropemaker St EC2 275 K6
Ropemaker St EC2 142 DR71
Ropemakers Flds E14 143 DZ73
Narrow St
Roper La SE1 279 N5
Roper St SE9 185 EM86
Roper Way, Mitch. 200 DG96
Ropers Av E4 101 EC50
Ropers Wk SW2 181 DN87
Brockwell Pk Gdns
Ropery St E3 143 DZ70
Ropewalk Ms E8 142 DT66
Middleton Rd
Ropley St E2 142 DU68
Rosa Alba Ms N5 122 DQ63
Kelross Rd
Rosa Av, Ashf. 174 BN91
Rosaline Rd SW6 159 CY80
Rosamond St SE26 182 DV90
Rosamun St, Sthl. 156 BY77
Rosamund Cl, S.Croy. 220 DR105
Rosary, The, Egh. 193 BD96
Rosary Cl, Houns. 156 BY82
Rosary Ct, Pot.B. 64 DB30
Rosary Gdns SW7 160 DC77
Rosary Gdns, Ashf. 175 BP91
Rosary Gdns, Bushey 95 CE45
Rosaville Rd SW6 159 CZ80
Roscoe St EC1 275 J5
Roscoff Cl, Edg. 96 CQ53
Rose All SE1 279 J2
Rose All SE1 142 DQ74
Rose & Crown Ct EC2 275 H8
Rose & Crown Yd SW1 277 L2
Rose Av E18 102 EH54
Rose Av, Grav. 191 GL88
Rose Av, Mitch. 200 DF95
Rose Av, Mord. 200 DC99
Rose Bk, Brwd. 108 FX48
Rose Bk Cotts, Wok. 226 AY122
Rose Bates Dr NW9 118 CN56
Rose Bushes, Epsom 233 CV116
Rose Ct E1 142 DS71
Sandy's Row
Rose Ct SE26 182 DV89
Rose Ct, Pnr. 116 BW55
Nursery Rd
Rose Ct, Wal.Cr. 66 DU27
Rose Dale, Orp. 205 EP103
Rose Dr, Chesh. 54 AS32
Rose End, Wor.Pk. 199 CX102
Rose Gdn Cl, Edg. 96 CL51
Rose Gdns W5 157 CK76
Rose Gdns, Felt. 175 BU89
Rose Gdns, Sthl. 136 CA70
Rose Gdns (Stanwell), Stai. 174 BK87
Diamedes Av
Rose Gdns, Wat. 75 BU43
Rose Glen NW9 118 CR56
Rose Glen, Rom. 127 FE60
Rose Hill, Dor. 263 CH136
Rose Hill (Burnham), Slou. 130 AG66
Rose Hill, Sutt. 200 DB103
Rose La, Rom. 126 EX55
Rose La (Ripley), Wok. 228 BJ121
Rose Lawn, Bushey 94 CC46
Rose Pk Cl, Hayes 136 BW70
Rose Sq SW3 276 A10
Rose Sq SW3 160 DD78
Rose St WC2 273 P10
Rose St (Northfleet), Grav. 190 GB86
Rose Vale, Hodd. 49 EA17
Rose Valley, Brwd. 108 FW48
Rose Vil, Dart. 188 FP87
Rose Wk, Pur. 219 DK111
Rose Wk, St.Alb. 43 CJ18
Rose Wk, Slou. 131 AP71
Birch Gro
Rose Wk, Surb. 198 CP99
Rose Wk, W.Wick. 203 ED103
Rose Wk, The, Rad. 77 CH37
Rose Way SE12 184 EG85
Rose Way, Edg. 96 CQ49
Roseacre, Oxt. 254 EG134
Roseacre Cl W13 137 CH71
Middlefielde
Roseacre Cl, Horn. 128 FM60
Roseacre Cl, Shep. 194 BN99
Roseacre Gdns (Chilworth), Guil. 259 BF140
Roseacre Gdns, Welw.G.C. 30 DC09
Roseacre Rd, Well. 166 EV83
Roseary Cl, West Dr. 154 BK77
Rosebank SE20 182 DV94
Rosebank, Epsom 216 CQ114
Rosebank, Wal.Abb. 68 EE33
Rosebank Av, Horn. 128 FJ64
Rosebank Av, Wem. 117 CF63
Rosebank Cl N12 98 DE50
Rosebank Cl, Tedd. 177 CG93
Rosebank Gdns E3 143 DZ68
Rosebank Gdns (Northfleet), Grav. 190 GE88
Rosebank Gro E17 123 DZ55
Rosebank Rd E17 123 EB58
Rosebank Rd W7 157 CE75
Rosebank Vil E17 123 EA56
Rosebank Wk NW1 141 DK66
Maiden La
Rosebank Wk SE18 164 EL77
Woodhill
Rosebank Way W3 138 CR72
Roseberry Cl, Upmin. 129 FT58
Roseberry Ct, Wat. 75 BU39
Grandfield Av
Roseberry Gdns N4 121 DP58
Roseberry Gdns, Dart. 188 FJ87
Roseberry Gdns, Orp. 205 ES104
Roseberry Gdns, Upmin. 129 FT59
Roseberry Pl E8 142 DT65
Roseberry St SE16 162 DV77
Rosebery Av E12 144 EL65
Rosebery Av EC1 274 D5
Rosebery Av EC1 141 DN70
Rosebery Av N17 100 DU54
Rosebery Av, Epsom 216 CS114
Rosebery Av, Har. 116 BZ63
Rosebery Av, N.Mal. 199 CT96
Rosebery Av, Sid. 185 ES87
Rosebery Av, Th.Hth. 202 DQ96
Rosebery Cl, Mord. 199 CX100
Rosebery Ct EC1 141 DN70
Rosebery Av
Rosebery Ct (Northfleet), Grav. 191 GF88
Rosebery Cres, Wok. 227 AZ121
Rosebery Gdns N8 121 DL57
Rosebery Gdns W13 137 CG72
Rosebery Gdns, Sutt. 218 DB105
Rosebery Ms N10 99 DJ54
Rosebery Ms SW2 181 DL86
Rosebery Rd
Rosebery Rd N9 100 DU48
Rosebery Rd N10 99 DJ54
Rosebery Rd SW2 181 DL86
Rosebery Rd, Bushey 94 CB45
Rosebery Rd, Epsom 232 CR119
Rosebery Rd, Grays 170 FY79
Rosebery Rd, Houns. 176 CC85
Rosebery Rd, Kings.T. 198 CP96
Rosebery Rd, Sutt. 217 CZ107
Rosebery Sq EC1 274 D5
Rosebery Sq, Kings.T. 198 CN96
Rosebine Av, Twick. 177 CD87
Rosebriar Cl, Wok. 228 BG116
Rosebriar Wk, Wat. 75 BT36
Rosebriars, Cat. 236 DS120
Rosebriars, Esher 214 CC106
Rosebury Rd SW6 160 DB82
Rosebury Sq, Wdf.Grn. 103 EN52
Rosebury Vale, Ruis. 115 BT60
Rosecourt Rd, Croy. 201 DM100
Rosecroft Av NW3 120 DA62
Rosecroft Cl, Orp. 206 EW100
Rosecroft Cl (Biggin Hill), West. 239 EM118
Lotus Rd
Rosecroft Dr, Wat. 75 BS36
Rosecroft Gdns NW2 119 CU62
Rosecroft Gdns, Twick. 177 CD88
Rosecroft Rd, Sthl. 136 CA70
Rosecroft Wk, Pnr. 116 BX57
Rosecroft Wk, Wem. 117 CK64
Rosedale, Ash. 231 CJ118
Rosedale, Cat. 236 DS123
Rosedale, Welw.G.C. 29 CZ05
Rosedale Av, Hayes 135 BR71
Rosedale Av (Cheshunt), Wal.Cr. 66 DT29
Rosedale Cl SE2 166 EV76
Finchale Rd
Rosedale Cl W7 157 CF75
Boston Rd
Rosedale Cl, Dart. 188 FP87
Rosedale Cl (Bricket Wd), St.Alb. 60 BY30
Rosedale Cl, Stan. 95 CH51
Rosedale Ct N5 121 DP63
Rosedale Gdns, Dag. 146 EV66
Rosedale Pl, Croy. 203 DX101
Rosedale Rd E7 124 EJ64
Rosedale Rd, Dag. 146 EV66
Rosedale Rd, Epsom 217 CU106
Rosedale Rd, Grays 170 GD78
Rosedale Rd, Rich. 158 CL84
Rosedale Rd, Rom. 105 FC54
Rosedale Ter W6 159 CV76
Dalling Rd
Rosedale Way (Cheshunt), Wal.Cr. 66 DU29
Rosedene NW6 139 CX67
Christchurch Av
Rosedene Av SW16 181 DM90
Rosedene Av, Croy. 201 DM101
Rosedene Av, Grnf. 136 CA69
Rosedene Av, Mord. 200 DA99
Rosedene Ct, Dart. 188 FJ87
Shepherds La
Rosedene Ct, Ruis. 115 BS60
Rosedene Gdns, Ilf. 125 EN56
Rosedene Ter E10 123 EB61
Rosedew Rd W6 159 CX79
Rosefield, Sev. 256 FG124
Rosefield Cl, Cars. 218 DE106
Rosefield Gdns E14 143 EA73
Rosefield Gdns (Ottershaw), Cher. 211 BD107
Rosefield Rd, Stai. 174 BG91
Roseford Ct W12 159 CX75
Rosehart Ms W11 140 DA72
Westbourne Gro
Rosehatch Av, Rom. 126 EX55
Roseheath, Hem.H. 39 BE19
Roseheath Rd, Houns. 176 BZ85
Rosehill (Claygate), Esher 215 CG107
Rosehill, Hmptn. 196 CA95
Rosehill Av, Sutt. 200 DC102
Rosehill Av, Wok. 226 AW116
Rosehill Cl, Hodd. 49 DZ17
Rosehill Ct, Hem.H. 40 BG22
Green End Rd
Rosehill Ct, Slou. 152 AU76
Yew Tree Rd
Rosehill Fm Meadow, Bans. 234 DB115
The Tracery
Rosehill Gdns, Abb.L. 59 BQ32
Rosehill Gdns, Grnf. 117 CF64
Rosehill Gdns, Sutt. 200 DB103
Rosehill Pk W, Sutt. 200 DC102
Rosehill Rd SW18 180 DC86
Rosehill Rd (Biggin Hill), West. 238 EJ117
Roseland Cl N17 100 DR52
Cavell Rd
Roselands Av, Hodd. 49 DZ15
Roseleigh Av N5 121 DP63
Roseleigh Cl, Twick. 177 CK86
Roseley Cotts, Harl. 35 EP11
Rosemary Av N3 98 DB54
Rosemary Av N9 100 DV46
Rosemary Av, Enf. 82 DR39
Rosemary Av, Houns. 156 BX82
Rosemary Av, Rom. 127 FF55
Rosemary Av, W.Mol. 196 CA97
Rosemary Cl, Croy. 201 DL100
Rosemary Cl, Harl. 36 EW11
Rosemary Cl, Oxt. 254 EG133
Rosemary Cl, S.Ock. 149 FW69
Rosemary Cl, Uxb. 134 BN71
Rosemary Ct, Horl. 268 DE147
Rosemary Cres, Guil. 242 AT130
Rosemary Dr E14 143 ED72
Rosemary Dr, Ilf. 124 EK57
Rosemary Gdns SW14 158 CQ83
Rosemary La
Rosemary Gdns, Chess. 216 CL105
Rosemary Gdns, Dag. 126 EZ60
Rosemary La SW14 158 CQ83
Rosemary La, Egh. 193 BB97
Rosemary La, Horl. 269 DH149
Rosemary Rd SE15 162 DT80
Rosemary Rd SW17 180 DC90
Rosemary Rd, Well. 165 ET81
Rosemary St N1 142 DR67
Shepperton Rd
Rosemead NW9 119 CT59
Rosemead, Cher. 194 BH101
Rosemead, Pot.B. 64 DC30
Rosemead Av, Felt. 175 BT89
Rosemead Av, Mitch. 201 DJ96
Rosemead Av, Wem. 118 CL64
Rosemead Cl, Red. 266 DD136
Rosemead Gdns, Brwd. 109 GD42
Rosemont Av N12 98 DC51
Rosemont Rd NW3 140 DC65
Rosemont Rd W3 138 CP73
Rosemont Rd, N.Mal. 198 CQ97
Rosemont Rd, Rich. 178 CL86
Rosemont Rd, Wem. 138 CL67
Rosemoor St SW3 276 D9
Rosemoor St SW3 160 DF77
Rosemount, Harl. 51 EP18
Rosemount Av, W.Byf. 212 BG113
Rosemount Cl, Wdf.Grn. 103 EM51
Chapelmount Rd
Rosemount Dr, Brom. 205 EM98
Rosemount Pt SE23 183 DX90
Dacres Rd
Rosemount Rd W13 137 CG72
Rosenau Cres SW11 160 DE81
Rosenau Rd SW11 160 DE81
Rosendale Rd SE21 182 DQ87
Rosendale Rd SE24 182 DQ87
Roseneath Av N21 99 DP46

Roseneath Cl, Orp. 224 EW108
Roseneath Rd SW11 180 DG86
Roseneath Wk, Enf. 82 DS42
Rosens Wk, Edg. 96 CP48
Rosenthal Rd SE6 183 EB86
Rosenthorpe Rd SE15 183 DX85
Rosepark Ct, Ilf. 103 EN54
Roseton St E14 163 EC75
Rosery, The, Croy. 203 DX100
Roses, The, Wdf.Grn. 102 EF52
Roses La, Wind. 151 AL82
Rosethorn Cl SW12 181 DJ87
Rosetrees, Guil. 259 BA135
Rosetta Cl SW8 161 DL80
Rosetti Ter, Dag. 126 EV63
Marlborough Rd
Roseveare Rd SE12 184 EJ91
Roseville Av, Houns. 176 CA85
Roseville Rd, Hayes 155 BU78
Rosevine Rd SW20 199 CW95
Rosewarne Cl, Wok. 226 AU118
Muirfield Rd
Roseway SE21 182 DR86
Rosewell Cl SE20 182 DV94
Rosewood, Dart. 187 FE91
Rosewood, Esher 197 CG103
Rosewood, Sutt. 218 DC110
Rosewood, Wok. 227 BA119
Rosewood Av, Grnf. 117 CG64
Rosewood Av, Horn. 127 FG64
Rosewood Cl, Sid. 186 EW90
Rosewood Ct, Brom. 204 EJ95
Rosewood Ct, Hem.H. 39 BE19
Rosewood Ct, Rom. 126 EW57
Rosewood Dr, Enf. 81 DN35
Rosewood Dr, Shep. 194 BM99
Rosewood Gdns SE13 163 EC82
Lewisham Rd
Rosewood Gro, Sutt. 200 DC103
Rosewood Sq W12 139 CU72
Primula St
Rosewood Ter SE20 182 DW94
Laurel Gro
Rosewood Way (Farnham Common), Slou. 111 AQ64
Rosher Cl E15 143 ED66
Rosherville Way, Grav. 190 GE87
Rosina St E9 123 DX64
Roskell Rd SW15 159 CX83
Rosken Gro (Farnham Royal), Slou. 131 AP68
Roslin Rd W3 158 CP76
Roslin Way, Brom. 184 EG92
Roslyn Cl, Brox. 49 DY21
Roslyn Cl, Mitch. 200 DD96
Roslyn Ct, Wok. 226 AU118
St. John's Rd
Roslyn Gdns, Rom. 105 FF54
Roslyn Rd N15 122 DR57
Rosmead Rd W11 139 CY73
Rosoman Pl EC1 274 E4
Rosoman St EC1 274 E3
Rosoman St EC1 141 DN69
Ross Av NW7 97 CY50
Ross Av, Dag. 126 EZ61
Ross Cl, Har. 94 CC52
Ross Cl, Hat. 45 CU15
Homestead Rd
Ross Cl, Hayes 155 BR77
Ross Ct SW15 179 CX87
Ross Cres, Wat. 75 BU35
Ross Par, Wall. 219 DH107
Ross Rd SE25 202 DR97
Ross Rd, Cob. 214 BW113
Ross Rd, Dart. 187 FG86
Ross Rd, Twick. 176 CB88
Ross Rd, Wall. 219 DJ106
Ross Way SE9 164 EL83
Ross Way, Nthwd. 93 BT49
Rossall Cl, Horn. 127 FG58
Rossall Cres NW10 138 CM69
Rossdale, Sutt. 218 DE106
Rossdale Dr N9 82 DW44
Rossdale Dr NW9 118 CQ60
Rossdale Rd SW15 159 CW84
Rosse Ms SE3 164 EH81
Rossendale St E5 122 DV61
Rossendale Way NW1 141 DJ66
Rossetti Gdns, Couls. 235 DM118
Rossetti Rd SE16 162 DV78
Rossgate, Hem.H. 40 BG18
Galley Hill
Rossignol Gdns, Cars. 200 DG103
Rossindel Rd, Houns. 176 CA85
Rossington Av, Borwd. 78 CL38
Rossington Cl, Enf. 82 DV38
Rossington St E5 122 DU61
Rossiter Cl, Slou. 152 AY77
Rossiter Flds, Barn. 79 CY44
Rossiter Rd SW12 181 DH88
Rossland Cl, Bexh. 187 FB85
Rosslare Cl, West. 255 ER125
Rosslyn Av E4 102 EF47
Rosslyn Av SW13 158 CS83
Rosslyn Av, Barn. 80 DE44
Rosslyn Av, Dag. 126 EZ59
Rosslyn Av, Felt. 175 BU86
Rosslyn Av, Rom. 106 FM54
Rosslyn Cl, Hayes 135 BR71
Morgans La
Rosslyn Cl, Sun. 175 BS93
Cadbury Rd
Rosslyn Cl, W.Wick. 204 EF104
Rosslyn Cres, Har. 117 CF57
Rosslyn Cres, Wem. 118 CL63
Rosslyn Gdns, Wem. 118 CL62
Rosslyn Cres
Rosslyn Hill NW3 120 DD63
Rosslyn Ms NW3 120 DD63
Rosslyn Hill
Rosslyn Pk, Wey. 213 BR105
Rosslyn Pk Ms NW3 120 DD64
Lyndhurst Rd
Rosslyn Rd E17 123 EC56
Rosslyn Rd, Bark. 145 ER66
Rosslyn Rd, Twick. 177 CJ86
Rosslyn Rd, Wat. 75 BV41
Rossmore Ct NW1 272 D4
Rossmore Rd NW1 272 C5
Rossmore Rd NW1 140 DE70
Rossway Dr, Bushey 76 CC43
Rosswood Gdns, Wall. 219 DJ107
Rostella Rd SW17 180 DD91
Rostrevor Av N15 122 DT58
Rostrevor Gdns, Hayes 135 BS74
Rostrevor Gdns, Iver 133 BD68
Rostrevor Gdns, Sthl. 156 BY78
Rostrevor Ms SW6 159 CZ81
Rostrevor Rd SW6 159 CZ81
Rostrevor Rd SW19 180 DA92
Roswell Cl (Cheshunt), Wal.Cr. 67 DY30
Rotary St SE1 278 F6
Roth Dr, Brwd. 109 GB47
Roth Wk N7 121 DM62
Durham Rd
Rothbury Av, Rain. 147 FH71
Rothbury Gdns, Islw. 157 CG80
Rothbury Rd E9 143 DZ66
Rothbury Wk N17 100 DU52
Rother Cl, Wat. 60 BW34
Rotherfield Rd, Cars. 218 DG105
Rotherfield Rd, Enf. 83 DX37
Rotherfield St N1 142 DQ66
Rotherham Wk SE1 278 F3
Rotherhill Av SW16 181 DK93
Rotherhithe New Rd SE16 162 DU78
Rotherhithe Old Rd SE16 163 DX77
Rotherhithe St SE16 162 DW75
Rotherhithe Tunnel E1 142 DW74
Rotherhithe Tunnel App E14 162 DW75
Rotherhithe Tunnel App SE16 162 DW75
Rothermere Rd, Croy. 219 DM106
Rothervale, Horl. 268 DF145
Rotherwick Hill W5 138 CM70
Rotherwick Rd NW11 120 DA59
Rotherwood Cl SW20 199 CY95
Rotherwood Rd SW15 159 CX83
Rothery St N1 141 DP67
Gaskin St
Rothery Ter SW9 161 DP80
Rothes Rd, Dor. 263 CH135
Rothesay Av SW20 199 CY96
Rothesay Av, Grnf. 137 CD65
Rothesay Av, Rich. 158 CP84
Rothesay Rd SE25 202 DS98
Rothsay Rd E7 144 EJ65
Rothsay St SE1 279 M6
Rothsay St SE1 162 DS76
Rothsay Wk E14 163 EA77
Charnwood Gdns
Rothschild Rd W4 158 CQ77
Rothschild St SE27 181 DP91
Rothwell Gdns, Dag. 146 EW66
Rothwell Rd, Dag. 146 EW67
Rothwell St NW1 140 DF67
Rotten Row SW1 276 F4
Rotten Row SW1 160 DF75
Rotten Row SW7 276 B4
Rotten Row SW7 160 DE75
Rotterdam Dr E14 163 EC76
Rouel Rd SE16 162 DU76
Rouge La, Grav. 191 GH88
Rougemont Av, Mord. 200 DA100
Rough Rew, Dor. 263 CH139
Roughdown Av, Hem.H. 40 BG23
Roughdown Rd, Hem.H. 40 BH23
Roughdown Vil Rd, Hem.H. 40 BG23
Roughetts La, Gdse. 252 DS129
Roughetts La, Red. 252 DS129
Roughlands, Wok. 227 BE115
Roughs, The, Nthwd. 93 BT48
Roughtallys, Epp. 70 EZ27
Roughwood Cl, Wat. 75 BS38
Roughwood La, Ch.St.G. 90 AY45
Round Gro, Croy. 203 DX101
Round Hill SE26 182 DW89
Round Oak Rd, Wey. 212 BM105
Roundacre SW19 179 CX89
Inner Pk Rd
Roundaway Rd, Ilf. 103 EM54
Roundcroft (Cheshunt), Wal.Cr. 66 DT26
Roundel Cl SE4 163 DZ84
Adelaide Av
Roundhay Cl SE23 183 DX89
Roundheads End (Forty Grn), Beac. 88 AH51
Roundhedge Way, Enf. 81 DM38
Roundhill, Wok. 227 BB119
Roundhill Dr, Enf. 81 DM42
Roundhill Dr, Wok. 227 BB118
Roundhill Way, Cob. 214 CB111
Roundhill Way, Guil. 242 AT134
Roundhills, Wal.Abb. 68 EE34
Roundings, The, Hert. 32 DV14
Roundlyn Gdns (St. Mary Cray), Orp. 206 EV98
Lynmouth Ri
Roundmead Av, Loug. 85 EN41
Roundmead Cl, Loug. 85 EN41
Roundmoor Dr (Cheshunt), Wal.Cr. 67 DY29
Roundshaw Cen, Wall. 219 DL108
Meteor Way
Roundtable Rd, Brom. 184 EF90
Roundthorn Way, Wok. 226 AT116
Roundtree Rd, Wem. 117 CH64
Roundway, Egh. 173 BC92
Roundway (Biggin Hill), West. 238 EK116
Norheads La
Roundway, The N17 100 DQ53
Roundway, The (Claygate), Esher 215 CF106
Roundway, The, Wat. 75 BT44
Roundways, Ruis. 115 BT62
Roundwood, Chis. 205 EP96
Roundwood, Kings L. 58 BL26
Roundwood Av, Brwd. 109 GA46
Roundwood Av, Uxb. 135 BQ74
Roundwood Cl, Ruis. 115 BR59
Roundwood Dr, Welw.G.C. 29 CW07
Roundwood Gro, Brwd. 109 GB45
Roundwood Lake, Brwd. 109 GB46
Roundwood Rd NW10 139 CT65
Roundwood Rd, Amer. 55 AS38
Roundwood Vw, Bans. 233 CX115
Roundwood Way, Bans. 233 CX115
Rounton Rd E3 143 EA70
Rounton Rd, Wal.Abb. 68 EE33
Roupell Rd SW2 181 DM88
Roupell St SE1 278 E3
Roupell St SE1 141 DN74
Rous Rd, Buck.H. 102 EL46
Rousden St NW1 141 DJ66
Rouse Gdns SE21 182 DS91
Rousebarn La, Rick. 75 BQ41
Routemaster Cl E13 144 EH69
Routh Ct, Felt. 175 BS88
Loxwood Cl
Routh Rd SW18 180 DE87
Routh St E6 145 EM71
Routledge Cl N19 121 DK60
Rover Av, Ilf. 103 ET51
Row Hill, Add. 211 BF107
Rowallan Rd SW6 159 CY80
Rowan Av E4 101 DZ51
Rowan Av, Egh. 173 BC92
Rowan Cl SW16 201 DJ95
Rowan Cl W5 158 CL75
Rowan Cl, Beac. 88 AH54
Rowan Cl, Guil. 242 AV131
Rowan Cl, Ilf. 125 ER64
Rowan Cl, N.Mal. 198 CS96
Rowan Cl (Shenley), Rad. 62 CL33
Juniper Gdns
Rowan Cl, Reig. 266 DC136
Rowan Cl, St.Alb. 44 CL20
Rowan Cl (Bricket Wd), St.Alb. 60 CA31
Rowan Cl, Stan. 95 CF51
Woodlands Dr
Rowan Cl, Wem. 117 CG62
Rowan Ct, Borwd. 78 CL39
Theobald St
Rowan Cres SW16 201 DJ95
Rowan Cres, Dart. 188 FJ88
Rowan Dr NW9 119 CU56
Rowan Dr, Brox. 67 DZ25
Rowan Gdns, Croy. 202 DT104
Radcliffe Rd
Rowan Gdns, Iver 133 BD68
Rowan Grn, Wey. 213 BR105
Rowan Grn E, Brwd. 109 FZ48
Rowan Grn W, Brwd. 109 FZ49
Rowan Gro, Couls. 235 DH121
Rowan Pl, Amer. 72 AT38
Rowan Pl, Hayes 135 BT73
West Av
Rowan Rd SW16 201 DJ96
Rowan Rd W6 159 CX77
Rowan Rd, Bexh. 166 EY83
Rowan Rd, Brent. 157 CH80
Rowan Rd, Swan. 207 FD97
Rowan Rd, West Dr. 154 BK77
Rowan Ter SE20 202 DU95
Sycamore Gro
Rowan Ter W6 159 CX77
Bute Gdns
Rowan Wk N2 120 DC58
Rowan Wk N19 121 DJ61
Bredgar Rd
Rowan Wk W10 139 CY70
Droop St
Rowan Wk, Barn. 80 DB43
Station Rd
Rowan Wk, Brom. 205 EM104
Rowan Wk, Hat. 45 CU21
Rowan Wk, Horn. 128 FK56
Rowan Way, Rom. 126 EW55
Rowan Way, Slou. 131 AP71
Rowan Way, S.Ock. 149 FX70
Rowanhurst Dr (Farnham Common), Slou. 111 AQ64
Rowans, Welw.G.C. 30 DA06
Rowans, The N13 99 DP48
Rowans, The (Chalfont St. Peter), Ger.Cr. 112 AW55
Rowans, The, Hem.H. 40 BG20
Rowans, The, S.Ock. 148 FQ74
Purfleet Rd
Rowans, The, Sun. 175 BT92
Rowans, The, Wok. 226 AY118
Rowans Cl, Long. 209 FX96
Rowans Way, Loug. 85 EM42
Rowantree Cl N21 100 DR46
Rowantree Rd N21 100 DR46
Rowantree Rd, Enf. 81 DP40
Rowanwood Av, Sid. 186 EU88
Rowanwood Ms, Enf. 81 DP40
Rowantree Rd
Rowbarns Way (East Horsley), Lthd. 245 BT130
Rowben Cl N20 98 DB46
Rowberry Cl SW6 159 CW80
Rowbury, Gdmg. 258 AU143
Rowcroft, Hem.H. 39 BE21
Rowcross St SE1 279 P10
Rowcross St SE1 162 DT78
Rowdell Rd, Nthlt. 136 CA67
Rowden Pk Gdns E4 101 EA51
Rowden Rd
Rowden Rd E4 101 EA51
Rowden Rd, Beck. 203 DY95
Rowden Rd, Epsom 216 CP105
Rowditch La SW11 160 DG82
Rowdon Av NW10 139 CV66
Rowdown Cres (New Addington), Croy. 221 ED109
Rowdowns Rd, Dag. 146 EZ67
Rowe Gdns, Bark. 145 ET68
Rowe La E9 122 DW64
Rowe Wk, Har. 116 CA62
Rowena Cres SW11 160 DE82
Rowfant Rd SW17 180 DG88
Rowhedge, Brwd. 109 GA48
Rowhill Rd E5 122 DV63
Rowhill Rd, Dart. 187 FF93
Rowhill Rd, Swan. 187 FF93
Rowhurst Av, Add. 212 BH107
Rowhurst Av, Lthd. 231 CF117
Rowington Cl W2 140 DB71
Rowland Av, Har. 117 CJ55
Rowland Cl, Wind. 151 AK83
Rowland Ct E16 144 EF70
Rowland Cres, Chig. 103 ES49
Rowland Gro SE26 182 DV90
Dallas Rd
Rowland Hill Av N17 100 DQ52
Rowland Hill St NW3 120 DE64
Rowland Wk (Havering-atte-Bower), Rom. 105 FE48
Rowland Way SW19 200 DB95
Hayward Cl
Rowland Way, Ashf. 175 BQ94
Littleton Rd
Rowlands Av, Pnr. 94 CA51
Rowlands Cl N6 120 DG58
North Hill
Rowlands Cl NW7 97 CU52
Rowlands Cl (Cheshunt), Wal.Cr. 67 DX30
Rowlands Flds (Cheshunt), Wal.Cr. 67 DX29
Rowlands Rd, Dag. 126 EZ61
Rowlatt Cl, Dart. 188 FJ91
Rowlatt Dr, St.Alb. 42 CA22
Rowlatt Rd, Dart. 188 FJ91
Whitehead Cl
Rowley Av, Sid. 186 EV87
Rowley Cl, Wat. 76 BY44
Lower Paddock Rd
Rowley Cl, Wem. 138 CM66
Rowley Cl (Pyrford), Wok. 228 BG116
Rowley Ct, Cat. 236 DR122
Fairbourne La
Rowley Gdns N4 122 DQ59
Rowley Gdns (Cheshunt), Wal.Cr. 67 DX28
Warwick Dr
Rowley Grn Rd, Barn. 79 CT43
Rowley Ind Pk W3 158 CP76
Rowley La, Barn. 79 CT43
Rowley La, Borwd. 78 CR39
Rowley La (Wexham), Slou. 132 AW67
Rowley Mead, Epp. 70 EW25
Rowley Rd N15 122 DQ57
Rowley Wk, Hem.H. 41 BQ15
Bayford Cl
Rowley Way NW8 140 DB67
Rowleys Rd, Hert. 32 DT08
Rowlheys Pl, West Dr. 154 BL76
Rowlls Rd, Kings.T. 198 CM97
Rowmarsh Cl (Northfleet), Grav. 190 GD91
Rowney Gdns, Dag. 146 EW65
Rowney Gdns, Saw. 36 EW07
Rowney Rd, Dag. 146 EV65
Rowney Wd, Saw. 36 EW06
Rowntree Clifford Cl E13 144 EH69
Liddon Rd
Rowntree Path SE28 146 EV73
Booth Cl
Rowntree Rd, Twick. 177 CE88
Rows, The, Harl. 35 ER14
East Gate
Rowse Cl E15 143 EC66
Rowsley Av NW4 119 CW55
Rowstock Gdns N7 121 DK64
Rowton Rd SE18 165 EQ80
Rowtown, Add. 211 BF108
Rowzill Rd, Swan. 187 FF93
Roxborough Av, Har. 117 CD59
Roxborough Av, Islw. 157 CF80
Roxborough Pk, Har. 117 CE59
Roxborough Rd, Har. 117 CD57
Roxbourne Cl, Nthlt. 136 BX65
Roxburgh Av, Upmin. 128 FQ62
Roxburgh Rd SE27 181 DP92
Roxburn Way, Ruis. 115 BT62
Roxby Pl SW6 160 DA79
Roxeth Ct, Ashf. 174 BN92
Roxeth Grn Av, Har. 116 CB62
Roxeth Gro, Har. 116 CB63
Roxeth Hill, Har. 117 CD61
Roxford Cl, Shep. 195 BS99
Roxley Rd SE13 183 EB86
Roxton Gdns, Croy. 221 EA106
Roxwell Cl, Slou. 131 AL74
Roxwell Gdns, Brwd. 109 GC43
Roxwell Rd W12 159 CU75
Roxwell Rd, Bark. 146 EU68
Roxwell Trd Pk E10 123 DY59
Roxwell Way, Wdf.Grn. 102 EJ52
Roxy Av, Rom. 126 EW59
Roy Gdns, Ilf. 125 ES56
Roy Gro, Hmptn. 176 CB93
Roy Rd, Nthwd. 93 BT52
Roy Sq E14 143 DY73
Narrow St
Royal Albert Dock E16 145 EM73
Royal Albert Roundabout E16 144 EL73
Royal Albert Way
Royal Albert Way E16 144 EK73
Royal Arc W1 277 K1
Royal Artillery Barracks SE18 165 EN78
Repository Rd
Royal Av SW3 276 D10
Royal Av SW3 160 DF78
Royal Av, Wal.Cr. 67 DY33
Royal Av, Wor.Pk. 198 CS103
Royal Circ SE27 181 DN90
Royal Cl N16 122 DS60
Manor Rd
Royal Cl SE8 163 DZ79
Royal Cl SW19 179 CX89
Queensmere Rd
Royal Cl, Ilf. 126 EU59
Royal Cl, Orp. 223 EP105
Royal Cl, Uxb. 134 BM72
Royal Cl, Wor.Pk. 198 CS103
Royal Coll St NW1 141 DJ66
Royal Ct EC3 142 DR72
Cornhill
Royal Ct SE16 163 DZ76
Royal Ct, Hem.H. 40 BL23
Royal Cres W11 139 CX74
Royal Cres, Ruis. 116 BY63
Royal Cres Ms W11 139 CX74
Queensdale Rd
Royal Docks Rd E6 145 EP72
Royal Dr N11 98 DG50
Royal Dr, Epsom 233 CV118
Royal Duchess Ms SW12 181 DH87
Dinsmore Rd
Royal Earlswood Pk, Red. 266 DG138
Royal Ex EC3 275 L9
Royal Ex EC3 142 DR72
Royal Ex Av EC3 275 L9
Royal Ex Bldgs EC3 275 L9
Royal Ex Steps EC3 142 DR72
Cornhill
Royal Gdns W7 157 CG76
Royal Herbert Pavilions SE18 165 EM81
Royal Hill SE10 163 EC80
Royal Horticultural Society Cotts (Wisley), Wok. 228 BL116
Wisley La
Royal Hosp Rd SW3 160 DF79
Royal La, Uxb. 134 BM69
Royal La, West Dr. 134 BM72
Royal London Est, The N17 100 DV51
Royal Ms, The SW1 277 J6
Royal Ms, The SW1 161 DH76
Royal Mint Ct EC3 142 DT73
Royal Mint Pl E1 142 DT73
Blue Anchor Yd
Royal Mint St E1 142 DT73
Royal Mt Ct, Twick. 177 CE90
Royal Naval Pl SE14 163 DZ80
Royal Oak Ct N1 142 DS69
Pitfield St
Royal Oak Pl SE22 182 DV86
Royal Oak Rd E8 142 DV65
Royal Oak Rd, Bexh. 186 EZ85
Royal Oak Rd, Wok. 226 AW118
Royal Opera Arc SW1 277 M2
Royal Opera Arc SW1 141 DK74
Royal Orchard Cl SW18 179 CY87
Royal Par SE3 164 EE82
Royal Par SW6 159 CY80
Dawes Rd
Royal Par W5 138 CL69
Western Av
Royal Par, Chis. 185 EQ94
Royal Par, Rich. 158 CN81
Station App
Royal Par Ms SE3 164 EF82
Royal Par
Royal Par Ms, Chis. 185 EQ94
Royal Pier Ms, Grav. 191 GH86
Royal Pier Rd
Royal Pier Rd, Grav. 191 GH86
Royal Pl SE10 163 EC80
Royal Rd E16 144 EK72
Royal Rd SE17 161 DP79
Royal Rd (Darenth), Dart. 188 FN92
Royal Rd, St.Alb. 43 CH20
Royal Rd, Sid. 186 EX90
Royal Rd, Tedd. 177 CD92
Royal Route, Wem. 118 CM63
Royal St SE1 278 C6
Royal St SE1 161 DM76
Royal Victor Pl E3 143 DX68
Royal Victoria Dock E16 144 EH73
Royal Victoria Patriotic Building SW18 180 DD86
Fitzhugh Gro
Royal Victoria Pl E16 144 EH74
Wesley Av
Royal Victoria Sq E16 144 EH73
Mace Gateway
Royal Wk, Wall. 201 DH104
Prince Charles Way
Royale Leisure Pk W3 138 CN70
Royalty Ms W1 273 M9
Royce Cl, Brox. 49 DZ21
Roycraft Av, Bark. 145 ET68
Roycraft Cl, Bark. 145 ET68
Roycroft Cl E18 102 EH53
Roycroft Cl SW2 181 DN88
Roydene Rd SE18 165 ES79
Roydon Cl SW11 161 DH81
Reform St
Roydon Cl, Loug. 102 EL45
Roydon Ct, Walt. 213 BU105
Roydon Lo Chalet Est, Harl. 34 EJ14
Roydon Mill Pk, Harl. 34 EG14
Roydon Rd, Harl. 34 EL14
Roydon Rd, Ware 34 EE11
Roydon St SW11 161 DH81
Southolm St
Roydonbury Ind Est, Harl. 50 EL15
Royle Cl (Chalfont St. Peter), Ger.Cr. 91 AZ52
Royle Cl, Rom. 127 FH57
Royle Cres W13 137 CG70
Royston Av E4 101 EA50
Royston Av, Sutt. 200 DD104
Royston Av, Wall. 219 DK105
Royston Av (Byfleet), W.Byf. 212 BL112
Royston Cl, Hert. 31 DP09
Royston Cl, Houns. 155 BV81
Royston Cl, Walt. 195 BU102
Royston Ct SE24 182 DQ86
Burbage Rd
Royston Ct, Rich. 158 CM81
Lichfield Rd
Royston Ct, Surb. 198 CN104
Hook Ri N
Royston Gdns, Ilf. 124 EK58
Royston Gro, Pnr. 94 BZ51
Royston Par, Ilf. 124 EK58
Royston Pk Rd, Pnr. 94 BZ51
Royston Rd SE20 203 DX95
Royston Rd, Dart. 187 FF86
Royston Rd, Rich. 178 CL85
Royston Rd, Rom. 106 FN52
Royston Rd, St.Alb. 43 CH21
Royston Rd (Byfleet), W.Byf. 212 BL112
Royston St E2 142 DW68
Royston Way, Slou. 130 AJ71
Roystons, The, Surb. 198 CP99
Rozel Ct N1 142 DS67
Rozel Rd SW4 161 DJ82
Rubastic Rd, Sthl. 155 BV76
Rubens Rd, Nthlt. 136 BW68
Rubens St SE6 183 DZ89
Rubeus Pl SW4 161 DL84
Dolman St
Rubin Pl, Enf. 83 EA37
Government Row
Ruby Cl, Slou. 151 AN75
Mitchell Cl
Ruby Ms E17 123 EA55
Ruby Rd
Ruby Rd E17 123 EA55
Ruby St SE15 162 DV79
Ruby Triangle SE15 162 DV79
Sandgate St
Ruckholt Cl E10 123 EB62
Ruckholt Rd E10 123 EA63
Rucklers La, Kings L. 58 BK27
Ruckles Way, Amer. 55 AQ40
Rucklidge Av NW10 139 CT68
Rudall Cres NW3 120 DD63
Willoughby Rd
Ruddington Cl E5 123 DY63
Ruddlesway, Wind. 151 AK81
Ruddock Cl, Edg. 96 CQ52
Ruddstreet Cl SE18 165 EP77
Ruden Way, Epsom 233 CV116
Rudge Ri, Add. 211 BF106
Rudland Rd, Bexh. 167 FB83
Rudloe Rd SW12 181 DJ87
Rudolf Pl SW8 161 DL79
Miles St
Rudolph Ct SE22 182 DU87
Rudolph Rd E13 144 EF68
Rudolph Rd NW6 140 DA68
Rudolph Rd, Bushey 76 CA44
Rudsworth Cl (Colnbrook), Slou. 153 BD80
Rudyard Gro NW7 96 CQ51
Rue de St. Lawrence, Wal.Abb. 67 EC34
Quaker La
Ruffets Wd, Grav. 191 GJ93
Ruffetts, The, S.Croy. 220 DV108
Ruffetts Cl, S.Croy. 220 DV108
Ruffetts Way, Tad. 233 CY118
Ruffle Cl, West Dr. 154 BL75
Rufford Cl, Har. 117 CG58
Rufford Cl, Wat. 75 BT37
Rufford St N1 141 DL67
Rufford Twr W3 138 CP74
Rufus Cl, Ruis. 116 BY62
Rufus St N1 275 M3
Rugby Av N9 100 DT46
Rugby Av, Grnf. 137 CD65
Rugby Av, Wem. 117 CH64
Rugby Cl, Har. 117 CE57
Rugby Gdns, Dag. 146 EW65
Rugby La, Sutt. 217 CX109
Nonsuch Wk
Rugby Rd NW9 118 CP56
Rugby Rd W4 158 CS75
Rugby Rd, Dag. 146 EV66
Rugby Rd, Twick. 177 CE86
Rugby St WC1 274 B5
Rugby St WC1 141 DM70
Rugby Way, Rick. 75 BP43
Rugg St E14 143 EA73
Rugged La, Wal.Abb. 68 EK33
Ruggles-Brise Rd, Ashf. 174 BK92
Ruislip Cl, Grnf. 136 CB70
Ruislip Ct, Ruis. 115 BT61
Courtfield Gdns
Ruislip Rd, Grnf. 136 CA69
Ruislip Rd, Nthlt. 136 BX69
Ruislip Rd, Sthl. 136 CA69
Ruislip Rd E W7 137 CE70
Ruislip Rd E W13 137 CD70
Ruislip Rd E, Grnf. 136 CA69

Ruislip St SW17 180 DF91
Rum Cl E1 142 DW73
Rumania Wk, Grav. 191 GM90
Rumballs Cl, Hem.H. 40 BN23
Rumballs Rd, Hem.H. 40 BN23
Rumbold Rd SW6 160 DB80
Rumbold Rd, Hodd. 49 EC15
Rumsey Cl, Hmptn. 176 BZ93
Rumsey Ms N4 121 DP62
Monsell Rd
Rumsey Rd SW9 161 DM83
Rumsley, Wal.Cr. 66 DU27
Runbury Circle NW9 118 CR61
Runcie Cl, St.Alb. 43 CG16
Runciman Cl, Orp. 224 EW110
Runcorn Cl N17 122 DV56
Runcorn Cres, Hem.H. 40 BM16
Runcorn Pl W11 139 CY73
Rundell Cres NW4 119 CV57
Rundells, Harl. 52 EU19
Runes Cl, Mitch. 200 DD98
Runham Rd, Hem.H. 40 BL22
Runnel Fld, Har. 117 CE62
Runnemede Rd, Egh. 173 BA91
Running Horse Yd, Brent. 158 CL79
Pottery Rd
Running Waters, Brwd. 109 GA49
Runnymede SW19 200 DD95
Runnymede Cl, Twick. 176 CB86
Runnymede Ct, Croy. 202 DT103
Runnymede Ct, Egh. 173 BA91
Runnymede Cres SW16 201 DK95
Runnymede Gdns, Grnf. 137 CD68
Runnymede Gdns, Twick. 176 CB86
Runnymede Rd, Twick. 176 CB86
Runrig Hill, Amer. 55 AS35
Runsley, Welw.G.C. 29 CZ06
Runtley Wd La (Sutton Grn), Guil. 243 AZ125
Runway, The, Ruis. 115 BV64
Rupack St SE16 162 DW75
St. Marychurch St
Rupert Av, Wem. 118 CL64
Rupert Ct W1 273 M10
Rupert Ct, W.Mol. 196 CA98
St. Peter's Rd
Rupert Gdns SW9 161 DP82
Rupert Rd N19 121 DK62
Holloway Rd
Rupert Rd NW6 139 CZ68
Rupert Rd W4 158 CS76
Rupert Rd, Guil. 258 AV135
Rupert St W1 273 M10
Rupert St W1 141 DK73
Rural Cl, Horn. 127 FH60
Rural Vale (Northfleet), Grav. 190 GE87
Rural Way SW16 181 DH94
Rural Way, Red. 250 DG134
Ruscoe Dr, Wok. 227 BA117
Pembroke Rd
Ruscoe Rd E16 144 EF72
Ruscombe Dr (Park St), St.Alb. 60 CB26
Ruscombe Gdns (Datchet), Slou. 152 AU80
Ruscombe Way, Felt. 175 BT87
Rush, The SW19 199 CZ95
Kingston Rd
Rush Cl, Ware 33 EC11
Rush Common Ms SW2 181 DM87
Rush Cft, Gdmg. 258 AU143
Rush Dr, Wal.Abb. 83 EC36
Rush Grn Gdns, Rom. 127 FC60
Rush Grn Rd, Rom. 127 FC60
Rush Gro St SE18 165 EM77
Rush Hill Ms SW11 160 DG83
Rush Hill Rd
Rush Hill Rd SW11 160 DG83
Rusham Pk Av, Egh. 173 AZ93
Rusham Rd SW12 180 DF86
Rusham Rd, Egh. 173 AZ93
Rushbrook Cres E17 101 DZ53
Rushbrook Rd SE9 185 EQ89
Rushburn (Wooburn Grn), H.Wyc. 110 AF57
Rushcroft Rd E4 101 EA52
Rushcroft Rd SW2 161 DN84
Rushden Cl SE19 182 DR94
Rushden Gdns NW7 97 CW51
Rushden Gdns, Ilf. 125 EN55
Rushdene SE2 166 EX76
Rushdene Av, Barn. 98 DE45
Rushdene Cl, Nthlt. 136 BW69
Rushdene Cres, Nthlt. 136 BW69
Rushdene Rd, Brwd. 108 FW45
Rushdene Rd, Pnr. 116 BX58
Rushdene Wk (Biggin Hill), West. 238 EK117
Rushdon Cl, Grays 170 GA76
Rushdon Cl, Rom. 127 FG57
Rushen Dr, Hert. 32 DW12
Rushen Wk, Cars. 200 DD102
Paisley Rd
Rushes Mead, Harl. 51 ES17
Rushes Mead, Uxb. 134 BJ67
Frays Waye
Rushet Rd, Orp. 206 EU96
Rushett Cl, T.Ditt. 197 CH102
Rushett Dr, Dor. 263 CH139
Rushett La, Chess. 215 CJ111
Rushett La, Epsom 215 CJ111
Rushett Rd, T.Ditt. 197 CH101
Rushetts Rd, Reig. 266 DC138
Rushey Cl, N.Mal. 198 CR98
Rushey Grn SE6 183 EB87
Rushey Hill, Enf. 81 DM42
Rushey Mead SE4 183 EA85
Rushfield, Pot.B. 63 CX33
Rushfield, Saw. 36 EY05
Rushford Rd SE4 183 DZ86
Rushgrove Av NW9 119 CT57
Rushleigh Av (Cheshunt), Wal.Cr. 67 DX31
Rushley Cl, Kes. 222 EK105
Rushmead E2 142 DV69
Florida St
Rushmead, Rich. 177 CH90
Rushmead Cl, Croy. 220 DT105
Rushmere Av, Upmin. 128 FQ62
Rushmere Ct, Wor.Pk. 199 CU103
The Av
Rushmere Ho SW15 179 CU88
Fontley Way
Rushmere La (Orchard Leigh), Chesh. 56 AU28
Rushmere Pl SW19 179 CX92
Rushmoor Cl, Guil. 242 AT131
Rushmoor Cl, Pnr. 115 BV56
Rushmoor Cl, Rick. 92 BK47
Rushmore Cl, Brom. 204 EL97
Rushmore Cres E5 123 DX63
Rushmore Rd
Rushmore Hill, Orp. 224 EW110
Rushmore Hill (Knockholt), Sev. 224 EX112
Rushmore Rd E5 122 DW63
Rusholme Av, Dag. 126 FA62
Rusholme Gro SE19 182 DS92
Rusholme Rd SW15 179 CY86
Rushout Av, Har. 117 CH58
Rushton Av, Wat. 75 BU35
Rushton Gro, Harl. 52 EX15
Rushton St N1 142 DR68
Rushworth Av NW4 119 CU55
Rushworth Gdns
Rushworth Gdns NW4 119 CU56
Rushworth Rd, Reig. 250 DA133
Rushworth St SE1 278 G4
Rushworth St SE1 161 DP75
Rushy Meadow La, Cars. 200 DE103
Ruskin Av E12 144 EL65
Ruskin Av, Felt. 175 BT86
Ruskin Av, Rich. 158 CN80
Ruskin Av, Upmin. 128 FQ59
Ruskin Av, Wal.Abb. 68 EE34
Ruskin Av, Well. 166 EU82
Ruskin Cl NW11 120 DB58
Ruskin Cl (Cheshunt), Wal.Cr. 66 DS26
Ruskin Dr, Orp. 205 ES104
Ruskin Dr, Well. 166 EU83
Ruskin Dr, Wor.Pk. 199 CV103
Ruskin Gdns W5 137 CK70
Ruskin Gdns, Har. 118 CM56
Ruskin Gdns, Rom. 105 FH52
Ruskin Gro, Dart. 188 FN85
Ruskin Gro, Well. 166 EU82
Ruskin Pk Ho SE5 162 DR83
Ruskin Rd N17 100 DT53
Ruskin Rd, Belv. 166 FA77
Ruskin Rd, Cars. 218 DF106
Ruskin Rd, Croy. 201 DP103
Ruskin Rd, Grays 171 GG77
Ruskin Rd, Islw. 157 CF83
Ruskin Rd, Sthl. 136 BY73
Ruskin Rd, Stai. 173 BF94
Ruskin Wk N9 100 DU47
Durham Rd
Ruskin Wk SE24 182 DQ85
Ruskin Wk, Brom. 205 EM100
Ruskin Way SW19 200 DD95
Rusland Av, Orp. 205 ER104
Rusland Hts, Har. 117 CE56
Rusland Pk Rd
Rusland Pk Rd, Har. 117 CE56
Rusper Cl NW2 119 CW62
Rusper Cl, Stan. 95 CJ49
Rusper Rd N22 100 DQ54
Rusper Rd, Dag. 146 EW65
Russell Av N22 99 DP54
Russell Av, St.Alb. 43 CD20
Russell Cl NW10 138 CQ66
Russell Cl SE7 164 EJ80
Russell Cl W4 159 CT79
Russell Cl, Amer. 72 AX39
Russell Cl, Beck. 203 EB97
Russell Cl, Bexh. 166 FA84
Russell Cl, Brwd. 108 FV45
Russell Cl, Dart. 167 FG83
Russell Cl, Nthwd. 93 BQ50
Russell Cl, Ruis. 116 BW61
Russell Cl, Tad. 249 CU125
Russell Cl, Wok. 226 AW115
Russell Ct SW1 277 L3
Russell Ct, Chesh. 54 AR29
Russell Ct, Guil. 242 AW131
Rowan Cl
Russell Ct, Lthd. 231 CH122
Russell Ct, St.Alb. 60 CA30
Russell Cres, Wat. 75 BT35
High Rd
Russell Dr (Stanwell), Stai. 174 BK86
Russell Gdns N20 98 DE47
Russell Gdns NW11 119 CY58
Russell Gdns W14 159 CY76
Russell Gdns, Rich. 177 CJ89
Russell Gdns, West Dr. 154 BN78
Russell Gdns Ms W14 159 CY75
Russell Grn Cl, Pur. 219 DN110
Russell Gro NW7 96 CS50
Russell Gro SW9 161 DN80
Russell Hill, Pur. 219 DM110
Russell Hill Pl, Pur. 219 DN111
Russell Hill Rd, Pur. 219 DN110
Russell Kerr Cl W4 158 CQ80
Burlington La
Russell La N20 98 DE47
Russell La, Wat. 75 BR36
Russell Mead (Harrow Weald), Har. 95 CF53
Russell Par NW11 119 CY58
Russell Gdns
Russell Pl NW3 120 DE64
Aspern Gro
Russell Pl SE16 163 DY76
Onega Gate
Russell Pl (Sutton at Hone), Dart. 208 FN95
Russell Pl, Hem.H. 40 BH23
Russell Rd E4 101 DZ49
Russell Rd E10 123 EB58
Russell Rd E16 144 EG72
Russell Rd E17 123 DZ55
Russell Rd N8 121 DK58
Russell Rd N13 99 DM51
Russell Rd N15 122 DS57
Russell Rd N20 98 DE47
Russell Rd NW9 119 CT58
Russell Rd SW19 180 DA94
Russell Rd W14 159 CY76
Russell Rd, Buck.H. 102 EH46
Russell Rd, Enf. 82 DT38
Russell Rd, Grav. 191 GK86
Russell Rd, Grays 170 GA77
Russell Rd, Mitch. 200 DE97
Russell Rd, Nthlt. 116 CC64
Russell Rd, Nthwd. 93 BQ49
Russell Rd, Shep. 195 BQ101
Russell Rd, Til. 170 GE81
Russell Rd, Twick. 177 CF86
Russell Rd, Walt. 195 BU100
Russell Rd, Wok. 226 AW115
Russell Sq WC1 273 P5
Russell Sq WC1 141 DK71
Russell Sq, Long. 209 FX97
Cavendish Sq
Russell St WC2 274 A10
Russell St WC2 141 DM72
Russell St, Hert. 32 DQ09
Russell St, Wind. 151 AQ81
Russell Wk, Rich. 178 CM86
Park Hill
Russell Way, Sutt. 218 DA106
Russell Way, Wat. 93 BV45
Russellcroft Rd, Welw.G.C. 29 CW08
Russells, Tad. 233 CX122
Russells Cres, Horl. 268 DG149
Russell's Footpath SW16 181 DL92
Russells Ride (Cheshunt), Wal.Cr. 67 DY31
Russet Cl, Horl. 269 DJ148
Carlton Tye
Russet Cl, Stai. 173 BF86
Russet Cl, Uxb. 135 BQ70
Uxbridge Rd
Russet Cl, Walt. 196 BX104
Russet Cres N7 121 DM64
Stock Orchard Cres
Russet Dr, Croy. 203 DY102
Russet Dr, Rad. 62 CL32
Russet Dr, St.Alb. 43 CJ21
Russet Way (North Holmwood), Dor. 263 CK140
Russets, The (Chalfont St. Peter), Ger.Cr. 90 AX54
Austenwood Cl
Russets Cl E4 101 ED49
Larkshall Rd
Russett Cl, Orp. 224 EV106
Russett Cl, Wal.Cr. 66 DS26
Russett Ct, Cat. 252 DU125
Russett Hill (Chalfont St. Peter), Ger.Cr. 112 AY55
Russett Way SE13 163 EB82
Conington Rd
Russett Way, Swan. 207 FD96
Russett Wd, Welw.G.C. 30 DD10
Russetts, Horn. 128 FL56
Russetts Cl, Wok. 227 AZ115
Russia Ct EC2 275 J8
Russia Dock Rd SE16 143 DY74
Russia La E2 142 DW68
Russia Row EC2 275 J9
Russia Wk SE16 163 DY75
Russington Rd, Shep. 195 BR100
Rust Sq SE5 162 DR80
Rusthall Av W4 158 CR77
Rusthall Cl, Croy. 202 DW100
Rustic Av SW16 181 DH94
Rustic Cl, Upmin. 129 FS60
Rustic Pl, Wem. 117 CK63
Rustic Wk E16 144 EH72
Lambert Rd
Rustington Wk, Mord. 199 CZ101
Ruston Av, Surb. 198 CP101
Ruston Gdns N14 80 DG44
Farm La
Ruston Ms W11 139 CY72
St. Marks Rd
Ruston Rd SE18 164 EL76
Ruston St E3 143 DZ67
Rutford Rd SW16 181 DL92
Ruth Cl, Stan. 118 CM56
Ruthen Cl, Epsom 216 CP114
Rutherford Cl, Borwd. 78 CQ40
Rutherford Cl, Sutt. 218 DD107
Rutherford Cl, Uxb. 134 BM70
Rutherford Cl, Wind. 151 AM81
Rutherford St SW1 277 M8
Rutherford St SW1 161 DK77
Rutherford Twr, Sthl. 136 CB72
Rutherford Way, Bushey 95 CD46
Rutherford Way, Wem. 118 CN63
Rutherglen Rd SE2 166 EU79
Rutherwick Cl, Horl. 268 DF148
Rutherwick Ri, Couls. 235 DL117
Rutherwick Twr, Horl. 268 DF148
Rutherwick Cl
Rutherwyk Rd, Cher. 193 BE101
Rutherwyke Cl, Epsom 217 CU107
Ruthin Cl NW9 118 CS58
Ruthin Rd SE3 164 EG79
Ruthven Av, Wal.Cr. 67 DX33
Ruthven St E9 143 DX67
Lauriston Rd
Rutland App, Horn. 128 FN57
Rutland Av, Sid. 186 EU87
Rutland Av, Slou. 131 AR71
Rutland Cl SW14 158 CQ83
Rutland Cl SW19 180 DE94
Rutland Rd
Rutland Cl, Ash. 232 CL117
Rutland Cl, Bex. 186 EX88
Rutland Cl, Chess. 216 CM107
Rutland Cl, Dart. 188 FK87
Rutland Cl, Epsom 216 CR110
Rutland Cl, Red. 250 DF133
Rutland Ct, Enf. 82 DW43
Rutland Dr, Horn. 128 FN57
Rutland Dr, Mord. 199 CZ100
Rutland Dr, Rich. 177 CK88
Rutland Gdns N4 121 DP58
Rutland Gdns SW7 276 C5
Rutland Gdns SW7 160 DE75
Rutland Gdns W13 137 CG71
Rutland Gdns, Croy. 220 DS105
Rutland Gdns, Dag. 126 EW64
Rutland Gdns, Hem.H. 40 BM19
Rutland Gdns Ms SW7 276 C5
Rutland Gate SW7 276 C5
Rutland Gate SW7 160 DE75
Rutland Gate, Belv. 167 FB78
Rutland Gate, Brom. 204 EF98
Rutland Gate Ms SW7 276 B5
Rutland Gro W6 159 CV78
Rutland Ms NW8 140 DB67
Boundary Rd
Rutland Ms E SW7 276 B6
Rutland Ms S SW7 276 B6
Rutland Ms W SW7 160 DE76
Ennismore St
Rutland Pk NW2 139 CW65
Rutland Pk SE6 183 DZ89
Rutland Pk Gdns NW2 139 CW65
Rutland Pk
Rutland Pk Mans NW2 139 CW65
Walm La
Rutland Pl EC1 275 H5
Rutland Pl, Bushey 95 CD46
The Rutts
Rutland Rd E7 144 EK66
Rutland Rd E9 142 DW67
Rutland Rd E11 124 EH57
Rutland Rd E17 123 EA58
Rutland Rd SW19 180 DE94
Rutland Rd, Har. 116 CC58
Rutland Rd, Hayes 155 BR77
Rutland Rd, Ilf. 125 EP63
Rutland Rd, Sthl. 136 CA71
Rutland Rd, Twick. 177 CD89
Rutland St SW7 276 C6
Rutland St SW7 160 DE76
Rutland Wk SE6 183 DZ89
Rutland Way, Orp. 206 EW100
Rutley Cl SE17 161 DP79
Royal Rd
Rutley Cl, Rom. 106 FK54
Pasteur Dr
Rutlish Rd SW19 200 DA95
Rutson Rd (Byfleet), W.Byf. 212 BM114
Rutter Gdns, Mitch. 200 DC98
Rutters Cl, West Dr. 154 BN75
Rutts, The, Bushey 95 CD46
Rutts Ter SE14 163 DX81
Ruvigny Gdns SW15 159 CX83
Ruxbury Rd, Cher. 193 BC100
Ruxley Cl, Epsom 216 CP106
Ruxley Cl, Sid. 186 EX93
Ruxley Cor Ind Est, Sid. 186 EX93
Ruxley Cres (Claygate), Esher 215 CH107
Ruxley Gdns, Shep. 195 BQ99
Ruxley La, Epsom 216 CR106
Ruxley Ms, Epsom 216 CP106
Ruxley Ridge (Claygate), Esher 215 CG108
Ruxton Cl, Swan. 207 FE97
Ryall Cl (Bricket Wd), St.Alb. 60 BY29
Ryalls Ct N20 98 DF48
Ryan Cl SE3 164 EJ84
Ryan Cl, Ruis. 115 BV60
Ryan Dr, Brent. 157 CG79
Ryan Way, Wat. 76 BW39
Ryarsh Cres, Orp. 223 ES105
Rycott Path SE22 182 DU87
Lordship La
Rycroft La, Sev. 256 FE130
Rycroft Way N17 122 DT55
Ryculff Sq SE3 164 EF82
Rydal Cl NW4 97 CY53
Rydal Cl, Pur. 220 DR113
Rydal Ct, Wat. 59 BV32
Grasmere Cl
Rydal Cres, Grnf. 137 CH69
Rydal Dr, Bexh. 166 FA81
Rydal Dr, W.Wick. 204 EE103
Rydal Gdns NW9 118 CS57
Rydal Gdns SW15 178 CS92
Rydal Gdns, Houns. 176 CB86
Rydal Gdns, Wem. 117 CJ60
Rydal Rd SW16 181 DK91
Rydal Way, Egh. 173 BB94
Rydal Way, Enf. 82 DW44
Rydal Way, Ruis. 116 BW63
Ryde, The, Hat. 45 CW16
Ryde, The, Stai. 194 BH95
Ryde Cl (Ripley), Wok. 228 BJ121
Ryde Heron (Knaphill), Wok. 226 AS117
Robin Hood Rd
Ryde Pl, Twick. 177 CJ86
Ryde Vale Rd SW12 181 DH89
Rydens Av, Walt. 196 BW103
Rydens Cl, Walt. 196 BW103
Rydens Gro, Walt. 214 BX105
Rydens Pk, Walt. 196 BX103
Rydens Rd
Rydens Rd, Walt. 196 BX103
Rydens Way, Wok. 227 BA120
Ryder Av, Hat. 44 CS20
Ryder Cl, Brom. 184 EH92
Ryder Cl, Bushey 76 CB44
Ryder Cl (Bovingdon), Hem.H. 57 BA28
Ryder Cl, Hert. 32 DV08
Ryder Ct SW1 277 L2
Ryder Dr SE16 162 DV78
Ryder Gdns, Rain. 147 FF65
Ryder Ms E9 122 DW64
Homerton High St
Ryder St SW1 277 L2
Ryder St SW1 141 DJ74
Ryder Yd SW1 277 L2
Ryders Ter NW8 140 DC68
Blenheim Ter
Rydes Av, Guil. 242 AT131
Rydes Cl, Wok. 227 BC120
Rydes Hill Cres, Guil. 242 AT130
Rydes Hill Rd, Guil. 242 AT132
Rydings, Wind. 151 AM83
Rydon St N1 142 DQ67
St. Paul St
Rydons Cl SE9 164 EL83
Rydon's La, Couls. 236 DQ120
Rydon's Wd Cl, Couls. 236 DQ120
Rydston Cl N7 141 DM66
Sutterton St
Rye, The N14 99 DJ45
Rye Cl, Bex. 187 FB86
Rye Cl, Guil. 242 AS132
Rye Cl, Horn. 128 FJ64
Rye Ct, Slou. 152 AU76
Alpha St S
Rye Cres, Orp. 206 EW102
Rye Fld, Ash. 231 CK116
Ashtead Wds Rd
Rye Fld, Orp. 206 EX102
Rye Hill Pk SE15 162 DW84
Rye Hill Rd, Epp. 52 EU23
Rye Hill Rd, Harl. 51 ES22
Rye La SE15 162 DU81
Rye La (Dunton Grn), Sev. 241 FG117
Rye Pk Ind Est, Hodd. 49 EC15
Salisbury Rd
Rye Pas SE15 162 DU83
Rye Rd SE15 163 DX84
Rye Rd, Hodd. 49 EB15
Rye Wk SW15 179 CX85
Chartfield Av
Rye Way, Edg. 96 CM51
Canons Dr
Ryebridge Cl, Lthd. 231 CG118
Ryebrook Rd, Lthd. 231 CG118
Ryecotes Mead SE21 182 DS88
Ryecroft, Grav. 191 GL92
Ryecroft, Harl. 51 EP15
Ryecroft, Hat. 45 CT20
Hazel Gro
Ryecroft, Wind. 151 AM83
Ryecroft Av, Ilf. 103 EP54
Ryecroft Av, Twick. 176 CB87
Ryecroft Cl, Hem.H. 41 BQ21
Poynders Hill
Ryecroft Ct, St.Alb. 44 CL20
Ryecroft Cres, Barn. 79 CV43
Ryecroft Rd SE13 183 EC85
Ryecroft Rd SW16 181 DN93
Ryecroft Rd, Chesh. 54 AN32
Ryecroft Rd, Orp. 205 ER100
Ryecroft Rd (Otford), Sev. 241 FG116
Ryecroft St SW6 160 DB81
Ryedale SE22 182 DV86
Ryedale Ct, Sev. 256 FE121
London Rd
Ryefield Av, Uxb. 135 BP66
Ryefield Cl, Hodd. 33 EC13
Ryefield Ct, Nthwd. 93 BU54
Ryefield Cres
Ryefield Cres, Nthwd. 93 BU54
Ryefield Par, Nthwd. 93 BU54
Ryefield Cres
Ryefield Path SW15 179 CU88
Ryefield Rd SE19 182 DQ93
Ryegates SE15 162 DV82
Caulfield Rd
Ryeland Cl, West Dr. 134 BL72
Ryelands, Horl. 269 DJ147
Ryelands, Welw.G.C. 29 CZ12
Ryelands Cl, Cat. 236 DS121
Ryelands Ct, Lthd. 231 CG118
Ryelands Cres SE12 184 EJ86
Ryelands Pl, Wey. 195 BS104
Ryfold Rd SW19 180 DA90
Ryhope Rd N11 99 DH49
Rykhill, Grays 171 GH76
Ryland Cl, Felt. 175 BT91
Ryland Ho, Croy. 202 DQ104
Ryland Rd NW5 141 DH65
Rylandes Rd NW2 119 CU62
Rylandes Rd, S.Croy. 220 DV109
Rylett Cres W12 159 CT76
Rylett Rd W12 159 CT75
Rylston Rd N13 100 DR48
Rylston Rd SW6 159 CZ79
Rymer Rd, Croy. 202 DS101
Rymer St SE24 181 DP86
Rymill Cl (Bovingdon), Hem.H. 57 BA28
Rymill St E16 145 EN74
Rysbrack St SW3 276 D6
Rysbrack St SW3 160 DF76
Rysted La, West. 255 EQ126
Rythe Cl, Chess. 215 CJ108
Nigel Fisher Way
Rythe Ct, T.Ditt. 197 CG101
Rythe Rd (Claygate), Esher 215 CD106
Ryvers Rd, Slou. 153 AZ76

S

Sabah Ct, Ashf. 174 BN91
Sabbarton St E16 144 EF72
Victoria Dock Rd
Sabella Ct E3 143 DZ68
Sabina Rd, Grays 171 GJ77
Sabine Rd SW11 160 DF83
Sable Cl, Houns. 156 BW83
Sable St N1 141 DP66
Canonbury Rd
Sach Rd E5 122 DV61
Sackville Av, Brom. 204 EG102
Sackville Cl, Har. 117 CD62
Sackville Cl, Sev. 257 FH122
Sackville Ct, Rom. 106 FL53
Sackville Cres
Sackville Cres, Rom. 106 FL53
Sackville Est SW16 181 DL90
Sackville Gdns, Ilf. 125 EM60
Sackville Rd, Dart. 188 FK89
Sackville Rd, Sutt. 218 DA108
Sackville St W1 277 L1
Sackville St W1 141 DJ73
Sackville Way SE22 182 DU88
Dulwich Common
Sacombe Rd, Hem.H. 39 BF18
Saddington St, Grav. 191 GH87
Saddle Yd W1 277 H2
Saddlebrook Pk, Sun. 175 BS94
Saddlers Cl (Arkley), Barn. 79 CV43
Saddlers Cl, Borwd. 78 CR44
Farriers Way
Saddlers Cl, Pnr. 94 CA51
Saddlers Mead, Harl. 52 EU16
Saddlers Ms SW8 161 DM81
Portland Gro
Saddlers Ms, Kings.T. 197 CJ95
Saddlers Ms, Wem. 117 CF63
The Boltons
Saddler's Pk (Eynsford), Dart. 208 FK104
Saddlers Path, Borwd. 78 CR43
Saddlers Way, Epsom 232 CR119
Saddlescombe Way N12 98 DA50
Saddleworth Rd, Rom. 106 FJ51
Saddleworth Sq, Rom. 106 FJ51
Sadleir Rd, St.Alb. 43 CE22
Sadler Cl, Mitch. 200 DF96
Sadler Cl (Cheshunt), Wal.Cr. 66 DQ25
Markham Rd
Sadlers Cl, Guil. 243 BD133
Sadlers Ride, W.Mol. 196 CC96
Sadlers Way, Hert. 31 DN09
Saffron Av E14 143 ED73
Saffron Cl NW11 119 CZ57
Saffron Cl, Croy. 201 DL100
Saffron Cl, Hodd. 49 DZ16
Saffron Cl (Datchet), Slou. 152 AV81
Saffron Ct, Felt. 175 BQ87
Staines Rd
Saffron Hill EC1 274 E5
Saffron Hill EC1 141 DN70
Saffron La, Hem.H. 40 BH19
Saffron Platt, Guil. 242 AU130
Saffron Rd, Grays 169 FW77
Saffron Rd, Rom. 105 FC54
Saffron St EC1 274 E6
Saffron Way, Surb. 197 CK102
Sage Cl E6 145 EM71
Bradley Stone Rd
Sage St E1 142 DW73
Cable St
Sage Way WC1 274 B3
Saigasso Cl E16 144 EK72
Royal Rd
Sail St SE11 278 C8
Sail St SE11 161 DM77
Sainfoin Rd SW17 180 DG89
Sainsbury Rd SE19 182 DS92
St. Agatha's Dr, Kings.T. 178 CM93
St. Agathas Gro, Cars. 200 DF102
St. Agnells Ct, Hem.H. 40 BN16
St. Agnells La, Hem.H. 40 BM15
St. Agnes Cl E9 142 DW67
Gore Rd
St. Agnes Pl SE11 161 DN79
St. Agnes Well EC1 142 DR70
Old St
St. Aidans Ct W13 157 CH75
St. Aidans Rd
St. Aidans Ct, Bark. 146 EV69
Choats Rd
St. Aidan's Rd SE22 182 DV86
St. Aidans Rd W13 157 CH75
St. Aidan's Way, Grav. 191 GL90
St. Albans Av E6 145 EM69
St. Alban's Av W4 158 CR77
St. Albans Av, Felt. 176 BX92
St. Albans Av, Upmin. 129 FS60
St. Albans Av, Wey. 194 BN104
St. Albans Cl NW11 120 DA60
St. Albans Cl, Grav. 191 GK90
St. Albans Cres N22 99 DN53
St. Alban's Cres, Wdf.Grn. 102 EG52
St. Albans Gdns, Grav. 191 GK90
St. Alban's Gdns, Tedd. 177 CG92
St. Albans Gro W8 160 DB76

St. Alban's Gro, Cars. 200 DE101
St. Albans Hill, Hem.H. 40 BL23
St. Albans La NW11 120 DA60
West Heath Dr
St. Albans La, Abb.L. 59 BT26
St. Alban's Pl N1 141 DP67
St. Albans Rd NW5 120 DG62
St. Albans Rd NW10 138 CS67
St. Albans Rd, Barn. 79 CY39
St. Albans Rd, Dart. 188 FM87
St. Albans Rd, Epp. 70 EX29
St. Albans Rd, Hem.H. 40 BN21
St. Albans Rd, Ilf. 125 ET60
St. Alban's Rd, Kings.T. 178 CL93
St. Albans Rd (Dancers Hill), Pot.B. 79 CV35
St. Albans Rd (South Mimms), Pot.B. 63 CV34
St. Albans Rd, Rad. 62 CQ30
St. Albans Rd, Reig. 250 DA133
St. Albans Rd (London Colney), St.Alb. 62 CN28
St. Albans Rd (Sandridge), St.Alb. 43 CF17
St. Alban's Rd, Sutt. 217 CZ105
St. Albans Rd, Wat. 75 BV40
St. Alban's Rd, Wdf.Grn. 102 EG52
St. Albans Rd E, Hat. 45 CV17
St. Albans Rd W, Hat. 44 CR18
St. Albans Rd W (Roe Grn), Hat. 45 CT17
St. Albans St SW1 277 M1
St. Alban's St, Wind. 151 AR81
St. Albans Ter W6 159 CY79
Margravine Rd
St. Alban's Vil NW5 120 DG62
Highgate Rd
St. Alfege Pas SE10 163 EC79
St. Alfege Rd SE7 164 EK79
St. Alphage Gdns EC2 275 J7
St. Alphage Highwalk EC2 142 DR71
London Wall
St. Alphage Wk, Edg. 96 CQ54
St. Alphege Rd N9 100 DW45
St. Alphonsus Rd SW4 161 DJ84
St. Amunds Cl SE6 183 EA91
St. Andrew Ms, Hert. 32 DQ09
St. Andrew St EC4 274 E7
St. Andrew St EC4 141 DN71
St. Andrew St, Hert. 32 DQ09
St. Andrews Av, Horn. 127 FG64
St. Andrews Av, Wem. 117 CG63
St. Andrews Av, Wind. 151 AM82
St. Andrew's Cl N12 98 DC49
Woodside Av
St. Andrews Cl NW2 119 CV62
St. Andrews Cl SE16 162 DV78
Ryder Dr
St. Andrews Cl SE28 146 EX72
St. Andrews Cl, Epp. 53 FC24
St. Andrew's Cl, Islw. 157 CD81
St. Andrews Cl, Reig. 266 DB135
St. Marys Rd
St. Andrews Cl, Ruis. 116 BX61
St. Andrew's Cl, Shep. 195 BR98
St. Andrew's Cl (Wraysbury), Stai. 172 AY87
St. Andrews Cl, Stan. 95 CJ54
St. Andrew's Cl (Old Windsor), Wind. 172 AU86
St. Andrews Cl, Wok. 226 AW117
St. Mary's Rd
St. Andrew's Ct SW18 180 DC89
Waynflete St
St. Andrews Ct, Wat. 75 BV39
St. Andrews Cres, Wind. 151 AM82
St. Andrews Dr, Orp. 206 EV100
St. Andrews Dr, Stan. 95 CJ53
St. Andrews Gdns, Cob. 214 BW113
St. Andrew's Gro N16 122 DR60
St. Andrew's Hill EC4 274 G10
St. Andrew's Hill EC4 141 DP73
St. Andrews Meadow, Harl. 51 ET16
St. Andrew's Ms N16 122 DS60
St. Andrews Ms SE3 164 EG80
Mycenae Rd
St. Andrews Pl NW1 273 J4
St. Andrews Pl NW1 141 DH70
St. Andrews Pl, Brwd. 109 FZ47
St. Andrews Rd E11 124 EE58
St. Andrews Rd E13 144 EH69
St. Andrews Rd E17 101 DX54
St. Andrews Rd N9 100 DW45
St. Andrews Rd NW9 118 CR60
St. Andrews Rd NW10 139 CV65
St. Andrews Rd NW11 119 CZ58
St. Andrews Rd W3 138 CS73
St. Andrews Rd W7 157 CE75
Church Rd
St. Andrews Rd W14 159 CY79
St. Andrews Rd, Cars. 200 DE104
St. Andrews Rd, Couls. 234 DG116
St. Andrews Rd, Croy. 220 DQ105
Lower Coombe St
St. Andrews Rd, Enf. 82 DR41
St. Andrew's Rd, Grav. 191 GJ87
St. Andrews Rd, Hem.H. 40 BJ24
West Valley Rd
St. Andrews Rd, Ilf. 125 EM59
St. Andrews Rd, Rom. 127 FD58
St. Andrews Rd, Sid. 186 EX90
St. Andrew's Rd, Surb. 197 CK100
St. Andrews Rd, Til. 170 GE81
St. Andrews Rd, Uxb. 134 BM66
St. Andrews Rd, Wat. 94 BX48
St. Andrews Sq W11 139 CY72
St. Marks Rd
St. Andrew's Sq, Surb. 197 CK100
St. Andrews Twr, Sthl. 136 CC73
St. Andrews Wk, Cob. 229 BV115
St. Andrews Way E3 143 EB70
St. Andrews Way, Oxt. 254 EL130
St. Andrews Way, Slou. 131 AK73
St. Anna Rd, Barn. 79 CX43
Sampson Av
St. Anne St E14 143 DZ72
Commercial Rd
St. Annes Av (Stanwell), Stai. 174 BK87
St. Annes Boul, Red. 251 DH132
St. Anne's Cl N6 120 DG62
Highgate W Hill
St. Annes Cl (Cheshunt), Wal.Cr. 66 DU28
St. Anne's Cl, Wat. 94 BW49
St. Anne's Ct W1 273 M9
St. Anne's Dr, Red. 250 DG133
St. Annes Dr N, Red. 250 DG132
St. Annes Gdns NW10 138 CM69
St. Anne's Mt, Red. 250 DG133
St. Annes Pk, Brox. 49 EA19
St. Annes Pas E14 143 DZ72
Newell St
St. Annes Ri, Red. 250 DG133
St. Annes Rd E11 123 ED61
St. Anne's Rd (London Colney), St.Alb. 61 CK27
St. Anne's Rd (Harefield), Uxb. 114 BJ55
St. Anne's Rd, Wem. 117 CK64
St. Anne's Row E14 143 DZ72
Commercial Rd
St. Anne's Way, Red. 250 DG133
St. Anne's Dr
St. Ann's, Bark. 145 EQ67
St. Anns Cl, Cher. 193 BF100
St. Ann's Cres SW18 180 DC86
St. Ann's Gdns NW5 140 DG65
Queen's Cres
St. Ann's Hill SW18 180 DB85
St. Anns Hill Rd, Cher. 193 BC100
St. Ann's La SW1 277 N6
St. Ann's Pk Rd SW18 180 DC86
St. Ann's Pas SW13 158 CS83
St. Anns Rd N9 100 DT47
St. Ann's Rd N15 121 DP57
St. Ann's Rd SW13 159 CT82
St. Anns Rd W11 139 CX73
St. Ann's Rd, Bark. *Axe St* 145 EQ67
St. Anns Rd, Cher. 193 BF100
St. Ann's Rd, Har. 117 CE58
St. Ann's Shop Cen, Har. 117 CE58
St. Ann's St SW1 277 N6
St. Ann's St SW1 161 DK76
St. Ann's Ter NW8 140 DD68
St. Anns Vil W11 139 CX74
St. Anns Way, S.Croy. 219 DP107
St. Anselm's Pl W1 273 H9
St. Anselms Rd, Hayes 155 BT75
St. Anthonys Av, Hem.H. 41 BP22
St. Anthonys Av, Wdf.Grn. 102 EJ51
St. Anthonys Cl E1 142 DU74
St. Anthonys Cl SW17 180 DE89
College Gdns
St. Anthonys Ct, Beac. 110 AJ55
Burkes Rd
St. Anthony's Way, Felt. 155 BT84
St. Antony's Rd E7 144 EH66
St. Arvans Cl, Croy. 202 DS104
St. Asaph Rd SE4 163 DX83
St. Aubyn's Av SW19 179 CZ92
St. Aubyns Av, Houns. 176 CA85
St. Aubyns Cl, Orp. 205 ET104
St. Aubyns Gdns, Orp. 205 ET103
St. Aubyn's Rd SE19 182 DT93
St. Audrey Av, Bexh. 166 FA82
St. Audreys Cl, Hat. 45 CV21
St. Audreys Grn, Welw.G.C. 29 CZ10
St. Augustine Rd, Grays 171 GH77
St. Augustine's Av W5 138 CL68
St. Augustines Av, Brom. 204 EL99
St. Augustine's Av, S.Croy. 220 DQ107
St. Augustines Av, Wem. 118 CL62
St. Augustines Cl, Brox. 49 DZ20
St. Augustines Dr, Brox. 49 DZ19
St. Augustine's Path N5 121 DP64
St. Augustines Rd NW1 141 DK66
St. Augustine's Rd, Belv. 166 EZ77
St. Austell Cl, Edg. 96 CM54
St. Austell Rd SE13 163 EC82
St. Awdry's Rd, Bark. 145 ER66
St. Awdry's Wk, Bark. 145 EQ66
Station Par
St. Barnabas Cl SE22 182 DS85
East Dulwich Gro
St. Barnabas Cl, Beck. 203 EC96
St. Barnabas Ct, Har. 94 CC53
St. Barnabas Gdns, W.Mol. 196 CA99
St. Barnabas Rd E17 123 EA58
St. Barnabas Rd, Mitch. 180 DG94
St. Barnabas Rd, Sutt. 218 DD106
St. Barnabas Rd, Wdf.Grn. 102 EH53
St. Barnabas St SW1 276 G10
St. Barnabas St SW1 160 DG78
St. Barnabas Ter E9 123 DX64
St. Barnabas Vil SW8 161 DL81
St. Bartholomews Cl SE26 182 DW91
St. Bartholomews Ct, Guil. 259 AZ135
St. Bartholomew's Rd E6 144 EL67
St. Bart's Cl, St.Alb. 43 CK21
St. Benedict's Av, Grav. 191 GK89
St. Benedict's Cl SW17 180 DG92
Church La
St. Benet's Cl SW17 180 DE89
College Gdns
St. Benet's Gro, Cars. 200 DC101
St. Benet's Pl EC3 275 L10
St. Benjamins Dr, Orp. 224 EW109
St. Bernards, Croy. 202 DS104
St. Bernard's Cl SE27 182 DR91
St. Gothard Rd
St. Bernard's Rd E6 144 EK67
St. Bernards Rd, St.Alb. 43 CD19
St. Bernards Rd, Slou. 152 AW76
St. Blaise Av, Brom. 204 EH96
St. Botolph Rd, Grav. 190 GC90
St. Botolph Row EC3 275 P9
St. Botolph St EC3 275 P9
St. Botolph St EC3 142 DT72
St. Botolph's Av, Sev. 256 FG124
St. Botolph's Rd, Sev. 256 FG124
St. Brelades Cl, Dor. 263 CG138
St. Brelades Pl, St.Alb. 43 CK16
Harvesters
St. Bride St EC4 274 F8
St. Bride St EC4 141 DP72
St. Bride's Av EC4 141 DP72
New Br St
St. Brides Av, Edg. 96 CM53
St. Brides Cl, Erith 166 EX75
St. Katherines Rd
St. Bride's Pas EC4 274 F9
St. Catherines, Wok. 226 AW119
St. Catherines Cl SW17 180 DE89
College Gdns
St. Catherines Cross (Bletchingley), Red. 252 DS134
St. Catherines Dr SE14 163 DX82
Kitto Rd
St. Catherines Dr, Guil. 258 AV138
St. Catherines Fm Ct, Ruis. 115 BQ58
St. Catherines Hill, Guil. 258 AW138
Portsmouth Rd
St. Catherine's Ms SW3 276 D8
St. Catherines Pk, Guil. 259 AZ136
St. Catherines Rd E4 101 EA47
St. Catherines Rd, Brox. 49 EA19
St. Catherines Rd, Ruis. 115 BR57
St. Catherines Twr E10 123 EB59
Kings Cl
St. Cecilia Rd, Grays 171 GH77
St. Cecilia's Cl, Sutt. 199 CY102
St. Chads Cl, Surb. 197 CJ101
St. Chad's Dr, Grav. 191 GL90
St. Chad's Gdns, Rom. 126 EY59
St. Chad's Pl WC1 274 A2
St. Chad's Pl WC1 141 DL69
St. Chad's Rd, Rom. 126 EY58
St. Chad's Rd, Til. 171 GG80
St. Chad's St WC1 274 A2
St. Chad's St WC1 141 DL69
St. Charles Ct, Wey. 212 BN106
St. Charles Pl W10 139 CY71
Chesterton Rd
St. Charles Pl, Wey. 212 BN106
St. Charles Rd, Brwd. 108 FV46
St. Charles Sq W10 139 CX71
St. Christopher Rd, Uxb. 134 BK71
St. Christopher's Cl, Islw. 157 CE81
St. Christopher's Dr, Hayes 135 BV73
St. Christophers Gdns, Th.Hth. 201 DN97
St. Christophers Ms, Wall. 219 DJ106
St. Christopher's Pl W1 272 G8
St. Clair Cl, Oxt. 253 EC130
St. Clair Cl, Reig. 250 DC134
St. Clair Dr, Wor.Pk. 199 CV104
St. Clair Rd E13 144 EH68
St. Clair's Rd, Croy. 202 DS103
St. Clare Business Pk, Hmptn. 176 CC93
St. Clare Cl, Ilf. 103 EM54
St. Clare St EC3 275 P9
St. Clement Cl, Uxb. 134 BK72
St. Clements Av, Grays 169 FU79
St. Clement's Cl (Northfleet), Grav. 191 GF90
Coldharbour Rd
St. Clements Ct EC4 142 DR73
Clements La
St. Clements Ct N7 141 DN65
Arundel Sq
St. Clements Ct, Purf. 168 FN77
Thamley
St. Clements Hts SE26 182 DU90
St. Clement's La WC2 274 C9
St. Clements Rd, Grays 169 FW80
St. Clements St N7 141 DN65
St. Cloud Rd SE27 182 DQ91
St. Columba's Cl, Grav. 191 GL90
St. Crispins Cl NW3 120 DE63
St. Crispins Cl, Sthl. 136 BZ73
St. Crispins Way (Ottershaw), Cher. 211 BC109
St. Cross Ct, Hodd. 49 EA19
St. Cross St EC1 274 E6
St. Cross St EC1 141 DN71
St. Cuthberts Cl, Egh. 172 AX92
St. Cuthberts Gdns, Pnr. 94 BZ52
Westfield Pk
St. Cuthberts Rd N13 99 DN51
St. Cuthberts Rd NW2 139 CZ65
St. Cuthberts Rd, Hodd. 33 EC14
St. Cyprian's St SW17 180 DF91
St. David Cl, Uxb. 134 BK71
St. Davids, Couls. 235 DM117
St. Davids Cl SE16 162 DV78
Masters Dr
St. Davids Cl, Hem.H. 41 BR21
St. Davids Cl, Iver 133 BD67
St. David's Cl, Reig. 250 DC133
St. Davids Cl, Wem. 118 CQ62
St. David's Cl, W.Wick. 203 EB101
St. David's Ct E17 123 EC55
St. David's Cres, Grav. 191 GK91
St. David's Dr, Brox. 49 DZ19
St. Davids Dr, Edg. 96 CM53
St. Davids Pl NW4 119 CV59
St. Davids Rd, Swan. 187 FF93
St. Davids Sq E14 163 EB78
St. Denis Rd SE27 182 DR91
St. Dionis Rd SW6 159 CZ82
St. Donatts Rd SE14 163 DZ81
St. Dunstan's All EC3 275 M10
St. Dunstans Av W3 138 CR73
St. Dunstans Cl, Hayes 155 BT77
St. Dunstan's Ct EC4 141 DN72
Fleet St
St. Dunstan's Dr, Grav. 191 GL91
St. Dunstans Gdns W3 138 CR73
St. Dunstans Av
St. Dunstan's Hill EC3 279 M1
St. Dunstan's Hill EC3 142 DS73
St. Dunstan's Hill, Sutt. 217 CY106
St. Dunstan's La EC3 279 M1
St. Dunstan's La, Beck. 203 EC100
St. Dunstan's Rd E7 144 EJ65
St. Dunstans Rd SE25 202 DT98
St. Dunstans Rd W6 159 CX78
St. Dunstans Rd W7 157 CE75
St. Dunstan's Rd, Felt. 175 BT90
St. Dunstans Rd, Houns. 156 BW82
St. Dunstans Rd, Ware 34 EK07
St. Edith Cl, Epsom 216 CQ114
St. Elizabeth Dr
St. Edmunds, Berk. 38 AW20
St. Edmunds Av, Ruis. 115 BR58
St. Edmunds Cl NW8 140 DF67
St. Edmunds Ter
St. Edmunds Cl SW17 180 DE89
College Gdns
St. Edmunds Cl, Erith 166 EX75
St. Katherines Rd
St. Edmunds Dr, Stan. 95 CG53
St. Edmund's La, Twick. 176 CB87
St. Edmunds Rd N9 100 DU45
St. Edmunds Rd, Dart. 168 FM84
St. Edmunds Rd, Ilf. 125 EM58
St. Edmunds Sq SW13 159 CW79
St. Edmunds Ter NW8 140 DE67
St. Edmunds Wk, St.Alb. 43 CJ21
St. Edmunds Way, Harl. 36 EW11
St. Edwards Cl NW11 120 DA58
St. Edwards Cl (New Addington), Croy. 221 ED111
St. Edwards Way, Rom. 127 FD57
St. Egberts Way E4 101 EC46
St. Elizabeth Dr, Epsom 216 CQ114
St. Elmo Cl, Slou. 131 AR70
St. Elmo Cres
St. Elmo Cres, Slou. 131 AR70
St. Elmo Rd W12 139 CT74
St. Elmos Rd SE16 163 DY75
St. Erkenwald Ms, Bark. 145 ER67
St. Erkenwald Rd
St. Erkenwald Rd, Bark. 145 ER67
St. Ermin's Hill SW1 277 M6
St. Ervans Rd W10 139 CY71
St. Ethelredas Dr, Hat. 45 CW18
St. Fabian Twr E4 101 DZ51
Iris Way
St. Faiths Cl, Enf. 82 DQ39
St. Faith's Rd SE21 181 DP88
St. Fidelis Rd, Erith 167 FD77
St. Fillans Rd SE6 183 EC88
St. Francis Av, Grav. 191 GL91
St. Francis Cl, Orp. 205 ES100
St. Francis Cl, Pot.B. 64 DC33
St. Francis Cl, Wat. 93 BV46
St. Francis Rd SE22 162 DS84
St. Francis Rd, Erith 167 FD77
West St
St. Francis Rd (Denham), Uxb. 113 BF58
St. Francis Way, Grays 171 GJ77
St. Francis Way, Ilf. 125 ES63
St. Frideswides Ms E14 143 EC72
Lodore St
St. Gabriel's Cl E11 124 EH60
St. Gabriels Rd NW2 119 CX64
St. George St W1 273 J9
St. George St W1 141 DH72
St. George Wf SW8 161 DL78
St. Georges Av E7 144 EH66
St. Georges Av N7 121 DK63
St. Georges Av NW9 118 CQ56
St. George's Av W5 157 CK75
St. Georges Av, Grays 170 GC77
St. Georges Av, Horn. 128 FM59
St. Georges Av, Sthl. 136 BZ73
St. George's Av, Wey. 213 BP107
St. Georges Cen, Har. 117 CE58
St. Georges Circ SE1 278 F6
St. Georges Circ SE1 161 DP76
St. Georges Cl NW11 119 CZ58
St. Georges Cl SE28 146 EX72
Redbourne Dr
St. George's Cl SW8 161 DJ81
Patmore Est
St. Georges Cl, Horl. 269 DH148
St. Georges Cl, Wem. 117 CG62
St. George's Cl, Wey. 213 BQ106
St. George's Cl, Wind. 151 AL81
St. Georges Ct E6 145 EM70
St. Georges Ct EC4 274 F8
St. Georges Ct SW7 160 DC76
Gloucester Rd
St. Georges Cres, Grav. 191 GK91
St. George's Cres, Slou. 131 AK73
St. George's Dr SW1 277 K10
St. George's Dr SW1 161 DH77
St. Georges Dr, Uxb. 114 BM62
St. Georges Dr, Wat. 94 BY48
St. George's Est, Amer. 72 AU39
St. Georges Flds W2 272 C9
St. Georges Flds W2 140 DE72
St. Georges Gdns, Epsom 217 CT114
Lynwood Rd
St. George's Gdns, Surb. 198 CP103
Hamilton Av
St. Georges Gro SW17 180 DD90
St. Georges Gro Est SW17 180 DD90
St. Georges Ind Est, Kings.T. 177 CK92
St. Georges La EC3 275 M10
St. George's Lo, Wey. 213 BR106
St. Georges Ms NW1 140 DF66
Regents Pk Rd
St. Georges Pl, Twick. 177 CG88
Church St
St. Georges Rd E7 144 EH65
St. Georges Rd E10 123 EC62
St. Georges Rd N9 100 DU48
St. Georges Rd N13 99 DM48
St. Georges Rd NW11 119 CZ58
St. Georges Rd SE1 278 E6
St. Georges Rd SE1 161 DN76
St. George's Rd SW19 179 CZ93
St. Georges Rd W4 158 CS75
St. Georges Rd W7 137 CF74
St. Georges Rd, Add. 212 BJ105
St. George's Rd, Beck. 203 EB95
St. Georges Rd, Brom. 205 EM96
St. Georges Rd, Dag. 126 EY64
St. Georges Rd, Enf. 82 DT38
St. George's Rd, Felt. 176 BX91
St. Georges Rd, Hem.H. 40 BJ24
St. Georges Rd, Ilf. 125 EM59
St. George's Rd, Kings.T. 178 CN94
St. George's Rd, Mitch. 201 DH97
St. Georges Rd, Orp. 205 ER100
St. Georges Rd, Red. 267 DK142
St. Georges Rd, Rich. 158 CM83
St. George's Rd, Sev. 257 FH122
St. George's Rd, Sid. 186 EX93
St. Georges Rd, Swan. 207 FF98
St. Georges Rd, Twick. 177 CH85
St. Georges Rd, Wall. 219 DH106
St. Georges Rd, Wat. 75 BV38
St. George's Rd, Wey. 213 BR107
St. Georges Rd W, Brom. 204 EL95
St. Georges Shop Cen, Grav. 191 GH86
St. Georges Sq E7 144 EH66
St. Georges Sq E14 143 DY73
Narrow St
St. Georges Sq SE8 163 DZ77
St. George's Sq SW1 277 M10
St. George's Sq SW1 161 DK78
St. George's Sq, N.Mal. 198 CS97
High St
St. George's Sq Ms SW1 161 DK78
St. Georges Ter NW1 140 DF66
Regents Pk Rd
St. Georges Wk, Croy. 202 DQ104
St. Georges Way SE15 162 DS79
St. Gerards Cl SW4 181 DJ85
St. German's Pl SE3 164 EG81
St. Germans Rd SE23 183 DY88
St. Giles Av, Dag. 147 FB66
St. Giles Av, Pot.B. 63 CV33
St. Giles Av, Uxb. 115 BQ63
St. Giles Cl, Dag. 147 FB66
St. Giles Av
St. Giles Cl, Orp. 223 ER106
St. Giles Ct WC2 141 DL72
St. Giles High St
St. Giles High St WC2 273 N8
St. Giles High St WC2 141 DK72
St. Giles Pas WC2 273 N9
St. Giles Rd SE5 162 DS80
St. Gilles Ho E2 143 DX68
St. Gothard Rd SE27 182 DR91
St. Gregory Cl, Ruis. 116 BW63
St. Gregorys Cres, Grav. 191 GL89
St. Helena Rd SE16 163 DX77
St. Helena St WC1 274 D3
St. Helens Cl, Uxb. 134 BK72
St. Helens Ct, Epp. 70 EU30
Hemnall St
St. Helens Ct, Rain. 147 FG70
St. Helens Cres SW16 201 DM95
St. Helens Rd
St. Helens Gdns W10 139 CX72
St. Helens Pl EC3 275 M8
St. Helens Rd SW16 201 DM95
St. Helen's Rd W13 137 CH74
Dane Rd
St. Helens Rd, Erith 166 EX75
St. Helens Rd, Ilf. 125 EM58
St. Helier Av, Mord. 200 DC101
St. Helier Rd (Sandridge), St.Alb. 43 CH15
St. Heliers Av, Houns. 176 CA85
St. Heliers Rd E10 123 EC58
St. Hildas Av, Ashf. 174 BL92
St. Hildas Cl NW6 139 CX66
St. Hildas Cl SW17 180 DE89
St. Hildas Cl, Horl. 269 DH148
St. Hilda's Rd SW13 159 CV79
St. Hilda's Way, Grav. 191 GK91
St. Huberts Cl, Ger.Cr. 112 AY60
St. Huberts La, Ger.Cr. 113 AZ61
St. Hughe's Cl SW17 180 DE89
College Gdns
St. Hughs Rd SE20 202 DV95
Ridsdale Rd
St. Ives Cl, Rom. 106 FM52
St. Ivians Dr, Rom. 127 FG55
St. James Av N20 98 DE48
St. James Av W13 137 CG74
St. James Av, Epsom 217 CT111
St. James Av, Sutt. 218 DA106
St. James Cl N20 98 DE48
St. James Cl SE18 165 EQ78
Congleton Gro
St. James Cl, Barn. 80 DD42
St. James Cl, Epsom 216 CS114
St. James Cl, N.Mal. 199 CT99
St. James Cl, Ruis. 116 BW61
St. James Cl, Wok. 226 AU118
St. James Ct, Green. 189 FT86
St. James Gdns, Rom. 126 EV56
St. James Gdns, Wem. 137 CK66
St. James Gate NW1 141 DK66
St. Paul's Cres
St. James Gro SW11 160 DF82
Reform St
St. James La, Green. 189 FS88
St. James Ms E14 163 EC76
St. James Ms E17 123 DY57
St. James's St
St. James Ms, Wey. 213 BP105
St. James Oaks, Grav. 191 GG87
Trafalgar Rd
St. James Pl, Dart. 188 FK86
Spital St
St. James Pl, Slou. 130 AJ72
Greenfern Av
St. James Rd E15 124 EF64
St. James Rd N9 100 DV47
Queens Rd
St. James Rd, Brwd. 108 FW48
St. James Rd, Cars. 200 DE104
St. James Rd, Kings.T. 198 CL96
St. James Rd, Mitch. 180 DG94
St. James Rd, Pur. 219 DP113
St. James Rd, Sev. 257 FH122
St. James Rd, Surb. 197 CK100
St. James Rd, Sutt. 218 DA106
St. James Rd (Cheshunt), Wal.Cr. 66 DQ28
St. James Rd, Wat. 75 BV43
St. James St W6 159 CW78
St. James Wk, Iver 153 BE75
St. James Way, Sid. 186 EY92
St. James's SE14 163 DY81
St. James's Av E2 142 DW68
St. James's Av, Beck. 203 DY97
St. James's Av, Grav. 191 GG87
St. James's Av (Hampton Hill), Hmptn. 176 CC92
St. James's Cl SW17 180 DF89
St. James's Dr
St. James's Cotts, Rich. 177 CK85
Paradise Rd
St. James's Ct SW1 277 L6
St. James's Ct SW1 161 DJ76
St. James's Cres SW9 161 DN83
St. James's Dr SW12 180 DF88
St. James's Dr SW17 180 DF88
St. James's Gdns W11 139 CY74
St. James's La N10 121 DH56
St. James's Mkt SW1 277 M1
St. James's Palace SW1 277 L4
St. James's Palace SW1 141 DJ74
St. James's Pk SW1 277 M4
St. James's Pk SW1 161 DK75
St. James's Pk, Croy. 202 DQ101
St. James's Pas EC3 275 N9
St. James's Pl SW1 277 K3
St. James's Pl SW1 141 DJ74
St. James's Rd SE1 162 DU78
St. James's Rd SE16 162 DU76
St. James's Rd, Croy. 201 DP101
St. James's Rd, Grav. 191 GG86
St. James's Rd (Hampton Hill), Hmptn. 176 CB92
St. James's Row EC1 274 E4
St. James's Sq SW1 277 L2
St. James's Sq SW1 141 DJ74
St. James's St E17 123 DY57
St. James's St SW1 277 K2
St. James's St SW1 141 DJ74
St. James's St, Grav. 191 GG86
St. James's Ter NW8 140 DF68
Prince Albert Rd
St. James's Ter Ms NW8 140 DF67
St. James's Wk EC1 274 F4
St. James's Wk EC1 141 DP70
St. Jeromes Gro, Hayes 135 BQ72
St. Joans Rd N9 100 DT46
St. John Fisher Rd, Erith 166 EX76
St. John St EC1 274 G5
St. John St EC1 141 DP70
St. Johns (North Holmwood), Dor. 263 CH140
St. John's, Red. 266 DE136
St. Johns Av N11 98 DF50
St. John's Av NW10 139 CT67
St. John's Av SW15 179 CX85
St. Johns Av, Brwd. 108 FX49
St. John's Av, Epsom 217 CT112
St. John's Av, Harl. 36 EW11
St. Johns Av, Lthd. 231 CH121
St. John's Ch Rd E9 122 DW64
St. John's Ch Rd, Dor. 262 BZ139
Coast Hill
St. Johns Cl N14 81 DJ44
Chase Rd
St. John's Cl SW6 160 DA80
Dawes Rd
St. John's Cl, Guil. 258 AU135
St. John's Rd
St. Johns Cl, Hem.H. 40 BH22
Anchor La
St. Johns Cl, Lthd. 231 CJ120
St. John's Cl, Pot.B. 64 DC33
St. Johns Cl, Rain. 147 FG66
St. John's Cl, Uxb. 134 BH67
St. John's Cl, Wem. 118 CL64
St. John's Cotts SE20 182 DW94
Maple Rd
St. Johns Cotts, Rich. 158 CL84
Kew Foot Rd
St. Johns Ct, Buck.H. 102 EH46
St. Johns Ct, Egh. 173 BA92
St. Johns Ct, Hert. 32 DR09
St. John's St
St. John's Ct, Islw. 157 CF82

St. Johns Ct, Nthwd. 93 BS53
Murray Rd
St. Johns Ct, St.Alb. 43 CH19
St. John's Ct, Wok. 226 AU119
St. Johns Hill Rd
St. John's Cres SW9 161 DN83
St. Johns Dr SW18 180 DB88
St. Johns Dr, Walt. 196 BW102
St. Johns Dr, Wind. 151 AM82
St. John's Est N1 275 L1
St. John's Est N1 142 DR68
St. John's Est SE1 279 P4
St. John's Gdns W11 139 CZ73
St. Johns Gro N19 121 DJ61
St. Johns Gro SW13 159 CT82
Terrace Gdns
St. Johns Gro, Rich. 158 CL84
Kew Foot Rd
St. John's Hill SW11 160 DD84
St. John's Hill, Couls. 235 DN117
St. John's Hill, Pur. 235 DN116
St. John's Hill, Sev. 257 FJ123
St. Johns Hill Gro SW11 160 DD84
St. Johns Hill Rd, Wok. 226 AU119
St. John's La EC1 274 F5
St. John's La EC1 141 DP70
St. John's La, Ware 33 EA09
St. John's Lye, Wok. 226 AT119
St. John's Ms W11 140 DA72
Ledbury Rd
St. John's Ms, Wok. 226 AU119
St. Johns Par, Sid. 186 EU91
St. John's Pk SE3 164 EF80
St. John's Pas SW19 179 CY93
Ridgway Pl
St. John's Path EC1 274 F5
St. Johns Pathway SE23 182 DW88
Devonshire Rd
St. John's Pl EC1 274 F5
St. Johns Ri, Wok. 226 AV119
St. John's Rd E4 101 EB48
St. Johns Rd E6 144 EL67
Ron Leighton Way
St. Johns Rd E16 144 EG72
St. John's Rd E17 101 EB54
St. John's Rd N15 122 DS58
St. Johns Rd NW11 119 CZ58
St. John's Rd SE20 182 DW94
St. John's Rd SW11 160 DE84
St. John's Rd SW19 179 CY94
St. John's Rd, Bark. 145 ES67
St. John's Rd, Cars. 200 DE104
St. Johns Rd, Croy. 201 DP104
Sylverdale Rd
St. John's Rd, Dart. 188 FQ87
St. John's Rd (Westcott), Dor. 262 CC137
St. Johns Rd, E.Mol. 197 CD98
St. John's Rd, Epp. 69 ET30
St. Johns Rd, Erith 167 FD78
St. John's Rd, Felt. 176 BY91
St. Johns Rd, Grav. 191 GK87
St. Johns Rd, Grays 171 GH78
St. John's Rd, Guil. 258 AT135
St. John's Rd, Har. 117 CF58
St. Johns Rd, Hem.H. 40 BG22
St. Johns Rd, Ilf. 125 ER59
St. John's Rd, Islw. 157 CF82
St. John's Rd, Kings.T. 197 CJ96
St. Johns Rd, Lthd. 231 CJ121
St. Johns Rd, Loug. 85 EM40
St. Johns Rd, N.Mal. 198 CQ97
St. John's Rd, Orp. 205 ER100
St. John's Rd, Red. 266 DF136
St. John's Rd, Rich. 158 CL84
St. Johns Rd, Rom. 105 FC50
St. John's Rd, Sev. 257 FH121
St. Johns Rd, Sid. 186 EV91
St. Johns Rd, Slou. 132 AU74
St. Johns Rd, Sthl. 156 BY76
St. John's Rd, Sutt. 200 DA103
St. Johns Rd, Uxb. 134 BH67
St. Johns Rd, Wat. 75 BV40
St. John's Rd, Well. 166 EV83
St. John's Rd, Wem. 117 CK63
St. John's Rd, Wind. 151 AN82
St. John's Rd, Wok. 226 AV118
St. John's Sq EC1 274 F5
St. John's St, Gdmg. 258 AT144
St. John's St, Hert. 32 DR09
St. Johns Ter E7 144 EH65
St. Johns Ter SE18 165 EQ79
St. Johns Ter SW15 178 CR91
Kingston Vale
St. Johns Ter W10 139 CX70
Harrow Rd
St. Johns Ter, Enf. 82 DR37
St. John's Ter, Red. 266 DF136
St. John's Ter Rd
St. John's Ter Rd, Red. 266 DF136
St. Johns Vale SE8 163 EA82
St. Johns Vil N19 121 DK61
St. John's Vil W8 160 DB76
St. Mary's Pl
St. Johns Wk, Harl. 36 EW11
Market St
St. Johns Way N19 121 DK60
St. Johns Well Ct, Berk. 38 AV18
St. Johns Well La, Berk. 38 AV18
St. John's Wd Ct NW8 272 A3
St. John's Wd High St NW8 272 A1
St. John's Wd High St NW8 140 DD68
St. John's Wd Pk NW8 140 DD67
St. John's Wd Rd NW8 140 DD70
St. John's Wd Ter NW8 140 DD68
St. Josephs Cl W10 139 CY71
Bevington Rd
St. Joseph's Cl, Orp. 223 ET105
St. Joseph's Ct SE7 164 EH79
St. Josephs Dr, Sthl. 136 BY74
St. Joseph's Gro NW4 119 CV56
St. Josephs Rd N9 100 DV45
St. Joseph's Rd, Wal.Cr. 67 DY33
St. Joseph's Vale SE3 163 ED82
St. Jude St N16 122 DS64
St. Judes Cl, Egh. 172 AW92
St. Jude's Rd E2 142 DV68
St. Jude's Rd, Egh. 172 AW90
St. Julians, Sev. 257 FN128
St. Julian's Cl SW16 181 DN91
St. Julian's Fm Rd SE27 181 DN91
St. Julian's Rd NW6 139 CZ66
St. Julians Rd, St.Alb. 43 CD22
St. Justin Cl, Orp. 206 EX97
St. Katharines Prec NW1 141 DH68
Outer Circle
St. Katharine's Way E1 142 DT74
St. Katherines Rd, Cat. 252 DU125
St. Katherines Rd, Erith 166 EX75
St. Katherine's Row EC3 275 N9
St. Katherine's Wk W11 139 CX73
Rifle Pl
St. Katherines Way, Berk. 38 AT16
St. Keverne Rd SE9 184 EL91
St. Kilda Rd W13 137 CG74
St. Kilda Rd, Orp. 205 ET102
St. Kilda's Rd N16 122 DR60
St. Kilda's Rd, Brwd. 108 FV45
St. Kilda's Rd, Har. 117 CE58
St. Kitts Ter SE19 182 DS92
St. Laurence Cl NW6 139 CX67
St. Laurence Cl, Orp. 206 EX97
St. Laurence Cl, Uxb. 134 BJ71
St. Laurence Dr, Brox. 49 DZ23
St. Laurence Way, Slou. 152 AU76
St. Lawrence Cl, Abb.L. 59 BS30
St. Lawrence Cl, Edg. 96 CM52
St. Lawrence Cl (Bovingdon), Hem.H. 57 BA27
St. Lawrence Dr, Pnr. 115 BV58
St. Lawrence Rd, Upmin. 128 FQ61
St. Lawrence St E14 143 EC74
St. Lawrence Ter W10 139 CY71
St. Lawrence Way SW9 161 DN82
St. Lawrence Way, Cat. 236 DQ123
St. Lawrence Way (Bricket Wd), St.Alb. 60 BZ30
St. Lawrence's Way, Reig. 250 DA134
Church St
St. Leonards Av E4 102 EE51
St. Leonards Av, Har. 117 CJ56
St. Leonards Av, Wind. 151 AQ82
St. Leonards Cl, Bushey 76 BY42
St. Leonards Cl, Grays 170 FZ79
St. Leonards Cl, Hert. 32 DS07
St. Leonard's Cl, Well. 166 EU83
Hook La
St. Leonards Ct N1 275 J2
St. Leonards Ct N1 142 DR69
St. Leonard's Gdns, Houns. 156 BY80
St. Leonards Gdns, Ilf. 125 EQ64
St. Leonards Hill, Wind. 151 AL84
St. Leonards Ri, Orp. 223 ES105
St. Leonards Rd E14 143 EB71
St. Leonards Rd NW10 138 CR70
St. Leonard's Rd SW14 158 CP83
St. Leonards Rd W13 137 CJ73
St. Leonards Rd, Amer. 55 AS35
St. Leonards Rd, Croy. 201 DP104
St. Leonards Rd, Epsom 233 CW119
St. Leonards Rd (Claygate), Esher 215 CF107
St. Leonards Rd, Hert. 32 DR07
St. Leonard's Rd, Surb. 197 CK99
St. Leonards Rd, T.Ditt. 197 CG100
St. Leonards Rd, Wal.Abb. 68 EE25
St. Leonards Rd, Wind. 151 AQ82
St. Leonards Sq NW5 140 DG65
St. Leonards Sq, Surb. 197 CK99
St. Leonard's Rd
St. Leonards St E3 143 EB69
St. Leonard's Ter SW3 160 DF78
St. Leonards Wk SW16 181 DM94
St. Leonards Wk, Iver 153 BF76
St. Leonards Way, Horn. 127 FH61
St. Loo Av SW3 160 DE79
St. Louis Rd SE27 182 DQ91
St. Loy's Rd N17 100 DS54
St. Lucia Dr E15 144 EF67
St. Luke Cl, Uxb. 134 BK72
St. Luke's Av SW4 161 DK84
St. Lukes Av, Enf. 82 DR38
St. Luke's Av, Ilf. 125 EP64
St. Lukes Cl EC1 142 DQ70
Old St
St. Luke's Cl SE25 202 DV100
St. Lukes Cl (Lane End), Dart. 189 FS92
St. Lukes Cl, Swan. 207 FD96
St. Luke's Est EC1 275 K3
St. Luke's Est EC1 142 DR69
St. Lukes Ms W11 139 CZ72
Basing St
St. Lukes Pas, Kings.T. 198 CM95
St. Lukes Rd W11 139 CZ71
St. Lukes Rd, Uxb. 134 BL66
St. Lukes Rd, Whyt. 236 DT118
Whyteleafe Hill
St. Lukes Rd (Old Windsor), Wind. 172 AU86
St. Lukes Sq E16 144 EF72
St. Lukes Sq, Guil. 259 AZ135
St. Luke's St SW3 276 B10
St. Luke's St SW3 160 DE78
St. Luke's Yd W9 139 CZ68
St. Malo Av N9 100 DW48
St. Margaret Dr, Epsom 216 CR114
St. Margarets, Bark. 145 ER67
St. Margarets, Guil. 243 AZ133
St. Margarets Av N15 121 DP56
St. Margarets Av N20 98 DC47
St. Margarets Av, Ashf. 175 BP91
St. Margarets Av, Har. 116 CC62
St. Margarets Av, Sid. 185 ER90
St. Margaret's Av, Sutt. 199 CY104
St. Margarets Av, Uxb. 134 BN70
St. Margarets Cl, Berk. 38 AX20
St. Margarets Cl, Dart. 189 FR89
St. Margarets Cl (Penn), H.Wyc. 88 AC47
St. Margarets Cl, Iver 133 BD68
St. Margarets Gate
St. Margarets Cl, Orp. 224 EV105
St. Margaret's Ct SE1 279 J3
St. Margarets Cres SW15 179 CV85
St. Margaret's Cres, Grav. 191 GL90
St. Margaret's Dr, Twick. 177 CH85
St. Margarets Gate, Iver 133 BD68
St. Margaret's Gro E11 124 EF62
St. Margaret's Gro SE18 165 EQ79
St. Margarets Gro, Twick. 177 CG86
St. Margarets La W8 160 DB76
St. Margarets Pas SE13 164 EE83
Church Ter
St. Margarets Rd E12 124 EJ61
St. Margaret's Rd N17 122 DS55
St. Margaret's Rd NW10 139 CW69
St. Margarets Rd SE4 163 DZ84
St. Margarets Rd W7 157 CE75
St. Margarets Rd, Couls. 235 DH121
St. Margarets Rd (South Darenth), Dart. 189 FS93
St. Margarets Rd, Edg. 96 CP50
St. Margaret's Rd (Northfleet), Grav. 190 GE89
St. Margarets Rd, Islw. 157 CH84
St. Margaret's Rd, Ruis. 115 BR58
St. Margarets Rd, Twick. 157 CH84
St. Margaret's Rd, Ware 33 EA13
St. Margarets Sq SE4 163 DZ84
Adelaide Av
St. Margaret's St SW1 277 P5
St. Margaret's St SW1 161 DK77
St. Margaret's Ter SE18 165 EQ78
St. Margarets Way, Hem.H. 41 BR20
St. Mark St E1 142 DT72
St. Marks Av (Northfleet), Grav. 191 GF87
St. Marks Cl SE10 163 EC80
Ashburnham Gro
St. Marks Cl W11 139 CY72
Lancaster Rd
St. Mark's Cl, Barn. 80 DB41
St. Marks Cl, Har. 117 CH59
Nightingale Av
St. Marks Cl (Colney Heath), St.Alb. 44 CP22
St. Marks Cres NW1 140 DG67
St. Mark's Gate E9 143 DZ66
Cadogan Ter
St. Mark's Gro SW10 160 DB79
St. Mark's Hill, Surb. 198 CL100
St. Mark's Pl SW19 179 CZ93
Wimbledon Hill Rd
St. Marks Pl W11 139 CY72
St. Marks Pl, Wind. 151 AQ82
St. Marks Ri E8 122 DT64
St. Marks Rd SE25 202 DU98
Coventry Rd
St. Mark's Rd W5 138 CL74
The Common
St. Marks Rd W7 157 CE75
St. Marks Rd W10 139 CX72
St. Marks Rd W11 139 CY72
St. Marks Rd, Brom. 204 EH97
St. Marks Rd, Enf. 82 DT44
St. Mark's Rd, Epsom 233 CW118
St. Marks Rd, Mitch. 200 DF96
St. Mark's Rd, Tedd. 177 CH94
St. Marks Rd, Wind. 151 AQ82
St. Marks Sq NW1 140 DG67
St. Martha's Av, Wok. 227 AZ121
St. Martin Cl, Uxb. 134 BK72
St. Martins App, Ruis. 115 BS59
St. Martins Av E6 144 EK68
St. Martins Av, Epsom 216 CS114
St. Martins Cl NW1 141 DJ67
St. Martins Cl, Enf. 82 DV39
St. Martins Cl, Epsom 216 CS113
Church Rd
St. Martins Cl, Erith 166 EX75
St. Helens Rd
St. Martins Cl (East Horsley), Lthd. 245 BS129
St. Martin's Cl, Wat. 94 BW49
Muirfield Rd
St. Martin's Cl, West Dr. 154 BK76
St. Martin's Rd
St. Martin's Ct WC2 141 DK73
St. Martin's La
St. Martin's Ct, Ashf. 174 BJ92
St. Martins Dr, Walt. 196 BW104
St. Martins Est SW2 181 DN88
St. Martin's La WC2 273 P10
St. Martin's La WC2 141 DL73
St. Martins La, Beck. 203 EB99
St. Martins Meadow (Brasted), West. 240 EW123
St. Martin's Ms WC2 277 P1
St. Martins Ms, Dor. 263 CG136
Church St
St. Martins Ms (Pyrford), Wok. 228 BG116
St. Martin's Pl WC2 277 P1
St. Martin's Pl WC2 141 DL73
St. Martins Rd N9 100 DV47
St. Martin's Rd SW9 161 DM82
St. Martins Rd, Dart. 188 FM86
St. Martin's Rd, West Dr. 154 BJ76
St. Martin's St WC2 277 N1
St. Martins Wk, Dor. 263 CH136
High St
St. Martins Way SW17 180 DC90
St. Martin's-le-Grand EC1 275 H8
St. Martin's-le-Grand EC1 142 DQ72
St. Mary Abbots Pl W8 159 CZ76
St. Mary Abbots Ter W14 159 CZ76
St. Mary at Hill EC3 279 M1
St. Mary at Hill EC3 142 DS73
St. Mary Av, Wall. 200 DG104
St. Mary Axe EC3 275 M9
St. Mary Axe EC3 142 DS72
St. Mary Rd E17 123 EA56
St. Mary St SE18 165 EM77
St. Marychurch St SE16 162 DW75
St. Marys, Bark. 145 ER67
St. Marys App E12 125 EM64
St. Marys Av E11 124 EH58
St. Mary's Av N3 97 CY54
St. Marys Av, Brwd. 109 GA43
St. Mary's Av, Brom. 204 EE97
St. Mary's Av, Nthwd. 93 BS50
St. Mary's Av (Stanwell), Stai. 174 BK87
St. Mary's Av, Tedd. 177 CF93
St. Mary's Av Cen, Sthl. 156 CB77
St. Mary's Av N, Sthl. 156 CB77
St. Mary's Av S, Sthl. 156 CB77
St. Mary's Cl N17 100 DT53
Kemble Rd
St. Marys Cl, Chess. 216 CM108
St. Marys Cl, Epsom 217 CU108
St. Mary's Cl, Grav. 191 GJ89
St. Marys Cl, Grays 170 GD79
Dock Rd
St. Mary's Cl (Fetcham), Lthd. 231 CD123
St. Marys Cl, Orp. 206 EV96
St. Mary's Cl, Oxt. 254 EE129
St. Mary's Cl (Stanwell), Stai. 174 BK87
St. Mary's Cl, Sun. 195 BU98
Green Way
St. Mary's Cl (Harefield), Uxb. 114 BH55
St. Marys Ct E6 145 EM70
St. Mary's Ct SE7 164 EK80
St. Mary's Ct W5 157 CK75
St. Mary's Rd
St. Marys Cres NW4 119 CV55
St. Mary's Cres, Hayes 135 BT73
St. Marys Cres, Islw. 157 CD80
St. Mary's Cres (Stanwell), Stai. 174 BK87
St. Marys Dr, Felt. 175 BQ87
St. Mary's Dr, Sev. 256 FE123
St. Mary's Gdns SE11 278 E8
St. Mary's Gdns SE11 161 DN77
St. Marys Gate W8 160 DB76
St. Marys Grn N2 120 DC55
Thomas More Way
St. Marys Grn (Biggin Hill), West. 238 EJ118
St. Mary's Gro N1 141 DP65
St. Mary's Gro SW13 159 CV83
St. Mary's Gro W4 158 CP79
St. Mary's Gro, Rich. 158 CM84
St. Marys Gro (Biggin Hill), West. 238 EJ118
St. Mary's La, Hert. 31 DM11
St. Mary's La, Upmin. 128 FN61
St. Marys Mans W2 140 DC71
St. Mary's Ms NW6 140 DB66
Priory Rd
St. Mary's Ms, Rich. 177 CJ89
Back La
St. Mary's Mt, Cat. 236 DT124
St. Marys Path N1 141 DP67
St. Mary's Pl SE9 185 EN86
Eltham High St
St. Mary's Pl W5 157 CK75
St. Mary's Rd
St. Mary's Pl W8 160 DB76
St. Marys Rd E10 123 EC62
St. Marys Rd E13 144 EH68
St. Marys Rd N8 121 DL56
High St
St. Marys Rd N9 100 DW46
St. Mary's Rd NW10 138 CS67
St. Mary's Rd NW11 119 CY59
St. Mary's Rd SE15 162 DW81
St. Mary's Rd SE25 202 DS97
St. Mary's Rd (Wimbledon) SW19 179 CY92
St. Mary's Rd W5 157 CK75
St. Mary's Rd, Barn. 98 DF45
St. Mary's Rd, Bex. 187 FC88
St. Marys Rd, E.Mol. 197 CD99
St. Mary's Rd, Grays 171 GH77
St. Mary's Rd, Green. 189 FS85
St. Mary's Rd, Hayes 135 BT73
St. Mary's Rd, Hem.H. 40 BK19
St. Marys Rd, Ilf. 125 EQ61
St. Marys Rd, Lthd. 231 CH122
St. Marys Rd, Reig. 266 DB135
St. Mary's Rd, Slou. 132 AY74
St. Mary's Rd, S.Croy. 220 DR110
St. Mary's Rd, Surb. 197 CK100
St. Marys Rd (Long Ditton), Surb. 197 CJ101
St. Marys Rd, Swan. 207 FD98
St. Mary's Rd (Denham), Uxb. 113 BF58
St. Mary's Rd (Harefield), Uxb. 114 BH56
St. Mary's Rd (Cheshunt), Wal.Cr. 66 DW29
St. Mary's Rd, Wat. 75 BV42
St. Marys Rd, Wey. 213 BR105
St. Mary's Rd, Wok. 226 AW117
St. Mary's Rd, Wor.Pk. 198 CS103
St. Marys Sq W2 140 DD71
St. Mary's Sq W5 157 CK75
St. Mary's Rd
St. Marys Ter W2 140 DD71
St. Marys Twr EC1 142 DQ70
St. Marys Vw, Har. 117 CJ57
St. Mary's Vw, Wat. 76 BW42
King St
St. Mary's Wk SE11 278 E8
St. Mary's Wk SE11 161 DN77
St. Mary's Wk, Hayes 135 BT73
St. Mary's Rd
St. Mary's Wk (Bletchingley), Red. 252 DR133
St. Marys Wk, St.Alb. 43 CH16
St. Mary's Way, Chesh. 54 AP31
St. Mary's Way, Chig. 103 EN50
St. Mary's Way (Chalfont St. Peter), Ger.Cr. 90 AX54
St. Mary's Way, Guil. 242 AS132
St. Matthew Cl, Uxb. 134 BK72
St. Matthew St SW1 277 M7
St. Matthew's Av, Surb. 198 CL102
St. Matthews Cl, Rain. 147 FG66
St. Matthews Cl, Wat. 76 BX44
St. Matthew's Dr, Brom. 205 EM97
St. Matthew's Rd SW2 161 DM84
St. Matthews Rd W5 138 CL74
The Common
St. Matthew's Rd, Red. 250 DF133
St. Matthew's Row E2 142 DU69
St. Matthias Cl NW9 119 CT57
St. Maur Rd SW6 159 CZ81
St. Mellion Cl SE28 146 EX72
Redbourne Dr
St. Merryn Cl SE18 165 ER80
St. Michael's All EC3 275 L9
St. Michaels Av N9 100 DW45
St. Michaels Av, Hem.H. 41 BP21
St. Michael's Av, Wem. 138 CN65
St. Michaels Cl E16 144 EK71
Fulmer Rd
St. Michael's Cl N3 97 CZ54
St. Michaels Cl N12 98 DE50
St. Michaels Cl, Brom. 204 EL97
St. Michaels Cl, Erith 166 EX75
St. Helens Rd
St. Michaels Cl, Harl. 35 ES14
St. Michaels Cl, S.Ock. 148 FQ73
St. Michaels Cl, Walt. 196 BW103
St. Michaels Cl, Wor.Pk. 199 CT103
St. Michael's Cres, Slou. 131 AK70
St. Michaels Cres, Pnr. 116 BY58
St. Michaels Dr, Wat. 59 BV33
St. Michaels Gdns W10 139 CY71
St. Lawrence Ter
St. Michael's Grn, Beac. 89 AL52
St. Michaels Rd NW2 119 CW63
St. Michael's Rd SW9 161 DM82
St. Michael's Rd, Ashf. 174 BN92
St. Michaels Rd, Brox. 49 DZ20
St. Michaels Rd, Cat. 236 DR122
St. Michaels Rd, Croy. 202 DQ102
St. Michaels Rd, Grays 171 GH78
St. Michaels Rd, Wall. 219 DJ107
St. Michaels Rd, Well. 166 EV83
St. Michaels Rd, Wok. 211 BD114
St. Michaels St W2 272 A8
St. Michaels St W2 140 DE71
St. Michaels St, St.Alb. 42 CB20
St. Michaels Ter N22 99 DL54
St. Michaels Way, Pot.B. 64 DB30
St. Mildred's Ct EC2 142 DR72
Poultry
St. Mildreds Rd SE12 184 EE87
St. Mildreds Rd, Guil. 243 AZ133
St. Monica's Rd, Tad. 233 CZ121
St. Nazaire Cl, Egh. 173 BC92
Mullens Rd
St. Neots Cl, Borwd. 78 CN38
St. Neots Rd, Rom. 106 FM52
St. Nicholas Av, Horn. 127 FG62
St. Nicholas Av (Bookham), Lthd. 246 CB125
St. Nicholas Cl, Amer. 72 AV39
St. Nicholas Cl, Borwd. 77 CK44
St. Nicholas Cl, Uxb. 134 BK72
St. Nicholas Cres (Pyrford), Wok. 228 BG116
St. Nicholas Dr, Sev. 257 FH126
St. Nicholas Dr, Shep. 194 BN101
St. Nicholas Glebe SW17 180 DG93
St. Nicholas Gro, Brwd. 109 GC50
St. Nicholas Hill, Lthd. 231 CH122
St. Nicholas Mt, Hem.H. 39 BF20
St. Nicholas Rd SE18 165 ET78
St. Nicholas Rd, Sutt. 218 DB106
St. Nicholas Rd, T.Ditt. 197 CF100
St. Nicholas St SE8 163 EA81
Lucas St
St. Nicholas Way, Sutt. 218 DB105
St. Nicolas La, Chis. 204 EL95
St. Ninian's Ct N20 98 DF48
St. Norbert Grn SE4 163 DY84
St. Norbert Rd SE4 163 DY84
St. Normans Way, Epsom 217 CU110
St. Olaf's Rd SW6 159 CY80
St. Olaves Cl, Stai. 173 BF94
St. Olaves Ct EC2 275 K9
St. Olave's Est SE1 279 N4
St. Olaves Gdns SE11 278 D8
St. Olaves Rd E6 145 EN67
St. Olave's Wk SW16 201 DJ96
St. Olav's Sq SE16 162 DW76
St. Omer Ridge, Guil. 259 BA135
St. Omer Rd, Guil. 259 BA135
St. Oswald's Pl SE11 161 DM78
St. Oswald's Rd SW16 201 DP95
St. Oswulf St SW1 277 N9
St. Pancras Way NW1 141 DJ66
St. Patrick's Ct, Wdf.Grn. 102 EE52
St. Patrick's Gdns, Grav. 191 GK90
St. Patricks Pl, Grays 171 GJ77
St. Paul Cl, Uxb. 134 BK71
St. Paul St N1 142 DQ67
St. Paul's All EC4 141 DP72
St. Paul's Chyd
St. Paul's Av NW2 139 CV65
St. Paul's Av SE16 143 DX74
St. Pauls Av, Har. 118 CM57
St. Pauls Av, Slou. 132 AT73
St. Paul's Chyd EC4 274 G9
St. Paul's Chyd EC4 141 DP72
St. Paul's Cl SE7 164 EK78
St. Paul's Cl W5 138 CM74
St. Pauls Cl, Add. 212 BG106
St. Paul's Cl, Ashf. 175 BQ92
St. Pauls Cl, Cars. 200 DE102
St. Pauls Cl, Chess. 215 CK105
St. Pauls Cl, Hayes 155 BR78
St. Paul's Cl, Houns. 156 BY82
St. Pauls Cl, S.Ock. 148 FQ73
St. Pauls Cl, Swans. 190 FY87
Swanscombe St
St. Paul's Ct W14 159 CX77
Colet Gdns
St. Pauls Ctyd SE8 163 EA80
Deptford High St
St. Pauls Cray Rd, Chis. 205 ER95
St. Paul's Cres NW1 141 DK66
St. Pauls Dr E15 123 ED64
St. Paul's Ms NW1 141 DK66
St. Paul's Cres
St. Paul's Pl N1 142 DR65
St. Pauls Pl, St.Alb. 43 CG20
St. Pauls Pl, S.Ock. 148 FQ73
St. Pauls Ri N13 99 DP51
St. Paul's Rd N1 141 DP65
St. Paul's Rd N17 100 DU52
St. Paul's Rd, Bark. 145 EQ67
St. Paul's Rd, Brent. 157 CK79
St. Paul's Rd, Erith 167 FC80
St. Pauls Rd, Hem.H. 40 BK19
St. Paul's Rd, Rich. 158 CM83
St. Paul's Rd, Stai. 173 BD92
St. Paul's Rd, Th.Hth. 202 DQ97
St. Pauls Rd, Wok. 227 BA117
St. Paul's Rd E, Dor. 263 CH137
St. Paul's Rd W, Dor. 263 CG137
St. Paul's Shrubbery N1 142 DR65
St. Pauls Sq, Brom. 204 EG96
St. Paul's Ter SE17 161 DP79
Westcott Rd
St. Pauls Twr E10 123 EB59
St. Pauls Wk, Kings.T. 178 CN94
Alexandra Rd
St. Pauls Way E3 143 DZ71
St. Pauls Way E14 143 DZ71
St. Pauls Way N3 98 DB52
St. Pauls Way, Wal.Abb. 67 ED33
Rochford Av
St. Pauls Way, Wat. 76 BW40
St. Pauls Wd Hill, Orp. 205 ES96
St. Peter's All EC3 275 L9
St. Peter's Av E2 142 DU68
St. Peter's Cl
St. Peter's Av E17 124 EE56
St. Peters Av N18 100 DU49
St. Peter's Cl E2 142 DU68
St. Peters Cl SW17 180 DE89
College Gdns
St. Peter's Cl, Barn. 79 CV43
St. Peters Cl, Bushey 95 CD46
St. Peters Cl, Chis. 185 ER94
St. Peters Cl (Chalfont St. Peter), Ger.Cr. 90 AY53
Lewis La
St. Peters Cl, Hat. 45 CU17
St. Peters Cl, Ilf. 125 ES56
St. Peters Cl, Rick. 92 BH46
St. Peter's Cl, Ruis. 116 BX61
St. Peters Cl, St.Alb. 43 CD19
St. Peter's Cl, Slou. 130 AH70
St. Peters Cl, Stai. 173 BF93
St. Peters Cl, Swans. 190 FZ87
St. Peters Cl (Old Windsor), Wind. 172 AU85
Church Rd
St. Peters Cl, Wok. 227 BC120
St. Peter's Ct NW4 119 CW57
St. Peters Ct SE3 164 EF84
Eltham Rd
St. Peters Ct SE4 163 DZ82
Wickham Rd
St. Peters Ct (Chalfont St. Peter), Ger.Cr. 90 AY53
High St
St. Peters Ct, W.Mol. 196 CA98
St. Peter's Gdns SE27 181 DN90
St. Peter's Gro W6 159 CU77
St. Peters La, Orp. 206 EU96
St. Peter's Pl W9 140 DB70
Shirland Rd
St. Peters Rd N9 100 DW46
St. Peter's Rd W6 159 CU78
St. Peters Rd, Brwd. 108 FV49
Crescent Rd
St. Peter's Rd, Croy. 220 DR105
St. Peter's Rd, Grays 171 GH77
St. Peter's Rd, Kings.T. 198 CN96
St. Peters Rd, St.Alb. 43 CE20
St. Peters Rd, Sthl. 136 CA71
St. Peters Rd, Twick. 177 CH85
St. Peters Rd, Uxb. 134 BK71
St. Peter's Rd, W.Mol. 196 CA98
St. Peters Rd, Wok. 227 BB121
St. Peter's Sq E2 142 DU68
St. Peter's Cl
St. Peter's Sq W6 159 CU78

St. Peters St N1 141 DP67
St. Peters St, St.Alb. 43 CD20
St. Peter's St, S.Croy. 220 DR106
St. Peters Ter SW6 159 CY80
St. Peter's Vil W6 159 CU77
St. Peter's Way N1 142 DS66
St. Peters Way W5 137 CK71
St. Peter's Way, Add. 194 BG104
St. Peter's Way, Cher. 211 BD105
St. Peters Way, Hayes 155 BR78
St. Peters Way, Rick. 73 BB43
St. Petersburgh Ms W2 140 DB73
St. Petersburgh Pl W2 140 DB73
St. Philip Sq SW8 161 DH82
St. Philip St SW8 161 DH82
St. Philip's Av, Wor.Pk. 199 CV103
St. Philips Gate, Wor.Pk. 199 CV103
St. Philip's Rd E8 142 DU65
St. Philips Rd, Surb. 197 CK100
St. Philip's Way N1 142 DQ67
Linton St
St. Pinnock Av, Stai. 194 BG95
St. Quentin Ho SW18 180 DD86
Fitzhugh Gro
St. Quentin Rd, Well. 165 ET83
St. Quintin Av W10 139 CW71
St. Quintin Gdns W10 139 CW71
St. Quintin Rd E13 144 EH68
St. Raphaels Ct, St.Alb. 43 CE19
Avenue Rd
St. Raphael's Way NW10 118 CQ64
St. Regis Cl N10 99 DH54
St. Ronan's Cl, Barn. 80 DD38
St. Ronans Cres, Wdf.Grn. 102 EG52
St. Rule St SW8 161 DJ82
St. Saviour's Est SE1 279 P6
St. Saviour's Est SE1 162 DT76
St. Saviours Pl, Guil. 242 AW134
Leas Rd
St. Saviour's Rd SW2 181 DM85
St. Saviours Rd, Croy. 202 DQ100
St. Saviours Vw, St.Alb. 43 CF19
Avenue Rd
St. Silas Pl NW5 140 DG65
St. Silas St Est NW5 140 DG65
St. Simon's Av SW15 179 CW85
St. Stephens Av E17 123 EC57
St. Stephens Av W12 159 CV75
St. Stephens Av W13 137 CH72
St. Stephen's Av, Ash. 232 CL116
St. Stephens Av, St.Alb. 42 CB22
St. Stephens Cl E17 123 EB57
St. Stephens Cl NW8 140 DE67
St. Stephens Cl, St.Alb. 42 CB23
St. Stephens Cl, Sthl. 136 CA71
St. Stephens Cres W2 140 DA72
St. Stephens Cres, Brwd. 109 GA49
St. Stephens Cres, Th.Hth. 201 DN97
St. Stephens Gdn Est W2 140 DA72
Shrewsbury Rd
St. Stephens Gdns SW15 179 CZ85
Manfred Rd
St. Stephens Gdns W2 140 DA72
St. Stephens Gdns, Twick. 177 CJ86
St. Stephens Gro SE13 163 EC83
St. Stephens Hill, St.Alb. 42 CC22
St. Stephens Ms W2 140 DA71
Chepstow Rd
St. Stephen's Par E7 144 EJ66
Green St
St. Stephen's Pas, Twick. 177 CJ86
Richmond Rd
St. Stephen's Rd E3 143 DZ68
St. Stephens Rd E6 144 EJ66
St. Stephen's Rd E17 123 EB57
Grove Rd
St. Stephens Rd W13 137 CH72
St. Stephen's Rd, Barn. 79 CX43
St. Stephens Rd, Enf. 83 DX37
St. Stephens Rd, Houns. 176 CA86
St. Stephen's Rd, West Dr. 134 BK74
St. Stephens Row EC4 275 K9
St. Stephens Ter SW8 161 DM80
St. Stephen's Wk SW7 160 DC77
St. Swithin's La EC4 275 K10
St. Swithin's La EC4 142 DR73
St. Swithun's Rd SE13 183 ED85
St. Teresa Wk, Grays 171 GH76
St. Theresa Cl, Epsom 216 CQ114
St. Theresa's Rd, Felt. 155 BT84
St. Thomas' Cl, Surb. 198 CM102
St. Thomas Cl, Wok. 226 AW117
St. Mary's Rd
St. Thomas Ct, Bex. 186 FA87
St. Thomas Dr (East Clandon), Guil. 244 BL131
The St
St. Thomas Dr, Orp. 205 EQ102
St. Thomas' Dr, Pnr. 94 BY53
St. Thomas Gdns, Ilf. 145 EQ65
St. Thomas Pl NW1 141 DK66
Maiden La
St. Thomas Rd E16 144 EG72
St. Thomas Rd N14 99 DK45
St. Thomas' Rd W4 158 CQ79
St. Thomas Rd, Belv. 167 FC75
St. Thomas Rd, Brwd. 108 FX47
St. Thomas Rd (Northfleet), Grav. 191 GF89
St. Thomas St SE1 279 K3
St. Thomas St SE1 142 DR74
St. Thomas Wk (Colnbrook), Slou. 153 BD80
St. Thomas's Av, Grav. 191 GH88
St. Thomas's Cl, Wal.Abb. 68 EH33
St. Thomas's Gdns NW5 140 DG65
Queen's Cres
St. Thomas's Ms, Guil. 259 AZ136
St. Catherines Pk
St. Thomas's Pl E9 142 DW66
St. Thomas's Rd N4 121 DN61
St. Thomas's Rd NW10 138 CS67
St. Thomas's Sq E9 142 DV66
St. Thomas's Way SW6 159 CZ80
St. Timothy's Ms, Brom. 204 EH95
Wharton Rd
St. Ursula Gro, Pnr. 116 BX57
St. Ursula Rd, Sthl. 136 CA72
St. Vincent Cl SE27 181 DP92
St. Vincent Dr, St.Alb. 43 CG23
St. Vincent Rd, Twick. 176 CC86
St. Vincent Rd, Walt. 195 BV104
St. Vincent St W1 272 G7
St. Vincents Av, Dart. 188 FN85
St. Vincents Rd, Dart. 188 FN86
St. Vincents Way, Pot.B. 64 DC33
St. Wilfrids Cl, Barn. 80 DE43
St. Wilfrids Rd, Barn. 80 DD43
St. Winefride's Av E12 125 EM64
St. Winifreds, Ken. 236 DQ115
St. Winifreds Cl, Chig. 103 EQ50
St. Winifred's Rd, Tedd. 177 CH93
St. Winifred's Rd (Biggin Hill), West. 239 EM118
St. Yon Ct, St.Alb. 43 CK20
Saints Cl SE27 181 DP91
Wolfington Rd
Saints Dr E7 124 EK64
Saints Wk, Grays 171 GJ77
Sakins Cft, Harl. 51 ET18
Sala Ho SE3 164 EH84
Pinto Way
Saladin Dr, Purf. 168 FN77
Salamanca Pl SE1 278 B9
Salamanca St SE1 278 A9
Salamanca St SE1 161 DM77
Salamander Cl, Kings.T. 177 CJ92
Salamander Quay (Harefield), Uxb. 92 BG52
Coppermill La
Salamons Way, Rain. 147 FE72
Salbrook Rd (Salfords), Red. 266 DG142
Salcombe Dr, Mord. 199 CX102
Salcombe Dr, Rom. 126 EZ58
Salcombe Gdns NW7 97 CW51
Salcombe Pk, Loug. 84 EK43
Salcombe Rd E17 123 DZ59
Salcombe Rd N16 122 DS64
Salcombe Rd, Ashf. 174 BL91
Salcombe Way, Hayes 135 BS69
Portland Rd
Salcombe Way, Ruis. 115 BU61
Salcot Cres (New Addington), Croy. 221 EC110
Salcote Rd, Grav. 191 GL92
Salcott Rd SW11 180 DE85
Salcott Rd, Croy. 201 DL104
Sale Pl W2 272 B7
Sale Pl W2 140 DE71
Sale St E2 142 DU70
Hereford St
Salehurst Cl, Har. 118 CL57
Salehurst Rd SE4 183 DZ86
Salem Pl, Croy. 202 DQ104
Salem Pl (Northfleet), Grav. 190 GD87
Salem Rd W2 140 DB73
Salesian Gdns, Cher. 194 BG102
Salford Rd SW2 181 DK88
Salfords Ind Est, Red. 267 DH143
Salfords Way, Red. 266 DG142
Salhouse Cl SE28 146 EW72
Rollesby Way
Salisbury Av N3 119 CZ55
Salisbury Av, Bark. 145 ES66
Salisbury Av, St.Alb. 43 CH19
Salisbury Av, Slou. 131 AQ70
Salisbury Av, Sutt. 217 CZ107
Salisbury Av, Swan. 207 FG98
Salisbury Cl SE17 279 K8
Salisbury Cl, Amer. 55 AS39
Salisbury Cl, Pot.B. 64 DC32
Salisbury Cl, Upmin. 129 FT61
Canterbury Av
Salisbury Cl, Wor.Pk. 199 CT104
Salisbury Ct EC4 274 F9
Salisbury Ct EC4 141 DP72
Salisbury Cres (Cheshunt), Wal.Cr. 67 DX32
Salisbury Gdns SW19 179 CY94
Salisbury Gdns, Buck.H. 102 EK47
Salisbury Gdns, Welw.G.C. 29 CZ10
Salisbury Hall Gdns E4 101 EA51
Salisbury Ho E14 143 EB72
Hobday St
Salisbury Ms SW6 159 CZ80
Dawes Rd
Salisbury Ms, Brom. 204 EL99
Salisbury Rd
Salisbury Pl SW9 161 DP80
Salisbury Pl W1 272 D6
Salisbury Pl W1 140 DF71
Salisbury Pl, W.Byf. 212 BJ111
Salisbury Rd E4 101 EA48
Salisbury Rd E7 144 EG65
Salisbury Rd E10 123 EC61
Salisbury Rd E12 124 EK64
Salisbury Rd E17 123 EC57
Salisbury Rd N4 121 DP57
Salisbury Rd N9 100 DU48
Salisbury Rd N22 99 DP53
Salisbury Rd SE25 202 DU100
Salisbury Rd SW19 179 CY94
Salisbury Rd W13 157 CG75
Salisbury Rd, Bans. 218 DB114
Salisbury Rd, Barn. 79 CY41
Salisbury Rd, Bex. 186 FA88
Salisbury Rd, Brom. 204 EL99
Salisbury Rd, Cars. 218 DF107
Salisbury Rd, Dag. 147 FB65
Salisbury Rd, Dart. 188 FQ88
Salisbury Rd, Enf. 83 DZ37
Salisbury Rd, Felt. 176 BW88
Salisbury Rd, Gdse. 252 DW131
Salisbury Rd, Grav. 191 GF88
Salisbury Rd, Grays 170 GC79
Salisbury Rd, Har. 117 CD57
Salisbury Rd, Hodd. 49 EC15
Salisbury Rd, Houns. 156 BW83
Salisbury Rd (Heathrow Airport), Houns. 175 BQ85
Salisbury Rd, Ilf. 125 ES61
Salisbury Rd, N.Mal. 198 CR97
Salisbury Rd, Pnr. 115 BU56
Salisbury Rd, Rich. 158 CL84
Salisbury Rd, Rom. 127 FH57
Salisbury Rd, Sthl. 156 BY77
Salisbury Rd, Uxb. 134 BH68
Salisbury Rd, Wat. 75 BV38
Salisbury Rd, Welw.G.C. 29 CZ10
Salisbury Rd, Wok. 226 AY119
Salisbury Rd, Wor.Pk. 199 CT104
Salisbury Sq EC4 274 E9
Salisbury Sq, Hat. 45 CW17
Park St
Salisbury Sq, Hert. 32 DR09
Railway St
Salisbury St NW8 272 B5
Salisbury St NW8 140 DE70
Salisbury St W3 158 CQ75
Salisbury Ter SE15 162 DW83
Salisbury Wk N19 121 DJ61
Salix Cl, Lthd. 230 CB123
Solebay St
Willow Vale
Salix Cl, Sun. 175 BV94
Oak Gro
Salix Rd, Grays 170 GD79
Salliesfield, Twick. 177 CD86
Sally Murrey Cl E12 125 EN63
Grantham Rd
Salmen Rd E13 144 EF68
Salmon Cl, Welw.G.C. 30 DA06
Salmon La E14 143 DY72
Salmon Meadow Footpath, Hem.H. 40 BK24
Salmon Rd, Belv. 166 FA78
Salmon Rd, Dart. 168 FM83
Salmon St E14 143 DZ72
Salmon La
Salmon St NW9 118 CP60
Salmond Cl, Stan. 95 CG51
Robb Rd
Salmonds Gro, Brwd. 109 GC50
Salmons La, Whyt. 236 DU119
Salmons La W, Cat. 236 DS120
Salmons Rd N9 100 DU46
Salmons Rd, Chess. 215 CK107
Salmons Rd (Effingham), Lthd. 245 BV129
Salomons Rd E13 144 EJ71
Chalk Rd
Salop Rd E17 123 DX58
Salt Box Hill, West. 222 EH113
Salt Box Rd, Guil. 242 AT129
Salt Hill Av, Slou. 131 AQ74
Salt Hill Dr, Slou. 131 AQ74
Salt Hill Way, Slou. 131 AQ74
Saltash Cl, Sutt. 217 CZ105
Saltash Rd, Ilf. 103 ER52
Saltash Rd, Well. 166 EW81
Saltcoats Rd W4 158 CS75
Saltcroft Cl, Wem. 118 CP60
Salter Cl, Har. 116 BZ62
Salter Rd SE16 143 DX74
Salter St E14 143 EA73
Salter St NW10 139 CU69
Salterford Rd SW17 180 DG93
Salters Cl, Berk. 38 AT17
Salters Cl, Rick. 92 BL46
Salters Gdns, Wat. 75 BU39
Salters Hall Ct EC4 275 K10
Salters Hill SE19 182 DR92
Salters Rd E17 123 ED56
Salters Rd W10 139 CX70
Salterton Rd N7 121 DL62
Saltford Cl, Erith 167 FE78
Salthill Cl, Uxb. 114 BL64
Saltley Cl E6 144 EL72
Dunnock Rd
Saltoun Rd SW2 161 DN84
Saltram Cl N15 122 DT56
Saltram Cres W9 139 CZ69
Saltwell St E14 143 EA73
Saltwood Cl, Orp. 224 EW105
Saltwood Gro SE17 162 DR78
Merrow St
Salusbury Rd NW6 139 CY67
Salutation Rd SE10 164 EE77
Salvia Gdns, Grnf. 137 CG68
Selborne Gdns
Salvin Rd SW15 159 CX83
Salway Cl, Wdf.Grn. 102 EF52
Salway Pl E15 144 EE65
Broadway
Salway Rd E15 143 ED65
Great Eastern Rd
Salwey Cres, Brox. 49 DZ20
Sam Bartram Cl SE7 164 EJ78
Samantha Cl E17 123 DZ59
Samantha Ms (Havering-atte-Bower), Rom. 105 FE48
Sambruck Ms SE6 183 EB88
Samels Ct W6 159 CU78
South Black Lion La
Samford St NW8 272 A5
Samford St NW8 140 DD70
Samian Gate, St.Alb. 42 BZ22
Mayne Av
Samos Rd SE20 202 DV96
Samphire Ct, Grays 170 GE80
Salix Rd
Sample Oak La (Chilworth), Guil. 259 BE140
Sampson Av, Barn. 79 CX43
Sampson Cl, Belv. 166 EX76
Carrill Way
Sampson St E1 142 DU74
Sampsons Ct, Shep. 195 BQ99
Linden Way
Sampsons Grn, Slou. 131 AM68
Samson St E13 144 EJ68
Samuel Cl E8 142 DT67
Pownall Rd
Samuel Cl SE14 163 DX79
Samuel Cl SE18 164 EL77
Samuel Gray Gdns, Kings.T. 197 CK95
Samuel Johnson Cl SW16 181 DN91
Curtis Fld Rd
Samuel Lewis Trust Dws E8 122 DU63
Amhurst Rd
Samuel Lewis Trust Dws N1 141 DN66
Liverpool Rd
Samuel Lewis Trust Dws SW3 276 B9
Samuel Lewis Trust Dws SW6 160 DA80
Samuel St SE15 162 DT80
Samuel St SE18 165 EM77
Samuels Cl W6 159 CU78
South Black Lion La
Sancroft Cl NW2 119 CV62
Sancroft Rd, Har. 95 CF54
Sancroft St SE11 278 C10
Sancroft St SE11 161 DM78
Sanctuary, The SW1 277 N5
Sanctuary, The, Bex. 186 EX86
Sanctuary, The, Mord. 200 DA100
Sanctuary Cl, Dart. 188 FJ86
Sanctuary Cl (Harefield), Uxb. 92 BJ52
Sanctuary Rd (Heathrow Airport), Houns. 174 BN86
Sanctuary St SE1 279 J5
Sandal Rd N18 100 DU50
Sandal Rd, N.Mal. 198 CR99
Sandal St E15 144 EE67
Sandale Cl N16 122 DR62
Stoke Newington Ch St
Sandall Cl W5 138 CL70
Sandall Rd NW5 141 DJ65
Sandall Rd W5 138 CL70
Sandalls Spring, Hem.H. 39 BF18
Sandalwood, Guil. 258 AV135
Sandalwood Av, Cher. 193 BD104
Sandalwood Cl E1 143 DY70
Solebay St
Sandalwood Dr, Ruis. 115 BQ59
Sandalwood Rd, Felt. 175 BV90
Sanday Cl, Hem.H. 41 BP22
Sandbach Pl SE18 165 EQ77
Sandbanks, Felt. 175 BT88
Sandbanks Hill (Bean), Dart. 189 FV93
Sandbourne Av SW19 200 DB97
Sandbourne Rd SE4 163 DY82
Sandbrook Cl NW7 96 CR51
Sandbrook Rd N16 122 DS62
Sandby Grn SE9 164 EL83
Sandcliff Rd, Erith 167 FD77
Sandcroft Cl N13 99 DP51
Sandcross La, Reig. 265 CZ137
Sandell St SE1 278 D4
Sandells Av, Ashf. 175 BQ91
Sandels Way, Beac. 89 AK51
Sandelswood End, Beac. 89 AK50
Sanders Cl (Hampton Hill), Hmptn. 176 CC92
Sanders Cl, Hem.H. 40 BM24
Sanders Cl (London Colney), St.Alb. 61 CK27
Sanders La NW7 97 CX52
Sanders Rd, Hem.H. 40 BM23
Sanders Way N19 121 DK60
Sussex Way
Sandersfield Gdns, Bans. 234 DA115
Sandersfield Rd, Bans. 234 DB115
Sanderson Av, Sev. 224 FA110
Sanderson Cl NW5 121 DH63
Sanderson Rd, Uxb. 134 BJ65
Sanderstead Av NW2 119 CY61
Sanderstead Cl SW12 181 DJ87
Atkins Rd
Sanderstead Ct Av, S.Croy. 220 DU113
Sanderstead Hill, S.Croy. 220 DS111
Sanderstead Rd E10 123 DY60
Sanderstead Rd, Orp. 206 EV100
Sanderstead Rd, S.Croy. 220 DR108
Sandes Pl, Lthd. 231 CG118
Sandfield Gdns, Th.Hth. 201 DP97
Sandfield Pas, Th.Hth. 202 DQ97
Sandfield Rd, St.Alb. 43 CG20
Sandfield Rd, Th.Hth. 201 DP97
Sandfield Ter, Guil. 258 AX135
Sandfields (Send), Wok. 227 BD124
Sandford Av N22 100 DQ52
Sandford Av, Loug. 85 EQ41
Sandford Cl E6 145 EM70
Sandford Ct N16 122 DS60
Sandford Rd E6 144 EL70
Sandford Rd, Bexh. 166 EY84
Sandford Rd, Brom. 204 EG98
Sandford St SW6 160 DB80
King's Rd
Sandgate Cl, Rom. 127 FD59
Sandgate La SW18 180 DE88
Sandgate Rd, Well. 166 EW80
Sandgate St SE15 162 DV79
Sandham Pt SE18 165 EP77
Troy Ct
Sandhills, Wall. 219 DK105
Sandhills La, Vir.W. 192 AY99
Sandhills Meadow, Shep. 195 BQ101
Sandhills Rd, Reig. 266 DA136
Sandhurst Av, Har. 116 CB58
Sandhurst Av, Surb. 198 CP101
Sandhurst Cl NW9 118 CN55
Sandhurst Cl, S.Croy. 220 DS109
Sandhurst Dr, Ilf. 125 ET63
Sandhurst Rd N9 82 DW44
Sandhurst Rd NW9 118 CN55
Sandhurst Rd SE6 183 ED88
Sandhurst Rd, Bex. 186 EX85
Sandhurst Rd, Orp. 206 EU104
Sandhurst Rd, Sid. 185 ET90
Sandhurst Rd, Til. 171 GJ82
Sandhurst Way, S.Croy. 220 DS108
Sandifield, Hat. 45 CU21
Sandiford Rd, Sutt. 199 CZ103
Sandiland Cres, Brom. 204 EF103
Sandilands, Croy. 202 DU103
Sandilands, Sev. 256 FD122
Sandilands Rd SW6 160 DB81
Sandison St SE15 162 DT83
Sandland St WC1 274 C7
Sandland St WC1 141 DM71
Sandlands Gro, Tad. 233 CU123
Sandlands Rd, Tad. 233 CU123
Sandlers End, Slou. 131 AP70
Sandling Ri SE9 185 EN90
Sandlings, The N22 99 DN54
Sandlings Cl SE15 162 DV82
Pilkington Rd
Sandmere Cl, Hem.H. 40 BN21
St. Albans Rd
Sandmere Rd SW4 161 DL84
Sandon Cl, Esher 197 CD101
Sandon Rd (Cheshunt), Wal.Cr. 66 DW30
Sandow Cres, Hayes 155 BT76
Sandown Av, Dag. 147 FC65
Sandown Av, Esher 214 CC106
Sandown Av, Horn. 128 FK61
Sandown Cl, Houns. 155 BU81
Sandown Ct, Sutt. 218 DB108
Grange Rd
Sandown Dr, Cars. 218 DG109
Sandown Gate, Esher 196 CC104
Sandown Ind Pk, Esher 196 CA103
Sandown Rd SE25 202 DV99
Sandown Rd, Couls. 234 DG116
Sandown Rd, Esher 214 CC105
Sandown Rd, Grav. 191 GJ93
Sandown Rd, Slou. 131 AM71
Sandown Rd, Wat. 76 BW38
Sandown Way, Nthlt. 136 BY65
Sandpiper Cl E17 101 DX53
Sandpiper Cl SE16 163 DZ75
Sandpiper Dr, Erith 167 FH80
Sandpiper Rd, S.Croy. 221 DX111
Sandpiper Rd, Sutt. 217 CZ106
Sandpiper Way, Orp. 206 EX98
Sandpipers, The, Grav. 191 GK89
Sandpit Hall Rd (Chobham), Wok. 210 AU112
Sandpit La (Pilgrim's Hatch), Brwd. 108 FT46
Sandpit La, St.Alb. 43 CJ18
Sandpit Pl SE7 164 EL78
Sandpit Rd, Brom. 184 EE92
Sandpit Rd, Dart. 168 FJ84
Sandpit Rd, Red. 266 DE135
Sandpit Rd, Welw.G.C. 29 CY11
Sandpits La (Penn), H.Wyc. 88 AC48
Sandpits Rd, Croy. 221 DX105
Sandpits Rd, Rich. 177 CK89
Sandra Cl N22 100 DQ53
New Rd
Sandra Cl, Houns. 176 CB85
Sandridge Cl, Har. 117 CE56
Sandridge Ct N4 122 DQ62
Queens Dr
Sandridge Rd, St.Alb. 43 CE18
Sandridge St N19 121 DJ61
Sandridgebury La, St.Alb. 43 CE16
Sandringham Av SW20 199 CY96
Sandringham Av, Harl. 50 EL15
Sandringham Cl SW19 179 CX88
Sandringham Cl, Enf. 82 DS40
Sandringham Cl, Ilf. 125 EQ55
Sandringham Cl, Wok. 228 BG116
Sandringham Ct W9 140 DC69
Maida Vale
Sandringham Ct, Slou. 131 AK72
Sandringham Cres, Har. 116 CA61
Sandringham Cres, St.Alb. 43 CJ15
Sandringham Dr, Ashf. 174 BK91
Sandringham Dr, Well. 165 ES82
Sandringham Gdns N8 121 DL58
Sandringham Gdns N12 98 DD51
Sandringham Gdns, Houns. 155 BU81
Sandringham Gdns, Ilf. 125 EQ55
Sandringham Ms W5 137 CK73
High St
Sandringham Pk, Cob. 214 BZ112
Sandringham Rd E7 124 EJ64
Sandringham Rd E8 122 DT64
Sandringham Rd E10 123 ED58
Sandringham Rd N22 122 DQ55
Sandringham Rd NW2 139 CV65
Sandringham Rd NW11 119 CY59
Sandringham Rd, Bark. 145 ET65
Sandringham Rd, Brwd. 108 FV43
Sandringham Rd, Brom. 184 EG92
Sandringham Rd (Heathrow Airport), Houns. 174 BL85
Sandringham Rd, Nthlt. 136 CA66
Sandringham Rd, Pot.B. 64 DB30
Sandringham Rd, Th.Hth. 202 DQ99
Sandringham Rd, Wat. 76 BW37
Sandringham Rd, Wor.Pk. 199 CU104
Sandringham Way, Wal.Cr. 67 DX34
Sandrock Pl, Croy. 221 DX105
Sandrock Rd SE13 163 EA83
Sandrock Rd (Westcott), Dor. 262 CB138
Sandroyd Way, Cob. 214 CA113
Sand's End La SW6 160 DB81
Sands Fm Dr (Burnham), Slou. 130 AJ70
Sands Way, Wdf.Grn. 102 EL51
Sandstone Pl N19 121 DH61
Sandstone Rd SE12 184 EH89
Sandtoft Rd SE7 164 EH79
Sandway Path, Orp. 206 EW98
Sandway Rd, Orp. 206 EW98
Sandwell Cres NW6 140 DA65
Sandwich St WC1 273 P3
Sandwich St WC1 141 DL69
Sandwick Cl NW7 97 CU52
Sandy Bk Rd, Grav. 191 GH88
Sandy Bury, Orp. 205 ER104
Sandy Cl, Hert. 31 DP09
Sandy Cl, Wok. 227 BB117
Sandy La
Sandy Dr, Cob. 214 CA111
Sandy Dr, Felt. 175 BS88
Sandy Hill Av SE18 165 EP78
Sandy Hill Rd SE18 165 EP78
Sandy Hill Rd, Wall. 219 DJ109
Sandy La, Bet. 264 CS135
Sandy La, Bushey 76 CC41
Sandy La, Cob. 214 BZ112
Sandy La (Bean), Dart. 189 FW89
Sandy La (Chadwell St. Mary), Grays 171 GH79
Sandy La (West Thurrock), Grays 169 FV79
London Rd
Sandy La, Guil. 258 AU139
Sandy La (Albury Heath), Guil. 260 BJ141
Sandy La (Shere), Guil. 260 BN139
Sandy La, Har. 118 CM58
Sandy La, Kings.T. 177 CG94
Sandy La, Lthd. 214 CA112
Sandy La, Mitch. 200 DG95
Sandy La, Nthwd. 93 BU50
Sandy La, Orp. 206 EU101
Sandy La (St. Paul's Cray), Orp. 206 EX95
Sandy La, Oxt. 253 EC129
Sandy La (Limpsfield), Oxt. 254 EH127
Sandy La (Bletchingley), Red. 251 DP132
Sandy La (Nutfield), Red. 267 DK135
Sandy La, Reig. 265 CW135
Sandy La, Rich. 177 CJ89
Sandy La, Sev. 257 FJ123
Sandy La, Sid. 186 EX94
Sandy La, S.Ock. 148 FM73
Sandy La, Sutt. 217 CY108
Sandy La (Kingswood), Tad. 233 CZ124
Sandy La, Tedd. 177 CG94
Sandy La, Vir.W. 192 AY98
Sandy La, Walt. 195 BV100
Sandy La, Wat. 76 CC41
Sandy La, West. 255 ER125
Sandy La, Wok. 227 BC116
Sandy La (Chobham), Wok. 210 AS109
Sandy La (Pyrford), Wok. 227 BF117
Sandy La (Send), Wok. 227 BC123
Sandy La Est, Rich. 177 CK89
Sandy La N, Wall. 219 DK106
Sandy La S, Wall. 219 DK107
Sandy Lo La, Nthwd. 93 BR47
Sandy Lo Rd, Rick. 93 BP47
Sandy Lo Way, Nthwd. 93 BS50
Sandy Mead, Maid. 150 AC78
Sandy Ridge, Chis. 185 EN93
Sandy Ri (Chalfont St. Peter), Ger.Cr. 90 AY53
Sandy Rd NW3 120 DB62
Sandy Rd, Add. 212 BG107
Sandy Way, Cob. 214 CA112
Sandy Way, Croy. 203 DZ104
Sandy Way, Walt. 195 BT102
Sandy Way, Wok. 227 BC117
Sandycombe Rd, Felt. 175 BU88
Sandycombe Rd, Rich. 158 CN83
Sandycombe Rd, Twick. 177 CJ86
Sandycroft SE2 166 EU79
Sandycroft, Epsom 217 CW110
Sandycroft Rd, Amer. 72 AV39
Sandyhill Rd, Ilf. 125 EP63
Sandymount Av, Stan. 95 CJ50
Sandy's Row E1 275 N7
Sandy's Row E1 142 DS71
Sanfoin End, Hem.H. 40 BN18
Sanford La N16 122 DT61
Lawrence Bldgs
Sanford St SE14 163 DY79
Sanford Ter N16 122 DT62
Sanford Wk N16 122 DT61
Sanford Ter
Sanford Wk SE14 163 DY79
Cold Blow La
Sanger Av, Chess. 216 CL106
Sanger Dr (Send), Wok. 227 BC123
Sangers Dr, Horl. 268 DF148
Sangers Wk, Horl. 268 DF148
Sangers Dr
Sangley Rd SE6 183 EB87
Sangley Rd SE25 202 DS98
Sangora Rd SW11 160 DD84
Sans Wk EC1 274 E4
Sans Wk EC1 141 DN70
Sansom Rd E11 124 EE61
Sansom St SE5 162 DR80
Santers La, Pot.B. 63 CY33
Santley St SW4 161 DM84

Santos Rd SW18 180 DA85
Santway, The, Stan. 95 CE50
Sanway Cl (Byfleet), W.Byf. 212 BL114
Sanway Rd (Byfleet), W.Byf. 212 BL114
Sapcote Trd Cen NW10 119 CT64
Saperton Wk SE11 278 C8
Saperton Wk SE11 161 DM77
Sapho Pk, Grav. 191 GM91
Saphora Cl, Orp. 223 ER106
Oleander Cl
Sappers Cl, Saw. 36 EZ05
Sapperton Ct EC1 275 H4
Sapphire Cl E6 145 EN72
Sapphire Cl, Dag. 126 EW60
Sapphire Rd SE8 163 DY77
Sappho Ct, Wok. 226 AS116
Langmans Way
Sara Ct, Beck. 203 EB95
Albemarle Rd
Sara Cres, Green. 169 FU84
Sara Pk, Grav. 191 GL91
Saracen Cl, Croy. 202 DR100
Saracen Ind Area, Hem.H. 41 BP18
Saracen St E14 143 EA72
Saracens Head, Hem.H. 40 BN19
Adeyfield Rd
Saracen's Head Yd EC3 275 P9
Sarah Ho SW15 159 CT84
Saratoga Rd E5 122 DW63
Sardinia St WC2 274 B9
Sarel Way, Horl. 269 DH146
Sargeant Cl, Uxb. 134 BK69
Ratcliffe Cl
Sarita Cl, Har. 95 CD54
Sarjant Path SW19 179 CX89
Queensmere Rd
Sark Cl, Houns. 156 CA80
Sark Ho, Enf. 83 DX38
Eastfield Rd
Sark Wk E16 144 EH72
Sarnesfield Ho SE15 162 DV79
Pencraig Way
Sarnesfield Rd, Enf. 82 DR41
Church St
Sarratt Bottom, Rick. 73 BE36
Sarratt La, Rick. 74 BH40
Sarratt Rd, Rick. 74 BM41
Sarre Av, Horn. 148 FJ65
Sarre Rd NW2 119 CZ64
Sarre Rd, Orp. 206 EW99
Sarsby Dr, Stai. 173 BA89
Feathers La
Sarsen Av, Houns. 156 BZ82
Sarsfeld Rd SW12 180 DF88
Sarsfield Rd, Grnf. 137 CH68
Sartor Rd SE15 163 DX84
Sarum Complex, Uxb. 134 BH68
Sarum Grn, Wey. 195 BS104
Sarum Pl, Hem.H. 40 BL16
Sarum Ter E3 143 DZ70
Satanita Cl E16 144 EK72
Fulmer Rd
Satchell Mead NW9 97 CT53
Satchwell Rd E2 142 DU69
Satinwood Ct, Hem.H. 40 BL22
Satis Ct, Epsom 217 CT111
Windmill Av
Saturn Way, Hem.H. 40 BM18
Sauls Grn E11 124 EE62
Napier Rd
Saunder Cl, Wal.Cr. 67 DX27
Welsummer Way
Saunders Cl E14 143 DZ73
Limehouse Causeway
Saunders Cl (Northfleet), Grav. 190 GE89
Saunders Copse, Wok. 226 AV122
Saunders La, Wok. 226 AS122
Saunders Ness Rd E14 163 EC78
Saunders Rd SE18 165 ET78
Saunders Rd, Uxb. 134 BM66
Saunders St SE11 278 D8
Saunders St SE11 161 DN77
Saunders Way SE28 146 EV73
Oriole Way
Saunders Way, Dart. 188 FM89
Saunderton Rd, Wem. 117 CH64
Saunton Av, Hayes 155 BT80
Saunton Rd, Horn. 127 FG61
Savage Gdns E6 145 EM72
Savage Gdns EC3 275 N10
Savay Cl (Denham), Uxb. 114 BG59
Savay La (Denham), Uxb. 114 BG58
Savernake Rd N9 82 DU44
Savernake Rd NW3 120 DF63
Savery Dr, Surb. 197 CJ101
Savile Cl, N.Mal. 198 CS99
Savile Cl, T.Ditt. 197 CF102
Savile Gdns, Croy. 202 DT103
Savile Row W1 273 K10
Savile Row W1 141 DJ73
Savill Cl (Cheshunt), Wal.Cr. 66 DQ25
Markham Rd
Savill Gdns SW20 199 CU97
Bodnant Gdns
Savill Row, Wdf.Grn. 102 EF51
Saville Cres, Ashf. 175 BR93
Saville Rd E16 144 EL74
Saville Rd W4 158 CR76
Saville Rd, Rom. 126 EZ58
Saville Rd, Twick. 177 CF88
Saville Row, Brom. 204 EF102
Saville Row, Enf. 83 DX40
Savona Cl SW19 179 CY94
Savona Est SW8 161 DJ80
Savona St SW8 161 DJ80
Savoy Av, Hayes 155 BS78
Savoy Bldgs WC2 278 B1
Savoy Cl E15 144 EE67
Arthingworth St
Savoy Cl, Edg. 96 CN50
Savoy Cl (Harefield), Uxb. 92 BK54
Savoy Ct WC2 278 A1
Savoy Hill WC2 278 B1
Savoy Pl WC2 278 A1
Savoy Pl WC2 141 DL73
Savoy Rd, Dart. 188 FK85
Savoy Row WC2 274 B10
Savoy Steps WC2 141 DM73
Savoy St
Savoy St WC2 274 B10
Savoy St WC2 141 DM73
Savoy Way WC2 278 B1
Savoy Wd, Harl. 51 EN20
Sawbill Cl, Hayes 136 BX71
Sawells, Brox. 49 DZ21
Sawkins Cl SW19 179 CY89
Sawley Rd W12 139 CU74
Sawpit La (East Clandon), Guil. 244 BL131
Sawtry Cl, Cars. 200 DE101
Sawtry Way, Borwd. 78 CN38
Sawyer Cl N9 100 DU47
Lion Rd
Sawyer St SE1 279 H4
Sawyer St SE1 162 DQ75
Sawyers Chase, Rom. 86 EV41
Sawyers Cl, Dag. 147 FC65
Sawyers Cl, Wind. 151 AL80
Sawyers Hall La, Brwd. 108 FW45
Sawyer's Hill, Rich. 178 CP87
Sawyers La, Borwd. 77 CH40
Sawyers La, Pot.B. 63 CX34
Sawyers Lawn W13 137 CF72
Sawyers Way, Hem.H. 40 BM20
Saxby Rd SW2 181 DL87
Saxham Rd, Bark. 145 ET67
Saxley, Horl. 269 DJ147
Ewelands
Saxlingham Rd E4 101 ED48
Saxon Av, Felt. 176 BZ89
Saxon Cl E17 123 EA59
Saxon Cl, Brwd. 109 GA48
Saxon Cl (Northfleet), Grav. 190 GC90
Saxon Cl, Rom. 106 FM54
Saxon Cl (Otford), Sev. 241 FF117
Saxon Cl, Slou. 153 AZ75
Saxon Cl, Surb. 197 CK100
Saxon Cl, Uxb. 134 BM71
Saxon Ct, Borwd. 78 CL40
Saxon Dr W3 138 CP72
Saxon Gdns, Maid. 130 AD70
Saxon Gdns, Sthl. 136 BY73
Saxon Rd
Saxon Pl (Horton Kirby), Dart. 208 FQ99
Saxon Rd E3 143 DZ68
Saxon Rd E6 145 EM70
Saxon Rd N22 99 DP53
Saxon Rd SE25 202 DR99
Saxon Rd, Ashf. 175 BR93
Saxon Rd, Brom. 184 EF94
Saxon Rd (Hawley), Dart. 188 FL91
Saxon Rd, Ilf. 145 EP65
Saxon Rd, Sthl. 136 BY74
Saxon Rd, Walt. 196 BX104
Saxon Rd, Wem. 118 CQ62
Saxon Shore Way, Grav. 191 GM86
Saxon Wk, Sid. 186 EW93
Saxon Way N14 81 DK44
Saxon Way, Reig. 249 CZ133
Saxon Way, Wal.Abb. 67 EC33
Saxon Way, West Dr. 154 BJ79
Saxon Way (Old Windsor), Wind. 172 AV86
Saxonbury Av, Sun. 195 BV97
Saxonbury Cl, Mitch. 200 DD97
Saxonbury Gdns, Surb. 197 CJ102
Saxonfield Cl SW2 181 DM87
Saxons, Tad. 233 CX121
Saxony Par, Hayes 135 BQ71
Saxton Cl SE13 163 ED83
Saxton Ms, Wat. 75 BU40
Dellfield Cl
Saxville Rd, Orp. 206 EV97
Sayer Cl, Green. 189 FU85
Sayers Cl (Fetcham), Lthd. 230 CC124
Sayers Gdns, Berk. 38 AU16
Sayers Wk, Rich. 178 CM87
Stafford Pl
Sayes Ct SE8 163 DZ78
Sayes Ct St
Sayes Ct, Add. 212 BJ106
Sayes Ct Fm Dr, Add. 212 BH106
Sayes Ct Rd, Orp. 206 EU98
Sayes Ct St SE8 163 DZ79
Sayes Gdns, Saw. 36 EZ05
Sayesbury La N18 100 DU50
Sayesbury Rd, Saw. 36 EX05
Sayward Cl, Chesh. 54 AR29
Scadbury Pk, Chis. 185 ET93
Scads Hill Cl, Orp. 205 ET100
Scafell Rd, Slou. 131 AM71
Scala St W1 273 L6
Scala St W1 141 DJ71
Scales Rd N17 122 DT55
Scammel Way, Wat. 75 BT44
Scampston Ms W10 139 CX72
Scampton Rd (Heathrow Airport), Houns. 174 BM86
Southampton Rd
Scandrett St E1 142 DV74
Scarba Wk N1 142 DR65
Marquess Rd
Scarborough Cl, Sutt. 217 CZ111
Scarborough Cl (Biggin Hill), West. 238 EJ118
Scarborough Rd E11 123 ED60
Scarborough Rd N4 121 DN59
Scarborough Rd N9 100 DW45
Scarborough Rd (Heathrow Airport), Houns. 175 BQ86
Southern Perimeter Rd
Scarborough St E1 142 DT72
West Tenter St
Scarborough Way, Slou. 151 AP75
Scarbrook Rd, Croy. 202 DQ104
Scarle Rd, Wem. 137 CK65
Scarlet Cl, Orp. 206 EV98
Scarlet Rd SE6 184 EE90
Scarlett Cl, Wok. 226 AT118
Bingham Dr
Scarlette Manor Way SW2 181 DN87
Papworth Way
Scarsbrook Rd SE3 164 EK83
Scarsdale Pl W8 160 DB76
Wrights La
Scarsdale Rd, Har. 116 CC62
Scarsdale Vil W8 160 DA76
Scarth Rd SW13 159 CT83
Scatterdells La, Kings L. 57 BF30
Scawen Cl, Cars. 218 DG105
Scawen Rd SE8 163 DY78
Scawfell St E2 142 DT68
Scaynes Link N12 98 DA50
Sceaux Est SE5 162 DS81
Sceptre Rd E2 142 DW69
Schofield Wk SE3 164 EH80
Dornberg Cl
Scholars Ms, Welw.G.C. 29 CX07
Scholars Rd E4 101 EC46
Scholars Rd SW12 181 DJ88
Scholars Wk (Chalfont St. Peter), Ger.Cr. 90 AY51
Scholars Wk, Guil. 258 AV135
Scholars Wk, Hat. 45 CU21
Scholars Way, Amer. 72 AT38
Scholefield Rd N19 121 DK60
Schonfeld Sq N16 122 DR61
School Cl, Guil. 242 AX132
School Cl (Essendon), Hat. 46 DF17
School La
School Cres (Crayford), Dart. 167 FF84
School Gdns, Berk. 39 BB17
School Grn La, Epp. 71 FC25
School Hill, Red. 251 DJ128
School Ho La, Tedd. 177 CH94
School La SE23 182 DV89
School La, Add. 212 BG105
School La (Amersham Old Town), Amer. 55 AM39
School La (Seer Grn), Beac. 89 AR51
School La, Bushey 94 CB45
School La, Cat. 252 DT126
School La, Ch.St.G. 90 AW47
School La, Chig. 103 ET49
School La (Bean), Dart. 189 FW90
School La (Horton Kirby), Dart. 208 FQ98
School La (Mickleham), Dor. 247 CJ127
School La (Westcott), Dor. 263 CD137
School La, Egh. 173 BA92
School La (Chalfont St. Peter), Ger.Cr. 90 AX54
School La (East Clandon), Guil. 244 BL131
School La, Harl. 35 ES12
School La, Hat. 45 CV17
School La (Essendon), Hat. 46 DE17
School La, Kings.T. 197 CJ95
School Rd
School La (Fetcham), Lthd. 231 CD122
School La (West Horsley), Lthd. 245 BP129
School La, Long. 209 FT100
School La, Ong. 53 FD17
School La, Pnr. 116 BY56
School La (Bricket Wd), St.Alb. 60 CA31
School La (Seal), Sev. 257 FM121
School La, Shep. 195 BP100
School La, Slou. 132 AT72
Lismore Pk
School La (Stoke Poges), Slou. 132 AV67
School La, Surb. 198 CN102
School La, Swan. 207 FH95
School La, Tad. 249 CU125
Chequers La
School La, Well. 166 EV83
School La (Tewin), Welw. 30 DE06
School La (Ockham), Wok. 229 BP122
School Mead, Abb.L. 59 BS32
School Pas, Kings.T. 198 CM96
School Pas, Sthl. 136 BZ74
School Rd E12 125 EM63
School Rd NW10 138 CR70
School Rd, Ashf. 175 BP93
School Rd, Chis. 205 EQ95
School Rd, Dag. 146 FA67
School Rd, E.Mol. 197 CD98
School Rd (Hampton Hill), Hmptn. 176 CC93
School Rd (Penn), H.Wyc. 88 AC47
School Rd (Wooburn Grn), H.Wyc. 110 AE57
School Rd, Houns. 156 CC83
School Rd, Kings.T. 197 CJ95
School Rd, Ong. 71 FG32
School Rd, Pot.B. 64 DC30
School Rd, West Dr. 154 BK79
School Rd Av (Hampton Hill), Hmptn. 176 CC93
School Row, Hem.H. 39 BF21
School Wk, Horl. 268 DE148
Thornton Cl
School Wk, Slou. 132 AV73
Grasmere Av
School Wk, Sun. 195 BT98
School Way N12 98 DC49
High Rd
School Way, Dag. 126 EW62
Schoolbell Ms E3 143 DY68
Arbery Rd
Schoolfield Rd, Grays 169 FU79
Schoolhouse Gdns, Loug. 85 EP42
Schoolhouse La E1 143 DX73
Schoolway N12 98 DD51
Schooner Cl E14 163 ED76
Schooner Cl SE16 163 DX75
Kinburn St
Schooner Cl, Bark. 146 EV69
Schooner Ct, Dart. 168 FQ84
Schroder Ct (Englefield Grn), Egh. 172 AV92
Schubert Rd SW15 179 CZ85
Schubert Rd, Borwd. 77 CK44
Scilla Ct, Grays 170 GD79
Scillonian Rd, Guil. 258 AU135
Sclater St E1 275 P4
Sclater St E1 142 DT70
Scoble Pl N16 122 DT63
Amhurst Rd
Scoles Cres SW2 181 DN88
Scope Way, Kings.T. 198 CL98
Scoresby St SE1 278 F3
Scoresby St SE1 141 DP74
Scorton Av, Grnf. 137 CG68
Scot Gro, Pnr. 94 BX52
Scotch Common W13 137 CG71
Scoter Cl, Wdf.Grn. 102 EH52
Mallards Rd
Scotia Rd SW2 181 DN87
Scotland Br Rd (New Haw), Add. 212 BG111
Scotland Grn N17 100 DU54
Scotland Grn Rd, Enf. 83 DX43
Scotland Grn Rd N, Enf. 83 DX42
Scotland Pl SW1 277 P2
Scotland Rd, Buck.H. 102 EJ46
Scotlands Dr (Farnham Common), Slou. 131 AP65
Scotney Cl, Orp. 223 EN105
Scotney Wk, Horn. 128 FK64
Bonington Rd
Scots Hill, Rick. 74 BM44
Scots Hill Cl, Rick. 74 BM44
Scots Hill
Scotscraig, Rad. 77 CF35
Scotsdale Cl, Orp. 205 ES98
Scotsdale Cl, Sutt. 217 CY108
Scotsdale Rd SE12 184 EH85
Scotshall La, Warl. 221 EC114
Scotsmill La, Rick. 74 BM44
Scotswood Cl, Beac. 89 AK50
Scotswood St EC1 274 E4
Scotswood Wk N17 100 DU52
Scott Av, Ware 33 EB11
Scott Cl SW16 201 DM95
Scott Cl, Epsom 216 CQ106
Scott Cl, Guil. 242 AU132
Scott Cl (Farnham Common), Slou. 111 AQ64
Scott Cl, West Dr. 154 BM77
Scott Ct W3 158 CQ75
Petersfield Rd
Scott Cres, Erith 167 FF81
Cloudesley Rd
Scott Cres, Har. 116 CB60
Scott Ellis Gdns NW8 140 DD69
Scott Fm Cl, T.Ditt. 197 CH102
Scott Gdns, Houns. 156 BX80
Scott Ho N18 100 DU50
Scott Lidgett Cres SE16 162 DU75
Scott Rd, Grav. 191 GK92
Scott Rd, Grays 171 GG77
Scott Russell Pl E14 163 EB78
Westferry Rd
Scott St E1 142 DV70
Scott Trimmer Way, Houns. 156 BY82
Scottes La, Dag. 126 EX60
Valence Av
Scotts Av, Brom. 203 ED96
Scotts Av, Sun. 175 BS94
Scotts Cl, Horn. 128 FJ64
Rye Cl
Scotts Cl, Stai. 174 BK88
Scotts Cl, Ware 33 DX07
Scotts Dr, Hmptn. 176 CB94
Scotts Fm Rd, Epsom 216 CQ107
Scotts La, Brom. 203 ED97
Scotts La, Walt. 214 BX105
Scotts Rd E10 123 EC60
Scotts Rd W12 159 CV75
Scotts Rd, Brom. 184 EG94
Scotts Rd, Sthl. 156 BW76
Scotts Rd, Ware 33 DX07
Scotts Vw, Welw.G.C. 29 CW10
Scotts Way, Sev. 256 FE122
Scotts Way, Sun. 175 BS93
Scott's Yd EC4 275 K10
Scottswood Cl, Bushey 76 BY40
Scottswood Rd
Scottswood Rd, Bushey 76 BY40
Scottwell Dr NW9 119 CT57
Scoulding Rd E16 144 EF72
Scouler St E14 143 ED73
Quixley St
Scout App NW10 118 CS63
Scout La SW4 161 DJ83
Old Town
Scout Way NW7 96 CR49
Scovell Cres SE1 279 H5
Scovell Rd SE1 279 H5
Scratchers La (Fawkham Grn), Long. 209 FR103
Scrattons Ter, Bark. 146 EX68
Scriven St E8 142 DT67
Scriveners Cl, Hem.H. 40 BL20
Scrooby St SE6 183 EB86
Scrubbitts Pk Rd, Rad. 77 CG35
Scrubbitts Sq, Rad. 77 CG36
The Dell
Scrubs La NW10 139 CU69
Scrubs La W10 139 CU69
Scrutton Cl SW12 181 DK87
Scrutton St EC2 275 M5
Scrutton St EC2 142 DS70
Scudamore La NW9 118 CQ55
Scudders Hill (Fawkham Grn), Long. 209 FV100
Scutari Rd SE22 182 DW85
Scylla Cres (Heathrow Airport), Houns. 175 BP87
Scylla Pl (St. John's), Wok. 226 AU119
Church Rd
Scylla Rd SE15 162 DV83
Scylla Rd (Heathrow Airport), Houns. 175 BP86
Seaborough Rd, Grays 171 GJ76
Seabright St E2 142 DV69
Bethnal Grn Rd
Seabrook Dr, W.Wick. 204 EE103
Seabrook Gdns, Rom. 126 FA59
Seabrook Rd, Dag. 126 EX62
Seabrook Rd, Kings L. 59 BR27
Seabrooke Ri, Grays 170 GB79
Seaburn Cl, Rain. 147 FE68
Seacole Cl W3 138 CR71
Seacourt Rd SE2 166 EX75
Seacourt Rd, Slou. 153 BB77
Seacroft Gdns, Wat. 94 BX48
Seafield Rd N11 99 DK49
Seaford Cl, Ruis. 115 BR61
Seaford Rd E17 123 EB55
Seaford Rd N15 122 DR57
Seaford Rd W13 137 CH74
Seaford Rd, Enf. 82 DS42
Seaford Rd (Heathrow Airport), Houns. 174 BK85
Seaford St WC1 274 A3
Seaford St WC1 141 DL69
Seaforth Av, N.Mal. 199 CV99
Seaforth Cl, Rom. 105 FE52
Seaforth Cres N5 122 DQ64
Seaforth Dr, Wal.Cr. 67 DX34
Seaforth Gdns N21 99 DM45
Seaforth Gdns, Epsom 217 CT105
Seaforth Gdns, Wdf.Grn. 102 EJ50
Seaforth Pl SW1 161 DJ76
Buckingham Gate
Seagrave Rd SW6 160 DA79
Seagrave Rd, Beac. 88 AJ51
Seagry Rd E11 124 EG58
Seagull Cl, Bark. 145 ES69
Seal Dr (Seal), Sev. 257 FM121
Seal Hollow Rd, Sev. 257 FJ124
Seal Rd, Sev. 257 FJ121
Seal St E8 122 DT63
Sealand Rd (Heathrow Airport), Houns. 174 BN86
Sealand Wk, Nthlt. 136 BY69
Wayfarer Rd
Seale Hill, Reig. 266 DA136
Seaman Cl (Park St), St.Alb. 61 CD25
Searches La, Abb.L. 59 BV28
Searchwood Rd, Warl. 236 DV118
Searle Pl N4 121 DM60
Evershot Rd
Searles Cl SW11 160 DE80
Searles Dr E6 145 EN71
Searles Rd SE1 279 L8
Searles Rd SE1 162 DR77
Sears St SE5 162 DR80
Seasprite Cl, Nthlt. 136 BX69
Seaton Av, Ilf. 125 ES64
Seaton Cl E13 144 EH70
New Barn St
Seaton Cl SE11 278 E10
Seaton Cl SE11 161 DN78
Seaton Cl SW15 179 CV88
Seaton Cl, Twick. 177 CD86
Seaton Dr, Ashf. 174 BL89
Seaton Gdns, Ruis. 115 BU62
Seaton Pt E5 122 DU63
Nolan Way
Seaton Rd, Dart. 187 FG87
Seaton Rd, Hayes 155 BR77
Seaton Rd, Hem.H. 40 BK23
Seaton Rd, Mitch. 200 DE96
Seaton Rd (London Colney), St.Alb. 61 CK26
Seaton Rd, Twick. 176 CC86
Seaton Rd, Well. 166 EW80
Seaton Rd, Wem. 138 CL68
Seaton St N18 100 DU50
Sebastian Av, Brwd. 109 GA44
Sebastian St EC1 274 G3
Sebastian St EC1 141 DP69
Sebastopol Rd N9 100 DU49
Sebbon St N1 141 DP66
Sebergham Gro NW7 97 CU52
Sebert Rd E7 124 EH64
Sebright Pas E2 142 DU68
Hackney Rd
Sebright Rd, Barn. 79 CX40
Sebright Rd, Hem.H. 40 BG21
Secker Cres, Har. 94 CC53
Secker St SE1 278 D3
Second Av E12 124 EL63
Second Av E13 144 EG69
Second Av E17 123 EA57
Second Av N18 100 DW49
Second Av NW4 119 CX56
Second Av SW14 158 CS83
Second Av W3 139 CT74
Second Av W10 139 CY70
Second Av, Dag. 147 FB67
Second Av, Enf. 82 DT43
Second Av, Grays 169 FU79
Second Av, Harl. 51 ER15
Second Av, Hayes 135 BT74
Second Av, Rom. 126 EW57
Second Av, Wal.Abb. 68 EH30
Breach Barn Mobile Home Pk
Second Av, Walt. 195 BV100
Second Av, Wat. 76 BX35
Second Av, Wem. 117 CK61
Second Cl, W.Mol. 196 CC98
Second Cres, Slou. 131 AQ71
Second Cross Rd, Twick. 177 CE89
Second Way, Wem. 118 CP63
Sedan Way SE17 279 M10
Sedcombe Cl, Sid. 186 EV91
Knoll Rd
Sedcote Rd, Enf. 82 DW43
Sedding St SW1 276 F8
Sedding St SW1 160 DG77
Seddon Highwalk EC2 142 DQ71
Beech St
Seddon Ho EC2 142 DQ71
The Barbican
Seddon Rd, Mord. 200 DD99
Seddon St WC1 274 C3
Sedge Ct, Grays 170 GE80
Sedge Grn, Harl. 50 EE20
Sedge Grn, Wal.Abb. 50 EE20
Sedge Rd N17 100 DW52
Sedgebrook Rd SE3 164 EK82
Sedgecombe Av, Har. 117 CJ57
Sedgefield Cl, Rom. 106 FM49
Sedgefield Cres, Rom. 106 FM49
Sedgeford Rd W12 139 CT74
Sedgehill Rd SE6 183 EA91
Sedgemere Av N2 120 DC55
Sedgemere Rd SE2 166 EW76
Sedgemoor Dr, Dag. 126 FA63
Sedgeway SE6 184 EF88
Sedgewick Av, Uxb. 135 BP66
Sedgewood Cl, Brom. 204 EF101
Sedgmoor Pl SE5 162 DS80
Sedgwick Rd E10 123 EC61
Sedgwick St E9 123 DX64
Sedleigh Rd SW18 179 CZ86
Sedlescombe Rd SW6 159 CZ79
Sedley (Southfleet), Grav. 190 GA93
Sedley Cl, Enf. 82 DV38
Sedley Gro (Harefield), Uxb. 114 BJ56
Sedley Pl W1 273 H9
Sedley Ri, Loug. 85 EM40
Sedum Cl NW9 118 CP57
Seedbed Cen, The, Harl. 51 EN16
Seeley Dr SE21 182 DS91
Seeleys, Harl. 36 EW12
Seeleys Cl, Beac. 88 AJ51
Seeleys La, Beac. 89 AK52
Seeleys Wk
Seeleys Rd, Beac. 88 AJ50
Seeleys Wk, Beac. 88 AJ52
Seelig Av NW9 119 CU59
Seely Rd SW17 180 DG93
Seer Grn La (Jordans), Beac. 90 AS52
Seer Mead (Seer Grn), Beac. 89 AR52
Seething La EC3 279 N1
Seething La EC3 142 DS73
Seething Wells La, Surb. 197 CJ100
Sefton Av NW7 96 CR50
Sefton Av, Har. 95 CD53
Sefton Cl, Orp. 205 ET98
Sefton Cl, St.Alb. 43 CF19
Blenheim Rd
Sefton Cl (Stoke Poges), Slou. 132 AT66
Sefton Paddock (Stoke Poges), Slou. 132 AU66
Sefton Pk (Stoke Poges), Slou. 132 AU66
Sefton Rd, Croy. 202 DU102
Sefton Rd, Epsom 216 CR110
Sefton Rd, Orp. 205 ET98
Sefton St SW15 159 CW82
Sefton Way, Uxb. 134 BJ72
Segal Cl SE23 183 DY87
Segrave Cl, Wey. 212 BN108
Sekforde St EC1 274 F5
Sekforde St EC1 141 DP70
Sekhon Ter, Felt. 176 CA90
Selah Dr, Swan. 207 FC95
Selan Gdns, Hayes 135 BV71
Selbie Av NW10 119 CT64
Selborne Av E12 125 EN63
Walton Rd
Selborne Av, Bex. 186 EY88
Selborne Gdns NW4 119 CU56
Selborne Gdns, Grnf. 137 CG67
Selborne Rd E17 123 DZ57
Selborne Rd N14 99 DL48
Selborne Rd N22 99 DM53
Selborne Rd SE5 162 DR82
Denmark Hill
Selborne Rd, Croy. 202 DS104
Selborne Rd, Ilf. 125 EN61
Selborne Rd, N.Mal. 198 CS96
Selborne Rd, Sid. 186 EV91
Selborne Wk E17 123 DZ56
Selborne Wk Shop Cen E17 123 DZ56
Selbourne Av (New Haw), Add. 212 BH110
Selbourne Av, Surb. 198 CM103
Selbourne Cl (New Haw), Add. 212 BH109
Selbourne Rd, Guil. 243 BA131
Selbourne Sq, Gdse. 252 DW130
Selby Av, St.Alb. 43 CD20
Selby Chase, Ruis. 115 BV61
Selby Cl E6 144 EL71
Linton Gdns

Sidney Rd, Wind. 150 AJ83
Sidney Sq E1 142 DW72
Sidney St E1 142 DV71
Sidworth St E8 142 DV66
Siebert Rd SE3 164 EG79
Siemens Rd SE18 164 EK76
Sigdon Rd E8 122 DU64
Sigers, The, Pnr. 115 BV58
Signmakers Yd NW1 141 DH67
Delancey St
Sigrist Sq, Kings.T. 198 CL95
Silbury Av, Mitch. 200 DE95
Silbury St N1 275 K2
Silchester Rd W10 139 CX72
Silecroft Rd, Bexh. 166 FA81
Silesia Bldgs E8 142 DV66
London La
Silex St SE1 278 G5
Silex St SE1 161 DP75
Silk Cl SE12 184 EG85
Silk Mill Ct, Wat. 93 BV45
Silk Mill Rd
Silk Mill Rd, Wat. 93 BV45
Silk Mills Cl, Sev. 257 FJ121
Silk Mills Path SE13 163 EC82
Lewisham Rd
Silk St EC2 275 J6
Silk St EC2 142 DQ71
Silkfield Rd NW9 118 CS57
Silkham Rd, Oxt. 253 ED127
Silkin Ho, Wat. 94 BW48
Silkmills Sq E9 143 DZ65
Silkmore La (West Horsley), Lthd. 244 BN125
Silkstream Rd, Edg. 96 CQ53
Silo Cl, Gdmg. 258 AT143
Silo Dr, Gdmg. 258 AT143
Silo Rd, Gdmg. 258 AT143
Silsden Cres, Ch.St.G. 90 AX48
London Rd
Silsoe Rd N22 99 DM54
Silver Birch Av E4 101 DZ51
Silver Birch Av, Epp. 70 EY27
Silver Birch Cl N11 98 DG51
Silver Birch Cl SE28 146 EU74
Silver Birch Cl (Woodham), Add. 211 BE112
Silver Birch Cl, Dart. 187 FE91
Silver Birch Cl, Uxb. 114 BL63
Silver Birch Gdns E6 145 EM70
Silver Birch Ms, Ilf. 103 EQ51
Fencepiece Rd
Silver Birches, Brwd. 109 GA46
Silver Cl SE14 163 DY80
Southerngate Way
Silver Cl, Har. 95 CD52
Silver Cl (Kingswood), Tad. 233 CY124
Silver Cres W4 158 CP77
Silver Dell, Wat. 75 BT35
Silver Hill, Ch.St.G. 90 AV47
Silver Jubilee Way, Houns. 155 BV82
Silver La, Pur. 219 DK112
Silver La, W.Wick. 203 ED103
Silver Pl W1 273 L10
Silver Rd SE13 163 EB83
Elmira St
Silver Rd W12 139 CX73
Silver Rd, Grav. 191 GL89
Silver Spring Cl, Erith 167 FB79
Silver St N18 100 DS49
Silver St, Enf. 82 DR41
Silver St, Rom. 86 EV41
Silver St, Wal.Abb. 67 EC34
Silver St (Cheshunt), Wal.Cr. 66 DR30
Silver Tree Cl, Walt. 195 BU104
Silver Wk SE16 143 DZ74
Silver Way, Rom. 127 FB55
Silver Way, Uxb. 135 BP68
Oakdene Rd
Silverbirch Wk NW3 140 DG65
Queen's Cres
Silvercliffe Gdns, Barn. 80 DE42
Silverdale SE26 182 DW91
Silverdale, Enf. 81 DL42
Silverdale Av, Ilf. 125 ES57
Silverdale Av (Oxshott), Lthd. 214 CC114
Silverdale Av, Walt. 195 BT104
Silverdale Cl W7 137 CE74
Silverdale Cl (Brockham), Bet. 264 CP138
Silverdale Cl, Nthlt. 116 BZ64
Silverdale Cl, Sutt. 217 CZ105
Silverdale Ct, Stai. 174 BH92
Silverdale Dr SE9 184 EL89
Silverdale Dr, Horn. 127 FH64
Silverdale Dr, Sun. 195 BV96
Silverdale Gdns, Hayes 155 BU75
Silverdale Rd E4 101 ED51
Silverdale Rd, Bexh. 167 FB82
Silverdale Rd, Bushey 76 BY43
Silverdale Rd, Hayes 155 BU75
Silverdale Rd (Petts Wd), Orp. 205 EQ98
Silverdale Rd (St. Paul's Cray), Orp. 206 EU97
Silverfield, Brox. 49 DZ22
Silverglade Business Pk, Chess. 215 CJ112
Silverhall St, Islw. 157 CG83
Silverholme Cl, Har. 117 CK59
Silverland St E16 145 EM74
Silverlea Gdns, Horl. 269 DJ149
Silverleigh Rd, Th.Hth. 201 DM98
Silverlocke Rd, Grays 170 GD79
Silvermead E18 102 EG52
Churchfields
Silvermere Av, Rom. 105 FB51
Silvermere Rd SE6 183 EB86
Silversmiths Way, Wok. 226 AW118
Silverstead La, West. 239 ER121
Silverston Way, Stan. 95 CJ51
Silverstone Cl, Red. 250 DF132
Goodwood Rd
Silverthorn Dr, Hem.H. 41 BP24
Silverthorn Gdns E4 101 EA47
Silverthorne Rd SW8 161 DH82
Silverton Rd W6 159 CX79
Silvertown Way E16 144 EF72
Silvertree La, Grnf. 137 CD69
Cowgate Rd
Silvertrees (Bricket Wd), St.Alb. 60 BZ30
West Riding
Silverwood Cl, Beck. 183 EA94
Silverwood Cl, Croy. 221 DZ109
Silverwood Cl, Nthwd. 93 BQ53
Silverwood Cotts (Shere), Guil. 260 BM138
Shere Rd
Silvester Rd SE22 182 DT85
Silvester St SE1 279 J5
Silvesters, Harl. 51 EM17
Silvocea Way E14 143 ED72
Silwood Est SE16 162 DW77
Silwood St SE16 162 DW77
Simla Cl SE14 163 DY79
Simla Ho SE1 279 L5
Simmil Rd (Claygate), Esher 215 CE106
Simmonds Ri, Hem.H. 40 BK22
Simmons Cl N20 98 DE46
Simmons Cl, Chess. 215 CJ108
Simmons Cl, Slou. 153 BA77
Common Rd
Simmons La E4 101 ED47
Simmons Pl, Stai. 173 BE92
Chertsey La
Simmons Rd SE18 165 EP78
Simmons Way N20 98 DE47
Simms Cl, Cars. 200 DE103
Simms Gdns N2 98 DC54
Tarling Rd
Simms Rd SE1 162 DU77
Simnel Rd SE12 184 EH87
Simon Cl W11 139 CZ73
Portobello Rd
Simon Dean (Bovingdon), Hem.H. 57 BA27
Simonds Rd E10 123 EA61
Simone Cl, Brom. 204 EK95
Simone Dr, Ken. 236 DQ116
Simons Cl (Ottershaw), Cher. 211 BC107
Simons Wk E15 123 ED64
Waddington St
Simons Wk (Englefield Grn), Egh. 172 AW94
Simplemarsh Ct, Add. 212 BH105
Simplemarsh Rd
Simplemarsh Rd, Add. 212 BG105
Simpson Cl N21 81 DL43
Macleod Rd
Simpson Dr W3 138 CR72
Simpson Rd, Houns. 176 BZ86
Simpson Rd, Rain. 147 FF65
Simpson Rd, Rich. 177 CJ91
Simpson St SW11 160 DD82
Simpsons Rd E14 143 EB73
Simpsons Rd, Brom. 204 EG97
Simrose Ct SW18 180 DA85
Wandsworth High St
Sims Cl, Rom. 127 FF56
Sims Wk SE3 164 EF84
Sinclair Ct, Beck. 183 EA94
Sinclair Dr, Sutt. 218 DB109
Sinclair Gdns W14 159 CX75
Sinclair Gro NW11 119 CX58
Sinclair Rd E4 101 DZ50
Sinclair Rd W14 159 CX75
Sinclair Way (Lane End), Dart. 189 FR91
Sinclare Cl, Enf. 82 DT39
Sincots Rd, Red. 250 DF134
Lower Br Rd
Sinderby Cl, Borwd. 78 CL39
Singapore Rd W13 137 CG74
Singer St EC2 275 L3
Single St (Berry's Grn), West. 239 EP115
Singles Cross La (Knockholt), Sev. 224 EW114
Singleton Cl SW17 180 DF94
Singleton Cl, Croy. 202 DQ101
St. Saviours Rd
Singleton Cl, Horn. 127 FF63
Carfax Rd
Singleton Rd, Dag. 126 EZ64
Singleton Scarp N12 98 DA50
Singlewell Rd, Grav. 191 GH89
Singret Pl (Cowley), Uxb. 134 BJ70
High St
Sinnott Rd E17 101 DX53
Sion Rd, Twick. 177 CH88
Sipson Cl, West Dr. 154 BN79
Sipson La, Hayes 154 BN79
Sipson La, West Dr. 154 BN79
Sipson Rd, West Dr. 154 BN78
Sipson Way, West Dr. 154 BN80
Sir Alexander Cl W3 139 CT74
Sir Alexander Rd W3 139 CT74
Sir Cyril Black Way SW19 180 DA94
Sir Francis Way, Brwd. 108 FV47
Sir Henry Peek's Dr, Slou. 131 AN65
Sir Thomas More Est SW3 160 DD79
Beaufort St
Sirdar Rd N22 121 DP55
Sirdar Rd W11 139 CX73
Sirdar Rd, Mitch. 180 DG93
Grenfell Rd
Sirdar Strand, Grav. 191 GM92
Sirinham Pt SW8 161 DM79
Sirius Rd, Nthwd. 93 BU50
Sise La EC4 275 K9
Siskin Cl, Borwd. 78 CN42
Siskin Cl, Bushey 76 BY42
Sisley Rd, Bark. 145 ES67
Sispara Gdns SW18 179 CZ86
Sissinghurst Rd, Croy. 202 DU101
Sissulu Ct E6 144 EJ67
Sister Mabel's Way SE15 162 DU80
Radnor Rd
Sisters Av SW11 160 DF84
Sistova Rd SW12 181 DH88
Sisulu Pl SW9 161 DN83
Sittingbourne Av, Enf. 82 DR44
Sitwell Gro, Stan. 95 CF50
Siverst Cl, Nthlt. 136 CB65
Sivill Ho E2 142 DT69
Siviter Way, Dag. 147 FB66
Siward Rd N17 100 DR53
Siward Rd SW17 180 DC90
Siward Rd, Brom. 204 EH97
Six Acres, Hem.H. 40 BN23
Six Acres Est N4 121 DN61
Six Bells La, Sev. 257 FJ126
Six Bridges Trd Est SE1 162 DU78
Sixth Av E12 125 EM63
Sixth Av W10 139 CY69
Sixth Av, Hayes 135 BT74
Sixth Av, Wat. 76 BX35
Sixth Cross Rd, Twick. 176 CC90
Skardu Rd NW2 119 CY64
Skarnings Ct, Wal.Abb. 68 EG33
Skeena Hill SW18 179 CY87
Skeet Hill La, Orp. 206 EY103
Skeffington Rd E6 145 EM67
Skelbrook St SW18 180 DB89
Skelgill Rd SW15 159 CZ84
Skelley Rd E15 144 EF66
Skelton Cl E8 142 DT65
Buttermere Wk
Skelton Cl, Beac. 110 AG55
Skelton Rd E7 144 EG65
Skeltons La E10 123 EB59
Skelwith Rd W6 159 CW79
Skenfrith Ho SE15 162 DV79
Commercial Way
Skerne Rd, Kings.T. 197 CK95
Skerries Ct (Langley), Slou. 153 BA77
Blacksmith Row
Sketchley Gdns SE16 163 DX78
Sketty Rd, Enf. 82 DS41
Skibbs La, Orp. 206 EZ103
Skid Hill La, Warl. 222 EF113
Skidmore Way, Rick. 92 BL46
Skiers St E15 144 EE67
Skiffington Cl SW2 181 DN88
Skillet Hill, Wal.Abb. 84 EH35
Skimpans Cl, Hat. 45 CX24
Skinner Ct E2 142 DV68
Parmiter St
Skinner Pl SW1 276 F9
Skinner St EC1 274 E3
Skinner St EC1 141 DN69
Skinners La EC4 275 J10
Skinners La, Ash. 231 CK118
Skinners La, Houns. 156 CB81
Skinney La (Horton Kirby), Dart. 209 FR97
Skip La (Harefield), Uxb. 114 BL60
Skippers Cl, Green. 189 FV85
Skips Cor, Epp. 71 FD25
Skipsea Ho SW18 180 DD86
Fitzhugh Gro
Skipsey Av E6 145 EM69
Skipton Cl N11 98 DG51
Ribblesdale Av
Skipton Dr, Hayes 155 BQ76
Skipton Way, Horl. 269 DH145
Skipworth Rd E9 142 DW67
Skomer Wk N1 142 DQ65
Clephane Rd
Sky Peals Rd, Wdf.Grn. 101 ED53
Skydmore Path, Slou. 131 AM69
Umberville Way
Skylark Rd (Denham), Uxb. 113 BC60
Skylines Village E14 163 EB75
Skyport Dr, West Dr. 154 BK80
Skys Wd Rd, St.Alb. 43 CH16
Slacksbury Hatch, Harl. 51 EP15
Helions Rd
Slade, The SE18 165 ES79
Slade Ct (Ottershaw), Cher. 211 BD107
Slade Ct, Rad. 77 CG35
Slade End, Epp. 85 ES36
Slade Gdns, Erith 167 FF81
Slade Grn Rd, Erith 167 FG80
Slade Ho, Houns. 176 BZ86
Slade Oak La, Ger.Cr. 113 BB55
Slade Oak La (Denham), Uxb. 113 BD59
Slade Rd (Ottershaw), Cher. 211 BD107
Slade Twr E10 123 EB61
Slade Wk SE17 161 DP79
Heiron St
Sladebrook Rd SE3 164 EK82
Sladedale Rd SE18 165 ES78
Slades Cl, Enf. 81 DN41
Slades Dr, Chis. 185 EQ90
Slades Gdns, Enf. 81 DN40
Slades Hill, Enf. 81 DN41
Slades Ri, Enf. 81 DN41
Slagrove Pl SE13 183 EB85
Slaidburn St SW10 160 DC79
Slaithwaite Rd SE13 163 EC84
Slaney Pl N7 121 DN64
Hornsey Rd
Slaney Rd, Rom. 127 FE57
Slapleys, Wok. 226 AX120
Slater Cl SE18 165 EN78
Woolwich New Rd
Slattery Rd, Felt. 176 BW88
Sleaford Grn, Wat. 94 BX48
Sleaford St SW8 161 DJ80
Sleapcross Gdns (Smallford), St.Alb. 44 CP21
Sleapshyde La (Smallford), St.Alb. 44 CP21
Sleddale, Hem.H. 40 BL17
Sledmere Ct, Felt. 175 BS88
Kilross Rd
Sleepers Fm Rd, Grays 171 GH75
Sleets End, Hem.H. 40 BH18
Slewins Cl, Horn. 128 FJ57
Slewins La, Horn. 128 FJ57
Slievemore Cl SW4 161 DK83
Voltaire Rd
Slimmons Dr, St.Alb. 43 CG16
Slines New Rd (Woldingham), Cat. 237 DZ119
Slines Oak Rd (Woldingham), Cat. 237 EA123
Slines Oak Rd, Warl. 237 EA119
Slingsby Pl WC2 273 P10
Slip, The, West. 255 EQ126
Slipe La, Brox. 49 DZ24
Slippers Hill, Hem.H. 40 BK19
Slippers Pl SE16 162 DV76
Slipshatch Rd, Reig. 265 CX138
Slipshoe St, Reig. 249 CZ134
West St
Sloane Av SW3 276 B9
Sloane Av SW3 160 DE77
Sloane Ct E SW3 276 F10
Sloane Ct W SW3 276 F10
Sloane Ct W SW3 160 DG78
Sloane Gdns SW1 276 F9
Sloane Gdns SW1 160 DG77
Sloane Gdns, Orp. 205 EQ104
Sloane Sq SW1 276 F9
Sloane Sq SW1 160 DF77
Sloane St SW1 276 E6
Sloane St SW1 160 DF75
Sloane Ter SW1 276 E8
Sloane Ter SW1 160 DF77
Sloane Wk, Croy. 203 DZ100
Sloansway, Welw.G.C. 29 CZ06
Slocock Hill, Wok. 226 AW117
Slocum Cl SE28 146 EW73
Slough La NW9 118 CQ58
Slough La (Buckland), Bet. 249 CU133
Slough La, Epp. 53 FD24
Slough La (Headley), Epsom 248 CQ125
Slough Rd, Iver 133 BC69
Slough Rd (Datchet), Slou. 152 AU78
Slough Rd (Eton), Wind. 151 AR78
Slough Trd Est, Slou. 131 AP72
Slowmans Cl (Park St), St.Alb. 60 CC28
Sly St E1 142 DV72
Cannon St Rd
Slyfield Ct, Guil. 242 AY130
Slyfield Grn
Slyfield Grn, Guil. 242 AX130
Slyfield Ind Est, Guil. 242 AY130
Smaldon Cl, West Dr. 154 BN76
Walnut Av
Small Acre, Hem.H. 39 BF20
Small Grains (Fawkham Grn), Long. 209 FV104
Smallberry Av, Islw. 157 CF82
Smallbrook Ms W2 140 DD72
Craven Rd
Smallcroft, Welw.G.C. 30 DB08
Smalley Cl N16 122 DT62
Smalley Rd Est N16 122 DT62
Smalley Cl
Smallfield Rd, Horl. 269 DH148
Smallford La (Smallford), St.Alb. 44 CP21
Smallholdings Rd, Epsom 217 CW114
Smallmead, Horl. 269 DH148
Small's Hill Rd (Leigh), Reig. 265 CU141
Smallwood Cl (Wheathampstead), St.Alb. 28 CL08
Smallwood Rd SW17 180 DD91
Smardale Rd SW18 180 DC85
Alma Rd
Smarden Cl, Belv. 166 FA78
Essenden Rd
Smarden Gro SE9 185 EM91
Smart Cl, Rom. 105 FH53
Smart St E2 143 DX69
Smarts Grn (Cheshunt), Wal.Cr. 66 DT27
Smarts Heath La, Wok. 226 AU123
Smarts Heath Rd, Wok. 226 AT123
Smarts La, Loug. 84 EK42
Smarts Pl N18 100 DU50
Fore St
Smart's Pl WC2 274 A8
Smarts Rd, Grav. 191 GH89
Smeaton Cl, Chess. 215 CK107
Merritt Gdns
Smeaton Cl, Wal.Abb. 68 EE32
Smeaton Rd SW18 180 DA87
Smeaton Rd, Enf. 83 EA37
Smeaton Rd, Wdf.Grn. 103 EM50
Smeaton St E1 142 DV74
Smedley St SW4 161 DK82
Smedley St SW8 161 DK82
Smeed Rd E3 143 EA66
Smiles Pl SE13 163 EC82
Smith Cl SE16 143 DX74
Smith Rd, Reig. 265 CZ137
Smith Sq SW1 277 P7
Smith Sq SW1 161 DL76
Smith St SW3 276 D10
Smith St SW3 160 DF78
Smith St, Surb. 198 CM100
Smith St, Wat. 76 BW42
Smith Ter SW3 160 DF78
Smitham Bottom La, Pur. 219 DJ111
Smitham Downs Rd, Pur. 219 DK113
Smithbarn Cl, Horl. 269 DH147
Tanyard Way
Smithers, The (Brockham), Bet. 264 CP136
Smithfield, Hem.H. 40 BK18
Smithfield St EC1 274 F7
Smithies Ct E15 123 EC64
Smithies Rd SE2 166 EV77
Smiths Caravan Site, Iver 133 BC74
Smith's Ct W1 273 L10
Smiths Cres (Smallford), St.Alb. 44 CP21
Smiths Fm Est, Nthlt. 136 CA68
Smiths La, Eden. 255 EQ133
Smiths La (Cheshunt), Wal.Cr. 66 DR26
Smiths La, Wind. 151 AL82
Smiths Pt E13 144 EG67
Brooks Rd
Smiths Yd SW18 180 DC89
Summerley St
Smith's Yd, Croy. 202 DQ104
St. Georges Wk
Smithson Rd N17 100 DR53
Smithwood Cl SW19 179 CY88
Smithy Cl (Lower Kingswood), Tad. 249 CZ126
Smithy La (Lower Kingswood), Tad. 249 CZ127
Smithy St E1 142 DW71
Smock Wk, Croy. 202 DQ100
Smoke La, Reig. 266 DB136
Smokehouse Yd EC1 274 G6
Smokehouse Yd EC1 141 DP71
Smug Oak Grn Business Cen, St.Alb. 60 CB30
Smug Oak La (Bricket Wd), St.Alb. 60 CB30
Smugglers Wk, Green. 189 FV85
Smugglers Way SW18 160 DB84
Smyrks Rd SE17 162 DS78
Smyrna Rd NW6 140 DA66
Smythe Rd (Sutton at Hone), Dart. 208 FN95
Smythe St E14 143 EB73
Snag La (Cudham), Sev. 223 ES109
Snakeley Cl (Loudwater), H.Wyc. 88 AC54
Snakes La, Barn. 81 DH41
Snakes La E, Wdf.Grn. 102 EJ51
Snakes La W, Wdf.Grn. 102 EG51
Snape Spur, Slou. 132 AS72
Snaresbrook Dr, Stan. 95 CK49
Snaresbrook Rd E11 124 EE56
Snarsgate St W10 139 CW71
Snatts Hill, Oxt. 254 EF129
Sneath Av NW11 119 CZ59
Snelling Av (Northfleet), Grav. 190 GE89
Snellings Rd, Walt. 214 BW106
Snells La, Amer. 72 AV39
Snells Pk N18 100 DT51
Snells Wd Ct, Amer. 72 AW40
Sneyd Rd NW2 119 CW63
Snipe Cl, Erith 167 FH80
Snodland Cl, Orp. 223 EN110
Mill La
Snow Hill EC1 274 F7
Snow Hill EC1 141 DP71
Snow Hill Ct EC1 274 G8
Snowberry Cl E15 123 ED63
Snowbury Rd SW6 160 DB82
Snowden Av, Uxb. 135 BP68
Snowden St EC2 275 M5
Snowden St EC2 142 DS70
Snowdon Cl, Wind. 151 AK83
Snowdon Cres, Hayes 155 BQ76
Snowdon Dr NW9 118 CS58
Snowdon Rd (Heathrow Airport), Houns. 175 BQ85
Southern Perimeter Rd
Snowdown Cl SE20 203 DX95
Snowdrop Cl, Hmptn. 176 CA93
Gresham Rd
Snowdrop Path, Rom. 106 FK52
Snowerhill Rd, Bet. 264 CS136
Snowhill Cotts, Chesh. 38 AT24
Snowman Ho NW6 140 DB67
Snowsfields SE1 279 L4
Snowsfields SE1 162 DR75
Snowshill Rd E12 124 EL64
Snowy Fielder Waye, Islw. 157 CH82
Soames St SE15 162 DT83
Soames Wk, N.Mal. 198 CS95
Socket La, Brom. 204 EH101
Soham Rd, Enf. 83 DZ37
Soho Cres (Wooburn Grn), H.Wyc. 110 AD59
Soho Mills Ind Est (Wooburn Grn), H.Wyc. 110 AD59
Soho Sq W1 273 M8
Soho Sq W1 141 DK72
Soho St W1 273 M8
Sojourner Truth Cl E8 142 DV65
Richmond Rd
Solander Gdns E1 142 DV73
Dellow St
Solar Way, Enf. 83 DZ36
Sole Fm Av (Bookham), Lthd. 246 BZ125
Sole Fm Cl (Bookham), Lthd. 230 BZ124
Sole Fm Rd (Bookham), Lthd. 246 BZ125
Solebay St E1 143 DY70
Solecote (Bookham), Lthd. 246 CA125
Solefields Rd, Sev. 257 FH128
Solent Ri E13 144 EG69
Solent Rd NW6 120 DA64
Solent Rd (Heathrow Airport), Houns. 174 BM86
Soleoak Dr, Sev. 257 FH127
Solesbridge Cl, Rick. 73 BF41
Solesbridge La
Solesbridge La, Rick. 74 BG40
Soley Ms WC1 274 D2
Solna Av SW15 179 CW85
Solna Rd N21 100 DR46
Solomon Av N9 100 DU49
Solomons Hill, Rick. 92 BK45
Northway
Solomon's Pas SE15 162 DV84
Solom's Ct Rd, Bans. 234 DE117
Solon New Rd SW4 161 DL84
Solon New Rd Est SW4 161 DL84
Solon New Rd
Solon Rd SW2 161 DL84
Solway, Hem.H. 40 BM18
Solway Cl E8 142 DT65
Buttermere Wk
Solway Cl, Houns. 156 BY83
Solway Rd N22 99 DP53
Solway Rd SE22 162 DU84
Somaford Gro, Barn. 80 DD44
Somali Rd NW2 119 CZ63
Somborne Ho SW15 179 CU87
Fontley Way
Somerby Cl, Brox. 49 EA21
Somerby Rd, Bark. 145 ER66
Somercoates Cl, Barn. 80 DE41
Somerden Rd, Orp. 206 EX101
Somerfield Cl, Tad. 233 CY119
Somerfield Rd N4 121 DP61
Somerford Cl, Pnr. 115 BU56
Somerford Gro N16 122 DT63
Somerford Gro N17 100 DU52
Somerford Gro Est N16 122 DT63
Somerford Gro
Somerford Pl, Beac. 89 AK52
Somerford St E1 142 DV70
Somerford Way SE16 163 DY75
Somerhill Av, Sid. 186 EV87
Somerhill Rd, Well. 166 EV82
Someries Rd, Hem.H. 39 BF18
Somerleyton Pas SW9 161 DP84
Somerleyton Rd SW9 161 DN84
Somers Cl NW1 141 DK68
Platt St
Somers Cl, Reig. 250 DA133
Somers Cres W2 272 B9
Somers Cres W2 140 DE72
Somers Ms W2 272 B9
Somers Pl SW2 181 DM87
Somers Pl, Reig. 250 DA133
Somers Rd E17 123 DZ56
Somers Rd SW2 181 DM86
Somers Rd, Hat. 45 CW24
Somers Rd, Reig. 249 CZ133
Somers Sq, Hat. 45 CW23
Somers Way, Bushey 94 CC45
Somersby Gdns, Ilf. 125 EM57
Somerset Av SW20 199 CV96
Somerset Av, Chess. 215 CK105
Somerset Av, Well. 185 ET85
Somerset Cl N17 100 DR54
Somerset Cl, Epsom 216 CS109
Somerset Cl, N.Mal. 198 CS100
Somerset Cl, Walt. 213 BV106
Queens Rd
Somerset Cl, Wdf.Grn. 102 EG53
Somerset Est SW11 160 DD81
Somerset Gdns N6 120 DG59
Somerset Gdns N17 100 DS52
Somerset Gdns SE13 163 EB82
Somerset Gdns SW16 201 DM97
Somerset Gdns, Horn. 128 FN60
Somerset Gdns, Tedd. 177 CE92
Somerset Ho SW19 179 CY90
Somerset Rd E17 123 EA57
Somerset Rd N17 122 DT55
Somerset Rd N18 100 DT50
Somerset Rd NW4 119 CW56
Somerset Rd SW19 179 CY91
Somerset Rd W4 158 CR76
Somerset Rd W13 137 CH74
Somerset Rd, Barn. 80 DB43
Somerset Rd, Brent. 157 CJ79
Somerset Rd, Dart. 187 FH86
Somerset Rd, Enf. 83 EA38
Somerset Rd, Har. 116 CC57
Somerset Rd, Kings.T. 198 CM96
Somerset Rd, Orp. 206 EU101
Somerset Rd, Red. 266 DD136
Somerset Rd, Sthl. 136 BZ71
Somerset Rd, Tedd. 177 CE92
Somerset Sq W14 159 CY75
Somerset Way, Iver 153 BF75
Somerset Waye, Houns. 156 BY79
Somersham, Welw.G.C. 30 DD09
Somersham Rd, Bexh. 166 EY82
Somerswey (Shalford), Guil. 258 AY142
Somerton Av, Rich. 158 CP83
Somerton Cl, Pur. 235 DN115
Somerton Rd NW2 119 CY62
Somerton Rd SE15 162 DV84
Somertons Cl, Guil. 242 AU131
Somertrees Av SE12 184 EH89
Somervell Rd, Har. 116 BZ64
Somerville Av SW13 159 CV79
Somerville Rd SE20 183 DX94
Somerville Rd, Cob. 214 CA114
Somerville Rd, Dart. 188 FM86
Somerville Rd, Rom. 126 EW58

Spear Ms SW5 160 DA77
Spearman St SE18 165 EN79
Spearpoint Gdns, Ilf. 125 ET56
Spears Rd N19 121 DL60
Speart La, Houns. 156 BY80
Spedan Cl NW3 120 DB62
Speed Highwalk EC2 142 DQ71
Beech St
Speed Ho EC2 275 K6
Speedbird Way, West Dr. 154 BH80
Speedgate Hill (Fawkham Grn), Long. 209 FU103
Speedwell Ct, Guil. 243 BB131
Speedwell Ct, Hem.H. 39 BE21
Campion Rd
Speedwell Ct, Grays 170 GE80
Speedwell St SE8 163 EA80
Comet St
Speedy Pl WC1 273 P3
Speer Rd, T.Ditt. 197 CF99
Speirs Cl, N.Mal. 199 CT100
Speke Ho SE5 162 DQ80
Speke Rd, Th.Hth. 202 DR96
Spekehill SE9 185 EM90
Speldhurst Cl, Brom. 204 EF99
Speldhurst Rd E9 143 DX66
Speldhurst Rd W4 158 CR76
Spellbrook Wk N1 142 DQ67
Basire St
Spelman St E1 142 DU71
Spelthorne Gro, Sun. 175 BT94
Spelthorne La, Ashf. 195 BQ95
Spence Av (Byfleet), W.Byf. 212 BL114
Spence Cl SE16 163 DZ75
Vaughan St
Spencer Av N13 99 DM51
Spencer Av, Hayes 135 BU71
Spencer Av (Cheshunt), Wal.Cr. 66 DS26
Spencer Cl N3 98 DA54
Spencer Cl NW10 138 CM69
Spencer Cl, Epsom 232 CS119
Spencer Cl, Orp. 205 ES103
Spencer Cl, Uxb. 134 BJ69
Spencer Cl, Wok. 211 BC113
Spencer Cl, Wdf.Grn. 102 EJ50
Spencer Ct NW8 140 DC68
Marlborough Pl
Spencer Dr N2 120 DC58
Spencer Gdns SE9 185 EM85
Spencer Gdns SW14 178 CQ85
Spencer Gdns (Englefield Grn), Egh. 172 AX92
Spencer Gate, St.Alb. 43 CE18
Spencer Hill SW19 179 CY93
Spencer Hill Rd SW19 179 CY94
Spencer Ms SW8 161 DM81
Lansdowne Way
Spencer Ms W6 159 CY79
Greyhound Rd
Spencer Pk SW18 180 DD85
Spencer Pas E2 142 DV68
Pritchard's Rd
Spencer Pl N1 141 DP66
Canonbury La
Spencer Pl, Croy. 202 DR101
Gloucester Rd
Spencer Ri NW5 121 DH63
Spencer Rd E6 144 EK67
Spencer Rd E17 101 EC53
Spencer Rd N8 121 DM57
Spencer Rd N11 99 DH49
Spencer Rd N17 100 DU53
Spencer Rd SW18 160 DD84
Spencer Rd SW20 199 CV95
Spencer Rd W3 138 CQ74
Spencer Rd W4 158 CQ80
Spencer Rd, Brom. 184 EE94
Spencer Rd, Cat. 236 DR121
Spencer Rd, Cob. 229 BV115
Spencer Rd, E.Mol. 196 CC99
Spencer Rd, Har. 95 CE54
Spencer Rd, Ilf. 125 ET60
Spencer Rd, Islw. 157 CD81
Spencer Rd, Mitch. 200 DG97
Spencer Rd (Beddington Corr), Mitch. 200 DG101
Spencer Rd, Rain. 147 FD69
Spencer Rd, Slou. 153 AZ76
Spencer Rd, S.Croy. 220 DS106
Spencer Rd, Twick. 177 CE90
Spencer Rd, Wem. 117 CJ61
Spencer St EC1 274 F3
Spencer St EC1 141 DP69
Spencer St, Grav. 191 GG87
Spencer St, Hert. 32 DS08
Spencer St, St.Alb. 43 CD20
Spencer St, Sthl. 156 BX75
Spencer Wk NW3 120 DC63
Hampstead High St
Spencer Wk SW15 159 CX84
Spencer Wk, Rick. 74 BJ43
Spencer Wk, Til. 171 GG82
Spencer Way, Hem.H. 40 BG17
Spencer Way, Red. 266 DG139
Spencers Cft, Harl. 52 EV17
Spenser Av, Wey. 212 BN108
Spenser Cres, Upmin. 128 FQ59
Spenser Gro N16 122 DS63
Spenser Ms SE21 182 DR88
Croxted Rd
Spenser Rd SE24 181 DN85
Spenser St SW1 277 L6
Spenser St SW1 161 DJ76
Spensley Wk N16 122 DR62
Clissold Rd
Speranza St SE18 165 ET78
Sperling Rd N17 100 DS54
Spert St E14 143 DY73
Spey St E14 143 EC71
Spey Way, Rom. 105 FE52
Speyhawk Pl, Pot.B. 64 DB29
Speyside N14 81 DJ44
Spezia Rd NW10 139 CU68
Sphere Ind Est, St.Alb. 43 CG21
Spice Quay Hts SE1 142 DT74
Shad Thames
Spicer Cl SW9 161 DP82
Spicer Cl, Walt. 196 BW100
Spicer St, St.Alb. 42 CC20
Spicers Fld (Oxshott), Lthd. 215 CD113
Spicers La, Harl. 36 EW11
Wayre St
Spicersfield (Cheshunt), Wal.Cr. 66 DU27
Spice's Yd, Croy. 220 DQ105
Spielman Rd, Dart. 168 FM84
Spiers Way, Horl. 269 DH150
Spigurnell Rd N17 100 DR53
Spikes Br Rd, Sthl. 136 BY72
Spilsby Cl NW9 96 CS54
Kenley Av
Spilsby Rd, Rom. 106 FK52
Spindle Cl SE18 164 EL76
Spindles, Til. 171 GG80
Spindlewood Gdns, Croy. 220 DS105
Spindlewoods, Tad. 233 CV122
Spindrift Av E14 163 EB77
Spinel Cl SE18 165 ET78
Spingate Cl, Horn. 128 FK64
Spinnaker Cl, Bark. 146 EV69
Spinnells Rd, Har. 116 BZ60
Spinners Wk, Wind. 151 AQ81
Spinney, Slou. 131 AP74
Spinney, The N21 99 DN45
Spinney, The SW16 181 DK90
Spinney, The, Barn. 80 DB40
Spinney, The, Beac. 111 AK55
Spinney, The, Berk. 38 AT20
Spinney, The, Brwd. 109 GC44
Spinney, The, Brox. 49 DZ19
Spinney, The, Chesh. 54 AR29
Spinney, The, Epsom 233 CV119
Spinney, The, Hert. 32 DT09
Spinney, The, Horl. 268 DG146
Spinney, The, Lthd. 214 CC112
Spinney, The (Great Bookham), Lthd. 230 CB124
Spinney, The, Pot.B. 64 DD31
Spinney, The, Pur. 219 DP111
Spinney, The, Sid. 186 EY92
Spinney, The, Stan. 96 CL49
Spinney, The, Sun. 195 BU95
Spinney, The, Sutt. 217 CW105
Spinney, The, Swan. 207 FE96
Spinney, The, Wat. 75 BU39
Spinney, The, Welw.G.C. 29 CY10
Spinney, The, Wem. 117 CG62
Spinney, The (Send), Wok. 244 BJ127
Spinney Cl, Beck. 203 EB98
Spinney Cl, Cob. 214 CA111
Spinney Cl, N.Mal. 198 CS99
Spinney Cl, Rain. 147 FE68
Spinney Cl, West Dr. 134 BL73
Yew Av
Spinney Cl, Wor.Pk. 199 CT103
Spinney Dr, Felt. 175 BQ87
Spinney Gdns SE19 182 DT92
Spinney Gdns, Dag. 126 EY64
Spinney Hill, Add. 211 BE106
Spinney Oak, Brom. 204 EL96
Spinney Oak (Ottershaw), Cher. 211 BD107
Spinney St, Hert. 32 DU09
Spinney Way (Cudham), Sev. 223 ER111
Spinneycroft, Lthd. 231 CD115
Spinneys, The, Brom. 205 EM96
Spinneys Dr, St.Alb. 42 CB22
Spinning Wk, The (Shere), Guil. 260 BN139
Spinning Wheel Mead, Harl. 52 EU18
Spire Cl, Grav. 191 GH88
Spire Grn Cen, Harl. 50 EL16
Flex Meadow
Spires, The, Dart. 188 FK89
Spires Shop Cen, The, Barn. 79 CY41
Spirit Quay E1 142 DU74
Smeaton St
Spital Heath, Dor. 263 CJ135
Spital La, Brwd. 108 FT48
Spital Sq E1 275 N6
Spital Sq E1 142 DS71
Spital St E1 142 DU70
Spital St, Dart. 188 FK86
Spital Yd E1 275 N6
Spitfire Est, Houns. 156 BW78
Spitfire Rd, Wall. 219 DM108
Lancastrian Rd
Spitfire Way, Houns. 156 BW78
Spode Wk NW6 140 DB65
Lymington Rd
Spondon Rd N15 122 DU56
Spook Hill (North Holmwood), Dor. 263 CH141
Spoonbill Way, Hayes 136 BX71
Spooner Wk, Wall. 219 DK106
Spooners Dr (Park St), St.Alb. 60 CC27
Spooners Ms W3 138 CR74
Churchfield Rd
Sporle Ct SW11 160 DD83
Sportsbank St SE6 183 EC87
Spottons Gro N17 100 DQ53
Gospatrick Rd
Spout Hill, Croy. 221 EA106
Spout La, Eden. 255 EQ134
Spout La, Stai. 174 BG85
Spout La N, Stai. 154 BH84
Spratt Hall Rd E11 124 EG58
Spratts All (Ottershaw), Cher. 211 BE107
Spratts La (Ottershaw), Cher. 211 BE107
Spray La, Twick. 177 CE86
Spray St SE18 165 EP77
Spreighton Rd, W.Mol. 196 CB98
Spriggs Oak, Epp. 70 EU29
Palmers Hill
Sprimont Pl SW3 276 D10
Sprimont Pl SW3 160 DF78
Spring Av, Egh. 172 AY93
Spring Bottom La, Red. 251 DN127
Spring Br Ms W5 137 CK73
Spring Br Rd
Spring Br Rd W5 137 CK73
Spring Cl, Barn. 79 CX43
Spring Cl, Borwd. 78 CN39
Spring Cl (Latimer), Chesh. 72 AX36
Spring Cl, Dag. 126 EX60
Spring Cl, Gdmg. 258 AS143
Spring Cl (Harefield), Uxb. 92 BK53
Spring Cotts, Surb. 197 CK99
St. Leonard's Rd
Spring Ct, Guil. 242 AV130
Dayspring
Spring Ct, Sid. 186 EU90
Station Rd
Spring Ct Rd, Enf. 81 DN38
Spring Cfts, Bushey 76 CA43
Spring Dr, Maid. 130 AE65
Spring Dr, Pnr. 115 BU58
Eastcote Rd
Spring Fm Cl, Rain. 148 FK69
Spring Gdns N5 122 DQ64
Grosvenor Av
Spring Gdns SE11 278 B10
Spring Gdns SW1 277 N2
Spring Gdns, Dor. 263 CG136
Spring Gdns (Wooburn Grn), H.Wyc. 110 AE55
Watery La
Spring Gdns, Horn. 127 FH63
Spring Gdns, Orp. 224 EV107
Spring Gdns, Rom. 127 FC57
Spring Gdns, Wall. 219 DJ106
Spring Gdns, Wat. 76 BW35
Spring Gdns, W.Mol. 196 CC99
Spring Gdns (Biggin Hill), West. 238 EJ118
Spring Gdns, Wdf.Grn. 102 EJ52
Spring Gdns Ind Est, Rom. 127 FC57
Spring Glen, Hat. 45 CT19
Spring Gro SE19 182 DT94
Alma Pl
Spring Gro W4 158 CN78
Spring Gro, Gdmg. 258 AS143
Spring Gro, Grav. 191 GH88
Spring Gro, Hmptn. 196 CB95
Plevna Rd
Spring Gro (Fetcham), Lthd. 230 CB123
Spring Gro, Loug. 84 EK44
Spring Gro, Mitch. 200 DG95
Spring Gro Cres, Houns. 156 CC81
Spring Gro Rd, Houns. 156 CC81
Spring Gro Rd, Islw. 156 CC81
Spring Gro Rd, Rich. 178 CM85
Spring Hill E5 122 DU59
Spring Hill SE26 182 DW91
Spring Hills, Harl. 35 EN14
Spring Lake, Stan. 95 CH49
Spring La E5 122 DV60
Spring La N10 120 DG55
Spring La SE25 202 DV100
Spring La, Hem.H. 39 BF18
Spring La, Oxt. 253 ED131
Spring La, Slou. 131 AM74
Spring La (Farnham Common), Slou. 131 AP66
Spring Ms W1 272 E6
Spring Ms, Epsom 217 CT109
Old Schools La
Spring Pk Av, Croy. 203 DX103
Spring Pk Dr N4 122 DQ60
Spring Pk Rd, Croy. 203 DX103
Spring Pas SW15 159 CX83
Embankment
Spring Path NW3 120 DD64
Spring Pl NW5 121 DH64
Spring Ri, Egh. 172 AY93
Spring Rd, Felt. 175 BT90
Spring Shaw Rd, Orp. 206 EU95
Spring St W2 140 DD72
Spring St, Epsom 217 CT109
Spring Ter, Rich. 178 CL85
Spring Vale, Bexh. 167 FB84
Spring Vale, Green. 189 FW86
Spring Vale Cl, Swan. 207 FF95
Spring Vale N, Dart. 188 FK87
Spring Vale S, Dart. 188 FK87
Spring Vw Rd, Ware 32 DW07
Spring Vil Rd, Edg. 96 CN52
Spring Wk E1 142 DU71
Old Montague St
Spring Wk, Brox. 48 DW22
Spring Wk, Horl. 268 DF148
Court Lo Rd
Spring Way, Hem.H. 41 BP18
Spring Wds, Vir.W. 192 AV98
Springall St SE15 162 DV80
Springate Fld, Slou. 152 AY75
Springbank N21 81 DM44
Springbank Av, Horn. 128 FJ64
Springbank Rd SE13 183 ED86
Springbank Wk NW1 141 DK66
St. Paul's Cres
Springbourne Ct, Beck. 203 EC95
Springclose La, Sutt. 217 CY107
Springcopse Rd, Reig. 266 DC135
Springcroft Av N2 120 DF56
Springdale Ms N16 122 DR63
Springdale Rd
Springdale Rd N16 122 DR63
Springfield E5 122 DV60
Springfield, Bushey 95 CD46
Springfield, Epp. 69 ET32
Springfield, Oxt. 253 ED130
Springfield Av N10 121 DJ55
Springfield Av SW20 199 CZ97
Springfield Av, Brwd. 109 GE45
Springfield Av, Hmptn. 176 CB93
Springfield Av, Swan. 207 FF98
Springfield Cl N12 98 DB50
Springfield Cl, Chesh. 54 AQ33
Springfield Cl, Pot.B. 64 DD31
Springfield Cl, Rick. 75 BP43
Springfield Cl, Stan. 95 CG48
Springfield Cl, Wind. 151 AP82
Springfield Cl (Knaphill), Wok. 226 AS118
Springfield Ct, Wall. 219 DH106
Springfield Rd
Springfield Dr, Ilf. 125 EQ58
Springfield Dr, Lthd. 231 CE119
Springfield Gdns E5 122 DV60
Springfield Gdns NW9 118 CR57
Springfield Gdns, Brom. 205 EM98
Springfield Gdns, Ruis. 115 BV60
Springfield Gdns, Upmin. 128 FQ62
Springfield Gdns, W.Wick. 203 EB103
Springfield Gdns, Wdf.Grn. 102 EJ52
Springfield Gro SE7 164 EJ79
Springfield Gro, Sun. 195 BT95
Springfield La NW6 140 DB67
Springfield La, Wey. 213 BP105
Springfield Meadows, Wey. 213 BP105
Springfield Mt NW9 118 CS57
Springfield Pl, N.Mal. 198 CQ98
Springfield Ri SE26 182 DV90
Springfield Rd E4 102 EE46
Springfield Rd E6 145 EM66
Springfield Rd E15 144 EE69
Springfield Rd E17 123 DZ58
Springfield Rd N11 99 DH50
Springfield Rd N15 122 DU56
Springfield Rd NW8 140 DC67
Springfield Rd SE26 182 DV92
Springfield Rd SW19 179 CZ92
Springfield Rd W7 137 CE74
Springfield Rd, Ashf. 174 BM92
Springfield Rd, Berk. 38 AT16
Springfield Rd, Bexh. 167 FB83
Springfield Rd, Brom. 205 EM98
Springfield Rd, Chesh. 54 AQ33
Springfield Rd (Westcott), Dor. 262 CB137
Springfield Rd, Epsom 217 CW110
Springfield Rd, Grays 170 GD75
Springfield Rd, Guil. 258 AY135
Springfield Rd, Har. 117 CE58
Springfield Rd, Hayes 136 BW74
Springfield Rd, Hem.H. 40 BM19
Springfield Rd, Kings.T. 198 CL97
Springfield Rd, St.Alb. 43 CG21
Springfield Rd (Smallford), St.Alb. 44 CP20
Springfield Rd, Slou. 153 BB80
Springfield Rd, Tedd. 177 CG92
Springfield Rd, Th.Hth. 202 DQ95
Springfield Rd, Twick. 176 CA88
Springfield Rd, Wall. 219 DH106
Springfield Rd (Cheshunt), Wal.Cr. 67 DY32
Springfield Rd, Wat. 59 BV33
Haines Way
Springfield Rd, Well. 166 EV83
Springfield Rd, Wind. 151 AP82
Springfield Wk NW6 140 DB67
Springfield Wk, Orp. 205 ER102
Place Fm Av
Springfields, Brox. 49 DZ19
Springfields, Wal.Abb. 68 EE34
Springfields, Welw.G.C. 29 CV11
Springfields Cl, Cher. 194 BH102
Springhall La, Saw. 36 EY07
Springhall Rd, Saw. 36 EY05
Springhaven Cl, Guil. 243 BA134
Springhead Enterprise Pk, Grav. 190 GC88
Springhead Rd, Erith 167 FF79
Springhead Rd (Northfleet), Grav. 190 GC87
Springhill Cl SE5 162 DR83
Springholm Cl (Biggin Hill), West. 238 EJ118
Springhurst Cl, Croy. 221 DZ105
Springle La, Hert. 33 DZ12
Springpark Dr, Beck. 203 EC97
Springpond Rd, Dag. 126 EY64
Springrice Rd SE13 183 ED86
Springs, The, Brox. 67 DY25
Springs, The, Hert. 32 DT08
Springshaw Cl, Sev. 256 FD123
Springside Ct, Guil. 242 AW133
Springvale Av, Brent. 157 CK78
Springvale Est W14 159 CY76
Blythe Rd
Springvale Retail Pk, Orp. 206 EW97
Springvale Ter W14 159 CX76
Springvale Way, Orp. 206 EW97
Springwater Cl SE18 165 EN81
Springway, Har. 117 CD59
Springwell Av NW10 139 CT67
Springwell Av, Rick. 92 BG47
Springwell Cl SW16 181 DN91
Etherstone Rd
Springwell Ct, Houns. 156 BX82
Springwell Hill (Harefield), Uxb. 92 BH51
Springwell La, Rick. 92 BG49
Springwell La (Harefield), Uxb. 92 BG49
Springwell Rd SW16 181 DN91
Springwell Rd, Houns. 156 BX81
Springwood (Cheshunt), Wal.Cr. 66 DU26
Springwood Cl (Harefield), Uxb. 92 BK53
Springwood Cres, Edg. 96 CP47
Springwood Wk, St.Alb. 43 CK17
Springwood Way, Rom. 127 FG57
Sprowston Ms E7 144 EG65
Sprowston Rd E7 124 EG64
Spruce Cl, Red. 250 DF133
Spruce Ct W5 158 CL76
Elderberry Rd
Spruce Hill, Harl. 51 ES20
Spruce Hills Rd E17 101 EC54
Spruce Pk, Brom. 204 EF98
Cumberland Rd
Spruce Rd (Biggin Hill), West. 238 EK116
Spruce Way (Park St), St.Alb. 60 CB27
Sprucedale Cl, Swan. 207 FE96
Sprucedale Gdns, Croy. 221 DX105
Sprucedale Gdns, Wall. 219 DK109
Sprules Rd SE4 163 DY82
Spur, The, Slou. 131 AK71
Spur, The (Cheshunt), Wal.Cr. 67 DX28
Welsummer Way
Spur Cl, Abb.L. 59 BR33
Spur Cl, Rom. 86 EV41
Spur Rd N15 122 DR56
Philip La
Spur Rd SE1 278 D4
Spur Rd SE1 161 DN75
Spur Rd SW1 277 K5
Spur Rd SW1 161 DJ75
Spur Rd, Bark. 145 EQ69
Spur Rd, Edg. 96 CL49
Spur Rd, Felt. 175 BV85
Spur Rd, Islw. 157 CH80
Spur Rd, Orp. 206 EU103
Spur Rd Est, Edg. 96 CM49
Spurfield, W.Mol. 196 CB97
Spurgate, Brwd. 109 GA47
Spurgeon Av SE19 202 DR95
Spurgeon Rd SE19 202 DR95
Spurgeon St SE1 279 K7
Spurgeon St SE1 162 DR76
Spurling Rd SE22 162 DT84
Spurling Rd, Dag. 146 EZ65
Spurrell Av, Bex. 187 FD91
Spurstowe Rd E8 142 DV65
Marcon Pl
Spurstowe Ter E8 122 DV64
Squadrons App, Horn. 148 FJ65
Square, The W6 159 CW78
Square, The, Berk. 39 BB16
Square, The, Brox. 49 DY23
High Rd Wormley
Square, The, Cars. 218 DG106
Square, The, Guil. 258 AT136
Orchard Rd
Square, The (Shere), Guil. 260 BN139
Square, The, Hayes 135 BR74
Square, The, Ilf. 125 EN59
Square, The, Rich. 177 CK85
Square, The, Saw. 36 EY05
Square, The, Sev. 256 FE122
Amherst Hill
Square, The, Swan. 207 FD97
Square, The, Wat. 75 BV37
The Harebreaks
Square, The, West Dr. 154 BH81
Square, The, West. 238 EJ120
Square, The, Wey. 213 BQ105
Square, The (Wisley), Wok. 228 BL116
Square, The, Wdf.Grn. 102 EG50
Square Rigger Row SW11 160 DC83
York Pl
Squarey St SW17 180 DC90
Squerryes Mede, West. 255 EQ127
Squire Gdns NW8 140 DD69
St. John's Wd Rd
Squires, The, Rom. 127 FC58
Squires Br Rd, Shep. 194 BM98
Squires Ct SW19 180 DA91
Squires Ct, Cher. 194 BH102
Springfields Cl
Squires Fld, Swan. 207 FF95
Squires La N3 98 DB54
Squires Mt NW3 120 DD62
East Heath Rd
Squires Rd, Shep. 194 BM98
Squires Wk, Ashf. 175 BR94
Napier Rd
Squires Way, Dart. 187 FD91
Squires Wd Dr, Chis. 184 EL94
Squirrel Chase, Hem.H. 39 BE19
Squirrel Cl, Houns. 156 BW82
Squirrel Keep, W.Byf. 212 BH112
Squirrel Ms W13 137 CG73
Squirrel Wd, W.Byf. 212 BH112
Squirrels, The SE13 163 ED83
Belmont Hill
Squirrels, The, Bushey 77 CD44
Squirrels, The, Hert. 32 DU09
Squirrels, The, Pnr. 116 BZ55
Squirrels, The, Welw.G.C. 30 DC10
Squirrels Chase, Grays 171 GG75
Hornsby La
Squirrels Cl N12 98 DC49
Woodside Av
Squirrels Cl, Uxb. 134 BN66
Squirrels Grn (Bookham), Lthd. 230 CA123
Squirrels Grn, Wor.Pk. 199 CT102
Squirrels Heath Av, Rom. 127 FH55
Squirrels Heath La, Horn. 128 FJ56
Squirrels Heath La, Rom. 128 FJ56
Squirrels Heath Rd, Rom. 128 FL55
Squirrels La, Buck.H. 102 EK48
Squirrels Trd Est, The, Hayes 155 BU76
Squirrels Way, Epsom 232 CR115
Squirries St E2 142 DU69
Stable Cl, Nthlt. 136 CA68
Stable La (Seer Grn), Beac. 89 AQ51
Stable Wk N2 98 DD53
Old Fm Rd
Stable Way W10 139 CW72
Latimer Rd
Stable Yd SW1 277 K4
Stable Yd SW9 161 DM82
Broomgrove Rd
Stable Yd SW15 159 CW83
Danemere St
Stable Yd Rd SW1 277 K3
Stable Yd Rd SW1 141 DJ74
Stables, The, Buck.H. 102 EJ45
Stables, The, Cob. 214 BZ114
Stables, The, Guil. 242 AX131
Old Fm Rd
Stables, The, Swan. 207 FH95
Stables End, Orp. 205 EQ104
Stables Ms SE27 182 DQ92
Stables Way SE11 278 D10
Stables Way SE11 161 DN78
Stacey Av N18 100 DW49
Stacey Cl E10 123 ED57
Halford Rd
Stacey Cl, Grav. 191 GL92
Stacey St N7 121 DN62
Stacey St WC2 273 N9
Stacey St WC2 141 DK72
Stack Rd (Horton Kirby), Dart. 209 FR97
Stackfield, Harl. 36 EU12
Stackhouse St SW3 276 D6
Stacklands, Welw.G.C. 29 CV11
Stacy Path SE5 162 DS80
Harris St
Stadium Rd NW2 119 CW59
Stadium Rd SE18 165 EM80
Stadium St SW10 160 DC80
Stadium Way, Dart. 187 FE85
Stadium Way, Harl. 35 EM14
Stadium Way, Wem. 118 CM63
Staff St EC1 275 L3
Staffa Rd E10 123 DY60
Stafford Av, Horn. 128 FK55
Stafford Av, Slou. 131 AQ70
Stafford Cl E17 123 DZ58
Stafford Cl N14 81 DJ43
Stafford Cl NW6 140 DA69
Stafford Cl, Cat. 236 DT123
Stafford Cl (Chafford Hundred), Grays 169 FW77
Stafford Cl, Green. 189 FT85
Stafford Cl, Maid. 130 AH72
Stafford Cl, Sutt. 217 CY107
Stafford Cl (Cheshunt), Wal.Cr. 66 DV29
Stafford Ct W8 160 DA76
Stafford Cross, Croy. 219 DM106
Stafford Dr, Brox. 49 EA20
Stafford Gdns, Croy. 219 DM106
Stafford Pl SW1 277 K6
Stafford Pl SW1 161 DJ76
Stafford Pl, Rich. 178 CM87
Stafford Rd E3 143 DZ68
Stafford Rd E7 144 EJ66
Stafford Rd NW6 140 DA69
Stafford Rd, Cat. 236 DT122
Stafford Rd, Croy. 219 DN105
Stafford Rd, Har. 94 CC52
Stafford Rd, N.Mal. 198 CQ97
Stafford Rd, Ruis. 115 BT63
Stafford Rd, Sid. 185 ES91
Stafford Rd, Wall. 219 DJ107
Stafford Sq, Wey. 213 BR105
Rosslyn Pk
Stafford St W1 277 K2
Stafford St W1 141 DJ74
Stafford Ter W8 160 DA76
Stafford Way, Sev. 257 FJ127
Staffords, Harl. 36 EY11
Staffords Pl, Horl. 269 DH150
Staffordshire St SE15 162 DU81
Stag Cl, Edg. 96 CQ54
Stag Grn Av, Hat. 45 CW16
Stag Hill, Guil. 258 AU135
Stag La NW9 96 CP54
Stag La SW15 179 CT89
Stag La, Berk. 38 AU18
Stag La, Buck.H. 102 EH47
Stag La, Edg. 96 CP54
Stag La, Rick. 73 BC44
Stag Leys, Ash. 232 CL120
Stag Leys Cl, Bans. 234 DD115
Stag Pl SW1 277 K6
Stag Pl SW1 161 DJ76
Stag Ride SW19 179 CT90
Stagbury Av, Couls. 234 DE118
Stagbury Cl, Couls. 234 DE119
Stagg Hill, Barn. 80 DD35
Stagg Hill, Pot.B. 80 DD35
Staggart Grn, Chig. 103 ET51
Stags Way, Islw. 157 CF79
Stainash Cres, Stai. 174 BH92
Stainash Par, Stai. 174 BH92
Kingston Rd
Stainbank Rd, Mitch. 201 DH97
Stainby Cl, West Dr. 154 BL76
Stainby Rd N15 122 DT56
Stainer Ho SE3 164 EJ84
Ryan Cl

Stainer Rd, Borwd. 77 CK39
Stainer St SE1 279 L3
Stainer St SE1 142 DR74
Staines Av, Sutt. 199 CX103
Staines Br, Stai. 173 BE92
Staines Bypass, Ashf. 174 BK92
Staines Bypass, Stai. 174 BH91
Staines Grn, Hert. 31 DK11
Staines La, Cher. 193 BF99
Staines La Cl, Cher. 193 BF100
Staines Rd, Cher. 193 BF97
Staines Rd, Felt. 175 BR87
Staines Rd, Houns. 156 CB83
Staines Rd, Ilf. 125 ER63
Staines Rd, Stai. 194 BH95
Staines Rd (Wraysbury), Stai. 172 AY87
Staines Rd, Twick. 176 CA90
Staines Rd E, Sun. 175 BU94
Staines Rd W, Ashf. 175 BP93
Staines Rd W, Sun. 175 BP93
Staines Wk, Sid. 186 EW93
Evry Rd
Stainford Cl, Ashf. 175 BR92
Stainforth Rd E17 123 EA56
Stainforth Rd, Ilf. 125 ER59
Staining La EC2 275 J8
Staining La EC2 142 DQ72
Stainmore Cl, Chis. 205 ER95
Stains Cl (Cheshunt), Wal.Cr. 67 DY28
Stainsbury St E2 142 DW68
Royston St
Stainsby Pl E14 143 EA72
Stainsby Rd
Stainsby Rd E14 143 EA72
Stainton Rd SE6 183 ED86
Stainton Rd, Enf. 82 DW39
Stainton Wk, Wok. 226 AW118
Inglewood
Stairfoot La (Chipstead), Sev. 256 FC122
Staithes Way, Tad. 233 CV120
Stakescorner Rd (Littleton), Guil. 258 AU142
Stalbridge St NW1 272 C6
Stalham St SE16 162 DV76
Stalisfield Pl, Orp. 223 EN110
Mill La
Stambourne Way SE19 182 DS94
Stambourne Way, W.Wick. 203 EC104
Stamford Brook Av W6 159 CT76
Stamford Brook Rd W6 159 CT76
Stamford Cl N15 122 DU56
Stamford Cl NW3 120 DC63
Heath St
Stamford Cl, Har. 95 CE52
Stamford Cl, Pot.B. 64 DD32
Stamford Cl, Sthl. 136 CA73
Stamford Cotts SW10 160 DB80
Billing St
Stamford Ct W6 159 CT77
Goldhawk Rd
Stamford Dr, Brom. 204 EF98
Stamford Gdns, Dag. 146 EW66
Stamford Grn Rd, Epsom 216 CP113
Stamford Gro E N16 122 DU60
Oldhill St
Stamford Gro W N16 122 DU60
Oldhill St
Stamford Hill N16 122 DT61
Stamford Hill Est N16 122 DT60
Stamford Rd E6 144 EL67
Stamford Rd N1 142 DS66
Stamford Rd N15 122 DU57
Stamford Rd, Dag. 146 EV67
Stamford Rd, Walt. 196 BX104
Kenilworth Dr
Stamford Rd, Wat. 75 BV40
Stamford St SE1 278 D3
Stamford St SE1 141 DN74
Stamp Pl E2 275 P2
Stamp Pl E2 142 DT69
Stanard Cl N16 122 DS59
Stanborough Av, Borwd. 78 CN37
Stanborough Cl, Borwd. 78 CN38
Stanborough Cl, Hmptn. 176 BZ93
Stanborough Cl, Welw.G.C. 29 CW10
Stanborough Grn, Welw.G.C. 29 CW11
Stanborough La Cycle Path, Welw.G.C. 29 CV12
Stanborough Pk, Wat. 75 BV35
Stanborough Pas E8 142 DT65
Abbot St
Stanborough Rd, Houns. 157 CD83
Stanborough Rd, Welw.G.C. 29 CV12
Stanbridge Pl N21 99 DP47
Stanbridge Rd SW15 159 CW83
Stanbrook Rd SE2 166 EV75
Stanbrook Rd, Grav. 191 GF88
Stanbury Av, Wat. 75 BS37
Stanbury Rd SE15 162 DV81
Stancroft NW9 118 CS56
Standale Gro, Ruis. 115 BQ57
Standard Ind Est E16 165 EM75
Standard Pl EC2 275 N3
Standard Rd NW10 138 CQ70
Standard Rd, Belv. 166 FA78
Standard Rd, Bexh. 166 EY84
Standard Rd, Enf. 83 DY38
Standard Rd, Houns. 156 BY83
Standard Rd, Orp. 223 EN110
Standen Av, Horn. 128 FK62
Standen Rd SW18 179 CZ87
Standfield, Abb.L. 59 BS31
Standfield Gdns, Dag. 146 FA65
Standfield Rd
Standfield Rd, Dag. 126 FA64
Standingford, Harl. 51 EP20
Standish Ho SE3 164 EJ84
Elford Cl
Standish Rd W6 159 CU77
Standlake Pt SE23 183 DX90
Standring Ri, Hem.H. 40 BH23
Stane Cl SW19 200 DB95
Hayward Cl
Stane St (Ockley), Dor. 247 CK127
Stane St, Lthd. 248 CL126
Stane Way SE18 164 EK80
Stane Way, Epsom 217 CU110
Stanfield Rd E3 143 DY68
Stanford Cl, Hmptn. 176 BZ93
Stanford Cl, Rom. 127 FB58
Stanford Cl, Ruis. 115 BQ58
Stanford Cl, Wdf.Grn. 102 EL50
Stanford Ct, Wal.Abb. 68 EG33
Stanford Gdns, S.Ock. 149 FR74
Stanford Ho, Bark. 146 EV68
Stanford Pl SE17 279 M9
Stanford Rd N11 98 DF50
Stanford Rd SW16 201 DK96
Stanford Rd W8 160 DB76
Stanford Rd, Grays 170 GD76
Stanford St SW1 277 M9
Stanford Way SW16 201 DK96
Stangate Cres, Borwd. 78 CS43
Stangate Gdns, Stan. 95 CH49
Stanger Rd SE25 202 DU98
Stanham Pl, Dart. 167 FG84
Crayford Way
Stanham Rd, Dart. 188 FJ85
Stanhope Av N3 119 CZ55
Stanhope Av, Brom. 204 EF102
Stanhope Av, Har. 95 CD53
Stanhope Cl SE16 163 DX75
Middleton Dr
Stanhope Gdns N4 121 DP58
Stanhope Gdns N6 121 DH58
Stanhope Gdns NW7 97 CT50
Stanhope Gdns SW7 160 DC77
Stanhope Gdns, Dag. 126 EZ62
Stanhope Gdns, Ilf. 125 EM60
Stanhope Gate W1 276 G2
Stanhope Gate W1 140 DG74
Stanhope Gro, Beck. 203 DZ99
Stanhope Heath (Stanwell), Stai. 174 BJ86
Stanhope Ms E SW7 160 DC77
Stanhope Ms S SW7 160 DC77
Gloucester Rd
Stanhope Ms W SW7 160 DC77
Stanhope Par NW1 273 K2
Stanhope Pk Rd, Grnf. 136 CC70
Stanhope Pl W2 272 D9
Stanhope Pl W2 140 DF72
Stanhope Rd E17 123 EB57
Stanhope Rd N6 121 DJ58
Stanhope Rd N12 98 DC50
Stanhope Rd, Barn. 79 CW44
Stanhope Rd, Bexh. 166 EY82
Stanhope Rd, Cars. 218 DG108
Stanhope Rd, Croy. 202 DS104
Stanhope Rd, Dag. 126 EZ61
Stanhope Rd, Grnf. 136 CC71
Stanhope Rd, Rain. 147 FG68
Stanhope Rd, St.Alb. 43 CF21
Stanhope Rd, Sid. 186 EU91
Stanhope Rd, Slou. 131 AK72
Stanhope Rd, Swans. 190 FZ85
Stanhope Rd, Wal.Cr. 67 DY33
Stanhope Row W1 277 H3
Stanhope St NW1 273 K3
Stanhope St NW1 141 DJ69
Stanhope Ter W2 272 A10
Stanhope Ter W2 140 DD73
Stanhope Way, Sev. 256 FD122
Stanhope Way (Stanwell), Stai. 174 BJ86
Stanhopes, Oxt. 254 EH128
Stanier Cl W14 159 CZ78
Aisgill Av
Stanier Ri, Berk. 38 AT16
Staniland Dr, Wey. 212 BM110
Stanlake Ms W12 139 CW74
Stanlake Rd W12 139 CV74
Stanlake Vil W12 139 CV74
Stanley Av, Bark. 145 ET68
Stanley Av, Beck. 203 EC96
Stanley Av, Chesh. 54 AP31
Stanley Av, Dag. 126 EZ60
Stanley Av, Grnf. 136 CC67
Stanley Av, N.Mal. 199 CU99
Stanley Av, Rom. 127 FG56
Stanley Av, St.Alb. 60 CA25
Stanley Av, Wem. 138 CL66
Stanley Cl SW8 161 DM79
Stanley Cl, Couls. 235 DM117
Stanley Cl, Green. 189 FS85
Stanley Cl, Horn. 128 FJ61
Stanley Rd
Stanley Cl, Rom. 127 FG56
Stanley Cl, Uxb. 134 BK67
Stanley Cl, Wem. 138 CL66
Stanley Cotts, Slou. 132 AT74
Stanley Ct, Cars. 218 DG108
Stanley Pk Rd
Stanley Cres W11 139 CZ73
Stanley Cres, Grav. 191 GK92
Stanley Dr, Hat. 45 CV20
Stanley Gdns NW2 119 CW64
Stanley Gdns W3 138 CS74
Stanley Gdns W11 139 CZ73
Stanley Gdns, Borwd. 78 CL39
Stanley Gdns, Mitch. 180 DG93
Ashbourne Rd
Stanley Gdns, S.Croy. 220 DU112
Stanley Gdns, Wall. 219 DJ107
Stanley Gdns, Walt. 214 BW107
Stanley Gdns Ms W11 139 CZ73
Stanley Cres
Stanley Gdns Rd, Tedd. 177 CE92
Stanley Grn E, Slou. 153 AZ77
Stanley Grn W, Slou. 153 AZ77
Stanley Gro SW8 160 DG82
Stanley Gro, Croy. 201 DN100
Stanley Hill, Amer. 55 AR40
Stanley Hill Av, Amer. 55 AR39
Stanley Horstead Twr E10 123 EB61
Oliver Rd
Stanley Pk Dr, Wem. 138 CM66
Stanley Pk Rd, Cars. 218 DF108
Stanley Pk Rd, Wall. 219 DH107
Stanley Pas NW1 273 P1
Stanley Rd E4 101 ED46
Stanley Rd E10 123 EB58
Stanley Rd E12 124 EL64
Stanley Rd E15 143 ED67
Stanley Rd E18 102 EF53
Stanley Rd N2 120 DD55
Stanley Rd N9 100 DT46
Stanley Rd N10 99 DH52
Stanley Rd N11 99 DK51
Stanley Rd N15 121 DP56
Stanley Rd NW9 119 CU59
West Hendon Bdy
Stanley Rd SW14 158 CP84
Stanley Rd SW19 180 DA94
Stanley Rd W3 158 CQ76
Stanley Rd, Ashf. 174 BL92
Stanley Rd, Brom. 204 EH98
Stanley Rd, Cars. 218 DG108
Stanley Rd, Croy. 201 DN101
Stanley Rd, Enf. 82 DS41
Stanley Rd (Northfleet), Grav. 190 GE88
Stanley Rd, Grays 170 GB78
Stanley Rd, Har. 116 CC61
Stanley Rd, Hert. 32 DS09
Stanley Rd, Horn. 128 FJ61
Stanley Rd, Houns. 156 CC84
Stanley Rd, Ilf. 125 ER61
Stanley Rd, Mitch. 180 DG94
Stanley Rd, Mord. 200 DA98
Stanley Rd, Nthwd. 93 BU53
Stanley Rd, Orp. 206 EU102
Stanley Rd, Sid. 186 EU90
Stanley Rd, Sthl. 136 BY73
Stanley Rd, Sutt. 218 DB107
Stanley Rd, Swans. 190 FZ86
Stanley Rd, Tedd. 177 CE91
Stanley Rd, Twick. 177 CD90
Stanley Rd, Wat. 76 BW41
Stanley Rd, Wem. 138 CM65
Stanley Rd, Wok. 227 AZ116
Stanley Rd N, Rain. 147 FE67
Stanley Rd S, Rain. 147 FF68
Stanley Sq, Cars. 218 DF109
Stanley St SE8 163 DZ80
Stanley St, Cat. 236 DQ122
Coulsdon Rd
Stanley Ter N19 121 DL61
Stanley Way, Orp. 206 EV99
Stanleycroft Cl, Islw. 157 CE81
Stanmer St SW11 160 DE81
Stanmore Chase, St.Alb. 43 CK21
Stanmore Gdns, Rich. 158 CM83
Stanmore Gdns, Sutt. 200 DC104
Stanmore Hall, Stan. 95 CH48
Stanmore Hill, Stan. 95 CG48
Stanmore Pk, Stan. 95 CH50
Stanmore Pl NW1 141 DH67
Arlington Rd
Stanmore Rd E11 124 EF60
Stanmore Rd N15 121 DP56
Stanmore Rd, Belv. 167 FC77
Stanmore Rd, Rich. 158 CM83
Stanmore Rd, Wat. 75 BV39
Stanmore St N1 141 DM67
Caledonian Rd
Stanmore Ter, Beck. 203 EA96
Stanmore Way, Loug. 85 EN39
Stanmount Rd, St.Alb. 60 CA25
Stannard Ms E8 142 DU65
Stannard Rd E8 142 DU65
Stannary Pl SE11 161 DN78
Stannary St SE11 161 DN79
Stannet Way, Wall. 219 DJ105
Stannington Path, Borwd. 78 CN39
Stansfeld Rd E6 144 EK71
Stansfield Rd SW9 161 DM83
Stansfield Rd, Houns. 155 BV82
Stansgate Rd, Dag. 126 FA61
Stanstead Cl, Brom. 204 EF99
Stanstead Dr, Hodd. 49 EB15
Stanstead Gro SE6 183 DZ88
Catford Hill
Stanstead Manor, Sutt. 218 DA107
Stanstead Rd E11 124 EH57
Stanstead Rd SE6 183 DX88
Stanstead Rd SE23 183 DX88
Stanstead Rd, Cat. 252 DR125
Stanstead Rd, Hert. 32 DT08
Stanstead Rd, Hodd. 49 EB16
Stanstead Rd (Heathrow Airport), Houns. 174 BM86
Stanstead Rd, Ware 32 DW09
Stansted Cl, Horn. 147 FH65
Stansted Cres, Bex. 186 EX88
Stanswood Gdns SE5 162 DS80
Sedgmoor Pl
Stanthorpe Cl SW16 181 DL92
Stanthorpe Rd
Stanthorpe Rd SW16 181 DL92
Stanton Av, Tedd. 177 CE92
Stanton Cl, Epsom 216 CP106
Stanton Cl, Orp. 206 EW101
Stanton Cl, St.Alb. 43 CK16
Stanton Cl, Wor.Pk. 199 CX102
Stanton Rd SE26 183 DZ91
Stanton Way
Stanton Rd SW13 159 CT82
Stanton Rd SW20 199 CX96
Stanton Rd, Croy. 202 DQ101
Stanton Sq SE26 183 DZ91
Stanton Way
Stanton Way SE26 183 DZ91
Stanton Way, Slou. 152 AY77
Stantons, Harl. 51 EP15
Stantons Wf (Bramley), Guil. 259 BA144
Stanway Cl, Chig. 103 ES50
Stanway Ct N1 142 DS68
Hoxton St
Stanway Gdns W3 138 CN74
Stanway Gdns, Edg. 96 CQ50
Stanway Rd, Wal.Abb. 68 EG33
Stanway St N1 142 DS68
Stanwell Cl (Stanwell), Stai. 174 BK86
Stanwell Gdns (Stanwell), Stai. 174 BK86
Stanwell Moor Rd, Stai. 174 BH85
Stanwell Moor Rd, West Dr. 154 BH81
Stanwell New Rd, Stai. 174 BH90
Stanwell Rd, Ashf. 174 BL91
Stanwell Rd, Felt. 175 BQ87
Stanwell Rd (Horton), Slou. 153 BA83
Stanwick Rd W14 159 CZ77
Stanworth St SE1 279 P5
Stanworth St SE1 162 DT75
Stanwyck Dr, Chig. 103 EQ50
Stanwyck Gdns, Rom. 105 FH50
Stapenhill Rd, Wem. 117 CH62
Staple Cl, Bex. 187 FD90
Staple Hill Rd (Chobham Common), Wok. 210 AS105
Staple Inn WC1 274 D7
Staple Inn Bldgs WC1 274 D7
Staple Inn Bldgs WC1 141 DN71
Staple La (Shere), Guil. 244 BK132
Staple St SE1 279 L5
Staple St SE1 162 DR75
Staple Tye, Harl. 51 EQ18
Staplefield Cl SW2 181 DL88
Staplefield Cl, Pnr. 94 BY52
Stapleford, Welw.G.C. 30 DC09
Stapleford Av, Ilf. 125 ES57
Stapleford Cl E4 101 EC48
Stapleford Cl SW19 179 CY87
Stapleford Cl, Kings.T. 198 CN97
Stapleford Ct, Sev. 256 FF123
Stapleford Gdns, Rom. 104 FA51
Stapleford Rd, Rom. 87 FB42
Stapleford Rd, Wem. 137 CK66
Stapleford Tawney, Ong. 71 FC32
Stapleford Tawney, Rom. 87 FD35
Stapleford Way, Bark. 146 EV69
Staplehurst Cl, Reig. 266 DC138
Staplehurst Rd SE13 184 EE85
Staplehurst Rd, Cars. 218 DE108
Staplehurst Rd, Reig. 266 DC138
Staples Cl SE16 143 DY74
Staples Cor NW2 119 CV60
Staples Cor Business Pk NW2 119 CV60
Staples Rd, Loug. 84 EL41
Stapleton Cl, Pot.B. 64 DD31
Stapleton Cres, Rain. 147 FG65
Stapleton Gdns, Croy. 219 DN106
Stapleton Hall Rd N4 121 DM59
Stapleton Rd SW17 180 DG90
Stapleton Rd, Bexh. 166 EZ80
Stapleton Rd, Borwd. 78 CN38
Stapleton Rd, Orp. 205 ET104
Stapley Rd, Belv. 166 FA78
Stapley Rd, St.Alb. 43 CD19
Stapylton Rd, Barn. 79 CY41
Star All EC3 275 N10
Star & Garter Hill, Rich. 178 CL88
Star Hill, Dart. 187 FE85
Star Hill, Wok. 226 AW119
Star Hill Rd (Dunton Grn), Sev. 240 EZ116
Star Home Ct, Ware 33 DY06
Star La E16 144 EE70
Star La, Couls. 234 DG122
Star La, Epp. 70 EU30
Star La, Orp. 206 EY98
Star Path, Nthlt. 136 CA68
Brabazon Rd
Star Pl E1 142 DT73
Thomas More St
Star Rd W14 159 CZ79
Star Rd, Islw. 157 CD82
Star Rd, Uxb. 135 BQ70
Star St E16 144 EF71
Star St W2 272 A8
Star St W2 140 DE71
Star St, Ware 33 DY06
Star Yd WC2 274 D8
Starboard Av, Green. 189 FV86
Starboard Way E14 163 EA76
Starch Ho La, Ilf. 103 ER54
Starcross St NW1 273 L3
Starcross St NW1 141 DJ69
Starfield Rd W12 159 CU75
Starkey Cl (Cheshunt), Wal.Cr. 66 DQ25
Shambrook Rd
Starlight Way, St.Alb. 43 CJ22
Starling Cl, Buck.H. 102 EG46
Starling Cl, Pnr. 116 BW55
Starling La (Cuffley), Pot.B. 65 DM28
Starling Ms SE28 165 ER75
Whinchat Rd
Starling Wk, Hmptn. 176 BY93
Oak Av
Starlings, The (Oxshott), Lthd. 214 CC113
Starmans Cl, Dag. 146 EY67
Starrock La (Chipstead), Couls. 234 DF120
Starrock Rd, Couls. 235 DH119
Starts Cl, Orp. 205 EN104
Starts Hill Av, Orp. 223 EP105
Starts Hill Rd, Orp. 205 EN104
Starveall Cl, West Dr. 154 BM76
Starwood Cl, W.Byf. 212 BJ111
Starwood Ct, Slou. 152 AW76
London Rd
State Fm Av, Orp. 223 EP105
Staten Gdns, Twick. 177 CF88
Statham Gro N16 122 DQ63
Green Las
Statham Gro N18 100 DS50
Station App (Highams Pk) E4 101 ED51
The Av
Station App E7 124 EH63
Woodford Rd
Station App (Snaresbrook) E11 124 EG57
High St
Station App N11 99 DH50
Friern Barnet Rd
Station App (Woodside Pk) N12 98 DB49
Station App (Stoke Newington) N16 122 DT61
Stamford Hill
Station App NW10 139 CT69
Station Rd
Station App SE1 278 C5
Station App SE1 161 DN75
Station App SE3 164 EH83
Kidbrooke Pk Rd
Station App (Mottingham) SE9 185 EM88
Station App (Lower Sydenham) SE26 183 DZ92
Worsley Br Rd
Station App (Sydenham) SE26 182 DW91
Sydenham Rd
Station App SW6 159 CY83
Station App SW16 181 DK92
Station App W7 137 CE74
Station App, Amer. 55 AQ38
Station App (Little Chalfont), Amer. 72 AX39
Chalfont Sta Rd
Station App, Ashf. 174 BL91
Station App, Barn. 80 DC42
Station App, Bex. 186 FA87
Bexley High St
Station App, Bexh. 166 EY82
Avenue Rd
Station App (Barnehurst), Bexh. 167 FC82
Station App (Hayes), Brom. 204 EG102
Station App, Buck.H. 102 EK49
Cherry Tree Ri
Station App, Chis. 205 EN95
Station App (Elmstead Wds), Chis. 184 EL93
Station App, Couls. 235 DK116
Station App (Chipstead), Couls. 234 DF118
Station App, Dart. 188 FL86
Station App (Crayford), Dart. 187 FF86
Station App, Dor. 247 CJ134
Station App (Theydon Bois), Epp. 85 ES36
Coppice Row
Station App, Epsom 216 CR113
Station App (Ewell E), Epsom 217 CV110
Station App (Ewell W), Epsom 217 CT109
Chessington Rd
Station App (Stoneleigh), Epsom 217 CU106
Station App (Hinchley Wd), Esher 197 CF104
Station App, Ger.Cr. 112 AY57
Station App, Grays 170 GA79
Station App, Grnf. 137 CD66
Station App, Guil. 258 AY135
Station App, Hmptn. 196 CA95
Milton Rd
Station App, Harl. 36 EW10
Station App, Har. 117 CE59
Station App, Hayes 155 BT75
Station App, Hem.H. 40 BG23
Station App, Horl. 269 DH148
Station App, Ken. 220 DQ114
Hayes La
Station App, Kings.T. 198 CN95
Station App, Lthd. 231 CG121
Station App (East Horsley), Lthd. 245 BS126
Station App (Oxshott), Lthd. 214 CC113
Station App, Loug. 84 EL43
Station App (Debden), Loug. 85 EQ42
Station App, Nthwd. 93 BS52
Station App, Orp. 205 ET103
Station App (Chelsfield), Orp. 224 EV106
Station App (St. Mary Cray), Orp. 206 EV98
Station App, Oxt. 254 EE128
Station App, Pnr. 116 BY55
Station App (Hatch End), Pnr. 94 CA52
Uxbridge Rd
Station App, Pur. 219 DN111
Whytecliffe Rd S
Station App, Rad. 77 CG35
Shenley Hill
Station App, Rich. 158 CN81
Station App, Rick. 73 BK42
Station App (South Ruislip), Ruis. 115 BV64
Station App, Shep. 195 BQ100
Station App, S.Croy. 220 DR109
Sanderstead Rd
Station App, Stai. 174 BG92
Station App, Sun. 195 BU95
Station App (Belmont), Sutt. 218 DB110
Brighton Rd
Station App (Cheam), Sutt. 217 CY108
Station App, Swan. 207 FE98
Station App, Upmin. 128 FQ61
Station App (Denham), Uxb. 113 BD59
Middle Rd
Station App, Vir.W. 192 AX98
Station App, Wal.Cr. 67 DY34
Station App (Cheshunt), Wal.Cr. 67 DZ30
Station App, Wat. 75 BT41
Cassiobury Pk Av
Station App (Carpenders Pk), Wat. 94 BX48
Prestwick Rd
Station App, Well. 165 ET82
Station App, Wem. 137 CH65
Station App, W.Byf. 212 BG112
Station App, West Dr. 134 BL74
Station App, Wey. 212 BN107
Station App, Whyt. 236 DU117
Station App, Wok. 227 AZ117
Station App E (Earlswood), Red. 266 DF136
Earlsbrook Rd
Station App N, Sid. 186 EU89
Station App Rd W4 158 CQ80
Station App Rd, Couls. 235 DK115
Station App Rd, Gat. 269 DH152
London Rd
Station App Rd, Tad. 233 CW122
Station App Rd, Til. 171 GG84
Station App W (Earlswood), Red. 266 DF136
Earlswood Rd
Station Av SW9 161 DP83
Coldharbour La
Station Av, Cat. 236 DU124
Station Av, Epsom 216 CS109
Station Av, N.Mal. 198 CS97
Station Av, Rich. 158 CN81
Station Av, Walt. 213 BU105
Station Cl N3 98 DA53
Station Cl (Woodside Pk) N12 98 DB49
Station Cl, Hmptn. 196 CB95
Station Cl, Hat. 63 CY26
Station Rd
Station Cl, Pot.B. 63 CZ31
Station Cres N15 122 DR56
Station Cres SE3 164 EG78
Station Cres, Ashf. 174 BK90
Station Cres, Wem. 137 CH65
Station Est, Beck. 203 DX98
Elmers End Rd
Station Est Rd, Felt. 175 BV88
Station Footpath, Kings L. 59 BP31
Station Gar Ms SW16 181 DK93
Estreham Rd
Station Gdns W4 158 CQ80
Station Gro, Wem. 138 CL65
Station Hill, Brom. 204 EG103
Station Ho Ms N9 100 DU49
Fore St
Station La, Horn. 128 FK62
Station Par E11 124 EG57
Station Par N14 99 DK46
High St
Station Par NW2 139 CW65
Station Par SW12 180 DG88
Balham High Rd
Station Par W3 138 CN72
Station Par, Ashf. 174 BM91
Woodthorpe Rd
Station Par, Bark. 145 EQ66
Station Par, Beac. 89 AK52
Station Par, Felt. 175 BV87
Station Par, Horn. 127 FH63
Rosewood Av
Station Par, Lthd. 245 BS126
Ockham Rd S
Station Par, Rich. 158 CN81
Station Par, Sev. 256 FG124
London Rd
Station Par (Denham), Uxb. 114 BG59
Station Par, Vir.W. 192 AX98
Station Pas E18 102 EH54
Maybank Rd
Station Path E8 142 DV65
Amhurst Rd
Station Path, Stai. 173 BF91
Station Pl N4 121 DN61
Seven Sisters Rd
Station Pl, Gdmg. 258 AT144
Summers Rd
Station Ri SE27 181 DP89
Norwood Rd
Station Rd (Chingford) E4 101 ED46
Station Rd E7 124 EG63
Station Rd E12 124 EK63
Station Rd E17 123 DY58
Station Rd N3 98 DA53
Station Rd N11 99 DH50
Station Rd N17 122 DU55
Hale Rd
Station Rd N19 121 DJ62
Station Rd N21 99 DP46
Station Rd N22 99 DM54
Station Rd NW4 119 CU58
Station Rd NW7 96 CS50
Station Rd NW10 139 CT68
Station Rd SE13 163 EC83
Station Rd SE20 182 DW93

Station Rd (Norwood Junct) SE25 202 DT98
Station Rd SW13 159 CU83
Station Rd SW19 200 DC95
Station Rd W5 138 CM72
Station Rd (Hanwell) W7 137 CE74
Station Rd, Add. 212 BJ105
Station Rd, Amer. 55 AQ38
Station Rd, Ashf. 174 BM91
Station Rd, Barn. 80 DB43
Station Rd, Beac. 89 AK52
Station Rd, Belv. 166 FA76
Station Rd, Berk. 38 AW18
Station Rd, Bet. 248 CS131
Station Rd, Bexh. 166 EY83
Station Rd, Borwd. 78 CN42
Station Rd, Brent. 157 CJ79
Station Rd, Brom. 204 EG95
Station Rd (Shortlands), Brom. 204 EE96
Station Rd, Brox. 49 DZ20
Station Rd, Cars. 218 DF105
Station Rd, Cat. 237 DZ123
Station Rd, Cher. 193 BF102
Station Rd, Chesh. 54 AP31
Station Rd, Chess. 216 CL106
Station Rd, Chig. 103 EP48
Station Rd (Stoke D'Abernon), Cob. 230 BY117
Station Rd (East Croydon), Croy. 202 DR103
Station Rd (West Croydon), Croy. 202 DQ102
Station Rd (Crayford), Dart. 187 FF86
Station Rd (Eynsford), Dart. 208 FK104
Station Rd (South Darenth), Dart. 208 FP96
Station Rd, Dor. 263 CG135
Station Rd, Edg. 96 CN51
Station Rd, Egh. 173 BA92
Station Rd, Epp. 70 EU31
Station Rd (North Weald Bassett), Epp. 71 FB27
Station Rd, Esher 197 CD103
Station Rd (Claygate), Esher 215 CD106
Station Rd, Ger.Cr. 112 AY57
Station Rd, Gdmg. 258 AT144
Station Rd (Betsham), Grav. 190 GA91
Station Rd (Northfleet), Grav. 190 GB86
Station Rd, Green. 189 FU85
Station Rd (Bramley), Guil. 259 AZ144
Station Rd (Gomshall), Guil. 261 BS139
Station Rd (Shalford), Guil. 258 AY140
Station Rd, Hmptn. 196 CA95
Station Rd, Harl. 36 EW11
Station Rd, Har. 117 CF59
Station Rd (North Harrow), Har. 116 CB57
Station Rd (Brookmans Pk), Hat. 63 CX25
Station Rd, Hayes 155 BT76
Station Rd, Hem.H. 40 BH22
Station Rd (Letty Grn), Hert. 30 DG12
Station Rd (Loudwater), H.Wyc. 88 AC53
Station Rd, Horl. 269 DH148
Station Rd, Houns. 156 CB84
Station Rd, Ilf. 125 EP62
Station Rd (Barkingside), Ilf. 125 ER55
Station Rd, Ken. 220 DQ114
Station Rd, Kings L. 59 BP29
Station Rd, Kings.T. 198 CN95
Station Rd (Hampton Wick), Kings.T. 197 CJ95
Station Rd, Lthd. 231 CG121
Station Rd, Loug. 84 EL42
Station Rd, Maid. 130 AF72
Station Rd (Motspur Pk), N.Mal. 199 CV99
Station Rd, Orp. 205 ET103
Station Rd (St. Paul's Cray), Orp. 206 EW98
Station Rd (Cuffley), Pot.B. 65 DM29
Station Rd, Rad. 77 CG35
Station Rd, Red. 250 DG133
Station Rd (Merstham), Red. 251 DJ128
Station Rd, Rick. 92 BK45
Station Rd (Chadwell Heath), Rom. 126 EX59
Station Rd (Gidea Pk), Rom. 127 FH56
Station Rd (Harold Wd), Rom. 106 FM53
Station Rd (Bricket Wd), St.Alb. 60 CA31
Station Rd (Smallford), St.Alb. 44 CP19
Station Rd (Dunton Grn), Sev. 241 FE120
Station Rd (Halstead), Sev. 224 EZ111
Station Rd (Otford), Sev. 241 FH116
Station Rd (Shoreham), Sev. 225 FG111
Station Rd, Shep. 195 BQ99
Station Rd, Sid. 186 EU91
Station Rd (Cippenham), Slou. 131 AL72
Station Rd (Langley), Slou. 153 BA76
Station Rd (Wraysbury), Stai. 173 AZ86
Station Rd, Sun. 175 BU94
Station Rd (Belmont), Sutt. 218 DA110
Station Rd, Swan. 207 FE98
Station Rd, Tedd. 177 CF92
Station Rd, T.Ditt. 197 CF101
Station Rd, Twick. 177 CF88
Station Rd, Upmin. 128 FQ61
Station Rd, Uxb. 134 BJ70
Station Rd, Wal.Cr. 67 EA34
Station Rd, Ware 33 DX06
Station Rd (St. Margarets), Ware 33 EA11
Station Rd, Wat. 75 BV40
Station Rd, W.Byf. 212 BG112
Station Rd, West Dr. 134 BL74
Station Rd, W.Wick. 203 EC102
Station Rd (Brasted), West. 240 EV123
Station Rd, Whyt. 236 DT118
Station Rd (Chobham), Wok. 210 AT111
Station Rd E, Oxt. 254 EE128
Station Rd N, Belv. 167 FB76
Station Rd N, Egh. 173 BA92
Station Rd N (Merstham), Red. 251 DJ128
Station Rd S (Merstham), Red. 251 DJ128
Station Rd W, Oxt. 254 EE129
Station Row (Shalford), Guil. 258 AY140
Station Sq (Petts Wd), Orp. 205 EQ99
Station Sq, Rom. 127 FH56
Station St E15 143 ED66
Station St E16 145 EP74
Station Ter NW10 139 CX68
Station Ter SE5 162 DQ81
Station Ter, Dor. 263 CG135
Chalkpit La
Station Ter (Park St), St.Alb. 61 CD26
Park St
Station Vw, Grnf. 137 CD67
Station Vw, Guil. 258 AW135
Station Way (Roding Valley), Buck.H. 102 EJ49
Station Way (Epsom), Epsom 216 CR113
Station Way (Claygate), Esher 215 CE107
Station Way, St.Alb. 43 CF20
Station Way (Cheam), Sutt. 217 CY107
Station Way, Welw.G.C. 29 CX08
Station Yd, Twick. 177 CG87
Stationers Hall Ct EC4 141 DP72
Ludgate Hill
Staunton Rd, Kings.T. 178 CL93
Staunton Rd, Slou. 131 AR71
Staunton St SE8 163 DZ79
Stave Yd Rd SE16 143 DY74
Staveley Cl E9 122 DW64
Churchill Wk
Staveley Cl N7 121 DL63
Penn Rd
Staveley Cl SE15 162 DV81
Asylum Rd
Staveley Gdns W4 158 CR81
Staveley Rd W4 158 CR80
Staveley Rd, Ashf. 175 BR93
Staveley Way (Knaphill), Wok. 226 AS117
Staverton Rd NW2 139 CW66
Staverton Rd, Horn. 128 FK58
Stavordale Rd N5 121 DP63
Stavordale Rd, Cars. 200 DC101
Stayne End, Vir.W. 192 AU98
Stayner's Rd E1 143 DX70
Stayton Rd, Sutt. 200 DA104
Stead St SE17 279 K9
Stead St SE17 162 DR77
Steadfast Rd, Kings.T. 197 CK95
Steam Fm La, Felt. 155 BT84
Stean St E8 142 DT67
Stebbing Ho W11 139 CX74
Stebbing Way, Bark. 146 EU68
Stebondale St E14 163 EC78
Stedham Pl WC1 273 P8
Stedman Cl, Bex. 187 FE90
Stedman Cl, Uxb. 114 BN62
Steed Cl, Horn. 127 FH61
Steedman St SE17 279 H9
Steeds Rd N10 98 DF53
Steeds Way, Loug. 84 EL41
Steele Av, Green. 189 FT85
Steele Rd E11 124 EE63
Steele Rd N17 122 DS55
Steele Rd NW10 138 CQ68
Steele Rd W4 158 CQ76
Steele Rd, Islw. 157 CG84
Steele Wk, Erith 167 FB79
Steeles Ms N NW3 140 DF65
Steeles Rd
Steeles Ms S NW3 140 DF65
Steeles Rd
Steeles Rd NW3 140 DF65
Steel's La E1 142 DW72
Devonport St
Steels La (Oxshott), Lthd. 214 CB114
Steelyard Pas EC4 142 DR73
Upper Thames St
Steen Way SE22 182 DS85
East Dulwich Gro
Steep Cl, Orp. 223 ET107
Steep Hill SW16 181 DK90
Steep Hill, Croy. 220 DS105
Steeplands, Bushey 94 CB45
Steeple Cl SW6 159 CY82
Steeple Cl SW19 179 CY92
Steeple Ct E1 142 DV70
Coventry Rd
Steeple Gdns, Add. 212 BH106
Weatherall Cl
Steeple Hts Dr (Biggin Hill), West. 238 EK117
Steeple Wk N1 142 DQ67
Basire St
Steeplestone Cl N18 100 DQ50
Steer Pl, Red. 266 DG143
Bonehurst Rd
Steerforth St SW18 180 DB89
Steers Mead, Mitch. 200 DF95
Steers Way SE16 163 DY75
Stella Rd SW17 180 DF93
Stellar Ho N17 100 DT51
Stelling Rd, Erith 167 FD80
Stellman Cl E5 122 DU62
Stembridge Rd SE20 202 DV96
Sten Cl, Enf. 83 EA38
Government Row
Stents La, Cob. 230 BZ120
Stepbridge Path, Wok. 226 AX117
Goldsworth Rd
Stepgates, Cher. 194 BH101
Stepgates Cl, Cher. 194 BH101
Stephan Cl E8 142 DU67
Stephen Av, Rain. 147 FG65
Stephen Cl, Egh. 173 BC93
Stephen Cl, Orp. 205 ET104
Stephen Ms W1 273 M7
Stephen Rd, Bexh. 167 FC83
Stephen St W1 273 M7
Stephen St W1 141 DK71
Stephendale Rd SW6 160 DB82
Stephens Cl, Rom. 106 FJ50
Stephen's Rd E15 144 EE67
Stephenson Av, Til. 171 GG81
Stephenson Dr, Wind. 151 AP80
Stephenson Rd E17 123 DY57
Stephenson Rd W7 137 CF72
Stephenson Rd, Twick. 176 CA87
Stephenson St E16 144 EE70
Stephenson St NW10 138 CS69
Stephenson Way NW1 273 L4
Stephenson Way NW1 141 DJ70
Stephenson Way, Wat. 76 BX41
Stephyns Chambers, Hem.H. 40 BJ21
Waterhouse St
Stepney Causeway E1 143 DX72
Stepney Grn E1 142 DW71
Stepney High St E1 143 DX71
Stepney Way E1 142 DV71
Sterling Av, Edg. 96 CM49
Sterling Av, Pnr. 116 BY59
Sterling Av, Wal.Cr. 67 DX34
Sterling Cl NW10 139 CU65
Sterling Cl, Pnr. 116 BX60
Sterling Gdns SE14 163 DY79
Sterling Ho SE3 164 EH84
Cambert Way
Sterling Ind Est, Dag. 127 FB63
Sterling Pl W5 158 CL77
Sterling Rd, Enf. 82 DR38
Sterling St SW7 276 C6
Sterling Way N18 100 DR50
Stern Cl, Bark. 146 EY69
Choats Rd
Sterndale Rd W14 159 CX76
Sterndale Rd, Dart. 188 FM87
Sterne St W12 159 CX75
Sternhall La SE15 162 DU83
Sternhold Av SW2 181 DK89
Sterry Cres, Dag. 126 FA64
Alibon Rd
Sterry Dr, Epsom 216 CS105
Sterry Dr, T.Ditt. 197 CE100
Sterry Gdns, Dag. 146 FA65
Sterry Rd, Bark. 145 ET67
Sterry Rd, Dag. 126 FA63
Sterry St SE1 279 K5
Sterry St SE1 162 DR75
Steucers La SE23 183 DY87
Steve Biko La SE6 183 EA91
Steve Biko Rd N7 121 DN62
Steve Biko Way, Houns. 156 CA83
Stevedale Rd, Well. 166 EW82
Stevedore St E1 142 DV74
Waterman Way
Stevenage Cres, Borwd. 78 CL39
Stevenage Ri, Hem.H. 40 BM16
Stevenage Rd E6 145 EN65
Stevenage Rd SW6 159 CX80
Stevens Av E9 142 DW65
Stevens Cl, Beck. 183 EA93
Stevens Cl, Bex. 187 FD91
Steven's Cl (Lane End), Dart. 189 FS92
Stevens Cl, Epsom 216 CS113
Upper High St
Stevens Cl, Hmptn. 176 BZ93
Stevens Cl, Pnr. 116 BW57
Bridle Rd
Stevens Grn, Bushey 94 CC46
Stevens La (Claygate), Esher 215 CG108
Stevens Pl, Pur. 219 DP113
Stevens Rd, Dag. 126 EV62
Stevens St SE1 279 N6
Steven's Wk, Croy. 221 DY111
Stevens Way, Chig. 103 ES49
Stevenson Cl, Barn. 80 DD44
Stevenson Cl, Erith 167 FH80
Stevenson Cres SE16 162 DV78
Stevenson Rd (Hedgerley), Slou. 111 AR61
Steventon Rd W12 139 CT73
Stew La EC4 275 H10
Steward Cl (Cheshunt), Wal.Cr. 67 DY30
Steward St E1 275 N7
Steward St E1 142 DS71
Stewards Cl, Epp. 70 EU33
Stewards Grn La, Epp. 70 EV32
Stewards Grn Rd, Epp. 70 EU33
Stewards Holte Wk N11 99 DH49
Coppies Gro
Stewards Wk, Rom. 127 FE57
Stewart, Tad. 233 CX121
Stewart Av, Shep. 194 BN98
Stewart Av, Slou. 132 AT71
Stewart Av, Upmin. 128 FP62
Stewart Cl NW9 118 CQ58
Stewart Cl, Abb.L. 59 BT32
Stewart Cl, Chis. 185 EP92
Stewart Cl, Hmptn. 176 BY92
Stewart Cl, Maid. 150 AD81
Stewart Cl, Wok. 226 AT117
Nethercote Av
Stewart Rainbird Ho E12 125 EN64
Stewart Rd E15 123 ED63
Stewart St E14 163 EC75
Stewart's Dr (Farnham Common), Slou. 111 AP64
Stewart's Gro SW3 276 A10
Stewart's Gro SW3 160 DD77
Stewart's Rd SW8 161 DJ80
Stewartsby Cl N18 100 DQ50
Steyne Rd W3 138 CQ74
Steyning Cl, Ken. 235 DP116
Steyning Gro SE9 185 EM91
Steyning Way, Houns. 156 BW84
Steynings Way N12 98 DA50
Steynton Av, Bex. 186 EX89
Stickland Rd, Belv. 166 FA77
Picardy Rd
Stickleton Cl, Grnf. 136 CB69
Stifford Hill (North Stifford), Grays 149 FX74
Stifford Hill, S.Ock. 149 FW73
Stifford Rd, S.Ock. 149 FR74
Stile Hall Gdns W4 158 CN78
Stile Hall Par W4 158 CN78
Chiswick High Rd
Stile Meadow, Beac. 89 AL52
Maxwell Rd
Stile Path, Sun. 195 BU97
Stile Rd, Slou. 152 AX76
Stilecroft, Harl. 52 EU17
Stilecroft Gdns, Wem. 117 CH62
Stiles Cl, Brom. 205 EM100
Stiles Cl, Erith 167 FB78
Riverdale Rd
Stillingfleet Rd SW13 159 CU79
Stillington St SW1 277 L8
Stillington St SW1 161 DJ77
Stillness Rd SE23 183 DY86
Stilton Cres NW10 138 CQ66
Stilton Path, Borwd. 78 CN38
Stilwell Dr, Uxb. 134 BM70
Stilwell Roundabout, Uxb. 134 BN73
Stipularis Dr, Hayes 136 BX70
Stirling Cl SW16 201 DJ95
Stirling Cl, Bans. 233 CZ117
Stirling Cl, Rain. 147 FH69
Stirling Cl, Uxb. 134 BJ69
Ferndale Cres
Stirling Cl, Wind. 151 AK82
Stirling Cor, Barn. 78 CR44
Stirling Cor, Borwd. 78 CR44
Stirling Dr, Orp. 224 EV106
Stirling Gro, Houns. 156 CC82
Stirling Rd E13 144 EH68
Stirling Rd E17 123 DY55
Stirling Rd N17 100 DU53
Stirling Rd N22 99 DP53
Stirling Rd SW9 161 DL82
Stirling Rd W3 158 CP76
Stirling Rd, Har. 117 CF55
Stirling Rd, Hayes 135 BV73
Stirling Rd (Heathrow Airport), Houns. 174 BM86
Stirling Rd, Slou. 131 AP72
Stirling Rd, Twick. 176 CA87
Stirling Rd Path E17 123 DY55
Stirling Wk, N.Mal. 198 CQ99
Stirling Wk, Surb. 198 CP100
Stirling Way, Abb.L. 59 BU32
Stirling Way, Borwd. 78 CR44
Stirling Way, Croy. 201 DL101
Stirling Way, Welw.G.C. 30 DE09
Stites Hill Rd, Couls. 235 DP120
Stiven Cres, Har. 116 BZ62
Stoat Cl, Hert. 32 DU09
Stoats Nest Rd, Couls. 219 DL114
Stoats Nest Village, Couls. 235 DL115
Stock Hill (Biggin Hill), West. 238 EK116
Stock La, Dart. 188 FJ91
Stock Orchard Cres N7 121 DM64
Stock Orchard St N7 121 DM64
Stock St E13 144 EG68
Stockbreach Cl, Hat. 45 CU17
Stockbreach Rd, Hat. 45 CU17
Stockbury Rd, Croy. 202 DW100
Stockdale Rd, Dag. 126 EZ61
Stockdales Rd (Eton Wick), Wind. 151 AM77
Stockdove Way, Grnf. 137 CF69
Stocker Gdns, Dag. 146 EW66
Stockers Fm Rd, Rick. 92 BK48
Stockers La, Wok. 227 AZ120
Stockfield, Horl. 269 DH147
Stockfield Av, Hodd. 49 EA15
Stockfield Rd SW16 181 DM90
Stockfield Rd (Claygate), Esher 215 CE106
Stockham's Cl, S.Croy. 220 DR111
Stockholm Ho E1 142 DU73
Stockholm Rd SE16 162 DW78
Stockholm Way E1 142 DU74
Stockhurst Cl SW15 159 CW82
Stocking La (Bayford), Hert. 47 DN18
Stockings La (Little Berkhamsted), Hert. 47 DK18
Stockingswater La, Enf. 83 DY41
Stockland Rd, Rom. 127 FD58
Stockley Cl, West Dr. 155 BP75
Stockley Fm Rd, West Dr. 155 BP76
Stockley Rd
Stockley Pk, Uxb. 135 BP74
Stockley Pk Roundabout, Uxb. 135 BP74
Stockley Rd, Uxb. 135 BP73
Stockley Rd, West Dr. 155 BP77
Stockport Rd SW16 201 DK95
Stockport Rd, Rick. 91 BC45
Stocks Cl, Horl. 269 DH149
Stocks Meadow, Hem.H. 40 BN19
Stocks Pl E14 143 DZ73
Grenade St
Stocksfield Rd E17 123 EC55
Stockton Cl, Barn. 80 DC42
Stockton Gdns N17 100 DQ52
Stockton Rd
Stockton Gdns NW7 96 CS48
Stockton Rd N17 100 DQ52
Stockton Rd N18 100 DU51
Stockton Rd, Reig. 266 DA137
Stockwell Av SW9 161 DM83
Stockwell Cl, Brom. 204 EH96
Stockwell Cl (Cheshunt), Wal.Cr. 66 DU28
Stockwell Gdns SW9 161 DM82
Stockwell Gdns Est SW9 161 DL82
Stockwell Grn SW9 161 DM82
Stockwell La SW9 161 DM82
Stockwell La (Cheshunt), Wal.Cr. 66 DU28
Stockwell Ms SW9 161 DM82
Stockwell Rd
Stockwell Pk Cres SW9 161 DM82
Stockwell Pk Est SW9 161 DN82
Stockwell Pk Rd SW9 161 DM81
Stockwell Pk Wk SW9 161 DM83
Stockwell Rd SW9 161 DM82
Stockwell St SE10 163 EC79
Stockwell Ter SW9 161 DM81
Stockwells, Maid. 130 AD70
Stocton Cl, Guil. 242 AW133
Stocton Rd, Guil. 242 AW133
Stodart Rd SE20 202 DW95
Stofield Gdns SE9 184 EK90
Aldersgrove Av
Stoford Cl SW19 179 CY87
Stoke Av, Ilf. 104 EU51
Stoke Cl (Stoke D'Abernon), Cob. 230 BZ116
Stoke Common Rd (Fulmer), Slou. 112 AU63
Stoke Ct Dr (Stoke Poges), Slou. 132 AS67
Stoke Flds, Guil. 258 AX135
Stoke Rd
Stoke Gdns, Slou. 132 AS74
Stoke Grn (Stoke Poges), Slou. 132 AU70
Stoke Gro, Guil. 242 AX134
Stoke Rd
Stoke Ms, Guil. 258 AX135
Stoke Rd
Stoke Newington Ch St N16 122 DR62
Stoke Newington Common N16 122 DT62
Stoke Newington High St N16 122 DT62
Stoke Newington Rd N16 122 DT64
Stoke Pk Av (Farnham Royal), Slou. 131 AQ69
Stoke Pl NW10 139 CT69
Stoke Poges La, Slou. 132 AS72
Stoke Rd, Cob. 230 BW115
Stoke Rd, Guil. 242 AX133
Stoke Rd, Kings.T. 178 CQ94
Stoke Rd, Rain. 148 FK68
Stoke Rd, Slou. 132 AT71
Stoke Rd, Walt. 196 BW104
Stoke Wd (Stoke Poges), Slou. 112 AT63
Stokenchurch St SW6 160 DB81
Stokers Cl, Gat. 268 DE151
Stokes Ridings, Tad. 233 CX123
Stokes Rd E6 144 EL70
Stokes Rd, Croy. 203 DX100
Stokesay, Slou. 132 AT73
Stokesby Rd, Chess. 216 CM107
Stokesheath Rd (Oxshott), Lthd. 215 CD111
Stokesley Ri (Wooburn Grn), H.Wyc. 110 AE55
Stokesley St W12 139 CT72
Stoll Cl NW2 119 CW62
Stomp Rd (Burnham), Slou. 130 AJ71
Stompond La, Walt. 195 BU103
Stonard Rd N13 99 DN48
Stonard Rd, Dag. 126 EV64
Stonards Hill, Epp. 70 EW31
Stonards Hill, Loug. 85 EM44
Stondon Pk SE23 183 DY87
Stondon Wk E6 144 EK68
Stone Bldgs WC2 274 C7
Stone Bldgs WC2 141 DM71
Stone Cl SW4 161 DJ82
Larkhall Ri
Stone Cl, Dag. 126 EZ61
Stone Cl, West Dr. 134 BM74
Stone Cres, Felt. 175 BT87
Stone Cross, Harl. 35 ER14
Post Office Rd
Stone Hall Gdns W8 160 DB76
St. Mary's Gate
Stone Hall Pl W8 160 DB76
St. Mary's Gate
Stone Hall Rd N21 99 DM45
Stone Ho Ct EC3 275 M8
Stone Lake Retail Pk SE7 164 EJ77
Stone Ness Rd, Grays 169 FV79
Stone Pk Av, Beck. 203 EA98
Stone Pl, Wor.Pk. 199 CU103
Stone Pl Rd, Green. 189 FS85
Stone Rd, Brom. 204 EF99
Stone St, Croy. 219 DN106
Stone St, Grav. 191 GH86
Stonebank, Welw.G.C. 29 CX08
Stonehills
Stonebanks, Walt. 195 BU101
Stonebridge Common E8 142 DT66
Mayfield Rd
Stonebridge Fld (Eton), Wind. 151 AP78
Stonebridge Flds (Shalford), Guil. 258 AX141
Stonebridge Pk NW10 138 CR66
Stonebridge Rd N15 122 DS57
Stonebridge Rd (Northfleet), Grav. 190 GA85
Stonebridge Way, Wem. 138 CP65
Stonebridge Wf (Shalford), Guil. 258 AX141
Stonechat Sq E6 144 EL71
Peridot St
Stonecot Cl, Sutt. 199 CY102
Stonecot Hill, Sutt. 199 CY102
Stonecourt Cl, Horl. 269 DJ148
Stonecroft Av, Iver 133 BE72
Stonecroft Cl, Barn. 79 CV42
Stonecroft Rd, Erith 167 FC80
Stonecroft Way, Croy. 201 DL101
Stonecrop Cl NW9 118 CR55
Stonecrop Rd, Guil. 243 BC132
Kingfisher Dr
Stonecross, St.Alb. 43 CE19
Stonecross Cl, St.Alb. 43 CE19
Stonecross
Stonecross Rd, Hat. 45 CV16
Stonecutter Ct EC4 141 DP72
Stonecutter St
Stonecutter St EC4 274 F8
Stonecutter St EC4 141 DP72
Stonefield Cl, Bexh. 166 FA83
Stonefield Cl, Ruis. 116 BY64
Stonefield St N1 141 DN67
Stonefield Way SE7 164 EK80
Greenbay Rd
Stonefield Way, Ruis. 116 BY63
Stonegate Cl, Orp. 206 EW97
Main Rd
Stonegrove, Edg. 96 CL49
Stonegrove Est, Edg. 96 CM49
Stonegrove Gdns, Edg. 96 CM50
Stonehall Av, Ilf. 124 EL58
Stoneham Rd N11 99 DJ51
Stonehill Cl SW14 178 CR85
Stonehill Cl (Bookham), Lthd. 246 CA125
Stonehill Cres (Ottershaw), Cher. 210 AY107
Stonehill Grn, Dart. 187 FC94
Stonehill Rd SW14 178 CQ85
Stonehill Rd W4 158 CN78
Wellesley Rd
Stonehill Rd (Ottershaw), Cher. 211 BA105
Stonehill Rd (Chobham), Wok. 210 AW108
Stonehill Wds Pk, Sid. 187 FB93
Stonehills, Welw.G.C. 29 CX09
Stonehills Ct SE21 182 DS90
Stonehorse Rd, Enf. 82 DW43
Stonehouse Gdns, Cat. 252 DS125
Stonehouse La, Purf. 169 FS79
Stonehouse La (Halstead), Sev. 224 EX109
Stonehouse Rd (Halstead), Sev. 224 EW110
Stoneings La (Knockholt), Sev. 239 ET118
Stonelea Rd, Hem.H. 40 BM23
Stoneleigh Av, Enf. 82 DV39
Stoneleigh Av, Wor.Pk. 217 CU105
Stoneleigh Bdy, Epsom 217 CU106
Stoneleigh Cl, Wal.Cr. 67 DX33
Stoneleigh Cres, Epsom 217 CT106
Stoneleigh Dr, Hodd. 33 EB14
Stoneleigh Pk, Wey. 213 BQ106
Stoneleigh Pk Av, Croy. 203 DX100
Stoneleigh Pk Rd, Epsom 217 CT107
Stoneleigh Pl W11 139 CX73
Stoneleigh Rd N17 122 DT55
Stoneleigh Rd, Cars. 200 DE101
Stoneleigh Rd, Ilf. 124 EL55
Stoneleigh Rd, Oxt. 254 EL130
Stoneleigh St W11 139 CX73
Stoneleigh Ter N19 121 DH61
Stonells Rd SW11 180 DF85
Chatham Rd
Stonemasons Cl N15 122 DR56
Stonenest St N4 121 DM60
Stones All, Wat. 75 BV42
Stones Cross Rd, Swan. 207 FC99
Stones End St SE1 279 H5
Stones End St SE1 162 DQ75
Stones La (Westcott), Dor. 262 CC137
Stones Rd, Epsom 216 CS112
Stoneswood Rd, Oxt. 254 EH130
Stonewall E6 145 EN71
Stonewood (Bean), Dart. 189 FW90
Stonewood Rd, Erith 167 FE78
Stoney All SE18 165 EN82
Stoney Brook, Guil. 242 AS133
Stoney Cft, Couls. 235 DK122
Netherne La
Stoney Gro, Chesh. 54 AR30
Stoney La E1 275 N8
Stoney La SE19 182 DT93
Church Rd
Stoney La, Hem.H. 39 BB23
Bourne End La
Stoney La (Bovingdon), Hem.H. 57 BB27
Stoney La, Kings L. 57 BE30
Stoney La (East Burnham), Slou. 131 AN67
Stoney Meade, Slou. 131 AP74
Weekes Dr

Stoney St SE1 279 **K2**
Stoney St SE1 142 DR74
Stoneyard La E14 143 EB73
Poplar High St
Stoneycroft, Hem.H. 40 BG20
Stoneycroft, Welw.G.C. 30 DA08
Stoneycroft Cl SE12 184 EF87
Stoneycroft Rd, Wdf.Grn. 102 EL51
Stoneydeep, Tedd. 177 CG91
Twickenham Rd
Stoneydown E17 123 DY56
Stoneydown Av E17 123 DY56
Stoneyfield Rd, Couls. 235 DM117
Stoneyfields Gdns, Edg. 96 CQ49
Stoneyfields La, Edg. 96 CQ50
Stoneylands Ct, Egh. 173 AZ92
Stoneylands Rd, Egh. 173 AZ92
Stonhouse St SW4 161 DK83
Stonny Cft, Ash. 232 CM117
Stonor Rd W14 159 CZ77
Stony La, Amer. 72 AY38
Stony Path, Loug. 85 EM40
Stony Wd, Harl. 51 ES16
Stonycroft Cl, Enf. 83 DY40
Brimsdown Av
Stonyrock La, Dor. 246 BY131
Stonyshotts, Wal.Abb. 68 EE34
Stoop Ct, W.Byf. 212 BH112
Stopes St SE15 162 DT80
Stopford Rd E13 144 EG67
Stopford Rd SE17 161 DP78
Store Rd E16 165 EN75
Store St E15 123 ED64
Store St WC1 273 **M7**
Store St WC1 141 DK71
Storers Quay E14 163 ED77
Storey Rd E17 123 DZ56
Storey Rd N6 120 DF58
Storey St E16 145 EN74
Storey St, Hem.H. 40 BK24
Storey's Gate SW1 277 **N5**
Storey's Gate SW1 161 DK75
Stories Ms SE5 162 DS82
Stories Rd SE5 162 DS83
Stork Rd E7 144 EF65
Storks Rd SE16 162 DU76
Storksmead Rd, Edg. 96 CS52
Stormont Rd N6 120 DF59
Stormont Rd SW11 160 DG83
Stormont Way, Chess. 215 CJ106
Stormount Dr, Hayes 155 BQ75
Stornaway Rd, Slou. 153 BC77
Stornaway Strand, Grav. 191 GM91
Stornoway, Hem.H. 41 BP22
Storr Gdns, Brwd. 109 GD43
Storrington Rd, Croy. 202 DT102
Stort Mill, Harl. 36 EV09
Stort Twr, Harl. 35 ET13
Stortford Rd, Hodd. 49 EB16
Story St N1 141 DM66
Carnoustie Dr
Stothard Pl EC2 142 DS71
Bishopsgate
Stothard St E1 142 DW70
Colebert Av
Stott Cl SW18 180 DD86
Stoughton Av, Sutt. 217 CX106
Stoughton Cl SE11 278 **C9**
Stoughton Cl SW15 179 CU88
Bessborough Rd
Stoughton Rd, Guil. 242 AU131
Stour Av, Sthl. 156 CA76
Stour Cl, Kes. 222 EJ105
Stour Cl, Slou. 151 AP76
Stour Rd E3 143 EA66
Stour Rd, Dag. 126 FA61
Stour Rd, Dart. 167 FG83
Stour Rd, Grays 171 GG78
Stour Way, Upmin. 129 FS58
Stourcliffe St W1 272 **D9**
Stourcliffe St W1 140 DF72
Stourhead Cl SW19 179 CX87
Castlecombe Dr
Stourhead Gdns SW20 199 CU97
Stourton Av, Felt. 176 BZ91
Stovell Rd, Wind. 151 AP80
Stow, The, Harl. 35 ET13
Stow Cres E17 101 DY52
Stowage SE8 163 EA79
Stowe Ct, Dart. 188 FQ87
Stowe Cres, Ruis. 115 BP58
Stowe Gdns N9 100 DT46
Stowe Pl N15 122 DS55
Stowe Rd W12 159 CV75
Stowe Rd, Orp. 224 EV105
Stowe Rd, Slou. 131 AL73
Stowell Av (New Addington), Croy. 221 ED110
Stowting Rd, Orp. 223 ES105
Stox Mead, Har. 95 CD53
Stracey Rd E7 124 EG63
Stracey Rd NW10 138 CR67
Strachan Pl SW19 179 CW93
Woodhayes Rd
Stradbroke Dr, Chig. 103 EN51
Stradbroke Gro, Buck.H. 102 EK46
Stradbroke Gro, Ilf. 124 EL55
Stradbroke Pk, Chig. 103 EP51
Stradbroke Rd N5 122 DQ63
Stradbrook Cl, Har. 116 BZ62
Stiven Cres
Stradella Rd SE24 182 DQ86
Strafford Av, Ilf. 103 EN54
Strafford Cl, Pot.B. 64 DA32
Strafford Gate
Strafford Gate, Pot.B. 64 DA32
Strafford Rd W3 158 CQ75
Strafford Rd, Barn. 79 CY41
Strafford Rd, Houns. 156 BZ83
Strafford Rd, Twick. 177 CG87
Strafford St E14 163 EA75
Strahan Rd E3 143 DY69
Straight, The, Sthl. 156 BX75
Straight Bit (Flackwell Heath), H.Wyc. 110 AC55
Straight Rd, Rom. 106 FJ52
Straight Rd (Old Windsor), Wind. 172 AU85
Straightsmouth SE10 163 EC80
Strait Rd E6 144 EL73
Straker's Rd SE15 162 DV84
Strand WC2 277 **P1**
Strand WC2 141 DL73
Strand Cl, Epsom 232 CR119
Strand Ct SE18 165 ES78
Strandfield Cl
Strand La WC2 274 **C10**
Strand on the Grn W4 158 CN79
Strand Pl N18 100 DR49
Strand Sch App W4 158 CN79
Thames Rd
Strandfield Cl SE18 165 ES78
Strangeways, Wat. 75 BS36
Strangways Ter W14 159 CZ76
Melbury Rd
Stranraer Gdns, Slou. 132 AS74
Stranraer Rd (Heathrow Airport), Houns. 174 BL86
Stranraer Way N1 141 DL66
Strasburg Rd SW11 161 DH81
Stratfield Dr, Brox. 49 DY19
Stratfield Pk Cl N21 99 DP45
Stratfield Rd, Borwd. 78 CN41
Stratfield Rd, Slou. 152 AU75
Stratford Av W8 160 DA76
Stratford Rd
Stratford Av, Uxb. 134 BM68
Stratford Cen, The E15 143 ED66
Stratford Cl, Bark. 146 EU66
Stratford Cl, Dag. 147 FC66
Stratford Cl, Slou. 131 AK70
Stratford Ct, N.Mal. 198 CR98
Kingston Rd
Stratford Dr (Wooburn Grn), H.Wyc. 110 AD59
Stratford Gro SW15 159 CX84
Stratford Ho Av, Brom. 204 EL97
Stratford Pl W1 273 **H9**
Stratford Pl W1 141 DH72
Stratford Rd E13 144 EF67
Stratford Rd NW4 119 CX56
Stratford Rd W8 160 DA76
Stratford Rd, Hayes 135 BV70
Stratford Rd (Heathrow Airport), Houns. 175 BP86
Stratford Rd, Sthl. 156 BY77
Stratford Rd, Th.Hth. 201 DN98
Stratford Rd, Wat. 75 BU40
Stratford Vil NW1 141 DJ66
Stratford Way, Hem.H. 40 BH23
Stratford Way (Bricket Wd), St.Alb. 60 BZ29
Stratford Way, Wat. 75 BT40
Strath Ter SW11 160 DE84
Strathan Cl SW18 179 CY86
Strathaven Rd SE12 184 EH86
Strathblaine Rd SW11 160 DD84
Strathbrook Rd SW16 181 DM94
Strathcona Av (Bookham), Lthd. 246 BY128
Strathcona Cl (Flackwell Heath), H.Wyc. 110 AC56
Strathcona Rd, Wem. 117 CK61
Strathcona Way (Flackwell Heath), H.Wyc. 110 AC56
Strathdale SW16 181 DM92
Strathdon Dr SW17 180 DD90
Strathearn Av, Hayes 155 BT80
Strathearn Av, Twick. 176 CB88
Strathearn Pl W2 272 **A10**
Strathearn Pl W2 140 DE73
Strathearn Rd SW19 180 DA92
Strathearn Rd, Sutt. 218 DA106
Stratheden Par SE3 164 EG80
Stratheden Rd
Stratheden Rd SE3 164 EG81
Strathfield Gdns, Bark. 145 ER65
Strathleven Rd SW2 181 DL85
Strathmore Cl, Cat. 236 DS121
Strathmore Gdns N3 98 DB53
Strathmore Gdns W8 140 DA74
Palace Gdns Ter
Strathmore Gdns, Edg. 96 CP54
Strathmore Gdns, Horn. 127 FF60
Strathmore Rd SW19 180 DA90
Strathmore Rd, Croy. 202 DQ101
Strathmore Rd, Tedd. 177 CE91
Strathnairn St SE1 162 DU77
Strathray Gdns NW3 140 DE65
Strathville Rd SW18 180 DB89
Strathyre Av SW16 201 DN97
Stratton Av, Enf. 82 DR37
Stratton Av, Wall. 219 DK109
Stratton Chase Dr, Ch.St.G. 90 AU47
Stratton Cl SW19 200 DA96
Stratton Cl, Bexh. 166 EY83
Stratton Cl, Edg. 96 CM51
Stratton Cl, Houns. 156 BZ81
Stratton Cl, Walt. 196 BW102
St. Johns Dr
Stratton Dr, Bark. 125 ET64
Stratton Gdns, Sthl. 136 BZ72
Stratton Rd SW19 200 DA96
Stratton Rd, Beac. 88 AH53
Stratton Rd, Bexh. 166 EY83
Stratton Rd, Rom. 106 FN50
Stratton Rd, Sun. 195 BT96
Stratton St W1 277 **J2**
Stratton St W1 141 DH74
Stratton Ter, West. 255 EQ127
High St
Stratton Wk, Rom. 106 FN50
Strattondale St E14 163 EC76
Strauss Rd W4 158 CR75
Straw Cl, Cat. 236 DQ123
Strawberry Fld, Hat. 45 CU21
Strawberry Flds, Swan. 207 FE95
Strawberry Flds, Ware 32 DV05
Strawberry Hill, Twick. 177 CF90
Strawberry Hill Cl, Twick. 177 CF90
Strawberry Hill Rd, Twick. 177 CF90
Strawberry La, Cars. 200 DF104
Strawberry Vale N2 98 DD53
Strawberry Vale, Twick. 177 CG90
Strawfields, Welw.G.C. 30 DB08
Strawmead, Hat. 45 CV16
Cob Mead
Strayfield Rd, Enf. 81 DP37
Streakes Fld Rd NW2 119 CU61
Stream Cl (Byfleet), W.Byf. 212 BK112
Stream La, Edg. 96 CP50
Streamdale SE2 166 EU79
Streamside, Slou. 131 AL74
Warner Cl
Streamside Cl N9 100 DT46
Streamside Cl, Brom. 204 EG98
Streamway, Belv. 166 FA79
Streatfield Av E6 145 EM67
Streatfield Rd, Har. 117 CK55
Streatham Cl SW16 181 DL89
Streatham Common N SW16 181 DL92
Streatham Common S SW16 181 DL93
Streatham Ct SW16 181 DL90
Streatham High Rd SW16 181 DL92
Streatham Hill SW2 181 DL89
Streatham Pl SW2 181 DL87
Streatham Rd SW16 200 DG95
Streatham Rd, Mitch. 200 DG95
Streatham St WC1 273 **N8**
Streatham St WC1 141 DK72
Streatham Vale SW16 181 DJ94
Streathbourne Rd SW17 180 DG89
Streatley Pl NW3 120 DC63
New End Sq
Streatley Rd NW6 139 CZ66
Street, The, Ash. 232 CL119
Street, The, Bet. 264 CS135
Street, The (Sheering), B.Stort. 37 FC07
Street, The (Horton Kirby), Dart. 208 FP98
Street, The (Albury), Guil. 260 BH139
Street, The (East Clandon), Guil. 244 BK131
Street, The (Shalford), Guil. 258 AY139
Street, The (West Clandon), Guil. 244 BH131
Street, The (Wonersh), Guil. 259 BA144
Street, The, Kings L. 58 BG31
Street, The (Effingham), Lthd. 246 BX127
Street, The (Fetcham), Lthd. 231 CD122
Street, The (West Horsley), Lthd. 245 BP129
Streeters La, Wall. 201 DK104
Streetfield Ms SE3 164 EG83
Streimer Rd E15 143 EC68
Strelley Way W3 138 CS73
Stretton Pl, Amer. 72 AT38
Stretton Rd, Croy. 202 DS101
Stretton Rd, Rich. 177 CJ89
Stretton Way, Borwd. 78 CL38
Strickland Av, Dart. 168 FL83
Strickland Row SW18 180 DD87
Strickland St SE8 163 EA82
Strickland Way, Orp. 223 ET105
Stride Rd E13 144 EF68
Stringers Av, Guil. 242 AX128
Stringer's Common, Guil. 242 AW129
Stringhams Copse (Ripley), Wok. 227 BF124
Stripling Way, Wat. 75 BU44
Strode Cl N10 98 DG52
Pembroke Rd
Strode Rd E7 124 EG63
Strode Rd N17 100 DS54
Strode Rd NW10 139 CU65
Strode Rd SW6 159 CX80
Strode St, Egh. 173 BA91
Strodes Coll La, Egh. 173 AZ92
Strodes Cres, Stai. 174 BJ92
Stroma Cl, Hem.H. 41 BQ22
Stroma Ct, Slou. 131 AK73
Lincoln Way
Strone Rd E7 144 EJ65
Strone Rd E12 144 EK65
Strone Way, Hayes 136 BY70
Strongbow Cres SE9 185 EM85
Strongbow Rd SE9 185 EM85
Strongbridge Cl, Har. 116 CA60
Stronsa Rd W12 159 CT75
Stronsay Cl, Hem.H. 41 BQ22
Northend
Strood Av, Rom. 127 FD60
Stroud Cl, Wind. 151 AK83
Stroud Cres SW15 179 CU90
Stroud Fld, Nthlt. 136 BY65
Stroud Gate, Har. 116 CB63
Stroud Grn Gdns, Croy. 202 DW101
Stroud Grn Rd N4 121 DM60
Stroud Grn Way, Croy. 202 DV101
Stroud Rd SE25 202 DU100
Stroud Rd SW19 180 DA90
Stroud Way, Ashf. 175 BP93
Courtfield Rd
Stroude Rd, Egh. 173 BA93
Stroude Rd, Vir.W. 192 AY98
Stroudes Cl, Wor.Pk. 198 CS101
Stroudley Wk E3 143 EB69
Strouds Cl (Chadwell Heath), Rom. 126 EV57
Stroudwater Pk, Wey. 213 BP107
Strouts Pl E2 275 **P2**
Struan Gdns, Wok. 226 AY115
Strutton Grd SW1 277 **M6**
Strutton Grd SW1 161 DK76
Struttons Av (Northfleet), Grav. 191 GF89
Strype St E1 275 **P7**
Stuart Av NW9 119 CU59
Stuart Av W5 138 CM74
Stuart Av, Brom. 204 EG102
Stuart Av, Har. 116 BZ62
Stuart Av, Walt. 195 BV102
Stuart Cl, Brwd. 108 FV43
Stuart Cl, Swan. 187 FF94
Stuart Cl, Uxb. 134 BN65
Stuart Cl, Wind. 151 AM82
Stuart Ct (Elstree), Borwd. 77 CK44
High St
Stuart Cres N22 99 DM53
Stuart Cres, Croy. 203 DZ104
Stuart Cres, Hayes 135 BQ72
Stuart Cres, Reig. 266 DA137
Stuart Evans Cl, Well. 166 EW83
Stuart Gro, Tedd. 177 CE92
Stuart Mantle Way, Erith 167 FD80
Stuart Pl, Mitch. 200 DF95
Stuart Rd NW6 140 DA69
Stuart Rd SE15 162 DW84
Stuart Rd SW19 180 DA90
Stuart Rd W3 138 CQ74
Stuart Rd, Bark. 145 ET66
Stuart Rd, Barn. 98 DE45
Stuart Rd, Grav. 191 GG86
Stuart Rd, Grays 170 GB78
Stuart Rd, Har. 95 CF54
Stuart Rd, Reig. 266 DA137
Stuart Rd, Rich. 177 CH89
Stuart Rd, Th.Hth. 202 DQ98
Stuart Rd, Warl. 236 DV120
Stuart Rd, Well. 166 EV81
Stuart Twr W9 140 DC69
Stuart Way, Stai. 174 BH93
Stuart Way, Vir.W. 192 AU97
Stuart Way (Cheshunt), Wal.Cr. 66 DV31
Stuart Way, Wind. 151 AL82
Stuarts Cl, Hem.H. 40 BK22
Marriotts Way
Stubbers La, Upmin. 149 FR65
Stubbins Hall La, Wal.Abb. 67 EB28
Stubbs Dr SE16 162 DV78
Stubbs End Cl, Amer. 55 AS37
Stubbs Hill (Knockholt), Sev. 224 EW113
Stubbs La (Lower Kingswood), Tad. 249 CZ128
Stubbs Ms, Dag. 126 EV63
Marlborough Rd
Stubbs Pt E13 144 EH70
Stubbs Way SW19 200 DD95
Brangwyn Cres
Stubbs Wd, Amer. 55 AS36
Stubs Cl, Dor. 263 CJ138
Stubs Hill
Stubs Hill, Dor. 263 CJ138
Stucley Pl NW1 141 DH66
Hawley Cres
Stucley Rd, Houns. 156 CC80
Stud Grn, Wat. 59 BV32
Studd St N1 141 DP67
Studdridge St SW6 160 DA82
Studholme Ct NW3 120 DA63
Studholme St SE15 162 DV80
Studio Pl SW1 276 **E5**
Studio Way, Borwd. 78 CQ40
Studios, The, Bushey 76 CA44
Studios Rd, Shep. 194 BM97
Studland SE17 279 **K10**
Studland Cl, Sid. 185 ET90
Studland Rd SE26 183 DX92
Studland Rd W7 137 CD72
Studland Rd, Kings.T. 178 CL93
Studland Rd (Byfleet), W.Byf. 212 BM113
Studland St W6 159 CV77
Studley Av E4 101 ED52
Studley Cl E5 123 DY64
Studley Ct, Sid. 186 EV92
Studley Dr, Ilf. 124 EK58
Studley Est SW4 161 DL81
Studley Gra Rd W7 157 CE75
Studley Rd E7 144 EH65
Studley Rd SW4 161 DL81
Studley Rd, Dag. 146 EX66
Stukeley Rd E7 144 EH66
Stukeley St WC2 274 **A8**
Stukeley St WC2 141 DL72
Stump Rd, Epp. 70 EW27
Stumps Hill La, Beck. 183 EA93
Stumps La, Whyt. 236 DS117
Stumpwell La (Penn), H.Wyc. 88 AD48
Sturdy Rd SE15 162 DV82
Sturge Av E17 101 EB54
Sturge St SE1 279 **H4**
Sturgeon Rd SE17 162 DQ78
Sturges Fld, Chis. 185 ER93
Sturgess Av NW4 119 CV59
Sturla Cl, Hert. 31 DP08
Millmead Way
Sturlas Way, Wal.Cr. 67 DX33
Sturmer Cl, St.Alb. 43 CJ21
Sturmer Way N7 121 DM64
Sturminster Cl, Hayes 136 BW72
Sturrock Cl N15 122 DR56
Sturry St E14 143 EB72
Sturt Ct, Guil. 243 BB132
Sturt St N1 275 **J1**
Sturt St N1 142 DQ68
Sturts La, Tad. 249 CT127
Stutfield St E1 142 DU72
Stychens Cl (Bletchingley), Red. 252 DQ133
Stychens La (Bletchingley), Red. 252 DQ132
Stylecroft Rd, Ch.St.G. 90 AX47
Styles End (Bookham), Lthd. 246 CB127
Styles Gdns SW9 161 DP83
Styles Way, Beck. 203 EC98
Styventon Pl, Cher. 193 BF101
Subrosa Dr, Red. 251 DH130
Succombs Hill, Warl. 236 DV120
Succombs Hill, Whyt. 236 DV120
Succombs Pl, Warl. 236 DV120
Sudbourne Rd SW2 181 DL85
Sudbrook Gdns, Rich. 177 CK90
Sudbrook La, Rich. 178 CL88
Sudbrooke Rd SW12 180 DF86
Sudbury E6 145 EN72
Newark Knok
Sudbury Av, Wem. 117 CK62
Sudbury Ct E5 123 DY63
Sudbury Ct Dr, Har. 117 CF62
Sudbury Ct Rd, Har. 117 CF62
Sudbury Cres, Brom. 184 EG93
Sudbury Cres, Wem. 117 CH64
Sudbury Cft, Wem. 117 CF63
Sudbury Gdns, Croy. 220 DS105
Langton Way
Sudbury Hts Av, Grnf. 117 CF64
Sudbury Hill, Har. 117 CE61
Sudbury Hill Cl, Wem. 117 CF63
Sudbury Rd, Bark. 125 ET64
Sudeley St N1 274 **G1**
Sudeley St N1 141 DP68
Sudicamps Ct, Wal.Abb. 68 EG33
Sudlow Rd SW18 160 DA84
Sudrey St SE1 279 **H5**
Suez Av, Grnf. 137 CF68
Suez Rd, Enf. 83 DY42
Suffield Cl, S.Croy. 221 DX112
Suffield Rd E4 101 EB48
Suffield Rd N15 122 DT57
Suffield Rd SE20 202 DW96
Suffolk Cl, Borwd. 78 CR43
Clydesdale Cl
Suffolk Cl, Horl. 268 DG149
Suffolk Cl (London Colney), St.Alb. 61 CJ25
Suffolk Cl, Slou. 131 AL72
Suffolk Ct E10 123 EA59
Suffolk Ct, Ilf. 125 ES58
Suffolk Dr, Guil. 243 BB129
Suffolk La EC4 275 **K10**
Suffolk Pk Rd E17 123 DY56
Suffolk Pl SW1 277 **N2**
Suffolk Rd E13 144 EF69
Suffolk Rd N15 122 DR58
Suffolk Rd NW10 138 CS66
Suffolk Rd SE25 202 DT98
Suffolk Rd SW13 159 CT80
Suffolk Rd, Bark. 145 ER66
Suffolk Rd, Dag. 127 FC64
Suffolk Rd, Dart. 188 FL86
Suffolk Rd, Enf. 82 DV43
Suffolk Rd, Grav. 191 GK86
Suffolk Rd, Har. 116 BZ58
Suffolk Rd, Ilf. 125 ES58
Suffolk Rd, Pot.B. 63 CY32
Suffolk Rd, Sid. 186 EW93
Suffolk Rd, Wor.Pk. 199 CT103
Suffolk St E7 124 EG64
Suffolk St SW1 277 **N2**
Suffolk Way, Horn. 128 FN56
Suffolk Way, Sev. 257 FJ125
Sugar Bakers Ct EC3 142 DS72
Creechurch La
Sugar Ho La E15 143 EC68
Sugar La, Berk. 39 AZ22
Sugar La, Hem.H. 39 BB22
Sugar Loaf Wk E2 142 DW69
Victoria Pk Sq
Sugar Quay Wk EC3 279 **N1**
Sugar Quay Wk EC3 142 DS73
Sugden Rd SW11 160 DG83
Sugden Rd, T.Ditt. 197 CH102
Sugden Way, Bark. 145 ET68
Sulgrave Gdns W6 159 CW75
Sulgrave Rd
Sulgrave Rd W6 159 CW75
Sulina Rd SW2 181 DL87
Sulivan Ct SW6 160 DA83
Sulivan Rd SW6 160 DA83
Sullivan Av E16 144 EK71
Sullivan Cl SW11 160 DE83
Sullivan Cl, Dart. 187 FH86
Sullivan Cl, Hayes 136 BW71
Sullivan Cl, W.Mol. 196 CA97
Victoria Av
Sullivan Cres (Harefield), Uxb. 92 BK54
Sullivan Rd SE11 278 **E8**
Sullivan Rd SE11 161 DP77
Sullivan Rd, Til. 171 GG81
Sullivan Way, Borwd. 77 CJ44
Sullivans Reach, Walt. 195 BT101
Sultan Rd E11 124 EH56
Sultan St SE5 162 DQ80
Sultan St, Beck. 203 DX96
Sumatra Rd NW6 120 DA64
Sumburgh Rd SW12 180 DG86
Sumburgh Way, Slou. 132 AS71
Summer Av, E.Mol. 197 CE99
Summer Ct, Hem.H. 40 BK18
Townsend
Summer Gdns, E.Mol. 197 CE99
Summer Gro, Borwd. 77 CK44
Summer Hill, Borwd. 78 CN43
Summer Hill, Chis. 205 EN96
Summer Hill Vil, Chis. 205 EN95
Summer Rd, E.Mol. 197 CE99
Summer Rd, T.Ditt. 197 CF99
Summer St EC1 274 **D5**
Summer Trees, Sun. 195 BV95
The Av
Summercourt Rd E1 142 DW72
Summerdale, Welw.G.C. 29 CX05
Summerene Cl SW16 181 DJ94
Summerfield, Ash. 231 CK119
Summerfield, Hat. 45 CU21
Summerfield Av NW6 139 CY68
Summerfield Cl, Add. 211 BF106
Spinney Hill
Summerfield Cl (London Colney), St.Alb. 61 CJ26
Summerfield La, Surb. 197 CK103
Summerfield Pl (Ottershaw), Cher. 211 BD107
Crawshaw Rd
Summerfield Rd W5 137 CH70
Summerfield Rd, Loug. 84 EK44
Summerfield Rd, Wat. 75 BU35
Summerfield St SE12 184 EF87
Summerfields Av N12 98 DE51
Summerhayes Cl, Wok. 210 AY114
Summerhays, Cob. 214 BX113
Summerhill Cl, Orp. 205 ES104
Summerhill Ct, St.Alb. 43 CF19
Avenue Rd
Summerhill Gro, Enf. 82 DS44
Summerhill Rd N15 122 DR56
Summerhill Rd, Dart. 188 FK87
Summerhill Way, Mitch. 200 DG95
Summerhouse Av, Houns. 156 BY81
Summerhouse Dr, Bex. 187 FD91
Summerhouse Dr, Dart. 187 FD91
Summerhouse La (Harefield), Uxb. 92 BG52
Summerhouse La, Wat. 76 CC40
Summerhouse La, West Dr. 154 BK79
Summerhouse Rd N16 122 DS61
Summerhouse Way, Abb.L. 59 BT30
Summerland Gdns N10 121 DH55
Summerlands Av W3 138 CQ73
Summerlands Rd, St.Alb. 43 CJ16
Summerlay Cl, Tad. 233 CY120
Summerlea, Slou. 131 AP74
Summerlee Av N2 120 DF56
Summerlee Gdns N2 120 DF56
Summerley St SW18 180 DB89
Summerly Av, Reig. 250 DA133
Burnham Dr
Summers Cl, Sutt. 218 DA108
Overton Rd
Summers Cl, Wem. 118 CP60
Summers Cl, Wey. 212 BN111
Summers La N12 98 DD52
Summers Rd, Gdmg. 258 AT144
Summers Rd (Burnham), Slou. 130 AJ69
Summers Row N12 98 DE51
Summersbury Dr (Shalford), Guil. 258 AY142
Summersby Rd N6 121 DH58
Summerstown SW17 180 DC90
Summerswood Cl, Ken. 236 DR116
Longwood Rd
Summerswood La, Borwd. 62 CS34
Summerton Way SE28 146 EX72
Summerville Gdns, Sutt. 217 CZ107
Summerwood Rd, Islw. 177 CF85
Summit, The, Loug. 85 EM39
Summit Av NW9 118 CR57
Summit Cl N14 99 DJ47
Summit Cl NW9 118 CR56
Summit Cl, Edg. 96 CN52
Summit Ct NW2 119 CY64
Summit Dr, Wdf.Grn. 102 EK54
Summit Est N16 122 DU59
Summit Pl, Wey. 212 BN108
Caenshill Rd
Summit Rd E17 123 EB56
Summit Rd, Nthlt. 136 CA66
Summit Rd, Pot.B. 63 CY30
Summit Way N14 99 DH47
Summit Way SE19 182 DS94
Sumner Av SE15 162 DT81
Sumner Rd
Sumner Cl (Fetcham), Lthd. 231 CD124
Sumner Cl, Orp. 223 EQ105
Sumner Est SE15 162 DT80
Sumner Gdns, Croy. 201 DN102
Sumner Pl SW7 276 **A9**
Sumner Pl SW7 160 DD77
Sumner Pl, Add. 212 BG106
Sumner Pl Ms SW7 276 **A9**
Sumner Rd SE15 162 DT80
Sumner Rd, Croy. 201 DN102
Sumner Rd, Har. 116 CC59
Sumner Rd S, Croy. 201 DN102
Sumner St SE1 278 **G2**
Sumner St SE1 142 DQ74
Sumners Fm Cl, Harl. 51 EN20
Sumpter Cl NW3 140 DC65
Sumpter Yd, St.Alb. 43 CD20
Sun All, Rich. 158 CL84
Kew Rd
Sun Ct EC3 275 **L9**
Sun Ct, Erith 167 FF82
Sun Hill (Fawkham Grn), Long. 209 FU104
Sun Hill, Wok. 226 AU121
Sun La SE3 164 EH80
Sun La, Grav. 191 GJ89
Sun Pas SE16 162 DU76
Frean St

Sun Pas, Wind. 151 AR81
Bachelors Acre
Sun Rd W14 159 CZ78
Sun Rd, Swans. 190 FZ86
Sun Sq, Hem.H. 40 BK19
High St
Sun St EC2 275 M7
Sun St EC2 142 DR71
Sun St, Saw. 36 EZ06
Sun St, Wal.Abb. 67 EC33
Sun St Pas EC2 275 M7
Sun Wk E1 142 DU74
Mews St
Sunbeam Cres W10 139 CW70
Sunbeam Rd NW10 138 CQ70
Sunbury Av NW7 96 CR50
Sunbury Av SW14 158 CR84
Sunbury Ct, Sun. 196 BX96
Sunbury Ct Island, Sun. 196 BX97
Sunbury Ct Ms, Sun. 196 BX96
Lower Hampton Rd
Sunbury Ct Rd, Sun. 196 BW96
Sunbury Cres, Felt. 175 BT91
Ryland Cl
Sunbury Cross Cen, Sun. 175 BT94
Sunbury Gdns NW7 96 CR50
Sunbury La SW11 160 DD81
Sunbury La, Walt. 195 BU100
Sunbury Lock Ait, Walt. 195 BV98
Sunbury Rd, Felt. 175 BT90
Sunbury Rd, Sutt. 199 CX104
Sunbury Rd (Eton), Wind. 151 AR79
Sunbury St SE18 165 EM76
Sunbury Way, Felt. 176 BW92
Suncroft Pl SE26 182 DW90
Sundale Av, S.Croy. 220 DW110
Sunderland Av, St.Alb. 43 CG18
Sunderland Ct SE22 182 DU87
Sunderland Mt SE23 183 DX89
Sunderland Rd
Sunderland Rd SE23 183 DX88
Sunderland Rd W5 157 CK76
Sunderland Ter W2 140 DB72
Sunderland Way E12 124 EK61
Sundew Av W12 139 CU73
Sundew Ct, Grays 170 GD79
Salix Rd
Sundew Rd, Hem.H. 39 BE21
Sundial Av SE25 202 DT97
Sundon Cres, Vir.W. 192 AV99
Sundorne Rd SE7 164 EJ78
Sundown Av, S.Croy. 220 DT111
Sundown Rd, Ashf. 175 BQ92
Sundra Wk E1 143 DX70
Beaumont Gro
Sundridge Av, Brom. 184 EK94
Sundridge Av, Chis. 184 EK94
Sundridge Av, Well. 165 ER82
Sundridge Cl, Dart. 188 FN86
Sundridge Ho, Brom. 184 EH92
Burnt Ash La
Sundridge La (Knockholt), Sev. 240 EV117
Sundridge Pl, Croy. 202 DU102
Inglis Rd
Sundridge Rd, Croy. 202 DT101
Sundridge Rd (Dunton Grn), Sev. 240 FA120
Sundridge Rd, Wok. 227 BA119
Sunfields Pl SE3 164 EH80
Sunflower Way, Rom. 106 FK53
Sunkist Way, Wall. 219 DL109
Sunland Av, Bexh. 166 EY84
Sunleigh Rd, Wem. 138 CL67
Sunley Gdns, Grnf. 137 CG67
Sunlight Cl SW19 180 DC93
Sunlight Sq E2 142 DV69
Sunmead Cl (Fetcham), Lthd. 231 CF122
Sunmead Rd, Hem.H. 40 BK18
Sunmead Rd, Sun. 195 BU97
Sunna Gdns, Sun. 195 BV96
Sunning Hill (Northfleet), Grav. 190 GE89
Sunningdale N14 99 DK50
Wilmer Way
Sunningdale Av W3 138 CS73
Sunningdale Av, Bark. 145 ER67
Sunningdale Av, Felt. 176 BY89
Sunningdale Av, Rain. 147 FH70
Sunningdale Av, Ruis. 116 BW60
Sunningdale Cl E6 145 EM69
Sunningdale Cl SE16 162 DV78
Ryder Dr
Sunningdale Cl SE28 146 EY72
Sunningdale Cl, Stan. 95 CG52
Sunningdale Cl, Surb. 198 CL103
Culsac Rd
Sunningdale Gdns NW9 118 CQ57
Sunningdale Gdns W8 160 DA76
Lexham Ms
Sunningdale Ms, Welw.G.C. 29 CY05
Sunningdale Rd, Brom. 204 EL98
Sunningdale Rd, Rain. 147 FG66
Sunningdale Rd, Sutt. 217 CZ105
Sunningfields Cres NW4 97 CV54
Sunningfields Rd NW4 97 CV54
Sunninghill Rd SE13 163 EB82
Sunnings La, Upmin. 148 FQ65
Sunningvale Av (Biggin Hill), West. 238 EJ115
Sunningvale Cl (Biggin Hill), West. 238 EK116
Sunny Bk SE25 202 DU97
Sunny Bk, Warl. 237 DY117
Sunny Cres NW10 138 CQ66
Sunny Cft, Harl. 51 ET18
Sunny Gdns Par NW4 97 CW54
Great N Way
Sunny Gdns Rd NW4 97 CV54
Sunny Hill NW4 119 CV55
Sunny Nook Gdns, S.Croy. 220 DR107
Selsdon Rd
Sunny Ri, Cat. 236 DR124
Sunny Rd, The, Enf. 83 DX39
Sunny Vw NW9 118 CR57
Sunny Way N12 98 DE52
Sunnybank, Epsom 232 CQ116
Sunnybank Rd, Pot.B. 64 DA33
Sunnybank Vil, Red. 252 DT132
Sunnycroft Gdns, Upmin. 129 FT59
Sunnycroft Rd SE25 202 DU97
Sunnycroft Rd, Houns. 156 CB82
Sunnycroft Rd, Sthl. 136 CA71
Sunnydale, Orp. 205 EN103
Sunnydale Gdns NW7 96 CR51
Sunnydale Rd SE12 184 EH85
Sunnydell, St.Alb. 60 CB26
Sunnydene Av E4 101 ED50
Sunnydene Av, Ruis. 115 BU61
Sunnydene Cl, Rom. 106 FM52
Sunnydene Gdns, Wem. 137 CJ65
Sunnydene Rd, Pur. 219 DP113
Sunnydene St SE26 183 DY91
Sunnyfield NW7 97 CT49
Sunnyfield, Hat. 45 CX15
Sunnyfield Rd, Chis. 206 EU97
Sunnyhill Cl E5 123 DY63
Sunnyhill Rd SW16 181 DL91
Sunnyhill Rd, Hem.H. 40 BH20
Sunnyhill Rd, Rick. 91 BD51
Sunnyhurst Cl, Sutt. 200 DA104
Sunnymead Av, Mitch. 201 DJ97
Sunnymead Rd NW9 118 CR59
Sunnymead Rd SW15 179 CV85
Sunnymede, Chig. 104 EV48
Sunnymede Av, Cars. 218 DD111
Sunnymede Av, Chesh. 54 AS28
Sunnymede Av, Epsom 216 CS109
Sunnymede Dr, Ilf. 125 EP56
Sunnyside NW2 119 CZ62
Sunnyside SW19 179 CY93
Sunnyside, Wal.Abb. 50 EF22
Sunnyside, Walt. 196 BW99
Sunnyside Cotts, Chesh. 56 AU26
Sunnyside Dr E4 101 EC45
Sunnyside Gdns, Upmin. 128 FQ61
Sunnyside Pas SW19 179 CY93
Sunnyside Pl SW19 179 CY93
Sunnyside
Sunnyside Rd E10 123 EA60
Sunnyside Rd N19 121 DK59
Sunnyside Rd W5 137 CK74
Sunnyside Rd, Chesh. 54 AP30
Sunnyside Rd, Epp. 69 ET32
Sunnyside Rd, Ilf. 125 EQ62
Sunnyside Rd, Tedd. 177 CD91
Sunnyside Rd E N9 100 DU48
Sunnyside Rd N N9 100 DT48
Sunnyside Rd S N9 100 DT48
Sunnyside Ter NW9 118 CR55
Edgware Rd
Sunray Av SE24 162 DR84
Sunray Av, Brwd. 109 GE44
Sunray Av, Brom. 204 EL100
Sunray Av, Surb. 198 CP103
Sunray Av, West Dr. 154 BK75
Sunrise Av, Horn. 128 FJ62
Sunrise Cl, Felt. 176 BZ90
Exeter Rd
Sunrise Cres, Hem.H. 40 BL23
Sunset Av E4 101 EB46
Sunset Av, Wdf.Grn. 102 EF49
Sunset Cl, Erith 167 FH81
Sunset Ct, Wdf.Grn. 102 EJ52
Navestock Cres
Sunset Dr (Havering-atte-Bower), Rom. 105 FH50
Sunset Gdns SE25 202 DT96
Sunset Rd SE5 162 DQ84
Sunset Rd SE28 166 EU75
Sunset Vw, Barn. 79 CY40
Sunshine Way, Mitch. 200 DF96
Sunstone Gro, Red. 251 DL129
Sunwell Cl SE15 162 DV81
Cossall Wk
Superior Dr, Orp. 223 ET107
Surbiton Ct, Surb. 197 CJ100
Surbiton Cres, Kings.T. 198 CL98
Surbiton Hall Cl, Kings.T. 198 CL98
Surbiton Hill Pk, Surb. 198 CN99
Surbiton Hill Rd, Surb. 198 CL98
Surbiton Par, Surb. 198 CL100
St. Mark's Hill
Surbiton Rd, Kings.T. 198 CL98
Surlingham Cl SE28 146 EX73
Surly Hall Wk, Wind. 151 AM81
Surma Cl E1 142 DV70
Surman Cres, Brwd. 109 GC45
Surmans Cl, Dag. 146 EV67
Goresbrook Rd
Surr St N7 121 DL64
Surrendale Pl W9 140 DA70
Surrey Av, Slou. 131 AQ71
Surrey Canal Rd SE14 162 DW79
Surrey Canal Rd SE15 162 DW79
Surrey Cres W4 158 CN78
Surrey Dr, Horn. 128 FN56
Surrey Gdns N4 122 DQ58
Finsbury Pk Av
Surrey Gdns (Effingham Junct), Lthd. 229 BT123
Surrey Gro SE17 162 DS78
Surrey Sq
Surrey Gro, Sutt. 200 DD104
Surrey Hills, Tad. 248 CP130
Surrey Hills Av, Tad. 248 CQ130
Surrey La SW11 160 DE81
Surrey La Est SW11 160 DE81
Surrey Lo SE1 278 D7
Surrey Ms SE27 182 DS91
Hamilton Rd
Surrey Mt SE23 182 DV88
Surrey Quays Retail Cen SE16 163 DX76
Surrey Quays Rd SE16 163 DX75
Surrey Rd SE15 183 DX85
Surrey Rd, Bark. 145 ES67
Surrey Rd, Dag. 127 FB64
Surrey Rd, Har. 116 CC57
Surrey Rd, W.Wick. 203 EB102
Surrey Row SE1 278 F4
Surrey Row SE1 161 DP75
Surrey Sq SE17 279 M10
Surrey Sq SE17 162 DS78
Surrey St E13 144 EH69
Surrey St WC2 274 C10
Surrey St WC2 141 DM73
Surrey St, Croy. 202 DQ104
Surrey Ter SE17 279 N10
Surrey Ter SE17 162 DS78
Surrey Twr SE20 182 DW94
Surrey Twrs, Add. 212 BJ106
Garfield Rd
Surrey Water Rd SE16 143 DX74
Surridge Cl, Rain. 148 FJ69
Surridge Gdns SE19 182 DR93
Hancock Rd
Susan Cl, Rom. 127 FC55
Susan Rd SE3 164 EH82
Susan Wd, Chis. 205 EN95
Susannah St E14 143 EB72
Sussex Av, Islw. 157 CE83
Sussex Av, Rom. 106 FM52
Sussex Border Path, Horl. 268 DF150
Sussex Cl N19 121 DL61
Cornwallis Rd
Sussex Cl, Ch.St.G. 90 AV47
Sussex Cl, Hodd. 49 EA16
Roman St
Sussex Cl, Ilf. 125 EM57
Sussex Cl, N.Mal. 198 CS98
Sussex Cl, Reig. 266 DD135
Sussex Cl, Slou. 152 AV75
Sussex Cl, Twick. 177 CH86
Westmorland Cl
Sussex Cres, Nthlt. 136 CA65
Sussex Gdns N4 122 DQ57
Sussex Gdns N6 120 DF57
Great N Rd
Sussex Gdns W2 140 DD72
Sussex Gdns, Chess. 215 CK107
Sussex Keep, Slou. 152 AV75
Sussex Cl
Sussex Ms SE6 183 EA87
Ravensbourne Pk
Sussex Ms E W2 272 A9
Sussex Ms W W2 272 A10
Sussex Pl NW1 272 D4
Sussex Pl NW1 140 DF70
Sussex Pl W2 272 A9
Sussex Pl W2 140 DD72
Sussex Pl W6 159 CW78
Sussex Pl, Erith 167 FB80
Sussex Pl, N.Mal. 198 CS98
Sussex Pl, Slou. 152 AV75
Sussex Ring N12 98 DA50
Sussex Rd E6 145 EN67
Sussex Rd, Brwd. 108 FV49
Sussex Rd, Cars. 218 DF107
Sussex Rd, Dart. 188 FN87
Sussex Rd, Erith 167 FB80
Sussex Rd, Har. 116 CC57
Sussex Rd, Mitch. 201 DL99
Lincoln Rd
Sussex Rd, N.Mal. 198 CS98
Sussex Rd, Orp. 206 EW100
Sussex Rd, Sid. 186 EV92
Sussex Rd, S.Croy. 220 DR107
Sussex Rd, Sthl. 156 BX76
Sussex Rd, Uxb. 115 BQ63
Sussex Rd, Wat. 75 BU38
Sussex Rd, W.Wick. 203 EB102
Sussex Sq W2 272 A10
Sussex Sq W2 140 DD73
Sussex St E13 144 EH69
Sussex St SW1 161 DH78
Sussex Wk SW9 161 DP84
Sussex Way N7 121 DL61
Sussex Way N19 121 DL60
Sussex Way, Barn. 80 DG43
Sussex Way (Denham), Uxb. 113 BF57
Sutcliffe Cl NW11 120 DB57
Sutcliffe Cl, Bushey 76 CC42
Sutcliffe Ho, Hayes 135 BU72
Sutcliffe Rd SE18 165 ES79
Sutcliffe Rd, Well. 166 EW82
Sutherland Av W9 140 DC69
Sutherland Av W13 137 CH72
Sutherland Av (Jacobs Well), Guil. 242 AX128
Sutherland Av, Hayes 155 BU77
Sutherland Av, Orp. 205 ET100
Sutherland Av (Cuffley), Pot.B. 65 DK28
Sutherland Av, Sun. 195 BT96
Sutherland Av, Well. 165 ES84
Sutherland Av (Biggin Hill), West. 238 EK117
Sutherland Cl, Barn. 79 CY42
Sutherland Cl, Green. 189 FT85
Sutherland Ct NW9 118 CP57
Sutherland Ct, Welw.G.C. 29 CZ08
Sutherland Dr SW19 200 DD95
Sutherland Dr (Burpham), Guil. 243 AZ131
Sutherland Gdns SW14 158 CS83
Sutherland Gdns, Sun. 195 BT96
Sutherland Av
Sutherland Gdns, Wor.Pk. 199 CV102
Sutherland Gro SW18 179 CY86
Sutherland Gro, Tedd. 177 CE92
Sutherland Pl W2 140 DA72
Sutherland Pt E5 122 DV63
Tiger Way
Sutherland Rd E17 101 DX54
Sutherland Rd N9 100 DU46
Sutherland Rd N17 100 DU52
Sutherland Rd W4 158 CS79
Sutherland Rd W13 137 CG72
Sutherland Rd, Belv. 166 FA76
Sutherland Rd, Croy. 201 DN101
Sutherland Rd, Enf. 83 DX43
Sutherland Rd, Sthl. 136 BZ72
Sutherland Rd Path E17 123 DX55
Sutherland Row SW1 277 J10
Sutherland Row SW1 161 DH78
Sutherland Sq SE17 162 DQ78
Sutherland St SW1 277 H10
Sutherland St SW1 161 DH78
Sutherland Wk SE17 162 DQ78
Sutherland Way (Cuffley), Pot.B. 65 DK28
Sutlej Rd SE7 164 EJ80
Sutterton St N7 141 DM65
Sutton Av, Slou. 152 AW75
Sutton Av, Wok. 226 AS119
Sutton Cl, Beck. 203 EB95
Albemarle Rd
Sutton Cl, Brox. 49 DY19
Sutton Cl, Loug. 102 EL45
Sutton Cl, Pnr. 115 BU57
Sutton Common Rd, Sutt. 199 CZ101
Sutton Ct W4 158 CQ79
Sutton Ct, Ware 33 DY06
Crane Mead
Sutton Ct Rd E13 144 EJ69
Sutton Ct Rd W4 158 CQ80
Sutton Ct Rd, Sutt. 218 DC107
Sutton Ct Rd, Uxb. 135 BP67
Sutton Cres, Barn. 79 CX43
Sutton Dene, Houns. 156 CB81
Sutton Est SW3 276 C10
Sutton Est SW3 160 DE78
Sutton Est W10 139 CW71
Sutton Est, The N1 141 DP66
Sutton Gdns, Bark. 145 ES67
Sutton Rd
Sutton Gdns, Croy. 202 DT99
Sutton Gdns, Red. 251 DK129
Sutton Grn, Bark. 145 ES67
Sutton Rd
Sutton Grn Rd (Sutton Grn), Guil. 242 AY126
Sutton Gro, Sutt. 218 DD105
Sutton Hall Rd, Houns. 156 CA80
Sutton Ho, Hem.H. 40 BL16
Sutton La, Bans. 234 DB115
Sutton La (Abinger Common), Dor. 261 BV143
Sutton La, Houns. 156 BZ83
Sutton La, Slou. 153 BC78
Sutton La, Sutt. 218 DB111
Sutton La N W4 158 CQ78
Sutton La S W4 158 CQ79
Sutton Par NW4 119 CW56
Church Rd
Sutton Pk (Sutton Grn), Guil. 243 AZ127
Sutton Pk Rd, Sutt. 218 DB107
Sutton Path, Borwd. 78 CN40
Stratfield Rd
Sutton Pl E9 122 DW64
Sutton Pl, Dart. 188 FN93
Sutton Pl (Abinger Hammer), Dor. 261 BT143
Sutton Pl, Slou. 153 BB79
Sutton Rd E13 144 EF70
Sutton Rd E17 101 DX53
Sutton Rd N10 98 DG54
Sutton Rd, Bark. 145 ES68
Sutton Rd, Houns. 156 CA81
Sutton Rd, St.Alb. 43 CH21
Sutton Rd, Wat. 76 BW41
Sutton Row W1 273 N8
Sutton Row W1 141 DK72
Sutton Sq E9 122 DW64
Urswick Rd
Sutton Sq, Houns. 156 BZ81
Sutton St E1 142 DW72
Sutton Way W10 139 CW71
Sutton Way, Houns. 156 BZ81
Suttons Av, Horn. 128 FJ62
Suttons Gdns, Horn. 128 FK62
Suttons La, Horn. 128 FK64
Sutton's Way EC1 275 J5
Swabey Rd, Slou. 153 BA77
Swaby Rd SW18 180 DC88
Swaffham Way N22 99 DP52
White Hart La
Swaffield Rd SW18 180 DB87
Swaffield Rd, Sev. 257 FJ122
Swain Cl SW16 181 DH93
Swain Rd, Th.Hth. 202 DQ99
Swain St NW8 272 B4
Swain St NW8 140 DE70
Swains Cl, West Dr. 154 BL75
Swains La N6 120 DG62
Swains Rd SW17 180 DF94
Swainson Rd W3 159 CT75
Swaisland Dr (Crayford), Dart. 187 FF85
Swaisland Rd, Dart. 187 FH85
Swakeleys Dr, Uxb. 114 BN63
Swakeleys Rd (Ickenham), Uxb. 114 BM62
Swale Cl, S.Ock. 148 FQ72
Swale Rd, Dart. 167 FG83
Swaledale Cl N11 98 DG51
Ribblesdale Av
Swaledale Rd, Dart. 188 FQ88
Swallands Rd SE6 183 EA90
Swallow Cl SE14 162 DW81
Swallow Cl, Bushey 94 CC46
Swallow Cl, Erith 167 FE81
Swallow Cl (Chafford Hundred), Grays 169 FW77
Swallow Cl, Green. 189 FT85
Swallow Cl, Rick. 92 BJ45
Swallow Cl, Stai. 173 BF91
Swallow Ct, Hert. 32 DQ09
Swallow Dr NW10 138 CR65
Kingfisher Way
Swallow Dr, Nthlt. 136 CA68
Swallow End, Welw.G.C. 29 CZ09
Swallow Gdns SW16 181 DK92
Swallow Gdns, Hat. 45 CU20
Swallow La (Mid Holmwood), Dor. 263 CH142
Swallow La, St.Alb. 43 CH23
Swallow Oaks, Abb.L. 59 BT31
Swallow Pas W1 273 J9
Swallow Pl W1 273 J9
Swallow St E6 144 EL71
Swallow St W1 277 L1
Swallow St, Iver 133 BD69
Swallow Wk, Horn. 147 FH65
Heron Flight Av
Swallowdale, Iver 133 BD69
Swallowdale, S.Croy. 221 DX109
Swallowdale La, Hem.H. 41 BP17
Swallowfield (Englefield Grn), Egh. 172 AV93
Heronfield
Swallowfield Rd SE7 164 EH78
Swallowfield Way, Hayes 155 BR75
Swallowfields (Northfleet), Grav. 190 GE90
Hillary Av
Swallowfields, Welw.G.C. 29 CZ09
Swallows, Harl. 36 EW11
Station Rd
Swallows, The, Welw.G.C. 29 CZ05
Swallowtail Cl, Orp. 206 EX98
Swan & Pike Rd, Enf. 83 EA38
Swan App E6 144 EL71
Swan Av, Upmin. 129 FT60
Swan Business Pk, Dart. 168 FK84
Swan Cl E17 101 DY53
Swan Cl, Chesh. 54 AP27
Swan Cl, Croy. 202 DS101
Swan Cl, Felt. 176 BY91
Swan Cl, Orp. 206 EU97
Swan Cl, Rick. 92 BK45
Parsonage Rd
Swan Ct SW3 160 DE78
Flood St
Swan Ct, Guil. 242 AX132
Swan Ct, Hem.H. 40 BJ21
Waterhouse St
Swan Dr NW9 96 CS54
Swan La EC4 279 K1
Swan La N20 98 DC48
Swan La, Dart. 187 FF87
Swan La, Guil. 258 AX135
Swan La, Loug. 102 EJ45
Swan Mead SE1 279 M7
Swan Mead SE1 162 DS76
Swan Mill Gdns, Dor. 247 CJ134
Swan Pas E1 142 DT73
Cartwright St
Swan Path E10 123 EC60
Jesse Rd
Swan Pl SW13 159 CT82
Swan Rd SE16 162 DW75
Swan Rd SE18 164 EK76
Swan Rd, Felt. 176 BY92
Swan Rd, Iver 133 BF72
Swan Rd, Sthl. 136 CB72
Swan Rd, West Dr. 154 BK75
Swan St SE1 279 J6
Swan St SE1 162 DQ76
Swan St, Islw. 157 CH83
Swan Ter, Wind. 151 AP80
Mill La
Swan Wk SW3 160 DF79
Swan Wk, Rom. 127 FE57
Swan Wk, Shep. 195 BS101
Swan Way, Enf. 83 DX40
Swan Yd N1 141 DP65
Highbury Sta Rd
Swanage Rd E4 101 EC52
Swanage Rd SW18 180 DC86
Swanage Waye, Hayes 136 BW72
Swanbourne Dr, Horn. 128 FJ64
Swanbridge Rd, Bexh. 166 FA81
Swandon Way SW18 160 DB84
Swanfield Rd, Wal.Cr. 67 DY33
Swanfield St E2 275 P3
Swanfield St E2 142 DT69
Swanhill, Welw.G.C. 30 DA06
Swanland Rd, Hat. 63 CV25
Swanland Rd, Pot.B. 63 CV33
Swanley Bar La, Pot.B. 64 DB28
Swanley Bypass, Sid. 207 FC97
Swanley Bypass, Swan. 207 FC97
Swanley Cen, Swan. 207 FE97
Swanley Cres, Pot.B. 64 DB29
Swanley La, Swan. 207 FF97
Swanley Rd, Well. 166 EW81
Swanley Village Rd, Swan. 207 FH95
Swanns Meadow (Bookham), Lthd. 246 CA126
Swans Cl, St.Alb. 44 CL21
Swanscombe Rd W4 158 CS78
Swanscombe Rd W11 139 CX74
Swanscombe St, Swans. 190 FY87
Swansea Ct E16 145 EP74
Fishguard Way
Swansea Rd, Enf. 82 DW42
Swansea Rd (Heathrow Airport), Houns. 175 BQ86
Southern Perimeter Rd
Swanshope, Loug. 85 EP40
Swansland Gdns E17 101 DY53
McEntee Av
Swanston Path, Wat. 94 BW48
Swanton Gdns SW19 179 CX88
Swanton Rd, Erith 167 FB80
Swanwick Cl SW15 179 CT87
Swanworth La (Mickleham), Dor. 247 CH128
Sward Rd, Orp. 206 EU100
Swaton Rd E3 143 EA70
Swaylands Rd, Belv. 166 FA79
Swaynes La, Guil. 243 BE134
Swaynesland Rd, Eden. 255 EM134
Swaythling Cl N18 100 DV49
Swaythling Ho SW15 179 CT86
Tunworth Cres
Sweden Gate SE16 163 DY76
Swedenborg Gdns E1 142 DU73
Sweeney Cres SE1 162 DT75
Sweeps Ditch Cl, Stai. 194 BG95
Sweeps La, Egh. 173 AZ92
Sweeps La, Orp. 206 EX99
Sweet Briar, Welw.G.C. 30 DA11
Sweet Briar Grn N9 100 DT48
Sweet Briar Gro N9 100 DT48
Sweet Briar La, Epsom 216 CR114
Sweet Briar Wk N18 100 DT49
Sweet La (Peaslake), Guil. 261 BR143
Sweetbriar Cl, Hem.H. 40 BG17
Sweetcroft La, Uxb. 134 BN66
Sweetmans Av, Pnr. 116 BX55
Sweets Way N20 98 DD47
Swete St E13 144 EG68
Swetenham Wk SE18 165 EQ78
Sandbach Pl
Sweyn Pl SE3 164 EG82
Sweyne Rd, Swans. 190 FY86
Sweyns, Harl. 52 EX17
Swievelands Rd (Biggin Hill), West. 238 EH119
Swift Cl E17 101 DY52
Swift Cl, Har. 116 CB61
Swift Cl, Hayes 135 BT72
Church Rd
Swift Cl, Upmin. 129 FS60
Swift Cl, Ware 33 EC12
Swift Rd, Felt. 176 BY90
Swift Rd, Sthl. 156 BZ76
Swift St SW6 159 CZ81
Swiftfields, Welw.G.C. 29 CZ08
Swiftsden Way, Brom. 184 EE93
Swiftsure Rd (Chafford Hundred), Grays 169 FW77
Swinbrook Rd W10 139 CY71
Swinburne Ct SE5 162 DR84
Basingdon Way
Swinburne Cres, Croy. 202 DW100
Swinburne Gdns, Til. 171 GH82
Swinburne Rd SW15 159 CU84
Swinderby Rd, Wem. 138 CL65
Swindon Cl, Ilf. 125 ES61
Salisbury Rd
Swindon Cl, Rom. 106 FM50
Swindon Gdns, Rom. 106 FM50
Swindon La, Rom. 106 FM50
Swindon Rd (Heathrow Airport), Houns. 175 BQ85
Swindon St W12 139 CV74
Swinfield Cl, Felt. 176 BY91
Swinford Gdns SW9 161 DP83
Swing Gate La, Berk. 38 AX22
Swingate La SE18 165 ES79
Swinnerton St E9 123 DY64
Swinton Cl, Wem. 118 CP60
Swinton Pl WC1 274 B2
Swinton Pl WC1 141 DM69
Swinton St WC1 274 B2
Swinton St WC1 141 DM69
Swires Shaw, Kes. 222 EK105
Swiss Av, Wat. 75 BS42
Swiss Cl, Wat. 75 BS41
Swiss Ter NW6 140 DD66
Swithland Gdns SE9 185 EN91
Sword Cl, Brox. 49 DX20
Swyncombe Av W5 157 CH77
Swynford Gdns NW4 119 CU56
Handowe Cl
Sybil Ms N4 121 DP58
Lothair Rd N
Sybil Phoenix Cl SE8 163 DX78
Sybil Thorndike Ho N1 142 DQ65
Clephane Rd
Sybourn St E17 123 DZ59
Sycamore App, Rick. 75 BQ43
Sycamore Av E3 143 DZ67
Sycamore Av W5 157 CK76
Sycamore Av, Hat. 45 CU19
Sycamore Av, Hayes 135 BS73
Sycamore Av, Sid. 185 ET86
Sycamore Av, Upmin. 128 FN62
Sycamore Cl E16 144 EE70
Clarence Rd
Sycamore Cl N9 100 DU49
Pycroft Way
Sycamore Cl SE9 184 EL89
Sycamore Cl W3 138 CS74
Bromyard Av
Sycamore Cl, Amer. 55 AR37
Sycamore Cl, Barn. 80 DD44
Sycamore Cl, Bushey 76 BY40
Sycamore Cl, Cars. 218 DF105
Sycamore Cl, Ch.St.G. 90 AU48
Sycamore Cl, Edg. 96 CQ49
Ash Cl

Sycamore Cl, Felt. 175 BU90
Sycamore Cl, Grav. 191 GK87
Sycamore Cl (Fetcham), Lthd. 231 CE123
Sycamore Cl, Loug. 85 EP40
Cedar Dr
Sycamore Cl, Nthlt. 136 BY67
Sycamore Cl, Wal.Cr. 66 DT27
Sycamore Cl, Wat. 75 BV35
Sycamore Cl, West Dr. 134 BM73
Whitethorn Av
Sycamore Ct, Surb. 198 CL101
Penners Gdns
Sycamore Dene, Chesh. 54 AR28
Sycamore Dr, Brwd. 108 FW46
Copperfield Gdns
Sycamore Dr (Park St), St.Alb. 61 CD27
Sycamore Dr, Swan. 207 FE97
Sycamore Fld, Harl. 51 EN19
Broadley Rd
Sycamore Gdns W6 159 CV75
Sycamore Gdns, Mitch. 200 DD96
Sycamore Gro NW9 118 CQ59
Sycamore Gro SE6 183 EC86
Sycamore Gro SE20 182 DU94
Sycamore Gro, N.Mal. 198 CR97
Sycamore Hill N11 98 DG51
Sycamore Ms SW4 161 DJ83
Sycamore Ri, Bans. 217 CX114
Sycamore Ri, Berk. 38 AX20
Sycamore Ri, Ch.St.G. 90 AU48
Sycamore Rd SW19 179 CW93
Sycamore Rd, Amer. 55 AR37
Sycamore Rd, Ch.St.G. 90 AU48
Sycamore Rd, Dart. 188 FK88
Sycamore Rd, Guil. 242 AX134
Sycamore Rd, Rick. 75 BQ43
Sycamore St EC1 275 H5
Sycamore Wk W10 139 CY70
Fifth Av
Sycamore Wk (Englefield Grn), Egh. 172 AV93
Sycamore Wk, Ilf. 125 EQ56
Civic Way
Sycamore Wk, Reig. 266 DC137
Sycamore Wk (George Grn), Slou. 132 AY72
Sycamore Way, S.Ock. 149 FX70
Sycamore Way, Tedd. 177 CJ93
Sycamore Way, Th.Hth. 201 DN99
Sycamores, The, Hem.H. 39 BF23
Sycamores, The, Rad. 61 CH34
The Av
Sycamores, The, S.Ock. 149 FR74
Dacre Av
Sydenham Av N21 81 DM43
Chadwick Av
Sydenham Av SE26 182 DV92
Sydenham Cl, Rom. 127 FF56
Sydenham Cotts SE12 184 EJ89
Sydenham Hill SE23 182 DV88
Sydenham Hill SE26 182 DU90
Sydenham Hill Est SE26 182 DU90
Sydenham Pk SE26 182 DW90
Sydenham Pk Rd SE26 182 DW90
Sydenham Ri SE23 182 DV89
Sydenham Rd SE26 182 DW92
Sydenham Rd, Croy. 202 DR101
Sydenham Rd, Guil. 258 AX136
Sydmons Ct SE23 182 DW87
Sydner Ms N16 122 DT63
Sydner Rd
Sydner Rd N16 122 DT63
Sydney Av, Pur. 219 DM112
Sydney Cl SW3 276 A9
Sydney Cl SW3 160 DD77
Sydney Cres, Ashf. 175 BP93
Sydney Gro NW4 119 CW57
Sydney Gro, Slou. 131 AQ72
Sydney Ms SW3 276 A9
Sydney Ms SW3 160 DD77
Sydney Pl SW7 276 A9
Sydney Pl SW7 160 DD77
Sydney Pl, Guil. 259 AZ135
Sydney Rd E11 124 EH58
Mansfield Rd
Sydney Rd N8 121 DN56
Sydney Rd N10 98 DG53
Sydney Rd SE2 166 EW76
Sydney Rd SW20 199 CX96
Sydney Rd W13 137 CG74
Sydney Rd, Bexh. 166 EX84
Sydney Rd, Enf. 82 DR42
Sydney Rd, Felt. 175 BU88
Sydney Rd, Guil. 259 AZ135
Sydney Rd, Ilf. 103 EQ54
Sydney Rd, Rich. 158 CL84
Sydney Rd, Sid. 185 ES91
Sydney Rd, Sutt. 218 DA105
Sydney Rd, Tedd. 177 CF92
Sydney Rd, Til. 171 GG82
Sydney Rd, Wat. 75 BS43
Sydney Rd, Wdf.Grn. 102 EG49
Sydney St SW3 276 B10
Sydney St SW3 160 DE77
Syke Cluan, Iver 153 BE75
Syke Ings, Iver 153 BE76
Sykes Dr, Stai. 174 BH92
Sykes Rd, Slou. 131 AP72
Sylvan Av N3 98 DA54
Sylvan Av N22 99 DM52
Sylvan Av NW7 97 CT51
Sylvan Av, Horn. 128 FL58
Sylvan Av, Rom. 126 EZ58
Sylvan Cl, Grays 170 FY77
Warren La
Sylvan Cl, Hem.H. 40 BN21
Sylvan Cl, Oxt. 254 EH129
Sylvan Cl, S.Croy. 220 DV110
Sylvan Cl, Wok. 227 BB117
Sylvan Ct N12 98 DB49
Sylvan Est SE19 202 DT95
Sylvan Gdns, Surb. 197 CK101
Sylvan Gro NW2 119 CX63
Sylvan Gro SE15 162 DV79
Sylvan Hill SE19 202 DS95
Sylvan Rd E7 144 EG65
Sylvan Rd E11 124 EG57
Sylvan Rd E17 123 EA57
Sylvan Rd SE19 202 DT95
Sylvan Rd, Ilf. 125 EQ61
Hainault St
Sylvan Wk, Brom. 205 EM97
Sylvan Way, Chig. 104 EV48
Sylvan Way, Dag. 126 EV62
Sylvan Way, Red. 266 DG135
Sylvan Way, Welw.G.C. 30 DC10
Sylvan Way, W.Wick. 222 EE105
Sylvana Cl, Uxb. 134 BM67
Sylvandale, Welw.G.C. 30 DC10
Sylverdale Rd, Croy. 201 DP104
Sylverdale Rd, Pur. 219 DP113
Sylvester Av, Chis. 185 EM93
Sylvester Gdns, Ilf. 104 EV50
Sylvester Path E8 142 DV65
Sylvester Rd
Sylvester Rd E8 142 DV65
Sylvester Rd E17 123 DZ59
Sylvester Rd N2 98 DC54
Sylvester Rd, Wem. 117 CJ64
Sylvestres (Riverhead), Sev. 256 FD121
Sylvestrus Cl, Kings.T. 198 CN95
Sylvia Av, Brwd. 109 GC47
Sylvia Av, Pnr. 94 BZ51
Sylvia Ct, Wem. 138 CP66
Harrow Rd
Sylvia Gdns, Wem. 138 CP66
Symes Ms NW1 141 DJ68
Camden High St
Symonds Ct (Cheshunt), Wal.Cr. 67 DX28
High St
Symons St SW3 276 E9
Symons St SW3 160 DF77
Symphony Ms W10 139 CY69
Third Av
Syon Gate Way, Brent. 157 CG80
Syon La, Islw. 157 CH80
Syon Pk Gdns, Islw. 157 CF80
Syon Vista, Rich. 157 CK81
Syracuse Av, Rain. 148 FL69
Syringa Ct, Grays 170 GD80
Sythwood, Wok. 226 AV117

T

Tabard Cen SE1 162 DR76
Prioress St
Tabard Gdn Est SE1 279 L5
Tabard Gdn Est SE1 162 DR75
Tabard St SE1 279 K5
Tabard St SE1 162 DR75
Tabarin Way, Epsom 233 CW116
Tabernacle Av E13 144 EG70
Barking Rd
Tabernacle St EC2 275 L5
Tabernacle St EC2 142 DR70
Tableer Av SW4 181 DK85
Tabley Rd N7 121 DL63
Tabor Gdns, Sutt. 217 CZ107
Tabor Gro SW19 179 CY94
Tabor Rd W6 159 CV76
Tabors Ct, Brwd. 109 FZ45
Shenfield Rd
Tabrums Way, Upmin. 129 FS59
Tachbrook Est SW1 161 DK78
Tachbrook Ms SW1 277 K8
Tachbrook Rd, Felt. 175 BT87
Tachbrook Rd, Sthl. 156 BX77
Tachbrook Rd, Uxb. 134 BJ68
Tachbrook St SW1 277 L9
Tachbrook St SW1 161 DJ77
Tack Ms SE4 163 EA83
Tadema Rd SW10 160 DC80
Tadlows Cl, Upmin. 128 FP64
Tadmor Cl, Sun. 195 BT98
Tadmor St W12 139 CX74
Tadorne Rd, Tad. 233 CW121
Tadworth Av, N.Mal. 199 CT99
Tadworth Cl, Tad. 233 CX122
Tadworth Par, Horn. 127 FH63
Maylands Av
Tadworth Rd NW2 119 CU61
Tadworth St, Tad. 233 CW123
Taeping St E14 163 EB77
Taffy's How, Mitch. 200 DE97
Taft Way E3 143 EB69
St. Leonards St
Tagalie Pl (Shenley), Rad. 62 CL32
Porters Pk Dr
Tagg's Island, Hmptn. 197 CD96
Tailworth St E1 142 DU71
Chicksand St
Tait Rd, Croy. 202 DS101
Takeley Cl, Rom. 105 FD54
Takeley Cl, Wal.Abb. 67 ED33
Takhar Ms SW11 160 DE82
Cabul Rd
Talacre Rd NW5 140 DG65
Talbot Av N2 120 DD55
Talbot Av, Slou. 153 AZ76
Talbot Av, Wat. 94 BY45
Talbot Cl N15 122 DT56
Talbot Cl, Reig. 266 DB135
Talbot Ct EC3 275 L10
Talbot Ct, Hem.H. 40 BK22
Crabtree La
Talbot Cres NW4 119 CU57
Talbot Gdns, Ilf. 126 EU61
Talbot Ho E14 143 EB72
Giraud St
Talbot Ho N7 121 DN62
Harvist Est
Talbot Pl SE3 164 EE82
Talbot Pl (Datchet), Slou. 152 AW81
Talbot Rd E6 145 EN68
Talbot Rd E7 124 EG63
Talbot Rd N6 120 DG58
Talbot Rd N15 122 DT56
Talbot Rd N22 99 DJ54
Talbot Rd SE22 162 DS84
Talbot Rd W2 139 CZ72
Talbot Rd W11 139 CZ72
Talbot Rd W13 137 CG73
Talbot Rd, Ashf. 174 BK92
Talbot Rd, Brom. 204 EH98
Masons Hill
Talbot Rd, Cars. 218 DG106
Talbot Rd, Dag. 146 EZ65
Talbot Rd, Har. 95 CF54
Talbot Rd, Hat. 45 CU15
Talbot Rd, Islw. 157 CG84
Talbot Rd, Rick. 92 BL46
Talbot Rd, Sthl. 156 BY77
Talbot Rd, Th.Hth. 202 DR98
Talbot Rd, Twick. 177 CE88
Talbot Rd, Wem. 117 CK64
Talbot Sq W2 272 A9
Talbot Sq W2 140 DD72
Talbot St, Hert. 32 DS09
Talbot Wk NW10 138 CS65
Garnet Rd
Talbot Wk W11 139 CY72
Talbot Yd SE1 279 K3
Talbrook, Brwd. 108 FT48
Taleworth Cl, Ash. 231 CK120
Taleworth Pk, Ash. 231 CK120
Taleworth Rd, Ash. 231 CK119
Talfourd Pl SE15 162 DT81
Talfourd Rd SE15 162 DT81
Talgarth Rd W6 159 CY78
Talgarth Rd W14 159 CY78
Talgarth Wk NW9 118 CS57
Talisman Cl, Ilf. 126 EV60
Talisman Sq SE26 182 DU91
Talisman Way, Epsom 233 CW116
Talisman Way, Wem. 118 CM62
Tall Elms Cl, Brom. 204 EF99
Tall Oaks, Amer. 55 AR37
Tall Trees SW16 201 DM97
Tall Trees (Colnbrook), Slou. 153 BE81
Tall Trees Cl, Horn. 128 FK58
Tallack Cl, Har. 95 CE52
College Hill Rd
Tallack Rd E10 123 DZ60
Tallents Cl (Sutton at Hone), Dart. 188 FP94
Tallis Cl E16 144 EH72
Tallis Gro SE7 164 EH79
Tallis St EC4 274 E10
Tallis St EC4 141 DN73
Tallis Vw NW10 138 CR65
Tallis Way, Borwd. 77 CK39
Tallon Rd, Brwd. 109 GE43
Tally Ho Cor N12 98 DC50
Tally Rd, Oxt. 254 EL131
Talma Gdns, Twick. 177 CE86
Talma Rd SW2 161 DN84
Talmage Cl SE23 182 DW87
Tyson Rd
Talman Gro, Stan. 95 CK51
Talus Cl, Purf. 169 FR77
Brimfield Rd
Talwin St E3 143 EB69
Tamar Cl E3 143 DZ67
Lefevre Wk
Tamar Cl, Upmin. 129 FS58
Tamar Dr, S.Ock. 148 FQ72
Tamar Grn, Hem.H. 40 BM15
Tamar Sq, Wdf.Grn. 102 EH51
Tamar St SE7 164 EL76
Woolwich Rd
Tamar Way N17 122 DU55
Tamar Way, Slou. 153 BB78
Tamarind Cl, Guil. 242 AU129
Tamarind Yd E1 142 DU74
Asher Way
Tamarisk Cl, St.Alb. 43 CD16
New Grns Av
Tamarisk Cl, S.Ock. 149 FW70
Tamarisk Rd, S.Ock. 149 FW69
Tamarisk Sq W12 139 CT73
Tamarisk Way, Slou. 151 AN75
Tamerton Sq, Wok. 226 AY119
Tamesis Gdns, Wor.Pk. 198 CS102
Tamesis Strand, Grav. 191 GL92
Tamian Way, Houns. 156 BW84
Tamworth Av, Wdf.Grn. 102 EE51
Tamworth La, Mitch. 201 DH96
Tamworth Pk, Mitch. 201 DH98
Tamworth Pl, Croy. 202 DQ103
Tamworth Rd, Croy. 201 DP103
Tamworth Rd, Hert. 32 DS08
Tamworth St SW6 160 DA79
Tancred Rd N4 121 DP58
Tandem Cen SW19 200 DD95
Prince George's Rd
Tandem Way SW19 200 DD95
Tandridge Ct, Cat. 236 DU122
Tandridge Dr, Orp. 205 ER102
Tandridge Gdns, S.Croy. 220 DT113
Tandridge Hill La, Gdse. 253 DZ128
Tandridge La (Tandridge), Oxt. 253 EA131
Tandridge Pl, Orp. 205 ER101
Tandridge Dr
Tandridge Rd, Warl. 237 DX119
Tanfield Av NW2 119 CT63
Tanfield Cl, Wal.Cr. 66 DU27
Tanfield Rd, Croy. 220 DQ105
Tangent Link, Rom. 106 FK53
Tangent Rd, Rom. 106 FK53
Ashton Rd
Tangier La (Eton), Wind. 151 AR79
Tangier Rd, Guil. 259 BA135
Tangier Rd, Rich. 158 CP83
Tangier Way, Tad. 233 CY117
Tangier Wd, Tad. 233 CY118
Tangle Tree Cl N3 98 DB54
Tanglebury Cl, Brom. 205 EM98
Tanglewood Cl (Longcross), Cher. 192 AV104
Tanglewood Cl, Croy. 202 DW104
Tanglewood Cl, Stan. 95 CE47
Tanglewood Cl, Uxb. 134 BN69
Tanglewood Cl, Wok. 227 BD116
Tanglewood Way, Felt. 175 BV90
Tangley Gro SW15 179 CT86
Tangley La, Guil. 242 AT130
Tangley Pk Rd, Hmptn. 176 BZ93
Tanglyn Av, Shep. 195 BP99
Tangmere Cres, Horn. 147 FH65
Tangmere Gdns, Nthlt. 136 BW68
Tangmere Gro, Kings.T. 177 CK92
Tangmere Way NW9 96 CS54
Tanhouse Rd, Oxt. 253 ED132
Tanhurst Wk SE2 166 EX76
Alsike Rd
Tank Hill Rd, Purf. 168 FN78
Tank La, Purf. 168 FN77
Tankerton Rd, Surb. 198 CM103
Tankerton St WC1 274 A3
Tankerville Rd SW16 181 DK93
Tankridge Rd NW2 119 CV61
Tanner Pt E13 *Pelly Rd* 144 EG67
Tanner St SE1 279 N5
Tanner St SE1 162 DS75
Tanner St, Bark. 145 EQ65
Tanners Cl, St.Alb. 42 CC19
Tanners Cl, Walt. 195 BV100
Tanners Cres, Hert. 32 DQ11
Tanners Dean, Lthd. 231 CJ122
Tanners End La N18 100 DS49
Tanners Hill SE8 163 DZ81
Tanners Hill, Abb.L. 59 BT31
Tanners La, Ilf. 125 EQ55
Tanners Meadow (Brockham), Bet. 264 CP138
Tanners Way, Ware 34 EJ06
Tanners Wd Cl, Abb.L. 59 BS32
Tanners Wd La
Tanners Wd La, Abb.L. 59 BS32
Tannersfield (Shalford), Guil. 258 AY142
Tannery, The, Red. 250 DE134
Oakdene Rd
Tannery Cl, Beck. 203 DX99
Tannery Cl, Dag. 127 FB62
Tannery La (Bramley), Guil. 258 AY144
Tannery La (Send), Wok. 227 BF122
Tannington Ter N5 121 DN62
Tannsfeld Rd SE26 183 DX92
Tannsfield Dr, Hem.H. 40 BM18
Tannsmore Cl, Hem.H. 40 BM18
Tansley Cl N7 121 DK64
Hilldrop Rd
Tanswell Est SE1 278 E5
Tanswell St SE1 278 D5
Tansy Cl E6 145 EN72
Tansy Cl, Guil. 243 BC132
Tansy Cl, Rom. 106 FL51
Tansycroft, Welw.G.C. 30 DB08
Tant Av E16 144 EF72
Tantallon Rd SW12 180 DG88
Tantony Gro, Rom. 126 EX55
Tanworth Cl, Nthwd. 93 BQ51
Tanworth Gdns, Pnr. 93 BV54
Tanyard La, Bex. 186 FA87
Bexley High St
Tanyard Way, Horl. 269 DH146
Tanys Dell, Harl. 36 EU12
Tanza Rd NW3 120 DF63
Tapestry Cl, Sutt. 218 DB108
Taplow NW3 140 DD66
Taplow SE17 162 DS78
Thurlow St
Taplow Common Rd (Burnham), Slou. 130 AG67
Taplow Rd N13 100 DQ49
Taplow Rd, Maid. 130 AG71
Taplow St N1 275 J1
Taplow St N1 142 DQ68
Tapners Rd, Bet. 265 CT139
Tapners Rd (Leigh), Reig. 265 CT139
Tapp St E1 142 DV70
Tappesfield Rd SE15 162 DW83
Tapster St, Barn. 79 CZ42
Taransay, Hem.H. 41 BP22
Taransay Wk N1 142 DR65
Marquess Rd
Tarbay La (Oakley Grn), Wind. 150 AH82
Tarbert Rd SE22 182 DS85
Tarbert Wk E1 142 DW73
Juniper St
Target Cl, Felt. 175 BS86
Tarham Cl, Horl. 268 DE146
Tariff Cres SE8 163 DZ77
Tariff Rd N17 100 DU51
Tarleton Gdns SE23 182 DV88
Tarling Cl, Sid. 186 EV90
Tarling Rd E16 144 EF72
Tarling Rd N2 98 DC54
Tarling St E1 142 DV72
Tarling St Est E1 142 DW72
Tarmac Way, West Dr. 154 BH80
Tarn St SE1 279 H7
Tarnbank, Enf. 81 DL43
Tarnwood Pk SE9 185 EM88
Tarnworth Rd, Rom. 106 FN50
Tarpan Way, Brox. 67 DZ26
Tarquin Ho SE26 182 DU91
Tarragon Cl SE14 163 DY80
Tarragon Dr, Guil. 242 AU129
Tarragon Gro SE26 183 DX93
Tarrant Pl W1 272 D7
Tarrant Pl W1 140 DF71
Tarrington Cl SW16 181 DK90
Tarry La SE8 163 DY77
Tartar Rd, Cob. 214 BW113
Tarver Rd SE17 161 DP78
Tarves Way SE10 163 EB80
Tash Pl N11 99 DH50
Woodland Rd
Tasker Cl, Hayes 155 BQ80
Tasker Ho, Bark. 145 ER68
Dovehouse Mead
Tasker Rd NW3 120 DF64
Tasker Rd, Grays 171 GH76
Tasman Ct E14 163 EB77
Westferry Rd
Tasman Ct, Sun. 175 BS94
Tasman Rd SW9 161 DL83
Tasman Wk E16 144 EK72
Royal Rd
Tasmania Ho, Til. 171 GG81
Hobart Rd
Tasmania Ter N18 100 DQ51
Tasso Rd W6 159 CY79
Tatam Rd NW10 138 CQ66
Tatchbury Ho SW15 179 CT86
Tunworth Cres
Tate & Lyle Jetty E16 164 EL75
Tate Cl, Lthd. 231 CJ123
Windmill Dr
Tate Rd E16 145 EM74
Newland St
Tate Rd (Chalfont St. Peter), Ger.Cr. 91 AZ50
Tate Rd, Sutt. 218 DA106
Tatnell Rd SE23 183 DY86
Tatsfield App Rd (Tatsfield), West. 238 EH123
Tatsfield Av, Wal.Abb. 49 ED23
Tatsfield La (Tatsfield), West. 239 EM121
Tattenham Cor Rd, Epsom 233 CT117
Tattenham Cres, Epsom 233 CU118
Tattenham Gro, Epsom 233 CV118
Tattenham Way, Tad. 233 CX118
Tattersall Cl SE9 184 EL85
Tattle Hill, Hert. 31 DL05
Tatton Cres N16 122 DT59
Clapton Common
Tatum St SE17 279 L9
Tatum St SE17 162 DR77
Tauber Cl, Borwd. 78 CM42
Tauheed Cl N4 122 DQ61
Taunton Av SW20 199 CV96
Taunton Av, Cat. 236 DT123
Taunton Av, Houns. 156 CC82
Taunton Cl, Bexh. 167 FD82
Taunton Cl, Ilf. 103 ET51
Taunton Cl, Sutt. 200 DA102
Taunton Dr N2 98 DC54
Taunton Dr, Enf. 81 DN41
Taunton La, Couls. 235 DN119
Taunton Ms NW1 272 D5
Taunton Pl NW1 272 D4
Taunton Pl NW1 140 DF70
Taunton Rd SE12 184 EE85
Taunton Rd (Northfleet), Grav. 190 GA85
Taunton Rd, Grnf. 136 CB67
Taunton Rd, Rom. 106 FJ49
Taunton Vale, Grav. 191 GK90
Taunton Way, Stan. 118 CL55
Tavern Cl, Cars. 200 DE101
Tavern La SW9 161 DN82
Taverner Sq N5 122 DQ63
Highbury Gra
Taverners, Hem.H. 40 BL18
Taverners Cl W11 139 CY74
Addison Av
Taverners Way E4 102 EE46
Douglas Rd
Taverners Way, Hodd. 49 EA17
Tavistock Av E17 123 DY55
Tavistock Av, Grnf. 137 CG68
Tavistock Av, St.Alb. 42 CC23
Tavistock Cl N16 122 DS64
Crossway
Tavistock Cl, Pot.B. 64 DD31
Tavistock Cl, Rom. 106 FK53
Tavistock Cl, St.Alb. 43 CD24
Tavistock Cl, Stai. 174 BK94
Tavistock Cres W11 139 CZ71
Tavistock Cres, Mitch. 201 DL98
Tavistock Gdns, Ilf. 125 ES63
Tavistock Gate, Croy. 202 DR102
Tavistock Gro, Croy. 202 DR101
Tavistock Ms E18 124 EG56
Avon Way
Tavistock Ms W11 139 CZ72
Lancaster Rd
Tavistock Pl E18 124 EG55
Avon Way
Tavistock Pl N14 99 DH45
Chase Side
Tavistock Pl WC1 273 N4
Tavistock Pl WC1 141 DL70
Tavistock Rd E7 124 EF63
Tavistock Rd E15 144 EF65
Tavistock Rd E18 124 EG55
Tavistock Rd N4 122 DR58
Tavistock Rd NW10 139 CT68
Tavistock Rd W11 139 CZ71
Tavistock Rd, Brom. 204 EF98
Tavistock Rd, Cars. 200 DD102
Tavistock Rd, Croy. 202 DR102
Tavistock Rd, Edg. 96 CN53
Tavistock Rd, Uxb. 115 BQ64
Tavistock Rd, Wat. 76 BX39
Tavistock Rd, Well. 166 EW81
Tavistock Rd, West Dr. 134 BK74
Tavistock Sq WC1 273 N4
Tavistock Sq WC1 141 DK70
Tavistock St WC2 274 A10
Tavistock St WC2 141 DL73
Tavistock Ter N19 121 DK62
Tavistock Twr SE16 163 DY76
Finland St
Tavistock Wk, Cars. 200 DD102
Tavistock Rd
Taviton St WC1 273 M4
Taviton St WC1 141 DK70
Tavy Cl SE11 278 E10
Tavy Cl SE11 161 DN78
Tawney Common, Epp. 70 FA32
Tawney Rd SE28 146 EV73
Tawneys Rd, Harl. 51 ES16
Tawny Av, Upmin. 128 FP64
Tawny Cl W13 137 CH74
Tawny Cl, Felt. 175 BU90
Chervil Cl
Tawny Way SE16 163 DX77
Tay Way, Rom. 105 FF53
Tayben Av, Twick. 177 CE86
Taybridge Rd SW11 160 DG83
Tayburn Cl E14 143 EC72
Tayfield Cl, Uxb. 115 BQ62
Tayler Cotts, Pot.B. 63 CT34
Crossoaks La
Tayles Hill, Epsom 217 CT110
Tayles Hill Dr
Tayles Hill Dr, Epsom 217 CT110
Taylifers, Harl. 51 EN20
Taylor Av, Rich. 158 CP82
Taylor Cl N17 100 DU52
Taylor Cl, Epsom 216 CN111
Williams Evans Rd
Taylor Cl (Hampton Hill), Hmptn. 176 CC92
Taylor Cl, Houns. 156 CC81
Taylor Cl, Orp. 223 ET105
Taylor Cl, Rom. 104 FA52
Taylor Cl, St.Alb. 43 CG16
Taylor Cl (Harefield), Uxb. 92 BJ53
High St
Taylor Ct E15 123 EC64
Clays La
Taylor Rd, Ash. 231 CK117
Taylor Rd, Mitch. 180 DE94
Taylor Rd, Wall. 219 DH106
Taylor Row, Dart. 188 FJ90
Taylor Row, Rom. 106 FJ48
Cummings Hall La
Taylors Av, Hodd. 49 EA18
Taylors Bldgs SE18 165 EP77
Spray St
Taylors Cl, Sid. 185 ET91
Taylors Grn W3 138 CS72
Long Dr
Taylors La NW10 138 CS66
Taylors La SE26 182 DV91
Taylors La, Barn. 79 CZ39
Taylors Rd, Chesh. 54 AR29
Taymount Ri SE23 182 DW89
Taynton Dr, Red. 251 DK129
Tayport Cl N1 141 DL66
Tayside Dr, Edg. 96 CP48
Taywood Rd, Nthlt. 136 BZ69
Teak Cl SE16 143 DY74
Teal Av, Orp. 206 EX98
Teal Cl E16 144 EK71
Fulmer Rd
Teal Cl, S.Croy. 221 DX111
Teal Ct, Wall. 219 DJ107
Carew Rd
Teal Dr, Nthwd. 93 BQ52
Teal Pl, Sutt. 217 CZ106
Sandpiper Rd
Teale St E2 142 DU68
Tealing Dr, Epsom 216 CR105
Teardrop Ind Est, Swan. 207 FH99
Teasel Cl, Croy. 203 DX102
Teasel Way E15 144 EE69
Teazle Meade, Epp. 70 EV25
Carpenters Arms La
Teazle Wd Hill, Lthd. 231 CE117
Teazlewood Pk, Lthd. 231 CG117
Tebworth Rd N17 100 DT52
Teck Cl, Islw. 157 CG82
Tedder Cl, Chess. 215 CJ106
Tedder Cl, Ruis. 115 BV64
West End Rd
Tedder Cl, Uxb. 134 BM66
Tedder Rd, Hem.H. 40 BN19
Tedder Rd, S.Croy. 220 DW108
Teddington Cl, Epsom 216 CR110
Teddington Lock, Tedd. 177 CH91
Teddington Pk, Tedd. 177 CF92
Teddington Pk Rd, Tedd. 177 CF91
Tedworth Gdns SW3 160 DF78
Tedworth Sq
Tedworth Sq SW3 160 DF78
Tee, The W3 138 CS72
Tee Side, Hert. 32 DV08
Tees Av, Grnf. 137 CE68
Tees Cl, Upmin. 129 FR59
Tees Dr, Rom. 106 FK48
Teesdale, Hem.H. 40 BL17
Teesdale Av, Islw. 157 CG81
Teesdale Cl E2 142 DV68
Teesdale Gdns SE25 202 DS96
Teesdale Gdns, Islw. 157 CG81
Teesdale Rd E11 124 EF58

Teesdale Rd, Dart. 188 FQ88
Teesdale Rd, Slou. 131 AM71
Teesdale St E2 142 DV68
Teesdale Yd E2 142 DV68
Teesdale St
Teeswater Ct, Erith 166 EX76
Middle Way
Teevan Cl, Croy. 202 DU101
Teevan Rd, Croy. 202 DU101
Teggs La, Wok. 227 BF116
Teignmouth Cl SW4 161 DK84
Teignmouth Cl, Edg. 96 CM54
Teignmouth Gdns, Grnf. 137 CG68
Teignmouth Rd NW2 119 CX64
Teignmouth Rd, Well. 166 EW82
Telcote Way, Ruis. 116 BW59
Woodlands Av
Telegraph Hill NW3 120 DB62
Telegraph La (Claygate), Esher 215 CF107
Telegraph Ms, Ilf. 126 EU60
Telegraph Path, Chis. 185 EP92
Telegraph Pl E14 163 EB77
Telegraph Rd SW15 179 CV87
Telegraph St EC2 275 K8
Telegraph Track, Cars. 218 DG110
Telemann Sq SE3 164 EH83
Telephone Pl SW6 159 CZ79
Lillie Rd
Telfer Cl W3 158 CQ75
Church Rd
Telferscot Rd SW12 181 DK88
Telford Av SW2 181 DL88
Telford Cl E17 123 DY59
Telford Cl SE19 182 DT93
St. Aubyn's Rd
Telford Cl, Wat. 76 BX35
Telford Ct, Guil. 258 AY135
Clandon Rd
Telford Ct, St.Alb. 43 CE21
Telford Dr, Slou. 151 AN75
Telford Dr, Walt. 196 BW101
Telford Rd N11 99 DJ51
Telford Rd NW9 119 CU58
West Hendon Bdy
Telford Rd SE9 185 ER89
Telford Rd W10 139 CY71
Telford Rd (London Colney), St.Alb. 61 CJ27
Telford Rd, Sthl. 136 CB73
Telford Rd, Twick. 176 CA87
Telford Ter SW1 161 DJ79
Telford Way W3 138 CS71
Telford Way, Hayes 136 BY71
Telfords Yd E1 142 DU73
The Highway
Telham Rd E6 145 EN68
Tell Gro SE22 162 DT84
Tellisford, Esher 214 CB105
Tellson Av SE18 164 EK81
Telscombe Cl, Orp. 205 ES103
Telston La (Otford), Sev. 241 FF117
Temeraire St SE16 162 DW75
Albion St
Temperance St, St.Alb. 42 CC20
Temperley Rd SW12 180 DG87
Tempest Av, Pot.B. 64 DC32
Tempest Mead (North Weald Bassett), Epp. 71 FB27
Tempest Rd, Egh. 173 BC93
Tempest Way, Rain. 147 FG65
Templar Dr SE28 146 EX72
Templar Dr, Grav. 191 GG92
Templar Ho NW2 139 CZ65
Shoot Up Hill
Templar Ho, Rain. 147 FD68
Chantry Way
Templar Pl, Hmptn. 176 CA94
Templar St SE5 161 DP82
Templars Av NW11 119 CZ58
Templars Cres N3 98 DA54
Templars Dr, Har. 95 CD51
Temple EC4 141 DN73
Temple Av EC4 274 E10
Temple Av EC4 141 DN73
Temple Av N20 98 DD45
Temple Av, Croy. 203 DZ103
Temple Av, Dag. 126 FA60
Temple Bk, Harl. 36 EV09
Temple Bar Rd, Wok. 226 AT119
Temple Cl E11 124 EE59
Wadley Rd
Temple Cl N3 97 CZ54
Cyprus Rd
Temple Cl SE28 165 EQ76
Temple Cl, Epsom 216 CR112
Temple Cl (Cheshunt), Wal.Cr. 66 DU31
Temple Cl, Wat. 75 BT40
Temple Ct E1 143 DX71
Rectory Sq
Temple Ct, Hert. 32 DR06
Temple Ct, Pot.B. 63 CY31
Temple Flds, Hert. 32 DR06
Temple Fortune Hill NW11 120 DA57
Temple Fortune La NW11 120 DA58
Temple Fortune Par NW11 119 CZ57
Finchley Rd
Temple Gdns N21 99 DP47
Barrowell Grn
Temple Gdns NW11 119 CZ58
Temple Gdns, Dag. 126 EX62
Temple Gdns, Rick. 93 BP49
Temple Gdns, Stai. 193 BF95
Temple Gro NW11 120 DA58
Temple Gro, Enf. 81 DP41
Temple Hill, Dart. 188 FM86
Temple Hill Sq, Dart. 188 FM85
Temple La EC4 274 E9
Temple Mead, Harl. 50 EH15
Temple Mead, Hem.H. 40 BK18
Temple Mead Cl, Stan. 95 CH51
Temple Mill La E15 123 EB63
Temple Pk, Uxb. 134 BN69
Temple Pl WC2 274 C10
Temple Pl WC2 141 DM73
Temple Rd E6 144 EL67
Temple Rd N8 121 DM56
Temple Rd NW2 119 CW63
Temple Rd W4 158 CQ76
Temple Rd W5 157 CK76
Temple Rd, Croy. 220 DR105
Temple Rd, Epsom 216 CR112
Temple Rd, Houns. 156 CB84
Temple Rd, Rich. 158 CM83
Temple Rd (Biggin Hill), West. 238 EK117
Temple Rd, Wind. 151 AR82
Temple Sheen SW14 178 CQ85
Temple Sheen Rd SW14 158 CP84
Temple St E2 142 DV68
Temple Vw, St.Alb. 42 CC18
Temple Way (Farnham Common), Slou. 111 AQ64
Temple Way, Sutt. 200 DD104
Temple W Ms SE11 278 F7
Temple W Ms SE11 161 DP76
Temple Wd Dr, Red. 250 DF130
Templecombe Ms, Wok. 227 BA116
Dorchester Ct
Templecombe Rd E9 142 DW67
Templecombe Way, Mord. 199 CY99
Templecroft, Ashf. 175 BR93
Templedene Av, Stai. 174 BH94
Templefield Cl, Add. 212 BH107
Templefields Enterprise Cen, Harl. 36 EU11
Templehof Av NW2 119 CW59
Templeman Cl, Pur. 235 DP116
Croftleigh Av
Templeman Rd W7 137 CF71
Templemead Cl W3 138 CS72
Templemere, Wey. 195 BR104
Templepan La, Rick. 74 BL37
Templer Av, Grays 171 GG77
Templeton Av E4 101 EA49
Templeton Cl N16 122 DS64
Truman's Rd
Templeton Cl SE19 202 DR95
Templeton Pl SW5 160 DA77
Templeton Rd N15 122 DR58
Templewood W13 137 CH71
Templewood, Welw.G.C. 29 CX06
Templewood Av NW3 120 DB62
Templewood Gdns NW3 120 DB62
Templewood La (Farnham Common), Slou. 111 AQ64
Templewood Pk, Slou. 112 AT63
Templewood Pt NW2 119 CZ61
Granville Rd
Tempsford, Welw.G.C. 30 DD09
Tempsford Av, Borwd. 78 CR42
Tempsford Cl, Enf. 82 DQ41
Gladbeck Way
Temsford Cl, Har. 94 CC54
Ten Acre, Wok. 226 AU118
Abercorn Way
Ten Acre La, Egh. 193 BC96
Ten Acres (Fetcham), Lthd. 231 CD124
Ten Acres Cl (Fetcham), Lthd. 231 CD124
Tenbury Cl E7 124 EK64
Romford Rd
Tenbury Ct SW2 181 DK88
Tenby Av, Har. 95 CH54
Tenby Cl N15 122 DT56
Hanover Rd
Tenby Cl, Rom. 126 EY58
Tenby Gdns, Nthlt. 136 CA65
Tenby Rd E17 123 DY57
Tenby Rd, Edg. 96 CM53
Tenby Rd, Enf. 82 DW41
Tenby Rd, Rom. 126 EY58
Tenby Rd, Well. 166 EX81
Tench St E1 142 DV74
Tenchleys La, Oxt. 254 EK131
Tenda Rd SE16 162 DV77
Roseberry St
Tendring Rd, Harl. 51 EQ17
Tendring Way, Rom. 126 EW57
Tenham Av SW2 181 DK88
Tenison Ct W1 273 K10
Tenison Way SE1 278 D3
Tenison Way SE1 141 DM74
Tennand Cl (Cheshunt), Wal.Cr. 66 DT26
Tenniel Cl W2 140 DC72
Porchester Gdns
Tenniel Cl, Guil. 242 AV132
Tennis Ct La, E.Mol. 197 CF97
Hampton Ct Way
Tennis St SE1 279 K4
Tennis St SE1 162 DR75
Tennison Av, Borwd. 78 CP43
Tennison Cl, Couls. 235 DP120
Tennison Rd SE25 202 DT98
Tenniswood Rd, Enf. 82 DT39
Tennyson Av E11 124 EG59
Tennyson Av E12 144 EL66
Tennyson Av NW9 118 CQ55
Tennyson Av, Grays 170 GB76
Tennyson Av, N.Mal. 199 CV99
Tennyson Av, Twick. 177 CF88
Tennyson Av, Wal.Abb. 68 EE34
Tennyson Cl, Enf. 83 DX43
Tennyson Cl, Felt. 175 BT86
Tennyson Cl, Well. 165 ET81
Tennyson Rd E10 123 EB61
Tennyson Rd E15 144 EE66
Tennyson Rd E17 123 DZ58
Tennyson Rd NW6 139 CZ67
Tennyson Rd NW7 97 CU50
Tennyson Rd SE20 183 DX94
Tennyson Rd SW19 180 DC93
Tennyson Rd W7 137 CF73
Tennyson Rd, Add. 212 BL105
Tennyson Rd, Ashf. 174 BL92
Tennyson Rd, Brwd. 109 GC45
Tennyson Rd, Dart. 188 FN85
Tennyson Rd, Houns. 156 CC82
Tennyson Rd, Rom. 106 FJ52
Tennyson Rd, St.Alb. 60 CA26
Tennyson St SW8 161 DH82
Tennyson Wk (Northfleet), Grav. 190 GD90
Tennyson Wk, Til. 171 GH82
Tennyson Way, Horn. 127 FF61
Tennyson Way, Slou. 131 AL70
Wordsworth Rd
Tensing Av (Northfleet), Grav. 190 GE90
Tensing Rd, Sthl. 156 CA76
Tent Peg La, Orp. 205 EQ99
Tent St E1 142 DV70
Tentelow La, Sthl. 156 CA78
Tenter Grd E1 275 P7
Tenter Pas E1 142 DT72
Mansell St
Tenterden Cl NW4 119 CX55
Tenterden Cl SE9 185 EM91
Tenterden Dr NW4 119 CX55
Tenterden Gdns NW4 119 CX55
Tenterden Gdns, Croy. 202 DU101
Tenterden Gro NW4 119 CX56
Tenterden Rd N17 100 DT52
Tenterden Rd, Croy. 202 DU101
Tenterden Rd, Dag. 126 EZ61
Tenterden St W1 273 J9
Tenterden St W1 141 DH72
Tenzing Rd, Hem.H. 40 BN20
Terborch Way SE22 182 DS85
East Dulwich Gro
Tercel Path, Chig. 104 EV49
Teredo St SE16 163 DX76
Terence Cl, Grav. 191 GM88
Terence Ct, Belv. 166 EZ79
Nuxley Rd
Terence Messenger Twr E10 123 EB61
Oliver Rd
Teresa Gdns, Wal.Cr. 66 DW34
Teresa Ms E17 123 EA56
Teresa Wk N10 121 DH57
Connaught Gdns
Terling Cl E11 124 EF62
Terling Rd, Dag. 126 FA61
Terling Wk N1 142 DQ67
Britannia Row
Terlings, The, Brwd. 108 FU48
Terminus Ho, Harl. 35 ER14
Terminus Pl SW1 277 J7
Terminus Pl SW1 161 DH76
Terminus St, Harl. 35 ER14
Tern Gdns, Upmin. 129 FS60
Tern Way, Brwd. 108 FS49
Terrace, The E4 102 EE48
Chingdale Rd
Terrace, The N3 97 CZ54
Hendon La
Terrace, The NW6 140 DA67
Terrace, The SW13 158 CS82
Terrace, The, Add. 212 BL106
Terrace, The, Dor. 263 CJ137
Terrace, The, Grav. 191 GH86
Terrace, The, Maid. 150 AC76
Terrace, The, Sev. 256 FD122
Terrace, The, Wdf.Grn. 102 EG51
Broadmead Rd
Terrace Gdns SW13 159 CT82
Terrace Gdns, Wat. 75 BV40
Terrace La, Rich. 178 CL86
Terrace Rd E9 142 DW66
Terrace Rd E13 144 EG67
Terrace Rd, Walt. 195 BU101
Terrace St, Grav. 191 GH86
Terrace Wk, Dag. 126 EY64
Terraces, The, Dart. 188 FQ87
Terrapin Rd SW17 181 DH90
Terretts Pl N1 141 DP66
Upper St
Terrick Rd N22 99 DL53
Terrick St W12 139 CV72
Terrilands, Pnr. 116 BZ55
Terront Rd N15 122 DQ57
Tersha St, Rich. 158 CM84
Tessa Sanderson Pl SW8 161 DH83
Tessa Sanderson Way, Grnf. 117 CD64
Lilian Board Way
Testard Rd, Guil. 258 AW136
Testers Cl, Oxt. 254 EH131
Testerton Wk W11 139 CX73
Testwood Rd, Wind. 151 AK81
Tetbury Pl N1 141 DP67
Upper St
Tetcott Rd SW10 160 DC80
Tetherdown N10 120 DG55
Tethys Rd, Hem.H. 40 BM17
Tetty Way, Brom. 204 EG96
Teversham La SW8 161 DL81
Teviot Av, S.Ock. 148 FQ72
Teviot Cl, Guil. 242 AU131
Teviot Cl, Well. 166 EV81
Teviot St E14 143 EC71
Tewin Cl, St.Alb. 43 CJ16
Tewin Ct, Welw.G.C. 29 CZ08
Tewin Rd, Hem.H. 41 BQ20
Tewin Rd, Welw.G.C. 29 CZ09
Tewkesbury Av SE23 182 DV88
Tewkesbury Av, Pnr. 116 BY57
Tewkesbury Cl N15 122 DR58
Tewkesbury Rd
Tewkesbury Cl, Loug. 84 EL44
Tewkesbury Cl (Byfleet), W.Byf. 212 BK111
Tewkesbury Gdns NW9 118 CP55
Tewkesbury Rd N15 122 DR58
Tewkesbury Rd W13 137 CG73
Tewkesbury Rd, Cars. 200 DD102
Tewkesbury Ter N11 99 DJ51
Tewson Rd SE18 165 ES78
Teynham Av, Enf. 82 DR44
Teynham Grn, Brom. 204 EG99
Teynton Ter N17 100 DQ53
Thackeray Av N17 100 DU54
Thackeray Av, Til. 171 GH81
Thackeray Cl SW19 179 CX94
Thackeray Cl, Har. 116 CA60
Thackeray Cl, Islw. 157 CG82
Thackeray Cl, Uxb. 135 BP72
Dickens Av
Thackeray Dr, Rom. 126 EU59
Thackeray Rd E6 144 EK68
Thackeray Rd SW8 161 DH82
Thackeray St W8 160 DB75
Thackrah Cl N2 98 DC54
Tarling Rd
Thakeham Cl SE26 182 DV92
Thalia Cl SE10 163 ED79
Thalmassing Cl, Brwd. 109 GB47
Thame Rd SE16 163 DX75
Thames Av SW10 160 DC81
Thames Av, Cher. 194 BG97
Thames Av, Dag. 147 FB70
Thames Av, Grnf. 137 CF68
Thames Av, Hem.H. 40 BM15
Thames Av, Wind. 151 AR80
Thames Bk SW14 158 CQ82
Thames Circle E14 163 EA77
Westferry Rd
Thames Cl, Cher. 194 BH101
Thames Cl, Hmptn. 196 CB96
Thames Cl, Rain. 147 FH72
Thames Ct, W.Mol. 196 CB96
Thames Cres W4 158 CS80
Corney Rd
Thames Ditton Island, T.Ditt. 197 CG99
Thames Dr, Grays 171 GG78
Thames Dr, Ruis. 115 BQ58
Thames Europort, Dart. 169 FS84
Thames Gate, Dart. 168 FN84
St. Edmunds Rd
Thames Gateway, Dag. 146 EZ68
Thames Gateway, Rain. 147 FG72
Thames Gateway, S.Ock. 168 FP75
Thames Mead, Wind. 151 AL81
Thames Meadow, Shep. 195 BR102
Thames Meadow, W.Mol. 196 CA96
Thames Path SE1 278 E1
Thames Path SE1 141 DN73
Thames Path SE7 164 EJ76
Thames Path SE10 164 EJ76
Thames Path W6 159 CW79
Thames Pl SW15 159 CX83
Thames Rd E16 144 EK74
Thames Rd W4 158 CN79
Thames Rd, Bark. 145 ET69
Thames Rd, Dart. 167 FF82
Thames Rd, Grays 170 GB80
Thames Rd, Slou. 153 BA77
Thames Side, Cher. 194 BJ100
Thames Side, Kings.T. 197 CK95
Thames Side, Stai. 194 BH96
Thames Side, Wind. 151 AR80
Thames St SE10 163 EB79
Thames St, Hmptn. 196 CB95
Thames St, Kings.T. 197 CK96
Thames St, Stai. 173 BE91
Thames St, Sun. 195 BV98
Thames St, Walt. 195 BT101
Thames St, Wey. 195 BP103
Thames St, Wind. 151 AR81
Thames Vw, Grays 171 GG78
Thames Village W4 158 CQ81
Thames Way, Grav. 190 GD88
Thames Wf E16 144 EF74
Thamesbank Pl SE28 146 EW72
Thamesdale (London Colney), St.Alb. 62 CM27
Thamesfield Ct, Shep. 195 BQ101
Thamesgate Cl, Rich. 177 CH91
Locksmeade Rd
Thameshill Av, Rom. 105 FC54
Thameside, Tedd. 177 CK94
Thameside Ind Est E16 164 EL75
Thameside Wk SE28 145 ET72
Thamesmead, Walt. 195 BU101
Thamesmead Spine Rd, Belv. 167 FB75
Thamesmere Dr SE28 146 EU73
Thamesvale Cl, Houns. 156 CA83
Thamley, Purf. 168 FN77
Thane Vil N7 121 DM62
Thane Wks N7 121 DM62
Thanescroft Gdns, Croy. 202 DS104
Thanet Dr, Kes. 204 EK104
Phoenix Dr
Thanet Pl, Croy. 220 DQ105
Thanet Rd, Bex. 186 FA87
Thanet Rd, Erith 167 FE80
Thanet St WC1 273 P3
Thanet St WC1 141 DL69
Thanington Ct SE9 185 ES86
Thanstead Copse (Loudwater), H.Wyc. 88 AC53
Thanstead Ct (Loudwater), H.Wyc. 88 AC53
Thant Cl E10 123 EB62
Tharp Rd, Wall. 219 DK106
Thatcham Gdns N20 98 DC45
Thatcher Cl, West Dr. 154 BL75
Classon Cl
Thatcher Ct, Dart. 188 FK87
Heath St
Thatchers Cl, Horl. 269 DH146
Wheatfield Way
Thatchers Cl, Loug. 85 EQ40
Thatchers Cft, Hem.H. 40 BL16
Thatchers Way, Islw. 177 CD85
Thatches Gro, Rom. 126 EY56
Thavies Inn EC1 274 E8
Thaxted Ct N1 275 K1
Thaxted Ct N1 142 DR68
Thaxted Grn, Brwd. 109 GC43
Thaxted Ho, Dag. 147 FB66
Thaxted Pl SW20 179 CX94
Thaxted Rd SE9 185 EQ89
Thaxted Rd, Buck.H. 102 EL45
Thaxted Wk, Rain. 147 FF67
Ongar Way
Thaxted Way, Wal.Abb. 67 ED33
Thaxton Rd W14 159 CZ79
Thayer St W1 272 G7
Thayer St W1 140 DG71
Thayers Fm Rd, Beck. 203 DY95
Thaynesfield, Pot.B. 64 DD31
Theatre Sq E15 143 ED65
Great Eastern Rd
Theatre St SW11 160 DF83
Theberton St N1 141 DN67
Theed St SE1 278 D3
Theed St SE1 141 DN74
Thele Av, Ware 33 ED11
Theleway Cl, Hodd. 33 EB14
Thellusson Way, Rick. 91 BF45
Thelma Cl, Grav. 191 GM92
Thelma Gdns SE3 164 EK81
Thelma Gdns, Felt. 176 BY90
Thelma Gro, Tedd. 177 CG93
Theobald Cres, Har. 94 CB53
Theobald Rd E17 123 DZ59
Theobald Rd, Croy. 201 DP103
Theobald St SE1 279 K7
Theobald St, Borwd. 78 CM40
Theobald St, Rad. 77 CH36
Theobalds Av N12 98 DC49
Theobalds Av, Grays 170 GC78
Theobalds Cl (Cuffley), Pot.B. 65 DM30
Theobalds Ct N4 122 DQ61
Queens Dr
Theobalds La (Cheshunt), Wal.Cr. 66 DV32
Theobalds Pk Rd, Enf. 81 DP35
Theobald's Rd WC1 274 B6
Theobald's Rd WC1 141 DM71
Theobalds Rd (Cuffley), Pot.B. 65 DL30
Theodora Way, Pnr. 115 BT55
Theodore Rd SE13 183 EC86
Thepps Cl (South Nutfield), Red. 267 DM137
Therapia La, Croy. 201 DL100
Therapia Rd SE22 182 DW86
Theresa Rd W6 159 CU77
Theresas Wk, S.Croy. 220 DR110
Sanderstead Rd
Therfield Ct N4 122 DQ61
Brownswood Rd
Therfield Rd, St.Alb. 43 CD16
Thermopylae Gate E14 163 EB77
Theseus Wk N1 274 G1
Thesiger Rd SE20 183 DX94
Thessaly Rd SW8 161 DJ80
Thetford Cl N13 99 DP51
Thetford Gdns, Dag. 146 EX66
Thetford Rd, Ashf. 174 BL91
Thetford Rd, Dag. 146 EX67
Thetford Rd, N.Mal. 198 CR100
Thetis Ter, Rich. 158 CN79
Kew Grn
Theydon Bower, Epp. 70 EU31
Theydon Ct, Wal.Abb. 68 EG33
Theydon Gdns, Rain. 147 FE66
Theydon Gate, Epp. 85 ES37
Coppice Row
Theydon Gro, Epp. 70 EU30
Theydon Gro, Wdf.Grn. 102 EJ51
Theydon Pk Rd, Epp. 85 ES39
Theydon Pl, Epp. 69 ET31
Theydon Rd E5 122 DW61
Theydon Rd, Epp. 69 ER34
Theydon St E17 123 DZ59
Thicket, The, West Dr. 134 BL72
Thicket Cres, Sutt. 218 DC105
Thicket Gro SE20 182 DU94
Anerley Rd
Thicket Gro, Dag. 146 EW65
Thicket Rd SE20 182 DU94
Thicket Rd, Sutt. 218 DC105
Thicketts, Sev. 257 FJ123
Thickthorne La, Stai. 174 BJ94
Thieves La, Hert. 31 DM10
Thieves La, Ware 32 DW08
Third Av E12 124 EL63
Third Av E13 144 EG69
Third Av E17 123 EA57
Third Av W3 139 CT74
Third Av W10 139 CY69
Third Av, Dag. 147 FB67
Third Av, Enf. 82 DT43
Third Av, Grays 169 FU79
Third Av, Harl. 51 EM16
Third Av, Hayes 135 BT74
Third Av, Rom. 126 EW58
Third Av, Wal.Abb. 68 EH30
Breach Barn Mobile Home Pk
Third Av, Wat. 76 BX35
Third Av, Wem. 117 CK61
Third Cl, W.Mol. 196 CB98
Third Cres, Slou. 131 AQ71
Third Cross Rd, Twick. 177 CD89
Third Way, Wem. 118 CP63
Thirkleby Cl, Slou. 131 AQ74
Thirleby Rd SW1 277 L7
Thirleby Rd SW1 161 DJ76
Thirleby Rd, Edg. 96 CR53
Thirlmere Av, Grnf. 137 CJ69
Thirlmere Av, Slou. 130 AJ71
Thirlmere Cl, Egh. 173 BB94
Keswick Rd
Thirlmere Dr, St.Alb. 43 CH22
Thirlmere Gdns, Nthwd. 93 BQ51
Thirlmere Gdns, Wem. 117 CJ60
Thirlmere Ho, Islw. 177 CF85
Summerwood Rd
Thirlmere Ri, Brom. 184 EF93
Thirlmere Rd N10 99 DH53
Thirlmere Rd SW16 181 DK91
Thirlmere Rd, Bexh. 167 FC82
Thirlstane, St.Alb. 43 CE19
Thirsk Cl, Nthlt. 136 CA65
Thirsk Rd SE25 202 DR98
Thirsk Rd SW11 160 DG83
Thirsk Rd, Borwd. 78 CN37
Thirsk Rd, Mitch. 180 DG94
Thirston Path, Borwd. 78 CN40
Thirza Rd, Dart. 188 FM86
Thistle Cl, Hem.H. 39 BE21
Thistle Gro SW10 160 DC78
Thistle Gro, Welw.G.C. 30 DC12
Thistle Mead, Loug. 85 EN41
Thistle Rd, Grav. 191 GL87
Thistlebrook SE2 166 EW76
Thistlebrook Ind Est SE2 166 EW75
Thistlecroft, Hem.H. 40 BH21
Thistlecroft Gdns, Stan. 95 CK53
Thistlecroft Rd, Walt. 214 BW105
Thistledene, T.Ditt. 197 CE100
Thistledene, W.Byf. 211 BF113
Thistledene Av, Har. 116 BY62
Thistledene Av, Rom. 105 FB50
Thistledown, Grav. 191 GK93
Thistlemead, Chis. 205 EP96
Thistles, The, Hem.H. 40 BH19
Thistlewaite Rd E5 122 DV62
Thistlewood Cl N7 121 DM61
Thistlewood Cres (New Addington), Croy. 221 ED112
Thistleworth Cl, Islw. 157 CD80
Thistley Cl N12 98 DE51
Summerfields Av
Thomas a'Beckett Cl, Wem. 117 CF63
Thomas Av, Cat. 236 DQ121
Thomas Baines Rd SW11 160 DD83
Thomas Cl, Brwd. 108 FY48
Thomas Cribb Ms E6 145 EN72
Woolwich Manor Way
Thomas Darby Ct W11 139 CY72
Thomas Dean Rd SE26 183 DZ91
Kangley Br Rd
Thomas Dinwiddy Rd SE12 184 EH89
Thomas Doyle St SE1 278 F6
Thomas Doyle St SE1 161 DP76
Thomas Dr, Grav. 191 GK89
Thomas Hardy Ho N22 99 DM52
Thomas La SE6 183 EA87
Thomas More Ho EC2 142 DQ71
The Barbican
Thomas More St E1 142 DU73
Thomas More Way N2 120 DC55
Thomas Pl W8 160 DB76
St. Mary's Pl
Thomas Rd E14 143 DZ72
Thomas Rd (Wooburn Grn), H.Wyc. 110 AD59
Thomas Rochford Way, Wal.Cr. 67 DZ27
Thomas Sims Ct, Horn. 127 FH64
Thomas St SE18 165 EP77
Thomas Wall Cl, Sutt. 218 DB106
Clarence Rd
Thompkins La (Farnham Royal), Slou. 131 AM66
Thompson Av, Rich. 158 CN83
Thompson Cl, Ilf. 125 EQ61
High Rd
Thompson Cl, Slou. 153 BA77
Thompson Cl, Sutt. 200 DA102
Barrington Rd
Thompson Rd SE22 182 DT86
Thompson Rd, Dag. 126 EZ62
Thompson Rd, Houns. 156 CB84
Thompson Rd, Uxb. 134 BL66
Thompson Way, Rick. 92 BG45
Thompson's Av SE5 162 DQ80
Thompsons Cl, Wal.Cr. 66 DT29
Thompson's La (High Beach), Loug. 84 EF39
Thomson Cres, Croy. 201 DN102
Thomson Rd, Har. 117 CE55
Thong La, Grav. 191 GM90
Thorburn Sq SE1 162 DU77
Thorburn Way SW19 200 DD95
Thoresby St N1 275 J2
Thoresby St N1 142 DQ69
Thorkhill Gdns, T.Ditt. 197 CG102
Thorkhill Rd, T.Ditt. 197 CH101
Thorley Cl, W.Byf. 212 BG114
Thorley Gdns, Wok. 212 BG114
Thorn Av, Bushey 94 CC46
Thorn Bk, Guil. 258 AU136
Thorn Cl, Brom. 205 EN100
Thorn Cl, Nthlt. 136 BZ69
Thorn Dr (George Grn), Slou. 132 AY72
Thorn Ho, Beck. 203 DY95
Thorn La, Rain. 148 FK68

Thorn Ter SE15 162 DW83
Nunhead Gro
Thornaby Gdns N18 100 DU51
Thornaby Pl (Wooburn Grn), H.Wyc. 110 AE55
Wootton Dr
Thornash Cl, Wok. 226 AW115
Thornash Rd, Wok. 226 AW115
Thornash Way, Wok. 226 AW115
Thornbank Cl, Stai. 174 BG85
Thornbridge Rd, Iver 133 BC67
Thornbrook, Epp. 70 EX25
Thornbury Av, Islw. 157 CD80
Thornbury Cl N16 122 DS64
Truman's Rd
Thornbury Cl, Hodd. 33 EB13
Thornbury Gdns, Borwd. 78 CQ42
Thornbury Rd SW2 181 DL86
Thornbury Rd, Islw. 157 CD81
Thornbury Sq N6 121 DJ60
Thornby Rd E5 122 DW62
Thorncliffe Rd SW2 181 DL86
Thorncliffe Rd, Sthl. 156 BZ78
Thorncombe Rd SE22 182 DS85
Thorncroft (Englefield Grn), Egh. 172 AW94
Thorncroft, Hem.H. 41 BP22
Thorncroft, Horn. 127 FH58
Thorncroft Cl, Couls. 235 DN120
Waddington Av
Thorncroft Dr, Lthd. 231 CH123
Thorncroft Rd, Sutt. 218 DB105
Thorncroft St SW8 161 DL80
Thorndales, Brwd. 108 FX49
Thorndean St SW18 180 DC89
Thornden Av N11 98 DG46
Thorndike, Slou. 131 AN71
Thorndike Av, Nthlt. 136 BX67
Thorndike Cl SW10 160 DC80
Thorndike St SW1 277 M10
Thorndike St SW1 161 DJ77
Thorndon Cl, Orp. 205 ET96
Thorndon Ct, Brwd. 107 FW51
Thorndon Gdns, Epsom 216 CS105
Thorndon Gate, Brwd. 109 GC50
Thorndon Rd, Orp. 205 ET96
Thorndyke Ct, Pnr. 94 BZ52
Westfield Pk
Thorne Cl E11 124 EE63
Thorne Cl E16 144 EG72
Thorne Cl, Ashf. 175 BQ94
Thorne Cl, Erith 167 FC79
Thorne Cl, Hem.H. 40 BH22
St. Johns Rd
Thorne Pas SW13 158 CS82
Thorne Rd SW8 161 DL80
Thorne St E16 144 EF72
Thorne St SW13 158 CS83
Thorneloe Gdns, Croy. 219 DN106
Thornes Cl, Beck. 203 EC97
Thornet Wd Rd, Brom. 205 EN97
Thorney Cres SW11 160 DD80
Thorney Hedge Rd W4 158 CP77
Thorney La N, Iver 133 BF74
Thorney La S, Iver 153 BF75
Thorney Mill Rd, Iver 154 BG76
Thorney Mill Rd, West Dr. 154 BG76
Thorney St SW1 277 P8
Thorney St SW1 161 DL77
Thorneycroft Cl, Walt. 196 BW100
Thorneycroft Dr, Enf. 83 EA38
Government Row
Thornfield Av NW7 97 CY53
Thornfield Rd W12 159 CV75
Thornfield Rd, Bans. 234 DA117
Thornford Rd SE13 183 EC85
Thorngate Rd W9 140 DA70
Thorngrove Rd E13 144 EH67
Thornham Gro E15 123 ED64
Thornham St SE10 163 EB79
Thornhaugh Ms WC1 273 N5
Thornhaugh St WC1 273 N6
Thornhaugh St WC1 141 DK70
Thornhill, Epp. 71 FC26
Thornhill Av SE18 165 ES80
Thornhill Av, Surb. 198 CL103
Thornhill Br Wf N1 141 DM67
Caledonian Rd
Thornhill Cl, Amer. 55 AP40
Thornhill Cres N1 141 DM66
Thornhill Gdns E10 123 EB61
Thornhill Gdns, Bark. 145 ES66
Thornhill Gro N1 141 DM66
Lofting Rd
Thornhill Rd E10 123 EB61
Thornhill Rd N1 141 DN66
Thornhill Rd, Croy. 202 DQ101
Thornhill Rd, Nthwd. 93 BQ49
Thornhill Rd, Surb. 198 CL103
Thornhill Rd, Uxb. 114 BM63
Thornhill Sq N1 141 DM66
Thornhill Way, Shep. 194 BN99
Thornlaw Rd SE27 181 DN91
Thornleas Pl (East Horsley), Lthd. 245 BS126
Station App
Thornley Cl N17 100 DU52
Thornley Dr, Har. 116 CB61
Thornley Pl SE10 164 EE78
Caradoc St
Thornridge, Brwd. 108 FV45
Thorns Meadow (Brasted), West. 240 EW123
Thornsbeach Rd SE6 183 EC88
Thornsett Pl SE20 202 DV96
Thornsett Rd SE20 202 DV96
Thornsett Rd SW18 180 DB89
Thornside, Edg. 96 CN51
High St
Thornton Av SW2 181 DK88
Thornton Av W4 158 CS77
Thornton Av, Croy. 201 DM100
Thornton Av, West Dr. 154 BM76
Thornton Cl, Guil. 242 AU130
Thornton Cl, Horl. 268 DE148
Thornton Cl, West Dr. 154 BM76
Thornton Ct SW20 199 CX99
Thornton Cres, Couls. 235 DN119
Thornton Dene, Beck. 203 EA96
Thornton Gdns SW12 181 DK88
Thornton Gro, Pnr. 94 CA51
Thornton Hill SW19 179 CY94
Thornton Pl W1 272 E6
Thornton Pl W1 140 DF71
Thornton Pl, Horl. 268 DE148
Thornton Rd E11 123 ED61
Thornton Rd N18 100 DW48
Thornton Rd SW12 181 DK87
Thornton Rd SW14 158 CR83
Thornton Rd SW19 179 CX93
Thornton Rd, Barn. 79 CY41
Thornton Rd, Belv. 167 FB77
Thornton Rd, Brom. 184 EG92
Thornton Rd, Cars. 200 DD102
Thornton Rd, Croy. 201 DM101
Thornton Rd, Ilf. 125 EP63
Thornton Rd, Pot.B. 64 DC30
Thornton Rd, Th.Hth. 201 DM101
Thornton Rd E SW19 179 CX93
Thornton Rd
Thornton Rd Retail Pk, Croy. 201 DM100
Thornton Row, Th.Hth. 201 DN99
London Rd
Thornton St SW9 161 DN82
Thornton St, Hert. 32 DR09
Thornton St, St.Alb. 42 CC19
Thornton Wk, Horl. 268 DE148
Thornton Pl
Thornton Way NW11 120 DB57
Thorntons Fm Av, Rom. 127 FD60
Thorntree Rd SE7 164 EK78
Thornville Gro, Mitch. 200 DC96
Thornville St SE8 163 EA81
Thornwood Cl E18 102 EH54
Thornwood Rd SE13 184 EE85
Thornwood Rd, Epp. 70 EV29
Thorogood Gdns E15 124 EE64
Thorogood Way, Rain. 147 FE67
Thorold Cl, S.Croy. 221 DX110
Thorold Rd N22 99 DL52
Thorold Rd, Ilf. 125 EP61
Thoroughfare, The, Tad. 249 CU125
Thorparch Rd SW8 161 DK81
Thorpe Bypass, Egh. 193 BB96
Thorpe Cl W10 139 CY72
Cambridge Gdns
Thorpe Cl (New Addington), Croy. 221 EC111
Thorpe Cl, Orp. 205 ES103
Thorpe Cres E17 101 DZ54
Thorpe Cres, Wat. 94 BW45
Thorpe Hall Rd E17 101 EC53
Thorpe Ind Est, Egh. 193 BC96
Thorpe Lea Rd, Egh. 173 BB93
Thorpe Lo, Horn. 128 FL59
Thorpe Rd E6 145 EM67
Thorpe Rd E7 124 EF63
Thorpe Rd E17 101 EC54
Thorpe Rd N15 122 DS58
Thorpe Rd, Bark. 145 ER66
Thorpe Rd, Cher. 193 BD99
Thorpe Rd, Kings.T. 178 CL94
Thorpe Rd, St.Alb. 43 CD21
Thorpe Rd, Stai. 173 BD93
Thorpebank Rd W12 139 CU74
Thorpedale Gdns, Ilf. 125 EN56
Thorpedale Rd N4 121 DL60
Thorpefield Cl, St.Alb. 43 CK17
Thorpes Cl, Guil. 242 AU131
Thorpeside Cl, Stai. 193 BE96
Thorpewood Av SE26 182 DV89
Thorpland Av, Uxb. 115 BQ62
Thorsden Cl, Wok. 226 AY118
Thorsden Ct, Wok. 226 AY118
Guildford Rd
Thorsden Way SE19 182 DS91
Oaks Av
Thorverton Rd NW2 119 CY62
Thoydon Rd E3 143 DY68
Thrale Rd SW16 181 DJ92
Thrale St SE1 279 J3
Thrale St SE1 142 DQ74
Thrasher Cl E8 142 DT67
Stean St
Thrawl St E1 142 DT71
Threadneedle St EC2 275 L9
Threadneedle St EC2 142 DR72
Three Arch Rd, Red. 266 DF138
Three Arches Pk, Red. 266 DF138
Three Barrels Wk EC4 275 J10
Three Cherry Trees La, Hem.H. 41 BP16
Three Cl La, Berk. 38 AW20
Three Colt St E14 143 DZ73
Three Colts Cor E2 142 DU70
Weaver St
Three Colts La E2 142 DV70
Three Cors, Bexh. 167 FB82
Three Cors, Hem.H. 40 BN22
Three Cups Yd WC1 274 C7
Three Forests Way, Chig. 104 EW48
Three Forests Way, Epp. 51 EM23
Three Forests Way, Harl. 50 EH18
Three Forests Way (Mark Hall N), Harl. 36 EU10
Three Forests Way, Loug. 84 EK38
The Clay Rd
Three Forests Way, Rom. 104 EW48
Three Forests Way, Wal.Abb. 84 EK36
Three Forests Way (Broadley Common), Wal.Abb. 50 EL21
Three Forests Way, Ware 34 EL12
Three Gates, Guil. 243 BC133
Three Gates Rd (Fawkham Grn), Long. 209 FU102
Three Horseshoes Rd, Harl. 51 EP17
Three Households, Ch.St.G. 90 AT49
Three Kings Rd, Mitch. 200 DG97
Three Kings Yd W1 273 H10
Three Kings Yd W1 141 DH73
Three Mill La E3 143 EC69
Three Oak La SE1 279 P4
Three Oaks Cl, Uxb. 114 BM62
Three Pears Rd, Guil. 243 BD134
Three Quays Wk EC3 279 N1
Three Quays Wk EC3 142 DS73
Threshers Bush, Harl. 36 FA14
Threshers Pl W11 139 CY73
Thriffwood SE26 182 DW90
Thrift, The (Bean), Dart. 189 FW90
Thrift Fm La, Borwd. 78 CP40
Thrift Grn, Brwd. 109 GA48
Knight's Way
Thrift La (Cudham), Sev. 239 ER117
Thrift Vale, Guil. 243 BD131
Thriftfield, Hem.H. 40 BK18
Thrifts Hall Fm Ms, Epp. 85 ET37
Abridge Rd
Thrifts Mead, Epp. 85 ES37
Thrigby Rd, Chess. 216 CM107
Throckmorten Rd E16 144 EH72
Throgmorton Av EC2 275 L8
Throgmorton Av EC2 142 DR72
Throgmorton St EC2 275 L8
Throgmorton St EC2 142 DR72
Throwley Cl SE2 166 EW76
Throwley Rd, Sutt. 218 DB106
Throwley Way, Sutt. 218 DB105
Thrums, The, Wat. 75 BV37
Thrupp Cl, Mitch. 201 DH96
Thrupps Av, Walt. 214 BX106
Thrupps La, Walt. 214 BX106
Thrush Av, Hat. 45 CU20
Thrush Grn, Har. 116 CA56
Thrush Grn, Rick. 92 BJ45
Thrush La (Cuffley), Pot.B. 65 DL28
Thrush St SE17 279 H10
Thruxton Way SE15 162 DT80
Daniel Gdns
Thumbswood, Welw.G.C. 30 DA12
Thumpers, Hem.H. 40 BL18
Thundercourt, Ware 33 DX05
Thunderer Rd, Dag. 146 EY70
Thundridge Cl, Welw.G.C. 30 DB10
Amwell Common
Thurbarn Rd SE6 183 EB92
Thurgood Rd, Hodd. 49 EA15
Thurland Rd SE16 162 DU76
Thurlby Cl, Har. 117 CG58
Gayton Rd
Thurlby Cl, Wdf.Grn. 103 EM50
Thurlby Rd SE27 181 DN91
Thurlby Rd, Wem. 137 CK65
Thurleigh Av SW12 180 DG86
Thurleigh Rd SW12 180 DG86
Thurleston Av, Mord. 199 CY99
Thurlestone Av N12 98 DF51
Thurlestone Av, Ilf. 125 ET63
Thurlestone Cl, Shep. 195 BQ100
Thurlestone Rd SE27 181 DN90
Thurloe Cl SW7 276 B8
Thurloe Cl SW7 160 DE76
Thurloe Gdns, Rom. 127 FF58
Thurloe Pl SW7 276 A8
Thurloe Pl SW7 160 DD77
Thurloe Pl Ms SW7 276 A8
Thurloe Sq SW7 276 B8
Thurloe Sq SW7 160 DE77
Thurloe St SW7 276 A8
Thurloe St SW7 160 DD77
Thurloe Wk, Grays 170 GA76
Thurlow Cl E4 101 EB51
Higham Sta Av
Thurlow Gdns, Ilf. 103 ER51
Thurlow Gdns, Wem. 117 CK64
Thurlow Hill SE21 182 DQ88
Thurlow Pk Rd SE21 181 DP88
Thurlow Rd NW3 120 DD64
Thurlow Rd W7 157 CG75
Thurlow St SE17 279 L10
Thurlow St SE17 162 DR78
Thurlow Ter NW5 120 DG64
Thurlstone Rd, Ruis. 115 BU62
Thurlton Ct, Wok. 226 AY116
Chobham Rd
Thurnby Ct, Twick. 177 CE90
Thurnham Way, Tad. 233 CW120
Thurrock Lakeside, Grays 169 FV77
Thurrock Pk Way, Til. 170 GD80
Thursby Rd, Wok. 226 AU118
Thursland Rd, Sid. 186 EY92
Thursley Cres (New Addington), Croy. 221 ED108
Thursley Gdns SW19 179 CX89
Thursley Rd SE9 185 EM90
Thurso Cl, Rom. 106 FP51
Thurso St SW17 180 DD91
Thurstan Rd SW20 179 CV94
Thurstans, Harl. 51 EQ20
Thurston Rd SE13 163 EB82
Thurston Rd, Slou. 131 AR72
Thurston Rd, Sthl. 136 BZ72
Thurston Rd Ind Est SE13 163 EB83
Jerrard St
Thurtle Rd E2 142 DT67
Thwaite Cl, Erith 167 FC79
Thyer Cl, Orp. 223 EQ105
Isabella Dr
Thyme Ct, Guil. 243 BB131
Mallow Cres
Thyra Gro N12 98 DB51
Tibbatts Rd E3 143 EB70
Tibbenham Wk E13 144 EF68
Tibberton Sq N1 142 DQ66
Popham Rd
Tibbets Cl SW19 179 CX88
Tibbet's Cor SW15 179 CX87
Tibbet's Cor Underpass SW15 179 CX87
West Hill
Tibbet's Ride SW15 179 CX87
Tibbles Cl, Wat. 76 BY35
Tibbs Hill Rd, Abb.L. 59 BT30
Tiber Gdns N1 141 DM67
Treaty St
Ticehurst Cl, Orp. 186 EU94
Grovelands Rd
Ticehurst Rd SE23 183 DY89
Tichborne, Rick. 91 BD50
Tichmarsh, Epsom 216 CQ110
Tickenhall Dr, Harl. 52 EX15
Tickford Cl SE2 166 EW75
Ampleforth Rd
Tidal Basin Rd E16 144 EF73
Tidenham Gdns, Croy. 202 DS104
Tideswell Rd SW15 179 CW85
Tideswell Rd, Croy. 203 EA104
Tideway Cl, Rich. 177 CH91
Locksmeade Rd
Tidey St E3 143 EA71
Tidford Rd, Well. 165 ET82
Tidworth Rd E3 143 EA70
Tidy's La, Epp. 70 EV29
Tiepigs La, Brom. 204 EE103
Tiepigs La, W.Wick. 204 EE103
Tierney Rd SW2 181 DL88
Tiger La, Brom. 204 EH98
Tiger Way E5 122 DV63
Tilbrook Rd SE3 164 EJ83
Tilburstow Hill Rd, Gdse. 252 DW132
Tilbury Cl SE15 162 DT80
Willowbrook Rd
Tilbury Cl, Orp. 206 EV96
Tilbury Docks, Til. 170 GE84
Tilbury Gdns, Til. 171 GG84
Tilbury Hotel Rd, Til. 171 GG84
Tilbury Mead, Harl. 52 EU17
Tilbury Rd E6 145 EM68
Tilbury Rd E10 123 EC59
Tildesley Rd SW15 179 CW86
Tile Fm Rd, Orp. 205 ER104
Tile Kiln Cl, Hem.H. 41 BP21
Tile Kiln Cres, Hem.H. 41 BP21
Tile Kiln La N6 121 DH60
Winchester Rd
Tile Kiln La N13 100 DQ50
Tile Kiln La, Bex. 187 FC89
Tile Kiln La, Hem.H. 40 BN21
Tile Kiln La (Harefield), Uxb. 115 BP59
Tile Yd E14 143 DZ72
Commercial Rd
Tilecroft, Welw.G.C. 29 CX06
Tilegate Rd, Harl. 51 ET17
Tilegate Rd, Ong. 53 FC19
Tilehouse Cl, Borwd. 78 CM41
Tilehouse La, Ger.Cr. 91 BE53
Tilehouse La, Rick. 91 BE53
Tilehouse La (Denham), Uxb. 113 BE58
Tilehouse Rd, Guil. 258 AY138
Tilehouse Way (Denham), Uxb. 113 BF59
Tilehurst La, Dor. 264 CL137
Tilehurst Pt SE2 166 EW75
Yarnton Way
Tilehurst Rd SW18 180 DD88
Tilehurst Rd, Sutt. 217 CY106
Tilekiln Cl, Wal.Cr. 66 DT29
Tiler's Wk, Reig. 266 DC138
Tiler's Way, Reig. 266 DC138
Tileyard Rd N7 141 DL66
Tilford Av (New Addington), Croy. 221 EC109
Tilford Gdns SW19 179 CX89
Tilia Cl, Sutt. 217 CZ106
Tilia Rd E5 122 DV63
Clarence Rd
Tilia Wk SW9 161 DP84
Moorland Rd
Till Av (Farningham), Dart. 208 FM102
Tiller Rd E14 163 EA76
Tillett Cl NW10 138 CQ65
Tillett Sq SE16 163 DY75
Howland Way
Tillett Way E2 142 DU69
Gosset St
Tilley La (Headley), Epsom 232 CQ123
Tillgate Common, Red. 252 DQ133
Tilling Rd NW2 119 CW60
Tilling Way, Wem. 117 CK61
Tillingbourne Gdns N3 119 CZ55
Tillingbourne Grn, Orp. 206 EU98
Tillingbourne Rd (Shalford), Guil. 258 AY140
Tillingbourne Way N3 119 CZ55
Tillingbourne Gdns
Tillingdown Hill, Cat. 236 DU122
Tillingdown La, Cat. 236 DV124
Tillingham Ct, Wal.Abb. 68 EG33
Tillingham Way N12 98 DA49
Tillman St E1 142 DV72
Bigland St
Tilloch St N1 141 DM66
Carnoustie Dr
Tillotson Rd N9 100 DT47
Tillotson Rd, Har. 94 CB52
Tillotson Rd, Ilf. 125 EN59
Tillwicks Rd, Harl. 52 EU17
Tilly's La, Stai. 173 BF91
Tilmans Mead (Farningham), Dart. 208 FM101
Tilney Ct EC1 275 J4
Tilney Dr, Buck.H. 102 EG47
Tilney Gdns N1 142 DR65
Tilney Rd, Dag. 146 EZ65
Tilney Rd, Sthl. 156 BW77
Tilney St W1 276 G2
Tilney St W1 140 DG74
Tilson Gdns SW2 181 DL87
Tilson Ho SW2 181 DL87
Tilson Gdns
Tilson Rd N17 100 DU53
Tilstone Av (Eton Wick), Wind. 151 AL78
Tilstone Cl (Eton Wick), Wind. 151 AL78
Tilsworth Rd, Beac. 110 AJ55
Tilsworth Wk, St.Alb. 43 CJ15
Sandringham Cres
Tilt Cl, Cob. 230 BY116
Tilt Meadow, Cob. 230 BY116
Tilt Rd, Cob. 230 BW115
Tilt Yd App SE9 185 EM86
Tilthams Cor Rd, Gdmg. 258 AV143
Tilthams Grn, Gdmg. 258 AV143
Tilton St SW6 159 CY79
Tiltwood, The W3 138 CQ73
Acacia Rd
Timber Cl, Chis. 205 EN96
Timber Cl (Bookham), Lthd. 246 CC126
Timber Cl, Wok. 211 BF114
Hacketts La
Timber Ct, Grays 170 GA79
Columbia Wf Rd
Timber Hill Rd, Cat. 236 DU124
Timber La, Cat. 236 DU124
Timber Hill Rd
Timber Mill Way SW4 161 DK83
Timber Orchard, Hert. 31 DN05
Timber Pond Rd SE16 163 DX75
Timber Ridge, Rick. 74 BK42
Timber St EC1 275 H4
Timbercroft, Epsom 216 CS105
Timbercroft, Welw.G.C. 29 CZ06
Timbercroft La SE18 165 ES79
Timberdene NW4 97 CX54
Timberdene Av, Ilf. 103 EP53
Timberham Fm Rd, Gat. 268 DD151
Timberham Way, Horl. 268 DE152
Timberhill, Ash. 232 CL119
Ottways La
Timberland Rd E1 142 DV72
Timberling Gdns, S.Croy. 220 DR109
Sanderstead Rd
Timberslip Dr, Wall. 219 DK109
Timbertop Rd (Biggin Hill), West. 238 EJ118
Timberwharf Rd N16 122 DU58
Timberwood, Slou. 111 AR62
Timbrell Pl SE16 143 DZ74
Silver Wk
Time Sq E8 122 DT64
Times Sq, Sutt. 218 DB106
Timothy Cl SW4 181 DJ85
Elms Rd
Timothy Cl, Bexh. 186 EY85
Timothy Ho, Erith 166 EY75
Kale Rd
Timothy Rd E3 143 DZ71
Timperley Gdns, Red. 250 DE132
Timplings Row, Hem.H. 40 BH18
Timsbury Wk SW15 179 CU88
Timsway, Stai. 173 BF92
Tindal St SW9 161 DP81
Tindale Cl, S.Croy. 220 DR111
Tindall Cl, Rom. 106 FM54
Tinderbox All SW14 158 CR83
Tine Rd, Chig. 103 ES50
Tingeys Top La, Enf. 81 DN36
Tinkers La, Wind. 151 AK82
Tinniswood Cl N5 121 DN64
Drayton Pk
Tinsey Cl, Egh. 173 BB92
Tinsley Rd E1 142 DW71
Tintagel Cl, Epsom 217 CT114
Tintagel Cl, Hem.H. 40 BK15
Tintagel Cres SE22 162 DT84
Tintagel Dr, Stan. 95 CK49
Tintagel Gdns SE22 162 DT84
Oxonian St
Tintagel Ho N9 100 DU48
Salisbury Rd
Tintagel Rd, Orp. 206 EW103
Tintagel Way, Wok. 227 BA116
Tintells La (West Horsley), Lthd. 245 BP128
Tintern Av NW9 118 CP55
Tintern Cl SW15 179 CY85
Tintern Cl SW19 180 DC94
Tintern Cl, Slou. 151 AQ76
Tintern Gdns N14 99 DL45
Tintern Path NW9 118 CS58
Ruthin Cl
Tintern Rd N22 100 DQ53
Tintern Rd, Cars. 200 DD102
Tintern St SW4 161 DL84
Tintern Way, Har. 116 CB60
Tinto Rd E16 144 EG70
Tinwell Ms, Borwd. 78 CQ43
Cranes Way
Tinworth St SE11 278 A10
Tinworth St SE11 161 DM78
Tippendell La (Park St), St.Alb. 60 CB26
Tippetts Cl, Enf. 82 DQ39
Tipthorpe Rd SW11 160 DG83
Tipton Cotts, Add. 212 BG105
Oliver Cl
Tipton Dr, Croy. 220 DS105
Tiptree Cl E4 101 EC48
Mapleton Rd
Tiptree Cl, Horn. 128 FN60
Tiptree Cres, Ilf. 125 EN55
Tiptree Dr, Enf. 82 DR42
Tiptree Est, Ilf. 125 EN55
Tiptree Rd, Ruis. 115 BV63
Tiree Cl, Hem.H. 41 BP22
Tirlemont Rd, S.Croy. 220 DQ108
Tirrell Rd, Croy. 202 DQ100
Tisbury Ct W1 141 DK73
Rupert St
Tisbury Rd SW16 201 DL96
Tisdall Pl SE17 279 L9
Tisdall Pl SE17 162 DR77
Titan Rd, Grays 170 GA78
Titan Rd, Hem.H. 40 BM17
Titchborne Row W2 272 C9
Titchfield Rd NW8 140 DF67
Titchfield Rd, Cars. 200 DD102
Titchfield Rd, Enf. 83 DY37
Titchfield Wk, Cars. 200 DD101
Titchfield Rd
Titchwell Rd SW18 180 DD87
Tite Hill, Egh. 172 AX92
Tite St SW3 160 DF78
Tithe Barn Cl, Kings.T. 198 CM95
Tithe Barn Cl, St.Alb. 42 CC23
Tithe Barn Ct, Abb.L. 59 BT29
Dairy Way
Tithe Barn Dr, Maid. 150 AE78
Tithe Barn Est, St.Alb. 42 CC24
Tithe Barn Way, Nthlt. 135 BV69
Tithe Cl NW7 97 CU53
Tithe Cl, Hayes 135 BT71
Gledwood Dr
Tithe Cl, Maid. 150 AC78
Tithe Cl, Walt. 195 BV100
Tithe Ct, Slou. 153 BA77
Tithe Fm Av, Har. 116 CA62
Tithe Fm Cl, Har. 116 CA62
Tithe La (Wraysbury), Stai. 173 BA86
Tithe Meadow, Wat. 75 BR44
Tithe Meadows, Vir.W. 192 AX100
Tithe Wk NW7 97 CU53
Tithebarns La (Send), Wok. 244 BG126
Tithelands, Harl. 51 EM18
Tithepit Shaw La, Warl. 236 DV115
Titian Av, Bushey 95 CE45
Titley Cl E4 101 EA50
Titmus Cl, Uxb. 135 BQ72
Titmuss Av SE28 146 EV73
Titmuss St W12 159 CW75
Goldhawk Rd
Titsey Hill (Titsey), Oxt. 238 EF123
Titsey Rd, Oxt. 254 EH125
Tiverton Av, Ilf. 125 EN55
Tiverton Dr SE9 185 EQ88
Tiverton Gro, Rom. 106 FN50
Tiverton Ho, Enf. 83 DX41
Tiverton Rd N15 122 DR58
Tiverton Rd N18 100 DS50
Tiverton Rd NW10 139 CX67
Tiverton Rd, Edg. 96 CM54
Tiverton Rd, Houns. 156 CC82
Tiverton Rd, Pot.B. 64 DD31
Tiverton Rd, Ruis. 115 BU62
Tiverton Rd, Th.Hth. 201 DN99
Willett Rd
Tiverton Rd, Wem. 138 CL68
Tiverton St SE1 279 H7
Tiverton St SE1 162 DQ76
Tiverton Way, Chess. 215 CJ106
Tivoli Ct SE16 163 DZ75
Tivoli Gdns SE18 164 EL77
Tivoli Rd N8 121 DK57
Tivoli Rd SE27 182 DQ92
Tivoli Rd, Houns. 156 BY84
Toad La, Houns. 156 BZ84
Tobacco Dock E1 142 DV73
Tobacco Quay E1 142 DV73
Wapping La
Tobago St E14 163 EA75
Manilla St
Tobin Cl NW3 140 DE66
Toby La E1 143 DY70
Toby Way, Surb. 198 CP103
Tockley Rd (Burnham), Slou. 130 AH69
Todd Cl, Rain. 148 FK70
Toddbrook, Harl. 51 EP16
Harberts Rd
Todds Cl, Horl. 268 DE146
Todds Wk N7 121 DM61
Andover Rd
Toft Av, Grays 170 GD77
Token Yd SW15 159 CY84
Montserrat Rd
Tokenhouse Yd EC2 275 K8
Tokyngton Av, Wem. 138 CN65
Toland Sq SW15 179 CU85
Tolcarne Dr, Pnr. 115 BV55
Toldene Ct, Couls. 235 DM120
Toley Av, Wem. 118 CL59
Toll Bar Ct, Sutt. 218 DB109
Tollbridge Cl W10 139 CY70
Kensal Rd
Tolldene Cl (Knaphill), Wok. 226 AS117
Robin Hood Rd
Tollers La, Couls. 235 DM119
Tollesbury Gdns, Ilf. 125 ER55
Tollet St E1 143 DX70
Tollgate, Guil. 243 BD133
Tollgate Av, Red. 266 DF139
Tollgate Cl, Rick. 73 BF41
Tollgate Dr SE21 182 DS89
Tollgate Dr, Hayes 136 BX73
Tollgate Gdns NW6 140 DB68
Tollgate Rd E6 144 EK71
Tollgate Rd E16 144 EJ71

Tollgate Rd, Dart. 189 FR87
Tollgate Rd, Dor. 263 CH139
Tollgate Rd, Hat. 44 CS24
Tollgate Rd (Colney Heath), St.Alb. 44 CS24
Tollgate Rd, Wal.Cr. 83 DX35
Tollhouse La, Wall. 219 DJ109
Tollhouse Way N19 121 DJ61
Tollington Pk N4 121 DM61
Tollington Pl N4 121 DM61
Tollington Rd N7 121 DM63
Tollington Way N7 121 DL62
Tollpit End, Hem.H. 40 BG17
Tolmers Av (Cuffley), Pot.B. 65 DL28
Tolmers Gdns (Cuffley), Pot.B. 65 DL29
Tolmers Ms (Newgate St), Hert. 65 DL25
Tolmers Pk (Newgate St), Hert. 65 DL25
Tolmers Rd (Cuffley), Pot.B. 65 DL27
Tolmers Sq NW1 273 L4
Tolpits Cl, Wat. 75 BT43
Tolpits La, Wat. 75 BT44
Tolpuddle Av E13 144 EJ67
Rochester Av
Tolpuddle St N1 141 DN68
Tolsford Rd E5 122 DV64
Tolson Rd, Islw. 157 CG83
Tolvaddon, Wok. 226 AU117
Cardingham
Tolverne Rd SW20 199 CW95
Tolworth Cl, Surb. 198 CP102
Tolworth Gdns, Rom. 126 EX57
Tolworth Pk Rd, Surb. 198 CM103
Tolworth Ri N, Surb. 198 CQ101
Elmbridge Av
Tolworth Ri S, Surb. 198 CQ102
Warren Dr S
Tolworth Rd, Surb. 198 CL103
Tolworth Twr, Surb. 198 CP103
Tom Coombs Cl SE9 164 EL84
Well Hall Rd
Tom Cribb Rd SE28 165 EQ76
Tom Gros Cl E15 123 ED64
Maryland St
Tom Hood Cl E15 123 ED64
Maryland St
Tom Jenkinson Rd E16 144 EG74
Tom Mann Cl, Bark. 145 ES67
Tom Nolan Cl E15 144 EE68
Tom Smith Cl SE10 164 EE79
Maze Hill
Tom Thumbs Arch E3 143 EA68
Malmesbury Rd
Tom Williams Ho SW6 159 CZ79
Clem Attlee Ct
Tomahawk Gdns, Nthlt. 136 BX69
Javelin Way
Tomkins Cl, Borwd. 78 CL39
Tallis Way
Tomkyns La, Upmin. 129 FR56
Tomlin Cl, Epsom 216 CR111
Tomlin Rd, Slou. 131 AL70
Tomlins Gro E3 143 EA69
Tomlins Orchard, Bark. 145 EQ67
Tomlins Ter E14 143 DZ71
Rhodeswell Rd
Tomlins Wk N7 121 DM61
Briset Way
Tomlinson Cl E2 142 DT69
Tomlinson Cl W4 158 CP78
Oxford Rd N
Tomlyns Cl, Brwd. 109 GE44
Tomo Ind Est, Uxb. 134 BJ72
Tompion St EC1 274 F3
Toms Cft, Hem.H. 40 BL21
Toms Hill, Kings L. 58 BJ33
Bucks Hill
Toms Hill, Rick. 74 BL36
Toms La, Abb.L. 59 BR28
Toms La, Kings L. 59 BP29
Tomsfield, Hat. 44 CS19
Tomswood Ct, Ilf. 103 EQ53
Tomswood Hill, Ilf. 103 EP52
Tomswood Rd, Chig. 103 EN51
Tonbridge Cl, Bans. 218 DF114
Tonbridge Cres, Har. 118 CL56
Tonbridge Ho SE25 202 DU97
Tonbridge Rd, Rom. 106 FK52
Tonbridge Rd, Sev. 257 FJ127
Tonbridge Rd, W.Mol. 196 BY98
Tonbridge St WC1 273 P2
Tonbridge St WC1 141 DL69
Tonbridge Wk WC1 141 DL69
Tonbridge St
Tonfield Rd, Sutt. 199 CZ102
Tonge Cl, Beck. 203 EA99
Tonsley Hill SW18 180 DB85
Tonsley Pl SW18 180 DB85
Tonsley Rd SW18 180 DB85
Tonsley St SW18 180 DB85
Tonstall Rd, Epsom 216 CR110
Tonstall Rd, Mitch. 200 DG96
Tony Cannell Ms E3 143 DZ69
Maplin St
Tooke Cl, Pnr. 94 BY53
Tookey Cl, Har. 118 CM59
Took's Ct EC4 274 D8
Tooley St SE1 279 L2
Tooley St SE1 142 DR74
Tooley St (Northfleet), Grav. 190 GD87
Toorack Rd, Har. 95 CD54
Toot Hill Rd, Ong. 71 FF29
Tooting Bec Gdns SW16 181 DK91
Tooting Bec Rd SW16 180 DG90
Tooting Bec Rd SW17 180 DG90
Tooting Gro SW17 180 DE92
Tooting High St SW17 180 DE93
Tootswood Rd, Brom. 204 EE99
Tooveys Mill Cl, Kings L. 58 BN28
Top Dartford Rd, Dart. 187 FF94
Top Dartford Rd, Swan. 187 FF94
Top Ho Ri E4 101 EC45
Parkhill Rd
Top Pk, Beck. 204 EE99
Top Pk, Ger.Cr. 112 AW58
Topaz Cl, Slou. 131 AP74
Pearl Gdns
Topaz Wk NW2 119 CX59
Marble Dr
Topcliffe Dr, Orp. 223 ER105
Topham Sq N17 100 DQ53
Topham St EC1 274 D4
Topiary, The, Ash. 232 CL120
Topiary Sq, Rich. 158 CM83
Topland Rd (Chalfont St. Peter), Ger.Cr. 90 AX52
Toplands Av, S.Ock. 148 FP74
Topley St SE9 164 EK84
Topmast Pt E14 163 EA75
Topp Wk NW2 119 CW61
Topping La, Uxb. 134 BK69
Topsfield Cl N8 121 DK57
Wolseley Rd
Topsfield Par N8 121 DL57
Tottenham La
Topsfield Rd N8 121 DL57
Topsham Rd SW17 180 DF90
Tor Gdns W8 160 DA75
Tor La, Wey. 213 BQ111
Tor Rd, Well. 166 EW81
Torbay Rd NW6 139 CZ66
Torbay Rd, Har. 116 BY61
Torbay St NW1 141 DH66
Hawley Rd
Torbitt Way, Ilf. 125 ET57
Torbridge Cl, Edg. 96 CL52
Torbrook Cl, Bex. 186 EY86
Torcross Dr SE23 182 DW89
Torcross Rd, Ruis. 115 BV62
Torin Ct (Englefield Grn), Egh. 172 AW92
Torland Dr (Oxshott), Lthd. 215 CD114
Tormead Cl, Sutt. 218 DA107
Tormead Rd, Guil. 243 AZ134
Tormount Rd SE18 165 ES79
Toronto Av E12 125 EM63
Toronto Dr, Horl. 269 DN148
Toronto Rd E11 123 ED63
Toronto Rd, Ilf. 125 EP60
Toronto Rd, Til. 171 GG82
Torquay Gdns, Ilf. 124 EK56
Torquay Spur, Slou. 131 AP70
Torquay St W2 140 DB71
Harrow Rd
Torr Rd SE20 183 DX94
Torrance Cl, Horn. 127 FH60
Torre Wk, Cars. 200 DE102
Torrens Cl, Guil. 242 AU131
Torrens Rd E15 144 EF65
Torrens Rd SW2 181 DM85
Torrens Sq E15 144 EE65
Torrens St EC1 274 E1
Torrens St EC1 141 DN68
Torrens Wk, Grav. 191 GL92
Torres Sq E14 163 EA78
Maritime Quay
Torriano Av NW5 121 DK64
Torriano Cotts NW5 121 DJ64
Torriano Av
Torriano Ms NW5 121 DK64
Torriano Av
Torridge Gdns SE15 162 DW84
Torridge Rd, Slou. 153 BB79
Torridge Rd, Th.Hth. 201 DP99
Torridge Wk, Hem.H. 40 BM15
The Dee
Torridon Cl, Wok. 226 AV117
Torridon Rd SE6 183 ED88
Torridon Rd SE13 183 ED87
Torrington Av N12 98 DD50
Torrington Cl N12 98 DD49
Torrington Cl (Claygate), Esher 215 CE107
Torrington Dr, Har. 116 CB63
Torrington Dr, Loug. 85 EQ42
Torrington Dr, Pot.B. 64 DD32
Torrington Gdns N11 99 DJ51
Torrington Gdns, Grnf. 137 CJ66
Torrington Gdns, Loug. 85 EQ42
Torrington Gro N12 98 DE50
Torrington Pk N12 98 DD50
Torrington Pl E1 142 DU74
Torrington Pl WC1 273 M6
Torrington Pl WC1 141 DK71
Torrington Rd E18 124 EG55
Torrington Rd, Berk. 38 AV19
Torrington Rd, Dag. 126 EZ60
Torrington Rd (Claygate), Esher 215 CE107
Torrington Rd, Grnf. 137 CJ67
Torrington Rd, Ruis. 115 BT62
Torrington Sq WC1 273 N5
Torrington Sq WC1 141 DK70
Torrington Sq, Croy. 202 DR101
Tavistock Gro
Torrington Way, Mord. 200 DA100
Tortoiseshell Way, Berk. 38 AT17
Torver Rd, Har. 117 CE56
Torver Way, Orp. 205 ER104
Torwood Cl, Berk. 38 AT19
Torwood La, Whyt. 236 DT120
Torwood Rd SW15 179 CU85
Toryhill Rd, Borwd. 78 CM39
Tothill St SW1 277 M5
Tothill St SW1 161 DK75
Totnes Rd, Well. 166 EV80
Totnes Wk N2 120 DD56
Tottan Ter E1 143 DX72
Tottenhall Rd N13 99 DN51
Tottenham Ct Rd W1 273 L5
Tottenham Ct Rd W1 141 DJ70
Tottenham Grn E N15 122 DT56
Tottenham La N8 121 DL57
Tottenham Ms W1 273 L6
Tottenham Rd N1 142 DS65
Tottenham St W1 273 L7
Tottenham St W1 141 DJ71
Totterdown St SW17 180 DF91
Totteridge Common N20 97 CU47
Totteridge Grn N20 98 DA47
Totteridge Ho SW11 160 DD82
Totteridge La N20 98 DA47
Totteridge Rd, Enf. 83 DX37
Totteridge Village N20 97 CY46
Totternhoe Cl, Har. 117 CJ57
Totton Rd, Th.Hth. 201 DN97
Toulmin Dr, St.Alb. 42 CC16
Toulmin St SE1 279 H5
Toulmin St SE1 162 DQ75
Toulon St SE5 162 DQ80
Tournay Rd SW6 159 CZ80
Toussaint Wk SE16 162 DU76
John Roll Way
Tovey Av, Hodd. 49 EA15
Tovey Cl (London Colney), St.Alb. 61 CK26
Tovey Cl, Wal.Abb. 50 EE23
Tovil Cl SE20 202 DU96
Towcester Rd E3 143 EB70
Tower, The, Couls. 235 DK122
Netherne La
Tower 42 EC2 275 M8
Tower 42 EC2 142 DS72
Tower Br E1 279 P3
Tower Br E1 142 DT74
Tower Br SE1 279 P3
Tower Br SE1 142 DT74
Tower Br App E1 279 P2
Tower Br App E1 142 DT74
Tower Br Piazza SE1 142 DT74
Horselydown La
Tower Br Rd SE1 279 M7
Tower Br Rd SE1 162 DS76
Tower Cen, Hodd. 49 EA17
Tower Cl NW3 120 DD64
Lyndhurst Rd
Tower Cl SE20 182 DV94
Tower Cl, Berk. 38 AU20
Tower Cl, Epp. 53 FD24
Tower Cl, Grav. 191 GL92
Tower Cl (Flackwell Heath), H.Wyc. 110 AC56
Tower Cl, Horl. 268 DF148
Tower Cl, Ilf. 103 EP51
Tower Cl, Orp. 205 ET103
Tower Cl, Wok. 226 AX117
Tower Ct WC2 273 P9
Tower Ct, Brwd. 108 FV47
Tower Cft (Eynsford), Dart. 208 FL103
High St
Tower Gdns (Claygate), Esher 215 CG108
Tower Gdns Rd N17 100 DQ53
Tower Gro, Wey. 195 BS103
Tower Hamlets Rd E7 124 EF63
Tower Hamlets Rd E17 123 EA55
Tower Hts, Hodd. 49 EA17
Amwell St
Tower Hill EC3 279 N1
Tower Hill EC3 142 DS73
Tower Hill, Brwd. 108 FW47
Tower Hill, Dor. 263 CH138
Tower Hill (Gomshall), Guil. 261 BQ140
Tower Hill, Kings L. 57 BE29
Tower Hill La (Gomshall), Guil. 261 BR141
Tower Hill La (Sandridge), St.Alb. 28 CM10
Tower Hill Ri (Gomshall), Guil. 261 BQ140
Tower Hill Rd, Dor. 263 CH138
Tower Hill Ter EC3 142 DS73
Byward St
Tower La, Wem. 117 CK62
Main Dr
Tower Ms E17 123 EA56
Tower Mill Rd SE15 162 DS79
Wells Way
Tower Pk Rd, Dart. 187 FE85
Tower Pier EC3 279 N2
Tower Pier EC3 142 DT74
Tower Pl EC3 279 N1
Tower Pt, Enf. 82 DR42
Tower Retail Pk, Dart. 187 FE85
Tower Ri, Rich. 158 CL83
Jocelyn Rd
Tower Rd NW10 139 CU66
Tower Rd (Coleshill), Amer. 55 AN43
Tower Rd, Belv. 167 FC77
Tower Rd, Bexh. 167 FB84
Tower Rd, Dart. 188 FJ86
Tower Rd, Epp. 69 ES30
Tower Rd, Orp. 205 ET103
Tower Rd, Tad. 233 CW123
Tower Rd, Twick. 177 CF90
Tower Rd, Ware 33 DY05
Tower Royal EC4 275 J10
Tower St WC2 273 N9
Tower St WC2 141 DK72
Tower St, Hert. 32 DQ07
Tower Ter N22 99 DM54
Mayes Rd
Tower Vw, Croy. 203 DX101
Towers, The, Ken. 236 DQ115
Towers Av (Hillingdon), Uxb. 135 BQ69
Towers Pl, Rich. 178 CL85
Eton St
Towers Rd, Grays 170 GC78
Towers Rd, Hem.H. 40 BL19
Towers Rd, Pnr. 94 BY53
Towers Rd, Sthl. 136 CA70
Towers Wk, Wey. 213 BP107
Towers Wd (South Darenth), Dart. 209 FR95
Towfield Rd, Felt. 176 BZ89
Towing Path, Guil. 258 AW138
Towing Path Wk N1 141 DL67
York Way
Town, The, Enf. 82 DR41
Town Br Ct, Chesh. 54 AP32
Water Meadow
Town Cen, Hat. 45 CU17
Town Ct Path N4 122 DQ60
Town End, Cat. 236 DS122
Town End Cl, Cat. 236 DS122
Town Fm Way (Stanwell), Stai. 174 BK87
Town La
Town Fld La, Ch.St.G. 90 AW48
Town Fld Way, Islw. 157 CG82
Town Hall App N16 122 DS63
Milton Gro
Town Hall App Rd N15 122 DT56
Town Hall Av W4 158 CR78
Town Hall Rd SW11 160 DF83
Town La (Wooburn Grn), H.Wyc. 110 AD59
Town La (Stanwell), Stai. 174 BK86
Town Meadow, Brent. 157 CK80
Town Mill Ms, Hert. 32 DQ09
Millbridge
Town Path, Egh. 173 BA92
Town Pier, Grav. 191 GH86
West St
Town Quay, Bark. 145 EP67
Town Rd N9 100 DV47
Town Sq, Erith 167 FE79
Pier Rd
Town Sq, Wok. 227 AZ117
Church St E
Town Sq Cres (Bluewater), Green. 189 FT87
Town Tree Rd, Ashf. 174 BN92
Towncourt Cres, Orp. 205 EQ99
Towncourt La, Orp. 205 ER100
Towney Mead, Nthlt. 136 BZ68
Towney Mead Ct, Nthlt. 136 BZ68
Towney Mead
Townfield, Chesh. 54 AP32
Townfield, Rick. 92 BJ45
Townfield Cor, Grav. 191 GJ88
Townfield Ct, Dor. 263 CG137
Horsham Rd
Townfield Rd, Dor. 263 CG137
Townfield Rd, Hayes 135 BT74
Townfield Sq, Hayes 135 BT73
Townfields, Hat. 45 CU17
Towngate, Cob. 230 BY115
Townholm Cres W7 157 CF76
Townley Ct E15 144 EF65
Townley Rd SE22 182 DS85
Townley Rd, Bexh. 186 EZ85
Townley St SE17 279 K10
Townmead, Red. 252 DR133
Townmead Rd SW6 160 DC82
Townmead Rd, Rich. 158 CP82
Townmead Rd, Wal.Abb. 67 EC34
Townsend, Hem.H. 40 BK18
Townsend Av N14 99 DK49
Townsend Av, St.Alb. 43 CE19
Townsend Dr, St.Alb. 43 CD18
Townsend Ind Est NW10 138 CR68
Townsend La NW9 118 CR59
Townsend La, Wok. 227 BB121
St. Peters Rd
Townsend Rd N15 122 DT57
Townsend Rd, Ashf. 174 BL92
Townsend Rd, Chesh. 54 AP30
Townsend Rd, Sthl. 136 BY74
Townsend St SE17 279 L9
Townsend St SE17 162 DR77
Townsend Way, Nthwd. 93 BT52
Townsend Yd N6 121 DH60
Townshend Cl, Sid. 186 EV93
Townshend Est NW8 140 DE68
Townshend Rd NW8 140 DE67
Townshend Rd, Chis. 185 EP92
Townshend Rd, Rich. 158 CM84
Townshend St, Hert. 32 DS09
Townshend Ter, Rich. 158 CM84
Townshott Cl (Bookham), Lthd. 246 CA126
Townslow La (Wisley), Wok. 228 BJ116
Townson Av, Nthlt. 135 BU69
Townson Way, Nthlt. 135 BU68
Townson Av
Towpath, Shep. 194 BM103
Towpath Wk E9 123 DZ64
Towpath Way, Croy. 202 DT100
Towton Rd SE27 182 DQ89
Toynbec Cl, Chis. 185 EP91
Beechwood Ri
Toynbee Rd SW20 199 CY95
Toynbee St E1 275 P7
Toynbee St E1 142 DT71
Toyne Way N6 120 DF58
Gaskell Rd
Tozer Wk, Wind. 151 AK83
Tracery, The, Bans. 234 DB115
Tracey Av NW2 119 CW64
Tracious Cl, Wok. 226 AV116
Sythwood
Tracious La, Wok. 226 AV116
Tracy Ct, Stan. 95 CJ52
Tracyes Rd, Harl. 52 EV17
Trade Cl N13 99 DN49
Trader Rd E6 145 EP72
Tradescant Rd SW8 161 DL80
Trading Est Rd NW10 138 CQ70
Trafalgar Av N17 100 DS51
Trafalgar Av SE15 162 DT78
Trafalgar Av, Brox. 49 DZ21
Trafalgar Av, Wor.Pk. 199 CX102
Trafalgar Business Cen, Bark. 145 ET70
Trafalgar Cl SE16 163 DY77
Greenland Quay
Trafalgar Ct E1 142 DW73
Glamis Rd
Trafalgar Ct, Cob. 213 BU113
Trafalgar Dr, Walt. 195 BV104
Trafalgar Gdns E1 143 DX71
Trafalgar Gdns W8 160 DB76
South End Row
Trafalgar Gro SE10 163 ED79
Trafalgar Pl E11 124 EG56
Trafalgar Pl N18 100 DU50
Trafalgar Rd SE10 163 ED79
Trafalgar Rd SW19 180 DB94
Trafalgar Rd, Dart. 188 FL89
Trafalgar Rd, Grav. 191 GG87
Trafalgar Rd, Rain. 147 FF68
Trafalgar Rd, Twick. 177 CD89
Trafalgar Sq SW1 277 N2
Trafalgar Sq SW1 141 DK74
Trafalgar Sq WC2 277 N2
Trafalgar Sq WC2 141 DK74
Trafalgar St SE17 279 K10
Trafalgar St SE17 162 DR78
Trafalgar Ter, Har. 117 CE60
Nelson Rd
Trafalgar Way E14 143 EC74
Trafalgar Way, Croy. 201 DM103
Trafford Cl E15 123 EB64
Trafford Cl, Ilf. 103 ET51
Trafford Cl, Rad. 62 CL32
Trafford Rd, Th.Hth. 201 DM99
Tralee Ct SE16 162 DV78
Masters Dr
Tramway Av E15 144 EE66
Tramway Av N9 100 DV45
Tramway Path, Mitch. 200 DF99
Tranby Pl E9 123 DX64
Homerton High St
Tranley Ms NW3 120 DE63
Fleet Rd
Tranmere Rd N9 100 DT45
Tranmere Rd SW18 180 DC89
Tranmere Rd, Twick. 176 CB87
Tranquil Dale (Buckland), Bet. 249 CT132
Tranquil Pas SE3 164 EF82
Tranquil Vale
Tranquil Ri, Erith 167 FE78
West St
Tranquil Vale SE3 164 EE82
Transay Wk N1 142 DR65
Marquess Rd
Transept St NW1 272 B7
Transept St NW1 140 DE71
Transmere Cl, Orp. 205 EQ100
Transmere Rd, Orp. 205 EQ100
Transom Cl SE16 163 DY77
Plough Way
Transom Sq E14 163 EB78
Transport Av, Brent. 157 CH78
Tranton Rd SE16 162 DU76
Trapps La, Chesh. 54 AR32
Traps Hill, Loug. 85 EM41
Traps La, N.Mal. 198 CS95
Trapstyle Rd, Ware 32 DU05
Trasher Mead, Dor. 263 CJ139
Travellers Cl, Hat. 45 CW23
Travellers La, Hat. 45 CU19
Travellers La (Welham Grn), Hat. 45 CW22
Travellers Way, Houns. 156 BW82
Travers Cl E17 101 DX53
Travers Rd N7 121 DN62
Travic Rd, Slou. 131 AM69
Travis Ct (Farnham Royal), Slou. 131 AP69
Treachers Cl, Chesh. 54 AP31
Treacy Cl, Bushey 94 CC47
Treadgold St W11 139 CX73
Treadway St E2 142 DV68
Treadwell Rd, Epsom 232 CS115
Treaty Cen, Houns. 156 CB83
Treaty Rd, Houns. 156 CB83
Hanworth Rd
Treaty St N1 141 DM67
Trebble Rd, Swans. 190 FY86
Trebeck St W1 277 H2
Trebellan Dr, Hem.H. 40 BM19
Trebovir Rd SW5 160 DA78
Treby St E3 143 DZ70
Trecastle Way N7 121 DK63
Carleton Rd
Tredegar Ms E3 143 DZ69
Tredegar Ter
Tredegar Rd E3 143 DZ68
Tredegar Rd N11 99 DK52
Tredegar Rd, Dart. 187 FG89
Tredegar Sq E3 143 DZ69
Tredegar Ter E3 143 DZ69
Trederwen Rd E8 142 DU67
Tredown Rd SE26 182 DW92
Tredwell Cl SW2 181 DM89
Hillside Rd
Tredwell Cl, Brom. 204 EL98
Tredwell Rd SE27 181 DP91
Tree Cl, Rich. 177 CK88
Tree Rd E16 144 EJ72
Tree Tops, Brwd. 108 FW46
Tree Way, Reig. 250 DB131
Treebourne Rd (Biggin Hill), West. 238 EJ117
Treebys Av, Guil. 242 AX128
Treelands (North Holmwood), Dor. 263 CJ139
Treen Av SW13 159 CT83
Treeside Cl, West Dr. 154 BK77
Treetops, Grav. 191 GH92
Treetops, Whyt. 236 DU118
Treetops Cl SE2 166 EY78
Treetops Cl, Nthwd. 93 BR50
Treetops Vw, Loug. 84 EJ44
Treeview Cl SE19 202 DS95
Treewall Gdns, Brom. 184 EH91
Trefgarne Rd, Dag. 126 FA61
Trefil Wk N7 121 DL63
Trefoil Ho, Erith 166 EY75
Kale Rd
Trefoil Rd SW18 180 DC85
Trefusis Wk, Wat. 75 BS39
Tregaron Av N8 121 DL58
Tregaron Gdns, N.Mal. 198 CS98
Avenue Rd
Tregarth Pl, Wok. 226 AT117
Tregarthen Pl, Lthd. 231 CJ121
Tregarvon Rd SW11 160 DG84
Tregelles Rd, Hodd. 33 EA14
Tregenna Av, Har. 116 BZ63
Tregenna Cl N14 81 DJ43
Tregenna Ct, Har. 116 CA63
Trego Rd E9 143 EA66
Tregony Rd, Orp. 223 ET105
Tregothnan Rd SW9 161 DL83
Tregunter Rd SW10 160 DC79
Trehearn Rd, Ilf. 103 ER52
Trehern Rd SW14 158 CR83
Treherne Ct SW9 161 DN81
Eythorne Rd
Treherne Ct SW17 180 DG91
Trehurst St E5 123 DY64
Trelawn Cl (Ottershaw), Cher. 211 BC108
Trelawn Rd E10 123 EC62
Trelawn Rd SW2 181 DN85
Trelawney Av, Slou. 152 AX76
Trelawney Cl E17 123 EB56
Orford Rd
Trelawney Est E9 142 DW65
Trelawney Gro, Wey. 212 BN107
Trelawney Rd, Ilf. 103 ER52
Trellick Twr W10 139 CZ70
Trellis Sq E3 143 DZ69
Malmesbury Rd
Treloar Gdns SE19 182 DR93
Hancock Rd
Tremadoc Rd SW4 161 DK84
Tremaine Cl SE4 163 EA82
Tremaine Gro, Hem.H. 40 BL16
Tremaine Rd SE20 202 DV96
Trematon Pl, Tedd. 177 CJ94
Tremlett Gro N19 121 DJ62
Tremlett Ms N19 121 DJ62
Trenance, Wok. 226 AU117
Cardingham
Trenance Gdns, Ilf. 126 EU62
Trench Yd Ct, Mord. 200 DB100
Green La
Trenchard Av, Ruis. 115 BV63
Trenchard Cl NW9 96 CS53
Fulbeck Dr
Trenchard Cl, Stan. 95 CG51
Trenchard Cl, Walt. 214 BW106
Trenchard Ct, Mord. 200 DB100
Green La
Trenchard St SE10 163 ED78
Trenches La, Slou. 133 BA73
Trenchold St SW8 161 DL79
Trenear Cl, Orp. 224 EU105
Trenham Dr, Warl. 236 DW116
Trenholme Cl SE20 182 DV94
Trenholme Ct, Cat. 236 DU122
Trenholme Rd SE20 182 DV94
Trenholme Ter SE20 182 DV94
Trenmar Gdns NW10 139 CV69
Trent Av W5 157 CJ76
Trent Av, Upmin. 129 FR58
Trent Cl, Rad. 62 CL32
Edgbaston Dr
Trent Gdns N14 81 DH44
Trent Rd SW2 181 DM85
Trent Rd, Buck.H. 102 EH46
Trent Rd, Slou. 153 BB79
Trent Way, Hayes 135 BS68
Trent Way, Wor.Pk. 199 CW104
Trentbridge Cl, Ilf. 103 ET51
Trentham Cres, Wok. 227 BA121
Trentham Dr, Orp. 206 EU98
Trentham Rd, Red. 266 DF136
Trentham St SW18 180 DA88
Trentwood Side, Enf. 81 DM41
Treport St SW18 180 DB87
Tresco Cl, Brom. 184 EE93
Tresco Gdns, Ilf. 126 EU61
Tresco Rd SE15 162 DV84
Tresco Rd, Berk. 38 AT19
Trescoe Gdns, Har. 116 BY59
Trescoe Gdns, Rom. 105 FC50
Tresham Cres NW8 272 B4
Tresham Cres NW8 140 DE70
Tresham Rd, Bark. 145 ET66
Tresham Wk E9 122 DW64
Churchill Wk
Tresilian Av N21 81 DM43
Tresilian Sq, Hem.H. 40 BM15
Tresillian Way, Wok. 226 AU116
Tressell Cl N1 141 DP66
Sebbon St
Tressillian Cres SE4 163 EA83
Tressillian Rd SE4 163 DZ84
Tresta Wk, Wok. 226 AU115

Trestis Cl, Hayes 136 BY71
Jollys La
Treston Ct, Stai. 173 BF92
Treswell Rd, Dag. 146 EY67
Tretawn Gdns NW7 96 CS49
Tretawn Pk NW7 96 CS49
Trevalga Way, Hem.H. 40 BL16
Trevanion Rd W14 159 CY78
Treve Av, Har. 116 CC59
Trevellance Way, Wat. 60 BW33
Trevelyan Av E12 125 EM63
Trevelyan Cl, Dart. 168 FM84
Trevelyan Cres, Har. 117 CK59
Trevelyan Gdns NW10 139 CW67
Trevelyan Rd E15 124 EF63
Trevelyan Rd SW17 180 DE92
Trevelyan Way, Berk. 38 AV17
Trevera Ct, Wal.Cr. 67 DY33
Eleanor Rd
Trevereux Hill, Oxt. 255 EM131
Treveris St SE1 278 F3
Treverton St W10 139 CX70
Treves Cl N21 81 DM43
Treville St SW15 179 CV87
Treviso Rd SE23 183 DX89
Farren Rd
Trevithick Cl, Felt. 175 BT88
Trevithick Dr, Dart. 168 FM84
Trevithick St SE8 163 EA78
Trevone Gdns, Pnr. 116 BY58
Trevor Cl, Barn. 80 DD43
Trevor Cl, Brom. 204 EF101
Trevor Cl, Har. 95 CF52
Kenton La
Trevor Cl, Islw. 177 CF85
Trevor Cl, Nthlt. 136 BW68
Trevor Cres, Ruis. 115 BT63
Trevor Gdns, Edg. 96 CR53
Trevor Gdns, Nthlt. 136 BW68
Trevor Gdns, Ruis. 115 BU63
Clyfford Rd
Trevor Pl SW7 276 C5
Trevor Pl SW7 160 DE75
Trevor Rd SW19 179 CY94
Trevor Rd, Edg. 96 CR53
Trevor Rd, Hayes 155 BS75
Trevor Rd, Wdf.Grn. 102 EG52
Trevor Sq SW7 276 D5
Trevor Sq SW7 160 DF75
Trevor St SW7 276 C5
Trevor St SW7 160 DE75
Trevor Wk SW7 160 DF75
Trevor Sq
Trevose Av, W.Byf. 211 BF114
Trevose Rd E17 101 ED53
Trevose Way, Wat. 94 BW48
Trewarden Av, Iver 133 BD68
Trewenna Dr, Chess. 215 CK106
Trewenna Dr, Pot.B. 64 DD32
Trewince Rd SW20 199 CW95
Trewint St SW18 180 DC89
Trewsbury Ho SE2 166 EX75
Hartslock Dr
Trewsbury Rd SE26 183 DX92
Triandra Way, Hayes 136 BX71
Triangle, The EC1 141 DP70
Goswell Rd
Triangle, The N13 99 DN49
Lodge Dr
Triangle, The, Bark. 145 EQ65
Tanner St
Triangle, The, Hmptn. 196 CC95
High St
Triangle, The, Kings.T. 198 CQ96
Kenley Rd
Triangle, The, Wok. 226 AW118
Triangle Ct E16 144 EK71
Tollgate Rd
Triangle Est SE11 161 DM78
Kennington La
Triangle Pas, Barn. 80 DC42
Station App
Triangle Pl SW4 161 DK84
Triangle Rd E8 142 DV67
Trident Cen, Wat. 76 BW39
Trident Gdns, Nthlt. 136 BX69
Jetstar Way
Trident Ind Est, Hodd. 49 EC17
Trident Ind Est (Colnbrook), Slou. 153 BE83
Trident Rd, Wat. 59 BT34
Trident St SE16 163 DX77
Trident Way, Sthl. 155 BV76
Trig La EC4 275 H10
Trigg's Cl, Wok. 226 AX119
Trigg's La, Wok. 226 AW118
Trigo Ct, Epsom 216 CR111
Blakeney Cl
Trigon Rd SW8 161 DM80
Trilby Rd SE23 183 DX89
Trim St SE14 163 DZ79
Trimmer Wk, Brent. 158 CL79
Trinder Gdns N19 121 DL60
Trinder Rd
Trinder Rd N19 121 DL60
Trinder Rd, Barn. 79 CW43
Trindles Rd (South Nutfield), Red. 267 DM136
Tring Av W5 138 CM74
Tring Av, Sthl. 136 BZ72
Tring Av, Wem. 138 CN65
Tring Cl, Ilf. 125 EQ57
Tring Cl, Rom. 106 FM49
Tring Gdns, Rom. 106 FL49
Tring Grn, Rom. 106 FM49
Tring Wk, Rom. 106 FL49
Tring Gdns
Tringham Cl (Ottershaw), Cher. 211 BC107
Trinidad Gdns, Dag. 147 FD66
Trinidad St E14 143 DZ73
Trinity Av N2 120 DD55
Trinity Av, Enf. 82 DT44
Trinity Buoy Wf E14 144 EF73
Trinity Ch Pas SW13 159 CV79
Trinity Ch Rd SW13 159 CV79
Trinity Ch Sq SE1 279 J6
Trinity Ch Sq SE1 162 DQ76
Trinity Chyd, Guil. 258 AX136
High St
Trinity Cl E8 142 DT65
Trinity Cl E11 124 EE61
Trinity Cl NW3 120 DD63
Hampstead High St
Trinity Cl SE13 163 ED84
Wisteria Rd
Trinity Cl, Brom. 204 EL102
Trinity Cl, Houns. 156 BY84
Trinity Cl, Nthwd. 93 BS51
Trinity Cl, S.Croy. 220 DS109
Trinity Cl (Stanwell), Stai. 174 BJ86
Trinity Cotts, Rich. 158 CM83
Trinity Rd
Trinity Ct N1 142 DS66
Downham Rd
Trinity Ct NW2 119 CW63
Anson Rd
Trinity Ct SE7 164 EK77
Charlton La
Trinity Cres SW17 180 DF89
Trinity Gdns E16 144 EF70
Cliff Wk
Trinity Gdns SW9 161 DM84
Trinity Gdns, Dart. 188 FK86
Summerhill Rd
Trinity Gro SE10 163 EC81
Trinity Gro, Hert. 32 DQ07
Trinity Hall Cl, Wat. 76 BW41
Trinity La, Wal.Cr. 67 DY32
Trinity Ms SE20 202 DV95
Trinity Ms W10 139 CX72
Cambridge Gdns
Trinity Ms, Hem.H. 41 BR21
Pancake La
Trinity Path SE26 182 DW90
Trinity Pl, Bexh. 166 EZ84
Trinity Pl, Wind. 151 AQ82
Trinity Ri SW2 181 DN88
Trinity Rd N2 120 DD55
Trinity Rd N22 99 DL53
Trinity Rd SW17 180 DF89
Trinity Rd SW18 180 DD85
Trinity Rd SW19 180 DA93
Trinity Rd, Grav. 191 GJ87
Trinity Rd, Hert. 32 DW12
Trinity Rd, Ilf. 125 EQ55
Trinity Rd, Rich. 158 CM83
Trinity Rd, Sthl. 136 BY74
Trinity Rd, Ware 33 DY05
Trinity Sq EC3 279 N1
Trinity Sq EC3 142 DS73
Trinity St E16 144 EG71
Vincent St
Trinity St SE1 279 J5
Trinity St SE1 162 DQ75
Trinity St, Enf. 82 DQ40
Trinity Wk NW3 140 DC65
Trinity Wk, Hem.H. 41 BR21
Pancake La
Trinity Wk, Hert. 32 DW12
Trinity Way E4 101 DZ51
Trinity Way W3 138 CS73
Trio Pl SE1 279 J5
Tripps Hill, Ch.St.G. 90 AU48
Tripps Hill Cl, Ch.St.G. 90 AU48
Tripton Rd, Harl. 51 ES16
Tristan Sq SE3 164 EE83
Tristram Cl E17 123 ED55
Tristram Rd, Brom. 184 EF91
Triton Sq NW1 273 K4
Triton Sq NW1 141 DJ70
Triton Way, Hem.H. 40 BM18
Tritton Av, Croy. 219 DL105
Tritton Rd SE21 182 DR90
Trittons, Tad. 233 CW121
Triumph Cl (Chafford Hundred), Grays 169 FW77
Triumph Cl, Hayes 155 BQ80
Triumph Ho, Bark. 146 EV69
Triumph Rd E6 145 EM72
Trivett Cl, Green. 189 FU85
Trocadero Shop Cen W1 141 DK73
Trodd's La, Guil. 259 BF135
Trojan Ct NW6 139 CY66
Willesden La
Trojan Way, Croy. 201 DM104
Trolling Down Hill, Dart. 188 FP89
Troon Cl SE16 162 DV78
Masters Dr
Troon Cl SE28 146 EX72
Fairway Dr
Troon St E1 143 DY72
Troopers Dr, Rom. 106 FK49
Trosley Av, Grav. 191 GH89
Trosley Rd, Belv. 166 FA79
Trossachs Rd SE22 182 DS85
Trothy Rd SE1 162 DU77
Monnow Rd
Trotsworth Av, Vir.W. 192 AX98
Trotsworth Ct, Vir.W. 192 AY98
Trott Rd N10 98 DF52
Trott St SW11 160 DE81
Trotter Way, Epsom 216 CN112
Abbots Av
Trotters Bottom, Barn. 79 CU37
Trotters Gap, Ware 33 ED11
Trotters La (Mimbridge), Wok. 210 AV112
Trotters Rd, Harl. 52 EU17
Trotts La, West. 255 EQ127
Trotwood, Chig. 103 ER51
Trotwood Cl, Brwd. 108 FY46
Middleton Rd
Troughton Rd SE7 164 EH78
Trout La, West Dr. 134 BJ73
Trout Ri, Rick. 74 BH41
Trout Rd, West Dr. 134 BK74
Troutbeck Cl, Slou. 132 AU73
Troutbeck Rd SE14 163 DY81
Troutstream Way, Rick. 74 BH42
Trouvere Pk, Hem.H. 40 BH18
Trouville Rd SW4 181 DJ86
Trowbridge Est E9 143 DZ65
Osborne Rd
Trowbridge Rd E9 143 DZ65
Trowbridge Rd, Rom. 106 FK51
Trowers Way, Red. 251 DH131
Trowley Ri, Abb.L. 59 BS31
Trowlock Av, Tedd. 177 CJ93
Trowlock Island, Tedd. 177 CK92
Trowlock Way, Tedd. 177 CK93
Troy Cl, Tad. 233 CV120
Troy Ct SE18 165 EP77
Troy Rd SE19 182 DR93
Troy Town SE15 162 DU83
Trubshaw Rd, Sthl. 156 CB76
Havelock Rd
Truesdale Dr (Harefield), Uxb. 114 BJ57
Truesdale Rd E6 145 EM72
Trulock Ct N17 100 DU52
Trulock Rd N17 100 DU52
Truman Cl, Edg. 96 CP52
Pavilion Way
Truman's Rd N16 122 DS64
Trump St EC2 275 J9
Trumper Way, Slou. 131 AM74
Trumper Way, Uxb. 134 BJ67
Trumpers Way W7 157 CE76
Trumpets Hill Rd, Reig. 265 CU135
Trumpington Dr, St.Alb. 43 CD23
Trumpington Rd E7 124 EF63
Trumps Grn Av, Vir.W. 192 AX100
Trumps Grn Cl, Vir.W. 192 AY99
Trumps Grn Rd
Trumps Grn Rd, Vir.W. 192 AX100
Trumps Mill La, Vir.W. 193 AZ100
Trundle St SE1 279 H4
Trundlers Way, Bushey 95 CE46
Trundleys Rd SE8 163 DX78
Trundleys Ter SE8 163 DX77
Trunks All, Swan. 207 FB96
Trunley Heath Rd (Bramley), Guil. 258 AW144
Truro Gdns, Ilf. 124 EL59
Truro Rd E17 123 DZ56
Truro Rd N22 99 DL52
Truro Rd, Grav. 191 GK90
Truro St NW5 140 DG65
Truro Wk, Rom. 106 FJ51
Saddleworth Rd
Truro Way, Hayes 135 BS69
Portland Rd
Truslove Rd SE27 181 DN92
Trussley Rd W6 159 CW76
Trust Rd, Wal.Cr. 67 DY34
Trust Wk SE21 181 DP88
Peabody Hill
Trustees Way (Denham), Uxb. 113 BF57
Trustons Gdns, Horn. 127 FG59
Tryfan Cl, Ilf. 124 EK57
Tryon Cres E9 142 DV67
Clermont Rd
Tryon St SW3 276 D10
Tryon St SW3 160 DF78
Trys Hill (Lyne), Cher. 193 AZ103
Trystings Cl (Claygate), Esher 215 CG107
Tuam Rd SE18 165 ER79
Tubbenden Cl, Orp. 205 ES103
Tubbenden Dr, Orp. 223 ER105
Tubbenden La, Orp. 205 ES104
Tubbenden La S, Orp. 223 ER106
Tubbs Rd NW10 139 CT68
Tubs Hill Par, Sev. 256 FG124
Tubwell Rd (Stoke Poges), Slou. 132 AV67
Tuck Rd, Rain. 147 FG65
Tucker Rd (Ottershaw), Cher. 211 BD107
Tucker St, Wat. 76 BW43
Tuckey Gro (Ripley), Wok. 227 BF124
Tudor Av, Hmptn. 176 CA93
Tudor Av, Rom. 127 FG55
Tudor Av (Cheshunt), Wal.Cr. 66 DU31
Tudor Av, Wat. 76 BX37
Tudor Av, Wor.Pk. 199 CV104
Tudor Circle, Gdmg. 258 AS144
Tudor Cl N6 121 DJ59
Tudor Cl NW3 120 DE64
Tudor Cl NW7 97 CU51
Tudor Cl NW9 118 CQ61
Tudor Cl SW2 181 DM86
Elm Pk
Tudor Cl, Ashf. 174 BL91
Tudor Cl, Bans. 233 CY115
Tudor Cl, Brwd. 109 FZ44
Tudor Cl, Chess. 216 CL106
Tudor Cl, Chig. 103 EN49
Tudor Cl, Chis. 205 EM95
Tudor Cl, Cob. 214 BZ113
Tudor Cl, Couls. 235 DN118
Tudor Cl, Dart. 187 FH86
Tudor Cl, Epsom 217 CT110
Tudor Cl (Northfleet), Grav. 190 GE88
Tudor Cl, Hat. 44 CS21
Tudor Cl, Horl. 269 DP148
Tudor Cl (Bookham), Lthd. 230 CA124
Tudor Cl, Pnr. 115 BU57
Tudor Cl, S.Croy. 236 DV115
Tudor Cl, Sutt. 217 CX106
Tudor Cl, Wall. 219 DJ108
Tudor Cl (Cheshunt), Wal.Cr. 66 DV31
Tudor Cl, Ware 34 EK07
Tudor Cl, Wok. 227 BA117
Tudor Cl, Wdf.Grn. 102 EH50
Tudor Ct E17 123 DY59
Tudor Ct, Borwd. 78 CL40
Tudor Ct, Felt. 176 BW91
Tudor Ct, Swan. 207 FC101
Tudor Ct N, Wem. 118 CN64
Tudor Ct S, Wem. 118 CN64
Tudor Cres, Enf. 81 DP39
Tudor Cres, Ilf. 103 EP51
Tudor Dr (Wooburn Grn), H.Wyc. 110 AD55
Tudor Dr, Kings.T. 178 CL92
Tudor Dr, Mord. 199 CX100
Tudor Dr, Rom. 127 FG56
Tudor Dr, Walt. 196 BX102
Tudor Dr, Wat. 76 BX38
Tudor Est NW10 138 CP68
Tudor Gdns NW9 118 CQ61
Tudor Gdns SW13 158 CS83
Treen Av
Tudor Gdns W3 138 CN72
Tudor Gdns, Har. 95 CD54
Tudor Rd
Tudor Gdns, Rom. 127 FG56
Tudor Gdns, Slou. 130 AJ71
Tudor Gdns, Twick. 177 CF88
Tudor Gdns, Upmin. 128 FQ61
Tudor Gdns, W.Wick. 203 EC104
Tudor Gro E9 142 DW66
Tudor Gro N20 98 DE48
Church Cres
Tudor Ho, Surb. 198 CN102
Lenelby Rd
Tudor La (Old Windsor), Wind. 172 AW87
Tudor Manor Gdns, Wat. 60 BX32
Tudor Ms, Rom. 127 FF57
Eastern Rd
Tudor Par, Rick. 92 BG45
Berry La
Tudor Pk, Amer. 55 AR37
Tudor Pl W1 273 M8
Tudor Pl, Mitch. 180 DE94
Tudor Ri, Brox. 49 DY21
Tudor Rd E4 101 EB51
Tudor Rd E6 144 EJ67
Tudor Rd E9 142 DV67
Tudor Rd N9 100 DV45
Tudor Rd SE19 182 DT94
Tudor Rd SE25 202 DV99
Tudor Rd, Ashf. 175 BR93
Tudor Rd, Bark. 145 ET67
Tudor Rd, Barn. 80 DA41
Tudor Rd, Beck. 203 EB97
Tudor Rd, Gdmg. 258 AS144
Tudor Rd, Hmptn. 176 CA94
Tudor Rd, Har. 95 CD54
Tudor Rd, Hayes 135 BR72
Tudor Rd (Hazlemere), H.Wyc. 88 AC45
Tudor Rd, Houns. 157 CD84
Tudor Rd, Kings.T. 178 CN94
Tudor Rd, Pnr. 94 BW54
Tudor Rd, St.Alb. 43 CE16
Tudor Rd (Wheathampstead), St.Alb. 28 CL07
Tudor Rd, Sthl. 136 BY73
Tudor Sq, Hayes 135 BR71
Tudor St EC4 274 E10
Tudor St EC4 141 DN73
Tudor Wk, Bex. 186 EY86
Tudor Wk, Lthd. 231 CF120
Tudor Wk, Wat. 76 BX37
Tudor Wk, Wey. 195 BP104
West Palace Gdns
Tudor Way N14 99 DK46
Tudor Way W3 158 CN75
Tudor Way, Hert. 31 DN09
Tudor Way, Orp. 205 ER100
Tudor Way, Rick. 92 BG46
Tudor Way, Uxb. 134 BN65
Tudor Way, Wal.Abb. 67 ED33
Tudor Way, Wind. 151 AL81
Tudor Well Cl, Stan. 95 CH50
Tudors, The, Reig. 250 DC131
Tudorwalk, Grays 170 GA76
Thurloe Wk
Tudway Rd SE3 164 EH83
Tufnail Rd, Dart. 188 FM86
Tufnell Pk Rd N7 121 DJ63
Tufnell Pk Rd N19 121 DJ63
Tufter Rd, Chig. 103 ET50
Tufton Gdns, W.Mol. 196 CB96
Tufton Rd E4 101 EA49
Tufton St SW1 277 N6
Tufton St SW1 161 DK76
Tugboat St SE28 165 ES75
Tugela Rd, Croy. 202 DR100
Tugela St SE6 183 DZ89
Tugmutton Cl, Orp. 223 EP105
Acorn Way
Tuilerie St E2 142 DU68
Tulip Cl E6 145 EM71
Bradley Stone Rd
Tulip Cl, Brwd. 108 FV43
Poppy Cl
Tulip Cl, Croy. 203 DX102
Tulip Cl, Hmptn. 176 BZ93
Partridge Rd
Tulip Cl, Rom. 106 FK51
Cloudberry Rd
Tulip Cl, Sthl. 156 CC75
Chevy Rd
Tulip Ct, Pnr. 116 BW55
Tulip Gdns, Ilf. 145 EP65
Tulip Tree Ct, Sutt. 218 DA111
The Cres
Tulip Way, West Dr. 154 BK76
Tull St, Mitch. 200 DF101
Tulse Cl, Beck. 203 EC97
Tulse Hill SW2 181 DN86
Tulse Hill Est SW2 181 DN86
Tulsemere Rd SE27 182 DQ89
Tulyar Cl, Tad. 233 CV120
Tumber St (Headley), Epsom 248 CQ125
Tumbler Rd, Harl. 52 EU17
Tumblewood Rd, Bans. 233 CY116
Tumbling Bay, Walt. 195 BU100
Tummons Gdns SE25 202 DS96
Tun Yd SW8 161 DH82
Peardon St
Tuncombe Rd N18 100 DS49
Tunfield Rd, Hodd. 33 EB14
Tunis Rd W12 139 CV74
Tunley Grn E14 143 DZ71
Burdett Rd
Tunley Rd NW10 138 CS67
Tunley Rd SW17 180 DG88
Tunmarsh La E13 144 EJ69
Tunmers End (Chalfont St. Peter), Ger.Cr. 90 AW53
Tunnan Leys E6 145 EN72
Tunnel Av SE10 163 ED75
Tunnel Est, Grays 169 FT77
Tunnel Gdns N11 99 DJ52
Tunnel Rd SE16 162 DW75
St. Marychurch St
Tunnel Rd, Reig. 250 DA133
Church St
Tunnel Wd Cl, Wat. 75 BT37
Tunnel Wd Rd, Wat. 75 BT37
Tunnmeade, Harl. 36 EU14
Tuns La, Slou. 151 AQ76
Tunsgate, Guil. 258 AX136
Tunsgate Sq Shop Cen, Guil. 258 AX136
High St
Tunstall Av, Ilf. 104 EU51
Tunstall Cl, Orp. 223 ES105
Tunstall Rd SW9 161 DM84
Tunstall Rd, Croy. 202 DS102
Tunstall Wk, Brent. 158 CL79
Tunstock Way, Belv. 166 EY76
Tunworth Cl NW9 118 CQ58
Tunworth Cres SW15 179 CT86
Tupelo Rd E10 123 EB61
Tuppers Ct (Albury), Guil. 260 BJ139
Tupwood Ct, Cat. 252 DU125
Tupwood La, Cat. 252 DU125
Tupwood Scrubbs Rd, Cat. 252 DU128
Turenne Cl SW18 160 DC84
Turfhouse La (Chobham), Wok. 210 AS109
Turin Rd N9 100 DW45
Turin St E2 142 DU69
Turkey Oak Cl SE19 202 DS95
Turkey St, Enf. 82 DV37
Turks Cl, Uxb. 134 BN69
Harlington Rd
Turk's Head Yd EC1 274 F6
Turks Row SW3 276 E10
Turks Row SW3 160 DF78
Turle Rd N4 121 DM60
Turle Rd SW16 201 DL96
Turlewray Cl N4 121 DM60
Turley Cl E15 144 EE67
Turmore Dale, Welw.G.C. 29 CW10
Turnagain La EC4 274 F8
Turnagain La, Dart. 187 FG90
Turnage Rd, Dag. 126 EY60
Turnberry Cl NW4 97 CX54
Turnberry Cl SE16 162 DV78
Ryder Dr
Turnberry Ct, Wat. 94 BW48
Turnberry Dr (Bricket Wd), St.Alb. 60 BY30
Turnberry Quay E14 163 EB76
Pepper St
Turnberry Way, Orp. 205 ER102
Turnbull Cl, Green. 189 FS87
Turnbury Cl SE28 146 EX72
Turnchapel Ms SW4 161 DH83
Cedars Rd
Turner Av N15 122 DS56
Turner Av, Mitch. 200 DF95
Turner Av, Twick. 176 CC90
Turner Cl NW11 120 DB58
Turner Cl SW9 161 DP81
Turner Cl, Guil. 243 AZ131
Turner Cl, Hayes 135 BQ68
Charville La
Turner Cl, Wem. 117 CK64
Turner Ct, Dart. 188 FJ85
Turner Dr NW11 120 DB58
Turner Pl SW11 180 DE85
Cairns Rd
Turner Rd E17 123 EC55
Turner Rd, Bushey 76 CC42
Turner Rd (Bean), Dart. 189 FV90
Turner Rd, Edg. 118 CM55
Turner Rd, N.Mal. 198 CR101
Turner Rd, Slou. 152 AW75
Turner Rd (Biggin Hill), West. 222 EJ112
Turner St E1 142 DV71
Turner St E16 144 EF72
Turners Cl, Stai. 174 BH92
Turners Gdns, Sev. 257 FJ128
Turners Hill, Hem.H. 40 BL21
Turners Hill (Cheshunt), Wal.Cr. 67 DX30
Turners La, Walt. 213 BV107
Turners Meadow Way, Beck. 203 DZ95
Turners Rd E3 143 DZ71
Turners Way, Croy. 201 DN103
Turners Wd NW11 120 DC59
Turners Wd Dr, Ch.St.G. 90 AX48
Turneville Rd W14 159 CZ79
Turney Rd SE21 182 DR87
Turneys Orchard, Rick. 73 BD43
Turnham Cl, Guil. 258 AW138
Turnham Grn Ter W4 158 CS77
Turnham Grn Ter Ms W4 158 CS77
Turnham Grn Ter
Turnham Rd SE4 183 DY85
Turnmill St EC1 274 E5
Turnmill St EC1 141 DN70
Turnoak Av, Wok. 226 AY120
Turnoak La, Wok. 226 AY119
Wych Hill La
Turnpike Pk, Wind. 151 AL84
Turnpike Cl SE8 163 DZ80
Amersham Vale
Turnpike Dr, Orp. 224 EW109
Turnpike Grn, Hem.H. 40 BL16
Turnpike Ho EC1 274 G3
Turnpike Ho EC1 141 DP69
Turnpike La N8 121 DM56
Turnpike La, Sutt. 218 DC106
Turnpike La, Til. 171 GK78
Turnpike La, Uxb. 134 BL69
Turnpike Link, Croy. 202 DS103
Turnpike Way, Islw. 157 CG81
Turnpin La SE10 163 EC79
Turnstone Cl E13 144 EG69
Turnstone Cl NW9 96 CS54
Kestrel Cl
Turnstone Cl, S.Croy. 221 DY110
Turnstone Cl (Ickenham), Uxb. 115 BP64
Turnstones, The, Grav. 191 GK89
Turnstones, The, Wat. 76 BY36
Turp Av, Grays 170 GC75
Turpentine La SW1 277 J10
Turpin Av, Rom. 104 FA52
Turpin Cl, Enf. 83 EA38
Government Row
Turpin La, Erith 167 FG80
Turpin Rd, Felt. 175 BT86
Staines Rd
Turpin Way N19 121 DK61
Elthorne Rd
Turpin Way, Wall. 219 DH108
Turpington Cl, Brom. 204 EL100
Turpington La, Brom. 204 EL101
Turpins Cl, Hert. 31 DM09
Turpins La, Wdf.Grn. 103 EM50
Turquand St SE17 279 J9
Turret Gro SW4 161 DJ83
Turton Rd, Wem. 118 CL64
Turton Way, Slou. 151 AR76
Turville Ct, Lthd. 246 CB125
Proctor Gdns
Turville St E2 275 P4
Tuscan Rd SE18 165 ER78
Tuskar St SE10 164 EE78
Tustin Est SE15 162 DW79
Tuttlebee La, Buck.H. 102 EG47
Tuxford Cl, Borwd. 78 CL38
Twankhams All, Epp. 70 EU30
Hemnall St
Tweed Cl, Berk. 38 AV18
Tweed Glen, Rom. 105 FD52
Tweed Grn, Rom. 105 FE52
Tweed La (Strood Grn), Bet. 264 CP139
Tweed Rd, Slou. 153 BA79
Tweed Way, Rom. 105 FD52
Tweedale Ct E15 123 EC64
Tweeddale Gro, Uxb. 115 BQ62
Tweeddale Rd, Cars. 200 DD102
Tweedmouth Rd E13 144 EH68
Tweedy Cl, Enf. 82 DT43
Tweedy Rd, Brom. 204 EG95
Tweenways, Chesh. 54 AR30
Tweezer's All WC2 274 D10
Twelve Acre Cl (Bookham), Lthd. 230 BZ124
Twelve Acres, Welw.G.C. 29 CY11
Twelvetrees Cres E3 143 EC70
Twentyman Cl, Wdf.Grn. 102 EG50
Twickenham Br, Rich. 177 CJ85
Twickenham Br, Twick. 177 CJ85
Twickenham Cl, Croy. 201 DM104
Twickenham Gdns, Grnf. 117 CG64
Twickenham Gdns, Har. 95 CE52
Twickenham Rd E11 123 ED61
Twickenham Rd, Felt. 176 BZ90
Twickenham Rd, Islw. 157 CG83
Twickenham Rd, Rich. 157 CJ84
Twickenham Rd, Tedd. 177 CG92
Twickenham Trd Est, Twick. 177 CF86
Twig Folly Cl E2 143 DX68
Roman Rd
Twigg Cl, Erith 167 FE80
Twilley St SW18 180 DB87
Twin Tumps Way SE28 146 EU73
Twinches La, Slou. 131 AP74
Twine Cl, Bark. 146 EV69
Thames Rd
Twine Ct E1 142 DW73
Twine Ter E3 143 DZ70
Ropery St
Twineham Grn N12 98 DA49
Tillingham Way
Twining Av, Twick. 176 CC90
Twinn Rd NW7 97 CY51
Twinoaks, Cob. 214 CA113
Twisden Rd NW5 121 DH63
Twisleton Ct, Dart. 188 FK86
Priory Hill

Twitchells La (Jordans), Beac. 90 AT51
Twitton La (Otford), Sev. 241 FD115
Twitton Meadows (Otford), Sev. 241 FE116
Two Acres, Welw.G.C. 29 CZ11
Two Dells La (Ashley Grn), Chesh. 38 AT24
Two Mile Dr, Slou. 151 AL75
Two Rivers Retail Pk, Stai. 173 BE91
Two Waters Rd, Hem.H. 40 BJ24
Twybridge Way NW10 138 CQ66
Twycross Ms SE10 164 EE77
Blackwall La
Twyford Abbey Rd NW10 138 CM69
Twyford Av N2 120 DF55
Twyford Av W3 138 CN73
Twyford Cres W3 138 CN74
Twyford Ho N15 122 DS58
Chisley Rd
Twyford Pl WC2 274 B8
Twyford Rd, Cars. 200 DD102
Twyford Rd, Har. 116 CB60
Twyford Rd, Ilf. 125 EQ64
Twyford Rd, St.Alb. 43 CJ16
Twyford St N1 141 DM67
Twyner Cl, Horl. 269 DK147
Twysdens Ter, Hat. 45 CW24
Dellsome La
Tyas Rd E16 144 EF70
Tybenham Rd SW19 200 DA97
Tyberry Rd, Enf. 82 DV41
Tyburn La, Har. 117 CE59
Tyburn Way W1 272 E10
Tyburn Way W1 140 DF73
Tyburns, The, Brwd. 109 GC47
Tycehurst Hill, Loug. 85 EM42
Tychbourne Dr, Guil. 243 BC131
Tydcombe Rd, Warl. 236 DW119
Tye Grn Village, Harl. 51 ET18
Tye La, Epsom 248 CR127
Tye La, Orp. 223 EQ106
Tye La, Tad. 249 CT128
Dorking Rd
Tyers Est SE1 279 M4
Tyers Est SE1 162 DS75
Tyers Gate SE1 279 M4
Tyers St SE11 278 B10
Tyers St SE11 161 DM78
Tyers Ter SE11 161 DM78
Tyeshurst Cl SE2 166 EY78
Tyfield Cl (Cheshunt), Wal.Cr. 66 DW30
Tykeswater La, Borwd. 77 CJ39
Tyle Grn, Horn. 128 FL56
Tyle Pl (Old Windsor), Wind. 172 AU85
Tylecroft Rd SW16 201 DL96
Tylehost, Guil. 242 AU130
Tylehurst Gdns, Ilf. 125 EQ64
Tyler Cl E2 142 DT68
Tyler Gdns, Add. 212 BJ105
Tyler Gro, Dart. 168 FM84
Spielman Rd
Tyler Rd, Sthl. 156 CB76
McNair Rd
Tyler St SE10 164 EE78
Tyler Way, Brwd. 108 FV46
Tylers Causeway, Hert. 47 DH23
Tylers Cl, Gdse. 252 DV130
Tylers Cl, Kings L. 58 BL28
Tylers Cl, Loug. 102 EL45
Tyler's Ct W1 273 M9
Tylers Cres, Horn. 128 FJ64
Tylers Gate, Har. 118 CL58
Tylers Grn Rd, Swan. 207 FC100
Tylers Hill Rd, Chesh. 56 AT30
Tylers Path, Cars. 218 DF105
Rochester Rd
Tylers Rd, Harl. 50 EJ19
Tylers Way, Wat. 77 CD42
Tylersfield, Abb.L. 59 BT31
Tylney Av SE19 182 DT92
Tylney Cft, Harl. 51 EP17
Tylney Rd E7 124 EJ63
Tylney Rd, Brom. 204 EK96
Tylsworth Cl, Amer. 55 AR38
Tymperley Ct SW19 179 CY88
Windlesham Gro
Tynan Cl, Felt. 175 BU88
Sandycombe Rd
Tyndale Ct E14 163 EB77
Tyndale La N1 141 DP66
Upper St
Tyndale Ter N1 141 DP66
Canonbury La
Tyndall Rd E10 123 EC61
Tyndall Rd, Well. 165 ET83
Tyne Cl, Upmin. 129 FR58
Tyne Gdns, S.Ock. 148 FQ73
Tyne St E1 142 DT72
Old Castle St
Tynedale (London Colney), St.Alb. 62 CM27
Thamesdale
Tynedale Cl, Dart. 189 FR88
Tynedale Rd (Strood Grn), Bet. 264 CP138
Tyneham Rd SW11 160 DG82
Tynemouth Cl E6 145 EP72
Covelees Wall
Tynemouth Dr, Enf. 82 DU38
Tynemouth Rd N15 122 DT56
Tynemouth Rd SE18 165 ET78
Tynemouth Rd, Mitch. 180 DG94
Tynemouth St SW6 160 DC82
Tynley Gro, Guil. 242 AX128
Type St E2 143 DX68
Typleden Cl, Hem.H. 40 BK18
Tyrawley Rd SW6 160 DB81
Tyre La NW9 118 CS56
Sheaveshill Av
Tyrell Cl, Har. 117 CE63
Tyrell Ct, Cars. 218 DF105
Tyrell Gdns, Wind. 151 AM83
Tyrell Ri, Brwd. 108 FW50
Tyrells Cl, Upmin. 128 FN61
Tyrols Rd SE23 183 DX88
Wastdale Rd
Tyron Way, Sid. 185 ES91
Tyrone Rd E6 145 EM68
Tyrrel Way NW9 119 CT59
Tyrrell Av, Well. 186 EU85
Tyrrell Rd SE22 162 DU84
Tyrrell Sq, Mitch. 200 DE95
Tyrrells Hall Cl, Grays 170 GD79
Tyrwhitt Av, Guil. 242 AV130
Tyrwhitt Rd SE4 163 EA83
Tysea Cl, Harl. 51 ET18
Tysea Hill, Rom. 105 FF45
Tysea Rd, Harl. 51 ET18
Tysoe Av, Enf. 83 DZ36
Tysoe St EC1 274 D3
Tyson Rd SE23 182 DW87
Tyssen Pas E8 142 DT65
Tyssen Pl, S.Ock. 149 FW69
Tyssen Rd N16 122 DT62
Tyssen St E8 142 DT65
Tyssen St N1 275 N1
Tythebarn Cl, Guil. 243 BB129
Dairyman's Wk
Tytherton Rd N19 121 DK62
Tyttenhanger Grn (Tyttenhanger), St.Alb. 43 CK23

U

Uamvar St E14 143 EB71
Uckfield Gro, Mitch. 200 DG95
Uckfield Rd, Enf. 83 DX37
Udall Gdns, Rom. 104 FA51
Udall St SW1 277 L9
Udney Pk Rd, Tedd. 177 CG92
Uffington Rd NW10 139 CU67
Uffington Rd SE27 181 DN91
Ufford Cl, Har. 94 CB52
Ufford Rd
Ufford Rd, Har. 94 CB52
Ufford St SE1 278 E4
Ufford St SE1 161 DN75
Ufton Gro N1 142 DR66
Ufton Rd N1 142 DR66
Uhura Sq N16 122 DS62
Ujima Ct SW16 181 DL91
Sunnyhill Rd
Ullathorne Rd SW16 181 DJ91
Ulleswater Rd N14 99 DL49
Ullin St E14 143 EC71
St. Leonards Rd
Ullswater Business Pk, Couls. 235 DL116
Ullswater Cl SW15 178 CR91
Ullswater Cl, Brom. 184 EE93
Ullswater Cl, Hayes 135 BS68
Ullswater Cl, Slou. 130 AJ71
Buttermere Av
Ullswater Ct, Har. 116 CA59
Oakington Av
Ullswater Cres SW15 178 CR91
Ullswater Cres, Couls. 235 DL116
Ullswater Rd SE27 181 DP89
Ullswater Rd SW13 159 CU80
Ullswater Rd, Hem.H. 41 BQ22
Ullswater Way, Horn. 127 FG64
Ulstan Cl (Woldingham), Cat. 237 EA123
Ulster Gdns N13 100 DQ49
Ulster Pl NW1 273 H5
Ulster Ter NW1 273 H4
Ulundi Rd SE3 164 EE79
Ulva Rd SW15 179 CX85
Ravenna Rd
Ulverscroft Rd SE22 182 DT85
Ulverston Rd E17 101 ED54
Ulverstone Rd SE27 181 DP89
Ulwin Av (Byfleet), W.Byf. 212 BL113
Ulysses Rd NW6 119 CZ64
Umberston St E1 142 DV72
Hessel St
Umberville Way, Slou. 131 AM70
Umbria St SW15 179 CU86
Umfreville Rd N4 121 DP58
Underacres Cl, Hem.H. 40 BN19
Undercliff Rd SE13 163 EA83
Underhill, Barn. 80 DA43
Underhill Pk Rd, Reig. 250 DA131
Underhill Pas NW1 141 DH67
Camden High St
Underhill Rd SE22 182 DV86
Underhill St NW1 141 DH67
Camden High St
Underne Av N14 99 DH47
Underriver Ho Rd (Underriver), Sev. 257 FP130
Undershaft EC3 275 M9
Undershaft EC3 142 DS72
Undershaw Rd, Brom. 184 EE90
Underwood (New Addington), Croy. 221 EC106
Underwood, The SE9 185 EM89
Underwood Rd E1 142 DU70
Underwood Rd E4 101 EB50
Underwood Rd, Cat. 252 DS126
Underwood Rd, Wdf.Grn. 102 EK52
Underwood Row N1 275 J2
Underwood Row N1 142 DQ69
Underwood St N1 275 J2
Underwood St N1 142 DQ69
Undine Rd E14 163 EB77
Undine St SW17 180 DF92
Uneeda Dr, Grnf. 137 CD67
Unicorn Ho, Brom. 204 EG97
Elmfield Rd
Unicorn Wk, Green. 189 FT85
Union Cl E11 123 ED63
Union Cotts E15 144 EE66
Welfare Rd
Union Ct EC2 275 M8
Union Ct, Rich. 178 CL85
Eton St
Union Dr E1 143 DY70
Canal Cl
Union Grn, Hem.H. 40 BK19
Church St
Union Gro SW8 161 DK82
Union Pk NW10 138 CQ69
Acton La
Union Rd N11 99 DK51
Union Rd SW4 161 DK82
Union Rd SW8 161 DK82
Union Rd, Brom. 204 EK99
Union Rd, Croy. 202 DQ101
Union Rd, Nthlt. 136 CA68
Union Rd, Wem. 138 CL65
Union Sq N1 142 DQ67
Union St E15 143 EC67
Union St SE1 278 G3
Union St SE1 141 DP74
Union St, Barn. 79 CY42
Union St, Kings.T. 197 CK96
Union Wk E2 275 N2
Unity Cl NW10 139 CU65
Unity Cl SE19 182 DQ92
Crown Dale
Unity Cl (New Addington), Croy. 221 EB109
Unity Rd, Enf. 82 DW37
Unity Trd Est, Wdf.Grn. 124 EK55
Unity Way SE18 164 EK76
Unity Wf SE1 162 DT75
Mill St
University Cl NW7 97 CT52
University Cl, Bushey 76 CA42
University Gdns, Bex. 186 EZ87
University Pl, Erith 167 FB80
Belmont Rd
University Rd SW19 180 DD93
University St WC1 273 L5
University St WC1 141 DJ70
University Way E16 145 EN73
University Way, Dart. 168 FJ84
Unstead La (Bramley), Guil. 258 AW144
Unstead Wd (Peasmarsh), Guil. 258 AW142
Unwin Av, Felt. 175 BS85
Unwin Cl SE15 162 DU79
Unwin Rd SW7 276 A6
Unwin Rd, Islw. 157 CE83
Up Cor, Ch.St.G. 90 AW47
Up Cor Cl, Ch.St.G. 90 AV47
Upbrook Ms W2 140 DC72
Chilworth St
Upcerne Rd SW10 160 DC80
Upchurch Cl SE20 182 DV94
Upcroft, Wind. 151 AP83
Upcroft Av, Edg. 96 CQ50
Updale Cl, Pot.B. 63 CY33
Updale Rd, Sid. 185 ET91
Upfield, Croy. 202 DV103
Upfield, Horl. 268 DG149
Upfield Cl, Horl. 268 DG150
Upfield Rd W7 137 CF70
Upfolds Grn, Guil. 243 BC130
Upgrove Manor Way SW2 181 DN87
Trinity Ri
Uphall Rd, Ilf. 125 EP64
Upham Pk Rd W4 158 CS77
Uphill Dr NW7 96 CS50
Uphill Dr NW9 118 CQ57
Uphill Gro NW7 96 CS49
Uphill Rd NW7 96 CS49
Upland Av, Chesh. 54 AP28
Upland Ct Rd, Rom. 106 FM54
Upland Dr, Hat. 64 DB25
Upland Ms SE22 182 DU85
Upland Rd
Upland Rd E13 144 EF70
Sutton Rd
Upland Rd SE22 182 DU85
Upland Rd, Bexh. 166 EZ83
Upland Rd, Cat. 237 EB120
Upland Rd, Epp. 69 ET25
Upland Rd, Harl. 35 ER12
Edinburgh Way
Upland Rd, S.Croy. 220 DR106
Upland Rd, Sutt. 218 DD108
Upland Way, Epsom 233 CW118
Uplands, Ash. 231 CK120
Uplands, Beck. 203 EA96
Uplands, Rick. 74 BM44
Uplands, Ware 33 DZ05
Uplands, Welw.G.C. 29 CW05
Uplands, The, Ger.Cr. 112 AY60
Uplands, The, Loug. 85 EM41
Uplands, The, Ruis. 115 BU60
Uplands, The (Bricket Wd), St.Alb. 60 BY30
Uplands Av E17 101 DX54
Blackhorse La
Uplands Business Pk E17 101 DX54
Uplands Cl SW14 178 CP85
Monroe Dr
Uplands Cl, Ger.Cr. 112 AY60
Uplands Cl, Sev. 256 FF123
Uplands Dr (Oxshott), Lthd. 215 CD113
Uplands End, Wdf.Grn. 102 EL52
Uplands Pk Rd, Enf. 81 DN41
Uplands Rd N8 121 DM57
Uplands Rd, Barn. 98 DG46
Uplands Rd, Brwd. 108 FY50
Uplands Rd, Ken. 236 DQ116
Uplands Rd, Orp. 206 EV102
Uplands Rd, Rom. 126 EX55
Uplands Rd, Wdf.Grn. 102 EL52
Uplands Way N21 81 DN43
Uplands Way, Sev. 256 FF123
Upminster Rd, Horn. 128 FM61
Upminster Rd, Upmin. 128 FM61
Upminster Rd N, Rain. 148 FJ69
Upminster Rd S, Rain. 147 FG70
Upminster Trd Pk, Upmin. 129 FX59
Upney Cl, Horn. 128 FJ64
Tylers Cres
Upney La, Bark. 145 ES65
Upnor Way SE17 279 N10
Uppark Dr, Ilf. 125 EQ58
Upper Abbey Rd, Belv. 166 EZ77
Upper Addison Gdns W14 159 CY75
Upper Ashlyns Rd, Berk. 38 AV20
Upper Bardsey Wk N1 142 DQ65
Clephane Rd
Upper Barn, Hem.H. 40 BM23
Upper Belgrave St SW1 276 G6
Upper Belgrave St SW1 160 DG76
Upper Belmont Rd, Chesh. 54 AP28
Upper Berkeley St W1 272 D9
Upper Berkeley St W1 140 DF72
Upper Beulah Hill SE19 202 DS95
Upper Bourne End La, Hem.H. 57 BA25
Upper Bray Rd, Maid. 150 AC77
Upper Brentwood Rd, Rom. 128 FJ56
Upper Br Rd, Red. 250 DE134
Upper Brighton Rd, Surb. 197 CK100
Upper Brockley Rd SE4 163 DZ82
Upper Brook St W1 276 F1
Upper Brook St W1 140 DG73
Upper Butts, Brent. 157 CJ79
Upper Caldy Wk N1 142 DQ65
Clephane Rd
Upper Camelford Wk W11 139 CY72
Lancaster Rd
Upper Cavendish Av N3 120 DA55
Upper Cheyne Row SW3 160 DE79
Upper Ch Hill, Green. 189 FS85
Upper Clabdens, Ware 33 DZ05
Upper Clapton Rd E5 122 DV60
Upper Clarendon Wk W11 139 CY72
Lancaster Rd
Upper Cornsland, Brwd. 108 FX48
Upper Ct Rd (Woldingham), Cat. 237 EA123
Upper Ct Rd, Epsom 216 CQ111
Upper Culver Rd, St.Alb. 43 CE18
Upper Dagnall St, St.Alb. 43 CD20
Upper Dengie Wk N1 142 DQ67
Popham Rd
Upper Dr, Beac. 89 AK50
Upper Dr (Biggin Hill), West. 238 EJ118
Upper Dunnymans, Bans. 217 CZ114
Basing Rd
Upper Edgeborough Rd, Guil. 259 AZ135
Upper Elmers End Rd, Beck. 203 DY98
Upper Fairfield Rd, Lthd. 231 CH121
Upper Fm Rd, W.Mol. 196 BZ98
Upper Forecourt, Gat. 269 DH152
Upper Fosters NW4 119 CW57
New Brent St
Upper George St, Chesh. 54 AQ30
Frances St
Upper Gladstone Rd, Chesh. 54 AQ30
Upper Grn E, Mitch. 200 DF97
Upper Grn Rd, Welw. 30 DE05
Upper Grn W, Mitch. 200 DF97
London Rd
Upper Grenfell Wk W11 139 CX73
Whitchurch Rd
Upper Grosvenor St W1 276 F1
Upper Grosvenor St W1 140 DG73
Upper Grotto Rd, Twick. 177 CF89
Upper Grd SE1 278 D2
Upper Grd SE1 141 DP74
Upper Gro SE25 202 DS98
Upper Gro Rd, Belv. 166 EZ79
Upper Guild Hall (Bluewater), Green. 189 FU88
Bluewater Parkway
Upper Guildown Rd, Guil. 258 AV137
Upper Gulland Wk N1 142 DQ65
Clephane Rd
Upper Hall Pk, Berk. 38 AX20
Upper Halliford Bypass, Shep. 195 BS99
Upper Halliford Grn, Shep. 195 BS98
Holmbank Dr
Upper Halliford Rd, Shep. 195 BS96
Upper Ham Rd, Kings.T. 177 CK91
Upper Ham Rd, Rich. 177 CK91
Upper Handa Wk N1 142 DR65
Clephane Rd
Upper Harley St NW1 272 G4
Upper Harley St NW1 140 DG70
Upper Hawkwell Wk N1 142 DQ67
Popham Rd
Upper Heath Rd, St.Alb. 43 CF18
Upper High St, Epsom 216 CS113
Upper Highway, Abb.L. 59 BR33
Upper Highway, Kings L. 59 BQ32
Upper Hill Ri, Rick. 74 BH44
Upper Hitch, Wat. 94 BY46
Upper Holly Hill Rd, Belv. 167 FB78
Upper Hook, Harl. 51 ES17
Upper James St W1 273 L10
Upper John St W1 273 L10
Upper Lattimore Rd, St.Alb. 43 CE20
Upper Lees Rd, Slou. 131 AP69
Upper Lismore Wk N1 142 DQ65
Clephane Rd
Upper Mall W6 159 CU78
Upper Manor Rd, Gdmg. 258 AS144
Upper Marlborough Rd, St.Alb. 43 CE20
Upper Marsh SE1 278 C6
Upper Marsh SE1 161 DM76
Upper Marsh La, Hodd. 49 EA18
Upper Mealines, Harl. 52 EU18
Upper Montagu St W1 272 D6
Upper Montagu St W1 140 DF71
Upper Mulgrave Rd, Sutt. 217 CZ108
Upper N St E14 143 EA71
Upper Paddock Rd, Wat. 76 BY44
Upper Palace Rd, E.Mol. 197 CD97
Upper Pk, Harl. 35 EP14
Upper Pk, Loug. 84 EK42
Upper Pk Rd N11 99 DH50
Upper Pk Rd NW3 120 DF64
Upper Pk Rd, Belv. 167 FB77
Upper Pk Rd, Brom. 204 EH95
Upper Pk Rd, Kings.T. 178 CN93
Upper Phillimore Gdns W8 160 DA75
Upper Pillory Down, Cars. 218 DG113
Upper Pines, Bans. 234 DF117
Upper Rainham Rd, Horn. 127 FF63
Upper Ramsey Wk N1 142 DR65
Clephane Rd
Upper Rawreth Wk N1 142 DQ67
Popham Rd
Upper Richmond Rd SW15 159 CY84
Upper Richmond Rd W SW14 158 CP84
Upper Richmond Rd W, Rich. 158 CN84
Upper Riding, Beac. 88 AG54
Upper Rd E13 144 EG69
Upper Rd (Denham), Uxb. 113 BD59
Upper Rd, Wall. 219 DK106
Upper Rose Gall (Bluewater), Green. 189 FU88
Bluewater Parkway
Upper Rose Hill, Dor. 263 CH137
Upper Ryle, Brwd. 108 FV45
Upper St. Martin's La WC2 273 P10
Upper Sales, Hem.H. 39 BF21
Upper Sawley Wd, Bans. 217 CZ114
Upper Selsdon Rd, S.Croy. 220 DT108
Upper Sheppey Wk N1 142 DQ66
Clephane Rd
Upper Sheridan Rd, Belv. 166 FA77
Coleman Rd
Upper Shirley Rd, Croy. 202 DW103
Upper Shot, Welw.G.C. 30 DA08
Upper Shott (Cheshunt), Wal.Cr. 66 DT26
Upper Sq, Islw. 157 CG83
Upper Sta Rd, Rad. 77 CG35
Upper Stonyfield, Harl. 51 EP15
Upper St N1 141 DN68
Upper St (Shere), Guil. 260 BM139
Upper Sunbury Rd, Hmptn. 196 BY95
Upper Sutton La, Houns. 156 CA80
Upper Swaines, Epp. 69 ET30
Upper Tachbrook St SW1 277 K8
Upper Tachbrook St SW1 161 DJ77
Upper Tail, Wat. 94 BY48
Upper Talbot Wk W11 139 CY72
Lancaster Rd
Upper Teddington Rd, Kings.T. 197 CJ95
Upper Ter NW3 120 DC62
Upper Thames St EC4 274 G10
Upper Thames St EC4 142 DQ73
Upper Thames Wk (Bluewater), Green. 189 FU88
Bluewater Parkway
Upper Tollington Pk N4 121 DN60
Upper Tooting Pk SW17 180 DF89
Upper Tooting Rd SW17 180 DF91
Upper Town Rd, Grnf. 136 CB70
Upper Tulse Hill SW2 181 DM87
Upper Vernon Rd, Sutt. 218 DD106
Upper Wk, Vir.W. 192 AY98
Upper Walthamstow Rd E17 123 ED56
Upper W St, Reig. 249 CZ134
Upper Wickham La, Well. 166 EV80
Upper Wimpole St W1 273 H6
Upper Wimpole St W1 140 DG71
Upper Woburn Pl WC1 273 N3
Upper Woburn Pl WC1 141 DK69
Upper Woodcote Village, Pur. 219 DK112
Upperfield Rd, Welw.G.C. 29 CZ11
Upperton Rd, Guil. 258 AW136
Upperton Rd, Sid. 185 ET92
Upperton Rd E E13 144 EJ69
Inniskilling Rd
Upperton Rd W E13 144 EJ69
Uppingham Av, Stan. 95 CH53
Upsdell Av N13 99 DN51
Upshire Rd, Wal.Abb. 68 EF32
Upshirebury Grn, Wal.Abb. 68 EK33
Horseshoe Hill
Upshott La, Wok. 227 BF117
Upstall St SE5 161 DP81
Upton, Wok. 226 AV117
Upton Av E7 144 EG66
Upton Av, St.Alb. 43 CD19
Upton Cl, Bex. 186 EZ86
Upton Cl (Park St), St.Alb. 61 CD25
Upton Cl, Slou. 152 AT76
Upton Ct SE20 182 DW94
Blean Gro
Upton Ct Rd, Slou. 152 AU76
Upton Dene, Sutt. 218 DB108
Upton Gdns, Har. 117 CH57
Upton La E7 144 EG66
Upton Lo Cl, Bushey 94 CC45
Upton Pk, Slou. 152 AT76
Upton Pk Rd E7 144 EH66
Upton Rd N18 100 DU50
Upton Rd SE18 165 EQ79
Upton Rd, Bex. 186 EZ86
Upton Rd, Bexh. 166 EY84
Upton Rd, Houns. 156 CA83
Upton Rd, Slou. 152 AU76
Upton Rd, Th.Hth. 202 DR96
Upton Rd, Wat. 75 BV42
Upton Rd S, Bex. 186 EZ86
Upway N12 98 DE52
Upway (Chalfont St. Peter), Ger.Cr. 91 AZ53
Upwood Rd SE12 184 EG86
Upwood Rd SW16 201 DL95
Uranus Rd, Hem.H. 40 BL18
Urban Av, Horn. 128 FJ62
Urlwin St SE5 162 DQ79
Urlwin Wk SW9 161 DN82
Urmston Dr SW19 179 CY88
Ursula Ms N4 122 DQ60
Portland Ri
Ursula St SW11 160 DE81
Urswick Gdns, Dag. 146 EY66
Urswick Rd
Urswick Rd E9 122 DW64
Urswick Rd, Dag. 146 EX66
Usborne Ms SW8 161 DM80
Usher Rd E3 143 DZ68
Usherwood Cl, Tad. 248 CP131
Usk Rd SW11 160 DC84
Usk Rd, S.Ock. 148 FQ72
Usk St E2 143 DX69
Utopia Village NW1 140 DG67
Chalcot Rd
Uvedale Cl (New Addington), Croy. 221 ED111
Uvedale Cres
Uvedale Cres (New Addington), Croy. 221 ED111
Uvedale Rd, Dag. 126 FA62
Uvedale Rd, Enf. 82 DR43
Uvedale Rd, Oxt. 254 EF129
Uverdale Rd SW10 160 DC80
Uxbridge Gdns, Felt. 176 BX89
Marlborough Rd
Uxbridge Rd W3 138 CL73
Uxbridge Rd W5 138 CL73
Uxbridge Rd W7 137 CF74
Uxbridge Rd W12 139 CU74
Uxbridge Rd W13 137 CF74
Uxbridge Rd, Felt. 176 BW89
Uxbridge Rd (Hampton Hill), Hmptn. 176 CA91
Uxbridge Rd, Har. 94 CC52
Uxbridge Rd, Hayes 136 BW73
Uxbridge Rd, Iver 132 AY71
Uxbridge Rd, Kings.T. 197 CK98
Uxbridge Rd, Pnr. 94 CB52
Uxbridge Rd, Rick. 91 BF47
Uxbridge Rd, Slou. 152 AU75
Uxbridge Rd, Sthl. 136 CA74
Uxbridge Rd, Stan. 95 CF51
Uxbridge Rd, Uxb. 135 BV72
Uxbridge St W8 140 DA74
Uxendon Cres, Wem. 118 CL60
Uxendon Hill, Wem. 118 CM60

V

Vache La, Ch.St.G. 90 AW47
Vache Ms, Ch.St.G. 90 AX46
Vaillant Rd, Wey. 213 BQ105
Val McKenzie Av N7 121 DN62
Parkside Cres
Valan Leas, Brom. 204 EE97
Valance Av E4 102 EF46
Vale, The N10 98 DG53
Vale, The N14 99 DK45
Vale, The NW11 119 CX62
Vale, The SW3 160 DD79
Vale, The W3 138 CR74
Vale, The, Brwd. 108 FW46
Vale, The, Couls. 219 DK114
Vale, The, Croy. 203 DX103
Vale, The, Felt. 175 BV86
Vale, The (Chalfont St. Peter), Ger.Cr. 90 AX53
Vale, The, Houns. 156 BY79
Vale, The, Ruis. 116 BW63
Vale, The, Sun. 175 BU93
Ashridge Way
Vale, The, Wdf.Grn. 102 EG52
Vale Av, Borwd. 78 CP43
Vale Border, Croy. 221 DX111
Vale Cl N2 120 DF55
Church Vale
Vale Cl W9 140 DC69
Maida Vale
Vale Cl, Brwd. 108 FT43
Vale Cl (Chalfont St. Peter), Ger.Cr. 90 AX53
Vale Cl, Orp. 223 EN105
Vale Cl, Wey. 195 BR104
Vale Cl, Wok. 226 AY116
The Larches
Vale Cotts SW15 178 CR91
Kingston Vale
Vale Ct W9 140 DC69
Maida Vale
Vale Ct, Wey. 195 BR104
Vale Cres SW15 178 CS90
Vale Cft (Claygate), Esher 215 CE108
Vale Cft, Pnr. 116 BY57
Vale Dr, Barn. 79 CZ42
Vale End SE22 162 DS84
Grove Vale

Vale Fm Rd, Wok. 226 AX117
Vale Gro N4 122 DQ59
Vale Gro W3 138 CR74
The Vale
Vale Gro, Slou. 152 AS76
Vale Ind Est, Wat. 93 BQ46
Vale La W3 138 CN71
Vale of Health NW3 120 DD62
East Heath Rd
Vale Par SW15 178 CR91
Kingston Vale
Vale Ri NW11 119 CZ60
Vale Ri, Chesh. 54 AQ28
Vale Rd E7 144 EH65
Vale Rd N4 122 DQ59
Vale Rd, Brom. 205 EN96
Vale Rd, Bushey 76 BY43
Vale Rd, Chesh. 54 AQ28
Vale Rd, Dart. 187 FH88
Vale Rd, Epsom 217 CT105
Vale Rd (Claygate), Esher 215 CE109
Vale Rd (Northfleet), Grav. 190 GD87
Vale Rd, Mitch. 201 DK97
Vale Rd, Sutt. 218 DB105
Vale Rd, Wey. 195 BR104
Vale Rd, Wind. 151 AM80
Vale Rd, Wor.Pk. 217 CT105
Vale Rd N, Surb. 198 CL103
Vale Rd S, Surb. 198 CL103
Vale Row N5 121 DP62
Gillespie Rd
Vale Royal N7 141 DL66
Vale St SE27 182 DR90
Vale Ter N4 122 DQ58
Valence Av, Dag. 126 EX62
Valence Circ, Dag. 126 EX62
Valence Dr (Cheshunt), Wal.Cr. 66 DU28
Valence Rd, Erith 167 FD80
Valence Wd Rd, Dag. 126 EX62
Valencia Rd, Stan. 95 CJ49
Valency Cl, Nthwd. 93 BT49
Valentia Pl SW9 161 DN84
Brixton Sta Rd
Valentine Av, Bex. 186 EY89
Valentine Ct SE23 183 DX89
Valentine Pl SE1 278 F4
Valentine Pl SE1 161 DP75
Valentine Rd E9 143 DX65
Valentine Rd, Har. 116 CC62
Valentine Row SE1 278 F5
Valentine Row SE1 161 DP75
Valentine Way, Ch.St.G. 90 AX48
Valentines Rd, Ilf. 125 EP60
Valentines Way, Rom. 127 FE61
Valentyne Cl (New Addington), Croy. 222 EE111
Valerian Way E15 144 EE69
Valerie Cl, St.Alb. 43 CH20
Valerie Ct, Bushey 94 CC45
Valerie Ct, Sutt. 218 DB108
Stanley Rd
Valeside, Hert. 31 DN10
Valeswood Rd, Brom. 184 EF92
Valetta Gro E13 144 EG68
Valetta Rd W3 158 CS75
Valette St E9 142 DV65
Valiant Cl, Nthlt. 136 BX69
Ruislip Rd
Valiant Cl, Rom. 104 FA54
Valiant Ho SE7 164 EJ78
Valiant Path NW9 96 CS52
Valiant Way E6 145 EM71
Vallance Rd E1 142 DU70
Vallance Rd E2 142 DU69
Vallance Rd N22 99 DJ54
Vallentin Rd E17 123 EC56
Valley, The, Guil. 258 AW138
Portsmouth Rd
Valley Av N12 98 DD49
Valley Cl, Dart. 187 FF86
Valley Cl, Hert. 32 DR10
Valley Cl, Loug. 85 EM44
Valley Cl, Pnr. 93 BV54
Alandale Dr
Valley Cl, Wal.Abb. 67 EC32
Valley Cl, Ware 32 DV05
Valley Ct, Cat. 236 DU122
Beechwood Gdns
Valley Ct, Ken. 220 DQ114
Hayes La
Valley Dr NW9 118 CN58
Valley Dr, Grav. 191 GK89
Valley Dr, Sev. 257 FH125
Valley Flds Cres, Enf. 81 DN40
Valley Gdns SW19 180 DD94
Valley Gdns, Wem. 138 CM66
Valley Grn, The, Welw.G.C. 29 CW08
Valley Gro SE7 164 EJ78
Valley Hill, Loug. 102 EL45
Valley Link Ind Est, Enf. 83 DY44
Valley Ms, Twick. 177 CG89
Cross Deep
Valley Ri, Wat. 59 BV33
Valley Rd SW16 181 DM91
Valley Rd, Belv. 167 FB77
Valley Rd, Berk. 38 AT17
Valley Rd, Brom. 204 EE96
Valley Rd, Dart. 187 FF86
Valley Rd, Erith 167 FD77
Valley Rd, Ken. 236 DR115
Valley Rd (Fawkham Grn), Long. 209 FV102
Valley Rd, Orp. 206 EV95
Valley Rd, Rick. 74 BG43
Valley Rd, St.Alb. 43 CE15
Valley Rd, Uxb. 134 BL68
Valley Rd, Welw.G.C. 29 CV10
Valley Side E4 101 EA47
Valley Side Par E4 101 EA47
Valley Side
Valley Vw, Barn. 79 CY44
Valley Vw, Chesh. 54 AN29
Valley Vw, Green. 189 FV86
Valley Vw (Cheshunt), Wal.Cr. 66 DQ28
Valley Vw (Biggin Hill), West. 238 EJ118
Valley Vw Gdns, Ken. 236 DS115
Godstone Rd
Valley Wk, Croy. 202 DW103
Valley Wk, Rick. 75 BQ43
Valley Way, Ger.Cr. 112 AW58
Valleyfield Rd SW16 181 DM92
Valleyside, Hem.H. 39 BF20
Valliere Rd NW10 139 CV69
Valliers Wd Rd, Sid. 185 ER88
Vallis Way W13 137 CG71
Vallis Way, Chess. 215 CK105
Valmar Rd SE5 162 DQ81
Valnay St SW17 180 DF92
Valognes Av E17 101 DY53
Valonia Gdns SW18 179 CZ86
Vambery Rd SE18 165 EQ79
Van Dyck Av, N.Mal. 198 CR101
Vanbrough Cres, Nthlt. 136 BW67
Vanbrugh Cl E16 144 EK71
Fulmer Rd
Vanbrugh Dr, Walt. 196 BW101
Vanbrugh Flds SE3 164 EF80
Vanbrugh Hill SE3 164 EF78
Vanbrugh Hill SE10 164 EF78
Vanbrugh Pk SE3 164 EF80
Vanbrugh Pk Rd SE3 164 EF80
Vanbrugh Pk Rd W SE3 164 EF80
Vanbrugh Rd W4 158 CR76
Vanbrugh Ter SE3 164 EF81
Vanburgh Cl, Orp. 205 ES102
Vancouver Cl, Epsom 216 CQ111
Vancouver Cl, Orp. 224 EU106
Vancouver Ct, Horl. 269 DN148
Vancouver Rd SE23 183 DY89
Vancouver Rd, Edg. 96 CP53
Vancouver Rd, Hayes 135 BV70
Vancouver Rd, Rich. 177 CJ91
Vanda Cres, St.Alb. 43 CF21
Vanderbilt Rd SW18 180 DC88
Vanderville Gdns N2 98 DC54
Tarling Rd
Vandome Cl E16 144 EH72
Vandon Pas SW1 277 L6
Vandon St SW1 277 L6
Vandon St SW1 161 DJ76
Vandy St EC2 275 M5
Vandyke Cl SW15 179 CX87
Vandyke Cl, Red. 250 DF131
Vandyke Cross SE9 184 EL85
Vane Cl NW3 120 DD63
Vane Cl, Har. 118 CM58
Vane St SW1 277 L8
Vanessa Cl, Belv. 166 FA78
Vanessa Wk, Grav. 191 GM92
Vanessa Way, Bex. 187 FD90
Vanguard Cl E16 144 EG71
Vanguard Cl, Croy. 201 DP102
Vanguard Cl, Rom. 105 FB54
Vanguard St SE8 163 EA81
Vanguard Way, Cat. 237 EB121
Slines Oak Rd
Vanguard Way, Wall. 219 DL108
Vanguard Way, Warl. 237 EB121
Vanneck Sq SW15 179 CU85
Vanner Pt E9 143 DX65
Wick Rd
Vanners Par (Byfleet), W.Byf. 212 BL113
Brewery La
Vanoc Gdns, Brom. 184 EG90
Vanquisher Wk, Grav. 191 GM90
Vansittart Est, Wind. 151 AQ81
Vansittart Rd E7 124 EF63
Vansittart Rd, Wind. 151 AP80
Vansittart St SE14 163 DY80
Vanston Pl SW6 160 DA80
Vant Rd SW17 180 DF92
Vantage Ms E14 143 EC74
Prestons Rd
Vantage Rd, Slou. 131 AP74
Summerlea
Vantorts Cl, Saw. 36 EY05
Vantorts Rd, Saw. 36 EY06
Varcoe Rd SE16 162 DV78
Varden St E1 142 DV72
Vardens Rd SW11 160 DD84
Vardon Cl W3 138 CR72
Varley Par NW9 118 CS56
Varley Rd E16 144 EH72
Varley Way, Mitch. 200 DD96
Varna Rd SW6 159 CY80
Varna Rd, Hmptn. 196 CB95
Varndell St NW1 273 K2
Varndell St NW1 141 DJ69
Varney Cl, Hem.H. 39 BF20
Varney Cl (Cheshunt), Wal.Cr. 66 DU27
Varney Rd, Hem.H. 39 BF20
Varsity Dr, Twick. 177 CE85
Varsity Row SW14 158 CQ82
William's La
Vartry Rd N15 122 DR58
Vassall Rd SW9 161 DN80
Vauban Est SE16 162 DU76
Vauban St SE16 162 DT76
Vaughan Av NW4 119 CU57
Vaughan Av W6 159 CT77
Vaughan Av, Horn. 128 FK63
Vaughan Cl, Hmptn. 176 BY93
Oak Av
Vaughan Gdns, Ilf. 125 EM59
Vaughan Gdns (Eton Wick), Wind. 151 AM77
Eton Wick Rd
Vaughan Rd E15 144 EF65
Vaughan Rd SE5 162 DQ83
Vaughan Rd, Har. 116 CC59
Vaughan Rd, T.Ditt. 197 CH101
Vaughan Rd, Well. 165 ET82
Vaughan St SE16 163 DZ75
Vaughan Way E1 142 DU73
Vaughan Way, Dor. 263 CG136
Vaughan Way, Slou. 131 AL70
Vaughan Williams Cl SE8 163 EA80
Watson's St
Vaux Cres, Walt. 213 BV107
Vauxhall Br SE1 161 DL78
Vauxhall Br SW1 161 DL78
Vauxhall Br Rd SW1 277 L8
Vauxhall Br Rd SW1 161 DJ77
Vauxhall Cl (Northfleet), Grav. 191 GF87
Vauxhall Gdns, S.Croy. 220 DQ107
Vauxhall Gdns Est SE11 161 DM78
Vauxhall Gro SW8 161 DM79
Vauxhall Pl, Dart. 188 FL87
Vauxhall Rd, Hem.H. 40 BN20
Vauxhall St SE11 161 DM78
Vauxhall Wk SE11 278 B10
Vauxhall Wk SE11 161 DM78
Vawdrey Cl E1 142 DW70
Veals Mead, Mitch. 200 DE95
Vectis Gdns SW17 181 DH93
Vectis Rd
Vectis Rd SW17 181 DH93
Veda Rd SE13 163 EA84
Vega Cres, Nthwd. 93 BT50
Vega Rd, Bushey 94 CC45
Vegal Cres (Englefield Grn), Egh. 172 AW92
Velde Way SE22 182 DS85
East Dulwich Gro
Veldene Way, Har. 116 BZ62
Velizy Av, Harl. 51 ER15
Velletri Ho E2 143 DX68
Vellum Dr, Cars. 200 DG104
Venables Cl, Dag. 127 FB63
Venables St NW8 272 A6
Venables St NW8 140 DD70
Vencourt Pl W6 159 CU78
Venetia Rd N4 121 DP58
Venetia Rd W5 157 CK75
Venetian Rd SE5 162 DQ82
Venette Cl, Rain. 147 FH71
Venn St SW4 161 DJ84
Venner Rd SE26 182 DW93
Venners Cl, Bexh. 167 FE82
Ventnor Av, Stan. 95 CH53
Ventnor Dr N20 98 DB48
Ventnor Gdns, Bark. 145 ES65
Ventnor Rd SE14 163 DX80
Ventnor Rd, Sutt. 218 DB108
Venton Cl, Wok. 226 AV117
Ventura Pk, St.Alb. 61 CF29
Venture Cl, Bex. 186 EY87
Venue St E14 143 EC71
Venus Hill (Bovingdon), Hem.H. 57 BA31
Venus Rd SE18 165 EM76
Veny Cres, Horn. 128 FK64
Ver Rd, St.Alb. 42 CC20
Vera Av N21 81 DN43
Vera Ct, Wat. 94 BX45
Vera Lynn Cl E7 124 EG63
Dames Rd
Vera Rd SW6 159 CY81
Verbena Cl E16 144 EF70
Pretoria Rd
Verbena Cl, S.Ock. 149 FW72
Verbena Cl, West Dr. 154 BK78
Magnolia St
Verbena Gdns W6 159 CU78
Verdant La SE6 184 EE88
Verdayne Av, Croy. 203 DX102
Verdayne Gdns, Warl. 236 DW116
Verderers Rd, Chig. 104 EU50
Verdun Rd SE18 166 EU79
Verdun Rd SW13 159 CU79
Verdure Cl, Wat. 60 BY32
Vere Rd, Loug. 85 EQ42
Vere St W1 273 H9
Vere St W1 141 DH72
Vereker Dr, Sun. 195 BU97
Vereker Rd W14 159 CY78
Verity Cl W11 139 CY72
Veritys, Hat. 45 CU18
Vermeer Gdns SE15 162 DW84
Elland Rd
Vermont Cl, Enf. 81 DP42
Vermont Rd SE19 182 DR93
Vermont Rd SW18 180 DB86
Vermont Rd, Slou. 131 AM70
Vermont Rd, Sutt. 200 DB104
Verney Cl, Berk. 38 AT18
Verney Gdns, Dag. 126 EY63
Verney Rd SE16 162 DU79
Verney Rd, Dag. 126 EY64
Verney Rd, Slou. 153 BA77
Verney St NW10 118 CR62
Verney Way SE16 162 DV78
Vernham Rd SE18 165 EQ79
Vernon Av E12 125 EM63
Vernon Av SW20 199 CX96
Vernon Av, Enf. 83 DY36
Vernon Av, Wdf.Grn. 102 EH52
Vernon Cl (Ottershaw), Cher. 211 BD107
Vernon Cl, Epsom 216 CQ107
Vernon Cl, Orp. 206 EV97
Vernon Cl, St.Alb. 43 CD21
Vernon Ct, Stan. 95 CH53
Vernon Dr
Vernon Cres, Barn. 80 DG44
Vernon Cres, Brwd. 109 GA48
Vernon Dr, Cat. 236 DQ122
Vernon Dr, Stan. 95 CG53
Vernon Dr (Harefield), Uxb. 92 BJ53
Vernon Ms E17 123 DZ56
Vernon Rd
Vernon Ms W14 159 CY77
Vernon St
Vernon Pl WC1 274 A7
Vernon Pl WC1 141 DL71
Vernon Ri WC1 274 C2
Vernon Ri WC1 141 DM69
Vernon Ri, Grnf. 117 CD64
Vernon Rd E3 143 DZ68
Vernon Rd E11 124 EE60
Vernon Rd E15 144 EE66
Vernon Rd E17 123 DZ57
Vernon Rd N8 121 DN55
Vernon Rd SW14 158 CR83
Vernon Rd, Bushey 76 BY43
Vernon Rd, Felt. 175 BT89
Vernon Rd, Ilf. 125 ET60
Vernon Rd, Rom. 105 FC50
Vernon Rd, Sutt. 218 DC106
Vernon Rd, Swans. 190 FZ86
Vernon Sq WC1 274 C2
Vernon St W14 159 CY77
Vernon Wk, Tad. 233 CX120
Vernon Way, Cat. 236 DQ122
Wellington Rd
Vernon Way, Guil. 242 AT133
Vernon Yd W11 139 CZ73
Portobello Rd
Veroan Rd, Bexh. 166 EY82
Verona Cl, Uxb. 134 BJ71
Verona Dr, Surb. 198 CL103
Verona Gdns, Grav. 191 GL91
Verona Rd E7 144 EG66
Upton La
Veronica Cl, Rom. 106 FJ52
Veronica Gdns SW16 201 DJ95
Veronica Rd SW17 181 DH90
Veronique Gdns, Ilf. 125 EP57
Verralls, Wok. 227 BB117
Verran Rd SW12 181 DH87
Balham Gro
Versailles Rd SE20 182 DU94
Verulam Av E17 123 DZ58
Verulam Av, Pur. 219 DJ112
Verulam Bldgs WC1 274 C6
Verulam Cl, Welw.G.C. 29 CZ09
Verulam Pas, Wat. 75 BV40
Verulam Rd, Grnf. 136 CA70
Verulam Rd, St.Alb. 42 CB19
Verulam St WC1 274 D6
Verwood Dr, Barn. 80 DF41
Verwood Rd, Har. 94 CC54
Veryan, Wok. 226 AU117
Veryan Cl, Orp. 206 EW98
Vesey Path E14 143 EB72
East India Dock Rd
Vespan Rd W12 159 CU75
Vesta Av, St.Alb. 42 CC23
Vesta Rd SE4 163 DY82
Vesta Rd, Hem.H. 40 BM18
Saturn Way
Vestris Rd SE23 183 DX89
Vestry Ms SE5 162 DS81
Vestry Rd E17 123 EB56
Vestry Rd SE5 162 DS81
Vestry St N1 275 K2
Vestry St N1 142 DR69
Vetch Cl, Felt. 175 BT87
Vevers Rd, Reig. 266 DB137
Vevey St SE6 183 DZ89
Vexil Cl, Purf. 169 FR77
Veysey Cl, Hem.H. 40 BH22
Halwick Cl
Veysey Gdns, Dag. 126 FA62
Viaduct Pl E2 142 DV69
Viaduct St
Viaduct Rd, Ware 33 DY06
Viaduct St E2 142 DV69
Viaduct Way, Welw.G.C. 29 CZ06
Vian Av, Enf. 83 DY35
Vian St SE13 163 EB83
Vibart Gdns SW2 181 DM87
Vibart Wk N1 141 DL67
Outram Pl
Vicarage Av SE3 164 EG81
Vicarage Av, Egh. 173 BB93
Vicarage Causeway, Hert. 32 DV11
Vicarage Cl (Seer Grn), Beac. 89 AQ52
Vicarage Cl, Brwd. 108 FS49
Vicarage Cl, Erith 167 FC79
Vicarage Cl, Hem.H. 40 BJ22
Vicarage Cl (Bookham), Lthd. 246 CA125
Vicarage Cl, Nthlt. 136 BZ66
Vicarage Cl, Pot.B. 64 DF30
Vicarage Cl, Ruis. 115 BR59
Vicarage Cl, St.Alb. 42 CC23
Vicarage Cl, Tad. 233 CY124
Vicarage Cl, Wor.Pk. 198 CS102
Vicarage Ct W8 160 DB75
Vicarage Gate
Vicarage Ct, Egh. 173 BB93
Vicarage Ct, Felt. 175 BQ87
Vicarage Cres SW11 160 DD81
Vicarage Cres, Egh. 173 BB92
Vicarage Dr SW14 178 CR85
Vicarage Dr, Bark. 145 EQ66
Vicarage Dr, Beck. 203 EA95
Vicarage Dr (Northfleet), Grav. 190 GC86
Vicarage Dr, Maid. 150 AC75
Vicarage Fm Rd, Houns. 156 BY82
Vicarage Fld Shop Cen, Bark. 145 EQ66
Vicarage Flds, Walt. 196 BW100
Vicarage Gdns SW14 178 CQ85
Vicarage Rd
Vicarage Gdns W8 140 DA74
Vicarage Gdns, Berk. 39 BB16
Vicarage Gdns, Mitch. 200 DE97
Vicarage Gate W8 160 DB75
Vicarage Gate, Guil. 258 AU136
Vicarage Gate Ms, Tad. 233 CY124
Vicarage Gro SE5 162 DR81
Vicarage Hill, West. 255 ER126
Vicarage La E6 145 EM69
Vicarage La E15 144 EE66
Vicarage La, Chig. 103 EQ47
Vicarage La (North Weald Bassett), Epp. 52 FA24
Vicarage La, Epsom 217 CU109
Vicarage La (Bovingdon), Hem.H. 57 BB26
Vicarage La, Horl. 268 DF147
Vicarage La, Ilf. 125 ER60
Vicarage La, Kings L. 58 BM29
Vicarage La, Lthd. 231 CH122
Vicarage La (Dunton Grn), Sev. 241 FD119
London Rd
Vicarage La (Laleham), Stai. 194 BH97
Vicarage La (Wraysbury), Stai. 172 AY88
Vicarage La (Send), Wok. 243 BC126
Vicarage Pk SE18 165 EQ78
Vicarage Path N8 121 DL59
Vicarage Pl, Slou. 152 AU76
Vicarage Rd E10 123 EB60
Vicarage Rd E15 144 EF66
Vicarage Rd N17 100 DU52
Vicarage Rd NW4 119 CU58
Vicarage Rd SE18 165 EQ78
Vicarage Rd SW14 178 CQ85
Vicarage Rd, Berk. 39 BA16
Vicarage Rd, Bex. 187 FB88
Vicarage Rd, Croy. 201 DN104
Vicarage Rd, Dag. 147 FB65
Vicarage Rd, Egh. 173 BB93
Vicarage Rd, Epp. 70 EW29
Vicarage Rd, Horn. 127 FG60
Vicarage Rd, Kings.T. 197 CK96
Vicarage Rd (Hampton Wick), Kings.T. 197 CJ95
Vicarage Rd, Stai. 173 BE91
Vicarage Rd, Sun. 175 BT92
Vicarage Rd, Sutt. 218 DB105
Vicarage Rd, Tedd. 177 CG92
Vicarage Rd, Twick. 177 CE89
Vicarage Rd (Whitton), Twick. 176 CC86
Vicarage Rd, Ware 33 DY06
Vicarage Rd, Wat. 75 BU44
Vicarage Rd, Wok. 227 AZ121
Vicarage Rd, Wdf.Grn. 102 EL52
Vicarage Sq, Grays 170 GA79
Vicarage Wk, Reig. 250 DB134
Chartway
Vicarage Way NW10 118 CR62
Vicarage Way, Ger.Cr. 113 AZ58
Vicarage Way, Har. 116 CA59
Vicarage Way (Colnbrook), Slou. 153 BC80
Vicarage Wd, Harl. 36 EU14
Vicars Br Cl, Wem. 138 CL68
Vicars Cl E9 142 DW67
Northiam St
Vicars Cl E15 144 EG67
Vicars Cl, Enf. 82 DS40
Vicars Hill SE13 163 EB84
Vicars Moor La N21 99 DN45
Vicars Oak Rd SE19 182 DS93
Vicars Rd NW5 120 DG64
Vicars Wk, Dag. 126 EV62
Viceroy Cl N2 120 DE56
Market Pl
Viceroy Ct NW8 140 DE68
Prince Albert Rd
Viceroy Par N2 120 DE55
High Rd
Viceroy Rd SW8 161 DL81
Vickers Cl, Wall. 219 DM108
Hurricane Rd
Vickers Dr N, Wey. 212 BL110
Vickers Dr S, Wey. 212 BL111
Vickers Rd, Erith 167 FD78
Vickers Way, Houns. 176 BY85
Victor App, Horn. 128 FK60
Abbs Cross Gdns
Victor Cl, Horn. 128 FK60
Victor Ct, Horn. 128 FK60
Victor Ct, Rain. 147 FD68
Askwith Rd
Victor Gdns, Horn. 128 FK60
Victor Gro, Wem. 138 CL66
Victor Rd NW10 139 CV69
Victor Rd SE20 183 DX94
Victor Rd, Har. 116 CC55
Victor Rd, Tedd. 177 CE91
Victor Rd, Wind. 151 AQ83
Victor Smith Ct, St.Alb. 60 CA31
Victor Vil N9 100 DR48
Victor Wk NW9 96 CS53
Victor Wk, Horn. 128 FK60
Abbs Cross Gdns
Victoria Arc SW1 161 DH76
Terminus Pl
Victoria Av E6 144 EK67
Victoria Av EC2 275 N7
Victoria Av N3 97 CZ53
Victoria Av, Barn. 80 DD42
Victoria Av, Grav. 191 GH87
Sheppy Pl
Victoria Av, Grays 170 GC75
Victoria Av, Houns. 176 BZ85
Victoria Av, Rom. 105 FB51
Victoria Av, S.Croy. 220 DQ110
Victoria Av, Surb. 197 CK101
Victoria Av, Uxb. 135 BP66
Victoria Av, Wall. 200 DG104
Victoria Av, Wem. 138 CP65
Victoria Av, W.Mol. 196 CA97
Victoria Cl, Barn. 80 DD42
Victoria Cl, Grays 170 GC75
Victoria Cl, Hayes 135 BR72
Commonwealth Av
Victoria Cl, Horl. 268 DG148
Victoria Cl, Rick. 92 BK45
Nightingale Rd
Victoria Cl, Wal.Cr. 67 DX30
Victoria Cl, W.Mol. 196 CA97
Victoria Av
Victoria Cl, Wey. 195 BR104
Victoria Cotts, Rich. 158 CM81
Victoria Ct, Wem. 138 CN65
Victoria Cres N15 122 DS57
Victoria Cres SE19 182 DS93
Victoria Cres SW19 179 CZ94
Victoria Cres, Iver 134 BG73
Victoria Dock Rd E16 144 EG73
Victoria Dr SW19 179 CX87
Victoria Dr (South Darenth), Dart. 209 FR96
Victoria Dr, Slou. 131 AL65
Victoria Embk EC4 278 B1
Victoria Embk EC4 141 DM73
Victoria Embk SW1 278 A4
Victoria Embk SW1 161 DL75
Victoria Embk WC2 278 B1
Victoria Embk WC2 161 DL75
Victoria Gdns W11 140 DA74
Victoria Gdns, Houns. 156 BY81
Victoria Gdns (Biggin Hill), West. 238 EJ115
Victoria Gate, Harl. 52 EW15
Victoria Gro N12 98 DC50
Victoria Gro W8 160 DC76
Victoria Gro Ms W2 140 DB73
Ossington St
Victoria Hill Rd, Swan. 207 FF95
Victoria Ind Est NW10 138 CS69
Victoria Ind Pk, Dart. 188 FL85
Victoria La, Barn. 79 CZ42
Victoria La, Hayes 155 BQ78
Victoria Ms NW6 140 DA67
Victoria Ms SW4 161 DH84
Victoria Ri
Victoria Ms SW18 180 DC88
Victoria Pk E9 143 DY66
Victoria Pk Rd E9 142 DW67
Victoria Pk Sq E2 142 DW69
Victoria Pas NW8 140 DD70
Cunningham Pl
Victoria Pas, Wat. 75 BV42
Victoria Pl SW1 161 DH77
Victoria Pl, Epsom 216 CS112
Victoria Pl, Rich. 177 CK85
Victoria Pt E13 144 EG68
Victoria Rd
Victoria Retail Pk, Ruis. 116 BY64
Victoria Ri SW4 161 DH83
Victoria Rd E4 102 EE46
Victoria Rd E11 124 EE63
Victoria Rd E13 144 EG68
Victoria Rd E17 101 EC54
Victoria Rd E18 102 EH54
Victoria Rd N4 121 DM59
Victoria Rd N9 100 DT49
Victoria Rd N15 122 DU56
Victoria Rd N18 100 DT49
Victoria Rd N22 99 DJ53
Victoria Rd NW4 119 CW56
Victoria Rd NW6 139 CZ67
Victoria Rd NW7 97 CT50
Victoria Rd NW10 138 CR71
Victoria Rd SW14 158 CR83
Victoria Rd W3 138 CR71
Victoria Rd W5 137 CH71
Victoria Rd W8 160 DC76
Victoria Rd, Add. 212 BK105
Victoria Rd, Bark. 145 EP65
Victoria Rd, Barn. 80 DD42
Victoria Rd, Berk. 38 AW20
Victoria Rd, Bexh. 166 FA84
Victoria Rd, Brwd. 108 FW49
Victoria Rd, Brom. 204 EK99
Victoria Rd, Buck.H. 102 EK47
Victoria Rd, Bushey 94 CB46
Victoria Rd, Chesh. 54 AQ31
Victoria Rd, Chis. 185 EN92
Victoria Rd, Couls. 235 DK115
Victoria Rd, Dag. 127 FB64
Victoria Rd, Dart. 188 FK85
Victoria Rd, Erith 167 FE79
Victoria Rd, Felt. 175 BV88
Victoria Rd (Northfleet), Grav. 191 GF88
Victoria Rd, Guil. 242 AY134
Victoria Rd, Horl. 268 DG148
Victoria Rd, Kings.T. 198 CM96
Victoria Rd, Mitch. 180 DE94
Victoria Rd, Red. 266 DG135
Victoria Rd, Rom. 127 FE58
Victoria Rd, Ruis. 116 BW64
Victoria Rd, Sev. 257 FH125
Victoria Rd, Sid. 185 ET90
Victoria Rd, Slou. 132 AV74
Victoria Rd (Farnham Common), Slou. 131 AQ65
Victoria Rd, Sthl. 156 BZ76
Victoria Rd, Stai. 173 BE90
Victoria Rd, Surb. 197 CK100
Victoria Rd, Sutt. 218 DD106
Victoria Rd, Tedd. 177 CG93
Victoria Rd, Twick. 177 CG87

Victoria Rd, Uxb. 134 BJ66
New Windsor St
Victoria Rd, Wal.Abb. 67 EC34
Victoria Rd, Wat. 75 BV38
Victoria Rd, Wey. 195 BR104
Victoria Rd (Eton Wick), Wind. 151 AM78
Victoria Rd, Wok. 226 AY117
Victoria Scott Ct, Dart. 167 FE83
Victoria Sq SW1 277 J6
Victoria Sta SW1 277 J8
Victoria Sta SW1 161 DH77
Victoria Steps, Brent. 158 CM79
Kew Br Rd
Victoria St E15 144 EE66
Victoria St SW1 277 K7
Victoria St SW1 161 DJ76
Victoria St, Belv. 166 EZ78
Victoria St (Englefield Grn), Egh. 172 AW93
Victoria St, St.Alb. 43 CD20
Victoria St, Slou. 152 AT75
Victoria St, Wind. 151 AQ81
Victoria Ter N4 121 DN60
Victoria Ter NW10 138 CS69
Old Oak La
Victoria Ter, Dor. 263 CG136
South St
Victoria Ter, Har. 117 CE60
Victoria Vil, Rich. 158 CM83
Victoria Way SE7 164 EH78
Victoria Way, Wey. 195 BR104
Victoria Way, Wok. 226 AY117
Victoria Wf E14 143 DY73
Victoria Yd E1 142 DU72
Fairclough St
Victorian Gro N16 122 DS62
Victorian Rd N16 122 DS62
Victors Cres, Brwd. 109 GB47
Victors Dr, Hmptn. 176 BY93
Victors Way, Barn. 79 CZ41
Victory Av, Mord. 200 DC99
Victory Business Cen, Islw. 157 CF83
Victory Cl, Grays 169 FX77
Victory Pk Rd, Add. 212 BJ105
Victory Pl E14 143 DY73
Northey St
Victory Pl SE17 279 J8
Victory Pl SE17 162 DQ77
Victory Pl SE19 182 DS93
Westow St
Victory Rd E11 124 EH56
Victory Rd SW19 180 DC94
Victory Rd, Berk. 38 AU18
Gossoms End
Victory Rd, Cher. 194 BG102
Victory Rd, Rain. 147 FG68
Victory Rd Ms SW19 180 DC94
Victory Rd
Victory Wk SE8 163 EA81
Ship St
Victory Way SE16 163 DY75
Victory Way, Dart. 168 FQ84
Victory Way, Houns. 156 BW78
Victory Way, Rom. 105 FB54
Vidler Cl, Chess. 215 CJ107
Merritt Gdns
Vienna Cl, Ilf. 124 EL55
View, The SE2 166 EY78
View Cl N6 120 DF59
View Cl, Chig. 103 ER50
View Cl, Har. 117 CD56
View Cl (Biggin Hill), West. 238 EJ116
View Rd N6 120 DF59
View Rd, Pot.B. 64 DC32
Viewfield Cl, Har. 118 CL59
Viewfield Rd SW18 179 CZ86
Viewfield Rd, Bex. 186 EW88
Viewland Rd SE18 165 ET78
Viewlands Av, West. 239 ES120
Viga Rd N21 81 DN44
Vigerons Way, Grays 171 GH77
Viggory La, Wok. 226 AW115
Vigilant Cl SE26 182 DU91
Vigilant Way, Grav. 191 GL92
Vignoles Rd, Rom. 126 FA59
Vigo St W1 277 K1
Vigo St W1 141 DJ73
Vigors Cft, Hat. 45 CT19
Viking Cl E3 143 DY68
Selwyn Rd
Viking Ct SW6 160 DA79
Viking Gdns E6 144 EL70
Jack Dash Way
Viking Pl E10 123 DZ60
Viking Rd (Northfleet), Grav. 190 GC90
Viking Rd, Sthl. 136 BY73
Viking Way, Brwd. 108 FV45
Viking Way, Erith 167 FC76
Viking Way, Rain. 147 FG70
Villa Ct, Dart. 188 FL89
Greenbanks
Villa Rd SW9 161 DN83
Villa St SE17 162 DR78
Villacourt Rd SE18 166 EU80
Village, The SE7 164 EJ79
Village, The (Bluewater), Green. 189 FT87
Village Arc E4 101 ED46
Station Rd
Village Cl E4 101 EC50
Village Cl NW3 120 DE64
Ornan Rd
Village Cl, Hodd. 49 ED15
Village Cl, Wey. 195 BR104
Oatlands Dr
Village Ct E17 123 EB57
Eden Rd
Village Gdns, Epsom 217 CT110
Village Grn Av (Biggin Hill), West. 238 EL117
Village Grn Rd, Dart. 167 FG84
Village Grn Way (Biggin Hill), West. 238 EL117
Main Rd
Village Hts, Wdf.Grn. 102 EF50
Village La (Hedgerley), Slou. 111 AR60
Village Ms NW9 118 CR61
Village Pk Cl, Enf. 82 DS44
Village Rd N3 97 CY53
Village Rd (Coleshill), Amer. 55 AM44
Village Rd, Egh. 193 BC97
Village Rd, Enf. 82 DS44
Village Rd (Denham), Uxb. 113 BF61
Village Rd (Dorney), Wind. 150 AH76
Village Row, Sutt. 218 DA108
Village Way NW10 118 CR63
Village Way SE21 182 DR86
Village Way, Amer. 72 AX40
Village Way, Ashf. 174 BM91
Village Way, Beck. 203 EA96
Village Way, Pnr. 116 BY59
Village Way, S.Croy. 220 DU113
Village Way E, Har. 116 BZ59
Villas Rd SE18 165 EQ77
Villier Ct, Uxb. 134 BK68
Villier St
Villier St, Uxb. 134 BK68
Villiers, The, Wey. 213 BR107
Villiers Av, Surb. 198 CM99
Villiers Av, Twick. 176 BZ88
Villiers Cl E10 123 EA61
Villiers Cl, Surb. 198 CM98
Villiers Ct N20 98 DC45
Buckingham Av
Villiers Cres, St.Alb. 43 CK17
Villiers Gro, Sutt. 217 CX109
Villiers Path, Surb. 198 CL99
Villiers Rd NW2 139 CU65
Villiers Rd, Beck. 203 DX96
Villiers Rd, Islw. 157 CE82
Villiers Rd, Kings.T. 198 CM97
Villiers Rd, Slou. 131 AR71
Villiers Rd, Sthl. 136 BZ74
Villiers Rd, Wat. 76 BY44
Villiers St WC2 277 P1
Villiers St WC2 141 DL73
Villiers St, Hert. 32 DS09
Vincam Cl, Twick. 176 CA87
Vince St EC1 275 L3
Vince St EC1 142 DR69
Vincent Av, Cars. 218 DD111
Vincent Av, Croy. 221 DY111
Vincent Av, Surb. 198 CP102
Vincent Cl SE16 163 DY75
Vincent Cl, Barn. 80 DA41
Vincent Cl, Brom. 204 EH98
Vincent Cl, Cher. 193 BE101
Vincent Cl, Couls. 234 DF120
Vincent Cl, Esher 196 CB104
Vincent Cl, Ilf. 103 EQ51
Vincent Cl (Fetcham), Lthd. 230 CB123
Vincent Cl, Sid. 185 ES88
Vincent Cl (Cheshunt), Wal.Cr. 67 DY28
Vincent Cl, West Dr. 154 BN79
Vincent Dr, Dor. 263 CG137
Vincent Dr, Shep. 195 BS97
Vincent Dr, Uxb. 134 BM67
Birch Cres
Vincent Gdns NW2 119 CT62
Vincent Grn, Couls. 234 DF120
High Rd
Vincent La, Dor. 263 CG136
Vincent Ms E3 143 EA68
Vincent Rd E4 101 ED51
Vincent Rd N15 122 DQ56
Vincent Rd N22 99 DN54
Vincent Rd SE18 165 EP77
Vincent Rd W3 158 CQ76
Vincent Rd, Cher. 193 BE101
Vincent Rd (Stoke D'Abernon), Cob. 230 BY116
Vincent Rd, Couls. 235 DJ116
Vincent Rd, Croy. 202 DS101
Vincent Rd, Dag. 146 EY66
Vincent Rd, Dor. 263 CG136
Vincent Rd, Houns. 156 BX82
Vincent Rd, Islw. 157 CD81
Vincent Rd, Kings.T. 198 CN97
Vincent Rd, Rain. 148 FJ70
Vincent Rd, Wem. 138 CM66
Vincent Row (Hampton Hill), Hmptn. 176 CC93
Vincent Sq SW1 277 L8
Vincent Sq SW1 161 DJ77
Vincent Sq (Biggin Hill), West. 222 EJ113
Vincent St E16 144 EF71
Vincent St SW1 277 M8
Vincent St SW1 161 DK77
Vincent Ter N1 141 DP68
Vincents Dr, Dor. 263 CG137
Nower Rd
Vincents Path, Nthlt. 136 BY65
Arnold Rd
Vincents Wk, Dor. 263 CG136
Arundel Rd
Vincenzo Cl, Hat. 45 CW23
Vine, The, Sev. 257 FH124
Vine Av, Sev. 257 FH124
Vine Cl, Stai. 174 BG85
Vine Cl, Surb. 198 CM100
Vine Cl, Sutt. 200 DC104
Vine Cl, Welw.G.C. 29 CY07
Vine Cl, West Dr. 154 BN77
Vine Ct E1 142 DU71
Whitechapel Rd
Vine Ct, Har. 118 CL58
Vine Ct Rd, Sev. 257 FJ124
Vine Gdns, Ilf. 125 EQ64
Vine Gate (Farnham Common), Slou. 131 AQ65
Vine Gro, Harl. 35 ER10
Vine Gro, Uxb. 134 BN66
Vine Hill EC1 274 D5
Vine La SE1 279 N3
Vine La, Uxb. 134 BM67
Vine Pl W5 138 CL74
The Common
Vine Pl, Houns. 156 CB84
Vine Rd E15 144 EF66
Vine Rd SW13 159 CT83
Vine Rd, E.Mol. 196 CC98
Vine Rd, Orp. 223 ET107
Vine Rd (Stoke Poges), Slou. 132 AT65
Vine Sq W14 159 CZ78
Vine St EC3 275 P10
Vine St W1 277 L1
Vine St, Rom. 127 FC57
Vine St, Uxb. 134 BK67
Vine St Br EC1 274 E5
Vine St Br EC1 141 DN70
Vine Way, Brwd. 108 FW46
Vine Yd SE1 279 J4
Vinegar All E17 123 EB56
Vinegar St E1 142 DV74
Reardon St
Vinegar Yd SE1 279 M4
Viner Cl, Walt. 196 BW100
Vineries, The N14 81 DJ44
Vineries, The, Enf. 82 DS41
Vineries Bk NW7 97 CV50
Vineries Cl, Dag. 146 FA65
Heathway
Vineries Cl, West Dr. 154 BN79
Vines Av N3 98 DB53
Viney Bk, Croy. 221 DZ109
Viney Rd SE13 163 EB83
Vineyard, The, Rich. 178 CL85
Vineyard, The, Ware 33 EA05
Vineyard, The, Welw.G.C. 29 CX07
Vineyard Av NW7 97 CY52
Vineyard Cl SE6 183 EA88
Vineyard Cl, Kings.T. 198 CM97
Vineyard Gro N3 98 DB53
Vineyard Hill, Pot.B. 64 DG29
Vineyard Hill Rd SW19 180 DA91
Vineyard Pas, Rich. 178 CL85
Paradise Rd
Vineyard Path SW14 158 CR83
Vineyard Rd, Felt. 175 BU90
Vineyard Row, Kings.T. 197 CJ95
Vineyard Wk EC1 274 D4
Vineyard Wk EC1 141 DN70
Vineyards Rd, Pot.B. 64 DG30
Vining St SW9 161 DN84
Vinlake Av, Uxb. 114 BM62
Vinson Cl, Orp. 206 EU102
Vintners Pl EC4 142 DQ73
Upper Thames St
Vintry Ms E17 123 EA56
Cleveland Pk Cres
Viola Av SE2 166 EV77
Viola Av, Felt. 176 BW86
Viola Av, Stai. 174 BK88
Viola Cl, S.Ock. 149 FW69
Viola Sq W12 139 CT73
Violet Av, Enf. 82 DR38
Violet Av, Uxb. 134 BM71
Violet Cl E16 144 EE70
Violet Cl, Wall. 201 DH102
Violet Gdns, Croy. 219 DP106
Violet Hill NW8 140 DC68
Violet La, Croy. 219 DP106
Violet Rd E3 143 EB70
Violet Rd E17 123 EA58
Violet Rd E18 102 EH54
Violet St E2 142 DV70
Three Colts La
Violet Way, Rick. 74 BJ42
Virgil Dr, Brox. 49 DZ23
Virgil Pl W1 272 D7
Virgil St SE1 278 C6
Virgil St SE1 161 DM76
Virginia Av, Vir.W. 192 AW99
Virginia Beeches, Vir.W. 192 AW97
Virginia Cl, Ash. 231 CK118
Skinners La
Virginia Cl, N.Mal. 198 CQ98
Willow Rd
Virginia Cl, Rom. 105 FC52
Virginia Cl, Stai. 194 BJ97
Blacksmiths La
Virginia Cl, Wey. 213 BQ107
Virginia Dr, Vir.W. 192 AW99
Virginia Gdns, Ilf. 103 EQ54
Virginia Pl, Cob. 213 BU114
Virginia Rd E2 275 P3
Virginia Rd E2 142 DT69
Virginia Rd, Th.Hth. 201 DP95
Virginia St E1 142 DU73
Virginia Wk SW2 181 DM86
Virginia Wk, Grav. 191 GK93
Viscount Cl N11 99 DH50
Viscount Dr E6 145 EM71
Viscount Gdns, W.Byf. 212 BL112
Viscount Gro, Nthlt. 136 BX69
Wayfarer Rd
Viscount Rd (Stanwell), Stai. 174 BK88
Viscount St EC1 275 H5
Viscount Way (Heathrow Airport), Houns. 155 BS84
Vista, The SE9 184 EK86
Vista, The, Sid. 185 ET92
Langdon Shaw
Vista Av, Enf. 83 DX40
Vista Dr, Ilf. 124 EK57
Vista Way, Har. 118 CL58
Viveash Cl, Hayes 155 BT76
Vivian Av NW4 119 CV57
Vivian Av, Wem. 118 CN64
Vivian Cl, Wat. 93 BU46
Vivian Comma Cl N4 121 DP62
Blackstock Rd
Vivian Gdns, Wat. 93 BU46
Vivian Gdns, Wem. 118 CN64
Vivian Rd E3 143 DY68
Vivian Sq SE15 162 DV83
Scylla Rd
Vivian Way N2 120 DD57
Vivien Cl, Chess. 216 CL108
Vivienne Cl, Twick. 177 CJ86
Vixen Dr, Hert. 32 DU09
Voce Rd SE18 165 ER80
Voewood Cl, N.Mal. 199 CT100
Vogan Cl, Reig. 266 DB137
Volt Av NW10 138 CR69
Volta Way, Croy. 201 DM102
Voltaire Rd SW4 161 DK83
Voltaire Way, Hayes 135 BS73
Judge Heath La
Voluntary Pl E11 124 EG58
Vorley Rd N19 121 DJ61
Voss Ct SW16 181 DL93
Voss St E2 142 DU69
Voyagers Cl SE28 146 EW72
Voysey Cl N3 119 CY55
Vulcan Cl E6 145 EN72
Vulcan Cl, Wall. 219 DM108
Vulcan Gate, Enf. 81 DN40
Vulcan Rd SE4 163 DZ82
Vulcan Sq E14 163 EA77
Britannia Rd
Vulcan Ter SE4 163 DZ82
Vulcan Way N7 141 DM65
Vulcan Way (New Addington), Croy. 222 EE110
Vyne, The, Bexh. 167 FB83
Vyner Rd W3 138 CR73
Vyner St E2 142 DV67
Vyners Way, Uxb. 114 BN64
Vyse Cl, Barn. 79 CW42

W

Wacketts (Cheshunt), Wal.Cr. 66 DU27
Spicersfield
Wadbrook St, Kings.T. 197 CK96
Wadding St SE17 279 K9
Wadding St SE17 162 DR77
Waddington Av, Couls. 235 DN120
Waddington Cl, Couls. 235 DP119
Waddington Cl, Enf. 82 DS42
Waddington Rd E15 123 ED64
Waddington Rd, St.Alb. 43 CD20
Waddington St E15 143 ED65
Waddington Way SE19 182 DQ94
Waddon Cl, Croy. 201 DN104
Waddon Ct Rd, Croy. 219 DN105
Waddon Marsh Way, Croy. 201 DM102
Waddon New Rd, Croy. 201 DP104
Waddon Pk Av, Croy. 201 DN104
Waddon Rd, Croy. 201 DN104
Waddon Way, Croy. 219 DN107
Wade, The, Welw.G.C. 29 CZ12
Wade Av, Orp. 206 EX101
Wade Dr, Slou. 131 AN74
Wades, The, Hat. 45 CU21
Wades Gro N21 99 DN45
Wades Hill N21 81 DN44
Wades La, Tedd. 177 CG92
High St
Wades Ms N21 99 DN45
Wades Hill
Wades Pl E14 143 EB73
Wadesmill Rd, Hert. 32 DQ06
Wadesmill Rd (Chapmore End), Ware 32 DQ06
Wadeson St E2 142 DV68
Wadeville Av, Rom. 126 EZ59
Wadeville Cl, Belv. 166 FA79
Wadham Av E17 101 EB52
Wadham Cl, Shep. 195 BQ101
Wadham Gdns NW3 140 DE67
Wadham Gdns, Grnf. 137 CD65
Wadham Rd E17 101 EB53
Wadham Rd SW15 159 CY84
Wadham Rd, Abb.L. 59 BT31
Wadhurst Cl SE20 202 DV96
Wadhurst Rd SW8 161 DJ81
Wadhurst Rd W4 158 CR76
Wadley Cl, Hem.H. 40 BM21
White Hart Dr
Wadley Rd E11 124 EE59
Wadsworth Business Cen, Grnf. 137 CJ68
Wadsworth Cl, Enf. 83 DX43
Wadsworth Cl, Grnf. 137 CJ68
Wadsworth Rd, Grnf. 137 CH68
Wager St E3 143 DZ70
Waggon Cl, Guil. 242 AS133
Waggon Ms N14 99 DJ46
Chase Side
Waggon Rd, Barn. 80 DC37
Waghorn Rd E13 144 EJ67
Waghorn Rd, Har. 117 CK55
Waghorn St SE15 162 DU83
Wagner St SE15 162 DW80
Wagon Rd, Barn. 80 DB36
Wagon Way, Rick. 74 BJ41
Wagstaff Gdns, Dag. 146 EW66
Wagtail Cl NW9 96 CS54
Swan Dr
Wagtail Gdns, S.Croy. 221 DY110
Wagtail Wk, Beck. 203 EC99
Wagtail Way, Orp. 206 EX98
Waid Cl, Dart. 188 FM86
Waights Ct, Kings.T. 198 CL95
Wain Cl, Pot.B. 64 DB29
Wainfleet Av, Rom. 105 FC54
Wainford Cl SW19 179 CX88
Windlesham Gro
Wainwright Av, Brwd. 109 GD44
Wainwright Gro, Islw. 157 CD84
Waite Davies Rd SE12 184 EF87
Waite St SE15 162 DT79
Waithman St EC4 274 F9
Wake Rd (High Beach), Loug. 84 EJ38
Wakefield Cl (Byfleet), W.Byf. 212 BL112
Wakefield Cres (Stoke Poges), Slou. 132 AT66
Wakefield Gdns SE19 182 DS94
Wakefield Gdns, Ilf. 124 EL58
Wakefield Ms WC1 274 A3
Wakefield Rd N11 99 DK50
Wakefield Rd N15 122 DT57
Wakefield Rd, Green. 189 FW85
Wakefield Rd, Rich. 177 CK85
Wakefield St E6 144 EK67
Wakefield St N18 100 DU50
Wakefield St WC1 274 A4
Wakefield St WC1 141 DL69
Wakefield Wk, Wal.Cr. 67 DY31
Wakeham St N1 142 DR65
Wakehams Hill, Pnr. 116 BZ55
Wakehurst Path, Wok. 211 BC114
Wakehurst Rd SW11 180 DE85
Wakelin Rd E15 144 EE68
Wakeling Rd W7 137 CF71
Wakeling St E14 143 DY72
Wakely Cl (Biggin Hill), West. 238 EJ118
Wakeman Rd NW10 139 CW69
Wakemans Hill Av NW9 118 CR57
Wakerfield Cl, Horn. 128 FM57
Wakering Rd, Bark. 145 EQ65
Wakerley Cl E6 145 EM72
Truesdale Rd
Wakley St EC1 274 F2
Wakley St EC1 141 DP68
Walberswick St SW8 161 DL80
Walbrook EC4 275 K10
Walbrook EC4 142 DR73
Walbrook Ho N9 100 DW46
Walbrook Wf EC4 142 DQ73
Upper Thames St
Walburgh St E1 142 DV72
Bigland St
Walburton Rd, Pur. 219 DJ113
Walcorde Av SE17 279 J9
Walcot Rd, Enf. 83 DZ40
Walcot Sq SE11 278 E8
Walcot Sq SE11 161 DN77
Walcott St SW1 277 L8
Waldair Ct E16 165 EP75
Barge Ho Rd
Waldair Wf E16 165 EP75
Waldeck Gro SE27 181 DP90
Waldeck Rd N15 121 DP56
Waldeck Rd SW14 158 CQ83
Lower Richmond Rd
Waldeck Rd W4 158 CN79
Waldeck Rd W13 137 CH72
Waldeck Rd, Dart. 188 FM86
Waldeck Ter SW14 158 CQ83
Lower Richmond Rd
Waldegrave Av, Tedd. 177 CF92
Waldegrave Rd
Waldegrave Ct, Upmin. 128 FP60
Waldegrave Gdns, Twick. 177 CF89
Waldegrave Gdns, Upmin. 128 FP60
Waldegrave Pk, Twick. 177 CF91
Waldegrave Rd N8 121 DN55
Waldegrave Rd SE19 182 DT94
Waldegrave Rd W5 138 CM72
Waldegrave Rd, Brom. 204 EL98
Waldegrave Rd, Dag. 126 EW61
Waldegrave Rd, Tedd. 177 CF91
Waldegrave Rd, Twick. 177 CF91
Waldegrove, Croy. 202 DT104
Waldemar Av SW6 159 CY81
Waldemar Av W13 137 CJ74
Waldemar Rd SW19 180 DA92
Walden Av N13 100 DQ49
Walden Av, Chis. 185 EM91
Walden Av, Rain. 147 FD68
Walden Cl, Belv. 166 EZ78
Walden Gdns, Th.Hth. 201 DM97
Walden Par, Chis. 185 EM93
Walden Rd
Walden Pl, Welw.G.C. 29 CX07
Walden Rd N17 100 DR53
Walden Rd, Chis. 185 EM93
Walden Rd, Horn. 128 FK58
Walden Rd, Welw.G.C. 29 CX07
Walden St E1 142 DV72
Walden Way NW7 97 CX51
Walden Way, Horn. 128 FK58
Walden Way, Ilf. 103 ES52
Waldenhurst Rd, Orp. 206 EX101
Waldens Cl, Orp. 206 EX101
Waldens Pk Rd, Wok. 226 AW116
Waldens Rd, Orp. 206 EY101
Waldens Rd, Wok. 226 AX117
Waldenshaw Rd SE23 182 DW88
Waldo Cl SW4 181 DJ85
Waldo Pl, Mitch. 180 DE94
Waldo Rd NW10 139 CU69
Waldo Rd, Brom. 204 EK97
Waldorf Cl, S.Croy. 219 DP109
Waldram Cres SE23 182 DW88
Waldram Pk Rd SE23 183 DX88
Waldram Pl SE23 182 DW88
Waldram Cres
Waldrist Way, Erith 166 EZ75
Waldron Gdns, Brom. 203 ED97
Waldron Ms SW3 160 DD79
Old Ch St
Waldron Rd SW18 180 DC90
Waldron Rd, Har. 117 CE60
Waldronhyrst, S.Croy. 219 DP105
Waldrons, The, Croy. 219 DP105
Waldrons, The, Oxt. 254 EF131
Waldrons Path, S.Croy. 220 DQ105
Waldstock Rd SE28 146 EU73
Waleran Cl, Stan. 95 CF51
Chenduit Way
Waleran Flats SE1 162 DS77
Old Kent Rd
Walerand Rd SE13 163 EC82
Wales Av, Cars. 218 DF106
Wales Cl SE15 162 DV80
Wales Fm Rd W3 138 CR71
Waleton Acres, Wall. 219 DJ107
Waley St E1 143 DX71
Walfield Av N20 98 DB45
Walford Cl, Harl. 36 EW12
Walford Rd N16 122 DS63
Walford Rd (North Holmwood), Dor. 263 CH140
Walford Rd, Uxb. 134 BJ68
Walfrey Gdns, Dag. 146 EY66
Walham Grn Ct SW6 160 DB80
Waterford Rd
Walham Gro SW6 160 DA80
Walham Ri SW19 179 CY93
Walham Yd SW6 160 DA80
Walham Gro
Walk, The, Horn. 128 FM61
Walk, The (Tandridge), Oxt. 253 EA133
Walk, The, Pot.B. 64 DA32
Walk, The, Sun. 175 BT94
Walk, The (Eton Wick), Wind. 151 AN78
Walkden Rd, Chis. 185 EN92
Walker Cl N11 99 DJ49
Walker Cl SE18 165 EQ77
Walker Cl W7 137 CE74
Walker Cl, Dart. 167 FF83
Walker Cl, Felt. 175 BT87
Westmacott Dr
Walker Cl, Hmptn. 176 BZ93
Fearnley Cres
Walker Ms SW2 181 DN85
Effra Rd
Walkers Ct E8 142 DU65
Wilton Way
Walkers Ct W1 273 M10
Walkers Pl SW15 159 CY83
Felsham Rd
Walkerscroft Mead SE21 182 DQ88
Walkfield Dr, Epsom 233 CV117
Walkford Way SE15 162 DT80
Daniel Gdns
Walkley Rd, Dart. 187 FH85
Walks, The N2 120 DD55
Walkwood End, Beac. 88 AJ54
Walkwood Ri, Beac. 110 AJ55
Walkynscroft SE15 162 DV82
Firbank Rd
Wall End Rd E6 145 EN66
Wall St N1 142 DR65
Wallace Cl SE28 146 EX73
Haldane Rd
Wallace Cl, Shep. 195 BR98
Wallace Cl, Uxb. 134 BL68
Grays Rd
Wallace Cres, Cars. 218 DF106
Wallace Flds, Epsom 217 CT112
Wallace Gdns, Swans. 190 FY86
Milton St
Wallace Rd N1 142 DQ65
Wallace Rd, Grays 170 GA76
Wallace Sq, Couls. 235 DH121
Brighton Rd
Wallace Wk, Add. 212 BJ105
Wallace Way N19 121 DK61
Giesbach Rd
Wallasey Cres, Uxb. 114 BN61
Wallbutton Rd SE4 163 DY82
Wallcote Av NW2 119 CX60
Walled Gdn, The, Bet. 264 CR135
Walled Gdn, The, Tad. 233 CX122
Heathcote
Wallenger Av, Rom. 127 FH55
Waller Dr, Nthwd. 93 BU54
Waller La, Cat. 236 DT123
Waller Rd SE14 163 DX81
Waller Rd, Beac. 89 AM53
Waller Way SE10 163 EB80
Greenwich High Rd
Wallers Cl, Dag. 146 EY67
Wallers Cl, Wdf.Grn. 103 EM51
Wallers Hoppit, Loug. 84 EL40
Wallers Way, Hodd. 33 EB14
Wallfield All, Hert. 32 DQ10
Wallflower St W12 139 CT73
Wallgrave Rd SW5 160 DB77
Wallhouse Rd, Erith 167 FH80
Wallingford Av W10 139 CX71
Wallingford Rd, Uxb. 134 BH68
Wallingford Wk, St.Alb. 43 CD23
Wallington Cl, Ruis. 115 BQ58
Wallington Cor, Wall. 219 DH105
Manor Rd N
Wallington Rd, Chesh. 54 AP30
Wallington Rd, Ilf. 125 ET59
Wallington Sq, Wall. 219 DH107
Woodcote Rd
Wallis All SE1 279 J5
Wallis Cl SW11 160 DD83
Wallis Cl, Dart. 187 FF90
Wallis Cl, Horn. 127 FH60

Warwick La, Rain. 148 FM68
Warwick La, Upmin. 148 FP68
Warwick La, Wok. 226 AU119
Warwick Pas EC4 274 G8
Warwick Pl W5 157 CK75
Warwick Rd
Warwick Pl W9 140 DC71
Warwick Pl (Northfleet), Grav. 190 GB85
Warwick Pl, Uxb. 134 BJ66
Warwick Pl N SW1 277 K9
Warwick Pl N SW1 161 DJ77
Warwick Quad Shop Mall, Red. 250 DG133
London Rd
Warwick Rd E4 101 EA50
Warwick Rd E11 124 EH57
Warwick Rd E12 124 EL64
Warwick Rd E15 124 EF65
Warwick Rd E17 101 DZ53
Warwick Rd N11 99 DK51
Warwick Rd N18 100 DS49
Warwick Rd SE20 202 DV97
Warwick Rd SW5 159 CZ77
Warwick Rd W5 157 CK75
Warwick Rd W14 159 CZ77
Warwick Rd, Ashf. 174 BL92
Warwick Rd, Barn. 80 DB42
Warwick Rd, Beac. 89 AK52
Warwick Rd, Borwd. 78 CR41
Warwick Rd, Couls. 219 DJ114
Warwick Rd (Holmwood), Dor. 263 CJ144
Warwick Rd, Enf. 83 DZ37
Warwick Rd, Houns. 155 BV83
Warwick Rd, Kings.T. 197 CJ95
Warwick Rd, N.Mal. 198 CQ97
Warwick Rd, Rain. 148 FJ70
Warwick Rd, Red. 250 DF133
Warwick Rd, St.Alb. 43 CF18
Warwick Rd, Sid. 186 EV92
Warwick Rd, Sthl. 156 BZ76
Warwick Rd, Sutt. 218 DC105
Warwick Rd, T.Ditt. 197 CF99
Warwick Rd, Th.Hth. 201 DN97
Warwick Rd, Twick. 177 CE88
Warwick Rd, Well. 166 EW83
Warwick Rd, West Dr. 134 BL74
Warwick Row SW1 277 J6
Warwick Row SW1 161 DH76
Warwick Sq EC4 274 G8
Warwick Sq SW1 277 K10
Warwick Sq SW1 161 DJ78
Warwick Sq Ms SW1 277 K9
Warwick Sq Ms SW1 161 DJ77
Warwick St W1 273 L10
Warwick St W1 141 DJ73
Warwick Ter SE18 165 ER79
Warwick Way SW1 277 K9
Warwick Way SW1 161 DJ77
Warwick Way, Rick. 75 BQ42
Warwick Wold Rd, Red. 251 DN128
Warwick Yd EC1 275 J5
Warwicks Bench, Guil. 258 AX136
Warwicks Bench La, Guil. 258 AY137
Warwicks Bench Rd, Guil. 258 AY137
Warwickshire Path SE8 163 DZ80
Wash, The, Hert. 32 DR09
Wash Hill (Wooburn Grn), H.Wyc. 110 AE60
Wash Hill Lea (Wooburn Grn), H.Wyc. 110 AD59
Wash La, Pot.B. 63 CV33
Wash Rd, Brwd. 109 GE44
Washington Av E12 124 EL63
Washington Av, Hem.H. 40 BM15
Washington Cl E3 143 EC72
Washington Cl, Reig. 250 DA131
Washington Dr, Slou. 131 AK73
Washington Dr, Wind. 151 AL83
Washington Rd E6 144 EJ66
St. Stephens Rd
Washington Rd E18 102 EF54
Washington Rd SW13 159 CU80
Washington Rd, Kings.T. 198 CN96
Washington Rd, Wor.Pk. 199 CV103
Washington Row, Amer. 55 AQ40
London Rd W
Washneys Rd, Orp. 224 EV113
Washpond La, Warl. 237 EC118
Wastdale Rd SE23 183 DX88
Wat Tyler Rd SE3 163 EC82
Wat Tyler Rd SE10 163 EC82
Watchfield Ct W4 158 CQ78
Watchgate (Lane End), Dart. 189 FR91
Watchlytes, Welw.G.C. 30 DC09
Watchmead, Welw.G.C. 30 DA09
Watcombe Cotts, Rich. 158 CN79
Watcombe Pl SE25 202 DV99
Albert Rd
Watcombe Rd SE25 202 DV99
Water Circ (Bluewater), Green. 189 FT88
Water End Rd, Berk. 39 BB17
Water Gdns, Stan. 95 CH51
Water Gdns, The W2 272 C8
Water Gdns, The W2 140 DE72
Water La E15 144 EE65
Water La EC3 279 M1
Water La N9 100 DV46
Water La NW1 141 DH66
Kentish Town Rd
Water La SE14 162 DW80
Water La, Berk. 38 AW19
Water La, Chesh. 54 AP32
Water La, Cob. 230 BY115
Water La (Abinger Hammer), Dor. 261 BV143
Water La (Albury), Guil. 260 BH137
Water La, Harl. 50 EL19
Water La (Bovingdon), Hem.H. 57 BA29
Water La, Hert. 32 DQ10
Water La, Ilf. 125 ES62
Water La, Kings L. 59 BP29
Water La, Kings.T. 197 CK95
Water La (Bookham), Lthd. 246 BY125
Water La (Titsey), Oxt. 254 EG126
Water La, Purf. 168 FN77
Water La, Red. 251 DP130
Water La, Rich. 177 CK85
Water La (Shoreham), Sev. 225 FF112
Water La, Sid. 186 EZ89
Water La, Twick. 177 CG88
The Embk
Water La, Wat. 76 BW42
Water La, West. 255 ER127
Water Lily Cl, Sthl. 156 CC75
Navigator Dr
Water Meadow, Chesh. 54 AP32
Water Ms SE15 162 DW84
Water Mill Way (South Darenth), Dart. 208 FP96
Water Rd, Wem. 138 CM67
Water Row, Ware 33 DX06
Water Side, Kings L. 58 BN29
Water St WC2 274 C10
Water Twr Cl, Uxb. 114 BL64
Water Twr Hill, Croy. 220 DR105
Water Twr Pl N1 141 DN67
Liverpool Rd
Water Vw, Horl. 269 DJ148
Carlton Tye
Waterbank Rd SE6 183 EB90
Waterbeach, Welw.G.C. 30 DD08
Waterbeach Cl, Slou. 131 AR72
Waterbeach Rd, Dag. 146 EW65
Waterbeach Rd, Slou. 131 AR72
Waterbrook La NW4 119 CW57
Watercress Pl N1 142 DS66
Hertford Rd
Watercress Rd (Cheshunt), Wal.Cr. 66 DR26
Watercress Way, Wok. 226 AV117
Watercroft Rd (Halstead), Sev. 224 EZ110
Waterdale, Hert. 32 DQ11
Waterdale Rd SE2 166 EU79
Waterdales (Northfleet), Grav. 190 GD88
Waterdell Pl, Rick. 92 BG47
Uxbridge Rd
Waterden Cl, Guil. 259 AZ135
Waterden Rd E15 123 EA64
Waterden Rd, Guil. 258 AY135
Waterend La (Wheathampstead), St.Alb. 28 CQ07
Waterend La, Welw. 28 CS06
Waterer Gdns, Tad. 233 CX118
Waterer Ri, Wall. 219 DK107
Waterfall Cl N14 99 DJ48
Waterfall Cl, Vir.W. 192 AU97
Waterfall Cotts SW19 180 DD93
Waterfall Rd N11 99 DH49
Waterfall Rd N14 99 DJ48
Waterfall Rd SW19 180 DD93
Waterfall Ter SW17 180 DE93
Waterfield, Rick. 91 BC45
Waterfield, Tad. 233 CV119
Waterfield, Welw.G.C. 30 DB08
Waterfield Cl SE28 146 EV74
Waterfield Cl, Belv. 166 FA76
Waterfield Dr, Warl. 236 DW119
Waterfield Gdns SE25 202 DS99
Waterfield Grn, Tad. 233 CW120
Waterfields, Lthd. 231 CH119
Waterfields Way, Wat. 76 BX42
Waterford Cl, Cob. 214 BY111
Waterford Common, Hert. 31 DP05
Waterford Grn, Welw.G.C. 30 DB09
Waterford Rd SW6 160 DB81
Watergardens, The, Kings.T. 178 CQ93
Watergate EC4 274 F10
Watergate, The, Wat. 94 BX47
Watergate St SE8 163 EA79
Watergate Wk WC2 278 A2
Waterglade Ind Pk, Grays 169 FT78
Waterhall Av E4 102 EE49
Waterhall Cl E17 101 DX53
Waterhead Cl, Erith 167 FE80
Waterhouse Cl E16 144 EK71
Waterhouse Cl NW3 120 DD64
Lyndhurst Rd
Waterhouse Cl W6 159 CX77
Great Ch La
Waterhouse La, Ken. 236 DQ119
Waterhouse La (Bletchingley), Red. 252 DT132
Waterhouse La (Kingswood), Tad. 233 CY121
Waterhouse Moor, Harl. 51 ET16
Waterhouse Sq EC1 274 D7
Waterhouse St, Hem.H. 40 BJ20
Wateridge Cl E14 163 EA76
Wateringbury Cl, Orp. 206 EV97
Waterloo Br SE1 278 B1
Waterloo Br SE1 141 DM73
Waterloo Br WC2 278 B1
Waterloo Br WC2 141 DM73
Waterloo Cl E9 122 DW64
Churchill Wk
Waterloo Cl, Felt. 175 BT88
Waterloo Est E2 142 DW68
Waterloo Gdns E2 142 DW68
Waterloo Gdns N1 141 DP66
Barnsbury St
Waterloo Gdns, Rom. 127 FD58
Waterloo Pas NW6 140 DA66
Waterloo Pl SW1 277 M2
Waterloo Pl SW1 141 DK74
Waterloo Pl, Rich. 178 CL85
Sheen Rd
Waterloo Pl (Kew), Rich. 158 CN79
Waterloo Rd E6 144 EJ66
Waterloo Rd E7 124 EF64
Wellington Rd
Waterloo Rd E10 123 EA59
Waterloo Rd NW2 119 CU60
Waterloo Rd SE1 278 D4
Waterloo Rd SE1 161 DN75
Waterloo Rd, Brwd. 108 FW46
Waterloo Rd, Epsom 216 CR112
Waterloo Rd, Ilf. 103 EQ54
Waterloo Rd, Rom. 127 FE57
Waterloo Rd, Sutt. 218 DD106
Waterloo Rd, Uxb. 134 BJ67
Waterloo St, Grav. 191 GJ87
Waterloo Ter N1 141 DP66
Waterlow Ct NW11 120 DB59
Heath Cl
Waterlow Rd N19 121 DJ60
Waterlow Rd, Reig. 266 DC135
Waterman Cl, Wat. 75 BV44
Waterman Ct, Slou. 131 AL74
Waterman St SW15 159 CX83
Waterman Way E1 142 DV74
Waterman's Cl, Kings.T. 178 CL94
Woodside Rd
Watermans Wk SE16 163 DY76
Watermans Way, Epp. 70 FA27
Watermark Way, Hert. 32 DT09
Watermead, Felt. 175 BS88
Watermead, Tad. 233 CV120
Watermead, Wok. 226 AT116
Watermead La, Cars. 200 DF101
Middleton Rd
Watermead Rd SE6 183 EC91
Watermead Way N17 122 DV55
Watermeadow Cl, Erith 167 FH81
Watermeadow La SW6 160 DC82
Watermen's Sq SE20 182 DW94
Watermill Cl, Rich. 177 CJ90
Watermill La N18 100 DS50
Watermill La, Hert. 32 DR06
Watermill La N, Hert. 32 DQ06
Watermill Way SW19 200 DC95
Watermill Way, Felt. 176 BZ89
Watermint Cl, Orp. 206 EX98
Wagtail Way
Watermint Quay N16 122 DU59
Waterperry La (Chobham), Wok. 210 AT110
Waters Dr, Rick. 92 BL46
Waters Dr, Stai. 173 BF90
Waters Gdns, Dag. 126 FA64
Waters Pl SW15 159 CW82
Danemere St
Waters Rd SE6 184 EE90
Waters Rd, Kings.T. 198 CP96
Waters Sq, Kings.T. 198 CP97
Watersedge, Epsom 216 CQ105
Watersfield Way, Edg. 95 CK52
Waterside, Beck. 203 EA95
Rectory Rd
Waterside, Berk. 38 AX19
Holliday St
Waterside, Chesh. 54 AQ32
Waterside, Dart. 187 FE85
Waterside (Wooburn Grn), H.Wyc. 110 AE56
Waterside, Horl. 268 DG146
Waterside, Rad. 61 CH34
Waterside (London Colney), St.Alb. 62 CL27
Waterside, Uxb. 134 BJ71
Waterside, Welw.G.C. 30 DA07
Waterside Cl E3 143 DZ67
Waterside Cl SE16 162 DU75
Bevington St
Waterside Cl, Bark. 126 EU63
Waterside Cl, Nthlt. 136 BZ69
Waterside Cl, Rom. 106 FN52
Waterside Cl, Surb. 198 CL103
Culsac Rd
Waterside Ct SE13 163 ED84
Weardale Rd
Waterside Ct, Kings L. 59 BP29
Water Side
Waterside Dr (Langley), Slou. 153 AZ75
Waterside Dr, Walt. 195 BU99
Waterside Ms, Guil. 242 AW132
Waterside Pl NW1 140 DG67
Princess Rd
Waterside Pl, Saw. 36 FA05
Waterside Pt SW11 160 DE80
Waterside Rd, Guil. 242 AX131
Waterside Rd, Sthl. 156 CA76
Waterside Trd Cen W7 157 CE76
Waterside Way SW17 180 DC91
Waterside Way, Wok. 226 AV118
Winnington Way
Watersmeet, Harl. 51 EP19
Watersmeet Cl, Guil. 243 BA129
Cotts Wd Dr
Watersmeet Way SE28 146 EW72
Waterson Rd, Grays 171 GH77
Waterson St E2 275 N2
Waterson St E2 142 DS69
Watersplash Cl, Kings.T. 198 CL97
Watersplash La, Hayes 155 BU77
Watersplash La, Houns. 155 BV78
Watersplash Rd, Shep. 194 BN98
Waterton Av, Grav. 191 GL87
Waterview Ho E14 143 DY71
Waterway Rd, Lthd. 231 CG122
Waterworks Cotts, Brox. 49 DY22
Waterworks La E5 123 DX61
Waterworks Rd SW2 181 DM86
Waterworks Yd, Croy. 202 DQ104
Surrey St
Watery La SW20 199 CZ96
Watery La (Lyne), Cher. 193 BD102
Watery La, Hat. 44 CS19
Watery La (Wooburn Grn), H.Wyc. 88 AE54
Watery La, Nthlt. 136 BW68
Watery La (Flamstead), St.Alb. 61 CK28
Watery La, Sid. 186 EV93
Wates Way, Brwd. 108 FX46
Wates Way, Mitch. 200 DF100
Wates Way Ind Est, Mitch. 200 DF100
Wates Way
Wateville Rd N17 100 DQ53
Watford Arches Retail Pk, Wat. 76 BX43
Lower High St
Watford Business Pk, Wat. 75 BS44
Watford Bypass, Borwd. 95 CG45
Watford Cl SW11 160 DE81
Petworth St
Watford Cl, Guil. 243 AZ134
Watford Fld Rd, Wat. 76 BW43
Watford Heath, Wat. 94 BX45
Watford Rd E16 144 EG71
Watford Rd, Borwd. 77 CJ44
Watford Rd, Har. 117 CG61
Watford Rd, Kings L. 59 BP32
Watford Rd, Nthwd. 93 BT51
Watford Rd, Rad. 77 CE36
Watford Rd, Rick. 75 BQ43
Watford Rd, St.Alb. 60 CA27
Watford Rd, Wem. 117 CG61
Watford Way NW4 119 CU56
Watford Way NW7 119 CU56
Wathen Rd, Dor. 263 CH135
Watkin Rd, Wem. 118 CP62
Watkins Ri, Pot.B. 64 DB32
The Wk
Watkinson Rd N7 141 DM65
Watling Av, Edg. 96 CR52
Watling Cl, Hem.H. 40 BL17
Watling Ct EC4 275 J9
Watling Ct, Borwd. 77 CK44
Watling Fm Cl, Stan. 95 CJ46
Watling Gdns NW2 139 CY65
Watling Knoll, Rad. 61 CF33
Watling St EC4 275 H9
Watling St EC4 142 DQ72
Watling St SE15 162 DS79
Dragon Rd
Watling St, Bexh. 167 FB84
Watling St, Borwd. 77 CJ40
Watling St, Dart. 188 FP87
Watling St, Grav. 190 GC90
Watling St, Rad. 61 CF32
Watling St, St.Alb. 60 CC25
Watling St Caravan Site (Travellers), St.Alb. 60 CC25
Watling Vw, St.Alb. 42 CC24
Watlings Cl, Croy. 203 DY100
Watlington Gro SE26 183 DY92
Watlington Rd, Harl. 36 EX11
Watney Mkt E1 142 DV72
Commercial Rd
Watney Rd SW14 158 CQ83
Watney St E1 142 DV72
Watneys Rd, Mitch. 201 DK99
Watson Av E6 145 EN66
Watson Av, St.Alb. 43 CF17
Watson Av, Sutt. 199 CY103
Watson Cl N16 122 DR64
Matthias Rd
Watson Cl SW19 180 DE93
Watson Cl, Grays 169 FU81
Watson Gdns, Rom. 106 FK54
Watson Rd (Westcott), Dor. 262 CC137
Watson St E13 144 EH68
Watson's Ms W1 272 C7
Watsons Rd N22 99 DM53
Watson's St SE8 163 EA80
Watsons Wk, St.Alb. 43 CE21
Watsons Yd NW2 119 CT61
North Circular Rd
Wattendon Rd, Ken. 235 DP116
Wattisfield Rd E5 122 DW62
Wattleton Rd, Beac. 89 AK54
Watton Rd, Ware 32 DW05
Watts Cl N15 122 DS57
Seaford Rd
Watts Cl, Tad. 233 CX122
Watts Cres, Purf. 168 FQ77
Watts Fm Par (Chobham), Wok. 210 AT110
Barnmead
Watts Gro E3 143 EB71
Watts La, Chis. 205 EP95
Watts La, Tad. 233 CX122
Watts La, Tedd. 177 CG92
Watts Mead, Tad. 233 CX122
Watts Pt E13 144 EG67
Brooks Rd
Watts Rd, T.Ditt. 197 CG101
Watts St E1 142 DV74
Watts St SE15 162 DT81
Watts Way SW7 276 A6
Wauthier Cl N13 99 DP50
Wavel Ms N8 121 DK56
Wavel Ms NW6 140 DB66
Acol Rd
Wavel Pl SE26 182 DT91
Sydenham Hill
Wavell Cl (Cheshunt), Wal.Cr. 67 DY27
Wavell Dr, Sid. 185 ES86
Wavell Gdns, Slou. 131 AM69
Wavell Rd, Beac. 89 AP54
Wavendene Av, Egh. 173 BB94
Wavendon Av W4 158 CR78
Waveney, Hem.H. 40 BM15
Waveney Av SE15 162 DV84
Waveney Cl E1 142 DU74
Kennet St
Waverley Av E4 101 DZ49
Waverley Av E17 123 ED55
Waverley Av, Ken. 236 DS116
Waverley Av, Surb. 198 CP100
Waverley Av, Sutt. 200 DB103
Waverley Av, Twick. 176 BZ88
Waverley Av, Wem. 118 CM64
Waverley Cl E18 102 EJ53
Waverley Cl, Brom. 204 EK99
Waverley Cl, Hayes 155 BR77
Waverley Cl, W.Mol. 196 CA99
Waverley Ct, Wok. 226 AY118
Waverley Cres SE18 165 ER78
Waverley Cres, Rom. 106 FJ52
Waverley Dr, Cher. 193 BD104
Waverley Dr, Vir.W. 192 AU97
Waverley Gdns E6 144 EL71
Oliver Gdns
Waverley Gdns NW10 138 CM69
Waverley Gdns, Bark. 145 ES68
Waverley Gdns, Grays 170 GA75
Waverley Gdns, Ilf. 103 EQ54
Waverley Gdns, Nthwd. 93 BU53
Waverley Gro N3 119 CY55
Waverley Ind Est, Har. 117 CD55
Waverley Pl N4 121 DP61
Adolphus Rd
Waverley Pl NW8 140 DD68
Waverley Pl, Lthd. 231 CH122
Church Rd
Waverley Rd E17 123 EC55
Waverley Rd E18 102 EJ53
Waverley Rd N8 121 DK58
Waverley Rd N17 100 DV52
Waverley Rd SE18 165 ER78
Waverley Rd SE25 202 DV98
Waverley Rd (Stoke D'Abernon), Cob. 214 CB114
Waverley Rd, Enf. 81 DP42
Waverley Rd, Epsom 217 CV106
Waverley Rd, Har. 116 BZ60
Waverley Rd (Oxshott), Lthd. 214 CB114
Waverley Rd, Rain. 147 FH69
Waverley Rd, St.Alb. 43 CD18
Waverley Rd, Slou. 131 AQ71
Waverley Rd, Sthl. 136 CA73
Waverley Rd, Wey. 212 BN106
Waverley Vil N17 100 DT54
Waverley Wk W2 140 DA71
Waverley Way, Cars. 218 DE107
Waverton Ho E3 143 DZ67
Waverton Rd SW18 180 DC87
Waverton St W1 276 G2
Waverton St W1 140 DG74
Wavertree Ct SW2 181 DM88
Streatham Hill
Wavertree Rd E18 102 EG54
Wavertree Rd SW2 181 DL88
Waxlow Cres, Sthl. 136 CA72
Waxlow Rd NW10 138 CQ68
Waxwell Cl, Pnr. 94 BX54
Waxwell La, Pnr. 94 BX54
Waxwell Ter SE1 278 C5
Way, The, Reig. 250 DD133
Way Volante, Grav. 191 GL91
Wayborne Gro, Ruis. 115 BQ58
Waycross Rd, Upmin. 129 FS58
Waye Av, Houns. 155 BU81
Wayfarer Rd, Nthlt. 136 BX70
Wayfarers Pk, Berk. 38 AT19
Wayfaring Grn, Grays 170 FZ78
Curling La
Wayfield Link SE9 185 ER86
Wayford St SW11 160 DE82
Wayland Av E8 122 DU64
Waylands, Hayes 135 BR71
Waylands, Swan. 207 FF98
Waylands Cl (Knockholt), Sev. 240 EY115
Waylands Mead, Beck. 203 EB95
Wayleave, The SE28 146 EV73
Waylett Pl SE27 181 DP90
Waylett Pl, Wem. 117 CK63
Wayman Ct E8 142 DV65
Wayne Cl, Orp. 205 ET104
Wayneflete Twr Av, Esher 196 CA104
Waynflete Av, Croy. 201 DP104
Waynflete Sq W10 139 CX73
Waynflete St SW18 180 DC89
Wayre, The, Harl. 36 EW11
Wayre St, Harl. 36 EW11
Wayside NW11 119 CY60
Wayside SW14 178 CQ85
Wayside, Croy. 221 EB107
Field Way
Wayside, Kings L. 58 BH30
Wayside, Pot.B. 64 DD33
Wayside, Rad. 61 CK33
Wayside, The, Hem.H. 41 BQ21
Wayside Av, Bushey 77 CD44
Wayside Av, Horn. 128 FK61
Wayside Cl N14 81 DJ44
Wayside Cl, Rom. 127 FF55
Wayside Commercial Est, Bark. 146 EU67
Wayside Ct, Twick. 177 CJ86
Wayside Ct, Wem. 118 CN62
Oakington Av
Wayside Ct, Wok. 226 AS116
Langmans Way
Wayside Gdns SE9 185 EM91
Wayside Gro
Wayside Gdns, Dag. 126 FA64
Wayside Gdns, Ger.Cr. 112 AX59
Wayside Gro SE9 185 EM91
Wayside Ms, Ilf. 125 EN57
Gaysham Av
Wayville Rd, Dart. 188 FP87
Weald, The, Chis. 185 EM93
Weald Br Rd, Epp. 53 FD24
Weald Cl SE16 162 DV78
Stevenson Cres
Weald Cl, Brwd. 108 FU48
Weald Cl, Brom. 204 EL103
Weald Cl (Istead Ri), Grav. 190 GE94
Weald Cl (Shalford), Guil. 258 AY140
Station Rd
Weald Hall La, Epp. 70 EW25
Weald La, Har. 95 CD54
Weald Pk Way, Brwd. 108 FS48
Weald Ri, Har. 95 CF52
Weald Rd, Brwd. 107 FR46
Weald Rd, Sev. 257 FH129
Weald Rd, Uxb. 134 BN68
Weald Sq E5 122 DV61
Rossington St
Weald Way, Cat. 252 DS128
Weald Way, Hayes 135 BS69
Weald Way, Reig. 266 DC138
Weald Way, Rom. 127 FB58
Wealdon Ct, Guil. 242 AT134
Humbolt Cl
Wealdstone Rd, Sutt. 199 CZ103
Wealdway, Grav. 191 GH93
Wealdwood Gdns, Pnr. 94 CB51
Highbanks Rd
Weale Rd E4 101 ED48
Weall Cl, Pur. 219 DM112
Weall Grn, Wat. 59 BV32
Wear Pl E2 142 DV69
Weardale Av, Dart. 188 FQ89
Weardale Gdns, Enf. 82 DR39
Weardale Rd SE13 163 ED84
Wearside Rd SE13 163 EB84
Weasdale Ct, Wok. 226 AT116
Roundthorn Way
Weatherall Cl, Add. 212 BH106
Weatherhill Cl, Horl. 269 DM148
Weatherhill Common, Horl. 269 DM147
Weatherhill Rd, Horl. 269 DM148
Weatherley Cl E3 143 DZ71
Weaver Cl E6 *Trader Rd* 145 EP73
Weaver Cl, Croy. 220 DT105
Weaver St E1 142 DU70
Weaver Wk SE27 181 DP91
Weavers Cl, Grav. 191 GG88
Weavers Cl, Islw. 157 CE84
Weavers La, Sev. 257 FJ121
Weavers Orchard (Southfleet), Grav. 190 GA93
Weavers Ter SW6 160 DA79
Weavers Way NW1 141 DK67
Webb Cl W10 139 CW70
Webb Cl, Chesh. 54 AP30
Webb Cl, Slou. 152 AX77
Webb Est E5 122 DU59
Webb Gdns E13 144 EG70
Kelland Rd
Webb Pl NW10 139 CT69
Old Oak La
Webb Rd SE3 164 EF79
Webb St SE1 279 M7
Webb St SE1 162 DS76
Webber Cl, Borwd. 77 CK44
Rodgers Cl
Webber Cl, Erith 167 FH80
Webber Row SE1 278 E6
Webber Row SE1 161 DP75
Webber St SE1 278 E4
Webber St SE1 161 DP75
Webb's All, Sev. 257 FJ125
Webbs Rd SW11 180 DF85
Webbs Rd, Hayes 135 BV69
Webbscroft Rd, Dag. 127 FB63
Webster Cl, Horn. 128 FK62
Webster Cl (Oxshott), Lthd. 214 CB114
Webster Cl, Wal.Abb. 68 EG33
Webster Gdns W5 137 CK74
Webster Rd E11 123 EC62
Webster Rd SE16 162 DU76
Websters Cl, Wok. 226 AU120
Wedderburn Rd NW3 120 DD64
Wedderburn Rd, Bark. 145 ES67
Wedgewood Cl, Epp. 70 EU30
Theydon Gro
Wedgewood Cl, Nthwd. 93 BQ51
Wedgewood Dr, Harl. 52 EX16
Wedgewood Wk NW6 120 DB64
Lymington Rd
Wedgewoods, West. 238 EJ121
Westmore Rd
Wedgwood Ms W1 273 N9
Wedgwood Pl, Cob. 213 BU114
Portsmouth Rd
Wedgwood Way SE19 182 DQ94
Wedhey, Harl. 51 EQ15
Wedlake Cl, Horn. 128 FL60
Wedlake St W10 139 CY70
Kensal Rd
Wedmore Av, Ilf. 103 EN53
Wedmore Gdns N19 121 DK61
Wedmore Ms N19 121 DK62
Wedmore St
Wedmore Rd, Grnf. 137 CD69
Wedmore St N19 121 DK62
Wednesbury Gdns, Rom. 106 FM52
Wednesbury Grn, Rom. 106 FM52
Wednesbury Gdns
Wednesbury Rd, Rom. 106 FM52
Weech Rd NW6 120 DA63
Weedington Rd NW5 120 DG64
Weedon Cl (Chalfont St. Peter), Ger.Cr. 90 AV53
Weedon La, Amer. 55 AN36

Weekes Dr, Slou. 131 AP74
Weekley Sq SW11 160 DD83
Thomas Baines Rd
Weigall Rd SE12 164 EG84
Weighhouse St W1 272 G9
Weighhouse St W1 140 DG72
Weighton Rd SE20 202 DW96
Weighton Rd, Har. 95 CD53
Weihurst Gdns, Sutt. 218 DD106
Weimar St SW15 159 CY83
Weind, The, Epp. 85 ES36
Weir Est SW12 181 DJ87
Weir Hall Av N18 100 DR51
Weir Hall Gdns N18 100 DR50
Weir Hall Rd N17 100 DR50
Weir Hall Rd N18 100 DR50
Weir Pl, Stai. 193 BE95
Weir Rd SW12 181 DJ87
Weir Rd SW19 180 DB90
Weir Rd, Bex. 187 FB87
Weir Rd, Cher. 194 BH101
Weir Rd, Walt. 195 BU100
Weirdale Av N20 98 DF47
Weir's Pas NW1 273 N2
Weir's Pas NW1 141 DK69
Weirside Gdns, West Dr. 134 BK74
Weiss Rd SW15 159 CX83
Welbeck Av, Brom. 184 EG91
Welbeck Av, Hayes 135 BV70
Welbeck Av, Sid. 186 EU88
Welbeck Cl N12 98 DD50
Torrington Pk
Welbeck Cl, Borwd. 78 CN41
Welbeck Cl, Epsom 217 CU108
Welbeck Cl, N.Mal. 199 CT99
Welbeck Rd E6 144 EK69
Welbeck Rd, Barn. 80 DD44
Welbeck Rd, Cars. 200 DE102
Welbeck Rd, Har. 116 CB60
Welbeck Rd, Sutt. 200 DD103
Welbeck St W1 273 H8
Welbeck St W1 140 DG71
Welbeck Wk, Cars. 200 DE102
Welbeck Rd
Welbeck Way W1 273 H8
Welbeck Way W1 141 DH72
Welby St SE5 161 DP81
Welch Ho, Enf. 83 DX37
Beaconsfield Rd
Welch Pl, Pnr. 94 BW53
Welclose St, St.Alb. 42 CC20
Welcomes Rd, Ken. 236 DQ116
Welcote Dr, Nthwd. 93 BR51
Weld Pl N11 99 DH50
Welden, Slou. 132 AW72
Welders La (Jordans), Beac. 90 AT52
Welders La (Chalfont St. Peter), Ger.Cr. 90 AT52
Weldon Cl, Ruis. 135 BV65
Weldon Dr, W.Mol. 196 BZ98
Weldon Way, Red. 251 DK129
Welfare Rd E15 144 EE66
Welford Cl E5 123 DX62
Denton Way
Welford Pl SW19 179 CY91
Welham Cl, Hat. 45 CW24
Welham Ct, Hat. 45 CW24
Dixons Hill Rd
Welham Manor, Hat. 45 CW24
Welham Rd SW16 180 DG92
Welham Rd SW17 180 DG92
Welhouse Rd, Cars. 200 DE102
Welkin Grn, Hem.H. 41 BQ19
Wood End Cl
Well App, Barn. 79 CW43
Well Cl SW16 181 DM91
Well Cl, Ruis. 116 BY62
Parkfield Cres
Well Cl, Wok. 226 AW117
Well Cottage Cl E11 124 EJ59
Well Ct EC4 275 J9
Well Ct SW16 181 DM91
Well Cft, Hem.H. 40 BH19
Gadebridge Rd
Well End Rd, Borwd. 78 CQ37
Well Fm Rd, Warl. 236 DU119
Well Gro N20 98 DC45
Well Hall Par SE9 165 EM84
Well Hall Rd
Well Hall Rd SE9 165 EM83
Well Hill, Orp. 225 FB107
Well Hill La, Orp. 225 FB108
Well Hill Rd, Sev. 225 FD107
Well La SW14 178 CQ85
Well La, Brwd. 108 FT41
Well La, Harl. 35 EN14
Well La, Wok. 226 AW117
Well Pas NW3 120 DD62
Well Path, Wok. 226 AW117
Well La
Well Rd NW3 120 DD62
Well Rd, Barn. 79 CW43
Well Rd, Pot.B. 64 DE28
Well Row, Hert. 47 DM17
Well St E9 142 DW66
Well St E15 144 EE65
Well Wk NW3 120 DD63
Well Way, Epsom 232 CN115
Wellacre Rd, Har. 117 CH58
Wellan Cl, Sid. 186 EV85
Welland Cl, Slou. 153 BA79
Welland Gdns, Grnf. 137 CF68
Welland Ms E1 142 DU74
Kennet St
Welland St SE10 163 EC79
Wellands, Hat. 45 CU16
Wellands Cl, Brom. 205 EM96
Wellbank, Maid. 130 AE70
Rectory Rd
Wellbrook Rd, Orp. 223 EN105
Wellbury Ter, Hem.H. 41 BQ20
Wellclose Sq E1 142 DU73
Wellclose St E1 142 DU73
The Highway
Wellcome Av, Dart. 168 FM84
Wellcroft Cl, Welw.G.C. 30 DA11
Wellcroft Rd, Slou. 131 AP74
Wellcroft Rd, Welw.G.C. 30 DA11
Welldon Cres, Har. 117 CE58
Wellen Ri, Hem.H. 40 BL23
Weller Cl, Amer. 55 AS37
Weller Rd, Amer. 55 AS37
Weller St SE1 279 H4
Wellers Cl, West. 255 EQ127
Weller's Ct N1 273 P1
Wellers Ct (Shere), Guil. 260 BN139
Wellers Gro (Cheshunt), Wal.Cr. 66 DU28
Wellesford Cl, Bans. 233 CZ117
Wellesley, Harl. 51 EN20
Wellesley Av W6 159 CV76
Wellesley Av, Iver 153 BF76
Wellesley Av, Nthwd. 93 BT50
Wellesley Ct W9 140 DC69
Maida Vale
Wellesley Ct Rd, Croy. 202 DR103
Wellesley Cres, Pot.B. 63 CY33
Wellesley Cres, Twick. 177 CE89
Wellesley Gro, Croy. 202 DR103
Wellesley Pk Ms, Enf. 81 DP40
Wellesley Pas, Croy. 202 DQ103
Wellesley Rd
Wellesley Path, Slou. 152 AU75
Wellesley Rd
Wellesley Pl NW1 273 M3
Wellesley Rd E11 124 EG57
Wellesley Rd E17 123 EA58
Wellesley Rd N22 99 DN54
Wellesley Rd NW5 120 DG64
Wellesley Rd W4 158 CN78
Wellesley Rd, Brwd. 108 FW46
Wellesley Rd, Croy. 202 DQ102
Wellesley Rd, Har. 117 CE57
Wellesley Rd, Ilf. 125 EP61
Wellesley Rd, Slou. 152 AU75
Wellesley Rd, Sutt. 218 DC107
Wellesley Rd, Twick. 177 CE90
Wellesley St E1 143 DX71
Wellesley Ter N1 275 J2
Wellesley Ter N1 142 DQ69
Welley Av (Wraysbury), Stai. 152 AY84
Welley Rd (Horton), Slou. 152 AY84
Welley Rd (Wraysbury), Stai. 152 AY84
Wellfield Av N10 121 DH55
Wellfield Cl, Hat. 45 CU17
Wellfield Gdns, Cars. 218 DE109
Wellfield Rd SW16 181 DL91
Wellfield Rd, Hat. 45 CU16
Wellfield Wk SW16 181 DM92
Wellfields, Loug. 85 EN41
Wellfit St SE24 161 DP83
Hinton Rd
Wellgarth, Grnf. 137 CH65
Wellgarth, Welw.G.C. 29 CY10
Wellgarth Rd NW11 120 DB60
Wellhouse La, Barn. 79 CW42
Wellhouse La, Bet. 264 CQ138
Wellhouse Rd, Beck. 203 DZ98
Welling High St, Well. 166 EV83
Welling Way SE9 165 ER83
Welling Way, Well. 165 ER83
Wellings Ho, Hayes 135 BV74
Wellington Av E4 101 EA47
Wellington Av N9 100 DV48
Wellington Av N15 122 DT58
Wellington Av, Houns. 176 CA85
Wellington Av, Pnr. 94 BZ53
Wellington Av, Sid. 186 EU86
Wellington Av, Vir.W. 192 AV99
Wellington Av, Wor.Pk. 217 CW105
Wellington Bldgs SW1 161 DH78
Ebury Br Rd
Wellington Cl SE14 163 DX81
Rutts Ter
Wellington Cl W11 140 DA72
Ledbury Rd
Wellington Cl, Dag. 147 FC66
Wellington Cl, Walt. 195 BT102
Hepworth Way
Wellington Cl, Wat. 94 BZ48
Highfield
Wellington Cotts, Lthd. 245 BS129
Wellington Ct NW8 140 DD68
Wellington Rd
Wellington Ct, Ashf. 174 BL92
Wellington Rd
Wellington Ct, Stai. 174 BL87
Clare Rd
Wellington Cres, N.Mal. 198 CQ97
Wellington Dr, Dag. 147 FC66
Wellington Dr, Pur. 219 DM110
Wellington Dr, Welw.G.C. 30 DC09
Wellington Gdns SE7 164 EJ79
Wellington Gdns, Twick. 177 CD91
Wellington Gro SE10 163 ED80
Crooms Hill
Wellington Hill (High Beach), Loug. 84 EH37
Wellington Ms SE7 164 EJ79
Wellington Ms SE22 162 DU84
Peckham Rye
Wellington Ms SW16 181 DK90
Woodbourne Av
Wellington Pk Est NW2 119 CU61
Wellington Pas E11 124 EG57
Wellington Rd
Wellington Pl N2 120 DE57
Great N Rd
Wellington Pl NW8 272 B1
Wellington Pl NW8 140 DE68
Wellington Pl, Brwd. 108 FW50
Wellington Pl, Brox. 48 DW23
Wellington Pl, Cob. 214 BZ112
Wellington Rd E6 145 EM68
Wellington Rd E7 124 EF63
Wellington Rd E10 123 DY60
Wellington Rd E11 124 EG57
Wellington Rd E17 123 DY56
Wellington Rd NW8 140 DD68
Wellington Rd NW10 139 CX69
Wellington Rd SW19 180 DA89
Wellington Rd W5 157 CJ76
Wellington Rd, Ashf. 174 BL92
Wellington Rd, Belv. 166 EZ78
Wellington Rd, Bex. 186 EX85
Wellington Rd, Brom. 204 EJ98
Wellington Rd, Cat. 236 DQ122
Wellington Rd, Croy. 201 DP101
Wellington Rd, Dart. 188 FJ86
Wellington Rd, Enf. 82 DS43
Wellington Rd, Epp. 70 FA27
Wellington Rd, Felt. 175 BS85
Wellington Rd, Hmptn. 177 CD92
Wellington Rd, Har. 117 CE55
Wellington Rd, Orp. 206 EV100
Wellington Rd, Pnr. 94 BZ53
Wellington Rd, St.Alb. 43 CH21
Wellington Rd (London Colney), St.Alb. 61 CK26
Wellington Rd, Til. 171 GG83
Wellington Rd, Twick. 177 CD92
Wellington Rd, Uxb. 134 BJ67
Wellington Rd, Wat. 75 BV40
Wellington Rd N, Houns. 156 BZ83
Wellington Rd S, Houns. 156 BZ84
Wellington Row E2 142 DT69
Wellington Sq SW3 276 D10
Wellington Sq SW3 160 DF78
Wellington St SE18 165 EN77
Wellington St WC2 274 A10
Wellington St WC2 141 DL73
Wellington St, Bark. 145 EQ67
Axe St
Wellington St, Grav. 191 GJ87
Wellington St, Hert. 31 DP08
Wellington St, Slou. 152 AT75
Wellington Ter E1 142 DV74
Wellington Ter W2 140 DB73
Notting Hill Gate
Wellington Ter, Har. 117 CD60
West St
Wellington Ter (Knaphill), Wok. 226 AS118
Victoria Rd
Wellington Way E3 143 EA69
Wellington Way, Horl. 268 DF146
Wellington Way, Wey. 212 BN110
Wellingtonia Av (Havering-atte-Bower), Rom. 105 FE48
Wellmeade Dr, Sev. 257 FH127
Wellmeadow Rd SE6 184 EE87
Wellmeadow Rd SE13 184 EE86
Wellmeadow Rd W7 157 CG77
Wellow Wk, Cars. 200 DD102
Wells, The N14 99 DK45
Wells Cl, Lthd. 230 CB124
Wells Cl, Nthlt. 136 BW69
Yeading La
Wells Cl, St.Alb. 42 CC19
Artisan Cres
Wells Cl, S.Croy. 220 DS106
Wells Cl (Cheshunt), Wal.Cr. 66 DQ25
Bloomfield Rd
Wells Cl, Wind. 151 AN80
Wells Dr NW9 118 CR60
Wells Gdns, Dag. 127 FB64
Wells Gdns, Ilf. 124 EL59
Wells Gdns, Rain. 147 FF65
Wells Ho Rd NW10 138 CS71
Wells Ms W1 273 L8
Wells Pk Rd SE26 182 DU90
Wells Path, Hayes 135 BS69
Wells Pl, Red. 251 DH130
Wells Ri NW8 140 DF67
Wells Rd W12 159 CW75
Wells Rd, Brom. 205 EM96
Wells Rd, Epsom 216 CN114
Wells Rd, Guil. 243 BC131
Wells Sq WC1 274 B3
Wells St W1 273 K7
Wells St W1 141 DJ72
Wells Ter N4 121 DN61
Wells Way SE5 162 DS79
Wells Way SW7 160 DD76
Wells Yd N7 121 DN64
Holloway Rd
Wellside Cl, Barn. 79 CW42
Wellside Gdns SW14 178 CQ85
Well La
Wellsmoor Gdns, Brom. 205 EN97
Wellsprings Cres, Wem. 118 CP62
Wellstead Av N9 101 DX45
Wellstead Rd E6 145 EN68
Wellstones, Wat. 75 BV41
Wellstones Yd, Wat. 75 BV41
Wellstones
Wellswood Cl, Hem.H. 41 BP19
Wellwood Cl, Couls. 219 DL114
The Vale
Wellwood Rd, Ilf. 126 EU60
Welsford St SE1 162 DU78
Welsh Cl E13 144 EG69
Welshpool Ho E8 142 DU67
Benjamin Cl
Welshpool St E8 142 DV67
Broadway Mkt
Welshside Wk NW9 118 CS58
Fryent Gro
Welstead Way W4 159 CT77
Welsummer Way, Wal.Cr. 67 DX27
Weltje Rd W6 159 CU77
Welton Rd SE18 165 ES80
Welwyn Av, Felt. 175 BT86
Welwyn Ct, Hem.H. 40 BM16
Welwyn Rd, Hert. 30 DG08
Welwyn St E2 142 DW69
Globe Rd
Welwyn Way, Hayes 135 BS70
Wembley Commercial Cen, Wem. 117 CK61
Wembley Hill Rd, Wem. 118 CM64
Wembley Pk Business Cen, Wem. 118 CP62
Wembley Pk Dr, Wem. 118 CM62
Wembley Pt, Wem. 138 CP66
Wembley Rd, Hmptn. 176 CA94
Wembley Way, Wem. 138 CP65
Wemborough Rd, Stan. 95 CJ52
Wembury Rd N6 121 DH59
Wemyss Rd SE3 164 EF82
Wend, The, Couls. 219 DK114
Wend, The, Croy. 221 DZ111
Wendela Cl, Wok. 227 AZ118
Wendela Ct, Har. 117 CE62
Wendell Rd W12 159 CT75
Wendle Ct SW8 161 DL79
Wendley Dr (New Haw), Add. 211 BF110
Wendling Rd, Sutt. 200 DD102
Wendon St E3 143 DZ67
Wendover SE17 162 DS78
Wendover Cl, Hayes 136 BY70
Kingsash Dr
Wendover Cl, St.Alb. 43 CJ15
Highview Gdns
Wendover Dr, N.Mal. 199 CT100
Wendover Gdns, Brwd. 109 GB47
Wendover Pl, Stai. 173 BD92
Wendover Rd NW10 139 CT68
Wendover Rd SE9 164 EK83
Wendover Rd, Brom. 204 EH97
Wendover Rd (Burnham), Slou. 130 AH71
Wendover Rd, Stai. 173 BC92
Wendover Way, Bushey 76 CC44
Wendover Way, Horn. 128 FJ64
Wendover Way, Orp. 206 EU100
Glendower Cres
Wendover Way, Well. 186 EU85
Wendron Cl, Wok. 226 AU118
Shilburn Way
Wendy Cl, Enf. 82 DT44
Wendy Cres, Guil. 242 AU132
Wendy Way, Wem. 138 CL67
Wengeo La, Ware 32 DV05
Wenham Gdns, Brwd. 109 GC44
Bannister Dr
Wenlack Cl (Denham), Uxb. 114 BG62
Lindsey Rd
Wenlock Ct N1 275 L1
Wenlock Gdns NW4 119 CU56
Rickard Cl
Wenlock Rd N1 275 H1
Wenlock Rd N1 142 DQ68
Wenlock Rd, Edg. 96 CP52
Wenlock St N1 275 J1
Wenlock St N1 142 DQ68
Wennington Rd E3 143 DX68
Wennington Rd, Rain. 147 FG70
Wensley Av, Wdf.Grn. 102 EF52
Wensley Cl N11 98 DG51
Pickering Gdns
Wensley Cl SE9 185 EM86
Wensley Cl, Rom. 104 FA50
Wensley Rd N18 100 DV51
Wensleydale, Hem.H. 40 BM17
Wensleydale Av, Ilf. 102 EL54
Wensleydale Gdns, Hmptn. 176 CB94
Wensleydale Pas, Hmptn. 196 CA95
Wensleydale Rd, Hmptn. 176 CA93
Wensum Way, Rick. 92 BK46
Wentbridge Path, Borwd. 78 CN38
Wentland Cl SE6 183 ED89
Wentland Rd SE6 183 ED89
Wentworth Av N3 98 DA52
Wentworth Av, Borwd. 78 CM43
Wentworth Av, Slou. 131 AN68
Wentworth Cl N3 98 DB52
Wentworth Cl SE28 146 EX72
Wentworth Cl, Ashf. 175 BP91
Reedsfield Rd
Wentworth Cl, Brom. 204 EG103
Hillside La
Wentworth Cl, Grav. 191 GG92
Wentworth Cl, Mord. 200 DA101
Wentworth Cl, Orp. 223 ES106
Wentworth Cl, Pot.B. 64 DA31
Strafford Gate
Wentworth Cl, Surb. 197 CK103
Wentworth Cl, Wat. 75 BT38
Wentworth Cl (Ripley), Wok. 228 BH121
Wentworth Cotts, Brox. 49 DY22
Wentworth Ct, Surb. 198 CL103
Culsac Rd
Wentworth Cres SE15 162 DU80
Wentworth Cres, Hayes 155 BR76
Wentworth Dr, Dart. 187 FG86
Wentworth Dr, Pnr. 115 BU57
Wentworth Dr, Vir.W. 192 AT98
Wentworth Gdns N13 99 DP49
Wentworth Hill, Wem. 118 CM60
Wentworth Ms E3 143 DZ70
Eric St
Wentworth Pk N3 98 DA52
Wentworth Pl, Grays 170 GD76
Wentworth Pl, Stan. 95 CH51
Greenacres Dr
Wentworth Rd E12 124 EK63
Wentworth Rd NW11 119 CZ58
Wentworth Rd, Barn. 79 CX41
Wentworth Rd, Croy. 201 DN101
Wentworth Rd, Hert. 32 DQ12
Wentworth Rd, Sthl. 156 BW77
Wentworth St E1 275 P8
Wentworth St E1 142 DT72
Wentworth Way, Pnr. 116 BY56
Wentworth Way, Rain. 147 FH69
Wentworth Way, S.Croy. 220 DU114
Wenvoe Av, Bexh. 167 FB82
Wernbrook St SE18 165 EQ79
Werndee Rd SE25 202 DU98
Werneth Hall Rd, Ilf. 125 EM55
Werrington St NW1 273 L1
Werrington St NW1 141 DJ68
Werter Rd SW15 159 CY84
Wescott Way, Uxb. 134 BJ68
Wesley Av E16 144 EG74
Wesley Av NW10 138 CR69
Wesley Av, Hert. 32 DR10
Hale Rd
Wesley Av, Houns. 156 BY82
Wesley Cl N7 121 DM61
Wesley Cl SE17 278 G9
Wesley Cl SE17 161 DP77
Wesley Cl, Har. 116 CC61
Wesley Cl, Horl. 268 DG146
Wesley Cl, Orp. 206 EW97
Wesley Cl, Reig. 265 CZ135
Wesley Cl (Cheshunt), Wal.Cr. 66 DQ28
Wesley Dr, Egh. 173 BA93
Wesley Hill, Chesh. 54 AP30
Wesley Rd E10 123 EC59
Wesley Rd NW10 138 CQ67
Wesley Rd, Hayes 135 BU73
Wesley Sq W11 139 CY72
Bartle Rd
Wesley St W1 272 G7
Wesleyan Pl NW5 121 DH63
Gordon Ho Rd
Wessels, Tad. 233 CX121
Wessex Av SW19 200 DA96
Wessex Cl, Ilf. 125 ES58
Wessex Cl, Kings.T. 198 CP95
Gloucester Rd
Wessex Cl, T.Ditt. 197 CF103
Wessex Dr, Erith 167 FE81
Wessex Dr, Pnr. 94 BY52
Wessex Gdns NW11 119 CY60
Wessex La, Grnf. 137 CD68
Wessex Rd (Heathrow Airport), Houns. 154 BK82
Wessex St E2 142 DW69
Wessex Way NW11 119 CY60
West Acres, Amer. 55 AR40
West App, Orp. 205 EQ99
West Arbour St E1 143 DX72
West Av E17 123 EB56
West Av N3 98 DA51
West Av NW4 119 CX57
West Av, Hayes 135 BT73
West Av (Penn), H.Wyc. 88 AC46
West Av, Pnr. 116 BZ58
West Av, Red. 266 DG140
West Av, St.Alb. 60 CB25
West Av, Sthl. 136 BZ73
West Av, Wall. 219 DL106
West Av, Walt. 213 BS109
West Av Rd E17 123 EA56
West Bk N16 122 DS59
West Bk, Bark. 145 EP67
Highbridge Rd
West Bk, Dor. 263 CF137
West Bk, Enf. 82 DQ40
West Barnes La SW20 199 CV96
West Barnes La, N.Mal. 199 CV97
West Burrowfield, Welw.G.C. 29 CX11
West Carriage Dr W2 276 A3
West Carriage Dr W2 140 DD73
West Cen St WC1 273 P8
West Cen Av W10 139 CV69
Harrow Rd
West Chantry, Har. 94 CB53
Chantry Rd
West Cl N9 100 DT48
West Cl, Ashf. 174 BL91
West Cl, Barn. 79 CV43
West Cl (Cockfosters), Barn. 80 DG42
West Cl, Grnf. 136 CC68
West Cl, Hmptn. 176 BY93
Oak Av
West Cl, Hodd. 49 EA16
West Cl, Rain. 147 FH70
West Cl, Wem. 118 CM60
West Common, Ger.Cr. 112 AX57
West Common Cl, Ger.Cr. 112 AY57
West Common Rd, Brom. 204 EG103
West Common Rd, Kes. 222 EH105
West Common Rd, Uxb. 114 BK64
West Cotts NW6 120 DA64
West Ct SE18 165 EM81
Prince Imperial Rd
West Ct, Wem. 117 CJ61
West Cres, Wind. 151 AM81
West Cres Rd, Grav. 191 GH86
West Cromwell Rd SW5 159 CZ77
West Cromwell Rd W14 159 CZ77
West Cross Cen, Brent. 157 CG79
West Cross Route W10 139 CX73
West Cross Route W11 139 CX73
West Cross Way, Brent. 157 CH79
West Dene, Sutt. 217 CY107
Park La
West Dene Dr, Rom. 106 FK50
West Down (Bookham), Lthd. 246 CB127
West Drayton Pk Av, West Dr. 154 BL76
West Drayton Rd, Uxb. 135 BQ71
West Dr SW16 181 DJ91
West Dr, Cars. 218 DD110
West Dr, Har. 95 CD51
West Dr (Cheam), Sutt. 217 CX109
West Dr, Tad. 233 CX118
West Dr, Vir.W. 192 AT101
West Dr, Wat. 75 BV36
West Dr Gdns, Har. 95 CD51
West Eaton Pl SW1 276 F8
West Eaton Pl SW1 160 DG77
West Eaton Pl Ms SW1 276 F8
West Ella Rd NW10 138 CS66
West End Av E10 123 EC57
West End Av, Pnr. 116 BX56
West End Cl NW10 138 CQ66
West End Ct, Pnr. 116 BX56
West End Ct (Stoke Poges), Slou. 132 AT67
West End Gdns, Esher 214 BZ106
West End Gdns, Nthlt. 136 BW68
Edward Cl
West End La NW6 140 DA67
West End La, Barn. 79 CX42
West End La, Esher 214 BZ107
West End La, Hat. 46 DC18
West End La, Hayes 155 BQ80
West End La, Pnr. 116 BX55
West End La (Stoke Poges), Slou. 132 AS67
West End Rd, Brox. 48 DS23
West End Rd, Nthlt. 136 BW66
West End Rd, Ruis. 115 BV64
West End Rd, Sthl. 136 BY74
West Fm Av, Ash. 231 CJ118
West Fm Cl, Ash. 231 CJ119
West Fm Dr, Ash. 231 CK119
West Gdn Pl W2 272 C9
West Gdns E1 142 DV73
West Gdns SW17 180 DE93
West Gdns, Epsom 216 CS110
West Gate W5 138 CL69
West Gate, Harl. 51 EQ15
West Gorse, Croy. 221 DY112
West Grn Pl, Grnf. 137 CD67
Uneeda Dr
West Grn Rd N15 122 DR56
West Gro SE10 163 EC81
West Gro, Walt. 213 BV105
West Gro, Wdf.Grn. 102 EJ51
West Halkin St SW1 276 F6
West Halkin St SW1 160 DG76
West Hall Rd, Rich. 158 CP81
West Hallowes SE9 184 EK88
West Ham La E15 144 EE66
West Ham Pk E7 144 EG66
West Hampstead Ms NW6 140 DB65
West Harding St EC4 274 E8
West Harold, Swan. 207 FD97
West Hatch Manor, Ruis. 115 BT60
West Heath, Oxt. 254 EG130
West Heath Av NW11 120 DA60
West Heath Cl NW3 120 DA62
West Heath Cl, Dart. 187 FF86
West Heath Rd
West Heath Dr NW11 120 DA60
West Heath Gdns NW3 120 DA62
West Heath La, Sev. 257 FH128
West Heath Rd NW3 120 DA61
West Heath Rd SE2 166 EX79
West Heath Rd, Dart. 187 FF86
West Hendon Bdy NW9 119 CT58
West Hill SW15 179 CX87
West Hill SW18 180 DA85
West Hill, Dart. 188 FK86
West Hill, Epsom 216 CQ113
West Hill, Har. 117 CE61
West Hill, Orp. 223 EM112
West Hill, Oxt. 253 ED130
West Hill, S.Croy. 220 DS110
West Hill, Wem. 118 CM60
West Hill Av, Epsom 216 CQ112
West Hill Bk, Oxt. 253 ED130
West Hill Ct N6 120 DG62
West Hill Dr, Dart. 188 FJ86
West Hill Pk N6 120 DF61
Merton La
West Hill Ri, Dart. 188 FK86
West Hill Rd SW18 180 DA86
West Hill Rd, Wok. 226 AX119
West Hill Way N20 98 DB46
West Holme, Erith 167 FC81
West Ho Cl SW19 179 CY88
West Hyde La (Chalfont St. Peter), Ger.Cr. 91 AZ52
West India Av E14 143 EA74
West India Dock Rd E14 143 DZ72
West Kent Av (Northfleet), Grav. 190 GC86
West Kentish Town Est NW5 120 DG64
West La SE16 162 DV75
West La (Abinger Hammer), Dor. 262 BX139
West Lo Av W3 138 CN74
West Mall W8 140 DA74
Palace Gdns Ter
West Malling Way, Horn. 128 FJ64
West Mead, Epsom 216 CS107
West Mead, Ruis. 116 BW63
West Mead, Welw.G.C. 30 DB12
West Meads, Guil. 258 AT135
West Mersea Cl E16 144 EH74
Hanameel St
West Ms N17 100 DV51
West Ms SW1 277 K9
West Mill, Grav. 191 GF86

Wetherby Way, Chess. 216 CL108
Wetherden St E17 123 DZ59
Wethered Dr (Burnham), Slou. 130 AH71
Wetherell Rd E9 143 DX67
Wetherill Rd N10 98 DG53
Wetherly Cl, Harl. 36 EZ11
Moor Hall Rd
Wettern Cl, S.Croy. 220 DS110
Purley Oaks Rd
Wetton Pl, Egh. 173 AZ92
Wexfenne Gdns, Wok. 228 BH116
Wexford Rd SW12 180 DF87
Wexham Pk La (Wexham), Slou. 132 AX70
Wexham Pl, Slou. 132 AX66
Framewood Rd
Wexham Rd, Slou. 132 AV71
Wexham St (Wexham), Slou. 132 AW67
Wexham Wds (Wexham), Slou. 132 AW71
Wey Av, Cher. 194 BG97
Wey Barton (Byfleet), W.Byf. 212 BM113
Wey Cl, W.Byf. 212 BH113
Broadoaks Cres
Wey Ct (New Haw), Add. 212 BK109
Wey Ct, Epsom 216 CQ105
Wey La, Chesh. 54 AP32
Wey Manor Rd (New Haw), Add. 212 BK109
Wey Meadows, Wey. 212 BL106
Wey Rd, Wey. 194 BM104
Wey Vw Ct, Guil. 258 AW135
Walnut Tree Cl
Weybank (Wisley), Wok. 228 BL116
Weybourne Pl, S.Croy. 220 DR110
Weybourne St SW18 180 DC89
Weybridge Business Pk, Add. 212 BL105
Weybridge Ct SE16 162 DU78
Argyle Way
Weybridge Pk, Wey. 213 BP106
Weybridge Pt SW11 160 DG82
Weybridge Rd, Add. 194 BL104
Weybridge Rd, Th.Hth. 201 DN98
Weybridge Rd, Wey. 212 BM105
Weybridge Trd Est, Add. 212 BL105
Weybrook Dr, Guil. 243 BB129
Weydown Cl SW19 179 CY88
Weydown Cl, Guil. 242 AU129
Weydown La, Guil. 242 AU129
Cumberland Av
Weyhill Rd E1 142 DU72
Commercial Rd
Weylands Cl, Walt. 196 BZ102
Weylands Pk, Wey. 213 BR107
Weylea Av, Guil. 243 BA131
Weylond Rd, Dag. 126 EZ62
Weyman Rd SE3 164 EJ81
Weymead Cl, Cher. 194 BJ102
Weymede (Byfleet), W.Byf. 212 BM112
Weymouth Av NW7 96 CS50
Weymouth Av W5 157 CJ76
Weymouth Cl E6 145 EP72
Covelees Wall
Weymouth Ct, Sutt. 218 DA108
Weymouth Ms W1 273 H6
Weymouth Ms W1 141 DH71
Weymouth Rd, Hayes 135 BS69
Weymouth St W1 272 G7
Weymouth St W1 141 DH71
Weymouth St, Hem.H. 40 BK24
Weymouth Ter E2 142 DT68
Weymouth Wk, Stan. 95 CG51
Weyside Cl (Byfleet), W.Byf. 212 BM112
Weyside Gdns, Guil. 242 AV132
Weyside Rd, Guil. 242 AV132
Weystone Rd, Add. 212 BM105
Weybridge Rd
Weyview Cl, Guil. 242 AW132
Whadcote St N4 121 DN61
Seven Sisters Rd
Whalebone Av, Rom. 126 EZ58
Whalebone Ct EC2 275 L8
Whalebone Gro, Rom. 126 EZ58
Whalebone La E15 144 EE66
West Ham La
Whalebone La N, Rom. 126 EY57
Whalebone La S, Dag. 126 EZ59
Whalebone La S, Rom. 126 EZ59
Whaley Rd, Pot.B. 64 DC33
Wharf La, Rick. 92 BL46
Wharf La, Twick. 177 CG88
Wharf La (Ripley), Wok. 228 BJ118
Wharf La (Send), Wok. 227 BC123
Wharf Pl E2 142 DU67
Wharf Rd E15 143 ED67
Wharf Rd N1 275 H1
Wharf Rd N1 142 DQ68
Wharf Rd, Brwd. 108 FW48
Wharf Rd, Brox. 49 DZ23
Wharf Rd, Enf. 83 DY44
Wharf Rd, Grav. 191 GL86
Wharf Rd, Grays 170 FZ79
Wharf Rd, Guil. 242 AW134
Wharf Rd, Hem.H. 40 BH22
Wharf Rd (Wraysbury), Stai. 172 AW87
Wharf Rd S, Grays 170 FZ79
Wharf St E16 144 EE71
Wharfdale Cl N11 98 DG51
Ribblesdale Av
Wharfdale Ct E5 123 DX63
Rushmore Rd
Wharfdale Rd N1 141 DL68
Wharfedale, Hem.H. 40 BL17
Wharfedale Gdns, Th.Hth. 201 DM98
Wharfedale Rd, Dart. 188 FQ88
Wharfedale St SW10 160 DB78
Wharfside Rd E16 144 EE71
Wharley Hook, Harl. 51 ET18
Wharncliffe Dr, Sthl. 137 CD74
Wharncliffe Gdns SE25 202 DS96
Wharncliffe Rd SE25 202 DS96
Wharton Cl NW10 138 CS65
Wharton Cotts WC1 141 DM69
Wharton St
Wharton Rd, Brom. 204 EH95
Wharton St WC1 274 C3
Wharton St WC1 141 DM69
Whateley Rd SE20 183 DX94
Whateley Rd SE22 182 DT85
Whateley Rd, Guil. 242 AV129
Whatley Av SW20 199 CY97
Whatman Rd SE23 183 DX87
Whatmore Cl, Stai. 174 BG86
Wheat Cl (Sandridge), St.Alb. 43 CG16
Wheat Knoll, Ken. 236 DQ116
Wheat Leys, St.Alb. 43 CJ18
Wheat Sheaf Cl E14 163 EB77
Wheatash Rd, Add. 194 BH103
Wheatbarn, Welw.G.C. 30 DB08
Wheatbutts, The (Eton Wick), Wind. 151 AM77
Wheatcroft (Cheshunt), Wal.Cr. 66 DV28
Wheatfield, Hat. 45 CV17
Crop Common
Wheatfield, Hem.H. 40 BK18
Wheatfield Way, Horl. 269 DH147
Wheatfield Way, Kings.T. 198 CL96
Wheatfields E6 145 EP72
Oxleas
Wheatfields, Enf. 83 DY40
Wheatfields, Harl. 36 EW09
Wheathill Rd SE20 202 DV97
Wheatlands, Houns. 156 CA79
Wheatlands Rd SW17 180 DG90
Stapleton Rd
Wheatlands Rd, Slou. 152 AW76
Wheatley Cl NW4 97 CU54
Wheatley Cl, Green. 189 FU85
Steele Av
Wheatley Cl, Horn. 128 FK57
Wheatley Cl, Saw. 36 EW06
Wheatley Cl, Welw.G.C. 30 DA11
Wheatley Cres, Hayes 135 BU73
Wheatley Gdns N9 100 DS47
Wheatley Ho SW15 179 CU87
Tangley Gro
Wheatley Rd, Islw. 157 CF83
Wheatley Rd, Welw.G.C. 29 CZ10
Wheatley St W1 272 G7
Wheatley Ter Rd, Erith 167 FF79
Wheatley Way (Chalfont St. Peter), Ger.Cr. 90 AY51
Wheatley's Ait, Sun. 195 BU99
Wheatsheaf Cl (Ottershaw), Cher. 211 BD107
Wheatsheaf Cl, Nthlt. 116 BY64
Wheatsheaf Cl, Wok. 226 AY116
Wheatsheaf Hill (Halstead), Sev. 224 EZ109
Wheatsheaf La SW6 159 CW80
Wheatsheaf La SW8 161 DL80
Wheatsheaf La, Stai. 173 BF94
Wheatsheaf Rd, Rom. 127 FF58
Wheatsheaf Rd, Ware 34 EK06
Wheatsheaf Ter SW6 159 CZ80
Wheatstone Cl, Mitch. 200 DE95
Wheatstone Rd W10 139 CY71
Wheel Fm Dr, Dag. 127 FC62
Wheeler Av (Penn), H.Wyc. 88 AC47
Wheeler Av, Oxt. 253 ED129
Wheeler Cl, Wdf.Grn. 103 EM50
Chigwell Rd
Wheeler Gdns N1 141 DL67
Outram Pl
Wheelers, Epp. 69 ET29
Wheelers Cl, Wal.Abb. 50 EE22
Wheelers Cross, Bark. 145 ER68
Wheelers Dr, Ruis. 115 BQ58
Wallington Cl
Wheelers Fm Gdns, Epp. 71 FB26
Wheelers La (Brockham), Bet. 264 CP136
Wheelers La, Epsom 216 CP113
Wheelers La, Hem.H. 40 BL22
Wheelers La, Horl. 269 DN149
Wheelers Orchard (Chalfont St. Peter), Ger.Cr. 90 AY51
Wheelock Cl, Erith 167 FB80
Wheelwright Cl, Bushey 76 CB44
Ashfield Av
Wheelwright St N7 141 DM66
Whelan Way, Wall. 201 DK104
Wheler St E1 275 P5
Wheler St E1 142 DT70
Whellock Rd W4 158 CS76
Whelpley Hill Pk (Whelpley Hill), Chesh. 56 AX26
Whenman Av, Bex. 187 FC89
Whernside Cl SE28 146 EW73
Wherwell Rd, Guil. 258 AW136
Whetstone Cl N20 98 DD47
Oakleigh Rd N
Whetstone Pk WC2 274 B8
Whetstone Rd SE3 164 EJ82
Whewell Rd N19 121 DL61
Whichcote Gdns, Chesh. 54 AR33
Pheasant Ri
Whichcote St SE1 278 D3
Whichert Cl (Knotty Grn), Beac. 88 AJ49
Whidborne Cl SE8 163 EA82
Cliff Ter
Whidborne St WC1 274 A3
Whidborne St WC1 141 DL69
Whielden Cl, Amer. 55 AP40
Whielden Gate (Winchmore Hill), Amer. 55 AL43
Whielden Grn, Amer. 55 AP40
Whielden La, Amer. 55 AL43
Whielden St, Amer. 55 AN41
Whieldon Gra (Church Langley), Harl. 52 EW15
Kiln La
Whiffins Orchard, Epp. 70 EX29
Whimbrel Cl SE28 146 EW73
Whimbrel Cl, S.Croy. 220 DR111
Whimbrel Way, Hayes 136 BX72
Whinchat Rd SE28 165 ER76
Whinfell Cl SW16 181 DK92
Whinfell Way, Grav. 191 GM91
Whinneys Rd (Loudwater), H.Wyc. 88 AC52
Whinyates Rd SE9 164 EL83
Whipley Cl, Guil. 243 BB129
Weybrook Dr
Whippendell Cl, Orp. 206 EV95
Whippendell Hill, Kings L. 58 BJ30
Whippendell Rd, Wat. 75 BU43
Whippendell Way, Orp. 206 EV95
Whipps Cross Rd E11 123 ED57
Whiskin St EC1 274 F3
Whiskin St EC1 141 DP69
Whisperwood, Rick. 74 BH41
Whisperwood Cl, Har. 95 CE52
Whistler Gdns, Edg. 96 CM54
Whistler Ms SE15 162 DT80
Commercial Way
Whistler Ms, Dag. 126 EV64
Fitzstephen Rd
Whistler St N5 121 DP63
Whistler Wk SW10 160 DD80
World's End Est
Whistlers Av SW11 160 DD80
Whiston Rd E2 142 DT68
Whit Hern Ct, Wal.Cr. 66 DW30
College Rd
Whitakers Way, Loug. 85 EM39
Whitbread Cl N17 100 DU53
Whitbread Rd SE4 163 DY84
Whitburn Rd SE13 163 EB84
Whitby Av NW10 138 CP69
Whitby Cl, Green. 189 FU85
Whitby Cl (Biggin Hill), West. 238 EH119
Whitby Gdns NW9 118 CN55
Whitby Gdns, Sutt. 200 DD103
Whitby Rd SE18 165 EM77
Whitby Rd, Har. 116 CC62
Whitby Rd, Ruis. 115 BV62
Whitby Rd, Slou. 131 AQ73
Whitby Rd, Sutt. 200 DD103
Whitby St E1 275 P4
Whitcher Cl SE14 163 DY79
Whitcher Pl NW1 141 DJ66
Rochester Rd
Whitchurch Av, Edg. 96 CM52
Whitchurch Cl, Edg. 96 CM51
Whitchurch Gdns, Edg. 96 CM51
Whitchurch La, Edg. 95 CK52
Whitchurch Rd W11 139 CX73
Whitchurch Rd, Rom. 106 FK49
Whitcomb Ct WC2 141 DK73
Whitcomb St
Whitcomb St WC2 277 N1
Whitcomb St WC2 141 DK73
White Acre NW9 96 CS54
White Av (Northfleet), Grav. 191 GF90
White Beam Way, Tad. 233 CU121
White Beams (Park St), St.Alb. 60 CC28
White Bear Pl NW3 120 DD63
New End Sq
White Br Av, Mitch. 200 DD98
White Butts Rd, Ruis. 116 BX62
White Ch La E1 142 DU72
White Ch Pas E1 142 DU72
White Ch La
White City Cl W12 139 CW73
White City Est W12 139 CV73
White City Rd W12 139 CV73
White Cl, Slou. 131 AR74
White Conduit St N1 141 DN68
Chapel Mkt
White Craig Cl, Pnr. 94 CA50
White Down Rd, Dor. 262 BW135
White Friars, Sev. 256 FG127
White Gdns, Dag. 146 FA65
White Gates, Horn. 128 FJ61
White Hall, Rom. 86 EV41
Market Pl
White Hart Cl, Ch.St.G. 90 AU48
White Hart Cl, Sev. 257 FJ128
White Hart Ct EC2 142 DS72
Bishopsgate
White Hart Ct (Ripley), Wok. 228 BJ121
White Hart Dr, Hem.H. 40 BM21
White Hart La N17 100 DR52
White Hart La N22 99 DN53
White Hart La NW10 139 CT65
Church Rd
White Hart La SW13 158 CS83
White Hart La, Rom. 104 FA53
White Hart Meadow, Beac. 89 AL54
White Hart Meadows (Ripley), Wok. 228 BJ121
White Hart Rd SE18 165 ES77
White Hart Rd, Hem.H. 40 BN21
White Hart Rd, Orp. 206 EU101
White Hart Rd, Slou. 151 AR76
White Hart Row, Cher. 194 BG101
Heriot Rd
White Hart Slip, Brom. 204 EG96
Market Sq
White Hart St SE11 278 E10
White Hart St SE11 161 DN78
White Hart Wd, Sev. 257 FJ129
White Hart Yd SE1 279 K3
White Hedge Dr, St.Alb. 42 CC19
White Heron Ms, Tedd. 177 CF93
White Hill, Beac. 110 AG55
White Hill, Chesh. 54 AQ31
White Hill (Chipstead), Couls. 234 DC124
White Hill, Hem.H. 39 BF21
White Hill, Nthwd. 92 BN51
White Hill, Rick. 92 BN51
White Hill, S.Croy. 220 DR109
St. Mary's Rd
White Hill, Welw. 29 CU05
White Hill Cl, Chesh. 54 AQ30
White Hill Cl, Berk. 38 AX18
Whitehill
White Hill Rd, Berk. 38 AV21
White Hill Rd, Chesh. 56 AX26
White Horse Dr, Epsom 216 CQ114
White Horse La E1 143 DX70
White Horse La (London Colney), St.Alb. 62 CL25
White Horse La (Ripley), Wok. 228 BJ121
White Horse Ms SE1 278 E6
White Horse Rd E1 143 DY72
White Horse Rd E6 145 EM69
White Horse Rd, Wind. 151 AK83
White Horse St W1 277 H3
White Horse St W1 141 DH74
White Horse Yd EC2 275 K8
White Ho Cl (Chalfont St. Peter), Ger.Cr. 90 AY52
White Ho Dr, Guil. 243 BB134
White Ho Dr, Stan. 95 CJ49
White Ho La (Jacobs Well), Guil. 242 AX129
White Ho La, Sev. 256 FF130
White Ho Rd, Sev. 256 FF130
White Kennett St E1 275 N8
White Knights Rd, Wey. 213 BQ108
White Knobs Way, Cat. 252 DU125
White La, Guil. 259 BC136
White La, Oxt. 238 EH123
White La, Warl. 238 EH123
White Lion Cl, Amer. 72 AU39
White Lion Ct EC3 275 M9
White Lion Hill EC4 274 G10
White Lion Hill EC4 141 DP73
White Lion Hos, Hat. 45 CU17
Robin Hood La
White Lion Rd, Amer. 72 AT38
White Lion Sq, Hat. 45 CU17
Robin Hood La
White Lion St N1 274 D1
White Lion St N1 141 DN68
White Lion St, Hem.H. 40 BK23
White Lion Wk Shop Cen, Guil. 258 AX136
High St
White Lo SE19 181 DP94
White Lo Cl N2 120 DE58
White Lo Cl, Sev. 257 FH123
White Lo Cl, Sutt. 218 DC108
White Lo Gdns, Red. 266 DG142
White Lyon Ct EC2 142 DQ70
Fann St
White Lyons Rd, Brwd. 108 FW47
White Oak Business Pk, Swan. 207 FE97
London Rd
White Oak Dr, Beck. 203 EC96
White Oak Gdns, Sid. 185 ET87
White Orchards N20 97 CZ45
White Orchards, Stan. 95 CG50
White Post Fld, Saw. 36 EX05
White Post Hill (Farningham), Dart. 208 FN101
White Post La E9 143 DZ66
White Post La SE13 163 EA83
White Post St SE15 162 DW80
White Rd E15 144 EE66
White Rd, Bet. 248 CN133
White Rd, Tad. 248 CN133
White Rose La, Wok. 227 AZ117
White Shack La, Rick. 74 BM37
White St, Sthl. 156 BX75
White Stubbs La, Brox. 47 DP21
White Stubbs La, Hert. 47 DK21
White Swan Ms W4 158 CS79
Bennett St
White Way, Lthd. 246 CB126
Whiteadder Way E14 163 EB77
Whitear Wk E15 143 ED65
Whitebarn La, Dag. 146 FA67
Whitebeam Av, Brom. 205 EN100
Whitebeam Cl SW9 161 DM80
Clapham Rd
Whitebeam Cl (Shenley), Rad. 62 CM33
Mulberry Gdns
Whitebeam Cl, Wal.Cr. 66 DS26
The Laurels
Whitebeam Dr, Reig. 266 DB137
Whitebeam Dr, S.Ock. 149 FW69
Whitebeam Twr E17 123 DY55
Hillyfield
Whitebeams, Hat. 45 CU21
Whiteberry Rd, Dor. 262 CB143
Whitebridge Cl, Felt. 175 BT86
Whitebroom Rd, Hem.H. 39 BE18
Whitechapel High St E1 142 DT72
Whitechapel Rd E1 142 DU71
Whitecote Rd, Sthl. 136 CB72
Whitecroft, Horl. 269 DH147
Woodhayes
Whitecroft, St.Alb. 43 CH23
Whitecroft, Swan. 207 FE96
Whitecroft Cl, Beck. 203 ED98
Whitecroft Way, Beck. 203 EC99
Whitecross Pl EC2 275 L6
Whitecross St EC1 275 J4
Whitecross St EC1 142 DQ70
Whitefield Av NW2 119 CW59
Whitefield Av, Pur. 235 DN116
Whitefield Cl SW15 179 CY86
Whitefield Cl, Orp. 206 EW97
Whitefields Rd (Cheshunt), Wal.Cr. 66 DW28
Whitefoot La, Brom. 183 EC91
Whitefoot Ter, Brom. 184 EE90
Whiteford Rd, Slou. 132 AS71
Whitefriars Av, Har. 95 CE54
Whitefriars Dr, Har. 95 CD54
Whitefriars St EC4 274 E9
Whitefriars St EC4 141 DN72
Whitegate Gdns, Har. 95 CF52
Whitegate Way, Tad. 233 CV120
Whitegates, Whyt. 236 DU119
Court Bushes Rd
Whitegates, Wok. 227 AZ120
Loop Rd
Whitegates Cl, Rick. 74 BN42
Whitehall SW1 277 P2
Whitehall SW1 141 DL74
Whitehall Cl, Chig. 104 EU48
Whitehall Cl, Uxb. 134 BJ67
Whitehall Cl, Wal.Abb. 50 EE22
Whitehall Ct SW1 277 P3
Whitehall Ct SW1 141 DL74
Whitehall Cres, Chess. 215 CK106
Whitehall Est, Harl. 50 EL16
Whitehall Fm La, Vir.W. 192 AY96
Whitehall Gdns E4 101 ED46
Whitehall Gdns SW1 277 P3
Whitehall Gdns W3 138 CN74
Whitehall Gdns W4 158 CP79
Whitehall La, Buck.H. 102 EG47
Whitehall La, Egh. 173 AZ94
Whitehall La, Erith 167 FF82
Whitehall La, Grays 170 GC78
Whitehall La (South Pk), Reig. 265 CZ138
Whitehall La (Wraysbury), Stai. 173 BA86
Whitehall Pk N19 121 DJ60
Whitehall Pk Rd W4 158 CP79
Whitehall Pl E7 124 EG64
Station Rd
Whitehall Pl SW1 277 P3
Whitehall Pl SW1 141 DL74
Whitehall Pl, Wall. 219 DH105
Bernard Rd
Whitehall Rd E4 102 EE47
Whitehall Rd W7 157 CG75
Whitehall Rd, Brom. 204 EK99
Whitehall Rd, Grays 170 GC77
Whitehall Rd, Har. 117 CE59
Whitehall Rd, Th.Hth. 201 DN99
Whitehall Rd, Uxb. 134 BK67
Whitehall Rd, Wdf.Grn. 102 EE47
Whitehall St N17 100 DT52
Whitehands Cl, Hodd. 49 DZ17
Whitehaven, Slou. 132 AT73
Whitehaven Cl, Brom. 204 EG98
Whitehaven St NW8 272 B5
Whitehead Cl N18 100 DR50
Whitehead Cl SW18 180 DC87
Whitehead Cl, Dart. 188 FJ90
Whitehead's Gro SW3 276 C10
Whitehead's Gro SW3 160 DE78
Whiteheart Av, Uxb. 135 BQ71
Whiteheath Av, Ruis. 115 BQ59
Whitehill, Berk. 38 AX18
Whitehill Cl, Berk. 38 AX18
Whitehill
Whitehill La, Grav. 191 GK90
Whitehill La, Red. 252 DR127
Whitehill La, Wok. 229 BQ123
Whitehill Par, Grav. 191 GJ90
Whitehill Pl, Vir.W. 192 AY99
Whitehill Rd, Dart. 187 FG85
Whitehill Rd, Grav. 191 GJ89
Whitehill Rd (Hook Grn), Grav. 209 FX96
Whitehill Rd, Long. 209 FX96
Whitehills Rd, Loug. 85 EN41
Whitehorse Hill, Chis. 185 EN91
Whitehorse La SE25 202 DR98
Whitehorse Rd, Croy. 202 DQ101
Whitehorse Rd, Th.Hth. 202 DR100
Whitehouse Av, Borwd. 78 CP41
Whitehouse Cl (Wooburn Grn), H.Wyc. 88 AE54
Whitehouse La, Abb.L. 59 BV26
Whitehouse La, Enf. 82 DQ39
Brigadier Hill
Whitehouse La (Wooburn Grn), H.Wyc. 88 AE54
Whitehouse Way N14 99 DH47
Whitehouse Way, Iver 133 BD69
Whitehouse Way, Slou. 152 AW76
Whitelands Av, Rick. 73 BC42
Whitelands Way, Rom. 106 FK54
Whiteleaf Rd, Hem.H. 40 BJ23
Whiteledges W13 137 CJ72
Whitelegg Rd E13 144 EF68
Whiteley, Wind. 151 AL80
Whiteley Rd SE19 182 DR92
Whiteleys Cotts W14 159 CZ77
Whiteleys Shop Cen W2 140 DB72
Whiteleys Way, Felt. 176 CA90
Whitemore Rd, Guil. 242 AX130
Whiteoaks, Bans. 218 DB113
Whiteoaks La, Grnf. 137 CD68
Whitepit La (Flackwell Heath), H.Wyc. 110 AE57
Whitepost Hill, Red. 250 DE134
Whites Av, Ilf. 125 ES58
Whites Cl, Green. 189 FW86
Whites Grds SE1 279 N5
Whites Grds SE1 162 DS75
Whites Grds Est SE1 279 N4
Whites La (Datchet), Slou. 152 AV79
White's Row E1 275 P7
White's Row E1 142 DT71
White's Sq SW4 161 DK84
Nelson's Row
Whitestile Rd, Brent. 157 CJ78
Whitestone La NW3 120 DC62
Heath St
Whitestone Wk NW3 120 DC62
North End Way
Whitestone Wk, Hem.H. 40 BG17
Fennycroft Rd
Whitethorn, Welw.G.C. 30 DB10
Whitethorn Av, Couls. 234 DG115
Whitethorn Av, West Dr. 134 BL73
Whitethorn Gdns, Croy. 202 DV103
Whitethorn Gdns, Enf. 82 DR43
Whitethorn Gdns, Horn. 128 FJ58
Whitethorn Pl, West Dr. 134 BM74
Whitethorn Av
Whitethorn St E3 143 EA70
Whitewaits, Harl. 35 ES14
Whiteways Ct, Stai. 174 BH94
Pavilion Gdns
Whitewebbs La, Enf. 82 DS35
Whitewebbs Pk, Enf. 82 DQ35
Whitewebbs Rd, Enf. 81 DP35
Whitewebbs Way, Orp. 205 ET95
Whitewood Cotts, West. 238 EJ120
Whitewood Rd, Berk. 38 AU19
Whitfield Cl, Guil. 242 AU131
Whitfield Pl W1 273 K5
Whitfield Rd E6 144 EJ66
Whitfield Rd SE3 163 ED81
Whitfield Rd, Bexh. 166 EZ80
Whitfield St W1 273 M7
Whitfield St W1 141 DK71
Whitfield Way, Rick. 91 BF46
Whitford Gdns, Mitch. 200 DF97
Whitgift Av, S.Croy. 220 DQ106
Whitgift Cen, Croy. 202 DQ103
Whitgift St SE11 278 B8
Whitgift St SE11 161 DM77
Whitgift St, Croy. 202 DQ104
Whiting Av, Bark. 145 EP66
Whitings, Ilf. 125 ER57
Whitings Rd, Barn. 79 CW43
Whitings Way E6 145 EN71
Whitland Rd, Cars. 200 DD102
Whitlars Dr, Kings L. 58 BM28
Whitley Cl, Abb.L. 59 BU32
Whitley Cl (Stanwell), Stai. 174 BL86
Whitley Rd N17 100 DS54
Whitley Rd, Hodd. 49 EB15
Whitlock Dr SW19 179 CY87
Whitman Rd E3 143 DY70
Mile End Rd
Whitmead Cl, S.Croy. 220 DS107
Whitmoor Common (Worplesdon), Guil. 242 AV127
Whitmoor La, Guil. 242 AX126
Whitmore Av, Rom. 106 FL54
Whitmore Cl N11 99 DH50
Whitmore Est N1 142 DS67
Whitmore Gdns NW10 139 CW68
Whitmore Rd N1 142 DS67
Whitmore Rd, Beck. 203 DZ97
Whitmore Rd, Har. 116 CC59
Whitmore Way, Horl. 268 DE147
Whitmores Cl, Epsom 232 CQ115
Whitmore's Wd, Hem.H. 41 BP19
Whitnell Way SW15 179 CX85
Whitney Av, Ilf. 124 EK56
Whitney Rd E10 123 EB59
Whitney Wk, Sid. 186 EY93
Whitstable Cl, Beck. 203 DZ95
Whitstable Cl, Ruis. 115 BS61
Chichester Av
Whitstable Ho W10 139 CX72
Whitstable Pl, Croy. 220 DQ105
Whitta Rd E12 124 EK63
Whittaker Av, Rich. 177 CK85
Hill St
Whittaker Rd E6 144 EJ66
Whittaker Rd, Slou. 131 AK70
Whittaker Rd, Sutt. 199 CZ104
Whittaker St SW1 276 F9
Whittaker St SW1 160 DG77
Whittaker Way SE1 162 DU77
Lynton Rd
Whittell Gdns SE26 182 DW90
Whittenham Cl, Slou. 132 AU74
Whittingstall Rd SW6 159 CZ81
Whittingstall Rd, Hodd. 49 EB15
Whittington Av EC3 275 M9
Whittington Av, Hayes 135 BT71
Whittington Ct N2 120 DF57
Whittington Ms N12 98 DC49
Fredericks Pl
Whittington Rd N22 99 DL52
Whittington Rd, Brwd. 109 GC44
Whittington Way, Pnr. 116 BY57
Whittle Cl E17 123 DY58
Whittle Cl, Sthl. 136 CB72
Whittle Parkway, Slou. 131 AK72
Whittle Rd, Houns. 156 BW80
Whittle Rd, Sthl. 156 CB75
Post Rd
Whittlebury Cl, Cars. 218 DF108
Whittlesea Cl, Har. 94 CC52
Whittlesea Path, Har. 94 CC53
Whittlesea Rd, Har. 94 CC53
Whittlesey St SE1 278 D3
Whitton Av E, Grnf. 117 CE64
Whitton Av W, Grnf. 116 CC64
Whitton Av W, Nthlt. 116 CC64

Witham Rd, Islw. 157 CD81
Witham Rd, Rom. 127 FH57
Withens Cl, Orp. 206 EW98
Wither Dale, Horl. 268 DE147
Witherby Cl, Croy. 220 DS106
Witheridge La (Knotty Grn), Beac. 88 AF48
Witheridge La (Penn), H.Wyc. 88 AF48
Witherings, The, Horn. 128 FL57
Witherington Rd N5 121 DN64
Withers Cl, Chess. 215 CJ107
Coppard Gdns
Withers Mead NW9 97 CT53
Witherston Way SE9 185 EN89
Withey Cl, Wind. 151 AL81
Withey Meadows, Horl. 268 DD150
Witheygate Av, Stai. 174 BH93
Withies, The, Lthd. 231 CH120
Withies, The (Knaphill), Wok. 226 AS117
Withy La, Ruis. 115 BQ57
Withy Mead E4 101 ED48
Withy Pl (Park St), St.Alb. 60 CC28
Withybed Cor, Tad. 233 CV123
Withycombe Rd SW19 179 CX87
Withycroft (George Grn), Slou. 132 AY72
Witley Cres (New Addington), Croy. 221 EC107
Witley Gdns, Sthl. 156 BZ77
Witley Pt SW15 179 CV88
Wanborough Dr
Witley Rd N19 121 DJ61
Holloway Rd
Witney Cl, Pnr. 94 BZ51
Witney Cl, Uxb. 114 BM63
Witney Path SE23 183 DX90
Wittenham Way E4 101 ED48
Wittering Cl, Kings.T. 177 CK92
Wittering Wk, Horn. 148 FJ65
Wittersham Rd, Brom. 184 EF92
Wivenhoe Cl SE15 162 DV83
Wivenhoe Ct, Houns. 156 BZ84
Wivenhoe Rd, Bark. 146 EU68
Wiverton Rd SE26 182 DW93
Wix Hill (West Horsley), Lthd. 245 BP130
Wix Hill Cl (West Horsley), Lthd. 245 BP131
Wix Rd, Dag. 146 EX67
Wixon Ho SE3 164 EJ84
Romero Sq
Wixs La SW4 161 DH84
Woburn Av, Epp. 85 ES37
Woburn Av, Horn. 127 FG63
Woburn Av, Pur. 219 DN111
High St
Woburn Cl SE28 146 EX72
Summerton Way
Woburn Cl SW19 180 DC93
Tintern Cl
Woburn Cl, Bushey 76 CC43
Woburn Ct SE16 162 DV78
Masters Dr
Woburn Hill, Add. 194 BJ103
Woburn Pl WC1 273 N4
Woburn Pl WC1 141 DL70
Woburn Rd, Cars. 200 DE102
Woburn Rd, Croy. 202 DQ102
Woburn Sq WC1 273 N5
Woburn Sq WC1 141 DK70
Woburn Wk WC1 273 N3
Woburn Wk WC1 141 DK69
Wodehouse Av SE5 162 DT81
Wodehouse Rd, Dart. 168 FN84
Wodeland Av, Guil. 258 AV136
Woffington Cl, Kings.T. 197 CJ95
Wokindon Rd, Grays 171 GH76
Woking Business Pk, Wok. 227 BB115
Woking Cl SW15 159 CT84
Woking Rd, Guil. 242 AX129
Wold, The (Woldingham), Cat. 237 EA122
Woldham Pl, Brom. 204 EJ98
Woldham Rd, Brom. 204 EJ98
Woldingham Rd (Woldingham), Cat. 236 DV120
Wolds Dr, Orp. 223 EN105
Wolf La, Wind. 151 AK83
Wolfe Cl, Brom. 204 EG100
Wolfe Cl, Hayes 135 BV69
Ayles Rd
Wolfe Cres SE7 164 EK78
Wolfe Cres SE16 163 DX75
Wolferton Rd E12 125 EM63
Wolffe Gdns E15 144 EF65
Wolffram Cl SE13 184 EE85
Wolfington Rd SE27 181 DP91
Wolfs Hill, Oxt. 254 EG131
Wolf's Row, Oxt. 254 EH130
Wolfs Wd, Oxt. 254 EG132
Wolftencroft Cl SW11 160 DD83
Wollaston Cl SE1 279 H8
Wolmer Cl, Edg. 96 CP49
Wolmer Gdns, Edg. 96 CN48
Wolseley Av SW19 180 DA89
Wolseley Gdns W4 158 CP79
Wolseley Rd E7 144 EH66
Wolseley Rd N8 121 DK58
Wolseley Rd N22 99 DM53
Wolseley Rd W4 158 CQ77
Wolseley Rd, Har. 117 CE55
Wolseley Rd, Mitch. 200 DG101
Wolseley Rd, Rom. 127 FD59
Wolseley St SE1 162 DT75
Wolsey Av E6 145 EN69
Wolsey Av E17 123 DZ55
Wolsey Av, T.Ditt. 197 CF99
Wolsey Av (Cheshunt), Wal.Cr. 66 DT29
Wolsey Business Pk, Wat. 93 BR45
Wolsey Cl SW20 179 CV94
Wolsey Cl, Houns. 156 CC84
Wolsey Cl, Kings.T. 198 CP95
Wolsey Cl, Sthl. 156 CC76
Wolsey Cl, Wor.Pk. 217 CU105
Wolsey Cres (New Addington), Croy. 221 EC108
Wolsey Cres, Mord. 199 CY101
Wolsey Dr, Kings.T. 178 CL92
Wolsey Dr, Walt. 196 BX102
Wolsey Gdns, Ilf. 103 EQ51
Wolsey Gro, Edg. 96 CR52
Wolsey Gro, Esher 214 CB105
Wolsey Ms NW5 141 DJ65
Wolsey Ms, Orp. 223 ET106
Osgood Av
Wolsey Pl Shop Cen, Wok. 226 AY117
Commercial Way
Wolsey Rd N1 122 DR64
Wolsey Rd, Ashf. 174 BL91
Wolsey Rd, E.Mol. 197 CD98
Wolsey Rd, Enf. 82 DV40
Wolsey Rd, Esher 214 CB105
Wolsey Rd (Hampton Hill), Hmptn. 176 CB93
Wolsey Rd, Hem.H. 40 BK21
Wolsey Rd, Nthwd. 93 BQ47
Wolsey Rd, Sun. 175 BT94
Wolsey St E1 142 DW71
Sidney St
Wolsey Wk, Wok. 226 AY117
Wolsey Way, Chess. 216 CN106
Wolsley Cl, Dart. 187 FE85
Wolstan Cl (Denham), Uxb. 114 BG62
Lindsey Rd
Wolstonbury N12 98 DA50
Wolvens La, Dor. 262 CA140
Wolvercote Rd SE2 166 EX75
Wolverley St E2 142 DV69
Bethnal Grn Rd
Wolverton SE17 279 L10
Wolverton Av, Kings.T. 198 CN95
Wolverton Cl, Horl. 268 DF150
Wolverton Gdns W5 138 CM73
Wolverton Gdns W6 159 CX77
Wolverton Gdns, Horl. 268 DF149
Wolverton Rd, Stan. 95 CH51
Wolverton Way N14 81 DJ43
Wolves La N13 99 DN52
Wolves La N22 99 DN52
Wombwell Gdns (Northfleet), Grav. 190 GE89
Womersley Rd N8 121 DM58
Wonersh Common (Wonersh), Guil. 259 BB141
Wonersh Common Rd (Wonersh), Guil. 259 BB142
Wonersh Way, Sutt. 217 CX109
Wonford Cl, Kings.T. 198 CS95
Wonford Cl, Tad. 249 CU126
Wonham La, Bet. 264 CS135
Wonham Way (Gomshall), Guil. 261 BR139
Wontford Rd, Pur. 235 DN115
Wontner Cl N1 142 DQ66
Greenman St
Wontner Rd SW17 180 DF89
Wooburn Cl, Uxb. 135 BP70
Aldenham Dr
Wooburn Common (Wooburn Grn), H.Wyc. 110 AH59
Wooburn Common Rd (Wooburn Grn), H.Wyc. 110 AH61
Wooburn Common Rd, Slou. 110 AH61
Wooburn Gra (Wooburn Grn), H.Wyc. 110 AD60
Wooburn Grn La, Beac. 110 AG56
Wooburn Ind Pk (Wooburn Grn), H.Wyc. 110 AD59
Wooburn Manor Pk (Wooburn Grn), H.Wyc. 110 AE58
Wooburn Ms (Wooburn Grn), H.Wyc. 110 AE58
Wooburn Town (Wooburn Grn), H.Wyc. 110 AE59
Wood Av, Purf. 168 FQ77
Wood Cl E2 142 DU70
Wood Cl NW9 118 CR59
Wood Cl, Bex. 187 FE90
Wood Cl, Har. 117 CD59
Wood Cl, Hat. 45 CV18
Wood Cl, Red. 266 DG143
Wood Cl, Wind. 151 AQ84
Wood Common, Hat. 45 CV15
Wood Cres, Hem.H. 40 BK21
Wood Dr, Chis. 184 EL93
Wood Dr, Sev. 256 FF126
Wood End, Hayes 135 BS72
Wood End (Park St), St.Alb. 60 CC28
Wood End Av, Har. 116 CB63
Wood End Cl, Hem.H. 41 BQ19
Wood End Cl, Nthlt. 117 CD64
Wood End Cl (Farnham Common), Slou. 111 AR62
Wood End Gdns, Nthlt. 116 CC64
Wood End Grn Rd, Hayes 135 BR71
Wood End La, Nthlt. 136 CB65
Wood End Rd, Har. 117 CD63
Wood End Way, Nthlt. 116 CC64
Wood Fm Rd, Hem.H. 40 BL20
Wood Grn Shop City N22 99 DN54
High Rd
Wood Grn Way (Cheshunt), Wal.Cr. 67 DY31
Wood Ho SW17 180 DE92
Laurel Cl
Wood Ho La, Brox. 48 DT21
Wood La N6 121 DH58
Wood La NW9 118 CS59
Wood La W12 139 CW72
Wood La, Cat. 236 DR124
Wood La, Dag. 126 EW63
Wood La (Lane End), Dart. 189 FR91
Wood La, Hem.H. 40 BK21
Wood La, Horn. 127 FG64
Wood La, Islw. 157 CF80
Wood La, Iver 133 BC71
Wood La, Ruis. 115 BR60
Wood La, Slou. 151 AM76
Wood La, Stan. 95 CG48
Wood La, Tad. 233 CZ116
Wood La, Ware 33 EA05
Wood La, Wey. 213 BQ109
Wood La, Wdf.Grn. 102 EF50
Wood La Cl, Iver 133 BB69
Wood La End, Hem.H. 40 BN19
Wood Lo Gdns, Brom. 184 EL94
Wood Lo La, W.Wick. 203 EC104
Wood Meads, Epp. 70 EU29
Wood Pt E16 144 EG71
Fife Rd
Wood Pond Cl (Seer Grn), Beac. 89 AQ51
Wood Retreat SE18 165 ER80
Wood Ride, Barn. 80 DD39
Wood Ride, Orp. 205 ER98
Wood Riding, Wok. 227 BF115
Pyrford Wds Rd
Wood Ri, Guil. 242 AS132
Wood Ri, Pnr. 115 BU57
Wood Rd, Gdmg. 258 AT144
Wood Rd, Shep. 194 BN98
Wood Rd (Biggin Hill), West. 238 EJ118
Wood St E16 144 EH73
Ethel Rd
Wood St E17 123 EC55
Wood St EC2 275 J9
Wood St EC2 142 DQ72
Wood St W4 158 CS78
Wood St, Barn. 79 CX42
Wood St, Grays 170 GC79
Wood St, Kings.T. 197 CK95
Wood St, Mitch. 200 DG101
Wood St, Red. 251 DJ129
Wood St, Swan. 208 FJ96
Wood Vale N10 121 DJ57
Wood Vale SE23 182 DV88
Wood Vale, Hat. 45 CV18
Wood Vale Est SE23 182 DW86
Wood Vw, Hem.H. 40 BH18
Wood Vw (Cuffley), Pot.B. 65 DL27
Wood Wk, Rick. 73 BE40
Wood Way, Beac. 88 AF54
Wood Way, Orp. 205 EN103
Wood Wf SE10 163 EB79
Woodall Cl E14 143 EB73
Lawless St
Woodall Rd, Enf. 83 DX44
Woodbank, Rick. 74 BJ44
Woodbank Av, Ger.Cr. 112 AX58
Woodbank Dr, Ch.St.G. 90 AX48
Woodbank Rd, Brom. 184 EF90
Woodbastwick Rd SE26 183 DX92
Woodberry Av N21 99 DN47
Woodberry Av, Har. 116 CB56
Woodberry Cl, Sun. 175 BU93
Ashridge Way
Woodberry Cres N10 121 DH55
Woodberry Down N4 122 DQ59
Woodberry Down, Epp. 70 EU29
Woodberry Down Est N4 122 DQ59
Woodberry Gdns N12 98 DC51
Woodberry Gro N4 122 DQ59
Woodberry Gro N12 98 DC51
Woodberry Gro, Bex. 187 FD90
Woodberry Way E4 101 EC46
Woodberry Way N12 98 DC51
Woodbine Cl, Harl. 51 EQ17
Linford End
Woodbine Cl, Twick. 177 CD89
Woodbine Cl, Wal.Abb. 84 EJ35
Woodbine Gro SE20 182 DV94
Woodbine Gro, Enf. 82 DR38
Woodbine La, Wor.Pk. 199 CW104
Woodbine Pl E11 124 EG58
Woodbine Rd, Sid. 185 ES88
Woodbine Ter E9 142 DW65
Morning La
Woodbines Av, Kings.T. 197 CK97
Woodborough Rd SW15 159 CV84
Woodbourne Av SW16 181 DK90
Woodbourne Cl SW16 181 DL90
Woodbourne Av
Woodbourne Dr (Claygate), Esher 215 CF107
Woodbourne Gdns, Wall. 219 DH108
Woodbridge Av, Lthd. 231 CG118
Woodbridge Cl N7 121 DM61
Woodbridge Cl NW2 119 CU62
Woodbridge Cl, Rom. 106 FK49
Woodbridge Ct, Wdf.Grn. 102 EL52
Woodbridge Gro, Lthd. 231 CG118
Woodbridge Hill, Guil. 242 AV133
Woodbridge Hill Gdns, Guil. 242 AU133
Woodbridge La, Rom. 106 FK48
Woodbridge Meadows, Guil. 242 AW133
Woodbridge Rd, Bark. 125 ET64
Woodbridge Rd, Guil. 242 AW133
Woodbridge St EC1 274 F4
Woodbridge St EC1 141 DP70
Woodbrook Gdns, Wal.Abb. 68 EE33
Woodbrook Rd SE2 166 EU79
Woodburn Cl NW4 119 CX57
Woodbury, B.End 110 AC59
Woodbury Cl E11 124 EH56
Woodbury Cl, Croy. 202 DT103
Woodbury Cl (Biggin Hill), West. 239 EM118
Woodbury Dr, Sutt. 218 DC110
Woodbury Hill, Loug. 84 EL41
Woodbury Hollow, Loug. 84 EL40
Woodbury Pk Rd W13 137 CH70
Woodbury Rd E17 123 EB56
Woodbury Rd, West. 239 EM118
Woodbury St SW17 180 DE92
Woodchester Pk (Knotty Grn), Beac. 88 AJ50
Woodchester Sq W2 140 DB71
Woodchurch Cl, Sid. 185 ER90
Woodchurch Dr, Brom. 184 EK94
Woodchurch Rd NW6 140 DA66
Woodclyffe Dr, Chis. 205 EN96
Woodcock Ct, Har. 118 CL59
Woodcock Dell Av, Har. 117 CK59
Woodcock Hill, Berk. 38 AS18
Woodcock Hill, Har. 117 CK59
Woodcock Hill, Rick. 92 BL50
Woodcock Hill (Sandridge), St.Alb. 44 CN15
Woodcocks E16 144 EJ71
Woodcombe Cres SE23 182 DW88
Woodcote, Guil. 258 AV138
Woodcote, Horl. 269 DJ147
The Fieldings
Woodcote Av NW7 97 CW51
Woodcote Av, Horn. 127 FG63
Woodcote Av, Th.Hth. 201 DP98
Woodcote Av, Wall. 219 DH108
Woodcote Cl, Enf. 82 DW44
Woodcote Cl, Epsom 216 CR114
Woodcote Cl, Kings.T. 178 CM92
Woodcote Cl (Cheshunt), Wal.Cr. 66 DW30
Woodcote Dr, Orp. 205 ER102
Woodcote Dr, Pur. 219 DK110
Woodcote End, Epsom 232 CR115
Woodcote Grn, Wall. 219 DJ109
Woodcote Grn Rd, Epsom 232 CQ116
Woodcote Gro, Couls. 219 DH112
Woodcote Gro Rd, Couls. 235 DK115
Woodcote Hurst, Epsom 232 CQ116
Woodcote La, Pur. 219 DK111
Woodcote Lawns, Chesh. 54 AN27
Little Hivings
Woodcote Ms, Loug. 102 EK45
Woodcote Ms, Wall. 219 DH107
Woodcote Pk Av, Pur. 219 DJ112
Woodcote Pk Rd, Epsom 232 CQ116
Woodcote Pl SE27 181 DP92
Woodcote Rd E11 124 EG59
Woodcote Rd, Epsom 216 CR114
Woodcote Rd, Pur. 219 DJ109
Woodcote Rd, Wall. 219 DH107
Woodcote Side, Epsom 232 CP115
Woodcote Valley Rd, Pur. 219 DK113
Woodcott Ho SW15 179 CU87
Ellisfield Dr
Woodcrest Rd, Pur. 219 DL113
Woodcrest Wk, Reig. 250 DE132
Woodcroft N21 99 DM46
Woodcroft SE9 185 EM90
Woodcroft, Grnf. 137 CG65
Woodcroft, Harl. 51 ER17
Woodcroft Av NW7 96 CS52
Woodcroft Av, Stan. 95 CF53
Woodcroft Av, Ware 33 ED11
Woodcroft Cres, Uxb. 135 BP67
Woodcroft Ms SE8 163 DY77
Croft St
Woodcroft Rd, Chesh. 54 AR28
Woodcroft Rd, Th.Hth. 201 DP99
Woodcutters Av, Grays 170 GC75
Woodedge Cl E4 102 EF46
Woodend SE19 182 DQ93
Woodend, Esher 196 CC103
Woodend, Lthd. 247 CJ125
Woodend, Sutt. 200 DC103
Woodend, The, Wall. 219 DH109
Woodend Cl, Wok. 226 AU119
Woodend Gdns, Enf. 81 DL42
Woodend Pk, Cob. 230 BX115
Woodend Rd E17 101 EC54
Wooder Gdns E7 124 EF63
Wooderson Cl SE25 202 DS98
Woodfall Av, Barn. 79 CZ43
Woodfall Dr, Dart. 167 FE84
Woodfall Rd N4 121 DN60
Woodfall St SW3 160 DF78
Woodfarrs SE5 162 DR84
Woodfield, Ash. 231 CK117
Woodfield Av NW9 118 CS56
Woodfield Av SW16 181 DK90
Woodfield Av W5 137 CJ70
Woodfield Av, Cars. 218 DG107
Woodfield Av, Grav. 191 GH88
Woodfield Av, Nthwd. 93 BS49
Woodfield Av, Wem. 117 CJ62
Woodfield Cl SE19 182 DQ94
Woodfield Cl, Ash. 231 CK117
Woodfield Cl, Couls. 235 DJ119
Woodfield Cl, Enf. 82 DS42
Woodfield Cl, Red. 250 DE133
Woodfield Cres W5 137 CJ70
Woodfield Dr, Barn. 98 DG46
Woodfield Dr, Hem.H. 41 BR22
Woodfield Dr, Rom. 127 FG56
Woodfield Gdns W9 139 CZ71
Woodfield Rd
Woodfield Gdns, Hem.H. 41 BQ22
Woodfield Gdns, N.Mal. 199 CT99
Woodfield Gro SW16 181 DK90
Woodfield Hill, Couls. 235 DH119
Woodfield La SW16 181 DK90
Woodfield La, Ash. 232 CL116
Woodfield La, Hat. 46 DD23
Woodfield La, Hert. 46 DD23
Woodfield Pk, Amer. 55 AN36
Woodfield Pl W9 139 CZ70
Woodfield Ri, Bushey 95 CD45
Woodfield Rd W5 137 CJ70
Woodfield Rd W9 139 CZ71
Woodfield Rd, Ash. 231 CK117
Woodfield Rd, Houns. 155 BV82
Woodfield Rd, Rad. 77 CG36
Woodfield Rd, T.Ditt. 197 CF103
Woodfield Rd, Welw.G.C. 29 CZ09
Woodfield Ter, Epp. 70 EW25
High Rd
Woodfield Ter (Harefield), Uxb. 92 BH54
Woodfield Way N11 99 DK52
Woodfield Way, Horn. 128 FK60
Woodfield Way, Red. 250 DE132
Woodfield Way, St.Alb. 43 CJ17
Woodfields, Sev. 256 FD122
Woodfields, The, S.Croy. 220 DT111
Woodfines, The, Horn. 128 FK58
Woodford Av, Ilf. 125 EM57
Woodford Av, Wdf.Grn. 124 EL55
Woodford Br Rd, Ilf. 124 EK55
Woodford Ct W12 159 CX75
Shepherds Bush Grn
Woodford Ct, Wal.Abb. 68 EG33
Woodford Cres, Pnr. 93 BV54
Woodford New Rd E17 124 EE56
Woodford New Rd E18 102 EE53
Woodford New Rd, Wdf.Grn. 102 EE53
Woodford Pl, Wem. 118 CL60
Woodford Rd E7 124 EH63
Woodford Rd E18 124 EG56
Woodford Rd, Wat. 75 BV40
Woodford Way, Slou. 131 AN69
Woodgate, Wat. 59 BV33
Woodgate Av, Chess. 215 CK106
Woodgate Av, Pot.B. 65 DH33
Woodgate Cres, Nthwd. 93 BU51
Woodgate Dr SW16 181 DK94
Woodgavil, Bans. 233 CZ116
Woodger Cl, Guil. 243 BC132
Kingfisher Dr
Woodger Rd W12 159 CW75
Goldhawk Rd
Woodgers Gro, Swan. 207 FF96
Woodget Cl E6 144 EL72
Remington Rd
Woodgrange Av N12 98 DD51
Woodgrange Av W5 138 CN74
Woodgrange Av, Enf. 82 DU44
Woodgrange Av, Har. 117 CJ57
Woodgrange Cl, Har. 117 CK57
Woodgrange Gdns, Enf. 82 DU44
Woodgrange Rd E7 124 EH63
Woodgrange Ter, Enf. 82 DU44
Great Cambridge Rd
Woodgreen Rd, Wal.Abb. 84 EJ35
Woodhall Av SE21 182 DT90
Woodhall Av, Pnr. 94 BY54
Woodhall Cl, Chess. 215 CK107
Ashlyns Way
Woodhall Cl, Hert. 32 DQ07
Woodhall Cl, Uxb. 114 BK64
Woodhall Ct, Welw.G.C. 29 CY10
Woodhall Cres, Horn. 128 FM59
Woodhall Dr SE21 182 DT90
Woodhall Dr, Pnr. 94 BX53
Woodhall Gate, Pnr. 94 BX52
Woodhall Ho SW18 180 DD86
Fitzhugh Gro
Woodhall La, Hem.H. 40 BL19
Woodhall La, Rad. 78 CL35
Woodhall La, Wat. 94 BX49
Woodhall La, Welw.G.C. 29 CY10
Woodhall Par, Welw.G.C. 29 CZ11
Woodhall Rd, Pnr. 94 BX52
Woodham Ct E18 124 EF56
Woodham La (New Haw), Add. 212 BG110
Woodham La, Wok. 211 BB114
Woodham Pk Rd (Woodham), Add. 211 BF109
Woodham Pk Way (Woodham), Add. 211 BF111
Woodham Ri, Wok. 211 AZ114
Woodham Rd SE6 183 EC90
Woodham Rd, Wok. 226 AY115
Woodham Way (Stanstead Abbotts), Ware 33 EC11
Woodham Waye, Wok. 211 BB113
Woodhatch Cl E6 144 EL72
Remington Rd
Woodhatch Rd, Red. 266 DB137
Woodhatch Rd, Reig. 266 DB137
Woodhatch Spinney, Couls. 235 DL116
Woodhaven Gdns, Ilf. 125 EQ55
Brandville Gdns
Woodhaw, Egh. 173 BB91
Woodhayes, Horl. 269 DH147
Woodhayes Rd SW19 179 CW94
Woodhead Dr, Orp. 205 ES103
Sherlies Av
Woodheyes Rd NW10 118 CR64
Woodhill SE18 164 EL77
Woodhill, Harl. 51 ES19
Woodhill (Send), Wok. 243 BE125
Woodhill Av, Ger.Cr. 113 BA58
Woodhill Cres, Har. 117 CK58
Woodhouse Av, Grnf. 137 CF68
Woodhouse Cl, Grnf. 137 CF68
Woodhouse Cl, Hayes 155 BS76
Woodhouse Eaves, Nthwd. 93 BU50
Woodhouse Gro E12 144 EL65
Woodhouse La (Holmbury St. Mary), Dor. 261 BU143
Woodhouse Rd E11 124 EF62
Woodhouse Rd N12 98 DD51
Woodhurst Av, Orp. 205 EQ100
Woodhurst Av, Wat. 76 BX35
Woodhurst Dr (Denham), Uxb. 113 BF57
Woodhurst La, Oxt. 254 EE130
Woodhurst Pk, Oxt. 254 EE130
Woodhurst Rd SE2 166 EU78
Woodhurst Rd W3 138 CQ73
Woodhyrst Gdns, Ken. 235 DP115
Firs Rd
Wooding Gro, Harl. 51 EP15
Woodington Cl SE9 185 EN86
Woodknoll Dr, Chis. 205 EM95
Woodland App, Grnf. 137 CG65
Woodland Av, Brwd. 109 GC43
Woodland Av, Hem.H. 40 BH21
Woodland Av, Slou. 131 AR73
Woodland Av, Wind. 151 AM84
Woodland Cl NW9 118 CQ58
Woodland Cl SE19 182 DS93
Woodland Hill
Woodland Cl, Brwd. 109 GC43
Woodland Cl, Epsom 216 CS107
Woodland Cl, Hem.H. 40 BH21
Woodland Cl (Ickenham), Uxb. 115 BP61
Woodland Cl, Wey. 213 BR105
Woodland Gro
Woodland Cl, Wdf.Grn. 102 EH48
Woodland Ct, Oxt. 253 ED128
Woodland Cres SE10 164 EE79
Woodland Cres SE16 163 DX75
Woodland Dr (East Horsley), Lthd. 245 BT127
Woodland Dr, St.Alb. 43 CJ18
Woodland Dr, Wat. 75 BT39
Woodland Gdns N10 121 DH57
Woodland Gdns, Islw. 157 CE82
Woodland Gdns, S.Croy. 220 DW111
Woodland Glade (Farnham Common), Slou. 111 AR62
Woodland Gro SE10 164 EE78
Woodland Gro, Epp. 70 EU31
Woodland Gro, Wey. 213 BR105
Woodland Hill SE19 182 DS93
Woodland La, Rick. 73 BD41
Woodland Mt, Hert. 32 DT09
Woodland Pl, Hem.H. 40 BH21
Woodland Pl, Rick. 73 BF42
Woodland Ri N10 121 DH56
Woodland Ri, Grnf. 137 CG65
Woodland Ri, Oxt. 254 EE130
Woodland Ri, Sev. 257 FL123
Woodland Ri, Welw.G.C. 29 CW07
Woodland Rd E4 101 EC46
Woodland Rd N11 99 DH50
Woodland Rd SE19 182 DS92
Woodland Rd, Hert. 32 DV12
Woodland Rd, Loug. 84 EL41
Woodland Rd, Rick. 91 BD50
Woodland Rd, Th.Hth. 201 DN98
Woodland St E8 142 DT65
Dalston La
Woodland Ter SE7 164 EL77
Woodland Vw, Chesh. 54 AR32
Woodland Vw, Gdmg. 258 AS142
Woodland Wk NW3 120 DE64
Woodland Wk SE10 164 EE78
Woodland Gro
Woodland Wk, Brom. 184 EE91
Woodland Way N21 99 DN47
Woodland Way NW7 96 CS51
Woodland Way SE2 166 EX77
Woodland Way, Abb.L. 59 BT27
Woodland Way, Cat. 252 DS128
Woodland Way, Croy. 203 DY102
Woodland Way, Epp. 85 ER35
Woodland Way, Green. 169 FU84
Woodland Way, Mitch. 180 DG94
Woodland Way, Mord. 199 CZ98
Woodland Way, Orp. 205 EQ98
Woodland Way, Pur. 219 DN113
Woodland Way, Surb. 198 CP103
Woodland Way (Kingswood), Tad. 233 CY122
Woodland Way (Cheshunt), Wal.Cr. 65 DP28
Woodland Way, W.Wick. 221 EB105
Woodland Way, Wey. 213 BR106
Woodland Way, Wdf.Grn. 102 EH48
Woodlands NW11 119 CY58
Woodlands SW20 199 CW98
Woodlands, Ger.Cr. 113 AZ57
Woodlands, Har. 116 CA56
Woodlands, Hat. 64 DB26
Woodlands, Horl. 269 DJ147
Woodlands, Rad. 61 CG34
Woodlands (Park St), St.Alb. 60 CC27
Woodlands, Wok. 226 AY118
Constitution Hill
Woodlands, The N14 99 DH46
Woodlands, The SE13 183 ED87
Woodlands, The SE19 182 DQ94
Woodlands, The, Amer. 55 AQ35
Woodlands, The, Beck. 203 EC95
Woodlands, The, Esher 196 CC103
Woodlands, The (Smallfield), Horl. 269 DP148
Woodlands, The, Islw. 157 CF82
Woodlands, The, Orp. 224 EV107
Woodlands, The, Wall. 219 DH109
Woodlands Av E11 124 EH60
Woodlands Av N3 98 DC52
Woodlands Av W3 138 CP74
Woodlands Av, Berk. 38 AW20
Woodlands Av, Horn. 128 FK57
Woodlands Av, N.Mal. 198 CQ95
Woodlands Av, Red. 266 DF135

Woodlands Av, Rom. 126 EY58
Woodlands Av, Ruis. 116 BX60
Woodlands Av, Sid. 185 ES88
Woodlands Av, W.Byf. 211 BF113
Woodlands Av, Wor.Pk. 199 CT103
Woodlands Cl NW11 119 CY57
Woodlands Cl, Borwd. 78 CP42
Woodlands Cl, Brom. 205 EM96
Woodlands Cl (Ottershaw), Cher. 211 BB110
Woodlands Cl (Claygate), Esher 215 CF108
Woodlands Cl, Ger.Cr. 113 BA58
Woodlands Cl, Grays 170 GE76
Woodlands Cl, Hodd. 49 EA18
Woodlands Cl (East Horsley), Lthd. 245 BT127
Woodlands Cl, Swan. 207 FF97
Woodlands Ct, Wok. 226 AY119
Constitution Hill
Woodlands Dr, Beac. 88 AJ51
Woodlands Dr, Hodd. 49 EA19
Woodlands Dr, Kings L. 59 BQ28
Woodlands Dr, Stan. 95 CF51
Woodlands Dr, Sun. 196 BW96
Woodlands Glade, Beac. 88 AJ51
Woodlands Gro, Couls. 234 DG117
Woodlands Gro, Islw. 157 CE82
Woodlands Hill, Beac. 111 AL58
Woodlands La (Stoke D'Abernon), Cob. 230 CA117
Woodlands Par, Ashf. 175 BQ93
Woodlands Pk, Add. 211 BF106
Woodlands Pk, Bex. 187 FC91
Woodlands Pk, Guil. 243 BB132
Woodlands Pk, Tad. 248 CP131
Woodlands Pk, Wok. 211 BC114
Blackmore Cres
Woodlands Pk Rd N15 121 DP57
Woodlands Pk Rd SE10 164 EE79
Woodlands Ri, Swan. 207 FF96
Woodlands Rd E11 124 EE61
Woodlands Rd E17 123 EC55
Woodlands Rd N9 100 DW46
Woodlands Rd SW13 159 CT83
Woodlands Rd, Bexh. 166 EY83
Woodlands Rd, Brom. 204 EL96
Woodlands Rd, Bushey 76 BY43
Woodlands Rd, Enf. 82 DR39
Woodlands Rd, Epsom 232 CN115
Woodlands Rd, Guil. 242 AX130
Woodlands Rd, Har. 117 CF57
Woodlands Rd, Hem.H. 58 BN27
Woodlands Rd, Hert. 32 DT09
Woodlands Rd, Ilf. 125 EQ62
Woodlands Rd, Islw. 157 CE82
Woodlands Rd, Lthd. 231 CD117
Woodlands Rd (Effingham), Lthd. 246 BY128
Woodlands Rd, Orp. 224 EU107
Woodlands Rd, Red. 266 DF136
Woodlands Rd, Rom. 127 FF55
Woodlands Rd (Harold Wd), Rom. 106 FN53
Woodlands Rd, Sthl. 136 BX74
Woodlands Rd, Surb. 197 CK101
Woodlands Rd, Vir.W. 192 AW98
Woodlands Rd, W.Byf. 211 BF114
Woodlands Rd E, Vir.W. 192 AW98
Woodlands Rd W, Vir.W. 192 AW97
Woodlands St SE13 183 ED87
Woodlands Vw, Dor. 263 CH142
Woodlands Vw (Badgers Mt), Sev. 224 FA110
Woodlands Way SW15 179 CZ85
Oakhill Rd
Woodlands Way, Ash. 232 CN116
Woodlands Way, Tad. 248 CQ130
Woodlawn Cl SW15 179 CZ85
Woodlawn Cres, Twick. 176 CB89
Woodlawn Dr, Felt. 176 BX89
Woodlawn Gro, Wok. 227 AZ115
Woodlawn Rd SW6 159 CX80
Woodlea Dr, Brom. 204 EE99
Woodlea Gro, Nthwd. 93 BQ51
Woodlea Rd N16 122 DS62
Woodleigh E18 102 EG53
Churchfields
Woodleigh Av N12 98 DE51
Woodleigh Gdns SW16 181 DL90
Woodley Cl SW17 180 DF94
Arnold Rd
Woodley Hill, Chesh. 54 AR34
Woodley La, Cars. 200 DD104
Woodley Rd, Orp. 206 EW103
Woodley Rd, Ware 33 DZ05
Woodman La E4 84 EE43
Woodman Path, Ilf. 103 ES51
Woodman Rd, Brwd. 108 FW50
Woodman Rd, Couls. 235 DJ115
Woodman Rd, Hem.H. 40 BL22
Woodman St E16 145 EN74
Woodmancote Gdns, W.Byf. 212 BG113
Woodmans Gro NW10 119 CT64
Woodmans Ms W12 139 CV71
Woodmansterne La, Bans. 234 DB115
Woodmansterne La, Cars. 218 DF112
Woodmansterne La, Wall. 219 DH111
Woodmansterne Rd SW16 181 DK94
Woodmansterne Rd, Cars. 218 DE109
Woodmansterne Rd, Couls. 235 DJ115
Woodmansterne St, Bans. 234 DE115
Woodmere SE9 185 EM88
Woodmere Av, Croy. 203 DX101
Woodmere Av, Wat. 76 BX38
Woodmere Cl SW11 160 DG83
Lavender Hill
Woodmere Cl, Croy. 203 DX101
Woodmere Gdns, Croy. 203 DX101
Woodmere Way, Beck. 203 ED99
Woodmill Ms, Hodd. 49 EB15
Whittingstall Rd
Woodmount, Swan. 207 FD101
Woodnook Rd SW16 181 DH92
Woodpecker Cl N9 82 DV44
Woodpecker Cl, Bushey 94 CC46
Woodpecker Cl, Cob. 214 BY112
Woodpecker Cl, Har. 95 CF53
Woodpecker Cl, Hat. 45 CT21
Woodpecker Mt, Croy. 221 DY109
Woodpecker Rd SE14 163 DY79
Woodpecker Rd SE28 146 EW73
Woodpecker Way, Wok. 226 AX123
Woodplace Cl, Couls. 235 DJ119
Woodplace La, Couls. 235 DJ118
Woodquest Av SE24 182 DQ85
Woodredon Cl, Harl. 50 EH16
Epping Rd
Woodredon Fm La, Wal.Abb. 84 EK35
Woodridden Hill, Wal.Abb. 84 EK35
Woodridge Cl, Enf. 81 DN39
Woodridge Way, Nthwd. 93 BS51
Woodridings Av, Pnr. 94 BZ53
Woodridings Cl, Pnr. 94 BY52
Woodriffe Rd E11 123 ED59
Woodrow SE18 165 EM77
Woodrow Av, Hayes 135 BT71
Woodrow Cl, Grnf. 137 CH66
Woodrow Ct N17 100 DV52
Heybourne Rd
Woodroyd Av, Horl. 268 DF149
Woodroyd Gdns, Horl. 268 DF150
Woodruff Av, Guil. 243 BA131
Woodrush Cl SE14 163 DY80
Southerngate Way
Woodrush Way, Rom. 126 EX56
Woods, The, Nthwd. 93 BU50
Woods, The, Rad. 61 CH34
Woods, The, Uxb. 115 BP63
Woods Av, Hat. 45 CU18
Wood's Bldgs E1 142 DV71
Whitechapel Rd
Woods Dr, Slou. 111 AM64
Woods Ms W1 272 E10
Woods Ms W1 140 DG73
Woods Pl SE1 279 N7
Woods Rd SE15 162 DV81
Woodseer St E1 142 DT71
Woodsford SE17 162 DR78
Portland St
Woodsford Sq W14 159 CY75
Woodshire Rd, Dag. 127 FB62
Woodshore Cl, Vir.W. 192 AV100
Woodside NW11 120 DA57
Woodside SW19 179 CZ93
Woodside, Borwd. 78 CM42
Woodside, Buck.H. 102 EJ47
Woodside, Epp. 70 EX27
Woodside, Hert. 32 DW12
Woodside (Flackwell Heath), H.Wyc. 110 AC57
Woodside (Fetcham), Lthd. 230 CB122
Woodside (West Horsley), Lthd. 245 BQ126
Woodside, Orp. 224 EU106
Woodside (Lower Kingswood), Tad. 249 CZ128
Woodside (Cheshunt), Wal.Cr. 66 DU31
Woodside, Walt. 195 BU102
Ashley Rd
Woodside, Wat. 75 BU36
Woodside Av N6 120 DF57
Woodside Av N10 120 DF57
Woodside Av N12 98 DC49
Woodside Av SE25 202 DV100
Woodside Av, Amer. 55 AR36
Woodside Av, Beac. 88 AJ52
Woodside Av, Chis. 185 EQ92
Woodside Av, Esher 197 CE101
Woodside Av (Flackwell Heath), H.Wyc. 110 AC57
Woodside Av, Walt. 213 BV105
Woodside Av, Wem. 138 CL67
Woodside Cl, Amer. 55 AR37
Woodside Cl, Beac. 88 AJ52
Woodside Cl, Bexh. 167 FD84
Woodside Cl, Brwd. 109 GD43
Woodside Cl, Cat. 236 DS124
Woodside Cl (Chalfont St. Peter), Ger.Cr. 90 AY54
Woodside Cl, Rain. 148 FJ70
Woodside Cl, Stan. 95 CH50
Woodside Cl, Surb. 198 CQ101
Woodside Cl, Wem. 138 CL67
Woodside Commercial Est, Epp. 70 EX26
Woodside Ct N12 98 DC49
Woodside Av
Woodside Ct Rd, Croy. 202 DU101
Woodside Cres, Horl. 269 DN148
Woodside Cres, Sid. 185 ES90
Woodside Dr, Dart. 187 FE91
Woodside End, Wem. 138 CL67
Woodside Gdns E4 101 EB50
Woodside Gdns N17 100 DS54
Woodside Gra Rd N12 98 DB49
Woodside Grn SE25 202 DV100
Woodside Gro N12 98 DC48
Woodside Hill (Chalfont St. Peter), Ger.Cr. 90 AY54
Woodside La N12 98 DB48
Woodside La, Bex. 186 EX86
Woodside La, Hat. 45 CZ21
Woodside Ms SE22 182 DT86
Heber Rd
Woodside Pk SE25 202 DU99
Woodside Pk Av E17 123 ED56
Woodside Pk Rd N12 98 DB49
Woodside Pl, Wem. 138 CL67
Woodside Rd E13 144 EJ70
Woodside Rd N22 99 DM52
Woodside Rd SE25 202 DV100
Woodside Rd, Abb.L. 59 BV31
Woodside Rd, Amer. 55 AR37
Woodside Rd, Beac. 88 AJ52
Woodside Rd, Bexh. 167 FD84
Woodside Rd, Brom. 204 EL99
Woodside Rd, Cob. 214 CA113
Woodside Rd, Guil. 242 AT133
Woodside Rd, Kings.T. 178 CL94
Woodside Rd, N.Mal. 198 CR96
Woodside Rd, Nthwd. 93 BT52
Woodside Rd, Pur. 219 DK113
Woodside Rd (Bricket Wd), St.Alb. 60 BZ30
Woodside Rd, Sev. 256 FG123
Woodside Rd (Sundridge), Sev. 240 EX124
Woodside Rd, Sid. 185 ES90
Woodside Rd, Sutt. 200 DC104
Woodside Rd, Wat. 59 BV31
Woodside Rd, Wdf.Grn. 102 EG49
Woodside Way, Croy. 202 DV100
Woodside Way (Penn), H.Wyc. 88 AC46
Woodside Way, Mitch. 201 DH95
Woodside Way, Red. 266 DG135
Woodside Way (White Bushes), Red. 266 DG140
Woodside Way, Vir.W. 192 AV97
Woodsome Lo, Wey. 213 BQ107
Woodsome Rd NW5 120 DG62
Woodspring Rd SW19 179 CY89
Woodstead Gro, Edg. 96 CL51
Woodstock (West Clandon), Guil. 244 BH128
Woodstock Av NW11 119 CY59
Woodstock Av W13 157 CG76
Woodstock Av, Islw. 177 CG85
Woodstock Av, Rom. 106 FP50
Woodstock Av, Slou. 152 AX77
Woodstock Av, Sthl. 136 BZ69
Woodstock Av, Sutt. 199 CZ101
Woodstock Cl, Bex. 186 EZ88
Woodstock Cl (Hertford Heath), Hert. 32 DV11
Hogsdell La
Woodstock Cl, Stan. 96 CL54
Woodstock Cl, Wok. 226 AY116
Woodstock Ct SE12 184 EG86
Woodstock Cres N9 82 DV44
Woodstock Dr, Uxb. 114 BL63
Woodstock Gdns, Beck. 203 EB95
Woodstock Gdns, Hayes 135 BT71
Woodstock Gdns, Ilf. 126 EU61
Woodstock Gro W12 159 CX75
Woodstock La N, Surb. 197 CJ103
Woodstock La S, Chess. 215 CJ105
Woodstock La S (Claygate), Esher 215 CH106
Woodstock Ms W1 272 G7
Woodstock Ri, Sutt. 199 CZ101
Woodstock Rd E7 144 EJ66
Woodstock Rd E17 101 ED54
Woodstock Rd N4 121 DN60
Woodstock Rd NW11 119 CZ59
Woodstock Rd W4 158 CS76
Woodstock Rd, Brox. 49 DY19
Woodstock Rd, Bushey 95 CE45
Woodstock Rd, Cars. 218 DG106
Woodstock Rd, Couls. 235 DH116
Chipstead Valley Rd
Woodstock Rd, Croy. 202 DR104
Woodstock Rd, Wem. 138 CM66
Woodstock Rd N, St.Alb. 43 CH18
Woodstock Rd S, St.Alb. 43 CH20
Woodstock St E16 144 EE72
Victoria Dock Rd
Woodstock St W1 273 H9
Woodstock Ter E14 143 EB73
Woodstock Way, Mitch. 201 DH96
Woodstone Av, Epsom 217 CU106
Woodsway (Oxshott), Lthd. 215 CE114
Woodsyre SE26 182 DT91
Woodthorpe Rd SW15 159 CV84
Woodthorpe Rd, Ashf. 174 BL91
Woodtree Cl NW4 97 CW54
Ashley La
Woodvale Av SE25 202 DT97
Woodvale Wk SE27 182 DQ92
Elder Rd
Woodvale Way NW11 119 CX62
The Vale
Woodview, Chess. 215 CJ111
Woodview, Grays 170 GE76
Woodview Av E4 101 EC49
Woodview Cl N4 121 DP59
Woodview Cl SW15 178 CR91
Woodview Cl, Orp. 205 EQ103
Crofton Rd
Woodview Cl, S.Croy. 220 DV114
Woodview Rd, Swan. 207 FC96
Woodville SE3 164 EH81
Woodville Cl SE12 184 EG85
Woodville Cl, Tedd. 177 CG91
Woodville Ct, Wat. 75 BU40
Woodville Gdns NW11 119 CX59
Woodville Gdns W5 138 CL72
Woodville Gdns, Ilf. 125 EP55
Woodville Gdns, Ruis. 115 BQ59
Woodville Gro, Well. 166 EU83
Woodville Pl, Cat. 236 DQ121
Woodville Pl, Grav. 191 GH87
Woodville Rd E11 124 EF60
Woodville Rd E17 123 DY56
Woodville Rd E18 102 EH54
Woodville Rd N16 122 DS64
Woodville Rd NW6 139 CZ68
Woodville Rd NW11 119 CX59
Woodville Rd W5 137 CK72
Woodville Rd, Barn. 80 DB41
Woodville Rd, Lthd. 231 CH120
Woodville Rd, Mord. 200 DA98
Woodville Rd, Rich. 177 CH90
Woodville Rd, Th.Hth. 202 DQ98
Woodville St SE18 164 EL77
Woodhill
Woodward Av NW4 119 CU57
Woodward Cl (Claygate), Esher 215 CF107
Woodward Cl, Grays 170 GB77
Woodward Gdns, Dag. 146 EW66
Woodward Rd
Woodward Gdns, Stan. 95 CF52
Woodward Hts, Grays 170 GB77
Woodward Rd, Dag. 146 EV66
Woodward Ter, Green. 189 FS86
Woodwarde Rd SE22 182 DS86
Woodwards, Harl. 51 EQ17
Woodway, Brwd. 109 GA46
Woodway, Guil. 243 BB133
Woodway Cres, Har. 117 CG58
Woodwaye, Wat. 94 BW45
Woodwell St SW18 180 DC85
Huguenot Pl
Woodwicks, Rick. 91 BD50
Woodyard, The, Epp. 70 EW28
Woodyard Cl NW5 120 DG64
Gillies St
Woodyard La SE21 182 DS87
Woodyates Rd SE12 184 EG86
Woodyers Cl (Wonersh), Guil. 259 BB144
Wool Rd SW20 179 CV93
Woolacombe Rd SE3 164 EJ81
Woolacombe Way, Hayes 155 BS77
Woolborough La (Outwood), Red. 267 DM143
Wooler St SE17 162 DR78
Woolf Cl SE28 146 EV74
Woolf Wk, Til. 171 GJ82
Coleridge Rd
Woolhampton Way, Chig. 104 EV48
Woolhams, Cat. 252 DT126
Woollam Cres, St.Alb. 42 CC16
Woollard St, Wal.Abb. 67 EC34
Woollaston Rd N4 121 DP58
Woollett Cl (Crayford), Dart. 167 FG84
Woolmans Cl, Brox. 49 DZ22
Woolmead Av NW9 119 CU59
Woolmer Cl, Borwd. 78 CN38
Woolmer Dr, Hem.H. 41 BQ20
Woolmer Gdns N18 100 DU50
Woolmer Rd N18 100 DU50
Woolmerdine Ct, Bushey 76 BX41
Woolmers La, Hert. 31 DH13
Woolmers Pk, Hert. 31 DH14
Woolmore St E14 143 EC73
Woolneigh St SW6 160 DB83
Woolpack Ho, Enf. 83 DX37
Woolstaplers Way SE16 162 DU77
Woolston Cl E17 101 DX54
Riverhead Cl
Woolstone Rd SE23 183 DY89
Woolwich Ch St SE18 164 EL76
Woolwich Common SE18 165 EN79
Woolwich Ferry Pier E16 165 EN75
Woolwich Foot Tunnel E16 165 EN75
Woolwich Foot Tunnel SE18 165 EN75
Woolwich Garrison SE18 165 EM79
Woolwich High St SE18 165 EN76
Woolwich Ind Est SE28 165 ES76
Hadden Rd
Woolwich Manor Way E6 145 EP72
Woolwich Manor Way E16 165 EP75
Woolwich Mkt SE18 165 EP77
Woolwich New Rd SE18 165 EN78
Woolwich Rd SE2 166 EX79
Woolwich Rd SE7 164 EG78
Woolwich Rd SE10 164 EF78
Woolwich Rd, Belv. 166 EX79
Woolwich Rd, Bexh. 166 FA84
Wooster Gdns E14 143 ED72
Wooster Ms, Har. 116 CC55
Fairfield Dr
Wooster Pl SE1 279 L8
Wooster Rd, Beac. 88 AJ51
Wootton Cl, Epsom 233 CT115
Wootton Cl, Horn. 128 FK57
Wootton Dr, Hem.H. 40 BM15
Wootton Dr (Wooburn Grn), H.Wyc. 110 AE55
Wootton Gro N3 98 DA53
Wootton St SE1 278 E4
Wootton St SE1 141 DN74
Worbeck Rd SE20 202 DV96
Worcester Av N17 100 DU52
Worcester Av, Upmin. 129 FT61
Worcester Cl NW2 119 CV62
Newfield Ri
Worcester Cl, Croy. 203 DZ103
Worcester Cl (Istead Ri), Grav. 191 GF94
Worcester Cl, Green. 169 FV84
Worcester Cl, Mitch. 201 DH97
Worcester Ct, Walt. 196 BW102
Rodney Rd
Worcester Cres NW7 96 CS48
Worcester Cres, Wdf.Grn. 102 EH50
Worcester Dr W4 158 CS75
Worcester Dr, Ashf. 175 BP93
Worcester Gdns SW11 180 DF85
Grandison Rd
Worcester Gdns, Grnf. 136 CC65
Worcester Gdns, Ilf. 124 EL59
Worcester Gdns, Slou. 151 AR75
Worcester Gdns, Wor.Pk. 198 CS104
Worcester Ms NW6 140 DB65
Lymington Rd
Worcester Pk Rd, Wor.Pk. 198 CQ104
Worcester Rd E12 125 EM63
Worcester Rd E17 101 DX54
Worcester Rd SW19 179 CZ92
Worcester Rd, Guil. 242 AT132
Worcester Rd, Hat. 45 CT17
Worcester Rd, Reig. 250 DA133
Worcester Rd, Sutt. 218 DB107
Worcester Rd, Uxb. 134 BJ71
Worcesters Av, Enf. 82 DU38
Wordsworth Av E12 144 EL65
Wordsworth Av E18 124 EF55
Wordsworth Av, Grnf. 137 CD68
Wordsworth Av, Ken. 236 DR115
Valley Rd
Wordsworth Cl, Rom. 106 FJ53
Wordsworth Cl, Til. 171 GJ82
Wordsworth Dr, Sutt. 217 CW105
Wordsworth Mead, Red. 250 DG132
Wordsworth Rd N16 122 DS63
Wordsworth Rd SE1 279 P9
Wordsworth Rd SE20 183 DX94
Wordsworth Rd, Add. 212 BK105
Wordsworth Rd, Hmptn. 176 BZ91
Wordsworth Rd, Slou. 131 AK70
Wordsworth Rd, Wall. 219 DJ107
Wordsworth Rd, Well. 165 ES81
Wordsworth Wk NW11 120 DA56
Wordsworth Way, Dart. 168 FN84
Wordsworth Way, West Dr. 154 BL77
Worfield St SW11 160 DE80
Worgan St SE11 278 B10
Worgan St SE11 161 DM78
Worgan St SE16 163 DX76
Workers Rd, Harl. 53 FB16
Workers Rd, Ong. 53 FG16
Worland Rd E15 144 EE66
World's End, Cob. 213 BU114
World's End Est SW10 160 DD80
Worlds End La N21 81 DM43
Worlds End La, Enf. 81 DM43
Worlds End La, Orp. 223 ET107
World's End Pas SW10 160 DD80
Riley St
World's End Pl SW10 160 DC80
King's Rd
Worley Rd, St.Alb. 42 CC19
Worlidge St W6 159 CW78
Worlingham Rd SE22 162 DT84
Wormholt Rd W12 139 CU73
Wormley Ct, Wal.Abb. 68 EG33
Winters Way
Wormley Lo Cl, Brox. 49 DZ23
Wormwood St EC2 275 M8
Wormwood St EC2 142 DS72
Wormyngford Ct, Wal.Abb. 68 EG33
Ninefields
Wornington Rd W10 139 CY71
Woronzow Rd NW8 140 DD67
Worple, The (Wraysbury), Stai. 173 AZ86
Worple Av SW19 179 CX94
Worple Av, Islw. 177 CG85
Worple Av, Stai. 174 BH93
Worple Cl, Har. 116 BZ60
Worple Rd SW19 179 CY94
Worple Rd SW20 199 CW96
Worple Rd, Epsom 216 CS114
Worple Rd, Islw. 157 CG84
Worple Rd, Lthd. 231 CH123
Worple Rd, Stai. 174 BH94
Worple Rd Ms SW19 179 CZ93
Worple St SW14 158 CR83
Worple Way, Har. 116 BZ60
Worple Way, Rich. 178 CL85
Worplesdon Rd, Guil. 242 AT129
Worrin Cl, Brwd. 109 FZ46
Worrin Rd, Brwd. 109 FZ47
Worsfold Cl (Send), Wok. 227 BB123
Worship St EC2 275 L5
Worship St EC2 142 DR70
Worships Hill, Sev. 256 FE123
Worslade Rd SW17 180 DD91
Worsley Br Rd SE26 183 DZ91
Worsley Br Rd, Beck. 183 DZ92
Worsley Rd E11 124 EE63
Worsopp Dr SW4 181 DJ85
Worsted Grn, Red. 251 DJ129
Worth Cl, Orp. 223 ES105
Worth Gro SE17 162 DR78
Merrow St
Worthfield Cl, Epsom 216 CR108
Worthies, The, Amer. 55 AP40
Worthing Cl E15 144 EE68
Mitre Rd
Worthing Cl, Grays 170 FY79
Worthing Rd, Houns. 156 BZ79
Worthington Cl, Mitch. 201 DH97
Worthington Rd, Surb. 198 CM102
Worthy Down Ct SE18 165 EN81
Prince Imperial Rd
Wortley Rd E6 144 EK66
Wortley Rd, Croy. 201 DN101
Worton Gdns, Islw. 157 CD82
Worton Hall Ind Est, Islw. 157 CE84
Worton Rd, Islw. 157 CE83
Worton Way, Houns. 157 CD82
Worton Way, Islw. 156 CC81
Wotton Dr, Dor. 262 BZ139
Wotton Grn, Orp. 206 EX98
Wotton Rd NW2 119 CW63
Wotton Rd SE8 163 DZ79
Wotton Way, Sutt. 217 CW110
Wouldham Rd E16 144 EF72
Wouldham Rd, Grays 170 FY79
Wrabness Way, Stai. 194 BH95
Wragby Rd E11 124 EE62
Wrampling Pl N9 100 DU46
Wrangley Ct, Wal.Abb. 68 EG33
Wrangthorn Wk, Croy. 219 DN105
Epsom Rd
Wray Av, Ilf. 125 EN55
Wray Cl, Horn. 128 FJ59
Wray Common, Reig. 250 DD132
Wray Common Rd, Reig. 250 DC133
Wray Cres N4 121 DL61
Wray La, Reig. 250 DC130
Wray Mill Pk, Reig. 250 DD132
Wray Pk Rd, Reig. 250 DB133
Wray Rd, Sutt. 217 CZ109
Wrayfield Av, Reig. 250 DC133
Wrayfield Rd, Sutt. 199 CX104
Wraylands Dr, Reig. 250 DD132
Wrays Way, Hayes 135 BS70
Balmoral Dr
Wraysbury Cl, Houns. 176 BY85
Dorney Way
Wraysbury Gdns, Stai. 173 BD89
Moor La
Wraysbury Rd, Stai. 173 BC90
Wrekin Rd SE18 165 EQ80
Wren Av NW2 119 CW64
Wren Av, Sthl. 156 BZ77
Wren Cl E16 144 EF72
Ibbotson Av
Wren Cl N9 101 DX46
Chaffinch Cl
Wren Cl, Orp. 206 EX97
Wren Cl, S.Croy. 221 DX109
Wren Ct, Slou. 153 BA76
New Rd
Wren Cres, Add. 212 BK106
Wren Cres, Bushey 94 CC46
Wren Dr, Wal.Abb. 68 EG34
Wren Dr, West Dr. 154 BK76
Wren Gdns, Dag. 126 EX64
Wren Gdns, Horn. 127 FF60
Wren Landing E14 143 DZ74
Cabot Sq
Wren Path SE28 165 ER76
Wren Pl, Brwd. 108 FX48
Wren Rd SE5 162 DR81
Wren Rd, Dag. 126 EX64
Wren Rd, Sid. 186 EW91
Wren St WC1 274 C4
Wren St WC1 141 DM70
Wren Ter, Ilf. 125 EN55
Tiptree Cres
Wren Wk, Til. 171 GH80
Wren Wd, Welw.G.C. 30 DB08
Wrens Av, Ashf. 175 BQ92
Wrens Cft (Northfleet), Grav. 190 GE91
Wrens Hill (Oxshott), Lthd. 230 CC115
Wrensfield, Hem.H. 40 BG21
Wrentham Av NW10 139 CX68
Wrenthorpe Rd, Brom. 184 EE91
Wrenwood Way, Pnr. 115 BV56
Wrestlers Cl, Hat. 45 CW15
Wrestlers Ct EC3 142 DS72
Camomile St
Wrexham Rd E3 143 EA68
Wrexham Rd, Rom. 106 FK48
Wricklemarsh Rd SE3 164 EH81
Wrigglesworth St SE14 163 DX80
Wright Cl, Swans. 189 FX86
Milton St
Wright Gdns, Shep. 194 BN99
Laleham Rd
Wright Rd N1 142 DS65
Burder Cl
Wright Rd, Houns. 156 BW80
Wright Sq, Wind. 150 AJ83
Wright Way
Wright Way, Wind. 150 AJ83
Wrights All SW19 179 CW93
Wrights Cl SE13 163 ED84
Wisteria Rd
Wrights Cl, Dag. 127 FB62
Wrights Grn SW4 161 DK84
Nelson's Row
Wrights La W8 160 DB76
Wrights Pl NW10 138 CQ65
Mitchell Way
Wrights Rd E3 143 DZ68
Wrights Rd SE25 202 DS97
Wrights Row, Wall. 219 DH105
Wrights Wk SW14 158 CR83
Wrightsbridge Rd, Brwd. 106 FN46
Wrigley Cl E4 101 ED50
Wriotsley Way, Add. 212 BG107
Coombelands La
Writtle Wk, Rain. 147 FF67
Wrotham Pk, Barn. 79 CZ36
Wrotham Rd NW1 141 DJ66
Agar Pl
Wrotham Rd W13 137 CH74
Mattock La
Wrotham Rd, Barn. 79 CY40
Wrotham Rd, Grav. 191 GH88
Wrotham Rd, Well. 166 EW81
Wroths Path, Loug. 85 EM39
Wrottesley Rd NW10 139 CU68
Wrottesley Rd SE18 165 EQ79
Wroughton Rd SW11 180 DF86
Wroughton Ter NW4 119 CW56
Wroxall Rd, Dag. 146 EW65
Wroxham Av, Hem.H. 40 BK22
Wroxham Gdns N11 99 DJ52
Wroxham Gdns, Enf. 81 DN35
Wroxham Gdns, Pot.B. 63 CX31
Wroxham Rd SE28 146 EX73
Wroxton Rd SE15 162 DV82
Wrythe Grn, Cars. 200 DF104
Wrythe Grn Rd
Wrythe Grn Rd, Cars. 200 DF104
Wrythe La, Cars. 200 DC102
Wulfstan St W12 139 CT72
Wulstan Pk, Pot.B. 64 DD32
Tempest Av

The following is a comprehensive listing of the railway stations which appear in this atlas. **Bold** references can be found within the Central London enlarged scale section (pages 272 - 279).

The following is a comprehensive listing of London Regional Transport Stations which appear in the atlas. **Bold** references can be found within the Central London enlarged scale section (pages 272 - 279). A London Underground map can be found on page 431. Restricted line services are indicated in brackets.

London Underground Line Abbreviations

Bak.	Bakerloo
Cen.	Central
Circ.	Circle
C.T.	Croydon Tramlink
D.L.R.	Docklands Light Railway
Dist.	District
E.L.	East London
H. & C.	Hammersmith & City
Jub.	Jubilee
Met.	Metropolitan
North.	Northern
Picc.	Piccadilly
Vic.	Victoria

Acton Town	*Dist.; Picc.*	158	CN75
Addington Village	*C.T.*	221	EA107
Addiscombe	*C.T.*	202	DU102
Aldgate	***Circ.; Met.***	**275**	**P8**
Aldgate East	*Dist.; H. & C.*	142	DT72
All Saints	*D.L.R.*	143	EB73
Alperton	*Picc.*	138	CL67
Amersham	*Met.*	55	AQ38
Ampere Way	*C.T.*	201	DM101
Angel	*North.*	141	DN68
Archway	*North.*	121	DJ61
Arena	*C.T.*	202	DW99
Arnos Grove	*Picc.*	99	DJ49
Arsenal	*Picc.*	121	DN62
Avenue Road	*C.T.*	203	DX96
Baker Street	***Bak.; Circ.; H. & C.; Jub.; Met.***	**272**	**E5**
Balham	*North.*	181	DH88
Bank	***Cen.; D.L.R.; North.***	**275**	**K9**
Barbican	***Circ.; H. & C.; Met.***	**274**	**G6**
Barking	*Dist.; (H. & C.)*	145	EQ66
Barkingside	*Cen.*	125	ER56
Barons Court	*Dist.; Picc.*	159	CY78
Bayswater	*Circ.; Dist.*	140	DB73
Beckenham Junction	*C.T.*	203	EA95
Beckenham Road	*C.T.*	203	DY95
Beckton	*D.L.R.*	145	EN71
Beckton Park	*D.L.R.*	145	EM73
Becontree	*Dist.*	146	EW66
Beddington Lane	*C.T.*	201	DJ100
Belgrave Walk	*C.T.*	200	DD97
Belsize Park	*North.*	120	DE64
Bermondsey	*Jub.*	162	DU76
Bethnal Green	*Cen.*	142	DW69
Birkbeck	*C.T.*	202	DW97
Blackfriars	***Circ.; Dist.***	**274**	**G10**
Blackhorse Lane	*C.T.*	202	DU101
Blackhorse Road	*Vic.*	123	DX56
Blackwall	*D.L.R.*	143	EC73
Bond Street	***Cen.; Jub.***	**272**	**G9**
Borough	***North.***	**279**	**J5**
Boston Manor	*Picc.*	157	CG77
Bounds Green	*Picc.*	99	DK51
Bow Church	*D.L.R.*	143	EA69
Bow Road	*Dist.; (H. & C.)*	143	DZ69
Brent Cross	*North.*	119	CX59
Brixton	*Vic.*	161	DN84
Bromley-by-Bow	*Dist.; (H. & C.)*	143	EB69
Buckhurst Hill	*Cen.*	102	EK47
Burnt Oak	*North.*	96	CQ53
Caledonian Road	*Picc.*	141	DL65
Camden Town	*North.*	141	DH67
Canada Water	*Jub.*	162	DW75
Canary Wharf	*D.L.R.; Jub.*	143	EA74
Canning Town	*D.L.R.; Jub.*	144	EE72
Cannon Street	***Circ.; Dist.***	**279**	**K1**
Canons Park	*Jub.*	96	CL52
Chalfont & Latimer	*Met.*	72	AW39
Chalk Farm	*North.*	140	DG66
Chancery Lane	***Cen.***	**274**	**D7**
Charing Cross	***Bak.; Jub.; North.***	**277**	**P2**
Chesham	*Met.*	54	AQ31
Chigwell	*(Cen.)*	103	EP49
Chiswick Park	*Dist.*	158	CQ77
Chorleywood	*Met.*	73	BD42
Church Street	*C.T.*	201	DP103
Clapham Common	*North.*	161	DJ84
Clapham North	*North.*	161	DL83
Clapham South	*North.*	181	DH86
Cockfosters	*Picc.*	80	DG42
Colindale	*North.*	118	CS55
Colliers Wood	*North.*	180	DD94
Coombe Lane	*C.T.*	220	DW106
Covent Garden	***Picc.***	**273**	**P10**
Crossharbour & London Arena	*D.L.R.*	163	EB76
Croxley	*Met.*	75	BP44
Custom House	*D.L.R.*	144	EH73
Cutty Sark	*D.L.R.*	163	EC79
Cyprus	*D.L.R.*	145	EN73
Dagenham East	*Dist.*	127	FC64
Dagenham Heathway	*Dist.*	146	EZ65
Debden	*Cen.*	85	EQ42
Deptford Bridge	*D.L.R.*	163	EA81
Devons Road	*D.L.R.*	143	EB70
Dollis Hill	*Jub.*	119	CU64
Dundonald Road	*C.T.*	179	CZ94
Ealing Broadway	*Cen.; Dist.*	137	CK73
Ealing Common	*Dist.; Picc.*	138	CM74
Earls Court	*Dist.; Picc.*	160	DA78
East Acton	*Cen.*	139	CT72
East Croydon	*C.T.*	202	DR103
East Finchley	*North.*	120	DE56
East Ham	*Dist.; (H. & C.)*	144	EL66
East India	*D.L.R.*	143	ED73
East Putney	*Dist.*	179	CY85
Eastcote	*Met.; Picc.*	116	BW59
Edgware	*North.*	96	CP51
Edgware Road	***Bak.; Circ.; Dist.; H. & C.***	**272**	**B7**
Elephant & Castle	***Bak.; North.***	**278**	**G8**
Elm Park	*Dist.*	127	FH63
Elmers End	*C.T.*	203	DX98
Elverson Road	*D.L.R.*	163	EB82
Embankment	***Bak.; Circ.; Dist.; North.***	**278**	**A2**
Epping	*Cen.*	70	EU31
Euston	***North.; Vic.***	**273**	**L2**
Euston Square	***Circ.; H. & C.; Met.***	**273**	**L4**
Fairlop	*Cen.*	103	ER53
Farringdon	***Circ.; H. & C.; Met.***	**274**	**E6**
Fieldway	*C.T.*	221	EB108
Finchley Central	*North.*	98	DA53
Finchley Road	*Jub.; Met.*	140	DC65
Finsbury Park	*Picc.; Vic.*	121	DN61
Fulham Broadway	*Dist.*	160	DA80
Gallions Reach	*D.L.R.*	145	EP72
Gants Hill	*Cen.*	125	EN58
George Street	*C.T.*	202	DQ103
Gloucester Road	*Circ.; Dist.; Picc.*	160	DC77
Golders Green	*North.*	120	DA59
Goldhawk Road	*H. & C.*	159	CW75
Goodge Street	***North.***	**273**	**L6**
Grange Hill	*(Cen.)*	103	ER49
Gravel Hill	*C.T.*	221	DY108
Great Portland Street	***Circ.; H. & C.; Met.***	**273**	**J5**
Green Park	***Jub.; Picc.; Vic.***	**277**	**K3**
Greenford	*Cen.*	137	CD67
Greenwich	*D.L.R.*	163	EB80
Gunnersbury	*Dist.*	158	CP78
Hainault	*(Cen.)*	103	ES52
Hammersmith	*Dist.; H. & C.; Picc.*	159	CW77
Hampstead	*North.*	120	DC63
Hanger Lane	*Cen.*	138	CM69
Harlesden	*Bak.*	138	CR68
Harrington Road	*C.T.*	202	DW97
Harrow & Wealdstone	*Bak.*	117	CE56
Harrow on the Hill	*Met.*	117	CE58
Hatton Cross	*Picc.*	155	BT84
Heathrow Terminal 4	*Picc.*	175	BP85
Heathrow Terminals 1,2,3	*Picc.*	155	BP83
Hendon Central	*North.*	119	CW57
Heron Quays (closed until 2003)	*D.L.R.*	143	EA74
High Barnet	*North.*	80	DA42
High Street Kensington	*Circ.; Dist.*	160	DB75
Highbury & Islington	*Vic.*	141	DP65
Highgate	*North.*	121	DH58
Hillingdon	*Met.; (Picc.)*	114	BN64
Holborn	***Cen.; Picc.***	**274**	**A7**
Holland Park	*Cen.*	139	CY74
Holloway Road	*Picc.*	121	DM64
Hornchurch	*Dist.*	128	FK62
Hounslow Central	*Picc.*	156	CA83
Hounslow East	*Picc.*	156	CC82
Hounslow West	*Picc.*	156	BY82
Hyde Park Corner	***Picc.***	**276**	**F4**
Ickenham	*Met.; (Picc.)*	115	BQ63
Island Gardens	*D.L.R.*	163	EC77
Kennington	***North.***	**278**	**F10**
Kensal Green	*Bak.*	139	CW69
Kensington (Olympia)	*(Dist.)*	159	CY76
Kentish Town	*North.*	121	DJ64
Kenton	*Bak.*	117	CH58
Kew Gardens	*Dist.*	158	CM81
Kilburn	*Jub.*	139	CZ65
Kilburn Park	*Bak.*	140	DA68
King Henry's Drive	*C.T.*	221	EB109
King's Cross St. Pancras	***Circ.; H. & C.; Met.; North.; Picc.; Vic.***	**274**	**A1**
Kingsbury	*Jub.*	118	CN57
Knightsbridge	***Picc.***	**276**	**D5**
Ladbroke Grove	*H. & C.*	139	CY72
Lambeth North	***Bak.***	**278**	**D5**
Lancaster Gate	*Cen.*	140	DD73
Latimer Road	*H. & C.*	139	CX73
Lebanon Road	*C.T.*	202	DS103
Leicester Square	***North.; Picc.***	**273**	**N10**
Lewisham	*D.L.R.*	163	EC83
Leyton	*Cen.*	123	EC62
Leytonstone	*Cen.*	124	EE60
Limehouse	*D.L.R.*	143	DY72
Liverpool Street	***Cen.; Circ.; H. & C.; Met.***	**275**	**M7**
Lloyd Park	*C.T.*	220	DT105
London Bridge	***Jub.; North.***	**279**	**M3**
Loughton	*Cen.*	84	EL43
Maida Vale	*Bak.*	140	DC69
Manor House	*Picc.*	121	DP59
Mansion House	***Circ.; Dist.***	**275**	**J10**
Marble Arch	***Cen.***	**272**	**E10**
Marylebone	***Bak.***	**272**	**D5**
Merton Park	*C.T.*	200	DA95
Mile End	*Cen.; Dist.; (H. & C.)*	143	DY69
Mill Hill East	*North.*	97	CX52
Mitcham	*C.T.*	200	DE98
Mitcham Junction	*C.T.*	200	DG99
Monument	***Circ.; Dist.; D.L.R.***	**275**	**L10**
Moor Park	*Met.*	93	BR48
Moorgate	***Circ.; H. & C.; Met.; North.***	**275**	**K7**
Morden	*North.*	200	DB97
Morden Road	*C.T.*	200	DB96
Mornington Crescent	*North.*	141	DH68
Mudchute	*D.L.R.*	163	EB77
Neasden	*Jub.*	118	CS64
New Addington	*C.T.*	221	EC110
New Cross	*E.L.*	163	DZ80
New Cross Gate	*E.L.*	163	DY80
Newbury Park	*Cen.*	125	ER58
North Acton	*Cen.*	138	CR70
North Ealing	*Picc.*	138	CM72
North Greenwich	*Jub.*	164	EE75
North Harrow	*Met.*	116	CA57
North Wembley	*Bak.*	117	CK62
Northfields	*Picc.*	157	CH76
Northolt	*Cen.*	136	CA66
Northwick Park	*Met.*	117	CG59
Northwood	*Met.*	93	BS52
Northwood Hills	*Met.*	93	BU54
Notting Hill Gate	*Cen.; Circ.; Dist.*	140	DA73
Oakwood	*Picc.*	81	DJ43
Old Street	***North.***	**275**	**K3**
Osterley	*Picc.*	157	CD80
Oval	*North.*	161	DN79
Oxford Circus	***Bak.; Cen.; Vic.***	**273**	**K8**
Paddington	*Bak.; Circ.; Dist.; H. & C.*	140	DC72
Park Royal	*Picc.*	138	CN70
Parsons Green	*Dist.*	159	CZ81
Perivale	*Cen.*	137	CG68
Phipps Bridge	*C.T.*	200	DC97
Piccadilly Circus	***Bak.; Picc.***	**277**	**L1**
Pimlico	***Vic.***	**277**	**M10**
Pinner	*Met.*	116	BY56
Plaistow	*Dist.; (H. & C.)*	144	EF68
Poplar	*D.L.R.*	143	EB73
Preston Road	*Met.*	118	CL60
Prince Regent	*D.L.R.*	144	EJ73
Pudding Mill Lane	*D.L.R.*	143	EB67
Putney Bridge	*Dist.*	159	CY83
Queen's Park	*Bak.*	139	CY68
Queensbury	*Jub.*	118	CM55
Queensway	*Cen.*	140	DB73
Ravenscourt Park	*Dist.*	159	CU77
Rayners Lane	*Met.; Picc.*	116	BZ59
Redbridge	*Cen.*	124	EK58
Reeves Corner	*C.T.*	201	DP103
Regent's Park	***Bak.***	**273**	**H5**
Richmond	*Dist.*	158	CL84
Rickmansworth	*Met.*	92	BK45
Roding Valley	*(Cen.)*	102	EK49
Rotherhithe	*E.L.*	162	DW75
Royal Albert	*D.L.R.*	144	EL73
Royal Oak	*H. & C.*	140	DB71
Royal Victoria	*D.L.R.*	144	EG73
Ruislip	*Met.; (Picc.)*	115	BS60
Ruislip Gardens	*Cen.*	115	BU63
Ruislip Manor	*Met.; (Picc.)*	115	BU60
Russell Square	***Picc.***	**273**	**P5**
St. James's Park	***Circ.; Dist.***	**277**	**M5**
St. John's Wood	*Jub.*	140	DD68
St. Paul's	***Cen.***	**275**	**H8**
Sandilands	*C.T.*	202	DT103
Seven Sisters	*Vic.*	122	DS57
Shadwell	*D.L.R.; E.L.*	142	DW73
Shepherd's Bush	*Cen.; H. & C.*	159	CW75
Shoreditch	*(E.L.)*	142	DT70
Sloane Square	***Circ.; Dist.***	**276**	**F9**
Snaresbrook	*Cen.*	124	EG57
South Ealing	*Picc.*	157	CJ76
South Harrow	*Picc.*	116	CC62
South Kensington	***Circ.; Dist.; Picc.***	**276**	**A8**
South Kenton	*Bak.*	117	CJ60
South Quay	*D.L.R.*	163	EB75
South Ruislip	*Cen.*	116	BW63
South Wimbledon	*North.*	180	DB94
South Woodford	*Cen.*	102	EG54
Southfields	*Dist.*	179	CZ88
Southgate	*Picc.*	99	DJ46
Southwark	***Jub.***	**278**	**F3**
Stamford Brook	*Dist.*	159	CT77
Stanmore	*Jub.*	95	CK50
Stepney Green	*Dist.; (H. & C.)*	143	DX70
Stockwell	*North.; Vic.*	161	DL81
Stonebridge Park	*Bak.*	138	CN66
Stratford	*Cen.; D.L.R.; Jub.*	143	EC66
Sudbury Hill	*Picc.*	117	CE63
Sudbury Town	*Picc.*	137	CH65
Surrey Quays	*E.L.*	163	DX76
Swiss Cottage	*Jub.*	140	DD66
Temple	***Circ.; Dist.***	**274**	**C10**
Therapia Lane	*C.T.*	201	DL101
Theydon Bois	*Cen.*	85	ET36
Tooting Bec	*North.*	180	DF90
Tooting Broadway	*North.*	180	DE92
Tottenham Court Road	***Cen.; North.***	**273**	**M8**
Tottenham Hale	*Vic.*	122	DV55
Totteridge & Whetstone	*North.*	98	DB47
Tower Gateway	*D.L.R.*	142	DT73
Tower Hill	***Circ.; Dist.***	**275**	**P10**
Tufnell Park	*North.*	121	DJ63
Turnham Green	*Dist.; Picc.*	158	CS77
Turnpike Lane	*Picc.*	121	DN55
Upminster	*Dist.*	128	FQ61
Upminster Bridge	*Dist.*	128	FN61
Upney	*Dist.*	145	ET66
Upton Park	*Dist.; (H. & C.)*	144	EH67
Uxbridge	*Met.; (Picc.)*	134	BK66
Vauxhall	*Vic.*	161	DL79
Victoria	***Circ.; Dist.; Vic.***	**277**	**J7**
Waddon Marsh	*C.T.*	201	DM102
Walthamstow Central	*Vic.*	123	EA56
Wandle Park	*C.T.*	201	DN103
Wanstead	*Cen.*	124	EH58
Wapping	*E.L.*	142	DW74
Warren Street	***North.; Vic.***	**273**	**L4**
Warwick Avenue	*Bak.*	140	DC70
Waterloo	***Bak.; Jub.; North.***	**278**	**D4**
Watford	*Met.*	75	BT41
Wellesley Road	*C.T.*	202	DQ103
Wembley Central	*Bak.*	118	CL64
Wembley Park	*Jub.; Met.*	118	CN62
West Acton	*Cen.*	138	CN72
West Brompton	*Dist.*	160	DA78
West Croydon	*C.T.*	202	DQ102
West Finchley	*North.*	98	DB51
West Ham	*Dist.; (H. & C.); Jub.*	144	EE69
West Hampstead	*Jub.*	140	DA65
West Harrow	*Met.*	116	CC58
West India Quay	*D.L.R.*	143	EA73
West Kensington	*Dist.*	159	CZ78
West Ruislip	*Cen.*	115	BQ61
Westbourne Park	*H. & C.*	139	CZ71
Westferry	*D.L.R.*	143	EA73
Westminster	***Circ.; Dist.***	**278**	**A5**
White City	*Cen.*	139	CW73
Whitechapel	*Dist.; E.L.; H. & C.*	142	DV71
Willesden Green	*Jub.*	139	CW65
Willesden Junction	*Bak.*	139	CT69
Wimbledon	*C.T.; Dist.*	179	CZ93
Wimbledon Park	*Dist.*	180	DA90
Wood Green	*Picc.*	99	DM54
Woodford	*Cen.*	102	EH51
Woodside	*C.T.*	202	DV100
Woodside Park	*North.*	98	DB49

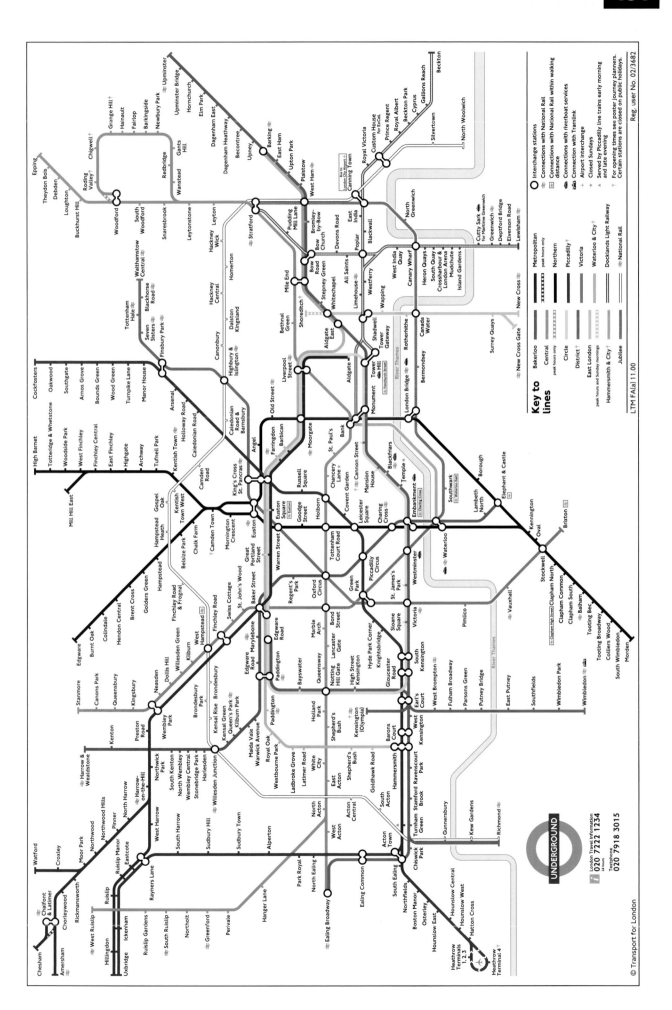

AYLESBURY VALE

DACORUM

38 39 40 41

ST.
ALBANS

42 43

28 29 30
WELWYN

HATFIELD
44 45 46

54 56 57 58 59 60 61 62 63 64

CHILTERN

55 72 73 74 75 76 77 78 79 80

THREE
RIVERS

WATFORD

HERTSMERE

WYCOMBE

88 89 90 91 92 93 94 95 96 97 98

BARNET

HARROW

HA

110 111 112 113 114 115 116 117 118 119 120

SOUTH BUCKS

HILLINGDON

BRENT

CAMDEN

130 131 132 133 134 135 136 137 138 139 140

SLOUGH

EALING

KENSINGTON &
CHELSEA

HAMMERSMITH &
FULHAM

WESTMINSTE

150 151 152 153 154 155 156 157 158 159 160

WINDSOR & MAIDENHEAD

HOUNSLOW

WOKINGHAM

172 173 174 175 176 177 178 179 180

SPELTHORNE

RICHMOND
UPON THAMES

WANDSWORTH

BRACKNELL
FOREST

192 193 194 195 196 197 198 199 200

RUNNYMEDE

KINGSTON
UPON THAMES

MERTON

SUTTON

ELMBRIDGE

EPSOM
& EWELL

210 211 212 213 214 215 216 217 218

SURREY HEATH

WOKING

226 227 228 229 230 231 232 233 234

HART

RUSHMOOR

REIGATE &
250
BANSTEAD

242 243 244 245 246 247 248 249

GUILDFORD

258 259 260 261 262 263 264 265 266

MOLE VALLEY

EAST
HANTS

268

WAVERLEY

CRAWLE

E

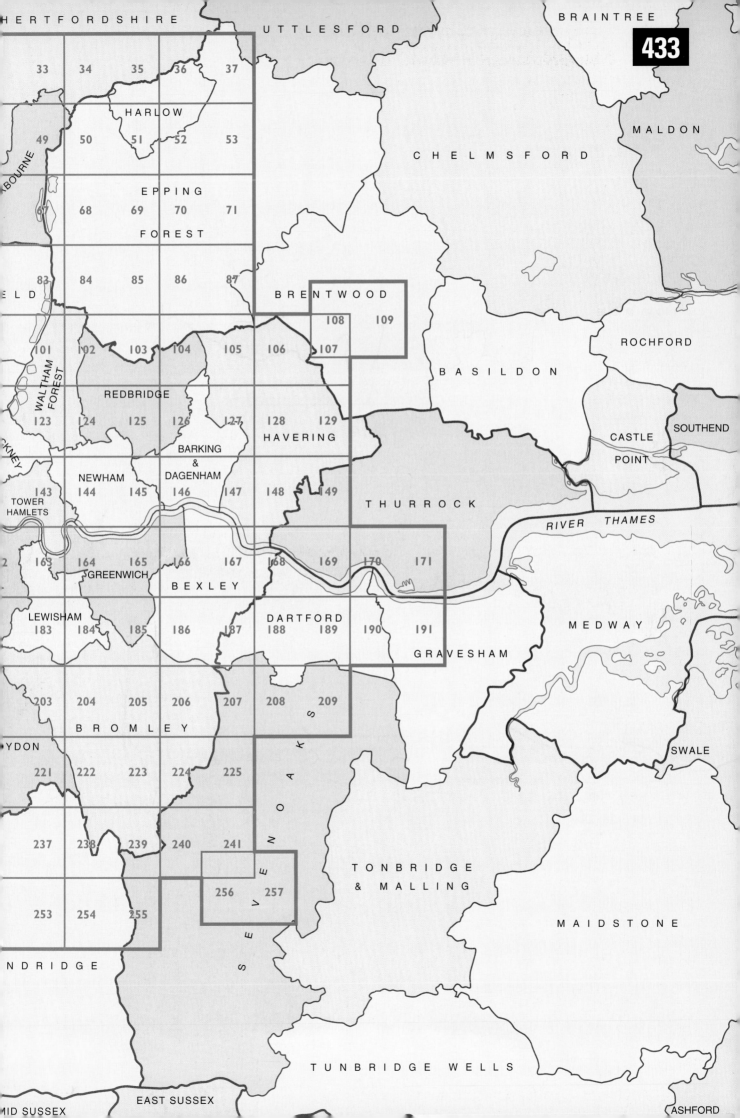